# Concise Oxford American Thesaurus

# Concise Oxford American Thesaurus

OXFORD UNIVERSITY PRESS

Oxford University Press, Inc., publishes works that further
Oxford University's objective of excellence
in research, scholarship, and education.

Oxford New York
Auckland Cape Town Dar es Salaam Hong Kong Karachi
Kuala Lumpur Madrid Melbourne Mexico City Nairobi
New Delhi Shanghai Taipei Toronto

With offices in
Argentina Austria Brazil Chile Czech Republic France Greece
Guatemala Hungary Italy Japan Poland Portugal Singapore
South Korea Switzerland Thailand Turkey Ukraine Vietnam



Published by Oxford University Press, Inc.
198 Madison Avenue, New York, New York, 10016
www.oup.com/us
www.askoxford.com



**Library of Congress Cataloging-in-Publication Data**

Concise Oxford American thesaurus.
p. cm.
ISBN-13: 978-0-19-530485-5 (acid-free paper)
ISBN-10: 0-19-530485-3 (acid-free paper)
1. English language—Synonyms and antonyms.
PE1591.C665 2006
423'.12—dc22

2005035868



10 9 8 7 6 5 4 3 2 1

Printed in the United States of America on acid-free paper

# *Contents*

# *Staff*

Erin McKean, *Editor in Chief*

Constance Baboukis, *Managing Editor*

Christine A. Lindberg, *Senior Project Editor*

Grant Barrett, *Assistant Editor*

Carol-June Cassidy, *Project Editor*

Sarah Hilliard, *Proofreader*

Elizabeth Jerabek, *Editorial Assistant*

# *Preface*

The *Concise Oxford American Thesaurus*, with more than 15,000 main entries and over 350,000 synonyms, is intended to be a useful, handy tool to help you enrich your writing and better express yourself. Sample sentences or phrases for virtually every sense keep you on the right track, helping you choose exactly what you want to say. Synonym studies show the subtle differences in meaning among a group of easily confused synonyms for even more precise guidance; and the back of the book holds the Oxford exclusive Language Guide, with information about grammar, usage, punctuation, frequently misspelled words, and much more.

Oxford lexicographers have arranged these entries to guide you quickly and easily, not only to the words you know you need, but even to ones you never knew existed. Here you will encounter wonderful words that will enhance your writing, enrich your vocabulary, and endear themselves to you for years to come.

Erin McKean<br>
Editor in Chief<br>
U.S. Dictionaries<br>
Oxford University Press

# *How To Use the Concise Oxford American Thesaurus*

## Entries

The synonyms in each entry are grouped in numbered sets. Major synonym sets correspond roughly to different senses of the word in a dictionary, and are identifiable by example phrases or sentences. Many sets also contain finer distinctions, which are signaled by semicolons.

The synonyms in each set that are closest in meaning to the entry word are given first, usually starting with a "core synonym" in SMALL CAPITALS. Some sets have more than one core synonym if two synonyms are very close to the entry word but neither covers the whole sense; for example, at *audience*, both *spectators* and *listeners* are given as core synonyms. Two different core synonyms may also emphasize slightly different aspects of the meaning of the entry word. For example, at *prosperous,* the first core synonym given is *thriving,* followed by a group of words closely related to that aspect of its meaning, such as *flourishing* and *successful.* Then, after a semicolon, a second core synonym, *affluent,* is given, with an allied group of synonyms such as *wealthy* and *rich.*

Phrases and idiomatic expressions are provided in bold form at the end of the entry for their principal word. For example, *make do* and *make off with* can be found with their synonyms at the end of the entry for *make.*

Most of the synonyms are standard English, but some are suitable only in certain contexts. These are grouped at the end of their synonym set and are given identifying labels, for example:

informal, e.g. *crummy, smacker, buck up.*

literary, e.g., *slumber, afire, besmear.*

archaic, e.g. *bootless, accouchement.*

historical, e.g. *schoolmarm, cablegram;* still used today, but only to refer to something that is no longer part of the modern world.

rare, e.g. *objurgation, exiguous.*

derogatory, e.g. *poetaster, guttersnipe.*

euphemistic, e.g. *physically challenged, adult.*

Antonyms are given for most entries, and many of these antonyms have entries of their own where a wider selection of words can be found.

## Features

Included in this thesaurus are many special features to help you distinguish just the word you need.

### *The Right Word*

These notes show fine distinctions in meaning among closely related synonyms, with expanded definitions and additional examples to help distinguish the right word from the list of synonyms.

### *Usage Notes*

Additional guidance on the finer points of English usage, including fifty notes from Bryan Garner, the author of *Garner's Modern American Usage.*

## An Important Note

Using an unfamiliar word simply because it is listed in a thesaurus can be a disaster. To avoid inappropriate collocations or embarrassing malapropisms, users should look up unfamiliar words in a dictionary before employing them. It is important to understand the connotations of *inveigle,* for instance, before using it as a synonym for *persuade.* Although the entries in the *Concise Oxford American Thesaurus* have been organized to make choosing the right word simpler, users should always have a good dictionary within reach.

**abandon** verb **1** *the party abandoned policies that made it unelectable* RENOUNCE, relinquish, dispense with, disclaim, forgo, disown, disavow, discard, wash one's hands of; give up, withdraw, drop, jettison, do away with; *informal* ax, ditch, dump, scrap, scrub, junk, deep-six; *formal* forswear, abjure. See note at RELINQUISH. ANTONYMS keep, retain.

**2** *by that time, she had abandoned painting* GIVE UP, stop, cease, drop, forgo, desist from, dispense with, have done with, abstain from, discontinue, break off, refrain from, set aside; *informal* cut out, kick, pack in, quit. ANTONYMS take up, continue.

**3** *he abandoned his wife and children* DESERT, leave, leave high and dry, turn one's back on, cast aside, break (up) with; jilt, strand, leave stranded, leave in the lurch, throw over; *informal* walk out on, run out on, dump, ditch; *literary* forsake.

**4** *the skipper gave the order to abandon ship* VACATE, leave, depart from, withdraw from, quit, evacuate.

**5** *a vast expanse of territory was abandoned to the invaders* RELINQUISH, surrender, give up, cede, yield, leave. ANTONYMS keep, claim.

**6** *she* ***abandoned herself to*** *the sensuousness of the music* INDULGE IN, give way to, give oneself up to, yield to, lose oneself to/in. ANTONYM control oneself.

▸ noun *at age sixty he had no less abandon than when he was twenty* UNINHIBITEDNESS, recklessness, lack of restraint, lack of inhibition, wildness, impulsiveness, impetuosity, immoderation, wantonness. ANTONYM self-control.

**abandoned** adjective **1** *an abandoned child* DESERTED, forsaken, cast aside/off; jilted, stranded, rejected; *informal* dumped, ditched.

**2** *an abandoned tin mine* UNUSED, disused, neglected, idle; deserted, unoccupied, uninhabited, empty.

**3** *an abandoned dance* UNINHIBITED, reckless, unrestrained, wild, unbridled, impulsive, impetuous; immoderate, wanton.

**abase** verb **1** *Dunlap had a reputation for openly abasing his employees* HUMBLE, humiliate, belittle, demean, lower, degrade, debase, cheapen, discredit, bring low. See note at HUMBLE.

**2** *I'd rather lose my job than continue to* ***abase myself*** grovel, kowtow, bow and scrape, toady, fawn; *informal* crawl, suck up to someone, lick someone's boots.

**abasement** noun *only a fiend delights in the abasement of his children* HUMILIATION, humbling, belittlement, lowering, degradation, debasement. ANTONYM pride.

**abashed** adjective *Iris was positively abashed when she rose only to realize another nominee had won the award* EMBARRASSED, ashamed, shamefaced, remorseful, conscience-stricken, mortified, humiliated, humbled, chagrined, crestfallen, sheepish, red-faced, blushing, put out of countenance, with one's tail between one's legs; taken aback, disconcerted, discomfited, fazed, disturbed; *informal* floored.

**abate** verb **1** *the storm had abated* SUBSIDE, die down/away/out, lessen, ease (off), let up, decrease, diminish, moderate, decline, fade, dwindle, recede, tail off, peter out, taper off, wane, ebb, weaken, come to an end; *archaic* remit. See note at ALLEVIATE. ANTONYM intensify.

**2** *nothing abated his crusading zeal* DECREASE, lessen, diminish, reduce, moderate, ease, soothe, dampen, calm, tone down, allay, temper. ANTONYM increase.

**abatement** noun **1** *the storm rages with no sign of abatement* SUBSIDING, dying down/away/out, lessening, easing (off), letup, decrease, moderation, decline, ebb.

**2** *noise abatement* DECREASE, reduction, lowering.

**abbey** noun *the brothers had been hiding refugees in the abbey's catacombs* MONASTERY, CONVENT, priory, cloister, friary, nunnery; *historical* charterhouse; *rare* cenobium.

**abbreviate** verb *please abbreviate your essays to a length of no more than two pages* SHORTEN, reduce, cut, contract, condense, compress, abridge, truncate, pare down, prune, shrink, telescope; summarize, abstract, précis, synopsize, digest, edit. ANTONYMS lengthen, expand, elongate.

**abbreviation** noun **1** *the abbreviation for 'teaspoon' is 'tsp.' or just 't.'* SHORTENED FORM, short form, contraction, acronym, initialism, symbol, diminutive; elision. ANTONYM full form.

**2** *'Desi Arnaz' was an abbreviation of the bandleader's full name, 'Desiderio Alberto Arnaz y de Acha III'* SHORTENING, reduction, cutting, contraction, condensation, abridgment, truncation, cropping, paring down. ANTONYM expansion.

**abdicate** verb **1** *the king abdicated in 1936* RESIGN, retire, stand down, step down, bow out, renounce the throne; *archaic* demit. ANTONYM be crowned.

**2** *Ferdinand abdicated the throne* RESIGN FROM, relinquish, renounce, give up, surrender, vacate, cede; *Law* disclaim; *formal* abjure. ANTONYM accede to.

**3** *the state abdicated all responsibility for their welfare* DISOWN, reject, renounce, give up, refuse, relinquish, repudiate, abandon, turn one's back on, wash one's hands of; forgo, waive; *formal* abjure; *literary* forsake. ANTONYMS accept, take on.

**abdication** noun **1** *Edward VIII's abdication* RESIGNATION, retirement; relinquishment, renunciation, surrender; *formal* abjuration; *archaic* demission. ANTONYM coronation.

**2** *an abdication of responsibility* DISOWNING, renunciation, rejection, refusal, relinquishment, repudiation, abandonment. ANTONYM acceptance.

**abdomen** noun *a firm abdomen* STOMACH, belly, gut, middle, intestines; *informal* tummy, insides, guts, maw, breadbasket, pot, paunch.

**abdominal** adjective *abdominal pains* GASTRIC, intestinal, stomach, stomachic, enteric, duodenal, visceral, celiac, ventral.

**abduct** verb *police were tipped off that Kiley was planning to abduct the congressman's wife* KIDNAP, carry off, seize, capture, run away/off with, make off with, spirit away; *informal* snatch, shanghai.

**aberrant** adjective *eating on the floor with the dogs is just one example of his aberrant behavior* DEVIANT, deviating, divergent, abnormal, atypical, anomalous, irregular; nonconformist, rogue; strange, odd, peculiar, uncommon, freakish, quirky; twisted, warped, perverted. ANTONYMS normal, typical.

**aberration** noun *a statistical aberration* ANOMALY, deviation, departure from the norm, divergence, abnormality, irregularity, variation, digression, freak, rogue, rarity, oddity, peculiarity, curiosity, quirk; mistake.

**abet** verb *I refused to abet the neighbors in their scheme to sabotage the construction site* ASSIST, aid, help, lend a hand to, support, back, encourage; cooperate with, collaborate with, work with, connive with, collude with, go along with, be in collusion with, be hand in glove with, side with; second, endorse, sanction; promote, incite, champion, further, expedite. ANTONYM hinder.

**abeyance** noun *expansion plans for the middle school are* ***in abeyance*** IN SUSPENSION, in a state of suspension, in a state of dormancy, in a state of uncertainty, in remission; pending, suspended, deferred, postponed, put off, put to one side, unresolved, up in the air; *informal* in cold storage, on ice, on the back burner. See note at LATENT.

**abhor** verb *I abhor the taste of liver* DETEST, hate, loathe, despise, execrate, regard with disgust, shrink from, recoil from, shudder at; *formal* abominate. See note at DESPISE. ANTONYMS love, admire.

**abhorrent** adjective *that slasher film was just one abhorrent scene after another* DETESTABLE, hateful, loathsome, despicable, abominable, execrable, repellent, repugnant, repulsive, revolting, disgusting, distasteful, horrible, horrid, horrifying, awful, heinous, reprehensible, obnoxious, odious, nauseating, offensive, contemptible. See note at OFFENSIVE. ANTONYM admirable.

**abide** verb **1** *he expected everybody to* ***abide by*** *the rules* COMPLY WITH, obey, observe, follow, keep to, hold to, conform to, adhere to, stick to, stand by, act in accordance with, uphold, heed, accept, go along with, acknowledge, respect, defer to. ANTONYMS flout, disobey.

**2** *informal I can't abide the smell of cigarettes* TOLERATE, bear, stand, put up with, endure, take, countenance; *informal* stomach; *formal* brook; *archaic* suffer. ANTONYMS enjoy, relish.

**3** *the memory of our parting will abide* CONTINUE, remain, survive, last, persist, stay, live on. ANTONYMS fade, disappear.

**abiding** adjective *theirs is an abiding friendship* ENDURING, lasting, persisting, long-lasting, lifelong, continuing, remaining, surviving, standing, durable, everlasting, perpetual, eternal, unending, constant, permanent, unchanging, steadfast, immutable. ANTONYMS short-lived, ephemeral.

**ability** noun **1** *the ability to read and write* CAPACITY, capability, potential, potentiality, power, faculty, aptness, facility; wherewithal, means.

**2** *the president's leadership ability* TALENT, skill, expertise, adeptness, aptitude, skillfulness, savoir faire, prowess, mastery, accomplishment; competence, proficiency; dexterity, adroitness, deftness, cleverness, flair, finesse, gift, knack, genius; qualification, resources; *informal* know-how.

**abject** adjective **1** *abject poverty* WRETCHED, miserable, hopeless, pathetic, pitiful, pitiable, piteous, sorry, woeful, lamentable, degrading, appalling, atrocious, awful.

**2** *an abject sinner* CONTEMPTIBLE, base, low, vile, worthless, debased, degraded, despicable, ignominious, mean, unworthy, ignoble.

**3** *an abject apology* OBSEQUIOUS, groveling, fawning, toadyish, servile, cringing, sycophantic, submissive, craven.

**abjure** verb *formal she has abjured the doctrines of her parents' faith* RENOUNCE, relinquish, reject, forgo, disavow, abandon, deny, repudiate, give up, wash one's hands of; eschew, abstain from, refrain from; *informal* kick, pack in; *Law* disaffirm; *literary* forsake; *formal* forswear, abnegate.

**ablaze** adjective **1** *several vehicles were ablaze* ON FIRE, alight, aflame, in flames, flaming, burning, fiery, blazing; *literary* afire, igneous.

**2** *every window was ablaze with light* LIT UP, alight, gleaming, glowing, aglow, illuminated, bright, shining, radiant, shimmering, sparkling, flashing, dazzling, luminous, incandescent.

**3** *his eyes were ablaze with fury* PASSIONATE, impassioned, aroused, excited, adrenalized, stimulated, eager, animated, intense, ardent, fiery, fervent, frenzied.

**able** adjective **1** *he will soon be able to resume his duties* CAPABLE OF, competent to, equal to, up to, fit to, prepared to, qualified to; allowed to, free to, in a position to. ANTONYM incapable.

**2** *an able student* INTELLIGENT, clever, talented, skillful, skilled, accomplished, gifted; proficient, apt, good, adroit, adept; capable, competent, efficient, effective. ANTONYM incompetent.

**able-bodied** adjective *we'll need at least six able-bodied men and women for the expedition* HEALTHY, FIT, in good health, robust, strong, sound, sturdy, vigorous, hardy, hale and hearty, athletic, muscular, strapping, burly, brawny, lusty; in good shape, in good trim, in fine fettle, fighting fit, as fit as a fiddle; *informal* husky; *dated* stalwart. ANTONYMS infirm, frail, disabled.

**abnegation** noun *formal* **1** *a serious abnegation of their responsibilities* RENUNCIATION, rejection, refusal, abandonment, abdication, surrender, relinquishment, repudiation, denial; *formal* abjuration. ANTONYM acceptance.

**2** *people capable of abnegation and unselfishness* SELF-DENIAL, self-sacrifice, abstinence, temperance, continence, asceticism, austerity, abstemiousness. ANTONYM self-indulgence.

**abnormal** adjective *an increased appetite during pregnancy is not abnormal | she speaks Spanish with a Swedish accent, which is pretty abnormal* UNUSUAL, uncommon, atypical, untypical, nontypical, unrepresentative, rare, isolated, irregular, anomalous, deviant, divergent, aberrant, freak, freakish; STRANGE, odd, peculiar, curious, bizarre, weird, queer; eccentric, idiosyncratic, quirky; unexpected, unfamiliar, unconventional, surprising, unorthodox, singular, exceptional, extraordinary, out of the ordinary, out of the way; unnatural, perverse, perverted, twisted, warped, unhealthy, distorted; *informal* freaky. ANTONYMS normal, typical, common.

**abnormality** noun **1** *born with a heart abnormality* MALFORMATION, deformity, irregularity, flaw, defect, anomaly.

**2** *the abnormality of such behavior* UNUSUALNESS, uncommonness, atypicality, irregularity, anomalousness, deviation, divergence, aberrance, aberration, freakishness; strangeness, oddness, peculiarity, unexpectedness, singularity.

**abode** noun *welcome to my humble abode* HOME, house, place of residence, accommodations; quarters, lodgings, domicile, rooms; address; *informal* pad, digs; *formal* dwelling, dwelling place, residence, habitation.

**abolish** verb *the governor never fulfilled his promise to abolish the state income tax* PUT AN END TO, get rid of, scrap, end, stop, terminate, ax, eradicate, eliminate, exterminate, destroy, annihilate, stamp out, obliterate, wipe out, extinguish, quash, expunge, extirpate; annul, cancel, invalidate, negate, nullify, void, dissolve; rescind, repeal, revoke, overturn; discontinue, remove, excise, drop, jettison; *informal* do away with, ditch, junk, scrub, dump; *formal* abrogate. ANTONYMS retain, create.

**abolition** noun *the abolition of slavery did not guarantee equality* SCRAPPING, ending, termination, eradication, elimination, extermination, abolishment, destruction, annihilation, obliteration, extirpation; annulment, cancellation, invalidation, nullification, dissolution; revocation, repeal, discontinuation, removal; *formal* abrogation.

**abominable** adjective *Caligula was among the most abominable figures in history* LOATHSOME, detestable, hateful, odious, obnoxious, despicable, contemptible, damnable, diabolical; disgusting, revolting, repellent, repulsive, offensive, repugnant, abhorrent, reprehensible, atrocious, horrifying, execrable, foul, vile, wretched, base, horrible, awful, dreadful, appalling, nauseating; horrid, nasty, disagreeable, unpleasant, distasteful; *informal* terrible, shocking, godawful; beastly; *dated* cursed, accursed. See note at OFFENSIVE. ANTONYMS good, admirable.

**abominate** verb *formal I truly abominate her use of coarse language* DETEST, loathe, hate, abhor, despise, execrate, shudder at, recoil from, shrink from, be repelled by. ANTONYMS like, love.

**abomination** noun **1** *in both wars, internment was an abomination* ATROCITY, disgrace, horror, obscenity, outrage, evil, crime, monstrosity, anathema, bane.

**2** *she looked upon his kitschy decor with abomination* DETESTATION, loathing, hatred, aversion, antipathy, revulsion, repugnance, abhorrence, odium, execration, disgust, horror, hostility. ANTONYMS liking, love.

**aboriginal** adjective **1** *the area's aboriginal inhabitants* INDIGENOUS, native; original, earliest, first; ancient, primitive, primeval, primordial; *rare* autochthonous.

**2** *Aboriginal soldiers serving in the Canadian forces* NATIVE, indigenous, First Nations, Indian, Inuit, Metis. See note at NATIVE.

▸ noun *the social structure of the aboriginals* NATIVE, aborigine, original inhabitant; *rare* autochthon, indigene.

**abort** verb *the crew aborted the takeoff* HALT, stop, end, ax, call off, cut short, discontinue, terminate, arrest, cancel, scrub; *informal* pull the plug on.

**abortion** noun *her first pregnancy resulted in a spontaneous abortion* TERMINATION, miscarriage.

**abortive** adjective *the abortive coup was crushed after two days of fighting* UNSUCCESSFUL, failed, vain, thwarted, futile, useless, worthless, ineffective, ineffectual, to no effect, inefficacious, fruitless, unproductive, unavailing, to no avail, sterile, nugatory; *archaic* bootless. ANTONYMS successful, fruitful.

**abound** verb **1** *cafés and bars abound in the narrow streets* BE PLENTIFUL, be abundant, be numerous, proliferate, superabound, be thick on the ground; *informal* grow on trees.

**2** *the stream **abounds with** trout and eels* BE FULL OF, overflow with, teem with, be packed with, be crowded with, be thronged with; be alive with, be crawling with, be overrun by/with, swarm with, bristle with, be infested with, be thick with; *informal* be stuffed with, be jam-packed with, be chockablock with, be chock-full of.

**about** preposition **1** *a book about needlecraft* REGARDING, concerning, with reference to, referring to, with regard to, with respect to, respecting, relating to, on, touching on, dealing with, relevant to, connected with, in connection with, on the subject of, in the matter of, apropos, re.

**2** *two hundred people were milling about the room* AROUND, round, throughout, over, through, on every side of.

▸ adverb **1** *there were babies crawling about in the grass* AROUND, here and there, to and fro, back and forth, from place to place, hither and thither, in all directions.

**2** *I knew he was somewhere about* NEAR, nearby, around, hereabouts, not far (off/away), close by, in the vicinity, in the neighborhood.

**3** *the explosion caused about $15,000 worth of damage* APPROXIMATELY, roughly, around, round about, in the region of, circa, of/on the order of, something like; or so, or thereabouts, there or thereabouts, more or less, give or take a few, not far off; *informal* in the ballpark of.

**4** *there's a lot of gossip about* AROUND, in circulation, in existence, current, going on, prevailing, prevalent, happening, in the air, abroad.

PHRASE: **about to** *I'm about to leave* (JUST) GOING TO, ready to, all set to, preparing to, getting ready to, intending to, soon to; on the point of, on the verge of, on the brink of, *informal* fixing to.

**above** preposition **1** *a tiny window above the door* OVER, higher (up) than; on top of, atop, on, upon. ANTONYMS below, under, beneath.

**2** *those above the rank of colonel* SUPERIOR TO, senior to, over, higher (up) than, more powerful than; in charge of, commanding. ANTONYMS below, junior to.

**3** *you must be above suspicion* BEYOND, not liable to, not open to, not vulnerable to, out of reach of; immune to, exempt from.

**4** *the Chinese valued pearls above gold* MORE THAN, over, before, rather than, in preference to, instead of.

**5** *an increase above the rate of inflation* GREATER THAN, more than, higher than, exceeding, in excess of, over, over and above, beyond, surpassing, upwards of. ANTONYMS below, less than.

▸ adverb **1** *in the darkness above, something moved* OVERHEAD, on/at the top, high up, on high, up above, (up) in the sky, high above one's head, aloft.

**2** *the two cases described above* EARLIER, previously, before, formerly.

▸ adjective *the above example* PRECEDING, previous, earlier, former, foregoing, prior, above-stated, above-mentioned, aforementioned, aforesaid.

PHRASE: **above all** *above all, deactivate the alarm before attempting to open the door* MOST IMPORTANTLY, before everything, beyond everything, first of all, most of all, chiefly, primarily, in the first place, first and foremost, mainly, principally, predominantly, especially, essentially, basically, in essence, at bottom; *informal* at the end of the day, when all is said and done.

**aboveboard** adjective *the proceedings were completely aboveboard* LEGITIMATE, lawful, legal, licit, honest, fair, open, frank, straight, overt, candid, forthright, unconcealed, trustworthy, unequivocal; *informal* legit, kosher, by the book, street legal, fair and square, square, on the level, on the up and up, upfront. ANTONYMS dishonest, shady.

**abrasion** noun **1** *his knees were marked up with abrasions* GRAZE, cut, scrape, scratch, gash, laceration, injury, contusion; sore, ulcer.

**2** *the metal is resistant to abrasion* EROSION, wearing away/down, corrosion, scraping, scouring.

**abrasive** adjective **1** *abrasive cleanser* CORROSIVE, corroding, erosive; caustic, harsh, scratching, coarse. ANTONYM gentle.

**2** *her abrasive manner* CAUSTIC, cutting, biting, acerbic; rough, harsh, hard, tough, sharp, grating, curt, brusque, stern, severe; wounding, nasty, cruel, callous, insensitive, unfeeling, unsympathetic, inconsiderate. ANTONYMS kind, gentle.

**abreast** adverb **1** *they walked three abreast* IN A ROW, side by side, alongside, level, beside each other, shoulder to shoulder.

**2** *try to keep **abreast of** current affairs* UP TO DATE WITH, up with, in touch with, informed about, acquainted with, knowledgeable about, conversant with, familiar with, au courant with, au fait with.

**abridge** verb *she was hired to abridge the works of Shakespeare for a children's book club* SHORTEN, cut, cut short, cut down, curtail, truncate, trim, crop, clip, pare down, prune; abbreviate, condense, contract, compress, reduce, decrease, shrink; summarize, sum up, abstract, précis, synopsize, give a digest of, put in a nutshell, edit; *rare* epitomize. ANTONYM lengthen.

**abridgment** noun *an abridgment of the full report* SUMMARY, abstract, synopsis, précis, outline, résumé, sketch, compendium, digest.

**abroad** adverb **1** *he regularly travels abroad* OVERSEAS, out of the country, to/in foreign parts, to/in a foreign country, to/in a foreign land.

**2** *rumors were abroad* IN CIRCULATION, circulating, widely current, everywhere, in the air, 'here, there, and everywhere'; about, around; at large.

**abrogation** noun *formal such a defense system would require amendment or abrogation of the 1972 antiballistic missile treaty* REPEAL, revocation, repudiation, rescinding, overturning, annulment, overruling, cancellation, invalidation, nullification, negation, dissolution, discontinuation; reversal, retraction, removal, withdrawal, abolition; *formal* rescission; *rare* deracination.

**abrupt** adjective **1** *an abrupt halt* | *an abrupt change of subject* SUDDEN, unexpected, without warning, unanticipated, unforeseen, precipitate, precipitous, surprising, startling; quick, swift, rapid, hurried, hasty, immediate, instantaneous. ANTONYMS gradual, unhurried.

**2** *an abrupt manner* CURT, brusque, blunt, short, sharp, terse, crisp, gruff, rude, discourteous, uncivil, snappish, unceremonious, offhand, rough, harsh; bluff, no-nonsense, to the point; *informal* snappy. ANTONYMS friendly, expansive.

**3** *abrupt, epigrammatic paragraphs* DISJOINTED, jerky, uneven, disconnected, inelegant. ANTONYMS smooth, flowing.

**4** *an abrupt slope* STEEP, sheer, precipitous, bluff, sharp, sudden; perpendicular, vertical, dizzy, vertiginous. ANTONYMS gradual, gentle.

**abscess** noun *the abscess is what's causing the pain* ULCER, ulceration, cyst, boil, blister, sore, pustule, carbuncle, pimple, wen, whitlow, canker; inflammation, infection, eruption.

**abscond** verb *it seems that the one they entrusted with their stolen goods has absconded* RUN AWAY, escape, bolt, flee, make off, take flight, take off, decamp; make a break for it, take to one's heels, make a quick getaway, beat a hasty retreat, run for it, make a run for it; disappear, vanish, slip away, split, steal away, sneak away; clear out, duck out; *informal* cut and run, skedaddle, skip, skip town, head for the hills, do a disappearing act, fly the coop, take French leave, vamoose, take a powder.

**absence** noun **1** *what excuse has he given for his absence this time?* | *an extended absence* NONATTENDANCE, nonappearance, absenteeism; TRUANCY, playing truant; leave, holiday, vacation, sabbatical. ANTONYMS presence, attendance.

**2** *the absence of suitable candidates* LACK, want, nonexistence, unavailability, deficiency, dearth; need. ANTONYMS presence, availability.

**absent** adjective **1** *she was absent from work* | *an absent parent* AWAY, off, out, nonattending, truant; off duty, on holiday, on leave; gone, missing, unavailable, nonexistent; *informal* AWOL, playing hooky. ANTONYM present.

**2** *an absent look* DISTRACTED, preoccupied, inattentive, vague, absorbed, abstracted, unheeding, oblivious, distrait, absentminded, dreamy, far away, in a world of one's own, lost in thought, in a brown study; blank, empty, vacant; *informal* miles away. ANTONYMS attentive, alert.

▸ verb (**absent oneself**) *Rose absented herself from the occasion* STAY AWAY, be absent, withdraw, retire, take one's leave, remove oneself.

**absentminded** adjective *I tend to be most absentminded in school* FORGETFUL, distracted, preoccupied, inattentive, vague, abstracted, daydreaming, unheeding, oblivious, distrait, in a brown study; lost in thought, moony, pensive, thoughtful, brooding; *informal* scatterbrained, out of it, out to lunch, miles away, having a mind/memory like a sieve, spacey. ANTONYMS alert, observant.

**absolute** adjective **1** *absolute silence* | *an absolute disgrace* COMPLETE, total, utter, out-and-out, outright, entire, perfect, pure, decided; thorough, thoroughgoing, undivided, unqualified, unadulterated, unalloyed, unmodified, unreserved, downright, undiluted, consummate, unmitigated, sheer, arrant, rank, dyed-in-the-wool. ANTONYMS partial, qualified.

**2** *the absolute truth* DEFINITE, certain, positive, unconditional, categorical, unquestionable, incontrovertible, undoubted, unequivocal, decisive, conclusive, confirmed, infallible. ANTONYMS partial, qualified.

**3** *absolute power* UNLIMITED, unrestricted, unrestrained, unbounded, boundless, infinite, ultimate, total, supreme, unconditional. ANTONYMS limited, conditional.

**4** *an absolute monarch* AUTOCRATIC, despotic, dictatorial, tyrannical, tyrannous, absolutist, authoritarian, arbitrary, autonomous, sovereign, autarchic, autarchical, omnipotent. ANTONYM constitutional.

**5** *absolute moral standards* UNIVERSAL, fixed, independent, nonrelative, nonvariable, absolutist. ANTONYMS relative, flexible.

**absolutely** adverb *you're absolutely right* COMPLETELY, totally, utterly, perfectly, entirely, wholly, fully, quite, thoroughly, unreservedly; definitely, certainly, positively, unconditionally, categorically, unquestionably, undoubtedly, without (a) doubt, without question, surely, unequivocally; exactly, precisely, decisively, conclusively, manifestly, in every way, in every respect, one hundred percent, every inch, to the hilt; *informal* dead. ANTONYMS partially, in no way.

▸ exclamation *informal* *"Have I made myself clear?" "Absolutely!"* YES, indeed, of course, definitely, certainly, quite, without (a) doubt, without question, unquestionably; affirmative, by all means. ANTONYM by no means.

**absolution** noun *Christianity* *Father, I am a sinful man in need of absolution* FORGIVENESS, pardon, exoneration, remission, dispensation, indulgence, clemency, mercy; discharge, acquittal; freedom, deliverance, release; vindication; *formal* exculpation; *archaic* shrift. ANTONYMS punishment, condemnation.

**absolve** verb **1** *this fact does not absolve you from responsibility* EXONERATE, discharge, acquit, vindicate; release, relieve, liberate, free, deliver, clear, exempt, let off; *formal* exculpate. ANTONYMS blame, condemn.

**2** *Christianity* *I* ***absolve*** *you* ***of*** *your sins* FORGIVE, pardon. ANTONYMS punish, condemn.

THE RIGHT WORD **absolve, acquit, exempt, exonerate, forgive, pardon, vindicate**

To varying degrees, all of these words mean to free from guilt or blame, and some are most frequently heard in a legal or political context. **Absolve** is the most general term, meaning to set free or release—not only from guilt or blame, but from a duty or obligation (*absolved from her promise to serve on the commit-*

*tee*) or from the penalties for their violation. **Pardon** is usually associated with the actions of a government or military official (*President Gerald Ford pardoned Richard Nixon following his resignation in the wake of the Watergate scandal*) and specifically refers to a release from prosecution or punishment. It is usually a legal official who decides to **acquit** someone—that is, release someone from a specific and formal accusation of wrongdoing (*the court acquitted the accused due to lack of evidence*). **Exonerate** suggests relief (its origin suggests the lifting of a burden), often in a moral sense, from a definite charge so that not even the suspicion of wrongdoing remains (*completely exonerated from the accusation of cheating*). A person who is **vindicated** is also off the hook, usually due to the examination of evidence (*she vindicated herself by producing the missing documents*). **Exempt** has less to do with guilt and punishment and more to do with duty and obligation (*exempt from paying taxes*). To **forgive**, however, is the most magnanimous act of all: It implies not only giving up on the idea that an offense should be punished, but also relinquishing any feelings of resentment or vengefulness (*"To err is human; to forgive divine"*).

---

**absorb** verb **1** *a spongelike material that absorbs water* SOAK UP, suck up, draw up/in, take up/in, blot up, mop up, sop up. ANTONYM exude.

**2** *she absorbed the information in silence* ASSIMILATE, digest, take in.

**3** *the company was absorbed into the new concern* INCORPORATE, assimilate, integrate, take, appropriate, subsume, include, co-opt, swallow up.

**4** *these roles absorb most of his time and energy* USE (UP), consume, take (up), occupy.

**5** *she was totally* ***absorbed in*** *her book* ENGROSS IN, captivate by, occupy with, preoccupy with, engage in, rivet by, grip by, hold by, interest in, intrigue by/with, immerse in, involve in, enthrall by, spellbind by, fascinate by/with.

**absorbent** adjective *absorbent towels* POROUS, spongy, spongelike, permeable, pervious, absorptive; *technical* spongiform. ANTONYM waterproof.

**absorbing** adjective *an absorbing spy novel* FASCINATING, interesting, captivating, gripping, engrossing, compelling, compulsive, enthralling, riveting, spellbinding, consuming, intriguing, thrilling, exciting; *informal* unputdownable. ANTONYMS boring, uninteresting.

**absorption** noun **1** *the absorption of water* SOAKING UP, sucking up; *technical* osmosis.

**2** *by 1543, Scottish fears of absorption by England were allayed* INCORPORATION, assimilation, integration, appropriation, inclusion.

**3** *her total* ***absorption in*** *the music* INVOLVEMENT IN, immersion in, raptness in, engrossment in, occupation with, preoccupation with, engagement in, captivation with, fascination with, enthrallment with.

**abstain** verb **1** *Benjamin* ***abstained from*** *wine* REFRAIN FROM, desist from, hold back from, forbear; give up, renounce, avoid, shun, eschew, forgo, go without, do without; refuse, decline; *informal* cut out; *formal* abjure. ANTONYM indulge in.

**2** *pregnant women are encouraged to abstain* NOT DRINK, be teetotal, take the pledge; *informal* be on the wagon. ANTONYM drink.

**3** *262 voted against, 38 abstained* NOT VOTE, decline to vote. ANTONYM vote.

**abstemious** adjective *the monks here have willingly chosen this abstemious life* SELF-DENYING, temperate, abstinent, moderate, self-disciplined, restrained, self-restrained, sober, austere, ascetic, puritanical, spartan, hair-shirt. ANTONYM self-indulgent.

**abstinence** noun **1** *AA endorses a path of abstinence* TEETOTALISM, temperance, sobriety, abstemiousness, abstention; *rare* nephalism.

**2** *of course abstinence is the most effective form of birth control, but is it the most realistic?* CELIBACY, chastity, virginity, self-restraint, self-denial. ANTONYM promiscuity.

**3** *three days of* ***abstinence from*** *solid food* REFRAINING FROM, desisting from, holding back from, withholding; RENUNCIATION OF, refusal of, declining, avoidance of, eschewal of, abjuration of; forgoing, shunning, going without, doing without. ANTONYM indulgence.

THE RIGHT WORD **abstinence, abnegation, abstemiousness, continence, forbearance, moderation, temperance**

---

**Abstinence** implies voluntary self-denial and is usually associated with the non-indulgence of an appetite (*total abstinence from cigarettes and alcohol*). **Abstemiousness** is the quality or habit of being abstinent; an abstemious person would be one who is moderate when it comes to eating and drinking. **Continence**, **temperance**, and **moderation** all imply various forms of self-restraint or self-denial: *moderation* is the avoidance of extremes or excesses (*he drank in moderation*); *temperance* is habitual moderation, or even total abstinence, particularly with regard to alcohol (*the nineteenth-century temperance movement*); and *continence* (in this regard) refers to self-restraint with regard to sexual activity. **Forbearance** is self-control, the patient endurance that characterizes deliberately holding back from action or response. **Abnegation** is the rejection or renunciation of something that is generally held in high esteem (*abnegation of the Christian Church*), although it can also mean to refuse or deny oneself a particular right, claim, or convenience (*abnegation of worldly goods*).

---

**abstract** adjective **1** *abstract concepts* THEORETICAL, conceptual, notional, intellectual, metaphysical, ideal, philosophical, academic; *rare* ideational. ANTONYMS actual, concrete.

**2** *abstract art* NONREPRESENTATIONAL, nonpictorial. ANTONYM representational.

▸ verb **1** *we'll be abstracting material for an online database* SUMMARIZE, précis, abridge, condense, compress, shorten, cut down, abbreviate, synopsize; *rare* epitomize.

**2** *he abstracted the art of tragedy from its context* EXTRACT, isolate, separate, detach.

▸ noun *an abstract of her speech* SUMMARY, synopsis, précis, résumé, outline, abridgment, digest, summation; wrap-up.

**abstracted** adjective *I apologize for being so abstracted when you were talking* ABSENTMINDED, distracted, preoccupied, in a world of one's own, with one's head in the clouds, daydreaming, dreamy, inattentive, thoughtful, pensive, lost in thought, deep in thought, immersed in thought, in a brown study, musing, brooding, absent, oblivious, moony, distrait; *informal* miles away, out to lunch. ANTONYM attentive.

**abstraction** noun **1** *philosophical abstractions* CONCEPT, idea, notion, thought, theory, hypothesis.

**2** *she sensed his momentary abstraction* ABSENTMINDEDNESS, distraction, preoccupation, dreaminess, inattentiveness, inattention, woolgathering; thoughtfulness, pensiveness.

**3** *the abstraction of metal from ore* EXTRACTION, removal, separation.

**abstruse** adjective *her abstruse arguments were hard to follow* OBSCURE, arcane, esoteric, little known, recherché, rarefied, recondite, difficult, hard, puzzling, perplexing, cryptic, enigmatic, Delphic, complex, complicated, involved, over/above one's head, incomprehensible, unfathomable, impenetrable, mysterious. See note at OBSCURE.

**absurd** adjective *what an absurd idea!* PREPOSTEROUS, ridiculous, ludicrous, farcical, laughable, risible, idiotic, stupid, foolish, silly, inane, imbecilic, insane, harebrained, cockamamie; unreasonable, irrational, illogical, nonsensical, incongruous, pointless, senseless; *informal* crazy, daft. ANTONYMS reasonable, sensible.

THE RIGHT WORD **absurd, foolish, ludicrous, preposterous, ridiculous, unreasonable**

We call something **absurd** when it is utterly inconsistent with what common sense or experience tells us (*she found herself in the absurd position of having to defend the intelligence of a cockroach*). **Ludicrous** applies to whatever is so incongruous that it provokes laughter or scorn (*a ludicrous suggestion that he might escape unnoticed if he dressed up as a woman*), and **ridiculous** implies that ridicule or mockery is the only appropriate response (*she tried to look younger, but succeeded only in making herself look ridiculous*). **Foolish** behavior shows a lack of intelligence or good judgment (*it was foolish to keep that much money under a mattress*), while **unreasonable** behavior implies that the person has intentionally acted contrary to good sense (*his response was totally unreasonable in view of the fact that he'd asked for their honest opinion*). **Preposterous** should be reserved for those acts or situations that are glaringly absurd or ludicrous. For example, it might be *unreasonable* to judge an entire nation on the basis of one tourist's experience and *foolish* to turn down an opportunity to visit that country on those grounds alone, but it would be *preposterous* to suggest that everyone who comes to the United States will be robbed at gunpoint.

**absurdity** noun *Milosevic spurned the evidence linking him to countless atrocities, calling the charges a supreme absurdity* PREPOSTEROUSNESS, ridiculousness, ludicrousness, incongruity, inappropriateness, risibility, idiocy, stupidity, foolishness, folly, silliness, inanity, insanity; unreasonableness, irrationality, illogicality, pointlessness, senselessness; *informal* craziness.

**abundance** noun *the abundance of donated funds was completely unexpected* PROFUSION, plentifulness, profuseness, copiousness, amplitude, lavishness, bountifulness, bounty; host, cornucopia, riot; plenty, quantities, scores, multitude; *informal* millions, sea, ocean(s), wealth, lot(s), heap(s), mass(es), stack(s), pile(s), load(s), bags, mountain(s), ton(s), slew, scads, oodles, gobs; *formal* plenitude. ANTONYMS lack, scarcity.

**abundant** adjective *an abundant supply of food* PLENTIFUL, copious, ample, profuse, rich, lavish, abounding, liberal, generous, bountiful, large, huge, great, bumper, overflowing, prolific, teeming; in plenty, in abundance; *informal* galore; *literary* plenteous, bounteous. See note at PREVALENT. ANTONYMS scarce, sparse.

**abuse** verb **1** *the judge abused his power* MISUSE, misapply, misemploy; exploit, take advantage of.

**2** *he was accused of abusing children* MISTREAT, maltreat, ill-treat, treat badly; molest, interfere with, indecently assault, sexually abuse, sexually assault; injure, hurt, harm, damage. ANTONYMS look after, nurture.

**3** *the referee was abused by players from both teams* INSULT, be rude to, swear at, curse, call someone names, taunt, badmouth, dis, shout at, revile, inveigh against, bawl out, vilify, slander, cast aspersions on. ANTONYMS compliment, flatter.

▸ noun **1** *the abuse of power* MISUSE, misapplication, misemployment; exploitation.

**2** *the abuse of children* MISTREATMENT, maltreatment, ill-treatment; molestation, interference, indecent assault, sexual abuse, sexual assault; injury, hurt, harm, damage. ANTONYMS care, nurturing.

**3** *the scheme is open to administrative abuse* CORRUPTION, injustice, wrongdoing, wrong, misconduct, misdeed(s), offense(s), crime(s), sin(s).

**4** *torrents of abuse* INSULTS, curses, jibes, expletives, swear words; swearing, cursing, name-calling; invective, vilification, vituperation, slander; *informal* trash talk; *archaic* contumely. ANTONYMS compliments, flattery.

**5** *alcohol abuse* ADDICTION, dependency, overuse, misuse, problems.

**abusive** adjective *such abusive language will not be tolerated in this workplace* INSULTING, rude, vulgar, offensive, disparaging, belittling, derogatory, opprobrious, disrespectful, denigratory, uncomplimentary, censorious, pejorative, vituperative; defamatory, slanderous, libelous, scurrilous, blasphemous; *informal* bitchy; *archaic* contumelious.

**abut** verb *two rows of forsythia abut one another where the driveway meets the sidewalk* ADJOIN, be adjacent to, butt against, border, neighbor, join, touch, meet, reach, be contiguous with.

**abysmal** adjective *informal some of the teaching was abysmal* VERY BAD, dreadful, awful, terrible, frightful, atrocious, disgraceful, deplorable, shameful, hopeless, lamentable; *informal* rotten, appalling, crummy, pathetic, pitiful, woeful, useless, lousy, dire, the pits.

**abyss** noun *a recurring nightmare in which he falls into an abyss* CHASM, gorge, ravine, canyon, fissure, rift, crevasse, hole, gulf, pit, cavity, void, bottomless pit.

**academic** adjective **1** *an academic institution* EDUCATIONAL, scholastic, instructional, pedagogical.

**2** *his academic turn of mind* SCHOLARLY, studious, literary, well-read, intellectual, clever, erudite, learned, educated, cultured, bookish, highbrow, pedantic, donnish, cerebral; *informal* brainy, inkhorn; *dated* lettered.

**3** *the debate has been largely academic* THEORETICAL, conceptual, notional, philosophical, hypothetical, speculative, conjectural, suppositional; impractical, unrealistic, ivory-tower.

▸ noun *a group of Russian academics* SCHOLAR, lecturer, teacher, tutor, professor, fellow, man/woman of letters, don, bluestocking; *informal* egghead, bookworm; *formal* pedagogue.

**accede** verb *formal* **1** *he* ***acceded to*** *the government's demands* AGREE TO, consent to, accept, assent to, acquiesce in, comply with, go along with, concur with, surrender to, yield to, give in to, give way to, defer to.

**2** *Elizabeth I* ***acceded to*** *the throne in 1558* SUCCEED TO, come to, assume, inherit, take.

**3** *Albania* ***acceded to*** *the IMF in 1990* JOIN, become a member of, sign on to, sign up for.

**accelerate** verb **1** *the car accelerated down the hill* SPEED UP, go faster, gain momentum, increase speed, pick up speed, gather speed, put on a spurt. ANTONYMS decelerate, slow down.

**2** *inflation started to accelerate* INCREASE, rise, go up, leap up, surge, escalate, spiral. ANTONYMS slow down, drop.

**3** *the university accelerated the planning process* HASTEN, expedite, precipitate, speed up, quicken, make faster, step up, advance, further, forward, promote, give a boost to, stimulate, spur on; *informal* crank up, fast-track. ANTONYMS slow down, delay.

**acceleration** noun **1** *the acceleration of the industrial process* HASTENING, precipitation, speeding up, quickening, stepping up, advancement, furtherance, boost, stimulation, spur.

**2** *an acceleration in the divorce rate* INCREASE, rise, leap, surge, escalation.

**accent** noun **1** *a Bronx accent* PRONUNCIATION, intonation, enunciation, articulation, inflection, tone, modulation, cadence, timbre, manner of speaking, delivery; brogue, burr, drawl, twang.

**2** *the accent is on the first syllable* STRESS, emphasis, accentuation, force, prominence; beat; *technical* ictus.

**3** *the accent is on comfort* EMPHASIS, stress, priority; importance, prominence.

**4** *an acute accent* MARK, diacritic, diacritical mark.

▸ verb *fabrics that accent the background colors in the room* FOCUS ATTENTION ON, draw attention to, point up, underline, underscore, accentuate, highlight, spotlight, foreground, feature, play up, bring to the fore, heighten, stress, emphasize.

**accentuate** verb *a haircut that accentuates your cheekbones* FOCUS ATTENTION ON, draw attention to, point up, underline, underscore, accent, highlight, spotlight, foreground, feature, play up, bring to the fore, heighten, stress, emphasize.

**accept** verb **1** *she accepted a pen as a present* RECEIVE, take, get, gain, obtain, acquire. ANTONYMS refuse, reject.

**2** *he accepted the job immediately* TAKE ON, undertake, assume, take responsibility for. ANTONYMS turn down, refuse.

**3** *she accepted an invitation to lunch* SAY YES TO, agree to. ANTONYMS turn down, refuse.

**4** *she was accepted as one of the family* WELCOME, greet, receive, receive favorably, embrace, adopt. ANTONYM reject.

**5** *he accepted Ellen's explanation* BELIEVE, regard as true, give credence to, credit, trust; *informal* buy, swallow. ANTONYMS reject, doubt.

**6** *we have agreed to accept his decision* GO ALONG WITH, agree to, consent to, acquiesce in, concur with, assent to, acknowledge, comply with, abide by, follow, adhere to, act in accordance with, defer to, yield to, surrender to, bow to, give in to, submit to, respect; *formal* accede to. ANTONYMS defy, go against.

**7** *she will just have to accept the consequences* TOLERATE, endure, put up with, bear, take, submit to, stomach, swallow; reconcile oneself to, resign oneself to, get used to, adjust to, learn to live with, make the best of; face up to.

**acceptable** adjective **1** *an acceptable standard of living* SATISFACTORY, adequate, reasonable, quite good, fair, decent, good enough, sufficient, sufficiently good, fine, not bad, all right, average, tolerable, passable, middling, moderate; *informal* OK, jake, so-so, 'comme ci, comme ça,' fair-to-middling.

**2** *the risk had seemed acceptable at the time* BEARABLE, tolerable, allowable, admissible, sustainable, justifiable, defensible.

**acceptance** noun **1** *the acceptance of an award* RECEIPT, receiving, taking, obtaining.

**2** *the acceptance of responsibility* UNDERTAKING, assumption.

**3** *acceptances to an invitation* YES, affirmative reply, confirmation.

**4** *her acceptance into the group* WELCOME, favorable reception, adoption.

**5** *his* ***acceptance of*** *Thom's promise* BELIEF IN, trust in, faith in, confidence in, credence in, giving of credence to.

**6** *their* ***acceptance of*** *the ruling* COMPLIANCE WITH, acquiescence in, agreement with, consent to, concurrence with, assent to, acknowledgment of, adherence to, deference to, surrender to, submission to, respect for, adoption of, buy-in to.

**7** *the acceptance of pain* TOLERATION, endurance, forbearance, sufferance.

**accepted** adjective *newspaper ads from the 1700s show that, even in New England, the brokering of slaves was an accepted practice* RECOGNIZED, acknowledged, established, traditional, orthodox, sanctioned; usual, customary, habitual, common, current, normal, general, prevailing, accustomed, familiar, wonted, popular, expected, routine, standard, stock.

**access** noun **1** *the building has a side access* ENTRANCE, entry, way in, means of entry; approach, means of approach.

**2** *they were denied access to the stadium* ADMISSION, admittance, entry, entrée, ingress, right of entry.

**3** *students have **access to** a photocopier* (THE) USE OF, permission to use/visit.

▸ verb **1** *the program is used to access data* RETRIEVE, gain access to, obtain; read.

**2** *you access the building from the south side* ENTER, approach, gain entry to.

**USAGE NOTE access**

Although the verb **access** is standard and common in computing and related terminology (*only subscribers may access the full text online*), the word is primarily a noun. Outside computing contexts, its use as a verb in the sense of 'approach or enter a place' is often regarded as nonstandard (*you must use a key card to access the lounge*). Even weaker is its use in an abstract sense ( *access the American dream*). It is usually clear enough to say 'enter' or 'gain access to.'

**accessible** adjective **1** *the village is accessible only on foot* | *an easily accessible reference tool* REACHABLE, attainable, approachable; obtainable, available; *informal* get-at-able.

**2** *his accessible style of writing* UNDERSTANDABLE, comprehensible, easy to understand, intelligible; *formal* exoteric.

**3** *Professor Cooper is very accessible* APPROACHABLE, friendly, agreeable, obliging, congenial, affable, cordial, welcoming, easygoing, pleasant.

**accession** noun **1** *the Queen's **accession to** the throne* SUCCESSION TO, assumption of, inheritance of.

**2** *accession to the Treaty of Rome was effected in 1971* ASSENT TO, consent to, agreement to; acceptance of, acquiescence in, compliance with, concurrence with.

**3** *recent museum accessions* ADDITION, acquisition, new item, gift, purchase.

**accessory** noun **1** *camera accessories such as tripods* ATTACHMENT, extra, addition, add-on, adjunct, appendage, appurtenance, fitment, supplement.

**2** *fashion accessories* ADORNMENT, embellishment, ornament, ornamentation, decoration; frills, trimmings.

**3** *two days after the murder, she was charged as an accessory* ACCOMPLICE, partner in crime, associate, collaborator, abettor, fellow conspirator, co-conspirator; henchman.

▸ adjective *an accessory gearbox* ADDITIONAL, extra, supplementary, supplemental, auxiliary, ancillary, secondary, subsidiary, reserve, add-on.

**accident** noun **1** *an accident at work* MISHAP, misadventure, unfortunate incident, mischance, misfortune, disaster, tragedy, catastrophe, calamity; *technical* casualty.

**2** *she was injured in a highway accident* CRASH, collision, smash, bump, car crash; wreck; *informal* smash-up, pileup, fender bender.

**3** *it is no accident that there is a similarity between them* (MERE) CHANCE, coincidence, twist of fate, freak; fluke, bit of luck, serendipity; fate, fortuity, fortune, providence, happenstance.

**accidental** adjective **1** *an accidental meeting* FORTUITOUS, chance, adventitious, fluky, coincidental, casual, serendipitous, random; unexpected, unforeseen, unanticipated, unlooked-for, unintentional, unintended, inadvertent, unplanned, unpremeditated, unthinking, unwitting. ANTONYM intentional.

**2** *the location is accidental and contributes nothing to the poem* INCIDENTAL, unimportant, by the way, by the by, supplementary, subsidiary, subordinate, secondary, accessory, peripheral, tangential, extraneous, extrinsic, irrelevant, nonessential, inessential. ANTONYM deliberate.

**THE RIGHT WORD accidental, adventitious, casual, contingent, fortuitous, incidental**

Things don't always go as planned, but there are many ways to describe the role that chance plays. **Accidental** applies to events that occur entirely by chance (*an accidental encounter with the candidate outside the men's room*); but it is so strongly influenced by the noun "accident" that it carries connotations of undesirable or possibly disastrous results (*an accidental miscalculation of the distance he had to jump*). A **casual** act or event is one that is random or unpremeditated (*a casual conversation with her son's teacher in the grocery store*), in which the role that chance plays is not always clear. Something that is **incidental** may or may not involve chance; it typically refers to what is secondary or nonessential (*incidental expenses in the budget*) or what occurs without design or regularity (*incidental lighting throughout the garden*). **Adventitious** also implies the lack of an essential relationship, referring to something that is a mere random occurrence (*adventitious circumstances that led to victory*). In contrast, **contingent** points to something that is entirely dependent on an uncertain event for its existence or occurrence (*travel plans that are contingent upon the weather*). **Fortuitous** refers to chance events of a fortunate nature; it is about as far as one can get from *accidental* (*a fortuitous meeting with the candidate outside the men's room just before the press conference*).

**acclaim** verb *the booklet has been widely acclaimed by teachers* PRAISE, applaud, cheer, commend, approve, welcome, pay tribute to, speak highly of, eulogize, compliment, celebrate, sing the praises of, rave about, heap praise on/upon, wax lyrical about, lionize, exalt, admire, hail, extol, honor, hymn; *informal* ballyhoo; *formal* laud. See note at PRAISE. ANTONYM criticize.

▸ noun *she has won acclaim for her commitment to democracy* PRAISE, applause, cheers, ovation, tribute, accolade, acclamation, salutes, plaudits, bouquets; approval, approbation, admiration, congratulations, commendation, kudos, welcome, homage; compliment, a pat on the back. ANTONYM criticism.

**acclamation** noun *the proposal was received with considerable acclamation* PRAISE, applause, cheers, ovation, tribute, accolade, acclaim, salutes, plaudits, bouquets; approval, admiration, approbation, congratulations, commendation, homage; compliment, a pat on the back. ANTONYM criticism.

PHRASE: **by acclamation** *she won reelection by acclamation* BY ORAL VOTE, by a verbal vote, without a ballot, by nonballot; *Canadian* without opposition, as the only candidate.

**acclimatize** verb *the panda Ling Ling will acclimatize to the environment in Mexico before choosing a mate* ADJUST, acclimate, adapt, accustom, accommodate, habituate, acculturate, assimilate, attune; get used, become inured, reconcile oneself, resign oneself; familiarize oneself; get one's bearings, become seasoned, become naturalized.

**accommodate** verb **1** *refugees were accommodated in army camps* LODGE, house, put up, billet, quarter, board, take in, shelter, give someone a roof over their head; harbor.

**2** *each cottage accommodates up to six people* HOLD, take, have room for.

**3** *our staff will make every effort to accommodate you* HELP, assist, aid, oblige; meet the needs/wants of, satisfy.

**4** *she tried to* ***accommodate herself to*** *her new situation* ADJUST TO, adapt to, accustom oneself to, habituate oneself to, acclimatize (oneself) to, acclimate (oneself) to, acculturate to, get (oneself) accustomed to, get used to, come to terms with.

**5** *the bank would be glad to accommodate you with a loan* PROVIDE, supply, furnish, grant.

**accommodating** adjective *her in-laws were far more accommodating than her own parents* OBLIGING, cooperative, helpful, eager to help, adaptable, amenable, considerate, unselfish, inclusionary, generous, willing, compliant, kindly, hospitable, neighborly, kind, friendly, pleasant, agreeable.

**accommodation** noun **1** **(accommodations)** *temporary accommodations* HOUSING, lodging(s), living quarters, quarters, rooms; place to stay, billet; shelter, roof over one's head; *informal* digs, pad; *formal* abode, residence, place of residence, dwelling, dwelling place, habitation.

**2** *lifeboat accommodations for 1,178 people* SPACE, room, seating; places.

**3** *an accommodation between the two parties was reached* ARRANGEMENT, understanding, settlement, accord, deal, bargain, compromise.

**4** *their accommodations to changing economic circumstances* ADJUSTMENT, adaptation, habituation, acclimatization, acclimation, acculturation; inurement.

**accompaniment** noun **1** *a musical accompaniment* BACKING, support, background, backup, soundtrack.

**2** *the wine makes a superb accompaniment to cheese* COMPLEMENT, supplement, addition, adjunct, appendage, companion, accessory.

**accompany** verb **1** *I accompanied my brother to the audition* GO WITH, travel with, keep someone company, tag along with, hang out with; partner, escort, chaperone, attend, show, see, usher, conduct.

**2** *the illness* ***is*** *often* ***accompanied by*** *nausea* OCCUR WITH, co-occur with, coexist with, go with, go together with, go hand in hand with, appear with, be attended by.

**3** *he accompanied the choir on the piano* BACK, play with, play for, support.

**accomplice** noun *police have reason to believe that Johnson had two accomplices, possibly his wife and brother* PARTNER IN CRIME, associate, accessory, abettor, confederate, collaborator, fellow conspirator, co-conspirator; henchman; *informal* sidekick.

**accomplish** verb *the planes accomplished their mission* FULFILL, achieve, succeed in, realize, attain, manage, bring about/off, carry out/through, execute, effect, perform, do, discharge, complete, finish, consummate, conclude; *informal* pull off, nail; *formal* effectuate.

**accomplished** adjective *an accomplished bassoonist* EXPERT, skilled, skillful, masterly, successful, virtuoso, master, consummate, complete, proficient, talented, gifted, adept, adroit, deft, dexterous, able, good, competent, capable, efficient, experienced, seasoned, trained, practiced, professional, polished, ready, apt; *informal* great, mean, nifty, crack, ace, wizard; *informal* crackerjack.

**accomplishment** noun **1** *the reduction of inflation was a remarkable accomplishment* ACHIEVEMENT, act, deed, exploit, performance, attainment, effort, feat, move, coup.

**2** *a poet of considerable accomplishment* EXPERTISE, skill, skillfulness, talent, adeptness, adroitness, deftness, dexterity, ability, prowess, mastery, competence, capability, proficiency, aptitude, artistry, art; *informal* know-how.

**accord** verb **1** *the national assembly accorded him more power* GIVE, grant, present, award, vouchsafe; confer on, bestow on, vest in, invest with. ANTONYM withhold.

**2** *his views* ***accorded with*** *mine* CORRESPOND TO, agree with, match up with, concur with, be consistent with, harmonize with, be in harmony with, be compatible with, chime in with, be in tune with, correlate with, dovetail with; conform to; suit, fit, parallel, match; *informal* square with, jibe with. ANTONYMS disagree, contrast.

▸ noun **1** *a peace accord* PACT, treaty, agreement, settlement, deal, entente, concordat, protocol, contract, convention.

**2** *the two sides failed to reach accord* AGREEMENT, consensus, unanimity, harmony, unison, unity; *formal* concord.

PHRASES: **of one's own accord** *Nels offered to fix the gate of his own accord* VOLUNTARILY, of one's own free will, of one's own volition, by choice; willingly, freely, readily.

**with one accord** *the committee decided with one accord to approve the drainage plans* UNANIMOUSLY, in complete agreement, with one mind, without exception, as one, of one voice, to a man.

**accordance** noun *a ballot held **in accordance with** union rules* IN AGREEMENT WITH, in conformity with, in line with, true to, in the spirit of, observing, following, heeding.

**according** adjective **1** *she had a narrow escape, **according to** the doctors* AS STATED BY, as claimed by, on the authority of, in the opinion of.

**2** *cook the rice **according to** the instructions* AS SPECIFIED BY, as per, in accordance with, in compliance with, in agreement with.

**3** *salary will be fixed **according to** experience* IN PROPORTION TO, proportional to, commensurate with, in relation to, relative to, in line with, corresponding to.

**accordingly** adverb **1** *they appreciated the danger and acted accordingly* APPROPRIATELY, correspondingly, suitably.

**2** *accordingly, he returned home to Kingston* THEREFORE, for that reason, consequently, so, as a result, as a consequence, in consequence, hence, thus, that being the case, ergo.

**accost** verb *police accosted him in the street* CONFRONT, call to, shout to, hail, address, speak to; approach, detain, stop, waylay; *informal* buttonhole, collar, bend someone's ear.

**account** noun **1** *an account of the extraordinary events* DESCRIPTION, report, version, story, narration, narrative, statement, explanation, exposition, delineation, portrayal, tale; chronicle, history, record, log; view, impression.

**2** *the firm's quarterly accounts* FINANCIAL RECORD, ledger, balance sheet, financial statement; **(accounts)** books.

**3** *I pay the account off in full each month* BILL, invoice, tally; debt, charges; *informal* tab.

**4** *his background is of no account* IMPORTANCE, import, significance, consequence, substance, note; *formal* moment.

**5** *efforts to keep our most important accounts happy* CLIENT, customer.

▸ verb *her visit could not be accounted a success* CONSIDER, regard as, reckon, hold to be, think, look on as, view as, see as, judge, adjudge, count, deem, rate.

PHRASES: **account for 1** *they must account for the delay* EXPLAIN, answer for, give reasons for, rationalize, justify.

**2** *taxes account for much of the price of gasoline* CONSTITUTE, make up, form, compose, represent.

**on account of** *I was invited on account of my friendship with her parents* BECAUSE OF, owing to, due to, as a consequence of, thanks to, by/in virtue of, in view of.

**on no account** *on no account sign a document without reading it* NEVER, under no circumstances, not for any reason.

**accountability** noun *there must be accountability for the expenditure of every public cent* RESPONSIBILITY, liability, answerability.

**accountable** adjective **1** *the government was held accountable for the food shortage* RESPONSIBLE, liable, answerable; to blame. See note at RESPONSIBLE.

**2** *the game's popularity is barely accountable* EXPLICABLE, explainable; understandable, comprehensible.

**accredited** adjective *an accredited preschool* OFFICIAL, appointed, recognized, authorized, approved, certified, licensed.

**accrue** verb **1** *financial benefits will **accrue from** restructuring* RESULT FROM, arise from, follow from, ensue from; be caused by, attend.

**2** *interest is added to the account as it accrues* ACCUMULATE, collect, build up, mount up, grow, increase.

**accumulate** verb *he has accumulated thousands of frequent-flier miles | mother whales transfer chemicals accumulated in their tissue to their offspring during gestation* GATHER, collect, assemble; amass, stockpile, pile up, heap up, store (up), hoard, cumulate, lay in/up; increase, mass, multiply, accrue, snowball; run up; *informal* stash (away). ANTONYM dissipate

**accumulation** noun *the accumulation of illegal funds | an accumulation of debris* BUILDUP, mass, pile, heap, stack, collection, stock, store, stockpile, reserve, hoard; amassing, gathering, cumulation, accrual, accretion.

**accuracy** noun *the accuracy of their lead story is being questioned* CORRECTNESS, precision, preciseness, exactness, exactitude; factuality, literalness, fidelity, faithfulness, truth, truthfulness, veracity, closeness, authenticity, realism, verisimilitude.

**accurate** adjective **1** *accurate information | an accurate representation of the situation* CORRECT, precise, exact, right, error-free, perfect; FACTUAL, fact-based, literal, faithful, true, truthful, true to life, authentic, realistic; *informal* on the mark, bang on, on the money, on the button; *formal* veracious.

**2** *an accurate shot* WELL-AIMED, on target, unerring, deadly, lethal, sure, true, on the mark.

**accursed** adjective *dated* **1** *that accursed woman* HATEFUL, detestable, loathsome, foul, abominable, damnable, odious, obnoxious, despicable, horrible, horrid, ghastly, awful, dreadful, terrible; annoying, irritating, vile, infuriating, exasperating; *informal* damned, damn, blasted, pesky, pestilential, infernal, beastly. ANTONYM pleasant.

**2** *literary he and his line are accursed* CURSED, damned, doomed, condemned, ill-fated, ill-omened, jinxed. ANTONYM blessed.

**accusation** noun *the Rwandan bishop has denied accusations of genocide* ALLEGATION, charge, claim, assertion, imputation; indictment, arraignment, incrimination, recrimination, inculpation; suit, lawsuit, impeachment; *informal* rap.

**accuse** verb **1** *four people were **accused of** assault* CHARGE WITH, indict for, arraign for; summons for, cite for, prefer charges against for; impeach for. ANTONYMS absolve, exonerate.

**2** *the companies were **accused of** causing job losses* BLAME FOR, lay/pin the blame on for, hold responsible for, inculpate for, hold accountable for; condemn for, criticize for, denounce for; *informal* point the finger at for. ANTONYMS defend, hold blameless.

**accustom** verb *she couldn't **accustom herself to** city life* ADAPT TO, adjust to, acclimatize to, acclimate to, habituate oneself to, accommodate oneself to, acculturate to; reconcile oneself to, become reconciled to, get used to, come to terms with, learn to live with, become inured to.

**accustomed** adjective 1 *his accustomed lifestyle* CUSTOMARY, usual, normal, habitual, regular, routine, ordinary, typical, traditional, established, common, general; *literary* wonted.

2 *she's **accustomed to** hard work* USED TO, habituated to, acclimatized to, no stranger to, familiar with, acquainted with, in the habit of, experienced in. ANTONYM unfamiliar.

**ace** noun *informal a snowboarding ace* EXPERT, master, genius, virtuoso, maestro, adept, past master, doyen, champion, star; *informal* demon, hotshot, wizard, pro, whiz; *informal* maven, crackerjack. ANTONYMS amateur, beginner.

▸ adjective *an ace tennis player* EXCELLENT, first-rate, first-class, marvelous, wonderful, magnificent, outstanding, superlative, formidable, virtuoso, masterly, expert, champion, consummate, skillful, adept; great, terrific, tremendous, superb, fantastic, sensational, fabulous; *informal* fab, crack, hotshot, A1, mean, demon, awesome, magic, tip-top, top-notch; killer, blue-ribbon, blue-chip, brilliant, wicked. ANTONYM mediocre.

**acerbic** adjective *soaring melodies built around acerbic lyrics* SHARP, sarcastic, sardonic, mordant, trenchant, cutting, razor-edged, biting, piercing, stinging, searing, scathing, caustic, bitter, acrimonious, astringent, abrasive, harsh, wounding, hurtful, unkind, cruel, virulent, vitriolic, venomous, malicious, vicious; *informal* bitchy; *rare* acidulous, mordacious. ANTONYMS mild, kind.

**ache** noun 1 *a stomachache* PAIN, cramp, twinge, pang; gnawing, stabbing, stinging, smarting; soreness, tenderness, irritation, discomfort.

2 *the ache in her heart* SORROW, sadness, misery, grief, anguish, suffering, pain, agony, torture, hurt.

▸ verb 1 *my legs were aching* HURT, be sore, be painful, be in pain, pain, throb, pound, twinge; smart, burn.

2 *her heart ached for poor Philippa* GRIEVE, sorrow, be in distress, be miserable, be in anguish, bleed.

3 *I **ached for** her affection* LONG FOR, yearn for, hunger for, thirst for, hanker for, pine for, itch for; crave, desire, covet.

**achieve** verb *the legal resources are inadequate to achieve our public health objectives* ATTAIN, reach, arrive at; realize, bring off/about, pull off, accomplish, carry off/out/through, fulfill, execute, perform, engineer, conclude, complete, finish, consummate; earn, win, gain, acquire, obtain, score, come by, get, secure, clinch, net; *informal* wrap up, wangle, swing; *formal* effectuate.

**achievement** noun 1 *the achievement of a high rate of economic growth* ATTAINMENT, realization, accomplishment, fulfillment, implementation, execution, performance; conclusion, completion, close, consummation.

2 *they felt justifiably proud of their achievement* ACCOMPLISHMENT, attainment, feat, performance, undertaking, act, action, deed, effort, exploit, success, triumph; work, handiwork.

**acid** adjective 1 *a slightly acid flavor* ACIDIC, SOUR, tart, bitter, sharp, acrid, pungent, acerbic, vinegary, acetic, acetous. ANTONYM sweet.

2 *acid remarks* ACERBIC, sarcastic, sharp, sardonic, scathing, cutting, razor-edged, biting, stinging, caustic, trenchant, mordant, bitter, acrimonious, astringent, harsh, abrasive, wounding, hurtful, unkind, vitriolic, venomous, waspish, spiteful, malicious; *informal* bitchy, catty; snarky. ANTONYM pleasant.

**acknowledge** verb 1 *the government acknowledged the need to begin talks* ADMIT, accept, grant, allow, concede, accede to, confess, own, recognize. ANTONYMS reject, deny.

2 *he did not acknowledge Colin, but hurried past* GREET, salute, address; nod to, wave to, raise one's hat to, say hello to. ANTONYM ignore.

3 *Douglas was glad to acknowledge her help* EXPRESS GRATITUDE FOR, show appreciation for, thank someone for.

4 *nobody acknowledged my letters* ANSWER, reply to, respond to. ANTONYM overlook.

**acknowledged** adjective *the acknowledged leader of the Turkish community* RECOGNIZED, accepted, approved, accredited, confirmed, declared, confessed, avowed.

**acknowledgment** noun 1 *acknowledgment of the need to take new initiatives* ACCEPTANCE, recognition, admission, concession, confession.

2 *a smile of acknowledgment* GREETING, welcome, salutation.

3 *she left without a word of acknowledgment* THANKS, gratitude, appreciation, recognition.

4 *I sent off the form, but there was no acknowledgment* ANSWER, reply, response.

**acme** noun *the acme of her career* PEAK, pinnacle, zenith, height, high point, crown, crest, summit, top, apex, apogee; climax, culmination. ANTONYM nadir.

**acolyte** noun *surrounded by eager acolytes* ASSISTANT, helper, attendant, aide, minion, underling, lackey, henchman; follower, disciple, supporter, votary; *informal* sidekick, groupie, hanger-on.

**acquaint** verb *this exercise will **acquaint** you **with** the food groups* FAMILIARIZE WITH, make familiar with, make aware of, inform of, advise of, apprise of, let know, get up to date on; brief on, prime on; *informal* fill in on, clue in on.

**acquaintance** noun 1 *a business acquaintance | friends and acquaintances* CONTACT, associate, ally, connection, colleague.

2 *my acquaintance with George* ASSOCIATION, relationship, contact; fellowship, companionship.

3 *the students had little **acquaintance with** the language* FAMILIARITY WITH, knowledge of, experience with/of, awareness of, understanding of, comprehension of, grasp of.

**acquiesce** verb *Bush wants to ensure that Beijing will* ***acquiesce in*** *a possible American war against Iraq* ACCEPT, consent to, agree to, allow, concede, assent to, concur with, give the nod to; comply with, cooperate with, give in to, bow to, yield to, submit to; *informal* go along with.

**acquiescence** noun *militia excesses were conducted with the acquiescence of the Indonesian police* CONSENT, agreement, acceptance, concurrence, assent, leave; compliance, concession, cooperation, buy-in; submission.

**acquiescent** adjective *the apolitical and acquiescent masses* COMPLIANT, complying, consenting, cooperative, willing, obliging, agreeable, amenable, tractable, persuadable, pliant, flexible, unprotesting; SUBMISSIVE, servile, subservient, obsequious, self-effacing, unassertive, yielding, biddable, docile, deferential; *rare* obeisant, longanimous.

**acquire** verb *the library's goal is to acquire eight new or upgraded computers in this fiscal year* OBTAIN, come by, get, receive, gain, earn, win, come into, be given; buy, purchase, procure, possess oneself of, secure, pick up, adopt; *informal* get one's hands on, get hold of, land, bag, cop, score. See note at GET. ANTONYMS lose, get rid of.

**acquisition** noun **1** *the boat is a new acquisition* PURCHASE, buy, gain, accession, addition, investment, possession.

**2** *the acquisition of funds* OBTAINING, acquirement, gaining, earning, winning, procurement, collection.

**acquisitive** adjective *his acquisitive wife has left him for a Denver architect* GREEDY, covetous, avaricious, possessive, grasping, grabbing, predatory, avid, rapacious, mercenary, materialistic; *informal* money-grubbing. See note at GREEDY.

**acquisitiveness** noun *their three children seem to possess none of the acquisitiveness so typical of Hollywood brats* GREED, greediness, covetousness, cupidity, possessiveness, avarice, avidity, rapaciousness, rapacity, materialism; *informal* affluenza.

**acquit** verb **1** *the jury acquitted her* CLEAR, exonerate, find innocent, absolve; discharge, release, free, set free; *informal* let off (the hook); *formal* exculpate. See note at ABSOLVE. ANTONYM convict.

**2** *the boys* ***acquitted themselves*** *well* BEHAVE (ONESELF), conduct oneself, perform, act; *formal* comport oneself.

**acquittal** noun *the acquittal of the defendants* CLEARING, exoneration, absolution; discharge, release, freeing; *formal* exculpation. ANTONYM conviction.

**acrid** adjective *the fruit's acrid taste was a bad surprise* PUNGENT, bitter, sharp, sour, tart, caustic, harsh, irritating, acid, acidic, vinegary, acetic, acetous; stinging, burning.

**acrimonious** adjective *a heated and acrimonious discussion* BITTER, angry, rancorous, caustic, acerbic, scathing, sarcastic, acid, harsh, sharp, cutting; virulent, spiteful, vicious, vitriolic, hostile, venomous, nasty, bad-tempered, ill-natured, mean, malign, malicious, malignant, waspish; *informal* bitchy, catty.

**acrimony** noun *the meeting ended with acrimony on both sides* BITTERNESS, anger, rancor, resentment, ill feeling, ill will, bad blood, animosity, hostility, enmity, antagonism, waspishness, spleen, malice, spite, spitefulness, peevishness, venom. ANTONYM goodwill.

**acrobatics** plural noun **1** *staggering feats of acrobatics* GYMNASTICS, tumbling; agility; *rare* funambulism.

**2** *the acrobatics required to negotiate an international contract* MENTAL AGILITY, skill, quick thinking, fancy footwork, alertness, inventiveness.

**act** verb **1** *the government must act to remedy the situation* TAKE ACTION, take steps, take measures, move, react.

**2** *he was* ***acting on*** *the orders of the party leader* FOLLOW, act in accordance with, obey, heed, comply with; fulfill, meet, discharge.

**3** *a real estate agent* ***acting for*** *a prospective buyer* REPRESENT, act on behalf of; stand in for, fill in for, deputize for, take the place of.

**4** *Alison began to act oddly* BEHAVE, conduct oneself, react; *formal* comport oneself.

**5** *the scents act as a powerful aphrodisiac* OPERATE, work, function, serve.

**6** *the drug* ***acted*** *directly* ***on*** *the blood vessels* AFFECT, have an effect on, work on; have an impact on, impact on, influence.

**7** *he acted in a highly successful film* PERFORM, play a part, play-act, take part, appear; *informal* tread the boards, ham it up.

**8** *we laughed, but most of us were just acting* PRETEND, play-act, put it on, fake it, feign it, dissemble, dissimulate.

▸ noun **1** *acts of kindness* | *a criminal act* DEED, action, feat, exploit, move, gesture, performance, undertaking, stunt, operation; achievement, accomplishment.

**2** *the act raised the tax on tobacco* LAW, decree, statute, bill, act of Congress, enactment, resolution, edict, dictum, ruling, measure; ordinance.

**3** *the first act of the play* DIVISION, section, subsection, part, segment.

**4** *a music hall act* PERFORMANCE, routine, number, sketch, skit, shtick, turn.

**5** *it was all just an act* PRETENSE, show, front, facade, masquerade, charade, posture, pose, affectation, sham, fake; *informal* put-on.

PHRASE: **act up** *informal* **1** *all children act up from time to time* MISBEHAVE, behave badly, be up to mischief, become unruly.

**2** *the engine was acting up* MALFUNCTION, go wrong, be defective, be faulty; *informal* be on the blink, be on the fritz.

**acting** noun *the theory and practice of acting* DRAMA, the theater, the stage, the performing arts, thespianism, dramatics, dramaturgy, stagecraft, theatricals; *informal* treading the boards.

▸ adjective *the bank's acting governor* TEMPORARY, interim, caretaker, pro tem, pro tempore, provisional, stopgap; deputy, stand-in, fill-in; *informal* pinch-hitting. ANTONYM permanent.

**action** noun 1 *there can be no excuse for their actions* DEED, act, move, undertaking, exploit, maneuver, endeavor, effort, exertion; behavior, conduct, activity.

2 *the need for local community action* MEASURES, steps, activity, movement, work, operation.

3 *a man of action* ENERGY, vitality, vigor, forcefulness, drive, initiative, spirit, liveliness, vim, pep; activity; *informal* get-up-and-go.

4 *the action of hormones on the pancreas* EFFECT, influence, working; power.

5 *he missed all the action while he was away* EXCITEMENT, activity, happenings, events, incidents; *informal* goings-on.

6 *twenty-nine men died in the action* FIGHTING, hostilities, battle, conflict, combat, warfare; engagement, clash, encounter, skirmish.

7 *a civil action for damages* LAWSUIT, legal action, suit, case, prosecution, litigation, proceedings.

**activate** verb *the alarm system can be activated remotely* OPERATE, switch on, turn on, start (up), set going, trigger (off), set in motion, initiate, actuate, energize; trip.

**active** adjective 1 *despite her illness she remained active* ENERGETIC, lively, sprightly, spry, mobile, vigorous, vital, dynamic, sporty; busy, occupied; *informal* on the go. ANTONYM listless.

2 *an active member of the union* HARD-WORKING, busy, industrious, diligent, tireless, contributing, effective, enterprising, involved, enthusiastic, keen, committed, devoted, zealous. ANTONYMS passive, indifferent.

3 *the mill was active until 1960* OPERATIVE, working, functioning, functional, operating, operational, in action, in operation, running; live; *informal* up and running. ANTONYM inoperative.

**activity** noun 1 *there was a lot of activity in the area* BUSTLE, hustle and bustle, busyness, action, liveliness, movement, life, stir, flurry; happenings, occurrences, proceedings, events, incidents; *informal* toing and froing, comings and goings.

2 *a wide range of activities* PURSUIT, occupation, interest, hobby, pastime, recreation, diversion; venture, undertaking, enterprise, project, scheme, business, entertainment; act, action, deed, exploit.

**actual** adjective *be honest—how much of this wild story is actual?* REAL, true, genuine, authentic, verified, attested, confirmed, definite, hard, plain, veritable; existing, existent, manifest, substantial, factual, de facto, bona fide; *informal* honest-to-goodness, real live. See note at GENUINE. ANTONYM notional.

**actually** adverb *believe it or not, George actually remembered our anniversary* REALLY, in (actual) fact, in point of fact, as a matter of fact, in reality, in actuality, in truth, if truth be told, to tell the truth; literally; truly, indeed; *archaic* in sooth.

**acumen** noun *noted for her business acumen* ASTUTENESS, shrewdness, acuity, sharpness, sharp-wittedness, cleverness, smartness, brains; judgment, understanding, awareness, sense, common sense, canniness, discernment, wisdom, wit, sagacity, perspicacity, insight, perception, penetration; savvy, know-how, horse sense, smarts, street smarts.

**acute** adjective 1 *acute food shortages* SEVERE, critical, drastic, dire, dreadful, terrible, awful, grave, bad, serious, desperate, dangerous. See note at CRUCIAL. ANTONYM negligible.

2 *acute stomach pains* SHARP, severe, stabbing, piercing, excruciating, agonizing, racking, keen, shooting, searing. See note at KEEN. ANTONYMS mild, dull.

3 *an acute mind* ASTUTE, shrewd, sharp, sharp-witted, razor-sharp, rapierlike, quick, quick-witted, agile, nimble, clever, intelligent, brilliant, keen, smart, canny, discerning, perceptive, perspicacious, penetrating, insightful, incisive, piercing, discriminating, sagacious, wise, judicious; *informal* on the ball, quick off the mark, quick on the uptake, streetwise, savvy. ANTONYM slow-witted.

4 *an acute sense of smell* KEEN, sharp, good, penetrating, discerning, sensitive. ANTONYMS poor, weak.

**acutely** adverb *our trust in you has become acutely shaken* EXTREMELY, exceedingly, very, markedly, severely, intensely, deeply, profoundly, keenly, painfully, desperately, tremendously, enormously, thoroughly, heartily; *informal* awfully, terribly; *slang* majorly. ANTONYM slightly.

**adage** noun *I should have remembered the old adage 'look before you leap'* SAYING, maxim, axiom, proverb, aphorism, saw, dictum, byword, precept, motto, truism, platitude, cliché, apophthegm, commonplace.

**adamant** adjective *he begged his mother to let him try out for the football team, but she was adamant* UNSHAKABLE, immovable, inflexible, unwavering, unswerving, uncompromising, insistent, resolute, resolved, determined, firm, steadfast; stubborn, unrelenting, diehard, unyielding, unbending, rigid, obdurate, inexorable, intransigent, (dead) set.

**adapt** verb 1 *we've adapted the procedures to suit their needs* MODIFY, alter, change, adjust, readjust, convert, redesign, restyle, refashion, remodel, reshape, revamp, rework, rejig, redo, reconstruct, reorganize; customize, tailor; improve, amend, refine, tweak.

2 *he has **adapted** well **to** his new home* ADJUST TO, acclimatize oneself to, acclimate to, accommodate oneself to, attune to, conform to, habituate oneself to, become habituated to, get used to, orient oneself in, reconcile oneself to, come to terms with, get one's bearings in, find one's feet in, acculturate to, assimilate to, blend in to, fit in to.

**adaptable** adjective 1 *competent and adaptable staff* FLEXIBLE, versatile, cooperative, accommodating, amenable.

2 *an adaptable piece of furniture* VERSATILE, modifiable, convertible, alterable, adjustable, changeable; multipurpose, all-purpose.

**adaptation** noun 1 *an adaptation of a Scandinavian folk tale* ALTERATION, modification, redesign, remodeling, revamping, reworking, reconstruction, conversion.

2 *the cubs' adaptation to the zoo environment* ADJUSTMENT,

acclimatization, acclimation, accommodations, habituation, acculturation, assimilation, integration.

**add** verb 1 *the back room was added in 1971* | *add more sugar to the mix* ATTACH, build on, join, append, affix, connect, annex; include, incorporate, throw in, toss in; admix. ANTONYM remove.

2 *they added all the numbers* TOTAL, add up, count, count up, compute, calculate, reckon, tally; *dated* cast up. ANTONYM subtract.

3 *the subsidies* ***added up to*** *$1,700* AMOUNT TO, come to, run to, make, total, equal, number.

4 *it all* ***adds up to*** *a deepening crisis* AMOUNT TO, constitute; signify, signal, mean, indicate, denote, point to, be evidence of, be symptomatic of; *informal* spell.

5 *her decision just* ***added to*** *his woe* INCREASE, magnify, amplify, augment, intensify, heighten, deepen; compound, reinforce; add fuel to the fire of, fan the flames of, rub salt on the wound of.

6 *she added that she had every confidence in Laura* GO ON TO SAY, state further, continue, carry on. PHRASE: **add up** *informal the situation just didn't add up* MAKE SENSE, stand to reason, hold up, hold water, ring true, be convincing.

**addendum** noun *we can add the list of sponsors as an addendum to the program* APPENDIX, codicil, postscript, afterword, tailpiece, rider, coda, supplement, *Law* adhesion; adjunct, appendage, addition, add-on, attachment.

**addict** noun 1 *stealing money for your next high, just like the addicts out in the street* | *a barbiturate addict* ABUSER, user, drug addict; *informal* junkie, druggie, -head, -freak, pill-popper, dope fiend.

2 *informal skiing addicts* ENTHUSIAST, fan, lover, devotee, aficionado; *informal* freak, buff, nut, fiend, bum, junkie, fanatic, maniac.

**addicted** adjective 1 *he was addicted to tranquilizers* DEPENDENT ON; *informal* hooked on, strung out on.

2 *she became* ***addicted to*** *the theater* DEVOTED TO, obsessed with, fixated on, dedicated to, fanatical about, passionate about, enamored of, a slave to; *informal* hooked on, wild about, mad about, crazy about, nuts about. ANTONYM indifferent.

**addiction** noun 1 *his heroin addiction* DEPENDENCY, dependence, habit, problem.

2 *a slavish* ***addiction to*** *fashion* DEVOTION TO, dedication to, obsession with, infatuation with, passion for, love of, mania for, enslavement to.

**addition** noun 1 *the soil is improved by the addition of compost* ADDING, incorporation, inclusion, introduction.

2 *an addition to the existing regulations* SUPPLEMENT, adjunct, addendum, adhesion, appendage, add-on, extra, attachment; rider, appurtenance. PHRASE: **in addition** 1 *the wind was frigid and, in addition, the sky threatened rain* ADDITIONALLY, as well, what's more, furthermore, moreover, also, into the bargain, to boot, likewise.

2 *three presidential hopefuls* ***in addition to*** *the vice president* BESIDES, as well as, along with, other than, apart from, on top of, plus, over and above, not to mention, to say nothing of.

**additional** adjective *six additional tables will be necessary to accommodate the entire crew* EXTRA, added, supplementary, supplemental, further, auxiliary, ancillary; more, other, another, new, fresh; *informal* bonus.

**additionally** adverb *additionally, there will be live entertainment every Thursday* ALSO, in addition, as well, too, besides, on top (of that), moreover, further, furthermore, what's more, over and above that, into the bargain, to boot, likewise; *archaic* withal.

**additive** noun *our flours have no additives* ADDED INGREDIENT, addition; preservative, coloring.

**address** noun 1 *the address on the envelope* inscription, superscription; directions, number.

2 *our officers arrived at the address* HOUSE, apartment, home; *formal* residence, dwelling, dwelling place, habitation, abode, domicile.

3 *her address to the board members* SPEECH, lecture, talk, monologue, dissertation, discourse, oration, peroration; *slang* spiel, chalk talk; sermon, homily, lesson; harangue.

▸ verb 1 *I addressed the envelope by hand* inscribe, superscribe.

2 *Rev. Lally addressed a crowded congregation* TALK TO, give a talk to, speak to, make a speech to, give a lecture to, lecture, hold forth to; PREACH TO, give a sermon to; *informal* buttonhole, collar.

3 *the question of how to address one's parents-in-law* CALL, name, designate; speak to; *formal* denominate.

4 *correspondence should be addressed to the Personnel Department* DIRECT, send, forward, communicate, convey, route, remit.

5 *the selectmen failed to address the issue of subsidies* ATTEND TO, apply oneself to, tackle, see to, deal with, confront, come to grips with, get down to, turn one's hand to, take in hand, undertake, concentrate on, focus on, devote oneself to.

**adduce** verb *evidence adduced to support their argument* CITE, quote, name, mention, instance, point out, refer to; put forward, present, offer, advance, propose, proffer.

**adept** adjective *an adept negotiator* EXPERT, proficient, accomplished, skillful, talented, masterly, masterful, consummate, virtuoso; adroit, dexterous, deft, artful; brilliant, splendid, marvelous, formidable, outstanding, first-rate, first-class, excellent, fine; *informal* great, top-notch, tip-top, A1, ace, mean, hotshot, crack, nifty, deadly; *informal* crackerjack. ANTONYM inept.

▸ noun *figure-skating adepts* EXPERT, past master, master, genius, maestro, doyen, virtuoso; *informal* wizard, demon, ace, hotshot, whiz, maven, crackerjack. ANTONYM amateur.

**adequacy** noun 1 *the adequacy of the existing services* SATISFACTORINESS, acceptability, acceptableness; sufficiency.

2 *he had deep misgivings about his own adequacy* CAPABILITY, competence, ability, aptitude, suitability; effectiveness, fitness; *formal* efficacy.

**adequate** adjective 1 *he lacked adequate financial resources* SUFFICIENT, enough, requisite.

2 *the company provides an adequate service* ACCEPTABLE, passable, reasonable, satisfactory, tolerable, fair, decent, quite good, pretty good, moderate, unexceptional, unremarkable, undistinguished, ordinary, average, not bad, all right, middling; *informal* OK, so-so, 'comme ci, comme ça,' fair-to-middling, nothing to write home about.

3 *the workstations were small but seemed* ***adequate to*** *the task* EQUAL TO, up to, capable of, suitable for, able to do, fit for, sufficient for.

**adhere** verb 1 *a dollop of cream adhered to her nose* STICK (FAST), cohere, cling, bond, attach; be stuck, be fixed, be glued, be cemented.

2 *they* ***adhere to*** *Judaic law* ABIDE BY, stick to, hold to, comply with, act in accordance with, conform to, submit to, hew to; follow, obey, heed, observe, respect, uphold, fulfill. ANTONYMS flout, ignore.

**adherent** noun *adherents of the Catholic faith* FOLLOWER, supporter, upholder, defender, advocate, disciple, votary, devotee, partisan, member, friend, stalwart; believer, true believer, worshiper; *rare* sectary. ANTONYM opponent.

**adhesive** noun *a spray adhesive* GLUE, fixative, gum, paste, cement, mucilage; *informal* stickum.

▸ adjective *adhesive paper* STICKY, tacky, gluey, gummed, stick-on, self-stick, gooey; viscous, viscid; *technical* adherent.

**adieu** noun & exclamation *with a cheery "adieu," they were gone* GOODBYE, farewell, until we meet again; bye-bye, bye, cheers, ciao, au revoir, adios, sayonara, so long, ta-ta, cheerio, toodle-oo.

**adjacent** adjective *adjacent angles* | *a patio* ***adjacent to*** *the greenhouse* ADJOINING, neighboring, next-door, abutting, contiguous, proximate; (**adjacent to**) close to, near, next to, by, by the side of, bordering on, beside, alongside, attached to, touching, cheek by jowl with.

**adjoining** adjective *adjoining hotel rooms* CONNECTING, connected, interconnecting, adjacent, ensuite, neighboring, bordering, next-door; contiguous, proximate; attached, touching.

**adjourn** verb 1 *the meeting was adjourned for lunch* SUSPEND, break off, discontinue, interrupt, prorogue, stay, recess.

2 *sentencing was adjourned until June 9* POSTPONE, put off, put back, defer, delay, hold over, shelve. See note at POSTPONE.

3 *they adjourned to the sitting room for liqueurs* WITHDRAW, retire, retreat, take oneself; *formal* repair, remove; *literary* betake oneself.

**adjournment** noun *if not now signed into law, the legislation will die with the adjournment of this Congress* SUSPENSION, discontinuation, interruption, postponement, deferment, deferral, stay, prorogation; break, pause, recess.

**adjudicate** verb *this court cannot proceed to* ***adjudicate on*** *a matter when the accused does not have a counsel* JUDGE, try, hear, examine, arbitrate, referee, umpire; pronounce on, give a ruling on, pass judgment on, decide, determine, settle, resolve.

**adjudication** noun *some newspapers do not publish the names of defendants in such cases until adjudication* JUDGMENT, decision, pronouncement, ruling, settlement, resolution, arbitration, finding, verdict, sentence; *Law* determination.

**adjunct** noun *the oral medication is used as an adjunct to the insulin* SUPPLEMENT, addition, extra, add-on, accessory, accompaniment, complement, appurtenance; attachment, appendage, addendum.

▸ adjective *an adjunct professor of entomology* SUBORDINATE, auxiliary, assistant; temporary, provisional.

**adjust** verb 1 *Nanfeldt never quite* ***adjusted to*** *military life* ADAPT TO, become accustomed to, get used to, accommodate oneself to, acclimatize to, acclimate to, orient oneself to, reconcile oneself to, habituate oneself to, assimilate to, familiarize oneself with; come to terms with, fit in with, find one's feet in.

2 *he adjusted the harness* MODIFY, alter, regulate, tune, fine-tune, calibrate, balance; adapt, arrange, rearrange, change, rejig, rework, revamp, remodel, reshape, convert, tailor, improve, enhance, customize; repair, fix, correct, rectify, overhaul, put right; *informal* tweak.

**adjustable** adjective *adjustable seats* ALTERABLE, adaptable, modifiable, convertible, changeable, variable, multiway, versatile.

**adjustment** noun 1 *a period of adjustment* ADAPTATION, accommodations, acclimatization, acclimation, habituation, acculturation, naturalization, assimilation.

2 *they had to make some adjustments to their strategy* MODIFICATION, alteration, regulation, adaptation, rearrangement, change, reconstruction, customization, refinement; repair, correction, amendment, overhaul, improvement.

**ad lib** verb *halfway through the speech, she started ad libbing* IMPROVISE, extemporize, speak impromptu, play it by ear, make it up as one goes along, wing it.

▸ adverb *she spoke ad lib* IMPROMPTU, extempore, without preparation, without rehearsal, extemporaneously; *informal* off the cuff, off the top of one's head; ad libitum.

▸ adjective *a live, ad lib commentary* IMPROMPTU, extempore, extemporaneous, extemporary, improvised, unprepared, unrehearsed, unscripted; *informal* off-the-cuff, spur-of-the-moment. ANTONYM rehearsed.

**administer** verb 1 *the union is administered by a central executive* | *Leighton administers an entire department* MANAGE, direct, control, operate, regulate, conduct, handle, run, organize, supervise, superintend, oversee, preside over, govern, rule, lead, head, steer; be in control of, be in charge of, be responsible for, be at the helm of; *informal* head up.

2 *the lifeboat crew administered first aid* DISPENSE, issue, give, provide, apply, allot, distribute, hand out, dole out, disburse.

3 *a gym shoe was used to administer punishment* INFLICT, mete out, deal out, deliver.

**administration** noun 1 *the day-to-day administration of the company* MANAGEMENT, direction, control, command, charge, conduct, operation, running, leadership, government, governing, superintendence, supervision, regulation, overseeing.

2 *the previous administration left a legacy of reckless spending* GOVERNMENT, cabinet, ministry, regime, executive, authority, directorate, council, leadership, management; parliament, congress, senate; rule, term of office, incumbency.

3 *the administration of anti-inflammatory drugs* PROVISION, issuing, issuance, application, dispensing, dispensation, distribution, disbursement.

**administrative** adjective *strong administrative skills* MANAGERIAL, management, directorial, executive, organizational, bureaucratic, supervisory, regulatory.

**administrator** noun *he became the team's top administrator in 1973* MANAGER, director, executive, controller, head, chief, leader, governor, superintendent, supervisor; *informal* boss.

**admirable** adjective *having done an admirable job of teaching preschoolers* COMMENDABLE, praiseworthy, laudable, estimable, meritorious, creditable, exemplary, honorable, worthy, deserving, respectable, worthwhile, good, sterling, fine, masterly, great. ANTONYM deplorable.

**admiration** noun *it is with much admiration that we dedicate tonight's concert to Dr. Woods* RESPECT, appreciation, (high) regard, esteem, veneration; commendation, acclaim, applause, praise, compliments, tributes, accolades, plaudits. ANTONYM scorn.

**admire** verb 1 *I admire your courage* ESTEEM, approve of, respect, think highly of, rate highly, hold in high regard, applaud, praise, commend, acclaim. See notes at ESTEEM, REVERE. ANTONYMS despise, disapprove of.

2 *we're just admiring your garden* DELIGHT IN, appreciate, take pleasure in.

**admirer** noun *a great admirer of William Finn* FAN, devotee, enthusiast, aficionado; supporter, adherent, follower, disciple.

**admissible** adjective *an admissible claim for damages* VALID, allowable, allowed, permissible, permitted, acceptable, satisfactory, justifiable, defensible, supportable, appropriate, well-founded, tenable, sound; legitimate, lawful, legal, licit; *informal* OK, legit, kosher.

**admission** noun 1 *membership entitles you to free admission* ADMITTANCE, entry, entrance, right of entry, access, right of access, ingress; entrée.

2 *the admission was $8* ENTRANCE FEE, entry charge, cover (charge), ticket.

3 *a written admission of guilt* CONFESSION, acknowledgment, mea culpa, acceptance, concession, disclosure, divulgence.

**admit** verb 1 *he unlocked the door to admit her* LET IN, allow entry, permit entry, take in, usher in, show in, receive, welcome. ANTONYM exclude.

2 *she was admitted to law school* ACCEPT TO/INTO, receive into, enroll in, enlist into, register into. ANTONYM expel.

3 *Paul admitted that he was angry* CONFESS, acknowledge, own, concede, grant, accept, allow; reveal, disclose, divulge; plead guilty. ANTONYM deny.

**admittance** noun *no one is granted admittance without a pass* ENTRY, right of entry, admission, entrance, access, right of access, ingress; entrée. See note at ADMISSION. ANTONYM exclusion.

**admonish** verb 1 *he was severely admonished by his father* REPRIMAND, rebuke, scold, reprove, reproach, upbraid, chastise, chide, berate, criticize, take to task, read the riot act to, rake/haul over the coals; dress down, bawl out, rap over the knuckles, give someone hell; chew out; *formal* castigate; *rare* reprehend. See note at REBUKE.

2 *she admonished him to drink less* ADVISE, recommend, counsel, urge, exhort, bid, enjoin; caution, warn; *formal* adjure.

**adolescence** noun *the lack of adequate sleep in adolescence is a growing health problem largely ignored by the public school system* TEENAGE YEARS, teens, youth; pubescence, puberty; *rare* juvenescence, juvenility.

**adolescent** noun *an awkward adolescent* TEENAGER, youngster, young person, youth, boy, girl; juvenile, minor; *informal* teen, teeny-bopper.

▸ adjective 1 *an adolescent boy* TEENAGE, pubescent, young; juvenile; *informal* teen.

2 *adolescent silliness* IMMATURE, childish, juvenile, infantile, puerile, jejune. See note at YOUTHFUL. ANTONYMS adult, mature.

**adopt** verb 1 *we adopted Sasha in 1996* TAKE AS ONE'S CHILD, be adoptive parents to, take in, take care of. ANTONYM abandon.

2 *they adopted local customs* ESPOUSE, take on/up, embrace, assume; appropriate, arrogate. See note at ADAPT. ANTONYMS abandon, reject.

3 *the people adopted him as their patron saint* CHOOSE, select, pick, vote for, elect, settle on, decide on, opt for; name, nominate, appoint. ANTONYM reject.

**adorable** adjective *adorable little kittens* LOVABLE, appealing, charming, cute, cuddly, sweet, enchanting, bewitching, captivating, engaging, endearing, dear, darling, delightful, lovely, beautiful, attractive, gorgeous, winsome, winning, fetching; *Scottish* bonny. ANTONYMS repulsive, hateful.

**adoration** noun **1** *the girl gazed at him with adoration* LOVE, devotion, care, fondness; admiration, high regard, awe, idolization, worship, hero-worship, adulation.

**2** *our day of prayer and adoration* WORSHIP, glory, glorification, praise, thanksgiving, homage, exaltation, veneration, reverence.

**adore** verb **1** *he adored his mother* LOVE DEARLY, love, be devoted to, dote on, hold dear, cherish, treasure, prize, think the world of; admire, hold in high regard, look up to, idolize, worship; *informal* put on a pedestal. ANTONYMS hate, detest.

**2** *we adore thee, Lord God* WORSHIP, glorify, praise, revere, reverence, exalt, extol, venerate, pay homage to; *formal* laud; *archaic* magnify. See note at REVERE.

**3** *informal I adore oysters* LIKE, love, be very fond of, be very keen on, be partial to, have a weakness for; delight in, relish, savor; *informal* be crazy about, be wild about, have a thing about/for/with, be hooked on. ANTONYMS hate, detest.

**adorn** verb *we'll adorn the hall with tiny lights and ropes of pine* DECORATE, embellish, ornament, enhance; beautify, prettify, grace, bedeck, deck (out), dress (up), trim, swathe, wreathe, festoon, garland, array, emblazon, titivate. ANTONYM disfigure.

**adornment** noun *why all the adornment just for a casual dinner party? | we purchased way more adornments than we could ever use* DECORATION, embellishment, ornamentation, ornament, enhancement; beautification, prettification; frill, accessory, doodad, fandangle, frippery; trimmings, finishing touches.

**adrift** adjective **1** *their empty boat was spotted adrift* DRIFTING, unmoored, unanchored.

**2** *adrift in a strange country* LOST, off course; disoriented, confused, at sea; drifting, rootless, unsettled, directionless, aimless, purposeless, without purpose.

**adroit** adjective *an adroit politician | adroit social commentary* SKILLFUL, adept, dexterous, deft, nimble, able, capable, skilled, expert, masterly, masterful, master, practiced, handy, polished, slick, proficient, accomplished, gifted, talented; quick-witted, quick-thinking, clever, smart, sharp, cunning, wily, resourceful, astute, shrewd, canny; *informal* nifty, crack, mean, ace, A1, clueful, on the ball, savvy, crackerjack. ANTONYMS inept, clumsy.

**adroitness** noun *there is an undeniable adroitness in his economic plan* SKILL, skillfulness, prowess, expertise, adeptness, dexterity, deftness, nimbleness, ability, capability, mastery, proficiency, accomplishment, artistry, art, facility, aptitude, flair, finesse, talent; quick-wittedness, cleverness, sharpness, cunning, astuteness, shrewdness, resourcefulness, savoir faire; *informal* know-how, savvy.

**adulation** noun *unspoiled by all the adulation he's received* HERO-WORSHIP, worship, idolization, adoration, admiration, veneration, awe, devotion, glorification, praise, flattery, blandishments.

**adult** adjective **1** *an adult woman* MATURE, grown-up, fully grown, full-grown, fully developed, of age, of legal age.

**2** *an adult movie* SEXUALLY EXPLICIT, pornographic, obscene, smutty, dirty, rude, erotic, sexy, suggestive, titillating; porn, porno, naughty, blue, X-rated.

**adulterate** verb *some of the drinks had been adulterated with tranquilizers* MAKE IMPURE, degrade, debase, spoil, taint, contaminate; doctor, tamper with, dilute, water down, weaken; bastardize, corrupt; *informal* cut, spike, lace, dope. See note at POLLUTE. ANTONYM purify.

**advance** verb **1** *the battalion advanced rapidly* MOVE FORWARD, proceed, press on, push on, push forward, make progress, make headway, gain ground, approach, come closer, draw nearer, near. ANTONYM retreat.

**2** *the court may advance the date of the hearing* BRING FORWARD, put forward, move forward. ANTONYM postpone.

**3** *the move advanced his career* PROMOTE, further, help, aid, assist, boost, strengthen, improve, benefit, foster. ANTONYMS impede, hinder.

**4** *our technology has advanced in the last few years* PROGRESS, make progress, make headway, develop, evolve, make strides, move forward (in leaps and bounds), move ahead; improve, thrive, flourish, prosper. ANTONYM stagnate.

**5** *the hypothesis I wish to advance in this article* PUT FORWARD, present, submit, suggest, propose, introduce, offer, adduce, moot. ANTONYM retract.

**6** *a relative advanced him some money* LEND, loan, put up, come up with. ANTONYM borrow.

▸ noun **1** *the advance of the aggressors* PROGRESS, forward movement; approach.

**2** *a significant medical advance* BREAKTHROUGH, development, step forward, step in the right direction, (quantum) leap; find, finding, discovery, invention.

**3** *share prices showed significant advances* INCREASE, rise, upturn, upsurge, upswing, growth; *informal* hike.

**4** *the writer is going to be given a huge advance* DOWN PAYMENT, retainer, prepayment, deposit, front money, money up front.

**5** *unwelcome sexual advances* PASS, proposition.

▸ adjective **1** *an advance party of settlers* PRELIMINARY, sent (on) ahead, first, exploratory; pilot, test, trial.

**2** *advance warning* EARLY, prior, beforehand.

PHRASE: **in advance** *rental skis and boots can be reserved in advance* BEFOREHAND, before, ahead of time, earlier, previously; in readiness.

**advanced** adjective **1** *advanced manufacturing techniques* STATE-OF-THE-ART, new, modern, developed, cutting-edge, leading-edge, up-to-date, up-to-the-minute, the newest, the latest; progressive, avant-garde, ahead of the times, pioneering, innovative, sophisticated.

2 *advanced further-education courses* HIGHER-LEVEL, higher. ANTONYM primitive.

**advancement** noun 1 *the advancement of computer technology* DEVELOPMENT, progress, evolution, growth, improvement, advance, furtherance; headway.

2 *employees must be offered opportunities for advancement* PROMOTION, preferment, career development, upgrading, a step up the ladder, progress, improvement, betterment, growth.

**advantage** noun 1 *the advantages of belonging to a union* BENEFIT, value, good point, strong point, asset, plus, bonus, boon, blessing, virtue; attraction, beauty, usefulness, helpfulness, convenience, advantageousness, profit. ANTONYMS disadvantage, drawback.

2 *they appeared to be gaining the advantage over their opponents* UPPER HAND, edge, lead, whip hand, trump card; superiority, dominance, ascendancy, supremacy, power, mastery; *informal* inside track, catbird seat.

3 *there is no advantage to be gained from delaying the process* BENEFIT, profit, gain, good; *informal* mileage. ANTONYM detriment.

**advantageous** adjective 1 *an advantageous position* SUPERIOR, dominant, powerful; good, fortunate, lucky, favorable. ANTONYM inferior.

2 *the arrangement is advantageous to both sides* BENEFICIAL, of benefit, helpful, of assistance, useful, of use, of value, of service, profitable, fruitful; convenient, expedient. ANTONYM detrimental.

**advent** noun *the advent of a new school year* ARRIVAL, appearance, emergence, materialization, occurrence, dawn, birth, rise, development; approach, coming. ANTONYM disappearance.

**adventitious** adjective *he felt that the conversation was not entirely adventitious* UNPLANNED, unpremeditated, accidental, chance, fortuitous, serendipitous, coincidental, casual, random. See note at ACCIDENTAL. ANTONYM premeditated.

**adventure** noun 1 *they set off in search of adventure* EXCITEMENT, thrill, stimulation; risk, danger, hazard, peril, uncertainty, precariousness.

2 *her recent adventures in Italy* EXPLOIT, escapade, deed, feat, experience.

**adventurous** adjective 1 *an adventurous traveler* DARING, daredevil, intrepid, venturesome, bold, fearless, brave, unafraid, unshrinking, dauntless; *informal* gutsy, spunky. ANTONYM cautious.

2 *adventurous activities* RISKY, dangerous, perilous, hazardous, precarious, uncertain; exciting, thrilling. ANTONYM tame.

**adversary** noun *once his devoted comrade at West Point, Arthur was now his adversary at Bull Run* OPPONENT, rival, enemy, antagonist, combatant, challenger, contender, competitor, opposer; opposition, competition, foe. ANTONYMS ally, supporter.

**adverse** adjective 1 *adverse weather conditions* UNFAVORABLE, disadvantageous, inauspicious, unpropitious, unfortunate, unlucky, untimely, untoward. ANTONYMS favorable, auspicious.

2 *the drug's adverse side effects* HARMFUL, dangerous, injurious, detrimental, hurtful, negative, deleterious. ANTONYM beneficial.

3 *an adverse response from the public* HOSTILE, UNFAVORABLE, antagonistic, unfriendly, ill-disposed, negative. See note at HOSTILE. ANTONYMS positive, friendly.

**adversity** noun *the studio made sure the public saw only the manufactured glamour and none of the real adversity of her private life* MISFORTUNE, ill luck, bad luck, trouble, difficulty, hardship, distress, disaster, suffering, affliction, sorrow, misery, tribulation, woe, pain, trauma; mishap, misadventure, accident, upset, reverse, setback, crisis, catastrophe, tragedy, calamity, trial, cross, burden, blow; hard times, trials and tribulations; *informal* ill wind.

**advertise** verb *you should advertise the contest on your local radio station* PUBLICIZE, make public, make known, announce, broadcast, proclaim, trumpet, call attention to, bill, promulgate; promote, market, beat/bang the drum for, huckster; *informal* push, plug, hype, boost; ballyhoo, flack.

**advertisement** noun *it looked like the phone bill, but it was just an advertisement* AD, announcement, notice; commercial, infomercial, promotion, endorsement, blurb, write-up; poster, leaflet, pamphlet, flyer, bill, handbill, handout, fact sheet, circular, bulletin, brochure, sign, placard, junk mail; *informal* plug.

**advice** noun *they give excellent advice on running a small business* GUIDANCE, counseling, counsel, help, direction; information, recommendations, guidelines, suggestions, hints, tips, pointers, ideas, opinions, views, input, words of wisdom.

**advisable** adjective *it is advisable to book a table in advance* JUDICIOUS, desirable, preferable, well, best, sensible, prudent, proper, appropriate, apt, suitable, fitting, wise, recommended, suggested; expedient, politic, advantageous, beneficial, profitable, in one's (best) interest.

**advise** verb 1 *her grandmother advised her about marriage* COUNSEL, give guidance, guide, offer suggestions, give hints, give tips, give pointers.

2 *he advised caution* ADVOCATE, recommend, suggest, urge, encourage, enjoin.

3 *you will be* ***advised of*** *the requirements* INFORM OF, notify about/of, give notice of, apprise of, warn of, forewarn of; acquaint with, make familiar with, keep posted about, update about/on; *informal* fill in on.

**advisory** adjective *she agreed to serve in an advisory role* CONSULTATIVE, advising. ANTONYM executive.

**advocacy** noun *his* ***advocacy of*** *animal rights* SUPPORT FOR, backing of, promotion of, championing of; argument for, push for; *informal* boosterism of.

**advocate** noun *an advocate of children's rights* CHAMPION, upholder, supporter, backer, promoter, proponent, exponent, spokesman, spokeswoman, spokesperson, campaigner, fighter, crusader; propagandist, apostle, apologist, booster, flag-bearer; *informal* libber. ANTONYM critic.

▸ verb *heart specialists advocate a diet low in cholesterol* RECOMMEND, prescribe, advise, urge; support, back, favor, espouse, endorse, uphold, subscribe to, champion, campaign on behalf of, speak for, argue for, lobby for, promote.

**aegis** noun *they had wrongly assumed that Lincoln Beach fell under the aegis of the Parks Department* PROTECTION, backing, support, patronage, sponsorship, charge, care, guidance, control, guardianship, trusteeship, agency, safeguarding, shelter, umbrella, aid, assistance; auspices.

**affable** adjective *he would have us believe that his sexual advances were merely the charming excesses of an affable rogue* FRIENDLY, amiable, genial, congenial, cordial, warm, pleasant, nice, likable, personable, charming, agreeable, sympathetic, simpatico, good-humored, good-natured, jolly, kindly, kind, courteous, civil, gracious, approachable, accessible, amenable, sociable, hail-fellow-well-met, outgoing, gregarious, neighborly. ANTONYM unfriendly.

**affair** noun **1** *what you do is your own affair* BUSINESS, concern, matter, responsibility, province, preserve; problem, worry.

**2** **(affairs)** *his financial affairs* TRANSACTIONS, concerns, matters, activities, dealings, undertakings, ventures, business.

**3** *the board admitted responsibility for the affair* EVENT, incident, happening, occurrence, eventuality, episode; case, matter, business.

**4** *his affair with Monica was over* RELATIONSHIP, love affair, affaire de coeur, romance, fling, flirtation, dalliance, liaison, involvement, intrigue, amour; *informal* hanky-panky.

**affect**[1] verb **1** *this development may have affected the judge's decision* HAVE AN EFFECT ON, influence, act on, work on, have an impact on, impact; change, alter, modify, transform, form, shape, sway, bias.

**2** *he was visibly affected by the experience* MOVE, touch, make an impression on, hit (hard), tug at someone's heartstrings; UPSET, trouble, distress, disturb, agitate, shake (up).

**3** *the disease affected his lungs* ATTACK, infect; hit, strike. See note at EMOTION.

**affect**[2] verb **1** *he deliberately affected a Republican stance* ASSUME, take on, adopt, embrace, espouse.

**2** *Paul affected an air of injured innocence* PRETEND, feign, fake, simulate, make a show of, make a pretense of, sham; *informal* put on, make like.

**affectation** noun **1** *the affectations of a prima donna* PRETENSION, pretentiousness, affectedness, artificiality, posturing, posing; airs (and graces).

**2** *an affectation of calm* FACADE, front, show, appearance, pretense, simulation, posture, pose.

**affected** adjective *that affected voice of his really grates on me* PRETENTIOUS, artificial, contrived, unnatural, stagy, studied, mannered, ostentatious; insincere, unconvincing, feigned, false, fake, sham, simulated; *informal* la-di-da, phony, pretend, put on. ANTONYMS natural, unpretentious, genuine.

**affecting** adjective *an affecting piece of music* TOUCHING, moving, emotive, emotional; stirring, soul-stirring, heartwarming; poignant, pathetic, pitiful, piteous, tear-jerking, heart-rending, gut-wrenching, heartbreaking, disturbing, distressing, upsetting, sad, haunting. See note at MOVING.

**affection** noun *the affection they share is obvious* FONDNESS, love, liking, tenderness, warmth, devotion, endearment, care, caring, attachment, friendship; warm feelings.

**affectionate** adjective *an affectionate handshake | golden retrievers are known for being affectionate* LOVING, fond, adoring, devoted, caring, doting, tender, warm, warmhearted, softhearted, friendly; demonstrative, cuddly; *informal* touchy-feely, lovey-dovey. ANTONYM cold.

**affiliate** verb *the college is* ***affiliated with*** *the University of Wisconsin* ASSOCIATE WITH, unite with, combine with, join (up) with, link up with, team up with, ally with, align with, band together with, federate with, amalgamate with, merge with; attach to, annex to, incorporate into, integrate into.

▸ noun *Conklin Textiles is their largest Midwest affiliate* PARTNER, branch, offshoot, subsidiary.

**affiliation** noun *the project's* ***affiliation with*** *the town's welfare department | the newspaper's obvious* ***affiliation to*** *the Republican party* ASSOCIATION WITH, connection with/to, alliance with/to, alignment with, link with/to, attachment to, tie with/to, relationship with/to, fellowship with, partnership with, coalition with, union with; amalgamation with, incorporation into, integration into, federation with, confederation with.

**affinity** noun **1** *her* ***affinity with*** *animals and birds | an* ***affinity for*** *opera* EMPATHY FOR, rapport with, sympathy for, accord with, harmony with, relationship with, bond with, fellow feeling for, closeness with/to, understanding of/for; liking of/for, fondness of/for; *informal* chemistry with. ANTONYMS aversion, dislike.

**2** *the semantic affinity between the two words* SIMILARITY, resemblance, likeness, kinship, relationship, association, link, analogy, similitude, correspondence. See note at LIKENESS. ANTONYMS dissimilitude, dissimilarity.

**affirm** verb **1** *he affirmed that they would lend military assistance* DECLARE, state, assert, proclaim, pronounce, attest, swear, avow, guarantee, pledge, give an undertaking; *formal* aver. ANTONYM deny.

**2** *the referendum affirmed the republic's right to secede* UPHOLD, support, confirm, ratify, endorse, sanction.

**affirmation** noun **1** *an affirmation of faith* DECLARATION, statement, assertion, proclamation, pronouncement, attestation; oath, avowal, guarantee, pledge; deposition; *formal* averment, asseveration. ANTONYM denial.

2 *the poem ends with an affirmation of pastoral values* CONFIRMATION, ratification, endorsement.

**affirmative** adjective *an affirmative answer* POSITIVE, assenting, consenting, corroborative, favorable. ANTONYM negative.

▸ noun *she took his grunt as an affirmative* AGREEMENT, acceptance, assent, acquiescence, concurrence; OK, yes, thumbs-up. ANTONYM disagreement.

**affix** verb 1 *he affixed a stamp to the envelope* STICK, glue, paste, gum; attach, fasten, fix; clip, tack, pin; tape. ANTONYM detach.

2 *formal affix your signature to the document* APPEND, add, attach.

**afflict** verb *arthritis can afflict people of all ages* TROUBLE, burden, distress, cause suffering to, beset, harass, worry, oppress; torment, pester, plague, blight, bedevil, rack, smite, curse; *archaic* ail.

**affliction** noun 1 *a common herb reputed to cure a variety of afflictions* DISORDER, disease, malady, complaint, ailment, illness, indisposition, handicap; scourge, plague, trouble.

2 *he bore his affliction with great dignity* SUFFERING, distress, pain, trouble, misery, wretchedness, hardship, misfortune, adversity, sorrow, torment, tribulation, woe.

**affluent** adjective *the affluent families of Newport* WEALTHY, rich, prosperous, well off, moneyed, well-to-do; propertied, substantial, of means, of substance, plutocratic; *informal* well-heeled, rolling in it, made of money, filthy rich, stinking rich, loaded, on easy street; upper-class, upscale. See note at WEALTHY. ANTONYMS poor, impoverished.

**afford** verb 1 *I can't afford a new car* PAY FOR, bear the expense of, have the money for, spare the price of.

2 *it took more time than he could afford* SPARE, allow (oneself).

3 *the rooftop terrace affords beautiful views* PROVIDE, supply, furnish, offer, give, make available, yield. See note at GIVE.

**affront** noun *an affront to public morality* INSULT, offense, indignity, slight, snub, put-down, provocation, injury; outrage, atrocity, scandal; *informal* slap in the face, kick in the teeth.

▸ verb *she was affronted by his familiarity* INSULT, offend, mortify, provoke, pique, wound, hurt; put out, irk, displease, bother, rankle, vex, gall; outrage, scandalize, disgust; *informal* put someone's back up, needle.

**afoot** adjective & adverb *evil plans are afoot* GOING ON, happening, around, about, abroad, stirring, circulating, in circulation, at large, in the air/wind; brewing, looming, in the offing, on the horizon.

**aforesaid** adjective *the policy insures the aforesaid items* PREVIOUSLY MENTIONED, aforementioned, aforenamed; foregoing, preceding, earlier, previous; above.

**afraid** adjective 1 *they ran away because they were afraid* FRIGHTENED, scared, terrified, fearful, petrified, scared witless, scared to death, terror-stricken, terror-struck, frightened out of one's wits, scared out of one's wits, shaking in one's shoes, shaking like a leaf; intimidated, alarmed, panicky; fainthearted, cowardly; *informal* scared stiff, in a cold sweat, spooked; chicken; *archaic* afeared, affrighted. ANTONYMS brave, confident.

2 *don't be afraid to ask questions* RELUCTANT, hesitant, unwilling, disinclined, loath, slow, chary, shy. ANTONYM confident.

3 *I'm afraid that your daughter is ill* SORRY, sad, distressed, regretful, apologetic. ANTONYM pleased.

**afresh** adverb *let's start afresh* ANEW, again, over again, once again, once more, another time.

**after** preposition 1 *she made a speech after the performance* FOLLOWING, subsequent to, at the close/end of, in the wake of; *formal* posterior to. ANTONYMS before, preceding.

2 *Guy shut the door after them* BEHIND, following. ANTONYM in front of.

3 *after the way he treated my sister, I never want to speak to him again* BECAUSE OF, as a result of, as a consequence of, in view of, owing to, on account of.

4 *is he still going to marry her, after all that's happened?* DESPITE, in spite of, regardless of, notwithstanding.

5 *the policeman ran after him* IN PURSUIT OF, in someone's direction, following. ANTONYMS away from, in front of.

6 *I'm after information, and I'm willing to pay for it* IN SEARCH OF, in quest of, in pursuit of, trying to find, looking for, hunting for; desirous of, wanting.

7 *they asked after Dad* ABOUT, concerning, regarding, with regard to, with respect to, with reference to.

8 *the village was named after a Roman officer* IN HONOR OF, as a tribute to.

▸ adverb 1 *the week after, we went to Madrid* LATER, afterward, after this/that, subsequently. ANTONYMS previously, before.

2 *porters were following on after with their bags* BEHIND, in the rear, at the back, in someone's wake. ANTONYMS ahead, in front.

PHRASE: **after all** *I couldn't stay mad—after all, we're best friends* ABOVE ALL, most important, most importantly, beyond everything, ultimately; *informal* when all is said and done, at the end of the day, when push comes to shove.

**afterlife** noun *they shared their personal beliefs about **the afterlife*** LIFE AFTER DEATH, the next world, the hereafter, the afterworld, eternity, kingdom come; immortality.

**aftermath** noun *the Red Cross is a prominent presence in the aftermath of last week's earthquake* REPERCUSSIONS, aftereffects, consequences, effects, results, fruits; wake.

**again** adverb 1 *her spirits lifted again* ONCE MORE, another time, afresh, anew.

2 *this can add half as much again to the price* EXTRA, in addition, additionally, on top.

3 *again, evidence was not always consistent* ALSO, furthermore; moreover, besides. PHRASE: **again and again** *I've warned you again and again about that loose step* REPEAT-

EDLY, over and over (again), time and (time) again, many times, many a time; often, frequently, continually, constantly.

**against** preposition **1** *a number of delegates were against the motion* OPPOSED TO, in opposition to, hostile to, averse to, antagonistic toward, inimical to, unsympathetic to, resistant to, at odds with, in disagreement with, dead set against; *informal* anti. ANTONYMS in favor of, pro.

**2** *he was swimming against the tide* IN OPPOSITION TO, counter to, contrary to, in the opposite direction to. ANTONYM with.

**3** *his age is against him* DISADVANTAGEOUS TO, unfavorable to, damaging to, detrimental to, prejudicial to, deleterious to, harmful to, injurious to, a drawback for. ANTONYM advantageous to.

**4** *she leaned against the wall* TOUCHING, in contact with, up against, on, adjacent to.

**age** noun **1** *he is 35 years of age | his wife is the same age* NUMBER OF YEARS, length of life; stage of life, generation, age group.

**2** *her hearing had deteriorated with age* ELDERLINESS, old age, oldness, senescence, dotage, seniority, maturity; one's advancing/advanced/declining years; *literary* eld; *archaic* caducity.

**3** *the Elizabethan age* ERA, epoch, period, time, eon.

**4** *informal* **(ages)** *you haven't been in touch with me for ages* A LONG TIME, days/months/years on end, an eternity, an eon; *informal* ages and ages, donkey's years, a coon's age, a month of Sundays, forever.

▸ verb **1** *Cabernet Sauvignon ages well* MATURE, mellow, ripen, season.

**2** *Leila has aged a lot since the last time I saw her* GROW/BECOME/GET OLD, mature, (cause to) decline, weather, fade; grow up, come of age. See note at MATURE.

**aged** adjective *an aged relative* ELDERLY, old, mature, older, senior, hoary, ancient, senescent, advanced in years, in one's dotage, long in the tooth, as old as the hills, past one's prime, not as young as one used to be, getting on, over the hill, no spring chicken. See note at OLD. ANTONYM young.

**agency** noun **1** *an advertising agency* BUSINESS, organization, company, firm, office, bureau.

**2** *the infection is caused by the agency of insects* ACTION, activity, means, effect, influence, force, power, vehicle, medium.

**3** *regional policy was introduced through the agency of the Board of Trade* INTERVENTION, intercession, involvement, good offices; auspices, aegis.

**agenda** noun **1** *the next topic on the agenda* LIST OF ITEMS, schedule, program, timetable, itinerary, lineup, list, plan.

**2** *their hidden agenda* PLAN, scheme, motive.

**agent** noun **1** *the sale was arranged through an agent* REPRESENTATIVE, emissary, envoy, go-between, proxy, negotiator, broker, liaison, spokesperson, spokesman, spokeswoman; *informal* rep.

**2** *a travel agent* AGENCY, business, organization, company, firm, bureau.

**3** *a CIA agent* SPY, secret agent, undercover agent, operative, fifth columnist, mole, Mata Hari; *informal* G-man.

**4** *the agents of destruction* PERFORMER, author, executor, perpetrator, producer, instrument, catalyst.

**5** *a cleansing agent* MEDIUM, means, instrument, vehicle.

**aggravate** verb **1** *the new law could aggravate the situation* WORSEN, make worse, exacerbate, inflame, compound; add fuel to the fire/flames, add insult to injury, rub salt in the wound. ANTONYMS alleviate, improve.

**2** *informal* *you don't have to aggravate people to get what you want* ANNOY, irritate, exasperate, bother, put out, nettle, provoke, antagonize, get on someone's nerves, ruffle (someone's feathers), try someone's patience; *informal* peeve, needle, bug, miff, get under someone's skin; tick off. ANTONYMS calm, conciliate.

**USAGE NOTE aggravate, aggravation**

Though documented as existing since the 1600s, *aggravate* for *annoy* or *irritate* has never gained the approval of stylists and should be avoided in formal writing. Strictly speaking, *aggravate* means "make worse; exacerbate": *writing a second apology might just aggravate the problem*. Even the eloquent American jurist Oliver Wendell Holmes, Jr., nodded once, using *aggravate* for *irritate* in a letter penned in 1895: "Our two countries aggravate each other from time to time."

In some contexts, it's genuinely difficult to tell whether the word *aggravating* is a present participle or an adjective—e.g.: "The City of Washington is notorious for aggravating allergies, and Mr. Clinton said he expected his to be more severe there than in Arkansas." (*New York Times*; Oct. 14, 1996.) The second half of that compound sentence suggests that the writer is using *aggravating* correctly. But taken alone, the phrase in the first half of the sentence ("Washington is notorious for aggravating allergies") could refer to either (1) making allergies worse (the preferred usage), or (2) allergies that are irritating or frustrating.

The confusion also occurs between the noun forms—e.g.: "Rush Limbaugh . . . has an extra tone of aggravation [read *irritation*] as he denounces the unyielding poll leads of 'the Schlickmeister' and 'noted hetero fun-seeker,' President Clinton." (*New York Times*; Sept. 25, 1996.)

Perhaps *exasperate* contributes to the misuse of *aggravate* (which sounds a bit like *exasperate*) in the sense of *irritate* (which is close in meaning to *exasperate*). Also, when *aggravate* is used in this sense it often implies something more intense than merely *irritate*. It is closer in meaning to *exasperate*. —*BG*

**aggravation** noun **1** *the recession led to the aggravation of unemployment problems* WORSENING, exacerbation, compounding.

**2** *informal* *it's not worth the aggravation* NUISANCE, annoyance, irritation, hassle, headache, trouble, difficulty, inconvenience, bother, pain, distress.

**aggregate** noun **1** *the specimen is an aggregate of rock and mineral fragments* COLLECTION, mass, agglomeration, conglomerate, assemblage; mixture, mix, combination, blend, accumulation; compound, alloy, amalgam.

**2** *he won with an aggregate of 325* TOTAL, sum total, sum, grand total.

▸ adjective *an aggregate score* TOTAL, combined, gross, overall, composite.

**aggression** noun **1** *an act of aggression* HOSTILITY, aggressiveness, belligerence, bellicosity, force, violence; pugnacity, pugnaciousness, militancy, warmongering; attack, assault.

**2** *he played the game with unceasing aggression* CONFIDENCE, self-confidence, boldness, determination, forcefulness, vigor, energy, zeal.

**aggressive** adjective **1** *aggressive behavior* HOSTILE, belligerent, bellicose, antagonistic, truculent; pugnacious, combative, two-fisted, violent; macho; confrontational; quarrelsome, argumentative. ANTONYMS meek, friendly.

**2** *aggressive foreign policy* WARMONGERING, warlike, warring, belligerent, bellicose, hawkish, militaristic; offensive, expansionist. ANTONYMS peaceable, peaceful.

**3** *an aggressive promotional drive* ASSERTIVE, pushy, forceful, vigorous, energetic, dynamic; bold, audacious; *informal* in-your-face, feisty. See note at BOLD. ANTONYMS submissive, diffident.

**aggressor** noun *England was the aggressor in a succession of wars* ATTACKER, assaulter, assailant; invader, instigator, warmonger.

**aggrieved** adjective **1** *the manager looked aggrieved at the suggestion* RESENTFUL, affronted, indignant, disgruntled, discontented, upset, offended, piqued, riled, nettled, vexed, irked, irritated, annoyed, put out, chagrined; *informal* peeved, miffed, in a huff, sore, steamed. ANTONYM pleased.

**2** *the aggrieved party* WRONGED, injured, mistreated, ill-treated, abused, harmed.

**aghast** adjective *eyewitnesses to the explosion were aghast* HORRIFIED, appalled, dismayed, thunderstruck, stunned, shocked, staggered; *informal* flabbergasted.

**agile** adjective **1** *she was as agile as a monkey* NIMBLE, lithe, supple, limber, acrobatic, fleet-footed, light-footed, light on one's feet; *literary* fleet, lightsome. ANTONYMS clumsy, stiff.

**2** *an agile mind* ALERT, sharp, acute, shrewd, astute, perceptive, quick-witted. ANTONYMS slow, dull.

**agitate** verb **1** *any mention of Clare agitates my grandmother* UPSET, perturb, fluster, ruffle, disconcert, unnerve, disquiet, disturb, distress, unsettle, unhinge; *informal* rattle, faze; discombobulate.

**2** *she agitated for the appointment of more women* CAMPAIGN, strive, battle, fight, struggle, push, press.

**3** *agitate the water to disperse the oil* STIR, whisk, churn, beat.

**agitator** noun *tell your band of agitators that my generals are heavily armed and most unsympathetic* TROUBLEMAKER, rabble-rouser, agent provocateur, demagogue, incendiary; revolutionary, firebrand, rebel, insurgent, subversive; *informal* disturber.

**agnostic** noun *Darrow was an avowed agnostic, legendary defense attorney, and Scopes's counsel* SKEPTIC, doubter, doubting Thomas, cynic; unbeliever, nonbeliever, rationalist; *rare* nullifidian. ANTONYMS believer, theist.

**ago** adverb *years ago, on this very site, was a small stone cottage* IN THE PAST, before, earlier, back, since, previously; *formal* heretofore.

**agog** adverb *tell us what happened—we're all agog!* EAGER, excited, impatient, keen, anxious, avid, in suspense, on tenterhooks, on the edge of one's seat, on pins and needles, waiting with bated breath.

**agonizing** adjective *agonizing pain* EXCRUCIATING, harrowing, racking, searing, extremely painful, acute, severe, torturous, tormenting, piercing; *informal* hellish.

**agony** noun *the agony was both mental and physical* PAIN, hurt, suffering, torture, torment, anguish, affliction, trauma; pangs, throes.

**agree** verb **1** *I agree with you* CONCUR, be of the same mind/opinion, see eye to eye, be in sympathy, be united, be as one man. ANTONYM differ.

**2** *they had **agreed to** a cease-fire* CONSENT TO, assent to, acquiesce to, accept, approve, say yes to, give one's approval to, give the nod to; *informal* OK; *formal* accede to. ANTONYM reject.

**3** *the plan and the drawing do not agree with each other* MATCH (UP), jibe, accord, correspond, chime in, conform, coincide, fit, tally, be in harmony/agreement, harmonize, be consistent/equivalent; *informal* square. ANTONYMS differ, contradict.

**4** *they **agreed on** a price* SETTLE ON, decide on, arrive at, work out, negotiate, reach an agreement on, come to terms on, strike a bargain on, make a deal on, shake hands on.

**agreeable** adjective **1** *an agreeable atmosphere of rural tranquility* PLEASANT, pleasing, enjoyable, pleasurable, nice, to one's liking, appealing, charming, delightful. See note at PLEASANT. ANTONYM unpleasant.

**2** *an agreeable fellow* LIKABLE, charming, amiable, affable, pleasant, nice, friendly, good-natured, sociable, genial, congenial, simpatico. ANTONYM unpleasant.

**3** *we should get together for a talk, if you're agreeable* WILLING, amenable, in accord/agreement, compliant, consenting. ANTONYM unwilling.

**agreement** noun **1** *all heads nodded in agreement* ACCORD, concurrence, consensus; assent, acceptance, consent, acquiescence, endorsement, like-mindedness.

**2** *an agreement on military cooperation* CONTRACT, compact, treaty, covenant, pact, accord, concordat, protocol.

**3** *there is some agreement between my view and that of the author* CORRESPONDENCE, consistency, compatibility, accord; similarity, resemblance, likeness, similitude. ANTONYM discord.

**agriculture** noun *the mechanization of agriculture* FARMING, cultivation, tillage, tilling, husbandry, land/farm management, horticulture; agribusiness, agronomy.

**aground** adverb & adjective *the ship was aground when we spotted it* GROUNDED, ashore, beached, stuck, shipwrecked, high and dry, on the rocks, on the ground/bottom.

**ahead** adverb **1** *he peered ahead, but could see nothing* FORWARD, toward the front, frontward, onward, along. ANTONYM behind.

**2** *he had ridden on ahead* IN FRONT, at the head, in the lead, at the fore, in the vanguard, in advance. ANTONYMS behind, at the back.

**3** *she was preparing herself for what lay ahead* IN THE FUTURE, in time, in time to come, in the fullness of time, at a later date, after this, henceforth, later on, in due course, next. ANTONYM in the past.

**4** *they are ahead by six points* LEADING, winning, in the lead, (out) in front, first, coming first. ANTONYMS trailing, losing.

PHRASE: **ahead of 1** *Blanche went ahead of the others* IN FRONT OF, before.

**2** *we have a demanding trip ahead of us* IN STORE FOR, waiting for.

**3** *two months ahead of schedule* IN ADVANCE OF, before, earlier than.

**aid** noun **1** *with the aid of his colleagues he prepared a manifesto* ASSISTANCE, support, help, backing, cooperation; a helping hand. ANTONYM hindrance.

**2** *humanitarian aid* RELIEF, charity, financial assistance, donations, contributions, subsidies, handouts, subvention, succor; *historical* alms.

▸ verb **1** *he provided an army to aid the King of England* HELP, assist, abet, come to someone's aid, give assistance, lend a hand, be of service; avail, succor, sustain. ANTONYM hinder.

**2** *certain teas can aid restful sleep* FACILITATE, promote, encourage, help, further, boost; speed up, hasten, accelerate, expedite. ANTONYMS discourage, hinder.

**aide** noun *an aide to the supervisor* ASSISTANT, helper, adviser, right-hand man, man/girl Friday, adjutant, deputy, second-in-command, second; subordinate, junior, underling, acolyte.

**ailing** adjective **1** *his ailing mother* ILL, sick, unwell, sickly, poorly, weak, indisposed, in poor/bad health, infirm, debilitated, diseased, delicate, valetudinarian, below par, bedridden; *informal* laid up, under the weather. ANTONYM healthy.

**2** *the country's ailing economy* FAILING, in poor condition, weak, poor, deficient. ANTONYM strong.

**ailment** noun *a common stomach ailment* ILLNESS, disease, sickness, disorder, condition, affliction, malady, complaint, infirmity; *informal* bug, virus.

**aim** verb **1** *he aimed the rifle* POINT, direct, train, sight, line up.

**2** *she **aimed at** the target* TAKE AIM AT, fix on, zero in on, draw a bead on.

**3** *undergraduates **aiming for** a degree* WORK TOWARD, be after, set one's sights on, try for, strive for, aspire to, endeavor to achieve; *formal* essay for.

**4** *this system is **aimed at** the home entertainment market* TARGET AT, intend for, destine for, direct at, design for, tailor for, market to, pitch to/at.

**5** *we aim to give you the best possible service* INTEND, mean, have in mind/view; plan, resolve, propose, design. See note at INTEND.

▸ noun *our aim is to develop gymnasts to the top level* OBJECTIVE, object, goal, end, target, design, desire, desired result, intention, intent, plan, purpose, object of the exercise; ambition, aspiration, wish, dream, hope, raison d'être.

**aimless** adjective **1** *Flavia set out on an aimless walk* PURPOSELESS, goalless, without purpose, haphazard, wandering, without goal, desultory. ANTONYM purposeful.

**2** *aimless men standing outside the bars* UNOCCUPIED, idle, at a loose end; purposeless, undirected. ANTONYM determined.

**air** noun **1** *hundreds of birds hovered in the air* SKY, atmosphere; heavens, ether.

**2** *open the windows to get some air into the room* BREEZE, draft, wind; breath/blast of air, gust of wind.

**3** *an air of defiance* EXPRESSION, appearance, look, impression, aspect, aura, mien, countenance, manner, bearing, tone.

**4** **(airs)** *putting on airs* AFFECTATIONS, pretension, pretentiousness, affectedness, posturing, airs and graces.

**5** *a traditional Scottish air* TUNE, melody, song; *literary* lay.

▸ verb **1** *a chance to air your views* EXPRESS, voice, make public, ventilate, articulate, state, declare, give expression/voice to; have one's say about.

**2** *the windows were opened to air the room* VENTILATE, freshen, refresh, cool.

**3** *the film was aired nationwide* BROADCAST, transmit, screen, show, televise, telecast.

**airily** adverb *the sparrow hopped airily along | the composer meant for the piece to be played airily* LIGHTLY, breezily, flippantly, casually, nonchalantly, heedlessly, without consideration. ANTONYM seriously.

**airtight** adjective **1** *an airtight container* SEALED, hermetically sealed, closed tight, shut tight.

**2** *an airtight alibi* INDISPUTABLE, unquestionable, incontrovertible, undeniable, incontestable, irrefutable, watertight, beyond dispute, beyond question, beyond doubt.

**airy** adjective **1** *the conservatory is light and airy* WELL VENTILATED, fresh; spacious, uncluttered; light, bright. ANTONYM stuffy.

**2** *an airy gesture* NONCHALANT, casual, breezy, flippant, insouciant, heedless. ANTONYM serious.

**3** *airy clouds* DELICATE, soft, fine, feathery, insubstantial. ANTONYMS heavy, dense.

**aisle** noun *there is no sitting allowed in the aisle* PASSAGE, passageway, gangway, walkway, corridor.

**ajar** adjective & adverb *with shutters ajar, we got only a glimpse of the morning sun | use the flatiron to keep the door ajar* SLIGHTLY OPEN, half open. ANTONYMS closed, wide open.

**akin** adjective *much of the vegetation here is akin to that of southern California* SIMILAR, related, close, near, corresponding, comparable, equivalent; connected, alike, analogous. ANTONYM unlike.

**alacrity** noun *I am confident that Liberia is going to move forward now with alacrity at the peace table* EAGERNESS, willingness, readiness; enthusiasm, ardor, avidity, fervor, keenness; promptness, haste, swiftness, dispatch, speed.

**alarm** noun **1** *we spun around in alarm* FEAR, anxiety, apprehension, trepidation, nervousness, unease, distress, agitation, consternation, disquiet, perturbation, fright, panic. ANTONYMS calmness, composure.

**2** *sound the alarm | a smoke alarm* WARNING, alert, distress signal; SIREN, bell, horn, whistle; *archaic* tocsin.

▸ verb *the news had alarmed her* FRIGHTEN, scare, panic, unnerve, distress, agitate, upset, disconcert, shock, dismay, disturb; *informal* rattle, spook, scare the living daylights out of. ANTONYMS calm, reassure.

**alarming** adjective *the latest statistics on deaths from AIDS are more than just a little alarming* FRIGHTENING, unnerving, shocking; distressing, upsetting, disconcerting, perturbing, worrisome, worrying, dismaying, disquieting, startling, disturbing; *informal* scary. ANTONYM reassuring.

**alarmist** noun *until I saw the map and radar photos of the hurricane, I thought he was being an alarmist* SCAREMONGER, doomster, doomsayer, Cassandra, Chicken Little. ANTONYM optimist.

**alcohol** noun *the doctor told him to avoid alcohol* LIQUOR, intoxicating drink/beverage(s), strong drink, alcoholic drink/beverage(s), drink, spirits; *informal* booze, hooch, the hard stuff, firewater, rotgut, moonshine, white lightning, grog, the demon rum, the bottle, the sauce; *technical* ethyl alcohol, ethanol. See tables at LIQUOR, COCKTAIL.

**alcoholic** adjective *alcoholic drinks* INTOXICATING, inebriating, containing alcohol, fermented; strong, hard, stiff; *formal* spirituous.

▸ noun *he is an alcoholic* DIPSOMANIAC, drunk, drunkard, heavy/hard/serious drinker, problem drinker, alcohol abuser, person with a drinking problem; tippler, sot, inebriate; *informal* boozer, lush, alky, boozehound, dipso, juicer, wino, barfly.

**alcove** noun *nestled on a cushion in the alcove, reading a book* RECESS, niche, nook, bay; arbor, bower.

**alert** adjective **1** *police have asked neighbors to stay alert* VIGILANT, watchful, attentive, observant, wide awake, circumspect; on the lookout, on one's guard, on one's toes, on the qui vive; *informal* heads-up, keeping one's eyes open/peeled, bright-eyed and bushy-tailed. See note at VIGILANT. ANTONYM inattentive.

**2** *mentally alert* QUICK-WITTED, sharp, bright, quick, keen, perceptive, wide awake, on one's toes; *informal* on the ball, quick on the uptake, all there, with it. ANTONYMS inattentive, slow-witted.

▸ noun **1** *a state of alert* VIGILANCE, watchfulness, attentiveness, alertness, circumspection.

**2** *a flood alert* WARNING, notification, notice; siren, alarm, signal, danger signal, distress signal.

▸ verb *police were alerted by a phone call* WARN, notify, apprise, forewarn, put on one's guard, put on the qui vive; *informal* tip off, clue in.

**alias** noun *he is known under several aliases* ASSUMED NAME, false name, pseudonym, sobriquet, incognito; pen name, stage name, nom de plume, nom de guerre; *rare* allonym, anonym.

▸ adverb *Lester Gillis, alias Baby Face Nelson* ALSO KNOWN AS, aka, also called, otherwise known as.

**alibi** noun *we've both got a good alibi for last night* DEFENSE, justification, explanation, reason; *informal* story, line.

**alien** adjective **1** *an alien landscape* UNFAMILIAR, unknown, strange, peculiar; exotic, foreign. ANTONYM familiar.

**2** *a vicious role* ***alien to*** *his nature* INCOMPATIBLE WITH, unusual for, opposed to, conflicting with, contrary to, in conflict with, at variance with, out of step with; *rare* oppugnant to. ANTONYM familiar.

**3** *alien beings* EXTRATERRESTRIAL, unearthly, otherworldly; Martian, Jovian, Venutian. ANTONYM earthly.

▸ noun **1** *an illegal alien* FOREIGNER, nonnative, immigrant, emigrant, émigré.

**2** *the alien's spaceship* EXTRATERRESTRIAL, ET; Martian, Jovian, Venutian; *informal* little green man.

**alienate** verb *was it the dispute over the inheritance that has alienated these two brothers?* ESTRANGE, divide, distance, put at a distance, isolate, cut off; set against, turn away, turn off, drive apart, marginalize, disunite, set at variance/odds, drive a wedge between.

**alienation** verb *my deep sense of alienation* ISOLATION, detachment, estrangement, distance, separation, division; cutting off, turning away. See note at SOLITUDE.

**alight**[1] verb **1** *he* ***alighted from*** *the train* GET OFF, step off, disembark from, pile out of; detrain, deplane; dismount. ANTONYMS get on, board.

**2** *a swallow alighted on a branch* LAND, come to rest, settle, perch, light. ANTONYM fly off.

**alight**[2] adjective **1** *the bales of hay were alight* BURNING, ablaze, aflame, on fire, in flames, blazing; *literary* afire.

**2** *her face was alight with laughter* LIT UP, gleaming, glowing, aglow, ablaze, bright, shining, resplendent, radiant.

**align** verb **1** *the desks are aligned in straight rows* LINE UP, put in order, put in rows/columns, straighten, place, position, situate, set, range.

**2** *he* ***aligned himself*** *with the workers* ALLY ONESELF, affiliate oneself, associate oneself, join, side, unite, combine oneself, join forces, form an alliance, team up, band together, throw in one's lot, make common cause.

**alike** adjective *all the doors looked alike* SIMILAR, (much) the same, indistinguishable, identical, uniform, interchangeable, cut from the same cloth; *informal* like (two) peas in a pod, like Tweedledum and Tweedledee, much of a muchness. ANTONYM different.

▸ adverb *great minds think alike* SIMILARLY, (just) the same, in the same way/manner/fashion, equally, likewise, identically.

**alimony** noun *he has failed to pay alimony for more than two years* FINANCIAL SUPPORT, maintenance, support; child support.

**alive** adjective **1** *he was last seen alive on Labor Day | when mastodons were alive* LIVING, live; breathing, vital, functioning; animate, sentient; existing; *informal* alive and kicking, in the land of the living, among the living; *archaic* quick. ANTONYMS dead, inanimate, extinct.

**2** *the association has kept her dream alive* IN EXISTENCE, existing, active, existent, extant, ongoing, abiding, functioning, in operation; current, contemporary; *informal* on the map. ANTONYMS inactive, obsolete.

**3** *it was Judith's great love that made Marty so alive* ANIMATED, lively, full of life, alert, active, energetic, vigorous, spry, sprightly, vital, vivacious, buoyant, exuberant, ebullient, zestful, spirited; *informal* full of beans, bright-eyed and bushy-tailed, chirpy, chipper, peppy, full of vim and vigor. ANTONYMS listless, lethargic.

**4** *the place was alive with mice* TEEMING, swarming, overrun, bristling, infested; crowded, packed; *informal* crawling, lousy; *rare* pullulating.

THE RIGHT WORD **alive, animate, animated, living, vital**

Dead is dead, but one can be **alive** to varying degrees The broadest of these terms describing what has life or shows signs of having it, *alive* can refer to what barely exists (*he was unconscious but still alive when they found him*) as well as to what is bursting with (literal or figurative) life (*her face was alive with excitement and anticipation*). **Living**, on the other hand, is more limited in scope and implies the condition of not being dead (*at 92, she was the oldest living member of the family*) or a state of continued existence or activity (*America's greatest living historian*). **Animate** has fewer connotations than *living* or *alive*; though rare, it is used to distinguish living organisms as opposed to dead ones (*one of the few animate creatures after the devastating explosion*). **Animated**, on the other hand, is used to describe inanimate things to which life or the appearance of life has been given (*an animated cartoon*), or things that are vigorous and lively (*an animated debate on the death penalty*). Anything that is essential to life is **vital** (*vital functions; vital organs*), but it can also be used to describe the energy, activity, and alertness of living things (*an aging but vital member of the historical society*).

**all** adjective **1** *all the children went home | all creatures need sleep* EACH OF, each one of, every one of, every single one of; every (single), each and every. ANTONYMS no, none of.

**2** *the sun shone all week* THE WHOLE OF THE, every bit of the, the complete, the entire. ANTONYM none of.

**3** *in all honesty | with all speed* COMPLETE, entire, total, full; greatest (possible), maximum. ANTONYMS no, little.

▸ pronoun **1** *all are welcome* EVERYONE, everybody, each person, every person. ANTONYMS none, nobody.

**2** *all of the cups were broken* EACH ONE, the sum, the total, the whole lot. ANTONYM none.

**3** *they took all of it* EVERYTHING, every part, the whole amount, the (whole) lot, the entirety. ANTONYMS none, nothing.

▸ adverb *he was dressed all in black* COMPLETELY, fully, entirely, totally, wholly, absolutely, utterly; in every respect, in all respects, without reservation, without exception. ANTONYM partly.

**allay** verb *nothing would allay his fears* REDUCE, diminish, decrease, lessen, assuage, alleviate, ease, relieve, soothe, soften, calm, take the edge off. See note at ALLEVIATE. ANTONYMS increase, intensify.

**allegation** noun *not one of the allegations against my client has been substantiated* CLAIM, assertion, charge, accusation, declaration, statement, contention, deposition, argument, affirmation, attestation, grievance; *formal* averment.

**allege** verb *both children allege that the babysitter had left them alone for hours at a time* CLAIM, assert, charge, accuse, declare, state, contend, argue, affirm, maintain, attest, testify, swear; *formal* aver.

**alleged** adjective *did Mr. Ramirez tell you what time this alleged crime took place?* SUPPOSED, so-called, claimed, professed, purported, ostensible, putative, unproven.

**allegiance** noun *allegiance to the queen* LOYALTY, faithfulness, fidelity, obedience, homage, devotion; *historical* fealty; *formal* troth. ANTONYMS disloyalty, treachery.

**allegorical** adjective *an allegorical painting* SYMBOLIC, metaphorical, figurative, representative, emblematic.

**allegory** noun *Saramago's latest novel is an allegory of social disintegration* PARABLE, analogy, metaphor, symbol, emblem.

**allergy** noun **1** *an allergy to feathers* HYPERSENSITIVITY, sensitivity, allergic reaction; anaphylaxis.

**2** *informal their allergy to free enterprise* AVERSION, antipathy, opposition, hostility, antagonism, dislike, distaste.

**alleviate** verb *use ice to alleviate the swelling* REDUCE, ease, relieve, take the edge off, deaden, dull, diminish, lessen, weaken, lighten, attenuate, mitigate, allay, assuage, palliate, damp, soothe, help, soften, temper. ANTONYM aggravate.

THE RIGHT WORD **alleviate, abate, allay, assuage, mitigate, relieve, temper**

To **alleviate** is to make something easier to endure (*alleviate the pain following surgery*); **allay** is often used interchangeably, but it also means to put to rest, to quiet or calm (*to allay their suspicions*). **Assuage** and *allay* both suggest the calming or satisfying of a desire or appetite, but *assuage* implies a more complete or permanent satisfaction (*we allay our hunger by nibbling hors d'oeuvres, but a huge dinner assuages our appetite*). To **relieve** implies reducing the misery or discomfort to the point where something is bearable (*relieve the monotony of the cross-country bus trip*) and **mitigate**, which comes from a Latin word meaning to soften, usually means to lessen in force or intensity (*mitigate the storm's impact*). **Abate** suggests a progressive lessening in degree or intensity (*her fever was abating*). To **temper** is to soften or moderate (*to temper justice with mercy*), but it can also mean the exact opposite: to harden or toughen something (*tempering steel; a body tempered by lifting weights*).

---

**alley** noun *he disappeared down an alley on his motorbike* PASSAGE, passageway, alleyway, back alley, back lane, laneway, backstreet, lane, path, pathway, walk, allée.

**alliance** noun **1** *a defense alliance* ASSOCIATION, union, league, confederation, federation, confederacy, coalition, consortium, affiliation, partnership.

**2** *an alliance between medicine and morality* RELATIONSHIP, affinity, association, connection.

**allied** adjective **1** *a group of allied nations* FEDERATED, confederated, associated, in alliance, in league, in partnership; unified, united, integrated. ANTONYM hostile.

**2** *agricultural and allied industries* ASSOCIATED, related, connected, interconnected, linked; similar, like, comparable, equivalent. ANTONYMS dissimilar, unrelated.

**allocate** verb *how funds will be allocated is dependent on which budget gets approved* ALLOT, assign, distribute, apportion, share out, portion out, dispense, deal out, dole out, give out, dish out, parcel out, ration out, divide up/out; *informal* divvy up.

**allocation** noun **1** *the efficient allocation of resources* ALLOTMENT, assignment, distribution, apportionment, sharing out, handing out, dealing out, doling out, giving out, dishing out, parceling out, rationing out, dividing up/out; *informal* divvying up.

**2** *our annual allocation of funds* ALLOWANCE, allotment, quota, share, ration, portion, grant, slice; *informal* cut.

**allot** verb *Councilwoman Crane has asked why so much tax revenue was* ***allotted to*** *park restoration* ALLOCATE TO, assign to, apportion to, distribute to, issue to, grant to; earmark for, designate for, set aside for; hand out to/for, deal out to/for, dish out to/for, dole out to/for, give out to/for; *informal* divvy up for.

**allotment** noun **1** *the allotment of shares by a company* ALLOCATION, assignment, distribution, apportionment, issuing, sharing out, handing out, dealing out, doling out, giving out, dishing out, parceling out, rationing out, dividing up/out; *informal* divvying up.

**2** *each member received an allotment of new shares* QUOTA, share, ration, grant, allocation, allowance, slice; *informal* cut.

**all out** adverb *I'm working all out to finish my novel* STRENUOUSLY, energetically, vigorously, hard, with all one's might (and main), at full speed, in high gear, eagerly, enthusiastically, industriously, diligently, assiduously, sedulously, indefatigably; *informal* like mad, like crazy. ANTONYM lackadaisically.

▸ adjective *an all-out attack* STRENUOUS, energetic, vigorous, forceful, forcible; spirited, mettlesome, plucky, determined, resolute, wholehearted, unrestrained, aggressive, eager, keen, enthusiastic, zealous, ardent, fervent. ANTONYM halfhearted.

**allow** verb **1** *we don't allow open fires at this campground* PERMIT, let, authorize, give permission for, give authorization for, sanction, license, enable, entitle; consent to, assent to, give one's consent to/for, give one's assent to/for, give one's blessing to/for, give the nod to, acquiesce to, agree to, approve; tolerate, brook; *informal* give the go-ahead to/for, give the thumbs up to/for, OK, give the OK to/for, give the green light to/for; *formal* accede to. ANTONYMS prevent, forbid.

**2** *allow an hour or so for driving* SET ASIDE, allocate, allot, earmark, designate, assign, leave.

**3** *she allowed that all people had their funny little ways* ADMIT, acknowledge, recognize, agree, accept, concede, grant. ANTONYM deny.

**allowable** adjective *the maximum allowable number of users* PERMISSIBLE, permitted, allowed, admissible, acceptable, legal, lawful, legitimate, licit, authorized, sanctioned, approved, in order; *informal* OK, legit. ANTONYM forbidden.

**allowance** noun **1** *your baggage allowance* PERMITTED AMOUNT/QUANTITY, allocation, allotment, quota, share, ration, grant, limit, portion, slice.

**2** *she spent her allowance on paperbacks* PAYMENT, pocket money, sum of money, contribution, grant, subsidy, stipend, maintenance, remittance, financial support, per diem.

**3** *a tax allowance* CONCESSION, reduction, decrease, discount. PHRASE: **make allowance(s) for** **1** *you must make allowances for delays* TAKE INTO CONSIDERATION, take into account, bear in mind, have regard to, provide for, plan for, make plans for, get ready for, allow for, make provision for, make preparations for, prepare for.

**2** *she made allowances for his faults* EXCUSE, make excuses for, forgive, pardon, overlook.

**alloy** noun *modern pewter is an alloy of tin, copper, and antimony* MIXTURE, mix, amalgam, fusion, meld, blend, compound, combination, composite, union; *technical* admixture.

**all right** adjective **1** *the tea was all right* SATISFACTORY, acceptable, adequate, fairly good, passable, reasonable; *informal* so-so, 'comme ci, comme ça,' OK, jake. ANTONYM unsatisfactory.

**2** *are you all right?* UNHURT, uninjured, unharmed, unscathed, in one piece, safe, safe and sound; well, fine, alive and well, OK. ANTONYMS hurt, in danger.

**3** *it's all right for you to go now* PERMISSIBLE, permitted, allowed, allowable, admissible, acceptable, legal, lawful, legitimate, licit, authorized, sanctioned, approved, in order, OK, legit. ANTONYM forbidden.

▸ adverb **1** *the system works all right* SATISFACTORILY, adequately, fairly well, passably, acceptably, reasonably; OK. ANTONYM unsatisfactorily.

**2** *it's him all right* DEFINITELY, certainly, unquestionably, undoubtedly, indubitably, undeniably, assuredly, for sure, without (a) doubt, beyond (any) doubt, beyond the shadow of a doubt; *archaic* in sooth, verily. ANTONYM possibly.

▸ exclamation *all right, I'll go* VERY WELL (THEN), fine, good, yes, agreed, right (then); *informal* OK, okey-dokey, roger, wilco. ANTONYM no.

**allude** verb *the prosecutor* ***alluded to*** *Dixon's past* REFER TO, touch on, suggest, hint at, imply, mention (in passing), make an allusion to; *formal* advert to.

**allure** noun *the allure of Paris* ATTRACTION, lure, draw, pull, appeal, allurement, enticement, temptation, charm, seduction, fascination. ANTONYM repulsion.

▸ verb *will sponsors be allured by such opportunities?* ATTRACT, lure, entice, tempt, appeal to, captivate, draw, win over, charm, seduce, inveigle, beguile, fascinate, whet the appetite of, make someone's mouth water. See note at TEMPT. ANTONYM repel.

**alluring** adjective *an alluring hostess* ENTICING, tempting, attractive, appealing, inviting, captivating, fetching, seductive; enchanting, charming, fascinating; *informal* come-hither.

**allusion** noun *the town's name is an* ***allusion to*** *its founding family* REFERENCE TO, mention of, suggestion of, hint to, intimation of, comment on, remark on.

**ally** noun *close political allies* ASSOCIATE, colleague, friend, confederate, partner, supporter. ANTONYMS enemy, opponent.

▸ verb **1** *he allied his racing experience with business acumen* COMBINE, marry, couple, merge, amalgamate, join, fuse. ANTONYM split.

**2** *the Catholic powers allied with Philip II* UNITE, combine, join (up), join forces, band together, team up, collaborate, side, align oneself, form an alliance, throw in one's lot, make common cause. ANTONYM split.

**almanac** noun *we consult the almanac for planting times* YEARBOOK, calendar, register, annual; manual, handbook.

**almighty** adjective **1** *I swear by almighty God* ALL-POWERFUL, omnipotent, supreme, preeminent. ANTONYM powerless.

**2** *informal an almighty explosion* VERY GREAT, huge, enormous, immense, colossal, massive, prodigious, stupendous, tremendous, monumental, mammoth, vast, gigantic, giant, mighty, Herculean, epic; very loud, deafening, ear-splitting, ear-piercing, booming, thundering, thunderous; *informal* whopping, thumping, astronomical, mega, monster, humongous, jumbo, ginormous. ANTONYM insignificant.

**almost** adverb *we're almost done with the attic* NEARLY, (just) about, more or less, practically, virtually, all but, as good as, close to, near, not quite, roughly, not far from, for all intents and purposes; approaching, bordering on, verging on; *informal* pretty near, pretty nearly, pretty much, pretty well; *literary* well-nigh, nigh on.

**alone** adjective & adverb **1** *she lived alone* | *he came to the party alone* BY ONESELF, on one's own, all alone, solitary, single, singly, solo, solus; unescorted, unaccompanied, partnerless, companionless, by one's lonesome. ANTONYMS with others, accompanied.

**2** *he managed the store alone* UNAIDED, unassisted, without help, without assistance, single-handedly, solo, on one's own. ANTONYM with help.

**3** *Klein felt terribly alone* LONELY, isolated, solitary, deserted, abandoned, forsaken, forlorn, friendless. ANTONYMS loved, wanted, among friends.

**4** *a house standing alone* APART, by itself/oneself, separate, detached, isolated. ANTONYM among others.

**5** *you alone inspire me* ONLY, solely, just; and no one else, and nothing else, and no one but, and nothing but.

**along** preposition **1** *she walked along the corridor* DOWN, from one end of —— to the other.

**2** *trees grew along the river bank* BESIDE, by the side of, on the edge of, alongside.

**3** *they'll stop along the way* ON, at a point on, in the course of.

▸ adverb **1** *Maurice moved along past the other exhibits* ONWARD, on, ahead, forward, forth.

**2** *I invited a friend along* AS COMPANY, with one, to accompany one, as a partner.

PHRASE: **along with** *he backpacked, along with Kate and Sean, across northern Vermont* TOGETHER WITH, accompanying, accompanied by; at the same time as; as well as, in addition to, plus, besides.

**aloof** adjective *part of their strategy is to remain aloof during the first stages of negotiation* DISTANT, detached, unfriendly, antisocial, unsociable, remote, unapproachable, formal, stiff, withdrawn, reserved, unforthcoming, uncommunicative, unsympathetic; *informal* standoffish. ANTONYMS familiar, friendly.

**aloud** adverb *please don't read aloud* AUDIBLY, out loud, for all to hear. ANTONYM silently.

**already** adverb **1** *Anna had already suffered a great deal* BY THIS/THAT TIME, by now/then, thus/so far, before now/then, until now/then, up to now/then.

**2** *is it 3 o'clock already?* AS EARLY AS THIS/THAT, as soon as this/that, so soon.

**also** adverb *she plays basketball also* | *gummy bears, candy corn, and also licorice whips* TOO, as well, besides, in addition, additionally, furthermore, further, moreover, into the bargain, on top (of that), what's more, to boot, equally; *informal* and all, likewise; *archaic* withal.

**alter** verb **1** *Eliot was persuaded to alter the opening passage to his sermon* CHANGE, make changes to, make different, make alterations to, adjust, make adjustments to, adapt, amend, modify, revise, revamp, rework, redo, refine, vary, transform; *informal* tweak; *technical* permute. ANTONYM preserve.

**2** *the state of affairs has altered* CHANGE, become different, undergo a change, undergo a sea change, adjust, adapt, transform, evolve. ANTONYM stay the same.

**alteration** noun *the library was lovely, but they had not anticipated such extensive alterations* CHANGE, adjustment, adaptation, modification, variation, revision, amendment; rearrangement, reordering, restyling, rejigging, reworking, revamping; sea change, transformation; *humorous* transmogrification.

**altercation** noun *an unruly passenger got into an altercation with the flight crew* ARGUMENT, quarrel, squabble, fight, shouting match, disagreement, contretemps, difference of opinion, falling-out, dispute, disputation, clash, fracas, wrangle, blowup, skirmish, run-in, war of words, donnybrook; *informal* tiff, scrap, spat, row, rhubarb. See note at QUARREL.

**alternate** verb **1** *rows of trees alternate with dense shrub* BE INTERSPERSED, occur in turn, rotate, follow one another; take turns, take it in turns, work/act in sequence; oscillate, fluctuate.

**2** *we could alternate the groups so that no one feels left out* GIVE TURNS TO, take in turn, rotate, take in rotation; swap, exchange, interchange.

▸ adjective **1** *she attended on alternate days* EVERY OTHER, every second.

**2** *place the leeks and noodles in alternate layers* ALTERNATING, interchanging, following in sequence, sequential, occurring in turns.

**3** *just in case, let's come up with a couple of alternate plans | an alternate crossing guard* ALTERNATIVE, other, another, second, different, substitute, replacement, deputy, relief, proxy, surrogate, cover, fill-in, stand-in, standby, emergency, reserve, backup, auxiliary, fallback; *informal* pinch-hitting.

**alternative** adjective **1** *an alternative route* DIFFERENT, other, another, second, possible, substitute, replacement, alternate; standby, emergency, reserve, backup, auxiliary, fallback.

**2** *an alternative lifestyle* UNORTHODOX, unconventional, nonstandard, unusual, uncommon, out of the ordinary, radical, revolutionary, nonconformist, avant-garde; *informal* off the wall, oddball, offbeat, way-out.

▸ noun *we have no alternative* OPTION, choice, other possibility; substitute, replacement.

**alternatively** adverb *alternatively, you can build your own barbecue* ON THE OTHER HAND, as an alternative, or; otherwise, instead, if not, then again, alternately.

**although** conjunction *although I'm not a fan of country music, I thoroughly enjoyed Vince Gill's performance* IN SPITE OF THE FACT THAT, despite the fact that, notwithstanding (the fact) that, even though/if, for all that, while; *chiefly Brit.* whilst.

**altitude** noun *clouds are classified according to form and altitude* HEIGHT, elevation, distance above the sea/ground; loftiness.

**altogether** adverb **1** *he wasn't altogether happy* COMPLETELY, totally, entirely, absolutely, wholly, fully, thoroughly, utterly, perfectly, one hundred percent, in all respects.

**2** *we have five offices altogether* IN ALL, all told, in toto.

**3** *altogether it was a great evening* ON THE WHOLE, overall, all in all, all things considered, on balance, on average, for the most part, in the main, in general, generally, by and large.

**altruistic** adjective *a team of altruistic doctors who left their lucrative practices to open a clinic in Zambia* UNSELFISH, selfless, compassionate, kind, public-spirited; charitable, benevolent, beneficent, philanthropic, humanitarian; *literary* bounteous.

**always** adverb **1** *he's always late* EVERY TIME, each time, at all times, all the time, without fail, consistently, invariably, regularly, habitually, unfailingly. ANTONYMS never, seldom, sometimes.

**2** *she's always complaining* CONTINUALLY, continuously, constantly, forever, perpetually, incessantly, ceaselessly, unceasingly, endlessly, the entire time; *informal* 24-7. ANTONYMS never, on and off.

**3** *the place will always be dear to me* FOREVER, for always, for good (and all), forevermore, for ever and ever, until the end of time, eternally, for eternity, until hell freezes over; *informal* for keeps, until the cows come home; *archaic* for aye. ANTONYM never.

**4** *you can always take it back to the shop* AS A LAST RESORT, no matter what, in any event, in any case, come what may.

**amalgamate** verb *the two departments were amalgamated | various companies amalgamated* COMBINE, merge, unite, fuse, blend, meld; join (together), join forces, band (together), link (up), team up, go into partnership; *literary* commingle. ANTONYM separate.

**amass** verb *the squirrels have amassed a huge quantity of acorns* GATHER, collect, assemble; accumulate, aggregate, stockpile, store (up), pile up, heap, cumulate, accrue, lay in/up, garner; *informal* stash (away). ANTONYM dissipate.

**amateur** noun **1** *the crew were all amateurs* NONPROFESSIONAL, nonspecialist, layman, layperson; dilettante; *informal* greenhorn. ANTONYM professional.

**2** *what a bunch of amateurs* BUNGLER, incompetent, bumbler. ANTONYM expert.

▸ adjective **1** *an amateur sportsman* NONPROFESSIONAL, nonspecialist, lay; dilettante.

**2** *their amateur efforts* INCOMPETENT, inept, unskillful, inexpert, amateurish, clumsy, maladroit, bumbling.

**amaze** verb *this shy, gawky teenager gets on the stage and amazes everyone with the best Elvis impersonation of the evening* ASTONISH, astound, surprise, stun, stagger, shock, stupefy, awe, stop someone in their tracks, leave open-mouthed, leave aghast, take someone's breath away, dumbfound; *informal* bowl over, flabbergast, blow away.

**amazement** noun *we watched in amazement as Yvonne took her first steps since the accident* ASTONISHMENT, surprise, shock, stupefaction, incredulity, disbelief, speechlessness, awe, wonder, wonderment.

**ambassador** noun **1** *the American ambassador* ENVOY, plenipotentiary, emissary, (papal) nuncio, representative, high commissioner, consul, consul general, diplomat; *archaic* legate.

**2** *a great ambassador for the sport* CAMPAIGNER, representative, promoter, champion, supporter, backer, booster.

**ambiguity** noun *the ambiguity of the rule made it impossible to follow* VAGUENESS, obscurity, abstruseness, doubtfulness, uncertainty; *formal* dubiety; ambivalence, equivocation, double meaning.

**ambiguous** adjective *an ambiguous explanation* EQUIVOCAL, ambivalent, open to debate/argument, arguable, debatable; obscure, unclear, imprecise, vague, abstruse, doubtful, dubious, uncertain. See note at DOUBTFUL. ANTONYM clear.

**ambition** noun **1** *young people with ambition* DRIVE, determination, enterprise, initiative, eagerness, motivation, resolve, enthusiasm, zeal, hunger, commitment, a sense of purpose; *informal* get-up-and-go.

**2** *her ambition was to become a diplomat* ASPIRATION, intention, goal, aim, objective, object, purpose, intent, plan, desire, wish, design, target, dream.

**ambitious** adjective **1** *an energetic and ambitious politician* ASPIRING, determined, forceful, pushy, enterprising, motivated, enthusiastic, energetic, zealous, committed, purposeful, power-hungry; *informal* go-getting, go-ahead. ANTONYMS lazy, laid-back.

**2** *he was ambitious to make it to the top* EAGER, determined, enthusiastic, anxious, hungry, impatient, striving.

**3** *an ambitious task* DIFFICULT, exacting, demanding, formidable, challenging, hard, arduous, onerous, tough; *archaic* toilsome. ANTONYM easy.

**ambivalent** adjective *the need to relocate has made her ambivalent about the promotion* EQUIVOCAL, uncertain, unsure, doubtful, indecisive, inconclusive, irresolute, of two minds, undecided, torn, in a quandary, on the fence, hesitating, wavering, vacillating, equivocating, blowing/running hot and cold; *informal* iffy. ANTONYMS unequivocal, certain.

**amble** verb *ambling through the park* STROLL, saunter, wander, ramble, promenade, walk, go for a walk, take a walk; *informal* mosey, toddle, tootle; *formal* perambulate.

**ambush** noun *the soldiers were killed in an ambush* SURPRISE ATTACK, trap; *archaic* ambuscade.

▸ verb *twenty youths ambushed the patrol car* ATTACK BY SURPRISE, surprise, pounce on, fall upon, lay a trap for, set an ambush for, lie in wait for, waylay, bushwhack; *archaic* ambuscade.

**amenable** adjective **1** *an amenable child* COOPERATIVE, acquiescent, compliant, accommodating, obliging, biddable, manageable, controllable, governable, persuadable, tractable, responsive, pliant, malleable, complaisant, easily handled; *rare* persuasible. ANTONYM uncooperative.

**2** *many cancers are amenable to treatment* SUSCEPTIBLE, receptive, responsive; *archaic* susceptive. ANTONYMS unresponsive, resistant.

**amend** verb *the membership application was recently amended* REVISE, alter, change, modify, qualify, adapt, adjust; edit, copyedit, rewrite, redraft, rephrase, reword, rework, revamp.

**amends** plural noun PHRASES: **make amends** *after all the pain I've caused, is it possible to make amends? | he's obviously trying to make amends for what he's done* MAKE GOOD, atone, make up, indemnify, expiate.
**make amends to** *it's up to you to make amends to those you've hurt* COMPENSATE, recompense, redress, indemnify, make it up to.

**amenity** noun *basic amenities* FACILITY, service, convenience, resource, appliance, aid, comfort, benefit, feature, advantage.

**amiable** adjective *you'll find that the folks in this department are genuinely amiable* FRIENDLY, affable, amicable, cordial; warm, warmhearted, good-natured, nice, pleasant, agreeable, likable, genial, good-humored, charming, easy to get along with, companionable, sociable, personable; *informal* chummy, simpatico. ANTONYMS unfriendly, disagreeable.

**amicable** adjective *the relationship between the kids and their stepfather is an amicable one* FRIENDLY, good-natured, cordial, easy, easygoing, neighborly, harmonious, cooperative, civilized. ANTONYM unfriendly.

**amid** preposition **1** *the jeep was concealed amid pine trees* IN THE MIDDLE OF, surrounded by, among, amongst; *literary* amidst, in the midst of.

**2** *the truce collapsed amid fears of a revolt* AT A TIME OF, in an atmosphere of, against a background of; as a result of.

**amiss** adjective *an inspection revealed nothing amiss* WRONG, awry, faulty, out of order, defective, flawed, unsatisfactory, incorrect, not right; inappropriate, improper. ANTONYMS right, in order.

PHRASE: **take something amiss** *we were only kidding, but I think he took it amiss* BE OFFENDED, take offense, be upset.

**ammunition** noun *police seized arms and ammunition* BULLETS, shells, projectiles, missiles, rounds, shot, slugs, cartridges, munitions; *informal* ammo.

**amnesty** noun *the governor has granted amnesty to seven of the prisoners* PARDON, pardoning, reprieve; grace; release, discharge.

**amok** PHRASE: **run amok** *the robot is running amok in Sector B* GO BERSERK, get out of control, rampage, riot, run riot, go on the rampage, behave like a maniac, behave wildly, behave uncontrollably, become violent, become destructive; *informal* raise hell, go postal.

**amorous** adjective *amorous advances* ROMANTIC, lustful, sexual, erotic, amatory, ardent, passionate, impassioned; in love, enamored, lovesick; *informal* lovey-dovey, kissy, smoochy, hot.

**amorphous** adjective *an amorphous lump of clay* SHAPELESS, formless, structureless, indeterminate; vague, nebulous, indefinite.

**amount** noun *a fair amount of roast beef | we sold a comparable amount in the second quarter* QUANTITY, number, total, aggregate, sum, quota, group, size, mass, weight, volume, bulk, lot, quantum. PHRASES: **the full amount** *we can't make a payment schedule until we know the full amount* THE GRAND TOTAL, the total, the aggregate; *informal* the whole kit and caboodle, the whole shebang, the whole nine yards.
**amount to 1** *the bill amounted to $50* ADD UP TO, come to, run (to), be, total.

**2** *a result that amounted to complete failure* CONSTITUTE, be tantamount to, come down to, boil down to; signify, signal, mean, indicate, suggest, denote, point to, be evidence of, be symptomatic of; *literary* betoken.

**3** *her relationships had never amounted to anything significant* BECOME, develop into, develop into, prove to be, turn out to be.

**ample** adjective **1** *there is ample time for discussion* ENOUGH, sufficient, adequate, plenty of, more than enough, enough and to spare. ANTONYM insufficient.

**2** *an ample supply of wine* PLENTIFUL, abundant, copious, profuse, rich, lavish, liberal, generous, bountiful, bounteous, large, huge, great, bumper; *literary* plenteous. ANTONYM meager.

**amplify** verb **1** *the sound from an electric guitar was meant to be amplified* MAKE LOUDER, louden, turn up, magnify, intensify, increase, boost, step up, raise. ANTONYM quieten.

**2** *these notes amplify our statement* EXPAND, enlarge upon, elaborate on, add to, supplement, develop, flesh out, add detail to, go into detail about. ANTONYM condense.

**amputate** verb *doctors had to amputate two fingers* CUT OFF, sever, remove (surgically), dismember, saw/chop off.

**amuse** verb **1** *the ugliest dog contest amused him* ENTERTAIN, make laugh, delight, divert, cheer (up), please, charm, tickle; *informal* tickle pink, crack up. ANTONYMS bore, depress.

**2** *he amused himself by writing poetry* OCCUPY, engage, busy, employ, distract, absorb, engross; interest, entertain, divert.

**amusement** noun **1** *we looked with amusement at the cartoon* MIRTH, merriment, lightheartedness, hilarity, glee, delight, gaiety, joviality, fun; enjoyment, pleasure, high spirits, cheerfulness.

**2** *I read the book for amusement* ENTERTAINMENT, pleasure, leisure, relaxation, fun, enjoyment, interest, diversion; *informal* R and R; *archaic* disport.

**3** *a wide range of amusements* ACTIVITY, entertainment, diversion; game, sport.

**amusing** adjective *an amusing story* ENTERTAINING, funny, comical, humorous, lighthearted, jocular, witty, mirthful, hilarious, droll, diverting; laughable; *informal* wacky, side-splitting, rib-tickling. ANTONYMS boring, solemn.

**analogous** adjective *their lab results were analogous* COMPARABLE, parallel, similar, like, akin, corresponding, related, kindred, equivalent. ANTONYM unrelated.

**analogy** noun *there's a thinly veiled analogy between his fiction and his real life* SIMILARITY, parallel, correspondence, likeness, resemblance, correlation, relation, kinship, equivalence, similitude, metaphor, simile. See note at LIKENESS. ANTONYM dissimilarity.

**analysis** noun *an interesting analysis of England's tax laws* EXAMINATION, investigation, inspection, survey, study, scrutiny; exploration, probe, research, review, evaluation, interpretation, dissection.

**analyze** verb *chemists are analyzing the substance* EXAMINE, inspect, survey, study, scrutinize, look over; investigate, explore, probe, research, go over (with a fine-tooth comb), review, evaluate, break down, dissect, anatomize.

**anarchic** adjective *an anarchic society has replaced the despotism* LAWLESS, without law and order, in disorder, in turmoil, unruly, disordered, disorganized, chaotic, turbulent; mutinous, rebellious.

**anarchist** noun *police said they arrested 10 self-styled anarchists* NIHILIST, insurgent, agitator, subversive, terrorist, revolutionary, revolutionist, insurrectionist.

**anarchy** noun *conditions are dangerously ripe for anarchy* LAWLESSNESS, nihilism, mobocracy, revolution, insurrection, disorder, chaos, mayhem, tumult, turmoil. ANTONYMS government, order.

**anathema** noun *a nation viewed as a sponsor of terrorism, which is anathema in the West* AN ABOMINATION, an outrage, an abhorrence, a disgrace, an evil, a bane, a bugbear, a bête noire; *adjectives* ABHORRENT, hateful, repugnant, odious, repellent, offensive.

**anatomy** noun *the anatomy of a frog* BODILY STRUCTURE, makeup, composition, constitution, form, structure.

**ancestor** noun **1** *he could trace his ancestors back to colonial Boston* FOREBEAR, forefather, predecessor, antecedent, progenitor, primogenitor. ANTONYMS descendant, successor.

**2** *the instrument is an ancestor of the lute* FORERUNNER, precursor, predecessor.

**ancestral** adjective *their ancestral hunting grounds* INHERITED, hereditary, familial; *rare* lineal.

**ancestry** noun *our Polish ancestry* ANCESTORS, forebears, forefathers, progenitors, antecedents; family tree; lineage, parentage, genealogy, descent, roots, stock, line.

**anchor** noun **1** *the anchor of the new coalition* MAINSTAY, cornerstone, linchpin, bulwark, foundation.

**2** *a TV news anchor* PRESENTER, announcer, anchorman, anchorwoman, broadcaster.

▸ verb **1** *the ship was anchored in the bay* MOOR, berth, be at anchor; *dated* harbor.

**2** *the fish anchors itself to the coral* SECURE, fasten, attach, affix, fix.

**ancient** adjective **1** *in ancient times* OF LONG AGO, early, prehistoric, primeval, primordial, primitive; *literary* of yore; *archaic* foregone. ANTONYMS recent, contemporary.

**2** *an ancient custom* OLD, very old, age-old, archaic, time-worn, time-honored, venerable. See note at OLD. ANTONYMS recent, new, modern.

**3** *informal I feel positively ancient* OLD, aged, elderly, antiquated, decrepit, antediluvian, in one's dotage; old-fashioned, out of date, outmoded, obsolete, passé, démodé; *informal* horse-and-buggy. ANTONYMS youthful, up to date.

**ancillary** adjective *the Administrative Procedures Act and ancillary documents* ADDITIONAL, auxiliary, supporting, helping, extra, supplementary, supplemental, accessory, attendant; subsidiary, secondary; *Medicine* adjuvant; *rare* adminicular.

**and** conjunction *coffee and a scone* TOGETHER WITH, along with, with, as well as, in addition to, also; besides, furthermore; *informal* plus.

**USAGE NOTE and**

It is rank superstition that this coordinating conjunction cannot properly begin a sentence:

• "Another stumbling-block to a certain type of academic mind is the conjunction *and*. It is often laid down as a rigid rule that a sentence should never begin with *and*. This was a point on which my own schoolmaster was inflexible. And quite recently a training college student whom I asked to comment on a passage from Malory condemned him for using 'the objectionable conjunction *and*.' And printers have an ugly trick of emasculating my meaning by turning my periods into commas because they happen to be followed by *and*. Taking down my Bible and opening it at random, I find that the eighth chapter of Exodus contains thirty-two sentences, twenty-five of which begin with *and*." (Philip Boswood Ballard, *Teaching and Testing English*; 1939.)

• "Many years ago schoolteachers insisted that it was improper to begin a sentence with *and*, but this convention is now outmoded. Innumerable respected writers use *and* at the beginning of a sentence." (William Morris and Mary Morris, *Harper Dictionary of Contemporary Usage*, 2d ed.; 1985.)

• "And the idea that *and* must not begin a sentence, or even a paragraph, is an empty superstition. The same goes for *but*. Indeed either word can give unimprovably early warning of the sort of thing that is to follow." (Kingsley Amis, *The King's English*; 1997.).

Schoolteachers may have laid down a prohibition against the initial *and* to counteract elementary-school students' tendency to begin every sentence with *and*. The same superstition has plagued *but* (see note at BUT). But the very best writers find occasion to begin sentences with *and*—e.g.: "And one had better make use of whatever beauty, elegance, riches the translator's language possesses, and hope that something emotionally, intellectually, aesthetically equivalent will emerge." (John Simon, *The Sheep from the Goats*; 1989.)

Oddly, *and* is frequently misused for *or* where a singular noun, or one of two nouns, is called for—e.g.: "While third-party candidates have mounted serious challenges for senator and governor in almost two dozen states this year, building an effective third-party apparatus is rare." (*New York Times*; Oct. 5, 1994.) The phrase should be "senator *or* governor"; as written, the sentence says that in each of almost 24 states, third-party candidates were running for *both* senator *and* governor—an idea belied by the context of the article.

Some writers have a tendency, especially in long enumerations, to omit *and* before the final element. To do so is often infelicitous: the reader is jarred by the abrupt period ending the sentence and may even wonder whether something has been omitted. One may occasionally omit *and* before the final element in an enumeration with a particular nuance in mind. Without *and*, the implication is that the series is incomplete—rhetoricians call this construction "asyndeton." With *and*, the implication is that the series is complete. This shade in meaning is increasingly subtle in modern prose. —*BG*

**anecdote** noun *amusing anecdotes* STORY, tale, narrative, incident; urban myth/legend; *informal* yarn.

**anemic** adjective **1** *his anemic face* COLORLESS, bloodless, pale, pallid, wan, ashen, gray, sallow, pasty-faced, whey-faced, peaked, sickly, etiolated.

**2** *an anemic description of her feelings* FEEBLE, weak, insipid, wishy-washy, vapid, bland; lame, tame, lackluster, spiritless, languid, lifeless, ineffective, ineffectual, etiolated; *informal* pathetic.

**anew** adverb *may we please begin anew?* AGAIN, afresh, another time, once more/again, over again.

**angel** noun **1** *an angel appeared in the heavens* MESSENGER OF GOD, divine/heavenly messenger, divine being. ANTONYMS devil, demon.

**2** *she's an absolute angel* SAINT, paragon of virtue; gem, treasure, darling, dear; *informal* star.

**3** *informal a financial angel* BACKER, sponsor, benefactor, fairy godmother, promoter, patron; *rare* Maecenas.

**angelic** adjective **1** *angelic beings* DIVINE, heavenly, celestial, holy, seraphic, cherubic; spiritual. ANTONYMS demonic, infernal.

**2** *Sophie's angelic appearance* INNOCENT, pure, virtuous, good, saintly, wholesome; beautiful.

**anger** noun *his face was livid with anger* RAGE, vexation, exasperation, displeasure, crossness, irritation, irritability, indignation, pique; annoyance, fury, wrath, ire, outrage, irascibility, ill temper/humor; *informal* slow burn, aggravation; *literary* choler. ANTONYMS pleasure, good humor.

▸ verb *she was angered by his terse reply* INFURIATE, irritate, exasperate, irk, vex, peeve, madden, put out; enrage, incense, annoy; rub the wrong way; *informal* make someone's blood boil, get someone's back up, make someone see red, get someone's dander up, rattle someone's cage, make someone's hackles rise; aggravate, get someone, rile, tick off, tee off, burn up. ANTONYMS pacify, placate.

**angle** noun **1** *the wall is sloping at an angle of 33°* GRADIENT, slant, inclination.

**2** *the angle of the roof* CORNER, intersection, point, apex.

**3** *consider the problem from a different angle* PERSPECTIVE, point of view, viewpoint, standpoint, position, aspect, slant, direction.

▸ verb **1** *Anna angled her camera toward the tree* TILT, slant, direct, turn.

**2** *angle your answer so that it is relevant* PRESENT, slant, orient, twist, bias.

**3** *he was angling for an invitation* TRY TO GET, seek to obtain, fish for, hope for, be after.

**angry** adjective **1** *Vivienne got angry* IRATE, mad, annoyed, cross, vexed, irritated, indignant, irked; furious, enraged, infuriated, in a temper, incensed, raging, fuming, seething, beside oneself, choleric, outraged; livid, apoplectic; *informal* hot under the collar, up in arms, in high dudgeon, foaming at the mouth, doing a slow burn, steamed up, in a lather, fit to be tied, seeing red; sore, bent out of shape, ticked off, teed off, PO'd; *literary* wrathful; *archaic* wroth. ANTONYM pleased.

**2** *an angry debate* HEATED, passionate, stormy, "lively"; bad-tempered, ill-tempered, ill-natured, acrimonious, bitter. ANTONYM good-humored.

PHRASE: **get angry** *my father almost never gets angry* LOSE ONE'S TEMPER, become enraged, go into a rage, go berserk, flare up; *informal* go crazy, go bananas, hit the roof, go through the roof, go up the wall, see red, go off the deep end, fly off the handle, blow one's top, blow a fuse/gasket, flip out, have a fit, foam at the mouth, explode, go ballistic, go postal, flip one's wig, blow one's stack, have a conniption.

**angst** noun *business leaders expressed their angst over war and recession* ANXIETY, fear, apprehension, worry, foreboding, trepidation, malaise, disquiet, disquietude, unease, uneasiness.

**anguish** noun *the anguish of the hostages' families* AGONY, pain, torment, torture, suffering, distress, angst, misery, sorrow, grief, heartache, desolation, despair; *literary* dolor. ANTONYM happiness.

**angular** adjective **1** *an angular shape* SHARP-CORNERED, pointed, V-shaped, Y-shaped. ANTONYMS rounded, curving.

**2** *an angular face* BONY, rawboned, lean, spare, thin, skinny, gaunt. ANTONYMS plump, curvy.

**animal** noun **1** *endangered animals* CREATURE, beast, living thing; *informal* critter, beastie; (**animals**) wildlife, fauna.

**2** *the man was an animal* BRUTE, beast, monster, devil, demon, fiend; *informal* swine, bastard, pig.

▸ adjective *a grunt of animal passion* CARNAL, fleshly, bodily, physical; brutish, beastly, bestial, unrefined, uncultured, coarse.

**animate** verb *a sense of excitement animated the whole school* ENLIVEN, vitalize, breathe (new) life into, energize, invigorate, revive, vivify, liven up; inspire, inspirit, exhilarate, thrill, excite, fire, arouse, rouse, quicken, stir; light a fire under. See note at QUICKEN. ANTONYM depress.

▸ adjective *an animate being* LIVING, alive, live, breathing; *archaic* quick. See note at ALIVE. ANTONYM inanimate.

**animated** adjective *an animated discussion | his animated walk* LIVELY, spirited, high-spirited, energetic, adrenalized, full of life, excited, enthusiastic, eager, alive, active, vigorous, vibrant, vital, vivacious, buoyant, exuberant, ebullient, effervescent, bouncy, bubbly, perky; *informal* bright-eyed and bushy-tailed, bright and breezy, chirpy, chipper, peppy; heated. See note at ALIVE. ANTONYMS lethargic, lifeless.

**annals** plural noun *the annals of the town's history* RECORDS, archives, chronicles, accounts, registers; *Law* muniments.

**annex** verb **1** *Charlemagne annexed northern Italy* TAKE OVER, take possession of, appropriate, seize, conquer, occupy.

**2** *ten amendments were annexed to the constitution* ADD, append, attach, tack on, tag on.

▸ noun *the new annex will house four classrooms and a computer lab* EXTENSION, addition; wing; ell.

**annihilate** verb *an ungodly tornado touched down, annihilating everything in its path* DESTROY, wipe out, obliterate, wipe off the face of the earth; eliminate, liquidate, defeat. See note at DESTROY. ANTONYM create.

**annotate** verb *annotate the text in Chapters 4 and 5* COMMENT ON, add notes/footnotes to, gloss, interpret, mark up.

**annotation** noun *the teacher's copy has annotations in the margins* NOTE, notation, comment, gloss, footnote; commentary, explanation, interpretation.

**announce** verb **1** *their financial results were announced* MAKE PUBLIC, make known, report, declare, divulge, state, give out, notify, publicize, broadcast, publish, advertise, circulate, proclaim, blazon.

**2** *Victor announced the guests* INTRODUCE, present, name.

**3** *strains of music announced her arrival* SIGNAL, indicate, give notice of, herald, proclaim; *literary* betoken.

THE RIGHT WORD **announce, blazon, declare, proclaim, promulgate, publish**

When you **announce** something, you communicate it in a formal and public manner, often for the first time (*to announce the arrival of the guest of honor*). But just how you go about announcing something depends on what you're trying to convey. If you want to make sure no one misses your message, use **blazon** (*signs along the highway blazoned the local farmers' complaints*). If you plan to make your views known to the general public through the medium of writing, use **publish** (*to publish a story on drunk driving in the local newspaper*). Use **proclaim** if you have something of great importance that you want to announce very formally and officially (*proclaim a national day of mourning*). Although **declare** also implies a very formal announcement (*declare war*), it can refer to any clear and explicit statement (*declare one's love*). **Promulgate** is usually associated with the communication of a creed, doctrine, or law (*promulgate the views of the Democratic Party*).

**announcement** noun **1** *an announcement by the dean* STATEMENT, report, declaration, proclamation, pronouncement, rescript; bulletin, communiqué.

**2** *the announcement of the decision* DECLARATION, notification, reporting, publishing, broadcasting, proclamation; *archaic* annunciation.

**announcer** noun *the announcer's voice sounds familiar* PRESENTER, anchorman, anchorwoman, anchor, anchorperson; news reader, newscaster, broadcaster; host, master of ceremonies; *informal* MC, emcee.

**annoy** verb *their barking dog annoys me | where the movie attempts to amuse, it only annoys* IRRITATE, vex, make angry/cross, anger, exasperate, irk, gall, pique, put out, antagonize, get on someone's nerves, get to, ruffle someone's feathers, make someone's hackles rise, nettle; rub the wrong way; *informal* aggravate, peeve, hassle, miff, rile, needle, frost, bug, get someone's goat, get someone's back up, get in someone's hair, give someone the gears, drive mad/crazy/bananas, drive around the bend, drive up the wall, tee off, tick off, burn up, rankle. See note at AGGRAVATE. ANTONYMS please, gratify.

**annoyance** noun **1** *much to his annoyance, Louise didn't even notice* IRRITATION, exasperation, vexation, indignation, anger, displeasure, chagrin; *informal* aggravation.

**2** *they found him an annoyance* NUISANCE, pest, bother, irritant, inconvenience, palaver; *informal* pain, pain in the neck/butt/ass, hassle; nudnik, burr under someone's saddle.

**annual** adjective **1** *the annual company picnic* YEARLY, once-a-year, every twelve months; year-end.

**2** *an annual subscription to the alumni newsletter* YEARLONG, twelve-month.

**annually** adverb *we renew our membership annually* YEARLY, once a year, each year, per annum, per year; every year.

**annul** verb *their parents wanted to get the marriage annulled* DECLARE INVALID, declare null and void, nullify, invalidate, void, disallow; repeal, reverse, rescind, revoke; *Law* vacate; *formal* abrogate; recall. See note at VOID. ANTONYMS restore, enact.

**anoint** verb *he was anointed and crowned* CONSECRATE, bless, ordain; *formal* hallow.

**anomalous** adjective *it's an anomalous birthmark* ABNORMAL, atypical, irregular, aberrant, heteroclite, exceptional, freak, freakish, odd, bizarre, peculiar, unusual, out of the ordinary; deviant, mutant. ANTONYMS normal, typical.

**anomaly** noun *the growth on the duck's bill is a harmless anomaly* ODDITY, peculiarity, abnormality, irregularity, inconsistency, incongruity, aberration, quirk, rarity.

**anonymous** adjective **1** *an anonymous donor* UNNAMED, of unknown name, nameless, incognito, unidentified, unknown, secret. ANTONYMS known, identified.

**2** *an anonymous letter* UNSIGNED, unattributed. ANTONYM signed.

**3** *an anonymous housing development* CHARACTERLESS, nondescript, impersonal, faceless.

**another** adjective *have another drink* ONE MORE, a further, an additional.

**answer** noun **1** *her answer was unequivocal* REPLY, response, rejoinder, reaction; retort, riposte; *informal* comeback. ANTONYM question.

**2** *a new filter is the answer* SOLUTION, remedy, key.

▸ verb **1** *Steve was about to answer* REPLY, respond, make a rejoinder, rejoin; retort, riposte, return.

**2** *she has yet to answer the charges* REBUT, defend oneself against.

**3** *a man answering this description* MATCH, fit, correspond to, be similar to.

**4** *we're trying to answer the needs of our audience* SATISFY, meet, fulfill, fill, measure up to.

**5** ***I answer to** the commissioner* REPORT TO, work for/under, be subordinate to, be accountable to, be answerable to, be responsible to.

**6** *he will answer for his crime* PAY, be punished, suffer; make amends, make reparation, atone.

**7** *the government has a lot to answer for* BE ACCOUNTABLE, be responsible, be liable, take the blame; *informal* take the rap.

**answerable** adjective *the ensign is answerable to the captain* ACCOUNTABLE, responsible, liable; subject. See note at RESPONSIBLE.

**antagonism** noun *a long history of antagonism between the two nations* HOSTILITY, friction, enmity, antipathy, animus, opposition, dissension, rivalry; acrimony, bitterness, rancor, resentment, animosity, aversion, dislike, ill feeling, ill will, bad blood. ANTONYMS rapport, friendship.

**antagonist** noun *only in our political life are we antagonists* ADVERSARY, opponent, enemy, foe, rival, competitor; (**antagonists**) opposition, competition. ANTONYM ally.

**antagonistic** adjective **1** *he was **antagonistic to** the reforms* HOSTILE TO, against, (dead) set against, opposed to, inimical to, antipathetic to, ill-disposed to, resistant to, in disagreement with; *informal* anti. ANTONYMS sympathetic, pro.

**2** *an antagonistic group of bystanders* HOSTILE, aggressive, belligerent, bellicose, pugnacious; *rare* oppugnant.

**antagonize** verb *have I done something to antagonize you?* AROUSE HOSTILITY IN, alienate; anger, annoy, provoke, vex, irritate; rub the wrong way; *informal* aggravate, rile, needle, rattle someone's cage, get someone's back up. ANTONYMS pacify, placate.

**antedate** verb *a civilization that antedates the Roman Empire* PRECEDE, predate, come/go before, be earlier than.

**antediluvian** adjective *her antediluvian attitudes* OUT OF DATE, outdated, outmoded, old-fashioned, antiquated, behind the times, passé. See note at OLD.

**anteroom** noun *guests will be met in the anteroom* ANTE-

CHAMBER, vestibule, lobby, foyer, outer room; *Architecture* narthex.

**anthem** noun *a patriotic anthem* HYMN, song, chorale, psalm, paean.

**anthology** noun *an anthology of American poetry* COLLECTION, selection, compendium, treasury, miscellany; *archaic* garland.

**anticipate** verb **1** *we don't anticipate any trouble* EXPECT, foresee, predict, be prepared for, bargain on, reckon on; *informal* figure on.

**2** *the defender must anticipate the attacker's moves* PREEMPT, forestall, second-guess; *informal* beat someone to the punch.

**3** *we enthusiastically anticipate your arrival* LOOK FORWARD TO, await, count the days until; *informal* lick one's lips over.

**anticipation** noun *her eyes sparkled with anticipation* EXPECTANCY, expectation, excitement, suspense. PHRASE: **in anticipation of** *we bought plenty of food in anticipation of holiday visitors* IN THE EXPECTATION OF, in preparation for, in case of, ready for.

**anticlimax** noun *for me, the anticlimax is when Reggie—for no apparent purpose to the plot—suddenly decides to quit school* LETDOWN, disappointment, comedown, nonevent; bathos.

**antics** plural noun *someday you'll be too old to get away with such antics* CAPERS, pranks, larks, hijinks, frolicking, skylarking, foolery, tomfoolery.

**antidote** noun **1** *the antidote to this poison* ANTITOXIN, antiserum, antivenin.

**2** *laughter is a good antidote to stress* REMEDY, cure, nostrum.

**antipathy** noun *I never encountered racial antipathy until I went to college* HOSTILITY, antagonism, animosity, aversion, animus, enmity, dislike, distaste, hatred, hate, abhorrence, loathing. ANTONYMS liking, affinity.

**antiquated** adjective *his views on single parenthood are antiquated* OUTDATED, out of date, outmoded, outworn, old, stale, behind the times, old-fashioned, anachronistic, old-fangled, antique, antediluvian, passé, démodé, obsolete; *informal* out of the ark, moldy, horse-and-buggy. See note at OLD. ANTONYMS modern, up to date.

**antique** noun *the zither is a lovely antique* COLLECTOR'S ITEM, period piece, antiquity, heirloom.

▸ adjective **1** *antique furniture* OLD, antiquarian, collectable, old-fashioned. ANTONYMS modern, new.

**2** *statues of antique gods* ANCIENT, of long ago; *literary* of yore.

**3** *antique work practices.* See ANTIQUATED. ANTONYMS modern, current.

**antiseptic** adjective **1** *an antiseptic substance* DISINFECTANT, germicidal, bactericidal, antibacterial, antibiotic.

**2** *antiseptic bandages* STERILE, aseptic, germ-free, uncontaminated, disinfected. See note at SANITARY. ANTONYM contaminated.

**3** *their antiseptic surroundings* CHARACTERLESS, colorless, soulless; clinical, institutional; dispassionate, detached. ANTONYM colorful.

▸ noun DISINFECTANT, germicide, bactericide.

**antisocial** adjective **1** *worrisome antisocial behavior* SOCIOPATHIC, distasteful, disruptive, rebellious, misanthropic, asocial.

**2** *I'm feeling a bit antisocial* UNSOCIABLE, unfriendly, uncommunicative, reclusive, withdrawn; standoffish. See note at UNSOCIABLE.

**antithesis** noun *friends of the actress say she is quite the antithesis of her giddy and frivolous character* (COMPLETE) OPPOSITE, converse, contrary, reverse, inverse, obverse, other side of the coin; *informal* flip side.

**anxiety** noun **1** *his anxiety grew* WORRY, concern, apprehension, apprehensiveness, uneasiness, unease, fearfulness, fear, disquiet, disquietude, inquietude, perturbation, agitation, angst, misgiving, nervousness, nerves, tension, tenseness; *informal* heebie-jeebies, butterflies (in one's stomach), jitteriness, the jitters, twitchiness. ANTONYMS calmness, serenity.

**2** *an anxiety to please* EAGERNESS, keenness, desire.

**anxious** adjective **1** *her fever has us all a little anxious* WORRIED, concerned, uneasy, apprehensive, fearful, perturbed, troubled, bothered, disturbed, distressed, disquieted, fretful, agitated, nervous, edgy, antsy, unquiet, on edge, tense, overwrought, worked up, keyed up, jumpy, worried sick, with one's stomach in knots, with one's heart in one's mouth; *informal* uptight, on tenterhooks, with butterflies in one's stomach, jittery, twitchy, in a dither, in a lather, in a tizzy, het up; strung out, having kittens; antsy, spooked, squirrelly. ANTONYMS carefree, unconcerned.

**2** *she was anxious for news* EAGER, keen, desirous, impatient.

### USAGE NOTE **anxious**

The word *anxious* has a range of meaning. As the adjective corresponding to *anxiety*, it has long meant "uneasy, disquieted." In the most unimpeachable uses, the word stays close to that association—e.g.: "The latest holdup is the EPA's final approval of the companies' plans to test for lead at the 150 homes . . . . Some residents are getting anxious." (*Atlanta Journal Constitution*; Sept. 13, 2002.)

Today the word typically encompasses both worry and anticipation—e.g.: "Creator and anchorman Brian Lamb, the prince of un-chic, tirelessly fields the remarks of obnoxious callers, preening journalists, and anxious authors." (*National Review*; Mar. 24, 1997.)

The word carries a sense of expectation, as when discussing a major life change. But when no sense of uneasiness is attached to the situation, *anxious* isn't the best word. In those instances, it displaces a word that might traditionally have been considered its opposite—namely, eager—e.g.: "Three years ago, the Latin music industry was caught up in crossover mania, anxious [read *eager*] to ride the popularity of singers such as Ricky Martin and Enrique Iglesias by selling their English-language albums to the American mainstream." (*Sun-Sentinel* [Fort Lauderdale]; Sept. 13, 2002.) —*BG*

**any** adjective **1** *is there any cake left?* SOME, a piece of, a part of, a bit of.

**2** *it doesn't make any difference* THE SLIGHTEST BIT OF, a scrap of, a shred of, a whit of, a particle of, an iota of, a jot of.

**3** *any job will do* WHICHEVER, no matter which, never mind which; *informal* any old.

▸ pronoun **1** *you don't know any of my friends* A SINGLE ONE, one, even one.

**2** *we no longer give to any, unless they represent one of our top five charities* ANYONE, anybody, any individual/person; any group

▸ adverb *is your father any better?* AT ALL, in the least, to any extent, in/to any degree.

**anyhow** adverb **1** *anyhow, it doesn't really matter.*

**2** *her clothes were strewn about anyhow* HAPHAZARDLY, carelessly, heedlessly, negligently, in a muddle; *informal* all over the place, every which way.

**apart** adverb **1** *the villages are two miles apart* AWAY FROM EACH OTHER, distant from each other.

**2** *Isabel stood apart* TO ONE SIDE, aside, separately, alone, by oneself/itself.

**3** *his parents are living apart* SEPARATELY, independently, on one's own.

**4** *the car was blown apart* TO PIECES, to bits, up; *literary* asunder. PHRASE: **apart from** *apart from the broken headlight, the car seems to be OK* EXCEPT FOR, but for, aside from, with the exception of, excepting, excluding, bar, barring, besides, other than; *informal* outside of; *formal* save.

**apartment** noun **1** *a rented apartment. informal* pad.

**2** *the royal apartments* SUITE (OF ROOMS), rooms, living quarters, accommodations.

**apathetic** adjective *an apathetic workforce* UNINTERESTED, INDIFFERENT, unconcerned, unmoved, uninvolved, disinterested, unemotional, emotionless, dispassionate, lukewarm, unmotivated, halfhearted; *informal* couldn't-care-less; *rare* Laodicean. See note at CARE.

**apathy** noun *widespread apathy among the voters* INDIFFERENCE, lack of interest, lack of enthusiasm, lack of concern, unconcern, uninterestedness, unresponsiveness, impassivity, dispassion, lethargy, languor, ennui; *rare* acedia.

**ape** noun PRIMATE, simian; monkey; *technical* anthropoid.

▸ verb *he aped Barbara's accent* IMITATE, mimic, copy, parrot, do an impression of, parody, mock; *informal* take off, send up. See note at IMITATE.

**aperture** noun *adjusting the aperture of the camera* OPENING, hole, gap, slit, slot, vent, crevice, chink, crack, interstice; *technical* orifice, foramen.

**apex** noun **1** *the apex of a pyramid* TIP, peak, summit, pinnacle, top, vertex. ANTONYM bottom.

**2** *the apex of his career* CLIMAX, culmination; peak, top, pinnacle, zenith, acme, apogee, high(est) point, capstone. ANTONYM nadir.

**aphrodisiac** noun LOVE POTION, philter; *informal* passion potion.

**apiece** adverb *the caps are $10 apiece* EACH, respectively, per item, individually; *informal* a pop, a throw, per; *formal* severally.

**aplomb** noun *the judges were especially impressed by her aplomb* POISE, self-assurance, self-confidence, calmness, composure, collectedness, levelheadedness, sangfroid, equilibrium, equanimity; *informal* unflappability.

**apocryphal** adjective *an apocryphal account of Jesus' childhood* FICTITIOUS, made-up, untrue, fabricated, false, spurious; unverified, unauthenticated, unsubstantiated; bogus. See note at SPURIOUS. ANTONYM authentic.

**apologetic** adjective *the students who defaced the lockers seemed truly apologetic* REGRETFUL, sorry, contrite, remorseful, rueful, penitent, repentant; conscience-stricken, compunctious, shamefaced, ashamed. ANTONYM unrepentant.

**apologize** verb *please allow me to apologize for my wrongful accusations* SAY (ONE IS) SORRY, express regret, be apologetic, make an apology, ask forgiveness, ask for pardon; *informal* eat one's words, eat humble pie.

**apology** noun **1** *I owe you an apology* EXPRESSION OF REGRET, one's regrets.

**2** *an* ***apology for*** *capitalism* DEFENSE OF, explanation of, justification of, vindication of, apologia for.

**apostle** noun **1** *the twelve apostles* DISCIPLE, follower.

**2** *the apostles of the Slavs* MISSIONARY, evangelist, proselytizer.

**3** *an apostle of capitalism* ADVOCATE, apologist, proponent, exponent, promoter, supporter, upholder, champion, booster.

**appall** verb *it doesn't take much to appall her* HORRIFY, shock, dismay, distress, outrage, scandalize; disgust, repel, revolt, sicken, nauseate, offend, make someone's blood run cold.

**appalling** adjective **1** *an appalling crime* SHOCKING, horrific, horrifying, horrible, terrible, awful, dreadful, ghastly, hideous, horrendous, frightful, atrocious, abominable, abhorrent, outrageous, gruesome, grisly, monstrous, heinous, egregious.

**2** *informal your schoolwork is appalling* BAD, dreadful, awful, terrible, frightful, atrocious, disgraceful, deplorable, hopeless, lamentable; *informal* rotten, crummy, pathetic, pitiful, woeful, useless, lousy, abysmal, dire.

**apparatus** noun **1** *laboratory apparatus* EQUIPMENT, gear, rig, tackle, gadgetry; appliance, instrument, machine, mechanism, device, contraption, gadget, gizmo, doohickey. See note at TOOL.

**2** *the apparatus of government* STRUCTURE, system, framework, organization, network.

**apparel** noun *formal the senator is noted for her snazzy ap-*

*parel* CLOTHES, clothing, garments, dress, attire, wear, garb, getup; *informal* gear, togs, duds, threads; *archaic* raiment, habit, habiliments.

**apparent** adjective **1** *their relief was all too apparent* EVIDENT, plain, obvious, clear, manifest, visible, discernible, perceptible; unmistakable, crystal clear, palpable, patent, blatant, writ large; *informal* as plain as the nose on one's face, written all over one's face. See note at OSTENSIBLE. ANTONYMS unclear, obscure.

**2** *his apparent lack of concern* SEEMING, ostensible, outward, superficial; supposed, alleged, professed. ANTONYM genuine.

**apparently** adverb *apparently, no one had ever told him that he had a half-sister in San Diego* SEEMINGLY, evidently, it seems (that), it appears (that), it would seem (that), it would appear (that), as far as one knows, by all accounts; ostensibly, outwardly, supposedly, on the face of it, so the story goes, so I'm told; allegedly, reputedly.

**apparition** noun *a monstrous apparition* GHOST, phantom, specter, spirit, wraith; vision, hallucination; *informal* spook, chimera; *literary* phantasm, revenant, shade, visitant; *rare* eidolon.

**appeal** verb **1** *police are appealing for information* ASK URGENTLY/EARNESTLY, make an urgent/earnest request, call, make a plea, plead.

**2** *Stuart* ***appealed to*** *me to help them* IMPLORE, beg, entreat, call on, plead with, exhort, ask, request, petition; *formal* adjure; *literary* beseech.

**3** *the idea of traveling* ***appealed to*** *me* ATTRACT, be attractive to, interest, take someone's fancy, fascinate, tempt, entice, allure, lure, draw, whet someone's appetite.

▸ noun **1** *an appeal for help* PLEA, urgent/earnest request, entreaty, cry, call, petition, supplication, cri de coeur.

**2** *the cultural appeal of the island* ATTRACTION, attractiveness, allure, charm; fascination, magnetism, drawing power, pull.

**3** *the court allowed the appeal* RETRIAL, reexamination.

**appear** verb **1** *a cloud of dust appeared on the horizon* BECOME VISIBLE, come into view, come into sight, materialize, pop up. ANTONYM vanish.

**2** *fundamental differences were beginning to appear* BE REVEALED, emerge, surface, manifest itself, become apparent, become evident, come to light; arise, crop up.

**3** *informal* *Bill still hadn't appeared* ARRIVE, turn up, put in an appearance, come, get here/there; *informal* show (up), roll in, blow in.

**4** *they* ***appear to be*** *completely devoted* SEEM TO BE, look to be, give the impression of being, come across as being, strike someone as being.

**5** *the paperback edition didn't appear for two years* BECOME AVAILABLE, come on the market, go on sale, come out, be published, be produced.

**6** *she appeared on Broadway* PERFORM, play, act.

**appearance** noun **1** *her disheveled appearance* LOOK(S), air, aspect, mien.

**2** *they tried to maintain a respectable appearance* IMPRESSION, air, image, show, outward show; semblance, facade, veneer, front, pretense.

**3** *the sudden appearance of her daughter* ARRIVAL, advent, coming, emergence, materialization.

**4** *the appearance of these symptoms* OCCURRENCE, manifestation, development.

**appease** verb **1** *an attempt to appease his critics* CONCILIATE, placate, pacify, mollify, propitiate, reconcile, win over. See note at PACIFY. ANTONYMS provoke, inflame.

**2** *I'd wasted a lot of money to appease my vanity* SATISFY, fulfill, gratify, indulge; assuage, relieve.

**appeasement** noun *a policy of appeasement* CONCILIATION, placation, concession, pacification, propitiation, reconciliation; fence-mending. ANTONYM provocation.

**append** verb *the teacher may append comments to the final report* ADD, attach, affix, tack on, tag on; *formal* subjoin.

**appendage** noun **1** *I am not just an appendage to the family* ADDITION, attachment, adjunct, addendum, appurtenance, accessory.

**2** *a pair of feathery appendages* PROTUBERANCE, projection; *technical* process.

**appendix** noun *there is a windchill table in the appendix* SUPPLEMENT, addendum, postscript, codicil; coda, epilogue, afterword, tailpiece, back matter; attachment.

**appertain** PHRASE: **appertain to** *how do these articles appertain to the topic of our discussion?* PERTAIN TO, be pertinent to, apply to, relate to, concern, be concerned with, have to do with, be relevant to, have reference to, have a bearing on, bear on; regard.

**appetite** noun **1** *a walk sharpens the appetite* HUNGER, ravenousness, hungriness; taste, palate.

**2** *my appetite for learning* CRAVING, longing, yearning, hankering, hunger, thirst, passion; enthusiasm, keenness, eagerness, desire; *informal* yen.

**appetizer** noun *tonight's featured appetizer is a dish of grilled oysters and roasted mushrooms* STARTER, first course, hors d'oeuvre, antipasto, amuse-gueule.

**appetizing** adjective **1** *an appetizing lunch* MOUTHWATERING, inviting, tempting; tasty, delicious, flavorful, toothsome, delectable, succulent; *informal* scrumptious, yummy, delish, lip-smacking. ANTONYMS bland, off-putting.

**2** *the least appetizing part of election campaigns* APPEALING, attractive, inviting, alluring. ANTONYM unappealing.

**applaud** verb **1** *the audience applauded* CLAP, give a standing ovation, put one's hands together; show one's appreciation; *informal* give someone a big hand. ANTONYM boo.

**2** *police have applauded the decision* PRAISE, commend, acclaim, salute, welcome, hail, celebrate, express admiration for, express approval of, look on with favor at, approve of, sing the praises of, pay tribute to, speak highly of, take one's hat off to, express respect for. ANTONYM criticize.

**applause** noun 1 *a massive round of applause* CLAPPING, hand clapping, (standing) ovation; acclamation.

2 *the museum's design won general applause* PRAISE, acclaim, acclamation, admiration, commendation, adulation, favor, approbation, approval, respect; compliments, accolades, tributes; *informal* props.

**appliance** noun *domestic appliances* DEVICE, machine, instrument, gadget, contraption, apparatus, utensil, implement, tool, mechanism, contrivance, labor-saving device; *informal* gizmo. See also note at TOOL.

**applicable** adjective *the laws applicable to the dispute* RELEVANT, appropriate, pertinent, appurtenant, apposite, germane, material, significant, related, connected; fitting, suitable, apt, befitting, useful, helpful. ANTONYMS inappropriate, irrelevant.

**applicant** noun *first-time applicants must have an appointment* CANDIDATE, interviewee, competitor, contestant, contender, entrant; claimant, suppliant, supplicant, petitioner, postulant; prospective student, prospective employee, job-seeker, job-hunter, auditioner.

**application** noun 1 *an application for a loan* REQUEST, appeal, petition, entreaty, plea, solicitation, supplication, requisition, suit, approach, claim, demand.

2 *the application of antiinflation policies* IMPLEMENTATION, use, exercise, employment, utilization, practice, applying, discharge, execution, prosecution, enactment; *formal* praxis.

3 *the argument is clearest in its application to the theater* RELEVANCE, relevancy, bearing, significance, pertinence, aptness, appositeness, germaneness, importance.

4 *the application of makeup* PUTTING ON, rubbing in, applying.

5 *a smelly application to relieve muscle pain* OINTMENT, lotion, cream, rub, salve, emollient, preparation, liniment, embrocation, balm, unguent, poultice.

6 *a vector graphics application* PROGRAM, software, routine.

**apply** verb 1 *more than 300 people* ***applied for*** *the job* PUT IN AN APPLICATION FOR, put in for, try (out) for, bid for, appeal for, petition for, sue for, register for, audition for; request, seek, solicit (for), claim, ask for, try to obtain.

2 *the third paragraph applies only to returning students* BE RELEVANT, have relevance, have a bearing, appertain, pertain, relate, concern, affect, involve, cover, deal with, touch; be pertinent, be appropriate, be significant.

3 *she applied some ointment* PUT ON, rub in, work in, spread, smear.

4 *a steady pressure should be applied* EXERT, administer, implement, use, exercise, employ, utilize, bring to bear. PHRASE: **apply oneself** *if Palermo applies himself, he has an excellent shot at the scholarship* BE DILIGENT, be industrious, be assiduous, show commitment, show dedication; work hard, exert oneself, make an effort, try hard, do one's best, give one's all, put one's shoulder to the wheel, put one's nose to the grindstone; strive, endeavor, struggle, labor, toil; pay attention, commit oneself, devote oneself; persevere, persist; *informal* put one's back into it, knuckle down, buckle down, hunker down.

**appoint** verb 1 *he was appointed chairman* NOMINATE, name, designate, install as, commission, engage, co-opt; select, choose, elect, vote in; *Military* detail. ANTONYM reject.

2 *the arbitrator shall appoint a date for the meeting* SPECIFY, determine, assign, designate, allot, set, fix, arrange, choose, decide on, establish, settle, ordain, prescribe, decree.

**appointment** noun 1 *a six o'clock appointment* MEETING, engagement, interview, arrangement, consultation, session; date, rendezvous, assignation; commitment, fixture.

2 *the appointment of directors* NOMINATION, naming, designation, installation, commissioning, engagement, co-option; selection, choosing, election, voting in; *Military* detailing.

3 *he held an appointment at the university* JOB, post, position, situation, employment, place, office; *dated* station.

**apportion** verb *the proceeds from the sale of the restaurant will be apportioned equally among the siblings* SHARE, divide, allocate, distribute, allot, assign, give out, hand out, mete out, deal out, dish out, dole out, parcel out, prorate; ration, measure out; split; *informal* divvy up.

**apposite** adjective *an apposite caption accompanies each photo* APPROPRIATE, suitable, fitting, apt, befitting; relevant, pertinent, appurtenant, to the point, applicable, germane, material, congruous, felicitous; *formal* ad rem. ANTONYM inappropriate.

**appraisal** noun 1 *an objective appraisal of the book* ASSESSMENT, evaluation, estimation, judgment, rating, gauging, sizing up, summing-up, consideration.

2 *a free insurance appraisal* VALUATION, estimate, estimation, quotation, pricing; survey.

**appraise** verb 1 *they appraised their handiwork* ASSESS, evaluate, judge, rate, gauge, review, consider; *informal* size up.

2 *the goods were appraised at $1,800* VALUE, price, estimate, quote; survey.

**appreciable** adjective *there is an appreciable amount of sugar in the lemonade* CONSIDERABLE, substantial, significant, sizable, goodly, fair, reasonable, marked; perceptible, noticeable, visible, discernible; *informal* tidy. See note at TANGIBLE. ANTONYM negligible.

**appreciate** verb 1 *I'd appreciate your advice* BE GRATEFUL FOR, be thankful for, be obliged for, be indebted for, be in your debt for, be appreciative of. ANTONYM disparage.

2 *the college appreciated her greatly* VALUE, treasure, admire, respect, hold in high regard, think highly of, think much of. See note at ESTEEM.

3 *we appreciate your difficulty* RECOGNIZE, acknowledge, re-

alize, know, be aware of, be conscious of, be sensitive to, understand, comprehend, grasp, fathom; *informal* be wise to.

**4** *a home that will appreciate in value* INCREASE, gain, grow, rise, go up, escalate, soar, rocket. ANTONYMS depreciate, decrease.

**appreciation** noun **1** *he showed his appreciation* GRATITUDE, thanks, gratefulness, thankfulness, recognition, sense of obligation. ANTONYM ingratitude.

**2** *her appreciation of literature* VALUING, treasuring, admiration, respect, regard, esteem, high opinion.

**3** *an appreciation of the difficulties involved* ACKNOWLEDGMENT, recognition, realization, knowledge, awareness, consciousness, understanding, comprehension. ANTONYM unawareness.

**4** *a critical appreciation of the professor's work* REVIEW, critique, criticism, critical analysis, assessment, evaluation, judgment, rating.

**appreciative** adjective **1** *we are* ***appreciative of*** *all your efforts* GRATEFUL FOR, thankful for, obliged for, indebted for, in someone's debt for. ANTONYM ungrateful.

**2** *an appreciative audience* SUPPORTIVE, encouraging, sympathetic, responsive; enthusiastic, admiring, approving, complimentary.

**apprehend** verb **1** *the thieves were quickly apprehended* ARREST, catch, capture, seize; take prisoner, take into custody, detain, put in jail, put behind bars, imprison, incarcerate; *informal* bag, collar, nab, nail, run in, bust, pick up, pull in.

**2** *they are slow to apprehend danger* APPRECIATE, recognize, discern, perceive, make out, take in, realize, grasp, understand, comprehend; *informal* get the picture.

**apprehension** noun **1** *he was filled with apprehension* ANXIETY, worry, unease, nervousness, nerves, misgivings, disquiet, concern, tension, trepidation, perturbation, consternation, angst, dread, alarm, fear, foreboding; *informal* butterflies, jitters, the willies, the creeps, the shivers, the heebie-jeebies. ANTONYM confidence.

**2** *the apprehension of a perpetrator* ARREST, capture, seizure; detention, imprisonment, incarceration; *informal* collar, nabbing, bagging, busting.

**apprehensive** adjective *dentists know that many of their patients are apprehensive* ANXIOUS, worried, uneasy, nervous, concerned, agitated, tense, afraid, scared, frightened, fearful; *informal* on tenterhooks. ANTONYM confident.

**apprentice** noun *she worked with the great violin maker as his apprentice* TRAINEE, learner, probationer, novice, beginner, starter, cadet, tenderfoot; pupil, student; *informal* rookie, newbie, greenhorn. See note at NOVICE. ANTONYM veteran.

**apprise** verb *we'll apprise you of any changes in your husband's condition* INFORM, tell, notify, advise, brief, make aware, enlighten, update, keep posted; *informal* clue in, fill in, bring up to speed.

**approach** verb **1** *she approached the altar* MOVE TOWARD, come/go toward, advance toward, inch toward, go/come/draw/move nearer, go/come/draw/move closer, near; close in, gain on; reach, arrive at. ANTONYM leave.

**2** *the trade deficit is approaching $20 million* BORDER ON, verge on, approximate, touch, nudge, near, come near to, come close to.

**3** *she approached him about leaving his job* SPEAK TO, talk to; make advances to, make overtures to, make a proposal to, sound out, proposition.

**4** *he approached the problem in the best way* TACKLE, set about, address oneself to, undertake, get down to, launch into, embark on, go about, come to grips with.

▸ noun **1** *a typical male approach* METHOD, procedure, technique, modus operandi, MO, style, way, manner; strategy, tactic, system, means.

**2** *the dog barked at the approach of any intruder* ADVANCE, coming, nearing; arrival, appearance; advent.

**3** *the approach to the castle* DRIVEWAY, drive, access road, road, avenue; way.

**appropriate** adjective *this isn't the appropriate time* SUITABLE, proper, fitting, apt, right; relevant, pertinent, apposite; convenient, opportune; seemly, befitting; *formal* ad rem; *archaic* meet. ANTONYM unsuitable.

▸ verb **1** *the barons appropriated church lands* SEIZE, commandeer, expropriate, annex, arrogate, sequestrate, sequester, take over, hijack;

**2** steal, take; *informal* swipe, nab, bag, pinch.

**3** *his images have been appropriated by advertisers* PLAGIARIZE, copy; poach, steal, borrow; *informal* rip off.

**4** *we are appropriating funds for these expenses* ALLOCATE, assign, allot, earmark, set aside, devote, apportion.

**approval** noun **1** *their proposals went to the board for approval* ACCEPTANCE, agreement, consent, assent, permission, leave; sanction, endorsement, ratification, authorization, validation; support, backing; *informal* the go-ahead, the green light, the nod, the rubber stamp, the OK, the say-so, the thumbs up. ANTONYM refusal.

**2** *Lily looked at him with approval* APPROBATION, appreciation, favor, liking, admiration, regard, esteem, respect, praise. ANTONYM dislike.

**approve** verb **1** *his boss doesn't* ***approve of*** *his lifestyle* AGREE WITH, endorse, support, back, uphold, subscribe to, recommend, advocate, be in favor of, favor, think well of, like, appreciate, go for, hold with, take kindly to; be pleased with, admire, applaud, praise. ANTONYMS condemn, disapprove.

**2** *the government approved the proposals* ACCEPT, agree to, consent to, assent to, give one's blessing to, bless, rubber-stamp; ratify, sanction, endorse, authorize, validate, pass; support, back; *informal* give the nod to, give the go-ahead to, give the green light to, give the OK to, give the thumbs-up to. ANTONYM refuse.

THE RIGHT WORD **approve, certify, commend, endorse, ratify, sanction**

There are a number of ways to show your support for something. The most general way is to **approve** it, a term that covers everything from simple, technical agreement (*to approve the plan*) to enthusiastic support (*she was quick to approve her son's decision to marry*). **Endorse** implies a more public and official expression of support and is used primarily in reference to things that require promotion or publicity (*endorse a political candidate*), while **commend** is to make a formal and usually public statement of approval or congratulation (*he was commended for his heroism*). **Sanction**, **certify**, and **ratify** imply that approval is not only official but that it makes something legal. To *sanction* is not only to *approve* but to authorize (*school authorities would not sanction the wearing of hats in class*), while *certify* implies conformity with certain standards (*certified to teach in the State of New York*). *Ratify* is usually confined to only the most official and authoritative settings. For example, an employer might *sanction* the idea of hiring a woman to perform a job that only men have performed in the past, and the woman in question might have to *certify* that she possesses the necessary training and qualifications. But to *ratify* a constitutional amendment granting equal rights to women requires a lengthy set of legislative procedures.

**approximate** adjective *approximate dimensions* ESTIMATED, rough, imprecise, inexact, indefinite, broad, loose; *informal* ballpark. ANTONYM precise.

▸ verb *the sound approximates that of a cow* RESEMBLE, be similar to, be not unlike; be/come close to, be/come near to, approach, border on, verge on.

**approximately** adverb *there are approximately 24 children per classroom* ROUGHLY, about, around, circa, more or less, in the neighborhood of, in the region of, of/on the order of, something like, around/round about, give or take (a few); near to, close to, nearly, almost, approaching; *informal* pushing, in the ballpark of. ANTONYM precisely.

**approximation** noun **1** *the figure is only an approximation* ESTIMATE, estimation, guess, rough calculation; *informal* guesstimate, ballpark figure.

**2** *an approximation to the truth* SEMBLANCE, resemblance, likeness, similarity, correspondence.

**appurtenances** plural noun *artist's studio with appurtenances for rent* ACCESSORIES, trappings, appendages, accoutrements, equipment, paraphernalia, impedimenta, bits and pieces, things; *informal* stuff.

**apropos** preposition *he was asked a question apropos his resignation* WITH REFERENCE TO, with regard to, with respect to, regarding, concerning, on the subject of, connected with, about, re.

▸ adjective *the word "conglomerate" was decidedly apropos* APPROPRIATE, pertinent, relevant, apposite, apt, applicable, suitable, germane, fitting, befitting, material; right on. ANTONYM inappropriate.

PHRASE: **apropos of nothing** *apropos of nothing, she started speaking only in rhyme* IRRELEVANTLY, arbitrarily, at random, for no reason, illogically.

**apt** adjective **1** *a very apt description of how I felt* SUITABLE, fitting, appropriate, befitting, relevant, germane, applicable, apposite. ANTONYM inappropriate.

**2** *they're apt to get a bit sloppy* INCLINED, given, likely, liable, disposed, predisposed, prone. ANTONYM unlikely.

**3** *an apt pupil* CLEVER, quick, bright, sharp, smart, intelligent, able, gifted, adept, astute. ANTONYM slow.

**aptitude** noun *an aptitude for higher mathematics* TALENT, gift, flair, bent, skill, knack, facility, ability, proficiency, capability, potential, capacity, faculty, genius.

**aquatic** adjective *seals and other aquatic mammals* MARINE, water, saltwater, freshwater, seawater, sea, oceanic, river; *technical* pelagic, thalassic.

**aqueduct** noun *our paper boats went through the aqueduct* CONDUIT, race, channel, chute, watercourse, sluice, sluiceway, spillway.

**arable** adjective *arable soil* FARMABLE, cultivable; fertile, productive.

**arbiter** noun **1** *an arbiter between Moscow and Washington.* See ARBITRATOR.

**2** *the great arbiter of fashion* AUTHORITY, judge, controller, director; master, expert, pundit.

**arbitrary** adjective **1** *an arbitrary decision* CAPRICIOUS, whimsical, random, chance, unpredictable; casual, wanton, unmotivated, motiveless, unreasoned, unsupported, irrational, illogical, groundless, unjustified; personal, discretionary, subjective. ANTONYMS reasoned, rational.

**2** *the arbitrary power of the prince* AUTOCRATIC, dictatorial, autarchic, undemocratic, despotic, tyrannical, authoritarian, high-handed; absolute, uncontrolled, unlimited, unrestrained. ANTONYM democratic.

**arbitrate** verb *a third and disinterested party was brought in to arbitrate* ADJUDICATE, judge, referee, umpire; mediate, conciliate, intervene, intercede; settle, decide, resolve, pass judgment.

**arbitration** noun *the council called for arbitration to settle the dispute* ADJUDICATION, judgment, arbitrament; mediation, mediatorship, conciliation, settlement, intervention.

**arbitrator** noun *the litigants met with a court-appointed arbitrator* ADJUDICATOR, arbiter, judge, referee, umpire; mediator, conciliator, intervenor, intercessor, go-between.

**arbor** noun *the arbor was overgrown with wisteria and bittersweet* BOWER, pergola; alcove, grotto, recess; gazebo.

**arc** noun *the arc of a circle* CURVE, arch, crescent, semicircle, half-moon; curvature, convexity.

▸ verb *I sent the ball arcing out over the river* CURL, curve; arch.

**arcade** noun **1** *a classical arcade* COLONNADE, gallery, cloister, loggia, portico, peristyle, stoa.

**2** *playing hooky at the arcade* VIDEO ARCADE, midway.

**arcane** adjective *processes as old and arcane as the language of the law* MYSTERIOUS, secret; enigmatic, esoteric, cryptic, obscure, abstruse, recondite, recherché, impenetrable, opaque.

**arch**[1] noun **1** *a stone arch* ARCHWAY, vault, span, dome.

**2** *the arch of his spine* CURVE, bow, bend, arc, curvature, convexity; hunch, crook.

▸ verb *she arched her eyebrows* CURVE, arc.

**arch**[2] adjective *an arch grin* MISCHIEVOUS, teasing, saucy, knowing, playful, roguish, impish, cheeky, tongue-in-cheek.

**arch-** combining form *his archenemy* CHIEF, principal, foremost, leading, main, major, prime, premier, greatest; *informal* number-one, numero uno. ANTONYM minor.

**archaic** adjective *archaic conventions* OBSOLETE, out of date, old-fashioned, outmoded, behind the times, bygone, anachronistic, antiquated, superannuated, antediluvian, old world, old-fangled; ancient, old, extinct, defunct; prehistoric; *literary* of yore. See note at OLD. ANTONYM modern.

**archetype** noun *the archetype of Southern hospitality* QUINTESSENCE, essence, representative, model, embodiment, prototype, stereotype; original, pattern, standard, paradigm. See note at MODEL.

**architect** noun **1** *the architect of St. Mary's Cathedral* DESIGNER, planner, draftsman.

**2** *Andrew was the architect of the plan* ORIGINATOR, author, creator, founder, father, founding father; engineer, inventor, mastermind; *literary* begetter.

**architecture** noun **1** *modern architecture* BUILDING DESIGN, building style, planning, building, construction; *formal* architectonics.

**2** *the architecture of a computer system* STRUCTURE, construction, organization, layout, design, build, anatomy, makeup; *informal* setup.

**arctic** adjective **1** **(Arctic)** *Arctic waters* POLAR, far northern, boreal; *literary* hyperborean.

**2** *arctic weather conditions* (BITTERLY) COLD, wintry, freezing, frozen, icy, glacial, hypothermic, gelid, subzero, polar, Siberian, bone-chilling. ANTONYMS Antarctic, tropical.

▸ noun **(the Arctic)** *a research station in the Arctic* FAR NORTH, High Arctic, North Pole, Arctic Circle, North of Sixty. ANTONYM Antarctic.

**ardent** adjective *an ardent soccer fan* PASSIONATE, fervent, zealous, fervid, wholehearted, vehement, intense, fierce, fiery; enthusiastic, keen, eager, avid, committed, dedicated; *literary* perfervid. See note at EAGER. ANTONYM apathetic.

**ardor** noun *approaching the project with ardor* PASSION, fervor, zeal, vehemence, intensity, verve, fire, emotion; enthusiasm, eagerness, avidity, gusto, keenness, dedication.

**arduous** adjective *an arduous journey* ONEROUS, taxing, difficult, hard, heavy, laborious, burdensome, strenuous, vigorous, back-breaking; demanding, tough, challenging, formidable; exhausting, tiring, punishing, grueling; uphill, steep; *informal* killing; toilsome. See note at HARD. ANTONYM easy.

**area** noun **1** *an inner-city area* DISTRICT, region, zone, sector, quarter, precinct; locality, locale, neighborhood, parish, patch; tract, belt; *informal* neck of the woods, turf.

**2** *specific areas of scientific knowledge* FIELD, sphere, discipline, realm, domain, sector, province, territory, line.

**3** *the dining area* SECTION, space; place, room.

**4** *the area of a circle* EXPANSE, extent, size, scope, compass; dimensions, proportions.

**arena** noun **1** *a hockey arena* STADIUM; amphitheater, coliseum; sportsplex; field, ring, court; bowl, park, ground; rink, ice rink; *historical* circus.

**2** *the political arena* SCENE, sphere, realm, province, domain, sector, forum, territory, world.

**argue** verb **1** *they argued that the government was to blame* CONTEND, assert, maintain, insist, hold, claim, reason, allege; *formal* aver, represent, opine.

**2** *the children are always arguing* QUARREL, disagree, squabble, bicker, fight, wrangle, dispute, feud, have words, cross swords, lock horns, be at each other's throats; *informal* spat.

**3** *it is hard to argue the point* DISPUTE, debate, discuss, controvert, deny, question.

**argument** noun **1** *he had an argument with Tony* QUARREL, disagreement, squabble, fight, dispute, wrangle, clash, altercation, feud, contretemps, disputation, falling-out; *informal* tiff, row, blowup, rhubarb.

**2** *arguments for the existence of God* REASONING, justification, explanation, rationalization; case, defense, vindication; evidence, reasons, grounds.

**3** *the argument of the book* THEME, topic, subject matter; summary, synopsis, précis, gist, outline.

**argumentative** adjective *the futility of dealing with argumentative people* QUARRELSOME, disputatious, captious, contrary, cantankerous, contentious; belligerent, bellicose, combative, antagonistic, truculent, pugnacious.

**arid** adjective **1** *an arid landscape* DRY, dried up, bone-dry, waterless, moistureless, parched, scorched, baked, thirsty, droughty, desert; BARREN, infertile. See note at DRY. ANTONYMS wet, fertile.

**2** *this town has an arid, empty feel* DREARY, dull, drab, dry, sterile, colorless, unstimulating, uninspiring, flat, boring, uninteresting, lifeless, emotionless, plain-vanilla. ANTONYM vibrant.

**arise** verb **1** *many problems arose* COME TO LIGHT, become apparent, appear, emerge, crop up, turn up, surface, spring up; occur; *literary* befall, come to pass.

**2** *injuries arising from defective products* RESULT, proceed, follow, ensue, derive, stem, originate; be caused by.

**3** *the beast arose* STAND UP, rise, get to one's feet, get up.

**aristocracy** noun *she was quite at home with the aristocracy*

NOBILITY, peerage, gentry, gentility, upper class, ruling class, elite, high society, establishment, haut monde; aristocrats, lords, ladies, peers, peers of the realm, nobles, noblemen, noblewomen; *informal* upper crust, top drawer, aristos. ANTONYM working class.

**aristocrat** noun *the son of aristocrats* NOBLEMAN, noblewoman, lord, lady, peer, peeress, peer of the realm, patrician, grandee; blue blood; *informal* aristo. ANTONYM commoner.

**aristocratic** adjective **1** *an aristocratic family* NOBLE, titled, upper-class, blue-blooded, high-born, well-born, elite; *informal* upper-crust, top-drawer. ANTONYM working-class.

**2** *an aristocratic manner* REFINED, polished, courtly, dignified, posh, decorous, gracious, fine; haughty, proud. ANTONYM vulgar.

**arm** noun **1** *an arm of the sea* INLET, creek, cove, fjord, bay; estuary, strait(s), sound, channel.

**2** *the political arm of the group* BRANCH, section, department, division, wing, sector, detachment, offshoot, extension.

**3** *the long arm of the law* REACH, power, authority, influence.

▸ verb *he armed himself with a revolver* EQUIP, provide, supply, furnish, issue, outfit, fit out.

**armada** noun *the world's largest armada of warships* FLEET, flotilla, squadron, navy.

**armaments** plural noun *a shortage of armaments* ARMS, weapons, weaponry, firearms, guns, ordnance, artillery, munitions, matériel, hardware.

**armistice** noun *the armistice was declared on November 11* TRUCE, cease-fire, peace, suspension of hostilities.

**armor** noun *a suit of armor | protected by his armor* PROTECTIVE COVERING, armor plate, shield; chain mail, coat of mail, panoply; carapace.

**armory** noun *a Civil War exhibition at the old armory* ARSENAL, arms depot, arms cache, ordnance depot, magazine, ammunition dump.

**arms** plural noun **1** *the illegal export of arms* WEAPONS, weaponry, firearms, guns, ordnance, artillery, armaments, munitions, matériel.

**2** *the family arms* CREST, emblem, coat of arms, heraldic device, insignia, escutcheon, shield.

**army** noun **1** *the invading army* ARMED FORCE, military force, land force, military, soldiery, infantry, militia; troops, soldiers; *archaic* host.

**2** *an army of tourists* CROWD, swarm, multitude, horde, mob, gang, throng, mass, flock, herd, pack.

**aroma** noun *the wonderful aroma of warm bread* SCENT, fragrance, perfume, smell, bouquet, balm, nose, odor, whiff; *literary* redolence. See note at SMELL.

**aromatic** adjective *aromatic wood chips* FRAGRANT, scented, perfumed, fragranced, odorous; *literary* redolent.

**around** adverb **1** *there were houses scattered around* ON EVERY SIDE, on all sides, throughout, all over (the place), everywhere; about, here and there.

**2** *he turned around* IN THE OPPOSITE DIRECTION, to face the other way, backward, to the rear.

**3** *there was no one around* NEARBY, near, about, close by, close, close at hand, at hand, in the vicinity, at close range.

▸ preposition **1** *the palazzo is built around a courtyard* ON ALL SIDES OF, about, encircling, surrounding, enclosing.

**2** *they drove around town* ABOUT, all over, in/to all parts of.

**3** *around three miles* APPROXIMATELY, about, around/round about, circa, roughly, something like, more or less, in the region of, in the neighborhood of, give or take (a few); nearly, close to, approaching; getting on for; *informal* in the ballpark of.

PHRASE: **around the clock 1** *we're working around the clock* DAY AND NIGHT, night and day, round the clock, all the time, [morning, noon, and night], continuously, nonstop, steadily, unremittingly; *informal* 24-7.

**2** *around-the-clock supervision* CONTINUOUS, round-the-clock, constant, nonstop, continual, uninterrupted.

**arouse** verb **1** *they had aroused his suspicion* INDUCE, prompt, trigger, stir up, bring out, kindle, fire, spark off, provoke, engender, cause, foster; *literary* enkindle. ANTONYM allay.

**2** *his ability to arouse the masses* STIR UP, rouse, galvanize, excite, electrify, stimulate, inspire, inspirit, move, fire up, whip up, get going, inflame, agitate, goad, incite; *rare* inspirit. See note at INCITE. ANTONYM pacify.

**3** *his touch aroused her* EXCITE, stimulate, titillate; *informal* turn on, get going, give a thrill to, light someone's fire. ANTONYM turn off.

**4** *she was aroused from her sleep* WAKE (UP), awaken, bring to, rouse; *literary* waken.

**arraign** verb **1** *he was* ***arraigned for*** *murder* INDICT FOR, prosecute for, put on trial for, bring to trial for, take to court for, lay/file/prefer charges against for, summons for, cite for; accuse of, charge with, incriminate with; *archaic* inculpate for. ANTONYM acquit.

**2** *they bitterly arraigned the government* CRITICIZE, censure, impugn, attack, condemn, chastise, lambaste, rebuke, admonish, remonstrate with, take to task, berate, reproach; *informal* knock, slam, blast, lay into; castigate, excoriate. ANTONYM praise.

**arrange** verb **1** *she arranged the flowers* ORDER, set out, lay out, array, position, dispose, present, display, exhibit; group, sort, organize, tidy.

**2** *they hoped to arrange a meeting* ORGANIZE, fix (up), plan, schedule, pencil in, contrive, settle on, decide, determine, agree.

**3** *he arranged the piece for a full orchestra* ADAPT, set, score, orchestrate, transcribe, instrument.

**arrangement** noun **1** *the arrangement of the furniture* POSITIONING, disposition, order, presentation, display; grouping, organization, alignment.

**2** **(arrangements)** *the arrangements for my trip* PREPARATIONS, plan(s), provision(s); planning, groundwork.

**3** *we had an arrangement* AGREEMENT, deal, understanding, bargain, settlement, pact, modus vivendi.

**4** *an arrangement of Beethoven's symphonies* ADAPTATION, orchestration, instrumentation.

**arrant** adjective *what arrant nonsense!* UTTER, complete, total, absolute, downright, outright, thorough, out-and-out, sheer, pure, unmitigated, unqualified; blatant, flagrant.

**array** noun **1** *a huge array of cars* RANGE, collection, selection, assortment, diversity, variety; arrangement, assemblage, lineup, formation; display, exhibition, exposition.

**2** *she arrived in silken array* DRESS, attire, clothing, garb, garments; finery, apparel.

▸ verb **1** *a buffet was arrayed on the table* ARRANGE, assemble, group, order, place, position, set out, exhibit, lay out, dispose; display.

**2** *he was arrayed in gray flannel* DRESS, attire, clothe, garb, deck (out), outfit, get up, turn out; *archaic* apparel.

**arrears** plural noun *rent arrears* MONEY OWING, outstanding payment(s), debt(s), liabilities, dues. ANTONYM credit.

PHRASE: **in arrears** *the personal accounts are fine, but the business is in arrears* BEHIND, behindhand, late, overdue, in the red, in debt.

**arrest** verb **1** *police arrested him for murder* APPREHEND, take into custody, take prisoner, imprison, incarcerate, detain, jail, put in jail; *informal* pick up, pull in, run in, pinch, bust, nab, collar. ANTONYM release.

**2** *the spread of the disease can be arrested* STOP, halt, check, block, hinder, restrict, limit, inhibit, impede, curb; prevent, obstruct; *literary* stay.

**3** *she tried to arrest his attention* ATTRACT, capture, catch, hold, engage; absorb, occupy, engross.

▸ noun **1** *a warrant for your arrest* DETENTION, apprehension, seizure, capture, takedown.

**2** *a cardiac arrest* STOPPAGE, halt, interruption.

**arresting** adjective *an arresting image* STRIKING, eye-catching, conspicuous, engaging, engrossing, fascinating, impressive, imposing, spectacular, dramatic, breathtaking, dazzling, stunning, awe-inspiring; remarkable, outstanding, distinctive. ANTONYM inconspicuous.

**arrival** noun **1** *they awaited Ruth's arrival* COMING, appearance, entrance, entry, approach. ANTONYM departure.

**2** *staff greeted the late arrivals* COMER, entrant, incomer; visitor, caller, guest.

**arrive** verb **1** *more police arrived* COME, turn up, get here/there, make it, appear, enter, present oneself, come along, materialize; *informal* show (up), roll in/up, blow in, show one's face. ANTONYM depart.

**2** *we* ***arrived at*** *his house* REACH, get to, come to, make it to, end up at; *informal* wind up at. ANTONYM leave.

**3** *they* ***arrived at*** *an agreement* REACH, achieve, attain, gain, accomplish; work out, draw up, put together, strike, settle on; *informal* clinch.

**4** *the wedding finally arrived* HAPPEN, occur, take place, come about; present itself, crop up; *literary* come to pass.

**5** *CD-ROMs arrived in the late eighties* EMERGE, appear, surface, come on the scene, dawn, be born, come into being, arise.

**6** *informal* *their Rolls Royce proved that they had arrived* SUCCEED, be a success, do well, reach the top, make good, prosper, thrive; *informal* make it, make one's mark, do all right for oneself.

**arrogant** adjective *success has made him arrogant* HAUGHTY, conceited, self-important, egotistic, full of oneself, superior; overbearing, pompous, bumptious, presumptuous, imperious, overweening; proud, immodest; *informal* high and mighty, too big for one's britches, too big for one's boots, bigheaded, puffed-up; *rare* hubristic. See note at PRIDE. ANTONYM modest.

**arrogate** verb *the Church* ***arrogated to itself*** *the power to create kings* ASSUME, take, claim, appropriate, seize, expropriate, wrest, usurp, commandeer.

**arrow** noun **1** *a bow and arrow* SHAFT, bolt, dart; *historical* quarrel.

**2** *the arrow pointed right* POINTER, indicator, marker, needle.

**arsenal** noun **1** *Britain's nuclear arsenal* WEAPONS, weaponry, arms, armaments.

**2** *mutineers broke into the arsenal* ARMORY, arms depot, arms cache, ordnance depot, magazine, ammunition dump.

**arson** noun *the fire is being treated as arson* PYROMANIA, incendiarism; *informal* torching.

**art** noun **1** *he studied art* FINE ART, artwork.

**2** *the art of writing* SKILL, craft, technique, knack, facility, ability, know-how.

**3** *she uses art to achieve her aims* CUNNING, artfulness, slyness, craftiness, guile; deceit, duplicity, artifice, wiles.

**artful** adjective **1** *artful politicians* SLY, crafty, cunning, wily, scheming, devious, Machiavellian, sneaky, tricky, conniving, designing, calculating; canny, shrewd; deceitful, duplicitous, disingenuous, underhanded; *informal* foxy, shifty; *archaic* subtle. ANTONYM ingenuous.

**2** *artful precision* SKILLFUL, clever, adept, adroit, skilled, expert.

**article** noun **1** *small household articles* ITEM, thing, object, artifact, commodity, product.

**2** *an article in the paper* REPORT, account, story, write-up, feature, item, piece, column, review, commentary.

**3** *the crucial article of the treaty* CLAUSE, section, subsection, point, item, paragraph, division, subdivision, part, portion.

**articulate** adjective *an articulate speaker* ELOQUENT, fluent, effective, persuasive, lucid, expressive, silver-tongued; intelligible, comprehensible, understandable. ANTONYM unintelligible.

▸ verb *they were unable to articulate their emotions* EXPRESS, voice, vocalize, put in words, communicate, state; air, ventilate, vent, pour out; utter, say, speak, enunciate, pronounce; *informal* come out with.

**artifice** noun *in our trade, artifice is an asset* TRICKERY, deceit, deception, duplicity, guile, cunning, artfulness, wiliness, craftiness, slyness, chicanery; fraud, fraudulence.

**artificial** adjective **1** *artificial flowers* SYNTHETIC, fake, imitation, mock, ersatz, faux, substitute, replica, reproduction; man-made, manufactured, fabricated, inorganic; plastic; *informal* pretend, phony. See note at SPURIOUS. ANTONYM natural.

**2** *an artificial smile* INSINCERE, feigned, false, unnatural, contrived, put-on, exaggerated, forced, labored, strained, hollow; *informal* pretend, phony, bogus. ANTONYM genuine.

**artisan** noun *artisans from around North America will demonstrate their crafts* CRAFTSMAN, craftswoman, craftsperson; skilled worker, technician; smith, wright, journeyman; *archaic* artificer.

**artist** noun **1** *a mural artist* DESIGNER, creator, originator, producer; old master.

**2** *the surgeon is an artist with the knife* EXPERT, master, maestro, past master, virtuoso, genius; *informal* pro, ace. ANTONYM novice.

**artistic** adjective **1** *he's very artistic* CREATIVE, imaginative, inventive, expressive; sensitive, perceptive, discerning; *informal* artsy. ANTONYM unimaginative.

**2** *artistic touches* AESTHETIC, aesthetically pleasing, beautiful, attractive, fine; decorative, ornamental; tasteful, stylish, elegant, exquisite. ANTONYM inelegant.

**artistry** noun *one immediately notices the sheer artistry in her music* CREATIVE SKILL, creativity, art, skill, talent, genius, brilliance, flair, proficiency, virtuosity, finesse, style; craftsmanship, workmanship.

**artless** adjective *there is a no-nonsense, artless flavor to his memoirs* NATURAL, ingenuous, naive, simple, innocent, childlike, guileless; candid, open, sincere, unaffected. ANTONYM scheming.

**as** conjunction **1** *she looked up as he entered the room* WHILE, just as, even as, (just) when, at the time that, at the moment that.

**2** *we all felt as Frank did* IN THE (SAME) WAY THAT, the (same) way; *informal* like.

**3** *do as you're told* WHAT, that which.

**4** *they were free, as the case had not been proved* BECAUSE, since, seeing that/as, in view of the fact that, owing to the fact that; *informal* on account of; *literary* for. See note at TOWARD.

**5** *try as she did, she couldn't smile* THOUGH, although, even though, in spite of the fact that, despite the fact that, notwithstanding that, for all that, albeit, however.

**6** *relatively short distances, as Hartford to New Haven* SUCH AS, like, for instance, e.g., for example.

**7** *I'm away a lot, as you know* WHICH, a fact which.

▸ preposition **1** *he was dressed as a policeman* LIKE, in the guise of, so as to appear to be.

**2** *I'm speaking to you as your friend* IN THE ROLE OF, being, acting as.

PHRASES: **as for/as to** *as for interior paint, I prefer a semigloss latex* CONCERNING, with respect to, on the subject of, in the matter of, as regards, with regard to, regarding, with reference to, re, in re, apropos to, vis-à-vis.

**as it were** *the guests were chosen, as it were, by an almost random process* SO TO SPEAK, in a manner of speaking, to some extent, so to say; *informal* sort of.

**as yet** *there is no sign of them as yet* SO FAR, thus far, yet, still, up till now, up to now.

**USAGE NOTE as to**

First, it must be said that *as to* is an all-purpose preposition to be avoided whenever a more specific preposition will do. But *as to* isn't always indefensible. The phrase is most justifiable when introducing something previously mentioned only cursorily: "As to concerns the fair might lose on-track business if it offered its signal to the OTBs, [Dun said]: 'I figured we were going to lose the handle either way.' (*Portland Press Herald* [ME]; Sept. 7, 1997.) In beginning sentences this way, *as to* is equivalent to the more colloquial *as for*. In effect, the phrase is a passable shorthand form of *regarding*, *with regard to*, or *on the question of*.

The phrase is also (minimally) defensible when used for *about*, but that word is stylistically preferable in most contexts. *As to* smells of jargon—e.g.: "The bill carries no presumptions as to [read *about*] the effect of incorporation." (*News & Observer* [Raleigh]; Mar. 17, 1997.)

The main problem with *as to* is that it doesn't clearly establish syntactic or conceptual relationships, so it can hamper comprehensibility. In each of the following examples, another preposition would more directly and forcefully express the thought:

• "There's no rule as to [read *about*] how long you have to wait before you can enjoy your creation." (*Florida Times-Union*; Aug. 14, 1997.)

• "It is always possible that your neighbor is not aware of how disturbing his or her behavior is and that he or she can be more sensitive to your concerns, or you can agree as to [read *on*] certain time parameters or (if music is the culprit) what is an acceptable volume level." (*San Diego Union-Tribune*; Aug. 24, 1997.)

• "The same is true as to [read *of*] other cases finding for leaders by applying the regulation." (*Bankruptcy Court Decisions*; Mar. 24, 1994.)

• "There is no change in the prior IRA rules with regard to an individual's participation in other qualifying retirement plans. As such, the rules remain the same as to [read *for*] the maximum amount of adjusted gross income a taxpayer can have before the IRA deduction begins to phase out." (*Gazette-Telegraph* [Colorado Springs]; Mar. 12, 1997.)

• "Some people are a little surprised as to [read *by* or *at*] how quickly Veniard has gotten to his present level." (*Florida Times-Union*; June 28, 199.).

• "During a trip to the Mars Pathfinder Mission Control Center in Pasadena this summer, House Aeronautics and Space Subcommittee member Sheila Jackson-Lee, D-Texas, inquired as to [read *into*] whether the Pathfinder Mission had taken pictures of the American flag planted by Neil Armstrong in 1969." (*San Francisco Chronicle*; Sept. 15, 1997.) (In this case, the better rewording of "inquired as to whether" would have been "asked whether.") —*BG*

---

**ascend** verb *ascending the stairs | we watched the missiles ascend* CLIMB, go up/upward, move up/upward, rise (up), clamber (up); mount, scale, conquer; take to the air, take off; rocket. ANTONYM descend.

**ascertain** verb *first let's ascertain when it was that you last saw Vince* FIND OUT, discover, get to know, work out, make out, fathom, learn, deduce, divine, discern, see, understand, comprehend; establish, determine, verify, confirm; figure out.

**ascetic** adjective *an ascetic life* AUSTERE, self-denying, abstinent, abstemious, self-disciplined, self-abnegating; simple, puritanical, monastic; reclusive, eremitic, hermitic; celibate, chaste. See note at SEVERE. ANTONYM sybaritic.

▸ noun *a desert ascetic* ABSTAINER, puritan, recluse, hermit, anchorite, solitary; fakir, Sufi, dervish, sadhu; *archaic* eremite. ANTONYM sybarite.

**ascribe** verb *much of our success can be* ***ascribed to*** *the generosity of the Fords* ATTRIBUTE TO, assign to, put down to, accredit to, credit to, chalk up to, impute to; blame on, lay at the door of; connect with, associate with.

**ashamed** adjective *I was too ashamed to return her call* SORRY, shamefaced, abashed, sheepish, guilty, contrite, remorseful, repentant, penitent, regretful, rueful, apologetic; EMBARRASSED, mortified, humiliated, chagrined, discomfited; *rare* compunctious. ANTONYMS proud, unabashed.

**ashen** adjective *an ashen complexion* PALE, wan, pasty, gray, ashy, colorless, sallow, pallid, anemic, white, waxen, ghostly, pale-faced, bloodless; *rare* etiolated, lymphatic. See note at PALE2.

**ashore** adverb *passengers may now go ashore* ON TO (THE) LAND, on to the shore, aground; shoreward, landward; on the shore, on (dry) land.

**aside** adverb **1** *they stood aside* TO ONE SIDE, to the side, on one side; apart, away, separately.

**2** *that aside, he seemed a nice man* APART, notwithstanding.

▸ noun *"Her parents died," he said in an aside* WHISPERED REMARK, confidential remark, stage whisper; digression, incidental remark, obiter dictum.

PHRASE: **aside from** *aside from the mess in the garage, this place is looking good* APART FROM, besides, in addition to, not counting, barring, other than, but (for), excluding, not including, except (for), excepting, leaving out, save (for).

**asinine** adjective *an asinine stunt* STUPID, foolish, brainless, mindless, senseless, idiotic, imbecilic, ridiculous, ludicrous, absurd, nonsensical, fatuous, silly, inane, witless, empty-headed; *informal* halfwitted, dimwitted, dumb, moronic. See note at STUPID. ANTONYMS intelligent, sensible.

**ask** verb **1** *he asked what time we opened* INQUIRE, query, want to know; question, interrogate, quiz. ANTONYM answer.

**2** *they want to ask a few questions* PUT FORWARD, pose, raise, submit. ANTONYM answer.

**3** *don't be afraid to* ***ask for*** *advice* REQUEST, demand; solicit, seek, crave, apply for, petition for, call for, appeal for, beg (for), sue for.

**4** *let's ask them to dinner* INVITE, bid, summon, have someone over/around.

**askance** adverb *they look askance at anything foreign* SUSPICIOUSLY, skeptically, cynically, mistrustfully, distrustfully, doubtfully, dubiously; disapprovingly, contemptuously, scornfully, disdainfully. ANTONYM approvingly.

**askew** adjective *the pictures are askew* CROOKED, lopsided, tilted, angled, at an angle, skew, skewed, slanted, aslant, awry, oblique, out of true, to/on one side, uneven, off-center, asymmetrical; *informal* cockeyed, wonky. ANTONYM straight.

**asleep** adjective **1** *she was asleep in bed* SLEEPING, in a deep sleep, napping, catnapping, dozing, drowsing; *informal* snoozing, catching some Zs, zonked, hibernating, dead to the world, comatose, in the land of Nod, in the arms of Morpheus; *literary* slumbering. ANTONYM awake.

**2** *my leg's asleep* NUMB, with no feeling, numbed, benumbed, dead, insensible; *rare* torpefied.

**aspect** noun **1** *the photos depict every aspect of life* FEATURE, facet, side, characteristic, particular, detail; angle, slant.

**2** *his face had a sinister aspect* APPEARANCE, look, air, cast, mien, demeanor, expression; atmosphere, mood, quality, ambience, feeling.

**asperity** noun *he replied with some asperity in his tone* HARSHNESS, sharpness, abrasiveness, roughness, severity, acerbity, astringency, tartness, sarcasm.

**aspersions** PHRASE: **cast aspersions on** *in saying this, I do not mean to cast aspersions on Senator Scofield* VILIFY, disparage, denigrate, defame, run down, impugn, belittle, criticize, condemn, decry, denounce, pillory; malign, slander, libel, discredit; *informal* pull apart, throw mud at, knock, bad-mouth, dis.

**asphyxiate** verb *they were nearly asphyxiated from the fumes* CHOKE (TO DEATH), suffocate, smother, stifle; throttle, strangle.

**aspiration** noun *his greatest aspiration is to win an Olympic gold medal* DESIRE, hope, dream, wish, longing, yearning; aim, ambition, expectation, goal, target.

**aspire** verb *Jen* ***aspires to*** *a career in veterinary medicine* DESIRE, hope for, dream of, long for, yearn for, set one's heart on, wish for, want, be desirous of; aim for, seek, pursue, set one's sights on.

**aspiring** adjective *an aspiring journalist* WOULD-BE, aspirant, hopeful, budding; potential, prospective, future; ambitious, determined, upwardly mobile; *informal* wannabe.

**ass** noun **1** *he rode on an ass* DONKEY, jackass, jenny; burro.
**2** *informal don't be a silly ass* FOOL, idiot, dolt, simpleton, imbecile; dimwit, halfwit, dummy, dum-dum, loon, jackass, cretin, jerk, fathead, blockhead, jughead, boob, bozo, buffoon, numbskull, numbnuts, lummox, dunce, moron, meatball, doofus, ninny, nincompoop, dipstick, lamebrain, chump, peabrain, thickhead, dumb-ass, wooden-head, pinhead, airhead, birdbrain; nitwit, twit, turkey, goofball, putz; *dated* tomfool, muttonhead.

**3** *informal I'm tired of sitting around on my big fat ass.* See BUTTOCKS.

**USAGE NOTE ass, arse**

*Arse* is the spelling of the British slang term—in the anatomical sense, that is, not in the horse sense. In American English, *ass* is the spelling for both meanings. There's a story behind this. Today *ass* means both (1) "donkey" and (2) "a person's bottom." Sense 1 is the historical one; sense 2 originated in the mid-eighteenth century as the result of a phonological change, as *arse* and *ass* became homophones. By the early nineteenth century, it was possible to engage in wordplay between the words—as in an 1802 cartoon ("Neddy [a donkey] Paces at Tunbridge Wells [in Kent, England]"), in which one female rider says to another, "I'll show my Ass against any Lady's at Wells." —*BG*

**assail** verb **1** *the army moved in to assail the enemy* ATTACK, assault, pounce on, set upon/about, fall on, charge, rush, storm; *informal* lay into, tear into, pitch into. See note at ATTACK.

**2** *she was assailed by doubts* PLAGUE, torment, rack, beset, dog, trouble, disturb, worry, bedevil, nag, vex.

**3** *critics assailed the policy* CRITICIZE, censure, attack, condemn, pillory, revile; *informal* knock, slam.

**assailant** noun *he recognized his assailant* ATTACKER, mugger, assaulter.

**assassin** noun *the presumed assassin, Oswald, was gunned down* MURDERER, killer, gunman; executioner; *informal* hit man, hired gun; *dated* homicide.

**assassinate** verb *a plot to assassinate the premier* MURDER, kill, slaughter; eliminate, execute; liquidate; *informal* hit, terminate, knock off; *literary* slay. See note at KILL.

**assault** verb **1** *he assaulted a police officer* ATTACK, hit, strike, punch, beat up, thump; pummel, pound, batter; *informal* clout, wallop, belt, clobber, hammer, bop, sock, deck, slug, plug, lay into, do over, rough up; *literary* smite.

**2** *they regrouped to assault the hill* ATTACK, assail, pounce on, set upon, strike, fall on, swoop on, rush, storm, besiege. See note at ATTACK.

**3** *he has no memory of assaulting the victim* RAPE, sexually assault, molest.

▸ noun **1** *he was charged with assault* BATTERY, violence; sexual assault, rape.

**2** *an assault on the city* ATTACK, strike, onslaught, offensive, charge, push, thrust, invasion, bombardment, sortie, incursion, raid, blitz, campaign.

**assay** noun *this brand of herbal supplement will undergo independent assay* EVALUATION, assessment, appraisal, analysis, examination, test/tests, testing, inspection, scrutiny.

▸ verb *gold is assayed to determine its purity* EVALUATE, assess, appraise, analyze, examine, test, inspect, scrutinize, probe.

**assemblage** noun *an assemblage of protestors* COLLECTION, accumulation, conglomeration, gathering, group, grouping, cluster, aggregation, mass, number; assortment, selection, array, miscellany.

**assemble** verb **1** *a crowd had assembled* GATHER, collect, get together, congregate, convene, meet, muster, rally. See note at GATHER. ANTONYM disperse.

**2** *he assembled the suspects* BRING TOGETHER, call together, gather, collect, round up, marshal, muster, summon; *formal* convoke. ANTONYM disperse.

**3** *how to assemble the kite* CONSTRUCT, build, fabricate, manufacture, erect, set up, put together, piece together, connect, join. ANTONYM dismantle.

**assembly** noun **1** *an assembly of civil servants* GATHERING, meeting, congregation, convention, rally, convocation, assemblage, group, body, crowd, throng, company; *informal* get-together.

**2** *the labor needed in car assembly* CONSTRUCTION, manufacture, building, fabrication, erection.

**assent** noun *they are likely to give their assent* AGREEMENT, acceptance, approval, approbation, consent, acquiescence, compliance, concurrence; sanction, endorsement, confirmation; permission, leave, blessing; *informal* the go-ahead, the nod, the green light, the OK, the thumbs up. ANTONYMS dissent, refusal.

▸ verb *he **assented to** the change* AGREE TO, accept, approve, consent to, acquiesce in, concur in, give one's blessing to; sanction, endorse, confirm; *informal* give the go-ahead to, give the nod to, give the green light to, give the OK to, OK, give the thumbs up to; *formal* accede to. ANTONYM refuse.

**assert** verb **1** *they asserted that all aboard were safe* DECLARE, maintain, contend, argue, state, claim, propound, proclaim, announce, pronounce, swear, insist, avow; *formal* aver, opine; *rare* asseverate.

**2** *we find it difficult to assert our rights* INSIST ON, stand up for, uphold, defend, contend, establish, press for, push for, stress. PHRASE: **assert oneself** *these abused spouses have lost the nerve to assert themselves in even the smallest of ways* BEHAVE CONFIDENTLY, SPEAK CONFIDENTLY, be assertive, put oneself forward, take a stand, make one's presence felt; *informal* put one's foot down.

**assertive** adjective *an assertive sales team* CONFIDENT, self-confident, bold, decisive, assured, self-assured, self-possessed, forthright, firm, emphatic; authoritative, strong-willed, forceful, insistent, determined, commanding; *informal* feisty, pushy. ANTONYM timid.

**assess** verb **1** *we need more time to assess the situation* EVAL-

UATE, judge, gauge, rate, estimate, appraise, consider, get the measure of, determine, analyze; *informal* size up.

2 *the damage was assessed at $5 million* VALUE, calculate, work out, determine, fix, cost, price, estimate.

**assessment** noun 1 *a teacher's assessment of the student's abilities* EVALUATION, judgment, rating, estimation, appraisal, analysis, opinion.

2 *some assessments valued the estate at $2 million* VALUATION, appraisal, calculation, costing, pricing, estimate.

**asset** noun 1 *he sees his age as an asset* BENEFIT, advantage, blessing, good point, strong point, selling point, strength, forte, virtue, recommendation, attraction, resource, boon, merit, bonus, plus, pro. ANTONYMS liability, handicap.

2 **(assets)** *the seizure of all their assets* PROPERTY, resources, estate, holdings, possessions, effects, goods, valuables, belongings, chattels. ANTONYM liability.

**assiduous** adjective *she was assiduous in pointing out every feature* DILIGENT, careful, meticulous, thorough, sedulous, attentive, conscientious, punctilious, painstaking, rigorous, particular; persevering. See note at BUSY.

**assign** verb 1 *a young doctor was assigned the task* ALLOCATE, allot, give, set to; charge with, entrust with.

2 *she was **assigned to** a new post* APPOINT TO, promote to, delegate to, commission to, post to, co-opt to; select for, choose for, install in; *Military* detail to.

3 *we **assign** large sums of money **to** travel budgets* EARMARK FOR, designate for, set aside for, reserve for, appropriate for, allot to/for, allocate for, apportion for.

4 *he **assigned** the opinion **to** the prince* ASCRIBE TO, attribute to, put down to, accredit to, credit to, chalk up to, impute to; pin on, lay at the door of.

5 *he may assign the money to a third party* TRANSFER, make over, give, pass, hand over, hand down, convey, consign.

**assignation** noun *their secret assignation* RENDEZVOUS, date, appointment, meeting; *literary* tryst.

**assignment** noun 1 *I'm going to finish this assignment tonight* TASK, piece of work, job, duty, chore, mission, errand, undertaking, exercise, business, endeavor, enterprise; project, homework.

2 *the assignment of tasks* ALLOCATION, allotment, issuance, designation; sharing out, apportionment, distribution, handing out, dispensation.

3 *the assignment of property* TRANSFER, making over, giving, hand down, consignment; *Law* conveyance, devise, attornment.

**assimilate** verb 1 *the amount of information he can assimilate* ABSORB, take in, acquire, soak up, pick up, grasp, comprehend, understand, learn, master; digest, ingest.

2 *many tribes were assimilated by Turkic peoples* SUBSUME, incorporate, integrate, absorb, engulf, acculturate; co-opt, adopt, embrace, admit.

3 *after arriving, it took us some time to assimilate* INTEGRATE, blend in.

**assist** verb 1 *I spend my time assisting the chef* HELP, aid, lend a (helping) hand to, oblige, accommodate, serve; collaborate with, work with; support, back (up), second; abet; *informal* pitch in with. ANTONYM hinder.

2 *the exchange rates assisted the firm's expansion* FACILITATE, aid, ease, expedite, spur, promote, boost, benefit, foster, encourage, stimulate, precipitate, accelerate, advance, further, forward. ANTONYM impede.

**assistance** noun *the governor has requested federal assistance* HELP, aid, support, backing, reinforcement, succor, relief, TLC, intervention, cooperation, collaboration; a (helping) hand, a good turn; social security, benefits; *informal* a break, a leg up; the dole. ANTONYM hindrance.

**assistant** noun *a photographer's assistant* HELPER, deputy, second-in-command, second, number two, right-hand man/woman, aide, attendant, mate, apprentice, junior, auxiliary, subordinate; hired hand, hired help, man/girl Friday; *informal* sidekick, gofer.

**associate** verb 1 *the colors that we associate with fire* LINK, connect, relate, identify, equate, bracket, set side by side.

2 *I was forced to associate with them* MIX, keep company, mingle, socialize, go around, rub shoulders, rub elbows, fraternize, consort, have dealings; *informal* hobnob, hang out/around.

3 *the firm is associated with a local charity* AFFILIATE, align, connect, join, attach, team up, be in league, ally; merge, integrate, confederate.

▸ noun *his business associate* PARTNER, colleague, coworker, workmate, comrade, ally, affiliate, confederate; connection, contact, acquaintance; collaborator; *informal* crony.

**assorted** adjective *the ribbons are available in assorted colors* VARIOUS, miscellaneous, mixed, varied, heterogeneous, varying, diverse, eclectic, multifarious, sundry; *literary* divers.

**assortment** noun *an assortment of antique buttons* MIXTURE, variety, array, mixed bag, mix, miscellany, selection, medley, diversity, hodgepodge, mishmash, potpourri, salmagundi, farrago, gallimaufry, omnium gatherum.

**assuage** verb 1 *a pain that could never be assuaged* RELIEVE, ease, alleviate, soothe, mitigate, allay, palliate, abate, suppress, subdue; moderate, lessen, diminish, reduce. See note at ALLEVIATE. ANTONYM aggravate.

2 *her hunger was quickly assuaged* SATISFY, gratify, appease, fulfill, indulge, relieve, slake, sate, satiate, quench, check. ANTONYM intensify.

**assume** verb 1 *I assumed he wanted me to keep the book* PRESUME, suppose, take it (as given), take for granted, take as read, conjecture, surmise, conclude, deduce, infer, reckon, reason, think, fancy, believe, understand, gather, figure.

2 *he assumed a Southern accent* AFFECT, adopt, impersonate, put on, simulate, feign, fake.

**3** *the disease may assume epidemic proportions* ACQUIRE, take on, come to have.

**4** *they are to assume more responsibility* ACCEPT, shoulder, bear, undertake, take on/up, manage, handle, deal with.

**5** *he assumed control of their finances* SEIZE, take (over), appropriate, commandeer, expropriate, hijack, wrest, arrogate, usurp.

**assumed** adjective *an assumed name* FALSE, fictitious, invented, made-up, fake, bogus, sham, spurious, make-believe, improvised, adopted; *informal* pretend, phony. ANTONYM genuine.

**assumption** noun **1** *an informed assumption* SUPPOSITION, presumption, belief, expectation, conjecture, speculation, surmise, guess, premise, hypothesis; conclusion, deduction, inference; *rare* illation, notion, impression.

**2** *the assumption of power by revolutionaries* SEIZURE, arrogation, appropriation, expropriation, commandeering, confiscation, hijacking, wresting.

**3** *the early assumption of community obligation* ACCEPTANCE, shouldering, tackling, undertaking.

**assurance** noun **1** *her calm assurance* SELF-CONFIDENCE, confidence, self-assurance, self-possession, nerve, poise, aplomb, levelheadedness; calmness, composure, sangfroid, equanimity; *informal* cool, unflappability. ANTONYM self-doubt.

**2** *you have my assurance* WORD OF HONOR, word, promise, pledge, vow, avowal, oath, bond, undertaking, guarantee, commitment.

**3** *there is no assurance of getting one's money back* GUARANTEE, certainty, certitude, surety, confidence, expectation. ANTONYM uncertainty.

**assure** verb **1** *we must assure him of our loyal support* REASSURE, convince, satisfy, persuade, guarantee, promise, tell; affirm, pledge, swear, vow.

**2** *he wants to assure a favorable vote* ENSURE, secure, guarantee, seal, clinch, confirm; *informal* sew up.

**assured** adjective **1** *an assured demeanor* CONFIDENT, self-confident, self-assured, self-possessed, poised, phlegmatic, levelheaded; calm, composed, equanimous, imperturbable, unruffled; *informal* unflappable, together. ANTONYM doubtful.

**2** *an assured supply of weapons* GUARANTEED, certain, sure, secure, reliable, dependable, sound; infallible, unfailing; *informal* sure-fire. ANTONYM uncertain.

**astonish** verb *the NYPD astonished many with the success of its aggressive crime-fighting tactics* AMAZE, astound, stagger, surprise, startle, stun, confound, dumbfound, strike dumb, boggle, stupefy, daze, shock, take aback, leave open-mouthed, leave aghast; *informal* flabbergast, blow away, bowl over, floor.

**astonishing** adjective *she's read an astonishing number of books* AMAZING, astounding, staggering, surprising, breathtaking; remarkable, extraordinary, incredible, unbelievable, phenomenal; *informal* mind-boggling.

**astonishment** noun *we stared in astonishment* AMAZEMENT, surprise, stupefaction, incredulity, disbelief, speechlessness, awe, wonder, wonderment.

**astound** verb *the dogs' tricks will astound you* AMAZE, astonish, stagger, surprise, startle, stun, confound, dumbfound, boggle, stupefy, shock, daze, take aback, leave open-mouthed, leave aghast; *informal* flabbergast, blow away, bowl over, floor.

**astounding** adjective *his speed and fitness were astounding* AMAZING, astonishing, staggering, surprising, breathtaking, remarkable, extraordinary, incredible, unbelievable, phenomenal; *informal* mind-boggling.

**astray** adverb **1** *the shots went astray* OFF TARGET, wide of the mark, awry, off course; amiss.

**2** *the older boys led him astray* INTO WRONGDOING, into error, into sin, into iniquity, away from the straight and narrow, off the right course.

**astringent** adjective **1** *the lotion has an astringent effect on pores* CONSTRICTING, constrictive, contracting; styptic.

**2** *her astringent words* SEVERE, sharp, stern, harsh, acerbic, acidulous, caustic, mordant, trenchant; scathing, spiteful, cutting, incisive, waspish.

**astronaut** noun SPACEMAN, SPACEWOMAN, cosmonaut, space traveler, space cadet.

**astute** adjective *an astute investor* SHREWD, sharp, acute, adroit, quick, clever, crafty, intelligent, bright, smart, canny, intuitive, perceptive, insightful, incisive, sagacious, wise; *informal* on the ball, quick on the uptake, savvy; heads-up. See note at KEEN. ANTONYM stupid.

**asunder** adverb *literary the fabric of society may be torn asunder* APART, up, in two; to pieces, to shreds, to bits.

**asylum** noun **1** *he appealed for political asylum* REFUGE, sanctuary, shelter, safety, protection, security, immunity; a safe haven.

**2** *he was confined to an asylum* PSYCHIATRIC HOSPITAL, mental hospital, mental institution, mental asylum; *informal* madhouse, loony bin, funny farm, nuthouse, bughouse; *dated* lunatic asylum; *archaic* bedlam.

**asymmetrical** adjective *the quilt pattern is asymmetrical* LOPSIDED, unsymmetrical, uneven, unbalanced, crooked, awry, askew, skew, misaligned; disproportionate, unequal, irregular; *informal* cockeyed, wonky.

**atheism** noun *atheism was not freely discussed in his community* NONBELIEF, disbelief, unbelief, irreligion, skepticism, doubt, agnosticism; nihilism.

**atheist** noun *why is it often assumed that a man of science is probably an atheist?* NONBELIEVER, disbeliever, unbeliever, skeptic, doubter, doubting Thomas, agnostic; nihilist. ANTONYM believer.

**athlete** noun *the school's top athletes* SPORTSMAN, sportswoman, sportsperson; jock; Olympian; runner.

**athletic** adjective **1** *his athletic physique* MUSCULAR, muscly, sturdy, strapping, well-built, strong, powerful, robust, able-bodied, vigorous, hardy, lusty, hearty, brawny, burly, broad-shouldered, Herculean; FIT, in good shape, in trim; *informal* sporty, husky, hunky, beefy; *literary* thewy. ANTONYM puny.

**2** *athletic events* SPORTING, sports; Olympic.

**athletics** plural noun SPORTS, sporting events, games, races; track and field events, track; contests; working out, exercising.

**atmosphere** noun **1** *the gases present in the atmosphere* AIR, aerospace; sky; *literary* heavens, firmament, blue, azure, ether.

**2** *the hotel has a relaxed atmosphere* AMBIENCE, air, mood, feel, feeling, character, tone, tenor, aura, quality, undercurrent, flavor; *informal* vibe.

**atom** noun **1** *they build tiny circuits atom by atom* PARTICLE, molecule, bit, piece, fragment, fraction.

**2** *there wasn't an atom of truth in the allegations* GRAIN, iota, jot, whit, mite, scrap, shred, ounce, scintilla, trace, smidgen, modicum.

**atone** verb *how shall I **atone for** my mistakes?* MAKE AMENDS FOR, make reparation for, make restitution for, make up for, compensate for, pay for, recompense for, expiate, redress, make good, offset; do penance for.

**atrocious** adjective **1** *atrocious cruelties* BRUTAL, barbaric, barbarous, savage, vicious, beastly; wicked, cruel, nasty, heinous, monstrous, vile, inhuman, black-hearted, fiendish, ghastly, horrible; abominable, outrageous, hateful, disgusting, despicable, contemptible, loathsome, odious, abhorrent, sickening, horrifying, unspeakable, execrable, egregious. ANTONYMS admirable, kindly.

**2** *the weather was atrocious* APPALLING, dreadful, terrible, very bad, unpleasant, miserable; *informal* abysmal, dire, rotten, lousy, godawful. ANTONYM superb.

**atrocity** noun *European ministers were appalled by scenes of alleged Kosovo atrocities* ABOMINATION, cruelty, enormity, outrage, horror, monstrosity, obscenity, violation, crime, abuse; barbarity, barbarism, brutality, savagery, inhumanity, wickedness, evil, iniquity.

**atrophy** verb *muscles atrophy in microgravity* WASTE AWAY, become emaciated, wither, shrivel (up), shrink; decay, decline, deteriorate, degenerate, weaken. ANTONYMS strengthen, flourish.

▸ noun *muscular atrophy* WASTING, emaciation, withering, shriveling, shrinking; decay, decline, deterioration, degeneration, weakening, debilitation, enfeeblement. ANTONYM strengthening.

**attach** verb **1** *a lead weight is attached to the cord* FASTEN, fix, affix, join, connect, link, couple, secure, make fast, tie, bind, chain; stick, adhere, glue, fuse; append. ANTONYM detach.

**2** *they attached importance to research* ASCRIBE, assign, attribute, accredit, impute.

**3** *the medical officer attached to HQ* ASSIGN, appoint, allocate, second; *Military* detail.

**attached** adjective **1** *I'm not interested in you—I'm attached* SPOKEN FOR, married, engaged, promised in marriage; going out, involved, seeing someone; *informal* hitched, spliced, shackled, going steady; *dated* betrothed; *formal* wed, wedded; *literary* affianced; *archaic* espoused. ANTONYM single.

**2** *she was very **attached to** her brother* FOND OF, devoted to; *informal* mad about, crazy about.

**attachment** noun **1** *he has a strong **attachment to** his mother* BOND WITH, closeness to/with, devotion to, loyalty to; fondness for, love for, affection for, feeling for; relationship with.

**2** *the shower had a massage attachment* ACCESSORY, fitting, extension, add-on, appendage.

**3** *the attachment of safety restraints* FIXING, fastening, linking, coupling, connection.

**attack** verb **1** *Chris had been brutally attacked* ASSAULT, assail, set upon, beat up; batter, pummel, punch; *informal* do over, work over, rough up.

**2** *they attacked along a 10-mile front* STRIKE, charge, pounce; bombard, shell, blitz, strafe, fire, besiege. ANTONYM defend.

**3** *the clergy attacked government policies* CRITICIZE, censure, condemn, pillory, savage, revile, vilify; *informal* knock, slam, blast, bash, lay into. ANTONYM praise.

**4** *they have to attack the problem soon* ADDRESS, attend to, deal with, confront, apply oneself to, get to work on, undertake, embark on; *informal* get cracking on.

▸ noun **1** *the attack began at dawn* ASSAULT, onslaught, offensive, strike, blitz, raid, charge, rush, invasion, incursion.

**2** *she wrote a hostile attack against him* CRITICISM, censure, rebuke, admonishment, reprimand; condemnation, denunciation, vilification; tirade, diatribe, polemic; *informal* roasting, caning, hatchet job. ANTONYMS defense, commendation.

**3** *an asthmatic attack* FIT, seizure, spasm, convulsion, paroxysm, outburst, bout.

**THE RIGHT WORD attack, assail, assault, beset, besiege, bombard, charge, molest, storm**

There is no shortage of "fighting words." **Attack** is the most general verb, meaning to set upon someone or something in a violent, forceful, or aggressive way (*the rebels attacked at dawn*); but it can also be used figuratively (*attack the government's policy*). **Assault** implies a greater degree of violence or viciousness and the infliction of more damage. As part of the legal term "assault and battery," it suggests an attempt or threat to injure someone physically. **Molest** is another word meaning to *attack* and is used today almost exclusively of sexual molestation (*she had been molested as a child*). **Charge** and **storm** are primarily military words, both suggesting a forceful assault on a fixed position. To *charge* is to make a violent onslaught (*the infantry charged the enemy camp*) and is often used as a command (*"Charge!" the general cried*). To *storm* means to take by force, with all the momentum and fury of a storm (*after days of planning, the soldiers stormed the castle*), but there is often the suggestion of a last-ditch, all-out effort to end a long siege or avoid defeat. To **assail** is to attack with repeated thrusts or blows, implying that victory depends not so much on force as on persistence. To **bombard** is to assail continuously with bombs or shells (*they bombarded the city without mercy for days*). **Besiege** means to surround with an armed force (*to* *besiege the capital city*). When used figuratively, its meaning comes close to that of *assail*, but with an emphasis on being hemmed in and enclosed rather than punished repeatedly (*besieged with fears*). **Beset** also means to attack on all sides (*beset by enemies*), but it is also used frequently in other contexts to mean set or placed upon (*a bracelet beset with diamonds*).

---

**attacker** noun *the attacker escaped with her purse* ASSAILANT, assaulter, aggressor; mugger, rapist, killer, murderer.

**attain** verb *attempts to attain a promotion* ACHIEVE, accomplish, reach, obtain, gain, procure, secure, get, hook, net, win, earn, acquire; realize, fulfill; *informal* clinch, bag, snag, wrap up. See note at GET.

**attainable** adjective *a challenging but attainable target* ACHIEVABLE, obtainable, accessible, within reach, securable, realizable; practicable, workable, realistic, reasonable, viable, feasible, possible; *informal* doable, get-at-able.

**attempt** verb *I attempted to answer the question* TRY, strive, aim, venture, endeavor, seek, undertake, make an effort; have a go at, try one's hand at; *informal* go all out, bend over backwards, bust a gut, hazard; *formal* essay; *archaic* assay.

▸ noun *an attempt to improve the economy* EFFORT, endeavor, try, venture, trial; *informal* crack, go, bid, shot, stab; *formal* essay; *archaic* assay.

**attend** verb **1** *they attended a carol service* BE PRESENT AT, sit in on, take part in; appear at, present oneself at, turn up at, visit, go to; *informal* show up at, show one's face at. ANTONYM miss.

**2** *he had not* ***attended to*** *the regulations* PAY ATTENTION TO, pay heed to, be attentive to, listen to; concentrate on, take note of, bear in mind, take into consideration, heed, observe, mark. ANTONYMS disregard, ignore.

**3** *the wounded were* ***attended to*** *nearby* CARE FOR, look after, minister to, see to; tend (to), treat, nurse, help, aid, assist, succor; *informal* doctor.

**4** *he* ***attended to*** *the boy's education* DEAL WITH, see to, manage, organize, sort out, handle, take care of, take charge of, take in hand, tackle. ANTONYM neglect.

**5** *the princess was attended by an usher* ESCORT, accompany, chaperone, squire, guide, lead, conduct, usher, shepherd; assist, help, serve, wait on.

**6** *her weakness* ***was attended with*** *a fever* BE ACCOMPANIED BY, occur with, coexist with, be associated with, connected with, be linked with; be produced by, originate from/in, stem from, result from, arise from.

**attendance** noun **1** *please confirm your attendance* PRESENCE, appearance.

**2** *the attendance was dismal* TURNOUT, audience, house, gate, box office; crowd, congregation, gathering. ANTONYM absence.

PHRASE: **in attendance** *three doctors are in attendance* PRESENT, here, there, at hand, available; assisting.

**attendant** noun *your attendant will be Edward* STEWARD, waiter, waitress, garçon, porter, servant, waitperson, stewardess; escort, companion, retainer, aide, lady-in-waiting, equerry, chaperone; manservant, valet, butler, maidservant, maid, footman; busboy, houseman; lackey.

▸ adjective *new discoveries and the attendant excitement* ACCOMPANYING, associated, related, connected, concomitant, coincident; resultant, resulting, consequent.

**attention** noun **1** *the issue needs further attention* CONSIDERATION, contemplation, deliberation, thought, study, observation, scrutiny, investigation, action.

**2** *he tried to attract the attention of a policeman* AWARENESS, notice, observation, heed, regard, scrutiny, surveillance.

**3** *adequate medical attention* CARE, treatment, ministration, succor, relief, aid, help, assistance.

**4** **(attentions)** *he was effusive in his attentions* OVERTURES, approaches, suit, wooing, courting; compliments, flattery; courtesy, politeness.

**attentive** adjective **1** *a bright and attentive scholar* PERCEPTIVE, observant, alert, acute, aware, heedful, vigilant; intent, focused, committed, studious, diligent, conscientious, earnest; wary, watchful; *informal* not missing a trick, on the ball.

**2** *the most attentive of husbands* CONSCIENTIOUS, considerate, thoughtful, kind, caring, solicitous, understanding, sympathetic, obliging, accommodating, courteous, gallant, chivalrous; dutiful, responsible. ANTONYM inconsiderate.

**attenuated** adjective **1** *attenuated fingers* THIN, slender, narrow, slim, skinny, spindly, bony; *rare* attenuate. ANTONYMS plump, broad.

**2** *his muscle activity was much attenuated* WEAKENED, reduced, lessened, decreased, diminished, impaired. ANTONYM strengthened.

**attest** verb *I can* ***attest to*** *her fitness as a mother* CERTIFY, corroborate, confirm, verify, substantiate, authenticate, evidence, demonstrate, show, prove; endorse, support, affirm, bear out, give credence to, vouch for; *formal* evince. ANTONYM disprove.

**attic** noun *the Christmas lights are in the attic* LOFT, garret.

**attire** noun *Thomas preferred formal attire* CLOTHING, clothes, garments, dress, wear, outfits, garb, costume; *informal* gear, duds, getup, threads; *formal* apparel; *archaic* raiment, habiliments.

▸ verb *she was attired in black crepe* DRESS, dress up, clothe, garb, robe, array, costume, swathe, deck, deck out, turn out, fit out, trick out; *archaic* apparel, invest, habit.

**attitude** noun **1** *you seem ambivalent in your attitude* VIEW, viewpoint, outlook, perspective, stance, standpoint, position, inclination, temper, orientation, approach, reaction; opinion, ideas, convictions, feelings, thinking.

**2** *an attitude of prayer* POSITION, posture, pose, stance, bearing.

**3** *their music is hard rock with plenty of attitude* HOSTILITY, anger, venom, vitriol, rancor, spunk, spirit; *informal* 'tude.

**attract** verb **1** *positive ions are attracted to the negatively charged terminal* DRAW, pull; magnetize. ANTONYM repel.

**2** *he was attracted by her smile* ENTICE, allure, lure, tempt, charm, win over, woo, engage, enthrall, enchant, entrance, captivate, beguile, bewitch, seduce. ANTONYM repel.

**attraction** noun **1** *the stars are held together by gravitational attraction* PULL, draw; magnetism. ANTONYM repulsion.

**2** *she had lost whatever attraction she once had* APPEAL, attractiveness, desirability, seductiveness, seduction, allure, animal magnetism; charisma, charm, beauty, good looks, eye-appeal. ANTONYM repulsion.

**3** *the fair offers sideshows and other attractions* ENTERTAINMENT, activity, diversion, interest.

**attractive** adjective **1** *a more attractive career* APPEALING, inviting, tempting, irresistible; agreeable, pleasing, interesting. See note at PLEASANT. ANTONYM uninviting.

**2** *she has no idea how attractive she is* GOOD-LOOKING, beautiful, pretty, handsome, lovely, stunning, striking, arresting, gorgeous, prepossessing, fetching, captivating, bewitching, beguiling, engaging, charming, enchanting, enticing, appealing, delightful, winning, photogenic, telegenic; sexy, seductive, alluring, tantalizing, irresistible, ravishing, desirable; *informal* drop-dead gorgeous, foxy; *literary* beauteous; *archaic* comely, fair. ANTONYM ugly.

**attribute** verb *they* ***attributed*** *their success* ***to*** *him* ASCRIBE TO, assign to, accredit to, credit to, impute to; put down to, chalk up to; hold responsible for, blame on, pin on; connect with, associate with.

▸ noun **1** *he has all the attributes of a top player* QUALITY, characteristic, trait, feature, element, aspect, property, sign, hallmark, mark, distinction.

**2** *the hourglass is the attribute of Father Time* SYMBOL, mark, sign, hallmark, trademark. See note at EMBLEM.

**attrition** noun **1** *the battle would result in further attrition of their already lame naval force* WEARING DOWN, WEARING AWAY, weakening, debilitation, enfeebling, sapping, attenuation; gradual loss.

**2** *the skull shows attrition of the teeth* ABRASION, friction, erosion, corrosion, corroding, grinding; wearing away, deterioration; *rare* detrition.

**attune** verb *we are finally attuned to city life* ACCUSTOM, adjust, adapt, acclimatize, condition, accommodate, assimilate; acclimate.

**auburn** adjective *auburn hair* REDDISH-BROWN, red-brown, Titian (red), tawny, russet, chestnut, copper, coppery, rufous, rust.

**audacious** adjective **1** *an audacious remark* IMPUDENT, impertinent, insolent, presumptuous, cheeky, irreverent, discourteous, disrespectful, insubordinate, ill-mannered, unmannerly, rude, brazen, shameless, pert, defiant, cocky, bold (as brass); *informal* fresh, lippy, mouthy, saucy, sassy, nervy, ballsy; *archaic* contumelious. ANTONYM polite.

**2** *his audacious exploits* BOLD, daring, fearless, intrepid, brave, courageous, valiant, heroic, plucky; daredevil, devil-may-care, reckless, madcap; venturesome, mettlesome; *informal* gutsy, spunky, ballsy; *literary* temerarious. See note at BOLD. ANTONYM timid.

**audacity** noun **1** *he had the audacity to contradict me* IMPUDENCE, impertinence, insolence, presumption, cheek, bad manners, effrontery, nerve, gall, defiance, temerity; *informal* chutzpah, sass. See note at TEMERITY.

**2** *a traveler of extraordinary audacity* BOLDNESS, daring, fearlessness, intrepidity, bravery, courage, heroism, pluck, grit; recklessness; spirit, mettle; *informal* guts, gutsiness, spunk, moxie.

**audible** adjective *the radio is barely audible* HEARABLE, perceptible, discernible, detectable, appreciable; clear, distinct, loud. ANTONYM faint.

**audience** noun **1** *the audience applauded* SPECTATORS, LISTENERS, viewers, onlookers, patrons; crowd, throng, congregation, turnout; house, gallery.

**2** *the radio station has a teenage audience* MARKET, PUBLIC, following, fans; listenership, viewership.

**3** *an audience with the Pope* MEETING, consultation, conference, hearing, reception, interview; *informal* meet-and-greet.

**audit** noun *an audit of the party accounts* INSPECTION, examination, verification, scrutiny, probe, investigation, assessment, appraisal, evaluation, review, analysis; *informal* going-over, once-over.

▸ verb *we audited their books* INSPECT, examine, survey, go through, scrutinize, check, probe, vet, investigate, inquire into, assess, verify, appraise, evaluate, review, analyze, study; *informal* give something a/the once-over, give something a going-over.

**augment** verb *moonlighting helps augment her income* INCREASE, add to, supplement, build up, enlarge, expand, extend, raise, multiply, swell, grow; magnify, amplify, escalate; improve, boost; *informal* up, jack up, hike up, bump up. ANTONYM decrease.

**augur** verb *Quebec's election on Monday may augur sovereignty sentiment* BODE, portend, herald, be a sign of, warn of, forewarn of, foreshadow, be an omen of, presage, indicate, signify, signal, promise, threaten, spell, denote; predict, prophesy; *literary* betoken, foretoken, forebode. See note at PREDICT.

**august** adjective *our august guests* DISTINGUISHED, respected, eminent, venerable, hallowed, illustrious, prestigious, renowned, celebrated, honored, acclaimed, esteemed, exalted; great, important, lofty, noble; imposing, impressive, awe-inspiring, stately, grand, dignified.

**aura** noun *an aura of sophistication* ATMOSPHERE, ambience, air, quality, character, mood, feeling, feel, flavor, tone, tenor; emanation; *informal* vibe.

**auspices** plural noun *talks were to be held under the auspices of the UN* PATRONAGE, aegis, umbrella, protection, keeping, care; support, backing, guardianship, trusteeship, guidance, supervision.

**auspicious** adjective *thanks for joining us on this auspicious occasion* FAVORABLE, propitious, promising, rosy, good, encouraging; opportune, timely, lucky, fortunate, providential, felicitous, advantageous. See note at OPPORTUNE.

**austere** adjective **1** *an outwardly austere man* SEVERE, stern, strict, harsh, steely, flinty, dour, grim, cold, frosty, unemotional, unfriendly; formal, stiff, reserved, aloof, forbidding; grave, solemn, serious, unsmiling, unsympathetic, unforgiving; hard, unyielding, unbending, inflexible; *informal* hard-boiled. See note at SEVERE. ANTONYM genial.

**2** *an austere life* ASCETIC, self-denying, self-disciplined, nonindulgent, frugal, spartan, puritanical, abstemious, abstinent, self-sacrificing, strict, temperate, sober, simple, restrained; celibate, chaste. ANTONYM immoderate.

**3** *the buildings were austere* PLAIN, simple, basic, functional, modest, unadorned, unembellished, unfussy, restrained; stark, bleak, bare, clinical, spartan, ascetic; *informal* no-frills, bare-bones. ANTONYM ornate.

**authentic** adjective **1** *an authentic document* GENUINE, real, bona fide, true, veritable; legitimate, lawful, legal, valid; *informal* the real McCoy, the real thing, kosher. See note at GENUINE. ANTONYM fake.

**2** *an authentic depiction of the situation* RELIABLE, dependable, trustworthy, authoritative, honest, faithful; accurate, factual, true, truthful; *formal* veridical, veracious. ANTONYM unreliable.

**authenticate** verb **1** *the evidence will authenticate his claim* VERIFY, validate, prove, substantiate, corroborate, confirm, support, back up, attest to, give credence to.

**2** *a mandate authenticated by the popular vote* VALIDATE, ratify, confirm, seal, sanction, endorse.

**authenticity** noun **1** *the authenticity of the painting* GENUINENESS, bona fides; legitimacy, legality, validity.

**2** *the authenticity of this account* RELIABILITY, dependability, trustworthiness, credibility; accuracy, truth, veracity, fidelity.

**author** noun **1** *modern Latin American authors* WRITER; novelist, playwright, poet, essayist, biographer; columnist, reporter; wordsmith; bard; *informal* scribe, scribbler.

**2** *the author of the peace plan* ORIGINATOR, creator, instigator, founder, father, architect, designer, deviser, producer; cause, agent.

**authoritarian** adjective *his authoritarian manner* AUTOCRATIC, dictatorial, despotic, tyrannical, draconian, oppressive, repressive, illiberal, undemocratic; disciplinarian, domineering, overbearing, high-handed, peremptory, imperious, strict, rigid, inflexible; *informal* bossy, iron-fisted. ANTONYMS democratic, liberal.

▸ noun *the army is dominated by authoritarians* AUTOCRAT, despot, dictator, tyrant; disciplinarian, martinet.

**authoritative** adjective **1** *authoritative information* RELIABLE, dependable, trustworthy, sound, authentic, valid, attested, verifiable; accurate. ANTONYM unreliable.

**2** *the authoritative edition* DEFINITIVE, most reliable, best; authorized, accredited, recognized, accepted, approved, standard, canonical.

**3** *his authoritative manner* ASSURED, confident, assertive; commanding, masterful, lordly; domineering, imperious, overbearing, authoritarian; *informal* bossy. ANTONYMS diffident, timid.

**authority** noun **1** *a rebellion against those in authority* POWER, jurisdiction, command, control, charge, dominance, rule, sovereignty, supremacy; influence; *informal* clout. See note at JURISDICTION.

**2** *the authority to arrest drug traffickers* AUTHORIZATION, right, power, mandate, prerogative, license, permission.

**3** **(authorities)** *they failed to report the theft to the authorities* OFFICIALS, officialdom; government, administration, establishment; police; *informal* the powers that be.

**4** *an authority on the stock market* EXPERT, specialist, aficionado, pundit, guru, sage.

**5** *on good authority* EVIDENCE, testimony, witness, attestation, word, avowal; *Law* deposition.

**authorize** verb **1** *they authorized further action* SANCTION, permit, allow, approve, consent to, assent to; ratify, endorse, validate; *informal* give the green light to, give the go-ahead to, OK, give the thumbs up to. ANTONYM forbid.

**2** *the troops were authorized to fire* EMPOWER, mandate, commission; entitle.

**autobiography** noun *Nixon's autobiography* MEMOIRS, life story, personal history.

**autocratic** adjective *autocratic governments* DESPOTIC, tyrannical, dictatorial, totalitarian, autarchic; undemocratic, one-party, monocratic; domineering, draconian, overbearing, high-handed, peremptory, imperious; harsh, rigid, inflexible, illiberal, oppressive, iron-fisted.

**autograph** noun *fans pestered him for his autograph* SIGNATURE; *informal* John Hancock.

▸ verb *Jack autographed copies of his book* SIGN, sign one's name to.

**automatic** adjective **1** *automatic garage doors* MECHANIZED, mechanical, automated, computerized, electronic, robotic; self-activating. ANTONYM manual.

**2** *an automatic reaction* INSTINCTIVE, involuntary, unconscious, reflex, knee-jerk, instinctual, subconscious; spontaneous, impulsive, unthinking; mechanical; *informal* gut. ANTONYMS conscious, deliberate.

**3** *he is the automatic choice for the team* INEVITABLE, unavoidable, inescapable, mandatory, compulsory; certain, definite, undoubted, assured.

**autonomy** noun *Filipinos voted on Muslim autonomy* SELF-GOVERNMENT, self-rule, home rule, self-determination, independence, sovereignty, freedom.

**available** adjective 1 *refreshments will be available | don't worry ladies, Bryan is still available* OBTAINABLE, accessible, at hand, at one's disposal, handy, convenient; on sale, procurable; untaken, unengaged, unused; *informal* up for grabs, on tap, gettable.

2 *I'll see if he's available* FREE, unoccupied; present, in attendance; contactable; unattached, single. ANTONYMS busy, engaged.

**avarice** noun *the job had become less about integrity and more about avarice* GREED, greediness, acquisitiveness, cupidity, covetousness, rapacity, materialism, mercenariness; *rare* pleonexia; *informal* money-grubbing, affluenza. See note at GREEDY. ANTONYM generosity.

**average** noun *the price is above the national average* MEAN, median, mode; norm, standard, rule, par.

▸ adjective 1 *the average temperature in May* MEAN, median, modal.

2 *a woman of average height* ORDINARY, standard, normal, typical, regular. See note at NORMAL.

3 *a very average director* MEDIOCRE, second-rate, undistinguished, ordinary, middle-of-the-road, unexceptional, unexciting, unremarkable, unmemorable, indifferent, pedestrian, lackluster, forgettable, amateurish; *informal* OK, so-so, 'comme ci, comme ça,' fair-to-middling, no great shakes, underwhelming, plain-vanilla. ANTONYMS outstanding, exceptional.

PHRASE: **on average** *on average, we get about two million visitors each year* NORMALLY, usually, ordinarily, generally, in general, for the most part, as a rule, typically; overall, by and large, on the whole.

**aversion** noun *an* ***aversion to*** *the use of force* DISLIKE OF, antipathy for, distaste for, abhorrence of, hatred of, odium of, loathing of, detestation of, hostility toward; reluctance toward, unwillingness for, disinclination toward. ANTONYM liking.

**avid** adjective *an avid reader of science fiction* KEEN, eager, enthusiastic, ardent, passionate, zealous, hard-core; devoted, dedicated, wholehearted, earnest. See note at EAGER. ANTONYM apathetic.

**avoid** verb 1 *I avoid situations that stress me out* KEEP AWAY FROM, STAY AWAY FROM, steer clear of, give a wide berth to, fight shy of. ANTONYM confront.

2 *he is trying to avoid responsibility* EVADE, dodge, sidestep, escape, run away from; *informal* duck, wriggle out of, get out of, cop out of. ANTONYM face up to.

3 *he jerked back to avoid a wild pitch* DODGE, duck, get out of the way of.

4 *you've been avoiding me all evening* SHUN, stay away from, evade, keep one's distance from, elude, hide from; ignore, give the cold shoulder. ANTONYM seek out.

5 *he should avoid drinking alcohol* REFRAIN FROM, abstain from, desist from, eschew. ANTONYM indulge in.

**aware** adjective 1 *she is* ***aware of*** *the dangers* CONSCIOUS OF, mindful of, informed about, acquainted with, familiar with, alive to, alert to; *informal* clued in to, wise to, in the know about, hip to; *formal* cognizant of; *archaic* ware of. ANTONYMS ignorant, oblivious.

2 *we need to be more environmentally aware* KNOWLEDGEABLE, enlightened, well-informed, au fait; *informal* clued in, tuned in, plugged in. ANTONYM ignorant.

**awe** noun *we watched in awe* WONDER, wonderment; admiration, reverence, respect, esteem; dread, fear.

**awful** adjective 1 *the place smelled awful* DISGUSTING, horrible, terrible, dreadful, ghastly, nasty, vile, foul, revolting, repulsive, repugnant, odious, sickening, nauseating; *informal* yucky, gross, beastly. ANTONYMS wonderful, lovely.

2 *an awful book* TERRIBLE, atrocious, dreadful, frightful, execrable, abominable; inadequate, inferior, substandard, lamentable; *informal* crummy, pathetic, rotten, woeful, lousy, appalling, abysmal. ANTONYMS good, excellent.

3 *an awful accident* SERIOUS, dreadful, grave, terrible, bad, critical ANTONYM minor.

4 *you look awful—go lie down* ILL, unwell, sick, queasy, nauseous; poorly; *informal* lousy, rotten, terrible, dreadful.

5 *I felt awful for getting so angry* REMORSEFUL, guilty, ashamed, contrite, sorry, regretful, repentant.

6 *archaic the awful sights of nature* AWE-INSPIRING, awesome, impressive; dread, fearful.

**awkward** adjective 1 *the box was awkward to carry* DIFFICULT, tricky; cumbersome, unwieldy. ANTONYM easy.

2 *an awkward time* INCONVENIENT, inappropriate, inopportune, unseasonable, difficult. ANTONYM convenient.

3 *he put her in a very awkward position* EMBARRASSING, uncomfortable, unpleasant, delicate, tricky, problematic, troublesome, thorny; humiliating, compromising; *informal* sticky, dicey, hairy.

4 *she felt awkward alone with him* UNCOMFORTABLE, uneasy, tense, nervous, edgy, unquiet; self-conscious, embarrassed. ANTONYMS relaxed, at ease.

5 *his awkward movements* CLUMSY, ungainly, uncoordinated, graceless, inelegant, gauche, gawky, wooden, stiff; unskillful, maladroit, inept, blundering; *informal* clodhopping, hamfisted, ham-handed, heavy-handed; *informal* all thumbs. ANTONYMS adroit, graceful.

**awry** adjective 1 *something was awry* AMISS, wrong; *informal* up.

2 *his wig looked awry* ASKEW, crooked, lopsided, tilted, skewed, skew, to one side, off-center, uneven; *informal* cockeyed, wonky. ANTONYMS straight, symmetrical.

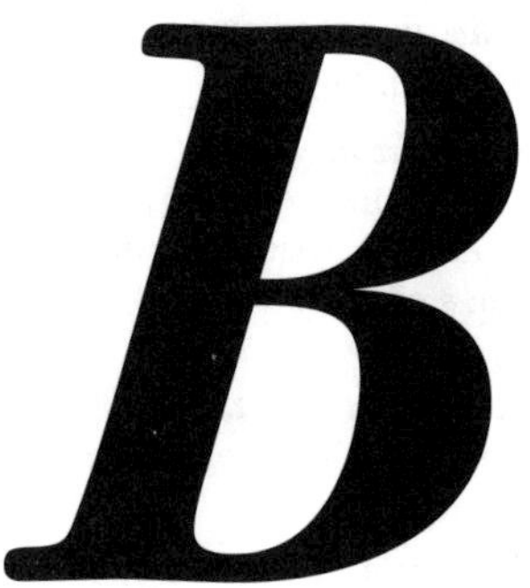

**babble** verb **1** *Betty babbled about the stupidest things* PRATTLE, rattle on, chatter, jabber, twitter, go on, run on, prate, ramble, burble, blather; *informal* gab, yap, yak, yabber, yatter, yammer, blabber, jaw, gas, shoot one's mouth off, run off at the mouth.

**2** *a brook babbled gently* BURBLE, murmur, gurgle, tinkle; *literary* plash.

▸ noun *his inarticulate babble* PRATTLE, chatter, jabber, prating, rambling, blather; *informal* gab, yabbering, yatter.

**babe** noun **1** *literary a babe in arms.* See BABY noun sense 1.

**2** *informal what a babe!* BEAUTY; *informal* hottie, looker, bombshell, heartthrob, knockout, fox, (piece of) arm candy, eyecatcher, dish, boy toy, hunk.

**babel** noun *I can't hear you above this babel* CLAMOR, din, racket, confused noise, tumult, uproar, hubbub; babble, babbling, shouting, yelling, screaming; *informal* hullabaloo.

**baby** noun **1** *a newborn baby* INFANT, newborn, child, tot, little one; *informal* rug rat; *Scottish* bairn; *literary* babe, babe in arms, suckling; papoose; *technical* neonate.

**2** *don't be such a baby* SISSY, wimp, wuss, milquetoast; pantywaist.

▸ adjective *baby carrots* MINIATURE, mini, little, small, small-scale, scaled-down, toy, pocket, vest-pocket, midget, dwarf; *informal* teeny, teeny-weeny, teensy, teensy-weensy, itsy-bitsy, itty-bitty, little-bitty, bite-sized. ANTONYM large.

▸ verb *her aunt babied her* PAMPER, mollycoddle, spoil, cosset, coddle, indulge, overindulge, nanny, pander to.

**babyish** adjective *she hated the babyish remarks he would make about her friends* CHILDISH, immature, infantile, juvenile, puerile, adolescent. ANTONYM mature.

**back** noun **1** *she's broken her back* SPINE, backbone, spinal column, vertebral column.

**2** *the back of the house* REAR, rear side, other side; *Nautical* stern. ANTONYM front.

**3** *the back of the line* END, tail end, rear end, rear, tail, tag end. ANTONYMS front, head.

**4** *the back of a postcard* REVERSE, other side, underside; verso; *informal* flip side. ANTONYMS front, face.

▸ adverb **1** *he pushed his chair back* BACKWARD, behind one, to one's rear, rearward; away, off. ANTONYM forward.

**2** *a few months back* AGO, earlier, previously, before, in the past.

▸ verb **1** *the government backed the initiative with $4 million* SPONSOR, finance, put up the money for, fund, subsidize, underwrite, be a patron of, act as guarantor of; *informal* foot the bill for, pick up the tab for; bankroll, stake.

**2** *most people backed the idea* SUPPORT, endorse, sanction, approve of, give one's blessing to, smile on, favor, advocate, promote, uphold, champion; vote for, ally oneself with, stand behind, stick by, side with, be on the side of, defend, take up the cudgels for; second; *informal* throw one's weight behind. ANTONYM oppose.

**3** *he backed the horse at 33–1* BET ON, gamble on, stake money on.

**4** *he backed out of the garage* REVERSE, draw back, step back, move backward, back off, pull back, retreat, withdraw, give ground, backtrack, retrace one's steps, recede. ANTONYMS move forward, advance.

▸ adjective **1** *the back seats* REAR, rearmost, backmost, hind, hindmost, hinder, posterior. ANTONYM front.

**2** *a back copy* PAST, old, previous, earlier, former, out of date. ANTONYM future.

PHRASES: **back away** *there's no need to back away—he's a very gentle dog* DRAW BACK, step back, move away, withdraw, retreat, pull back, give ground; shrink back, cower, quail, quake.
**back down** *all your begging is useless because I am not going to back down* GIVE IN, concede defeat, surrender, yield, submit, climb down, concede, reconsider; backtrack, backpedal.
**back out of** *Charlie's backed out of the original agreement* RENEGE ON, go back on, withdraw from, pull out of, retreat from, fail to honor, abandon, default on, repudiate, backpedal on.
**back someone up** *I was surprised when it turned out to be Dina who backed me up* SUPPORT, stand by, give one's support to, side with, be on someone's side, take someone's side, take someone's part; vouch for.
**back something up** *can you back up that statement with any real evidence?* SUBSTANTIATE, corroborate, confirm, support, bear out, endorse, bolster, reinforce, lend weight to.
**behind someone's back** *the takeover was planned behind the plant manager's back* SECRETLY, without someone's knowl-

edge, on the sly, slyly, sneakily, covertly, surreptitiously, furtively.

**backbiting** noun *the backbiting between Democrats and Republicans has become tiresome* MALICIOUS TALK, spiteful talk, slander, libel, defamation, abuse, character assassination, disparagement, denigration, vilification, vituperation, calumny; slurs, aspersions; *informal* bitching, bitchiness, cattiness, mudslinging, bad-mouthing, dissing.

**backbone** noun **1** *an injured backbone* SPINE, spinal column, vertebral column, vertebrae; back; *Anatomy* dorsum, rachis.

**2** *the infantry is the backbone of our army* MAINSTAY, cornerstone, foundation, chief support, buttress, pillar, tower of strength.

**3** *he has enough backbone to see us through* STRENGTH OF CHARACTER, strength of will, firmness, resolution, resolve, determination, fortitude, pluck, pluckiness, nerve, courage, mettle, spirit, moral fiber; *informal* guts, spunk, grit, true grit.

**backer** noun **1** *the backers of the proposition* SUPPORTER, defender, advocate, promoter, proponent; seconder; booster.

**2** *$3 million was provided by the project's backers* SPONSOR, investor, underwriter, financier, patron, benefactor, benefactress; *informal* angel.

**backfire** verb *Bernard's plan backfired* REBOUND, boomerang, come back; fail, miscarry, go wrong; *informal* blow up in someone's face.

**background** noun **1** *a background of palm trees* BACKDROP, backcloth, surrounding(s), setting, scene.

**2** *students from many different backgrounds* SOCIAL CIRCUMSTANCES, family circumstances; environment, class, culture, tradition; upbringing.

**3** *her nursing background* EXPERIENCE, record, history, past, training, education, grounding, knowledge; backstory.

**4** *the political background* CIRCUMSTANCES, context, conditions, situation, environment, milieu, scene, scenario. PHRASE: **in the background** *maybe there was a sugar daddy in the background* BEHIND THE SCENES, out of the public eye, out of the spotlight, out of the limelight, backstage; inconspicuous, unobtrusive, unnoticed.

**backhanded** adjective *a backhanded compliment* INDIRECT, ambiguous, oblique, equivocal; double-edged, two-edged, left-handed; tongue-in-cheek. ANTONYM direct.

**backing** noun **1** *he has the backing of his colleagues* SUPPORT, help, assistance, aid; approval, endorsement, sanction, blessing.

**2** *financial backing* SPONSORSHIP, funding, patronage; money, investment, funds, finance; grant, contribution, subsidy.

**3** *musical backing* ACCOMPANIMENT; harmony, obbligato.

**backlash** noun *the move provoked a backlash from union leaders* ADVERSE REACTION, adverse response, counterblast, comeback, repercussion; retaliation, reprisal.

**backlog** noun *Stella's been gone for one day and there's already a backlog of messages* ACCUMULATION, logjam, pileup, pile, mountain.

**backpedal** verb *they agreed to the peace initiative, but soon after they backpedaled* CHANGE ONE'S MIND, backtrack, back down, climb down, (do an) about-face, reverse course, do a U-turn, renege, go back (on), back out (of), fail to honor something, withdraw, default (on).

**backslide** verb *many things can cause dieters to backslide* RELAPSE, lapse, regress, weaken, lose one's resolve, give in to temptation, go astray, leave the straight and narrow, fall off the wagon. ANTONYM persevere.

**backslider** noun *I'll have no backslider like you in my family* RECIDIVIST, regressor; defector, deserter, turncoat, apostate, fallen angel.

**backward** adjective **1** *a backward look* REARWARD, to/toward the rear, to/toward the back, behind one, reverse. ANTONYM forward.

**2** *the decision was a backward step* RETROGRADE, retrogressive, regressive, for the worse, in the wrong direction, downhill, negative. ANTONYM progressive.

**3** *an economically backward country* UNDERDEVELOPED, undeveloped; primitive, unsophisticated, benighted. ANTONYMS advanced, sophisticated.

**4** *he was not backward in displaying his talents* HESITANT, reticent, reluctant; shy, diffident, bashful, timid; unwilling, afraid, loath, averse. ANTONYMS bold, confident.

▸ adverb (also **backwards**) **1** *Penny glanced backward* TOWARD THE REAR, rearward, behind one. ANTONYM forward.

**2** *count backward from twenty to ten* IN REVERSE, in reverse order; *informal* ass-backward, bass-ackward. ANTONYM forward.

**USAGE NOTE backward, backwards**

In British English, the spelling **backwards** is more common than **backward**. In American English, the adverb form is sometimes spelled **backwards** ( *the ladder fell backwards*), but the adjective is almost always **backward** ( *a backward glance*). Directional words using the suffix *-ward* tend to have no *s* ending in American English, although **backwards** is more common than *afterwards*, *towards*, or *forwards*. The *s* ending often (but not always) appears in the phrases *backwards and forwards* and *bending over backwards*.

**backwash** noun **1** *a ship's backwash* WAKE, wash, slipstream.

**2** *the backwash of the Cuban missile crisis* REPERCUSSIONS, reverberations, aftereffects, aftermath, fallout.

**backwoods** plural noun *they're bringing cable TV to the backwoods* BACK OF BEYOND, remote areas, wilds, bush, bush country, bushland, hinterlands, backwater; backcountry, backlands; middle of nowhere; *informal* sticks, boondocks, boonies, tall timbers.

**bacteria** plural noun *a different strain of bacteria* MICROORGANISMS, microbes, germs, bacilli, pathogens, prokaryotes; *informal* bugs.

**bad** adjective **1** *bad workmanship* SUBSTANDARD, poor, inferior, second-rate, second-class, unsatisfactory, inadequate, unacceptable, not up to scratch, not up to par, deficient, imperfect, defective, faulty, shoddy, amateurish, careless, negligent, miserable, sorry; incompetent, inept, inexpert, ineffectual; awful, atrocious, appalling, execrable, deplorable, terrible, abysmal, godawful; *informal* crummy, rotten, pathetic, useless, woeful, bum, lousy, not up to snuff. ANTONYMS good, excellent, skilled.

**2** *the alcohol had a really bad effect on me* HARMFUL, damaging, detrimental, injurious, hurtful, inimical, destructive, ruinous, deleterious; unhealthy, unwholesome. ANTONYMS good, beneficial.

**3** *the bad guys* WICKED, evil, sinful, immoral, morally wrong, corrupt, base, black-hearted, reprobate, amoral; criminal, villainous, nefarious, iniquitous, dishonest, dishonorable, unscrupulous, unprincipled; *informal* crooked, dirty; *dated* dastardly. ANTONYM virtuous.

**4** *you bad girl!* BADLY BEHAVED, naughty, ill-behaved, disobedient, wayward, willful, self-willed, defiant, unruly, insubordinate, undisciplined. ANTONYM well-behaved.

**5** *bad news* UNPLEASANT, disagreeable, unwelcome; unfortunate, unlucky, unfavorable; terrible, dreadful, awful, grim, distressing. ANTONYM good.

**6** *a bad time to arrive* INAUSPICIOUS, unfavorable, inopportune, unpropitious, unfortunate, disadvantageous, adverse, inappropriate, unsuitable, untoward. ANTONYMS good, auspicious.

**7** *a bad accident* SEVERE, serious, grave, critical, acute; *formal* grievous. ANTONYMS minor, slight.

**8** *the meat's bad* ROTTEN, decayed, decomposed, decomposing, putrid, putrefied, off, moldy; sour, spoiled, rancid, rank, unfit for human consumption; (of an egg) addled, (of beer) skunky. ANTONYM fresh.

**9** *if you still feel bad, stay in bed.* See ILL adjective sense 1.

**10** *a bad knee* INJURED, wounded, diseased; *dated* game.

**11** *I felt bad about leaving them* GUILTY, conscience-stricken, remorseful, guilt-ridden, ashamed, contrite, sorry, full of regret, regretful, shamefaced. ANTONYM unrepentant.

**12** *a bad check* INVALID, worthless; counterfeit, fake, false, bogus, fraudulent; *informal* phony, dud. ANTONYM valid.

**13** *bad language* OFFENSIVE, vulgar, crude, foul, obscene, rude, coarse, smutty, dirty, filthy, indecent, indecorous; blasphemous, profane. PHRASE: **not bad** *hey, this curried octopus is not bad | the movie's not bad, but the book's much better* ALL RIGHT, adequate, good enough, pretty good, reasonable, fair, decent, average, tolerable, acceptable, passable, middling, moderate, fine; *informal* OK, so-so, 'comme ci, comme ça,' fair-to-middling, satisfactory.

**badge** noun **1** *the badge on her jacket was earned in combat* pin, brooch, button, emblem, crest.

**2** *a badge of success* SIGN, symbol, indication, signal, mark; hallmark, trademark.

**badger** verb *stop badgering us* PESTER, harass, bother, plague, torment, hound, nag, harry, tease, go on at; *informal* hassle, bug, get on someone's case.

**badly** adverb **1** *the job had been very badly done* POORLY, incompetently, ineptly, inexpertly, inefficiently, imperfectly, deficiently, defectively, unsatisfactorily, inadequately, incorrectly, faultily, shoddily, amateurishly, carelessly, negligently; abominably; *informal* crummily, pitifully, woefully. ANTONYM well.

**2** *try not to think badly of me* UNFAVORABLY, ill, critically, disapprovingly.

**3** *stop behaving badly* NAUGHTILY, disobediently, willfully, reprehensibly, mischievously.

**4** *he had been badly treated* CRUELLY, wickedly, unkindly, harshly, shamefully; unfairly, unjustly, wrongly, improperly.

**5** *it turned out badly* UNSUCCESSFULLY, unfavorably, adversely, unfortunately, unhappily, unluckily.

**6** *some of the victims are badly hurt* SEVERELY, seriously, gravely, acutely, critically; *formal* grievously. ANTONYM slightly.

**7** *she badly needs help* DESPERATELY, sorely, intensely, seriously, very much, greatly, exceedingly.

**baffle** verb *his explanations baffle the class* PERPLEX, puzzle, bewilder, mystify, bemuse, confuse, confound, disconcert; *informal* flummox, faze, stump, make someone scratch their head, be all Greek to, floor, discombobulate. See note at THWART. ANTONYM enlighten.

**bag** noun **1** *I dug around in my bag for a lipstick* HANDBAG, purse, shoulder bag, clutch bag/purse, minaudière; sack, pouch; *historical* reticule.

**2** *she began to unpack her bags* SUITCASE, case, valise, portmanteau, grip, overnighter; backpack, rucksack, knapsack, haversack, carryall, kit bag, duffel bag; satchel; **(bags)** luggage, baggage.

**3** *informal mystery novels just aren't my bag* INTEREST, preoccupation, concern; *informal* thing.

▸ verb **1** *locals bagged the most fish* CATCH, land, capture, trap, snare, ensnare; kill, shoot.

**2** *he bagged seven medals* GET, secure, obtain, acquire, pick up; win, achieve, attain; commandeer, grab, appropriate, take; *informal* get one's hands on, land, net.

**baggage** noun *leave your baggage with the inspectors* LUGGAGE, suitcases, cases, bags.

**baggy** adjective *baggy pants* LOOSE-FITTING, loose, roomy, full, ample, voluminous, billowing; oversized, shapeless, ill-fitting, tentlike, sacklike. ANTONYMS tight, form-fitting.

**bail** noun *he was released on bail* SURETY, security, assurance, indemnity, indemnification; bond, guarantee, pledge; *archaic* gage. PHRASES: **bail out** *the pilot bailed out* EJECT, parachute to safety; desert, get out, escape.
**bail someone/something out** *the state was called in to bail out the foundering housing project* RESCUE, save, relieve; finance, help (out), assist, aid; *informal* save someone's bacon/neck/skin.

**bait** noun **1** *the fish let go of the bait* LURE, decoy, fly, troll, jig, plug.

**2** *was she the bait to lure him into a trap?* ENTICEMENT, lure, decoy, snare, trap, siren, carrot, attraction, draw, magnet, incentive, temptation, inducement; *informal* come-on.

▸ verb *he was baited at school* TAUNT, tease, goad, pick on, torment, persecute, plague, harry, bother, harass, hound; *informal* needle.

**bake** verb **1** *bake the fish for 15–20 minutes* COOK, oven-bake, roast, dry-roast.

**2** *the earth was baked by the sun* SCORCH, burn, sear, parch, dry (up), desiccate; broil.

**balance** noun **1** *I tripped and lost my balance* STABILITY, equilibrium, steadiness, footing. ANTONYM instability.

**2** *political balance in broadcasting* FAIRNESS, justice, impartiality, evenhandedness, egalitarianism, equal opportunity; parity, equity, equilibrium, equipoise, evenness, symmetry, correspondence, uniformity, equality, equivalence, comparability. ANTONYM imbalance.

**3** *this stylistic development provides a balance to the rest of the work* COUNTERBALANCE, counterweight, stabilizer, compensation.

**4** *the food was weighed on a balance* SCALE(S), weighing machine.

**5** *the balance of the rent* REMAINDER, outstanding amount, rest, residue, difference, remaining part.

▸ verb **1** *she balanced the book on her head* STEADY, stabilize, poise, level.

**2** *he balanced his radical remarks with more familiar declarations* COUNTERBALANCE, balance out, offset, even out/up, counteract, compensate for, make up for.

**3** *their income and expenditure do not balance* CORRESPOND, agree, tally, match up, concur, coincide, be in agreement, be consistent, equate, be equal.

**4** *you need to balance cost against benefit* WEIGH, weigh up, compare, evaluate, consider, assess, appraise, judge.

PHRASES: **in the balance** *thanks to these dismal sales figures, everyone's job is in the balance* UNCERTAIN, undetermined, unsettled, unresolved, unsure, pending, in limbo, up in the air, at a turning point, critical, at a critical stage, at a crisis.

**on balance** *on balance, I'd say the scenery for Act II is coming along great* OVERALL, all in all, all things considered, taking everything into consideration/account, by and large, on average.

**balcony** noun **1** *the balcony of the hotel* veranda, terrace, balustrade, patio.

**2** *the applause from the balcony* GALLERY, dress circle, loge, upper tier, upper deck; choir loft; *informal* gods.

**bald** adjective **1** *a bald head* HAIRLESS, smooth, shaven, depilated; bald-headed; *informal* chrome-domed; *technical* glabrous; *archaic* bald-pated. ANTONYMS hairy, hirsute.

**2** *a few bald bushes* LEAFLESS, bare, uncovered. ANTONYMS lush, leafy.

**3** *the bald prairie* TREELESS, naked, barren. See note at NAKED. ANTONYM lush.

**4** *a bald statement* PLAIN, simple, unadorned, unvarnished, unembellished, undisguised, unveiled, stark, severe, austere, brutal, harsh; blunt, direct, forthright, plain-spoken, straight, straightforward, candid, honest, truthful, realistic, frank, outspoken; *informal* upfront. ANTONYM vague.

**balderdash** noun . See NONSENSE sense 1.

**bale** noun *a bale of cotton* BUNDLE, bunch, pack, package, parcel.

**baleful** adjective *she saw her rival's reddened, baleful face* MENACING, threatening, unfriendly, hostile, antagonistic, evil, evil-intentioned, vindictive, wicked, nasty, bitter, acrimonious, malevolent, malicious, malignant, malign, sinister; harmful, injurious, dangerous, destructive, noxious, pernicious, deadly, venomous, poisonous, vitriolic; *literary* malefic, maleficent. ANTONYMS benevolent, friendly.

**balk** verb **1** ***I balk at** paying that much* BE UNWILLING TO (BE), draw the line at, be reluctant to (be), hesitate over; eschew, resist, refuse to (be), take exception to; draw back from, flinch from, shrink from, recoil from, demur from, hate to (be). ANTONYM accept.

**2** *they were balked by traffic* IMPEDE, obstruct, thwart, hinder, prevent, check, stop, curb, halt, bar, block, forestall, frustrate. See note at THWART. ANTONYM assist.

**ball** noun **1** *a ball of dough* SPHERE, globe, orb, globule, spherule, spheroid, ovoid.

**2** *a musket ball* BULLET, pellet, slug, projectile.

**3** *a costume ball* DANCE, dinner dance, masked ball, formal, prom, masquerade; *informal* hop, bop.

**4** *everyone had a ball* GOOD TIME, blast, riot.

**ballad** noun *a ballad sung by Burl Ives* SONG, folk song, chantey, ditty, canzone; poem, tale, saga.

**ballast** noun *the third balloonist appears to be in need of ballast* STABILIZER, counterbalance, counterweight.

**balloon** noun *sailing by in a balloon* hot-air balloon, barrage balloon; airship, dirigible, Zeppelin, blimp; weather balloon.

▸ verb **1** *her long skirt ballooned in the wind* SWELL (OUT), puff out/up, bulge (out), bag, belly (out), fill (out), billow (out), distend.

**2** *the company's debt has ballooned* INCREASE RAPIDLY, soar, rocket, shoot up, escalate, mount, surge, spiral; *informal* go through the ceiling, go through the roof, skyrocket. ANTONYM plummet.

**ballot** noun *the ballot results will be announced soon* VOTE, poll, election, referendum, plebiscite; show of hands.

**ballyhoo** noun *informal after all the ballyhoo, the movie was a flop* PUBLICITY, advertising, promotion, marketing, propaganda, push, puffery, buildup, boosting; fuss, excitement; *informal* hype, spiel, hullabaloo, splash.

**balm** noun **1** *skin balm* OINTMENT, lotion, cream, salve, liniment, embrocation, rub, gel, emollient, unguent, balsam, moisturizer; *dated* pomade; *archaic* unction. ANTONYMS astringent, irritant.

**2** *balm for troubled spirits* RELIEF, comfort, ease, succor, consolation, cheer, solace. ANTONYMS exacerbation, misery.

**balmy** adjective *the balmy breezes of the West Indies* MILD, gentle, temperate, summery, calm, tranquil, clement, fine, pleasant, benign, soothing, soft. ANTONYMS harsh, wintry.

**bamboozle** verb *informal*. See TRICK verb.

**ban** verb **1** *smoking was banned* PROHIBIT, forbid, veto, proscribe, disallow, outlaw, make illegal, embargo, bar, debar, block, stop, suppress, interdict; *Law* enjoin, restrain. See note at PROHIBIT. ANTONYM permit.

**2** *Gary was banned from the playground* EXCLUDE, banish, expel, eject, evict, drive out, force out, oust, remove, get rid of; *informal* boot out, kick out. ANTONYM admit.

▸ noun **1** *a ban on soliciting* PROHIBITION, veto, proscription, embargo, bar, suppression, stoppage, interdict, interdiction, moratorium, injunction.

**2** *a ban from international competition* EXCLUSION, banishment, expulsion, ejection, eviction, removal.

**banal** adjective *banal lyrics* TRITE, hackneyed, clichéd, platitudinous, vapid, commonplace, ordinary, common, stock, conventional, stereotyped, overused, overdone, overworked, stale, worn out, timeworn, tired, threadbare, hoary, hack, unimaginative, humdrum, ho-hum, unoriginal, uninteresting, dull, trivial; *informal* old hat, corny, cornball, played out; *dated* dime-store; *rare* truistic, bromidic. ANTONYM original.

**banality** noun **1** *the banality of most sitcoms* TRITENESS, vapidity, staleness, unimaginativeness, lack of originality, prosaicness, dullness; *informal* corniness. ANTONYM originality.

**2** *they exchanged banalities* PLATITUDE, cliché, truism, old chestnut, stock phrase, bromide, commonplace. ANTONYMS epigram, witticism.

**band**[1] noun **1** *a band around her waist* BELT, sash, girdle, strap, tape, ring, hoop, loop, circlet, circle, cord, tie, string, thong, ribbon, fillet, strip; *literary* cincture.

**2** *the sweater is white with a green band* STRIPE, strip, streak, line, bar, swathe; *technical* stria, striation.

**band**[2] noun **1** *a band of robbers* GROUP, gang, mob, pack, troop, company, party, crew, body, working party, posse; team, side, lineup; association, society, club, circle, fellowship, partnership, guild, lodge, order, fraternity, confraternity, sodality, brotherhood, sisterhood, sorority, union, alliance, affiliation, institution, league, federation, clique, set, coterie; *informal* bunch.

**2** *the band played on* (MUSICAL) GROUP, pop group, ensemble, orchestra; *informal* combo.

▸ verb *local people* ***banded together*** JOIN (UP), team up, join forces, pool resources, get together; amalgamate, unite, form an alliance, form an association, affiliate, federate. ANTONYM split up.

**bandage** noun *she had a bandage on her foot* DRESSING, covering, gauze, compress, plaster, tourniquet; *trademark* Band-Aid, *trademark* Ace bandage.

▸ verb *she bandaged my knee* BIND, bind up, dress, cover, wrap, swaddle, strap (up).

**bandit** noun *masked bandits held up the train* ROBBER, thief, outlaw, gunman, crook, mugger, gangster, raider, freebooter, hijacker, looter, marauder; *dated* desperado; *literary* brigand; *historical* rustler, highwayman, reaver.

**bandy**[1] adjective *bandy legs* BOWED, curved, bent; bowlegged, bandy-legged. ANTONYM straight.

**bandy**[2] verb **1** *a figure of $40,000 has been* ***bandied about*** | *what's the latest story being* ***bandied about?*** TOSS AROUND/ABOUT, put about, spread (around), discuss, rumor, mention, repeat; *literary* bruit about/abroad.

**2** *I'm not going to bandy words with you* EXCHANGE, swap, trade.

**bane** noun *scurvy was the bane of these seafarers* SCOURGE, plague, curse, blight, pest, nuisance, headache, nightmare, trial, hardship, cross to bear, burden, thorn in one's flesh/side, bitter pill, affliction, trouble, misery, woe, tribulation, misfortune, pain.

**bang** noun **1** *the door slammed with a bang* THUD, thump, bump, crack, crash, smack, boom, clang, clap, knock, tap, clunk; stamp, stomp, bam, kaboom, kapow, wham, whump, whomp; report, explosion, detonation.

**2** *a nasty bang on the head* BLOW, knock, thump, bump, hit, smack, bonk, crack, bash, whack, thwack.

▸ verb **1** *he banged the table with his fist* HIT, strike, beat, thump, hammer, knock, rap, pound, thud, punch, bump, smack, slap, slam, cuff, pummel, buffet, bash, whack, thwack, clobber, clout, clip, wallop, belt, bop, sock, whomp, bust, slug, whale.

**2** *fireworks banged in the air* GO BANG, thud, thump, boom, clap, pound, crack, crash, explode, detonate, burst, blow up.

▸ adverb *informal the library is bang in the center of town* | *the train arrived bang on time* PRECISELY, exactly, right, directly, immediately, squarely, dead; promptly, prompt, dead on, sharp, on the dot; *informal* smack, slap, smack dab, plumb, on the button, on the nose.

**bangle** noun *the familiar jingle of Nana's silver bangles* BRACELET, wristlet, anklet, armlet.

**banish** verb **1** *he was banished for his crime* EXILE, expel, deport, eject, expatriate, ostracize, extradite, repatriate, transport; cast out, oust, evict, throw out, exclude, shut out, ban. ANTONYMS admit, readmit.

**2** *he tried to banish his fear* DISPEL, dismiss, disperse, scatter, dissipate, drive away, chase away, shut out, quell, allay. ANTONYM engender.

**bank**[1] noun **1** *the bank of the great river* EDGE, side, shore, coast, embankment, bankside, levee, border, verge, boundary, margin, rim, fringe; *literary* marge, skirt.

**2** *a grassy bank* SLOPE, rise, incline, gradient, ramp; mound, ridge, hillock, hummock, knoll; bar, reef, shoal, shelf; accumulation, pile, heap, mass, drift.

**3** *a bank of switches* ARRAY, row, line, tier, group, series.

▸ verb **1** *they **banked up** the earth* PILE (UP), heap (up), stack (up); accumulate, amass, assemble, put together.

**2** *the aircraft banked* TILT, LEAN, tip, slant, incline, angle, slope, list, camber, pitch, dip, cant.

**bank**[2] noun **1** *money in the bank* FINANCIAL INSTITUTION, merchant bank, savings bank, finance company, trust company, credit union.

**2** *a blood bank* STORE, reserve, accumulation, stock, stockpile, supply, pool, fund, cache, hoard, deposit; storehouse, reservoir, repository, depository.

▸ verb *I banked the money* DEPOSIT, pay in, invest, lay away.

PHRASE: **bank on** *can the senator bank on your support?* RELY ON, depend on, count on, place reliance on, bargain on, plan on; anticipate, expect; be confident of, be sure of, pin one's hopes/faith on, figure on.

**bankrupt** adjective **1** *the company was declared bankrupt* INSOLVENT, failed, ruined, in debt, owing money, in the red, in arrears, in receivership; *informal* bust, belly up, broke, cash-strapped, flat broke. ANTONYMS solvent, in the black.

**2** *this government is **bankrupt of** ideas* BEREFT OF, devoid of, empty of, destitute of; completely lacking in, without, in need of, wanting. ANTONYM teeming with.

▸ verb *the strike nearly bankrupted the union* RUIN, impoverish, reduce to penury/destitution, bring to ruin, bring someone to their knees, wipe out, break; *rare* beggar, pauperize.

**bankruptcy** noun *many companies were facing bankruptcy* INSOLVENCY, liquidation, failure, ruin, financial ruin, collapse, receivership. ANTONYM solvency.

**banner** noun **1** *students waved banners* SIGN, placard, poster, notice.

**2** *banners fluttered above the troops* FLAG, standard, ensign, color(s), pennant, banderole, guidon; *Nautical* burgee.

**banquet** noun *the awards banquet* FEAST, dinner; *informal* spread, blowout. ANTONYM snack.

**banter** noun *a brief exchange of banter* REPARTEE, witty conversation, raillery, wordplay, cut and thrust, kidding, ribbing, badinage, joshing.

▸ verb *sightseers were bantering with the guards* JOKE, jest, quip; *informal* josh, wisecrack.

**baptism** noun **1** *the baptism ceremony* CHRISTENING, naming.

**2** *his baptism as a politician* INITIATION, debut, introduction, inauguration, launch, rite of passage.

**baptize** verb **1** *he was baptized as a baby* CHRISTEN.

**2** *they were baptized into the church* ADMIT, initiate, enroll, recruit, convert.

**3** *he was baptized Enoch* NAME, give the name, call, dub; *formal* denominate.

**bar** noun **1** *an iron bar* ROD, pole, stick, batten, shaft, rail, paling, spar, strut, crosspiece, beam.

**2** *a bar of chocolate* BLOCK, slab, cake, tablet, brick, loaf, wedge, ingot.

**3** *your drinks are on the bar* COUNTER, table, buffet, stand.

**4** *she had a drink in a bar* TAVERN, cocktail lounge, barroom, taproom, pub, after-hours club, lounge, nightclub, speakeasy, roadhouse, beer hall, boîte, club, inn, rathskeller, cantina, bodega; singles bar, sports bar; *informal* watering hole, gin mill, dive, nineteenth hole, *Brit.* public house; *historical* saloon, alehouse.

**5** *a bar to promotion* OBSTACLE, impediment, hindrance, obstruction, block, hurdle, barrier, stumbling block. ANTONYM aid.

**6** *members of the Bar* LAWYERS, barristers, advocates, counsel, counselors; *chiefly Brit.* solicitors.

**7** *the bar across the river mouth* SANDBAR, sandbank, shoal, shallow, reef.

▸ verb **1** *they have barred the door* BOLT, lock, fasten, secure, block, barricade, obstruct. ANTONYMS open, unlock.

**2** *I was barred from entering* PROHIBIT, debar, preclude, forbid, ban, interdict, inhibit; exclude, keep out; obstruct, hinder, block; *Law* enjoin. ANTONYMS accept, admit.

▸ preposition *everyone bar me.* See EXCEPT preposition.

**barb** noun **1** *the hook has a nasty barb* SPIKE, prong, spur, thorn, needle, prickle, spine, quill.

**2** *the barbs from his critics* INSULT, sneer, jibe, cutting remark, shaft, slight, brickbat, slur, jeer, taunt; *informal* dig, put-down; (**barbs**) abuse, disparagement, scoffing, scorn, sarcasm, goading.

**barbarian** noun *the city was besieged by barbarians* SAVAGE, heathen, brute, beast, wild man/woman; ruffian, thug, lout, vandal, boor, hoodlum, hooligan, Neanderthal, troglodyte; philistine; *informal* roughneck, lowlife.

▸ adjective *the barbarian hordes* SAVAGE, uncivilized, barbaric, primitive, heathen, vulgar, wild, brutish, Neanderthal. ANTONYM civilized.

**barbaric** adjective *barbaric crimes* BRUTAL, barbarous, brutish, bestial, savage, vicious, wicked, cruel, ruthless, merciless, villainous, murderous, heinous, monstrous, vile, inhuman, infernal, dark, fiendish, diabolical. ANTONYM civilized.

**barbarity** noun *the barbarity of slavery* BRUTALITY, brutalism, cruelty, bestiality, barbarism, barbarousness, savagery, viciousness, wickedness, villainy, baseness, inhumanity; atrocity. ANTONYM benevolence.

**barbarous** adjective. See BARBARIC.

**barbecue** noun *a backyard barbecue* COOKOUT, wiener/wienie/weenie roast; BBQ.

▸ verb *they barbecued some steaks* GRILL, spit-roast, broil, char-broil.

**bare** adjective **1** *a giggling bare infant in her arms* NAKED, unclothed, undressed, uncovered, stripped, having nothing on, nude, in the nude, stark naked; *informal* without a stitch on, buck-naked, butt-naked, mother-naked, in one's birthday suit, in the raw, in the altogether, in the buff. See note at NAKED. ANTONYM clothed.

**2** *a bare room* EMPTY, unfurnished, cleared; stark, austere, spartan, unadorned, unembellished, unornamented, plain. ANTONYMS furnished, embellished.

**3** *a cupboard* ***bare of*** *food* EMPTY OF, devoid of, bereft of; without, lacking, wanting, free from. ANTONYM containing.

**4** *a bare landscape* BARREN, bleak, exposed, desolate, stark, arid, desert, lunar; treeless, deforested, bald. ANTONYM lush.

**5** *the bare facts* PLAIN, essential, fundamental, basic, straightforward, simple, pure, stark, bald, cold, hard, brutal, harsh.

**6** *a bare lead in the race* MERE, no more than, simple; slim, slight, slender, paltry, minimum. ANTONYM comfortable.

▸ verb *he bared his arm* UNCOVER, strip, lay bare, undress, unclothe, denude, expose. ANTONYM cover.

**barefaced** adjective *a barefaced lie* FLAGRANT, blatant, glaring, obvious, undisguised, unconcealed, naked; shameless, unabashed, unashamed, impudent, audacious, unblushing, brazen.

**barely** adverb *former hurricane Patricia was barely at tropical storm force* HARDLY, scarcely, just, only just, narrowly, by a very small margin, by the narrowest of margins, by the skin of one's teeth, by a hair's breadth, by a nose; almost not; *informal* by a whisker. ANTONYM easily.

**bargain** noun **1** *this binder is a bargain at $1.98* GOOD BUY, (good) value for the money, surprisingly cheap; *informal* steal, deal, giveaway, best buy. ANTONYM rip-off.

**2** *I'll make a bargain with you* AGREEMENT, arrangement, understanding, deal; contract, pact, compact; pledge, promise.

▸ verb *they bargained over the contract* HAGGLE, negotiate, discuss terms, hold talks, deal, barter, dicker; *formal* treat.

PHRASES: **bargain for/on** *a whole new roof is more than we bargained for* EXPECT, anticipate, be prepared for, allow for, plan for, reckon with, take into account, take into consideration, contemplate, imagine, envisage, foresee, predict; count on, rely on, depend on, bank on, plan on, reckon on, figure on.

**in(to) the bargain** *we went to pick out one puppy and came home with two more in the bargain* ALSO, as well, in addition, additionally, besides, on top of that, over and above that, to boot, for good measure.

**barge** noun *a barge carrying lumber and dry goods* lighter, canal boat, wherry, scow.

▸ verb *he* ***barged into*** *us* PUSH, shove, force, elbow, shoulder, jostle, bulldoze, muscle.

PHRASE: **barge in** *sorry for barging in* BURST IN, break in, butt in, cut in, interrupt, intrude, encroach; *informal* horn in.

**bark**[1] noun *the bark of a dog* WOOF, yap, yelp, bay.

▸ verb **1** *the collie barked* WOOF, yap, yelp, bay.

**2** *"Get out!" he barked* SAY BRUSQUELY, say abruptly, say angrily, snap; shout, bawl, cry, yell, roar, bellow, thunder; *informal* holler. ANTONYM whisper.

**bark**[2] noun *the bark of a tree* RIND, skin, peel, covering; integument; cork; *technical* cortex.

**barn** noun *the loft in the barn* OUTBUILDING, shed, cowshed, shelter; stable, stall, outhouse; *archaic* grange, garner.

**baron** noun **1** *she married a baron* LORD, noble, nobleman, aristocrat, peer.

**2** *a steel baron* MAGNATE, tycoon, mogul, captain of industry, nabob, mandarin.

**barracks** plural noun *confined to the barracks* GARRISON, camp, encampment, depot, billet, quarters, fort, cantonment.

**barrage** noun **1** *an artillery barrage* BOMBARDMENT, cannonade; gunfire, shelling; salvo, volley, fusillade; *historical* broadside.

**2** *a barrage of criticism* DELUGE, stream, storm, torrent, onslaught, flood, shower, spate, tide, avalanche, hail, blaze; abundance, mass, profusion.

**barrel** noun *oak barrels* CASK, keg, butt, vat, tun, drum, hogshead, kilderkin, barrique, pipe; *historical* firkin.

▸ verb *barreling down the road* CHARGE, plow, stampede, rush, go headlong; zoom.

**barren** adjective **1** *barren land* UNPRODUCTIVE, infertile, unfruitful, sterile, arid, desert. See note at NAKED. ANTONYM fertile.

**2** *archaic a barren woman* INFERTILE, sterile, childless; *technical* infecund. ANTONYM fertile.

**3** *a barren exchange of courtesies* POINTLESS, futile, worthless, profitless, valueless, unrewarding, purposeless, useless, vain, aimless, hollow, empty, vacuous, vapid. ANTONYM fruitful.

**barricade** noun *a barricade across the street* BARRIER, roadblock, blockade; obstacle, obstruction.

▸ verb *they barricaded the building* SEAL (UP), close up, block off, shut off/up; defend, protect, fortify.

**barrier** noun **1** *the barrier across the entrance* FENCE, railing, barricade, hurdle, bar, blockade, roadblock.

**2** *a barrier to international trade* OBSTACLE, obstruction, hurdle, stumbling block, bar, block, impediment, hindrance, curb.

**barter** verb **1** *they bartered grain for salt* TRADE, swap, exchange, sell.

**2** *you can barter for souvenirs* HAGGLE, bargain, negotiate, discuss terms, deal, dicker; *formal* treat.

**base**[1] noun **1** *the base of the tower* FOUNDATION, bottom, foot, support, stand, pedestal, plinth. ANTONYM top.

**2** *the system uses existing technology as its base* BASIS, foundation, bedrock, starting point, source, origin, root(s), core, key component, heart, backbone.

3 *the troops returned to their base* HEADQUARTERS, camp, site, station, settlement, post, center, starting point.

▸ verb 1 *he based his idea on a movie* FOUND, build, construct, form, ground, root; use as a basis; **(be based on)** derive from, spring from, stem from, originate in, have its origin in, issue from.

2 *the company was based in Quebec* LOCATE, situate, position, install, station, site, establish; garrison.

**base**2 adjective *base motives* SORDID, ignoble, low, low-minded, mean, immoral, improper, unseemly, unscrupulous, unprincipled, dishonest, dishonorable, shameful, bad, wrong, evil, wicked, iniquitous, sinful. ANTONYM noble.

**baseless** adjective *baseless accusations* GROUNDLESS, unfounded, ill-founded, without foundation; unsubstantiated, unproven, unsupported, uncorroborated, unconfirmed, unverified, unattested; unjustified, unwarranted; speculative, conjectural; unsound, unreliable, spurious, specious, trumped up, fabricated, untrue. ANTONYM valid.

**bashful** adjective *the superhero's alter ego is a sweetly bashful science dork* SHY, reserved, diffident, inhibited, retiring, reticent, reluctant, shrinking; hesitant, timid, apprehensive, nervous, wary, demure, coy, blushing. ANTONYMS bold, confident.

**basic** adjective 1 *basic human rights* FUNDAMENTAL, essential, primary, principal, cardinal, elementary, elemental, quintessential, intrinsic, central, pivotal, critical, key, focal; vital, necessary, indispensable. ANTONYMS secondary, unimportant.

2 *basic cooking facilities* PLAIN, simple, unsophisticated, straightforward, adequate; unadorned, undecorated, unornamented, without frills; spartan, stark, severe, austere, limited, meager, rudimentary, patchy, sketchy, minimal; unfussy, homely, homespun, meat-and-potatoes, bread-and-butter; rough, rough and ready, crude, makeshift. ANTONYM elaborate.

**basically** adverb *he's basically a well-behaved dog* FUNDAMENTALLY, essentially, in essence; firstly, first of all, first and foremost, primarily; at heart, at bottom, au fond; principally, chiefly, above all, most of all, mostly, mainly, on the whole, by and large, substantially; intrinsically, inherently; *informal* at the end of the day, when all is said and done.

**basics** plural noun *this woodworking class is recommended for those who already know the basics* FUNDAMENTALS, essentials, rudiments, (first) principles, foundations, preliminaries, groundwork; essence, basis, core; *informal* nitty-gritty, brass tacks, nuts and bolts, meat and potatoes, bread and butter, ABCs.

**basin** noun 1 *she poured water into the basin* BOWL, dish, pan; sink, washtub.

2 *a basin among low hills* VALLEY, hollow, dip, depression.

**basis** noun 1 *the basis of his method* FOUNDATION, support, base; reasoning, rationale, defense; reason, grounds, justification, motivation.

2 *the basis of discussion* STARTING POINT, base, point of departure, beginning, premise, fundamental point/principle, principal constituent, main ingredient, cornerstone, core, heart, thrust, essence, kernel, nub.

3 *on a part-time basis* FOOTING, condition, status, position; arrangement, system, method.

**bask** verb 1 *I basked in the sun* LAZE, lie, lounge, relax, sprawl, loll, wallow; sunbathe, sun oneself.

2 *she's* ***basking in*** *all the glory* REVEL IN, delight in, luxuriate in, wallow in, take pleasure in, rejoice in, glory in, indulge oneself in; enjoy, relish, savor, lap up.

**basket** noun *baskets decorated with ribbons* hamper, creel, pannier, bushel; wicker basket.

**bass** adjective *his beautiful bass voice* LOW, deep, low-pitched, resonant, sonorous, rumbling, booming, resounding; baritone. ANTONYM high.

**bastard** noun 1 *archaic* *he had fathered a bastard* ILLEGITIMATE CHILD, child born out of wedlock; *dated* love child, byblow; natural child/son/daughter.

2 *informal* *he's a real bastard* SCOUNDREL, villain, rogue, rascal, weasel, snake, snake in the grass, miscreant, good-for-nothing, reprobate; *informal* lowlife, creep, nogoodnik, scamp, scalawag, jerk, beast, rat, ratfink, louse, swine, dog, skunk, heel; slimeball, son of a bitch, SOB, scumbag, scumbucket, scuzzball, scuzzbag, dirtbag, sleazeball, sleazebag; *dated* hound, cad; *archaic* blackguard, knave, varlet, whoreson.

▸ adjective 1 *archaic* *a bastard child* ILLEGITIMATE, born out of wedlock; *dated* natural.

2 *a bastard socialism* ADULTERATED, alloyed, impure, inferior; hybrid, mongrel, patchwork.

**bastardize** verb *it is unthinkable that I would bastardize my values* ADULTERATE, corrupt, contaminate, weaken, dilute, taint, pollute, debase, distort.

**bastion** noun 1 *fortified with ditches and bastions* PROJECTION, outwork, breastwork, barbican; *Architecture* bartizan.

2 *a bastion of respectability* STRONGHOLD, bulwark, defender, support, supporter, guard, protection, protector, defense, prop, mainstay.

**batch** noun *when can we expect the next batch of invoices?* GROUP, quantity, lot, bunch, mass, cluster, raft, set, collection, bundle, pack; consignment, shipment.

**bath** noun 1 *he lay soaking in the bath* BATHTUB, tub, hot tub, whirlpool, sauna, steam bath, Turkish bath; *trademark* Jacuzzi.

2 *give it a bath* WASH, soak, cleansing, soaking, scrubbing, ablutions; dip; shower.

**bathe** verb 1 *she bathed and dressed* HAVE/TAKE A BATH, wash; shower.

**2** *I bathed in the local swimming pool* SWIM, go swimming, take a dip.

**3** *they bathed his wounds* CLEAN, cleanse, wash, rinse, wet, soak, immerse.

**4** *the room was bathed in light* SUFFUSE, permeate, pervade, envelop, flood, cover, wash, fill; *literary* mantle.

**bathing suit** noun *bring a bathing suit and a towel* SWIMSUIT; bikini, monokini, maillot, swimming trunks, swim trunks; swimwear.

**bathos** noun *the story ends with such a stroke of bathos, you're not sure whether to laugh or scream* ANTICLIMAX, letdown, disappointment, disillusionment; absurdity; *informal* comedown.

**bathroom** noun *excuse me, where's the bathroom?* WASHROOM, toilet, ladies'/men's room, restroom, lavatory, powder room, comfort station; urinal; *informal* facilities; little girls'/boys' room, can, john; *Brit.* water closet; *Brit. informal* WC, loo, ladies'/gents'; *Military* latrine; *Nautical* head; *dated* commode, privy, outhouse.

**baton** noun **1** *the conductor's baton* STICK, rod, staff, wand.

**2** *police batons* TRUNCHEON, club, billy club, cudgel, bludgeon, stick, nightstick, blackjack, mace; *Irish* shillelagh.

**battalion** noun **1** *an infantry battalion* regiment, brigade, force, division, squadron, squad, company, section, detachment, contingent, legion, corps, cohort.

**2** *a battalion of supporters.* See CROWD noun sense 1.

**batten** noun *two boards joined with battens* BAR, bolt, rail, shaft; board, strip.

▸ verb *Stephen was* ***battening down*** *the shutters* FASTEN, fix, secure, clamp (down), lash, make fast, nail (down), seal.

**batter** verb *they took turns battering the effigy* PUMMEL, pound, hit repeatedly, buffet, thrash, beat up, clobber, trounce, rain blows on; *informal* knock around/about, beat the living daylights out of, give someone a good hiding, lay into, lace into, do over, rough up.

**battered** adjective *a battered boat drifted to shore* DAMAGED, shabby, run-down, worn out, beat-up, falling to pieces, falling apart, dilapidated, rickety, ramshackle, crumbling, the worse for wear, on its last legs; ABUSED.

**battery** noun **1** *insert fresh batteries* STORAGE CELL, cell.

**2** *a gun battery* EMPLACEMENT, artillery unit; cannonry, ordnance.

**3** *a battery of equipment* ARRAY, series, set, bank, group, row, line, lineup, collection.

**4** *a battery of tests* SERIES, sequence, cycle, string, succession.

**5** *assault and battery* VIOLENCE, assault, mugging.

**battle** noun **1** *he was killed in the battle* FIGHT, armed conflict, clash, struggle, skirmish, engagement, fray, duel; war, campaign, crusade; fighting, warfare, combat, action, hostilities; *informal* scrap, dogfight, shoot-out; brawl.

**2** *a battle at the office* CONFLICT, clash, contest, competition, struggle, turf war; disagreement, argument, altercation, dispute, controversy, tug-of-war.

▸ verb **1** *he has been battling cancer* FIGHT, combat, contend with; resist, withstand, stand up to, confront; war with, feud with; struggle with, strive against.

**2** *Mark battled his way to the podium* FORCE, push, elbow, shoulder, fight; struggle, labor.

**battle-ax** noun **1** *a severe blow from a battle-ax* POLEAX, ax, pike, halberd, tomahawk.

**2** *informal she's a real battle-ax.* See HARRIDAN.

**battle cry** noun **1** *the army's battle cry* WAR CRY, war whoop, rallying call/cry; rebel yell.

**2** *the battle cry of the feminist movement* SLOGAN, motto, watchword, catchphrase, mantra.

**battlefield** noun *what were Vietnam battlefields then are now tourist sites* BATTLEGROUND, field of battle, field of operations, combat zone, theater of war, arena of war, front.

**battlement** noun *the battlements were abandoned* CASTELLATION, crenellation, parapet, rampart, balustrade, bulwark, wall, bastion, fortification.

**batty** adjective *informal*. See MAD sense 1. See also note at MAD.

**bauble** noun *gift-shop baubles* TRINKET, knickknack, ornament, frippery, gewgaw, gimcrack, bibelot, kickshaw, tchotchke.

**bawdy** adjective *bawdy jokes* RIBALD, indecent, risqué, racy, rude, spicy, sexy, suggestive, titillating, naughty, improper, indelicate, indecorous, off-color, earthy, barnyard, broad, locker-room, Rabelaisian; pornographic, obscene, vulgar, crude, coarse, lewd, dirty, filthy, smutty, unseemly, salacious, prurient, lascivious, licentious, X-rated, blue, raunchy; *euphemistic* adult. ANTONYMS clean, innocent.

**bawl** verb **1** *"Come on!" he bawled* SHOUT, yell, roar, bellow, screech, scream, shriek, howl, whoop, bark, trumpet, thunder; *informal* yammer, holler. ANTONYM whisper.

**2** *the children continued to bawl* CRY, sob, weep, shed tears, wail, whine, howl, squall; *rare* ululate. PHRASE: **bawl someone out** *informal.* See REPRIMAND.

**bay**[1] noun *ships were anchored in the bay* COVE, inlet, estuary, indentation, gulf, bight, basin, fjord, arm; natural harbor, anchorage.

**bay**[2] noun *there was a bay set into the wall* ALCOVE, recess, niche, nook, oriel, opening, hollow, cavity, inglenook; compartment.

**bay**[3] verb *coyotes baying at the moon* HOWL, bark, yelp, yap, cry, bellow, roar. PHRASE: **at bay** *the smoke did little to keep the mosquitoes at bay* AT A DISTANCE, away, off, at arm's length.

**bayonet** noun *a man armed with a bayonet* sword, knife, blade, spear, lance, pike, javelin.

**bazaar** noun **1** *a Turkish bazaar* MARKET, marketplace, mart, exchange, souk.

2 *the church bazaar* RUMMAGE SALE, garage sale, yard sale; fundraiser, charity event; flea market, swap meet; fair, carnival.

**be** verb 1 *there was once a king* EXIST, have being, have existence; live, be alive, have life, breathe, draw breath, be extant.

2 *the trial is tomorrow at half past one* OCCUR, happen, take place, come about, arise, crop up, transpire, fall, materialize, ensue; *literary* come to pass, befall, betide.

3 *the bed is over there* BE SITUATED, be located, be found, be present, be set, be positioned, be placed, be installed.

4 *it has been like this for hours* REMAIN, stay, last, continue, survive, endure, persist, prevail; wait, linger, hold on, hang on.

**beach** noun *a sandy beach* SEASIDE, seashore, shore, coast, waterfront, lakeshore, coastline, coastal region, littoral, seaboard, foreshore, water's edge; sands; *literary* strand.

▸ verb *they beached the boat* LAND, ground, strand, run aground, run ashore.

**beached** adjective *rescuing the beached whale* STRANDED, grounded, aground, ashore, marooned, high and dry, stuck, washed up, washed ashore.

**beacon** noun *the beacon penetrated the fog* LIGHTHOUSE; signal light, signal fire, danger signal, bonfire, warning light, warning fire; spotlight, searchlight.

**bead** noun 1 *a string of beads* BALL, pellet, pill, globule, sphere, spheroid, oval, ovoid, orb, round; **(beads)** necklace, rosary, chaplet.

2 *beads of sweat* DROPLET, drop, blob, dot, dewdrop, teardrop. PHRASE: **draw/get a bead on** *I drew a bead on the figure in the attic window* AIM AT, fix on, focus on, zero in on, sight.

**beak** noun *a bird's beak* BILL, nib, mandible.

**beam** noun 1 *an oak beam* JOIST, lintel, rafter, purlin; spar, girder, balk, timber, two-by-four, plank; support, strut; scantling, transom, stringer, collar beam, I-beam.

2 *a beam of light coming from the window* RAY, shaft, stream, streak, pencil, finger; flash, gleam, glow, glimmer, glint, flare.

3 *the beam on her face* GRIN, smile, happy expression, bright look. ANTONYM frown.

▸ verb 1 *the signal is* ***beamed out*** BROADCAST, transmit, relay, emit, send/put out, disseminate; direct, aim.

2 *the sun* ***beamed down*** SHINE, radiate, give off light, glare, gleam.

3 *he beamed broadly* GRIN, smile, smirk; *informal* be all smiles. ANTONYM frown.

**bear** verb 1 *I come bearing gifts* CARRY, bring, transport, move, convey, take, fetch, deliver, tote, lug.

2 *the bag bore my name* DISPLAY, exhibit, be marked with, show, carry, have.

3 *will it bear his weight?* SUPPORT, carry, hold up, prop up.

4 *they can't bear the cost alone* SUSTAIN, carry, support, shoulder, absorb, take on.

5 *she bore no grudge* HARBOR, foster, entertain, nurse, nurture, brood over.

6 *such a solution does not bear close scrutiny* WITHSTAND, stand up to, stand, put up with, take, cope with, handle, sustain, accept.

7 *I can't bear having him around* ENDURE, tolerate, put up with, stand, abide, submit to, experience, undergo, go through, countenance, brave, weather, stomach; *informal* hack, swallow; *formal* brook; *archaic* suffer.

8 *she bore a son* GIVE BIRTH TO, bring forth, deliver, be delivered of, have, produce, spawn, birth; *informal* drop; *literary* beget.

9 *a shrub that bears yellow berries* PRODUCE, yield, give forth, give, grow, provide, supply.

10 *bear left at the junction* VEER, curve, swerve, fork, diverge, deviate, turn, bend. PHRASES: **bear oneself** *if you bear yourself like a bum, expect to treated as a bum* CONDUCT ONESELF, carry oneself, acquit oneself, act, behave, perform; *formal* comport oneself.

**bear down on** *we knew that Sherman's men would be bearing down on us by dawn* ADVANCE ON, close in on, move in on, converge on.

**bear fruit** *we're always amazed when one of her crazy ideas actually bears fruit* YIELD RESULTS, get results, succeed, meet with success, be successful, be effective, be profitable, work, go as planned; *informal* pay off, come off, pan out, do the trick.

**bear something in mind** *the meals are free, but please bear in mind that you are expected to tip the servers* TAKE INTO ACCOUNT, take into consideration, remember, consider, be mindful, mind, mark, heed.

**bear on** *I fail to see how Hugh's personal problem bears on our final decision* BE RELEVANT TO, appertain to, pertain to, relate to, have a bearing on, have relevance to, apply to, be pertinent to.

**bear something out** *we're hoping you can bear out his statement* CONFIRM, corroborate, substantiate, endorse, vindicate, give credence to, support, ratify, warrant, uphold, justify, prove, authenticate, verify.

**bear with** *if you'll just bear with us, I'm sure the lights will be back on soon* BE PATIENT WITH, show forbearance toward, make allowances for, tolerate, put up with, endure.

**bear witness/testimony to** *the majestic windows bear witness to the architect's fascination with natural light* TESTIFY TO, be evidence of, be proof of, attest to, evidence, prove, vouch for; demonstrate, show, establish, indicate, reveal, bespeak.

**bearable** adjective *volunteer staff can make a hospital stay bearable* TOLERABLE, endurable, supportable, sustainable, sufferable, brookable; acceptable, admissible, manageable. ANTONYM intolerable.

**beard** noun *a black beard* FACIAL HAIR, whiskers, stubble, five o'clock shadow, bristles; goatee, imperial, Vandyke.

▸ verb *it was up to me to beard the bully* CONFRONT, face, challenge, brave, come face to face with, meet head on; defy, oppose, stand up against, dare, throw down the gauntlet to.

**bearded** adjective *bearded men* UNSHAVEN, whiskered, whiskery, bewhiskered; stubbly, bristly. ANTONYM clean-shaven.

**bearer** noun **1** *a lantern-bearer* CARRIER, porter.

**2** *the bearer of bad news* MESSENGER, agent, conveyor, carrier, emissary.

**3** *the bearer of the documents* HOLDER, possessor, owner.

**bearing** noun **1** *a man of military bearing* POSTURE, stance, carriage, gait, deportment; *formal* comportment.

**2** *a regal bearing* DEMEANOR, manner, air, aspect, attitude, behavior, mien, style.

**3** *this has no bearing on the matter* RELEVANCE, pertinence, connection, appositeness, germaneness, importance, significance, application.

**4** *a bearing of 15°* DIRECTION, orientation, course, trajectory, heading, tack, path, line, run.

**5** *he tormented her beyond bearing* ENDURANCE, tolerance, toleration.

**6** **(bearings)** *I lost my bearings* ORIENTATION, sense of direction; whereabouts, location, position.

**beast** noun **1** *the beasts of the forest* ANIMAL, creature; *informal* critter, varmint.

**2** *he is a cruel beast* MONSTER, brute, savage, barbarian, animal, swine, pig, ogre, fiend, demon, devil.

**beastly** adjective **1** *politics is a beastly profession* AWFUL, horrible, rotten, nasty, foul, objectionable, unpleasant, disagreeable, offensive, vile, abominable, hateful, detestable, terrible, godawful. ANTONYM pleasant.

**2** *he was beastly to her* UNKIND, malicious, mean, nasty, unpleasant, unfriendly, spiteful, cruel, vicious, base, foul, malevolent, despicable, contemptible, horrible, horrid, rotten. ANTONYM kind.

**beat** verb **1** *they were beaten with truncheons* HIT, strike, batter, thump, bang, hammer, punch, knock, thrash, pound, pummel, slap, smack, rain blows on; assault, attack, abuse; cudgel, club, birch; *informal* wallop, belt, bash, whack, thwack, clout, clobber, slug, tan, bop, sock, deck, plug, beat the living daylights out of; *dated* chastise.

**2** *the waves* ***beat upon*** *the shore* BREAK ON/UPON/AGAINST, dash against; lash against, strike, lap (upon), wash against; splash on/upon/against, roll upon; *literary* plash upon/against, lave against.

**3** *the metal is beaten into a die* HAMMER, forge, form, shape, mold, work, stamp, fashion, model.

**4** *her heart was still beating* PULSATE, pulse, palpitate, vibrate, throb; pump, pound, thump, thud, hammer, drum; pitter-patter.

**5** *the eagle beat its wings* FLAP, flutter, thresh, thrash, wave, vibrate, oscillate.

**6** *beat the cream into the mixture* WHISK, mix, blend, whip.

**7** *she beat a path through the grass* TREAD, tramp, trample, wear, flatten, press down.

**8** *the team they need to beat* DEFEAT, conquer, win against, get the better of, vanquish, trounce, rout, overpower, overcome, subdue; *informal* lick, thrash, whip, wipe the floor with, clobber, cream, shellac, skunk.

**9** *he beat the record* SURPASS, exceed, better, improve on, go one better than, eclipse, transcend, top, trump, cap.

▸ noun **1** *the song has a good beat* RHYTHM, pulse, meter, time, measure, cadence; stress, accent.

**2** *the beat of hooves* POUNDING, banging, thumping, thudding, booming, hammering, battering, crashing.

**3** *the beat of her heart* PULSE, pulsating, vibration, throb, palpitation, reverberation; pounding, thump, thud, hammering, drumming; pitter-patter.

**4** *a cop on his beat* CIRCUIT, round, route, way, path.

▸ adjective *informal phew, I'm beat!* See EXHAUSTED sense 1.

PHRASES: **beat a (hasty) retreat.** See RETREAT verb sense 1.

**beat it** *informal.* See RUN verb sense 2.

**beat someone up** *he just snapped and started beating up his abusive father* ASSAULT, attack, mug, thrash, do over, work over, rough up, lay into, lace into, sail into, beat the living daylights out of, let someone have it, beat up on, knock around/about.

**beaten** adjective **1** *the beaten team* DEFEATED, losing, unsuccessful, conquered, bettered, vanquished, trounced, routed, overcome, overwhelmed, overpowered, overthrown, bested, subdued, quashed, crushed, broken, foiled, hapless, luckless; *informal* licked, thrashed, losingest, clobbered. ANTONYMS victorious, winning.

**2** *a beaten dog* ABUSED, battered, maltreated, ill-treated, mistreated, misused, downtrodden; ASSAULTED, thumped, whacked, hit, thrashed, pummeled, smacked, drubbed; *informal* walloped, belted, bashed, clobbered, knocked around/about, roughed up.

**3** *gradually stir in the beaten eggs* WHISKED, whipped, stirred, mixed, blended; frothy, foamy.

**4** *a beaten path* TRODDEN, trampled; well-trodden, much trodden, well-used, much traveled, worn, well-worn. ANTONYM untouched.

PHRASE: **off the beaten track/path** *we tried to find a campsite off the beaten track* OUT OF THE WAY, isolated, quiet, private, remote, unfrequented, outlying, secluded, hidden, backwoods, in the back of beyond, in the middle of nowhere, in the hinterlands; *informal* in the sticks. ANTONYMS busy, popular.

**beatific** adjective **1** *a beatific smile* RAPTUROUS, joyful, ecstatic, seraphic, blissful, serene, happy, beaming.

**2** *a beatific vision* BLESSED, exalted, sublime, heavenly, holy, divine, celestial, paradisical, glorious.

**beatitude** noun *the everlasting beatitude* BLESSEDNESS, benediction, grace; bliss, ecstasy, exaltation, supreme happiness, divine joy, divine rapture; saintliness, sainthood.

**beau** noun *dated* **1** *Sally and her beau* BOYFRIEND, sweetheart, lover, darling, partner, significant other, escort, young man, admirer, suitor; *informal* main squeeze, boy toy.

2 *an eighteenth-century beau* DANDY, fop; *dated* swell, coxcomb, popinjay.

**beautiful** adjective *beautiful fashion models* | *a beautiful crystal vase* ATTRACTIVE, pretty, handsome, good-looking, alluring, prepossessing; lovely, charming, delightful, appealing, engaging, winsome; ravishing, gorgeous, stunning, arresting, glamorous, bewitching, beguiling; graceful, elegant, exquisite, aesthetic, artistic, decorative, magnificent; *informal* divine, drop-dead gorgeous, easy on the eye, killer, cute, foxy; *formal* beauteous; *archaic* comely, fair. ANTONYM ugly.

**beautify** verb *efforts to beautify the town center* ADORN, embellish, enhance, decorate, ornament, garnish, gild, smarten up, prettify, enrich, glamorize, spruce up, spiff up, deck (out), trick out, grace; *informal* do up. ANTONYM spoil.

**beauty** noun 1 *the beauty of the scenery* ATTRACTIVENESS, prettiness, good looks, comeliness, allure; loveliness, charm, appeal, eye-appeal, heavenliness; winsomeness, grace, elegance, exquisiteness; splendor, magnificence, grandeur, impressiveness, decorativeness; gorgeousness, glamour; *literary* beauteousness, pulchritude. ANTONYM ugliness.

2 *she is a beauty* BEAUTIFUL WOMAN, belle, vision, Venus, goddess, beauty queen, picture; *informal* babe, hottie, looker, good looker, beaut, siren, doll, arm candy, lovely, stunner, knockout, bombshell, dish, peach, eyeful, fox. ANTONYM hag.

3 *the beauty of this plan* ADVANTAGE, attraction, strength, benefit, boon, blessing, good thing, strong point, virtue, merit, selling point. ANTONYM drawback.

**becalmed** adjective *the boats remained becalmed* MOTIONLESS, still, at a standstill, at a halt, unmoving, stuck.

**because** conjunction *your photos won because they're the best* SINCE, as, in view of the fact that, inasmuch as, owing to the fact that, seeing that/as; *informal* on account of, cuz; *literary* for. ANTONYM despite.

PHRASE: **because of** *because of her exceptionally high scores, she was able to start at Level 3* ON ACCOUNT OF, as a result of, as a consequence of, owing to, due to; thanks to, by/in virtue of; *formal* by reason of.

**beckon** verb 1 *the guard beckoned to Benny* GESTURE, signal, wave, gesticulate, motion.

2 *the countryside beckons you* ENTICE, invite, tempt, coax, lure, charm, attract, draw, call.

**become** verb 1 *she became rich* GROW, get, turn, come to be, get to be; *literary* wax.

2 *he became a tyrant* TURN INTO, change into, be transformed into, be converted into.

3 *he became Louisiana's attorney general* BE APPOINTED (AS), be assigned as, be nominated, be elected (as), be made.

4 *the dress becomes her* SUIT, flatter, look good on; set off, show to advantage; *informal* do something for.

5 *it ill becomes him to preach the gospel during a board meeting* BEFIT, suit, behoove. PHRASE: **become of** *whatever became of the guy who designed your terrace?* HAPPEN TO, be the fate of, be the lot of, overtake; *literary* befall, betide. See note at HAPPEN.

**becoming** adjective *that suit's very becoming* FLATTERING, attractive, lovely, pretty, handsome, fetching; stylish, elegant, chic, fashionable, tasteful; *archaic* comely.

**bed** noun 1 *she got into her bed* cot, cradle, crib, berth; brass bed, bunk bed, camp bed, canopy bed, captain's bed, daybed, featherbed; *trademark* Hide-A-Bed, Murphy bed, sofa bed, spool bed, trundle bed, waterbed, divan, futon, four-poster; *informal* the sack, the hay.

2 *a flower bed* PATCH, plot, border, strip.

3 *built on a bed of stones* BASE, foundation, support, prop, substructure, substratum.

4 *a river bed* BOTTOM, floor, ground. PHRASE: **go to bed** *time to go to bed* RETIRE, call it a day; go to sleep, have/take a nap, get some sleep; *informal* hit the sack, hit the hay, turn in, go (to) beddy-bye, crash, catch forty winks, get some shut-eye, catch some Zs, beat the sheets, meet the sandman, go to slumberland; *literary* slumber.

**bedeck** verb *a church bedecked with flowers* DECORATE, adorn, ornament, embellish, furnish, garnish, trim, deck, grace, enrich, dress up, trick out; swathe, wreathe, festoon; *informal* do up.

**bedevil** verb *past mistakes that continue to bedevil her* | *he accused Congress of allowing "single-interest-group" politics to bedevil U.S. foreign policy* AFFLICT, torment, beset, assail, beleaguer, plague, blight, rack, oppress, harry, curse, dog; harass, distress, trouble, worry, torture; frustrate, vex, annoy, irritate, irk.

**bedlam** noun *there was bedlam in the stadium* UPROAR, pandemonium, commotion, mayhem, confusion, disorder, chaos, anarchy, lawlessness; furor, upheaval, hubbub, hoopla, turmoil, riot, ruckus, rumpus, tumult, hullabaloo. ANTONYM calm.

**bedraggled** adjective *the bedraggled search party* DISHEVELED, disordered, untidy, unkempt, tousled, disarranged, in a mess, mussed. ANTONYMS neat, clean.

**bedridden** adjective *Jake will be bedridden for weeks* CONFINED TO BED, sick in bed, laid up, immobilized, flat on one's back.

**bedrock** noun 1 *we're digging till we hit bedrock* SUBSTRATUM, substructure, understructure, solid foundation, base, rock base.

2 *the bedrock of our society* CORE, basis, base, foundation, roots, heart, backbone, principle, essence, nitty-gritty; *informal* nuts and bolts.

**beef** noun 1 *there's plenty of beef on him* MUSCLE, brawn, bulk; strength, power.

2 *his beef was about the cost* COMPLAINT, criticism, objection, cavil, quibble, grievance, grumble, gripe, grouse.

▸ verb **1** *security was being **beefed up*** TOUGHEN UP, strengthen, build up, reinforce, consolidate, augment, improve.

**2** *they're constantly beefing about the neighbor's dog* COMPLAIN, grumble, whine, carp, bitch, gripe, bellyache.

**beefy** adjective *informal the beefy right fielder* MUSCULAR, brawny, hefty, burly, hulking, strapping, well-built, hard-bodied, solid, stalwart, strong, powerful, heavy, robust, sturdy; *informal* hunky, husky. ANTONYM puny.

**beer** noun *pizza and beer* ALE, brew; *informal* brewski, suds, pint.

**befall** verb *literary* **1** *the same fate befell him* HAPPEN TO, overtake, come upon, be visited on.

**2** *tell us what befell* HAPPEN, occur, take place, come about, transpire, materialize; ensue, follow, result; *informal* go down; *literary* come to pass, betide.

**befitting** preposition *this is an automobile befitting your fine taste* IN KEEPING WITH, as befits, appropriate to, fit for, suitable for, suited to, proper to, right for, compatible with, consistent with, in character with; *archaic* meet for.

**before** preposition **1** *he dressed up before going out* PRIOR TO, previous to, earlier than, preparatory to, in preparation for, preliminary to, in anticipation of, in expectation of; in advance of, ahead of, leading up to, on the eve of; *rare* anterior to. ANTONYM after.

**2** *he appeared before the judge* IN FRONT OF, in the presence of, in the sight of.

**3** *death before dishonor* IN PREFERENCE TO, rather than, sooner than.

▸ adverb *she has ridden before* PREVIOUSLY, before now/then, until now/then, up to now/then; earlier, formerly, hitherto, in the past, in days gone by; *formal* heretofore.

**beforehand** adverb *bring any notes you compiled beforehand* IN ADVANCE, ahead of time, in readiness; before, before now/then, earlier (on), previously, already, sooner. ANTONYM afterward.

**befriend** verb *a charming story in which the toys befriend one another* MAKE FRIENDS WITH, make a friend of; look after, keep an eye on; be of service to, lend a helping hand to, help, protect; side with, stand by, encourage.

**befuddled** adjective *befuddled from the anesthesia* CONFUSED, muddled, addled, bewildered, disorientated, fazed, perplexed, dazed, dizzy, stupefied, groggy, muzzy, foggy, fuddled, fuzzy, dopey, woozy, befogged, mixed up, discombobulated. ANTONYM clear.

**beg** verb **1** *he begged on the streets* PANHANDLE, ask for money, seek charity, seek alms; *informal* sponge, cadge, scrounge, bum, mooch.

**2** *we **begged for** mercy* ASK FOR, request, plead for, appeal for, call for, sue for, solicit, seek, press for.

**3** *he begged her not to go* IMPLORE, entreat, plead with, appeal to, supplicate, pray to, importune; ask, request, call on, petition; *literary* beseech.

THE RIGHT WORD **beg, entreat, plead, beseech, implore, importune, petition, solicit**

How badly do you want something? You can **beg** for it, which implies a humble and earnest approach. If you **entreat**, you're trying to get what you want by ingratiating yourself (*she entreated her mother to help her prepare for the exam*). To **plead** involves more urgency (*he pleaded with the judge to spare his life*) and is usually associated with the legal system (*she was advised to plead guilty*). **Beseech** also suggests urgency, as well as an emotional appeal (*he beseeched her to tell the truth*). **Implore** is still stronger, suggesting desperation or great distress (*the look in his mother's eyes implored him to have mercy*). If you really want to get your way, you can **importune**, which means to *beg* not only urgently but persistently and to risk making a pest of yourself (*he importuned her daily to accept his invitation*). **Petition** suggests an appeal to authority (*to petition the government to repeal an unjust law*), while **solicit** suggests petitioning in a courteous, formal way (*soliciting financial support for the school carnival*).

**beget** verb **1** *literary he begat a son* FATHER, sire, have, bring into the world, give life to, bring into being, spawn.

**2** *violence begets violence* CAUSE, give rise to, lead to, result in, bring about, create, produce, generate, engender, spawn, occasion, bring on, precipitate, prompt, provoke, kindle, trigger, spark off, touch off, stir up, whip up, induce, inspire, promote; *literary* enkindle.

**beggar** noun *he never turned any beggar from his door* PANHANDLER, mendicant, tramp, vagrant, vagabond, hobo; *informal* scrounger, sponger, cadger, freeloader, bum, moocher, mooch.

**begin** verb **1** *we began work* START, commence, set about, go about, embark on, launch into, get down to, take up; initiate, set in motion, institute, inaugurate, get ahead with; *informal* get cracking on, get going on. ANTONYM cease.

**2** *he began by saying hello* OPEN, lead off, get underway, get going, get off the ground, start, start off, go ahead, commence; *informal* start the ball rolling, kick off, get the show on the road, fire away, take the plunge. ANTONYMS finish, conclude.

**3** *when did the illness begin?* APPEAR, arise, become apparent, make an appearance, spring up, crop up, turn up, come into existence, come into being, originate, start, commence, develop; *literary* come to pass. ANTONYM disappear.

**beginner** noun *a yoga video for beginners* NOVICE, newcomer, fledgling, neophyte, starter, learner, student, apprentice, trainee; recruit, raw recruit, initiate, freshman; tenderfoot, tyro; postulant, novitiate; *informal* rookie, newbie, cub, greenhorn, new kid (on the block). See note at NOVICE. ANTONYMS expert, veteran.

**beginning** noun **1** *the beginning of socialism* DAWN, birth, inception, conception, origination, genesis, emergence, rise, start, commencement, starting point, launch, onset, outset; day one; *informal* kickoff. ANTONYM end.

**2** *the beginning of the article* OPENING, introduction, start, first part, preamble, opening statement. ANTONYMS end, conclusion.

3 (**beginnings**) *the therapy has its beginnings in China* ORIGIN, source, roots, starting point, birthplace, cradle, spring, fountainhead; genesis, creation; *literary* fount, well spring.

**begrudge** verb 1 *she begrudged Brian his affluence* ENVY, resent, grudge.

2 *don't begrudge the cost* RESENT, feel aggrieved about, feel bitter about, be annoyed about, be resentful of, grudge, mind, object to, take exception to, regret.

**beguile** verb 1 *she was beguiled by his beauty* CHARM, attract, enchant, entrance, win over, woo, captivate, bewitch, spellbind, dazzle, hypnotize, mesmerize, seduce. See note at TEMPT. ANTONYM repel.

2 *the program has been beguiling children for years* ENTERTAIN, amuse, delight, please, occupy, absorb, engage, distract, divert, fascinate, enthrall, engross. ANTONYM bore.

**behalf** PHRASE: **on behalf of/on someone's behalf** 1 *I am writing on behalf of my client* AS A REPRESENTATIVE OF, as a spokesperson for, for, in the name of, in place of, on the authority of, at the behest of.

2 *a campaign on behalf of recycling* IN THE INTERESTS OF, in support of, for, for the benefit of, for the good of, for the sake of.

**behave** verb 1 *she behaved badly* CONDUCT ONESELF, act, acquit oneself, bear oneself; *formal* comport oneself; *archaic* deport oneself.

2 *the children behaved themselves* ACT CORRECTLY, act properly, conduct oneself well, be well-behaved, be good; be polite, show good manners, mind one's manners. ANTONYM misbehave.

**behavior** noun 1 *his behavior was inexcusable* CONDUCT, deportment, bearing, actions, doings; manners, ways; *formal* comportment.

2 *the behavior of these organisms* FUNCTIONING, action, performance, operation, working, reaction, response.

**behead** verb *dissidents were beheaded* DECAPITATE, cut/chop/lop someone's head off, guillotine.

**behest** noun *the plan is being pushed through the legislature at the behest of Congressman DeLay* INSTRUCTION, requirement, demand, insistence, bidding, request, wish, desire, will; command, injunction, order, decree, ruling, directive, mandate; *informal* say-so; *rare* rescript.

**behind** preposition 1 *he hid behind a tree* AT THE BACK/REAR OF, beyond, on the far/other side of, in back of. ANTONYM in front of.

2 *a guard ran behind him* AFTER, following, at the back/rear of, (hard) on the heels of, in the wake of. ANTONYM ahead of.

3 *he was behind the bombings* RESPONSIBLE FOR, at the bottom of, the cause of, the source of, the organizer of; to blame for, culpable of, guilty of.

4 *we're behind you all the way* SUPPORTING, backing, for, on the side of, in agreement with; financing; *informal* rooting for.

▸ adverb 1 *a man followed behind* AFTER, afterward, at the back/end, in the rear. ANTONYMS in front, ahead.

2 *I looked behind* OVER ONE'S SHOULDER, to/toward the back, to/toward the rear, backward. ANTONYM ahead.

3 *we're behind, so don't stop* LATE, running late, behind schedule, behindhand, not on time, behind time.

4 *he was behind with his subscription* IN ARREARS, overdue; late, unpunctual, behindhand.

▸ noun *informal he sat on his behind.* See BUTTOCKS.

PHRASE: **put something behind one** *they put last night's loss to the Orioles behind them* CONSIGN TO THE PAST, put down to experience, regard as water under the bridge, forget about, ignore.

**behold** verb *literary no eyes beheld them* SEE, observe, view, look at, watch, survey, witness, gaze at/upon, regard, contemplate, inspect, eye; catch sight of, glimpse, spot, spy, notice; *informal* clap eyes on, have/take a gander at, get a load of, eyeball; *literary* espy, descry.

▸ exclamation *archaic behold, the prince returns!* LOOK, see; *archaic* lo.

**beholden** adjective *he is beholden to no one in his determination to defend Malaysia's rights* INDEBTED, in someone's debt, obligated, under an obligation; grateful, owing a debt of gratitude.

**behoove** verb 1 *it behooves me to go* BE INCUMBENT ON, be obligatory for, be required of, be expected of, be appropriate for.

2 *it ill behooves them to comment* BEFIT, become, suit.

**beige** adjective *beige curtains* FAWN, pale brown, buff, sand, sandy, oatmeal, khaki, biscuit, coffee, coffee-colored, café au lait, camel, ecru.

**being** noun 1 *she is warmed by his very being* EXISTENCE, living, life, reality, actuality.

2 *God is alive in the being of man* SOUL, spirit, nature, essence, inner being, inner self, psyche; heart, bosom, breast; *Philosophy* quiddity, pneuma.

3 *an enlightened being* CREATURE, life form, living entity, living thing, soul, living soul, individual, person, human being, human.

**belabor** verb *don't belabor the point* OVERELABORATE, labor, dwell on, harp on about, hammer away at; overdo, overplay, overdramatize, make too much of, place too much emphasis on; *informal* beat to death, drag out, make a big thing of, blow out of proportion. ANTONYM understate.

**belated** adjective *a belated anniversary dinner* LATE, overdue, behindhand, behind time, behind schedule, delayed, tardy, unpunctual. ANTONYM early.

**belch** verb 1 *onions make me belch* BURP.

2 *the furnace belched flames* EMIT, give off, give out, pour out, discharge, disgorge, spew out, spit out, vomit, gush, cough up.

▸ noun *he gave a loud belch* BURP; *formal* eructation.

**beleaguered** adjective **1** *the beleaguered garrison* BESIEGED, under siege, blockaded, surrounded, encircled, beset, hemmed in, under attack.

**2** *a beleaguered government* HARD-PRESSED, troubled, in difficulties, under pressure, under stress, with one's back to the wall, in a tight corner, in a tight spot, up against it; beset, assailed.

**belie** verb *his eyes belied his words* CONTRADICT, be at odds with, call into question, show/prove to be false, disprove, debunk, discredit, controvert, negate; *formal* confute. ANTONYMS testify to, reveal.

**belief** noun **1** *it's my belief that age is irrelevant* OPINION, view, conviction, judgment, thinking, way of thinking, idea, impression, theory, conclusion, notion. See note at OPINION.

**2** *belief in God* FAITH, trust, reliance, confidence, credence. ANTONYMS disbelief, doubt.

**3** *traditional beliefs* IDEOLOGY, principle, ethic, tenet, canon; doctrine, teaching, dogma, article of faith, creed, credo.

**believable** adjective *contestant number 3 tells the most believable anecdotes | she was completely believable in her role as a federal marshal* CREDIBLE, plausible, likely, tenable, able to hold water, conceivable, imaginable, convincing, creditable, probable, possible, feasible, reasonable, rational, sound, within the bounds of possibility, with a ring of truth. ANTONYM inconceivable.

THE RIGHT WORD **believable, cogent, convincing, credible, creditable, plausible, valid**

**Believable** is the most general of these terms, used to describe anything we accept as true, even in the absence of absolute proof (*a believable story about why she was late*). **Credible** also means worthy of belief or confidence and is often used interchangeably with *believable*, but it goes one step further: a *credible* excuse is one that is supported by known facts. **Creditable**, often confused with *credible*, at one time meant worthy of belief but nowadays is used to mean respectable or decent, deserving of honor, reputation, or esteem (*leading a creditable life*). Something that is **convincing** is *believable* because it overcomes doubts or opposition (*a convincing performance*), while something that is **plausible** may appear to be convincing or believable on the surface, but may not be so upon closer examination. **Valid** means legally sound, just, or authoritative; a *valid* criticism seldom provokes opposition. **Cogent**, on the other hand, means having the power to convince; a *cogent* argument is believable because of its clear, forceful, or incisive presentation.

**believe** verb **1** *I don't believe you* BE CONVINCED BY, trust, have confidence in, consider honest, consider truthful.

**2** *do you believe that story?* REGARD AS TRUE, accept, be convinced by, give credence to, credit, trust, put confidence in; *informal* swallow, buy, go for.

**3** *I believe he worked for you* THINK, be of the opinion that, have an idea that, imagine, suspect, suppose, assume, presume, take it, conjecture, surmise, conclude, deduce, understand, be given to understand, gather, fancy, guess, dare say; *informal* reckon, figure; *archaic* ween. ANTONYM doubt.

PHRASE: **believe in 1** *she believed in God* BE CONVINCED OF THE EXISTENCE OF, be sure of the existence of.

**2** *I believe in lots of exercise* HAVE FAITH IN, pin one's faith on, trust in, have every confidence in, cling to, set (great) store by, value, be convinced by, be persuaded by; subscribe to, approve of; *informal* swear by.

**believer** noun *a cause with few believers* DEVOTEE, adherent, disciple, follower, supporter. ANTONYMS infidel, skeptic.

**belittle** verb *Mr. Reese had been warned on two previous occasions to stop belittling his students* DISPARAGE, denigrate, run down, deprecate, depreciate, downgrade, play down, trivialize, minimize, make light of, pooh-pooh, treat lightly, scoff at, sneer at; *formal* derogate; *rare* misprize. ANTONYMS praise, magnify.

**belligerent** adjective **1** *a belligerent attitude* HOSTILE, aggressive, threatening, antagonistic, warlike, warmongering, hawkish, pugnacious, bellicose, truculent, confrontational, contentious, militant, combative; *informal* spoiling for a fight, trigger-happy, scrappy. See note at HOSTILE. ANTONYMS peaceable, friendly.

**2** *belligerent nations* WARRING, at war, combatant, fighting, battling. ANTONYMS peaceful, neutral.

**bellow** verb *she bellowed in his ear* ROAR, shout, bawl, thunder, trumpet, boom, bark, yell, shriek, howl, scream; raise one's voice; *informal* holler. ANTONYM whisper.

▸ noun *a bellow of pain* ROAR, shout, bawl, bark, yell, yelp, shriek, howl, scream. ANTONYM whisper.

**belly** noun *he scratched his belly* STOMACH, abdomen, paunch, middle, midriff, girth; *informal* tummy, tum, breadbasket, gut, guts, insides, pot, potbelly, beer belly, spare tire.

▸ verb *her skirt bellied out* BILLOW (OUT), bulge (out), balloon (out), bag (out); distend. ANTONYMS sag, flap.

**belong** verb **1** *the house belongs to his mother* BE OWNED BY, be the property of, be the possession of, be held by, be in the hands of.

**2** *I belong to a book club* BE A MEMBER OF, be in, be affiliated to/with, be allied to, be associated with, be linked to, be an adherent of.

**3** *the atlas belongs with the reference books* BE CLASSED, be classified, be categorized, be included, have a place, be located, be situated, be found, lie.

**4** *she doesn't belong here* FIT IN, be suited to, have a rightful place, have a home; *informal* go, click.

**belongings** plural noun *she could fit all her belongings in one bag* POSSESSIONS, effects, worldly goods, assets, chattels, property; *informal* gear, tackle, kit, things, stuff.

**beloved** adjective *her beloved brother* DARLING, dear, dearest, precious, adored, much loved, cherished, treasured, prized, highly regarded, admired, esteemed, worshiped, revered, venerated, idolized. ANTONYM hated.

▸ noun *he watched his beloved* SWEETHEART, love, darling, dearest, lover, girlfriend, boyfriend, young lady, young man, beau, lady friend; *informal* steady, main squeeze, swain; *archaic* paramour, doxy.

**below** preposition **1** *the water rushed below them* BENEATH, under, underneath, further down than, lower than. ANTONYMS above, over.

**2** *the result is below average* LESS THAN, lower than, under, not as much as, smaller than. ANTONYMS above, more than.

**3** *a captain is below a major* LOWER THAN, under, inferior to, subordinate to, subservient to. ANTONYM above.

▸ adverb **1** *I could see what was happening below* FURTHER DOWN, lower down, in a lower position, underneath, beneath.

**2** *read the statements below* UNDERNEATH, following, further on, at a later point.

**belt** noun **1** *the belt of her coat* SASH, girdle, strap, cummerbund, band; *literary* cincture; *historical* baldric.

**2** *farmers in the cotton belt* REGION, area, district, zone, sector, territory; tract, strip, stretch.

▸ verb **1** *she belted them in* FASTEN, tie, bind; *literary* gird.

**2** *informal a guy belted him in the face* HIT, strike, smack, slap, bang, beat, punch, thump; *informal* clout, bash, whack, thwack, wallop, sock, clobber, bop, larrup, slug; *archaic* smite.

PHRASE: **below the belt** *bringing up Dana's past to the boss was below the belt* UNFAIR, unjust, unacceptable, inequitable; unethical, unprincipled, immoral, unscrupulous, unsporting, sneaky, dishonorable, dishonest, underhanded; *informal* low-down, dirty.

**bemoan** verb *it does no good to bemoan the loss of that job* LAMENT, bewail, mourn, grieve over, sorrow over, regret, cry over; deplore, complain about; *archaic* plain over. See note at MOURN. ANTONYMS rejoice at, applaud.

**bemused** adjective *bemused expressions on their faces* BEWILDERED, confused, puzzled, perplexed, baffled, mystified, nonplussed, muddled, befuddled, dumbfounded, at sea, at a loss, taken aback, disoriented, disconcerted; *informal* flummoxed, bamboozled, clueless, fazed, discombobulated.

**bench** noun **1** *he sat on a bench* PEW, stall, settle, seat; bleacher.

**2** *a laboratory bench* WORKBENCH, work table, worktop, work surface, counter.

**3** *the bench heard the evidence* JUDGES, magistrates, judiciary; court.

▸ verb *the coach benched him for two games* SIDELINE, sit out, cut.

**benchmark** noun *the settlement became the benchmark for all future negotiations* STANDARD, point of reference, gauge, guide, guideline, guiding principle, norm, touchstone, yardstick, barometer, indicator, measure, model, exemplar, pattern, criterion, specification, convention.

**bend** verb **1** *the frames can be bent to fit your face* CURVE, angle, hook, bow, arch, flex, crook, hump, warp, contort, distort, deform. ANTONYM straighten.

**2** *the highway bends to the left* TURN, curve, incline, swing, veer, deviate, diverge, fork, change course, curl, loop.

**3** *he bent down to tie his shoe* STOOP, bow, crouch, hunch, lean down/over. ANTONYM straighten up.

**4** *they want to bend me to their will* MOLD, shape, manipulate, direct, force, press, influence, incline, sway.

▸ noun *he came to a bend in the road* CURVE, turn, corner, jog, kink, dogleg, oxbow, zigzag, angle, arc, crescent, twist, crook, deviation, deflection, loop, hairpin turn, hairpin.

PHRASE: **bend over backwards** *informal we've bent over backwards to give you a second chance* TRY ONE'S HARDEST, do one's best, do one's utmost, do all one can, give one's all, make every effort; *informal* do one's damnedest, go all out, pull out all the stops, bust a gut, move heaven and earth.

**beneath** preposition **1** *we sat beneath the trees* UNDER, underneath, below, at the foot of, at the bottom of; lower than. ANTONYM above.

**2** *made to feel beneath them* INFERIOR TO, below, not so important as, lower in status than, subordinate to, subservient to. ANTONYM above.

**3** *such an attitude was beneath her* UNWORTHY OF, unbecoming to, degrading to, below. ANTONYM above.

▸ adverb *sand with rock beneath* UNDERNEATH, below, further down, lower down. ANTONYM above.

**benediction** noun **1** *the priest pronounced the benediction* BLESSING, prayer, invocation; grace, benedicite.

**2** *filled with heavenly benediction* BLESSEDNESS, beatitude, bliss, grace.

**benefactor, benefactress** noun *an anonymous benefactor* PATRON, supporter, backer, sponsor; donor, contributor, subscriber; *informal* angel.

**beneficial** adjective *ladybugs and other species beneficial to the garden | this information has been highly beneficial* ADVANTAGEOUS, favorable, helpful, useful, of use, of benefit, of assistance, valuable, of value, profitable, rewarding, gainful. ANTONYMS detrimental, disadvantageous.

**beneficiary** noun *her beneficiaries include several godchildren | about three in five Medicare beneficiaries do not have dependable drug coverage* HEIR, heiress, inheritor, legatee; recipient, receiver, payee, donee, assignee; *Law* devisee, grantee.

**benefit** noun **1** *for the benefit of others* GOOD, sake, welfare, well-being, advantage, comfort, ease, convenience; help, aid, assistance, service; profit. ANTONYM detriment.

**2** *the benefits of working for a large firm* ADVANTAGE, reward, merit, boon, blessing, virtue; bonus; value; *informal* perk; *formal* perquisite. ANTONYMS drawback, disadvantage.

**3** *have you applied for this benefit?* SOCIAL SECURITY, welfare, assistance, employment insurance, unemployment, food stamps; charity, donations, gifts, financial assistance.

**4** *we have four tickets for tonight's benefit* FUNDRAISER, fundraising event, charity affair, charity event.

▸ verb 1 *the deal benefited them both* BE ADVANTAGEOUS TO, be beneficial to, be of advantage to, be to the advantage of, profit, do good to, be of service to, serve, be useful to, be of use to, be helpful to, be of help to, help, aid, assist, be of assistance to; better, improve, strengthen, boost, advance, further. ANTONYM damage.

2 *they may **benefit from** the scheme* PROFIT FROM, gain from, reap benefits from, reap reward(s) from, make money from; make the most of, exploit, turn to one's advantage, put to good use, do well out of; *informal* cash in on, make a killing from. ANTONYM suffer.

**benevolence** noun *the benevolence of local businesses* KINDNESS, kindheartedness, bigheartedness, goodness, goodwill, charity, altruism, humanitarianism, compassion, philanthropy; generosity, magnanimity, munificence, unselfishness, openhandedness, beneficence; *literary* bounty, bounteousness. See note at MERCY. ANTONYMS spite, miserliness.

**benevolent** adjective 1 *a benevolent patriarch* KIND, kindly, kindhearted, bighearted, good-natured, good, benign, compassionate, caring, altruistic, humanitarian, philanthropic; generous, magnanimous, munificent, unselfish, openhanded, beneficent; *literary* bounteous. ANTONYMS unkind, tightfisted.

2 *a benevolent institution* CHARITABLE, nonprofit, not-for-profit; *formal* eleemosynary.

**benign** adjective 1 *a benign grandfatherly role* KINDLY, kind, warmhearted, good-natured, friendly, warm, affectionate, agreeable, genial, congenial, cordial, approachable, tenderhearted, gentle, sympathetic, compassionate, caring, well-disposed, benevolent. ANTONYMS unfriendly, hostile.

2 *a benign climate* TEMPERATE, mild, gentle, balmy, soft, pleasant, favorable; healthy, wholesome, salubrious. ANTONYMS harsh, unhealthy, unfavorable.

3 *Medicine* *a benign tumor* HARMLESS, nonmalignant, noncancerous; *Medicine* benignant. ANTONYM malignant.

**bent** adjective *the bucket had a bent handle* TWISTED, crooked, warped, contorted, deformed, misshapen, out of shape, irregular; bowed, arched, curved, angled, hooked, kinked; *informal* pretzeled.

▸ noun *an artistic bent* INCLINATION, leaning, tendency; talent, gift, flair, aptitude, facility, skill, capability, capacity; predisposition, disposition, instinct, orientation, predilection, proclivity, propensity.

PHRASE: **bent on** *he's bent on going to law school* INTENT ON, determined on, set on, insistent on, resolved on, hell-bent on; committed to, single-minded about, obsessed with, fanatical about, fixated on.

**bequeath** verb *I **bequeath** the northern campgrounds **to** the Yellow Birch Fishing Club* LEAVE TO, leave in one's will to, hand on/down to, will to, make over to, pass on to, entrust to, grant to, transfer to; donate to, give to; endow on, bestow on, confer on; *Law* demise to, devise to, convey to.

**bequest** noun *they received a bequest of more than $300,000* LEGACY, inheritance, endowment, settlement; estate, heritage; bestowal; *Law* devise; *Law, dated* hereditament.

**berate** verb *she berates him so often, he barely hears the words anymore* SCOLD, rebuke, reprimand, reproach, reprove, admonish, chide, criticize, upbraid, take to task, read someone the riot act, haul over the coals; castigate; *informal* tell off, give someone a talking-to, give someone what for, dress down, give someone a dressing-down, give someone a tongue-lashing, rap over the knuckles, bawl out, come down on, tear into, blast; ream out, chew out, zing, take to the woodshed; *dated* call down, rate; *rare* reprehend. See note at SCOLD. ANTONYM praise.

**bereavement** noun *slowly getting over his bereavement* LOSS, deprivation, dispossession, privation; grief, sorrow, sadness, suffering.

**bereft** adjective *are you totally **bereft of** common sense?* DEPRIVED OF, robbed of, stripped of, devoid of, bankrupt of; wanting, in need of, lacking, without; *informal* minus, sans, clean out of.

**berserk** adjective *one of the inmates is berserk* FRENZIED, raving, wild, out of control, amok, on the rampage, frantic, crazy, raging, insane, out of one's mind, hysterical, mad, crazed, maniacal, manic; *informal* bananas, bonkers, nuts, loco, hyper, postal.

**berth** noun 1 *a four-berth cabin* BUNK, bed, cot, couch, hammock.

2 *the vessel left its berth* MOORING, dock, slip, anchorage; wharf, pier, jetty, quay.

▸ verb *they berthed at a jetty in Ram's Head Bay* DOCK, moor, land, tie up, make fast.

PHRASE: **give someone/something a wide berth** *they learned to give those gang members a wide berth* AVOID, shun, keep away from, stay away from, steer clear of, keep at arm's length, have nothing to do with; dodge, sidestep, circumvent, skirt around.

**beseech** verb *literary* *we beseech your help in permitting us the right to live in a country where human rights are respected* IMPLORE, beg, entreat, importune, plead with, appeal to, exhort, call on, supplicate, importune, pray to, ask, request, petition; *rare* obtest, impetrate, obsecrate. See note at BEG.

**beset** verb 1 *he is beset by fears* PLAGUE, bedevil, assail, beleaguer, afflict, torment, rack, oppress, trouble, worry, harass, dog, harry.

2 *they were beset by enemy forces* SURROUND, besiege, hem in, shut in, fence in, box in, encircle. See note at ATTACK.

**beside** preposition 1 *Kate walked beside him* ALONGSIDE, by/at the side of, next to, parallel to, abreast of, at someone's elbow; adjacent to, next door to, cheek by jowl with; bordering, abutting, neighboring.

2 *beside Paula, she felt clumsy* COMPARED WITH/TO, in comparison with/to, by comparison with, next to, against, contrasted with, in contrast to/with. PHRASES: **beside oneself** *she was beside herself with worry* DISTRAUGHT, overcome, out of

one's mind, frantic, desperate, distracted, at one's wits' end, frenzied, wound up, worked up; hysterical, unhinged, mad, crazed.

**beside the point.** See POINT[1] .

**besides** preposition *who did you ask besides Mary?* IN ADDITION TO, as well as, over and above, above and beyond, on top of; apart from, other than, aside from, but for, save for, not counting, excluding, not including, except, with the exception of, excepting, leaving aside; *informal* outside of.

▸ adverb 1 *there's a lot more besides* IN ADDITION, as well, too, also, in/into the bargain, on top of that, to boot; *archaic* therewithal.

2 *besides, he's always late* FURTHERMORE, moreover, further; anyway, anyhow, in any case, be that as it may; *informal* what's more, anyways.

**besiege** verb 1 *the Romans besieged Carthage* LAY SIEGE TO, beleaguer, blockade, surround; *archaic* invest.

2 *fans besieged his hotel* SURROUND, mob, crowd around, swarm around, throng around, encircle. See note at ENCIRCLE.

3 *guilt besieged him* OPPRESS, torment, torture, rack, plague, afflict, haunt, harrow, hound, beset, beleaguer, trouble, bedevil, prey on.

4 *he was besieged with requests* OVERWHELM, inundate, deluge, flood, swamp, snow under; bombard.

**besmirch** verb *literary* *I'm not trying to besmirch the victim, but the woman had an extensive history of drug-related arrests* SULLY, tarnish, blacken, drag through the mud/mire, stain, taint, smear, disgrace, dishonor, bring discredit to, damage, debase, ruin; slander, malign, defame; *literary* besmear, smirch; *archaic* breathe on. ANTONYMS honor, enhance.

**besotted** adjective *the poor boy is so obviously besotted with Miss O'Toole* INFATUATED WITH, smitten with, in love with, head over heels in love with, obsessed with; doting on, greatly enamored of; *informal* swept off one's feet by, crazy about, mad about, wild about, carrying a torch for, gaga about/for/over, stuck on, gone on.

**bespeak** verb *a tree-lined road which bespoke money* INDICATE, be evidence of, be a sign of, denote, point to, testify to, evidence, reflect, demonstrate, show, manifest, display, signify; reveal, betray; *informal* spell; *literary* betoken. ANTONYM belie.

**best** adjective 1 *the best hotel in Rhode Island* FINEST, greatest, top, foremost, leading, preeminent, premier, prime, first, chief, principal, supreme, of the highest quality, superlative, par excellence, unrivaled, second to none, without equal, nonpareil, unsurpassed, peerless, matchless, unparalleled, unbeaten, unbeatable, optimum, optimal, ultimate, incomparable, ideal, perfect; highest, record-breaking; *informal* star, number-one, a cut above the rest, top-drawer, the Cadillac of, the Rolls-Royce of. ANTONYM worst.

2 *do whatever you think best* MOST ADVANTAGEOUS, most useful, most suitable, most fitting, most appropriate; most prudent, most sensible, most advisable.

▸ adverb 1 *the best-dressed man* TO THE HIGHEST STANDARD, in the best way. ANTONYM worst.

2 *the food he liked best* MOST, to the highest/greatest degree. ANTONYM least.

3 *this is best done at home* MOST ADVANTAGEOUSLY, most usefully, most suitably, most fittingly, most appropriately; most sensibly, most prudently, most wisely; better.

▸ noun 1 *only the best will do* FINEST, choicest, top, cream, choice, prime, elite, crème de la crème, flower, jewel in the crown, nonpareil; *informal* tops, pick of the bunch.

2 *she dressed in her best* BEST CLOTHES, finery, Sunday best; *informal* glad rags.

3 *give her my best* BEST WISHES, regards, kind/kindest regards, greetings, compliments, felicitations, respects; love.

▸ verb *informal* *she was not to be bested* DEFEAT, beat, get the better of, outdo, outwit, outsmart, worst, be more than a match for, prevail over, vanquish, trounce, triumph over; surpass, outclass, outshine, put someone in the shade, overshadow, eclipse; *informal* lick.

PHRASES: **do one's best** *we'll do our best to make sure you get a good education* DO ONE'S UTMOST, try one's hardest, make every effort, do all one can, give one's all; *informal* bend over backwards, do one's damnedest, go all out, pull out all the stops, bust a gut, break one's neck, move heaven and earth.

**had best** *you had best check the pantry for moths* OUGHT TO, should.

**bestial** adjective *Stanley's bestial behavior* SAVAGE, brutish, brutal, barbarous, barbaric, cruel, vicious, violent, inhuman, subhuman; depraved, degenerate, perverted, debauched, immoral, warped. ANTONYMS civilized, humane.

**bestow** verb *the honor* ***bestowed upon*** *him* CONFER ON, grant, accord, afford, endow someone with, vest in, present, award, give, donate to, entrust with, vouchsafe. See note at GIVE.

**bet** verb 1 *he bet $10 on the favorite* WAGER, gamble, stake, risk, venture, hazard, chance; put/lay money, speculate.

2 *informal* *I bet it was your idea* BE CERTAIN, be sure, be convinced, be confident; expect, predict, forecast, guess.

▸ noun 1 *a $20 bet* WAGER, gamble, stake, ante.

2 *informal* *my bet is that they'll lose* PREDICTION, forecast, guess; opinion, belief, feeling, view, theory.

3 *informal* *your best bet is to go early* OPTION, choice, alternative, course of action, plan.

**betoken** verb *literary* 1 *a small gift betokening regret* INDICATE, be a sign of, be evidence of, evidence, manifest, mean, signify, denote, represent, show, demonstrate, bespeak.

2 *the blue sky betokened a day of good weather* FORETELL, signal, give notice of, herald, proclaim, prophesy, foreshadow, presage, be a harbinger of, portend, augur, be an omen of, be a sign of, be a warning of, warn of, bode; *literary* foretoken, forebode.

**betray** verb **1** *he betrayed his own brother* BE DISLOYAL TO, be unfaithful to, double-cross, cross, break faith with, inform on/against, give away, denounce, sell out, stab in the back, break one's promise to; *informal* rat on, fink on, sell down the river, squeal on, rat on/out, finger. ANTONYM be loyal to.

**2** *he betrayed a secret* REVEAL, disclose, divulge, tell, give away, leak; unmask, expose, bring out into the open; let slip, let out, let drop, blurt out; *informal* blab, spill, kiss and tell. ANTONYMS conceal, hide.

**betrayal** noun *betrayal in the workplace | the CIA leak was a serious act of betrayal* DISLOYALTY, treachery, bad faith, faithlessness, falseness, duplicity, deception, double-dealing; breach of faith, breach of trust, stab in the back; double-cross, sellout; *literary* perfidy. ANTONYM loyalty.

**betrothal** noun *dated the betrothal was announced on St. Swithin's Day* ENGAGEMENT, marriage contract; *archaic* espousal.

**better** adjective **1** *better facilities* SUPERIOR, finer, of higher quality; preferable; *informal* a cut above, head and shoulders above, ahead of the pack/field. ANTONYMS worse, inferior.

**2** *there couldn't be a better time* MORE ADVANTAGEOUS, more suitable, more fitting, more appropriate, more useful, more valuable, more desirable. ANTONYM worse.

**3** *are you better?* HEALTHIER, fitter, stronger; well, cured, healed, recovered; recovering, on the road to recovery, making progress, improving; *informal* on the mend. ANTONYMS worse, sicker.

▸ adverb **1** *I played better today* TO A HIGHER STANDARD, in a superior/finer way.

**2** *this may suit you better* MORE, to a greater degree/extent.

**3** *the money could be better spent* MORE WISELY, more sensibly, more suitably, more fittingly, more advantageously.

▸ verb **1** *he bettered the record* SURPASS, improve on, beat, exceed, top, cap, trump, eclipse.

**2** *refugees who want to better their lot* IMPROVE, ameliorate, raise, advance, further, lift, upgrade, enhance. ANTONYM worsen.

**betterment** noun *Musharraf spoke of his desire for the betterment of Pakistan and its people* IMPROVEMENT, amelioration, advancement, change for the better, furtherance, upgrading, enhancement; reform, rectification.

**between** preposition **1** *Philip stood between his parents* IN THE SPACE SEPARATING, in the middle of, with one on either side; amid, amidst; *archaic* betwixt.

**2** *the bond between Amy and her mother* CONNECTING, linking, joining; uniting, allying; among.

**bevel** noun *the bevel that borders the mirror* SLOPE, slant, angle, cant, miter, chamfer, bezel.

**beverage** noun *soda and other beverages* DRINK, liquid refreshment; *humorous* libation; *archaic* potation.

**bevy** noun *a bevy of Vegas headliners* GROUP, crowd, herd, flock, horde, army, galaxy, assemblage, throng, company, gathering, band, body, pack, covey; knot, cluster; *informal* bunch, gaggle, posse.

**bewail** verb *they bewailed the loss of their cherished freedoms* LAMENT, bemoan, mourn, grieve over, sorrow over, cry over; deplore, complain about, wail about; *archaic* plain over. ANTONYMS rejoice at, applaud.

**beware** verb *there are loose rocks underfoot, so beware!* BE ON YOUR GUARD, watch out, look out, be alert, be on the lookout, keep your eyes open/peeled, keep an eye out, keep a sharp lookout, be on the qui vive; take care, be careful, be cautious, watch your step; *Golf* fore.

**bewilder** verb *Sally's words bewildered him* BAFFLE, mystify, bemuse, perplex, puzzle, addle, confuse, confound; *informal* flummox, faze, stump, beat, fox, make someone scratch their head, be all Greek to, floor, discombobulate. ANTONYM enlighten.

**bewildered** adjective *she looked completely bewildered* BAFFLED, mystified, bemused, perplexed, puzzled, confused, nonplussed, dumbfounded, at sea, at a loss, disorientated, taken aback; *informal* flummoxed, bamboozled; discombobulated.

**bewitch** verb **1** *the villagers were certain that Ramara had bewitched him* CAST/PUT A SPELL ON, enchant; possess, curse, hex; *archaic* witch.

**2** *we were bewitched by the surroundings* CAPTIVATE, enchant, entrance, enrapture, charm, beguile, delight, fascinate, enthrall. ANTONYM repel.

**beyond** preposition **1** *beyond the trees* ON THE FAR SIDE OF, on the other side of, further away than, behind, past, after, over.

**2** *inflation beyond 10 percent* GREATER THAN, more than, exceeding, in excess of, above, over and above, above and beyond, upwards of.

**3** *little beyond food was provided* APART FROM, except, other than, besides; *informal* outside of; *formal* save.

▸ adverb *a house with a garden beyond* FURTHER AWAY, further off.

**bias** noun **1** *he accused the media of bias* PREJUDICE, partiality, partisanship, favoritism, unfairness, one-sidedness; bigotry, intolerance, discrimination, leaning, tendency, inclination, predilection. ANTONYM impartiality.

**2** *a dress cut on the bias* DIAGONAL, cross, slant, angle.

▸ verb *this may have biased the result* PREJUDICE, influence, color, sway, weight, predispose; distort, skew, slant.

THE RIGHT WORD **bias, bigotry, intolerance, narrow-mindedness, parochialism, partiality, prejudice, provincialism**

**Bias** is a predisposition either for or against something; one can have a *bias* against police officers or a *bias* for French food and wines. **Partiality**, on the other hand, is a favorable *bias* (*the partiality of parents for their own children; the partiality of Americans for fast food*), while **prejudice** implies a preconceived and usually negative judgment or opinion (*a decision motivated by* *racial prejudice*). **Bigotry** is an even stronger term, referring to an intense dislike and often violent hatred for the members of a particular race, religion, or ethnic group. **Narrow-mindedness** also points to rigidly preconceived ideas, but implies that they are the result of lack of education or understanding, rather than outright hostility (*her parents' narrow-mindedness prevented her from meeting any boys her age*). **Parochialism** is another term meaning excessive narrowness of mind (from "parochial," pertaining to a parish or parishes; that is, concerned mainly about local issues), while **provincialism** is narrow-mindedness that results from lack of exposure to cultural or intellectual activity, characteristic of a province or non-urban area. **Intolerance** is a broad term used to describe the inability to put up with almost anything (*parents' intolerance of their children's misbehavior*).

---

**biased** adjective *a biased view of the situation* PREJUDICED, partial, partisan, one-sided, blinkered; bigoted, intolerant, discriminatory; distorted, warped, twisted, skewed. See note at IMPARTIAL. ANTONYM impartial.

**Bible** noun **1** *he read the Bible* (HOLY) SCRIPTURES, Holy Writ, Good Book, Book of Books.

**2** *informal* (**bible**) *the taxi driver's bible* HANDBOOK, manual, ABCs, companion, guide, primer, vade mecum; *rare* enchiridion.

**bicker** verb *they never bickered before they were married* QUARREL, argue, squabble, wrangle, fight, disagree, dispute, spar, have words, be at each other's throats, lock horns; *informal* scrap, spat. ANTONYM agree.

**bicycle** noun *her first bicycle was a Schwinn* BIKE, cycle, two-wheeler, mountain bike, ten-speed, racing bike, recumbent; *historical* penny-farthing, ordinary, velocipede.

**bid**[1] verb **1** *we bid $650 for the antique table* OFFER, make an offer of, put in a bid of, put up, tender, proffer, propose.

**2** *she is* ***bidding for*** *a place on the UConn team* TRY TO OBTAIN, try to get, make a pitch for, make a bid for.

▸ noun **1** *a bid of $3,000* OFFER, tender, proposal.

**2** *a bid to cut crime* ATTEMPT, effort, endeavor, try; *informal* crack, go, shot, stab; *formal* essay.

**bid**[2] verb **1** *she bid him farewell* WISH; utter.

**2** *literary* *I did as he bade me* ORDER, command, tell, instruct, direct, enjoin, charge.

**3** *literary* *he bade his companions enter* INVITE TO, ask to, request to.

**bidding** noun *let's make it clear that I am not here at your bidding* COMMAND, order, instruction, decree, injunction, demand, mandate, direction, summons, call; wish, desire; request; *literary* behest; *archaic* hest.

**big** adjective **1** *a big building* LARGE, sizable, substantial, great, huge, immense, enormous, extensive, colossal, massive, mammoth, vast, tremendous, gigantic, giant, monumental, mighty, gargantuan, elephantine, titanic, mountainous, Brobdingnagian; towering, tall, high, lofty; outsize, oversized; goodly; capacious, voluminous, spacious; king-size(d), man-size, family-size(d), economy-size(d); *informal* jumbo, whopping, mega, humongous, monster, astronomical, ginormous; *formal* commodious. ANTONYMS small, little.

**2** *clothing for big people* WELL-BUILT, sturdy, brawny, burly, broad-shouldered, muscular, muscly, rugged, Herculean, bulky, hulking, strapping, thickset, stocky, solid, hefty, large; tall, huge, gigantic; fat, stout, portly, plump, fleshy, paunchy, corpulent, obese; full-figured, big-boned, buxom; roly-poly, rotund, well-fed; *informal* hunky, beefy, husky; *literary* thewy. ANTONYMS small, slight, diminutive.

**3** *my big sister* ELDER, older; grown-up, adult, mature, grown.

**4** *a big decision* IMPORTANT, significant, major, momentous, weighty, consequential, far-reaching, key, vital, critical, crucial, life-and-death. ANTONYMS unimportant, minor, trivial.

**5** *informal* *a big man in the government* POWERFUL, important, prominent, influential, high-powered, leading, preeminent; major-league. ANTONYMS unimportant, obscure.

**6** *informal* *she has big plans* AMBITIOUS, far-reaching, grandiose, on a grand scale. ANTONYM modest.

**7** *he's got a big heart* GENEROUS, kind, kindly, caring, compassionate, loving.

**8** *informal* *East Coast bands are big across the country* POPULAR, successful, in demand, sought-after, all the rage; *informal* hot, in, cool, trendy, now, hip. PHRASE: **too big for one's britches/boots** *informal* *sudden popularity has made Scully too big for his britches* CONCEITED, full of oneself, cocky, arrogant, cocksure, above oneself, self-important, puffed-up; vain, self-satisfied, pleased with oneself, smug, complacent; *informal* bigheaded; *literary* vainglorious.

**bigot** noun *he was denounced as an anti-Catholic bigot* CHAUVINIST, partisan, sectarian; racist, sexist, homophobe, dogmatist, jingoist. See note at ZEALOT.

**bigoted** adjective *his bigoted father-in-law* PREJUDICED, biased, partial, one-sided, sectarian, discriminatory; opinionated, dogmatic, intolerant, narrow-minded, blinkered, illiberal; racist, sexist, chauvinistic, jingoistic; warped, twisted, distorted. See note at BIAS. ANTONYM open-minded.

**bigwig** noun *informal* *the company bigwigs are flying in for the annual meeting* VIP, (very) important person, notable, dignitary, grandee; celebrity; *informal* somebody, heavyweight, big shot, big gun, big cheese, big fish, big kahuna, big wheel, top gun. ANTONYM nonentity.

**bilious** adjective **1** *I felt bilious* NAUSEOUS, sick, queasy, nauseated, green around the gills; *rare* qualmish. ANTONYM well.

**2** *his bilious disposition.* See IRRITABLE.

**3** *a bilious green and pink color scheme* NAUSEATING, sickly, distasteful, dreadful; lurid, garish, loud. ANTONYMS subtle, muted.

**bilk** verb *informal.* See SWINDLE verb.

**bill**[1] noun **1** *a bill for $60* INVOICE, account, statement, list of charges; check, tab; *archaic* reckoning, score.

**2** *a congressional bill* DRAFT LAW, proposed piece of legislation, proposal, measure.

**3** *a $20 bill* BANKNOTE, note.

**4** *he had been posting bills* POSTER, advertisement, ad, public notice, announcement; flyer, leaflet, handbill.

▸ verb **1** *please bill me for the work* INVOICE, charge, debit, send a statement to.

**2** *the concert went ahead as billed* ADVERTISE, announce; schedule, program, timetable; slate.

**3** *he was* ***billed as*** *the new Sean Connery* DESCRIBE AS, call, style, label, dub; promote as, publicize as, talk up as, hype as.

**bill**2 noun *a bird's bill* BEAK, neb; *technical* mandibles.

**billet** noun *the troop's billet* QUARTERS, rooms; accommodations, lodging, housing; barracks, cantonment.

▸ verb *two soldiers were billeted here* ACCOMMODATE, quarter, put up, lodge, house; station, garrison.

**billow** noun **1** *billows of smoke* CLOUD, mass.

**2** *archaic the billows that break upon the shore* WAVE, roller, breaker.

▸ verb **1** *her dress billowed around her* PUFF UP/OUT, balloon (out), swell, fill (out), belly out.

**2** *smoke billowed from the chimney* SWIRL, spiral, roll, undulate, eddy; pour, flow.

**bin** noun *the onions go in a bin* CONTAINER, receptacle, holder; drum, canister, box, caddy, can, crate, chest, tin.

**bind** verb **1** *they bound our hands and feet* TIE (UP), fasten (together), hold together, secure, make fast, attach; rope, strap, lash, fetter, truss, hog-tie, tether. ANTONYMS untie, release.

**2** *the experience had* ***bound*** *them* ***together*** UNITE, join, bond, knit together, draw together, yoke together. ANTONYM separate.

**3** *we were bound by a rigid timetable* CONSTRAIN, restrict, restrain, trammel, tie hand and foot, tie down, fetter, shackle, hog-tie; hamper, hinder, inhibit.

**4** *the edges are bound in a contrasting color* TRIM, hem, edge, border, fringe; finish; *archaic* purfle.

▸ noun *we're in a terrible bind* PREDICAMENT, awkward situation, difficult situation, quandary, dilemma, plight, spot, tight spot; *informal* Catch-22, fix, hole.

**binding** adjective *the agreement is binding* IRREVOCABLE, unalterable, inescapable, unbreakable, contractual; compulsory, obligatory, mandatory, incumbent.

**binge** noun **1** *she was afraid that Howie was on another of his all-night binges* DRINKING BOUT, debauch; *informal* bender, jag, toot, session; *dated* souse; *literary* bacchanal, bacchanalia; *archaic* wassail.

**2** *a two-day shopping binge* SPREE; *informal* splurge, spendfest, orgy.

▸ verb *we binged on all the free food* OVERINDULGE, overeat, gorge; *informal* pig out.

**biography** noun *an unauthorized biography of Pat Nixon* LIFE STORY, life history, life, memoir; *informal* bio.

**bird** noun *feeding the birds* fowl; chick, fledgling, nestling; *informal* feathered friend, birdie; budgie; *technical* (**birds**) avifauna.

**birth** noun **1** *Nick arrived just in time for the birth* CHILDBIRTH, delivery, nativity, birthing; blessed/happy event; *formal* parturition; *dated* confinement; *archaic* accouchement, childbed. ANTONYM death.

**2** *the birth of science* BEGINNING(S), emergence, genesis, dawn, dawning, rise, start, onset, commencement. ANTONYMS demise, end.

**3** *he is of noble birth* ANCESTRY, lineage, blood, descent, parentage, family, extraction, origin, genealogy, heritage, stock, kinship. PHRASE: **give birth to** *she gave birth to twins* HAVE, bear, produce, be delivered of, bring into the world; birth; *informal* drop; *dated* mother; *archaic* bring forth.

**birthmark** noun *a birthmark shaped like an apple* BEAUTY SPOT/MARK, mole, blemish, nevus.

**birthright** noun *the presidency of this firm is my birthright* PATRIMONY, inheritance, heritage; right, due, prerogative, privilege; primogeniture.

**bisect** verb *bisect the exterior angle* CUT IN HALF, halve, divide/cut/split in two, split down the middle; cross, intersect.

**bit** noun **1** *a bit of bread* PIECE, portion, segment, section, part; chunk, lump, hunk, slice; fragment, scrap, shred, crumb, grain, speck; spot, drop, pinch, dash, soupçon, modicum; morsel, mouthful, bite, sample; iota, jot, tittle, whit, atom, particle, trace, touch, suggestion, hint, tinge; snippet, snatch, smidgen, tad. ANTONYM lot.

**2** *wait a bit* MOMENT, minute, second, (little) while; *informal* sec, jiffy, jiff. PHRASES: **a bit** *he's a bit forgetful* SOMEWHAT, fairly, slightly, rather, quite, a little, moderately; *informal* pretty, sort of, kind of, kinda.

**bit by bit** *bit by bit, the truth came out* GRADUALLY, little by little, in stages, step by step, piecemeal, slowly.

**in a bit** *I'll see you in a bit* SOON, in a (little) while, in a second, in a minute, in a moment, shortly, in no time, before you know it, before long, directly; *informal* in a jiffy/jiff, in two shakes, in a snap; *literary* ere long, anon.

**bitch** noun *informal* **1** *she's such a bitch* WITCH, shrew, vixen, she-devil, hellcat, harridan, termagant, virago, harpy; *archaic* grimalkin.

**2** *a bitch of a job* NIGHTMARE; *informal* bastard, bummer, —— from hell, stinker.

▸ verb *they bitched about the price of oil* COMPLAIN, whine, grumble, grouse; *informal* whinge, moan, grouch, gripe.

**bitchy** adjective *informal*. See SPITEFUL.

**bite** verb **1** *the dog bit his arm* SINK ONE'S TEETH INTO, chew, munch, crunch, chomp, tear at, snap at.

**2** *the acid* ***bites into*** *the copper* CORRODE, eat into, eat away at, burn (into), etch, dissolve.

**3** *a hundred or so retailers should bite* ACCEPT, agree, respond; be lured, be enticed, be tempted; take the bait.

▸ noun **1** *he took a bite of his sandwich* MUNCH, chew, nibble, nip, snap.

**2** *he ate it in two bites* MOUTHFUL, piece, bit, morsel.

**3** *let's go out for* ***a bite*** A SNACK, a light meal, a quick meal; refreshments; *informal* a little something.

**4** *we came back from the picnic covered in insect bites* STING.

**5** *the appetizer had a fiery bite* PIQUANCY, pungency, spiciness, strong flavor, tang, zest, sharpness, tartness; *informal* kick, punch, edge, zing.

**biting** adjective **1** *biting comments* VICIOUS, harsh, cruel, savage, cutting, sharp, bitter, scathing, caustic, acid, acrimonious, acerbic, stinging; vitriolic, hostile, spiteful, venomous, mean, nasty; *informal* bitchy, catty. ANTONYMS mild, gentle.

**2** *the biting wind* FREEZING, icy, arctic, glacial; bitter, piercing, penetrating, raw, wintry. ANTONYMS mild, balmy.

**bitter** adjective **1** *a bitter aftertaste* SHARP, acid, acidic, acrid, tart, sour, biting, unsweetened, vinegary; *technical* acerbic. ANTONYM sweet.

**2** *a bitter woman* RESENTFUL, embittered, aggrieved, begrudging, rancorous, spiteful, jaundiced, ill-disposed, sullen, sour, churlish, morose, petulant, peevish, with a chip on one's shoulder. ANTONYMS magnanimous, content.

**3** *a bitter blow* PAINFUL, unpleasant, disagreeable, nasty, cruel, awful, distressing, upsetting, harrowing, heartbreaking, heart-rending, agonizing, traumatic, tragic, chilling; *formal* grievous. ANTONYM welcome.

**4** *a bitter wind* FREEZING, icy, arctic, glacial; biting, piercing, penetrating, raw, wintry. ANTONYMS warm, balmy.

**5** *a bitter dispute* ACRIMONIOUS, virulent, angry, rancorous, spiteful, vicious, vitriolic, savage, ferocious, hate-filled, venomous, poisonous, acrid, nasty, ill-natured. ANTONYM amicable.

**bitterness** noun **1** *the bitterness of the medicine* SHARPNESS, acidity, acridity, tartness, sourness, harshness; *technical* acerbity. ANTONYM sweetness.

**2** *there was no bitterness between them* RESENTMENT, rancor, indignation, grudge, spite, sullenness, sourness, churlishness, moroseness, petulance, pique, peevishness; ACRIMONY, hostility, malice, virulence, antipathy, antagonism, enmity, animus, friction, vitriol, hatred, loathing, venom, poison, nastiness, ill feeling, ill will, bad blood. ANTONYMS magnanimity, contentment, goodwill.

**3** *the bitterness of war* TRAUMA, pain, agony, grief; unpleasantness, disagreeableness, nastiness; heartache, heartbreak, distress, desolation, despair, tragedy. ANTONYM delight.

**bizarre** adjective *bizarre sculptures* STRANGE, peculiar, odd, funny, curious, outlandish, outré, abnormal, eccentric, unconventional, unusual, unorthodox, queer, extraordinary; *informal* weird, wacky, bizarro, oddball, way out, kooky, freaky, off the wall, offbeat. ANTONYMS normal, conventional.

**black** adjective **1** *a black horse* DARK, pitch-black, jet-black, coal-black, ebony, sable, inky. ANTONYM white.

**2** *a black night* UNLIT, dark, starless, moonless, wan; *literary* tenebrous, Stygian. ANTONYMS clear, bright.

**3** *thirty-seven percent of our advanced-study students are black.* See note below.

**4** *the blackest day of the war* TRAGIC, disastrous, calamitous, catastrophic, cataclysmic, fateful, wretched, woeful, awful, terrible; *formal* grievous. ANTONYM joyful.

**5** *Mary was in a black mood* MISERABLE, unhappy, sad, wretched, broken-hearted, heartbroken, grief-stricken, grieving, sorrowful, sorrowing, anguished, desolate, despairing, disconsolate, downcast, dejected, sullen, cheerless, melancholy, morose, gloomy, glum, mournful, doleful, funereal, dismal, forlorn, woeful, abject; *informal* blue; *literary* dolorous. ANTONYM cheerful.

**6** *black humor* CYNICAL, macabre, weird, unhealthy, ghoulish, morbid, perverted, gruesome; *informal* sick.

**7** *a black look* ANGRY, vexed, cross, irritated, incensed. See also ANGRY sense 1. ANTONYM pleased.

**8** *archaic a black deed.* WICKED, evil, heinous, villainous, bad. See also WICKED sense 1. ANTONYM virtuous.

PHRASES: **black out** *he blacked out from the pain* FAINT, lose consciousness, pass out, swoon; *informal* go out.

**black something out** *we blacked out our homes during the war* DARKEN, shade, turn off the lights in; keep the light out of.

**in the black** *our business is finally in the black* SOLVENT, debt-free, out of debt, in credit, financially sound, able to pay one's debts, creditworthy.

**black and white** **1** *a black-and-white picture* MONOCHROME, gray-scale.

**2** *I wish to see the proposals in black and white* IN PRINT, printed, written down, set down, on paper, recorded, on record, documented.

**3** *in black-and-white terms* CATEGORICAL, unequivocal, absolute, uncompromising, unconditional, unqualified, unambiguous, clear, clear-cut.

USAGE NOTE **black**

**Black**, designating Americans of African heritage, became the most widely used and accepted term in the 1960s and 1970s, replacing **Negro**. It is not usually capitalized: *black Americans*. Through the 1980s, the more formal **African American** replaced **black** in much usage, but both are now generally acceptable. **Afro-American**, an earlier alternative to **black**, is heard mostly in anthropological and cultural contexts. **Colored people**, common earlier in the twentieth century, is now usually regarded as derogatory, although the phrase survives in the full name of the NAACP, the National Association for the Advancement of Colored People. An inversion, **people of color**, has gained some favor, but is also used in reference to other nonwhite ethnic groups: *a gathering spot for African Americans and other people of color interested in reading about their cultures.*

**blackball** verb *Zabel could not support the group's intention to blackball Curtis* REJECT, debar, bar, ban, vote against, blacklist, exclude, shut out; ostracize, expel. ANTONYM admit.

**blacken** verb **1** *they blackened their faces* BLACK, darken; dirty, make sooty, make smoky, stain, grime, soil. ANTONYMS whiten, clean.

**2** *the sky blackened* GROW/BECOME BLACK, darken, dim, grow dim, cloud over. ANTONYMS lighten, brighten.

**3** *someone has blackened my name* SULLY, tarnish, besmirch, drag through the mud/mire, stain, taint, smear, disgrace, dishonor, bring discredit to, damage, ruin; slander, defame. ANTONYMS clear, honor.

**blacklist** verb *the club blacklisted Edwards soon after his arrest* BOYCOTT, ostracize, blackball, spurn, avoid, embargo, steer clear of, ignore; stigmatize; refuse to employ.

**blackmail** noun *he was accused of blackmail* EXTORTION; *informal* hush money; *formal* exaction.

▸ verb **1** *he was blackmailing the murderer* EXTORT MONEY FROM, threaten; *informal* demand hush money from.

**2** *she blackmailed me to work for her* COERCE, pressurize, pressure, force; *informal* lean on, put the screws on, twist someone's arm.

**blackout** noun **1** *there must have been a blackout—all the clocks are blinking* POWER FAILURE, power outage, brownout.

**2** *a news blackout* SUPPRESSION, silence, censorship, gag order, reporting restrictions.

**3** *he had a blackout* FAINTING SPELL, faint, loss of consciousness, passing out, swoon, collapse; *Medicine* syncope.

**blame** verb **1** *he always blames others* HOLD RESPONSIBLE, hold accountable, condemn, accuse, find/consider guilty, assign fault/liability/guilt to, indict, point the finger at, finger, incriminate; *archaic* inculpate. ANTONYM absolve.

**2** *they **blame** youth crime **on** unemployment* ASCRIBE TO, attribute to, impute to, lay at the door of, put down to; *informal* pin on.

▸ noun *he was cleared of all blame* | *Ullman took the blame* RESPONSIBILITY, guilt, accountability, liability, culpability, fault; *informal* rap.

**blameless** adjective *the company conceded that it was not entirely blameless* INNOCENT, guiltless, above reproach, irreproachable, unimpeachable, in the clear, exemplary, perfect, virtuous, pure, impeccable, faultless; *informal* squeaky clean, *trademark* Teflon. ANTONYM blameworthy.

**blameworthy** adjective *there is no longer any doubt that Otis is the blameworthy individual* CULPABLE, reprehensible, indefensible, inexcusable, guilty, criminal, delinquent, wrong, evil, wicked; to blame, at fault, reproachable, responsible, answerable, erring, errant, in the wrong. ANTONYM blameless.

**blanch** verb **1** *the moonlight blanches her hair* TURN PALE, whiten, lighten, wash out, fade. ANTONYM darken.

**2** *his face blanched* PALE, turn pale, turn white, whiten, lose its color, lighten, fade. ANTONYMS color, darken.

**3** *blanch the spinach leaves* SCALD, boil briefly.

**bland** adjective **1** *bland food* TASTELESS, flavorless, insipid, weak, watery, spiceless; *informal* wishy-washy. ANTONYMS tangy, tasty.

**2** *a bland film* UNINTERESTING, dull, boring, tedious, monotonous, monochrome, dry, drab, dreary, wearisome; unexciting, unimaginative, uninspiring, uninspired, lackluster, vapid, flat, stale, trite; *informal* blah, plain-vanilla, white-bread, banal, commonplace, humdrum, ho-hum, vacuous, wishy-washy. ANTONYMS interesting, stimulating.

**3** *a bland expression* UNEMOTIONAL, emotionless, dispassionate, passionless; inexpressive, cool, impassive; expressionless, blank, wooden, stony, deadpan, hollow, undemonstrative, imperturbable. ANTONYMS emotional, expressive.

**blandishments** plural noun *the blandishments of advertisers* FLATTERY, cajolery, coaxing, wheedling, persuasion, palaver, honeyed words, smooth talk, blarney; *informal* sweet talk, soft soap, buttering up, smarm.

**blank** adjective **1** *a blank sheet of paper* EMPTY, unmarked, unused, clear, free, bare, clean, plain. ANTONYM full.

**2** *a blank face* EXPRESSIONLESS, deadpan, wooden, stony, impassive, unresponsive, poker-faced, vacuous, empty, glazed, fixed, lifeless, inscrutable. ANTONYM expressive.

**3** *"What?" said Maxim, looking blank* BAFFLED, mystified, puzzled, perplexed, stumped, at a loss, stuck, bewildered, dumbfounded, nonplussed, bemused, lost, uncomprehending, at sea, confused; *informal* flummoxed, bamboozled.

**4** *a blank refusal* OUTRIGHT, absolute, categorical, unqualified, complete, flat, straight, positive, certain, explicit, unequivocal, clear, clear-cut.

▸ noun *leave a blank where the address will go* SPACE, gap, blank space, empty space; lacuna.

**blanket** noun *a blanket of cloud* COVERING, layer, coating, carpet, overlay, cloak, mantle, veil, pall, shroud.

▸ adjective *blanket coverage* complete, total, comprehensive, overall, general, mass, umbrella, inclusive, all-inclusive, all-around, wholesale, outright, across-the-board, sweeping, indiscriminate, thorough; universal, international, worldwide, global, nationwide, countrywide, coast-to-coast. ANTONYMS partial, piecemeal.

▸ verb *snow blanketed the mountains* COVER, coat, carpet, overlay; cloak, shroud, swathe, envelop; *literary* mantle.

**blare** verb *sirens blared* BLAST, sound loudly, trumpet, bray, clamor, boom, blat, roar, thunder, bellow, resound. ANTONYM murmur.

▸ noun *the blare of the siren* BLAST, trumpeting, clamor, boom, roar, thunder, bellow, blat. ANTONYM murmur.

**blaspheme** verb *would you dare to blaspheme in the House of* *the Lord?* SWEAR, curse, take the Lord's name in vain; *informal* cuss; *archaic* execrate.

**blasphemous** adjective *a blasphemous mock communion* SACRILEGIOUS, profane, irreligious, irreverent, impious, ungodly, godless. ANTONYM reverent.

**blasphemy** noun *the nuns would punish me at least three times a week for my blasphemy* PROFANITY, sacrilege, irreligion, irreverence, taking the Lord's name in vain, swearing, curse, cursing, impiety, desecration; *archaic* execration. ANTONYM reverence.

**blast** noun **1** *the blast from the bomb* SHOCK WAVE, pressure wave.

**2** *Friday's blast killed two people* EXPLOSION, detonation, discharge, burst.

**3** *a sudden blast of cold air* GUST, rush, gale, squall, wind, draft, waft, puff.

**4** *the shrill blast of the trumpets* BLARE, wail, roar, screech, shriek, hoot, honk, beep.

**5** *we had a blast* GOOD TIME, ball, riot.

▸ verb **1** *bombers were blasting enemy airfields* BLOW UP, bomb, blow to pieces, dynamite, shell, explode.

**2** *guns were **blasting away*** FIRE, shoot, blaze, let fly, discharge.

**3** *he blasted his horn* HONK, beep, toot, sound.

**4** *radios blasting out pop music* BLARE, boom, roar, thunder, bellow, pump, shriek, screech.

**5** *informal the opposition blasted the government over the deal.* See BERATE.

PHRASE: **blast off** *the rocket blasted off at 8:02* BE LAUNCHED, take off, lift off, leave the ground, become airborne, take to the air.

**blatant** adjective *it was a blatant lie* FLAGRANT, glaring, obvious, undisguised, unconcealed, open; shameless, barefaced, naked, unabashed, unashamed, unblushing, brazen. ANTONYMS inconspicuous, shamefaced.

**blaze** noun **1** *firemen fought the blaze* FIRE, flames, conflagration, inferno, holocaust; forest fire, wildfire, bush fire.

**2** *a blaze of light* GLARE, gleam, flash, burst, flare, streak, radiance, brilliance, beam.

▸ verb **1** *the fire blazed for hours* BURN, be alight, be on fire, be in flames, flame.

**2** *headlights blazed* SHINE, flash, flare, glare, gleam, glint, dazzle, glitter, glisten.

**blazon** verb *their name is blazoned across the sails* DISPLAY, exhibit, present, spread, emblazon, plaster; announce, proclaim. See note at ANNOUNCE.

**bleach** verb *the blinds had been bleached by the sun* TURN WHITE, whiten, turn pale, blanch, lighten, fade, decolorize, peroxide. ANTONYM darken.

▸ noun *a bottle of bleach* chlorine bleach; *trademark* Clorox.

**bleak** adjective **1** *a bleak landscape* BARE, exposed, desolate, stark, desert, lunar, open, empty, windswept; treeless, without vegetation, denuded. ANTONYM lush.

**2** *the future is bleak* UNPROMISING, unfavorable, unpropitious, inauspicious; discouraging, disheartening, depressing, dreary, dim, gloomy, black, dark, grim, hopeless, somber. ANTONYM promising.

**3** *a bleak wind* COLD, bitter, biting, raw, freezing, icy.

**bleary** adjective *his eyes were bleary from exhaustion* BLURRED, blurry, unfocused; fogged, clouded, dull, misty, watery, rheumy; *archaic* blear. ANTONYM clear.

**bleed** verb **1** *his arm was bleeding* LOSE BLOOD, hemorrhage.

**2** *the doctor bled him* DRAW BLOOD FROM; *Medicine* exsanguinate; *archaic* phlebotomize.

**3** *one color bled into another* FLOW, run, seep, filter, percolate, leach.

**4** *sap was bleeding from the trunk* FLOW, run, ooze, seep, exude, weep.

**5** *the country was **bled dry** by poachers* DRAIN, sap, deplete, milk, exhaust.

**6** *my heart **bleeds for** them* GRIEVE FOR, ache for, sorrow for, mourn for, lament for, feel for, suffer for; sympathize with, pity.

**blemish** noun **1** *not a blemish marred her skin* IMPERFECTION, flaw, defect, fault, deformity, discoloration, disfigurement; bruise, scar, pit, pock, pimple, blackhead, wart, scratch, cut, gash; mark, streak, spot, smear, speck, blotch, smudge, smut; birthmark, mole; *Medicine* stigma.

**2** *the mayor's record is not without blemish* DEFECT, fault, failing, flaw, imperfection, foible, vice; shortcoming, weakness, deficiency, limitation; taint, blot, stain, dishonor, disgrace. ANTONYM virtue.

▸ verb **1** *nothing blemished the coast* MAR, spoil, impair, disfigure, blight, deface, mark, scar; ruin. ANTONYM enhance.

**2** *his reign has been blemished by controversy* SULLY, tarnish, besmirch, blacken, blot, taint; spoil, mar, ruin, disgrace, damage, degrade, dishonor; *formal* vitiate.

**blend** verb **1** *blend the ingredients until smooth* MIX, mingle, combine, merge, fuse, meld, coalesce, integrate, intermix; stir, whisk, fold in; *technical* admix; *literary* commingle.

**2** *the new buildings blend with the older ones* HARMONIZE, go (well), fit (in), be in tune, be compatible; coordinate, match, complement.

▸ noun *a blend of bananas, raisins, and ginger* MIXTURE, mix, combination, amalgamation, amalgam, union, marriage, fusion, meld, synthesis, concoction; *technical* admixture.

**bless** verb **1** *the chaplain blessed the couple* ASK/INVOKE GOD'S FAVOR FOR, give a benediction for; CONSECRATE, sanctify, dedicate (to God), make holy, make sacred; *formal* hallow. ANTONYM curse.

**2** *bless the name of the Lord* PRAISE, worship, glorify, honor, exalt, pay homage to, venerate, reverence, hallow; *archaic* magnify.

3 *the gods* ***blessed*** *us* ***with*** *magical voices* ENDOW WITH, bestow with, furnish with, accord, give, favor with, grace with; confer on; *literary* endue with.

4 *I bless the day you came here* GIVE THANKS FOR, be grateful for, thank; appreciate. ANTONYM rue.

**blessed** adjective 1 *a blessed place* HOLY, sacred, hallowed, consecrated, sanctified; ordained, canonized, beatified. ANTONYM cursed.

2 *blessed are the meek* FAVORED, fortunate, lucky, privileged, enviable, happy. ANTONYM wretched.

**blessing** noun 1 *may God give us his blessing* PROTECTION, favor. ANTONYM condemnation.

2 *a special blessing from the priest* BENEDICTION, invocation, prayer, intercession; grace. ANTONYM anathema.

3 *she gave the plan her blessing* SANCTION, endorsement, approval, approbation, favor, consent, assent, agreement; backing, support; *informal* thumbs up, OK, nod.

4 *it was a blessing they didn't have far to go* GODSEND, boon, advantage, benefit, help, bonus, plus; stroke of luck, unmixed blessing, (lucky) break, windfall; *literary* benison. ANTONYM affliction.

**blight** noun 1 *potato blight* DISEASE, canker, infestation, fungus, mildew, mold.

2 *the blight of aircraft noise* AFFLICTION, scourge, bane, curse, plague, menace, misfortune, woe, trouble, ordeal, trial, nuisance, pest. ANTONYM blessing.

▸ verb 1 *a tree blighted by leaf curl* INFECT, mildew; kill, destroy.

2 *scandal blighted the careers of several politicians* RUIN, wreck, spoil, mar, frustrate, disrupt, undo, end, scotch, destroy, shatter, devastate, demolish; *informal* mess up, foul up, stymie.

**blind** adjective 1 *he has been blind since birth* SIGHTLESS, unsighted, visually impaired, visionless, unseeing; partially sighted, purblind; *informal* as blind as a bat. ANTONYM sighted.

2 *the government must be blind* IMPERCEPTIVE, unperceptive, insensitive, slow, obtuse, uncomprehending; stupid, unintelligent; *informal* dense, dim, thick, dumb, dopey, dozy. ANTONYM perceptive.

3 *he was* ***blind to*** *her shortcomings* UNMINDFUL OF, mindless of, careless of, heedless of, oblivious to, insensible to, unconcerned about, indifferent to. ANTONYM mindful.

4 *blind acceptance of conventional opinion* UNCRITICAL, unreasoned, unthinking, unconsidered, mindless, undiscerning, indiscriminate. ANTONYM discerning.

5 *a blind rage* IMPETUOUS, impulsive, uncontrolled, uncontrollable, wild, unrestrained, immoderate, intemperate, irrational, unbridled.

▸ verb 1 *he was blinded in a car crash* MAKE BLIND, deprive of sight, render sightless; put someone's eyes out.

2 *he was blinded by his faith* DEPRIVE OF JUDGMENT, deprive of perception, deprive of reason, deprive of sense.

3 *they try to blind you with science* OVERAWE, intimidate, daunt, deter, discourage, cow, subdue, dismay; disquiet, discomfit, unsettle, disconcert; disorient, stun, stupefy, confuse, bewilder, bedazzle, confound, perplex, overwhelm; *informal* faze, psych out.

▸ noun 1 *a window blind* SHADE, screen, sunshade, shutter, curtain, awning, canopy; louver, jalousie; Venetian blind, miniblind, vertical blind.

2 *some crook had sent the basketball tickets as a blind* DECEPTION, smokescreen, front, facade, cover, pretext, masquerade, feint, camouflage; trick, ploy, ruse, machination.

**blindly** adverb *they blindly followed Moscow policy* UNCRITICALLY, unthinkingly, mindlessly, indiscriminately.

**blink** verb 1 *his eyes did not blink* flutter, flicker, wink, bat.

2 *several red lights began to blink* FLASH, flicker, wink.

3 *no one even blinks at the estimated cost* BE SURPRISED, look twice; *informal* boggle.

4 *after a tense standoff, the union blinked* BACK DOWN, give in, knuckle under, submit, relent.

**bliss** noun 1 *she gave a sigh of bliss* JOY, happiness, pleasure, delight, ecstasy, elation, rapture, euphoria. See note at RAPTURE. ANTONYM misery.

2 *religions promise perfect bliss after death* BLESSEDNESS, benediction, beatitude, glory, heavenly joy, divine happiness; heaven, paradise. ANTONYM hell.

**blister** noun 1 *a blister on each heel* vesicle, vesication; pustule, abscess.

2 *check for blisters in the wall covering* BUBBLE, swelling, bulge, protuberance.

**blistering** adjective 1 *blistering heat* INTENSE, extreme, ferocious, fierce; SCORCHING, searing, blazing, burning, fiery; *informal* boiling, baking, roasting, sweltering. ANTONYMS mild, icy.

2 *a blistering attack on the government* SAVAGE, vicious, fierce, bitter, harsh, scathing, devastating, caustic, searing, vitriolic. ANTONYM mild.

3 *a blistering pace* VERY FAST, breakneck; *informal* blinding. ANTONYM leisurely.

**blithe** adjective 1 *a blithe disregard for the rules* CASUAL, indifferent, unconcerned, unworried, untroubled, uncaring, careless, heedless, thoughtless; nonchalant, blasé. ANTONYM thoughtful.

2 *literary his blithe, smiling face* HAPPY, cheerful, jolly, merry, joyful, joyous, blissful, ecstatic, euphoric, elated; *dated* gay. ANTONYM sad.

**blitz** noun 1 *the 1940 blitz on London* BOMBARDMENT, bombing, onslaught, barrage; attack, assault, raid, strike, blitzkrieg.

2 *an expensive new marketing blitz* CAMPAIGN, effort, operation, undertaking.

**blizzard** noun SNOWSTORM, whiteout, snow squall, snowfall; nor'easter, northeaster.

**blob** noun **1** *a blob of cold gravy* DROP, droplet, globule, bead, bubble; *informal* glob.

**2** *a blob of ink* SPOT, dab, blotch, blot, dot, smudge; *informal* splotch.

**bloc** noun *a free-trade bloc* ALLIANCE, coalition, federation, confederation, league, union, partnership, axis, body, association, group.

**block** noun **1** *a block of cheese* CHUNK, hunk, lump, wedge, cube, brick, slab, bar, piece.

**2** *an apartment block* BUILDING, complex, structure, development.

**3** *a block of shares* BATCH, group, set, quantity.

**4** *a block to Third World development* OBSTACLE, bar, barrier, impediment, hindrance, check, hurdle, stumbling block, handicap, deterrent. ANTONYM aid.

**5** *a block in the pipe* BLOCKAGE, obstruction, stoppage, clog, congestion, occlusion, clot.

▸ verb **1** *weeds can block drainage ditches* CLOG (UP), stop up, choke, plug, obstruct, gum up, dam up, congest, jam, close; *informal* gunge up; *technical* occlude. ANTONYM open.

**2** *picket lines blocked access to the factory* HINDER, hamper, obstruct, impede, inhibit, restrict, limit; halt, stop, bar, check, prevent. ANTONYM facilitate.

**3** *he blocked a shot on the goal line* STOP, deflect, fend off, hold off, repel, parry, repulse.

PHRASES: **block something off** *the bridge was blocked off* CLOSE UP, shut off, seal off, barricade, bar, obstruct.
**block something out** *trees blocked out the light* CONCEAL, keep out, blot out, exclude, obliterate, blank out, stop.

**blockade** noun **1** *a naval blockade of the island* SIEGE; *rare* besiegement.

**2** *they erected blockades in the streets* BARRICADE, barrier, roadblock; obstacle, obstruction.

▸ verb *rebels blockaded the capital* BARRICADE, block off, shut off, seal; BESIEGE, surround.

**blockage** noun *a blockage of leaves in the storm drain* OBSTRUCTION, stoppage, block, occlusion, clog, congestion.

**blockhead** noun *informal*. See IDIOT.

**blood** noun **1** *he had lost too much blood* PLASMA, vital fluid, gore; *literary* lifeblood, ichor.

**2** *a woman of noble blood* ANCESTRY, lineage, bloodline, descent, parentage, family, birth, extraction, origin, genealogy, heritage, stock, kinship.

**blood-curdling** adjective *a blood-curdling scream* TERRIFYING, frightening, bone-chilling, spine-tingling, chilling, hair-raising, horrifying, alarming; eerie, sinister, horrible; *informal* spooky.

**bloodless** adjective **1** *a bloodless revolution* NONVIOLENT, peaceful, peaceable, pacifist. ANTONYMS bloody, violent.

**2** *his face was bloodless* ANEMIC, pale, wan, pallid, ashen, colorless, chalky, waxen, white, gray, pasty, drained, drawn, deathly. ANTONYM ruddy.

**3** *a bloodless production* FEEBLE, spiritless, lifeless, listless, halfhearted, unenthusiastic, lukewarm. ANTONYM powerful.

**bloodshed** noun *another day of bloodshed in Beirut* SLAUGHTER, massacre, killing, wounding; carnage, butchery, bloodletting, bloodbath; violence, fighting, warfare; *literary* slaying.

**bloodthirsty** adjective *bloodthirsty Vikings* MURDEROUS, homicidal, violent, vicious, barbarous, barbaric, savage, brutal, cutthroat; fierce, ferocious, inhuman.

**bloody** adjective **1** *his bloody nose* BLEEDING.

**2** *bloody medical waste* BLOODSTAINED, blood-soaked, gory; *archaic* sanguinary.

**3** *a bloody civil war* VICIOUS, ferocious, savage, fierce, brutal, murderous, barbarous, gory; *archaic* sanguinary.

**4** *Brit. informal* *a bloody nuisance!* See DAMNED sense 2.

**bloom** noun **1** *orchid blooms* FLOWER, blossom, floweret, floret.

**2** *a girl in the bloom of youth* PRIME, perfection, acme, peak, height, heyday; salad days.

**3** *the bloom of her skin* RADIANCE, luster, sheen, glow, freshness; BLUSH, rosiness, pinkness, color.

▸ verb **1** *the geraniums bloomed* FLOWER, blossom, open; mature. ANTONYM wither.

**2** *their health bloomed in the mountain air* FLOURISH, thrive, prosper, progress, burgeon; *informal* be in the pink. ANTONYM decline.

**blossom** noun *pink blossoms* FLOWER, bloom, floweret, floret.

▸ verb **1** *the trilliums have blossomed* BLOOM, flower, open, unfold; mature. ANTONYM fade.

**2** *the whole region had blossomed* DEVELOP, grow, mature, progress, evolve; flourish, thrive, prosper, bloom, burgeon. ANTONYM decline.

PHRASE: **in blossom** *the cactus is in blossom* IN FLOWER, flowering, blossoming, blooming, in (full) bloom, abloom, open, out; *formal* inflorescent.

**blot** noun **1** *an ink blot* SPOT, dot, mark, blotch, smudge, patch, dab; *informal* splotch.

**2** *the only blot on a clean campaign* BLEMISH, taint, stain, blight, flaw, fault; disgrace, dishonor.

▸ verb **1** *blot the excess water* SOAK UP, absorb, sponge up, mop up; dry up/out; dab, pat.

**2** *he had blotted our name forever* TARNISH, taint, stain, blacken, sully, mar; dishonor, disgrace, besmirch. ANTONYM honor.

PHRASE: **blot something out** **1** *Mary blotted out her picture* ERASE, obliterate, delete, efface, rub out, blank out, expunge, eradicate; cross out, strike out, wipe out.

2 *clouds were starting to blot out the stars* CONCEAL, hide, obscure, exclude, obliterate; shadow, eclipse.

**blotch** noun 1 *pink flowers with dark blotches* PATCH, smudge, dot, spot, blot, dab, daub; *informal* splotch.

2 *his face was covered in blotches* PATCH, mark, freckle, birthmark, discoloration, eruption, nevus.

▸ verb *her face was blotched and swollen* SPOT, mark, smudge, streak, blemish.

**blow** verb 1 *the icy wind blew around us* GUST, bluster, puff, blast, roar, rush, storm.

2 *his ship was blown on to the rocks* SWEEP, carry, toss, drive, push, force.

3 *leaves blew across the road* DRIFT, flutter, waft, float, glide, whirl, move.

4 *he blew a smoke ring* EXHALE, puff, breathe out; emit, expel, discharge, issue.

5 *he blew a trumpet* SOUND, blast, toot, pipe, trumpet; play.

6 *a rear tire had blown* BURST, explode, blow out, split, rupture, puncture.

7 *informal he blew his money on gambling* SQUANDER, waste, misspend, throw away, fritter away, go through, lose, lavish, dissipate, use up; spend recklessly; *informal* splurge.

8 *informal don't blow this opportunity* SPOIL, ruin, bungle, mess up, fudge, muff; WASTE, lose, squander; *informal* botch, screw up, foul up.

9 *his cover was blown* EXPOSE, reveal, uncover, disclose, divulge, unveil, betray, leak.

▸ noun 1 *a blow on the head* KNOCK, BANG, hit, punch, thump, smack, crack, rap, karate chop; *informal* whack, thwack, bonk, bash, clout, sock, wallop.

2 *losing his wife must have been a blow* SHOCK, surprise, bombshell, thunderbolt, jolt; calamity, catastrophe, disaster, upset, setback.

3 *a blow on the guard's whistle* TOOT, blast, blare; whistle.

PHRASES: **blow out** 1 *the matches will not blow out in a strong wind* BE EXTINGUISHED, go out, be put out, stop burning.

2 *the front tire blew out.* See BLOW verb sense 6.

3 *the windows blew out* SHATTER, rupture, crack, smash, splinter, disintegrate; burst, explode, fly apart; *informal* bust.
**blow something out** *blow the candles out* EXTINGUISH, put out, snuff, douse, quench, smother.
**blow over** *the storm will blow over soon* ABATE, subside, drop off, lessen, ease (off), let up, diminish, fade, dwindle, slacken, recede, tail off, peter out, pass, die down, fizzle out; *dated* remit.
**blow up** 1 *a truckload of shells blew up* EXPLODE, detonate, go off, ignite, erupt.

2 *he blows up over every little thing* LOSE ONE'S TEMPER, get angry, rant and rave, go berserk, flare up, erupt; *informal* go mad, go crazy, go wild, hit the roof, fly off the handle.

3 *a crisis blew up* BREAK OUT, erupt, flare up, boil over; emerge, arise.

**blow something up** 1 *they blew the plane up* BOMB, blast, destroy; explode, detonate.

2 *blow up the balloons* INFLATE, pump up, fill up, puff up, swell, expand.

3 *I blew the picture up on a photocopier* ENLARGE, magnify, expand, increase.
**blow out of proportion** *it was an innocent passing remark that he's blown out of proportion* EXAGGERATE, overstate, overstress, overestimate, magnify, amplify; aggrandize, embellish, elaborate.

**blowout** noun 1 *the steering is automatic in the event of blowouts* PUNCTURE, flat tire, burst tire; *informal* flat.

2 *informal this meal is our last real blowout* FEAST, banquet, celebration, party; *informal* shindig, do, binge.

3 *the game turned into a 17–3 blowout* ROUT, whitewash, walkover, landslide.

**bludgeon** noun *hooligans wielding bludgeons* CUDGEL, club, stick, truncheon, baton; nightstick, billy club, blackjack.

▸ verb *he was bludgeoned to death* BATTER, cudgel, club, beat, thrash; clobber, pummel.

**blue** adjective 1 *bright blue eyes* sky blue, azure, cobalt, sapphire, navy, powder blue, midnight blue, Prussian blue, electric blue, indigo, royal blue, ice-blue, baby blue, air force blue, robin's egg blue, peacock blue, ultramarine, aquamarine, steel blue, slate blue, cyan; *chiefly Brit.* Oxford blue, Cambridge blue; *literary* cerulean.

2 *informal Mom was feeling a bit blue* DEPRESSED, down, sad, unhappy, melancholy, miserable, gloomy, dejected, dispirited, downhearted, downcast, despondent, low, glum; *informal* down in the dumps. ANTONYM happy.

**blueprint** noun 1 *blueprints of the aircraft* PLAN, design, diagram, drawing, sketch, map, layout, representation.

2 *a blueprint for similar measures in other countries* MODEL, plan, template, framework, pattern, example, guide, prototype, pilot.

**blues** plural noun *informal a fit of blues* DEPRESSION, sadness, unhappiness, melancholy, misery, sorrow, gloom, dejection, despondency, despair; the doldrums, the dumps, a blue funk.

**bluff**[1] noun *this threat was dismissed as a bluff* DECEPTION, front, subterfuge, pretense, posturing, sham, fake, deceit, feint, hoax, facade, fraud, charade; trick, ruse, scheme, machination; *informal* put-on.

▸ verb 1 *they are bluffing to hide their guilt* PRETEND, sham, fake, feign, lie, hoax, pose, posture, masquerade, dissemble.

2 *I managed to bluff the board into believing me* DECEIVE, delude, mislead, trick, fool, hoodwink, dupe, hoax, beguile, gull; *informal* con, kid.

**bluff**[2] adjective *a bluff man* PLAIN-SPOKEN, straightforward, blunt, direct, no-nonsense, frank, open, candid, forthright, unequivocal; hearty, genial, good-natured; *informal* upfront. See note at BRUSQUE.

**bluff**[3] noun *an impregnable high bluff* CLIFF, promontory, ridge, headland, crag, bank, height, peak, escarpment, scarp, overhang; *rare* eminence.

**blunder** noun *he shook his head at his blunder* MISTAKE, error, gaffe, slip, oversight, faux pas, misstep, infelicity; *informal* botch, slip-up, boo-boo, blooper, boner, flub. See note at MISTAKE.

▸ verb **1** *the government admitted it had blundered* MAKE A MISTAKE, err, miscalculate, bungle, trip up, be wrong; *informal* slip up, screw up, blow it, goof.

**2** *she blundered down the steps* STUMBLE, lurch, stagger, flounder, struggle, fumble, grope.

**blunt** adjective **1** *a blunt knife* UNSHARPENED, dull, worn, edgeless. ANTONYM sharp.

**2** *the leaf is broad with a blunt tip* ROUNDED, flat, obtuse, stubby. ANTONYM pointed.

**3** *a blunt message* STRAIGHTFORWARD, frank, plain-spoken, candid, direct, bluff, forthright, unequivocal; BRUSQUE, abrupt, curt, terse, bald, brutal, harsh; stark, unadorned, undisguised, unvarnished; *informal* upfront. See note at BRUSQUE. ANTONYM subtle.

▸ verb **1** *ebony blunts tools very rapidly* DULL, make less sharp. ANTONYM sharpen.

**2** *age hasn't blunted my passion for life* DULL, deaden, dampen, numb, weaken, sap, cool, temper, allay, abate; diminish, reduce, decrease, lessen, deplete. ANTONYM intensify.

**blur** verb **1** *tears blurred her vision* CLOUD, fog, obscure, dim, make hazy, unfocus, soften; *literary* bedim; *archaic* blear. ANTONYMS sharpen, focus.

**2** *movies blur the difference between villains and victims* OBSCURE, make vague, confuse, muddle, muddy, obfuscate, cloud, weaken.

▸ noun *a blur on the horizon* INDISTINCT SHAPE, smudge; haze, cloud, mist.

**blurred** adjective *a blurred photograph* INDISTINCT, blurry, fuzzy, hazy, misty, foggy, shadowy, faint; unclear, vague, indefinite, unfocused, obscure, nebulous.

**blurt** PHRASE: **blurt something out** *he blurted out his story* BURST OUT WITH, exclaim, call out; DIVULGE, disclose, reveal, betray, let slip, give away; *informal* blab, gush, let on, spill the beans (about), let the cat out of the bag (about).

**blush** verb *Joan blushed at the compliment* REDDEN, turn/go pink, turn/go red, flush, color, burn up; feel shy, feel embarrassed.

▸ noun *a blush spread across his face* FLUSH, rosiness, pinkness, bloom, (high) color.

**bluster** verb **1** *he started blustering about the general election* RANT, rave, thunder, bellow, sound off; be overbearing; *informal* throw one's weight around/about.

**2** *storms bluster in from the sea* BLAST, gust, storm, roar, rush.

▸ noun *his bluster turned to cooperation* RANTING, thundering, hectoring, bullying; bombast, bravado, bumptiousness, braggadocio.

**blustery** adjective *a blustery autumn day* STORMY, gusty, blowy, windy, squally, wild, tempestuous, turbulent; howling, roaring. ANTONYM calm.

**board** noun **1** *a wooden board* PLANK, beam, panel, slat, batten, timber, lath.

**2** *the board of directors* COMMITTEE, council, panel, directorate, commission, executive, group.

**3** *your room and board will be free* FOOD, meals, provisions, diet, table, bread, rations; keep, maintenance; *informal* grub, nosh, eats, chow.

▸ verb **1** *he boarded the aircraft* GET ON, go aboard, enter, mount, ascend; embark, emplane, entrain; catch; *informal* hop on.

**2** *a number of students boarded with them* LODGE, live, reside, be housed, room; *informal* be put up.

**3** *they run a facility for boarding dogs* ACCOMMODATE, lodge, take in, put up, house; keep, feed, cater for, billet.

PHRASE: **board something up/over** *shoreline residents are boarding up their windows* COVER UP/OVER, close up, shut up, seal.

**boast** verb **1** *his mother had been boasting about him* BRAG, crow, swagger, swank, gloat, show off; exaggerate, overstate; *informal* talk big, blow one's own horn, lay it on thick.

**2** *the hotel boasts a fine restaurant* POSSESS, have, own, enjoy, pride oneself/itself on.

▸ noun **1** *everyone has tired of listening to your boast* BRAG, self-praise; exaggeration, overstatement, grandiloquence, fanfaronade.

**2** *the hall is the boast of the county* PRIDE, joy, wonder, delight, treasure, gem.

**boastful** adjective *in the first debate he came across as aggressive and boastful* BRAGGING, swaggering, bumptious, puffed up, full of oneself; cocky, conceited, arrogant, egotistical; *informal* swanky, bigheaded, blowhard; *literary* vainglorious. ANTONYM modest.

**boat** noun *a rowing boat* VESSEL, craft, watercraft, ship; *literary* keel.

▸ verb *they were out boating for hours* SAIL, yacht, paddle, row, cruise.

**bob** verb *the bottle bobbed in the water* MOVE UP AND DOWN, bounce, toss, skip, dance, jounce; wobble, jiggle, joggle, jolt, jerk; NOD, incline, dip; wag, waggle.

**bode** verb *it's that unsettling kind of silence that bodes danger* AUGUR, portend, herald, be a sign of, warn of, foreshadow, be an omen of, presage, indicate, signify, promise, threaten, spell, denote, foretell; prophesy, predict; *literary* betoken, forebode.

**bodily** adjective *bodily sensations* PHYSICAL, corporeal, corporal, somatic, fleshly; concrete, real, actual, tangible. ANTONYMS spiritual, mental.

**body** noun **1** *the human body* FIGURE, frame, form, physique, anatomy, skeleton; soma; *informal* bod.

**2** *he was hit by shrapnel in the head and body* TORSO, trunk.

**3** *the body was exhumed* CORPSE, carcass, skeleton, remains; *informal* stiff; *Medicine* cadaver.

**4** *the body of the essay* MAIN PART, central part, core, heart.

**5** *a body of water* EXPANSE, mass, area, stretch, tract, sweep, extent.

**6** *a growing body of evidence* QUANTITY, amount, volume, collection, mass, corpus.

**7** *the representative body of the employers* ASSOCIATION, organization, group, party, company, society, circle, syndicate, guild, corporation, contingent.

**8** *add body to your hair* FULLNESS, thickness, substance, bounce, lift, shape. PHRASE: **body and soul** *these young men and women belong to the Corps, body and soul* COMPLETELY, entirely, totally, utterly, fully, thoroughly, wholeheartedly, unconditionally, to the hilt.

THE RIGHT WORD **body, cadaver, carcass, corpse, cremains, remains**

The problem of what to call the human **body** after it has departed this life is a delicate one. Although a *body* can be either dead or alive, human or animal, a **corpse** is most definitely a dead human body and a **carcass** is the body of a dead animal. The issue has been confused, of course, by the figurative use of *carcass* as a term of contempt (*"Get your carcass out of bed and come down here!"*). While *carcass* is often used humorously, there's nothing funny about *corpse*, a no-nonsense term for a lifeless physical body (*the battlefield was littered with corpses*). A funeral director is likely to prefer the term **remains**, which is a euphemism for the body of the deceased (*he had his wife's remains shipped home for burial*), or **cremains**, if the body has been cremated. A medical student, on the other hand, is much more likely to use the term **cadaver**, which is a corpse that is dissected in a laboratory for scientific study.

**bog** noun *the bogs were alive with chirring insects and croaking frogs* MARSH, swamp, muskeg, mire, quagmire, morass, slough, fen, wetland, bogland. PHRASE: **bogged down** *bogged down with endless paperwork* MIRED, stuck, entangled, ensnared, embroiled; hampered, hindered, impeded, delayed, stalled, detained; swamped, overwhelmed.

**boggle** verb **1** *this data makes the mind boggle* MARVEL, wonder.

**2** *it boggles my mind* BAFFLE, astonish, astound, amaze, stagger, overwhelm.

**bogus** adjective *a bogus insurance claim | a bogus lottery ticket* FAKE, spurious, false, fraudulent, sham, deceptive; COUNTERFEIT, forged, feigned; make-believe, dummy, pseudo, phony, pretend, fictitious. ANTONYM genuine.

**bohemian** noun *he is an artist and a Bohemian* NONCONFORMIST, free spirit, dropout; hippie, beatnik; *informal* boho. ANTONYM conservative.

▸ adjective *a Bohemian student life* UNCONVENTIONAL, nonconformist, unorthodox, avant-garde, irregular, offbeat, alternative; artistic; *informal* boho, artsy, artsy-fartsy, way-out. ANTONYM conventional.

**boil**[1] verb **1** *boil the potatoes* BRING TO A BOIL, simmer, parboil, poach; cook.

**2** *the soup is boiling* SIMMER, bubble, stew.

**3** *a huge cliff with the sea boiling below* CHURN, seethe, froth, foam; *literary* roil.

▸ noun *bring the stock to a boil* BOILING POINT, rolling boil.

PHRASES: **boil something down** *you have to boil down a lot of tomatoes to make just a few tablespoons of tomato paste* CONDENSE, reduce, concentrate, distill, thicken, compress. ANTONYM dilute.

**boil down to** *it all boils down to how much money you're willing to spend* COME DOWN TO, amount to, add up to, be in essence.

**boil**[2] noun *a boil on her neck* SWELLING, spot, pimple, blister, pustule, eruption, carbuncle, wen, abscess, ulcer; *technical* furuncle.

**boiling** adjective **1** *boiling water* AT BOILING POINT, at 212 degrees Fahrenheit, at 100 degrees Celsius/centigrade; very hot, piping hot; bubbling. ANTONYMS freezing, ice-cold.

**2** *informal* *it was a boiling day* VERY HOT, scorching, blistering, sweltering, sultry, torrid; *informal* broiling, roasting, baking, sizzling. ANTONYMS cold, freezing.

**boisterous** adjective **1** *a boisterous game of handball* LIVELY, animated, exuberant, spirited, rambunctious; rowdy, unruly, wild, uproarious, unrestrained, undisciplined, uninhibited, uncontrolled, rough, disorderly, riotous, knockabout; noisy, loud, clamorous. See note at VOCIFEROUS. ANTONYMS restrained, quiet.

**2** *a boisterous wind* BLUSTERY, gusty, windy, stormy, wild, squally, tempestuous; howling, roaring; *informal* blowy. ANTONYM calm.

**bold** adjective **1** *bold adventurers* DARING, intrepid, brave, courageous, valiant, valorous, fearless, dauntless, audacious, daredevil; adventurous, heroic, plucky, spirited, confident, assured; *informal* gutsy, spunky, feisty; *literary* temerarious. ANTONYMS timid, unadventurous.

**2** *don't be so bold in public* IMPUDENT, insolent, impertinent, brazen, brash, disrespectful, presumptuous, forward; cheeky, fresh.

**3** *a bold pattern* STRIKING, vivid, bright, strong, eye-catching, prominent; gaudy, lurid, garish. ANTONYM pale.

**4** *departure times are in bold type* HEAVY, thick, pronounced, conspicuous. ANTONYMS light, roman.

THE RIGHT WORD **bold, aggressive, audacious, bumptious, brazen, intrepid, presumptuous**

Is walking up to an attractive stranger and asking him or her to have dinner with you tonight a **bold** move or merely an **aggressive** one? Both words suggest assertive, confident behavior that is a little on the shameless side, but *bold* has a wider range of application. It can suggest self-confidence that borders on impudence (*to be so bold as to call the president by his first name*), but it can also be used to describe a daring temperament that is either courageous or defiant (*a bold investigator* *who would not give up*). *Aggressive* behavior, on the other hand, usually falls within a narrower range, somewhere between menacing (*aggressive attacks on innocent villagers*) and just plain pushy (*an aggressive salesperson*). **Brazen** implies a defiant lack of modesty (*a brazen stare*), and **presumptuous** goes even further, suggesting over-confidence to the point of causing offense (*a presumptuous request for money*). **Bumptious** behavior can also be offensive, but it is usually associated with the kind of cockiness that can't be helped (*a bumptious young upstart*). An **audacious** individual is bold to the point of recklessness (*an audacious explorer*), which brings it very close in meaning to **intrepid**, suggesting fearlessness in the face of the unknown (*the intrepid settlers of the Great Plains*).

---

**bolster** verb *an occasional word of thanks would really bolster the staff's morale* STRENGTHEN, reinforce, boost, fortify, renew; support, sustain, buoy up, prop up, shore up, maintain, aid, help; augment, increase. ANTONYM undermine.

**bolt** noun **1** *the bolt on the shed door* BAR, LOCK, catch, latch, fastener, deadbolt.

**2** *nuts and bolts* RIVET, pin, peg, screw.

**3** *a bolt whirred over my head* ARROW, quarrel, dart, shaft.

**4** *a bolt of lightning* FLASH, thunderbolt, shaft, streak, burst, flare.

**5** *Mark made a bolt for the door* DASH, dart, run, sprint, leap, bound.

**6** *a bolt of cloth* ROLL, reel, spool; quantity, amount.

▸ verb **1** *he bolted the door* LOCK, bar, latch, fasten, secure.

**2** *the lid was bolted down* RIVET, pin, peg, screw; fasten, fix.

**3** *Anna bolted from the room* DASH, dart, run, sprint, hurtle, careen, rush, fly, shoot, bound; flee; *informal* tear, scoot, leg it.

**4** *he* ***bolted down*** *his breakfast* GOBBLE UP, gulp down, wolf down, guzzle (down), devour; *informal* demolish, polish off, shovel in/down, scarf up.

PHRASES: **a bolt (from) out of the blue** *the department shutdown came as a bolt out of the blue* SHOCK, surprise, bombshell, thunderbolt, revelation.
**bolt upright** *in Scene 2, the corpse is supposed to sit suddenly bolt upright* STRAIGHT, rigidly, stiffly. ANTONYM slouching.

**bomb** noun **1** *they saw bombs bursting on the runway* EXPLOSIVE, incendiary (device); missile, projectile; *dated* blockbuster, bombshell.

**2** *countries with the bomb* NUCLEAR WEAPONS, nuclear bombs, atom bombs, A-bombs.

**3** *informal their next film was a bomb* FAILURE, flop, megaflop, fiasco, bust, dud, washout, debacle, turkey, dog, clunker.

▸ verb **1** *their headquarters were bombed* BOMBARD, blast, shell, blitz, strafe, pound; attack, assault; blow up, destroy, demolish, flatten, devastate.

**2** *informal the show bombed at the box office* FAIL, flop, fall flat, founder.

**bombard** verb **1** *gun batteries bombarded the islands* SHELL, pound, blitz, strafe, bomb; assail, attack, assault, batter, blast, pelt. See note at ATTACK.

**2** *we were bombarded with information* INUNDATE, swamp, flood, deluge, snow under; besiege, overwhelm.

**bona fide** adjective *the table is definitely an imitation Chippendale, but the chairs are bona fide | a bona fide endorsement* AUTHENTIC, genuine, real, true, actual; legal, legitimate, lawful, valid, proper; *informal* legit, the real McCoy. See note at GENUINE. ANTONYM bogus.

**bonanza** noun *those grisly murders of 1872 turned into quite a bonanza for the town, which has thrived as a center of tourism ever since* WINDFALL, godsend, boon, blessing, bonus, stroke of luck, jackpot.

**bond** noun **1** *the bond between Moira and her son* RELATIONSHIP, tie, link, friendship, fellowship, partnership, association, affiliation, alliance, attachment.

**2** *the prisoner struggled with his bonds* CHAINS, fetters, shackles, manacles, irons, restraints.

**3** *you've broken your bond* PROMISE, pledge, vow, oath, word (of honor), guarantee, assurance; agreement, contract, pact, bargain, deal.

▸ verb *the extensions are bonded to your hair* JOIN, fasten, fix, affix, attach, secure, bind, stick, fuse.

**bondage** noun *our own freedom is not so gratifying when we must look upon the bondage of others* SLAVERY, enslavement, servitude, subjugation, subjection, oppression, domination, exploitation, persecution; enthrallment, thraldom; *historical* serfdom, vassalage. ANTONYM liberty.

**bonus** noun **1** *the extra space is a real bonus* BENEFIT, advantage, boon, blessing, godsend, stroke of luck, asset, attraction; *informal* plus, pro, perk, gravy; *formal* perquisite. ANTONYM disadvantage.

**2** *she's on a good salary and she gets a bonus* GRATUITY, gift, present, reward, prize, lagniappe; incentive, inducement, handout; *informal* sweetener. See note at PRESENT3 . ANTONYM penalty.

**bony** adjective *his pale, bony face* GAUNT, ANGULAR, skinny, thin, lean, spare, spindly, skin-and-bones, skeletal, emaciated, underweight; *informal* like a bag of bones; *rare* starveling, macilent, gracile. ANTONYM plump.

**book** noun **1** *Nadine and Ian have recommended some good books* VOLUME, tome, publication, title; novel, storybook, anthology, treatise, manual; paperback, hardback, pocket book, e-book.

**2** *he scribbled in his book* NOTEBOOK, notepad, pad, memo pad, exercise book, workbook; logbook, ledger, journal, diary.

**3** *enter a $400 deposit in the book | the council had to balance its books* LEDGER, account book, record book, balance sheet; (**books**) ACCOUNTS, records.

▸ verb **1** *Dan and Veronica booked a table at the restaurant* RESERVE, make a reservation for, prearrange, order; *formal* bespeak.

**2** *we booked a number of events for the festival* ARRANGE, program, schedule, timetable, line up, pencil in, slate.

PHRASE: **by the book** *he's a cop who does everything by the book* ACCORDING TO THE RULES, within the law, lawfully, legally, legitimately; honestly, fairly; *informal* on the level, fair and square.

**bookish** adjective *Swann was always the bookish one in our group* STUDIOUS, scholarly, academic, intellectual, highbrow, erudite, learned, lettered, educated, well-read, knowledgeable; cerebral, serious, earnest; pedantic.

**boom** noun **1** *the boom of the thunder* REVERBERATION, resonance, thunder, echoing, crashing, drumming, pounding, roar, rumble, explosion.

**2** *an unprecedented boom in sales* UPTURN, upsurge, upswing, increase, advance, growth, boost, escalation, improvement, spurt. ANTONYM slump.

▸ verb **1** *thunder boomed overhead* REVERBERATE, resound, resonate; rumble, thunder, blare, echo; crash, roll, clap, explode, bang.

**2** *a voice boomed at her* BELLOW, roar, thunder, shout, bawl; *informal* holler. ANTONYM whisper.

**3** *the market continued to boom* FLOURISH, burgeon, thrive, prosper, progress, improve, pick up, expand, mushroom, snowball. ANTONYM slump.

**boomerang** verb *their tax-evading scheme boomeranged, and now they're facing serious legal trouble* BACKFIRE, recoil, reverse, rebound, ricochet; be self-defeating; *informal* blow up in one's face.

**boon** noun *their help was such a boon* BLESSING, godsend, bonus, plus, benefit, advantage, help, aid, asset; stroke of luck, windfall. ANTONYM curse.

**boor** noun *a civilized affair guaranteed to separate the boors from the gentlemen* LOUT, oaf, ruffian, thug, yahoo, barbarian, Neanderthal, brute, beast, lubber; *informal* clod, roughneck, troglodyte, pig, peasant.

**boorish** adjective *we will not tolerate such boorish behavior from our officers* COARSE, uncouth, rude, ill-bred, ill-mannered, uncivilized, unrefined, rough, thuggish, loutish, oafish, lubberly, lumpen; vulgar, unsavory, gross, brutish, Neanderthal; *informal* cloddish. ANTONYM refined.

**boost** noun **1** *a boost to one's morale | just the boost I needed* UPLIFT, lift, spur, encouragement, help, inspiration, stimulus, pick-me-up; *informal* shot in the arm.

**2** *a boost in sales* INCREASE, expansion, upturn, upsurge, upswing, rise, escalation, improvement, advance, growth, boom; hike, jump. ANTONYM decrease.

▸ verb **1** *he phoned to boost her spirits* IMPROVE, raise, uplift, increase, enhance, encourage, heighten, help, promote, foster, stimulate, invigorate, revitalize; *informal* buck up.

**2** *they used advertising to boost sales* INCREASE, raise, escalate, improve, strengthen, inflate, push up, promote, advance, foster, stimulate, maximize; facilitate, help, assist, aid; jump-start; *informal* hike, bump up. ANTONYM decrease.

**boot** noun *muddy boots.*

▸ verb **1** *his shot was booted away by the goalkeeper* KICK, punt; propel, drive.

**2** ***boot up*** *your computer* START UP, fire up, reboot.

PHRASE: **give someone the boot** *informal.* See DISMISS sense 1.

**booth** noun **1** *booths for different vendors* STALL, stand, kiosk.

**2** *a phone booth* CUBICLE, kiosk, box, enclosure.

**booty** noun *divvying up the booty* LOOT, plunder, pillage, haul, spoils, stolen goods, ill-gotten gains, pickings; *informal* swag.

**bordello** noun *she's currently on Broadway, playing the feisty madam of a bordello* BROTHEL, whorehouse; *informal* cathouse; *euphemistic* massage parlor; *dated* bawdy house, house of ill repute; *Law, dated* disorderly house.

**border** noun **1** *the border of a medieval manuscript* EDGE, MARGIN, perimeter, circumference, periphery; rim, fringe, verge; sides.

**2** *the Canadian border* FRONTIER, boundary; borderline, perimeter; marches, bounds.

▸ verb **1** *the fields were bordered by hedges* SURROUND, enclose, encircle, circle, edge, fringe, bound, flank.

**2** *the straps are bordered with gold braid* EDGE, fringe, hem; trim, pipe, finish.

**3** *the property* ***bordered on*** *the state park* ADJOIN, abut, be next to, be adjacent to, be contiguous with, touch, join, meet, reach.

PHRASE: **border on** *his tone bordered on contempt* VERGE ON, approach, come close to, be comparable to, approximate to, be tantamount to, be similar to, resemble.

THE RIGHT WORD **border, brim, brink, edge, margin, rim, verge**

A **border** is the part of a surface that is nearest to its boundary (*a rug with a flowered border*)—although it may also refer to the boundary line itself (*the border between Vermont and New Hampshire*). A **margin** is a *border* of a definite width that is usually distinct in appearance from what it encloses; but unlike *border*, it usually refers to the blankness or emptiness that surrounds something (*the margin on a printed page*). While *border* and *margin* usually refer to something that is circumscribed, **edge** may refer to only a part of the perimeter (*the edge of the lawn*) or the line where two planes or surfaces converge (*the edge of the table*). *Edge* can also connote sharpness (*the edge of a knife*) and can be used metaphorically to suggest tension, harshness, or keenness (*there was an edge in her voice; take the edge off their nervousness*). **Verge** may also be used metaphorically to describe the extreme limit of something (*on the verge of a nervous breakdown*), but in a more literal sense, it sometimes is used of the line or narrow space that marks the limit or termination of something (*the verge of a desert or forest*). **Brink** denotes the edge of something very steep or an abrupt division between land and water (*the brink of the river*), or metaphorically the very final limit before an abrupt change (*on the brink of disaster*). **Rim** and **brim** apply only to things that are circular or curving. But while *rim* describes the edge or lip of a rounded or cylindrical shape (*the rim of a glass*), *brim* refers to the inner side of the rim when the container is completely full (*a cup filled to the brim with steaming coffee*). However, when one speaks of the *brim* of a hat, it comes closer to the meaning of *margin* or *border*.

---

**bore** verb **1** *the movie bored us* STULTIFY, pall on, stupefy, weary, tire, fatigue, send to sleep, leave cold; bore to death, bore to tears; *informal* turn off.

**2** *bore a hole in the ceiling* DRILL, pierce, perforate, puncture, punch, cut; tunnel, burrow, mine, dig, gouge, sink.

▸ noun *you can be such a bore* TEDIOUS PERSON/THING, tiresome person/thing, dull person/thing, yawn, bother, nuisance, wet blanket.

**boredom** noun *his eyes were glassy with boredom* WEARINESS, ennui, apathy, unconcern; frustration, dissatisfaction, restlessness, restiveness, lethargy, lassitude; tedium, dullness, monotony, repetitiveness, flatness, dreariness; *informal* deadliness.

**boring** adjective *a boring one-man play* TEDIOUS, dull, monotonous, repetitive, unrelieved, unvaried, unimaginative, uneventful; characterless, featureless, colorless, lifeless, insipid, uninteresting, unexciting, uninspiring, unstimulating; unreadable, unwatchable; jejune, flat, bland, dry, stale, tired, banal, lackluster, stodgy, vapid, monochrome, dreary, humdrum, mundane; mind-numbing, wearisome, tiring, tiresome, irksome, trying, frustrating; *informal* deadly, ho-hum, dullsville, dull as dishwater, plain-vanilla.

**borrow** verb **1** *we borrowed a lot of money* take as a loan; lease, hire; *informal* scrounge, bum, cadge, mooch. ANTONYM lend.

**2** *informal they "borrowed" all of his tools* TAKE, help oneself to, appropriate, commandeer, abscond with, carry off; steal, purloin; *informal* filch, rob, swipe, nab, rip off, lift, "liberate", pinch, heist.

**3** *adventurous chefs borrow foreign techniques* ADOPT, take on, acquire, embrace. ANTONYM impart.

**bosom** noun **1** *the gown was set low over her bosom* BUST, chest; breasts, mammary glands; *informal* boobs, knockers, mammaries, bazooms.

**2** *literary the family took Gill into its bosom* PROTECTION, shelter, safety, refuge; heart.

**3** *love was kindled within his bosom* HEART, breast, soul, core, spirit.

▸ adjective *bosom friends* CLOSE, intimate, inseparable, faithful, constant, devoted; good, best, favorite.

**boss** noun *the boss of a large company* HEAD, chief, director, president, principal, chief executive, chair, manager; supervisor, foreman, overseer, controller; employer, owner, proprietor; *informal* number one, kingpin, boss man, boss lady, top dog, bigwig, big cheese, head honcho, big kahuna.

▸ verb *you have no right to* ***boss me around*** ORDER AROUND, dictate to, lord it over, bully, push around, domineer, dominate, pressurize, browbeat; call the shots for, lay down the law on, bulldoze, walk all over, railroad.

**bossy** adjective *we're hiding from his bossy sister* DOMINEERING, pushy, overbearing, imperious, officious, high-handed, authoritarian, dictatorial, controlling; *informal* high and mighty. ANTONYM submissive.

**botch** verb *examiners botched the test scores* BUNGLE, mismanage, mishandle, make a mess of, mess up, make a hash of, muff, fluff, foul up, screw up, flub.

**bother** verb **1** *no one bothered her* DISTURB, trouble, inconvenience, pester, badger, harass, molest, plague, nag, hound, harry, annoy, upset, irritate, hassle, bug, get in someone's hair, get on someone's case, get under a someone's skin, ruffle someone's feathers, rag on, ride.

**2** *the incident was too small to bother about* MIND, care, concern oneself, trouble oneself, worry oneself; *informal* give a damn, give a hoot.

**3** *there was something bothering him* WORRY, trouble, concern, perturb, disturb, disquiet, disconcert, unnerve; fret, upset, distress, agitate, gnaw at, weigh down; *informal* rattle.

▸ noun **1** *I don't want to put you to any bother* TROUBLE, effort, exertion, inconvenience, fuss, pains.

**2** *the food was such a bother to cook* NUISANCE, hassle, pain in the neck, headache, pest, palaver, rigmarole, job, trial, drag, chore, inconvenience, trouble, problem.

**bottle** noun **1** *a bottle of whiskey* carafe, flask, decanter, canteen, vessel, pitcher, flagon, magnum, carboy, demijohn.

**2** *informal a world blurred by the bottle.* See ALCOHOL. PHRASE: **bottle something up** *don't bottle up your emotions* SUPPRESS, repress, restrain, withhold, hold in, rein in, inhibit, smother, stifle, contain, conceal, hide, cork, keep a lid on.

**bottleneck** noun *there's a bottleneck at the intersection of I-91 and I-84* TRAFFIC JAM, jam, congestion, tie-up, holdup, snarl-up, gridlock, logjam, constriction, narrowing, restriction, obstruction, blockage, choke point.

**bottom** noun **1** *the bottom of the stairs* FOOT, lowest part, lowest point, base; foundation, substructure, underpinning. ANTONYM top.

**2** *the bottom of the car* UNDERSIDE, underneath, undersurface, undercarriage, underbelly.

**3** *the bottom of Lake Ontario* FLOOR, bed. ANTONYM surface.

**4** *the bottom of the standings in the Eastern League* LOWEST POSITION, lowest level. ANTONYM top.

**5** *I enjoyed the horseback ride, except for my sore bottom* REAR, rear end, backside, seat, buttocks, rump, derrière; *informal* cheeks, behind, butt, fanny, keister, tush, tail, buns, caboose, duff, heinie, ass, fundament, posterior, gluteus maximus, sit-upon, stern; *Brit. informal* bum, arse; *Anatomy* nates.

**6** *police got to the bottom of the mystery* ORIGIN, cause, root, source, basis, foundation; heart, kernel; essence.

▸ adjective *she sat on the bottom step* LOWEST, last, bottommost; *technical* basal. ANTONYMS highest, top.

**bottomless** adjective **1** *the bottomless pits of hell* FATHOMLESS, unfathomable, endless, infinite, immeasurable.

**2** *George's appetite was bottomless* UNLIMITED, limitless, boundless, infinite, inexhaustible, endless, never-ending, everlasting; vast, huge, enormous. ANTONYM limited.

**bough** noun *snow-laden pine boughs* BRANCH, limb, arm, offshoot.

**boulder** noun *a natural formation of boulders* ROCK, stone.

**boulevard** noun *the third right off of the boulevard* AVENUE, street, road, drive, thoroughfare, way.

**bounce** verb **1** *the ball bounced* REBOUND, spring back, ricochet, jounce, carom; reflect.

**2** *William bounced down the stairs* BOUND, leap, jump, spring, bob, hop, skip, trip, prance.

▸ noun **1** *he reached the door in a single bounce* BOUND, leap, jump, spring, hop, skip.

**2** *she had lost her bounce* VITALITY, vigor, energy, vivacity, liveliness, animation, sparkle, verve, spirit, enthusiasm, dynamism; cheerfulness, happiness, buoyancy, optimism; exuberance, ebullience; *informal* get-up-and-go, pep, zing.

PHRASE: **bounce back** *despite our optimistic predictions, sales never bounced back* RECOVER, revive, rally, pick up, be on the mend; perk up, cheer up, brighten up, liven up; *informal* buck up.

**bouncing** adjective *can we expect a bouncing economy within the next five years?* VIGOROUS, thriving, flourishing, blooming; HEALTHY, strong, robust, fit, in fine fettle; *informal* in the pink.

**bound**[1] adjective **1** *his bound ankles* TIED, chained, fettered, shackled, secured, tied up.

**2** *she seemed bound to win* CERTAIN, sure, very likely, destined, fated, doomed.

**3** *you're bound by the law to keep quiet* OBLIGATED, obliged, compelled, required, constrained, forced.

**4** *the unrest was* ***bound up*** *with the region's economic stagnation* CONNECTED, linked, tied, united, allied.

**bound**[2] verb *hares bound in the fields* LEAP, jump, spring, bounce, hop; skip, bob, dance, prance, gambol, gallop.

▸ noun *he crossed the room with a single bound* LEAP, jump, spring, bounce, hop.

**bound**[3] verb **1** *corporate freedom is bounded by law* LIMIT, restrict, confine, circumscribe, demarcate, delimit.

**2** *the garden is bounded by a hedge* ENCLOSE, surround, encircle, circle, border; close in/off, hem in. PHRASE: **out of bounds** *this building is out of bounds for all nonmilitary personnel | harassment of our waitresses is strictly out of bounds* OFF LIMITS, restricted, closed off; forbidden, banned, proscribed, illegal, illicit, unlawful, unacceptable, taboo; *informal* no go; *rare* non licet.

**boundary** noun **1** *the boundary between Alaska and the Yukon Territory* BORDER, frontier, borderline, partition; fenceline.

**2** *the boundary between art and advertising* DIVIDING LINE, divide, division, borderline, cutoff point.

**3** *the boundary of his estate* BOUNDS, confines, limits, margins, edges, fringes; border, periphery, perimeter.

**4** (**boundaries**) *the boundaries of acceptable behavior* LIMITS, parameters, bounds, confines; ambit, compass.

**boundless** adjective *the pups have boundless energy* LIMITLESS, unlimited, unbounded, untold, immeasurable, abundant; inexhaustible, endless, infinite, interminable, unfailing, ceaseless, everlasting. ANTONYM limited.

**bountiful** adjective **1** *their bountiful patron* GENEROUS, magnanimous, munificent, openhanded, unselfish, unstinting, lavish; benevolent, beneficent, charitable, philanthropic; *rare* eleemosynary, benignant. ANTONYMS mean, stingy.

**2** *a bountiful supply of fresh food* ABUNDANT, plentiful, ample, copious, bumper, superabundant, inexhaustible, prolific, profuse; lavish, generous, handsome, rich; *informal* whopping; *literary* plenteous. ANTONYM meager.

**bouquet** noun **1** *her bridal bouquet* BUNCH OF FLOWERS, posy, nosegay, spray, corsage, boutonniere.

**2** *bouquets go to Ann for a well-planned event* COMPLIMENT, commendation, tribute, accolade; praise, congratulations, applause.

**3** *the Chardonnay has a fine bouquet* AROMA, nose, smell, fragrance, perfume, scent, odor. See note at SMELL.

**bourgeois** adjective **1** *a bourgeois family* MIDDLE-CLASS, propertied; CONVENTIONAL, conservative, conformist; provincial, suburban, small-town; *informal* white-bread. ANTONYMS proletarian, unconventional.

**2** *bourgeois decadence* CAPITALISTIC, materialistic, money-oriented, commercial. ANTONYM communist.

▸ noun *a proud bourgeois* MEMBER OF THE MIDDLE CLASS, property owner.

**bout** noun **1** *a bout of dysentery* ATTACK, fit, spasm, paroxysm, convulsion, eruption, outburst; period, session, spell.

**2** *he is fighting his fifth bout* CONTEST, match, fight, prizefight, competition, event, meeting.

**bovine** adjective **1** *large, bovine eyes* COWLIKE, calflike, taurine.

**2** *an expression of bovine amazement* STUPID, slow, ignorant, unintelligent, imperceptive, vacuous, mindless, witless, doltish, dumb, dense, dim, dimwitted, dopey, birdbrained, peabrained, dozy.

▸ noun *a beautiful bovine* COW, heifer, bull, bullock, calf, ox, bison.

**bow**[1] verb **1** *the officers bowed* INCLINE THE BODY, incline the head, nod, salaam, kowtow, curtsy, bob, genuflect.

**2** *the government* ***bowed to*** *foreign pressure* YIELD TO, submit to, give in to, surrender to, succumb to, capitulate to, defer to, conform to; comply with, accept, heed, observe.

▸ noun *a perfunctory bow* OBEISANCE, salaam, bob, curtsy, nod; *archaic* reverence.

PHRASE: **bow out** *Elwood decided to bow out before the New Hampshire primary* WITHDRAW, resign, retire, step down, pull out, back out; give up, quit, leave, pack it in.

**bow**2 noun *the bow of the tanker* PROW, front, stem, nose, head, cutwater.

**bow**3 noun **1** *she tied a bow in her hair* LOOP, knot; ribbon.

**2** *he bent the rod into a bow* ARC, curve, bend; crescent, half-moon.

**3** *an archer's bow* LONGBOW, crossbow; *Archery* recurve.

**bowdlerize** verb *the English translation was bowdlerized beyond recognition* EXPURGATE, censor, blue-pencil, cut, edit; purge, sanitize, water down; *informal* clean up.

**bowel** noun **1** (also **bowels**) *a disorder of the bowels* INTESTINE(S), entrails, innards, small intestine, large intestine, colon; *informal* guts, insides, viscera.

**2** (**bowels**) *the bowels of the ship* INTERIOR, inside, core, belly; depths, recesses; *informal* innards.

**bower** noun *a rose-scented bower* ARBOR, pergola, grotto, alcove, sanctuary; gazebo.

**bowl** noun **1** *she cracked two eggs into a bowl* DISH, basin, pot, crock, mortar; container, vessel, receptacle; *rare* jorum, porringer.

**2** *the Hollywood Bowl* STADIUM, arena, amphitheater, colosseum.

▸ verb PHRASE: **bowl someone over 1** *the explosion bowled us over* KNOCK DOWN/OVER, fell, floor, prostrate.

**2** *informal I have been bowled over by your generosity* OVERWHELM, astound, astonish, overawe, awe, dumbfound, stagger, stun, amaze, daze, shake, take aback, leave aghast; *informal* floor, flabbergast, blow away.

**box**1 noun *a box of cigars* CARTON, pack, packet; case, crate, chest, coffer, casket; container, receptacle.

▸ verb *Muriel* ***boxed up*** *his clothes* PACKAGE, pack, parcel, wrap, bundle, crate, bin.

PHRASE: **box something/someone in** *those two vans have boxed in my car* HEM IN, fence in, close in, shut in; trap, confine, imprison, intern; surround, enclose, encircle, circle.

**box**2 verb **1** *he began boxing professionally* FIGHT, prizefight, spar; brawl; *informal* scrap.

**2** *he boxed my ears* STRIKE, smack, cuff, hit, thump, slap, swat, punch, jab, wallop; *informal* belt, bop, sock, clout, clobber, whack, slug; *literary* swinge, smite.

**boxer** noun *a professional boxer* FIGHTER, pugilist, prizefighter, kick-boxer; *informal* bruiser, scrapper.

**boy** noun *the tallest boy in our class* LAD, schoolboy, male child, youth, young man, laddie, stripling. See also CHILD.

**boycott** verb *they boycotted the elections* SPURN, snub, shun, avoid, abstain from, wash one's hands of, turn one's back on, reject, veto. ANTONYM support.

▸ noun *a boycott of imported lumber* BAN, veto, embargo, prohibition, sanction, restriction; avoidance, rejection, refusal.

**boyfriend** noun *her old boyfriend was at the reunion* LOVER, sweetheart, beloved, darling, dearest, young man, man friend, man, guy, escort, suitor; PARTNER, significant other, companion; *informal* fella, (main) squeeze, flame, steady, toy boy, boy toy, sugar daddy; *literary* swain; *dated* beau; *archaic* paramour.

**boyish** adjective *his boyish good looks* YOUTHFUL, young, childlike, adolescent, teenage; immature, juvenile, infantile, childish, babyish, puerile.

**brace** noun *the aquarium is supported by wooden braces* PROP, beam, joist, batten, rod, post, strut, stay, support, stanchion, bracket.

▸ verb **1** *the plane's wing is braced by a system of rods* SUPPORT, shore up, prop up, hold up, buttress, underpin; strengthen, reinforce.

**2** *he braced his hand on the railing* STEADY, secure, stabilize, fix, poise; tense, tighten.

**3** *brace yourself for disappointment* PREPARE, get ready, gear up, nerve, steel, galvanize, gird, strengthen, fortify; *informal* psych oneself up.

**bracelet** noun *gold bracelets* BANGLE, band, circlet, armlet, wristlet, anklet.

**bracing** adjective *a bracing jog through the snowy field* INVIGORATING, refreshing, stimulating, energizing, exhilarating, reviving, restorative, rejuvenating, revitalizing, rousing, fortifying, strengthening; FRESH, brisk, keen.

**bracket** noun **1** *each speaker is fixed on a separate bracket* SUPPORT, prop, stay, batten, joist; rest, mounting, rack, frame.

**2** *put the words in brackets* PARENTHESIS, square bracket; *Printing* brace.

**3** *a higher tax bracket* GROUP, category, grade, classification, set, division, order.

**brackish** adjective *several species of crab inhabit the brackish water* SLIGHTLY SALTY, saline, salt, briny.

**brag** verb *he liked to brag about his business connections* BOAST, crow, swagger, swank, bluster, gloat, show off; blow one's own horn, sing one's own praises; *informal* talk big, lay it on thick.

**braggart** noun *Jeff is a prodigious braggart and a liar* BOASTER, bragger, swaggerer, egotist; *informal* big head, loudmouth, show-off, showboat, blowhard.

**braid** noun *her hair is in braids* PLAIT, pigtail, twist; cornrows, dreadlocks.

▸ verb **1** *she began to braid her hair* PLAIT, entwine, intertwine, interweave, weave, twist, twine.

**2** *the sleeves are braided in scarlet* TRIM, edge, border, pipe, hem, fringe.

**brain** noun **1** *the disease attacks certain cells in the brain* CEREBRUM, cerebral matter, encephalon; *informal* gray matter.

**2** (also **brains**) *success requires brains as well as brawn* INTELLIGENCE, intellect, brainpower, IQ, cleverness, wit(s), reasoning, wisdom, acumen, discernment, judgment, understanding, sense; *informal* gray matter, savvy; smarts.

**3** *informal* (**brains**) *Janice is the brains of the family* CLEVER PERSON, intellectual, intellect, thinker, mind, scholar; genius, Einstein; *informal* egghead, brainiac, rocket scientist. ANTONYM dunce.

**brainy** adjective *informal behind every successful machine is a brainy scientist* CLEVER, intelligent, smart, bright, brilliant, gifted; intellectual, erudite, academic, scholarly, studious, bookish. ANTONYM stupid.

**brake** noun *a brake on research* CURB, check, restraint, restriction, constraint, control, limitation.

▸ verb *she braked at the traffic lights* SLOW DOWN, slow, decelerate, reduce speed, stop. ANTONYM accelerate.

**branch** noun **1** *the branches of a tree* BOUGH, limb, arm, offshoot.

**2** *a branch of the river* TRIBUTARY, feeder, side stream, fork, side channel, influent.

**3** *the judicial branch of government* DIVISION, subdivision, section, subsection, subset, department, sector, part, side, wing.

**4** *the corporation's New York branch* OFFICE, bureau, agency; subsidiary, affiliate, offshoot, satellite.

▸ verb **1** *the place where the road branches* FORK, bifurcate, divide, subdivide, split.

**2** *narrow paths* ***branched off*** *the road* DIVERGE FROM, deviate from, split off from; fan out from, radiate from.

PHRASE: **branch out** *the company is branching out into the European market* EXPAND, open up, extend; diversify, broaden one's horizons.

**brand** noun **1** *a new brand of margarine* MAKE, line, label, marque; type, kind, sort, variety; trade name, trademark, proprietary name.

**2** *her particular brand of humor* TYPE, kind, sort, variety, class, category, genre, style, ilk, stripe.

**3** *the brand on a sheep* IDENTIFICATION, marker, earmark.

▸ verb **1** *the letter M was branded on each animal* MARK, stamp, burn, sear.

**2** *the scene was branded on her brain* ENGRAVE, stamp, etch, imprint.

**3** *the media branded us as communists* STIGMATIZE, mark out; denounce, discredit, vilify; label.

**brandish** verb *brandishing a sword* FLOURISH, wave, shake, wield; swing, swish; display, flaunt, show off.

**brash** adjective *a brash man* SELF-ASSERTIVE, pushy, cocksure, cocky, self-confident, arrogant, bold, audacious, brazen, bumptious, overweening, puffed-up; forward, impudent, insolent, rude. ANTONYM meek.

**brassy** adjective *we're not at all pleased with your brassy new friends* BRAZEN, forward, bold, self-assertive, pushy, cocksure, cocky, cheeky, saucy, brash; shameless, immodest; loud, vulgar, showy, ostentatious; *informal* flashy. ANTONYMS demure, modest.

**brat** noun *now that I've met his two little brats, I'm not so sure about this relationship* BADLY BEHAVED CHILD, spoiled child; rascal, wretch, imp, scamp, scapegrace, whippersnapper; minx; *informal* monster, horror, hellion; *archaic* jackanapes.

**bravado** noun *his bravado seems so phony and overplayed* BOLDNESS, swaggering, bluster; machismo; boasting, bragging, bombast, braggadocio; *informal* showing off.

**brave** adjective **1** *they put up a brave fight* COURAGEOUS, valiant, valorous, intrepid, heroic, lionhearted, bold, fearless, gallant, daring, plucky, audacious; unflinching, unshrinking, unafraid, dauntless, doughty, mettlesome, stouthearted, spirited; *informal* game, gutsy, spunky. ANTONYM cowardly.

**2** *literary his medals made a brave show* SPLENDID, magnificent, impressive, fine, handsome.

▸ noun *dated an Indian brave* WARRIOR, soldier, fighter.

▸ verb *fans braved freezing temperatures to see them play* ENDURE, put up with, bear, withstand, weather, suffer, go through; face, confront, defy.

**bravery** noun *the bravery witnessed here today will never be forgotten* COURAGE, valor, intrepidity, nerve, daring, fearlessness, audacity, boldness, dauntlessness, stoutheartedness, heroism; backbone, grit, true grit, pluck, spine, spirit, mettle; *informal* guts, balls, cojones, spunk.

**bravo** exclamation *chants of "Bravo!" went on for several minutes* WELL DONE, splendid, congratulations, brava; encore, take a bow; *informal* attaboy, attagirl.

**brawl** noun *a drunken brawl* FIGHT, skirmish, scuffle, tussle, fray, melee, free-for-all, donnybrook; fisticuffs; *informal* scrap, set-to.

▸ verb *he ended up brawling with photographers* FIGHT, skirmish, scuffle, tussle, exchange blows, grapple, wrestle; *informal* scrap.

**brawn** noun *he has certainly developed his brawn since high school* PHYSICAL STRENGTH, muscle(s), burliness, huskiness, toughness, power, might; vigor, punch; *informal* beef, beefiness.

**brawny** adjective *the brawny young hunks at the gym* STRONG, muscular, muscly, well-built, hard-bodied, powerful, mighty, Herculean, strapping, burly, sturdy, husky, rugged; hefty, solid; *informal* beefy, hunky. ANTONYMS puny, weak.

**bray** verb **1** *a donkey brayed* NEIGH, whinny, hee-haw.

**2** *Billy brayed with laughter* ROAR, bellow, trumpet.

**brazen** adjective *brazen defiance* BOLD, SHAMELESS, unashamed, unabashed, unembarrassed; defiant, impudent, impertinent, cheeky, saucy, insolent, in-your-face; barefaced, blatant, flagrant. See note at BOLD. ANTONYM timid.

PHRASE: **brazen it out** *we were shaking in our boots, but we brazened it out* PUT ON A BOLD FRONT, stand one's ground, be defiant, be unrepentant, be unabashed.

**breach** noun **1** *a clear breach of the regulations* CONTRAVENTION, violation, infringement, infraction, transgression, neglect; *Law* delict.

**2** *a breach between government and Church* RIFT, schism, division, gulf, chasm; disunion, estrangement, discord, dissension, disagreement; split, break, rupture, scission.

**3** *a breach in the sea wall* BREAK, rupture, split, crack, fracture; opening, gap, hole, fissure.

▸ verb **1** *the river breached its bank* BREAK (THROUGH), burst (through), rupture; *informal* bust (through).

**2** *the changes breached union rules* BREAK, contravene, violate, infringe; defy, disobey, flout, fly in the face of; *Law* infract.

**bread** noun **1** *have some bread with your soup* rye (bread), pumpernickel, French bread, Italian bread, focaccia, pita (bread), cornbread, soda bread.

**2** *his job puts bread on the table.* See FOOD sense 1.

**3** *informal I hate doing this, but I need the bread.* See MONEY sense 1.

**breadth** noun **1** *a breadth of 100 meters* WIDTH, broadness, wideness, thickness; span; diameter.

**2** *the breadth of his knowledge* RANGE, extent, scope, depth, reach, compass, scale, degree.

**break** verb **1** *the mirror broke* SHATTER, smash, crack, snap, fracture, fragment, splinter, fall to bits, fall to pieces; split, burst; *informal* bust.

**2** *she had broken her leg* FRACTURE, crack. ANTONYM mend.

**3** *the bite had barely broken the skin* PIERCE, puncture, penetrate, perforate; cut.

**4** *the coffee machine has broken* STOP WORKING, break down, give out, go wrong, malfunction, crash; *informal* go kaput, conk out, go/be on the blink, go/be on the fritz, give up the ghost.

**5** *traders who break the law* CONTRAVENE, violate, fail to observe, fail to comply with, infringe, breach; defy, flout, disobey, fly in the face of. ANTONYMS abide by, keep.

**6** *his concentration was broken* INTERRUPT, disturb, interfere with.

**7** *they broke for coffee* STOP, pause, have a rest, recess; *informal* take a breather, take five. ANTONYM resume.

**8** *a pile of carpets broke his fall* CUSHION, soften the impact of, take the edge off.

**9** *the movie broke box-office records* EXCEED, surpass, beat, better, cap, top, outdo, outstrip, eclipse.

**10** *habits are difficult to break* GIVE UP, relinquish, drop; *informal* kick, shake, quit.

**11** *the strategies used to break the union* DESTROY, crush, quash, defeat, vanquish, overcome, overpower, overwhelm, suppress, cripple; weaken, subdue, cow, undermine.

**12** *her self-control finally broke* GIVE WAY, crack, cave in, yield, go to pieces.

**13** *four thousand dollars wouldn't break him* BANKRUPT, ruin, pauperize.

**14** *he tried to break the news gently* REVEAL, disclose, divulge, impart, tell; announce, release.

**15** *he broke the encryption code* DECIPHER, decode, decrypt, unravel, work out; *informal* figure out.

**16** *the day broke fair and cloudless* DAWN, begin, start, emerge, appear.

**17** *a political scandal broke* ERUPT, break out.

**18** *the weather broke* CHANGE, alter, shift.

**19** *waves broke against the rocks* CRASH, dash, beat, pound, lash.

**20** *her voice broke as she relived the experience* FALTER, quaver, quiver, tremble, shake.

▸ noun **1** *the magazine has been published without a break since 1950* INTERRUPTION, interval, gap, hiatus; discontinuation, suspension, disruption, cutoff; stop, stoppage, cessation.

**2** *a break in the weather* CHANGE, alteration, variation.

**3** *let's have a break* REST, respite, recess; stop, pause; interval, intermission; *informal* breather, time out, down time; coffee break.

**4** *a weekend break* TIME OFF, vacation, holiday, leave, getaway.

**5** *a break in diplomatic relations* RIFT, schism, split, breakup, severance, rupture.

**6** *the actress got her first break in 1951* OPPORTUNITY, chance, opening.

PHRASES: **break away 1** *she attempted to break away* ESCAPE, get away, run away, flee, make off; break free, break loose, get out of someone's clutches; *informal* cut and run.

**2** *a group* ***broke away from*** *the main party* LEAVE, secede from, split off from, separate from, part company with, defect from; *Politics* cross the floor from.

**break down 1** *his van broke down.* See BREAK verb sense 4.

**2** *pay negotiations broke down* FAIL, collapse, founder, fall through, disintegrate; *informal* fizzle out.

**3** *Vicky broke down, sobbing loudly* BURST INTO TEARS; lose control, be overcome, go to pieces, crumble, disintegrate; *informal* crack up, lose it.

**break something down 1** *the police broke the door down* KNOCK DOWN, kick down, smash in, pull down, tear down, demolish.

**2** *break big tasks down into smaller parts* DIVIDE, separate.

**3** *graphs show how the information can be broken down* ANALYZE, categorize, classify, sort out, itemize, organize; dissect.

**break in 1** *thieves broke in and took her checkbook* COMMIT BURGLARY, break and enter; force one's way in.

**2** *"I don't want to interfere," Mrs. Hendry broke in* INTERRUPT, butt in, cut in, interject, interpose, intervene, chime in.

**break someone in** *it's Edgar's responsibility to break in the new cooks* TRAIN, initiate; *informal* show someone the ropes.

**break into 1** *thieves broke into a house on Park Street* BURGLE, burglarize, rob; force one's way into.

**2** *Phil broke into the discussion* INTERRUPT, butt into, cut in on, intervene in.

**3** *he broke into a song* BURST INTO, launch into.

**break off** *the cup handle just broke off* SNAP OFF, come off, become detached, become separated.

**break something off 1** *I broke off a branch from the tree* SNAP OFF, pull off, sever, detach.

**2** *they threatened to break off diplomatic relations* END, terminate, stop, cease, call a halt to, finish, dissolve; SUSPEND, discontinue; *informal* pull the plug on.

**break out 1** *he* ***broke out of*** *the detention center* ESCAPE FROM, abscond from, flee from; get free of.

**2** *fighting broke out* FLARE UP, start suddenly, erupt, burst out.

**break up 1** *the meeting broke up* END, finish, stop, terminate; adjourn; recess.

**2** *the crowd began to break up* DISPERSE, scatter, disband, part company.

**3** *Danny and I broke up last year* SPLIT UP, separate, part, part company; divorce.

**4** *informal* *the whole cast broke up* BURST OUT LAUGHING, crack up, dissolve into laughter.

**break something up 1** *police tried to break up the crowd* DISPERSE, scatter, disband.

**2** *I'm not going to let you break up my marriage* WRECK, ruin, destroy.

**breakable** adjective *pack the breakable items in bubble wrap* FRAGILE, delicate, flimsy, destructible, brittle, easily broken, easily damaged; *formal* frangible. ANTONYM shatterproof.

**breakdown** noun **1** *the breakdown of the negotiations* FAILURE, collapse, disintegration, foundering.

**2** *on the death of her father she suffered a breakdown* NERVOUS BREAKDOWN, collapse; *informal* crack-up.

**3** *the breakdown of the computer system* MALFUNCTION, failure, crash.

**4** *a breakdown of the figures* ANALYSIS, classification, examination, investigation, dissection.

**breaker** noun *breakers crashed against the cliff* WAVE, roller, comber, whitecap; *informal* (big) kahuna.

**break-in** noun *the break-in occurred just before midnight* BURGLARY, robbery, theft, raid, breaking and entering, forced entry, break and enter.

**breakneck** adjective *the breakneck pace of change* EXTREMELY FAST, rapid, speedy, high-speed, lightning, whirlwind.

**breakthrough** noun *the breakthroughs that will lead us to the cure for this disease cannot happen without adequate funding* ADVANCE, development, step forward, success, improvement; discovery, innovation, revolution; progress, headway. ANTONYM setback.

**breakup** noun **1** *the breakup of negotiations* END, dissolution; breakdown, failure, collapse, disintegration.

**2** *their breakup was very amicable* SEPARATION, split, parting, divorce; estrangement, rift.

**breakwater** noun *she found a submerged breakwater, constructed of parallel stone walls filled with rubble* SEA WALL, jetty, barrier, mole, bulwark, groin, pier.

**breast** noun **1** *a baby at her breast* mammary gland, mamma; **(breasts)** BOSOM(S), bust, chest; *informal* boobs, knockers, bazooms, hooters.

**2** *feelings of frustration were rising up in his breast* HEART, bosom, soul, core.

**breath** noun **1** *I took a deep breath* INHALATION, inspiration, gulp of air; exhalation, expiration; *Medicine* respiration.

**2** *a breath of wind* PUFF, waft, faint breeze.

**3** *a breath of scandal* HINT, suggestion, trace, touch, whisper, murmur, suspicion, whiff, undertone.

**4** *there was no breath left in him* LIFE, life force. PHRASE: **take someone's breath away** *his solo on the sax took our breath away* ASTONISH, astound, amaze, stun, startle, stagger, shock, take aback, dumbfound, jolt, shake up; awe, overawe, thrill, flabbergast, blow away, bowl over, stop someone in their tracks, leave someone speechless.

**breathe** verb **1** *she breathed deeply* inhale and exhale, respire, draw breath; puff, pant, blow, gasp, wheeze, huff; *Medicine* inspire, expire.

**2** *at least I'm still breathing* BE ALIVE, be living, live.

**3** *she would breathe new life into the firm* INSTILL, infuse, inject, inspire, impart, imbue.

**4** *"Together at last," she breathed* WHISPER, murmur, purr, sigh, say.

**breather** noun *we could all use a breather* BREAK, REST, respite, breathing space, pause, interval, recess.

**breathless** adjective **1** *Will arrived flushed and breathless* OUT OF BREATH, panting, puffing, gasping, wheezing, hyperventilating; winded, short of breath.

**2** *the crowd was breathless with anticipation* AGOG, openmouthed, waiting with bated breath, on the edge of one's seat, on tenterhooks, in suspense; excited, impatient.

**breathtaking** adjective *the breathtaking view from the tower* SPECTACULAR, magnificent, wonderful, awe-inspiring, awesome, astounding, astonishing, amazing, stunning, incredible; thrilling, exciting; *informal* sensational, out of this world, jaw-dropping; *literary* wondrous.

**breed** verb **1** *elephants breed readily in captivity* REPRODUCE, produce/bear/generate offspring, procreate, multiply, propagate; mate.

**2** *she was born and bred in the village* BRING UP, rear, raise, nurture.

**3** *the political system bred discontent* CAUSE, bring about, give rise to, lead to, produce, generate, foster, result in; stir up; *literary* beget.

▸ noun **1** *a breed of cow* VARIETY, stock, strain; type, kind, sort.

**2** *a new breed of journalist* TYPE, kind, sort, variety, class, brand, genre, generation.

**breeding** noun **1** *the birds pair for breeding* REPRODUCTION, procreation; mating.

**2** *the breeding of laboratory rats* REARING, raising, nurturing.

**3** *her aristocratic breeding* UPBRINGING, rearing; parentage, family, pedigree, blood, birth, ancestry.

**4** *people of rank and breeding* (GOOD) MANNERS, gentility, refinement, cultivation, polish, urbanity; *informal* class. ANTONYMS bad manners, vulgarity.

**breeze** noun **1** *a breeze ruffled the leaves* GENTLE WIND, puff of air, gust, cat's paw; *Meteorology* light air; *literary* zephyr.

**2** *informal getting your child in and out of the seat is a breeze* EASY TASK, child's play, nothing; *informal* piece of cake, cinch, snap, kids' stuff, cakewalk, five-finger exercise, duck soup.

▸ verb *informal Roger breezed into her office* SAUNTER, stroll, sail, cruise.

**breezy** adjective **1** *a bright, breezy day* WINDY, fresh, brisk, airy; blowy, blustery, gusty.

**2** *his breezy manner* JAUNTY, CHEERFUL, cheery, brisk, carefree, easy, casual, relaxed, *informal* , lighthearted, lively, buoyant, blithe spirited, sunny, jovial; *informal* upbeat, bright-eyed and bushy-tailed; *dated* gay.

**brevity** noun **1** *the report is notable for its brevity* CONCISENESS, concision, succinctness, economy of language, pithiness, incisiveness, shortness, compactness. ANTONYM verbosity.

**2** *the brevity of human life* SHORTNESS, briefness, transience, ephemerality, impermanence. ANTONYMS lengthiness, permanence.

**brew** verb **1** *this beer is brewed in Oshkosh* FERMENT, make.

**2** *I'll brew some tea* PREPARE, infuse, make, steep, stew.

**3** *there's trouble brewing* DEVELOP, loom, threaten, impend, be imminent, be on the horizon, be in the offing.

▸ noun **1** *a home brew* BEER, ale.

**2** *a piping hot brew* DRINK, beverage; tea, coffee.

**3** *a dangerous brew of political turmoil and violent conflict* MIXTURE, mix, blend, combination, amalgam, mishmash, hodgepodge.

**bribe** verb *he used his wealth to bribe officials* BUY OFF, pay off, suborn; *informal* grease someone's palm, fix, square.

▸ noun *she accepted bribes* INDUCEMENT, incentive, payola; *informal* payoff, kickback, boodle, sweetener.

**bridal** adjective *the bridal party* WEDDING, nuptial, marriage, matrimonial, marital, conjugal.

**bride** noun *Ben's lovely bride* WIFE, marriage partner; newlywed.

**bridge** noun **1** *a bridge over the river* VIADUCT, overpass, fixed link, aqueduct.

**2** *a bridge between rival groups* LINK, connection, bond, tie.

▸ verb **1** *a walkway bridged the highway* SPAN, cross (over), extend across, traverse, arch over.

**2** *an attempt to bridge the gap between cultures* JOIN, link, connect, unite; straddle; overcome, reconcile.

**bridle** noun *a horse's bridle* HARNESS, headgear; hackamore.

▸ verb **1** *military officials bridled at Washington's insistence that they not buy these Russian-made missiles* BRISTLE, take offense, take umbrage, be affronted, be offended, get angry.

**2** *he bridled his indignation* CURB, restrain, hold back, control, check, rein in/back; suppress, stifle; *informal* keep a/the lid on.

**brief** adjective **1** *a brief account* CONCISE, succinct, short, pithy, incisive, abridged, condensed, compressed, abbreviated, compact, thumbnail, capsule, potted; *formal* compendious. ANTONYMS lengthy, long-winded.

**2** *a brief visit* SHORT, flying, fleeting, hasty, hurried, quick, cursory, perfunctory; temporary, short-lived, momentary, transient; *informal* quickie. ANTONYMS long, lengthy.

**3** *a pair of brief shorts* SKIMPY, scanty, short; revealing.

**4** *the boss was rather brief with him* BRUSQUE, abrupt, curt, short, blunt, sharp.

▸ noun **1** *a lawyer's brief* SUMMARY, case, argument, contention; dossier.

**2** *a brief of our requirements* OUTLINE, summary, synopsis, précis, sketch, digest.

▸ verb *employees were briefed about the decision* INFORM, tell, update, notify, advise, apprise; prepare, prime, instruct; *informal* fill in, clue in, put in the picture.

**briefing** noun *a press briefing* CONFERENCE, meeting, interview; orientation; *informal* backgrounder, Q & A session.

**briefly** adverb **1** *Henry paused briefly* MOMENTARILY, temporarily, for a moment, fleetingly.

**2** *briefly, the plot is as follows* IN SHORT, in brief, to make/cut a long story short, in a word, in sum, in a nutshell, in essence.

**brigade** noun **1** *a brigade of soldiers* UNIT, contingent, battalion, regiment, division, squadron, company, platoon, section, corps, troop.

**2** *the volunteer ambulance brigade* SQUAD, team, group, band, party, crew, force, outfit.

**brigand** noun *literary*. See BANDIT.

**bright** adjective **1** *the bright surface of the metal* SHINING, brilliant, dazzling, beaming, glaring; sparkling, flashing, glittering, scintillating, gleaming, glowing, luminous, radiant; shiny, lustrous, glossy. ANTONYMS dull, dark.

**2** *a bright morning* SUNNY, sunshiny, cloudless, clear, fair, fine. ANTONYMS cloudy, overcast.

**3** *bright crayons* VIVID, brilliant, intense, strong, bold, glowing, rich; gaudy, lurid, garish; COLORFUL, vibrant; *dated* gay. ANTONYM drab.

**4** *a bright guitar sound* CLEAR, vibrant, pellucid; high-pitched.

5 *a bright young graduate* CLEVER, intelligent, quick-witted, smart, canny, astute, intuitive, perceptive; ingenious, resourceful; gifted, brilliant; *informal* brainy. ANTONYMS dimwitted, stupid.

6 *a bright smile* HAPPY, cheerful, cheery, jolly, merry, sunny, beaming; lively, exuberant, buoyant, bubbly, bouncy, perky, chirpy; *dated* gay. ANTONYM cheerless.

7 *a bright future* PROMISING, rosy, optimistic, hopeful, favorable, propitious, auspicious, encouraging, good, golden. ANTONYMS dismal, pessimistic.

▸ adverb *literary the moon shone bright* BRIGHTLY, brilliantly, intensely.

THE RIGHT WORD **bright, brilliant, effulgent, luminous, lustrous, radiant, refulgent, resplendent, shining**

Looking for just the right word to capture the quality of the light on a moonlit night or a summer day? All of these adjectives describe an intense, steady light emanating (or appearing to emanate) from a source. **Bright** is the most general term, applied to something that gives forth, reflects, or is filled with light (*a bright and sunny day*; *a bright star*). **Brilliant** light is even more intense or dazzling (*the brilliant diamond on her finger*), and **resplendent** is a slightly more formal, even poetic, way of describing a striking brilliance (*the sky was resplendent with stars*). Poets also prefer adjectives like **effulgent** and **refulgent**, both of which can be applied to an intense, pervading light, sometimes from an unseen source (*her effulgent loveliness*); but *refulgent* specifically refers to reflected light (*a chandelier of refulgent crystal pendants*). **Radiant** is used to describe the power of giving off light, either literally or metaphorically (*a radiant June day*; *the bride's radiant face*); it describes a steady, warm light that is emitted in all directions. Like *radiant*, **luminous** suggests sending forth light, but light of the glow-in-the-dark variety (*the luminous face of the alarm clock*). While diamonds are known for being *brilliant*, fabrics like satin and surfaces like polished wood, which reflect light and take on a gloss or sheen, are often called **lustrous**. If none of these words captures the exact quality of the light you're trying to describe, you can always join the masses and use **shining**, a word that has been overworked to the point of cliché (*my knight in shining armor*).

**brighten** verb 1 *sunshine brightened the room* ILLUMINATE, light up, lighten, make bright, make brighter, cast/shed light on; *formal* illume.

2 *Sarah* ***brightened up*** *as she thought of her mother's words* CHEER UP, perk up, rally; be enlivened, feel heartened, be uplifted, be encouraged, take heart; *informal* buck up, pep up.

**brilliance** noun 1 *a philosopher of great brilliance* GENIUS, intelligence, wisdom, sagacity, intellect; talent, ability, prowess, skill, expertise, aptitude; flair, finesse, panache; greatness.

2 *the brilliance and beauty of Paris* SPLENDOR, magnificence, grandeur, resplendence.

3 *the brilliance of the sunshine* BRIGHTNESS, vividness, intensity; sparkle, glitter, glittering, glow, blaze, luminosity, radiance.

**brilliant** adjective 1 *a brilliant student* BRIGHT, intelligent, clever, smart, astute, intellectual; gifted, talented, able, adept, skillful; elite, superior, first-class, first-rate, excellent; *informal* brainy. ANTONYM stupid.

2 *his brilliant career* SUPERB, glorious, illustrious, impressive, remarkable, exceptional. ANTONYM unremarkable.

3 *a shaft of brilliant light* BRIGHT, shining, blazing, dazzling, vivid, intense, gleaming, glaring, luminous, radiant; *literary* irradiant, coruscating. See note at BRIGHT. ANTONYMS obscure, dark.

4 *brilliant green* VIVID, intense, bright, bold, dazzling. ANTONYMS dull, dark.

**brim** noun 1 *the brim of his hat* peak, visor, shield, shade; fringe.

2 *the cup was filled to its brim* RIM, lip, brink, edge, margin. See note at BORDER.

**bring** verb 1 *he brought a tray* CARRY, fetch, bear, take; convey, transport, tote; move, haul, shift, lug.

2 *Seth brought his bride to the club* ESCORT, conduct, guide, lead, usher, show, shepherd.

3 *the wind changed and brought rain* CAUSE, produce, create, generate, precipitate, lead to, give rise to, result in; stir up, whip up, promote; *literary* beget.

4 *the police contemplated bringing charges* PUT FORWARD, prefer, lay, submit, present, initiate, institute.

5 *this job brings him a regular salary* EARN, make, fetch, bring in, yield, net, gross, return, produce; command, attract.
PHRASES: **bring about** *the events that brought about her death* CAUSE, produce, give rise to, result in, lead to, occasion, bring to pass; provoke, generate, engender, precipitate, bring on; *formal* effectuate.
**bring around** 1 *she administered CPR and brought him around* WAKE UP, return to consciousness, rouse, bring to.

2 *we would have brought him around, given time* PERSUADE, convince, win over, sway, influence.
**bring back** 1 *the smell brought back memories* REMIND ONE OF, put one in mind of, bring/call to mind, conjure up, evoke, summon up.

2 *bring back capital punishment* REINTRODUCE, reinstate, reestablish, revive, resurrect.
**bring down** 1 *he was brought down by his own teammate* TRIP, knock over, knock down; foul.

2 *I couldn't bear to bring her down* DEPRESS, sadden, upset, get down, dispirit, dishearten, discourage.

3 *we will bring down the price* DECREASE, reduce, lower, cut, drop; *informal* slash.

4 *the unrest brought down the government* UNSEAT, overturn, topple, overthrow, depose, oust.
**bring forward** *why wasn't this brought forward at the last meeting?* PROPOSE, suggest, advance, raise, present, move, submit, lodge.
**bring in** *the event brings in a million dollars each year.* See BRING sense 5.

**bring on** *what could have brought on this fever?* See BRING ABOUT.

**bring out 1** *they were bringing out a new magazine* LAUNCH, establish, begin, start, found, set up, instigate, inaugurate, market; publish, print, issue, produce.

**2** *the shawl brings out the color of your eyes* ACCENTUATE, highlight, emphasize, accent, set off.

**bring oneself to** *she could not bring herself to complain* FORCE ONESELF TO, make oneself, bear to.

**bring up 1** *she and Lenny brought up her brother's four children* REAR, raise, care for, look after, nurture, provide for.

**2** *I wonder if he'll bring up the matter of the grocery bill* MENTION, allude to, touch on, raise, broach, introduce; voice, air, suggest, propose, submit, put forward, bring forward.

**brink** noun **1** *the brink of the abyss* EDGE, verge, margin, rim, lip; border, boundary, perimeter, periphery, limit(s).

**2** *two countries on the brink of war* VERGE, threshold, point, edge. See note at BORDER.

**brisk** adjective **1** *a brisk pace* QUICK, rapid, fast, swift, speedy, hurried; energetic, lively, vigorous. ANTONYMS slow, sluggish.

**2** *business was brisk at the bar* BUSY, bustling, lively, hectic; good. ANTONYM slow.

**3** *a brisk breeze* BRACING, fresh, crisp, invigorating, refreshing, stimulating, energizing; biting, keen, chilly, cold; *informal* nippy. ANTONYM sultry.

**bristle** noun **1** *the bristles on his chin* HAIR, whisker; (**bristles**) stubble, five o'clock shadow; *Zoology* seta/setae.

**2** *a hedgehog's bristles* SPINE, prickle, quill, barb.

▸ verb **1** *the hair on the back of his neck bristled* RISE, stand up, stand on end; *literary* horripilate.

**2** *she bristled at his tone* TAKE OFFENSE, bridle, take umbrage, be affronted, be offended; get angry, be irritated.

**3** *the roof bristled with antennas* ABOUND, overflow, be full, be packed, be crowded, be jammed, be covered; *informal* be thick, be jam-packed, be chock-full.

**bristly** adjective **1** *bristly little bushes* PRICKLY, spiky, thorny, scratchy, brambly.

**2** *the bristly skin of his cheek* STUBBLY, hairy, fuzzy, unshaven, whiskered, whiskery; scratchy, rough, coarse, prickly; *Biology* setaceous, hispid. ANTONYM smooth.

**brittle** adjective **1** *glass is a brittle material* BREAKABLE, fragile, delicate; splintery; *formal* frangible. ANTONYMS flexible, resilient.

**2** *a brittle laugh* HARSH, hard, sharp, grating. ANTONYM soft.

**3** *a brittle young woman* EDGY, anxious, unstable, high-strung, tense, excitable, jumpy, skittish, neurotic; *informal* uptight. ANTONYM relaxed.

**broach** verb **1** *I broached the matter with my parents* BRING UP, raise, introduce, talk about, mention, touch on, air.

**2** *he broached a barrel of beer* PIERCE, puncture, tap; OPEN, uncork; *informal* crack open.

**broad** adjective **1** *a broad flight of steps* WIDE. ANTONYM narrow.

**2** *the leaves are two inches broad* WIDE, across, in breadth, in width.

**3** *a broad expanse of prairie* EXTENSIVE, vast, immense, great, spacious, expansive, sizable, sweeping, rolling.

**4** *a broad range of opportunities* COMPREHENSIVE, inclusive, extensive, wide, all-embracing, eclectic, unlimited. ANTONYM limited.

**5** *this report gives a broad outline* GENERAL, nonspecific, unspecific, rough, approximate, basic; loose, vague. ANTONYM detailed.

**6** *a broad hint* OBVIOUS, unsubtle, explicit, direct, plain, clear, straightforward, bald, patent, transparent, undisguised, overt. ANTONYM subtle.

**7** *a broad Latvian accent* PRONOUNCED, noticeable, strong, thick. ANTONYM slight.

**8** *he was attacked in broad daylight* FULL, complete, total; clear, bright.

**broadcast** verb **1** *the show will be broadcast worldwide* TRANSMIT, relay, air, beam, show, televise, telecast, webcast, simulcast, cablecast, screen.

**2** *the result was broadcast far and wide* REPORT, announce, publicize, proclaim; spread, circulate, air, blazon, trumpet. See note at SCATTER.

▸ noun *radio and television broadcasts* PROGRAM, show, production, transmission, telecast, webcast, simulcast, screening.

**broaden** verb **1** *her smile broadened* WIDEN, expand, stretch (out), draw out, spread; deepen.

**2** *the government tried to broaden its political base* EXPAND, enlarge, extend, widen, swell; increase, augment, add to, amplify; develop, enrich, improve, build on.

**broad-minded** adjective *our broad-minded English professor* LIBERAL, tolerant, open-minded, freethinking, progressive, permissive, unprejudiced, unbiased, unbigoted. ANTONYM intolerant.

**broadside** noun **1** *historical the gunners fired broadsides* SALVO, volley, cannonade, barrage, blast, fusillade.

**2** *a broadside against the economic reforms* CRITICISM, censure, polemic, diatribe, tirade; attack, onslaught; *literary* philippic.

**brochure** noun *college recruitment brochures* BOOKLET, pamphlet, leaflet, flyer, handbill, catalog, handout, prospectus, fact sheet, folder.

**broil** verb *broil the lamb chops* GRILL, toast, barbecue; cook.

**broiling** adjective *the sweaty nights and broiling days* HOT, scorching, roasting, baking, boiling (hot), blistering, sweltering, parching, searing, blazing, sizzling, burning (hot), sultry, torrid, tropical, like an oven, like a furnace. ANTONYMS cold, cool.

**broke** adjective *have you so easily forgotten what it's like to be* *broke?* PENNILESS, moneyless, bankrupt, insolvent, ruined, down-and-out, without a penny to one's name, without a cent, without one red cent, without two pennies to rub together; poor, poverty-stricken, impoverished, impecunious, penurious, indigent, in penury, needy, destitute; *informal* cleaned out, flat broke, strapped (for cash), bust, busted, hard up, stone broke, as poor as a church mouse.

**broken** adjective **1** *a broken bottle* SMASHED, shattered, fragmented, splintered, crushed, snapped; in bits, in pieces; destroyed, disintegrated; cracked, split; *informal* in smithereens. ANTONYM whole.

**2** *a broken arm* FRACTURED, damaged, injured.

**3** *this TV's broken* INOPERATIVE, not working, malfunctioning, faulty, defective, in disrepair, damaged, out of order, broken-down, down; *informal* on the blink, on the fritz, kaput, bust, busted, conked out, acting up, done for. ANTONYMS working, fixed.

**4** *broken skin* CUT, ruptured, punctured, perforated.

**5** *a broken marriage* FAILED, ended.

**6** *broken promises* FLOUTED, violated, infringed, contravened, disregarded, ignored, unkept. ANTONYMS kept, honored.

**7** *he was left a broken man* DEFEATED, beaten, subdued; DEMORALIZED, dispirited, discouraged, crushed, humbled; dishonored, ruined.

**8** *a night of broken sleep* INTERRUPTED, disturbed, fitful, disrupted, discontinuous, intermittent, unsettled, troubled. ANTONYM uninterrupted.

**9** *he pressed on over the broken ground* UNEVEN, rough, irregular, bumpy; rutted, pitted. ANTONYM smooth.

**10** *she spoke in broken English* HALTING, hesitating, disjointed, faltering, imperfect. ANTONYM perfect.

**broken-down** adjective **1** *a broken-down hotel* DILAPIDATED, run-down, ramshackle, tumbledown, in disrepair, beat-up, battered, crumbling, deteriorated, gone to rack and ruin; *informal* fleabag.

**2** *a broken-down car* DEFECTIVE, broken, faulty; not working, malfunctioning, inoperative, nonfunctioning; *informal* kaput, conked out, done for.

**broken-hearted** adjective *his broken-hearted family* HEARTBROKEN, grief-stricken, desolate, devastated, despondent, inconsolable, disconsolate, miserable, depressed, melancholy, wretched, sorrowful, forlorn, heavy-hearted, woeful, doleful, downcast, woebegone, sad, down; *informal* down in/at the mouth; *literary* heartsick. ANTONYM overjoyed.

**broker** noun *a top Wall Street broker* DEALER, agent; middleman, intermediary, mediator; liaison; stockbroker.

▸ verb *an agreement brokered by the secretariat* ARRANGE, organize, orchestrate, work out, settle, clinch, bring about; negotiate, mediate.

**brooch** noun *her great aunt's ivory brooch* pin, clip, clasp, badge; *historical* fibula.

**brood** noun **1** *the bird flew to feed its brood* OFFSPRING, young, progeny; family, hatch, clutch.

**2** *informal Gill was the youngest of the brood* FAMILY; children, offspring, youngsters, progeny; *informal* kids.

▸ verb **1** *once the eggs are laid, the male broods them* INCUBATE, hatch.

**2** *he slumped in his armchair, brooding* WORRY, fret, agonize, mope, sulk; think, ponder, contemplate, meditate, muse, ruminate.

**brook**[1] noun *a babbling brook* STREAM, creek, streamlet, rivulet, rill, brooklet, runnel; *Brit.* bourn, burn, beck.

**brook**[2] verb *formal we brook no violence* TOLERATE, allow, stand, bear, abide, put up with, endure; accept, permit, countenance; *informal* stomach, stand for, hack; *archaic* suffer.

**brothel** noun *young girls from Nepal are sold to the owners of these brothels* WHOREHOUSE, bordello, massage parlor, cathouse, bagnio; *dated* bawdy house, house of ill repute; *Law, dated* disorderly house.

**brother** noun **1** *then Steve and his brother Dan showed up* SIBLING; *informal* bro, sib.

**2** *they were brothers in crime* COMRADE, colleague, partner, associate, fellow, friend; *informal* pal, chum, mate.

**3** *a brother of the order* MONK, cleric, friar, religious, monastic.

**brotherhood** noun **1** *the ideals of justice and brotherhood* COMRADESHIP, fellowship, brotherliness, fraternalism, kinship; camaraderie, friendship.

**2** *a masonic brotherhood* SOCIETY, fraternity, association, alliance, union, league, guild, order, body, community, club, lodge, circle.

**brotherly** adjective **1** *brotherly rivalry* FRATERNAL, sibling.

**2** *brotherly love* FRIENDLY, comradely; affectionate, amicable, kind, devoted, loyal.

**brow** noun **1** *the doctor wiped his brow* FOREHEAD, temple; *Zoology* frons.

**2** *heavy black brows* EYEBROW.

**3** *the brow of the hill* SUMMIT, peak, top, crest, crown, head, pinnacle, apex.

**browbeat** verb *they browbeat the witness into changing her testimony* BULLY, intimidate, force, coerce, compel, hector, dragoon, bludgeon, pressure, pressurize, tyrannize, terrorize, menace; harass, harry, hound; *informal* bulldoze, railroad.

**brown** adjective *she has brown eyes* hazel, chocolate-colored, coffee-colored, cocoa-colored, nut-brown; brunette; sepia, mahogany, umber, burnt sienna; beige, buff, tan, fawn, camel, café au lait, caramel, chestnut.

**browse** verb **1** *I visited all the little boutiques, just to browse* LOOK AROUND, window-shop, peruse.

**2** *she* ***browsed through*** *the newspaper* SCAN (THROUGH), skim through, glance through, look through, peruse; thumb through, leaf through, flick through; dip into.

**3** *three cows were browsing in the meadow* GRAZE, feed, nibble, crop; ruminate.

**4** *he spent hours browsing online* SURFING, go from site to site.

**bruise** noun *a bruise across her forehead* CONTUSION, lesion, mark, black-and-blue mark, discoloration, blackening; injury; swelling, lump, bump, welt; *Medicine* ecchymosis.

▸ verb **1** *her face was badly bruised* injure, mark, discolor.

**2** *every one of the apples is bruised* MARK, discolor, blemish; damage, spoil.

**3** *Eric's ego was bruised* UPSET, offend, insult, affront, hurt, wound, injure, crush.

**brunette** adjective *a brunette woman* BROWN-HAIRED, dark, dark-haired.

**brunt** noun *the brunt of the downsizing was felt most by the warehouse crew* FULL FORCE, force, impact, shock, burden, pressure, weight; effect, repercussions, consequences.

**brush** noun **1** *a styling brush | camel-hair brushes | a brush and dustpan* hairbrush; toothbrush; paintbrush; scrub brush; whisk broom, sweeper, broom.

**2** *he gave the seat a brush with his hand* SWEEP, wipe, dust.

**3** *the brush of his lips against her cheek* TOUCH, stroke, skim, graze, nudge, contact; kiss.

**4** *a brush with the law* ENCOUNTER, clash, confrontation, conflict, altercation, incident; *informal* run-in.

▸ verb **1** *she brushed her hair* GROOM, comb, neaten, tidy, smooth, arrange, fix, do; curry.

**2** *she felt his lips brush her cheek* TOUCH, stroke, caress, skim, sweep, graze, contact; kiss.

**3** *she brushed a wisp of hair away* PUSH, move, sweep, clear.

PHRASES: **brush something aside** *she brushed aside his repeated warnings* DISREGARD, ignore, dismiss, shrug off, wave aside; overlook, pay no attention to, take no notice of, neglect, forget about, turn a blind eye to, turn a deaf ear to; reject, spurn; laugh off, make light of, trivialize; *informal* pooh-pooh.

**brush someone off** *he tried to help, but she brushed him off* REBUFF, dismiss, spurn, reject; slight, scorn, disdain; ignore, disregard, snub, turn one's back on, give someone the cold shoulder, freeze out; jilt, cast aside, discard.

**brush up (on)** *I'm brushing up on my French before our trip to Paris* RELEARN, read up (on), go over, study; improve, sharpen (up), polish up; hone, refine, perfect; *informal* bone up (on).

**brusque** adjective *his brusque manners* CURT, abrupt, blunt, short, sharp, terse, peremptory, gruff; offhand, discourteous, impolite, rude; *informal* snappy. ANTONYM polite.

THE RIGHT WORD **brusque, blunt, bluff, curt, gruff, surly**

**Brusque**, which comes from an Italian word meaning rude, describes an abruptness of speech or manner that is not necessarily meant to be rude (*a brusque handshake*; *a brusque reply*). **Curt** is more deliberately unfriendly, suggesting brevity and coldness of manner (*a curt dismissal*). There's nothing wrong with being **blunt**, although it implies an honesty and directness that can border on tactlessness (*a blunt reply to his question about where the money went*). Someone who is **bluff** is usually more likable, possessing a frank, hearty manner that may be a little too outspoken but is seldom offensive (*a bluff man who rarely minced words*). Exhibiting **gruff** or **surly** behavior will not win friends, since both words suggest bad temper if not rudeness. But *gruff* is used to describe a rough or grouchy disposition and, like *bluff*, is applied more often to a man. Anyone who has had to deal with an overworked store clerk while shopping during the holidays knows the meaning of *surly*, which is worse than *gruff*. It describes not only a sour disposition but an outright hostility toward people, and it can apply to someone of either sex (*that surly woman at the customer service desk*).

**brutal** adjective **1** *a brutal attack* SAVAGE, cruel, vicious, ferocious, brutish, barbaric, barbarous, wicked, murderous, bloodthirsty, cold-blooded, callous, heartless, ruthless, merciless, sadistic; heinous, monstrous, abominable, atrocious. See note at CRUELTY. ANTONYMS gentle, humane.

**2** *brutal honesty* UNSPARING, unstinting, unembellished, unvarnished, bald, naked, stark, blunt, direct, straightforward, frank, outspoken, forthright, plain-spoken; complete, total.

**brute** noun *a callous brute* SAVAGE, beast, monster, animal, barbarian, fiend, ogre; sadist; thug, lout, ruffian; *informal* swine, pig.

▸ adjective *brute strength* PHYSICAL, bodily; crude, violent.

**bubble** noun *the bubbles rose in the glass* globule, bead, blister; air pocket; (**bubbles**) sparkle, fizz, effervescence, froth, head.

▸ verb **1** *the champagne bubbled nicely on the tongue* SPARKLE, fizz, effervesce, foam, froth.

**2** *the milk was bubbling above the flame* BOIL, simmer, seethe, gurgle.

**3** *she was* ***bubbling over*** *with enthusiasm* OVERFLOW, brim over, be filled, gush.

**bubbly** adjective **1** *a bubbly wine* SPARKLING, bubbling, fizzy, effervescent, gassy, aerated, carbonated; spumante, frothy, foamy. ANTONYM flat.

**2** *she was bubbly and full of life* VIVACIOUS, animated, ebullient, exuberant, lively, high-spirited, zestful; sparkling, bouncy, buoyant, carefree; merry, happy, cheerful, perky, sunny, bright; *informal* upbeat, chirpy. ANTONYMS dull, listless.

▸ noun *informal a bottle of bubbly* CHAMPAGNE, sparkling wine, spumante, cava.

**buck** verb *it takes guts to buck the system* RESIST, oppose, defy, fight, kick against. PHRASES: **buck up** *informal don't worry, I'll buck up soon* CHEER UP, perk up, take heart, pick up, bounce back.

**buck someone up** *informal how can we buck you up, pal?* CHEER UP, buoy up, perk up, hearten, uplift, encourage, enliven, give someone a lift; *informal* pep up; *rare* inspirit.

**bucket** noun **1** *a bucket of cold water* PAIL, scuttle, can, tin, tub; ice bucket, wine cooler.

**2** *informal everyone wept buckets* FLOODS, gallons, oceans.

**buckle** noun *a belt buckle* CLASP, clip, catch, hasp, fastener.

▸ verb **1** *he buckled the belt around his waist* FASTEN, do up, hook, strap, secure, clasp, clip.

**2** *the front axle buckled* WARP, bend, twist, curve, distort, contort, deform; bulge, arc, arch; crumple, collapse, give way.

PHRASE: **buckle down** *Isaac finally began to buckle down in his junior year* GET (DOWN) TO WORK, set to work, get down to business; work hard, apply oneself, make an effort, be industrious, be diligent, focus.

**bucolic** adjective *their farm had been used as the bucolic setting for two major motion pictures* RUSTIC, rural, pastoral, country, countryside; *literary* Arcadian, sylvan, georgic.

**bud** noun *fresh buds* SPROUT, shoot, blossom; *Botany* plumule.

▸ verb *trees began to bud* SPROUT, shoot, germinate.

**budding** adjective *a budding artist* PROMISING, up-and-coming, rising, in the making, aspiring, emerging, fledgling, developing, blossoming; *informal* would-be, wannabe.

**budge** verb **1** *the horses wouldn't budge* MOVE, shift, stir, go.

**2** *I couldn't budge the door* DISLODGE, shift, move, reposition.

**3** *they refuse to budge on the issue* GIVE IN, give way, yield, change one's mind, acquiesce, compromise, do a U-turn.

**budget** noun **1** *your budget for the week* FINANCIAL PLAN, forecast; accounts, statement.

**2** *a cut in the defense budget* ALLOWANCE, allocation, quota; grant, award, funds, resources, capital.

▸ verb **1** *we have to budget $7,000 for the work* ALLOCATE, allot, allow, earmark, designate, set aside.

**2** *budget your finances* SCHEDULE, plan, cost, estimate; ration.

▸ adjective *a budget hotel* CHEAP, inexpensive, economy, affordable, low-cost, low-price, cut-rate, discount, bargain, downmarket. ANTONYM expensive.

**buff** adjective *a plain buff envelope* BEIGE, yellowish, yellowish-brown, light brown, fawn, sandy, wheaten, biscuit, camel.

▸ verb *he buffed the glass* POLISH, burnish, shine, clean, rub.

▸ noun *informal a film buff* ENTHUSIAST, fan, devotee, lover, admirer; expert, aficionado, authority, pundit; *informal* freak, nut, fanatic, fiend, addict, junkie, bum.

PHRASE: **in the buff** *informal.* See NAKED sense 1.

**buffer** noun *a buffer against market fluctuations* CUSHION, bulwark, shield, barrier, guard, safeguard.

▸ verb *she tried to buffer the children from the troubles* SHIELD, protect, defend, cushion, insulate, screen, guard.

**buffet**[1] noun **1** *a sumptuous buffet* SMORGASBORD, self-serve meal, serve-yourself meal, spread.

**2** *the plates are kept in the buffet* SIDEBOARD, cabinet, cupboard.

**buffet**[2] verb **1** *rough seas buffeted the coast* BATTER, pound, lash, strike, hit.

**2** *he has been buffeted by bad publicity* AFFLICT, trouble, harm, burden, bother, beset, harass, assail, harry, plague, torment, blight, bedevil.

**buffoon** noun **1** *archaic the king's buffoon* CLOWN, jester, fool, comic, comedian, wag, wit, merry-andrew, harlequin, Punchinello, Pierrot.

**2** *they regarded him as a buffoon* FOOL, idiot, dolt, dunce, dunderhead, dullard, ignoramus, dummy, simpleton, jackass; *informal* chump, blockhead, jughead, boob, bozo, doofus, nincompoop, numbskull, numbnuts, dope, twit, nitwit, halfwit, birdbrain. See also ASS sense 2.

**bug** noun **1** *bugs were crawling everywhere* INSECT, mite; *informal* creepy-crawly, beastie.

**2** *informal a stomach bug* ILLNESS, ailment, disorder, infection, disease, sickness, complaint, upset, condition; bacterium, germ, virus.

**3** *informal he caught the journalism bug* OBSESSION, enthusiasm, craze, fad, mania, passion, fixation.

**4** *the bug planted in his phone* LISTENING DEVICE, hidden microphone, wire, wiretap, tap.

**5** *a bug in the software* FAULT, error, defect, flaw; virus; *informal* glitch, gremlin.

▸ verb **1** *her conversations were bugged* RECORD, eavesdrop on, spy on, overhear; wiretap, tap, monitor.

**2** *informal she really bugs me.* See ANNOY.

**bugbear** noun *pseudoscience is a perennial bugbear for legitimate researchers* PET PEEVE, hate, bête noire, anathema, aversion, bugaboo; bane, bane of one's life/existence, irritant, irritation, vexation, thorn in one's flesh/side; nightmare, torment; *informal* pain, pain in the neck, hang-up.

**build** verb **1** *they were building a tree house* CONSTRUCT, erect, put up, assemble; make, form, create, fashion, model, shape.

**2** *they are building a business strategy* ESTABLISH, found, set up, institute, inaugurate, initiate.

**3** *the pressure was building* INCREASE, mount, intensify, escalate, grow, rise.

▸ noun *a man of slim build* PHYSIQUE, frame, body, figure, form, shape, stature, proportions; *informal* vital statistics.

PHRASES: **build something in/into** *emergency procedures must be built into every plan* INCORPORATE IN/INTO, include in, absorb into, subsume into, assimilate into.

**build on** *we are now in a position to build on all the wonderful legwork that our staff has accomplished* EXPAND ON, enlarge on, develop, elaborate, flesh out, embellish, amplify; refine, improve, perfect.

**build up** *the traffic continues to build up* INCREASE, grow, mount (up), intensify, escalate; strengthen.

**build something up 1** *he built up a huge business* ESTABLISH, set up, found, institute, start, create; develop, expand, enlarge.

**2** *she built up her stamina* BOOST, strengthen, increase, improve, augment, raise, enhance, swell; *informal* beef up.

**3** *I have built up a collection of prints* ACCUMULATE, amass, collect, gather; stockpile, hoard.

**building** noun 1 *a brick building* STRUCTURE, construction, edifice, erection; property, premises, establishment.

2 *the building of power stations* CONSTRUCTION, erection, fabrication, assembly.

**buildup** noun 1 *the buildup of military strength* INCREASE, growth, expansion, escalation, development, proliferation.

2 *the buildup of carbon dioxide* ACCUMULATION, accretion.

3 *the buildup for the World Cup* PUBLICITY, promotion, advertising, marketing; *informal* hype, ballyhoo, brouhaha, to-do.

**built-in** adjective 1 *a built-in cupboard* integrated, integral, incorporated.

2 *built-in advantages* INHERENT, intrinsic, inbuilt, innate; essential, implicit, basic, fundamental, deep-rooted.

**bulge** noun 1 *a bulge in the tire* SWELLING, bump, lump, protuberance, prominence, tumescence.

2 *informal a bulge in the population* SURGE, upsurge, rise, increase, escalation.

▸ verb *his eyes were bulging* SWELL, stick out, puff out, balloon (out), bug out, fill out, belly, distend, tumefy, intumesce; project, protrude, stand out.

THE RIGHT WORD **bulge, project, protrude, protuberate**

While all of these verbs mean to extend outward, beyond the normal line or surface of something, it is almost impossible not to associate the word **bulge** with the human body (*a stomach that bulges over a waistband, muscles that bulge beneath a shirt*). *Bulge* suggests a swelling out that is quite noticeable or even abnormal, and that may be the result of internal pressure, although a brick wall can *bulge*, as can a bicep muscle. **Protuberate** is a less common word meaning to swell or stick out, but it does not necessarily imply that anything is abnormal or radically wrong (*he was so thin that his knees protuberated*). To **protrude** is to thrust forth in an unexpected way or to stick out in a way that is abnormal or disfiguring (*her eyes protruded from her skull*). **Project** is the least upsetting of all these words, probably because it is used less often with reference to the human body. Anything that juts out abruptly beyond the rest of a surface is said to *project* (*the balcony projected from the south side of the house*).

**bulk** noun 1 *the sheer bulk of the bags* SIZE, volume, dimensions, proportions, mass, scale, magnitude, immensity, vastness.

2 *the bulk of entrants were women* MAJORITY, main part, major part, lion's share, preponderance, generality; most, almost all. ANTONYM minority.

**bulky** adjective *bulky items* LARGE, big, huge, sizable, substantial, massive; king-size, economy-size(d), outsize, oversized, considerable, voluminous; CUMBERSOME, unmanageable, unwieldy, ponderous, heavy, weighty; *informal* jumbo, whopping, hulking, humongous, ginormous. ANTONYMS small, slight.

**bulldoze** verb 1 *they plan to bulldoze the park* DEMOLISH, knock down, tear down, pull down, flatten, level, raze, clear.

2 *he bulldozed his way through* FORCE, push, shove, barge, elbow, shoulder, jostle, muscle; plunge, crash, sweep, bundle.

3 *informal she tends to bulldoze everyone* BULLY, browbeat, intimidate, dragoon, domineer, hector, pressurize, tyrannize, strong-arm, push around, walk all over; railroad, steamroller, lean on, boss.

**bullet** noun *the bullet was taken to the police lab* ball, shot, cartridge; *informal* slug; **(bullets)** lead, ammunition, ammo.

**bulletin** noun 1 *a news bulletin* REPORT, dispatch, story, press release, newscast, flash; statement, announcement, message, communication, communiqué.

2 *the society's monthly bulletin* NEWSLETTER, proceedings; newspaper, magazine, digest, gazette, review; tipsheet.

**bullish** adjective *another bullish candidate has thrown her hat into the ring* CONFIDENT, positive, assertive, self-assertive, assured, self-assured, bold, determined; optimistic, buoyant, sanguine; *informal* feisty, upbeat.

**bully** noun *the school bully* PERSECUTOR, oppressor, tyrant, tormentor, intimidator; tough guy, thug, ruffian, strong-arm.

▸ verb 1 *the others bully him* PERSECUTE, oppress, tyrannize, browbeat, harass, torment, intimidate, strong-arm, dominate; *informal* push around, bullyrag.

2 *she was bullied into helping* COERCE, pressure, pressurize, press, push; force, compel; badger, goad, prod, browbeat, intimidate, dragoon, strong-arm; *informal* bulldoze, railroad, lean on.

**bulwark** noun 1 *ancient bulwarks* WALL, rampart, fortification, parapet, stockade, palisade, barricade, embankment, earthwork.

2 *a bulwark of liberty* PROTECTOR, defender, protection, guard, defense, supporter, buttress; mainstay, bastion, stronghold.

**bum**[1] noun *informal* 1 *the bums sleeping on the sidewalk.* See TRAMP noun sense 1.

2 *you lazy bum* IDLER, loafer, slacker, good-for-nothing, ne'er-do-well, layabout, lounger, shirker; loser.

3 *a ski bum* ENTHUSIAST, fan, aficionado, lover, freak, nut, buff, fanatic, addict.

▸ verb 1 *that summer he bummed around Montreal* LOAF, lounge, idle, wander, drift, meander, dawdle; *informal* mooch, lollygag.

2 *they bummed money off him* BEG, borrow; *informal* scrounge, cadge, sponge, mooch.

▸ adjective *a bum deal* CRUMMY, rotten, pathetic, lousy, pitiful; BAD, poor, second-rate, tinpot, third-rate, second-class, unsatisfactory, inadequate, unacceptable; dreadful, awful, terrible, deplorable, lamentable. ANTONYM excellent.

**bum**[2] noun *Brit. informal next time I go skating, I'm tying a pillow to my bum!* See BUTTOCKS.

**bumbling** adjective *the bumbling Inspector Clouseau* BLUNDERING, bungling, inept, clumsy, maladroit, awkward, muddled, klutzy; oafish, clodhopping, lumbering; botched, ham-handed, ham-fisted. ANTONYMS efficient, debonair.

**bump** noun **1** *I landed with a bump* BANG, crash, smash, smack, crack, jolt, thud, thump; *informal* whack, thwack, bash, bonk, wallop.

**2** *a bump in the road | the bump on his head* HUMP, lump, ridge, bulge, knob, protuberance; swelling.

▸ verb **1** *cars **bumped into** each other* HIT, crash into, smash into, smack into, slam into, bang into, knock into, run into, plow into; ram into, collide with, strike.

**2** *a cart bumping along the road* BOUNCE, jolt, jerk, rattle, shake.

**3** *she got bumped in favor of a rookie* DISPLACE, demote, dislodge, supplant.

PHRASE: **bump into** *informal you'll never guess who we bumped into at the theater* MEET, meet by chance, encounter, run into/across, come across, chance on, happen on.

**bumpkin** noun *he was very bright, but a bit of a bumpkin* YOKEL, peasant, provincial, rustic, country cousin, hayseed, hillbilly, hick, rube.

**bumptious** adjective *our bumptious cousin thinks she's God's gift to men* SELF-IMPORTANT, conceited, arrogant, self-assertive, pushy, pompous, overbearing, cocky, swaggering; proud, haughty, overweening, egotistical; *informal* snooty, uppity. See note at BOLD. ANTONYM modest.

**bumpy** adjective **1** *a bumpy road* UNEVEN, rough, rutted, rutty, pitted, potholed, holey; lumpy, rocky. ANTONYMS smooth, level.

**2** *a bumpy ride* BOUNCY, rough, uncomfortable, jolting, lurching, jerky, jarring, bone-shaking. ANTONYMS smooth, comfortable.

**bunch** noun **1** *a bunch of flowers* BOUQUET, posy, nosegay, spray, corsage; wreath, garland.

**2** *a bunch of grapes | a bunch of keys* CLUSTER, clump; knot; group, assemblage.

**3** *informal we invited the whole bunch* GROUP, set, circle, company, collection, bevy, band, party; gang, crew, pack; crowd, throng, multitude.

**4** *informal I bought **a bunch of** used books* AN ASSORTMENT OF, a bundle of, a collection of; many, lots of, a lot of, loads of, a load of, tons of, a ton of, an abundance of.

▸ verb **1** *he bunched the reins in his hand* BUNDLE, clump, cluster, group, gather; pack.

**2** *her skirt bunched at the waist* GATHER, ruffle, pucker, fold, pleat.

**3** *the runners **bunched up** behind him* CLUSTER, huddle, gather, congregate, collect, amass, group, crowd.

**bundle** noun *a bundle of clothes* BUNCH, roll, clump, wad, parcel, sheaf, bale, bolt; package; pile, stack, heap, mass; *informal* load.

▸ verb **1** *she bundled up her things* TIE, pack, parcel, wrap, roll, fold, bind, bale, package.

**2** *she was bundled in furs* WRAP, envelop, clothe, cover, muffle, swathe, swaddle, shroud, drape, enfold.

**3** *informal he was bundled into a van* shove, push, thrust, manhandle, hurry, rush.

**bungle** verb *they bungled the robbery* MISHANDLE, mismanage, mess up, spoil, ruin, blunder; *informal* botch, muff, fluff, make a hash of, foul up, screw up, flub, goof up.

**bungling** adjective *the work of a bungling amateur* INCOMPETENT, blundering, amateurish, inept, unskillful, maladroit, clumsy, klutzy, awkward, bumbling; *informal* ham-handed, ham-fisted.

**bunk** noun **1** *there were twelve bunks per dormitory* BERTH, cot, bed.

**2** *informal the idea was sheer bunk.* See NONSENSE sense 1. See also note at NONSENSE

**bunkum** noun *informal, dated*. See NONSENSE sense 1.

**buoy** noun *a mooring buoy* FLOAT, marker; bellbuoy, nun buoy, sonobuoy.

▸ verb *the party was buoyed by an election victory* CHEER, cheer up, hearten, rally, invigorate, uplift, lift, encourage, stimulate, inspirit; *informal* pep up, perk up, buck up. ANTONYM depress.

**buoyant** adjective **1** *a buoyant substance* ABLE TO FLOAT, floating, floatable. ANTONYM leaden.

**2** *a buoyant mood* CHEERFUL, cheery, happy, lighthearted, carefree, bright, merry, joyful, bubbly, bouncy, sunny, jolly; lively, jaunty, high-spirited, perky; optimistic, confident, positive; *informal* peppy, upbeat. ANTONYMS depressed, optimistic.

**burden** noun **1** *a financial burden* ENCUMBRANCE, strain, care, problem, worry, difficulty, trouble, millstone; RESPONSIBILITY, onus, charge, duty, obligation, liability.

**2** *they shouldered their burdens* LOAD, weight, cargo, freight.

▸ verb *she thought nothing of burdening us with yet another mouth to feed* LOAD, charge, weigh down, encumber, hamper; overload, overburden; OPPRESS, trouble, worry, harass, upset, distress; haunt, afflict, strain, stress, tax, overwhelm.

**bureau** noun **1** *an oak bureau* DRESSER, chest of drawers, cabinet, tallboy, highboy.

**2** *the tourism bureau* AGENCY, service, office, business, company, firm; DEPARTMENT, division, branch, section.

**bureaucracy** noun **1** *the ranks of the bureaucracy* CIVIL SERVICE, government, administration; establishment, system, powers that be; ministries, authorities.

**2** *unnecessary bureaucracy* RED TAPE, rules and regulations, protocol, officialdom, paperwork.

**bureaucrat** noun *Washington bureaucrats* OFFICIAL, officeholder, administrator, public servant, civil servant, functionary; mandarin; *derogatory* apparatchik, bean counter, paper shuffler.

**burgeon** verb *the toy industry is burgeoning* FLOURISH,

thrive, prosper, improve, develop; expand, escalate, swell, grow, boom, mushroom, snowball, rocket.

**burglar** noun *the burglar escaped through the bedroom window* ROBBER, housebreaker, cat burglar, thief, raider, looter, safecracker, intruder, prowler; *informal* second-story man, yegg.

**burglary** noun **1** *serving time for burglary* HOUSEBREAKING, breaking and entering, theft, stealing, robbery, larceny, thievery, looting, pilferage.

**2** *a series of burglaries* BREAK-IN, theft, robbery, raid; *informal* heist.

**burial** noun *a private burial at Vineyard Point Cemetery* BURYING, interment, committal, entombment; funeral, obsequies; *formal* inhumation; *archaic* sepulture. See note at INTERMENT. ANTONYM exhumation.

**burlesque** noun *a rather risqué burlesque* PARODY, caricature, satire, lampoon, skit, farce; sendup, takeoff, spoof; striptease, strip. See note at CARICATURE.

**burly** adjective *his burly bodyguards* STRAPPING, well-built, sturdy, brawny, strong, muscular, muscly, thickset, blocky, big, hefty, bulky, stocky, stout, Herculean; *informal* hunky, beefy, husky, hulking; *literary* stalwart, thewy; *technical* mesomorphic. ANTONYM puny.

**burn** verb **1** *the shed was burning* BE ON FIRE, be alight, be ablaze, blaze, go up, go up in smoke, be in flames, be aflame; smolder, glow.

**2** *he burned the letters* SET FIRE TO, set on fire, set alight, light, ignite, touch off; incinerate; *informal* torch.

**3** *I burned my dress with the iron* SCORCH, singe, sear, char, blacken, brand, sizzle; scald.

**4** *her face burned* BE HOT, be warm, be feverish, be on fire; blush, redden, go red, flush, color.

**5** *she **is burning with** curiosity* BE CONSUMED BY/WITH, be eaten up by/with, be obsessed by/with, be tormented by/with, be beside oneself with.

**6** *the energy they **burn up*** CONSUME, use up, expend, go/get through, eat up; dissipate. ANTONYM conserve.

THE RIGHT WORD **burn, cauterize, char, scald, scorch, sear, singe**

If you're not an experienced cook, you're likely to **burn** your vegetables, **char** your meat, and, if you put your face too close to the stove, you might even **singe** your eyebrows. All of these verbs mean to injure or bring about a change in something by exposing it to fire or intense heat. *Burn*, which is the most comprehensive term, can mean to change only slightly (*she burned her face by staying out in the sun*) or to destroy completely (*the factory was burned to the ground*). To *char* is to reduce a substance to carbon or charcoal (*the beams in the ceiling were charred by the fire*). Like *char*, **singe** and **scorch** mean to burn only partially or superficially (*scorched the blouse while ironing it*; *singe the chicken before cooking it*). *Singeing* is often done deliberately to remove the hair, bristles, or feathers from the carcass of an animal or bird. **Scald** refers specifically to burning with, or as if with, a hot liquid or steam (*the cook scalded herself when she spilled the boiling water*); it can also mean to parboil or heat to a temperature just below boiling ( *scald the milk to make the sauce*). **Sear** is also a term used in cooking, where it means to brown the outside of a piece of meat by subjecting it briefly to intense heat to seal in the juices. When it's human flesh that's being seared in surgery, the correct verb is **cauterize**, which means to burn for healing purposes (*the doctor cauterized the wound to ward off infection*).

**burning** adjective **1** *burning coals* BLAZING, flaming, fiery, ignited, glowing, red-hot, smoldering, igneous; raging, roaring.

**2** *burning desert sands* EXTREMELY HOT, red-hot, fiery, blistering, scorching, searing, sweltering, torrid; *informal* baking, boiling (hot), broiling, roasting, sizzling. ANTONYM freezing.

**3** *a burning desire* INTENSE, passionate, deep-seated, profound, wholehearted, strong, ardent, fervent, urgent, fierce, eager, frantic, consuming, uncontrollable.

**4** *burning issues* IMPORTANT, crucial, significant, vital, essential, pivotal; urgent, pressing, compelling, critical.

**burnish** verb *marks can be removed by burnishing the metal* POLISH, shine, buff, rub, gloss.

**burp** verb *informal cucumbers make me burp* BELCH; *formal* eructate; *rare* eruct; *archaic* bolk, rout, ruck.

▸ noun *he let out a loud burp* BELCH; *formal* eructation; *rare* ventosity; *archaic* bolk.

**burrow** noun *a rabbits' burrow* HOLE, tunnel, warren, dugout; lair, set, den, earth.

▸ verb *the mouse burrows a hole* TUNNEL, dig (out), excavate, grub, mine, bore, channel; hollow out, gouge out.

**burst** verb **1** *one balloon burst* SPLIT OPEN, rupture, break, tear.

**2** *a shell burst in the distance* EXPLODE, blow up, detonate, go off.

**3** *water burst through the hole* BREAK, erupt, surge, gush, rush, stream, flow, pour, spill; spout, spurt, jet, spew.

**4** *he burst into the room* BARGE, charge, plunge, plow, hurtle, career, careen, rush, dash, tear.

**5** *they **burst into** tears* BREAK OUT IN, launch into, erupt in, have a fit of.

▸ noun **1** *mortar bursts* EXPLOSION, detonation, blast, eruption, bang.

**2** *a burst of gunfire* VOLLEY, salvo, fusillade, barrage, discharge; hail, rain.

**3** *a burst of activity* OUTBREAK, eruption, flare-up, blaze, attack, fit, rush, gale, storm, surge, upsurge, spurt.

PHRASE: **burst out** *"I don't care!" she burst out* EXCLAIM, blurt, cry, shout, yell; *dated* ejaculate.

**bury** verb **1** *the dead were buried* INTER, lay to rest, entomb; *informal* put six feet under; *literary* inhume. ANTONYM exhume.

**2** *she buried her face in her hands* HIDE, conceal, cover, enfold, engulf, tuck, cup, sink; *literary* enshroud. ANTONYM reveal.

**3** *the bullet buried itself in the wood* EMBED, sink, implant, submerge; drive into. ANTONYM extract.

**4** *he buried himself in his work* ABSORB, engross, immerse, occupy, engage, busy, involve.

**bush** noun **1** *a rose bush* SHRUB, brier; (**bushes**) undergrowth, shrubbery.

**2** *out in the bush* WILDS, wilderness, forest, woodland, timberland, bush country, bushland; backwoods, hinterland(s), backcountry, backlands; *informal* the sticks, boondocks, boonies.

**bushy** adjective *Groucho's trademark greasepaint mustache and bushy eyebrows* THICK, shaggy, unruly, fuzzy, bristly, fluffy, woolly; luxuriant. ANTONYMS sleek, wispy.

**business** noun **1** *Bill's business is electrical engineering* WORK, line of work, occupation, profession, career, employment, job, position; vocation, calling; field, sphere, trade, métier, craft; *informal* biz, racket, game.

**2** *whom do you do business with?* TRADE, trading, commerce, dealing, traffic, merchandising; dealings, transactions, negotiations.

**3** *her own business* COMPANY, firm, concern, enterprise, venture, organization, operation, corporation, undertaking; office, agency, franchise, practice; *informal* outfit.

**4** *none of your business* CONCERN, affair, responsibility, duty, function, obligation; problem, worry; *informal* beeswax, bailiwick.

**5** *this thing about the disappearing furniture is a strange business* AFFAIR, matter, thing, case, circumstance, situation, event, incident, happening, occurrence; episode.

**businesslike** adjective *our meetings are usually conducted in a more businesslike fashion* PROFESSIONAL, efficient, competent, methodical, disciplined, systematic, orderly, organized, structured, practical, pragmatic, routine, slick.

**bust**[1] noun **1** *an empire waistline accentuates the bust* CHEST, bosom, breasts.

**2** *a bust of Caesar* SCULPTURE, carving, effigy, statue; head and shoulders.

**bust**[2] verb *informal* **1** *I didn't mean to bust your DVD player* BREAK, smash, fracture, shatter, crack, disintegrate, snap; split, burst.

**2** *he promised to bust the counterfeit ring* OVERTHROW, destroy, topple, bring down, ruin, break, overturn, overcome, defeat, get rid of, oust, dislodge.

**3** *they were busted for drugs.* See ARREST verb sense 1.

▸ noun *a cache of guns was discovered in the bust* RAID, search; *informal* takedown, shakedown.

PHRASE: **go bust** *their flower shop went bust* FAIL, collapse, fold, go under, founder; go bankrupt, go into receivership, go into liquidation, be wound up; *informal* crash, go broke, go belly up, flop, bomb.

**bustle** verb *people bustled about* RUSH, dash, hurry, scurry, scuttle, hustle, scamper, scramble; run, tear, charge; *informal* scoot, beetle, buzz, zoom.

▸ noun *the bustle of the market* ACTIVITY, action, liveliness, hustle and bustle, excitement; tumult, hubbub, whirl, commotion; *informal* toing and froing, comings and goings.

**bustling** adjective *the mall is bustling with holiday shoppers* BUSY, crowded, swarming, teeming, thronged; buzzing, abuzz, buzzy, hectic, lively. ANTONYM deserted.

**busy** adjective **1** *the campaign volunteers have been busy* OCCUPIED, engaged, involved, employed, working, hard at work; rushed off one's feet, hard-pressed, swamped, up to one's neck; on the job, absorbed, engrossed, immersed, preoccupied; *informal* (as) busy as a bee, on the go, hard at it. ANTONYM idle.

**2** *sorry, she's busy at the moment* UNAVAILABLE, engaged, occupied; working, in a meeting, on duty; *informal* tied up. ANTONYM free.

**3** *the busy streets of Toronto* HECTIC, active, lively; crowded, bustling, abuzz, swarming, teeming, full, thronged.

**4** *a busy design* ORNATE, overelaborate, overblown, overwrought, overdone, fussy, cluttered, overworked. ANTONYMS restrained, quiet.

▸ verb *he busied himself with paperwork* OCCUPY, involve, engage, concern, absorb, engross, immerse, preoccupy; distract, divert.

THE RIGHT WORD **busy, assiduous, diligent, engaged, industrious, sedulous**

There are varying degrees of busyness. **Busy** implies actively and attentively involved in work or a pastime (*too busy to come to the phone*). It can also be used to describe intensive activity of any kind (*a busy intersection*; *a busy day*). Someone who is **engaged** is also *busy*, but in a more focused way (*engaged in compiling a dictionary*). **Diligent** is used to describe earnest and constant effort, and it often connotes enjoyment of or dedication to what one is doing (*diligent efforts to rescue injured animals*). To be **industrious** is to be more focused still, often with a definite goal in mind (*an industrious employee working for a promotion*). **Sedulous** also applies to goal-oriented activity, but it suggests more close care and perseverance than *industrious* does (*a sedulous investigation of the accident*). The award for concentrated effort goes to the person who is **assiduous**, which suggests painstaking preoccupation with a specific task (*an assiduous student is the one most likely to win his or her teacher's favor*).

**busybody** noun *I was labeled a snob because I didn't care to belong to her nest of busybodies* MEDDLER, interferer, mischief-maker, troublemaker; gossip, scandalmonger; eavesdropper; *informal* kibitzer, buttinsky, snoop, snooper, Nosy Parker, yenta.

**but** conjunction **1** *he stumbled but didn't fall* YET, nevertheless, nonetheless, even so, however, still, notwithstanding, despite that, in spite of that, for all that, all the same, just the same; though, although.

**2** *this one's expensive, but this one isn't* WHEREAS, conversely, but then, then again, on the other hand, by/in contrast, on the contrary.

▸ preposition *everyone but him* EXCEPT (FOR), apart from,

other than, besides, aside from, with the exception of, bar, excepting, excluding, leaving out, save (for), saving.

▸ adverb *he is but a shadow of his former self* ONLY, just, simply, merely, no more than, nothing but; a mere.

PHRASE: **but for** *I would not have survived but for your selfless courage* EXCEPT FOR, if it were not for, were it not for, barring, notwithstanding.

### USAGE NOTE but

It is a gross canard that beginning a sentence with *but* is stylistically slipshod. In fact, doing so is highly desirable in any number of contexts, as many stylebooks have said (many correctly pointing out that *but* is more effective than *however* at the beginning of a sentence)—e.g.:

• "The group of Adversative conjunctions represented by BUT (called Arrestive) very often fulfil [sic] the office of relating consecutive sentences. . . . An entire paragraph is not unfrequently devoted to arresting or preventing a seeming inference from one preceding, and is therefore appropriately opened by But, Still, Nevertheless, &c." (Alexander Bain, *English Composition and Rhetoric*, 4th ed.; 1877.)

• "*But* (not followed by a comma) always heads its turning sentence; *Nevertheless* usually does (followed by a comma). I am sure, however, that *however* is always better buried in the sentence between commas; *But* is for the quick turn; the inlaid *however* for the more elegant sweep." (Sheridan Baker, *The Practical Stylist*;1962.)

• "Of the many myths concerning 'correct' English, one of the most persistent is the belief that it is somehow improper to begin a sentence with *and*, *but*, *for*, *or*, or *nor*. The construction is, of course, widely used today and has been widely used for generations, for the very good reason that it is an effective means of achieving coherence between sentences and between larger units of discourse, such as paragraphs." (R. W. Pence and D. W. Emery, *A Grammar of Present-Day English*, 2d ed.; 1963.)

• "I can't overstate how much easier it is for readers to process a sentence if you start with *but* when you're shifting direction." (William Zinsser, *On Writing Well*, 6th ed.; 1998.)

• "If you want to begin a sentence by contradicting the last, use *but* instead of *however*." (Christopher Lasch, *Plain Style*; 2002.)

Good writers often begin sentences with *but* and have always done so. Samples from twentieth- and twenty-first-century writers follow:

• "But such simplicity of instinct is scarcely possible for human beings." (Bertrand Russell, *Education and the Good Life*; 1926.)

• "But it must not be assumed that intelligent thinking can play no part in the formation of the goal and of ethical judgments." (Albert Einstein, "Science and Religion" (1939), in *Ideas and Opinions*; 1954.)

• "But he had got used to that and it did not disquiet him." (Ursula K. Le Guin, *The Other Wind*; 2001.)

These are not good writers on bad days. No: they were having good days. In 1963, researcher Francis Christensen found that 8.75% of the sentences in the work of first-rate writers—including H. L. Mencken, Lionel Trilling, and Edmund Wilson—began with coordinating conjunctions (i.e., *and* and *but*). In *The New York Times* (front page during the 1990s) and *U.S. News & World Report* (in 1997), the figure is about the same. To the professional rhetorician, these figures aren't at all surprising.

All this enthusiasm for the construction, though, needs to be tempered to this extent: don't start consecutive sentences with *but*. Also, putting this subordinating conjunction twice in one sentence invariably makes the sentence unwieldy and less easy to read—e.g.: "But this opening misleads because the focus dissipates as the play progresses and the scattershot climax drips with sentiment but is ultimately unsatisfying." (*Pittsburgh Post-Gazette*; Oct. 10, 1997.) (A possible revision: "But this opening misleads because the focus dissipates as the play progresses. Although the scattershot climax drips with sentiment, it's ultimately unsatisfying.")

The surprisingly common misuse of *but* for *and* often betrays the writer's idiosyncratic prejudice. That is, if you write that someone is "attractive but smart," you're suggesting that this combination of characteristics is atypical—e.g.: "Billy's father . . . is a man of sterling rectitude, poor but honest [read *poor and honest*], determined to pass his upcoming naturalization exams." (*Chicago Tribune*; Oct. 24, 1997.) Is the writer really suggesting that poor people are typically dishonest?

The use of *but* in a negative sense after a pronoun has long caused confusion. Is it "No one but she" or "No one but her"? When *but* is a preposition (meaning "except"), the objective *her* (or *him*) follows. But when *but* is a conjunction, the nominative *she* (or *he*) is proper. The correct form depends on the structure of the sentence. If the verb precedes the *but* phrase, the objective case should be used: "None of the defendants were convicted but him." But if the *but* phrase precedes the verb, the nominative case is proper: "None of the defendants but he were convicted." That sentence is considered equivalent to "None of the defendants were convicted, but he was convicted." (Although that rewording doesn't seem to make literal sense—given that he was one of the defendants—it serves to show the grammar of the sentence excepting him from the absolute word *none*.) *But* thus acts as a conjunction when it precedes the verb in a sentence, as in this one from Thomas Jefferson: "Nobody but we of the craft can understand the diction, and find out what [the statute] means." Here the subject of *can understand* is *nobody*, and the *but* heads the understood clause: "nobody can understand, but we can understand."

The logic here is based on syntax: the native English speaker instinctively rejects as alien-sounding the constructions *me know* in "No one but you and I know what is on these notice boards" and *him knew* in "No one but he knew what this had cost him." —*BG*

---

**butch** adjective *informal a butch haircut* MASCULINE, manly; mannish, manlike; *informal* macho. ANTONYM effeminate.

**butcher** noun **1** *a butcher's shop* MEAT SELLER, meat vendor, meat trader.

**2** *a Nazi butcher* MURDERER, slaughterer, killer, assassin; *literary* slayer; *dated* cutthroat, homicide.

▸ verb **1** *the goat was butchered* SLAUGHTER, cut up, carve up.

**2** *they butchered 150 people* MASSACRE, murder, slaughter, kill, destroy, exterminate, assassinate; *literary* slay.

**3** *the studio butchered the film* SPOIL, ruin, mutilate, mangle, mess up, wreck; *informal* make a hash of, screw up, botch.

**butt** noun **1** *the butt of a joke* TARGET, victim, object, subject, dupe; laughingstock.

**2** *the butt of a gun* STOCK, end, handle, hilt, haft, helve.

**3** *a cigarette butt* STUB, end, tail end, stump, remnant.

**4** *informal sitting on his butt.* See BUTTOCKS.

▸ verb **1** *the shop* **butts up against** *the house* ADJOIN, abut, be next to, be adjacent to, border (on), be connected to; join, touch.

2 *students butting everyone with their backpacks* RAM, head-butt, bunt; bump, buffet, push, shove. PHRASE: **butt in** *I've asked you not to butt in when your father and I are talking* INTERRUPT, break in, cut in, chime in, interject, intervene, interfere, interpose; *informal* poke one's nose in, put one's oar in.

**buttocks** plural noun *stand with your heels and buttocks against the wall* BACKSIDE, rear end, rear, seat, bottom, rump, cheeks, behind, derrière; *informal* butt, fanny, keister, tush, tail, buns, heinie, ass, caboose; fundament, posterior, haunches, gluteus maximus, sit-upon, stern, wazoo; *Brit. informal* bum, arse; *Anatomy* nates. See note at ASS.

**button** noun 1 *shirt buttons* FASTENER, stud, toggle; hook, catch, clasp, snap fastener, pin.

2 *press the button* SWITCH, knob, control; lever, handle; icon, box.

**buttonhole** verb *informal*. See ACCOST.

**buttress** noun 1 *stone buttresses* PROP, support, abutment, brace, shore, pier, reinforcement, stanchion.

2 *a buttress against social collapse* SAFEGUARD, defense, protection, guard; support, prop; bulwark.

▸ verb *authority was buttressed by religion* STRENGTHEN, reinforce, fortify, support, bolster, shore up, underpin, cement, uphold, prop up, defend, sustain, back up.

**buxom** adjective *a buxom lingerie model* LARGE-BREASTED, big-breasted, bosomy, big-bosomed; shapely, ample, plump, rounded, full-figured, voluptuous, curvaceous, Rubenesque; *informal* busty, built, stacked, chesty, well-endowed, curvy.

**buy** verb *they bought a new house* PURCHASE, acquire, obtain, get, pick up; take, procure, pay for; invest in; *informal* get hold of, snatch up, snap up, grab, score. ANTONYM sell.

▸ noun *informal a good buy* PURCHASE, investment, acquisition, gain; deal, value, bargain.

**buzz** noun 1 *the buzz of the bees* HUM, humming, buzzing, murmur, drone.

2 *the buzz of the doorbell* RING, purr, note, tone, beep, bleep, warble, alarm, warning sound.

3 *informal give me a buzz* CALL, ring, phone call, telephone call.

4 *informal the buzz is that he's gone.* See RUMOR.

5 *informal get a buzz out of flying* THRILL, stimulation, glow, tingle; *informal* kick, rush, high, charge.

▸ verb 1 *bees buzzed* HUM, drone, bumble, murmur.

2 *the intercom was buzzing* PURR, warble, sound, ring, beep, bleep.

3 *informal he buzzed around the mall* BUSTLE, scurry, scuttle, hurry, rush, race, dash, tear, chase; *informal* scoot, beetle, whiz, zoom, zip.

4 *the town is buzzing with excitement* HUM, throb, vibrate, pulse, bustle, be abuzz. PHRASE: **buzz off** *I told that little pest to buzz off* SCRAM, go away, be gone/begone, be off; *informal* get lost, take a hike, beat it, bug off, go fly a kite, go suck an egg, vamoose.

**by** preposition 1 *I broke it by forcing the lid* THROUGH, as a result of, because of, by dint of, by way of, via, by means of; with the help of, with the aid of, by virtue of.

2 *be there by midday* NO LATER THAN, in good time for, at, before.

3 *a house by the lake* NEXT TO, beside, alongside, by/at the side of, adjacent to, side by side with; near, close to, neighboring, adjoining, bordering, overlooking; connected to, contiguous with, attached to.

4 *go by the building* PAST, in front of, beyond.

5 *all right by me* ACCORDING TO, with, as far as —— is concerned.

▸ adverb *people hurried by* PAST, on, along.

PHRASES: **by and by** *by and by, you'll learn the routine* EVENTUALLY, ultimately, finally, in the end, one day, some day, sooner or later, in time, in a while, in the long run, in the fullness of time, in time to come, at length, in the future, in due course, over the long haul.

**by oneself** *I built the fireplace by myself* ALONE, on one's own, singly, separately, solitarily, unaccompanied, companionless, unattended, unescorted, solo; unaided, unassisted, without help, by one's own efforts, under one's own steam, independently, single-handed(ly), on one's own initiative; *informal* by one's lonesome.

**bygone** adjective *it recaptures a bygone era* PAST, former, olden, earlier, previous, one-time, long-ago, of old, ancient, antiquated; departed, dead, extinct, defunct, out of date, outmoded; *literary* of yore. ANTONYMS present, recent.

**bypass** noun *follow the signs for the bypass* DETOUR, alternate route, alternative route, diversion, shortcut.

▸ verb 1 *bypass the farm* GO AROUND, go past, make a detour around; avoid.

2 *an attempt to bypass the problem* AVOID, evade, dodge, escape, elude, circumvent, get around, shortcut around, skirt, sidestep, steer clear of; *informal* duck.

3 *they bypassed the regulations* IGNORE, pass over, neglect, go over the head of; *informal* short-circuit.

**bystander** noun *bystanders witnessed the accident* ONLOOKER, looker-on, passerby, nonparticipant, observer, spectator, eyewitness, witness, watcher, gawker; *informal* rubbernecker.

**byword** noun 1 *their office was a byword for delay* PERFECT EXAMPLE, classic case, model, exemplar, embodiment, incarnation, personification, epitome.

2 *'vigor' was the byword of the Kennedy years* SLOGAN, motto, maxim, mantra, catchword, watchword, formula; middle name; proverb, adage, saying, dictum.

**cab** noun *she hailed a cab* TAXI, taxicab, hack; rickshaw, trishaw, pedicab.

**cabal** noun *a cabal of dissidents* CLIQUE, faction, coterie, cell, sect, junta, camarilla; lobby (group), pressure group. See note at PLOT.

**cabaret** noun **1** *the evening's cabaret* ENTERTAINMENT, show, floor show, performance.

**2** *the cabarets of New Orleans* NIGHTCLUB, dinner theater, club, boîte, café; *informal* nightspot, clip joint, honky-tonk.

**cabin** noun *a cabin by the lake* COTTAGE, log cabin, shack, chantey, hut; chalet; cabana; *historical* camboose.

**cabinet** noun **1** *a walnut cabinet* CUPBOARD, bureau, bookcase, chest of drawers, sideboard, buffet, dresser, credenza, highboy, tallboy, wardrobe, chiffonier, armoire, wall unit; china cabinet, file cabinet, medicine cabinet.

**2** *a meeting of the new cabinet* COUNCIL, administration, ministry, executive, senate.

**cable** noun **1** *a thick cable moored the ship* ROPE, cord, line, guy, wire; hawser, stay, bridle; choker.

**2** *electric cables* WIRE, lead; power line, hydro line, transmission line.

**cache** noun *a cache of arms* HOARD, store, stockpile, stock, supply, reserve; arsenal; *informal* stash.

**cachet** noun *for more than fifty years, their winery enjoyed the cachet that others could only envy* PRESTIGE, status, standing, clout, kudos, snob value, stature, preeminence, eminence; street credibility.

**cackle** verb **1** *the geese cackled at him* SQUAWK, cluck, gabble.

**2** *Noel cackled with glee* LAUGH LOUDLY, guffaw, chortle, chuckle.

**cacophony** noun *despite the cacophony, Rita slept on* DIN, racket, noise, clamor, discord, dissonance, discordance, uproar.

**cad** noun *dated*. See BASTARD noun sense 2.

**cadaver** noun *Medicine each student is assigned a cadaver* CORPSE, body, dead body, remains, carcass; *informal* stiff; *archaic* corse. See note at BODY.

**cadaverous** adjective *his cadaverous face* (DEATHLY) PALE, pallid, ashen, gray, whey-faced, sallow, wan, anemic, bloodless, etiolated, corpselike, deathlike; bony, skeletal, emaciated, skin-and-bones, haggard, gaunt, drawn, pinched, hollow-cheeked, hollow-eyed; *informal* like a bag of bones, anorexic. ANTONYMS rosy, plump.

**cadence** noun *there is a musical cadence in her speech* INTONATION, modulation, lilt, accent, inflection; rhythm, tempo, meter, beat, pulse; *Music* resolution.

**cafeteria** noun LUNCHROOM, luncheonette, lunch counter; snack bar, canteen, café; *informal* caf.

**cage** noun *animals in cages* ENCLOSURE, pen, pound; coop, hutch; birdcage, aviary; corral.

▸ verb *many animals are caged* CONFINE, shut in/up, pen, coop up, fence in, immure, impound, corral.

**cajole** verb *I hate it when he cajoles me to go out with his friends* PERSUADE, wheedle, coax, talk into, prevail on, sweet-talk, butter up, soft-soap, seduce, inveigle.

**cake** noun **1** *cakes from the bakery* cupcake, sponge cake, angel food cake, layer cake, fruitcake, gingerbread, shortcake.

**2** *a cake of soap* BAR, block, brick, slab, tablet, lump.

▸ verb **1** *boots caked with mud* COAT, encrust, plaster, cover.

**2** *the blood was beginning to cake* CLOT, congeal, coagulate, solidify, set, inspissate.

**calamitous** adjective *their calamitous adventure became legendary* DISASTROUS, catastrophic, cataclysmic, devastating, dire, tragic; *literary* direful.

**calamity** noun *she has survived more calamities in the past three months than most people experience in a lifetime* DISASTER, catastrophe, tragedy, cataclysm, adversity, tribulation, affliction, misfortune, misadventure. ANTONYM godsend.

**calculate** verb **1** *the interest is calculated on a daily basis* COMPUTE, work out, reckon, figure; add up/together, count up, tally, total, tote, tot up.

**2** *his words were calculated to wound her* INTEND, mean, aim, design.

**3** *we had **calculated on** a quiet Sunday* EXPECT, count on, anticipate, reckon on, bargain on, figure on.

**calculated** adjective *a vicious and calculated assault* DELIB-

ERATE, premeditated, planned, preplanned, preconceived, intentional, intended, willful; *Law* prepense. ANTONYM unintentional.

**calculating** adjective *a crime that only a calculating mind could have planned* CUNNING, crafty, wily, shrewd, sly, scheming, devious, designing, conniving, Machiavellian; *informal* foxy; *archaic* subtle. ANTONYM ingenuous.

**calculation** noun **1** *the calculation of the overall cost* COMPUTATION, reckoning, adding up, counting up, working out, figuring, totaling up, totting up.

**2** *political calculations* ASSESSMENT, judgment; forecast, projection, prediction.

**caliber** noun **1** *a man of his caliber* QUALITY, merit, distinction, stature, excellence, preeminence; ability, expertise, talent, capability, capacity, proficiency.

**2** *questions about the caliber of the officiating* STANDARD, level, quality.

**3** *the caliber of a gun* BORE, diameter, gauge.

**call** verb **1** *"Wait for me!" she called* CRY OUT, cry, shout, yell, hail, bellow, roar, bawl, vociferate; *informal* holler.

**2** *I'll call you tomorrow* PHONE, telephone, get someone on the phone, give someone a call, give someone a ring, give someone a buzz.

**3** *dinner's ready—call the kids* SUMMON, send for, assemble, muster, invite, order.

**4** *the vice president called a meeting* CONVENE, summon, assemble; *formal* convoke.

**5** *they called their son Liam* NAME, christen, baptize; designate, style, term, dub; *formal* denominate.

**6** *yes, I would call him a friend* DESCRIBE AS, regard as, look on as, consider to be.

▸ noun **1** *I heard calls from the auditorium* CRY, shout, yell, roar, scream, exclamation, vociferation; *informal* holler.

**2** *the call of the loon* CRY, song, sound.

**3** *I'll give you a call tomorrow* PHONE CALL, telephone call, ring; *informal* buzz.

**4** *he paid a call on Harold* VISIT, social call.

**5** *a call for party unity* APPEAL, request, plea, entreaty.

**6** *the last call for passengers on flight 701* SUMMONS, request.

**7** *there's no call for expensive wine here* DEMAND, desire, market.

**8** *the call of the sea* ATTRACTION, appeal, lure, allure, spell, pull, draw.

**9** *it's your call* DECISION, ruling, judgment, verdict.

PHRASES: **call for** *desperate times call for desperate measures* REQUIRE, need, necessitate; justify, warrant.
**call off** *we had to call off the trip to Maryland* CANCEL, abandon, scrap, drop, ax, scrub, nix; end, terminate.
**call on 1** *I might call on her later* VISIT, pay a visit to, go and see, drop in on, pop in on, visit with.

**2** *he called on the government to hold a plebiscite* APPEAL TO, ask, request, petition, urge, exhort.

**3** *we are able to call on qualified staff* HAVE RECOURSE TO, avail oneself of, draw on, make use of.
**call the shots** *if she's gonna call the shots from now on, I'm not gonna stick around* BE IN CHARGE, be in control, be the boss, be at the helm/wheel, be in the driver's seat, pull the strings, run the show, rule the roost.
**call to mind** *this calls to mind the last constitutional debate* EVOKE, bring to mind, call up, conjure up.
**call up 1** *Roland called me up to ask me out.* See CALL verb sense 2.

**2** *they called up the reservists* ENLIST, recruit, conscript; draft.

**3** *he was called up from the minors* SELECT, pick, choose.
**on call** *Dr. Merton is on call this evening* ON DUTY, on standby, available.

**calling** noun *when I was four, I knew my calling was photography* PROFESSION, occupation, vocation, call, summons, career, work, employment, job, business, trade, craft, line, line of work; *informal* bag; *archaic* employ.

**callous** adjective *his callous disregard for other people's feelings* HEARTLESS, unfeeling, uncaring, cold, cold-hearted, hard, as hard as nails, hard-hearted, insensitive, lacking compassion, hard-bitten, hard-nosed, hard-edged, unsympathetic. ANTONYMS kind, compassionate.

**callow** adjective *she toyed with the emotions of Laughton when he was a callow and insecure young man* IMMATURE, inexperienced, juvenile, adolescent, naive, green, raw, untried, unworldly, unsophisticated; *informal* wet behind the ears. See notes at GULLIBLE, RUDE, YOUTHFUL. ANTONYM mature.

**calm** adjective **1** *she seemed very calm* SERENE, tranquil, relaxed, unruffled, unperturbed, unflustered, untroubled; equable, even-tempered; placid, unexcitable, unemotional, phlegmatic; composed, 'calm, cool, and collected,' coolheaded, self-possessed; *informal* unflappable, unfazed, nonplussed. ANTONYMS excited, nervous, upset.

**2** *the night was calm* WINDLESS, still, tranquil, serene, quiet. ANTONYMS windy, stormy.

**3** *the calm waters of the lake* TRANQUIL, still, smooth, glassy, like a millpond; *literary* stilly. ANTONYMS rough, stormy.

▸ noun **1** *calm prevailed* TRANQUILITY, stillness, calmness, quiet, quietness, quietude, peace, peacefulness.

**2** *his usual calm deserted him* COMPOSURE, coolness, calmness, self-possession, sangfroid; serenity, tranquility, equanimity, equability, placidness, placidity; *informal* cool, unflappability.

▸ verb **1** *I tried to **calm** him **down*** SOOTHE, pacify, placate, mollify, appease, conciliate, quiet (down), relax. ANTONYMS excite, upset.

**2** *she forced herself to **calm down*** COMPOSE ONESELF, recover/regain one's composure, control oneself, pull oneself together, simmer down, cool down/off, take it easy; *informal* get a grip, keep one's shirt on, chill (out), cool one's jets, hang/stay loose, decompress.

THE RIGHT WORD **calm, halcyon, peaceful, placid, serene, tranquil**

We usually speak of the weather or the sea as **calm**, meaning free from disturbance or storm. When applied to people and their feelings or moods, *calm* implies an unruffled state, often under disturbing conditions (*to remain calm in the face of disaster*). **Halcyon** is another adjective associated with the weather (*the halcyon days of summer*); it comes from the name of a mythical bird, usually identified with the kingfisher, that builds its nest on the sea and possesses a magical power to calm the winds and waves. **Peaceful** also suggests a lack of turbulence or disorder, although it is usually applied to situations, scenes, and activities rather than to people (*a peaceful gathering of protesters*; *a peaceful resolution to their problems*). **Serene, tranquil**, and **placid** are more often used to describe human states of being. *Serene* suggests a lofty and undisturbed calmness (*he died with a serene look on his face*), while *tranquil* implies an intrinsic calmness (*they led a tranquil life in the country*). **Placid** usually refers to a prevailing tendency and is sometimes used disparagingly to suggest a lack of responsiveness or a dull complacency (*with her placid disposition, she seldom got involved in family arguments*).

**calumny** noun *voters were tired of the candidates' endless barrage of calumny* SLANDER, defamation (of character), character assassination, libel; vilification, traducement, obloquy, verbal abuse; *informal* mudslinging, trash-talk; *rare* contumely. See note at MALIGN.

**camaraderie** noun *he enjoyed the camaraderie of army life* FRIENDSHIP, comradeship, fellowship, companionship, fraternity, conviviality; mutual support, team spirit, esprit de corps.

**camouflage** noun **1** *pieces of mossy turf served for camouflage* DISGUISE, concealment, cover, screen.

**2** *her indifference was merely camouflage* A FACADE, a front, a false front, a smokescreen, a cover-up, a mask, a blind, a screen, a masquerade, a dissimulation, a pretense.

▸ verb *the van was camouflaged with branches* DISGUISE, hide, conceal, keep hidden, mask, screen, cover (up).

**camp**[1] noun **1** *a kids' camp* CAMPSITE, campground, encampment, bivouac.

**2** *the liberal and conservative camps* FACTION, wing, group, lobby, caucus, bloc, party, coterie, sect, cabal.

▸ verb *they camped in a field* PITCH TENTS, set up camp, encamp, bivouac.

**camp**[2] adjective *informal* **1** *the camp humor became tiresome after the first twenty minutes* EXAGGERATED, theatrical, affected; *informal* over the top, OTT, camped up, hammy.

**2** *a highly camp actor* EFFEMINATE, effete, mincing; *informal* campy. ANTONYM macho.

PHRASE: **camp it up** *he camped it up for the cameras* POSTURE, behave theatrically/affectedly, overact; *informal* ham it up.

**campaign** noun **1** *Napoleon's Russian campaign* MILITARY OPERATION(S), maneuver(s); crusade, war, battle, offensive, attack.

**2** *the campaign to reduce vehicle emissions* CRUSADE, drive, push, struggle; operation, strategy, battle plan.

▸ verb **1** *they are campaigning for political reform* CRUSADE, fight, battle, push, press, strive, struggle, lobby.

**2** *she campaigned as a political outsider* RUN FOR OFFICE, stand for office, canvass, barnstorm, electioneer, stump, go on the hustings.

**can** noun *a bag of empty cans for recycling* tin can, aluminum can; canister; spray can; garbage can, trash can.

▸ verb *informal he was canned after being caught stealing office supplies* FIRE, dismiss, ax, let go, lay off, sack.

**canal** noun **1** *barges chugged up the canal* INLAND WATERWAY, watercourse, channel.

**2** *the ear canal* DUCT, tube, passage.

**cancel** verb **1** *the meeting was canceled* CALL OFF, abandon, scrap, drop, ax, scrub, nix.

**2** *his visa has been canceled* ANNUL, invalidate, nullify, declare null and void, void; revoke, rescind, retract, countermand, withdraw; *Law* vacate.

**3** *rising unemployment* ***cancelled out*** *earlier economic gains* NEUTRALIZE, counterbalance, counteract, balance (out), countervail, compensate for; negate, nullify, wipe out.

**cancer** noun **1** *most skin cancers are curable if detected early* MALIGNANT GROWTH, cancerous growth, tumor, malignancy; *technical* carcinoma, sarcoma, melanoma, lymphoma, myeloma.

**2** *the cancer of slavery spread across the continent* EVIL, blight, scourge, poison, canker, plague; *archaic* pestilence.

**candid** adjective **1** *his responses were remarkably candid* FRANK, outspoken, forthright, blunt, open, honest, truthful, sincere, direct, plain-spoken, straightforward, ingenuous, bluff; *informal* upfront, on the level, on the up and up. ANTONYM guarded.

**2** *candid shots* UNPOSED, informal, uncontrived, impromptu, natural.

**candidate** noun *candidates should be computer-literate* APPLICANT, job applicants, job-seeker, interviewee; contender, contestant, nominee.

**candle** noun *hand-dipped white candles* taper, votive candle; *archaic* glim.

**candor** noun *I'm not sure he appreciated my candor* FRANKNESS, openness, honesty, candidness, truthfulness, sincerity, forthrightness, directness, plain-spokenness, bluntness, straightforwardness, outspokenness; *informal* telling it like it is.

**candy** noun *chocolate candy* bonbon, confectionery, sweet.

**cane** noun **1** *a silver-topped cane* WALKING STICK, staff; alpenstock; crook, pikestaff.

**2** *he was beaten with a cane* STICK, rod, birch; *historical* ferule.

▸ verb *Matthew was caned for bullying* BEAT, strike, hit, flog, thrash, lash, birch, flagellate; *informal* belt, whale.

**canker** noun **1** *this plant is susceptible to canker* FUNGAL DISEASE, plant rot; blight.

**2** *ear cankers* ULCER, ulceration, infection, sore, abscess, noma.

**3** *racism remains a canker.* See CANCER sense 2.

**cannibal** noun *overblown tales of savage cannibals* MAN-EATER, people-eater; *rare* anthropophagite, anthropophagist.

**cannon** noun *a Civil War cannon sits near the entrance to the armory* MOUNTED GUN, field gun, piece of artillery; mortar, howitzer; *historical* culverin, falconet.

▸ verb *the couple behind* ***cannoned into*** *us* COLLIDE WITH, hit, run into, crash into, plow into.

**cannonade** noun *the distant cannonade kept us alert all night* BOMBARDMENT, shelling, gunfire, artillery fire, barrage, pounding.

**canny** adjective *canny investors* SHREWD, astute, smart, sharp, sharp-witted, discerning, penetrating, discriminating, perceptive, perspicacious, wise, worldly-wise, sagacious; cunning, crafty, wily, as sharp as a tack, savvy; *dated* long-headed. ANTONYM foolish.

**canon** noun **1** *the canons of fair play and equal opportunity* PRINCIPLE, rule, law, tenet, precept; standard, convention, criterion, measure.

**2** *a set of ecclesiastical canons* LAW, decree, edict, statute, dictate, decretal.

**3** *the Shakespeare canon* LIST OF WORKS, works, writings, oeuvre.

**canopy** noun *the canopy gave us some relief from the sun* AWNING, shade, sunshade; marquee; chuppah.

**cant**[1] noun **1** *religious cant* HYPOCRISY, sanctimoniousness, sanctimony, pietism.

**2** *thieves' cant* SLANG, jargon, idiom, argot, patois, speech, terminology, language; *informal* lingo, -speak, -ese. See note at DIALECT.

**cant**[2] verb *the deck canted some twenty degrees* TILT, lean, slant, slope, incline; tip, list, bank, heel.

▸ noun *the cant of the walls* SLOPE, slant, tilt, angle, inclination.

**cantankerous** adjective. See GRUMPY.

**canvass** verb **1** *he's canvassing for the Green Party* CAMPAIGN, electioneer, stump, barnstorm.

**2** *they promised to canvass all members* POLL, question, ask, survey, interview.

**3** *they're canvassing support* SEEK, try to obtain.

**canyon** noun *burros can be negotiated through the canyon* RAVINE, gorge, gully, defile, couloir; chasm, abyss, gulf, gulch, coulee.

**cap** noun **1** *his cap blew off in the wind.* See the table at HAT.

**2** *a white plastic cap* LID, top; stopper, cork, bung.

**3** *the cap on spending* LIMIT, upper limit, ceiling; curb, check.

▸ verb **1** *mountains capped with snow* TOP, crown, cover, coat.

**2** *his breakaway goal capped a great game* ROUND OFF, crown, top off, be a fitting climax to.

**3** *they tried to cap each other's stories* BEAT, better, improve on, surpass, outdo, outshine, outstrip, top, upstage.

**4** *budgets will be capped* SET A LIMIT ON, limit, restrict; curb, control.

**capability** noun *her professional capabilities* | *their capability and willingness to tackle tough issues* ABILITY, capacity, power, potential; competence, proficiency, adeptness, aptitude, faculty, wherewithal, experience, skill, skillfulness, talent, flair; *informal* know-how.

**capable** adjective *a capable young woman* COMPETENT, able, efficient, effective, proficient, accomplished, adept, handy, experienced, skillful, skilled, talented, gifted; *informal* useful. ANTONYM incompetent.

PHRASE: **be capable of** *I'm capable of looking after myself* HAVE THE ABILITY TO, be equal to (the task of), be up to, have what it takes to (be).

**capacious** adjective *a capacious hotel suite* ROOMY, spacious, ample, big, large, sizable, generous; *formal* commodious. ANTONYMS cramped, small.

**capacity** noun **1** *the capacity of the freezer* VOLUME, size, magnitude, dimensions, measurements, proportions.

**2** *his capacity to inspire trust.* See CAPABILITY.

**3** *in his capacity as head librarian* POSITION, post, job, office; role, function.

**cape**[1] noun *a woolen cape* CLOAK, mantle, cope, wrap, stole, poncho, shawl, tippet, capelet; *historical* pelisse, mantelet.

**cape**[2] noun *the ship rounded the cape* HEADLAND, promontory, point, spit, head, foreland, horn, hook.

**caper** verb *children were capering about* SKIP, dance, romp, frisk, gambol, cavort, prance, frolic, leap, hop, jump, rollick.

▸ noun **1** *she did a little caper* DANCE, skip, hop, leap, jump.

**2** *informal I'm too old for this kind of caper* STUNT, monkey business, escapade, prank, trick, mischief, foolery, tomfoolery, antics, hijinks, skylarking, lark, shenanigans.

**capital** noun **1** *Warsaw is the capital of Poland* FIRST CITY, seat of government, metropolis.

**2** *she had the capital to pull off the deal* MONEY, finance(s), funds, wherewithal, means, assets, wealth, resources, investment capital; *informal* cash, dough, bread, loot, bucks.

**3** *he wrote the name in capitals* CAPITAL LETTERS, uppercase letters, block letters; *informal* caps.

**capitalism** noun *the capitalism of emerging nations* FREE ENTERPRISE, private enterprise, the free market. ANTONYM communism.

**capitalist** noun *a capitalist who made his fortune in textiles*

FINANCIER, investor, industrialist; magnate, tycoon, entrepreneur, businessman, businesswoman.

**capitalize** verb *the capacity to capitalize new ventures* FINANCE, fund, underwrite, provide capital for, back; *informal* bankroll, stake, grubstake. PHRASE: **capitalize on** *she tried to capitalize on Sam's misfortune by offering him a high-interest loan* TAKE ADVANTAGE OF, profit from, make the most of, exploit; *informal* cash in on.

**capitulate** verb *the rebels had been forced to capitulate* SURRENDER, give in/up, yield, concede defeat, give up the struggle, submit, knuckle under; lay down one's arms, raise/show the white flag, throw in the towel. ANTONYMS resist, hold out.

**caprice** noun **1** *his wife's caprices* WHIM, whimsy, vagary, fancy, fad, quirk, eccentricity, foible.

**2** *the staff tired of his caprice* FICKLENESS, changeableness, volatility, capriciousness, unpredictability.

**capricious** adjective *the capricious workings of fate* FICKLE, inconstant, changeable, variable, mercurial, volatile, unpredictable, temperamental; whimsical, fanciful, flighty, quirky, faddish. ANTONYM consistent.

**capsize** verb *gale-force winds capsized their small craft* OVERTURN, turn over, turn upside down, upend, flip/tip/keel over, turn turtle; *Nautical* pitchpole; *archaic* overset. ANTONYM right.

**capsule** noun **1** *he swallowed a capsule* PILL, tablet, lozenge, pastille, drop; *informal* tab.

**2** *a space capsule* MODULE, craft, probe.

**captain** noun **1** *the ship's captain* COMMANDER, master; *informal* skipper.

**2** *the team captain* LEADER, head; *informal* boss, skipper.

**3** *a captain of industry* MAGNATE, tycoon, industrialist; chief, head, leader, principal; *informal* boss, number one, bigwig, big shot, big gun, big cheese, big kahuna, honcho, top dog, top banana.

▸ verb *a vessel captained by a cutthroat* COMMAND, run, be in charge of, control, manage, govern; *informal* skipper.

**caption** noun *the captions are written in German* TITLE, heading, wording, head, legend, subtitle; rubric, slogan.

**captivate** verb *audiences are captivated by his energy* ENTHRALL, charm, enchant, bewitch, fascinate, beguile, entrance, enrapture, delight, attract, allure; engross, mesmerize, spellbind, hypnotize. ANTONYMS repel, bore.

**captive** noun *release the captives* PRISONER, convict, detainee, inmate, abductee; prisoner of war, POW, internee; *informal* jailbird, con, yardbird, lifer.

▸ adjective *captive wild animals* CONFINED, caged, incarcerated, locked up; jailed, imprisoned, in prison, interned, detained, in captivity, under lock and key, behind bars.

**captivity** noun *these creatures will languish in captivity* IMPRISONMENT, confinement, internment, incarceration, detention, custody. ANTONYM freedom.

**capture** verb **1** *the spy was captured in Moscow* CATCH, apprehend, seize, arrest; take prisoner, take captive, imprison, detain, put/throw in jail, put behind bars, put under lock and key, incarcerate; *informal* nab, collar, bag, pick up. ANTONYM free.

**2** *guerrillas captured a strategic district* OCCUPY, invade, conquer, seize, take, take over, take possession of.

**3** *the music captured the atmosphere of a summer morning* EXPRESS, reproduce, represent, encapsulate.

**4** *the tales of pirates captured the children's imaginations* ENGAGE, attract, catch, seize, hold.

▸ noun *he tried to evade capture* ARREST, apprehension, seizure, being taken prisoner, being taken captive, imprisonment.

**car** noun **1** *he drove up in his car* AUTOMOBILE, motor vehicle, vehicle; *dated* motorcar; *informal* auto, wheels, gas guzzler; jalopy, lemon, junker, clunker, Tin Lizzie, rustbucket.

**2** *the dining car* CARRIAGE, coach.

**carafe** noun *a carafe of hot coffee* FLASK, jug, pitcher, decanter, flagon.

**caravan** noun *a refugee caravan* CONVOY, procession, column, train, cavalcade.

**carcass** noun *a mule carcass* CORPSE, dead body, body, remains; *Medicine* cadaver; *informal* stiff, roadkill; *archaic* corse. See note at BODY.

**card** noun **1** *a piece of stiff card* CARDBOARD, pasteboard, board, Bristol board.

**2** *I'll send her a card* GREETING CARD, postcard, notecard.

**3** *she produced her card* IDENTIFICATION (CARD), ID, credentials, pass, key card; business card, calling card.

**4** *she paid with her card* CREDIT CARD, debit card, bank card, charge card, gold card, platinum card; phone card; *informal* plastic.

**5** *the cards were dealt* PLAYING CARD; tarot card; **(cards)** deck/pack of cards.

**6** *informal she's such a card!* ECCENTRIC, character; JOKER, wit, wag, jester, clown, comedian; *informal* laugh, scream, hoot, riot, jokester.

**cardinal** adjective *you've broken one of the cardinal rules* FUNDAMENTAL, basic, main, chief, primary, crucial, pivotal, prime, principal, paramount, preeminent, highest, key, essential. ANTONYM unimportant.

**care** noun **1** *the care of the child* SAFEKEEPING, SUPERVISION, custody, charge, protection, control, responsibility; guardianship, wardship. ANTONYM neglect.

**2** *handle with care* CAUTION, carefulness, heedfulness, heed, attention, attentiveness. ANTONYM carelessness.

**3** *she chose her words with care* DISCRETION, judiciousness, forethought, thought, regard, heed, mindfulness; accuracy, precision, discrimination. ANTONYM carelessness.

**4** *the cares of the day* WORRY, anxiety, trouble, concern, stress, pressure, strain; sorrow, woe, hardship.

**5** *care for the elderly* HELP, aid, assistance, succor, support; concern, consideration, thought, regard, solicitude; *informal* TLC. ANTONYM disregard.

▸ verb *the teachers didn't care about our work* BE CONCERNED, worry (oneself), trouble oneself, concern oneself, bother, mind, be interested; *informal* give a damn, give a hoot.

PHRASE: **care for 1** *he cares for his children* LOVE, be fond of, be devoted to, treasure, adore, dote on, think the world of, worship, idolize.

**2** *would you care for a cup of coffee?* LIKE, want, desire, fancy, feel like.

**3** *Hospice cares for the terminally ill* LOOK AFTER, take care of, tend (to), attend to, minister to, nurse; be responsible for, keep safe, keep an eye on.

USAGE NOTE **couldn't care less**

*Couldn't care less* is the correct and logical phrasing, not *could care less*—e.g.: "The American people could care less [read *couldn't care less*] who's White House Chief of Staff." (George Will, on "This Week with David Brinkley"; July 3, 1994.) If you *could care less*, you're saying that you do care some. Invariably, though, writers and speakers who use the phrase mean that they don't care at all. Although some apologists argue that *could care less* is meant to be sarcastic and not to be taken literally, a more plausible explanation is that the *-n't* of *couldn't* has been garbled in sloppy speech and sloppy writing. As American linguist Atcheson L. Hench explains: "A listener has not heard the whole phrase; he has heard a slurred form. *Couldn't care* has two dental stops practically together, *dnt*. This is heard only as *d* and slurring results. The outcome is *I c'd care less*." (*American Speech*, 159; 1973.) *—BG*

**career** noun **1** *a business career* PROFESSION, occupation, job, vocation, calling, employment, line, line of work, walk of life, métier.

**2** *a checkered career* HISTORY, existence, life, course, passage, path.

▸ adjective *a career politician* PROFESSIONAL, permanent, full-time.

**carefree** adjective *she's nothing like her carefree mother* UNWORRIED, untroubled, blithe, airy, nonchalant, insouciant, happy-go-lucky, free and easy, easygoing, relaxed, mellow; *informal* laid-back, loosey-goosey. ANTONYM careworn.

**careful** adjective **1** *be careful when you go up the stairs* CAUTIOUS, heedful, alert, attentive, watchful, vigilant, wary, on guard, circumspect. See note at VIGILANT. ANTONYM careless.

**2** *she'd always been careful with money* PRUDENT, thrifty, frugal, economical, economizing, scrimping, abstemious, sensible; mean, miserly, penny-pinching, parsimonious, niggardly; *informal* stingy. ANTONYM extravagant.

**3** *careful consideration of the facts* ATTENTIVE, conscientious, painstaking, meticulous, diligent, deliberate, assiduous, sedulous, scrupulous, punctilious, methodical; *informal* persnickety. ANTONYM inattentive.

**careless** adjective **1** *careless motorists* INATTENTIVE, incautious, negligent, absentminded, remiss; heedless, irresponsible, impetuous, reckless, foolhardy; cavalier, supercilious, devil-may-care. ANTONYMS careful, attentive.

**2** *careless work* SHODDY, slapdash, slipshod, slovenly, negligent, lax, slack, disorganized, hasty, hurried; *informal* sloppy, slaphappy. ANTONYM meticulous.

**3** *a careless remark* THOUGHTLESS, insensitive, indiscreet, unguarded, incautious, inadvertent. ANTONYM judicious.

**4** *she carried on,* ***careless of*** *the time* HEEDLESS OF, unconcerned with, indifferent to, oblivious to.

**caress** verb *his hands caressed her back* STROKE, touch, fondle, brush, pet; hug, embrace; nuzzle.

**caretaker** noun JANITOR, custodian, superintendent, maintenance man/woman; curator; concierge, attendant, porter; *informal* super.

▸ adjective *a caretaker government* TEMPORARY, short-term, provisional, substitute, acting, interim, pro tem, stand-in, fill-in, stopgap. ANTONYM permanent.

**cargo** noun *they work on the docks loading cargo* FREIGHT, load, haul, consignment, delivery, shipment; goods, merchandise, payload, lading.

**caricature** noun *a caricature of the Baldwin brothers* CARTOON, parody, satire, lampoon, burlesque; *informal* sendup, takeoff.

▸ verb *she has turned to caricaturing her fellow actors* PARODY, satirize, lampoon, make fun of, burlesque, mimic; *informal* send up, take off.

THE RIGHT WORD **caricature, burlesque, lampoon, mimicry, parody, travesty**

Skilled writers and artists who want to poke fun at someone or something have a number of weapons at their disposal. An artist might come up with a **caricature**, which is a drawing or written piece that exaggerates its subject's distinguishing features or peculiarities (*the cartoonist's caricature of the presidential candidate*). A **parody** is similar to a caricature in purpose, but is used of written work, or performances that ridicule an author or performer's work by imitating its language and style for comic effect (*a parody of the scene between Romeo and Juliet*). While a *parody* concentrates on distorting the content of the original work, a **travesty** retains the subject matter but imitates the style in a grotesque or absurd way (*their version of the Greek tragedy was a travesty*). A **lampoon** is a strongly satirical piece of writing that attacks or ridicules an individual or an institution; it is more commonly used as a verb (*to lampoon the government in a local newspaper*). While a *caricature*, a *parody*, and a *travesty* must have an original to imitate, a **burlesque** can be an independent creation or composition; it is a comic or satiric imitation, often a theatrical one, that treats a serious subject lightly or a trivial subject with mock seriousness (*the play was a burlesque of Homer's great epic*). **Mimicry** is something you don't have to be an artist, a writer, or an actor to be good at. Anyone who successfully imitates another person's speech or gestures is a good mimic or impressionist, whether the intent is playful or mocking (*he showed an early talent for mimicry; entertaining his parents with imitations of their friends*).

**carnage** noun *an unforgettable scene of carnage* SLAUGHTER, massacre, mass murder, butchery, bloodbath, bloodletting, gore; holocaust, pogrom, ethnic cleansing.

**carnal** adjective *his carnal desires* SEXUAL, sensual, erotic, lustful, lascivious, libidinous, lecherous, licentious; physical, bodily, corporeal, fleshly. ANTONYM spiritual.

**carnival** noun **1** *the town's carnival* FESTIVAL, fiesta, fête, gala, jamboree, celebration, fest.

**2** *he worked at a carnival* FAIR, amusement park, fun fair, ex, amusement show, circus, big top, midway.

**carol** noun *children sang carols* CHRISTMAS SONG, hymn, canticle.

**carouse** verb *it was pretty stupid to carouse the night before an exam* DRINK AND MAKE MERRY, go on a drinking bout, go on a spree; revel, celebrate, roister; *informal* party, booze, go boozing, binge, go on a binge, go on a bender, paint the town red, rave, whoop it up; *archaic* wassail.

**carp** verb *they could always find something to carp about* COMPLAIN, cavil, grumble, grouse, whine, bleat, nag; *informal* gripe, grouch, beef, bellyache, moan, bitch, whinge, kvetch. ANTONYM praise.

**carpenter** noun *you'll need a carpenter to repair those joists* WOODWORKER, cabinetmaker.

**carpet** noun **1** *a Turkish carpet* RUG, mat, floor covering.

**2** *a carpet of wildflowers* COVERING, blanket, layer, cover, cloak, mantle.

▸ verb *the gravel was carpeted in moss* COVER, coat, overlay, overspread, blanket.

**carriage** noun **1** *a horse and carriage* COACH, coach-and-four, stagecoach; hansom, hackney, gig, surrey.

**2** *a railroad carriage* COACH, car, passenger car; flatcar, boxcar.

**carry** verb **1** *she carried the box into the kitchen* CONVEY, transfer, move, take, bring, bear, lug, tote, fetch, cart.

**2** *a cruise line carrying a million passengers a year* TRANSPORT, convey, move, handle.

**3** *satellites carry the signal across the country* TRANSMIT, conduct, relay, communicate, convey, dispatch, beam.

**4** *the dinghy can carry the weight of the baggage* SUPPORT, sustain, stand; prop up, shore up, bolster.

**5** *managers carry most of the responsibility* BEAR, accept, assume, undertake, shoulder, take on (oneself).

**6** *she was carrying twins* BE PREGNANT WITH, bear, expect; *technical* be gravid with.

**7** *she carried herself with assurance* CONDUCT, bear, hold; act, behave, acquit; *formal* comport.

**8** *a resolution was carried* APPROVE, vote for, accept, endorse, ratify, pass; agree to, assent to, rubber-stamp; *informal* OK, give the thumbs up to.

**9** *I carried the whole audience* WIN OVER, sway, convince, persuade, influence; motivate, stimulate.

**10** *today's paper carried an article on housing policy* PUBLISH, print, communicate, distribute; broadcast, transmit.

**11** *we carry a wide range of linens* SELL, stock, keep, keep in stock, offer, have, have for sale, retail, supply.

**12** *most toxins carry warnings* DISPLAY, bear, exhibit, show, be marked with.

**13** *it carries a penalty of two years' imprisonment* ENTAIL, involve, result in, occasion, have as a consequence.

**14** *his voice carried across the field* BE AUDIBLE, travel, reach.
PHRASES: **be/get carried away** *I'm afraid I get a bit carried away* LOSE SELF-CONTROL, get overexcited, go too far; *informal* flip, lose it.
**carry something off** *she carried off four awards* WIN, secure, gain, achieve, collect; *informal* land, net, bag, scoop.
**carry on 1** *they carried on arguing* CONTINUE, keep (on), go on; persist in, persevere in, stick with/at.

**2** *informal she was carrying on with other men* HAVE AN AFFAIR, commit adultery, have a fling, play around, mess around, fool around.

**3** *informal I was always carrying on* MISBEHAVE, behave badly, get up to mischief, cause trouble, get up to no good, be naughty; clown around, fool around, mess around, act up.

**4** *we carried on a conversation* ENGAGE IN, conduct, undertake, be involved in, carry out, perform.
**carry out 1** *operations were carried out in secret* CONDUCT, perform, implement, execute.

**2** *I carried out my promise to her* FULFILL, carry through, honor, redeem, make good; keep, observe, abide by, comply with, adhere to, stick to, keep faith with.

**cart** noun **1** *a horse-drawn cart.*

**2** *carts lined up at the checkout* SHOPPING CART, handcart, pushcart.

▸ verb *informal he had the wreckage carted away* TRANSPORT, convey, haul, move, shift, take; carry, lug.

**carton** noun *a carton of empty whiskey bottles* BOX, package, cardboard box, container, pack, packet.

**cartoon** noun **1** *a cartoon of the defense secretary* CARICATURE, parody, lampoon, satire; *informal* takeoff, sendup.

**2** *he was reading cartoons* COMIC STRIP, comic, funnies, graphic novel.

**3** *they watched cartoons on television* ANIMATED FILM, animation; *informal* toon.

**cartridge** noun **1** *a toner cartridge* CASSETTE, canister, container, magazine.

**2** *a rifle cartridge* BULLET, round, shell, charge, shot.

**carve** verb **1** *she carved horn handles* SCULPT, sculpture; cut, hew, whittle; form, shape, fashion.

**2** *I carved my initials on the tree* ENGRAVE, etch, incise, score.

**3** *he carved the roast chicken* SLICE, cut up; chop. PHRASE: **carved in stone** *these are merely suggestions, they're not carved in stone* UNALTERABLE, immutable, unchangeable, irreversible, irrevocable.

**cascade** noun *a roaring cascade* WATERFALL, cataract, falls, rapids, white water.

▸ verb *rain cascaded from the roof* POUR, gush, surge, spill, stream, flow, issue, spurt.

**case**[1] noun **1** *a classic case of overreaction* INSTANCE, occurrence, manifestation, demonstration, exposition, exhibition; example, illustration, specimen, sample, exemplification.

**2** *if that is the case, I will have to find somebody else* SITUATION, position, state of affairs, lay of the land; circumstances, conditions, facts; way things stand; *informal* score.

**3** *the officers on the case* INVESTIGATION, inquiry, examination, exploration, probe, search, inquest.

**4** *only urgent cases were admitted for immediate examination* PATIENT, sick person, invalid, sufferer, victim.

**5** *she lost her case* LAWSUIT, (legal) action, legal dispute, suit, trial, legal/judicial proceedings, litigation.

**6** *a strong case* ARGUMENT, contention, reasoning, logic, defense, justification, vindication, exposition, thesis.

**case**[2] noun **1** *a cigarette case* CONTAINER, box, canister, receptacle, holder.

**2** *a seed case* CASING, cover, covering, sheath, sheathing, envelope, sleeve, jacket, integument.

**3** *a case of wine* CRATE, box, pack.

**4** *a glass display case* CABINET, cupboard, buffet.

▸ verb *informal a thief casing the joint* RECONNOITER, inspect, examine, survey, explore, check out.

**cash** noun **1** *a wallet stuffed with cash* MONEY, currency, hard cash; notes, bank notes, bills; coins, change; *informal* dough, bread, loot, moolah, bucks, dinero, lucre. ANTONYMS check, credit.

**2** *a lack of cash* FINANCE(S), money, resources, funds, assets, the means, the wherewithal.

▸ verb *the bank cashed her check* EXCHANGE, change, convert into cash/money; honor, pay, accept.

PHRASE: **cash in on** *the band is cashing in on merchandising* TAKE ADVANTAGE OF, exploit, milk; make money from, profit from, make a killing from.

**cashier** noun *the cashier took the check* CHECKOUT GIRL/BOY/PERSON, clerk; bank clerk, teller, banker, treasurer, bursar, purser.

**casino** noun *playing the slots in her favorite casino* GAMBLING ESTABLISHMENT, gambling club, gambling den, gaming house.

**cask** noun *casks of ale for the crew* BARREL, keg, butt, tun, vat, drum, hogshead; *historical* firkin.

**casket** noun **1** *the casket of a dead soldier* COFFIN, sarcophagus; *informal* box; *humorous* wooden overcoat.

**2** *a small casket of jewels* BOX, chest, case, container, receptacle.

**cast** verb **1** *he cast the stone into the stream* THROW, toss, fling, pitch, hurl, lob; *informal* chuck.

**2** *fishermen cast their nets* SPREAD, throw, open out.

**3** *she cast a fearful glance over her shoulder* DIRECT, shoot, throw, send.

**4** *each citizen cast a vote* REGISTER, record, enter, file, vote.

**5** *the fire cast a soft light* EMIT, give off, send out, radiate.

**6** *the figures cast shadows* FORM, create, produce; project, throw.

**7** *the stags' antlers are cast each year* SHED, lose, discard, slough off.

**8** *a figure cast by hand* MOLD, fashion, form, shape, model; sculpt, sculpture, forge.

**9** *they were cast as extras* CHOOSE, select, pick, name, nominate.

▸ noun **1** *a cast of the writer's hand* MOLD, die, matrix, shape, casting, model.

**2** *a cast of the dice* THROW, toss, fling, pitch, hurl, lob; *informal* chuck.

**3** *an inquiring cast of mind* TYPE, sort, kind, character, variety, class, style, stamp, nature.

**4** *the cast of our spring musical* ACTORS, performers, players, company, troupe; dramatis personae, characters.

PHRASE: **cast aside** *cast aside the pages marked with an "X"* DISCARD, reject, throw away/out, get rid of, dispose of, abandon.

**caste** noun *she could not marry outside her caste* CLASS, social class, social order, rank, level, stratum, echelon, status; *dated* estate, station.

**castigate** verb *Leopold castigated his son for leaving the archbishop's service* REPRIMAND, rebuke, admonish, chastise, chide, censure, upbraid, reprove, reproach, scold, berate, take to task, lambaste, give someone a piece of one's mind; *informal* rake/haul over the coals, tell off, give someone an earful, give someone a tongue-lashing, give someone a roasting, rap someone on the knuckles, slap someone's wrist, dress down, bawl out, give someone hell, blow up at, lay into, blast, zing, have a go at, give someone what for, chew out, ream out; *rare* reprehend. ANTONYMS praise, commend.

**castle** noun *a drafty old Scottish castle* FORTRESS, fort, stronghold, fortification, keep, citadel.

**casual** adjective **1** *a casual attitude to life* INDIFFERENT, apathetic, uncaring, unconcerned; lackadaisical, blasé, nonchalant, insouciant, offhand, flippant; easygoing, free and easy, blithe, carefree, devil-may-care; *informal* laid-back, loosey-goosey, Type-B. ANTONYMS careful, concerned.

**2** *a casual remark* OFFHAND, spontaneous, unpremeditated, unthinking, unconsidered, impromptu, throwaway, unguarded; *informal* off-the-cuff. ANTONYM premeditated.

**3** *a casual glance* CURSORY, perfunctory, superficial, passing, fleeting; hasty, brief, quick. ANTONYMS careful, thorough.

**4** *a casual acquaintance* SLIGHT, superficial. ANTONYMS intimate, close.

**5** *casual work* TEMPORARY, part-time, freelance, impermanent, irregular, occasional. ANTONYMS permanent, full-time.

**6** *casual sex* PROMISCUOUS, extramarital, free.

**7** *a casual meeting changed his life* CHANCE, accidental, unplanned, unintended, unexpected, unforeseen, unanticipated, fortuitous, serendipitous, adventitious. See note at ACCIDENTAL. ANTONYMS intentional, planned.

**8** *a casual shirt* INFORMAL, comfortable, leisure, everyday; *informal* sporty. ANTONYMS formal, dressy.

**9** *the inn's casual atmosphere* RELAXED, friendly, informal, unceremonious, easygoing, free and easy; *informal* laid-back. ANTONYM formal.

**casualty** noun *a casualty of war | a record of the casualties* VICTIM, fatality, loss, MIA; **(casualties)** dead and injured, missing in action, missing.

**cat** noun *their pet cats* FELINE, tomcat, tom, kitten, mouser; *informal* pussy (cat), puss, kitty; alley cat; *archaic* grimalkin.

**catacombs** plural noun *they unearthed the catacombs of an apparently prominent family* UNDERGROUND CEMETERY, crypt, vault, tomb, ossuary.

**catalog** noun **1** *a library catalog* DIRECTORY, register, index, list, listing, record, archive, inventory.

**2** *a mail-order catalog* BROCHURE, mailer, wish book.

▸ verb *the collection is fully cataloged* CLASSIFY, categorize, systematize, index, list, archive, make an inventory of, inventory, record, itemize.

**catapult** verb *the boulder was catapulted into the sea* PROPEL, launch, hurl, fling, send flying, fire, blast, shoot.

**cataract** noun *the glistening cataract made a spectacular backdrop for our photo shoot* WATERFALL, cascade, falls, rapids, white water.

**catastrophe** noun *the flood of '82 was the worst catastrophe in the town's history* DISASTER, calamity, cataclysm, holocaust, havoc, ruin, ruination, tragedy; adversity, blight, trouble, trial, tribulation.

**catcall** noun *the young comics have to learn how to withstand the inevitable catcalls* WHISTLE, boo, hiss, jeer, raspberry, taunt; **(catcalls)** scoffing, abuse, taunting, derision.

**catch** verb **1** *he caught the ball* SEIZE, grab, snatch, take hold of, grasp, grip, trap, clutch, clench; receive, get, intercept. ANTONYM drop.

**2** *we've caught the thief* CAPTURE, seize; apprehend, arrest, take prisoner/captive, take into custody; trap, snare, ensnare; net, hook, land; *informal* nab, collar, run in, bust. ANTONYM release.

**3** *her heel caught in a hole* BECOME TRAPPED, become entangled, snag.

**4** *she caught the last bus* BE IN TIME FOR, make, get; board, get on, step aboard. ANTONYM miss.

**5** *they were caught siphoning gas* DISCOVER, find, come upon/across, stumble on, chance on; surprise, catch red-handed, catch in the act.

**6** *it caught his imagination* ENGAGE, capture, attract, draw, grab, grip, seize; hold, absorb, engross.

**7** *she caught a trace of aftershave* PERCEIVE, notice, observe, discern, detect, note, make out. ANTONYM miss.

**8** *I couldn't catch what she was saying* HEAR, perceive, discern, make out; understand, comprehend, grasp, apprehend; *informal* get, get the drift of, figure out.

**9** *it caught the flavor of the sixties* EVOKE, conjure up, call to mind, recall, encapsulate, capture.

**10** *the blow caught her on the side of her face* HIT, strike, slap, smack, bang. ANTONYM miss.

**11** *he caught malaria* BECOME INFECTED WITH, contract, get, fall ill with, be taken ill with, develop, come down with, be struck down with. ANTONYM escape.

**12** *the kindling wouldn't catch* IGNITE, start burning, catch fire, kindle.

▸ noun **1** *he inspected the catch* HAUL, net, bag, yield.

**2** *he secured the catch* LATCH, lock, fastener, clasp, hasp.

**3** *it looks great, but there's a catch* SNAG, disadvantage, drawback, stumbling block, hitch, fly in the ointment, pitfall, complication, problem, hiccup, difficulty; trap, trick, snare; *informal* catch-22.

PHRASES: **catch on 1** *radio soon caught on* BECOME POPULAR, become fashionable, take off, boom, flourish, thrive.

**2** *I caught on fast* UNDERSTAND, comprehend, learn, see the light; *informal* latch on, get the picture, get the message, get wise.

**catch up to** *police didn't catch up to Swanson until he stopped for gas and food in Great Neck* REACH; be even with; gain on, close in on.

**catching** adjective *informal my rash is not catching* INFECTIOUS, contagious; communicable, transmittable, transmissible, infective.

**catchy** adjective *I'm not sure what their product is, but they've got a catchy little jingle* MEMORABLE, unforgettable, haunting; appealing, popular; singable, melodious, tuneful, foot-tapping.

**categorical** adjective *a categorical assurance that annual premiums would not increase* UNQUALIFIED, unconditional, unequivocal, absolute, explicit, express, unambiguous, definite, direct, downright, outright, emphatic, positive, point-blank, conclusive, without reservations, out-and-out. ANTONYMS qualified, equivocal.

**categorize** verb *we should first categorize them by years of experience* CLASSIFY, class, group, grade, rate, designate; order, arrange, sort, rank; file, catalog, list, index; typecast, pigeonhole, stereotype.

**category** noun *his music doesn't fit into any conventional category* CLASS, classification, group, grouping, bracket, heading, set; type, sort, kind, variety, species, breed, brand, make, model; grade, order, rank; *informal* pigeonhole.

**cater** verb **1** *we* ***cater for*** *vegetarians* PROVIDE FOOD FOR, feed, serve, cook for.

**2** *a resort* ***catering to*** *older travelers* SERVE, provide for, meet the needs/wants of, accommodate; satisfy, indulge, pander to, gratify.

**3** *he seemed to* ***cater to*** *all tastes* TAKE INTO ACCOUNT, take into consideration, allow for, consider, bear in mind, make provision for, have regard for.

**catharsis** noun *the hope was that hypnosis would bring about a catharsis* EMOTIONAL RELEASE, relief, release, venting; purging, purgation, purification, cleansing; *Psychoanalysis* abreaction.

**catholic** adjective *her musical tastes are quite catholic* UNIVERSAL, diverse, diversified, wide, broad, broad-based, eclectic, liberal, latitudinarian; comprehensive, all-encompassing, all-embracing, all-inclusive. See note at UNIVERSAL. ANTONYM narrow.

**cattle** plural noun COWS, bovines, oxen, bulls; stock, livestock.

**catty** adjective *informal*. See SPITEFUL.

**caucus** noun **1** *the conservative caucus* MEMBERS, party, faction, camp, bloc, group, set, band, ring, cabal, coterie, pressure group.

**2** *caucuses will be held in eleven states* MEETING, assembly, gathering, congress, conference, convention, rally, convocation.

**cause** noun **1** *the cause of the fire* SOURCE, root, origin, beginning(s), starting point; mainspring, base, basis, foundation, fountainhead; originator, author, creator, producer, agent. ANTONYMS effect, result.

**2** *there is no cause for alarm* REASON, grounds, justification, call, need, necessity, occasion; excuse, pretext.

**3** *the cause of human rights* | *a good cause* PRINCIPLE, ideal, belief, conviction; object, end, aim, objective, purpose, mission; charity.

**4** *he went to plead his cause* CASE, suit, lawsuit, action, dispute.

▸ verb *this disease can cause blindness* BRING ABOUT, give rise to, lead to, result in, create, produce, generate, engender, spawn, bring on, precipitate, prompt, provoke, trigger, make happen, induce, inspire, promote, foster; *literary* beget, enkindle. ANTONYM result from.

**caustic** adjective **1** *a caustic cleaner* CORROSIVE, corroding, abrasive, mordant, acid.

**2** *a caustic comment* SARCASTIC, cutting, biting, mordant, sharp, bitter, scathing, derisive, sardonic, ironic, scornful, trenchant, acerbic, abrasive, vitriolic, acidulous.

**caution** noun *proceed with caution* CARE, carefulness, heedfulness, heed, attention, attentiveness, alertness, watchfulness, vigilance, circumspection, discretion, prudence.

▸ verb *you were cautioned against taking such rash action* ADVISE, warn, counsel; admonish, exhort.

**cautious** adjective *a cautious driver* CAREFUL, heedful, attentive, alert, watchful, vigilant, circumspect, prudent; cagey, canny. See note at VIGILANT. ANTONYM reckless.

**cavalcade** noun *bystanders cheered as the cavalcade passed by* PROCESSION, parade, motorcade, cortège.

**cavalier** noun *archaic foot soldiers and cavaliers* HORSEMAN, equestrian; cavalryman, trooper, knight.

▸ adjective *a cavalier disregard for danger* OFFHAND, indifferent, casual, dismissive, insouciant, unconcerned; supercilious, patronizing, condescending, disdainful, scornful, contemptuous; *informal* couldn't-care-less, devil-may-care.

**cavalry** plural noun *he rode with the cavalry during the Mexican War* MOUNTED TROOPS, cavalrymen, troopers, horse; *historical* dragoons, lancers, hussars.

**cave** noun *the caves at the bottom of the cliff* CAVERN, grotto, underground chamber; cellar, vault, crypt. PHRASE: **cave in 1** *the roof caved in* COLLAPSE, fall in/down, give, give way, crumble, subside.

**2** *the manager caved in to their demands* YIELD, surrender, capitulate, submit, give in, back down, make concessions, throw in the towel.

**caveat** noun *he added the caveat that the results still had to be corroborated* WARNING, caution, admonition; proviso, condition, stipulation, provision, clause, rider, qualification.

**caveman** , **cavewoman** noun *were these the drawings of a caveman?* CAVE DWELLER, troglodyte, primitive man/woman, prehistoric man/woman; Neanderthal.

**cavern** noun *the crude stone steps led down to a dank and cold cavern* LARGE CAVE, grotto, underground chamber/gallery, vault.

**cavernous** adjective *dinner was served in a cavernous hall* VAST, huge, large, immense, spacious, roomy, airy, capacious, voluminous, extensive, deep; hollow, gaping, yawning; *formal* commodious. ANTONYM small.

**cavil** verb *He caviled at the cost.* See CARP.

**cavity** noun *microscopic photos show a surface erose with nodes and cavities* SPACE, chamber, hollow, hole, pocket, pouch; orifice, aperture; socket, gap, crater, pit.

**cease** verb **1** *hostilities had ceased* COME TO AN END, come to a halt, end, halt, stop, conclude, terminate, finish, draw to a close, be over. ANTONYMS start, continue.

**2** *they ceased all military activity* BRING TO AN END, bring to a halt, end, halt, stop, conclude, terminate, finish, wind up, discontinue, suspend, break off; *informal* leave off. ANTONYMS start, continue.

PHRASE: **without cease** *they have worked without cease on these prototypes* CONTINUOUSLY, incessantly, unendingly, unremittingly, without a pause, without a break, on and on.

**ceaseless** adjective *a ceaseless flow of questions* CONTINUAL, constant, continuous; incessant, unceasing, unending, endless, never-ending, interminable, nonstop, uninterrupted, unremitting, relentless, unrelenting, unrelieved, sustained, persistent, eternal, perpetual. ANTONYM intermittent.

**cede** verb *the library has ceded ten parking spaces to the hearing clinic* SURRENDER, concede, relinquish, yield, part with, give up; hand over, deliver up, give over, make over, transfer; abandon, forgo, sacrifice; *literary* forsake. See note at RELINQUISH.

**ceiling** noun *a ceiling was to be set on prices* UPPER LIMIT, maximum, limitation.

**celebrate** verb **1** *they were celebrating their wedding anniversary* COMMEMORATE, observe, mark, keep, honor, remember, memorialize.

**2** *let's all celebrate!* ENJOY ONESELF, have fun, have a good time, have a party, revel, roister, carouse, make merry; *informal* party, go out on the town, paint the town red, whoop it up, make whoopee, live it up, have a ball.

**3** *he was celebrated for his achievements* PRAISE, extol, glorify, eulogize, reverence, honor, pay tribute to; *formal* laud.

**celebrated** adjective *a celebrated hero* ACCLAIMED, admired, highly rated, lionized, revered, honored, esteemed, exalted, vaunted, well-thought-of, ballyhooed; eminent, great, distinguished, prestigious, illustrious, preeminent, estimable, notable, of note, of repute; *formal* lauded. ANTONYM unsung.

**celebration** noun **1** *the celebration of his 50th birthday* COMMEMORATION, observance, marking, keeping.

**2** *a birthday celebration for the twins* PARTY, gathering, festivities, festival, féte, carnival, gala, jamboree, function; *informal* do, bash, shindig, rave.

**3** *the celebration of the Eucharist* OBSERVANCE, performance, officiation, solemnization.

**celebrity** noun **1** *a sports celebrity* FAMOUS PERSON, VIP, very important person, personality, name, big name, famous name, household name, star, superstar; *informal* celeb, somebody, someone, megastar. ANTONYM nonentity.

**2** *his celebrity grew* FAME, prominence, renown, eminence, preeminence, stardom, popularity, distinction, note, notability, prestige, stature, repute, reputation. ANTONYM obscurity.

**celestial** adjective **1** *a celestial body* (IN) SPACE, heavenly, astronomical, extraterrestrial, stellar, astral, planetary. ANTONYMS earthly, terrestrial.

**2** *celestial beings* HEAVENLY, holy, saintly, divine, godly, godlike, ethereal, otherworldly; immortal, angelic, seraphic, cherubic. ANTONYMS mundane, hellish.

**cell** noun **1** *a prison cell* ROOM, cubicle, chamber; dungeon, oubliette, lockup.

**2** *each cell of the honeycomb* COMPARTMENT, cavity, hole, hollow, section.

**3** *terrorist cells* UNIT, faction, arm, section, ring, coterie, group.

**cement** noun *don't step in the wet cement* MORTAR, grout, concrete; ADHESIVE, glue, fixative, gum, paste; superglue; mucilage.

▸ verb *he cemented the sample to a microscope slide* STICK, bond; fasten, fix, affix, attach, secure, bind, glue, gum, paste.

**cemetery** noun *we gather at the cemetery on Memorial Day* GRAVEYARD, churchyard, burial ground, burying ground, necropolis, memorial park/garden; *informal* boneyard; *historical* potter's field; *archaic* God's acre.

**censor** noun *the film censors* EXPURGATOR, bowdlerizer; examiner, inspector, editor.

▸ verb *letters home were censored* CUT, delete parts of, make cuts in, blue-pencil; edit, expurgate, bowdlerize, sanitize; *informal* clean up.

**censorious** adjective *the appointment of censorious watchdogs over the broadcasters* HYPERCRITICAL, overcritical, fault-finding, disapproving, condemnatory, denunciatory, deprecatory, disparaging, reproachful, reproving, censuring, captious, carping, sitting in judgment. ANTONYM complimentary.

**censure** verb *he was censured for his conduct.* See REPRIMAND verb. See also note at REBUKE.

▸ noun *a note of censure* CONDEMNATION, criticism, attack, abuse; reprimand, rebuke, admonishment, reproof, upbraiding, disapproval, reproach, scolding, obloquy; *informal* flak, dressing-down, tongue-lashing; *formal* excoriation, castigation. See note at CENSOR. ANTONYM approval.

**center** noun *the center of the town* MIDDLE, nucleus, heart, core, hub; middle point, midpoint, halfway point, mean, median. ANTONYM edge.

▸ verb *the story centers on a doctor* FOCUS, concentrate, pivot, hinge, revolve, be based.

**USAGE NOTE center on**

The construction **center on** (as opposed to *center on*, or *revolve around*) has been denounced as incorrect and illogical since it first appeared in the mid-nineteenth century. Although the phrase is common, it defies geometry by confusing the orbit with the fixed point: *the earth revolves around (or its revolution centers on) the sun*. A careful writer will use a precise expression, such as *centers on*, *revolves around*, *concerns*, or *involves*.

**central** adjective **1** *occupying a central position* MIDDLE, center, halfway, midway, mid, median, medial, mean; *Anatomy* mesial. ANTONYMS side, extreme.

**2** *central Fargo* INNER, innermost, middle, mid; downtown. ANTONYM outer.

**3** *their central campaign issue* MAIN, chief, principal, primary, leading, foremost, first, most important, predominant, dominant, key, crucial, vital, essential, basic, fundamental, core, prime, premier, paramount, major, overriding; *informal* number-one. ANTONYMS minor, subordinate.

**centralize** verb *the state is to centralize its communications network* CONCENTRATE, consolidate, amalgamate, condense, unify, streamline, focus; *Brit.* rationalize. ANTONYM devolve.

**ceramics** plural noun *an exhibit of Armenian ceramics* POTTERY, pots, china, terra cotta.

**ceremonial** adjective *a ceremonial occasion* FORMAL, official, state, public; ritual, ritualistic, prescribed, stately, courtly, solemn. See note at FORMAL. ANTONYM informal.

**ceremonious** adjective *a ceremonious affair at the White House* DIGNIFIED, majestic, imposing, impressive, solemn, ritualistic, stately, formal; courtly, regal, imperial, elegant, grand, glorious, splendid, magnificent, resplendent, portentous; *informal* starchy. See note at FORMAL.

**ceremony** noun **1** *a wedding ceremony* RITUAL, rite, ceremonial, observance; service, sacrament, liturgy, worship, celebration.

**2** *the new queen was proclaimed with due ceremony* POMP, protocol, formalities, niceties, decorum, etiquette, punctilio, politesse.

**certain** adjective **1** *I'm certain he's guilty* SURE, confident, positive, convinced, in no doubt, satisfied, assured, persuaded. ANTONYM doubtful.

**2** *it is certain that more changes are in the offing* UNQUESTIONABLE, sure, definite, beyond question, not in doubt, indubitable, undeniable, irrefutable, indisputable; obvious, evident, recognized, confirmed, accepted, acknowledged, undisputed, undoubted, unquestioned. ANTONYMS doubtful, possible, unthinkable.

**3** *they are certain to win* SURE, very likely, bound, destined. ANTONYM unlikely.

**4** *certain defeat* INEVITABLE, assured, destined, predestined; unavoidable, inescapable, inexorable, ineluctable; *informal* in the bag. ANTONYMS possible, unlikely.

**5** *there is no certain cure for this* RELIABLE, dependable, trustworthy, foolproof, tried and tested, effective, guaranteed, sure, unfailing, infallible; *informal* sure-fire, idiot-proof, goof-proof. ANTONYM unreliable.

**6** *a certain sum of money* DETERMINED, definite, fixed, established, precise. ANTONYMS undefined, undetermined.

**7** *a certain lady* PARTICULAR, specific, individual, special.

**8** *to a certain extent that is true* MODERATE, modest, medium, middling; limited, small. ANTONYM great.

**certainly** adverb *this is certainly a forgery* UNQUESTIONABLY, surely, assuredly, definitely, beyond/without question, without doubt, indubitably, undeniably, irrefutably, indisputably; obviously, patently, evidently, plainly, clearly, unmistakably, undisputedly, undoubtedly; *informal* sure as shootin', for sure. ANTONYM possibly.

▸ exclamation *"May I have one?" "Certainly."* YES, definitely, absolutely, sure, by all means, indeed, of course, naturally; affirmative; *informal* OK, okay.

**certainty** noun **1** *she knew with certainty that he was telling the truth* CONFIDENCE, sureness, positiveness, conviction, certitude, assurance. ANTONYM doubt.

**2** *he accepted defeat as a certainty* INEVITABILITY, foregone conclusion; *informal* sure thing, sure bet, no-brainer. ANTONYMS impossibility, possibility.

**certificate** noun *do you have any type of certificate that proves your ownership?* GUARANTEE, certification, document, authorization, registration, authentication, credentials, accreditation, license, diploma.

**certify** verb **1** *the aircraft was certified as airworthy* VERIFY, guarantee, attest, validate, confirm, substantiate, endorse, vouch for, testify to; provide evidence, give proof, prove, demonstrate.

**2** *a certified hospital* ACCREDIT, recognize, license, authorize, approve, warrant. See note at APPROVE.

**cessation** noun *the cessation of hostilities* END, ending, termination, stopping, halting, ceasing, finish, finishing, stoppage, conclusion, winding up, discontinuation, abandonment, suspension, breaking off, cutting short. ANTONYMS start, resumption.

**chafe** verb **1** *the collar chafed his neck* ABRADE, graze, rub against, gall, scrape, scratch; *Medicine* excoriate.

**2** *material chafed by the rock* WEAR AWAY/DOWN, erode, abrade, scour, scrape away.

**3** *the bank chafed at the restrictions* BE ANGRY, be annoyed, be irritated, fume, be exasperated, be frustrated.

**chaff** noun **1** *separating the chaff from the grain* HUSKS, hulls, pods, shells, bran, shucks.

**2** *the proposals were so much chaff* GARBAGE, dross, rubbish, trash; *informal* junk, crap, schlock.

**3** *good-natured chaff* BANTER, repartee, teasing, ragging, joking, jesting, raillery, badinage, wisecracks, witticism(s); *informal* kidding, ribbing; *formal* persiflage.

▸ verb *the pleasure of chaffing your buddies* TEASE, make fun of, poke fun at, make sport of; *informal* rib, razz, kid, josh, have on, pull someone's leg, pull/jerk/yank someone's chain, goof on.

**chagrin** noun *Sean showed up at the party, to everyone's chagrin* ANNOYANCE, irritation, vexation, exasperation, displeasure, dissatisfaction, discontent; anger, rage, fury, wrath, indignation, resentment; embarrassment, mortification, humiliation, shame. ANTONYM delight.

**chain** noun **1** *he was held in chains* FETTERS, shackles, irons, leg irons, manacles, handcuffs; *informal* cuffs, bracelets; *historical* bilboes.

**2** *a chain of events* SERIES, succession, string, sequence, train, course.

▸ verb *she chained her bicycle to the railing* SECURE, fasten, tie, tether, hitch; restrain, shackle, fetter, manacle, handcuff.

**chair** noun *he sat down on a chair* SEAT.

▸ verb *she chairs the economic committee* PRESIDE OVER, take the chair of; lead, direct, run, manage, control, be in charge of.

**chalk** PHRASE: **chalk something up 1** *he has chalked up another success* ACHIEVE, attain, accomplish, gain, earn, win, succeed in making, make, get, obtain, rack up.

**2** *I forgot completely—chalk it up to age* ATTRIBUTE, assign, ascribe, put down; blame on, pin on, lay at the door of.

**chalky** adjective **1** *chalky skin* PALE, bloodless, pallid, colorless, wan, ashen, white, pasty.

**2** *chalky bits at the bottom of the glass* POWDERY, gritty, granular.

**challenge** noun **1** *he accepted the challenge* DARE, provocation; summons.

**2** *a challenge to his leadership* TEST, questioning, dispute, stand, opposition, confrontation.

**3** *it was proving quite a challenge* PROBLEM, difficult task, test, trial.

▸ verb **1** *we challenged their statistics* QUESTION, disagree with, dispute, take issue with, protest against, call into question, object to.

**2** *he challenged one of my men to a duel* DARE, summon, throw down the gauntlet to.

**3** *changes that would challenge them* TEST, tax, strain, make demands on; stretch, stimulate, inspire, excite.

USAGE NOTE **challenged**

The use of **challenged** with a preceding adverb, e.g., **physically challenged**, originally intended to give a more positive tone than such terms as **disabled** or **handicapped**, arose in the U.S. in the 1980s. Despite the originally serious intention, the term rapidly became stalled by uses whose intention was to make fun of the attempts at euphemism and whose tone was usually clearly ironic: examples include **cerebrally challenged**, **follicularly challenged**, etc.

**chamber** noun **1** *a debating chamber* ROOM, hall, assembly room, auditorium.

**2** archaic *we slept safely in our chamber* BEDROOM, room; *literary* bower; *historical* boudoir; *archaic* bedchamber.

**3** *the left chamber of the heart* COMPARTMENT, cavity; *Anatomy* auricle, ventricle.

**champion** noun **1** *the world champion* WINNER, titleholder, defending champion, gold medalist, titleist; prizewinner, victor; *informal* champ, number one, king.

**2** *a champion of change* ADVOCATE, proponent, promoter, supporter, defender, upholder, backer, exponent; campaigner, lobbyist, crusader, apologist, booster, flag-bearer.

**3** *historical* *the king's champion* KNIGHT, man-at-arms, warrior.

▸ verb *championing the rights of refugees* ADVOCATE, promote, defend, uphold, support, back, stand up for, take someone's part; campaign for, lobby for, fight for, crusade for, stick up for. ANTONYM oppose.

**chance** noun **1** *there was a chance he might be released* POSSIBILITY, prospect, probability, likelihood, likeliness, expectation, anticipation; risk, threat, danger.

**2** *I gave her a chance to answer* OPPORTUNITY, opening, occasion, turn, time, window (of opportunity); *informal* shot.

**3** *Nichola took an awful chance* RISK, gamble, venture, speculation, long shot, shot in the dark.

**4** *pure chance* ACCIDENT, coincidence, serendipity, fate, destiny, fortuity, providence, happenstance; good fortune, luck, good luck, fluke.

▸ adjective *a chance discovery* ACCIDENTAL, fortuitous, adventitious, fluky, coincidental, serendipitous; unintentional, unintended, inadvertent, unplanned. ANTONYM intentional.

▸ verb **1** *I chanced to meet him* HAPPEN. See note at HAPPEN.

**2** *she chanced another look* RISK, hazard, venture, try; *formal* essay.

PHRASES: **by chance** *we found a signed first edition completely by chance* FORTUITOUSLY, by accident, accidentally, coincidentally, serendipitously; unintentionally, inadvertently.

**chance on/upon** *if you should chance upon a Willie McCovey card, please let me know* COME ACROSS/UPON, run across/into, happen on, light on, stumble on, find by chance, meet (by chance), bump into.

**chancy** adjective *informal* *these investments seem too chancy for me* RISKY, unpredictable, uncertain, precarious; unsafe, insecure, tricky, high-risk, hazardous, perilous, parlous; *informal* dicey, hairy. ANTONYM predictable.

**change** verb **1** *this could change the face of television | things have changed* ALTER, make/become different, adjust, adapt, amend, modify, revise, refine; reshape, refashion, redesign, restyle, revamp, rework, remodel, reorganize, reorder; vary, transform, transfigure, transmute, metamorphose, evolve; *informal* tweak, doctor, rejig; *technical* permute. ANTONYMS preserve, stay the same.

**2** *they've changed places* EXCHANGE, substitute, swap, switch, replace, alternate, interchange. ANTONYM keep.

▸ noun **1** *a change of plan* ALTERATION, modification, variation, revision, amendment, adjustment, adaptation; remodeling, reshaping, rearrangement, reordering, restyling, reworking; metamorphosis, transformation, evolution, mutation; *informal* transmogrification.

**2** *a change of government* EXCHANGE, substitution, swap, switch, changeover, replacement, alternation, interchange.

**3** *I don't have any change* COINS, loose/small change, silver; cash, petty cash; formal specie.

PHRASE: **have a change of heart** See HEART.

**changeable** adjective **1** *the weather will be changeable | changeable moods* VARIABLE, inconstant, varying, changing, fluctuating, irregular; erratic, inconsistent, unstable, unsettled, turbulent, protean; fickle, capricious, temperamental, volatile, mercurial, unpredictable, blowing hot and cold; *informal* up and down. ANTONYM constant.

**2** *the colors are changeable* ALTERABLE, adjustable, modifiable, variable, mutable, exchangeable, interchangeable, replaceable. ANTONYM invariable.

**channel** noun **1** *sailing the North Channel* STRAIT(S), sound, narrows, passage, sea passage.

**2** *the water ran down a channel* DUCT, gutter, conduit, trough, culvert, sluice, spillway, race, drain.

**3** *a channel for their extraordinary energy* USE, medium, vehicle, way of harnessing; release (mechanism), safety valve, vent.

**4** *a channel of communication* MEANS, medium, instrument, mechanism, agency, vehicle, route, avenue.

▸ verb **1** *she* ***channeled out*** *a groove* HOLLOW OUT, gouge (out), cut (out).

**2** *many countries channel their aid through charities* CONVEY, transmit, conduct, direct, guide, relay, pass on, transfer.

**chant** noun **1** *the protesters' chants* SHOUT, cry, call, rallying call, cheer, slogan.

**2** *the melodious chant of the monks* INCANTATION, intonation, singing, song, plainsong, recitative.

▸ verb **1** *protesters were chanting slogans* SHOUT, chorus, repeat.

**2** *the choir chanted Psalm 118* SING, intone, incant.

**chaos** noun *police were called in to quell the chaos* DISORDER, disarray, disorganization, confusion, mayhem, bedlam, pandemonium, havoc, turmoil, tumult, commotion, disruption, upheaval, uproar, maelstrom; muddle, mess, shambles, free-for-all; anarchy, lawlessness, entropy; *informal* hullabaloo, hoopla, all hell broken loose. ANTONYM order.

**chaotic** adjective *the whole town was chaotic* DISORDERLY, disordered, in disorder, in chaos, in disarray, disorganized, topsy-turvy, in pandemonium, in turmoil, in an uproar; in a muddle, in a mess, messy, in a shambles; anarchic, lawless.

**chap** verb *my skin chapped in the wind* BECOME RAW, become sore, become inflamed, chafe, crack.

**chapter** noun **1** *the first chapter of the book* SECTION, division, part, portion.

**2** *a new chapter in our history* PERIOD, phase, page, stage, epoch, era.

**3** *a local chapter of the American Cancer Society* BRANCH, division, subdivision, section, department, lodge, wing, arm.

**4** *the cathedral chapter* GOVERNING BODY, council, assembly, convocation, synod, consistory.

**char** verb *the steaks should be slightly charred* SCORCH, burn, singe, sear, blacken; *informal* toast. See note at BURN.

**character** noun **1** *a forceful character* | *the character of a town* PERSONALITY, nature, disposition, temperament, temper, mentality, makeup; features, qualities, properties, traits; spirit, essence, identity, ethos, complexion, tone, feel, feeling.

**2** *a woman of character* INTEGRITY, honor, moral strength, moral fiber, rectitude, uprightness; fortitude, strength, backbone, resolve, grit, willpower; *informal* guts, gutsiness.

**3** *a stain on his character* REPUTATION, name, good name, standing, stature, position, status.

**4** *informal a bit of a character* ECCENTRIC, oddity, madcap, crank, individualist, nonconformist, rare bird, free spirit; *informal* oddball.

**5** *a boorish character* PERSON, man, woman, soul, creature, individual, customer.

**6** *the characters develop throughout the play* PERSONA, role, part; **(characters)** dramatis personae.

**7** *thirty characters per line* LETTER, figure, symbol, sign, mark.

**characteristic** noun *interesting characteristics* ATTRIBUTE, feature, quality, essential quality, property, trait, aspect, element, facet; mannerism, habit, custom, idiosyncrasy, peculiarity, quirk, oddity, foible.

▸ adjective *his characteristic eloquence* TYPICAL, usual, normal, predictable, habitual; distinctive, particular, special, especial, peculiar, idiosyncratic, defining, singular, unique.

**characterize** verb **1** *the period was characterized by scientific advancement* DISTINGUISH, make distinctive, mark, typify, set apart.

**2** *the women are characterized as prophets of doom* PORTRAY, depict, present, represent, describe; categorize, class, style, brand.

**charade** noun *our entire relationship is a charade* FARCE, pantomime, travesty, mockery, parody, pretense, act, masquerade.

**charge** verb **1** *he didn't charge much* ASK IN PAYMENT, ask, levy, demand, want, exact; bill, invoice.

**2** *the subscription will be charged to your account* BILL, debit from, take from.

**3** *two men were charged with theft* ACCUSE, indict, arraign; prosecute, try, put on trial, inculpate.

**4** *they charged him with reforming the system* ENTRUST, burden, encumber, saddle, tax.

**5** *the cavalry charged the tanks* ATTACK, storm, assault, assail, fall on, swoop on, descend on; *informal* lay into, tear into. See note at ATTACK.

**6** *we charged into the crowd* RUSH, storm, stampede, push, plow, launch oneself, go headlong, steam, barrel, zoom.

**7** *his work was charged with energy* SUFFUSE, pervade, permeate, saturate, infuse, imbue, load, fill.

**8** *I charge you to stop* ORDER, command, direct, instruct, enjoin; *formal* adjure; *literary* bid.

▸ noun **1** *all customers pay a charge* FEE, payment, price, tariff, amount, sum, fare, levy.

**2** *he pleaded guilty to the charge* ACCUSATION, allegation, indictment, arraignment.

**3** *an infantry charge* ATTACK, assault, offensive, onslaught, drive, push, thrust.

**4** *the child was in her charge* CARE, protection, safekeeping, control; custody, guardianship, wardship; hands.

5 *his charge was to save the business* DUTY, responsibility, task, job, assignment, mission, function; *informal* marching orders.

6 *the safety of my charge* WARD, protégé, dependent.

7 *the judge gave a careful charge to the jury* INSTRUCTION, direction, directive, order, command, dictate, exhortation.

8 *informal I get a real charge out of working hard* THRILL, tingle, glow; excitement, stimulation, enjoyment, pleasure; *informal* kick, buzz, rush.

PHRASE: **in charge of** *I'm in charge of museum security* RESPONSIBLE FOR, in control of, in command of, at the helm/wheel of; MANAGING, running, administering, directing, supervising, overseeing, controlling.

**charitable** adjective 1 *charitable activities* PHILANTHROPIC, humanitarian, altruistic, benevolent, public-spirited; nonprofit; *formal* eleemosynary.

2 *charitable people* BIGHEARTED, generous, openhanded, free-handed, munificent, bountiful, beneficent; *literary* bounteous.

3 *he was charitable in his judgments* MAGNANIMOUS, generous, liberal, tolerant, easygoing, broad-minded, considerate, sympathetic, lenient, indulgent, forgiving, kind.

**charity** noun 1 *a children's charity* NONPROFIT ORGANIZATION, voluntary organization, charitable institution; fund, trust, foundation.

2 *we don't need charity* FINANCIAL ASSISTANCE, aid, welfare, relief, financial relief; handouts, gifts, presents, largesse; *historical* alms.

3 *his actions are motivated by charity* PHILANTHROPY, humanitarianism, humanity, altruism, public-spiritedness, social conscience, benevolence, beneficence, munificence.

4 *show a bit of charity* GOODWILL, compassion, consideration, concern, kindness, kindheartedness, tenderness, tenderheartedness, sympathy, indulgence, tolerance, leniency, caritas; *literary* bounteousness. See note at MERCY.

**charlatan** noun *Doc Brimley didn't go to no fancy halls of ivy, but he was no charlatan* QUACK, sham, fraud, fake, impostor, hoaxer, cheat, deceiver, double-dealer, swindler, fraudster, mountebank; *informal* phony, shark, con man, con artist, scam artist, flimflammer, bunco artist, snake oil salesman; *dated* confidence man/woman. See note at QUACK.

**charm** noun 1 *people were captivated by her charm* ATTRACTIVENESS, beauty, glamour, loveliness; appeal, allure, desirability, seductiveness, magnetism, charisma.

2 *these traditions retain a lot of charm* APPEAL, drawing power, attraction, allure, fascination.

3 *magical charms* SPELL, incantation, conjuration, magic formula, magic word, mojo, hex.

4 *a lucky charm* TALISMAN, fetish, amulet, mascot, totem, juju.

▸ verb 1 *he charmed them with his singing* DELIGHT, please, win (over), attract, captivate, allure, lure, dazzle, fascinate, enchant, enthrall, enrapture, seduce, spellbind.

2 *he charmed his mother into agreeing* COAX, cajole, wheedle; *informal* sweet-talk, soft-soap; *archaic* blandish.

**charming** adjective *a charming inn on the cape* | *their charming daughter* DELIGHTFUL, pleasing, pleasant, agreeable, likable, endearing, lovely, lovable, adorable, appealing, attractive, good-looking, prepossessing; alluring, delectable, ravishing, winning, winsome, fetching, captivating, enchanting, entrancing, fascinating, seductive; *informal* heavenly, divine, gorgeous; *literary* beauteous; *archaic* fair, comely. ANTONYM repulsive.

**chart** noun 1 *check your ideal weight on the chart* GRAPH, table, diagram, histogram; bar chart, pie chart, flow chart; *Computing* graphic.

2 (**charts**) *the song hit the charts at number twelve* top twenty, top ten, list, listing; *dated* hit parade.

▸ verb 1 *the changes were charted accurately* TABULATE, plot, graph, record, register, represent; make a chart/diagram of.

2 *the book charted his progress* FOLLOW, trace, outline, describe, detail, record, document, chronicle, log.

**charter** noun 1 *a royal charter* AUTHORITY, authorization, sanction, dispensation, consent, permission; permit, license, warrant, franchise.

2 *the UN Charter* CONSTITUTION, code, canon; fundamental principles, rules, laws.

3 *the charter of a yacht* HIRE, hiring, lease, leasing, rent, rental, renting; booking, reservation, reserving.

▸ verb *they chartered a bus* HIRE, lease, rent; book, reserve.

**chary** adjective *he was chary of broaching the subject* WARY, cautious, circumspect, heedful, careful, on one's guard; distrustful, mistrustful, skeptical, suspicious, dubious, hesitant, reluctant, leery, canny, nervous, apprehensive, uneasy; *informal* cagey, iffy.

**chase** verb 1 *the cat chased the mouse* PURSUE, run after, give chase to, follow; hunt, track, trail; *informal* tail.

2 *chasing young girls* PURSUE, run after, make advances to, flirt with; *informal* come on to, hit on; *dated* woo, court, romance, set one's cap for/at, make love to.

3 *she* ***chased away*** *the donkeys* DRIVE AWAY, drive off, send away, scare off; *informal* shoo (away), send packing.

4 *she* ***chased away*** *all thoughts of him* DISPEL, banish, dismiss, drive away, shut out, put out of one's mind.

▸ noun *they gave up the chase* PURSUIT, hunt, trail.

**chasm** noun 1 *a deep chasm* GORGE, abyss, canyon, ravine, gully, gulf, defile, couloir, crevasse, fissure, crevice, gulch, coulee.

2 *the chasm between their views* BREACH, gulf, rift; difference, separation, division, dissension, schism, scission.

**chassis** noun *the chassis of the car is in mint condition* FRAMEWORK, frame, structure, substructure, shell, casing.

**chaste** adjective 1 *her determination to remain chaste* VIRGINAL, virgin, intact, maidenly, unmarried, unwed; celibate, abstinent, self-restrained, self-denying, continent; innocent, virtuous, pure, pure as the driven snow, sinless, undefiled, unsullied, immaculate; *literary* vestal. ANTONYMS promiscuous, immoral.

**2** *a chaste kiss on the cheek* NONSEXUAL, platonic, innocent. ANTONYM passionate.

**3** *the dark, chaste interior* PLAIN, simple, bare, unadorned, undecorated, unornamented, unembellished, functional, no-frills, austere. ANTONYM ostentatious.

**USAGE NOTE chaste, celibate**

*Chaste* (= untainted by unlawful sexual intercourse; virtuous; sexually continent) is a word that applies to males and females alike—e.g.: "As a young and chaste boy, Yava said, he would often be called on to help construct the sand painting, lending the power of his purity." (*Phoenix Gazette*; June 4, 1993.) Unfortunately, however, a bias pervades the word's usual applications so that it typically refers to women and girls—e.g.: "One view is that a fallen woman who has fully reformed is chaste, while another is that chastity before marriage means physical virginity—a woman can be seduced only once. There is nothing unchaste about marital intercourse and hence, under either view, a widow or divorcee may be an unmarried female of previously chaste character." (Rollin M. Perkins and Ronald N. Boyce, *Criminal Law*, 3d ed.; 1982.)

There is also some confusion about the sense of *chaste*, as opposed to *celibate*. A person who is *chaste* is innocent of unlawful sex—that is, does not engage in sex with anyone other than the person's spouse. So, in both secular law and church law, a person who frequently has sex, but only with his or her spouse, is *chaste*. By contrast, a person who is *celibate* (in the word's original sense and still the only definition in the *Oxford English Dictionary*) abstains from marrying—and sex, too, but only as a consequence of the choice not to marry. The times have passed that meaning by, and today this traditional sense is obsolescent at best. It may remain current with the vow of celibacy that Catholic priests make (i.e., a promise not to marry). But it is almost universally understood, even in that context, to mean "abstaining from sex"—e.g.: "His case underscores the growing debate within the church over whether there is a place in the priesthood for gay men, even celibate ones." (*Boston Globe*; Nov. 25, 2002.) And while many word extensions result in the loss of a useful and unique term, here the shift in meaning of *celibate* has resulted in the creation of a term that has no good substitute—especially since *chaste* sounds archaic, carries outdated connotations about sex, and has drifted toward becoming gender-specific. *—BG*

**chasten** verb **1** *both men were chastened* SUBDUE, humble, cow, squash, deflate, abase; *informal* flatten, take down a peg or two, put someone in their place, cut down to size, settle someone's hash.

**2** *archaic the Heaven that chastens us.* See CHASTISE.

**chastise** verb *the staff were chastised for arriving late* SCOLD, upbraid, berate, reprimand, reprove, rebuke, admonish, chide, censure, lambaste, castigate, lecture, give someone a piece of one's mind, give someone a tongue-lashing, take to task, rake/haul over the coals; *informal* tell off, dress down, bawl out, blow up at, give someone an earful, give someone a roasting, come down on someone like a ton of bricks, slap someone's wrist, rap over the knuckles, give someone hell, give someone what for, chew out, ream out, zing; *archaic* chasten; *rare* reprehend. ANTONYM praise.

**chastity** noun *a vow of chastity* CELIBACY, chasteness, virginity, abstinence, self-restraint, self-denial, continence; innocence, purity, virtue, morality.

**chat** noun *I popped in for a chat* TALK, conversation, chitchat, gossip, chatter, heart-to-heart, tête-à-tête; *informal* jaw, confab, chinwag, rap, bull session; *formal* confabulation, colloquy. See note at CONVERSATION.

▸ verb *they chatted with their guests* TALK, gossip, chatter, speak, converse, engage in conversation, tittle-tattle, prattle (on), jabber, babble; *informal* gas, jaw, chew the fat, yap, yak, yatter, yammer, shoot the breeze; *formal* confabulate.

**chatter** noun *she tired him with her chatter* CHAT, talk, gossip, chitchat, jabbering, jabber, prattling, prattle, babbling, babble, tittle-tattle, blathering, blather; *informal* yammering, yattering, yapping, jawing, chewing the fat; *formal* confabulation, colloquy.

▸ verb *they chattered excitedly.*

**chatterbox** noun *informal he was the office chatterbox* TALKER, chatterer, prattler; *informal* windbag, bigmouth, gasbag, blabbermouth, motormouth.

**chatty** adjective **1** *he was a chatty person* TALKATIVE, communicative, expansive, unreserved, gossipy, gossiping, garrulous, loquacious, voluble, verbose; *informal* mouthy, talky, gabby, motormouthed. ANTONYM taciturn.

**2** *a chatty letter* CONVERSATIONAL, gossipy, informal, casual, familiar, friendly; *informal* newsy. ANTONYM formal.

**chauvinism** noun *they have a tendency toward small-mindedness and chauvinism* JINGOISM, excessive patriotism, blind patriotism, excessive nationalism, sectarianism, isolationism, flag-waving; xenophobia, racism, ethnocentrism, ethnocentricity; PARTISANSHIP partiality, prejudice, bias, discrimination, bigotry; male chauvinism, antifeminism, misogyny, sexism. See note at JINGOISM.

**USAGE NOTE chauvinism, jingoism**

Most traditionally, *chauvinism* (/**shoh**-vuh-niz-um/) refers to fanatical patriotism. The word is an eponym from Nicolas Chauvin, a French soldier who was ridiculed for being excessively devoted to Napoleon. By metaphorical extension, the word was broadened to denote excessive pride in people like oneself, especially in reference to males. Today *male chauvinism*, which (as a phrase, not a phenomenon) dates back to the late 1960s, is something of a cliché, being the word's most frequent application. Indeed, some writers have come to use *chauvinism* as if it were synonymous with *male chauvinism*—e.g.: "He betrayed his chauvinism by expressing surprise that I [Diane McFarlin] was an editor." (*Sarasota Herald-Tribune*; Nov. 8, 1998.) To the linguistic traditionalist, these uses (or misuses) are arrant nonsense

The void left by the shift in the meaning of *chauvinism* from national pride to supposed sexual superiority has been filled by *jingoism*. Essentially synonymous with *chauvinism* in its traditional sense, *jingoism* has the added layer of xenophobic and aggressive attitudes toward foreign policy—e.g.: "Gilmour goes overboard in trying to rationalize and justify Kipling's racism and jingoism. He argues, for example, that 'white' in *The White Man's Burden* does not refer to skin color but rather to 'civilization and character' and that Kipling's imperialistic beliefs were essentially humane and benevolent rather than based on greed, paternalism and self-interest." (*Houston Chronicle*; June 23, 2002.). Sometimes the word takes on an even softer sense, suggesting a provincialism or regionalism that is broader than national sovereignty—e.g.: "The prime minister's evident glee that the BA order had gone to a 'European' company is mere jingoism at bottom." (*Wall Street Journal Europe*; Aug. 27, 1998.) —*BG*

---

**cheap** adjective **1** *cheap tickets* INEXPENSIVE, low-priced, low-cost, economical, competitive, affordable, reasonable, reasonably priced, budget, economy, bargain, downmarket, cut-rate, reduced, discounted, discount, rock-bottom, giveaway, bargain-basement, low-end, dirt cheap. ANTONYM expensive.

**2** *cheap furniture* POOR-QUALITY, second-rate, third-rate, tinpot, substandard, low-grade, inferior, vulgar, shoddy, trashy, tawdry, meretricious, cheapjack, gimcrack, pinchbeck; *informal* rubbishy, chintzy, cheapo, junky, tacky, cheesy, ticky-tacky, kitsch, kitschy, two-bit, dime-store, schlocky. ANTONYM high-class.

**3** *she was too cheap to contribute to the fund* MISERLY, stingy, parsimonious, tightfisted, niggardly, chintzy, frugal, penny-pinching, cheeseparing. ANTONYM generous.

**4** *the cheap exploitation of suffering* DESPICABLE, contemptible, immoral, unscrupulous, unprincipled, unsavory, distasteful, vulgar, ignoble, shameful. ANTONYM admirable.

**5** *he made me feel cheap* ASHAMED, humiliated, mortified, debased, degraded.

**cheapen** verb **1** *Hetty never cheapened herself* DEMEAN, debase, degrade, lower, humble, devalue, abase, discredit, disgrace, dishonor, shame, humiliate, mortify, prostitute.

**2** *cheapening the cost of exports* REDUCE, lower (in price), cut, mark down, discount; *informal* slash.

**cheat** verb **1** *customers were cheated* SWINDLE, defraud, deceive, trick, scam, dupe, hoodwink, double-cross, gull; *informal* rip off, con, fleece, shaft, hose, sting, bilk, diddle, rook, gyp, finagle, bamboozle, flimflam, put one over on, pull a fast one on, sucker, stiff, hornswoggle; *formal* mulct; *literary* cozen.

**2** *the boy cheated death* AVOID, escape, evade, elude; foil, frustrate, thwart.

**3** *it's not the first time her husband has cheated* COMMIT ADULTERY, be unfaithful, stray; *informal* two-time, play around; *archaic* cuckold.

▸ noun *a liar and a cheat* SWINDLER, cheater, fraudster, trickster, deceiver, hoaxer, double-dealer, double-crosser, sham, fraud, fake, charlatan, quack, crook, snake oil salesman, mountebank; *informal* con man, con artist, scam artist, shark, sharper, phony, flimflammer, bunco artist; *dated* confidence man/woman.

**check** verb **1** *troops checked all vehicles* | *I checked her background* EXAMINE, inspect, look at/over, scrutinize, survey; study, investigate, research, probe, look into, inquire into; *informal* check out, give something a once-over.

**2** *he checked that the gun was cocked* MAKE SURE, confirm, verify.

**3** *two defeats checked their progress* HALT, stop, arrest, cut short; bar, obstruct, hamper, impede, inhibit, frustrate, foil, thwart, curb, block, stall, hold up, retard, delay, slow down; *literary* stay.

**4** *her tears could not be checked* SUPPRESS, repress, restrain, control, curb, rein in, stifle, hold back, choke back; *informal* keep a lid on.

▸ noun **1** *a check of the records* EXAMINATION, inspection, scrutiny, perusal, study, investigation, probe, analysis; test, trial, monitoring; checkup; *informal* once-over, look-see.

**2** *a check on the abuse of authority* CONTROL, restraint, constraint, curb, limitation.

**3** *write a check in the amount of $150* bank draft; traveler's check, certified check, bank check; paycheck.

**4** *the waitress arrived with the check* BILL, account, invoice, statement, tab.

PHRASES: **check in** *I checked in at two o'clock sharp* REPORT (ONE'S ARRIVAL), sign in, register.

**check out 1** *we'll be checking out in the morning* LEAVE, vacate, depart; pay the bill, settle up.

**2** *the police checked out dozens of leads* INVESTIGATE, look into, inquire into, probe, research, examine, go over; assess, analyze, evaluate; follow up; *informal* give something a once-over, scope out.

**3** *she checked herself out in the mirror* LOOK AT, survey, regard, inspect, contemplate; *informal* eyeball.

**keep in check** *I try to keep my temper in check* CURB, restrain, hold back, keep a tight rein on, rein in/back; control, govern, master, suppress, stifle; *informal* keep a lid on.

**checkered** adjective **1** *a checkered tablecloth* CHECKED, plaid, tartan, multicolored, many-colored.

**2** *a checkered history* VARIED, mixed, up and down, full of ups and downs, vicissitudinous; unstable, irregular, erratic, inconstant.

**checkup** noun *I saw the doctor for my annual checkup* EXAMINATION, inspection, evaluation, analysis, survey, probe, test, appraisal; check, health check; *informal* once-over, going-over.

**cheek** noun *that's enough of your cheek!* See IMPUDENCE.

**cheeky** adjective. See IMPUDENT.

**cheep** verb *the summer sounds of bees buzzing and birds cheeping* CHIRP, chirrup, twitter, tweet, peep, chitter, chirr, trill, warble, sing.

**cheer** noun **1** *the cheers of the crowd* HURRAY, hurrah, whoop, bravo, shout, roar; hosanna, alleluia; **(cheers)** applause, acclamation, clamor, acclaim, ovation. ANTONYM boo.

**2** *a time of cheer* HAPPINESS, joy, joyousness, cheerfulness, cheeriness, gladness, merriment, gaiety, jubilation, jollity, jolliness, high spirits, joviality, jocularity, conviviality, lightheartedness; merrymaking, pleasure, rejoicing, revelry. ANTONYM sadness.

**3** *Christmas cheer* FARE, food, foodstuffs, eatables, provender; drink, beverages; *informal* eats, nibbles, nosh, grub, chow; *formal* victuals, comestibles.

▸ verb **1** *they cheered their team* APPLAUD, hail, salute, shout for, root for, hurrah, hurray, acclaim, clap for; encourage, support; bring the house down for, holler for, give someone a big hand, put one's hands together for. ANTONYM boo.

**2** *the bad weather did little to cheer me* RAISE SOMEONE'S SPIRITS, make happier, brighten, buoy up, enliven, exhilarate, hearten, gladden, uplift, perk up, boost, encourage, inspirit; *informal* buck up. ANTONYM depress.

PHRASES: **cheer on** *my friends were there to cheer me on* ENCOURAGE, urge on, spur on, drive on, motivate, inspire, fire (up), inspirit, light a fire under.
**cheer up** *Leslie cheered up as soon as the grades were posted* PERK UP, brighten (up), become more cheerful, liven up, rally, revive, bounce back, take heart; *informal* buck up.

**cheerful** adjective **1** *he arrived looking cheerful* HAPPY, jolly, merry, bright, glad, sunny, joyful, joyous, lighthearted, in good/high spirits, sparkling, bubbly, exuberant, buoyant, ebullient, elated, gleeful; breezy, cheery, jaunty, animated, radiant, smiling; jovial, genial, good-humored; carefree, unworried, untroubled, without a care in the world; *informal* upbeat, chipper, chirpy, peppy, bright-eyed and bushy-tailed, full of beans; *dated* gay; *formal* blithe, jocund. ANTONYM sad.

**2** *a cheerful room* PLEASANT, attractive, agreeable, cheering, bright, sunny, happy, friendly, welcoming. ANTONYMS drab, dreary.

**cheerless** adjective *visitors often remarked that the interior of the castle was more cheerless than they had expected* GLOOMY, dreary, dull, dismal, bleak, drab, somber, dark, dim, dingy, funereal; austere, stark, bare, comfortless, unwelcoming, uninviting; miserable, wretched, joyless, depressing, disheartening, dispiriting.

**cheers** exclamation *informal from Bertie's table we could hear the clinking of glasses and a rousing "Cheers!"* HERE'S TO YOU, good health, your health, skol, prosit, salut, l'chaim; *informal* bottoms up, down the hatch, here's mud in your eye.

**cheery** adjective. See CHEERFUL sense 1.

**chef** noun *he was Mitterand's personal chef* COOK, food preparer; chef de cuisine, pastry chef, sous-chef, short-order cook, cordon bleu cook; *informal* cookie.

**cherish** verb **1** *a woman he could cherish* ADORE, hold dear, love, dote on, be devoted to, revere, esteem, admire; think the world of, set great store by, hold in high esteem; care for, tend to, look after, protect, preserve, keep safe.

**2** *I cherish her letters* TREASURE, prize, value highly, hold dear.

**3** *they cherished dreams of glory* HARBOR, entertain, possess, hold (on to), cling to, keep in one's mind, foster, nurture.

**cherub** noun **1** *she was borne up to heaven by cherubs* ANGEL, seraph.

**2** *a cherub of 18 months* BABY, infant, toddler, little angel, (tiny) tot; *literary* babe, babe in arms.

**chest** noun **1** *a bullet wound in the chest* BREAST, upper body, torso, trunk; *technical* thorax.

**2** *her matronly chest* BUST, bosom; breasts.

**3** *an oak chest* BOX, case, casket, crate, trunk, coffer, strongbox. PHRASE: **get off one's chest** *informal I've known what really happened for years, and I'd like to finally get it off my chest* CONFESS, disclose, divulge, reveal, make known, make public, make a clean breast of, bring into the open, tell all about, get a load off one's mind.

**chew** verb *Carolyn chewed a mouthful of toast* munch, chomp, champ, crunch, nibble, gnaw, eat, consume; *formal* MASTICATE, manducate. PHRASES: **chew over** *go home and chew it over* MEDITATE ON, ruminate on, think about/over/through, mull over, consider, ponder on, deliberate on, reflect on, muse on, dwell on, give thought to, turn over in one's mind; brood over, puzzle over, rack one's brains about; *informal* kick around, bat around; *formal* cogitate about.
**chew the fat** *informal.* See CHAT verb.

**chic** adjective *a chic yellow belt* STYLISH, elegant, sophisticated, dressy, smart; fashionable, high-fashion, in vogue, up-to-date, up-to-the-minute, contemporary, à la mode, chi-chi, au courant; dapper, dashing, trim; *informal* trendy, with it, happening, snappy, snazzy, modish, du jour, in, funky, natty, swish, fly, spiffy, kicky, tony. ANTONYM unfashionable.

**chicanery** noun *we didn't catch on to his chicanery until it was too late* TRICKERY, deception, deceit, deceitfulness, duplicity, dishonesty, deviousness, unscrupulousness, underhandedness, subterfuge, fraud, fraudulence, swindling, cheating, duping, hoodwinking; *informal* crookedness, monkey business, hanky-panky, shenanigans, skulduggery, monkeyshines; *archaic* management, knavery.

**chide** verb *he wasn't expecting her to chide him right there in front of everyone* SCOLD, chastise, upbraid, berate, reprimand, reprove, rebuke, admonish, censure, lambaste, lecture, give someone a piece of one's mind, take to task, rake/haul over the coals; *informal* tell off, dress down, bawl out, blow up at, give someone an earful, give someone a roasting, give someone a tongue-lashing, come down on someone like a ton of bricks, slap someone's wrist, rap over the knuckles, give someone hell, take to the woodshed, have a go at, give someone what for, chew out, ream out; *formal* castigate; *archaic* chasten; *rare* reprehend. See note at SCOLD. ANTONYM praise.

**chief** noun **1** *a Wampanoag chief* LEADER, chieftain, grand chief, sachem, sagamore, head, headman, ruler, overlord, master, commander, seigneur, liege lord, liege, potentate, cacique.
**2** *the chief of the central bank* HEAD, principal, chief executive, chief executive officer; CEO, president, chair, chairman,

chairwoman, chairperson, governor, director, manager; employer, proprietor; *informal* big cheese, big shot, bigwig, skipper, numero uno, honcho, head honcho, boss, padrone.

▸ adjective **1** *the chief rabbi* HEAD, leading, principal, premier, highest, foremost, supreme, arch. ANTONYM subordinate.

**2** *their chief aim* MAIN, principal, most important, primary, prime, first, cardinal, central, key, crucial, essential, predominant, preeminent, paramount, overriding, number-one. ANTONYMS secondary, minor.

**chiefly** adverb *we are interested chiefly in waterfront properties* MAINLY, in the main, primarily, principally, predominantly, mostly, for the most part; usually, habitually, typically, commonly, generally, on the whole, largely, by and large, almost always.

**child** noun *a well-behaved child* | *his estate goes directly to his children* YOUNGSTER, little one, boy, girl; baby, newborn, infant, toddler; cherub, angel; schoolboy, schoolgirl; minor, junior, preteen; son, daughter, descendant; *informal* kid, kiddie, tot, tyke, young 'un, lad, rug rat, ankle-biter; *derogatory* brat, guttersnipe, urchin, gamin, gamine; *literary* babe, babe in arms; (**children**) offspring, progeny, issue, brood, descendants.

**childbirth** noun *complications during childbirth have been drastically reduced* LABOR, delivery, giving birth, birthing, child-bearing; *formal* parturition; *dated* confinement; *literary* travail; *archaic* lying-in, accouchement, childbed.

**childhood** noun *born into a war-torn environment, they are subject to experiences inappropriate for anyone's childhood* YOUTH, early years, early life, infancy, babyhood, boyhood, girlhood, prepubescence, minority; springtime of life, salad days; *formal* nonage, juvenescence. ANTONYM adulthood.

**childish** adjective **1** *childish behavior* IMMATURE, babyish, infantile, juvenile, puerile; silly, inane, jejune, foolish, irresponsible. ANTONYM mature.

**2** *a round childish face* CHILDLIKE, youthful, young, young-looking, girlish, boyish, baby. ANTONYM adult.

**childlike** adjective **1** *his grandmother looked almost childlike* YOUTHFUL, young, young-looking, girlish, boyish.

**2** *geniuses tend to be rather childlike* INNOCENT, artless, guileless, unworldly, unsophisticated, naive, ingenuous, trusting, unsuspicious, unwary, credulous, gullible; unaffected, without airs, uninhibited, natural, spontaneous; *informal* wet behind the ears.

**chill** noun **1** *a chill in the air* COLDNESS, chilliness, coolness, iciness, rawness, bitterness, nip. ANTONYM warmth.

**2** *he had **a chill*** A COLD, (the) sniffles, (the) shivers, (the) flu/influenza, a fever; *archaic* (the) grippe.

**3** *the chill in their relations* UNFRIENDLINESS, lack of warmth, lack of understanding, chilliness, coldness, coolness. ANTONYM friendliness.

▸ verb **1** *the dessert is best chilled* MAKE COLD, make colder, cool (down/off); refrigerate, ice. ANTONYM warm.

**2** *his quiet tone chilled Ruth* SCARE, frighten, petrify, terrify, alarm; make someone's blood run cold, chill to the bone, make someone's flesh crawl; *informal* scare the pants off; *archaic* affright. ANTONYMS comfort, reassure.

▸ adjective *a chill wind* COLD, chilly, cool, fresh; wintry, frosty, icy, ice-cold, icy-cold, glacial, polar, arctic, raw, bitter, bitterly cold, biting, freezing, frigid, gelid, hypothermic; *informal* nippy.

PHRASE: **chill out** *informal a place to chill out.* See RELAX sense 1.

**chilly** adjective **1** *the weather had turned chilly* COOL, cold, crisp, fresh, wintry, frosty, brisk, icy, ice-cold, icy-cold, chill, glacial, polar, arctic, raw, bitter, bitterly cold, freezing, frigid, gelid, hypothermic; *informal* nippy. ANTONYM warm.

**2** *a chilly reception* UNFRIENDLY, unwelcoming, cold, cool, frosty, gelid; *informal* standoffish, offish. ANTONYMS warm, friendly.

**chime** verb **1** *the bells began to chime* RING, peal, toll, sound; ding, dong, clang, boom, bong; *literary* knell.

**2** *the clock chimed eight o'clock* STRIKE, sound.

▸ noun *the chimes of the bells* PEAL, pealing, ringing, carillon, toll, tolling; ding-dong, clanging, tintinnabulation; *literary* knell.

PHRASE: **chime in** *"Yes, you do that," Doreen chimed in* INTERJECT, interpose, interrupt, butt in, cut in, join in.

**china** noun **1** *a cup made of fine china* PORCELAIN.

**2** *a table laid with the best china* DISHES, plates, cups and saucers, tableware, chinaware, dinner service; *chiefly Brit.* crockery.

**chink** noun *a chink in the curtains* OPENING, gap, space, hole, aperture, crack, fissure, crevice, cranny, cleft, split, slit, slot.

▸ verb *the glasses chinked* JINGLE, jangle, clink, tinkle.

**chip** noun **1** *wood chips* FRAGMENT, sliver, splinter, shaving, paring, flake.

**2** *a chip in the glass* NICK, crack, scratch, notch; flaw, fault.

**3** *chiefly Brit. fish and chips* French fries, fries, home fries, frites, pommes frites.

**4** *gambling chips* COUNTER, token, check.

▸ verb **1** *a stone chipped my windshield* NICK, crack, scratch; damage.

**2** *the plaster had chipped* BREAK (OFF), crack, crumble.

**3** *chip the flint to the required shape* WHITTLE, hew, chisel, carve.

PHRASES: **chip away at** *chipping away at their defenses* erode, wear down, wear away, whittle down, corrode, gnaw away at.

**chip in** *we can afford the new dishwasher if everybody chips in* CONTRIBUTE, make a contribution, make a donation, pay; *informal* fork out, shell out, cough up, kick in.

**chirp** verb *winter is officially over when I hear the robins* *chirping* TWEET, twitter, cheep, peep, chitter, chirrup, chirr; sing, warble, trill.

**chit-chat** noun *informal we ran into each other at the pharmacy and had a little chitchat* SMALL TALK, chatter, gossip, chat, chatting, prattle.

**chivalrous** adjective **1** *his chivalrous treatment of women* GALLANT, gentlemanly, honorable, respectful, considerate; courteous, polite, gracious, well-mannered, mannerly; *archaic* gentle. ANTONYM rude.

**2** *chivalrous pursuits* KNIGHTLY, noble, chivalric; brave, courageous, bold, valiant, valorous, heroic, daring, intrepid. ANTONYM cowardly.

**chivalry** noun **1** *acts of chivalry* GALLANTRY, gentlemanliness, courtesy, courteousness, politeness, graciousness, mannerliness, good manners. ANTONYM rudeness.

**2** *the values of chivalry* KNIGHT ERRANTRY, courtly manners, knightliness, courtliness, nobility; bravery, courage, boldness, valour, heroism, daring, intrepidity; bushido.

**choice** noun **1** *it's your choice | freedom of choice* SELECTION, election, choosing, picking; decision, say, vote.

**2** *you have no other choice* OPTION, alternative, possible course of action.

**3** *an extensive choice of wines* RANGE, variety, selection, assortment.

**4** *the critics' choice* PREFERENCE, selection, pick, favorite.

▸ adjective *choice plums* SUPERIOR, first-class, first-rate, prime, premier, grade A, best, finest, excellent, select, quality, high-quality, top, top-quality, high-grade, prize, fine, special; hand-picked, carefully chosen; *informal* tip-top, A1, top-notch, blue-ribbon, blue-chip. ANTONYM inferior.

**choke** verb **1** *Christopher started to choke* GAG, retch, cough, fight for breath.

**2** *thick dust choked her* SUFFOCATE, asphyxiate, smother, stifle.

**3** *she had been choked to death* STRANGLE, throttle; asphyxiate, suffocate; *informal* strangulate.

**4** *the gutters were choked with leaves* CLOG (UP), stop up, block, obstruct, plug, bung up; *technical* occlude.

**5** *the Rangers choked in the playoffs* UNDERACHIEVE, underperform, disappoint, lose, collapse, fall apart. PHRASE: **choke back** *we could see that he was choking back tears* SUPPRESS, hold back, fight back, bite back, swallow, check, restrain, control, repress, smother, stifle; *informal* keep a lid on.

**choose** verb **1** *we chose a quiet country inn* SELECT, pick (out), opt for, settle on, decide on, fix on, take; appoint, name, nominate, vote for, elect.

**2** *I'll stay as long as I choose* WISH, want, desire, feel/be inclined, please, like, see fit.

**choosy** adjective *my cat Kiki was never too choosy when it came to leftovers* FUSSY, finicky, fastidious, overparticular, difficult/hard to please, demanding; *informal* picky, persnickety.

**chop** verb **1** *chop the potatoes into small pieces* CUT UP, cut into pieces, chop up, cube, dice, hash.

**2** *they were out back chopping wood* CHOP UP, cut up, cut into pieces, hew, split.

**3** *four fingers were* ***chopped off*** SEVER, cut off, hack off, slice off, lop off, saw off, shear off.

**4** *they chopped down large areas of rain forest* CUT DOWN, fell, hack down, clear-cut, harvest.

**5** *their training courses were chopped* CUT, ax, abolish, scrap, slash, cancel, terminate, ditch, dump, pull the plug on.

**choppy** adjective *sailing on choppy waters* ROUGH, turbulent, heavy, heaving, stormy, tempestuous, squally; uneven. ANTONYM calm.

**chore** noun **1** *he was not accustomed to doing the chores that were now expected of him* TASK, job, duty, errand; **(chores)** work, domestic work, drudgery.

**2** *informal spending the afternoon with Millie was a chore* drag, bore, pain.

**chortle** verb *they were chortling behind their hands, as if we didn't notice* CHUCKLE, laugh, giggle, titter, tee-hee, snigger.

**chorus** noun **1** *the chorus sang powerfully* CHOIR, ensemble, choral group, choristers, (group of) singers, voices, glee club.

**2** *Nancy sang the chorus* REFRAIN. PHRASE: **in chorus** *at least on the library parking issue, we were in chorus* IN UNISON, together, simultaneously, as one, united; in concert, in harmony.

**christen** verb **1** *she was christened Sara* BAPTIZE, name, give the name of, call.

**2** *a group who were christened "The Magic Circle"* CALL, name, dub, style, term, designate, label, nickname, give the name of; *formal* denominate.

**chronic** adjective **1** *a chronic illness* PERSISTENT, long-standing, long-term; incurable; *Medicine* immedicable. ANTONYM acute.

**2** *chronic economic problems* CONSTANT, continuing, ceaseless, unabating, unending, persistent, long-lasting; severe, serious, acute, grave, dire. ANTONYM temporary.

**3** *a chronic liar* INVETERATE, hardened, dyed-in-the-wool, incorrigible; compulsive; *informal* pathological. ANTONYM occasional.

**USAGE NOTE chronic**

**Chronic** is often used to mean 'habitual, inveterate,' e.g., *a chronic liar.* Some consider this use incorrect. The precise meaning of **chronic** is 'persisting for a long time,' and it is used chiefly of illnesses or other problems: *more than one million people in the United States have chronic bronchitis.*

**chronicle** noun *a chronicle of the region's past* RECORD, written account, history, annals, archive(s); log, diary, journal.

▸ verb *the events that followed have been chronicled* RECORD, put on record, write down, set down, document, register, report.

**chronological** adjective *put these eight historical events in chronological order, beginning with the earliest* SEQUENTIAL, consecutive, in sequence, in order (of time).

**chubby** adjective *look how chubby Dad was as a baby!* PLUMP, fat, rotund, portly, dumpy, chunky, well-upholstered, well-rounded; *informal* roly-poly, tubby, pudgy, blubbery, big-boned, full-figured; zaftig, corn-fed. ANTONYM skinny.

**chuck** verb *informal* 1 *he chucked the letter onto the table* THROW, toss, fling, hurl, pitch, cast, lob.

2 *I chucked the old comics* THROW AWAY/OUT, discard, dispose of, get rid of, dump, scrap, jettison; *informal* ditch, junk, deep-six, trash.

3 *Mary chucked him for another guy* LEAVE, throw over, finish with, break off with, jilt; *informal* dump, ditch.

**chuckle** verb *Adam chuckled to himself as he drove away* GIGGLE, chortle, titter, tee-hee, snicker, snigger.

**chum** noun *informal he's having lunch with a few of his old army chums* FRIEND, buddy, bud, pal; companion, sidekick, intimate; playmate, classmate, schoolmate, workmate; mate; crony; amigo, compadre. ANTONYMS enemy, stranger.

**chunk** noun *a chunk of cheese* LUMP, hunk, wedge, block, slab, square, nugget, brick, cube, bar, cake.

**church** noun 1 *a village church* PLACE OF WORSHIP, house of God, house of worship; cathedral, abbey, chapel, basilica; synagogue, mosque.

2 *the Methodist Church* DENOMINATION, ecclesial community; creed, faith.

**churlish** adjective *it seemed churlish to refuse her invitation* RUDE, ill-mannered, ill-bred, discourteous, impolite, unmannerly, uncivil, unchivalrous; inconsiderate, uncharitable, surly, sullen. ANTONYM polite.

**churn** verb 1 *Mae churned the milk* STIR, agitate, beat, whip, whisk.

2 *the sea churned* HEAVE, boil, swirl, toss, seethe; *literary* roil.

3 *propellers churned up the water* DISTURB, stir up, agitate; *literary* roil. PHRASE: **churn out** *they churn out at least twenty romance novels a year* PRODUCE, make, turn out; *informal* crank out.

**cigarette** noun *he's outside, having a cigarette informal* smoke, butt, ciggie/ciggy, cancer stick, coffin nail; *Brit. informal* fag.

**cinema** noun 1 *chiefly Brit. the local cinema* MOVIE THEATER, theater, multiplex, movie house; *historical* nickelodeon.

2 *Italian cinema* FILMS, movies, pictures, motion pictures.

**cipher** noun 1 *information in cipher* CODE, secret writing, cryptograph, cryptogram.

2 *dated a row of ciphers* ZERO, 0, nil, naught/nought.

**circle** noun 1 *a circle of gold stars* RING, band, hoop, circlet; halo, disc; *technical* annulus.

2 *her circle of friends* GROUP, set, company, coterie, clique; crowd, band; *informal* gang, bunch, crew.

3 *I don't move in such illustrious circles* SPHERE, world, milieu; society.

▸ verb 1 *seagulls circled above* WHEEL, move around, revolve, rotate, whirl, spiral.

2 *satellites circling the earth* GO AROUND, travel around, circumnavigate; orbit, revolve around.

3 *the abbey was circled by a wall* SURROUND, encircle, ring, enclose, encompass; *literary* gird.

**circuit** noun 1 *two circuits of the course* LAP, turn, round, circle.

2 *a racing circuit* TRACK, racetrack, raceway, running track, course.

3 *the judge's circuit* TOUR, tour of duty, rounds, regular journey; *informal* beat.

**circuitous** adjective 1 *a circuitous route* ROUNDABOUT, indirect, winding, meandering, serpentine, tortuous. ANTONYMS direct, straight.

2 *a circuitous discussion* INDIRECT, oblique, roundabout, circumlocutory, periphrastic. ANTONYM to the point.

**circular** adjective *a circular window* ROUND, disk-shaped, ring-shaped, annular. See note at ROUND.

▸ noun *handing out circulars at the mall* LEAFLET, pamphlet, handbill, flyer, mailer, folder.

**circulate** verb 1 *the news was widely circulated* SPREAD (AROUND/ABOUT), communicate, disseminate, make known, make public, broadcast, publicize, advertise, propagate, promulgate; distribute, give out, pass around.

2 *fresh air circulates freely* FLOW, course, move around.

3 *they circulated among their guests* SOCIALIZE, mingle.

**circumference** noun 1 *the circumference of the pit* PERIMETER, border, boundary; edge, rim, verge, margin, fringe; *literary* marge.

2 *the circumference of his arm* GIRTH, width.

**circumlocution** noun *when you've finished your circumlocution, maybe you could just get to the point* PERIPHRASIS, discursiveness, long-windedness, verbosity, verbiage, wordiness, prolixity, redundancy, pleonasm, tautology, repetitiveness, repetitiousness.

**circumscribe** verb *the power of the local agency has been circumscribed by the national organization* RESTRICT, limit, keep within bounds, curb, confine, restrain; regulate, control.

**THE RIGHT WORD circumscribe, encircle, enclose, encompass, envelop, surround**

Strictly speaking, to **circumscribe** is to draw a line around something to mark its limits or boundary (*a square circumscribed by a circle*). Beyond the realm of geometry, however, it suggests something that is hemmed in on all sides (*a lake circumscribed by mountains*). **Encompass** is used when something is set within a circle or within limits (*a road that encompassed the grounds of the estate*; *a view that encompassed the harbor*). **Surround** is a less formal word for *circumscribe*, but it can also refer to an undesirable, threatening, or dangerous situation (*surrounded by angry demonstrators; surrounded by skyscrapers*). **Encircle** is similar to *surround* in meaning, but it suggests a tight or quite circular clustering around a central object (*a bowl of fruit encircled by flowers*) or a deliberate attempt to surround someone or something for a definite reason (*to encircle the enemy camp*). **Envelop** is the right word if something is surrounded to the point where it can barely be seen (*a lonely figure enveloped in fog*) or if it is surrounded by layers or folds of an amorphous material (*enveloped in soft cotton to prevent breakage*). **Enclose** is very similar to *envelop*, but it suggests that something has been especially designed to fit around something else for protection or containment (*a ship model enclosed in a glass case*).

---

**circumspect** adjective *she would have to be circumspect in her dealings with Catherine* CAUTIOUS, wary, careful, chary, guarded, on one's guard; watchful, alert, attentive, heedful, vigilant, leery; *informal* cagey, playing one's cards close to one's chest. See note at VIGILANT. ANTONYM unguarded.

**circumstances** plural noun **1** *favorable economic circumstances* SITUATION, conditions, state of affairs, position; events, turn of events, incidents, occurrences, happenings; factors, context, background, environment.

**2** *Jane explained* ***the circumstances*** *to him* THE FACTS, the details, the particulars, how things stand, the lay of the land; *informal* what's what, the score.

**3** *reduced circumstances* FINANCIAL POSITION, lot, lifestyle; resources, means, finances, income.

**circumstantial** adjective **1** *they have only circumstantial evidence* INDIRECT, inferred, deduced, conjectural; inconclusive, unprovable.

**2** *a circumstantial account* DETAILED, particularized, comprehensive, thorough, exhaustive; explicit, specific.

**citadel** noun *they were prisoners within their own citadel* FORTRESS, fort, stronghold, fortification, castle; *archaic* hold.

**citation** noun **1** *a citation from an eighteenth-century text* QUOTATION, quote, extract, excerpt, passage, line; reference, allusion.

**2** *a citation for gallantry* COMMENDATION, mention, honorable mention.

**3** *Law a traffic citation* SUMMONS, TICKET, subpoena, writ, court order.

**cite** verb **1** *cite the passage in full* QUOTE, reproduce.

**2** *he cited the case of Roe v. Wade* REFER TO, make reference to, mention, allude to, adduce, instance; specify, name.

**3** *he has been cited many times* COMMEND, pay tribute to, praise.

**4** *Law the writ cited four of the signatories* SUMMON, summons, serve with a summons, serve with a writ, subpoena.

**citizen** noun **1** *a Japanese citizen* NATIONAL, subject, passport holder, native.

**2** *the citizens of Amsterdam* INHABITANT, resident, native, townsman, townswoman, townsperson, denizen; taxpayer; burgher.

**city** noun *Phoenix is my favorite city in the Southwest* TOWN, municipality, metropolis, megalopolis, megacity; conurbation, urban area, metropolitan area, urban municipality; borough, township; *informal* burg.

**civic** adjective *they encourage their children to participate in civic affairs* MUNICIPAL, city, town, urban, metropolitan; public, civil, community, local.

**civil** adjective **1** *a civil marriage* SECULAR, nonreligious, lay; *formal* laic. ANTONYM religious.

**2** *civil aviation* NONMILITARY, civilian. ANTONYM military.

**3** *a civil war* INTERNAL, domestic, interior, national. ANTONYMS international, foreign.

**4** *he behaved in a civil manner* POLITE, courteous, well-mannered, well-bred, chivalrous, gallant; cordial, genial, pleasant, affable; gentlemanly, ladylike. ANTONYMS discourteous, rude.

**civilian** noun *family members and other civilians were quickly evacuated from the post* NONCOMBATANT, nonmilitary person, ordinary citizen, private citizen; *informal* civvy.

**civility** noun **1** *he treated me with civility* COURTESY, courteousness, politeness, good manners, graciousness, consideration, respect, politesse, comity. ANTONYMS disrespect, rudeness.

**2** *she didn't waste time on civilities* POLITE REMARK, politeness, courtesy; formality.

**civilization** noun **1** *a higher stage of civilization* HUMAN DEVELOPMENT, advancement, progress, enlightenment, culture, refinement, sophistication.

**2** *ancient civilizations* CULTURE, society, nation, people.

**civilize** verb *they were trying to civilize people who strongly resented the intrusion* ENLIGHTEN, edify, improve, educate, instruct, refine, cultivate, polish, socialize, humanize.

**civilized** adjective *his civilized behavior | a civilized society* POLITE, courteous, well-mannered, civil, gentlemanly, ladylike, mannerly; cultured, cultivated, refined, polished, sophisticated; enlightened, educated, advanced, developed. ANTONYMS rude, unsophisticated.

**clad** adjective *he's clad in a hunting outfit* DRESSED, clothed, attired, got up, garbed, rigged out, togged out, costumed; *archaic* appareled; **(clad in)** wearing, sporting.

**claim** verb **1** *Davies claimed that she was lying* ASSERT, declare, profess, maintain, state, hold, affirm, avow; argue, contend, allege; *formal* aver.

**2** *no one claimed the items* LAY CLAIM TO, assert ownership of, formally request.

**3** *you can claim compensation* REQUEST, ask for, apply for; demand, exact.

**4** *the fire claimed four lives* TAKE, result in the loss of, cause the loss of.

▸ noun **1** *her claim that she was unaware of the problem* ASSERTION, declaration, profession, affirmation, avowal, protestation; contention, allegation.

**2** *a claim for damages* REQUEST, application; demand, petition.

**3** *we have first* ***claim on*** *their assets* ENTITLEMENT TO, title to, right to.

**claimant** noun *the claimant was a passenger on the derailed train* APPLICANT, candidate, supplicant; petitioner, plaintiff, litigant, appellant.

**clairvoyance** noun *I'm not sure how much confidence I have in Miss ZuZu's clairvoyance* ESP, extrasensory perception, sixth sense, psychic powers, second sight; telepathy.

**clamber** verb *Frankie clambered up to the top bunk* SCRAMBLE, climb, scrabble, claw one's way.

**clammy** adjective **1** *his clammy hands* MOIST, damp, sweaty, sticky; slimy, slippery. ANTONYM dry.

**2** *the clammy atmosphere* DAMP, dank, wet; humid, close, muggy, heavy.

**clamor** noun **1** *her voice rose above the clamor* DIN, racket, rumpus, loud noise, uproar, tumult, shouting, yelling, screaming, roaring; commotion, brouhaha, hue and cry, hubbub, hullabaloo, hoopla.

**2** *the clamor for her resignation* DEMAND(S), call(s), urging.

**3** *the clamor of the workers* PROTESTS, complaints, outcry.

▸ verb **1** *clamoring crowds* YELL, shout loudly, bay, scream, roar.

**2** *scientists are* ***clamoring for*** *a ban* DEMAND, call for, press for, push for, lobby for.

**clamp** noun *if the clamp is too loose, its function becomes useless* BRACE, vice, press, clasp; *Music* capo (tasto); *Climbing* jumar.

▸ verb **1** *the sander is clamped on to the workbench* FASTEN, secure, fix, attach; screw, bolt.

**2** *a pipe was clamped between his teeth* CLENCH, grip, hold, press, clasp.

PHRASE: **clamp down on** *they promised to clamp down on the drug trafficking in this neighborhood* SUPPRESS, prevent, stop, put a stop/end to, stamp out; crack down on, limit, restrict, control, keep in check.

**clampdown** noun *informal Barone's clampdown on graft rooted out a lot of unexpected dirt in the department* SUPPRESSION, prevention, stamping out; crackdown, restriction, restraint, curb, check.

**clan** noun **1** *the Macleod clan* GROUP OF FAMILIES, sept; family, house, dynasty, tribe; *Anthropology* kinship group.

**2** *a clan of art collectors* GROUP, set, circle, clique, coterie; crowd, band; *informal* gang, bunch.

**clandestine** adjective *their clandestine meetings* SECRET, covert, furtive, surreptitious, stealthy, cloak-and-dagger, hole-and-corner, closet, backstairs, backroom; hush-hush. See note at SECRET.

**clang** noun *the clang of the church bells* REVERBERATION, ringing, ring, ding-dong, bong, peal, chime, toll.

▸ verb *the huge bells clanged* REVERBERATE, resound, ring, bong, peal, chime, toll.

**clank** noun *the clank of rusty chains* JANGLING, clanging, rattling, clinking, jingling; clang, jangle, rattle, clangor, clink, jingle.

▸ verb *I could hear the chain clanking* JANGLE, rattle, clink, clang, jingle.

**clannish** adjective *your daughter is part of a very clannish group of girls* CLIQUEY, cliquish, insular, exclusive; unfriendly, unwelcoming.

**clap** verb **1** *the audience clapped* APPLAUD, clap one's hands, give someone a round of applause, put one's hands together; *informal* give someone a big hand.

**2** *he clapped Owen on the back* SLAP, strike, hit, smack, thump; pat; *informal* whack, thwack.

**3** *the dove clapped its wings* FLAP, beat, flutter.

▸ noun **1** *everybody gave him a clap* ROUND OF APPLAUSE, handclap; *informal* hand.

**2** *a clap on the shoulder* SLAP, blow, smack, thump; pat; *informal* whack, thwack.

**3** *a clap of thunder* CRACK, crash, bang, boom; thunderclap.

**claptrap** noun *sentimental claptrap.* See NONSENSE sense 1.

**clarify** verb **1** *their report clarified the situation* MAKE CLEAR, shed/throw light on, elucidate, illuminate; EXPLAIN, explicate, define, spell out, clear up. ANTONYM confuse.

**2** *clarify the butter* PURIFY, refine; filter, fine.

THE RIGHT WORD **clarify, construe, elucidate, explain, explicate, interpret**

When a biology teacher gets up in front of a class and tries to **explain** how two brown-eyed parents can produce a blue-eyed child, the purpose is to make an entire process or sequence of events understandable. In a less formal sense, to *explain* is to make a verbal attempt to justify certain actions or to make them understood (*she tried to explain why she was so late*). That same teacher might **clarify** a particular exam question that almost everyone in the class got wrong—a word that means to make an earlier event, situation, or statement clear. **Elucidate** is a more formal word meaning to *clarify*, but where the root of the latter refers to clearness, the root of the former refers to light; to *elucidate* is to shed light on something through explanation, illustration, etc. (*the principal's comments were an attempt to elucidate the school's policy on cheating*). A teacher who **explicates** something discusses a complex subject in a point-by-point manner (*to explicate a poem*). If a personal judgment is inserted in making such an explication, the correct word is **interpret** (*to interpret a poem's symbolic meanings*). To **construe** is to make a careful interpretation of something, especially where the meaning is ambiguous. For example, when a class misbehaves in front of a visitor, the teacher is likely to *construe* that behavior as an attempt to cause embarrassment or ridicule.

**clarity** noun **1** *the clarity of his account* LUCIDITY, lucidness, clearness, coherence; *formal* perspicuity. ANTONYMS vagueness, obscurity.

2 *the clarity of the image* SHARPNESS, clearness, crispness, definition. ANTONYM blurriness.

3 *the crystal clarity of the water* LIMPIDITY, limpidness, clearness, transparency, translucence, pellucidity. ANTONYMS murkiness, opacity.

**clash** noun 1 *clashes between armed gangs* CONFRONTATION, skirmish, fight, battle, engagement, encounter, conflict.

2 *an angry clash* ARGUMENT, altercation, confrontation, shouting match; contretemps, quarrel, disagreement, dispute, run-in.

3 *a clash of tweeds and a striped shirt* MISMATCH, discordance, discord, lack of harmony.

4 *the clash of cymbals* STRIKING, bang, clang, crash.

▸ verb 1 *protesters clashed with police* FIGHT, skirmish, contend, come to blows, come into conflict; do battle.

2 *the mayor clashed with union leaders* DISAGREE, differ, wrangle, dispute, cross swords, lock horns, be at loggerheads.

3 *her red scarf clashed with her coat* BE INCOMPATIBLE, not match, not go, be discordant.

4 *she clashed the cymbals together* BANG, strike, clang, crash.

**clasp** verb 1 *Ruth clasped his hand* GRASP, grip, clutch, hold tightly; take hold of, seize, grab.

2 *he clasped Joanne in his arms* EMBRACE, hug, enfold, fold, envelop; hold, squeeze.

▸ noun 1 *a gold clasp* FASTENER, fastening, catch, clip, pin; buckle, hasp.

2 *his tight clasp* EMBRACE, hug, cuddle; grip, grasp.

**class** noun 1 *a hotel of the first class* CATEGORY, grade, rating, classification, group, grouping.

2 *a new class of heart drug* KIND, sort, type, variety, genre, brand; species, genus, breed, strain, stripe.

3 *the middle class* SOCIAL DIVISION, social stratum, rank, level, echelon, group, grouping, income group; social status; *dated* estate; *archaic* condition.

4 *a math class* LESSON, period; seminar, tutorial, workshop, study group.

5 *informal a woman of class* STYLE, stylishness, elegance, chic, sophistication, taste, refinement, quality, excellence.

▸ verb *the 12-seater is classed as a commercial vehicle* CLASSIFY, categorize, group, grade; order, sort, codify; bracket, designate, label, pigeonhole.

▸ adjective *informal a class player* CLASSY, decent, gracious, respectable, noble.

**classic** adjective 1 *the classic work on the subject* DEFINITIVE, authoritative; outstanding, first-rate, first-class, best, finest, excellent, superior, masterly.

2 *a classic example of Norman design* TYPICAL, archetypal, quintessential, vintage; model, representative, perfect, prime, textbook. ANTONYM atypical.

3 *a classic style* SIMPLE, elegant, understated; traditional, timeless, ageless.

▸ noun *a classic of the genre* DEFINITIVE EXAMPLE, model, epitome, paradigm, exemplar; great work, masterpiece.

**classical** adjective 1 *classical mythology* ancient Greek, Hellenic, Attic; Latin, ancient Roman.

2 *classical music* TRADITIONAL, long-established; serious, highbrow. ANTONYM modern.

3 *a classical style* SIMPLE, pure, restrained, plain, austere; well-proportioned, harmonious, balanced, symmetrical, elegant. See note at CLASSIC.

**classification** noun 1 *the classification of diseases* CATEGORIZATION, categorizing, classifying, grouping, grading, ranking, organization, sorting, codification, systematization.

2 *a series of classifications* CATEGORY, class, group, grouping, grade, grading, ranking.

**classify** verb *we can classify the students into two groups* CATEGORIZE, group, grade, rank, rate, order, organize, range, sort, type, codify, bracket, systematize, systemize; catalog, list, file, index, lump.

**clatter** verb *the cups clattered on the tray* RATTLE, clank, clink, clunk, clang.

**clause** noun *a new clause in the treaty* SECTION, paragraph, article, subsection; stipulation, condition, proviso, rider.

**claw** noun 1 *a bird's claw* TALON, nail; *technical* unguis.

2 *a crab's claw* PINCER, nipper; *technical* chela.

▸ verb *her fingers clawed his shoulders* SCRATCH, lacerate, tear, rip, scrape, graze, dig into.

**clay** noun 1 *the soil is mainly clay* EARTH, soil, loam.

2 *potter's clay* china clay, kaolin, adobe, ball clay, argil, pug; fireclay.

**clean** adjective 1 *keep the wound clean* WASHED, scrubbed, cleansed, cleaned; spotless, unsoiled, unstained, unsullied, unblemished, immaculate, pristine, dirt-free; hygienic, sanitary, disinfected, sterilized, sterile, aseptic, decontaminated; laundered; *informal* squeaky clean, as clean as a whistle. ANTONYM dirty.

2 *a clean sheet of paper* BLANK, empty, clear, plain; unused, new, pristine, fresh, unmarked. ANTONYM used.

3 *clean air* PURE, clear, fresh, crisp, refreshing; unpolluted, uncontaminated. ANTONYM polluted.

4 *a clean life* VIRTUOUS, good, upright, upstanding; honorable, respectable, reputable, decent, righteous, moral, exemplary; innocent, pure, chaste; *informal* squeaky clean. ANTONYM guilty.

5 *the firm is clean* INNOCENT, guiltless, blameless, guilt-free, crime-free, above suspicion; *informal* squeaky clean. ANTONYMS dirty, polluted.

6 *a good clean fight* FAIR, honest, sporting, sportsmanlike, honorable, according to the rules; *informal* on the level. ANTONYMS dirty, unfair.

**7** *informal they are trying to stay clean* SOBER, teetotal, dry, nondrinking; DRUG-FREE, off drugs; *informal* on the wagon.

**8** *a clean cut* NEAT, smooth, crisp, straight, precise. ANTONYM ragged.

**9** *a clean break* COMPLETE, thorough, total, absolute, conclusive, decisive, final, irrevocable. ANTONYM partial.

**10** *clean lines* SIMPLE, elegant, graceful, streamlined, smooth. ANTONYMS complex, elaborate.

▸ adverb *informal I clean forgot* COMPLETELY, entirely, totally, fully, quite, utterly, absolutely.

▸ verb **1** *Dad cleaned the windows* WASH, cleanse, wipe, sponge, scrub, mop, rinse, scour, swab, hose down, sluice (down), disinfect; shampoo; *literary* lave. ANTONYMS dirty, soil.

**2** *I got my clothes cleaned* LAUNDER, dry-clean.

**3** *she cleaned the fish* GUT, draw, dress; *formal* eviscerate.

PHRASES: **clean out** *informal those grifters cleaned him out* BANKRUPT, ruin, make insolvent, make penniless, wipe out.
**come clean** *informal if you don't come clean, they're going to pin all of this on Kerry* TELL THE TRUTH, tell all, make a clean breast of it; confess, own up, admit guilt, admit to one's crimes/sins; *informal* fess up.

**cleanse** verb **1** *the wound was cleansed* CLEAN (UP), wash, bathe, rinse, disinfect.

**2** *cleansing the environment of traces of lead* RID, clear, free, purify, purge.

**clear** adjective **1** *clear instructions* UNDERSTANDABLE, comprehensible, intelligible, plain, uncomplicated, explicit, lucid, coherent, simple, straightforward, unambiguous, clear-cut, crystal clear; *formal* perspicuous. ANTONYM vague.

**2** *a clear case of harassment* OBVIOUS, evident, plain, crystal clear; sure, definite, unmistakable, manifest, indisputable, patent, incontrovertible, irrefutable, beyond doubt, beyond question; palpable, visible, discernible, conspicuous, overt, blatant, glaring; as plain as day, as plain as the nose on one's face. ANTONYMS vague, possible.

**3** *clear water* TRANSPARENT, limpid, pellucid, translucent, crystal clear; unclouded. ANTONYMS murky, opaque.

**4** *a clear blue sky* BRIGHT, cloudless, unclouded, without a cloud in the sky. ANTONYM cloudy.

**5** *her clear complexion* UNBLEMISHED, spot-free. ANTONYMS spotty, pimply.

**6** *Rosa's clear voice* DISTINCT, bell-like, as clear as a bell. ANTONYM muffled.

**7** *the road was clear* | *a clear view* UNOBSTRUCTED, unblocked, passable, unrestricted, open, unhindered. ANTONYMS limited, obstructed.

**8** *a clear conscience* UNTROUBLED, undisturbed, unperturbed, unconcerned, having no qualms; peaceful, at peace, tranquil, serene, calm, easy. ANTONYM guilty.

▸ adverb **1** *stand clear of the doors* AWAY FROM, apart from, at a (safe) distance from, out of contact with.

**2** *Tommy's voice came loud and clear* DISTINCTLY, clearly, as clear as a bell, plainly, audibly.

**3** *he has time to get clear away* COMPLETELY, entirely, fully, wholly, totally, utterly; *informal* clean.

▸ verb **1** *the sky cleared briefly* BRIGHTEN (UP), lighten, clear up, become bright/brighter, become light/lighter, become sunny.

**2** *the drizzle had cleared* DISAPPEAR, go away, end; peter out, fade, wear off, decrease, lessen, diminish.

**3** *together they cleared the table* EMPTY, unload, unburden, strip.

**4** *clearing drains* UNBLOCK, unstop.

**5** *staff cleared the building* EVACUATE, empty; leave.

**6** *Karen cleared the dirty dishes* REMOVE, take away, carry away, tidy up.

**7** *I cleared the bar on my first attempt* GO OVER, pass over, sail over; jump (over), vault (over), leap (over), hurdle.

**8** *he was cleared by an appeals court* ACQUIT, declare innocent, find not guilty; absolve, exonerate; *informal* let off (the hook); *formal* exculpate.

**9** *I was cleared to work on the atomic project* AUTHORIZE, give permission, permit, allow, pass, accept, endorse, license, sanction, give approval, give consent; *informal* OK, give the OK, give the thumbs up, give the green light, give the go-ahead.

**10** *I cleared $50,000 profit* NET, make/realize a profit of, take home, pocket; gain, earn, make, get, bring in, pull in.

PHRASES: **clear out 1** *informal we were told to clear out immediately.* See LEAVE[1] sense 1.

**2** *we cleared out the junk room* EMPTY (OUT); tidy (up), clean up, clear up.

**3** *clear out the old equipment* GET RID OF, throw out/away, discard, dispose of, dump, scrap, jettison; *informal* chuck (out), deep-six, ditch, trash.
**clear up 1** *I hope it clears up before the party.* See CLEAR verb sense 1.

**2** *we've cleared up the problem* SOLVE, resolve, straighten out, find an/the answer to; get to the bottom of, explain; *informal* crack, figure out.

**clearance** noun **1** *slum clearance* REMOVAL, clearing, demolition.

**2** *you must have clearance to enter* AUTHORIZATION, permission, consent, approval, blessing, leave, sanction, license, dispensation, assent, agreement, endorsement; *informal* the green light, the go-ahead, the thumbs up, the OK, the say-so.

**3** *the clearance of a debt* REPAYMENT, payment, paying (off), settling, discharge.

**4** *there is plenty of clearance* SPACE, room, room to spare, margin, leeway.

**clear-cut** adjective *a clear-cut objective* DEFINITE, distinct, clear, well-defined, precise, specific, explicit, unambiguous, unequivocal, black and white, cut and dried. ANTONYM vague.

**clearly** adverb **1** *write clearly* INTELLIGIBLY, plainly, distinctly, comprehensibly, with clarity; legibly, audibly; *formal* perspicuously.

2 *clearly, substantial changes are needed* OBVIOUSLY, evidently, patently, unquestionably, undoubtedly, without doubt, indubitably, plainly, undeniably, incontrovertibly, irrefutably, doubtless, it goes without saying, needless to say.

**USAGE NOTE clearly**

Exaggerators like this word, along with its cousins (*obviously*, *undeniably*, *undoubtedly*, and the like). Often a statement prefaced with one of these words is conclusory, and sometimes even exceedingly dubious. As a result—though some readers don't consciously realize it—*clearly* and its ilk are 'weasel words'—that is, unnecessary words that supposedly intensify the meaning of a statement, but actually weaken it. Just how much *clearly* can weaken a statement is evident in the following example, in which the author uses the word to buttress a claim about his own state of mind: "Clearly, I am not to be convinced that this is a small matter." (Stephen White, *The Written Word*; 1984.) —*BG*

**cleave**[1] verb 1 *cleaving wood for the fire* SPLIT (OPEN), cut (up), hew, hack, chop up; *literary* rive.

2 *cleaving a path through the traffic* PLOW, drive, bulldoze, carve.

**cleave**[2] PHRASE: **cleave to** *literary* 1 *her tongue clove to the roof of her mouth* STICK (FAST), adhere, be attached.

2 ***cleaving** too closely **to** Moscow's line* ADHERE TO, hold to, abide by, be loyal to, be faithful to.

**cleaver** noun *the butcher's cleaver* CHOPPER, hatchet, ax, knife; butcher's knife, kitchen knife.

**cleft** noun 1 *a deep cleft in the rocks* SPLIT, slit, crack, fissure, crevice, rift, break, fracture, rent, breach.

2 *the cleft in his chin* DIMPLE.

▸ adjective *a cleft tail* SPLIT, divided, cloven, bifid.

**clemency** noun *a fallen dictator who now seeks the clemency he withheld from others* MERCY, mercifulness, leniency, mildness, indulgence, quarter; compassion, humanity, pity, sympathy. See note at MERCY. ANTONYM ruthlessness.

**clench** verb 1 *he stood there clenching his hands* SQUEEZE TOGETHER, clamp together, close/shut tightly; make into a fist.

2 *he clenched the iron bar* GRIP, grasp, grab, clutch, clasp, hold tightly, seize, press, squeeze.

**clergy** noun *a group of clergy who want to promote religious tolerance* CLERICS, clergymen, clergywomen, churchmen, churchwomen, priests, ecclesiastics, men/women of God; ministry, priesthood, holy orders, the church, the cloth. ANTONYM laity.

**clerical** adjective 1 *typing, filing, and other clerical jobs* OFFICE, desk, back-room; administrative, secretarial; white-collar.

2 *her clerical duties as the associate pastor* ECCLESIASTICAL, church, priestly, religious, spiritual, sacerdotal; holy, divine. ANTONYM secular.

**clever** adjective 1 *a clever young woman* INTELLIGENT, bright, smart, astute, sharp, quick-witted, shrewd; talented, gifted, brilliant, capable, able, competent, apt; educated, learned, knowledgeable, wise; *informal* brainy, clueful, savvy. ANTONYM stupid.

2 *a clever scheme* INGENIOUS, canny, cunning, crafty, artful, slick, neat. ANTONYMS ill-advised, foolish.

3 *she was clever with her hands* SKILLFUL, dexterous, adroit, adept, deft, nimble, handy; skilled, talented, gifted.

4 *a clever remark* WITTY, amusing, droll, humorous, funny. ANTONYM witless.

**click** noun *the click of the timer* CLACK, snap, pop, tick; clink.

▸ verb 1 *cameras clicked* SNAP, clack, tick, pop; clink.

2 *informal that night it clicked* BECOME CLEAR, fall into place, come home, make sense, dawn, register, get through, sink in.

3 *informal we just clicked* TAKE TO EACH OTHER, get along, be compatible, be like-minded, feel a rapport, see eye to eye; *informal* hit it off, be on the same wavelength.

4 *informal this issue hasn't clicked with the voters* GO DOWN WELL, prove popular, be a hit, succeed.

**client** noun *the waiting room was designed to put the clients at ease* CUSTOMER, buyer, purchaser, shopper, consumer, user; patient; patron, regular; **(clients)** clientele, patronage, public, market; *Law* vendee.

**cliff** noun *the cliffs of the Southwest are breathtaking* PRECIPICE, rock face, crag, bluff, ridge, escarpment, scar, scarp, ledge, overhang.

**climate** noun 1 *the mild climate* WEATHER CONDITIONS, weather; atmospheric conditions.

2 *they come from a colder climate* REGION, area, zone, country, place; *literary* clime.

3 *the political climate* ATMOSPHERE, mood, feeling, ambience, tenor; tendency, ethos, attitude; milieu; *informal* vibe(s).

**climax** noun *the climax of his career* PEAK, pinnacle, height, high(est) point, top; acme, zenith; culmination, crowning point, crown, crest; highlight, high spot, high-water mark. ANTONYM nadir.

▸ verb *the event will climax with a concert* CULMINATE, peak, reach a pinnacle, come to a crescendo, come to a head.

**climb** verb 1 *we climbed the hill* ASCEND, mount, scale, scramble up, clamber up, shinny up; go up, walk up; conquer, gain. ANTONYM descend.

2 *the plane climbed* RISE, ascend, go up, gain altitude. ANTONYMS descend, dive.

3 *the road climbs steeply* SLOPE UPWARD, rise, go uphill, incline upward. ANTONYM drop.

4 *the shares climbed to $10.77* INCREASE, rise, go up; shoot up, soar, rocket. ANTONYMS decrease, fall.

5 *he climbed through the ranks* ADVANCE, rise, move up, progress, work one's way (up).

6 *he climbed out of his car* CLAMBER, scramble; step.

▸ noun *a steep climb* ASCENT, clamber. ANTONYM descent.

PHRASE: **climb down** *Sandy climbed down the ladder* DESCEND, go/come down, move down, shinny down.

**clinch** verb 1 *he clinched the deal* SECURE, settle, conclude, close, pull off, bring off, complete, confirm, seal, finalize; *informal* sew up, wrap up.

2 *these findings clinched the matter* SETTLE, decide, determine; resolve; *informal* sort out.

3 *Wisconsin State clinched the title* WIN, secure; be victorious, come first, triumph, prevail. ANTONYM lose.

4 *the boxers clinched* GRAPPLE, wrestle, struggle, scuffle.

**cling** verb *rice grains tend to cling together* STICK, adhere, hold, cohere, bond, bind. PHRASE: **cling (on) to** 1 *she clung to him* HOLD ON TO, clutch, grip, grasp, clasp, attach oneself to, hang on to; embrace, hug.

2 *they clung to their beliefs* ADHERE TO, hold to, stick to, stand by, abide by, cherish, remain true to, have faith in; *informal* swear by, stick with.

**clinic** noun *we took Ralph to the clinic for stitches* MEDICAL CENTER, health center, doctor's office.

**clinical** adjective 1 *he seemed so clinical* DETACHED, impersonal, dispassionate, objective, uninvolved, distant, remote, aloof, removed, cold, indifferent, neutral, unsympathetic, unfeeling, unemotional. ANTONYM emotional.

2 *the room was clinical* PLAIN, simple, unadorned, unembellished, stark, austere, spartan, bleak, bare; clean; functional, utilitarian, basic, institutional, impersonal, characterless. ANTONYM luxurious.

**clip**[1] noun 1 *a briefcase clip* FASTENER, clasp, hasp, catch, hook, buckle, lock.

2 *a mother-of-pearl clip* BROOCH, pin, badge.

3 *his clip was empty* MAGAZINE, cartridge, cylinder.

▸ verb *he clipped the pages together* FASTEN, attach, fix, join; pin, staple, tack.

**clip**[2] verb 1 *I clipped the hedge* TRIM, prune, cut, snip, shorten, crop, shear, pare; lop; neaten, shape.

2 *clip the coupon below* REMOVE, cut out, snip out, tear out, detach.

3 *his trailer clipped a parked van* HIT, strike, touch, graze, glance off, run into.

4 *Mom clipped his ear* HIT, cuff, strike, smack, slap, box; *informal* clout, whack, wallop, clobber, sock.

▸ noun 1 *I gave the dog a clip* TRIM, cut, crop, haircut; shear.

2 *a film clip* EXTRACT, excerpt, snippet, cutting, fragment; trailer.

3 *informal a clip to the ear* SMACK, cuff, slap; *informal* clout, whack, wallop, sock.

4 *informal the truck went at a good clip* SPEED, rate, pace, velocity; *informal* lick.

PHRASE: **clip someone's wings** *if you try to clip her wings, neither one of you will ever be happy* RESTRICT SOMEONE'S FREEDOM, impose limits on, keep under control, stand in the way of; obstruct, impede, frustrate, thwart, fetter, hamstring, handcuff.

**clique** noun *almost no one from her clique showed up at the reunion* COTERIE, set, circle, ring, in-crowd, group; club, society, fraternity, sorority; cabal, caucus; *informal* gang.

**cloak** noun 1 *the cloak over his shoulders* CAPE, poncho, serape, shawl, mantle, wrap, pelisse, burnoose, cope, robe, cowl, djellaba, tippet; cassock, chasuble, pallium; *historical* cardinal.

2 *a cloak of secrecy* COVER, veil, mantle, shroud, screen, mask, shield, blanket.

▸ verb *a peak cloaked in mist* CONCEAL, hide, cover, veil, shroud, mask, obscure, cloud; envelop, swathe, surround.

**clock** noun *a grandfather clock* TIMEPIECE, timekeeper, timer; chronometer, chronograph.

▸ verb *informal his fastball was clocked at 92 mph* TIME, measure.

**clog** noun *dancing in clogs takes a lot of practice* SABOT, wooden shoe.

▸ verb *the pipes were clogged* BLOCK, obstruct, congest, jam, choke, bung up, plug, stop up, fill up, gunge up.

**cloister** noun 1 *the convent's shadowed cloisters* WALKWAY, covered walk, arcade, loggia, gallery.

2 *I was educated in the cloister* ABBEY, monastery, friary, convent, priory, nunnery.

**cloistered** adjective *the cloistered life of a writer* SECLUDED, sequestered, sheltered, protected, insulated; shut off, isolated, confined, incommunicado; solitary, monastic, reclusive.

**close**[1] adjective 1 *the town is* ***close to*** *Joliette* NEAR, adjacent to; in the vicinity of, in the neighborhood of, within reach of; neighboring, adjoining, abutting, alongside, on the doorstep, a stone's throw (away) from/to, 'a hop, skip, and a jump from'; nearby, at close quarters to; *informal* within spitting distance from/to; *archaic* nigh to. ANTONYMS far, distant.

2 *flying in close formation* DENSE, compact, tight, close-packed, packed, solid; crowded, cramped, congested. ANTONYM sparse.

3 *I was* ***close to*** *tears* NEAR, on the verge of, on the brink of, on the point of.

4 *a very close match* EVENLY MATCHED, even, with nothing to choose between them, neck and neck; *informal* even-steven. ANTONYM one-sided.

5 *close relatives* IMMEDIATE, direct, near. ANTONYM distant.

6 *close friends* INTIMATE, dear, bosom; close-knit, tight-knit, inseparable, attached, devoted, faithful; special, good, best, fast, firm; *informal* (as) thick as thieves. ANTONYM casual.

7 *a close resemblance* STRONG, marked, distinct, pronounced. ANTONYM slight.

8 *a close examination* CAREFUL, detailed, thorough, minute, searching, painstaking, meticulous, rigorous, scrupulous, conscientious; attentive, focused. ANTONYM casual.

9 *keep a close eye on them* VIGILANT, watchful, keen, alert.

10 *a close translation* STRICT, faithful, exact, precise, literal; word for word, verbatim. ANTONYM loose.

11 *the weather was hot and close* HUMID, muggy, stuffy, airless, heavy, sticky, sultry, oppressive, stifling. ANTONYM fresh.

**close**[2] verb 1 *she closed the door* SHUT, pull (shut), push (shut), slam; fasten, secure. ANTONYM open.

2 *close the hole* BLOCK (UP/OFF), stop up, plug, seal (up/off), shut up/off, cork, stopper, bung (up); clog (up), choke, obstruct. ANTONYMS open, unblock.

3 *the enemy was closing fast* CATCH UP, close in, creep up, near, approach, gain on someone.

4 *the gap is closing* NARROW, reduce, shrink, lessen, get smaller, diminish, contract. ANTONYM widen.

5 *his arms closed around her* MEET, join, connect; form a circle.

6 *he closed the meeting* END, conclude, finish, terminate, wind up, break off, halt, discontinue, dissolve; adjourn, suspend. ANTONYMS open, begin.

7 *the factory is to close* SHUT DOWN, close down, cease production, cease trading, go out of business, go bankrupt, go into receivership, go into liquidation; *informal* fold, go bust. ANTONYM open.

8 *he closed a deal* CLINCH, settle, secure, seal, confirm, establish; transact, pull off; complete, conclude, fix, agree, finalize; *informal* wrap up.

▸ noun *the close of the talks* END, finish, conclusion, termination, cessation, completion, resolution, climax, denouement; *informal* outro. ANTONYM beginning.

**closet** noun *a clothes closet* CABINET, cupboard, wardrobe, armoire, locker.

▸ adjective *a closet Sherlock Holmes fan* SECRET, covert, private; surreptitious, clandestine, underground, furtive.

▸ verb *David was closeted in his den* SHUT AWAY, sequester, seclude, cloister, confine, isolate.

**closure** noun *the closure of rural schools* CLOSING DOWN, shutdown; termination, discontinuation, cessation, finish, conclusion; failure; *informal* folding.

**clot** noun *blood clots* LUMP, clump, mass; thrombus, thrombosis, embolus; *informal* glob, gob.

▸ verb *the blood is likely to clot* COAGULATE, set, congeal, curdle, thicken, solidify.

**cloth** noun 1 *a maker of cloth* FABRIC, material; textile(s), soft goods.

2 *a cloth to wipe the table* RAG, wipe, duster, sponge; towel; chamois.

**clothe** verb 1 *they were clothed in silk* DRESS, attire, robe, garb, array, costume, swathe, deck (out), turn out, fit out, rig (out); *informal* get up; *archaic* apparel, habit, invest.

2 *a valley clothed in conifers* COVER, blanket, carpet; envelop, swathe.

**clothes** plural noun *his clothes are too big for him* CLOTHING, garments, attire, garb, dress, wear, costume; *informal* gear, togs, duds, threads, getup; *formal* apparel; *archaic* raiment, habiliments, vestments.

**clothing** noun. See CLOTHES.

**cloud** noun . 1 *dark clouds* storm cloud, cloudbank, cloud cover; mackerel sky.

2 *a cloud of exhaust smoke* MASS, billow; pall, mantle, blanket.

▸ verb 1 *the sky clouded* BECOME CLOUDY, cloud over, become overcast, lower, blacken, darken.

2 *the sand is churned up, clouding the water* MAKE CLOUDY, make murky, dirty, darken, blacken.

3 *anger clouded my judgment* CONFUSE, muddle, obscure, fog, muddy, mar.

PHRASE: **on cloud nine** *Amy was on cloud nine when she passed the bar exam* ECSTATIC, rapturous, joyful, elated, blissful, euphoric, in seventh heaven, walking on air, transported, in raptures, delighted, thrilled, overjoyed, over the moon, on top of the world, tickled pink.

**cloudy** adjective 1 *a cloudy sky* OVERCAST, clouded; dark, gray, black, leaden, murky; somber, dismal, heavy, gloomy; sunless, starless; hazy, misty, foggy. ANTONYMS clear, bright.

2 *cloudy water* MURKY, muddy, milky, dirty, opaque, turbid. ANTONYM clear.

3 *his eyes grew cloudy* TEARFUL, teary, weepy, lachrymose; moist, watery; misty, blurred. ANTONYMS clear, dry.

**clout** *informal* noun 1 *a clout on the ear* SMACK, slap, thump, punch, blow, hit, cuff, box, clip; *informal* whack, wallop.

2 *her clout in the business world* INFLUENCE, power, weight, sway, leverage, control, say; dominance, authority; *informal* teeth, muscle.

▸ verb *he clouted me* HIT, strike, punch, smack, slap, cuff, thump, buffet; *informal* wallop, belt, whack, clobber, sock, bop,

**clown** noun 1 *a circus clown* COMEDIAN; jester, fool, zany.

2 *the class clown* JOKER, comedian, comic, humorist, wag, wit, prankster, jester, buffoon; *informal* laugh, kidder, wisecracker.

3 *bureaucratic clowns* FOOL, idiot, dolt, ass, simpleton, ignoramus; bungler, blunderer; *informal* moron, meatball, bozo, jackass, chump, numbskull, numbnuts, nincompoop, halfwit, bonehead, knucklehead, fathead, birdbrain, twit, nitwit, twerp.

▸ verb *Harvey* ***clowned around*** FOOL AROUND, play the fool, play around, monkey around; joke (around), jest; *informal* mess around, horse around.

**cloying** adjective *her romance novels are too cloying for my taste* SICKLY, syrupy, saccharine, oversweet; sickening, nauseating; mawkish, sentimental, twee; *informal* over the top, mushy, slushy, sloppy, gooey, cheesy, corny, cornball, sappy.

**club**[1] noun **1** *a canoeing club* SOCIETY, association, organization, institution, group, circle, band, body, ring, crew; alliance, league, union.

**2** *the city has great clubs* NIGHTCLUB, disco, discotheque, bar.

**3** *the top club in the league* TEAM, squad, side, lineup, franchise.

**club**[2] noun *a wooden club* CUDGEL, truncheon, bludgeon, baton, stick, mace, bat, blackjack, nightstick.

▸ verb *he was clubbed with an iron bar* CUDGEL, bludgeon, bash, beat, hit, strike, batter, belabor; *informal* clout, clobber.

**clue** noun **1** *give me just one clue | police are searching for clues* HINT, indication, sign, signal, pointer, trace, indicator; lead, tip, tipoff; **(clues)** EVIDENCE, information.

**2** *a crossword clue* QUESTION, problem, puzzle, riddle, poser, conundrum. PHRASES: **clue in** *informal if you're missing any of the facts, we can clue you in* INFORM, notify, make aware, prime; keep up to date, keep posted; *informal* tip off, give the lowdown, fill in on, put in the picture, put wise, get/keep up to speed.

**not have a clue** *informal you expect me to explain her motives, but I do not have a clue* HAVE NO IDEA, be ignorant, not have an inkling; be baffled, be mystified, be at a loss; *informal* be clueless, not have the faintest/foggiest/slightest idea.

**clump** noun **1** *a clump of trees* CLUSTER, thicket, group, bunch, assemblage.

**2** *a clump of earth* LUMP, clod, mass, wad, glob, gob.

▸ verb **1** *galaxies clump together* CLUSTER, group, collect, gather, assemble, congregate, mass.

**2** *they were clumping around upstairs* STAMP, stomp, clomp, tramp, lumber; thump, thud, bang; *informal* galumph.

**clumsy** adjective **1** *she was terribly clumsy* AWKWARD, uncoordinated, ungainly, graceless, inelegant; inept, maladroit, unskillful, unhandy, accident-prone, like a bull in a china shop, all thumbs; *informal* ham-fisted, butterfingered, having two left feet, klutzy. ANTONYM graceful.

**2** *a clumsy contraption* UNWIELDY, cumbersome, bulky, awkward. ANTONYM elegant.

**3** *a clumsy remark* GAUCHE, awkward, graceless; unsubtle, uncouth, boorish, crass; tactless, insensitive, thoughtless, undiplomatic, indelicate, ill-judged. ANTONYM tactful.

**cluster** noun **1** *clusters of berries* BUNCH, clump, mass, knot, group, clutch, bundle, truss.

**2** *a cluster of spectators* CROWD, group, knot, huddle, bunch, throng, flock, pack, band; *informal* gang, gaggle.

▸ verb *they clustered around the television* CONGREGATE, gather, collect, group, assemble; huddle, crowd, flock.

**clutch**[1] verb *she clutched his arm* GRIP, grasp, clasp, cling to, hang on to, clench, hold. PHRASE: **clutch at** *she saved herself by clutching at a branch* REACH FOR, snatch at, make a grab for, catch at, claw at.

**clutch**[2] noun **1** *a clutch of eggs* GROUP, batch.

**2** *a clutch of awards* GROUP, collection; raft, armful; *informal* load, bunch, ton.

**clutches** plural noun *she's married to a hateful man who has her in his clutches* POWER, control, domination, command, rule, tyranny; hands, hold, grip, grasp, claws, jaws, tentacles; custody.

**clutter** noun **1** *a clutter of toys* MESS, jumble, litter, heap, tangle, muddle, hodgepodge.

**2** *a desk full of clutter* DISORDER, chaos, disarray, untidiness, mess, confusion; litter, rubbish, junk.

▸ verb *the garden was cluttered with tools* LITTER, mess up, disarrange; be strewn, be scattered; *literary* bestrew.

**coach**[1] noun **1** *an air-conditioned coach shuttled us to the casino* BUS, minibus; *dated* omnibus.

**2** *chiefly Brit. a railroad coach* CAR, carriage, wagon, compartment, van, Pullman.

**3** *a coach and horses* HORSE-DRAWN CARRIAGE, hackney, hansom, gig, landau, brougham.

**coach**[2] noun *a football coach* INSTRUCTOR, trainer, manager; teacher, tutor, mentor, guru.

▸ verb *she coached Richard in math* INSTRUCT, teach, tutor, school, educate; drill; train.

**coagulate** verb *a drug that helps the blood to coagulate* CONGEAL, clot, thicken, jell; solidify, harden, set, dry.

**coalesce** verb *the puddles had coalesced into shallow streams* MERGE, unite, join together, combine, fuse, mingle, blend; amalgamate, consolidate, integrate, homogenize, converge.

**coalition** noun *the ruling four-party coalition* ALLIANCE, union, partnership, bloc, caucus; federation, league, association, confederation, consortium, syndicate, combine; amalgamation, merger.

**coarse** adjective **1** *coarse blankets* ROUGH, scratchy, prickly, wiry. ANTONYM soft.

**2** *his coarse features* LARGE, rough, rough-hewn, heavy; ugly. ANTONYM delicate.

**3** *a coarse boy* OAFISH, loutish, boorish, uncouth, rude, impolite, ill-mannered, uncivil; vulgar, common, rough, uncultured, crass. ANTONYMS sophisticated, refined.

**4** *a coarse innuendo* VULGAR, crude, rude, off-color, dirty, filthy, smutty, indelicate, improper, unseemly, crass, tasteless, lewd, prurient, blue, farmyard.

**coarsen** verb **1** *hands coarsened by work* ROUGHEN, toughen, harden. ANTONYM soften.

**2** *I had been coarsened by the army* DESENSITIZE, dehumanize; dull, deaden. ANTONYM refine.

**coast** noun *the houses along the coast* SEABOARD, coastal region, coastline, seashore, shore, foreshore, shoreline, seaside, waterfront, littoral; *literary* strand.

▸ verb *the car coasted down a hill* FREEWHEEL, cruise, taxi, drift, glide, sail.

**coat** noun **1** *a winter coat* OVERCOAT, jacket.

**2** *a dog's coat* FUR, hair, wool, fleece; hide, pelt, skin.

**3** *a coat of paint* LAYER, covering, coating, skin, film, wash; plating, glaze, varnish, veneer, patina; deposit.

▸ verb *the tube was coated with wax* COVER, paint, glaze, varnish, wash; surface, veneer, laminate, plate, face; daub, smear, cake, plaster.

**coating** noun. See COAT noun sense 3.

**coax** verb *you have to coax some of the children to speak* PERSUADE, wheedle, cajole, get around; beguile, seduce, inveigle, maneuver; *informal* sweet-talk, soft-soap, butter up, twist someone's arm.

**cock** noun *strutting around like a barnyard cock* ROOSTER, cockerel, capon.

▸ verb **1** *he cocked his head* TILT, tip, angle, incline, dip.

**2** *she cocked her little finger* BEND, flex, crook, curve.

**3** *the dog cocked its leg* LIFT, raise, hold up.

**cocky** adjective *military school has certainly made him less cocky* ARROGANT, conceited, overweening, overconfident, cocksure, self-important, egotistical, presumptuous, boastful, self-assertive; bold, forward, insolent, cheeky, puffed-up. ANTONYM modest.

**coddle** verb *your sons are too old for you to be coddling them* PAMPER, cosset, mollycoddle; spoil, indulge, overindulge, pander to; baby, mother, wait on hand and foot. ANTONYM neglect.

**code** noun **1** *a secret code* CIPHER, key; hieroglyphics; cryptogram.

**2** *a strict social code* MORALITY, convention, etiquette, protocol, value system.

**3** *the penal code* LAW(S), rules, regulations; constitution, system.

**coerce** verb *he was coerced into giving evidence* PRESSURE, pressurize, press, push, constrain; force, compel, oblige, browbeat, bludgeon, bully, threaten, intimidate, dragoon, twist someone's arm; *informal* railroad, squeeze, lean on. See note at COMPEL.

**coffer** noun **1** *every church had a coffer* STRONGBOX, money box, cashbox, money chest, treasure chest, safe; casket, box.

**2** **(coffers)** *the government coffers* FUND(S), reserves, resources, money, finances, wealth, cash, capital, purse; treasury, exchequer; *informal* pork barrel.

**coffin** noun *a simple pine coffin* casket; sarcophagus; *informal* box; *humorous* wooden overcoat.

**cogent** adjective *a cogent argument* CONVINCING, compelling, strong, forceful, powerful, potent, weighty, effective; valid, sound, plausible, telling; impressive, persuasive, eloquent, credible, influential; conclusive, authoritative; logical, reasoned, rational, reasonable, lucid, coherent, clear. See note at BELIEVABLE.

**cogitate** verb *formal I may have to* ***cogitate on*** *that one for a bit* THINK ABOUT/ON/OVER, contemplate, consider, mull over, meditate on, muse on/over, ponder, reflect on, deliberate on/over, ruminate on/over; dwell on, brood on, chew over; *informal* put on one's thinking cap for.

**cognate** adjective *formal the cognate words in English and German* ASSOCIATED, related, connected, allied, linked; similar, like, alike, akin, kindred, comparable, parallel, corresponding, analogous.

**cognition** noun *the head injury has impaired his speech and cognition* PERCEPTION, discernment, apprehension, learning, understanding, comprehension, insight; reasoning, thinking, thought.

**cognizant** adjective *formal*. See AWARE sense 1.

**cohabit** verb *her brother James and this Marilyn Monroe lookalike are cohabiting in Soho* LIVE TOGETHER, live as a couple; *informal* shack up; *dated* live in sin.

**coherent** adjective *the patient's speech is more coherent today* LOGICAL, reasoned, reasonable, rational, sound, cogent, consistent, consilient; clear, lucid, articulate; intelligible, comprehensible. ANTONYM muddled.

**cohort** noun **1** *a Roman army cohort* UNIT, force, corps, division, brigade, battalion, regiment, squadron, company, troop, contingent, legion, phalanx.

**2** *the 1940–44 birth cohort of women* GROUP, grouping, category, class, set, division, batch, list; age group, generation.

**3** *a party thrown by her departmental cohorts* COLLEAGUE, companion, associate, friend.

**coil** noun *coils of rope* LOOP, twist, turn, curl, convolution; spiral, helix, corkscrew.

▸ verb *he coiled her hair around his finger* WIND, loop, twist, curl, curve, bend, twine, entwine; spiral, corkscrew.

**coin** noun **1** *coins in my pocket* penny, nickel, dime, quarter; piece.

**2** *large amounts of coin* COINAGE, coins, specie; change, loose change, small change; silver, gold.

▸ verb **1** *dimes were coined* MINT, stamp, strike, cast, punch, die, mold, forge, make.

**2** *he coined the term* INVENT, create, make up, conceive, originate, think up, dream up.

**coincide** verb **1** *the events coincided* OCCUR SIMULTANEOUSLY, happen together, be concurrent, concur, coexist.

**2** *their interests do not always coincide* CORRESPOND, tally, agree, accord, concur, match, fit, be consistent, equate, harmonize, be compatible, dovetail, correlate; *informal* square. ANTONYM differ.

**coincidence** noun **1** *too close to be mere coincidence* ACCIDENT, chance, serendipity, fortuity, providence, happenstance, fate; a fluke.

**2** *the coincidence of inflation and unemployment* CO-OCCURRENCE, coexistence, conjunction, simultaneity, contemporaneity, concomitance.

3 *a coincidence of interests* CORRESPONDENCE, agreement, accord, concurrence, consistency, conformity, harmony, compatibility.

**coincidental** adjective 1 *a coincidental resemblance* ACCIDENTAL, chance, fluky, random; fortuitous, adventitious, serendipitous; unexpected, unforeseen, unintentional, inadvertent, unplanned.

2 *the coincidental disappearance of the two men* SIMULTANEOUS, concurrent, coincident, contemporaneous, concomitant.

**cold** adjective 1 *a cold day* CHILLY, chill, cool, freezing, icy, snowy, wintry, frosty, frigid, gelid; bitter, biting, raw, bone-chilling, nippy, arctic. ANTONYM hot.

2 *I'm very cold* CHILLY, chilled, cool, freezing, frozen, shivery, numb, benumbed; hypothermic. ANTONYM hot.

3 *a cold reception* UNFRIENDLY, inhospitable, unwelcoming, forbidding, cool, frigid, frosty, glacial, lukewarm, indifferent, unfeeling, unemotional, formal, stiff. ANTONYMS friendly, warm.

**cold-blooded** adjective *a cold-blooded killer* CRUEL, callous, sadistic, inhuman, inhumane, pitiless, merciless, ruthless, unforgiving, unfeeling, uncaring, heartless; savage, brutal, barbaric, barbarous; cold, cold-hearted, unemotional.

**collaborate** verb 1 *they collaborated on the project* CO-OPERATE, join forces, team up, band together, work together, participate, combine, ally; pool resources, put —— heads together.

2 *they collaborated with the enemy* COLLUDE, conspire, fraternize, co-operate, consort, sympathize; *informal* be in cahoots.

**collaborator** noun 1 *his collaborator on the book* CO-WORKER, partner, associate, colleague, confederate; assistant.

2 *a wartime collaborator* QUISLING, fraternizer, collaborationist, colluder, (enemy) sympathizer; traitor, fifth columnist.

**collapse** verb 1 *the roof collapsed* CAVE IN, fall in, subside, fall down, give (way), crumple, buckle, sag, slump.

2 *he collapsed last night* FAINT, pass out, black out, lose consciousness, keel over, swoon; *informal* conk out.

3 *he collapsed in tears* BREAK DOWN, go to pieces, lose control, be overcome, crumble; *informal* crack up.

4 *peace talks collapsed* BREAK DOWN, fail, fall through, fold, founder, miscarry, come to grief, be unsuccessful; end; *informal* flop, fizzle out.

▸ noun 1 *the collapse of the roof* CAVE-IN, subsidence.

2 *her collapse on stage* FAINTING FIT, faint, blackout, loss of consciousness, swoon; *Medicine* syncope.

3 *the collapse of the talks* BREAKDOWN, failure, disintegration; end.

4 *he suffered a collapse* BREAKDOWN, nervous breakdown, personal crisis, psychological trauma; *informal* crack-up.

**collar** noun 1 *a shirt collar* NECKBAND, choker; *historical* ruff, gorget, bertha.

2 *a collar around the pipe* RING, band, collet, sleeve, flange.

▸ verb *informal* 1 *he collared a thief* APPREHEND, arrest, catch, capture, seize; take prisoner, take into custody, detain; *informal* nab, pinch, bust, pick up, pull in.

2 *she collared me in the street* ACCOST, waylay, hail, approach, detain, stop, halt, catch, confront, importune; *informal* buttonhole.

**collate** verb 1 *the system is used to collate information* COLLECT, gather, accumulate, assemble; combine, aggregate, put together; arrange, organize.

2 *we must collate these two sources* COMPARE, contrast, set side by side, juxtapose, weigh against.

**collateral** noun *she put up her house as collateral for the loan* SECURITY, surety, guarantee, guaranty, insurance, indemnity, indemnification; backing.

**colleague** noun *Dr. Clinton's colleagues started a scholarship fund in his name* COWORKER, fellow worker, workmate, teammate, associate, partner, collaborator, ally, confederate.

**collect** verb 1 *he collected the rubbish | she collects Hummel figurines* GATHER, accumulate, assemble; amass, stockpile, pile up, heap up, store (up), hoard, save; mass, accrue. See note at GATHER. ANTONYMS squander, distribute.

2 *a crowd collected in the square* GATHER, assemble, meet, muster, congregate, convene, converge, flock together. ANTONYM disperse.

3 *I must collect the children* FETCH, go/come to get, call for, meet. ANTONYMS take, drop off.

4 *they collect money for charity* RAISE, appeal for, ask for, solicit; obtain, acquire, gather. ANTONYMS give away, distribute.

5 *he paused to* ***collect himself*** RECOVER, regain one's composure, pull oneself together, steady oneself; *informal* get a grip (on oneself). ANTONYMS disperse, distribute.

6 *she collected her thoughts* GATHER, summon (up), muster, get together, marshal. ANTONYMS disperse, distribute.

**collected** adjective *she is the most collected gymnast on the team* CALM, cool, self-possessed, self-controlled, composed, poised; serene, tranquil, relaxed, unruffled, unperturbed, untroubled; placid, quiet, sedate, phlegmatic; *informal* unfazed, nonplussed, together, laid-back. ANTONYMS excited, hysterical.

**collection** noun 1 *a collection of stolen items* HOARD, pile, heap, stack, stock, store, stockpile; accumulation, reserve, supply, bank, pool, fund, mine, reservoir.

2 *a collection of shoppers* GROUP, crowd, body, assemblage, gathering, throng; knot, cluster; multitude, bevy, party, band, horde, pack, flock, swarm, mob; *informal* gang, load, gaggle.

3 *a collection of Victorian dolls* SET, series; array, assortment.

4 *a collection of short stories* ANTHOLOGY, selection, compendium, treasury, compilation, miscellany, potpourri.

5 *a collection for the poor* DONATIONS, contributions, gifts, subscription(s); *historical* alms.

6 *a church collection* OFFERING, offertory, tithe.

**collective** adjective *our collective interests* COMMON, shared, joint, combined, mutual, communal, pooled; united, allied, cooperative, collaborative. ANTONYM individual.

**college** noun **1** *a college of technology* SCHOOL, academy, university, polytechnic, institute, seminary, conservatoire, conservatory.

**2** *the college of physicians* ASSOCIATION, society, club, institute, body, fellowship, guild, lodge, order, fraternity, league, union, alliance.

**collide** verb **1** *the trains* ***collided with*** *each other* CRASH INTO, hit, strike, impact, run into, bump into, meet head-on, cannon into, plow into, barrel into.

**2** *in her work, politics and metaphysics collide* CONFLICT, clash; differ, diverge, disagree, be at odds, be incompatible.

**collision** noun **1** *a collision in the passing lane* CRASH, accident, impact, smash, bump, hit, fender bender, wreck, pileup.

**2** *a collision between two ideas* CONFLICT, clash; disagreement, incompatibility, contradiction.

**colloquial** adjective *she just loved the colloquial expressions of her Southern in-laws* INFORMAL, conversational, everyday, nonliterary; unofficial, idiomatic, slangy, vernacular, popular, demotic. ANTONYM formal.

**collusion** noun *there has been collusion between the security forces and paramilitary groups* CONSPIRACY, connivance, complicity, intrigue, plotting, secret understanding, collaboration, scheming.

**colonize** verb *the Germans colonized Tanganyika in 1885* SETTLE (IN), people, populate; occupy, take over, seize, capture, subjugate.

**colonnade** noun *we took a stroll through the colonnade* ROW OF COLUMNS; portico, gallery, stoa, peristyle; arcade.

**colony** noun **1** *a French colony* SETTLEMENT, dependency, protectorate, satellite, territory, outpost, province.

**2** *an artists' colony* COMMUNITY, commune; quarter, district, ghetto.

**color** noun **1** *the lights changed color* HUE, shade, tint, tone, coloration.

**2** *oil color* PAINT, pigment, colorant, dye, stain, tint, wash.

**3** *the color in her cheeks* REDNESS, pinkness, rosiness, ruddiness, blush, flush, bloom.

**4** *people of every color* SKIN COLORING, skin tone, coloring; race, ethnic group.

**5** *anecdotes add color to the text* VIVIDNESS, life, liveliness, vitality, excitement, interest, richness, zest, spice, piquancy, impact, force; *informal* oomph, pizzazz, punch, kick; *literary* salt.

▸ verb **1** *the wood was colored blue* TINT, dye, stain, paint, pigment, wash.

**2** *she colored* BLUSH, redden, go pink, go red, flush.

**3** *the experience colored her outlook* INFLUENCE, affect, taint, warp, skew, distort, bias, prejudice.

**4** *they color evidence to make a story sell* EXAGGERATE, overstate, embroider, embellish, dramatize, enhance, varnish; falsify, misreport, manipulate.

**colorful** adjective **1** *a colorful picture* BRIGHTLY COLORED, vivid, vibrant, brilliant, radiant, rich; gaudy, glaring, garish; multicolored, multicolor, rainbow, varicolored, harlequin, polychromatic, psychedelic, neon, jazzy.

**2** *a colorful account* VIVID, graphic, lively, animated, dramatic, fascinating, interesting, stimulating, scintillating, evocative.

**colorless** adjective **1** *a colorless liquid* UNCOLORED, white, bleached; *literary* achromatic. ANTONYM colored.

**2** *her colorless face* PALE, pallid, wan, anemic, bloodless, ashen, white, waxen, pasty, peaked, sickly, drained, drawn, ghostly, deathly. ANTONYM rosy.

**3** *a colorless personality* UNINTERESTING, dull, boring, tedious, dry, dreary; unexciting, bland, weak, insipid, vapid, vacuous, feeble, wishy-washy, lame, lifeless, spiritless, anemic, bloodless; nondescript, characterless, plain-vanilla. ANTONYM colorful.

**colossal** adjective *a colossal building | we made some colossal mistakes* HUGE, massive, enormous, gigantic, giant, mammoth, vast, immense, monumental, prodigious, mountainous, titanic, towering, king-size(d), economy-size(d); *informal* monster, whopping, humongous, jumbo, ginormous. ANTONYM tiny.

**column** noun **1** *arches supported by massive columns* PILLAR, post, support, upright, baluster, pier, pile, pilaster, stanchion; obelisk, monolith; Doric column, Ionic column, Corinthian column, Tuscan column.

**2** *a column in the paper* ARTICLE, piece, item, story, report, account, write-up, feature, review, notice, editorial.

**3** *we walked in a column* LINE, file, queue, procession, train, cavalcade, convoy.

**coma** noun *doctors do not expect him to come out of the coma* state of unconsciousness; *Medicine* persistent vegetative state.

**comatose** adjective **1** *he was comatose after the accident* UNCONSCIOUS, in a coma, insensible, insensate.

**2** *informal she lay comatose in the sun* INERT, inactive, lethargic, sluggish, torpid, languid; somnolent, sleeping, dormant.

**comb** verb **1** *she combed her hair* GROOM, brush, untangle, smooth, straighten, neaten, tidy, arrange; curry.

**2** *police combed the area* SEARCH, scour, explore, sweep, probe, hunt through, forage through, poke around in, go over, go over with a fine-tooth comb; leave no stone unturned.

**combat** noun *he was killed in combat* BATTLE, fighting, action, hostilities, conflict, war, warfare.

▸ verb *they tried to combat the disease* FIGHT, battle, tackle, attack, counter, resist, withstand; impede, block, thwart, inhibit; stop, halt, prevent, check, curb.

**combatant** noun **1** *a combatant in the war* FIGHTER, soldier, serviceman, servicewoman, warrior, trooper.

**2** *combatants in the computer market* CONTENDER, adversary, opponent, competitor, challenger, rival.

▸ adjective *combatant armies* WARRING, at war, opposing, belligerent, fighting, battling.

**combative** adjective *Mosley's combative language* PUGNACIOUS, aggressive, antagonistic, quarrelsome, argumentative, contentious, hostile, truculent, belligerent, bellicose, militant; *informal* spoiling for a fight. ANTONYM conciliatory.

**combination** noun **1** *a combination of ancient and modern* AMALGAMATION, amalgam, merger, merging, blend, mixture, mix, fusion, marriage, coalition, integration, incorporation, synthesis, composite; *informal* combo.

**2** *he acted in combination with his brother* COOPERATION, collaboration, association, union, partnership, league.

**combine** verb **1** *he combines comedy with tragedy* AMALGAMATE, integrate, incorporate, merge, mix, fuse, blend; bind, join, marry, unify. See note at JOIN.

**2** *teachers combined to tackle the problem* CO-OPERATE, collaborate, join forces, get together, unite, team up, throw in one's lot; *informal* gang up.

**combustible** adjective *piles of combustible material* INFLAMMABLE, flammable, incendiary, ignitable.

**combustion** noun *the combustion of fossil fuels* BURNING; kindling, ignition.

**come** verb **1** *come and listen* MOVE NEARER, move closer, approach, advance, draw close/closer, draw near/nearer; proceed; *archaic* draw nigh. ANTONYM go away.

**2** *they came last night* ARRIVE, get here/there, make it, appear, come on the scene; approach, enter, turn up, come along, materialize; *informal* show (up), roll in/up, blow in, show one's face. ANTONYM leave.

**3** *they* ***came to*** *a stream* REACH, arrive at, get to, make it to; come across, run across, happen on/upon, chance on/upon, come upon, stumble on/upon; end up at, wind up at.

**4** *the dress* ***comes to*** *her ankles* EXTEND TO, stretch to, reach, come as far as.

**5** *she* ***comes from*** *Italy* BE FROM, be a native of, hail from, originate in; live in, reside in.

**6** *attacks came without warning* HAPPEN, occur, take place, come about, transpire, fall, present itself, crop up, materialize, arise, arrive, appear; ensue, follow; *literary* come to pass, befall.

**7** *the shoes come in black and brown* BE AVAILABLE, be for sale; be made, be produced. PHRASES: **come about** *the change came about in 1989* HAPPEN, occur, take place, transpire, fall; crop up, materialize, arise, arrive, appear, surface; ensue, follow; *literary* come to pass, befall.

**come across 1** *they came across his friends* MEET/FIND BY CHANCE, meet, run into, run across, come upon, chance on/upon, stumble on/upon, happen on/upon; discover, encounter, find, locate; *informal* bump into.

**2** *the emotion comes across* BE COMMUNICATED, be perceived, get across, be clear, be understood, register, sink in, strike home.

**3** *she came across as cool* SEEM, appear, look, sound, look to be.

**come along 1** *the puppies are coming along nicely* PROGRESS, develop, shape up; come on, turn out; improve, get better, pick up, rally, recover.

**2** *come along!* HURRY (UP), be quick, get a move on, come on, look lively, speed up, move faster; *informal* get moving, get cracking, step on it, move it, shake a leg, make it snappy; *dated* make haste.

**come apart** *if the straw is too short, the bales will come apart* BREAK APART, break up, fall to bits/pieces, fall apart, disintegrate, come unstuck, separate, split, tear.

**come around 1** *the smelling salts helped him come around* REGAIN CONSCIOUSNESS, recover consciousness, come to, come to one's senses, recover, revive, awake, wake up.

**2** *I* ***came around to*** *her view* BE CONVERTED TO, be won over by, agree with, change one's mind to, be persuaded by; give way to, yield to, relent to.

**3** *Friday the 13th comes around every few months* OCCUR, take place, happen, come up, crop up, arise; recur, reoccur, return, reappear.

**4** *come around for a drink* VISIT, stop by, drop by/in/over, come over, pop in/over.

**come back** *are you coming back before dinner?* RETURN, get back, arrive home, come home; come again.

**come between** *I let my drinking come between me and my family* ALIENATE, estrange, separate, divide, split up, break up, disunite, set at odds.

**come by** *where did you ever come by such a magnificent horse?* OBTAIN, acquire, gain, get, find, pick up, procure, secure; buy, purchase; *informal* get one's hands on, get hold of, bag, score, swing.

**come down** *the report comes down against a zoning variance in the wetlands* DECIDE, conclude, settle; choose, opt, plump.

**come down on** *she came down on him like a ton of bricks.* See REPRIMAND verb.

**come down to** *it comes down to two choices: stay in school or find another place to live* AMOUNT TO, add up to, constitute, boil down to, be equivalent to.

**come down with** *the whole family has come down with chicken pox* FALL ILL WITH, fall sick with, be taken ill with, show symptoms of, become infected with, get, catch, develop, contract, fall victim to.

**come forward** *Vera is always the first to come forward* VOLUNTEER, offer one's services, make oneself available.

**come in** *you can't come in without a pass* ENTER, gain admission, cross the threshold.

**come into** *Jerry came into a small fortune when his grandfather died* INHERIT, be left, be willed, be bequeathed.

**come off** *if you make this meeting come off, you're probably looking at a promotion* SUCCEED, work, turn out well, work out, go as planned, produce the desired result, get results.

**come on** *the new bookcases are coming on nicely* PROGRESS, develop, shape up, take shape, come along, turn out; improve.

**come out** 1 *it came out that he'd been to Rome* BECOME KNOWN, become apparent, come to light, emerge, transpire; get out, be discovered, be uncovered, be revealed, leak out, be disclosed.

2 *my book is coming out* BE PUBLISHED, be issued, be released, be brought out, be printed, go on sale.

3 *the flowers have come out* BLOOM, flower, open.

4 *it will come out all right* END, finish, conclude, work out, turn out; *informal* pan out.

5 *the councilman came out voluntarily* disclose one's homosexuality; *informal* come out of the closet.

**come out with** *I didn't really mean to come out with those stupid remarks* UTTER, say, let out, blurt out, burst out with; issue, present.

**come through** 1 *we came through it OK* SURVIVE, get through, ride out, weather, live through, pull through; withstand, stand up to, endure, surmount, overcome; *informal* stick out.

2 *you **came through for** us* HELP, be there for.

**come to** 1 *the bill came to $17.50* AMOUNT TO, add up to, total, run to, equal.

2 *I came to in the ambulance* REGAIN CONSCIOUSNESS, recover consciousness, come around, come to one's senses, recover, revive, awake, wake up.

**come up** *whatever comes up, we'll be ready* ARISE, occur, happen, come about, transpire, emerge, surface, crop up, turn up, pop up.

**come up to** 1 *she came up to his shoulder* REACH, come to, be as tall as, extend to.

2 *he never came up to her expectations* MEASURE UP TO, match up to, live up to, fulfill, satisfy, meet, equal, compare with; be good enough for; *informal* hold a candle to.

**come up with** *Miranda has come up with a terrific idea* PRODUCE, devise, think up; propose, put forward, submit, suggest, recommend, advocate, introduce, moot.

**comeback** noun 1 *he made a determined comeback* RESURGENCE, recovery, return, rally, upturn.

2 *informal one of my best comebacks* RETORT, riposte, return, rejoinder; answer, reply, response.

**comedian , comedienne** noun 1 *a famous comedian* COMIC, comedienne, funny man, funny woman, humorist, gagster, stand-up.

2 *Dad was such a comedian* JOKER, jester, wit, wag, comic, wisecracker, jokester; prankster, clown, fool, buffoon; *informal* laugh, hoot, riot; *informal, dated* card.

**comedown** noun *informal* 1 *a bit of a comedown for a sergeant* LOSS OF STATUS, loss of face, humiliation, belittlement, demotion, degradation, disgrace.

2 *it's such a comedown after Christmas* ANTICLIMAX, letdown, disappointment, disillusionment, deflation, decline.

**comedy** noun 1 *he excels in comedy* LIGHT ENTERTAINMENT, comic theater, farce, situation comedy, satire, pantomime, comic opera; burlesque, slapstick; *informal* sitcom. ANTONYMS tragedy, drama.

2 *the comedy in their work* HUMOR, fun, funny side, comical aspect, absurdity, drollness, farce. ANTONYM gravity.

**comely** adjective *archaic*. See ATTRACTIVE sense 2.

**come-on** noun *informal the $200 rebate is a come-on for prospective car buyers* INDUCEMENT, incentive, attraction, lure, pull, draw, enticement, bait, carrot, temptation; fascination, charm, appeal, allure.

**comeuppance** noun *informal the bad guys always get their comeuppance in the final scene* JUST DESERTS, just punishment, due, retribution, requital, what's coming to one.

**comfort** noun 1 *travel in comfort* EASE, relaxation, repose, serenity, tranquility, contentment, coziness; luxury, opulence, prosperity; bed of roses.

2 *words of comfort* CONSOLATION, solace, condolence, sympathy, commiseration; support, reassurance, cheer.

▸ verb *a friend tried to comfort her* CONSOLE, solace, condole with, commiserate with, sympathize with; support, succor, ease, reassure, soothe, calm; cheer, hearten, uplift. ANTONYMS distress, depress.

**comfortable** adjective 1 *a comfortable lifestyle* PLEASANT, free from hardship; affluent, well-to-do, luxurious, opulent. ANTONYM harsh.

2 *a comfortable room* COZY, snug, warm, pleasant, agreeable; restful, homelike, homely; *informal* comfy. ANTONYM spartan.

3 *comfortable clothes* LOOSE, loose-fitting, casual; *informal* comfy.

4 *a comfortable pace* LEISURELY, unhurried, relaxed, easy, gentle, sedate, undemanding, slow; *informal* laid-back.

5 *they feel comfortable with each other* AT EASE, relaxed, secure, safe, unworried, contented, happy. ANTONYMS vulnerable, tense.

**comforting** adjective *Anne gave her a comforting hug* CONSOLING, sympathetic, compassionate, solicitous, tender, warm, caring, loving; supportive, reassuring, soothing, calming; cheering, heartening, encouraging.

**comic** adjective *a comic play* HUMOROUS, funny, droll, amusing, hilarious, uproarious; comical, farcical, silly, slapstick, zany; witty, jocular; *informal* priceless, side-splitting, rib-tickling; *informal, dated* killing. ANTONYM serious.

▸ noun 1 *a professional comic* COMEDIAN, comedienne, funny man/woman, humorist, wit; joker, clown; *informal* kidder, wisecracker.

2 *the paper no longer runs his favorite Sunday comic* comic strip, cartoon, comic book; *informal* funny.

**comical** adjective 1 *he could be quite comical* FUNNY, comic, humorous, droll, witty, jocular, hilarious, amusing, diverting, entertaining; *informal* jokey, wacky, waggish, side-splitting, rib-tickling, priceless, a scream, a laugh; *informal, dated* killing, a card, a caution. ANTONYM sensible.

2 *they look comical in those suits* SILLY, absurd, ridiculous,

laughable, risible, ludicrous, preposterous, foolish; *informal* wacky, crazy. ANTONYM sensible.

**coming** adjective *the coming election* FORTHCOMING, imminent, impending, approaching; future, expected, anticipated; close, at hand, in store, in the offing, in the pipeline, on the horizon, on the way; *informal* in the cards.

▸ noun *the coming of spring* APPROACH, advance, advent, arrival, appearance, emergence, onset.

**command** verb **1** *he commanded his men to retreat* ORDER, tell, direct, instruct, call on, require; *literary* bid.

**2** *Jones commanded a tank squadron* BE IN CHARGE OF, be in command of, be the leader of; head, lead, control, direct, manage, supervise, oversee; *informal* head up.

**3** *they command great respect* RECEIVE, get, gain, secure.

▸ noun **1** *officers shouted commands* ORDER, instruction, directive, direction, commandment, injunction, decree, edict, demand, stipulation, requirement, exhortation, bidding, request.

**2** *he had 160 men under his command* AUTHORITY, control, charge, power, direction, dominion, guidance; leadership, rule, government, management, supervision, jurisdiction.

**3** *a brilliant command of Italian* KNOWLEDGE, mastery, grasp, comprehension, understanding.

**commandeer** verb *dozens of private homes were commandeered by the army* SEIZE, take, requisition, appropriate, expropriate, sequestrate, sequester, confiscate, annex, take over, claim, preempt; hijack, arrogate, help oneself to; *informal* walk off with; *Law* distrain.

**commander** noun *he is commander of an intelligence unit in Bogota* LEADER, head, chief, overseer, controller; commander-in-chief, C in C, commanding officer, CO, officer; *informal* boss, boss man, skipper, numero uno, number one, top dog, kingpin, head honcho, big kahuna.

**commanding** adjective **1** *a commanding position* DOMINANT, dominating, controlling, superior, powerful, prominent, advantageous, favorable.

**2** *a commanding voice* AUTHORITATIVE, masterful, assertive, firm, emphatic, insistent, imperative; peremptory, imperious, dictatorial; *informal* bossy.

**commemorate** verb *an annual festival to commemorate the liberation of our town* CELEBRATE, pay tribute to, pay homage to, honor, salute, toast; remember, recognize, acknowledge, observe, mark.

**commemorative** adjective *a commemorative coin that depicts the raising of the flag on Iwo Jima* MEMORIAL, remembrance; celebratory.

**commence** verb *the meeting will commence at noon* BEGIN, start; get the ball rolling, get going, get underway, get off the ground, set about, embark on, launch into, lead off; open, initiate, inaugurate; *informal* kick off, get the show on the road. ANTONYM conclude.

**commend** verb **1** *we should commend him* PRAISE, compliment, congratulate, applaud, salute, honor; sing the praises of, pay tribute to, take one's hat off to, pat on the back; *formal* laud. See note at PRAISE. ANTONYM criticize.

**2** *I commend her to you without reservation* RECOMMEND, suggest, propose; endorse, advocate, vouch for, speak for, support, back. See note at APPROVE.

**3** *formal I commend them to your care* ENTRUST, trust, deliver, commit, hand over, give, turn over, consign, assign.

**commendable** adjective *he tackled the tests with commendable zeal* ADMIRABLE, praiseworthy, creditable, laudable, estimable, meritorious, exemplary, noteworthy, honorable, respectable, fine, excellent. ANTONYM reprehensible.

**commendation** noun **1** *letters of commendation* PRAISE, congratulation, appreciation; acclaim, credit, recognition, respect, esteem, admiration, homage, tribute.

**2** *a commendation for bravery* AWARD, accolade, prize, honor, honorable mention, mention, citation.

**commensurate** adjective **1** *they had privileges but commensurate duties* EQUIVALENT, equal, corresponding, correspondent, comparable, proportionate, proportional.

**2** *a salary* ***commensurate with*** *your qualifications* APPROPRIATE TO, in keeping with, in line with, consistent with, corresponding to, according to, relative to; dependent on, based on.

**comment** noun **1** *their comments on her appearance* REMARK, observation, statement, utterance; pronouncement, judgment, reflection, opinion, view; criticism.

**2** *a great deal of comment* DISCUSSION, debate; interest.

**3** *a comment in the margin* NOTE, annotation, footnote, gloss, commentary, explanation.

▸ verb **1** *they* ***commented on*** *the food* REMARK ON, speak about, talk about, discuss, mention.

**2** *"It will soon be night," he commented* REMARK, observe, reflect, say, state, declare, announce; interpose, interject.

**commentary** noun **1** *the soccer commentary* NARRATION, description, account, report, review.

**2** *textual commentary* EXPLANATION, elucidation, interpretation, exegesis, analysis; assessment, appraisal, criticism; notes, comments.

**commentator** noun **1** *a television commentator* NARRATOR, announcer, presenter, anchor, anchorman, anchorwoman; reporter, journalist, newscaster, sportscaster; *informal* talking head.

**2** *a political commentator* ANALYST, pundit, monitor, observer; writer, speaker.

**commerce** noun **1** *industry and commerce* TRADE, trading, buying and selling, business, dealing, traffic; (financial) transactions, dealings.

**2** *dated human commerce* RELATIONS, dealings, socializing, communication, association, contact, intercourse.

**commercial** adjective **1** *a vessel built for commercial purposes*

TRADE, trading, business, private enterprise, mercantile, sales.

2 *a commercial society* PROFIT-ORIENTED, money-oriented, materialistic, mercenary.

▸ noun *a TV commercial* ADVERTISEMENT, promotion, display; *informal* ad, plug, infomercial.

**commission** noun 1 *the dealer's commission* PERCENTAGE, brokerage, share, portion, dividend, premium, fee, consideration, bonus; *informal* cut, take, rake-off, slice.

2 *the commission of building a palace* TASK, employment, job, project, mission, assignment, undertaking; duty, charge, responsibility; *informal* marching orders.

3 *items made under state commission* WARRANT, license, sanction, authority.

4 *an independent commission* COMMITTEE, board, council, panel, directorate, delegation.

5 *the commission of an offense* PERPETRATION, committing, committal, execution.

▸ verb 1 *he was commissioned to paint a portrait* ENGAGE, contract, charge, employ, hire, recruit, retain, appoint, enlist, book, sign up.

2 *they commissioned a sculpture* ORDER; authorize; *formal* bespeak.

PHRASES: **in commission** *the new bathrooms are now in commission* IN SERVICE, in use; working, functional, operative, up and running, in operation, in working order.
**out of commission** *more than half of our original computers are out of commission* NOT IN SERVICE, not in use, unserviceable; not working, inoperative, out of order, malfunctioning, broken, down.

**commit** verb 1 *he committed a murder* CARRY OUT, do, perpetrate, engage in, enact, execute, effect, accomplish; be responsible for; *informal* pull off.

2 *she was committed to their care* ENTRUST, consign, assign, deliver, give, hand over, relinquish; *formal* commend.

3 *they committed themselves to the project* PLEDGE, devote, apply, give, dedicate.

4 *the judge committed him to prison* CONSIGN, send, deliver, confine.

5 *her husband had her committed* HOSPITALIZE, confine, institutionalize, put away; certify.

**commitment** noun 1 *the pressure of his commitments* RESPONSIBILITY, obligation, duty, tie, liability; task; engagement, arrangement.

2 *her commitment to her students* DEDICATION, devotion, allegiance, loyalty, faithfulness, fidelity.

3 *he made a commitment* VOW, promise, pledge, oath; contract, pact, deal; decision, resolution.

**commodious** adjective *formal a commodious armchair* ROOMY, capacious, spacious, ample, generous, sizable, large, big, extensive. ANTONYM cramped.

**commodity** noun *Australian wools are among our most popular foreign commodities* ITEM, material, product, article, object; import, export.

**common** adjective 1 *the common folk* ORDINARY, normal, average, unexceptional; simple.

2 *a very common art form* USUAL, ordinary, familiar, regular, frequent, recurrent, everyday; standard, typical, conventional, stock, commonplace, run-of-the-mill; *informal* garden variety. See note at PREVALENT. ANTONYM unusual.

3 *a common belief* WIDESPREAD, general, universal, popular, mainstream, prevalent, prevailing, rife, established, conventional, traditional, orthodox, accepted. See note at UNIVERSAL. ANTONYM rare.

4 *the common good* COLLECTIVE, communal, community, public, popular, general; shared, combined. ANTONYMS individual, private.

5 *they are far too common* UNCOUTH, vulgar, coarse, rough, boorish, unladylike, ungentlemanly, ill-bred, uncivilized, unrefined, unsophisticated; lowly, low-born, low-class, inferior, proletarian, plebeian. ANTONYM refined.

**common sense** noun *well, at least you had the common sense to call 911* GOOD SENSE, sense, native wit, sensibleness, judgment, levelheadedness, prudence, discernment, canniness, astuteness, shrewdness, wisdom, insight, perception, perspicacity; practicality, capability, resourcefulness, enterprise; *informal* horse sense, gumption, savvy, smarts, street smarts. ANTONYM folly.

**commotion** noun *what's all that commotion in the parking lot?* DISTURBANCE, uproar, tumult, rumpus, ruckus, brouhaha, hoopla, furor, hue and cry, fuss, stir, storm; turmoil, disorder, confusion, chaos, mayhem, havoc, pandemonium; unrest, fracas, riot, breach of the peace, donnybrook; *informal* ruction, ballyhoo, hoo-ha, to-do, hullabaloo.

**communal** adjective 1 *the kitchen was communal* SHARED, joint, common. ANTONYM private.

2 *they farm on a communal basis* COLLECTIVE, cooperative, community, communalist, combined. ANTONYM individual.

**commune** noun *she lives in a commune* COLLECTIVE, cooperative, communal settlement, kibbutz.

▸ verb 1 *we pray to commune with God* COMMUNICATE, speak, talk, converse, interface.

2 *she likes to **commune with** nature* EMPATHIZE WITH, identify with, have a rapport with, feel at one with; relate to, feel close to.

**communicable** adjective *the spread of communicable diseases* CONTAGIOUS, INFECTIOUS, transmittable, transmissible, transferable, spreadable; *informal* catching.

**communicate** verb 1 *he communicated the news to his boss* CONVEY, tell, impart, relay, transmit, pass on, announce, report, recount, relate, present; divulge, disclose, mention; spread, disseminate, promulgate, broadcast.

2 *they communicate daily* BE IN TOUCH, be in contact, have

dealings, interface, interact, commune, meet, liaise; talk, speak, converse; *informal* have a confab, powwow.

3 *learn how to communicate better* GET ONE'S MESSAGE ACROSS, explain oneself, be understood, get through to someone.

4 *the disease is communicated easily* TRANSMIT, transfer, spread, carry, pass on.

5 *each bedroom communicates with a bathroom* CONNECT WITH, join up with, open on to, lead into.

**communication** noun 1 *the communication of news* TRANSMISSION, conveyance, divulgence, disclosure; dissemination, promulgation, broadcasting.

2 *there was no communication between them* CONTACT, dealings, relations, connection, association, socializing, intercourse; correspondence, dialogue, talk, conversation, discussion.

3 *an official communication* MESSAGE, statement, announcement, report, dispatch, communiqué, letter, bulletin, correspondence.

**communicative** adjective *we find that abused children tend to be less communicative than other children* FORTHCOMING, expansive, expressive, unreserved, uninhibited, vocal, outgoing, frank, open, candid; talkative, chatty, loquacious; *informal* gabby.

**communion** noun 1 *a sense of communion with others* AFFINITY, fellowship, kinship, friendship, fellow feeling, togetherness, closeness, harmony, understanding, rapport, connection, communication, empathy, accord, unity. See note at CONVERSATION.

2 *Christ's presence at Communion* THE EUCHARIST, Holy Communion, the Lord's Supper, Mass.

**community** noun 1 *work done for the community* PUBLIC, general public, populace, people, citizenry, population, collective; residents, inhabitants, citizens.

2 *a suburban community* DISTRICT, region, zone, area, locality, locale, neighborhood; *informal* neck of the woods, hood.

3 *concerns in the immigrant community* GROUP, body, set, circle, clique, faction; *informal* gang, bunch.

4 *a monastic community* BROTHERHOOD, sisterhood, fraternity, sorority, sodality; order, congregation, abbey, convent.

**commute** verb 1 *they commute by train* TRAVEL TO AND FROM WORK, travel to and fro, travel back and forth.

2 *his sentence was commuted* REDUCE, lessen, lighten, shorten, cut, attenuate, moderate. ANTONYMS increase, uphold.

3 *knight service was commuted for a payment* EXCHANGE, change, substitute, swap, trade, switch.

**commuter** noun *commuters may see an increase in train fares this spring* DAILY TRAVELER, traveler, passenger; *informal* straphanger.

**compact**[1] adjective 1 *a compact rug* DENSE, close-packed, tightly packed; thick, tight, firm. ANTONYM loose.

2 *a compact camera* SMALL, little, petite, miniature, mini, small-scale; *informal* teeny, teeny-weeny; little-bitty, itty-bitty; *Scottish* wee. ANTONYM large.

3 *her overview is compact* CONCISE, succinct, condensed, brief, pithy; short and sweet; *informal* snappy; *formal* compendious. ANTONYM rambling.

▸ verb *the snow has been compacted* COMPRESS, condense, pack down, press down, tamp (down), flatten.

**compact**[2] noun *the warring states signed a compact* TREATY, pact, accord, agreement, contract, bargain, deal, settlement, covenant, concordat; pledge, promise, bond.

**companion** noun 1 *Harry and his companion* ASSOCIATE, partner, escort, compatriot, confederate; friend, intimate, confidant, confidante, comrade; *informal* pal, chum, crony, sidekick, mate, buddy, amigo, compadre.

2 *a lady's companion* ATTENDANT, aide, helper, assistant, valet, equerry, lady-in-waiting; chaperone; minder.

3 *the tape is a companion to the book* COMPLEMENT, counterpart, twin, match; accompaniment, supplement, addition, adjunct, accessory.

4 *The Gardener's Companion* HANDBOOK, manual, guide, reference book, ABC, primer, vade mecum; *informal* bible.

**companionship** noun *the volunteers do various errands for our elderly clients and provide some much-appreciated companionship* FRIENDSHIP, fellowship, closeness, togetherness, amity, intimacy, rapport, camaraderie, brotherhood, sisterhood; company, society, social contact.

**company** noun 1 *an oil company* FIRM, business, corporation, establishment, agency, office, bureau, institution, organization, concern, enterprise; conglomerate, consortium, syndicate, multinational; *informal* outfit.

2 *I enjoy his company* COMPANIONSHIP, friendship, fellowship, amity, camaraderie; society, association.

3 *I'm expecting company* GUESTS, house guests, visitors, callers, people; someone.

4 *a company of poets* GROUP, crowd, party, band, assembly, cluster, flock, herd, troupe, throng, congregation; *informal* bunch, gang.

5 *a company of infantry* UNIT, section, detachment, troop, corps, squad, squadron, platoon, battalion, division.

**comparable** adjective 1 *comparable incomes* SIMILAR, close, near, approximate, akin, equivalent, commensurate, proportional, proportionate; like, matching, homologous.

2 *nobody is* ***comparable with*** *him* EQUAL TO, as good as, in the same league as, able to hold a candle to, on a par with, on a level with; a match for.

**comparative** adjective *the left the city for the comparative quiet of the country* RELATIVE, in/by comparison.

**compare** verb 1 *we compared the data sets* CONTRAST, juxtapose, collate, differentiate. See note at CONTRAST.

2 *he was* ***compared to*** *Wagner* LIKEN TO, equate to, analogize to; class with, set side by side with.

**3** *the porcelain* ***compares with*** *Dresden's fine china* BE AS GOOD AS, be comparable to, bear comparison with, be the equal of, match up to, be on a par with, be in the same league as, come close to, hold a candle to, be not unlike; match, resemble, emulate, rival, approach. PHRASE: **beyond compare** *their peach cobbler is beyond compare* WITHOUT EQUAL, second to none, in a class of one's own; peerless, matchless, unmatched, incomparable, inimitable, supreme, outstanding, consummate, unique, singular, perfect.

**comparison** noun **1** *a comparison of the results* JUXTAPOSITION, collation, differentiation.

**2** *there's no comparison between them* RESEMBLANCE, likeness, similarity, correspondence, correlation, parallel, parity, comparability.

**compartment** noun **1** *a secret compartment* SECTION, part, bay, recess, chamber, cavity; pocket.

**2** *they put science and religion in separate compartments* DOMAIN, field, sphere, department; category, pigeonhole, bracket, group, set.

**compass** noun *faith cannot be defined within the compass of human thought* SCOPE, range, extent, reach, span, breadth, ambit, limits, parameters, bounds. See note at RANGE.

**compassion** noun *have you no compassion for a fellow human being?* PITY, sympathy, empathy, fellow feeling, care, concern, solicitude, sensitivity, warmth, love, tenderness, mercy, leniency, tolerance, kindness, humanity, charity. See note at MERCY. ANTONYMS indifference, cruelty.

**compassionate** adjective *a compassionate concern for the victims* SYMPATHETIC, empathetic, understanding, caring, solicitous, sensitive, warm, loving; merciful, lenient, tolerant, considerate, kind, humane, charitable, bighearted.

**compatible** adjective **1** *they were never compatible* WELL SUITED, suited, well matched, like-minded, in tune, in harmony; reconcilable.

**2** *her bruising is compatible with a fall* CONSISTENT, congruous, congruent; in keeping.

**compatriot** noun *Sampras defeated his compatriot Agassi in the final* FELLOW COUNTRYMAN, fellow countrywoman, countryman, countrywoman, fellow citizen.

**compel** verb **1** *he compelled them to leave their land* FORCE, pressure, press, push, urge; dragoon, browbeat, bully, intimidate, strong-arm; oblige, require, make; *informal* lean on, put the screws on.

**2** *they can compel compliance* EXACT, extort, demand, insist on, force, necessitate.

THE RIGHT WORD **compel, coerce, constrain, force, necessitate, oblige**

A parent faced with a rebellious teenager may try to **compel** him to do his homework by threatening to take away his allowance. *Compel* commonly implies the exercise of authority, the exertion of great effort, or the impossibility of doing anything else (*compelled to graduate from high school by her eagerness to leave home*). It typically requires a personal object, although it is possible to *compel* a reaction or response (*she compels admiration*). **Force** is a little stronger, suggesting the exertion of power, energy, or physical strength to accomplish something or to subdue resistance (*his mother forced him to confess that he'd broken the basement window*). **Coerce** can imply the use of force, but often stops short of using it (*she was coerced into obedience by the threat of losing her telephone privileges*). **Constrain** means *compel*, but by means of restriction, confinement, or limitation (*constrained from dating by his parents' strictness*). **Necessitate** and **oblige** make an action necessary by imposing certain conditions that demand a response (*Her mother's illness obliged her to be more cooperative; it also necessitated giving up her social life*).

**compelling** adjective **1** *a compelling performance* ENTHRALLING, captivating, gripping, riveting, spellbinding, mesmerizing, absorbing, irresistible. ANTONYM boring.

**2** *a compelling argument* CONVINCING, persuasive, cogent, irresistible, powerful, strong, weighty, plausible, credible, sound, valid, telling, conclusive, irrefutable, unanswerable. ANTONYM weak.

**compensate** verb **1** *you must compensate for what you did* MAKE AMENDS, make up, make reparation, recompense, atone, requite, pay; expiate, make good, rectify.

**2** *we agreed to compensate him for his loss* RECOMPENSE, repay, pay back, reimburse, remunerate, recoup, requite, indemnify.

**3** *his flair* ***compensated for*** *his faults* BALANCE (OUT), counterbalance, counteract, offset, make up for, cancel out, neutralize, negative.

**compensation** noun *my client has not received compensation for the legal fees incurred in 1998* RECOMPENSE, repayment, reimbursement, remuneration, requital, indemnification, indemnity, redress; damages; *informal* comp.

**compete** verb **1** *they competed in a tennis tournament* TAKE PART, participate, play, be a competitor, be involved; enter.

**2** *they had to* ***compete with*** *other firms* CONTEND WITH, vie with, battle (with), wrangle with, jockey with, go head to head with; strive against, pit oneself against; challenge, take on.

**3** *no one can* ***compete with*** *Elaine* RIVAL, challenge, keep up with, keep pace with, compare with, match, be in the same league as, come near to, come close to, touch; *informal* hold a candle to.

**competence** noun **1** *my technical competence* CAPABILITY, ability, competency, proficiency, accomplishment, expertise, adeptness, skill, prowess, mastery, talent; *informal* savvy, know-how.

**2** *the competence of the system* ADEQUACY, appropriateness, suitability, fitness; effectiveness; *formal* efficacy.

**3** *matters within the competence of the courts* AUTHORITY, power, control, jurisdiction, ambit, scope.

**competent** adjective **1** *a competent carpenter* CAPABLE, able, proficient, adept, adroit, accomplished, complete, skillful, skilled, credentialed, gifted, talented, expert; good, excellent; *informal* great, mean, wicked, nifty, ace.

**2** *she spoke competent French* ADEQUATE, acceptable, satisfactory, reasonable, fair, decent, not bad, all right, average, tolerable, passable, moderate, middling; *informal* OK, okay, so-so, 'comme ci, comme ça'. ANTONYM inadequate.

**3** *the court was not competent to hear the case* FIT, suitable, suited, appropriate; qualified, empowered, authorized. ANTONYM unfit.

**competition** noun **1** *Stephanie won the competition* CONTEST, tournament, match, game, heat, fixture, event.

**2** *I'm not interested in competition* RIVALRY, competitiveness, vying; conflict, feuding, fighting; *informal* keeping up with the Joneses.

**3** *we must stay ahead of the competition* OPPOSITION, other side, field; enemy; challengers, opponents, rivals, adversaries; *literary* foe.

**competitive** adjective **1** *a competitive player* AMBITIOUS, zealous, keen, pushy, combative, aggressive. ANTONYM apathetic.

**2** *a highly competitive industry* RUTHLESS, aggressive, fierce; Darwinian; *informal* dog-eat-dog, cutthroat.

**3** *competitive prices* REASONABLE, moderate; low, inexpensive, cheap, budget, bargain, reduced, discount; rock-bottom, bargain-basement, downmarket. ANTONYM exorbitant.

**competitor** noun **1** *the competitors in the race* CONTESTANT, contender, challenger, participant, entrant; runner, player. ANTONYM spectator.

**2** *our European competitors* RIVAL, challenger, opponent, adversary; competition, opposition. ANTONYM ally.

**compilation** noun *a compilation of their greatest hits* COLLECTION, selection, anthology, treasury, compendium, album, corpus; potpourri.

**compile** verb *he compiled a dossier of patients with tropical diseases* ASSEMBLE, put together, make up, collate, compose, organize, arrange; gather, collect.

**complacent** adjective *in this competitive field we can't afford to be complacent* SMUG, self-satisfied, self-congratulatory, self-regarding; gloating, triumphant, proud; pleased, satisfied, content, contented.

**complain** verb *his dogs were always roaming until someone finally complained* PROTEST, grumble, whine, bleat, carp, cavil, grouse, make a fuss; object, speak out, criticize, find fault; *informal* kick up a fuss, raise a stink, bellyache, moan, snivel, beef, bitch, sound off, gripe, kvetch.

**complaint** noun **1** *they lodged a complaint* PROTEST, objection, grievance, grouse, cavil, quibble, grumble; charge, accusation, criticism; jeremiad; *informal* beef, gripe, whinge; *Law* plaint.

**2** *little cause for complaint* PROTESTATION, objection, exception, grievance, grumbling; criticism, fault-finding, condemnation, disapproval, dissatisfaction; *informal* grousing, bellyaching, nitpicking.

**3** *a kidney complaint* DISORDER, disease, infection, affliction, illness, ailment, sickness; condition, problem, upset, trouble.

**complement** noun **1** *the perfect complement to the food* ACCOMPANIMENT, companion, addition, supplement, accessory, trimming.

**2** *a full complement of lifeboats* AMOUNT, total, contingent, capacity, allowance, quota.

▸ verb *this sauce complements the dessert* ACCOMPANY, go with, round off, set off, suit, harmonize with; enhance, complete.

**complementary** adjective *decorating in complementary colors and patterns* HARMONIOUS, compatible, corresponding, matching, twin; supportive, reciprocal, interdependent. See note at COMPLEMENT. ANTONYM incompatible.

**complete** adjective **1** *the complete interview* ENTIRE, whole, full, total; uncut, unabridged.

**2** *their research was complete* FINISHED, ended, concluded, completed, finalized; accomplished, achieved, discharged, settled, done; *informal* wrapped up, sewn up, polished off. ANTONYM unfinished.

**3** *a complete fool* ABSOLUTE, out-and-out, utter, total, real, downright, thoroughgoing, veritable, prize, perfect, unqualified, unmitigated, sheer, arrant, full-out. ANTONYM partial.

▸ verb **1** *he had to complete his training* FINISH, end, conclude, finalize, wind up; *informal* wrap up, sew up, polish off.

**2** *the outfit was completed with a veil* FINISH OFF, round off, top off, crown, cap, complement.

**3** *complete the application form* FILL IN/OUT, answer.

**completely** adverb *he'd always been completely honest with her* TOTALLY, entirely, wholly, thoroughly, fully, utterly, absolutely, perfectly, unreservedly, unconditionally, quite, altogether, downright; in every way, in every respect, one hundred percent, every inch, to the hilt; *informal* dead, deadly, to the max.

**completion** noun *the money ran out before the project's completion* REALIZATION, accomplishment, achievement, fulfillment, consummation, finalization, resolution; finish, end, conclusion, close, cessation.

**complex** adjective **1** *a complex situation* COMPLICATED, involved, intricate, convoluted, elaborate, impenetrable, Gordian; difficult, knotty, tricky, thorny. ANTONYM simple.

**2** *a complex structure* COMPOUND, composite, multiplex.

▸ noun **1** *a complex of roads* NETWORK, system, nexus, web, tissue; combination, aggregation.

**2** *informal he had a complex about losing his hair* OBSESSION, fixation, preoccupation; neurosis; *informal* hang-up, thing, bee in one's bonnet.

**complexion** noun **1** *a pale complexion* SKIN, skin color, skin tone; pigmentation.

**2** *this puts an entirely new complexion on things* PERSPECTIVE, angle, slant, interpretation; appearance, light, look.

**3** *governments of all complexions* TYPE, kind, sort; nature, character, stamp, ilk, kidney.

**complexity** noun *an issue of great complexity* COMPLICATION, problem, difficulty; twist, turn, intricacy.

**compliance** noun **1** ***compliance with*** *international law* OBEDIENCE TO, observance of, adherence to, conformity to, respect for. ANTONYM violation.

**2** *he mistook her silence for compliance* ACQUIESCENCE, agreement, assent, consent, acceptance; complaisance, pliability, docility, meekness, submission. ANTONYM defiance.

**complicate** verb *involvement with Adam could only complicate her life* MAKE (MORE) DIFFICULT, make complicated, mix up, confuse, muddle; *informal* mess up, screw up, snarl up. ANTONYM simplify.

**complicated** adjective *the complicated election process* COMPLEX, intricate, involved, convoluted, tangled, impenetrable, knotty, tricky, thorny, labyrinthine, tortuous, Gordian; confusing, bewildering, perplexing. ANTONYM straightforward.

**complication** noun **1** *a complication concerning ownership* DIFFICULTY, problem, obstacle, hurdle, stumbling block; drawback, snag, catch, hitch; *informal* fly in the ointment, headache.

**2** *the complication of life in our society* COMPLEXITY, complicatedness, intricacy, convolutedness.

**complicity** noun *they've been accused of complicity in the destruction of damning evidence* COLLUSION, involvement, collaboration, connivance; conspiracy; *informal* being in cahoots.

**compliment** noun **1** *an unexpected compliment | he enjoyed the compliments* FLATTERING REMARK, tribute, accolade, commendation, bouquet, pat on the back; **(compliments)** praise, acclaim, admiration, flattery, blandishments, honeyed words. ANTONYM insult.

**2** **(compliments)** *my compliments on your cooking* CONGRATULATIONS, commendations, praise; *informal* props, kudos.

**3** **(compliments)** *Margaret sends her compliments* GREETINGS, regards, respects, good wishes, best wishes, salutations, felicitations.

▸ verb *they complimented his performance* PRAISE, pay tribute to, speak highly/well of, flatter, wax lyrical about, make much of, commend, acclaim, applaud, salute, honor; congratulate someone on. See note at COMPLEMENT. ANTONYM criticize.

**complimentary** adjective **1** *complimentary remarks* FLATTERING, appreciative, congratulatory, admiring, approving, commendatory, favorable, glowing, adulatory; *informal* rave. ANTONYM derogatory.

**2** *complimentary tickets* FREE, free of charge, gratis, for nothing; courtesy; *informal* on the house. See note at COMPLEMENT.

**comply** verb *Myra* ***complied with*** *his wishes* ABIDE BY, observe, obey, adhere to, conform to, hew to, follow, respect; agree to, assent to, go along with, yield to, submit to, defer to; satisfy, fulfill. ANTONYMS ignore, disobey.

**component** noun *the components of electronic devices* PART, piece, bit, element, constituent, ingredient, building block; unit, module, section.

▸ adjective *the molecule's component elements* CONSTITUENT, integral; basic, essential.

**compose** verb **1** *a poem composed by Shelley* WRITE, formulate, devise, make up, think up, produce, invent, concoct; pen, author, draft; score, orchestrate, choreograph.

**2** *compose a still life* ORGANIZE, arrange, set out.

**3** *the subcommittee is composed of ten senators* MAKE UP, constitute, form. PHRASE: **compose oneself** *you have to compose yourself before you take the stand* CALM DOWN, control oneself, regain one's composure, pull oneself together, collect oneself, steady oneself, keep one's head, relax; *informal* get a grip, keep one's cool, cool one's jets, decompress.

**composed** adjective *she remained composed throughout the ordeal* CALM, collected, cool, cool as a cucumber, 'cool, calm, and collected', self-controlled, self-possessed; serene, tranquil, relaxed, at ease, unruffled, unperturbed, untroubled; equable, even-tempered, imperturbable; *informal* unflappable, together, laid-back. ANTONYM excited.

**composite** adjective *a composite structure* COMPOUND, complex; combined, blended, mixed.

▸ noun *a composite of plastic and metal* AMALGAMATION, amalgam, combination, compound, fusion, synthesis, mixture, blend; alloy.

**composition** noun **1** *the composition of the council* MAKEUP, constitution, configuration, structure, formation, form, framework, fabric, anatomy, organization; *informal* setup.

**2** *a literary composition* WORK, work of art, creation, opus, oeuvre, piece, arrangement.

**3** *we all participated in the composition of the school song* WRITING, creation, formulation, invention, concoction, orchestration.

**4** *a school composition* ESSAY, paper, study, piece of writing, theme.

**5** *the composition of the painting* ARRANGEMENT, disposition, layout; proportions, balance, symmetry.

**6** *an adhesive composition* MIXTURE, compound, amalgam, blend, mix.

**compost** noun *all of our organic garbage is converted to compost* FERTILIZER, mulch, manure, bone meal, fish meal, blood meal, guano; humus, peat; plant food, top-dressing.

**composure** noun *most people would have lost their composure after such a disappointing defeat* SELF-CONTROL, self-possession, calm, equanimity, equilibrium, serenity, tranquility; aplomb, poise, presence of mind, sangfroid; imperturbability, placidness, impassivity; *informal* cool.

**compound** noun **1** *a compound of two elements* AMALGAM, amalgamation, combination, composite, blend, mixture, mix, fusion, synthesis; alloy.

2 *they were contained in the compound* ENCLOSURE, pound, coop; estate, cloister.

▸ adjective *a compound substance* COMPOSITE, complex; blended, fused, combined. ANTONYM simple.

▸ verb 1 *soap compounded with disinfectant* MIX, combine, blend, amalgamate, fuse, synthesize.

2 *his illness compounds their problems* AGGRAVATE, exacerbate, worsen, add to, augment, intensify, heighten, increase, magnify; complicate. ANTONYM alleviate.

PHRASE: **compounded of** *a smell compounded of dust and mold* COMPOSED OF, made up of, formed from.

**comprehend** verb 1 *Katie couldn't comprehend his message* UNDERSTAND, grasp, take in, see, apprehend, follow, make sense of, fathom, get to the bottom of; unravel, decipher, interpret; *informal* work out, figure out, make head(s) or tail(s) of, get one's head around, get the drift of, catch on to, get.

2 *formal a divine order comprehending all men* COMPRISE, include, encompass, embrace, involve, contain. ANTONYM exclude.

**comprehensible** adjective *the information must be accurate and comprehensible* INTELLIGIBLE, understandable, accessible; lucid, coherent, clear, plain, explicit, unambiguous, straightforward, fathomable. ANTONYM opaque.

**comprehension** noun *matters that seemed beyond her comprehension* UNDERSTANDING, grasp, conception, apprehension, cognition, ken, knowledge, awareness, perception; interpretation. ANTONYM ignorance.

**comprehensive** adjective *a comprehensive review of our defense policy* INCLUSIVE, all-inclusive, complete; thorough, full, extensive, all-embracing, exhaustive, detailed, in-depth, encyclopedic, universal, catholic; far-reaching, radical, sweeping, across the board, wholesale; broad, wide-ranging; *informal* wall-to-wall. ANTONYM limited.

**compress** verb 1 *the skirt can be compressed into a small bag* SQUEEZE, press, squash, crush, cram, jam, stuff; tamp, pack, compact; constrict; *informal* scrunch.

2 *the text was compressed* ABRIDGE, condense, shorten, cut, abbreviate, truncate; summarize, précis. ANTONYM expand.

**comprise** verb 1 *the country comprises twenty states* CONSIST OF, be made up of, be composed of, contain, encompass, incorporate; include; *formal* comprehend.

2 *informal this breed comprises half the herd* MAKE UP, constitute, form, compose; account for. See note at INCLUDE.

**compromise** noun 1 *they reached a compromise* AGREEMENT, understanding, settlement, terms, deal, trade-off, bargain; middle ground, happy medium, balance.

2 *a happy marriage needs compromise* GIVE AND TAKE, concession, cooperation. ANTONYM intransigence.

▸ verb 1 *we compromised* MEET EACH OTHER HALFWAY, come to an understanding, make a deal, make concessions, find a happy medium, strike a balance; give and take.

2 *his actions could compromise his reputation* UNDERMINE, weaken, damage, harm; jeopardize, prejudice; discredit, dishonor, shame, embarrass.

**compulsion** noun 1 *he is under no compulsion to go* OBLIGATION, constraint, coercion, duress, pressure, intimidation.

2 *a compulsion to tell the truth* URGE, impulse, need, desire, drive; obsession, fixation, addiction; temptation.

**compulsive** adjective 1 *a compulsive desire* IRRESISTIBLE, uncontrollable, compelling, overwhelming, urgent; obsessive.

2 *compulsive eating* OBSESSIVE, obsessional, addictive, uncontrollable.

3 *a compulsive liar* INVETERATE, chronic, incorrigible, incurable, hardened, hopeless, persistent; obsessive, addicted, habitual; *informal* pathological.

4 *it's compulsive viewing* FASCINATING, compelling, gripping, riveting, engrossing, enthralling, captivating.

**compulsory** adjective *the wearing of seat belts is compulsory* OBLIGATORY, mandatory, required, requisite, necessary, essential; imperative, unavoidable, enforced, demanded, prescribed. ANTONYM optional.

**compunction** noun *she had no compunction about deceiving them* SCRUPLES, misgivings, qualms, worries, unease, uneasiness, doubts, reluctance, reservations; guilt, regret, contrition, self-reproach. See note at QUALMS.

**compute** verb *we compute our expenses at the close of each day* CALCULATE, work out, reckon, determine, evaluate, quantify; add up, count up, tally, total, totalize, tot up.

**comrade** noun *we became comrades back in 1943, working in a field hospital in the Philippines* COMPANION, friend; colleague, associate, partner, coworker, workmate; *informal* pal, crony, mate, chum, buddy.

**con** verb *informal we got conned.* See SWINDLE.

▸ noun 1 *an ex-con.* See CONVICT.

2 *a public relations con.* See SWINDLE.

**concave** adjective *a small concave area now filled with rainwater* INCURVATE, curved inward, hollow, depressed, sunken; indented, recessed. ANTONYM convex.

**conceal** verb 1 *clouds concealed the sun* HIDE, screen, cover, obscure, block out, blot out, mask, shroud, secrete. ANTONYM reveal.

2 *he concealed his true feelings* HIDE, cover up, disguise, mask, veil; keep secret, draw a veil over; suppress, repress, bottle up; *informal* keep a lid on, keep under one's hat. ANTONYMS reveal, confess.

**concealed** adjective *another piece of concealed evidence was disclosed to Sgt. Kahn* HIDDEN, not visible, out of sight, invisible, covered, disguised, camouflaged, obscured; private, secret.

**concealment** noun **1** *the concealment of his weapon* HIDING, secretion.

**2** *the deliberate concealment of facts* SUPPRESSION, hiding, cover-up, hushing up; whitewash.

**concede** verb **1** *I had to concede that I'd overreacted* ADMIT, acknowledge, accept, allow, grant, recognize, own, confess; agree. ANTONYM deny.

**2** *he conceded the Auvergne to the king* SURRENDER, yield, give up, relinquish, cede, hand over. ANTONYM retain.

PHRASE: **concede defeat** *Colonel Morris vowed never to concede defeat* CAPITULATE, give in, give, surrender, yield, give up, submit, raise the white flag; back down, climb down; *informal* throw in the towel.

**conceited** adjective *she's too conceited to think she might not get the lead role* VAIN, narcissistic, self-centered, egotistic, egotistical, egocentric; proud, arrogant, boastful, full of oneself, self-important, immodest, swaggering; self-satisfied, smug; supercilious, haughty, snobbish; *informal* bigheaded, too big for one's britches, stuck-up, high and mighty, uppity, snotty; *literary* vainglorious.

**conceivable** adjective *is there any conceivable justification for betraying your family?* IMAGINABLE, possible; plausible, tenable, credible, believable, thinkable, feasible; understandable, comprehensible.

**conceive** verb **1** *they were unable to conceive* BECOME PREGNANT, become impregnated.

**2** *the project was conceived in 1977* THINK UP, think of, dream up, devise, formulate, design, originate, create, develop; *informal* cook up, hatch.

**3** *I can hardly conceive what it must be like* IMAGINE, envisage, visualize,

**4** picture, think, envision; grasp, appreciate, apprehend; *formal* ideate.

**concentrate** verb **1** *the government concentrated its efforts* FOCUS, direct, center, centralize. ANTONYM dissipate.

**2** *she* ***concentrated on*** *the movie* FOCUS ON, pay attention to, keep one's mind on, devote oneself to; be absorbed in, be engrossed in, be immersed in.

**3** *troops concentrated on the horizon* COLLECT, gather, congregate, converge, mass, cluster, rally. ANTONYM disperse.

**4** *the liquid is filtered and concentrated* CONDENSE, boil down, reduce, thicken. ANTONYM dilute.

▸ noun *a fruit concentrate* EXTRACT, decoction, distillation.

**concentrated** adjective **1** *a concentrated effort* STRENUOUS, concerted, intensive, intense; *informal* all-out. ANTONYM half-hearted.

**2** *a concentrated solution* CONDENSED, reduced, evaporated, thickened; undiluted, strong. ANTONYM diluted.

**concentration** noun **1** *a task requiring concentration* CLOSE ATTENTION, attentiveness, application, single-mindedness, tunnel vision, absorption. ANTONYM inattention.

**2** *the concentration of effort* FOCUSING, centralization.

**3** *concentrations of seals* GATHERING, cluster, mass, congregation, assemblage.

**concept** noun *Freud's concept of the superego* IDEA, notion, conception, abstraction; theory, hypothesis; belief, conviction, opinion; image, impression, picture. See note at IDEA.

**conception** noun **1** *from conception until natural death* INCEPTION OF PREGNANCY, conceiving, fertilization, impregnation, insemination.

**2** *the product's conception* INCEPTION, genesis, origination, creation, invention; beginning, origin.

**3** *his original conception* PLAN, scheme, project, proposal; intention, aim, idea. See note at IDEA.

**4** *my conception of democracy* IDEA, concept, notion, understanding, abstraction; theory, hypothesis; perception, image, impression.

**5** *they had no conception of our problems* UNDERSTANDING, comprehension, appreciation, grasp, knowledge; idea, inkling; *informal* clue.

**concern** verb **1** *the report concerns the war* BE ABOUT, deal with, have to do with, cover; discuss, go into, examine, study, review, analyze; relate to, pertain to.

**2** *that doesn't concern you* AFFECT, involve, be relevant to, apply to, have a bearing on, impact on; be important to, interest.

**3** *I won't* ***concern myself with*** *your affairs* INVOLVE ONESELF IN, take an interest in, busy oneself with, devote one's time to, bother oneself with.

**4** *one thing still concerns me* WORRY, disturb, trouble, bother, perturb, unsettle, make anxious.

▸ noun **1** *a voice full of concern* ANXIETY, worry, disquiet, apprehensiveness, unease, consternation. ANTONYM peace of mind.

**2** *his concern for others* SOLICITUDE, consideration, care, sympathy, regard. ANTONYM indifference.

**3** *housing is the concern of the council* RESPONSIBILITY, business, affair, charge, duty, job; province, preserve; problem, worry; *informal* bag, bailiwick.

**4** *issues that are of concern to women* INTEREST, importance, relevance, significance.

**5** *Aboriginal concerns* AFFAIR, issue, matter, question, consideration.

**6** *a publishing concern* COMPANY, business, firm, organization, operation, corporation, establishment, house, office, agency; *informal* outfit.

**concerned** adjective **1** *her mother looked concerned* WORRIED, anxious, upset, perturbed, troubled, distressed, uneasy, apprehensive, agitated.

**2** *he is concerned about your welfare* SOLICITOUS, caring; attentive to, considerate of.

**3** *all concerned parties* INTERESTED, involved, affected; connected, related, implicated.

**concerning** preposition *we have new information concerning his disappearance* ABOUT, regarding, relating to, with reference to, referring to, with regard to, as regards, with respect to, respecting, dealing with, on the subject of, in connection with, re, apropos of.

**concert** noun *a concert at Woolsey Hall featuring a pianist from Estonia* MUSICAL PERFORMANCE, show, production, presentation; recital; *informal* gig. PHRASE: **in concert** *we must take stronger action in concert with our European allies* TOGETHER, jointly, in combination, in collaboration, in cooperation, in league, side by side; in unison.

**concerted** adjective **1** *make a concerted effort* STRENUOUS, vigorous, intensive, intense, concentrated; *informal* all-out. ANTONYM halfhearted.

**2** *concerted action* JOINT, united, collaborative, collective, combined, cooperative. ANTONYM individual.

**concession** noun **1** *the government made several concessions* COMPROMISE, allowance, exception.

**2** *a concession of failure* ADMISSION, acknowledgment, acceptance, recognition, confession. ANTONYM denial.

**3** *the concession of territory* SURRENDER, relinquishment, sacrifice, handover. ANTONYMS retention, acquisition.

**4** *tax concessions* REDUCTION, cut, discount, deduction, decrease; rebate; *informal* break.

**5** *a fast-food concession* STAND, kiosk, stall, counter, vendor.

**6** *a logging concession* RIGHT, privilege; license, permit, franchise, warrant, authorization.

**conciliate** verb **1** *he tried to conciliate the peasantry* APPEASE, placate, pacify, mollify, assuage, soothe, humor, reconcile, win over, make peace with. See note at PACIFY. ANTONYM provoke.

**2** *he conciliated in the dispute* MEDIATE, act as peacemaker, arbitrate; pour oil on troubled waters.

**conciliatory** adjective *a conciliatory gesture* PROPITIATORY, placatory, appeasing, pacifying, mollifying, peacemaking.

**concise** adjective *a concise account* SUCCINCT, pithy, incisive, brief, short and to the point, short and sweet; abridged, condensed, compressed, abbreviated, compact; *informal* snappy. See note at TERSE. ANTONYMS lengthy, wordy.

**conclave** noun *a conclave of American and Japanese business leaders* (PRIVATE) MEETING, gathering, assembly, conference, council, summit; *informal* parley, powwow, get-together.

**conclude** verb **1** *the meeting concluded at ten* FINISH, end, draw to a close, be over, stop, cease. ANTONYMS commence, start, begin.

**2** *she concluded the press conference* BRING TO AN END, close, wind up, terminate, dissolve; *informal* wrap up. ANTONYMS open, start, begin.

**3** *an attempt to conclude a cease-fire* NEGOTIATE, broker, agree, come to terms on, settle, clinch, finalize, tie up; bring about, arrange, effect, engineer; *informal* sew up.

**4** *I concluded that he was rather unpleasant* DEDUCE, infer, gather, judge, decide, conjecture, surmise, extrapolate, figure, reckon.

**conclusion** noun **1** *the conclusion of his speech* END, ending, finish, close, termination, windup, cessation; culmination, denouement, peroration, coda; *informal* outro. ANTONYM beginning.

**2** *the conclusion of a trade agreement* NEGOTIATION, brokering, settlement, completion, arrangement, resolution.

**3** *his conclusions have been verified* DEDUCTION, inference, interpretation, reasoning; opinion, judgment, verdict; assumption, presumption, supposition; *rare* illation. PHRASE: **in conclusion** *in conclusion, I'd like to remind you that Mr. Clark will be signing books in the cafeteria* FINALLY, in closing, to conclude, last but not least; to sum up, in short, to make a long story short.

**conclusive** adjective **1** *conclusive proof* INCONTROVERTIBLE, undeniable, indisputable, irrefutable, unquestionable, unassailable, convincing, certain, decisive, definitive, definite, positive, categorical, unequivocal; airtight, watertight. ANTONYM unconvincing.

**2** *a conclusive win* EMPHATIC, resounding, convincing. ANTONYM narrow.

**concoct** verb **1** *he planned to concoct a dessert* PREPARE, make, assemble; *informal* fix, rustle up.

**2** *this story she has concocted* MAKE UP, dream up, fabricate, invent, trump up; formulate, hatch, brew, cook up.

**concoction** noun **1** *a concoction containing gin and vodka* MIXTURE, brew, preparation, potion.

**2** *a strange concoction of folk pop and Gregorian chant* BLEND, mixture, mix, combination, hybrid.

**3** *her story is an improbable concoction* FABRICATION, invention, falsification; *informal* fairy tale.

**concomitant** adjective *formal the rise of urbanism brought a concomitant risk of crime* ATTENDANT, accompanying, associated, related, connected; resultant, consequent. ANTONYM unrelated.

**concord** noun *council meetings rarely ended in concord* AGREEMENT, harmony, accord, consensus, concurrence, unity. ANTONYM discord.

**concrete** adjective **1** *concrete objects* SOLID, material, real, physical, tangible, palpable, substantial, visible, existing. ANTONYMS abstract, imaginary.

**2** *concrete proof* DEFINITE, firm, positive, conclusive, definitive; real, genuine, bona fide. ANTONYM vague.

**concubine** noun *archaic she was the reluctant concubine of Prince Percival* MISTRESS, courtesan, kept woman; lover; *archaic* paramour, doxy; *historical* hetaera.

**concur** verb **1** *we concur with this view* AGREE, be in agreement, go along, fall in, be in sympathy; see eye to eye, be of the same mind, be of the same opinion. ANTONYM disagree.

**2** *the two events concurred* COINCIDE, be simultaneous, be concurrent, coexist.

**concurrent** adjective **1** *nine concurrent life sentences* SIMULTANEOUS, coincident, contemporaneous, parallel.

**2** *concurrent lines* CONVERGENT, converging, meeting, intersecting.

**concussion** noun **1** *he suffered a concussion* temporary unconsciousness; brain injury.

**2** *the concussion of the blast* FORCE, impact, shock, jolt.

**condemn** verb **1** *he condemned the suspended players* CENSURE, criticize, denounce, revile, blame, chastise, berate, reprimand, rebuke, reprove, take to task, find fault with; *informal* slam, blast, lay into; *formal* castigate. ANTONYM praise.

**2** *he was condemned to death* SENTENCE; convict, find guilty. ANTONYM acquit.

**3** *the house has been condemned* DECLARE UNFIT, declare unsafe.

**4** *her mistake had condemned her* INCRIMINATE, implicate; *archaic* inculpate.

**5** *his illness condemned him to a lonely life* DOOM, destine, damn; consign, assign.

**condensation** noun **1** *windows misty with condensation* MOISTURE, water droplets, steam.

**2** *the condensation of the vapor* PRECIPITATION, liquefaction, deliquescence.

**3** *a condensation of recent literature* ABRIDGMENT, summary, synopsis, précis, digest.

**4** *the condensation of the report* SHORTENING, abridgment, abbreviation, summarization.

**condense** verb **1** *the water vapor condenses* PRECIPITATE, liquefy, become liquid, deliquesce. ANTONYM vaporize.

**2** *he condensed the play* ABRIDGE, shorten, cut, abbreviate, compact; summarize, synopsize, précis; truncate, curtail. ANTONYMS lengthen, expand.

**condescend** verb **1** *don't* ***condescend to*** *your reader* PATRONIZE, talk down to, look down one's nose at, look down on, put down.

**2** *he condescended to see us* DEIGN, stoop, descend, lower oneself, demean oneself; vouchsafe, see fit, consent.

**condescending** adjective *she looked us up and down in a condescending manner* PATRONIZING, supercilious, superior, snobbish, snobby, disdainful, lofty, haughty; *informal* snooty, stuck-up.

**condition** noun **1** *check the condition of your wiring* STATE, shape, order.

**2** *they lived in appalling conditions* CIRCUMSTANCES, surroundings, environment, situation, setup, setting, habitat.

**3** *she was in top condition* FITNESS, health, form, shape, trim, fettle.

**4** *a liver condition* DISORDER, problem, complaint, illness, disease, ailment, sickness, affliction, infection, upset.

**5** *a condition of membership* STIPULATION, constraint, prerequisite, precondition, requirement, rule, term, specification, provision, proviso.

▸ verb **1** *their choices are conditioned by the economy* CONSTRAIN, control, govern, determine, decide; affect, touch; form, shape, guide, sway, bias.

**2** *our minds are conditioned by habit* TRAIN, teach, educate, guide; accustom, adapt, habituate, mold, inure.

**3** *condition the boards with water* TREAT, prepare, prime, temper, process, acclimatize, acclimate, season.

**4** *a product to condition your skin* IMPROVE, nourish, tone (up), moisturize.

**conditional** adjective **1** *their approval is* ***conditional on*** *success* SUBJECT TO, dependent on, contingent on, based on, determined by, controlled by, tied to.

**2** *a conditional offer* CONTINGENT, dependent, qualified, with reservations, limited, provisional, provisory.

**condom** noun *using a condom is only one part of safe sex* CONTRACEPTIVE, prophylactic, sheath; *trademark* Trojan; *informal* rubber; *chiefly Brit. informal* French letter.

**condone** verb *we cannot condone such dreadful behavior* DISREGARD, accept, allow, let pass, turn a blind eye to, overlook, forget; forgive, pardon, excuse, let go. ANTONYM condemn.

**conducive** adjective *a environment that is* ***conducive to*** *learning* FAVORABLE TO, beneficial to, advantageous to, opportune to, propitious to, encouraging to, promising to, convenient for, good for, helpful, instrumental in, productive of, useful for. ANTONYM unfavorable.

**conduct** noun **1** *they complained about her conduct* BEHAVIOR, performance, demeanor; actions, activities, deeds, doings, exploits; habits, manners; *formal* comportment.

**2** *the conduct of the elections* MANAGEMENT, running, direction, control, supervision, regulation, administration, organization, coordination, orchestration, handling.

▸ verb **1** *the election was conducted lawfully* MANAGE, direct, run, administer, organize, coordinate, orchestrate, handle, control, oversee, supervise, regulate, carry out/on.

**2** *he was conducted through the corridors* ESCORT, guide, lead, usher, show; shepherd, see, bring, take, help.

**3** *aluminum conducts heat* TRANSMIT, convey, carry, transfer, impart, channel, relay; disseminate, diffuse, radiate.

PHRASE: **conduct oneself** *I am proud of the way they conducted themselves* BEHAVE, act, acquit oneself, bear oneself; *formal* comport oneself.

**conduit** noun *spring water enters the brewery through a conduit* CHANNEL, duct, pipe, tube, gutter, trench, culvert, cut, sluice, spillway, flume, chute.

**confederacy** noun *a confederacy of Indian tribes* FEDERATION, confederation, alliance, league, association, coalition, consortium, syndicate, group, circle; bloc, axis.

**confederate** adjective *confederate councils* ALLIED, in alliance, in league, cooperating, associated, united, combined, amalgamated.

▸ noun *he was a confederate of the James brothers* ASSOCIATE, partner, accomplice, helper, assistant, ally, collaborator, colleague.

**confer** verb **1** *she went to confer with her colleagues* CONSULT, talk, speak, converse, have a chat, have a tête-à-tête, parley; *informal* have a confab, powwow.

**2** *she **conferred** a knighthood **on** him* BESTOW ON, present to, grant to, award to, decorate with, honor with, give to, endow with, extend to. See note at GIVE.

**conference** noun **1** *an international conference* CONGRESS, meeting, convention, seminar, colloquium, symposium, forum, summit.

**2** *he gathered them for a conference* DISCUSSION, consultation, debate, talk, conversation, dialogue, chat, tête-à-tête, parley; *informal* confab; *formal* confabulation.

**confess** verb **1** *he confessed that he had done it* ADMIT, acknowledge, reveal, disclose, divulge, avow, declare, profess; own up, tell all. ANTONYM deny.

**2** *they could not make him confess* OWN UP, plead guilty, accept the blame; tell the truth, tell all, make a clean breast of it; *informal* come clean, spill the beans, let the cat out of the bag, get something off one's chest, let on, fess up.

**3** *I confess I don't know* ACKNOWLEDGE, admit, concede, grant, allow, own, declare, affirm.

**confession** noun *they soon got a confession out of him* ADMISSION, acknowledgment, profession; revelation, disclosure, divulgence, avowal; guilty plea.

**confide** verb **1** *he confided his fears to his mother* REVEAL, disclose, divulge, lay bare, betray, impart, declare, intimate, uncover, expose, vouchsafe, tell; confess, admit, give away; *informal* blab, spill.

**2** *I need him to **confide in*** OPEN ONE'S HEART TO, unburden oneself to, confess to, tell all to.

**confidence** noun **1** *I have little confidence in these figures* TRUST, belief, faith, credence, conviction. ANTONYMS skepticism, distrust.

**2** *she's brimming with confidence* SELF-ASSURANCE, self-confidence, self-possession, assertiveness; poise, aplomb, phlegm; courage, boldness, mettle, nerve. ANTONYMS uncertainty, doubt.

**3** *the girls exchanged confidences* SECRET, confidentiality, intimacy.

**confidential** adjective **1** *a confidential chat* PRIVATE, personal, intimate, quiet; secret, sensitive, classified, restricted, unofficial, unrevealed, undisclosed, unpublished; *informal* hush-hush, mum; *formal* sub rosa; *archaic* privy.

**2** *a confidential friend* TRUSTED, trustworthy, trusty, faithful, reliable, dependable; close, bosom, intimate.

**confidentially** adverb *I thought we were speaking confidentially* PRIVATELY, in private, in confidence, between ourselves/themselves, off the record, quietly, secretly, in secret, behind closed doors; between you and me and the lamppost; *formal* sub rosa.

**confine** verb **1** *they were confined in the house* ENCLOSE, incarcerate, imprison, intern, impound, hold captive, trap; shut in/up, keep, lock in/up, coop (up); fence in, hedge in, wall in/up.

**2** *he confined his remarks to the weather* RESTRICT, limit.

**confinement** noun **1** *solitary confinement* IMPRISONMENT, internment, incarceration, custody, captivity, detention, restraint; house arrest.

**2** *the confinement of an animal* CAGING, enclosure; quarantine.

**3** *dated she went to the hospital for her confinement* LABOR, delivery, birthing; birth, childbirth; *formal* parturition; *archaic* lying-in, childbed.

**confirm** verb **1** *records confirm the latest evidence* CORROBORATE, verify, prove, validate, authenticate, substantiate, justify, vindicate; support, uphold, back up. ANTONYMS contradict, repudiate.

**2** *he confirmed that help was on the way* AFFIRM, reaffirm, assert, assure someone, repeat; promise, guarantee. ANTONYM deny.

**3** *his appointment was confirmed by the president* RATIFY, validate, sanction, endorse, formalize, authorize, warrant, accredit, approve, accept. ANTONYM revoke.

**confirmation** noun **1** *independent confirmation of the deaths* CORROBORATION, verification, proof, testimony, endorsement, authentication, substantiation, evidence.

**2** *confirmation of your appointment* RATIFICATION, approval, authorization, validation, sanction, endorsement, formalization, accreditation, acceptance.

**confirmed** adjective *he's a confirmed gambler* ESTABLISHED, long-standing, committed, dyed-in-the-wool, through and through; staunch, loyal, faithful, devoted, dedicated, steadfast; habitual, compulsive, persistent; unapologetic, unashamed, inveterate, chronic, incurable; *informal* card-carrying.

**confiscate** verb *the guards confiscated his camera* IMPOUND, seize, commandeer, requisition, appropriate, expropriate, sequester, sequestrate, take (away); *Law* distrain. ANTONYM return.

**conflagration** noun *the conflagration spread rapidly through the wooden buildings* FIRE, blaze, flames, inferno, firestorm.

**conflict** noun **1** *industrial conflicts* DISPUTE, quarrel, squabble, disagreement, dissension, clash; discord, friction, strife, antagonism, hostility, disputation, contention; feud, schism. ANTONYM agreement.

**2** *the Vietnam conflict* WAR, campaign, battle, fighting, (armed) confrontation, engagement, encounter, struggle, hostilities; warfare, combat. ANTONYM peace.

**3** *a conflict between his business and domestic life* CLASH, incompatibility, incongruity, friction; mismatch, variance, difference, divergence, contradiction, inconsistency. ANTONYM harmony.

▸ verb *their interests sometimes conflict* CLASH, be incompatible, vary, be at odds, be in conflict, differ, diverge, disagree, contrast, collide.

**conflicting** adjective *the two suspects gave conflicting stories* CONTRADICTORY, incompatible, inconsistent, irreconcilable, incongruous, contrary, opposite, opposing, antithetical, clashing, discordant, divergent; at odds.

**conform** verb **1** *visitors have to **conform to** our rules* COMPLY WITH, abide by, obey, observe, follow, keep to, stick to, adhere to, uphold, heed, accept, go along with, fall in with, respect, defer to; satisfy, meet, fulfill. ANTONYM flout.

**2** *they refuse to conform* FOLLOW CONVENTION, be conventional, fit in, adapt, adjust, follow the crowd; comply, acquiesce, toe the line, follow the rules; submit, yield; *informal* play it by the book, play by the rules. ANTONYM rebel.

**3** *goods must **conform to** their description* MATCH, fit, suit, answer, agree with, be like, correspond to, be consistent with, measure up to, tally with, square with. ANTONYM differ.

**conformist** noun *he was too much of a conformist to wear anything but a suit* TRADITIONALIST, conservative, stickler, formalist, diehard, reactionary; *informal* stick-in-the-mud, stuffed shirt. ANTONYMS eccentric, rebel.

**confound** verb **1** *the figures confounded analysts* AMAZE, astonish, dumbfound, stagger, surprise, startle, stun, throw, shake, discompose, bewilder, bedazzle, baffle, mystify, bemuse, perplex, puzzle, confuse; take aback, shake up, catch off balance; *informal* flabbergast, blow someone's mind, blow away, flummox, faze, stump, beat, fox, discombobulate.

**2** *he has always confounded expectations* CONTRADICT, counter, invalidate, negate, go against, quash, explode, demolish, shoot down, destroy, disprove; *informal* poke holes in.

**confront** verb **1** *Jones confronted the intruder* CHALLENGE, face (up to), come face to face with, meet, accost; stand up to, brave; tackle; *informal* collar. ANTONYM avoid.

**2** *the problems that confront us* TROUBLE, bother, burden, distress, worry, oppress, annoy, strain, stress, tax, torment, plague, blight, curse; face, beset.

**3** *they must confront their problems* TACKLE, address, face, come to grips with, grapple with, take on, attend to, see to, deal with, take care of, handle, manage. ANTONYM avoid.

**4** *she confronted him with the evidence* PRESENT, face.

**confrontation** noun *I've been trying to avoid a confrontation with his new girlfriend* CONFLICT, clash, fight, battle, encounter, faceoff, engagement, skirmish; hostilities, fighting; *informal* set-to, run-in, dust-up, showdown.

**confuse** verb **1** *don't confuse students with too much detail* BEWILDER, baffle, mystify, bemuse, perplex, puzzle, confound; *informal* flummox, faze, stump, fox, discombobulate, bedazzle. ANTONYM enlighten.

**2** *the authors have confused the issue* COMPLICATE, muddle, jumble, garble, blur, obscure, cloud. ANTONYM simplify.

**3** *some people **confuse** strokes **with** heart attacks* MISTAKE FOR, take for, misinterpret as; mix up with, muddle up with, confound with.

**confused** adjective **1** *they are confused about what is going on* BEWILDERED, bemused, puzzled, perplexed, baffled, mystified, nonplussed, muddled, dumbfounded, at sea, at a loss, taken aback, disoriented, disconcerted; *informal* flummoxed, clueless, fazed, discombobulated.

**2** *her confused elderly mother* DEMENTED, bewildered, muddled, addled, befuddled, disoriented, disorientated; unbalanced, unhinged; senile. ANTONYM lucid.

**3** *a confused recollection* VAGUE, unclear, indistinct, imprecise, blurred, hazy, woolly, shadowy, dim; imperfect, sketchy. ANTONYMS clear, precise.

**4** *a confused mass of bones* DISORDERLY, disordered, disorganized, disarranged, out of order, untidy, muddled, jumbled, mixed up, chaotic, topsy-turvy; *informal* shambolic. ANTONYM neat.

**confusing** adjective *the instructions are confusing* BEWILDERING, baffling, unclear, perplexing, puzzling, mystifying, disconcerting; ambiguous, misleading, inconsistent, contradictory; unaccountable, inexplicable, impenetrable, unfathomable; complex, complicated.

**confusion** noun **1** *there is confusion about the new system* UNCERTAINTY, incertitude, unsureness, doubt, ignorance; *formal* dubiety. ANTONYM certainty.

**2** *she stared in confusion* BEWILDERMENT, bafflement, perplexity, puzzlement, mystification, befuddlement; shock, daze, wonder, wonderment, astonishment; *informal* head-scratching, discombobulation.

**3** *I could not live in this kind of confusion* DISORDER, disarray, disorganization, untidiness, chaos, mayhem; turmoil, tumult, disruption, upheaval, uproar, muddle, mess, shambles; *informal* three-ring circus. ANTONYM order.

**4** *a confusion of boxes* JUMBLE, muddle, mess, heap, tangle; *informal* shambles. See note at JUMBLE.

**congeal** verb *the gravy is starting to congeal* COAGULATE, clot, thicken, jell, cake, set, curdle.

**congenial** adjective **1** *very congenial people* HOSPITABLE, genial, personable, agreeable, friendly, pleasant, likable, amiable, nice; companionable, sociable, sympathetic, comradely, convivial, simpatico; LIKE-MINDED, compatible, kindred, well-suited. See note at PLEASANT. ANTONYM disagreeable.

**2** *a congenial environment* PLEASANT, pleasing, agreeable, enjoyable, pleasurable, nice, appealing, satisfying, gratifying, delightful, relaxing, welcoming, hospitable; suitable, well-suited, favorable. ANTONYM unpleasant.

**congenital** adjective **1** *congenital defects* INBORN, inherited, hereditary, innate, inbred, constitutional, inbuilt, natural, inherent. See note at INHERENT. ANTONYM acquired.

**2** *a congenital liar* INVETERATE, compulsive, persistent, chronic, regular, habitual, obsessive, confirmed; incurable, incorrigible, irredeemable, hopeless; unashamed, shameless, pathological.

**congested** adjective *the tunnels are congested with holiday traffic* CROWDED, overcrowded, full, overflowing, packed, jammed, thronged, teeming, swarming; obstructed, blocked, clogged, choked; *informal* snarled up, gridlocked, jam-packed. ANTONYM clear.

**congestion** noun *the congestion on I-95 is especially bad near exit 34* CROWDING, overcrowding; obstruction, blockage; traffic jam, bottleneck; *informal* snarl-up, gridlock.

**conglomerate** noun **1** *the conglomerate was broken up* CORPORATION, company, business, multinational, combine, group, consortium, partnership; firm.

**2** *a conglomerate of disparate peoples* MIXTURE, mix, combination, amalgamation, union, marriage, fusion, composite, synthesis; miscellany, hodgepodge. See note at JUMBLE.

▸ adjective *a conglomerate mass* AGGREGATE, agglomerate, amassed, combined.

▸ verb *the debris conglomerated into planets* COALESCE, unite, join, combine, merge, fuse, consolidate, amalgamate, integrate, mingle, intermingle.

**congratulate** verb **1** *she congratulated him on his marriage* SEND ONE'S BEST WISHES TO, wish someone good luck, wish someone joy; drink to someone's health, toast. ANTONYM curse.

**2** *they are to be congratulated* PRAISE, commend, applaud, salute, honor; pay tribute to, regard highly, pat on the back, take one's hat off to. ANTONYM criticize.

PHRASE: **congratulate oneself** *you should **congratulate yourself on** this wonderful accomplishment* TAKE PRIDE IN, feel proud of, flatter oneself on, pat oneself on the back for; take/feel satisfaction in, take pleasure in, glory in, bask in, delight in.

**congratulations** plural noun **1** *her congratulations on their wedding* GOOD WISHES, best wishes, compliments, felicitations.

**2** *you all deserve congratulations* PRAISE, commendation, applause, salutes, honor, acclaim, cheers; approval, admiration, compliments, bouquets, kudos, adulation; a pat on the back.

▸ exclamation *Congratulations! You did it!* BRAVO, brava, mazel tov, kudos; *informal* congrats, attaboy, attagirl, way to go.

**congregate** verb *war protesters congregated in front of the recruiting office* ASSEMBLE, gather, collect, come together, convene, rally, rendezvous, muster, meet, cluster, group. See note at GATHER. ANTONYM disperse.

**congregation** noun **1** *the chapel congregation* PARISHIONERS, parish, churchgoers, flock, faithful, followers, believers, fellowship, communicants, laity, brethren, membership; throng, company, assemblage, audience.

**2** *congregations of birds* GATHERING, assembly, flock, swarm, bevy, pack, group, body, crowd, mass, multitude, horde, host, mob, throng.

**congress** noun **1** *a congress of mathematicians* CONFERENCE, convention, seminar, colloquium, symposium, forum, meeting, assembly, gathering, rally, summit.

**2** *elections for the new Congress* LEGISLATURE, legislative assembly, senate, house, house of representatives, parliament, convocation, diet, council, chamber.

**conjecture** noun *the information is merely conjecture* SPECULATION, guesswork, surmise, fancy, presumption, assumption, theory, postulation, supposition; inference, (an) extrapolation; an estimate; *informal* a guesstimate, a shot in the dark, a ballpark figure. ANTONYM fact.

▸ verb *I conjectured that the game was over* GUESS, speculate, surmise, infer, fancy, imagine, believe, think, suspect, presume, assume, hypothesize, suppose. ANTONYM know.

**conjugal** adjective *the conjugal bond must be a two-way relationship* MARITAL, matrimonial, nuptial, marriage, bridal; *Law* spousal; *literary* connubial.

**conjunction** noun **1** *a theory that the Americas were formed by a conjunction of floating islands* COMING TOGETHER, convergence, union, confluence.

**2** *a conjunction of planets* CO-OCCURRENCE, concurrence, coincidence, coexistence, simultaneity, contemporaneity, concomitance, synchronicity, synchrony. PHRASE: **in conjunction with** *in conjunction with our Native American Day, there will be an exhibit of Pequot art in the gymnasium* TOGETHER WITH, along with, accompanying, accompanied by; as well as, in addition to, plus.

**conjure** verb **1** *he conjured a cigarette out of the air* PRODUCE, make appear, materialize, summon.

**2** *the picture that his words **conjured up*** BRING TO MIND, call to mind, evoke, summon up, recall, recreate; echo, allude to, suggest, awaken.

**connect** verb **1** *electrodes were connected to the device* ATTACH, join, fasten, fix, affix, couple, link, secure, hitch; stick, adhere, fuse, pin, screw, bolt, clamp, clip, hook (up); add, append. See note at JOIN.

**2** *rituals **connected with** Easter* ASSOCIATE WITH, link to/with, couple with; identify with, equate with, relate to.

**connection** noun **1** *the connection between commerce and art* LINK, relationship, relation, interconnection, interdependence, association; bond, tie, tie-in, correspondence, parallel, analogy.

**2** *a poor connection in the plug* ATTACHMENT, joint, fastening, coupling.

**3** *he has the right connections* CONTACT, friend, acquaintance, ally, colleague, associate; relation, relative, kin. PHRASE: **in connection with** *a man is being questioned in connection with the murder* REGARDING, concerning, with reference to, with regard to, with respect to, respecting, relating to, in relation to, on, connected with, on the subject of, in the matter of, apropos, re.

**connive** verb *it is now known that at least two of the directors connived with Officer Cutler in the cover-up* CONSPIRE, collude, collaborate, intrigue, be hand in glove, plot, scheme; *informal* be in cahoots.

**conniving** adjective *his conniving brother planned the whole dirty affair* SCHEMING, cunning, crafty, calculating, devious, wily, sly, tricky, artful, guileful; manipulative, Machiavellian, disingenuous, deceitful, underhanded, treacherous; *informal* foxy.

**connoisseur** noun *a connoisseur of fine wines* EXPERT, authority, specialist, pundit, savant; arbiter of taste, aesthete; gourmet, epicure, gastronome; *informal* buff, maven.

**connotation** noun *there was a connotation of distrust in his voice* OVERTONE, undertone, undercurrent, implication, hidden meaning, nuance, hint, echo, vibrations, association, intimation, suggestion, suspicion, insinuation.

**conquer** verb **1** *the Franks conquered the Visigoths* DEFEAT, beat, vanquish, trounce, triumph over, be victorious over, get the better of, worst; overcome, overwhelm, overpower, overthrow, subdue, subjugate, quell, quash, crush, rout; *informal* lick, best, hammer, clobber, thrash, paste, demolish, annihilate, wipe the floor with, walk all over, make mincemeat of, massacre, slaughter, cream, shellac, skunk.

**2** *Peru was conquered by Spain* SEIZE, take (over), appropriate, subjugate, capture, occupy, invade, annex, overrun.

**3** *the first men to conquer Mount Everest* CLIMB, ascend, mount, scale, top, crest.

**4** *the way to conquer fear* OVERCOME, get the better of, control, master, get a grip on, deal with, cope with, surmount, rise above, get over; quell, quash, beat, triumph over; *informal* lick.

**conqueror** noun *they may have uncovered the burial ground of legendary conqueror Genghis Khan* VANQUISHER, conquistador; victor, winner, champion, conquering hero.

**conquest** noun **1** *the conquest of the Aztecs* DEFEAT, vanquishment, annihilation, overthrow, subjugation, rout, mastery, crushing; victory over, triumph over.

**2** *their conquest of the valley* SEIZURE, takeover, capture, occupation, invasion, acquisition, appropriation, subjugation, subjection.

**3** *the conquest of K2* ASCENT, climbing, scaling.

**4** *she's his latest conquest* CATCH, acquisition, prize, slave; admirer, fan, worshiper; lover, boyfriend, girlfriend.

**conscience** noun *her conscience would not allow her to remain silent* SENSE OF RIGHT AND WRONG, moral sense, inner voice; morals, standards, values, principles, ethics, beliefs; compunction, scruples, qualms.

**conscience-stricken** adjective *the conscience-stricken teens who set fire to the gazebo* GUILT-RIDDEN, remorseful, ashamed, shamefaced, apologetic, sorry; chastened, contrite, guilty, regretful, rueful, repentant, penitent, abashed, sheepish, compunctious. ANTONYM unrepentant.

**conscientious** adjective *even Douglas, the most conscientious worker in our department, was laid off* DILIGENT, industrious, punctilious, painstaking, sedulous, assiduous, dedicated, careful, meticulous, thorough, attentive, hard-working, studious, rigorous, particular; religious, strict. ANTONYM casual.

**conscious** adjective **1** *the patient was conscious* AWARE, awake, alert, responsive, sentient, compos mentis.

**2** *he became conscious of people talking* AWARE, mindful, sensible; *formal* cognizant; *rare* regardful. ANTONYM unaware.

**3** *a conscious effort* DELIBERATE, intentional, intended, purposeful, purposive, knowing, considered, calculated, willful, premeditated, planned, volitional.

**conscript** verb *they were conscripted into the army* CALL UP, enlist, recruit, draft; *historical* press, impress.

▸ noun *an army conscript* compulsorily enlisted soldier, recruit, draftee. ANTONYM volunteer.

**consecrate** verb *the bishop had consecrated two cathedrals in his time* SANCTIFY, bless, make holy, make sacred; dedicate to God, devote, reserve, set apart; anoint, ordain; *formal* hallow. See note at DIVINE.

**consecutive** adjective *share prices fell for three consecutive days* SUCCESSIVE, succeeding, following, in succession, running, in a row, one after the other, back-to-back, continuous, straight, uninterrupted.

**consensus** noun **1** *there was consensus among delegates* AGREEMENT, harmony, concurrence, accord, unity, unanimity, solidarity; *formal* concord. ANTONYM disagreement.

**2** *the consensus was that they should act* GENERAL OPINION, majority opinion, common view.

**consent** noun *the consent of all members* AGREEMENT, assent, acceptance, approval, approbation; permission, authorization, sanction, leave; backing, endorsement, support; *informal* go-ahead, thumbs up, green light, OK. ANTONYM dissent.

▸ verb *she **consented to** surgery* AGREE TO, assent to, yield to, give in to, submit to; allow, give permission for, sanction, accept, approve, go along with. ANTONYM forbid.

**consequence** noun **1** *a consequence of inflation* RESULT, upshot, outcome, effect, repercussion, ramification, corollary, concomitant, aftermath, aftereffect; fruit(s), product, by-product, end result; *informal* payoff; *Medicine* sequela. ANTONYM cause.

**2** *the past is of no consequence* IMPORTANCE, import, significance, account, substance, note, mark, prominence, value, concern, interest; *formal* moment.

**consequent** adjective *heavy rains and consequent flash flooding are tonight's lead stories* RESULTING, resultant, ensuing, consequential; following, subsequent, successive; attendant, accompanying, concomitant; collateral, associated, related.

**consequently** adverb *the doctor has had two emergencies this morning and consequently is running behind schedule* AS A RESULT, as a consequence, so, thus, therefore, ergo, accordingly, hence, for this/that reason, because of this/that, on this/that account; inevitably, necessarily.

**conservation** noun *the conservation of tropical forests* PRESERVATION, protection, safeguarding, safekeeping; care, guardianship, husbandry, supervision; upkeep, maintenance, repair, restoration; ecology, environmentalism.

**conservative** adjective **1** *the conservative wing of the party* RIGHT-WING, reactionary, traditionalist; Republican; *Brit.* Tory; *informal* redneck. ANTONYM socialist.

**2** *our more conservative neighbors may object to the modern architecture being proposed* TRADITIONALIST, traditional, conventional, orthodox, old-fashioned, dyed-in-the-wool, hidebound, unadventurous, set in one's ways; moderate, middle-of-the-road, buttoned-down; *informal* stick-in-the-mud. ANTONYM radical.

**3** *he wore a conservative blue suit* CONVENTIONAL, sober, modest, plain, unobtrusive, restrained, subtle, low-key, demure; *informal* square, straight. ANTONYM ostentatious.

**4** *a conservative estimate* LOW, cautious, understated, moderate, reasonable.

▸ noun *liberals and conservatives have found common ground* RIGHT-WINGER, reactionary, rightist, diehard; Republican; *Brit.* Tory.

**conservatory** noun **1** *a frost-free conservatory* SUMMER HOUSE, belvedere; glasshouse, greenhouse, hothouse.

**2** *a teaching job at the conservatory* CONSERVATOIRE, music school, drama school.

**conserve** verb *fossil fuel should be conserved* PRESERVE, protect, save, safeguard, keep, look after; sustain, prolong, perpetuate; store, reserve, husband. ANTONYM squander.

▸ noun *cherry conserve* JAM, preserve, jelly, marmalade.

**consider** verb **1** *Isabel considered her choices* THINK ABOUT, contemplate, reflect on, examine, review; mull over, ponder, deliberate on, chew over, meditate on, ruminate on; assess, evaluate, appraise; *informal* size up.

**2** *I consider him irresponsible* DEEM, think, believe, judge, adjudge, rate, count, find; regard as, hold to be, reckon to be, view as, see as.

**3** *he considered the ceiling* LOOK AT, contemplate, observe, regard, survey, view, scrutinize, scan, examine, inspect; *informal* check out, eyeball.

**4** *the inquiry will consider those issues* TAKE INTO CONSIDERATION, take account of, make allowances for, bear in mind, be mindful of, remember, mind, mark, respect, heed, note, make provision for. ANTONYM ignore.

**considerable** adjective **1** *a considerable amount of money* SIZABLE, substantial, appreciable, significant; goodly, fair, hefty, handsome, decent, worthwhile; ample, plentiful, abundant, great, large, generous; *informal* tidy, not to be sneezed at. ANTONYM paltry.

**2** *considerable success* MUCH, great, a lot of, lots of, a great deal of, plenty of, a fair amount of. ANTONYM minor.

**3** *a considerable player in the game of politics* DISTINGUISHED, noteworthy, important, significant, prominent, eminent, influential, illustrious; renowned, celebrated, acclaimed. ANTONYM insignificant.

**considerably** adverb *alcoholic drinks vary considerably in strength* GREATLY, much, very much, a great deal, a lot, lots; significantly, substantially, appreciably, markedly, noticeably; *informal* plenty, seriously.

**considerate** adjective *the doorman was considerate enough to call her when the mail was delivered* ATTENTIVE, thoughtful, solicitous, mindful, heedful; obliging, accommodating, helpful, cooperative, patient; kind, unselfish, compassionate, sympathetic, caring, charitable, altruistic, generous; polite, sensitive, tactful.

**consideration** noun **1** *your case needs careful consideration* THOUGHT, deliberation, reflection, contemplation, rumination, meditation; examination, inspection, scrutiny, analysis, discussion; attention, regard; *formal* cogitation.

**2** *his health is the prime consideration* FACTOR, issue, matter, concern, detail, aspect, feature.

**3** *firms should show more consideration* ATTENTIVENESS, concern, care, thoughtfulness, solicitude; kindness, understanding, respect, sensitivity, tact, discretion; compassion, charity, benevolence. PHRASE: **take into consideration** *the company was willing to take her extended illness into consideration* CONSIDER, give thought to, take into account, allow for, provide for, plan for, make provision for, accommodate, bargain for, reckon with; foresee, anticipate.

**considering** preposition *considering his size, he was speedy* BEARING IN MIND, taking into consideration, taking into account, keeping in mind, in view of, in light of.

▸ adverb *informal he's been lucky, considering* ALL THINGS CONSIDERED, all in all, on the whole, at the end of the day, when all is said and done.

**consign** verb **1** *he was **consigned to** Sing Sing* SEND TO, deliver to, hand over to, turn over to, sentence to; confine in, imprison in, incarcerate in, lock up in; **(consign to prison/jail)** *informal* put away, put behind bars, send up the river.

**2** *the picture was consigned to the gallery* ASSIGN, allocate, place, put, remit, commit.

**3** *the package was consigned by a local company* SEND (OFF), courier, dispatch, transmit, convey, mail, post, ship.

**4** *I consigned her picture to the garbage can* DEPOSIT, commit, banish, relegate.

**consignment** adjective *a consignment clothing shop* SECONDHAND, used, preowned, castoff, hand-me-down.

▸ noun *Dexter has to initial the paperwork for any consignment* DELIVERY, shipment, load, boatload, truckload, cargo; batch; goods.

**consist** verb **1** *the exhibition **consists of** 180 drawings* BE COMPOSED OF, be made up of, be formed of; comprise, contain, include, incorporate.

**2** *style **consists in** the choices that writers make* BE INHERENT IN, lie in, reside in, be present in, be contained in; be expressed by.

**consistency** noun **1** *the trend shows a degree of consistency*

UNIFORMITY, constancy, regularity, evenness, steadiness, stability, equilibrium; dependability, reliability.

2 *mix until the batter is of pouring consistency* THICKNESS, density, viscosity, heaviness, texture; firmness, solidity.

**consistent** adjective 1 *consistent opinion-poll evidence* CONSTANT, regular, uniform, steady, stable, even, unchanging, undeviating, unfluctuating; dependable, reliable, predictable. ANTONYM irregular.

2 *her injuries were* ***consistent with*** *a knife attack* COMPATIBLE WITH, congruous with, consonant with, in tune with, in line with, reconcilable with; corresponding to, conforming to. ANTONYM incompatible.

**consolation** noun *I realize that mere words are of little consolation* COMFORT, solace, sympathy, compassion, pity, commiseration, empathy; relief, help, support, moral support, encouragement, reassurance.

**console** verb *she tried to console him* COMFORT, solace, sympathize with, commiserate with, show compassion for, condole with; help, support, cheer (up), hearten, encourage, reassure, soothe. ANTONYM upset.

**consolidate** verb 1 *we consolidated our position in the market* STRENGTHEN, secure, stabilize, reinforce, fortify; enhance, improve.

2 *consolidate the results into an action plan* COMBINE, unite, merge, integrate, amalgamate, fuse, synthesize, bring together, unify. See note at JOIN.

**consonant** PHRASE: **consonant with** *these findings are consonant with recent research* IN AGREEMENT WITH, consistent with, in accordance with, in harmony with, compatible with, congruous with, in tune with.

**consort** noun *the queen and her consort* PARTNER, life partner, companion, mate; spouse, husband, wife, helpmate.

▸ verb *he consorted with other women* ASSOCIATE, keep company, mix, go around, spend time, socialize, fraternize, have dealings; *informal* run around, hang around/out, be thick.

**conspicuous** adjective *a tropical vine with conspicuous blossoms* EASILY SEEN, clear, visible, noticeable, discernible, perceptible, detectable; obvious, manifest, evident, apparent, marked, pronounced, prominent, patent, crystal clear; striking, eye-catching, overt, blatant; distinct, recognizable, unmistakable, inescapable; *informal* as plain as the nose on one's face, standing/sticking out like a sore thumb. See note at NOTICEABLE.

**conspiracy** noun 1 *a conspiracy to manipulate the results* PLOT, scheme, plan, machination, ploy, trick, ruse, subterfuge; *informal* racket. See note at PLOT.

2 *conspiracy to commit murder* PLOTTING, collusion, intrigue, connivance, machination, collaboration; treason.

**conspirator** noun *is there any credible evidence of a conspirator working with Oswald?* PLOTTER, schemer, intriguer, colluder, collaborator, conniver.

**conspire** verb 1 *they admitted conspiring to steal cars* PLOT, scheme, plan, intrigue, machinate, collude, connive, collaborate, work hand in glove; *informal* be in cahoots.

2 *circumstances conspired against them* ACT TOGETHER, work together, combine, unite, join forces; *informal* gang up.

**constancy** noun 1 *constancy between lovers* FIDELITY, faithfulness, loyalty, commitment, dedication, devotion; dependability, reliability, trustworthiness.

2 *the constancy of Henry's views* STEADFASTNESS, resolution, resolve, firmness, fixedness; determination, perseverance, tenacity, doggedness, staunchness, staying power, obstinacy.

3 *the constancy of their doubt* CONSISTENCY, permanence, persistence, durability, endurance; uniformity, immutability, regularity, stability, steadiness.

**constant** adjective 1 *the constant background noise* CONTINUAL, continuous, persistent, sustained, around/round-the-clock; ceaseless, unceasing, perpetual, incessant, never-ending, eternal, endless, unabating, nonstop, unrelieved; interminable, unremitting, relentless. See note at RESOLUTE. ANTONYMS fitful, inconstant.

2 *a constant speed* CONSISTENT, regular, steady, uniform, even, invariable, unvarying, unchanging, undeviating, unfluctuating. ANTONYM variable.

3 *a constant friend* FAITHFUL, loyal, devoted, true, fast, firm, unswerving; steadfast, staunch, dependable, trustworthy, trusty, reliable, dedicated, committed. ANTONYM fickle.

4 *constant vigilance* STEADFAST, steady, resolute, determined, tenacious, dogged, unwavering, unflagging.

▸ noun *dread of cancer has been a constant* UNCHANGING FACTOR, given.

**constantly** adverb *the language is constantly in flux* ALWAYS, all the time, continually, continuously, persistently; around/round the clock, night and day, 'morning, noon, and night'; endlessly, nonstop, incessantly, unceasingly, perpetually, eternally, forever; interminably, unremittingly, relentlessly; *informal* 24-7. ANTONYM occasionally.

**consternation** noun *much to his colleagues' consternation, Victor was awarded the job in Paris* DISMAY, perturbation, distress, disquiet, discomposure; surprise, amazement, astonishment; alarm, panic, fear, fright, shock. ANTONYM satisfaction.

**constituent** adjective *constituent parts* COMPONENT, integral; elemental, basic, essential, inherent.

▸ noun 1 *representatives must listen to their constituents* VOTER, elector, member of a constituency.

2 *the constituents of tobacco* COMPONENT, ingredient, element; part, piece, bit, unit; section, portion.

**constitute** verb 1 *farmers constituted 10 percent of the population* AMOUNT TO, add up to, account for, form, make up, compose.

2 *this constitutes a breach of copyright* BE EQUIVALENT TO, be, embody, be tantamount to, be regarded as.

3 *the courts were constituted in 1875* INAUGURATE, establish,

initiate, found, create, set up, start, form, organize, develop; commission, charter, invest, appoint, install, empower.

**constitution** noun **1** *the constitution guarantees our rights* CHARTER, social code, law; bill of rights; rules, regulations, fundamental principles.

**2** *the chemical constitution of the dye* COMPOSITION, makeup, structure, construction, arrangement, configuration, formation, anatomy.

**3** *she has the constitution of an ox* HEALTH, physical condition, fettle; physique.

**constitutional** adjective **1** *constitutional powers* LEGAL, lawful, legitimate, authorized, permitted; sanctioned, ratified, warranted, constituted, statutory, chartered, vested, official; by law.

**2** *a constitutional weakness* INHERENT, intrinsic, innate, fundamental, essential, organic; congenital, inborn, inbred.

▸ noun *dated* *she went out for a constitutional.* See WALK noun sense 1.

**constrain** verb **1** *he felt constrained to explain* COMPEL, force, drive, impel, oblige, coerce, prevail on, require; press, push, pressure. See note at COMPEL.

**2** *prices were constrained by government controls* RESTRICT, limit, curb, check, restrain, contain, rein in, hold back, keep down.

**constrained** adjective *she was uncharacteristically constrained whenever her in-laws were visiting* UNNATURAL, awkward, self-conscious, forced, stilted, strained; restrained, reserved, reticent, guarded. ANTONYM relaxed.

**constraint** noun **1** *financial constraints* RESTRICTION, limitation, curb, check, restraint, control, damper, rein; hindrance, impediment, obstruction, handicap.

**2** *they were able to talk without constraint* INHIBITION, uneasiness, embarrassment; restraint, reticence, guardedness, formality; self-consciousness, awkwardness, stiltedness.

**constrict** verb **1** *fat constricts the blood vessels* NARROW, make narrower, tighten, compress, contract, squeeze, strangle, strangulate; *archaic* straiten. ANTONYMS expand, dilate.

**2** *fear of crime constricts many people's lives* RESTRICT, impede, limit, inhibit, obstruct, interfere with, hinder, hamper.

**construct** verb **1** *a new high-rise was being constructed* BUILD, erect, put up, set up, raise, establish, assemble, manufacture, fabricate, create, make. ANTONYM demolish.

**2** *he constructed a faultless argument* FORMULATE, form, put together, create, devise, design, compose, work out; fashion, mold, shape, frame.

**construction** noun **1** *the construction of a new airport* BUILDING, erection, putting up, setting up, establishment; assembly, manufacture, fabrication, creation.

**2** *the station was a spectacular construction* STRUCTURE, building, edifice, pile.

**3** *you could put an honest construction on their conduct* INTERPRETATION, reading, meaning, explanation, explication, construal; *informal* take, spin.

**constructive** adjective *constructive criticism* USEFUL, helpful, productive, positive, encouraging; practical, valuable, profitable, worthwhile.

**consul** noun *he was posing as the French consul* AMBASSADOR, diplomat, chargé d'affaires, attaché, envoy, emissary, plenipotentiary.

**consult** verb **1** *you need to consult a lawyer* SEEK ADVICE FROM, ask, take counsel from, call on/upon, speak to, turn to, have recourse to; *informal* pick someone's brains.

**2** *the government must consult with interested parties* CONFER, have discussions, talk things over, exchange views, communicate, parley, deliberate; *informal* put their heads together.

**3** *she consulted her diary* REFER TO, turn to, look at.

**consultant** noun *she freelanced as a communications consultant* ADVISER, expert, specialist, authority, pundit.

**consultation** noun **1** *the need for further consultation with industry* DISCUSSION, dialogue, discourse, debate, negotiation, deliberation.

**2** *a 30-minute consultation* MEETING, talk, discussion, interview, audience, hearing; appointment, session; *formal* confabulation, colloquy.

**consume** verb **1** *vast amounts of food and drink were consumed* EAT, devour, ingest, swallow, gobble up, wolf down, guzzle, feast on, snack on; DRINK, gulp down, imbibe; *informal* tuck into, put away, polish off, dispose of, pig out on, down, swill, scarf (down/up).

**2** *natural resources are being consumed at an alarming rate* USE (UP), utilize, expend; deplete, exhaust; waste, squander, drain, dissipate, fritter away.

**3** *the fire consumed fifty houses* DESTROY, demolish, lay waste, wipe out, annihilate, devastate, gut, ruin, wreck.

**4** *Carolyn was consumed with guilt* EAT UP, devour, obsess, grip, overwhelm; absorb, preoccupy.

**consumer** noun *if you're a satisfied consumer, we've done our job* | *they provide what consumers ask for* PURCHASER, buyer, customer, shopper; user, end user; client, patron; (**the consumer** or **consumers**) the public, the market.

**consuming** adjective *his consuming passion for opera* ABSORBING, compelling, compulsive, obsessive, overwhelming; intense, ardent, strong, powerful, burning, raging, fervid, profound, deep-seated.

**consummate** verb *the deal was finally consummated* COMPLETE, conclude, finish, accomplish, achieve; execute, carry out, perform; *informal* sew up, wrap up; *formal* effectuate.

▸ adjective *his consummate skill* | *a consummate politician* SUPREME, superb, superlative, superior, accomplished, expert, proficient, skillful, skilled, masterly, master, first-class, talented, gifted, polished, practiced, perfect, ultimate; complete, total, utter, absolute, pure.

**consumption** noun **1** *food unfit for human consumption* EATING, drinking, ingestion.

**2** *the consumption of fossil fuels* USE, using up, utilization, expending, depletion; waste, squandering, dissipation.

**contact** noun **1** *a disease transmitted through casual contact* TOUCH, touching; proximity, exposure.

**2** *foreign diplomats were asked to avoid all contact with him* COMMUNICATION, correspondence, touch; association, connection, intercourse, relations, dealings; *archaic* traffic.

**3** *he had many contacts in Germany* CONNECTION, acquaintance, associate, friend.

▸ verb *anyone with information should contact the police* GET IN TOUCH WITH, communicate with, make contact with, approach, notify; telephone, phone, call, speak to, talk to, write to, get hold of.

**contagious** adjective *the disease is highly contagious* INFECTIOUS, communicable, transmittable, transmissible, spreadable; *informal* catching; *dated* infective.

**contain** verb **1** *the archive contains much unpublished material* INCLUDE, comprise, take in, incorporate, involve, encompass, embrace; consist of, be made up of, be composed of.

**2** *the boat contained four people* HOLD, carry, accommodate, seat.

**3** *he must contain his anger* RESTRAIN, curb, rein in, suppress, repress, stifle, subdue, quell, swallow, bottle up, hold in, keep in check; control, master.

**container** noun *a container of leftover beets* RECEPTACLE, vessel, canister, can, box, holder, repository.

**contaminate** verb *the river was contaminated with photographic chemicals* POLLUTE, adulterate; defile, debase, corrupt, taint, infect, foul, spoil, soil, stain, sully; poison; *literary* befoul. See note at POLLUTE. ANTONYM purify.

**contemplate** verb **1** *she contemplated her image in the mirror* LOOK AT, view, regard, examine, inspect, observe, survey, study, scrutinize, scan, stare at, gaze at, eye.

**2** *he contemplated his fate* THINK ABOUT, ponder, reflect on, consider, mull over, muse on, dwell on, deliberate over, meditate on, ruminate on, chew over, brood on/about, turn over in one's mind; *formal* cogitate.

**3** *he was contemplating action for damages* CONSIDER, think about, have in mind, intend, propose; envisage, foresee.

**contemplation** noun **1** *the contemplation of beautiful objects* VIEWING, examination, inspection, observation, survey, study, scrutiny.

**2** *the monks sat in quiet contemplation* THOUGHT, reflection, meditation, consideration, rumination, deliberation, reverie, introspection, brown study; *formal* cogitation, cerebration.

**contemplative** adjective *a peaceful, contemplative mood* THOUGHTFUL, pensive, reflective, meditative, musing, ruminative, introspective, brooding, deep/lost in thought, in a brown study.

**contemporary** adjective **1** *contemporary sources* OF THE TIME, of the day, contemporaneous, concurrent, coeval, coexisting, coexistent.

**2** *contemporary society* MODERN, present-day, present, current, present-time.

**3** *a very contemporary design* MODERN, up-to-date, up-to-the-minute, fashionable; modish, latest, recent; *informal* trendy, with it, du jour. ANTONYMS old-fashioned, out of date.

▸ noun *Chaucer's contemporaries* PEER, fellow; *formal* compeer.

**contempt** noun **1** *she regarded him with contempt* SCORN, disdain, disrespect, scornfulness, contemptuousness, derision; disgust, loathing, hatred, abhorrence. ANTONYM respect.

**2** *he is guilty of contempt of court* DISRESPECT, disregard, slighting. ANTONYM respect.

**contemptible** adjective *what they said to poor old Mr. Ortiz was contemptible* DESPICABLE, detestable, hateful, reprehensible, deplorable, unspeakable, disgraceful, shameful, ignominious, abject, low, mean, cowardly, unworthy, discreditable, petty, worthless, shabby, cheap, beyond contempt, beyond the pale, sordid; *archaic* scurvy. ANTONYM admirable.

**contemptuous** adjective *the contemptuous look on your face says it all* SCORNFUL, disdainful, disrespectful, insulting, insolent, derisive, mocking, sneering, scoffing, withering, scathing, snide; condescending, supercilious, haughty, proud, superior, arrogant, dismissive, aloof; *informal* high and mighty, snotty, sniffy. ANTONYM respectful.

**contend** verb **1** *the pilot had to contend with torrential rain* COPE WITH, face, grapple with, deal with, take on, pit oneself against.

**2** *three main groups were contending for power* COMPETE, vie, contest, fight, battle, tussle, go head to head; strive, struggle.

**3** *he contends that the judge was wrong* ASSERT, maintain, hold, claim, argue, insist, state, declare, profess, affirm; allege; *formal* aver.

**content**[1] adjective *she seemed content with life* CONTENTED, satisfied, pleased, gratified, fulfilled, happy, cheerful, glad; unworried, untroubled, at ease, at peace, tranquil, serene. ANTONYMS discontented, dissatisfied.

▸ verb *her reply seemed to content him* SATISFY, please; soothe, pacify, placate, appease, mollify.

▸ noun *a time of content.* See CONTENTMENT.

**content**[2] noun **1** *foods with a high fiber content* AMOUNT, proportion, quantity.

**2 (contents)** *the contents of a vegetarian sausage* CONSTITUENTS, ingredients, components, elements.

**3 (contents)** *the book's table of contents* CHAPTERS, sections, divisions.

**4** *the content of the essay* SUBJECT MATTER, subject, theme, argument, thesis, message, thrust, substance, matter, material, text, ideas.

**contented** adjective *a contented man.* See CONTENT[1] adjective.

**contention** noun **1** *a point of contention* DISAGREEMENT, dispute, disputation, argument, discord, conflict, friction, strife, dissension, disharmony. ANTONYM agreement.

**2** *we questioned the validity of his contention* ARGUMENT, claim, plea, submission, allegation, assertion, declaration; opinion, stand, position, view, belief, thesis, case. PHRASE: **in contention** *the sisters are in contention for the top ranking* IN COMPETITION, competing, contesting, contending, vying; striving, struggling.

**contentious** adjective **1** *a contentious issue* CONTROVERSIAL, disputable, debatable, disputed, open to debate, vexed.

**2** *a contentious debate* HEATED, vehement, fierce, violent, intense, impassioned.

**3** *contentious people.* See QUARRELSOME.

**contentment** noun *finally being alone brought her a contentment she'd never known* CONTENTEDNESS, content, satisfaction, gratification, fulfillment, happiness, pleasure, cheerfulness; ease, comfort, well-being, peace, equanimity, serenity, tranquility.

**contest** noun **1** *a boxing contest* COMPETITION, match, tournament, game, meet, event, trial, bout, heat, race.

**2** *the contest for the party leadership* FIGHT, battle, tussle, struggle, competition, race.

▸ verb **1** *he intended to contest the seat* COMPETE FOR, contend for, vie for, fight for, try to win, go for.

**2** *we contested the decision* OPPOSE, object to, challenge, take a stand against, take issue with, question, call into question.

**3** *the issues have been hotly contested* DEBATE, argue about, dispute, quarrel over.

**contestant** noun *the celebrity contestants play for their favorite charities* COMPETITOR, participant, player, contender, candidate, aspirant, hopeful, entrant.

**context** noun **1** *the wider historical context* CIRCUMSTANCES, conditions, factors, state of affairs, situation, background, scene, setting.

**2** *a quote taken out of context* FRAME OF REFERENCE, contextual relationship; text, subject, theme, topic.

**contiguous** adjective *the contiguous Gulf states* ADJACENT, neighboring, adjoining, bordering, next-door; abutting, connecting, touching, in contact, proximate.

**contingency** noun *we've tried to imagine and provide for all possible contingencies* EVENTUALITY, (chance) event, incident, happening, occurrence, juncture, possibility, fortuity, accident, chance, emergency.

**contingent** adjective **1** *the merger is* ***contingent on*** *government approval* DEPENDENT ON, conditional on, subject to, determined by, hinging on, resting on.

**2** *contingent events* CHANCE, accidental, fortuitous, possible, unforeseeable, unpredictable, random, haphazard. See note at ACCIDENTAL.

▸ noun **1** *a contingent of Japanese businessmen* GROUP, party, body, band, company, cohort, deputation, delegation; *informal* bunch, gang.

**2** *a contingent of soldiers* DETACHMENT, unit, group.

**continual** adjective *a service disrupted by continual breakdowns* FREQUENT, repeated, recurrent, recurring, intermittent, regular. ANTONYMS occasional, sporadic.

**USAGE NOTE continual, continuous**

*Continual* = frequently recurring; intermittent—e.g.: "And [the police are] removing [the homeless]—by police rides to the edge of town, by continual issuing of citations for camping, by mass towing of vehicles and by routine discarding of people's belongings." (*USA Today*; Dec. 3, 1997.) *Continuous* = occurring without interruption; unceasing—e.g.: "Crow Canyon archaeologists want to study the twelfth- and thirteenth-century village to determine exactly when it was inhabited and whether it was occupied continuously or intermittently." (*Santa Fe New Mexican*; Sept. 8, 1996.) A good mnemonic device is to think of the *-ous* ending as being short for "one uninterrupted sequence."

The two words are frequently confused, usually with *continuous* horning in where *continual* belongs—e.g.:

• "Minutes after the arrest, Wayne Forrest, a Deputy Attorney General helping prosecute the case, told the presiding judge, Charles R. DiGisi, that the sheriff's office had been engaged in a 'continuous [read *continual*] course of misconduct' in the Spath case." (*New York Times*; Jan. 18, 1992.)

• "Continuous [read *Continual*] interruptions are frustrating because it often means [read *they often mean*] you have to warm up all over again or don't get a complete workout." (*Montgomery Advertiser*; Jan. 1, 1996.)

The two-word phrase *almost continuous* is correctly replaced by the single-word *continual*—e.g.: "The antidepressant Prozac has been in the news almost continuously [read *continually*] since it was introduced in Belgium in 1986." (*Tampa Tribune*; Nov. 24, 1996.)

A related mistake is to use *continuous* for something that happens at regular (e.g., annual) intervals—e.g.: "The White House tree-lighting ceremony has been held continuously [read *annually*] since 1923." (*Herald-Sun* [Durham, NC]; Dec. 6, 1996.) —*BG*

**continually** adverb **1** *security measures are continually updated and improved* FREQUENTLY, regularly, repeatedly, recurrently, again and again, time and (time) again; constantly. ANTONYMS occasionally, sporadically.

**2** *patients were monitored continually* CONSTANTLY, continuously, around/round the clock, day and night, night and day, 'morning, noon, and night', without a break, nonstop; all the time, the entire time, always, forever, at every turn, incessantly, ceaselessly, endlessly, perpetually, eternally, 24-7. ANTONYMS occasionally, sporadically.

**continuance** noun **1** *concerned with the continuance of life.* See CONTINUATION.

**2** *the prosecution sought a continuance* ADJOURNMENT, postponement, deferment, stay.

**continuation** noun *the continuation of our relationship seems futile* CARRYING ON, continuance, extension, prolongation, protraction, perpetuation. ANTONYM end.

**continue** verb **1** *he was unable to continue with his job* CARRY ON, proceed, go on, keep on, persist, press on, persevere; *informal* stick, soldier on. ANTONYM stop.

**2** *discussions continued throughout the night* GO ON, carry on, last, extend, be prolonged, run on, drag on. ANTONYMS stop, cease.

**3** *we are keen to continue this relationship* MAINTAIN, keep up, sustain, keep going, keep alive, preserve. ANTONYMS suspend, break off.

**4** *his willingness to continue in office* REMAIN, stay, carry on, keep going.

**5** *we continued our conversation after supper* RESUME, pick up, take up, carry on with, return to, recommence. ANTONYM end.

**continuity** noun *a breakdown in the continutiy of care* CONTINUOUSNESS, uninterruptedness, flow, progression.

**continuous** adjective *the rain has been continuous since early this morning* UNCEASING, uninterrupted, unbroken, constant, ceaseless, incessant, steady, sustained, solid, continuing, ongoing, without a break, nonstop, around/round-the-clock, persistent, unremitting, relentless, unrelenting, unabating, unrelieved, without respite, endless, unending, never-ending, perpetual, everlasting, eternal, interminable; consecutive, rolling, running; *archaic* without surcease. See note at CONTINUAL. ANTONYMS momentary, temporary.

**contort** verb *her face was contorted with grief* TWIST, bend out of shape, distort, misshape, warp, buckle, deform.

**contour** noun *the contour of the moon's surface* OUTLINE, shape, form; lines, curves, figure; silhouette, profile.

**contraband** noun **1** *contraband was suspected* SMUGGLING, illegal traffic, black marketeering, bootlegging; the black market.

**2** *they confiscated the contraband* STOLEN GOODS, swag, bootleg.

▸ adjective *contraband goods* SMUGGLED, black-market, bootleg, under the counter, illegal, illicit, unlawful; prohibited, banned, proscribed, forbidden; *informal* hot.

**contraceptive** noun *what type of contraceptive did you use?* BIRTH CONTROL; prophylactic, condom, birth control pill, the pill, diaphragm, the sponge, female condom, IUD, cervical cap, morning-after pill, BC/BCP; *trademark* Plan B.

**contract** noun *a legally binding contract* AGREEMENT, commitment, arrangement, settlement, understanding, compact, covenant, bond; deal, bargain; *Law* indenture.

▸ verb **1** *the market for such goods began to contract* SHRINK, get smaller, decrease, diminish, reduce, dwindle, decline. ANTONYMS expand, increase.

**2** *her stomach muscles contracted* TIGHTEN, tense, flex, constrict, draw in, narrow. ANTONYM relax.

**3** *she contracted her brow* WRINKLE, knit, crease, purse, pucker.

**4** *his name was soon contracted to "Rob"* SHORTEN, abbreviate, cut, reduce; elide. ANTONYMS expand, lengthen.

**5** *the company contracted to rebuild the stadium* UNDERTAKE, pledge, promise, covenant, commit oneself, engage, agree, enter an agreement, make a deal.

**6** *she contracted rubella* DEVELOP, catch, get, pick up, come down with, be struck down by, be stricken with, succumb to.

**7** *he contracted a debt of $3,300* INCUR, run up.

PHRASE: **contract out** *trash collection is contracted out by the town* SUBCONTRACT, outsource, farm out.

**contraction** noun **1** *the contraction of the industry* SHRINKING, shrinkage, decline, decrease, diminution, dwindling.

**2** *the contraction of muscles* TIGHTENING, tensing, flexing.

**3** *my contractions started at midnight* LABOR PAINS, labor; cramps.

**4** *"goodbye" is a contraction of "God be with you"* ABBREVIATION, short form, shortened form, elision, diminutive.

**contradict** verb **1** *he contradicted the government's account of the affair* DENY, rebut, dispute, challenge, counter, controvert; *formal* gainsay. ANTONYMS confirm, agree with.

**2** *nobody dared to contradict him* ARGUE AGAINST, go against, challenge, oppose; *formal* gainsay.

**3** *this research contradicts previous assertions* CONFLICT WITH, be at odds with, be at variance with, be inconsistent with, run counter to, disagree with. ANTONYMS corroborate, support.

**contradiction** noun **1** *the contradiction between his faith and his lifestyle* CONFLICT, clash, disagreement, opposition, inconsistency, mismatch, variance. ANTONYM agreement.

**2** *a contradiction of his statement* DENIAL, refutation, rebuttal, countering. ANTONYMS confirmation, reaffirmation.

**contradictory** adjective *their contradictory accounts angered the lieutenant* OPPOSED, in opposition, opposite, antithetical, contrary, contrasting, conflicting, at variance, at odds, opposing, clashing, divergent, discrepant, different; inconsistent, incompatible, irreconcilable. See note at OPPOSITE.

**contraption** noun *he's driving around the yard in another one of his wild contraptions* DEVICE, gadget, apparatus, machine, appliance, mechanism, invention, contrivance; *informal* gizmo, widget, doohickey.

**contrary** adjective **1** *contrary views* OPPOSITE, opposing, opposed, contradictory, clashing, conflicting, antithetical, incompatible, irreconcilable. See note at OPPOSITE. ANTONYMS compatible, same.

**2** *she was sulky and contrary* PERVERSE, awkward, difficult, uncooperative, unhelpful, obstructive, disobliging, recalcitrant, willful, self-willed, stubborn, obstinate, defiant, mulish, pigheaded, intractable; *formal* refractory; *archaic* froward. ANTONYMS cooperative, accommodating.

▸ noun *in fact, the contrary is true* OPPOSITE, reverse, converse, antithesis.

PHRASE: **contrary to** *contrary to what we had predicted, the lemon potatoes were very popular* IN CONFLICT WITH, against, at variance with, at odds with, in opposition to, counter to, incompatible with.

**contrast** noun **1** *the contrast between rural and urban trends* DIFFERENCE, dissimilarity, disparity, distinction, contradistinction, divergence, variance, variation, differentiation; contradiction, incongruity, opposition, polarity. ANTONYM similarity.

**2** *Jane was a complete contrast to Sarah* OPPOSITE, antithesis; foil, complement.

▸ verb **1** *a view that* ***contrasts with*** *his earlier opinion* DIFFER FROM, be at variance with, be contrary to, conflict with, go against, be at odds with, be in opposition to, disagree with, clash with. ANTONYMS resemble, echo.

**2** *people* ***contrasted*** *her* ***with*** *her sister* COMPARE WITH/TO, set side by side with, juxtapose with/to; measure against; distinguish from, differentiate from. ANTONYM liken.

**contravene** verb **1** *he contravened several laws* BREAK, breach, violate, infringe; defy, disobey, flout. ANTONYMS comply with, uphold.

**2** *the prosecution contravened the rights of the individual* CONFLICT WITH, be in conflict with, be at odds with, be at variance with, run counter to.

**contretemps** noun *her little contretemps with Terry* ARGUMENT, quarrel, squabble, disagreement, difference of opinion, dispute; *informal* tiff, set-to, run-in, spat, row.

**contribute** verb **1** *the government contributed a million dollars* GIVE, donate, put up, subscribe, hand out, grant, bestow, present, provide, supply, furnish; *informal* chip in, pitch in, fork out, shell out, cough up, kick in, ante up, pony up.

**2** *an article contributed by Dr. Clouson* SUPPLY, provide, submit.

**3** *numerous factors contribute to job satisfaction* PLAY A PART IN, be instrumental in, be a factor in, have a hand in, be conducive to, make for, lead to, cause.

**contribution** noun **1** *voluntary financial contributions* DONATION, gift, offering, present, handout, grant, subsidy, allowance, endowment, subscription; *formal* benefaction.

**2** *contributions from local authors* ARTICLE, piece, story, item, chapter, paper, essay.

**contributor** noun **1** *the magazine's regular contributors* WRITER, columnist, correspondent.

**2** *campaign contributors* DONOR, benefactor, subscriber, supporter, backer, patron, sponsor.

**contrite** adjective *Joey was so contrite we had to conceal our amusement* REMORSEFUL, repentant, penitent, regretful, sorry, apologetic, rueful, sheepish, hangdog, ashamed, chastened, shamefaced, conscience-stricken, guilt-ridden.

**contrivance** noun **1** *a mechanical contrivance* DEVICE, gadget, machine, appliance, contraption, apparatus, mechanism, implement, tool, invention; *informal* gizmo, widget, doohickey.

**2** *her matchmaking contrivances* SCHEME, stratagem, tactic, maneuver, move, plan, ploy, gambit, wile, trick, ruse, plot, machination.

**contrive** verb *his opponents contrived a cabinet crisis* BRING ABOUT, engineer, manufacture, orchestrate, stage-manage, create, devise, concoct, construct, plan, fabricate, plot, hatch; *informal* wangle, set up.

**contrived** adjective *the story's contrived ending is a big letdown* FORCED, strained, studied, artificial, affected, put-on, phony, pretended, false, feigned, fake, manufactured, unnatural; labored, overdone, elaborate. ANTONYM natural.

**control** noun **1** *China retained control over the region* JURISDICTION, sway, power, authority, command, dominance, government, mastery, leadership, rule, sovereignty, supremacy, ascendancy; charge, management, direction, supervision, superintendence.

**2** *strict import controls* RESTRAINT, constraint, limitation, restriction, check, curb, brake, rein; regulation.

**3** *her control deserted her* SELF-CONTROL, self-restraint, self-possession, composure, calmness; *informal* cool.

**4** *easy-to-use controls* SWITCH, knob, button, dial, handle, lever.

**5** *mission control* HEADQUARTERS, HQ, base, center of operations, command post, nerve center.

▸ verb **1** *one family had controlled the company since its formation* BE IN CHARGE OF, run, manage, direct, administer, head, preside over, supervise, superintend, steer; command, rule, govern, lead, dominate, hold sway over, be at the helm; *informal* head up, be in the driver's seat, run the show.

**2** *she struggled to control her temper* RESTRAIN, keep in check, curb, check, contain, hold back, bridle, rein in, suppress, repress, master.

**3** *public spending was controlled* LIMIT, restrict, curb, cap, constrain; *informal* put the brakes on.

**controversial** adjective *controversial issues such as abortion* CONTENTIOUS, disputed, at issue, disputable, debatable, arguable, vexed, tendentious; *informal* hot.

**controversy** noun *being drawn into the political controversy* DISAGREEMENT, dispute, argument, debate, dissension, contention, disputation, altercation, wrangle, wrangling, quarrel, quarreling, war of words, storm; cause célèbre; *informal* hot potato, minefield.

**contusion** noun *a minor contusion on his elbow* BRUISE, discoloration, injury.

**conundrum** noun **1** *the conundrums facing policy-makers* PROBLEM, difficult question, difficulty, quandary, dilemma; *informal* poser.

**2** *Rod enjoyed conundrums and crosswords* RIDDLE, puzzle, word game; *informal* brainteaser. See note at RIDDLE.

**convalescence** noun *a long period of convalescence* RECU-

PERATION, recovery, return to health, rehabilitation, improvement.

**convene** verb **1** *he convened a secret meeting* SUMMON, call, call together, order; *formal* convoke.

**2** *the committee convened for its final session* ASSEMBLE, gather, meet, come together, congregate. See note at GATHER.

**convenience** noun **1** *the convenience of the arrangement* EXPEDIENCE, advantage, propitiousness, timeliness; suitability, appropriateness.

**2** *for convenience, the handset is wall-mounted* EASE OF USE, usability, usefulness, utility, serviceability, practicality.

**3** *the kitchen has all the modern conveniences* APPLIANCE, device, labor-saving device, gadget; amenity; *informal* gizmo.

**convenient** adjective **1** *a convenient time* SUITABLE, appropriate, fitting, fit, suited, opportune, timely, well-timed, favorable, advantageous, seasonable, expedient.

**2** *a hotel that's* ***convenient for*** *public transit* NEAR (TO), close to, within easy reach of, well situated for, handy for, not far from, just around the corner from; *informal* a stone's throw from, within spitting distance of.

**convent** noun *even the hardest work at the convent gave her sense of peace and fulfillment* NUNNERY, MONASTERY, priory, abbey, cloister, religious community.

**convention** noun **1** *social conventions* CUSTOM, usage, practice, tradition, way, habit, norm; rule, code, canon, punctilio; propriety, etiquette, protocol; *formal* praxis; **(conventions)** mores.

**2** *a convention signed by 74 countries* AGREEMENT, accord, protocol, compact, pact, treaty, concordat, entente; contract, bargain, deal.

**3** *the party's biennial convention* CONFERENCE, meeting, congress, assembly, gathering, summit, convocation, synod, conclave.

**conventional** adjective **1** *the conventional wisdom of the day* ORTHODOX, traditional, established, accepted, received, mainstream, prevailing, prevalent, accustomed, customary. ANTONYM unorthodox.

**2** *a conventional railroad* NORMAL, standard, regular, ordinary, usual, traditional, typical, common.

**3** *a very conventional woman* CONSERVATIVE, traditional, traditionalist, conformist, bourgeois, old-fashioned, of the old school, small-town, suburban; *informal* straight, buttoned-down, square, stick-in-the-mud, fuddy-duddy. ANTONYMS radical, Bohemian.

**4** *a conventional piece of work* UNORIGINAL, formulaic, predictable, stock, unadventurous, unremarkable; *informal* humdrum, run-of-the-mill. ANTONYM original.

**converge** verb **1** *the tracks converge at Union Station* MEET, intersect, cross, connect, link up, coincide, join, unite, merge. ANTONYM diverge.

**2** *5,000 protesters* ***converged on*** *Capitol Hill* CLOSE IN ON, bear down on, approach, move toward. ANTONYMS diverge, leave.

**conversant** adjective *the students are* ***conversant with*** *a wide range of math skills* FAMILIAR WITH, acquainted with, au fait with, au courant with, at home with, well versed in, well-informed about, knowledgeable about, informed about, abreast of, up-to-date on; *informal* up to speed on, in the loop about; *formal* cognizant of.

**conversation** noun *he may have overheard our conversation* DISCUSSION, talk, chat, gossip, tête-à-tête, heart-to-heart, exchange, dialogue; *informal* confab, jaw, chitchat, chinwag, gabfest; *formal* confabulation, colloquy.

THE RIGHT WORD **conversation, chat, colloquy, communion, dialogue, parley, tête-á-tête**

It is nearly impossible for most people to get through a day without having a **conversation** with someone, even if it's only a **chat** with the mailman. Although *conversation* can and does take place in all sorts of contexts, both formal and informal, the word usually implies a relaxed, casual exchange. A *chat* is the least formal of all conversations, whether it's a father talking to his son about girls or two women having a **tête-á-tête** (French for "head to head," meaning a confidential conversation) about their wayward husbands. Men, of course, often complain that women don't understand the meaning of **dialogue**, which is a two-way conversation that may involve opposing points of view. Argument is even more likely to play a role in a **parley**, which formally is a discussion between enemies regarding the terms of a truce. A **colloquy** is the most formal of all conversations (*a colloquy on nuclear disarmament*); it can also be used to jocularly describe a guarded exchange (*a brief colloquy with the arresting officer*). **Communion** is a form of conversation as well—one that may take place on such a profound level that no words are necessary (*communion with nature*).

**conversational** adjective **1** *conversational English* INFORMAL, chatty, relaxed, friendly; colloquial, idiomatic.

**2** *a conversational man* TALKATIVE, chatty, communicative, forthcoming, expansive, loquacious, garrulous.

**converse**[1] verb *they conversed in low voices* TALK, speak, chat, have a conversation, discourse, communicate; *informal* chew the fat, jaw, visit, shoot the breeze; *formal* confabulate.

**converse**[2] noun *the converse is also true* OPPOSITE, reverse, obverse, contrary, antithesis, other side of the coin, flip side.

**conversion** noun **1** *the conversion of waste into energy* CHANGE, changing, transformation, metamorphosis, transfiguration, transmutation, sea change; *humorous* transmogrification.

**2** *the conversion of the building* ADAPTATION, alteration, modification, reconstruction, rebuilding, redevelopment, redesign, renovation, rehabilitation.

**3** *his religious conversion* REBIRTH, regeneration, reformation.

**convert** verb **1** *plants convert the sun's energy into chemical energy* CHANGE, turn, transform, metamorphose, transfigure, transmute; *humorous* transmogrify; *technical* permute.

**2** *the factory was converted into lofts* ADAPT, turn, change, alter, modify, rebuild, reconstruct, redevelop, refashion, redesign, restyle, revamp, renovate, rehabilitate; *informal* do up, rehab.

3 *they sought to convert sinners* PROSELYTIZE, evangelize, bring to God, redeem, save, reform, re-educate, cause to see the light.

▸ noun *Christian converts* PROSELYTE, neophyte, new believer; *Christianity* catechumen.

**convey** verb 1 *taxis conveyed guests to the station* TRANSPORT, carry, bring, take, fetch, bear, move, ferry, shuttle, shift, transfer.

2 *he conveyed the information to me* COMMUNICATE, pass on, make known, impart, relay, transmit, send, hand on/off, relate, tell, reveal, disclose.

3 *it's impossible to convey how I felt* EXPRESS, communicate, get across/over, put across/over, indicate, say.

4 *he conveys an air of competence* PROJECT, exude, emit, emanate.

**conveyance** noun 1 *the conveyance of agricultural produce* TRANSPORTATION, transport, carriage, carrying, transfer, movement, delivery; haulage, portage, cartage, shipment.

2 *formal three-wheeled conveyances* VEHICLE, means/method of transport.

**convict** verb *he was convicted of sexual assault* FIND GUILTY, sentence. ANTONYM acquit.

▸ noun *two escaped convicts* PRISONER, inmate; criminal, offender, lawbreaker, felon; *informal* jailbird, con, crook, lifer, yardbird.

**conviction** noun 1 *his conviction for murder* DECLARATION OF GUILT, sentence, judgment. ANTONYM acquittal.

2 *his political convictions* BELIEF, opinion, view, thought, persuasion, idea, position, stance, article of faith. See note at OPINION.

3 *she spoke with conviction* CERTAINTY, certitude, assurance, confidence, sureness, no shadow of a doubt. ANTONYM uncertainty.

**convince** verb 1 *he convinced me that I was wrong* MAKE CERTAIN, persuade, satisfy, prove to; assure, put/set someone's mind at rest.

2 *I convinced her to marry me* PERSUADE, induce, prevail on/upon, get, talk into, win over, cajole, inveigle.

THE RIGHT WORD **convince, persuade**

Although it is common to see **convince** and **persuade** used interchangeably, there are distinctions in meaning that careful writers and speakers try to preserve. **Convince** derives from a Latin word meaning 'to conquer, overcome.' **Persuade** derives from a Latin word meaning 'to advise, make appealing, sweeten.' One can **convince** or **persuade** someone with facts or arguments, but, in general, *convincing* is limited to the mind, while *persuasion* results in action (just as *dissuasion* results in nonaction): *the prime minister convinced the council that delay was pointless*; *the senator persuaded her colleagues to pass the legislation.*

**convincing** adjective 1 *a convincing argument* COGENT, persuasive, plausible, powerful, potent, strong, forceful, compelling, irresistible, telling, conclusive. See note at BELIEVABLE.

2 *a convincing 5–0 win* RESOUNDING, emphatic, decisive, conclusive.

**convivial** adjective *our convivial host* FRIENDLY, genial, affable, amiable, congenial, agreeable, good-humored, cordial, warm, sociable, outgoing, gregarious, companionable, clubby, hail-fellow-well-met, cheerful, jolly, jovial, lively; enjoyable, festive.

**convocation** noun 1 *the students gathered for their convocation* GRADUATION (CEREMONY), commencement.

2 *a convocation of church leaders* ASSEMBLY, gathering, meeting, conference, convention, congress, council, symposium, colloquium, conclave, synod.

**convolution** noun 1 *crosses adorned with elaborate convolutions* TWIST, turn, coil, spiral, twirl, curl, helix, whorl, loop, curlicue; *Architecture* volute.

2 *the convolutions of the plot* COMPLEXITY, intricacy, complication, twist, turn, entanglement.

**convoy** noun *a convoy of vehicles* GROUP, fleet, cavalcade, motorcade, cortège, caravan, line, train.

▸ verb *the ship was convoyed by army gunboats* ESCORT, accompany, attend, flank; protect, defend, guard.

**convulse** verb *his whole body convulsed* SHAKE UNCONTROLLABLY, go into spasms, shudder, jerk, thrash about.

**convulsion** noun 1 *she had convulsions* FIT, seizure, paroxysm, spasm, attack; *Medicine* ictus.

2 **(convulsions)** *the audience collapsed in convulsions* FITS OF LAUGHTER, paroxysms of laughter, uncontrollable laughter; *informal* hysterics.

3 *the political convulsions of the period* UPHEAVAL, eruption, cataclysm, turmoil, turbulence, tumult, disruption, agitation, disturbance, unrest, disorder.

**cook** verb 1 *Scott cooked dinner* PREPARE, make, put together; *informal* fix, rustle up.

2 *informal he's been cooking the books* FALSIFY, alter, doctor, tamper with, interfere with, massage, manipulate, fiddle.

3 *informal* **(cookin'/cooking)** *we just stopped by to see what's cookin'* HAPPENING, going on, taking place, occurring; *informal* going down.

▸ noun CHEF, food preparer, short-order cook, pastry chef; chef de cuisine, sous-chef, cordon bleu cook; *informal* cookie.

PHRASE: **cook up** *informal he cooked up an alibi so ludicrous that even his own attorney laughed* CONCOCT, devise, contrive, fabricate, trump up, hatch, plot, plan, invent, make up, think up, dream up.

**cool** adjective 1 *a cool breeze* CHILLY, chill, cold, bracing, brisk, crisp, fresh, refreshing, invigorating, nippy. ANTONYMS warm, hot.

**2** *a cool response* UNENTHUSIASTIC, lukewarm, tepid, indifferent, uninterested, apathetic, halfhearted; unfriendly, distant, remote, aloof, cold, chilly, frosty, unwelcoming, unresponsive, uncommunicative, undemonstrative, standoffish. ANTONYMS enthusiastic, friendly.

**3** *his ability to keep cool in a crisis* CALM, 'calm, cool, and collected', composed, as cool as a cucumber, collected, coolheaded, levelheaded, self-possessed, controlled, self-controlled, poised, serene, tranquil, unruffled, unperturbed, unmoved, untroubled, imperturbable, placid, phlegmatic; *informal* unflappable, together, laid-back. ANTONYMS panic-stricken, agitated.

**4** *a cool lack of morality* BOLD, audacious, nerveless; brazen, shameless, unabashed.

**5** *informal she thinks she's so cool* FASHIONABLE, stylish, chic, up-to-the-minute, sophisticated; *informal* trendy, funky, with it, hip, big, happening, groovy, phat, kicky, fly.

**6** *informal a cool song.* See EXCELLENT.

▸ noun **1** *the cool of the evening* CHILL, chilliness, coldness, coolness. ANTONYM warmth.

**2** *Ken lost his cool* SELF-CONTROL, control, composure, self-possession, calmness, equilibrium, calm; aplomb, poise, sangfroid, presence of mind.

▸ verb **1** *cool the sauce in the fridge* CHILL, refrigerate. ANTONYM heat.

**2** *her reluctance did nothing to cool his interest* LESSEN, moderate, diminish, reduce, dampen. ANTONYMS inflame, arouse.

**3** *Simon's ardor had cooled* SUBSIDE, lessen, diminish, decrease, abate, moderate, die down, fade, dwindle, wane. ANTONYM intensify.

**4** *after a while, she* ***cooled off*** CALM DOWN, recover/regain one's composure, compose oneself, control oneself, pull oneself together, simmer down.

**coop** noun *a chicken coop* PEN, run, cage, hutch, enclosure.

▸ verb *he hates being* ***cooped up*** *at home* CONFINE, shut in/up, cage (in), pen up/in, keep, detain, trap, incarcerate, immure.

**cooperate** verb **1** *police and social services cooperated in the operation* COLLABORATE, work together, work side by side, pull together, band together, join forces, team up, unite, combine, pool resources, make common cause, liaise.

**2** *he was happy to cooperate* BE OF ASSISTANCE, assist, help, lend a hand, be of service, do one's bit; *informal* play ball.

**cooperation** noun **1** *cooperation between management and workers* COLLABORATION, joint action, combined effort, teamwork, partnership, coordination, liaison, association, synergy, synergism, give and take, compromise.

**2** *thank you for your cooperation* ASSISTANCE, helpfulness, help, helping hand, aid.

**cooperative** adjective **1** *a cooperative effort* COLLABORATIVE, collective, combined, common, joint, shared, mutual, united, concerted, coordinated.

**2** *pleasant and cooperative staff* HELPFUL, eager to help, glad to be of assistance, obliging, accommodating, willing, amenable, adaptable.

▸ noun *a housing cooperative* | *a farm cooperative* COMPLEX, commune, collective; joint venture, cooperative enterprise; credit union; pool; *informal* CO-OP.

**coordinate** verb **1** *exhibitions coordinated by a team of international scholars* ORGANIZE, arrange, order, systematize, harmonize, correlate, synchronize, bring together, fit together, dovetail.

**2** *care workers coordinate at a local level* CO-OPERATE, liaise, collaborate, work together, negotiate, communicate, be in contact.

**3** *floral designs coordinate with the decor* MATCH, complement, set off; harmonize, blend, fit in, go.

**cope** verb **1** *she couldn't cope on her own* MANAGE, survive, subsist, look after oneself, fend for oneself, carry on, get by/through, bear up, hold one's own, keep one's end up, keep one's head above water; *informal* make it, hack it.

**2** *his inability to cope with the situation* DEAL WITH, handle, manage, address, face (up to), confront, tackle, come to grips with, get through, weather, come to terms with.

**copious** adjective *she took copious notes* ABUNDANT, superabundant, plentiful, ample, profuse, full, extensive, generous, bumper, lavish, fulsome, liberal, overflowing, in abundance, many, numerous; *informal* galore; *literary* plenteous. See note at PREVALENT. ANTONYM sparse.

**copse** noun *tall firs form a copse at the back of the house* THICKET, grove, wood, coppice, stand, bush, woodlot, brake, brush; *archaic* hurst, holt, boscage.

**copy** noun **1** *a copy of the report* DUPLICATE, facsimile, photocopy; transcript; reprint; *trademark* Xerox; *dated* carbon (copy), mimeograph, mimeo.

**2** *a copy of a sketch by Leonardo da Vinci* REPLICA, reproduction, replication, print, imitation, likeness; counterfeit, forgery, fake; *informal* knockoff.

▸ verb **1** *each form had to be copied* DUPLICATE, photocopy, xerox, run off, reproduce, replicate; *dated* mimeograph.

**2** *portraits copied from original paintings by Reynolds* REPRODUCE, replicate; forge, fake, counterfeit.

**3** *their sound was copied by a lot of jazz players* IMITATE, reproduce, emulate, follow, echo, mirror, parrot, mimic, ape; plagiarize, steal; *informal* rip off. See note at IMITATE.

**cord** noun *a two-foot cotton cord* STRING, thread, thong, lace, ribbon, strap, tape, tie, line, rope, cable, wire, ligature; twine, yarn; braid, braiding; elastic, bungee (cord).

**cordial** adjective *a cordial welcome* FRIENDLY, warm, genial, affable, amiable, pleasant, fond, affectionate, warmhearted, good-natured, gracious, hospitable, welcoming, hearty.

▸ noun *fruit cordial* LIQUEUR, drink.

**cordon** noun *a cordon of 500 police* BARRIER, line, row, chain, ring, circle; picket line.

▸ verb *troops **cordoned off** the area* CLOSE OFF, shut off, seal off, fence off, separate off, isolate, enclose, surround.

**core** noun 1 *the earth's core* CENTER, interior, middle, nucleus; recesses, bowels, depths; *informal* innards; *literary* midst.

2 *the core of the argument* HEART, heart of the matter, nucleus, nub, kernel, marrow, meat, essence, quintessence, crux, gist, pith, substance, basis, fundamentals; *informal* nitty-gritty, brass tacks, nuts and bolts.

▸ adjective *the core issue* CENTRAL, key, basic, fundamental, principal, primary, main, chief, crucial, vital, essential; *informal* number-one. ANTONYM peripheral.

**cork** noun *the cork from the wine bottle went flying across the room* STOPPER, stop, plug, peg, spigot, spile.

**corner** noun 1 *the cart lurched around the corner* BEND, curve, crook, dog-leg; turn, turning, jog, junction, fork, intersection; hairpin turn.

2 *a charming corner of Italy* DISTRICT, region, area, section, quarter, part; *informal* neck of the woods.

3 *he found himself in a tight corner* PREDICAMENT, plight, tight spot, mess, can of worms, muddle, difficulty, problem, dilemma, quandary; *informal* pickle, jam, stew, fix, hole, hot water, bind.

▸ verb 1 *he was eventually cornered by police dogs* DRIVE INTO A CORNER, bring to bay, cut off, block off, trap, hem in, pen in, surround, enclose; capture, catch.

2 *crime syndicates have cornered the stolen car market* GAIN CONTROL OF, take over, control, dominate, monopolize; capture; *informal* sew up.

**corny** adjective *informal most of our outdoors play was inspired by those corny TV westerns* BANAL, trite, hackneyed, commonplace, clichéd, predictable, hoary, stereotyped, platitudinous, tired, stale, overworked, overused, well-worn; mawkish, sentimental, cloying, syrupy, sugary, saccharine; *informal* cheesy, schmaltzy, mushy, sloppy, cutesy, soppy, cornball, hokey.

**corollary** noun *job losses are the unfortunate corollary of budget cutting* CONSEQUENCE, result, end result, upshot, effect, repercussion, product, by-product, offshoot.

**coronet** noun. See CROWN noun sense 1.

**corporation** noun *the chairman of the corporation* COMPANY, firm, business, concern, operation, house, organization, agency, trust, partnership; conglomerate, group, chain, multinational; *informal* outfit, setup.

**corps** noun 1 *an army corps* UNIT, division, detachment, section, company, contingent, squad, squadron, regiment, battalion, brigade, platoon.

2 *a corps of trained engineers* GROUP, body, band, cohort, party, gang, pack; team, crew.

**corpse** noun *the corpse was stolen from the morgue* DEAD BODY, body, carcass, skeleton, remains, mortal remains; *informal* stiff; *Medicine* cadaver. See note at BODY.

**corpulent** adjective *they provide ample seating for their corpulent clients* FAT, obese, overweight, plump, portly, stout, chubby, paunchy, beer-bellied, heavy, bulky, chunky, well-upholstered, well padded, well covered, meaty, fleshy, rotund, broad in the beam; *informal* tubby, pudgy, beefy, porky, roly-poly, blubbery, corn-fed; *rare* abdominous. ANTONYM thin.

**correct** adjective 1 *the correct answer* RIGHT, accurate, true, exact, precise, unerring, faithful, strict, faultless, flawless, error-free, perfect, letter-perfect, word-perfect; *informal* on the mark, on the nail, bang on, (right) on the money, on the button. ANTONYMS wrong, inaccurate.

2 *correct behavior* PROPER, seemly, decorous, decent, respectable, right, suitable, fit, fitting, befitting, appropriate, apt; approved, accepted, conventional, customary, traditional, orthodox, comme il faut. ANTONYM improper.

▸ verb 1 *proofread your work and correct any mistakes* RECTIFY, put right, set right, right, amend, emend, remedy, repair.

2 *an attempt to correct the trade imbalance* COUNTERACT, offset, counterbalance, compensate for, make up for, neutralize.

3 *the thermostat needs correcting* ADJUST, regulate, fix, set, standardize, normalize, calibrate, fine-tune.

**corrective** adjective *corrective shoes* REMEDIAL, therapeutic, restorative, curative, reparative, rehabilitative.

**correctly** adverb 1 *the questions were answered correctly* ACCURATELY, right, unerringly, precisely, faultlessly, flawlessly, perfectly, without error; *dated* aright.

2 *she behaved correctly at all times* PROPERLY, decorously, with decorum, decently, suitably, fittingly, appropriately, well.

**correlate** verb 1 *postal codes **correlate with** geographic location* CORRESPOND TO/WITH, match, parallel, agree with, tally with, tie in with, be consistent with, be compatible with, be consonant with, coordinate with, dovetail (with), relate to, conform to; *informal* square with, jibe with. ANTONYM contrast.

2 *we can correlate good health and physical fitness* CONNECT, analogize, associate, relate, compare, set side by side.

**correlation** noun *the correlation between smoking and lung cancer* CONNECTION, association, link, tie-in, tie-up, relation, relationship, interrelationship, interdependence, interaction, interconnection; correspondence, parallel.

**correspond** verb 1 *their policies do not **correspond with** their statements* CORRELATE WITH, agree with, be in agreement with, be consistent with, be compatible with, be consonant with, accord with, be in tune with, concur with, coincide with, tally with, tie in with, dovetail (with), fit in with; match, parallel; *informal* square with, jibe with.

2 *a rank corresponding to the American rank of corporal* BE EQUIVALENT, be analogous, be comparable, equate.

3 *Debbie and I corresponded for years* EXCHANGE LETTERS, write, communicate, keep in touch, keep in contact.

**correspondence** noun 1 *there is some correspondence be-*

*tween the two variables* CORRELATION, agreement, consistency, compatibility, consonance, conformity, similarity, resemblance, parallel, comparability, accord, concurrence, coincidence.

2 *his private correspondence* LETTERS, messages, missives, mail, post; communication.

**correspondent** noun *the paper's foreign correspondent* REPORTER, journalist, columnist, writer, contributor, newspaperman, newspaperwoman, commentator; *informal* stringer, newshound.

**corridor** noun *the conference room is at the end of the corridor* PASSAGE, passageway, aisle, gangway, hall, hallway, gallery, arcade.

**corroborate** verb *the witness can corroborate Brueller's story* CONFIRM, verify, endorse, ratify, authenticate, validate, certify; support, back up, uphold, bear out, bear witness to, attest to, testify to, vouch for, give credence to, substantiate, sustain. ANTONYM contradict.

**corrode** verb 1 *the iron had corroded* RUST, become rusty, tarnish; wear away, disintegrate, crumble, perish, spoil; oxidize.

2 *acid rain corrodes buildings* WEAR AWAY, eat away (at), gnaw away (at), erode, abrade, consume, destroy.

**corrosive** adjective *corrosive chemicals* CAUSTIC, corroding, erosive, abrasive, burning, stinging; destructive, damaging, harmful, harsh.

**corrugated** adjective *panels of corrugated fiberglass* RIDGED, fluted, grooved, furrowed, crinkled, crinkly, puckered, creased, wrinkled, wrinkly, crumpled; *technical* striated.

**corrupt** adjective 1 *a corrupt official | corrupt practices* DISHONEST, unscrupulous, dishonorable, unprincipled, unethical, amoral, untrustworthy, venal, underhanded, double-dealing, fraudulent, bribable, criminal, illegal, unlawful, nefarious; *informal* crooked, shady, dirty, sleazy. ANTONYMS honest, law-abiding.

2 *the earth was corrupt in God's sight* IMMORAL, depraved, degenerate, reprobate, vice-ridden, perverted, debauched, dissolute, dissipated, bad, wicked, evil, base, sinful, ungodly, unholy, irreligious, profane, impious, impure; *informal* warped. See note at DEPRAVED. ANTONYM moral.

3 *a corrupt text* IMPURE, bastardized, debased, adulterated. ANTONYM pure.

▸ verb 1 *a book that might corrupt its readers* DEPRAVE, pervert, debauch, degrade, warp, lead astray, defile, pollute, sully.

2 *the apostolic writings had been corrupted* ALTER, tamper with, interfere with, bastardize, debase, adulterate.

**corruption** noun 1 *political corruption* DISHONESTY, unscrupulousness, double-dealing, fraud, fraudulence, misconduct, crime, criminality, wrongdoing; bribery, venality, extortion, profiteering, payola; *informal* graft, grift, crookedness, sleaze. ANTONYM honesty.

2 *his fall into corruption* IMMORALITY, depravity, vice, degeneracy, perversion, debauchery, dissoluteness, decadence, wickedness, evil, sin, sinfulness, ungodliness; *formal* turpitude. ANTONYMS morality, purity.

3 *these figures have been subject to corruption* ALTERATION, bastardization, debasement, adulteration.

**corset** noun *dated* GIRDLE, panty girdle, foundation garment, foundation, corselette; *historical* stays.

**cosmetic** adjective *most of the changes were merely cosmetic* SUPERFICIAL, surface, skin-deep, outward, exterior, external.

▸ noun (**cosmetics**) *a new range of cosmetics* MAKEUP, beauty products, beauty aids; *informal* war paint; *rare* maquillage.

**cosmic** adjective 1 *cosmic bodies* EXTRATERRESTRIAL, in space, from space.

2 *an epic of cosmic dimensions* VAST, huge, immense, enormous, massive, colossal, prodigious, immeasurable, incalculable, unfathomable, fathomless, measureless, infinite, limitless, boundless.

**cosmonaut** noun. See ASTRONAUT.

**cosmopolitan** adjective 1 *the student body has a cosmopolitan character* MULTICULTURAL, multiracial, international, worldwide, global.

2 *a cosmopolitan audience* WORLDLY, worldly-wise, well travelled, experienced, unprovincial, cultivated, cultured, sophisticated, suave, urbane, glamorous, fashionable; *informal* jet-setting, cool, hip, stylish. See note at URBANE.

**cost** noun 1 *the cost of the equipment* PRICE, asking price, market price, selling price, unit price, fee, tariff, fare, toll, levy, charge, rental; value, valuation, quotation, rate, worth; *informal, humorous* damage.

2 *the human cost of the conflict* SACRIFICE, loss, expense, penalty, toll, price.

3 (**costs**) *we need to make $10,000 to cover our costs* EXPENSES, disbursements, overheads, running costs, operating costs, fixed costs; expenditure, spending, outlay.

▸ verb 1 *the chair costs $186* BE PRICED AT, sell for, be valued at, fetch, come to, amount to; *informal* set someone back, go for.

2 *the proposal has not yet been costed* PUT A PRICE ON, price, value, put a value on, put a figure on.

**costly** adjective 1 *costly machinery* EXPENSIVE, dear, high-priced, highly priced, overpriced; *informal* steep, pricey, costing an arm and a leg, costing the earth. ANTONYMS cheap, inexpensive.

2 *a costly mistake* CATASTROPHIC, disastrous, calamitous, ruinous; damaging, harmful, injurious, deleterious, woeful, awful, terrible, dreadful; *formal* grievous. ANTONYM beneficial.

**costume** noun *each contestant wore a costume depicting her state* OUTFIT, garments, (set of) clothes, ensemble; dress, clothing, attire, garb, uniform, livery; *informal* getup, gear, togs, threads; *formal* apparel; *archaic* habit, habiliments, raiment.

**coterie** noun *a coterie of kindred spirits* CLIQUE, set, circle, inner circle, crowd, in-crowd, band, community, gang.

**cottage** noun *summers up at Anna and Renzo's cottage* CABIN, lodge; bungalow, country house; shack, chantey.

**couch** noun *she seated herself on the couch* SOFA, divan, settee, love seat, chesterfield, daybed, davenport, studio couch.

▸ verb *his reply was couched in deferential terms* EXPRESS, phrase, word, frame, put, formulate, style, convey, say, state, utter.

**cough** verb *he coughed loudly* HACK, hawk, bark, clear one's throat, hem.

▸ noun *a loud cough* HACK, bark.

PHRASE: **cough up** *we need to cough up the rent by next Thursday* PAY, pay up, come up with, hand over, dish out, part with; fork out, shell out, lay out, ante up, pony up.

**council** noun **1** *the town council* LOCAL AUTHORITY, municipal authority, local government, administration, executive, chamber, assembly, corporation.

**2** *the Student Council* ADVISORY BODY, board, committee, brain trust, commission, assembly, panel; synod, convocation.

**3** *that evening, she held a family council* meeting, gathering, conference, conclave, assembly.

**counsel** noun **1** *his wise counsel* ADVICE, guidance, counseling, direction, information; hints, recommendations, suggestions, guidelines, tips, pointers, warnings.

**2** *the counsel for the defense* LAWYER, advocate, attorney, attorney-at-law, counselor; *chiefly Brit.* solicitor, barrister.

▸ verb *he counseled the team to withdraw from the deal* ADVISE, recommend, direct, advocate, encourage, urge, warn, caution; guide, give guidance.

**counselor** noun *I discussed college choices with my counselor* ADVISER, consultant, guide, mentor; expert, specialist.

**count** verb **1** *Vern counted the money again* ADD UP, add together, reckon up, total, tally, calculate, compute, tot up; census; *formal* enumerate; *dated* cast up.

**2** *a company with 250 employees, not counting overseas staff* INCLUDE, take into account, take account of, take into consideration, allow for.

**3** *I count it a privilege to be asked* CONSIDER, think, feel, regard, look on as, view as, hold to be, judge, deem, account.

**4** *it's your mother's feelings that count* MATTER, be of consequence, be of account, be significant, signify, be important, carry weight.

▸ noun **1** *at last count, the committee had 57 members* CALCULATION, computation, reckoning, tally; *formal* enumeration.

**2** *her white blood cell count* AMOUNT, number, total.

PHRASES: **count on/upon 1** *you can count on me* RELY ON, depend on, bank on, trust (in), be sure of, have (every) confidence in, believe in, put one's faith in, take for granted, take as read.

**2** *they hadn't counted on his indomitable spirit* EXPECT, reckon on, anticipate, envisage, allow for, be prepared for, bargain for/on, figure on.

**down for the count** *informal* See UNCONSCIOUS adjective sense 1.

**countenance** noun *his strikingly handsome countenance* FACE, features, physiognomy, profile; (facial) expression, look, appearance, aspect, mien; *informal* mug, puss; *literary* visage, lineaments.

▸ verb *he would not countenance the use of force* TOLERATE, permit, allow, agree to, consent to, give one's blessing to, go along with, hold with, put up with, endure, stomach, swallow, stand for; *formal* brook.

**counter**[1] noun *the sugar is in a canister on the counter* WORK SURFACE, countertop, work table; bar; checkout (counter).

**counter**[2] verb **1** *workers countered accusations of dishonesty* RESPOND TO, parry, hit back at, answer, retort to.

**2** *the second argument is more difficult to counter* OPPOSE, dispute, argue against/with, contradict, controvert, negate, counteract; challenge, contest; *formal* gainsay, confute. ANTONYM support.

▸ adjective *a counter bid* OPPOSING, opposed, opposite.

PHRASE: **counter to** *nearly all of his proposals are counter to our original agreement* AGAINST, in opposition to, contrary to, at variance with, in defiance of, in contravention of, in conflict with, at odds with.

**counteract** verb **1** *new measures to counteract drug trafficking* PREVENT, thwart, frustrate, foil, impede, curb, hinder, hamper, check, put a stop to, put/bring a end to, defeat. ANTONYM encourage.

**2** *a drug to counteract the side effects* OFFSET, counterbalance, balance (out), cancel out, even out, counterpoise, countervail, compensate for, make up for, remedy; neutralize, nullify, negate, invalidate. ANTONYMS enhance, exacerbate.

**counterbalance** verb *the risk is counterbalanced by the potential high yields* COMPENSATE FOR, make up for, offset, balance (out), even out, counterpoise, counteract, equalize, neutralize; nullify, negate, undo.

**counterfeit** adjective *counterfeit $100 bills* FAKE, faked, bogus, forged, imitation, spurious, substitute, ersatz, phony. See note at SPURIOUS. ANTONYM genuine.

▸ noun *the notes were counterfeits* FAKE, forgery, copy, reproduction, imitation; fraud, sham; *informal* phony, knockoff. ANTONYM original.

▸ verb **1** *his signature was hard to counterfeit* FAKE, forge, copy, reproduce, imitate.

**2** *he grew tired of counterfeiting interest* FEIGN, simulate, pretend, fake, sham.

**countermand** verb *orders were being issued and then countermanded* REVOKE, rescind, reverse, undo, repeal, retract, withdraw, quash, overturn, overrule, cancel, annul, invalidate, nullify, negate; *Law* disaffirm, discharge, vacate; *formal* abrogate. ANTONYM uphold.

**counterpart** noun *the minister held talks with his French counterpart* EQUIVALENT, opposite number, peer, equal, coequal, parallel, complement, analog, match, twin, mate, fellow, brother, sister; *formal* compeer.

**countless** adjective *bringing relief to countless patients* INNUMERABLE, numerous, untold, a legion of, without number, numberless, unnumbered, limitless, multitudinous, incalculable; *informal* umpteen, no end of, a slew of, loads of, stacks of, heaps of, masses of, oodles of, zillions of, gazillions of; *literary* myriad. ANTONYM few.

**country** noun **1** *foreign countries* NATION, (sovereign) state, kingdom, realm, territory, province, principality, palatinate, duchy.

**2** *he risked his life for his country* HOMELAND, native land, fatherland, motherland, the land of one's fathers.

**3** *every election year, these guys claim to know what* ***the country*** *wants* THE PEOPLE, the public, the population, the populace, citizenry, the nation, the body politic; the electors, the voters, the taxpayers, the grass roots; *informal* John Q. Public, Joe Blow, Joe Schmo.

**4** *thickly forested country* TERRAIN, land, territory, parts; landscape, scenery, setting, surroundings, environment.

**5** *she hated living in the country* COUNTRYSIDE, greenbelt, great outdoors; rural areas, back woods, back of beyond, hinterland, bush, backcountry; *informal* sticks, middle of nowhere, boondocks, boonies; *Austral.* outback.

▸ adjective *country pursuits* RURAL, countryside, outdoor, rustic, pastoral, bucolic; *literary* sylvan, Arcadian, georgic. ANTONYM urban.

**countryside** noun **1** *beautiful unspoiled countryside* LANDSCAPE, scenery, surroundings, setting, environment; country, terrain, land.

**2** *I was brought up in the countryside.* See COUNTRY noun sense 5.

**county** noun *families from neighboring counties* REGION, province, administrative unit, territory, district, area.

**coup** noun **1** *a violent military coup* SEIZURE OF POWER, coup d'état, putsch, overthrow, takeover, deposition; revolution, palace revolution, rebellion, revolt, insurrection, mutiny, insurgence, uprising.

**2** *a major publishing coup* SUCCESS, triumph, feat, accomplishment, achievement, scoop, master stroke, stroke of genius.

**couple** noun **1** *the next couple is a sister act from Trenton* PAIR, duo, twosome, two; *archaic* twain, brace.

**2** *a honeymoon couple* HUSBAND AND WIFE, twosome, partners, lovers; *informal* item.

**3** *I have* ***a couple of*** *things to do* SOME, a few, a handful of, one or two.

▸ verb **1** *a sense of hope* ***coupled with*** *a sense of loss* COMBINE WITH, accompany with, mix with, incorporate with, link with, associate with, connect with/to, ally with; add to, join to; *formal* conjoin with.

**2** *a cable is coupled to one of the wheels* CONNECT, attach, join, fasten, fix, link, secure, tie, bind, strap, rope, tether, truss, lash, hitch, yoke, chain, hook (up). ANTONYM detach.

**coupon** noun **1** *grocery coupons* VOUCHER, token, ticket; *informal* comp, rain check.

**2** *fill in the coupon below* FORM, tear-off card.

**courage** noun *the courage of firefighters is just awesome* BRAVERY, courageousness, pluck, pluckiness, valour, fearlessness, intrepidity, nerve, daring, audacity, boldness, grit, true grit, hardihood, heroism, gallantry; *informal* guts, spunk, moxie, cojones, balls. ANTONYM cowardice.

THE RIGHT WORD **courage, fortitude, guts, nerve, pluck, resolution, tenacity**

**Courage** is what makes someone capable of facing extreme danger and difficulty without retreating (*the courage to confront the enemy head-on*). It implies not only bravery and a dauntless spirit but the ability to endure in times of adversity (*a mother's courage in the face of her loss*). Someone who has **guts**, a slang word indicating an admirable display of courage when it really counts (*having the guts to stand up to one's boss*), might also be described as having "intestinal fortitude," a cliché that is more formal and means the same thing. **Fortitude** is the most formal of any of these words; it suggests firmness or strength of mind rather than physical bravery (*the fortitude to stand up for his beliefs*). **Resolution** also implies firmness of mind rather than fearlessness, but the emphasis is on the determination to achieve a goal in spite of opposition or interference (*a woman of strong resolution, not easily held back by her male superiors*). **Tenacity** goes one step beyond *resolution*, adding stubborn persistence and unwillingness to acknowledge defeat (*the tenacity of a bulldog*). **Nerve** and **pluck** are informal words. *Pluck* connotes high spirits, conviction, and eagerness (*the pluck to volunteer her time even after she'd been laid off*), while *nerve* is the cool, unflappable daring with which someone takes a calculated risk (*the nerve to take over the controls and land the plane safely*). *Nerve* can also refer to brashness or even rudeness in social situations (*She had the nerve to go to his house without calling first*).

**courageous** adjective *these Special Olympians are among the most courageous individuals on the planet* BRAVE, plucky, fearless, valiant, valorous, intrepid, heroic, lionhearted, bold, daring, daredevil, audacious, undaunted, unflinching, unshrinking, unafraid, dauntless, indomitable, doughty, mettlesome, venturesome, stouthearted, gallant; *informal* game, gutsy, spunky, ballsy. ANTONYM cowardly.

**courier** noun *the documents were sent by courier* MESSENGER, runner; letter carrier, mail carrier, delivery man/woman; delivery service.

**course** noun **1** *the island was not far off our course* ROUTE, way, track, direction, tack, path, line, trail, trajectory, bearing, heading, orbit.

**2** *the course of history* PROGRESSION, development, progress, advance, evolution, flow, movement, sequence, order, succession, rise, march, passage, passing.

**3** *what is the best course to adopt?* PROCEDURE, plan, plan of action, course of action, line of action, MO, modus operandi, practice, approach, technique, way, means, policy, strategy, program; *formal* praxis.

**4** *a waterlogged course* RACECOURSE, raceway, racetrack, track, ground.

**5** *I'm taking a French course* CLASS, course of study, program of study, curriculum, syllabus; classes, lectures, studies.

**6** *a course of antibiotics* PROGRAM, series, sequence, system, schedule, regimen.

▸ verb *tears coursed down her cheeks* FLOW, pour, stream, run, rush, gush, cascade, flood, roll.

PHRASES: **in due course** *I look forward to hearing from you in due course* AT THE APPROPRIATE TIME, when the time is ripe, in time, in the fullness of time, in the course of time, at a later date, by and by, sooner or later, in the end, eventually.
**of course** *there are, of course, exceptions to the rule* NATURALLY, as might be expected, as you/one would expect, needless to say, certainly, to be sure, as a matter of course, obviously, it goes without saying; *informal* natch.

**court** noun **1** *the court found him guilty* COURT OF LAW, bench, bar, judicature, tribunal; *chiefly Brit.* law court, chancery.

**2** *the court of Louis IX* ROYAL HOUSEHOLD, retinue, entourage, train, suite, courtiers, attendants.

**3** *she made her way to the queen's court* ROYAL RESIDENCE, palace, castle, château.

▸ verb **1** *a newspaper editor who was courted by senior politicians* CURRY FAVOR WITH, cultivate, try to win over, make up to, ingratiate oneself with; *informal* suck up to, butter up.

**2** *he was busily courting public attention* SEEK, pursue, go after, strive for, solicit.

**3** *he has often courted controversy* RISK, invite, attract, bring on oneself.

**4** *dated he's courting her sister* GO OUT WITH, pursue, run after, chase; *informal* date, see, go steady with; *dated* woo, set one's cap for, romance, seek the hand of.

**courteous** adjective *our courteous staff is available 24 hours a day* POLITE, well-mannered, civil, respectful, well-behaved, well-bred, well-spoken, mannerly; gentlemanly, chivalrous, gallant; gracious, obliging, considerate, pleasant, cordial, urbane, polished, refined, courtly, civilized. ANTONYM rude.

**courtesan** noun *archaic*. See PROSTITUTE noun.

**courtesy** noun *our customers will be treated with courtesy* POLITENESS, courteousness, good manners, civility, respect, respectfulness; chivalry, gallantry; graciousness, consideration, thought, thoughtfulness, cordiality, urbanity, courtliness.

**courtier** noun *the princess's courtiers* ATTENDANT, lord, lady, lady-in-waiting, steward, page, squire.

**courtly** adjective *he gave a courtly bow* REFINED, polished, suave, cultivated, civilized, elegant, urbane, debonair; polite, civil, courteous, gracious, well-mannered, well-bred, chivalrous, gallant, gentlemanly, ladylike, aristocratic, dignified, decorous, formal, stately, ceremonious. ANTONYM uncouth.

**courtship** noun **1** *a whirlwind courtship* ROMANCE, love affair, affair; engagement.

**2** *his courtship of Emma* WOOING, courting, suit, pursuit.

**courtyard** noun *India and I met in the courtyard for lunch* QUADRANGLE, cloister, square, plaza, piazza, close, enclosure, yard; *informal* quad.

**cove** noun *a small sandy cove* BAY, inlet, fjord, anchorage.

**covenant** noun *a breach of the covenant* CONTRACT, agreement, undertaking, commitment, guarantee, warrant, pledge, promise, bond, indenture; pact, deal, settlement, arrangement, understanding.

▸ verb *the landlord covenants to repair the property* UNDERTAKE, contract, guarantee, pledge, promise, agree, engage, warrant, commit oneself, bind oneself.

**cover** verb **1** *she covered her face with a towel* PROTECT, shield, shelter; hide, conceal, veil. ANTONYMS expose, reveal.

**2** *his car was covered in mud* CAKE, coat, encrust, plaster, smother, daub, bedaub.

**3** *snow covered the fields* BLANKET, overlay, overspread, carpet, coat; *literary* mantle.

**4** *a course covering all aspects of the business* DEAL WITH, consider, take in, include, involve, comprise, incorporate, embrace.

**5** *the trial was covered by several newspapers* REPORT ON, write about, describe, commentate on, publish/broadcast details of.

**6** *he turned on the radio to cover the noise of the air conditioner* MASK, disguise, hide, camouflage, muffle, block out, stifle, smother.

**7** *I'm covering for Jill* STAND IN FOR, fill in for, deputize for, take over from, relieve, take the place of, sit in for, understudy, hold the fort; *informal* sub for, pinch-hit for.

**8** *can you make enough to cover your costs?* PAY (FOR), be enough for, fund, finance; pay back, make up for, offset.

**9** *your home is covered against damage and loss* INSURE, protect, secure, underwrite, assure, indemnify.

**10** *we covered ten miles each day* TRAVEL, journey, go, do, traverse.

▸ noun **1** *a protective cover* | *a manhole cover.* See COVERING sense 1.

**2** *a book cover* BINDING, jacket, dust jacket, dust cover, wrapper.

**3** **(covers)** *she pulled the covers over her head* BEDDING, bedclothes, sheets, blankets.

**4** *a thick cover of snow* COATING, coat, covering, layer, carpet, blanket, overlay, dusting, film, sheet, veneer, crust, skin, cloak, mantle, veil, pall, shroud.

**5** *panicking onlookers ran for cover* SHELTER, protection, refuge, sanctuary, haven, hiding place.

**6** *there is considerable game cover around the lake* UNDERGROWTH, vegetation, greenery, woodland, trees, bushes, brush, scrub, plants; covert, thicket, copse.

**7** *the company was a cover for an international swindle* FRONT, facade, smokescreen, screen, blind, camouflage, disguise, mask, cloak.

**8** *on weekends there's a cover to get in the bar* COVER CHARGE, entry charge, entrance fee, admission charge, price of admission.

PHRASE: **cover up** *the government has tried to cover up the army's role* CONCEAL, hide, keep secret, hush up, draw a veil over, suppress, sweep under the carpet, gloss over, keep dark; *informal* whitewash, keep a/the lid on.

**coverage** noun **1** *up-to-the-minute coverage of the situation* REPORTAGE, reporting, description, treatment, handling, presentation, investigation, commentary; reports, articles, pieces, stories, ink.

**2** *your policy provides coverage against damage by fire* INSURANCE, protection, security, assurance, indemnification, indemnity, compensation.

**covering** noun **1** *a plastic covering* AWNING, canopy, tarpaulin, cowling, cowl, casing, housing; wrapping, wrapper, cover, envelope, sheath, sleeve, jacket, lid, top, cap.

**2** *a covering of snow* LAYER, coating, coat, carpet, blanket, overlay, topping, dusting, film, sheet, veneer, crust, skin, cloak, mantle, veil.

▸ adjective *a covering letter* ACCOMPANYING, explanatory, introductory, prefatory.

**coverlet** noun *a queen-size flannel coverlet* BEDSPREAD, bedcover, cover, throw, duvet, quilt, eiderdown, comforter; *dated* counterpane.

**covert** adjective *covert plans to sell arms* SECRET, furtive, clandestine, surreptitious, stealthy, cloak-and-dagger, hole-and-corner, backstairs, backroom, hidden, under-the-table, concealed, private, undercover, underground; *informal* hush-hush. See note at SECRET. ANTONYM overt.

**covet** verb *even with all they have, they covet the wealth of others* DESIRE, yearn for, crave, have one's heart set on, want, wish for, long for, hanker after/for, hunger after/for, thirst for.

**covetous** adjective *this covetous man will never be satisfied* GRASPING, greedy, acquisitive, desirous, possessive, envious, green with envy, green-eyed. See notes at GREEDY, JEALOUS.

**cow** verb *has he cowed you all with his threats?* INTIMIDATE, daunt, browbeat, bully, tyrannize, scare, terrorize, frighten, dishearten, unnerve, subdue; *informal* psych out, bulldoze.

**coward** noun *the cowards were the first to give up* WEAKLING, milksop, namby-pamby, mouse; *informal* chicken, scaredy-cat, yellow-belly, sissy, baby, candy-ass, milquetoast. ANTONYM hero.

**cowardly** adjective *he made a cowardly dash for the exit, leaving everyone else behind* FAINT-HEARTED, lily-livered, spineless, chicken-hearted, craven, timid, timorous, fearful, pusillanimous; *informal* yellow, chicken, weak-kneed, gutless, yellow-bellied, wimpish, wimpy. See note at BRAVERY. ANTONYM brave.

**cowboy** noun *cowboys on horseback* CATTLEMAN, cowhand, cowman, cowherd, herder, herdsman, drover, stockman, rancher, gaucho, vaquero; *informal* cowpuncher, cowpoke, broncobuster; *dated* buckaroo.

▸ adjective *informal a cowboy pilot* MAVERICK, original, nonconformist, unorthodox, rebel, rebellious.

**cower** verb *they cowered at the sound of gunfire* CRINGE, shrink, crouch, recoil, flinch, pull back, draw back, tremble, shake, quake, blench, quail, grovel. See note at WINCE.

**coy** adjective *her coy demeanor is just an act* ARCH, simpering, coquettish, flirtatious, kittenish; demure, shy, modest, bashful, reticent, diffident, self-effacing, shrinking, timid. ANTONYM brazen.

**cozen** verb *literary*. See TRICK verb.

**cozy** adjective **1** *a cozy country cottage* SNUG, comfortable, warm, homelike, homey, homely, welcoming; safe, sheltered, secure, down-home, homestyle; *informal* comfy, toasty, snug as a bug (in a rug).

**2** *a cozy chat* INTIMATE, relaxed, informal, friendly.

**crabbed** adjective **1** *her crabbed handwriting* CRAMPED, ill-formed, bad, illegible, unreadable, indecipherable, hieroglyphic; shaky, spidery.

**2** *a crabbed old man.* See CRABBY.

**crabby** adjective *sorry, I didn't mean to be so crabby* IRRITABLE, cantankerous, irascible, bad-tempered, grumpy, grouchy, crotchety, tetchy, testy, crusty, curmudgeonly, ill-tempered, ill-humored, peevish, cross, fractious, pettish, crabbed, prickly, waspish; *informal* snappish, snappy, cranky, ornery. ANTONYM affable.

**crack** noun **1** *a crack in the glass* SPLIT, break, chip, fracture, rupture; crazing.

**2** *a crack between two rocks* SPACE, gap, crevice, fissure, cleft, breach, rift, cranny, chink, interstice.

**3** *the crack of a rifle* BANG, report, explosion, detonation, pop; clap, crash.

**4** *a crack on the head* BLOW, bang, hit, knock, rap, punch, thump, bump, smack, slap; *informal* bash, whack, thwack, clout, wallop, clip, bop.

**5** *informal we'll have a crack at it* ATTEMPT, try; *informal* go, shot, stab, whack; *formal* essay.

**6** *informal cheap cracks about her clothes* JOKE, witticism, quip; jibe, barb, taunt, sneer, insult; *informal* gag, wisecrack, funny, dig.

▸ verb **1** *the glass cracked in the heat* BREAK, split, fracture, rupture, snap.

**2** *she cracked him across the forehead* HIT, strike, smack, slap, beat, thump, knock, rap, punch; *informal* bash, whack, thwack, clobber, clout, clip, wallop, belt, bop, sock, boff, bust, slug.

**3** *the witnesses cracked* BREAK DOWN, give way, cave in, go to pieces, crumble, lose control, yield, succumb.

**4** *informal* *the naval code proved harder to crack* DECIPHER, interpret, decode, break, solve, resolve, work out, find the key to; *informal* figure out.

▸ adjective *a crack shot* EXPERT, skilled, skillful, formidable, virtuoso, masterly, consummate, excellent, first-rate, first-class, marvelous, wonderful, magnificent, outstanding, superlative; deadly; *informal* great, superb, fantastic, ace, hotshot, mean, demon, brilliant, crackerjack, bang-up. ANTONYM incompetent.

PHRASES: **crack down on** *a campaign to crack down on crime* SUPPRESS, prevent, stop, put a stop to, put an end to, stamp out, eliminate, eradicate; clamp down on, get tough on, come down hard on, limit, restrain, restrict, check, keep in check, control, keep under control.

**crack up** *informal* *I feel as if I'm about to crack up* BREAK DOWN, have a breakdown, lose control, go to pieces, go out of one's mind, go mad; *informal* lose it, fall/come apart at the seams, go crazy, freak out.

**cracked** adjective **1** *a cracked cup* CHIPPED, broken, crazed, fractured, splintered, split; damaged, defective, flawed, imperfect.

**2** *informal* *you're cracked!* See MAD sense 1.

**crackle** verb *bits of dried mosses crackled in the fire* SIZZLE, fizz, hiss, crack, snap, sputter, crepitate.

**cradle** noun **1** *the baby's cradle* CRIB, bassinet, cot, rocker.

**2** *the cradle of democracy* BIRTHPLACE, fount, fountainhead, source, spring, fountain, origin, place of origin, seat; *literary* wellspring.

▸ verb *she cradled his head in her arms* HOLD, support, pillow, cushion, shelter, protect; rest, prop (up).

**craft** noun **1** *a player with plenty of craft* SKILL, skillfulness, ability, capability, competence, art, talent, flair, artistry, dexterity, craftsmanship, expertise, proficiency, adroitness, adeptness, deftness, virtuosity.

**2** *the historian's craft* ACTIVITY, occupation, profession, work, line of work, pursuit.

**3** *she used craft to get what she wanted* CUNNING, craftiness, guile, wiliness, artfulness, deviousness, slyness, trickery, duplicity, dishonesty, deceit, deceitfulness, deception, intrigue, subterfuge; wiles, ploys, ruses, schemes, stratagems, tricks.

**4** *a sailing craft* VESSEL, ship, boat; *literary* bark/barque.

**craftsmanship** noun *a fine example of modern craftsmanship* WORKMANSHIP, artistry, craft, art, handiwork, work; skill, skillfulness, expertise, technique.

**crafty** adjective *a couple of crafty rogues* CUNNING, wily, guileful, artful, devious, sly, tricky, scheming, calculating, designing, sharp, shrewd, astute, canny; duplicitous, dishonest, deceitful; *informal* foxy. ANTONYM honest.

**crag** noun *the crag is a popular nesting site for eagles* CLIFF, bluff, ridge, precipice, height, peak, tor, escarpment, scarp.

**cram** verb **1** *closets crammed with clothes* FILL, stuff, pack, jam, fill to overflowing, fill to the brim, overload; crowd, overcrowd.

**2** *they all crammed into the car* CROWD, pack, pile, squash, squish, squeeze, wedge oneself, force one's way.

**3** *he crammed his clothes into a suitcase* THRUST, push, shove, force, ram, jam, stuff, pack, pile, squash, compress, squeeze, wedge.

**4** *most of the students are cramming for exams* STUDY, review, bone up.

**cramp** noun *stomach cramps* MUSCLE/MUSCULAR SPASM, pain, shooting pain, pang, stitch; *Medicine* hyperkinesis.

▸ verb *tighter rules will cramp economic growth* HINDER, impede, inhibit, hamper, constrain, hamstring, interfere with, restrict, limit, shackle; slow down, check, arrest, curb, retard.

**cramped** adjective **1** *cramped accommodations* CONFINED, uncomfortable, restricted, constricted, small, tiny, narrow; crowded, packed, congested; *archaic* strait. ANTONYM spacious.

**2** *cramped handwriting* SMALL, crabbed, illegible, unreadable, indecipherable, hieroglyphic.

**crane** noun *the cargo is lifted by a crane* DERRICK, winch, hoist, davit, windlass; block and tackle.

**cranium** noun *a blow to his cranium* SKULL, head, brain case; *informal* noggin, brainpan.

**crank**[1] verb *you crank the engine by hand* START, turn (over), get going. PHRASE: **crank up** *informal* *crank up the volume, Steve* INCREASE, intensify, amplify, heighten, escalate, add to, augment, build up, expand, extend, raise; speed up, accelerate; up, jack up, hike up, step up, bump up, pump up.

**crank**[2] noun *they're nothing but a bunch of cranks* ECCENTRIC, oddity, madman/madwoman, lunatic; *informal* oddball, freak, weirdo, crackpot, loony, nut, nutcase, head case, maniac, screwball, kook.

**cranky** adjective *informal* *the children were tired and cranky.* See CRABBY.

**cranny** noun *every little cranny was filled with drifted snow* CHINK, crack, crevice, slit, split, fissure, rift, cleft, opening, gap, aperture, cavity, hole, hollow, niche, corner, nook, interstice.

**crash** verb **1** *the car **crashed into** a tree* SMASH INTO, collide with, be in collision with, hit, strike, ram, cannon into, plow into, meet head-on, run into, impact.

**2** *he crashed his car* SMASH, wreck; *informal* total.

**3** *waves **crashed against** the shore* DASH AGAINST, batter, pound, lash (against), slam (against), be hurled against.

**4** *thunder crashed overhead* BOOM, crack, roll, clap, explode, bang, blast, blare, resound, reverberate, rumble, thunder, echo.

**5** *informal* *his clothing company crashed* COLLAPSE, fold, fail, go under, go bankrupt, become insolvent, cease trading, go into receivership, go into liquidation; *informal* go broke, go bust, go belly up.

▸ noun **1** *a crash on the highway* ACCIDENT, collision, road traffic accident, derailment, wreck; *informal* pileup, smash-up, rear-ender.

**2** *a loud crash* BANG, smash, smack, crack, bump, thud, clatter, clunk, clang; report, detonation, explosion; noise, racket, clangor, din.

**3** *the stock market crash* COLLAPSE, failure, bankruptcy.

▸ adjective *a crash course* INTENSIVE, concentrated, rapid, short; accelerated, immersion.

**crass** adjective *crass assumptions about women* STUPID, insensitive, mindless, thoughtless, ignorant, witless, oafish, boorish, asinine, coarse, gross, graceless, tasteless, tactless, clumsy, heavy-handed, blundering. ANTONYM intelligent.

**crate** noun *a crate for their good china* CASE, packing case, chest, box; container, receptacle.

**crater** noun *the crater has become a lake* HOLLOW, bowl, basin, hole, cavity, depression; *Geology* caldera.

**crave** verb *he craved professional recognition* LONG FOR, yearn for, desire, want, wish for, hunger for, thirst for, sigh for, pine for, hanker after, covet, lust after, ache for, set one's heart on, dream of, be bent on; *informal* have a yen for, have a jones for, itch for, be dying for.

**craven** adjective *a craven surrender* COWARDLY, lily-livered, faint-hearted, chicken-hearted, spineless, timid, timorous, fearful, pusillanimous, weak, feeble; *informal* yellow, chicken, weak-kneed, gutless, yellow-bellied, wimpish; contemptible, abject, ignominious. ANTONYM brave.

**craving** noun *a craving for chocolate* LONGING, yearning, desire, want, wish, hankering, hunger, thirst, appetite, greed, lust, ache, need, urge; *informal* yen, itch, jones.

**crawl** verb **1** *they crawled under the table* CREEP, worm one's way, go on all fours, go on hands and knees, wriggle, slither, squirm, scrabble.

**2** *informal I'm not going to go **crawling to** him* GROVEL TO, ingratiate oneself with, be obsequious to, kowtow to, pander to, toady to, truckle to, bow and scrape to, dance attendance on, curry favor with, make up to, fawn on/over; *informal* suck up to, lick someone's boots, butter up.

**3** *the place was **crawling with** soldiers* BE FULL OF, overflow with, teem with, be packed with, be crowded with, be alive with, be overrun with, swarm with, be bristling with, be infested with, be thick with; *informal* be lousy with, be jam-packed with, be chock-full of.

**craze** noun *the latest fitness craze* FAD, fashion, trend, vogue, enthusiasm, mania, passion, rage, obsession, compulsion, fixation, fetish, fancy, taste, fascination, preoccupation; *informal* thing.

**crazed** adjective *a crazed murderer* MAD, insane, out of one's mind, deranged, demented, certifiable, psychopathic, lunatic; wild, raving, berserk, manic, maniac, frenzied; *informal* crazy, mental, out of one's head, raving mad, psycho. See also CRAZY sense 1. ANTONYM sane.

**crazy** adjective *informal* **1** *he was acting like a crazy person* MAD, insane, out of one's mind, deranged, demented, not in one's right mind, crazed, lunatic, non compos mentis, unhinged, mad as a hatter, mad as a March hare; *informal* mental, nutty, nutty as a fruitcake, off one's rocker, not right in the head, round/around the bend, raving mad, batty, bonkers, cuckoo, loopy, ditzy, loony, bananas, loco, with a screw loose, touched, gaga, not all there, out to lunch, crackers, nutso, out of one's tree, wacko, gonzo. ANTONYM sane.

**2** *Andrea had a crazy idea* STUPID, foolish, idiotic, silly, absurd, ridiculous, ludicrous, preposterous, farcical, laughable, risible, nonsensical, imbecilic, harebrained, cockamamie, half-baked, impracticable, unworkable, ill-conceived, senseless; *informal* cockeyed, daft, kooky. ANTONYM sensible.

**3** *he's **crazy about** her* PASSIONATE ABOUT, (very) keen on, enamored of, infatuated with, smitten with, devoted to; (very) enthusiastic about, fanatical about; *informal* wild about, mad about, nuts about, hog-wild about, gone on. ANTONYMS indifferent, apathetic.

**creak** verb *the rusty gate creaked in the wind* SQUEAK, grate, rasp; groan, complain.

**cream** noun **1** *skin creams* LOTION, ointment, moisturizer, emollient, unguent, cosmetic; salve, rub, embrocation, balm, liniment.

**2** *the cream of the crop* BEST, finest, pick, flower, crème de la crème, elite. ANTONYM dregs.

▸ adjective *a cream dress* OFF-WHITE, whitish, cream-colored, creamy, ivory, yellowish-white, ecru.

**crease** noun **1** *pants with knife-edge creases* FOLD, line, ridge; pleat, tuck; furrow, groove, corrugation.

**2** *the creases at the corners of her eyes* WRINKLE, line, crinkle, pucker; **(creases)** crow's feet.

▸ verb *her skirt was creased and stained* CRUMPLE, wrinkle, crinkle, line, scrunch up, rumple, ruck up.

**create** verb **1** *she has created a work of stunning originality* PRODUCE, generate, bring into being, make, fabricate, fashion, build, construct; design, devise, originate, frame, develop, shape, form, forge.

**2** *regular socializing creates good team spirit* BRING ABOUT, give rise to, lead to, result in, cause, breed, generate, engender, produce, make for, promote, foster, sow the seeds of, contribute to. ANTONYM destroy.

**3** *the governments planned to create a free-trade zone* ESTABLISH, found, initiate, institute, constitute, inaugurate, launch, set up, form, organize, develop.

**creation** noun **1** *the creation of a coalition government* ESTABLISHMENT, formation, foundation, initiation, institution, inauguration, constitution; production, generation, fabrication, fashioning, building, construction, origination, development. ANTONYM destruction.

**2** *the whole of creation* THE WORLD, the universe, the cosmos; the living world, the natural world, nature, life, living things.

**3** *Margaret Atwood's literary creations* WORK, work of art, production, opus, oeuvre; achievement, intellectual property; *informal* brainchild.

**creative** adjective *our students are encouraged to be creative* INVENTIVE, imaginative, innovative, experimental, original; artistic, expressive, inspired, visionary; enterprising, resourceful.

THE RIGHT WORD **creative, inventive, original, resourceful, imaginative, ingenious**

Everyone likes to think that he or she is **creative**, which is used to describe the active, exploratory minds possessed by artists, writers, and inventors (*a creative approach to problem-solving*). Today, however, *creative* has become an advertising buzzword (*creative cooking, creative hair-styling*) that simply means new or different. **Original** is more specific and limited in scope. Someone who is *original* comes up with things that no one else has thought of (*an original approach to constructing a doghouse*), or thinks in an independent and creative way (*a highly original filmmaker*). **Imaginative** implies having an active and creative imagination, which often means that the person visualizes things quite differently than the way they appear in the real world (*imaginative illustrations for a children's book*). The practical side of *imaginative* is **inventive**; the *inventive* person figures out how to make things work (*an inventive solution to the problem of getting a wheelchair into a van*). But where an *inventive* mind tends to comes up with solutions to problems it has posed for itself, a **resourceful** mind deals successfully with externally imposed problems or limitations (*A resourceful child can amuse herself with simple wooden blocks*). Someone who is **ingenious** is both *inventive* and *resourceful*, with a dose of cleverness thrown in (*the ingenious idea of using recycled plastic to create a warm, fleecelike fabric*).

**creator** noun **1** *the creator of the series* AUTHOR, writer, designer, deviser, maker, producer; originator, inventor, architect, mastermind, prime mover; *literary* begetter.

**2** (**the Creator**) *the Sabbath is kept to honor the Creator.* See GOD sense 1.

**creature** noun **1** *the earth and its creatures* ANIMAL, beast, brute; living thing, living being; *informal* critter, varmint.

**2** *you're such a lazy creature!* PERSON, individual, human being, character, soul, wretch, customer; *informal* devil, beggar, sort, type.

**3** *the boss's truckling creatures* LACKEY, minion, hireling, servant, puppet, tool, cat's paw, pawn; *informal* stooge, yes-man.

**credence** noun **1** *the government placed little credence in the scheme* BELIEF, faith, trust, confidence, reliance.

**2** *later reports lent credence to this view* CREDIBILITY, plausibility, believability; *archaic* credit.

**credentials** plural noun *checking the driver's credentials* DOCUMENTS, documentation, papers, identity papers, bona fides, ID, ID card, identity card, passport, proof of identity; certificates, diplomas, certification, references.

**credibility** noun **1** *the whole tale lacks credibility* PLAUSIBILITY, believability, tenability, probability, feasibility, likelihood, credence; authority, cogency.

**2** *does he possess the moral credibility the party is looking for?* TRUSTWORTHINESS, reliability, dependability, integrity; reputation, status.

**credible** adjective *only one of the so-called witnesses could provide a credible story* BELIEVABLE, plausible, tenable, able to hold water, conceivable, likely, probable, possible, feasible, reasonable, with a ring of truth, persuasive. See note at BELIEVABLE.

**credit** noun **1** *he never got the credit he deserved* PRAISE, commendation, acclaim, acknowledgment, recognition, kudos, glory, esteem, respect, thanks, admiration, tributes, gratitude, appreciation; *informal* bouquets, brownie points, marks.

**2** *the speech did his credit no good* REPUTATION, repute, image, name, good name, character, prestige, standing, status, estimation, credibility.

**3** *archaic* *his theory has been given very little credit* CREDENCE, belief, faith, trust, reliance, confidence.

**4** *she bought her new car on credit* LOAN, advance, financing; installments; *informal* plastic.

▸ verb **1** *the wise will seldom credit all they hear* BELIEVE, accept, give credence to, trust, have faith in; *informal* buy, swallow, fall for, take something as gospel (truth).

**2** *the scheme's success can be credited to the team's frugality* ASCRIBE, attribute, assign, accredit, chalk up, put down.

**creditable** adjective *her forty years of creditable stage work* COMMENDABLE, praiseworthy, laudable, admirable, honorable, estimable, meritorious, worthy, deserving, respectable. See note at BELIEVABLE. ANTONYM deplorable.

**credulous** adjective *he sold 'miracle' cures to desperate and credulous clients* GULLIBLE, naive, too trusting, easily taken in, impressionable, unsuspecting, unsuspicious, unwary, unquestioning; innocent, ingenuous, inexperienced, unsophisticated, unworldly, wide-eyed; *informal* born yesterday, wet behind the ears. See note at GULLIBLE. ANTONYM suspicious.

**creed** noun **1** *people of many creeds and cultures* FAITH, religion, religious belief, religious persuasion, church, denomination, sect.

**2** *his political creed* SYSTEM OF BELIEF, set of beliefs, beliefs, principles, articles of faith, ideology, credo, doctrine, teaching, dogma, tenets, canons.

**creek** noun *marsh marigolds grow along the creek* STREAM, river, brook, rivulet, freshet, runnel, rill, tributary, watercourse, bourn; *informal* crick. PHRASE: **up a/the creek** *when I saw the condition of the spare tire, I knew we were up a creek* IN TROUBLE, in difficulty/difficulties, in a mess, in a predicament; *informal* in a pickle, in a jam, in a fix.

**creep** verb *Tim crept out of the house* TIPTOE, steal, sneak, slip, slink, sidle, pad, edge, inch; skulk, prowl.

▸ noun *informal* *he's such a creep!* See BASTARD noun sense 2.

**creeps** PHRASE: **give someone the creeps** *informal Pam says he's a nice guy, but he still gives me the creeps* REPEL, repulse, revolt, disgust, sicken, nauseate, make someone's flesh creep, make someone's skin crawl; scare, frighten, terrify, horrify; *informal* gross out, freak out, creep out.

**creepy** adjective *informal the old apple trees look creepy in the dim moonlight* FRIGHTENING, eerie, disturbing, sinister, weird, hair-raising, menacing, threatening, eldritch; *informal* spooky, scary, freaky.

**crescent** noun *she carved a small crescent into the lid of the box* HALF-MOON, sickle-shape, lunula, lunette; arc, curve, bow.

**crest** noun **1** *the bird's crest* COMB, plume, tuft of feathers.

**2** *the crest of the hill* SUMMIT, peak, top, tip, pinnacle, brow, crown, apex.

**3** *our family crest* INSIGNIA, regalia, badge, emblem, heraldic device, coat of arms, arms.

**crestfallen** adjective *he was crestfallen after his mediocre performance at the tryouts* DOWNHEARTED, downcast, despondent, disappointed, disconsolate, disheartened, discouraged, dispirited, dejected, depressed, desolate, in the doldrums, sad, glum, gloomy, dismayed, doleful, miserable, unhappy, woebegone, forlorn; *informal* blue, bummed, in a blue funk, down in/at the mouth, down in the dumps. ANTONYM cheerful.

**crevice** noun *the termites crawled into a crevice* CRACK, fissure, cleft, chink, interstice, cranny, nook, slit, split, rift, fracture, breach; opening, gap, hole.

**crew** noun **1** *the ship's crew* SAILORS, mariners, hands, ship's company, ship's complement.

**2** *a crew of cameramen and sound engineers* TEAM, group, company, unit, corps, party, gang.

**3** *informal they were a motley crew* CROWD, group, band, gang, mob, pack, troop, swarm, herd, posse; *informal* bunch, tribe.

**crib** noun **1** *the baby's crib* CRADLE, cot, bassinet.

**2** *the oxen's crib* MANGER, stall, feeding trough.

▸ verb *informal she cribbed the plot from a Shakespeare play* COPY, plagiarize, poach, appropriate, steal, "borrow"; *informal* rip off, lift, pinch.

**crick** noun *a crick in my neck* KINK, pinch, knot, strain, stiffness.

**crime** noun **1** *kidnapping is a very serious crime* OFFENSE, unlawful act, illegal act, felony, misdemeanor, misdeed, wrong; *informal* no-no.

**2** *the increase in crime* LAWBREAKING, delinquency, wrongdoing, criminality, misconduct, illegality, villainy; *informal* crookedness; *Law* malfeasance.

**3** *a crime against humanity* SIN, evil, immoral act, wrong, atrocity, abomination, disgrace, outrage. See note at SIN.

**criminal** noun *a convicted criminal* LAWBREAKER, offender, villain, delinquent, felon, convict, malefactor, wrongdoer, culprit, miscreant; thief, burglar, robber, armed robber, gunman, gangster, terrorist; *informal* crook, con, jailbird, hood, yardbird, perp; *Law* malfeasant.

▸ adjective **1** *criminal conduct* UNLAWFUL, illegal, illicit, lawless, felonious, delinquent, fraudulent, actionable, culpable; villainous, nefarious, corrupt, wrong, bad, evil, wicked, iniquitous; *informal* crooked; *Law* malfeasant. ANTONYM lawful.

**2** *informal a criminal waste of taxpayers' money* DEPLORABLE, shameful, reprehensible, disgraceful, inexcusable, unforgivable, unconscionable, unpardonable, outrageous, monstrous, shocking, scandalous, wicked. ANTONYM commendable.

**crimp** verb *crimp the edges of the pie crust* PLEAT, flute, corrugate, ruffle, fold, crease, crinkle, pucker, gather; pinch, compress, press together, squeeze together.

**cringe** verb **1** *she cringed as he bellowed in her ear* COWER, shrink, recoil, shy away, flinch, blench, draw back; shake, tremble, quiver, quail, quake.

**2** *it makes me cringe when I think of it* WINCE, shudder, squirm, feel embarrassed, feel mortified. See note at WINCE.

**crinkly** adjective *a stiff, crinkly fabric* WRINKLED, wrinkly, crinkled, creased, crumpled, rumpled, crimped, corrugated, fluted, puckered, furrowed; wavy.

**cripple** verb **1** *the accident crippled her* DISABLE, paralyze, immobilize, make lame, incapacitate, handicap, leave someone a paraplegic/quadriplegic.

**2** *the company had been crippled by the recession* DEVASTATE, ruin, destroy, wipe out; paralyze, hamstring, bring to a standstill, put out of action, sideline, put out of business, bankrupt, break, bring someone to their knees.

**crippled** adjective *crippled soldiers* DISABLED, paralyzed, incapacitated, physically handicapped, lame, immobilized, bedridden, in a wheelchair, paraplegic, quadriplegic; *euphemistic* physically challenged.

**crisis** noun **1** *the situation had reached a crisis* CRITICAL POINT, turning point, crossroads, watershed, head, moment of truth, zero hour, point of no return, Rubicon, doomsday; *informal* crunch; *Medicine* climacteric. See note at CRUCIAL.

**2** *the current economic crisis* EMERGENCY, disaster, catastrophe, calamity; predicament, plight, mess, trouble, dire straits, difficulty, extremity.

**crisp** adjective **1** *Sarah ordered scrambled eggs and crisp bacon* CRUNCHY, crispy, brittle, crumbly, friable, breakable; firm, dry. ANTONYM soft.

**2** *Grace and Elijah enjoyed the crisp autumn day* INVIGORATING, bracing, brisk, fresh, refreshing, exhilarating, tonic, energizing; cool, chill, chilly, cold, nippy. ANTONYM sultry.

**3** *Ms. Stevens's answers were crisp and to the point* BRISK, decisive, businesslike, no-nonsense, incisive, to the point, matter of fact, brusque; terse, succinct, concise, brief, short, short and sweet, laconic, snappy. ANTONYMS soft, sultry, rambling.

**4** *crisp white bed linen* SMOOTH, uncreased, ironed; starched. ANTONYM wrinkled.

**criterion** noun *academic ability is not the sole criterion for allocating funds* STANDARD, specification, measure, gauge, test, scale, benchmark, yardstick, touchstone, barometer; principle, rule, law, canon.

**critic** noun **1** *a literary critic* REVIEWER, commentator, evaluator, analyst, judge, pundit.

**2** *critics of the government* DETRACTOR, attacker, fault-finder, backseat driver, gadfly.

**critical** adjective **1** *a highly critical report* CENSORIOUS, condemnatory, condemning, denunciatory, disparaging, disapproving, scathing, fault-finding, judgmental, accusatory, negative, unfavorable; *informal* nitpicking, picky. ANTONYM complimentary.

**2** *a critical essay* EVALUATIVE, analytical, interpretative, expository, explanatory.

**3** *the situation is critical* GRAVE, serious, dangerous, risky, perilous, hazardous, precarious, touch-and-go, in the balance, uncertain, parlous, desperate, dire, acute, life-and-death. ANTONYM safe.

**4** *the choice of materials is critical for product safety* CRUCIAL, vital, essential, of the essence, all-important, paramount, fundamental, key, pivotal, decisive, deciding, climacteric. ANTONYM unimportant.

**criticism** noun **1** *she was stung by his criticism* CENSURE, condemnation, denunciation, disapproval, disparagement, opprobrium, fault-finding, attack, broadside, stricture, recrimination; *informal* flak, bad press, panning, put down, knock, slam, brickbats, potshot(s); *formal* excoriation.

**2** *literary criticism* EVALUATION, assessment, appraisal, analysis, judgment; commentary, interpretation, explanation, explication, elucidation.

**criticize** verb *must you criticize everything she does?* FIND FAULT WITH, censure, denounce, condemn, attack, lambaste, pillory, rail against, inveigh against, arraign, cast aspersions on, pour scorn on, disparage, denigrate, give bad press to, run down; *informal* knock, pan, maul, slam, roast, hammer, lay into, lace into, flay, crucify, take apart, pull to pieces, pick holes in, pummel, trash, nitpick; *formal* excoriate. ANTONYM praise.

**critique** noun *a critique of North American culture* ANALYSIS, evaluation, assessment, appraisal, appreciation, criticism, review, study, commentary, exposition, exegesis.

**croak** verb **1** *"Thank you," I croaked* RASP, squawk, caw, wheeze, gasp.

**2** *informal I thought that old mule croaked years ago.* See DIE sense 1.

**crock** noun **1** *a crock of honey* POT, jar; jug, pitcher, ewer; container, receptacle, vessel.

**2** *chiefly Brit.* **(crocks)** *a pile of dirty crocks.* See CROCKERY.

**3** *informal his story was a total crock* LIE, falsehood, fib, made-up story, invention, fabrication, deception, (piece of) fiction; (little) white lie, half-truth; *informal* tall tale, whopper.

**crockery** noun *chiefly Brit. a sink filled with crockery* DISHES, china, tableware; plates, bowls, cups, saucers; *chiefly Brit.* crocks.

**crony** noun *informal he's playing pool with his cronies* FRIEND, companion, bosom friend, intimate, confidant, confidante, familiar, associate, accomplice, comrade; *informal* pal, chum, sidekick, partner in crime, buddy, amigo, compadre, mate; *archaic* compeer.

**crook** noun **1** *informal a small-time crook* CRIMINAL, lawbreaker, offender, villain, delinquent, felon, convict, malefactor, culprit, wrongdoer; rogue, scoundrel, shyster, cheat, scam artist, swindler, racketeer, confidence trickster, snake oil salesman; thief, robber, burglar; *informal* shark, con man, con, jailbird, hood, yardbird; *Law* malfeasant.

**2** *the crook of a tree branch* BEND, fork, curve, angle.

▸ verb *he crooked his finger and called the waiter* COCK, flex, bend, curve, curl.

**crooked** adjective **1** *narrow, crooked streets* WINDING, twisting, zigzag, meandering, tortuous, serpentine. ANTONYM straight.

**2** *a crooked spine* BENT, twisted, misshapen, deformed, malformed, contorted, out of shape, wry, warped, bowed, distorted.

**3** *the picture over the bed looked crooked* LOPSIDED, askew, awry, off-center, uneven, out of line, asymmetrical, tilted, at an angle, aslant, slanting, cockeyed, wonky.

**4** *informal a crooked cop crooked deals* DISHONEST, unscrupulous, unprincipled, untrustworthy, corrupt, corruptible, venal; criminal, illegal, unlawful, nefarious, fraudulent; *informal* shady, dodgy, hinky. ANTONYMS law-abiding, honest.

**croon** verb *she'd sit by the old phonograph for hours, listening to Rudy Vallee croon* SING SOFTLY, hum, warble, trill.

**crop** noun **1** *some farmers lost their entire crop* HARVEST, year's growth, yield; fruits, produce.

**2** *a bumper crop of mail* BATCH, lot, assortment, selection, collection, supply, intake.

**3** *a rider's crop* WHIP, switch, cane, stick.

▸ verb **1** *she's had her hair cropped* CUT SHORT, cut, clip, shear, shave, lop off, chop off, hack off; dock, bob.

**2** *a flock of sheep were cropping the turf* GRAZE ON, browse on, feed on, nibble, eat.

**3** *the hay was cropped several times this summer* HARVEST, reap, mow; gather (in), collect, pick, bring home.

PHRASE: **crop up** *things kept cropping up to delay their work* HAPPEN, occur, arise, turn up, spring up, pop up, emerge, materialize, surface, appear, come to light, present itself; *literary* come to pass, befall.

**cross** noun **1** *a bronze cross* CRUCIFIX, rood.

**2** *we all have our crosses to bear* BURDEN, trouble, worry, trial, tribulation, affliction, curse, bane, misfortune, adversity, hardship, vicissitude; millstone, albatross, thorn in one's flesh/side; misery, woe, pain, sorrow, suffering; *informal* hassle, headache.

**3** *a cross between a yak and a cow* HYBRID, hybridization, cross-breed, half-breed, mongrel; mixture, amalgam, blend, combination.

▸ verb **1** *they crossed the hills on foot* TRAVEL ACROSS, traverse, range over; negotiate, navigate, cover.

**2** *a lake crossed by a fine stone bridge* SPAN, bridge; extend across, stretch across, pass over.

**3** *the point where the two roads cross* INTERSECT, meet, join, connect, crisscross.

**4** *no one dared cross him* OPPOSE, resist, defy, obstruct, impede, hinder, hamper; contradict, argue with, quarrel with, stand up to, take a stand against, take issue with; *formal* gainsay.

**5** *the breed was crossed with the similarly colored Holstein* HYBRIDIZE, cross-breed, interbreed, cross-fertilize, cross-pollinate.

▸ adjective *Jane was getting cross* ANGRY, annoyed, irate, irritated, in a bad mood, vexed, irked, piqued, out of humor, put out, displeased; irritable, short-tempered, bad-tempered, snappish, snappy, crotchety, grouchy, grumpy, fractious, testy, crabby, cranky, mad, hot under the collar, peeved, riled, on the warpath, up in arms, steamed up, sore, bent out of shape, teed off, ticked off, pissed off. ANTONYM pleased.

PHRASE: **cross out** *looking at the manager's starting lineup, it seems that Mitchell's name has been crossed out* DELETE, strike out, ink out, score out, edit out, cancel, obliterate.

**cross-examine** verb *when McCoy cross-examines a witness, it's not a pretty sight* INTERROGATE, question, cross-question, quiz, catechize, give someone the third degree; *informal* grill, pump, put someone through the wringer.

**crossing** noun **1** *there should be a traffic light at this crossing* INTERSECTION, crossroads, junction, interchange.

**2** *a short ferry crossing* JOURNEY, passage, voyage, trip.

**crotchety** adjective *it's the dreadful arthritis that has made him so crotchety* BAD-TEMPERED, irascible, irritable, grumpy, grouchy, cantankerous, short-tempered, tetchy, testy, curmudgeonly, ill-tempered, ill-humored, ill-natured, cross-grained, peevish, cross, fractious, pettish, waspish, crabbed, crabby, crusty, prickly, touchy, snappish, snappy, cranky, ornery. ANTONYM good-humored.

**crouch** verb *the umpire crouches just enough to get a good view of the strike zone* SQUAT, bend (down), hunker down, scrunch down, hunch over, stoop, kneel (down); duck, cower.

**crow** verb **1** *a cock crowed* CRY, squawk, screech, caw, call.

**2** *crowing about your success* BOAST, brag, trumpet, swagger, swank, gloat, show off, preen oneself, sing one's own praises; *informal* talk big, blow one's own horn.

**crowd** noun **1** *a crowd of people* THRONG, horde, mass, multitude, host, army, battalion, herd, flock, drove, swarm, sea, troupe, pack, press, crush, mob, rabble; collection, company, gathering, assembly, audience, assemblage, congregation; *informal* gaggle, bunch, gang, posse.

**2** *she wanted to stand out from the crowd* MAJORITY, multitude, common people, populace, general public, masses, rank and file, hoi polloi; *informal* Joe Public, John Q. Public.

**3** *he's been hanging round with a bad crowd* SET, group, circle, clique, coterie; camp; *informal* gang, crew, lot.

**4** *the spectacle attracted a capacity crowd* AUDIENCE, spectators, listeners, viewers; house, turnout, attendance, gate; congregation.

▸ verb **1** *reporters crowded around her* CLUSTER, flock, swarm, mill, throng, huddle, gather, assemble, congregate, converge.

**2** *the guests all crowded into the dining room* SURGE, push one's way, jostle, elbow one's way; squeeze, pile, cram.

**3** *stop crowding me* pressure; harass, hound, pester, harry, badger, nag; *informal* hassle, lean on.

**crowded** adjective *the pizza place is crowded after every home game | a crowded bus | our villa was crowded with uninvited guests* PACKED, full, mobbed, filled to capacity, full to bursting, congested, overcrowded, overflowing, teeming, swarming, thronged, populous, overpopulated; busy; *informal* jam-packed, stuffed, chockablock, chock-full, bursting at the seams, wall-to-wall, standing room only, SRO; (**crowded with**) full of; *informal* crawling with, lousy with. ANTONYM deserted.

**crown** noun **1** *a jeweled crown* CORONET, diadem, circlet, tiara; *literary* coronal.

**2** *the world heavyweight crown* TITLE, award, accolade, distinction; trophy, cup, medal, plate, shield, belt, prize; laurels, bays, palm(s).

**3** *he and his family were loyal servants of the Crown* MONARCH, sovereign, king, queen, emperor, empress; monarchy, royalty; *informal* royals.

**4** *the crown of the hill* TOP, crest, summit, peak, pinnacle, tip, head, brow, apex.

▸ verb **1** *David II was crowned in 1331* ENTHRONE, install; invest, induct.

**2** *a teaching post at Harvard crowned his career* ROUND OFF, cap, be the climax of, be the culmination of, top off, consummate, perfect, complete, put the finishing touch(es) on/to.

**3** *a steeple crowned by a gilded cross* TOP, cap, tip, head, surmount.

**4** *informal someone crowned him with a poker.* See HIT verb sense 1.

**crucial** adjective **1** *negotiations were at a crucial stage* PIVOTAL, critical, key, climacteric, decisive, deciding; life-and-death. ANTONYMS minor, unimportant.

**2** *confidentiality is crucial in this case* ALL-IMPORTANT, of the utmost importance, of the essence, critical, preeminent, paramount, essential, vital. ANTONYM unimportant.

THE RIGHT WORD **crucial, acute, critical, deciding, pressing, urgent**

In any emergency or crisis situation, there is usually a turning point. Such an event is called **critical** if it determines the outcome of a situation (*a critical point in the nuclear disarmament negotiations; a critical election for the Democratic Party*). **Crucial** can also refer to a turning point, but it emphasizes the necessity of something happening before a result can be achieved (*the battle was crucial to their victory*), while *critical* suggests more of a balance between positive and negative outcomes (*a critical debate on foreign policy*). **Acute** describes the intensification of a situation that is rapidly approaching a climax (*an acute shortage of O-negative blood*), while **deciding** refers to something that forces a certain outcome (*a deciding factor in his recovery*). **Pressing** and **urgent** are milder words. A situation that is *pressing* may be chronic rather than *acute* (*a pressing need for changes in the political system*), while an *urgent* situation may be approaching a crisis without reference to a specific turning point (*an urgent meeting between the two presidents*). While *urgent* expresses more intensity than *pressing*, neither adjective conveys the same sense of intensity as *crucial*, *critical*, or *acute*.

**crucify** verb **1** *two thieves were crucified with Jesus* NAIL TO A CROSS; execute, put to death, kill.

**2** *she had been crucified by his boastful admission of adultery* DEVASTATE, crush, shatter, cut to the quick, wound, pain, harrow, torture, torment, agonize, persecute.

**3** *informal the fans would crucify us if we lost.* See CRITICIZE.

**crude** adjective **1** *crude oil* UNREFINED, unpurified, unprocessed, untreated; unmilled, unpolished; coarse, raw, natural. ANTONYM refined.

**2** *a crude barricade* PRIMITIVE, simple, basic, homespun, rudimentary, rough, rough and ready, rough-hewn, make-do, makeshift, improvised, unfinished, jury-rigged, jerry-built, slapdash; *dated* rude. ANTONYM sophisticated.

**3** *crude jokes* VULGAR, rude, naughty, suggestive, bawdy, off-color, indecent, obscene, offensive, lewd, salacious, licentious, ribald, coarse, uncouth, indelicate, tasteless, crass, smutty, dirty, filthy, scatological; *informal* blue. See note at RUDE. ANTONYMS decent, inoffensive.

**cruel** adjective **1** *a cruel man* BRUTAL, savage, inhuman, barbaric, barbarous, brutish, bloodthirsty, murderous, vicious, sadistic, wicked, evil, fiendish, diabolical, monstrous, abominable; callous, ruthless, merciless, pitiless, remorseless, uncaring, heartless, stony-hearted, hard-hearted, cold-blooded, cold-hearted, unfeeling, unkind, inhumane; *dated* dastardly; *literary* fell. See note at KIND. ANTONYM compassionate.

**2** *her death was a cruel blow* HARSH, severe, bitter, harrowing, heartbreaking, heart-rending, painful, agonizing, traumatic; *formal* grievous. ANTONYM mild.

**cruelty** noun *he treated her with cruelty* BRUTALITY, savagery, inhumanity, barbarity, barbarousness, brutishness, sadism, bloodthirstiness, viciousness, wickedness; lack of compassion, callousness, ruthlessness.

**cruise** noun *a cruise to the islands* BOAT TRIP, sea trip; voyage, journey.

▸ verb **1** *she cruised across the Atlantic* SAIL, voyage, journey.

**2** *a taxi cruised past* DRIVE SLOWLY, drift; *informal* mosey, toodle.

**crumb** noun *we haven't got a crumb of evidence* FRAGMENT, bit, morsel, particle, speck, scrap, shred, sliver, atom, grain, trace, tinge, mite, iota, jot, whit, ounce, scintilla, soupçon; *informal* smidgen, tad, titch.

**crumble** verb *the old barn is slowly crumbling* DISINTEGRATE, fall apart, fall to pieces, fall down, break up, collapse, fragment; decay, fall into decay, deteriorate, degenerate, go to rack and ruin, decompose, rot, molder, perish.

**crumple** verb **1** *she crumpled the note in her fist* CRUSH, scrunch up, screw up, squash, squeeze.

**2** *his pants were dirty and crumpled* CREASE, wrinkle, crinkle, rumple.

**3** *her resistance crumpled* COLLAPSE, give way, cave in, go to pieces, break down, crumble, be overcome.

**crunch** verb *she hungrily crunched the apple* MUNCH, chomp, bite into.

▸ noun *informal when the crunch comes, she'll be forced to choose* MOMENT OF TRUTH, critical point, crux, crisis, decision time, zero hour, point of no return; showdown.

**crusade** noun **1** *the medieval crusades* HOLY WAR; jihad.

**2** *a crusade against crime* CAMPAIGN, drive, push, movement, effort, struggle; battle, war, offensive.

▸ verb *she likes crusading for the cause of the underdog* CAMPAIGN, fight, do battle, battle, take up arms, work, strive, struggle, agitate, lobby, champion, promote.

**crusader** noun *she was a crusader against domestic violence* CAMPAIGNER, fighter, champion, advocate; reformer.

**crush** verb **1** *essential oils are released when the herbs are crushed* SQUASH, squeeze, press, compress; pulp, mash, macerate, mangle; flatten, trample on, tread on; *informal* smush.

**2** *your dress will get crushed* CREASE, crumple, rumple, wrinkle, crinkle, scrunch (up).

**3** *crush the cookies with a rolling pin* PULVERIZE, pound, grind, break up, smash, crumble; mill; *technical* comminute.

**4** *he crushed her in his arms* HUG, squeeze, hold tight, embrace, enfold.

**5** *the new regime crushed all popular uprisings* SUPPRESS, put down, quell, quash, stamp out, put an end to, overcome, overpower, defeat, triumph over, break, repress, subdue, extinguish.

**6** *Alan was crushed by her words* MORTIFY, humiliate, abash, chagrin, deflate, flatten, demoralize, squash; devastate, shatter; *informal* shoot down in flames, knock the stuffing out of.

▸ noun **1** *the crush of people* CROWD, throng, horde, swarm, sea, mass, pack, press, mob.

2 *informal a teenage crush* INFATUATION, obsession, love, passion; *informal* puppy love.

**crust** noun *a thin crust will form where the twig was snapped off* COVERING, layer, coating, cover, coat, sheet, thickness, film, skin, topping; incrustation, scab.

**crusty** adjective 1 *crusty French bread* CRISP, crispy, well baked; crumbly, brittle, friable. ANTONYMS soft, soggy.

2 *a crusty old man* IRRITABLE, cantankerous, irascible, bad-tempered, ill-tempered, grumpy, grouchy, crotchety, short-tempered, testy, crabby, curmudgeonly, peevish, cross, fractious, pettish, crabbed, prickly, waspish, peppery, cross-grained; *informal* snappish, cranky, ornery. ANTONYMS affable, good-natured.

**cry** verb 1 *Mandy started to cry* WEEP, shed tears, sob, wail, cry one's eyes out, bawl, howl, snivel, whimper, squall, mewl, bleat; lament, grieve, mourn, keen; *informal* boo-hoo, blubber, turn on the waterworks; *literary* pule. ANTONYM laugh.

2 *"Wait!" he cried* CALL, shout, exclaim, sing out, yell, shriek, scream, screech, bawl, bellow, roar, vociferate, squeal, yelp, holler; *dated* ejaculate. ANTONYM whisper.

▸ noun 1 *Leonora had a good cry* SOB, weep, crying fit, crying jag; *Technical* vagitus.

2 *a cry of despair* CALL, shout, exclamation, yell, shriek, scream, screech, bawl, bellow, roar, howl, yowl, squeal, yelp, interjection, holler; *dated* ejaculation.

3 *they've issued a cry for help* APPEAL, plea, entreaty, cry from the heart, cri de cœur.

**crypt** noun *the fraternity pledges had to spend the night in a crypt* TOMB, vault, mausoleum, burial chamber, sepulcher, catacomb, ossuary, undercroft.

**cub** noun 1 *a lioness and her cubs* (**cubs**) YOUNG, offspring, pups; *archaic* whelps.

2 *don't waste our top writer's time with a routine story—give it to one of the cubs* | *a cub reporter* TRAINEE, apprentice, probationer, novice, tyro, learner, beginner, tenderfoot; *informal* rookie, newbie, greenhorn. ANTONYM veteran.

**cubbyhole** noun *the glass-partitioned cubbyhole he called an office* SMALL ROOM, booth, cubicle; den; *informal* cubby.

**cube** noun 1 *I like my ice to be in conventional cubes* HEXAHEDRON, cuboid, parallelepiped.

2 *a cube of soap* BLOCK, lump, chunk, brick.

**cuddle** verb 1 *she picked up the baby and cuddled him* HUG, embrace, clasp, hold tight, hold/fold in one's arms, snuggle.

2 *the pair were kissing and cuddling* EMBRACE, hug, caress, pet, fondle; *informal* canoodle, smooch; *informal, dated* spoon, bill and coo.

3 *I cuddled up to him* SNUGGLE, nestle, curl, nuzzle.

**cuddly** adjective *a cute and cuddly teddy bear* HUGGABLE, soft, warm, cuddlesome, snuggly, cushy; attractive, endearing, lovable.

**cudgel** noun *a thick wooden cudgel* CLUB, bludgeon, stick, truncheon, baton, mace, blackjack, billy club, nightstick, shillelagh.

▸ verb *the victim was cudgeled to death* BLUDGEON, club, beat, batter, bash.

**cue** noun *the blinking blue light is my cue to lower the volume* SIGNAL, sign, indication, prompt, reminder; nod, word, gesture.

**USAGE NOTE cue, queue**

---

Though pronounced the same, these words have different meanings. *Cue* = (1) a signal to begin; a hint; or (2) a stick used in billiards, pool, or shuffleboard. *Queue* = (1) a line of people or things waiting their turn; or (2) a hanging braid of hair. Not surprisingly, the two are sometimes confused—e.g.:

- "Like most birds, teal don't start their migration based on air temperatures, but take their queue [read *cue*] to head south from the shortening hours of daylight." (*Times-Picayune* [New Orleans]; Sept. 25, 1994.)
- "People were forced to stand in long cues [read *queues*] at five emergency water stations in Amagasaki." (*Daily Yomiuri* [English language/Japan]; Jan. 19, 1995.)

To *cue up* a videotape, an audiotape, or a compact disc is to have it ready for playing at a particular point—e.g.: "His brother cued up the tape, the rousing theme song from 'Rocky.' (*Hartford Courant*; Sept. 17, 1996.)

To *queue up* is to line up—e.g.: "Florida State students queued up for probably the most prized ticket they would ever use." (*Sports Illustrated*; Dec. 2, 1996.)

The braid of hair is spelled *queue*, not *cue*—e.g.: "Instructed by French dancing masters in the stately steps and deep curtsies of the minuet, the young men had indeed to mind their pieds (feet) and queues (pigtails) to keep from losing their balance or their huge wigs." (*Press-Enterprise* [Riverside, CA]; Nov. 15, 1995.) —*BG*

---

**cuff** verb *Chris cuffed him on the head* HIT, strike, slap, smack, thump, beat, punch; *informal* clout, wallop, belt, whack, thwack, bash, clobber, bop, sock, boff, slug; *archaic* smite. PHRASE: **off the cuff** *informal* 1 *an off-the-cuff remark* IMPROMPTU, extempore, ad lib; unrehearsed, unscripted, unprepared, improvised, spontaneous, unplanned.

2 *I spoke off the cuff* WITHOUT PREPARATION, without rehearsal, impromptu, ad lib; *informal* off the top of one's head.

**cuisine** noun *authentic Vietnamese cuisine* COOKING, cookery, food, dishes.

**cul-de-sac** noun *this is not a through street, it's a cul-de-sac* DEAD END, no exit; blind alley.

**culminate** verb *two hours and ten minutes of toe-tapping merriment culminating in the grandest musical finale on Broadway* COME TO A CLIMAX, come to a head, peak, climax, reach a pinnacle; build up to, lead up to; end with, finish with, conclude with.

**culmination** noun *the gold medal at Nagano was the culmination of her amateur career* CLIMAX, pinnacle, peak, high point, highest point, height, high-water mark, top, summit, crest, apex, zenith, crowning moment, apotheosis, apogee; consummation, completion, finish, conclusion. ANTONYM nadir.

**culpable** adjective *I hold you personally culpable* TO BLAME, guilty, at fault, in the wrong, answerable, accountable, responsible, blameworthy, censurable. ANTONYM innocent.

**culprit** noun *police are doing all they can to catch the culprit* GUILTY PARTY, offender, wrongdoer, perpetrator, miscreant; criminal, malefactor, felon, lawbreaker, delinquent; *informal* baddy, crook, perp.

**cult** noun **1** *a religious cult* SECT, denomination, group, movement, church, persuasion, body, faction.

**2** *the* ***cult of*** *eternal youth in Hollywood* OBSESSION WITH, fixation on, mania for, passion for, idolization of, devotion to, worship of, veneration of.

**cultivate** verb **1** *the peasants cultivated the land* TILL, plow, dig, hoe, farm, work, fertilize, mulch, weed.

**2** *they were encouraged to cultivate basic food crops* GROW, raise, rear, plant, sow.

**3** *Tessa tried to cultivate her as a friend* WIN SOMEONE'S FRIENDSHIP, woo, court, curry favor with, ingratiate oneself with; *informal* get in good with someone, butter up, suck up to.

**4** *he wants to cultivate his mind* IMPROVE, better, refine, elevate; educate, train, develop, enrich.

**cultivated** adjective *believe it or not, Mrs. Cleasby, there are some cultivated young ladies in the Ozarks* CULTURED, educated, well-read, civilized, enlightened, discerning, discriminating, refined, polished; sophisticated, urbane, cosmopolitan.

**cultural** adjective **1** *cultural differences* ETHNIC, racial, folk; societal, lifestyle.

**2** *cultural achievements* AESTHETIC, artistic, intellectual; educational, edifying, civilizing.

**culture** noun **1** *exposing their children to culture* THE ARTS, the humanities, intellectual achievement; literature, music, painting, philosophy, the performing arts.

**2** *a man of culture* INTELLECTUAL/ARTISTIC AWARENESS, education, cultivation, enlightenment, discernment, discrimination, good taste, taste, refinement, polish, sophistication.

**3** *Afro-Caribbean culture* CIVILIZATION, society, way of life, lifestyle; customs, traditions, heritage, habits, ways, mores, values.

**4** *the culture of crops* CULTIVATION, farming; agriculture, husbandry, agronomy.

**cultured** adjective *she got her love of art and music from her mother, a vibrant and cultured woman* CULTIVATED, intellectually/artistically aware, artistic, enlightened, civilized, educated, well-educated, well-read, well-informed, learned, knowledgeable, discerning, discriminating, refined, polished, sophisticated; *informal* artsy. ANTONYM ignorant.

**culvert** noun *they were concerned with the foul smell from the water in the culvert* CHANNEL, conduit, watercourse, trough; drain, gutter, ditch.

**cumbersome** adjective **1** *a cumbersome diving suit* UNWIELDY, unmanageable, awkward, clumsy, inconvenient, incommodious; bulky, large, heavy, hefty, weighty, burdensome; *informal* hulking, clunky. See note at HEAVY. ANTONYM manageable.

**2** *cumbersome procedures* COMPLICATED, complex, involved, inefficient, unwieldy, slow. ANTONYM straightforward.

**cumulative** adjective *the effects of pollution are cumulative* INCREASING, accumulative, growing, mounting; collective, aggregate, amassed.

**cunning** adjective *a cunning scheme* CRAFTY, wily, artful, guileful, devious, sly, scheming, designing, calculating, Machiavellian; shrewd, astute, clever, canny; deceitful, deceptive, duplicitous, foxy; *archaic* subtle. ANTONYM honest.

▸ noun *his political cunning* GUILE, craftiness, deviousness, slyness, trickery, duplicity; shrewdness, astuteness.

**cup** noun **1** *a cup and saucer* teacup, coffee cup, demitasse; mug; *historical* chalice.

**2** *the winner was presented with a silver cup* TROPHY, loving cup, award, prize.

**cupboard** noun *there are clean potholders in the cupboard* CABINET, sideboard, buffet; dresser, armoire, credenza, chiffonier, closet, wardrobe, commode.

**cupidity** noun *he did not really see her cupidity until they'd been married for several years* GREED, avarice, avariciousness, acquisitiveness, covetousness, rapacity, materialism, Mammonism; *informal* money-grubbing. ANTONYM generosity.

**cur** noun **1** *a mangy cur* MONGREL, mutt.

**2** *informal Neil was beginning to feel like a cur.* See BASTARD noun sense 2.

**curative** adjective *the natives have used these curative herbs for centuries* HEALING, therapeutic, medicinal, remedial, corrective, restorative, tonic, health-giving.

**curb** noun *a curb on public spending* RESTRAINT, restriction, check, brake, rein, control, limitation, limit, constraint; *informal* crackdown; *literary* trammel.

▸ verb *he tried to curb his temper* RESTRAIN, hold back/in, keep back, repress, suppress, fight back, bite back, keep in check, check, control, rein in, contain, bridle, subdue; *informal* keep a/the lid on.

**curdle** verb *the milk was left out so long that it curdled* CLOT, coagulate, congeal, solidify, thicken; turn, sour, ferment.

**cure** verb **1** *after a long course of treatment, he was cured* HEAL, restore to health, make well/better; *archaic* cleanse.

**2** *economic equality cannot cure all social ills* RECTIFY, remedy, put/set right, right, fix, mend, repair, heal, make better; solve, sort out, be the answer/solution to; eliminate, end, put an end to.

**3** *the farmers cured their own bacon* PRESERVE, smoke, salt, dry, pickle.

▸ noun **1** *a cure for cancer* REMEDY, medicine, medication, medicament, antidote, antiserum; treatment, therapy; *archaic* physic.

2 *interest rate cuts are not the cure for the problem* SOLUTION, answer, antidote, nostrum, panacea, cure-all; *informal* quick fix, magic bullet, silver bullet.

**curio** noun *a dusty old room full of forgotten curios* TRINKET, knickknack, bibelot, ornament, bauble; objet d'art, collector's item, rarity, curiosity, oddity, kickshaw, tchotchke.

**curiosity** noun 1 *his evasiveness roused my curiosity* INTEREST, spirit of inquiry, inquisitiveness.

2 *the shop is a treasure trove of curiosities.* See CURIO.

**curious** adjective 1 *she was curious to know what had happened* INTRIGUED, interested, eager to know, dying to know, agog; inquisitive. ANTONYM uninterested.

2 *her curious behavior* STRANGE, odd, peculiar, funny, unusual, bizarre, weird, eccentric, queer, unexpected, unfamiliar, extraordinary, abnormal, out of the ordinary, anomalous, surprising, incongruous, unconventional, offbeat, unorthodox. ANTONYM ordinary.

**curl** verb 1 *smoke curled up from his cigarette* SPIRAL, coil, wreathe, twirl, swirl; wind, curve, bend, twist, twist and turn, loop, meander, snake, corkscrew, zigzag.

2 *Ruth curled her arms around his neck* WIND, twine, entwine, wrap.

3 *she washed and curled my hair* CRIMP, perm, wave.

4 *they curled up together on the sofa* NESTLE, snuggle, cuddle.

▸ noun 1 *the tangled curls of her hair* RINGLET, corkscrew, kink, wave.

2 *a curl of smoke* SPIRAL, coil, twirl, swirl, twist, corkscrew, curlicue, helix.

**curly** adjective *thick, curly hair* WAVY, curling, curled, ringlety, crimped, permed, frizzy, kinky, corkscrew. ANTONYM straight.

**currency** noun 1 *foreign currency* MONEY, legal tender, cash, banknotes, bills, notes, coins, coinage, specie.

2 *a term that has gained new currency* PREVALENCE, circulation, exposure; acceptance, popularity.

**current** adjective 1 *current events* CONTEMPORARY, present-day, modern, present, contemporaneous; topical, in the news, live, burning. ANTONYM past.

2 *the idea is still current* PREVALENT, prevailing, common, accepted, in circulation, circulating, on everyone's lips, popular, widespread. ANTONYM obsolete.

3 *a current driver's license* VALID, usable, up-to-date. ANTONYM expired.

4 *the current prime minister* INCUMBENT, present, in office, in power; reigning. ANTONYMS past, former.

▸ noun 1 *a current of air* FLOW, stream, backdraft, slipstream; airstream, thermal, updraft, draft; undercurrent, undertow, tide.

2 *the current of human life* COURSE, progress, progression, flow, tide, movement.

3 *the current of opinion* TREND, drift, direction, tendency.

**curse** noun 1 *she put a curse on him* MALEDICTION, hex, jinx; *formal* imprecation; *literary* anathema; (**a curse**) the evil eye.

2 *the curse of racism* EVIL, blight, scourge, plague, cancer, canker, poison.

3 *the curse of unemployment* AFFLICTION, burden, cross to bear, bane.

4 *muffled curses* OBSCENITY, swear word, expletive, oath, profanity, four-letter word, dirty word, blasphemy; *informal* cuss, cuss word; *formal* imprecation. See note at OATH.

▸ verb 1 *it seemed as if the family had been cursed* PUT A CURSE ON, put the evil eye on, anathematize, damn, hex, jinx; *archaic* imprecate.

2 *she was cursed with feelings of inadequacy* AFFLICT, trouble, plague, bedevil.

3 *drivers cursed and honked their horns* SWEAR, blaspheme, take the Lord's name in vain; *informal* cuss; *archaic* execrate.

**cursed** adjective *a cursed city* UNDER A CURSE, damned, doomed, ill-fated, ill-starred, jinxed, blighted; *literary* accursed, star-crossed.

**cursory** adjective *a cursory inspection* PERFUNCTORY, desultory, casual, superficial, token; hasty, quick, hurried, rapid, brief, passing, fleeting. See note at SUPERFICIAL. ANTONYM thorough.

**curt** adjective *after a curt response to Mary's accusation, he grabbed his coat and headed for the door* TERSE, brusque, abrupt, clipped, blunt, short, monosyllabic, summary; snappish, snappy, sharp, tart; gruff, offhand, unceremonious, ungracious, rude, impolite, discourteous, uncivil. See note at BRUSQUE. ANTONYM expansive.

**curtail** verb 1 *economic policies designed to curtail spending* REDUCE, cut, cut down, decrease, lessen, pare down, trim, retrench; restrict, limit, curb, rein in; *informal* slash. ANTONYM increase.

2 *his visit was curtailed* SHORTEN, cut short, truncate. ANTONYM lengthen.

**curtain** noun *he drew the curtains* DRAPE, drapery; window treatment, window hanging, screen, blind(s), shade; valance, café curtain.

▸ verb *the bed was* ***curtained off*** *from the rest of the room* CONCEAL, hide, screen, shield; separate, isolate.

**curve** noun *the serpentine curves of the river* BEND, turn, loop, curl, twist, hook; arc, arch, bow, undulation, curvature, meander.

▸ verb *the road curved back on itself* BEND, turn, loop, wind, meander, undulate, snake, spiral, twist, coil, curl; arc, arch.

**curved** adjective *use a large curved needle for the upholstery* BENT, arched, bowed, crescent, curving, wavy, sinuous, serpentine, meandering, undulating, curvilinear, curvy. ANTONYM straight.

**cushion** noun *a cushion against inflation* PROTECTION, buffer, shield, defense, bulwark.

▸ verb 1 *she cushioned her head on her arms* SUPPORT, cradle, prop (up), rest.

2 *to cushion the blow, wages and pensions were increased* SOFTEN, lessen, diminish, decrease, mitigate, temper, allay, alleviate, take the edge off, dull, deaden.

3 *residents are cushioned from the outside world* PROTECT, shield, shelter, cocoon.

**custody** noun *the parent who has custody of the child* CARE, guardianship, charge, keeping, safekeeping, wardship, responsibility, protection, tutelage; custodianship, trusteeship. PHRASE: **in custody** *the carjacker is in custody* IN PRISON, in jail, imprisoned, incarcerated, locked up, under lock and key, interned, detained; on remand; *informal* behind bars, doing time, inside.

**custom** noun 1 *his unfamiliarity with the local customs* TRADITION, practice, usage, observance, way, convention, formality, ceremony, ritual; sacred cow, unwritten rule; mores; *formal* praxis.

2 *it is our custom to visit the Adirondacks in October* HABIT, practice, routine, way, wont; policy, rule.

**customarily** adverb *we customarily leave at least a fifteen-percent tip* USUALLY, traditionally, normally, as a rule, generally, ordinarily, commonly; habitually, routinely. ANTONYM occasionally.

**customary** adjective 1 *customary social practices* USUAL, traditional, normal, conventional, familiar, accepted, routine, established, time-honored, regular, prevailing. ANTONYM unusual.

2 *her customary good sense* USUAL, accustomed, habitual, wonted. ANTONYM unusual.

**customer** noun *Mr. Kanter is one of our best customers* CONSUMER, buyer, purchaser, patron, client, subscriber; shopper.

**customs** plural noun. See TAX noun sense 1.

**cut** verb 1 *the knife slipped and cut his finger* GASH, slash, lacerate, sever, slit, pierce, penetrate, wound, injure; scratch, graze, nick, incise, score; lance.

2 *cut the pepper into small pieces* CHOP, cut up, slice, dice, cube, mince; carve, hash.

3 *cut back the new growth to about half its length | he should get his hair cut* TRIM, snip, clip, crop, barber, shear, shave; pare; prune, lop, dock; mow.

4 *I went to cut some flowers* PICK, pluck, gather; *literary* cull.

5 *lettering had been cut into the stonework* CARVE, engrave, incise, etch, score; chisel, whittle.

6 *the government cut public spending* REDUCE, cut back/down on, decrease, lessen, retrench, trim, slim down; rationalize, downsize, lower, slash, chop.

7 *the text has been substantially cut* SHORTEN, abridge, condense, abbreviate, truncate; edit; bowdlerize, expurgate.

8 *you need to cut at least ten lines per page* DELETE, remove, take out, excise, blue-pencil, chop.

9 *oil supplies to the area had been cut* DISCONTINUE, break off, suspend, interrupt; stop, end, put an end to.

10 *the point where the line cuts the vertical axis* CROSS, intersect, bisect; meet, join.

11 *she was suspended for cutting classes* SKIP, miss, play truant from; *informal* ditch, play hooky from.

▸ noun 1 *a cut on his jaw* GASH, slash, laceration, incision, wound, injury; scratch, graze, nick.

2 *a cut of beef* piece, section.

3 *informal the directors are demanding their cut* SHARE, portion, bit, quota, percentage; *informal* slice, piece of the pie, piece of the action.

4 *his hair was in need of a cut* HAIRCUT, trim, clip, crop.

5 *a smart cut of the whip* BLOW, slash, stroke.

6 *he followed this with the unkindest cut of all* INSULT, slight, affront, slap in the face, jibe, barb, cutting remark, put-down, dig.

7 *a cut in interest rates* REDUCTION, cutback, decrease, lessening, rollback.

8 *the elegant cut of his jacket* STYLE, design; tailoring, lines, fit.

PHRASES: **cut back** *if profits don't soon improve, we'll have to find ways to cut back | they cut back on medical benefits* ECONOMIZE, downsize, pull/draw in one's horns, tighten one's belt, slim down, scale down; **(cut back on)** cut, cut down, decrease, lessen, retrench, reduce, trim; *informal* slash.

**cut down** 1 *24 hectares of trees were cut down* FELL, chop down, hack down, saw down, hew.

2 *he was cut down in his prime* KILL, slaughter, shoot down, mow down, gun down; *informal* take out, blow away; *literary* slay.

**cut and dried** *the answers to such questions are not always cut and dried* DEFINITE, decided, settled, explicit, specific, precise, unambiguous, clear-cut, unequivocal, black and white, hard and fast.

**cut in** *excuse me for cutting in, but Glenda says that dinner's ready* INTERRUPT, butt in, break in, interject, interpose, chime in.

**cut off** 1 *how did this doll's arm get cut off?* SEVER, chop off, hack off; amputate.

2 *oil and gas supplies were cut off* DISCONTINUE, break off, disconnect, suspend; stop, end, bring to an end.

3 *a community cut off from the mainland by the floodwaters* ISOLATE, separate, keep apart; seclude, closet, cloister, sequester.

**cut out** 1 *the lifeboat's engines cut out* STOP WORKING, stop, fail, give out, break down; *informal* die, give up the ghost, conk out.

2 *cut out all the diseased wood* REMOVE, take out, excise, extract; snip out, clip out.

3 *it's best to cut out alcohol altogether* GIVE UP, refrain from, abstain from, go without; *informal* quit, lay off, knock off.

**cut out of** *his mother cut him out of her will* EXCLUDE FROM, leave out of, omit from, eliminate from.

**cut short** 1 *they cut short their vacation* BREAK OFF, shorten, truncate, curtail, terminate, end, stop, abort, bring to an untimely end.

**2** *several award recipients were cut short during their acceptance speeches* INTERRUPT, cut off, butt in on, break in on.

**cut-rate** adjective *sorry, but I'm not interested in cut-rate tires* CHEAP, marked down, reduced, discount, bargain.

**cutthroat** noun *dated a band of robbers and cutthroats* MURDERER, killer, assassin; *informal* hit man.

▸ adjective *cutthroat competition between rival firms* RUTHLESS, merciless, fierce, intense, aggressive, dog-eat-dog.

**cutting** noun **1** *plant cuttings* SCION, slip; graft.

**2** *fabric cuttings* PIECE, bit, fragment; trimming.

▸ adjective **1** *a cutting remark* HURTFUL, wounding, barbed, pointed, scathing, acerbic, mordant, caustic, acid, sarcastic, sardonic, snide, spiteful, malicious, mean, nasty, cruel, unkind; *informal* bitchy, catty. ANTONYMS friendly, pleasant.

**2** *cutting winter winds* ICY, icy-cold, freezing, arctic, Siberian, glacial, hypothermic, bitter, chilling, chilly, chill; biting, piercing, penetrating, raw, keen, sharp. ANTONYMS balmy, warm.

**cycle** noun **1** *the cycle of birth, death, and rebirth* ROUND, rotation; pattern, rhythm.

**2** *the painting is one of a cycle of seven* SERIES, sequence, succession, run; set.

▸ verb *Patrick cycled 10 miles each day* RIDE (A BICYCLE), bike, pedal.

**cyclone** noun. See STORM noun sense 1.

**cynic** noun *he was a cynic who deflated all the hopeful aspirations of his children* SKEPTIC, doubter, doubting Thomas; pessimist, prophet of doom, doomsayer, Cassandra, Chicken Little. ANTONYMS idealist, Pollyanna.

**cynical** adjective *losing her job after fifteen years of loyal service had left her bitter and cynical* SKEPTICAL, doubtful, distrustful, suspicious, disbelieving; pessimistic, negative, world-weary, disillusioned, disenchanted, jaundiced, sardonic. ANTONYM idealistic.

**cynicism** noun *theirs was a childhood of absent parents and broken promises, so cynicism was hardly a surprise* SKEPTICISM, doubt, distrust, mistrust, suspicion, disbelief; pessimism, negativity, world-weariness, disenchantment. ANTONYM idealism.

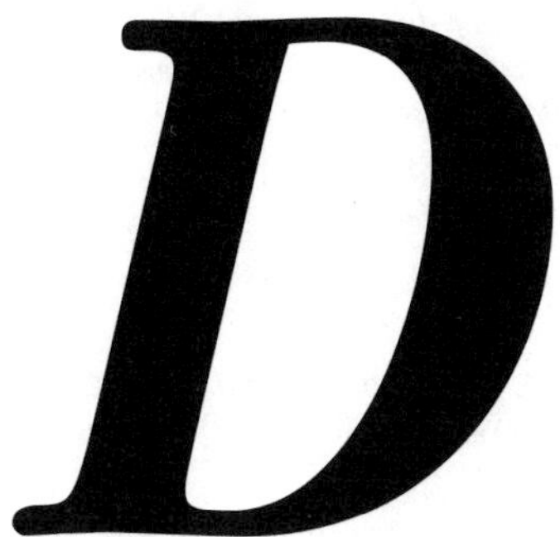

**dab** verb *she dabbed disinfectant on the cut* PAT, press, touch, blot, mop, swab; daub, apply, wipe, stroke.

▸ noun **1** *a dab of glue* DROP, spot, smear, splash, speck, taste, trace, touch, hint, bit; *informal* smidgen, tad, lick.

**2** *apply concealer with light dabs* PAT, touch, blot, wipe.

**dabble** verb **1** *they dabbled their feet in rock pools* SPLASH, dip, paddle, trail; immerse.

**2** *he* ***dabbled in*** *politics* TOY WITH, dip into, flirt with, tinker with, trifle with, play with, dally with.

**dabbler** noun *I'm no expert astronomer, just a dabbler* AMATEUR, dilettante, layman, layperson; trifler, nonprofessional, nonspecialist. ANTONYM professional.

**daft** adjective **1** *a daft idea* ABSURD, preposterous, ridiculous, ludicrous, farcical, laughable; idiotic, stupid, foolish, silly, inane, fatuous, harebrained, cockamamie, half-baked, crazy, cockeyed. ANTONYM sensible.

**2** *are you daft?* SIMPLEMINDED, stupid, idiotic, slow, witless, feebleminded, empty-headed, vacuous, vapid; unhinged, insane, mad; *informal* thick, dim, dopey, dumb, dimwitted, halfwitted, birdbrained, pea-brained, slow on the uptake, soft in the head, brain-dead, not all there, touched, crazy, mental, nuts, batty, bonkers, crackers, dumb-ass.

**daily** adjective *a daily event* EVERYDAY, day-to-day, quotidian, diurnal, circadian.

▸ adverb *the museum is open daily* EVERY DAY, once a day, day after day, diurnally.

**dainty** adjective **1** *a dainty china cup* DELICATE, fine, neat, elegant, exquisite. ANTONYM unwieldy.

**2** *a dainty morsel* TASTY, delicious, choice, palatable, luscious, mouthwatering, delectable, toothsome; appetizing, inviting, tempting; *informal* scrumptious, yummy, finger-licking, melt-in-your-mouth. ANTONYMS tasteless, unpalatable.

**3** *a dainty eater* FASTIDIOUS, fussy, finicky, particular, discriminating; *informal* choosy, persnickety, picky. ANTONYM undiscriminating.

▸ noun *homemade dainties* DELICACY, tidbit, fancy, luxury, treat; nibble, appetizer; confection, bonbon, goody; *archaic* sweetmeat.

**dais** noun *each speaker is allowed ten minutes on the dais* PLATFORM, stage, podium, rostrum, stand; soapbox.

**dale** noun *the green lushness of the dale in springtime* VALLEY, vale; hollow, basin, gully, gorge, ravine, glen; *literary* dell.

**dally** verb **1** *don't dally on the way to work* DAWDLE, delay, loiter, linger, waste time; lag, trail, straggle, fall behind; amble, meander, drift; *informal* dilly-dally; *archaic* tarry. See note at LOITER. ANTONYM hurry.

**2** *he likes dallying with film stars* TRIFLE, toy, amuse oneself, flirt, play fast and loose, philander, carry on, play around.

**dam** noun *the dam burst* BARRAGE, barrier, wall, embankment, barricade, obstruction.

▸ verb *the river was dammed* BLOCK (UP), obstruct, bung up, close; *technical* occlude.

**damage** noun **1** *did the thieves do any damage?* HARM, destruction, vandalism; injury, impairment, desecration, vitiation, detriment; ruin, havoc, devastation.

**2** *informal what's the damage?* COST, price, expense, charge, total.

**3** **(damages)** *she won $4,300 in damages* COMPENSATION, recompense, restitution, redress, reparation(s); indemnification, indemnity.

▸ verb *the parcel had been damaged* HARM, deface, mutilate, mangle, impair, injure, disfigure, vandalize; tamper with, sabotage; ruin, destroy, wreck, trash; *formal* vitiate. ANTONYM repair.

**damn** verb **1** *they were all damning him* CURSE, put the evil eye on, anathematize, hex, jinx. ANTONYM bless.

**2** *we are not going to damn the new product before we try it* CONDEMN, censure, criticize, attack, denounce, revile; find fault with, deprecate, disparage; *informal* slam, lay into, blast. ANTONYMS acclaim, praise.

▸ noun *informal it's not worth a damn* JOT, whit, iota, rap, scrap, bit; *informal* hoot, two hoots; *dated* a tinker's damn.

▸ exclamation *Damn! I forgot the keys.* DARN, damn it, dammit, drat, shoot, blast, doggone (it), goddammit, hell, rats.

PHRASE: **give a damn** *the only thing she gives a damn about is herself* CARE, mind, concern oneself; *informal* give a hoot.

**damnable** adjective *a damnable nuisance* UNPLEASANT,

disagreeable, objectionable, horrible, horrid, awful, nasty, dreadful, terrible; annoying, irritating, maddening, exasperating; hateful, detestable, loathsome, abominable, beastly.

**damned** adjective **1** *damned souls* CURSED, doomed, lost, condemned to hell; anathematized; *literary* accursed.

**2** *informal this damned car won't start* BLASTED, damn, damnable, confounded, rotten, wretched; *informal* blessed, bloody; *dated* accursed.

**damning** adjective *Erlich's family was stunned to hear the damning new evidence against her* INCRIMINATING, condemnatory, damnatory; damaging, derogatory; conclusive, strong.

**damp** adjective *her hair was damp* MOIST, moistened, wettish, dampened, dampish; humid, steamy, muggy, clammy, sweaty, sticky, dank, moisture-laden, wet, wetted; rainy, drizzly, showery, misty, foggy, vaporous, dewy. ANTONYM dry.

▸ noun *the damp in the air* MOISTURE, dampness, humidity, wetness, wet, water, condensation, steam, vapor; clamminess, dankness; rain, dew, drizzle, precipitation, spray; perspiration, sweat. ANTONYM dryness.

▸ verb **1** *sweat damped his hair.* See DAMPEN sense 1.

**2** *nothing damped my enthusiasm.* See DAMPEN sense 2.

**dampen** verb **1** *the rain dampened her face* MOISTEN, damp, wet, dew, water; *literary* bedew. ANTONYM dry.

**2** *nothing could dampen her enthusiasm* LESSEN, decrease, diminish, reduce, moderate, damp, put a damper on, throw cold water on, cool, discourage; suppress, extinguish, quench, stifle, curb, limit, check, restrain, inhibit, deter. ANTONYM heighten.

**damper** noun *the presence of the wretched Inez puts a damper on our fun* CURB, check, restraint, restriction, limit, limitation, constraint, rein, brake, control, impediment; chill, pall, gloom.

**dampness** noun See DAMP noun.

**damsel** noun *literary* See GIRL sense 2.

**dance** verb **1** *he danced with Katherine* sway, trip, twirl, whirl, pirouette, gyrate; *informal* bop, disco, rock, boogie, shake a leg, hoof it, cut a/the rug, trip the light fantastic, get down, mosh, groove.

**2** *little girls danced around me* CAPER, cavort, frisk, frolic, skip, prance, gambol, jig; leap, jump, hop, bounce.

**3** *flames danced in the fireplace* FLICKER, leap, dart, play, flit, quiver; twinkle, shimmer.

▸ noun **1** *they met at a dance* BALL, masquerade, prom, hoedown, disco; *dated* hop, sock hop.

**2** *the last dance had been played* (PIECE OF) DANCE MUSIC.

**dandy** noun *he became something of a dandy* FOP, man about town, glamour boy, rake; *informal* sharp dresser, snappy dresser, trendy, dude, pretty boy; *informal, dated* swell; *dated* beau; *archaic* buck, coxcomb, popinjay.

▸ adjective *informal our trip was dandy.* See EXCELLENT.

**danger** noun **1** *an element of danger* PERIL, hazard, risk, jeopardy; perilousness, riskiness, precariousness, uncertainty, instability, insecurity. ANTONYM safety.

**2** *that car is a danger on the roads* MENACE, hazard, threat, risk; *informal* death trap, widow-maker.

**3** *a serious danger of fire* POSSIBILITY, chance, risk, probability, likelihood, fear, prospect.

**dangerous** adjective **1** *a dangerous animal* MENACING, threatening, treacherous; savage, wild, vicious, murderous, desperate. ANTONYM harmless.

**2** *dangerous wiring* HAZARDOUS, perilous, risky, high-risk, unsafe, unpredictable, precarious, insecure, touch-and-go, chancy, treacherous; *informal* dicey, hairy. ANTONYM safe.

**dangle** verb **1** *a chain dangled from his belt* HANG (DOWN), droop, swing, sway, wave, trail, stream.

**2** *he dangled the keys* WAVE, swing, jiggle, brandish, flourish.

**3** *he dangled money in front of the locals* OFFER, hold out; entice someone with, tempt someone with.

**dangling** adjective *her dangling earrings* HANGING, drooping, droopy, suspended, pendulous, pendent, trailing, flowing, tumbling.

**dank** adjective *the dank basement* DAMP, musty, chilly, clammy, moist, wet, unaired, humid. ANTONYM dry.

**dapper** adjective *doesn't Norm look dapper in his new suit?* SMART, spruce, trim, debonair, neat, well-dressed, well-groomed, well turned out, elegant, chic, dashing; *informal* snazzy, snappy, natty, sharp, spiffy, fly. ANTONYM scruffy.

**dapple** verb *we dappled the wall by gently flicking the paintbrushes* DOT, spot, fleck, streak, speck, speckle, mottle, marble.

**dappled** adjective *a dappled horse* SPECKLED, blotched, blotchy, spotted, spotty, dotted, mottled, marbled, flecked, freckled; piebald, pied, brindle, pinto, tabby, calico; patchy, variegated; *informal* splotchy.

**dare** verb **1** *everyone wanted to say something, but nobody dared* BE BRAVE ENOUGH, have the courage; venture, have the nerve, have the temerity, be so bold as, have the audacity; risk, hazard, take the liberty, stick one's neck out, go out on a limb.

**2** *she dared him to go* CHALLENGE, defy, invite, bid, provoke, goad; throw down the gauntlet.

▸ noun *she accepted the dare* CHALLENGE, provocation, goad; gauntlet, invitation.

**USAGE NOTE dare**

It's been called "one of the subtlest and most variegated verbs in the language" (Robert W. Burchfield, *Points of View*; 1992) and also "one of the trickiest" (William Safire, "Love That Dare," *New York Times*; May 17, 1987). The subtleties arise because *dare* is both an ordinary verb (*he dares you to pick up the snake*) and a modal verb (*he dare not do it himself*). And the form it takes (*dares* vs. *dare* in those examples) changes with that grammatical function.

When *dare* is used as a full verb, it behaves just like most other verbs: it takes an *-s* with a third-person singular subject (*Robert always speaks his mind bluntly and dares anyone to disagree*). The form is identifiable by the presence of an explicit infinitive (with *to*) after *dare* (here, *to disagree*).

*Dare* was an Old English modal. When it is used as an auxiliary verb (like the modern modals *will*, *must*, and, more closely, *ought*), the infinitive either is missing its *to* (*dare he disagree with Robert?*) or is missing altogether but understood (*he dare not!*). This occurs chiefly, but not only, in interrogative or negative sentences. In those sentences, the form *dares*—although sometimes used mistakenly in striving for correctness—would be unidiomatic, because *dare* in this usage behaves like other uninflected modals (*will he disagree with Robert?* ¦ *he must not*)

As a modal verb, *dare* raises an interesting question of tense: in reference to past time, should one write (1) "Although challenged to do it, he dare not," or (2) "Although challenged to do it, he dared not"? The *Oxford English Dictionary* endorses the first and calls the second "careless," but that advice was written when that part of the great dictionary was published in 1894 (and the dandy but now archaic *durst* was still available). More recent grammarians are more lenient—e.g.: "As a modal, *dare* exhibits abnormal time reference in that it can be used, without inflection, for past as well as present time: 'The king was so hot-tempered that no one dare tell him the bad news.' The main verb form *dared (to)* might also occur here." (Randolph Quirk et al., *A Comprehensive Grammar of the English Language*; 1985.)

These more modern grammarians' analyses are borne out by actual usage—e.g.: "Mayo said he dared not declare it a little blue heron without confirmation from others." (*Hartford Courant*; Dec. 23, 2001.)

It is odd, however, to see the past-tense form in the set phrase *how dare you*—e.g.: " 'How dared you!' Jon shouted, waving his arms for emphasis. 'That dish was ours, the property of the entire Order! How dared you even think to appropriate it for your own uses!" (Patricia C. Wrede, *Mairelon the Magician*; 1991.)

The form *durst*, which is a past indicative and past subjunctive along with *dared*, is obsolete in American English. In British English, it still occurs rarely, always in a negative sentence or conditional clause in which there is an infinitive either understood or having no *to* (*none durst answer him*).

The exclamatory construction *How dare he do that!* is an idiomatic phrasing of the interrogative *How (does/did he) dare (to) do that?* The subject/actor (*he*) appears after the verb (*dare*) and is always in the nominative case—e.g.: "How dare she tell taxpayers to take on more responsibility to help neighborhood kids? How dare she be right?" (*Cincinnati Enquirer*; Aug. 18, 2002.) —*BG*

---

**daredevil** noun *a young daredevil crashed his car* THRILL-SEEKER, adventurer, madcap, exhibitionist, swashbuckler; stuntman; *informal* show-off.

▸ adjective *a daredevil skydiver* DARING, bold, audacious, intrepid, fearless, madcap, dauntless; heedless, reckless, rash, impulsive, impetuous, foolhardy, incautious, imprudent, harum-scarum. ANTONYMS cowardly, cautious.

**daring** adjective *a daring attack* BOLD, audacious, intrepid, venturesome, fearless, brave, unafraid, undaunted, dauntless, valiant, valorous, heroic, dashing; madcap, rash, reckless, heedless; *informal* gutsy, spunky, ballsy.

▸ noun *his sheer daring* BOLDNESS, audacity, temerity, fearlessness, intrepidity, bravery, courage, valor, heroism, pluck, spirit, mettle; recklessness, rashness, foolhardiness; *informal* nerve, guts, spunk, grit, moxie, sand, balls.

**dark** adjective **1** *a dark night* BLACK, pitch-black, jet-black, inky; unlit, unilluminated; starless, moonless; dingy, gloomy, dusky, shadowy, shady; *literary* Stygian. ANTONYM bright.

**2** *a dark secret* MYSTERIOUS, secret, hidden, concealed, veiled, covert, clandestine; enigmatic, arcane, esoteric, obscure, abstruse, impenetrable, incomprehensible, cryptic.

**3** *dark hair* BRUNETTE, dark brown, chestnut, sable, jet-black, ebony. ANTONYM blond/blonde.

**4** *dark skin* SWARTHY, dusky, olive, brown, black, ebony; tanned, bronzed. ANTONYM pale.

**5** *dark days* TRAGIC, disastrous, calamitous, catastrophic, cataclysmic; dire, awful, terrible, dreadful, horrible, horrendous, atrocious, nightmarish, harrowing; wretched, woeful. ANTONYM happy.

**6** *dark thoughts* GLOOMY, dismal, pessimistic, negative, downbeat, bleak, grim, fatalistic, black, somber; despairing, despondent, hopeless, cheerless, melancholy, glum, grave, morose, mournful, doleful. ANTONYM optimistic.

**7** *a dark look* MOODY, brooding, sullen, dour, scowling, glowering, angry, forbidding, threatening, ominous.

**8** *dark deeds* EVIL, wicked, sinful, immoral, bad, iniquitous, ungodly, unholy, base; vile, unspeakable, sinister, foul, monstrous, shocking, atrocious, abominable, hateful, despicable, odious, horrible, heinous, execrable, diabolical, fiendish, murderous, barbarous, black; sordid, degenerate, depraved; dishonorable, dishonest, unscrupulous; *informal* lowdown, dirty, crooked, shady. ANTONYMS virtuous, good.

▸ noun **1** *he's afraid of the dark* DARKNESS, blackness, gloom, murkiness, shadow, shade; dusk, twilight, gloaming. ANTONYM light.

**2** *she went out after dark* NIGHT, nighttime, darkness; nightfall, evening, twilight, sunset. ANTONYMS dawn, day.

PHRASE: **in the dark** *informal* *all those months that Luis was running guns for the Contras, his family was completely in the dark* UNAWARE, ignorant, incognizant, oblivious, uninformed, unenlightened, unacquainted, unconversant.

**darken** verb **1** *the sky darkened* GROW DARK, blacken, dim, cloud over, lower; shade, fog.

**2** *his mood darkened* BLACKEN, become angry, become annoyed; sadden, become gloomy, become unhappy, become depressed, become dejected, become dispirited, become troubled.

**darkness** noun **1** *lights shone in the darkness* DARK, blackness, gloom, dimness, murkiness, shadow, shade; dusk, twilight, gloaming.

**2** *darkness fell* NIGHT, nighttime, dark.

**3** *the forces of darkness* EVIL, wickedness, sin, iniquity, immorality; devilry, the Devil.

**darling** noun **1** *good night, my darling* DEAR, dearest, love, lover, sweetheart, sweet, beloved; *informal* honey, hon, angel, pet, sweetie, sugar, babe, baby, treasure.

2 *the darling of the media* FAVORITE, pet, idol, hero, heroine; *informal* blue-eyed boy/girl, fair-haired boy.

▸ adjective 1 *his darling wife* DEAR, dearest, precious, adored, loved, beloved, cherished, treasured, esteemed, worshiped.

2 *a darling little hat* ADORABLE, appealing, charming, cute, sweet, enchanting, bewitching, endearing, dear, delightful, lovely, beautiful, attractive, gorgeous, fetching; *Scottish* bonny.

**darn** verb *he was darning his socks* MEND, repair, reinforce; sew up, stitch, patch.

▸ exclamation *oh, darn!* See DAMN.

**dart** noun 1 *a poisoned dart* SMALL ARROW, missile, projectile, flechette.

2 *she made a dart for the door* DASH, rush, run, bolt, break, start, charge, sprint, bound, leap, dive; scurry, scamper, scramble.

▸ verb 1 *Karl darted across the road* DASH, rush, tear, run, bolt, fly, shoot, charge, race, sprint, bound, leap, dive, gallop, scurry, scamper, scramble; *informal* scoot.

2 *he darted a glance at her* DIRECT, cast, throw, shoot, send, flash.

**dash** verb 1 *he dashed home* RUSH, race, run, sprint, bolt, dart, gallop, career, charge, shoot, hurtle, careen, fly, speed, zoom, scurry, scuttle, scamper; *informal* tear, belt, scoot, zip, whip, hotfoot it, leg it, bomb, barrel. ANTONYM dawdle.

2 *he dashed the glass to the ground* HURL, smash, crash, slam, throw, toss, fling, pitch, cast, project, propel, send; *informal* chuck, heave, sling, peg.

3 *rain dashed against the walls* BE HURLED, crash, smash; batter, strike, beat, pound, lash.

4 *her hopes were dashed* SHATTER, destroy, wreck, ruin, crush, devastate, demolish, blight, overturn, scotch, spoil, frustrate, thwart, check; *informal* blow a hole in, scuttle. ANTONYM raise.

▸ noun 1 *a dash for the door* RUSH, race, run, sprint, bolt, dart, leap, charge, bound, break; scramble.

2 *a dash of salt* PINCH, touch, sprinkle, taste, spot, drop, dab, speck, smattering, sprinkling, splash, bit, modicum, little; *informal* smidgen, tad, lick.

3 *he led off with such dash* VERVE, style, flamboyance, gusto, zest, confidence, self-assurance, élan, flair, vigor, vivacity, sparkle, brio, panache, éclat, vitality, dynamism; *informal* pizzazz, pep, oomph.

**dashing** adjective 1 *a dashing pilot* DEBONAIR, devil-may-care, raffish, sporty, spirited, lively, dazzling, energetic, animated, exuberant, flamboyant, dynamic, bold, intrepid, daring, adventurous, plucky, swashbuckling; romantic, attractive, gallant.

2 *he looked exceptionally dashing* STYLISH, smart, elegant, chic, dapper, spruce, trim, debonair; fashionable, modish, voguish; *informal* trendy, with it, hip, sharp, snazzy, classy, natty, swish, fly, spiffy.

**dastardly** adjective *dated their dastardly plan to kidnap Hayes* WICKED, evil, heinous, villainous, diabolical, fiendish, barbarous, cruel, black, dark, rotten, vile, monstrous, abominable, despicable, degenerate, sordid; bad, base, mean, low, dishonorable, dishonest, unscrupulous, unprincipled; *informal* lowdown, dirty, shady, rascally, crooked; beastly. ANTONYM noble.

USAGE NOTE **dastard, dastardly**

*Dastard* (= coward) is commonly muddled because of the sound association with its harsher rhyme, *bastard*. Although English usage authority H. W. Fowler insisted that *dastard* should be reserved for "one who avoids all personal risk," modern American writers tend to use it as a printable euphemism for the more widely objectionable epithet—e.g.: "Samuel Ramey is the dastard of the piece, the treacherous, lecherous, murderous Assur." (*Los Angeles Times*; May 22, 1994.) British writers, on the other hand, have remained truer to the word's original sense—e.g.: "Last week I moved house from London to Brighton but like a genuine spineless dastard I flatly denied its implications on personal relationships to the last." (*Times* [London]; Feb. 8, 1994.) Recent American dictionaries record one meaning of *dastard* as being "dishonorable, despicable" or "treacherously underhanded." So the new meaning should probably now be considered standard.

Like the noun form, the adjective *dastardly* has been subjected to slipshod extension. Although most dictionaries define it merely as "cowardly," it is now often used as if it meant "sneaky and underhanded; treacherous"—e.g.: "He's b-a-a-a-c-k. Dastardly J. R. Ewing and his oft-manipulated clan rise from TV dustdom to air three times a day on TNN, Cable Channel 37, beginning Monday." (*Tulsa World*; Sept. 27, 1996.) —*BG*

**data** plural noun (often as singular) *a lack of data on the drug's side effects* FACTS, figures, statistics, details, particulars, specifics; information, intelligence, material, input; *informal* info.

USAGE NOTE **data**

Whether you write "data are" or "data is," you're likely to make some readers raise their eyebrows. Technically a plural, *data* has, since the 1940s, been increasingly treated as a mass noun taking a singular verb. But in more or less formal contexts it is preferably treated as a plural—e.g.: "The data are derived from tests performed on expectant mothers." (*Economist*; Mar. 24, 2001.) Many writers use it as a singular, however, risking their credibility with some readers (admittedly a shrinking minority)—e.g.: "No data is offered to suggest that women are being adversely hit by the dearth of articles." (*Globe and Mail* [Canada]; Aug. 24, 1993.)

In the context of computing and related disciplines, the singular use of *data* is common and comfortable—e.g.: "Every time you synchronize your PDA, the data gets backed up to your PC." (PCWorld.com; Feb. 8, 2001.) In one particular use, *data* is rarely treated as a singular: when it begins a clause and is not preceded by the definite article—e.g.: "Data over the last two years suggest that the rate at which gay men get AIDS has finally begun to flatten out." (*New York Times*; Feb. 5, 1989.)

*Datum*, the "true" singular, is sometimes used when a single piece of information is referred to—e.g.: "We accept the law as a necessary datum, but that is not to say that we are required to accept it in abeyance of our critical faculties." (F. R. Leavis, *The*

*Common Pursuit*; 1952.) Still, in nonscientific contexts, *datum* is likely to sound pretentious.

Because *data* can be either a plural count noun or a singular mass noun, both *many data* and *much data* are correct—e.g.:

• "Numerous expert and representative interests are consulted, and many data assembled, often over a long period." (Carleton K. Allen, *Law in the Making*, 7th ed.; 1964.)

• "But much of the data in present personnel files is highly subjective." (William O. Douglas, *Points of Rebellion*; 1970.) As Albert C. Baugh, a historian of the English language, put it in 1962, "A student with one year of Latin [knows] that *data* and *phenomena* are plural." Whatever you do, if you use *data* in a context in which its number becomes known, you'll bother some of your readers. Perhaps 50 years from now—maybe sooner, maybe later—everybody will accept it as a collective. But not yet. —*BG*

---

**date** noun **1** *the only date he has to remember* DAY, day of the month, occasion, time; year; anniversary.

**2** *a later date is suggested for this artifact* AGE, time, period, era, epoch, century, decade, year.

**3** *a lunch date* APPOINTMENT, meeting, engagement, rendezvous, assignation; commitment.

**4** *informal he's my date for tonight* PARTNER, escort, girlfriend, boyfriend, steady.

▸ verb **1** *the sculpture can be dated accurately* ASSIGN A DATE TO, ascertain the date of, put a date on.

**2** *the building **dates from** the sixteenth century* WAS MADE IN, was built in, originates in, comes from, belongs to, goes back to.

**3** *the best films don't date* BECOME OLD-FASHIONED, become outmoded, become dated, show its age.

**4** *informal he's dating Jill* GO OUT WITH, take out, go around with, be involved with, see, go steady with; *dated* woo, court.

PHRASE: **to date** *this is all the information we have to date* SO FAR, thus far, yet, as yet, up to now, till now, until now, up to the present (time), hitherto.

**dated** adjective *the graphics look somewhat dated* OLD-FASHIONED, outdated, outmoded, passé, behind the times, archaic, obsolete, antiquated; unfashionable, unstylish, untrendy; crusty, old world, prehistoric, antediluvian; *informal* old hat, out, uncool. ANTONYM modern.

**daub** verb *he daubed a rock with paint* SMEAR, bedaub, plaster, splash, spatter, splatter, cake, cover, smother, coat.

▸ noun *daubs of paint* SMEAR, smudge, splash, blot, spot, patch, blotch, splotch.

**daunt** verb *wintry conditions did not daunt the runners* DISCOURAGE, deter, demoralize, put off, dishearten, dispirit; intimidate, abash, take aback, throw, cow, overawe, awe, frighten, scare, unman, dismay, disconcert, discompose, perturb, unsettle, unnerve; throw off balance; *informal* rattle, faze, shake up. ANTONYM hearten.

**dawdle** verb **1** *they dawdled over breakfast* LINGER, dally, take one's time, be slow, waste time, idle; delay, procrastinate, stall, dilly-dally, lollygag; *archaic* tarry. See note at LOITER. ANTONYM hurry.

**2** *Ruth dawdled home* AMBLE, stroll, trail, walk slowly, move at a snail's pace; *informal* mosey, toodle. ANTONYMS hurry, speed.

**dawn** noun **1** *we got up at dawn* DAYBREAK, sunrise, first light, daylight; first thing in the morning, sun-up. ANTONYM dusk.

**2** *the dawn of civilization* BEGINNING, start, birth, inception, origination, genesis, emergence, advent, appearance, arrival, dawning, rise, origin, onset; unfolding, development, infancy; *informal* kickoff. ANTONYM end.

▸ verb **1** *Thursday dawned crisp and sunny* BEGIN, break, arrive, emerge. ANTONYM end.

**2** *a bright new future has dawned* BEGIN, start, commence, be born, appear, arrive, emerge; arise, rise, break, unfold, develop. ANTONYM end.

**3** *the reality dawned on him* OCCUR TO, come to, strike, hit, enter someone's mind, register with, enter someone's consciousness, cross someone's mind, suggest itself.

**day** noun **1** *I stayed for **a day*** A TWENTY-FOUR-HOUR PERIOD, twenty-four hours.

**2** *enjoy the beach during the day* DAYTIME, daylight; waking hours. ANTONYM night.

**3** *the leading architect of the day* PERIOD, time, age, era, generation.

**4** *in his day he had great influence* HEYDAY, prime, time; peak, height, zenith, ascendancy; youth, springtime, salad days. ANTONYM decline.

PHRASES: **day after day** *day after day, we learn of new allegations* REPEATEDLY, again and again, over and over (again), time and (time) again, frequently, often, time after time; 'day in, day out', night and day, all the time; persistently, recurrently, constantly, continuously, continually, relentlessly, regularly, habitually, unfailingly, always, oftentimes; *informal* 24-7; *literary* oft, ofttimes.

**day by day 1** *day by day they were forced to retreat* GRADUALLY, slowly, progressively; bit by bit, inch by inch, little by little.

**2** *they follow the news day by day* DAILY, every day, day after day; diurnally.

**daybreak** noun *we'll be packed and ready to go by daybreak* DAWN, crack of dawn, sunrise, first light; daylight, sunup. ANTONYM nightfall.

**daydream** noun **1** *she was lost in **a daydream*** (A) REVERIE, a trance, (a) fantasy, a vision, fancy, (a) brown study; inattentiveness, woolgathering, preoccupation, absorption, self-absorption, absentmindedness, abstraction.

**2** *winning the lottery is just **a daydream*** A DREAM, a pipe dream, a fantasy, a castle in the air, a fond hope; wishful thinking; *informal* pie in the sky.

▸ verb *stop daydreaming!* DREAM, muse, stare into space; fantasize, build castles in the air.

**daylight** noun **1** *do the test in daylight* NATURAL LIGHT, sunlight. ANTONYM darkness.

**2** *she went there only in daylight* DAYTIME, day; broad daylight. ANTONYM nighttime.

**3** *police moved in at daylight* DAWN, daybreak, (the) break of day, (the) crack of dawn, sunrise, first light, early morning, sunup. ANTONYM nightfall.

**daze** verb **1** *he was dazed by his fall* STUN, stupefy; knock unconscious, knock out; *informal* knock the stuffing out of.

**2** *she was dazed by the revelations* ASTOUND, amaze, astonish, startle, dumbfound, stupefy, overwhelm, stagger, shock, confound, bewilder, bedazzle, take aback, shake up; *informal* flabbergast, bowl over, blow away.

▸ noun *she is in a daze* STUPOR, trance, haze; spin, whirl, muddle, jumble.

**dazzle** verb **1** *she was dazzled by the headlights* BLIND TEMPORARILY, deprive of sight.

**2** *I was dazzled by the exhibition* OVERWHELM, overcome, impress, move, stir, affect, touch, awe, overawe, leave speechless, take someone's breath away; spellbind, hypnotize; *informal* bowl over, blow away, knock out.

▸ noun **1** *dazzle can be a problem to sensitive eyes* GLARE, brightness, brilliance, shimmer, radiance, shine.

**2** *the dazzle of the limelight* SPARKLE, glitter, brilliance, glory, splendor, magnificence, glamour; attraction, lure, allure, draw, appeal; *informal* razzle-dazzle, razzmatazz.

**dead** adjective **1** *my parents are dead* PASSED ON/AWAY, expired, departed, gone, no more; late, lost, lamented; perished, fallen, slain, slaughtered, killed, murdered; lifeless, extinct; *informal* (as) dead as a doornail, six feet under, pushing up daisies; *formal* deceased; *euphemistic* with God, asleep. ANTONYMS alive, living.

**2** *patches of dead ground* BARREN, lifeless, bare, desolate, sterile. ANTONYMS fertile, lush.

**3** *a dead language* OBSOLETE, extinct, defunct, disused, abandoned, discarded, superseded, vanished, forgotten; archaic, antiquated, ancient; *literary* of yore. ANTONYMS modern, current.

**4** *the phone was dead* NOT WORKING, out of order, inoperative, inactive, in disrepair, broken, malfunctioning, defective; *informal* kaput, conked out, on the blink, on the fritz, bust, busted. ANTONYM in working order.

**5** *a dead leg* NUMB, numbed, deadened, desensitized, unfeeling; paralyzed, crippled, incapacitated, immobilized, frozen.

**6** *she has dead eyes* EMOTIONLESS, unemotional, unfeeling, impassive, unresponsive, indifferent, dispassionate, inexpressive, wooden, stony, cold; deadpan, flat; blank, vacant. ANTONYM passionate.

**7** *his affection for her was dead* EXTINGUISHED, quashed, stifled; finished, over, gone, no more; a thing of the past, ancient history.

**8** *a dead town* UNEVENTFUL, uninteresting, unexciting, uninspiring, dull, boring, flat, quiet, sleepy, slow, lackluster, lifeless; *informal* one-horse, dullsville. ANTONYM lively.

**9** *dead silence* COMPLETE, absolute, total, utter, out-and-out, thorough, unmitigated. ANTONYM partial.

**10** *a dead shot* UNERRING, unfailing, impeccable, sure, true, accurate, precise; deadly, lethal, bang on. ANTONYM poor.

▸ adverb **1** *he was dead serious* COMPLETELY, absolutely, totally, utterly, deadly, perfectly, entirely, quite, thoroughly; definitely, certainly, positively, categorically, unquestionably, undoubtedly, surely; in every way, one hundred percent.

**2** *flares were seen dead ahead* DIRECTLY, exactly, precisely, immediately, right, straight, due, squarely; *informal* smack dab.

**3** *informal it's dead easy*. See VERY.

**deaden** verb **1** *surgeons tried to deaden the pain* NUMB, dull, blunt, suppress; alleviate, mitigate, diminish, reduce, lessen, ease, soothe, relieve, assuage, kill. ANTONYM intensify.

**2** *the wood paneling deadened any noise* MUFFLE, mute, smother, stifle, dull, dampen; silence, quieten, soften; cushion, buffer, absorb. ANTONYM amplify.

**3** *laughing might deaden us to the moral issue* DESENSITIZE, numb, anesthetize; harden (one's heart), toughen, inure. ANTONYM sensitize.

**deadlock** noun *the negotiations reached a deadlock* STALEMATE, impasse, standoff, logjam; standstill, halt, stop, full stop, dead end.

**deadly** adjective **1** *these drugs can be deadly* FATAL, lethal, mortal, death-dealing, life-threatening; dangerous, injurious, harmful, detrimental, deleterious, unhealthy; noxious, toxic, poisonous; *literary* deathly. ANTONYMS harmless, beneficial.

**2** *deadly enemies* MORTAL, irreconcilable, implacable, unappeasable, unforgiving, remorseless, merciless, pitiless; bitter, hostile, antagonistic.

**3** *I noticed their deadly seriousness* INTENSE, great, marked, extreme. ANTONYM mild.

**4** *he was deadly pale* DEATHLY, ghostly, ashen, white, pallid, wan, pale; ghastly.

**5** *his aim is deadly* UNERRING, unfailing, impeccable, perfect, flawless, faultless; sure, true, precise, accurate, exact, bang on. ANTONYMS inaccurate, poor.

**6** *informal life here can be deadly*. See BORING.

▸ adverb *deadly calm* COMPLETELY, absolutely, totally, utterly, perfectly, entirely, wholly, quite, dead, thoroughly; in every way, one hundred percent, to the hilt.

**deaf** adjective **1** *she is deaf and blind* HEARING IMPAIRED, hard of hearing; *informal* deaf as a post.

**2** *she was* ***deaf to*** *their pleading* UNMOVED BY, untouched by, unaffected by, indifferent to, unresponsive to, unconcerned by; unaware of, oblivious to, incognizant of, impervious to.

**deafen** verb *they were deafened by the explosion* MAKE DEAF, deprive of hearing, impair someone's hearing.

**deafening** adjective *the deafening noise from the construction site* VERY LOUD, very noisy, overloud, ear-splitting, overwhelming, almighty, mighty, tremendous; booming, thunderous, roaring, resounding, resonant, reverberating. ANTONYM quiet.

**deal** noun *completion of the deal* AGREEMENT, understanding, pact, bargain, covenant, contract, treaty; arrangement, compromise, settlement; terms; transaction, sale, account; *Law* indenture.

▸ verb 1 *how to* ***deal with*** *difficult children* COPE WITH, handle, manage, treat, take care of, take charge of, take in hand, sort out, tackle, take on; control; act toward, behave toward.

2 *the article* ***deals with*** *advances in chemistry* CONCERN, be about, have to do with, discuss, consider, cover, pertain to; tackle, study, explore, investigate, examine, review, analyze.

3 *the company* ***deals in*** *high-tech goods* TRADE IN, buy and sell; sell, purvey, supply, stock, market, merchandise; traffic, smuggle; *informal* push, flog.

4 *the cards were dealt* DISTRIBUTE, give out, share out, divide out, hand out, pass out, pass around, dole out, dispense, allocate; *informal* divvy up.

5 *the court dealt a blow to government reforms* DELIVER, administer, dispense, inflict, give, impose; aim.

PHRASE: **a great deal/a good deal** *under a great deal of pressure | there's a good deal of unfinished work here* A LOT, a large amount, a fair amount, much, plenty; *informal* lots, loads, heaps, bags, masses, tons, stacks.

**dealer** noun 1 *an antique dealer* TRADER, merchant, salesman, saleswoman, seller, vendor, purveyor, peddler, hawker; buyer, merchandiser, distributor, supplier, shopkeeper, retailer, wholesaler.

2 *a drug dealer* TRAFFICKER, supplier.

**dealing** noun 1 *dishonest dealing* BUSINESS METHODS, business practices, business, commerce, trading, transactions; behavior, conduct, actions.

2 **(dealings)** *Canada's dealings with China* RELATIONS, relationship, association, connections, contact, intercourse; negotiations, bargaining, transactions; trade, trading, business, commerce, traffic; *informal* truck, doings.

**dean** noun 1 *students must have the consent of the dean* FACULTY HEAD, department head, college head, provost, university official; chief, director, principal, president, chancellor, governor.

2 *the dean of Russian literature* DOYEN/DOYENNE, elder statesman, grande dame, grand old man, veteran.

**dear** adjective 1 *a dear friend* BELOVED, loved, adored, cherished, precious; esteemed, respected, worshiped; close, intimate, bosom, best. ANTONYM hated.

2 *her pictures were too dear to part with* PRECIOUS, treasured, valued, prized, cherished, special.

3 *such a dear man* ENDEARING, adorable, lovable, appealing, engaging, charming, captivating, winsome, lovely, nice, pleasant, delightful, sweet, darling. ANTONYM disagreeable.

4 *the meals are rather dear* EXPENSIVE, costly, high-priced, overpriced, exorbitant, extortionate; *informal* pricey, steep, stiff. ANTONYMS inexpensive, cheap.

▸ noun 1 *don't worry, my dear* DARLING, dearest, love, beloved, sweetheart, sweet, precious, treasure; *informal* sweetie, sugar, honey, hon, baby, pet.

2 *he's such a dear* LOVABLE PERSON; darling, sweetheart, pet, angel, gem, treasure, star.

**dearly** adverb 1 *I love my son dearly* VERY MUCH, a great deal, greatly, deeply, profoundly, extremely; fondly, devotedly, tenderly.

2 *our freedom has been bought dearly* AT GREAT COST, at a high price, with much suffering, with much sacrifice.

**dearth** noun *a dearth of trained specialists* LACK, scarcity, shortage, shortfall, want, deficiency, insufficiency, inadequacy, paucity, sparseness, scantiness, rareness; absence. See note at LACK. ANTONYM surfeit.

**death** noun 1 *her father's death* DEMISE, dying, end, passing, loss of life; eternal rest, quietus; murder, assassination, execution, slaughter, massacre; *informal* curtains; *formal* decease; *archaic* expiry. ANTONYM life.

2 *the death of their dream* END, finish, termination, extinction, extinguishing, collapse, destruction, eradication, obliteration. ANTONYM birth.

3 *Death gestured toward a grave* THE GRIM REAPER, the Dark Angel, the Angel of Death. PHRASE: **put to death** *the czar and his family were put to death* EXECUTE, hang, behead, guillotine, decapitate, electrocute, shoot, gas, crucify, stone; kill, murder, assassinate, eliminate, terminate, exterminate, destroy; *informal* bump off, polish off, do away with, do in, knock off, string up, take out, croak, stiff, blow away, ice, rub out, waste, whack, smoke; *literary* slay.

**deathless** adjective *our deathless souls* IMMORTAL, undying, imperishable, indestructible; enduring, everlasting, eternal; timeless, ageless. ANTONYMS mortal, ephemeral.

**debacle** noun *the Watergate break-in became a debacle of the highest order* FIASCO, failure, catastrophe, disaster, mess, ruin; downfall, collapse, defeat; *informal* foul-up, screw-up, hash, botch, washout, snafu.

**debar** verb 1 *women were debarred from the club* EXCLUDE, ban, bar, disqualify, declare ineligible, preclude, shut out, lock out, keep out, reject, blackball. ANTONYM admit.

2 *the unions were debarred from striking* PREVENT, prohibit, proscribe, disallow, ban, interdict, block, stop; *Law* enjoin, estop. ANTONYM allow.

**debase** verb 1 *the moral code has been debased* DEGRADE, devalue, demean, cheapen, prostitute, discredit, drag down, tarnish, blacken, blemish; disgrace, dishonor, shame; damage, harm, undermine. See notes at DEPRAVED, HUMBLE. ANTONYM enhance.

2 *the added copper debases the silver* REDUCE IN VALUE, reduce in quality, depreciate; contaminate, adulterate, pollute, taint, sully, corrupt; dilute, alloy.

**debatable** adjective *the historical accuracy of this account is debatable* ARGUABLE, disputable, questionable, open to question, controversial, contentious; doubtful, dubious, uncertain, unsure, unclear; borderline, inconclusive, moot, unsettled, unresolved, unconfirmed, undetermined, undecided, up in the air, iffy.

**debate** noun *a debate on the reforms* DISCUSSION, discourse, parley, dialogue; argument, dispute, wrangle, war of words; argumentation, disputation, dissension, disagreement, contention, conflict; negotiations, talks; *informal* confab, powwow.

▸ verb **1** *they will debate the future of rail transport* DISCUSS, talk over/through, talk about, thrash out, hash out, argue, dispute; *informal* kick around, bat around.

**2** *he debated whether to call her* CONSIDER, think over/about, chew over, mull over, ponder, revolve, deliberate, contemplate, muse, meditate; *formal* cogitate.

**debauched** adjective *a fleet commanded by debauched young men* DISSOLUTE, dissipated, degenerate, corrupt, depraved, sinful, unprincipled, immoral; lascivious, lecherous, lewd, lustful, libidinous, licentious, promiscuous, loose, wanton, abandoned; decadent, profligate, intemperate, sybaritic. ANTONYM wholesome.

**debauchery** noun a life of self-absorption and debauchery DISSIPATION, degeneracy, corruption, vice, depravity; immodesty, indecency, perversion, iniquity, wickedness, sinfulness, impropriety, immorality; lasciviousness, salaciousness, lechery, lewdness, lust, promiscuity, wantonness, profligacy; decadence, intemperance, sybaritism; *formal* turpitude.

**debilitate** verb *can't you see how these drugs have debilitated you?* WEAKEN, enfeeble, enervate, devitalize, sap, drain, exhaust, weary, fatigue, prostrate; undermine, impair, indispose, incapacitate, cripple, disable, paralyze, immobilize; *informal* knock out, do in. See note at WEAK. ANTONYM invigorate.

**debility** noun *Sam's obvious debility came as a shock to us* FRAILTY, weakness, enfeeblement, enervation, devitalization, lassitude, exhaustion, weariness, fatigue, prostration; incapacity, indisposition, infirmity, illness, sickness, sickliness; *Medicine* asthenia.

**debonair** adjective *as debonair as Cary Grant* SUAVE, urbane, sophisticated, cultured, self-possessed, self-assured, confident, charming, gracious, courteous, gallant, chivalrous, gentlemanly, refined, polished, well-bred, genteel, dignified, courtly; well-groomed, elegant, stylish, smart, dashing; *informal* smooth, sharp, cool, slick, fly. ANTONYM unsophisticated.

**debris** noun *the irrigation channels were blocked with debris* DETRITUS, refuse, rubbish, waste, litter, scrap, dross, chaff, flotsam and jetsam; rubble, wreckage; remains, scraps, dregs, trash, garbage, dreck, junk.

**debt** noun **1** *he couldn't pay his debts* BILL, account, dues, arrears, charges; financial obligation, outstanding payment; check, tab.

**2** *his debt to the author* INDEBTEDNESS, obligation; gratitude, appreciation, thanks. PHRASES: **in debt** *the medical bills left them hopelessly in debt* OWING MONEY, in arrears, behind with payments, overdrawn; insolvent, bankrupt, ruined; *informal* in the red.

**in someone's debt** *Chris would be forever in his debt* INDEBTED TO, beholden to, obliged to, duty-bound to, honor-bound to, obligated to; grateful (to), thankful (to), appreciative (of).

**debunk** verb *even the most successful hoax will eventually be debunked* EXPLODE, deflate, quash, discredit, disprove, contradict, controvert, invalidate, negate; challenge, call into question, poke holes in; *formal* confute. ANTONYM confirm.

**debut** noun *her acting debut was in a forgettable play in Pittsburgh* FIRST APPEARANCE, first performance, launch, coming out, entrance, premiere, introduction, inception, inauguration; *informal* kickoff.

**decadence** noun **1** *the decadence of modern society* DISSIPATION, degeneracy, debauchery, corruption, depravity, vice, sin, moral decay, immorality; immoderateness, intemperance, licentiousness, self-indulgence, hedonism. ANTONYM morality.

**2** *the decadence of nations* DETERIORATION, fall, decay, degeneration, decline, degradation, retrogression. ANTONYM rise.

**decadent** adjective **1** *decadent city life* DISSOLUTE, dissipated, degenerate, corrupt, depraved, sinful, unprincipled, immoral; licentious, abandoned, profligate, intemperate; sybaritic, hedonistic, pleasure-seeking, self-indulgent.

**2** *the decadent empire* DECLINING, decaying, ebbing, degenerating, deteriorating.

**decamp** verb **1** *he decamped with the profits* ABSCOND, make off, run off/away, flee, bolt, take flight, disappear, vanish, steal away, sneak away, escape, make a run for it, leave, depart; *informal* split, scram, vamoose, cut and run, do a disappearing act, head for the hills, go AWOL, take a powder, go on the lam.

**2** *archaic the armies decamped* STRIKE ONE'S TENTS, break camp, move on.

**decant** verb *the wine was decanted into a flask* POUR OFF, draw off, siphon off, drain, tap; transfer.

**decapitate** verb *traitors were publicly decapitated* BEHEAD, guillotine, put on the block.

**decay** verb **1** *the corpses had decayed* DECOMPOSE, rot, putrefy, go bad, go off, spoil, fester, perish, deteriorate; degrade, break down, molder, shrivel, wither.

**2** *the cities continue to decay* DETERIORATE, degenerate, decline, go downhill, slump, slide, go to rack and ruin, go to seed; disintegrate, fall to pieces, fall into disrepair; fail, collapse; *informal* go to pot, go to the dogs, go into/down the toilet.

▸ noun **1** *signs of decay* DECOMPOSITION, putrefaction, festering; rot, mold, mildew, fungus.

**2** *tooth decay* ROT, corrosion, decomposition; caries, cavities, holes.

**3** *the decay of American values* DETERIORATION, degeneration, debasement, degradation, decline, weakening, atrophy; crumbling, disintegration, collapse.

**decease** noun *formal her decease was imminent* DEATH, dying, demise, end, passing, loss of life, quietus; *informal* curtains, croaking, snuffing; *archaic* expiry.

**deceased** adjective *formal his deceased relatives* DEAD, expired, departed, gone, no more, passed on/away; late, lost, lamented; perished, fallen, slain, slaughtered, killed, murdered; lifeless, extinct; *informal* (as) dead as a doornail, six feet under, pushing up daisies; *euphemistic* with God, asleep.

**deceit** noun **1** *her endless deceit* DECEPTION, deceitfulness, duplicity, double-dealing, fraud, cheating, trickery, chicanery, deviousness, slyness, wiliness, guile, bluff, lying, pretense, treachery; *informal* crookedness, monkey business, monkeyshines. ANTONYM honesty.

**2** *their life is a deceit* SHAM, fraud, pretense, hoax, fake, blind, artifice; trick, stratagem, device, ruse, scheme, dodge, machination, deception, subterfuge; cheat, swindle; *informal* con, setup, scam, flimflam, bunco. See note at FICTION.

**deceitful** adjective **1** *a deceitful woman* DISHONEST, untruthful, mendacious, insincere, false, disingenuous, untrustworthy, unscrupulous, unprincipled, two-faced, duplicitous, double-dealing, underhanded, crafty, cunning, sly, scheming, calculating, treacherous, Machiavellian, sneaky, tricky, foxy, crooked.

**2** *a deceitful allegation* FRAUDULENT, counterfeit, fabricated, invented, concocted, made up, trumped up, untrue, false, bogus, fake, spurious, fallacious, deceptive, misleading; *euphemistic* economical with the truth.

**deceive** verb **1** *she was deceived by a con man* SWINDLE, defraud, cheat, trick, hoodwink, hoax, dupe, take in, mislead, delude, fool, outwit, lead on, inveigle, beguile, double-cross, gull; *informal* con, bamboozle, do, gyp, diddle, rip off, shaft, pull a fast one on, take for a ride, pull the wool over someone's eyes, sucker, snooker, stiff.

**2** *he deceived her with another woman* BE UNFAITHFUL TO, cheat on, betray, play someone false; *informal* two-time.

**decelerate** verb *decelerate when approaching the curve* SLOW DOWN, slow up, ease up, slack up, reduce speed, brake.

**decency** noun **1** *standards of taste and decency* PROPRIETY, decorum, good taste, respectability, dignity, correctness, good form, etiquette; morality, virtue, modesty, delicacy.

**2** *he didn't have the decency to tell me* COURTESY, politeness, good manners, civility, respect; consideration, thoughtfulness, tact, diplomacy.

**decent** adjective **1** *a decent burial* PROPER, correct, appropriate, apt, fitting, suitable; respectable, dignified, decorous, seemly; nice, tasteful; conventional, accepted, standard, traditional, orthodox; comme il faut.

**2** *a very decent fellow* HONORABLE, honest, trustworthy, dependable; respectable, upright, clean-living, virtuous, good; obliging, helpful, accommodating, unselfish, generous, kind, thoughtful, considerate; neighborly, hospitable, pleasant, agreeable, amiable. ANTONYMS dishonest, disobliging.

**3** *a job with decent pay* SATISFACTORY, reasonable, fair, acceptable, adequate, sufficient, ample; not bad, all right, tolerable, passable, suitable; *informal* OK, okay, up to snuff. ANTONYM unsatisfactory.

**deception** noun **1** *they obtained money by deception* DECEIT, deceitfulness, duplicity, double-dealing, fraud, cheating, trickery, chicanery, deviousness, slyness, wiliness, guile, bluff, lying, pretense, treachery; *informal* crookedness, monkey business, monkeyshines.

**2** *it was all a deception* TRICK, deceit, sham, fraud, pretense, hoax, fake, blind, artifice; stratagem, device, ruse, scheme, dodge, machination, subterfuge; cheat, swindle; *informal* con, setup, scam, flimflam, bunco.

**deceptive** adjective **1** *distances are very deceptive* MISLEADING, illusory, illusionary, specious; ambiguous; distorted; *literary* illusive.

**2** *deceptive practices* DECEITFUL, duplicitous, fraudulent, counterfeit, underhanded, cunning, crafty, sly, guileful, scheming, treacherous, Machiavellian; disingenuous, untrustworthy, unscrupulous, unprincipled, dishonest, insincere, false; *informal* crooked, sharp, shady, sneaky, tricky, foxy.

USAGE NOTE **deceptively**

---

**Deceptively** belongs to a very small set of words whose meaning is genuinely ambiguous in that it can be used in similar contexts to mean both one thing and also its complete opposite. A *deceptively smooth surface* is one that appears smooth but in fact is not smooth at all, while a *deceptively spacious room* is one that does not look spacious but is in fact *more* spacious than it appears. But what is a *deceptively steep gradient*? Or a person who is described as *deceptively strong*? To avoid confusion, use with caution (or not at all) unless the context makes clear in what way the thing modified is not what it first appears to be.

---

**decide** verb **1** *she decided to become a writer* RESOLVE, determine, make up one's mind, make a decision; elect, choose, opt, plan, aim, have the intention, have in mind.

**2** *research to decide a variety of questions* SETTLE, resolve, determine, work out, answer; *informal* sort out, figure out.

**3** *the court is to decide the case* ADJUDICATE, arbitrate, adjudge, judge; hear, try, examine; sit in judgment on, pronounce on, give a verdict on, rule on.

**decided** adjective **1** *they have a decided advantage* DISTINCT, clear, marked, pronounced, obvious, striking, noticeable, unmistakable, patent, manifest; definite, certain, positive, emphatic, undeniable, indisputable, unquestionable; assured, guaranteed.

**2** *he was very decided* DETERMINED, resolute, firm, strong-minded, strong-willed, emphatic, dead set, unwavering, unyielding, unbending, inflexible, unshakable, unrelenting, obstinate, stubborn, rock-ribbed.

**3** *our future is decided* SETTLED, established, resolved, determined, agreed, designated, chosen, ordained, prescribed; set, fixed; *informal* sewn up, wrapped up.

**decidedly** adverb *they were decidedly hostile to one another* DISTINCTLY, clearly, markedly, obviously, noticeably, unmistakably, patently, manifestly; definitely, certainly, positively, absolutely, downright, undeniably, unquestionably; extremely, exceedingly, exceptionally, particularly, especially, very; *informal* terrifically, devilishly, ultra, mega, majorly, ever so, dead, real, mighty, awful.

**deciding** adjective *the deciding factor may be the size of your budget* DETERMINING, decisive, conclusive, key, pivotal, crucial, critical, significant, major, chief, principal, prime. See note at CRUCIAL.

**decipher** verb **1** *he deciphered the code* DECODE, decrypt, break, work out, solve, interpret, unscramble, translate; make sense of, get to the bottom of, unravel; *informal* crack, figure out. ANTONYM encode.

**2** *the writing was hard to decipher* MAKE OUT, discern, perceive, read, follow, fathom, make sense of, interpret, understand, comprehend, grasp.

**decision** noun **1** *they came to a decision* RESOLUTION, conclusion, settlement, commitment, resolve, determination; choice, option, selection.

**2** *the judge's decision* VERDICT, finding, ruling, recommendation, judgment, judgment call, pronouncement, adjudication, order, rule, resolve; findings, results; *Law* determination.

**3** *his order had a ring of decision* DECISIVENESS, determination, resolution, resolve, firmness; strong-mindedness, purpose, purposefulness.

**decisive** adjective **1** *a decisive man* RESOLUTE, firm, strong-minded, strong-willed, determined; purposeful, forceful, dead set, unwavering, unyielding, unbending, inflexible, unshakable, obstinate, stubborn, rock-ribbed. See note at RESOLUTE.

**2** *the decisive factor* DECIDING, conclusive, determining; key, pivotal, critical, crucial, significant, influential, major, chief, principal, prime.

**deck** verb **1** *the street was decked with streamers* DECORATE, bedeck, adorn, ornament, trim, trick out, garnish, cover, hang, festoon, garland, swathe, wreathe; embellish, beautify, prettify, enhance, grace, set off; *informal* get up, do up, tart up; *literary* bejewel, bedizen, caparison.

**2** *Ingrid was* ***decked out*** *in blue* DRESS (UP), clothe, attire, garb, robe, drape, turn out, fit out, outfit, costume; *informal* doll up, get up, do up, gussy up.

**3** *he got up from the table and decked me.* See HIT verb sense 1.

▸ noun *they were lounging on the deck* TERRACE, balcony, veranda, porch, patio.

**declaim** verb **1** *a preacher declaiming from the pulpit* MAKE A SPEECH, give an address, give a lecture, deliver a sermon; speak, hold forth, orate, preach, lecture, sermonize, moralize; *informal* sound off, spout, speechify, preachify.

**2** *they loved to hear Garfield declaim his poetry* RECITE, read aloud, read out loud, read out; deliver; *informal* spout.

**3** *he* ***declaimed against*** *the evils of society* SPEAK OUT AGAINST, rail against, inveigh against, fulminate against, rage against, thunder against; rant about, expostulate against; condemn, criticize, attack, decry, disparage.

**declamation** noun *he delivered a passionate declamation* SPEECH, address, lecture, sermon, homily, discourse, oration, recitation, disquisition, monologue.

**declaration** noun **1** *they issued a declaration* ANNOUNCEMENT, statement, communication, pronouncement, proclamation, communiqué, edict, advisory.

**2** *the declaration of war* PROCLAMATION, notification, announcement, revelation, disclosure, broadcasting.

**3** *a declaration of faith* ASSERTION, profession, affirmation, acknowledgment, revelation, disclosure, manifestation, confirmation, testimony, validation, certification, attestation; pledge, avowal, vow, oath, protestation.

**declare** verb **1** *she declared her political principles* PROCLAIM, announce, state, reveal, air, voice, articulate, express, vent, set forth, publicize, broadcast; *informal* come out with, shout from the rooftops. See note at ANNOUNCE.

**2** *he declared that they were guilty* ASSERT, maintain, state, affirm, contend, argue, insist, hold, profess, claim, avow, swear; *formal* aver.

**3** *his speech* ***declared*** *him* ***to be*** *a gentleman* SHOW TO BE, reveal as, confirm as, prove to be, attest to someone's being.

**decline** verb **1** *she declined all invitations* TURN DOWN, reject, brush aside, refuse, rebuff, spurn, repulse, dismiss; forgo, deny oneself, pass up; abstain from, say no to; *informal* give the thumbs down to, give something a miss. ANTONYM accept.

**2** *the number of traders has declined* DECREASE, reduce, lessen, diminish, dwindle, contract, shrink, fall off, tail off; drop, fall, go down, slump, plummet; *informal* nosedive, take a header, crash. ANTONYM increase.

**3** *standards steadily declined* DETERIORATE, degenerate, decay, crumble, collapse, slump, slip, slide, go downhill, worsen; weaken, wane, ebb; *informal* go to pot, go to the dogs, go into/down the toilet. ANTONYM rise.

▸ noun **1** *a decline in profits* REDUCTION, decrease, downturn, downswing, devaluation, depreciation, diminution, ebb, drop, slump, plunge; *informal* nosedive, crash.

**2** *forest decline* DETERIORATION, degeneration, degradation, shrinkage; death, decay.

PHRASE: **in decline** *sadly, our volunteer program is in decline* DECLINING, decaying, crumbling, collapsing, failing; disappearing, dying, moribund; *informal* on its last legs, on the way out.

**decompose** verb **1** *the carcasses will not decompose in these subzero temperatures* DECAY, rot, putrefy, go bad, go off, spoil, fester, perish, deteriorate; degrade, break down, molder, shrivel, wither.

2 *some minerals decompose rapidly* BREAK UP, fragment, disintegrate, crumble, dissolve; break down, decay.

**decomposition** noun 1 *an advanced state of decomposition* DECAY, putrefaction, putrescence, putridity.

2 *the decomposition of granite* DISINTEGRATION, dissolution; breaking down, decay.

**decor** noun *the decor in the family room is just awful* DECORATION, furnishing, ornamentation; color scheme.

**decorate** verb 1 *the door was decorated with a wreath* ORNAMENT, adorn, trim, embellish, garnish, furnish, enhance, grace, prettify; festoon, garland, bedeck.

2 *he started to decorate his home* PAINT, WALLPAPER, paper; refurbish, furbish, renovate, redecorate; *informal* do up, spruce up, do over, fix up, give something a facelift.

3 *he was decorated for courage* GIVE A MEDAL TO, honor, cite, reward.

**decoration** noun 1 *a ceiling with rich decoration* ORNAMENTATION, adornment, trimming, embellishment, garnishing, gilding; beautification, prettification; enhancements, enrichments, frills, accessories, trimmings, finery, frippery.

2 *internal decoration.* See DECOR.

3 *a Christmas tree decoration* ORNAMENT, bauble, trinket, knickknack, spangle; trimming, tinsel.

4 *a decoration won on the battlefield* MEDAL, award, star, ribbon; laurel, trophy, prize.

**decorative** adjective *mirrors were used as decorative features* ORNAMENTAL, embellishing, garnishing; fancy, ornate, attractive, pretty, showy. ANTONYM functional.

**decorous** adjective *he behaved toward her in a decorous manner* PROPER, seemly, decent, becoming, befitting, tasteful; correct, appropriate, suitable, fitting; tactful, polite, well-mannered, genteel, respectable; formal, restrained, modest, demure, gentlemanly, ladylike. ANTONYM unseemly.

**decorum** noun 1 *he had acted with decorum* PROPRIETY, seemliness, decency, good taste, correctness; politeness, courtesy, good manners; dignity, respectability, modesty, demureness. ANTONYM impropriety.

2 *a breach of decorum* ETIQUETTE, protocol, good form, custom, convention; formalities, niceties, punctilios, politeness. ANTONYM impropriety.

**decoy** noun *a decoy to distract their attention* LURE, bait, red herring; enticement, inducement, temptation, attraction, carrot; snare, trap.

▸ verb *he was decoyed to the mainland* LURE, entice, allure, tempt; entrap, snare, trap.

**decrease** verb 1 *pollution levels decreased* LESSEN, reduce, drop, diminish, decline, dwindle, fall off; die down, abate, subside, tail off, ebb, wane; plummet, plunge. ANTONYM increase.

2 *decrease the amount of fat in your body* REDUCE, lessen, lower, cut (back/down), curtail; slim down, tone down, deplete, minimize, slash. ANTONYM increase.

▸ noun *a decrease in crime* REDUCTION, drop, decline, downturn, cut, falloff, cutback, diminution, ebb, wane. ANTONYM increase.

**decree** noun 1 *a presidential decree* ORDER, edict, command, commandment, mandate, proclamation, dictum, fiat; law, bylaw, statute, act; *formal* ordinance.

2 *a court decree* JUDGMENT, verdict, adjudication, ruling, resolution, decision.

▸ verb *he decreed that a stadium should be built* ORDER, command, rule, dictate, pronounce, proclaim, ordain; direct, decide, determine.

**decrepit** adjective 1 *a decrepit old man* FEEBLE, infirm, weak, weakly, frail; disabled, incapacitated, crippled, doddering, tottering; old, elderly, aged, ancient, senile; *informal* past it, over the hill, no spring chicken. See note at WEAK. ANTONYMS strong, fit.

2 *a decrepit house* DILAPIDATED, rickety, run-down, tumbledown, beat-up, ramshackle, derelict, ruined, in (a state of) disrepair, gone to rack and ruin; battered, decayed, crumbling, deteriorating. ANTONYM sound.

**decry** verb *she decried the double standards* DENOUNCE, condemn, criticize, censure, attack, rail against, run down, pillory, lambaste, vilify, revile; disparage, deprecate, cast aspersions on; *informal* slam, blast, knock. ANTONYM praise.

**dedicate** verb 1 *she dedicated her life to the sick* DEVOTE, commit, pledge, give, surrender, sacrifice; set aside, allocate, consign.

2 *a book dedicated to his muse* INSCRIBE, address; assign.

3 *the chapel was dedicated to the Virgin Mary* DEVOTE, assign; bless, consecrate, sanctify; *formal* hallow.

**dedicated** adjective 1 *a dedicated socialist* COMMITTED, devoted, staunch, firm, steadfast, resolute, unwavering, loyal, faithful, true, dyed-in-the-wool; wholehearted, enthusiastic, single-minded, keen, earnest, zealous, ardent, passionate, fervent; *informal* card-carrying, hardcore. ANTONYM indifferent.

2 *data is accessed by a dedicated machine* EXCLUSIVE, custom built, customized.

**dedication** noun 1 *athletic excellence requires dedication* COMMITMENT, application, diligence, industry, resolve, enthusiasm, zeal, conscientiousness, perseverance, persistence, tenacity, drive, staying power; hard work, effort. ANTONYMS apathy, laziness.

2 *her dedication to the job* DEVOTION, commitment, loyalty, adherence, allegiance. ANTONYM indifference.

3 *the book has a dedication to her husband* INSCRIPTION, address, message.

4 *the dedication of the church* BLESSING, consecration, sanctification, benediction.

**deduce** verb *we can deduce from the evidence that Harding* *was indeed present at the time of the murder* CONCLUDE, reason, work out, infer; glean, divine, intuit, understand, assume, presume, conjecture, surmise, reckon; *informal* figure out.

**deduct** verb *we'll deduct ten percent from the total* SUBTRACT, take away, take off, debit, dock, discount; abstract, remove, knock off. ANTONYM add.

**deduction** noun **1** *the deduction of tax* SUBTRACTION, removal, debit, abstraction.

**2** *gross pay, before deductions* SUBTRACTION.

**3** *she was right in her deduction* CONCLUSION, inference, supposition, hypothesis, assumption, presumption; suspicion, conviction, belief, reasoning; *archaic* illation.

**deed** noun **1** *kindly deeds* ACT, action; feat, exploit, achievement, accomplishment, endeavor, undertaking, enterprise.

**2** *unity must be established in deed and word* FACT, reality, actuality.

**3** *a deed to the property* LEGAL DOCUMENT, contract, indenture, instrument.

**deem** verb *many of these campaigns have been deemed successful* CONSIDER, regard as, judge, adjudge, hold to be, view as, see as, take for, class as, count, find, suppose, reckon; think, believe to be, feel to be; *formal* esteem.

**deep** adjective **1** *a deep ravine* CAVERNOUS, yawning, gaping, huge, extensive; bottomless, fathomless, unfathomable. ANTONYM shallow.

**2** *two inches deep* IN DEPTH, downward, inward, in vertical extent.

**3** *deep affection* INTENSE, heartfelt, wholehearted, deep-seated, deep-rooted; sincere, genuine, earnest, enthusiastic, great. ANTONYMS insincere, superficial.

**4** *a deep sleep* SOUND, heavy, intense.

**5** *a deep thinker* PROFOUND, serious, philosophical, complex, weighty; abstruse, esoteric, recondite, mysterious, obscure; intelligent, intellectual, learned, wise, scholarly; discerning, penetrating, perceptive, insightful.

**6** *he was deep in concentration* RAPT, absorbed, engrossed, preoccupied, immersed, lost, gripped, intent, engaged.

**7** *a deep mystery* OBSCURE, mysterious, secret, unfathomable, opaque, abstruse, recondite, esoteric, enigmatic, arcane; puzzling, baffling, mystifying, inexplicable.

**8** *his deep voice* LOW-PITCHED, low, bass, rich, powerful, resonant, booming, sonorous. ANTONYM high.

**9** *a deep red* DARK, intense, rich, strong, bold, warm. ANTONYM light.

▸ noun **1** *literary creatures of deep* SEA, ocean; *informal* drink, briny; *literary* profound.

**2** *the deep of night* MIDDLE, midst; depths, dead, thick.

▸ adverb **1** *I dug deep* FAR DOWN, way down, to a great depth.

**2** *he brought them deep into woodland* FAR, a long way, a great distance.

**deepen** verb **1** *his love for her had deepened* GROW, increase, intensify, strengthen, heighten, amplify, augment; *informal* step up.

**2** *they deepened the hole* DIG OUT, dig deeper, excavate.

**deeply** adverb *I am deeply grateful* PROFOUNDLY, greatly, enormously, extremely, very much; strongly, powerfully, intensely, keenly, acutely; thoroughly, completely, entirely; *informal* well, seriously, majorly.

**deface** verb *the kids were caught defacing a school building with spray paint* VANDALIZE, disfigure, mar, spoil, ruin, sully, damage, blight, impair, trash.

**de facto** adverb *the republic is de facto two states* IN PRACTICE, in effect, in fact, in reality, really, actually. ANTONYM de jure.

▸ adjective *de facto control* ACTUAL, real, effective. ANTONYM de jure.

**defamation** noun *he sued the newspaper for defamation* LIBEL, slander, calumny, character assassination, vilification; scandalmongering, malicious gossip, aspersions, muckraking, abuse; disparagement, denigration; smear, slur; *informal* mudslinging.

**defamatory** adjective *the candidates abused the debate forum by exchanging defamatory remarks* LIBELOUS, slanderous, calumnious, scandalmongering, malicious, vicious, backbiting, muckraking; abusive, disparaging, denigratory, insulting; *informal* mudslinging, bitchy, catty.

**defame** verb *she has defamed my character* LIBEL, slander, malign, cast aspersions on, smear, traduce, give someone a bad name, run down, speak ill of, vilify, besmirch, stigmatize, disparage, denigrate, discredit, decry; *informal* do a hatchet job on, drag through the mud, slur; *informal* badmouth, dis; *formal* calumniate. See note at MALIGN. ANTONYM compliment.

**default** noun **1** *the incidence of defaults on loans* NONPAYMENT, failure to pay, bad debt.

**2** *Browne lost the case by default* INACTION, omission, lapse, neglect, negligence, disregard; failure to appear, absence, nonappearance.

▸ verb **1** *the customer defaulted* FAIL TO PAY, not pay, renege, back out; go back on one's word; *informal* welsh, bilk.

**2** *the program will default to its own style* REVERT, select automatically.

**defeat** verb **1** *the army that defeated the rebels* BEAT, conquer, win against, triumph over, get the better of, vanquish; rout, trounce, overcome, overpower, crush, subdue; *informal* lick, thrash, whip, wipe the floor with, make mincemeat of, clobber, slaughter, demolish, cream, skunk, nose out.

**2** *these complex plans defeat their purpose* THWART, frustrate, foil, ruin, scotch, debar, derail; obstruct, impede, hinder, hamper; *informal* put the kibosh on, stymie, scuttle.

**3** *the motion was defeated* REJECT, overthrow, throw out, dismiss, outvote, turn down; *informal* give the thumbs down.

**4** *how to make it work defeats me* BAFFLE, perplex, bewilder, mystify, bemuse, confuse, confound, throw; *informal* beat, flummox, faze, stump.

▸ noun **1** *a crippling defeat* LOSS, conquest, vanquishment; rout, trouncing; downfall; *informal* thrashing, hiding, drubbing, licking, pasting, massacre, slaughter. ANTONYM victory.

**2** *the defeat of his plans* FAILURE, downfall, collapse, ruin; rejection, frustration, abortion, miscarriage; undoing, reverse. ANTONYM success.

**defeatist** adjective *a defeatist attitude* PESSIMISTIC, fatalistic, negative, cynical, despondent, despairing, hopeless, bleak, gloomy. ANTONYM optimistic.

▸ noun PESSIMIST, fatalist, cynic, prophet of doom, doomster; misery, killjoy, worrier; *informal* quitter, wet blanket, worrywart. ANTONYM optimist.

**defecate** verb *nobody wants to see dogs defecating on the beach* EXCRETE FECES, have a bowel movement, have a BM, evacuate one's bowels, relieve oneself, go to the bathroom; *informal* do/go number two, poop, take a crap, take a dump.

**defect**[1] noun *he spotted a defect in my work* FAULT, flaw, imperfection, deficiency, weakness, weak spot, inadequacy, shortcoming, limitation, failing; kink, deformity, blemish; mistake, error; *informal* glitch; *Computing* bug.

**defect**[2] verb *his chief intelligence officer defected* DESERT, change sides, turn traitor, rebel, renege; abscond, quit, jump ship, escape; break faith; secede from, revolt against; *Military* go AWOL; *Politics* cross the floor; *literary* forsake.

**defection** noun *his defection to the United States* DESERTION, absconding, decamping, flight; apostasy, secession; treason, betrayal, disloyalty; *literary* perfidy.

**defective** adjective **1** *a defective seat belt* FAULTY, flawed, imperfect, shoddy, inoperative, malfunctioning, out of order, unsound; in disrepair, broken; *informal* on the blink, on the fritz. ANTONYM perfect.

**2** *these methods are defective* LACKING, wanting, deficient, inadequate, insufficient.

**defector** noun *Cuban defectors sought refuge in Miami* DESERTER, turncoat, traitor, renegade, Judas, quisling; *informal* rat.

**defend** verb **1** *a fort built to defend the border* PROTECT, guard, safeguard, secure, shield; fortify, garrison, barricade; uphold, support, watch over. ANTONYM attack.

**2** *he defended his policy* JUSTIFY, vindicate, argue for, support, make a case for, plead for; excuse, explain. ANTONYMS attack, criticize.

**3** *the manager defended his players* SUPPORT, back, stand by, stick up for, stand up for, argue for, champion, endorse; *informal* throw one's weight behind. ANTONYM criticize.

**defendant** noun *does the defendant have counsel?* ACCUSED, prisoner (at the bar); appellant, litigant, respondent; suspect. ANTONYM plaintiff.

**defender** noun **1** *defenders of the environment* PROTECTOR, guard, guardian, preserver; custodian, watchdog, keeper, overseer.

**2** *a defender of colonialism* SUPPORTER, upholder, backer, champion, advocate, apologist, proponent, exponent, promoter; adherent, believer.

**defense** noun **1** *the defense of the fortress* PROTECTION, guarding, security, fortification; resistance, deterrent.

**2** *the enemy's defenses* BARRICADE, fortification; fortress, keep, rampart, bulwark, bastion.

**3** *he spoke in defense of his boss* VINDICATION, justification, support, advocacy, endorsement; apology, explanation, exoneration.

**4** *more spending on defense* ARMAMENTS, weapons, weaponry, arms; the military, the armed forces.

**5** *the prisoner's defense* VINDICATION, explanation, mitigation, justification, rationalization, excuse, alibi, reason; plea, pleading; testimony, declaration, case.

**defenseless** adjective **1** *defenseless animals* VULNERABLE, helpless, powerless, impotent, weak, susceptible. ANTONYM resilient.

**2** *the country is wholly defenseless* UNDEFENDED, unprotected, unguarded, unshielded, unarmed; vulnerable, assailable, exposed, insecure. ANTONYM well-protected.

**defensible** adjective **1** *a defensible attitude* JUSTIFIABLE, arguable, tenable, defendable, supportable; plausible, sound, sensible, reasonable, rational, logical; acceptable, valid, legitimate; excusable, pardonable, understandable. ANTONYM untenable.

**2** *a defensible territory* SECURE, safe, fortified; invulnerable, impregnable, impenetrable, unassailable. ANTONYM vulnerable.

**defensive** adjective **1** *troops in defensive positions* DEFENDING, protective; wary, watchful.

**2** *a defensive response* SELF-JUSTIFYING, oversensitive, prickly, paranoid, neurotic; *informal* uptight.

**defer**[1] verb *the committee will defer its decision* POSTPONE, put off, delay, hold over, hold off (on), put back; shelve, suspend, stay, put over, table; *informal* put on ice, put on the back burner, back-burner, put in cold storage, mothball. See note at POSTPONE.

**defer**[2] verb *they* ***deferred to*** *Joseph's judgment* YIELD TO, submit to, give way to, give in to, surrender to, capitulate to, acquiesce to; respect, honor.

**deference** noun *his writings show excessive deference to the wealthy* RESPECT, respectfulness, dutifulness; submissiveness, submission, obedience, surrender, accession, capitulation, acquiescence, complaisance, obeisance. See note at HONOR. ANTONYM disrespect.

**deferential** adjective *the hotel's deferential treatment of its elite clientele* RESPECTFUL, humble, obsequious; dutiful, obedient, submissive, subservient, yielding, acquiescent, complaisant, compliant, tractable, biddable, docile.

**deferment** noun *they sought a temporary deferment of the loan payments* POSTPONEMENT, deferral, suspension, delay, adjournment, interruption, pause; respite, stay, moratorium, reprieve, grace.

**defiance** noun *he wasn't used to such outspoken defiance* RESISTANCE, opposition, noncompliance, disobedience, insubordination, dissent, recalcitrance, subversion, rebellion; contempt, disregard, scorn, insolence, truculence. ANTONYM obedience.

**defiant** adjective *he is defiant in the face of critics* INTRANSIGENT, resistant, obstinate, uncooperative, noncompliant, recalcitrant; obstreperous, truculent, dissenting, disobedient, insubordinate, subversive, rebellious, mutinous, feisty. ANTONYM cooperative.

**deficiency** noun **1** *a vitamin deficiency* INSUFFICIENCY, lack, shortage, want, dearth, inadequacy, deficit, shortfall; scarcity, paucity, absence, deprivation, shortness. ANTONYM surplus.

**2** *the team's big deficiency* DEFECT, fault, flaw, imperfection, weakness, weak point, inadequacy, shortcoming, limitation, failing. ANTONYM strength.

**deficient** adjective **1** *a diet deficient in vitamin A* LACKING, wanting, inadequate, insufficient, limited, poor, scant; low.

**2** *deficient leadership* DEFECTIVE, faulty, flawed, inadequate, imperfect, shoddy, weak, inferior, unsound, substandard, second-rate, poor.

**deficit** noun *a large deficit in the federal budget* SHORTFALL, deficiency, shortage, debt, arrears; negative amount, loss. ANTONYM surplus.

**defile** verb **1** *her capacity for love had been defiled* SPOIL, sully, mar, impair, debase, degrade; poison, taint, tarnish; destroy, ruin. ANTONYM purify.

**2** *the sacred bones were defiled* DESECRATE, profane, violate; contaminate, pollute, debase, degrade, dishonor. See note at POLLUTE. ANTONYM sanctify.

**3** archaic *she was defiled by a married man* RAPE, violate; *literary* ravish; *dated* deflower.

**definable** adjective *she had no definable illness* DETERMINABLE, ascertainable, known, definite, clear-cut, precise, exact, specific.

**define** verb **1** *the dictionary defines it succinctly* EXPLAIN, expound, interpret, elucidate, describe, clarify; give the meaning of, put into words.

**2** *he defined the limits of the law* DETERMINE, establish, fix, specify, designate, decide, stipulate, set out; demarcate, delineate.

**3** *the farm buildings defined against the fields* OUTLINE, delineate, silhouette.

**definite** adjective **1** *a definite answer* EXPLICIT, specific, express, precise, exact, clear-cut, direct, plain, outright; fixed, established, confirmed, concrete. See note at DEFINITIVE. ANTONYM vague.

**2** *definite evidence* CERTAIN, sure, positive, conclusive, decisive, firm, concrete, unambiguous, unequivocal, clear, unmistakable, proven; guaranteed, assured, cut and dried. ANTONYMS uncertain, ambiguous.

**3** *she had a definite dislike for dogs* UNMISTAKABLE, certain, unequivocal, unambiguous, undisputed, decided, marked, distinct. ANTONYMS vague, slight.

**4** *a definite geographical area* FIXED, marked, demarcated, delimited, stipulated, particular. ANTONYM indeterminate.

**definitely** adverb *it was definitely a case of exploiting child labor* CERTAINLY, surely, for sure, unquestionably, without doubt, without question, undoubtedly, indubitably, positively, absolutely; undeniably, unmistakably, plainly, clearly, obviously, patently, palpably, transparently, unequivocally.

**definition** noun **1** *the definition of "intelligence"* MEANING, denotation, sense; interpretation, explanation, elucidation, description, clarification, illustration.

**2** *the definition of the picture* CLARITY, visibility, sharpness, crispness, acuteness; resolution, focus, contrast.

**definitive** adjective **1** *a definitive decision* CONCLUSIVE, final, ultimate; unconditional, unqualified, absolute, categorical, positive, definite.

**2** *the definitive guide* AUTHORITATIVE, exhaustive, best, finest, consummate; classic, standard, recognized, accepted, official.

**deflate** verb **1** *he deflated the tires* LET DOWN, flatten, void; puncture. ANTONYM inflate.

**2** *the balloon deflated* GO DOWN, collapse, shrink, contract. ANTONYMS inflate, expand.

**3** *the news had deflated him* SUBDUE, humble, cow, chasten; dispirit, dismay, discourage, dishearten; squash, crush, bring down, take the wind out of someone's sails, knock the stuffing out of. ANTONYM aggrandize.

**4** *the budget deflated the economy* REDUCE, slow down, diminish; devalue, depreciate, depress. ANTONYM inflate.

**deflect** verb **1** *she wanted to deflect attention from herself* TURN ASIDE/AWAY, divert, avert, sidetrack; distract, draw away; block, parry, fend off, stave off.

**2** *the ball deflected off the wall* BOUNCE, glance, ricochet, carom; diverge, deviate, veer, swerve, slew.

**deform** verb *shoes that will not cramp or deform the toes* DISFIGURE, bend out of shape, contort, buckle, warp; damage, impair.

**deformed** adjective *a deformed skeleton* MISSHAPEN, distorted, dysmorphic, malformed, contorted, out of shape; twisted, crooked, warped, buckled, gnarled; crippled, humpbacked, hunchbacked, disfigured, grotesque; injured, damaged, mutilated, mangled.

**deformity** noun *a brace used to correct spinal deformities* MALFORMATION, misshapenness, distortion, crookedness; imperfection, abnormality, irregularity; disfigurement; defect, flaw, blemish.

**defraud** verb *they defrauded thousands of investors* SWINDLE, cheat, rob, embezzle; deceive, dupe, hoodwink, double-cross, trick; *informal* con, do, sting, diddle, rip off, shaft, bilk, rook, gyp, pull a fast one on, put one over on, sucker, snooker, stiff.

**deft** adjective *a deft piece of footwork | his deft handling of the situation* SKILLFUL, adept, adroit, dexterous, agile, nimble, handy; able, capable, skilled, proficient, accomplished, expert, polished, slick, professional, masterly; clever, shrewd, astute, canny, sharp; *informal* nifty, neat. ANTONYM clumsy.

**defunct** adjective *the original contract is defunct* DISUSED, unused, inoperative, nonfunctioning, unusable, obsolete; no longer existing, discontinued; extinct. ANTONYMS working, extant.

**defy** verb **1** *he defied local law* DISOBEY, go against, flout, fly in the face of, disregard, ignore; break, violate, contravene, breach, infringe. ANTONYM obey.

**2** *his actions defy belief* ELUDE, escape, defeat; frustrate, thwart, baffle.

**3** *he glowered, defying her to mock him* CHALLENGE, dare.

**degeneracy** noun *the sexual degeneracy and intellectual deterioration of the time* CORRUPTION, decadence, moral decay, dissipation, dissolution, profligacy, vice, immorality, sin, sinfulness, ungodliness; debauchery; *formal* turpitude.

**degenerate** adjective **1** *a degenerate form of classicism* DEBASED, degraded, corrupt, impure; *formal* vitiated. ANTONYM pure.

**2** *her degenerate brother* CORRUPT, decadent, dissolute, dissipated, debauched, reprobate, profligate; sinful, ungodly, immoral, unprincipled, amoral, dishonorable, disreputable, unsavory, sordid, low, ignoble. See note at DEPRAVED. ANTONYM moral.

▸ noun *a group of degenerates* REPROBATE, debauchee, profligate, libertine, roué.

▸ verb **1** *their quality of life had degenerated* DETERIORATE, decline, slip, slide, worsen, lapse, slump, go downhill, regress, retrogress; go to rack and ruin; *informal* go to pot, go to the dogs, hit the skids, go into/down the toilet. ANTONYM improve.

**2** *the muscles started to degenerate* WASTE (AWAY), atrophy, weaken.

**degradation** noun **1** *poverty brings with it degradation* HUMILIATION, shame, loss of self-respect, abasement, indignity, ignominy.

**2** *the degradation of women* DEMEANING, debasement, discrediting.

**3** *the degradation of the tissues* DETERIORATION, degeneration, atrophy, decay; breakdown.

**degrade** verb **1** *prisons should not degrade prisoners* DEMEAN, debase, cheapen, devalue; shame, humiliate, humble, mortify, abase, dishonor; dehumanize, brutalize. See note at HUMBLE. ANTONYM dignify.

**2** *the polymer will not degrade* BREAK DOWN, deteriorate, degenerate, decay.

**degraded** adjective **1** *I feel so degraded* HUMILIATED, demeaned, cheapened, cheap, ashamed. ANTONYM proud.

**2** *his degraded sensibilities* DEGENERATE, corrupt, depraved, dissolute, dissipated, debauched, immoral, base, sordid. ANTONYMS pure, moral.

**degrading** adjective *accepting our assistance should not be a degrading experience* HUMILIATING, demeaning, shameful, mortifying, ignominious, undignified, inglorious, wretched.

**degree** noun **1** *to a high degree* LEVEL, standard, grade, mark; amount, extent, measure; magnitude, intensity, strength; proportion, ratio.

**2** *she completed her degree in three years* DIPLOMA, academic program; baccalaureate, bachelor's, master's, doctorate, Ph.D. PHRASES: **by degrees** *rivalries and prejudice were by degrees fading out* GRADUALLY, little by little, bit by bit, inch by inch, step by step, slowly; piecemeal.

**to a degree** *without proper instruction, you can operate the machinery only to a degree* TO SOME EXTENT, to a certain extent, up to a point, somewhat.

**dehydrate** verb **1** *alcohol dehydrates the skin* DRY (OUT), desiccate, dehumidify, effloresce. See note at DRY. ANTONYM hydrate.

**2** *frogs can dehydrate quickly* DRY UP/OUT, lose water.

**deify** verb **1** *she was deified by the early Romans* WORSHIP, revere, venerate, reverence, hold sacred; immortalize.

**2** *he was deified by the press* IDOLIZE, lionize, extol, hero-worship; idealize, glorify, aggrandize, put on a pedestal. ANTONYM demonize.

**deign** verb *he'll never deign to return to his father's house* CONDESCEND, stoop, lower oneself, demean oneself, humble oneself; consent, vouchsafe; *informal* come down from one's high horse.

**deity** noun *everyone cracked up when Coolidge said she worshiped a deity named Grover* GOD, goddess, divine being, supreme being, divinity, immortal; creator, demiurge; godhead.

**dejected** adjective *the dejected look on Thomas's face* DOWNCAST, downhearted, despondent, disconsolate, dispirited, crestfallen, disheartened; depressed, crushed, desolate, heartbroken, in the doldrums, sad, unhappy, doleful, melancholy, miserable, woebegone, forlorn, wretched, glum, gloomy; *informal* blue, down in/at the mouth, down in the dumps, in a blue funk. ANTONYM cheerful.

**delay** verb **1** *we were delayed by the traffic* DETAIN, hold up, make late, slow up/down, bog down; hinder, hamper, impede, obstruct.

**2** *they delayed no longer* LINGER, dally, drag one's feet, be slow, hold back, dawdle, waste time; procrastinate, stall, hang fire, mark time, temporize, hesitate, dither, shilly-shally, dilly-dally; *archaic* tarry. ANTONYM hurry.

**3** *he may delay the cut in interest rates* POSTPONE, put off, defer, hold over, shelve, suspend, stay; reschedule, put over, push back, table; *informal* put on ice, back-burner, put on the back burner, put in cold storage. See note at POSTPONE. ANTONYM advance.

▸ noun **1** *drivers will face lengthy delays* HOLDUP, wait, detainment; hindrance, impediment, obstruction, setback.

**2** *the delay of his trial* POSTPONEMENT, deferral, deferment, stay, respite; adjournment.

**3** *I set off without delay* PROCRASTINATION, stalling, hesitation, dithering, dallying, lollygagging, dawdling.

**delectable** adjective **1** *a delectable meal* DELICIOUS, mouthwatering, appetizing, flavorful, toothsome, palatable; succulent, luscious, tasty; *informal* scrumptious, delish, yummy, finger-licking, lip-smacking, melt-in-your-mouth. ANTONYM unpalatable.

**2** *the delectable Ms. Davis* DELIGHTFUL, pleasant, lovely, captivating, charming, enchanting, appealing, beguiling; beautiful, attractive, ravishing, gorgeous, stunning, alluring, sexy, seductive, desirable, luscious; *informal* divine, heavenly, dreamy. ANTONYM unattractive.

**delectation** noun *chiefly humorous they had all manner of goodies for our delectation* ENJOYMENT, gratification, delight, pleasure, satisfaction, relish; entertainment, amusement, titillation.

**delegate** noun *union delegates* REPRESENTATIVE, envoy, emissary, commissioner, agent, deputy, commissary; spokesperson, spokesman, spokeswoman; ambassador, plenipotentiary.

▸ verb **1** *she must delegate routine tasks* ASSIGN, entrust, pass on, hand on/over, turn over, devolve, depute, transfer.

**2** *they were delegated to negotiate with the Slavs* AUTHORIZE, commission, depute, appoint, nominate, mandate, empower, charge, choose, designate, elect.

**delegation** noun **1** *the delegation from South Africa* DEPUTATION, legation, mission, diplomatic mission, commission; delegates, representatives, envoys, emissaries, deputies; contingent.

**2** *the delegation of tasks to others* ASSIGNMENT, entrusting, giving, devolution, deputation, transference.

**delete** verb *the offending paragraph was deleted* REMOVE, cut out, take out, edit out, expunge, excise, eradicate, cancel; cross out, strike out, blue-pencil, ink out, scratch out, obliterate, white out; rub out, erase, efface, wipe out, blot out; *Printing* dele. ANTONYM add.

**deleterious** adjective *the deleterious effects of smoking* HARMFUL, damaging, detrimental, injurious; adverse, disadvantageous, unfavorable, unfortunate, undesirable, bad. ANTONYM beneficial.

**deliberate** adjective **1** *a deliberate attempt to provoke him* INTENTIONAL, calculated, conscious, intended, planned, studied, knowing, willful, purposeful, purposive, premeditated, preplanned; voluntary, volitional. ANTONYMS accidental, unintentional.

**2** *small, deliberate steps* CAREFUL, cautious; measured, regular, even, steady. ANTONYM hasty.

**3** *a deliberate worker* METHODICAL, systematic, careful, painstaking, meticulous, thorough. ANTONYM careless.

▸ verb *she* ***deliberated on*** *his words* THINK ABOUT/OVER, ponder, consider, contemplate, reflect on, muse on, meditate on, ruminate on, mull over, give thought to, brood over, dwell on, think on.

**deliberately** adverb **1** *he deliberately hurt me* INTENTIONALLY, on purpose, purposely, by design, knowingly, wittingly, consciously, purposefully; willfully; *Law* with malice aforethought.

**2** *he walked deliberately down the aisle* CAREFULLY, cautiously, slowly, steadily, evenly.

**deliberation** noun **1** *after much deliberation, I accepted* THOUGHT, consideration, reflection, contemplation, meditation, rumination; *formal* cogitation.

**2** *he replaced the glass with deliberation* CARE, carefulness, caution, steadiness.

**delicacy** noun **1** *the fabric's delicacy* FINENESS, exquisiteness, daintiness, airiness; flimsiness, gauziness, silkiness.

**2** *the children's delicacy* SICKLINESS, ill health, frailty, fragility, weakness, debility; infirmity, valetudinarianism.

**3** *the delicacy of the situation* DIFFICULTY, trickiness; sensitivity, ticklishness, awkwardness.

**4** *treat this matter with delicacy* CARE, sensitivity, tact, discretion, diplomacy, subtlety, sensibility.

**5** *an Australian delicacy* CHOICE FOOD, gourmet food, treat, luxury, specialty.

**delicate** adjective **1** *delicate embroidery* FINE, exquisite, intricate, dainty; flimsy, gauzy, filmy, floaty, diaphanous, wispy, insubstantial. ANTONYMS coarse, crude.

**2** *a delicate shade of blue* SUBTLE, soft, muted; pastel, pale, light. ANTONYMS bold, lurid, vibrant.

**3** *delicate china cups* FRAGILE, breakable, frail; *formal* frangible. ANTONYMS strong, durable.

**4** *his wife is delicate* SICKLY, unhealthy, frail, feeble, weak, debilitated; unwell, infirm; *formal* valetudinarian. ANTONYMS strong, robust, healthy.

**5** *a delicate issue* DIFFICULT, tricky, sensitive, ticklish, awkward, problematic, touchy, prickly, thorny; embarrassing; *informal* sticky, dicey.

**6** *the matter required delicate handling* CAREFUL, sensitive, tactful, diplomatic, discreet, kid-glove. ANTONYMS inept, clumsy.

**7** *his delicate palate* DISCRIMINATING, discerning; FASTIDIOUS, fussy, finicky, dainty; *informal* picky, choosy, persnickety.

**8** *a delicate mechanism* SENSITIVE, precision, precise.

**delicious** adjective **1** *Ezio's delicious sausages* DELECTABLE, mouthwatering, appetizing, tasty, flavorful, toothsome, palatable; succulent, luscious; *informal* scrumptious, delish, yummy, finger-licking, nummy, lip-smacking, melt-in-your-mouth. ANTONYM unpalatable.

**2** *a delicious languor stole over her* DELIGHTFUL, exquisite, lovely, pleasurable, pleasant; *informal* heavenly, divine. ANTONYM unpleasant.

**delight** verb **1** *her manners delighted him* PLEASE GREATLY, charm, enchant, captivate, entrance, thrill; gladden, gratify, appeal to; entertain, amuse, divert; *informal* send, tickle pink, bowl over. ANTONYMS dismay, disgust, displease.

**2** *Meg* ***delighted in*** *his touch* TAKE PLEASURE IN, revel in, luxuriate in, wallow in, glory in; adore, love, relish, savor, lap up; *informal* get a kick out of, get a thrill out of, get a charge out of, dig. ANTONYMS loathe, dislike.

▸ noun *she squealed with delight* PLEASURE, happiness, joy, glee, gladness; excitement, amusement; bliss, rapture, elation, euphoria. ANTONYM displeasure.

**delighted** adjective *a delighted child | the Fitzgeralds were delighted with the kitchen remodeling* PLEASED, glad, happy, thrilled, overjoyed, ecstatic, elated; on cloud nine, walking on air, in seventh heaven, jumping for joy; enchanted, charmed; amused, diverted; gleeful; *informal* over the moon, tickled pink, as pleased as punch, on top of the world, blissed out, on a high.

**delightful** adjective **1** *a delightful evening* PLEASANT, lovely, pleasurable, enjoyable; amusing, entertaining, diverting; gratifying, satisfying; marvelous, wonderful, splendid, sublime, thrilling; *informal* great, super, fabulous, fab, terrific, heavenly, divine, grand, brilliant, peachy, ducky.

**2** *the delightful Sally* CHARMING, enchanting, captivating, bewitching, appealing; sweet, endearing, cute, lovely, adorable, delectable, delicious, gorgeous, ravishing, beautiful, pretty; *informal* dreamy, divine.

**delineate** verb **1** *the aims of the study as delineated by the boss* DESCRIBE, set forth/out, present, outline, sketch, depict, represent; map out, define, specify, identify.

**2** *a section delineated in red pen* OUTLINE, trace, block in, mark (out/off), delimit.

**delinquency** noun **1** *teenage delinquency* CRIME, wrongdoing, lawbreaking, lawlessness, misconduct, misbehavior; misdemeanors, offenses, misdeeds.

**2** *formal**grave delinquency on the host's part* NEGLIGENCE, dereliction of duty, irresponsibility.

**delinquent** adjective **1** *delinquent teenagers* LAWLESS, lawbreaking, criminal; errant, badly behaved, troublesome, difficult, unruly, disobedient, uncontrollable. ANTONYM well-behaved.

**2** *formal delinquent parents face tough penalties* NEGLIGENT, neglectful, remiss, irresponsible, lax, slack, derelict. ANTONYM dutiful.

▸ noun *young delinquents* OFFENDER, wrongdoer, malefactor, lawbreaker, culprit, criminal; hooligan, vandal, mischief-maker, ruffian, hoodlum, lowlife, punk; young offender.

**delirious** adjective **1** *she was delirious but had lucid intervals* INCOHERENT, raving, babbling, irrational; feverish, frenzied; deranged, demented, unhinged, mad, insane, out of one's mind.

**2** *the crowd was delirious during the concert* ECSTATIC, euphoric, elated, thrilled, overjoyed, beside oneself, walking on air, on cloud nine, in seventh heaven, carried away, transported, rapturous; hysterical, wild, frenzied; *informal* blissed out, over the moon, on a high.

**delirium** noun **1** *she had fits of delirium* DERANGEMENT, dementia, madness, insanity; incoherence, irrationality, hysteria, feverishness, hallucination. ANTONYM lucidity.

**2** *the delirium of desire* ECSTASY, rapture, transports, wild emotion, passion, wildness, excitement, frenzy, feverishness, fever; euphoria, elation.

**deliver** verb **1** *the parcel was delivered to his house* BRING, take, convey, carry, transport, courier; send, dispatch, remit.

**2** *the money was* ***delivered up*** *to the official* HAND OVER, turn over, make over, sign over; surrender, give up, yield, cede; consign, commit, entrust, trust.

**3** *he was delivered from his enemies* SAVE, rescue, free, liberate, release, extricate, emancipate, redeem.

**4** *the court delivered its verdict* UTTER, give, make, read, broadcast; pronounce, announce, declare, proclaim, hand down, return, set forth.

**5** *she delivered a deadly blow to his head* ADMINISTER, deal, inflict, give; *informal* land.

**6** *he delivered the ball* THROW, pitch, hurl, launch, cast, lob, aim.

**7** *the trip delivered everything she wanted* PROVIDE, supply, furnish.

**8** *we must* ***deliver on*** *our commitments* FULFILL, live up to, carry out, carry through, make good on.

**9** *she returned home to deliver her child* GIVE BIRTH TO, bear, have, bring into the world, birth; *informal* drop; *dated* be delivered of.

**deliverance** noun **1** *their deliverance from prison* LIBERATION, release, delivery, discharge, rescue, emancipation; salvation; *informal* bailout.

**2** *the tone he adopted for such deliverances* UTTERANCE, statement, announcement, pronouncement, declaration, proclamation; lecture, speech.

**delivery** noun **1** *the delivery of the goods* CONVEYANCE, carriage, transportation, transport, distribution; dispatch, remittance; haulage, shipment.

**2** *we get several deliveries a day* CONSIGNMENT, load, shipment.

**3** *the midwife had assisted at four deliveries* BIRTH, childbirth; *formal* parturition.

**4** *her delivery was stilted* SPEECH, pronunciation, enunciation, articulation, elocution; utterance, recitation, recital, execution.

**delude** verb *Arthur's children were convinced that his young bride was deluding him* MISLEAD, deceive, fool, take in, trick, dupe, hoodwink, gull, lead on; *informal* con, pull the wool over someone's eyes, lead up the garden path, take for a ride, sucker, snooker.

**deluge** noun **1** *homes were swept away by the deluge* FLOOD, torrent, spate.

**2** *the deluge turned the field into a swamp* DOWNPOUR, torrential rain; thunderstorm, thundershower, rainstorm, cloudburst.

**3** *a deluge of complaints* BARRAGE, volley; flood, torrent, avalanche, stream, spate, rush, outpouring, niagara.

▸ verb **1** *homes were deluged by the rains* FLOOD, inundate, submerge, swamp, drown.

**2** *we have been deluged with calls* INUNDATE, overwhelm, overrun, flood, swamp, snow under, engulf, bombard.

**delusion** noun *was her belief in his fidelity just a delusion?* MISAPPREHENSION, misconception, misunderstanding, mistake, error, misinterpretation, misconstruction, misbelief; fallacy, illusion, fantasy.

**deluxe** adjective *deluxe accommodations* LUXURIOUS, luxury, sumptuous, palatial, opulent, lavish; grand, high-class, quality, exclusive, choice, fancy; expensive, costly, upscale, upmarket; high-end, top-line, top-notch, five-star; *informal* plush, posh, classy, ritzy, swanky, pricey, swank. ANTONYMS basic, cheap.

**delve** verb **1** *she* ***delved into*** *her pocket* RUMMAGE (AROUND/ABOUT) IN, search, hunt in, scrabble around in, root around/about in, ferret (about/around) in, fish about/around in, dig into/in; go through, rifle through.

**2** *we must* ***delve into*** *the matter more deeply* INVESTIGATE, inquire into, probe, explore, research, look into, go into.

**demagogue** noun *he was drawn into a circle of campus demagogues* RABBLE-ROUSER, agitator, political agitator, soapbox orator, firebrand, fomenter, provocateur.

**demand** noun **1** *I gave in to her demands* REQUEST, call, command, order, dictate, ultimatum, stipulation.

**2** *the demands of a young family* REQUIREMENT, need, desire, wish, want; claim, imposition.

**3** *there is a big demand for such toys* MARKET, call, appetite, desire.

▸ verb **1** *workers demanded wage increases* CALL FOR, ask for, request, push for, hold out for; insist on, claim.

**2** *Harvey demanded that I tell him the truth* ORDER, command, enjoin, urge; *literary* bid.

**3** *"Where is she?" he demanded* ASK, inquire, question, interrogate; challenge.

**4** *an activity demanding detailed knowledge* REQUIRE, need, necessitate, call for, involve, entail.

**5** *they demanded complete anonymity* INSIST ON, stipulate, make a condition of; expect, look for.

PHRASE: **in demand** *the clerk at Buchanan's said that red kitchen accessories were suddenly in demand* SOUGHT-AFTER, desired, coveted, wanted, requested; marketable, desirable, popular, all the rage, at a premium, big, trendy, hot.

**demanding** adjective **1** *a demanding task* DIFFICULT, challenging, taxing, exacting, tough, hard, onerous, burdensome, formidable; arduous, uphill, rigorous, grueling, back-breaking, punishing. ANTONYMS easy, effortless.

**2** *a demanding child* NAGGING, clamorous, importunate, insistent; trying, tiresome, hard to please; *informal* high-maintenance. ANTONYM easygoing.

**demarcation** noun **1** *clear demarcation of function* SEPARATION, distinction, differentiation, division, delimitation, definition.

**2** *territorial demarcations* BOUNDARY, border, borderline, frontier; dividing line, divide.

**demean** verb *such actions demean him in the eyes of the public* DEBASE, lower, degrade, discredit, devalue; cheapen, abase, humble, humiliate, disgrace, dishonor. See note at HUMBLE. ANTONYM dignify.

**demeanor** noun *his normally calm demeanor* MANNER, air, attitude, appearance, look; bearing, carriage; behavior, conduct; *formal* comportment.

**demented** adjective *many of her patients were too demented to benefit from group therapy* MAD, insane, deranged, out of one's mind, crazed, lunatic, unbalanced, unhinged, disturbed, non compos mentis; *informal* crazy, mental, psycho, off one's rocker, nutty, around the bend, raving mad, batty, cuckoo, loopy, loony, bananas, screwy, touched, gaga, not all there, out to lunch, bonkers, crackers, cracked, buggy, nutso, squirrelly, wacko. ANTONYM sane.

**dementia** noun *her failing memory is not necessarily a symptom of dementia* MENTAL ILLNESS, madness, insanity, derangement, lunacy.

**demise** noun **1** *her tragic demise* DEATH, dying, passing, loss of life, end, quietus; *formal* decease; *archaic* expiry. ANTONYM birth.

**2** *the demise of the Ottoman empire* END, breakup, disintegration, fall, downfall, collapse. ANTONYM start.

**democracy** noun *a democracy in Iraq is quite unlikely for now or any time soon* REPRESENTATIVE GOVERNMENT, elective government; self-government, government by the people; republic, commonwealth. ANTONYM dictatorship.

**democratic** adjective *a young democratic government* ELECTED, representative, popular, parliamentary; egalitarian, classless; self-governing, autonomous, republican.

**demolish** verb **1** *they demolished the building* KNOCK DOWN, pull down, tear down, bring down, destroy, flatten, raze (to the ground), level, bulldoze, topple; blow up; dismantle, disassemble. See note at DESTROY. ANTONYM construct.

**2** *he demolished her credibility* DESTROY, ruin, wreck; refute, disprove, discredit, overturn, explode; *informal* poke holes in. ANTONYMS confirm, strengthen.

3 *informal* *our team was demolished.* See TROUNCE.

4 *informal* *she demolished a bagel.* See DEVOUR sense 1.

**demon** noun 1 *the demons from hell* DEVIL, fiend, evil spirit; incubus, succubus. ANTONYM angel.

2 *the man was a demon* MONSTER, ogre, fiend, devil, brute, savage, beast, barbarian, animal. ANTONYM saint.

3 *she's a demon on the tennis court* PRO, ace, expert, genius, master, virtuoso, maestro, past master, marvel; star; *informal* hotshot, whiz, buff.

**demonstrable** adjective *the demonstrable links between French and American art* VERIFIABLE, provable, attestable; verified, proven, confirmed; obvious, clear, clear-cut, evident, apparent, manifest, patent, distinct, noticeable; unmistakable, undeniable.

**demonstrate** verb 1 *his findings demonstrate that boys commit more crimes than girls* SHOW, indicate, determine, establish, prove, confirm, verify, corroborate, substantiate.

2 *she was asked to demonstrate quilting* GIVE A DEMONSTRATION OF, show how something is done; display, show, illustrate, exemplify, demo.

3 *his work demonstrated an analytical ability* REVEAL, bespeak, indicate, signify, signal, denote, show, display, exhibit; bear witness to, testify to; imply, intimate, give away.

4 *they demonstrated against the government* PROTEST, rally, march; stage a sit-in, picket, strike, walk out; mutiny, rebel.

**demonstration** noun 1 *a dubious demonstration of God's existence* PROOF, substantiation, confirmation, affirmation, corroboration, verification, validation; evidence, indication, witness, testament.

2 *a demonstration of woodcarving* EXHIBITION, presentation, display, exposition, teach-in, demo, expo.

3 *his paintings are a demonstration of his talent* MANIFESTATION, indication, sign, mark, token, embodiment; expression.

4 *an anti-racism demonstration* PROTEST, march, rally, lobby, sit-in; stoppage, strike, walkout, picket (line); *informal* demo.

**demonstrative** adjective 1 *a very demonstrative family* EXPRESSIVE, open, forthcoming, communicative, unreserved, emotional, effusive, gushing; affectionate, cuddly, loving, warm, friendly, approachable; *informal* touchy-feely, lovey-dovey, huggy. ANTONYM reserved.

2 *the successes are demonstrative of their skill* INDICATIVE, suggestive, illustrative.

3 *demonstrative evidence of his theorem* CONVINCING, definite, positive, telling, conclusive, certain, decisive; incontrovertible, irrefutable, undeniable, indisputable, unassailable. ANTONYM inconclusive.

**demoralize** verb *the celebratory fuss made about young Browning's promotion has demoralized many of the older employees* DISHEARTEN, dispirit, deject, cast down, depress, dismay, daunt, discourage, unman, unnerve, crush, shake, throw, cow, subdue; break someone's spirit, knock the stuffing out of. ANTONYM hearten.

**demote** verb *Calvin was demoted to second lieutenant* DOWNGRADE, relegate, declass, reduce in rank; depose, unseat, displace, oust; *Military* cashier. ANTONYM promote.

**demur** verb *Steve demurred when the suggestion was made* OBJECT, take exception, take issue, protest, cavil, dissent; voice reservations, be unwilling, be reluctant, balk, think twice; drag one's heels, refuse; *informal* boggle, kick up a fuss.

▸ noun *they accepted without demur* OBJECTION, protest, protestation, complaint, dispute, dissent, opposition, resistance; reservation, hesitation, reluctance, disinclination; doubts, qualms, misgivings, second thoughts; a murmur, a word. See note at QUALMS.

**demure** adjective *a demure Victorian miss* MODEST, unassuming, meek, mild, reserved, retiring, quiet, shy, bashful, diffident, reticent, timid, shrinking, coy; decorous, decent, seemly, ladylike, respectable, proper, virtuous, pure, innocent, chaste; sober, sedate, staid, prim, goody-goody, straitlaced. ANTONYM brazen.

**den** noun 1 *the mink left its den* LAIR, set, earth, burrow, hole, dugout, covert, shelter, hiding place, hideout.

2 *a notorious drinking den* HAUNT, site, nest, pit, hole; hotbed; *informal* joint, dive.

3 *he scribbled a letter in his den* STUDY, studio, library; family room, living room; sanctum, retreat, sanctuary, hideaway.

**denial** noun 1 *the reports met with a denial* CONTRADICTION, refutation, rebuttal, repudiation, disclaimer; negation, dissent.

2 *the denial of insurance to certain people* REFUSAL, withholding; rejection, rebuff, repulse, veto, turndown; *formal* declination.

3 *the denial of worldly values* RENUNCIATION, eschewal, repudiation, disavowal, rejection, abandonment, surrender, relinquishment.

**denigrate** verb *it amused him to denigrate his guests* DISPARAGE, belittle, deprecate, decry, cast aspersions on, criticize, attack; speak ill of, give someone a bad name, defame, slander, libel; run down, abuse, insult, revile, malign, vilify, slur; *informal* badmouth, dis, pull to pieces. ANTONYM extol.

**denizen** noun *formal* *the denizens of Grant's Hollow were a quirky lot* INHABITANT, resident, townsman, townswoman, native, local; occupier, occupant, dweller; *archaic* burgher.

**denomination** noun 1 *a Christian denomination* RELIGIOUS GROUP, sect, cult, movement, body, branch, persuasion, order, school; church.

2 *they demanded bills in small denominations* VALUE, unit, size.

**denote** verb 1 *the headdresses denoted warriors* DESIGNATE, indicate, be a mark of, signify, signal, symbolize, represent, mean; typify, characterize, distinguish, mark, identify.

2 *his manner denoted an inner strength* SUGGEST, point to,

smack of, indicate, show, reveal, intimate, imply, convey, betray, bespeak, spell.

**denouement** noun **1** *the film's denouement* FINALE, final scene, epilogue, coda, end, ending, finish, close; culmination, climax, conclusion, resolution, solution. ANTONYM beginning.

**2** *the debate had an unexpected denouement* OUTCOME, upshot, consequence, result, end; *informal* payoff. ANTONYM origin.

**denounce** verb **1** *the Pope denounced abortion* CONDEMN, criticize, attack, censure, decry, revile, vilify, discredit, damn, reject; proscribe; malign, rail against, run down, slur; *informal* knock, slam, hit out at, lay into; *formal* castigate. ANTONYM praise.

**2** *he was denounced as a traitor* EXPOSE, betray, inform on; incriminate, implicate, cite, name, accuse.

**dense** adjective **1** *a dense forest* THICK, close-packed, tightly packed, closely set, close-set, crowded, crammed, compact, solid, tight; overgrown, jungly, impenetrable, impassable. ANTONYM sparse.

**2** *dense smoke* THICK, heavy, opaque, soupy, murky, smoggy; concentrated, condensed. ANTONYMS thin, light.

**3** *informal they were dense enough to believe me* STUPID, unintelligent, ignorant, brainless, mindless, foolish, slow, witless, simpleminded, empty-headed, vacuous, vapid, idiotic, imbecilic; *informal* thick, dim, moronic, dumb, dopey, dozy, wooden-headed, lamebrained, birdbrained, pea-brained; daft. See note at STUPID. ANTONYM clever.

**deny** verb **1** *the report was denied by witnesses* CONTRADICT, controvert, repudiate, challenge, counter, contest, oppose, rebut; *informal* poke holes in; *formal* gainsay. ANTONYM confirm.

**2** *he denied the request* REFUSE, turn down, reject, rebuff, repulse, decline, veto, dismiss; *informal* give the thumbs down to, give the red light to, nix. ANTONYM accept.

**3** *she had to deny her parents* RENOUNCE, eschew, repudiate, disavow, disown, wash one's hands of, reject, discard, cast aside, abandon, give up; *formal* forswear; *literary* forsake.

**deodorant** noun *an underarm deodorant* ANTIPERSPIRANT, body spray, perfume, scent; *informal* roll-on.

**depart** verb **1** *James departed after lunch* LEAVE, go (away), withdraw, absent oneself, abstract oneself, quit, exit, decamp, retreat, retire; make off, run off/away; set off/out, get underway, be on one's way; *informal* make tracks, clear off/out, take off, split. ANTONYM arrive.

**2** *the budget departed from the norm* DEVIATE, diverge, digress, drift, stray, veer; differ, vary.

**departed** adjective *her dear departed father* DEAD, expired, gone, no more, passed on/away; perished, fallen; *informal* six feet under, pushing up daisies; *formal* deceased; with God, asleep.

**department** noun **1** *the public health department* DIVISION, section, sector, unit, branch, arm, wing; office, bureau, agency, ministry.

**2** *the food is Kay's department* DOMAIN, territory, province, area, line; responsibility, duty, function, business, affair, charge, task, concern; *informal* baby, bag, bailiwick.

**departure** noun **1** *he tried to delay her departure* LEAVING, going, leave-taking, withdrawal, exit, egress, retreat.

**2** *a departure from the norm* DEVIATION, divergence, digression, shift; variation, change.

**3** *an exciting departure for filmmakers* CHANGE, innovation, novelty, rarity.

**depend** verb **1** *her career **depends on** a good reference* BE CONTINGENT ON, be conditional on, be dependent on, hinge on, hang on, rest on, rely on; be decided by.

**2** *my family **depends on** me* RELY ON, lean on; count on, bank on, trust (in), have faith in, believe in; pin one's hopes on.

**dependable** adjective *a dependable worker* RELIABLE, trustworthy, trusty, faithful, loyal, unfailing, sure, steadfast, stable; honorable, sensible, responsible.

**dependence** noun See DEPENDENCY.

**dependency** noun **1** *her **dependency on** her husband* DEPENDENCE ON, reliance on; need for.

**2** *the association of retirement with dependency* HELPLESSNESS, dependence, weakness, defenselessness, vulnerability. ANTONYM independence.

**3** *drug dependency* ADDICTION, dependence, reliance; craving, compulsion, fixation, obsession; abuse.

**dependent** adjective **1** *your placement is **dependent on** her decision* CONDITIONAL ON, contingent on, based on; subject to, determined by, influenced by.

**2** *the army is **dependent on** volunteers* RELIANT ON, relying on, counting on; sustained by.

**3** *she is **dependent on** drugs* ADDICTED TO, reliant on; *informal* hooked on.

**4** *he is ill and dependent* RELIANT, needy; helpless, weak, infirm, invalid, incapable; debilitated, disabled.

▸ noun *providing for his dependents* CHILD, minor; ward, charge, protégé; relative; **(dependents)** offspring, progeny.

**depict** verb **1** *the painting depicts the Last Supper* PORTRAY, represent, picture, illustrate, delineate, reproduce, render; draw, paint; *literary* limn.

**2** *the process depicted by Darwin's theory* DESCRIBE, detail, relate; present, set forth, set out, outline, delineate; represent, portray, characterize.

**deplete** verb *the food supply has been depleted* EXHAUST, use up, consume, expend, drain, empty, milk; reduce, decrease, diminish; slim down, cut back. ANTONYM augment.

**depletion** noun *the depletion of our natural resources* EXHAUSTION, use, consumption, expenditure; reduction, decrease, diminution; impoverishment.

**deplorable** adjective **1** *your conduct is deplorable* DISGRACE-

FUL, shameful, dishonorable, unworthy, inexcusable, unpardonable, unforgivable; reprehensible, despicable, abominable, contemptible, execrable, heinous, beyond the pale. ANTONYM admirable.

**2** *the garden is in a deplorable state* LAMENTABLE, regrettable, unfortunate, wretched, atrocious, awful, terrible, dreadful, diabolical; sorry, poor, inadequate; *informal* appalling, dire, abysmal, woeful, lousy; *formal* grievous. ANTONYM excellent.

**deplore** verb **1** *we deplore violence* ABHOR, find unacceptable, frown on, disapprove of, take a dim view of, take exception to; detest, despise; condemn, denounce. ANTONYMS applaud, admire.

**2** *he deplored their lack of flair* REGRET, lament, mourn, rue, bemoan, bewail, complain about, grieve over, sigh over. ANTONYM applaud.

**deploy** verb **1** *forces were deployed at strategic points* POSITION, station, post, place, install, locate, situate, site, establish; base; distribute, dispose.

**2** *she deployed all her skills* USE, utilize, employ, take advantage of, exploit; bring into service, call on, turn to, resort to.

**deport** verb **1** *they were fined and deported* EXPEL, banish, exile, transport, expatriate, extradite, repatriate; evict, oust, throw out; *informal* kick out, boot out, send packing. ANTONYM admit.

**2** *archaic he deported himself with dignity.* See BEHAVE sense 1.

**deportment** noun *unprofessional deportment* BEHAVIOR, conduct, performance; manners, practices, actions.

**depose** verb **1** *the president was deposed* OVERTHROW, unseat, dethrone, topple, remove, supplant, displace; dismiss, oust, drum out, throw out, expel, eject; *informal* chuck out, boot out, get rid of, show someone the door.

**2** *Law a witness deposed that he had seen me* SWEAR, testify, attest, assert, declare, claim.

**deposit** noun **1** *a thick deposit of ash* ACCUMULATION, sediment; layer, covering, coating, blanket.

**2** *a copper deposit* SEAM, vein, lode, layer, stratum, bed, pipe.

**3** *they paid a deposit* DOWN PAYMENT, advance payment, prepayment, installment, retainer, stake.

▸ verb **1** *she deposited her books on the table* PUT (DOWN), place, set (down), unload, rest; drop; *informal* dump, park, plonk, plunk.

**2** *the silt deposited by floodwater* LEAVE (BEHIND), precipitate, dump; wash up, cast up.

**3** *the gold was deposited at the bank* HOUSE, bank, store, stow, put away; *informal* stash, squirrel away.

**deposition** noun **1** *Law depositions from witnesses* STATEMENT, affidavit, attestation, affirmation, assertion; allegation, declaration; testimony, evidence; *rare* asseveration.

**2** *the deposition of calcium* DEPOSITING, accumulation, buildup, precipitation.

**depository** noun *a book depository* REPOSITORY, cache, store, storeroom, storehouse, warehouse; vault, strongroom, safe, treasury; container, receptacle.

**depot** noun **1** *the bus depot* TERMINAL, terminus, station, garage; headquarters, base.

**2** *an arms depot* STOREHOUSE, warehouse, store, repository, depository, cache; arsenal, magazine, armory, ammunition dump, drop-off.

**deprave** verb *young minds depraved by pornography* CORRUPT, lead astray, warp, subvert, pervert, debauch, debase, degrade, defile, sully, pollute.

**depraved** adjective *the depraved patrons of these sex shops* CORRUPT, perverted, deviant, degenerate, debased, immoral, unprincipled; debauched, dissolute, licentious, lecherous, prurient, indecent, sordid; wicked, sinful, vile, iniquitous, nefarious; *informal* warped, twisted, sick.

THE RIGHT WORD **depraved, corrupt, debased, degenerate, perverted, vile**

There are many terms to describe the dark side of human nature. Someone who preys on young children would be considered **depraved**, a term that means totally immoral and implies a warped character or a twisted mind (*a depraved man who stole money from his own mother and eventually murdered her*). While *depraved* suggests an absolute condition, **degenerate** is a relative term that implies deterioration from a mental, moral, or physical standard (*her degenerate habits eventually led to her arrest for possession of drugs*). **Corrupt** also suggests a deterioration or loss of soundness, particularly through a destructive or contaminating influence. But unlike *depraved*, which usually applies to the lower end of the human spectrum, people in high positions are often referred to as *corrupt* (*a corrupt politician from a prominent family*). To say that someone or something is **debased** suggests a lowering in quality, value, dignity, or character (*debased by having to spend time in prison*). **Perverted** and **vile** are the strongest of these words describing lack of moral character. *Perverted* suggests a distortion of someone or something from what is right, natural, or true; in a moral sense, it means to use one's appetites or natural desires for other ends than those which are considered normal or natural (*a perverted individual who never should have been left alone with young children*). Most people find criminals who prey on either very old or very young victims to be **vile**, a more general term for whatever is loathsome, repulsive, or utterly despicable (*a vile killer who deserved the maximum sentence*).

**depravity** noun *the depravity of white slavers* CORRUPTION, vice, perversion, deviance, degeneracy, immorality, debauchery, dissipation, profligacy, licentiousness, lechery, prurience, obscenity, indecency; wickedness, sin, iniquity; *formal* turpitude.

**deprecate** verb **1** *the school deprecates this behavior* DEPLORE, abhor, disapprove of, frown on, take a dim view of, take exception to, detest, despise; criticize, censure. ANTONYMS praise, overrate.

**2** *he deprecates the value of television.* See DEPRECIATE sense 3.

USAGE NOTE **deprecate, depreciate**

The first of these has increasingly encroached on the figurative senses of the second, while the second has retreated into financial contexts. *Deprecate* means "disapprove earnestly"—e.g.: " 'Well,' he admitted, deprecatingly, 'one can't suppress one's natural instincts altogether; even if one's reason and self-interest are all the other way.' " (Dorothy L. Sayers, *Gaudy Night*; 1936)

*Depreciate*, transitively, means "belittle, disparage"; and intransitively, "fall in value" (used in reference to assets or investments).

The familiar phrase *self-deprecating* is, literally speaking, a virtual impossibility, except perhaps for those suffering from extreme neuroses. Thus *self-depreciating*, with *depreciate* in its transitive sense, has historically been viewed as the correct phrase—e.g.: "Sadly, Grizzard did not have the self-depreciating humor of a Jeff Foxworthy, the self-proclaimed redneck comedian." (*St. Louis Post-Dispatch*; July 25, 1996.)

Unfortunately, though, the form *self-deprecating*—despite its mistaken origins—is now 50 times as common in print as *self-depreciating*. Speakers of American English routinely use *self-deprecating*. However grudgingly, we must accord to it the status of standard English—e.g.: "He's smart, articulate, funny, alternately self-deprecating and proud of his success." (*Los Angeles Times*; Sept. 1, 1996.) —*BG*

**deprecatory** adjective **1** *deprecatory remarks* DISAPPROVING, censorious, critical, scathing, damning, condemnatory, denunciatory, disparaging, denigrating, derogatory, negative, unflattering; disdainful, derisive, snide.

**2** *a deprecatory smile* APOLOGETIC, rueful, regretful, sorry, remorseful, contrite, penitent, repentant; shamefaced, sheepish.

**depreciate** verb **1** *these cars will depreciate quickly* DECREASE IN VALUE, lose value, fall in price.

**2** *the decision to depreciate property* DEVALUE, cheapen, reduce, lower in price, mark down, discount.

**3** *they depreciate the importance of art* BELITTLE, disparage, denigrate, decry, deprecate, underrate, undervalue, underestimate, diminish, trivialize; disdain, sneer at, scoff at, scorn; *informal* knock, badmouth, sell short, pooh-pooh. See note at DEPRECATE. ANTONYM overrate.

**depreciation** noun *we are concerned about the depreciation of residential properties* DEVALUATION, devaluing, decrease in value, lowering in value, reduction in value, cheapening, markdown, reduction; decline, downturn, downswing, drop, slump, plunge, tumble, nosedive, crash.

**depredation** noun *the depredation of the barbarian invasion* PLUNDERING, plunder, looting, pillaging, robbery; devastation, destruction, damage, rape; ravages, raids.

**depress** verb **1** *the news depressed him* SADDEN, dispirit, cast down, get down, dishearten, demoralize, crush, shake, desolate, weigh down, oppress; upset, distress, grieve, haunt, harrow; *informal* give someone the blues. ANTONYM cheer (up).

**2** *new economic policies depressed sales* SLOW DOWN, reduce, lower, weaken, impair; limit, check, inhibit, restrict. ANTONYM encourage.

**3** *foreign imports will depress domestic prices* REDUCE, lower, cut, cheapen, keep down, discount, deflate, depreciate, devalue, diminish, ax, slash. ANTONYM raise.

**4** *depress each lever in turn* PRESS, push, hold down; thumb, tap; operate, activate. ANTONYM lift.

**depressant** noun *they were found guilty of drugging Jefferson's horse with depressants* SEDATIVE, tranquilizer, calmative, sleeping pill, soporific, opiate, hypnotic; *informal* downer, trank/tranq; *trademark* Valium; *Medicine* neuroleptic. ANTONYM stimulant.

**depressed** adjective **1** *he felt lonely and depressed* SAD, unhappy, miserable, gloomy, glum, melancholy, dejected, disconsolate, downhearted, downcast, down, despondent, dispirited, low, heavy-hearted, morose, dismal, desolate; tearful, upset; *informal* blue, down in the dumps, down in/at the mouth. ANTONYM cheerful.

**2** *a depressed economy* WEAK, enervated, devitalized, impaired; inactive, flat, slow, slack, sluggish, stagnant. ANTONYM strong.

**3** *depressed prices* REDUCED, low, cut, cheap, marked down, discounted, discount; *informal* slashed. ANTONYM inflated.

**4** *a depressed part of town* POVERTY-STRICKEN, poor, disadvantaged, underprivileged, deprived, needy, distressed; rundown, slummy. ANTONYM prosperous.

**5** *the removal of the tree left a depressed patch of ground* SUNKEN, hollow, concave, indented, recessed. ANTONYM raised.

**depressing** adjective **1** *depressing thoughts* UPSETTING, distressing, painful, heartbreaking; dismal, bleak, black, somber, gloomy, grave, unhappy, melancholy, sad; wretched, doleful; *informal* morbid, blue.

**2** *a depressing room* GLOOMY, bleak, dreary, grim, drab, somber, dark, dingy, funereal, cheerless, joyless, comfortless, uninviting.

**depression** noun **1** *she seems to be suffering from depression* UNHAPPINESS, sadness, melancholy, melancholia, misery, sorrow, woe, gloom, despondency, low spirits, a heavy heart, despair, desolation, hopelessness; upset, tearfulness; *informal* the dumps, the doldrums, the blues, a funk, a blue funk; *Psychiatry* dysthymia, seasonal affective disorder, SAD.

**2** *an economic depression* RECESSION, slump, decline, downturn, standstill; stagnation; the Great Depression; *Economics* stagflation.

**3** *a depression in the ground* HOLLOW, indentation, dent, cavity, concavity, dip, pit, hole, sinkhole, trough, crater; basin, bowl.

**deprivation** noun **1** *unemployment and deprivation* POVERTY, impoverishment, penury, privation, hardship, destitution; need, want, distress, indigence, beggary, ruin; straitened circumstances. ANTONYM wealth.

**2** *deprivation of political rights* DISPOSSESSION, withholding, withdrawal, removal, divestment, expropriation, seizure, confiscation; denial, forfeiture, loss; absence, lack. ANTONYM possession.

**deprive** verb *Adams was* ***deprived of*** *her civil rights* DISPOSSESS OF, strip of, divest of, relieve of, deny, rob of; cheat out of; *informal* do out of.

**deprived** adjective *society's deprived classes* DISADVANTAGED, underprivileged, poverty-stricken, impoverished, poor, destitute, needy, unable to make ends meet.

**depth** noun **1** *the depth of the caves* DEEPNESS, distance downward, distance inward; drop, vertical extent; *archaic* profundity. ANTONYM shallowness.

**2** *the depth of his knowledge* EXTENT, range, scope, breadth, width; magnitude, scale, degree.

**3** *her lack of depth* PROFUNDITY, deepness, wisdom, understanding, intelligence, sagacity, discernment, penetration, insight, astuteness, acumen, shrewdness; *formal* perspicuity. ANTONYM shallowness.

**4** *a work of great depth* COMPLEXITY, intricacy; profundity, gravity, weight. ANTONYM triviality.

**5** *depth of color* INTENSITY, richness, deepness, vividness, strength, brilliance.

**6** **(depths)** *the depths of the sea* DEEPEST PART, bottom, floor, bed; abyss. ANTONYM surface.

PHRASE: **in depth** *choose one aspect of the case and investigate it in depth* THOROUGHLY, extensively, comprehensively, rigorously, exhaustively, completely, fully; meticulously, scrupulously, painstakingly.

**deputation** noun *a deputation on behalf of disabled veterans* DELEGATION, legation, commission, committee, mission, diplomatic mission; contingent, group, party.

**depute** verb **1** *he was deputed to handle negotiations.* See DESIGNATE sense 1.

**2** *the judge deputed smaller cases to others.* See DELEGATE verb sense 1.

**deputy** noun *he handed over his duties to his deputy* SECOND, second-in-command, number two; substitute, stand-in, fill-in, relief, understudy, locum tenens; representative, proxy, agent, spokesperson; *informal* sidekick, locum.

▸ adjective *her deputy editor* ASSISTANT, substitute, stand-in, acting, reserve, fill-in, caretaker, temporary, provisional, stopgap, surrogate, interim; *informal* second-string.

**deranged** adjective *her deranged cousin has finally been locked up* INSANE, mad, disturbed, unbalanced, unhinged, unstable, irrational; crazed, demented, berserk, frenzied, lunatic, certifiable; non compos mentis; *informal* touched, crazy, wacko, mental, psycho. ANTONYM rational.

**derelict** adjective **1** *a derelict building* DILAPIDATED, ramshackle, run-down, tumbledown, in ruins, falling apart; rickety, creaky, deteriorating, crumbling; neglected, untended, gone to rack and ruin.

**2** *a derelict airfield* DISUSED, abandoned, deserted, discarded, rejected, neglected, untended.

**3** *he was derelict in his duty* NEGLIGENT, neglectful, remiss, lax, careless, sloppy, slipshod, slack, irresponsible, delinquent.

▸ noun *the derelicts who survive on the streets* TRAMP, vagrant, vagabond, down and out, homeless person, drifter; beggar, mendicant; outcast; *informal* bag lady, hobo, bum.

**dereliction** noun **1** *buildings were reclaimed from dereliction* DILAPIDATION, disrepair, deterioration, ruin, rack and ruin; abandonment, neglect, disuse.

**2** *dereliction of duty* NEGLIGENCE, neglect, delinquency, failure; carelessness, laxity, sloppiness, slackness, irresponsibility; oversight, omission.

**deride** verb *the kid I used to deride in junior high is now my boss* RIDICULE, mock, scoff at, jibe at, make fun of, poke fun at, laugh at, hold up to ridicule, pillory; disdain, disparage, denigrate, dismiss, slight; sneer at, scorn, insult; *informal* knock, pooh-pooh. ANTONYM praise.

**derision** noun *Quincy's memoirs incited the derision of his siblings* MOCKERY, ridicule, jeers, sneers, taunts; disdain, disparagement, denigration, disrespect, insults; scorn, contempt; lampooning, satire.

**derisive** adjective *shouting derisive comments* MOCKING, jeering, scoffing, teasing, derisory, snide, sneering; disdainful, scornful, contemptuous, taunting, insulting; scathing, sarcastic.

**derisory** adjective **1** *a derisory sum* INADEQUATE, insufficient, tiny, small; trifling, paltry, pitiful, miserly, miserable; negligible, token, nominal; ridiculous, laughable, ludicrous, preposterous, insulting; *informal* measly, stingy, lousy, pathetic, piddling, piffling, mingy.

**2** *derisory calls from the crowd.* See DERISIVE.

**derivation** noun **1** *the derivation of theories from empirical observation* DERIVING, induction, deduction, inference; extraction, eliciting.

**2** *the derivation of a word* ORIGIN, etymology, root, etymon, provenance, source; origination, beginning, foundation, basis, cause; development, evolution.

**derivative** adjective *her poetry was derivative* IMITATIVE, unoriginal, uninventive, unimaginative, uninspired; copied, plagiarized, plagiaristic, secondhand; trite, hackneyed, clichéd, stale, stock, banal; *informal* copycat, cribbed, old hat. ANTONYM original.

▸ noun *a derivative of opium* BY-PRODUCT, subsidiary product; spin-off.

**derive** verb **1** *he derives consolation from his poetry* OBTAIN, get, take, gain, acquire, procure, extract, attain, glean.

**2** *"coffee"* ***derives from*** *the Turkish "kahveh"* ORIGINATE IN, stem from, descend from, spring from, be taken from.

**3** *his fortune* ***derives from*** *real estate* ORIGINATE IN, be rooted in; stem from, come from, spring from, proceed from, issue from.

**derogate** verb *formal* **1** *his contribution was derogated by crit-*

*ics* DISPARAGE, denigrate, belittle, deprecate, deflate; decry, discredit, cast aspersions on, run down, criticize; defame, vilify, abuse, insult, attack, pour scorn on; *informal* drag through the mud, knock, slam, bash, badmouth, dis. ANTONYM praise.

**2** *the act would* ***derogate from*** *the king's majesty* DETRACT FROM, devalue, diminish, reduce, lessen, depreciate; demean, cheapen. ANTONYMS improve, increase.

**3** *behaviors that* ***derogate from*** *the norm* DEVIATE FROM, diverge from, depart from, digress from, stray from; differ from, vary from; conflict with, be incompatible with.

**derogatory** adjective *a derogatory remark* DISPARAGING, denigratory, deprecatory, disrespectful, demeaning; critical, pejorative, negative, unfavorable, uncomplimentary, unflattering, insulting; offensive, personal, abusive, rude, nasty, mean, hurtful; defamatory, slanderous, libelous; *informal* bitchy, catty. See note at OFFENSE. ANTONYM complimentary.

**descend** verb **1** *the plane started descending* GO DOWN, come down; drop, fall, sink, dive, plummet, plunge, nosedive. ANTONYMS ascend, climb.

**2** *she descended the stairs* CLIMB DOWN, go down, come down. ANTONYMS ascend, climb.

**3** *the road descends to a village* SLOPE, dip, slant, go down, fall away.

**4** *she saw Herb* ***descend from*** *the bus* ALIGHT FROM, disembark, get down from, get off, dismount. ANTONYMS climb aboard, board.

**5** *they would not descend to such mean tricks* STOOP, lower oneself, demean oneself, debase oneself; resort, be reduced.

**6** *the army descended into chaos* DEGENERATE, deteriorate, decline, sink, slide, fall.

**7** *they* ***descended on*** *the fortress* COME IN FORCE ON/UPON, arrive in hordes on; attack, assail, assault, storm, invade, swoop (down) on, charge.

**8** *he* ***is descended from*** *a Flemish family* BE A DESCENDANT OF, originate from, issue from, spring from, derive from.

**9** *his estates descended to his son* BE HANDED DOWN, be passed down; be inherited by.

**descent** noun **1** *the plane began its descent* DIVE, drop; fall, pitch, nosedive.

**2** *their descent of the mountain* DOWNWARD CLIMB.

**3** *a steep descent* SLOPE, incline, dip, drop, gradient, declivity, slant; hill.

**4** *his descent into alcoholism* DECLINE, slide, fall, degeneration, deterioration, regression.

**5** *she is of Italian descent* ANCESTRY, parentage, ancestors, family, antecedents; extraction, origin, derivation, birth; lineage, line, genealogy, heredity, stock, pedigree, blood, bloodline; roots, origins.

**6** *the descent of property* INHERITANCE, succession.

**7** *the sudden descent of the cavalry* ATTACK, assault, raid, onslaught, charge, thrust, push, drive, incursion, foray.

**describe** verb **1** *he described his experiences* REPORT, recount, relate, tell of, set out, chronicle; detail, catalog, give a rundown of; explain, illustrate, discuss, comment on.

**2** *she described him as a pathetic figure* DESIGNATE, pronounce, call, label, style, dub; characterize, class; portray, depict, brand, paint; *literary* limn.

**3** *the pen described a circle* DELINEATE, mark out, outline, trace, draw.

**description** noun **1** *a description of my travels* ACCOUNT, report, rendition, explanation, illustration; chronicle, narration, narrative, story, commentary; portrayal, portrait; details.

**2** *the description of horse racing as "the sport of kings"* DESIGNATION, labeling, naming, dubbing, pronouncement; characterization, classification, branding; portrayal, depiction.

**3** *vehicles of every description* SORT, variety, kind, type, category, order, breed, class, designation, specification, genre, genus, brand, make, character, ilk, stripe.

**descriptive** adjective *descriptive prose* ILLUSTRATIVE, expressive, graphic, detailed, lively, vivid, striking; explanatory, explicative.

**descry** verb *literary* See NOTICE verb. See also note at DISTINGUISH.

**desecrate** verb *invaders desecrated the temple* VIOLATE, profane, defile, debase, degrade, dishonor; vandalize, damage, destroy, deface.

**desert**[1] verb **1** *his wife deserted him* ABANDON, leave, turn one's back on; throw over, jilt, break up with; leave high and dry, leave in the lurch, leave behind, strand; *informal* walk out on, run out on, drop, dump, ditch; *literary* forsake.

**2** *his allies were deserting the cause* RENOUNCE, repudiate, relinquish, wash one's hands of, abandon, turn one's back on, betray, disavow; *formal* abjure; *literary* forsake.

**3** *soldiers deserted in droves* ABSCOND, defect, run away, make off, decamp, flee, turn tail, take French leave, depart, quit, jump ship; *Military* go AWOL.

**desert**[2] noun *an expanse of desert* WASTELAND, wastes, wilderness, wilds, barren land; dust bowl.

▸ adjective **1** *desert conditions* ARID, dry, moistureless, parched; scorched, hot; barren, bare, stark, infertile, unfruitful, dehydrated, sterile. ANTONYM fertile.

**2** *an uncharted desert island* UNINHABITED, empty, lonely, desolate, bleak; wild, uncultivated.

**deserted** adjective **1** *a deserted wife* ABANDONED, thrown over, jilted, cast aside; neglected, stranded, marooned, forlorn, bereft; *informal* dumped, ditched, dropped; *literary* forsaken.

**2** *a deserted village* EMPTY, uninhabited, unoccupied, unpeopled, abandoned, evacuated, vacant; untenanted, tenantless, neglected; desolate, lonely, godforsaken. ANTONYM populous.

**deserter** noun *deserters were shot in full view of their fellow soldiers* ABSCONDER, runaway, fugitive, truant, escapee; renegade, defector, turncoat, traitor.

**desertion** noun **1** *McKinley's desertion of her family* ABANDONMENT, leaving, jilting.

**2** *the desertion of the president's colleagues* DEFECTION; betrayal, renunciation, repudiation, apostasy; *formal* abjuration.

**3** *soldiers were prosecuted for desertion* ABSCONDING, running away, truancy, going absent without leave, taking French leave, escape; defection, treason; *Military* going AWOL.

**deserve** verb *the book deserves our greatest praise* MERIT, earn, warrant, rate, justify, be worthy of, be entitled to, have a right to, be qualified for.

**deserved** adjective *they clinched a deserved victory* WELL-EARNED, merited, warranted, justified, justifiable; rightful, due, right, just, fair, fitting, appropriate, suitable, proper, apt; *archaic* meet.

**deserving** adjective **1** *the deserving workers* WORTHY, meritorious, commendable, praiseworthy, admirable, estimable, creditable; respectable, decent, honorable, righteous.

**2** *a lapse deserving punishment* MERITING, warranting, justifying, suitable for, worthy of.

**design** noun **1** *a design for the offices* PLAN, blueprint, drawing, sketch, outline, map, plot, diagram, draft, representation, scheme, model.

**2** *tableware with a gold design* PATTERN, motif, device; style, composition, makeup, layout, construction, shape, form.

**3** *his design of reaching the top* INTENTION, aim, purpose, plan, intent, objective, object, goal, end, target; hope, desire, wish, dream, aspiration, ambition.

▸ verb **1** *the church was designed by Hicks* PLAN, outline, map out, draft, draw.

**2** *they designed a new engine* INVENT, originate, create, think up, come up with, devise, formulate, conceive; make, produce, develop, fashion; *informal* dream up.

**3** *this paper is designed to provoke discussion* INTEND, aim; devise, contrive, purpose, plan; tailor, fashion, adapt, gear; mean, destine. See note at INTEND.

PHRASE: **by design** *things worked out more by accident than by design* DELIBERATELY, intentionally, on purpose, purposefully; knowingly, wittingly, consciously, calculatedly.

**designate** verb **1** *she designated her successor* APPOINT, nominate, depute, delegate; select, choose, pick, elect, name, identify, assign.

**2** *the building was designated a historical site* CLASSIFY, class, label, tag; name, call, entitle, term, dub; *formal* denominate.

**designation** noun **1** *the designation of a leader* APPOINTMENT, nomination, naming, selection, election.

**2** *the designation of wildlife preserves* CLASSIFICATION, specification, definition, earmarking, pinpointing.

**3** *the designation "Generalissimo"* TITLE, name, epithet, tag; nickname, byname, sobriquet; *informal* moniker, handle; *formal* denomination, appellation.

**designer** noun **1** *a designer of office furniture* CREATOR, planner, deviser, inventor, originator; maker; architect, builder.

**2** *young designers made the dress* COUTURIER, tailor, dressmaker.

**designing** adjective *he couldn't compete with the designing young executives he encountered in Washington* SCHEMING, calculating, conniving; cunning, crafty, artful, wily, devious, guileful, manipulative; treacherous, sly, underhanded, deceitful, double-dealing; *informal* crooked, foxy.

**desirability** noun **1** *the desirability of the property* APPEAL, attractiveness, allure; agreeableness, worth, excellence.

**2** *they debated the desirability of gay marriage* ADVISABILITY, advantage, expedience, benefit, merit, value, profit, profitability.

**3** *her obvious desirability* ATTRACTIVENESS, sexual attraction, beauty, good looks; charm, seductiveness; *informal* sexiness.

**desirable** adjective **1** *a desirable location* ATTRACTIVE, sought-after, in demand, popular, desired, covetable, coveted, enviable; appealing, agreeable, pleasant; valuable, good, excellent; *informal* to die for.

**2** *it is desirable that they should meet* ADVANTAGEOUS, advisable, wise, sensible, recommendable; helpful, useful, beneficial, worthwhile, profitable, preferable. ANTONYM disadvantageous.

**3** *a very desirable woman* SEXUALLY ATTRACTIVE, attractive, beautiful, pretty, appealing; seductive, alluring, enchanting, beguiling, captivating, bewitching, irresistible; *informal* sexy, beddable. ANTONYMS unattractive, ugly.

**desire** noun **1** *a desire to see the world* WISH, want, aspiration, fancy, inclination, impulse; yearning, longing, craving, hankering, hunger; eagerness, enthusiasm, determination; *informal* yen, itch, jones.

**2** *his eyes glittered with desire* LUST, sexual attraction, passion, sensuality, sexuality; lasciviousness, lechery, salaciousness, libidinousness; *informal* the hots, raunchiness, horniness.

▸ verb **1** *they desired peace* WANT, wish for, long for, yearn for, crave, hanker after, be desperate for, be bent on, covet, aspire to; fancy; *informal* have a yen for, have a jones for, yen for, hanker after/for.

**2** *she desired him* BE ATTRACTED TO, lust after, burn for, be infatuated by; *informal* fancy, have the hots for, have a crush on, be mad about, be crazy about.

**desired** adjective **1** *cut the cloth to the desired length* REQUIRED, necessary, proper, right, correct; appropriate, suitable; preferred, chosen, selected.

**2** *the desired results* WISHED FOR, wanted, coveted; sought-after, longed for, yearned for; *informal* must-have.

**desirous** adjective *he was* ***desirous of*** *change* EAGER FOR, desiring, anxious for, keen for, craving, yearning for, longing for, hungry for; ambitious for, aspiring to; covetous of, envious of; *informal* dying for, itching for.

**desist** verb *manufacturers were ordered to* ***desist from*** *dumping chemicals in the river* ABSTAIN FROM, refrain from, forbear from, hold back from, keep from; stop, cease, discontinue, suspend, give up, break off, drop, dispense with, eschew; *informal* lay off, quit. ANTONYM continue.

**desolate** adjective **1** *the desolate prairie* BLEAK, stark, bare, dismal, grim; wild, inhospitable; deserted, uninhabited, godforsaken, abandoned, unpeopled, untenanted, empty, barren; unfrequented, unvisited, isolated, remote. ANTONYM populous.

**2** *the news of Rudolph's disappearance left them desolate* MISERABLE, despondent, depressed, disconsolate, devastated, despairing, inconsolable, broken-hearted, grief-stricken, crushed, bereft; sad, unhappy, downcast, down, dejected, forlorn, upset, distressed; *informal* blue, cut up. ANTONYM joyful.

▸ verb **1** *droughts desolated the plains* DEVASTATE, ravage, ruin, lay waste to; level, raze, demolish, wipe out, obliterate.

**2** *she was desolated by the loss of her husband* DISHEARTEN, depress, sadden, cast down, make miserable, weigh down, crush, upset, distress, devastate; *informal* shatter.

**desolation** noun **1** *the desolation of the Gobi Desert* BLEAKNESS, starkness, barrenness, sterility; wildness; isolation, loneliness, remoteness. See note at SOLITUDE.

**2** *a feeling of utter desolation* MISERY, sadness, unhappiness, despondency, sorrow, depression, grief, woe; broken-heartedness, wretchedness, dejection, devastation, despair, anguish, distress.

**despair** noun *let me help you during this time of your despair* HOPELESSNESS, disheartenment, discouragement, desperation, distress, anguish, unhappiness; despondency, depression, disconsolateness, melancholy, misery, wretchedness; defeatism, pessimism. ANTONYMS hope, joy.

▸ verb *don't despair if you can't find a job right away* LOSE HOPE, abandon hope, give up, lose heart, lose faith, be discouraged, be despondent, be demoralized, resign oneself; be pessimistic.

**despairing** adjective *a despairing look came over his face* HOPELESS, in despair, dejected, depressed, despondent, disconsolate, gloomy, miserable, wretched, desolate, inconsolable; disheartened, discouraged, demoralized, devastated, suicidal; defeatist, pessimistic.

**desperado** noun *dated a band of armed desperados* BANDIT, criminal, outlaw, lawbreaker, villain, renegade; robber, cutthroat, gangster, pirate.

**desperate** adjective **1** *a desperate look* DESPAIRING, hopeless; anguished, distressed, wretched, desolate, forlorn, distraught, fraught; out of one's mind, at one's wits' end, beside oneself, at the end of one's rope/tether.

**2** *a desperate attempt to escape* LAST-DITCH, last-gasp, eleventh-hour, do-or-die, final; frantic, frenzied, wild; futile, hopeless, doomed.

**3** *a desperate shortage of teachers* GRAVE, serious, critical, acute, risky, precarious; dire, awful, terrible, dreadful; urgent, pressing, crucial, vital, drastic, extreme; *informal* chronic.

**4** *they were* ***desperate for*** *food* IN GREAT NEED OF, urgently requiring, in want of; eager for, longing for, yearning for, hungry for, crying out for; *informal* dying for.

**5** *a desperate act* VIOLENT, dangerous, lawless; reckless, rash, hasty, impetuous, foolhardy, incautious, hazardous, risky; do-or-die.

**desperately** adverb **1** *he screamed desperately for help* IN DESPERATION, in despair, despairingly, in anguish, in distress; wretchedly, hopelessly, desolately, forlornly.

**2** *they are desperately ill* SERIOUSLY, critically, gravely, severely, acutely, dangerously, perilously; very, extremely, dreadfully; hopelessly, irretrievably; *informal* terribly.

**3** *he desperately wanted to talk* URGENTLY, pressingly; intensely, eagerly.

**desperation** noun *her family failed to see her state of desperation* HOPELESSNESS, despair, distress; anguish, agony, torment, misery, wretchedness; discouragement, disheartenment.

**despicable** adjective *despicable crimes* CONTEMPTIBLE, loathsome, hateful, detestable, reprehensible, abhorrent, abominable, awful, heinous; odious, vile, low, mean, abject, shameful, ignominious, shabby, ignoble, disreputable, discreditable, unworthy; *informal* dirty, rotten, lowdown, lousy; beastly; *archaic* scurvy. ANTONYM admirable.

**despise** verb *he despised weakness* DETEST, hate, loathe, abhor, execrate, deplore, dislike; scorn, disdain, look down on, deride, sneer at, revile; spurn, shun; *formal* abominate; *archaic, or literary* contemn. ANTONYM adore.

THE RIGHT WORD **despise, abhor, contemn, detest, disdain, loathe, scorn**

It's one thing to dislike someone; it's quite another to **despise** or **detest** the person. Both are strong words, used to describe extreme dislike or hatred. *Detest* is probably the purest expression of hatred (*she detested the woman who had raised her, and longed to find her own mother*), while *despise* suggests looking down with great contempt and regarding the person as mean, petty, weak, or worthless (*he despised men whose only concern was their own safety*). **Disdain** carries even stronger connotations of superiority, often combined with self-righteousness (*to disdain anyone lacking a college education*). **Scorn** is a stronger word for *disdain*, and it implies an attitude of not only contempt but of haughty rejection or refusal (*to scorn the woman he'd once loved*). To **loathe** something is to feel utter disgust toward it (*he grew to loathe peanut butter and jelly sandwiches*) and to **abhor** it is to feel a profound, shuddering, repugnance (*she abhorred the very idea of asking her husband for the money*). **Contemn** is a more literary word meaning to treat with disdain, scorn, or contempt.

**despite** preposition *despite his lack of enthusiasm, Zachary had a pretty good time* IN SPITE OF, notwithstanding, regardless of, in the face of, for all, even with.

**despoil** verb **1** *a village despoiled by invaders* PLUNDER, pillage, rob, ravage, raid, ransack, rape, loot, sack; devastate, lay waste, ruin. See note at RAVAGE.

2 *the thief despoiled him of all he had* ROB, strip, deprive, dispossess, denude, divest, relieve, clean out.

**despondency** noun *the despondency of the refugees was captured in this documentary* HOPELESSNESS, despair, discouragement, low spirits, wretchedness; melancholy, gloom, misery, desolation, disappointment, disheartenment, dejection, sadness, unhappiness; *informal* blues, heartache.

**despondent** adjective *they were tired and despondent* DISHEARTENED, discouraged, dispirited, downhearted, downcast, crestfallen, down, low, disconsolate, despairing, wretched; melancholy, gloomy, morose, dismal, woebegone, miserable, depressed, dejected, sad; *informal* blue, down in/at the mouth, down in the dumps. ANTONYMS hopeful, cheerful.

**despot** noun *when one despot is deposed for another, the cycle of repression continues* TYRANT, oppressor, dictator, absolute ruler, totalitarian, autocrat; *informal* slave driver.

**despotic** adjective *a despotic regime* AUTOCRATIC, dictatorial, totalitarian, absolutist, undemocratic, unaccountable; one-party, autarchic, monocratic; tyrannical, tyrannous, oppressive, repressive, draconian, illiberal. ANTONYM democratic.

**destination** noun *our original destination was Richmond* JOURNEY'S END, end of the line; terminus, stop, stopping place, port of call; goal, purpose, target, end.

**destined** adjective 1 *he is destined to lead a charmed life* FATED, ordained, predestined, meant; certain, sure, bound, assured, likely; doomed.

2 *computers destined for Pakistan* HEADING, bound, en route, scheduled; intended, meant, designed, designated, allotted, reserved.

**destiny** noun 1 *master of his own destiny* FUTURE, fate, fortune, doom; lot; *archaic* portion.

2 *she believed their meeting was destiny* FATE, providence; predestination; God's will, kismet, the stars; luck, fortune, chance; karma, serendipity.

**destitute** adjective 1 *she was left destitute* PENNILESS, poor, impoverished, poverty-stricken, impecunious, without a cent/penny (to one's name); needy, in straitened circumstances, distressed, badly off; *informal* hard up, broke, flat broke, strapped (for cash), without a red cent, dirt poor. ANTONYM rich.

2 *we were* ***destitute of*** *clothing* DEVOID OF, bereft of, deprived of, in need of; lacking, without, deficient in, wanting.

**destroy** verb 1 *their offices were destroyed by bombing* DEMOLISH, knock down, level, raze (to the ground), fell; wreck, ruin, shatter; blast, blow up, dynamite, explode, bomb. ANTONYMS build, reconstruct.

2 *the new highway would destroy the conservation area* SPOIL, ruin, wreck, disfigure, blight, mar, impair, deface, scar, injure, harm, devastate, damage, wreak havoc on; *informal* total. ANTONYMS restore, preserve.

3 *illness destroyed his career* WRECK, ruin, spoil, disrupt, undo, upset, put an end to, put a stop to, terminate, frustrate, blight, crush, quash, dash, scotch; devastate, demolish, scuttle, sabotage; *informal* mess up, foul up, put the kibosh on, fry, do for, blow a hole in; *archaic* bring to naught. ANTONYMS bolster, help.

4 *the horse had to be destroyed* KILL, put down, put to sleep, slaughter, terminate, exterminate, euthanize.

5 *we will destroy the enemy* ANNIHILATE, wipe out, obliterate, wipe off the face of the earth, eliminate, eradicate, liquidate, finish off, erase; kill, slaughter, massacre, exterminate; *informal* take out, rub out, snuff out, waste, fry, nuke, zap. ANTONYM spare.

THE RIGHT WORD **destroy, annihilate, demolish, eradicate, exterminate, extirpate, raze**

If you're interested in getting rid of something, you've got a number of options at your disposal. **Destroy** is a general term covering any force that wrecks, ruins, kills, etc. (*to destroy an ant hill by pouring boiling water on it*). If it's a building, you'll want to **demolish** or **raze** it, two words that are generally applied only to very large things. *Raze* is used almost exclusively with structures; it means to bring something down to the level of the ground (*they razed the apartment building to make way for the new hospital*). *Demolish* implies pulling or smashing something to pieces; when used with regard to buildings, it conjures up a vision of complete wreckage and often a heap of rubble (*their new house was demolished by the first hurricane of the season*). But unlike *raze*, *demolish* can also be applied to nonmaterial things (*to demolish the theory with a few simple experiments*). If you **eradicate** something, you eliminate it completely, literally or figuratively, pull it out by the roots (*to eradicate smallpox with a vaccine*) and prevent its reappearance. **Extirpate**, like *eradicate*, implies the utter destruction of something (*the species was extirpated from the park by the flooding*). If you're dealing with cockroaches, you'll probably want to **exterminate** them, which means to wipe out or kill in great numbers. Or better yet, you'll want to **annihilate** them, which is the most extreme word in this group and literally means to reduce to nothingness.

**destruction** noun 1 *the destruction by allied bombers* DEMOLITION, wrecking, ruination, blasting, bombing; wreckage, ruins.

2 *the destruction of the countryside* DEVASTATION, ruination, blighting, disfigurement, impairment, scarring, harm, desolation.

3 *the destruction of cattle* SLAUGHTER, killing, putting down, extermination, termination.

4 *the destruction of the enemies' forces* ANNIHILATION, obliteration, elimination, eradication, liquidation; killing, slaughter, massacre, extermination.

**destructive** adjective 1 *the most destructive war* DEVASTATING, ruinous, disastrous, catastrophic, calamitous, cataclysmic; harmful, damaging, detrimental, deleterious, injurious, crippling; violent, savage, fierce, brutal, deadly, lethal.

**2** *destructive criticism* NEGATIVE, hostile, vicious, unfriendly; unhelpful, obstructive, discouraging.

**desultory** adjective *the desultory interest you have in your child's welfare is appalling* CASUAL, cursory, superficial, token, perfunctory, half-hearted, lukewarm; random, aimless, erratic, unmethodical, unsystematic, chaotic, inconsistent, irregular, intermittent, sporadic, fitful. ANTONYM keen.

**detach** verb *he detached the lamp from its bracket* UNFASTEN, disconnect, disengage, separate, uncouple, remove, loose, unhitch, unhook, free, pull off, cut off, break off. ANTONYM attach.

PHRASE: **detach oneself from 1** *she detached herself from the crowd* FREE ONESELF FROM, separate oneself from, segregate oneself from; move away from, split off from; leave, abandon.

**2** *he has detached himself from his family* DISSOCIATE ONESELF FROM, divorce oneself from, alienate oneself from, separate (oneself) from, segregate oneself from, isolate oneself from, cut oneself off from; break away from, disaffiliate oneself from, defect from; leave, quit, withdraw from, break with.

**detached** adjective **1** *a detached collar* UNFASTENED, disconnected, separated, separate, loosened; untied, unhitched, undone, unhooked, unbuttoned; free, severed, cut off.

**2** *a detached observer* DISPASSIONATE, disinterested, objective, uninvolved, outside, neutral, unbiased, unprejudiced, impartial, nonpartisan; indifferent, aloof, remote, distant, impersonal; *informal* cool.

**3** *a detached house* STANDING ALONE, separate.

**detachment** noun **1** *she looked on everything with detachment* OBJECTIVITY, dispassion, disinterest, open-mindedness, neutrality, impartiality; indifference, aloofness.

**2** *a detachment of soldiers* UNIT, detail, squad, troop, contingent, outfit, task force, patrol, crew; platoon, company, corps, regiment, brigade, battalion.

**3** *retinal detachment* LOOSENING, disconnection, disengagement, separation; removal.

**detail** noun **1** *the picture is correct in every detail* PARTICULAR, respect, feature, characteristic, attribute, specific, aspect, facet, part, unit, component, constituent; fact, piece of information, point, element, circumstance, consideration.

**2** *that's just a detail* UNIMPORTANT POINT, trivial fact, triviality, technicality, nicety, subtlety, trifle, fine point, incidental, inessential, nothing.

**3** *records with a considerable degree of detail* PRECISION, exactness, accuracy, thoroughness, carefulness, scrupulousness, particularity.

**4** *a guard detail* UNIT, detachment, squad, troop, contingent, outfit, task force, patrol.

**5** *I got kitchen detail* DUTY, task, job, chore, charge, responsibility, assignment, function, mission, engagement, occupation, undertaking, errand.

▸ verb **1** *the report details our objections* DESCRIBE, explain, expound, relate, catalog, list, spell out, itemize, particularize, identify, specify; state, declare, present, set out, frame; cite, quote, instance, mention, name.

**2** *troops were detailed to prevent their escape* ASSIGN, allocate, appoint, delegate, commission, charge; send, post; nominate, vote, elect, co-opt.

PHRASE: **in detail** *this will be examined in detail in the next chapter* THOROUGHLY, in depth, exhaustively, minutely, closely, meticulously, rigorously, scrupulously, painstakingly, carefully; completely, comprehensively, fully, extensively.

**detailed** adjective *a detailed description of the assailants* COMPREHENSIVE, full, complete, thorough, exhaustive, all-inclusive; elaborate, minute, intricate; explicit, specific, precise, exact, accurate, meticulous, painstaking; itemized, blow-by-blow. ANTONYM general.

**detain** verb **1** *they were detained for questioning* HOLD, take into custody, take (in), confine, imprison, lock up, put in jail, intern; arrest, apprehend, seize; *informal* pick up, run in, haul in, nab, collar. ANTONYM release.

**2** *don't let me detain you* DELAY, hold up, make late, keep, slow up/down; hinder, hamper, impede, obstruct.

**detect** verb **1** *no one detected the smell of gas* NOTICE, perceive, discern, be aware of, note, make out, spot, recognize, distinguish, remark, identify, diagnose; catch, sense, see, smell, scent, taste.

**2** *they are responsible for detecting fraud* DISCOVER, uncover, find out, turn up, unearth, dig up, root out, expose, reveal.

**3** *the hackers were detected* CATCH, hunt down, track down, find, expose, reveal, unmask, smoke out; apprehend, arrest; *informal* nail.

**detection** noun **1** *the detection of methane* DISCERNMENT, perception, awareness, recognition, identification, diagnosis; sensing, sight, smelling, tasting.

**2** *the detection of insider trading* DISCOVERY, uncovering, unearthing, exposure, revelation.

**3** *he managed to escape detection* CAPTURE, identification, exposure; apprehension, arrest; notice.

**detective** noun *they hired a detective to track down Polk's former partner* INVESTIGATOR, private investigator, private detective, police detective, operative; *informal* private eye, PI, sleuth, snoop, shamus, gumshoe, Sherlock; *informal, dated* dick, private dick.

**detention** noun *he was released after spending a year in detention* CUSTODY, imprisonment, confinement, incarceration, internment, detainment, captivity; arrest, house arrest; quarantine; punishment, discipline.

**deter** verb **1** *the high cost deterred many* DISCOURAGE, dissuade, put off, scare off; dishearten, demoralize, daunt, intimidate. ANTONYM encourage.

**2** *the presence of a guard deters crime* PREVENT, stop, avert, fend off, stave off, ward off, block, halt, check; hinder, impede, hamper, obstruct, foil, forestall, counteract, inhibit, curb. ANTONYM encourage.

**detergent** noun *laundry detergent* CLEANER, cleanser, cleaning agent; soap, soap powder, dish soap, soap flakes.

**deteriorate** verb **1** *his health deteriorated* WORSEN, decline, degenerate; fail, slump, slip, go downhill, wane, ebb; *informal* go to pot. ANTONYM improve.

**2** *these materials deteriorate if stored wrongly* DECAY, degrade, degenerate, break down, decompose, rot, go off, spoil, perish; break up, disintegrate, crumble, fall apart.

**deterioration** noun **1** *a deterioration in market conditions* DECLINE, collapse, failure, drop, downturn, slump, *informal* slip, retrogression.

**2** *deterioration of the main structure* DECAY, degradation, degeneration, breakdown, decomposition, rot; atrophy, weakening; breakup, disintegration, dilapidation; entropy.

**determination** noun **1** *it took great determination to win* RESOLUTION, resolve, willpower, strength of character, single-mindedness, purposefulness, intentness; staunchness, perseverance, persistence, tenacity, staying power; strong-mindedness, backbone; stubbornness, doggedness, obstinacy; spirit, courage, pluck, grit, stout-heartedness; *informal* guts, spunk, balls, moxie; *formal* pertinacity.

**2** *the determination of the rent* SETTING, specification, settlement, designation, arrangement, establishment, prescription.

**3** *the determination of the speed of light* CALCULATION, discovery, ascertainment, establishment, deduction, divination, diagnosis, discernment, verification, confirmation.

**determine** verb **1** *chromosomes determine the sex of the embryo* CONTROL, decide, regulate, direct, dictate, govern; affect, influence, mold.

**2** *he determined to sell* RESOLVE, decide, make up one's mind, choose, elect, opt; *formal* purpose.

**3** *the sum will be determined by an accountant* SPECIFY, set, fix, decide on, settle, assign, designate, arrange, choose, establish, ordain, prescribe, decree.

**4** *determine the composition of the fibers* ASCERTAIN, find out, discover, learn, establish, calculate, work out, make out, deduce, diagnose, discern; check, verify, confirm; *informal* figure out.

**determined** adjective **1** *he was determined to have his way* INTENT ON, bent on, set on, insistent on, resolved to, firm about, committed to; single-minded about, obsessive about.

**2** *a very determined man* RESOLUTE, purposeful, purposive, adamant, single-minded, unswerving, unwavering, undaunted, intent, insistent; steadfast, staunch, stalwart; persevering, persistent, indefatigable, tenacious; strong-minded, strong-willed, unshakable, steely, four-square, dedicated, committed; stubborn, dogged, obstinate, inflexible, intransigent, unyielding, immovable, rock-ribbed; *formal* pertinacious. See note at RESOLUTE.

**determining** adjective *money is the determining factor* DECIDING, decisive, conclusive, final, definitive, key, pivotal, crucial, critical, major, chief, prime.

**deterrent** noun *the high rate of interest is a deterrent to first-time home buyers* DISINCENTIVE, discouragement, damper, curb, check, restraint; obstacle, hindrance, impediment, obstruction, block, barrier, inhibition. ANTONYM incentive.

**detest** verb *the only vegetable I truly detest is turnip* ABHOR, hate, loathe, despise, shrink from, be unable to bear, find intolerable, dislike, disdain, have an aversion to; *formal* abominate. See note at DESPISE. ANTONYM love.

**detestable** adjective *civilized people must not tolerate such detestable inhumanity* ABHORRENT, hateful, loathsome, despicable, abominable, execrable, repellent, repugnant, repulsive, revolting, disgusting, distasteful, horrible, horrid, awful; heinous, reprehensible, obnoxious, odious, offensive, contemptible. See note at OFFENSIVE.

**detonate** verb **1** *the charge detonated on impact* EXPLODE, go off, blow up, shatter, erupt; ignite; bang, blast, boom.

**2** *they detonated the bomb* SET OFF, explode, discharge, let off, touch off, trigger; ignite, kindle.

**detour** noun *the detour will add another twenty minutes to the trip* DIVERSION, circuitous route, indirect route, scenic route; bypass; digression, deviation, shortcut.

**detract** verb *my reservations should not* ***detract from*** *the book's excellence* BELITTLE, take away from, diminish, reduce, lessen, minimize, play down, trivialize, decry, depreciate, devalue, deprecate.

**detractor** noun *detractors never deterred me from pursuing my art* CRITIC, disparager, denigrator, deprecator, belittler, attacker, fault-finder, backbiter; slanderer, libeler; *informal* knocker.

**detriment** noun *local merchants fear the detriment to business that one of these superstores could bring about* HARM, damage, injury, hurt, impairment, loss, disadvantage, disservice, mischief. ANTONYM benefit.

**detrimental** adjective *erosion can have a detrimental effect on our water* HARMFUL, damaging, injurious, hurtful, inimical, deleterious, destructive, ruinous, disastrous, bad, malign, adverse, undesirable, unfavorable, unfortunate; unhealthy, unwholesome. ANTONYM benign.

**detritus** noun *areas littered with military detritus* DEBRIS, waste, refuse, rubbish, litter, scrap, flotsam and jetsam, rubble; remains, remnants, fragments, scraps, dregs, leavings, sweepings, dross, scum, trash, garbage; *informal* dreck.

**devastate** verb **1** *the city was devastated by an earthquake* DESTROY, ruin, wreck, lay waste, ravage, demolish, raze (to the ground), level, flatten; *informal* trash, total. See note at RAVAGE.

**2** *he was devastated by the news* SHATTER, shock, stun, daze, dumbfound, traumatize, crush, overwhelm, overcome, distress.

**devastating** adjective **1** *a devastating cyclone* DESTRUCTIVE, ruinous, disastrous, catastrophic, calamitous, cataclysmic; harmful, damaging, injurious, detrimental; crippling, violent, savage, fierce, dangerous, fatal, deadly, lethal.

2 *devastating news* SHATTERING, shocking, traumatic, overwhelming, crushing, distressing, terrible.

3 *informal he presented devastating arguments* INCISIVE, highly effective, penetrating, cutting; withering, blistering, searing, scathing, fierce, savage, stinging, biting, caustic, harsh, unsparing.

**devastation** noun 1 *the hurricane left a trail of devastation* DESTRUCTION, ruin, desolation, havoc, wreckage; ruins, ravages.

2 *the devastation of Prussia* DESTRUCTION, wrecking, ruination; demolition, annihilation; despoliation, plunder, pillaging, plundering.

3 *the devastation you have caused the family* SHOCK, trauma, distress, stress, strain, pain, anguish, suffering, upset, agony, misery, heartache.

**develop** verb 1 *the industry developed rapidly* GROW, expand, spread; advance, progress, evolve, mature; prosper, thrive, flourish, blossom. See note at MATURE.

2 *a plan was developed* INITIATE, instigate, set in motion; originate, invent, form, establish, generate.

3 *children should develop their talents* EXPAND, augment, broaden, supplement, reinforce; enhance, refine, improve, polish, perfect.

4 *a fight developed* START, begin, emerge, erupt, break out, burst out, arise, break, unfold, happen.

5 *he developed the symptoms last week* FALL ILL WITH, be stricken with, succumb to; contract, catch, get, pick up, come down with, become infected with.

**development** noun 1 *the development of the firm* EVOLUTION, growth, maturation, expansion, enlargement, spread, progress; success.

2 *the development of an idea* FORMING, establishment, initiation, instigation, origination, invention, generation.

3 *keep abreast of developments* EVENT, occurrence, happening, circumstance, incident, situation, issue.

4 *a housing development* COMPLEX, site.

**deviant** adjective *deviant behavior* ABERRANT, abnormal, atypical, anomalous, irregular, nonstandard; nonconformist, perverse, uncommon, unusual; freakish, strange, odd, peculiar, bizarre, eccentric, idiosyncratic, unorthodox, exceptional; warped, perverted; *informal* kinky, quirky. ANTONYM normal.

▸ noun *we were seen as deviants* NONCONFORMIST, eccentric, maverick, individualist; outsider, misfit; *informal* oddball, weirdo, freak, screwball, kook, odd duck.

**deviate** verb *do not* ***deviate from*** *the original plan* DIVERGE FROM, digress from, drift from, stray from, veer from, swerve from; get sidetracked from, branch off from; differ from, vary from, run counter to, go in opposition to, contrast with.

**deviation** noun *the slightest deviation could prove disastrous* DIVERGENCE, digression, departure; difference, variation, variance; aberration, abnormality, irregularity, anomaly, inconsistency, discrepancy.

**device** noun 1 *a device for measuring pressure* IMPLEMENT, gadget, utensil, tool, appliance, apparatus, instrument, machine, mechanism, contrivance, contraption; *informal* gizmo, widget, doohickey.

2 *an ingenious legal device* PLOY, tactic, move, stratagem, scheme, plot, plan, trick, ruse, maneuver, machination, contrivance, expedient, dodge, wile.

3 *their shields bear his device* EMBLEM, symbol, logo, badge, crest, insignia, coat of arms, escutcheon, seal, mark, design, motif; monogram, hallmark, trademark.

**devil** noun 1 *God and* **the Devil** SATAN, Beelzebub, Lucifer, the Prince of Darkness, the Evil One; *informal* Old Nick.

2 *he drove out the devils from their bodies* EVIL SPIRIT, demon, fiend, bogie; *informal* spook.

3 *look what the cruel devil has done* BRUTE, beast, monster, fiend; villain, sadist, barbarian, ogre.

4 *he's a naughty little devil* RASCAL, rogue, imp, fiend, monkey, wretch; *informal* monster, horror, scamp, tyke, varmint.

5 *informal the poor devils looked ill* WRETCH, unfortunate, creature, soul, person, fellow; *informal* thing, beggar.

**devilish** adjective 1 *a devilish grin* DIABOLICAL, fiendish, demonic, satanic, demoniac, demoniacal; hellish, infernal; MISCHIEVOUS, wicked, impish, roguish.

2 *a devilish job* DIFFICULT, tricky, ticklish, troublesome, thorny, awkward, problematic.

**devil-may-care** adjective *devil-may-care stunt pilots* RECKLESS, rash, incautious, heedless, impetuous, impulsive, daredevil, hotheaded, wild, foolhardy, audacious, nonchalant, casual, breezy, flippant, insouciant, happy-go-lucky, easygoing, unworried, untroubled, unconcerned, harum-scarum.

**devious** adjective 1 *the devious ways in which they bent the rules* UNDERHANDED, deceitful, dishonest, dishonorable, unethical, unprincipled, immoral, unscrupulous, fraudulent, dubious, unfair, treacherous, duplicitous; crafty, cunning, calculating, artful, conniving, scheming, sly, wily; sneaky, furtive, secret, clandestine, surreptitious, covert, snide; *informal* crooked, shady, dirty, lowdown.

2 *a devious route around the coast* CIRCUITOUS, roundabout, indirect, meandering, winding, tortuous.

**devise** verb *they have devised a way to recycle contaminated oil* CONCEIVE, think up, dream up, work out, formulate, concoct; design, invent, coin, originate; compose, construct, fabricate, create, produce, develop; discover, hit on; hatch, contrive; *informal* cook up.

**devoid** adjective *your argument is* ***devoid of*** *logic* FREE OF, empty of, vacant of, bereft of, deprived of, destitute of, bankrupt of; lacking, without, wanting; *informal* minus.

**devolve** verb *the move would devolve responsibility to local units* DELEGATE, depute, pass (down/on), download, hand down/over/on, transfer, transmit, assign, consign, convey, entrust, turn over, give, cede, surrender, relinquish, deliver; bestow, grant.

**devote** verb ALLOCATE, assign, allot, commit, give (over), apportion, consign, pledge; dedicate, consecrate; set aside, earmark, reserve, designate.

**devoted** adjective LOYAL, faithful, true, staunch, steadfast, constant, committed, dedicated, devout; fond, loving, affectionate, caring, admiring.

**devotee** noun **1** *a devotee of rock music* ENTHUSIAST, fan, lover, aficionado, admirer; *informal* buff, bum, freak, nut, fiend, fanatic, addict, maniac.

**2** *devotees thronged the temple* FOLLOWER, adherent, supporter, advocate, disciple, votary, member, stalwart, fanatic, zealot; believer, worshiper.

**devotion** noun **1** *her devotion to her husband* LOYALTY, faithfulness, fidelity, constancy, commitment, adherence, allegiance, dedication; fondness, love, admiration, affection, care.

**2** *a life of devotion* DEVOUTNESS, piety, religiousness, spirituality, godliness, holiness, sanctity.

**3** *morning devotions* RELIGIOUS WORSHIP, worship, religious observance; prayers; prayer meeting, church service.

**devour** verb **1** *he devoured his meal* EAT HUNGRILY, eat greedily, gobble (up/down), guzzle, gulp (down), bolt (down), gorge oneself on, wolf (down), feast on, consume, eat up; *informal* demolish, dispose of, make short work of, polish off, shovel down, stuff oneself with, pig out on, put away; *informal* scarf (down/up).

**2** *flames devoured the house* CONSUME, engulf, envelop; destroy, demolish, lay waste, devastate; gut, ravage, ruin, wreck.

**3** *he was devoured by remorse* AFFLICT, plague, bedevil, trouble, harrow, rack; consume, swallow up, overcome, overwhelm.

**devout** adjective **1** *a devout Christian* PIOUS, religious, devoted, dedicated, reverent, God-fearing; holy, godly, saintly, faithful, dutiful, righteous, churchgoing, orthodox.

**2** *a devout family man* DEDICATED, devoted, committed, loyal, faithful, staunch, genuine, firm, steadfast, unwavering, sincere, wholehearted, keen, enthusiastic, zealous, passionate, ardent, fervent, active, sworn, pledged; *informal* card-carrying, true blue.

**dexterity** noun **1** *painting china demanded dexterity* DEFTNESS, adeptness, adroitness, agility, nimbleness, handiness, ability, talent, skill, proficiency, expertise, experience, efficiency, mastery, delicacy, knack, artistry, finesse.

**2** *his political dexterity* SHREWDNESS, astuteness, acumen, acuity, intelligence; ingenuity, inventiveness, cleverness, smartness; canniness, sense, discernment, insight, understanding, penetration, perception, perspicacity, discrimination; cunning, artfulness, craftiness; *informal* horse sense, savvy, street smarts.

**dexterous** adjective **1** *a dexterous flick of the wrist* DEFT, adept, adroit, agile, nimble, neat, handy, able, capable, skillful, skilled, proficient, expert, practiced, polished; efficient, effortless, slick, professional, masterly; *informal* nifty, mean, ace. ANTONYM clumsy.

**2** *his dexterous accounting abilities* SHREWD, ingenious, inventive, clever, intelligent, brilliant, smart, sharp, acute, astute, canny, intuitive, discerning, perceptive, insightful, incisive, judicious; cunning, artful, crafty, wily; *informal* on the ball, quick off the mark, quick on the uptake, brainy, savvy. ANTONYM stupid.

**diadem** noun *the queen's jeweled diadem* CROWN, coronet, tiara, circlet, chaplet; *literary* coronal.

**diagnose** verb *perhaps he diagnosed the condition incorrectly* IDENTIFY, determine, distinguish, recognize, detect, pinpoint.

**diagnosis** noun **1** *the diagnosis of celiac disease* IDENTIFICATION, detection, recognition, determination, discovery, pinpointing.

**2** *the results confirmed his diagnosis* OPINION, judgment, verdict, conclusion.

**diagonal** adjective *the diagonal stripes on the wall make me dizzy* CROSSWISE, crossways, slanting, slanted, aslant, oblique, angled, at an angle; cater-cornered, kitty-cornered.

**diagram** noun *Jackson's diagrams show the dramatic effects of erosion since 1948* DRAWING, line drawing, sketch, representation, draft, illustration, picture, plan, outline, delineation, figure; *Computing* graphic.

**dialect** noun *the island dialect was influenced by the Spanish in the sixteenth century* REGIONAL LANGUAGE, local language, local speech, vernacular, patois, idiom; regionalisms, localisms; *informal* lingo.

THE RIGHT WORD **dialect, argot, cant, jargon, lingo, slang, vernacular**

When a New York City cab driver calls out the window, "Hey, wassa madda wichoo?" he is using the **vernacular**, which is the authentic, natural pattern of speech among those belonging to a certain community. In some areas of London, on the other hand, one might hear the Cockney **dialect**, which is a form or variety of a language that is confined to a specific group or locality; it has its own pronunciation, usage, and vocabulary, and may persist for generations or even centuries (*he spoke in the dialect of the Appalachian backwoodsman*). A teenager who tells his parents to "Chill out" is using **slang**, which is a very informal language that includes "substitute" vocabulary ("wheels" for *car*, "rug" for *toupee*), grammatical distortions, and other departures from formal or polite usage. **Argot** refers to the slang of a group that feels threatened by the hostility of society as a whole; it traditionally refers to the slang used by criminals and thieves, although it may refer to any peculiar language that a clique or other closely knit group uses to communicate with each other. At one time **cant** was a synonym for *argot*, but now it usually refers to pompous, inflated language or the hackneyed use of words and phrases by members of a particular class or profession (*the cant of the fashion industry*). In contrast to *cant*, which can at least be understood, **jargon** is nearly impossible for the average person to decipher. This term refers to the technical or highly specialized language used by members of an occupational or professional group (*medical jargon, the jargon of the theater*). If you are frustrated because you can't understand the language used by a particular class or group, you're apt to refer to their way of talking as **lingo**, which is a term for any language that is not readily understood (*she tried to reason with the cab driver, but she couldn't understand his lingo*).

---

**dialectic** noun *feminism has of course contributed to this dialectic* DISCUSSION, debate, dialogue, logical argument, reasoning, argumentation, polemics; *formal* ratiocination.

**dialogue** noun **1** *a book consisting of a series of dialogues* CONVERSATION, talk, discussion, interchange, discourse; chat, tête-à-tête, heart-to-heart; *informal* confab, chinwag; *formal* colloquy, confabulation. See note at CONVERSATION.

**2** *they called for a serious political dialogue* DISCUSSION, exchange, debate, exchange of views, talk, consultation, conference, parley; talks, negotiations; *informal* powwow, skull session.

**diameter** noun *the diameter of the hole is less than two inches* BREADTH, width, thickness; caliber, bore, gauge.

**diametrical**, **diametric** adjective *politically, Taylor was in diametrical opposition to her parents* DIRECT, absolute, complete, exact, extreme, polar, antipodal.

**diaphanous** adjective *a diaphanous dress* SHEER, fine, delicate, light, thin, insubstantial, floaty, flimsy, filmy, silken, chiffony, gossamer, gossamer-thin, gauzy; translucent, transparent, see-through. ANTONYMS thick, opaque.

**diarrhea** noun *an outbreak of diarrhea in the camp* loose stools; *informal* the runs, the trots, the squirts, Montezuma's revenge, turista; *Medicine* dysentery; *archaic* the flux. ANTONYM constipation.

**diary** noun **1** *he put the date in his diary* APPOINTMENT BOOK, engagement book, organizer, personal organizer, daybook, PDA.

**2** *her World War II diaries* JOURNAL, memoir, chronicle, log, logbook, history, annal, record.

**diatribe** noun *he launched into a diatribe against the Catholic Church* TIRADE, harangue, onslaught, attack, polemic, denunciation, broadside, fulmination, condemnation, censure, criticism; *informal* blast; *literary* philippic.

**dicey** adjective *informal refueling at sea is a bit dicey in bad weather* RISKY, uncertain, unpredictable, touch-and-go, precarious, unsafe, dangerous, fraught with danger, hazardous, perilous, high-risk, difficult; *informal* chancy, hairy, iffy, gnarly. ANTONYM safe.

**dictate** verb **1** *the president's attempts to dictate policy* PRESCRIBE, lay down, impose, set down, order, command, decree, ordain, direct, determine, decide, control, govern.

**2** *you are in no position to* **dictate to** *me* GIVE ORDERS TO, order around/about, lord it over; lay down the law to; *informal* boss around/about, push around/about; (**dictate to someone**) throw one's weight around/about.

**3** *choice is often dictated by availability* DETERMINE, control, govern, decide, influence, affect.

▸ noun *the dictates of his superior* ORDER, command, commandment, decree, edict, ruling, dictum, diktat, directive, direction, instruction, pronouncement, mandate, requirement, stipulation, injunction, demand; *formal* ordinance; *literary* behest.

**dictator** noun *a regime that has survived under one dictator for more than forty years* AUTOCRAT, absolute ruler, despot, tyrant, oppressor, autarch.

**dictatorial** adjective **1** *a dictatorial regime* AUTOCRATIC, undemocratic, totalitarian, authoritarian, autarchic, despotic, tyrannical, tyrannous, absolute, unrestricted, unlimited, unaccountable, arbitrary; *informal* iron-fisted. ANTONYM democratic.

**2** *his dictatorial manner* DOMINEERING, autocratic, authoritarian, oppressive, imperious, officious, overweening, overbearing, peremptory, dogmatic, high and mighty; severe, strict; *informal* bossy, high-handed. ANTONYM meek.

**dictatorship** noun *growing up in the shadow of dictatorship* ABSOLUTE RULE, undemocratic rule, despotism, tyranny, autocracy, autarchy, authoritarianism, totalitarianism, fascism; oppression, repression. ANTONYM democracy.

**diction** noun **1** *his careful diction* ENUNCIATION, articulation, elocution, locution, pronunciation, speech, intonation, inflection; delivery.

**2** *her diction was archaic* PHRASEOLOGY, phrasing, turn of phrase, wording, language, usage, vocabulary, terminology, expressions, idioms.

**dictionary** noun *dictionaries created by Oxford's American lexicographers* LEXICON, wordbook, word list, glossary; thesaurus.

**dictum** noun **1** *he received the dictum with evident reluctance* PRONOUNCEMENT, proclamation, direction, injunction, dictate, command, commandment, order, decree, edict, mandate, diktat.

**2** *the old dictum "might is right"* SAYING, maxim, axiom, proverb, adage, aphorism, saw, precept, epigram, motto, truism, commonplace, platitude; expression, phrase, tag.

**didactic** adjective *the didactic photojournalism of Jacob Riis* INSTRUCTIVE, instructional, educational, educative, informative, informational, edifying, improving, preceptive, pedagogic, moralistic.

**die** verb **1** *her father died last year* PASS AWAY, pass on, lose one's life, expire, breathe one's last, meet one's end, meet one's death, lay down one's life, perish, go the way of all flesh, go to one's last resting place, go to meet one's maker, cross the great divide, slip away; *informal* give up the ghost, kick the bucket, croak, buy it, turn up one's toes, cash in one's chips, bite the big one, check out, buy the farm; *archaic* depart this life. ANTONYMS live, survive.

2 *the wind had **died down*** ABATE, subside, drop, lessen, ease (off), let up, moderate, fade, dwindle, peter out, wane, ebb, relent, weaken; melt away, dissolve, vanish, disappear; *archaic* remit. ANTONYM intensify.

3 *informal the engine died* FAIL, cut out, give out, stop, break down, stop working; *informal* conk out, go kaput, give up the ghost.

4 *informal she's dying to meet you* LONG, yearn, burn, ache; *informal* itch.

**diehard** adjective *a diehard hockey fan* HARDLINE, reactionary, ultraconservative, conservative, traditionalist, dyed-in-the-wool, intransigent, inflexible, uncompromising, rigid, entrenched, set in one's ways; staunch, steadfast.

**diet**[1] noun *health problems related to your diet* SELECTION OF FOOD, food, foodstuffs; *informal* grub, nosh.

▸ verb *she dieted for most of her life* BE ON A DIET, eat sparingly; lose weight, watch one's weight, reduce, slenderize.

**diet**[2] noun *the diet's lower house* LEGISLATIVE ASSEMBLY, legislature, congress, senate, parliament, council, assembly.

**differ** verb 1 *the second set of data **differed from** the first* CONTRAST WITH, be different from, be dissimilar to, be unlike, vary from, diverge from, deviate from, conflict with, run counter to, be incompatible with, be at odds with, go against, contradict. ANTONYM resemble.

2 *the two sides differed over this issue* DISAGREE, conflict, be at variance, be at odds, be in dispute, not see eye to eye. ANTONYM agree.

**difference** noun 1 *the difference between the two sets of data* DISSIMILARITY, contrast, distinction, differentiation, variance, variation, divergence, disparity, deviation, polarity, gulf, gap, imbalance, contradiction, contradistinction. ANTONYM similarity.

2 *we've had our differences in the past* DISAGREEMENT, difference of opinion, dispute, argument, quarrel, wrangle, contretemps, altercation; *informal* tiff, set-to, run-in, spat, row.

3 *I am willing to pay the difference* BALANCE, remainder, rest, remaining amount, residue.

**different** adjective 1 *people with different lifestyles* DISSIMILAR, unalike, unlike, contrasting, contrastive, divergent, differing, varying, disparate; poles apart, incompatible, mismatched, conflicting, clashing. ANTONYM similar.

2 *suddenly everything in her life was different* CHANGED, altered, transformed, new, unfamiliar, unknown, strange. ANTONYM the same.

3 *two different occasions* DISTINCT, separate, individual, discrete, independent. ANTONYMS similar, related.

4 *informal he wanted to try something different* UNUSUAL, out of the ordinary, unfamiliar, novel, new, fresh, original, unconventional, exotic, uncommon. ANTONYM ordinary.

**differential** adjective *technical* 1 *the differential achievements of boys and girls* DIFFERENT, dissimilar, contrasting, unalike, divergent, disparate, contrastive. ANTONYM similar.

2 *the differential features of benign and malignant tumors* DISTINCTIVE, distinguishing. ANTONYM similar.

**differentiate** verb 1 *he was unable to differentiate between fantasy and reality* DISTINGUISH, discriminate, make/draw a distinction, tell the difference, tell apart. See note at DISTINGUISH.

2 *this differentiates their business from all other booksellers* MAKE DIFFERENT, distinguish, set apart, single out, separate, mark off.

**difficult** adjective 1 *a very difficult job* HARD, strenuous, arduous, laborious, tough, onerous, burdensome, demanding, punishing, grueling, back-breaking, exhausting, tiring, fatiguing, wearisome; *informal* hellish, killing; *archaic* toilsome. ANTONYM easy.

2 *she found math very difficult* HARD, complicated, complex, involved, impenetrable, unfathomable, over/above one's head, beyond one, puzzling, baffling, perplexing, confusing, mystifying; problematic, intricate, knotty, thorny, ticklish. See note at HARD. ANTONYMS simple, straightforward.

3 *a difficult child* TROUBLESOME, tiresome, trying, exasperating, awkward, demanding, perverse, contrary, recalcitrant, unmanageable, obstreperous, unaccommodating, unhelpful, uncooperative, disobliging; hard to please, fussy, finicky; *formal* refractory. See note at DOCILE. ANTONYM accommodating.

4 *you've come at a difficult time* INCONVENIENT, awkward, inopportune, unfavorable, unfortunate, inappropriate, unsuitable, untimely, ill-timed. ANTONYM convenient.

5 *the family has been through a difficult year* BAD, tough, grim, dark, black, hard, adverse, distressing; straitened. ANTONYM happy.

**difficulty** noun 1 *the difficulty of balancing motherhood with a career* STRAIN, trouble, problems, toil, struggle, laboriousness, arduousness; *informal* hassle, stress. ANTONYM ease.

2 *the project has met with one difficulty after another* PROBLEM, complication, snag, hitch, pitfall, handicap, impediment, hindrance, obstacle, hurdle, stumbling block, obstruction, barrier; *informal* fly in the ointment, headache; growing pains.

3 **(difficulties)** *Charles got into difficulties* TROUBLE, predicament, plight, hard times, dire straits; quandary, dilemma; *informal* deep water, a fix, a jam, a spot, a scrape, a stew, a hole, a pickle.

**diffidence** noun *her diffidence was out of place in this outgoing group* SHYNESS, bashfulness, modesty, self-effacement, meekness, unassertiveness, timidity, humility, hesitancy, reticence, insecurity, self-doubt, uncertainty, self-consciousness.

**diffident** adjective *underneath his diffident exterior was a passionate temperament* SHY, bashful, modest, self-effacing, unassuming, meek, unconfident, unassertive, timid, timorous, humble, shrinking, reticent, hesitant, insecure, self-doubting, doubtful, uncertain, unsure, self-conscious; *informal* mousy. ANTONYM confident.

**diffuse** verb *such ideas were diffused widely in the 1970s* SPREAD, spread around, send out, disseminate, scatter, disperse, distribute, put about, circulate, communicate, purvey, propagate, transmit, broadcast, promulgate. See note at SCATTER.

▸ adjective **1** *a diffuse community centered on the church* SPREAD OUT, scattered, dispersed, diasporic.

**2** *a diffuse narrative* VERBOSE, wordy, prolix, long-winded, long-drawn-out, discursive, rambling, wandering, meandering, maundering, digressive, circuitous, roundabout, circumlocutory, periphrastic.

**diffusion** noun *the diffusion of Marxist ideas* SPREAD, dissemination, scattering, dispersal, diaspora, distribution, circulation, propagation, transmission, broadcasting, promulgation.

**dig** verb **1** *she began to dig the heavy clay soil* TURN OVER, work, break up; till, harrow, plow, shovel.

**2** *he took a spade and dug a hole* EXCAVATE, dig out, quarry, hollow out, scoop out, gouge out; cut, bore, tunnel, burrow, mine.

**3** *the bodies were hastily* ***dug up*** EXHUME, disinter, unearth.

**4** *Winnie dug her elbow into his ribs* POKE, prod, jab, stab, shove, ram, push, thrust, drive.

**5** *he'd been* ***digging into*** *my past* DELVE INTO, probe into, search into, inquire into, look into, investigate, research, examine, scrutinize, check up on; *informal* check out.

**6** ***I dug up*** *some disturbing information* UNCOVER, discover, find (out), unearth, dredge up, root out, ferret out, turn up, reveal, bring to light, expose.

**7** *informal, dated I dig talking with him.* See ENJOY verb sense 1.

▸ noun **1** *a dig in the ribs* POKE, prod, jab, stab, shove, push.

**2** *informal they're always making digs at each other* SNIDE REMARK, cutting remark, jibe, jeer, taunt, sneer, insult, barb, insinuation; *informal* wisecrack, crack, put-down.

**digest** verb *Liz digested this information* ASSIMILATE, absorb, take in, understand, comprehend, grasp; consider, think about, reflect on, ponder, contemplate, mull over.

▸ noun *a digest of their findings* SUMMARY, synopsis, abstract, précis, résumé, summation; compilation; *informal* wrap-up.

**dignified** adjective *a dignified and courteous butler* STATELY, noble, courtly, majestic, distinguished, proud, august, lofty, exalted, regal, lordly, imposing, impressive, grand; solemn, serious, grave, formal, proper, ceremonious, decorous, reserved, composed, sedate.

**dignify** verb *shall we dignify their arrival with some music?* ENNOBLE, enhance, distinguish, add distinction to, honor, grace, exalt, magnify, glorify, elevate.

**dignitary** noun *the studio is being visited by a bunch of foreign dignitaries* WORTHY, personage, VIP, grandee, notable, pillar of society, luminary, leading light, big name; *informal* heavyweight, bigwig, top brass, top dog, big gun, big shot, big cheese, big chief, supremo, big wheel, big kahuna, big enchilada, top banana.

**dignity** noun **1** *the dignity of the proceedings* STATELINESS, nobility, majesty, regality, courtliness, augustness, loftiness, lordliness, grandeur; solemnity, gravity, gravitas, formality, decorum, propriety, sedateness.

**2** *he had lost his dignity* SELF-RESPECT, pride, self-esteem, self-worth.

**digress** verb *I have digressed from the original plan* DEVIATE, go off on a tangent, get off the subject, get sidetracked, lose the thread, turn aside/away, depart, drift, stray, wander.

**digression** noun *a book full of long digressions* DEVIATION, detour, diversion, departure, divergence, excursus; aside, incidental remark.

**dilapidated** adjective *a row of dilapidated houses* RUNDOWN, tumbledown, ramshackle, broken-down, in disrepair, shabby, battered, beat-up, rickety, shaky, unsound, crumbling, in ruins, ruined, decayed, decaying, decrepit; neglected, uncared-for, untended, the worse for wear, falling to pieces, falling apart, gone to rack and ruin, gone to seed.

**dilate** verb **1** *her nostrils dilated* ENLARGE, widen, expand, distend. ANTONYM contract.

**2** *Diane dilated on the joys of her married life* EXPATIATE, expound, enlarge, elaborate, speak/write at length. ANTONYM contract.

**dilatory** adjective **1** *he had been dilatory in appointing an executor* SLOW, tardy, unhurried, sluggish, sluggardly, snaillike, lazy. ANTONYMS fast, prompt.

**2** *dilatory procedural tactics* DELAYING, stalling, temporizing, procrastinating, time-wasting, filibustering.

**dilemma** noun *a discussion with a colleague resolved her dilemma* QUANDARY, predicament, Catch-22, vicious circle, plight, mess, muddle; difficulty, problem, trouble, perplexity, confusion, conflict; *informal* no-win situation, fix, tight spot, tight corner, can of worms.

USAGE NOTE **dilemma**

**Dilemma** should be reserved for reference to a predicament in which a difficult choice must be made between undesirable alternatives: *You see his dilemma? If he moves to London, he may never see his parents again. But if he stays in Seattle, he may be giving up the best job offer of his life.* The weakened use of *dilemma* to mean simply "a difficult situation or problem" (*the dilemma of a teacher shortage*) is recorded as early as the first part of the seventeenth century, but many regard this use as unacceptable and it should be avoided in written English.

**dilettante** noun *there is no room for the dilettante in this business* DABBLER, amateur, nonprofessional, nonspecialist, layman, layperson. ANTONYM professional.

**diligence** noun *they set about their tasks with diligence* CONSCIENTIOUSNESS, assiduousness, assiduity, hard work, application, concentration, effort, care, industriousness, rigor, meticulousness, thoroughness; perseverance, persistence, tenacity, dedication, commitment, tirelessness, indefatigability, doggedness.

**diligent** adjective *diligent workers* INDUSTRIOUS, hardworking, assiduous, conscientious, particular, punctilious, meticulous, painstaking, rigorous, careful, thorough, sedulous, earnest; persevering, persistent, tenacious, zealous, dedicated, committed, unflagging, untiring, tireless, indefatigable, dogged; *archaic* laborious. See note at BUSY. ANTONYM lazy.

**dilly-dally** verb *informal we can't dilly-dally when there are critical decisions to be made* WASTE TIME, dally, dawdle, loiter, linger, take one's time, delay, temporize, stall, procrastinate, pussyfoot around, drag one's feet; dither, hesitate, falter, vacillate, waver, hem and haw; *informal* shilly-shally, lollygag, let the grass grow under one's feet; *archaic* tarry. ANTONYM hurry.

**dilute** verb **1** *strong bleach can be diluted with water* MAKE WEAKER, weaken, water down; thin out, thin; doctor, adulterate; *informal* cut.

**2** *the original plans have been diluted* WEAKEN, moderate, tone down, water down.

**dim** adjective **1** *the dim light* FAINT, weak, feeble, soft, pale, dull, subdued, muted. ANTONYM bright.

**2** *long dim corridors* DARK, badly lit, ill-lit, dingy, dismal, gloomy, murky; *literary* tenebrous. ANTONYM bright.

**3** *a dim figure* INDISTINCT, ill-defined, unclear, vague, shadowy, nebulous, obscured, blurred, blurry, fuzzy. ANTONYM distinct.

**4** *dim memories* VAGUE, imprecise, imperfect, unclear, indistinct, sketchy, hazy, blurred, shadowy. ANTONYMS clear, distinct.

**5** *informal is she a bit dim?* See STUPID sense 1.

**6** *their prospects for the future looked dim* GLOOMY, unpromising, unfavorable, discouraging, disheartening, depressing, dispiriting, hopeless. ANTONYM encouraging.

▸ verb **1** *the lights were dimmed* TURN DOWN, lower, soften, subdue, mute; *literary* bedim. ANTONYM turn up.

**2** *my memories have not dimmed with time* FADE, become vague, dwindle, blur. ANTONYM sharpen.

**3** *the fighting dimmed hopes of peace* DIMINISH, reduce, lessen, weaken, undermine. ANTONYM intensify.

**dimension** noun **1** *the dimensions of the room* SIZE, measurements, proportions, extent; length, width, breadth, depth, area, volume, capacity; footage, acreage.

**2** *the dimension of the problem* SIZE, scale, extent, scope, magnitude; importance, significance.

**3** *the cultural dimensions of the problem* ASPECT, feature, element, facet, side.

**diminish** verb **1** *the pain will gradually diminish* DECREASE, lessen, decline, reduce, subside, die down, abate, dwindle, fade, slacken off, moderate, let up, ebb, wane, recede, die away/out, peter out; *archaic* remit. ANTONYM increase.

**2** *new legislation diminished the courts' authority* REDUCE, decrease, lessen, curtail, cut, cut down/back, constrict, restrict, limit, curb, check; weaken, blunt, erode, undermine, sap. ANTONYM increase.

**3** *she lost no opportunity to diminish him* BELITTLE, disparage, denigrate, defame, deprecate, run down; decry, demean, cheapen, devalue; *formal* derogate. ANTONYM boost.

**diminution** noun *a diminution of freedom reduces the quality of life* REDUCTION, decrease, lessening, decline, dwindling, moderation, fading, fade-out, weakening, ebb.

**diminutive** adjective *a diminutive breed of parrot* TINY, small, little, petite, elfin, minute, miniature, mini, minuscule, compact, pocket, toy, midget, undersized, short; *informal* teeny, weeny, teeny-weeny, teensy-weensy, itty-bitty, itsy-bitsy, baby, pint-sized, knee-high to a grasshopper, little-bitty; *Scottish* wee. See note at SMALL. ANTONYM enormous.

**din** noun *he shouted above the din* NOISE, racket, rumpus, ruckus, cacophony, babel, hubbub, tumult, uproar, commotion, clatter; shouting, yelling, screaming, caterwauling, clamor, clangor, outcry; *informal* hullabaloo. ANTONYM silence.

▸ verb **1** *she had had the evils of drink dinned into her* INSTILL, inculcate, drive, drum, hammer, drill, ingrain; indoctrinate, brainwash.

**2** *the sound dinning in my ears* BLARE, blast, clang, clatter, crash, clamor.

**dine** verb **1** *we dined at a restaurant* HAVE DINNER, have supper, eat; *dated* sup, break bread.

**2** *they dined on lobster* EAT, feed on, feast on, banquet on, partake of; *informal* tuck into, chow down on.

**dingy** adjective *their secret hiding place was a dingy room in the basement* GLOOMY, dark, dull, badly/poorly lit, murky, dim, dismal, dreary, drab, somber, grim, cheerless; dirty, grimy, shabby, faded, worn, dowdy, seedy, run-down; *informal* grungy. ANTONYM bright.

**dinky** adjective *informal as usual, he made a dinky contribution* TRIFLING, trivial, insignificant, unimportant, negligible, of no account.

**dinner** noun *dinner will be served on the terrace* EVENING MEAL, supper, main meal; lunch, midday meal; feast, banquet, dinner party; *informal* spread; *humorous* din-din; *formal* repast.

**dip** verb **1** *he dipped a rag in the water* IMMERSE, submerge, plunge, duck, dunk, lower, sink.

**2** *the sun dipped below the horizon* SINK, set, drop, go/drop down, fall, descend; disappear, vanish. ANTONYM rise.

**3** *the president's popularity has dipped* DECREASE, fall, drop, fall off, decline, diminish, dwindle, slump, plummet, plunge. ANTONYMS rise, increase.

4 *the road dipped* SLOPE DOWN, descend, go down; drop away, fall, sink. ANTONYM rise.

5 *you might have to* ***dip into*** *your savings* DRAW ON, use, make use of, have recourse to, spend.

▸ noun 1 *a relaxing dip in the pool* SWIM, bathe; splash, paddle.

2 *give the fish a ten-minute dip in a salt bath* IMMERSION, plunge, ducking, dunking.

3 *chicken satay with peanut dip* SAUCE, dressing.

4 *the hedge at the bottom of the dip* SLOPE, incline, decline, descent; hollow, concavity, depression, basin, indentation.

5 *a dip in sales* DECREASE, fall, drop, downturn, decline, falling-off, slump, reduction, diminution, ebb.

**diplomacy** noun 1 *diplomacy failed to win them independence* STATESMANSHIP, statecraft, negotiation(s), discussion(s), talks, dialogue; international relations, foreign affairs.

2 *Jack's quiet diplomacy* TACT, tactfulness, sensitivity, discretion, subtlety, finesse, delicacy, savoir faire, politeness, thoughtfulness, care, judiciousness, prudence.

**diplomat** noun *a British diplomat working in Germany* AMBASSADOR, attaché, consul, chargé d'affaires, envoy, nuncio, emissary, plenipotentiary; *archaic* legate.

**diplomatic** adjective 1 *diplomatic activity* AMBASSADORIAL, consular.

2 *he tried to be diplomatic* TACTFUL, sensitive, subtle, delicate, polite, discreet, thoughtful, careful, judicious, prudent, politic, clever, skillful. ANTONYM tactless.

**dire** adjective 1 *the dire economic situation* TERRIBLE, dreadful, appalling, frightful, awful, atrocious, grim, alarming; grave, serious, disastrous, calamitous, ruinous, hopeless, irretrievable, wretched, desperate, parlous; *formal* grievous.

2 *he was in dire need of help* URGENT, desperate, pressing, crying, sore, grave, serious, extreme, acute, drastic.

3 *dire warnings of fuel shortages* OMINOUS, gloomy, grim, dismal, unpropitious, inauspicious, unfavorable, pessimistic.

**direct** adjective 1 *the most direct route* STRAIGHT, undeviating, unswerving; shortest, quickest.

2 *a direct flight* NONSTOP, unbroken, uninterrupted, through.

3 *he is very direct* FRANK, candid, straightforward, honest, open, blunt, plain-spoken, outspoken, forthright, downright, no-nonsense, matter-of-fact, not afraid to call a spade a spade; *informal* upfront.

4 *direct contact with the president* FACE TO FACE, personal, immediate, firsthand.

5 *a direct quotation* VERBATIM, word for word, to the letter, faithful, exact, precise, accurate, correct.

6 *the direct opposite* EXACT, absolute, complete, diametrical.

▸ verb 1 *an economic elite directed the nation's affairs* MANAGE, govern, run, administer, control, conduct, handle, be in charge/control of, preside over, lead, head, rule, be at the helm of; supervise, superintend, oversee, regulate, orchestrate, coordinate; *informal* run the show, call the shots, be in the driver's seat.

2 *was that remark* ***directed at*** *me?* AIM AT, target at, address to, intend for, mean for, design for.

3 *a man in uniform directed them to the hall* GIVE DIRECTIONS, show the way, guide, lead, conduct, accompany, usher, escort.

4 *the judge directed the jury to return a 'not guilty' verdict* INSTRUCT, tell, command, order, charge, require; *literary* bid.

**direction** noun 1 *a northerly direction* WAY, route, course, line, run, bearing, orientation.

2 *the direction of my research* ORIENTATION, inclination, leaning, tendency, bent, bias, preference; drift, tack, attitude, tone, tenor, mood, current, trend.

3 *his direction of the project* ADMINISTRATION, management, conduct, handling, running, supervision, superintendence, regulation, orchestration; control, command, rule, leadership, guidance.

4 *explicit directions about nursing care* INSTRUCTION, order, command, prescription, rule, regulation, requirement.

**directive** noun *a directive from the front office* INSTRUCTION, direction, command, order, charge, injunction, prescription, rule, ruling, regulation, law, dictate, decree, dictum, edict, mandate, fiat; *formal* ordinance.

**directly** adverb 1 *they flew directly to New York* STRAIGHT, right, as the crow flies, by a direct route.

2 *I went directly after breakfast* IMMEDIATELY, at once, instantly, right away, straightaway, posthaste, without delay, without hesitation, forthwith; quickly, speedily, promptly; *informal* pronto.

3 *the houses directly opposite* EXACTLY, right, immediately; diametrically; *informal* bang.

4 *she spoke simply and directly* FRANKLY, candidly, openly, bluntly, forthrightly, without beating around the bush.

**director** noun *the director of the museum* ADMINISTRATOR, manager, chairman, chairwoman, chairperson, chair, head, chief, principal, leader, governor, president; managing director, chief executive (officer), CEO; supervisor, controller, overseer; *informal* boss, kingpin, top dog, head honcho, numero uno.

**dirge** noun *a lone bagpiper played the woeful dirge* ELEGY, lament, burial hymn, threnody, requiem, funeral march; *Irish* keen.

**dirt** noun 1 *his face was streaked with dirt* GRIME, filth; dust, soot, smut; muck, mud, mire, sludge, slime, ooze, dross; smudges, stains; *informal* crud, yuck, grunge; *Brit.* gunge.

2 *the packed dirt of the road* EARTH, soil, loam, clay, silt; ground.

3 *informal dog dirt.* See EXCREMENT.

4 *informal they tried to dig up dirt on the president* A SCANDAL, gossip, revelations, a rumor, rumors; information.

**dirty** adjective 1 *a dirty sweatshirt* | *dirty water* SOILED, grimy, grubby, filthy, mucky, stained, unwashed, greasy, smeared, smeary, spotted, smudged, cloudy, muddy, dusty, sooty; unclean, sullied, impure, tarnished, polluted, contaminated, defiled, foul, unhygienic, unsanitary; *informal* cruddy, yucky, icky, grotty, grungy; *literary* befouled, besmirched, begrimed. ANTONYM clean.

**2** *a dirty joke* INDECENT, obscene, rude, naughty, vulgar, smutty, coarse, crude, filthy, bawdy, suggestive, ribald, racy, salacious, risqué, offensive, off-color, lewd, pornographic, explicit, X-rated; *informal* blue, triple-X, XXX; *euphemistic* adult. ANTONYM clean.

**3** *dirty tricks* DISHONEST, deceitful, unscrupulous, dishonorable, unsporting, ungentlemanly, below the belt, unfair, unethical, unprincipled; crooked, double-dealing, underhanded, sly, crafty, devious, sneaky. ANTONYMS honest, decent.

**4** *informal a dirty cheat* DESPICABLE, contemptible, hateful, vile, low, mean, unworthy, worthless, beyond contempt, sordid; *informal* rotten; *archaic* scurvy. ANTONYMS trustworthy, decent.

**5** *a dirty look* MALEVOLENT, resentful, hostile, black, dark; angry, cross, indignant, annoyed, disapproving; *informal* peeved.

▸ verb *he dirtied her nice clean towels* SOIL, stain, muddy, blacken, mess up, mark, spatter, bespatter, smudge, smear, splatter; sully, pollute, foul, defile; *literary* befoul, besmirch, begrime. ANTONYM clean.

**disability** noun *my disability makes getting into bed a slow process* HANDICAP, disablement, incapacity, impairment, infirmity, defect, abnormality; condition, disorder, affliction.

**disable** verb **1** *an injury that could disable somebody for life* INCAPACITATE, put out of action, debilitate; handicap, cripple, lame, maim, immobilize, paralyze.

**2** *the bomb squad disabled the device* DEACTIVATE, defuse, disarm.

**3** *he was disabled from holding public office* DISQUALIFY, prevent, preclude.

**disabled** adjective **1** *a disabled athlete* HANDICAPPED, incapacitated; debilitated, infirm, out of action; crippled, lame, paralyzed, immobilized, bedridden, paraplegic, quadriplegic, in a wheelchair; *euphemistic* physically challenged, differently abled. ANTONYM able-bodied.

**2** *a disabled cargo ship* BROKEN DOWN, out of service, out of commission, wrecked. ANTONYM functioning.

**disabuse** verb *it isn't easy to **disabuse** people **of** something they've been taught to believe in* DISILLUSION ABOUT, undeceive about, set straight on/about, open someone's eyes about, correct on, enlighten on/about, disenchant about, shatter someone's illusions about.

**disadvantage** noun *the long commute is a big disadvantage of this job* DRAWBACK, snag, downside, stumbling block, fly in the ointment, catch, hindrance, obstacle, impediment; flaw, defect, weakness, fault, handicap, con, trouble, difficulty, problem, complication, nuisance; *informal* minus. ANTONYM benefit.

**disadvantaged** adjective *disadvantaged families will not be helped by these measures* DEPRIVED, underprivileged, depressed, in need, needy, poor, impoverished, indigent, hard up.

**disadvantageous** adjective *this puts us in a disadvantageous position* UNFAVORABLE, adverse, unfortunate, unlucky, bad; detrimental, prejudicial, deleterious, harmful, damaging, injurious, hurtful; inconvenient, inopportune, ill-timed, untimely, inexpedient.

**disaffected** adjective *a plot by disaffected soldiers* DISSATISFIED, disgruntled, discontented, malcontent, frustrated, alienated; disloyal, rebellious, mutinous, seditious, dissident, up in arms; hostile, antagonistic, unfriendly. See note at SOLITUDE. ANTONYM contented.

**disagree** verb **1** *no one was willing to **disagree with** him* TAKE ISSUE WITH, challenge, contradict, oppose; be at variance with, be at odds with, not see eye to eye with, differ with, dissent from, be in dispute with, debate with, argue with, quarrel with, wrangle with, clash with, be at loggerheads with, cross swords with, lock horns with; *formal* gainsay.

**2** *their accounts disagree on details* DIFFER, be dissimilar, be different, vary, diverge; contradict each other, conflict, clash, contrast.

**3** *the spicy food **disagreed with** her* MAKE ILL, make unwell, nauseate, sicken, upset.

**disagreeable** adjective **1** *a disagreeable smell* UNPLEASANT, displeasing, nasty, offensive, off-putting, obnoxious, objectionable, horrible, horrid, dreadful, frightful, abominable, odious, repugnant, repulsive, repellent, revolting, disgusting, foul, vile, nauseating, sickening, unpalatable. ANTONYM pleasant.

**2** *a disagreeable man* BAD-TEMPERED, ill-tempered, curmudgeonly, cross, crabbed, irritable, grumpy, peevish, sullen, prickly; unfriendly, unpleasant, nasty, mean, mean-spirited, ill-natured, rude, surly, discourteous, impolite, brusque, abrupt, churlish, disobliging. ANTONYM pleasant.

**disagreement** noun **1** *there was some disagreement over possible solutions* DISSENT, dispute, difference of opinion, variance, controversy, discord, contention, division.

**2** *a heated disagreement* ARGUMENT, debate, quarrel, wrangle, squabble, falling-out, altercation, dispute, disputation, war of words, contretemps; *informal* tiff, set-to, blowup, spat, row.

**3** *the disagreement between the results of the two assessments* DIFFERENCE, dissimilarity, variation, variance, discrepancy, disparity, divergence, deviation, nonconformity; incompatibility, contradiction, conflict, clash, contrast.

**disallow** verb *Nguyen's testimony will be disallowed* REJECT, refuse, dismiss, say no to; ban, bar, block, debar, forbid, prohibit; cancel, invalidate, overrule, quash, overturn, countermand, reverse, throw out, set aside; *informal* give the thumbs down to, veto, nix. See note at PROHIBIT.

**disappear** verb **1** *by 4 o'clock the mist had disappeared* VANISH, pass from sight, be lost to view/sight, recede from view;

fade (away), melt away, clear, dissolve, disperse, evaporate, dematerialize; *literary* evanesce. ANTONYM materialize.

**2** *this way of life has disappeared* DIE OUT, die, cease to exist, come to an end, end, pass away, pass into oblivion, perish, vanish. ANTONYM survive.

**disappoint** verb **1** *I'm sorry to have disappointed you* LET DOWN, fail, dissatisfy, dash someone's hopes; upset, dismay, sadden, disenchant, disillusion, shatter someone's illusions, disabuse. ANTONYMS please, satisfy.

**2** *his hopes were disappointed* THWART, frustrate, foil, dash, put a damper on; *informal* throw cold water on. ANTONYM fulfill.

**disappointed** adjective *it was hard to look into those disappointed faces* UPSET, saddened, let down, cast down, disheartened, downhearted, downcast, depressed, dispirited, discouraged, despondent, dismayed, crestfallen, distressed, chagrined; disenchanted, disillusioned; displeased, discontented, dissatisfied, frustrated, disgruntled; *informal* choked, bummed (out), miffed, cut up. ANTONYM pleased.

**disappointing** adjective *a pretty good movie up until the disappointing ending* REGRETTABLE, unfortunate, sorry, discouraging, disheartening, dispiriting, depressing, dismaying, upsetting, saddening; unsatisfactory; *informal* not all it's cracked up to be.

**disappointment** noun **1** *his disappointment in the outcome was obvious* SADNESS, regret, dismay, sorrow; dispiritedness, despondency, distress, chagrin; disenchantment, disillusionment; displeasure, dissatisfaction, disgruntlement. ANTONYM satisfaction.

**2** *the trip was a bit of a disappointment* LETDOWN, nonevent, anticlimax, washout; *informal* bummer.

**disapproval** noun *their strong disapproval of the law* DISAPPROBATION, objection, dislike; dissatisfaction, disfavor, displeasure, distaste; criticism, censure, condemnation, denunciation, deprecation; *informal* thumbs down.

**disapprove** verb **1** *he* ***disapproved of*** *gamblers* OBJECT TO, have a poor opinion of, look down one's nose at, take exception to, dislike, take a dim view of, look askance at, frown on, be against, not believe in; deplore, criticize, censure, condemn, denounce, decry, deprecate.

**2** *the board disapproved the plan* REJECT, veto, refuse, turn down, disallow, throw out, dismiss, rule against; *informal* nix.

**disarm** verb **1** *the UN must disarm the country* DEMILITARIZE, demobilize.

**2** *the militia refused to disarm* LAY DOWN ONE'S ARMS, demilitarize; *literary* beat one's swords into plowshares.

**3** *police disarmed the bomb* DEFUSE, disable, deactivate, put out of action, make harmless.

**4** *the warmth in his voice disarmed her* WIN OVER, charm, persuade, thaw; mollify, appease, placate, pacify, conciliate, propitiate.

**disarmament** noun *the public wanted peace and disarmament* DEMILITARIZATION, demobilization, decommissioning; arms reduction, arms limitation, arms control; the zero option.

**disarming** adjective *a disarming smile* WINNING, charming, irresistible, persuasive, beguiling; conciliatory, mollifying.

**disarrange** verb *every year the festival gets bigger, and every year the town gets more disarranged* DISORDER, throw into disarray/disorder, put out of place, disorganize, disturb, displace; mess up, make untidy, make a mess of, jumble, mix up, muddle, turn upside-down, scatter; dishevel, tousle, rumple; *informal* turn topsy-turvy, make a shambles of, muss up.

**disarray** noun *the room was in disarray* DISORDER, confusion, chaos, untidiness, disorganization, dishevelment, mess, muddle, clutter, jumble, tangle, shambles. See note at JUMBLE. ANTONYM tidiness.

**disaster** noun **1** *a subway disaster* CATASTROPHE, calamity, cataclysm, tragedy, act of God, holocaust; accident.

**2** *a string of personal disasters* MISFORTUNE, mishap, misadventure, mischance, setback, reversal, stroke of bad luck, blow. ANTONYM blessing.

**3** *informal the film was a disaster* FAILURE, fiasco, catastrophe, debacle; *informal* flop, megaflop, dud, bomb, washout, dog, turkey, dead loss. ANTONYM success.

**disastrous** adjective *a series of disastrous floods* CATASTROPHIC, calamitous, cataclysmic, tragic; devastating, ruinous, harmful, dire, terrible, awful, shocking, appalling, dreadful; black, dark, unfortunate, unlucky, ill-fated, ill-starred, inauspicious; *formal* grievous.

**disavowal** noun *it's a complete disavowal of responsibility* DENIAL, rejection, repudiation, renunciation, disclaimer.

**disband** verb *the unit was scheduled to disband* BREAK UP, disperse, demobilize, dissolve, scatter, separate, go separate ways, part company. ANTONYM assemble.

**disbelief** noun **1** *she stared at him in disbelief* INCREDULITY, astonishment, amazement, surprise, incredulousness; skepticism, doubt, doubtfulness, dubiousness; cynicism, suspicion, distrust, mistrust; *formal* dubiety.

**2** *I guess I'll burn in hell for my disbelief* ATHEISM, nonbelief, unbelief, godlessness, irreligion, agnosticism, nihilism.

**disbelieve** verb *we've learned to disbelieve most of Hubert's explanations* NOT BELIEVE, give no credence to, discredit, discount, doubt, distrust, mistrust, be incredulous, be unconvinced; reject, repudiate, question, challenge; *informal* take with a pinch of salt.

**disbeliever** noun *they promised to pray for us disbelievers* UNBELIEVER, nonbeliever, atheist, nihilist; skeptic, doubter, agnostic, doubting Thomas, cynic.

**disburse** verb *the proceeds were disbursed weekly* PAY OUT, spend, expend, dole out, dish out, hand out, part with, donate, give; *informal* fork out/over, shell out, lay out, ante up, pony up.

**discard** verb *his old suit has been discarded* DISPOSE OF, throw away/out, get rid of, toss out, jettison, scrap, dispense with, cast aside/off, throw on the scrap heap; reject, repudiate, abandon, drop, have done with, shed; *informal* chuck, dump, ditch, junk, trash, deep-six. ANTONYM keep.

**discern** verb *they could discern a slender figure, probably a woman, slowly approaching* PERCEIVE, make out, pick out, detect, recognize, notice, observe, see, spot; identify, determine, distinguish; *literary* descry, espy. See note at DISTINGUISH.

**discernible** adjective *in the fog our flares may be barely discernible* VISIBLE, detectable, noticeable, perceptible, observable, distinguishable, recognizable, identifiable; apparent, evident, distinct, appreciable, clear, obvious, manifest, conspicuous.

**discerning** adjective *some real treasures for the discerning collector* DISCRIMINATING, judicious, shrewd, clever, astute, intelligent, sharp, selective, sophisticated, tasteful, sensitive, perceptive, percipient, perspicacious, wise, aware, knowing; *informal* clueful.

**discharge** verb **1** *after his third violation, Vance was discharged* DISMISS, eject, expel, throw out, give someone notice; release, let go, fire, terminate; *Military* cashier; *informal* sack, give someone the sack, boot out, give someone the boot, turf out, give someone their marching orders, show someone the door, send packing, pink-slip, give some the (old) heave-ho. ANTONYMS recruit, engage.

**2** *he was discharged from prison* RELEASE, free, set free, let go, liberate, let out. ANTONYM imprison.

**3** *oil is routinely discharged from ships* SEND OUT, release, eject, let out, pour out, void, give off.

**4** *the swelling will burst and discharge pus* EMIT, exude, ooze, leak. ANTONYM absorb.

**5** *he accidentally discharged the gun* FIRE, shoot, let off; set off, trigger, explode, detonate.

**6** *the ferry was discharging passengers* UNLOAD, offload, put off; remove. ANTONYM load.

**7** *they discharged their duties efficiently* CARRY OUT, perform, execute, conduct, do; fulfill, accomplish, achieve, complete.

**8** *the executor must discharge the funeral expenses* PAY, pay off, settle, clear, honor, meet, liquidate, defray, make good; *informal* square.

▸ noun **1** *his discharge from the service* DISMISSAL, release, removal, ejection, expulsion; *Military* cashiering; *informal* the sack, the boot, the ax, a/the pink slip.

**2** *her discharge from prison* RELEASE, liberation.

**3** *a discharge of diesel oil into the river* LEAK, leakage, emission, release, flow.

**4** *a watery discharge from the eyes* EMISSION, secretion, excretion, seepage, suppuration; pus, matter; *Medicine* exudate.

**5** *a single discharge of his gun* SHOT, firing, blast; explosion, detonation.

**6** *the discharge of their duties* CARRYING OUT, performance, performing, execution, conduct; fulfillment, accomplishment, completion.

**7** *the discharge of all debts* PAYMENT, repayment, settlement, clearance, meeting, liquidation.

**disciple** noun **1** *the disciples of Jesus* APOSTLE, follower.

**2** *a disciple of Rousseau* FOLLOWER, adherent, believer, admirer, devotee, acolyte, votary; pupil, student, learner; upholder, supporter, advocate, proponent, apologist.

**disciplinarian** noun *Mr. Chips was the antithesis of the stern disciplinarian that the boys had come to expect* MARTINET, hard taskmaster, authoritarian, stickler for discipline; tyrant, despot, ramrod; *informal* slave driver.

**discipline** noun **1** *a lack of proper parental discipline* CONTROL, training, teaching, instruction, regulation, direction, order, authority, rule, strictness, a firm hand; routine, regimen, drill, drilling.

**2** *he was able to maintain discipline among his men* GOOD BEHAVIOR, orderliness, control, obedience; self-control, self-discipline, self-government, self-restraint.

**3** *sociology is a fairly new discipline* FIELD (OF STUDY), branch of knowledge, subject, area; specialty.

▸ verb **1** *she had disciplined herself to ignore the pain* TRAIN, drill, teach, school, coach; regiment.

**2** *she learned to discipline her emotions* CONTROL, restrain, regulate, govern, keep in check, check, curb, keep a tight rein on, rein in, bridle, tame, bring into line.

**3** *he was disciplined by management* PUNISH, penalize, bring to book; reprimand, rebuke, reprove, chastise, upbraid; *informal* dress down, give someone a dressing-down, rap on/over the knuckles, give someone a roasting, call (up) on the carpet; *formal* castigate.

**disclaimer** noun **1** *a disclaimer of responsibility* DENIAL, refusal, rejection. ANTONYMS acceptance, acknowledgment.

**2** *Law a deed of disclaimer* RENUNCIATION, relinquishment, resignation, abdication; repudiation, abjuration, disavowal.

**disclose** verb **1** *the information must not be disclosed to anyone* REVEAL, make known, divulge, tell, impart, communicate, pass on, vouchsafe; release, make public, broadcast, publish, report, unveil; leak, betray, let slip, let drop, give away; *informal* let on, blab, spill the beans, let the cat out of the bag; *archaic* discover, unbosom. ANTONYM conceal.

**2** *exploratory surgery disclosed an aneurysm* UNCOVER, reveal, show, expose, bring to light.

**disclosure** noun **1** *she was embarrassed by this unexpected disclosure* REVELATION, declaration, announcement, news, report; leak.

**2** *the disclosure of official information* PUBLISHING, broadcasting; revelation, communication, release, uncovering, unveiling, exposure, exposé; leakage.

**discolor** verb *smoke will discolor the fabric* STAIN, mark, soil, dirty, streak, smear, spot, tarnish, sully, spoil, mar, blemish; blacken, char; fade, bleach.

**discoloration** noun *a brown discoloration on the skin* STAIN, mark, streak, spot, blotch, tarnishing; blemish, flaw, defect, bruise, contusion; birthmark, nevus; liver spot, age spot; *informal* splotch.

**discomfit** verb *her kiss on the cheek discomfited him even more* EMBARRASS, abash, disconcert, discompose, discomfort, take aback, unsettle, unnerve, put someone off their game, ruffle, confuse, fluster, agitate, disorient, upset, disturb, perturb, distress; chagrin, mortify; *informal* faze, rattle, discombobulate.

**discomfiture** noun *I admit we were somewhat amused by his discomfiture* EMBARRASSMENT, unease, uneasiness, awkwardness, discomfort, discomposure, abashment, confusion, agitation, nervousness, disorientation, perturbation, distress; chagrin, mortification, shame, humiliation; *informal* discombobulation.

**discomfort** noun **1** *abdominal discomfort* PAIN, aches and pains, soreness, tenderness, irritation, stiffness; ache, twinge, pang, throb, cramp.

**2** *the discomforts of life at sea* INCONVENIENCE, difficulty, bother, nuisance, vexation, drawback, disadvantage, trouble, problem, trial, tribulation, hardship; *informal* hassle.

**3** *she was unable to hide her discomfort* EMBARRASSMENT, discomfiture, unease, uneasiness, awkwardness, discomposure, confusion, nervousness, perturbation, distress, anxiety; chagrin, mortification, shame, humiliation.

▸ verb *his purpose was to discomfort the president.* See DISCOMFIT.

**discomposure** noun *she laughed to cover her discomposure* AGITATION, discomfiture, discomfort, uneasiness, unease, confusion, disorientation, perturbation, distress, nervousness; anxiety, worry, consternation, disquiet, disquietude; embarrassment, abashment, chagrin, loss of face; *informal* discombobulation.

**disconcert** verb *Sheila's unexpected appearance disconcerted him* UNSETTLE, discomfit, throw/catch off balance, take aback, rattle, unnerve, disorient, perturb, disturb, perplex, confuse, bewilder, baffle, fluster, ruffle, shake, upset, agitate, worry, dismay, surprise, take by surprise, startle, put someone off (their game), distract; *informal* throw, faze, discombobulate.

**disconcerting** adjective *the intense scrutiny was disconcerting* UNSETTLING, unnerving, discomfiting, disturbing, perturbing, troubling, upsetting, worrying, alarming, distracting, off-putting; confusing, bewildering, perplexing.

**disconnect** verb **1** *the trucks were disconnected from the train* DETACH, disengage, uncouple, decouple, unhook, unhitch, undo, unfasten, unyoke. ANTONYM attach.

**2** *she felt as if she were disconnected from the real world* SEPARATE, cut off, divorce, sever, isolate, divide, part, disengage, dissociate, disassociate, remove.

**3** *an engineer disconnected the power source* DEACTIVATE, shut off, turn off, switch off, unplug.

**disconnected** adjective **1** *a world that seemed disconnected from reality* DETACHED, separate, separated, divorced, cut off, isolated, dissociated, disengaged; apart.

**2** *a disconnected narrative* DISJOINTED, incoherent, garbled, confused, jumbled, mixed up, rambling, wandering, disorganized, uncoordinated, ill-thought-out.

**disconsolate** adjective *his partner had to face the disconsolate investors on his own* SAD, unhappy, doleful, woebegone, dejected, downcast, downhearted, despondent, dispirited, crestfallen, cast down, depressed, down, disappointed, disheartened, discouraged, demoralized, low-spirited, forlorn, in the doldrums, melancholy, miserable, long-faced, glum, gloomy; *informal* blue, choked, down in/at the mouth, down in the dumps, in a blue funk; *literary* dolorous. ANTONYM cheerful.

**discontent** noun *the workers' discontent could no longer be overlooked* DISSATISFACTION, disaffection, discontentment, discontentedness, disgruntlement, grievances, unhappiness, displeasure, bad feelings, resentment, envy; restlessness, unrest, uneasiness, unease, frustration, irritation, annoyance; *informal* a chip on one's shoulder. ANTONYM satisfaction.

**discontented** adjective *discontented parents attended the meeting in record numbers* DISSATISFIED, disgruntled, fed up, disaffected, discontent, malcontent, unhappy, aggrieved, displeased, resentful; restless, frustrated, irritated, annoyed; *informal* fed up (to the teeth), teed off, ticked off. ANTONYM satisfied.

**discontinue** verb *ferry service was discontinued* STOP, end, terminate, put an end to, put a stop to, finish, call a halt to, cancel, drop, abandon, dispense with, do away with, get rid of, ax, abolish; suspend, interrupt, break off, withdraw; *informal* cut, pull the plug on, scrap, nix.

**discord** noun **1** *stress resulting from family discord* STRIFE, conflict, friction, hostility, antagonism, antipathy, enmity, bad feeling, ill feeling, bad blood, argument, quarreling, squabbling, bickering, wrangling, feuding, contention, disagreement, dissension, dispute, difference of opinion, disunity, division, opposition; infighting. ANTONYMS accord, harmony.

**2** *the music faded in discord* DISSONANCE, discordance, disharmony, cacophony. ANTONYM harmony.

**discordant** adjective **1** *the messages from Washington and Ottawa were discordant* DIFFERENT, in disagreement, at variance, at odds, divergent, discrepant, contradictory, contrary, in conflict, conflicting, opposite, opposed, opposing, clashing; incompatible, inconsistent, irreconcilable. ANTONYMS harmonious, compatible.

**2** *discordant sounds* INHARMONIOUS, tuneless, off-key, dissonant, harsh, jarring, grating, jangling, jangly, strident, shrill, screeching, screechy, cacophonous; sharp, flat. ANTONYMS harmonious, dulcet.

**discount** noun *students get a 10 percent discount* REDUCTION, deduction, markdown, price cut, cut, rebate.

▸ verb **1** *I'd heard rumors, but I discounted them* DISREGARD, pay no attention to, take no notice of, take no account of, dismiss, ignore, overlook, disbelieve, reject; *informal* take with a pinch of salt, pooh-pooh. ANTONYM believe.

2 *the actual price is discounted in many stores* REDUCE, mark down, cut, lower; *informal* knock down. ANTONYM increase.

3 *show your card and they'll discount 40 percent* DEDUCT, take off, rebate; *informal* knock off, slash off. ANTONYM add.

**discourage** verb 1 *we want to* ***discourage*** *children* ***from*** *smoking* DETER FROM, dissuade from, disincline from, put off, talk out of; advise against, urge against; *archaic* discountenance from. ANTONYM encourage.

2 *she was discouraged by his hostile tone* DISHEARTEN, dispirit, demoralize, cast down, depress, disappoint; put off, unnerve, daunt, intimidate, cow, crush. ANTONYMS encourage, hearten.

3 *he sought to discourage further conversation* PREVENT, stop, put a stop to, avert, fend off, stave off, ward off; inhibit, hinder, check, curb, put a damper on, throw cold water on. ANTONYM encourage.

**discouraged** adjective *Doug must be feeling pretty discouraged* DISHEARTENED, dispirited, demoralized, deflated, disappointed, let down, disconsolate, despondent, dejected, cast down, downcast, depressed, crestfallen, dismayed, low-spirited, gloomy, glum, pessimistic, unenthusiastic; put off, daunted, intimidated, cowed, crushed; *informal* down in/at the mouth, down in the dumps, unenthused, bummed.

**discouraging** adjective *most reports from the area are discouraging* DEPRESSING, demoralizing, disheartening, dispiriting, disappointing, gloomy, off-putting; unfavorable, unpromising, inauspicious. ANTONYM encouraging.

**discourse** noun 1 *they prolonged their discourse outside the door* DISCUSSION, conversation, talk, dialogue, conference, debate, consultation; parley, powwow, chat, confab; *formal* confabulation, colloquy.

2 *a discourse on critical theory* ESSAY, treatise, dissertation, paper, study, critique, monograph, disquisition, tract; lecture, address, speech, oration; sermon, homily.

▸ verb 1 *he discoursed at length on his favorite topic* HOLD FORTH, expatiate, pontificate; talk, give a talk, give a speech, lecture, sermonize, preach; *informal* spout, sound off; *formal* perorate.

2 *Edward was discoursing with his friends* CONVERSE, talk, speak, debate, confer, consult, parley, chat.

**discourteous** adjective *it would be discourteous to ignore her* RUDE, impolite, ill-mannered, bad-mannered, disrespectful, uncivil, unmannerly, unchivalrous, ungentlemanly, unladylike, ill-bred, churlish, boorish, crass, ungracious, graceless, uncouth; insolent, impudent, cheeky, audacious, presumptuous; curt, brusque, blunt, offhand, unceremonious, short, sharp; ignorant. ANTONYM polite.

**discourtesy** noun *these parents seemed unfazed by the discourtesy of their children* RUDENESS, impoliteness, bad manners, incivility, disrespect, ungraciousness, churlishness, boorishness, ill breeding, uncouthness, crassness; insolence, impudence, impertinence; curtness, brusqueness, abruptness.

**discover** verb 1 *firemen discovered a body in the debris* FIND, locate, come across/upon, stumble on, chance on, light on, bring to light, uncover, unearth, turn up; track down.

2 *eventually, I discovered the truth* FIND OUT, learn, realize, recognize, fathom, see, ascertain, work out, dig up/out, ferret out, root out; *informal* figure out, dope out.

3 *scientists discovered a new way of dating fossil crustaceans* HIT ON, come up with, invent, originate, devise, design, contrive, conceive of; pioneer, develop.

**discoverer** noun *the discoverer of penicillin* ORIGINATOR, inventor, creator, deviser, designer; pioneer, explorer.

**discovery** noun 1 *the discovery of the body* FINDING, location, uncovering, unearthing.

2 *the discovery that she was pregnant* REALIZATION, recognition; revelation, disclosure.

3 *the discovery of new drugs* INVENTION, origination, devising; pioneering.

4 *he failed to take out a patent on his discoveries* FIND, finding; invention, breakthrough, innovation.

**discredit** verb 1 *an attempt to discredit him and his company* BRING INTO DISREPUTE, disgrace, dishonor, damage the reputation of, blacken the name of, put/show in a bad light, reflect badly on, compromise, stigmatize, smear, tarnish, taint, slur.

2 *that theory has been discredited* DISPROVE, invalidate, explode, refute; *informal* debunk, poke holes in; *formal* confute.

▸ noun 1 *crimes that brought discredit on the administration* DISHONOR, disrepute, disgrace, shame, humiliation, ignominy, infamy, notoriety; censure, blame, reproach, opprobrium; stigma; *dated* disesteem. ANTONYM honor.

2 *the ships were a discredit to the country* DISGRACE, source of shame, reproach. ANTONYM glory.

**discreet** adjective 1 *discreet inquiries* CAREFUL, circumspect, cautious, wary, chary, guarded; tactful, diplomatic, prudent, judicious, strategic, politic, delicate, sensitive, kid-glove.

2 *discreet lighting* UNOBTRUSIVE, inconspicuous, subtle, low-key, understated, subdued, muted, soft, restrained.

**discrepancy** noun *the discrepancy between the two sets of figures* DIFFERENCE, disparity, variance, variation, deviation, divergence, disagreement, inconsistency, dissimilarity, mismatch, discordance, incompatibility, conflict. ANTONYM correspondence.

**discrete** adjective *discrete units of sound* SEPARATE, distinct, individual, detached, unattached, disconnected, discontinuous, disjunct, disjoined. ANTONYM connected.

**discretion** noun 1 *you can rely on his discretion* CIRCUMSPECTION, carefulness, caution, wariness, chariness, guardedness; TACT, tactfulness, diplomacy, delicacy, sensitivity, prudence, judiciousness.

2 *his sentence would be determined at the discretion of the court* CHOICE, option, preference, disposition, volition; pleasure, liking, wish, will, inclination, desire.

**discretionary** adjective *a discretionary service charge* OPTIONAL, voluntary, at one's discretion, elective. ANTONYM compulsory.

**discriminate** verb 1 *he cannot discriminate between fact and fiction* DIFFERENTIATE, distinguish, draw a distinction, tell the difference, tell apart; separate, separate the sheep from the goats, separate the wheat from the chaff. See note at DISTINGUISH.

2 *existing employment policies* ***discriminate against*** *women* BE BIASED AGAINST, be prejudiced against; treat differently, treat unfairly, put at a disadvantage, single out; victimize.

**discriminating** adjective *she had discriminating tastes* DISCERNING, perceptive, astute, shrewd, judicious, perspicacious, insightful, keen; selective, fastidious, tasteful, refined, sensitive, cultivated, cultured, artistic, aesthetic. ANTONYM indiscriminate.

**discrimination** noun 1 *racial discrimination* PREJUDICE, bias, bigotry, intolerance, narrow-mindedness, unfairness, inequity, favoritism, one-sidedness, partisanship; sexism, chauvinism, misogyny, racism, racialism, anti-Semitism, heterosexism, ageism, classism; *in South Africa, historical* apartheid. ANTONYM impartiality.

2 *a bland man with no discrimination* DISCERNMENT, judgment, perception, perceptiveness, perspicacity, acumen, astuteness, shrewdness, judiciousness, insight; selectivity, (good) taste, fastidiousness, refinement, sensitivity, cultivation, culture.

**discriminatory** adjective *the decision against Ms. Rodriquez was discriminatory* PREJUDICIAL, biased, prejudiced, preferential, unfair, unjust, invidious, inequitable, weighted, one-sided, partisan; sexist, chauvinistic, chauvinist, racist, racialist, anti-Semitic, ageist, classist. ANTONYM impartial.

**discursive** adjective 1 *dull, discursive prose* RAMBLING, digressive, meandering, wandering, maundering, diffuse, long, lengthy, wordy, verbose, long-winded, prolix; circuitous, roundabout, circumlocutory; *informal* waffly. ANTONYM concise.

2 *an elegant discursive style* FLUENT, flowing, fluid, eloquent, expansive. ANTONYM terse.

**discuss** verb 1 *I discussed the matter with my wife* TALK OVER, talk about, talk through, converse about, debate, confer about, deliberate about, chew over, consider, consider the pros and cons of, thrash out; *informal* kick around, hash out, bat around.

2 *the third chapter discusses this topic in detail* EXAMINE, explore, study, analyze, go into, deal with, treat, consider, concern itself with, tackle.

**discussion** noun 1 *a long discussion with her husband* CONVERSATION, talk, dialogue, discourse, conference, debate, exchange of views, consultation, deliberation; powwow, chat, tête-à-tête, heart-to-heart, huddle; negotiations, parley; *informal* confab, chitchat, rap (session), skull session, bull session; *formal* confabulation, colloquy.

2 *the book's candid discussion of sexual matters* EXAMINATION, exploration, analysis, study; treatment, consideration.

**disdain** noun *she looked at him with disdain* CONTEMPT, scorn, scornfulness, contemptuousness, derision, disrespect; disparagement, condescension, superciliousness, hauteur, haughtiness, arrogance, snobbishness, indifference, distaste, dislike, disgust. ANTONYM respect.

▸ verb 1 *she disdained vulgar exhibitionism* SCORN, deride, pour scorn on, regard with contempt, sneer at, sniff at, curl one's lip at, look down one's nose at, look down on; despise; *informal* turn up one's nose at, pooh-pooh. See note at DESPISE.

2 *we disdained his invitation* SPURN, reject, refuse, rebuff, disregard, ignore, snub; decline, turn down, brush aside.

**disdainful** adjective *Tyler was offended by his disdainful expression* CONTEMPTUOUS, scornful, derisive, sneering, withering, slighting, disparaging, disrespectful, condescending, patronizing, supercilious, haughty, superior, arrogant, proud, snobbish, lordly, aloof, indifferent, dismissive; *informal* high and mighty, hoity-toity, sniffy, snotty; *archaic* contumelious. ANTONYM respectful.

**disease** noun *herbal preparations to treat tropical diseases* ILLNESS, sickness, ill health; infection, ailment, malady, disorder, complaint, affliction, condition, indisposition, upset, problem, trouble, infirmity, disability, defect, abnormality; pestilence, plague, cancer, canker, blight; *informal* bug, virus; *dated* contagion.

**diseased** adjective *the diseased trees have been marked with red paint* UNHEALTHY, ill, sick, unwell, ailing, sickly, unsound; infected, septic, contaminated, blighted, rotten, bad, abnormal.

**disembark** verb *passengers are asked to disembark in single file* GET OFF, step off, leave, pile out; go ashore, debark, detrain, deplane; land, arrive, alight.

**disembodied** adjective *disembodied faces floated through the smoky mist* BODILESS, incorporeal, discarnate, spiritual; intangible, insubstantial, impalpable; ghostly, spectral, phantom, wraithlike.

USAGE NOTE **disembodied, dismembered**

*Disembodied* = separated from the physical body, esp. as a spirit. The word is stretched too far when used to describe a body part severed from the torso—e.g.: "Having said all that, did we really need to see the disembodied [read *severed*] heads? In a word: yuck. We got the idea with the hacksaw and the meat cleaver, thanks." (*Arizona Republic*; Nov. 21, 2002.)

*Dismembered* = (1) (of bodily limbs) cut from the torso; or (2) (of a torso) characterized by having had limbs cut off. This term does not work well with heads—e.g.: "In a flurry of recent TV appearances promoting his new book on families, the former vice president has been seen . . . floating as a dismembered [read *detached*] head in a jar on the Fox cartoon show 'Futurama,' where he's dubbed 'the inventor of the environment.' " (*Christian Science Monitor*, Nov. 19, 2002.) —*BG*

---

**disembowel** verb *we cleaned and disemboweled the game before returning to the campsite* GUT, draw, remove the guts from; *formal* eviscerate.

**disenchanted** adjective *disenchanted with politics, he retired from the foreign service* DISILLUSIONED, disappointed, disabused, let down, fed up, dissatisfied, discontented; cynical, soured, jaundiced, sick, indifferent, blasé.

**disenchantment** noun *the disenchantment of a first love gone sour* DISILLUSIONMENT, disappointment, dissatisfaction, discontent, discontentedness, rude awakening; cynicism.

**disengage** verb **1** *I disengaged his hand from mine* REMOVE, detach, disentangle, extricate, separate, release, free, loosen, loose, disconnect, unfasten, unclasp, uncouple, undo, unhook, unhitch, untie, unyoke. ANTONYM attach.

**2** *UN forces* ***disengaged from*** *the country* WITHDRAW FROM, leave, pull out of, quit, retreat from. ANTONYM enter.

**disentangle** verb **1** *Allen was disentangling a coil of rope* UNTANGLE, unravel, untwist, unwind, undo, untie, straighten out, smooth out; comb.

**2** *he disentangled his fingers from her hair* EXTRICATE, extract, free, remove, disengage, untwine, release, loosen, detach, unfasten, unclasp, disconnect.

**disfavor** noun *the disfavor of his fellow students* DISAPPROVAL, disapprobation; dislike, displeasure, distaste, dissatisfaction, low opinion; *dated* disesteem.

**disfigure** verb *junkyards disfigure the landscape* MAR, spoil, deface, scar, blemish, uglify; damage, injure, impair, blight, mutilate, deform, maim, ruin; vandalize. ANTONYM adorn.

**disfigurement** noun **1** *the disfigurement of Victorian buildings* DEFACEMENT, spoiling, scarring, uglification, mutilation, damage, vandalizing, ruin.

**2** *a permanent facial disfigurement* BLEMISH, flaw, defect, imperfection, discoloration, blotch; scar, pockmark; deformity, malformation, abnormality, injury, wound.

**disgorge** verb **1** *the combine disgorged a stream of grain* POUR OUT, discharge, eject, throw out, emit, expel, spit out, spew out, belch forth, spout; vomit, regurgitate.

**2** *they were made to disgorge all the profits* SURRENDER, relinquish, hand over, give up, turn over, yield; *informal* cough up, fork over.

**disgrace** noun **1** *he brought disgrace on the family* DISHONOR, shame, discredit, ignominy, degradation, disrepute, ill repute, infamy, scandal, stigma, opprobrium, obloquy, condemnation, vilification, contempt, disrespect; humiliation, embarrassment, loss of face; *dated* disesteem. ANTONYM honor.

**2** *the unemployment figures are a disgrace* SCANDAL, outrage; discredit, reproach, affront, insult; stain, blemish, blot, black mark; *informal* crime, sin. ANTONYM credit.

▸ verb **1** *you have disgraced the family name* BRING SHAME ON, shame, dishonor, discredit, bring into disrepute, degrade, debase, defame, stigmatize, taint, sully, tarnish, besmirch, stain, blacken, drag through the mud/mire. ANTONYM honor.

**2** *he was publicly disgraced* DISCREDIT, dishonor, stigmatize; humiliate, cause to lose face, chasten, humble, demean, put someone in their place, take down a peg or two, cut down to size. ANTONYM honor.

PHRASE: **in disgrace** *Benjamin couldn't bear to return home in disgrace* OUT OF FAVOR, unpopular, under a cloud, disgraced; *informal* in the doghouse.

**disgraceful** adjective *they caught Warren's disgraceful behavior on videotape* SHAMEFUL, shocking, scandalous, deplorable, despicable, contemptible, beyond contempt, beyond the pale, dishonorable, discreditable, reprehensible, base, mean, low, blameworthy, unworthy, ignoble, shabby, inglorious, outrageous, abominable, atrocious, appalling, dreadful, terrible, disgusting, shameless, vile, odious, monstrous, heinous, iniquitous, unspeakable, loathsome, sordid, nefarious; *archaic* scurvy. ANTONYM admirable.

**disgruntled** adjective *poor service was the primary complaint of these disgruntled customers* DISSATISFIED, discontented, aggrieved, resentful, fed up, displeased, unhappy, disappointed, disaffected; angry, irate, annoyed, cross, exasperated, indignant, vexed, irritated, piqued, irked, put out, peeved, miffed, bummed, aggravated, hacked off, riled, peed off, PO'd, hot under the collar, in a huff, cheesed off, shirty, sore, teed off, ticked off.

**disguise** verb *his controlled voice disguised his true feelings* CAMOUFLAGE, conceal, hide, cover up, dissemble, mask, screen, shroud, veil, cloak; gloss over, put up a smokescreen to hide/mask. ANTONYM expose.

PHRASE: **disguise oneself as** *Eleanor disguised herself as a man* DRESS UP AS, pretend to be, pass oneself off as, impersonate, pose as; *formal* personate.

**disgust** noun *a look of disgust* REVULSION, repugnance, aversion, distaste, nausea, abhorrence, loathing, detestation, odium, horror; contempt, outrage. ANTONYM delight.

▸ verb **1** *the hospital food disgusted me* REVOLT, repel, repulse, sicken, nauseate, turn someone's stomach; *informal* turn off, gross out.

**2** *Toby's foul language disgusted her* OUTRAGE, shock, horrify, appall, scandalize, offend.

**disgusting** adjective **1** *the food was disgusting* REVOLTING, repellent, repulsive, sickening, nauseating, stomach-churning, stomach-turning, off-putting, unpalatable, distasteful, foul, nasty, vomitous; *informal* yucky, icky, gross. ANTONYMS delicious, appealing.

**2** *I find racism disgusting* ABHORRENT, loathsome, offensive, appalling, outrageous, objectionable, shocking, horrifying, scandalous, monstrous, unspeakable, shameful, vile, odious, obnoxious, detestable, hateful, sickening, contemptible, despicable, deplorable, abominable, beyond the pale; *informal* gross, ghastly, sick. ANTONYM commendable.

**dish** noun **1** *a china dish* BOWL, plate, platter, salver, paten; container, receptacle, casserole, tureen; *archaic* trencher, charger; *historical* porringer.

**2** *vegetarian dishes* RECIPE, meal, course; **(dishes)** food, fare.

**3** *informal* *she's quite a dish.* See BEAUTY sense 2. PHRASE: **dish out** *they dished out free coffee and bagels to the volunteers* DISTRIBUTE, dispense, issue, hand out/around, give out, pass out/around; deal out, dole out, share out, allocate, allot, apportion.

**dishearten** verb *poor reviews disheartened the young author* DISCOURAGE, dispirit, demoralize, cast down, depress, disappoint, dismay, dash someone's hopes; put off, deter, unnerve, daunt, intimidate, cow, crush. ANTONYM encourage.

**disheveled** adjective *long and disheveled hair* UNTIDY, unkempt, scruffy, messy, in a mess, disordered, disarranged, rumpled, bedraggled; uncombed, tousled, tangled, tangly, knotted, knotty, shaggy, straggly, windswept, wind-blown, wild; slovenly, slatternly, blowsy, frowzy, mussed (up), mussy. ANTONYM tidy.

**dishonest** adjective *accused of dishonest business practices* FRAUDULENT, corrupt, swindling, cheating, double-dealing; underhanded, crafty, cunning, devious, treacherous, unfair, unjust, dirty, unethical, immoral, dishonorable, untrustworthy, unscrupulous, unprincipled, amoral; criminal, illegal, unlawful; false, untruthful, deceitful, deceiving, lying, mendacious; *informal* crooked, hinky, shady, tricky, sharp, shifty; *literary* perfidious.

**dishonesty** noun *Richard was a victim of his business manager's dishonesty* FRAUD, fraudulence, corruption, cheating, chicanery, double-dealing, deceit, deception, duplicity, lying, falseness, falsity, falsehood, untruthfulness; craft, cunning, trickery, artifice, underhandedness, subterfuge, skulduggery, treachery, untrustworthiness, unscrupulousness, criminality, misconduct; *informal* crookedness, dirty tricks, shenanigans; *literary* perfidy. ANTONYM probity.

**dishonor** noun *the incident brought dishonor upon the police department* DISGRACE, shame, discredit, humiliation, degradation, ignominy, scandal, infamy, disrepute, ill repute, loss of face, disfavor, ill favor, debasement, opprobrium, obloquy; stigma; *dated* disesteem.

▸ verb *his family name has been dishonored* DISGRACE, shame, discredit, bring into disrepute, humiliate, degrade, debase, lower, cheapen, drag down, drag through the mud, blacken the name of, give a bad name to; sully, stain, taint, besmirch, smear, mar, blot, stigmatize.

**dishonorable** adjective *dishonorable conduct cost Major Pierce her commission* DISGRACEFUL, shameful, disreputable, discreditable, degrading, ignominious, ignoble, blameworthy, contemptible, despicable, reprehensible, shabby, shoddy, sordid, sorry, base, low, improper, unseemly, unworthy; unprincipled, unscrupulous, corrupt, untrustworthy, treacherous, traitorous; *informal* shady, dirty; *literary* perfidious; *archaic* scurvy.

**disillusion** verb *we pretended to have a happy marriage because we didn't want to disillusion the children* DISABUSE, enlighten, set straight, open someone's eyes; disenchant, shatter someone's illusions, disappoint, make sadder and wiser. ANTONYM deceive.

**disincentive** noun *high interest rates are a disincentive to investment* DETERRENT, discouragement, damper, brake, curb, check, restraint, inhibitor; obstacle, impediment, hindrance, obstruction, block, barrier.

**disinclination** noun *they show a disinclination to face the truth* RELUCTANCE, unwillingness, lack of enthusiasm, indisposition, hesitancy; aversion, dislike, distaste; objection, demur, resistance, opposition. ANTONYM enthusiasm.

**disinclined** adjective *she was disinclined to abandon the old ways* RELUCTANT, unwilling, unenthusiastic, unprepared, indisposed, ill-disposed, not in the mood, hesitant; loath, averse, antipathetic, resistant, opposed. ANTONYM willing.

**disinfect** verb *use bleach to disinfect your kitchen surfaces* STERILIZE, sanitize, clean, cleanse, purify, decontaminate; fumigate. ANTONYM contaminate.

**disinfectant** noun *vinegar is a natural disinfectant* ANTISEPTIC, germicide, sterilizer, cleanser, decontaminant; fumigant.

**disingenuous** adjective *that innocent, teary-eyed look is just part of a disingenuous act* INSINCERE, dishonest, untruthful, false, deceitful, duplicitous, lying, mendacious; hypocritical.

**disinherit** verb *Harrison's parents disinherited him when he joined a neo-Nazi cult* CUT SOMEONE OUT OF ONE'S WILL, cut off, dispossess; disown, repudiate, reject, cast off/aside, wash one's hands of, have nothing more to do with, turn one's back on; *informal* cut off without a penny.

**disintegrate** verb *steam causes the substance to disintegrate* BREAK UP, break apart, fall apart, fall to pieces, fragment, fracture, shatter, splinter; explode, blow up, blow apart, fly apart; crumble, deteriorate, decay, decompose, rot, molder, perish, dissolve, collapse, go to rack and ruin, degenerate; *informal* bust, be smashed to smithereens.

**disinterested** adjective **1** *disinterested advice* UNBIASED, unprejudiced, impartial, neutral, nonpartisan, detached, uninvolved, objective, dispassionate, impersonal, clinical; open-minded, fair, just, equitable, balanced, evenhanded, with no ax to grind.

**2** *he looked at her with disinterested eyes* UNINTERESTED, indifferent, incurious, uncurious, unconcerned, unmoved, unresponsive, impassive, passive, detached, unenthusiastic, lukewarm, bored, apathetic; *informal* couldn't-care-less.

USAGE NOTE **disinterested, uninterested**

*Disinterest* = (1) impartiality or freedom from bias or from chance of financial benefit; or (2) lack of concern or attention. Leading writers and editors almost unanimously reject sense 2, for which *uninterest* is the better term. Given the overlapping nouns, writers have found it difficult to keep the past-participial adjectives entirely separate, and many have given up the fight to preserve the distinction between them. But the distinction is still best recognized and followed because *disinterested* captures a nuance that no other word quite does. Many influential writers have urged the preservation of its traditional sense. The typically understated A. R. Orage rhapsodized over the word: "No word in the English language is more difficult [than *disinterestedness*] to define or better worth attempting to define. Somewhere or other in its capacious folds it contains all the ideas of ethics and even, I should say, of religion . . . . I venture to say that whoever has understood the meaning of 'disinterestedness' is not far off understanding the goal of human culture." (*Readers and Writers: 1917–1921*; 1922.)

A *disinterested* observer is not merely "impartial" but has nothing to gain from taking a stand on the issue in question. The illustrative quotation that follows deals with journalists' disinterest: "In the film, Wexler's directorial debut, a cameraman portrayed by Robert Forster must wrestle with being a disinterested observer or becoming emotionally involved with what he sees through his lens." (*Los Angeles Times*; Aug. 26, 1996.)

Yet *disinterested* is frequently used (or, in traditionalists' eyes, misused) for *uninterested*—e.g.: "On a day when seeded players fell by the wayside like overripe tomatoes, Agassi looked sickly and almost disinterested [read *uninterested*]." (*Toronto Sun*; June 25, 1996.) —*BG*

---

**disjointed** adjective *the discussion was too disjointed to follow* UNCONNECTED, disconnected, disunited, discontinuous, fragmented, disorganized, disordered, muddled, mixed up, jumbled, garbled, incoherent, confused; rambling, wandering.

**dislike** verb *a man she had always disliked* FIND DISTASTEFUL, regard with distaste, be averse to, have an aversion to, have no liking/taste for, disapprove of, object to, take exception to; hate, detest, loathe, abhor, despise, be unable to bear/stand, shrink from, shudder at, find repellent; *informal* be unable to stomach; *formal* abominate.

▸ noun *she viewed the other woman with dislike* DISTASTE, aversion, disfavor, disapproval, disapprobation, enmity, animosity, hostility, antipathy, antagonism; hate, hatred, detestation, loathing, disgust, repugnance, abhorrence, disdain, contempt.

**dislocate** verb **1** *she dislocated her hip* PUT OUT OF JOINT; *informal* put out; *Medicine* luxate.

**2** *trade was dislocated by a famine* DISRUPT, disturb, throw into disarray, throw into confusion, play havoc with, interfere with, disorganize, upset, disorder; *informal* mess up.

**dislodge** verb **1** *replace any stones you dislodge* DISPLACE, knock out of place/position, move, shift; knock over, upset.

**2** *economic sanctions failed to dislodge the dictator* REMOVE, force out, drive out, oust, eject, get rid of, evict, unseat, depose, topple, drum out; *informal* kick out, boot out.

**disloyal** adjective *once judged disloyal, you will never be welcome in this group* UNFAITHFUL, faithless, false, false-hearted, untrue, inconstant, untrustworthy, unreliable, undependable, fickle; treacherous, traitorous, subversive, seditious, unpatriotic, two-faced, double-dealing, double-crossing, deceitful; dissident, renegade; adulterous; *informal* backstabbing, two-timing; *literary* perfidious.

**disloyalty** noun *the investigation uncovered more cases of disloyalty than anyone had originally suspected* UNFAITHFULNESS, infidelity, inconstancy, faithlessness, fickleness, unreliability, untrustworthiness, betrayal, falseness; duplicity, double-dealing, treachery, treason, subversion, sedition, dissidence; adultery; *informal* backstabbing, two-timing; *literary* perfidy, perfidiousness.

**dismal** adjective **1** *a dismal look* GLOOMY, glum, melancholy, morose, doleful, woebegone, forlorn, dejected, depressed, dispirited, downcast, despondent, disconsolate, miserable, sad, unhappy, sorrowful, desolate, wretched; *informal* blue, down in the dumps, down in/at the mouth; *literary* dolorous. ANTONYM cheerful.

**2** *a dismal hall* DINGY, dim, dark, gloomy, dreary, drab, dull, bleak, cheerless, depressing, uninviting, unwelcoming. ANTONYMS cheerful, bright.

**3** *informal a dismal performance.* See POOR sense 2.

**dismantle** verb *the old opera house was dismantled* TAKE APART, pull apart, pull to pieces, disassemble, break up, break down, strip (down); knock down, pull down, demolish. ANTONYMS assemble, build.

**dismay** verb *he was dismayed by the change in his friend* APPALL, horrify, shock, shake (up); disconcert, take aback, alarm, unnerve, unsettle, throw off balance, discompose; disturb, upset, distress; *informal* rattle, faze. ANTONYMS encourage, please.

▸ noun *they greeted his decision with dismay* ALARM, shock, surprise, consternation, concern, perturbation, disquiet, discomposure, distress. ANTONYMS pleasure, relief.

**dismiss** verb **1** *the president dismissed five aides* GIVE SOMEONE THEIR NOTICE, get rid of, discharge, terminate; lay off; *informal* sack, give someone the sack, fire, boot out, give someone the boot, give someone their marching orders, show someone the door, can, pink-slip; *Military* cashier. ANTONYM engage.

**2** *the guards were dismissed* SEND AWAY, let go; disband, dissolve, discharge. See note at EJECT. ANTONYM assemble.

**3** *he dismissed all morbid thoughts* BANISH, set aside, disregard, shrug off, put out of one's mind; reject, deny, repudiate, spurn. ANTONYM entertain.

**dismissal** noun **1** *the threat of dismissal* TERMINATION, discharge, one's notice; redundancy, laying off; *informal* the sack, sacking, firing, the boot, the ax, one's marching orders, the pink slip; *Military* cashiering. ANTONYM recruitment.

**2** *a condescending dismissal* REJECTION, repudiation, repulse, nonacceptance; *informal* kiss-off. ANTONYM acceptance.

**disobedient** adjective *he had never been punished for being disobedient* INSUBORDINATE, unruly, wayward, badly behaved, naughty, delinquent, disruptive, troublesome, rebellious, defiant, mutinous, recalcitrant, uncooperative, truculent, willful, intractable, obstreperous; *archaic* contumacious.

**disobey** verb *she was put on report for willfully disobeying a superior officer* DEFY, go against, flout, contravene, infringe, transgress, violate; disregard, ignore, pay no heed to.

**disobliging** adjective *our disobliging neighbors* UNHELPFUL, uncooperative, unaccommodating, unreasonable, awkward, difficult; discourteous, uncivil, unfriendly. ANTONYM helpful.

**disorder** noun **1** *he hates disorder* UNTIDINESS, disorderliness, mess, disarray, chaos, confusion; clutter, jumble; a muddle, a shambles. ANTONYM tidiness.

**2** *incidents of public disorder* UNREST, disturbance, disruption, upheaval, turmoil, mayhem, pandemonium; violence, fighting, rioting, lawlessness, anarchy; breach of the peace, fracas, rumpus, ruckus, melee. ANTONYMS order, peace.

**3** *a blood disorder* DISEASE, infection, complaint, condition, affliction, malady, sickness, illness, ailment, infirmity, irregularity.

**disorderly** adjective **1** *a disorderly desk* UNTIDY, disorganized, messy, cluttered; in disarray, in a mess, in a jumble, in a muddle, at sixes and sevens; *informal* shambolic, like a bomb went off. ANTONYM tidy.

**2** *disorderly behavior* UNRULY, boisterous, rough, rowdy, wild, riotous; disruptive, troublesome, undisciplined, lawless, unmanageable, uncontrollable, out of hand, out of control. ANTONYM peaceful.

**disorganized** adjective **1** *a disorganized toolbox* DISORDERLY, disordered, unorganized, jumbled, muddled, untidy, messy, chaotic, topsy-turvy, haphazard, ragtag; in disorder, in disarray, in a mess, in a muddle, in a shambles, shambolic. ANTONYM orderly.

**2** *muddled and disorganized* UNMETHODICAL, unsystematic, undisciplined, badly organized, inefficient; haphazard, careless, slapdash; *informal* sloppy, hit-and-miss. ANTONYM organized.

**disown** verb *he has been disowned by his parents* REJECT, cast off/aside, abandon, renounce, deny; turn one's back on, wash one's hands of, have nothing more to do with; *literary* forsake.

**disparage** verb *they disparage Lawrence and his achievements* BELITTLE, denigrate, deprecate, trivialize, make light of, undervalue, underrate, play down; ridicule, deride, mock, scorn, scoff at, sneer at; run down, defame, discredit, speak badly of, cast aspersions on, impugn, vilify, traduce, criticize, slur; *informal* pick holes in, knock, slam, pan, badmouth, dis, pooh-pooh; *formal* calumniate, derogate. ANTONYMS praise, overrate.

**disparity** noun *a disparity between their stories* DISCREPANCY, inconsistency, imbalance; variance, variation, divergence, gap, gulf; difference, dissimilarity, contrast. ANTONYM similarity.

**dispassionate** adjective **1** *a calm, dispassionate manner* UNEMOTIONAL, emotionless, impassive, cool, calm, 'calm, cool, and collected', unruffled, unperturbed, composed, self-possessed, self-controlled, unexcitable; *informal* laid-back. ANTONYM emotional.

**2** *a dispassionate analysis* OBJECTIVE, detached, neutral, disinterested, impartial, nonpartisan, unbiased, unprejudiced; scientific, analytical. ANTONYM biased.

**dispatch** verb **1** *all the messages were dispatched* SEND (OFF), post, mail, forward, transmit, e-mail.

**2** *the business was dispatched in the morning* DEAL WITH, finish, conclude, settle, discharge, perform; expedite, push through; *informal* make short work of.

**3** *the hero dispatched a host of villains* KILL, put to death, take/end the life of; slaughter, butcher, massacre, wipe out, exterminate, eliminate; murder, assassinate, execute; *informal* bump off, do in, do away with, take out, blow away, ice, rub out, waste; *literary* slay. See note at KILL.

▸ noun **1** *files ready for dispatch* SENDING, posting, mailing, e-mailing.

**2** *efficiency and dispatch* PROMPTNESS, speed, speediness, swiftness, rapidity, briskness, haste, hastiness; *literary* fleetness, celerity.

**3** *the latest dispatch from the front* COMMUNICATION, communiqué, bulletin, report, statement, letter, message; news, intelligence; *informal* memo, info, story, lowdown, scoop; *literary* tidings.

**4** *the capture and dispatch of the rogue bull* KILLING, slaughter, massacre, extermination, elimination; murder, assassination, execution; *literary* slaying.

**dispel** verb *allow me to dispel your fears* BANISH, eliminate, drive away/off, get rid of; relieve, allay, ease, quell. See note at SCATTER.

**dispensable** adjective *any goods deemed dispensable will not be allowed on board* EXPENDABLE, disposable, replaceable, inessential, nonessential, noncore; unnecessary, redundant, superfluous, surplus to requirements.

**dispensation** noun **1** *the dispensation of supplies* DISTRIBUTION, supply, supplying, issue, issuing, handing out, doling out, dishing out, sharing out, dividing out; division, allocation, allotment, apportionment.

**2** *the dispensation of justice* ADMINISTRATION, administering, delivery, discharge, dealing out, meting out.

**3** *a dispensation from the Pope* EXEMPTION, immunity, exception, exoneration, reprieve, remission.

**4** *the new constitutional dispensation* SYSTEM, order, arrangement, organization.

**dispense** verb **1** *servants dispensed the drinks* DISTRIBUTE, pass around, hand out, dole out, dish out, share out; allocate, supply, allot, apportion.

**2** *the soldiers dispensed summary justice* ADMINISTER, deliver, issue, discharge, deal out, mete out.

3 *dispensing medicines* PREPARE, make up; supply, provide, sell.

4 *the Pope dispensed him from his impediment* EXEMPT, excuse, except, release, let off, reprieve, absolve. PHRASE: **dispense with 1** *let's dispense with the formalities* WAIVE, omit, drop, leave out, forgo; do away with, give something a miss.

2 *he dispensed with his crutches* GET RID OF, throw away/out, dispose of, discard; manage without, cope without; *informal* ditch, scrap, dump, deep-six, chuck.

**disperse** verb 1 *the crowd began to disperse | police dispersed the demonstrators* BREAK UP, split up, disband, scatter, leave, go their separate ways; drive away/off, chase away. ANTONYM assemble.

2 *the fog finally dispersed* DISSIPATE, dissolve, melt away, fade away, clear, lift.

3 *seeds dispersed by birds* SCATTER, disseminate, distribute, spread, broadcast. See note at SCATTER. ANTONYM gather.

**displace** verb 1 *roof tiles displaced by gales* DISLODGE, dislocate, move, shift, reposition; move out of place, knock out of place/position. ANTONYM replace.

2 *the director was displaced* DEPOSE, dislodge, unseat, remove (from office), dismiss, eject, oust, expel, force out, drive out; overthrow, topple, bring down; *informal* boot out, give someone the boot, show someone the door, bump. ANTONYM reinstate.

3 *English displaced the local language* REPLACE, take the place of, supplant, supersede. See note at REPLACE.

**display** noun 1 *a display of lights* EXHIBITION, exposition, array, arrangement, presentation, demonstration; spectacle, show, parade, pageant.

2 *they vied to outdo each other in display* OSTENTATION, showiness, extravagance, flamboyance, lavishness, splendor; *informal* swank, flashiness, glitziness.

3 *his display of concern* MANIFESTATION, expression, show.

▸ verb 1 *the paintings are displayed in the art gallery* EXHIBIT, show, put on show/view; arrange, array, present, lay out, set out.

2 *the play displays his many theatrical talents* SHOW OFF, parade, flaunt, reveal; publicize, make known, call/draw attention to. ANTONYM hide.

3 *she displayed a caustic sense of humor* MANIFEST, show evidence of, reveal; demonstrate, show; *formal* evince. ANTONYM conceal.

**displease** verb *I'd never seen his mom when she wasn't displeased about something* ANNOY, irritate, anger, irk, vex, pique, gall, nettle; put out, upset, aggravate, peeve, needle, bug, rile, miff; *informal* tee off, tick off, piss off.

**displeasure** noun *the scowl on his face indicated displeasure* ANNOYANCE, irritation, crossness, anger, vexation, pique, rancor; dissatisfaction, discontent, discontentedness, disgruntlement, disapproval; *informal* aggravation. ANTONYM satisfaction.

**disposable** adjective 1 *disposable plates* THROWAWAY, expendable, single-use.

2 *disposable income* AVAILABLE, usable, spendable.

**disposal** noun 1 *garbage ready for disposal* THROWING AWAY, discarding, jettisoning, scrapping, recycling; *informal* dumping, ditching, chucking, deep-sixing.

2 *the disposal of the troops in two lines* ARRANGEMENT, arranging, positioning, placement, lining up, disposition, grouping. PHRASE: **at someone's disposal** *the van will be at your disposal all weekend* FOR USE BY, in reserve for, in the hands of, in the possession of.

**dispose** verb 1 *he disposed the pictures in sequence* ARRANGE, place, put, position, array, set up, form; marshal, gather, group.

2 *the experience disposed him to be kind* INCLINE, encourage, persuade, predispose, make willing, prompt, lead, motivate; sway, influence. PHRASE: **dispose of 1** *the waste was disposed of* THROW AWAY/OUT, get rid of, discard, jettison, scrap, junk; *informal* dump, ditch, chuck, trash, deep-six.

2 *he had disposed of all his assets* PART WITH, give away, hand over, deliver up, transfer; sell, auction.

3 *informal she disposed of a fourth cupcake.* See CONSUME sense 1.

**disposed** adjective 1 *they are philanthropically disposed* INCLINED, predisposed, minded.

2 *we are not disposed to argue* WILLING, inclined, prepared, ready, minded, in the mood.

3 *he was disposed to be cruel* LIABLE, apt, inclined, likely, predisposed, prone, tending; capable of.

**disposition** noun 1 *a nervous disposition* TEMPERAMENT, nature, character, constitution, makeup, mentality.

2 *his disposition to generosity* INCLINATION, tendency, proneness, propensity, proclivity.

3 *the disposition of the armed forces* ARRANGEMENT, positioning, placement, configuration; setup, lineup, layout, array; marshaling, mustering, grouping; *Military* dressing.

4 *Law the disposition of the company's property* DISTRIBUTION, disposal, allocation, transfer; sale, auction.

**dispossess** verb *the peasants have been dispossessed of their land* DIVEST, strip, rob, cheat (out), deprive; *informal* do out.

**disproportionate** adjective *the sentence is* ***disproportionate to*** *the offense committed* OUT OF PROPORTION TO, not appropriate to, inappropriate to, not commensurate with, incommensurate with, relatively too large/small for; inordinate for, unreasonable for, excessive for, undue for.

**disprove** verb *Wesley's version of the story should be easy to disprove* REFUTE, prove false, falsify, debunk, negate, invalidate, contradict, confound, controvert, discredit; *informal* poke holes in, blow out of the water, shoot down; *formal* confute.

**disputable** adjective *some of these figures are disputable* DEBATABLE, open to debate, open to discussion, open to question, arguable, contestable, moot, questionable, doubtful; *informal* iffy.

**disputation** noun *we'll have no religious disputation in this house* DEBATE, discussion, dispute, argument, arguing, altercation, dissension, disagreement, controversy; polemics.

**dispute** noun **1** *a subject of dispute* DEBATE, discussion, disputation, argument, controversy, disagreement, quarreling, dissension, conflict, friction, strife, discord. ANTONYM agreement.

**2** *they have settled their dispute* QUARREL, argument, altercation, squabble, falling-out, disagreement, difference of opinion, clash, wrangle; *informal* tiff, spat, blowup, scrap, row, rhubarb. See note at QUARREL. ANTONYM agreement.

▸ verb **1** *George disputed with him* DEBATE, discuss, exchange views; quarrel, argue, disagree, clash, fall out, wrangle, bicker, squabble; *informal* have words, have a tiff, have a spat.

**2** *they disputed his proposals* CHALLENGE, contest, question, call into question, impugn, quibble over, contradict, controvert, argue about, disagree with, take issue with; *formal* gainsay. ANTONYM accept.

**disquiet** noun *grave public disquiet* UNEASE, uneasiness, worry, anxiety, anxiousness, concern, disquietude; perturbation, consternation, upset, malaise, angst; agitation, restlessness, fretfulness; *informal* jitteriness. ANTONYM calm.

▸ verb *I was disquieted by the news* PERTURB, agitate, upset, disturb, unnerve, unsettle, discompose, disconcert; make uneasy, worry, make anxious; trouble, concern, make fretful, make restless.

**disregard** verb *Annie disregarded the remark* IGNORE, take no notice of, pay no attention/heed to; overlook, turn a blind eye to, turn a deaf ear to, shut one's eyes to, gloss over, brush aside, shrug off; *informal* sneeze at. See note at NEGLECT. ANTONYM heed.

▸ noun *blithe disregard for the rules* INDIFFERENCE, nonobservance, inattention, heedlessness, neglect. ANTONYM attention.

**disrepair** noun *the outbuildings are in disrepair* DILAPIDATION, decrepitude, shabbiness, collapse, ruin; abandonment, neglect, disuse.

**disreputable** adjective **1** *he fell into disreputable company* OF BAD REPUTATION, infamous, notorious, louche; dishonorable, dishonest, untrustworthy, unwholesome, villainous, corrupt, immoral; unsavory, slippery, seedy, sleazy; *informal* crooked, shady, shifty, dodgy. ANTONYMS respectable, smart.

**2** *filthy and disreputable* SCRUFFY, shabby, down-at-heel, down-at-the-heel(s), seedy, untidy, unkempt, disheveled. ANTONYMS respectable, smart.

**disrepute** noun *she had brought the family name into disrepute* DISGRACE, shame, dishonor, infamy, notoriety, ignominy, bad reputation; humiliation, discredit, ill repute, low esteem, opprobrium, obloquy. ANTONYM honor.

**disrespect** noun **1** *disrespect for authority* CONTEMPT, lack of respect, scorn, disregard, disdain. ANTONYM esteem.

**2** *he meant no disrespect to anybody* DISCOURTESY, rudeness, impoliteness, incivility, ill/bad manners; insolence, impudence, impertinence. ANTONYM esteem.

**disrespectful** adjective *no one had ever heard him utter a disrespectful word* DISCOURTEOUS, rude, impolite, uncivil, ill-mannered, bad-mannered; insolent, impudent, impertinent, cheeky, flippant, insubordinate. ANTONYM polite.

**disrupt** verb **1** *the strike disrupted public transit* THROW INTO CONFUSION, throw into disorder, throw into disarray, cause confusion/turmoil in, play havoc with; disturb, interfere with, upset, unsettle; obstruct, impede, hold up, delay, interrupt, suspend; *informal* throw a (monkey) wrench into the works of.

**2** *the explosion disrupted the walls of the crater* DISTORT, damage, buckle, warp; shatter; *literary* sunder.

**disruptive** adjective *he's the most disruptive student in the school* TROUBLESOME, unruly, badly behaved, rowdy, disorderly, undisciplined, wild; unmanageable, uncontrollable, uncooperative, out of control/hand, obstreperous, truculent; *formal* refractory. ANTONYM well-behaved.

**dissatisfaction** noun *widespread dissatisfaction with the new law* DISCONTENT, discontentment, disaffection, disquiet, unhappiness, malaise, disgruntlement, vexation, annoyance, irritation, anger; disapproval, disapprobation, disfavor, displeasure.

**dissatisfied** adjective *no one could handle a dissatisfied customer better than Angie* DISCONTENTED, malcontent, unsatisfied, disappointed, disaffected, unhappy, displeased; disgruntled, aggrieved, vexed, annoyed, irritated, angry, exasperated, fed up. ANTONYM contented.

**dissect** verb **1** *the body was dissected* ANATOMIZE, cut up/open, dismember; vivisect.

**2** *the text of the gospels was dissected* ANALYZE, examine, study, scrutinize, pore over, investigate, go over with a fine-tooth comb.

**dissection** noun **1** *the dissection of corpses* CUTTING UP/OPEN, dismemberment; autopsy, postmortem, necropsy, anatomy, vivisection.

**2** *a thorough dissection of their policies* ANALYSIS, examination, study, scrutiny, investigation; evaluation, assessment.

**disseminate** verb *much of our funding is used to disseminate information where it is most needed* SPREAD, circulate, distribute, disperse, promulgate, propagate, publicize, communicate, pass on, put about, make known. See note at SCATTER.

**dissension** noun *there was dissension within the cabinet* DISAGREEMENT, difference of opinion, dispute, dissent, conflict, friction, strife, discord, antagonism, infighting; argument, debate, controversy, disputation, contention.

**dissent** verb *two members dissented* DIFFER, disagree, demur, fail to agree, be at variance/odds, take issue; decline/refuse to support, protest, object, dispute, challenge, quibble. ANTONYMS agree, accept.

▸ noun *murmurs of dissent* DISAGREEMENT, difference of opinion, argument, dispute; disapproval, objection, protest, opposition, defiance; conflict, friction, strife, infighting. ANTONYM agreement.

**dissenter** noun *a chorus of criticism from dissenters* DISSIDENT, objector, protester, disputant; rebel, renegade, maverick, independent; apostate, heretic.

**dissertation** noun *a fascinating dissertation on the fall of Communism* ESSAY, thesis, treatise, paper, study, discourse, disquisition, tract, monograph.

**disservice** noun *the posting of inaccurate information does a great disservice to the patrons* UNKINDNESS, bad turn, ill turn, disfavor; injury, harm, hurt, damage, wrong, injustice. ANTONYM favor.

**dissident** noun *a jailed dissident* DISSENTER, objector, protester; rebel, revolutionary, recusant, subversive, agitator, insurgent, insurrectionist, refusenik. ANTONYM conformist.

▸ adjective *dissident intellectuals* DISSENTING, disagreeing; opposing, objecting, protesting, rebellious, rebelling, revolutionary, recusant, nonconformist, dissentient. ANTONYM conforming.

**dissimilar** adjective *families of dissimilar backgrounds* DIFFERENT, differing, unalike, variant, diverse, divergent, heterogeneous, disparate, unrelated, distinct, contrasting; *literary* divers.

**dissimilarity** noun *the enzymes' structural dissimilarity* DIFFERENCE(S), variance, diversity, heterogeneity, disparateness, disparity, distinctness, contrast, nonuniformity, divergence.

**dissipate** verb **1** *his anger dissipated* DISAPPEAR, vanish, evaporate, dissolve, melt away, melt into thin air, be dispelled; disperse, scatter; *literary* evanesce. See note at SCATTER.

**2** *he dissipated his fortune* SQUANDER, fritter (away), misspend, waste, be prodigal with, spend recklessly/freely, spend like water; expend, use up, consume, run through, go through (like water); *informal* blow, splurge.

**dissipated** adjective *it was in college that he became a dissipated young man* DISSOLUTE, debauched, decadent, intemperate, profligate, self-indulgent, wild, depraved; licentious, promiscuous; drunken. ANTONYM ascetic.

**dissociate** verb *the word "spiritual" has become dissociated from religion* SEPARATE, detach, disconnect, sever, cut off, divorce; isolate, alienate, disassociate. ANTONYM relate.

PHRASE: **dissociate oneself from 1** *he dissociated himself from the Catholic Church* BREAK AWAY FROM, end relations with, sever connections with; withdraw from, quit, leave, disaffiliate from, resign from, pull out of, drop out of, defect from.

**2** *he dissociated himself from the statement* DISOWN, reject, disagree with, distance oneself from.

**dissolute** adjective *the problems of dissolute teens have become epidemic* DISSIPATED, debauched, decadent, intemperate, profligate, self-indulgent, wild, depraved; licentious, promiscuous; drunken. ANTONYM ascetic.

**dissolution** noun **1** *the dissolution of the legislative session* CESSATION, conclusion, end, ending, termination, winding up/down, discontinuation, suspension, disbanding; prorogation, recess.

**2** *technical the dissolution of a polymer in a solvent* DISSOLVING, liquefaction, melting, deliquescence; breaking up, decomposition, disintegration.

**3** *the dissolution of the empire* DISINTEGRATION, breaking up; decay, collapse, demise, extinction.

**dissolve** verb **1** *sugar dissolves in water* GO INTO SOLUTION, break down; liquefy, deliquesce, disintegrate.

**2** *his hopes dissolved* DISAPPEAR, vanish, melt away, evaporate, disperse, dissipate, disintegrate; dwindle, fade (away), wither; *literary* evanesce.

**3** *the crowd dissolved* DISPERSE, disband, break up, scatter, go in different directions.

**4** *the assembly was dissolved* DISBAND, disestablish, bring to an end, end, terminate, discontinue, close down, wind up/down, suspend; prorogue, adjourn.

**5** *their marriage was dissolved* ANNUL, nullify, void, invalidate, overturn, revoke. PHRASE: **dissolve into/in** *she dissolved into tears* BURST INTO, break (down) into, be overcome with.

**dissuade** verb *his colleagues did nothing to* ***dissuade*** *him* ***from*** *quitting* DISCOURAGE FROM, deter from, prevent from, divert from, stop from; talk out of, persuade against, advise against, argue out of. ANTONYM encourage.

**distance** noun **1** *they measured the distance* INTERVAL, space, span, gap, extent; length, width, breadth, depth; range, reach.

**2** *our perception of distance* REMOTENESS; closeness.

**3** *there is a distance between them* ALOOFNESS, remoteness, detachment, unfriendliness; reserve, reticence, restraint, formality; *informal* standoffishness.

▸ verb *he distanced himself from her* WITHDRAW, detach, separate, dissociate, disassociate, isolate, put at a distance.

PHRASE: **in the distance** *there was a cabin in the distance* FAR AWAY/OFF, afar, just in view; on the horizon; *dated* yonder.

**distant** adjective **1** *distant parts of the world* FARAWAY, far-off, far, far-flung, remote, out of the way, outlying, extrasolar. ANTONYM near.

**2** *the distant past* LONG AGO, bygone, olden; ancient, prehistoric; *literary* of yore, olden. ANTONYM recent.

**3** *half a mile distant* AWAY, off, apart.

**4** *a distant memory* VAGUE, faint, dim, indistinct, unclear, indefinite, sketchy, hazy. ANTONYMS strong, clear.

**5** *a distant family connection* REMOTE, indirect, slight. ANTONYM close.

**6** *father was always distant* ALOOF, reserved, remote, detached, unapproachable; withdrawn, reticent, taciturn, uncommunicative, undemonstrative, unforthcoming, unresponsive, unfriendly; *informal* standoffish. ANTONYMS friendly, close.

7 *a distant look in his eyes* DISTRACTED, absentminded, faraway, detached, distrait, vague; *informal* spacey. ANTONYM attentive.

**distaste** noun *they make little secret of their* ***distaste for*** *returning exiles now looking for power* DISLIKE FOR, aversion to/toward, disinclination to/toward, disapproval of, disapprobation of, disdain for, repugnance at/toward, hatred for/of, loathing of. ANTONYM liking.

**distasteful** adjective 1 *distasteful behavior* UNPLEASANT, disagreeable, displeasing, undesirable; objectionable, offensive, unsavory, unpalatable, obnoxious; disgusting, repellent, repulsive, revolting, repugnant, abhorrent, loathsome, vile. ANTONYMS agreeable, pleasant.

2 *their eggs are distasteful to predators* UNPALATABLE, unsavory, unappetizing, inedible, disgusting. ANTONYM tasty.

**distended** adjective *a distended abdomen* SWOLLEN, bloated, dilated, engorged, enlarged, inflated, expanded, extended, bulging, protuberant.

**distill** verb 1 *the water was distilled* PURIFY, refine, filter, treat, process; evaporate and condense.

2 *oil distilled from marjoram* EXTRACT, press out, squeeze out, express.

3 *whiskey is distilled from barley* BREW, ferment.

4 *the solvent is distilled to leave the oil* BOIL DOWN, reduce, concentrate, condense; purify, refine.

**distinct** adjective 1 *two distinct categories* DISCRETE, separate, different, unconnected; precise, specific, distinctive, individual, contrasting. ANTONYM overlapping.

2 *the tail has distinct black tips* CLEAR, well-defined, unmistakable, easily distinguishable; recognizable, visible, obvious, pronounced, prominent, striking. ANTONYMS indistinct, indefinite.

**distinction** noun 1 *class distinctions* DIFFERENCE, contrast, dissimilarity, variance, variation; division, differentiation, dividing line, gulf, gap. ANTONYM similarity.

2 *a painter of distinction* IMPORTANCE, significance, note, consequence; renown, fame, celebrity, prominence, eminence, preeminence, repute, reputation; merit, worth, greatness, excellence, quality. ANTONYM mediocrity.

3 *he had served with distinction* HONOR, credit, excellence, merit.

**distinctive** adjective *the distinctive design in the lace* DISTINGUISHING, characteristic, typical, individual, particular, peculiar, unique, exclusive, special. ANTONYM common.

**distinctly** adverb 1 *there's something distinctly odd about him* DECIDEDLY, markedly, definitely; clearly, noticeably, obviously, plainly, evidently, unmistakably, manifestly, patently.

2 *Laura spoke quite distinctly* CLEARLY, plainly, intelligibly, audibly, unambiguously.

**distinguish** verb 1 *distinguishing reality from fantasy* DIFFERENTIATE, tell apart, discriminate between, tell the difference between.

2 *he could distinguish shapes in the dark* DISCERN, see, perceive, make out; detect, recognize, identify; *literary* descry, espy.

3 *this is what distinguishes history from other disciplines* SEPARATE, set apart, make distinctive, make different; single out, mark off, characterize. PHRASE: **distinguish oneself** *she distinguished herself in the air corps* ATTAIN DISTINCTION, be successful, bring fame/honor to oneself, become famous.

THE RIGHT WORD **distinguish, descry, differentiate, discern, discriminate**

What we **discern** we see apart from all other objects (*to discern the lighthouse beaming on the far shore*). **Descry** puts even more emphasis on the distant or unclear nature of what we're seeing (*the lookout was barely able to descry a man approaching in the dusk*). To **discriminate** is to perceive the differences between or among things that are very similar; it may suggest that some aesthetic evaluation is involved (*to discriminate between two painters' styles*). **Distinguish** requires making even finer distinctions among things that resemble each other even more closely (*unable to distinguish the shadowy figures moving through the forest*). *Distinguish* can also mean recognizing by some special mark or outward sign (*the sheriff could be distinguished by his silver badge*). **Differentiate**, on the other hand, suggests the ability to perceive differences between things that are easily confused. In contrast to *distinguish*, *differentiate* suggests subtle differences that must be compared in some detail (*the color of her dress was difficult to differentiate from the color of the chair in which she was seated; it took a sharp eye to distinguish where her skirt ended and the upholstery began*) If you have trouble *differentiating* among these closely related verbs, you're not alone.

**distinguishable** adjective *the differences between the original and the copy were only slightly distinguishable* DISCERNIBLE, recognizable, identifiable, detectable.

**distinguished** adjective *our distinguished guests* EMINENT, famous, renowned, prominent, well-known; esteemed, respected, illustrious, acclaimed, celebrated, great; notable, important, influential. ANTONYMS unknown, obscure.

**distinguishing** adjective *does he have any distinguishing features, such as a scar or a birthmark?* DISTINCTIVE, differentiating, characteristic, typical, peculiar, singular, unique.

**distract** verb *let's not distract Dionne while she's painting* DIVERT, sidetrack, draw away, disturb, put off.

**distracted** adjective 1 *she seemed distracted today* PREOCCUPIED, inattentive, vague, abstracted, distrait, absentminded, faraway, in a world of one's own; bemused, confused, bewildered; troubled, harassed, worried, anxious; *informal* miles away, not with it. ANTONYM attentive.

2 *she was distracted with worry* CRAZED, mad, insane, wild, out of one's head, crazy.

**distraction** noun 1 *a distraction from the real issues* DIVERSION, interruption, disturbance, interference, hindrance.

**2** *frivolous distractions* AMUSEMENT, entertainment, diversion, recreation, leisure pursuit, divertissement.

**3** *he was driven to distraction* FRENZY, hysteria, mental distress, madness, insanity, mania; agitation, perturbation.

**distress** noun **1** *she concealed her distress* ANGUISH, suffering, pain, agony, torment, heartache, heartbreak; misery, wretchedness, sorrow, grief, woe, sadness, unhappiness, desolation, despair. ANTONYM happiness.

**2** *a ship in distress* DANGER, peril, difficulty, trouble, jeopardy, risk. ANTONYM safety.

**3** *the distress of the refugees* HARDSHIP, adversity, poverty, deprivation, privation, destitution, indigence, impoverishment, penury, need, dire straits. ANTONYM prosperity.

▸ verb *he was distressed by the trial* CAUSE ANGUISH TO, cause suffering to, pain, upset, make miserable; trouble, worry, bother, perturb, disturb, disquiet, agitate, harrow, torment. ANTONYMS calm, please.

**distressing** adjective *the news was terribly distressing* UPSETTING, worrying, disturbing, disquieting, painful, traumatic, agonizing, harrowing; sad, saddening, heartbreaking, heart-rending; *informal* gut-wrenching. ANTONYM comforting.

**distribute** verb **1** *the proceeds were distributed among his creditors* GIVE OUT, deal out, dole out, dish out, hand out/around; allocate, allot, apportion, share out, divide out/up, parcel out. ANTONYM collect.

**2** *the newsletter is distributed free* CIRCULATE, issue, hand out, deliver.

**3** *more than 130 different species are distributed worldwide* DISPERSE, scatter, spread.

**distribution** noun **1** *the distribution of charity* GIVING OUT, dealing out, doling out, handing out/around, issue, issuing, dispensation; allocation, allotment, apportioning, sharing out, dividing up/out, parceling out.

**2** *the geographical distribution of plants* DISPERSAL, dissemination, spread; placement, position, location, disposition.

**3** *centers of food distribution* SUPPLY, supplying, delivery, transport, transportation.

**4** *the statistical distribution of the problem* FREQUENCY, prevalence, incidence, commonness.

**district** noun *the most respected contractor in our district* NEIGHBORHOOD, area, region, locality, locale, community, quarter, sector, zone, territory; ward; *informal* neck of the woods.

**distrust** noun *the general distrust of authority* MISTRUST, suspicion, wariness, chariness, leeriness, lack of trust, lack of confidence; skepticism, doubt, doubtfulness, cynicism; misgivings, qualms, disbelief; *formal* dubiety.

▸ verb *Louise distrusted him* MISTRUST, be suspicious of, be wary/chary of, be leery of, regard with suspicion, suspect; be skeptical of, have doubts about, doubt, be unsure of/about, have misgivings about, wonder about, disbelieve (in).

**disturb** verb **1** *let's go somewhere where we won't be disturbed* INTERRUPT, intrude on, butt in on, barge in on; distract, disrupt, bother, trouble, pester, harass; *informal* hassle.

**2** *don't disturb his papers* DISARRANGE, muddle, rearrange, disorganize, disorder, mix up, interfere with, throw into disorder/confusion, turn upside down.

**3** *waters disturbed by winds* AGITATE, churn up, stir up; *literary* roil.

**4** *he wasn't disturbed by the allegations* PERTURB, trouble, concern, worry, upset; agitate, fluster, discomfit, disconcert, dismay, distress, discompose, unsettle, ruffle.

**disturbance** noun **1** *we are concerned about the disturbance to local residents* DISRUPTION, distraction, interference; bother, trouble, inconvenience, upset, annoyance, irritation, intrusion, harassment, hassle.

**2** *disturbances among the peasantry* RIOT, fracas, upheaval, brawl, street fight, melee, free-for-all, ruckus, rumpus, rumble, ruction.

**3** *emotional disturbance* TROUBLE, perturbation, distress, worry, upset, agitation, discomposure, discomfiture; neurosis, illness, sickness, disorder, complaint.

**disturbed** adjective **1** *disturbed sleep* DISRUPTED, interrupted, fitful, intermittent, broken.

**2** *the children seemed disturbed* TROUBLED, distressed, upset, distraught; unbalanced, unstable, disordered, dysfunctional, maladjusted, neurotic, unhinged; *informal* screwed up, mixed up.

**disturbing** adjective *he gave us some disturbing information* WORRYING, perturbing, troubling, upsetting; distressing, discomfiting, disconcerting, disquieting, unsettling, dismaying, alarming, frightening.

**disuse** noun *many of the mills fell into disuse* NONUSE, nonemployment, lack of use; neglect, abandonment, desertion, obsolescence; *formal* desuetude.

**disused** adjective *a disused building* UNUSED, no longer in use, unemployed, idle; abandoned, deserted, vacated, unoccupied, uninhabited.

**ditch** noun *she rescued a cat from the ditch* TRENCH, trough, channel, dike, drain, gutter, gully, watercourse, conduit; *Archaeology* fosse.

▸ verb **1** *they started ditching the coastal areas* DIG A DITCH IN, trench, excavate, drain.

**2** *informal* *she ditched her old curtains* THROW OUT, throw away, discard, get rid of, dispose of, do away with, deep-six, shed; abandon, drop, shelve, scrap, jettison, throw on the scrap heap; *informal* dump, junk, chuck, pull the plug on, trash.

**3** *informal* *she ditched her husband.* See ABANDON verb sense 3.

**diurnal** adjective *the patient's moods are determined by diurnal events* DAILY, everyday, quotidian, occurring every/each day.

**divan** noun *have a rest on the divan* SETTEE, sofa, couch, chesterfield; sofa bed, daybed, studio couch.

**dive** verb **1** *they dived into the clear water | the plane was diving toward the ground* PLUNGE, nosedive, jump head first, bellyflop; plummet, fall, drop, pitch, dive-bomb.

**2** *the islanders dive for oysters* SWIM UNDER WATER; snorkel, scuba dive.

**3** *they dove for cover* LEAP, jump, lunge, launch oneself, throw oneself, go headlong, duck.

▸ noun **1** *a dive into the pool* PLUNGE, swan dive, nosedive, jump, bellyflop; plummet, fall, drop, swoop, pitch.

**2** *a sideways dive* LUNGE, spring, jump, leap.

**3** *informal John got into a fight in some dive* SLEAZY BAR/NIGHTCLUB, seedy bar/nightclub; *informal* (drinking) joint, hole.

**diverge** verb **1** *the two roads diverged* SEPARATE, part, fork, divide, split, bifurcate, go in different directions. ANTONYM converge.

**2** *areas where our views diverge* DIFFER, be different, be dissimilar; disagree, be at variance, be at odds, conflict, clash. ANTONYM agree.

**3** *he diverged from his script* DEVIATE, digress, depart, veer, stray; stray from the point, get off the subject.

**divergence** noun **1** *the divergence of the human and ape lineages* SEPARATION, dividing, parting, forking, bifurcation.

**2** *a marked political divergence* DIFFERENCE, dissimilarity, variance, disparity; disagreement, incompatibility, mismatch.

**3** *divergence from standard behavior* DEVIATION, digression, departure, shift, straying; variation, change, alteration.

**divergent** adjective *divergent points of view* DIFFERING, varying, different, dissimilar, unalike, disparate, contrasting, contrastive; conflicting, incompatible, contradictory, at odds, at variance. ANTONYM similar.

**divers** adjective *literary Mr. Roosevelt's divers areas of expertise* SEVERAL, many, numerous, multiple, manifold, multifarious, multitudinous; sundry, miscellaneous, assorted, various; *literary* myriad.

**diverse** adjective *managing data from diverse databases* VARIOUS, sundry, manifold, multiple; varied, varying, miscellaneous, assorted, mixed, diversified, divergent, heterogeneous, a mixed bag of; different, differing, distinct, unlike, dissimilar; *literary* divers, myriad.

**diversify** verb **1** *farmers looking for ways to diversify* BRANCH OUT, expand, extend operations.

**2** *a plan aimed at diversifying the economy* VARY, bring variety to; modify, alter, change, transform; expand, enlarge.

**diversion** noun **1** *the diversion of 19 rivers* REROUTING, redirection, deflection, deviation, divergence.

**2** *traffic diversions* DETOUR, bypass, deviation, alternative route.

**3** *the noise created a diversion* DISTRACTION, disturbance, smokescreen, feint.

**4** *a city full of diversions* ENTERTAINMENT, amusement, pastime, delight, divertissement; fun, recreation, rest and relaxation, pleasure; *informal* R and R; *dated* sport.

**diversity** noun *a diversity of design styles* VARIETY, miscellany, assortment, mixture, mix, mélange, range, array, multiplicity; variation, variance, diversification, heterogeneity, difference, contrast. ANTONYM uniformity.

**divert** verb **1** *a plan to divert the Fraser River* REROUTE, redirect, change the course of, deflect, channel.

**2** *he diverted her from her studies* DISTRACT, sidetrack, disturb, draw away, be a distraction, put off.

**3** *the story diverted them* AMUSE, entertain, distract, delight, enchant, interest, fascinate, absorb, engross, rivet, grip, hold the attention of.

**diverting** adjective *a diverting musical* ENTERTAINING, amusing, enjoyable, pleasing, agreeable, delightful, appealing; interesting, fascinating, intriguing, absorbing, riveting, compelling; humorous, funny, witty, comical. ANTONYM boring.

**divest** verb *he intends to* ***divest*** *you* ***of*** *your power* DEPRIVE OF, strip of, dispossess of, rob of, cheat out of, trick out of.

**divide** verb **1** *he divided his estate into separate holdings* SPLIT (UP), cut up, carve up; dissect, bisect, halve, quarter; *literary* sunder. ANTONYMS unify, join, converge.

**2** *a curtain divided her cabin from the galley* SEPARATE, segregate, partition, screen off, section off, split off. ANTONYMS unify, join, converge.

**3** *the stairs divide at the mezzanine* DIVERGE, separate, part, branch (off), fork, split (in two), bifurcate. ANTONYMS unify, join, converge.

**4** *Jack* ***divided up*** *the cash* SHARE OUT, allocate, allot, apportion, portion out, ration out, parcel out, deal out, dole out, dish out, distribute, dispense; *informal* divvy up.

**5** *he aimed to divide his opponents* DISUNITE, drive apart, break up, split up, set at variance, set at odds; separate, isolate, estrange, alienate; *literary* tear asunder. ANTONYMS unify, unite.

**6** *living things are divided into three categories* CLASSIFY, sort (out), categorize, order, group, grade, rank. ANTONYM combine.

▸ noun *the sectarian divide* BREACH, gulf, gap, split; borderline, boundary, dividing line.

**dividend** noun **1** *an annual dividend* SHARE, portion, premium, return, gain, profit, commission; *informal* cut.

**2** *the research will produce dividends in the future* BENEFIT, advantage, gain; bonus, extra, plus.

**divine** adjective **1** *a divine being* GODLY, angelic, seraphic, saintly, beatific; heavenly, celestial, supernal, holy. ANTONYM mortal.

**2** *divine worship* RELIGIOUS, holy, sacred, sanctified, consecrated, blessed, devotional.

**3** *informal this food is divine.* See EXCELLENT.

▸ noun *dated puritan divines* THEOLOGIAN, clergyman, clergywoman, member of the clergy, churchman, churchwoman, cleric, minister, man/woman of the cloth, preacher, priest; *informal* reverend.

▸ verb **1** *Fergus divined how afraid she was* GUESS, surmise, conjecture, deduce, infer; discern, intuit, perceive, recognize, see, realize, appreciate, understand, grasp, comprehend; *informal* figure (out), savvy.

**2** *they divined that this was an auspicious day* FORETELL, predict, prophesy, forecast, foresee, prognosticate. See note at PREDICT.

THE RIGHT WORD **divine, holy, sacred, hallowed, consecrated**

**Holy** is the only one of these words associated with religion and worship that may be applied directly to the Supreme Being. Something that is *holy* is regarded with the highest reverence because of its connection with God or a god (*Christmas is a holy day in the Christian calendar*). Something that is **sacred**, on the other hand, is set apart as *holy* or is dedicated to some exalted purpose (*sacred music*) but may derive its holiness from a human source rather than from God (*a sacred oath between brothers*). In its strictest sense, **divine** means associated with or derived from God (*the divine right of kings*), but it has also been used to describe anything that is admirable or treasured (*her wedding dress was divine*). **Hallowed** and **consecrated** refer to what has been made sacred or holy, with *hallowed* connotating intrinsic holiness (*they walked on hallowed ground*) and *consecrated* meaning blessed by a formal rite or formally dedicated to some religious use (*the old building had been consecrated as a church*).

**divinity** noun **1** *they denied Christ's divinity* DIVINE NATURE, godliness, deity, godhead, holiness.

**2** *the study of divinity* THEOLOGY, religious studies, religion, scripture.

**3** *a female divinity* DEITY, god, goddess, divine being, supreme being.

**division** noun **1** *the division of the island | cell division* DIVIDING (UP), breaking up, breakup, carving up, splitting, dissection, bisection; partitioning, separation, segregation.

**2** *the division of his assets* SHARING OUT, dividing up, parceling out, dishing out, allocation, allotment, apportionment; splitting up, carving up; *informal* divvying up.

**3** *the division between nomadic and urban cultures* DIVIDING LINE, divide, boundary, borderline, border, demarcation line.

**4** *each class is divided into nine divisions* SECTION, subsection, subdivision, category, class, group, grouping, set, subset, family.

**5** *an independent division of the company* DEPARTMENT, branch, arm, wing, sector, section, subsection, subdivision, subsidiary.

**6** *the causes of social division* DISUNITY, disunion, conflict, discord, disagreement, dissension, disaffection, estrangement, alienation, isolation.

**divisive** adjective *a divisive scheme to set his rivals against each other* ALIENATING, estranging, isolating, schismatic. ANTONYM unifying.

**divorce** noun **1** *she wants a divorce* DISSOLUTION, annulment, (official) separation. ANTONYM marriage.

**2** *a growing divorce between the church and people* SEPARATION, division, split, disunity, estrangement, alienation; schism, gulf, chasm. ANTONYM unity.

▸ verb **1** *her parents have divorced* DISSOLVE ONE'S MARRIAGE, annul one's marriage, end one's marriage, get a divorce.

**2** *religion cannot be divorced from morality* SEPARATE, disconnect, divide, dissociate, disassociate, detach, isolate, alienate, set apart, cut off.

**divulge** verb *he refused to divulge Father O'Neill's whereabouts* DISCLOSE, reveal, tell, communicate, pass on, publish, broadcast, proclaim; expose, uncover, make public, give away, let slip; *informal* spill the beans about, let on about, let the cat out of the bag about. ANTONYM conceal.

**dizzy** adjective **1** *she felt dizzy* GIDDY, lightheaded, faint, unsteady, shaky, muzzy, wobbly; *informal* woozy.

**2** *dizzy heights* CAUSING DIZZINESS, causing giddiness, vertiginous.

**do** verb **1** *she does most of the manual work* CARRY OUT, undertake, discharge, execute, perform, accomplish, achieve; bring about/off, engineer; *informal* pull off; *formal* effectuate.

**2** *they can do as they please* ACT, behave, conduct oneself, acquit oneself; *formal* comport oneself.

**3** *regular coffee will do* SUFFICE, be adequate, be satisfactory, fill/fit the bill, serve one's purpose, meet one's needs.

**4** *the boys will do the dinner* PREPARE, make, get ready, see to, arrange, organize, be responsible for, be in charge of; *informal* fix.

**5** *the company is doing a new range of footwear | a portrait I am doing* MAKE, create, produce, turn out, design, manufacture; paint, draw, sketch; *informal* knock off.

**6** *each room was done in a different color* DECORATE, furnish, ornament, deck out, trick out; *informal* do up.

**7** *the maid did her hair* STYLE, arrange, adjust; brush, comb, wash, dry, cut; *informal* fix.

**8** *I am doing a show to raise money* PUT ON, present, produce; perform in, act in, take part in, participate in.

**9** *you've done me a favor* GRANT, pay, render, give.

**10** *show me how to do these equations* WORK OUT, figure out, calculate; solve, resolve.

**11** *she's doing archaeology* STUDY, learn, take a course in.

**12** *what does he do?* HAVE AS A JOB, have as a profession, be employed at, earn a living at.

**13** *he is doing well at college* GET ON/ALONG, progress, fare, manage, cope; succeed, prosper.

**14** *he was doing 25 mph over the speed limit* DRIVE AT, travel at, move at.

**15** *the cyclists do 30 kilometers per day* TRAVEL (OVER), journey, cover, traverse, achieve, notch up, log; *informal* chalk up.

16 *informal we're doing Scotland this summer* VISIT, tour, sightsee in.

▸ noun *informal he invited us to a grand do* PARTY, reception, gathering, celebration, function, social event/occasion, social, soiree; *informal* bash, shindig.

PHRASES: **do away with** 1 *they want to do away with the old customs* ABOLISH, get rid of, discard, remove, eliminate, discontinue, stop, end, terminate, put an end to, put a stop to, dispense with, drop, abandon, give up; *informal* scrap, ditch, dump, deep-six.

2 *informal she tried to do away with her husband.* See KILL verb sense 1.

**do in** *informal* 1 *the poor devil's been done in.* See KILL verb sense 1.

2 *the long walk home did me in* WEAR OUT, tire out, exhaust, fatigue, weary, overtire, drain; *informal* take it out of.

3 *I did my back in* INJURE, hurt, damage.

**do out of** *informal she nearly succeeded in doing Martin out of his inheritance* SWINDLE OUT OF, cheat out of, trick out of, deprive of; *informal* con out of, diddle out of.

**do up** 1 *she did up her bootlace* FASTEN, tie (up), lace, knot; make fast, secure.

2 *informal he's had his house done up* RENOVATE, refurbish, refit, redecorate, decorate, revamp, make over, modernize, improve, spruce up, smarten up; *informal* give something a facelift, rehab.

**do without** *we learned to do without many of the luxuries we had become accustomed to* FORGO, dispense with, abstain from, refrain from, eschew, give up, cut out, renounce, manage without; *formal* forswear.

**docile** adjective *his docile children do everything he asks of them* COMPLIANT, obedient, pliant, dutiful, submissive, deferential, unassertive, cooperative, amenable, accommodating, biddable, malleable. See note at OBEDIENT. ANTONYMS disobedient, willful.

**dock**[1] noun *his boat was moored at the dock* HARBOR, marina, port, anchorage; wharf, quay, pier, jetty, landing stage.

▸ verb *the ship docked* MOOR, berth, put in, tie up, anchor.

**dock**[2] verb 1 *they docked the money from his salary* DEDUCT, subtract, remove, debit, take off/away, garnishee; *informal* knock off.

2 *workers had their pay docked* REDUCE, cut, decrease.

3 *the dog's tail was docked* CUT OFF, cut short, shorten, crop, lop; remove, amputate, detach, sever, chop off, take off.

**docket** noun 1 *he opened a new docket for the account* FILE, dossier, folder.

2 *I looked my name up on the docket* LIST, index; schedule, agenda, program, timetable.

▸ verb *docket the package* DOCUMENT, record, register; label, tag, tab, mark.

**doctor** noun *Claudio went to see a doctor* PHYSICIAN, MD, medical practitioner, clinician; general practitioner, GP; medic, intern; *informal* doc, medico, quack, sawbones.

▸ verb 1 *informal he doctored their wounds* TREAT, medicate, cure, heal; tend, attend to, minister to, care for, nurse.

2 *he doctored Stephen's drink* ADULTERATE, contaminate, tamper with, lace; *informal* spike, dope.

3 *the reports have been doctored* FALSIFY, tamper with, interfere with, alter, change; forge, fake; *informal* cook, fiddle with.

**doctrinaire** adjective *doctrinaire Marxists* DOGMATIC, rigid, inflexible, uncompromising; authoritarian, intolerant, fanatical, zealous, extreme.

**doctrine** noun *the doctrine of the Trinity* CREED, credo, dogma, belief, teaching, ideology; tenet, maxim, canon, principle, precept.

**document** noun *their lawyer drew up a document* OFFICIAL PAPER, legal paper, certificate, deed, contract, legal agreement; *Law* instrument, indenture.

▸ verb *many aspects of school life have been documented* RECORD, register, report, log, chronicle, archive, put on record, write down; detail, note, describe.

**documentary** adjective 1 *documentary evidence* RECORDED, documented, registered, written, chronicled, archived, on record, on paper, in writing.

2 *a documentary film* FACTUAL, nonfictional.

▸ noun *a documentary about rural West Virginia* FACTUAL PROGRAM, factual film; program, film, broadcast.

**dodder** verb *doddering along the sidewalk* TOTTER, teeter, toddle, hobble, shuffle, shamble, falter.

**doddering**, **doddery** adjective *a doddering patient who needs constant supervision* TOTTERING, tottery, staggering, shuffling, shambling, faltering, shaky, unsteady, wobbly; feeble, frail, weak.

**dodge** verb 1 *she dodged into a crowded restaurant* DART, bolt, dive, lunge, leap, spring.

2 *he could easily dodge the two cops* ELUDE, evade, avoid, escape, run away from, lose, shake (off), jink; *informal* give someone the slip, ditch.

3 *the mayor tried to dodge the debate* AVOID, evade, get out of, back out of, sidestep, do an end run; *informal* duck, wriggle out of.

▸ noun 1 *a dodge to the right* DART, bolt, dive, lunge, leap, spring.

2 *a clever dodge* | *a tax dodge* RUSE, ploy, scheme, tactic, stratagem, subterfuge, trick, hoax, wile, cheat, deception, blind; swindle, fraud; *informal* scam, con, bunco, grift.

**doer** noun 1 *the doer of unspeakable deeds* PERFORMER, perpetrator, executor, accomplisher, agent.

2 *Daniel is a thinker more than a doer* WORKER, organizer, man/woman of action; *informal* mover and shaker, busy bee.

**doff** verb *literary he doffed his cap as we walked past* TAKE OFF, remove, strip off, pull off; raise, lift, tip; *dated* divest oneself of. ANTONYM don.

**dog** noun **1** *she went for a walk with her dog* hound, canine; mongrel, cur; pup, puppy; *informal* doggy/doggie, pooch.

**2** *informal you black-hearted dog!* See BASTARD noun sense 2.

**3** *informal you're a lucky dog!* See FELLOW sense 1.

▸ verb **1** *they dogged him the length of the country* PURSUE, follow, track, trail, shadow, hound; *informal* tail.

**2** *the scheme was dogged by bad weather* PLAGUE, beset, bedevil, beleaguer, blight, trouble.

**dogged** adjective *what he lacks in natural talent he makes up for in dogged spirit* TENACIOUS, determined, resolute, resolved, purposeful, persistent, persevering, single-minded, tireless; strong-willed, steadfast, staunch; *formal* pertinacious. See note at STUBBORN. ANTONYM halfhearted.

**dogma** noun *a dogma of the Sikh religion* TEACHING, belief, tenet, principle, precept, maxim, article of faith, canon; creed, credo, set of beliefs, doctrine, ideology.

**dogmatic** adjective *your being so dogmatic does not attract me to your religious philosophy* OPINIONATED, peremptory, assertive, insistent, emphatic, adamant, doctrinaire, authoritarian, imperious, dictatorial, uncompromising, unyielding, inflexible, rigid.

**doing** noun **1** *the doing of the act constitutes the offense* PERFORMANCE, performing, carrying out, execution, implementation, implementing, achievement, accomplishment, realization, completion; *formal* effectuation.

**2** *an account of his doings in Boston* EXPLOIT, activity, act, action, deed, feat, achievement, accomplishment; *informal* caper.

**3** *that would take some doing* EFFORT, exertion, work, hard work, application, labor, toil, struggle.

**doldrums** plural noun *winter doldrums* DEPRESSION, melancholy, gloom, gloominess, downheartedness, dejection, despondency, low spirits, despair; inertia, apathy, listlessness, blahs, blue funk, blues. PHRASE: **in the doldrums** *overseas stocks are in the doldrums* INACTIVE, quiet, slow, slack, sluggish, stagnant.

**dole** verb *we dole out fresh soup and bread every afternoon* DEAL OUT, share out, divide up, allocate, allot, distribute, dispense, hand out, give out, dish out/up, divvy up.

**doleful** adjective *her doleful eyes* MOURNFUL, woeful, sorrowful, sad, unhappy, depressed, gloomy, morose, melancholy, miserable, forlorn, wretched, woebegone, despondent, dejected, disconsolate, downcast, crestfallen, downhearted; *informal* blue, down in/at the mouth, down in the dumps; *literary* dolorous, heartsick. ANTONYM cheerful.

**doll** noun **1** *the child was hugging a doll* FIGURE, figurine, action figure, model; toy, plaything; *informal* dolly.

**2** *informal she was quite a doll.* See BEAUTY sense 2. PHRASE: **doll oneself up** *informal you don't need to doll yourself up for me* DRESS UP; *informal* do oneself up, dress up to the nines, put on one's glad rags.

**dolor** noun *literary* See MISERY sense 1.

**dolt** noun See IDIOT.

**domain** noun **1** *they extended their domain* REALM, kingdom, empire, dominion, province, territory, land.

**2** *the domain of art* FIELD, area, sphere, discipline, province, world.

**dome** noun *the distinctive dome of the cathedral* CUPOLA, vault, arched roof, rotunda.

**domestic** adjective **1** *domestic commitments* FAMILY, home, household.

**2** *she was not at all domestic* stay-at-home, home-loving, homey, housewifely; *humorous* domesticated.

**3** *small domestic animals* DOMESTICATED, tame, pet, household.

**4** *the domestic car industry* NATIONAL, home, internal.

**5** *domestic plants* NATIVE, indigenous.

▸ noun *they worked as domestics* SERVANT, domestic worker, domestic help, maid, housemaid, cleaner, cleaning lady, housekeeper.

**domesticated** adjective **1** *domesticated animals* TAME, tamed, pet, domestic, trained. ANTONYM wild.

**2** *domesticated crops* CULTIVATED, naturalized. ANTONYMS foreign, wild.

**3** *humorous I'm happily domesticated.* See DOMESTIC sense 2.

**domicile** noun *formal changes of domicile* RESIDENCE, home, house, address, residency, lodging, accommodations; *informal* digs; *formal* dwelling (place), abode, habitation.

▸ verb *he **is domiciled** in Australia* IS SETTLED, live, make one's home, take up residence.

**dominant** adjective **1** *the dominant classes* PRESIDING, ruling, governing, controlling, commanding, ascendant, supreme, authoritative. ANTONYM subservient.

**2** *he has a dominant personality* ASSERTIVE, authoritative, forceful, domineering, commanding, controlling, pushy. ANTONYM submissive.

**3** *the dominant issues in psychology* MAIN, principal, prime, premier, chief, foremost, primary, predominant, paramount, prominent; central, key, crucial, core; *informal* number-one. ANTONYM secondary.

**dominate** verb **1** *the Russians dominated Iran in the nineteenth century* CONTROL, influence, exercise control over, command, be in command of, be in charge of, rule, govern, direct, have ascendancy over, have mastery over; *informal* head up, be in the driver's seat, be at the helm of, rule the roost (in), wear the pants (in), have someone in one's hip pocket; *literary* sway.

**2** *it dominates the sports scene* PREDOMINATE, prevail, reign, be prevalent, be paramount, be preeminent; *informal* kick butt.

**3** *the village is dominated by the viaduct* OVERLOOK, command, tower above/over, loom over.

**domination** noun *she was put off by the male domination sanctioned by her boyfriend's family* RULE, government, sovereignty, control, command, authority, power, dominion, dominance, mastery, supremacy, superiority, ascendancy, sway.

**domineer** verb *his mother had always sought out men she could domineer* BROWBEAT, bully, intimidate, push around/about, order about/around, lord it over; dictate to, be overbearing, have under one's thumb, rule with a rod of iron; *informal* boss about/around, walk all over.

**domineering** adjective *a domineering father and a meek mother had turned her against the idea of marriage* OVERBEARING, authoritarian, imperious, high-handed, autocratic; masterful, dictatorial, despotic, oppressive, iron-fisted, strict, harsh, bossy.

**dominion** noun **1** *France had dominion over Laos* SUPREMACY, ascendancy, dominance, domination, superiority, predominance, preeminence, hegemony, authority, mastery, control, command, power, sway, rule, government, jurisdiction, sovereignty, suzerainty. See note at JURISDICTION.

**2** *a British dominion* DEPENDENCY, colony, protectorate, territory, province, possession; *historical* tributary.

**don** verb *he donned an overcoat* PUT ON, get dressed in, dress (oneself) in, get into, slip into/on.

**donate** verb *the proceeds were donated to the American Red Cross* GIVE, give/make a donation of, contribute, make a contribution of, gift, pledge, grant, bestow; *informal* chip in, pitch in, kick in. See note at GIVE.

**donation** noun *a tax-deductible donation* GIFT, contribution, present, pledge, handout, grant, offering; *formal* benefaction; *historical* alms. See note at PRESENT[3] .

**done** adjective **1** *the job is done* FINISHED, ended, concluded, complete, completed, accomplished, achieved, fulfilled, discharged, executed; *informal* wrapped up, sewn up, polished off. ANTONYM incomplete.

**2** *is the meat done?* COOKED (THROUGH), ready. ANTONYMS raw, underdone.

**3** *those days are done* OVER, over and done with, at an end, finished, ended, concluded, terminated, no more, dead, gone, in the past. ANTONYMS to come, ongoing.

**4** *informal* *that's just not done* PROPER, seemly, decent, respectable, right, correct, in order, fitting, appropriate, acceptable, the done thing. PHRASES: **be/have done with** *she was done with him* BE/HAVE FINISHED WITH, be through with, want no more to do with.

**done for** *informal* *if you get caught, you'll be done for* RUINED, finished, destroyed, undone, doomed, lost; *informal* washed up.

**donkey** noun **1** *the cart was drawn by a donkey* ASS, jackass, jenny; mule, hinny, burro.

**2** *informal* *you silly donkey!* See FOOL noun sense 1.

**donor** noun *an anonymous donor* GIVER, contributor, benefactor, benefactress; supporter, backer, patron, sponsor, friend, member; *informal* angel.

**doom** noun **1** *his impending doom* DESTRUCTION, downfall, ruin, ruination; extinction, annihilation, death.

**2** *archaic* *the day of doom* JUDGMENT DAY, the Last Judgment, doomsday, Armageddon.

▸ verb *we were doomed to fail* DESTINE, fate, predestine, preordain, foredoom, mean; condemn, sentence.

**doomed** adjective *a doomed voyage* ILL-FATED, ill-starred, cursed, jinxed, foredoomed, damned; *literary* star-crossed.

**door** noun *many a weary traveler has walked through that door* DOORWAY, portal, opening, entrance, entry, exit. PHRASE: **out of doors** *if the weather's nice, we'll have our dinner out of doors* OUTSIDE, outdoors, in/into the open air, alfresco.

**dope** noun *informal* **1** *he was caught smuggling dope* (ILLEGAL) DRUGS, narcotics; cannabis, heroin, cocaine.

**2** *what a dope!* See FOOL noun sense 1.

**3** *give me the dope on Mr. Dixon.* See INTELLIGENCE sense 2.

▸ verb **1** *the horse was doped* DRUG, administer drugs/narcotics to, tamper with, interfere with; sedate.

**2** *they doped his drink* ADD DRUGS TO, tamper with, adulterate, contaminate, lace; *informal* spike, doctor.

**dormant** adjective *the tubers lie dormant in the soil until spring* ASLEEP, sleeping, resting; INACTIVE, passive, inert, latent, quiescent. See note at LATENT. ANTONYMS awake, active.

**dose** noun *do not exceed the prescribed dose* MEASURE, measurement, portion, dosage, shot; *informal* hit, fix.

**dot** noun *a pattern of tiny dots* SPOT, speck, fleck, speckle; decimal point, period, pixel.

▸ verb **1** *spots of rain dotted his shirt* SPOT, fleck, mark, stipple, freckle, sprinkle; *literary* bestrew, besprinkle.

**2** *the streets are dotted with restaurants* SCATTER, pepper, sprinkle, strew.

PHRASE: **on the dot** *informal* *ring the bell at 1:15 on the dot* PRECISELY, exactly, sharp, prompt, dead on, on the stroke of ——; *informal* on the button, on the nose.

**dotage** noun *the memoirs she began in her dotage* DECLINING YEARS, winter of one's life, autumn of one's life; advanced years, old age; *literary* eld.

**dote** PHRASE: **dote on** *she doted on the boy* ADORE, love dearly, be devoted to, idolize, treasure, cherish, worship, hold dear; indulge, spoil, pamper.

**doting** adjective *all her doting admirers* ADORING, loving, besotted, infatuated; affectionate, fond, devoted, caring; uxorious.

**double** adjective **1** *a double garage* | *double yellow lines* DUAL, duplex, twin, binary, duplicate, in pairs, coupled, twofold. ANTONYM single.

**2** *a double helping* DOUBLED, twofold.

**3** *a double meaning* AMBIGUOUS, equivocal, dual, two-edged, double-edged, ambivalent, cryptic, enigmatic. ANTONYM unambiguous.

**4** *a double life* DECEITFUL, double-dealing, two-faced, dual; hypocritical, false, duplicitous, insincere, deceiving, dissembling, dishonest. ANTONYMS simple, honest.

▸ adverb *we had to pay double* TWICE (OVER), twice the amount, doubly.

▸ noun **1** *if it's not her, it's her double* LOOK-ALIKE, twin, clone, duplicate, exact likeness, replica, copy, facsimile, doppelgänger; *informal* spitting image, dead ringer.

**2** *she used a double for the stunts* STAND-IN, substitute.

▸ verb **1** *they doubled his salary* MULTIPLY BY TWO, increase twofold.

**2** *the bottom sheet had been doubled up* FOLD (BACK/UP/DOWN/OVER/UNDER), turn back/up/down/over/under, tuck back/up/down/under.

**3** *the kitchen can double as a dining room* FUNCTION, do, (also) serve.

PHRASE: **on the double** *hold tight, we'll be there on the double* VERY QUICKLY, as fast as one's legs can carry one, at a run, at a gallop, fast, swiftly, rapidly, speedily, at full speed, at full tilt, as fast as possible; *informal* like (greased) lightning, like the wind, like a bat out of hell, lickety-split, PDQ (pretty damn quick).

**double-cross** verb *he was double-crossing his family behind their backs* BETRAY, cheat, defraud, trick, hoodwink, mislead, deceive, swindle, be disloyal to, be unfaithful to, play false; *informal* sell down the river.

**double-dealing** noun *your double-dealing will eventually be your undoing* DUPLICITY, treachery, betrayal, double-crossing, unfaithfulness, untrustworthiness, infidelity, bad faith, disloyalty, breach of trust, fraud, underhandedness, cheating, dishonesty, deceit, deceitfulness, deception, falseness; *informal* crookedness. ANTONYM honesty.

**double entendre** noun *much of the comedy is derived from racy double entendres* AMBIGUITY, double meaning, innuendo, play on words.

**doubt** noun **1** *there was some doubt as to the caller's identity* UNCERTAINTY, unsureness, indecision, hesitation, dubiousness, suspicion, confusion; queries, questions; *formal* dubiety. See note at UNCERTAINTY. ANTONYM certainty.

**2** *a weak leader racked by doubt* INDECISION, hesitation, uncertainty, insecurity, unease, uneasiness, apprehension; hesitancy, vacillation, irresolution. ANTONYMS confidence, conviction.

**3** *there is doubt about their motives* SKEPTICISM, distrust, mistrust, doubtfulness, suspicion, cynicism, uneasiness, apprehension, wariness, chariness, leeriness; reservations, misgivings, suspicions; *formal* dubiety. ANTONYM trust.

▸ verb **1** *they doubted my story* DISBELIEVE, distrust, mistrust, suspect, have doubts about, be suspicious of, have misgivings about, have qualms about, feel uneasy about, feel apprehensive about, query, question, challenge. ANTONYM trust.

**2** *I doubt whether he will come* THINK SOMETHING UNLIKELY, have (one's) doubts about, question, query, be dubious. ANTONYM be confident.

**3** *stop doubting and believe!* BE UNDECIDED, have doubts, be irresolute, be ambivalent, be doubtful, be unsure, be uncertain, be of two minds, hesitate, shilly-shally, waver, vacillate. ANTONYM believe.

PHRASES: **in doubt 1** *the issue was in doubt* DOUBTFUL, uncertain, open to question, unconfirmed, unknown, undecided, unresolved, in the balance, up in the air; *informal* iffy.

**2** *if you are in doubt, ask for advice* IRRESOLUTE, hesitant, vacillating, dithering, wavering, ambivalent; doubtful, unsure, uncertain, of two minds, shilly-shallying, undecided, in a quandary, in a dilemma; *informal* sitting on the fence.

**no doubt** *he's no doubt read the note by now* DOUBTLESS, undoubtedly, indubitably, doubtlessly, without (a) doubt; unquestionably, undeniably, incontrovertibly, irrefutably; unequivocally, clearly, plainly, obviously, patently.

**doubter** noun *this is his chance to confound the doubters* SKEPTIC, doubting Thomas, nonbeliever, unbeliever, disbeliever, cynic, scoffer, questioner, challenger, dissenter. ANTONYM believer.

**doubtful** adjective **1** *I was doubtful about going* IRRESOLUTE, hesitant, vacillating, dithering, wavering, in doubt, unsure, uncertain, of two minds, shilly-shallying, undecided, in a quandary, in a dilemma, blowing hot and cold. ANTONYMS confident, decisive.

**2** *at this point, the verdict is still doubtful* IN DOUBT, uncertain, open to question, unsure, unconfirmed, not definite, unknown, undecided, unresolved, debatable, in the balance, up in the air; *informal* iffy. ANTONYM certain.

**3** *the whole trip is looking rather doubtful* UNLIKELY, improbable, dubious, impossible. ANTONYM probable.

**4** *they are doubtful of the methods used* DISTRUSTFUL, mistrustful, suspicious, wary, chary, leery, apprehensive; skeptical, unsure, ambivalent, dubious, cynical. ANTONYM trusting.

**5** *this decision is of doubtful validity* QUESTIONABLE, arguable, debatable, controversial, contentious; *informal* iffy. ANTONYM sound.

THE RIGHT WORD **doubtful, ambiguous, dubious, enigmatic, equivocal, problematic, questionable**

If you are **doubtful** about the outcome of a situation, you might be understandably **dubious** about getting involved in it. While all of these adjectives express suspicion, indecision, or a lack of clarity, *doubtful* carries such strong connotations of uncertainty that the thing being described is as good as worthless, unsound, invalid, unlikely, or doomed to fail (*it was doubtful that the plane could land safely*). *Dubious* is not quite as strong, suggesting suspicion, mistrust, or hesitation (*a dubious reputation*). It can also mean inclined to doubt or full of hesitation. If you're *doubtful* about the outcome of a particular situation, it means that you are fairly certain it will not turn out well. If you're *dubious*, on the other hand, it means that you're wavering or hesitating in your opinion. **Questionable** may merely imply the existence of doubt (*a questionable excuse*), but like *dubious*, it also has connotations of dishonesty and immorality (*a place *where questionable activities were going on*). **Problematic**, in contrast to both *dubious* and *questionable*, is free from any suggestion of moral judgment or suspicion. It is applied to things that are genuinely uncertain, and to outcomes that are as likely to be positive as negative (*getting everyone in the family to agree could be problematic*). **Ambiguous** and **equivocal** refer to lack of clarity. But while *ambiguous* can refer to either an intentional or unintentional lack of clarity (*her ambiguous replies to our questions*), *equivocal* suggests an intentional wish to remain unclear (*his equivocal responses indicated that he wasn't keen to cooperate*). It can also mean capable of different interpretations (*an equivocal statement that could be taken to mean opposite things*). Something that is **enigmatic** is likely to be intentionally unclear as well (*an enigmatic statement designed to provoke controversy*), although *enigmatic* can also mean perplexing or mysterious.

---

**doubtless** adverb *Henry was doubtless glad of the opportunity* UNDOUBTEDLY, indubitably, doubtlessly, no doubt; unquestionably, indisputably, undeniably, incontrovertibly, irrefutably; certainly, surely, of course, indeed.

**dour** adjective *they were barely acknowledged by the dour receptionist* STERN, unsmiling, unfriendly, severe, forbidding, gruff, surly, grim, sullen, solemn, austere, stony. See note at GLUM. ANTONYMS cheerful, friendly.

**dovetail** verb **1** *the ends of the logs were dovetailed* JOINT, join, fit together, splice, mortise, tenon.

**2** *this will dovetail well with the company's existing activities* FIT IN, go together, be consistent, match, conform, harmonize, be in tune, correspond; *informal* square, jibe.

**dowdy** adjective *a makeover that took her from dowdy to wowdy* UNFASHIONABLE, frumpy, old-fashioned, outmoded, out-of-date, inelegant, shabby, frowzy. ANTONYM fashionable.

**down**[1] adverb **1** *they went down in the elevator* TOWARD A LOWER POSITION, downward, downstairs. ANTONYM up.

**2** *she fell down* TO THE GROUND, to the floor, over. ANTONYM up.

▸ preposition **1** *the elevator plunged down the shaft* TO A LOWER POSITION IN, to the bottom of.

**2** *I walked down the street* ALONG, to the other end of, from one end of —— to the other.

**3** *down the years* THROUGHOUT, through, during.

▸ adjective **1** *I'm feeling a bit down* DEPRESSED, sad, unhappy, melancholy, miserable, wretched, sorrowful, gloomy, dejected, downhearted, despondent, dispirited, low; *informal* blue, down in the dumps, down in/at the mouth. ANTONYM elated.

**2** *the computer is down* NOT WORKING, inoperative, malfunctioning, out of order, broken; not in service, out of action, out of commission; *informal* conked out, bust, busted, (gone) kaput, on the fritz, on the blink. ANTONYM working.

▸ verb *informal* **1** *antiaircraft missiles downed the fighter jet* KNOCK DOWN/OVER, knock to the ground, bring down, topple; *informal* deck, floor, flatten.

**2** *he downed his beer* DRINK (UP/DOWN), gulp (down), guzzle, quaff, drain, chugalug, slug, finish off; *informal* knock back, put away, scarf (down/up).

▸ noun *the ups and downs of running a business* SETBACKS, upsets, reverses, reversals, mishaps, vicissitudes; *informal* glitches.

PHRASE: **be down on** *informal why do you have to be down on your parents all the time?* DISAPPROVE OF, be against, feel antagonism to, be hostile to, feel ill will toward; *informal* have it in for.

**down**[2] noun *goose down* SOFT FEATHERS, fine hair; fluff, fuzz, floss, lint.

**downbeat** adjective *the mood is decidedly downbeat* PESSIMISTIC, gloomy, negative, defeatist, cynical, bleak, fatalistic, dark, black; despairing, despondent, depressed, dejected, demoralized, hopeless, melancholy, glum.

**downcast** adjective *it's too nice a day to be looking so downcast* DESPONDENT, disheartened, discouraged, dispirited, downhearted, crestfallen, down, low, disconsolate, despairing; sad, melancholy, gloomy, glum, morose, doleful, dismal, woebegone, miserable, depressed, dejected; *informal* blue, down in/at the mouth, down in the dumps. ANTONYM elated.

**downfall** noun *the shah's downfall* UNDOING, ruin, ruination; defeat, conquest, deposition, overthrow; nemesis, destruction, annihilation, elimination; end, collapse, fall, crash, failure; debasement, degradation, disgrace; Waterloo. ANTONYM rise.

**downgrade** verb **1** *plans to downgrade three workers* DEMOTE, lower, reduce/lower in rank; relegate. ANTONYM promote.

**2** *I won't downgrade their achievement* DISPARAGE, denigrate, detract from, run down, belittle; *informal* badmouth, dis. ANTONYM praise.

**downhearted** adjective *of the children, little Robbie was the most downhearted* DESPONDENT, disheartened, discouraged, dispirited, downcast, crestfallen, down, low, disconsolate, wretched; melancholy, gloomy, glum, morose, doleful, dismal, woebegone, miserable, depressed, dejected, sorrowful, sad; *informal* blue, down in/at the mouth, down in the dumps. ANTONYM elated.

**downpour** noun *they met when huddled under an awning during a sudden downpour* RAINSTORM, cloudburst, deluge, shower; thunderstorm, thundershower; torrential/pouring rain.

**downright** adjective **1** *downright lies* COMPLETE, total, absolute, utter, thorough, out-and-out, outright, sheer, arrant, pure, real, veritable, categorical, unmitigated, unadulterated, unalloyed, unequivocal.

**2** *her downright attitude.* See FORTHRIGHT.

▸ adverb *that's downright dangerous* THOROUGHLY, utterly, positively, profoundly, really, completely, totally, entirely; unquestionably, undeniably, in every respect, through and through; *informal* plain.

**down-to-earth** adjective *I guess we weren't expecting the son of those weirdos to be so charming and down-to-earth* PRACTICAL, sensible, realistic, matter-of-fact, responsible, reasonable, rational, logical, balanced, sober, pragmatic, levelheaded, commonsensical, sane. ANTONYM idealistic.

**downtrodden** adjective *thousands of downtrodden families arrived at the border, only to be turned away* OPPRESSED, subjugated, persecuted, repressed, tyrannized, crushed, enslaved, exploited, victimized, bullied; disadvantaged, underprivileged, powerless, helpless; abused, maltreated.

**downward** adjective *profits are in a downward trend* DESCENDING, downhill, falling, sinking, dipping; earthbound, earthward.

**dowry** noun *Belinda's dowry included an acre of fertile pasture and two young mules* MARRIAGE SETTLEMENT, (marriage) portion; *archaic* dot.

**doze** verb *she was dozing at her desk when the supervisor walked by* CATNAP, nap, drowse, sleep lightly, rest; *informal* snooze, catch forty winks, get some shut-eye, catch some Zs; *literary* slumber.

▸ noun *a little doze before dinner might be just what you need* CATNAP, nap, siesta, light sleep, drowse, rest; *informal* snooze, forty winks; *literary* slumber.

PHRASE: **doze off** *the guy in front of us would doze off between all the musical numbers* FALL ASLEEP, go to sleep, drop off; *informal* nod off, drift off, sack out, conk out.

**drab** adjective **1** *a drab interior* COLORLESS, gray, dull, washed out, muted, lackluster; dingy, dreary, dismal, cheerless, gloomy, somber. ANTONYMS bright, cheerful.

**2** *a drab existence* UNINTERESTING, dull, boring, tedious, monotonous, dry, dreary; unexciting, unimaginative, uninspiring, insipid, lackluster, flat, stale, wishy-washy, colorless; lame, tired, sterile, anemic, barren, tame; middle-of-the-road, run-of-the-mill, mediocre, nondescript, characterless, mundane, unremarkable, humdrum, plain-vanilla. ANTONYM interesting.

**draft**[1] noun **1** *the draft of his speech* PRELIMINARY VERSION, rough outline, plan, skeleton, abstract; main points, bare bones.

**2** *a draft of the building* PLAN, blueprint, design, diagram, drawing, sketch, map, layout, representation.

**3** *a bank draft* CHECK, order, money order, bill of exchange.

**draft**[2] noun **1** *the draft made Robyn shiver* CURRENT OF AIR, rush of air; waft, wind, breeze, gust, puff, blast; *informal* blow.

**2** *a deep draft of beer* GULP, drink, swallow, mouthful, slug; *informal* swig, swill.

**drag** verb **1** *she dragged the chair backward* HAUL, pull, tug, heave, lug, draw; trail, trawl, tow; *informal* yank.

**2** *the day dragged* BECOME TEDIOUS, pass slowly, creep along, hang heavy, wear on, go on too long, go on and on.

▸ noun **1** *the drag of the air brakes* PULL, resistance, tug.

**2** *informal work can be a drag* BORE, nuisance, bother, trouble, pest, annoyance, trial, chore, vexation; *informal* pain, pain in the neck, headache, hassle.

PHRASES: **drag on** *their feud has dragged on for years* PERSIST, continue, go on, carry on, extend, run on, be protracted, endure, prevail.

**drag out** *let's not drag out the Q&A session with issues that can't be addressed at this point* PROLONG, protract, draw out, spin out, string out, extend, lengthen, carry on, keep going, continue.

**dragoon** noun *historical the dragoons charged* CAVALRYMAN, mounted soldier; *historical* knight, chevalier, hussar; *archaic* cavalier.

▸ verb *he dragooned his friends into participating* COERCE, pressure, press, push; force, compel, impel; hound, harass, nag, harry, badger, goad, pester; browbeat, bludgeon, bully, twist someone's arm, strong-arm; *informal* railroad.

**drain** verb **1** *a valve for draining the tank* EMPTY (OUT), void, clear (out), evacuate, unload. ANTONYM fill.

**2** *drain off any surplus liquid* DRAW OFF, extract, withdraw, remove, siphon off, pour out, pour off; milk, bleed, tap, void, filter, discharge.

**3** *the water drained away to the sea* FLOW, pour, trickle, stream, run, rush, gush, flood, surge; leak, ooze, seep, dribble, issue, filter, bleed, leach.

**4** *more people would just drain our resources* USE UP, exhaust, deplete, consume, expend, get through, sap, strain, tax; milk, bleed. ANTONYM replenish.

▸ noun **1** *the drain filled with water* SEWER, channel, conduit, ditch, culvert, duct, pipe, gutter, trough; sluice, spillway, race, flume, chute.

**2** *a drain on the battery* STRAIN, pressure, burden, load, tax, demand.

**drama** noun **1** *a television drama* PLAY, show, piece, theatrical work, dramatization.

**2** *he is studying drama* ACTING, the theater, the stage, the performing arts, dramatic art(s), stagecraft.

**3** *she liked to create a drama* INCIDENT, scene, spectacle, crisis; excitement, thrill, sensation; disturbance, commotion, turmoil; dramatics, theatrics.

**dramatic** adjective **1** *dramatic art* THEATRICAL, theatric, thespian, stage, dramaturgical; *formal* histrionic.

**2** *a dramatic increase* CONSIDERABLE, substantial, sizable, goodly, fair, marked, noticeable, measurable, perceptible, obvious, appreciable; significant, notable, noteworthy, remarkable, extraordinary, exceptional, phenomenal; *informal* tidy. ANTONYM insignificant.

**3** *dramatic scenes set in the city* EXCITING, stirring, action-packed, sensational, spectacular; startling, unexpected, tense, gripping, riveting, fascinating, thrilling, hair-raising; rousing, lively, electrifying, impassioned, moving. ANTONYM boring.

**4** *dramatic headlands* STRIKING, impressive, imposing, spectacular, breathtaking, dazzling, sensational, awesome, awe-inspiring, remarkable, outstanding, incredible, phenomenal. ANTONYM unimpressive.

**5** *a dramatic gesture* EXAGGERATED, theatrical, ostentatious, actressy, stagy, showy, splashy, melodramatic, overdone, histrionic, affected, mannered, artificial; *informal* hammy, ham, campy. ANTONYMS natural, unaffected.

**dramatist** noun *Fonda plays the part of dramatist Lillian Hellman* PLAYWRIGHT, writer, scriptwriter, screenwriter, scenarist, dramaturge.

**dramatize** verb **1** *the novel was dramatized* TURN INTO A PLAY/MOVIE/MOTION PICTURE/FILM, adapt for the stage/ screen.

**2** *the tabloids dramatized the event* EXAGGERATE, overdo, overstate, hyperbolize, magnify, amplify, inflate; sensationalize, embroider, color, aggrandize, embellish, elaborate; *informal* blow up (out of all proportion).

**drape** verb **1** *she draped a shawl around her* WRAP, wind, swathe, sling, hang.

**2** *the chair was draped with dirty laundry* COVER, envelop, swathe, shroud, deck, festoon, overlay, cloak, wind, enfold, sheathe.

**3** *he draped one leg over the arm of his chair* DANGLE, hang, suspend, droop, drop.

**drastic** adjective *drastic measures were necessary* EXTREME, serious, desperate, radical, far-reaching, momentous, substantial; heavy, severe, harsh, rigorous; oppressive, draconian. ANTONYM moderate.

**draw** verb **1** *he drew the house* SKETCH, make a drawing (of), delineate, outline, draft, rough out, illustrate, render, represent, trace; portray, depict.

**2** *she drew her chair closer to the fire* PULL, haul, drag, tug, heave, lug, trail, tow; *informal* yank.

**3** *the train drew into the station* MOVE, go, come, proceed, progress, travel, advance, pass, drive; inch, roll, glide, cruise; forge, sweep; back.

**4** *she drew the curtains* CLOSE, shut, lower; open, part, pull back, pull open, fling open, raise.

**5** *the doctor drew some fluid off the knee* DRAIN, extract, withdraw, remove, suck, pump, siphon, milk, bleed, tap.

**6** *he drew his gun* PULL OUT, take out, produce, fish out, extract, withdraw; unsheathe.

**7** *I drew on my line of credit* WITHDRAW, take out.

**8** *while I draw breath* BREATHE IN, inhale, inspire, respire.

**9** *she was drawing huge audiences* ATTRACT, interest, win, capture, catch, engage, lure, entice; absorb, occupy, rivet, engross, fascinate, mesmerize, spellbind, captivate, enthrall, grip.

**10** *what conclusion can we draw?* DEDUCE, infer, conclude, derive, gather, glean.

▸ noun **1** *the match ended in a draw* TIE, dead heat, stalemate.

**2** *the draw of the city* ATTRACTION, lure, allure, pull, appeal, glamour, enticement, temptation, charm, seduction, fascination, magnetism.

PHRASES: **draw on** *you can always draw on your carpentry skills* CALL ON, have recourse to, avail oneself of, turn to, look to, fall back on, rely on, exploit, use, employ, utilize, bring into play.

**draw out 1** *he drew out a gun.* See DRAW verb sense 6.

**2** *they always drew out their goodbyes* PROLONG, protract, drag out, spin out, string out, extend, lengthen.

**3** *you'll have to carefully draw him out with specific questions* ENCOURAGE TO TALK, put at ease.

**draw up 1** *a car drew up beside us* STOP, pull up, halt, come to a standstill, brake, park; arrive.

**2** *we drew up a list* COMPOSE, formulate, frame, write down, draft, prepare, think up, devise, work out; create, invent, design.

**3** *he drew up his forces in battle array* ARRANGE, marshal, muster, assemble, group, order, range, rank, line up, dispose, position, array.

**drawback** noun *one of the drawbacks of the bigger screen is a slight loss in resolution* DISADVANTAGE, snag, downside, stumbling block, catch, hitch, pitfall, fly in the ointment; weak spot/point, weakness, imperfection; handicap, limitation, trouble, difficulty, problem, complication; hindrance, obstacle, impediment, obstruction, inconvenience, discouragement, deterrent; *informal* minus, hiccup, (monkey) wrench in the works. ANTONYM benefit.

**drawing** noun **1** *a drawing of our poodles, Skibby and Popo* SKETCH, picture, illustration, representation, portrayal, delineation, depiction, composition, study; diagram, outline, design, plan.

**2** *she won the Christmas drawing* RAFFLE, lottery, sweepstake, sweep, ballot, lotto.

**drawl** verb *by the time he drawls a complete sentence, I'll be old and gray* SAY SLOWLY, speak slowly; drone.

**drawn** adjective *she looked pale and drawn* PINCHED, haggard, drained, wan, hollow-cheeked; fatigued, tired, exhausted; tense, stressed, strained, worried, anxious, harassed, fraught; *informal* hassled.

**dread** verb *I used to dread going to school* FEAR, be afraid of, worry about, be anxious about, have forebodings about; be terrified by, tremble/shudder at, shrink from, quail from, flinch from; *informal* get cold feet about.

▸ noun *she was filled with dread* FEAR, apprehension, trepidation, anxiety, worry, concern, foreboding, disquiet, unease, angst; fright, panic, alarm; terror, horror; *informal* the jitters, the creeps, the shivers, the heebie-jeebies. ANTONYM confidence.

▸ adjective *the dread disease* AWFUL, frightful, terrible, horrible, dreadful; feared, frightening, alarming, terrifying, dire, dreaded.

**dreadful** adjective **1** *a dreadful accident* TERRIBLE, frightful, horrible, grim, awful, dire; horrifying, alarming, shocking, distressing, appalling, harrowing; ghastly, fearful, horrendous; tragic, calamitous; *formal* grievous. ANTONYM mild.

2 *a dreadful meal* UNPLEASANT, disagreeable, nasty; frightful, shocking, awful, abysmal, atrocious, disgraceful, deplorable, very bad, repugnant; poor, inadequate, inferior, unsatisfactory, distasteful; *informal* pathetic, woeful, crummy, rotten, sorry, third-rate, lousy, godawful. ANTONYMS pleasant, agreeable.

3 *you're a dreadful flirt* OUTRAGEOUS, shocking; inordinate, immoderate, unrestrained.

**dream** noun 1 *I awoke from my dreams* REM sleep; nightmare; vision, fantasy, hallucination.

2 *she went around in a dream* DAYDREAM, reverie, trance, daze, stupor, haze.

3 *he realized his childhood dream* AMBITION, aspiration, hope; goal, aim, objective, grail, intention, intent, target; desire, wish, yearning; daydream, fantasy, pipe dream.

4 *he's an absolute dream* DELIGHT, joy, marvel, wonder, gem, treasure; beauty, vision.

▸ verb 1 *she dreamed about her own funeral* HAVE A DREAM, have a nightmare.

2 *I* ***dreamt of*** *making the Olympic team* FANTASIZE ABOUT, daydream about; WISH FOR, hope for, long for, yearn for, hanker after, set one's heart on; aspire to, aim for, set one's sights on.

3 *she's always dreaming* DAYDREAM, be in a trance, be lost in thought, be preoccupied, be abstracted, stare into space, muse, be in la-la land.

4 *I wouldn't dream of being late* THINK, consider, contemplate, conceive.

▸ adjective *his dream home* IDEAL, perfect, fantasy.

PHRASE: **dream up** *I dreamed up some new excuse* THINK UP, invent, concoct, devise, hatch, contrive, create, work out, come up with; *informal* cook up.

**dreamer** noun *part of me will always be a dreamer* FANTASIST, daydreamer; romantic, sentimentalist, idealist, wishful thinker, Don Quixote; Utopian, visionary. ANTONYM realist.

**dreamland** noun 1 *I drift off to dreamland* SLEEP; *humorous* the land of Nod.

2 *they must be living in dreamland* THE LAND OF MAKE-BELIEVE, fairyland, cloudland, la-la land, never-never land, paradise, Utopia, heaven, Shangri-La.

**dreamy** adjective 1 *a dreamy expression* DAYDREAMING, dreaming; pensive, thoughtful, reflective, meditative, ruminative; lost in thought, preoccupied, distracted, rapt, inattentive, woolgathering, vague, absorbed, absentminded, with one's head in the clouds, in a world of one's own; *informal* miles away. ANTONYMS alert, attentive.

2 *you and your ideas are a bit too dreamy for me* IDEALISTIC, romantic, starry-eyed, impractical, unrealistic, Utopian, quixotic; *chiefly Brit. informal* airy-fairy. ANTONYMS realistic, practical.

3 *a dreamy recollection* DREAMLIKE, vague, dim, hazy, shadowy, faint, indistinct, unclear. ANTONYMS clear, sharp.

4 *informal* *Tasha's friend Rick is really dreamy* ATTRACTIVE, handsome, good-looking; appealing, lovely, delightful; *informal* heavenly, divine, gorgeous, hot, cute. ANTONYMS unattractive, ugly.

**dreary** adjective 1 *the dreary hours spent in a jail cell* DULL, drab, uninteresting, flat, tedious, wearisome, boring, unexciting, unstimulating, uninspiring, soul-destroying; humdrum, monotonous, uneventful, unremarkable, featureless, ho-hum. ANTONYM exciting.

2 *she thought of dreary things* SAD, miserable, depressing, gloomy, somber, grave, mournful, melancholic, joyless, cheerless. ANTONYM cheerful.

3 *a dreary day* GLOOMY, dismal, dull, dark, dingy, murky, overcast; depressing, somber. ANTONYM bright.

**dregs** plural noun 1 *the dregs from a bottle of wine* SEDIMENT, deposit, residue, accumulation, sludge, lees, grounds, remains; *technical* residuum.

2 *the dregs of humanity* SCUM, refuse, riffraff, outcasts, deadbeats; underclass, untouchables, lowest of the low, great unwashed, hoi polloi; *informal* trash.

**drench** verb *the rain has drenched us to the bone* SOAK, saturate, wet through, permeate, douse, souse; drown, swamp, inundate, flood; steep, bathe.

**dress** verb 1 *he dressed quickly* PUT ON CLOTHES, clothe oneself, get dressed.

2 *she was dressed in a suit* CLOTHE, attire, garb, deck out, trick out, costume, array, robe; *informal* get up, doll up.

3 *they dress for dinner every day* WEAR FORMAL CLOTHES, wear evening dress, dress up.

4 *dressing the house for the holidays* DECORATE, trim, deck, adorn, ornament, embellish, beautify, prettify; festoon, garland, garnish.

5 *they dressed his wounds* BANDAGE, cover, bind, wrap, swathe; doctor, care for.

6 *dress the chicken* PREPARE, get ready; clean.

7 *the field was dressed with manure* FERTILIZE, enrich, manure, mulch, compost, top-dress.

8 *he dressed Michelle's hair* STYLE, groom, arrange, do; comb, brush; preen, primp; *informal* fix.

9 *Military* *the battalion dressed its ranks* LINE UP, align, straighten, arrange, order, dispose; fall in.

▸ noun 1 *a long blue dress* gown, robe, shift, frock.

2 *fancy dress* CLOTHES, clothing, garments, attire; costume, outfit, ensemble, garb; *informal* gear, getup, togs, duds, glad rags, threads, Sunday best; *formal* apparel; *archaic* raiment.

PHRASES: **dress down** 1 *even the execs dress down on Fridays* DRESS INFORMALLY, dress casually.

2 *never dress down an employee in front of his colleagues.* See REPRIMAND verb.

**dress up** 1 *Angela loved dressing up* DRESS SMARTLY, dress formally, wear evening dress; *informal* doll oneself up, put on one's glad rags, gussy oneself up.

2 *Hugh dressed up as Santa Claus* DISGUISE ONESELF, dress; put on fancy dress, put on a costume.

**dressing** noun 1 *salad dressing* SAUCE, condiment, dip.

2 *they put fresh dressings on her burns* BANDAGE, covering, plaster, gauze, lint, compress; *trademark* Band-Aid.

3 *an organic dressing for the vegetable garden* FERTILIZER, manure, compost, dung, guano; bone meal, blood meal, fish meal; mulch; top-dressing.

**dressmaker** noun *her dressmaker was the young widow of Colonel Wilcox* TAILOR, seamstress, needlewoman; clothier; couturier, designer.

**dribble** verb 1 *the baby started to dribble* DROOL, slaver, slobber, salivate, drivel.

2 *rainwater dribbled down her face* TRICKLE, drip, fall, drizzle; ooze, seep.

3 *dribble the ball* BOUNCE.

▸ noun 1 *there was dribble on his chin* SALIVA, spittle, spit, slaver, slobber, drool.

2 *a dribble of sweat* TRICKLE, drip, driblet, stream, drizzle; drop, splash.

**drift** verb 1 *his raft drifted down the river* BE CARRIED, be borne; float, bob, waft, meander.

2 *the guests drifted away* WANDER, meander, stray, putter, dawdle.

3 *don't allow your attention to drift* STRAY, digress, deviate, diverge, veer, get sidetracked.

4 *snow drifted over the path* PILE UP, bank up, heap up, accumulate, gather, amass.

▸ noun 1 *a drift from the country to urban areas* MOVEMENT, shift, flow, transfer, relocation, gravitation.

2 *the pilot had not noticed any drift* DEVIATION, digression.

3 *he caught her drift* GIST, essence, meaning, sense, substance, significance; thrust, import, tenor; implication, intention; direction, course.

4 *a drift of deep snow* PILE, heap, bank, mound, mass, accumulation.

**drill** noun 1 *a hydraulic drill* DRILLING TOOL, boring tool, auger, (brace and) bit, gimlet, awl, bradawl.

2 *they learned military drills* TRAINING, instruction, coaching, teaching; (physical) exercises, workout.

3 *Estelle knew the drill* PROCEDURE, routine, practice, regimen, program, schedule; method, system.

▸ verb 1 *drill the piece of wood* BORE A HOLE IN, make a hole in; bore, pierce, puncture, perforate.

2 *a sergeant drilling new recruits* TRAIN, instruct, coach, teach, discipline; exercise, put someone through their paces.

3 *his mother had drilled politeness into him* INSTILL, hammer, drive, drum, din, implant, ingrain; teach, indoctrinate, brainwash.

**drink** verb 1 *she drank her coffee* SWALLOW, gulp down, quaff, guzzle, imbibe, sip, consume; *informal* swig, down, knock back, put away, swill, chug.

2 *he never drank* DRINK ALCOHOL, tipple, indulge; carouse; *informal* hit the bottle, booze, booze it up, knock a few back, get tanked up, go on a bender, bend one's elbow.

3 *let's **drink to** success* TOAST, salute.

▸ noun 1 *he took a sip of his drink* BEVERAGE, liquid refreshment; bracer, nightcap, nip; *humorous* libation; *archaic* potation.

2 *she turned to drink* ALCOHOL, liquor, alcoholic drink; *informal* booze, hooch, the hard stuff, firewater, rotgut, moonshine, the bottle, the sauce.

3 *she took a drink of her wine* SWALLOW, gulp, sip, draft, slug; *informal* swig, swill.

4 *informal he fell into **the drink*** THE SEA, the ocean, the water; *informal* the briny, Davy Jones's locker; *literary* the deep.

PHRASE: **drink something in** *I'll just sit here and drink in the scenery* ABSORB, assimilate, digest, ingest, take in; be rapt in, be lost in, be fascinated by, pay close attention to.

**drinkable** adjective *running low on drinkable water* POTABLE, fit to drink, palatable; pure, clean, safe, unpolluted, untainted, uncontaminated.

**drinker** noun *I had no idea he was such a drinker.* See DRUNK noun.

**drip** verb 1 *there was a faucet dripping* DRIBBLE, leak.

2 *sweat dripped from his chin* DROP, dribble, trickle, drizzle, run, splash, plop; leak, emanate, issue.

▸ noun 1 *a bucket to catch the drips* DROP, dribble, spot, trickle, splash.

2 *informal that drip who fancies you* bore; ninny, milksop, namby-pamby; *informal* creep; wimp, sissy, wuss, candy-ass, pantywaist.

**drive** verb 1 *I can't drive a car* OPERATE, handle, manage; pilot, steer.

2 *he drove to the police station* TRAVEL BY CAR, motor.

3 *I'll drive you to the airport* CHAUFFEUR, run, give someone a lift/ride, take, ferry, transport, convey, carry.

4 *the engine drives the front wheels* POWER, propel, move, push.

5 *he drove a nail into the board* HAMMER, screw, ram, sink, plunge, thrust, propel, knock.

6 *she drove her cattle to market* IMPEL, urge; herd, round up, shepherd.

7 *a desperate mother driven to crime* FORCE, compel, prompt, precipitate; oblige, coerce, pressure, goad, spur, prod.

8 *he drove his staff extremely hard* WORK, push, tax, exert.

▸ noun 1 *an afternoon drive* EXCURSION, outing, trip, jaunt, tour; ride, run, journey; *informal* spin.

2 *the house has a long drive* DRIVEWAY, approach, access road.

**3** *sexual drive* URGE, appetite, desire, need; impulse, instinct.

**4** *she lacked the drive to succeed* MOTIVATION, ambition, single-mindedness, willpower, dedication, doggedness, tenacity; enthusiasm, zeal, commitment, aggression, spirit; energy, vigor, verve, vitality, pep; *informal* getup-and-go.

**5** *an anticorruption drive* CAMPAIGN, crusade, movement, effort, push, appeal.

PHRASE: **drive at** *I can see what you're driving at, but you're wrong* SUGGEST, imply, hint at, allude to, intimate, insinuate, indicate; refer to, mean, intend; *informal* get at.

**drivel** noun *he was talking complete drivel* NONSENSE, twaddle, claptrap, balderdash, gibberish, rubbish, mumbo-jumbo, garbage; *informal* poppycock, piffle, tripe, bull, hogwash, baloney, codswallop, flapdoodle, jive, guff, bushwa; *informal, dated* tommyrot, bunkum. See note at NONSENSE.

▸ verb *you always* ***drivel on*** TALK NONSENSE, talk rubbish, babble, ramble, gibber, blather, prattle, gabble, waffle.

**driver** verb *the driver failed to signal* MOTORIST, chauffeur; pilot, operator.

**drizzle** noun **1** *they shivered in the drizzle* FINE RAIN, light shower, spray, mist.

**2** *a drizzle of syrup* TRICKLE, dribble, drip, stream, rivulet; sprinkle, sprinkling.

▸ verb **1** *it's beginning to drizzle* RAIN LIGHTLY, shower, spot, spit, sprinkle.

**2** *drizzle the cream over the fruit* TRICKLE, drip, dribble, pour, splash, sprinkle.

**droll** adjective *a droll remark that started everyone laughing* FUNNY, humorous, amusing, comic, comical, mirthful, hilarious; clownish, farcical, zany, quirky; jocular, lighthearted, facetious, witty, whimsical, wry, tongue-in-cheek; *informal* waggish, wacky, side-splitting, rib-tickling. ANTONYM serious.

**drone** verb **1** *a plane droned overhead* HUM, buzz, whirr, vibrate, murmur, rumble, purr.

**2** *he* ***droned on*** *about right and wrong* SPEAK BORINGLY, go on and on, talk at length; intone, pontificate; *informal* spout, sound off, jaw, spiel, speechify.

▸ noun **1** *the drone of aircraft taking off* HUM, buzz, whirr, vibration, murmur, purr.

**2** *drones supported by taxpayers' money* HANGER-ON, parasite, leech, passenger, bottom feeder; idler, loafer, layabout, good-for-nothing, do-nothing; *informal* lazybones, scrounger, sponger, freeloader, slacker.

**droop** verb **1** *the dog's tail is drooping* HANG (DOWN), dangle, sag, flop; wilt, sink, slump, drop.

**2** *his eyelids were drooping* CLOSE, shut, fall.

**3** *the news made her droop* BE DESPONDENT, lose heart, give up hope, become dispirited, become dejected; flag, languish, wilt.

**drop** verb **1** *Eric dropped the box* LET FALL, let go of, lose one's grip on; release, unhand, relinquish. ANTONYMS lift, hold on to.

**2** *water drops from the cave roof* DRIP, fall, dribble, trickle, run, plop, leak.

**3** *a plane dropped out of the sky* FALL, descend, plunge, plummet, dive, nosedive, tumble, pitch. ANTONYM rise.

**4** *she dropped to her knees* FALL, sink, collapse, slump, tumble. ANTONYM rise.

**5** *informal I was so tired I thought I would drop* COLLAPSE, faint, pass out, black out, swoon, keel over; *informal* conk out.

**6** *the track drops from the ridge* SLOPE DOWNWARD, slant downward, descend, go down, fall away, sink, dip. ANTONYM lift.

**7** *the exchange rate dropped* DECREASE, lessen, reduce, diminish, depreciate; fall, decline, dwindle, sink, slump, plunge, plummet, drop off. ANTONYM increase.

**8** *you can drop algebra if you wish* GIVE UP, drop out of, finish with, withdraw from; discontinue, end, stop, cease, halt; abandon, forgo, relinquish, dispense with, have done with; *informal* pack in, quit. ANTONYMS take up, continue.

**9** *he was dropped from the team* EXCLUDE, discard, expel, oust, throw out, leave out; dismiss, discharge, let go; *informal* boot out, kick out. ANTONYMS pick, keep.

**10** *he dropped his unsuitable friends* ABANDON, desert, throw over; renounce, disown, turn one's back on, wash one's hands of; reject, give up, cast off; neglect, shun; *literary* forsake. ANTONYM keep.

**11** *he dropped all reference to compensation* OMIT, leave out, eliminate, take out, delete, cut, erase. ANTONYMS insert, include.

**12** *the taxi* ***dropped*** *her* ***off*** DELIVER, bring, take, convey, carry, transport; leave, unload. ANTONYM pick up.

**13** *drop the gun on the ground* PUT, place, deposit, set, lay, leave; *informal* pop, plonk. ANTONYM pick up.

**14** *she dropped names* MENTION, refer to, hint at; bring up, raise, broach, introduce; show off.

**15** *the team has yet to drop a point* LOSE, concede, give away. ANTONYMS gain, win.

▸ noun **1** *a drop of water* DROPLET, blob, globule, bead, bubble, tear, dot; *informal* glob; **(drops of water/rain)** *rare* stillicide.

**2** *it needs a drop of oil* SMALL AMOUNT, little, bit, dash, spot; dribble, driblet, sprinkle, trickle, splash; dab, speck, smattering, sprinkling, modicum; *informal* smidgen, tad. ANTONYM great deal.

**3** *a lemon drop* CANDY, lozenge, pastille.

**4** *a small drop in profits* DECREASE, reduction, decline, fall-off, downturn, slump; cut, cutback, curtailment; depreciation. ANTONYM increase.

**5** *I walked to the edge of the drop* CLIFF, abyss, chasm, gorge, gully, precipice; slope, descent, incline.

PHRASES: **drop back/behind** *he dropped back and was soon lost in the crowd* FALL BACK/BEHIND, get left behind, lag behind; straggle, linger, dawdle, dally, hang back, loiter, bring/take up the rear, dilly-dally.

**drop off 1** *trade dropped off sharply.* See DROP verb sense 7.

**2** *she kept dropping off* FALL ASLEEP, doze (off), nap, catnap, drowse; *informal* nod off, drift off, snooze, take forty winks.

**drop out of** *he dropped out of his studies.* See DROP verb sense 8.

**drought** noun *this year's drought was devastating to cotton growers* DRY SPELL, lack of rain, shortage of water.

**drove** noun **1** *a drove of cattle* HERD, flock, pack.

**2** *they came in droves* CROWD, swarm, horde, multitude, mob, throng, host, mass, army, herd.

**drown** verb **1** *he nearly drowned* SUFFOCATE IN WATER, inhale water; go to a watery grave.

**2** *the valleys were drowned* FLOOD, submerge, immerse, inundate, deluge, swamp, engulf.

**3** *his voice was **drowned out** by the music* MAKE INAUDIBLE, overpower, overwhelm, override; muffle, deaden, stifle, extinguish.

**drowsy** adjective **1** *the pills made her drowsy* SLEEPY, dozy, groggy, somnolent; tired, weary, fatigued, exhausted, yawning, nodding; lethargic, sluggish, torpid, listless, languid; *informal* snoozy, dopey, yawny, dead beat, all in, dog-tired, bone-weary. ANTONYM alert.

**2** *a drowsy afternoon* SOPORIFIC, sleep-inducing, sleepy, somniferous; narcotic, sedative, tranquilizing; lulling, soothing. ANTONYM invigorating.

**drubbing** noun **1** *I gave him a good drubbing* BEATING, thrashing, walloping, thumping, battering, pounding, pummeling, slapping, punching, pelting; *informal* hammering, licking, clobbering, belting, bashing, pasting, tanning, kicking.

**2** *informal New York's 8–1 drubbing by Anaheim.* See DEFEAT noun sense 1.

**drudge** noun *a household drudge* MENIAL WORKER, slave, lackey, servant, laborer, worker, cog; *informal* gofer, runner, bottle-washer, serf.

▸ verb *archaic he drudged in the fields.* See TOIL verb sense 1.

**drudgery** noun *she swore her daughters would never be condemned to a life of drudgery* HARD WORK, menial work, donkey work, toil, labor; chores. See note at LABOR.

**drug** noun **1** *drugs prescribed by doctors* MEDICINE, medication, medicament, pharmaceutical; remedy, cure, antidote.

**2** *she was under the influence of drugs* NARCOTIC, stimulant, hallucinogen; *informal* dope.

▸ verb **1** *he was drugged* ANESTHETIZE, narcotize; poison; knock out, stupefy; *informal* dope.

**2** *she drugged his coffee* ADD DRUGS TO, tamper with, adulterate, contaminate, lace, poison; *informal* dope, spike, doctor.

**drugged** adjective *they found Tom and his drugged friends camped out in the living room* STUPEFIED, insensible, befuddled; delirious, hallucinating, narcotized; anesthetized, knocked out; *informal* stoned, coked, high (as a kite), doped, tripping, spaced out, wasted, wrecked. ANTONYM sober.

**drum** noun **1** *the beat of a drum* percussion instrument; bongo, tom-tom, snare drum, kettledrum, bodhrán; *historical* tambour.

**2** *the steady drum of raindrops* BEAT, rhythm, patter, tap, pounding, thump, thud, rattle, pitter-patter, pit-a-pat, rat-a-tat, thrum.

**3** *a drum of radioactive waste* CANISTER, barrel, cylinder, tank, bin, can; container.

▸ verb **1** *she drummed her fingers on the desk* TAP, beat, rap, thud, thump; tattoo, thrum.

**2** *the rules were drummed into us at school* INSTILL, drive, din, hammer, drill, implant, ingrain, inculcate.

PHRASES: **drum out of** *Kazwell was running the organization into the ground, until the other members drummed him out* EXPEL, dismiss, throw out, oust; drive out, get rid of; exclude, banish; *informal* give someone the boot, boot out, kick out, give someone their marching orders, show someone the door, send packing.

**drum up** *leaflets were distributed in hopes of drumming up support for the campaign* ROUND UP, gather, collect; summon, attract; canvass, solicit, petition.

**drunk** adjective *he was so drunk he couldn't stand up* INTOXICATED, inebriated, inebriate, impaired, drunken, tipsy, under the influence; *informal* plastered, smashed, bombed, sloshed, sozzled, sauced, lubricated, well-oiled, wrecked, juiced, blasted, stinko, blitzed, half-cut, fried, wasted, hopped up, gassed, polluted, pissed, tanked (up), soaked, out of one's head/skull, loaded, trashed, hammered, soused, buzzed, befuddled, besotted, pickled, pixilated, canned, cockeyed, blotto, blind drunk, roaring drunk, dead drunk, punch-drunk, ripped, stewed, tight, merry, the worse for wear, far gone, pie-eyed, in one's cups, three sheets to the wind; *Brit. informal* bladdered, lashed; *literary* crapulous. ANTONYM sober.

▸ noun *a brilliant artist, he was also a tortured drunk* DRUNKARD, inebriate, drinker, tippler, imbiber, sot; heavy drinker, problem drinker, alcoholic, dipsomaniac; *informal* boozer, soak, lush, wino, alky, rummy, barfly; *archaic* toper. ANTONYM teetotaler.

THE RIGHT WORD **drunk, blotto, drunken, inebriated, intoxicated, tight, tipsy**

Anyone who is obviously or legally under the influence of alcohol is said to be **drunk**. **Drunken** means the same thing, but only *drunk* should be used predicatively, that is, after a linking verb (*she was drunk*) while *drunken* is more often used to modify a noun (*a drunken sailor*) and, in some cases, to imply habitual drinking to excess. *Drunken* is also used to modify nouns that do not refer to a person (*a drunken celebration*). To say **intoxicated** or **inebriated** is a more formal and less offensive way of calling someone *drunk*, with *intoxicated* implying that the individual is only slightly drunk, and *inebriated* implying drunkenness to the point of excitement or exhilaration (*the streets were filled with inebriated revelers*). **Tight** and **tipsy** are two of the more common slang expressions (there are literally hundreds more) meaning *drunk*. Like *intoxicated*, *tipsy* implies that someone is only slightly drunk, while *tight* implies obvious drunkenness but without any loss of muscular coordination. An elderly woman who has had one sherry too many might be described as *tipsy*, but someone who has been drinking all evening and is still able to stand up and give a speech might be described as *tight*. Either condition is preferable to being **blotto**, a word that means drunk to the point of incomprehensibility or unconsciousness.

---

**drunken** adjective 1 *drunken revelers.* See DRUNK adjective. See also note at DRUNK.

2 *a drunken all-night party* DEBAUCHED, dissipated, carousing, roistering, intemperate, unrestrained, uninhibited, abandoned; bacchanalian, Bacchic; *informal* boozy.

**drunkenness** noun *his bouts of drunkenness* INTOXICATION, inebriation, insobriety, tipsiness, impairment; intemperance, overindulgence, debauchery; heavy drinking, alcoholism, dipsomania.

**dry** adjective 1 *the dry desert* ARID, parched, droughty, scorched, baked; waterless, moistureless, rainless; dehydrated, desiccated, thirsty, bone dry. ANTONYM wet.

2 *dry leaves* PARCHED, dried, withered, shriveled, wilted, wizened; crisp, crispy, brittle; dehydrated, desiccated. ANTONYM fresh.

3 *the rolls were dry* HARD, stale, old, past its best. ANTONYMS moist, fresh.

4 *a dry well* WATERLESS, empty.

5 *I'm really dry* THIRSTY, dehydrated; *informal* parched, gasping.

6 *it was dry work* THIRSTY, thirst-making; hot; strenuous, arduous.

7 *dry toast* UNBUTTERED, butterless, plain.

8 *the dry facts* BARE, simple, basic, fundamental, stark, bald, hard, straightforward. ANTONYM embellished.

9 *a dry debate* DULL, uninteresting, boring, unexciting, tedious, tiresome, wearisome, dreary, monotonous; unimaginative, sterile, flat, bland, lackluster, stodgy, prosaic, humdrum, mundane; *informal* deadly. ANTONYMS lively, interesting.

10 *a dry sense of humor* WRY, subtle, laconic, sharp; ironic, sardonic, sarcastic, cynical; satirical, mocking, droll; *informal* waggish.

11 *a dry response to his cordial advance* UNEMOTIONAL, indifferent, impassive, cool, cold, emotionless; reserved, restrained, impersonal, formal, stiff, wooden. ANTONYMS emotional, expressive.

12 *this is a dry state* TEETOTAL, prohibitionist, alcohol-free, nondrinking, abstinent, sober; *informal* on the wagon.

13 *dry white wine* CRISP, sharp, piquant, tart, bitter. ANTONYM sweet.

▸ verb 1 *the sun dried the ground* PARCH, scorch, bake; dehydrate, desiccate, dehumidify. ANTONYM moisten.

2 *dry the leaves completely* DEHYDRATE, desiccate; wither, shrivel. ANTONYM moisten.

3 *he dried the spills with a paper towel* TOWEL, rub; mop up, blot up, soak up, absorb.

4 *she dried her eyes* WIPE, rub, dab.

5 *methods of drying meat* DESICCATE, dehydrate; preserve, cure, smoke.

PHRASES: **dry out** *she dried out on her thirtieth birthday and has been sober ever since* GIVE UP DRINKING, give up alcohol, become a teetotaler, go on the wagon.

**dry up** *foreign investment may dry up* DWINDLE, subside, peter out, wane, taper off, ebb, come to a halt/end, run out, give out, disappear, vanish.

THE RIGHT WORD **dry, arid, dehydrated, dessicated, parched, sere**

---

Almost anything lacking in moisture (in relative terms)—whether it's a piece of bread, the basement of a house, or the state of Arizona—may be described as **dry**, a word that also connotes a lack of life or spirit (*a dry lecture on cell division*). **Arid**, on the other hand, applies to places or things that have been deprived of moisture and are therefore extremely or abnormally *dry* (*one side of the island was arid*); it is most commonly used to describe a desertlike region or climate that is lifeless or barren. **Desiccated** is used as a technical term for something from which moisture has been removed, and in general use it suggests lifelessness, although it is applied very often to people who have lost their vitality (*a desiccated old woman who never left her house*) or to animal and vegetable products that have been completely deprived of their vital juices (*desiccated oranges hanging limply from the tree*). **Dehydrated** is very close in meaning to *desiccated* and is often the preferred adjective when describing foods from which the moisture has been extracted (*they lived on dehydrated fruit*). *Dehydrated* may also refer to an unwanted loss of moisture (*the virus had left him seriously dehydrated*), as may the less formal term **parched**, which refers to an undesirable or uncomfortable lack of water in either a human being or a place (*parched with thirst*; *the parched landscape*). **Sere** is associated primarily with places and means *dry* or *arid* (*a harsh, sere land where few inhabitants could survive*).

---

**dual** adjective *a futuristic car with dual engines* DOUBLE, twofold, binary; duplicate, twin, matching, paired, coupled. ANTONYM single.

**dub** verb 1 *he was dubbed "the world's sexiest man"* NICKNAME, call, name, label, christen, term, tag, entitle, style; designate, characterize, nominate; *formal* denominate.

2 *she dubbed him "Sir Elton John"* KNIGHT, invest.

**dubiety** noun *formal the dubiety of Henry's fate* DOUBTFULNESS, uncertainty, unsureness, incertitude; ambiguity, ambivalence, confusion; hesitancy, doubt. See note at UNCERTAINTY.

**dubious** adjective 1 *I was rather dubious about the idea* DOUBTFUL, uncertain, unsure, hesitant; undecided, indefinite, unresolved, up in the air; vacillating, irresolute; skeptical, suspicious; *informal* iffy. See note at DOUBTFUL. ANTONYMS certain, definite.

2 *dubious business practices* SUSPICIOUS, suspect, untrustworthy, unreliable, questionable; *informal* shady, fishy. ANTONYM trustworthy.

**duck** noun *a pair of ducks were nesting on the edge of our pond male* drake; *female* duck; *young* duckling.

**duct** noun *a ventilation duct* TUBE, channel, canal, vessel; conduit, culvert; pipe, pipeline, outlet, inlet, flue, shaft, vent; *Anatomy* ductus.

**ductile** adjective **1** *ductile metals* PLIABLE, pliant, flexible, supple, plastic, tensile; soft, malleable, workable, bendable; *informal* bendy. ANTONYM brittle.

**2** *efforts to keep the oppressed people ductile* DOCILE, obedient, submissive, meek, mild, lamblike; willing, accommodating, amenable, cooperative, compliant, malleable, tractable, biddable, persuadable. ANTONYM intransigent.

**dud** noun *their new product is a dud* FAILURE, flop, letdown, disappointment; *informal* washout, lemon, no-hoper, nonstarter, dead loss, clunker. ANTONYM success.

▸ adjective **1** *a dud typewriter* DEFECTIVE, faulty, unsound, inoperative, broken, malfunctioning; *informal* bust, busted, kaput, conked out. ANTONYM sound.

**2** *a dud $50 bill* COUNTERFEIT, fraudulent, forged, fake, faked, false, bogus; invalid, worthless; *informal* phony. ANTONYM genuine.

**dudgeon** PHRASE: **in high dudgeon** *the sponsors from Cleveland stormed out in high dudgeon* INDIGNANTLY, resentfully, angrily, furiously; in a temper, in anger, with displeasure; *informal* in a huff, seeing red.

**due** adjective **1** *their fees were due* OWING, owed, payable; outstanding, overdue, unpaid, unsettled, undischarged, delinquent.

**2** *the chancellor's statement is due today* EXPECTED, anticipated, scheduled for, awaited; required.

**3** *the respect due to a great artist* DESERVED BY, merited by, warranted by; appropriate to, fit for, fitting for, right for, proper to.

**4** *he drove without due care* PROPER, correct, rightful, suitable, appropriate, apt; adequate, sufficient, enough, satisfactory, requisite.

▸ noun **1** *he attracts more criticism than is his due* RIGHTFUL TREATMENT, fair treatment, just punishment; right, entitlement; just deserts; *informal* comeuppance.

**2** *members have paid their dues* FEE, subscription, charge; payment, contribution.

▸ adverb *he hiked due north* DIRECTLY, straight, exactly, precisely, dead.

PHRASE: **due to 1** *her death was due to an infection* ATTRIBUTABLE TO, caused by, ascribed to, because of, put down to.

**2** *the train was canceled due to staff shortages* BECAUSE OF, owing to, on account of, as a consequence of, as a result of, thanks to, in view of; *formal* by reason of.

**USAGE NOTE due to**

The use of **due to** as a prepositional phrase meaning 'because of,' as in *he had to retire due to an injury* first appeared in print in 1897, and traditional grammarians have opposed this prepositional usage for a century on the grounds that it is a misuse of the adjectival phrase **due to** in the sense of 'attributable to, likely or expected to' (*the train is due to arrive at 11:15*), or 'payable to' ( *render unto Caesar what is due to Caesar*). Nevertheless, this prepositional usage is now widespread and common in all types of literature and must be regarded as standard English.

Avoid the wordy phrase **due to the fact that** and use *because* instead, especially in writing.

---

**duel** noun **1** *he was killed in a duel* AFFAIR OF HONOR; single combat; (sword) fight, confrontation, face-off, shoot-out.

**2** *a chess duel* CONTEST, match, game, meet, encounter.

▸ verb *they dueled with swords* FIGHT A DUEL, fight, battle, combat, contend.

**dulcet** adjective *the dulcet sounds of the zither* SWEET, soothing, mellow, honeyed, mellifluous, euphonious, pleasant, agreeable; melodious, melodic, lilting, lyrical, silvery, golden. ANTONYM harsh.

**dull** adjective **1** *a dull novel* UNINTERESTING, boring, tedious, monotonous, unrelieved, unvaried, unimaginative, uneventful; characterless, featureless, colorless, lifeless, insipid, unexciting, uninspiring, unstimulating, jejune, flat, bland, dry, stale, tired, banal, lackluster, ho-hum, stodgy, dreary, humdrum, mundane; mind-numbing, wearisome, tiring, tiresome, irksome, dullsville. ANTONYM interesting.

**2** *a dull morning* OVERCAST, cloudy, gloomy, dark, dismal, dreary, somber, gray, murky, sunless. ANTONYMS sunny, bright.

**3** *dull colors* DRAB, dreary, somber, dark, subdued, muted, lackluster, faded, washed out, muddy, dingy. ANTONYM bright.

**4** *a dull sound* MUFFLED, muted, quiet, soft, faint, indistinct; stifled, suppressed. ANTONYMS loud, resonant.

**5** *the chisel became dull* BLUNT, unsharpened, edgeless, worn down. ANTONYM sharp.

**6** *a rather dull child* UNINTELLIGENT, stupid, slow, witless, vacuous, empty-headed, stunned, brainless, mindless, foolish, idiotic; *informal* dense, dim, moronic, halfwitted, thick, dumb, dopey, dozy, bovine, slow on the uptake, woodenheaded, fat-headed. See note at STUPID. ANTONYM clever.

**7** *her cold made her feel dull* SLUGGISH, lethargic, enervated, listless, languid, torpid, slow, sleepy, drowsy, weary, tired, fatigued; apathetic; *informal* dozy, dopey, yawny, logy. ANTONYM lively.

▸ verb **1** *the pain was dulled by drugs* LESSEN, decrease, diminish, reduce, dampen, blunt, deaden, allay, ease, soothe, assuage, alleviate. ANTONYM intensify.

**2** *sleep dulled her mind* NUMB, benumb, deaden, desensitize, stupefy, daze. ANTONYM enliven.

**3** *rain dulled the sky* DARKEN, blacken, dim, veil, obscure, shadow, fog. ANTONYM brighten.

**4** *the somber atmosphere dulled her spirit* DAMPEN, lower, depress, crush, sap, extinguish, smother, stifle. ANTONYMS raise, brighten.

**duly** adverb **1** *the document was duly signed* PROPERLY, correctly, appropriately, suitably, fittingly.

**2** *he duly arrived to collect Alice* AT THE RIGHT TIME, on time, punctually.

**dumb** adjective **1** *she stood dumb while he shouted* MUTE, speechless, tongue-tied, silent, at a loss for words; taciturn, uncommunicative, untalkative, tight-lipped, close-mouthed; *informal* mum.

**2** *informal he is not as dumb as you'd think* STUPID, unintelligent, ignorant, dense, brainless, mindless, foolish, slow, dull, simple, empty-headed, stunned, vacuous, vapid, idiotic, half-baked, imbecilic, bovine; *informal* thick, dim, moronic, dopey, dozy, thickheaded, fat-headed, birdbrained, pea-brained; daft. See note at STUPID. ANTONYM clever.

**dumbfound** verb *she was dumbfounded by Bruce's actions* ASTONISH, astound, amaze, stagger, surprise, startle, stun, confound, stupefy, daze, take aback, stop someone in their tracks, strike dumb, leave open-mouthed, leave aghast; *informal* flabbergast, floor, bowl over.

**dummy** noun **1** *a store-window dummy* MANNEQUIN, model, figure.

**2** *the book is just a dummy* MOCK-UP, imitation, likeness, look-alike, representation, substitute, sample; replica, reproduction; counterfeit, sham, fake, forgery; *informal* dupe.

**3** *informal you're a dummy.* See IDIOT.

▸ adjective *a dummy attack on the airfield* SIMULATED, feigned, pretended, practice, trial, mock, make-believe; *informal* pretend, phony, virtual. ANTONYM real.

**dump** noun **1** *take the garbage to the dump* TRANSFER STATION, garbage dump, landfill (site), rubbish heap, dumping ground; dustheap, slag heap.

**2** *informal the house is a dump* HOVEL, shack, slum; mess; hole, pigsty.

▸ verb **1** *he dumped his bag on the table* PUT DOWN, set down, deposit, place, unload; drop, throw down; *informal* park, plonk (down), plunk (down).

**2** *they will dump asbestos at the site* DISPOSE OF, get rid of, throw away/out, discard, jettison; *informal* ditch, junk, deep-six.

**3** *informal he dumped her* ABANDON, desert, leave, jilt, break up with, finish with, throw over; *informal* walk out on, rat on, drop, ditch.

**dumps** PHRASE: **down in the dumps** *informal why so down in dumps, Mrs. Herbert?* UNHAPPY, sad, depressed, gloomy, glum, melancholy, miserable, dejected, despondent, dispirited, downhearted, downcast, down, low, heavy-hearted, dismal, desolate; tearful, upset, blue, down in/at the mouth.

**dun** adjective *a dun cow* GRAYISH-BROWN, brownish, mousy, muddy, khaki, umber.

**dunce** noun *Uncle Abraham was a bit of a dunce, but most people got along with him* FOOL, idiot, stupid person, simpleton, ignoramus, dullard; *informal* dummy, dumbo, thickhead, nitwit, dimwit, halfwit, moron, cretin, imbecile, dope, boob, chump, numbskull, numbnuts, nincompoop, fathead, airhead, birdbrain, peabrain, ninny, ass, doofus, goof, meatball, schmuck, bozo, lummox. ANTONYM genius.

**dungeon** noun *the castle dungeon is now a tourist attraction* UNDERGROUND PRISON, oubliette; cell, jail, lockup.

**duplicate** noun *a duplicate of the invoice* COPY, photocopy, facsimile, reprint; replica, reproduction, clone; *dated* carbon copy; *informal* dupe; *trademark* Xerox.

▸ adjective *duplicate keys* MATCHING, identical, twin, corresponding, equivalent.

▸ verb **1** *she will duplicate the newsletter* COPY, photocopy, xerox, reproduce, replicate, reprint, run off; *dated* mimeograph.

**2** *a feat difficult to duplicate* REPEAT, do again, redo, replicate.

**duplicity** noun *he got caught up in the duplicity of his crooked partners* DECEITFULNESS, deceit, deception, double-dealing, underhandedness, dishonesty, fraud, fraudulence, sharp practice, chicanery, trickery, subterfuge, skulduggery, treachery; *informal* crookedness, shadiness, dirty tricks, shenanigans, monkey business; *literary* perfidy. ANTONYM honesty.

**durable** adjective **1** *durable carpets* HARDWEARING, long-lasting, heavy-duty, industrial-strength, tough, resistant, imperishable, indestructible, strong, sturdy. ANTONYM delicate.

**2** *a durable peace* LASTING, long-lasting, long-term, enduring, persistent, abiding; stable, secure, firm, deep-rooted, permanent, undying, everlasting. ANTONYM short-lived.

**duress** noun *their confessions were extracted under duress* COERCION, compulsion, force, pressure, intimidation, constraint; threats; *informal* arm-twisting.

**during** conjunction *the museum is closed during December* THROUGHOUT, through, in, in the course of, for the time of.

**dusk** noun *we launch the patrol boats at dusk* TWILIGHT, nightfall, sunset, sundown, evening, close of day; semidarkness, gloom, murkiness; *literary* gloaming, eventide. ANTONYM dawn.

**dusky** adjective **1** *the dusky countryside* SHADOWY, dark, dim, gloomy, murky, shady; unlit, unilluminated; sunless, moonless. ANTONYM bright.

**2** *dated a dusky complexion* DARK-SKINNED, dark, olive-skinned, swarthy, ebony, black; tanned, bronzed, coppery, brown. ANTONYM fair.

**dust** noun **1** *the desk was covered in dust* DIRT, grime, filth, smut, soot; fine powder.

**2** *they fought in the dust* EARTH, soil, dirt; ground.

▸ verb **1** *she dusted her mantelpiece* WIPE, clean, brush, sweep, mop.

**2** *dust the cake with powdered sugar* SPRINKLE, scatter, powder, dredge, sift, cover, strew.

**dusty** adjective **1** *the floor was dusty* DIRTY, grimy, grubby, unclean, soiled, mucky, sooty; undusted; *informal* grungy, cruddy. ANTONYM clean.

**2** *dusty sandstone* POWDERY, crumbly, chalky, friable; granular, gritty, sandy.

**3** *a dusty pink* MUTED, dull, faded, pale, pastel, subtle; grayish, darkish, dirty. ANTONYM bright.

**dutiful** adjective *Clarence's dutiful niece* CONSCIENTIOUS, responsible, dedicated, devoted, attentive; obedient, compliant, submissive, biddable; deferential, reverent, reverential, respectful, good. See note at OBEDIENT. ANTONYM remiss.

**duty** noun **1** *she was free of any duty* RESPONSIBILITY, obligation, commitment; allegiance, loyalty, faithfulness, fidelity, homage.

**2** *it was his duty to attend the king* JOB, task, assignment, mission, function, charge, place, role, responsibility, obligation; *dated* office.

**3** *the duty was raised on alcohol* TAX, levy, tariff, excise, toll, fee, payment, rate, countervail; dues. PHRASES: **off duty** *I'll be off duty at midnight* NOT WORKING, at leisure, on leave, off (work), free.
**on duty** *there is always a supervisor on duty* WORKING, at work, busy, occupied, engaged; *informal* on the job.

**dwarf** noun **1** *she married a dwarf who worked in her father's circus* SMALL PERSON, short person; midget, pygmy, manikin, homunculus.

**2** *the wizard captured the dwarf* GNOME, goblin, hobgoblin, troll, imp, elf, brownie, leprechaun.

▸ adjective *dwarf conifers* MINIATURE, small, little, tiny, toy, pocket, diminutive, baby, pygmy, stunted, undersized, undersize; *informal* mini, teeny, teeny-weeny, itsy-bitsy, pint-sized, little-bitty, vertically challenged; *Scottish* wee. ANTONYM giant.

▸ verb **1** *the buildings dwarf the trees* DOMINATE, tower over, loom over, overshadow, overtop.

**2** *her progress was dwarfed by her sister's success* OVERSHADOW, outshine, surpass, exceed, outclass, outstrip, outdo, top, trump, transcend; diminish, minimize.

**dwell** verb *formal gypsies dwell in these caves* RESIDE, live, be settled, be housed, lodge, stay; *informal* put up; *formal* abide, be domiciled. PHRASE: **dwell on** *I'm not one to dwell on the past* LINGER OVER, mull over, muse on, brood about/over, think about; be preoccupied by, be obsessed by, eat one's heart out over; harp on about, discuss at length.

**dwelling** noun *formal their dwellings were simple but pristine, both inside and out* RESIDENCE, home, house, accommodations; quarters, rooms, lodgings; *informal* place, pad, digs; *formal* abode, domicile, habitation.

**dwindle** verb **1** *the population dwindled* DIMINISH, decrease, reduce, lessen, shrink; fall off, tail off, drop, fall, slump, plummet; disappear, vanish, die out; *informal* nosedive. ANTONYM increase.

**2** *her career dwindled* DECLINE, deteriorate, fail, slip, slide, fade, go downhill, go to rack and ruin; *informal* go to pot, go to the dogs, hit the skids, go down the tubes, go down the drain, go down the toilet. ANTONYM flourish.

**dye** noun *a blue dye* COLORANT, coloring, color, dyestuff, pigment, tint, stain, wash.

▸ verb *the gloves were dyed* COLOR, tint, pigment, stain, wash.

**dyed-in-the-wool** adjective *a dyed-in-the-wool socialist* INVETERATE, confirmed, entrenched, established, long-standing, deep-rooted, diehard; complete, absolute, thorough, thoroughgoing, out-and-out, true blue; firm, unshakable, staunch, steadfast, committed, devoted, dedicated, loyal, unswerving, full bore; *informal* card-carrying.

**dying** adjective **1** *his dying aunt* TERMINALLY ILL, at death's door, on one's deathbed, near death, fading fast, expiring, moribund, not long for this world, in extremis; *informal* on one's last legs, having one foot in the grave.

**2** *a dying art form* DECLINING, vanishing, fading, ebbing, waning; *informal* on the way out. ANTONYM thriving.

**3** *her dying words* FINAL, last; deathbed. ANTONYM first.

▸ noun *he took her dying very hard* DEATH, demise, passing, loss of life, quietus; *formal* decease.

**dynamic** adjective *he was eclipsed by his more dynamic colleagues* ENERGETIC, spirited, active, lively, zestful, vital, vigorous, forceful, powerful, positive; high-powered, aggressive, bold, enterprising; magnetic, passionate, fiery, high-octane; *informal* go-getting, peppy, full of get-up-and-go, full of vim and vigor, gutsy, spunky, feisty, go-ahead. ANTONYM half-hearted.

**dynasty** noun *the fourth king of the Shang dynasty* BLOODLINE, line, ancestral line, lineage, house, family, ancestry, descent, succession, genealogy, family tree; regime, rule, reign, empire, sovereignty.

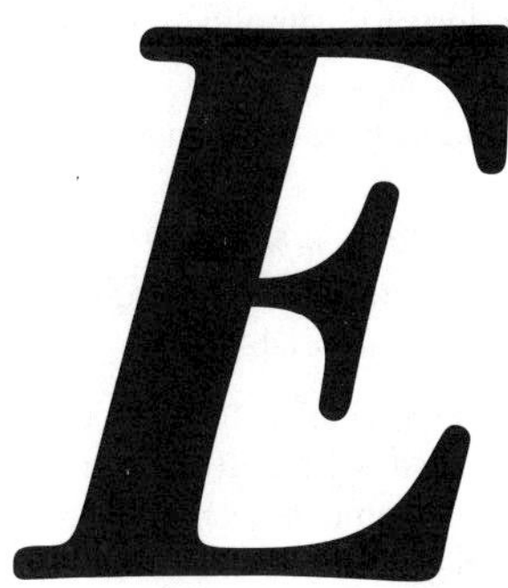

**each** pronoun *there are 47 books and each must be read* EVERY ONE, each one, each and every one, all, the whole lot.

▸ adjective *he visited each month* EVERY, each and every, every single.

▸ adverb *they gave $10 each* APIECE, per person, per capita, from each, individually, respectively, severally.

**eager** adjective **1** *small eager faces* KEEN, enthusiastic, avid, fervent, ardent, motivated, wholehearted, dedicated, committed, earnest; *informal* gung-ho. ANTONYM apathetic.

**2** *we were eager for news* ANXIOUS, impatient, longing, yearning, wishing, hoping, hopeful; on the edge of one's seat, on tenterhooks, on pins and needles; *informal* itching, gagging, dying. ANTONYM uninterested.

THE RIGHT WORD **eager, ardent, avid, enthusiastic, fervent, keen, zealous**

You've heard of the "eager beaver"? Anyone who has a strong interest or an impatient desire to pursue or become involved in something is called **eager** (*eager to get started; an eager learner*). Someone who is especially *eager* might be called **avid**, a word that implies greed or insatiable desire (*an avid golfer, he was never at home on weekends*). **Ardent** combines eagerness with intense feelings of passion or devotion (*an ardent lover; an ardent theatergoer*), while **fervent** suggests an eagerness that is ready, at least figuratively, to boil over (*their fervent pleas could not be ignored*). Anyone who is deeply interested in something or who shows a spirited readiness to act is called **keen** (*he was keen on bicycling*), while **zealous** implies the kind of eagerness that pushes all other considerations aside (*a zealous environmentalist*). **Enthusiastic** may connote participation rather than expectation: One can be *eager* to take a trip to Switzerland, an *ardent* student of Swiss history, and an *avid* outdoorsperson who is *keen* on hiking, but one is usually called *enthusiastic* about a trip to Switzerland when it is under way or is over; *enthusiastic* also very often applies to someone who outwardly and forcefully expresses eagerness.

**eagerness** noun *the eagerness of potential buyers* KEENNESS, enthusiasm, avidity, fervor, zeal, wholeheartedness, earnestness, commitment, dedication; impatience, desire, longing, yearning, hunger, appetite, ambition, yen.

**ear** noun **1** *an infection of the ear* inner ear, middle ear, outer ear.

**2** *he had the ear of the president* ATTENTION, notice, heed, regard, consideration.

**3** *he has an ear for a good song* APPRECIATION, discrimination, perception. PHRASE: **play it by ear** *until we know all the facts, we'll have to play it by ear* IMPROVISE, extemporize, ad lib; make it up as one goes along, think on one's feet, wing it, fly by the seat of one's pants.

**early** adjective **1** *early copies of the book* ADVANCE, forward; initial, preliminary, first; pilot, trial. ANTONYM late.

**2** *an early death* UNTIMELY, premature, unseasonable, before time.

**3** *early man* PRIMITIVE, ancient, prehistoric, primeval; *literary* of yore. ANTONYM modern.

**4** *an early official statement* PROMPT, timely, quick, speedy, rapid, fast. ANTONYM overdue.

▸ adverb **1** *Rachel has to get up early* IN THE EARLY MORNING; at dawn, at daybreak, at first light. ANTONYM late.

**2** *they hoped to leave school early* BEFORE THE USUAL TIME; prematurely, too soon, ahead of time, ahead of schedule; *literary* betimes.

**earmark** verb *the cash had been earmarked for the firm* SET ASIDE, keep (back), reserve; designate, assign, mark; allocate, allot, devote, pledge, give over.

▸ noun *he has all the earmarks of a leader* CHARACTERISTICS, attribute, feature, hallmark, quality.

**earn** verb **1** *they earned $20,000* BE PAID, take home, gross, net; receive, get, make, obtain, collect, bring in; *informal* pocket, bank, rake in.

**2** *he has earned their trust* DESERVE, merit, warrant, justify, be worthy of; gain, win, secure, establish, obtain, procure, get, acquire; *informal* clinch. ANTONYM lose.

**earnest** adjective **1** *he is dreadfully earnest* SERIOUS, solemn, grave, sober, humorless, staid, intense; committed, dedicated, keen, diligent, zealous; thoughtful, cerebral, deep, profound. ANTONYMS frivolous, apathetic.

**2** *earnest prayer* DEVOUT, heartfelt, wholehearted, sincere, impassioned, fervent, ardent, intense, urgent. ANTONYM half-hearted.

PHRASE: **in earnest 1** *we are in earnest about stopping crime* SERIOUS, sincere, wholehearted, genuine; committed, firm, resolute, determined.

**2** *he started writing in earnest* ZEALOUSLY, purposefully, determinedly, resolutely; passionately, wholeheartedly.

**earnings** plural noun *their combined earnings paid for this house* INCOME, wages, salary, stipend, pay, payment, fees; revenue, yield, profit, takings, proceeds, avails, dividends, return, remuneration.

**earth** noun **1** *the moon orbits the earth* WORLD, globe, planet.

**2** *a trembling of the earth* LAND, ground, terra firma; floor.

**3** *he plowed the earth* SOIL, clay, loam; dirt, sod, turf; ground.

**4** *the earth rejoiced* HUMANITY, humankind, mankind, (all) people; *humorous* earthlings.

**5** *the fox's earth* DEN, lair, set, burrow, warren, hole; retreat, shelter, hideout, hideaway.

**earthenware** noun *her original line of earthenware* POTTERY, stoneware; china, porcelain; pots, crockery.

**earthly** adjective **1** *the earthly environment* TERRESTRIAL, telluric. ANTONYM extraterrestrial.

**2** *the promise of earthly delights* WORLDLY, temporal, mortal, human; material; carnal, fleshly, bodily, physical, corporeal, sensual. ANTONYMS spiritual, heavenly.

**3** *informal there is no earthly explanation for this* FEASIBLE, possible, likely, conceivable, imaginable.

**earthy** adjective **1** *an earthy smell* SOIL-LIKE, dirtlike.

**2** *she was a simple, earthy girl* DOWN-TO-EARTH, unsophisticated, unrefined, simple, plain, unpretentious, natural.

**3** *Emma's earthy language* BAWDY, ribald, off-color, racy, rude, vulgar, lewd, crude, foul, coarse, uncouth, unseemly, indelicate, indecent, obscene; *informal* blue, locker-room, barnyard.

**ease** noun **1** *he defeated them all with ease* EFFORTLESSNESS, no trouble, simplicity; deftness, adroitness, proficiency, mastery. ANTONYM difficulty.

**2** *his ease of manner* NATURALNESS, casualness, informality, amiability, affability; unconcern, composure, nonchalance, insouciance. ANTONYMS stiffness, formality.

**3** *he couldn't find any ease* PEACE, calm, tranquility, serenity; repose, restfulness, quiet, security, comfort. ANTONYMS trouble, disturbance.

**4** *a life of ease* AFFLUENCE, wealth, prosperity, luxury, plenty; comfort, contentment, enjoyment, well-being. ANTONYMS poverty, hardship.

▸ verb **1** *the alcohol eased his pain* RELIEVE, alleviate, mitigate, soothe, palliate, moderate, dull, deaden, numb; reduce, lighten, diminish. ANTONYM aggravate.

**2** *the rain* ***eased off*** ABATE, subside, die down, let up, slack off, diminish, lessen, peter out, relent, come to an end. ANTONYM worsen.

**3** *work helped to ease her mind* CALM, pacify, soothe, comfort, console, quieten; hearten, gladden, uplift, encourage.

**4** *we want to ease their adjustment* FACILITATE, expedite, assist, help, aid, advance, further, forward, simplify. ANTONYM hinder.

**5** *he eased out the cork* GUIDE, maneuver, inch, edge; slide, slip, squeeze.

PHRASE: **at ease/at one's ease** *she felt completely at ease in their mountain retreat* RELAXED, calm, serene, tranquil, unworried, contented, content, happy; comfortable.

**easy** adjective **1** *the task was very easy* UNCOMPLICATED, undemanding, unchallenging, effortless, painless, trouble-free, facile, simple, straightforward, elementary; *informal* easy as pie, a piece of cake, child's play, kids' stuff, a cinch, no sweat, a breeze, smooth sailing, duck soup, a snap. ANTONYMS difficult, challenging.

**2** *easy babies* DOCILE, manageable, amenable, tractable, compliant, pliant, acquiescent, obliging, cooperative, easygoing. ANTONYMS difficult, demanding.

**3** *an easy target* VULNERABLE, susceptible, defenseless; naive, gullible, trusting. ANTONYMS streetwise, savvy.

**4** *Dave's easy manner* NATURAL, casual, informal, unceremonious, unreserved, uninhibited, unaffected, easygoing, amiable, affable, genial, good-humored; carefree, nonchalant, unconcerned, laid-back. ANTONYM formal.

**5** *an easy life* CALM, tranquil, serene, quiet, peaceful, untroubled, contented, relaxed, comfortable, secure, safe; *informal* cushy. ANTONYMS stressful, chaotic.

**6** *an easy pace* LEISURELY, unhurried, comfortable, undemanding, easygoing, gentle, sedate, moderate, steady. ANTONYM demanding.

**7** *informal people think she's easy* PROMISCUOUS, unchaste, loose, wanton, abandoned, licentious, debauched; *informal* sluttish, slutty, whorish. ANTONYM chaste.

**easygoing** adjective *Fred was easygoing and a pleasure to work with* RELAXED, even-tempered, placid, mellow, mild, happy-go-lucky, carefree, free and easy, nonchalant, insouciant, imperturbable; amiable, considerate, undemanding, patient, tolerant, lenient, broad-minded, understanding; good-natured, pleasant, agreeable; *informal* laid-back, unflappable, Type-B, low-maintenance. ANTONYMS tense; intolerant.

**eat** verb **1** *we ate a hearty breakfast* CONSUME, devour, ingest, partake of; gobble (up/down), bolt (down), wolf (down); swallow, chew, munch, chomp; *informal* guzzle, nosh, put away, chow down on, tuck into, demolish, dispose of, polish off, pig out on, scarf (down).

**2** *we ate at a local restaurant* HAVE A MEAL, consume food, feed, snack; breakfast, lunch, dine; feast, banquet; *informal* graze, nosh; *dated* sup.

**3** *acidic water can* ***eat away at*** *pipes* ERODE, corrode, wear away/down/through, burn through, consume, dissolve, disintegrate, crumble, decay; damage, destroy.

**eavesdrop** verb *sorry, I refuse to* ***eavesdrop on*** *Kenny for you* LISTEN IN ON, spy on; monitor, tap, wiretap, record, overhear; *informal* snoop on, bug.

**ebb** verb **1** *the tide ebbed* RECEDE, go out, retreat, flow back, fall back/away, subside. ANTONYM come in.

**2** *his courage began to ebb* DIMINISH, dwindle, wane, fade away, peter out, decline, flag, let up, decrease, weaken, disappear. ANTONYMS increase, intensify.

▸ noun **1** *the ebb of the tide* RECEDING, retreat, subsiding.

**2** *the ebb of the fighting* ABATEMENT, subsiding, easing, dying down, de-escalation, decrease, decline, diminution.

**ebony** adjective *his ebony eyes* BLACK, jet-black, pitch-black, coal-black, sable, inky, sooty, raven, dark.

**ebullience** noun *the director's ebullience inspires the cast* EXUBERANCE, buoyancy, cheerfulness, cheeriness, merriment, jollity, sunniness, jauntiness, lightheartedness, high spirits, elation, euphoria, jubilation; animation, sparkle, vivacity, enthusiasm, perkiness; *informal* chirpiness, bounciness, pep.

**ebullient** adjective *in an ebullient mood* EXUBERANT, buoyant, cheerful, joyful, cheery, merry, jolly, sunny, jaunty, lighthearted, elated; animated, sparkling, vivacious, irrepressible; *informal* bubbly, bouncy, peppy, upbeat, chirpy, smiley, full of beans; *dated* gay. ANTONYM depressed.

**eccentric** adjective *eccentric behavior* UNCONVENTIONAL, uncommon, abnormal, irregular, aberrant, anomalous, odd, queer, strange, peculiar, weird, bizarre, outlandish, freakish, extraordinary; idiosyncratic, quirky, nonconformist, outré; *informal* way out, offbeat, freaky, oddball, wacky, kooky. ANTONYM conventional.

▸ noun *he was something of an eccentric* ODDITY, odd fellow, character, individualist, individual, free spirit; misfit; *informal* oddball, odd duck, weirdo, freak, nut, head case, crank, wacko, kook, screwball, crackpot.

**eccentricity** noun *Sidney's eccentricity was more charming than alarming* UNCONVENTIONALITY, singularity, oddness, strangeness, weirdness, quirkiness, freakishness; peculiarity, foible, idiosyncrasy, caprice, whimsy, quirk; *informal* nuttiness, screwiness, freakiness, kookiness.

**ecclesiastic** noun *a high ecclesiastic.* See CLERGY.

**echelon** noun *he reached the upper echelons of government* LEVEL, rank, grade, step, rung, tier, position, order.

**echo** noun **1** *a faint echo of my shout* REVERBERATION, reflection, ringing, repetition, repeat.

**2** *the scene she described was an echo of the photograph* DUPLICATE, copy, replica, imitation, mirror image, double, match, parallel; *informal* look-alike, spitting image, dead ringer.

**3** *a faint echo of their love* TRACE, vestige, remnant, ghost, shadow, memory, recollection, remembrance; reminder, sign, mark, token, souvenir, indication, suggestion, hint; evidence.

▸ verb **1** *his laughter echoed around the room* REVERBERATE, resonate, resound, reflect, ring, vibrate.

**2** *Bill echoed Rex's words* REPEAT, restate, reiterate; copy, imitate, parrot, mimic; reproduce, recite, quote, regurgitate; *informal* recap.

**eclectic** adjective *an eclectic mix of party music* WIDE-RANGING, broad-based, extensive, comprehensive, encyclopedic; varied, diverse, catholic, all-embracing, multifaceted, multifarious, heterogeneous, miscellaneous, assorted.

**eclipse** noun **1** *the eclipse of the sun* BLOTTING OUT, blocking, covering, obscuring, concealing, darkening; *Astronomy* occultation.

**2** *the eclipse of the empire* DECLINE, fall, failure, decay, deterioration, degeneration, weakening, collapse.

▸ verb **1** *the sun was eclipsed by the moon* BLOT OUT, block, cover, obscure, hide, conceal, obliterate, darken; shade; *Astronomy* occult.

**2** *the system was eclipsed by new methods* OUTSHINE, overshadow, surpass, exceed, outclass, outstrip, outdo, top, trump, transcend, upstage.

**economic** adjective **1** *economic reform* FINANCIAL, monetary, budgetary, fiscal; commercial.

**2** *an economic alternative to carpeting* CHEAP, inexpensive, low-cost, economical, cut-rate, discount, bargain. ANTONYM expensive.

**economical** adjective **1** *an economical car* CHEAP, inexpensive, low-cost, budget, economy, economic; cut-rate, discount, bargain. ANTONYM expensive.

**2** *a very economical shopper* THRIFTY, provident, prudent, sensible, frugal, sparing, abstemious; mean, parsimonious, penny-pinching, miserly, stingy. ANTONYM spendthrift.

THE RIGHT WORD **economical, frugal, miserly, parsimonious, provident, sparing, thrifty**

If you don't like to spend money unnecessarily, you may simply be **economical**, which means that you manage your finances wisely and avoid any unnecessary expenses. If you're **thrifty**, you're both industrious and clever in managing your resources (*a thrifty shopper who never leaves home without her coupons*). **Frugal**, on the other hand, means that you tend to be sparing with money—sometimes getting a little carried away in your efforts—by avoiding any form of luxury or lavishness (*too frugal to take a taxi, even at night*). If you're **sparing**, you exercise such restraint in your spending that you sometimes deprive yourself (*sparing to the point where she allowed herself only one new item of clothing a season*). If you're **provident**, however, you're focused on providing for the future (*never one to be provident, she spent her allowance the day she received it*). **Miserly** and **parsimonious** are both used to describe frugality in its most extreme form. But while being *frugal* might be considered a virtue, being *parsimonious* is usually considered to be a fault or even a vice (*they could have been generous with their wealth, but they chose to lead a parsimonious life*). And no one wants to be called *miserly*, which implies being stingy out of greed rather than need (*so miserly that he reveled in his riches while those around him were starving*).

**economize** verb *they economized by growing their own vegetables* SAVE (MONEY), cut costs; cut back, make cutbacks, retrench, budget, make economies, be thrifty, be frugal, scrimp, cut corners, tighten one's belt, watch the/one's pennies.

**economy** noun **1** *the nation's economy* WEALTH, (financial) resources; financial system, financial management.

**2** *one can combine good living with economy* THRIFT, thriftiness, providence, prudence, careful budgeting, economizing, saving, scrimping, restraint, frugality, abstemiousness. ANTONYM extravagance.

**ecstasy** noun *the ecstasy of loving him* RAPTURE, bliss, elation, euphoria, transports, rhapsodies; joy, jubilation, exultation. See note at RAPTURE. ANTONYM misery.

**ecstatic** adjective *the news of Sophie's safe return made them ecstatic* ENRAPTURED, elated, in raptures, euphoric, rapturous, joyful, overjoyed, blissful; on cloud nine, in seventh heaven, beside oneself with joy, jumping for joy, delighted, thrilled, exultant; *informal* over the moon, on top of the world, blissed out.

**eddy** noun *small eddies at the river's edge* SWIRL, whirlpool, vortex, maelstrom.

▸ verb *cold air eddied around her* SWIRL, whirl, spiral, wind, circulate, twist; flow, ripple, stream, surge, billow.

**edge** noun **1** *the edge of the lake* BORDER, boundary, extremity, fringe, margin, side; lip, rim, brim, brink, verge; perimeter, circumference, periphery, limits, bounds. See note at BORDER. ANTONYM middle.

**2** *she had an edge in her voice* SHARPNESS, severity, bite, sting, asperity, acerbity, acidity, trenchancy; sarcasm, acrimony, malice, spite, venom. ANTONYM kindness.

**3** *they have an edge over their rivals* ADVANTAGE, lead, head start, the whip hand, the upper hand; superiority, dominance, ascendancy, supremacy, primacy; *informal* inside track. ANTONYM disadvantage.

▸ verb **1** *poplars edged the orchard* BORDER, fringe, verge, skirt; surround, enclose, encircle, circle, encompass, bound.

**2** *a nightie edged with lace* TRIM, pipe, band, decorate, finish; border, fringe; bind, hem.

**3** *he edged closer to the fire* CREEP, inch, work one's way, pick one's way, ease oneself; sidle, steal, slink.

PHRASE: **on edge** *they were always on edge when Uncle Herman visited.* See EDGY sense 1.

**edgy** adjective **1** *everyone was edgy as the deadline approached* TENSE, nervous, on edge, anxious, apprehensive, uneasy, unsettled; twitchy, jumpy, keyed up, restive, skittish, neurotic, insecure; irritable, touchy, tetchy, testy, crotchety, prickly; *informal* uptight, wired, snappy, strung out. ANTONYM calm.

**2** *an edgy new novel* CUTTING-EDGE, on-the-edge, fringe, avant-garde, innovative, original, offbeat; gritty. ANTONYM conventional.

**edible** adjective *these berries may not be edible* SAFE TO EAT, fit for human consumption, wholesome, good to eat; consumable, digestible, palatable; *formal* comestible.

**edict** noun *rules established by government edict* DECREE, order, command, commandment, mandate, proclamation, pronouncement, dictate, fiat, promulgation; law, statute, act, bill, ruling, injunction; *formal* ordinance.

**edification** noun *formal I read Latin for my own personal edification* EDUCATION, instruction, tuition, teaching, training, tutelage, guidance; enlightenment, cultivation, information; improvement, development.

**USAGE NOTE edification**

In the phrase *for your edification* (= for your moral or intellectual instruction), the word *edification* is sometimes misused to mean "for your enjoyment" or the like—e.g.:

• "Dennis has come to the Tishomingo Lodge and Casino to perform daredevil dives for the edification [read *thrill*] of the casino guests." (*Rocky Mountain News* [Denver]; Feb. 15, 2002.)

• "Everyone says vaguely snotty things about each other and hidden cameras record, for our edification [read *titillation*], sundry couples' first kisses." (*Daily News of Los Angeles*; June 2, 2002.)

• "Quinn and his best friend Creedy (Gerard Butler) reenact the climactic light-saber battle between Luke Skywalker and Darth Vader for the edification [read *enjoyment*] of the local children." (*Austin American-Statesman*; July 12, 2002.) —*BG*

**edifice** noun *the imposing new edifice on Whitfield Street* BUILDING, structure, construction, erection, pile, complex; property, development, premises.

**edify** verb *formal students who have no desire to be edified should leave my classroom and take up thumb-twiddling* EDUCATE, instruct, teach, school, tutor, train, guide; enlighten, inform, cultivate, develop, improve, better.

**edit** verb **1** *she edited the text* CORRECT, check, copyedit, improve, emend, polish; modify, adapt, revise, rewrite, reword, rework, redraft; shorten, condense, cut, abridge; *informal* clean up, blue-pencil.

**2** *this volume was edited by a consultant* SELECT, choose, assemble, organize, put together.

**3** *he edited the school newspaper* BE THE EDITOR OF, direct, run, manage, head, lead, supervise, oversee, preside over; *informal* be the boss of.

**edition** noun *the latest edition includes candid photos from the peace rally* ISSUE, number, volume, impression, publication; version, revision.

**educate** verb *it's nearly impossible to educate children who hate being in school* TEACH, school, tutor, instruct, coach, train, drill; guide, inform, enlighten; inculcate, indoctrinate; *formal* edify.

**educated** adjective *her assistant was an educated and creative young man* INFORMED, literate, schooled, tutored, well-read, learned, knowledgeable, enlightened; intellectual, academic, erudite, scholarly, cultivated, cultured; *dated* lettered.

**education** noun **1** *the education of young children* TEACHING, schooling, tuition, tutoring, instruction, coaching, training, tutelage, guidance; indoctrination, inculcation, enlightenment; *formal* edification.

**2** *a woman of some education* LEARNING, knowledge, literacy, scholarship, enlightenment.

**educational** adjective 1 *a stuffy educational establishment* ACADEMIC, scholastic, school, learning, teaching, pedagogic, instructional.

2 *an educational experience* INSTRUCTIVE, instructional, educative, informative, illuminating, pedagogic, enlightening, didactic, heuristic; *formal* edifying.

**educator** noun *Mr. Chips is one of the most beloved educators in fiction* TEACHER, tutor, instructor, schoolteacher; educationalist, educationist; lecturer, professor; guide, mentor, guru; *formal* pedagogue; *dated* schoolmaster, schoolmistress, schoolmarm; *archaic* schoolman.

**eerie** adjective *eerie sounds from the swamp* UNCANNY, sinister, ghostly, unnatural, unearthly, supernatural, otherworldly; strange, abnormal, odd, weird, freakish; creepy, scary, spooky, freaky, frightening; bone-chilling, spine-chilling, hair-raising, blood-curdling, terrifying.

**efface** verb 1 *the chalk drawings were effaced by the rain* ERASE, eradicate, expunge, blot out, rub out, wipe out, remove, eliminate; delete, cancel, obliterate.

2 *he attempted to* ***efface himself*** MAKE ONESELF INCONSPICUOUS, keep out of sight, keep out of the limelight, lie low, keep a low profile, withdraw (oneself).

**effect** noun 1 *the effect of these changes* RESULT, consequence, upshot, outcome, repercussions, ramifications; end result, conclusion, culmination, corollary, concomitant, aftermath; fruit(s), product, by-product, payoff; *Medicine* sequela. ANTONYM cause.

2 *the effect of the drug* IMPACT, action, effectiveness, influence; power, potency, strength; success; *formal* efficacy.

3 *the new rules come into effect tomorrow* FORCE, operation, enforcement, implementation, effectiveness; validity, lawfulness, legality, legitimacy.

4 *some words to that effect* SENSE, meaning, theme, drift, import, intent, intention, tenor, significance, message; gist, essence, spirit.

5 **(effects)** *the dead man's effects* BELONGINGS, possessions, goods, worldly goods, chattels, goods and chattels; property, paraphernalia; *informal* gear, tackle, things, stuff.

▸ verb *they effected many changes* ACHIEVE, accomplish, carry out, realize, manage, bring off, execute, conduct, engineer, perform, do, perpetrate, discharge, complete, consummate; cause, bring about, create, produce, make; provoke, occasion, generate, engender, actuate, initiate; *formal* effectuate.

PHRASES: **in effect** *the battle had, in effect, already been won* REALLY, in reality, in truth, in fact, in actual fact, effectively, essentially, in essence, practically, to all intents and purposes, all but, as good as, more or less, almost, nearly, just about; *informal* pretty much; *literary* well-nigh, nigh on.

**take effect** 1 *these measures will take effect in May* COME INTO FORCE, come into operation, become operative, begin, become valid, become law, apply, be applied.

2 *the drug started to take effect* WORK, act, be effective, produce results.

**effective** adjective 1 *an effective treatment* SUCCESSFUL, effectual, potent, powerful; helpful, beneficial, advantageous, valuable, useful; *formal* efficacious. ANTONYMS ineffective, weak.

2 *a more effective argument* CONVINCING, compelling, strong, forceful, potent, weighty, sound, valid; impressive, persuasive, plausible, credible, authoritative; logical, reasonable, lucid, coherent, cogent, eloquent; *formal* efficacious. ANTONYM weak.

3 *the new law will become effective next week* OPERATIVE, in force, in effect; valid, official, lawful, legal, binding; *Law* effectual. ANTONYM invalid.

4 *Korea was under effective Japanese control* VIRTUAL, practical, essential, actual, implicit, tacit. ANTONYM theoretical.

THE RIGHT WORD **effective, effectual, efficacious, efficient**

All of these adjectives mean producing or capable of producing a result, but they are not interchangeable. Use **effective** when you want to describe something that produces a definite effect or result (*an effective speaker who was able to rally the crowd's support*) and **efficacious** when it produces the desired effect or result (*an efficacious remedy that cured her almost immediately*). If something produces the desired effect or result in a decisive manner, use **effectual** (*an effectual recommendation that got him the job*), an adjective that is often employed when looking back after an event is over (*an effectual strategy that finally turned the tide in their favor*). Reserve the use of **efficient** for when you want to imply skill and economy of energy in producing the desired result (*so efficient in her management of the company that layoffs were not necessary*). When applied to people, *efficient* means capable or competent (*an efficient homemaker*) and places less emphasis on the achievement of results and more on the skills involved.

**effectiveness** noun *we were impressed by the effectiveness of the nontoxic pesticide* SUCCESS, productiveness, potency, power; benefit, advantage, value, virtue, usefulness; *formal* efficacy.

**effectual** adjective 1 *effectual political action* EFFECTIVE, successful, productive, constructive; worthwhile, helpful, beneficial, advantageous, valuable, useful; *formal* efficacious. See note at EFFECTIVE.

2 *Law an effectual document* VALID, authentic, bona fide, genuine, official; lawful, legal, legitimate, binding, legally binding, contractual.

**effeminate** adjective *an effeminate bartender* WOMANISH, effete, foppish, unmanly, feminine; *informal* camp, campy, flaming. ANTONYM manly.

**effervescence** noun 1 *wines of uniform effervescence* FIZZ, fizziness, sparkle, gassiness, carbonation, aeration, bubbliness.

2 *his cheeky effervescence* VIVACITY, liveliness, animation, high spirits, ebullience, exuberance, buoyancy, sparkle, gaiety, jollity, cheerfulness, perkiness, breeziness, enthusiasm, irrepressibility, vitality, zest, energy, dynamism, pep, bounce, spunk.

**effervescent** adjective **1** *an effervescent drink* FIZZY, sparkling, carbonated, aerated, gassy, bubbly. ANTONYMS flat, still.

**2** *effervescent young people* VIVACIOUS, lively, animated, high-spirited, bubbly, ebullient, buoyant, sparkling, scintillating, lighthearted, jaunty, happy, jolly, cheery, cheerful, perky, sunny, enthusiastic, irrepressible, vital, zestful, energetic, dynamic; *informal* bright-eyed and bushy-tailed, peppy, bouncy, upbeat, chirpy, full of beans. ANTONYM depressed.

**effete** adjective **1** *effete trendies* AFFECTED, pretentious, precious, mannered, overrefined; ineffectual; *informal* la-di-da. ANTONYM unpretentious.

**2** *an effete young man* EFFEMINATE, unmanly, girlish, feminine; soft, timid, cowardly, lily-livered, spineless, pusillanimous; *informal* sissy, wimpish, wimpy. ANTONYM manly.

**3** *the fabric of society is effete* WEAK, enfeebled, enervated, worn out, exhausted, finished, drained, spent, powerless, ineffectual. ANTONYM powerful.

**efficacious** adjective *formal a change in diet may be quite efficacious* EFFECTIVE, effectual, successful, productive, constructive, potent; helpful, beneficial, advantageous, valuable, useful. See note at EFFECTIVE.

**efficacy** noun *formal the efficacy of prescription drugs* EFFECTIVENESS, success, productiveness, potency, power; benefit, advantage, value, virtue, usefulness.

**efficiency** noun **1** *we need to make changes to improve efficiency* ORGANIZATION, order, orderliness, regulation, coherence; productivity, effectiveness.

**2** *I compliment you on your efficiency* COMPETENCE, capability, ability, proficiency, adeptness, expertise, professionalism, skill, effectiveness.

**efficient** adjective **1** *efficient techniques* ORGANIZED, methodical, systematic, logical, orderly, businesslike, streamlined, productive, effective, cost-effective, labor-saving. See note at EFFECTIVE. ANTONYM disorganized.

**2** *an efficient secretary* COMPETENT, capable, able, proficient, adept, skillful, skilled, effective, productive, organized, businesslike. ANTONYM incompetent.

**effigy** noun *protestors threw water-balloon "bombs" at an effigy of the president* STATUE, statuette, sculpture, model, dummy, figurine; likeness, image; bust.

**effluent** noun *the effluent from papermaking contains may contaminants* (LIQUID) WASTE, sewage, waste water, effluvium, outflow, discharge, emission.

**effort** noun **1** *they made an effort to work together* ATTEMPT, try, endeavor; *informal* crack, shot, stab; *formal* essay.

**2** *his score was a fine effort* ACHIEVEMENT, accomplishment, attainment, result, feat; undertaking, enterprise, work; triumph, success, coup.

**3** *the job requires little effort* EXERTION, energy, work, endeavor, application, labor, power, muscle, toil, strain; *informal* sweat, elbow grease.

**effortless** adjective *he makes the most complex dance moves look effortless* EASY, undemanding, unchallenging, painless, simple, uncomplicated, straightforward, elementary; fluent, natural; *informal* as easy as pie, child's play, kids' stuff, a cinch, no sweat, a breeze, duck soup, a snap. ANTONYM difficult.

**effrontery** noun *Stearns had the effrontery to counter the admiral's directive* IMPUDENCE, impertinence, cheek, insolence, cockiness, audacity, temerity, presumption, nerve, gall, shamelessness, impoliteness, disrespect, bad manners; *informal* brass, face, chutzpah, sauce, sass. See note at TEMERITY.

**effusion** noun **1** *an effusion of poisonous gas* OUTFLOW, outpouring, rush, current, flood, deluge, emission, discharge, emanation; spurt, surge, jet, stream, torrent, gush, flow.

**2** *reporters' flamboyant effusions* OUTBURST, outpouring, gushing, rhapsody; wordiness, verbiage.

**effusive** adjective *effusive compliments* GUSHING, gushy, unrestrained, extravagant, fulsome, demonstrative, lavish, enthusiastic, lyrical; expansive, wordy, verbose, over the top. See note at SENTIMENTAL. ANTONYM restrained.

**egg** noun *the eggs are suspended in a gelatinous mass* OVUM; gamete, germ cell; **(eggs)** roe, spawn, seed. PHRASE: **egg someone on** *Earl didn't really want to enter the talent contest, but his friends egged him on* URGE, goad, incite, provoke, push, drive, prod, prompt, induce, impel, spur on; encourage, exhort, motivate, galvanize.

**egghead** noun *informal Frances fits right in with all the chess-club eggheads* INTELLECTUAL, thinker, academic, scholar, sage; bookworm, highbrow; expert, genius, mastermind; *informal* brain, whiz, brainiac, rocket scientist. ANTONYM dunce.

**ego** noun *the defeat was a bruise to his ego* SELF-ESTEEM, self-importance, self-worth, self-respect, self-image, self-confidence.

**egotism, egoism** noun *Darla's egotism will always thwart her chances for a lasting relationship* SELF-CENTEREDNESS, egomania, egocentricity, self-interest, selfishness, self-seeking, self-serving, self-regard, self-love, narcissism, self-admiration, vanity, conceit, self-importance; boastfulness. See also note at PRIDE.

THE RIGHT WORD **egotism, conceit, egoism, narcissism, solipsism, vanity**

Is the handsome, arrogant, successful politician who thinks the world revolves around him an egoist or an egotist? **Egotism** is a negative term that combines extreme self-preoccupation with a tendency to show off or attract attention, while **egoism** is a more neutral term for those who are preoccupied with their own needs and interests but do not necessarily consider themselves superior (*the egoism of teenagers is well-documented*). There is nothing neutral about **conceit**, which carries strong connotations of superiority and a failure to see oneself realistically (*he was so rich and powerful that conceit came easily*). **Vanity**, on the other hand, is not based so much on feelings of superiority as it is on a love for oneself and a craving for the admiration of others (*his vanity drove him to cosmetic surgery*). **Narcissism** and **solipsism** were once considered technical terms drawn from psychology and philosophy, respectively, but nowadays they are also in the general language. *Narcissism* means self-love and preoccupation with one's physical or mental attributes (*the beautiful young actress had a reputation for narcissism*), while *solipsism* refers to someone who is completely wrapped up in his or her own concerns (*the solipsism of the theoretical mathematician*).

---

**egotist, egoist** noun *boxing is a sport that breeds egotists* SELF-SEEKER, egocentric, egomaniac, narcissist; boaster, braggart; *informal* show-off, big head, showboat.

**egotistic, egoistic** adjective *Archie's egotistic lifestyle has alienated many people over the years* SELF-CENTERED, selfish, egocentric, egomaniacal, self-interested, self-seeking, self-absorbed, narcissistic, vain, conceited, self-important; boastful.

**egregious** adjective *an egregious error of judgment* SHOCKING, appalling, terrible, awful, horrendous, frightful, atrocious, abominable, abhorrent, outrageous; monstrous, heinous, dire, unspeakable, shameful, unforgivable, intolerable, dreadful; *formal* grievous. ANTONYM marvelous.

**egress** noun **1** *the egress from the gallery was blocked* EXIT, way out, escape route. ANTONYM entrance.

**2** *a means of egress* DEPARTURE, exit, withdrawal, retreat, exodus; escape. ANTONYM entry.

**ejaculate** verb **1** *the male ejaculates* EMIT SEMEN, climax, have an orgasm, orgasm; *informal* come.

**2** *dated "What?" he ejaculated* EXCLAIM, cry out, call out, yell, blurt out, come out with.

**ejaculation** noun **1** *the ejaculation of fluid* EMISSION, ejection, discharge, release, expulsion.

**2** *premature ejaculation* EMISSION OF SEMEN, climax, orgasm.

**3** *dated the conversation consisted of ejaculations* EXCLAMATION, interjection; call, shout, yell.

**eject** verb **1** *the volcano ejected ash* EMIT, spew out, discharge, give off, send out, belch, vent; expel, release, disgorge, spout, vomit, throw up.

**2** *the pilot had time to eject* BAIL OUT, escape, get out.

**3** *they were ejected from the hall* EXPEL, throw out, turn out, cast out, remove, oust; evict, banish; *informal* kick out, boot out, chuck out, give someone the bum's rush. ANTONYM admit.

**4** *he was ejected from his post* DISMISS, remove, discharge, oust, expel, ax, throw out, force out, drive out; *informal* sack, fire, send packing, boot out, kick out, chuck out, give someone their marching orders, show someone the door. ANTONYM appoint.

THE RIGHT WORD **eject, dismiss, evict, expel, oust**

---

Want to get rid of someone? You can **eject** him or her, which means to throw or cast out (*he was ejected from the meeting room*). If you hope the person never comes back, use **expel**, a verb that suggests driving someone out of a country, an organization, etc., for all time (*to be expelled from school*); it can also imply the use of voluntary force (*to expel air from the lungs*). If you exercise force or the power of law to get rid of someone or something, **oust** is the correct verb (*ousted after less than two years in office*). If as a property owner you are turning someone out of a house or a place of business, you'll want to **evict** the person (*she was evicted for not paying the rent*). **Dismiss** is by far the mildest of these terms, suggesting that you are rejecting or refusing to consider someone or something (*to dismiss a legal case*). It is also commonly used of loss of employment (*dismissed from his job for excessive tardiness*).

---

**ejection** noun **1** *the ejection of electrons* EMISSION, discharge, expulsion, release; elimination.

**2** *their ejection from the grounds* EXPULSION, removal; eviction, banishment, exile.

**3** *his ejection from office* DISMISSAL, removal, discharge, expulsion.

**eke** verb *I had to **eke out** my remaining funds* HUSBAND, use sparingly, be thrifty with, be frugal with, be sparing with, use economically; *informal* go easy on. ANTONYM squander.

PHRASE: **eke out a living** *they barely eked out a living* SUBSIST, survive, get by, scrape by, make ends meet, keep body and soul together, keep the wolf from the door, keep one's head above water.

**elaborate** adjective **1** *an elaborate plan* COMPLICATED, complex, intricate, involved; detailed, painstaking, careful; tortuous, convoluted, serpentine, Byzantine. ANTONYMS simple, plain.

**2** *an elaborate plasterwork ceiling* ORNATE, decorated, embellished, adorned, ornamented, fancy, fussy, busy, ostentatious, extravagant, showy, baroque, rococo, florid; *informal* fancy-schmancy. ANTONYMS simple, plain.

▸ verb *both sides refused to **elaborate on** their reasons* EXPAND ON, enlarge on, add to, flesh out, put flesh on the bones of, add detail to, expatiate on; develop, fill out, embellish, embroider, enhance, amplify.

**elapse** verb *how much time has elapsed?* PASS, go by/past, wear on, slip by/away/past, roll by/past, slide by/past, steal by/past, tick by/past.

**elastic** adjective **1** *elastic material* STRETCHY, elasticized, stretchable, springy, flexible, pliant, pliable, supple, yielding, plastic, resilient. See note at FLEXIBLE. ANTONYM rigid.

**2** *an elastic concept of nationality* ADAPTABLE, flexible, adjustable, accommodating, variable, fluid, versatile. ANTONYM inflexible.

▸ noun *buying elastics for her hair* RUBBER BAND, elastic band, scrunchie.

**elasticity** noun **1** *the skin's natural elasticity* STRETCHINESS, flexibility, pliancy, suppleness, plasticity, resilience, springiness, give.

**2** *the elasticity of the term* ADAPTABILITY, flexibility, adjustability, fluidity, versatility.

**elated** adjective *Sally and Marv were elated at the idea of becoming grandparents* THRILLED, delighted, overjoyed, ecstatic, euphoric, very happy, joyous, gleeful, jubilant, beside oneself, exultant, rapturous, in raptures, walking on air, on cloud nine, in seventh heaven, jumping for joy, in transports of delight; *informal* on top of the world, over the moon, on a high, tickled pink. ANTONYM miserable.

**elation** noun *the declaration of peace is indeed cause for our greatest elation* EUPHORIA, ecstasy, happiness, delight, transports of delight, joy, joyousness, glee, jubilation, exultation, bliss, rapture.

**elbow** verb *he elbowed his way through the crowd* PUSH, shove, force, shoulder, jostle, barge, muscle, bulldoze.

**elbow room** noun *the committee desires more elbow room within the confines of the organization* ROOM TO MANEUVER, room, space, breathing space, personal space, scope, opportunity, freedom, play, free rein, license, latitude, leeway.

**elder** adjective *his elder brother* OLDER, senior, big.

▸ noun *the native elders* LEADER, senior figure, patriarch, father.

**elderly** adjective *her elderly mother* AGED, old, advanced in years, aging, long in the tooth, past one's prime; gray-haired, grizzled, hoary; in one's dotage, decrepit, doddering, doddery, senescent; *informal* getting on, past it, over the hill, no spring chicken. ANTONYM youthful.

▸ noun (**the elderly**) *health care for the elderly* OLD PEOPLE, the aged, senior citizens; geriatrics, seniors; retired people, retirees, golden agers; *informal* oldsters, geezers.

**elect** verb **1** *a new president was elected* VOTE FOR, VOTE IN, return, cast one's vote for; choose, pick, select.

**2** *she elected to stay behind* CHOOSE, decide, opt, vote.

▸ adjective *the president-elect* FUTURE, -to-be, designate, chosen, elected, coming, next, appointed.

▸ noun (**the elect**) *it is not the elect who need better health care and safer schools* THE CHOSEN, the elite, the favored; the crème de la crème.

**election** noun *announcing the results of the election* BALLOT, vote, popular vote, ballot box; poll(s); acclamation; primary.

**elector** noun *my thanks to the faithful electors who brought me to this place* VOTER, member of the electorate, constituent.

**electric** adjective **1** *an electric kettle* ELECTRIC-POWERED, electrically operated, battery-operated.

**2** *the atmosphere was electric* EXCITING, charged, electrifying, thrilling, heady, dramatic, intoxicating, dynamic, stimulating, galvanizing, rousing, stirring, moving; tense, knife-edge, explosive, volatile.

**electrify** verb *lecturers who electrify their students* EXCITE, thrill, stimulate, arouse, rouse, inspire, stir (up), exhilarate, intoxicate, galvanize, move, fire (with enthusiasm), fire someone's imagination, invigorate, animate; startle, jolt, shock, light a fire under; *informal* give someone a thrill, give someone a charge.

**elegance** noun **1** *he was attracted by her elegance* STYLE, stylishness, grace, gracefulness, taste, tastefulness, sophistication; refinement, dignity, beauty, poise, charm, culture; suaveness, urbanity, panache.

**2** *the elegance of the idea* NEATNESS, simplicity; ingenuity, cleverness, inventiveness.

**elegant** adjective **1** *an elegant black outfit* STYLISH, graceful, tasteful, sophisticated, classic, chic, smart, fashionable, modish; refined, dignified, poised, beautiful, lovely, charming, artistic, aesthetic; cultivated, polished, cultured; dashing, debonair, suave, urbane. ANTONYM gauche.

**2** *an elegant solution* NEAT, simple, effective; ingenious, clever, deft, intelligent, inventive. ANTONYMS messy, unwieldy.

**elegiac** adjective *an elegiac piece for small orchestra* MOURNFUL, melancholic, melancholy, plaintive, sorrowful, sad, lamenting, doleful; funereal, dirgelike; nostalgic, valedictory, poignant; *literary* dolorous. ANTONYM cheerful.

**elegy** noun *an elegy for his father* LAMENT, requiem, threnody, dirge; *literary* plaint; *Irish* keen.

**element** noun **1** *an essential element of the game* COMPONENT, constituent, part, section, portion, piece, segment, bit; aspect, factor, feature, facet, ingredient, strand, detail, point; member, unit, module, item.

**2** *there is an element of truth in this stereotype* TRACE, touch, hint, smattering, soupçon.

**3** (**elements**) *the elements of political science* BASICS, essentials, principles, first principles; foundations, fundamentals, rudiments; *informal* nuts and bolts, ABCs.

**4** (**elements**) *I braved the elements* WEATHER, climate, meteorological conditions, atmospheric conditions; wind, rain, snow.

**elemental** adjective **1** *the elemental principles of accounting* BASIC, primary, fundamental, essential, root, underlying; rudimentary.

**2** *elemental forces* NATURAL, atmospheric, meteorological, environmental, climatic.

**elementary** adjective **1** *an elementary astronomy course* BASIC, rudimentary, fundamental; preparatory, introductory, initiatory, entry-level; *informal* 101. ANTONYM advanced.

**2** *a lot of the work is elementary* EASY, simple, straightforward, uncomplicated, undemanding, painless, child's play, plain sailing; *informal* as easy as pie, as easy as ABC, a piece of cake, no sweat, kids' stuff. ANTONYMS complicated, difficult.

**elephantine** adjective *a tropical plant with elephantine leaves* ENORMOUS, huge, gigantic, very big, massive, giant, immense, tremendous, colossal, mammoth, gargantuan, vast, prodigious, monumental, titanic; hulking, bulky, heavy, weighty, ponderous, lumbering; *informal* jumbo, whopping, humongous, monster, ginormous. ANTONYM tiny.

**elevate** verb **1** *we need a breeze to elevate the kite* RAISE, lift (up), raise up/aloft, upraise; hoist, hike up, haul up. ANTONYM lower.

**2** *he was elevated to senior writer* PROMOTE, upgrade, advance, move up, raise, prefer; ennoble, exalt, aggrandize; *informal* move up the ladder. ANTONYM demote.

**elevated** adjective **1** *an elevated highway* RAISED, upraised, high up, aloft; overhead.

**2** *elevated language* LOFTY, grand, exalted, fine, sublime; inflated, pompous, bombastic, orotund. ANTONYMS lowly, base.

**3** *the gentry's elevated status* HIGH, higher, high-ranking, of high standing, lofty, superior, exalted, eminent; grand, noble. ANTONYMS lowly, humble.

**elevation** noun **1** *his elevation to the directorship* PROMOTION, upgrading, advancement, advance, preferment, aggrandizement; ennoblement; *informal* step up the ladder.

**2** *15,000–30,000 feet in elevation* ALTITUDE, height.

**3** *elevations in excess of 8,000 feet* HEIGHT, hill, mountain, mount; *formal* eminence.

**4** *elevation of thought* GRANDEUR, greatness, nobility, loftiness, majesty, sublimity.

**elf** noun *elves inhabit the great hollow trees* PIXIE, fairy, sprite, imp, brownie; dwarf, gnome, goblin, hobgoblin; leprechaun, puck, troll.

**elfin** adjective *her elfin little brother charmed all the aunts and uncles* ELFLIKE, elfish, elvish, pixielike; puckish, impish, playful, mischievous; dainty, delicate, small, petite, slight, little, tiny, diminutive.

**elicit** verb *your sarcastic remarks will no doubt elicit a negative response* OBTAIN, draw out, extract, bring out, evoke, call forth, bring forth, induce, prompt, generate, engender, trigger, provoke; *formal* educe.

**elite** noun *hobnobbing with Southport's elite* BEST, pick, cream, crème de la crème, flower, nonpareil, elect; high society, jet set, beautiful people, beau monde, haut monde, glitterati; aristocracy, nobility, upper class. ANTONYM dregs.

**elixir** noun *a homemade elixir purported to enhance virility* POTION, concoction, brew, philter, decoction, mixture; medicine, tincture; extract, essence, concentrate, distillate, distillation; *literary* draft.

**elliptical** adjective **1** *an elliptical shape* OVAL, egg-shaped, elliptic, ovate, ovoid, oviform, ellipsoidal.

**2** *elliptical phraseology* CRYPTIC, abstruse, ambiguous, obscure, oblique, Delphic; terse, concise, succinct, compact, economic, laconic, sparing, abridged.

**elocution** noun *the producers brought in a teacher to help with her elocution* PRONUNCIATION, enunciation, articulation, diction, speech, intonation, vocalization, modulation; phrasing, delivery, public speaking.

**elongate** verb **1** *an exercise that elongates the muscles* LENGTHEN, extend, stretch (out). ANTONYM shorten.

**2** *the high notes were elongated* PROLONG, protract, draw out, sustain. ANTONYM shorten.

**eloquence** noun *the eloquence of his sermons* FLUENCY, articulateness, expressiveness, silver tongue, persuasiveness, forcefulness, power, potency, effectiveness; oratory, rhetoric, grandiloquence, magniloquence; *informal* gift of the gab, way with words.

**eloquent** adjective **1** *an eloquent speaker* FLUENT, articulate, expressive, silver-tongued; persuasive, strong, forceful, powerful, potent, well-expressed, effective, lucid, vivid, graphic; smooth-tongued, glib. ANTONYM inarticulate.

**2** *her glance was more eloquent than words* EXPRESSIVE, meaningful, suggestive, revealing, telling, significant, indicative.

**elsewhere** adverb *the negatives are stored in one place, and the prints are stored elsewhere* SOMEWHERE ELSE, in/at/to another place, in/at/to a different place, hence; not here, not present, absent, away, abroad, out. ANTONYM here.

**elucidate** verb *Sherwood's diaries may help elucidate his motives* EXPLAIN, make clear, illuminate, throw/shed light on, clarify, clear up, sort out, unravel, spell out; interpret, explicate; gloss. See note at CLARIFY. ANTONYM confuse.

**elucidation** noun *the manual provides elucidation useful to the beginner* EXPLANATION, clarification, illumination; interpretation, explication; gloss.

**elude** verb *Holbrook eluded the police for several weeks* EVADE, avoid, get away from, dodge, escape from, run from, run away from; lose, shake off, give the slip to, slip away from, throw off the scent; *informal* slip through someone's fingers, slip through the net.

**elusive** adjective **1** *her elusive husband* DIFFICULT TO FIND; evasive, slippery; *informal* always on the move.

**2** *an elusive quality* INDEFINABLE, intangible, impalpable, ambiguous.

**Elysium** noun *Greek Mythology* *human souls conveyed to Elysium* HEAVEN, paradise, the Elysian fields; eternity, the afterlife, the next world, the hereafter; *Scandinavian Mythology* Valhalla; *Classical Mythology* the Islands of the Blessed; *Arthurian Legend* Avalon.

**emaciated** adjective *emaciated bodies* THIN, skeletal, bony, gaunt, wasted; scrawny, skinny, scraggy, skin and bones, rawboned, sticklike, waiflike; starved, underfed, undernourished, underweight, half-starved; cadaverous, shriveled, shrunken, withered; *informal* anorexic, like a bag of bones. ANTONYM fat.

**emanate** verb **1** *warmth emanated from the fireplace* ISSUE, spread, radiate, be sent forth/out.

**2** *the proposals emanated from a committee* ORIGINATE, stem, derive, proceed, spring, issue, emerge, flow, come.

**3** *he emanated an air of power* EXUDE, emit, radiate, give off/out, send out/forth.

**emanation** noun **1** *an emanation of his tortured personality* PRODUCT, consequence, result, fruit.

**2** *radon gas emanation* DISCHARGE, emission, radiation, effusion, outflow, outpouring, flow, leak; *technical* efflux.

**emancipate** verb *the young Cowles emancipated his father's serfs* FREE, liberate, set free, release, deliver, discharge; unchain, unfetter, unshackle, untie, unyoke; *rare* disenthrall. ANTONYM enslave.

**emasculate** verb *the opposition emasculated the committee's proposal* WEAKEN, enfeeble, debilitate, erode, undermine, cripple; remove the sting from, pull the teeth out of; *informal* water down.

**embalm** verb **1** *his body had been embalmed* PRESERVE, mummify, lay out.

**2** *the poem ought to embalm his memory* PRESERVE, conserve, enshrine, immortalize.

**embargo** noun *an embargo on oil sales* BAN, bar, prohibition, stoppage, interdict, proscription, veto, moratorium; restriction, restraint, block, barrier, impediment, obstruction; boycott.

▸ verb *arms sales were embargoed* BAN, bar, prohibit, stop, interdict, debar, proscribe, outlaw; restrict, restrain, block, obstruct; boycott. ANTONYM allow.

**embark** verb **1** *the passengers were not allowed to embark until 4:30* BOARD SHIP, go on board, go aboard; *informal* hop on, jump on.

**2** *he* ***embarked on*** *a new career* BEGIN, start, commence, undertake, set about, take up, turn one's hand to, get down to; enter into, venture into, launch into, plunge into, engage in, settle down to; *informal* get cracking on, get going on, have a go/crack/shot at.

**embarrass** verb *his parents would show up drunk and embarrass him* MORTIFY, shame, put someone to shame, humiliate, abash, chagrin, make uncomfortable, make self-conscious; discomfit, disconcert, discompose, upset, distress; *informal* show up, discombobulate.

**embarrassed** adjective *the officer's flashlight caught a pair of embarrassed teens in the back seat* MORTIFIED, red-faced, blushing, abashed, shamed, ashamed, shamefaced, humiliated, chagrined, awkward, self-conscious, uncomfortable, sheepish; discomfited, disconcerted, upset, discomposed, flustered, agitated, distressed; shy, bashful, tongue-tied; *informal* with egg on one's face, wishing the earth would swallow one up.

**embarrassing** adjective *many embarrassing moments have been preserved on videotape* HUMILIATING, shaming, shameful, mortifying, ignominious; awkward, uncomfortable, cringeworthy, compromising; disconcerting, discomfiting, upsetting, distressing.

**embarrassment** noun **1** *he was scarlet with embarrassment* MORTIFICATION, humiliation, shame, shamefacedness, chagrin, awkwardness, self-consciousness, sheepishness, discomfort, discomfiture, discomposure, agitation, distress; shyness, bashfulness.

**2** *his current financial embarrassment* DIFFICULTY, predicament, plight, problem, mess, imbroglio; *informal* bind, jam, pickle, fix, scrape.

**3** *an embarrassment of riches* SURPLUS, excess, overabundance, superabundance, glut, surfeit, superfluity; abundance, profusion, plethora.

**embassy** noun **1** *the Italian embassy* CONSULATE, legation.

**2** *historical the king sent an embassy to the rebels* ENVOY, representative, delegate, emissary; delegation, deputation, legation, mission, diplomatic mission.

**embed, imbed** verb *rhinestones are then embedded in the leather trim* IMPLANT, plant, set, fix, lodge, root, insert, place; sink, drive, hammer, ram.

**embellish** verb **1** *weapons embellished with precious metal* DECORATE, adorn, ornament; beautify, enhance, grace; trim, garnish, gild; deck, bedeck, festoon, emblazon; *literary* bejewel, bedizen.

**2** *the legend was embellished in later retellings* ELABORATE, embroider, expand on, exaggerate.

**embellishment** noun **1** *architectural embellishments* DECORATION, ornamentation, adornment; beautification, enhancement, trimming, trim, garnishing, gilding.

**2** *we wanted the truth, not romantic embellishments* ELABORATION, addition, exaggeration.

**embezzle** verb *he's accused of embezzling donated funds* MISAPPROPRIATE, steal, thieve, pilfer, purloin, appropriate, defraud someone of, siphon off, pocket, help oneself to; abstract; *informal* rob, rip off, skim, line one's pockets with, pinch.

**embezzlement** noun *four corporate managers were indicted for embezzlement* MISAPPROPRIATION, theft, stealing, robbery, thieving, pilfering, purloining, pilferage, appropriation, swindling; fraud, larceny.

**emblazon** verb **1** *shirts emblazoned with the company name* ADORN, decorate, ornament, embellish; inscribe.

**2** *a flag with a hammer and sickle emblazoned on it* DISPLAY, depict, show.

**emblem** noun *their emblem is an eagle perched atop a cannon* SYMBOL, representation, token, image, figure, mark, sign; crest, badge, device, insignia, stamp, seal, heraldic device, coat of arms, shield; logo, trademark, brand.

THE RIGHT WORD **emblem, attribute, image, sign, symbol, token, type**

When it comes to representing or embodying the invisible or intangible, you can't beat a **symbol**. It applies to anything that serves as an outward sign of something immaterial or spiritual (*the cross as a symbol of salvation*; *the crown as a symbol of monarchy*), although the association between the symbol and what it represents does not have to be based on tradition or convention and may, in fact, be quite arbitrary (*the annual gathering at the cemetery became a symbol of the family's long and tragic history*). An **emblem** is a visual symbol or pictorial device that represents the character or history of a family, a nation, or an office (*the eagle is an emblem of the United States*). It is very close in meaning to **attribute**, which is an object that is conventionally associated with either an individual, a group, or an abstraction (*the spiked wheel as an attribute of St. Catherine; the scales as an attribute of Justice*). An **image** is also a visual representation or embodiment, but in a much broader sense (*veins popping, he was the image of the angry father*). **Sign** is often used in place of *symbol* to refer to a simple representation of an agreed-upon meaning (*the upraised fist as a sign of victory; the white flag as a sign of surrender*), but a *symbol* usually embodies a wider range of meanings, while a *sign* can be any object, event, or gesture from which information can be deduced (*her faltering voice was a sign of her nervousness*). A **token**, on the other hand, is something offered as a symbol or reminder (*he gave her his class ring as a token of his devotion*) and a **type**, particularly in a religious context, is a symbol or representation of something not present (*Jerusalem as the type of heaven; the paschal lamb as the type of Christ*).

---

**embodiment** noun *the embodiment of the hippie culture* PERSONIFICATION, incarnation, realization, manifestation, avatar, expression, representation, actualization, symbol, symbolization, materialization; paradigm, epitome, paragon, soul, model; type, essence, quintessence, exemplification, example, exemplar, ideal; *formal* reification.

**embody** verb **1** *he embodies the spirit of industrial capitalism* PERSONIFY, realize, manifest, symbolize, represent, express, concretize, incarnate, epitomize, stand for, typify, exemplify; *formal* reify, hypostatize.

**2** *the changes embodied in the gun control legislation* INCORPORATE, include, contain, encompass; assimilate, consolidate, integrate, organize, systematize; combine.

**embolden** verb *emboldened by the brandy, he walked over to her table* FORTIFY, make brave/braver, encourage, hearten, strengthen, brace, stiffen the resolve of, lift the morale of; rouse, stir, stimulate, cheer, rally, fire, animate, inspirit, invigorate; *informal* buck up. See note at ENCOURAGE. ANTONYM dishearten.

**embrace** verb **1** *he embraced her warmly* HUG, take/hold in one's arms, hold, cuddle, clasp to one's bosom, clasp, squeeze, clutch; caress; enfold, enclasp, encircle, envelop, entwine oneself around; *informal* canoodle, clinch.

**2** *most states have embraced the concept* WELCOME, welcome with open arms, accept, take up, take to one's heart, adopt; espouse, support, back, champion.

**3** *the faculty embraces a wide range of departments* INCLUDE, take in, comprise, contain, incorporate, encompass, cover, involve, embody, subsume, comprehend.

▸ noun *a fond embrace* HUG, cuddle, squeeze, clinch, caress, clasp; bear hug.

**embroider** verb **1** *a cushion embroidered with a pattern of golden keys* SEW, stitch; decorate, adorn, ornament, embellish.

**2** *she embroidered her stories with colorful detail* ELABORATE, embellish, enlarge on, exaggerate, touch up, dress up, gild, color; *informal* jazz up.

**embroidery** noun **1** *the girls were taught embroidery* NEEDLEWORK, needlepoint, needlecraft, sewing, tatting, crewel work, tapestry.

**2** *fanciful embroidery of the facts* ELABORATION, embellishment, adornment, ornamentation, coloring, enhancement; exaggeration, overstatement, hyperbole.

**embryonic** adjective **1** *an embryonic chick* FETAL, unborn, unhatched; in utero.

**2** *an embryonic prodemocracy movement* RUDIMENTARY, undeveloped, unformed, immature, incomplete, incipient, inchoate; fledgling, budding, nascent, emerging, developing, early, germinal. ANTONYM mature.

**emend** verb *the editors select letters for publication and may emend content at their own discretion* CORRECT, rectify, repair, fix; improve, enhance, polish, refine, amend; edit, rewrite, revise, copyedit, redraft, recast, rephrase, reword, rework, alter, change, modify; *rare* redact.

**emerge** verb **1** *a policeman emerged from the alley* COME OUT, appear, come into view, become visible, surface, materialize, manifest oneself, issue, come forth.

**2** *several unexpected facts emerged* BECOME KNOWN, become apparent, be revealed, come to light, come out, turn up, transpire, unfold, prove to be the case.

**emergence** noun *the emergence of a new generation* APPEARANCE, arrival, coming, materialization; advent, inception, dawn, birth, origination, start, development, rise.

**emergency** noun **1** *a military emergency* CRISIS, urgent situation, extremity, exigency; accident, disaster, catastrophe, calamity; difficulty, plight, predicament, danger.

**2** *get her down to emergency right away* emergency room, ER.

▸ adjective **1** *an emergency meeting* URGENT, crisis; impromptu, extraordinary.

**2** *emergency supplies* RESERVE, standby, backup, fallback, in reserve.

**emergent** adjective *an emergent democracy* EMERGING, developing, rising, dawning, budding, embryonic, infant, fledgling, nascent, incipient, inchoate.

**emigrate** verb *her Swedish ancestors emigrated in 1901* MOVE ABROAD, move overseas, leave one's country, migrate; relocate, resettle; defect. ANTONYM immigrate.

**emigration** noun *the main incentive for emigration was the promise of higher wages* MOVING ABROAD, moving overseas, expatriation, migration; exodus, diaspora; relocation, resettling; defection.

**eminence** noun **1** *his eminence as a scientist* FAME, celebrity, illustriousness, distinction, renown, preeminence, notability, greatness, prestige, importance, reputation, repute, note; prominence, superiority, stature, standing.

**2** *various legal eminences* IMPORTANT PERSON, dignitary, luminary, worthy, grandee, notable, notability, personage, leading light, VIP; *informal* somebody, someone, big shot, big gun, heavyweight.

**3** *formal the hotel's eminence above the sea* ELEVATION, height, rise.

**eminent** adjective **1** *an eminent man of letters* ILLUSTRIOUS, distinguished, renowned, esteemed, preeminent, notable, noteworthy, great, prestigious, important, influential, affluential, outstanding, noted, of note; famous, celebrated, prominent, well-known, lionized, acclaimed, exalted, revered, august, venerable. ANTONYM unknown.

**2** *the eminent reasonableness of their claims* OBVIOUS, clear, conspicuous, marked, singular, signal; total, complete, utter, absolute, thorough, perfect, downright, sheer.

**eminently** adverb *this vehicle is eminently suitable for rough terrain* VERY, greatly, highly, exceedingly, extremely, particularly, exceptionally, supremely, uniquely; obviously, clearly, conspicuously, markedly, singularly, signally, outstandingly, strikingly, notably, surpassingly; totally, completely, utterly, absolutely, thoroughly, perfectly, downright.

**emissary** noun *Clinton praised King Hussein as a bold emissary for peace* ENVOY, ambassador, delegate, attaché, consul, plenipotentiary; agent, representative, deputy; messenger, courier; nuncio.

**emission** noun *controlling the emission of carbon dioxide* DISCHARGE, release, outpouring, outflow, leak, excretion, secretion, ejection; emanation, radiation, effusion, ejaculation, disgorgement, issuance.

**emit** verb **1** *the hydrocarbons emitted from vehicle exhausts* DISCHARGE, release, give out/off, pour out, send forth, throw out, void, vent, issue; leak, ooze, excrete, disgorge, secrete, eject, ejaculate; spout, belch, spew out; emanate, radiate, exude. ANTONYM absorb.

**2** *he emitted a loud cry* UTTER, voice, let out, produce, give vent to, come out with, vocalize.

**emolument** noun *formal his name alone is worth the emolument they're willing to offer* SALARY, pay, payment, wage(s), earnings, allowance, stipend, honorarium, reward, premium; fee, charge, consideration; income, profit, gain, return.

**emotion** noun **1** *she was good at hiding her emotions* FEELING, sentiment; reaction, response.

**2** *overcome by emotion, she turned away* PASSION, strength of feeling, warmth of feeling.

**3** *responses based purely on emotion* INSTINCT, intuition, gut feeling; sentiment, the heart.

THE RIGHT WORD **emotion, affect, feeling, passion, sentiment**

A **feeling** can be almost any subjective reaction or state—pleasant or unpleasant, strong or mild, positive or negative—that is characterized by an emotional response (*a feeling of insecurity*; *a feeling of pleasure*). An **emotion** is a very intense feeling, which often involves a physical as well as a mental response and implies outward expression or agitation (*to be overcome with emotion*) **Passion** suggests a powerful or overwhelming emotion, with connotations of sexual love (*their passion remained undiminished after 30 years of marriage*) or intense anger (*a passion for revenge*). There is more intellect and less feeling in **sentiment**, which is often applied to an emotion inspired by an idea (*political sentiments*; *antiwar sentiments*). *Sentiment* also suggests a refined or slightly artificial feeling (*a speech marked by sentiment rather than passion*). **Affect** is a formal psychological term that refers to an observed emotional state (*heavily sedated, he spoke without affect*).

**emotional** adjective **1** *an emotional young man* PASSIONATE, hot-blooded, ardent, fervent, excitable, temperamental, melodramatic, tempestuous; demonstrative, responsive, tender, loving, feeling, sentimental, sensitive. ANTONYMS cold, apathetic.

**2** *he paid an emotional tribute to his wife* POIGNANT, moving, touching, affecting, powerful, stirring, emotive, heartrending, heartwarming, impassioned, dramatic; haunting, pathetic, sentimental; *informal* tear-jerking. ANTONYM unfeeling.

**3** *during the speech we all became a little emotional* TEARFUL, teary-eyed, sad, choked up, weepy; *formal, literary* lachrymose. ANTONYM dry-eyed.

**4** *their emotional needs are often ignored* SPIRITUAL, inner, psychological, psychic, of the heart. ANTONYM material.

**emotionless** adjective *emotionless faces* UNEMOTIONAL, unfeeling, dispassionate, passionless, unexpressive, inexpressive, cool, cold, cold-blooded, impassive, indifferent, detached, remote, aloof; toneless, flat, dead, expressionless, blank, wooden, stony, deadpan, vacant, poker-faced.

**emotive** adjective **1** *a highly emotive book.* See EMOTIONAL sense 2.

**2** *an emotive issue* CONTROVERSIAL, contentious, inflammatory; sensitive, delicate, difficult, problematic, touchy, awkward, prickly, ticklish.

**empathize** verb *John could* ***empathize with*** *the survivors* IDENTIFY WITH, sympathize with, be in sympathy with, understand, share the feelings of, be in tune with; be on the same wavelength as, talk the same language as; relate to, feel for, have insight into; *informal* put oneself in someone else's shoes.

**emperor** noun *the emperor of Japan* RULER, sovereign, king, monarch, potentate; *historical* czar, kaiser, mikado, khan.

**emphasis** noun **1** *the curriculum gave more emphasis to reading and writing* PROMINENCE, importance, significance, value; stress, weight, accent, attention, priority, preeminence, urgency, force.

**2** *the emphasis is on the word "little"* STRESS, accent, accentuation, weight, prominence; beat; *Prosody* ictus.

**emphasize** verb *the profile emphasizes Orgento's dedication to feeding the hungry* STRESS, underline, highlight, focus attention on, point up, lay stress on, draw attention to, spotlight, foreground, play up, make a point of; bring to the fore, insist on, belabor; accent, accentuate, underscore; *informal* press home, rub it in. ANTONYM understate.

**emphatic** adjective **1** *an emphatic denial* VEHEMENT, firm, wholehearted, forceful, forcible, energetic, vigorous, direct, assertive, insistent; certain, definite, out-and-out, one hundred percent; decided, determined, categorical, unqualified, unconditional, unequivocal, unambiguous, absolute, explicit, downright, outright, clear. ANTONYMS hesitant, tentative.

**2** *an emphatic victory* CONCLUSIVE, decisive, decided, unmistakable; resounding, telling; *informal* thundering. ANTONYM narrow.

**empire** noun **1** *the Ottoman Empire* KINGDOM, realm, domain, territory, imperium; commonwealth; power, world power, superpower.

**2** *a worldwide shipping empire* ORGANIZATION, corporation, multinational, conglomerate, consortium, company, business, firm, operation.

**3** *his dream of empire* POWER, rule, ascendancy, supremacy, command, control, authority, sway, dominance, domination, dominion.

**employ** verb **1** *she employed a chauffeur* HIRE, engage, recruit, take on, secure the services of, sign up, sign, put on the payroll, enroll, appoint; retain, contract; indenture, apprentice. ANTONYM dismiss.

**2** *Julio was employed in carving a stone figure* OCCUPY, engage, involve, keep busy, tie up; absorb, engross, immerse.

**3** *the team employed subtle psychological tactics* USE, utilize, make use of, avail oneself of; apply, exercise, practice, put into practice, exert, bring into play, bring to bear; draw on, resort to, turn to, have recourse to.

**employed** adjective *it is a myth that most employed people have adequate health insurance for their families* WORKING, in work, in employment, holding down a job; earning, wage-earning, waged, breadwinning.

**employee** noun *each employee receives a Thanksgiving turkey | the slowdown has been a hard blow to our employees* WORKER, member of staff, staffer; blue-collar worker, white-collar worker, laborer, hand, hired hand; wage earner; *informal* desk jockey; **(employees)** personnel, staff, workforce, human resources.

**employer** noun **1** *his employer gave him a glowing reference* MANAGER, boss, proprietor, director, chief executive, chief, president, head man, head woman; *informal* boss man, skipper; padrone.

**2** *the largest private-sector employer in Ohio* COMPANY, firm, business, organization, manufacturer.

**employment** noun **1** *she found employment as a clerk* WORK, service, labor; a job, a post, a position, a situation, an occupation, a profession, a trade, a line of work, a calling, a vocation, a craft, a pursuit; *archaic* employ.

**2** *the employment of children* HIRING, hire, engagement, taking on; apprenticing.

**3** *the employment of nuclear weapons* USE, utilization, application, exercise.

**emporium** noun *a furniture emporium* STORE, shop, outlet, retail outlet, superstore, megastore, department store, chain store, supermarket; establishment.

**empower** verb **1** *the act empowered police to arrest dissenters* AUTHORIZE, entitle, permit, allow, license, sanction, warrant, commission, delegate, qualify, enable, equip. ANTONYM forbid.

**2** *movements to empower the poor* EMANCIPATE, unshackle, set free, liberate. ANTONYM enslave.

**emptiness** noun *she had filled an emptiness in his life* VOID, vacuum, empty space, vacuity, gap, vacancy, hole, lack.

**empty** adjective **1** *an empty house* VACANT, unoccupied, uninhabited, untenanted, bare, desolate, deserted, abandoned; clear, free. ANTONYM full.

**2** *an empty threat* MEANINGLESS, hollow, idle, vain, futile, worthless, useless, nugatory, insubstantial, ineffective, ineffectual. ANTONYMS meaningful, serious.

**3** *without her, my life is empty* FUTILE, pointless, purposeless, worthless, meaningless, valueless, of no value, useless, of no use, aimless, senseless, hollow, barren, insignificant, inconsequential, trivial. ANTONYM worthwhile.

**4** *his eyes were empty* BLANK, expressionless, vacant, deadpan, wooden, stony, impassive, absent, glazed, fixed, lifeless, emotionless, unresponsive. ANTONYM expressive.

▸ verb **1** *I emptied the dishwasher* UNLOAD, unpack, void; clear, evacuate. ANTONYMS fill, load.

**2** *he emptied out the contents of the case* REMOVE, take out, extract, tip out, pour out, dump out, drain.

**empty-headed** adjective *they treat her like some empty-headed bimbo* STUPID, foolish, silly, unintelligent, idiotic, brainless, witless, vacuous, stunned, vapid, featherbrained, birdbrained, harebrained, scatterbrained, thoughtless, imbecilic; *informal* halfwitted, dumb, dim, airheaded, brain-dead, dippy, dizzy, dopey, flaky, soft in the head, slow on the uptake, ditzy, dumb-ass. ANTONYM intelligent.

**enable** verb *the brace will enable you to walk more steadily* ALLOW, permit, let, give the means, equip, empower, make able, fit; make possible, facilitate; authorize, entitle, qualify; *formal* capacitate. ANTONYM prevent.

**enact** verb **1** *the charter was enacted in 1982* PASS, make law, legislate; approve, ratify, sanction, authorize; impose, lay down, bring down. ANTONYM repeal.

**2** *members of the church enacted the Nativity* ACT OUT, act, perform, appear in, stage, mount, put on, present.

**enactment** noun **1** *the enactment of a Bill of Rights* PASSING; ratification, sanction, approval, authorization; imposition.

**2** *congressional enactments* ACT, law, bylaw, ruling, rule, regulation, statute, measure; *formal* ordinance; **(enactments)** legislation.

**enamored** adjective *she was secretly* ***enamored of*** *the prince* IN LOVE WITH, infatuated with, besotted with, smitten with, captivated by, enchanted by, fascinated by, bewitched by, beguiled by; keen on, taken with; *informal* mad about, crazy about, wild about, bowled over by, stuck on, hot for, sweet on, carrying a torch for, moonstruck by; *literary* ensorcelled by.

**encampment** noun *Dolan and Martini reached the encamp-*

*ment only minutes before daybreak* CAMP, military camp, bivouac, cantonment; campsite, camping ground; tents.

**encapsulate** verb **1** *their conclusions are encapsulated in one sentence* SUMMARIZE, sum up, give the gist of, put in a nutshell; capture, express.

**2** *seeds encapsulated in resin* ENCLOSE, encase, contain, envelop, enfold, sheath, cocoon, surround.

**enchant** verb *these tales are sure to enchant your little ones | mermaids enchanted the sailors* CAPTIVATE, charm, delight, enrapture, entrance, enthrall, beguile, bewitch, spellbind, fascinate, hypnotize, mesmerize, rivet, grip, transfix; *rare* ensorcell; *informal* bowl someone over. ANTONYM bore.

**enchanter** noun *an evil enchanter named Norg* WIZARD, witch, sorcerer, warlock, magician, necromancer, magus; witch doctor, medicine man, shaman; *archaic* mage; *rare* thaumaturge.

**enchanting** adjective *an enchanting ballerina* CAPTIVATING, charming, delightful, bewitching, beguiling, adorable, lovely, attractive, appealing, engaging, winning, fetching, winsome, alluring, disarming, seductive, irresistible, fascinating; *dated* taking.

**enchantment** noun **1** *a race of giants skilled in enchantment* MAGIC, witchcraft, sorcery, wizardry, necromancy; charms, spells, incantations, mojo; *rare* thaumaturgy.

**2** *the enchantment of the garden by moonlight* ALLURE, delight, charm, beauty, attractiveness, appeal, fascination, irresistibility, magnetism, pull, draw, lure.

**3** *being with him was sheer enchantment* BLISS, ecstasy, heaven, rapture, joy.

**enchantress** noun *the enchantress put a curse on all the young men of Underwood Village* WITCH, sorceress, magician, fairy; Circe, siren.

**encircle** verb *". . . and the smoke, it encircled his head like a wreath"* SURROUND, enclose, circle, girdle, ring, encompass; close in, shut in, fence in, wall in, hem in, confine; *literary* gird, engirdle. See note at CIRCUMSCRIBE.

**enclose** verb **1** *tall trees enclosed the campsite* SURROUND, circle, ring, girdle, encompass, encircle; confine, close in, shut in, corral, fence in, wall in, hedge in, hem in; *literary* gird, engirdle. See note at CIRCUMSCRIBE.

**2** *please enclose a stamped addressed envelope* INCLUDE, insert, put in; send.

**enclosure** noun *they drove the donkeys into the enclosure* PADDOCK, fold, pen, compound, stockade, ring, yard; sty, coop, corral.

**encompass** verb **1** *the apartment buildings encompass common recreational grounds, complete with swimming pool and tennis court* SURROUND, enclose, encircle, circumscribe, bound, border; *literary* gird, engird; *rare* compass. See note at CIRCUMSCRIBE.

**2** *the debates encompassed a vast range of subjects* COVER, embrace, include, incorporate, take in, contain, comprise, involve, deal with, range across; *formal* comprehend.

**encounter** verb **1** *I encountered a teacher I used to know* MEET, meet by chance, run into, come across/upon, stumble across/on/upon, chance on/upon, happen on/upon; *informal* bump into.

**2** *we encountered a slight problem* EXPERIENCE, hit, run into, come up against, face, be faced with, confront.

▸ noun **1** *an unexpected encounter* MEETING, chance meeting.

**2** *a violent encounter between police and demonstrators* BATTLE, fight, clash, confrontation, struggle, skirmish, engagement; *informal* run-in, set-to, scrap.

**encourage** verb **1** *the players were encouraged by the crowd's response* HEARTEN, cheer, buoy up, uplift, inspire, motivate, spur on, stir, stir up, fire up, stimulate, invigorate, vitalize, revitalize, embolden, fortify, rally; *informal* buck up, pep up, give a shot in the arm to. ANTONYM discourage.

**2** *she had encouraged him to go* PERSUADE, coax, urge, press, push, pressure, pressurize, prod, goad, egg on, prompt, influence, sway; *informal* put ideas into one's head. ANTONYM dissuade.

**3** *the municipal government must encourage local businesses* SUPPORT, back, champion, promote, further, foster, nurture, cultivate, strengthen, stimulate; help, assist, aid, boost, fuel. ANTONYM hinder.

**THE RIGHT WORD encourage, embolden, foster, hearten, inspire, instigate, stimulate**

To **encourage** is to give active help or to raise confidence to the point where one dares to do what is difficult (*encouraged by her teacher, she set her sights on attending Harvard*). **Embolden** also entails giving confidence or boldness, but it implies overcoming reluctance or shyness (*success as a public speaker emboldened her to enter politics*). To **hearten** is to put one's heart into or to renew someone's spirit (*heartened by the news of his recovery*), and to **inspire** is to infuse with confidence, resolution, or enthusiasm (*inspired by her mother's example, she started exercising regularly*). To **foster** is to encourage by nurturing or extending aid (*to foster the growth of small businesses by offering low-interest loans*); in some contexts, *foster* suggests an unwise or controversial kind of help (*to foster rebellion among local farmers*). **Instigate** also implies that what is being encouraged is not necessarily desirable (*to instigate a fight*), while **stimulate** is a more neutral term meaning to rouse to action or effort (*to stimulate the growth of crops; to stimulate an interest in literature*).

**encouragement** noun **1** *she needed a bit of encouragement* HEARTENING, cheering up, inspiration, motivation, stimulation, fortification; support, morale-boosting, a boost, a shot in the arm.

**2** *they required no encouragement to get back to work* PERSUASION, coaxing, urging, pep talk, pressure, prodding, prompting; spur, goad, inducement, incentive, bait, motive; *informal* carrot.

**3** *the encouragement of foreign investment* SUPPORT, backing, championship, championing, sponsoring, promotion, furtherance, furthering, fostering, nurture, cultivation; help, assistance, boosterism.

**encroach** verb *she didn't want to* ***encroach on*** *his privacy* INTRUDE ON, trespass on, impinge on, obtrude on, impose oneself on, invade, infiltrate, interrupt, infringe on, violate, interfere with, disturb; *informal* horn in on, muscle in on; *archaic* entrench on.

**encroachment** noun *the* ***encroachment on*** *their territory* INTRUSION ON, trespass on, invasion of, infiltration of, incursion into, appropriation of; infringement of, impingement on.

**encumber** verb **1** *her movements were encumbered by her heavy skirts* HAMPER, hinder, obstruct, impede, cramp, inhibit, restrict, limit, constrain, restrain, bog down, retard, slow (down); inconvenience, disadvantage, handicap. See note at HINDER.

**2** *they are encumbered with debt* BURDEN, load, weigh down, saddle; overwhelm, tax, stress, strain, overload, overburden.

**encumbrance** noun **1** *he soon found the old equipment a great encumbrance* HINDRANCE, obstruction, obstacle, impediment, constraint, handicap, inconvenience, nuisance, disadvantage, drawback; *literary* trammel; *archaic* cumber.

**2** *she knew she was an encumbrance to him* BURDEN, responsibility, obligation, liability, weight, load, stress, strain, pressure, trouble, worry; millstone, albatross, cross to bear; *informal* ball and chain.

**encyclopedic** adjective *his encyclopedic knowledge of food* COMPREHENSIVE, complete, thorough, thoroughgoing, full, exhaustive, in-depth, wide-ranging, all-inclusive, all-embracing, all-encompassing, universal, vast; *formal* compendious.

**end** noun **1** *the end of the road* EXTREMITY, furthermost part, limit; margin, edge, border, boundary, periphery; point, tip, tail end, tag end, terminus. ANTONYMS beginning, middle.

**2** *the end of the novel* CONCLUSION, termination, ending, finish, close, resolution, climax, finale, culmination, denouement; epilogue, coda, peroration. ANTONYM beginning.

**3** *wealth is a means and not an end in itself* AIM, goal, purpose, objective, object, holy grail, target; intention, intent, design, motive; aspiration, wish, desire, ambition.

**4** *the commercial end of the business* ASPECT, side, section, area, field, part, share, portion, segment, province.

**5** *his end might come at any time* DEATH, dying, demise, passing, expiry, quietus; doom, extinction, annihilation, extermination, destruction; downfall, ruin, ruination, Waterloo; *informal* curtains; *formal* decease. ANTONYM birth.

▸ verb **1** *the show* ***ended with*** *a wedding scene* FINISH WITH, conclude with, terminate with, come to an end with, draw to a close with, close with, stop with, cease with; culminate in, climax with, build up to, lead up to, come to a head with. ANTONYMS begin, start.

**2** *she ended their relationship* BREAK OFF, call off, bring to an end, put an end to, stop, finish, terminate, discontinue, curtail; dissolve, cancel, annul; *informal* can, ax. See note at BEGIN. ANTONYM begin.

**endanger** verb *the pollutants endanger the fish* IMPERIL, jeopardize, risk, put at risk, put in danger, expose to danger; threaten, pose a threat to, be a danger to, be detrimental to, damage, injure, harm; *archaic* peril.

**endearing** adjective *the baby ducklings are endearing* LOVABLE, adorable, cute, sweet, dear, delightful, lovely, charming, appealing, attractive, engaging, winning, captivating, enchanting, beguiling, winsome.

**endearment** noun **1** *his murmured endearments* TERM OF AFFECTION, term of endearment, pet name; **(endearments)** sweet nothings, sweet talk.

**2** *he spoke to her without endearment* AFFECTION, fondness, tenderness, feeling, sentiment, warmth, love, liking, care.

**endeavor** verb *the company endeavored to expand its activities* TRY, attempt, seek, undertake, aspire, aim, set out; strive, struggle, labor, toil, work, exert oneself, apply oneself, do one's best, do one's utmost, give one's all, be at pains; *informal* have a go, have a shot, have a stab, give something one's best shot, do one's damnedest, go all out, bend over backwards; *formal* essay.

▸ noun **1** *an endeavor to build a more buoyant economy* ATTEMPT, try, bid, effort, venture; *informal* go, crack, shot, stab; *formal* essay.

**2** *several days of endeavor* EFFORT, exertion, striving, struggling, laboring, toil, struggle, labor, hard work, application, industry; pains; *informal* sweat, 'blood, sweat, and tears', elbow grease; *literary* travail.

**3** *an extremely unwise endeavor* UNDERTAKING, enterprise, venture, exercise, activity, exploit, deed, act, action, move; scheme, plan, project; *informal* caper.

**ending** noun *a happy ending* END, finish, close, closing, conclusion, resolution, summing-up, windup, denouement, finale; cessation, stopping, termination, discontinuation. ANTONYM beginning.

**endless** adjective **1** *a woman with endless energy* UNLIMITED, limitless, infinite, inexhaustible, boundless, unbounded, untold, immeasurable, measureless, incalculable; abundant, abounding, great; bottomless, ceaseless, unceasing, unending, without end, everlasting, constant, continuous, continual, interminable, unfading, unfailing, perpetual, eternal, enduring, lasting. See note at ETERNAL. ANTONYMS limited, transient.

**2** *as children we played endless games* COUNTLESS, innumerable, untold, legion, numberless, unnumbered, numerous, very many, manifold, multitudinous, multifarious; a great number of, infinite numbers of, a multitude of; *informal* umpteen, no end of, loads of, stacks of, heaps of, masses of, oodles of, scads of, zillions of, gazillions of; *literary* myriad, divers. ANTONYM few.

**endorse** verb **1** *endorse a product* SUPPORT, back, agree with, approve (of), favor, subscribe to, recommend, champion, stick up for, uphold, affirm, sanction; *informal* throw one's weight behind, okay. See note at APPROVE. ANTONYM oppose.

2 *endorse a check* COUNTERSIGN, sign, autograph, authenticate; *rare* chirographate.

**endorsement** noun *the proposal won their overwhelming endorsement* SUPPORT, backing, approval, seal of approval, agreement, recommendation, championship, patronage, affirmation, sanction; *informal* buy-in.

**endow** verb 1 *the CEO endowed a hospital for sick kids* FINANCE, fund, pay for, provide for, subsidize, support financially, put up the money for; establish, found, set up, institute.

2 *nature endowed fish with gills* PROVIDE, supply, furnish, equip, invest, favor, bless, grace, gift; give, bestow; *literary* endue.

**endowment** noun 1 *the endowment of a Chair of Botany* FUNDING, financing, subsidizing; establishment, foundation, institution.

2 *her will contained a generous endowment* BEQUEST, legacy, inheritance; gift, present, grant, award, donation, contribution, subsidy, settlement; *formal* benefaction.

3 *his natural endowments* QUALITY, characteristic, feature, attribute, facility, faculty, ability, talent, gift, strength, aptitude, capability, capacity.

**endurance** noun 1 *she pushed him beyond the limit of his endurance* TOLERATION, tolerance, sufferance, forbearance, patience, acceptance, resignation, stoicism.

2 *the race is a test of endurance* STAMINA, staying power, fortitude, perseverance, persistence, tenacity, doggedness, grit, indefatigability, resolution, determination; *formal* pertinacity.

**endure** verb 1 *he endured years of pain* UNDERGO, go through, live through, experience, meet, encounter; cope with, deal with, face, suffer, tolerate, put up with, brave, bear, withstand, sustain, weather; *Brit.* thole.

2 *I cannot endure such behavior* TOLERATE, bear, put up with, suffer, take, abide; *informal* hack, stand for, stomach, swallow, hold with; *formal* brook.

3 *our love will endure forever* LAST, live, live on, go on, survive, abide, continue, persist, persevere, remain, stay. ANTONYM fade.

**enduring** adjective *our enduring faith* LASTING, long-lasting, abiding, durable, continuing, persisting, eternal, perennial, permanent, unending, everlasting; constant, stable, steady, steadfast, fixed, firm, unwavering, unfaltering, unchanging; *literary* amaranthine. ANTONYM short-lived.

**enemy** noun *he and his brother have been enemies for years | the enemy would strike at dawn* OPPONENT, adversary, foe, rival, antagonist, combatant, challenger, competitor, opposer; **(the enemy)** the opposition, the competition, the other side, the opposing side. ANTONYMS ally, friend.

**energetic** adjective 1 *an energetic teacher* ACTIVE, lively, dynamic, zestful, spirited, animated, vital, vibrant, bouncy, bubbly, exuberant, ebullient, perky, frisky, sprightly, tireless, indefatigable, enthusiastic; *informal* peppy, feisty, full of beans, bright-eyed and bushy-tailed. ANTONYMS lethargic, inactive.

2 *energetic exercises* VIGOROUS, strenuous, brisk; hard, arduous, demanding, taxing, tough, rigorous. ANTONYM gentle.

3 *an energetic advertising campaign* FORCEFUL, vigorous, high-powered, all-out, determined, bold, powerful, potent; intensive, hard-hitting, pulling no punches, aggressive, high-octane; *informal* punchy, in-your-face. ANTONYM halfhearted.

**energize** verb 1 *people are energized by his ideas* ENLIVEN, liven up, animate, vitalize, invigorate, perk up, excite, electrify, stimulate, stir up, fire up, rouse, motivate, move, drive, spur on, encourage, galvanize; *informal* pep up, buck up, jump-start, kick-start, give a shot in the arm to, turbocharge.

2 *floor sensors energized by standing passengers* ACTIVATE, trigger, trip, operate, actuate, switch on, turn on, start, start up, power.

**energy** noun *a good night's sleep will restore their energy* VITALITY, vigor, life, liveliness, animation, vivacity, spirit, spiritedness, verve, enthusiasm, zest, vibrancy, spark, sparkle, effervescence, ebullience, exuberance, buoyancy, sprightliness; strength, stamina, forcefulness, power, dynamism, drive; fire, passion, ardor, zeal; *informal* zip, zing, pep, pizzazz, punch, bounce, oomph, moxie, mojo, go, get-up-and-go, vim and vigor, feistiness.

**enervate** verb *the hot weather enervated her* EXHAUST, tire, fatigue, weary, wear out, devitalize, drain, sap, weaken, enfeeble, debilitate, incapacitate, prostrate; *informal* knock out, do in, shatter. ANTONYM invigorate.

**enfold** verb 1 *the summit was enfolded in white cloud* ENVELOP, engulf, sheathe, swathe, swaddle, cocoon, shroud, veil, cloak, drape, cover; surround, enclose, encase, encircle; *literary* enshroud, mantle.

2 *he enfolded her in his arms* CLASP, hold, fold, wrap, squeeze, clutch, gather; embrace, hug, cuddle; *literary* embosom.

**enforce** verb 1 *the sheriff enforced the law* IMPOSE, apply, administer, implement, bring to bear, discharge, execute, prosecute.

2 *they cannot enforce cooperation between the parties* FORCE, compel, coerce, exact, extort; *archaic* constrain.

**enforced** adjective *an enforced break from work* COMPULSORY, obligatory, mandatory, involuntary, forced, imposed, required, requisite, stipulated, prescribed, contractual, binding, necessary, unavoidable, inescapable. ANTONYM voluntary.

**enfranchise** verb 1 *women were enfranchised in Manitoba in 1916* GIVE THE VOTE TO, give suffrage to, grant suffrage to.

2 *historical he enfranchised his slaves* EMANCIPATE, liberate, free, set free, release; unchain, unyoke, unfetter, unshackle.

**engage** verb 1 *tasks that engage children's interest* CAPTURE, catch, arrest, grab, snag, draw, attract, gain, win, hold, grip, captivate, engross, absorb, occupy. ANTONYM lose.

2 *he engaged a landscaper to do the job* EMPLOY, hire, recruit,

take on, secure the services of, put on the payroll, enroll, appoint. ANTONYM dismiss.

3 *he engaged to pay them $10,000* CONTRACT, promise, agree, pledge, vow, covenant, commit oneself, bind oneself, undertake, enter into an agreement.

4 *the chance to **engage in** many social activities* PARTICIPATE IN, take part in, join in, become involved in, go in for, partake in/of, share in, play a part/role in; have a hand in, be a party to, enter into.

5 *infantry units engaged the enemy* FIGHT, do battle with, wage war on/against, attack, take on, set upon, clash with, skirmish with; encounter, meet.

6 *he engaged the gears* INTERLOCK, interconnect, mesh, intermesh, fit together, join, join together, unite, connect, couple. ANTONYM disengage.

**engaged** adjective 1 *he's otherwise engaged* BUSY, occupied, unavailable; *informal* tied up. See note at BUSY. ANTONYMS free, unoccupied.

2 *she's engaged to an American guy* BETROTHED, promised in marriage, pledged in marriage; attached; *informal* spoken for; *literary* affianced; *archaic* plighted, espoused. ANTONYM unattached.

**engagement** noun 1 *they broke off their engagement* MARRIAGE CONTRACT; *dated* betrothal; *archaic* espousal.

2 *a social engagement* APPOINTMENT, meeting, arrangement, commitment; date, assignation, rendezvous; *literary* tryst.

3 *the first engagement of the war* BATTLE, fight, clash, confrontation, encounter, conflict, skirmish; warfare, action, combat, hostilities; *informal* dogfight.

**engaging** adjective 1 *an engaging young person* CHARMING, appealing, attractive, pretty, delightful, lovely, pleasing, pleasant, agreeable, likable, winsome, enchanting, captivating. ANTONYM unappealing.

2 *an engaging story* INTERESTING, engrossing, gripping, involving, absorbing, fascinating. ANTONYM boring.

**engender** verb 1 *his works engendered considerable controversy* CAUSE, be the cause of, give rise to, bring about, occasion, lead to, result in, produce, create, generate, arouse, rouse, inspire, provoke, prompt, kindle, trigger, spark, stir up, whip up, induce, incite, instigate, foment; *literary* beget, enkindle.

2 *archaic he engendered six children* FATHER, sire, bring into the world, spawn, breed; *literary* beget.

**engine** noun 1 *a power-generating engine* MOTOR, machine, mechanism; jet, turbojet, turboprop, turbofan, turbine, generator.

2 *the main engine of change* CAUSE, agent, instrument, originator, initiator, generator.

3 *historical engines of war* DEVICE, contraption, apparatus, machine, appliance, mechanism, implement, instrument, tool.

**engineer** noun 1 *a structural engineer* designer, planner, builder.

2 *the ship's engineer* OPERATOR, driver, controller.

3 *the prime engineer of the approach* ORIGINATOR, deviser, designer, architect, inventor, developer, creator; mastermind.

▸ verb *he engineered a takeover deal* BRING ABOUT, arrange, pull off, bring off, contrive, maneuver, manipulate, negotiate, organize, orchestrate, choreograph, mount, stage, mastermind, originate, manage, stage-manage, coordinate, control, superintend, direct, conduct; *informal* wangle.

**engrave** verb 1 *my name was engraved on the ring* CARVE, inscribe, cut (in), incise, chisel, chase, score, notch, etch, imprint, impress.

2 *the image was engraved in his memory* FIX, set, imprint, stamp, brand, impress, embed, etch.

**engraving** noun *an engraving of a clipper ship* ETCHING, print, impression, lithograph; plate, dry point, woodcut, linocut.

**engross** verb *Poppa's stories will engross them* ABSORB, engage, rivet, grip, hold, interest, involve, occupy, preoccupy; fascinate, captivate, enthrall, intrigue.

**engrossed** adjective *Leopold is **engrossed in** his stamp collection* ABSORBED IN, involved in, interested in, engaged in, occupied by/with, preoccupied by/with, immersed in, caught up in, riveted by, gripped by, rapt in, fascinated by/with, intent on, captivated by, enthralled by/with, intrigued by/with.

**engrossing** adjective *an engrossing murder mystery* ABSORBING, interesting, riveting, gripping, captivating, compelling, fascinating, intriguing, enthralling, engaging; *informal* unputdownable.

**engulf** verb *waves engulfed the sand castles* INUNDATE, flood, deluge, immerse, swamp, swallow up, submerge; bury, envelop, overwhelm.

**enhance** verb *background music will enhance the mood* INCREASE, add to, intensify, heighten, magnify, amplify, inflate, strengthen, build up, supplement, augment, boost, raise, lift, elevate, exalt; improve, enrich, complement. ANTONYM diminish.

**enigma** noun *how it works is an enigma to me* MYSTERY, puzzle, riddle, conundrum, paradox, problem, quandary; a closed book; *informal* poser. See note at RIDDLE.

**enigmatic** adjective *photos of his wife, the enigmatic artist Georgia O'Keeffe* MYSTERIOUS, inscrutable, puzzling, mystifying, baffling, perplexing, impenetrable, unfathomable, sphinxlike, Delphic, oracular; cryptic, elliptical, ambiguous, equivocal, paradoxical, obscure, oblique, secret. See note at DOUBTFUL.

**enjoin** verb *I enjoin you to admit your mistake* URGE, encourage, admonish, press; instruct, direct, require, order, command, tell, call on, demand, charge; *formal* adjure; *literary* bid. See note at PROHIBIT.

**enjoy** verb 1 *he enjoys playing the piano* LIKE, love, be fond of, be entertained by, take pleasure in, be keen on, delight in, appreciate, relish, revel in, adore, lap up, savor, luxuriate in, bask in; *informal* get a kick out of, get a thrill out of, dig. ANTONYMS dislike, hate.

**2** *she had always enjoyed good health* BENEFIT FROM, have the benefit of; be blessed with, be favored with, be endowed with, be possessed of, possess, own, boast. ANTONYMS dislike, lack.

PHRASE: **enjoy oneself** *she travels just to enjoy herself* HAVE FUN, have a good time, have the time of one's life; make merry, celebrate, revel, disport; *informal* party, love life, have a ball, have a whale of a time, whoop it up, let one's hair down.

**enjoyable** adjective *a most enjoyable movie* ENTERTAINING, amusing, agreeable, pleasurable, diverting, engaging, delightful, to one's liking, pleasant, congenial, convivial, lovely, fine, good, great, delicious, delectable, satisfying, gratifying; marvelous, wonderful, magnificent, splendid; *informal* super, fantastic, fabulous, fab, terrific, magic, killer. See note at PLEASANT.

**enjoyment** noun *he has brought enjoyment to millions* PLEASURE, fun, entertainment, amusement, diversion, recreation, relaxation; delight, happiness, merriment, joy, gaiety, jollity; satisfaction, gratification, liking, relish, gusto; *humorous* delectation.

**enlarge** verb **1** *they enlarged the scope of their research* EXTEND, expand, grow, add to, amplify, augment, magnify, build up, supplement; widen, broaden, stretch, lengthen; elongate, deepen, thicken. ANTONYM reduce.

**2** *the lymph glands had enlarged* SWELL, distend, bloat, bulge, dilate, tumefy, blow up, puff up, balloon. ANTONYM shrink.

**3** *he **enlarged on** this subject* ELABORATE ON, expand on, add to, build on, flesh out, add detail to, expatiate on; develop, fill out, embellish, embroider.

**enlargement** noun *the enlargement of the park* EXPANSION, extension, growth, amplification, augmentation, addition, magnification, widening, broadening, lengthening; elongation, deepening, thickening; swelling, distension, dilation.

**enlighten** verb *please enlighten us about the latest developments* INFORM, tell, make aware, open someone's eyes, notify, illuminate, apprise, brief, update, bring up to date; disabuse, set straight; *informal* put in the picture, clue in, fill in, put wise, bring up to speed.

**enlightened** adjective *without a free press there cannot be an enlightened people* INFORMED, well-informed, aware, sophisticated, advanced, developed, liberal, open-minded, broad-minded, educated, knowledgeable, wise; civilized, refined, cultured, cultivated. ANTONYM benighted.

**enlightenment** noun *sharing her musical enlightenment with her children* INSIGHT, understanding, awareness, wisdom, education, learning, knowledge; illumination, awakening, instruction, teaching; sophistication, advancement, development, open-mindedness, broad-mindedness; culture, refinement, cultivation, civilization.

**enlist** verb **1** *he **enlisted in** the scouts* JOIN UP WITH, join, enroll in, sign up for, volunteer for.

**2** *he was enlisted in the army* RECRUIT, call up, enroll, sign up; conscript; draft, induct; *archaic* levy.

**3** *he enlisted the help of a friend* OBTAIN, engage, secure, win, get, procure.

**enliven** verb **1** *a meeting enlivened by her wit and vivacity* LIVEN UP, spice up, add spice to, ginger up, vitalize, leaven; *informal* perk up, pep up. See note at QUICKEN.

**2** *the visit had enlivened my mother* CHEER UP, brighten up, liven up, raise someone's spirits, uplift, gladden, buoy up, animate, vivify, vitalize, invigorate, restore, revive, refresh, rejuvenate, stimulate, rouse, boost, exhilarate, light a fire under; *informal* perk up, buck up, pep up.

**en masse** adverb *the angry audience walked out en masse* (ALL) TOGETHER, as a group, as one, en bloc, as a whole, wholesale; unanimously, with one voice.

**enmity** noun *a world free from enmity between nations and races* HOSTILITY, animosity, antagonism, friction, antipathy, animus, acrimony, bitterness, rancor, resentment, aversion, ill feeling, bad feeling, ill will, bad blood, hatred, hate, loathing, odium; malice, spite, spitefulness, venom, malevolence. ANTONYM friendship.

**ennoble** verb *the original vision of the modern Olympic Games was to ennoble and strengthen sports* DIGNIFY, honor, exalt, elevate, raise, enhance, add dignity to, distinguish; magnify, glorify, aggrandize. ANTONYM demean.

**ennui** noun *an ennui bred of long familiarity* BOREDOM, tedium, listlessness, lethargy, lassitude, languor, weariness, enervation; malaise, dissatisfaction, melancholy, depression, world-weariness, Weltschmerz.

**enormity** noun **1** *the enormity of the task* IMMENSITY, hugeness; size, extent, magnitude, greatness.

**2** *the enormity of his crimes* WICKEDNESS, evil, vileness, baseness, depravity; outrageousness, monstrousness, hideousness, heinousness, horror, atrocity; villainy, cruelty, inhumanity, mercilessness, brutality, savagery, viciousness.

**3** *the enormities of the regime* OUTRAGE, horror, evil, atrocity, barbarity, abomination, monstrosity, obscenity, iniquity; crime, sin, violation, wrong, offense, disgrace, injustice, abuse.

**USAGE NOTE enormity**

This word is imprecisely used to mean 'great size,' as in *it is difficult to comprehend the enormity of the continent,* but the original and preferred meaning is 'extreme wickedness,' as in *the enormity of the mass murders.* To indicate enormous size, the words *enormousness, immensity, vastness, hugeness,* etc., are preferable.

**enormous** adjective *enormous waves battered the shore* HUGE, vast, immense, gigantic, very big, great, giant, massive, colossal, mammoth, tremendous, mighty, monumental, epic, prodigious, mountainous, king-size(d), economy-size(d), titanic, towering, elephantine, gargantuan, Brobdingnagian; *in-*

*formal* mega, monster, whopping, humongous, jumbo, astronomical, ginormous. ANTONYM tiny.

**enormously** adverb **1** *an enormously important factor* VERY, extremely, really, exceedingly, exceptionally, tremendously, immensely, hugely; singularly, particularly, eminently; *informal* terrifically, awfully, seriously, desperately, ultra, damn, damned, darn, darned; real, mighty. ANTONYMS slightly, moderately.

**2** *prices vary enormously* CONSIDERABLY, greatly, widely, very much, a great deal, a lot. ANTONYMS slightly, not at all.

**enough** adjective *they had enough food* SUFFICIENT, adequate, ample, the necessary; *informal* plenty of. ANTONYM insufficient.

▸ pronoun *there's enough for everyone* SUFFICIENT, plenty, a sufficient amount, an adequate amount, as much as necessary; a sufficiency, an ample supply; one's fill.

**enrage** verb *the scheme is bound to enrage union members* ANGER, infuriate, incense, madden, inflame; antagonize, provoke, exasperate; *informal* drive mad/crazy, drive up the wall, make someone see red, make someone's blood boil, make someone's hackles rise, get someone's back up, get someone's dander up; *informal* tick off, piss off, burn up. ANTONYM placate.

**enraged** adjective *an enraged mob* FURIOUS, infuriated, very angry, irate, incensed, raging, incandescent, fuming, ranting, raving, seething, beside oneself; *informal* mad, hopping mad, wild, livid, boiling, apoplectic, hot under the collar, on the warpath, foaming at the mouth, steamed up, fit to be tied, pissed off, PO'd; *literary* wrathful. ANTONYM calm.

**enrapture** verb *enraptured by the music* DELIGHT, enchant, captivate, charm, enthrall, entrance, bewitch, beguile, transport, thrill, excite, exhilarate, intoxicate, take someone's breath away; *informal* bowl over, blow someone's mind; *literary* ravish.

**enrich** verb *enrich the soil with nitrogen* ENHANCE, improve, better, add to, augment; supplement, complement; boost, elevate, raise, lift, refine. ANTONYM spoil.

**enroll** verb **1** *they both **enrolled for** the course* REGISTER FOR, sign up/on for, put one's name down for, apply for, volunteer for; enter, join.

**2** *280 new members were enrolled* ACCEPT, admit, take on, register, sign on/up, recruit, engage; empanel.

**en route** adverb *he was en route from Delaware to Illinois* ON THE WAY, in transit, during the journey, along/on the road, on the move; coming, going, proceeding, traveling.

**ensconce** verb *Agnes ensconced herself in their bedroom* SETTLE, install, plant, position, seat, sit; establish, nestle; hide away, tuck away; *informal* park, plonk.

**ensemble** noun **1** *a Bulgarian folk ensemble* GROUP, band; company, troupe, cast, chorus, corps; *informal* combo.

**2** *the buildings present a charming provincial ensemble* WHOLE, entity, unit, body, set, combination, composite, package; sum, total, totality, entirety, aggregate.

**3** *a pink and black ensemble* OUTFIT, costume, suit; separates, coordinates; *informal* getup.

**enshrine** verb *the following rights should be enshrined in the treaty* PRESERVE, entrench, set down, lay down, set in stone, embody, incorporate, contain, include, treasure, immortalize, cherish.

**enshroud** verb *literary gray clouds enshrouded the city* ENVELOP, veil, shroud, swathe, cloak, cloud, enfold, surround, bury; cover, conceal, obscure, blot out, hide, mask; *literary* mantle.

**ensign** noun *the ship flew a Greek ensign* FLAG, standard, color(s), banner, pennant, pennon, streamer, banderole.

**ensnare** verb *the larvae construct pits to ensnare their prey* CAPTURE, catch, trap, entrap, snare, net; entangle, embroil, enmesh.

**ensue** verb *Evelyn showed up unexpectedly and a fierce argument ensued* RESULT, follow, develop, proceed, succeed, emerge, stem, arise, derive, issue; occur, happen, take place, come next/after, transpire, supervene; *formal* eventuate; *literary* come to pass, befall.

**ensure** verb **1** *ensure that the surface is completely clean* MAKE SURE, make certain, see to it; check, confirm, establish, verify.

**2** *legislation to ensure equal opportunities for all* SECURE, guarantee, assure, certify, safeguard, set the seal on, clinch, entrench.

**entail** verb *first, we'll need to know exactly what the job entails* INVOLVE, necessitate, require, need, demand, call for; mean, imply; cause, produce, result in, lead to, give rise to, occasion.

**entangle** verb **1** *their parachutes became entangled* TWIST, intertwine, entwine, tangle, ravel, snarl, knot, coil, mat.

**2** *the fish are easily entangled in fine nets* CATCH, capture, trap, snare, ensnare, entrap, enmesh.

**3** *he was entangled in a lawsuit* INVOLVE, implicate, embroil, mix up, catch up, bog down, mire.

**entanglement** noun **1** *their entanglement in the war* INVOLVEMENT, embroilment.

**2** *romantic entanglements* AFFAIR, relationship, love affair, romance, amour, fling, dalliance, liaison, involvement, intrigue; complication.

**enter** verb **1** *police entered the house from the side* GO IN/INTO, come in/into, get in/into, set foot in, cross the threshold of, gain access to, infiltrate, access. ANTONYM leave.

**2** *a bullet entered his chest* PENETRATE, pierce, puncture, perforate; *literary* transpierce. ANTONYM leave.

**3** *he entered politics in 1979* GET INVOLVED IN, join, throw oneself into, engage in, embark on, take up; participate in, take part in, play a part/role in, contribute to. ANTONYM leave.

**4** *the planning entered a new phase* REACH, move into, get to, begin, start, commence. ANTONYM finish.

**5** *they entered the military at eighteen* JOIN, become a member of, enroll in/for, enlist in, volunteer for, sign up for; take up. ANTONYM leave.

**6** *she entered a cooking competition* SIGN ON/UP FOR, put one's name down for, register for, enroll in/for, go in for; compete in, take part in, participate in.

**7** *the cashier entered the details in a ledger* RECORD, write, set down, put down, take down, note, jot down; put on record, minute, register, log. ANTONYM erase.

**8** *please enter your password* KEY (IN), type (in).

**9** Law *he entered a plea of guilty* SUBMIT, register, lodge, record, file, put forward, present. ANTONYM withdraw.

**enterprise** noun **1** *a joint enterprise* UNDERTAKING, endeavor, venture, exercise, activity, operation, task, business, proceeding; project, scheme, plan, program, campaign.

**2** *we want candidates with enterprise* INITIATIVE, resourcefulness, imagination, entrepreneurialism, ingenuity, inventiveness, originality, creativity; quick-wittedness, cleverness; enthusiasm, dynamism, drive, ambition, energy; boldness, daring, courage, leadership; *informal* gumption, get-up-and-go, oomph.

**3** *a profit-making enterprise* BUSINESS, company, firm, venture, organization, operation, concern, corporation, establishment, partnership; *informal* outfit, setup.

**enterprising** adjective *an enterprising farmer is now charging visitors* RESOURCEFUL, entrepreneurial, imaginative, ingenious, inventive, creative; quick-witted, clever, bright, sharp, sharp-witted; enthusiastic, dynamic, proactive, ambitious, energetic; bold, daring, courageous, adventurous; *informal* go-ahead, take-charge, self-motivated. ANTONYM unimaginative.

**entertain** verb **1** *she wrote plays to entertain them* AMUSE, divert, delight, please, charm, cheer, interest; *informal* bring the house down; engage, occupy, absorb, engross. ANTONYM bore.

**2** *he entertains foreign visitors* RECEIVE, host, play host/hostess to, invite (around/round/over), throw a party for; wine and dine, feast, cater for, feed, treat, welcome, féte.

**3** *we don't entertain much* RECEIVE GUESTS, have people around/round/over, have company, throw/have a party.

**4** *I would never entertain such an idea* CONSIDER, give consideration to, contemplate, think about, give thought to; countenance, tolerate, support; *formal* brook. ANTONYM reject.

**entertainer** noun *a family of entertainers* PERFORMER, artiste, artist.

**entertaining** adjective *Ben is an entertaining companion* DELIGHTFUL, enjoyable, diverting, amusing, pleasing, agreeable, appealing, engaging, interesting, fascinating, absorbing, compelling; humorous, funny, comical; *informal* fun.

**entertainment** noun **1** *he reads for entertainment* AMUSEMENT, pleasure, leisure, recreation, relaxation, fun, enjoyment, interest, diversion.

**2** *an entertainment for the emperor* SHOW, performance, presentation, production, extravaganza, spectacle, pageant.

**enthrall** verb *the exhibit of Calder's early mobiles enthralled us* CAPTIVATE, charm, enchant, bewitch, fascinate, beguile, entrance, delight; win, ensnare, absorb, engross, rivet, grip, transfix, hypnotize, mesmerize, spellbind. ANTONYM bore.

**enthralling** adjective *her travel journals are enthralling* FASCINATING, entrancing, enchanting, bewitching, captivating, charming, beguiling, delightful; absorbing, engrossing, compelling, riveting, gripping, exciting, spellbinding; *informal* unputdownable.

**enthuse** verb **1** *I **enthused about** the idea* RAVE ABOUT, be enthusiastic about, gush over, wax lyrical about, be effusive about, get all worked up about, rhapsodize about; praise to the skies, extol; *informal* go wild/mad/crazy about/over/for, ballyhoo.

**2** *he enthuses people* MOTIVATE, inspire, stimulate, encourage, spur (on), galvanize, rouse, excite, stir (up), fire; *rare* inspirit.

**USAGE NOTE enthuse**

The verb **enthuse** is a back-formation from the noun **enthusiasm** and, like many verbs formed from nouns in this way, it is regarded by traditionalists as unacceptable. **Enthuse** has been in the language for more than 150 years, but, before using the word in formal writing, be aware that readers familiar with its Greek meaning may find casual usage misguided or irritating. **Enthusiasm** derives from a word originally meaning 'to become inspired or possessed by a god' (*en* 'in' + *theos* 'god'). From the traditionalist point of view, *inspired* or *excited* is preferable to *enthused*.

**enthusiasm** noun **1** *she worked with enthusiasm* EAGERNESS, keenness, ardor, fervor, passion, zeal, zest, gusto, energy, verve, vigor, vehemence, fire, spirit, avidity; wholeheartedness, commitment, willingness, devotion, earnestness; *informal* get-up-and-go. ANTONYMS apathy, half-heartedness.

**2** *he responded to the proposal with enthusiasm* INTEREST, admiration, approval, support, encouragement. ANTONYMS apathy, disinterest.

**3** *they put their enthusiasms to good use* INTEREST, passion, obsession, mania; inclination, preference, penchant, predilection, fancy; pastime, hobby, recreation, pursuit.

**enthusiast** noun *a railroad enthusiast* FAN, devotee, aficionado, lover, admirer, follower; expert, connoisseur, authority, pundit; *informal* buff, bum, freak, fanatic, nut, fiend, addict, maniac; geek, eager beaver. See note at ZEALOT.

**enthusiastic** adjective *an enthusiastic supporter of Latin American baseball* EAGER, keen, avid, ardent, fervent, passionate, ebullient, zealous, vehement; excited, wholehearted, committed, devoted, fanatical, earnest; *informal* hog-wild, can-do, gung-ho, rah-rah, psyched. See note at EAGER.

**entice** verb *he tried to entice us by promising a screen test at his studio* TEMPT, lure, allure, attract, appeal to; invite, persuade, convince, beguile, coax, woo, court; seduce, lead on; *informal* sweet-talk. See note at TEMPT.

**enticement** noun *on my budget, I have to resist the enticement of colorful packaging and clever advertising* LURE, temptation, allure, attraction, appeal, draw, pull, bait; charm, seduction, fascination; *informal* come-on.

**entire** adjective **1** *I devoted my entire life to him* WHOLE, complete, total, full; undivided. ANTONYM partial.

**2** *only one of the vases is entire* INTACT, unbroken, undamaged, unimpaired, unscathed, unspoiled, perfect, in one piece. ANTONYMS partial, broken.

**3** *they are in entire agreement* ABSOLUTE, total, utter, out-and-out, thorough, wholehearted; unqualified, unreserved, outright. ANTONYMS partial, qualified.

**entirely** adverb **1** *that's entirely out of the question* ABSOLUTELY, completely, totally, wholly, utterly, quite; altogether, in every respect, thoroughly, downright, one hundred percent.

**2** *a gift entirely for charitable purposes* SOLELY, only, exclusively, purely, merely, just, alone.

**entirety** noun *I'll give you ten bucks for the entirety* WHOLE, total, aggregate, totality, sum total. ANTONYM part.

PHRASE: **in its entirety** *we heard his miserable life story, in its entirety* COMPLETELY, entirely, totally, fully, wholly; in every respect, in every way, one hundred percent, all the way, every inch, to the hilt, to the core.

**entitle** verb **1** *this pass entitles you to visit the museum* QUALIFY, make eligible, authorize, allow, permit; enable, empower.

**2** *a chapter entitled "Comedy and Tragedy"* TITLE, name, call, label, head, designate, dub; *formal* denominate.

**entity** noun **1** *a single entity* BEING, creature, individual, organism, life form; person; body, object, article, thing.

**2** *the distinction between entity and nonentity* EXISTENCE, being; life, living, animation; substance, essence, reality, actuality.

**entourage** noun *Elvis's entourage* RETINUE, escort, cortège, train, suite; court, staff, bodyguard(s); attendants, companions, retainers; *informal* posse.

**entrails** plural noun *the entrails are removed by the butcher* INTESTINES, bowels, guts, viscera, internal organs, vital organs; offal; *informal* insides, innards.

**entrance**[1] noun **1** *the main entrance* ENTRY, way in, entryway, entranceway, access, approach; door, portal, gate; opening, mouth; entrance hall, foyer, lobby, porch. ANTONYM exit.

**2** *the entrance of Mrs. Salter* APPEARANCE, arrival, entry, ingress, coming. ANTONYMS exit, departure.

**3** *he was refused entrance* ADMISSION, admittance, entry, right of entry, access, ingress.

**entrance**[2] verb **1** *I was entranced by her beauty* ENCHANT, bewitch, beguile, captivate, mesmerize, hypnotize, spellbind; enthrall, engross, absorb, fascinate; stun, stupefy, overpower, electrify; charm, dazzle, delight; *informal* bowl over, knock out.

**2** *Orpheus entranced the wild beasts* CAST A SPELL ON, bewitch, hex, spellbind, hypnotize, mesmerize.

**entrant** noun **1** *university entrants* NEW MEMBER, new arrival, beginner, newcomer, freshman, recruit; novice, neophyte, tenderfoot; *informal* rookie, newbie, greenhorn.

**2** *a prize will be awarded to the best entrant* COMPETITOR, contestant, contender, participant; candidate, applicant.

**entrap** verb **1** *fishing lines can entrap wildlife* TRAP, snare, snag, ensnare, entangle, enmesh; catch, capture.

**2** *he was entrapped by an undercover policeman* ENTICE, lure, inveigle; bait, decoy, trap; lead on, trick, deceive, dupe, hoodwink, sting; *informal* set up, frame.

**entreat** verb *my lord, I entreat you to believe me* IMPLORE, beg, plead with, pray, ask, request; bid, enjoin, appeal to, call on, petition, solicit, importune; *literary* beseech. See note at BEG.

**entreaty** noun *he ignored Gert's entreaties* PLEA, appeal, request, petition; suit, application, claim; solicitation, supplication; prayer.

**entrench** verb *post-Communist countries strive to entrench their new press freedoms* ESTABLISH, settle, lodge, set, root, install, plant, embed, seat; enshrine; *informal* dig (oneself) in.

**entrenched** adjective *they tend to cling to entrenched attitudes* INGRAINED, established, confirmed, fixed, firm, deep-seated, deep-rooted; unshakable, indelible, ineradicable, inexorable.

**entrepreneur** noun *a newsletter for young entrepreneurs* BUSINESSMAN/BUSINESSWOMAN, enterpriser, speculator, tycoon, magnate, mogul; dealer, trader; promoter, impresario; *informal* wheeler-dealer, whiz kid, mover and shaker, go-getter, high flyer, hustler, idea man/person.

**entrust** verb **1** *he was entrusted with the task* CHARGE, invest, endow; burden, encumber, saddle.

**2** *the powers* ***entrusted to*** *the treasury department* ASSIGN TO, confer on, bestow on, vest in, consign to; delegate to, depute to, devolve to; give to, grant to, vouchsafe to.

**3** *she entrusted them to the hospital* HAND OVER, give custody of, turn over, commit, consign, deliver; *formal* commend.

**entry** noun **1** *my moment of entry* APPEARANCE, arrival, entrance, ingress, coming. ANTONYMS departure, exit.

**2** *the entry to the building.* See ENTRANCE[1] sense 1.

**3** *he was refused entry* ADMISSION, admittance, entrance, access, ingress.

**4** *entries in the cash book* ITEM, record, note, listing; memo, memorandum; account.

**5** *data entry* RECORDING, archiving, logging, documentation, capture, keying.

**6** *we must pick a winner from the entries* CONTESTANT, competitor, contender, entrant, participant; candidate, applicant; submission, entry form, application.

**entwine** verb *her hair was entwined with ropes of pearls* WIND AROUND, twist around, coil around; weave, intertwine, interlace, interweave; entangle, tangle; twine, braid, plait, wreathe, knit.

**enumerate** verb **1** *he enumerated four objectives* LIST, itemize, set out, give; cite, name, specify, identify, spell out, detail, particularize.

**2** *they enumerated voters* CALCULATE, compute, count, add up, tally, total, number, quantify; reckon, work out, tot up.

**enunciate** verb **1** *she enunciated each word slowly* PRONOUNCE, articulate; say, speak, utter, voice, vocalize, sound.

**2** *a document enunciating the policy* EXPRESS, state, put into words, declare, profess, set forth, assert, affirm; put forward, air, proclaim.

**envelop** verb *enveloped in a blanket, safe in his mother's arms* SURROUND, cover, enfold, engulf, encircle, encompass, cocoon, sheathe, swathe, enclose; cloak, screen, shield, veil, shroud. See note at CIRCUMSCRIBE.

**envelope** noun *she tore open the envelope* WRAPPER, wrapping, sleeve, cover, covering, casing, package.

**enviable** adjective *of the three candidates, St. Clair has the enviable advantage of experience* DESIRABLE, desired, favored, sought-after, admirable, covetable, attractive; fortunate, lucky; *informal* to die for.

**envious** adjective *she felt envious of her friend's beauty* JEALOUS, covetous, desirous; grudging, begrudging, resentful; bitter. See note at JEALOUS.

**environment** noun **1** *birds from many environments* HABITAT, territory, domain; surroundings, environs, conditions.

**2** *the hospital environment* SITUATION, SETTING, milieu, background, backdrop, scene, location; context, framework; sphere, world, realm; ambience, atmosphere.

**3** **(the environment)** *the impact of pesticides on the environment* THE NATURAL WORLD, nature, the earth, the planet, the ecosystem, the biosphere, Mother Nature; wildlife, flora and fauna, the countryside.

**environmentalist** noun *environmentalists and industrialists must unite to save the world's forests* CONSERVATIONIST, preservationist, ecologist, nature lover; *informal* tree hugger, green, greenie.

**environs** plural noun *the environs of Milwaukee* SURROUNDINGS, surrounding area, vicinity, purlieu; locality, neighborhood, district, region; precincts.

**envisage** verb *can you envisage the factories of the future?* IMAGINE, contemplate, visualize, envision, picture; conceive of, think of; foresee.

**envoy** noun *a UN envoy has visited the home of Myanmar's opposition leader* AMBASSADOR, emissary, diplomat, consul, attaché, chargé d'affaires, plenipotentiary; nuncio; representative, delegate, proxy, surrogate, liaison, spokesperson; agent, intermediary, mediator; *informal* go-between; *historical* legate.

**envy** noun **1** *a pang of envy* JEALOUSY, covetousness; resentment, bitterness, discontent; the green-eyed monster.

**2** *the firm is the envy of Europe* FINEST, best, pride, top, cream, jewel, flower, leading light, the crème de la crème.

▸ verb **1** *I admired and envied her* BE ENVIOUS OF, be jealous of; begrudge, be resentful of.

**2** *we envied her lifestyle* COVET, desire, aspire to, wish for, want, long for, yearn for, hanker after, crave.

**ephemeral** adjective *last year's ephemeral fashions* TRANSITORY, transient, fleeting, passing, short-lived, momentary, brief, short; temporary, impermanent, short-term; fly-by-night. See note at TEMPORARY. ANTONYM permanent.

**epic** noun **1** *the epics of Homer* HEROIC POEM; story, saga, legend, romance, chronicle, myth, fable, tale.

**2** *a big Hollywood epic* long film; *informal* blockbuster.

▸ adjective **1** *a traditional epic poem* HEROIC, long, grand, monumental, Homeric, Miltonian.

**2** *their epic journey* AMBITIOUS, heroic, grand, great, Herculean; very long, monumental; adventurous.

**epicure** noun *this Caribbean island will help you meet your own inner epicure* GOURMET, gastronome, gourmand, connoisseur; *informal* foodie.

**epicurean** noun *a generous, life-loving epicurean* HEDONIST, sensualist, pleasure-seeker, sybarite, voluptuary, bon vivant, bon viveur; epicure, gourmet, gastronome, connoisseur, gourmand.

▸ adjective *epicurean excesses* HEDONISTIC, sensualist, pleasure-seeking, self-indulgent, good-time, sybaritic, voluptuary, lotus-eating; decadent, unrestrained, extravagant, intemperate, immoderate; gluttonous, gourmandizing. See note at SENSUOUS.

**epidemic** noun **1** *an epidemic of typhoid* OUTBREAK, plague, pandemic, epizootic.

**2** *a joyriding epidemic* SPATE, rash, wave, eruption, outbreak, craze; flood, torrent; upsurge, upturn, increase, growth, rise.

▸ adjective *the craze is now epidemic* RIFE, rampant, widespread, wide-ranging, extensive, pervasive; global, universal, ubiquitous; endemic, pandemic, epizootic.

THE RIGHT WORD **epidemic, endemic, pandemic**

A disease that quickly and severely affects a large number of people and then subsides is an **epidemic**: *throughout the Middle Ages, successive epidemics of the plague killed millions.* **Epidemic** is also used as an adjective: *she studied the causes of epidemic cholera.* A disease that is continually present in an area and affects a relatively small number of people is **endemic**: *malaria is endemic in* (or *to*) *hot, moist climates*. A **pandemic** is a widespread epidemic that may affect entire continents or even the world: *the pandemic of 1918 ushered in a* *period of frequent epidemics of gradually diminishing severity.* Thus, from an epidemiologist's point of view, the Black Death in Europe and AIDS in sub-Saharan Africa are pandemics rather than epidemics.

---

**epigram** noun *a collection of humorous epigrams from old gravestones* WITTICISM, quip, jest, pun, bon mot; saying, maxim, adage, aphorism, apophthegm, epigraph; *informal* one-liner, wisecrack, (old) chestnut. See note at SAYING.

**epigrammatic** adjective *her epigrammatic verses* CONCISE, succinct, pithy, aphoristic; incisive, short and sweet; witty, clever, quick-witted, piquant, sharp, gnomic, laconic; *informal* snappy. ANTONYM expansive.

**epilogue** noun *the book is summarized in the epilogue* AFTERWORD, postscript, PS, coda, codicil, appendix, tailpiece, supplement, addendum, postlude, rider, back matter; conclusion. ANTONYM prologue.

**episode** noun **1** *the best episode of his career* INCIDENT, event, occurrence, happening; occasion, experience, adventure, exploit; matter, affair, thing; interlude, chapter.

**2** *the final episode of the series* INSTALLMENT, chapter, passage; part, portion, section, component; program, show.

**3** *an episode of illness* PERIOD, spell, bout, attack, phase; *informal* patch.

**episodic** adjective **1** *episodic wheezing* INTERMITTENT, sporadic, periodic, fitful, irregular, spasmodic, occasional. ANTONYM continuous.

**2** *an episodic account of the war* IN EPISODES, in installments, in sections, in parts.

**epistle** noun *formal the historical backdrop of St. Paul's epistles* LETTER, missive, communication, dispatch, note, line; news, correspondence.

**epitaph** noun *the epitaphs on their tombstones* ELEGY, commemoration, obituary; inscription, legend.

**epithet** noun *Marion is better known by his epithet, the 'Swamp Fox'* SOBRIQUET, nickname, byname, title, name, label, tag; description, designation; *informal* moniker, handle; *formal* appellation, denomination.

**epitome** noun *Cary Grant will always be the epitome of the debonair man* PERSONIFICATION, embodiment, incarnation, paragon; essence, quintessence, archetype, paradigm; exemplar, model, soul, example; height.

**epitomize** verb *a nation that has come to epitomize socialism* EMBODY, encapsulate, typify, exemplify, represent, manifest, symbolize, illustrate, sum up; personify; *formal* reify.

**epoch** noun *England's Tudor epoch* ERA, age, period, time, span, stage; eon.

**equable** adjective **1** *an equable man* EVEN-TEMPERED, calm, composed, collected, self-possessed, relaxed, easygoing; nonchalant, insouciant, mellow, mild, tranquil, placid, stable, levelheaded; imperturbable, unexcitable, untroubled, well-balanced, serene; *informal* unflappable, together, laid-back. ANTONYMS temperamental, excitable.

**2** *an equable climate* STABLE, constant, uniform, unvarying, consistent, unchanging, changeless; moderate, temperate. ANTONYMS uneven, extreme.

**equal** adjective **1** *lines of equal length* IDENTICAL, uniform, alike, like, the same, equivalent; matching, even, comparable, similar, corresponding. See note at SAME. ANTONYM different.

**2** *fares* ***equal to*** *a month's wages* EQUIVALENT TO, identical to, amounting to; proportionate to; commensurate with, on a par with. ANTONYMS more than, less than.

**3** *equal treatment before the law* UNBIASED, impartial, nonpartisan, fair, just, equitable; unprejudiced, nondiscriminatory, egalitarian; neutral, objective, disinterested. ANTONYM discriminatory.

**4** *an equal contest* EVENLY MATCHED, even, balanced, level; on a par, on an equal footing; *informal* fifty-fifty, neck and neck. ANTONYM uneven.

▸ noun *they did not treat him as their equal* EQUIVALENT, peer, fellow, coequal, like; counterpart, match, parallel.

▸ verb **1** *two plus two equals four* BE EQUAL TO, be equivalent to, be the same as; come to, amount to, make, total, add up to.

**2** *he equaled the world record* MATCH, reach, parallel, be level with, measure up to.

**3** *the fable equals that of any other poet* BE AS GOOD AS, be a match for, measure up to, equate with; be in the same league as, rival, compete with.

PHRASE: **equal to** *trust me, I am equal to the task* CAPABLE OF, fit for, up to, good enough for, strong enough for; suitable for, suited to, appropriate for.

**equality** noun **1** *we promote equality for women* FAIRNESS, equal rights, equal opportunities, equity, egalitarianism; impartiality, evenhandedness; justice.

**2** *equality between supply and demand* PARITY, similarity, comparability, correspondence; likeness, resemblance; uniformity, evenness, balance, equilibrium, consistency, homogeneity, agreement, congruence, symmetry.

**equalize** verb *attempts to equalize their earnings* MAKE EQUAL, make even, even out/up, level, regularize, standardize, balance, square, match; bring into line.

**equanimity** noun *she confronted the daily crises with equanimity* COMPOSURE, calm, level-headedness, self-possession, coolheadedness, presence of mind; serenity, tranquility, phlegm, imperturbability, equilibrium; poise, assurance, self-confidence, aplomb, sangfroid, nerve; *informal* cool. ANTONYM anxiety.

**equate** verb **1** *he equates criticism with treachery* IDENTIFY, compare, liken, associate, connect, link, relate, class, bracket.

**2** *the rent equates to $24 per square foot* CORRESPOND, be equivalent, amount; equal.

**3** *moves to equate supply and demand* EQUALIZE, balance, even out/up, level, square, tally, match; make equal, make even, make equivalent.

**equation** noun **1** *a quadratic equation* MATHEMATICAL PROBLEM, sum, calculation, question.

**2** *the equation of success with riches* IDENTIFICATION, association, connection, matching; equivalence, correspondence, agreement, comparison.

**3** *other factors came into the equation* SITUATION, problem, case, question; quandary, predicament.

**equatorial** adjective *equatorial regions* TROPICAL, hot, humid, sultry. ANTONYM polar.

**equestrian** adjective *an equestrian statue* ON HORSEBACK, mounted, riding.

▸ noun *tracks for equestrians* RIDER, horseback rider, horseman, horsewoman, jockey.

**equilibrium** noun **1** *the equilibrium of the economy* BALANCE, symmetry, equipoise, parity, equality; stability. ANTONYM imbalance.

**2** *his equilibrium was never shaken* COMPOSURE, calm, equanimity, sangfroid; level-headedness, coolheadedness, imperturbability, poise, presence of mind; self-possession, self-command; impassivity, placidity, tranquility, serenity; *informal* cool. ANTONYMS nervousness, agitation.

**equip** verb **1** *the boat was equipped with a flare gun* PROVIDE, furnish, supply, issue, stock, provision, arm, endow, rig.

**2** *the course will equip them for the workplace* PREPARE, qualify, suit, train, ready.

**equipment** noun *taking inventory of our equipment* APPARATUS, paraphernalia, articles, appliances, impedimenta; tools, utensils, implements, instruments, hardware, gadgets, gadgetry; stuff, things; kit, tackle, rig; resources, supplies; trappings, appurtenances, accoutrements; *informal* gear; *dated* equipage; *Military* matériel, baggage.

**equitable** adjective *a plan to distribute the burden of taxes in an equitable way* FAIR, just, impartial, evenhanded, unbiased, unprejudiced, egalitarian; disinterested, objective, neutral, nonpartisan, open-minded; *informal* fair and square. ANTONYM unfair.

**equity** noun **1** *the equity of Finnish society* FAIRNESS, justness, impartiality, egalitarianism; objectivity, balance, open-mindedness.

**2** *he owns 25% of the equity in the property* VALUE, worth; ownership, rights, proprietorship.

**equivalence** noun *equivalence of birth and death rates in human populations is rare* EQUALITY, sameness, interchangeability, comparability, correspondence; uniformity, similarity, likeness, nearness.

**equivalent** adjective *a degree or equivalent qualification* EQUAL, identical; similar, comparable, corresponding, analogous, homologous, commensurate, parallel, synonymous; approximate, near. See note at SAME.

▸ noun *the Australian press is touting her as the equivalent of Dolly Parton* COUNTERPART, parallel, alternative, match, analog, twin, clone, opposite number; equal, peer; version; *rare* coequal.

**equivocal** adjective *an equivocal statement* AMBIGUOUS, indefinite, noncommittal, vague, imprecise, inexact, inexplicit, hazy; unclear, cryptic, enigmatic, pettifogging; ambivalent, uncertain, unsure, indecisive. See note at DOUBTFUL. ANTONYM definite.

**equivocate** verb *you have equivocated too often in the past* PREVARICATE, be evasive, be noncommittal, be vague, be ambiguous, dodge the question, beat around the bush, hedge; vacillate, shilly-shally, waver; temporize, hesitate, stall, hem and haw; *informal* pussyfoot around, sit on the fence; *rare* tergiversate. See note at LIE[1].

**era** noun *the Roosevelt era* EPOCH, age, period, phase, time, span, eon; generation.

**eradicate** verb *a total of three monthly applications will eradicate the termites* ELIMINATE, get rid of, remove, obliterate; exterminate, destroy, annihilate, kill, wipe out; abolish, stamp out, extinguish, quash; erase, efface, excise, expunge, expel; *informal* zap, nuke, wave goodbye to. See note at DESTROY.

**erase** verb **1** *they erased his name from all lists* DELETE, rub out, wipe off, blot out, cancel; efface, expunge, excise, remove, obliterate, eliminate, cut.

**2** *the old differences in style were erased* DESTROY, wipe out, obliterate, eradicate, abolish, stamp out, quash.

**erect** adjective **1** *she held her body erect* UPRIGHT, straight, vertical, perpendicular; standing. ANTONYMS bent, flaccid.

**2** *an erect penis* ENGORGED, enlarged, swollen, tumescent; hard, stiff, rigid. ANTONYM limp.

**3** *the dog's fur was erect* BRISTLING, standing on end, upright. ANTONYM flat.

▸ verb *erecting a new barn* BUILD, construct, put up; assemble, put together, fabricate. ANTONYMS demolish, dismantle.

**erection** noun **1** *the erection of a house* CONSTRUCTION, building, assembly, fabrication, elevation.

**2** *a bleak concrete erection* BUILDING, structure, edifice, construction, pile.

**3** *a normal erection* ERECT PENIS, phallus; tumescence; *informal, vulgar* boner, hard-on.

**erode** verb *waves and weather are seriously eroding the north side of the island* WEAR AWAY/DOWN, abrade, grind down, crumble; weather; eat away at, dissolve, corrode, rot, decay; undermine, weaken, deteriorate, destroy.

**erosion** noun *erosion has dramatically affected the topography here over the past two hundred years* WEARING AWAY, abrasion, attrition; weathering; dissolution, corrosion, decay; deterioration, disintegration, destruction.

**erotic** adjective *erotic literature* SEXY, sexually arousing, sexually stimulating, titillating, suggestive; pornographic, sexually explicit, lewd, smutty, hard-core, soft-core, dirty, racy, risqué, ribald, naughty; sexual, sensual, amatory; seductive, alluring, tantalizing; *informal* blue, X-rated, steamy, raunchy, bootylicious; *euphemistic* adult.

**err** verb *the judge had erred in not allowing new evidence* MAKE A MISTAKE, be wrong, be in error, be mistaken, blunder, fumble, be incorrect, miscalculate, get it wrong; sin, lapse; *informal* slip up, screw up, foul up, goof, make a booboo, drop the ball, bark up the wrong tree.

**errand** noun *one of my errands is to stop at the pharmacy for batteries* TASK, job, chore, assignment; collection, delivery; mission, undertaking.

**errant** adjective **1** *the errant officers were suspended* OFFENDING, guilty, culpable, misbehaving, delinquent, lawbreaking; troublesome, unruly, wayward, disobedient. ANTONYMS innocent, law-abiding.

**2** *archaic a knight errant* TRAVELING, wandering, itinerant, roaming, roving, voyaging. ANTONYM sedentary.

**erratic** adjective *the test results were too erratic for useful analysis* UNPREDICTABLE, inconsistent, changeable, variable, inconstant, irregular, fitful, unstable, turbulent, unsettled, changing, varying, fluctuating, mutable; unreliable, undependable, volatile, spasmodic, mercurial, capricious, fickle, temperamental, moody. ANTONYM consistent.

**erring** adjective *the jury agreed that the erring party should pay full restitution* OFFENDING, guilty, culpable, misbehaving, errant, delinquent, lawbreaking, aberrant, deviant.

**erroneous** adjective *an erroneous accusation* WRONG, incorrect, mistaken, in error, inaccurate, untrue, false, fallacious; unsound, specious, faulty, flawed; *informal* way out, full of holes. ANTONYM correct.

**error** noun *leaving the door unlocked was my error* MISTAKE, inaccuracy, miscalculation, blunder, oversight; fallacy, misconception, delusion; misprint, erratum; *informal* slip-up, boo-boo, goof. See note at MISTAKE. PHRASE: **in error** *millions of tax dollars were collected in error* WRONGLY, by mistake, mistakenly, incorrectly; accidentally, by accident, inadvertently, unintentionally, by chance.

**ersatz** adjective *ersatz coffee* ARTIFICIAL, substitute, imitation, synthetic, fake, false, faux, mock, simulated; pseudo, sham, bogus, spurious, counterfeit; manufactured, manmade; *informal* phony, wannabe. See note at SPURIOUS. ANTONYM genuine.

**erudite** adjective *our erudite cousin, Norma* LEARNED, scholarly, educated, knowledgeable, well-read, well-informed, intellectual; intelligent, clever, academic, literary; bookish, highbrow, sophisticated, cerebral; *informal* brainy; *dated* lettered. See note at KNOWLEDGE. ANTONYM ignorant.

**erupt** verb **1** *the volcano erupted* EMIT LAVA, become active, flare up; explode.

**2** *fighting erupted* BREAK OUT, flare up, start suddenly; ensue, arise, happen.

**3** *a boil erupted on her temple* APPEAR, break out, flare up, come to a head, suppurate, emerge.

**eruption** noun **1** *a volcanic eruption* DISCHARGE, ejection, emission; explosion.

**2** *an eruption of violence* OUTBREAK, flare-up, upsurge, outburst, explosion; wave, spate.

**3** *a skin eruption* RASH, outbreak, breakout, inflammation.

**escalate** verb **1** *prices have escalated* INCREASE RAPIDLY, soar, rocket, shoot up, mount, spiral, climb, go up, inflate; *informal* go through the ceiling, go through the roof, skyrocket. ANTONYM plunge.

**2** *the dispute escalated* GROW, develop, mushroom, increase, heighten, intensify, accelerate. ANTONYM shrink.

**escapade** noun *famous for his flying escapades* EXPLOIT, stunt, caper, antic(s), spree, shenanigan, hijinks; adventure, venture, mission; deed, feat, trial, experience; incident, occurrence, event.

**escape** verb **1** *he escaped from prison* RUN AWAY/OFF, get out, break out, break free, make a break for it, bolt, flee, take flight, make off, take off, abscond, take to one's heels, make one's getaway, make a run for it; disappear, vanish, slip away, sneak away; *informal* cut and run, skedaddle, vamoose, fly the coop, take French leave, go on the lam.

**2** *he escaped his pursuers* GET AWAY FROM, escape from, elude, avoid, dodge, shake off; *informal* give someone the slip.

**3** *they escaped injury* AVOID, evade, dodge, elude, miss, cheat, sidestep, circumvent, steer clear of; *informal* duck.

**4** *lethal gas escaped* LEAK (OUT), seep (out), discharge, emanate, issue, flow (out), pour (out), gush (out), spurt (out), spew (out).

▸ noun **1** *his escape from prison* GETAWAY, breakout, jailbreak, bolt, flight; disappearance, vanishing act.

**2** *a narrow* ***escape from*** *death* AVOIDANCE OF, evasion of, circumvention of.

**3** *a gas escape* LEAK, leakage, spill, seepage, discharge, effusion, emanation, outflow, outpouring; gush, stream, spurt.

**4** *an escape from boredom* DISTRACTION, diversion.

**escapism** noun *romance novels offer a form of escapism that many people thoroughly enjoy* FANTASY, fantasizing, daydreaming, daydreams, reverie; imagination, flight(s) of fancy, pipe dreams, wishful thinking, woolgathering; *informal* pie in the sky. ANTONYM realism.

**eschew** verb *he firmly eschewed political involvement* ABSTAIN FROM, refrain from, give up, forgo, shun, renounce, steer clear of, have nothing to do with, fight shy of; relinquish, reject, disavow, abandon, spurn, wash one's hands of, drop; *informal* kick, pack in; *formal* forswear, abjure.

**escort** noun **1** *a police escort* GUARD, bodyguard, protector, minder, attendant, chaperone; entourage, retinue, cortège; protection, defense, convoy.

**2** *her escort for the evening* COMPANION, partner; *informal* date; *formal* attendant.

3 *an agency dealing with escorts* PAID COMPANION, hostess; geisha; gigolo.

▸ verb *he escorted her down the aisle* CONDUCT, accompany, guide, lead, usher, shepherd, bring, take; drive, walk.

**esoteric** adjective *in attendance were more than 50 antiques dealers brimming with esoteric knowledge* ABSTRUSE, obscure, arcane, recherché, rarefied, recondite, abstract; enigmatic, inscrutable, cryptic, Delphic; complex, complicated, incomprehensible, opaque, impenetrable, mysterious.

**especial** adjective 1 *especial care is required* PARTICULAR, special, extra special, superior, exceptional, extraordinary; unusual, out of the ordinary, uncommon, remarkable, singular.

2 *her especial brand of charm* DISTINCTIVE, individual, special, particular, distinct, peculiar, personal, own, unique, specific.

**especially** adverb 1 *complaints poured in, especially from Toronto* MAINLY, mostly, chiefly, principally, largely; substantially, particularly, primarily, generally, usually, typically.

2 *a committee especially for the purpose* EXPRESSLY, specially, specifically, exclusively, just, particularly, explicitly.

3 *he is especially talented* EXCEPTIONALLY, particularly, specially, very, extremely, singularly, strikingly, distinctly, unusually, extraordinarily, uncommonly, uniquely, remarkably, outstandingly, really; *informal* seriously, majorly.

**espionage** noun *an American pilot suspected of espionage* SPYING, infiltration; eavesdropping, surveillance, reconnaissance, intelligence, undercover work.

**espousal** noun *Will's recent espousal of neo-Nazism has distressed his family and perplexed his friends* ADOPTION, embracing, acceptance; support, championship, encouragement, defense; sponsorship, promotion, endorsement, advocacy, approval.

**espouse** verb *do you espouse the political beliefs of your parents?* ADOPT, embrace, take up, accept, welcome; support, back, champion, favor, prefer, encourage; promote, endorse, advocate. ANTONYM reject.

**espy** verb *literary he espied a niche up in the rocks* CATCH SIGHT OF, glimpse, see, spot, spy, notice, observe, discern, pick out, detect; *literary* behold.

**essay** noun 1 *he wrote an essay* ARTICLE, composition, study, paper, dissertation, thesis, discourse, treatise, disquisition, monograph; commentary, critique, theme.

2 *formal his first essay in telecommunications* ATTEMPT, effort, endeavor, try, venture, trial, experiment, undertaking.

**essence** noun 1 *the very essence of economics* QUINTESSENCE, soul, spirit, nature; core, heart, crux, nucleus, substance; principle, fundamental quality, sum and substance, warp and woof, reality, actuality; *informal* nitty-gritty.

2 *essence of ginger* EXTRACT, concentrate, distillate, elixir, decoction, juice, tincture; scent, perfume, oil. PHRASES: **in essence** *in essence, his essays are the products of an indoctrinated young mind* ESSENTIALLY, basically, fundamentally, primarily, principally, chiefly, predominantly, substantially; above all, first and foremost; effectively, virtually, to all intents and purposes; intrinsically, inherently.

**of the essence** *absolute secrecy is of the essence.* See ESSENTIAL adjective sense 1.

**essential** adjective 1 *it is essential to remove the paint* CRUCIAL, necessary, key, vital, indispensable, important, all-important, of the essence, critical, imperative, mandatory, compulsory, obligatory; urgent, pressing, paramount, preeminent, high-priority, nonnegotiable; *informal* must-have. See note at NECESSARY. ANTONYMS unimportant, optional.

2 *the essential simplicity of his style* BASIC, inherent, fundamental, quintessential, intrinsic, underlying, characteristic, innate, primary, elementary, elemental; central, pivotal, vital. See note at INHERENT. ANTONYM secondary.

▸ noun 1 *an essential for broadcasters* NECESSITY, prerequisite, requisite, requirement, need; condition, precondition, stipulation; sine qua non; *informal* must, must-have.

2 *the essentials of the job* FUNDAMENTALS, basics, rudiments, first principles, foundations, bedrock; essence, basis, core, kernel, crux, sine qua non; *informal* nitty-gritty, brass tacks, nuts and bolts, meat and potatoes.

**establish** verb 1 *they established an office in Moscow* SET UP, start, initiate, institute, form, found, create, inaugurate; build, construct, install.

2 *evidence to establish his guilt* PROVE, demonstrate, show, indicate, signal, exhibit, manifest, attest to, evidence, determine, confirm, verify, certify, substantiate.

**established** adjective 1 *established practice* ACCEPTED, traditional, orthodox, habitual, set, fixed, official; usual, customary, common, normal, general, prevailing, accustomed, familiar, expected, routine, typical, conventional, standard.

2 *an established composer* WELL-KNOWN, recognized, esteemed, respected, famous, prominent, noted, renowned.

**establishment** noun 1 *the establishment of a democracy* FOUNDATION, institution, formation, inception, creation, installation; inauguration, start, initiation.

2 *a dressmaking establishment* BUSINESS, firm, company, concern, enterprise, venture, organization, operation; factory, plant, store, shop, office, practice; *informal* outfit, setup.

3 *educational establishments* INSTITUTION, place, premises, foundation, institute.

4 **(the Establishment)** *they dare to poke fun at the Establishment* THE AUTHORITIES, the powers that be, the system, the ruling class; the hierarchy, the oligarchy; *informal* Big Brother.

**estate** noun 1 *the Knowltons' estate* PROPERTY, grounds, garden(s), park, parkland, land(s), landholding, manor, territory; *historical* seigneury.

2 *a coffee estate* PLANTATION, farm, holding; forest, vineyard; ranch.

3 *he left an estate worth $610,000* ASSETS, capital, wealth,

riches, holdings, fortune; property, effects, possessions, belongings; *Law* goods and chattels.

**esteem** noun *she was held in high esteem* RESPECT, admiration, acclaim, approbation, appreciation, favor, recognition, honor, reverence; estimation, regard, opinion.

▸ verb **1** *such ceramics are highly esteemed* RESPECT, ADMIRE, value, regard, acclaim, appreciate, like, prize, treasure, favor, revere.

**2** *formal I would esteem it a favor if you could speak to him.* See DEEM.

THE RIGHT WORD **esteem, admire, appreciate, prize, regard, respect**

If you're a classical music aficionado, you might **appreciate** a good symphony orchestra, **admire** someone who plays the oboe, and **esteem** the works of Beethoven above all other classical composers. All three of these verbs are concerned with recognizing the worth of something, but in order to *appreciate* it, you have to understand it well enough to judge it critically. If you *admire* something, you appreciate its superiority (*to admire a pianist's performance*), while *esteem* goes one step further, implying that your admiration is of the highest degree (*a musician esteemed throughout the music world*). You **prize** what you value highly or cherish, especially if it is a possession (*she prized her Stradivarius violin*), while **regard** is a more neutral term meaning to look at or to have a certain mental view of something, either favorable or unfavorable (*to regard him as a great musician*; *to regard her as a ruthless competitor*). To **respect** is to have a deferential regard for someone or something because of its worth or value (*to respect the conductor's interpretation of the music*).

**estimate** verb **1** *estimate the cost* CALCULATE ROUGHLY, approximate, guess; evaluate, judge, gauge, reckon, rate, determine; *informal* guesstimate, ballpark.

**2** *we estimate it to be worth $50,000* CONSIDER, believe, reckon, deem, judge, rate, gauge.

▸ noun **1** *an estimate of the cost* ROUGH CALCULATION, approximation, estimation, rough guess; costing, quotation, valuation, evaluation; *informal* guesstimate.

**2** *his estimate of Paul's integrity* EVALUATION, estimation, judgment, rating, appraisal, opinion, view.

**estimation** noun **1** *an estimation of economic growth* ESTIMATE, approximation, rough calculation, rough guess, evaluation; *informal* guesstimate, ballpark figure.

**2** *she rated highly in Janice's estimation* ASSESSMENT, evaluation, judgment, perception; esteem, opinion, view.

**estrange** verb *Arafat was urged not to estrange the Bush White House* ALIENATE, antagonize, turn away, drive away, distance; sever, set at odds with; drive a wedge between (oneself and).

**estrangement** noun *the estrangement between Vita and her family* ALIENATION, antagonism, antipathy, disaffection, hostility, unfriendliness; variance, difference; parting, separation, divorce, breakup, split, breach, schism. See note at SOLITUDE.

**estuary** noun *we paddled down the estuary, observing herons and ospreys* (RIVER) MOUTH, delta; *archaic* embouchure, debouchure, debouchment, discharge, disemboguement.

**et cetera** adverb *they make their own linguini, fettuccini, ziti, lasagna, et cetera* AND SO ON, and so forth, and the rest, and/or the like, and suchlike, among others, et al., etc.; *informal* and what have you, and whatnot, and on and on, yadda yadda yadda.

**etch** verb *the metal is etched with a dilute acid* ENGRAVE, carve, inscribe, incise, chase, score, print, mark.

**etching** noun *Picasso's etchings were often relatively large and bold* ENGRAVING, print, impression, block, plate; woodcut, linocut.

**eternal** adjective **1** *eternal happiness* EVERLASTING, never-ending, endless, perpetual, undying, immortal, abiding, permanent, enduring, infinite, boundless, timeless; amaranthine. ANTONYM transient.

**2** *eternal vigilance* CONSTANT, continual, continuous, perpetual, persistent, sustained, unremitting, relentless, unrelieved, uninterrupted, unbroken, never-ending, nonstop, around/round-the-clock, endless, ceaseless. ANTONYM intermittent.

THE RIGHT WORD **eternal, endless, everlasting, interminable, never-ending, unending**

There are some things in life that seem to exist beyond the boundaries of time. **Endless** is the most informal and has the broadest scope of all these adjectives. It can mean without end in time (*an endless argument*) or space (*the endless universe*), and it implies never stopping, or going on continuously as if in a circle (*to consult an endless succession of doctors*). **Unending** is a less formal word used to describe something that endures or has no end, and it can be used either in an approving sense (*unending devotion*) or a disapproving one (*unending conflict*). **Never-ending** is a more emphatic term than *unending*; it, too, can be used in either a positive or a negative sense (*a never-ending delight*; *a never-ending source of embarrassment*). In contrast, **interminable** is almost always used in a disapproving or negative sense for something that lasts a long time (*interminable delays in construction*). **Everlasting** refers to something that will continue to exist once it is created, while **eternal** implies that it has always existed and will continue to exist in the future. In Christian theology, for example, believers in the *eternal* God look forward to *everlasting* life.

**eternally** adverb **1** *I shall be eternally grateful* FOREVER, permanently, perpetually, (for) evermore, for ever and ever, for eternity, in perpetuity, enduringly; forevermore; *informal* until the cows come home; *archaic* for aye.

**2** *the drummer is eternally complaining* CONSTANTLY, continually, continuously, always, all the time, persistently, repeatedly, regularly; day and night, night and day, nonstop; endlessly, incessantly, perpetually; interminably, relentlessly; *informal* 24-7.

**eternity** noun **1** *the memory will remain for eternity* EVER, all time, perpetuity.

**2** *Theology souls destined for eternity* THE AFTERLIFE, everlasting life, life after death, the hereafter, the afterworld, the next world; heaven, paradise, immortality.

**3** *informal I waited an eternity for you* A LONG TIME, an age, ages, a lifetime; hours, years, eons; forever; *informal* donkey's years, a month of Sundays, a coon's age.

**ethereal** adjective *melodic phrases of ethereal beauty* DELICATE, exquisite, dainty, elegant, graceful; fragile, airy, fine, subtle; unearthly. ANTONYMS substantial, earthly.

**ethical** adjective **1** *an ethical dilemma* MORAL, social, behavioral. See note at MORAL.

**2** *an ethical investment policy* MORAL, right-minded, principled, irreproachable; righteous, high-minded, virtuous, good, morally correct; clean, lawful, just, honorable, reputable, respectable, noble, worthy; praiseworthy, commendable, admirable, laudable; whiter than white, saintly, impeccable, politically correct; *informal* squeaky clean, PC.

**ethics** plural noun *your so-called newspaper is clearly not burdened by a sense of ethics* MORAL CODE, morals, morality, values, rights and wrongs, principles, ideals, standards (of behavior), value system, virtues, dictates of conscience.

**ethnic** adjective *a wide spectrum of ethnic groups* RACIAL, race-related, ethnological; cultural, national, tribal, ancestral, traditional.

**ethos** noun *responsibility for the ethos of the school* SPIRIT, character, atmosphere, climate, mood, feeling, tenor, essence; disposition, rationale, morality, moral code, value system, principles, standards, ethics.

**etiquette** noun *the article includes tips on etiquette* PROTOCOL, manners, accepted behavior, rules of conduct, decorum, good form; courtesy, propriety, formalities, niceties, punctilios; custom, convention; *Computing* netiquette; *informal* the done thing; *formal* politesse.

**eulogize** verb *the police eulogized the positive effect of speed cameras* EXTOL, acclaim, sing the praises of, praise to the skies, wax lyrical about, rhapsodize about, rave about, enthuse about, ballyhoo, hype. See note at PRAISE. ANTONYM criticize.

**eulogy** noun *a graveside eulogy* ACCOLADE, panegyric, paean, tribute, compliment, commendation; praise, acclaim; plaudits, bouquets; *formal* encomium. ANTONYM attack.

**euphemism** noun *'influential person' is the local euphemism for underworld don* POLITE TERM, indirect term, circumlocution, substitute, alternative, understatement, genteelism.

**euphemistic** adjective *the textbooks reportedly use the euphemistic term 'advance' instead of 'invade' to describe Japan's takeover of the Korean Peninsula* POLITE, substitute, mild, understated, indirect, neutral, evasive; diplomatic, inoffensive, genteel; periphrastic, circumlocutory, mealy-mouthed.

**euphonious** adjective *the euphonious chorus of songbirds* PLEASANT-SOUNDING, sweet-sounding, mellow, mellifluous, dulcet, sweet, honeyed, lyrical, silvery, golden, lilting, soothing; harmonious, melodious; *informal* easy on the ear. ANTONYM cacophonous.

**euphoria** noun *the euphoria of victory* ELATION, happiness, joy, delight, glee; excitement, exhilaration, jubilation, exultation; ecstasy, bliss, rapture. See note at RAPTURE. ANTONYM misery.

**euphoric** adjective *they received a euphoric welcome* ELATED, happy, joyful, delighted, gleeful; excited, exhilarated, jubilant, exultant; ecstatic, blissful, rapturous, transported, on cloud nine, in seventh heaven; *informal* on top of the world, over the moon, on a high.

**euthanasia** noun *both veterinarians recommended euthanasia as the most merciful procedure* MERCY KILLING, assisted suicide; *rare* quietus.

**evacuate** verb **1** *local residents were evacuated* REMOVE, clear, move out, take away, shift.

**2** *they evacuated the bombed town* LEAVE, vacate, abandon, desert, move out of, quit, withdraw from, retreat from, decamp from, flee, depart from, escape from.

**3** *police evacuated the area* CLEAR, empty.

**4** *patients couldn't evacuate their bowels* EMPTY (OUT), void, open, move, purge; defecate.

**5** *he evacuated the contents of his stomach* EXPEL, eject, discharge, excrete, void, empty (out), vomit up.

**evade** verb **1** *they evaded the guards* ELUDE, avoid, dodge, escape (from), steer clear of, keep at arm's length, sidestep; lose, leave behind, shake off; *informal* give someone the slip. ANTONYMS confront, run into.

**2** *he evaded the question* AVOID, dodge, sidestep, bypass, shirk, hedge, skirt around, fudge, be evasive about; *informal* duck. ANTONYM face.

**evaluate** verb *the house was most recently evaluated in 2002* ASSESS, judge, gauge, rate, estimate, appraise, analyze, examine, get the measure of; *informal* size up, check out.

**evaluation** noun *proper evaluation of the results is critical* ASSESSMENT, appraisal, judgment, gauging, rating, estimation, consideration; analysis, examination, test, review.

**evanescent** adjective *literary operating on an evanescent budget* VANISHING, fading, evaporating, melting away, disappearing; ephemeral, fleeting, short-lived, short-term, transitory, transient, fugitive, temporary. See note at TEMPORARY. ANTONYM permanent.

**evangelical** adjective **1** *evangelical Christianity* SCRIPTURAL, biblical; fundamentalist.

**2** *an evangelical preacher* EVANGELISTIC, evangelizing, missionary, crusading, proselytizing; *informal* Bible-thumping.

**evangelist** noun *the first evangelist I ever heard of was Billy Graham* PREACHER, missionary, gospeler, proselytizer, crusader; *informal* Bible-thumper.

**evangelistic** adjective. See EVANGELICAL sense 2.

**evangelize** verb *his calling is to evangelize the downtrodden* *in these poor neighborhoods* | *evangelizing in the West Indies* CONVERT, proselytize, redeem, save, preach to, recruit; act as a missionary, missionize, crusade, campaign.

**evaporate** verb **1** *the water evaporated* VAPORIZE, become vapor, volatilize; dry up. ANTONYM condense.

**2** *the rock salt is washed and evaporated* DRY OUT, dehydrate, desiccate, dehumidify. ANTONYM wet.

**3** *the feeling has evaporated* END, pass, pass away, fizzle out, peter out, wear off, vanish, fade, disappear, dissolve, melt away. ANTONYM materialize.

**evasion** noun **1** *the evasion of immigration control* AVOIDANCE, elusion, circumvention, dodging, sidestepping.

**2** *she grew tired of all the evasion* PREVARICATION, evasiveness, beating around the bush, hedging, pussyfooting, hemming and hawing, equivocation, vagueness, temporization; *rare* tergiversation.

**evasive** adjective *the judge was infuriated by the defendant's evasive answers* EQUIVOCAL, prevaricating, elusive, ambiguous, noncommittal, vague, inexplicit, unclear; roundabout, indirect; *informal* cagey, shifty, slippery. See note at FRANK.

**eve** noun **1** *the **eve of** the election* DAY BEFORE, evening before, night before; period (just) before.

**2** *literary a winter's eve* EVENING, night; end of day, close of day; twilight, dusk, sunset, sundown, nightfall; *literary* eventide, evenfall, gloaming. ANTONYM morning.

**even** adjective **1** *an even surface* FLAT, smooth, uniform, featureless; unbroken, undamaged; level, plane. ANTONYM bumpy.

**2** *an even temperature* UNIFORM, constant, steady, stable, consistent, unvarying, unchanging, regular. ANTONYMS variable, irregular.

**3** *they all have an even chance* EQUAL, the same, identical, like, alike, similar, comparable, parallel. ANTONYM unequal.

**4** *the score was even* TIED, drawn, level, all square, balanced; neck and neck; *informal* even-steven. ANTONYM unequal.

**5** *an even disposition* EVEN-TEMPERED, balanced, stable, equable, placid, calm, composed, poised, cool, relaxed, easy, imperturbable, unexcitable, unruffled, untroubled; *informal* together, laid-back, unflappable. ANTONYMS excitable, moody.

▸ verb **1** *the canal bottom was **evened out*** FLATTEN, level (off/out), smooth (off/out), plane; make uniform, make regular.

**2** ***even up** the portions* EQUALIZE, make equal, balance, square; standardize, regularize, homogenize.

▸ adverb **1** *it got even colder* STILL, yet, more, all the more.

**2** *even the best hitters missed the ball* SURPRISINGLY, unexpectedly, paradoxically.

**3** *she is afraid, even ashamed, to ask for help* INDEED, you could say, veritably, in truth, actually, or rather; *dated* nay.

**4** *she could **not even** afford food* NOT SO MUCH AS, hardly, barely, scarcely.

PHRASES: **even as** *we laugh even as we empathize with his discomfort* WHILE, whilst, as, just as, at the very time that, during the time that.

**even so** *I feel better, but the doubts persist even so* NEVERTHELESS, nonetheless, all the same, just the same, anyway, anyhow, still, yet, however, notwithstanding, despite that, in spite of that, for all that, be that as it may, in any event, at any rate; *informal* anyhoo, anyways.

**get even** *Waite thinks he's struck the final blow, but I'll get even* HAVE ONE'S REVENGE, avenge oneself, take vengeance, even the score, settle the score, hit back, give as good as one gets, pay someone back, repay someone, reciprocate, retaliate, take reprisals, exact retribution; give someone their just deserts; *informal* give someone a taste of their own medicine, settle someone's hash; *literary* be revenged.

**evenhanded** adjective *for reasons we have yet to analyze, our older teachers are far more evenhanded than the younger ones* FAIR, just, equitable, impartial, unbiased, unprejudiced, nonpartisan, nondiscriminatory; disinterested, detached, objective, neutral. ANTONYM biased.

**evening** noun *they met in town nearly every evening* NIGHT, late afternoon, end of day, close of day; twilight, dusk, nightfall, sunset, sundown; *literary* eve, eventide, evenfall, gloaming.

**event** noun **1** *an annual event* OCCURRENCE, happening, proceeding, incident, affair, circumstance, occasion, phenomenon; function, gathering; *informal* bash.

**2** *the team lost the event* COMPETITION, contest, tournament, round, heat, match, fixture; race, game, bout. PHRASES: **in any event** *we may not join you for dinner, but in any event we'll see you at the theater* REGARDLESS, whatever happens, come what may, no matter what, at any rate, in any case, anyhow, anyway, even so, still, nevertheless, nonetheless; *informal* anyways, anyhoo.

**in the event** *in the event, they squabbled and the plan fell through* AS IT TURNED OUT, as it happened, in the end; as a result, as a consequence.

**eventful** adjective *a long and eventful day* BUSY, action-packed, full, lively, active, hectic, strenuous; momentous, significant, important, historic, consequential, fateful. ANTONYM dull.

**eventual** adjective *the eventual outcome of the competition* FINAL, ultimate, concluding, closing, end; resulting, ensuing, consequent, subsequent.

**eventuality** noun *it is impossible to anticipate every eventuality* EVENT, incident, occurrence, happening, development, phenomenon, situation, circumstance, case, contingency, chance, likelihood, possibility, probability; outcome, result.

**eventually** adverb *the culprit will be caught eventually* IN THE END, in due course, by and by, in time, after some time, after a bit, finally, at last, over the long haul; ultimately, in the long run, at the end of the day, one day, some day, sometime, at some point, sooner or later.

**eventuate** verb *formal* **1** *you never know what might eventuate.* See HAPPEN sense 1.

**2** *the fight* ***eventuated in*** *his death* RESULT IN, end in, lead to, give rise to, bring about, cause.

**ever** adverb **1** *the best I've ever done* AT ANY TIME, at any point, on any occasion, under any circumstances, on any account; up till now, until now.

**2** *he was ever the optimist* ALWAYS, forever, eternally, until hell freezes over, until the cows come home.

**3** *an ever increasing rate of crime* CONTINUALLY, constantly, always, endlessly, perpetually, incessantly, unremittingly.

**4** *will she ever learn?* AT ALL, in any way.

**everlasting** adjective **1** *everlasting love* ETERNAL, endless, never-ending, perpetual, undying, abiding, enduring, infinite, boundless, timeless. See note at ETERNAL. ANTONYM transient.

**2** *his everlasting complaints* CONSTANT, continual, continuous, persistent, relentless, unrelieved, uninterrupted, unabating, endless, interminable, never-ending, nonstop, incessant. ANTONYM occasional.

**every** adjective **1** *he exercised every day* EACH, each and every, every single.

**2** *we make every effort to satisfy our clients* ALL POSSIBLE, the utmost.

**everyday** adjective **1** *the everyday demands of a baby* DAILY, day-to-day, quotidian.

**2** *everyday drugs like acetaminophen* COMMONPLACE, ordinary, common, usual, regular, familiar, conventional, run-of-the-mill, standard, stock; household, domestic; *informal* garden variety. ANTONYM unusual.

**everything** pronoun *everything is half price* EACH ITEM, each thing, every single thing, the lot, the whole lot; all; *informal* the whole kit and caboodle, the whole shebang, the whole schmear, the whole ball of wax, the whole nine yards. ANTONYM nothing.

**everywhere** adverb *McDonald's restaurants are found everywhere* ALL OVER, all around, ubiquitously, in every nook and cranny, far and wide, near and far, high and low, 'here, there, and everywhere'; throughout the land, the world over, worldwide, globally; *informal* all over the place, everyplace, all over the map. ANTONYM nowhere.

**evict** verb *Leonard took no pleasure in evicting tenants* EXPEL, eject, oust, remove, dislodge, turn out, throw out, drive out; dispossess, expropriate; *informal* chuck out, kick out, boot out, bounce, give someone the (old) heave-ho, throw someone out on their ear, give someone the bum's rush, give someone their walking papers. See note at EJECT.

**eviction** noun *a notice of eviction was left in the mailbox* EXPULSION, ejection, ousting, removal, dislodgment, displacement, banishment; dispossession, expropriation; *Law* ouster.

**evidence** noun **1** *they found evidence of his plotting* PROOF, confirmation, verification, substantiation, corroboration, affirmation, attestation.

**2** *the court accepted her evidence* TESTIMONY, statement, attestation, declaration, avowal, submission, claim, contention, allegation; *Law* deposition, representation, affidavit.

**3** *evidence of a struggle* SIGNS, indications, pointers, marks, traces, suggestions, hints; manifestation.

▸ verb *the rise of racism is evidenced here* INDICATE, show, reveal, display, exhibit, manifest; testify to, confirm, prove, substantiate, endorse, bear out; *formal* evince. ANTONYM disprove.

PHRASE: **in evidence** *team spirit was in evidence* NOTICEABLE, conspicuous, obvious, perceptible, visible, on view, on display, plain to see; palpable, tangible, unmistakable, undisguised, prominent, striking, glaring; *informal* as plain as the nose on your face, sticking out like a sore thumb, staring someone in the face.

**evident** adjective *the fact that he loves his family is evident* OBVIOUS, apparent, noticeable, conspicuous, perceptible, visible, discernible, clear, clear-cut, plain, manifest, patent; palpable, tangible, distinct, pronounced, marked, striking, glaring, blatant; unmistakable, indisputable; *informal* as plain as the nose on your face, sticking out like a sore thumb, as clear as day.

**evidently** adverb **1** *he was evidently dismayed* OBVIOUSLY, clearly, plainly, visibly, manifestly, patently, distinctly, markedly; unmistakably, undeniably, undoubtedly.

**2** *evidently, she believed herself superior* SEEMINGLY, apparently, as far as one can tell, from all appearances, on the face of it; it seems (that), it appears (that).

**evil** adjective **1** *an evil deed* WICKED, bad, wrong, immoral, sinful, foul, vile, dishonorable, corrupt, iniquitous, depraved, reprobate, villainous, nefarious, vicious, malicious; malevolent, sinister, demonic, devilish, diabolical, fiendish, dark; monstrous, shocking, despicable, atrocious, heinous, odious, contemptible, horrible, execrable; *informal* lowdown, dirty. ANTONYMS good, virtuous.

**2** *an evil spirit* CRUEL, mischievous, pernicious, malignant, malign, baleful, vicious; destructive, harmful, hurtful, injurious, detrimental, deleterious, inimical, bad, ruinous. ANTONYMS good, beneficial.

**3** *an evil smell* UNPLEASANT, disagreeable, nasty, horrible, foul, disgusting, filthy, vile, noxious. ANTONYM pleasant.

▸ noun **1** *the evil in our midst* WICKEDNESS, bad, badness, wrongdoing, sin, ill, immorality, vice, iniquity, degeneracy, corruption, depravity, villainy, nefariousness, malevolence; devil; *formal* turpitude.

**2** *nothing but evil would ensue* HARM, pain, misery, sorrow, suffering, trouble, disaster, misfortune, catastrophe, affliction, woe, hardship.

**3** *the evils of war* ABOMINATION, atrocity, obscenity, outrage, enormity, crime, monstrosity, barbarity.

**evince** verb *formal his letters evince the excitement he felt*

REVEAL, show, make plain, manifest, indicate, display, exhibit, demonstrate, evidence, attest to; convey, communicate, proclaim, bespeak; *informal* ooze. ANTONYM conceal.

**evocative** adjective *evocative photos from our childhood* REMINISCENT, suggestive, redolent; expressive, vivid, graphic, powerful, haunting, moving, poignant.

**evoke** verb *the music evoked some forgotten memories* BRING TO MIND, put one in mind of, conjure up, summon (up), invoke, elicit, induce, kindle, stimulate, stir up, awaken, arouse, call forth; recall, echo, capture.

**evolution** noun **1** *the evolution of Bolshevism* DEVELOPMENT, advancement, growth, rise, progress, expansion, unfolding; transformation, adaptation, modification, revision.

**2** *his interest in evolution* DARWINISM, natural selection.

**evolve** verb *our little tea party evolved into an all-night bash* DEVELOP, progress, advance; mature, grow, expand, spread; alter, change, transform, adapt, metamorphose; *humorous* transmogrify.

**exacerbate** verb *each party blames the other for exacerbating the problem* AGGRAVATE, worsen, inflame, compound; intensify, increase, heighten, magnify, add to, amplify, augment; *informal* add fuel to the fire/flames. See note at EXASPERATE. ANTONYM reduce.

**exact** adjective **1** *an exact description* PRECISE, accurate, correct, faithful, close, true; literal, strict, faultless, perfect, impeccable; explicit, detailed, minute, meticulous, thorough; *informal* on the nail, on the mark, bang on, on the money, on the button. ANTONYM inaccurate.

**2** *an exact manager* CAREFUL, meticulous, painstaking, punctilious, conscientious, scrupulous, exacting; methodical, organized, orderly. ANTONYM careless.

▸ verb **1** *she exacted high standards from them* DEMAND, require, insist on, request, impose, expect; extract, compel, force, squeeze.

**2** *they exacted a terrible vengeance on him* INFLICT, impose, administer, apply.

**exacting** adjective **1** *an exacting training routine* DEMANDING, stringent, testing, challenging, onerous, arduous, laborious, taxing, grueling, punishing, hard, tough. ANTONYM easy.

**2** *an exacting boss* STRICT, stern, severe, firm, demanding, tough, harsh; inflexible, uncompromising, unyielding, unsparing; *informal* persnickety. ANTONYM easygoing.

**exactly** adverb **1** *it's exactly as I expected it to be* PRECISELY, entirely, absolutely, completely, totally, just, quite, in every way, in every respect, one hundred percent, every inch; *informal* to a T, on the money.

**2** *write the quotation out exactly* ACCURATELY, precisely, correctly, unerringly, faultlessly, perfectly; verbatim, word for word, letter for letter, to the letter, faithfully.

▸ exclamation *"She escaped?" "Exactly."* PRECISELY, yes, that's right, just so, quite so, quite, indeed, absolutely; *informal* you got it.

PHRASE: **not exactly** *I'm not exactly a spring chicken* BY NO MEANS, not at all, in no way, certainly not; not really.

**exaggerate** verb *the conflict was exaggerated by the media* OVERSTATE, overemphasize, overestimate, magnify, amplify, aggrandize, inflate; embellish, embroider, elaborate, overplay, dramatize; hyperbolize, stretch the truth; *informal* lay it on thick, make a mountain out of a molehill, blow out of all proportion, blow up, make a big thing of. ANTONYM understate.

**exaggerated** adjective *an exaggerated account of my exploits* OVERSTATED, inflated, magnified, amplified, aggrandized, excessive; hyperbolic, elaborate, overdone, overplayed, overblown, over-dramatized, melodramatic, sensational; *informal* over the top.

**exaggeration** noun *his testimony was a laughable mix of contradiction and exaggeration* OVERSTATEMENT, overemphasis, magnification, amplification, aggrandizement; dramatization, elaboration, embellishment, embroidery, hyperbole, overkill, gilding the lily.

**exalt** verb **1** *they exalted their hero* EXTOL, praise, acclaim, esteem; pay homage to, revere, venerate, worship, lionize, idolize, look up to; *informal* put on a pedestal, laud. ANTONYMS disparage, despise.

**2** *this power exalts the peasant* ELEVATE, promote, raise, advance, upgrade, ennoble, dignify, aggrandize. ANTONYM lower.

**3** *his works exalt the emotions* UPLIFT, elevate, inspire, excite, stimulate, enliven, exhilarate. ANTONYM depress.

**exaltation** noun **1** *a heart full of exaltation* ELATION, joy, rapture, ecstasy, bliss, happiness, delight, gladness.

**2** *their exaltation of Shakespeare* PRAISE, acclamation, reverence, veneration, worship, adoration, idolization, lionization.

**exalted** adjective **1** *his exalted office* HIGH, high-ranking, elevated, superior, lofty, eminent, prestigious, illustrious, distinguished, esteemed.

**2** *his exalted aims* NOBLE, lofty, high-minded, elevated; inflated, pretentious.

**3** *she felt spiritually exalted* ELATED, exultant, jubilant, joyful, rapturous, ecstatic, blissful, transported, happy, exuberant, exhilarated; *informal* high.

**exam** noun. See EXAMINATION sense 3.

**examination** noun **1** *artifacts spread out for examination* SCRUTINY, inspection, perusal, study, investigation, consideration, analysis, appraisal, evaluation.

**2** *a medical examination* INSPECTION, checkup, assessment, appraisal; probe, test, scan; *informal* once-over, overhaul.

**3** *a school examination* TEST, exam, quiz, assessment; oral, midterm, final; paper, term paper.

**4** *Law* *the examination of witnesses* INTERROGATION, questioning, cross-examination, inquisition.

**examine** verb **1** *they examined the bank records* INSPECT, scrutinize, investigate, look at, study, scan, sift (through), probe, appraise, analyze, review, survey; *informal* check out.

2 *students were examined after a year* TEST, quiz, question; assess, appraise.

3 Law *name the witnesses to be examined* INTERROGATE, question, quiz, cross-examine; catechize, give the third degree to, probe, sound out; *informal* grill, pump.

**example** noun 1 *a fine example of Chinese porcelain* SPECIMEN, sample, exemplar, exemplification, instance, case, illustration, case in point.

2 *we must follow their example* PRECEDENT, lead, model, pattern, exemplar, ideal, standard, template, paradigm; role model, object lesson. See note at MODEL.

3 *he was hanged as an example to others* WARNING, caution, lesson, deterrent, admonition; moral. PHRASE: **for example** *she's met several Hall of Famers—for example, Brooks Robinson and Johnny Mize* FOR INSTANCE, e.g., by way of illustration, such as, as, like; in particular, case in point, namely, viz., to wit.

**exasperate** verb *her bratty children exasperate their teachers* INFURIATE, incense, anger, annoy, irritate, madden, enrage, antagonize, provoke, irk, vex, get on someone's nerves, ruffle someone's feathers, rub the wrong way; *informal* aggravate, rile, bug, needle, get someone's back up, get someone's goat, tee off, tick off. ANTONYM please.

**exasperation** noun *she provoked exasperation among her colleagues* IRRITATION, annoyance, vexation, anger, fury, rage, ill humor, crossness, testiness, tetchiness; disgruntlement, discontent, displeasure, chagrin; *informal* aggravation.

**excavate** verb 1 *she excavated a narrow tunnel* DIG, dig out, bore, hollow out, scoop out; burrow, tunnel, sink, gouge.

2 *numerous artifacts have been excavated* UNEARTH, dig up, uncover, reveal; disinter, exhume.

**excavation** noun 1 *the excavation of a grave* UNEARTHING, digging up; disinterment, exhumation.

2 *the excavation of a moat* DIGGING, hollowing out, boring, channeling.

3 *implements found in the excavations* HOLE, pit, trench, trough; archaeological site.

**exceed** verb 1 *the cost will exceed $400* BE MORE THAN, be greater than, be over, go beyond, overreach, top.

2 *Brazil exceeds the U.S. in fertile land* SURPASS, outdo, outstrip, outshine, outclass, transcend, top, cap, beat, excel, better, eclipse, overshadow; *informal* best, leave standing, be head and shoulders above.

**exceedingly** adverb *an exceedingly comfortable home* EXTREMELY, exceptionally, especially, tremendously, very, really, truly, awfully, seriously, totally, completely; *formal* most; *informal* mega, ultra, real, mighty; *archaic* exceeding.

**excel** verb 1 *he excelled at football* SHINE, be excellent, be outstanding, be skillful, be talented, be preeminent, reign supreme; stand out, be the best, be unparalleled, be unequaled, be second to none, be unsurpassed.

2 *she excelled him in her work* SURPASS, outdo, outshine, outclass, outstrip, beat, top, transcend, exceed, better, pass, eclipse, overshadow; *informal* best, be head and shoulders above, be a cut above.

**excellence** noun *a center of medical excellence* DISTINCTION, quality, superiority, brilliance, greatness, merit, caliber, eminence, preeminence, supremacy; skill, talent, virtuosity, accomplishment, mastery.

**excellent** adjective *a cruise ship with excellent accommodations* VERY GOOD, superb, outstanding, exceptional, marvelous, wonderful, magnificent; preeminent, perfect, matchless, unbeatable, peerless, supreme, prime, first-rate, first-class, superlative, splendid, fine, beautiful, exemplary; *informal* A1, ace, great, terrific, tremendous, fantastic, fabulous, splendiferous, fab, top-notch, dandy, divine, blue-ribbon, blue-chip, bang-up, skookum, class, awesome, magic, wicked, mean, cool, out of this world, hunky-dory, A-OK, brilliant, killer. ANTONYMS inferior, poor.

**except** preposition *every day except Monday* EXCLUDING, not including, excepting, omitting, not counting, but, besides, apart from, aside from, barring, bar, other than, saving; with the exception of, save for; *informal* outside of. ANTONYM including.

▸ verb *lawyers are all crooks, present company excepted* EXCLUDE, omit, leave out, count out, disregard; exempt. ANTONYM include.

**exception** noun *this case is an exception* ANOMALY, irregularity, deviation, special case, isolated example, peculiarity, abnormality, oddity; misfit, aberration; *informal* freak; bad apple. PHRASES: **take exception to** *Lydia took exception to their criticism of her husband* OBJECT TO, take offense at, take umbrage at, demur at, disagree with; resent, argue against, protest against, oppose, complain about, shudder at; *informal* kick up a fuss about, raise a stink about.
**with the exception of** *all of the sopranos, with the exception of Dia, will wear black dresses with red sashes.* See EXCEPT preposition.

**exceptionable** adjective *formal*. See OBJECTIONABLE.

**exceptional** adjective 1 *the drought was exceptional* UNUSUAL, uncommon, abnormal, atypical, extraordinary, out of the ordinary, rare, unprecedented, unexpected, surprising; strange, odd, freakish, anomalous, peculiar, weird; *informal* freaky, something else. ANTONYMS normal, usual.

2 *her exceptional ability* OUTSTANDING, extraordinary, remarkable, special, excellent, phenomenal, prodigious; unequaled, unparalleled, unsurpassed, peerless, matchless, nonpareil, first-rate, first-class; *informal* A1, top-notch. ANTONYM average.

**excerpt** noun *an excerpt from the poem* EXTRACT, part, section, piece, portion, snippet, clip, bit, sample; reading, citation, quotation, quote, line, passage.

▸ verb *a portion of her play was excerpted for the magazine* QUOTE, extract, cite.

**excess** noun 1 *an excess of calcium* SURPLUS, surfeit, overabundance, superabundance, superfluity, glut. ANTONYMS lack, dearth.

2 *the excess is turned into fat* REMAINDER, rest, residue; leftovers, remnants; surplus, extra, difference.

3 *a life of excess* OVERINDULGENCE, intemperance, immoderation, profligacy, lavishness, extravagance, decadence, self-indulgence. ANTONYMS moderation, restraint.

▸ adjective *excess skin oils* SURPLUS, superfluous, redundant, unwanted, unneeded, excessive; extra.

PHRASE: **in excess of** *the book sold in excess of 10,000 copies* MORE THAN, over, above, upwards of, beyond.

**excessive** adjective 1 *excessive alcohol consumption* IMMODERATE, intemperate, imprudent, overindulgent, unrestrained, uncontrolled, lavish, extravagant; superfluous.

2 *the cost is excessive* EXORBITANT, extortionate, unreasonable, outrageous, undue, uncalled for, extreme, inordinate, unwarranted, disproportionate, too much, de trop; *informal* over the top.

**excessively** adverb *her father had excessively high standards* INORDINATELY, unduly, unnecessarily, unreasonably, ridiculously, overly; very, extremely, exceedingly, exceptionally, impossibly; immoderately, intemperately; ad nauseam.

**exchange** noun 1 *the exchange of ideas* INTERCHANGE, trade, trading, swapping, traffic, trafficking.

2 *a broker on the exchange* STOCK EXCHANGE, money market; bourse.

3 *an acrimonious exchange* CONVERSATION, dialogue, talk, discussion, chat; debate, argument, altercation, row; *formal* confabulation, colloquy.

▸ verb *we exchanged shirts* TRADE, swap, switch, change, interchange.

PHRASES: **exchange blows** *they exchanged blows out in the parking lot* FIGHT, brawl, scuffle, tussle; *informal* scrap, have a set-to.
**exchange words** *the children would tearfully listen from upstairs when their parents exchanged words* ARGUE, quarrel, squabble, have an argument, have a disagreement.

**excise**[1] noun *the excise on liquor* DUTY, tax, levy, tariff.

**excise**[2] verb 1 *the tumors were excised* CUT OUT/OFF/AWAY, take out, extract, remove; *technical* resect.

2 *all unnecessary detail should be excised* DELETE, cross out/through, strike out, score out, cancel, put a line through; erase, scratch; *informal* ditch, nix, kill; *Printing* dele.

**excitable** adjective *the horses are very excitable* TEMPERAMENTAL, mercurial, volatile, emotional, sensitive, highstrung, unstable, nervous, tense, edgy, jumpy, twitchy, uneasy, neurotic; *informal* uptight, wired. ANTONYM placid.

**excite** verb 1 *the prospect of a vacation excited me* THRILL, exhilarate, animate, enliven, rouse, stir, stimulate, galvanize, electrify, inspirit; *informal* buck up, pep up, give someone a buzz, give someone a kick, give someone a charge. ANTONYMS bore, depress.

2 *she wore a chiffon nightgown to excite him* AROUSE, arouse sexually, stimulate, titillate, inflame; *informal* turn someone on, get someone going. ANTONYM turn off.

3 *his clothes excited envy* PROVOKE, stir up, rouse, arouse, kindle, trigger (off), spark (off), incite, cause; *literary* enkindle.

**excited** adjective 1 *they were excited about the prospect* THRILLED, exhilarated, animated, enlivened, electrified; enraptured, intoxicated, feverish, adrenalized, enthusiastic; *informal* high, high as a kite, fired up, psyched.

2 *excited lovers* AROUSED, sexually aroused, stimulated, titillated, inflamed; *informal* turned on, hot, horny, sexed up.

**excitement** noun 1 *the excitement of seeing a leopard in the wild* THRILL, pleasure, delight, joy; *informal* kick, buzz, charge, high.

2 *excitement in her eyes* EXHILARATION, elation, animation, enthusiasm, eagerness, anticipation, feverishness; *informal* pep, vim, zing.

3 *their excitement was mutual* AROUSAL, sexual arousal, passion, stimulation, titillation.

**exciting** adjective 1 *an exciting story* THRILLING, exhilarating, action-packed, stirring, rousing, stimulating, intoxicating, electrifying, invigorating; gripping, compelling, powerful, dramatic.

2 *an exciting encounter with her lover* AROUSING, sexually arousing, stimulating, sexually stimulating, titillating, erotic, sexual, sexy; *informal* raunchy, steamy.

**exclaim** verb *"Well, I never!" she exclaimed* CRY OUT, cry, declare, blurt out; call, call out, shout, yell; *dated* ejaculate.

**exclamation** noun *an exclamation of amazement* CRY, call, shout, yell, interjection.

**exclude** verb 1 *women were excluded from many scientific societies* KEEP OUT, deny access to, shut out, debar, disbar, bar, ban, prohibit, ostracized. ANTONYMS admit, accept.

2 *the clause excluded any judicial review* ELIMINATE, rule out, preclude, foreclose; *formal* except. ANTONYM allow for.

3 *the price excludes postage* BE EXCLUSIVE OF, not include. ANTONYM include.

4 *he excluded his own name from the list* LEAVE OUT/OFF, omit, miss out. ANTONYM include.

**exclusive** adjective 1 *an exclusive club* SELECT, chic, high-class, elite, fashionable, stylish, elegant, premier, grade A; expensive, upscale, upmarket, high-toned; *informal* posh, ritzy, classy, tony.

2 *a room for your exclusive use* SOLE, unshared, unique, only, individual, personal, private. ANTONYM partial.

3 *prices* ***exclusive of*** *sales tax* NOT INCLUDING, excluding, leaving out, omitting, excepting. ANTONYM inclusive.

4 *mutually exclusive alternatives* INCOMPATIBLE, irreconcilable.

▸ noun *a six-page exclusive* SCOOP, exposé, special.

**excoriate** verb 1 *Medicine the skin had been excoriated*

ABRADE, rub away, rub raw, scrape, scratch, chafe; strip away, skin.

2 *formal he was excoriated in the press.* See CRITICIZE.

**excrement** noun *cleaning up the ferrets' excrement* FECES, excreta, stools, droppings; waste matter, ordure, dung; *informal* poop, poo, dirt, turds, caca.

**excrescence** noun 1 *an excrescence on his leg* GROWTH, lump, swelling, nodule, outgrowth.

2 *the new buildings were an excrescence* EYESORE, blot on the landscape, monstrosity.

**excrete** verb *waste products are excreted from the body* EXPEL, pass, void, discharge, eject, evacuate; defecate, urinate. ANTONYM ingest.

**excruciating** adjective *excruciating pain* AGONIZING, severe, acute, intense, violent, racking, searing, piercing, stabbing, raging; unbearable, unendurable; *informal* splitting, killing.

**excursion** noun *a lovely excursion to Nassau* TRIP, outing, jaunt, expedition, journey, tour; day trip, day out, side trip, drive, run, ride; *informal* junket, spin, sortie. See note at JOURNEY.

**excusable** adjective *it's an excusable mistake* FORGIVABLE, pardonable, defensible, justifiable; venial. ANTONYM unforgivable.

**excuse** verb 1 *eventually she excused him* FORGIVE, pardon, absolve, exonerate, acquit; *informal* let someone off (the hook); *formal* exculpate. ANTONYMS punish, blame.

2 *such conduct can never be excused* JUSTIFY, defend, condone, vindicate; forgive, overlook, disregard, ignore, tolerate, sanction. ANTONYM condemn.

3 *she has been excused from her duties* LET OFF, release, relieve, exempt, absolve, free.

▸ noun 1 *that's no excuse for stealing* JUSTIFICATION, defense, reason, explanation, mitigating circumstances, mitigation, vindication.

2 *an excuse to get away* PRETEXT, ostensible reason, pretense; *informal* story, alibi.

3 *informal that pathetic* ***excuse for*** *a man!* TRAVESTY OF, poor specimen of; *informal* apology for.

**execrable** adjective *an execrable piece of work* APPALLING, atrocious, lamentable, egregious, awful, dreadful, terrible; disgusting, deplorable, disgraceful, frightful, reprehensible, abhorrent, loathsome, odious, hateful, vile, abysmal, lousy, godawful. ANTONYM admirable.

**execute** verb 1 *he was convicted and executed* PUT TO DEATH, kill; hang, behead, guillotine, electrocute, send to the (electric) chair, shoot, put before a firing squad; *informal* string up, fry. See note at KILL.

2 *the corporation executed a series of financial deals* CARRY OUT, accomplish, bring off/about, achieve, complete, engineer, conduct; *informal* pull off; *formal* effectuate.

3 *a well-executed act* PERFORM, present, render; stage.

**execution** noun 1 *the execution of the plan* IMPLEMENTATION, carrying out, accomplishment, bringing off/about, engineering, attainment, realization.

2 *the execution of the play* PERFORMANCE, presentation, rendition, rendering, staging.

3 *thousands were sentenced to execution* CAPITAL PUNISHMENT, the death penalty; the gibbet, the gallows, the noose, the rope, the scaffold, the guillotine, the firing squad, the electric chair, the chair.

**executioner** noun *today he meets his executioner* HANGMAN; *historical* headsman.

**executive** adjective *executive powers* ADMINISTRATIVE, decision-making, managerial; lawmaking.

▸ noun 1 *top-level bank executives* CHIEF, head, director, senior official, senior manager, CEO, chief executive officer; *informal* boss, exec, suit, big cheese.

2 *the executive has increased in number* ADMINISTRATION, management, directorate; government, legislative body.

**exegesis** noun *the exegesis of ancient texts* INTERPRETATION, explanation, exposition, explication.

**exemplar** noun *Luciano is an exemplar of decorum* EPITOME, perfect example, paragon, ideal, exemplification, textbook example, embodiment, essence, quintessence; paradigm, model, role model, template.

**exemplary** adjective 1 *her exemplary behavior* PERFECT, ideal, model, faultless, flawless, impeccable, irreproachable; excellent, outstanding, admirable, commendable, laudable, above/beyond reproach; textbook. ANTONYM deplorable.

2 *exemplary jail sentences* DETERRENT, cautionary, warning, admonitory; *rare* monitory.

3 *her works are exemplary of cutting-edge feminism* REPRESENTATIVE, illustrative, characteristic, typical.

**exemplify** verb 1 *this story exemplifies current trends* TYPIFY, epitomize, be a typical example of, represent, be representative of, symbolize.

2 *he exemplified his point with an anecdote* ILLUSTRATE, give an example of, demonstrate.

**exempt** adjective *they are* ***exempt from*** *all charges* FREE FROM, not liable to, not subject to, exempted from, excepted from, excused of/from, absolved of. ANTONYM subject to.

▸ verb *he had been exempted from military service* EXCUSE, free, release, exclude from, give/grant immunity, spare, absolve from; *informal* let off (the hook), grandfather. See note at ABSOLVE.

**exemption** noun *exemption from the road tax* IMMUNITY, exception, dispensation, indemnity, exclusion, freedom, release, relief, absolution.

**exercise** noun 1 *exercise improves your heart* PHYSICAL ACTIVITY, a workout, working out; gymnastics, sports, games, physical education, physical training, aerobics, body conditioning, calisthenics; *informal* phys ed.

2 *Mr. Nixon's translation exercises* TASK, piece of work, problem, assignment, activity; *Music* étude.

3 *the exercise of professional skill* USE, utilization, employment; practice, application.

4 **(exercises)** *military exercises* MANEUVERS, operations; war games.

▸ verb 1 *she exercised every day* WORK OUT, do exercises, train; *informal* pump iron.

2 *he must learn to exercise patience* USE, employ, make use of, utilize; practice, apply.

**exert** verb 1 *he exerted considerable pressure on me* BRING TO BEAR, apply, exercise, employ, use, utilize, deploy.

2 *Geoff had been* ***exerting himself*** STRIVE, try hard, make an/every effort, endeavor, do one's best, do one's utmost, give one's all, push oneself, drive oneself, work hard; *informal* go all out, pull out all the stops, bend/lean over backwards, do one's damnedest, do one's darnedest, move heaven and earth, bust one's chops.

**exertion** noun 1 *she was panting with exertion* EFFORT, strain, struggle, toil, endeavor, hard work, labor; *literary* travail.

2 *the exertion of pressure* USE, application, exercise, employment, utilization.

**exhaust** verb 1 *the effort had exhausted him* TIRE OUT, wear out, overtire, fatigue, weary, tire, drain, run someone into the ground; *informal* do in, take it out of one, wipe out, knock out, burn out, poop, tucker out. ANTONYMS invigorate, refresh.

2 *the country has exhausted its reserves* USE UP, run through, go through, consume, finish, deplete, spend, empty, drain, run out of; *informal* blow. ANTONYM replenish.

3 *we've exhausted the subject* TREAT THOROUGHLY, say all there is to say about, do to death, overwork.

**exhausted** adjective 1 *I worked until I was exhausted* TIRED OUT, worn out, weary, dead-tired, dog-tired, bone-tired, ready to drop, drained, fatigued, enervated; *informal* beat, done in, all in, bushed, zonked, bagged, knocked out, wiped out, burned out, pooped, tuckered out, tapped out, fried, whipped. See note at TIRED.

2 *exhausted reserves* USED UP, consumed, finished, spent, depleted; empty, drained.

**exhausting** adjective *an exhausting day of moving furniture* TIRING, wearying, taxing, fatiguing, wearing, enervating, draining; arduous, strenuous, onerous, demanding, grueling; *informal* killing, murderous.

**exhaustion** noun 1 *sheer exhaustion forced Mona to give up* EXTREME TIREDNESS, overtiredness, fatigue, weariness, burnout.

2 *the exhaustion of fuel reserves* CONSUMPTION, depletion, using up, expenditure; draining, emptying.

**exhaustive** adjective *an exhaustive study of Icelandic history* COMPREHENSIVE, all-inclusive, complete, full, full-scale, encyclopedic, sweeping, thorough, in-depth; detailed, meticulous, painstaking. ANTONYM perfunctory.

**exhibit** verb 1 *the paintings were exhibited at the Wadsworth* PUT ON DISPLAY/SHOW, display, show, put on public view, showcase; set out, lay out, array, arrange.

2 *Luke exhibited signs of jealousy* SHOW, reveal, display, manifest; express, indicate, demonstrate, present; *formal* evince.

▸ noun 1 *exhibit A is a handwritten letter* OBJECT, item, piece, showpiece; display; evidence.

2 *people flocked to the exhibit.* See EXHIBITION sense 1.

**exhibition** noun 1 *an exhibition of Inuit sculpture* (PUBLIC) DISPLAY, show, showing, presentation, demonstration, exposition, showcase, exhibit.

2 *a convincing exhibition of concern* DISPLAY, show, demonstration, manifestation, expression.

**exhilarate** verb *the fireworks display exhilarated us* THRILL, excite, intoxicate, elate, delight, enliven, animate, invigorate, energize, vitalize, stimulate; *informal* give someone a thrill, give someone a buzz, give someone a charge.

**exhilaration** noun *a feeling of exhilaration* ELATION, euphoria, exultation, exaltation, joy, happiness, delight, joyousness, jubilation, rapture, ecstasy, bliss.

**exhort** verb *Clinton exhorted state legislatures to beef up educational standards and help put welfare recipients to work* URGE, encourage, call on, enjoin, charge, press; bid, appeal to, entreat, implore, beg; *formal* adjure; *literary* beseech. See note at INCITE.

**exhortation** noun 1 *no amount of exhortation had any effect* URGING, encouragement, persuasion, pressure; warning.

2 *the government's exhortations to voters* ENTREATY, appeal, call, charge, injunction; admonition, warning.

**exhume** verb *the district attorney is requesting that Baker's body be exhumed* DISINTER, dig up, unearth. ANTONYM bury.

**exigency** noun 1 *the exigencies of the continuing war* NEED, demand, requirement, necessity.

2 *financial exigency* URGENCY, crisis, difficulty, pressure.

**exiguous** adjective *formal Bob Cratchit's exiguous wages* MEAGER, inadequate, insufficient, small, scanty, paltry, negligible, modest, deficient, miserly, niggardly, beggarly; *informal* measly, stingy, piddling. ANTONYMS ample, generous.

**exile** noun 1 *his exile from the land of his birth* BANISHMENT, expulsion, expatriation, deportation.

2 *political exiles* ÉMIGRÉ, expatriate; displaced person, refugee, deportee; *informal* expat; *historical* DP.

▸ verb *he was exiled from his country* EXPEL, banish, expatriate, deport, drive out, throw out, outlaw.

**exist** verb 1 *animals existing in the distant past* LIVE, be alive, be living; be; happen.

2 *the liberal climate that existed during his presidency* PREVAIL, occur, be found, be in existence; be the case.

**3** *she had to exist on a low income* SURVIVE, subsist, live, support oneself; manage, make do, get by, scrape by, make ends meet.

**existence** noun **1** *the industry's continued existence* ACTUALITY, being, existing, reality; survival, continuation.

**2** *her suburban existence* WAY OF LIFE, way of living, life, lifestyle. PHRASE: **in existence** *there are millions of unidentified species in existence.* See EXISTENT.

**existent** adjective *species that are no longer existent* IN EXISTENCE, alive, existing, living, extant; surviving, remaining, undestroyed.

**exit** noun **1** *the fire exit* WAY OUT, door, egress, escape route; doorway, gate, gateway, portal. ANTONYM entrance.

**2** *take the second exit* TURNING, turnoff, turn, junction.

**3** *his sudden exit* DEPARTURE, leaving, withdrawal, going, decamping, retreat; flight, exodus, escape. ANTONYM arrival.

▸ verb *the doctor had just exited* LEAVE, go (out), depart, withdraw, retreat. ANTONYM enter.

**exodus** noun *the exodus of refugees from Albania* MASS DEPARTURE, withdrawal, evacuation, leaving; migration, emigration; flight, escape, fleeing.

**exonerate** verb **1** *the inquiry exonerated them* ABSOLVE, clear, acquit, find innocent, discharge; *formal* exculpate. See note at ABSOLVE. ANTONYMS charge, convict.

**2** *Pope Clement V exonerated the king from his oath* RELEASE, discharge, free, liberate; excuse, exempt, except, dispense; *informal* let off. ANTONYM hold to.

**exorbitant** adjective *exorbitant interest rates* EXTORTIONATE, excessively high, excessive, prohibitive, outrageous, unreasonable, inflated, unconscionable, huge, enormous; *informal* steep, stiff, sky-high, over the top, rip-off. ANTONYM reasonable.

**exotic** adjective **1** *exotic birds* FOREIGN, nonnative, tropical; introduced, imported. ANTONYM native.

**2** *exotic places* FOREIGN, faraway, far-off, far-flung, distant. ANTONYMS familiar, nearby.

**3** *Carlotta's exotic appearance* STRIKING, colorful, eye-catching, flamboyant; unusual, unconventional, out of the ordinary, foreign-looking, extravagant, outlandish, orchidaceous; *informal* offbeat, off the wall. ANTONYM conventional.

**expand** verb **1** *metals expand when heated* INCREASE IN SIZE, become larger, enlarge; swell, dilate, inflate; lengthen, stretch, thicken, fill out. ANTONYMS shrink, contract.

**2** *the company is expanding* GROW, become/make larger, become/make bigger, increase in size, increase in scope, upsize; extend, augment, broaden, widen, develop, diversify, build up; branch out, spread, proliferate. ANTONYMS shrink, scale down.

**3** *the senator* ***expanded on*** *the proposals* ELABORATE ON, enlarge on, go into detail about, flesh out, develop, expatiate on.

**4** *she learned to expand and flourish among new acquaintances* RELAX, unbend, become relaxed, grow friendlier, loosen up. ANTONYMS tense up, clam up.

**expanse** noun *an expanse of wheat and barley* AREA, stretch, sweep, tract, swathe, belt, region; sea, carpet, blanket, sheet.

**expansion** noun **1** *expansion and contraction of blood vessels* ENLARGEMENT, increase in size, swelling, dilation; lengthening, elongation, stretching, thickening. ANTONYM contraction.

**2** *the expansion of the company* GROWTH, increase in size, enlargement, extension, development; spread, proliferation, multiplication. ANTONYM reduction in size.

**3** *an expansion of a lecture given last year* ELABORATION, enlargement, amplification, development. ANTONYMS abridgment, summary.

**expansive** adjective **1** *expansive grassland* EXTENSIVE, sweeping, rolling.

**2** *expansive coverage* WIDE-RANGING, extensive, broad, wide, comprehensive, thorough, full-scale.

**3** *Bethany became engagingly expansive* COMMUNICATIVE, forthcoming, sociable, friendly, outgoing, affable, chatty, talkative, garrulous, effusive, loquacious, voluble.

**expatiate** verb *he expatiated on the topic of volunteerism* SPEAK/WRITE AT LENGTH, go into detail, expound, dwell, dilate, expand, enlarge, elaborate; *formal* perorate.

**expatriate** noun *expatriates working overseas* EMIGRANT, nonnative, émigré, migrant; *informal* expat. ANTONYM national.

▸ adjective *expatriate workers* EMIGRANT, living abroad, nonnative, foreign, émigré; *informal* expat. ANTONYMS indigenous, native.

▸ verb *he was expatriated* EXILE, deport, banish, expel. ANTONYM repatriate.

**expect** verb **1** *I expect she'll be late* SUPPOSE, presume, think, believe, imagine, assume, surmise; *informal* guess, reckon, figure.

**2** *a 10 percent rise was expected* ANTICIPATE, await, look for, hope for, look forward to; contemplate, bargain for/on, bank on; predict, forecast, envisage, envision.

**3** *we expect total loyalty* REQUIRE, ask for, call for, want, insist on, demand.

**expectancy** noun **1** *feverish expectancy* ANTICIPATION, expectation, eagerness, excitement.

**2** *life expectancy* LIKELIHOOD, probability, outlook, prospect.

**expectant** adjective **1** *expectant fans* EAGER, excited, psyched, agog, waiting with bated breath, hopeful; in suspense, on tenterhooks.

**2** *an expectant mother* PREGNANT; *informal* expecting, with a bun in the oven; *chiefly Brit. informal* preggers; *technical* gravid; *dated* in the family way; *archaic* with child.

**expectation** noun **1** *her expectations were unrealistic* SUPPOSITION, assumption, presumption, conjecture, surmise, calculation, prediction, hope.

2 *tense with expectation* ANTICIPATION, expectancy, eagerness, excitement, suspense.

**expecting** adjective *informal*. See EXPECTANT sense 2.

**expedient** adjective *a politically expedient strategy* CONVENIENT, advantageous, in one's own interests, useful, of use, beneficial, of benefit, helpful; practical, pragmatic, politic, prudent, wise, judicious, sensible.

▸ noun *a temporary expedient* MEASURE, means, method, stratagem, scheme, plan, move, tactic, maneuver, device, contrivance, ploy, machination, dodge.

**expedite** verb *our legal assistants can help expedite the paperwork* SPEED UP, accelerate, hurry, hasten, step up, quicken, precipitate, dispatch; advance, facilitate, ease, make easier, further, promote, aid, push through, urge on, boost, stimulate, spur on, help along, catalyze, fast-track. ANTONYM delay.

**expedition** noun 1 *an expedition to the South Pole* JOURNEY, voyage, tour, odyssey; exploration, safari, trek, hike. See note at JOURNEY.

2 *informal a shopping expedition* TRIP, excursion, outing, jaunt.

3 *all members of the expedition* GROUP, team, party, crew, band, squad.

**expeditious** adjective *an expeditious review* SPEEDY, swift, quick, rapid, fast, brisk, efficient; prompt, punctual, immediate, instant; *literary* fleet. ANTONYM slow.

**expel** verb 1 *the opposition leader was expelled from her party* THROW OUT, eject, bar, ban, debar, drum out, oust, remove, get rid of, dismiss; *Military* cashier; *informal* chuck out, sling out, kick out, boot out, give someone the bum's rush. See note at EJECT. ANTONYM admit.

2 *he was expelled from the country* BANISH, exile, deport, evict, expatriate, drive out, throw out.

3 *Dolly expelled a hiss* LET OUT, discharge, eject, issue, send forth.

**expend** verb 1 *they had already expended $75,000* SPEND, pay out, disburse, dole out, get through, waste, fritter (away), dissipate; *informal* fork out, dish out, shell out, lay out, cough up, blow, splurge, ante up. ANTONYMS save, conserve.

2 *children expend a lot of energy* USE UP, use, utilize, consume, eat up, deplete, get through, burn through. ANTONYM conserve.

**expendable** adjective 1 *an accountant decided Mathers was expendable* DISPENSABLE, replaceable, nonessential, inessential, unnecessary, noncore, unneeded, not required, superfluous, disposable. ANTONYMS indispensable, essential.

2 *an expendable satellite launcher* DISPOSABLE, throwaway, single-use.

**expenditure** noun 1 *the expenditure of funds* SPENDING, paying out, outlay, use, disbursement, doling out, waste, wasting, frittering (away), dissipation. ANTONYMS saving, conservation.

2 *reducing public expenditure* COSTS, spending, payments, expenses, overheads. ANTONYM income.

**expense** noun 1 *the expense of entertaining* COST, price, charge, outlay, fee, tariff, levy, payment; *informal, humorous* damage.

2 **(expenses)** *regular expenses* OVERHEAD, costs, outlay, expenditure(s), charges, bills, payment(s); incidentals.

3 *tax cuts come at the expense of social programs* SACRIFICE, cost, loss.

**expensive** adjective *an expensive meal* COSTLY, high-priced, dear; overpriced, exorbitant, extortionate; *informal* steep, pricey, costing an arm and a leg, big-ticket, costing the earth. ANTONYMS cheap, economical.

**experience** noun 1 *qualifications and experience* SKILL, knowledge, practical knowledge, understanding; background, record, history; maturity, worldliness, sophistication; *informal* know-how.

2 *an enjoyable experience* INCIDENT, occurrence, event, happening, episode; adventure, exploit, escapade.

3 *his first **experience of** business* INVOLVEMENT IN, participation in, contact with, acquaintance with, exposure to, observation of, awareness of, insight into.

▸ verb *some policemen experience harassment* UNDERGO, encounter, meet, come into contact with, come across, come up against, face, be faced with.

**experienced** adjective 1 *an experienced pilot* KNOWLEDGEABLE, skillful, skilled, expert, accomplished, adept, adroit, master, consummate; proficient, trained, competent, capable, well trained, well versed; seasoned, practiced, mature, veteran. ANTONYM novice.

2 *she deluded herself that she was experienced* WORLDLY WISE, worldly, sophisticated, suave, urbane, mature, knowing; *informal* streetwise, street smart. ANTONYM naive.

**experiment** noun 1 *carrying out experiments* TEST, investigation, trial, examination, observation; assessment, evaluation, appraisal, analysis, study.

2 *these results have been established by experiment* RESEARCH, experimentation, observation, analysis, testing.

▸ verb *they experimented with new ideas* CONDUCT EXPERIMENTS, carry out trials/tests, conduct research; test, trial, do tests on, try out, assess, appraise, evaluate.

**experimental** adjective 1 *the experimental stage* EXPLORATORY, investigational, trial, test, pilot; speculative, conjectural, hypothetical, tentative, preliminary, untested, untried.

2 *experimental music* INNOVATIVE, innovatory, new, original, radical, avant-garde, cutting-edge, alternative, unorthodox, unconventional; *informal* way-out.

**expert** noun *she is an art expert* SPECIALIST, authority, pundit; adept, maestro, virtuoso, master, past master, wizard; connoisseur, aficionado; *informal* ace, buff, pro, techie, whiz, hotshot, maven, crackerjack.

▸ adjective *an expert chess player* SKILLFUL, skilled, adept, accomplished, talented, fine; master, masterly, brilliant, virtuoso, magnificent, outstanding, great, exceptional, excellent, first-class, first-rate, superb; proficient, good, able, capable, experienced, practiced, knowledgeable; *informal* ace, crack, mean. ANTONYM incompetent.

**expertise** noun *a high level of expertise in psychiatry is required* SKILL, skillfulness, expertness, prowess, proficiency, competence; knowledge, mastery, ability, aptitude, facility, capability; *informal* know-how.

**expiate** verb *the desire to expiate his sins* ATONE FOR, make amends for, make up for, do penance for, pay for, redress, redeem, offset, make good.

**expire** verb **1** *my contract has expired* RUN OUT, become invalid, become void, lapse; END, finish, stop, come to an end, terminate.

**2** *the spot where he expired* DIE, pass away/on, breathe one's last; *informal* kick the bucket, bite the dust, croak, buy it, buy the farm; *dated* depart this life.

**3** *technical* *the breath is then expired* BREATHE OUT, exhale, blow out, expel.

**explain** verb **1** *a technician explained the procedure* DESCRIBE, give an explanation of, make clear, make intelligible, spell out, put into words; elucidate, expound, explicate, clarify, throw/shed light on; gloss, interpret. See note at CLARIFY.

**2** *nothing could explain his newfound wealth* ACCOUNT FOR, give an explanation for, give a reason for; justify, give a justification for, give an excuse for, vindicate, legitimize.

**explanation** noun **1** *an explanation of the ideas contained in the essay* CLARIFICATION, simplification; description, report, statement; elucidation, exposition, expounding, explication; gloss, interpretation, commentary, exegesis.

**2** *I owe you an explanation* ACCOUNT, reason; justification, excuse, alibi, defense, vindication, story, answers.

**explanatory** adjective *write two or three explanatory paragraphs* EXPLAINING, descriptive, describing, illustrative, interpretive, instructive, expository.

**expletive** noun *she let out an expletive and slammed the phone down* SWEAR WORD, obscenity, profanity, oath, curse, four-letter word, dirty word; *informal* cuss word, cuss; *formal* imprecation; (**expletives**) bad language, foul language, strong language, swearing.

**explicable** adjective *it is our understanding of history that makes the present more explicable* EXPLAINABLE, understandable, comprehensible, accountable, intelligible, interpretable.

**explicate** verb *I'm not sure anyone could fully explicate the works of Joyce* EXPLAIN, make explicit, clarify, make plain/clear, spell out, untangle; interpret, translate, elucidate, expound, illuminate, throw light on. See note at CLARIFY.

**explicit** adjective **1** *explicit instructions* CLEAR, plain, straightforward, crystal clear, easily understandable; precise, exact, specific, unequivocal, unambiguous; detailed, comprehensive, exhaustive. ANTONYM vague.

**2** *sexually explicit material* GRAPHIC, uncensored, candid, full-frontal, hard-core.

**explode** verb **1** *a bomb has exploded* BLOW UP, detonate, go off, burst (apart), fly apart, erupt.

**2** *exploding the first atomic device* DETONATE, set off, let off, discharge. ANTONYMS disarm, defuse.

**3** *he exploded in anger* LOSE ONE'S TEMPER, blow up, get angry, become enraged, get mad; *informal* fly off the handle, hit the roof, blow one's cool/top/stack, go wild, go bananas, go ballistic, see red, go off the deep end, go crackers, go postal.

**4** *the city's population is exploding* INCREASE SUDDENLY/RAPIDLY, mushroom, snowball, escalate, multiply, burgeon, rocket, skyrocket.

**5** *exploding the myths about men* DISPROVE, refute, invalidate, negate, discredit, debunk, dispel, belie, give the lie to; *informal* poke holes in, blow out of the water; *formal* confute. ANTONYM confirm.

**exploit** verb **1** *we should exploit this new technology* UTILIZE, harness, use, make use of, turn/put to good use, make the most of, capitalize on, benefit from; *informal* cash in on.

**2** *exploiting the workers* TAKE ADVANTAGE OF, abuse, impose on, treat unfairly, misuse, ill-treat; *informal* walk (all) over, take for a ride, rip off.

▸ noun *his exploits brought him notoriety* FEAT, deed, act, adventure, stunt, escapade; achievement, accomplishment, attainment; *informal* lark, caper.

**exploration** noun **1** *the exploration of space* INVESTIGATION, study, survey, research, inspection, examination, scrutiny, observation; consideration, analysis, review.

**2** *explorations into the mountains* EXPEDITION, trip, journey, voyage; *archaic* peregrination; (**explorations**) travels.

**exploratory** adjective *exploratory surgery* INVESTIGATIVE, investigational, explorative, probing, fact-finding; experimental, trial, tentative, test, preliminary, provisional.

**explore** verb **1** *they explored all the possibilities* INVESTIGATE, look into, consider; examine, research, survey, scrutinize, study, review, go over with a fine-tooth comb; *informal* check out.

**2** *a rare chance to explore the Galapagos Islands* TRAVEL OVER/IN/THROUGH, tour, range over; survey, take a look at, inspect, investigate, reconnoiter, wander through.

**explorer** noun *the street is named after Peary, the Arctic explorer* TRAVELER, discoverer, voyager, adventurer; surveyor, scout, prospector.

**explosion** noun **1** *Edward heard the explosion* DETONATION, eruption, blowing up; bang, blast, boom, kaboom.

**2** *an explosion of anger* OUTBURST, flare-up, outbreak, eruption, storm, rush, surge; fit, paroxysm, attack.

**3** *the explosion of human populations* SUDDEN/RAPID INCREASE, mushrooming, snowballing, escalation, multiplication, burgeoning, rocketing, skyrocketing.

**explosive** adjective **1** *explosive gases* VOLATILE, inflammable, flammable, combustible, incendiary.

**2** *Biff's explosive temper* FIERY, stormy, violent, volatile, angry, passionate, tempestuous, turbulent, touchy, irascible, hotheaded, short-tempered.

**3** *an explosive situation* TENSE, charged, highly charged, overwrought; dangerous, perilous, hazardous, sensitive, delicate, unstable, volatile.

**4** *explosive population growth* SUDDEN, dramatic, rapid; mushrooming, snowballing, escalating, rocketing, skyrocketing, accelerating.

▸ noun *stocks of explosives* BOMB, incendiary (device).

**exponent** noun *the new premier is an exponent of free trade* ADVOCATE, supporter, proponent, upholder, backer, defender, champion; promoter, propagandist, campaigner, fighter, crusader, enthusiast, apologist; *informal* cheerleader, booster. ANTONYMS critic, opponent.

**export** verb **1** *exporting raw materials* SELL OVERSEAS/ABROAD, send overseas/abroad, ship overseas/abroad, market overseas/abroad, trade internationally. ANTONYM import.

**2** *she is trying to export her ideas to Japan* TRANSMIT, spread, disseminate, circulate, communicate, pass on; *literary* bruit about/abroad.

**expose** verb **1** *at low tide, the sands are exposed* REVEAL, uncover, lay bare. ANTONYM cover.

**2** *he was* ***exposed to*** *asbestos* MAKE VULNERABLE TO, subject to, lay open to, put at risk of/from, put in jeopardy of/from. ANTONYM protect.

**3** *they were* ***exposed to*** *liberal ideas* INTRODUCE TO, bring into contact with, make aware of, familiarize with, acquaint with. ANTONYM keep away.

**4** *he was exposed as a liar* UNCOVER, reveal, unveil, unmask, detect, find out; discover, bring to light, bring into the open, make known; denounce, condemn; *informal* spill the beans on, blow the whistle on.

**exposed** adjective *an exposed hillside* UNPROTECTED, unsheltered, open to the elements/weather; vulnerable, defenseless, undefended. ANTONYM sheltered.

**exposition** noun **1** *a lucid exposition* EXPLANATION, description, elucidation, explication, interpretation; account, commentary, appraisal, assessment, discussion, exegesis.

**2** *the exposition will feature 200 exhibits* EXHIBITION, fair, trade fair, trade show, show, expo, display, presentation, demonstration, exhibit.

**expository** adjective *expository dialogue* EXPLANATORY, descriptive, describing, explicatory, explicative, interpretative, exegetical.

**expostulate** verb *Jim* ***expostulated with*** *the teacher's opinion to no avail* REMONSTRATE WITH, disagree with, argue with, take issue with, protest against, reason against, express disagreement with, raise objections to, rail against.

**exposure** noun **1** *the exposure of the lizard's vivid blue tongue* REVEALING, revelation, uncovering, baring, laying bare.

**2** *exposure to harmful chemicals* SUBJECTION, vulnerability, laying open.

**3** *suffering from exposure* HYPOTHERMIA, cold, frostbite.

**4** ***exposure to*** *great literature* INTRODUCTION TO, experience of/with, contact with, familiarity with, acquaintance with, awareness of.

**5** *the exposure of a banking scandal* UNCOVERING, revelation, disclosure, unveiling, unmasking, discovery, detection; denunciation, condemnation.

**6** *we're getting a lot of exposure* PUBLICITY, coverage, publicizing, advertising, public interest/attention, media interest/attention, ink; *informal* hype, face time.

**7** *a southern exposure* OUTLOOK, aspect, view; position, setting, location.

**expound** verb **1** *he expounded his theories* PRESENT, put forward, set forth, propose, propound; explain, give an explanation of, detail, spell out, describe.

**2** *a treatise expounding Chomsky's theories* EXPLAIN, interpret, explicate, elucidate; comment on, give a commentary on. PHRASE: **expound on** *he expounded on the virtues of books* ELABORATE ON, expand on, expatiate on, discuss at length.

**express**[1] verb **1** *community leaders expressed their anger* COMMUNICATE, convey, indicate, show, demonstrate, reveal, make manifest, put across/over, get across/over; articulate, put into words, utter, voice, give voice to; state, assert, proclaim, profess, air, make public, give vent to; *formal* evince.

**2** *all the juice is expressed* SQUEEZE OUT, press out, extract. PHRASE: **express oneself** *he had difficulty expressing himself* COMMUNICATE ONE'S THOUGHTS/OPINIONS/VIEWS, put thoughts into words, speak one's mind, say what's on one's mind.

**express**[2] adjective *an express bus* RAPID, swift, fast, quick, speedy, high-speed; nonstop, direct. ANTONYMS slow, local.

**expression** noun **1** *the free expression of opposition views* UTTERANCE, uttering, voicing, pronouncement, declaration, articulation, assertion, setting forth; dissemination, circulation, communication, spreading, promulgation.

**2** *an expression of sympathy* INDICATION, demonstration, show, exhibition, token; communication, illustration, revelation.

**3** *an expression of harassed fatigue* LOOK, appearance, air, manner, countenance, mien.

**4** *a timeworn expression* IDIOM, phrase, idiomatic expression; proverb, saying, adage, maxim, axiom, aphorism, saw, motto, platitude, cliché.

**5** *these pieces are very different in expression* EMOTION, feeling, spirit, passion, intensity; style, intonation, tone.

**6** *essential oils obtained by expression* SQUEEZING, pressing, extraction, extracting.

**expressionless** adjective **1** *his face was expressionless* IN-

SCRUTABLE, deadpan, poker-faced; blank, vacant, emotionless, unemotional, inexpressive; glazed, stony, wooden, impassive. ANTONYM expressive.

**2** *a flat, expressionless tone* DULL, dry, toneless, monotonous, boring, tedious, flat, wooden, unmodulated, unvarying, devoid of feeling/emotion. ANTONYMS interesting, lively.

**expressive** adjective **1** *an expressive shrug* ELOQUENT, meaningful, demonstrative, suggestive. ANTONYM expressionless.

**2** *an expressive song* EMOTIONAL, full of emotion/feeling, passionate, poignant, moving, stirring, evocative, powerful, emotionally charged. ANTONYM unemotional.

**3** *his diction is very expressive of his upbringing* INDICATIVE, demonstrative, revealing.

**expressly** adverb **1** *he was expressly forbidden to discuss the matter* EXPLICITLY, clearly, directly, plainly, distinctly, unambiguously, unequivocally; absolutely; specifically, categorically, pointedly, emphatically.

**2** *a machine expressly built for spraying paint* SOLELY, specifically, particularly, specially, exclusively, just, only, explicitly.

**expropriate** verb *legislation to expropriate land from absentee landlords* SEIZE, take away, take over, take, appropriate, take possession of, requisition, commandeer, claim, acquire, sequestrate, confiscate; *Law* distrain.

**expulsion** noun **1** *expulsion from the party* REMOVAL, debarment, dismissal, exclusion, discharge, ejection, drumming out. ANTONYM admission.

**2** *the expulsion of bodily wastes* DISCHARGE, ejection, excretion, voiding, evacuation, elimination, passing.

**expunge** verb *a moment that cannot be expunged from his memory* ERASE, remove, delete, rub out, wipe out, efface; cross out, strike out, blot out, destroy, obliterate, scratch, eradicate, eliminate, deep-six.

**expurgate** verb *a book that had been expurgated for use in schools* CENSOR, bowdlerize, blue-pencil, cut, edit; clean up, sanitize, make acceptable, make palatable, water down, tame.

**exquisite** adjective **1** *exquisite antique glass* BEAUTIFUL, lovely, elegant, fine; magnificent, superb, excellent, wonderful, ornate, well-crafted, well-made, perfect; delicate, fragile, dainty, subtle.

**2** *exquisite taste* DISCRIMINATING, discerning, sensitive, selective, fastidious; refined, cultivated, cultured, educated.

**3** *exquisite agony* INTENSE, acute, keen, piercing, sharp, severe, racking, excruciating, agonizing, harrowing, searing; unbearable, unendurable.

**extant** adjective *extant manuscripts* STILL EXISTING, in existence, existent, surviving, remaining, undestroyed.

**extempore** adjective *an extempore speech* IMPROMPTU, spontaneous, unscripted, ad lib, extemporary, extemporaneous; improvised, unrehearsed, unplanned, unprepared, off the top of one's head; *informal* off-the-cuff; *formal* ad libitum. ANTONYM rehearsed.

▸ adverb *he was speaking extempore* SPONTANEOUSLY, extemporaneously, ad lib, without preparation, without rehearsal, off the top of one's head; *informal* off the cuff; *formal* ad libitum.

**extemporize** verb *jazz musicians extemporize freely* IMPROVISE, ad lib, play it by ear, think on one's feet; *informal* wing it, fly by the seat of one's pants.

**extend** verb **1** *he attempted to extend his dominions* EXPAND, enlarge, increase, make larger, make bigger; lengthen, widen, broaden. ANTONYMS reduce, shrink.

**2** *the garden extends down to the road* CONTINUE, carry on, run on, stretch (out), reach, lead.

**3** *we have extended our range of services* WIDEN, expand, broaden; augment, supplement, increase, add to, enhance, develop. ANTONYM narrow.

**4** *extending the life of the charter* PROLONG, lengthen, increase; stretch out, protract, spin out, string out. ANTONYM shorten.

**5** *extend your arms and legs* STRETCH OUT, spread out, reach out, straighten out.

**6** *he extended a hand in greeting* HOLD OUT, reach out, hold forth; offer, give, outstretch, proffer.

**7** *we wish to extend our thanks to Mr. Bayes* OFFER, proffer, give, grant, bestow, accord. PHRASE: **extend to** *her tolerance did not always extend to her staff* INCLUDE, take in, incorporate, encompass.

**extended** adjective *an extended legal battle* PROLONGED, protracted, long-lasting, long-drawn-out, spun out, long, dragged out, strung out, lengthy; *informal* marathon.

**extension** noun **1** *they are planning a new extension* ADDITION, adjunct, annex, wing, supplementary building, ell, add-on.

**2** *an extension of knowledge* EXPANSION, increase, enlargement, widening, broadening, deepening; augmentation, enhancement, development, growth, continuation.

**3** *an extension of opening hours* PROLONGATION, lengthening, increase.

**4** *I need an extension on my essay* POSTPONEMENT, more/extra time, deferral, delay.

**extensive** adjective **1** *a mansion with extensive grounds* LARGE, large-scale, sizable, substantial, considerable, ample, expansive, great, vast.

**2** *extensive knowledge* COMPREHENSIVE, thorough, exhaustive; broad, wide, wide-ranging, catholic, eclectic.

**extent** noun **1** *two acres in extent* AREA, size, expanse, length; proportions, dimensions.

**2** *the full extent of her father's illness* DEGREE, scale, level, magnitude, scope; size, breadth, width, reach, range.

**extenuating** adjective *a just decision must allow for extenuating circumstances* MITIGATING, excusing, exonerative, palliative, justifying, justificatory, vindicating; *formal* exculpatory.

**exterior** adjective *the exterior walls* OUTER, outside, outermost, outward, external. ANTONYM interior.

▸ noun *the exterior of the building* OUTSIDE, outer surface, external surface, outward appearance, facade.

**exterminate** verb *they were hired to exterminate the carpenter ants* KILL, put to death, take/end the life of, dispatch; slaughter, butcher, massacre, wipe out, eliminate, eradicate, annihilate; murder, assassinate, execute, slay; *informal* do away with, bump off, do in, take out, blow away, ice, rub out, waste. See note at DESTROY.

**external** adjective **1** *an external wall* OUTER, outside, outermost, outward, exterior. ANTONYM internal.

**2** *an external examiner* OUTSIDE, independent, nonresident, from elsewhere. ANTONYM in-house.

**extinct** adjective **1** *an extinct species* VANISHED, lost, died out, no longer existing, no longer extant, wiped out, destroyed, gone. ANTONYM extant.

**2** *an extinct volcano* INACTIVE. ANTONYM dormant.

**extinction** noun *efforts to save the California condor from extinction* DYING OUT, disappearance, vanishing; extermination, destruction, elimination, eradication, annihilation.

**extinguish** verb **1** *the fire was extinguished* DOUSE, put out, stamp out, smother, beat out. ANTONYM light.

**2** *all hope was extinguished* DESTROY, end, finish off, put an end to, bring to an end, terminate, remove, annihilate, wipe out, erase, eliminate, eradicate, obliterate; *informal* take out, rub out. ANTONYM start up.

**extol** verb *nutritionists extol the virtues of fiber* PRAISE ENTHUSIASTICALLY, go into raptures about/over, wax lyrical about, sing the praises of, praise to the skies, acclaim, exalt, eulogize, adulate, rhapsodize over, rave about, enthuse about/over; *informal* go wild about, go on about, ballyhoo; *formal* laud; *archaic* panegyrize. See note at PRAISE. ANTONYM criticize.

**extort** verb *he was convicted of extorting money from local residents* FORCE, extract, exact, wring, wrest, screw, squeeze, obtain by threat(s), blackmail someone for; *informal* put the bite on someone for; soak, rook.

**extortion** noun *arrested on a charge of extortion* BLACKMAIL, shakedown; *formal* exaction.

**extortionate** adjective *extortionate prices* EXORBITANT, excessively high, excessive, outrageous, unreasonable, inordinate, inflated, exacting, harsh, severe, oppressive; *informal* over the top; grasping, bloodsucking, avaricious, greedy, moneygrubbing.

**extra** adjective *extra income* ADDITIONAL, more, added, supplementary, further, auxiliary, ancillary, subsidiary, secondary, bonus.

▸ adverb **1** *working extra hard* EXCEPTIONALLY, particularly, specially, especially, very, extremely; unusually, extraordinarily, uncommonly, remarkably, outstandingly, amazingly, incredibly, really, awfully, terribly; *informal* seriously, mucho, majorly.

**2** *we charge extra for cheese* IN ADDITION, additionally, as well, also, too, besides, on top (of that); *archaic* withal.

▸ noun **1** *an optional extra* ADDITION, supplement, adjunct, addendum, add-on, bonus.

**2** *a group of tourists were hired as extras for the scene on the bus* WALK-ON, supernumerary, spear carrier.

**extract** verb **1** *he extracted the videocassette* TAKE OUT, draw out, pull out, remove, withdraw; free, release, extricate. ANTONYM insert.

**2** *extracting money* WREST, exact, wring, screw, squeeze, obtain by force, obtain by threat(s), extort, blackmail someone for; *informal* put the bite on someone for.

**3** *the roots are crushed to extract the juice* SQUEEZE OUT, express, press out, obtain. ANTONYMS add, infuse.

**4** *the figures are extracted from the report* EXCERPT, select, reproduce, copy, take. ANTONYM insert.

**5** *ideas extracted from a variety of theories* DERIVE, develop, evolve, deduce, infer, obtain; *formal* educe.

▸ noun **1** *an extract from his article* EXCERPT, passage, citation, quotation; **(excerpts)** analects.

**2** *an extract of the ginseng root* DECOCTION, distillation, distillate, abstraction, concentrate, essence, juice.

**extraction** noun **1** *the extraction of gallstones* REMOVAL, taking out, drawing out, pulling out, withdrawal; freeing, release, extrication. ANTONYM insertion.

**2** *the extraction of grape juice* SQUEEZING, expressing, pressing, obtaining.

**3** *a man of Irish extraction* DESCENT, ancestry, parentage, ancestors, family, antecedents; lineage, line, origin, derivation, birth; genealogy, heredity, stock, pedigree, blood, bloodline; roots, origins; *rare* filiation, stirps.

**extradite** verb *the Russians extradited him to Germany* DEPORT, send, ship, deliver, hand over; repatriate.

**extradition** noun *detainees awaiting extradition* DEPORTATION, repatriation, expulsion.

**extraneous** adjective **1** *extraneous considerations* IRRELEVANT, immaterial, beside the point, unrelated, unconnected, inapposite, inapplicable, superfluous.

**2** *extraneous noise* EXTERNAL, outside, exterior.

**extraordinary** adjective **1** *an extraordinary coincidence* REMARKABLE, exceptional, amazing, astonishing, astounding, sensational, stunning, incredible, unbelievable, phenomenal; striking, outstanding, momentous, impressive, singular, memorable, unforgettable, unique, noteworthy; out of the ordinary, unusual, uncommon, rare, surprising; *informal* fantastic, terrific, tremendous, stupendous, awesome; *literary* wondrous.

**2** *extraordinary speed* VERY GREAT, tremendous, enormous, immense, prodigious, stupendous, monumental.

**extravagance** noun 1 *a fit of extravagance* PROFLIGACY, improvidence, wastefulness, prodigality, lavishness.

2 *the costliest brand is an extravagance* LUXURY, indulgence, self-indulgence, treat, extra, nonessential.

3 *the extravagance of the decor* ORNATENESS, elaborateness, embellishment, ornamentation; ostentation, overelaborateness, excessiveness, exaggeration, outrageousness, immoderation, excess.

**extravagant** adjective 1 *an extravagant lifestyle* SPENDTHRIFT, profligate, improvident, wasteful, prodigal, lavish. ANTONYM thrifty.

2 *extravagant gifts* EXPENSIVE, costly, lavish, high-priced, high-cost; valuable, precious; *informal* pricey, costing the earth. ANTONYM cheap.

3 *extravagant prices* EXORBITANT, extortionate, excessive, high, unreasonable. ANTONYMS reasonable, low.

4 *extravagant praise* EXCESSIVE, immoderate, exaggerated, gushing, unrestrained, effusive, fulsome. See note at PROFUSE. ANTONYM moderate.

5 *decorated in an extravagant style* ORNATE, elaborate, decorated, ornamented, fancy; overelaborate, gaudy, garish, ostentatious, exaggerated, baroque, rococo; *informal* lavish, flashy, glitzy. ANTONYM plain.

**extravaganza** noun *a star-studded extravaganza to raise funds for AIDS research* SPECTACULAR, display, spectacle, show, pageant, gala; blowout, barn-burner.

**extreme** adjective 1 *extreme danger* UTMOST, very great, greatest, greatest possible, maximum, maximal, highest, supreme, great, acute, enormous, severe, high, exceptional, extraordinary. ANTONYM slight.

2 *extreme measures* DRASTIC, serious, desperate, dire, radical, far-reaching, momentous, consequential; heavy, sharp, severe, austere, harsh, tough, strict, rigorous, oppressive, draconian. ANTONYM mild.

3 *extreme views* RADICAL, extremist, immoderate, fanatical, revolutionary, rebel, subversive, militant, far-right, far-left. ANTONYM moderate.

4 *extreme sports* DANGEROUS, hazardous, risky, high-risk, adventurous. ANTONYMS tame, safe.

5 *the extreme north* FURTHEST, farthest, furthermost, far, very, utmost; *archaic* outmost. ANTONYM near.

▸ noun 1 *the two extremes* OPPOSITE, antithesis, side of the coin, (opposite) pole, antipode.

2 *this attitude is taken to its extreme in the following quote* LIMIT, extremity, highest/greatest degree, maximum, height, top, zenith, peak, ne plus ultra.

PHRASE: **in the extreme** *David was generous in the extreme.* See EXTREMELY.

**extremely** adverb *even on the hottest days, the caverns are extremely cold* VERY, exceedingly, exceptionally, especially, extraordinarily, in the extreme, tremendously, immensely, vastly, hugely, intensely, acutely, singularly, uncommonly, unusually, decidedly, particularly, supremely, highly, remarkably, really, truly, mightily; *informal* terrifically, awfully, terribly, devilishly, majorly, seriously, mega, ultra, damn, damned, ever so, real, mighty, awful, way, darned, gosh-darn; *archaic* exceeding. ANTONYMS slightly, barely.

**extremist** noun *the attack was carried out by a group of right-wing extremists* FANATIC, radical, zealot, fundamentalist, hard-liner, militant, activist; *informal* ultra. See note at ZEALOT. ANTONYM moderate.

**extremity** noun 1 *the eastern extremity* LIMIT, end, edge, side, farthest point, boundary, border, frontier; perimeter, periphery, margin; *literary* bourn, marge.

2 *she lost feeling in her extremities* FINGERS AND TOES, hands and feet, limbs.

3 *the extremity of the violence* INTENSITY, magnitude, acuteness, ferocity, vehemence, fierceness, violence, severity, seriousness, strength, power, powerfulness, vigor, force, forcefulness.

4 *in extremity he will send for her* DIRE STRAITS, trouble, difficulty, hard times, hardship, adversity, misfortune, distress; (a) crisis, an emergency, (a) disaster, (a) catastrophe, calamity; a predicament, a plight, mess, a dilemma; *informal* a fix, a pickle, a jam, a spot, a bind, a hole, a sticky situation, hot water, deep water.

**extricate** verb *there's always someone who can extricate these wealthy little brats from their run-ins with the law* EXTRACT, free, release, disentangle, get out, remove, withdraw, disengage; *informal* get someone/oneself off the hook.

**extrinsic** adjective *climate, geography, and other extrinsic factors* EXTERNAL, extraneous, exterior, outside, outward. ANTONYM intrinsic.

**extrovert** noun *like many extroverts, he was unhappy inside* OUTGOING PERSON, sociable person, socializer, life of the party. ANTONYM introvert.

▸ adjective *Raj's extrovert personality* OUTGOING, extroverted, sociable, gregarious, genial, affable, friendly, unreserved. ANTONYM introverted.

**extrude** verb *machines extrude the plastics that become jars and bottles* FORCE OUT, thrust out, express, eject, expel, release, emit.

**exuberant** adjective 1 *exuberant guests dancing on the terrace* EBULLIENT, buoyant, cheerful, jaunty, lighthearted, high-spirited, exhilarated, excited, elated, exultant, euphoric, joyful, cheery, merry, jubilant, vivacious, enthusiastic, irrepressible, energetic, animated, full of life, lively, vigorous, adrenalized; *informal* bubbly, bouncy, chipper, chirpy, full of beans; *literary* blithe. ANTONYM gloomy.

2 *an exuberant welcome* EFFUSIVE, extravagant, fulsome, expansive, gushing, gushy, demonstrative. ANTONYM restrained.

3 *an exuberant coating of mosses* LUXURIANT, lush, rich, dense, thick, abundant, profuse, plentiful, prolific. ANTONYM meager.

**exude** verb **1** *milkweed exudes a milky sap* GIVE OFF/OUT, discharge, release, emit, issue; ooze, weep, secrete, excrete.

**2** *slime exudes from the fungus* OOZE, seep, issue, escape, discharge, flow, leak.

**3** *he exuded self-confidence* EMANATE, radiate, ooze, emit; display, show, evince, exhibit, manifest, transmit, embody.

**exult** verb **1** *her opponents exulted when she left* REJOICE, be joyful, be happy, be delighted, be elated, be ecstatic, be overjoyed, be jubilant, be rapturous, be in raptures, be thrilled, jump for joy, be on cloud nine, be in seventh heaven; celebrate, cheer; *informal* be over the moon, be on top of the world; *literary* joy; *archaic* jubilate. ANTONYM sorrow.

**2** *he* ***exulted in*** *his triumph* REJOICE AT/IN, take delight in, find/take pleasure in, find joy in, enjoy, revel in, glory in, delight in, relish, savor; be/feel proud of, congratulate oneself on. ANTONYM sorrow.

**exultant** adjective *the exultant winners waved to the crowd* JUBILANT, thrilled, triumphant, delighted, exhilarated, happy, overjoyed, joyous, joyful, gleeful, excited, rejoicing, ecstatic, euphoric, elated, rapturous, in raptures, enraptured, on cloud nine, in seventh heaven; *rare* exilient; *informal* over the moon, jumping for joy.

**exultation** noun *a gold medalist filled with exultation* JUBILATION, rejoicing, happiness, pleasure, joy, gladness, delight, glee, elation, cheer, euphoria, exhilaration, delirium, ecstasy, rapture, exuberance.

**eye** noun **1** *he rubbed his eyes* EYEBALL; *informal* peeper, baby blues; *literary* or *humorous* orb.

**2** *sharp eyes* EYESIGHT, vision, sight, powers of observation, perception, visual perception.

**3** *an eye for a bargain* APPRECIATION, awareness, alertness, perception, consciousness, feeling, instinct, intuition, nose.

**4** *his thoughtful eye* WATCH, observance, gaze, stare, regard; observation, surveillance, vigilance, contemplation, scrutiny.

**5** **(eyes)** *to desert was despicable in their eyes* OPINION, thinking, way of thinking, mind, view, viewpoint, point of view, attitude, standpoint, perspective, belief, judgment, assessment, analysis, estimation.

**6** *the eye of a needle* HOLE, opening, aperture, eyelet, slit, slot.

**7** *the eye of the storm* CENTER, middle, heart, core, hub, thick.

▸ verb *I saw him intently eyeing that antique car* LOOK AT, observe, view, gaze at, stare at, regard, contemplate, survey, scrutinize, consider, glance at; watch, keep an eye on, keep under observation; ogle, leer at, make eyes at; *informal* have/take a gander at, check out, size up, eyeball; *literary* behold.

PHRASES: **lay/set/clap eyes on** *informal have you ever laid your eyes on a more beautiful sailboat?* SEE, observe, notice, spot, spy, catch sight of, glimpse, catch/get a glimpse of; *literary* behold, espy, descry.

**see eye to eye** *even best friends can't expect to see eye to eye on everything* AGREE, concur, be in agreement, be of the same mind/opinion, be in accord, think as one; be on the same wavelength, get on/along.

**eye-catching** adjective *eye-catching designs adorn each door* STRIKING, arresting, conspicuous, dramatic, impressive, spectacular, breathtaking, dazzling, amazing, stunning, sensational, remarkable, distinctive, unusual, out of the ordinary.

**eyesight** noun *my eyesight is perfect* SIGHT, vision, faculty of sight, ability to see, visual perception, perception.

**eyesore** noun *what's left of the old factory is a danger and an eyesore* MONSTROSITY, blot (on the landscape), mess, scar, blight, disfigurement, blemish, ugly sight.

**eyewitness** noun *several eyewitnesses were questioned by the police* OBSERVER, onlooker, witness, bystander, spectator, watcher, viewer, passerby, gawker; *literary* beholder.

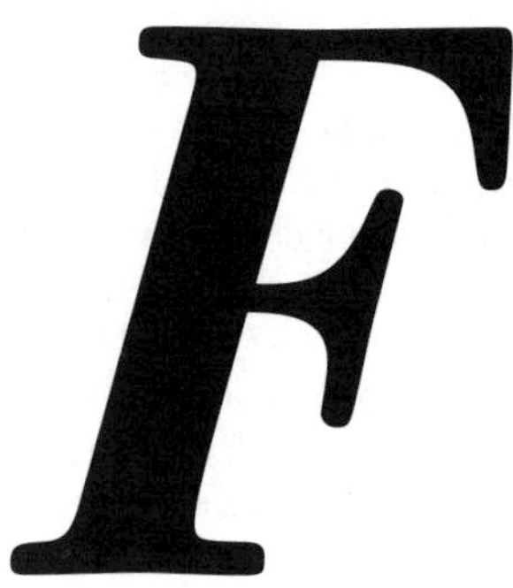

**fable** noun **1** *the fable of the wary fox* MORAL TALE, tale, parable, allegory.

**2** *the fables of ancient Greece* MYTH, legend, saga, epic, folk tale, folk story, fairy tale, mythos, folklore, mythology. See note at FICTION.

**fabric** noun **1** *the finest silk fabric* CLOTH, material, textile, tissue.

**2** *the fabric of society* STRUCTURE, infrastructure, framework, frame, form, composition, construction, foundations, warp and woof.

**fabricate** verb **1** *he fabricated research data* FALSIFY, fake, counterfeit, cook; invent, make up. See note at LIE[1].

**2** *fabricating a pack of lies* CONCOCT, make up, dream up, invent, trump up; *informal* cook up.

**3** *you will have to fabricate an exhaust system* MAKE, create, manufacture, produce; construct, build, assemble, put together, form, fashion.

**fabulous** adjective **1** *fabulous wealth* TREMENDOUS, stupendous, prodigious, phenomenal, remarkable, exceptional; astounding, amazing, fantastic, breathtaking, staggering, unthinkable, unimaginable, incredible, unbelievable, unheard of, untold, undreamed of, beyond one's wildest dreams; *informal* mind-boggling, mind-blowing, jaw-dropping.

**2** *informal we had a fabulous time.* See EXCELLENT.

**3** *a fabulous horselike beast* MYTHICAL, legendary, mythic, mythological, fabled, folkloric, fairy-tale; fictitious, imaginary, imagined, made up.

**face** noun **1** *a beautiful face* COUNTENANCE, physiognomy, features; *informal* mug; puss; *literary* visage; *archaic* front.

**2** *her face grew sad* (FACIAL) EXPRESSION, look, appearance, air, manner, bearing, countenance, mien.

**3** *he made a face at the sourness of the drink* GRIMACE, scowl, wry face, wince, frown, glower, pout, moue.

**4** *a cube has six faces* SIDE, aspect, flank, surface, plane, facet, wall, elevation.

**5** *a watch face* DIAL, display.

**6** *changing the face of the industry* APPEARANCE, outward appearance, aspect, nature, image.

**7** *he put on a brave face* FRONT, show, display, act, appearance, facade, exterior, mask, masquerade, pretense, pose, veneer.

**8** *criticism should never cause the recipient to lose face* RESPECT, honor, esteem, regard, admiration, approbation, acclaim, approval, favor, appreciation, popularity, prestige, standing, status, dignity; self-respect, self-esteem.

▸ verb **1** *the hotel faces the sea* LOOK OUT ON, front on to, look toward, be facing, look over/across, overlook, give on to, be opposite (to).

**2** *you'll just have to face the facts* ACCEPT, become reconciled to, get used to, become accustomed to, adjust to, acclimatize oneself to; learn to live with, cope with, deal with, come to terms with, become resigned to.

**3** *he faces a humiliating rejection* BE CONFRONTED BY, be faced with, encounter, experience, come into contact with, come up against.

**4** *the problems facing our police force* BESET, worry, distress, trouble, bother, confront; harass, oppress, vex, irritate, exasperate, strain, stress, tax; torment, plague, blight, bedevil, curse; *formal* discommode.

**5** *he faced the challenge boldly* BRAVE, face up to, encounter, meet, meet head-on, confront; oppose, resist, withstand.

**6** *a wall faced with stucco* COVER, clad, veneer, overlay, surface, dress, put a facing on, laminate, coat, line.

PHRASES: **face to face** *the two men stood face to face* FACING (EACH OTHER), opposite (each other), across from each other.

**on the face of it** *on the face on it, the peace talks are going quite well* OSTENSIBLY, to all appearances, to all intents and purposes, at first glance, on the surface, superficially; apparently, seemingly, outwardly, it seems (that), it would seem (that), it appears (that), it would appear (that), as far as one can see/tell, by all accounts.

**facet** noun **1** *the many facets of the gem* SURFACE, face, side, plane.

**2** *other facets of his character* ASPECT, feature, side, dimension, characteristic, detail, point, ingredient, strand; component, constituent, element.

**facetious** adjective *unfortunately, they took my facetious remarks seriously* FLIPPANT, flip, glib, frivolous, tongue-in-cheek, ironic, sardonic, joking, jokey, jocular, playful, sportive, teasing, mischievous; witty, amusing, funny, droll, comic, comical, lighthearted, jocose. ANTONYM serious.

**facile** adjective **1** *a facile explanation* SIMPLISTIC, superficial, oversimplified; shallow, glib, jejune, naive; dime-store.

**2** *he achieved a facile victory* EFFORTLESS, easy, undemanding, unexacting, painless, trouble-free.

**USAGE NOTE facile**

Always meaning "easy" in one sense or another, *facile* may connote either proficiency or shallowness. The writer must achieve clarity through context. Sometimes the word connotes the ease that comes with artistic mastery—e.g.: "Nicolai Dobrev played the jester, a noble baritone with a facile instrument." (*Boston Herald*; Mar. 30, 2002.) More often, it connotes triteness or oversimplification—e.g.: "But most mental health experts say closure is no holy grail, only rendered so by people seeking facile solutions to complex problems." (*Christian Science Monitor*; Mar. 28, 2002.) —*BG*

**facilitate** verb *private funding has facilitated our research* MAKE EASY/EASIER, ease, make possible, make smooth/smoother, smooth the way for; enable, assist, help (along), aid, oil the wheels of, expedite, speed up, accelerate, forward, advance, promote, further, encourage, catalyze, be a catalyst for. ANTONYM impede.

**facility** noun **1** *parking facilities* PROVISION, space, means, potential, equipment.

**2** *the facilities consisted of an old wooden outhouse* WASHROOM, toilet, restroom, bathroom.

**3** *a wealth of local facilities* AMENITY, resource, service, advantage, convenience, benefit.

**4** *a medical facility* ESTABLISHMENT, center, place, station, location, premises, site, post, base; *informal* joint, outfit, setup.

**5** *his facility for drawing* APTITUDE, talent, gift, flair, bent, skill, knack, genius; ability, proficiency, competence, capability, capacity, faculty; expertness, adeptness, prowess, mastery, artistry.

**facing** noun **1** *green velvet facings* COVERING, trimming, lining, interfacing.

**2** *brick facing on a concrete core* SIDING, facade, cladding, veneer, skin, surface, front, coating, covering, dressing, overlay, lamination, plating.

**facsimile** noun *a facsimile of the manuscript* COPY, reproduction, duplicate, photocopy, replica, likeness, print, reprint, printout, offprint, fax; *trademark* Xerox; *dated* carbon copy, photostat, mimeograph. ANTONYM original.

**fact** noun **1** *it is a fact that the water is polluted* REALITY, actuality, certainty; truth, verity, gospel. ANTONYMS lie, fiction.

**2** *every fact was double-checked* DETAIL, piece of information, particular, item, specific, element, point, factor, feature, characteristic, ingredient, circumstance, aspect, facet; **(facts)** information.

**3** *an accessory after the fact* EVENT, happening, occurrence, incident, act, deed. PHRASE: **in fact** *Mr. Hartmann was in fact present at the time of the shooting* ACTUALLY, in actuality, in actual fact, really, in reality, in point of fact, as a matter of fact, as it happens, in truth, to tell the truth; *archaic* in sooth, verily.

**faction** noun **1** *a faction of the party* CLIQUE, coterie, caucus, cabal, bloc, camp, group, grouping, sector, section, wing, arm, branch, set; ginger group, pressure group.

**2** *the council was split by faction* INFIGHTING, dissension, dissent, dispute, discord, strife, conflict, friction, argument, disagreement, controversy, quarreling, wrangling, bickering, squabbling, disharmony, disunity, schism.

**factious** adjective *factious parties have weakened the movement* DIVIDED, split, schismatic, discordant, conflicting, argumentative, disagreeing, disputatious, quarreling, quarrelsome, clashing, warring, at loggerheads, at odds, rebellious, mutinous. ANTONYM harmonious.

**factor** noun *this had been a key factor in his decision to withdraw* ELEMENT, part, component, ingredient, strand, constituent, point, detail, item, feature, facet, aspect, characteristic, consideration, influence, circumstance.

**factory** noun *jobs in the factories were getting harder to find* PLANT, works, yard, mill, workshop, shop; *informal* sweatshop.

**factotum** noun *back then, these wealthy college boys made sure their personal factotums were just a whistle away* HANDYMAN, jack of all trades; assistant, man Friday, gal/girl Friday; gofer; *informal* Mr./Ms. Fix-It.

**factual** adjective *a factual report from the chairman* TRUTHFUL, true, accurate, authentic, historical, genuine, fact-based; true-to-life, correct, exact, honest, faithful, literal, verbatim, word for word, well-documented, unbiased, objective, unvarnished; *formal* veridical. ANTONYM fictitious.

**faculty** noun **1** *the faculty of speech* POWER, capability, capacity, facility, wherewithal, means; **(faculties)** senses, wits, reason, intelligence.

**2** *an unusual faculty for unearthing contributors* ABILITY, proficiency, competence, capability, potential, capacity, facility; aptitude, talent, gift, flair, bent, skill, knack, genius; expertise, expertness, adeptness, adroitness, dexterity, prowess, mastery, artistry.

**3** *conflict between students and faculty* STAFF, teachers, professors, instructors.

**4** *the arts faculty* DEPARTMENT, school, division, section.

**fad** noun *when I was a kid, no fad was more apparent than the coonskin cap* CRAZE, vogue, trend, fashion, mode, enthusiasm, passion, obsession, mania, rage, compulsion, fixation, fetish, fancy, whim, fascination; *informal* thing.

**fade** verb **1** *the paintwork has faded* BECOME PALE, become bleached, become washed out, lose color, discolor; grow dull, grow dim, lose luster. ANTONYM brighten.

**2** *sunlight had faded the picture* BLEACH, wash out, make pale, blanch, whiten. ANTONYMS brighten, enhance.

**3** *remove the flower heads as they fade* WITHER, wilt, droop, shrivel, die.

**4** *the afternoon light began to fade* DIM, grow dim, grow faint, fail, dwindle, die away, wane, disappear, vanish, decline, melt away; *literary* evanesce. ANTONYM increase.

**5** *the Communist movement was **fading away*** DECLINE, die out, diminish, deteriorate, decay, crumble, collapse, fail, fall, sink, slump, go downhill; *informal* go to pot, go to the dogs; *archaic* retrograde. ANTONYM thrive.

**fail** verb **1** *the enterprise had failed* BE UNSUCCESSFUL, not succeed, fall through, fall flat, collapse, founder, backfire, meet with disaster, come to nothing, come to naught; *informal* flop, bomb. ANTONYM succeed.

**2** *he has failed the final French examination* BE UNSUCCESSFUL IN, not pass; not make the grade on; *informal* FLUNK, botch, blow, screw up, bungle. ANTONYM pass.

**3** *at his lowest point, his friends failed him* LET DOWN, disappoint; desert, abandon, betray, be disloyal to; *literary* forsake. ANTONYM support.

**4** *the crops failed* DIE, wither; be deficient, be insufficient, be inadequate. ANTONYM thrive.

**5** *daylight failed* FADE, dim, die away, wane, disappear, vanish.

**6** *the ventilation system failed* BREAK DOWN, break, stop working, cut out, crash; malfunction, go wrong, develop a fault; *informal* conk out, go on the blink, go on the fritz. ANTONYM work.

**7** *Joe's health was failing* DETERIORATE, degenerate, decline, fade, wane, ebb. ANTONYM improving.

**8** *900 businesses are failing a week* COLLAPSE, crash, go under, go bankrupt, go into receivership, go into liquidation, cease trading; *informal* fold, flop, go bust, go broke, go belly-up. ANTONYM thrive.

PHRASE: **without fail** *without fail, Carlos leaves for lunch at 12:05 every day* WITHOUT EXCEPTION, unfailingly, regularly, invariably, predictably, conscientiously, religiously, whatever happened.

**failing** noun *Deborah accepted him despite his failings* FAULT, shortcoming, weakness, imperfection, defect, flaw, frailty, foible, idiosyncrasy, vice. ANTONYM strength.

▸ preposition *failing financial assistance, you will be bankrupt* IN THE ABSENCE OF, lacking, barring, absent, without.

**failure** noun **1** *the failure of the assassination attempt* LACK OF SUCCESS, nonfulfillment, defeat, collapse, foundering. ANTONYM success.

**2** *all his schemes had been a failure* FIASCO, debacle, catastrophe, disaster; *informal* flop, megaflop, washout, dead loss, snafu, clinker, dud, no-go. ANTONYM success.

**3** *she was regarded as a failure* LOSER, underachiever, ne'er-do-well, disappointment; *informal* no-hoper, dead loss, dud, write-off. ANTONYM success.

**4** *his failure in duty* NEGLIGENCE, dereliction; omission, oversight.

**5** *a crop failure* INADEQUACY, insufficiency, deficiency, dearth, scarcity, shortfall.

**6** *the failure of the camera* BREAKING DOWN, breakdown, malfunction; crash.

**7** *company failures* COLLAPSE, crash, bankruptcy, insolvency, liquidation, closure. ANTONYM success.

**faint** adjective **1** *a faint mark* INDISTINCT, vague, unclear, indefinite, ill-defined, imperceptible, unobtrusive; pale, light, faded. ANTONYM clear.

**2** *a faint cry* QUIET, muted, muffled, stifled; feeble, weak, whispered, murmured, indistinct; low, soft, gentle. ANTONYM loud.

**3** *a faint possibility* SLIGHT, slender, slim, small, tiny, negligible, remote, vague, unlikely, improbable; *informal* minuscule. ANTONYM great.

**4** *faint praise* UNENTHUSIASTIC, halfhearted, weak, feeble. ANTONYM strong.

**5** *I suddenly felt faint* DIZZY, giddy, lightheaded, unsteady; *informal* woozy.

▸ verb *she thought he would faint* PASS OUT, lose consciousness, black out, keel over, swoon; *informal* flake out, conk out, zonk out, go out like a light.

▸ noun *a dead faint* BLACKOUT, fainting fit, loss of consciousness, swoon; *Medicine* syncope.

**faint-hearted** adjective *come now, my faint-hearted friend, I'll get you to safety* TIMID, timorous, nervous, easily scared, fearful, afraid; cowardly, craven, spineless, pusillanimous, lily-livered; *informal* chicken, chicken-hearted, yellow-bellied, gutless, sissy, wimpy, wimpish. ANTONYM brave.

**faintly** adverb **1** *Maria called his name faintly* INDISTINCTLY, softly, gently, weakly; in a whisper, in a murmur, in a low voice. ANTONYM loudly.

**2** *he looked faintly bewildered* SLIGHTLY, vaguely, somewhat, quite, fairly, rather, a little, a bit, a touch, a shade; *informal* sort of, kind of, kinda. ANTONYM extremely.

**fair**[1] adjective **1** *the courts were generally fair* JUST, equitable, honest, upright, honorable, trustworthy; impartial, unbiased, unprejudiced, nonpartisan, neutral, evenhanded; lawful, legal, legitimate; *informal* legit, on the level; on the up and up. ANTONYMS unjust, biased.

**2** *fair weather* FINE, dry, bright, clear, sunny, cloudless; warm, balmy, clement, benign, pleasant. ANTONYM inclement.

**3** *fair winds* FAVORABLE, advantageous, benign; on one's side, in one's favor. ANTONYM unfavorable.

**4** *fair hair* BLOND/BLONDE, yellowish, golden, flaxen, light, light brown, ash blond. ANTONYM dark.

**5** *Hermione's fair skin* PALE, light, light-colored, white, creamy. ANTONYM dark.

**6** *archaic the fair maiden's heart.* See BEAUTIFUL.

**7** *the restaurant was fair* REASONABLE, passable, tolerable, satisfactory, acceptable, respectable, decent, all right, good enough, pretty good, not bad, average, middling; *informal* OK, so-so, 'comme ci, comme ça'. PHRASE: **fair and square** *face it, I beat you fair and square* HONESTLY, fairly, without cheating, without foul play, by the book; lawfully, legally, legitimately; *informal* on the level, on the up and up.

**fair**[2] noun **1** *a country fair* CARNIVAL, festival, exhibition; midway.

**2** *an antiques fair* MARKET, bazaar, flea market, exchange, sale; *dated* emporium.

**3** *a new art fair* EXHIBITION, exhibit, display, show, presentation, exposition.

**fairly** adverb **1** *all students were treated fairly* JUSTLY, equitably, impartially, without bias, without prejudice, evenhandedly; lawfully, legally, legitimately, by the book; equally, the same.

**2** *the pipes are in fairly good condition* REASONABLY, passably, tolerably, adequately, moderately, quite, relatively, comparatively; *informal* pretty, kind of, kinda, sort of.

**fair-minded** adjective *all you can do now is pray for a fair-minded jury* FAIR, just, evenhanded, equitable, impartial, nonpartisan, unbiased, unprejudiced; honest, honorable, trustworthy, upright, decent; *informal* on the level; on the up and up.

**fairy** noun *we were gleefully certain that little fairies inhabited our woods* SPRITE, pixie, elf, imp, brownie, puck, leprechaun; *literary* faerie, fay.

**fairy tale, fairy story** noun **1** *the movie was inspired by a fairy tale* FOLK TALE, folk story, traditional story, myth, legend, fantasy, fable.

**2** *informal she accused him of telling fairy tales* LIE, white lie, fib, half-truth, untruth, falsehood, tall tale, story, fabrication, invention, fiction; *informal* whopper, cock-and-bull story.

**faith** noun **1** *he justified his boss's faith in him* TRUST, belief, confidence, conviction; optimism, hopefulness, hope. ANTONYM mistrust.

**2** *she gave her life for her faith* RELIGION, church, sect, denomination, (religious) persuasion, (religious) belief, ideology, creed, teaching, doctrine. PHRASES: **break faith with** *our own chairman has broken faith with this organization* BE DISLOYAL TO, be unfaithful to, be untrue to, betray, play someone false, break one's promise to, fail, let down; double-cross, deceive, cheat, stab in the back.
**keep faith with** *Mrs. Grimes has always kept faith with everyone in my department* BE LOYAL TO, be faithful to, be true to, stand by, stick by, keep one's promise to.

**faithful** adjective **1** *his faithful assistant* LOYAL, constant, true, devoted, true-blue, unswerving, staunch, steadfast, dedicated, committed; trusty, trustworthy, dependable, reliable. See note at RESOLUTE. ANTONYMS traitorous, unreliable.

**2** *a faithful copy* ACCURATE, precise, exact, errorless, unerring, faultless, true, close, strict; realistic, authentic; *informal* on the mark, bang on, on the money. ANTONYM inaccurate.

**faithless** adjective **1** *her faithless lover* UNFAITHFUL, disloyal, inconstant, false, untrue, adulterous, traitorous; fickle, flighty, untrustworthy, unreliable, undependable; deceitful, two-faced, double-crossing; *informal* cheating, two-timing, backstabbing; *literary* perfidious.

**2** *a faithless society* UNBELIEVING, nonbelieving, irreligious, disbelieving, agnostic, atheistic; pagan, heathen.

**fake** noun **1** *the sculpture was a fake* FORGERY, counterfeit, copy, pirate(d) copy, sham, fraud, hoax, imitation, mock-up, dummy, reproduction; *informal* phony, rip-off, knockoff, dupe.

**2** *that doctor is a fake* CHARLATAN, fraud, fraudster, mountebank, sham, quack, humbug, impostor, hoaxer, cheat, trickster; *informal* phony, con man, con artist, scam artist. See note at QUACK.

▸ adjective **1** *fake $50 bills* COUNTERFEIT, forged, fraudulent, sham, imitation, pirate(d), false, bogus; invalid, inauthentic; *informal* phony, dud. ANTONYM genuine.

**2** *fake diamonds* IMITATION, artificial, synthetic, simulated, reproduction, replica, ersatz, faux, man-made, dummy, false, mock, bogus; *informal* pretend, phony, pseudo. ANTONYM genuine.

**3** *a fake accent* FEIGNED, faked, put-on, assumed, invented, affected, pseudo; unconvincing, artificial, mock; *informal* phony. ANTONYM authentic.

▸ verb **1** *the certificate was faked* FORGE, counterfeit, falsify, mock up, copy, pirate, reproduce, replicate; doctor, alter, tamper with.

**2** *she faked a yawn* FEIGN, pretend, simulate, put on, affect.

**fall** verb **1** *bombs began to fall* DROP, descend, come down, go down; plummet, plunge, sink, dive, tumble; cascade. ANTONYM rise.

**2** *he tripped and fell* TOPPLE OVER, tumble over, keel over, fall down/over, go head over heels, go headlong, collapse, take a spill, pitch forward; trip, stumble, slip; *informal* come a cropper. ANTONYM get up.

**3** *the river began to fall* SUBSIDE, recede, ebb, flow back, fall away, go down, sink. ANTONYMS rise, flood.

**4** *inflation will fall* DECREASE, decline, diminish, fall off, drop off, lessen, dwindle; plummet, plunge, slump, sink; depreciate, cheapen, devalue; *informal* go through the floor, nosedive, take a header, crash. ANTONYMS rise, increase.

**5** *the Mogul empire fell* DECLINE, deteriorate, degenerate, go downhill, go to rack and ruin; decay, wither, fade, fail; *informal* go to the dogs, go to pot, go down the toilet. ANTONYMS rise, flood, increase, flourish.

**6** *those who fell in the war* DIE, perish, lose one's life, be killed, be slain, be lost, meet one's death; *informal* bite the dust, croak, buy it, buy the farm. ANTONYM flourish.

**7** *the town* ***fell to*** *the barbarians* SURRENDER TO, yield to, submit to, give in to, capitulate to, succumb to; be taken by, be defeated by, be conquered by, be overwhelmed by. ANTONYM resist.

**8** *Easter falls on April 11th* OCCUR, take place, happen, come about; arise; *literary* come to pass.

**9** *night fell* COME, arrive, appear, arise, materialize.

**10** *she fell ill* BECOME, grow, get, turn.

**11** *more tasks may **fall to** him* BE THE RESPONSIBILITY OF, be the duty of, be borne by, be one's job; come someone's way.

▸ noun **1** *an accidental fall* TUMBLE, trip, spill, topple, slip; collapse; *informal* nosedive, header, cropper.

**2** *a fall in sales* DECLINE, falloff, drop, decrease, cut, dip, reduction, downswing; plummet, plunge, slump; *informal* nosedive, crash. ANTONYM increase.

**3** *the fall of the Roman Empire* DOWNFALL, collapse, ruin, ruination, failure, decline, deterioration, degeneration; destruction, overthrow, demise. ANTONYMS increase, rise, ascent.

**4** *the fall of the city* SURRENDER, capitulation, yielding, submission; defeat. ANTONYM rise.

**5** *a steep fall down to the ocean* DESCENT, declivity, slope, slant, incline, downgrade. ANTONYM ascent.

**6** *the fall of man* SIN, wrongdoing, transgression, error, offense, lapse, fall from grace, original sin.

**7** (**falls**) *rafting trips below the falls* WATERFALL, cascade, cataract; rapids, white water.

PHRASES: **fall apart** *the old teacup fell apart in my hands* FALL TO PIECES, fall to bits, come apart (at the seams); disintegrate, fragment, break up, break apart, crumble, decay, perish; *informal* bust.

**fall asleep** *I almost fell asleep at work* DOZE OFF, drop off, go to sleep; *informal* nod off, go off, drift off, crash, conk out, go out like a light, sack out.

**fall away** *the ground here falls away abruptly* SLOPE DOWN, slope, slant down, go down, drop, drop away, descend, dip, sink, plunge.

**fall back** *the troops were ordered to fall back* RETREAT, withdraw, back off, draw back, pull back, pull away, move away.

**fall back on** *I can always fall back on my career in landscaping* RESORT TO, turn to, look to, call on, have recourse to; rely on, depend on, lean on.

**fall behind 1** *the other walkers fell behind* LAG, lag behind, trail, trail behind, be left behind, drop back, bring up the rear; straggle, dally, dawdle, hang back.

**2** *they fell behind on their payments* GET INTO DEBT, get into arrears, default, be in the red.

**fall for 1** *she fell for John* FALL IN LOVE WITH, become infatuated with, lose one's heart to, take a fancy to, be smitten with/by, be attracted to; *informal* have the hots for.

**2** *she won't fall for that trick* BE DECEIVED BY, be duped by, be fooled by, be taken in by, believe, trust, be convinced by; *informal* go for, buy, swallow (hook, line, and sinker).

**fall in 1** *the roof fell in* COLLAPSE, cave in, crash in, fall down; give way, crumble, disintegrate.

**2** *the soldiers fell in* GET IN FORMATION, get in line, line up, take one's position.

**3** *he fell in with a bad crowd* GET INVOLVED, take up, join up, go around, make friends; *informal* hang, hang out.

**fall off.** See FALL verb sense 4.

**fall on** *the army fell on the rebels* ATTACK, assail, assault, fly at, set about, set upon; pounce upon, ambush, surprise, rush, storm, charge; *informal* jump, lay into, have a go at.

**fall out** *let's not fall out over something so silly* QUARREL, argue, row, fight, squabble, bicker, have words, disagree, be at odds, clash, wrangle, cross swords, lock horns, be at loggerheads, be at each other's throats; *informal* scrap.

**fall short** *we sincerely hope that our fund-raising efforts will not fall short* BE DEFICIENT, be inadequate, be insufficient, be wanting, be lacking, disappoint; *informal* not come up to scratch, not come up to snuff.

**fall short of** *the results fell short of what was expected* FAIL TO MEET, fail to reach, fail to live up to.

**fall through** *the deal fell through* FAIL, be unsuccessful, come to nothing, miscarry, abort, go awry, collapse, founder, come to grief; *informal* fizzle out, flop, fold, come a cropper, go over like a lead balloon.

**fallacious** adjective *we almost printed his fallacious information* ERRONEOUS, false, untrue, wrong, incorrect, flawed, inaccurate, mistaken, misinformed, misguided; specious, spurious, bogus, fictitious, fabricated, made up; groundless, unfounded, ill-founded, unproven, unsupported, uncorroborated; *informal* phony, full of holes. ANTONYM correct.

**fallacy** noun *the fallacy that Abner Doubleday invented the game of baseball* MISCONCEPTION, misbelief, delusion, mistaken impression, error, misapprehension, misinterpretation, misconstruction, mistake; untruth, inconsistency, myth.

**fallen** adjective **1** *fallen heroes* DEAD, perished, killed, slain, slaughtered, murdered; lost, late, lamented, departed, gone; *formal* deceased.

**2** *dated fallen women* IMMORAL, loose, promiscuous, unchaste, sinful, impure, sullied, tainted, dishonored, ruined.

**fallible** adjective *what good is a fallible security system?* ERROR-PRONE, errant, liable to err, open to error; imperfect, flawed, weak.

**fallow** adjective **1** *fallow farmland* UNCULTIVATED, unplowed, untilled, unplanted, unsown; unused, dormant, resting, empty, bare. ANTONYM cultivated.

**2** *a fallow trading period* INACTIVE, dormant, quiet, slack, slow, stagnant; barren, unproductive. ANTONYM busy.

**false** adjective **1** *a false report* INCORRECT, untrue, wrong, erroneous, fallacious, flawed, distorted, inaccurate, imprecise; untruthful, fictitious, concocted, fabricated, invented, made up, trumped up, unfounded, spurious; counterfeit, forged, fraudulent. ANTONYMS correct, truthful.

**2** *a false friend* FAITHLESS, unfaithful, disloyal, untrue, inconstant, treacherous, traitorous, two-faced, double-crossing, deceitful, dishonest, duplicitous, untrustworthy, unreliable; untruthful; *informal* cheating, two-timing, backstabbing; *literary* perfidious. ANTONYM faithful.

**3** *false pearls.* See FAKE adjective, sense 2.

**falsehood** noun **1** *a downright falsehood* LIE, untruth, fib, falsification, fabrication, invention, fiction, story, cock-and-bull story, flight of fancy; half truth; *informal* tall story, tall tale, fairy tale, whopper. See note at FICTION. ANTONYM truth.

**2** *he accused me of falsehood* LYING, mendacity, untruthfulness, fibbing, fabrication, invention, perjury, telling stories; deceit, deception, pretense, artifice, double-crossing, treachery; *literary* perfidy. ANTONYM honesty.

**falsify** verb **1** *she falsified the accounts* FORGE, fake, counterfeit, fabricate; alter, change, doctor, tamper with, fudge, manipulate, adulterate, corrupt, misrepresent, misreport, distort, warp, embellish, embroider; *informal* cook.

**2** *the theory is falsified by the evidence* DISPROVE, refute, debunk, negate, negative, invalidate, contradict, controvert, confound, demolish, discredit; *informal* poke holes in, blow out of the water; *formal* confute.

**falter** verb **1** *the government faltered* HESITATE, delay, drag one's feet, stall; waver, vacillate, waffle, be indecisive, be irresolute, blow hot and cold, hem and haw; *informal* sit on the fence, dilly-dally, shilly-shally.

**2** *she faltered over his name* STAMMER, stutter, stumble; hesitate, flounder.

**3** *the economy was faltering* STRUGGLE, stumble, flounder, founder, be in difficulty.

**fame** noun *a designer of international fame* RENOWN, celebrity, stardom, popularity, prominence; note, distinction, esteem, importance, account, consequence, greatness, eminence, prestige, stature, repute; notoriety, infamy. ANTONYM obscurity.

**familiar** adjective **1** *a familiar task* WELL-KNOWN, recognized, accustomed; common, commonplace, everyday, day-to-day, ordinary, habitual, usual, customary, routine, standard, stock, mundane, run-of-the-mill; *literary* wonted.

**2** *are you **familiar with** the subject?* ACQUAINTED WITH, conversant with, versed in, knowledgeable of, well-informed in/of; skilled in, proficient in; at home with, no stranger to, au fait with, au courant with; *informal* up on, in the know about.

**3** *a familiar atmosphere* INFORMAL, casual, relaxed, easy, comfortable; friendly, unceremonious, unreserved, open, natural, unpretentious. ANTONYM formal.

**4** *he is too familiar with the teachers* PRESUMPTUOUS, overfamiliar, disrespectful, forward, bold, impudent, impertinent. ANTONYM formal.

**familiarity** noun **1** *her **familiarity with** Asian politics* ACQUAINTANCE WITH, awareness of, experience with/of, insight into, knowledge of, understanding of, comprehension of, grasp of, skill in, proficiency in.

**2** *she was affronted by his familiarity* PRESUMPTION, overfamiliarity, presumptuousness, forwardness, boldness, audacity, cheek, impudence, impertinence, disrespect; liberties.

**3** *our familiarity allows us to tease one another* CLOSENESS, intimacy, attachment, affinity, friendliness, friendship, amity; *informal* chumminess.

**familiarize** verb *let me **familiarize** you **with** our new phone setup* MAKE CONVERSANT WITH, make familiar with, acquaint with; accustom to, habituate to, instruct in, teach in, educate in, school in, prime in, introduce to; brief in/about; *informal* put in the picture about/with, give the lowdown on, fill in on, get up to speed on/with.

**family** noun **1** *I met his family* RELATIVES, relations, kin, next of kin, kinsfolk, kindred, one's (own) flesh and blood, nearest and dearest, people, connections; extended family, in-laws; clan, tribe; *informal* folks.

**2** *he had the right kind of family* ANCESTRY, parentage, pedigree, genealogy, background, family tree, descent, lineage, bloodline, blood, extraction, stock; forebears, forefathers, antecedents, roots, origins.

**3** *she is married with **a family*** CHILDREN, little ones, youngsters; offspring, progeny, descendants, scions, heirs; a brood; *Law* issue; *informal* kids, kiddies, tots.

**4** *the warbler family* TAXONOMIC GROUP, order, class, genus, species; stock, strain, line; *Zoology* phylum.

**famine** noun *a nation threatened by famine* FOOD SHORTAGES, scarcity of food; starvation, malnutrition. ANTONYM plenty.

**famished** adjective *the hikers were famished by the time they reached camp* RAVENOUS, hungry, starving, starved, empty, unfed; *informal* peckish. ANTONYM full.

**famous** adjective *an exhibit featuring the artwork of famous actors* WELL KNOWN, prominent, famed, popular; renowned, noted, eminent, distinguished, esteemed, celebrated, respected; of distinction, of repute; illustrious, acclaimed, great, legendary, lionized; having one's name in lights; notorious, infamous. ANTONYM unknown.

**fan**[1] noun *a ceiling fan* VENTILATOR, blower, air conditioner.

▸ verb **1** *she fanned her face* COOL, aerate, ventilate; freshen, refresh.

**2** *they fanned public fears* INTENSIFY, increase, agitate, inflame, exacerbate; stimulate, stir up, whip up, fuel, kindle, spark, arouse.

**3** *the police squad **fanned out*** SPREAD (OUT), branch (out); outspread.

**fan**[2] noun *a basketball fan* ENTHUSIAST, devotee, admirer, lover; supporter, follower, disciple, adherent, zealot; expert, connoisseur, aficionado; *informal* buff, bum, fiend, freak, nut, addict, junkie, fanatic, groupie.

**fanatic** noun **1** *a religious fanatic* ZEALOT, extremist, militant, dogmatist, devotee, adherent; sectarian, bigot, partisan, radical, diehard; *informal* maniac. See note at ZEALOT.

**2** *informal a hockey fanatic.* See FAN[2].

**fanatical** adjective **1** *they are fanatical about their faith* ZEALOUS, extremist, extreme, militant, dogmatic, radical, diehard; intolerant, single-minded, blinkered, inflexible, uncompromising, hardcore.

**2** *he was fanatical about tidiness* ENTHUSIASTIC, eager, keen, overkeen, fervent, ardent, passionate; obsessive, obsessed, fixated, compulsive; *informal* wild, gung-ho, nuts, crazy, hog-wild.

**fanciful** adjective **1** *a fanciful story* FANTASTIC, far-fetched, unbelievable, extravagant; ridiculous, absurd, preposterous; imaginary, made-up, make-believe, mythical, fabulous; *informal* tall, hard to swallow. ANTONYM literal.

**2** *a fanciful girl* IMAGINATIVE, inventive; whimsical, impractical, dreamy, quixotic; out of touch with reality, in a world of one's own. ANTONYM down-to-earthl.

**3** *a fanciful building* ORNATE, exotic, fancy, imaginative, extravagant, fantastic; curious, bizarre, eccentric, unusual. ANTONYM practical.

**fancy** verb **1** *she fancied him.* See LIKE[1] sense 1.

**2** *I fancied I could see lights* THINK, imagine, believe, be of the opinion, be under the impression; reckon.

▸ adjective *fancy clothes* ELABORATE, ornate, ornamental, decorative, adorned, embellished, intricate; ostentatious, showy, flamboyant; luxurious, lavish, extravagant, expensive; *informal* flashy, jazzy, ritzy, snazzy, posh, classy; fancy-schmancy. ANTONYM plain.

▸ noun *she took a fancy to you* LIKING, taste, inclination; urge, wish, whim, impulse, notion, whimsy, hankering, craving; *informal* yen, itch.

**fanfare** noun **1** *a fanfare announced her arrival* TRUMPET CALL, flourish, fanfaronade; *archaic* trump.

**2** *the project was greeted with great fanfare* FUSS, commotion, show, display, ostentation, flashiness, pageantry, splendor; *informal* ballyhoo, hype, pizzazz, razzle-dazzle, glitz.

**fantastic** adjective **1** *a fantastic car* MARVELOUS, wonderful, sensational, outstanding, superb, super, excellent, first-rate, first-class, dazzling, out of this world, breathtaking; *informal* great, terrific, fabulous, ace, magic, cool, wicked, awesome, brilliant, killer. ANTONYM ordinary.

**2** *a fantastic notion* FANCIFUL, extravagant, extraordinary, irrational, wild, absurd, far-fetched, nonsensical, incredible, unbelievable, unthinkable, implausible, improbable, unlikely, doubtful, dubious; strange, peculiar, odd, queer, weird, eccentric, whimsical, capricious; visionary, romantic; *informal* crazy, cockeyed, off the wall. ANTONYM rational.

**3** *fantastic shapes* STRANGE, weird, bizarre, outlandish, queer, peculiar, grotesque, freakish, surreal, exotic; elaborate, ornate, intricate. ANTONYM ordinary.

**4** *his fantastic accuracy* TREMENDOUS, remarkable, great, terrific, impressive, outstanding, phenomenal.

**fantasy** noun **1** *a mix of fantasy and realism* IMAGINATION, fancy, invention, make-believe; creativity, vision; daydreaming, reverie. ANTONYMS realism, truth.

**2** *his fantasy about being famous* DREAM, daydream, pipe dream, fanciful notion, wish; fond hope, chimera, delusion, illusion; *informal* pie in the sky.

**far** adverb **1** *we walked far that afternoon* A LONG WAY, a great distance, a good way; afar.

**2** *her charm far outweighs any flaws* MUCH, considerably, markedly, immeasurably, greatly, significantly, substantially, appreciably, noticeably; to a great extent, by a long way, by far, by a mile, easily. ANTONYM slightly.

▸ adjective **1** *far places* DISTANT, faraway, far-off, remote, out of the way, far-flung, outlying. ANTONYMS near, neighboring.

**2** *the far side of the campus* FURTHER, more distant; opposite. ANTONYM near.

PHRASES: **by far** *this is by far the best essay we've read today* BY A GREAT AMOUNT, by a good deal, by a long way, by a mile, far and away; undoubtedly, without doubt, without question, positively, absolutely, easily; significantly, substantially, appreciably, much.

**far and near** *people came from far and near in hopes of witnessing a miracle* EVERYWHERE, 'here, there, and everywhere,' far and wide, all over (the world), throughout the land, worldwide; *informal* all over the place; all over the map.

**far from** *staff were far from happy* NOT, not at all, nowhere near; the opposite of, the antithesis of, anything but.

**go far** *we always knew that Rudy would go far* BE SUCCESSFUL, succeed, prosper, flourish, thrive, get on, get on in the world, make good, set the world on fire; *informal* make a name for oneself, make one's mark, go places, do all right for oneself, find a place in the sun.

**go too far** *one of these days, you're going to go too far and they're going to haul you away* GO TO EXTREMES, go overboard, overdo it, go over the top, not know when to stop.

**so far 1** *nobody has noticed so far* UP TO THIS POINT, up to now, as yet, thus far, hitherto, up to the present, to date.

**2** *his liberalism only extends so far* TO A CERTAIN EXTENT, up to a point, to a degree, within reason, within limits.

**farce** noun **1** *the stories approach farce* SLAPSTICK COMEDY, slapstick, burlesque, vaudeville, buffoonery. ANTONYM tragedy.

**2** *the trial was a farce* MOCKERY, travesty, absurdity, sham, pretense, masquerade, charade, joke, waste of time; *informal* shambles.

**farcical** adjective **1** *the idea is farcical* RIDICULOUS, preposterous, ludicrous, absurd, laughable, risible, nonsensical; senseless, pointless, useless; silly, foolish, idiotic, stupid, harebrained, cockamamie; *informal* crazy, daft.

**2** *farcical goings-on* MADCAP, zany, slapstick, comic, comical, clownish, amusing; hilarious, uproarious; *informal* wacky.

**fare** noun **1** *we paid the fare* TICKET PRICE; price, cost, charge, fee, toll, tariff; transport cost.

**2** *the taxi picked up a fare* PASSENGER, traveler, customer.

**3** *they eat simple fare* FOOD, meals, sustenance, nourishment, nutriment, foodstuffs, provender, eatables, provisions; cooking, cuisine; diet; *informal* grub, nosh, eats, chow; *formal* comestibles, victuals.

**4** *typical Hollywood fare* OFFERING(S), wares; menu.

▸ verb *how are you faring?* GET ON, get along, cope, manage, do, muddle through/along, survive; *informal* make out.

**farewell** exclamation *farewell, New York* GOODBYE, so long, bye, bye-bye, see you (later), cheers; adieu, au revoir, ciao, adios, sayonara; bon voyage; *informal, dated* toodle-oo.

▸ noun *an emotional farewell* GOODBYE, valediction, adieu; leave-taking, parting, departure; send-off.

**far-fetched** adjective *a far-fetched story about alien abduction* IMPROBABLE, unlikely, implausible, unconvincing, dubious, doubtful, incredible, unbelievable, unthinkable; contrived, fanciful, unrealistic, ridiculous, absurd, preposterous; *informal* hard to swallow, fishy.

**farm** noun *a farm of 100 acres* RANCH, farmstead, plantation, estate, family farm, dairy farm, hobby farm; farmland, market garden.

▸ verb **1** *he farmed locally* WORK THE LAND, be a farmer, cultivate the land; rear livestock.

**2** *they farm the land* CULTIVATE, till, work, plow, dig, plant.

**3** *the family farms sheep* BREED, rear, keep, raise, tend.

PHRASE: **farm something out** *we farmed out the warehouse construction to another firm* CONTRACT OUT, outsource, subcontract, delegate.

**farmer** noun *the independent Tennessee farmers have been hurt by this careless legislation* AGRICULTURIST, agronomist, rancher, smallholder, peasant; farmhand, *historical* habitant, grazier.

**farming** noun *her family's been in farming since the 1700s* AGRICULTURE, cultivation, ranching, land management, farm management; husbandry; agronomy, agribusiness.

**farsighted** adjective *reaping the benefits of her farsighted investments* PRESCIENT, visionary, percipient, shrewd, discerning, judicious, canny, prudent.

**farther** adverb *he'd like to live even farther from the city* MORE FAR, farther away, further, further away, more remote, more distant, more removed.

▸ adjective *the farther side of the field* MORE DISTANT, more remote, remoter, farther away/off, further, further (away/off); far, other, opposite.

**farthest** adjective *the farthest island in the chain is uninhabited* MOST DISTANT, most remote, remotest, farthest away, furthest, furthest away, farthermost, furthermost; (most) outlying, (most) outer, outermost, extreme, uttermost, ultimate; *archaic* outmost. ANTONYM nearest.

▸ adverb *Charlie threw his discus the farthest* MOST DISTANT, farthest away, furthest, furthest away, at/for the greatest distance. See note at FARTHER.

**fascinate** verb *the space program fascinates me* INTEREST, captivate, engross, absorb, enchant, enthrall, entrance, transfix, rivet, mesmerize, engage, compel; lure, tempt, entice, draw; charm, attract, intrigue, divert, entertain. ANTONYM bore.

**fascinating** adjective *the book is a fascinating study of Southern schools during the Civil War* INTERESTING, captivating, engrossing, absorbing, enchanting, enthralling, spellbinding, riveting, engaging, compelling, compulsive, gripping, thrilling; alluring, tempting, irresistible; charming, attractive, intriguing, diverting, entertaining.

**fascination** noun *crime and criminals are topics of endless fascination* INTEREST, preoccupation, passion, obsession, compulsion; allure, lure, charm, attraction, intrigue, appeal, pull, draw.

**fashion** noun **1** *the fashion for tight clothes* VOGUE, trend, craze, rage, mania, fad; style, look; tendency, convention, custom, practice; *informal* thing.

**2** *the world of fashion* CLOTHES, clothing design, couture; the garment industry; *informal* the rag trade.

**3** *it needs to be run in a sensible fashion* MANNER, way, method, mode, style; system, approach.

▸ verb *the model was fashioned from lead* CONSTRUCT, build, make, manufacture, fabricate, tailor, contrive; cast, shape, form, mold, sculpt; forge, hew.

PHRASES: **after a fashion** *the arrangement worked after a fashion* TO A CERTAIN EXTENT, in a way, somehow, somehow or other, in a manner of speaking, in its way.
**in fashion** *are these hideous shoes really in fashion?* FASHIONABLE, in vogue, up-to-date, up-to-the-minute, all the rage, chic, à la mode; *informal* trendy, with it, cool, in, the in thing, hot, big, hip, happening, now, sharp, groovy, tony, fly.
**out of fashion** *sorry, Dad, that necktie is completely out of fashion* UNFASHIONABLE, dated, old-fashioned, out of date, outdated, outmoded, behind the times; unstylish, untrendy, unpopular, passé, démodé; *informal* old hat, out, square, uncool.

**fashionable** adjective *a fashionable spa in Newport* IN VOGUE, voguish, in fashion, popular, up-to-date, up-to-the-minute, modern, all the rage, du jour, modish, à la mode, trendsetting; stylish, chic; *informal* trendy, classy, with it, cool, in, hot, big, hip, happening, now, snazzy, spiffy, tony, fly.

**fast**[1] adjective **1** *a fast pace* SPEEDY, quick, swift, rapid; fast-moving, fast-paced, high-speed, turbo, sporty; accelerated, express, blistering, breakneck, pell-mell; hasty, hurried; *informal* nippy, zippy, blinding, supersonic; *literary* fleet. ANTONYM slow.

**2** *he held the door fast* SECURE, fastened, tight, firm, closed, shut; immovable, unbudgeable. ANTONYM loose.

**3** *a fast color* INDELIBLE, lasting, permanent, stable. ANTONYM temporary.

**4** *fast friends* LOYAL, devoted, faithful, firm, steadfast, staunch, true, bosom, inseparable; constant, enduring, unswerving.

**5** *a fast woman* PROMISCUOUS, licentious, dissolute, debauched, impure, unchaste, wanton, abandoned, of easy virtue; sluttish, whorish; intemperate, immoderate, shameless, sinful, immoral; *informal* easy; *dated* loose. ANTONYM chaste.

▸ adverb **1** *she drove fast* QUICKLY, rapidly, swiftly, speedily, briskly, at speed, at full tilt; hastily, hurriedly, in a hurry, posthaste, pell-mell; like a shot, like a flash, on the double, at the speed of light; *informal* lickety-split, PDQ (pretty damn quick), nippily, like (greased) lightning, hell-bent for leather, like mad, like the wind, like a bat out of hell; *literary* apace. ANTONYM slowly.

**2** *his wheels were stuck fast* SECURELY, firmly, immovably, fixedly.

**3** *he's fast asleep* DEEPLY, sound, completely.

**4** *she lived fast and dangerously* WILDLY, dissolutely, intemperately, immoderately, recklessly, self-indulgently, extravagantly.

**fast**[2] verb *we must fast and pray* EAT NOTHING, abstain from food, refrain from eating, go without food, go hungry, starve oneself; go on a hunger strike. ANTONYM eat.

▸ noun *a five-day fast* PERIOD OF FASTING, period of abstinence; hunger strike; diet. ANTONYM feast.

**fasten** verb **1** *he fastened the door* BOLT, lock, secure, make fast, chain, seal. ANTONYM unlock.

**2** *they fastened splints to his leg* ATTACH, fix, affix, clip, pin, tack; stick, bond, join. ANTONYM remove.

**3** *he fastened his horse to a tree* TIE, tie up, bind, tether, truss, fetter, lash, hitch, anchor, strap, rope. ANTONYM untie.

**4** *the dress fastens at the front* BUTTON (UP), zip (up), do up, close. ANTONYM undo.

**5** *his gaze fastened on me* FOCUS, fix, be riveted, concentrate, zero in, zoom in, direct at.

**6** *blame had been **fastened on** the underling* ASCRIBE TO, attribute to, assign to, chalk up to; pin on, lay at the door of.

**7** *critics **fastened on** the end of the report* SINGLE OUT, concentrate on, focus on, pick out, fix on, seize on.

**fastidious** adjective *he was fastidious about personal hygiene* SCRUPULOUS, punctilious, painstaking, meticulous; perfectionist, fussy, finicky, overparticular; critical, overcritical, hypercritical, hard to please, exacting, demanding; *informal* persnickety, nitpicking, choosy, picky, anal. ANTONYM lax.

**fat** adjective **1** *a fat man* PLUMP, stout, overweight, large, chubby, portly, flabby, paunchy, potbellied, beer-bellied, meaty, of ample proportions, heavyset; obese, corpulent, fleshy, gross; *informal* plus-sized, big-boned, tubby, roly-poly, well-upholstered, beefy, porky, blubbery, chunky, pudgy. ANTONYMS thin, skinny.

**2** *fat bacon* FATTY, greasy, oily, oleaginous; *formal* pinguid. ANTONYM lean.

**3** *a fat book* THICK, big, chunky, bulky, substantial, voluminous; long. ANTONYM thin.

**4** *informal a fat salary* LARGE, substantial, sizable, considerable; generous, lucrative. ANTONYM small.

▸ noun **1** *exercises to burn away the fat* FATTY TISSUE, adipose tissue, cellulite; blubber; flab; *informal* spare tire, love handles.

**2** *eggs fried in sizzling fat* COOKING OIL, grease; lard, suet, butter, margarine.

**fatal** adjective **1** *a fatal disease* DEADLY, lethal, mortal, death-dealing; terminal, incurable, untreatable, inoperable, malignant; *literary* deathly. ANTONYMS harmless, superficial.

**2** *a fatal mistake* DISASTROUS, devastating, ruinous, catastrophic, calamitous, dire; costly; *formal* grievous. ANTONYMS harmless, beneficial.

**fatalism** noun *Paulette's fatalism made her come across as pretty morose* PASSIVE ACCEPTANCE, resignation, stoicism, acceptance of the inevitable; pessimism, defeatism, negativism, negative thinking, doom and gloom; predeterminism.

**fatality** noun *news of this fatality has spread quickly* DEATH, casualty, mortality, victim; fatal accident.

**fate** noun **1** *what has fate in store for me?* DESTINY, providence, the stars, chance, luck, serendipity, fortune, kismet, karma.

**2** *my fate was in their hands* FUTURE, destiny, outcome, end, lot.

**3** *a similar fate would befall other killers* DEATH, demise, end; retribution, sentence.

**4** *Mythology* (**the Fates**) *the Fates will decide* the weird sisters; the Parcae, the Moirai, the Norns; 'Clotho, Lachesis, and Atropos'.

▸ verb (**be fated**) *his daughter was fated to face the same problem* BE PREDESTINED, be preordained, be destined, be meant, be doomed; be sure, be certain, be bound, be guaranteed.

**fateful** adjective **1** *that fateful day* DECISIVE, critical, crucial, pivotal; momentous, important, key, significant, historic, portentous; *informal* earth-shattering, earth-shaking. See note at OMINOUS. ANTONYMS unimportant, trivial.

**2** *their fateful defeat in 1812* DISASTROUS, ruinous, calamitous, devastating, tragic, terrible.

**father** noun **1** *his mother and father* DAD; daddy, pop, pa, dada, papa; old man, patriarch, paterfamilias.

**2** *literary the religion of my fathers* ANCESTOR, forefather, forebear, predecessor, antecedent, progenitor, primogenitor. ANTONYM descendant.

**3** *the father of democracy* ORIGINATOR, initiator, founder, inventor, creator, maker, author, architect.

**4** *the city fathers* LEADER, elder, patriarch, official.

**5** (**Father**) *our heavenly Father* GOD, Lord, Lord God.

**6** (often **Father**) *ask the father to pray for you* PRIEST, pastor, parson, clergyman, cleric, minister, preacher; *informal* reverend, padre.

▸ verb PARENT, be the father of, bring into the world, spawn, sire, breed; *literary* beget; *archaic* engender.

**fatherland** noun *returning to his fatherland after forty years* NATIVE LAND, native country, homeland, mother country, motherland, land of one's birth.

**fatherly** adjective *she appreciated his fatherly advice* PATERNAL, fatherlike; protective, supportive, encouraging, affectionate, caring, sympathetic, indulgent.

**fathom** verb **1** *Charlotte tried to fathom her cat's expression* UNDERSTAND, comprehend, work out, make sense of, grasp, divine, puzzle out, get to the bottom of; interpret, decipher, decode; *informal* make head(s) or tail(s) of, crack.

2 *fathoming the ocean* MEASURE THE DEPTH OF, sound, plumb.

**fatigue** noun TIREDNESS, weariness, sleepiness, drowsiness, exhaustion, enervation, languor, lethargy, torpor, prostration. ANTONYM energy.

▸ verb *the troops were fatigued* TIRE (OUT), exhaust, wear out, drain, weary, wash out, overtire, prostrate, enervate; *informal* knock out, take it out of, do in, poop, bush, wear to a frazzle. See note at TIRED. ANTONYM invigorate.

**fatness** noun *persons with varying degrees of fatness were chosen for the stress tests* PLUMPNESS, stoutness, heaviness, chubbiness, portliness, rotundity, flabbiness, paunchiness; obesity, corpulence; *informal* tubbiness, pudginess. ANTONYM thinness.

**fatten** verb 1 *fattening livestock* MAKE FAT/FATTER, feed (up), build up.

2 *we're sending her home to* ***fatten up*** PUT ON WEIGHT, gain weight, get heavier, grow fatter, fill out. ANTONYMS lose weight, slim down.

**fatty** adjective *avoid fatty foods* GREASY, oily, fat, oleaginous; high-fat. ANTONYM lean.

**fatuous** adjective *the irritation of fatuous questions* SILLY, foolish, stupid, inane, idiotic, vacuous, asinine; pointless, senseless, ridiculous, ludicrous, absurd; *informal* dumb, daft. ANTONYM sensible.

**fault** noun 1 *he has his faults* DEFECT, failing, imperfection, flaw, blemish, shortcoming, weakness, frailty, foible, vice. ANTONYMS merit, strength.

2 *engineers have located the fault* DEFECT, flaw, imperfection, bug; error, mistake, inaccuracy; *informal* glitch, gremlin.

3 *it was not my fault* RESPONSIBILITY, liability, culpability, blameworthiness, guilt.

4 *don't blame one child for another's faults* MISDEED, wrongdoing, offense, misdemeanor, misconduct, indiscretion, peccadillo, transgression; *informal* no-no. See note at SIN.

▸ verb *you couldn't fault any of the players* FIND FAULT WITH, criticize, attack, censure, condemn, reproach; complain about, quibble about, moan about; *informal* knock, slam, gripe about, beef about, pick holes in.

PHRASES: **at fault** *no one is at fault* TO BLAME, blameworthy, culpable; responsible, guilty, in the wrong.

**to a fault** *Katherine is very giving, sometimes to a fault* EXCESSIVELY, unduly, immoderately, overly, needlessly.

THE RIGHT WORD **fault, blemish, defect, failing, flaw, foible, shortcoming**

No one is perfect. But when it comes to cataloguing your own imperfections, it's best to start with your **foibles**—the slight weaknesses or eccentricities for which you will be most quickly forgiven. You also have a good chance of being forgiven for your **shortcomings**, which are not necessarily damaging to others (*his ardent devotion to his dog was a shortcoming that was readily overlooked*). **Failing** suggests a more severe shortcoming, usually with more serious consequences (*chronic tardiness was one of her failings*), but a *failing* can also be a weakness of character that you're not responsible for and perhaps not even aware of (*pride is a common failing among those who have met with great success early in life*). **Fault** also implies failure—but not necessarily a serious failure—to reach moral perfection (*his major fault was his outspokenness*). While *fault* usually indicates something inherent in your nature rather than external to it, a **flaw** can be either superficial (*a flaw in his otherwise immaculate appearance*) or profound (*a personality flaw that made her impossible to work with*), and it can refer to things as well as people (*a flaw in the table's finish*). A **blemish** is usually a physical flaw (*a facial blemish*), although it can be anything that disfigures or mars the perfection or someone or something (*a blemish on her otherwise spotless academic record*). You can get rid of a blemish and even overcome your shortcomings, but a **defect** is a flaw so serious that you may never be able to get rid of it (*a defect in his hearing*).

**fault-finding** noun *he came to expect nothing but fault-finding from his wife* CRITICISM, captiousness, caviling, quibbling; complaining, grumbling, carping, moaning; *informal* nitpicking, griping, grousing, bellyaching. ANTONYM praise.

**faultless** adjective *speaking faultless English* PERFECT, flawless, without fault, error-free, impeccable, accurate, precise, exact, correct, exemplary. ANTONYM flawed.

**faulty** adjective 1 *a faulty electric blanket* MALFUNCTIONING, broken, damaged, defective, not working, out of order; *informal* on the blink, acting up, kaput, bust, busted, on the fritz. ANTONYM working.

2 *her logic is faulty* DEFECTIVE, flawed, unsound, inaccurate, incorrect, erroneous, fallacious, wrong. ANTONYM sound.

**faux pas** noun *excuse my faux pas* MISTAKE, blunder, gaffe, indiscretion, impropriety, solecism, barbarism; *informal* booboo, blooper. See note at MISTAKE.

**favor** noun 1 *will you do me a favor?* SERVICE, good turn, good deed, kindness, act of kindness, courtesy. ANTONYM disservice.

2 *she looked on him with favor* APPROVAL, approbation, goodwill, kindness, benevolence. ANTONYM disapproval.

3 *they showed favor to one of the players* FAVORITISM, bias, partiality, partisanship.

4 *you shall receive the king's favor* PATRONAGE, backing, support, assistance.

▸ verb 1 *she favors the modest option* PREFER, lean toward, opt for, tend toward, be in favor of; approve (of), advocate, support, ANTONYM oppose.

2 *he favors his son over his daughter* TREAT PARTIALLY, be biased toward, prefer.

3 *the conditions favored the other team* BENEFIT, advantage, help, assist, aid, be of service to, do a favor for. ANTONYM hinder.

4 *he favored Lucy with a smile* OBLIGE, honor, gratify, humor, indulge.

PHRASE: **in favor of** *we're in favor of a strike* ON THE SIDE OF, pro, (all) for, giving support to, approving of, sympathetic to.

**favorable** adjective **1** *a favorable assessment of his ability* APPROVING, commendatory, complimentary, flattering, glowing, enthusiastic; good, pleasing, positive; *informal* rave. ANTONYM critical.

**2** *conditions are favorable* ADVANTAGEOUS, beneficial, in one's favor, good, right, suitable, fitting, appropriate; propitious, auspicious, promising, encouraging. ANTONYM disadvantageous.

**3** *a favorable reply* POSITIVE, affirmative, assenting, agreeing, approving; encouraging, reassuring. ANTONYM negative.

**favorite** adjective *his favorite aunt* BEST-LOVED, most-liked, favored, dearest; preferred, chosen, choice.

▸ noun **1** *Brutus was Caesar's favorite* (FIRST) CHOICE, pick, preference, pet, darling, the apple of one's eye; *informal* blue-eyed boy/girl, golden boy/girl, fair-haired boy/girl.

**2** *the favorite in the first race* EXPECTED WINNER, probable winner, odds-on favorite, top seed, top pick, front runner.

**favoritism** noun *we want one rule for everyone and no favoritism* PARTIALITY, partisanship, preferential treatment, favor, prejudice, bias, inequality, unfairness, discrimination.

**fawn** verb *they were **fawning over** the president* BE OBSEQUIOUS TO, be sycophantic to, curry favor with, flatter, play up to, crawl to, ingratiate oneself with, dance attendance on; *informal* suck up to, be all over, brown-nose, toady.

**fawning** adjective *her fawning personal staff* OBSEQUIOUS, servile, sycophantic, flattering, ingratiating, unctuous, oleaginous, groveling, crawling; *informal* bootlicking, smarmy, sucky, brown-nosing, toadying.

**fear** noun **1** *he felt fear at entering the house* TERROR, fright, fearfulness, horror, alarm, panic, agitation, trepidation, dread, consternation, dismay, distress; anxiety, worry, angst, unease, uneasiness, apprehension, apprehensiveness, nervousness, nerves, perturbation, foreboding; *informal* the creeps, the shivers, the willies, the heebie-jeebies, jitteriness, twitchiness, butterflies (in the stomach).

**2** *she overcame her fears* PHOBIA, aversion, antipathy, dread, bugbear, nightmare, horror, terror; anxiety, neurosis; *informal* hang-up.

**3** *there's no fear of my leaving you alone* LIKELIHOOD, likeliness, prospect, possibility, chance, probability; risk, danger.

▸ verb **1** *she feared her husband* BE AFRAID OF, be fearful of, be scared of, be apprehensive of, dread, live in fear of, be terrified of; be anxious about, worry about, feel apprehensive about.

**2** *he fears heights* HAVE A PHOBIA ABOUT, have a horror of, take fright at.

**3** *he feared to tell them* BE TOO AFRAID, be too scared, hesitate, dare not.

**4** *they **feared for** his health* WORRY ABOUT, feel anxious about, feel concerned about, have anxieties about.

**5** *all who fear the Lord* STAND IN AWE OF, revere, reverence, venerate, respect.

**6** *I fear that you may be right* SUSPECT, have a (sneaking) suspicion, be inclined to think, be afraid, have a hunch, think it likely.

**fearful** adjective **1** *they are fearful of being overheard* AFRAID, frightened, scared (stiff), scared to death, terrified, petrified; alarmed, panicky, nervous, tense, apprehensive, uneasy, worried (sick), anxious; *informal* jittery, jumpy.

**2** *the guards were fearful* NERVOUS, trembling, quaking, cowed, daunted; timid, timorous, faint-hearted; *informal* jittery, jumpy, twitchy, keyed up, in a cold sweat, a bundle of nerves; *informal* spooked.

**3** *a fearful accident* HORRIFIC, terrible, dreadful, awful, appalling, frightful, ghastly, horrible, horrifying, horrendous, terribly bad, shocking, atrocious, abominable, hideous, monstrous, gruesome.

**fearfully** adverb *she opened the door fearfully* APPREHENSIVELY, uneasily, nervously, timidly, timorously, hesitantly, with one's heart in one's mouth.

**fearless** adjective *fearless warriors* BOLD, brave, courageous, intrepid, valiant, valorous, gallant, plucky, lionhearted, heroic, daring, audacious, indomitable, doughty; unafraid, undaunted, unflinching; *informal* gutsy, spunky, ballsy, feisty. ANTONYMS timid, cowardly.

**fearsome** adjective *the crocodile's teeth were a fearsome sight* FRIGHTENING, scary, horrifying, terrifying, menacing, chilling, spine-chilling, hair-raising, alarming, unnerving, daunting, formidable, forbidding, dismaying, disquieting, disturbing.

**feasible** adjective *a feasible solution* PRACTICABLE, practical, workable, achievable, attainable, realizable, viable, realistic, sensible, reasonable, within reason; suitable, possible, expedient; *informal* doable. ANTONYM impractical.

**feast** noun **1** *a wedding feast* BANQUET, celebration meal, lavish dinner; entertainment; revels, festivities; *informal* blowout, spread.

**2** *the feast of St. Stephen* (RELIGIOUS) FESTIVAL, feast day, saint's day, holy day, holiday.

**3** *a feast for the eyes* TREAT, delight, joy, pleasure.

▸ verb **1** *they **feasted on** lobster* GORGE ON, dine on, eat one's fill of, overindulge in, binge on; eat, devour, consume, partake of; *informal* stuff one's face with, stuff oneself with, pig out on, chow down on.

**2** *they feasted the returning heroes* HOLD A BANQUET FOR, throw a party for, wine and dine, entertain lavishly, regale, treat, fête.

**feat** noun *his gaining access to the imperial palace was no small feat* ACHIEVEMENT, accomplishment, attainment, coup, triumph; undertaking, enterprise, venture, operation, exercise, endeavor, effort, performance, exploit.

**feather** noun *the size and markings of this feather would indi-*

*cate a barred owl* PLUME, quill, flight feather, tail feather; *Ornithology* covert, plumule; **(feathers)** plumage, feathering, down.

**feature** noun **1** *a typical feature of French music* CHARACTERISTIC, attribute, quality, property, trait, hallmark, trademark; aspect, facet, factor, ingredient, component, element, theme; peculiarity, idiosyncrasy, quirk.

**2** *her delicate features* FACE, countenance, physiognomy; *informal* mug, kisser; puss, pan; *literary* visage, lineaments.

**3** *she made a feature of her garden sculptures* CENTERPIECE, (special) attraction, highlight, focal point, focus (of attention).

**4** *she writes features at the newspaper* ARTICLE, piece, item, report, story, column, review, commentary, write-up.

**5** *tonight's feature stars Clint Eastwood* MOVIE, film; main show, main event; *informal* flick, pic.

▸ verb **1** *PBS is featuring a week of live concerts* PRESENT, promote, make a feature of, give prominence to, focus attention on, spotlight, highlight.

**2** *she is to feature in a major advertising campaign* STAR, appear, participate, play a part.

**feces** plural noun *the feces were examined for parasites* EXCREMENT, bodily waste, waste matter, ordure, dung, manure; excreta, stools, droppings; dirt, filth, muck, mess, night soil; *informal* poop, pooh, doo-doo, turds, poo, caca.

**fecund** adjective *the fecund wheat fields* FERTILE, fruitful, productive, high-yielding; rich, lush, flourishing, thriving. See note at FERTILE. ANTONYM barren.

**federation** noun *a federation of Protestant denominations* CONFEDERATION, confederacy, league; combination, alliance, coalition, union, syndicate, guild, consortium, partnership, cooperative, association, amalgamation; *informal* federacy.

**fee** noun *for the quality of work, I think the fee was reasonable* PAYMENT, wage, salary, allowance; price, cost, charge, tariff, rate, amount, sum, figure; **(fees)** remuneration, dues, earnings, pay; *formal* emolument.

**feeble** adjective **1** *he was very old and feeble* WEAK, weakly, weakened, frail, infirm, delicate, sickly, ailing, unwell, poorly, enfeebled, enervated, debilitated, incapacitated, decrepit, etiolated. See note at WEAK. ANTONYM strong.

**2** *a feeble argument* INEFFECTIVE, ineffectual, inadequate, unconvincing, implausible, unsatisfactory, poor, weak, flimsy. ANTONYM effective.

**3** *he's too feeble to stand up to his boss* COWARDLY, craven, faint-hearted, spineless, spiritless, lily-livered, chinless; timid, timorous, fearful, unassertive, weak, ineffectual, wishy-washy; *informal* wimpy, sissy, sissified, gutless, chicken. ANTONYMS forceful, brave.

**4** *a feeble light* FAINT, dim, weak, pale, soft, subdued, muted. ANTONYM strong.

**feeble-minded** adjective *he's not as feebleminded as he pretends to be* STUPID, idiotic, imbecilic, foolish, witless, doltish, empty-headed, vacuous; *informal* halfwitted, moronic, dumb, dim, dopey, dippy; daft. ANTONYM clever.

**feed** verb **1** *feed the kids* GIVE FOOD TO, provide (food) for, cater for, cook for.

**2** *feed the baby* NURSE, breast-feed, suckle; bottle-feed.

**3** *too many cows feeding in a small area* GRAZE, browse, crop, pasture; eat, consume food, chow down.

**4** *the birds* ***feed on*** *a varied diet* LIVE ON/OFF, exist on, subsist on, eat, consume.

**5** *feeding one's self-esteem* STRENGTHEN, fortify, support, bolster, reinforce, boost, fuel, encourage.

**6** *she fed secrets to the Russians* SUPPLY, provide, give, deliver, furnish, issue, pass on.

▸ noun *feed for goats and sheep* FODDER, food, forage, pasturage, herbage, provender; *formal* comestibles.

**feel** verb **1** *she felt the fabric* TOUCH, stroke, caress, fondle, finger, thumb, handle.

**2** *she felt a breeze on her back* PERCEIVE, sense, detect, discern, notice, be aware of, be conscious of.

**3** *you will not feel any pain* EXPERIENCE, undergo, go through, bear, endure, suffer.

**4** *he felt his way toward the door* GROPE, fumble, scrabble, pick.

**5** *feel the temperature of the water* TEST, try (out), check, assess.

**6** *he feels that he should go to the meeting* BELIEVE, think, consider (it right), be of the opinion, hold, maintain, judge; *informal* reckon, figure.

**7** *I feel that he is only biding his time* SENSE, have a (funny) feeling, get the impression, have a hunch, intuit.

**8** *the air feels damp* SEEM, appear, strike one as.

▸ noun **1** *the divers worked by feel* (SENSE OF) TOUCH, tactile sense, feeling (one's way).

**2** *the feel of the paper* TEXTURE, surface, finish; weight, thickness, consistency, quality.

**3** *the feel of a room* ATMOSPHERE, ambience, aura, mood, feeling, air, impression, character, tenor, spirit, flavor; *informal* vibrations, vibes.

**4** *a feel for languages* APTITUDE, knack, flair, bent, talent, gift, faculty, ability.

PHRASES: **feel for** *tell your mother we certainly feel for her* SYMPATHIZE WITH, be sorry for, pity, feel pity for, feel sympathy for, feel compassion for, be moved by; commiserate with, condole with.

**feel like** *I feel like some lemon meringue pie* WANT, would like, wish for, desire, fancy, feel in need of, long for; *informal* yen for, be dying for.

**feeler** noun **1** *the fish has two feelers on its head* ANTENNA, tentacle, tactile/sensory organ; *Zoology* antennule.

**2** *the committee put out feelers* TENTATIVE INQUIRY/PROPOSAL, advance, approach, overture, probe.

**feeling** noun **1** *assess the fabric by feeling* (SENSE OF) TOUCH, feel, tactile sense, using one's hands.

**2** *a feeling of nausea* SENSATION, sense, consciousness.

**3** *I had a feeling that I would win* SUSPICION, sneaking suspicion, notion, inkling, hunch, funny feeling, feeling in one's bones, fancy, idea; presentiment, premonition; *informal* gut feeling.

**4** *the strength of her feeling* LOVE, affection, fondness, tenderness, warmth, warmness, emotion, sentiment; passion, ardor, desire. See note at EMOTION.

**5** *a rush of feeling* COMPASSION, sympathy, empathy, fellow feeling, concern, solicitude, solicitousness, tenderness, love; pity, sorrow, commiseration.

**6** *he had hurt her feelings* SENSIBILITIES, sensitivities, self-esteem, pride.

**7** *my feeling is that it is true* OPINION, belief, view, impression, intuition, instinct, hunch, estimation, guess.

**8** *a feeling of peace* ATMOSPHERE, ambience, aura, air, feel, mood, impression, spirit, quality, flavor; *informal* vibrations, vibes.

▸ adjective *a feeling man* SENSITIVE, warm, warmhearted, tender, tenderhearted, caring, sympathetic, kind, compassionate, understanding, thoughtful.

**feign** verb **1** *she lay still and feigned sleep* SIMULATE, fake, sham, affect, give the appearance of, make a pretense of.

**2** *he's not really ill, he's only feigning* PRETEND, put it on, fake, sham, bluff, masquerade, play-act; *informal* kid.

**felicitations** plural noun *on the occasion of your marriage, felicitations from us all* CONGRATULATIONS, good wishes, best wishes, regards, kind regards, blessings, compliments, respects.

**felicitous** adjective **1** *his nickname was particularly felicitous* APT, well-chosen, fitting, suitable, appropriate, apposite, pertinent, germane, relevant. ANTONYM inappropriate.

**2** *the room's only felicitous feature* FAVORABLE, advantageous, good, pleasing. ANTONYM unfortunate.

**feline** adjective *she moved with feline grace* CATLIKE, graceful, sleek, sinuous.

▸ noun *her pet feline* CAT, kitten; *informal* puss, pussy (cat), kitty (cat); *archaic* grimalkin.

**fell** verb **1** *all the dead sycamores had to be felled* CUT DOWN, chop down, hack down, saw down, clear.

**2** *she felled him with one punch* KNOCK DOWN/OVER, knock to the ground, strike down, bring down, bring to the ground, prostrate; knock out, knock unconscious; *informal* deck, floor, flatten, down, lay out, KO.

**fellow** noun **1** *informal he's a decent sort of fellow* MAN, boy; person, individual, soul; *informal* guy, character, customer, joe, devil, bastard, chap, dude, hombre; *dated* dog.

**2** *he exchanged glances with his fellows* COMPANION, friend, comrade, partner, associate, coworker, colleague; peer, equal, contemporary, confrere; *informal* chum, pal, buddy. PHRASE: **fellow feeling** *the fellow feeling he had for his jilted brother came from recent experience* SYMPATHY, empathy, feeling, compassion, care, concern, solicitude, solicitousness, warmth, tenderness, (brotherly) love; pity, sorrow, commiseration.

**fellowship** noun **1** *a community bound together in fellowship* COMPANIONSHIP, companionability, sociability, comradeship, camaraderie, friendship, mutual support; togetherness, solidarity; *informal* chumminess.

**2** *the church fellowship* ASSOCIATION, society, club, league, union, guild, affiliation, alliance, fraternity, confraternity, brotherhood, sorority, sodality, benevolent society.

**female** adjective *female attributes* FEMININE, womanly, ladylike. ANTONYM male.

▸ noun *the author was a female.* See WOMAN sense 1.

**feminine** adjective **1** *a very feminine young woman* WOMANLY, ladylike; girlish; soft, delicate, gentle, graceful; *informal* girly. ANTONYM masculine.

**2** *he seemed slightly feminine* EFFEMINATE, womanish, unmanly, effete, epicene; *informal* sissy, sissified, wimpy. ANTONYM manly.

**fence** noun **1** *a gap in the fence* BARRIER, fencing, enclosure, barricade, stockade, palisade, fenceline; railing.

**2** *informal a fence dealing mainly in jewelry* RECEIVER (OF STOLEN GOODS), dealer.

▸ verb **1** *they fenced off many acres* ENCLOSE, surround, circumscribe, encircle, circle, encompass; *archaic* compass.

**2** *he* ***fenced in*** *his chickens* CONFINE, pen in, coop up, shut in/up, separate off; enclose, surround, corral.

**3** *she fences as a hobby* SWORD-FIGHT; duel.

PHRASE: **(sitting) on the fence** *informal voters tend to shy away from candidates who are on the fence* UNDECIDED, uncommitted, uncertain, unsure, vacillating, wavering, dithering, hesitant, doubtful, ambivalent, of two minds, in a quandary, hemming and hawing, wishy-washy; neutral, impartial, nonpartisan.

**fend** verb *they were unable to* ***fend off*** *the invasion* WARD OFF, head off, stave off, hold off, repel, repulse, resist, fight off, defend oneself against, prevent, stop, block, intercept, hold back. PHRASE: **fend for oneself** *the children were forced to fend for themselves* TAKE CARE OF ONESELF, look after oneself, provide for oneself, manage (by oneself), cope alone, stand on one's own two feet.

**ferment** verb **1** *the beer continues to ferment* UNDERGO FERMENTATION, brew; effervesce, fizz, foam, froth.

**2** *an environment that ferments disorder* CAUSE, bring about, give rise to, generate, engender, spawn, instigate, provoke, incite, excite, stir up, whip up, foment; *literary* beget, enkindle.

▸ noun *a ferment of revolutionary upheaval* FEVER, furor, frenzy, tumult, storm, rumpus; turmoil, upheaval, unrest, disquiet, uproar, agitation, turbulence, disruption, confusion, disorder, chaos, mayhem; *informal* hoo-ha, to-do.

**ferocious** adjective **1** *ferocious animals* FIERCE, savage, wild, predatory, aggressive, dangerous. ANTONYMS gentle, tame.

**2** *a ferocious attack* BRUTAL, vicious, violent, bloody, barbaric, savage, sadistic, ruthless, cruel, merciless, heartless, bloodthirsty, murderous; *literary* fell. ANTONYM gentle.

**3** *informal a ferocious headache* INTENSE, strong, powerful, fierce, severe, extreme, acute, unbearable, raging; *informal* hellish. ANTONYM mild.

**ferret** verb **1** *she ferreted in her handbag* RUMMAGE, feel around, grope around, forage around, fish around/about, poke around/about; search through, hunt through, rifle through.

**2** ***ferreting out*** *misdemeanors* UNEARTH, uncover, discover, detect, search out, bring to light, track down, dig up, root out, nose out, snoop around for.

**ferry** noun *the Block Island ferry from New London* PASSENGER BOAT, passenger ship, ferry boat, car ferry; ship, boat, vessel; *historical* packet, packet boat.

▸ verb *the new cars were ferried to the island* TRANSPORT, convey, carry, ship, run, take, bring, shuttle.

**fertile** adjective **1** *the soil is fertile* FECUND, fruitful, productive, high-yielding, rich, lush.

**2** *fertile couples* ABLE TO CONCEIVE, able to have children; *technical* fecund. ANTONYM barren.

**3** *a fertile brain* IMAGINATIVE, inventive, innovative, creative, visionary, original, ingenious; productive, prolific. ANTONYM unimaginative.

THE RIGHT WORD **fertile, fecund, fruitful, prolific**

A **fertile** woman is one who has the power to produce offspring, just as *fertile* soil produces crops and a *fertile* imagination produces ideas. This adjective pertains to anything in which seeds (or thoughts) can take root and grow. A woman with ten children might be described as **fecund**, which means that she is not only capable of producing many offspring but has actually done it. A woman can be *fertile*, in other words, without necessarily being *fecund*. **Fruitful**, whose meaning is very close to that of *fecund* when used to describe plants and may replace *fertile* in reference to soil or land, pertains specifically to something that promotes fertility or fecundity (*a fruitful downpour*). It can also apply in a broader sense to anything that bears or promotes results (*a fruitful idea*; *a fruitful discussion*). While it's one thing to call a woman with a large family *fecund*, **prolific** is more usually applied to animals or plants in the literal sense of fertility, and suggests reproducing in great quantity or with rapidity. Figuratively, prolific is often used of highly productive creative efforts (*a prolific author with 40 titles published*).

**fertilize** verb **1** *the field was fertilized* FEED, mulch, compost, green manure, manure, dress, top-dress, add fertilizer to.

**2** *these orchids are fertilized by insects* POLLINATE, cross-pollinate, cross-fertilize, fecundate.

**fertilizer** noun *we use only organic fertilizer* MANURE, plant food, compost, dressing, top dressing, dung.

**fervent** adjective *a fervent prayer* IMPASSIONED, passionate, intense, vehement, ardent, sincere, fervid, heartfelt; enthusiastic, zealous, fanatical, hardcore, wholehearted, avid, eager, keen, committed, dedicated, devout; *literary* perfervid. See note at EAGER. ANTONYM apathetic.

**fervid** adjective *fervid protestations of love* FERVENT, ardent, passionate, impassioned, intense, vehement, wholehearted, heartfelt, sincere, earnest; *literary* perfervid.

**fervor** noun *even the smallest of tasks he tackled with fervor* PASSION, ardor, intensity, zeal, vehemence, emotion, warmth, earnestness, avidity, eagerness, keenness, enthusiasm, excitement, animation, vigor, energy, fire, spirit, zest, fervency. ANTONYM apathy.

**fester** verb **1** *his deep wound festered* SUPPURATE, become septic, become infected, form pus, weep; *Medicine* be purulent; *archaic* rankle.

**2** *the garbage festered* ROT, molder, decay, decompose, putrefy, go bad, spoil, deteriorate.

**3** *their resentment festered* RANKLE, eat away, gnaw away, brew, smolder.

**festival** noun **1** *the town's fall festival* FAIR, carnival, fiesta, jamboree, celebrations, festivities, fest.

**2** *fasting precedes the festival* HOLY DAY, feast day, saint's day, commemoration, day of observance.

**festive** adjective *a festive mood* JOLLY, merry, joyous, joyful, happy, jovial, lighthearted, cheerful, jubilant, convivial, high-spirited, mirthful, uproarious; celebratory, holiday, carnival; Christmassy; *archaic* festal.

**festivity** noun **1** (**festivities**) *food plays an important part in the festivities* CELEBRATION, festival, entertainment, party, jamboree; merrymaking, feasting, revelry, jollification; revels, fun and games; *informal* bash.

**2** *the festivity of Opening Day* JUBILATION, merriment, gaiety, cheerfulness, cheer, joyfulness, jollity, conviviality, high spirits, revelry.

**festoon** noun *festoons of paper flowers* GARLAND, chain, lei, swathe, swag, loop.

▸ verb *the room was festooned with streamers* DECORATE, adorn, ornament, trim, deck (out), hang, loop, drape, swathe, garland, wreathe, bedeck; *informal* do up/out, get up, trick out; *literary* bedizen.

**fetch** verb **1** *he went to fetch a doctor* (GO AND) GET, go for, call for, summon, pick up, collect, bring, carry, convey, transport.

**2** *the land could fetch a million dollars* SELL FOR, bring in, raise, realize, yield, make, command, cost, be priced at; *informal* go for, set one back, pull in.

**fetching** adjective *give this note to the fetching young lady in the blue dress* ATTRACTIVE, appealing, sweet, pretty, good-looking, lovely, delightful, charming, prepossessing, captivating, enchanting, irresistible; *Scottish* bonny; *informal* divine, heavenly; killer; *archaic* comely, fair.

**fetish** noun **1** *he developed a bodybuilding fetish* FIXATION, obsession, compulsion, mania; weakness, fancy, fascination, fad; *informal* thing, hang-up.

**2** *an African fetish* JUJU, talisman, charm, amulet; totem, idol, image, effigy.

**fetter** verb **1** *the captive was fettered* SHACKLE, manacle, handcuff, clap in irons, put in chains, chain (up); *informal* cuff; *literary* enfetter.

**2** *these obligations fetter the company's powers* RESTRICT, restrain, constrain, limit; hinder, hamper, impede, obstruct, hamstring, inhibit, check, curb, trammel; *informal* hog-tie.

**fetters** plural noun *bound by fetters of iron* SHACKLES, manacles, handcuffs, irons, leg irons, chains, restraints; *informal* cuffs, bracelets; *historical* bilboes.

**fettle** noun *my, you certainly are in fine fettle* SHAPE, trim, fitness, physical fitness, health, state of health; condition, form, repair, state of repair, order, working order.

**fetus** noun *an ultrasonic photo of the fetus* EMBRYO, unborn baby/child.

**feud** noun *tribal feuds* VENDETTA, conflict; rivalry, hostility, enmity, strife, discord; quarrel, argument, falling out. See note at QUARREL.

▸ verb *he feuded with his teammates* QUARREL, fight, argue, bicker, squabble, fall out, dispute, clash, differ, be at odds; *informal* scrap.

**fever** noun **1** *he developed a fever* FEVERISHNESS, high temperature, febrility; *Medicine* pyrexia; *informal* TEMPERATURE.

**2** *a fever of excitement* FERMENT, frenzy, furor; ecstasy, rapture.

**3** *Stanley Cup fever* EXCITEMENT, frenzy, agitation, passion.

**feverish** adjective **1** *she's really feverish* FEBRILE, fevered, hot, burning; *informal* having a temperature.

**2** *feverish excitement* FRENZIED, frenetic, hectic, agitated, excited, restless, nervous, worked up, overwrought, frantic, furious, hysterical, wild, uncontrolled, unrestrained.

**few** adjective **1** *police are revealing few details* NOT MANY, hardly any, scarcely any; a small number of, a small amount of, one or two, a handful of; little. See note at LESS. ANTONYM many.

**2** *comforts here are few* SCARCE, scant, meager, insufficient, in short supply; thin on the ground, few and far between, infrequent, uncommon, rare; negligible. ANTONYM plentiful.

▸ pronoun **(a few)** *there weren't many biscuits, but we saved you a few* A SMALL NUMBER, a handful, one or two, a couple, two or three; not many, hardly any.

**fiasco** noun *the picnic was a fiasco* FAILURE, disaster, catastrophe, debacle, shambles, farce, mess, wreck; *informal* flop, washout, snafu. ANTONYM success.

**fib** noun *you're telling a fib* LIE, untruth, falsehood, made-up story, invention, fabrication, deception, (piece of) fiction; (little) white lie, half-truth; *informal* tall story/tale, whopper. See note at LIE[1]. ANTONYM truth.

**fiber** noun **1** *fibers from the murderer's sweater* THREAD, strand, filament; *technical* fibril.

**2** *natural fibers* MATERIAL, cloth, fabric.

**3** *fiber in the diet* ROUGHAGE, bulk.

**fickle** adjective *the fickle Loretta has a different boyfriend every month* CAPRICIOUS, changeable, variable, volatile, mercurial; inconstant, undependable, unsteady, unfaithful, faithless, flighty, giddy, skittish; fair-weather; *technical* labile; *literary* mutable. ANTONYM constant.

**fiction** noun **1** *the popularity of South American fiction* NOVELS, stories, (creative) writing, (prose) literature; *informal* lit.

**2** *the president dismissed the allegation as absolute fiction* FABRICATION, invention, lies, fibs, untruth, falsehood, fantasy, nonsense. ANTONYM fact.

THE RIGHT WORD **fiction, deception, fable, fabrication, falsehood, figment**

If a young child tells you there is a dinosaur under his bed, you might assume that his story is a **fiction**, but it is probably a **figment**. A *fiction* is a story that is invented either to entertain or to deceive (*her excuse was ingenious, but it was pure fiction*), while *figment* suggests the operation of fancy or imagination (*a figment of his imagination*). If a child hides his sandwich under the sofa cushions and tells you that a dinosaur ate it, this would be a **fabrication**, which is a story that is intended to deceive. Unlike a *figment*, which is mostly imagined, a *fabrication* is a false but thoughtfully constructed story in which some truth is often interwoven (*the city's safety record was a fabrication designed to lure tourists downtown*). A **falsehood** is basically a lie—a statement or story that one knows to be false but tells with intent to deceive (*a deliberate falsehood about where the money had come from*). A **deception**, on the other hand, is an act that deceives but not always intentionally (*a foolish deception designed to prevent her parents from worrying*). A **fable** is a fictitious story that deals with events or situations that are clearly fantastic, impossible, or incredible. It often gives animals or inanimate objects the power to speak and conveys a lesson of practical wisdom, as in *Aesop's Fables*.

**fictional** adjective *fictional characters* FICTITIOUS, fictive, invented, imaginary, made up, make-believe, unreal, fabricated, mythical. ANTONYM real.

**fictitious** adjective **1** *a fictitious name* FALSE, fake, fabricated, sham; bogus, spurious, assumed, affected, adopted, feigned, invented, made up; *informal* pretend, phony. ANTONYM genuine.

**2** *a fictitious character*. See FICTIONAL.

**fiddle** *informal* noun *she played the fiddle* VIOLIN, viola.

▸ verb **1** *he fiddled with a coaster* FIDGET, play, toy, twiddle, fuss, fool about/around; finger, thumb, handle; *informal* mess around/about.

**2** *he fiddled with the dials* ADJUST, tinker, play around, meddle, interfere.

**3** *fiddling the figures* FALSIFY, manipulate, massage, rig, distort, misrepresent, doctor, alter, tamper with, interfere with; *informal* fix, flimflam, cook (the books).

**fidelity** noun **1** *fidelity to her husband* FAITHFULNESS, loyalty, constancy; trueheartedness, trustworthiness, dependability, reliability; *formal* troth. ANTONYMS infidelity, disloyalty.

**2** *fidelity to your king* LOYALTY, allegiance, obedience; *historical* homage, fealty. ANTONYM disloyalty.

**3** *the fidelity of the reproduction* ACCURACY, exactness, precision, preciseness, correctness; strictness, closeness, faithfulness, authenticity. ANTONYM inaccuracy.

**fidget** verb **1** *the audience began to fidget* MOVE RESTLESSLY, wriggle, squirm, twitch, jiggle, shuffle, be agitated; *informal* be jittery.

**2** *she fidgeted with her scarf* PLAY, fuss, toy, twiddle, fool around; *informal* fiddle, mess around.

▸ noun **1** *his convulsive fidgets* TWITCH, wriggle, squirm, jiggle, shuffle, tic, spasm.

**2** *what a fidget you are!* FLIBBERTIGIBBET, restless person, bundle of nerves.

**fidgety** adjective *why is the dog so fidgety?* RESTLESS, restive, on edge, uneasy, antsy, nervous, keyed up, anxious, agitated; *informal* jittery, twitchy.

**field** noun **1** *a large plowed field* MEADOW, pasture, paddock, grassland, pastureland; *literary* lea, sward; *archaic* glebe.

**2** *a soccer field* PLAYING FIELD, ground, sports field; *Brit.* pitch.

**3** *the field of biotechnology* AREA, sphere, discipline, province, department, domain, sector, branch, subject; *informal* bailiwick.

**4** *your field of vision* SCOPE, range, sweep, reach, extent.

**5** *she is well ahead of the field* COMPETITORS, entrants, competition; applicants, candidates, possibles.

▸ verb **1** *she fielded the ball* CATCH, stop, retrieve; return, throw back.

**2** *they can field an army of about one million* DEPLOY, position, range, dispose.

**3** *he fielded some awkward questions* DEAL WITH, handle, cope with, answer, reply to, respond to.

▸ adjective **1** *field experience* PRACTICAL, hands-on, applied, experiential, empirical. ANTONYM theoretical.

**2** *field artillery* MOBILE, portable, transportable, movable, maneuverable, light.

**fiend** noun **1** *a fiend had taken possession of him* DEMON, devil, evil spirit; *informal* spook.

**2** *a fiend bent on global evildoing* VILLAIN, beast, brute, barbarian, monster, ogre, sadist, evildoer, swine.

**3** *informal a drug fiend* ADDICT, abuser, user; *informal* junkie, ——head, ——freak.

**4** *informal a fitness fiend* ENTHUSIAST, maniac; devotee, fan, lover, fanatic, addict, buff, freak, nut.

**fiendish** adjective **1** *a fiendish torturer* WICKED, cruel, vicious, evil, malevolent, villainous; brutal, savage, barbaric, barbarous, inhuman, murderous, ruthless, merciless; *dated* dastardly.

**2** *a fiendish plot* CUNNING, clever, ingenious, crafty, canny, wily, devious, shrewd; *informal* sneaky.

**3** *a fiendish puzzle* DIFFICULT, complex, challenging, complicated, intricate, involved, knotty, thorny, tricky.

**fierce** adjective **1** *a fierce black mastiff* FEROCIOUS, savage, vicious, aggressive. ANTONYM gentle.

**2** *fierce competition* AGGRESSIVE, cutthroat, competitive; keen, intense, strong, relentless. ANTONYM mild.

**3** *fierce, murderous jealousy* INTENSE, powerful, vehement, passionate, impassioned, fervent, fervid, ardent. ANTONYM mild.

**4** *a fierce wind* POWERFUL, strong, violent, forceful; stormy, blustery, gusty, tempestuous. ANTONYMS gentle, mild.

**5** *a fierce pain* SEVERE, extreme, intense, acute, awful, dreadful; excruciating, agonizing, piercing. ANTONYM mild.

**fight** verb **1** *two men were fighting* BRAWL, exchange blows, attack each other, assault each other, hit each other, punch each other; struggle, grapple, wrestle; *informal* scrap, have a set-to, roughhouse, engage in fisticuffs.

**2** *they fought in the First World War* (DO) BATTLE, go to war, take up arms, be a soldier; engage, meet, clash, skirmish.

**3** *a war fought for freedom* ENGAGE IN, wage, conduct, prosecute, undertake.

**4** *they are always fighting* QUARREL, argue, bicker, squabble, fall out, have a fight, have a row, wrangle, be at odds, disagree, differ, have words, bandy words, be at each other's throats, be at loggerheads; *informal* scrap.

**5** *fighting against wage reductions* CAMPAIGN, strive, battle, struggle, contend, crusade, agitate, lobby, push, press.

**6** *they will fight the decision* OPPOSE, contest, contend with, confront, challenge, combat, dispute, quarrel with, argue against/with, strive against, struggle against.

**7** *Tyler fought the urge to stick his tongue out* REPRESS, restrain, suppress, stifle, smother, hold back, fight back, keep in check, curb, control, rein in, choke back; *informal* keep the lid on.

▸ noun **1** *a fight outside a club* BRAWL, fracas, melee, rumpus, skirmish, sparring match, struggle, scuffle, altercation, clash, disturbance; fisticuffs; *informal* scrap, set-to, donnybrook.

**2** *a heavyweight fight* BOXING MATCH, bout, match.

**3** *Japan's fight against Russia* BATTLE, engagement, clash, conflict, struggle; war, campaign, crusade, action, hostilities.

**4** *a fight with my girlfriend* ARGUMENT, quarrel, squabble, row, wrangle, disagreement, falling-out, contretemps, altercation, dispute; *informal* tiff, spat, scrap, cat fight, blowup.

**5** *their fight for control of the company* STRUGGLE, battle, campaign, push, effort.

**6** *she had no fight left in her* WILL TO RESIST, resistance, spirit, courage, pluck, pluckiness, grit, strength, backbone, determination, resolution, resolve, resoluteness, aggression, aggressiveness; *informal* guts, spunk, moxie.

PHRASES: **fight back 1** *if the enemy attacks, we will fight back* RETALIATE, counterattack, strike back, hit back, respond, reciprocate, return fire, give tit for tat.

**2** *Russ fought back tears.* See FIGHT verb sense 7.

**fight off** *they tried in vain to fight off the swarming locusts* REPEL, repulse, beat off/back, ward off, fend off, keep/hold at bay, drive away/back, force back.

**fighter** noun **1** *a guerrilla fighter* SOLDIER, fighting man/woman, warrior, combatant, serviceman, servicewoman, trooper, mercenary; *archaic* man-at-arms.

**2** *the fighter was knocked to the ground* BOXER, pugilist, prizefighter; wrestler.

**3** *enemy fighters* WARPLANE, armed aircraft.

**figurative** adjective *the example given was meant to be figurative* METAPHORICAL, nonliteral, symbolic, allegorical, representative, emblematic. ANTONYM literal.

**figure** noun **1** *the production figure* STATISTIC, number, quantity, amount, level, total, sum; (**figures**) data, information.

**2** *the second figure was 9* DIGIT, numeral, numerical symbol.

**3** *he can't put a figure on it* PRICE, cost, amount, value, valuation.

**4** (**figures**) *I'm good with figures* ARITHMETIC, mathematics, math, calculations, computation, numbers.

**5** *her petite figure* PHYSIQUE, build, frame, body, proportions, shape, form.

**6** *a dark figure emerged* SILHOUETTE, outline, shape, form.

**7** *a figure of authority* PERSON, personage, individual, man, woman, character, personality; representative, embodiment, personification, epitome.

**8** *life-size figures* HUMAN REPRESENTATION, effigy, model, statue.

**9** *geometrical figures* SHAPE, pattern, design, motif.

**10** *see figure 4* DIAGRAM, illustration, drawing, picture, plate.

▸ verb **1** *a beast figuring in Egyptian legend* FEATURE, appear, be featured, be mentioned, be referred to, have prominence, crop up.

**2** *a way to figure the values* CALCULATE, work out, total, reckon, compute, determine, assess, put a figure on, crunch the numbers, tot up.

**3** *informal* *I figured that I didn't have a chance* SUPPOSE, think, believe, consider, expect, take it, suspect, sense; assume, dare say, conclude, take it as read, presume, deduce, infer, extrapolate, gather, guess.

**4** *"Charlotte's late." "That figures."* MAKE SENSE, seem reasonable, stand to reason, be to be expected, be logical, follow, ring true.

PHRASES: **figure on** *they figured on paying about $100* PLAN ON, count on, rely on, bank on, bargain on, depend on, pin one's hopes on; anticipate, expect to (be).

**figure out** *he tried to figure out how to switch on the lamp* WORK OUT, fathom, puzzle out, decipher, ascertain, make sense of, think through, get to the bottom of; understand, comprehend, see, grasp, get the hang of, get the drift of; *informal* crack; *Brit. informal* twig.

**figurehead** noun **1** *the president was just a figurehead* TITULAR HEAD, nominal leader, leader in name only, front man, cipher, token, mouthpiece, puppet, instrument.

**2** *the figurehead on the ship* CARVING, bust, sculpture, image, statue.

**filament** noun *the fragile filament inside the bulb* FIBER, thread, strand; *technical* fibril.

**file**[1] noun **1** *he opened the file* FOLDER, portfolio, binder, document case.

**2** *we have files on all the major companies* DOSSIER, document, record, report; data, information, documentation, annals, archives.

**3** *the computer file was searched* DATA, document, text.

**4** *the director needed updating on the Uecker file* DOSSIER, department, front.

▸ verb **1** *file the documents correctly* CATEGORIZE, classify, organize, put in place/order, order, arrange, catalog, record, store, archive.

**2** *Debbie has filed for divorce* APPLY, register, ask.

**3** *two women have filed a civil suit against him* BRING, press, lodge, place; *formal* prefer.

**file**[2] noun *a file of boys* LINE, column, row, string, chain, procession, queue.

▸ verb *we filed out into the parking lot* WALK IN A LINE, march, parade, troop.

**file**[3] verb *she filed her nails* SMOOTH, buff, rub (down), polish, shape; scrape, abrade, rasp, sandpaper.

**filigree** noun *decorated with gold filigree* TRACERY, fretwork, latticework, scrollwork, lacework, quilling.

**fill** verb **1** *he filled a bowl with cereal* MAKE FULL, fill up, fill to the brim, top up, charge. ANTONYM empty.

**2** *guests filled the parlor* CROWD INTO, throng, pack (into), occupy, squeeze into, cram (into); overcrowd, overfill.

**3** *he was filling his shelves* STOCK, pack, load, supply, replenish, restock, refill.

**4** *fill all the holes with a spackling compound* BLOCK UP, stop (up), plug, seal, caulk. ANTONYM unblock.

**5** *the perfume filled the room* PERVADE, permeate, suffuse, be diffused through, penetrate, infuse, perfuse.

**6** *he was going to fill a government post* OCCUPY, hold, take up; *informal* hold down.

**7** *we had just filled a big order* CARRY OUT, complete, fulfill, execute, discharge. PHRASES: **fill in** *while Mr. Grant is on vacation, Luis will be filling in* SUBSTITUTE, deputize, stand in, cover, take over, act as stand-in, take the place of; *informal* sub, step into someone's shoes/boots, pinch-hit.

**fill in on** *when we get home, you can fill us in on the details* INFORM OF, advise of, tell about, acquaint with, apprise of, brief on, update with; *informal* put in the picture about, bring up to speed on.

**fill something in/out** *fill in these forms | he filled out the questionnaire* COMPLETE, answer.

**fill out** *the puppies will begin to fill out once they start getting proper nutrition* GROW FATTER, become plumper, flesh out, put on weight, gain weight, get heavier.

**film** noun **1** *a film of sweat* LAYER, coat, coating, covering, cover, sheet, patina, overlay.

**2** *Emma was watching a film* MOVIE, picture, feature film, motion picture; *informal* flick, pic; *dated* moving picture, talkie.

**3** *she would like to work in film* MOVIES, cinema, pictures, the motion picture industry.

▸ verb **1** *he immediately filmed the next scene* RECORD (ON FILM), shoot, capture on film, video.

**2** *his eyes had* ***filmed over*** CLOUD (OVER), mist (over), haze (over); become blurred, blur; *archaic* blear.

**filmy** adjective *a filmy black blouse* DIAPHANOUS, transparent, see-through, translucent, sheer, gossamer; delicate, fine, light, thin, silky. ANTONYMS thick, opaque.

**filter** noun *a carbon filter* STRAINER, sifter; riddle; gauze, netting.

▸ verb **1** *the farmers filter the water* SIEVE, strain, sift, filtrate, clarify, purify, refine, treat.

**2** *the rain had filtered through her jacket* SEEP, percolate, leak, trickle, ooze.

**filth** noun **1** *stagnant pools of filth* DIRT, muck, grime, mud, mire, sludge, slime, ooze; excrement, excreta, dung, manure, ordure, sewage; rubbish, refuse, dross; pollution, contamination, filthiness, uncleanness, foulness, nastiness, garbage, crud, grunge, gunge, trash.

**2** *I felt sick after reading that filth* PORNOGRAPHY, pornographic literature/films, dirty books, smut, obscenity, indecency; *informal* porn, porno.

**filthy** adjective **1** *the room was filthy* DIRTY, grimy, muddy, slimy, unclean, mucky; foul, squalid, sordid, nasty, soiled, sullied; polluted, contaminated, unhygienic, unsanitary; *informal* cruddy, grungy; *literary* besmirched; *formal* feculent. ANTONYM clean.

**2** *his face was filthy* UNWASHED, unclean, dirty, grimy, smeared, grubby, muddy, mucky, black, blackened, stained; *literary* begrimed. ANTONYM clean.

**3** *filthy jokes* OBSCENE, indecent, dirty, smutty, rude, improper, coarse, bawdy, vulgar, lewd, racy, raw, off-color, earthy, barnyard, locker-room, ribald, risqué, "adult", pornographic, explicit; *informal* blue, porn, porno, X-rated. ANTONYMS clean, polite.

**4** *you filthy brute!* DESPICABLE, contemptible, nasty, low, base, mean, vile, obnoxious; *informal* dirty (rotten), lowdown, no-good.

**5** *he was in a filthy mood* BAD, foul, bad-tempered, ill-tempered, irritable, grumpy, grouchy, cross, fractious, peevish; *informal* cranky, ornery. ANTONYM good.

▸ adverb *filthy rich* VERY, extremely, tremendously, immensely, remarkably, excessively, exceedingly; *informal* stinking, awfully, terribly, seriously, mega, majorly, ultra, damn.

**final** adjective **1** *the final year of study* LAST, closing, concluding, finishing, end, terminating, ultimate, eventual. ANTONYM first.

**2** *their decisions are final* IRREVOCABLE, unalterable, absolute, conclusive, irrefutable, incontrovertible, indisputable, unchallengeable, binding. ANTONYM provisional.

▸ noun *the Stanley Cup final* DECIDER, clincher, final game/match. ANTONYM qualifier.

**finale** noun *the show's spectacular finale* CLIMAX, culmination; end, ending, finish, close, conclusion, termination; denouement, last act, final scene. ANTONYM beginning.

**finality** noun *an answer delivered with finality* CONCLUSIVENESS, decisiveness, decision, definiteness, definitiveness, certainty, certitude; irrevocability, irrefutability.

**finalize** verb *they had yet to finalize a peace treaty* CONCLUDE, complete, clinch, settle, work out, secure, wrap up, wind up, put the finishing touches to; reach an agreement on, agree on, come to terms on; *informal* sew up.

**finally** adverb **1** *she finally got her man to the altar* EVENTUALLY, ultimately, in the end, after a long time, at (long) last; in the long run, in the fullness of time.

**2** *finally, wrap the ribbon around the edge* LASTLY, last, in conclusion, to conclude, to end.

**3** *this should finally dispel that common misconception* CONCLUSIVELY, irrevocably, decisively, definitively, for ever, for good, once and for all.

**finance** noun **1** *he knows about finance* FINANCIAL AFFAIRS, money matters, fiscal matters, economics, money management, commerce, business, investment.

**2** *short-term finance* FUNDS, assets, money, capital, resources, cash, reserves, revenue, income; funding, backing, sponsorship.

▸ verb *the project was financed by grants* FUND, pay for, back, capitalize, endow, subsidize, invest in; underwrite, guarantee, sponsor, support, bankroll.

**financial** adjective *our financial picture has improved* MONETARY, money, economic, pecuniary, fiscal, banking, commercial, business, investment.

THE RIGHT WORD **financial, monetary, pecuniary, fiscal**

What's the difference between a **financial** crisis and a **fiscal** one? It all depends on who's having trouble with money and the scale of the difficulties. *Financial* usually applies to money matters involving large sums or transactions of considerable importance (*the auction was a financial success*). *Fiscal* refers specifically to the financial affairs of a government, organization, or corporation (*the end of the company's fiscal year*), while

**pecuniary** refers to money matters of a more personal or practical nature and is preferred to *financial* when money is being discussed on a smaller scale (*pecuniary motives, pecuniary assistance, pecuniary difficulties*). Of all these words, **monetary** refers most directly to money as such and is often used when discussing the coinage, distribution, and circulation of money (*the European monetary system; the monetary unit of a country*).

---

**find** verb **1** *I found the book I wanted* LOCATE, spot, pinpoint, unearth, obtain; search out, nose out, track down, root out; come across/upon, run across/into, chance on, light on, happen on, stumble on, encounter; *informal* bump into; *literary* espy.

**2** *they say they've found a cure for rabies* DISCOVER, invent, come up with, hit on.

**3** *the police found her purse* RETRIEVE, recover, get back, regain, repossess. ANTONYM lose.

**4** *I hope you find peace* OBTAIN, acquire, get, procure, come by, secure, gain, earn, achieve, attain.

**5** *I found the courage to speak* SUMMON (UP), gather, muster (up), screw up, call up.

**6** *caffeine **is found** in coffee and tea* BE (PRESENT), occur, exist, be existent, appear.

**7** *you'll find that it's a lively area* DISCOVER, become aware, realize, observe, notice, note, perceive, learn.

**8** *I find their decision strange* CONSIDER, think, believe to be, feel to be, look on as, view as, see as, judge, deem, regard as.

**9** *he was found guilty* JUDGE, adjudge, adjudicate, deem, rule, declare, pronounce.

**10** *her barb found its mark* ARRIVE AT, reach, attain, achieve; hit, strike.

▸ noun **1** *an archaeological find* DISCOVERY, acquisition, asset.

**2** *this table is a real find* GOOD BUY, bargain; godsend, boon.

PHRASE: **find out** *let us know what you find out about the theft* DISCOVER, become aware, learn, detect, discern, perceive, observe, notice, note, get/come to know, realize; bring to light, reveal, expose, unearth, disclose; *informal* figure out, cotton on, catch on, get wise (to), savvy; *Brit. informal* twig.

**finding** noun **1** *the finding of the leak* DISCOVERY, location, locating, detection, detecting, uncovering.

**2** *the tribunal's findings* CONCLUSION, decision, verdict, pronouncement, judgment, ruling, rule, decree, order, recommendation, resolve; *Law* determination.

**fine**[1] adjective **1** *fine wines* EXCELLENT, first-class, first-rate, great, exceptional, outstanding, quality, superior, splendid, magnificent, exquisite, choice, select, prime, supreme, superb, wonderful, superlative, of high quality, second to none; *informal* A1, top-notch, blue-ribbon, blue-chip, splendiferous. ANTONYM poor.

**2** *a fine citizen* WORTHY, admirable, praiseworthy, laudable, estimable, upright, upstanding, respectable.

**3** *the initiative is fine, but it's not enough on its own* ALL RIGHT, acceptable, suitable, good (enough), passable, satisfactory, adequate, reasonable, tolerable; *informal* OK. ANTONYM unsatisfactory.

**4** *I feel fine* IN GOOD HEALTH, well, healthy, all right, (fighting) fit, as fit as a fiddle, blooming, thriving, in good shape, in good condition, in fine fettle; *informal* OK, in the pink. ANTONYM ill.

**5** *a fine day* FAIR, dry, bright, clear, sunny, without a cloud in the sky, warm, balmy, summery. ANTONYM inclement.

**6** *a fine old house* IMPRESSIVE, imposing, striking, splendid, grand, majestic, magnificent, stately.

**7** *fine clothes* ELEGANT, stylish, expensive, smart, chic, fashionable; fancy, sumptuous, lavish, opulent; *informal* flashy, swanky, ritzy, plush.

**8** *a fine mind* KEEN, quick, alert, sharp, bright, brilliant, astute, clever, intelligent, perspicacious. ANTONYM slow.

**9** *fine china* DELICATE, fragile, dainty. ANTONYM coarse.

**10** *fine hair* THIN, light, delicate, wispy, flyaway. ANTONYM thick.

**11** *a fine point* SHARP, keen, acute, sharpened, razor-sharp. ANTONYMS thick, blunt.

**12** *fine material* SHEER, light, lightweight, thin, flimsy; diaphanous, filmy, gossamer, silky, transparent, translucent, see-through. ANTONYMS thick, coarse.

**13** *fine sand* FINE-GRAINED, powdery, powdered, dusty, ground, crushed; *technical* comminuted. ANTONYM coarse.

**14** *fine detailed work* INTRICATE, delicate, detailed, elaborate, dainty, meticulous.

**15** *a fine distinction* SUBTLE, ultra-fine, nice, hair-splitting, nitpicking.

**16** *people's finer feelings* ELEVATED, lofty, exalted, noble; refined, sensitive, cultivated, cultured, civilized, sophisticated. ANTONYM coarse.

**17** *fine taste* DISCERNING, discriminating, refined, cultivated, cultured, critical. ANTONYM vulgar.

▸ adverb *informal you're doing fine* WELL, all right, not badly, satisfactorily, adequately, nicely, tolerably; *informal* OK, good. ANTONYM badly.

**fine**[2] noun *heavy fines* (FINANCIAL) PENALTY, sanction, fee, charge.

▸ verb *they were fined for breaking environmental laws* PENALIZE, impose a fine on, charge.

**finery** noun *all dressed up in her finery* REGALIA, best clothes, best, Sunday best; *informal* glad rags.

**finesse** noun **1** *masterly finesse* SKILL, skillfulness, expertise, subtlety, flair, panache, élan, polish, artistry, virtuosity, mastery.

**2** *a modicum of finesse* TACT, tactfulness, discretion, diplomacy, delicacy, sensitivity, perceptiveness, savoir faire.

**3** *a clever finesse* WINNING MOVE, trick, stratagem, ruse, maneuver, artifice, machination.

**finger** noun *he wagged his finger at the cat* DIGIT, thumb, index finger, forefinger; *informal* pinkie.

▸ verb 1 *she fingered her brooch uneasily* TOUCH, feel, handle, stroke, rub, caress, fondle, toy with, play (around) with, fiddle with.

2 *no one fingered the culprit* IDENTIFY, recognize, pick out, spot; inform on, point the finger at; *informal* rat on, squeal on, tell on, blow the whistle on, snitch on.

**finicky** adjective *their fancy words and finicky manners* FUSSY, fastidious, punctilious, over-particular, difficult, exacting, demanding; *informal* picky, choosy, persnickety; *archaic* nice.

**finish** verb 1 *Mrs. Porter had just finished the task* COMPLETE, end, conclude, stop, cease, terminate, bring to a conclusion/end/close, wind up; crown, cap, round off, put the finishing touches to; accomplish, discharge, carry out, do, get done, fulfill; *informal* wrap up, sew up, polish off. ANTONYM start.

2 *Sarah has finished school* LEAVE, give up, drop; stop, discontinue, have done with, complete; *informal* pack in, quit. ANTONYMS begin, continue.

3 *Hitch finished his dinner* CONSUME, eat, devour, drink, finish off, polish off, gulp (down); use (up), exhaust, empty, drain, get through, run through; *informal* down. ANTONYM start.

4 *the program has finished* END, come to an end, stop, conclude, come to a conclusion/end/close, cease. ANTONYMS start, begin.

5 *some items were finished in a black lacquer* VARNISH, lacquer, veneer, coat, stain, wax, shellac, enamel, glaze.

▸ noun 1 *the finish of filming* END, ending, completion, conclusion, close, closing, cessation, termination; final part/stage, finale, denouement; *informal* sewing up, polishing off. ANTONYMS start, beginning.

2 *a gallop to the finish* FINISHING LINE, finishing post, tape.

3 *an antiquated paint finish* VENEER, lacquer, lamination, glaze, coating, covering; surface, texture.

PHRASE: **finish off** 1 *the executioners finished them off* KILL, take/end the life of, execute, terminate, exterminate, liquidate, get rid of; *informal* wipe out, do in, bump off, take out, dispose of, do away with, ice, rub out, waste.

2 *financial difficulties finished off the business* OVERWHELM, overcome, defeat, get the better of, worst, bring down; *informal* drive to the wall, best.

**finished** adjective 1 *the finished job* COMPLETED, concluded, terminated, over (and done with), at an end; accomplished, executed, discharged, fulfilled, done; *informal* wrapped up, sewn up, polished off; *formal* effectuated. ANTONYM incomplete.

2 *a finished performance* ACCOMPLISHED, polished, flawless, faultless, perfect; expert, proficient, masterly, impeccable, virtuoso, skillful, skilled, professional. ANTONYMS crude, unpolished.

3 *he was finished* RUINED, defeated, beaten, wrecked, doomed, bankrupt, broken; *informal* washed up, through.

**finite** adjective *there is a finite amount of water in the system* LIMITED, restricted, determinate, fixed.

**fire** noun 1 *a fire broke out* BLAZE, conflagration, inferno; flames, burning, combustion; forest fire, wildfire, brush fire.

2 *he lacked fire* DYNAMISM, energy, vigor, animation, vitality, vibrancy, exuberance, zest, élan; passion, ardor, zeal, spirit, verve, vivacity, vivaciousness; enthusiasm, eagerness, gusto, fervor, fervency; *informal* pep, vim, go, get-up-and-go, oomph.

3 *rapid machine-gun fire* GUNFIRE, firing, flak, bombardment.

4 *they directed their fire at the state legislature* CRITICISM, censure, condemnation, denunciation, opprobrium, admonishments, brickbats; hostility, antagonism, animosity; *informal* flak.

▸ verb 1 *howitzers firing shells* LAUNCH, shoot, discharge, let fly with.

2 *someone fired a gun* SHOOT, discharge, let off, set off.

3 *informal he was fired* DISMISS, discharge, give someone their notice, lay off, let go, get rid of, ax, cashier; *informal* sack, give someone the sack, boot out, give someone the boot, give someone their marching orders, pink-slip; *Brit.* make redundant.

4 *the engine fired* START, get started, get going.

5 *the stories fired my imagination* STIMULATE, stir up, excite, awaken, arouse, rouse, inflame, animate, inspire, motivate.

PHRASES: **catch fire** *it was amazing that neither of the adjoining buildings caught fire* IGNITE, catch light, burst into flames, go up in flames.
**on fire** 1 *the restaurant was on fire* BURNING, alight, ablaze, blazing, aflame, in flames; *literary* afire.

2 *she was on fire with passion* ARDENT, passionate, fervent, excited, eager, enthusiastic.

**firebrand** noun *a group of political firebrands* RADICAL, revolutionary, agitator, rabble-rouser, incendiary, subversive, troublemaker.

**fireproof** adjective *fireproof coveralls* NONFLAMMABLE, incombustible, fire resistant, flame resistant, flame retardant, heatproof. ANTONYM inflammable.

**fireworks** plural noun 1 *there are fireworks after every Friday night game* PYROTECHNICS, firecrackers.

2 *his stubbornness has produced some fireworks* UPROAR, trouble, mayhem, fuss; tantrums, hysterics.

**firm**[1] adjective 1 *the ground is fairly firm* HARD, solid, unyielding, resistant; solidified, hardened, compacted, compressed, dense, stiff, rigid, frozen, set. ANTONYMS soft, yielding.

2 *firm foundations* SECURE, secured, stable, steady, strong, fixed, fast, set, taut, tight; immovable, irremovable, stationary, motionless. ANTONYM unstable.

3 *a firm handshake* STRONG, vigorous, sturdy, forceful. ANTONYM limp.

4 *I was very firm about what I wanted | a firm supporter* RES-

OLUTE, determined, decided, resolved, steadfast; adamant, emphatic, insistent, single-minded, in earnest, wholehearted; unfaltering, unwavering, unflinching, unswerving, unbending; hardline, committed, dyed-in-the-wool. ANTONYM irresolute.

**5** *firm friends* CLOSE, good, intimate, inseparable, dear, special, fast; constant, devoted, loving, faithful, long-standing, steady, steadfast, rock-steady. ANTONYM distant.

**6** *firm plans* DEFINITE, fixed, settled, decided, established, confirmed, agreed; unalterable, unchangeable, irreversible. ANTONYM indefinite.

**firm**[2] noun *an accounting firm* COMPANY, business, concern, enterprise, organization, corporation, conglomerate, office, bureau, agency, consortium; *informal* outfit, setup.

**firmament** noun *literary gazing up to* ***the firmament*** THE SKY, heaven; the heavens, the skies; *literary* the empyrean, the welkin.

**first** adjective **1** *the first chapter* EARLIEST, initial, opening, introductory. ANTONYMS last, closing.

**2** *first principles* FUNDAMENTAL, basic, rudimentary, primary; key, cardinal, central, chief, vital, essential.

**3** *our first priority* FOREMOST, principal, highest, greatest, paramount, top, uppermost, prime, chief, leading, main, major; overriding, predominant, prevailing, central, core, dominant; *informal* number-one. ANTONYM last.

**4** *first prize* TOP, best, prime, premier, winner's, winning.

▸ adverb **1** *the room they had first entered* AT FIRST, to begin with, first of all, at the outset, initially.

**2** *she would eat first* BEFORE ANYTHING ELSE, first and foremost, now.

**3** *she wouldn't go—she'd die first!* IN PREFERENCE, sooner, rather.

▸ noun *it was a first for both of us* NOVELTY, new experience; unknown territory.

**first-hand** adjective *her firsthand experience in grant writing* DIRECT, immediate, personal, hands-on, experiential, empirical, evidence-based, eye-witness. ANTONYMS vicarious, indirect.

**first-rate** adjective *they have done a first-rate job* TOP-QUALITY, high-quality, top-grade, first-class, second to none, fine; superlative, excellent, superb, outstanding, exceptional, exemplary, marvelous, magnificent, splendid; *informal* top-notch, blue-ribbon, blue-chip, ace, A1, super, great, terrific, tremendous, bang-up, skookum, fantastic, killer.

**fiscal** adjective *figures for the past fiscal year show a trend of improvement* budgetary; financial, economic, monetary, money. See note at FINANCIAL.

**fish** noun *we caught enough fish to live on for a week.*

▸ verb **1** *we can fish in Putnam's Pond* GO FISHING, angle, cast, trawl, troll, seine.

**2** *she fished for her purse* SEARCH, delve, look, hunt; grope, fumble, ferret (about/around), root around/about, rummage (around/about).

**3** *I'm not* ***fishing for*** *compliments* TRY TO GET, seek to obtain, solicit, angle for, aim for, hope for, cast around/about for, be after.

PHRASE: **fish out** *I fished my earring out of the cake batter* PULL OUT, haul out, remove, extricate, extract, retrieve; rescue from, save from.

**fisherman** noun *a favorite vacation spot for fishermen* ANGLER, fisher, fisheries worker.

**fishy** adjective **1** *a fishy smell* FISHLIKE, piscine.

**2** *round fishy eyes* EXPRESSIONLESS, inexpressive, vacant, lackluster, glassy.

**3** *informal there was something fishy going on* SUSPICIOUS, questionable, dubious, doubtful, suspect; odd, queer, peculiar, strange; *informal* funny, shady, crooked, sketchy.

**fission** noun *the radioactive materials absorb neutrons and undergo fission* SPLITTING, division, dividing, rupture, breaking, severance. ANTONYM fusion.

**fissure** noun *the flood was blamed on an unreported fissure in the dam* OPENING, crevice, crack, cleft, breach, crevasse, chasm; break, fracture, fault, rift, rupture, split.

**fit**[1] adjective **1** *fit for human habitation* | *he is a fit subject for such a book* SUITABLE, good enough; relevant, pertinent, apt, appropriate, suited, apposite, fitting; *archaic* meet. ANTONYM unsuitable.

**2** *is he fit to look after a child?* COMPETENT, able, capable; ready, prepared, qualified, trained, equipped. ANTONYM incapable.

**3** *informal you look fit to commit murder!* READY, prepared, all set, in a fit state, likely, about; *informal* psyched up.

**4** *he looked tanned and fit* HEALTHY, well, in good health, in (good) shape, in (good) trim, in good condition, fighting fit, as fit as a fiddle; athletic, muscular, well-built, strong, robust, hale and hearty, in the pink. ANTONYM unwell.

▸ verb **1** *have your carpets fitted professionally* LAY, position, place, put in place/position, fix.

**2** *cameras fitted with a backlight button* EQUIP, provide, supply, fit out, furnish.

**3** *concrete slabs were* ***fitted together*** JOIN, connect, put together, piece together, attach, unite, link (together), slot together.

**4** *a sentence that fits her crimes* MATCH, suit, be appropriate to, correspond to, tally with, go with, accord with, correlate to, be congruous with, be congruent with, be consonant with.

**5** *an MA fits you for a professional career* QUALIFY, prepare, make ready, train, groom.

▸ noun *the degree of fit between a school's philosophy and practice* CORRELATION, correspondence, agreement, consistency, equivalence, match, similarity, compatibility, concurrence.

PHRASE: **fit in** *he never fit in with the academic crowd* CONFORM, be in harmony, blend in, be in line, be assimilated into.

**fit**[2] noun **1** *an epileptic fit* CONVULSION, spasm, paroxysm, seizure, attack; *Medicine* ictus.

**2** *a fit of the giggles* OUTBREAK, outburst, attack, bout, spell.

**3** *my mother would have a fit if she knew* TANTRUM, fit of temper, outburst of anger/rage, frenzy; *informal* blowout, hissy fit, conniption (fit). PHRASE: **in/by fits and starts** *she writes in fits and starts yet manages to complete a new book almost every year.* SPASMODICALLY, intermittently, sporadically, erratically, irregularly, fitfully, haphazardly.

**fitful** adjective *a fitful night's sleep* INTERMITTENT, sporadic, spasmodic, broken, disturbed, disrupted, patchy, irregular, uneven, unsettled; *informal* herky-jerky.

**fitness** noun **1** *marathon running requires tremendous fitness* GOOD HEALTH, strength, robustness, vigor, athleticism, toughness, physical fitness, muscularity; good condition, good shape, well-being.

**2** *his fitness for active service* SUITABILITY, capability, competence, ability, aptitude; readiness, preparedness, eligibility.

**fitted** adjective *a fitted sheet* SHAPED, contoured, fitting tightly, fitting well.

**fitting** noun **1** *bathroom fittings* FURNISHINGS, furniture, fixtures, equipment, appointments, appurtenances.

**2** *the fitting of catalytic converters* INSTALLATION, installing, putting in, fixing.

▸ adjective *a fitting conclusion* APT, appropriate, suitable, apposite; fit, proper, right, seemly, correct; *archaic* meet. ANTONYM unsuitable.

**fix** verb **1** *he fixed my washing machine* REPAIR, mend, put right, put to rights, get working, restore (to working order); overhaul, service, renovate, recondition.

**2** *signs were fixed to utility poles* FASTEN, attach, affix, secure; join, connect, couple, link; install, implant, embed; stick, glue, pin, nail, screw, bolt, clamp, clip.

**3** *his words are fixed in my memory* STICK, lodge, embed, burned, branded.

**4** *his eyes were fixed on the ground* FOCUS, direct, level, point, train.

**5** *informal Laura was fixing her hair* ARRANGE, put in order, adjust; style, groom, comb, brush; *informal* do.

**6** *informal Chris will fix supper* PREPARE, cook, make, get; *informal* rustle up, whip up.

**7** *let's fix a date for the meeting* DECIDE ON, select, choose, resolve on; determine, settle, set, arrange, establish, allot; designate, name, appoint, specify.

**8** *chemicals are used to fix the dye* MAKE PERMANENT, make fast, set.

**9** *informal the fight was fixed* RIG, arrange fraudulently; tamper with, influence; *informal* fiddle.

**10** *informal don't tell anybody, or I'll fix you!* GET ONE'S REVENGE ON, avenge oneself on, get even with, get back at, take reprisals against, punish, deal with; sort someone out.

**11** *the cat has been fixed* CASTRATE, neuter, geld, spay, desex, sterilize; *informal* doctor, alter.

▸ noun *informal* **1** *they are in a bit of a fix* PREDICAMENT, plight, difficulty, awkward situation, corner, tight spot; mess, mare's nest, dire straits; *informal* pickle, jam, hole, scrape, bind, sticky situation.

**2** *he needed his fix* DOSE; *informal* hit.

**3** *a quick fix for the coal industry* SOLUTION, answer, resolution, way out, remedy, cure, placebo; *informal* magic bullet, band-aid solution.

**4** *the result was a complete fix* FRAUD, swindle, trick, charade, sham; *informal* setup, fiddle.

PHRASE: **fix up** *informal we need to get Dolly fixed up with a job* PROVIDE, supply, furnish.

**fixation** noun *his sports fixation has gotten intolerable* OBSESSION, preoccupation, mania, addiction, compulsion; *informal* thing, bug, craze, fad.

**fixture** noun **1** *fixtures and fittings* FIXED APPLIANCE, installation, unit.

**2** *she's a fixture at the bar* RESIDENT, lifer, permanent feature; *informal* part of the furniture.

**fizz** verb *the soda really fizzes when you first open the bottle* EFFERVESCE, sparkle, bubble, froth; *literary* spume.

▸ noun **1** *the fizz in champagne* EFFERVESCENCE, sparkle, fizziness, bubbles, bubbliness, gassiness, carbonation, froth.

**2** *informal their set is a little lacking in fizz* EBULLIENCE, exuberance, liveliness, life, vivacity, animation, vigor, energy, verve, dash, spirit, sparkle, zest, fire; *informal* pizzazz, pep, zip, oomph.

**3** *the fizz of the static* CRACKLE, crackling, buzz, buzzing, hiss, hissing, white noise; *literary* susurration.

**fizzle** verb *the loudspeaker fizzled* CRACKLE, buzz, hiss, fizz, crepitate.

▸ noun **1** *electric fizzle.* See FIZZ noun sense 3.

**2** *the whole thing turned out to be a fizzle* FAILURE, fiasco, debacle, disaster; *informal* flop, washout, letdown, dead loss, snafu.

PHRASE: **fizzle out** *the viewers' enthusiasm pretty much fizzled out after the first season* PETER OUT, die off, ease off, cool off, flatline; tail off, wither away, wind down.

**fizzy** adjective *fizzy root beer* EFFERVESCENT, sparkling, carbonated, gassy, bubbly, frothy; spumante, frizzante. ANTONYMS still, flat.

**flabbergast** verb *informal*. See ASTONISH.

**flabby** adjective **1** *his flabby stomach* SOFT, loose, flaccid, slack, untoned, drooping, sagging. ANTONYM firm.

**2** *a flabby child* FAT, fleshy, overweight, plump, chubby, portly, rotund, broad in the beam, of ample proportions, obese, corpulent; *informal* tubby, roly-poly, well-upholstered. ANTONYM thin.

**flaccid** adjective **1** *a flaccid muscle* SOFT, loose, flabby, slack, lax; drooping, sagging. ANTONYM firm.

**2** *his play seemed flaccid* LACKLUSTER, lifeless, listless, uninspiring, unanimated, tame, dull, vapid. ANTONYM spirited.

**flag**[1] noun *he raised the flag* BANNER, standard, ensign, pennant, banderole, streamer, jack, gonfalon; colors; Stars and Stripes, Old Glory, Union Jack; Jolly Roger; *Canadian* Red Ensign, Maple Leaf.

▸ verb *flag the misspelled words* INDICATE, identify, point out, mark, label, tag, highlight.

PHRASE: **flag down** *we had no luck flagging down a cab* HAIL, wave down, signal to stop, stop, halt.

**flag**[2] verb **1** *they were flagging toward the finish* TIRE, grow tired/weary, weaken, grow weak, wilt, droop, fade, run out of steam. ANTONYM revive.

**2** *my energy flags in the afternoon* FADE, decline, wane, ebb, diminish, decrease, lessen, dwindle; wither, melt away, peter out, die away/down. ANTONYM increase.

**flagrant** adjective *it was a flagrant distortion of the facts* BLATANT, glaring, obvious, overt, conspicuous, barefaced, shameless, brazen, undisguised, unconcealed; outrageous, scandalous, shocking, disgraceful, dreadful, terrible, gross.

**flagstone** noun *the landscapers unearthed a beautiful flagstone walkway, perhaps laid a hundred years ago* PAVING SLAB, paving stone, slab, flag.

**flail** verb **1** *he fell headlong, his arms flailing* WAVE, swing, thrash about, flap about.

**2** *I was flailing about in the water* FLOUNDER, struggle, thrash, writhe, splash.

**3** *he flailed their shoulders with his cane* THRASH, beat, strike, flog, whip, lash, scourge, cane; *informal* wallop, whack.

**flair** noun **1** *a flair for publicity* APTITUDE, talent, gift, instinct, (natural) ability, facility, skill, bent, feel, knack.

**2** *she dressed with flair* STYLE, stylishness, panache, dash, élan, poise, elegance; taste, good taste, discernment, discrimination; *informal* class, pizzazz.

**flake**[1] noun **1** *flakes of pastry* SLIVER, wafer, shaving, paring; chip, scale; fragment, scrap, shred; *technical* lamina.

**2** *informal Geoff can be such a flake* DITZ, space cadet, airhead, fool, scatterbrain.

▸ verb *the paint was flaking* PEEL (OFF), chip, blister, come off (in layers).

**flake**[2] PHRASE: **flake out** *informal she flaked out in her chair* FALL ASLEEP, go to sleep, drop off; collapse, faint, pass out, lose consciousness, black out, swoon; *informal* conk out, nod off, sack out.

**flamboyant** adjective **1** *her flamboyant personality* EXUBERANT, confident, lively, animated, vibrant, vivacious. ANTONYMS modest, restrained.

**2** *a flamboyant cravat* COLORFUL, brightly colored, bright, vibrant, vivid; dazzling, eye-catching, bold; showy, ostentatious, gaudy, garish, lurid, loud; *informal* jazzy, flashy. ANTONYMS dull, restrained.

**3** *a flamboyant architectural style* ELABORATE, ornate, fancy; baroque, rococo. ANTONYM simple.

**flame** noun **1** (**flames**) *a sheet of flames* FIRE, blaze, conflagration, inferno.

**2** (**flames**) *the flames of her anger* PASSION, warmth, ardor, fervor, fervency, fire, intensity.

**3** *informal an old flame* SWEETHEART, boyfriend, girlfriend, lover, partner; *informal* beau; *dated* steady.

▸ verb **1** *logs crackled and flamed* BURN, blaze, be ablaze, be alight, be on fire, be in flames, be aflame.

**2** *Erica's cheeks flamed* BECOME RED, go red, blush, flush, redden, grow pink/crimson/scarlet, color, glow.

PHRASE: **in flames** *the cabin was in flames* ON FIRE, burning, alight, flaming, blazing, ignited; *literary* afire.

**flame-proof** adjective *flame-proof gloves* NONFLAMMABLE, noninflammable, flame-resistant, fire-resistant, flame-retardant. ANTONYM flammable.

**flaming** adjective **1** *a flaming bonfire* BLAZING, ablaze, burning, on fire, in flames, aflame; *literary* afire.

**2** *flaming hair* BRIGHT, brilliant, vivid; red, reddish-orange, ginger, titian.

**3** *a flaming altercation* FURIOUS, violent, vehement, frenzied, angry, passionate.

**4** *in a flaming temper* FURIOUS, enraged, fuming, seething, incensed, infuriated, angry, raging, livid; *literary* wrathful.

**flank** noun **1** *the horse's flanks* SIDE, haunch, quarter, thigh.

**2** *the southern flank of the army* SIDE, wing.

▸ verb *the garden is flanked by two rivers* EDGE, bound, line, border, fringe.

**flap** verb **1** *the mallards flapped their wings* BEAT, flutter, agitate, wave, wag, swing.

**2** *the flag flapped in the breeze* FLUTTER, fly, blow, swing, sway, ripple, stir.

▸ noun **1** *pockets with buttoned flaps* FOLD, overlap, covering.

**2** *a few flaps of the wing* FLUTTER, fluttering, beat, beating, waving.

**3** *informal I'm in a desperate flap* PANIC, fluster, state, dither, twitter, stew, tizzy.

**4** *informal she created a flap with her controversial statement* FUSS, commotion, stir, hubbub, storm, uproar; controversy, brouhaha, furor; *informal* to-do, ballyhoo, hoo-ha.

**flare** noun **1** *the flare of the match* BLAZE, flash, dazzle, burst, flicker.

**2** *a flare set off by the crew* DISTRESS SIGNAL, rocket, beacon, light, signal.

**3** *a flare of anger* BURST, rush, eruption, explosion, spasm, access.

▸ verb **1** *the wick flared* BLAZE, flash, flare up, flame, burn; glow, flicker.

**2** *her nostrils flared* SPREAD, broaden, widen; dilate.

PHRASE: **flare up 1** *the wooden houses flared up like matchsticks* BURN, blaze, go up in flames.

**2** *his injury has flared up again* RECUR, reoccur, reappear; break out, start suddenly, erupt.

**3** *I flared up at him* LOSE ONE'S TEMPER, become enraged, fly into a temper, go berserk; *informal* blow one's top, fly off the handle, go mad, go bananas, hit the roof, go off the deep end, flip out, explode, have a fit, go crackers, flip one's wig, blow one's stack, go ballistic, go postal, have a conniption fit.

**flash** verb **1** *a torch flashed* LIGHT UP, shine, flare, blaze, gleam, glint, sparkle, burn; blink, wink, flicker, shimmer, twinkle, glimmer, glisten, scintillate; *literary* glister, coruscate.

**2** *informal he was flashing his money around* SHOW OFF, flaunt, flourish, display, parade.

**3** *informal he flashed at me* EXPOSE ONESELF.

**4** *racing cars flashed past* ZOOM, streak, tear, shoot, dash, dart, fly, whistle, hurtle, careen, rush, bolt, race, speed, career, whiz, whoosh, buzz; *informal* belt, zap, bomb; barrel.

▸ noun **1** *a flash of light* FLARE, blaze, burst; gleam, glint, sparkle, flicker, shimmer, twinkle, glimmer.

**2** *a basic uniform with no flashes* EMBLEM, insignia, badge; stripe, bar, chevron, brevet, wings.

**3** *a sudden flash of inspiration* BURST, outburst, wave, rush, surge, flush.

▸ adjective *informal a flash sports car.* See FLASHY.

PHRASE: **in/like a flash** *the police were there in a flash* INSTANTLY, suddenly, abruptly, immediately, all of a sudden; quickly, rapidly, swiftly, speedily; in an instant/moment, in a (split) second, in a trice, in the blink of an eye; *informal* in a jiff, in a jiffy.

**flashy** adjective *informal a flashy outfit for the dance number* OSTENTATIOUS, flamboyant, showy, conspicuous, extravagant, expensive; vulgar, tasteless, brash, lurid, garish, loud, gaudy; *informal* snazzy, fancy, swanky, flash, jazzy, glitzy. ANTONYM understated.

**flask** noun *a flask of warm brandy* BOTTLE, container; hip flask, vacuum flask; *trademark* Thermos.

**flat** adjective **1** *a flat surface* LEVEL, horizontal; smooth, even, uniform, regular, plane. ANTONYMS vertical, uneven.

**2** *the sea was flat* CALM, still, pacific, tranquil, glassy, undisturbed, without waves, like a millpond. ANTONYM choppy.

**3** *a flat wooden box* SHALLOW, low-sided. ANTONYM deep.

**4** *flat sandals* LOW, low-heeled, without heels.

**5** *the teacher's flat voice* MONOTONOUS, toneless, droning, boring, dull, tedious, uninteresting, unexciting, soporific; bland, dreary, colorless, featureless, emotionless, expressionless, lifeless, spiritless, lackluster, plain-vanilla. ANTONYMS exciting, emotional.

**6** *he felt too flat to get out of bed* DEPRESSED, dejected, dispirited, despondent, downhearted, disheartened, low, low-spirited, down, unhappy, blue; without energy, enervated, sapped, weary, tired out, worn out, exhausted, drained; *informal* down in the dumps. ANTONYMS cheerful, energized.

**7** *the market was flat* SLOW, inactive, sluggish, slack, quiet, depressed. ANTONYM busy.

**8** *a flat tire* DEFLATED, punctured, burst. ANTONYM inflated.

**9** *a flat fee* FIXED, set, regular, unchanging, unvarying, invariable.

**10** *a flat denial* OUTRIGHT, direct, absolute, definite, positive, straight, plain, explicit; firm, resolute, adamant, assertive, emphatic, categorical, unconditional, unqualified, unequivocal.

▸ adverb **1** *she lay down flat on the floor* STRETCHED OUT, outstretched, spread-eagle, sprawling, prone, supine, prostrate, recumbent.

**2** *informal she turned me down flat* OUTRIGHT, absolutely, firmly, resolutely, adamantly, emphatically, insistently, categorically, unconditionally, unequivocally.

▸ noun **(flats)** *they race their bikes across the flats* TIDAL FLATS, mud flats, tideland, intertidal area.

PHRASE: **flat out** *I'd been working flat out* HARD, as hard as possible, for all one's worth, to the limit, all out; at full speed, as fast as possible, at full tilt, full bore, full throttle, in high gear; *informal* like crazy, like mad, like the wind, firing on all cylinders, like a bat out of hell.

**flatten** verb **1** *Flynn flattened the crumpled paper* MAKE FLAT, make even, smooth (out/off), level (out/off).

**2** *the cows flattened the grass* COMPRESS, press down, crush, squash, compact, trample.

**3** *tornadoes can flatten buildings in seconds* DEMOLISH, raze (to the ground), tear down, knock down, destroy, wreck, devastate, obliterate; *informal* total.

**4** *informal Griff flattened him with a single punch* KNOCK DOWN/OVER, knock to the ground, fell, prostrate; *informal* floor, deck.

**flatter** verb **1** *it amused him to flatter her* COMPLIMENT, praise, express admiration for, say nice things about, fawn over; cajole, humor, flannel, blarney; *informal* sweet-talk, soft-soap, brown-nose, butter up, play up to, slobber over; *formal* laud. ANTONYM insult.

**2** *I was flattered to be asked* HONOR, gratify, please, delight; *informal* tickle pink. ANTONYM offend.

**3** *a hairstyle that flattered her* SUIT, become, look good on, go well with; *informal* do something for. ANTONYM clash with.

**flattering** adjective **1** *flattering remarks* COMPLIMENTARY, praising, favorable, commending, admiring, applauding, appreciative, good; fulsome, honeyed, sugary, cajoling, silver-tongued, honey-tongued; fawning, oily, obsequious, ingratiating, servile, sycophantic; *informal* sweet-talking, soft-soaping, crawling, bootlicking; *formal* encomiastic.

**2** *it was very flattering to be nominated* PLEASING, gratifying, honoring, gladdening.

**3** *her most flattering dress* BECOMING, enhancing.

**flattery** noun *she's simply not vain enough to fall for your flattery* PRAISE, adulation, compliments, blandishments, honeyed words; fawning, blarney, cajolery; *formal* encomium; *informal* sweet talk, soft soap, snow job, buttering up, toadying.

**flatulence** noun **1** *medications that help with flatulence* (INTESTINAL) GAS, wind; *informal* farting, tooting; *formal* flatus.

**2** *the flatulence of his latest recordings* POMPOSITY, pompousness, pretension, pretentiousness, grandiloquence, bombast, turgidity.

**flaunt** verb *he flaunts his young wife as if she were the prize heifer at the county fair* SHOW OFF, display ostentatiously, make a (great) show of, put on show/display, parade; brag about, crow about, vaunt; *informal* flash.

**USAGE NOTE flaunt, flout**

Confusion about these terms is so distressingly common that some dictionaries have thrown in the towel and now treat *flaunt* as a synonym of *flout*. *Flout* means "contravene or disregard; treat with contempt." *Flaunt* means "show off or parade something in an ostentatious manner," but is often incorrectly used for *flout*, perhaps because it is misunderstood as a telescoped version of *flout* and *taunt*—e.g.: "In Washington, the White House issued a statement that deplored the Nigerian Government's 'flaunting [read *flouting*] of even the most basic international norms and universal standards of human rights.' " (*New York Times*; Nov. 11, 1995.)

Of course, *flaunt* is more often used correctly—e.g.: "He donates millions to religious and charitable groups, yet flaunts his own wealth." (*Fortune*; Aug. 18, 1997.) *Flout*, meanwhile, almost never causes a problem. Here it's correctly used: "A record rider turnout, fueled by the mayor's earlier pledge to end the escort and crack down on cyclists flouting traffic laws, poured into the streets on an improvised route." (*San Francisco Examiner*; Aug. 3, 1997.) But the rare mistake of misusing *flout* for *flaunt* does sometimes occur—e.g.: "Mr. Talton was soon joined by almost two dozen other conservative Republicans who filed en masse into the clerk's office to flout [read *flaunt*] their disapproval for their colleague and fellow party member." (*Dallas Morning News*; May 25, 2000.)

One federal appellate judge who misused *flaunt* for *flout* in a published opinion—only to be corrected by judges who later quoted him—appealed to *Webster's Third New International Dictionary of the English Language*, which accepts as standard any usage that can be documented with any frequency. The judge then attempted to justify his error and pledged to persist in it. Seeking refuge in a nonprescriptive dictionary, however, merely ignores the all-important distinction between formal contexts, in which strict standards of usage must apply, and informal contexts, in which venial faults of grammar or usage may, if we are lucky, go unnoticed (or unmentioned). —*BG*

**flavor** noun **1** *the flavor of prosciutto* TASTE, savor, tang.

**2** *cilantro gives a distinctive flavor to the sauce* FLAVORING, seasoning, tastiness, tang, relish, bite, piquancy, pungency, spice, spiciness, zest; *informal* zing, zip.

**3** *a strong international flavor* CHARACTER, quality, feel, feeling, ambience, atmosphere, aura, air, mood, tone; spirit, essence, nature.

**4** *this excerpt will give a flavor of the report* IMPRESSION, suggestion, hint, taste.

▸ verb *spices for flavoring food* ADD FLAVOR TO, add flavoring to, season, spice (up), add piquancy to, ginger up, enrich; *informal* pep up.

PHRASE: **flavor of the month** *informal sure, it's great to be flavor of the month, but where will you be a year from now?* ALL THE RAGE, the latest thing, the fashion, in vogue; a one-hit wonder; *informal* hot, in.

**flavoring** noun **1** *this cheese is often combined with other flavorings* SEASONING, spice, herb, additive; condiment, dressing.

**2** *vanilla flavoring* EXTRACT, flavor, essence, concentrate, distillate.

**flaw** noun *the reactor's design flaw | a flaw in his character* DEFECT, blemish, fault, imperfection, deficiency, weakness, weak spot/point/link, inadequacy, shortcoming, limitation, failing, foible; *literary* hamartia; *Computing* bug; *informal* glitch. See note at FAULT. ANTONYM strength.

**flawless** adjective *a flawless performance* PERFECT, unblemished, unmarked, unimpaired; whole, intact, sound, unbroken, undamaged, mint, pristine; impeccable, immaculate, consummate, accurate, correct, faultless, error-free, unerring; exemplary, model, ideal, copybook; *Theology* inerrant. ANTONYM flawed.

**fleck** noun *flecks of pale blue* SPOT, mark, dot, speck, speckle, freckle, patch, smudge, streak, blotch, dab; *informal* splotch; *rare* macula.

▸ verb *the deer's flanks were flecked with white* SPOT, mark, dot, speckle, bespeckle, freckle, stipple, stud, bestud, blotch, mottle, streak, splash, spatter, bespatter, scatter, sprinkle; *informal* splotch.

**flee** verb **1** *she fled to her room* RUN (AWAY/OFF), run for it, make a run for it, dash, take flight, be gone, make off, take off, take to one's heels, make a break for it, bolt, beat a (hasty) retreat, make a quick exit, make one's getaway, escape; *informal* beat it, clear off/out, vamoose, skedaddle, split, leg it, turn tail, scram, light out, cut out, peel out; *archaic* fly.

**2** *they fled the country* RUN AWAY FROM, leave hastily, escape from; *informal* skip; *archaic* fly.

**fleece** noun *a sheep's fleece* WOOL, coat.

▸ verb *informal we were fleeced by a scalper.* See SWINDLE verb.

**fleecy** adjective *a fleecy robe* FLUFFY, woolly, downy, soft, fuzzy, furry, velvety, shaggy; *technical* floccose, pilose. ANTONYM coarse.

**fleet**[1] noun *the fleet set sail* NAVY, naval force, (naval) task force, armada, flotilla, squadron, convoy.

**fleet**[2] adjective *literary as fleet as a greyhound* NIMBLE, agile, lithe, lissome, acrobatic, supple, light-footed, light on one's feet, spry, sprightly; quick, fast, swift, rapid, speedy, brisk, smart; *informal* zippy, twinkle-toed.

**fleeting** adjective *ours was a fleeting romance* BRIEF, short,

short-lived, quick, momentary, cursory, transient, ephemeral, fugitive, passing, transitory; *literary* evanescent. See note at TEMPORARY. ANTONYM lasting.

**flesh** noun **1** *you need more flesh on your bones* MUSCLE, meat, tissue, brawn; *informal* beef.

**2** *she carries too much flesh* FAT, weight; *Anatomy* adipose tissue; *informal* blubber, flab.

**3** *a fruit with juicy flesh* PULP, soft part, marrow, meat.

**4** *the pleasures of the flesh* THE BODY, human nature, physicality, carnality, animality; sensuality, sexuality. PHRASES: **one's (own) flesh and blood** *how can you deny your own flesh and blood?* FAMILY, relative(s), relation(s), blood relation(s), kin, kinsfolk, kinsman, kinsmen, kinswoman, kinswomen, kindred, nearest and dearest, people; *informal* folks.

**flesh out 1** *he really fleshed out for his latest movie role* PUT ON WEIGHT, gain weight, get heavier, grow fat/fatter, fatten up, get fat, fill out.

**2** *the story line should be fleshed out a bit* EXPAND (ON), elaborate on, add to, build on, add flesh to, put flesh on (the bones of), add detail to, expatiate on, supplement, reinforce, augment, fill out, enlarge on.

**in the flesh** *look, it's Sean Penn, in the flesh* IN PERSON, before one's (very) eyes, in front of one; in real life, live; physically, bodily, in bodily/human form, incarnate.

**flex** verb **1** *you must flex your elbow* BEND, crook, hook, cock, angle, double up. ANTONYM straighten.

**2** *Rachel flexed her cramped muscles* TIGHTEN, tauten, tense (up), tension, contract. ANTONYM relax.

**flexible** adjective **1** *flexible tubing* PLIABLE, supple, bendable, pliant, plastic; elastic, stretchy, whippy, springy, resilient, bouncy; *informal* bendy. ANTONYM rigid.

**2** *a flexible arrangement* ADAPTABLE, adjustable, variable, versatile, open-ended, open, free. ANTONYM inflexible.

**3** *the need to be flexible toward tenants* ACCOMMODATING, amenable, willing to compromise, cooperative, tolerant, easygoing. ANTONYM intransigent.

THE RIGHT WORD **flexible, elastic, limber, pliable, pliant, resilient, supple**

If you can bend over and touch your toes, you are **flexible**. But a dancer or gymnast is **limber**, an adjective that specifically applies to a body that has been brought into condition through training (*to stay limber, she did yoga every day*). *Flexible* applies to whatever can be bent without breaking, whether or not it returns to its original shape (*a flexible plastic hose; a flexible electrical conduit*); it does not necessarily refer, as *limber* does, to the human body. Unlike *flexible*, **resilient** implies the ability to spring back into shape after being bent or compressed, or to recover one's health or spirits quickly (*so young and resilient that she was back at work in a week*). **Elastic** is usually applied to substances or materials that are easy to stretch or expand and that quickly recover their shape or size (*pants with an elastic waist*), while **supple** is applied to whatever is easily bent, twisted, or folded without breaking or cracking (*a soft, supple leather*). When applied to the human body, *supple* suggests the ability to move effortlessly. **Pliant** and **pliable** may used to describe either people or things that are easily bent or manipulated. *Pliant* suggests a tendency to bend without force or pressure from the outside, while *pliable* suggests the use of force or submission to another's will. A *pliant* person is merely adaptable, but a *pliable* person is easy to influence and eager to please.

**flick** noun *a flick of the wrist* JERK, snap, flip, whisk.

▸ verb **1** *he flicked the switch* CLICK, snap, flip, jerk.

**2** *the horse flicked its tail* SWISH, twitch, wave, wag, waggle, shake.

PHRASE: **flick through** *flick through the pages and try to find a hairstyle you like* THUMB (THROUGH), leaf through, flip through, skim through, scan, look through, browse through, dip into, glance at/through, peruse, run one's eye over.

**flicker** verb **1** *the lights flickered* GLIMMER, glint, flare, dance, gutter; twinkle, sparkle, blink, wink, flash, scintillate; *literary* glister, coruscate.

**2** *his eyelids flickered* FLUTTER, quiver, tremble, shiver, shudder, spasm, jerk, twitch.

**flight** noun **1** *the history of flight* AVIATION, flying, air transport, aerial navigation, aeronautics.

**2** *a flight to Rome* AIRPLANE/PLANE TRIP, air trip, trip/journey by air.

**3** *the flight of a baseball* TRAJECTORY, path through the air, track, orbit.

**4** *a flight of birds* FLOCK, skein, covey, swarm, cloud.

**5** *his headlong flight from home* ESCAPE, getaway, hasty departure, exit, exodus, decamping, breakout, bolt, disappearance.

**6** *a flight of stairs* STAIRCASE, set of steps, set of stairs. PHRASES: **put someone to flight** *the king's infantry put our demoralized militia to flight* CHASE AWAY/OFF, drive back/away/off/out, scatter (to the four winds), disperse, repel, repulse, rout, stampede, scare off; *informal* send packing.

**take flight** *the cowards took flight as the enemy approached* FLEE, run (away/off), run for it, make a run for it, be gone, make off, take off, take to one's heels, make a break for it, bolt, beat a (hasty) retreat, make a quick exit, make one's getaway, escape; *informal* beat it, clear off/out, vamoose, skedaddle, split, leg it, turn tail, scram, light out, bug out, cut out, peel out; *archaic* fly.

**flighty** adjective *his flighty sister has changed her college major four times* FICKLE, inconstant, mercurial, whimsical, capricious, skittish, volatile, impulsive; irresponsible, giddy, reckless, wild, careless, thoughtless. ANTONYMS steady, responsible.

**flimsy** adjective **1** *a flimsy building* INSUBSTANTIAL, fragile, breakable, frail, shaky, unstable, wobbly, tottery, rickety, ramshackle, makeshift; jerry-built, badly built, shoddy, chintzy, gimcrack. ANTONYM sturdy.

**2** *a flimsy garment* THIN, light, fine, filmy, floaty, diaphanous, sheer, delicate, insubstantial, wispy, gossamer, gauzy. ANTONYM thick.

**3** *flimsy evidence* WEAK, feeble, poor, inadequate, insufficient, thin, unsubstantial, unconvincing, implausible, unsatisfactory. ANTONYM sound.

**flinch** verb **1** *he flinched at the noise* WINCE, start, shudder, quiver, jerk, shy. See note at WINCE.

**2** *she never **flinched from** her duty* SHRINK FROM, recoil from, shy away from, swerve from, demur from; dodge, evade, avoid, duck, balk at, jib at, quail at, fight shy of.

**fling** verb *he flung the ax into the river* THROW, toss, sling, hurl, cast, pitch, lob; *informal* chuck, heave.

▸ noun **1** *a birthday fling* GOOD TIME, spree, bit of fun, night on the town; fun and games, revels, larks; *informal* binge.

**2** *she had a brief fling with him* AFFAIR, love affair, relationship, romance, affaire (de cœur), amour, flirtation, dalliance, liaison, entanglement, involvement, attachment.

**flip** verb **1** *the wave **flipped** the dinghy **over** | the plane flipped on to its back* OVERTURN, turn over, tip over, roll (over), upturn, capsize; upend, invert, knock over; keel over, topple over, turn turtle; *archaic* overset.

**2** *he flipped the key through the air* THROW, flick, toss, fling, sling, pitch, cast, spin, lob; *informal* chuck; *dated* shy.

**3** *I flipped the transmitter switch* FLICK, click, snap. PHRASE: **flip through** *mindlessly flipping through the magazine* THUMB (THROUGH), leaf through, flick through, skim through, scan, look through, browse through, glance at/through, peruse, run one's eye over.

**flippant** adjective *a flippant remark* FRIVOLOUS, facetious, tongue-in-cheek; disrespectful, irreverent, cheeky, impudent, impertinent; *informal* flip, waggish. ANTONYMS serious, respectful.

**flirt** verb **1** *it amused him to **flirt with** her* TRIFLE WITH, toy with, tease, lead on.

**2** *those conservatives who **flirted with** fascism* DABBLE IN, toy with, trifle with, amuse oneself with, play with, tinker with, dip into, scratch the surface of.

**3** *he is **flirting with** danger* COURT, risk, not fear, invite.

▸ noun *Anna was quite a flirt* TEASE, trifler, philanderer, coquette, heartbreaker.

**flirtatious** adjective *her blatantly flirtatious manner* COQUETTISH, flirty, kittenish, teasing.

**float** verb **1** *oil floats on water* STAY AFLOAT, stay on the surface, be buoyant, be buoyed up. ANTONYM sink.

**2** *the balloon floated in the air* HOVER, levitate, be suspended, hang, defy gravity.

**3** *a cloud floated across the moon* DRIFT, glide, sail, slip, slide, waft. ANTONYM rush.

**4** *they have just floated that idea* SUGGEST, put forward, come up with, submit, moot, propose, advance, test the popularity of; *informal* run something up the flagpole (to see who salutes). ANTONYM withdraw.

**floating** adjective **1** *floating seaweed* BUOYANT, on the surface, afloat, drifting. ANTONYM sunken.

**2** *floating helium balloons* HOVERING, levitating, suspended, hanging, defying gravity. ANTONYM grounded.

**3** *floating voters* UNCOMMITTED, undecided, of two minds, torn, split, uncertain, unsure, wavering, vacillating, indecisive, blowing hot and cold, undeclared; *informal* sitting on the fence. ANTONYM committed.

**4** *a floating population* UNSETTLED, transient, temporary, variable, fluctuating; migrant, wandering, nomadic, on the move, migratory, traveling, drifting, roving, roaming, itinerant, vagabond. ANTONYM settled.

**5** *a floating exchange rate* VARIABLE, changeable, changing, fluid, fluctuating. ANTONYM fixed.

**flock** noun **1** *a flock of sheep* HERD, drove.

**2** *a flock of birds* FLIGHT, congregation, covey, clutch.

**3** *flocks of people* CROWD, throng, horde, mob, rabble, mass, multitude, host, army, pack, swarm, sea; *informal* gaggle.

▸ verb **1** *people flocked around McCartney* GATHER, collect, congregate, assemble, converge, mass, crowd, throng, cluster, swarm.

**2** *tourists flock to the place* STREAM, go in large numbers, swarm, crowd, troop.

**flog** verb *the thief was flogged* WHIP, scourge, flagellate, lash, birch, switch, cane, thrash, beat; tan someone's hide.

**flood** noun **1** *a flood warning* INUNDATION, swamping, deluge, high water; torrent, overflow, flash flood, freshet, spate.

**2** *a flood of tears* OUTPOURING, torrent, rush, stream, gush, surge, cascade.

**3** *a flood of complaints* SUCCESSION, series, string, chain; barrage, volley, battery; avalanche, torrent, stream, tide, spate, storm, shower, cascade. ANTONYM trickle.

▸ verb **1** *the whole town was flooded* INUNDATE, swamp, deluge, immerse, submerge, drown, engulf.

**2** *the river could flood* OVERFLOW, burst its banks, brim over, run over.

**3** *imports are flooding the domestic market* GLUT, swamp, saturate, oversupply.

**4** *refugees flooded in* POUR, stream, flow, surge, swarm, pile, crowd. ANTONYM trickle.

**floor** noun **1** *he sat on the floor* GROUND, flooring.

**2** *the second floor* STORY, level, deck, tier.

▸ verb **1** *he floored his attacker* KNOCK DOWN, knock over, bring down, fell, prostrate; *informal* lay out.

**2** *informal the question floored him* BAFFLE, defeat, confound, perplex, puzzle, mystify; *informal* beat, flummox, stump, fox.

**flop** verb **1** *he flopped into a chair* COLLAPSE, slump, crumple, subside, sink, drop.

**2** *his hair flopped over his eyes* HANG (DOWN), dangle, droop, sag, loll.

**3** *informal the play flopped* BE UNSUCCESSFUL, fail, not work, fall flat, founder, misfire, backfire, be a disappointment, do badly, lose money, be a disaster; *informal* bomb, tank, flame out, come a cropper, bite the dust, blow up in someone's face. ANTONYM succeed.

▸ noun *informal the play was a flop* FAILURE, disaster, debacle, catastrophe, loser; *informal* washout, also-ran, dog, lemon, nonstarter, clinker, turkey. ANTONYM success.

**florid** adjective **1** *a florid complexion* RUDDY, red, red-faced, rosy, rosy-cheeked, pink; flushed, blushing, high-colored; *archaic* sanguine. ANTONYM pale.

**2** *florid plasterwork* ORNATE, fancy, elaborate, embellished, curlicued, extravagant, flamboyant, baroque, rococo, fussy, busy. ANTONYM plain.

**3** *florid prose* FLOWERY, flamboyant, high-flown, high-sounding, grandiloquent, ornate, fancy, bombastic, elaborate, turgid, pleonastic; *informal* highfalutin; *rare* fustian. ANTONYM plain.

**flotsam** noun *search and salvage crews are gathering flotsam by the boatfuls* WRECKAGE, cargo, remains; debris, detritus, waste, dross, refuse, scrap, trash, garbage, rubbish; *informal* dreck, junk.

**flounder** verb **1** *people were floundering in the water* STRUGGLE, thrash, flail, twist and turn, splash, stagger, stumble, reel, lurch, blunder, squirm, writhe.

**2** *she floundered, not knowing quite what to say* STRUGGLE, be out of one's depth, have difficulty, be confounded, be confused; *informal* scratch one's head, be flummoxed, be clueless, be foxed, be fazed, be floored, be beaten.

**3** *more firms are floundering* STRUGGLE FINANCIALLY, be in dire straits, face financial ruin, be in difficulties, face bankruptcy/insolvency, founder. ANTONYM prosper.

**flourish** verb **1** *ferns flourish in the shade* GROW, thrive, prosper, do well, burgeon, increase, multiply, proliferate; spring up, shoot up, bloom, blossom, bear fruit, burst forth, run riot. ANTONYMS die, wither.

**2** *the arts flourished* THRIVE, prosper, bloom, be in good health, be vigorous, be in its heyday; progress, make progress, advance, make headway, develop, improve; evolve, make strides, move forward (in leaps and bounds), expand; *informal* be in the pink, go places, go great guns, get somewhere. ANTONYM decline.

**3** *he flourished the sword at them* BRANDISH, wave, shake, wield; swing, twirl, swish; display, exhibit, flaunt, show off.

**flout** verb *countless retailers flout the law by selling cigarettes to children* DEFY, refuse to obey, disobey, break, violate, fail to comply with, fail to observe, contravene, infringe, breach, commit a breach of, transgress against; ignore, disregard. See note at FLAUNT. ANTONYM observe.

**flow** verb **1** *the water flowed down the channel* RUN, course, glide, drift, circulate; trickle, seep, ooze, dribble, drip, drizzle, spill; stream, swirl, surge, sweep, gush, cascade, pour, roll, rush.

**2** *many questions flow from today's announcement* RESULT, proceed, arise, follow, ensue, derive, stem, accrue; originate, emanate, spring, emerge; be caused by, be brought about by, be produced by, be consequent on.

▸ noun *a good flow of water* MOVEMENT, motion, current, flux, circulation; trickle, ooze, percolation, drip; stream, swirl, surge, gush, rush, spate, tide.

**flower** noun **1** *blue flowers* BLOOM, blossom, floweret, floret.

**2** *the flower of the nation's youth* BEST, finest, pick, choice, cream, crème de la crème, elite. ANTONYM dregs.

**flowery** adjective **1** *flowery fabrics* FLORAL, flower-patterned.

**2** *flowery language* FLORID, flamboyant, ornate, fancy, convoluted; high-flown, high-sounding, magniloquent, grandiloquent, baroque, orotund, overblown, pleonastic; *informal* highfalutin, purple, fancy-dancy, fancy-schmancy; *rare* fustian. ANTONYM plain.

**flowing** adjective **1** *long flowing hair* LOOSE, free, unconfined, draping. ANTONYMS stiff, curly.

**2** *the new model will have soft, flowing lines* SLEEK, streamlined, aerodynamic, smooth, clean; elegant, graceful; *technical* faired. ANTONYM jagged.

**3** *he writes in an easy, flowing style* FLUENT, fluid, free-flowing, effortless, easy, natural, smooth. ANTONYMS stilted, halting.

**fluctuate** verb *profits fluctuate from month to month* VARY, change, differ, shift, alter, waver, swing, oscillate, alternate, rise and fall, go up and down, seesaw, yo-yo, be unstable.

**fluctuation** noun *a natural fluctuation in temperature* VARIATION, change, shift, alteration, swing, movement, oscillation, alternation, rise and fall, seesawing, yo-yoing, instability, unsteadiness. ANTONYM stability.

**flue** noun *periodically check the flue for obstructions* DUCT, tube, shaft, vent, pipe, passage, channel, conduit; funnel, chimney, smokestack.

**fluent** adjective **1** *a fluent campaign speech* ARTICULATE, eloquent, expressive, communicative, coherent, cogent, illuminating, vivid, well-written/spoken. ANTONYM inarticulate.

**2** *fluent in French* ARTICULATE; **(be fluent in)** have a (good) command of.

**3** *a very fluent running style* FREE-FLOWING, smooth, effortless, easy, natural, fluid; graceful, elegant; regular, rhythmic. ANTONYM jerky.

**fluff** noun **1** *fluff on her sleeve* FUZZ, lint, dust, dustballs, dust bunnies.

**2** *informal he only made a few fluffs* MISTAKE, error, slip, misstep, flub, slip of the tongue; wrong note, slip-up; *formal* lapsus linguae.

▸ verb *informal Penney fluffed the shot* | *he fluffed his only line* FUMBLE, make a mess of, bungle, miss, deliver badly, muddle up, forget; *informal* mess up, make a hash of, botch, foul up, screw up, flub, goof up. ANTONYM succeed in.

**fluffy** adjective *the gloves have a fluffy lining* FLEECY, woolly, fuzzy, hairy, feathery, downy, furry; soft. ANTONYM rough.

**fluid** noun *the fluid seeps up the tube* LIQUID, watery substance, solution. ANTONYM solid.

▸ adjective **1** *a fluid substance* FREE-FLOWING; liquid, liquefied, melted, molten, runny, running. ANTONYM solid.

**2** *his plans were still fluid* ADAPTABLE, flexible, adjustable, open-ended, open, open to change, changeable, variable. ANTONYM firm.

**3** *the fluid state of affairs* FLUCTUATING, changeable, subject/likely to change, shifting, ever-shifting, inconstant; unstable, unsettled, turbulent, volatile, mercurial, protean. ANTONYM static.

**4** *he stood up in one fluid movement* SMOOTH, fluent, flowing, effortless, easy, continuous, seamless; graceful, elegant. ANTONYM jerky.

**fluke** noun *what a nice fluke, finding you here* CHANCE, coincidence, accident, twist of fate; piece of luck, stroke of good luck/fortune, serendipity.

**flunky** noun **1** *a flunky brought us drinks* SERVANT, lackey, steward, butler, footman, valet, attendant, page.

**2** *government flunkies searched his offices* MINION, lackey, hireling, subordinate, underling, servant; creature, instrument, cat's paw; *informal* stooge, gofer.

**flurry** noun **1** *snow flurries* SWIRL, whirl, eddy, billow, shower, gust.

**2** *a flurry of activity* BURST, outbreak, spurt, fit, spell, bout, rash, eruption; fuss, stir, bustle, hubbub, commotion, disturbance, furor; *informal* to-do, flap.

**3** *a flurry of imports* SPATE, wave, flood, deluge, torrent, stream, tide, avalanche; series, succession, string, outbreak, rash, explosion, run, rush. ANTONYMS dearth, trickle.

**flush**[1] verb **1** *Shane flushed in embarrassment* BLUSH, redden, go pink, go red, go crimson, go scarlet, color (up). ANTONYM pale.

**2** *fruit helps to flush toxins from the body* RINSE, wash, sluice, swill, cleanse, clean.

**3** *they flushed out the snipers* DRIVE, chase, force, dislodge, expel, frighten, scare.

▸ noun **1** *a flush crept over her face* BLUSH, reddening, high color, color, rosiness, pinkness, ruddiness, bloom. ANTONYM paleness.

**2** *the flush of youth* BLOOM, glow, freshness, radiance, vigor, rush.

**flush**[2] adjective *informal* **1** *the company was* ***flush with*** *cash* WELL SUPPLIED WITH, well provided with, well stocked with, replete with, overflowing with, bursting with, brimming with, loaded with, overloaded with, teeming with, stuffed with, swarming with, thick with, solid with; full of, abounding in, rich in, abundant in; *informal* awash with, jam-packed with, chock-full of. ANTONYM bereft.

**2** *the years when cash was flush* PLENTIFUL, abundant, in abundance, copious, ample, profuse, superabundant; *informal* galore; *literary* plenteous, bounteous. See note at WEALTHY. ANTONYMS lacking, low.

**flushed** adjective **1** *flushed faces* RED, pink, ruddy, glowing, reddish, pinkish, rosy, florid, high-colored, healthy-looking, aglow, burning, feverish; blushing, red-faced, embarrassed, shamefaced. ANTONYM pale.

**2** *flushed with success* ELATED, excited, thrilled, exhilarated, happy, delighted, overjoyed, joyous, gleeful, jubilant, exultant, ecstatic, euphoric, rapturous; *informal* blissed out, over the moon, high, on a high. ANTONYM dismayed.

**fluster** verb *she was flustered by his presence* UNSETTLE, make nervous, unnerve, agitate, ruffle, upset, bother, put on edge, disquiet, disturb, worry, perturb, disconcert, confuse, throw off balance, confound; *informal* rattle, faze, put into a flap, throw into a tizzy, discombobulate. ANTONYM calm.

▸ noun *I was in a terrible fluster* STATE OF AGITATION, state of anxiety, nervous state, panic, frenzy, fret; *informal* dither, flap, tizz, tizzy, twitter, state, sweat. ANTONYM state of calm.

**flutter** verb **1** *butterflies fluttered around* FLIT, hover, flitter, dance.

**2** *a tern was fluttering its wings* FLAP, move up and down, beat, quiver, agitate, vibrate, whiffle.

**3** *she fluttered her eyelashes* FLICKER, bat.

**4** *flags fluttered* FLAP, wave, ripple, undulate, quiver; fly.

**5** *her heart fluttered* BEAT WEAKLY, beat irregularly, palpitate, miss/skip a beat, quiver, go pit-a-pat; *Medicine* exhibit arrhythmia.

▸ noun **1** *the flutter of wings* BEATING, flapping, quivering, agitation, vibrating.

**2** *a flutter of dark eyelashes* FLICKER, bat.

**3** *the flutter of the flags* FLAPPING, waving, rippling.

**4** *a flutter of nervousness* TREMOR, wave, rush, surge, flash, stab, flush, tremble, quiver, shiver, frisson, chill, thrill, tingle, shudder, ripple, flicker.

**fly** verb **1** *a bird flew overhead* TRAVEL THROUGH THE AIR, wing its way, wing, glide, soar, wheel; hover, hang; take wing, take to the air, mount.

**2** *they flew to Paris* TRAVEL BY AIRPLANE/PLANE, travel by air, jet.

**3** *military planes flew in food supplies* TRANSPORT BY AIRPLANE/PLANE, transport by air, airlift, lift, jet.

**4** *he could fly a plane* PILOT, operate, control, maneuver, steer.

**5** *the ship was flying a red flag* DISPLAY, show, exhibit, bear; have hoisted, have run up.

**6** *flags flew in the town* FLUTTER, flap, wave.

**7** *doesn't time fly?* GO QUICKLY, fly by/past, pass swiftly, slip past, rush past.

**8** *the runners flew by.* See SPEED verb sense 1.

**9** *archaic the beaten army had to fly.* See FLEE sense 1.

PHRASES: **fly at** *he flew at Rodriguez with fire in his eyes* ATTACK, assault, pounce on, set upon, set about, let fly at, turn

on, round on, lash out at, hit out at, fall on; *informal* lay into, tear into, lace into, sail into, pitch into, let someone have it, jump, have a go at, light into.
**let fly.** See LET.

**flying** adjective **1** *a flying beetle* WINGED; AIRBORNE, in the air, in flight.

**2** *a flying visit* BRIEF, short, lightning, fleeting, hasty, rushed, hurried, quick, whistle-stop, cursory, perfunctory; *informal* quickie. ANTONYM long.

**foam** noun *the foam on the waves* FROTH, spume, surf; fizz, effervescence, bubbles, head; lather, suds.

▸ verb *the water foamed* FROTH, spume; fizz, effervesce, bubble; lather; ferment, rise; boil, seethe, simmer.

**focus** noun **1** *schools are a focus of community life* CENTER, focal point, central point, center of attention, hub, pivot, nucleus, heart, cornerstone, linchpin, cynosure.

**2** *the focus is on helping people* EMPHASIS, accent, priority, attention, concentration.

**3** *the main focus of this chapter* SUBJECT, theme, concern, subject matter, topic, issue, thesis, point, thread; substance, essence, gist, matter.

**4** *the resulting light beams are brought to a focus at the eyepiece* FOCAL POINT, point of convergence.

▸ verb **1** *she focused her binoculars on the tower* BRING INTO FOCUS; aim, point, turn.

**2** *the investigation will* ***focus on*** *areas of social need* CONCENTRATE ON, center on, zero in on, zoom in on; address itself to, pay attention to, pinpoint, revolve around, have as its starting point.

PHRASES: **in focus** *submit only those snapshots that are in focus* SHARP, crisp, distinct, clear, well-defined, well focused.
**out of focus** *the shots are slightly out of focus, which gives them an eerie quality* BLURRED, unfocused, indistinct, blurry, fuzzy, hazy, misty, cloudy, lacking definition, nebulous.

**foe** noun *a well-armed foe* ENEMY, adversary, opponent, rival, antagonist, combatant, challenger, competitor, opposer, opposition, competition, other side. ANTONYM friend.

**fog** noun *we can't set sail in this fog* MIST, smog, murk, haze, ice fog; *archaic* sea smoke; *literary* brume, fume.

▸ verb **1** *the windshield* ***fogged up*** | *his breath fogged the glass* STEAM UP, mist over, cloud over, film over, make/become misty. ANTONYM clear.

**2** *his brain was fogged with sleep* MUDDLE, daze, stupefy, fuddle, befuddle, bewilder, confuse, befog; *literary* bedim, becloud.

**foggy** adjective **1** *the weather was foggy* MISTY, smoggy, hazy, murky. ANTONYM clear.

**2** *she was foggy with sleep* | *a foggy memory* MUDDLED, fuddled, befuddled, confused, at sea, bewildered, dazed, stupefied, numb, groggy, fuzzy, bleary; dark, dim, hazy, shadowy, cloudy, blurred, obscure, vague, indistinct, unclear; *informal* dopey, woolly, woozy, out of it. ANTONYM lucid.

**foible** noun *tolerating each other's foibles* WEAKNESS, failing, shortcoming, flaw, imperfection, blemish, fault, defect, limitation; quirk, kink, idiosyncrasy, eccentricity, peculiarity. See note at FAULT. ANTONYM strength.

**foil**[1] verb *their escape attempt was foiled* THWART, frustrate, counter, balk, impede, obstruct, hamper, euchre, hinder, snooker, cripple, scotch, derail, scupper, scuttle, smash; stop, block, prevent, defeat; *informal* do for, put paid to, stymie, cook someone's goose. See note at THWART. ANTONYM assist.

**foil**[2] noun *Abbott was the perfect foil to Costello* CONTRAST, complement, antithesis, relief.

**foist** verb *why are you trying to* ***foist*** *your crummy old furniture* ***on*** *me?* IMPOSE ON, force on, thrust on, offload on, unload on, dump on, palm off on; pass off on; saddle someone with, land someone with.

**fold**[1] verb **1** *I folded the cloth* DOUBLE (OVER/UP), crease, turn under/up/over, bend; tuck, gather, pleat.

**2** *fold the cream into the chocolate mixture* MIX, blend, stir gently, incorporate.

**3** *he folded her in his arms* ENFOLD, wrap, envelop; take, gather, clasp, squeeze, clutch; embrace, hug, cuddle, cradle.

**4** *the firm folded last year* FAIL, collapse, founder; go bankrupt, become insolvent, cease trading, go into receivership, go into liquidation, be closed (down), be shut (down); *informal* crash, go bust, go broke, go under, go belly up.

▸ noun *there was a fold in the paper* CREASE, wrinkle, crinkle, pucker, furrow; pleat, gather.

**fold**[2] noun **1** *the sheep were in their fold* ENCLOSURE, pen, paddock, pound, compound, ring, corral; sheepfold.

**2** *they welcomed Joe back into the fold* COMMUNITY, group, body, company, mass, flock, congregation, assembly.

**folder** noun *it's the blue folder labeled "Taxes"* FILE, binder, portfolio, envelope, sleeve, wallet.

**foliage** noun *the plant is grown for its striking foliage* LEAVES, leafage; greenery, vegetation, verdure.

**folk** noun *informal* **1** *the local folk* PEOPLE, individuals, 'men, women, and children,' (living) souls, mortals; citizenry, inhabitants, residents, populace, population; *formal* denizens.

**2** *my folks came from the north* PARENTS, RELATIVES, relations, blood relations, family, nearest and dearest, people, kinsfolk, kinsmen, kinswomen, kin, kith and kin, kindred, flesh and blood.

**folklore** noun *Adrian is fascinated by the local folklore* MYTHOLOGY, lore, oral history, tradition, folk tradition; legends, fables, myths, folk tales, folk stories, old wives' tales; mythos.

**follow** verb **1** *we'll let the others follow* COME BEHIND, come after, go behind, go after, walk behind. ANTONYM lead.

**2** *he was expected to follow his father in the business* SUCCEED, replace, take the place of, take over from; *informal* step into someone's shoes, fill someone's shoes/boots.

**3** *people used to* ***follow*** *the band* ***around*** ACCOMPANY, go along with, go around with, travel with, escort, attend, trail around with, string along with; *informal* tag along with. ANTONYM lead.

**4** *the KGB followed her everywhere* SHADOW, trail, stalk, track, dog, hound; *informal* tail.

**5** *follow the instructions* OBEY, comply with, conform to, adhere to, stick to, keep to, hew to, act in accordance with, abide by, observe, heed, pay attention to. ANTONYM flout.

**6** *penalties may* ***follow from*** *such behaviour* RESULT FROM, arise from, be a consequence of, be caused by, be brought about by, be a result of, come after, develop from, ensue from, emanate from, issue from, proceed from, spring from, flow from, originate from, stem from. ANTONYM lead to.

**7** *I couldn't follow what he said* UNDERSTAND, comprehend, apprehend, take in, grasp, fathom, appreciate, see; *informal* make head(s) or tail(s) of, get, figure out, savvy, wrap/get one's head around, wrap/get one's mind around, get the drift of. ANTONYM misunderstand.

**8** *she followed her mentor in her poetic style* IMITATE, copy, mimic, ape, reproduce, mirror, echo; emulate, take as a pattern, take as an example, take as a model, adopt the style of, model oneself on, take a leaf out of someone's book.

**9** *he follows the Pacers* BE A FAN OF, be a supporter of, support, be a follower of, be an admirer of, be a devotee of, be devoted to. ANTONYM dislike.

PHRASES: **follow through** *they lack the resources to follow the project through* COMPLETE, bring to completion, see something through; continue with, carry on with, keep on with, keep going with, stay with; *informal* stick something out.

**follow up** *I've got a hunch and I'm going to follow it up* INVESTIGATE, research, look into, dig into, delve into, make inquiries into, inquire about, ask questions about, pursue, chase up; *informal* check out, scope out.

**follower** noun **1** *the president's closest followers* ACOLYTE, assistant, attendant, companion; henchman, minion, lackey, servant; *informal* hanger-on, sidekick. ANTONYM leader.

**2** *a follower of Christ* DISCIPLE, apostle, supporter, defender, champion; believer, true believer, worshiper. ANTONYM opponent.

**3** *followers of winter sports* FAN, enthusiast, admirer, devotee, lover, supporter, adherent.

**following** noun *his devoted following* ADMIRERS, supporters, backers, fans, adherents, devotees, advocates, patrons, public, audience, circle, retinue, train. ANTONYM opposition.

▸ adjective **1** *the following day* NEXT, ensuing, succeeding, subsequent. ANTONYM preceding.

**2** *the following questions* below, further on; these; *formal* hereunder, hereinafter. ANTONYMS preceding, aforementioned.

**folly** noun *the folly of youth* FOOLISHNESS, foolhardiness, stupidity, idiocy, lunacy, madness, rashness, recklessness, imprudence, injudiciousness, irresponsibility, thoughtlessness, indiscretion; *informal* craziness. ANTONYM wisdom.

**foment** verb *accused of fomenting civil unrest* INSTIGATE, incite, provoke, agitate, excite, stir up, whip up, encourage, urge, fan the flames of. See note at INCITE.

**fond** adjective **1** *she was* ***fond of*** *dancing* KEEN ON, partial to, addicted to, enthusiastic about, passionate about; attached to, attracted to, enamored of, in love with, having a soft spot for; *informal* into, hooked on, gone on, sweet on, struck on. ANTONYM indifferent.

**2** *her fond husband* ADORING, devoted, doting, loving, caring, affectionate, warm, tender, kind, attentive, uxorious. ANTONYM unfeeling.

**3** *a fond hope* UNREALISTIC, naive, foolish, overoptimistic, deluded, delusory, absurd, vain, Panglossian. ANTONYM realistic.

**fondle** verb *gently fondling the puppies | a priest who had inappropriately fondled several children* CARESS, stroke, pat, pet, finger, tickle, play with; maul, molest; *informal* paw, grope, feel up, touch up, cop a feel of.

**fondness** noun **1** *they look at each other with such fondness* AFFECTION, love, liking, warmth, tenderness, kindness, devotion, endearment, attachment, friendliness. ANTONYM hatred.

**2** *a fondness for spicy food* LIKING, love, taste, partiality, keenness, inclination, penchant, predilection, relish, passion, appetite; weakness, soft spot; *informal* thing, yen, jones. ANTONYM dislike.

**food** noun **1** *French food* NOURISHMENT, sustenance, nutriment, fare; bread, daily bread; cooking, cuisine; foodstuffs, edibles, provender, refreshments, meals, provisions, rations; solids; *informal* eats, eatables, nosh, grub, chow, vittles; *formal* comestibles; *literary* viands; *dated* victuals; *archaic* commons, meat, aliment.

**2** *food for the cattle* FODDER, feed, provender, forage.

**fool** noun **1** *you've acted like a complete fool* IDIOT, ass, blockhead, dunce, dolt, ignoramus, imbecile, cretin, dullard, simpleton, moron, clod; *informal* nitwit, halfwit, dope, ninny, nincompoop, chump, dimwit, dingbat, dipstick, goober, coot, goon, dumbo, dummy, ditz, dumdum, fathead, numbskull, numbnuts, dunderhead, thickhead, airhead, flake, lamebrain, zombie, nerd, peabrain, birdbrain, jughead, jerk, donkey, twit, goat, dork, twerp, schmuck, bozo, boob, turkey, schlep, chowderhead, dumbhead, goofball, goof, goofus, galoot, lummox, klutz, putz, schlemiel, sap, meatball, dumb cluck.

**2** *she made a fool of me* LAUGHINGSTOCK, dupe, butt, gull, cat's paw; *informal* stooge, sucker, fall guy, sap.

**3** *historical* *the fool in King James's court* JESTER, court jester, clown, buffoon, joker, zany.

▸ verb **1** *he'd been fooled by a mere child* DECEIVE, trick, hoax, dupe, take in, mislead, delude, hoodwink, sucker, bluff, gull; swindle, defraud, cheat, double-cross; *informal* con, bamboozle, pull a fast one on, take for a ride, pull the wool over someone's eyes, put one over on, have on, diddle, fiddle, sting, shaft, snooker, stiff, euchre, hornswoggle; *literary* cozen.

2 *I'm not fooling, I promise* PRETEND, make believe, feign, put on an act, act, sham, fake; joke, jest; *informal* kid; have someone on.

PHRASE: **fool around 1** *someone's been fooling around with the controls* FIDDLE, play (around), toy, trifle, meddle, tamper, interfere, monkey (around); *informal* mess (around).

2 *informal* *my husband's been fooling around* PHILANDER, womanize, flirt, have an affair, commit adultery, cheat; *informal* play around, mess around, carry on, play the field, sleep around.

**foolery** noun *the foolery in this dormitory has gotten out of hand* CLOWNING, fooling, tomfoolery, buffoonery, silliness, foolishness, stupidity, idiocy; antics, capers; *informal* larks, shenanigans, didoes; *archaic* harlequinade.

**foolhardy** adjective *their foolhardy plans* RECKLESS, rash, irresponsible, impulsive, hotheaded, impetuous, bullheaded, daredevil, devil-may-care, madcap, harebrained, precipitate, hasty, overhasty; *literary* temerarious. See note at TEMERITY. ANTONYM prudent.

**foolish** adjective *don't let your foolish impulses get you into trouble* STUPID, silly, idiotic, witless, brainless, mindless, unintelligent, thoughtless, half-baked, imprudent, incautious, injudicious, unwise; ill-advised, ill-considered, impolitic, rash, reckless, foolhardy, daft; *informal* dumb, dim, dimwitted, halfwitted, thick, harebrained, crack-brained, crackpot, pea-brained, wooden-headed, dumb-ass, chowderheaded. See note at ABSURD. ANTONYMS sensible, wise.

**foolishness** noun *I regretted my foolishness* FOLLY, stupidity, idiocy, imbecility, silliness, inanity, thoughtlessness, imprudence, injudiciousness, lack of foresight, lack of sense, irresponsibility, indiscretion, foolhardiness, rashness, recklessness. ANTONYMS sense, wisdom.

**foolproof** adjective *a foolproof security system* INFALLIBLE, dependable, reliable, trustworthy, certain, sure, guaranteed, safe, sound, tried and tested; watertight, airtight, flawless, perfect; *informal* sure-fire, idiot-proof, goof-proof; *formal* efficacious. ANTONYM flawed.

**foot** noun **1** (**feet**) *my feet hurt* *informal* tootsies, dogs, boats; *Brit. informal* trotters.

**2** *the animal's foot* paw, hoof, pad; *Brit.* trotter.

**3** *the foot of the hill* BOTTOM, base, lowest part; end; foundation. PHRASE: **foot the bill** *informal as usual, the taxpayers will have to foot the bill* PAY (THE BILL), settle up; *informal* pick up the tab, pick up the check, cough up (the money/dough), fork out (the money/dough), shell out (the money/dough).

**footing** noun **1** *Natalie lost her footing* FOOTHOLD, toehold, grip, purchase.

**2** *a solid financial footing* BASIS, base, foundation.

**3** *on an equal footing* STANDING, status, position; condition, arrangement, basis; relationship, terms.

**footstep** noun **1** *he heard a footstep* FOOTFALL, step, tread, stomp, stamp.

**2** *footsteps in the sand* FOOTPRINT, footmark, mark, impression; (**footsteps**) track(s), spoor.

**fop** noun *he was known as quite a fop in the old neighborhood, always dressed to the nines and whistling a cheery tune* DANDY, man about town, poseur; *informal* snappy dresser, trendoid, hipster; *archaic* coxcomb, popinjay.

**forage** verb *Colonel Kendricks sent out a small party to forage for provisions* HUNT, search, look, rummage around, ferret, root about/around, nose around/about, scavenge.

▸ noun **1** *forage for the horses* FODDER, feed, food, provender.

**2** *a nightly forage for food* HUNT, search, look, quest, rummage, scavenge.

**forbear** verb *can you **forbear from** drinking?* REFRAIN FROM, abstain from, desist from, keep from, restrain oneself from, stop oneself from, hold back from, withhold from; resist the temptation to (be); eschew, avoid, decline to (be). ANTONYM persist.

**forbearance** noun *we are proud of the forbearance you have demonstrated during these difficult weeks* TOLERANCE, patience, resignation, endurance, fortitude, stoicism; leniency, clemency, indulgence; restraint, self-restraint, self-control. See note at ABSTINENCE.

**forbid** verb *the law forbids gender discrimination* PROHIBIT, ban, outlaw, make illegal, veto, proscribe, disallow, embargo, bar, debar, interdict; *Law* enjoin, restrain. See also note at PROHIBIT. ANTONYM permit.

**forbidding** adjective **1** *a forbidding manner* HOSTILE, unwelcoming, unfriendly, off-putting, unsympathetic, unapproachable, grim, stern, hard, tough, frosty. ANTONYM friendly.

**2** *the dark castle looked forbidding* THREATENING, ominous, menacing, sinister, brooding, daunting, formidable, fearsome, frightening, chilling, disturbing, disquieting. See note at OMINOUS. ANTONYM inviting.

**force** noun **1** *he pushed with all his force* STRENGTH, power, energy, might, effort, exertion; impact, pressure, weight, impetus. ANTONYM weakness.

**2** *they used force to achieve their aims* COERCION, compulsion, constraint, duress, oppression, harassment, intimidation, threats; *informal* arm-twisting, bullying tactics.

**3** *the force of the argument* COGENCY, potency, weight, effectiveness, soundness, validity, strength, power, significance, influence, authority; *informal* punch; *formal* efficacy. ANTONYM weakness.

**4** *a force for good* AGENCY, power, influence, instrument, vehicle, means.

**5** *a peace-keeping force* BODY, body of people, group, outfit, party, team; detachment, unit, squad; *informal* bunch.

▸ verb **1** *he was forced to pay* COMPEL, coerce, make, constrain, oblige, impel, drive, pressurize, pressure, press, push, press-gang, bully, dragoon, bludgeon; *informal* put the screws on, lean on, twist someone's arm. See note at COMPEL.

**2** *the door had to be forced* BREAK OPEN, burst open, knock down, smash down, kick in.

**3** *water was forced through a hole* PROPEL, push, thrust, shove, drive, press, pump.

**4** *they forced a confession out of the kids* EXTRACT, elicit, exact, extort, wrest, wring, drag, screw, squeeze.

PHRASE: **in force 1** *the law is now in force* EFFECTIVE, in operation, operative, operational, in action, valid.

**2** *her fans were out in force* IN GREAT NUMBERS, in hordes, in full strength.

**forced** adjective **1** *forced entry* VIOLENT, forcible.

**2** *forced repatriation* ENFORCED, forcible, compulsory, obligatory, mandatory, involuntary, imposed, required, stipulated, dictated, ordained, prescribed. ANTONYM voluntary.

**3** *a forced smile* STRAINED, unnatural, artificial, false, feigned, simulated, contrived, labored, stilted, studied, mannered, affected, unconvincing, insincere, hollow; *informal* phony, pretend, put on. ANTONYM natural.

**forceful** adjective **1** *a forceful personality* DYNAMIC, energetic, assertive, authoritative, vigorous, powerful, strong, pushy, driving, determined, insistent, commanding, dominant, domineering; *informal* bossy, in-your-face, go-ahead, feisty. ANTONYMS weak, submissive.

**2** *a forceful argument* COGENT, convincing, compelling, strong, powerful, potent, weighty, effective, well-founded, telling, persuasive, irresistible, eloquent, coherent. ANTONYMS weak, unconvincing.

**forcible** adjective **1** *forcible entry* FORCED, violent.

**2** *forcible repatriation.* See FORCED sense 2.

**forebear** noun ANCESTOR, forefather, antecedent, progenitor, primogenitor. ANTONYM descendant.

**forebode** verb *literary* *the scarlet sky forebodes the visitation of mischief* PRESAGE, augur, portend, herald, warn of, forewarn of, foreshadow, be an omen of, indicate, signify, signal, promise, threaten, spell, denote; *literary* betoken, foretoken. See note at OMINOUS.

**foreboding** noun **1** *a feeling of foreboding* APPREHENSION, anxiety, trepidation, disquiet, unease, uneasiness, misgiving, suspicion, worry, fear, fearfulness, dread, alarm; *informal* the willies, the heebie-jeebies, the jitters, the creeps. ANTONYM calm.

**2** *their forebodings proved justified* PREMONITION, presentiment, bad feeling, sneaking suspicion, funny feeling, intuition; *archaic* presage.

**forecast** verb *they forecast record profits* PREDICT, prophesy, prognosticate, foretell, foresee, forewarn of. See note at PREDICT.

▸ noun *a gloomy forecast* PREDICTION, prophecy, forewarning, prognostication, augury, divination, prognosis.

**forefather** noun. See FOREBEAR.

**forefront** noun *her first CD propelled her to the forefront of the music scene* VANGUARD, van, spearhead, head, lead, front, fore, front line, cutting edge, avant-garde. ANTONYMS rear, background.

**foregoing** adjective *the foregoing circumstances are no longer applicable to this argument* PRECEDING, aforesaid, aforementioned, previously mentioned, earlier, above; previous, prior, antecedent. ANTONYM following.

**foregone** PHRASE: **a foregone conclusion** *a rental increase is a foregone conclusion* CERTAINTY, inevitability, matter of course, predictable result; *informal* sure thing, no-brainer.

**foreground** noun **1** *the foreground of the picture* FRONT, fore.

**2** *in the foreground of the political drama* FOREFRONT, vanguard, van, spearhead, head, lead, front, fore, front line, cutting edge.

**foreign** adjective **1** *foreign branches of American banks* OVERSEAS, exotic, distant, external, alien, nonnative. ANTONYMS domestic, native.

**2** *the concept is very foreign to us* UNFAMILIAR, unknown, unheard of, strange, alien; novel, new. ANTONYM familiar.

**foreigner** noun *her unease with foreigners* ALIEN, nonnative, stranger, outsider; immigrant, landed immigrant, refugee, settler, newcomer. ANTONYM native.

**foreman, forewoman** noun *report any injury to the foreman* SUPERVISOR, overseer, superintendent, team leader; foreperson; captain; ramrod, straw boss.

**foremost** adjective *the foremost impressionist of his age* LEADING, principal, premier, prime, top, top-level, greatest, best, supreme, preeminent, outstanding, most important, most prominent, most influential, most illustrious, most notable; ranking, number-one, star. ANTONYM minor.

**forerunner** noun **1** *archosaurs were the forerunners of dinosaurs* PREDECESSOR, precursor, antecedent, ancestor, forebear; prototype. ANTONYM descendant.

**2** *a headache may be the forerunner of other complaints* PRELUDE, herald, harbinger, precursor, sign, signal, indication, warning.

**foresee** verb *I foresee much good fortune in your future* ANTICIPATE, predict, forecast, expect, envisage, envision, see; foretell, prophesy, prognosticate; *literary* foreknow.

**foreshadow** verb *those things that foreshadow war are sadly upon us* SIGNAL, indicate, signify, mean, be a sign of, suggest, herald, be a harbinger of, warn of, portend, prefigure, presage, promise, point to, anticipate; *informal* spell; *literary* forebode, foretoken, betoken, adumbrate; *archaic* foreshow. See note at PREDICT.

**foresight** noun *my lack of foresight has cost me dearly* FORETHOUGHT, planning, farsightedness, vision, anticipation, prudence, care, caution, precaution, readiness, preparedness. ANTONYM hindsight.

**forest** noun *the cooling shade of the forest* WOOD(S), woodland, timberland, trees, bush, plantation; jungle, rain forest, pinewood; *archaic* greenwood; taiga, boreal forest, Carolinian forest, Acadian forest.

**forestall** verb *they were unable to forestall Roosevelt's reelection* PREEMPT, get in before; anticipate, second-guess; nip in the bud, thwart, frustrate, foil, stave off, ward off, fend off, avert, preclude, obviate, prevent; *informal* beat someone to it.

**forestry** noun *a college degree in forestry* FOREST MANAGEMENT, tree growing, agroforestry; *technical* arboriculture, silviculture, dendrology.

**foretell** verb **1** *the locals can foretell a storm* PREDICT, forecast, prophesy, prognosticate; foresee, anticipate, envisage, envision, see. See note at PREDICT.

**2** *dreams can foretell the future* INDICATE, foreshadow, prefigure, anticipate, warn of, point to, signal, portend, augur, presage, be an omen of; *literary* forebode, foretoken, betoken; *archaic* foreshow.

**forethought** noun *without forethought, you'll just keep stumbling through life* ANTICIPATION, planning, forward planning, provision, precaution, prudence, care, caution; foresight, farsightedness, vision. ANTONYMS impulse, recklessness.

**forever** adverb **1** *their love would last forever* FOR ALWAYS, evermore, for ever and ever, for good, for all time, until the end of time, until hell freezes over, eternally, forevermore, perpetually, in perpetuity; *informal* until the cows come home, until kingdom come; *archaic* for aye.

**2** *he was forever banging into things* ALWAYS, continually, constantly, perpetually, incessantly, endlessly, persistently, repeatedly, regularly; nonstop, day and night, 'morning, noon, and night'; all the time, the entire time; *informal* 24–7. ANTONYMS never, occasionally.

**forewarn** verb *the building would have been torched if the authorities had not been forewarned* WARN, warn in advance, give advance warning, give fair warning, give notice, apprise, inform; alert, caution, put someone on their guard; *informal* tip off.

**foreword** noun *he wrote the foreword to one of her books* PREFACE, introduction, prologue, preamble; *informal* intro, lead-in; *formal* exordium, prolegomenon, proem. ANTONYM conclusion.

**forfeit** verb *latecomers will forfeit their places* LOSE, be deprived of, surrender, relinquish, sacrifice, give up, yield, renounce, forgo; *informal* pass up, lose out on. ANTONYM retain.

▸ noun *they are liable to a forfeit* PENALTY, sanction, punishment, penance; fine; confiscation, loss, relinquishment, forfeiture, surrender; *Law* sequestration.

**forge**[1] verb **1** *smiths forged swords* HAMMER OUT, beat into shape, fashion.

**2** *they forged a partnership* BUILD, construct, form, create, establish, set up.

**3** *he forged her signature* FAKE, falsify, counterfeit, copy, imitate, reproduce, replicate, simulate.

**forge**[2] verb *they forged through swamps* ADVANCE STEADILY, advance gradually, press on, push on, soldier on, march on, push forward, make progress, make headway. PHRASE: **forge ahead** *Jack's horse forged ahead and took the lead* ADVANCE RAPIDLY, progress quickly, make rapid progress, increase speed.

**forgery** noun **1** *guilty of forgery* COUNTERFEITING, falsification, faking, copying, pirating.

**2** *the painting was a forgery* FAKE, counterfeit, fraud, sham; imitation, replica, copy, pirate copy; *informal* phony.

**forget** verb **1** *he forgot where he was* FAIL TO REMEMBER, fail to recall, fail to think of; *informal* disremember. ANTONYM remember.

**2** *I never forget my briefcase* LEAVE BEHIND, fail to take/bring.

**3** *I forgot to close the door* NEGLECT, fail, omit.

**4** *you can forget that idea* STOP THINKING ABOUT, put out of one's mind, shut out, blank out, pay no heed to, not worry about, ignore, overlook, take no notice of; abandon, say goodbye to, deep-six.

**forgetful** adjective **1** *I'm so forgetful these days* ABSENT-MINDED, amnesic, amnesiac, vague, disorganized, dreamy, abstracted; *informal* scatterbrained, having a mind/memory like a sieve. ANTONYM reliable.

**2** ***forgetful of** the time* HEEDLESS OF, careless of, unmindful of; inattentive to, negligent about, oblivious to, unconcerned about, indifferent to, not bothered about. ANTONYM heedful.

**forgetfulness** noun **1** *his excuse was forgetfulness* ABSENT-MINDEDNESS, amnesia, poor memory, a lapse of memory, vagueness, abstraction; *informal* scattiness. ANTONYM reliability.

**2** *a forgetfulness of duty* NEGLECT, heedlessness, carelessness, disregard; inattention, obliviousness, lack of concern, indifference. ANTONYM heed.

**forgive** verb **1** *she would not forgive him* PARDON, excuse, exonerate, absolve; make allowances for, feel no resentment toward, feel no malice toward, harbor no grudge against, bury the hatchet with; let bygones be bygones; *informal* let off (the hook); *formal* exculpate. See note at ABSOLVE. ANTONYMS blame, resent.

**2** *you must forgive his rude conduct* EXCUSE, overlook, disregard, ignore, pass over, make allowances for, allow; turn a blind eye to, turn a deaf ear to, wink at, indulge, tolerate. ANTONYM punish.

**forgiveness** noun *we beg your forgiveness* PARDON, absolution, exoneration, remission, dispensation, indulgence, clemency, mercy; reprieve, amnesty; *archaic* shrift. ANTONYMS mercilessness, punishment.

**forgiving** adjective *Cromwell was not renowned for his forgiving nature* MERCIFUL, lenient, compassionate, magnanimous, humane, softhearted, forbearing, tolerant, indulgent, understanding. ANTONYMS merciless, vindictive.

**forgotten** adjective *Vivaldi's operas are largely forgotten* UNREMEMBERED, out of mind, past recollection, beyond/past recall, consigned to oblivion; left behind; neglected, overlooked, ignored, disregarded, unrecognized. ANTONYM remembered.

**fork** verb *the road forks at the south end of the lake* SPLIT, branch (off), divide, subdivide, separate, part, diverge, go in different directions, bifurcate; *technical* divaricate, ramify.

**forked** adjective *the hawk's distinctive forked tail* SPLIT, branching, branched, bifurcate(d), Y-shaped, V-shaped, pronged, divided; *technical* divaricate. ANTONYM straight.

**forlorn** adjective **1** *he sounded forlorn* UNHAPPY, sad, miserable, sorrowful, dejected, despondent, disconsolate, wretched, abject, down, downcast, dispirited, downhearted, crestfallen, depressed, melancholy, gloomy, glum, mournful, despairing, doleful, woebegone; *informal* blue, down in/at the mouth, down in the dumps; *rare* lachrymose. ANTONYM happy.

**2** *a forlorn garden* DESOLATE, deserted, abandoned, forsaken, forgotten, neglected. ANTONYM cared for.

**3** *a forlorn attempt* HOPELESS, vain, with no chance of success; useless, futile, pointless, purposeless, unavailing, nugatory; *archaic* bootless. ANTONYMS hopeful, sure-fire.

**form** noun **1** *the general form of the landscape | form is less important than content* SHAPE, configuration, formation, structure, construction, arrangement, appearance, exterior, outline, format, layout, design.

**2** *the human form* BODY, shape, figure, stature, build, frame, physique, anatomy; *informal* vital statistics.

**3** *the infection takes different forms* MANIFESTATION, appearance, embodiment, incarnation, semblance, shape, guise.

**4** *sponsorship is a form of advertising* KIND, sort, type, class, classification, category, variety, genre, brand, style; species, genus, family.

**5** *put the mixture into a form* MOLD, cast, shape, matrix, die.

**6** *what is the form here?* ETIQUETTE, social practice, custom, usage, use, modus operandi, habit, wont, protocol, procedure, rules, convention, tradition, fashion, style; *formal* praxis.

**7** *you have to fill in a form* QUESTIONNAIRE, document, coupon, paper, sheet.

**8** *in top form* FITNESS, condition, fettle, shape, trim, health.

▸ verb **1** *the pads are formed from mild steel* MAKE, construct, build, manufacture, fabricate, assemble, put together; create, produce, concoct, devise, contrive, frame, fashion, shape.

**2** *he formed a plan* FORMULATE, devise, conceive, work out, think up, lay, draw up, put together, produce, fashion, concoct, forge, hatch, incubate, develop; *informal* dream up.

**3** *they plan to form a company* SET UP, establish, found, launch, float, create, bring into being, institute, start (up), get going, initiate, bring about, inaugurate. ANTONYM dissolve.

**4** *a mist was forming* MATERIALIZE, come into being/existence, crystallize, emerge, spring up, develop; take shape, appear, loom, show up, become visible. ANTONYM disappear.

**5** *the horse may form bad habits* ACQUIRE, develop, get, pick up, contract, slip into, get into. ANTONYMS avoid, break.

**6** *the warriors formed themselves into a diamond pattern* ARRANGE, draw up, line up, assemble, organize, sort, order, range, array, dispose, marshal, deploy.

**7** *the parts of society form an integrated whole* CONSTITUTE, make, make up, compose, add up to.

**8** *the city formed a natural meeting point* CONSTITUTE, serve as, act as, function as, perform the function of, do duty for, make.

**9** *teachers form the minds of children* DEVELOP, mold, shape, train, teach, instruct, educate, school, drill, discipline, prime, prepare, guide, direct, inform, enlighten, inculcate, indoctrinate, edify.

PHRASE: **good form** *it is not good form to leave visitors on their own* GOOD MANNERS, manners, polite behavior, correct behavior, convention, etiquette, protocol; *informal* the done thing.

**formal** adjective **1** *a formal dinner* CEREMONIAL, ceremonious, ritualistic, ritual, conventional, traditional; stately, courtly, solemn, dignified; elaborate, ornate, dressy; black-tie. ANTONYM informal.

**2** *a very formal manner* ALOOF, reserved, remote, detached, unapproachable; stiff, prim, stuffy, staid, ceremonious, correct, proper, decorous, conventional, precise, exact, punctilious, unbending, inflexible, straitlaced; *informal* buttoned-down, standoffish. ANTONYMS informal, casual.

**3** *a formal garden* SYMMETRICAL, regular, orderly, arranged, methodical, systematic. ANTONYM informal.

**4** *formal permission* OFFICIAL, legal, authorized, approved, validated, certified, endorsed, documented, sanctioned, licensed, recognized, authoritative. ANTONYMS informal, unofficial.

**5** *formal education* CONVENTIONAL, mainstream; school, institutional. ANTONYM informal.

THE RIGHT WORD **formal, ceremonial, ceremonious, pompous, proper, punctilious**

**Formal** suggests a suit-and-tie approach to certain situations—reserved, conventional, obeying all the rules (*an engraved invitation to a formal dinner requiring black tie or evening gown*). **Proper**, in this regard, implies scrupulously correct behavior that observes rules of etiquette (*the proper way to serve a guest; the proper spoon for dessert*). **Punctilious** behavior observes all the proper formalities (a *"punctilio"* is a detail or fine point), but may verge on the annoying (*her punctilious attention to the correct placement of silverware made setting the table an ordeal*). Someone (usually a man) who likes to show off just how *formal* and *proper* he can be runs the risk of becoming the most dreaded dinner guest of all: the **pompous** ass. *Pompous* individuals may derive more than the normal amount of pleasure from participating in **ceremonial** acts or events, which are those performed according to set rules, but **ceremo-**

**nious** suggests a less negative and more ritualized approach to formality (*the Japanese woman could not have been more ceremonious than when she was carrying out the ceremonial serving of tea*).

---

**formality** noun **1** *the formality of the occasion* CEREMONY, ceremoniousness, ritual, conventionality, red tape, protocol, decorum; stateliness, courtliness, solemnity. ANTONYM informality.

**2** *his formality was off-putting* ALOOFNESS, reserve, remoteness, detachment, unapproachability; stiffness, primness, stuffiness, staidness, correctness, decorum, punctiliousness, inflexibility; *informal* standoffishness. ANTONYM informality.

**3** **(formalities)** *we keep the formalities to a minimum* OFFICIAL PROCEDURE, bureaucracy, red tape, paperwork.

**4** *the medical examination is just a formality* ROUTINE, routine practice, normal procedure.

**formation** noun **1** *the formation of the island's sand ridges* EMERGENCE, coming into being, genesis, development, evolution, shaping, origination. ANTONYMS destruction, disappearance.

**2** *the formation of a new government* ESTABLISHMENT, setting up, start, initiation, institution, foundation, inception, creation, inauguration, launch, flotation. ANTONYM dissolution.

**3** *the aircraft were flying in tight formation* CONFIGURATION, arrangement, pattern, array, alignment, positioning, disposition, order.

**formative** adjective **1** *at a formative stage* DEVELOPMENTAL, developing, growing, malleable, impressionable, susceptible.

**2** *a formative influence* DETERMINING, controlling, influential, guiding, decisive, forming, shaping, determinative.

**former** adjective **1** *the former bishop* ONE-TIME, erstwhile, sometime, ex-, late; PREVIOUS, foregoing, preceding, earlier, prior, past, last. ANTONYMS future, next.

**2** *in former times* EARLIER, old, past, bygone, olden, long-ago, gone by, long past, of old; *literary* of yore. ANTONYMS future, present.

**3** *the former of the two* FIRST-MENTIONED, first. ANTONYM latter.

**formerly** adverb *this is Mr. Kane, formerly of Kane Industries* PREVIOUSLY, earlier, before, until now/then, hitherto, née, once, once upon a time, at one time, in the past; *formal* heretofore.

**formidable** adjective **1** *a formidable curved dagger* INTIMIDATING, forbidding, daunting, disturbing, alarming, frightening, disquieting, brooding, awesome, fearsome, ominous, foreboding, sinister, menacing, threatening, dangerous. ANTONYMS pleasant-looking, comforting.

**2** *a formidable task* ONEROUS, arduous, taxing, difficult, hard, heavy, laborious, burdensome, strenuous, back-breaking, uphill, Herculean, monumental, colossal; demanding, tough, challenging, exacting; *formal* exigent; *archaic* toilsome. ANTONYM easy.

**3** *a formidable pianist* CAPABLE, able, proficient, adept, adroit, accomplished, seasoned, skillful, skilled, gifted, talented, masterly, virtuoso, expert, knowledgeable, qualified; impressive, powerful, mighty, terrific, tremendous, great, complete, redoubtable; *informal* mean, wicked, deadly, nifty, crack, ace, magic, crackerjack. ANTONYM weak.

**formula** noun **1** *a legal formula* FORM OF WORDS, set expression, phrase, saying, aphorism.

**2** *a peace formula* RECIPE, prescription, blueprint, plan, method, procedure, technique, system; template.

**3** *a formula for removing grease* PREPARATION, concoction, mixture, compound, creation, substance.

**formulate** verb **1** *the miners formulated a plan* DEVISE, conceive, work out, think up, lay, draw up, put together, form, produce, fashion, concoct, contrive, forge, hatch, prepare, develop; *informal* dream up.

**2** *this is how Marx formulated his question* EXPRESS, phrase, word, put into words, frame, couch, put, articulate, convey, say, state, utter.

**fornication** noun *formal* *the nuns warned us about the spiritual price one pays for fornication* EXTRAMARITAL SEX, extramarital relations, adultery, infidelity, unfaithfulness, cuckoldry; premarital sex; *informal* hanky-panky.

**forsake** verb *literary* **1** *he forsook his wife* ABANDON, desert, leave, leave high and dry, turn one's back on, cast aside, break (up) with; jilt, strand, leave stranded, leave in the lurch, throw over; *informal* walk out on, run out on, dump, ditch, can. ANTONYMS return to, stay with.

**2** *I won't forsake my vegetarian principles* RENOUNCE, abandon, relinquish, dispense with, disclaim, disown, disavow, discard, wash one's hands of; give up, drop, jettison, do away with, ax; *informal* ditch, scrap, scrub, junk; *formal* forswear. ANTONYM keep (to).

**forswear** verb *formal* *we are formally forswearing the use of chemical weapons* RENOUNCE, relinquish, reject, forgo, disavow, abandon, deny, repudiate, give up, wash one's hands of; eschew, abstain from, refrain from; *informal* kick, pack in, quit, swear off; *Law* disaffirm; *literary* forsake; *formal* abjure, abnegate. ANTONYMS adhere to, persist with, take up.

**fort** noun *dozens of settlers in the area sought refuge within the confines of the fort* FORTRESS, castle, citadel, blockhouse, stronghold, redoubt, fortification, bastion; fastness.

**forte** noun *acting had always been her forte* STRENGTH, strong point, specialty, strong suit, talent, special ability, skill, bent, gift, métier; *informal* thing. ANTONYM weakness.

**forth** adverb **1** *smoke billowed forth* OUT, outside, away, off, ahead, forward, into view; into existence.

**2** *from that day forth* ONWARD, onwards, on, forward; for ever, into eternity; until now.

**forthcoming** adjective **1** *forthcoming events* IMMINENT, impending, coming, upcoming, approaching, future; close, (close) at hand, in store, in the wind, in the air, in the offing, in the pipeline, on the horizon, on the way, on us, about to happen. ANTONYMS past, current.

**2** *no reply was forthcoming* AVAILABLE, ready, at hand, accessible, obtainable, at someone's disposal, obtained, given, vouchsafed to someone; *informal* up for grabs, on tap. ANTONYM unavailable.

**3** *he was not very forthcoming about himself* COMMUNICATIVE, talkative, chatty, loquacious, vocal; expansive, expressive, unreserved, uninhibited, outgoing, frank, open, candid; *informal* gabby. ANTONYM uncommunicative.

**forthright** adjective *a forthright statement to the press about her involvement in the cover-up* FRANK, direct, straightforward, honest, candid, open, sincere, outspoken, straight, blunt, plain-spoken, no-nonsense, downright, bluff, matter-of-fact, to the point; *informal* upfront. ANTONYMS secretive, evasive.

**forthwith** adverb *all hostages are to be released forthwith* IMMEDIATELY, at once, instantly, directly, right away, straightaway, posthaste, without delay, without hesitation; quickly, speedily, promptly; *informal* pronto. ANTONYM sometime.

**fortification** noun *fortifications loomed ominously along the high banks of the river* RAMPART, wall, defense, bulwark, palisade, stockade, redoubt, earthwork, bastion, parapet, barricade.

**fortify** verb **1** *the knights fortified their citadel* BUILD DEFENSES AROUND, strengthen, secure, protect. ANTONYMS weaken, expose.

**2** *the wall had been fortified* STRENGTHEN, reinforce, toughen, consolidate, bolster, shore up, brace, buttress. ANTONYM weaken.

**3** *I'll have a drink to fortify me* INVIGORATE, strengthen, energize, enliven, liven up, animate, vitalize, rejuvenate, restore, revive, refresh; *informal* pep up, buck up, give a shot in the arm to. ANTONYMS sedate, subdue.

**fortitude** noun COURAGE, bravery, endurance, resilience, mettle, moral fiber, strength of mind, strength of character, strong-mindedness, backbone, spirit, grit, true grit, doughtiness, steadfastness; *informal* guts. See note at COURAGE. ANTONYM faint-heartedness.

**fortress** noun *the fortress fell into the hands of the French* FORT, castle, citadel, blockhouse, stronghold, redoubt, fortification, bastion; fastness.

**fortuitous** adjective **1** *a fortuitous resemblance* CHANCE, adventitious, unexpected, unanticipated, unpredictable, unforeseen, unlooked-for, serendipitous, casual, incidental, coincidental, random, accidental, inadvertent, unintentional, unintended, unplanned, unpremeditated. See note at ACCIDENTAL. ANTONYM predictable.

**2** *the Red Wings were saved by a fortuitous rebound* LUCKY, fluky, fortunate, providential, advantageous, timely, opportune, serendipitous, heaven-sent. ANTONYM unlucky.

---

USAGE NOTE **fortuitous**

The traditional, etymological meaning of **fortuitous** is 'happening by chance': a *fortuitous meeting* is a chance meeting, which might turn out to be either a good thing or a bad thing. In modern uses, however, **fortuitous** tends more often to be used to refer to fortunate outcomes, and the word has become more or less a synonym for 'lucky' or 'fortunate.' This use is frowned upon as being not etymologically correct and is best avoided except in informal contexts.

---

**fortunate** adjective **1** *he was fortunate that the punishment was so slight* LUCKY, favored, blessed, blessed with good luck, in luck, having a charmed life, charmed; *informal* sitting pretty. ANTONYM unfortunate.

**2** *in a fortunate position* FAVORABLE, advantageous, providential, auspicious, welcome, heaven-sent, beneficial, propitious, fortuitous, opportune, happy, felicitous. ANTONYM unfavorable.

**3** *the society gives generously to less fortunate people* WEALTHY, rich, affluent, prosperous, well off, moneyed, well-to-do, well-heeled, opulent, comfortable; favored, privileged. ANTONYM underprivileged.

**fortune** noun **1** *fortune favored him* CHANCE, accident, coincidence, serendipity, destiny, fortuity, providence, happenstance.

**2** *a change of fortune* LUCK, fate, destiny, predestination, the stars, serendipity, karma, kismet, lot.

**3** **(fortunes)** *an upswing in the team's fortunes* CIRCUMSTANCES, state of affairs, condition, position, situation; plight, predicament.

**4** *he made his fortune in steel* WEALTH, riches, substance, property, assets, resources, means, possessions, treasure, estate.

**5** *informal* *this dress cost **a fortune*** A HUGE AMOUNT, a vast sum, a king's ransom, millions, billions; *informal* a small fortune, a mint, a bundle, a pile, a wad, an arm and a leg, a pretty penny, a tidy sum, big money, big bucks, gazillions, megabucks, top dollar. ANTONYM pittance.

**fortune teller** noun *for two bucks you could get a reading from a gypsy fortune teller* CLAIRVOYANT, crystal-gazer, psychic, prophet, seer, oracle, soothsayer, augur, diviner, sibyl; palmist, palm-reader.

**forum** noun **1** *forums were held for staff to air grievances* MEETING, assembly, gathering, rally, conference, seminar, convention, symposium, colloquium, caucus; *informal* get-together; *formal* colloquy.

**2** *a forum for discussion* SETTING, place, scene, context, stage, framework, backdrop; medium, means, apparatus, auspices.

**3** *the Roman forum* PUBLIC MEETING PLACE, marketplace, agora.

**forward** adverb **1** *the traffic moved forward* AHEAD, forward, onward, onwards, on, further.

2 *the winner stepped forward* TOWARD THE FRONT, out, forth, into view.

3 *from that day forward* ONWARD, onwards, on, forth; for ever, into eternity; until now.

▸ adjective 1 *in a forward direction* MOVING FORWARD, moving forward, moving ahead, onward, advancing, progressing, progressive. ANTONYM backward.

2 *the fortress served as the Austrian army's forward base against the Russians* FRONT, advance, foremost, head, leading, frontal. ANTONYM rear.

3 *forward planning* FUTURE, forward-looking, for the future, prospective.

4 *the girls seemed very forward* BOLD, BRAZEN, brazen-faced, barefaced, brash, shameless, immodest, audacious, daring, presumptuous, familiar, overfamiliar, pert; *informal* fresh. ANTONYM shy.

▸ verb 1 *my mother forwarded me your e-mail* SEND ON, mail on, redirect, re-address, pass on.

2 *the goods were forwarded by sea* SEND, dispatch, transmit, carry, convey, deliver, ship.

**forward-looking** adjective *the forward-looking countries of Europe forged ahead* PROGRESSIVE, enlightened, dynamic, pushing, bold, enterprising, ambitious, pioneering, innovative, modern, avant-garde, positive, reforming, radical; *informal* go-ahead, go-getting. ANTONYM backward-looking.

**forwards** adverb. See FORWARD adverb.

**fossil** noun *we could detect fossils in the cornerstone of the building* PETRIFIED REMAINS, petrified impression, remnant, relic.

**foster** verb 1 *he fostered the arts* ENCOURAGE, promote, further, stimulate, advance, forward, cultivate, nurture, strengthen, enrich; help, aid, abet, assist, contribute to, support, back, be a patron of. See note at ENCOURAGE. ANTONYMS neglect, suppress.

2 *they started fostering children* BRING UP, rear, raise, care for, take care of, look after, nurture, provide for; mother, parent.

**foul** adjective 1 *a foul stench* DISGUSTING, revolting, repulsive, repugnant, abhorrent, loathsome, offensive, sickening, nauseating, nauseous, stomach-churning, stomach-turning, distasteful, obnoxious, objectionable, odious, noxious, vomitous; *informal* ghastly, gruesome, gross, putrid, yucky, skanky, beastly; *literary* miasmic, noisome, mephitic. ANTONYM fragrant.

2 *a pile of foul laundry* DIRTY, filthy, mucky, grimy, grubby, muddy, muddied, unclean, unwashed; squalid, sordid, soiled, sullied, scummy; rotten, defiled, decaying, putrid, putrefied, smelly, fetid; *informal* cruddy, yucky, icky; *rare* feculent. ANTONYM clean.

3 *he had been foul to her* UNKIND, malicious, mean, nasty, unpleasant, unfriendly, spiteful, cruel, vicious, base, malevolent, despicable, contemptible; *informal* horrible, horrid, rotten; beastly. ANTONYMS pleasant, kind.

4 *foul weather* INCLEMENT, unpleasant, disagreeable, bad; rough, stormy, squally, gusty, windy, blustery, wild, blowy, rainy, wet. ANTONYM fair.

5 *foul drinking water* CONTAMINATED, polluted, infected, tainted, impure, filthy, dirty, unclean; *rare* feculent. ANTONYM clean.

6 *a foul deed* EVIL, wicked, bad, wrong, immoral, sinful, vile, dishonorable, corrupt, iniquitous, depraved, villainous, nefarious, vicious, malicious; malevolent, sinister, demonic, devilish, diabolical, fiendish, dark; monstrous, shocking, despicable, atrocious, heinous, odious, contemptible, horrible, execrable; *informal* lowdown, dirty. ANTONYM righteous.

7 *foul language* VULGAR, crude, coarse, filthy, dirty, obscene, indecent, indelicate, naughty, lewd, smutty, ribald, salacious, scatological, offensive, abusive. ANTONYM mild.

8 *a foul tackle* ILLEGAL; unfair, unsporting, unsportsmanlike, below the belt, dirty. ANTONYM fair.

▸ verb 1 *the river had been fouled with waste* DIRTY, infect, pollute, contaminate, poison, taint, sully, soil, stain, blacken, muddy, splash, spatter, smear, blight, defile, make filthy. ANTONYM clean up.

2 *the vessel had fouled her nets* TANGLE UP, entangle, snarl, catch, entwine, enmesh, twist. ANTONYM disentangle.

**found** verb 1 *she founded her company in 2002* ESTABLISH, set up, start (up), begin, get going, institute, inaugurate, launch, float, form, create, bring into being, originate, develop. ANTONYMS dissolve, liquidate.

2 *they founded a new city* BUILD, construct, erect, put up; plan, lay plans for. ANTONYMS abandon, demolish.

PHRASE: **be founded on** *our relationship must be founded on trust* BE BASED ON, be built on, be constructed on; be grounded in, be rooted in; rest, hinge, depend.

**foundation** noun 1 *the foundations of a building* FOOTING, foot, base, substructure, infrastructure, underpinning; bottom, bedrock, substratum.

2 *the report has a scientific foundation* BASIS, starting point, base, point of departure, beginning, premise; principles, fundamentals, rudiments; cornerstone, core, heart, thrust, essence, kernel.

3 *there was no foundation for the claim* JUSTIFICATION, grounds, defense, reason, rationale, cause, basis, motive, excuse, call, pretext, provocation.

4 *an educational foundation* ENDOWED INSTITUTION, charitable body, funding agency, source of funds, endowment.

**founder**[1] noun *the founder of modern physics* ORIGINATOR, creator, (founding) father, prime mover, architect, engineer, designer, developer, pioneer, author, planner, inventor, mastermind; *literary* begetter.

**founder**[2] verb 1 *the ship foundered* SINK, go to the bottom, go down, be lost at sea.

2 *the scheme foundered* FAIL, be unsuccessful, not succeed, fall flat, fall through, collapse, backfire, meet with disaster, come to nothing, come to naught; *informal* flatline, flop, bomb. ANTONYM succeed.

**3** *their horses foundered in the river* STUMBLE, trip, trip up, lose one's balance, lose/miss one's footing, slip, stagger, lurch, totter, fall, tumble, topple, sprawl, collapse.

**foundling** noun *it was during the Depression that Mrs. Aronson took in eight little foundlings and raised them as her own* ABANDONED INFANT, waif, stray, orphan, outcast.

**fountain** noun **1** *a fountain of water* JET, spray, spout, spurt, well, fount, cascade.

**2** *a fountain of knowledge* SOURCE, fount, font, well; reservoir, fund, mass, mine.

**foyer** noun *you may hang your coats in the foyer* ENTRANCE HALL, hall, hallway, entrance, entry, entranceway, entryway, porch, reception area, atrium, concourse, lobby, narthex.

**fracas** noun *the fracas in the alley drew the attention of a passing patrol car* DISTURBANCE, brawl, melee, rumpus, skirmish, struggle, scuffle, scrum, clash, fisticuffs, altercation; *informal* scrap, dust-up, set-to, donnybrook.

**fraction** noun **1** *a fraction of the population* PART, subdivision, division, portion, segment, slice, section, sector; proportion, percentage, ratio, measure. ANTONYM whole.

**2** *only a fraction of the collection* TINY PART, fragment, snippet, snatch, smattering, selection. See note at FRAGMENT.

**3** *he moved a fraction closer* TINY AMOUNT, little, bit, touch, soupçon, trifle, mite, shade, jot; *informal* smidgen, smidge, tad.

**fractious** adjective **1** *fractious children* GRUMPY, bad-tempered, irascible, irritable, crotchety, grouchy, cantankerous, short-tempered, tetchy, testy, curmudgeonly, ill-tempered, ill-humored, peevish, cross, waspish, crabby, crusty, prickly, touchy; *informal* snappish, cranky, ornery. ANTONYMS contented, affable.

**2** *the fractious opposition party* WAYWARD, unruly, uncontrollable, unmanageable, out of hand, obstreperous, difficult, headstrong, recalcitrant, intractable; disobedient, insubordinate, disruptive, disorderly, undisciplined; contrary, willful; *formal* refractory; *archaic* contumacious. ANTONYM dutiful.

**fracture** noun **1** *the risk of vertebral fracture* BREAKING, breakage, cracking, fragmentation, splintering, rupture.

**2** *tiny fractures in the rock* CRACK, split, fissure, crevice, break, rupture, breach, rift, cleft, chink, interstice; crazing.

▸ verb *the glass fractured* BREAK, crack, shatter, splinter, split, rupture; *informal* bust.

**fragile** adjective **1** *fragile porcelain* BREAKABLE, easily broken; delicate, dainty, fine, flimsy; eggshell; *formal* frangible. ANTONYMS durable, robust.

**2** *the fragile cease-fire* TENUOUS, shaky, insecure, unreliable, vulnerable, flimsy. ANTONYM durable.

**3** *she is still very fragile* WEAK, delicate, frail, debilitated; ill, unwell, ailing, poorly, sickly, infirm, enfeebled. ANTONYM strong.

**fragment** noun **1** *meteorite fragments* PIECE, bit, particle, speck; chip, shard, sliver, splinter; shaving, paring, snippet, scrap, flake, shred, wisp, morsel.

**2** *a fragment of conversation* SNATCH, snippet, scrap, bit.

▸ verb *explosions caused the granite to fragment* BREAK UP, break, break into pieces, crack open/apart, shatter, splinter, fracture; disintegrate, fall to pieces, fall apart.

**THE RIGHT WORD fragment, fraction, part, piece, portion, section, segment**

The whole is equal to the sum of its **parts**—*part* being a general term for any of the components of a whole. But how did the whole come apart? **Fragment** suggests that breakage has occurred (*fragments of pottery*) and often refers to a brittle substance such as glass or pottery. **Segment** suggests that the whole has been separated along natural or pre-existing lines of division (*a segment of an orange*), and **section** suggests a substantial and clearly separate *part* that fits closely with other parts to form the whole (*a section of a bookcase*). **Fraction** usually suggests a less substantial but still clearly delineated *part*(*a fraction of her income*), and a **portion** is a *part* that has been allotted or assigned to someone (*her portion of the program*). Finally, the very frequently used **piece** is any *part* that is separate from the whole.

**fragrance** noun **1** *the fragrance of spring flowers* SWEET SMELL, scent, perfume, bouquet; aroma, redolence, nose. See note at SMELL.

**2** *a bottle of fragrance* PERFUME, scent, eau de toilette, toilet water; eau de cologne, cologne; aftershave.

**fragrant** adjective *an infusion of fragrant herbs* SWEET-SCENTED, sweet-smelling, scented, perfumed, aromatic, odoriferous, odiferous, perfumy; *literary* redolent. ANTONYM smelly.

**frail** adjective **1** *a frail old lady* WEAK, delicate, feeble, enfeebled, debilitated; infirm, ill, ailing, unwell, sickly, poorly, in poor health. See note at WEAK. ANTONYMS strong, fit.

**2** *a frail structure* FRAGILE, breakable, easily damaged, delicate, flimsy, insubstantial, unsteady, unstable, rickety; *formal* frangible. ANTONYMS sturdy, robust.

**frailty** noun **1** *the frailty of old age* INFIRMITY, weakness, enfeeblement, debility; fragility, delicacy; ill health, sickliness. ANTONYM strength.

**2** *his many frailties* WEAKNESS, fallibility; weak point, flaw, imperfection, defect, failing, fault, shortcoming, deficiency, inadequacy, limitation. ANTONYM strength.

**frame** noun **1** *a tubular metal frame* FRAMEWORK, structure, substructure, skeleton, chassis, shell, casing, body, bodywork; support, scaffolding, foundation, infrastructure.

**2** *his tall, slender frame* BODY, figure, form, shape, physique, build, size, proportions.

**3** *a picture frame* SETTING, mount, mounting.

▸ verb **1** *he had the picture framed* MOUNT, set in a frame.

**2** *the legislators who frame the regulations* FORMULATE, draw up, draft, plan, shape, compose, put together, form, devise, create, establish, conceive, think up, originate; *informal* dream up.

PHRASE: **frame of mind** *what was your frame of mind at the* *time just preceding the accident?* MOOD, state of mind, humor, temper, disposition.

**frame-up** noun *informal he spent six years behind bars, the victim of a clever frame-up* CONSPIRACY, plot; trick, trap, entrapment; *informal* put-up job, setup.

**framework** noun **1** *a metal framework* FRAME, substructure, infrastructure, structure, skeleton, chassis, shell, body, bodywork; support, scaffolding, foundation.

**2** *the framework of society* STRUCTURE, shape, fabric, order, scheme, system, organization, construction, configuration, composition, warp and woof; *informal* makeup.

**franchise** noun **1** *the extension of the franchise to women* SUFFRAGE, the vote, the right to vote, voting rights, enfranchisement.

**2** *the company lost its TV franchise* WARRANT, charter, license, permit, authorization, permission, sanction, privilege.

**frank** adjective **1** *he was quite frank with me* CANDID, direct, forthright, plain, plain-spoken, straight, straightforward, explicit, to the point, matter-of-fact; open, honest, truthful, sincere; outspoken, bluff, blunt, unsparing, not afraid to call a spade a spade; *informal* upfront. ANTONYM evasive.

**2** *she looked at the child with frank admiration* OPEN, undisguised, unconcealed, naked, unmistakable, clear, obvious, transparent, patent, manifest, evident, perceptible, palpable; blatant, barefaced, flagrant. ANTONYM concealed.

**frankly** adverb **1** *frankly, I couldn't care less* TO BE FRANK, to be honest, to tell you the truth, to be truthful, in all honesty, as it happens.

**2** *he stated the case quite frankly* CANDIDLY, directly, plainly, straightforwardly, forthrightly, openly, honestly, without beating about the bush, without mincing one's words, without prevarication, point-blank; bluntly, outspokenly, with no holds barred.

**frantic** adjective *the families of the missing passengers were frantic* PANIC-STRICKEN, panicky, beside oneself, at one's wits' end, distraught, overwrought, worked up, agitated, distressed; frenzied, wild, frenetic, fraught, feverish, hysterical, desperate; *informal* in a state, in a tizzy, wound up, het up, in a flap, tearing one's hair out. ANTONYM calm.

**fraternity** noun **1** *a spirit of fraternity* BROTHERHOOD, fellowship, kinship, friendship, (mutual) support, solidarity, community, union, togetherness; sisterhood.

**2** *the teaching fraternity* PROFESSION, body of workers; band, group, set, circle.

**3** *a college fraternity* SOCIETY, club, association; group, set.

**fraternize** verb *the musicians were told not to fraternize with the dancers* ASSOCIATE, mix, consort, socialize, keep company, rub elbows; *informal* hang around, hang out, run around, hobnob, be thick with.

**fraud** noun **1** *he was arrested for fraud* FRAUDULENCE, cheating, swindling, embezzlement, deceit, deception, double-dealing, chicanery, sharp practice.

**2** *social insurance frauds* SWINDLE, racket, deception, trick, cheat, hoax; *informal* scam, con, rip-off, sting, gyp, fiddle, bunco, hustle, grift.

**3** *they exposed him as a fraud* IMPOSTOR, fake, sham, charlatan, quack, mountebank; swindler, gonif, snake oil salesman, fraudster, racketeer, cheat, confidence trickster; *informal* phony, con man, con artist, scam artist.

**fraudulent** adjective *a fraudulent stock transaction* DISHONEST, cheating, swindling, corrupt, criminal, illegal, unlawful, illicit; deceitful, double-dealing, duplicitous, dishonorable, unscrupulous, unprincipled; *informal* crooked, shady, dirty. ANTONYM honest.

**fraught** adjective **1** *their world is* ***fraught with*** *danger* FULL OF, filled with, rife with; attended by, accompanied by.

**2** *she sounded a bit fraught* ANXIOUS, worried, stressed, upset, distraught, overwrought, worked up, antsy, agitated, distressed, distracted, desperate, frantic, panic-stricken, panic-struck, panicky; beside oneself, at one's wits' end, at the end of one's tether/rope; *informal* wound up, in a state, in a flap, in a cold sweat, tearing one's hair out, having kittens.

**fray** verb **1** *cheap fabric soon frays* UNRAVEL, wear, wear thin, wear out/through, become worn.

**2** *her nerves were frayed* STRAIN, tax, overtax, put on edge.

**freak** noun **1** *a genetically engineered freak* ABERRATION, abnormality, irregularity, oddity; monster, monstrosity, mutant; freak of nature.

**2** *the accident was a complete freak* ANOMALY, aberration, rarity, oddity, unusual occurrence; fluke, twist of fate.

**3** *informal they were dismissed as a bunch of freaks* ODDITY, eccentric, misfit; crank, lunatic; *informal* oddball, weirdo, nutcase, nut, wacko, kook.

**4** *informal a fitness freak* ENTHUSIAST, fan, devotee, lover, aficionado; *informal* fiend, nut, fanatic, addict, maniac.

▸ adjective *a freak storm* | *a freak result* UNUSUAL, anomalous, aberrant, atypical, unrepresentative, irregular, fluky, exceptional, unaccountable, bizarre, queer, peculiar, odd, freakish; unpredictable, unforeseeable, unexpected, unanticipated, surprising; rare, singular, isolated. ANTONYM normal.

▸ verb *informal he* ***freaked out*** GO CRAZY, go mad, go out of one's mind, go to pieces, crack, snap, lose control; panic, become hysterical; *informal* lose it, lose one's cool, crack up, go ape, go postal.

**free** adjective **1** *admission is free* WITHOUT CHARGE, free of charge, for nothing; complimentary, gratis; *informal* for free, on the house.

**2** *she was* ***free of*** *any pressures* UNENCUMBERED BY, unaffected by, clear of, without, rid of; exempt from, not liable to, safe from, immune to, excused from; *informal* sans, minus.

**3** *I'm free this afternoon* UNOCCUPIED, not busy, available, between appointments; off duty, off work, off; on vacation, on leave; at leisure, with time on one's hands, with time to spare. ANTONYMS busy, occupied, unavailable.

**4** *the bathroom's free now* VACANT, empty, available, unoccupied, not taken, not in use. ANTONYM occupied.

**5** *a citizen of a free nation* INDEPENDENT, self-governing, self-governed, self-ruling, self-determining, nonaligned, sovereign, autonomous; democratic. ANTONYM dependent.

**6** *the killer is still free* ON THE LOOSE, at liberty, at large; loose, unconfined, unbound, untied, unchained, untethered, unshackled, unfettered, unrestrained. ANTONYM captive.

**7** *you are free to leave* ALLOWED, permitted; ABLE, in a position to. ANTONYM unable.

**8** *the free flow of water* UNIMPEDED, unobstructed, unrestricted, unhampered, clear, open, unblocked. ANTONYM obstructed.

**9** *she was free with her money* GENEROUS, liberal, open-handed, unstinting, bountiful; lavish, extravagant, prodigal. ANTONYM mean.

**10** *his free and hearty manner* FRANK, open, candid, direct, plain-spoken; unrestrained, unconstrained, free and easy, uninhibited.

▸ verb **1** *three of the hostages were freed* RELEASE, set free, let go, liberate, discharge, deliver; set loose, let loose, turn loose, untie, unchain, unfetter, unshackle, unleash; *literary* disenthrall. ANTONYMS confine, lock up.

**2** *the victims were freed by firefighters* EXTRICATE, release, get out, pull out, pull free; rescue, set free. ANTONYM trap.

**3** *they wish to be freed from all legal ties* EXEMPT, except, excuse, relieve, unburden, disburden.

PHRASES: **free and easy** *the restaurant's free and easy atmosphere* EASYGOING, relaxed, casual, informal, unceremonious, unforced, natural, open, spontaneous, uninhibited, friendly; tolerant, liberal; *informal* laid-back.
**a free hand** *he was allowed a free hand in appointing new staff* FREE REIN, carte blanche, freedom, liberty, license, latitude, leeway, a blank check.

**freedom** noun **1** *a desperate bid for freedom* LIBERTY, liberation, release, deliverance, delivery, discharge; *literary* disenthrallment; *historical* manumission. See note at LIBERTY. ANTONYM captivity.

**2** *revolution was the only path to freedom* INDEPENDENCE, self-government, self-determination, self-rule, home rule, sovereignty, nonalignment, autonomy; democracy. ANTONYM dependence.

**3** *freedom from local political accountability* EXEMPTION, immunity, dispensation; impunity. ANTONYM liability.

**4** *freedom to choose your course of treatment* RIGHT, entitlement, privilege, prerogative; scope, latitude, leeway, flexibility, space, breathing space, room, elbow room; license, leave, free rein, a free hand, carte blanche, a blank check. ANTONYM restriction.

**freeze** verb **1** *the stream had frozen* ICE OVER, ice up, solidify. ANTONYMS thaw, melt.

**2** *my fingers froze* become frozen, become frostbitten. ANTONYMS thaw, warm up.

**3** *the campers stifled in summer and froze in winter* BE VERY COLD, be numb with cold, turn blue with cold, shiver, be chilled to the bone/marrow. ANTONYM overheat.

**4** *she froze in horror* STOP DEAD, stop in one's tracks, stop, stand (stock) still, go rigid, become motionless, become paralyzed. ANTONYM run away.

**5** *the price of gasoline was frozen* FIX, hold, peg, set; limit, restrict, cap, confine, regulate; hold/keep down. ANTONYM change.

PHRASE: **freeze out** *informal she was frozen out by her husband's relatives* EXCLUDE, leave out, shut out, cut out, ignore, ostracize, spurn, snub, shun, turn one's back on, cold-shoulder, give someone the cold shoulder, leave out in the cold.

**freezing** adjective **1** *a freezing wind* BITTER, bitterly cold, icy, chill, frosty, glacial, wintry, subzero, hypothermic; raw, biting, piercing, bone-chilling, penetrating, cutting, numbing; arctic, polar, Siberian. ANTONYM balmy.

**2** *you must be freezing* FROZEN, extremely cold, numb with cold, chilled to the bone/marrow, frozen stiff, shivery, shivering; *informal* frozen to death. ANTONYM hot.

**freight** noun **1** *freight carried by rail* GOODS, cargo, load, consignment, delivery, shipment; merchandise.

**2** *our reliance on air freight* TRANSPORTATION, transport, conveyance, carriage, portage, haulage.

**frenzied** adjective *frenzied holiday shoppers* FRANTIC, wild, frenetic, hectic, fraught, feverish, fevered, mad, crazed, manic, intense, furious, uncontrolled, out of control. ANTONYM calm.

**frenzy** noun **1** *the crowd whipped itself into a state of frenzy* HYSTERIA, madness, mania, delirium, feverishness, fever, wildness, agitation, turmoil, tumult; wild excitement, euphoria, elation, ecstasy.

**2** *a frenzy of anger* FIT, paroxysm, spasm, bout.

**frequency** noun *the frequency of errors* RATE OF OCCURRENCE, incidence, amount, commonness, prevalence; *Statistics* distribution.

**frequent** adjective **1** *frequent bouts of chest infection* RECURRENT, recurring, repeated, periodic, continual, one after another, successive; many, numerous, lots of, several. ANTONYM few.

**2** *a frequent business traveler* HABITUAL, regular. ANTONYM occasional.

▸ verb *he frequented chic nightclubs* VISIT, patronize, spend time in, visit regularly, be a regular visitor to, haunt; *informal* hang out at.

**frequenter** noun *a* ***frequenter of*** *Ed's Bar & Grill* HABITUÉ OF, patron of, regular at, regular visitor to, regular customer at/of, regular client of, familiar face at.

**frequently** adverb *he frequently attends church* REGULARLY, often, very often, all the time, habitually, customarily, routinely; many times, a lot, many a time, lots of times, again and again, time and again, over and over again, repeatedly, recurrently, continually, oftentimes; *literary* oft, ofttimes.

**fresh** adjective 1 *fresh fruit* NEWLY PICKED, garden-fresh, crisp, unwilted; raw, natural, unprocessed. ANTONYMS stale, processed.

2 *a fresh sheet of paper* CLEAN, blank, empty, clear, white; unused, new, pristine, unmarked, untouched. ANTONYM used.

3 *a fresh approach* NEW, recent, latest, up-to-date, modern, modernistic, ultra-modern, newfangled; original, novel, different, innovative, unusual, unconventional, unorthodox; radical, revolutionary; *informal* offbeat. ANTONYM old.

4 *fresh recruits* YOUNG, youthful; new, inexperienced, naive, untrained, unqualified, untried, raw; *informal* wet behind the ears. ANTONYM experienced.

5 *he felt fresh and happy to be alive* REFRESHED, rested, restored, revived; (as) fresh as a daisy, energetic, vigorous, invigorated, full of vim and vigor, lively, vibrant, spry, sprightly, bright, alert, perky; *informal* full of beans, raring to go, bright-eyed and bushy-tailed, chirpy, chipper. ANTONYM tired.

6 *her fresh complexion* HEALTHY, healthy-looking, clear, bright, youthful, blooming, glowing, unblemished; fair, rosy, rosy-cheeked, pink, ruddy. ANTONYM healthy.

7 *the night air was fresh* COOL, crisp, refreshing, invigorating, tonic; pure, clean, clear, uncontaminated, untainted. ANTONYMS stale, stifling.

8 *a fresh wind* CHILLY, chill, cool, cold, brisk, bracing, invigorating; strong; *informal* nippy. ANTONYMS sultry, warm.

9 *informal don't get fresh with me* IMPUDENT, sassy, saucy, brazen, shameless, forward, bold, cheeky, impertinent, insolent, presumptuous, disrespectful, rude, pert, (as) bold as brass; *informal* lippy, mouthy. ANTONYM polite.

**freshen** verb 1 *this will freshen your breath* REFRESH, deodorize, cleanse; revitalize, restore.

2 *she went to **freshen up** before dinner* WASH, wash up, bathe, shower; tidy oneself (up), spruce oneself up, smarten oneself up, groom oneself, primp oneself; *informal* titivate oneself, doll oneself up; *formal, humorous* perform one's ablutions.

3 *the waitress freshened their coffee* REFILL, top up, fill up, replenish.

**fret** verb 1 *she was fretting about Jonathan* WORRY, be anxious, feel uneasy, be distressed, be upset, upset oneself, concern oneself; agonize, sigh, pine, brood, eat one's heart out.

2 *his absence began to fret her* TROUBLE, bother, concern, perturb, disturb, disquiet, disconcert, distress, upset, alarm, panic, agitate; *informal* eat away at.

**fretful** adjective *the long wait in traffic was making us fretful* DISTRESSED, upset, miserable, unsettled, uneasy, ill at ease, uncomfortable, edgy, agitated, worked up, tense, stressed, restive, fidgety, antsy; querulous, irritable, cross, fractious, peevish, petulant, out of sorts, bad-tempered, irascible, grumpy, crotchety, captious, testy, tetchy, cranky, het up, uptight, twitchy, crabby.

**friction** noun 1 *a lubrication system that reduces friction* ABRASION, rubbing, chafing, grating, rasping, scraping; resistance, drag.

2 *there was considerable friction between father and son* DISCORD, strife, conflict, disagreement, dissension, dissent, infighting, opposition, contention, dispute, disputation, arguing, argument, quarreling, bickering, squabbling, wrangling, fighting, feuding, rivalry; hostility, animosity, antipathy, enmity, antagonism, resentment, acrimony, bitterness, bad feeling, ill feeling, ill will, bad blood. ANTONYM harmony.

**friend** noun 1 *a close friend* COMPANION, soul mate, intimate, confidante, confidant, familiar, alter ego, second self, playmate, playfellow, classmate, schoolmate, workmate; ally, associate; sister, brother; best friend, kindred spirit, bosom buddy, bosom friend; *informal* pal, chum, sidekick, crony, main man, mate, buddy, bud, amigo, compadre, homeboy, homegirl, homie; *archaic* compeer. ANTONYM enemy.

2 *the friends of the National Ballet* PATRON, backer, supporter, benefactor, benefactress, sponsor; well-wisher, defender, champion; *informal* angel.

**friendless** adjective *caring for those who are poor and friendless* ALONE, all alone, by oneself, solitary, lonely, with no one to turn to, lone, without friends, companionless, unbefriended, unpopular, unwanted, unloved, abandoned, rejected, forsaken, shunned, spurned, forlorn, lonesome. ANTONYM popular.

**friendliness** noun *her host's friendliness* AFFABILITY, amiability, geniality, congeniality, bonhomie, cordiality, good nature, good humor, warmth, affection, demonstrativeness, conviviality, joviality, companionability, sociability, gregariousness, camaraderie, neighborliness, hospitableness, approachability, accessibility, openness, kindness, kindliness, sympathy, amenability, benevolence.

**friendly** adjective 1 *a friendly woman* AFFABLE, amiable, genial, congenial, cordial, warm, affectionate, demonstrative, convivial, companionable, sociable, gregarious, outgoing, comradely, neighborly, hospitable, approachable, easy to get on with, accessible, communicative, open, unreserved, easygoing, good-natured, kindly, benign, amenable, agreeable, obliging, sympathetic, well-disposed, benevolent; *informal* chummy, buddy-buddy.

2 *friendly conversation* AMICABLE, congenial, cordial, pleasant, easy, relaxed, casual, informal, unceremonious; close, intimate, familiar. ANTONYM hostile.

3 *a friendly wind swept the boat to the shore* FAVORABLE, advantageous, helpful; lucky, providential. ANTONYM unfavorable.

4 *a kid-friendly hotel* COMPATIBLE, suited, adapted, appropriate.

**friendship** noun 1 *lasting friendships* RELATIONSHIP, close relationship, attachment, mutual attachment, association, bond, tie, link, union.

2 *old ties of love and friendship* AMITY, camaraderie, friendliness, comradeship, companionship, fellowship, fellow feel-

ing, closeness, affinity, rapport, understanding, harmony, unity; intimacy, mutual affection. ANTONYM enmity.

**fright** noun **1** *she was paralyzed with fright* FEAR, fearfulness, terror, horror, alarm, panic, dread, trepidation, dismay, nervousness, apprehension, apprehensiveness, perturbation, disquiet; *informal* jitteriness, twitchiness.

**2** *the experience gave everyone* ***a fright*** A SCARE, a shock, a surprise, a turn, a jolt, a start; the shivers, the shakes; *informal* the jitters, the heebie-jeebies, the willies, the creeps, a cold sweat, butterflies (in one's stomach).

**3** *informal she looked an absolute fright* UGLY SIGHT, eyesore, monstrosity; *informal* mess, sight, state, blot on the landscape.

**frighten** verb *the fighting in the streets frightened us* SCARE, startle, alarm, terrify, petrify, shock, chill, panic, shake, disturb, dismay, unnerve, unman, intimidate, terrorize, cow, daunt; strike terror into, put the fear of God into, chill someone to the bone/marrow, make someone's blood run cold; *informal* scare the living daylights out of, scare stiff, scare someone out of their wits, scare witless, scare to death, scare the pants off, spook, make someone's hair stand on end, make someone jump out of their skin, give someone the heebie-jeebies, make someone's hair curl, scare the bejesus out of; *archaic* affright.

**frightful** adjective *the house was in a frightful mess* HORRIBLE, horrific, ghastly, horrendous, serious, awful, dreadful, terrible, nasty, grim, dire, unspeakable; alarming, shocking, terrifying, harrowing, appalling, fearful; hideous, gruesome, grisly; *informal* horrid; *formal* grievous.

**frigid** adjective **1** *a frigid January night* VERY COLD, bitterly cold, bitter, freezing, frozen, frosty, icy, gelid, chilly, chill, wintry, bleak, subzero, arctic, Siberian, bone-chilling, polar, glacial, hypothermic; *informal* nippy. ANTONYMS hot, tropical.

**2** *frigid politeness* STIFF, formal, stony, wooden, unemotional, passionless, unfeeling, indifferent, unresponsive, unenthusiastic, austere, distant, aloof, remote, reserved, unapproachable; frosty, cold, icy, cool, unsmiling, forbidding, unfriendly, unwelcoming, hostile; *informal* offish, standoffish. ANTONYM friendly.

**frill** noun **1** *a full skirt with a wide frill* RUFFLE, flounce, ruff, furbelow, jabot, peplum, ruche, ruching, fringe; *archaic* purfle.

**2** *a comfortable apartment with no-frills* OSTENTATION, ornamentation, decoration, embellishment, fanciness, fuss, chichi, gilding, excess; trimmings, extras, additions, nonessentials, luxuries, extravagances, superfluities.

**fringe** noun **1** *the city's northern fringe* PERIMETER, periphery, border, borderline, margin, rim, outer edge, edge, extremity, limit; outer limits, limits, borders, bounds, outskirts; *literary* marge. ANTONYM middle.

**2** *the curtains with the yellow fringe* EDGING, edge, border, trimming, frill, flounce, ruffle; tassels; *archaic* purfle.

▸ adjective *fringe theater* UNCONVENTIONAL, unorthodox, alternative, avant-garde, experimental, innovative, left-field, innovatory, radical, extreme; peripheral; off-off Broadway; *informal* offbeat, way out. ANTONYM mainstream.

▸ verb **1** *a robe of gold, fringed with black velvet* TRIM, edge, hem, border, bind, braid; decorate, adorn, ornament, embellish, finish; *archaic* purfle.

**2** *the lake is fringed by a belt of trees* BORDER, edge, bound, skirt, line, surround, enclose, encircle, circle, girdle, encompass, ring; *literary* gird.

**frisk** verb **1** *the spaniels frisked around my ankles* FROLIC, gambol, cavort, caper, scamper, skip, dance, romp, trip, prance, leap, spring, hop, jump, bounce.

**2** *the officer frisked him* SEARCH, check, inspect.

**frisky** adjective *frisky squirrels* LIVELY, bouncy, bubbly, perky, active, energetic, animated, zestful, full of vim and vigor; playful, coltish, skittish, spirited, high-spirited, in high spirits, exuberant; *informal* full of beans, zippy, peppy, bright-eyed and bushy-tailed; *literary* frolicsome.

**fritter** verb *he* ***frittered away*** *his inheritance* SQUANDER, waste, misuse, misspend, dissipate; overspend, spend like water, be prodigal with, run through, get through; *informal* blow, splurge, pour/throw down the drain. ANTONYM save.

**frivolity** noun *everyone needs a little frivolity now and again* LIGHTHEARTEDNESS, levity, joking, jocularity, gaiety, fun, frivolousness, silliness, foolishness, flightiness, skittishness; superficiality, shallowness, flippancy, vacuity, empty-headedness.

**frivolous** adjective **1** *a frivolous girl* SKITTISH, flighty, giddy, silly, foolish, superficial, shallow, irresponsible, thoughtless, featherbrained, empty-headed, peabrained, birdbrained, vacuous, vapid; *informal* dizzy, dippy, ditzy, flaky. ANTONYMS sensible, serious.

**2** *frivolous remarks* FLIPPANT, glib, facetious, joking, jokey, lighthearted; fatuous, inane, senseless, thoughtless; *informal* flip. ANTONYM serious.

**3** *new rules to stop frivolous lawsuits* TIME-WASTING, pointless, trivial, trifling, minor, petty, insignificant, unimportant. ANTONYM important.

**frolic** verb *children frolicked on the sand* PLAY, amuse oneself, romp, disport oneself, frisk, gambol, cavort, caper, cut capers, scamper, skip, dance, prance, leap about, jump about; *dated* sport.

▸ noun *the youngsters enjoyed their frolic* ANTIC, caper, game, romp, escapade; **(frolics)** fun, fun and games, hijinks, merrymaking, amusement, skylarking.

**front** noun **1** *the front of the boat* FORE, foremost part, forepart, anterior, forefront, nose, head; bow, prow; foreground. ANTONYMS rear, back.

**2** *the store's front* FRONTAGE, face, facing, facade; window.

**3** *the battlefield surgeons who work at the front* FRONT LINE, firing line, vanguard, van; trenches.

**4** *the front of the line* HEAD, beginning, start, top, lead. ANTONYM back.

**5** *she kept up a brave front* APPEARANCE, air, face, manner, demeanor, bearing, pose, exterior, veneer, (outward) show, act, pretense, affectation.

**6** *the shop was a front for his real business* COVER, cover-up, false front, blind, disguise, facade, mask, cloak, screen, smokescreen, camouflage.

▸ adjective *the front runners* LEADING, lead, first, foremost; in first place. ANTONYM last.

▸ verb *the houses **fronted on** a reservoir* OVERLOOK, look out on/over, face (toward), lie opposite (to); have a view of, command a view of.

PHRASE: **in front** *it looks as if Carson is now in front* AHEAD, to/at the fore, at the head, up ahead, in the vanguard, in the van, in the lead, leading, coming first; *informal* up front.

**frontier** noun *the lakes sit astride the U.S.-Canadian frontier* BORDER, boundary, borderline, dividing line, demarcation line; perimeter, limit, edge, rim, bounds.

**frost** noun **1** *bushes covered with frost* ICE CRYSTALS, ice, rime, verglas; hoarfrost, ground frost, black frost; *informal* Jack Frost; *archaic* hoar.

**2** *there was frost in his tone* COLDNESS, coolness, frostiness, ice, iciness, frigidity; hostility, unfriendliness, stiffness, aloofness; *informal* standoffishness.

**frosty** adjective **1** *a frosty morning* FREEZING, cold, icy-cold, bitter, bitterly cold, chill, wintry, frigid, glacial, hypothermic, arctic; frozen, icy, gelid; *informal* nippy; *literary* rimy.

**2** *her frosty gaze* COLD, frigid, icy, glacial, unfriendly, inhospitable, unwelcoming, forbidding, hostile, stony, stern, steely, hard.

**froth** noun *the froth on top of his beer* FOAM, head; bubbles, frothiness, fizz, effervescence; lather, suds; scum; *literary* spume.

▸ verb *the liquid frothed up* BUBBLE, fizz, effervesce, foam, lather; churn, seethe; *literary* spume.

**frothy** adjective **1** *a frothy liquid* FOAMING, foamy, bubbling, bubbly, fizzy, sparkling, effervescent, gassy, carbonated; sudsy; *literary* spumy.

**2** *a frothy daytime show* LIGHTWEIGHT, light, superficial, shallow, slight, insubstantial; trivial, trifling, frivolous.

**frown** verb **1** *she frowned at him* SCOWL, glower, glare, lower, make a face, look daggers, give someone a black look; knit/furrow one's brows; *informal* give someone a dirty look. ANTONYM smile.

**2** *public displays of affection were **frowned on*** DISAPPROVE OF, view with disfavor, dislike, look askance at, not take kindly to, take a dim view of, take exception to, object to, have a low opinion of.

**frozen** adjective **1** *the frozen ground* ICY, ice-covered, icebound, frosty, frosted, gelid; frozen solid, hard, (as) hard as iron; *literary* rimy. ANTONYM thawed.

**2** *his hands were frozen* FREEZING, icy, very cold, chilled to the bone/marrow, numb, numbed, frozen stiff, frostbitten; *informal* frozen to death. ANTONYMS hot, boiling.

**frugal** adjective **1** *a hard-working, frugal woman* THRIFTY, economical, careful, cautious, prudent, provident, unwasteful, sparing, scrimping; abstemious, abstinent, austere, self-denying, ascetic, monkish, spartan; parsimonious, miserly, niggardly, cheeseparing, penny-pinching, close-fisted; *informal* tightfisted, tight, stingy. See note at ECONOMICAL. ANTONYM extravagant.

**2** *their frugal breakfast* MEAGER, scanty, scant, paltry, skimpy; plain, simple, spartan, inexpensive, cheap, economical. ANTONYM lavish.

**fruitful** adjective **1** *a fruitful tree* FERTILE, fecund, prolific, high-yielding; fruit-bearing, fruiting. See note at FERTILE. ANTONYM barren.

**2** *fruitful discussions* PRODUCTIVE, constructive, useful, of use, worthwhile, helpful, beneficial, valuable, rewarding, profitable, advantageous, gainful, successful, effective, effectual, well-spent. ANTONYM futile.

**fruition** noun *when the project comes to its fruition, you will be favorably impressed* FULFILLMENT, realization, actualization, materialization, achievement, attainment, accomplishment, resolution; success, completion, consummation, conclusion, close, finish, perfection, maturity, maturation, ripening, ripeness; implementation, execution, performance.

**fruitless** adjective *fruitless negotiations* FUTILE, vain, in vain, to no avail, to no effect, idle; pointless, useless, worthless, wasted, hollow; ineffectual, ineffective, inefficacious; unproductive, unrewarding, frustrating, profitless, unsuccessful, unavailing, barren, for naught; abortive; *archaic* bootless. ANTONYM productive.

**frustrate** verb **1** *his plans were frustrated* THWART, defeat, foil, block, stop, put a stop to, counter, spoil, check, balk, disappoint, forestall, dash, scotch, quash, crush, derail, snooker; obstruct, impede, hamper, hinder, hamstring, stand in the way of; *informal* stymie, foul up, screw up, put the kibosh on, do for; *informal* scuttle. ANTONYMS help, facilitate.

**2** *the delays frustrated her* EXASPERATE, infuriate, annoy, anger, vex, irritate, irk, try someone's patience; disappoint, discontent, dissatisfy, discourage, dishearten, dispirit; *informal* aggravate, bug, miff. ANTONYM please.

**frustration** noun **1** *he clenched his fists in frustration* EXASPERATION, annoyance, anger, vexation, irritation; disappointment, dissatisfaction, discontentment, discontent; *informal* aggravation.

**2** *the frustration of her attempts to introduce changes* THWARTING, defeat, prevention, foiling, blocking, spoiling, circumvention, forestalling, disappointment, derailment; obstruction, hampering, hindering; failure, collapse.

**fuddy-duddy** noun *informal* *stop being such a fuddy-duddy and listen to the kids' music* (OLD) FOGEY, conservative, traditionalist, conformist; fossil, dinosaur, troglodyte, mossback, museum piece, stick-in-the-mud, square, stuffed shirt, dodo.

**fudge** verb **1** *the mayor tried to fudge the issue* EVADE, avoid, dodge, skirt, duck, gloss over; hedge on, prevaricate about, vacillate on, be noncommittal on, stall on, beat around the bush about, equivocate on, hem and haw on; *informal* cop out on, sit on the fence about; *rare* tergiversate about.

**2** *the government has been fudging figures* ADJUST, manipulate, massage, put a spin on, juggle, misrepresent, misreport, bend; tamper with, tinker with, interfere with, doctor, falsify, distort; *informal* cook, fiddle with.

**fuel** noun **1** *the car ran out of fuel* GAS, gasoline, diesel, petroleum, propane; power source; *Brit.* petrol.

**2** *she added more fuel to the fire* FIREWOOD, wood, kindling, logs; coal, coke, anthracite; oil, kerosene, propane, lighter fluid; heat source.

**3** *we all need fuel to keep our bodies going* NOURISHMENT, food, sustenance, nutriment, nutrition.

**4** *his antics added fuel to the opposition's cause* ENCOURAGEMENT, ammunition, stimulus, incentive; provocation, goading.

▸ verb **1** *power stations fueled by low-grade coal* POWER, fire, charge.

**2** *the rumors fueled anxiety among opposition* FAN, feed, stoke up, inflame, intensify, stimulate, encourage, provoke, incite, whip up; sustain, keep alive.

**fugitive** noun *a hunted fugitive* ESCAPEE, runaway, deserter, absconder; refugee.

▸ adjective **1** *a fugitive criminal* ESCAPED, runaway, on the run, on the loose, at large; wanted; *informal* AWOL, on the lam.

**2** *the fugitive nature of life* FLEETING, transient, transitory, ephemeral, fading, momentary, short-lived, short, brief, passing, impermanent, here today and gone tomorrow; *literary* evanescent.

**fulfill** verb **1** *she fulfilled a lifelong ambition to visit Israel* ACHIEVE, attain, realize, actualize, make happen, succeed in, bring to completion, bring to fruition, satisfy.

**2** *she failed to fulfill her duties* CARRY OUT, perform, accomplish, execute, do, discharge, conduct; complete, finish, conclude, perfect.

**3** *they fulfilled the criteria* MEET, satisfy, comply with, conform to, fill, answer.

**fulfilled** adjective *the new job has me feeling fulfilled* SATISFIED, content, contented, happy, pleased; serene, placid, untroubled, at ease, at peace. ANTONYM discontented.

**full** adjective **1** *her glass was full* FILLED, filled up, filled to capacity, filled to the brim, brimming, brimful. ANTONYM empty.

**2** *streets **full of** people* CROWDED WITH, packed with, crammed with, congested with; teeming with, swarming with, thick with, thronged with, overcrowded with, overrun with; abounding with, bursting with, overflowing with; *informal* jam-packed with, wall-to-wall with, stuffed with, chockablock with, chock-full of, bursting at the seams with, packed to the gunwales with, awash with. ANTONYM empty.

**3** *all the seats were full* OCCUPIED, taken, in use, unavailable. ANTONYMS empty, unoccupied.

**4** *I'm full* REPLETE, full up, satisfied, well-fed, sated, satiated, surfeited; gorged, glutted; *informal* stuffed. ANTONYM hungry.

**5** *she'd had a full life* EVENTFUL, interesting, exciting, lively, action-packed, busy, energetic, active. ANTONYM uneventful.

**6** *a full list of available facilities* COMPREHENSIVE, thorough, exhaustive, all-inclusive, all-encompassing, all-embracing, in depth; complete, entire, whole, unabridged, uncut. ANTONYMS selective, incomplete.

**7** *a fire engine driven at full speed* MAXIMUM, top, greatest, highest. ANTONYM low.

**8** *she had a full figure* PLUMP, well-rounded, rounded, buxom, shapely, ample, curvaceous, voluptuous, womanly, Junoesque; *informal* busty, curvy, well-upholstered, well-endowed, zaftig. ANTONYM thin.

**9** *a full skirt* LOOSE-FITTING, loose, baggy, voluminous, roomy, capacious, billowing. ANTONYMS tight, tight-fitting.

**10** *his full baritone voice* RESONANT, rich, sonorous, deep, vibrant, full-bodied, strong, fruity, clear. ANTONYM thin.

**11** *the full flavor of a Bordeaux* RICH, intense, full-bodied, strong, deep. ANTONYMS watery, thin.

▸ adverb **1** *she looked full into his face* DIRECTLY, right, straight, squarely, square, dead, point-blank; *informal* bang, plumb.

**2** *you knew full well I was leaving* VERY, perfectly, quite; *informal* darn, damn, damned, darned; *chiefly Brit.* bloody.

PHRASES: **in full** *my letter was published in full* IN ITS ENTIRETY, in toto, in total, unabridged, uncut.
**to the full** *live your life to the full* FULLY, thoroughly, completely, to the utmost, to the limit, to the maximum, for all one's worth.

**full-grown** adjective *how full-grown men can act so childishly is beyond me* ADULT, mature, grown-up, of age; fully grown, fully developed, fully fledged, in one's prime, in full bloom, ripe. ANTONYM infant.

**fullness** noun **1** *the fullness of the information they provide* COMPREHENSIVENESS, completeness, thoroughness, exhaustiveness, all-inclusiveness.

**2** *the fullness of her body* PLUMPNESS, roundedness, roundness, shapeliness, curvaceousness, voluptuousness, womanliness; *informal* curviness.

**3** *the recording has a fullness and warmth* RESONANCE, richness, intensity, depth, vibrancy, strength, clarity, three-dimensionality. PHRASE: **in the fullness of time** *in the fullness of time, Ricardo would realize they were right* IN DUE COURSE, when the time is ripe, eventually, in time, in time to come, one day, some day, sooner or later; ultimately, finally, in the end.

**full-scale** adjective **1** *a full-scale model* FULL-SIZE, life-size. ANTONYM small-scale.

**2** *a full-scale public inquiry* THOROUGH, comprehensive, extensive, exhaustive, complete, all-out, all-encompassing, all-inclusive, all-embracing, thoroughgoing, wide-ranging, sweeping, in-depth, far-reaching. ANTONYM partial.

**fully** adverb **1** *I fully agree with him* COMPLETELY, entirely, wholly, totally, quite, utterly, perfectly, altogether, thoroughly, in all respects, in every respect, without reservation, without exception, to the hilt. ANTONYMS partly, nearly.

**2** *fully two minutes must have passed* AT LEAST, no less than, no fewer than, easily, without exaggeration. ANTONYM nearly.

**fulminate** verb *homeowners fulminated against the tax hikes* PROTEST, rail against, rage about, rant about, thunder about, storm about, vociferate against, declaim, inveigh against, speak out against, make/take a stand against; denounce, decry, condemn, criticize, censure, disparage, attack, execrate; *informal* mouth off about; *formal* excoriate.

**fulmination** noun *the fulminations of media moralists* PROTEST, objection, complaint, rant, tirade, diatribe, harangue, invective, railing, obloquy; denunciation, condemnation, criticism, censure, attack, broadside, brickbats; *formal* excoriation; *literary* philippic.

**fulsome** adjective *he paid fulsome tribute to his secretary* EXCESSIVE, extravagant, overdone, immoderate, inordinate, over-appreciative, flattering, adulatory, fawning, unctuous, ingratiating, cloying, saccharine; enthusiastic, effusive, rapturous, glowing, gushing, profuse, generous, lavish; *informal* over the top, smarmy.

**fumble** verb **1** *she fumbled for her keys* GROPE, fish, search blindly, scrabble around.

**2** *he fumbled about in the dark* STUMBLE, blunder, flounder, lumber, stagger, totter, lurch; **(fumble about/around)** feel one's way, grope one's way.

**3** *the quarterback fumbled the ball* MISS, drop, mishandle, bobble.

**4** *she fumbled her lines* MESS UP, make a mess of, bungle, mismanage, mishandle, spoil; *informal* make a hash of, fluff, botch, muff, flub.

▸ noun *a fumble from the goaltender* SLIP, mistake, error, gaffe; *informal* slip-up, boo-boo.

**fume** noun **(fumes) 1** *a fire giving off toxic fumes* SMOKE, vapor, gas, effluvium; exhaust; pollution.

**2** *stale wine fumes* SMELL, odor, stink, reek, stench, fetor, funk; *literary* miasma.

▸ verb **1** *fragments of lava were fuming and sizzling* EMIT SMOKE, emit gas, smoke; *archaic* reek.

**2** *Elsa was still fuming at his arrogance* BE FURIOUS, be enraged, be very angry, seethe, be livid, be incensed, boil, be beside oneself, spit; rage, rant and rave; *informal* be hot under the collar, foam at the mouth, see red.

**fumigate** verb *the prisoners' quarters are fumigated once a month* DISINFECT, purify, sterilize, sanitize, decontaminate, cleanse, clean out. ANTONYM soil.

**fun** noun **1** *I joined in with the fun | did you have fun?* ENJOYMENT, entertainment, amusement, pleasure; jollification, merrymaking; recreation, diversion, leisure, relaxation; a good time, a great time; *informal* R and R (rest and recreation), a ball. ANTONYM boredom.

**2** *she's full of fun* MERRIMENT, cheerfulness, cheeriness, jollity, joviality, jocularity, high spirits, gaiety, mirth, laughter, hilarity, glee, gladness, lightheartedness, levity. ANTONYM misery.

**3** *he became a figure of fun* RIDICULE, derision, mockery, laughter, scorn, contempt, jeering, sneering, jibing, teasing, taunting. ANTONYM respect.

▸ adjective *informal a fun evening* ENJOYABLE, entertaining, amusing, diverting, pleasurable, pleasing, agreeable, interesting.

PHRASES: **in fun** *the teasing was all in fun* PLAYFUL, in jest, as a joke, tongue in cheek, lighthearted, for a laugh.

**make fun of** *the kids who made fun of Marty were total jerks* TEASE, poke fun at, ridicule, mock, laugh at, taunt, jeer at, scoff at, deride; parody, lampoon, caricature, satirize; *informal* rib, kid, have on, pull someone's leg, send up, rag on, razz.

**USAGE NOTE fun**

The use of **fun** as an adjective meaning 'enjoyable,' as in *we had a fun evening*, is not fully accepted in standard English and should only be used in informal contexts. There are signs, however, that this situation is changing, given the recent appearance in American English of comparative and superlative forms **funner** and **funnest**, formed as if **fun** were a normal adjective. The adjectival forms **funner** and **funnest** have not 'arrived' in all the dictionaries, however, and if employed at all, they should be used sparingly and not in formal written English.

**function** noun **1** *the main function of the machine* PURPOSE, task, use, role.

**2** *my function was to select and train the recruits* RESPONSIBILITY, duty, role, concern, province, activity, assignment, obligation, charge; task, job, mission, undertaking, commission; capacity, post, situation, office, occupation, employment, business.

**3** *a function attended by local dignitaries* SOCIAL EVENT, party, social occasion, affair, gathering, reception, soiree, jamboree, gala, meet-and-greet; *informal* do, bash, shindig.

▸ verb **1** *the electrical system had ceased to function* WORK, go, run, be in working/running order, operate, be operative.

**2** *the museum **functions as** an educational center* ACT AS, serve as, operate as; perform as, work as, play the role of, do duty as.

**functional** adjective **1** *a small functional kitchen* PRACTICAL, useful, utilitarian, utility, workaday, serviceable; minimalist, plain, simple, basic, modest, unadorned, unostentatious, no-frills, without frills; impersonal, characterless, soulless, institutional, clinical.

**2** *the machine is now fully functional* WORKING, in working order, functioning, in service, in use; going, running, operative, operating, in operation, in commission, in action; *informal* up and running.

**functionary** noun *a Capitol Hill functionary* OFFICIAL, officeholder, public servant, civil servant, bureaucrat, administrator, apparatchik; *informal* bean counter.

**fund** noun **1** *an emergency fund for refugees* COLLECTION, kitty, reserve, pool, purse; endowment, foundation, trust, grant, investment; savings, nest egg; *informal* stash.

**2** (**funds**) *I was very short of funds* MONEY, cash, ready money; wealth, means, assets, resources, savings, capital, reserves, the wherewithal; *informal* dough, bread, loot.

**3** *his fund of stories* STOCK, store, supply, accumulation, collection, bank, pool; mine, reservoir, storehouse, treasury, treasure house, hoard, repository; *informal* pork barrel.

▸ verb *the agency was funded by a federal grant* FINANCE, pay for, back, capitalize, sponsor, put up the money for, subsidize, underwrite, endow, support, maintain; *informal* foot the bill for, pick up the tab for, bankroll, stake.

**fundamental** adjective *fundamental principles* BASIC, underlying, core, foundational, rudimentary, elemental, elementary, basal, root; primary, prime, cardinal, first, principal, chief, key, central, vital, essential, important, indispensable, necessary, crucial, pivotal, critical; structural, organic, constitutional, inherent, intrinsic. ANTONYMS secondary, unimportant.

**fundamentally** adverb *she was, fundamentally, a good person* ESSENTIALLY, in essence, basically, at heart, at bottom, deep down, au fond; primarily, above all, first and foremost, first of all; *informal* at the end of the day, when all is said and done, when you get right down to it.

**fundamentals** plural noun *the fundamentals of the job* BASICS, essentials, rudiments, foundations, basic principles, first principles, preliminaries; crux, crux of the matter, heart of the matter, essence, core, heart, base, bedrock; *informal* nuts and bolts, nitty-gritty, brass tacks, ABC, meat and potatoes.

**funeral** noun **1** *he'd attended a funeral* BURIAL, interment, entombment, committal, inhumation, laying to rest; cremation; obsequies, last offices, memorial service; *archaic* sepulture.

**2** *informal* *ignore my advice if you like—it's your funeral* RESPONSIBILITY, problem, worry, concern, business, affair; *informal* headache.

**funereal** adjective **1** *the funereal atmosphere* SOMBER, gloomy, mournful, melancholy, lugubrious, sepulchral, miserable, doleful, woeful, sad, sorrowful, cheerless, joyless, bleak, dismal, depressing, dreary; grave, solemn, serious; *literary* dolorous. ANTONYM cheerful.

**2** *funereal colors* DARK, black, drab.

**fungus** noun *the fungus will flourish in a dark, moist environment* MUSHROOM, toadstool; mold, mildew, rust; *Biology* saprophyte.

**funny** adjective **1** *a funny movie* | *these guys are really funny* AMUSING, humorous, witty, comic, comical, droll, facetious, jocular, jokey; hilarious, hysterical, riotous, uproarious; entertaining, diverting, sparkling, scintillating; silly, farcical, slapstick; *informal* side-splitting, rib-tickling, laugh-a-minute, wacky, zany, off the wall, a scream, rich, priceless; *informal, dated* killing. ANTONYMS serious, unamusing.

**2** *a funny coincidence* STRANGE, peculiar, odd, queer, weird, bizarre, curious, freakish, freak, quirky; mysterious, mystifying, puzzling, perplexing; unusual, uncommon, anomalous, irregular, abnormal, exceptional, singular, out of the ordinary, extraordinary.

**3** *there's something funny about him* SUSPICIOUS, suspect, dubious, untrustworthy, questionable; *informal* shady, sketchy, fishy. ANTONYM trustworthy.

**furious** adjective **1** *she was furious when she learned about it* ENRAGED, infuriated, very angry, irate, incensed, raging, incandescent, fuming, ranting, raving, seething, beside oneself, outraged; *informal* mad, hopping mad, wild, livid, boiling, apoplectic, hot under the collar, on the warpath, foaming at the mouth, steamed up, fit to be tied; *literary* wrathful. ANTONYM calm.

**2** *a furious debate* HEATED, hot, passionate, fiery, "lively"; fierce, vehement, violent, wild, unrestrained, tumultuous, turbulent, tempestuous, stormy. ANTONYM calm.

**furnish** verb **1** *the bedrooms are elegantly furnished* FIT OUT, provide with furniture, appoint, outfit.

**2** *grooms furnished us with horses for our journey* SUPPLY, provide, equip, provision, issue, kit out, present, give, offer, afford, purvey, bestow; *informal* fix up.

**furniture** noun *most of the bedroom furniture is mahogany* FURNISHINGS, fittings, movables, appointments, effects; *Law* chattels; *informal* stuff, things.

**furor** noun *her memoirs caused a furor* COMMOTION, uproar, outcry, fuss, upset, brouhaha, foofaraw, palaver, pother, tempest, agitation, pandemonium, disturbance, hubbub, rumpus, tumult, turmoil; stir, excitement; *informal* song and dance, to-do, hoo-ha, hullabaloo, ballyhoo, flap, stink.

**furrow** noun **1** *furrows in a plowed field* GROOVE, trench, rut, trough, channel, hollow.

**2** *the furrows on either side of her mouth* WRINKLE, line, crease, crinkle, crow's foot, corrugation.

▸ verb *his brow furrowed* WRINKLE, crease, line, crinkle, pucker, screw up, scrunch up, corrugate.

**further** adverb **1** *further information* ADDITIONAL, more, extra, supplementary, supplemental, other; new, fresh.

**2** *further, it gave him an excellent excuse not to attend.* See FURTHERMORE.

**3** *she's transferring to a school further from home.* See FARTHER.

▸ adjective *the further end of the hall.* See FARTHER.

▸ verb *an attempt to further his career* PROMOTE, advance, forward, develop, facilitate, aid, assist, help, help along, lend a hand to, abet; expedite, hasten, speed up, catalyze, accelerate, step up, spur on, oil the wheels of, give a push to, boost, encourage, cultivate, nurture, foster. See note at FARTHER. ANTONYM impede.

**furtherance** noun *the furtherance of his business interests* PROMOTION, furthering, advancement, forwarding, development, facilitation, aiding, assisting, helping, abetting; hastening, acceleration, boosting, encouragement, cultivation, nurturing, fostering. ANTONYM hindrance.

**furthermore** adverb *furthermore, you'll have access to a better library* MOREOVER, further, what's more, also, additionally, in addition, besides, as well, too, to boot, on top of that, over and above that, into the bargain, by the same token; *archaic* withal.

**furthest** adjective *the furthest car on the left is mine.* See FARTHEST.

▸ adverb *Lynda had to walk the furthest.* See FARTHEST. See note at FARTHER.

**furtive** adjective *they met in seedy dives to craft their furtive plans* SECRETIVE, secret, surreptitious, clandestine, hidden, covert, conspiratorial, cloak-and-dagger, backroom, backstairs, sly, sneaky, under-the-table; sidelong, sideways, oblique, indirect; *informal* hush-hush, shifty. See note at SECRET. ANTONYM open.

**fury** noun **1** *she exploded with fury* RAGE, anger, wrath, outrage, spleen, temper; crossness, indignation, umbrage, annoyance, exasperation; *literary* ire, choler. ANTONYM good humor.

**2** *the fury of the storm* FIERCENESS, ferocity, violence, turbulence, tempestuousness, savagery; severity, intensity, vehemence, force, forcefulness, power, strength. ANTONYM mildness.

**3** *she turned on her mother like a fury* VIRAGO, hellcat, termagant, spitfire, vixen, shrew, harridan, dragon, gorgon; **(Furies)** *Greek Mythology* Eumenides.

**fuse** verb **1** *a band that fuses rap with rock* COMBINE, amalgamate, put together, join, unite, marry, blend, merge, meld, mingle, integrate, intermix, intermingle, synthesize; coalesce, compound, alloy; *technical* admix; *literary* commingle. ANTONYM separate.

**2** *metal fused to a base of colored glass* BOND, stick, bind, weld, solder; melt, smelt. ANTONYM disconnect.

**fuss** noun **1** *what's all the fuss about?* ADO, excitement, agitation, pother, stir, commotion, confusion, disturbance, brouhaha, uproar, furor, palaver, foofaraw, tempest in a teapot, much ado about nothing; bother, fluster, flurry, bustle; *informal* hoo-ha, to-do, ballyhoo, song and dance, performance, pantomime.

**2** *they settled in with very little fuss* BOTHER, trouble, inconvenience, effort, exertion, labor; *informal* hassle.

**3** *he didn't put up a fuss* PROTEST, complaint, objection, grumble, grouse; *informal* gripe.

▸ verb *he was still **fussing over** his clothes* WORRY ABOUT, fret about, be anxious about, be agitated about, make a big thing out of; *informal* flap about, be in a tizzy over/about, be in a stew over/about.

**fussy** adjective **1** *he's very fussy about what he eats* FINICKY, particular, overparticular, fastidious, discriminating, selective, dainty; hard to please, difficult, exacting, demanding; faddish; *informal* persnickety, choosy, picky.

**2** *a fussy, frilly bridal gown* OVERELABORATE, overdecorated, ornate, fancy, overdone; busy, cluttered.

**futile** adjective *they piled on thousands of sandbags in a futile attempt to hold back the river* FRUITLESS, vain, pointless, useless, ineffectual, ineffective, inefficacious, to no effect, of no use, in vain, to no avail, unavailing; unsuccessful, failed, thwarted; unproductive, barren, unprofitable, abortive; impotent, hollow, empty, forlorn, idle, hopeless; *archaic* bootless. ANTONYM useful.

**futility** noun *the futility of his actions* FRUITLESSNESS, pointlessness, uselessness, vanity, ineffectiveness, inefficacy; failure, barrenness, unprofitability; impotence, hollowness, emptiness, forlornness, hopelessness.

**future** noun **1** *his plans for **the future*** THE TIME TO COME, the time ahead; what lies ahead, (the) coming times. ANTONYM past.

**2** *she knew her future lay in acting* DESTINY, fate, fortune; prospects, expectations, chances.

▸ adjective **1** *a future date* LATER, to come, following, ensuing, succeeding, subsequent, coming.

**2** *his future wife* TO BE, destined; intended, planned, prospective.

PHRASE: **in future** *in future, let's bring plenty of extra batteries* FROM NOW ON, after this, in the future, from this day forward, hence, henceforward, subsequently, in time to come, down the road; *formal* hereafter.

**fuzzy** adjective **1** *her fuzzy hair* FRIZZY, fluffy, woolly; downy, soft.

**2** *a fuzzy picture* BLURRY, blurred, indistinct, unclear, bleary, misty, distorted, out of focus, unfocused, lacking definition, nebulous; ill-defined, indefinite, vague, hazy, imprecise, inexact, loose, woolly.

**3** *my mind was fuzzy* CONFUSED, muddled, addled, fuddled, befuddled, groggy, disoriented, disorientated, mixed up, fazed, foggy, dizzy, stupefied, benumbed.

**gad** verb *informal she's been **gadding about** in Europe* GALLIVANT ABOUT, traipse around, flit around, run around, travel around, roam (about/around).

**gadabout** noun *informal Marc and Patty linked up with some other gadabouts in Paris* PLEASURE-SEEKER; traveler, globe-trotter, wanderer, drifter.

**gadget** noun *Everett had to buy every new gadget on the market* APPLIANCE, apparatus, instrument, implement, tool, utensil, contrivance, contraption, machine, mechanism, device, labor-saving device, convenience, invention; *informal* gizmo, widget.

**gaffe** noun *I made some real gaffes at work* BLUNDER, mistake, error, slip, faux pas, indiscretion, impropriety, miscalculation, gaucherie, solecism; *informal* slip-up, howler, boo-boo, fluff, flub, blooper, goof.

**gag**[1] verb **1** *a dirty rag was used to gag her mouth* SMOTHER, block, plug, stifle, stop up, muffle.

**2** *the government tried to gag its critics* SILENCE, muzzle, mute, muffle, suppress, stifle; censor, curb, check, restrain, fetter, shackle, restrict.

**3** *the stench made her gag* RETCH, heave, dry-heave.

▸ noun *his scream was muffled by the gag* MUZZLE, tie, restraint.

**gag**[2] noun *informal a film full of lame gags* JOKE, jest, witticism, quip, pun, play on words, double entendre; practical joke, stunt, lark; *informal* crack, wisecrack, one-liner.

**gaiety** noun **1** *the gaiety of Susannah's youth had been supplanted by the cares of widowhood* CHEERFULNESS, lightheartedness, happiness, merriment, glee, gladness, joy, joie de vivre, joyfulness, joyousness, delight, high spirits, good spirits, good humor, cheeriness, jollity, mirth, joviality, exuberance, elation; liveliness, vivacity, animation, effervescence, sprightliness, zest, zestfulness; *informal* chirpiness, bounce, pep; *literary* blitheness. ANTONYM misery.

**2** *the hotel restaurant was a scene of gaiety* MERRYMAKING, festivity, fun, fun and games, frolics, revelry, jollification, celebration, pleasure; *informal* partying; *dated* sport.

**gain** verb **1** *he gained a scholarship to the college* OBTAIN, get, secure, acquire, come by, procure, attain, achieve, earn, win, garner, capture, clinch, pick up, carry off, reap; *informal* land, net, bag, scoop, wangle, swing, walk away/off with. See note at GET. ANTONYM lose.

**2** *they stood to gain from the deal* PROFIT, make money, reap benefits, benefit, do well; *informal* make a killing. ANTONYM lose.

**3** *the dog gained weight* PUT ON, increase in. ANTONYM lose.

**4** *the others were **gaining on** us* CATCH UP WITH/ON, catch someone up, catch, close (in) on, near.

**5** *we finally gained the ridge* REACH, arrive at, get to, come to, make, attain, set foot on; *informal* hit, wind up at.

▸ noun **1** *his gain from the deal* PROFIT, advantage, benefit, reward; percentage, takings, yield, return, winnings, receipts, proceeds, dividend, interest; *informal* pickings, cut, take, divvy, slice, piece of the pie. ANTONYM loss.

**2** *a price gain of 7.5 percent* INCREASE, rise, increment, augmentation, addition. ANTONYM decrease.

PHRASE: **gain time** *the district attorney had run out of plausible ways to gain time* PLAY FOR TIME, stall, procrastinate, delay, temporize, hold back, hang back, hang fire, dally, drag one's feet.

**gainful** adjective *a gainful investment* PROFITABLE, paid, well-paid, remunerative, lucrative, moneymaking; rewarding, fruitful, worthwhile, useful, productive, constructive, beneficial, advantageous, valuable.

**gainsay** verb *formal it was difficult to gainsay his claim* DENY, dispute, disagree with, argue with, dissent from, contradict, repudiate, challenge, oppose, contest, counter, controvert, rebut. ANTONYM confirm.

**gait** noun *there was a new liveliness to her gait* WALK, step, stride, pace, tread, bearing, carriage; *formal* comportment.

**gala** noun *the annual summer gala* FÊTE, fair, festival, carnival, pageant, jubilee, jamboree, party, garden party, celebration; festivities.

▸ adjective *a gala occasion* FESTIVE, celebratory, merry, joyous, joyful; diverting, entertaining, enjoyable, spectacular.

**galaxy** noun *the search for life in other galaxies* STAR SYSTEM, solar system, constellation; stars, heavens.

**gale** noun **1** *a howling gale.* See STORM noun sense 1.

2 *gales of laughter* PEAL, howl, hoot, shriek, scream, roar; outburst, burst, fit, paroxysm, explosion.

**gall**[1] noun 1 *she had the gall to ask for money* EFFRONTERY, impudence, impertinence, cheek, cheekiness, insolence, audacity, temerity, presumption, cockiness, nerve, shamelessness, disrespect, bad manners; *informal* face, chutzpah; sauce, sass. See note at TEMERITY.

2 *scholarly gall was poured on this work* BITTERNESS, resentment, rancor, bile, spleen, malice, spite, spitefulness, malignity, venom, vitriol, poison.

**gall**[2] noun 1 *this was a gall that she frequently had to endure* IRRITATION, irritant, annoyance, vexation, nuisance, provocation, bother, torment, plague, thorn in one's side/flesh; *informal* aggravation, bore, headache, hassle, pain, pain in the neck, pain in the butt.

2 *a bay horse with a gall on its side* SORE, ulcer, ulceration; abrasion, scrape, scratch, graze, chafe.

▸ verb *it galled him that he had to wake early* IRRITATE, annoy, vex, anger, infuriate, exasperate, irk, pique, nettle, put out, displease, antagonize, get on someone's nerves, make someone's hackles rise, rub the wrong way; *informal* aggravate, peeve, miff, rile, needle, get (to), bug, get someone's goat, get/put someone's back up, get someone's dander up, drive mad/crazy, drive round/around the bend, drive up the wall, tee off, tick off, rankle.

**gallant** adjective 1 *his gallant countrymen* BRAVE, courageous, valiant, valorous, bold, plucky, daring, fearless, intrepid, heroic, lionhearted, stouthearted, doughty, mettlesome, dauntless, undaunted, unflinching, unafraid; *informal* gutsy, spunky. ANTONYM cowardly.

2 *her gallant companion* CHIVALROUS, princely, gentlemanly, honorable, courteous, polite, mannerly, attentive, respectful, gracious, considerate, thoughtful. ANTONYM discourteous.

**gallantry** noun 1 *he received medals for gallantry* BRAVERY, courage, courageousness, valor, pluck, pluckiness, nerve, daring, boldness, fearlessness, dauntlessness, intrepidity, heroism, mettle, grit, stoutheartedness; *informal* guts, spunk, moxie.

2 *she acknowledged his selfless gallantry* CHIVALRY, chivalrousness, gentlemanliness, courtesy, courteousness, politeness, good manners, attentiveness, graciousness, respectfulness, respect.

**galling** adjective *his hypocrisy was galling* ANNOYING, irritating, vexing, vexatious, infuriating, maddening, irksome, provoking, exasperating, trying, tiresome, troublesome, bothersome, displeasing, disagreeable; *informal* aggravating.

**gallivant** verb *my days of gallivanting are long past* FLIT, jaunt, run; roam, wander, travel, rove; *informal* gad.

**gallop** verb *Paul galloped across the clearing* RUSH, race, run, sprint, bolt, dart, dash, career, charge, shoot, hurtle, careen, hare, fly, speed, zoom, streak; *informal* tear, belt, pelt, scoot, zip, whip, hotfoot it, hightail it, bomb, barrel. ANTONYM amble.

**gallows** plural noun 1 *the wooden gallows* GIBBET, scaffold, gallows tree.

2 *they were condemned to* ***the gallows*** HANGING, being hanged, the noose, the rope, the gibbet, the scaffold, execution.

**galore** adjective *up in the attic were old trunks and hatboxes galore* APLENTY, in abundance, in profusion, in great quantities, in large numbers, by the dozen; to spare; everywhere, all over (the place); *informal* by the truckload.

**galvanize** verb *the reverend's words galvanized our group into action* JOLT, shock, startle, impel, stir, spur, prod, urge, motivate, stimulate, electrify, excite, rouse, arouse, awaken; invigorate, fire, animate, vitalize, energize, exhilarate, thrill, catalyze, inspire, light a fire under; *informal* give someone a shot in the arm.

**gambit** noun *the most ambitious financial gambit in history* STRATAGEM, scheme, plan, tactic, maneuver, move, course/line of action, device; machination, ruse, trick, ploy, wangle.

**gamble** verb 1 *he started to gamble more often* BET, place/lay a bet on something, stake money on something, back the horses, game; *informal* play the ponies.

2 *investors are gambling that the British pound will fall* TAKE A CHANCE, take a risk; *informal* stick one's neck out, go out on a limb.

▸ noun 1 *his grandfather enjoyed a gamble* BET, wager, speculation; game of chance.

2 *I took a gamble and it paid off* RISK, chance, hazard, shot in the dark, leap of faith; pig in a poke, pot luck; *rare* salto.

**gambol** verb *lambs gamboled in the pasture* FROLIC, frisk, cavort, caper, skip, dance, romp, prance, leap, hop, jump, spring, bound, bounce; play; *dated* sport.

**game** noun 1 *Andrew and his friends invented a new game* PASTIME, diversion, entertainment, amusement, distraction, divertissement, recreation, sport, activity.

2 *the team hasn't lost a game all season* MATCH, contest, tournament, meet; final, playoff.

3 *I spoiled his little game* SCHEME, plot, ploy, stratagem, strategy, gambit, tactics; trick, device, maneuver, wile, dodge, ruse, machination, contrivance, subterfuge; prank, practical joke; *informal* scam; *archaic* shift.

4 *she lived off fish and game* WILD ANIMALS, wild fowl, big game.

▸ adjective 1 *they weren't game enough to join in* BRAVE, courageous, plucky, bold, daring, intrepid, valiant, stouthearted, mettlesome; fearless, dauntless, undaunted, unflinching; *informal* gutsy, spunky.

2 *I need a bit of help—are you game?* WILLING, prepared, ready, disposed, of a mind; eager, keen, enthusiastic, up for it.

▸ verb *they were drinking and gaming all evening* GAMBLE, bet, place/lay bets.

**gamut** noun *the complete gamut of human emotion* RANGE,

spectrum, span, scope, sweep, compass, area, breadth, reach, extent, catalog, scale; variety. See note at RANGE.

**gang** noun **1** *a gang of tough-looking boys* BAND, group, crowd, pack, horde, throng, mob, herd, swarm, troop, cluster; company, gathering; *informal* posse, bunch, gaggle, load.

**2** *informal Shania was one of our gang* CIRCLE, social circle, social set, group, clique, in-crowd, coterie, cabal, lot, ring; *informal* crew, rat pack.

**3** *a gang of workmen* CREW, team, group, squad, shift, detachment, unit.

▸ verb *they all* ***ganged up*** *to put me down* CONSPIRE, cooperate, collude, work together, act together, combine, join forces, team up, get together, unite, ally.

**gangster** noun *Prohibition was a boon era for gangsters* HOODLUM, gang member, racketeer, robber, ruffian, thug, tough, villain, lawbreaker, criminal; gunman; Mafioso; *informal* mobster, crook, lowlife, hit man, hood; *dated* desperado.

**gap** noun **1** *a gap in the shutters* OPENING, aperture, space, breach, chink, slit, slot, vent, crack, crevice, cranny, cavity, hole, orifice, interstice, perforation, break, fracture, rift, rent, fissure, cleft, divide.

**2** *a gap between meetings* PAUSE, intermission, interval, interlude, break, breathing space, breather, respite, hiatus, recess.

**3** *a gap in our records* OMISSION, blank, lacuna, void, vacuity.

**4** *the gap between rich and poor* CHASM, gulf, rift, split, separation, breach; contrast, difference, disparity, divergence, imbalance.

**gape** verb **1** *she gaped at him in astonishment* STARE, stare open-mouthed, stare in wonder, goggle, gaze, ogle; *informal* rubberneck, gawk.

**2** *a padded coat that gaped at every seam* OPEN WIDE, open up, yawn; part, split.

**garb** noun *men and women in riding garb* CLOTHES, clothing, garments, attire, dress, costume, outfit, wear, uniform, livery, regalia; *informal* gear, getup, togs, duds; *formal* apparel; *archaic* raiment, habiliment, vestments.

▸ verb *both men were garbed in black* DRESS, clothe, attire, fit out, turn out, deck (out), costume, robe; *informal* get up; *archaic* apparel.

**garbage** noun **1** *the garbage is taken to landfill sites* TRASH, rubbish, refuse, waste, detritus, litter, junk, scrap; scraps, leftovers, remains, slops; *informal* crap.

**2** *most of what he says is garbage* NONSENSE, balderdash, claptrap, twaddle, blather; dross, rubbish; *informal* hogwash, baloney, tripe, jive, bilge, bull, crap, bunk, poppycock, piffle, bunkum.

**garble** verb *the message was garbled in transmission* MIX UP, muddle, jumble, confuse, obscure, distort, scramble; misstate, misquote, misreport, misrepresent, mistranslate, misinterpret, misconstrue, twist.

**gargantuan** adjective *a gargantuan wedding cake* HUGE, enormous, vast, gigantic, very big, giant, massive, colossal, mammoth, immense, mighty, monumental, mountainous, titanic, towering, tremendous, elephantine, king-size(d), economy-size(d), prodigious; *informal* mega, monster, whopping, humongous, jumbo, ginormous. ANTONYM tiny.

**garish** adjective *garish party decorations* GAUDY, lurid, loud, harsh, glaring, violent, showy, glittering, brassy, brash; tasteless, in bad taste, tawdry, vulgar, unattractive, bilious; *informal* flash, flashy, tacky, tinselly, neon. ANTONYM drab.

**garland** noun *a garland of flowers* FESTOON, lei, wreath, ring, circle, swag; coronet, crown, coronal, chaplet, fillet.

▸ verb *gardens garlanded with colored lights* FESTOON, wreathe, swathe, hang; adorn, ornament, embellish, decorate, deck, trim, dress, bedeck, array; *literary* bedizen.

**garment** noun *the brown tweed is a lovely garment | all of her garments seem to be red* ITEM OF CLOTHING, article of clothing; *informal* getup; (**garments**) clothes, clothing, dress, garb, outfit, costume, attire; *informal* gear, togs, duds, threads; *formal* apparel.

**garner** verb *Edward garnered ideas from his travels* GATHER, collect, accumulate, amass, assemble, reap.

**garnish** verb *garnish the dish with chopped parsley* DECORATE, adorn, ornament, trim, dress, embellish; enhance, grace, beautify, prettify, add the finishing touch to.

▸ noun *keep a few sprigs for a garnish* DECORATION, adornment, trim, trimming, ornament, ornamentation, embellishment, enhancement, finishing touch; *Cooking* chiffonade.

**garret** noun *there were two straw beds in the garret* LOFT, attic, mansard.

**garrison** noun **1** *the enemy garrison had been burned alive* TROOPS, militia, soldiers, forces; armed force, military detachment, unit, platoon, brigade, squadron, battalion, corps.

**2** *forces from three garrisons* FORTRESS, fort, fortification, stronghold, citadel, camp, encampment, cantonment, command post, base, station; barracks.

▸ verb **1** *French infantry garrisoned the town* DEFEND, guard, protect, barricade, shield, secure; man, occupy.

**2** *troops were garrisoned in various regions* STATION, post, put on duty, deploy, assign, install; base, site, place, position; billet.

**garrulous** adjective **1** *a garrulous old man* TALKATIVE, loquacious, voluble, verbose, chatty, chattering, gossipy; effusive, expansive, forthcoming, conversational, communicative; *informal* mouthy, gabby, gassy, windy, having the gift of the gab, motormouthed. See note at TALKATIVE. ANTONYMS taciturn, reticent.

**2** *his garrulous reminiscences* LONG-WINDED, wordy, verbose, prolix, long, lengthy, rambling, wandering, maundering, meandering, digressive, diffuse, discursive; gossipy, chatty; *informal* windy, gassy. ANTONYM concise.

**gash** noun *a gash on his forehead* LACERATION, cut, wound, injury, slash, tear, incision; slit, split, rip, rent; scratch, scrape, graze, abrasion; *Medicine* lesion.

▸ verb *he gashed his hand on some broken glass* LACERATE, cut (open), wound, injure, hurt, slash, tear, gouge, puncture, slit, split, rend; scratch, scrape, graze, abrade.

**gasp** verb **1** *I gasped in surprise* CATCH ONE'S BREATH, draw in one's breath, gulp; exclaim, cry (out).

**2** *she collapsed on the ground, gasping* PANT, puff, wheeze, breathe hard, choke, fight for breath.

▸ noun *a gasp of dismay* GULP; exclamation, cry; sharp inhalation.

**gastric** adjective *gastric pain* STOMACH, intestinal, enteric, duodenal, celiac, abdominal, ventral.

**gate** noun *they barged through the gate without stopping* GATEWAY, doorway, entrance, entryway; exit, egress, opening; door, portal; barrier, turnstile.

**gather** verb **1** *we gathered in the hotel lobby* CONGREGATE, assemble, meet, collect, come/get together, convene, muster, rally, converge; cluster together, crowd, mass, flock together. ANTONYM scatter.

**2** *she* ***gathered*** *her family* ***together*** SUMMON, call together, bring together, assemble, convene, rally, round up, muster, marshal. ANTONYM disperse.

**3** *knickknacks he had gathered over the years* COLLECT, accumulate, amass, garner, accrue; store, stockpile, hoard, put away/by, lay by/in; *informal* stash away, squirrel away.

**4** *they gathered corn from the fields* HARVEST, reap, crop; pick, pluck; collect.

**5** *the show soon gathered a fanatical following* ATTRACT, draw, pull, pull in, collect, pick up.

**6** *I gather that environmentalism is the hot issue* UNDERSTAND, be given to understand, believe, be led to believe, think, conclude, deduce, infer, assume, take it, surmise, fancy; hear, hear tell, learn, discover.

**7** *he gathered her to his chest* CLASP, clutch, pull, embrace, enfold, hold, hug, cuddle, squeeze; *literary* embosom.

**8** *his tunic was gathered at the waist* PLEAT, shirr, pucker, tuck, fold, ruffle.

THE RIGHT WORD **gather, assemble, collect, congregate, convene, marshal, muster**

**Gather** is the most general of these terms meaning to come or bring together. It implies bringing widely scattered things or people to one place but with no particular arrangement (*to gather shells at the beach; to gather the family in the living room*). **Collect**, on the other hand, implies both selectivity (*to collect evidence for the trial*) and organization (*to collect butterflies as a hobby*). To *gather* one's thoughts means to bring them together because they have been previously scattered; to *collect* one's thoughts is to organize them. **Assemble** pertains to objects or people who are brought together for a purpose (*to assemble data for a report; to assemble Congress so that legislation will be passed*), while **congregate** may be more spontaneous, done as a free choice (*people congregated in front of the palace, hoping to catch a glimpse of the queen*). **Convene** is a formal word meaning to *assemble* or meet in a body (*to convene an international conference on the subject of global warming*) **Marshal** and **muster** are usually thought of as military terms. *Muster* implies bringing together the parts or units of a force (*troops mustered for inspection*), and *marshal* suggests a very orderly and purposeful arrangement (*to marshal the allied forces along the battle front*).

**gathering** noun **1** *she rose to address the gathering* ASSEMBLY, meeting, convention, rally, turnout, congress, convocation, conclave, council, synod, forum; congregation, audience, crowd, group, throng, mass, multitude; *informal* get-together; *formal* concourse.

**2** *the gathering of data for a future book* COLLECTING, collection, garnering, amassing, compilation, accumulation, accrual, cumulation, building up.

**gauche** adjective *Rose was embarrassed by her gauche relatives* AWKWARD, gawky, inelegant, graceless, ungraceful, ungainly, maladroit, klutzy, inept; lacking in social grace(s), unsophisticated, uncultured, uncultivated, unrefined, raw, inexperienced, unworldly. ANTONYMS elegant, sophisticated.

**gaudy** adjective *the motel rooms were clean but howlingly gaudy* GARISH, lurid, loud, overbright, glaring, harsh, violent, showy, glittering, brassy, ostentatious; tasteless, in bad taste, tawdry, vulgar, unattractive, bilious; *informal* flash, flashy, tacky, kitsch, kitschy. ANTONYMS drab, tasteful.

**gauge** noun **1** *the temperature gauge* MEASURING DEVICE, measuring instrument, meter, measure; indicator, dial, scale, display.

**2** *exports are an important gauge of economic activity* MEASURE, indicator, barometer, point of reference, guide, guideline, touchstone, yardstick, benchmark, criterion, test, litmus test.

**3** *guitar strings of a different gauge* SIZE, diameter, thickness, width, breadth; measure, capacity, magnitude; bore, caliber.

▸ verb **1** *astronomers can gauge the star's intrinsic brightness* MEASURE, calculate, compute, work out, determine, ascertain; count, weigh, quantify, put a figure on, pin down.

**2** *it is difficult to gauge how effective the ban was* ASSESS, evaluate, determine, estimate, form an opinion of, appraise, get the measure of, judge, guess; *informal* guesstimate, size up.

**gaunt** adjective **1** *a gaunt, graying man* HAGGARD, drawn, thin, lean, skinny, spindly, spare, bony, angular, rawboned, pinched, hollow-cheeked, scrawny, scraggy, as thin as a rail, cadaverous, skeletal, emaciated, skin-and-bones; wasted, withered, etiolated; *informal* like a bag of bones; *dated* spindleshanked. See note at THIN. ANTONYM plump.

**2** *the gaunt ruin of the dark tower* BLEAK, stark, desolate, bare, gloomy, dismal, somber, grim, stern, harsh, forbidding, uninviting, cheerless. ANTONYM cheerful.

**gawk** verb *informal I somehow managed not to gawk at his gorgeous roommate* GAPE, goggle, gaze, ogle, stare, stare openmouthed; *informal* rubberneck.

**gawky** adjective *how can you convince a fourteen-year-old boy that he will not always be so gawky?* AWKWARD, ungainly, gangling, maladroit, clumsy, klutzy, inelegant, uncoordinated, graceless, ungraceful; unconfident, unsophisticated. ANTONYM graceful.

**gay** adjective **1** *gay men and women* HOMOSEXUAL, lesbian; *informal* queer.

**2** *dated her children were all chubby and gay.* See CHEERFUL sense 1.

▸ noun See HOMOSEXUAL.

USAGE NOTE **gay**

**Gay** meaning 'homosexual,' dating back to the 1930s (if not earlier), became established in the 1960s as the term preferred by homosexual men to describe themselves. It is now the standard accepted term throughout the English-speaking world. As a result, the centuries-old other senses of **gay** meaning either 'carefree' or 'bright and showy,' once common in speech and literature, are much less frequent. The word **gay** cannot be readily used unselfconsciously today in these older senses without sounding old-fashioned or arousing a sense of double entendre, despite concerted attempts by some to keep them alive.

**Gay** in its modern sense typically refers to men (**lesbian** being the standard term for homosexual women), but in some contexts it can be used of both men and women.

**gaze** verb *he **gazed at** her* STARE AT, look fixedly at, gape at, goggle at, eye, look at, study, scrutinize, take a good look at; ogle, leer at; *informal* gawk at, rubberneck, eyeball.

▸ noun *her piercing gaze* STARE, fixed look, gape; regard, inspection, scrutiny.

**gazette** noun *it's in this week's gazette* NEWSPAPER, paper, journal, periodical, organ, newsletter, bulletin; *informal* rag.

**gear** noun *informal* **1** *his fishing gear* EQUIPMENT, apparatus, paraphernalia, articles, appliances, impedimenta; tools, utensils, implements, instruments, gadgets; stuff, things; kit, rig, tackle, odds and ends, bits and pieces, trappings, appurtenances, accoutrements, regalia; *archaic* equipage.

**2** *I'll go back to the hotel and pick up my gear* BELONGINGS, possessions, effects, personal effects, property, paraphernalia, odds and ends, bits and pieces, bags, baggage, luggage; *Law* chattels; *informal* things, stuff.

**3** *police in riot gear* CLOTHES, clothing, garments, outfits, attire, garb; dress, wear; *informal* togs, duds, getup, threads; *formal* apparel.

**gelatinous** adjective *stir over low heat until the mixture becomes gelatinous* JELLYLIKE, glutinous, viscous, viscid, mucilaginous, sticky, gluey, gummy, slimy; *informal* gooey, gunky.

**geld** verb *Mitch selects the horses that are to be gelded* CASTRATE, neuter, fix, alter, desex, doctor.

**gem** noun **1** *rubies and other gems* JEWEL, gemstone, stone, precious stone, semiprecious stone; solitaire, cabochon; *archaic* bijou.

**2** *the gem of the collection* BEST, finest, pride, prize, treasure, flower, pearl, jewel in the crown; pick, choice, cream, the crème de la crème, elite, acme; *informal* one in a million, bee's knees.

**genealogy** noun *our genealogy has been difficult to determine* LINEAGE, line, line of descent, family tree, bloodline; pedigree, ancestry, extraction, heritage, parentage, birth, family, dynasty, house, stock, blood, roots.

**general** adjective **1** *this is suitable for general use* WIDESPREAD, common, extensive, universal, wide, popular, public, mainstream; established, conventional, traditional, orthodox, accepted. See note at UNIVERSAL. ANTONYM restricted.

**2** *a general pay increase* COMPREHENSIVE, overall, across the board, blanket, umbrella, mass, wholesale, sweeping, broad-ranging, inclusive, companywide; universal, global, worldwide, nationwide. ANTONYM localized.

**3** *general knowledge* MISCELLANEOUS, mixed, assorted, diversified, composite, heterogeneous, eclectic. ANTONYM specialist.

**4** *the general practice* USUAL, customary, habitual, traditional, normal, conventional, typical, standard, regular; familiar, accepted, prevailing, routine, run-of-the-mill, established, everyday, ordinary, common. ANTONYM exceptional.

**5** *a general description* BROAD, imprecise, inexact, rough, loose, approximate, unspecific, vague, woolly, indefinite; *informal* ballpark. ANTONYM detailed.

**generality** noun **1** *the debate has moved on from generalities* GENERALIZATION, general statement, general principle, sweeping statement; abstraction, extrapolation. ANTONYM specific.

**2** *the generality of this principle* UNIVERSALITY, comprehensiveness, all-inclusiveness, broadness.

**generally** adverb **1** *summers were generally hot* NORMALLY, in general, as a rule, by and large, more often than not, almost always, mainly, mostly, for the most part, predominantly, on the whole; usually, habitually, customarily, typically, ordinarily, commonly.

**2** *popular opinion veers generally to the left* OVERALL, in general terms, generally speaking, all in all, broadly, on average, basically, effectively.

**3** *the method was generally accepted* WIDELY, commonly, extensively, universally, popularly.

**generate** verb **1** *moves to generate extra business* CAUSE, give rise to, lead to, result in, bring about, create, make, produce, engender, spawn, precipitate, prompt, provoke, trigger, spark off, stir up, induce, promote, foster.

**2** *captive animals may not **generate offspring*** PROCREATE, breed, reproduce, father offspring, sire offspring, mother offspring, spawn offspring, create offspring, produce offspring, have offspring; *literary* beget offspring; *archaic* engender offspring.

**generation** noun **1** *people of the same generation* AGE, age group, peer group.

**2** (**generations**) *generations ago* AGES, years, eons, a long time, an eternity; *informal* donkey's years.

**3** *the next generation of computers* CROP, batch, wave, range.

4 *the generation of novel ideas* CREATION, production, initiation, origination, inception, inspiration.

5 *human generation* PROCREATION, reproduction, breeding; creation.

**generic** adjective 1 *a generic classification for similar offenses* GENERAL, common, collective, nonspecific, inclusive, all-encompassing, broad, comprehensive, blanket, umbrella. See note at UNIVERSAL. ANTONYM specific.

2 *generic drugs are cheaper than brand-name ones* UNBRANDED, nonproprietary, no-name. ANTONYM specific.

**generosity** noun 1 *the generosity of our host* LIBERALITY, lavishness, magnanimity, munificence, openhandedness, freehandedness, unselfishness; kindness, benevolence, altruism, charity, big-heartedness, goodness; *literary* bounteousness.

2 *the generosity of the food portions* ABUNDANCE, plentifulness, copiousness, lavishness, liberality, largeness.

**generous** adjective 1 *she is generous with money* LIBERAL, lavish, magnanimous, munificent, giving, openhanded, freehanded, bountiful, unselfish, ungrudging, free, indulgent, prodigal; *literary* bounteous. ANTONYMS mean, stingy.

2 *it was generous of them to offer* MAGNANIMOUS, kind, benevolent, altruistic, charitable, noble, big-hearted, honorable, good; unselfish, self-sacrificing. ANTONYMS mean, selfish.

3 *a generous amount of fabric* LAVISH, plentiful, copious, ample, liberal, large, great, abundant, profuse, bumper, opulent, prolific; *informal* galore; *literary* bounteous, plenteous. ANTONYM meager.

**genesis** noun 1 *the hatred had its genesis in something dark* ORIGIN, source, root, beginning, start.

2 *the genesis of his neurosis* FORMATION, development, evolution, emergence, inception, origination, creation, formulation, propagation.

**genial** adjective *my genial colleagues* FRIENDLY, affable, cordial, amiable, warm, easygoing, approachable, sympathetic; good-natured, good-humored, cheerful; neighborly, hospitable, companionable, comradely, sociable, convivial, outgoing, gregarious; *informal* chummy. ANTONYM unfriendly.

**genius** noun 1 *the world knew of his genius* BRILLIANCE, intelligence, intellect, ability, cleverness, brains, erudition, wisdom, fine mind; artistry, flair. ANTONYM stupidity.

2 *she has a genius for organization* TALENT, gift, flair, aptitude, facility, knack, bent, ability, expertise, capacity, faculty; strength, forte, brilliance, skill, artistry.

3 *he is a genius* BRILLIANT PERSON, gifted person, mastermind, Einstein, intellectual, great intellect, brain, mind; prodigy; *informal* egghead, bright spark, brainiac, rocket scientist. ANTONYM dunce.

**genre** noun *historical fiction is my favorite genre of literature* CATEGORY, class, classification, group, set, list; type, sort, kind, breed, variety, style, model, school, stamp, cast, ilk.

**genteel** adjective *she never quite fit in with Harold's genteel family* REFINED, respectable, decorous, mannerly, well-mannered, courteous, polite, proper, correct, seemly; well-bred, cultured, sophisticated, ladylike, gentlemanly, dignified, gracious; affected. See note at URBAN. ANTONYM uncouth.

**gentility** noun *an air of old-fashioned gentility* REFINEMENT, distinction, breeding, sophistication; respectability, punctiliousness, decorum, good manners, politeness, civility, courtesy, graciousness, correctness; affectation, ostentation.

**gentle** adjective 1 *his manner was gentle* KIND, tender, sympathetic, considerate, understanding, compassionate, benevolent, good-natured; humane, lenient, merciful, clement; mild, placid, serene, sweet-tempered. ANTONYM brutal.

2 *a gentle breeze* LIGHT, soft. ANTONYM strong.

3 *a gentle slope* GRADUAL, slight, easy. ANTONYM steep.

4 *archaic a woman of gentle birth.* See NOBLE adjective sense 1.

**gentlemanly** adjective *gentlemanly manners came naturally to him* CHIVALROUS, gallant, honorable, noble, courteous, civil, mannerly, polite, gracious, considerate, thoughtful; well-bred, cultivated, cultured, refined, suave, urbane. ANTONYM rude.

**genuine** adjective 1 *a genuine Picasso* AUTHENTIC, real, actual, original, bona fide, true, veritable; attested, undisputed; *informal* the real McCoy, honest-to-goodness, honest-to-God, the real thing, kosher. ANTONYM bogus.

2 *a genuine person* SINCERE, honest, truthful, straightforward, direct, frank, candid, open; artless, natural, unaffected; *informal* straight, upfront, on the level, on the up and up. ANTONYM insincere.

THE RIGHT WORD **genuine, actual, authentic, bona fide, legitimate, veritable**

A car salesperson might claim that the seats of that pricey sedan you're considering are made from **genuine** leather, a word that applies to anything that is really what it is claimed or represented to be. If you're in the market for a Model T Ford, however, you'll want to make sure that the car is **authentic**, which emphasizes formal proof or documentation that an object is what it is claimed to be. Use **bona fide** when sincerity is involved (*a bona fide offer*), and **legitimate** when you mean lawful or in accordance with established rules, principles, and standards (*a legitimate business*). **Veritable** implies correspondence with the truth but not necessarily a literal or strict correspondence with reality (*a veritable supermarket for car-buyers*). How will it feel to drive that Mercedes out of the showroom? You won't know until you're the **actual** owner of the car—a word that means existing in fact rather than in the imagination.

**genus** noun 1 *Biology a large genus of plants* SUBDIVISION, division, group, subfamily.

2 *a new genus of music* TYPE, sort, kind, genre, style, variety, category, class; breed, brand, family, stamp, cast, ilk.

**germ** noun 1 *this detergent kills germs* MICROBE, microorganism, bacillus, bacterium, virus; *informal* bug.

2 *a fertilized germ* EMBRYO, bud; seed, spore, ovule; egg, ovum.

3 *the germ of an idea* START, beginning(s), seed, embryo, bud,

root, rudiment; origin, source, potential; core, nucleus, kernel, essence.

**germane** adjective *your question is not germane to the topic at hand* RELEVANT, pertinent, applicable, apposite, material; apropos, appropriate, apt, fitting, suitable; connected, related, akin. ANTONYM irrelevant.

**germinate** verb **1** *the grain is allowed to germinate* SPROUT, shoot (up), bud; develop, grow, spring up; *dated* vegetate.

**2** *the idea began to germinate* DEVELOP, take root, grow, incubate, emerge, evolve, mature, expand, advance, progress.

**gestation** noun **1** *a gestation of thirty days* PREGNANCY, incubation; development, maturation.

**2** *the law underwent a period of gestation* DEVELOPMENT, evolution, formation, emergence, origination.

**gesticulate** verb *they frantically gesticulated to get someone's attention* GESTURE, signal, motion, wave, sign.

**gesture** noun **1** *a gesture of surrender* SIGNAL, sign, motion, indication, gesticulation; show.

**2** *a symbolic gesture* ACTION, act, deed, move.

▸ verb *he gestured to her* SIGNAL, motion, gesticulate, wave, indicate, give a sign.

**get** verb **1** *where did you get that hat?* ACQUIRE, obtain, come by, receive, gain, earn, win, come into, take possession of, be given; buy, purchase, procure, secure; gather, collect, pick up, hook, net, land; achieve, attain; *informal* get one's hands on, get one's mitts on, get hold of, grab, bag, score. ANTONYM give.

**2** *I got your letter* RECEIVE, be sent, be in receipt of, be given. ANTONYM send.

**3** *your tea's getting cold* BECOME, grow, turn, go.

**4** *get the children from school* FETCH, collect, go for, call for, pick up, bring, deliver, convey, ferry, transport. ANTONYM leave.

**5** *the chairman gets $650,000 a year* EARN, be paid, take home, bring in, make, receive, collect, gross; *informal* pocket, bank, rake in, net, bag.

**6** *have the police got their man?* APPREHEND, catch, arrest, capture, seize; take prisoner, take into custody, detain, put in jail, put behind bars, imprison, incarcerate; *informal* collar, grab, nab, nail, run in, pinch, bust, pick up, pull in.

**7** *I got a taxi* TRAVEL BY/ON/IN; take, catch, use.

**8** *she got the flu* SUCCUMB TO, develop, come/go down with, get sick with, fall victim to, be struck down with, be afflicted by/with; become infected with, catch, contract, fall ill with, be taken ill with.

**9** *I got a pain in my arm* EXPERIENCE, suffer, be afflicted with, sustain, feel, have.

**10** *I got him on the radio* CONTACT, get in touch with, communicate with, make contact with, reach; phone, call, radio; speak to, talk to; *informal* get hold of.

**11** *I didn't get what he said* HEAR, discern, distinguish, make out, perceive, follow, take in.

**12** *I don't get the joke* UNDERSTAND, comprehend, grasp, see, fathom, follow, perceive, apprehend, unravel, decipher; *informal* get the drift of, catch on to, latch on to, figure out.

**13** *we got there early* ARRIVE, reach, come, make it, turn up, appear, come on the scene, approach, enter, present oneself, come along, materialize, show one's face; *informal* show (up), roll in/up, blow in.

**14** *we got her to go* PERSUADE, induce, prevail on/upon, influence.

**15** *I'd like to get to meet him* CONTRIVE, arrange, find a way, manage; *informal* work it, fix it.

**16** *I'll get supper* PREPARE, get ready, cook, make, assemble, muster, concoct; *informal* fix, rustle up.

**17** *informal* *I'll get him for that* TAKE REVENGE ON, exact/wreak revenge on, get one's revenge on, avenge oneself on, take vengeance on, get even with, pay back, get back at, exact retribution on, give someone their just deserts.

**18** *you really got me with that third question* BAFFLE, perplex, puzzle, bewilder, mystify, bemuse, confuse, confound; *informal* flummox, faze, stump, beat, fox, discombobulate.

**19** *what gets me is how neurotic she is* ANNOY, irritate, exasperate, anger, irk, vex, provoke, incense, infuriate, madden, try someone's patience, ruffle someone's feathers; *informal* aggravate, peeve, miff, rile, get to, needle, get someone's back up, get on someone's nerves, get someone's goat, drive mad, make someone see red, tee off, tick off. PHRASES: **get about** *he uses a wheelchair to get about* MOVE ABOUT, move around, travel.
**get across** *a photo will help you get the message across* COMMUNICATE, impart, convey, transmit, make clear, express.
**get ahead** *the desire to get ahead* PROSPER, flourish, thrive, do well; succeed, make it, advance, get on in the world, go up in the world, make good, become rich; *informal* go places, get somewhere, make the big time.
**get along 1** *can't you try to get along with his family?* BE FRIENDLY, be compatible, get on; agree, see eye to eye, concur, be in accord; *informal* hit it off, be on the same wavelength.
**2** *she was getting along well at school* FARE, manage, progress, advance, get on, get by, do, cope; succeed.
**get around** *Toby really gets around* TRAVEL, circulate, socialize, do the rounds.
**get at 1** *it's difficult to get at the pipes* ACCESS, get to, reach, touch.
**2** *she had been got at by enemy agents* CORRUPT, suborn, influence, bribe, buy off, pay off; *informal* fix, square.
**3** *informal* *what are you getting at?* IMPLY, suggest, intimate, insinuate, hint, mean, drive at, allude to.
**get away** *the prisoners got away* ESCAPE, run away/off, break out, break free, break loose, bolt, flee, take flight, make off, take off, decamp, abscond, make a run for it; slip away, sneak away; *informal* cut and run, skedaddle, do a disappearing act.
**get away with** *he's been getting away with every kind of wrongdoing since he was three* ESCAPE BLAME FOR, escape punishment for.
**get back 1** *they should get back before dawn* RETURN, come home, come back.

**2** *she got her gloves back from the lost and found* RETRIEVE, regain, win back, recover, recoup, reclaim, repossess, recapture, redeem; find (again), trace.

**get back at** *she wasted years of her life thinking about getting back at her ex-husband* TAKE REVENGE ON, exact/wreak revenge on, avenge oneself on, take vengeance on, get even with, pay back, retaliate on/against, exact retribution on, give someone their just deserts.

**get by** *he had just enough money to get by* MANAGE, cope, survive, exist, subsist, muddle through/along, scrape by, make ends meet, make do, keep the wolf from the door; *informal* make out.

**get down** *her poetry always gets me down* DEPRESS, sadden, make unhappy, make gloomy, dispirit, dishearten, demoralize, discourage, crush, weigh down, oppress; upset, distress; *informal* give someone the blues, make someone fed up.

**get off 1** *Sally got off the bus* STEP OFF, alight (from), dismount (from), descend (from), disembark (from), leave, exit.

**2** *informal he was arrested but got off* ESCAPE PUNISHMENT, be acquitted, be absolved, be cleared, be exonerated.

**get on 1** *we got on the train* BOARD, enter, step aboard, climb on, mount, ascend, catch; *informal* hop on, jump on.

**2** *how are you getting on?* FARE, manage, progress, get along, do, cope, get by, survive, muddle through/along; succeed, prosper; *informal* make out.

**get on with** *she got on with her job* CONTINUE (WITH), proceed with, go ahead with, carry on with, go on with, press on with, persist with/in, persevere with; keep at; *informal* stick with/at.

**get out** *the news got out* BECOME KNOWN, become common knowledge, come to light, emerge, transpire; come out, be uncovered, be revealed, be divulged, be disseminated, be disclosed, be reported, be released, leak out.

**get out of** *how do you plan to get out of this mess?* EVADE, dodge, shirk, avoid, escape, sidestep; *informal* duck (out of), wriggle out of, cop out of.

**get over 1** *I just got over the flu* RECOVER FROM, recuperate from, get better after, shrug off, survive.

**2** *we tried to get over this problem* OVERCOME, surmount, get the better of, master, find an/the answer to, get a grip on, deal with, cope with, sort out, take care of, crack, rise above; *informal* lick.

**get together 1** *get together the best writers* COLLECT, gather, assemble, bring together, rally, muster, marshal, congregate, convene, amass; *formal* convoke.

**2** *we must get together soon* MEET, meet up, rendezvous, see each other, socialize.

**get up** *he seldom gets up before noon* GET OUT OF BED, rise, stir, rouse oneself; *informal* surface; *formal* arise.

THE RIGHT WORD **get, acquire, attain, gain, obtain, procure, secure**

**Get** is a very broad term meaning to come into possession of. You can *get* something by fetching it (*get some groceries*), by receiving it (*get a birthday gift*), by earning it (*get interest on a bank loan*), or by any of a dozen other familiar means. It is such a common, over-used word that many writers try to substitute **obtain** for it whenever possible, perhaps because it sounds less colloquial. But it can also sound pretentious (*all employees were required to obtain an annual physical exam*) and should be reserved for contexts where the emphasis is on seeking something out (*to obtain blood samples*). **Acquire** often suggests a continued, sustained, or cumulative acquisition (*to acquire poise as one matures*), but it can also hint at deviousness (*to acquire the keys to the safe*). Use **procure** if you want to emphasize the effort involved in bringing something to pass (*procure a mediated divorce settlement*) or if you want to imply maneuvering to possess something (*procure a reserved parking space*). But beware: *Procure* is so often used to describe the act of obtaining partners to gratify the lust of others (*to procure a prostitute*) that it has acquired somewhat unsavory overtones. **Gain** also implies effort, usually in *getting* something advantageous or profitable (*gain entry, gain victory*). In a similar vein, **secure** underscores the difficulty involved in bringing something to pass and the desire to place it beyond danger (*secure a permanent peace; secure a lifeline*). **Attain** should be reserved for achieving a high goal or desirable result (*If she attains the summit of Mt. Everest, she will secure for herself a place in mountaineering history*).

**getaway** noun *he made his getaway in broad daylight* ESCAPE, breakout, bolt for freedom, flight; disappearance, vanishing act.

**get-together** noun *a friendly get-together at Pete's house* PARTY, meeting, gathering, social event, social; *informal* do, bash.

**getup** noun *informal check out Stacey's wild getup* OUTFIT, clothes, costume, ensemble, suit, clothing, dress, attire, garments, garb; *informal* gear, togs, duds, threads; *formal* apparel.

**get-up-and-go** noun *informal your grandfather has more getup-and-go than you do* DRIVE, initiative, enterprise, enthusiasm, eagerness, ambition, motivation, dynamism, energy, gusto, vim, vigor, vitality, verve, fire, fervor, zeal, commitment, spirit; *informal* gumption, oomph, pep. ANTONYM apathy.

**ghastly** adjective **1** *a ghastly stabbing* TERRIBLE, horrible, grim, awful, dire; frightening, terrifying, horrifying, alarming; distressing, shocking, appalling, harrowing; dreadful, frightful, horrendous, monstrous, gruesome, grisly; *informal* gut-wrenching. ANTONYM pleasant.

**2** *informal a ghastly building* UNPLEASANT, objectionable, disagreeable, distasteful, awful, terrible, dreadful, detestable, insufferable, vile; *informal* horrible, horrid. ANTONYM charming.

**3** *a ghastly pallor* PALE, white, pallid, pasty, wan, bloodless, peaked, ashen, gray, waxy, blanched, drained, pinched, green, sickly, ghostly, ghostlike; *informal* like death warmed over. ANTONYMS ruddy, healthy.

**ghost** noun **1** *his ghost haunts the crypt* SPECTER, phantom, wraith, spirit, presence; apparition; *informal* spook. See also the table at SPIRIT.

**2** *the ghost of a smile* TRACE, hint, suggestion, impression, suspicion, tinge; glimmer, semblance, shadow, whisper.

**ghostly** adjective *a ghostly vision at the end of the hallway*

SPECTRAL, ghostlike, phantom, wraithlike, phantasmal, phantasmic; unearthly, unnatural, supernatural; insubstantial, shadowy; eerie, weird, uncanny; frightening, spine-chilling, hair-raising, blood-curdling, bone-chilling, terrifying, chilling, sinister; *informal* creepy, scary, spooky.

**giant** noun *the mythical giant of the forest* COLOSSUS, behemoth, Brobdingnagian, mammoth, monster, leviathan, titan; giantess; *informal* jumbo, whopper. ANTONYM dwarf.

▸ adjective *a giant balloon* HUGE, colossal, massive, enormous, gigantic, very big, mammoth, vast, immense, monumental, mountainous, titanic, towering, elephantine, king-size(d), economy-size(d), gargantuan, Brobdingnagian; substantial, hefty; *informal* mega, monster, whopping, humongous, jumbo, hulking, bumper, ginormous. ANTONYM miniature.

**gibberish** noun *am I going deaf, or is she speaking gibberish?* NONSENSE, garbage, balderdash, blather, rubbish; *informal* drivel, gobbledygook, mumbo-jumbo, tripe, hogwash, baloney, bilge, bull, bunk, guff, eyewash, piffle, twaddle, poppycock.

**giddy** adjective **1** *just one beer would make him feel giddy* DIZZY, lightheaded, faint, weak, vertiginous; unsteady, shaky, wobbly; *informal* woozy. ANTONYM steady.

**2** *she was young and giddy* FLIGHTY, silly, frivolous, skittish, irresponsible, flippant, whimsical, capricious; featherbrained, scatty, thoughtless, heedless, carefree; *informal* dippy, ditzy, flaky. ANTONYM sensible.

**gift** noun **1** *he gave the staff a gift* PRESENT, handout, donation, offering, bestowal, bonus, award, endowment; tip, gratuity; largesse; *informal* freebie, perk; *formal* benefaction. See note at PRESENT[3].

**2** *Marlin possessed a gift for interior design* TALENT, flair, aptitude, facility, knack, bent, ability, expertise, capacity, capability, faculty; endowment, strength, genius, brilliance, skill, artistry.

▸ verb *he gifted a composition to the orchestra* PRESENT, give, bestow, confer, donate, endow, award, accord, grant; hand over, make over.

**gifted** adjective *a gifted young percussionist* TALENTED, skillful, skilled, accomplished, expert, consummate, master(ly), virtuoso, first-rate, able, apt, adept, proficient; intelligent, clever, bright, brilliant; precocious; *informal* crack, top-notch, ace. ANTONYM inept.

**gigantic** adjective *the new houses on Long Hill Road are gigantic* HUGE, enormous, vast, extensive, very big, very large, giant, massive, colossal, mammoth, immense, monumental, mountainous, titanic, towering, elephantine, king-size(d), economy-size(d), gargantuan; *informal* mega, monster, whopping, humongous, jumbo, hulking, bumper, ginormous. ANTONYM tiny.

**giggle** noun & verb *she suppressed a giggle | he giggled at the picture* TITTER, snigger, snicker, tee-hee, chuckle, chortle, laugh.

**gigolo** noun *she was mortified to learn her husband had been a gigolo in LA when he was twenty-something* PLAYBOY, escort, male escort, paid escort; lover; *informal* toy boy.

**gild** verb **1** *she gilded the picture frame* GOLD-PLATE; cover with gold, paint gold.

**2** *he tends to gild the truth* ELABORATE, embellish, embroider; camouflage, disguise, dress up, color, exaggerate, expand on; *informal* jazz up.

**gimcrack** adjective *they lived in gimcrack villas you'd be afraid to sneeze in* SHODDY, jerry-built, flimsy, insubstantial, thrown together, makeshift; inferior, poor-quality, second-rate, cheap, cheapjack; tawdry, kitsch, kitschy, chintzy, trashy, dime-store; *informal* tacky, junky, cheapo, schlocky.

**gimmick** noun *the trivia contest was a gimmick to sell more newspapers* PUBLICITY STUNT, contrivance, scheme, stratagem, ploy; *informal* shtick.

**gingerly** adverb *he stepped gingerly on to the ice* CAUTIOUSLY, carefully, with care, warily, charily, circumspectly, delicately; heedfully, watchfully, vigilantly, attentively; hesitantly, timidly. ANTONYM recklessly.

**gird** verb **1** *the island was girded by rocks* SURROUND, enclose, encircle, circle, encompass, border, bound, edge, skirt, fringe; close in, confine.

**2** *they girded themselves for war* PREPARE, get ready, gear up; nerve, steel, galvanize, brace, fortify; *informal* psych oneself up.

**girdle** noun **1** *her stockings were held up by her girdle* CORSET, panty girdle, corselet, foundation garment; truss.

**2** *a diamond-studded girdle* BELT, sash, cummerbund, waistband, strap, band, girth, cord.

▸ verb *a garden girdled the house* SURROUND, enclose, encircle, circle, encompass, circumscribe, border, bound, skirt, edge; *literary* gird.

**girl** noun **1** *a five-year-old girl* FEMALE CHILD, daughter; schoolgirl; *Scottish* lass, lassie. See also CHILD.

**2** *he settled down with a nice girl* YOUNG WOMAN, young lady, miss, mademoiselle; *Scottish* lass, lassie; *informal* chick, gal, grrrl, babe; *literary* maid, damsel, ingenue.

**3** *his girl left him* GIRLFRIEND.

**girth** noun **1** *a tree ten feet in girth* CIRCUMFERENCE, perimeter; width, breadth.

**2** *he tied the towel around his girth* STOMACH, midriff, middle, abdomen, belly, gut; *informal* tummy, tum.

**3** *a horse's girth* cinch.

**gist** noun *the gist of her essay is an indictment of the religious right* ESSENCE, substance, central theme, heart of the matter, nub, kernel, marrow, meat, burden, crux; thrust, drift, sense, meaning, significance, import; *informal* nitty-gritty.

**give** verb **1** *she gave them $2000* PRESENT WITH, provide with, supply with, furnish with, let someone have; hand (over to), offer, proffer; award, grant (to), bestow on/upon, accord, confer on, make over to; donate to, contribute to. ANTONYMS receive, take.

**2** *can I give him a message?* CONVEY TO, pass on to, impart to, communicate to, transmit to; send, deliver (to), relay to; tell (to).

**3** *a baby given into their care* ENTRUST, commit, consign, assign; *formal* commend.

**4** *she gave her life for them* SACRIFICE, give up, relinquish; devote, dedicate.

**5** *he gave her time to think* ALLOW, permit, grant, accord; offer.

**6** *this leaflet gives our opening times* SHOW, display, set out, indicate, detail, list.

**7** *they gave no further trouble* CAUSE, make, create, occasion.

**8** *garlic gives flavor* PRODUCE, yield, afford, impart, lend.

**9** *she gave a party* ORGANIZE, arrange, throw, host, hold, have, provide.

**10** *Dominic gave a bow* PERFORM, execute, make, do.

**11** *she gave a shout* UTTER, let out, emit, produce, make.

**12** *he gave Larry a beating* ADMINISTER, deliver, deal, inflict, impose.

**13** *the door gave* GIVE WAY, cave in, collapse, break, fall apart; bend, buckle.

▸ noun *informal there isn't enough give in the jacket* ELASTICITY, flexibility, stretch, stretchiness; slack, play.

PHRASES: **give away 1** *he refused to believe that his own sister had given him away* BETRAY, inform on; *informal* rat on, blow the whistle on, sell down the river, rat out, finger.

**2** *his face gave little away* REVEAL, disclose, divulge, let slip, leak, let out.

**3** *Kellie gave away all of her possessions* DONATE, make a gift of, confer, contribute, will, bequeath; distribute; sacrifice; get rid of, dispose of, relent, throw in the towel/sponge.

**give in** *in the end, Dolan was forced to give in* CAPITULATE, concede defeat, admit defeat, give up, surrender, yield, submit, back down, give way, defer, relent, throw in the towel.

**give off** *the lantern gives off a powerful glow* EMIT, produce, send out, throw out; discharge, release, exude, vent.

**give out 1** *the gas reserves have finally given out* RUN OUT, be used up, be consumed, be exhausted, be depleted; fail, flag; dry up.

**2** *thousands of leaflets were given out* DISTRIBUTE, issue, hand out, pass around, dispense; dole out, dish out, mete out; allocate, allot.

**give up.** *when did you give up drinking?* STOP, cease, discontinue, desist from, abstain from, cut out, renounce, forgo; resign from, stand down from; *informal* quit, kick, swear off, leave off, pack in, lay off.

THE RIGHT WORD **give, afford, award, bestow, confer, donate, grant**

You **give** a birthday present, **grant** a favor, **bestow** charity, and **confer** an honor. While all of these verbs mean to convey something or transfer it from one's own possession to that of another, the circumstances surrounding that transfer dictate which word is the best one. *Give* is the most general, meaning to pass over, deliver, or transmit something (*give him encouragement*). *Grant* implies that a request or desire has been expressed, and that the receiver is dependent on the giver's discretion (*grant permission for the trip*). **Award** suggests that the giver is in some sense a judge, and that the thing given is deserved (*award a scholarship*), while *bestow* implies that something is given as a gift and may imply condescension on the part of the giver (*bestow a large sum of money on a needy charity*). To *confer* is to give an honor, a privilege, or a favor; it implies that the giver is a superior (*confer a knighthood; confer a college degree*). **Donate** implies that the giving is to a public cause or charity (*donate a painting to the local art museum*), and to **afford** is to give or bestow as a natural consequence (the window afforded a fine view of the mountains).

**giver** noun *Lynette threw her indolent nephews out of the house, vowing that her days as the "family giver" were over* DONOR, contributor, donator, benefactor, benefactress, provider; supporter, backer, patron, sponsor, subscriber.

**glacial** adjective **1** *glacial conditions* FREEZING, cold, icy, ice-cold, subzero, frozen, gelid, wintry; arctic, polar, Siberian, hypothermic; bitter, biting, raw; *literary* chill. ANTONYMS tropical, hot.

**2** *Beverly's tone was glacial* UNFRIENDLY, hostile, unwelcoming; frosty, icy, cold, chilly. ANTONYMS warm, friendly.

**3** *they proceeded at a glacial pace* SLOW, lugubrious, unhurried, leisurely, steady, sedate, slow-moving, plodding, dawdling, sluggish, sluggardly, lead-footed. ANTONYMS fast, brisk.

**glad** adjective **1** *I'm really glad you're coming* PLEASED, happy, delighted, thrilled, overjoyed, elated, gleeful; gratified, grateful, thankful; *informal* tickled pink, over the moon. ANTONYMS dismayed, annoyed.

**2** *I'd be glad to help* WILLING, eager, happy, pleased, delighted; ready, prepared. ANTONYMS unwilling, reluctant.

**3** *glad tidings* PLEASING, welcome, happy, joyful, cheering, heartening, gratifying. ANTONYMS unwelcome, distressing.

**gladden** verb *it gladdens us to see you so happy* DELIGHT, please, make happy, elate; cheer, cheer up, hearten, buoy up, give someone a lift, uplift; gratify; *informal* tickle someone pink, buck up. ANTONYM sadden.

**gladly** adverb *we gladly accepted the senator's invitation* WITH PLEASURE, happily, cheerfully; willingly, readily, eagerly, freely, ungrudgingly; *archaic* fain, lief.

**glamorous** adjective **1** *a glamorous woman* BEAUTIFUL, attractive, lovely, bewitching, enchanting, beguiling; elegant, chic, stylish, fashionable; charming, charismatic, appealing, alluring, seductive; *informal* classy, glam. ANTONYMS dowdy, drab.

**2** *a glamorous lifestyle* EXCITING, thrilling, stimulating; dazzling, glittering, glossy, colorful, exotic; *informal* ritzy, glitzy, jet-setting. ANTONYMS boring, dull.

**glamour** noun **1** *she had undeniable glamour* BEAUTY, allure, attractiveness; elegance, chic, style; charisma, charm, magnetism, desirability.

2 *the glamour of show business* ALLURE, attraction, fascination, charm, magic, romance, mystique, exoticism, spell; excitement, thrill; glitter, bright lights; *informal* glitz, glam, tinsel.

**glance** verb 1 *Rachel glanced at him* LOOK BRIEFLY, look quickly, peek, peep; glimpse; *informal* have a gander.

2 *I **glanced through** the report* READ QUICKLY, scan, skim through, leaf through, flip through, thumb through, browse (through); dip into.

3 *a bullet **glanced off** the ice* RICOCHET OFF, rebound off, be deflected off, bounce off; graze, clip.

4 *sunlight glanced off her hair* REFLECT, flash, gleam, glint, glitter, glisten, glimmer, shimmer.

▸ noun *a glance at his watch* PEEK, peep, brief look, quick look, glimpse; *informal* gander.

PHRASE: **at first glance** *at first glance, the plastic stemware could have been mistaken for crystal* ON THE FACE OF IT, on the surface, at first sight, to the casual eye, to all appearances; apparently, seemingly, outwardly, superficially, it would seem, it appears, as far as one can see/tell, by all accounts.

**glare** verb 1 *she glared at him* SCOWL, glower, stare angrily, look daggers, frown, lower, give someone a black look, look threateningly; *informal* give someone a dirty look.

2 *the sun glared out of the sky* BLAZE, beam, shine brightly, be dazzling, be blinding.

▸ noun 1 *a cold glare* SCOWL, glower, angry stare, frown, black look, threatening look; *informal* dirty look.

2 *the harsh glare of the lights* BLAZE, dazzle, shine, beam; radiance, brilliance, luminescence.

**glaring** adjective 1 *glaring lights* DAZZLING, blinding, blazing, strong, bright, harsh. ANTONYMS soft, dim.

2 *a glaring omission* OBVIOUS, conspicuous, unmistakable, inescapable, unmissable, striking; flagrant, blatant, outrageous, gross; overt, patent, transparent, manifest; *informal* standing/sticking out like a sore thumb. ANTONYMS inconspicuous, minor.

**glass** noun 1 *a glass of water* TUMBLER, drinking vessel; goblet, flute, schooner, chalice.

2 *we sell china and glass* GLASSWARE, stemware, crystal, crystalware.

**glasses** plural noun *Hale looks older in his glasses* EYEGLASSES, eyewear, spectacles; *informal* specs; bifocals.

**glassy** adjective 1 *the glassy surface of the lake* SMOOTH, mirrorlike, gleaming, shiny, glossy, polished, vitreous; slippery, icy; clear, transparent, translucent; calm, still, flat. ANTONYM rough.

2 *a glassy stare* EXPRESSIONLESS, glazed, blank, vacant, fixed, motionless; emotionless, impassive, lifeless, wooden, vacuous. ANTONYM expressive.

**glaze** verb 1 *the pots are glazed when dry* VARNISH, enamel, lacquer, japan, shellac, paint; gloss.

2 *pastry glazed with caramel* COVER, coat; ice, frost.

3 *his eyes glazed over* BECOME GLASSY, go blank; mist over, film over.

▸ noun 1 *pottery with a blue glaze* VARNISH, enamel, lacquer, finish, coating; luster, shine, gloss.

2 *a cake with an apricot glaze* COATING, topping; icing, frosting.

**gleam** verb *the new silver tea service positively gleams* SHINE, glimmer, glint, glitter, shimmer, sparkle, twinkle, flicker, wink, glisten, flash; *literary* glister.

▸ noun 1 *a gleam of light* GLIMMER, glint, shimmer, twinkle, sparkle, flicker, flash; beam, ray, shaft.

2 *the gleam of brass* SHINE, luster, gloss, sheen; glint, glitter, glimmer, sparkle; brilliance, radiance, glow; *literary* glister.

3 *a gleam of hope* GLIMMER, flicker, ray, spark, trace, suggestion, hint, sign.

**glee** noun *Agnes clapped her hands together with glee* DELIGHT, pleasure, happiness, joy, gladness, elation, euphoria; amusement, mirth, merriment; excitement, gaiety, exuberance; relish, triumph, jubilation, satisfaction, gratification. ANTONYM disappointment.

**gleeful** adjective *the gleeful bunch over there must have been rooting for the Patriots* DELIGHTED, pleased, joyful, happy, glad, overjoyed, elated, euphoric; amused, mirthful, merry, exuberant; jubilant; *informal* over the moon.

**glib** adjective *glib phrases rolled off his tongue* SLICK, pat, fast-talking, smooth-talking; disingenuous, insincere, facile, shallow, superficial, flippant; smooth, silver-tongued, urbane; *informal* flip, sweet-talking. See note at TALKATIVE. ANTONYM sincere.

**glide** verb 1 *a gondola glided past* SLIDE, slip, sail, float, drift, flow; coast, freewheel, roll; skim, skate.

2 *seagulls gliding over the waves* SOAR, wheel, plane; fly.

3 *he glided out of the door* SLIP, steal, slink.

**glimmer** verb *moonlight glimmered on the lawn* GLEAM, shine, glint, flicker, shimmer, glisten, glow, twinkle, sparkle, glitter, wink, flash; *literary* glister.

▸ noun 1 *a glimmer of light* GLEAM, glint, flicker, shimmer, glow, twinkle, sparkle, flash, ray.

2 *a glimmer of hope* GLEAM, flicker, ray, trace, sign, suggestion, hint.

**glimpse** noun *a glimpse of her face* BRIEF LOOK, quick look; glance, peek, peep; sight, sighting.

▸ verb *he glimpsed a figure* CATCH SIGHT OF, notice, discern, spot, spy, sight, pick out, make out; *literary* espy, descry.

**glint** verb *the diamond glinted* SHINE, gleam, catch the light, glitter, sparkle, twinkle, wink, glimmer, shimmer, glisten, flash; *literary* glister.

▸ noun *the glint of the silver* GLITTER, gleam, sparkle, twinkle, glimmer, flash.

**glisten** verb *the sea glistened in the morning light* SHINE, sparkle, twinkle, glint, glitter, glimmer, shimmer, wink, flash; *literary* glister.

**glitter** verb *crystal glittered in the candlelight* SHINE, sparkle, twinkle, glint, gleam, shimmer, glimmer, wink, flash, catch the light; *literary* glister.

▸ noun **1** *the glitter of light on the water* SPARKLE, twinkle, glint, gleam, shimmer, glimmer, flicker, flash; brilliance, luminescence.

**2** *the glitter of show business* GLAMOUR, excitement, thrills, attraction, appeal; dazzle; *informal* razzle-dazzle, razzmatazz, glitz, ritziness.

**gloat** verb *Richard's been gloating ever since he won the lottery* DELIGHT, relish, take great pleasure, revel, rejoice, glory, exult, triumph, crow; boast, brag, be smug, congratulate oneself, preen oneself, pat oneself on the back; rub one's hands together; *informal* rub it in.

**global** adjective **1** *the global economy* WORLDWIDE, international, world, intercontinental.

**2** *a global view of the problem* COMPREHENSIVE, overall, general, all-inclusive, all-encompassing, encyclopedic, universal, blanket; broad, far-reaching, extensive, sweeping.

**globe** noun **1** *every corner of the globe* WORLD, earth, planet.

**2** *the sun is a globe* SPHERE, orb, ball, spheroid, round.

**globule** noun *a globule of gravy on the tablecloth* DROPLET, drop, bead, tear, ball, bubble, pearl; *informal* blob, glob.

**gloom** noun **1** *she peered into the gloom* DARKNESS, dark, dimness, blackness, murkiness, shadows, shade; dusk, twilight, gloaming. ANTONYM light.

**2** *his gloom deepened* DESPONDENCY, depression, dejection, melancholy, melancholia, downheartedness, unhappiness, sadness, glumness, gloominess, misery, sorrow, woe, wretchedness; despair, pessimism, hopelessness; *informal* the blues, the dumps. ANTONYM happiness.

**gloomy** adjective **1** *a gloomy room* DARK, shadowy, sunless, dim, somber, dingy, dismal, dreary, murky, unwelcoming, cheerless, comfortless, funereal; *literary* Stygian. ANTONYMS bright, sunny.

**2** *Joanna looked gloomy* DESPONDENT, downcast, downhearted, dejected, dispirited, disheartened, discouraged, demoralized, crestfallen; depressed, desolate, low, sad, unhappy, glum, melancholy, miserable, woebegone, mournful, forlorn, morose; *informal* blue, down in/at the mouth, down in the dumps; *literary* dolorous. ANTONYMS happy, cheerful.

**3** *gloomy forecasts about the economy* PESSIMISTIC, depressing, downbeat, disheartening, disappointing; unfavorable, bleak, bad, black, somber, grim, cheerless, hopeless. ANTONYMS upbeat, optimistic.

**glorify** verb **1** *they gather to glorify God* PRAISE, extol, exalt, worship, revere, reverence, venerate, pay homage to, honor, adore, thank, give thanks to; *formal* laud; *archaic* magnify.

**2** *a poem to glorify the memory of the dead* ENNOBLE, exalt, elevate, dignify, enhance, augment, promote; praise, celebrate, honor, extol, lionize, acclaim, applaud, hail; glamorize, idealize, romanticize, enshrine, immortalize; *formal* laud. ANTONYM dishonor.

**glorious** adjective **1** *a glorious victory* ILLUSTRIOUS, celebrated, famous, acclaimed, distinguished, honored; outstanding, great, magnificent, noble, triumphant. ANTONYM undistinguished.

**2** *glorious views* WONDERFUL, marvelous, magnificent, superb, sublime, spectacular, lovely, fine, delightful; *informal* super, great, stunning, fantastic, terrific, tremendous, sensational, heavenly, divine, gorgeous, fabulous, fab, awesome, ace, killer; *literary* wondrous, beauteous. ANTONYMS miserable, horrid.

**glory** noun **1** *a sport that won him glory* RENOWN, fame, prestige, honor, distinction, kudos, eminence, acclaim, praise; celebrity, recognition, reputation; *informal* bouquets. ANTONYMS shame, obscurity.

**2** *glory to the Lord* PRAISE, worship, adoration, veneration, honor, reverence, exaltation, homage, thanksgiving, thanks.

**3** *a house restored to its former glory* MAGNIFICENCE, splendor, resplendence, grandeur, majesty, greatness, nobility; opulence, beauty, elegance. ANTONYMS lowliness, modesty.

**4** *the glories of Vermont* WONDER, beauty, delight, marvel, phenomenon; sight, spectacle.

▸ verb *we* ***gloried in*** *our independence* TAKE PLEASURE IN, revel in, rejoice in, delight in; relish, savor; congratulate oneself on, be proud of, boast about, bask in; *informal* get a kick out of, get a thrill out of.

**gloss**[1] noun **1** *the gloss of her hair* SHINE, sheen, luster, gleam, patina, brilliance, shimmer. See note at POLISH.

**2** *beneath the gloss of success* FACADE, veneer, surface, show, camouflage, disguise, mask, smokescreen; window dressing.

▸ verb **1** *she glossed her lips* MAKE GLOSSY, shine; glaze, polish, burnish.

**2** *he tried to* ***gloss over*** *his problems* CONCEAL, cover up, hide, disguise, mask, veil; shrug off, brush aside, play down, minimize, understate, make light of; *informal* brush under the carpet.

**gloss**[2] noun *glosses in the margin* EXPLANATION, interpretation, exegesis, explication, elucidation; annotation, note, footnote, commentary, comment, rubric; translation, definition; *historical* scholium.

▸ verb *difficult words are glossed in a footnote* EXPLAIN, interpret, explicate, define, elucidate; annotate; translate, paraphrase.

**glossy** adjective **1** *a glossy wooden floor* SHINY, gleaming, lustrous, brilliant, shimmering, glistening, satiny, sheeny, smooth, glassy; polished, lacquered, glazed. ANTONYMS dull, lusterless.

**2** *a glossy magazine* EXPENSIVE, high-quality; stylish, fashionable, glamorous; attractive, artistic, upmarket; *informal* classy, ritzy, glitzy. ANTONYMS downmarket, cheap.

**glow** verb **1** *lights glowed from the windows* SHINE, radiate, gleam, glimmer, flicker, flare; luminesce.

**2** *a fire glowed in the hearth* RADIATE HEAT, smolder, burn.

**3** *she glowed with embarrassment* FLUSH, blush, redden, color (up), go pink, go scarlet; burn.

**4** *she glowed with pride* TINGLE, thrill; beam.

▸ noun **1** *the glow of the fire* RADIANCE, light, shine, gleam, glimmer, incandescence, luminescence; warmth, heat.

**2** *a glow spread over her face* FLUSH, blush, rosiness, pinkness, redness, high color; bloom, radiance. ANTONYM pallor.

**3** *a warm glow deep inside her* HAPPINESS, contentment, pleasure, satisfaction.

**glower** verb *she glowered at him* SCOWL, glare, look daggers, frown, lower, give someone a black look; *informal* give someone a dirty look.

▸ noun *the glower on his face* SCOWL, glare, frown, black look; *informal* dirty look.

**glowing** adjective **1** *glowing coals* BRIGHT, shining, radiant, glimmering, flickering, twinkling, incandescent, luminous, luminescent; lit (up), lighted, illuminated, ablaze; aglow, smoldering.

**2** *his glowing cheeks* ROSY, pink, red, flushed, blushing; radiant, blooming, ruddy, florid; hot, burning.

**3** *glowing colors* VIVID, vibrant, bright, brilliant, rich, intense, strong, radiant, warm.

**4** *a glowing report* COMPLIMENTARY, favorable, enthusiastic, positive, commendatory, admiring, lionizing, rapturous, rhapsodic, adulatory; fulsome; *informal* rave.

**glue** noun *a tube of glue* ADHESIVE, fixative, gum, paste, cement; epoxy, epoxy resin, size, sizing, mucilage, stickum.

▸ verb **1** *the planks were glued together* STICK, gum, paste; affix, fix, cement, bond.

**2** *informal she* ***is glued to*** *the television* BE RIVETED TO, be gripped by, be hypnotized by, be mesmerized by.

**glum** adjective *Gary sure looks glum today* GLOOMY, downcast, downhearted, dejected, despondent, crestfallen, disheartened; depressed, desolate, unhappy, doleful, melancholy, miserable, woebegone, mournful, forlorn, in the doldrums, morose; *informal* blue, down in/at the mouth, in a blue funk, down in the dumps. ANTONYM cheerful.

THE RIGHT WORD **glum, doleful, dour, lugubrious, melancholy, saturnine, sullen**

All happy people are alike, to paraphrase Tolstoy, but each unhappy person is unhappy in his or her own way. A **sullen** person is gloomy, untalkative, and ill-humored by nature; a **glum** person is usually silent because of low spirits or depressing circumstances (*to be glum in the face of a plummeting stock market*). **Melancholy** suggests a more or less chronic sadness (*her melancholy was the result of an unhappy childhood*), while a person who is **saturnine** has a forbiddingly gloomy and taciturn nature (*his request was met with a saturnine and scornful silence*). **Dour** refers to a grim and bitter outlook or disposition (*a dour old woman who never smiled*), and **doleful** implies a mournful sadness (*the child's doleful expression as his parents left*). Someone or something described as **lugubrious** is mournful or gloomy in an affected or exaggerated way (*lugubrious songs about lost love*).

**glut** noun *a glut of cars* SURPLUS, excess, surfeit, superfluity, overabundance, superabundance, oversupply, plethora. ANTONYM dearth.

▸ verb *the factories are glutted* OVERLOAD, cram, cram full, overfill, oversupply, saturate, flood, inundate, deluge, swamp, congest; *informal* stuff.

**glutinous** adjective *a glutinous white liquid* STICKY, viscous, viscid, tacky, gluey, gummy, treacly; adhesive; *informal* gooey, cloggy, gloppy.

**glutton** noun *I can barely stomach being at the same table with that glutton* GOURMAND, overeater, big eater, gorger, gobbler; *informal* pig, greedy pig, guzzler.

**gluttonous** adjective *doesn't anyone ever feed those gluttonous children?* GREEDY, gourmandizing, voracious, insatiable, wolfish; *informal* piggish, piggy. See note at GREEDY.

**gluttony** noun *the gluttony you displayed last evening was reprehensible* GREED, greediness, overeating, gourmandism, gourmandizing, voracity, insatiability; *informal* piggishness.

**gnarled** adjective **1** *a gnarled tree trunk* KNOBBLY, knotty, knotted, gnarly, lumpy, bumpy, nodular; twisted, bent, crooked, distorted, contorted.

**2** *gnarled hands* TWISTED, bent, misshapen; arthritic; rough, wrinkled, wizened.

**gnash** verb *she wailed and gnashed her teeth* GRIND, grate, rasp, grit; *archaic* gristbite.

**gnaw** verb **1** *the dog gnawed at a bone* CHEW, chomp, champ, bite, munch, crunch; nibble.

**2** *the pressures are* ***gnawing away at*** *their independence* ERODE, wear away, wear down, eat away (at); consume, devour.

**3** *the doubts* ***gnawed at*** *her* NAG, plague, torment, torture, trouble, distress, worry, haunt, oppress, burden, hang over, bother, fret; niggle at.

**go** verb **1** *he's gone into town* MOVE, proceed, make one's way, advance, progress, pass; walk, travel, journey; *literary* betake oneself.

**2** *the road goes to Michigan Avenue* EXTEND, stretch, reach; lead.

**3** *the money will go to charity* BE GIVEN, be donated, be granted, be presented, be awarded; be devoted; be handed (over).

**4** *it's time to go* LEAVE, depart, go away, withdraw, absent oneself, make an exit, exit; set off, start out, get underway, be on one's way; decamp, retreat, retire, make off, clear out, run off, run away, flee, make a move; *informal* make tracks, push off, beat it, take off, skedaddle, scram, split, scoot. ANTONYMS arrive, come.

**5** *how quickly the years* **go by** PASS, elapse, slip by/past, roll by/past, tick away; fly by/past.

**6** *a golden age that has gone for good* DISAPPEAR, vanish, be no more, cease to exist, come to an end, be over, run its course, fade away; finish, end, cease. ANTONYM return.

**7** *when your money* **is gone**, *you'll come crawling back* BE USED UP, be spent, be exhausted, be consumed, be drained, be depleted.

**8** *I'd like to see my grandchildren before I go* DIE, pass away, pass on, lose one's life, expire, breathe one's last, perish, go to meet one's maker; *informal* give up the ghost, kick the bucket, croak, buy it, bite the big one, buy the farm, check out; *archaic* decease, depart this life.

**9** *the bridge went suddenly* COLLAPSE, give way, fall down, cave in, crumble, disintegrate.

**10** *his hair had gone gray* BECOME, get, turn, grow.

**11** *he heard the bell go* MAKE A SOUND, sound, reverberate, resound; ring, chime, peal, toll, clang.

**12** *everything went well* TURN OUT, work out, develop, come out; result, end (up); *informal* pan out.

**13** *those colors don't go* MATCH, be harmonious, harmonize, blend, be suited, be complementary, coordinate, be compatible. ANTONYM clash.

**14** *my car won't go* FUNCTION, work, run, operate.

**15** *where does the cutlery go?* BELONG, be kept.

**16** *this all goes to prove my point* CONTRIBUTE, help, serve; incline, tend.

▸ noun **1** *her second go* ATTEMPT, try, effort, bid, endeavor; *informal* shot, stab, crack, bash, whirl, whack; *formal* essay.

**2** *he has plenty of go in him* ENERGY, vigor, vitality, life, liveliness, spirit, verve, enthusiasm, zest, vibrancy, sparkle; stamina, dynamism, drive, push, determination; *informal* pep, punch, oomph, get-up-and-go.

PHRASES: **go about** *Ruth went about with her housework* SET ABOUT, begin, embark on, start, commence, address oneself to, get down to, get to work on, get going on, undertake; approach, tackle, attack; *informal* get cracking on/with.

**go along with** *I'm willing to go along with that idea* AGREE TO/WITH, fall in with, comply with, cooperate with, acquiesce in, assent to, follow; submit to, yield to, defer to.

**go around 1** *the wheels were going around* SPIN, revolve, turn, rotate, whirl.

**2** *a nasty rumor is going around* BE SPREAD, be circulated, be put about, circulate, be broadcast.

**go away.** See GO verb sense 4.

**go back on** *she went back on her promise* RENEGE ON, break, fail to honor, default on, repudiate, retract; do an about-face; *informal* cop out (of).

**go by** *we have to go by his decision* OBEY, abide by, comply with, keep to, conform to, follow, heed, defer to, respect.

**go down 1** *the ship went down* SINK, founder, go under.

**2** *interest rates are going down* DECREASE, get lower, fall, drop, decline; plummet, plunge, slump.

**3** *informal they went down in the first round* LOSE, be beaten, be defeated.

**4** *his name will go down in history* BE REMEMBERED, be recorded, be commemorated, be immortalized.

**go far** *stick with your aunts' company and you'll go far* BE SUCCESSFUL, succeed, be a success, do well, get on, get somewhere, get ahead, make good; *informal* make a name for oneself, make one's mark.

**go for 1** *I went for the tuna* CHOOSE, pick, opt for, select, decide on, settle on.

**2** *the dog went for her* ATTACK, assault, hit, strike, beat up, assail, set upon, rush at, lash out at; *informal* lay into, rough up, have a go at, beat up on.

**3** *she goes for younger men* BE ATTRACTED TO, like, fancy; prefer, favor, choose; *informal* have a thing about.

**go in for** *until I got to San Juan, I'd never gone in for water sports* TAKE PART IN, participate in, engage in, get involved in, join in, enter into, undertake; practice, pursue; espouse, adopt, embrace.

**go into** *you should have gone into the subject more thoroughly* INVESTIGATE, examine, inquire into, look into, research, probe, explore, delve into; consider, review, analyze.

**go off** *the bomb went off* EXPLODE, detonate, blow up.

**go on 1** *the lecture went on for hours* LAST, continue, carry on, run on, proceed; endure, persist; take.

**2** *she went on about her cruise* TALK AT LENGTH, ramble, rattle on, chatter, prattle, blather, twitter; *informal* gab, yak, yabber, yatter, run off at the mouth, mouth off.

**3** *I'm not sure what went on* HAPPEN, take place, occur, transpire; *informal* go down; *literary* come to pass, betide.

**go out 1** *the lights went out* BE TURNED OFF, be extinguished; stop burning.

**2** *he's* **going out with** *Kate* SEE, date, take out, be someone's boyfriend/girlfriend, be involved with; *informal* go steady with, go with; *dated* court, woo, step out with.

**go over 1** *go over the figures* EXAMINE, study, scrutinize, inspect, look at/over, scan, check; analyze, appraise, review.

**2** *we are going over our lines* REHEARSE, practice, read through, run through.

**go through 1** *the terrible things she has gone through* UNDERGO, experience, face, suffer, be subjected to, live through, endure, brave, bear, tolerate, withstand, put up with, cope with, weather.

**2** *she went through hundreds of dollars* SPEND, use up, run through, get through, expend, deplete, burn up; waste, squander, fritter away.

**3** *she went through Sue's bag* SEARCH, look through, hunt through, rummage in/through, rifle through.

**4** *I have to go through the report* EXAMINE, study, scrutinize, inspect, look over, scan, check; analyze, appraise, review.

**5** *the deal has gone through* BE COMPLETED, be concluded, be brought off; be approved, be signed, be rubber-stamped, be given the green light.

**go under** *another local restaurant has gone under* GO BANK-

RUPT, be shut (down), go into receivership, go into liquidation, become insolvent, be liquidated, cease trading; fail; *informal* go broke, go belly up, fold.

**go without 1** *I went without breakfast* ABSTAIN FROM, refrain from, forgo, do without, deny oneself.

**2** *the children did not go without* BE DEPRIVED, be in want, go short, go hungry, be in need.

**goad** noun **1** *he applied his goad to the cows* PROD, spike, staff, crook, rod.

**2** *a goad to political change* STIMULUS, incentive, encouragement, inducement, fillip, spur, prod, prompt, catalyst; motive, motivation.

▸ verb *we were goaded into action* PROVOKE, spur, prod, egg on, hound, badger, incite, rouse, stir, move, stimulate, motivate, prompt, induce, encourage, urge, inspire; impel, pressure, dragoon.

**go-ahead** *informal* noun *they gave the go-ahead for the scheme* PERMISSION, consent, leave, license, dispensation, warrant, clearance; authorization, assent, agreement, approval, endorsement, sanction, blessing, nod; *informal* thumbs up, OK, green light.

▸ adjective *go-ahead companies* ENTERPRISING, resourceful, innovative, ingenious, original, creative; progressive, pioneering, modern, forward-looking, enlightened; enthusiastic, ambitious, entrepreneurial, high-powered; bold, daring, audacious, adventurous, dynamic; *informal* go-getting.

**goal** noun *I never numbered wealth as one of my goals* OBJECTIVE, aim, end, target, design, intention, intent, plan, purpose; (holy) grail; ambition, aspiration, wish, dream, brass ring, desire, hope.

**goat** noun **1** *a herd of goats* billy goat, nanny goat, kid.

**2** *be careful of that old goat* LECHER, libertine, womanizer, seducer, Don Juan, Casanova, Lothario, Romeo; pervert, debauchee, rake; *informal* lech, dirty old man, ladykiller, wolf.

**gobble** verb *must you gobble your food so?* | *he* ***gobbled down*** *every last crumb* | *the dogs* ***gobbled up*** *their kibble* EAT GREEDILY, EAT HUNGRILY, guzzle, bolt, gulp (down), devour, wolf (down), gorge (oneself) on; *informal* tuck into, put away, pack away, demolish, polish off, shovel in/down, stuff one's face with, pig out on; *informal* scoff (down/up), scarf (down/up), inhale; *rare* gluttonize, gourmandize, ingurgitate.

**gobbledygook, gobbledegook** noun *informal a letter full of legal gobbledygook* GIBBERISH, claptrap, nonsense, rubbish, balderdash, blather, garbage; *informal* mumbo-jumbo, drivel, tripe, hogwash, baloney, bilge, bull, bunk, guff, eyewash, piffle, twaddle, poppycock, phooey, hooey.

**go-between** noun *history will recognize Carter's skills as a go-between* INTERMEDIARY, middleman, agent, broker, liaison, contact; negotiator, interceder, intercessor, mediator.

**goblet** noun *the goblets go on the right* WINE GLASS, water glass, chalice; glass, tumbler, cup, beaker.

**goblin** noun *the goblins of Yekov would make their surreptitious jaunts into town every third moon* HOBGOBLIN, gnome, dwarf, troll, imp, elf, brownie, fairy, pixie, leprechaun.

**god** noun **1** **(God)** *a gift from God* THE LORD, the Almighty, the Creator, the Maker, the Godhead; Allah, Jehovah, Yahweh; (God) the Father, (God) the Son, the Holy Ghost/Spirit, the Holy Trinity; the Great Spirit, Gitchi Manitou; *humorous* the Man Upstairs.

**2** *sacrifices to appease the gods* DEITY, goddess, divine being, celestial being, divinity, immortal, avatar.

**3** *wooden gods* IDOL, graven image, icon, totem, talisman, fetish, juju.

**godforsaken** adjective *this godforsaken town holds no future for you* WRETCHED, miserable, dreary, dismal, depressing, grim, cheerless, bleak, desolate, gloomy; deserted, neglected, isolated, remote, backward. ANTONYM charming.

**godless** adjective **1** *a godless society* ATHEISTIC, unbelieving, agnostic, skeptical, heretical, faithless, irreligious, ungodly, unholy, impious, profane; infidel, heathen, idolatrous, pagan; satanic, devilish. ANTONYM religious.

**2** *godless pleasures* IMMORAL, wicked, sinful, wrong, evil, bad, iniquitous, corrupt; irreligious, sacrilegious, profane, blasphemous, impious; depraved, degenerate, debauched, perverted, decadent; impure. ANTONYM virtuous.

**godlike** adjective *the godlike giants of Roman mythology* DIVINE, godly, superhuman; angelic, seraphic; spiritual, heavenly, celestial; sacred, holy, saintly.

**godly** adjective *their claims of a godly agenda do not jibe with their hateful activities* RELIGIOUS, devout, pious, reverent, believing, God-fearing, saintly, holy, prayerful, spiritual, churchgoing.

**godsend** noun *the state subsidies have been a godsend to our preschool center* BOON, blessing, bonus, plus, benefit, advantage, help, aid, asset; stroke of luck, windfall, manna (from heaven). ANTONYM curse.

**goings-on** plural noun *the goings-on at his Hollywood parties have become legendary* EVENTS, happenings, affairs, business; mischief, misbehavior, misconduct, funny business; *informal* monkey business, hanky-panky, shenanigans.

**gold** noun **1** *she won the gold* GOLD MEDAL, first prize.

**2** *he struck gold* PAY DIRT, the jackpot, the bull's-eye.

**golden** adjective **1** *her golden hair* BLOND/BLONDE, yellow, fair, flaxen, tow-colored. ANTONYMS dark, raven.

**2** *a golden time* SUCCESSFUL, prosperous, flourishing, thriving; favorable, providential, lucky, fortunate; happy, joyful, glorious. ANTONYMS unsuccessful, unhappy.

**3** *a golden opportunity* EXCELLENT, fine, superb, splendid; special, unique; favorable, opportune, promising, bright, full of promise; advantageous, profitable, valuable, providential.

**4** *the golden girl of tennis* FAVORITE, favored, popular, admired, beloved, pet; acclaimed, applauded, praised; brilliant, consummate, gifted; *informal* blue-eyed; *formal* lauded.

**good** adjective **1** *a good product* FINE, superior, quality; excellent, superb, outstanding, magnificent, exceptional, marvelous, wonderful, first-rate, first-class, sterling; satisfactory, acceptable, not bad, all right; *informal* great, OK, A1, jake, hunky-dory, ace, terrific, fantastic, fabulous, fab, top-notch, blue-chip, blue-ribbon, bang-up, killer, class, awesome, wicked; smashing, brilliant. ANTONYM bad.

**2** *a good person* VIRTUOUS, righteous, upright, upstanding, moral, ethical, high-minded, principled; exemplary, law-abiding, irreproachable, blameless, guiltless, unimpeachable, honorable, scrupulous, reputable, decent, respectable, noble, trustworthy; meritorious, praiseworthy, admirable; whiter than white, saintly, saintlike, angelic; *informal* squeaky clean. ANTONYM wicked.

**3** *the children are good at school* WELL-BEHAVED, obedient, dutiful, polite, courteous, respectful, deferential, compliant. ANTONYM naughty.

**4** *a good thing to do* RIGHT, correct, proper, decorous, seemly; appropriate, fitting, apt, suitable; convenient, expedient, favorable, opportune, felicitous, timely; *archaic* meet.

**5** *a good driver* CAPABLE, able, proficient, adept, adroit, accomplished, skillful, skilled, talented, masterly, virtuoso, expert; *informal* great, mean, wicked, nifty, ace, crackerjack. ANTONYM inept.

**6** *a good friend* CLOSE, intimate, dear, bosom, special, best, firm, valued, treasured; loving, devoted, loyal, faithful, constant, reliable, dependable, trustworthy, trusty, true, unfailing, staunch.

**7** *the dogs are in good condition* HEALTHY, fine, sound, tiptop, hale and hearty, fit, robust, sturdy, strong, vigorous. ANTONYMS poor, ill.

**8** *a good time was had by all* ENJOYABLE, pleasant, agreeable, pleasurable, delightful, great, nice, lovely; amusing, diverting, jolly, merry, lively; *informal* super, fantastic, fabulous, fab, terrific, grand, brilliant, killer, peachy, ducky. ANTONYMS unpleasant, terrible.

**9** *it was good of you to come* KIND, kindhearted, good-hearted, thoughtful, generous, charitable, magnanimous, gracious; altruistic, unselfish, selfless. ANTONYMS unkind, thoughtless.

**10** *a good time to call* CONVENIENT, suitable, appropriate, fitting, fit; opportune, timely, favorable, advantageous, expedient, felicitous, happy, providential. ANTONYM inconvenient.

**11** *bananas are good for you* WHOLESOME, healthy, healthful, nourishing, nutritious, nutritional, beneficial, salubrious. ANTONYMS bad, unhealthy.

**12** *are these eggs good?* EDIBLE, safe to eat, fit for human consumption; fresh, wholesome, consumable; *formal* comestible. ANTONYMS bad, inedible.

**13** *good food* DELICIOUS, tasty, mouthwatering, appetizing, flavorful, delectable, toothsome, palatable; succulent, luscious; *informal* scrumptious, delish, yummy, lip-smacking, finger-licking, nummy, melt-in-your-mouth.

**14** *a good reason* VALID, genuine, authentic, legitimate, sound, bona fide; convincing, persuasive, telling, potent, cogent, compelling. ANTONYM unconvincing.

**15** *we waited a good hour* WHOLE, full, entire, complete, solid.

**16** *a good number of them* CONSIDERABLE, sizable, substantial, appreciable, significant; goodly, fair, reasonable; plentiful, abundant, great, large, generous; *informal* tidy. ANTONYM small.

**17** *wear your good clothes* BEST, finest, nicest; special, party, Sunday, formal, dressy, smart, smartest. ANTONYMS casual, everyday.

**18** *good weather* FINE, fair, dry; bright, clear, sunny, cloudless; calm, windless; warm, mild, balmy, clement, pleasant, nice. ANTONYMS bad, inclement.

▸ noun **1** *issues of good and evil* VIRTUE, righteousness, goodness, morality, integrity, rectitude; honesty, truth, honor, probity; propriety, worthiness, merit; blamelessness, purity. ANTONYM wickedness.

**2** *it's all for your good* BENEFIT, advantage, profit, gain, interest, welfare, well-being; enjoyment, comfort, ease, convenience; help, aid, assistance, service; behalf. ANTONYM disadvantage.

▸ exclamation *good, that's settled* FINE, very well, all right, right, all right then, yes, agreed; *informal* okay, OK, okey-dokey.

PHRASES: **for good** *those days are gone for good* FOREVER, permanently, for always, evermore, forevermore, for ever and ever, for eternity, never to return, forevermore; *informal* for keeps, until the cows come home, until hell freezes over; *archaic* for aye.

**make good 1** *if I don't get away from my family, I'll never make good* SUCCEED, be successful, be a success, do well, get ahead, reach the top; prosper, flourish, thrive; *informal* make it, make the grade, make a name for oneself, make one's mark, get somewhere, arrive.

**2** *he promised to make good any damage* REPAIR, mend, fix, put right, see to; restore, remedy, rectify.

**3** *they made good their escape* EFFECT, conduct, perform, implement, execute, carry out; achieve, accomplish, succeed in, realize, attain, engineer, bring about, bring off.

**4** *he will make good his promise* FULFILL, carry out, implement, discharge, honor, redeem; keep, observe, abide by, comply with, stick to, heed, follow, be bound by, live up to, stand by, adhere to.

**goodbye** exclamation *Goodbye! See you all next year!* FAREWELL, adieu, au revoir, ciao, adios; bye, bye-bye, so long, see you later, see you, sayonara; bon voyage; cheers; *informal* toodle-oo. ANTONYM hello.

▸ noun (often **goodbyes**) *we said our goodbyes at the door* PARTING, leave-taking, send-off.

**good-for-nothing** adjective *a good-for-nothing bum* USELESS, worthless, incompetent, inefficient, inept, ne'er-do-well; lazy, idle, slothful, indolent, shiftless; *informal* no-good, lousy. ANTONYM worthy.

▸ noun *lazy good-for-nothings* NE'ER-DO-WELL, layabout, do-nothing, idler, loafer, lounger, sluggard, shirker, underachiever; *informal* slacker, lazybones, couch potato.

**good-humored** adjective *Disney insisted on hiring only the most good-humored of personnel* GENIAL, affable, cordial, friendly, amiable, easygoing, approachable, good-natured, cheerful, cheery; companionable, comradely, sociable, convivial; *informal* chummy. ANTONYM grumpy.

**good-looking** adjective *a good-looking couple* ATTRACTIVE, beautiful, pretty, handsome, lovely, stunning, striking, arresting, gorgeous, prepossessing, fetching, captivating, bewitching, beguiling, engaging, charming, enchanting, appealing, delightful; sexy, seductive, alluring, tantalizing, irresistible, ravishing, desirable; *Scottish* bonny; *informal* hot, easy on the eye, drop-dead gorgeous, cute, foxy, bodacious; *literary* beauteous; *archaic* comely, fair. ANTONYM ugly.

**goodly** adjective *I'll bet he paid a goodly sum for that car* LARGE, largish, sizable, substantial, considerable, respectable, significant, decent, generous, handsome; *informal* tidy, serious. ANTONYM paltry.

**good-natured** adjective *the crowd was rowdy but good-natured* WARMHEARTED, friendly, amiable; neighborly, benevolent, kind, kindhearted, generous, unselfish, considerate, thoughtful, obliging, helpful, supportive, charitable; understanding, sympathetic, easygoing, accommodating. ANTONYM malicious.

**goodness** noun **1** *she must have seen some goodness in him* VIRTUE, good, righteousness, morality, integrity, rectitude; honesty, truth, truthfulness, honor, probity; propriety, decency, respectability, nobility, worthiness, worth, merit, trustworthiness; blamelessness, purity.

**2** *the neighbor's goodness toward us* KINDNESS, kindliness, tenderheartedness, humanity, mildness, benevolence, graciousness; tenderness, warmth, affection, love, goodwill; sympathy, compassion, care, concern, understanding, tolerance, generosity, charity, leniency, clemency, magnanimity.

**3** *slow cooking retains the food's goodness* NUTRITIONAL VALUE, nutrients, wholesomeness, nourishment.

THE RIGHT WORD **goodness, morality, probity, rectitude, virtue**

Of all these words denoting moral excellence, **goodness** is the broadest in meaning. It describes an excellence so well established that it is thought of as inherent or innate and is associated with kindness, generosity, helpfulness, and sincerity (*she has more goodness in her little finger than most people have in their whole body*). **Morality**, on the other hand, is moral excellence based on a code of ethical conduct or religious teaching (*his behavior was kept in line by fear of punishment rather than morality*). Although it is often used as a synonym for *goodness*, **virtue** suggests moral excellence that is acquired rather than innate and that is consciously or steadfastly maintained, often in spite of temptations or evil influences (*her virtue was as unassailable as her noble character*). **Rectitude** is used to describe strict adherence to the rules of just or right behavior and carries strong connotations of sternness and self-discipline (*he had a reputation for rectitude and insisted on absolute truthfulness*). **Probity** describes an honesty or integrity that has been tried and proved (*as mayor, she displayed a probity that was rare in a politician*).

**goods** plural noun **1** *he dispatched the goods* MERCHANDISE, wares, stock, commodities, produce, products, articles; imports, exports.

**2** *the dead woman's goods* PROPERTY, possessions, worldly possessions, effects, chattels, valuables; *informal* things, stuff, junk, gear, bits and pieces.

**goodwill** noun *your acts of goodwill have not gone unnoticed* BENEVOLENCE, compassion, goodness, kindness, consideration, charity; cooperation, collaboration; friendliness, amity, thoughtfulness, decency, sympathy, understanding, neighborliness. ANTONYM hostility.

**gorge** noun *the river runs through a gorge* RAVINE, canyon, gully, defile, couloir; chasm, gulf; gulch, coulee.

▸ verb **1** *they gorged themselves on cake* STUFF, cram, fill; glut, satiate, overindulge, overfill; *informal* pig out.

**2** *vultures* ***gorged on*** *the flesh* DEVOUR, guzzle, gobble, gulp (down), wolf (down); *informal* demolish, polish off, scoff (down), down, stuff one's face with; scarf (down/up).

**gorgeous** adjective **1** *a gorgeous woman.* See GOOD-LOOKING.

**2** *a gorgeous view* SPECTACULAR, splendid, superb, wonderful, grand, impressive, awe-inspiring, awesome, amazing, stunning, breathtaking, incredible; *informal* sensational, fabulous, fantastic.

**3** *gorgeous uniforms* RESPLENDENT, magnificent, sumptuous, luxurious, elegant, opulent; dazzling, brilliant. ANTONYM drab.

**gory** adjective **1** *a gory ritual slaughter* GRISLY, gruesome, violent, bloody, brutal, savage; ghastly, frightful, horrid, fearful, hideous, macabre, horrible, horrific; shocking, appalling, monstrous, unspeakable; *informal* blood-and-guts.

**2** *gory pieces of flesh* BLOODY, bloodstained, bloodsoaked.

**gospel** noun **1** **(the Gospel)** *the Gospel according to John* CHRISTIAN TEACHING, Christian doctrine, Christ's teaching; the word of God, the good news, the New Testament.

**2** *don't treat this as gospel* THE TRUTH; fact, actual fact, reality, actuality, factuality, the case, a certainty.

**3** *her gospel of nonviolence* DOCTRINE, dogma, teaching, principle, ethic, creed, credo, ideology, ideal; belief, tenet, canon.

**gossamer** noun *her dress swirled like gossamer* COBWEBS; silk, gauze, chiffon.

▸ adjective *a gossamer veil* GAUZY, gossamery, fine, diaphanous, delicate, filmy, floaty, chiffony, cobwebby, wispy, thin, light, insubstantial, flimsy; translucent, transparent, see-through, sheer.

**gossip** noun **1** *tell me all the gossip* RUMOR(S), tittle-tattle, whispers, canards, tidbits; scandal, hearsay; *informal* dirt, buzz, scuttlebutt.

**2** *she's such a gossip* SCANDALMONGER, gossipmonger, tattler, busybody, muckraker, flibbertigibbet.

▸ verb *she gossiped about Dean's wife* SPREAD RUMORS, spread gossip, talk, whisper, tell tales, tittle-tattle, tattle; *informal* dish the dirt.

**govern** verb **1** *he governs the province* RULE, preside over, reign over, control, be in charge of, command, lead, dominate; run, head, administer, manage, regulate, oversee, supervise; *informal* be in the driver's seat of.

**2** *the rules governing social behavior* DETERMINE, decide, control, regulate, direct, rule, dictate, shape; affect, influence, sway, act on, mold, modify, impact on.

**government** noun **1** *the government announced further cuts* ADMINISTRATION, executive, regime, authority, powers that be, directorate, council, leadership; cabinet, ministry; *informal* feds; (**the government**) Washington.

**2** *her job was the government of the district* RULE, governing, running, leadership, control, administration, regulation, management, supervision.

**gown** noun *a blue gown with seed pearls on the bodice* DRESS, evening gown, prom dress, prom gown, wedding gown; frock, shift; robe, dressing gown.

**grab** verb **1** *Jessica grabbed his arm* SEIZE, grasp, snatch, take hold of, grip, clasp, clutch; take; *informal* glom on to.

**2** *informal I'll grab another drink* GET, acquire, obtain; buy, purchase, procure; secure, snap up; gather, collect, garner; achieve, attain; *informal* get one's hands on, get one's mitts on, get hold of, bag, score, nab.

▸ noun *she made a grab for his gun* LUNGE, snatch.

PHRASE: **up for grabs** *informal dozens of prizes are up for grabs* AVAILABLE, obtainable, to be had, for the taking; for sale, on the market; *informal* for the asking, on tap, gettable.

**grace** noun **1** *the grace of a ballerina* ELEGANCE, poise, gracefulness, finesse; suppleness, agility, nimbleness, lightfootedness. ANTONYMS inelegance, stiffness.

**2** *he at least had the grace to look sheepish* COURTESY, decency, (good) manners, politeness, decorum, respect, tact. ANTONYM effrontery.

**3** *she fell from grace* FAVOR, approval, approbation, acceptance, esteem, regard, respect; goodwill. ANTONYM disfavor.

**4** *he lived there by grace of the king* FAVOR, goodwill, generosity, kindness, indulgence; *formal* benefaction.

**5** *they have five days' grace to decide* DEFERMENT, deferral, postponement, suspension, adjournment, delay, pause; respite, stay, moratorium, reprieve.

**6** *who would like to say this evening's grace?* BLESSING, prayer of thanks, thanksgiving, benediction.

▸ verb **1** *the occasion was graced by the president* DIGNIFY, distinguish, honor, favor; enhance, ennoble, glorify, elevate, aggrandize, upgrade.

**2** *a mosaic graced the floor* ADORN, embellish, decorate, ornament, enhance; beautify, prettify, enrich, bedeck.

**graceful** adjective *our dancers must be both muscular and graceful* ELEGANT, fluid, fluent, natural, neat; agile, supple, nimble, light-footed.

**gracious** adjective **1** *a gracious hostess* COURTEOUS, polite, civil, chivalrous, well-mannered, mannerly, decorous; tactful, diplomatic; kind, benevolent, considerate, thoughtful, obliging, accommodating, indulgent, magnanimous; friendly, amiable, cordial, hospitable. ANTONYM rude.

**2** *gracious colonial buildings* ELEGANT, stylish, tasteful, graceful; comfortable, luxurious, sumptuous, opulent, grand, high-class; *informal* swanky, plush. ANTONYMS shabby, crude.

**3** *God's gracious intervention* MERCIFUL, compassionate, kind; forgiving, lenient, clement, forbearing, humane, tenderhearted, sympathetic; indulgent, generous, magnanimous, benign, benevolent. ANTONYM cruel.

**grade** noun **1** *a higher grade of steel* CATEGORY, set, class, classification, grouping, group, bracket.

**2** *his job is of the lowest grade* RANK, level, echelon, standing, position, class, status, order; step, rung, stratum, tier.

**3** *she got the best grades in the class* MARK, score; assessment, evaluation, appraisal.

**4** *he's in grade 5* YEAR; class.

**5** *a steep grade.* See GRADIENT.

▸ verb **1** *eggs are graded by size* CLASSIFY, class, categorize, bracket, sort, group, arrange, pigeonhole; rank, evaluate, rate, value.

**2** *the essays have been graded* SCORE, mark, assess, judge, evaluate, appraise.

**3** *the colors grade into one another* BLEND, shade, merge, pass.

PHRASE: **make the grade** *informal he lacked the experience to make the grade* QUALIFY, be up to scratch, come up to standard, pass, pass muster, measure up; succeed, win through; *informal* be up to snuff, cut it, cut the mustard.

**gradient** noun **1** *the gradient of Miller's Hill Road is less steep than it was fifty years ago* SLOPE, incline, hill, rise, ramp, bank; declivity, grade.

**2** *the gradient of the line* STEEPNESS, angle, slant, slope, inclination.

**gradual** adjective **1** *a gradual transition* SLOW, measured, unhurried, cautious; piecemeal, step-by-step, progressive, continuous, systematic, steady. ANTONYMS abrupt, sudden.

**2** *a gradual slope* GENTLE, moderate, slight, easy. ANTONYM steep.

**gradually** adverb *the icicles gradually got longer throughout the day | gradually add the flour mixture* SLOWLY, slowly but surely, cautiously, gently, gingerly; piecemeal, little by little, bit by bit, inch by inch, by degrees; progressively, systematically; regularly, steadily.

**graduate** verb **1** *he wants to teach when he graduates* GET ONE'S DIPLOMA, get one's degree, pass one's exams, complete/finish one's studies.

**2** *she wants to graduate to serious drama* PROGRESS, advance, move up.

**3** *a thermometer graduated in Fahrenheit* CALIBRATE, mark off, measure out, grade.

**graft**[1] noun **1** *grafts may die from lack of water* SCION, cutting, shoot, offshoot, bud, sprout, sprig.

**2** *a skin graft* TRANSPLANT, implant.

▸ verb **1** *graft a bud onto the stem* AFFIX, join, insert, splice.

**2** *tissue is grafted on to the cornea* TRANSPLANT, implant.

**3** *a mansion grafted on to a farmhouse* ATTACH, add, join.

**graft**[2] noun *sweeping measures to curb official graft* CORRUPTION, bribery, dishonesty, deceit, fraud, unlawful practices, illegal means, payola; *informal* palm-greasing, hush money, kickbacks, crookedness. ANTONYM honesty.

**grain** noun **1** *the local farmers grow grain* CEREAL, cereal crops.

**2** *a grain of wheat* KERNEL, seed, grist.

**3** *grains of sand* GRANULE, particle, speck, mote, mite; bit, piece; scrap, crumb, fragment, morsel.

**4** *a grain of truth* TRACE, hint, tinge, suggestion, shadow; bit, soupçon; scintilla, ounce, iota, jot, whit, scrap, shred; *informal* smidgen, smidge, tad.

**5** *the grain of the lumber* TEXTURE, surface, finish; weave, pattern.

**grand** adjective **1** *a grand hotel* MAGNIFICENT, imposing, impressive, awe-inspiring, splendid, resplendent, majestic, monumental; palatial, stately, large; luxurious, sumptuous, lavish, opulent, upmarket, upscale; *informal* fancy, posh, plush, classy, swanky, five-star. ANTONYMS inferior, unimpressive.

**2** *a grand scheme* AMBITIOUS, bold, epic, big, extravagant.

**3** *a grand old lady* AUGUST, distinguished, illustrious, eminent, esteemed, honored, venerable, dignified, respectable; preeminent, prominent, notable, renowned, celebrated, famous; aristocratic, noble, regal, blue-blooded, high-born, patrician; *informal* upper-crust. ANTONYMS ordinary, humble.

**4** *a grand total of $2,000* COMPLETE, comprehensive, all-inclusive, inclusive; final. ANTONYM partial.

**5** *the grand staircase* MAIN, principal, central, prime; biggest, largest. ANTONYMS minor, secondary.

**6** *informal you're doing a grand job* EXCELLENT, very good, marvelous, first-class, first-rate, wonderful, outstanding, sterling, fine, splendid, superb, terrific, fabulous, great; *informal* super, ace, killer; smashing, brilliant. ANTONYM poor.

▸ noun *informal a check for ten grand* THOUSAND DOLLARS; *informal* thou, K/Ks; G/Gs, gee/gees.

**grandeur** noun *the grandeur of the Rockies | the grandeur of a royal wedding* SPLENDOR, magnificence, impressiveness, glory, resplendence, majesty, greatness; stateliness, pomp, ceremony.

**grandfather** noun **1** *his grandfather lives here informal* granddad, grandad, grandpa, gramps, grampy, granddaddy, grandaddy, poppa.

**2** *the grandfather of modern liberalism* FOUNDER, inventor, originator, creator, initiator; father, founding father, pioneer.

**3** *our pioneering grandfathers* FOREFATHER, forebear, ancestor, progenitor, antecedent.

▸ verb *federal funding was eliminated for these air-polluting road projects, but a loophole has grandfathered the previously funded projects* EXEMPT, excuse, free, exclude, grant immunity to, spare, absolve; *informal* let off (the hook).

**grandiloquent** adjective *grandiloquent speeches* POMPOUS, bombastic, magniloquent, pretentious, ostentatious, high-flown, orotund, florid, flowery; overwrought, overblown, overdone; *informal* highfalutin, purple. ANTONYM understated.

**grandiose** adjective **1** *the court's grandiose facade* MAGNIFICENT, impressive, grand, imposing, awe-inspiring, splendid, resplendent, majestic, glorious, elaborate; palatial, stately, luxurious, opulent; *informal* plush, swanky, flash. ANTONYMS humble, unimpressive.

**2** *a grandiose plan* AMBITIOUS, bold, overambitious, extravagant, high-flown, flamboyant; *informal* over the top. ANTONYMS humble, modest.

**grandmother** noun *informal* grandma, gramma, granny, grannie, gran, nana.

**grant** verb **1** *he granted them leave of absence* ALLOW, accord, permit, afford, vouchsafe. ANTONYM refuse.

**2** *he granted them $20,000* GIVE, award, bestow on, confer on, present with, provide with, endow with, supply with. See note at GIVE.

**3** *I grant that the difference is not absolute* ADMIT, accept, concede, yield, allow, appreciate, recognize, acknowledge, confess; agree. ANTONYM deny.

▸ noun *a grant from the council* ENDOWMENT, subvention, award, donation, bursary, allowance, subsidy, contribution, handout, allocation, gift; scholarship.

**granule** noun *minute granules of gold* GRAIN, particle, fragment, bit, crumb, morsel, mote, speck.

**graph** noun *use graphs to analyze your data* CHART, diagram; bar chart, pie chart, histogram, scatter diagram.

▸ verb *we graphed the new prices* PLOT, trace, draw up, delineate.

**graphic** adjective **1** *a graphic representation of language* VISUAL, symbolic, pictorial, illustrative, diagrammatic; drawn, written.

**2** *a graphic account of the war* VIVID, explicit, expressive, detailed; uninhibited, powerful, colorful, rich, lurid, shocking; realistic, descriptive, illustrative; telling, effective. ANTONYM vague.

▸ noun *Computing this printer's good enough for graphics* PICTURE, illustration, image; diagram, graph, chart; **(graphics)** art, visual art.

THE RIGHT WORD **graphic, pictorial, picturesque, vivid**

A photograph of a car accident on the front page of a newspaper might be described as **graphic**, while a photograph of a mountain village would be called **picturesque**. Both adjectives are used to describe things that have visual impact or that produce a strong, clear impression, but *graphic* means having the power to evoke a strikingly lifelike representation, whether it is in pictures or in words (*the driving instructor gave them a graphic description of what happens in a 50-mph head-on collision*). **Vivid** is a more general term suggesting something that is felt, seen, heard, or apprehended with a sense of intense reality (*the vivid colors of the landscape; a vivid memory of the horrors of war*). Something that is **pictorial** aims to present a vivid picture (*a pictorial writing style*), while **picturesque** usually applies to scenes, pictures, etc. that are visually striking because they are panoramic, quaint, or unusual (*from a distance the village looked picturesque, but up close it was seen to be rundown*).

---

**grapple** verb **1** *the policemen grappled with him* WRESTLE, struggle, tussle; brawl, fight, scuffle, battle.

**2** *he grappled his prey* SEIZE, grab, catch, catch hold of, take hold of, grasp.

**3** *she is* ***grappling with*** *her problems* TACKLE, confront, face, deal with, cope with, come to grips with; apply oneself to, devote oneself to.

**grasp** verb **1** *she grasped his hands* GRIP, clutch, clasp, hold, clench; catch, seize, grab, snatch, latch on to. ANTONYM release.

**2** *everybody grasped the important points* UNDERSTAND, comprehend, follow, take in, perceive, see, apprehend, assimilate, absorb; *informal* get, catch on to, figure out, get one's head around, take on board.

**3** *he grasped the opportunity* TAKE ADVANTAGE OF, act on; seize, leap at, snatch, jump at, pounce on. ANTONYMS miss, overlook.

▸ noun **1** *his grasp on her hand* GRIP, hold; clutch, clasp, clench.

**2** *his domineering mother's grasp* CONTROL, power, clutches, command, domination, rule, tyranny.

**3** *a prize lay within their grasp* REACH, scope, power, limits, range; sights.

**4** *your grasp of history* UNDERSTANDING, comprehension, perception, apprehension, awareness, grip, knowledge; mastery, command.

**grate** verb **1** *she grated the cheese* SHRED, pulverize, mince, grind, granulate, crush, crumble.

**2** *her bones grated together* GRIND, rub, rasp, scrape, jar, grit, creak.

**3** *the tune is beginning to grate* IRRITATE, set someone's teeth on edge, jar; annoy, nettle, chafe, fret; *informal* aggravate, get on someone's nerves, get under someone's skin, get someone's goat.

**grateful** adjective *we were all grateful to Rita* THANKFUL, appreciative; indebted, obliged, obligated, in someone's debt, beholden.

**gratify** verb **1** *it gratified him to be seen with her* PLEASE, gladden, make happy, delight, make someone feel good, satisfy; *informal* tickle pink, buck up. See note at PLEASANT. ANTONYM displease.

**2** *he gratified her desires* SATISFY, fulfill, indulge, comply with, pander to, cater to, give in to, satiate, feed, accommodate. ANTONYM frustrate.

**grating** adjective **1** *the chair made a grating noise* SCRAPING, scratching, grinding, rasping, jarring.

**2** *a grating voice* HARSH, raucous, strident, piercing, shrill, screechy; discordant, cacophonous; hoarse, rough, gravelly. ANTONYMS harmonious, pleasing.

**3** *it's written in grating language* IRRITATING, annoying, infuriating, irksome, maddening, displeasing, tiresome; jarring, unsuitable, inappropriate; *informal* aggravating. ANTONYMS pleasing, appropriate.

**gratis** adverb *the room was provided gratis, courtesy of the casino* FREE, free of charge, without charge, for nothing, at no cost, gratuitously; *informal* on the house, for free.

**gratitude** noun *Chip was miffed by his nephew's lack of gratitude* GRATEFULNESS, thankfulness, thanks, appreciation, indebtedness; recognition, acknowledgment, credit.

**gratuitous** adjective *there was one moment of nudity in the movie, and it was ridiculously gratuitous* UNJUSTIFIED, uncalled for, unwarranted, unprovoked, undue; indefensible, unjustifiable; needless, unnecessary, inessential, unmerited, groundless, senseless, wanton, indiscriminate; excessive, immoderate, inordinate, inappropriate. ANTONYM necessary.

**gratuity** noun *I'm not allowed to accept this gratuity* TIP, gift, present, donation, reward, handout; bonus, extra; baksheesh. See note at PRESENT3.

**grave**1 noun *she left flowers at his grave* BURIAL SITE, gravesite, cemetery plot, tomb, sepulcher, vault, burial chamber, mausoleum, crypt; last resting place.

**grave**2 adjective **1** *a grave matter* SERIOUS, important, weighty, profound, significant, momentous; critical, acute, urgent, pressing; dire, terrible, awful, dreadful; *formal* exigent. ANTONYM trivial.

**2** *Jackie looked grave* SOLEMN, serious, sober, unsmiling, grim, somber; severe, stern, dour. ANTONYM cheerful.

**graveyard** noun *he visits the graveyard every Sunday* CEMETERY, burial ground, burying ground, necropolis, columbarium, memorial park/garden; *informal* boneyard; *historical* potter's field.

**gravitate** verb *take her to a bar, and she automatically gravitates to the lowlifes* MOVE, head, drift, be drawn, be attracted; tend, lean, incline.

**gravity** noun **1** *the gravity of the situation* SERIOUSNESS, importance, significance, weight, consequence, magnitude;

acuteness, urgency, exigence; awfulness, dreadfulness; *formal* moment.

2 *the gravity of his demeanor* SOLEMNITY, seriousness, somberness, sobriety, soberness, severity, grimness, humorlessness, dourness; gloominess.

**gray** adjective 1 *a gray suit* silvery, silver-gray, gunmetal, slate, charcoal, smoky.

2 *his gray hair* WHITE, silver, hoary.

3 *a gray day* CLOUDY, overcast, dull, sunless, gloomy, dreary, dismal, somber, bleak, murky. ANTONYMS sunny, bright.

4 *her face looked gray* ASHEN, wan, pale, pasty, pallid, colorless, bloodless, white, waxen; sickly, peaked, drained, drawn, deathly. ANTONYM ruddy.

5 *the gray daily routine* CHARACTERLESS, colorless, nondescript, insipid, jejune, unremarkable, flat, bland, dry, stale; dull, uninteresting, boring, tedious, monotonous, monochrome. ANTONYM lively.

6 *their policy regarding unmarried couples is a gray area* AMBIGUOUS, unclear, uncertain, doubtful, indefinite, indistinct, indeterminate, debatable, open to question. ANTONYMS black and white, certain.

▸ verb *the population grayed* AGE, grow old, mature.

**graze**[1] verb *the deer grazed* FEED, eat, nibble, browse.

**graze**[2] verb 1 *she grazed her knuckles on the box* SCRAPE, abrade, skin, scratch, chafe, bark, scuff, rasp; cut, nick.

2 *his shot grazed the far post* TOUCH, brush, shave, skim, kiss, scrape, clip, glance off.

▸ noun *grazes on the skin* SCRATCH, scrape, abrasion, cut; *Medicine* trauma.

**greasy** adjective 1 *a plate of greasy food* FATTY, oily, buttery, oleaginous; *formal* pinguid. ANTONYM lean.

2 *greasy hair* OILY. ANTONYM dry.

3 *the pole was very greasy* SLIPPERY, slick, slimy, slithery, oily; *informal* slippy. ANTONYM dry.

4 *a greasy little man* INGRATIATING, obsequious, sycophantic, fawning, toadying, groveling; effusive, gushing, gushy; unctuous, oily; *informal* smarmy, slimy, bootlicking.

**great** adjective 1 *they showed great interest* CONSIDERABLE, substantial, significant, appreciable, special, serious; exceptional, extraordinary. ANTONYM little.

2 *a great expanse of water* LARGE, big, extensive, expansive, broad, wide, sizable, ample; vast, immense, huge, enormous, massive; *informal* humongous, whopping, ginormous. ANTONYM small.

3 *you great fool!* ABSOLUTE, total, utter, out-and-out, downright, thoroughgoing, complete; perfect, positive, prize, sheer, arrant, unqualified, consummate, veritable.

4 *great writers* PROMINENT, eminent, important, distinguished, illustrious, celebrated, honored, acclaimed, admired, esteemed, revered, renowned, notable, famous, famed, well-known; leading, top, major, principal, first-rate, matchless, peerless, star. ANTONYM minor.

5 *the great navies in world history* POWERFUL, dominant, influential, strong, potent, formidable, redoubtable; leading, important, foremost, major, chief, principal. ANTONYM minor.

6 *a great castle* MAGNIFICENT, imposing, impressive, awe-inspiring, grand, splendid, majestic, sumptuous, resplendent. ANTONYM modest.

7 *a great sportsman* EXPERT, skillful, skilled, adept, accomplished, talented, fine, masterly, master, brilliant, virtuoso, marvelous, outstanding, first-class, superb; *informal* crack, ace, A1, class. ANTONYM poor.

8 *a great fan of rugby* ENTHUSIASTIC, eager, keen, zealous, devoted, ardent, fanatical, passionate, dedicated, committed. ANTONYM unenthusiastic.

9 *we had a great time* ENJOYABLE, delightful, lovely, pleasant, congenial; exciting, thrilling; excellent, marvelous, wonderful, fine, splendid, very good; *informal* terrific, fantastic, fabulous, splendiferous, fab, super, grand, cool, hunky-dory, killer, swell. ANTONYM bad.

**greatly** adverb *your donations are greatly appreciated* VERY MUCH, considerably, substantially, appreciably, significantly, markedly, sizably, seriously, materially, profoundly; enormously, vastly, immensely, tremendously, mightily, abundantly, extremely, exceedingly; *informal* plenty, majorly. ANTONYM slightly.

**greatness** noun 1 *a child destined for greatness* EMINENCE, distinction, illustriousness, repute, high standing; importance, significance; celebrity, fame, prominence, renown.

2 *her greatness as a writer* GENIUS, prowess, talent, expertise, mastery, artistry, virtuosity, skill, proficiency; flair, finesse; caliber, distinction.

**greedy** adjective 1 *a greedy eater* GLUTTONOUS, ravenous, voracious, intemperate, self-indulgent, insatiable, wolfish; *informal* piggish, piggy.

2 *a greedy capitalist* AVARICIOUS, acquisitive, covetous, grasping, materialistic, mercenary, possessive; *informal* money-grubbing, money-grabbing, grabby.

3 *she is greedy for an award* EAGER, avid, hungry, craving, longing, yearning, hankering; impatient, anxious; *informal* dying, itching.

**THE RIGHT WORD greedy, acquisitive, covetous, avaricious, rapacious, gluttonous**

The desire for money and the things it can buy is often associated with Americans. But not all Americans are **greedy**, which implies an insatiable desire to possess or acquire something, beyond what one needs or deserves (*greedy for profits*). Someone who is *greedy* for food might be called **gluttonous**, which emphasizes consumption as well as desire (*a gluttonous appetite for sweets*), but *greedy* is a derogatory term only when the object of longing is itself evil or when it cannot be possessed without harm to oneself or others (*a reporter greedy for information*). A *greedy* child may grow up to be an **avaricious** adult, which implies a fanatical greediness for money or other valuables. **Rapacious** is an even stronger term, with an emphasis on taking things by force (*so rapacious in his desire for land that he forced dozens of families from their homes*). **Acquisitive**, on the other hand, is a more neutral word suggesting a willingness to exert effort in acquiring things (*an acquisitive woman who filled her house with antiques and artwork*), and not necessarily material things (*a probing, acquisitive mind*). **Covetous**, in contrast to *acquisitive*, implies an intense desire for something as opposed to the act of acquiring or possessing it. It is often associated with the Ten Commandments (*Thou shalt not covet thy neighbor's wife*) and suggests a longing for something that rightfully belongs to another.

---

**green** adjective 1 *a green scarf* viridescent; olive, jade, pea green, emerald (green), lime (green), sea green; *literary* virescent, glaucous.

2 *a green island* VERDANT, grassy, leafy, verdurous. ANTONYM barren.

3 **(Green)** *he promotes Green issues* ENVIRONMENTAL, ecological, conservation, ecocentric, eco-.

4 *a green alternative to diesel* ENVIRONMENTALLY FRIENDLY, nonpolluting, ecological; ozone-friendly. ANTONYM polluting.

5 *green bananas* UNRIPE, immature. ANTONYM ripe.

6 *green firewood* UNSEASONED, not aged; pliable, supple. ANTONYMS seasoned, dry.

7 *the new lieutenant was green* INEXPERIENCED, unversed, callow, immature; new, raw, unseasoned, untried; inexpert, untrained, unqualified, ignorant; simple, unsophisticated, unpolished; naive, innocent, ingenuous, credulous, gullible, unworldly; *informal* wet behind the ears, born yesterday. ANTONYM experienced.

8 *he went green* PALE, wan, pallid, ashen, ashen-faced, pasty, pasty-faced, gray, whitish, washed out, blanched, drained, pinched, sallow; sickly, nauseous, ill, sick, unhealthy. ANTONYM ruddy.

▸ noun 1 *a canopy of green over the road* FOLIAGE, greenery, plants, leaves, leafage, vegetation.

2 *a village green* PARK, common, grassy area, lawn, sward.

3 *eat your* **greens** VEGETABLES, leafy vegetables, salad; *informal* veggies.

4 **(Green)** *Greens are against multinationals* ENVIRONMENTALIST, conservationist, preservationist, nature lover, eco-activist; *informal, derogatory* tree hugger, greenie.

**green light** noun *he was given the green light to implement his proposals* AUTHORIZATION, permission, approval, assent, consent, sanction; leave, clearance, warranty, agreement, imprimatur, one's blessing, the seal/stamp of approval, the rubber stamp, the nod; authority, license, dispensation, empowerment, freedom, liberty; *informal* the OK, the go-ahead, the thumbs up, the say-so. ANTONYM the red light, refusal.

**greet** verb 1 *she greeted Hank cheerily* SAY HELLO TO, address, salute, hail; welcome, meet, receive.

2 *the decision was greeted with outrage* RECEIVE, acknowledge, respond to, react to, take.

**greeting** noun 1 *he shouted a greeting* HELLO, salute, salutation, address; welcome; acknowledgment. ANTONYM farewell.

2 **(greetings)** *birthday greetings* BEST WISHES, good wishes, congratulations, felicitations; compliments, regards, respects.

**gregarious** adjective 1 *he was fun-loving and gregarious* SOCIABLE, company-loving, convivial, companionable, outgoing, friendly, affable, amiable, genial, warm, comradely; *informal* chummy. ANTONYM unsociable.

2 *gregarious fish* SOCIAL, living in groups.

**grief** noun 1 *he was overcome with grief* SORROW, misery, sadness, anguish, pain, distress, heartache, heartbreak, agony, torment, affliction, suffering, woe, desolation, dejection, despair; mourning, mournfulness, bereavement, lamentation; *literary* dolor, dole. ANTONYM joy.

2 *informal* *the police gave me a lot of grief* TROUBLE, annoyance, bother, irritation, vexation, harassment; *informal* aggravation, hassle.

**grievance** noun 1 *social and economic grievances* INJUSTICE, wrong, injury, ill, unfairness; affront, insult, indignity.

2 *students voiced their grievances* COMPLAINT, criticism, objection, grumble, grouse; ill feeling, bad feeling, resentment, bitterness, pique; *informal* gripe; *Brit.* whinge, moan, grouch, niggle, beef, bone to pick.

**grieve** verb 1 *she grieved for her father* MOURN, lament, sorrow, be sorrowful; cry, sob, weep, shed tears, weep and wail, beat one's breast. See note at MOURN. ANTONYM rejoice.

2 *it grieved me to leave her* SADDEN, upset, distress, pain, hurt, wound, break someone's heart, make someone's heart bleed. ANTONYM please.

**grievous** *formal* adjective 1 *his death was a grievous blow* SERIOUS, severe, grave, bad, critical, dreadful, terrible, awful, crushing, calamitous; painful, agonizing, traumatic, wounding, damaging, injurious; sharp, acute. ANTONYMS slight, trivial.

2 *a grievous sin* HEINOUS, grave, deplorable, shocking, appalling, atrocious, gross, dreadful, egregious, iniquitous. ANTONYMS venial, trivial.

**grim** adjective 1 *his grim expression* STERN, forbidding, uninviting, unsmiling, dour, formidable, harsh, steely, flinty, stony; cross, churlish, surly, sour, ill-tempered; fierce, ferocious, threatening, menacing, implacable, ruthless, merciless. ANTONYMS amiable, pleasant.

2 *grim humor* BLACK, dark, mirthless, bleak, cynical. ANTONYM lighthearted.

3 *the asylum holds some grim secrets* DREADFUL, dire, ghastly, horrible, horrendous, horrid, terrible, awful, appalling, frightful, shocking, unspeakable, grisly, gruesome, hideous, macabre; depressing, distressing, upsetting, worrying, unpleasant.

4 *a grim little hovel* BLEAK, dreary, dismal, dingy, wretched, miserable, depressing, cheerless, comfortless, joyless, gloomy, uninviting; *informal* godawful. ANTONYM cheery.

5 *grim determination* RESOLUTE, determined, firm, decided,

steadfast, dead set; obstinate, stubborn, obdurate, unyielding, intractable, uncompromising, unshakable, unrelenting, relentless, dogged, tenacious. ANTONYM irresolute.

**grimace** noun *his mouth twisted into a grimace* SCOWL, frown, sneer; face.

▸ verb *Nina grimaced at Joe* SCOWL, frown, sneer, glower, lower; make a face, make faces. ANTONYM smile.

**grime** noun *her skirt was smeared with grime* DIRT, filth, grunge, mud, mire, smut, soot, dust; *informal* muck, crud, gunge.

▸ verb *concrete grimed by diesel exhaust* BLACKEN, dirty, stain, soil; *literary* begrime, besmirch.

**grimy** adjective *grimy old rags* DIRTY, grubby, grungy, mucky, soiled, stained, smeared, filthy, smutty, sooty, dusty, muddy; *informal* yucky, cruddy; *literary* besmirched, begrimed. ANTONYM clean.

**grin** verb *Liam grinned at us* SMILE, smile broadly, beam, smile from ear to ear, grin like a Cheshire cat; smirk; *informal* be all smiles.

▸ noun *a silly grin* SMILE, broad smile; smirk. See note at SMILE. ANTONYMS frown, scowl.

**grind** verb **1** *the sandstone is ground into powder* CRUSH, pound, pulverize, mill, granulate, crumble, smash, press; *technical* triturate, comminute.

**2** *a knife being ground on a wheel* SHARPEN, whet, hone, file, strop; smooth, polish, sand, sandpaper.

**3** *one tectonic plate grinds against another* RUB, grate, scrape, rasp.

▸ noun *the daily grind* DRUDGERY, toil, hard work, labor, exertion, chores, slog; *informal* sweat; *literary* travail. See note at LABOR.

PHRASE: **grind out** *the composing department grinds out hundreds of pages a day* PRODUCE, generate, crank out, turn out; *informal* churn out.

**grip** verb **1** *she gripped the edge of the table* GRASP, clutch, hold, clasp, take hold of, clench, grab, seize, cling to; squeeze, press; *informal* glom on to. ANTONYMS release, hold lightly.

**2** *Harry was gripped by a sneezing fit* AFFLICT, affect, take over, beset, rack, convulse.

**3** *we were gripped by the drama* ENGROSS, enthrall, absorb, rivet, spellbind, hold spellbound, bewitch, fascinate, hold, mesmerize, enrapture; interest. ANTONYMS bore, repel.

▸ noun **1** *a tight grip* GRASP, hold.

**2** *the wheels lost their grip on the road* TRACTION, purchase, friction, adhesion, resistance.

**3** *he was in the grip of an obsession* CONTROL, power, hold, stranglehold, chokehold, clutches, command, mastery, influence.

**4** *I had a pretty good **grip on** the situation* UNDERSTANDING OF, comprehension of, grasp of, command of, perception of, awareness of, apprehension of, conception of; *formal* cognizance of.

**5** *a leather grip* TRAVEL BAG, traveling bag, suitcase, bag, overnight bag, flight bag.

PHRASE: **come to grips with** *you need to come to grips with the divorce* DEAL WITH, cope with, handle, grasp, tackle, undertake, take on, grapple with, face, face up to, confront.

**gripe** *informal* verb *he's always griping about something* COMPLAIN, grumble, grouse, protest, whine, bleat; *informal* moan, bellyache, beef, bitch, kvetch; *Brit.* whinge, kvetch.

▸ noun *employees' gripes* COMPLAINT, grumble, grouse, grievance, objection; cavil, quibble, niggle; *informal* moan, beef, kvetch; *Brit.* whinge.

**gripping** adjective *a gripping spy novel* ENGROSSING, enthralling, absorbing, riveting, captivating, spellbinding, bewitching, fascinating, compulsive, compelling, mesmerizing; thrilling, exciting, action-packed, dramatic, stimulating; *informal* unputdownable, page-turning. ANTONYM boring.

**grisly** adjective *the grisly details of the crime* GRUESOME, ghastly, frightful, horrid, horrifying, fearful, hideous, macabre, spine-chilling, horrible, horrendous, grim, awful, dire, dreadful, terrible, horrific, shocking, appalling, abominable, loathsome, abhorrent, odious, monstrous, unspeakable, disgusting, repulsive, repugnant, revolting, repellent, sickening; *informal* gross.

**grit** noun **1** *the grit from the paths* SAND, dust, dirt; gravel, pebbles, stones.

**2** *just the grit we're looking for in a candidate* COURAGE, bravery, pluck, mettle, backbone, spirit, strength of character, strength of will, moral fiber, steel, nerve, fortitude, toughness, hardiness, resolve, resolution, determination, tenacity, perseverance, endurance; *informal* guts, spunk.

▸ verb *Gina gritted her teeth* CLENCH, clamp together, shut tightly; grind, gnash.

**gritty** adjective **1** *a gritty floor* SANDY, gravelly, pebbly, stony; powdery, dusty.

**2** *a gritty performance* COURAGEOUS, brave, plucky, mettlesome, stouthearted, valiant, bold, spirited, intrepid, tough, determined, resolute, purposeful, dogged, tenacious; *informal* gutsy, spunky, feisty.

**3** *a gritty look at urban life* REALISTIC, uncompromising, tough, true-to-life, unidealized, graphic, sordid.

**groan** verb **1** *she groaned and rubbed her stomach* MOAN, whimper, cry, call out.

**2** *they were groaning about the management* COMPLAIN, grumble, grouse; *informal* moan, niggle, beef, bellyache, bitch, gripe.

**3** *the old wooden door groaned* CREAK, squeak; grate, rasp.

▸ noun **1** *a groan of anguish* MOAN, cry, whimper.

**2** *their moans and groans* COMPLAINT, grumble, grouse, objection, protest, grievance; *informal* grouch, moan, beef, gripe.

**3** *the groan of the elevator* CREAKING, creak, squeak, grating, grinding.

**groggy** adjective *the sedative made him groggy* DAZED, stupefied, in a stupor, befuddled, fuddled, dizzy, disoriented, disorientated, punch-drunk, shaky, unsteady, wobbly, weak, faint, muzzy; *informal* dopey, woozy, not with it.

**groom** verb **1** *she groomed her pony* CURRY, brush, comb, clean, rub down.

**2** *his dark hair was carefully groomed* BRUSH, comb, arrange, do; tidy, spruce up, smarten up, preen, primp; *informal* fix.

**3** *they were groomed for stardom* PREPARE, prime, ready, condition, tailor; coach, train, instruct, drill, teach, school.

▸ noun **1** *a groom took his horse* STABLE HAND, stableman, stable boy, stable girl; *historical* equerry.

**2** *the bride and groom* BRIDEGROOM; newly married man, newlywed.

**groove** noun *water trickled down the grooves* FURROW, channel, trench, trough, canal, gouge, hollow, indentation, rut, gutter, cutting, cut, fissure; *Carpentry* rabbet.

**grope** verb **1** *she groped for her glasses* FUMBLE, scrabble, fish, ferret, rummage, feel, search, hunt.

**2** *informal one of the men started groping her* FONDLE, touch; *informal* paw, maul, feel up, touch up.

**gross** adjective **1** *the child was pale and gross* OBESE, corpulent, overweight, fat, big, large, fleshy, flabby, portly, bloated; *informal* porky, pudgy, tubby, blubbery, roly-poly. ANTONYM slender.

**2** *men of gross natures* BOORISH, coarse, vulgar, loutish, oafish, thuggish, brutish, philistine, uncouth, crass, common, unrefined, unsophisticated, uncultured, uncultivated; *informal* cloddish. ANTONYM refined.

**3** *informal the place smelled gross* DISGUSTING, repellent, repulsive, abhorrent, loathsome, foul, nasty, obnoxious, sickening, nauseating, stomach-churning, unpalatable; vomitous; *informal* yucky, icky, gut-churning. ANTONYMS pleasant, lovely.

**4** *a gross distortion of the truth* FLAGRANT, blatant, glaring, obvious, overt, naked, barefaced, shameless, brazen, audacious, undisguised, unconcealed, patent, transparent, manifest, palpable; out and out, utter, complete. ANTONYM minor.

**5** *their gross income* TOTAL, whole, entire, complete, full, overall, combined, aggregate; before deductions, before tax, pretax. ANTONYM net.

▸ verb *she grosses over a million dollars a year* EARN, make, bring in, take, get, receive, collect; *informal* rake in.

**grotesque** adjective **1** *a grotesque creature* MALFORMED, deformed, misshapen, misproportioned, distorted, twisted, gnarled, mangled, mutilated; ugly, unsightly, monstrous, hideous, freakish, unnatural, abnormal, strange, odd, peculiar; *informal* weird, freaky. ANTONYM normal.

**2** *grotesque mismanagement of funds* OUTRAGEOUS, monstrous, shocking, appalling, preposterous; ridiculous, ludicrous, farcical, unbelievable, incredible.

**ground** noun **1** *she collapsed on the ground* FLOOR, earth, terra firma; flooring; *informal* deck.

**2** *the soggy ground* EARTH, soil, dirt, clay, loam, turf, clod, sod; land, terrain.

**3 (grounds)** *the mansion's grounds* ESTATE, lawn(s), yard(s), gardens, park, parkland, land, acres, property, surroundings, holding, territory; *archaic* demesne.

**4 (grounds)** *grounds for dismissal* REASON, cause, basis, base, foundation, justification, rationale, argument, premise, occasion, excuse, pretext, motive, motivation.

**5 (grounds)** *coffee grounds* SEDIMENT, precipitate, settlings, dregs, lees, deposit, residue.

▸ verb **1** *the boat grounded on a sandbar* RUN AGROUND, run ashore, beach, land.

**2** *an assertion grounded on results of several studies* BASE, found, establish, root, build, construct, form.

**3** *they were grounded in classics and history* INSTRUCT, coach, teach, tutor, educate, school, train, drill, prime, prepare; familiarize with, acquaint with.

PHRASES: **hold one's ground** *he tried to dissuade me with his negative remarks, but I held my ground* STAND FIRM, stand fast, make a stand, stick to one's guns, dig in one's heels.
**gain ground** *we failed to gain ground in that last campaign* ADVANCE, progress, make headway; catch up, close in.

**groundless** adjective *groundless accusations* BASELESS, without basis, without foundation, ill-founded, unfounded, unsupported, uncorroborated, unproven, empty, idle, unsubstantiated, unwarranted, unjustified, unjustifiable, without cause, without reason, without justification, unreasonable, irrational, illogical, misguided.

**groundwork** noun *their predecessors did all the groundwork and got none of the credit* PRELIMINARY WORK, preliminaries, preparations, spadework, legwork, donkey work; planning, arrangements, organization, homework; basics, essentials, fundamentals, underpinning, foundation.

**group** noun **1** *the exhibits were divided into three distinct groups* CATEGORY, class, classification, grouping, set, lot, batch, bracket, type, sort, kind, variety, family, species, genus, breed; grade, grading, rank, status.

**2** *a group of tourists* CROWD, party, body, band, company, gathering, congregation, assembly, collection, cluster, flock, pack, troop, gang; *informal* bunch, pile.

**3** *a coup attempt by a group within the legislature* FACTION, division, section, clique, coterie, circle, set, ring, camp, bloc, caucus, cabal, fringe movement, splinter group.

**4** *the women's group* ASSOCIATION, club, society, league, guild, circle, union, sorority, fraternity.

**5** *a small group of trees* CLUSTER, knot, collection, mass, clump.

**6** *a local singing group* BAND, ensemble, act; *informal* combo, outfit.

▸ verb **1** *patients were grouped according to their symptoms* CATEGORIZE, classify, class, catalog, sort, bracket, pigeonhole, grade, rate, rank; prioritize, triage.

**2** *extra chairs were grouped around the table* PLACE, arrange, assemble, organize, range, line up, dispose.

**3** *the two parties* ***grouped together*** UNITE, join together/up, team up, gang up, join forces, get together, ally, form an alliance, affiliate, combine, marry, merge, pool resources; collaborate, work together, pull together, cooperate.

**grouse** verb *she groused about the food* GRUMBLE, complain, protest, whine, bleat, carp, cavil, make a fuss; *informal* moan, bellyache, gripe, beef, bitch, grouch, sound off, kvetch.

▸ noun *our biggest grouse was about the noise* GRUMBLE, complaint, grievance, objection, cavil, quibble; *informal* moan, beef, gripe, grouch.

**grovel** verb **1** *George groveled at his feet, begging for mercy* PROSTRATE ONESELF, lie, kneel, cringe.

**2** *she was not going to* ***grovel to*** *him* BE OBSEQUIOUS TO, fawn on, kowtow to, bow and scrape to, toady to, truckle to, abase oneself to, humble oneself to; curry favor with, flatter, dance attendance on, make up to, play up to, ingratiate oneself with; *informal* crawl to, suck up to, lick someone's boots.

**grow** verb **1** *the boys had grown* GET BIGGER, get taller, get larger, increase in size. ANTONYM shrink.

**2** *sales and profits continue to grow* INCREASE, swell, multiply, snowball, mushroom, balloon, build up, mount up, pile up; *informal* skyrocket. ANTONYM decline.

**3** *flowers grew among the rocks* SPROUT, germinate, shoot up, spring up, develop, bud, burst forth, bloom, flourish, thrive, burgeon.

**4** *he grew vegetables* CULTIVATE, produce, propagate, raise, rear, nurture, tend; farm.

**5** *the family business grew* EXPAND, extend, develop, progress, make progress; flourish, thrive, burgeon, prosper, succeed, boom. ANTONYMS fail, decline.

**6** *the modern fable grew from an ancient myth* ORIGINATE, stem, spring, arise, emerge, issue; develop, evolve.

**7** *Leonora grew bored* BECOME, get, turn, begin to feel.

**growl** verb *why is your dog growling at us?* SNARL, bark, yap, bay.

**grown-up** noun *she wanted to be treated like a grown-up* ADULT, (grown) woman, (grown) man, mature woman, mature man. ANTONYM child.

▸ adjective *she has two grown-up daughters* ADULT, mature, of age; fully grown, full-grown, fully developed.

**growth** noun **1** *population growth* INCREASE, expansion, augmentation, proliferation, multiplication, enlargement, mushrooming, snowballing, rise, escalation, buildup. ANTONYM decrease.

**2** *the growth of plants* DEVELOPMENT, maturation, growing, germination, sprouting; blooming. ANTONYM withering.

**3** *the marked growth of local enterprises* EXPANSION, extension, development, progress, advance, advancement, headway, spread; rise, success, boom, upturn, upswing. ANTONYMS failure, decline.

**4** *a growth on his jaw* TUMOR, malignancy, cancer; lump, excrescence, outgrowth, swelling, nodule; cyst, polyp.

**grub** noun **1** *a small black grub* LARVA; maggot; caterpillar.

**2** *informal we'll grab some grub on the way.* See FOOD sense 1.

▸ verb **1** *they* ***grubbed up*** *the weeds* DIG UP, unearth, uproot, root up/out, pull up/out, tear out.

**2** *he began grubbing around in the trash* RUMMAGE, search, hunt, delve, dig, scrabble, ferret, root, rifle, fish, poke.

**grubby** adjective *his grubby work clothes* DIRTY, grimy, filthy, mucky, unwashed, stained, soiled, smeared, spotted, muddy, dusty, sooty; unhygienic, unsanitary; *informal* cruddy, yucky; *literary* befouled, begrimed. ANTONYM clean.

**grudge** noun *a former employee with a grudge* GRIEVANCE, resentment, bitterness, rancor, pique, umbrage, dissatisfaction, disgruntlement, bad feelings, hard feelings, ill feelings, ill will, animosity, antipathy, antagonism, enmity, animus; *informal* a chip on one's shoulder.

▸ verb *he grudges the time the meetings use up* BEGRUDGE, resent, feel aggrieved about, be resentful of, mind, object to, take exception to, take umbrage at.

**grueling** adjective *a grueling hike through the snow* EXHAUSTING, tiring, fatiguing, wearying, taxing, draining, debilitating; demanding, exacting, difficult, hard, arduous, strenuous, laborious, back-breaking, harsh, severe, stiff, stressful, punishing, crippling; *informal* killing, murderous, hellish.

**gruesome** adjective *Arnie's gruesome Halloween mask frightened the little kids* GRISLY, ghastly, frightful, horrid, horrifying, hideous, horrible, horrendous, grim, awful, dire, dreadful, terrible, horrific, shocking, appalling, disgusting, repulsive, repugnant, revolting, repellent, sickening; loathsome, abhorrent, odious, monstrous, unspeakable; *informal* sick, gross. ANTONYM pleasant.

**gruff** adjective **1** *a gruff reply* | *his gruff exterior* ABRUPT, brusque, curt, short, blunt, bluff, no-nonsense; laconic, taciturn; surly, churlish, grumpy, crotchety, curmudgeonly, crabby, cross, bad-tempered, short-tempered, ill-natured, crusty, tetchy, bearish, ungracious, unceremonious; *informal* grouchy. See note at BRUSQUE. ANTONYMS friendly, courteous.

**2** *a gruff voice* ROUGH, guttural, throaty, gravelly, husky, croaking, rasping, raspy, growly, hoarse, harsh; low, thick. ANTONYMS mellow, soft.

**grumble** verb *they grumbled about the disruption* COMPLAIN, grouse, whine, mutter, bleat, carp, cavil, protest, make a fuss; *informal* moan, bellyache, beef, bitch, grouch, sound off, gripe, kvetch; *Brit.* whinge.

▸ noun *his customers' grumbles* COMPLAINT, grievance, protest, cavil, quibble, criticism, grouse; *informal* grouch, moan, beef, bitch, gripe.

**grumpy** adjective *Matthau's grumpy old man was a tour de force* BAD-TEMPERED, crabby, ill-tempered, short-tempered, crotchety, tetchy, testy, waspish, prickly, touchy, irritable, irascible, crusty, cantankerous, curmudgeonly, bearish, surly, ill-natured, churlish, ill-humored, peevish, pettish, cross, fractious, disagreeable, snappish; *informal* grouchy, snappy, cranky, shirty, ornery. ANTONYM good-humored.

**guarantee** noun **1** *all repairs have a one-year guarantee* WARRANTY.

**2** *a guarantee that the hospital will stay open* PROMISE, assurance, word (of honor), pledge, vow, oath, bond, commitment, covenant.

**3** *banks usually demand* ***a guarantee*** *for loans* COLLATERAL, security, surety, a guaranty, earnest.

▸ verb **1** *he agreed to guarantee the loan* UNDERWRITE, put up collateral for.

**2** *can you guarantee that he wasn't involved?* PROMISE, swear, swear to the fact, pledge, vow, undertake, give one's word, give an assurance, give an undertaking, take an oath.

**guard** verb **1** *infantry guarded the barricaded bridge* PROTECT, stand guard over, watch over, keep an eye on; cover, patrol, police, defend, shield, safeguard, keep safe, secure.

**2** *the prisoners were guarded by armed men* KEEP UNDER SURVEILLANCE, keep under guard, keep watch over, mind.

**3** *forest wardens must* ***guard against*** *poachers* BEWARE OF, keep watch for, be alert to, keep an eye out for, be on the lookout for, be on the alert for.

▸ noun **1** *border guards* SENTRY, sentinel, security guard, watchman, night watchman; protector, defender, guardian; lookout, watch; garrison.

**2** *her prison guard* WARDEN, warder, keeper; jailer; *informal* screw; *archaic* turnkey.

**3** *he let his guard slip and they escaped* VIGILANCE, vigil, watch, surveillance, watchfulness, caution, heed, attention, care, wariness.

**4** *a metal guard* SAFETY GUARD, safety device, protective device, shield, screen, fender; bumper, buffer.

PHRASES: **off (one's) guard** *the explosion from the furnace room caught everyone off guard* UNPREPARED, unready, inattentive, unwary, with one's defenses down, cold, unsuspecting; *informal* napping, asleep at the wheel.
**on one's guard** *homeowners should be on their guard* VIGILANT, alert, on the alert, wary, watchful, cautious, careful, heedful, chary, circumspect, on the lookout, on the qui vive, on one's toes, prepared, ready, wide awake, attentive, observant, keeping one's eyes peeled.

**guarded** adjective *they showed guarded enthusiasm for the proposal* CAUTIOUS, careful, circumspect, wary, chary, on one's guard, reluctant, reticent, noncommittal, restrained, reserved; *informal* buttoned-up, cagey.

**guardian** noun *Linwood has been my guardian since I was three* PROTECTOR, defender, preserver, custodian, warden, guard, keeper; conservator, curator, caretaker, steward, trustee.

**guerrilla** noun *the communications canter was raided by leftist guerrillas from the north* FREEDOM FIGHTER, irregular, member of the resistance, partisan; rebel, radical, revolutionary, revolutionist; terrorist.

**guess** verb **1** *he guessed she was about 40* ESTIMATE, hazard a guess, reckon, gauge, judge, calculate; hypothesize, postulate, predict, speculate, conjecture, surmise; *informal* guesstimate.

**2** *informal I guess I owe you an apology* SUPPOSE, think, imagine, expect, suspect, dare say; *informal* reckon, figure.

▸ noun *my guess was right* HYPOTHESIS, theory, prediction, postulation, conjecture, surmise, estimate, belief, opinion, reckoning, judgment, supposition, speculation, suspicion, impression, feeling; *informal* guesstimate, shot in the dark.

**guesswork** noun *the educated guesswork we rely on in our research* GUESSING, conjecture, surmise, supposition, assumptions, presumptions, speculation, hypothesizing, theorizing, prediction; approximations, rough calculations; hunches; *informal* guesstimates, ballpark figures.

**guest** noun **1** *I have two guests coming to dinner* VISITOR, house guest, caller; company; *archaic* visitant. ANTONYM host.

**2** *hotel guests* PATRON, client, visitor, boarder, lodger, roomer. ANTONYMS host, landlord, landlady.

▸ adjective *a guest speaker* INVITED, featured, special.

**guidance** noun **1** *she looked to her father for guidance* ADVICE, counsel, direction, instruction, enlightenment, information; recommendations, suggestions, tips, hints, pointers, guidelines.

**2** *work continued under the guidance of a project supervisor* DIRECTION, control, leadership, management, supervision, superintendence, charge; handling, conduct, running, overseeing.

**guide** noun **1** *our guide took us back to the hotel* ESCORT, attendant, tour guide, docent, cicerone; usher, chaperone; *historical* dragoman.

**2** *she is an inspiration and a guide* ADVISER/ADVISOR, mentor, counselor; guru.

**3** *the light acted as a guide for shipping* POINTER, marker, indicator, signpost, mark, landmark; guiding light, sign, signal, beacon.

**4** *the techniques outlined are meant as a guide* MODEL, pattern, blueprint, template, example, exemplar; standard, touchstone, measure, benchmark, yardstick, gauge.

**5** *a pocket guide to the Aleutians.* GUIDEBOOK.

▸ verb **1** *he guided her to her seat* LEAD, conduct, show, show the way, usher, shepherd, direct, steer, pilot, escort, accompany, attend; see, take, help, assist.

**2** *the chairperson must guide the meeting* DIRECT, steer, control, manage, command, lead, conduct, run, be in charge of, have control of, pilot, govern, preside over, superintend, supervise, oversee; handle, regulate.

**3** *he was always there to guide me* ADVISE, counsel, give advice to, direct, give direction to.

**guideline** noun *the zoning commission's strict guidelines* RECOMMENDATION, instruction, direction, suggestion, advice; regulation, rule, principle, guiding principle; standard, criterion, measure, gauge, yardstick, benchmark, touchstone; procedure, parameter.

**guild** noun *the copper craftsmen have formed a guild* ASSOCIATION, society, union, league, organization, company, cooperative, fellowship, club, order, lodge, brotherhood, fraternity, sisterhood, sorority.

**guile** noun *Georgia was the only one among us not taken in by Owen's guile* CUNNING, craftiness, craft, artfulness, art, artifice, wiliness, slyness, deviousness; wiles, ploys, schemes, stratagems, maneuvers, tricks, subterfuges, ruses; deception, deceit, duplicity, underhandedness, double-dealing, trickery. ANTONYM honesty.

**guileless** adjective *how can you take advantage of someone so sweet and guileless?* ARTLESS, ingenuous, naive, open, genuine, natural, simple, childlike, innocent, unsophisticated, unworldly, unsuspicious, trustful, trusting; honest, truthful, sincere, straightforward. ANTONYM scheming.

**guilt** noun **1** *the proof of his guilt* CULPABILITY, guiltiness, blameworthiness; wrongdoing, wrong, criminality, misconduct, sin. ANTONYM innocence.

**2** *a terrible feeling of guilt* SELF-REPROACH, self-condemnation, shame, a guilty conscience, pangs of conscience; remorse, remorsefulness, regret, contrition, contriteness, compunction. ANTONYM innocence.

**guiltless** adjective *the victims here are these guiltless children* INNOCENT, blameless, not to blame, without fault, above reproach, above suspicion, in the clear, unimpeachable, irreproachable, faultless, sinless, spotless, immaculate, unsullied, uncorrupted, undefiled, untainted, unblemished, untarnished, impeccable; *informal* squeaky clean, whiter than white, as pure as the driven snow. ANTONYM guilty.

**guilty** adjective **1** *the guilty party* CULPABLE, to blame, at fault, in the wrong, blameworthy, responsible; erring, errant, delinquent, offending, sinful, criminal; *archaic* peccant. ANTONYM innocent.

**2** *I still feel guilty about it* ASHAMED, guilt-ridden, conscience-stricken, remorseful, sorry, contrite, repentant, penitent, regretful, rueful, abashed, shamefaced, sheepish, hangdog; in sackcloth and ashes. ANTONYM unrepentant.

**guise** noun **1** *the god appeared in the guise of a swan* LIKENESS, outward appearance, appearance, semblance, form, shape, image; disguise.

**2** *additional payments were made under the guise of consulting fees* PRETENSE, disguise, front, facade, cover, blind, screen, smokescreen.

**gulf** noun **1** *our ship sailed into the gulf* INLET, bay, bight, cove, fjord, estuary, sound.

**2** *the ice gave way and a gulf widened slowly* HOLE, crevasse, fissure, cleft, split, rift, pit, cavity, chasm, abyss, void; ravine, gorge, canyon, gully.

**3** *a growing gulf between rich and poor* DIVIDE, division, separation, gap, breach, rift, split, chasm, abyss; difference, contrast, polarity.

**gullet** noun *the bird's gullet* ESOPHAGUS, throat, maw, pharynx; crop, craw; *archaic* throttle, gorge.

**gullible** adjective *he was a swindler who preyed on gullible elderly widows* CREDULOUS, naive, overtrusting, overtrustful, easily deceived, easily taken in, exploitable, dupable, impressionable, unsuspecting, unsuspicious, unwary, ingenuous, innocent, inexperienced, unworldly, green; *informal* wet behind the ears, born yesterday. ANTONYM suspicious.

THE RIGHT WORD **gullible, callow, credulous, ingenuous, naïve, trusting, unsophisticated**

Some people will believe anything. Those who are truly **gullible** are the easiest to deceive, which is why they so often make fools of themselves. Those who are merely **credulous** might be a little too quick to believe something, but they usually aren't stupid enough to act on it. **Trusting** suggests the same willingness to believe (*a trusting child*), but it isn't necessarily a bad way to be (*a person so trusting he completely disarmed his enemies*). No one likes to be called **naïve** because it implies a lack of street smarts (*she's so naïve she'd accept a ride from a stranger*), but when applied to things other than people, it can describe a simplicity and absence of artificiality that is quite charming (*the naïve style in which nineteenth-century American portraits were often painted*). Most people would rather be thought of as **ingenuous**, meaning straightforward and sincere (*an ingenuous confession of the truth*), because it implies the simplicity of a child without the negative overtones. **Callow**, however, comes down a little more heavily on the side of immaturity and almost always goes hand-in-hand with youth. Whether young or old, someone who is **unsophisticated** suffers because of lack of experience.

**gully** noun **1** *a steep icy gully* RAVINE, canyon, gorge, pass, defile, couloir, gulch, coulee, draw.

**2** *water runs from the drainpipe into a gully* CHANNEL, conduit, trench, ditch, drain, culvert, cut, gutter.

**gulp** verb **1** *she gulped her juice* SWALLOW, guzzle (down), quaff, swill down, down; *informal* swig, knock back, chug, chugalug. ANTONYM sip.

**2** *he* ***gulped down*** *the rest of his meal* GOBBLE (DOWN), guzzle (down), devour, bolt down, wolf down; *informal* put away, demolish, polish off, shovel in/down, scoff (down). ANTONYM nibble.

**3** *Lisa* ***gulped back*** *her tears* CHOKE BACK, fight back, hold back/in, suppress, stifle, smother.

▸ noun *a gulp of cold beer* MOUTHFUL, swallow, draft; *informal* swig.

**gum** noun *photographs stuck down with gum* GLUE, adhesive, fixative, paste, epoxy, epoxy resin, mucilage.

▸ verb *the receipts were gummed into a book* STICK, glue, paste; fix, affix, attach, fasten.

PHRASE: **gum up** *check to see if the valves are gummed up* CLOG (UP), choke (up), stop up, plug; obstruct; *informal* bung up, gunge up; *technical* occlude.

**gumption** noun *informal we never thought Clarence would have the gumption to stand up to the committee—and actually get what he wanted* INITIATIVE, resourcefulness, enterprise, ingenuity, imagination; astuteness, shrewdness, acumen, sense, common sense, wit, mother wit, practicality; spirit, backbone, pluck, mettle, nerve, courage, wherewithal; *informal* getup-and-go, spunk, oomph, moxie, savvy, horse sense, (street) smarts.

**gun** noun *the illegal trafficking of drugs and guns* FIREARM, pistol, revolver, rifle, shotgun, carbine, automatic, handgun, semiautomatic, machine gun, Uzi; weapon; *informal* piece, gat, heater.

**gunman** noun *a lone gunman apparently hid in the stairwell for several hours* ARMED ROBBER, gangster, terrorist; sniper, gunfighter; assassin, murderer, killer; *informal* hit man, hired gun, gunslinger, mobster, shootist, hood.

**gurgle** verb *the water swirled and gurgled* BABBLE, burble, tinkle, bubble, ripple, murmur, purl, splash; *literary* plash.

▸ noun *the gurgle of a small brook* BABBLING, tinkling, bubbling, rippling, trickling, murmur, murmuring, purling, splashing; *literary* plashing.

**guru** noun **1** *a Hindu guru and mystic* SPIRITUAL TEACHER, teacher, tutor, sage, mentor, spiritual leader, leader, master; *Hinduism* swami, maharishi. ANTONYM disciple.

**2** *a management guru* EXPERT, authority, pundit, leading light, master, specialist; *informal* whiz. ANTONYM amateur.

**gush** verb **1** *water gushed through the weir* SURGE, burst, spout, spurt, jet, stream, rush, pour, spill, well out, cascade, flood; flow, run, issue.

**2** *everyone gushed about the script* ENTHUSE, rave, be enthusiastic, be effusive, rhapsodize, go into raptures, wax lyrical, praise to the skies; *informal* go mad, go wild, go crazy.

▸ noun *a gush of water* SURGE, stream, spurt, jet, spout, outpouring, outflow, burst, rush, cascade, flood, torrent; *technical* efflux.

**gust** noun **1** *a sudden gust of wind* FLURRY, blast, puff, blow, rush; squall.

**2** *gusts of laughter* OUTBURST, burst, eruption, fit, paroxysm; gale, peal, howl, hoot, shriek, roar.

▸ verb *wind gusted around the chimneys* BLOW, bluster, flurry, roar.

**gusto** noun *neighbors remembered the slain soldier as a friendly kid who played sports with gusto* ENTHUSIASM, relish, appetite, enjoyment, delight, glee, pleasure, satisfaction, appreciation, liking; zest, zeal, fervor, verve, keenness, avidity. ANTONYMS apathy, distaste.

**gut** noun **1** *he had an ache in his gut* STOMACH, belly, abdomen, solar plexus; intestines, bowels; *informal* tummy, tum, insides, innards.

**2** *fish heads and guts* ENTRAILS; intestines, viscera; offal; gurry; *informal* insides, innards.

**3** *informal* **(guts)** *Nicola had the guts to say what she felt* COURAGE, bravery, backbone, nerve, pluck, spirit, boldness, audacity, daring, grit, fearlessness, feistiness, toughness, determination; *informal* spunk, moxie. See note at COURAGE.

▸ adjective *informal a gut feeling* INSTINCTIVE, instinctual, intuitive, deep-seated; knee-jerk, automatic, involuntary, spontaneous, unthinking, visceral.

▸ verb **1** *clean, scale, and gut the trout* REMOVE THE GUTS FROM, disembowel, draw; *formal* eviscerate.

**2** *the church was gutted by fire* DEVASTATE, destroy, demolish, wipe out, lay waste, ravage, consume, ruin, wreck.

**gutter** noun *gutters clogged with leaves* DRAIN, sluice, sluiceway, culvert, spillway, sewer; channel, conduit, pipe; rain gutter; trough, trench, ditch, furrow, cut.

**guttural** adjective *the man who called had a guttural voice* THROATY, husky, gruff, gravelly, growly, growling, croaky, croaking, harsh, rough, rasping, raspy; deep, low, thick.

**guy** noun *informal he's a handsome guy* MAN, fellow, gentleman; youth, boy; *informal* lad, fella, gent, chap, dude, joe, Joe Blow, Joe Schmo, hombre.

**guzzle** verb *she* ***guzzled down*** *the orange juice* GULP DOWN, swallow, quaff, down, swill; *informal* knock back, swig, slug.

**gypsy** noun *a caravan of gypsies* ROMANY, Rom, traveler, nomad, rover, roamer, wanderer.

**gyrate** verb *the disk gyrates atop an aluminum pole* ROTATE, revolve, wheel, turn around, whirl, circle, pirouette, twirl, swirl, spin, swivel.

**habit** noun **1** *it was his habit to go for a run every morning* CUSTOM, practice, routine, wont, pattern, convention, way, norm, tradition, matter of course, rule, usage.

**2** *her many irritating habits* MANNERISM, way, quirk, foible, trick, trait, idiosyncrasy, peculiarity, singularity, oddity, eccentricity, feature; tendency, propensity, inclination, bent, proclivity, disposition, predisposition.

**3** *his cocaine habit* ADDICTION, dependence, dependency, craving, fixation, compulsion, obsession, weakness; *informal* monkey on one's back.

**4** *a monk's habit* GARMENT(S), dress, garb, clothes, clothing, attire, outfit, costume; *informal* gear; *formal* apparel. PHRASES:
**habit of mind** *a scientific habit of mind* DISPOSITION, temperament, character, nature, makeup, constitution, frame of mind, bent.
**in the habit of** *they were in the habit of phoning each other daily* ACCUSTOMED TO, used to, given to, wont to, inclined to.

**habitable** adjective *it's not the Ritz, but it's habitable* FIT TO LIVE IN, inhabitable, fit to occupy, in good repair, livable; *formal* tenantable.

**habitat** noun *the habitat of the spotted turtle has been greatly diminished* NATURAL ENVIRONMENT, natural surroundings, home, domain, haunt; *formal* habitation.

**habitation** noun **1** *a house fit for human habitation* OCCUPANCY, occupation, residence, residency, living in, tenancy.

**2** *formal* *his main habitation* RESIDENCE, place of residence, house, home, seat, lodging place, billet, quarters, living quarters, rooms, accommodations; *informal* pad, digs; *formal* dwelling, dwelling place, abode, domicile.

**habitual** adjective **1** *her father's habitual complaints* CONSTANT, persistent, continual, continuous, perpetual, nonstop, recurrent, repeated, frequent; interminable, incessant, ceaseless, endless, never-ending; *informal* eternal. ANTONYMS occasional, infrequent.

**2** *habitual drinkers* INVETERATE, confirmed, compulsive, obsessive, incorrigible, hardened, ingrained, dyed-in-the-wool, chronic, regular; addicted; *informal* pathological. ANTONYM occasional.

**3** *his habitual secretiveness* CUSTOMARY, accustomed, regular, usual, normal, set, fixed, established, routine, common, ordinary, familiar, traditional, typical, general, characteristic, standard, time-honored; *literary* wonted. ANTONYM unaccustomed.

**habituate** verb *poverty had habituated their children to a life of hopelessness* ACCUSTOM, make used, familiarize, adapt, adjust, attune, acclimatize, acculturate, condition; inure, harden; acclimate.

**hack**[1] verb *Stuart hacked the padlock off* CUT, chop, hew, lop, saw; slash. PHRASE: **hack it** *informal* *he tried to run his own commercial fishing outfit, but he couldn't hack it* COPE, manage, get on/by, carry on, come through, muddle along/through; stand it, tolerate it, bear it, endure it, put up with it; *informal* handle it, abide it, stick it out.

**hack**[2] noun **1** *a tabloid hack* JOURNALIST, reporter, newspaperman, newspaperwoman, writer; *informal* journo, scribbler; *archaic* penny-a-liner.

**2** *office hacks* DRUDGE, menial, menial worker, factotum; *informal* gofer.

**hackle** PHRASE: **make someone's hackles rise** *Julie's compulsive criticizing made her sister's hackles rise* ANNOY, irritate, exasperate, anger, incense, infuriate, irk, nettle, vex, put out, provoke, gall, antagonize, get on someone's nerves, ruffle someone's feathers, rankle with; rub the wrong way; *informal* aggravate, peeve, needle, rile, make someone see red, make someone's blood boil, get someone's back up, get someone's goat, get someone's dander up, bug, tee off, tick off, burn up.

**hackneyed** adjective *your hackneyed arguments fail to persuade anyone* OVERUSED, overdone, overworked, worn out, timeworn, platitudinous, vapid, stale, tired, threadbare; trite, banal, hack, clichéd, hoary, commonplace, common, ordinary, stock, conventional, stereotyped, predictable; unimaginative, unoriginal, uninspired, prosaic, dull, boring, pedestrian, run-of-the-mill, boilerplate, routine; *informal* old hat, cheesy, corny, played out. ANTONYM original.

**hag** noun *we'd all heard tales of a wizened hag who lived alone on the far side of the mountain* CRONE, old woman, gorgon; *informal* witch, crow, cow, old bag.

**haggard** adjective *he looked terrible, all pale and haggard* DRAWN, tired, exhausted, drained, careworn, unwell, unhealthy, spent, washed out, run-down; gaunt, pinched, peaked, hollow-cheeked, hollow-eyed, thin, emaciated, wasted, cadaverous; pale, wan, gray, ashen. ANTONYM healthy.

**haggle** verb *John spent nearly every Saturday morning haggling at flea markets and garage sales* BARTER, bargain, negotiate, dicker, quibble, wrangle; beat someone down, drive a hard bargain.

**hail**[1] verb **1** *a friend hailed him from the upper deck* CALL OUT TO, shout to, address; greet, say hello to, salute.

**2** *he hailed a cab* FLAG DOWN, wave down, signal to.

**3** *critics hailed the film as a masterpiece* ACCLAIM, praise, applaud, rave about, extol, eulogize, hymn, lionize, sing the praises of, make much of, glorify, cheer, salute, toast, ballyhoo; *formal* laud.

**4** *Rick* ***hails from*** *Australia* COME FROM, be from, be a native of, have one's roots in.

**hail**[2] noun *a hail of bullets* BARRAGE, volley, shower, rain, torrent, burst, stream, storm, avalanche, onslaught; bombardment, cannonade, battery, blast, salvo; *historical* broadside.

▸ verb *tons of dust hailed down on us* BEAT, shower, rain, fall, pour; pelt, pepper, batter, bombard, assail.

**hair** noun **1** *her thick black hair* LOCKS, curls, ringlets, mane, mop; shock of hair, head of hair; tresses.

**2** *I like your hair* HAIRSTYLE, haircut, cut, coiffure; *informal* hairdo, do, coif.

**3** *a dog with short, blue-gray hair* FUR, wool; coat, fleece, pelt; mane. PHRASES: **a hair's breadth** *she won by a hair's breadth* THE NARROWEST OF MARGINS, a narrow margin, the skin of one's teeth, a split second, a nose, a whisker.

**let one's hair down** *informal even the chairman of the board has to let his hair down once in a while* ENJOY ONESELF, have a good time, have fun, make merry, let oneself go; *informal* have a ball, whoop it up, paint the town red, live it up, have a whale of a time, let it all hang out.

**make someone's hair stand on end** *the truth about Corrine would make your hair stand on end* HORRIFY, shock, appall, scandalize, stun; make someone's blood run cold; *informal* make someone's hair curl, turn someone's hair white.

**split hairs** *you missed the point because you were so busy splitting hairs* QUIBBLE, cavil, carp, niggle; *informal* nitpick; *archaic* pettifog.

**hair-raising** adjective *the hair-raising stories we would tell around the campfire* TERRIFYING, frightening, petrifying, alarming, chilling, horrifying, shocking, spine-chilling, bloodcurdling, bone-chilling, white-knuckle, fearsome, nightmarish; eerie, sinister, weird, ghostly, unearthly; eldritch; *informal* hairy, spooky, scary, creepy.

**hairy** adjective **1** *animals with hairy coats* SHAGGY, bushy, long-haired; woolly, furry, fleecy, fuzzy; *Botany & Zoology* pilose.

**2** *his hairy face* BEARDED, bewhiskered, mustachioed; unshaven, stubbly, bristly; *formal* hirsute.

**3** *informal a hairy situation* RISKY, dangerous, perilous, hazardous, touch-and-go; tricky, ticklish, difficult, awkward; *informal* dicey, sticky.

**halcyon** adjective *the halcyon days of our youth* HAPPY, golden, idyllic, carefree, blissful, joyful, joyous, contented; flourishing, thriving, prosperous, successful; serene, calm, tranquil, peaceful. See note at CALM.

**hale** adjective *fair weather and a hale crew* HEALTHY, fit, fighting fit, well, in good health, bursting with health, in fine fettle, strong, robust, vigorous, hardy, sturdy, hearty, lusty, able-bodied; *informal* in the pink, as right as rain. ANTONYM unwell.

**half** adjective *a half grapefruit* HALVED, bisected, divided in two. ANTONYM whole.

▸ adverb **1** *the chicken is half cooked* PARTIALLY, partly, incompletely, inadequately, insufficiently; in part, part, slightly. ANTONYMS fully, completely.

**2** *I'm half inclined to believe you* TO A CERTAIN EXTENT/DEGREE, to some extent/degree, (up) to a point, in part, partly, in some measure. ANTONYM fully.

▸ noun *the first half of the show* PORTION, section, part, period; 50 percent.

**half-baked** adjective **1** *half-baked theories* ILL-CONCEIVED, hare-brained, cockamamie, ill-judged, impractical, unrealistic, unworkable, ridiculous, absurd; *informal* crazy, crackpot, cockeyed. ANTONYM sensible.

**2** *her half-baked nephew* FOOLISH, stupid, silly, idiotic, simpleminded, feebleminded, empty-headed, featherbrained, featherheaded, brainless, witless, unintelligent, ignorant; *informal* dim, dopey, dumb, thick, halfwitted, dimwitted, birdbrained, dozy. ANTONYM sensible.

**half-hearted** adjective *the halfhearted applause was not exactly encouraging* UNENTHUSIASTIC, cool, lukewarm, tepid, apathetic, indifferent, uninterested, unconcerned, languid, listless; perfunctory, cursory, superficial, desultory, feeble, lackluster. ANTONYM enthusiastic.

**halfway** adjective *the halfway point* MIDWAY, middle, mid, central, center, intermediate; *Anatomy* medial, mesial.

▸ adverb **1** *he started running down the passage and then stopped halfway* MIDWAY, in the middle, in the center; partway, part of the way.

**2** *she seemed halfway friendly* TO SOME EXTENT/DEGREE, in some measure, relatively, comparatively, moderately, somewhat, (up) to a point; just about, almost, nearly.

PHRASE: **meet someone halfway** *I was willing to meet him halfway* COMPROMISE, come to terms, reach an agreement, make a deal, make concessions, find the middle ground, strike a balance; give and take.

**halfwit** noun *informal*. See FOOL noun sense 1.

**halfwitted** adjective *informal*. See STUPID sense 1.

**hall** noun **1** *hang your coat in the hall* ENTRANCE HALL, hallway, entry, entrance, lobby, foyer, vestibule; atrium, concourse; passageway, passage, corridor, entryway.

2 *we booked a hall for the wedding* BANQUET HALL, community center, assembly room, meeting room, chamber; auditorium, concert hall, theater.

**hallmark** noun 1 *the hallmark on silver* ASSAY MARK, official mark, stamp of authenticity.

2 *tiny bubbles are the hallmark of fine champagnes* MARK, distinctive feature, characteristic, sign, sure sign, telltale sign, badge, stamp, trademark, indication, indicator, calling card.

**hallucinate** verb *the fever made her hallucinate* HAVE HALLUCINATIONS, see things, be delirious, fantasize; *informal* trip, see pink elephants.

**hallucination** noun *are you sure that what you saw wasn't a hallucination?* DELUSION, illusion, figment of the imagination, vision, apparition, mirage, chimera, fantasy; (**hallucinations**) delirium, phantasmagoria; *informal* trip, pink elephants.

**halo** noun *a stunning depiction of the angel's halo* RING OF LIGHT, nimbus, aureole, glory, crown of light, corona; *technical* halation; *rare* gloriole.

**halt** verb 1 *Jen halted and turned around* STOP, come to a halt, come to a stop, come to a standstill; pull up, draw up. ANTONYMS start, go.

2 *a further strike has halted production* STOP, bring to a stop, put a stop to, bring to an end, put an end to, terminate, end, wind up; suspend, break off, arrest; impede, check, curb, stem, block, stall, hold back; *informal* pull the plug on, put the kibosh on. ANTONYMS start, continue.

▸ noun 1 *the car drew to a halt* STOP, standstill.

2 *a halt in production* STOPPAGE, stopping, discontinuation, break, suspension, pause, interval, interruption, hiatus; cessation, termination, close, end.

**halting** adjective 1 *a halting conversation* | *halting English* HESITANT, faltering, hesitating, stumbling, stammering, stuttering; broken, imperfect. ANTONYM fluent.

2 *his halting gait* UNSTEADY, awkward, faltering, stumbling, limping, hobbling. ANTONYMS steady, nimble.

**hammer** noun *a hammer and chisel* mallet, beetle, gavel, sledgehammer, jackhammer.

▸ verb 1 *the alloy is hammered into a circular shape* BEAT, forge, shape, form, mold, fashion, make.

2 *Sally **hammered at** the door* BATTER, pummel, beat, bang, pound; strike, hit, knock on, thump on; cudgel, bludgeon, club; *informal* bash, wallop, clobber, whack, thwack.

3 *they **hammered away at** their nonsmoking campaign* WORK HARD AT, labor at, slog away at, plod away at, grind away at, slave away at, work like a dog on, put one's nose to the grindstone for; persist with, persevere with, press on with; *informal* stick at, plug away at, work one's tail off on/for, soldier on with.

4 *antiracism had been **hammered into** her* DRUM INTO, instill in, inculcate into, knock into, drive into; drive home to, impress upon; ingrain into.

5 *informal we've hammered them twice this season.* See TROUNCE.

PHRASE: **hammer out** *the committee sat for three hours hammering out a new budget* THRASH OUT, work out, agree on, sort out, decide on, bring about, effect, produce, broker, negotiate, reach an agreement on.

**hamper**[1] noun *a picnic hamper* BASKET, pannier, wickerwork basket; box, container.

**hamper**[2] verb *the search was hampered by fog* HINDER, obstruct, impede, inhibit, retard, balk, thwart, foil, curb, delay, set back, slow down, hobble, hold up, interfere with; restrict, constrain, trammel, block, check, curtail, frustrate, cramp, bridle, handicap, cripple, hamstring, shackle, fetter; *informal* stymie, hog-tie, throw a (monkey) wrench in the works of. See note at HINDER. ANTONYM help.

**hamstring** verb 1 *cattle were killed or hamstrung* CRIPPLE, lame, disable, incapacitate.

2 *he felt hamstrung by the regulations.* See HAMPER[2].

**hand** noun 1 *big, strong hands* palm, fist; *informal* paw, mitt, duke, hook, meathook.

2 *the clock's second hand* POINTER, indicator, needle, arrow, marker.

3 (**hands**) *the frontier posts remained in government hands* CONTROL, power, charge, authority; command, responsibility, guardianship, management, care, supervision, jurisdiction; possession, keeping, custody; clutches, grasp, thrall; disposal; *informal* say-so.

4 *let me give you **a hand*** HELP, a helping hand, assistance, aid, support, succor, relief; a good turn, a favor.

5 *a document written in his own hand* HANDWRITING, writing, script, calligraphy.

6 *a ranch hand* WORKER, workman, laborer, operative, hired hand, roustabout, peon; cowboy.

▸ verb *she handed each of us an envelope* PASS, give, let someone have; throw, toss; present to.

PHRASES: **at hand** *the time for courage is at hand* IMMINENT, approaching, coming, about to happen, on the horizon; impending.

**big hand** *informal her fans gave her a big hand* ROUND OF APPLAUSE, clap, handclap, ovation, standing ovation; applause, handclapping.

**close at hand** *keep the manual close at hand* READILY AVAILABLE, available, handy, to hand, within reach, accessible, close, close by, near, nearby, at the ready, at one's fingertips, at one's disposal, convenient; *informal* get-at-able.

**hand down** *this bracelet has been handed down from four generations* PASS ON, pass down; bequeath, will, leave, make over, give, gift, transfer; *Law* demise, devise.

**hand in glove** *working hand in glove with their former adversaries* IN CLOSE COLLABORATION, in close association, in close cooperation, very closely, in partnership, in league, in collusion; *informal* in cahoots, in bed.

**hand out** *volunteers were asked to hand out pamphlets* DIS-

TRIBUTE, give out, pass out/around, dole out, dish out, deal out, mete out, issue, dispense; allocate, allot, apportion, disburse; circulate, disseminate.

**hand over** *they handed over the stolen goods to the authorities* YIELD, give, give up, pass, grant, entrust, surrender, relinquish, cede, turn over, deliver up, forfeit, sacrifice.

**hands down** *we won hands down* EASILY, effortlessly, with ease, with no trouble, without effort; *informal* by a mile, no sweat.

**try one's hand at** *I regret that I never tried my hand at water-skiing* HAVE A GO AT, make an attempt at, have a shot at; attempt, try, try out, give something a try; *informal* have a stab at, give something a whirl; *formal* essay.

**handbag** noun *a leather handbag* PURSE, bag, shoulder bag, clutch purse, evening bag; pocketbook; *historical* reticule.

**handbill** noun *annoyed by the handbills on our windshield* NOTICE, advertisement, flyer, leaflet, circular, handout, pamphlet, brochure, fact sheet; *informal* ad.

**handbook** noun *the handbook explains our late-fee policy* MANUAL, instructions, instruction manual, how-to guide; almanac, companion, directory, compendium; guide, guidebook, vade mecum.

**handcuff** verb *Martini was handcuffed to the radiator* MANACLE, shackle, fetter; restrain, clap/put someone in irons; *informal* cuff.

**handcuffs** plural noun *when her lawyer came, Paula was still in handcuffs* MANACLES, shackles, irons, fetters, bonds, restraints; *informal* cuffs, bracelets.

**handful** noun **1** ***a handful of*** *bad apples* A FEW, a small number of, a small amount of, a small quantity of, one or two, some, not many, a scattering of, a trickle of.

**2** *informal* *the child is a real handful* NUISANCE, problem, bother, irritant, thorn in someone's flesh/side; *informal* pest, headache, pain, pain in the neck, pain in the butt.

**handicap** noun **1** *a visual handicap* DISABILITY, physical abnormality, mental abnormality, defect, impairment, affliction, deficiency, dysfunction.

**2** *a handicap to the competitiveness of the industry* IMPEDIMENT, hindrance, obstacle, barrier, bar, obstruction, encumbrance, constraint, restriction, check, block, curb; disadvantage, drawback, stumbling block, difficulty, shortcoming, limitation; ball and chain, albatross, millstone (around someone's neck), burden, liability; *literary* trammel. ANTONYMS benefit, advantage.

▸ verb *lack of funding handicapped the research* HAMPER, impede, hinder, impair, hamstring; restrict, check, obstruct, block, curb, bridle, hold back, constrain, trammel, limit, encumber; *informal* stymie. ANTONYMS help, advance.

**handiwork** noun *the jewelry is the handiwork of Chinese smiths* CREATION, product, work, achievement; handicraft, craft, craftwork.

**handle** verb **1** *the equipment must be handled with care* HOLD, pick up, grasp, grip, lift; feel, touch, finger; *informal* paw.

**2** *a car that is easy to handle* CONTROL, drive, steer, operate, maneuver, manipulate.

**3** *she handled the problems well* DEAL WITH, manage, tackle, take care of, take charge of, attend to, see to, sort out, apply oneself to, take in hand; respond to, field.

**4** *the advertising company that is handling the account* ADMINISTER, manage, control, conduct, direct, guide, supervise, oversee, be in charge of, take care of, look after.

**5** *the traders handled goods manufactured in the Rhineland* TRADE IN, deal in, buy, sell, supply, peddle, traffic in, purvey, hawk, tout, market.

▸ noun *the knife's handle* HAFT, shank, stock, shaft, grip, handgrip, hilt, helve, butt; knob.

**handout** noun **1** (**handouts**) *she existed on handouts* CHARITY, aid, benefit, financial support, donations, subsidies, welfare; *historical* alms.

**2** *a photocopied handout* LEAFLET, pamphlet, brochure, fact sheet; handbill, flyer, notice, circular.

**hand-picked** adjective *six hand-picked contestants will be flown to Ireland for the finals* SPECIALLY CHOSEN, selected, invited; select, elite; choice.

**handsome** adjective **1** *a handsome man* GOOD-LOOKING, attractive, striking, gorgeous; *informal* hunky, drop-dead gorgeous, hot, cute. ANTONYM ugly.

**2** *a handsome woman of 30* STRIKING, imposing, prepossessing, elegant, stately, dignified, statuesque, good-looking, attractive, personable. ANTONYM plain.

**3** *a handsome profit* SUBSTANTIAL, considerable, sizable, princely, large, big, ample, bumper; *informal* tidy, whopping, not to be sneezed at, ginormous. ANTONYM meager.

**handwriting** noun *barely legible handwriting* WRITING, script, hand, pen; penmanship, calligraphy, chirography; *informal* scrawl, scribble, chicken scratch.

**handy** adjective **1** *a handy reference tool* USEFUL, convenient, practical, easy-to-use, well-designed, user-friendly, user-oriented, helpful, functional, serviceable. ANTONYM inconvenient.

**2** *keep your credit card handy* READILY AVAILABLE, available, at hand, near at hand, within reach, accessible, ready, close, close by, near, nearby, at the ready, at one's fingertips; *informal* get-at-able.

**3** *he's handy with a needle and thread* SKILLFUL, skilled, dexterous, deft, nimble-fingered, adroit, able, adept, proficient, capable; good with one's hands; *informal* nifty. ANTONYM inept.

**hang** verb **1** *lights hung from the trees* BE SUSPENDED, dangle, hang down, be pendent, swing, sway.

**2** *hang the pictures at eye level* PUT UP, fix, attach, affix, fasten, post, display, suspend, pin up, nail up.

**3** *the room was hung with streamers* DECORATE, adorn,

drape, festoon, deck out, trick out, bedeck, array, garland, swathe, cover, ornament; *literary* bedizen.

4 *he was hanged for murder* STRING UP, send to the gallows.

5 *a pall of smoke hung over the city* HOVER, float, drift, be suspended. PHRASES: **hang around** *informal* 1 *they spent their time hanging around in bars* LOITER, linger, wait around, waste time, kill time, mark time, while away the/one's time, cool one's heels, twiddle one's thumbs; frequent, be a regular visitor to, haunt; *informal* hang out in.

2 *she's hanging around with a gang of marketing types* ASSOCIATE, mix, keep company, socialize, fraternize, consort, rub elbows; *informal* hang out, run around, be thick, hobnob.

**hang on** 1 *he* ***hung on to*** *her coat* HOLD ON TO, hold fast to, grip, clutch, grasp, hold tightly to, cling to.

2 *her future hung on their decision* DEPEND ON, be dependent on, turn on, hinge on, rest on, be contingent on, be determined by, be decided by.

3 *I'll hang on as long as I can* PERSEVERE, hold out, hold on, go on, carry on, keep on, keep going, keep at it, continue, persist, stay with it, struggle on, plod on; *informal* soldier on, stick to/at it, stick it out, hang in there.

4 *informal hang on, let me think* WAIT, wait a minute, wait a second, hold on, stop; hold the line/phone; *informal* hold your horses, sit tight, wait a sec.

**hang over someone** *the threat of budget cuts is hanging over us* BE IMMINENT, threaten, be close, be impending, impend, loom, be on the horizon.

**hangdog** adjective *his hangdog expression betrayed his alleged confidence* SHAMEFACED, sheepish, abashed, ashamed, guilty-looking, abject, cowed, dejected, downcast, crestfallen, woebegone, disconsolate. ANTONYM unabashed.

**hanger-on** noun *here comes Mr. Bigshot and his creepy hangers-on* FOLLOWER, flunky, toady, camp follower, sycophant, parasite, leech, bottom feeder; henchman, minion, lackey, vassal; acolyte; cohort; *informal* groupie, sponger, freeloader, passenger, sidekick.

**hang-up** noun *Louie has a hang-up about dirty windows* NEUROSIS, phobia, preoccupation, fixation, obsession, idée fixe; inhibition, mental block, psychological block, block, difficulty; *informal* complex, thing, bee in one's bonnet.

**hank** noun *a hank of yarn* COIL, skein, length, roll, loop, twist, piece; lock, ringlet, curl.

**hanker** verb *I hanker to go home* YEARN, long, crave, desire, wish, want, hunger, thirst, lust, ache, pant, be eager, be desperate, be eating one's heart out; fancy, pine; *informal* be dying, have a yen, itch.

**hankering** noun *I had a sudden hankering for a BLT* LONGING, yearning, craving, desire, wish, hunger, thirst, urge, ache, lust, appetite, fancy; *informal* yen, itch; *archaic* appetency. ANTONYM aversion.

**haphazard** adjective *Shelley's haphazard piles of laundry* RANDOM, unplanned, unsystematic, unmethodical, disorganized, disorderly, irregular, indiscriminate, chaotic, hit-and-miss, arbitrary, aimless, careless, casual, slapdash, slipshod; chance, accidental; *informal* higgledy-piggledy.

**hapless** adjective *the hapless victims of exploitation* UNFORTUNATE, unlucky, luckless, out of luck, ill-starred, ill-fated, jinxed, cursed, doomed; unhappy, forlorn, wretched, miserable, woebegone; *informal* down on one's luck; *literary* star-crossed. ANTONYM lucky.

**happen** verb 1 *remember what happened last time he was here* OCCUR, take place, come about; ensue, result, transpire, materialize, arise, crop up, come up, present itself, supervene; *informal* go down; *formal* eventuate; *literary* come to pass, betide.

2 *I wonder what* ***happened to*** *Joe?* BECOME OF; *literary* befall, betide.

3 *they happened to be in* CHANCE, have the good/bad luck.

4 *she* ***happened on*** *a blue jay's nest* DISCOVER, find, find by chance, come across, chance on, stumble on, hit on.

THE RIGHT WORD **happen, befall, occur, transpire**

When things **happen**, they come to pass either for a reason or by chance (*it happened the day after school started; she happened upon the scene of the accident*), but the verb is more frequently associated with chance (*it happened to be raining when we got there*). **Occur** can also refer either to something that comes to pass either accidentally or as planned, but it should only be used interchangeably with *happen* when the subject is a definite or actual event (*the tragedy occurred last winter*). Unlike *happen*, *occur* also carries the implication of something that presents itself to sight or mind (*it never occurred to me that he was lying*). **Transpire** is a more formal (and some would say undesirable) word meaning to *happen* or *occur*, and it conveys the sense that something has leaked out or become known (*he told her exactly what had transpired while she was away*). While things that *happen*, *occur*, or *transpire* can be either positive or negative, when something **befalls** it is usually unpleasant (*he had no inkling of the disaster that would befall him when he got home*).

**happening** noun *bizarre happenings* OCCURRENCE, event, incident, proceeding, affair, doing, circumstance, phenomenon, episode, experience, occasion, development, eventuality.

▸ adjective *informal a happening nightspot* FASHIONABLE, modern, popular, new, latest, up-to-date, up-to-the-minute, in fashion, in vogue, le dernier cri; *informal* trendy, funky, hot, cool, with it, hip, in, big, now, groovy. ANTONYM old-fashioned.

**happily** adverb 1 *he smiled happily* CONTENTEDLY, cheerfully, cheerily, merrily, delightedly, joyfully, joyously, gaily, gleefully.

2 *I will happily do as you ask* GLADLY, willingly, readily, freely, cheerfully, ungrudgingly, with pleasure; *archaic* fain.

3 *happily, we are living in enlightened times* FORTUNATELY, luckily, thankfully, mercifully, by good luck, by good fortune, as luck would have it; thank goodness, thank God, thank heavens, thank the Lord.

**happiness** noun *trying to rediscover the happiness we once knew* PLEASURE, contentment, satisfaction, cheerfulness, merriment, gaiety, joy, joyfulness, joviality, jollity, glee, delight, good spirits, lightheartedness, well-being, enjoyment; exuberance, exhilaration, elation, ecstasy, jubilation, rapture, bliss, blissfulness, euphoria, transports of delight.

**happy** adjective **1** *Melissa looked happy and excited* CHEERFUL, cheery, merry, joyful, jovial, jolly, jocular, gleeful, carefree, untroubled, delighted, smiling, beaming, grinning, in good spirits, in a good mood, lighthearted, pleased, contented, content, satisfied, gratified, buoyant, radiant, sunny, blithe, joyous, beatific; thrilled, elated, exhilarated, ecstatic, blissful, euphoric, overjoyed, exultant, rapturous, in seventh heaven, on cloud nine, walking on air, jumping for joy, jubilant; *informal* chirpy, over the moon, on top of the world, tickled pink, on a high, as happy as a clam; *formal* jocund. ANTONYM sad.

**2** *we will be happy to advise you* GLAD, pleased, delighted; willing, ready, disposed. ANTONYM unwilling.

**3** *a happy coincidence* FORTUNATE, lucky, favorable, advantageous, opportune, timely, well-timed, convenient. ANTONYM unfortunate.

**happy-go-lucky** adjective *what's wrong with letting your children be happy-go-lucky?* EASYGOING, carefree, casual, free and easy, devil-may-care, blithe, nonchalant, insouciant, blasé, unconcerned, untroubled, unworried, lighthearted, laid-back. ANTONYM anxious.

**harangue** noun *a ten-minute harangue* TIRADE, diatribe, lecture, polemic, rant, fulmination, broadside, attack, onslaught; criticism, condemnation, censure, admonition, sermon; declamation, speech; *informal* blast; *literary* philippic.

▸ verb *he harangued his erstwhile colleagues* RANT AT, hold forth to, lecture, shout at; berate, criticize, attack; *informal* sound off at, mouth off to.

**harass** verb **1** *tenants who harass their neighbors* PERSECUTE, intimidate, hound, harry, plague, torment, bully, bedevil; pester, bother, worry, disturb, trouble, provoke, stress; *informal* hassle, bug, ride, give someone a hard time, get on someone's case.

**2** *they were sent to harass the enemy flanks* HARRY, attack, beleaguer, set upon, assail.

**harassed** adjective *the job left her totally harassed* STRESSED, stressed out, strained, worn out, hard-pressed, careworn, worried, troubled, beleaguered, under pressure, at the end of one's tether, at the end of one's rope; *informal* hassled. ANTONYM carefree.

**harbinger** noun *I long to see the robins, crocuses, and other harbingers of spring* HERALD, sign, indication, signal, portent, omen, augury, forewarning, presage; forerunner, precursor, messenger; *literary* foretoken.

**harbor** noun **1** *a picturesque harbor* PORT, dock, haven, marina; mooring, moorage, anchorage; waterfront.

**2** *a safe harbor for me* REFUGE, haven, safe haven, shelter, sanctuary, retreat, place of safety, port in a storm.

▸ verb **1** *he is harboring a dangerous criminal* SHELTER, conceal, hide, shield, protect, give sanctuary to; take in, put up, accommodate, house.

**2** *Rose had harbored a grudge against him* BEAR, nurse, nurture, cherish, entertain, foster, hold on to, cling to.

**hard** adjective **1** *hard ground* FIRM, solid, rigid, stiff, resistant, unbreakable, inflexible, impenetrable, unyielding, solidified, hardened, compact, compacted, dense, close-packed, compressed; steely, tough, strong, stony, rocklike, flinty, as hard as stone; frozen; *literary* adamantine. ANTONYM soft.

**2** *hard physical work* ARDUOUS, strenuous, tiring, fatiguing, exhausting, wearying, back-breaking, grueling, heavy, laborious; difficult, taxing, exacting, testing, challenging, demanding, punishing, tough, formidable, onerous, rigorous, uphill, Herculean; *informal* murderous, killing, hellish; *formal* exigent; *archaic* toilsome. ANTONYM easy.

**3** *hard workers* DILIGENT, hard-working, industrious, sedulous, assiduous, conscientious, energetic, keen, enthusiastic, zealous, earnest, persevering, persistent, unflagging, untiring, indefatigable; studious. ANTONYM lazy.

**4** *a hard problem* DIFFICULT, puzzling, perplexing, baffling, bewildering, mystifying, knotty, thorny, problematic, complicated, complex, intricate, involved; insoluble, unfathomable, impenetrable, incomprehensible, unanswerable. ANTONYM simple.

**5** *times are hard* HARSH, grim, difficult, bad, bleak, dire, tough, austere, unpleasant, uncomfortable, straitened, spartan; dark, distressing, painful, awful. ANTONYM comfortable.

**6** *a hard taskmaster* STRICT, harsh, firm, severe, stern, tough, rigorous, demanding, exacting; callous, unkind, unsympathetic, cold, heartless, hard-hearted, unfeeling; intransigent, unbending, uncompromising, inflexible, implacable, stubborn, obdurate, unyielding, unrelenting, unsparing, grim, ruthless, merciless, pitiless, cruel; standing no nonsense, ruling with a rod of iron. ANTONYMS kind, easygoing.

**7** *a hard winter* BITTERLY COLD, cold, bitter, harsh, severe, bleak, freezing, icy, icy-cold, arctic. ANTONYM mild.

**8** *a hard blow* FORCEFUL, heavy, strong, sharp, smart, violent, powerful, vigorous, mighty, hefty, tremendous. ANTONYMS light, gentle.

**9** *hard facts* RELIABLE, definite, true, confirmed, substantiated, undeniable, indisputable, unquestionable, verifiable. ANTONYMS unverified, questionable.

**10** *hard cider* ALCOHOLIC, strong, intoxicating, potent; *formal* spirituous. ANTONYM nonalcoholic.

**11** *hard drugs* ADDICTIVE, habit-forming; strong, harmful.

▸ adverb **1** *George pushed the door hard* FORCEFULLY, forcibly, roughly, powerfully, strongly, heavily, sharply, vigorously, energetically, with all one's might, with might and main. ANTONYM gently.

**2** *they worked hard* DILIGENTLY, industriously, assiduously, conscientiously, sedulously, busily, enthusiastically, energetically, doggedly, steadily; *informal* like mad, like crazy.

**3** *this prosperity has been hard won* WITH DIFFICULTY, with effort, after a struggle, painfully, laboriously. ANTONYM easily.

**4** *her death hit him hard* SEVERELY, badly, acutely, deeply, keenly, seriously, profoundly, gravely; *formal* grievously. ANTONYM slightly.

**5** *it was raining hard* HEAVILY, strongly, in torrents, in sheets; steadily; *informal* cats and dogs, buckets. ANTONYM lightly.

**6** *my mother looked hard at me* CLOSELY, attentively, intently, critically, carefully, keenly, searchingly, earnestly, sharply. ANTONYM casually.

PHRASES: **hard and fast** *get used to it—the curfew here is hard and fast* DEFINITE, fixed, set, strict, rigid, binding, clear-cut, cast-iron, ironclad; inflexible, immutable, unchangeable, incontestable.

**hard by** CLOSE TO, right by, beside, near (to), nearby, not far from, a stone's throw from, on the doorstep of; *informal* within spitting distance of, 'a hop, skip, and jump away from.'

**hard feelings** *I had no idea that our separation had left him with such hard feelings* RESENTMENT, animosity, ill feeling, ill will, bitterness, bad blood, resentfulness, rancor, malice, acrimony, antagonism, antipathy, animus, friction, anger, hostility, hate, hatred.

**hard up** *informal this administration ignores the families that are hard up* POOR, short of money, badly off, impoverished, impecunious, in reduced circumstances, unable to make ends meet; penniless, destitute, poverty-stricken; *informal* broke, strapped for cash, strapped.

THE RIGHT WORD **hard, arduous, difficult, laborious, trying**

For the student who doesn't read well, homework is **hard** work, which means that it demands great physical or mental effort. An English assignment to write an essay might be particularly **difficult**, meaning that it not only requires effort but skill. Where *hard* suggests toil, *difficult* emphasizes complexity (*a difficult math problem*). Memorizing long lists of vocabulary words would be **laborious**, which is even more restrictive than *hard* and suggests prolonged, wearisome toil with no suggestion of the skill required and no reference to the complexity of the task. Reading *War and Peace*, however, would be an **arduous** task, because it would require a persistent effort over a long period of time. A school assignment may be *difficult*, but is usually not *arduous*; that is, it may require skill rather than perseverance. It may also be *arduous* without being particularly *difficult*, as when a student is asked to write "I will not throw spitballs" five hundred times. A student who is new to a school may find it especially **trying**, which implies that it taxes the individual's patience, skill, or capabilities.

**hard-bitten** adjective *a hard-bitten FBI agent* HARDENED, tough, cynical, unsentimental, hardheaded, case-hardened, as tough as nails; *informal* hard-nosed, hard-edged, hard-boiled. ANTONYM sentimental.

**hard-boiled** adjective *informal*. See HARD-BITTEN.

**hard-core** adjective *hard-core socialists* DIEHARD, staunch, dedicated, committed, steadfast, dyed-in-the-wool, long-standing; hardline, extreme, entrenched, radical, intransigent, uncompromising, rigid.

**harden** verb **1** *this glue will harden in four hours* SOLIDIFY, set, congeal, clot, coagulate, stiffen, thicken, cake, cure, inspissate; freeze, crystallize; ossify, calcify, petrify. ANTONYM liquefy.

**2** *their suffering had hardened them* TOUGHEN, desensitize, inure, case-harden, harden someone's heart; deaden, numb, benumb, anesthetize; brutalize. ANTONYM soften.

**hardened** adjective **1** *he was hardened to the violence he had seen* INURED, desensitized, deadened; accustomed, habituated, acclimatized, used.

**2** *a hardened criminal* INVETERATE, seasoned, habitual, chronic, compulsive, confirmed, dyed-in-the-wool; incorrigible, incurable, irredeemable, unregenerate.

**hardheaded** adjective *a hardheaded jurist* UNSENTIMENTAL, practical, pragmatic, businesslike, realistic, sensible, rational, clear-thinking, coolheaded, down-to-earth, matter-of-fact, no-nonsense, with both feet on the ground; tough, hard-bitten; shrewd, astute, sharp, sharp-witted; *informal* hard-nosed, hard-edged, hard-boiled. ANTONYMS idealistic, sentimental.

**hard-hearted** adjective *he's not nearly as hard-hearted as he pretends to be* UNFEELING, heartless, cold, hard, callous, unsympathetic, uncaring, unloving, unconcerned, indifferent, unmoved, unkind, uncharitable, unemotional, cold-hearted, cold-blooded, mean-spirited, stony-hearted, having a heart of stone, as hard as nails, cruel. ANTONYM compassionate.

**hard-hitting** adjective *a hard-hitting ad campaign* UNCOMPROMISING, blunt, forthright, frank, honest, direct, tough; critical, unsparing, strongly worded, straight-talking, pulling no punches, not mincing one's words, not beating around/about the bush.

**hardiness** noun *in New England, you should select plants for their hardiness* ROBUSTNESS, strength, toughness, ruggedness, sturdiness, resilience, stamina, vigor; healthiness, good health. ANTONYM frailty.

**hardline** adjective *one of President Mugabe's key hardline allies* UNCOMPROMISING, strict, extreme, tough, diehard, immoderate, inflexible, intransigent, firm, intractable, unyielding, undeviating, unwavering, single-minded, not giving an inch; *rare* indurate. ANTONYMS moderate, flexible.

**hardly** adverb *we hardly know each other* SCARCELY, barely, only just, slightly.

**hard-pressed** adjective **1** *the hard-pressed infantry* UNDER ATTACK, hotly pursued, harried.

**2** *the hard-pressed construction industry* IN DIFFICULTIES, under pressure, troubled, beleaguered, harassed, with one's back to/against the wall, in a tight corner, in a tight spot, between a rock and a hard place; overburdened, overworked, overloaded, stressed-out; *informal* up against it.

**hardship** noun *by age six, she was a refugee and no stranger to hardship* PRIVATION, deprivation, destitution, poverty, austerity, penury, want, need, neediness, impecuniousness; misfortune, distress, suffering, affliction, trouble, pain, misery, wretchedness, tribulation, adversity, trials, trials and tribulations, dire straits; *literary* travails. ANTONYMS prosperity, ease.

**hard-working** adjective *even the hard-working employees got stiffed at bonus time* DILIGENT, industrious, conscientious, assiduous, sedulous, painstaking, persevering, unflagging, untiring, tireless, indefatigable, studious; keen, enthusiastic, zealous, busy, with one's shoulder to the wheel, with one's nose to the grindstone. ANTONYM lazy.

**hardy** adjective *our tiny frail baby has grown into a strapping hardy man* ROBUST, healthy, fit, strong, sturdy, tough, rugged, hearty, lusty, vigorous, hale and hearty, fit as a fiddle, fighting fit, in fine fettle, in good health, in good condition; *dated* stalwart. ANTONYM delicate.

**hare-brained** adjective **1** *a hare-brained scheme* ILL-JUDGED, rash, foolish, foolhardy, reckless, madcap, wild, silly, stupid, ridiculous, absurd, idiotic, asinine, imprudent, impracticable, unworkable, unrealistic, unconsidered, half-baked, ill-thought-out, ill-advised, ill-conceived; *informal* crackpot, cockeyed, crazy, daft. ANTONYM sensible.

**2** *a hare-brained kid* FOOLISH, silly, idiotic, unintelligent, empty-headed, scatterbrained, featherbrained, birdbrained, peabrained, brainless, giddy; *informal* dippy, dizzy, flaky, dopey, dotty, airheaded. ANTONYM intelligent.

**hark** verb *literary hark, I hear a warning note* LISTEN, lend an ear, pay attention, attend, mark; *archaic* hearken, give ear. PHRASE: **hark back to** *why hark back to such unpleasant memories?* RECALL, call to mind, bring to mind, look back on, evoke, put one in mind of.

**harlequin** noun *historical the gaily garbed harlequins of his court* JESTER, joker, merry-andrew.

▸ adjective *a harlequin pattern* MULTICOLORED, many-colored, colorful, parti-colored, varicolored, many-hued, rainbow, variegated, jazzy, kaleidoscopic, psychedelic, polychromatic, checkered; *archaic* motley.

**harlot** noun *archaic stay off that street, unless you want to be mistaken for a harlot* PROSTITUTE, whore, fille de joie, call girl; promiscuous woman; *informal* hooker, hustler, tramp; *dated* streetwalker, hussy, lady of the evening, tart, pro, member of the oldest profession, scarlet woman, loose woman, fallen woman, cocotte, wanton; *archaic* strumpet, courtesan, trollop, doxy, trull.

**harm** noun **1** *the voltage is not sufficient to cause harm* INJURY, hurt, pain, trauma; damage, impairment, mischief. ANTONYM benefit.

**2** *I can't see any harm in it* EVIL, wrong, ill, wickedness, iniquity, sin. ANTONYM good.

▸ verb **1** *he's never harmed anybody in his life* INJURE, hurt, wound, lay a finger on, maltreat, mistreat, misuse, ill-treat, ill-use, abuse, molest.

**2** *this could harm her Olympic prospects* DAMAGE, hurt, spoil, mar, do mischief to, impair.

**harmful** adjective *the harmful rays of the sun* DAMAGING, injurious, detrimental, dangerous, deleterious, unfavorable, negative, disadvantageous, unhealthy, unwholesome, hurtful, baleful, destructive; noxious, hazardous, poisonous, toxic, deadly, lethal; bad, evil, malign, malignant, malevolent, corrupting, subversive, pernicious. ANTONYM beneficial.

**harmless** adjective **1** *a harmless substance* SAFE, innocuous, benign, gentle, mild, wholesome, nontoxic, nonpoisonous, nonirritant, nonirritating, hypoallergenic; nonaddictive. ANTONYMS dangerous, toxic.

**2** *he seems harmless enough* INOFFENSIVE, innocuous, unobjectionable, unexceptionable. ANTONYM objectionable.

**harmonious** adjective **1** *harmonious music* TUNEFUL, melodious, melodic, sweet-sounding, mellifluous, dulcet, lyrical; euphonious, euphonic, harmonic, polyphonic; *informal* easy on the ear. ANTONYM discordant.

**2** *their harmonious relationship* FRIENDLY, amicable, cordial, amiable, congenial, easy, peaceful, peaceable, cooperative; compatible, sympathetic, united, attuned, in harmony, in rapport, in tune, in accord, of one mind, seeing eye to eye. ANTONYM hostile.

**3** *a harmonious blend of traditional and modern* CONGRUOUS, coordinated, balanced, in proportion, compatible, well-matched, well-balanced; *literary* consilient. ANTONYM incongruous.

**harmonize** verb **1** *colors that harmonize in a pleasing way* COORDINATE, go together, match, blend, mix, balance; be compatible, be harmonious, suit each other. ANTONYM clash.

**2** *a plan to harmonize tax laws across the country* COORDINATE, systematize, correlate, integrate, synchronize, make consistent, homogenize, bring in line, bring in tune.

**harmony** noun **1** *musical harmony* EUPHONY, polyphony; tunefulness, melodiousness, mellifluousness. ANTONYM dissonance.

**2** *the harmony of the whole structure* BALANCE, symmetry, congruity, consonance, coordination, compatibility. ANTONYM incongruity.

**3** *the villagers live together in harmony* ACCORD, agreement, peace, peacefulness, amity, amicability, friendship, fellowship, cooperation, understanding, consensus, unity, sympathy, rapport, like-mindedness; unison, union, concert, oneness, synthesis; *formal* concord. ANTONYM disagreement.

**harness** noun *a horse's harness* TACK, tackle, equipment; trappings; yoke; *archaic* equipage.

▸ verb **1** *he harnessed his horse* HITCH UP, put in harness, yoke, couple.

**2** *attempts to harness solar energy* CONTROL, exploit, utilize, use, employ, make use of, put to use; channel, mobilize, apply, capitalize on.

**harp** PHRASE: **harp on about** *the way she harps on about his* *shortcomings, it's a wonder he can stand to be with her* KEEP ON ABOUT, go on about, keep talking about, dwell on, make an issue of; labor the point of.

**harridan** noun *Steve tried to scare us with stories of the evil harridan Miss Duffy, who in reality was the sweetest teacher in Coolidge Elementary* SHREW, termagant, virago, harpy, vixen, nag, hag, crone, dragon, ogress; fishwife, hellcat, she-devil, gorgon; martinet, tartar; *informal* old bag, old bat, battle-ax, witch; *archaic* scold.

**harrowing** adjective *a harrowing experience for the hostages* DISTRESSING, distressful, traumatic, upsetting; shocking, disturbing, painful, haunting, appalling, horrifying.

**harry** verb **1** *they harried the retreating enemy* ATTACK, assail, assault; charge, rush, strike, set upon; bombard, shell, strafe.

**2** *the government was harried by a new lobby* HARASS, hound, bedevil, torment, pester, bother, worry, badger, nag, plague; *informal* hassle, bug, lean on, give someone a hard time.

**harsh** adjective **1** *a harsh voice* GRATING, jarring, rasping, strident, raucous, brassy, discordant, unharmonious, unmelodious; screeching, shrill; rough, coarse, hoarse, gruff, croaky. ANTONYMS soft, dulcet.

**2** *harsh colors* GLARING, bright, dazzling; loud, garish, gaudy, lurid, bold. ANTONYM subdued.

**3** *his harsh rule over them* CRUEL, savage, barbarous, despotic, dictatorial, tyrannical, tyrannous; ruthless, merciless, pitiless, relentless, unmerciful; severe, strict, intolerant, illiberal, iron-fisted; hard-hearted, heartless, unkind, inhuman, inhumane. ANTONYMS kind, enlightened.

**4** *they took harsh measures to end the crisis* SEVERE, stringent, draconian, firm, stiff, hard, stern, rigorous, grim, uncompromising; punitive, cruel, brutal. ANTONYM lenient.

**5** *harsh words* RUDE, discourteous, uncivil, impolite; unfriendly, sharp, bitter, abusive, unkind, disparaging; abrupt, brusque, curt, gruff, short, surly, offhand. ANTONYM friendly.

**6** *harsh conditions* AUSTERE, grim, spartan, hard, comfortless, inhospitable, stark, bleak, desolate. ANTONYM comfortable.

**7** *a harsh winter* HARD, severe, cold, bitter, bleak, freezing, icy; arctic, polar, Siberian. ANTONYMS balmy, mild.

**8** *harsh detergents* ABRASIVE, strong, caustic; coarse, rough. ANTONYMS gentle, mild.

**harum-scarum** adjective *the rules were too restrictive for a couple of harum-scarum teens like Bella and Maud* RECKLESS, impetuous, impulsive, imprudent, rash, wild; daredevil, madcap, hotheaded, hare-brained, foolhardy, incautious, careless, heedless; *informal* devil-may-care; *literary* temerarious. See note at SUPERFICIAL. ANTONYM cautious.

**harvest** noun **1** *we all helped with the harvest* HARVESTING, reaping, picking, collecting.

**2** *a poor harvest* YIELD, crop, vintage; fruits, produce.

**3** *the experiment yielded a meager harvest* RETURN, result, fruits; product, output, effect; consequence.

▸ verb **1** *he harvested the wheat* GATHER (IN), bring in, reap, pick, collect.

**2** *she harvested many honors* ACQUIRE, obtain, gain, get, earn; accumulate, amass, gather, collect; *informal* land, net, bag, rake in, scoop up.

**hash** noun *a whole hash of excuses* MIXTURE, assortment, variety, array, mix, miscellany, selection, medley, mishmash, ragbag, gallimaufry, potpourri, hodgepodge. PHRASE: **make a hash of** *informal he was sorry to have made such a hash of the travel arrangements* BUNGLE, fluff, flub, mess up, make a mess of; mismanage, mishandle, ruin, wreck; botch, muff, muck up, foul up, screw up, blow.

**hassle** noun *informal* **1** *parking is such a hassle* INCONVENIENCE, bother, nuisance, problem, trouble, struggle, difficulty, annoyance, irritation, thorn in one's side/flesh, fuss; *informal* aggravation, stress, headache, pain, pain in the neck.

**2** *she got into a hassle with that guy.* See QUARREL noun.

▸ verb *they were hassling him to pay up* HARASS, pester, nag, keep on at, badger, hound, harry, bother, torment, plague; *informal* bug, give someone a hard time, get on someone's case, breathe down someone's neck.

**haste** noun *working with feverish haste* SPEED, hastiness, hurriedness, swiftness, rapidity, quickness, briskness; *formal* expedition. ANTONYM delay.

PHRASE: **in haste** *the curtains look as if they were hung in haste* QUICKLY, rapidly, fast, speedily, with urgency, in a rush, in a hurry.

**hasten** verb **1** *we hastened back home* HURRY, rush, dash, race, fly, shoot; scurry, scramble, dart, bolt, sprint, run, gallop; go fast, go quickly, go like lightning, go hell-bent for leather; *informal* tear, scoot, zip, zoom, belt, hotfoot it, bomb, hightail, barrel; *dated* make haste. ANTONYMS dawdle, crawl.

**2** *chemicals can hasten aging* SPEED UP, accelerate, quicken, precipitate, advance, hurry on, step up, spur on, catalyze; facilitate, aid, assist, boost. ANTONYMS slow down, delay.

**hasty** adjective **1** *hasty steps* QUICK, hurried, fast, swift, rapid, speedy, brisk; *literary* fleet. ANTONYM slow.

**2** *hasty decisions* RASH, impetuous, impulsive, reckless, precipitate, spur-of-the-moment, premature, unconsidered, unthinking; *literary* temerarious. ANTONYM considered.

**hat** noun *please remove your hat* CAP, beret, bonnet.

**hatch** verb **1** *the duck hatched her eggs* INCUBATE, brood.

**2** *the plot that you* ***hatched up*** *last night* DEVISE, conceive, concoct, brew, invent, plan, design, formulate; think up, dream up; *informal* cook up.

**hatchet** noun *a small hatchet with an oak handle* AX, tomahawk, cleaver, mattock.

**hate** verb **1** *they hate each other* LOATHE, detest, despise, dislike, abhor, execrate; be repelled by, be unable to bear/stand, find intolerable, recoil from, shrink from; *formal* abominate. ANTONYM love.

**2** *I hate to bother you* BE SORRY, be reluctant, be loath, be unwilling, be disinclined; regret, dislike.

▸ noun **1** *feelings of hate* HATRED, loathing, detestation, dislike, distaste, abhorrence, abomination, execration, aversion; hostility, enmity, animosity, antipathy, revulsion, disgust, contempt, odium. ANTONYM love.

**2** *a hate of mine is filling in forms* PEEVE, pet peeve, bugbear, bane, bête noire, bogey, aversion, thorn in one's flesh/side, bugaboo. ANTONYM love.

**hateful** adjective *his hateful letters were presented as evidence* DETESTABLE, horrible, horrid, unpleasant, awful, nasty, disagreeable, despicable, objectionable, insufferable, revolting, loathsome, abhorrent, abominable, execrable, odious, disgusting, distasteful, obnoxious, offensive, vile, heinous, ghastly, beastly, godawful. ANTONYM delightful.

**hatred** noun *he finally overcame the hatred he felt for his unfaithful wife* LOATHING, hate, detestation, dislike, distaste, abhorrence, abomination, execration; aversion, hostility, ill will, ill feeling, enmity, animosity, antipathy; revulsion, disgust, contempt, odium.

**haughty** adjective *he is both haughty and disdainful* PROUD, arrogant, vain, conceited, snobbish, superior, self-important, pompous, supercilious, condescending, patronizing; scornful, contemptuous, disdainful; full of oneself, above oneself; *informal* stuck-up, snooty, hoity-toity, uppity, uppish, bigheaded, high and mighty, la-di-da. ANTONYM humble.

**haul** verb **1** *she hauled the basket along* DRAG, pull, tug, heave, lug, hump, draw, tow; *informal* yank.

**2** *a contract to haul coal* TRANSPORT, convey, carry, ship, ferry, move.

▸ noun *the thieves abandoned their haul* BOOTY, loot, plunder; spoils, stolen goods, ill-gotten gains; *informal* swag, boodle.

**haunt** verb **1** *a ghost haunts this house* APPEAR IN, materialize in; visit.

**2** *he haunts street markets* FREQUENT, patronize, visit regularly; loiter in, linger in; *informal* hang out in.

**3** *the sight haunted me for years* TORMENT, disturb, trouble, worry, plague, burden, beset, beleaguer; prey on, weigh on, gnaw at, nag at, weigh heavily on, obsess; *informal* bug.

▸ noun *a favorite haunt of artists* HANGOUT, stomping ground, stamping ground, meeting place; territory, domain, resort, retreat, spot.

**haunting** adjective *the haunting background music* EVOCATIVE, emotive, affecting, moving, touching, stirring, powerful; poignant, nostalgic, wistful, elegiac; memorable, indelible, unforgettable.

**have** verb **1** *he had a new car* POSSESS, own, be in possession of, be the owner of; be blessed with, boast, enjoy; keep, retain, hold, occupy.

**2** *the apartment has five rooms* COMPRISE, consist of, contain, include, incorporate, be composed of, be made up of; encompass; *formal* comprehend.

**3** *they had dinner together* EAT, consume, devour, partake of; drink, imbibe, quaff; *informal* demolish, dispose of, put away, scoff (down), scarf (down/up).

**4** *she had a letter from Mark* RECEIVE, get, be given, be sent, obtain, acquire, come by, take receipt of. ANTONYMS send, give.

**5** *we've decided to have a party* ORGANIZE, arrange, hold, give, host, throw, put on, lay on, set up, fix up.

**6** *she's going to have a baby* GIVE BIRTH TO, bear, be delivered of, bring into the world, produce; *informal* drop; *archaic* beget.

**7** *we are having guests for dinner* ENTERTAIN, be host to, cater for, receive; invite over, ask over/around, wine and dine; accommodate, put up.

**8** *he had trouble finding the restaurant* EXPERIENCE, encounter, face, meet, find, run into, go through, undergo.

**9** *I have a headache* BE SUFFERING FROM, be afflicted by, be affected by, be troubled with.

**10** *I had a good time* EXPERIENCE; enjoy.

**11** *many of them have doubts* HARBOR, entertain, feel, nurse, nurture, sustain, maintain.

**12** *he had little patience* MANIFEST, show, display, exhibit, demonstrate.

**13** *she had them line up according to height* MAKE, ask to, request to, get to, tell to, require to, induce to, prevail upon to; order to, command to, direct to, force to.

**14** *I can't have you insulting me* TOLERATE, endure, bear, support, accept, put up with, go along with, take, countenance; permit to, allow to; *informal* stand, abide, stomach; *formal* brook.

**15** *I* ***have to*** *get up at six* MUST, be obliged to, be required to, be compelled to, be forced to, be bound to.

**16** *informal I'd been had* TRICK, fool, deceive, cheat, dupe, take in, hoodwink, swindle; *informal* con, diddle, rip off, shaft, hose, sucker, snooker. PHRASES: **have had it** *informal* **1** *they admit that they've had it* HAVE NO CHANCE, have no hope, have failed, be finished, be defeated, have lost; *informal* have flopped, have come a cropper, have bought the farm.

**2** *if you tell anyone, you've had it* BE IN TROUBLE, be in for a scolding; *informal* be in hot water, be in deep doo-doo, be toast, be dead meat.

**have on** *she had a blue dress on* BE WEARING, be dressed in, be clothed in, be attired in, be decked out in, be robed in.

**haven** noun **1** *a safe haven* REFUGE, retreat, shelter, sanctuary, asylum; port in a storm, oasis, sanctum.

**2** *they stopped in a small haven* ANCHORAGE, harbor, harborage, port, moorage, mooring; cove, inlet, bay.

**haversack** noun *they looked like little soldiers with their khaki haversacks* KNAPSACK, backpack, rucksack, pack.

**havoc** noun **1** *the hurricane caused havoc* DEVASTATION, destruction, damage, desolation, ruination, ruin; disaster, catastrophe.

**2** *hyperactive children create havoc* DISORDER, chaos, disruption, mayhem, bedlam, pandemonium, turmoil, tumult, uproar; commotion, furor, a three-ring circus; *informal* hullabaloo.

**hawk** noun *every October we meet at Dobbs' Hill to watch the red-tailed hawks.*

**hay** noun *soon the barns will be filled with hay* FORAGE, dried grass, silage, fodder, straw, herbage. PHRASE: **make hay while the sun shines** *Jack was a firm believer in making hay while the sun shines* MAKE THE MOST OF AN OPPORTUNITY, take advantage of something, strike while the iron is hot, seize the day, carpe diem.

**haywire** adjective *informal the binding machine has gone haywire | by midnight, the negotiations were completely haywire* OUT OF CONTROL, erratic, faulty, malfunctioning, out of order; chaotic, confused, disorganized, disordered, topsy-turvy; *informal* on the blink, on the fritz.

**hazard** noun **1** *the hazards of radiation* DANGER, risk, peril, threat, menace; problem, pitfall.

**2** *literary the laws of hazard* CHANCE, probability, fortuity, luck, fate, destiny, fortune, providence.

▸ verb **1** *he hazarded a guess* VENTURE, advance, put forward, volunteer, float; conjecture, speculate, surmise; *formal* opine.

**2** *it's too risky to hazard money on* RISK, jeopardize, gamble, stake, bet, chance; endanger, imperil.

**hazardous** adjective *a hazardous construction site* RISKY, dangerous, unsafe, perilous, precarious, fraught with danger; unpredictable, uncertain, chancy, high-risk, insecure, touch-and-go; *informal* dicey, hairy. ANTONYMS safe, certain.

**haze** noun **1** *a thick haze on the sea* MIST, fog, cloud; smoke, vapor, steam.

**2** *a haze of euphoria* BLUR, daze, confusion, muddle, befuddlement.

**hazy** adjective **1** *a hazy day* MISTY, foggy, cloudy, overcast; smoggy, murky.

**2** *hazy memories* VAGUE, indistinct, unclear, faint, dim, nebulous, shadowy, blurred, fuzzy, confused.

**head** noun **1** *she scratched her head thoughtfully* skull, cranium, crown; *informal* nut, noodle, noggin, dome.

**2** *he had to use his head* BRAIN(S), brainpower, intellect, intelligence; wit(s), wisdom, mind, sense, reasoning, common sense; *informal* savvy, gray matter, smarts.

**3** *she had a good head for business* APTITUDE, faculty, talent, gift, capacity, ability; mind, brain.

**4** *the head of the church* LEADER, chief, controller, governor, superintendent, commander, captain; director, manager; principal, president, premier; chieftain, headman, sachem; CEO; *informal* boss, boss man, kingpin, top dog, Mr. Big, skipper, ringleader, numero uno, head honcho, big kahuna.

**5** *the head of the line* FRONT, beginning, start, fore, forefront; top.

**6** *the head of the river* SOURCE, origin, headspring, headwater; *literary* wellspring.

**7** *beer with **a head*** FROTH, foam, bubbles, spume, fizz, effervescence; suds.

▸ adjective *the head waiter* CHIEF, principal, leading, main, first, foremost, prime, premier, senior, top, highest, supreme, superior, top-ranking, ranking. ANTONYM subordinate.

▸ verb **1** *the procession was headed by the mayor* LEAD, be at the front of; be first, lead the way.

**2** *Dr. Jones heads a research team* COMMAND, control, lead, run, manage, direct, supervise, superintend, oversee, preside over, rule, govern, captain; *informal* be the boss of.

**3** *she was **heading for** the exit* MOVE TOWARD, make for, aim for, go in the direction of, be bound for, make a beeline for; set out for, start out for.

PHRASES: **at the head of** *Stasha will now be at the head of the department* IN CHARGE OF, controlling, commanding, leading, managing, running, directing, supervising, overseeing; at the wheel of, at the helm of.

**come to a head** *the violence came to a head after two civilians were killed* REACH A CRISIS, come to a climax, reach a critical point, reach a crossroads.

**go to someone's head** **1** *the wine has gone to my head* INTOXICATE SOMEONE, befuddle someone, make someone drunk; *informal* make someone woozy; *formal* inebriate someone.

**2** *her victory went to her head* MAKE SOMEONE CONCEITED, make someone full of themselves, turn someone's head, puff someone up.

**head off** **1** *he went to head off the cars* INTERCEPT, divert, deflect, redirect, reroute, draw away, turn away.

**2** *they headed off a confrontation* FORESTALL, avert, ward off, fend off, stave off, hold off, nip in the bud, keep at bay; prevent, avoid, stop.

**keep one's head** *Richie kept his head throughout the confrontation* KEEP/STAY CALM, keep one's self-control, maintain one's composure; *informal* keep one's cool, keep one's shirt on, keep it together, cool one's jets.

**lose one's head** *you cannot lose your head in the courtroom* LOSE CONTROL, lose one's composure, lose one's equilibrium, go to pieces; panic, get flustered, get confused, get hysterical; *informal* lose one's cool, freak out, crack up.

**headache** noun **1** *I've got a headache* PAIN IN THE HEAD, migraine; neuralgia; *informal* head.

**2** *informal their behavior was a headache for the teacher* NUISANCE, trouble, problem, bother, bugbear, pest, worry, inconvenience, vexation, irritant, thorn in one's side; *informal* aggravation, hassle, pain (in the neck).

**heading** noun **1** *chapter headings* TITLE, caption, legend, subtitle, subheading, rubric, headline.

**2** *this topic falls under four main headings* CATEGORY, division, classification, class, section, group, grouping, subject, topic.

**headlong** adverb **1** *he fell headlong into the tent* HEAD FIRST, on one's head. ANTONYM feet first.

**2** *she rushed headlong to join the craze* WITHOUT THINKING, without forethought, precipitously, impetuously, rashly, recklessly, carelessly, heedlessly, hastily, head first. ANTONYM cautiously.

▸ adjective *a headlong dash* BREAKNECK, whirlwind; reckless, precipitate, precipitous, hasty, careless, heedless, head-first. ANTONYM cautious.

**head-on** adjective **1** *a head-on collision* DIRECT, full on.

**2** *a head-on confrontation* DIRECT, face to face, personal; *informal* eyeball to eyeball.

**headquarters** plural noun *the report was immediately dispatched to headquarters* THE HEAD OFFICE, the main office, HQ, the base, the nerve center, the war room, mission control, the command post.

**headstone** noun *the heavy salt air up here is erosive to these old headstones* GRAVESTONE, tombstone, stone, grave marker, monument, memorial.

**headstrong** adjective *our middle child is the most headstrong* WILLFUL, strong-willed, stubborn, obstinate, unyielding, obdurate; contrary, perverse, wayward, unruly; *formal* refractory. ANTONYM tractable.

**headway** PHRASE: **make headway** *critics charge that the ground troops are making no headway in their purported mission* MAKE PROGRESS, progress, make strides, gain ground, advance, proceed, move, get ahead, come along, take shape.

**heady** adjective **1** *heady wine* POTENT, intoxicating, strong; alcoholic, vinous; *formal* spirituous. ANTONYM nonalcoholic.

**2** *the heady days of my youth* EXHILARATING, exciting, thrilling, stimulating, invigorating, electrifying, rousing; *informal* mind-blowing. ANTONYM boring.

**heal** verb **1** *he heals sick people* MAKE BETTER, make well, cure, treat, restore to health. ANTONYM make worse.

**2** *his knee had healed* GET BETTER, get well, be cured, recover, mend, improve. ANTONYM get worse.

**3** *time will heal the pain of grief* ALLEVIATE, ease, assuage, palliate, relieve, help, lessen, mitigate, attenuate, allay. ANTONYM aggravate.

**4** *we tried to heal the rift* PUT RIGHT, set right, repair, remedy, resolve, correct, settle; conciliate, reconcile, harmonize; *informal* patch up. ANTONYM worsen.

**health** noun **1** *he was restored to health* WELL-BEING, healthiness, fitness, good condition, good shape, fine fettle; strength, vigor, wellness. ANTONYM illness.

**2** *bad health forced him to retire* PHYSICAL STATE, physical shape, condition, constitution.

**healthy** adjective **1** *a healthy baby* WELL, in good health, fine, fit, in good trim, in good shape, in fine fettle, in tip-top shape; blooming, thriving, hardy, robust, strong, vigorous, fighting fit, fit as a fiddle, the picture of health; *informal* OK, in the pink, right as rain. ANTONYM ill.

**2** *a healthy diet* HEALTH-GIVING, healthful, good for one; wholesome, nutritious, nourishing; beneficial, salubrious. ANTONYM unwholesome.

**heap** noun **1** *a heap of boxes* PILE, stack, mound, mountain, mass, quantity, load, lot, jumble; collection, accumulation, assemblage, store, hoard.

**2** *informal we have **heaps of** room **a heap of** troubles* A LOT OF, a fair amount of, much, plenty of, a good deal of, a great deal of, an abundance of, a wealth of, a profusion of; (a great) many, a large number of, numerous, scores of; *informal* hundreds of, thousands of, millions of, a load of, loads of, a pile of, piles of, oodles of, stacks of, lots of, masses of, scads of, reams of, oceans of, miles of, tons of, zillions of.

▸ verb *she heaped logs on the fire* PILE UP, pile, stack up, stack, make a mound of; assemble, collect.

PHRASE: **heap on/upon** *they heaped praise on her* SHOWER ON, lavish on, load on; bestow on, confer on, give, grant, vouchsafe, favor with.

**hear** verb **1** *she can't hear* PERCEIVE SOUND; have hearing.

**2** *she could hear men's voices* PERCEIVE, make out, discern, catch, get, apprehend; overhear.

**3** *I heard that radio show* LISTEN TO, catch.

**4** *they heard that I had moved* BE INFORMED, be told, find out, discover, learn, gather, glean, ascertain, get word, get wind.

**5** *a jury heard the case* TRY, judge; adjudicate (on), adjudge, pass judgment on.

**6** *I totally hear what you're saying* ACKNOWLEDGE, understand, sympathize with, recognize, get, perceive.

**hearing** noun **1** *the wolf's acute hearing* ABILITY TO HEAR, auditory perception, sense of hearing, aural faculty.

**2** *she moved out of hearing* EARSHOT, hearing distance, hearing range, auditory range.

**3** *I had a fair hearing* CHANCE TO SPEAK, opportunity to be heard; interview, audience.

**4** *he gave evidence at the hearing* TRIAL, court case, inquiry, inquest, tribunal; investigation, inquisition.

**hearsay** noun *that's all hearsay, and I don't care to listen to such tripe* RUMOR, gossip, tittle-tattle, idle talk; stories, tales; *informal* the grapevine, scuttlebutt, loose lips.

**heart** noun **1** *my heart stopped beating informal* ticker.

**2** *he poured out his heart* EMOTIONS, feelings, sentiments; soul; love, affection, passion.

**3** *she has no heart* COMPASSION, sympathy, humanity, feeling(s), fellow feeling, tenderness, softness, empathy, understanding; kindness, goodwill.

**4** *they may lose heart* ENTHUSIASM, keenness, eagerness, spirit, determination, resolve, purpose, courage, nerve, willpower, fortitude; *informal* guts, spunk.

**5** *the heart of the city* CENTER, middle, hub, core, nucleus, eye, bosom. ANTONYM edge.

**6** *the heart of the matter* ESSENCE, crux, core, nub, root, gist, meat, marrow, pith, substance, kernel; *informal* nitty-gritty. ANTONYM peripherals.

PHRASES: **after one's own heart** *Lucie was always a girl after my own heart* LIKE-MINDED, of the same mind, kindred, compatible, congenial, sharing one's tastes; *informal* on the same wavelength.

**at heart** *he's a good kid at heart* DEEP DOWN, basically, fundamentally, essentially, in essence, intrinsically; really, actually, truly, in fact; *informal* when you get right down to it.

**by heart** *I know the lyrics by heart* FROM MEMORY, down pat, by rote, word for word, verbatim, word-perfect.

**do one's heart good** *it does my heart good to see the children getting along* CHEER ONE (UP), please one, gladden one, make one happy, delight one, hearten one, gratify one, make one feel good, give one a lift; *informal* tickle someone pink.

**eat one's heart out** *Adam will eat his heart out when he hears about Julia's engagement* PINE, long, ache, brood, mope, fret, sigh, sorrow, yearn, agonize; grieve, mourn, lament.

**from the bottom of one's heart** *everything in that poem I meant from the bottom of my heart* SINCERELY, earnestly, fervently, passionately, truly, genuinely, heartily, with all sincerity.

**give/lose one's heart to** *so, which young lady have you given your heart to this week?* FALL IN LOVE WITH, fall for, be smitten by; *informal* fall head over heels for, be swept off one's feet by, develop a crush on.

**have a change of heart** *it seems that the Smiths have had a change of heart about selling their house* CHANGE ONE'S MIND, flip-flop, change one's tune, have second thoughts, have a rethink, think again, think twice; *informal* get cold feet, do a U-turn, pull a U-ey.

**have a heart** *come on, have a heart and let Sandy keep the puppy* BE COMPASSIONATE, be kind, be merciful, be lenient, be sympathetic, be considerate, have mercy.

**heart and soul** *the volunteers were into the campaign heart and soul* WHOLEHEARTEDLY, enthusiastically, eagerly, zealously; absolutely, completely, entirely, fully, utterly, to the hilt, one hundred percent.

**take heart** *your cards and letters helped us to take heart* BE ENCOURAGED, be heartened, be comforted; cheer up, brighten up, perk up, liven up, revive.

**with one's heart in one's mouth** *she slowly made her way down the dark cellar stairs with her heart in her mouth* IN ALARM, in fear, fearfully, apprehensively, on edge, with trepidation, in suspense, in a cold sweat, with bated breath, on tenterhooks; *informal* with butterflies in one's stomach, in a state, in a stew, in a sweat.

**heartache** noun *a life of heartache* ANGUISH, grief, suffering, distress, unhappiness, misery, sorrow, sadness, heartbreak, via dolorosa, pain, hurt, agony, angst, despondency, despair, woe, desolation. ANTONYM happiness.

**heartbreaking** adjective *heartbreaking news from the doctor* DISTRESSING, upsetting, disturbing, heart-rending, sad, tragic, painful, traumatic, agonizing, harrowing; pitiful, poignant, plaintive, moving, tearjerker, tearjerking, gut-wrenching. ANTONYM comforting.

**heartbroken** adjective *the disqualified gymnasts were heartbroken* ANGUISHED, devastated, broken-hearted, heavy-hearted, grieving, grief-stricken, inconsolable, crushed, shattered, desolate, despairing; upset, distressed, miserable, sorrowful, sad, downcast, disconsolate, crestfallen, despondent; *informal* down in the dumps.

**heartburn** noun *the chest pains may indicate something more serious than heartburn* INDIGESTION, dyspepsia, acid reflux, pyrosis.

**hearten** verb *the letter from Daphne will hearten him* CHEER (UP), encourage, raise someone's spirits, boost, buoy up, perk up, inspirit, uplift, elate; comfort, reassure; *informal* buck up, pep up. See note at ENCOURAGE.

**heartfelt** adjective *her heartfelt confession* SINCERE, genuine, from the heart; earnest, profound, deep, wholehearted, ardent, fervent, passionate, enthusiastic, eager; honest, bona fide. ANTONYM insincere.

**heartily** adverb **1** *we heartily welcome the changes* WHOLEHEARTEDLY, sincerely, genuinely, warmly, profoundly, with all one's heart; eagerly, enthusiastically, earnestly, ardently.

**2** *they were heartily sick of her* VERY, extremely, thoroughly, completely, absolutely, really, exceedingly, immensely, most, downright, quite, seriously; *informal* real, mighty.

**heartless** adjective *Amelia had known more than her share of heartless men* UNFEELING, unsympathetic, unkind, uncaring, unconcerned, insensitive, inconsiderate, hard-hearted, stony-hearted, cold-hearted, mean-spirited; cold, callous, cruel, merciless, pitiless, inhuman. ANTONYM compassionate.

**heart-rending** adjective *their heart-rending testimonies had the audience in tears* DISTRESSING, upsetting, disturbing, heartbreaking, sad, tragic, painful, traumatic, harrowing; pitiful, poignant, plaintive, moving, tearjerker, tearjerking, gut-wrenching.

**heartsick** adjective *literary we were heartsick when we read the story of his misfortune* DESPONDENT, dejected, depressed, desolate, downcast, forlorn, unhappy, sad, upset, miserable, wretched, woebegone, inconsolable, grieving, grief-stricken, heavy-hearted, broken-hearted.

**heart-to-heart** adjective *a heart-to-heart chat* INTIMATE, personal, man-to-man, woman-to-woman; candid, honest, truthful, sincere.

▸ noun *they had a long heart-to-heart* PRIVATE CONVERSATION, tête-à-tête, one-to-one, chat, talk, word; *informal* confab.

**heartwarming** adjective *tonight's heartwarming episode reunites Dan's family for a memorable Thanksgiving* TOUCHING, moving, heartening, stirring, uplifting, pleasing, cheering, gladdening, encouraging, gratifying. ANTONYM distressing.

**hearty** adjective **1** *a hearty character* EXUBERANT, jovial, ebullient, cheerful, uninhibited, effusive, lively, loud, animated, vivacious, energetic, spirited, dynamic, enthusiastic, eager; warm, cordial, friendly, affable, amiable, good natured. ANTONYM introverted.

**2** *hearty congratulations* WHOLEHEARTED, heartfelt, sincere, genuine, real, true; earnest, fervent, ardent, enthusiastic. ANTONYM halfhearted.

**3** *a hearty woman of sixty-five* ROBUST, healthy, hardy, fit, flourishing, blooming, fighting fit, fit as a fiddle; vigorous, sturdy, strong; *informal* full of vim. ANTONYM frail.

**4** *a hearty meal* SUBSTANTIAL, large, ample, sizable, filling, generous, square, solid; healthy. ANTONYM light.

**heat** noun **1** *a plant sensitive to heat* WARMTH, hotness, warmness, high temperature; hot weather, warm weather, sultriness, mugginess, humidity; heat wave, hot spell. ANTONYM cold.

**2** *he took the heat out of the dispute* PASSION, intensity, vehemence, warmth, fervor, fervency; enthusiasm, excitement, agitation; anger, fury. ANTONYM apathy.

**3** *a female bear in heat* ESTRUS, season, sexual receptivity.

▸ verb **1** *the food was heated* WARM, warm up, heat up, make hot, make warm; reheat, cook, microwave; *informal* nuke, zap. ANTONYMS cool, chill.

**2** *the pipes expand as they* ***heat up*** BECOME HOT, become warm, get hotter, get warmer, increase in temperature. ANTONYM cool (down).

**3** *he calmed down as quickly as he had* ***heated up*** BECOME IMPASSIONED, become excited, become animated; get angry, become enraged.

**heated** adjective **1** *a heated swimming pool* WARM, hot; thermal.

**2** *a heated argument* VEHEMENT, passionate, impassioned, animated, spirited, lively, intense, fiery; angry, bitter, furious, fierce, stormy, tempestuous.

**3** *Robert grew heated as he spoke of the risks* EXCITED, animated, inflamed, worked up, wound up, keyed up; *informal* het up, in a state.

**heathen** noun **1** *the evangelist preached to the heathens* PAGAN, infidel, idolater, heretic, unbeliever, disbeliever, nonbeliever, atheist, agnostic, skeptic; *archaic* paynim. ANTONYM believer.

**2** *heathens who spoil good whiskey with ice* PHILISTINE, boor, oaf, ignoramus, lout, yahoo, vulgarian, plebeian; *informal* pleb, peasant.

▸ adjective *a heathen practice* PAGAN, infidel, idolatrous, heathenish; unbelieving, nonbelieving, atheistic, agnostic, heretical, faithless, godless, irreligious, ungodly, unholy; barbarian, barbarous, uncivilized, uncultured, primitive, ignorant, philistine.

**heave** verb **1** *she heaved the sofa backward* HAUL, pull, lug, drag, draw, tug, heft; *informal* hump, yank.

**2** *informal she heaved a brick at him* THROW, fling, cast, toss, hurl, lob, pitch; *informal* chuck, sling.

**3** *he heaved a sigh of relief* LET OUT, breathe, give, sigh; emit, utter.

**4** *the sea heaved* RISE AND FALL, roll, swell, surge, churn, seethe, swirl.

**5** *she heaved into the sink* RETCH, gag; vomit, be sick, get sick; *informal* throw up, puke, hurl, spew, barf, upchuck, ralph.

**heaven** noun **1** *the good will have a place in heaven* PARADISE, nirvana, Zion; the hereafter, the next world, the next life, Elysium, the Elysian Fields, Valhalla; *literary* the empyrean. ANTONYMS hell, purgatory.

**2** *a good book is my idea of heaven* BLISS, ecstasy, rapture, contentment, happiness, delight, joy, seventh heaven; paradise, Utopia, nirvana. ANTONYM misery.

**3** **(the heavens)** *he observed the heavens* THE SKY, the skies, the upper atmosphere, the stratosphere, space; *literary* the firmament, the vault of heaven, the blue, the (wild/wide) blue yonder, the welkin, the empyrean, the azure, the upper regions, the sphere, the celestial sphere. PHRASES: **in seventh heaven** *we're all in seventh heaven with this new swimming pool* ECSTATIC, euphoric, thrilled, elated, delighted, overjoyed, on cloud nine, walking on air, jubilant, rapturous, jumping for joy, transported, delirious, blissful; *informal* over the moon, on top of the world, on a high, tickled pink, as happy as a clam.

**move heaven and earth** *I'm going to get this promotion, even if I have to move heaven and earth to do it* TRY ONE'S HARDEST, do one's best, do one's utmost, do all one can, give one's all, spare no effort, put oneself out; strive, exert oneself, work hard; *informal* bend over backwards, do one's damnedest, pull out all the stops, go all out, bust a gut.

**heavenly** adjective **1** *heavenly choirs* DIVINE, holy, celestial, supernal; angelic, seraphic, cherubic; *literary* empyrean. ANTONYMS mortal, infernal.

**2** *heavenly constellations* CELESTIAL, cosmic, stellar, astral; planetary; extraterrestrial, superterrestrial. ANTONYMS terrestrial, earthly.

**3** *informal a heavenly morning* DELIGHTFUL, wonderful, glorious, perfect, excellent, sublime, idyllic, first-class, first-rate; blissful, pleasurable, enjoyable; exquisite, beautiful, lovely, gorgeous, enchanting; *informal* divine, super, great, fantastic, fabulous, terrific. ANTONYM dreadful.

**heavily** adverb **1** *Dad walked heavily* LABORIOUSLY, slowly, ponderously, woodenly, stiffly; with difficulty, painfully, awkwardly, clumsily. ANTONYMS easily, quickly.

**2** *we were heavily defeated* DECISIVELY, conclusively, roundly, soundly; utterly, completely, thoroughly. ANTONYM narrowly.

**3** *he drank heavily* EXCESSIVELY, to excess, immoderately, copiously, inordinately, intemperately, a great deal, too much, overmuch. ANTONYM moderately.

**4** *the area is heavily planted with trees* DENSELY, closely, thickly. ANTONYMS lightly, sparsely.

**5** *I became heavily involved in politics* DEEPLY, very, extremely, greatly, exceedingly, tremendously, profoundly; *informal* seriously, ever so.

**heavy** adjective **1** *a heavy box* WEIGHTY, hefty, substantial, ponderous; solid, dense, leaden; burdensome; *informal* hulking, weighing a ton. ANTONYM light.

**2** *a heavy man* OVERWEIGHT, fat, obese, corpulent, large, bulky, stout, stocky, portly, plump, paunchy, fleshy; *informal* hulking, tubby, beefy, porky, pudgy. ANTONYM thin.

**3** *a heavy blow to the head* FORCEFUL, hard, strong, violent, powerful, vigorous, mighty, hefty, sharp, smart, severe. ANTONYM gentle.

**4** *a gardener did the heavy work for me* ARDUOUS, hard, physical, laborious, difficult, strenuous, demanding, tough, onerous, back-breaking, grueling; *archaic* toilsome. ANTONYM easy.

**5** *a heavy burden of responsibility* ONEROUS, burdensome, demanding, challenging, difficult, formidable, weighty; worrisome, stressful, trying, crushing, oppressive. ANTONYMS undemanding, moderate.

**6** *heavy fog* DENSE, thick, soupy, murky, impenetrable. ANTONYMS light, wispy.

**7** *a heavy sky* OVERCAST, cloudy, clouded, gray, dull, gloomy, murky, dark, black, stormy, leaden, lowering. ANTONYMS sunny, bright.

**8** *heavy rain* TORRENTIAL, relentless, copious, teeming, severe. ANTONYMS light, intermittent.

**9** *heavy soil* CLAYEY, muddy, sticky, wet. ANTONYMS friable, dry.

**10** *a heavy fine* SIZABLE, hefty, substantial, colossal, big, considerable; stiff; *informal* tidy, whopping, steep, astronomical. ANTONYM small.

**11** *heavy seas* TEMPESTUOUS, turbulent, rough, wild, stormy, choppy, squally. ANTONYM calm.

**12** *heavy fighting* INTENSE, fierce, vigorous, relentless, all-out, severe, serious. ANTONYM halfhearted.

**13** *a heavy drinker* IMMODERATE, excessive, intemperate, overindulgent, unrestrained, uncontrolled. ANTONYM moderate.

**14** *a heavy meal* SUBSTANTIAL, filling, hearty, large, big, ample, sizable, generous, square, solid. ANTONYM light.

**15** *their diet is* ***heavy on*** *vegetables* ABOUNDING IN, abundant in, lavish with, profuse with, unstinting with, using a lot of. ANTONYM light on.

**16** *he felt heavy and very tired* LETHARGIC, listless, sluggish, torpid, languid, apathetic, logy. ANTONYMS energetic, animated.

**17** *a heavy heart* SAD, sorrowful, melancholy, gloomy, downcast, downhearted, heartbroken, dejected, disconsolate, demoralized, despondent, depressed, crestfallen, desolate, down; *informal* blue; *literary* dolorous. ANTONYM cheerful.

**18** *these poems are rather heavy* TEDIOUS, difficult, dull, dry, serious, heavy going, dreary, boring, turgid, uninteresting.

**19** *branches heavy with blossoms* LADEN, loaded, covered, filled, groaning, bursting, teeming, abounding.

**20** *a heavy crop* BOUNTIFUL, plentiful, abundant, large, bumper, rich, copious, considerable, sizable, profuse; *informal* whopping; *literary* plenteous. ANTONYM meager.

**21** *he has heavy features* COARSE, rough, rough-hewn, unrefined; rugged, craggy. ANTONYM delicate.

THE RIGHT WORD **heavy, burdensome, cumbersome, massive, ponderous, weighty**

Trying to move a refrigerator out of a third-floor apartment is difficult because it is **cumbersome**, which means that it is so heavy and bulky that it becomes unwieldy or awkward to handle. Cartons filled with books, on the other hand, are merely **heavy**, which implies greater density and compactness than the average load. A huge oak dining table might be described as **massive**, which stresses largeness and solidity rather than weight, while something that is **ponderous** is too large or too *massive* to move, or to be moved quickly (*a ponderous printing press*). Most of these terms can be used figuratively as well. *Heavy*, for example, connotes a pressing down on the mind, spirits, or senses (*heavy with fatigue; a heavy heart*) and *ponderous* implies a dull and labored quality (*a novel too ponderous to read*). **Burdensome**, which refers to something that is not only *heavy* but must be carried or supported, is even more likely to be used in an abstract way to describe something that is difficult but can, with effort, be managed (*a burdensome task*). Both a package and a problem may be described as **weighty**, meaning actually (as opposed to relatively) heavy; but it is more commonly used to mean very important or momentous (*weighty matters to discuss*).

**heavy-handed** adjective **1** *they are heavy-handed with the equipment* CLUMSY, awkward, maladroit, unhandy, inept, unskillful; *informal* ham-handed, ham-fisted, all thumbs. ANTONYM dexterous.

**2** *heavy-handed policing* INSENSITIVE, oppressive, overbearing, high-handed, harsh, stern, severe, tyrannical, despotic, ruthless, merciless; tactless, undiplomatic, inept. ANTONYM sensitive.

**heckle** verb *he was heckled by the drunk in the back of the room* JEER, taunt, jibe at, shout down, boo, hiss, harass; *informal* give someone a hard time. ANTONYM cheer.

**hectic** adjective *the trip to the airport was hectic* FRANTIC, frenetic, frenzied, feverish, manic, busy, active, fast and furious, fast-paced; lively, brisk, bustling, buzzing, abuzz. ANTONYM leisurely.

**hedge** noun **1** *high hedges* HEDGEROW, bushes; windbreak.

**2** *an excellent hedge against a fall in the dollar* SAFEGUARD, protection, shield, screen, guard, buffer, cushion; insurance, security.

**3** *his analysis is full of hedges* EQUIVOCATION, evasion, fudge, quibble, qualification; temporizing, uncertainty, prevarication, vagueness.

▸ verb **1** *fields hedged with forsythia* SURROUND, enclose, encircle, ring, border, edge, bound.

**2** *she was* ***hedged in*** *by her limited education* CONFINE, restrict, limit, hinder, obstruct, impede, constrain, trap; hem in.

**3** *he hedged at every new question* PREVARICATE, equivocate, vacillate, quibble, hesitate, stall, dodge the issue, be noncommittal, be evasive, be vague, beat around the bush, pussyfoot around, mince one's words; hem and haw; *informal* sit on the fence, duck the question.

4 *the company hedged its position on the market* SAFEGUARD, protect, shield, guard, cushion; cover, insure.

**heed** verb *heed the warnings* PAY ATTENTION TO, take notice of, take note of, pay heed to, attend to, listen to; bear in mind, be mindful of, mind, mark, consider, take into account, follow, obey, adhere to, abide by, observe, take to heart, be alert to. ANTONYM disregard.

▸ noun *he paid no heed* ATTENTION, notice, note, regard; consideration, thought, care.

**heedful** adjective *the governor is about to deliver a statement regarding the hurricane, and it is imperative that everyone is heedful* ATTENTIVE, careful, mindful, cautious, prudent, circumspect; alert, aware, wary, chary, watchful, vigilant, on guard, on the alert.

**heedless** adjective *the evacuation warnings were clear, but he was heedless and didn't get out in time* UNMINDFUL, taking no notice, paying no heed, unheeding, disregardful, neglectful, oblivious, inattentive, blind, deaf; incautious, imprudent, rash, reckless, foolhardy, improvident, unwary.

**heel**[1] noun 1 *shoes with low heels* wedge, stiletto.

2 *the heel of a loaf* TAIL END, end, crust, remnant, remainder, remains.

3 *informal you're such a heel to have left Liz at the altar* SCOUNDREL, rogue, rascal, reprobate, miscreant; *informal* beast, rat, louse, swine, snake, scumbag, scumbucket, scuzzball, sleazeball, sleazebag, stinker.

**heel**[2] verb *the ship heeled to starboard* LEAN OVER, list, careen, tilt, tip, incline, keel over.

**heft** verb *Doug helped us heft the kegs up into the truck* LIFT, lift up, raise, raise up, heave, hoist, haul; carry, lug, tote; *informal* cart, hump, schlep.

▸ noun *the heft of the urn surprised us* WEIGHT, heaviness, bulk.

**hefty** adjective 1 *a hefty young man* BURLY, heavy, sturdy, strapping, bulky, brawny, husky, strong, muscular, large, big, solid, well-built; portly, stout; *informal* hulking, hunky, beefy. ANTONYMS slight, gaunt.

2 *a hefty kick* POWERFUL, violent, hard, forceful, heavy, mighty. ANTONYM feeble.

3 *hefty loads of lumber* HEAVY, weighty, bulky, big, large, substantial, massive, ponderous; unwieldy, cumbersome, burdensome, hulking. ANTONYM light.

4 *a hefty fine* SUBSTANTIAL, sizable, considerable, stiff, extortionate, large, excessive; *informal* steep, astronomical, whopping. ANTONYMS paltry, small.

**height** noun 1 *the height of the wall* SIZE, tallness, extent upward, vertical measurement, elevation, stature, altitude. ANTONYM width.

2 *the mountain heights* SUMMIT, top, peak, crest, crown, tip, cap, pinnacle, apex, brow, ridge. ANTONYM base.

3 *the height of their fame* HIGHEST POINT, crowning moment, peak, acme, zenith, apogee, pinnacle, climax, high-water mark. ANTONYM nadir.

4 *the height of bad manners* EPITOME, acme, zenith, quintessence, very limit; ultimate, utmost; ne plus ultra.

5 **(heights)** *he is terrified of heights* HIGH PLACES, high ground; precipices, cliffs.

**heighten** verb 1 *the roof had to be heightened* RAISE, make higher, lift (up), elevate. ANTONYM lower.

2 *her pleasure was heightened by guilt* INTENSIFY, increase, enhance, add to, augment, boost, strengthen, deepen, magnify, amplify, aggravate, reinforce. ANTONYM reduce.

**heinous** adjective *heinous crimes* ODIOUS, wicked, evil, atrocious, monstrous, abominable, detestable, contemptible, reprehensible, despicable, egregious, horrific, terrible, awful, abhorrent, loathsome, hideous, unspeakable, execrable; iniquitous, villainous, beyond the pale. ANTONYM admirable.

**helix** noun *the teacher's crude drawing of a DNA double helix* SPIRAL, coil, corkscrew, curl, curlicue, twist, gyre, whorl, convolution; *technical* volute, volution.

**hell** noun 1 *they feared hell* THE NETHERWORLD, the Inferno, the infernal regions, the abyss; eternal damnation, perdition; hellfire, fire and brimstone; Hades, Sheol, Acheron, Gehenna, Tophet; *literary* the pit. ANTONYM heaven.

2 *he made her life hell* A MISERY, torture, agony, a torment, a nightmare, an ordeal; anguish, wretchedness, woe. ANTONYM paradise.

PHRASES: **give hell** *informal* 1 *when I found out, I gave him hell* REPRIMAND SEVERELY, rebuke, admonish, chastise, castigate, chide, upbraid, reprove, scold, berate, remonstrate with, reprehend, take to task, lambaste; read the riot act, give a piece of one's mind, rake/haul over the coals; *informal* tell off, dress down, give an earful, give a roasting, rap over the knuckles, let have it, bawl out, come down hard on, lay into, blast, chew out.

2 *she gave me hell when I was her assistant* HARASS, hound, plague, harry, bother, trouble, bully, intimidate, pick on, victimize, terrorize; *informal* hassle, give a hard time.

**raise hell** *informal* 1 *they were hollering and raising hell* CAUSE A DISTURBANCE, cause a commotion, be noisy, run riot, run wild, go on the rampage, be out of control; *informal* raise the roof.

2 *he raised hell with the planners* REMONSTRATE, expostulate, be angry, be furious; argue; *informal* kick up a fuss, raise a stink.

**hellish** adjective 1 *the hellish face of Death* INFERNAL, Hadean, chthonic; diabolical, fiendish, satanic, demonic; evil, wicked. ANTONYM angelic.

2 *informal a hellish week* HORRIBLE, rotten, awful, terrible, dreadful, ghastly, horrid, vile, foul, appalling, atrocious, horrendous, frightful; difficult, unpleasant, nasty, disagreeable; stressful, taxing, tough, hard, frustrating, fraught, traumatic, grueling; *informal* murderous, lousy; beastly, hellacious. ANTONYM wonderful.

**helm** noun *he took the helm* TILLER, wheel; steering gear, rudder. PHRASE: **at the helm** *Judith will be at the helm while I am in New Jersey* IN CHARGE, in command, in control, responsible, in authority, at the wheel, in the driver's seat, in the saddle, holding the reins, running the show, calling the shots.

**help** verb **1** *can you help me please?* ASSIST, aid, lend a (helping) hand to, give assistance to, come to the aid of; be of service to, be of use to; do someone a favor, do someone a service, do someone a good turn, bail someone out, come to someone's/the rescue, give someone a leg up; *informal* get someone out of a tight spot, save someone's bacon, save someone's skin. ANTONYM hinder.

**2** *this credit card helps cancer research* SUPPORT, contribute to, give money to, donate to; promote, boost, back; further the interests of, bankroll. ANTONYM impede.

**3** *sore throats are helped by lozenges* RELIEVE, soothe, ease, alleviate, make better, improve, assuage, lessen; remedy, cure, heal. ANTONYM worsen.

▸ noun **1** *I'll take help wherever I can find it | this may be of help to you* ASSISTANCE, aid, a helping hand, support, succor, advice, guidance; benefit, use, advantage, service, comfort; *informal* a shot in the arm.

**2** *he sought help for his eczema* RELIEF, alleviation, improvement, assuagement, healing; a remedy, a cure, a restorative.

**3** *they treated the help badly* DOMESTIC WORKER, domestic servant, cleaner, cleaning lady, housekeeper, maid, hired help, helper.

▸ exclamation *we heard the faint cries of "Help!" in the distance* SOS, mayday.

PHRASES: **cannot help** *he could not help laughing* BE UNABLE TO STOP, be unable to refrain from, be unable to keep from.
**help oneself to** *Tara helped herself to one of the photo albums that we left on the table* STEAL, take, appropriate, borrow, liberate, pocket, lift, purloin, commandeer; *informal* swipe, nab, filch, walk off with, run off with, pinch.

**helper** noun *the teachers' helpers are treated to a picnic lunch at the end of each school year* ASSISTANT, aide, helpmate, helpmeet, deputy, auxiliary, second, right-hand man/woman, attendant, acolyte; coworker, workmate, teammate, associate, colleague, partner; *informal* sidekick.

**helpful** adjective **1** *the staff are helpful* OBLIGING, eager to please, kind, accommodating, supportive, cooperative; sympathetic, boosterish, neighborly, charitable. ANTONYMS unsympathetic, unobliging.

**2** *we found your comments helpful* USEFUL, of use, beneficial, valuable, profitable, advantageous, fruitful, worthwhile, constructive; informative, instructive. ANTONYM useless.

**3** *a helpful new tool* HANDY, useful, convenient, practical, easy-to-use, functional, serviceable; *informal* neat, nifty. ANTONYM inconvenient.

**helping** noun *the helpings are very generous* PORTION, serving, piece, slice, share, ration, allocation; *informal* dollop.

**helpless** adjective *the cubs are born blind and helpless* DEPENDENT, incapable, powerless, impotent, weak; defenseless, vulnerable, exposed, unprotected, open to attack; paralyzed, disabled. ANTONYM independent.

**helpmate, helpmeet** noun *he thanked his wife of twenty years for being his helpmate and best friend* HELPER, assistant, attendant; supporter, friend, companion; spouse, partner, life partner, mate, husband, wife.

**helter-skelter** adverb *they ran helter-skelter down the hill* HEADLONG, pell-mell, hotfoot, posthaste, hastily, hurriedly, at full tilt, hell-bent for leather; recklessly, precipitately, heedlessly, wildly; *informal* like a bat out of hell, like the wind, like greased lightning, lickety-split.

▸ adjective *a helter-skelter collection of houses* DISORDERED, disorderly, chaotic, muddled, jumbled, untidy, haphazard, disorganized, topsy-turvy; *informal* higgledy-piggledy. ANTONYM orderly.

**hem** noun *the hem of her dress* EDGE, edging, border, trim, trimming. PHRASES: **hem in 1** *a bay hemmed in by pine trees* SURROUND, border, edge, encircle, circle, ring, enclose, skirt, fringe, encompass, corral.

**2** *we were hemmed in by the rules* RESTRICT, confine, trap, hedge in, fence in; constrain, restrain, limit, curb, check.
**hem and haw** *they hem and haw every time we ask for an explanation* HESITATE, dither, vacillate, be indecisive, equivocate, waver; *informal* blow hot and cold, shilly-shally.

**hence** adverb *the amount of traffic—and hence the amount of pollution—will be reduced* CONSEQUENTLY, as a consequence, for this reason, therefore, ergo, thus, so, accordingly, as a result, because of that, that being so.

**henceforth, henceforward** adverb *henceforth, we will accept only photo IDs* FROM NOW ON, as of now, in (the) future, hence, subsequently, from this day on, from this day forth; *formal* hereafter.

**henchman** noun *he leaves all the dirty work to his henchmen* RIGHT-HAND MAN, assistant, aide, helper; underling, minion, man Friday, lackey, flunky, stooge; bodyguard; *informal* sidekick, crony, heavy, goon.

**henpecked** adjective *the prosecution characterized him as a henpecked husband who finally snapped* BROWBEATEN, downtrodden, bullied, dominated, subjugated, oppressed, intimidated; meek, timid, cringing, long-suffering; *informal* under someone's thumb. ANTONYM domineering.

**herald** noun **1** *historical a herald announced the armistice* MESSENGER, courier; proclaimer, announcer, crier.

**2** *the first herald of spring* HARBINGER, sign, indicator, indication, signal, prelude, portent, omen; forerunner, precursor; *literary* foretoken.

▸ verb **1** *shouts heralded their approach* PROCLAIM, announce, broadcast, publicize, declare, trumpet, blazon, advertise.

**2** *the speech heralded a policy change* SIGNAL, indicate, announce, spell, presage, augur, portend, promise, foretell; usher in, pave the way for, be a harbinger of; *literary* foretoken, betoken.

**Herculean** adjective **1** *a Herculean task* ARDUOUS, grueling, laborious, back-breaking, onerous, strenuous, difficult, formidable, hard, tough, huge, massive, uphill; demanding, exhausting, taxing; *archaic* toilsome. ANTONYM easy.

**2** *his Herculean build* STRONG, muscular, muscly, powerful, robust, solid, strapping, brawny, burly; *informal* hunky, beefy, hulking. ANTONYM puny.

**herd** noun **1** *a herd of cows* drove, flock, pack, fold; group, collection.

**2** *a herd of actors* CROWD, group, bunch, horde, mob, host, pack, multitude, throng, swarm, company.

**3** *they consider themselves above the herd* COMMON PEOPLE, masses, rank and file, crowd, commonality, plebeians; hoi polloi, mob, proletariat, rabble, riffraff, great unwashed; *informal* proles, plebs.

▸ verb **1** *we herded the sheep into the pen* DRIVE, shepherd, guide; round up, gather, collect, corral.

**2** *we all herded into the room* CROWD, pack, flock; cluster, huddle.

**3** *they herd reindeer* TEND, look after, keep, watch (over), mind, guard.

**here** adverb **1** *they lived here* AT/IN THIS PLACE, at/in this spot, at/in this location.

**2** *I am here now* PRESENT, in attendance, attending, at hand; available. ANTONYM absent.

**3** *come here tomorrow* TO THIS PLACE, to this spot, to this location, over here, nearer, closer; *literary* hither.

**4** *here is your opportunity* NOW, at this moment, at this point, at this point in time, at this juncture, at this stage. PHRASE: **here and there 1** *clumps of crabgrass here and there* IN VARIOUS PLACES, in different places; at random.

**2** *they darted here and there* BACK AND FORTH, around, about, to and fro, hither and thither, in all directions.

**hereafter** adverb *formal* *nothing I say hereafter is intended to offend* FROM NOW ON, after this, as of now, from this moment forth, from this day forth, from this day forward, subsequently, in (the) future, hence, henceforth, henceforward; *formal* hereinafter.

▸ noun **(the hereafter)** *our preparation for the hereafter* LIFE AFTER DEATH, the afterlife, the afterworld, the next world; eternity, heaven, paradise.

**hereditary** adjective **1** *a hereditary right* INHERITED; bequeathed, willed, handed-down, passed-down, passed-on, transferred; ancestral, family, familial.

**2** *a hereditary disease* GENETIC, congenital, inborn, inherited, inbred, innate; in the family, in the blood, in the genes.

**heredity** noun *heredity is a major factor in the diagnosis of many conditions* CONGENITAL TRAITS, genetic makeup, genes; ancestry, descent, extraction, parentage.

**heresy** noun *an age in which scientists were often accused of heresy* DISSENSION, dissent, nonconformity, heterodoxy, unorthodoxy, apostasy, blasphemy, freethinking; agnosticism, atheism, nonbelief; idolatry, paganism.

**heretic** noun *heretics were banished or put to death* DISSENTER, nonconformist, apostate, freethinker, iconoclast; agnostic, atheist, nonbeliever, unbeliever, idolater, idolatress, pagan, heathen; *archaic* paynim. ANTONYMS conformist, believer.

**heritage** noun **1** *they stole his heritage* INHERITANCE, birthright, patrimony; legacy, bequest.

**2** *Hawaii's cultural heritage* TRADITION, history, past, background; culture, customs.

**3** *his Greek heritage* ANCESTRY, lineage, descent, extraction, parentage, roots, background, heredity.

**hermit** noun *just because I prefer to live alone doesn't make me a hermit* RECLUSE, solitary, loner, ascetic, marabout, troglodyte; *historical* anchorite, anchoress; *archaic* eremite.

**hero** noun **1** *the heroes of Guadalcanal* BRAVE PERSON, brave man/woman, man/woman of courage, man/woman of the hour, lionheart, warrior, knight; champion, victor, conqueror. ANTONYMS coward, loser.

**2** *a football hero* STAR, superstar, megastar, idol, celebrity, luminary; ideal, paragon, shining example, demigod; favorite, darling; *informal* celeb. ANTONYMS unknown, nobody.

**3** *the hero of the film* (MALE) PROTAGONIST, principal (male) character, principal (male) role, main character, title character, starring role, star part; (male) lead, lead actor, leading man. ANTONYMS villain, supporting character, supporting role.

**heroic** adjective *firefighters perform heroic acts every single day* BRAVE, courageous, valiant, valorous, lionhearted, superhuman, intrepid, bold, fearless, daring, audacious; unafraid, undaunted, dauntless, doughty, plucky, manly, stout-hearted, mettlesome; gallant, chivalrous, noble; *informal* gutsy, spunky, ballsy.

**heroine** noun **1** *she's a heroine—she saved my baby | the heroines of the air corps* BRAVE WOMAN, hero, woman of courage, woman of the hour; victor, winner, conqueror. ANTONYMS coward, loser.

**2** *the literary heroine of Moscow* STAR, superstar, megastar, idol, celebrity, luminary; ideal, paragon, shining example; favorite, darling, queen; *informal* celeb. ANTONYMS unknown, nobody.

**3** *the film's heroine* (FEMALE) PROTAGONIST, principal (female) character, principal (female) role, main character, title character; (female) lead, lead actress, leading lady; prima donna, diva. ANTONYMS villain, supporting character, supporting role.

**heroism** noun *an award for his heroism* BRAVERY, courage, valor, intrepidity, boldness, daring, audacity, fearlessness, dauntlessness, pluck, stout-heartedness, lionheartedness; backbone, spine, grit, spirit, mettle; gallantry, chivalry; *informal* guts, spunk, balls, cojones, moxie.

**hero-worship** noun *the hero-worship of his fans soon became unsettling to him* IDOLIZATION, adulation, admiration, lionization, idealization, worship, adoration, veneration.

**hesitancy** noun. See HESITATION.

**hesitant** adjective **1** *she is hesitant about buying* UNCERTAIN, undecided, unsure, doubtful, dubious, skeptical; tentative, nervous, reluctant, gun-shy; indecisive, irresolute, hesitating, dithering, vacillating, wavering, waffling, blowing hot and cold; ambivalent, of two minds, hemming and hawing; *informal* iffy. ANTONYMS certain, decisive.

**2** *a hesitant child* LACKING CONFIDENCE, diffident, timid, shy, bashful, insecure, tentative. ANTONYM confident.

**hesitate** verb **1** *she hesitated, unsure of what to say* PAUSE, delay, wait, shilly-shally, dither, stall, temporize; be of two minds, be uncertain, be unsure, be doubtful, be indecisive, hedge, equivocate, fluctuate, vacillate, waver, waffle, have second thoughts, think twice; *informal* dilly-dally, blow hot and cold, get cold feet, hem and haw.

**2** *don't hesitate to contact me* BE RELUCTANT, be unwilling, be disinclined, scruple; have misgivings about, have qualms about, shrink from, demur from, think twice about, balk at; *informal* miss a beat.

**hesitation** noun *she answered without hesitation* HESITANCY, uncertainty, unsureness, doubt, doubtfulness, dubiousness; irresolution, irresoluteness, indecision, indecisiveness, hesitance; equivocation, vacillation, waffling, wavering, second thoughts; dithering, stalling, dawdling, temporization, delay; reluctance, disinclination, unease, ambivalence; *informal* cold feet; *formal* dubiety.

**hew** verb **1** *the logs are freshly hewn* CHOP, hack, cut, lop, ax, cleave, split; fell.

**2** *steps had been hewn into the rock wall* CUT, carve, chisel, shape, fashion, sculpt.

**heyday** noun *during his heyday, he was quite the matinee idol* PRIME, peak, height, pinnacle, summit, apex, acme, zenith, climax, high point; day, time, bloom, flowering; prime of life, salad days, halcyon days, glory days.

**hiatus** noun *the spring hiatus gave us time to rethink our next project* PAUSE, break, gap, lacuna, interval, intermission, interlude, interruption, suspension, lull, respite, time out, time off, recess; *informal* breather, letup.

**hibernate** verb **1** *bears hibernate in winter* LIE DORMANT, lie torpid, sleep; overwinter.

**2** *he wanted to hibernate in front of a fire for the night* HOLE UP, escape, withdraw, retreat, cocoon.

**hidden** adjective **1** *a hidden camera* CONCEALED, secret, undercover, invisible, unseen, out of sight, closeted, covert; secluded, tucked away; camouflaged, disguised, masked, cloaked. ANTONYM visible.

**2** *a hidden meaning* OBSCURE, unclear, veiled, clouded, shrouded, concealed; cryptic, mysterious, secret, abstruse, arcane; ulterior, deep, subliminal, coded. ANTONYMS clear, obvious.

**hide**[1] verb **1** *he hid the money* CONCEAL, secrete, put out of sight; camouflage; lock up, stow away, tuck away, squirrel away, cache; *informal* stash. ANTONYMS flaunt, expose.

**2** *they hid in an air vent* CONCEAL ONESELF, sequester oneself, hide out, take cover, keep out of sight; lie low, go underground; *informal* hole up.

**3** *clouds hid the moon* OBSCURE, block out, blot out, obstruct, cloud, shroud, veil, blanket, envelop, eclipse. ANTONYM reveal.

**4** *he could not hide his dislike* CONCEAL, keep secret, cover up, keep quiet about, hush up, bottle up, suppress, curtain, bury; disguise, dissemble, mask, camouflage; *informal* keep under one's hat, keep a/the lid on. ANTONYM disclose.

**hide**[2] noun *the hide should be tanned quickly* SKIN, pelt, coat; leather.

**hideaway** noun *the cabin in Maine is our hideaway* RETREAT, refuge, hiding place, hideout, den, bolt-hole, shelter, sanctuary, sanctum; hermitage, secret place.

**hidebound** adjective *hidebound traditionalists* CONSERVATIVE, reactionary, conventional, orthodox; fundamentalist, diehard, hardline, dyed-in-the-wool, set in one's ways, unyielding, inflexible; narrow-minded, small-minded, intolerant, uncompromising, rigid; prejudiced, bigoted. ANTONYM liberal.

**hideous** adjective *the scenes were too hideous to watch* UGLY, repulsive, repellent, unsightly, revolting, gruesome, grotesque, monstrous, ghastly; *informal* as ugly as sin; awful, terrible, appalling, dreadful, frightful, horrible, horrendous, horrific, horrifying, shocking, sickening, unspeakable, abhorrent, heinous, abominable, foul, vile, odious, execrable. ANTONYMS beautiful, pleasant.

**hideout** noun *the gang had a hideout up in the mountains* HIDING PLACE, hideaway, retreat, refuge, shelter, safe house, sanctuary, sanctum.

**hierarchy** noun *in the corporate hierarchy, Curt is about six levels below the CEO* PECKING ORDER, order, ranking, chain of command, grading, gradation, ladder, scale, range.

**high** adjective **1** *a high mountain* TALL, lofty, towering, soaring, elevated, giant, big; multistory, high-rise. ANTONYMS short, low.

**2** *a high position in the government* HIGH-RANKING, high-level, leading, top, top-level, prominent, preeminent, foremost, senior; influential, powerful, important, elevated, prime, premier, exalted, ranking; *informal* top-notch, chief. ANTONYMS low-ranking, lowly.

**3** *high principles* HIGH-MINDED, noble, lofty, moral, ethical, honorable, exalted, admirable, upright, honest, virtuous, righteous. ANTONYM amoral.

**4** *high prices* INFLATED, excessive, unreasonable, expensive, costly, exorbitant, extortionate, prohibitive, dear; *informal* steep, stiff, pricey. ANTONYMS reasonable, low.

**5** *high winds* STRONG, powerful, violent, intense, extreme, forceful; BLUSTERY, gusty, stiff, squally, tempestuous, turbulent, howling, roaring. ANTONYMS light, calm.

**6** *the high life* LUXURIOUS, lavish, extravagant, grand, opulent; sybaritic, hedonistic, epicurean, decadent; upmarket, upscale; *informal* fancy, classy, swanky. ANTONYM abstemious.

**7** *I have a high opinion of you* FAVORABLE, good, positive, approving, admiring, complimentary, commendatory, flattering, glowing, adulatory, rapturous. ANTONYM unfavorable.

**8** *a high note | his high voice* HIGH-PITCHED, high-frequency; soprano, treble, falsetto, shrill, sharp, piercing, penetrating. ANTONYMS low, low-pitched, deep.

**9** *informal they were high before they even got to the party* INTOXICATED, inebriated, drugged, on drugs, stupefied, befuddled, delirious, hallucinating; *informal* STONED, wired, hopped up, high as a kite, tripping, hyped up, doped up, coked, spaced out, wasted, wrecked. ANTONYMS sober, straight.

**10** ***high in*** *fiber* ELEVATED IN, rich in, ample in, loaded with, plentiful in, full of; *informal* chock-full of, jam-packed with. ANTONYM deficient.

▸ noun *prices were at a rare high* HIGH LEVEL, high point, peak, high-water mark; pinnacle, zenith, acme, height. ANTONYM low.

▸ adverb *a jet flew high overhead* AT GREAT HEIGHT, high up, far up, way up, at altitude; in the air, in the sky, on high, aloft, overhead. ANTONYM low.

PHRASES: **high and dry** *we track down these guys who have left their wives and children high and dry* DESTITUTE, helpless, in the lurch, in difficulties; abandoned, stranded, marooned.
**high and low** *I searched high and low for my keys* EVERYWHERE, all over, all around, far and wide, 'here, there, and everywhere,' extensively, thoroughly, widely, in every nook and cranny; *informal* all over the place, all over the map.
**high and mighty** *informal he feels high and mighty just because he was lucky enough to keep his job* SELF-IMPORTANT, condescending, patronizing, pompous, disdainful, supercilious, superior, snobbish, snobby, haughty, conceited, above oneself; *informal* stuck-up, puffed up, snooty, hoity-toity, la-di-da, uppity, full of oneself, too big for one's britches/boots.
**on a high** *informal she was obviously on a high after Joey proposed* ECSTATIC, euphoric, exhilarated, delirious, elated, ebullient, thrilled, overjoyed, beside oneself, walking on air, on cloud nine, in seventh heaven, jumping for joy, in raptures, in high spirits, exultant, jubilant; excited, overexcited; *informal* blissed out, over the moon, on top of the world.

**high-born** adjective *her high-born father had given up his inheritance to marry a lowly seamstress* NOBLE, aristocratic, well-born, titled, patrician, blue-blooded, upper-class, genteel; *informal* upper-crust, top-drawer; *archaic* gentle. ANTONYM lowly.

**highbrow** adjective *his work has a highbrow following* INTELLECTUAL, scholarly, bookish, well-read, literary, cultured, academic, educated, lettered, sophisticated, erudite, learned, cerebral; *informal* brainy, egghead, inkhorn. ANTONYM lowbrow.

▸ noun *highbrows who hate rap music* INTELLECTUAL, scholar, academic, bluestocking, bookish person, thinker; *informal* egghead, brain, bookworm, brainiac.

**high-class** adjective *the casino's high-class hotel* SUPERIOR, upper-class, first-rate; excellent, select, elite, choice, premier, top, top-flight; luxurious, deluxe, upscale, high-quality, top-quality, upmarket; *informal* top-notch, blue-ribbon, five-star, top-drawer, A1, ritzy, tony, classy, posh.

**highfalutin** adjective *informal*. See PRETENTIOUS.

**high-flown** adjective *one of his high-flown ideas finally panned out* GRAND, extravagant, elaborate, flowery, lofty, ornate, overblown, overdone, overwrought, grandiloquent, magniloquent, grandiose, orotund, inflated, high-sounding; affected, pretentious, bombastic, pompous, turgid; *informal* windy, purple, highfalutin, la-di-da. ANTONYM plain.

**high-handed** adjective *I'll not be subordinate to any high-handed individual, male or female* IMPERIOUS, arbitrary, peremptory, arrogant, haughty, domineering, supercilious, pushy, overbearing, heavy-handed, lordly, magisterial; inflexible, rigid; autocratic, authoritarian, dictatorial, tyrannical; *informal* bossy, high and mighty. ANTONYM modest.

**highland** noun *Peru's Andean highland* UPLANDS, highlands, mountains, hills, heights, moors; upland, tableland, plateau.

**highlight** noun *the highlight of his career* HIGH POINT, best part, climax, peak, pinnacle, height, acme, zenith, summit, crowning moment, high-water mark, centerpiece. ANTONYM nadir.

▸ verb *he has highlighted shortcomings in the plan* SPOTLIGHT, call attention to, point out, single out, focus on, underline, feature, play up, show up, bring out, accentuate, accent, give prominence to, zero in on, stress, emphasize.

**highly** adverb **1** *a highly dangerous substance* VERY, extremely, exceedingly, particularly, most, really, thoroughly, decidedly, distinctly, exceptionally, immensely, greatly, inordinately, singularly, extraordinarily; *informal* awfully, terribly, majorly, seriously, supremely, desperately, hugely, ultra, oh-so, damn, damned; real, mighty, awful; *dated* frightfully. ANTONYM slightly.

**2** *he was highly regarded* FAVORABLY, well, appreciatively, admiringly, approvingly, positively, glowingly, enthusiastically. ANTONYM unfavorably.

**high-minded** adjective *high-minded civil libertarians* HIGH-PRINCIPLED, principled, honorable, moral, upright, upstanding, right-minded, noble, good, honest, decent, ethical, righteous, virtuous, worthy, idealistic. ANTONYM unprincipled.

**high-powered** adjective *high-powered career women* DYNAMIC, ambitious, energetic, assertive, enterprising, vigorous; forceful, powerful, potent, aggressive; *informal* go-getting, high-octane.

**high-pressure** adjective **1** *high-pressure sales tactics* FORCEFUL, insistent, persistent, pushy; intensive, high-powered, aggressive, coercive, compelling, not taking no for an answer.

**2** *a high-pressure job* DEMANDING, stressful, nerve-racking, tense, pressured.

**high-priced** adjective *high-priced luxury cars* EXPENSIVE, costly, dear, big-ticket, high-end; overpriced, exorbitant, extortionate; *informal* pricey, steep, stiff.

**high-sounding** adjective. See HIGH-FLOWN.

**high-spirited** adjective *a high-spirited horse* LIVELY, spirited, full of fun, fun-loving, animated, zestful, bouncy, bubbly, sparkling, vivacious, buoyant, cheerful, joyful, exuberant, ebullient, jaunty, irrepressible; *informal* chirpy, peppy, full of beans; *literary* frolicsome.

**high spirits** plural noun *the high spirits of these young competitors is indeed infectious* LIVELINESS, vitality, spirit, zest, energy, bounce, sparkle, vivacity, buoyancy, cheerfulness, good humor, joy, joyfulness, exuberance, ebullience, joie de vivre; *informal* pep, zing.

**high-strung** adjective *a high-strung woman answered the phone and started accusing me of harassing her* NERVOUS, excitable, agitated, temperamental, sensitive, unstable; brittle, on edge, edgy, jumpy, jittery, restless, anxious, tense, stressed, overwrought, neurotic; *informal* worked up, uptight, twitchy, wired, wound up, het up, strung out. ANTONYM easygoing.

**hijack** verb *two flight attendants thwarted Girard's attempt to hijack the plane* COMMANDEER, seize, take over, take control; skyjack, carjack; appropriate, expropriate, confiscate, co-opt.

**hike** noun *a five-mile hike* WALK, trek, tramp, trudge, slog, footslog, march; ramble.

▸ verb *they hiked across the island* WALK, trek, tramp, tromp, trudge, slog, footslog, march; ramble, rove, traipse; *informal* hoof it, leg it.

PHRASE: **hike up 1** *Roy hiked up his trousers* HITCH UP, pull up, hoist, lift, raise; *informal* yank up.

**2** *they hiked up the price* INCREASE, raise, up, put up, boost up, mark up, push up, inflate; *informal* jack up, bump up.

**hilarious** adjective *the final scene is hilarious* VERY FUNNY, hysterically funny, hysterical, uproarious, riotous, rollicking, farcical, rib-tickling; humorous, comic, amusing, entertaining jocular, jovial, laughable; *informal* side-splitting, gut-busting, knee-slapping, thigh-slapping, priceless, a scream, a hoot.

**hilarity** noun *we always enjoy a great deal of hilarity when we get together* AMUSEMENT, mirth, laughter, merriment, lightheartedness, levity, fun, humor, jocularity, jollity, gaiety, delight, glee, exuberance, high spirits; comedy.

**hill** noun **1** *the top of the hill* HIGH GROUND, prominence, hillock, foothill, hillside, rise, mound, mount, knoll, butte, hummock, mesa; bank, bluff, ridge, slope, incline, gradient; (**hills**) heights, highland(s), downs, elevation; *Geology* drumlin; *formal* eminence.

**2** *a hill of garbage* HEAP, pile, stack, mound, mountain, mass.

**hillock** noun *the lovely green hillocks in the distance* MOUND, small hill, prominence, elevation, rise, knoll, hummock, hump, dune; bank, ridge, knob; *formal* eminence.

**hilt** noun *the hilt of his sword* HANDLE, haft, handgrip, grip, shaft, shank, helve. PHRASE: **to the hilt** *we will support our leaders to the hilt* COMPLETELY, fully, wholly, totally, absolutely, entirely, utterly, unreservedly, unconditionally, in every respect, in all respects, one hundred percent, every inch, to the full, to the maximum extent, all the way, body and soul, heart and soul.

**hind** adjective *the left hind leg* BACK, rear, hinder, hindmost, posterior; dorsal. ANTONYMS fore, front.

**hinder** verb *budget cuts have hindered our progress* HAMPER, obstruct, impede, inhibit, retard, balk, prevent, thwart, foil, curb, delay, arrest, interfere with, set back, slow down, hobble, hold back, hold up, stop, halt; restrict, restrain, constrain, block, check, curtail, frustrate, cramp, handicap, cripple, hamstring; *informal* stymie, throw a wrench in the works. See note at PROHIBIT. ANTONYM facilitate.

THE RIGHT WORD **encumber, hamper, impede, obstruct, prevent**

If you're about to set off on a cross-country trip by car and wake up to find that a foot of snow has fallen overnight, it would be correct to say that the weather has **hindered** you. But if you're trying to drive through a snowstorm and are forced to creep along at a snail's pace behind a snowplow, it would be correct to say you were **impeded**. To *hinder* is to delay or hold something back, especially something that is under way or is about to start (*she entered college but was hindered by poor study habits*); it connotes a thwarting of progress, either deliberate or accidental. *Impede*, on the other hand, means to slow the progress of someone or something by a deliberate act; it implies that the obstacles are more serious and suggests that movement or progress is so slow that it is painful or frustrating (*the shoes were so tight they impeded his circulation*). Both **hamper** and **encumber** involve hindering by outside forces. To *hamper* is to impede by placing restraints on someone or something so as to make action difficult (*hampered by family responsibilities*), while **encumber** means to hinder by the placing of a burden (*encumbered with several heavy suitcases*). To **obstruct** is to place obstacles in the way, often bringing progress or movement to a complete halt (*obstruct traffic; obstruct justice*). **Prevent** suggests precautionary or restraining measures (*the police prevented him from entering the burning building*) and is also used to describe a nonhuman agency or cause that hinders something (*the snow prevented us from leaving that day*).

**hindrance** noun *bad weather was the primary hindrance to our rescue efforts* IMPEDIMENT, obstacle, barrier, bar, obstruction, handicap, block, hurdle, restraint, restriction, limitation, encumbrance, interference; complication, delay, drawback, setback, difficulty, inconvenience, snag, catch, hitch, check, stumbling block; *informal* fly in the ointment, hiccup, wrench in the works. ANTONYM help.

**hinge** verb *our future **hinges on** the election* DEPEND ON, hang on, rest on, turn on, center on, pivot on, be contingent on, be dependent on, be conditional on; be determined by, be decided by, revolve around.

**hint** noun **1** *a hint that he would leave* CLUE, inkling, suggestion, indication, indicator, sign, signal, pointer, intimation, insinuation, innuendo, mention, whisper.

**2** *handy hints about painting* TIP, suggestion, pointer, clue, guideline, recommendation; advice, help; *informal* how-to.

**3** *a hint of mint* TRACE, touch, suspicion, suggestion, dash, soupçon, tinge, modicum, whiff, taste, undertone; *informal* smidgen, tad, speck.

▸ verb *what are you **hinting at**?* IMPLY, insinuate, intimate, suggest, indicate, signal; allude to, refer to, drive at, mean; *informal* get at.

**hippie** noun *yesterday's hippies are today's ad execs* FLOWER CHILD, Bohemian, beatnik, long-hair, free spirit, nonconformist, dropout.

**hire** verb **1** *they hire labor in line with demand* EMPLOY, engage, recruit, appoint, take on, sign up, enrolll, commission, enlist, contract. ANTONYMS dismiss, lay off.

**2** *we hired a car* RENT, lease, charter, let, sublet.

**hiss** verb **1** *the escaping gas hissed* FIZZ, fizzle, whistle, wheeze; *rare* sibilate.

**2** *the audience hissed* JEER, catcall, boo, heckle, whistle, hoot; scoff, jibe.

▸ noun **1** *the hiss of the steam* FIZZ, fizzing, whistle, hissing, sibilance, wheeze, pfft; *rare* sibilation.

**2** *the speaker received hisses* JEER, catcall, boo, whistle; abuse, scoffing, taunting, derision.

**historic** adjective *the historic first flight at Kitty Hawk* SIGNIFICANT, notable, important, momentous, consequential, memorable, newsworthy, unforgettable, remarkable; famous, famed, celebrated, renowned, legendary; landmark, sensational, groundbreaking, epoch-making, red-letter, earth-shattering. ANTONYM insignificant.

USAGE NOTE **historic, historical**

**Historical,** meaning "of or relating to or occurring in history," is called upon for use far more frequently than historic. **Historic** means "historically significant" *the Alamo is a historic building*. An event that makes history is historic; momentous happenings or developments are historic—e.g.: "The Supreme Court's historic decision about whether mentally competent, dying patients and their doctors have the right to hasten death won't be known for months." (*USA Today,* Jan. 10, 1997). A documented fact, event, or development—perhaps having no great importance—is *historical.* E.g.: "Despite the historical data, some people just don't feel comfortable knowing their loan's rate can drift up 5 or 6 points." (Chicago Sun-Times, Jan. 24, 1997). Examples of *historic* used incorrectly for *historical* could easily run for several pages—e.g.: "The Sunday Trading Act, which formally became law yesterday, removes historic [read *historical*] anomalies of the kind that allowed shopkeepers to sell pornographic magazines but not Bibles on the Sabbath, and instant but not ground coffee." (*Times* (London), Aug. 27, 1994). "The odds are now on a further easing of monetary policy and there is a good historic [read *historical*] correlation between falling interest rates and a rising stock market." (*Financial Times,* June 13, 1996). "Rape is also an historic [read a *historical*] soldiers' sport." (*Harper's Magazine,* Jan. 2003). The far less common mistake is misusing *historical* for *historic*—e.g.: "Gary Pinkel didn't know what to expect after Toledo and Nevada found themselves going into a historical [read *historic*] overtime in the Las Vegas Bowl." (*Austin Am.-Statesman,* Dec. 16, 1995). —*BG*

**historical** adjective **1** *historical evidence* DOCUMENTED, recorded, chronicled, archival; authentic, factual, actual, true. ANTONYMS mythical, legendary.

**2** *historical figures* PAST, bygone, ancient, old, former; *literary* of yore. See note at HISTORIC. ANTONYM contemporary.

**history** noun **1** *my interest in history* THE PAST, former times, historical events, the olden days, the old days, bygone days, long ago, yesterday, antiquity; *literary* days of yore, yesteryear.

**2** *a history of the Boxer Rebellion* CHRONICLE, archive, record, diary, report, narrative, account, study, tale, story, saga; memoir.

**3** *she gave details of her history* BACKGROUND, past, life story, biography, experiences, backstory; antecedents.

**hit** verb **1** *she hit her child* STRIKE, slap, smack, spank, cuff, punch, thump, swat; beat, thrash, batter, pound, pummel, box someone's ears; whip, flog, cane; *informal* whack, wallop, bash, bop, clout, clip, clobber, sock, swipe, crown, beat the living daylights out of, knock someone around, belt, tan, lay into, let someone have it, deck, floor, slug; *literary* smite.

**2** *a car hit the barrier* CRASH INTO, run into, smash into, smack into, knock into, bump into, plow into, collide with, meet head-on, impact.

**3** *informal spending will hit $180 million* REACH, touch, arrive at, rise to, climb to.

**4** *it hit me that I had forgotten* OCCUR TO, strike, dawn on, come to; enter one's head, cross one's mind, come to mind, spring to one's mind.

▸ noun **1** *he received a hit from behind* BLOW, thump, punch, knock, bang, cuff, slap, smack, spank, tap, crack, stroke, welt, karate chop; impact, collision, bump, crash; *informal* whack, thwack, wallop, bash, belt, clout, sock, swipe, clip, slug.

**2** *he directed many big hits* SUCCESS, box-office success, sellout, winner, triumph, sensation; best seller; *informal* smash, smash hit, megahit, knockout, crowd-pleaser, chart-topper, chart-buster, wow, biggie, number one. ANTONYM failure.

PHRASES: **hit back** *if you're gonna come after me with lies and innuendo, I'm gonna hit back* RETALIATE, respond, reply, react, counter, defend oneself.

**hit hard** *the tragedy hit her hard* DEVASTATE, affect badly, hurt, harm, leave a mark on; upset, shatter, crush, shock, overwhelm, traumatize.

**hit home** *the documentary on teen suicide painfully hit home*

HAVE THE INTENDED EFFECT, strike home, hit the mark, register, be understood, get through, sink in.
**hit it off** *informal Mark and Mika hit it off almost immediately* GET ON WELL, get along, get on, be friends, be friendly, be compatible, be well matched, feel a rapport, see eye to eye, take to each other, warm to each other; *informal* click, get on like a house on fire, be on the same wavelength.
**hit on/upon** 1 *he hit on the truth | Cagney hit upon a great idea for the finale* DISCOVER, come up with, think of, conceive of, dream up, work out, invent, create, devise, design, pioneer; uncover, stumble on, happen upon, chance on, light on, come upon.

2 *he tried to hit on me* FLIRT WITH, show interest in, make eyes at, come on to, make advances to/toward.

**hitch** verb 1 *Tom hitched the pony to his cart* HARNESS, yoke, couple, fasten, connect, attach, tether, tie.

2 *she hitched the blanket around her* PULL, jerk, tug, hike, lift, raise, yank, shift.

3 *informal they hitched a ride informal* THUMB, hitchhike.

▸ noun *it went without a hitch* PROBLEM, difficulty, snag, catch, setback, hindrance, obstacle, obstruction, complication, impediment, stumbling block, barrier; holdup, interruption, delay; *informal* headache, glitch, hiccup.

**hither** adverb *literary*. See HERE sense 3.

**hitherto** adverb *hitherto a part of French West Africa, Benin achieved independence in 1960* PREVIOUSLY, formerly, earlier, before, beforehand; so far, thus far, to date, as yet, until now, until then, till now, till then, up to now, up to then; *formal* heretofore.

**hit-or-miss, hit-and-miss** adjective *even his approach to finding a job is hit-or-miss* ERRATIC, haphazard, disorganized, undisciplined, unmethodical, uneven; careless, slapdash, slipshod, casual, cursory, lackadaisical, random, aimless, undirected, indiscriminate; *informal* sloppy. ANTONYM meticulous.

**hoard** noun *a secret hoard of gold* CACHE, stockpile, stock, store, collection, supply, reserve, reservoir, fund, accumulation; treasury, treasure house, treasure trove; *informal* stash.

▸ verb *they hoarded rations* STOCKPILE, store, store up, stock up on, put aside, put by, lay by, lay up, set aside, stow away, buy up; cache, amass, collect, save, gather, garner, accumulate, squirrel away, put aside for a rainy day; *informal* stash away, salt away. ANTONYM squander.

**hoarse** adjective *voices hoarse from shouting* ROUGH, harsh, throaty, gruff, husky, growly, gravelly, grating, scratchy, raspy, rasping, raucous, croaky, croaking, with a frog in one's throat. ANTONYMS mellow, clear.

**hoary** adjective 1 *hoary cobwebs* GRAYISH-WHITE, gray, white, snowy, silver, silvery; frosty; *literary* rimy.

2 *a hoary old man* GRAY-HAIRED, white-haired, silver-haired, grizzled; elderly, aged, old, ancient, venerable *informal* over the hill. ANTONYM young.

**hoax** noun *the Piltdown man was perhaps the most successful hoax of the twentieth century* PRACTICAL JOKE, joke, jest, prank, trick; ruse, deception, fraud, bluff, confidence trick; *informal* con, spoof, scam, setup.

**hobble** verb *Luke hobbled into the post office* LIMP, walk with difficulty, walk lamely, move unsteadily, walk haltingly; shamble, totter, dodder, stagger, falter, stumble, lurch.

**hobby** noun *writing poetry is just one of my hobbies* PASTIME, leisure activity, leisure pursuit; sideline, side interest, diversion, avocation; recreation, entertainment, amusement.

**hobgoblin** noun *he believed there were hobgoblins under his bed* GOBLIN, imp, sprite, elf, brownie, pixie, puck, leprechaun, gnome; bogey, bugbear, bogeyman.

**hobnob** verb *informal she sought out every opportunity to hobnob with the rich and famous* ASSOCIATE, mix, fraternize, socialize, keep company, spend time, go around, mingle, consort, network, rub shoulders, rub elbows; *informal* hang around/out, be thick, schmooze.

**hocus-pocus** noun 1 *a little hocus-pocus and—presto!—the tiger disappears* MAGIC, sleight of hand, conjuring, witchcraft, wizardry, sorcery; deception, sham, devilry, trickery; *informal* scam.

2 *she dismissed it as so much hocus-pocus* NONSENSE, rubbish, garbage, balderdash, malarkey, baloney, bunk, hogwash, bull, hokum.

**hodgepodge** noun *a rambling hodgepodge of Chinese modern and art deco* MIXTURE, mix, mixed bag, assortment, random collection, conglomeration, jumble, ragbag, grab bag, miscellany, medley, salmagundi, potpourri, patchwork, pastiche; mélange, mishmash, hash, confusion, farrago, gallimaufry. See note at JUMBLE.

**hog** noun *a prize-winning hog* PIG, sow, swine, porker, piglet, boar; *informal* piggy.

▸ verb *informal he hogged the limelight* MONOPOLIZE, dominate, take over, corner, control. ANTONYM share.

**hogwash** noun *informal*. See NONSENSE sense 1.

**hoi polloi** noun *in days long past, the royal family would not have deigned to commune with the hoi polloi* MASSES, common people, populace, public, multitude, rank and file, lower order(s), plebeians, proletariat; mob, herd, rabble, riffraff, great unwashed; *informal* plebs, proles; *historical* third estate.

**hoist** verb *we hoisted the mainsail* RAISE, raise up, lift, lift, haul up, heave up, jack up, hike up, winch up, pull up, heft up, upraise, uplift, elevate, erect. ANTONYM lower.

▸ noun *a mechanical hoist* LIFTING GEAR, crane, winch, block and tackle, pulley, windlass, derrick; *Nautical* sheerlegs.

**hold** verb 1 *she held a suitcase* CLASP, clutch, grasp, grip, clench, cling to, hold on to; carry, bear. ANTONYMS release, let go of.

2 *I wanted to hold her* EMBRACE, hug, clasp, cradle, enfold, squeeze, fold in one's arms, cling to.

**3** *do you hold a degree?* POSSESS, have, own, bear, carry, have to one's name.

**4** *the branch held my weight* SUPPORT, bear, carry, take, keep up, sustain, prop up, shore up.

**5** *the police were holding him* DETAIN, hold in custody, imprison, lock up, put behind bars, put in prison, put in jail, incarcerate, keep under lock and key, confine, constrain, intern, impound; *informal* put away. ANTONYMS release, let go.

**6** *try to hold the audience's attention* MAINTAIN, keep, occupy, engross, absorb, interest, captivate, fascinate, enthrall, rivet, mesmerize, transfix; engage, catch, capture, arrest. ANTONYM lose.

**7** *he held a senior post* OCCUPY, have, fill; *informal* hold down.

**8** *the tank holds 250 gallons* TAKE, contain, accommodate, fit; have a capacity of, have room for.

**9** *the court held that there was no evidence* MAINTAIN, consider, take the view, believe, think, feel, deem, be of the opinion; judge, rule, decide; *informal* reckon; *formal* opine, esteem.

**10** *let's hope the good weather holds* PERSIST, continue, carry on, go on, hold out, keep up, last, endure, stay, remain. ANTONYM end.

**11** *the offer still holds* BE AVAILABLE, be valid, hold good, stand, apply, remain, exist, be the case, be in force, be in effect.

**12** *they held a meeting* CONVENE, call, summon; conduct, have, organize, run; *formal* convoke. ANTONYM disband.

**13** *hold your fire* STOP, halt, restrain, check, cease, discontinue; *informal* break off, give up; hold back, suppress, repress, refrain from using, stifle, withhold. ANTONYM resume.

▸ noun **1** *she kept a hold on my hand* GRIP, grasp, clasp, clutch.

**2** *Tom had a hold over his father* INFLUENCE, power, control, dominance, authority, command, leverage, sway, mastery, dominion.

**3** *the military tightened their hold on the capital* CONTROL, grip, power, stranglehold, chokehold, dominion, authority.

PHRASES: **get hold of** *informal I'll try to get hold of Stevenson this evening* CONTACT, get in touch with, communicate with, make contact with, reach, notify; phone, call, speak to, talk to.

**hold back 1** *if you feel like singing, don't hold back* HESITATE, pause, stop oneself, restrain oneself, desist, forbear.

**2** *Jane held back her tears* SUPPRESS, fight back, choke back, stifle, smother, subdue, rein in, repress, curb, control, keep a tight rein on; *informal* keep a lid on.

**3** *don't hold anything back from me* WITHHOLD, hide, conceal, keep secret, keep hidden, keep quiet about, keep to oneself, hush up; *informal* sit on, keep under one's hat.

**4** *you'll never make it in music if you keep letting your parents hold you back* HINDER, hamper, impede, obstruct, inhibit, hobble, check, curb, block, thwart, balk, hamstring, restrain, frustrate, stand in someone's way.

**hold dear** *she holds this house dear* CHERISH, treasure, prize, appreciate, adore, value highly, care for/about; *informal* put on a pedestal.

**hold down 1** *they will hold down inflation* KEEP DOWN, keep low, freeze, fix.

**2** *informal she held down two jobs* OCCUPY, have, do, fill.

**3** *the people can be held down only so long* OPPRESS, repress, suppress, subdue, subjugate, keep down, keep under, tyrannize, dominate.

**hold forth** *he was holding forth on the qualities of good wine* SPEAK AT LENGTH, talk at length, go on, sound off; declaim, spout, pontificate, orate, preach, sermonize; *informal* speechify, drone on.

**hold off 1** *the rain held off* STAY AWAY, keep off, not come, delay.

**2** *we held off the swarms of ants as long as we could* RESIST, repel, repulse, rebuff, parry, deflect, fend off, stave off, ward off, keep at bay.

**hold on 1** *hold on, I'll be right there* WAIT, wait a minute, just a moment, just a second; stay here, stay put; hold the line; *informal* just a sec, hang on, sit tight, hold your horses.

**2** *if only they could hold on just a little longer* KEEP GOING, persevere, survive, last, continue, struggle on, carry on, go on, hold out, see it through, stay the course; *informal* soldier on, stick it out, hang in there.

**hold on to 1** *he held on to the chair* CLUTCH, hang on to, clasp, grasp, grip, cling to.

**2** *they can't hold on to their staff* RETAIN, keep, hang on to.

**hold one's own.** See OWN.

**hold out 1** *the small band of weary soldiers held out until reinforcements arrived* PERSIST, last, remain; persevere, continue.

**2** *Celia held out her hands* EXTEND, proffer, offer, present; outstretch, reach out, stretch out, put out.

**hold over** *the family gathering was held over until late January* POSTPONE, put off, put back, delay, defer, suspend, shelve, put over, table, take a rain check on; *informal* put on ice, put on the back burner, put in cold storage, mothball.

**hold up 1** *the argument doesn't hold up* BE CONVINCING, be logical, hold water, bear examination, be sound.

**2** *they held up the trophy* DISPLAY, hold aloft, exhibit, show (off), flourish, brandish; *informal* flash.

**3** *concrete pillars hold up the bridge* SUPPORT, bear, carry, take, keep up, prop up, shore up, buttress.

**4** *our flight was held up for hours* DELAY, detain, make late, set back, keep back, retard, slow up.

**5** *a lack of cash has held up progress* OBSTRUCT, impede, hinder, hamper, inhibit, arrest, balk, thwart, curb, hamstring, frustrate, foil, interfere with, stop; *informal* stymie, hog-tie.

**6** *two gunmen held up the bank* ROB; *informal* stick up.

**hold water.** See WATER.

**with no holds barred** *you can tell us everything that happened, with no holds barred* CANDIDLY, honestly, frankly, directly, openly, bluntly; *informal* point-blank, without mincing one's words.

**holder** noun **1** *a knife holder* CONTAINER, receptacle, case, casing, cover, covering, housing, sheath; stand, rest, rack.

**2** *are you the holder of a major credit card?* BEARER, owner, possessor, keeper; custodian.

**holdup** noun **1** *I ran into a series of holdups* DELAY, setback, hitch, snag, obstruction, difficulty, problem, trouble, stumbling block; *informal* tie-up, logjam; traffic jam, gridlock, bottleneck, roadblock; snarl-up, glitch, hiccup.

**2** *a bank holdup* ROBBERY, raid, armed robbery, armed raid; theft, burglary, mugging; *informal* stickup, heist.

**hole** noun **1** *a hole in the roof* OPENING, aperture, gap, space, orifice, vent, chink, breach, break; crack, leak, rift, rupture; puncture, perforation, cut, split, gash, slit, rent, tear, crevice, fissure.

**2** *a hole in the ground* PIT, ditch, trench, cavity, crater, depression, indentation, hollow; well, borehole, excavation, dugout; cave, cavern, pothole.

**3** *the gopher's hole* BURROW, lair, den, earth, set; retreat, shelter.

**4** *there are holes in their argument* FLAW, fault, defect, weakness, shortcoming, inconsistency, discrepancy, loophole; error, mistake.

**5** *informal I was living in a real hole* HOVEL, slum, shack; *informal* dump, dive, pigsty, hole in the wall, rathole, sty.

**6** *informal she has dug herself into a hole* PREDICAMENT, difficult situation, awkward situation, corner, tight corner, quandary, dilemma; crisis, emergency, difficulty, trouble, plight, dire straits, imbroglio; *informal* fix, jam, mess, bind, scrape, spot, tight spot, pickle, sticky situation, can of worms, hot water. PHRASES: **hole up 1** *the bears hole up in winter* HIBERNATE, lie dormant.

**2** *informal the snipers holed up in a farmhouse* HIDE (OUT), conceal oneself, secrete oneself, shelter, take cover, lie low.

**poke holes in** *informal it was pretty easy to poke holes in Dr. Delvecchio's theories* FIND FAULT WITH, pick apart, deconstruct, query, quibble with; deflate, puncture.

**in the hole** *the diner was in the hole within six months after Abdul's sons took over* IN DEBT, in arrears, in deficit, overdrawn, behind; *informal* in the red.

**holiday** noun **1** *Presidents' Day is a federal holiday* DAY OF OBSERVANCE, festival, feast day, féte, fiesta, celebration, anniversary, jubilee; saint's day, holy day.

**2** *chiefly Brit. Sara and Lou's ten-day holiday* VACATION, break, rest, respite, recess; time off, time out, leave, furlough, sabbatical; trip, tour, journey, voyage; *informal* getaway; *formal* sojourn.

**holier-than-thou** adjective *you will never sell your opinions to me with that holier-than-thou attitude* SANCTIMONIOUS, self-righteous, smug, self-satisfied; priggish, pious, pietistic, Pharisaic. ANTONYM humble.

**hollow** adjective **1** *each fiber has a hollow core* EMPTY, void, unfilled, vacant. ANTONYM solid.

**2** *hollow cheeks* SUNKEN, gaunt, deep-set, concave, depressed, indented; *rare* incurvate.

**3** *a hollow sound* DULL, low, flat, toneless, expressionless; muffled, muted.

**4** *a hollow victory* MEANINGLESS, empty, valueless, worthless, useless, pyrrhic, nugatory, futile, fruitless, profitless, pointless. ANTONYM worthwhile.

**5** *a hollow promise* INSINCERE, hypocritical, feigned, false, sham, deceitful, cynical, spurious, untrue, two-faced; *informal* phony, pretend. ANTONYM sincere.

▸ noun **1** *a hollow under the tree* HOLE, pit, cavity, crater, trough, bowl, cave, cavern; depression, indentation, dip, dent; niche, nook, cranny, recess.

**2** *the village lay in a hollow* VALLEY, vale, dale, basin, glen. *literary* dell.

▸ verb *a tunnel hollowed out of a mountain* GOUGE, scoop, dig, shovel, cut; excavate, channel.

**holocaust** noun *fears of a nuclear holocaust* CATACLYSM, disaster, catastrophe; destruction, devastation, annihilation; massacre, slaughter, mass murder, extermination, extirpation, carnage, butchery; genocide, ethnic cleansing, pogrom.

**holy** adjective **1** *holy men* SAINTLY, godly, saintlike, pious, pietistic, religious, devout, God-fearing, spiritual; righteous, good, virtuous, angelic, sinless, pure, numinous, beatific; canonized, beatified, ordained. See note at DIVINE. ANTONYMS sinful, irreligious.

**2** *a Jewish holy place* SACRED, consecrated, hallowed, sanctified, sacrosanct, venerated, revered, divine, religious, blessed, dedicated. ANTONYM cursed.

**home** noun **1** *they fled their homes* RESIDENCE, place of residence, house, apartment, flat, bungalow, cottage; accommodations, property, quarters, rooms, lodgings; a roof over one's head; address, place; *informal* pad, digs; hearth, nest; *formal* domicile, abode, dwelling, dwelling place, habitation.

**2** *an Italian stonemason far from his home.* See HOMELAND.

**3** *a home for the elderly* INSTITUTION, nursing home, retirement home, rest home; children's home; hospice, shelter, refuge, retreat, asylum, hostel, halfway house.

**4** *the home of fine wines* ORIGIN, source, cradle, fount, fountainhead.

▸ adjective **1** *the home market* DOMESTIC, internal, local, national, interior. ANTONYMS foreign, international.

**2** *home movies* | *the sale of home produce* HOMEMADE, homegrown, family.

PHRASES: **at home 1** *I was at home all day* IN, in one's house, present, available, indoors, inside, here.

**2** *she felt very much at home* AT EASE, comfortable, relaxed, content; in one's element, on one's own turf.

**3** *he is **at home with** mathematics* CONFIDENT WITH, conversant with, proficient in; used to, familiar with, au fait with, au courant with, skilled in, experienced in, well versed in.

**bring home to someone** *Sylvia's overdose brought home to them the fragility of their own lives* MAKE SOMEONE REALIZE, make someone understand, make someone aware, make clear to someone; drive home to someone, impress upon someone, draw attention to, focus attention on, underline, highlight, spotlight, emphasize, stress; *informal* clue someone in to.

**hit home.** See HIT HOME at HIT.

**home free** *when the inspector at the third checkpoint nodded at Mitchell, I knew we were home free | I passed the final flag with so much stamina that I knew I was home free* SAFE, secure, out of danger, off the hook; assured of success, the winner, victorious; *informal* golden.

**home in on** *the reporters immediately wanted to home in on his broken engagement* FOCUS ON, concentrate on, zero in on, center on, fix on; highlight, spotlight, target, underline, pinpoint, track, zoom in on.

**nothing to write home about** *informal the amusement park was enjoyable enough, but nothing to write home about* UNEXCEPTIONAL, mediocre, ordinary, commonplace, indifferent, average, middle-of-the-road, run-of-the-mill, garden variety; boring, mundane, humdrum, ho-hum; tolerable, passable, adequate, fair; *informal* OK, so-so, 'comme ci, comme ça,' plain-vanilla, no great shakes, not so hot.

**homeland** noun *she left her homeland to settle in Japan with her husband's family* NATIVE LAND, country of origin, home, birthplace, hometown; roots, fatherland, motherland, mother country, land of one's fathers; the old country.

**homeless** adjective *homeless people* OF NO FIXED ADDRESS, without a roof over one's head, on the streets, vagrant, displaced, dispossessed, destitute, down-and-out.

▸ noun *charities for the homeless* PEOPLE OF NO FIXED ADDRESS, vagrants, down-and-outs, street people, tramps, vagabonds, itinerants, transients, migrants, derelicts, drifters, hoboes; *informal* bag ladies, bums.

**homely** adjective *she's rather homely* UNATTRACTIVE, plain, unprepossessing, unlovely, ill-favored, ugly; *informal* not much to look at. ANTONYM attractive.

**homeowner** noun *homeowners in the Scotch Hill section have drafted a petition against the proposed landfill on Fuller Drive* OWNER, householder, resident, occupant, proprietor.

**homespun** adjective *homespun rural philosophy* UNSOPHISTICATED, plain, simple, basic, unpolished, unrefined, rustic, folksy; coarse, rough, crude, rudimentary, bush-league. ANTONYM sophisticated.

**homicidal** adjective *his homicidal tendencies went undetected for years* MURDEROUS, violent, brutal, savage, ferocious, vicious, bloody, bloodthirsty, barbarous, barbaric; deadly, lethal, mortal; *literary* fell; *archaic* sanguinary.

**homicide** noun *we're investigating a homicide that took place in this building* MURDER, killing, slaughter, butchery, massacre; assassination, execution, extermination; patricide, matricide, infanticide; *literary* slaying.

**homily** noun *a guest preacher delivered today's homily* SERMON, lecture, discourse, address, lesson, talk, speech, oration.

**homogeneous** adjective *should the members of a society become so homogeneous that any trace of cultural diversity vanishes?* UNIFORM, identical, unvaried, consistent, indistinguishable, homologous, homogenized; alike, similar, the same, much the same, all of a piece, melting-pot. ANTONYM different.

**homogenize** verb *my job is to homogenize all you precious little 'individuals' into one fighting machine* MAKE UNIFORM, make similar, standardize, unite, integrate, fuse, merge, blend, meld, coalesce, amalgamate, combine. ANTONYM diversify.

**homosexual** adjective *we decided to march with our homosexual friends* GAY, lesbian, homoerotic, same-sex; *informal* queer, camp, pink, lavender, homo; *literary* Uranian. See note at GAY. ANTONYM heterosexual.

▸ noun *she has a serious crush on William, who, unfortunately for her, is a homosexual* GAY, lesbian; *informal* queer, queen, dyke, butch, femme; *literary* Uranian. ANTONYM heterosexual.

**honest** adjective **1** *an honest man* UPRIGHT, honorable, moral, ethical, principled, righteous, right-minded, respectable; virtuous, good, decent, fair, law-abiding, high-minded, upstanding, incorruptible, truthful, trustworthy, reliable, conscientious, scrupulous, reputable; *informal* on the level, trusty. ANTONYMS unscrupulous, dishonest.

**2** *I haven't been honest with you* TRUTHFUL, sincere, candid, frank, open, forthright, ingenuous, straight; straightforward, plain-speaking, matter-of-fact; *informal* upfront, aboveboard, on the level. ANTONYM insincere.

**3** *an honest mistake* GENUINE, true, bona fide, legitimate; *informal* legit, honest-to-goodness.

**honestly** adverb **1** *he earned the money honestly* FAIRLY, lawfully, legally, legitimately, honorably, decently, ethically, in good faith, by the book; openly, on the level, aboveboard.

**2** *we honestly believe this is for the best* SINCERELY, genuinely, truthfully, truly, wholeheartedly; really, frankly, actually, seriously, to be honest, to tell you the truth, to be frank, in all honesty, in all sincerity; *informal* Scout's honor.

▸ exclamation *Honestly! I don't know what to do with you!* FOR HEAVEN'S SAKE, for goodness' sake, for Pete's sake, really, sheesh, jeepers.

**honesty** noun **1** *I can attest to his honesty* INTEGRITY, uprightness, honorableness, honor, morality, morals, ethics, principles, high principles, righteousness, right-mindedness; virtue, goodness, probity, high-mindedness, fairness, incorruptibility, truthfulness, trustworthiness, reliability, dependability, rectitude.

**2** *they spoke with honesty about their fears* SINCERITY, candor, frankness, directness, bluntness, truthfulness, truth, openness, straightforwardness.

**honor** noun **1** *a man of honor* INTEGRITY, honesty, uprightness, ethics, morals, morality, principles, high principles, righteousness, high-mindedness; virtue, goodness, decency, probity, character, good character, scrupulousness, worth, fairness, justness, trustworthiness, reliability, dependability. ANTONYMS unscrupulousness, dishonor.

**2** *a mark of honor* DISTINCTION, recognition, privilege, glory, kudos, cachet, prestige, merit, credit; importance, illustriousness, notability; respect, esteem, approbation. ANTONYM disgrace.

**3** *our honor is at stake* REPUTATION, name, good name, good credit, character, esteem, repute, image, standing, stature, status, popularity.

**4** *he was welcomed with honor* ACCLAIM, acclamation, applause, accolades, adoration, tributes, compliments, salutes, bouquets; homage, praise, veneration, glory, reverence, adulation, exaltation; *dated* laud. ANTONYM contempt.

**5** *she had the honor of meeting the first lady* PRIVILEGE, pleasure, pride, joy; compliment, favor, distinction. ANTONYM shame.

**6** *military honors* ACCOLADE, award, reward, prize, decoration, distinction, medal, ribbon, star, laurel.

**7** *dated* *she died defending her honor* CHASTITY, virginity, maidenhead, purity, innocence, modesty; *archaic* virtue, maidenhood.

▸ verb **1** *we should honor our parents* ESTEEM, respect, admire, defer to, look up to; appreciate, value, cherish, adore; reverence, revere, venerate, worship; *informal* put on a pedestal. ANTONYM disrespect.

**2** *they were honored at a special ceremony* APPLAUD, acclaim, praise, salute, recognize, celebrate, commemorate, commend, hail, lionize, exalt, eulogize, pay homage to, pay tribute to, sing the praises of; *formal* laud. ANTONYMS disgrace, criticize.

**3** *he honored the contract* FULFILL, observe, keep, obey, heed, follow, carry out, discharge, implement, execute, effect; keep to, abide by, adhere to, comply with, conform to, be true to, live up to. ANTONYM disobey.

THE RIGHT WORD **honor, deference, homage, obeisance, reverence**

The Ten Commandments instruct us to "**Honor** thy father and mother." But what does *honor* entail? While all of these nouns describe the respect or esteem that one shows to another, *honor* implies acknowledgment of a person's right to such respect (*honor one's ancestors; honor the dead*). **Homage** is honor with praise or tributes added, and it connotes a more worshipful attitude (*pay homage to the king*). **Reverence** combines profound respect with love or devotion (*he treated his wife with reverence*), while **deference** suggests courteous regard for a superior, often by yielding to the person's status or wishes (*show deference to one's elders*). **Obeisance** is a show of honor or reverence by an act or gesture of submission or humility, such as a bow or a curtsy (*the schoolchildren were instructed to pay obeisance when the Queen arrived*).

**honorable** adjective **1** *an honorable man* HONEST, moral, ethical, principled, righteous, right-minded; decent, respectable, estimable, virtuous, good, upstanding, upright, worthy, noble, fair, just, truthful, trustworthy, law-abiding, reliable, reputable, creditable, dependable. See note at MORAL. ANTONYM crooked.

**2** *an honorable career* ILLUSTRIOUS, distinguished, eminent, great, glorious, renowned, acclaimed, prestigious, noble, creditable, admirable. ANTONYM deplorable.

**honorarium** noun *each technical adviser receives an annual honorarium of $500* FEE, payment, consideration, allowance, stipend; remuneration, pay, expenses, compensation, recompense, reward; *formal* emolument.

**honorary** adjective *she has received honorary diplomas from eleven colleges and universities worldwide* TITULAR, symbolic, in name only, ceremonial, nominal, unofficial, token.

**hood** noun *they wore sunglasses and hoods to disguise themselves* HEAD COVERING, cowl, snood, headscarf, amice.

**hoodlum** noun *he was roughed up by a bunch of hoodlums* THUG, lout, delinquent, vandal, ruffian, hooligan, lowlife; gangster, crook, mobster, criminal; *informal* tough, bruiser, goon, hood, punk, rowdy.

**hoodwink** verb *Jimmy was hoodwinked by his own brother* DECEIVE, trick, dupe, outwit, fool, delude, inveigle, cheat, take in, hoax, mislead, lead on, defraud, double-cross, swindle, gull, scam; *informal* con, bamboozle, hornswoggle, fleece, do, have, sting, gyp, shaft, rip off, lead up the garden path, pull a fast one on, put one over on, take for a ride, pull the wool over someone's eyes, sucker, snooker; *literary* cozen.

**hook** noun **1** *she hung her jacket on the hook* PEG, coat rack.

**2** *the dress has six hooks* FASTENER, fastening, catch, clasp, hasp, clip, pin.

**3** *I had a fish on the end of my hook* FISHHOOK, barb, gaff, snare, snag.

**4** *a right hook to the chin* PUNCH, blow, hit, cuff, thump, smack; *informal* belt, bop, sock, clout, whack, wallop, slug; *informal* boff.

▸ verb **1** *they hooked baskets onto the ladder* ATTACH, hitch, fasten, fix, secure, clasp. See note at PAIR.

**2** *he hooked his thumbs in his belt* CURL, bend, crook, loop, curve.

**3** *he hooked a 24-pound pike* CATCH, land, net, take; bag, snare, trap.

PHRASES: **by hook or by crook** *I'll get to Hollywood by hook or by crook* BY ANY MEANS, somehow (or other), no matter how, in one way or another, by fair means or foul.

**hook, line, and sinker** *they believed her phony alibi hook, line, and sinker* COMPLETELY, totally, utterly, entirely, wholly, absolutely, through and through, one hundred percent, 'lock, stock, and barrel.'

**off the hook** *informal* *Mr. Lee paid the fine, so now Tammy is off the hook* OUT OF TROUBLE, in the clear, free, home free; acquitted, cleared, reprieved, exonerated, absolved; *informal* let off.

**hooked** adjective **1** *a hooked nose* CURVED, hook-shaped, hooklike, aquiline, angular, bent, crooked. ANTONYM straight.

**2** *informal* *he is* ***hooked on*** *reality TV* KEEN ON, enthusiastic about, addicted to, obsessed with, infatuated with, fixated on, fanatical about; *informal* mad about, crazy about, wild about, nuts about.

**3** *she had the audience hooked* CAPTIVATED, enthralled, entranced, bewitched, charmed. ANTONYM indifferent.

**hooligan** noun *I want you to stop hanging around with those hooligans* TROUBLEMAKER, delinquent, juvenile delinquent, mischief-maker, vandal; rowdy, ruffian, yahoo.

**hoop** noun *a simple gold hoop* RING, band, circle, circlet, bracelet, (hoop) earring, loop; *technical* annulus.

**hoot** noun **1** *the hoot of an owl* SCREECH, shriek, call, cry.

**2** *hoots of derision* SHOUT, yell, cry, snort, howl, shriek, whoop, whistle; boo, hiss, jeer, catcall.

**3** *informal the party was a hoot* GOOD TIME, scream, laugh, blast, riot, giggle, barrel of laughs; *dated* caution.

▸ verb **1** *an owl hooted* SCREECH, shriek, cry, call.

**2** *they hooted in disgust* SHOUT, yell, cry, howl, shriek, whistle; boo, hiss, jeer, heckle, catcall.

PHRASE: **give a hoot** *informal obviously you don't give a hoot about clean air* CARE, be concerned, mind, be interested, be bothered, trouble oneself about; *informal* give a damn.

**hop** verb **1** *he hopped over the fence* JUMP, bound, spring, bounce, leap, vault.

**2** *informal she hopped over the Atlantic* GO, dash; travel, journey; jet, fly; *informal* pop, whip, nip.

▸ noun **1** *the rabbit had a hop around* JUMP, bound, bounce, leap, spring.

**2** *informal a short hop by taxi* JOURNEY, distance, ride, drive, run, trip, jaunt; flight; *informal* hop, skip, and a jump.

**hope** noun **1** *I had high hopes* ASPIRATION, desire, wish, expectation, ambition, aim, goal, plan, design; dream, daydream, pipe dream.

**2** *a life filled with hope* HOPEFULNESS, optimism, expectation, expectancy; confidence, faith, trust, belief, conviction, assurance; promise, possibility. ANTONYM pessimism.

**3** *have we any hope of winning?* CHANCE, prospect, likelihood, probability, possibility; *informal* shot.

▸ verb **1** *he's* ***hoping for*** *a medal* EXPECT, anticipate, look for, be hopeful of, pin one's hopes on, want; wish for, long for, dream of.

**2** *we're hoping to address the issue* AIM, intend, be looking, have the intention, have in mind, plan, aspire.

**hopeful** adjective **1** *he remained hopeful* OPTIMISTIC, full of hope, confident, positive, buoyant, sanguine, expectant, bullish, cheerful, lighthearted; *informal* upbeat.

**2** *hopeful signs* PROMISING, encouraging, heartening, inspiring, reassuring, auspicious, favorable, optimistic, propitious, bright, rosy.

▸ noun *the Democratic hopeful for 2004* CANDIDATE, aspirant, prospect, possibility; nominee, competitor, contender; *informal* up-and-comer.

**hopefully** adverb **1** *he rode on hopefully* OPTIMISTICALLY, full of hope, confidently, buoyantly, sanguinely; expectantly.

**2** *hopefully it will finish soon* IF ALL GOES WELL, God willing, with luck, with any luck; most likely, probably; conceivably, feasibly; *informal* knock on wood, fingers crossed.

### USAGE NOTE **hopefully**

Four points about this word: First, it was widely condemned from the 1960s to the 1980s. Briefly, the objections are that (1) *hopefully* properly means "in a hopeful manner" and shouldn't be used in the radically different sense "I hope" or "it is to be hoped"; (2) if the extended sense is accepted, the original sense will be forever lost; and (3) in constructions such as "Hopefully, it won't rain this afternoon," the writer illogically ascribes an emotion (*hopefulness*) to a nonperson. *Hopefully* isn't analogous to *curiously* (= it is a curious fact that), *fortunately* (= it is a fortunate thing that), and *sadly* (= it is a sad fact that). How so? Unlike all those other sentence adverbs, *hopefully* can't be resolved into any longer expression involving the word *hopeful*—but only *hope* (e.g., *it is to be hoped that* or *I hope that*).

Second, whatever the merits of those arguments, the battle is now over. *Hopefully* is now a part of American English, and it has all but lost its traditional meaning—e.g.: "Hopefully, one day we will all grow older." (*San Diego Union-Tribune*; Nov. 26, 1997.) Sometimes, the word is genuinely ambiguous (if the original meaning is considered still alive)—e.g.: "Dave Krieg will take the snaps and, hopefully, hand off to RB Garrison Hearst." (*USA Today*; Sept. 1, 1995.) (Is Krieg hoping for the best when Hearst runs? Or is the writer hoping that Krieg won't pass the football or hand off to another running back?) Indeed, the original meaning of *hopefully* is alive, even if moribund—e.g.: "Officials recently have pointed hopefully to signs of increased usage of the garage." (*Boston Globe*; Oct. 9, 1994.)

Third, some stalwarts continue to condemn the word, so that anyone using it in the new sense is likely to have a credibility problem with some readers—e.g.

- "Professor Michael Dummett, an Oxford logician, condemns the new usage of *hopefully* because only a person can be hopeful, and in many such cases there is nobody around in the sentence to be hopeful." (*Daily Telegraph* [UK]; Dec. 11, 1996.)
- "Although various adverbs may be used to modify entire clauses, *hopefully* isn't among them—yet. I only hope I won't have to concede that it is until I'm an old, old woman." (Barbara Wallraff, *Word Court*; 2000.)

Fourth, though the controversy swirling around this word has subsided, any use of it is likely to distract some readers. Avoid it in all senses if you're concerned with your credibility: if you use it in the traditional way, many readers will think it odd; if you use it in the newish way, a few readers will tacitly tut-tut you.

Throughout the late twentieth century, the common wisdom was that the use of *hopefully* as a sentence adverb had begun sometime around the early 1930s. Then, in 1999, a lexicographic scholar named Fred Shapiro, using computer-assisted research, traced it back to Cotton Mather's 1702 book, *Magnalia Christi Americana*, in this sentence: "Chronical diseases, which evidently threaten his Life, might hopefully be relieved by his removal." The evidence then skips to 1851, then to the 1930s. —*BG*

---

**hopeless** adjective **1** *she felt weary and hopeless* DESPAIRING, desperate, wretched, forlorn, pessimistic, defeatist, resigned;

dejected, downhearted, despondent, demoralized; *archaic* woebegone.

**2** *a hopeless case* IRREMEDIABLE, beyond hope, lost, beyond repair, irreparable, irreversible; helpless, incurable; impossible, no-win, unwinnable, futile, unworkable, impracticable, useless; *archaic* bootless.

**3** *Joseph was hopeless at tennis* BAD, awful, terrible, dreadful, horrible, atrocious; inferior, incompetent, inadequate, unskilled; *informal* pathetic, useless, lousy, rotten.

**4** *a hopeless romantic* INCURABLE, incorrigible, chronic, compulsive; complete, utter, absolute, total, out-and-out; inveterate, confirmed, established, dyed-in-the-wool.

**horde** noun *a horde of fans stormed the playing field* CROWD, mob, pack, gang, group, troop, army, legion, swarm, mass, herd, rabble; throng, multitude, host, band, flock, drove, press, crush; *informal* crew, tribe, pile.

**horizon** noun **1** *the sun rose above the horizon* SKYLINE.

**2** *she wanted to broaden her horizons* OUTLOOK, perspective, perception; range of experience, range of interests, scope, prospect, ambit, compass, orbit. PHRASE: **on the horizon** *a better life for us is on the horizon* IMMINENT, impending, due, close, near, approaching, coming, forthcoming, at hand, on the way, about to happen, upon us, in the offing, in the pipeline, in the air, in the wings, in the cards, just around the corner, coming down the pike; brewing, looming, threatening, menacing.

**horizontal** adjective **1** *a horizontal surface* level, flat, plane, smooth, even; straight, parallel. ANTONYM vertical.

**2** *she was horizontal on the bed* FLAT, supine, prone, prostrate, recumbent. ANTONYM upright.

**3** *a horizontal move* LATERAL, sideways.

**horrendous** adjective. See HORRIBLE.

**horrible** adjective **1** *a horrible murder* DREADFUL, awful, terrible, shocking, appalling, horrifying, horrific, horrendous, horrid, hideous, grisly, ghastly, gruesome, gory, harrowing, heinous, vile, unspeakable; nightmarish, macabre, spine-chilling, blood-curdling; loathsome, monstrous, abhorrent, hateful, hellish, execrable, abominable, atrocious, sickening, foul. ANTONYMS pleasant, agreeable.

**2** *informal a horrible little man* NASTY, horrid, disagreeable, unpleasant, detestable, awful, dreadful, terrible, appalling, horrendous, foul, repulsive, repugnant, repellent, ghastly; obnoxious, hateful, odious, hideous, objectionable, insufferable, vile, loathsome, abhorrent; *informal* frightful, godawful. ANTONYMS pleasant, agreeable.

**horrid** adjective. See HORRIBLE.

**horrify** verb **1** *she horrified us with ghastly tales* FRIGHTEN, scare, terrify, petrify, paralyze, alarm, panic, terrorize, fill with fear, scare someone out of their wits, frighten the living daylights out of, make someone's hair stand on end, make someone's blood run cold, give someone the creeps; *informal* scare the pants off, spook; *archaic* affright.

**2** *he was horrified by her remarks* SHOCK, appall, outrage, scandalize, offend; disgust, revolt, nauseate, sicken.

**horror** noun **1** *children screamed in horror* TERROR, fear, fright, alarm, panic; dread, trepidation. ANTONYM delight.

**2** *to her horror she found herself alone* DISMAY, consternation, perturbation, alarm, distress; disgust, outrage, shock. ANTONYM satisfaction.

**3** *the horror of the tragedy* AWFULNESS, frightfulness, savagery, barbarity, hideousness; atrocity, outrage.

**4** *informal he's a little horror* RASCAL, devil, imp, monkey; *informal* terror, scamp, scalawag, tyke, varmint.

**5** *informal her new dress is a horror* EYESORE, monstrosity, abomination, blot, disgrace, mess, sight. ANTONYM beauty.

**horse** noun *Nadine boards and grooms horses* EQUINE, mount, charger, cob, nag; pony; foal, yearling, colt, stallion, gelding, mare, filly; bronco; *dated* stepper; *archaic* steed. PHRASE: **horse around** *informal they knew better than to horse around when their father came home* FOOL AROUND, play, have fun, clown around, monkey around.

**horseplay** noun *the brothers' horseplay was not looked on too kindly by Aunt Smitty* TOMFOOLERY, fooling around, roughhousing, clowning, buffoonery, fun; pranks, antics, hijinks; *informal* shenanigans, monkey business.

**horse sense** noun *informal*. See COMMON SENSE.

**horticulture** noun *your gardener apparently knows very little about horticulture* GARDENING, landscaping, cultivation; floriculture, arboriculture, agriculture.

**hosanna** noun *the people's hosannas greeted him as he rode into the city* SHOUT OF PRAISE, alleluia, hurrah, hurray, hooray, cheer, paean.

**hose** noun **1** *a flexible green hose.* See PIPE noun sense 1.

**2** *some new black dress hose.* See HOSIERY.

**hosiery** noun *rinsing out some hosiery* STOCKINGS, tights, nylons, hose, pantyhose, leotards; socks.

**hospitable** adjective *my hospitable in-laws* WELCOMING, friendly, congenial, genial, sociable, convivial, cordial, courteous; gracious, well-disposed, amenable, helpful, obliging, accommodating, neighborly, warm, kind, generous, bountiful.

**hospital** noun *the hospitals were overwhelmed with cases of influenza* INFIRMARY, medical center, health center, clinic, sanatorium, hospice; *Military* field hospital; *dated* asylum.

**hospitality** noun *we found nothing but hospitality among the Ukrainians* FRIENDLINESS, hospitableness, warm reception, welcome, helpfulness, neighborliness, warmth, kindness, congeniality, geniality, cordiality, courtesy, amenability, generosity, entertainment, catering, food.

**host**[1] noun **1** *the host greeted the guests* PARTY-GIVER, hostess, entertainer. ANTONYM guest.

**2** *the host of a TV series* PRESENTER, anchor, anchorman, anchorwoman, announcer, master of ceremonies, ringmaster; *informal* emcee.

▸ verb **1** *Diane hosted a dinner party* GIVE, have, hold, throw, put on, provide, arrange, organize.

**2** *Jack hosted the show* PRESENT, introduce, front, anchor, announce; *informal* emcee.

**3** *she hosted her colleagues from overseas* ENTERTAIN, play host/hostess to; receive, welcome; take in, house, provide accommodations for, put up.

**host**[2] noun **1** *a host of memories* MULTITUDE, lot, abundance, wealth, profusion; *informal* load, heap, mass, pile, ton, number; *literary* myriad.

**2** *a host of movie stars* CROWD, throng, group, flock, herd, swarm, horde, mob, army, legion, pack, tribe, troop; assemblage, congregation, gathering.

**hostage** noun *all of the hostages were released unharmed* CAPTIVE, prisoner, inmate, detainee, internee; victim, abductee, prey; human shield, pawn, instrument.

**hostile** adjective **1** *a hostile attack* UNFRIENDLY, unkind, bitter, unsympathetic, malicious, vicious, rancorous, venomous, poisonous, virulent; antagonistic, aggressive, confrontational, belligerent, truculent, vitriolic; bellicose, pugnacious, warlike. ANTONYMS friendly, mild.

**2** *hostile conditions* UNFAVORABLE, adverse, bad, harsh, grim, hard, tough, brutal, fierce, inhospitable, forbidding, menacing, threatening. ANTONYM favorable.

**3** *they are* ***hostile to*** *the idea* OPPOSED TO, averse to, antagonistic to, ill-disposed to, disapproving of, unsympathetic to, antipathetic to; opposing, against, inimical to; *informal* anti, down on.

THE RIGHT WORD **hostile, adverse, bellicose, belligerent, inimical**

Few people have trouble recognizing hostility when confronted with it. Someone who is **hostile** displays an attitude of intense ill will and acts like an enemy (*the audience grew hostile after waiting an hour for the show to start*). Both **bellicose** and **belligerent** imply a readiness or eagerness to fight, but the former is used to describe a state of mind or temper (*after drinking all night, he was in a bellicose mood*), while the latter is normally used to describe someone who is actively engaged in hostilities (*the belligerent brothers were at it again*). While *hostile* and *belligerent* usually apply to people, **adverse** and **inimical** are used describe tendencies or influences. *Inimical* means having an antagonistic tendency (*remarks that were inimical to everything she believed in*), and *adverse* means turned toward something in opposition (*an adverse wind; under adverse circumstances*). Unlike *hostile*, *adverse* and *inimical* need not connote the involvement of human feeling.

**hostility** noun **1** *he glared at her with hostility* ANTAGONISM, unfriendliness, enmity, malevolence, malice, unkindness, rancor, venom, hatred, loathing; resentment, animosity, antipathy, acrimony, ill will, ill feeling; aggression, belligerence.

**2** *their hostility to the present regime* OPPOSITION, antagonism, aversion, resistance, dissidence.

**3** **(hostilities)** *a cessation of hostilities* FIGHTING, conflict, armed conflict, combat, aggression, warfare, war, bloodshed, violence.

**hot** adjective **1** *hot food* HEATED, piping hot, sizzling, steaming, roasting, boiling (hot), searing, scorching, scalding, burning, red-hot. ANTONYMS cold, chilled.

**2** *a hot day* VERY WARM, balmy, summery, tropical, scorching, broiling, searing, blistering; sweltering, torrid, sultry, humid, muggy, close, boiling, baking, roasting. ANTONYMS cold, chilly.

**3** *she felt very hot* FEVERISH, fevered, febrile; burning, flushed, sweaty; *rare* pyretic.

**4** *a hot chili* SPICY, spiced, highly seasoned, peppery, fiery, strong; piquant, pungent, aromatic, zesty. ANTONYM mild.

**5** *hot competition* FIERCE, intense, keen, competitive, cutthroat, dog-eat-dog, ruthless, aggressive, strong. ANTONYM weak.

**6** *informal hot gossip* NEW, fresh, recent, late, up to date, up-to-the-minute; just out, hot off the press(es), real-time. ANTONYMS old, stale.

**7** *informal this band is hot* POPULAR, in demand, sought-after, in favor; fashionable, in vogue, all the rage; *informal* big, in, now, hip, trendy, cool. ANTONYMS out of fashion, unpopular.

**8** *she thought Mark was hot* GOOD-LOOKING, sexy, attractive, gorgeous, handsome, beautiful; *archaic* comely, fair. ANTONYM unappealing.

**9** *hot goods* STOLEN, illegally obtained, purloined, pilfered, illegal, illicit, unlawful; smuggled, fenced, bootleg, contraband. ANTONYM lawful.

**10** *her dancing made him hot* AROUSED, sexually aroused, excited, stimulated, titillated, inflamed; *informal* turned on, hot to trot. ANTONYM frigid.

PHRASES: **blow hot and cold** *when it comes to her romantic interest in him, she blows hot and cold* VACILLATE, dither, shilly-shally, waver, be indecisive, change one's mind, be undecided, be uncertain, be unsure, hem and haw.

**hot and heavy** *isn't it a bit too soon for them to be so hot and heavy with each other?* intense, ardent, passionate, fervid.

**have the hots for** *Liza admits that she has the hots for Ryan* be (sexually) attracted to, desire, lust after; *informal* have a crush on, have a thing for, be crazy about.

**hot on the heels/trail of** *the marketing mavens are hot on the heels of this latest craze* CLOSE BEHIND, directly after, right after, straight after, hard on the heels of, following closely.

**hot under the collar** *informal.* See ANGRY sense 1.

**hotbed** noun *a hotbed of crime* BREEDING GROUND, den, nest, stronghold, flash point, cradle, seedbed.

**hot-blooded** adjective *he's not exactly the hot-blooded Latin lover I thought he'd be* PASSIONATE, amorous, amatory, ardent, fervid, lustful, libidinous, lecherous, sexy, virile; *informal* horny. ANTONYM cold.

**hotel** noun *we booked separate rooms at the hotel* INN, motel, boarding house, guest house, bed and breakfast, B&B, hostel, lodge, accommodations, lodging.

**hotfoot** PHRASE: **hotfoot it** *informal we'd better hotfoot it to the airport* HURRY, dash, run, rush, race, sprint, bolt, dart, career, careen, charge, shoot, hurtle, fly, speed, zoom, streak; *informal* tear, belt, scoot, clip, leg it, go like a bat out of hell, bomb, hightail it; *archaic* hie.

**hotheaded** adjective *Desi could camp it up as the hotheaded Cuban bandleader* IMPETUOUS, impulsive, headstrong, reckless, rash, irresponsible, foolhardy, madcap, devil-may-care; excitable, volatile, explosive, fiery, hot-tempered, quick-tempered, unruly.

**hothouse** noun **1** *tomatoes grew in the hothouse* GREENHOUSE, conservatory.

**2** *society was becoming a hothouse of narcissism* BREEDING GROUND, hotbed, seedbed.

▸ adjective *the school has a hothouse atmosphere* INTENSE, oppressive, stifling; overprotected, sheltered, insular, isolated, shielded; sensitive.

**hound** noun *take the hounds out for a run* DOG, hunting dog, canine, mongrel, cur; *informal* doggy, pooch, mutt, pup.

▸ verb **1** *she was hounded by the press* PURSUE, chase, follow, shadow, be hot on someone's heels, hunt (down), stalk, track, trail, tail, dog; harass, hassle, persecute, harry, pester, bother, badger, torment, bedevil; *informal* bug, give someone a hard time, devil.

**2** *they hounded him out of office* FORCE, drive, pressure, pressurize, push, urge, coerce, impel, dragoon, strong-arm; nag, bully, browbeat; *informal* bulldoze, railroad, hustle.

**house** noun **1** *a new development with 200 houses* RESIDENCE, home, place of residence; homestead; a roof over one's head; *formal* habitation, dwelling (place), abode, domicile.

**2** *you'll wake the whole house!* HOUSEHOLD, family, occupants; clan, tribe; *informal* brood.

**3** *the house of Windsor* FAMILY, clan, tribe; dynasty, line, bloodline, lineage, ancestry, family tree.

**4** *a printing house* FIRM, business, company, corporation, enterprise, establishment, institution, organization, operation; *informal* outfit, setup.

**5** *the country's upper house* LEGISLATIVE ASSEMBLY, legislative body, legislature, chamber, council, congress, senate, parliament, diet.

**6** *the house applauded* AUDIENCE, crowd, spectators, viewers, listeners; assembly, congregation.

**7** *they filled the house* theater, auditorium, amphitheater, hall, gallery, stalls.

▸ verb **1** *they can house twelve employees* ACCOMMODATE, provide accommodations for, give someone a roof over their head, lodge, quarter, board, billet, take in, sleep, put up; harbor, shelter.

**2** *this panel houses the main switch* CONTAIN, hold, store; cover, protect, enclose.

PHRASE: **on the house** *informal drinks are on the house* FREE, free of charge, without charge, at no cost, for nothing, gratis; complimentary; *informal* for free, comp.

**household** noun *the household was asleep* FAMILY, house, occupants, residents, ménage; clan, tribe; *informal* brood.

▸ adjective *household goods* DOMESTIC, family; everyday, ordinary, common, commonplace, regular, practical, workaday.

**housing** noun **1** *they invested in housing* HOUSES, homes, residences, apartment buildings, condominiums; accommodations, lodging, living quarters, shelter; *formal* dwellings, dwelling places, habitations.

**2** *the housing for the antenna* CASING, covering, case, cover, holder, sheath, jacket, shell, carapace, capsule.

**hovel** noun *living in the most dismal hovels* SHACK, slum, chantey, hut; *informal* dump, hole, dive, pigsty.

**hover** verb **1** *helicopters hovered overhead* BE SUSPENDED, be poised, hang, levitate, float; fly.

**2** *she hovered anxiously nearby* LINGER, loiter, wait (around); *informal* hang around/about, stick around.

**however** adverb **1** *however, gaining weight is not inevitable* NEVERTHELESS, nonetheless, but, still, yet, though, although, even so, for all that, despite that, in spite of that; anyway, anyhow, be that as it may, all the same, having said that, notwithstanding; *informal* still and all.

**2** *however you look at it* IN WHATEVER WAY, regardless of how, no matter how.

**howl** noun **1** *the howl of a wolf* BAYING, howling, bay, cry, yowl, bark, yelp.

**2** *a howl of anguish* WAIL, cry, yell, yelp, yowl; bellow, roar, shout, shriek, scream, screech.

▸ verb **1** *dogs howled in the distance* BAY, cry, yowl, bark, yelp.

**2** *a baby started to howl* WAIL, cry, yell, yowl, bawl, bellow, shriek, scream, screech, caterwaul; *informal* holler.

**3** *the movie was so funny, we just howled* LAUGH, guffaw, roar; be doubled up, split one's sides; *informal* crack up, be in stitches, be rolling in the aisles, be on the floor.

**hub** noun **1** *the hub of the wheel* PIVOT, axis, fulcrum, center, middle.

**2** *the hub of family life* CENTER, core, heart, middle, focus, focal point, central point, nucleus, kernel, nerve center, polestar. ANTONYM periphery.

**huddle** verb **1** *they huddled together* CROWD, cluster, gather, bunch, throng, flock, herd, collect, group, congregate, mass; press, pack, squeeze. ANTONYM disperse.

**2** *he huddled beneath the sheets* CURL UP, snuggle, nestle, hunch up.

▸ noun **1** *a huddle of passengers* CROWD, cluster, bunch, knot, group, throng, flock, press, pack; collection, assemblage; *informal* gaggle.

**2** *the team went into a huddle* CONSULTATION, discussion, debate, talk, parley, meeting, conference; *informal* confab, powwow.

**hue** noun *a lovely hue of lilac* COLOR, shade, tone, tint, tinge.

**huff** noun *he ran out in a huff* BAD MOOD, fit of pique, temper, tantrum, rage; *informal* snit, state, grump, hissy fit.

**hug** verb **1** *they hugged each other* EMBRACE, cuddle, squeeze, clasp, clutch, cradle, cling to, hold close, hold tight, take/fold someone in one's arms, clasp someone to one's bosom.

**2** *our route hugged the coastline* FOLLOW CLOSELY, keep close to, stay near to, follow the course of.

**3** *we hugged the comforting thought* CLING TO, hold on to, cherish, hold dear; harbor, nurse, foster, retain, keep in mind.

▸ noun *there were hugs as we left* EMBRACE, cuddle, squeeze, bear hug, clasp, hold, clinch.

**huge** adjective *a huge battleship* ENORMOUS, vast, immense, large, big, great, massive, colossal, prodigious, gigantic, gargantuan, mammoth, monumental; giant, towering, elephantine, mountainous, monstrous, titanic; epic, Herculean, Brobdingnagian; *informal* jumbo, mega, monster, king-size(d), economy-size(d), oversized, super-size(d), whopping, humongous, honking, hulking, astronomical, cosmic, ginormous. ANTONYM tiny.

**hulk** noun **1** *the rusting hulks of ships* WRECK, shipwreck, wreckage, ruin, derelict; shell, skeleton, hull.

**2** *a great hulk of a man* GIANT, lump, blob, clod; oaf; *informal* clodhopper, ape, gorilla, lummox, lubber.

**hulking** adjective *informal a hulking black dog lumbered down the stairs* LARGE, big, heavy, sturdy, burly, brawny, hefty, strapping; bulky, weighty, massive, ponderous; clumsy, awkward, ungainly, lumbering, lumpish, oafish; *informal* beefy, clunky, clodhopping. ANTONYM small.

**hull** noun **1** *the ship's hull* FRAMEWORK, body, shell, frame, skeleton, structure; fuselage.

**2** *seed hulls* SHELL, husk, pod, case, covering, integument, calyx, shuck; *Botany* pericarp, legume.

**hullabaloo** noun *informal the hullabaloo outside the police station attracted reporters by the dozen* FUSS, commotion, hue and cry, uproar, outcry, clamor, storm, furor, hubbub, ruckus, brouhaha; pandemonium, mayhem, tumult, turmoil, hurly-burly, rumpus, palaver; *informal* hoo-ha, to-do, song and dance, stink.

**hum** verb **1** *the engine was humming* PURR, drone, murmur, buzz, thrum, whine, whir, throb, vibrate, rumble.

**2** *she hummed a tune* sing, croon, murmur, drone.

**3** *the workshops are humming* BE BUSY, be active, be lively, buzz, bustle, be a hive of activity, throb, pulsate; *informal* be happening.

▸ noun *a low hum of conversation* MURMUR, drone, purr, buzz, mumble.

**human** adjective **1** *they're only human* MORTAL, flesh and blood; fallible, weak, frail, imperfect, vulnerable, susceptible, erring, error-prone; physical, bodily, fleshly.

**2** *the human side of politics* COMPASSIONATE, humane, kind, considerate, understanding, sympathetic, tolerant; approachable, accessible.

**3** *in human form* ANTHROPOMORPHIC, anthropoid, humanoid, hominid.

▸ noun *the link between humans and animals* PERSON, human being, personage, mortal, member of the human race; man, woman; individual, soul, living soul, being; Homo sapiens; earthling.

**humane** adjective *the humane treatment of animals* COMPASSIONATE, kind, considerate, understanding, sympathetic, tolerant; lenient, forbearing, forgiving, merciful, mild, gentle, tender, clement, benign, humanitarian, benevolent, charitable; warmhearted, tenderhearted, softhearted. ANTONYM cruel.

**humanitarian** adjective **1** *a humanitarian act* COMPASSIONATE, humane; unselfish, altruistic, generous, magnanimous, benevolent, merciful, kind, sympathetic. ANTONYM selfish.

**2** *a humanitarian organization* CHARITABLE, philanthropic, public-spirited, socially concerned, welfare; *rare* eleemosynary.

▸ noun *Mrs. Roosevelt would be most gratified to be remembered as a humanitarian* PHILANTHROPIST, altruist, benefactor, patron, social reformer, good Samaritan; do-gooder; *archaic* philanthrope.

**humanities** plural noun *if higher education becomes any more driven by corporate objectives, the humanities will be grappling for survival* ARTS, liberal arts, literature, philosophy; classics, classical studies, classical literature.

**humanity** noun **1** *humanity evolved from the apes* HUMANKIND, mankind, man, people, human beings, humans, the human race, mortals; Homo sapiens.

**2** *the humanity of Christ* HUMAN NATURE, humanness, mortality.

**3** *he praised them for their humanity* COMPASSION, brotherly love, fraternity, fellow feeling, philanthropy, humaneness, kindness, consideration, understanding, sympathy, tolerance; leniency, mercy, mercifulness, clemency, pity, tenderness; benevolence, charity, goodness, magnanimity, generosity.

**humble** adjective **1** *her bearing was humble* MEEK, deferential, respectful, submissive, diffident, self-effacing, unassertive; unpresuming, modest, unassuming, self-deprecating; subdued, chastened. ANTONYMS proud, overbearing.

**2** *a humble background* LOWLY, working-class, lower-class, poor, undistinguished, mean, modest, ignoble, low-born, plebeian, underprivileged; common, ordinary, simple, inferior, unremarkable, insignificant, inconsequential. ANTONYM noble.

**3** *my humble abode* MODEST, plain, simple, ordinary, unostentatious, unpretentious. ANTONYM grand.

▸ verb *he had to humble himself to ask for my help* HUMILIATE, abase, demean, lower, degrade, debase; mortify, shame, abash; *informal* cut down to size, deflate, make eat humble pie, take down a peg or two, settle someone's hash, make eat crow.

THE RIGHT WORD **humble, abase, debase, degrade, demean, humiliate**

While all of these verbs mean to lower in one's own estimation or in the eyes of others, there are subtle distinctions among them. **Humble** and **humiliate** sound similar, but *humiliate* emphasizes shame and the loss of self-respect and usually takes place in public (*humiliated by her tearful outburst*), while *humble* is a milder term implying a lowering of one's pride or rank (*to humble the arrogant professor by pointing out his mistake*). **Abase** suggests groveling or a sense of inferiority and is usually used reflexively (*got down on his knees and abased himself before the king*), while **demean** is more likely to imply a loss of dignity or social standing (*refused to demean herself by marrying a common laborer*). When used to describe things, **debase** means a deterioration in the quality or value of something (*a currency debased by the country's political turmoil*), but in reference to people it connotes a weakening of moral standards or character (*debased himself by accepting bribes*). **Degrade** is even stronger, suggesting the destruction of a person's character through degenerate or shameful behavior (*degraded by long association with criminals*).

**humdrum** adjective *they were quite wrong in assuming that the lighthouse keeper led a lonely and humdrum life* MUNDANE, dull, dreary, boring, tedious, monotonous, prosaic; unexciting, uninteresting, uneventful, unvaried, repetitive, unremarkable; routine, ordinary, everyday, day-to-day, workaday, quotidian, run-of-the-mill, commonplace, garden variety, pedestrian; *informal* plain-vanilla, ho-hum. ANTONYMS remarkable, exciting.

**humidity** noun *a climate of warm temperatures and high humidity* MUGGINESS, humidness, closeness, sultriness, stickiness, steaminess, airlessness, stuffiness, clamminess; dampness, damp, dankness, moisture, moistness, wetness, dewiness. ANTONYMS freshness, aridity.

**humiliate** verb *he was humiliated in front of the whole school* EMBARRASS, mortify, humble, shame, put to shame, disgrace, chagrin; discomfit, chasten, abash, deflate, crush, squash; abase, debase, demean, degrade, lower; belittle, cause to feel small, cause to lose face; *informal* show up, put down, cut down to size, take down (a peg or two), put someone in their place, make someone eat crow. See note at HUMBLE.

**humiliation** noun *the humiliation of having been left at the altar* EMBARRASSMENT, mortification, shame, indignity, ignominy, disgrace, discomfiture, dishonor, degradation, discredit, belittlement, opprobrium; loss of face; *informal* blow to one's pride/ego, slap in the face, kick in the teeth, comedown. ANTONYM honor.

**humility** noun *he accepted the award with sincere humility* MODESTY, humbleness, meekness, diffidence, unassertiveness; lack of pride, lack of vanity; servility, submissiveness. ANTONYM pride.

**humor** noun **1** *the humor of the film* COMEDY, comical aspect, funny side, fun, amusement, funniness, hilarity, jocularity; absurdity, ludicrousness, drollness; satire, irony, farce.

**2** *the stories are spiced up with humor* JOKES, joking, jests, jesting, quips, witticisms, bon mots, funny remarks, puns, sallies, badinage; wit, wittiness, funniness, comedy, drollery; *informal* gags, wisecracks, cracks, kidding, waggishness, one-liners. See note at WIT.

**3** *his good humor was infectious* MOOD, temper, disposition, temperament, nature, state of mind, frame of mind; spirits.

▸ verb *she was always humoring him* INDULGE, accommodate, pander to, cater to, yield to, give way to, give in to, go along with; pamper, spoil, baby, overindulge, mollify, placate, gratify, satisfy.

**humorist** noun *the sports editor was looking for a humorist to write a brief daily column during the course of the Olympic Games* COMIC WRITER, wit, wag; comic, funny man/woman, comedian, comedienne, stand-up comic, joker, jester, clown, wisecracker; *informal* cutup.

**humorous** adjective *a humorous account of our expedition* AMUSING, funny, comic, comical, entertaining, diverting, witty, jocular, jocose, lighthearted, tongue-in-cheek, wry, facetious, laughable, risible; hilarious, uproarious, riotous, zany, farcical, droll; *informal* priceless, side-splitting, gut-busting, rib-tickling, knee-slapping, thigh-slapping. ANTONYM serious.

**hump** noun *the hump made her look old and slouchy* PROTUBERANCE, prominence, lump, bump, knob, protrusion, projection, bulge, swelling, hunch; growth, outgrowth.

**hunch** verb **1** *he hunched his shoulders* ARCH, curve, hump, bend, bow. ANTONYM straighten.

**2** *I **hunched up** as small as I could* CROUCH, huddle, curl; hunker down, bend, stoop, slouch, squat, duck. ANTONYM stretch (out).

▸ noun **1** *the hunch on his back* PROTUBERANCE, hump, lump, bump, knob, protrusion, prominence, bulge, swelling; growth, outgrowth.

**2** *my hunch is that he'll be back* FEELING, feeling in one's bones, guess, suspicion, impression, conjecture, inkling, idea, sense, notion, fancy, intuition, premonition, presentiment; *informal* gut feeling, gut instinct.

**hunger** noun **1** *she was faint with hunger* LACK OF FOOD, hungriness, ravenousness, emptiness; starvation, malnutrition, famine, malnourishment, undernourishment.

**2** *a hunger for news* DESIRE, craving, longing, yearning, hankering, appetite, thirst; want, need; *informal* itch, yen. PHRASE: **hunger after/for** *all actors hunger after such a role* DESIRE, crave, covet; long for, yearn for, pine for, ache for, hanker after, thirst for, lust for; want, need; *informal* have a yen for, itch for, be dying for.

**hungry** adjective **1** *I was really hungry* RAVENOUS, empty, in need of food, hollow, faint from/with hunger; starving, starved, famished; malnourished, undernourished, underfed;

*informal* peckish, able to eat a horse; *archaic* esurient. ANTONYM full.

**2** *they are hungry for success* EAGER, keen, avid, longing, yearning, aching, pining, greedy, covetous; craving, hankering; *informal* itching, dying, hot. ANTONYM indifferent.

**hunk** noun **1** *a hunk of bread* CHUNK, piece, wedge, block, slab, lump, square; gobbet.

**2** *informal he's such a hunk* GOOD-LOOKING MAN, heartthrob, macho man; *informal* babe, stud, studmuffin, dreamboat, (male) specimen, looker, beefcake, chick magnet, babe magnet, he-man, hottie.

**hunt** verb **1** *they hunted deer* CHASE, stalk, pursue, course, run down; track, trail, follow, hound, shadow; *informal* tail.

**2** *police are **hunting for** her* SEARCH FOR, look for, look high and low for, scour the area for, sweep the area for, comb the area for; seek, try to find; scout around, rummage around/about, root around/about, fish around/about.

▸ noun **1** *the thrill of the hunt* CHASE, pursuit.

**2** *police have stepped up their hunt* SEARCH, look, quest, manhunt.

**hurdle** noun **1** *his leg hit a hurdle* FENCE, jump, barrier, barricade, bar, railing, rail.

**2** *the final hurdle to overcome* OBSTACLE, difficulty, problem, barrier, bar, snag, stumbling block, impediment, obstruction, complication, hindrance, hitch; *informal* headache, hiccup, glitch, fly in the ointment, wrench in the works.

**hurl** verb **1** *he hurled an eraser at her head* THROW, toss, fling, pitch, cast, lob, bowl, launch, catapult; project, propel, let fly, fire; *informal* chuck, heave, sling, peg; *dated* shy.

**2** *informal she felt like she was going to hurl.* See VOMIT.

**hurricane** noun. See STORM noun sense 1.

**hurried** adjective **1** *a hurried greeting* QUICK, fast, swift, rapid, speedy, brisk, hasty, abrupt; cursory, perfunctory, brief, short, fleeting, flying, passing, superficial, slapdash. ANTONYMS slow, leisurely.

**2** *a hurried decision* HASTY, rushed, speedy, quick, expeditious; impetuous, impulsive, precipitate, precipitous, rash, incautious, imprudent, spur-of-the-moment. ANTONYM considered.

**hurry** verb **1** *hurry or you'll be late* BE QUICK, hurry up, hurry it up, hasten, speed up, speed it up, press on, push on; run, dash, rush, race, fly; scurry, scramble, scuttle, sprint; *informal* get a move on, move it, step on it, get cracking, get moving, shake a leg, hightail it, chop-chop, tear, zip, zoom, hotfoot it, leg it, get the lead out; *dated* make haste; *archaic* hie. ANTONYMS dawdle, move slowly.

**2** *she hurried him out* HUSTLE, hasten, push, urge, drive, spur, goad, prod.

▸ noun *in all the hurry, we forgot* RUSH, haste, flurry, hustle and bustle, confusion, commotion, hubbub, turmoil; race, scramble, scurry.

**hurt** verb **1** *my back hurts* BE PAINFUL, be sore, be tender, cause pain, cause discomfort; ache, smart, sting, burn, throb; *informal* be killing (one).

**2** *Dad hurt his leg* INJURE, wound, damage, abuse, disable, incapacitate, maim, mutilate, wrench; bruise, cut, gash, graze, scrape, scratch, lacerate. ANTONYM heal.

**3** *his words hurt her* DISTRESS, pain, wound, sting, upset, sadden, devastate, grieve, mortify; cut to the quick. ANTONYMS please, comfort.

**4** *high interest rates are hurting the economy* HARM, damage, be detrimental to, weaken, blight, impede, jeopardize, undermine, ruin, wreck, sabotage, cripple. ANTONYMS improve, benefit.

▸ noun *she apologized for the hurt she had caused* DISTRESS, pain, suffering, injury, grief, misery, anguish, agony, trauma, woe, upset, sadness, sorrow; harm, damage, trouble. ANTONYM joy.

▸ adjective **1** *my hurt hand* INJURED, wounded, bruised, grazed, cut, gashed, battered, sore, painful, aching, smarting, throbbing. ANTONYM healed.

**2** *Anne's hurt expression* PAINED, injured, distressed, anguished, upset, sad, mortified, offended; *informal* miffed, peeved, sore. ANTONYM pleased.

**hurtful** adjective *the effects of hurtful remarks may last a lifetime* UPSETTING, distressing, wounding, painful, injurious; unkind, cruel, nasty, mean, malicious, spiteful, vindictive; cutting, barbed, poisonous; *informal* catty, bitchy.

**husband** noun *Chris's husband is a South American businessman* SPOUSE, partner, life partner, mate, consort, man, helpmate, helpmeet; groom, bridegroom; *informal* hubby, old man, one's better half, other half, significant other.

**husbandry** noun **1** *farmers have new methods of husbandry* FARM MANAGEMENT, land management, farming, agriculture, agronomy; cultivation; animal husbandry, ranching.

**2** *the careful husbandry of their resources* CONSERVATION, management; economy, thrift, thriftiness, frugality.

**hush** verb *will somebody please hush those kids in the back row?* SILENCE, quiet, quiet down, shush; soothe, calm, pacify; gag, muzzle, muffle, mute; *informal* shut up.

▸ exclamation *someone's coming, everybody hush!* BE QUIET, keep quiet, quiet, quiet down, be silent, stop talking, hold your tongue; *informal* shut up, shh, hush up, shut your mouth, shut your face, shut your trap, button your lip, pipe down, put a sock in it, give it a rest, save it, not another word.

▸ noun *a hush descended* SILENCE, quiet, quietness; stillness, peace, peacefulness, calm, lull, tranquility. ANTONYM noise.

PHRASE: **hush up** *management took steps to hush up the dangers* KEEP SECRET, conceal, hide, suppress, cover up, keep quiet about; obscure, veil, sweep under the carpet; *informal* sit on, keep under one's hat.

**hush-hush** adjective *informal*. See SECRET adjective sense 1.

**husk** noun *the husk of the coconut* SHELL, hull, pod, case, covering, integument, shuck; *Botany* pericarp, legume.

**husky** adjective **1** *a husky voice* THROATY, gruff, gravelly, hoarse, croaky, rough, guttural, harsh, rasping, raspy; deep. ANTONYMS shrill, soft.

**2** *Paddy was a husky guy* STRONG, muscular, muscly, muscle-bound, big, brawny, hefty, burly, hulking, strapping, thickset, solid, powerful, heavy, robust, sturdy, stalwart, blocky, Herculean, well-built; *informal* beefy, hunky; *literary* thewy. ANTONYM puny.

**hussy** noun *in this farcical version, Juliet is portrayed as a shameless hussy* MINX, coquette, tease, seductress, Lolita, Jezebel; slut, harlot, loose woman; *informal* floozy, tart, vamp, tramp; *dated* trollop; *archaic* jade, strumpet.

**hustle** verb **1** *I was hustled away* MANHANDLE, push, shove, thrust, frogmarch, whisk, bundle.

**2** *we'll have to hustle to catch the bus* rush, hurry, be quick, hasten; speed up, press on; *informal* get a move on, step on it, get moving, get cracking, shake a leg.

**3** *if you want it, you'll have to hustle for it* WORK, work hard, strive, endeavor, apply oneself, exert oneself; *informal* pull out all the stops.

**4** *informal don't be hustled into joining some cause you don't believe in* COERCE, force, compel, pressure, pressurize, badger, pester, hound, harass, nag, harry, urge, goad, prod, spur; browbeat, bulldoze, bludgeon, steamroller, strong-arm; *informal* railroad, fast-talk. PHRASE: **hustle and bustle** *I need the hustle and bustle of the city* ACTIVITY, bustle, tumult, hubbub, action, liveliness, animation, excitement, agitation, commotion, flurry, whirl; *informal* ballyhoo, hoo-ha, hullabaloo.

**hut** noun *we spent two nights in a rustic little hut near the village* SHACK, chantey, cabin, log cabin, shelter, shed, lean-to, hovel; hovel; cabana.

**hybrid** noun *a hybrid between a brown and an albino mouse* CROSS, cross-breed, mixed breed, half-breed, half-blood; mixture, blend, amalgamation, combination, composite, compound, fusion.

▸ adjective *a hybrid organization* COMPOSITE, cross-bred, interbred, mongrel; heterogeneous, mixed, blended, compound, amalgamated, hyphenated.

**hygiene** noun *they teach preschoolers the fundamentals of personal hygiene* CLEANLINESS, sanitation, sterility, purity, disinfection; public health, environmental health.

**hygienic** adjective *keeping the kitchen hygienic* SANITARY, clean, germ-free, disinfected, sterilized, sterile, antiseptic, aseptic, unpolluted, uncontaminated, salubrious, healthy, wholesome, purified; *informal* squeaky clean. See note at SANITARY. ANTONYM unsanitary.

**hymn** noun *singing the old familiar hymns* RELIGIOUS SONG, song of praise, anthem, canticle, chorale, psalm, paean, carol; spiritual.

**hype** *informal* noun *her work relies on hype and headlines* PUBLICITY, advertising, promotion, marketing, exposure; *informal* ballyhoo, promo.

▸ verb *a stunt to hype a new product* PUBLICIZE, advertise, promote, push, boost, merchandise, build up; *informal* plug.

**hyperbole** noun *the media hyperbole that accompanied their championship series* EXAGGERATION, overstatement, magnification, embroidery, embellishment, excess, overkill, rhetoric; *informal* purple prose, puffery. ANTONYM understatement.

**hypnotic** adjective *hypnotic music* MESMERIZING, mesmeric, spellbinding, entrancing, bewitching, irresistible, magnetic, compelling, enthralling, captivating, charming; soporific, sleep-inducing, sedative, numbing; *Medicine* stupefacient.

**hypnotize** verb **1** *he had been hypnotized as a stunt* MESMERIZE, put into a trance.

**2** *they were hypnotized by the dancers* ENTRANCE, mesmerize, spellbind, enthrall, transfix, captivate, bewitch, charm, enrapture, grip, rivet, absorb, fascinate, magnetize.

**hypocrisy** noun *must politics be the perennial benchmark of hypocrisy?* DISSIMULATION, false virtue, cant, posturing, affectation, speciousness, empty talk, insincerity, falseness, deceit, dishonesty, mendacity, pretense, duplicity; sanctimoniousness, sanctimony, pietism, piousness; *informal* phoniness, fraud. ANTONYM sincerity.

**hypocrite** noun *I've been made to feel inadequate my whole life by someone who turns out to be a total hypocrite* PRETENDER, dissembler, deceiver, liar, pietist, sanctimonious person, plaster saint; *informal* phony, fraud, sham, fake.

**hypothesis** noun *his 'steady state' hypothesis of the origin of the universe* THEORY, theorem, thesis, conjecture, supposition, postulation, postulate, proposition, premise, assumption; notion, concept, idea, possibility.

**hypothetical** adjective *the scenario I suggested was strictly hypothetical* THEORETICAL, speculative, conjectured, conjectural, notional, suppositional, supposed, putative, assumed; academic. ANTONYM actual.

**hysteria** noun *his fictional account of an alien invasion caused not-so-fictional hysteria among the radio audience* FRENZY, feverishness, hysterics, fit of madness, derangement, mania, delirium; panic, alarm, distress. ANTONYM calm.

**hysterical** adjective **1** *Janet became hysterical* OVERWROUGHT, overemotional, out of control, frenzied, frantic, wild, feverish, crazed; beside oneself, driven to distraction, distraught, agitated, berserk, manic, delirious, unhinged, deranged, out of one's mind, raving; *informal* in a state.

**2** *informal her attempts to dance were hysterical* HILARIOUS, uproarious, very funny, very amusing, comical, farcical; *informal* hysterically funny, priceless, side-splitting, rib-tickling, gut-busting, knee-slapping, thigh-slapping, a scream, a hoot, a barrel of laughs; *dated* killing.

**ice** noun **1** *a roof covered with ice* FROZEN WATER, icicles; black ice, frost, rime, glaze.

**2** *the ice in her voice* COLDNESS, coolness, frost, frostiness, iciness; hostility, unfriendliness; stiffness, aloofness. ANTONYMS warmth, friendliness.

▸ verb **1** *the lake has* ***iced over*** FREEZE, FREEZE OVER, turn into ice, harden, solidify; *archaic* glaciate. ANTONYM thaw.

**2** *she had iced the cake* FROST, cover with icing, glaze.

PHRASES: **on ice** *informal.* See PENDING adjective sense 1.

**on thin ice** *we're standing on thin ice by testing Russia's patience* IN A RISKY SITUATION, at risk, in peril, imperiled, living dangerously, living on the edge.

**icing** noun *a cake with pink icing* GLAZE, frosting, topping, fondant, piping.

**icon** noun **1** *an icon of the Blessed Virgin* IMAGE, idol, portrait, picture, representation, likeness, symbol, sign; figure, statue.

**2** *he became a teen icon* IDOL, paragon, hero, heroine; celebrity, superstar, star; favorite, darling.

**icy** adjective **1** *icy roads* FROZEN, frozen over, iced over, frosty, frosted, ice-bound, ice-covered, iced up; slippery; *literary* rimy.

**2** *an icy wind* FREEZING, cold, chill, chilly, chilling, nippy, frigid, frosty, biting, cutting, bitter, raw, arctic, wintry, glacial, Siberian, hypothermic, polar, gelid. ANTONYMS hot, warm.

**3** *an icy voice* UNFRIENDLY, hostile, forbidding, unwelcoming, inhospitable; cold, cool, chilly, frigid, frosty, glacial, gelid; haughty, stern, hard. ANTONYM friendly.

**idea** noun **1** *the idea of death scares her* CONCEPT, notion, conception, thought; image, visualization; hypothesis, postulation.

**2** *our idea is to open a new shop* PLAN, scheme, design, proposal, proposition, suggestion, brainchild, vision; aim, intention, purpose, objective, object, goal, target.

**3** *Liz had other ideas on the subject* THOUGHT, theory, view, opinion, feeling, belief, attitude, conclusion; *informal* take.

**4** *I had an idea that it might happen* SENSE, feeling, suspicion, inkling, hunch, clue, theory, notion, impression; *dated* fancy.

**5** *I get the idea* MEANING, significance, sense, import, essence, gist, drift; point, aim, intention, purport, implication; design, motive.

**6** *an idea of the cost* ESTIMATE, estimation, approximation, guess, conjecture, rough calculation; *informal* guesstimate.

THE RIGHT WORD **idea, concept, conception, impression, notion, thought**

If you have an **idea** it might refer to something perceived through the senses (*I had no idea it was so cold out*), to something visualized (*the idea of a joyous family outing*), or to something that is the product of the imagination (*a great idea for raising money*). *Idea* is a comprehensive word that applies to almost any aspect of mental activity. A **thought**, on the other hand, is an idea that is the result of meditation, reasoning, or some other intellectual activity (*she hadn't given much thought to the possibility of losing*). A **notion** is a vague or capricious idea, often without any sound basis (*he had a notion that he could get there by hitchhiking*). A widely held idea of what something is or should be is a **concept** (*the concept of loyalty was beyond him*), while a **conception** is a concept that is held by an individual or small group and that is often colored by imagination and feeling (*her conception of marriage as a romantic ideal*). An idea that is triggered by something external is an **impression**, a word that suggests a half-formed mental picture or superficial view (*he made a good impression; she had the impression that everything would be taken care of*).

**ideal** adjective **1** *ideal flying weather* PERFECT, best possible, consummate, supreme, excellent, flawless, faultless, exemplary, classic, model, ultimate, quintessential. ANTONYM bad.

**2** *an ideal concept* ABSTRACT, theoretical, conceptual, notional; hypothetical, speculative, conjectural, suppositional. ANTONYM concrete.

**3** *an ideal world* UNATTAINABLE, unachievable, impracticable, chimerical; unreal, fictitious, hypothetical, theoretical, ivory-towered, imaginary, illusory, idealized, idyllic, visionary, Utopian, fairy-tale. ANTONYMS attainable, real.

▸ noun **1** *no woman could be the ideal he imagined for himself* PERFECTION, paragon, epitome, shining example, ne plus ultra, nonpareil, dream.

**2** *an ideal to aim at* MODEL, pattern, exemplar, standard, example, paradigm, archetype, prototype; yardstick, lodestar. See note at MODEL.

**3** *a liberal ideal* PRINCIPLE, standard, value, belief, conviction, persuasion; **(ideals)** morals, morality, ethics, ideology, creed.

**idealist** noun *the title character is a liberal idealist set up to lose a senatorial election* UTOPIAN, visionary, wishful thinker, pipe-dreamer, fantasist, romantic, dreamer, daydreamer, stargazer; Walter Mitty, Don Quixote; *rare* fantast.

**idealistic** adjective *some say I'm drawing a wildly idealistic portrait of what the Church can become* UTOPIAN, visionary, romantic, quixotic, dreamy, unrealistic, impractical, starry-eyed; fanciful; *informal* with one's head in the clouds; *chiefly Brit. informal* airy-fairy.

**ideally** adverb *ideally, it would be a good thing to provide rehabilitation* IN A PERFECT WORLD; preferably, if possible, by choice, by preference, as a matter of choice, rather; all things being equal, theoretically, hypothetically, in theory, in principle, on paper.

**identical** adjective **1** *wearing identical badges* INDISTINGUISHABLE, (exactly) the same, uniform, twin, duplicate, interchangeable, synonymous, undifferentiated, homogeneous, of a piece, cut from the same cloth; alike, like, matching, like (two) peas in a pod; similar. ANTONYMS different, unlike.

**2** *I used the identical technique* SAME, very same, selfsame, very, one and the same; aforementioned, aforesaid, aforenamed, above, above-stated; foregoing, preceding. ANTONYM different.

**identification** noun **1** *the identification of the suspect* RECOGNITION, singling out, pinpointing, naming; discerning, distinguishing; *informal* fingering.

**2** *early identification of problems* DETERMINATION, establishment, ascertainment, discovery, diagnosis, divination; verification, confirmation.

**3** *may I see your identification?* ID, (identity/identification) papers, bona fides, documents, credentials; ID card, identity card, pass, badge, warrant, license, permit, passport.

**4** *the identification of Nonconformity with Victorian values* ASSOCIATION, link, linkage, connection, tie, interconnection, interrelation, interdependence.

**5** *his identification with the music is evident* EMPATHY, rapport, relationship, fellow feeling, sympathetic cord.

**identify** verb **1** *the driver was identified by two witnesses* RECOGNIZE, single out, pick out, spot, point out, pinpoint, put one's finger on, put a name to, name, know; discern, distinguish; remember, recall, recollect; *informal* finger; *formal* espy.

**2** *I identified four problem areas* DETERMINE, establish, ascertain, make out, diagnose, discern, distinguish; verify, confirm; *informal* figure out, get a fix on, peg.

**3** *they identify professional sports with wealth and glamour* ASSOCIATE, link, connect, relate, bracket, couple; mention in the same breath as, put side by side with.

**4** *Peter* ***identifies with*** *the hero* EMPATHIZE WITH, be in tune with, have a rapport with, feel at one with, sympathize with; be on the same wavelength as, speak the same language as; understand, relate to, feel for.

**identity** noun **1** *the identity of the owner* NAME, ID; specification.

**2** *she was afraid of losing her identity* INDIVIDUALITY, self, selfhood; personality, character, originality, distinctiveness, differentness, singularity, uniqueness.

**3** *a case of mistaken identity* IDENTIFICATION, recognition, naming, singling out.

**ideology** noun *the party has to jettison outdated ideology and give up its stranglehold on power* BELIEFS, ideas, ideals, principles, ethics, morals; doctrine, creed, credo, faith, teaching, theory, philosophy; tenets, canon(s); conviction(s), persuasion; *informal* ism.

**idiocy** noun *a seventeenth-century antidote to idiocy was to rub the forehead with beaver testicles* STUPIDITY, folly, foolishness, foolhardiness, ignorance; madness, insanity, lunacy, nonsense; silliness, brainlessness, thoughtlessness, senselessness, irresponsibility, imprudence, ineptitude, inanity, absurdity, ludicrousness, fatuousness; *informal* craziness. ANTONYM sense.

**idiom** noun *these musicians all work in the gospel idiom* LANGUAGE, mode of expression, turn of phrase, style, speech, locution, diction, usage, phraseology, phrasing, phrase, vocabulary, terminology, parlance, jargon, argot, cant, patter, tongue, vernacular; *informal* lingo.

**idiosyncrasy** noun *traveling with her own fruitcake is one of the queen's idiosyncrasies | Fenway's Green Monster is perhaps the most recognizable ballpark idiosyncrasy* PECULIARITY, oddity, eccentricity, mannerism, trait, singularity, quirk, tic, whim, vagary, caprice, kink; fetish, foible, crotchet, habit, characteristic; individuality; unorthodoxy, unconventionality.

**idiot** noun *informal that idiot was driving way too fast* FOOL, ass, halfwit, dunce, dolt, ignoramus, cretin, moron, imbecile, simpleton; *informal* dope, ninny, nincompoop, chump, dimwit, dumbo, dummy, dum-dum, loon, dork, sap, jackass, blockhead, jughead, bonehead, knucklehead, fathead, numbskull, numbnuts, dumb-ass, doofus, clod, dunderhead, ditz, lummox, dipstick, thickhead, meathead, meatball, woodenhead, airhead, pinhead, lamebrain, peabrain, birdbrain, jerk, nerd, donkey, nitwit, twit, boob, twerp, schmuck, bozo, turkey, chowderhead, dingbat. ANTONYM genius.

**idiotic** adjective *her latest comedy is fanciful without being idiotic* STUPID, silly, foolish, witless, brainless, mindless, thoughtless, unintelligent; imprudent, unwise, ill-advised, ill-considered, half-baked, foolhardy; absurd, senseless, pointless, nonsensical, inane, fatuous, ridiculous; *informal* dumb, dim, dimwitted, halfwitted, dopey, hare-brained, pea-brained, wooden-headed, thickheaded, dumb-ass.

**idle** adjective **1** *an idle person* LAZY, indolent, slothful, work-shy, shiftless, inactive, sluggish, lethargic, listless; slack, lax, lackadaisical, good-for-nothing; *rare* otiose. ANTONYM industrious.

**2** *being idle won't pay the bills* UNEMPLOYED, jobless, out-of-work, redundant, between jobs, workless, unwaged, unoccupied. ANTONYM employed.

**3** *they left the machine idle* INACTIVE, unused, unoccupied, unemployed, disused; not in use, out of use, out of action, inoperative, nonfunctioning, out of service. ANTONYM working.

**4** *their idle hours* UNOCCUPIED, spare, empty, vacant, unfilled, available. ANTONYMS busy, full.

**5** *idle remarks* FRIVOLOUS, trivial, trifling, vain, minor, petty, lightweight, shallow, superficial, insignificant, unimportant, worthless, paltry, niggling, peripheral, inane, fatuous; unnecessary, time-wasting. ANTONYMS meaningful, serious.

**6** *idle threats* EMPTY, meaningless, pointless, worthless, vain, hollow, insubstantial, futile, ineffective, ineffectual; groundless, baseless. ANTONYM serious.

▸ verb **1** *Lily idled on the window seat* DO NOTHING, be inactive, vegetate, take it easy, mark time, twiddle one's thumbs, kill time, languish, laze, lounge, loll, loaf, loiter; *informal* hang around, veg out, bum around, lollygag. See note at LOITER.

**2** *he let the engine idle* RUN IN NEUTRAL, run.

**idol** noun **1** *idols deemed un-Islamic were summarily destroyed* ICON, representation of a god, image, effigy, statue, figure, figurine, fetish, totem; graven image, false god, golden calf.

**2** *a teen idol* HERO, HEROINE, star, superstar, icon, celebrity; favorite, darling, pet, beloved; *informal* pinup, heartthrob, dreamboat, golden boy/girl.

**idolatry** noun *the prophets railed against idolatry* IDOLIZATION, fetishization, fetishism, idol worship, adulation, adoration, reverence, veneration, glorification, lionization, hero-worshiping.

**idolize** verb *the kids idolize their fighter-pilot father* HERO-WORSHIP, worship, revere, venerate, deify, lionize; stand in awe of, reverence, look up to, admire, adore, exalt; *informal* put on a pedestal. See note at REVERE.

**if** conjunction **1** *if the rain holds off, we can walk* ON (THE) CONDITION THAT, provided (that), providing (that), presuming (that), supposing (that), assuming (that), as long as, given that, in the event that.

**2** *if I miss curfew, she lays down the law* WHENEVER, every time.

**3** *a useful, if unintended innovation* ALTHOUGH, albeit, but, yet, while; even though, despite being; *chiefly Brit.* whilst.

▸ noun *there is one if in all this* UNCERTAINTY, doubt; condition, stipulation, provision, proviso, constraint, precondition, requirement, specification, restriction.

**iffy** adjective *informal* **1** *an iffy neighborhood* DUBIOUS, doubtful, questionable, shaky; substandard, second-rate, inferior; sketchy.

**2** *the date was a bit iffy* UNCERTAIN, undecided, unsettled, unsure, unresolved, in doubt, dubious, ambivalent; *informal* up in the air, borderline.

**ignite** verb **1** *he escaped moments before the gas ignited* CATCH FIRE, burst into flames, combust; be set off, explode. ANTONYM go out.

**2** *his cigarette ignited the blanket* LIGHT, set fire to, set on fire, set alight, kindle, spark, touch off; *informal* set/put a match to. ANTONYM extinguish.

**3** *the campaign failed to ignite voter interest* AROUSE, kindle, trigger, spark, instigate, excite, provoke, stimulate, animate, stir up, whip up, rally, jump-start, incite, fuel. ANTONYM dampen.

**ignominious** adjective *Wahid made an ignominious exit after 21 months in power* HUMILIATING, undignified, embarrassing, mortifying; ignoble, inglorious; disgraceful, shameful, dishonorable, discreditable. ANTONYM glorious.

**ignominy** noun *the Braves face the ignominy of losing three straight games to the league's worst team* SHAME, humiliation, embarrassment, mortification; disgrace, dishonor, discredit, degradation, scandal, infamy, indignity, ignobility, loss of face. ANTONYM honor.

**ignorance** noun **1** *our* ***ignorance of*** *Islam* INCOMPREHENSION OF, unawareness of, unconsciousness of, unfamiliarity with, inexperience with, lack of knowledge about, lack of information about; *informal* cluelessness about. ANTONYMS understanding, familiarity.

**2** *both ignorance and poverty contribute to the growing problem of forced child labor* LACK OF KNOWLEDGE, lack of education, unenlightenment, illiteracy; lack of intelligence, stupidity, foolishness, idiocy. ANTONYMS knowledge, education.

**ignorant** adjective **1** *the plight of these ignorant children should be an international concern* UNEDUCATED, unknowledgeable, untaught, unschooled, untutored, untrained, illiterate, unlettered, unlearned, unread, uninformed, unenlightened, benighted; inexperienced, unworldly, unsophisticated. ANTONYM educated.

**2** *they were* ***ignorant of*** *working-class life* WITHOUT KNOWLEDGE OF, unaware of, unconscious of, oblivious to, incognizant of, unfamiliar with, unacquainted with, uninformed about, ill-informed about, unenlightened about, unconversant with, inexperienced in/with, naive about, green about; *informal* in the dark about, clueless about. ANTONYM knowledgeable.

THE RIGHT WORD **ignorant, illiterate, uneducated, uninformed, unlearned, unlettered, untutored**

Someone who knows nothing about growing things might be called **ignorant** by a farmer who never went to high school but has spent his life in the fields. Although all of these adjectives refer to a lack of knowledge, *ignorant* refers to a lack of knowledge in general (*a foolish, ignorant person*) or to a lack of knowledge of some particular subject (*ignorant of the fine points of financial management*). A professor of art history might refer to someone who doesn't know how to look at a painting as **uneducated** or **untutored**, both of which refer to a lack of formal education in schools (*she was very bright but basically uneducated, and completely untutored in the fine arts*). Someone who cannot read or write is **illiterate**, a term that may also denote a failure to display civility or cultivated behavior (*the professor routinely referred to his students as illiterate louts*). Someone who is **unlettered** lacks a knowledge of fine literature (*a scientist who was highly trained but unlettered*); it also implies being able to read and write, but with no skill in either of these areas. **Unlearned** is similar to *ignorant* in that it refers to a lack of learning in general or in a specific subject (*an unlearned man who managed to become a millionaire*), but it does not carry the same negative connotations. **Uninformed** refers to a lack of definite information or data. For example, one can be highly intelligent and well educated but still *uninformed* about the latest developments in earthquake prediction.

---

**ignore** verb **1** *he ignored the customers* DISREGARD, take no notice of, pay no attention to, pay no heed to; turn a blind eye to, turn a deaf ear to, tune out. See note at NEGLECT. ANTONYM pay attention to.

**2** *he was ignored by the journalists* SNUB, slight, spurn, shun, disdain, look right through, pass over, look past; *informal* give someone the brush-off, give someone the cold shoulder. ANTONYM acknowledge.

**3** *doctors ignored her husband's instructions* SET ASIDE, pay no attention to, take no account of; break, contravene, fail to comply with, fail to observe, disregard, disobey, breach, defy, flout; *informal* pooh-pooh. ANTONYM obey.

**ill** adjective **1** *she was feeling rather ill* UNWELL, sick, not (very) well, ailing, poorly, sickly, peaked, indisposed, infirm; out of sorts, not oneself, bad, off, in a bad way, far gone; bedridden, valetudinarian; queasy, nauseous, nauseated; *informal* under the weather, laid up, rotten, crummy, lousy, pukey, dizzy, woozy, green around the gills, like death warmed over. ANTONYMS well, healthy.

**2** *the ill effects of smoking* HARMFUL, damaging, detrimental, deleterious, adverse, injurious, hurtful, destructive, pernicious, dangerous; unhealthy, unwholesome, poisonous, noxious; *literary* malefic, maleficent. ANTONYMS good, beneficial.

**3** *ill feelings had divided them for years* HOSTILE, antagonistic, acrimonious, inimical, antipathetic; unfriendly, unsympathetic, unkind; resentful, spiteful, malicious, vindictive, malevolent, bitter. ANTONYMS friendly, warm.

**4** *an ill omen* UNLUCKY, adverse, unfavorable, unfortunate, unpropitious, inauspicious, unpromising, infelicitous, ominous, sinister; *literary* direful. ANTONYM auspicious.

**5** *ill manners* RUDE, discourteous, impolite, improper; impertinent, insolent, impudent, uncivil, disrespectful; *informal* ignorant. ANTONYMS good, polite.

**6** *the ill management of the front office* BAD, poor, incompetent, unsatisfactory, inadequate, inexpert, deficient. ANTONYMS good, competent.

▸ noun **1** **(ills)** *the ills of society* PROBLEMS, troubles, evils, difficulties, misfortunes, trials, tribulations; worries, anxieties, concerns; *informal* headaches, hassles; *archaic* travails.

**2** *he wished them no ill* HARM, hurt, injury, damage, pain, trouble, misfortune, suffering, distress.

**3** **(ills)** *the body's ills* ILLNESSES, ailments, disorders, complaints, afflictions, sicknesses, diseases, maladies, infirmities.

▸ adverb **1** *such behavior ill becomes a chief executive* POORLY, badly, imperfectly. ANTONYM well.

**2** *the look on her face boded ill for her opponents* UNFAVORABLY, adversely, badly, inauspiciously. ANTONYMS well, auspiciously.

**3** *he can ill afford the loss of income* BARELY, scarcely, hardly, only just, (only) with difficulty, just possibly. ANTONYM easily.

**4** *we are ill prepared for another flood* INADEQUATELY, unsatisfactorily, insufficiently, imperfectly, poorly, badly. ANTONYMS well, satisfactorily.

PHRASES: **ill at ease** *Ritchie was cautioned not to appear ill at ease in the courtroom* AWKWARD, uneasy, uncomfortable, embarrassed, self-conscious, out of place, inhibited, gauche; restless, restive, fidgety, discomfited, worried, anxious, on edge, edgy, nervous, tense, high-strung; *informal* twitchy, jittery, discombobulated, antsy.
**speak ill of** *we never heard him once speak ill of his ex-wife* DENIGRATE, disparage, criticize, be critical of, speak badly of, be malicious about, blacken the name of, run down, insult, abuse, attack, revile, malign, vilify, slur; *informal* badmouth, dis, bitch about, slag; *formal* derogate; *rare* asperse.

**ill-advised** adjective *an ill-advised business venture* UNWISE, injudicious, misguided, imprudent, ill-considered, ill-judged, impolitic; foolhardy, foolish, hare-brained, rash, reckless, irresponsible; *informal* crazy, idiotic, crackpot, madcap. ANTONYMS wise, judicious.

**ill-bred** adjective. See ILL-MANNERED.

**ill-defined** adjective *an ill-defined property line* | *the ill-defined messages in his art* VAGUE, indistinct, unclear, imprecise, nebulous, shadowy, obscure; blurred, fuzzy, hazy, woolly.

**ill-disposed** adjective *the court may be **ill-disposed to** foreign companies* HOSTILE TO, antagonistic to, unfriendly to, unsympathetic to, antipathetic to, inimical to, unfavorable to, adverse to, averse to, at odds with; *informal* anti, down on. ANTONYM friendly.

**illegal** adjective *illegal campaign contributions* UNLAWFUL, illicit, illegitimate, criminal, felonious; unlicensed, unauthorized, unsanctioned; outlawed, banned, forbidden, prohibited, proscribed, taboo; contraband, black-market, bootleg; *Law* malfeasant; *informal* crooked, shady, sketchy. ANTONYMS lawful, legitimate.

**illegible** adjective *nearly a billion prescriptions are rechecked each year because of physicians' illegible handwriting* UNREADABLE, indecipherable, unintelligible, incomprehensible, hieroglyphic; scrawled, scribbled, crabbed, cramped.

**illegitimate** adjective **1** *illegitimate share trading* ILLEGAL, unlawful, illicit, criminal, felonious; unlicensed, unauthorized, unsanctioned; prohibited, outlawed, banned, forbidden, proscribed; fraudulent, corrupt, dishonest; *Law* malfeasant; *informal* crooked, shady. ANTONYMS legal, lawful.

**2** *dated her illegitimate children* BORN OUT OF WEDLOCK, bastard, unfathered; *archaic* natural, misbegotten; **(illegitimate child)** love child. ANTONYM legitimate.

**ill-fated** adjective *an ill-fated rebellion* DOOMED, blighted, damned, cursed, accursed, ill-starred, unlucky, hapless, jinxed; disastrous, unfortunate; *literary* star-crossed.

**ill-favored** adjective *he was particularly ill-favored after a night of drunken debauchery* UNATTRACTIVE, plain, ugly, homely, unprepossessing, displeasing; *informal* not much to look at. ANTONYM attractive.

**illicit** adjective **1** *illicit drugs* ILLEGAL, unlawful, illegitimate, criminal, felonious; outlawed, banned, forbidden, prohibited, proscribed; unlicensed, unauthorized, unsanctioned; contraband, black-market, bootleg; *Law* malfeasant. ANTONYMS lawful, legal.

**2** *an illicit love affair* TABOO, forbidden, impermissible, unacceptable, adulterous; secret, clandestine, furtive. ANTONYM aboveboard.

**illiteracy** noun **1** *for these villagers, poverty and illiteracy go hand in hand* INABILITY TO READ OR WRITE.

**2** *technological illiteracy* IGNORANCE, unawareness, inexperience, unenlightenment, lack of knowledge, lack of education; *informal* cluelessness; *literary* nescience.

**illiterate** adjective **1** *an illiterate peasant* UNABLE TO READ OR WRITE, unlettered.

**2** *too many voters are politically illiterate* IGNORANT, unknowledgeable, unenlightened, uneducated, unschooled, untaught, untutored, untrained, uninstructed, uninformed, unread, unlearned; *informal* clueless; *literary* nescient. See note at IGNORANT.

**ill-judged** adjective. See ILL-ADVISED.

**ill-mannered** adjective *we never encountered the ill-mannered locals you had warned us about* BAD-MANNERED, discourteous, rude, impolite, uncivil, abusive, disagreeable; insolent, impertinent, impudent, cheeky, presumptuous, audacious, disrespectful; badly behaved, ill-behaved, boorish, loutish, oafish, uncouth, uncivilized, unmannered, ill-bred, vulgar, crass; *informal* ignorant. See note at RUDE. ANTONYM polite.

**ill-natured** adjective *Cinderella's ill-natured stepsisters* MEAN, nasty, spiteful, malicious, disagreeable; poisonous, venomous, bitter; ill-tempered, bad-tempered, moody, irritable, irascible, surly, sullen, peevish, petulant, fractious, cross, crabbed, crabby, tetchy, testy, grouchy, waspish; *informal* bitchy. ANTONYMS good-natured, sweet.

**illness** noun *more than fifty students have been diagnosed with the same illness* SICKNESS, disease, ailment, complaint, disorder, malady, affliction, indisposition; ill health, poor health, infirmity; infection, virus; *informal* bug; *dated* contagion. ANTONYM good health.

**illogical** adjective *it is illogical to assume that there will never be a cure for Parkinson's disease* IRRATIONAL, unreasonable, unsound, unreasoned, unjustifiable, groundless, unfounded; incorrect, erroneous, invalid, spurious, faulty, flawed, fallacious, unscientific; specious, sophistic, casuistic; absurd, preposterous, untenable; *informal* full of holes, off the wall. ANTONYM logical.

**ill-starred** adjective. See ILL-FATED.

**ill-tempered** adjective *retirement didn't suit Uncle Luke, who soon became sullen and ill-tempered* BAD-TEMPERED, short-tempered, quick-tempered, ill-humored, moody; in a (bad) mood, cross, irritable, irascible, tetchy, testy, crotchety, touchy, cantankerous, curmudgeonly, peevish, fractious, waspish, prickly, pettish; grumpy, grouchy, crabbed, crabby, disagreeable, splenetic, dyspeptic, choleric; *informal* snappish, snippy, short-fused, on a short fuse, soreheaded, cranky, ornery, bitchy.

**ill-timed** adjective *our ill-timed vacation landed us in the worst-hit area during the hurricane* UNTIMELY, mistimed, badly timed; premature, hasty; inconvenient, inopportune; in, unsuitable, malapropos; unfavorable, unfortunate. ANTONYMS timely, opportune.

**illuminate** verb **1** *the bundle was illuminated by the torch* LIGHT (UP), lighten, throw light on, brighten, shine on, irradiate; *literary* illumine, illume, enlighten. ANTONYM darken.

**2** *the manuscripts were illuminated* DECORATE, illustrate, embellish, adorn, ornament.

**3** *documents often illuminate people's thought processes* CLARIFY, elucidate, explain, reveal, shed light on, give insight into, demystify; exemplify, illustrate; *informal* spell out. ANTONYMS confuse, conceal.

**illuminating** adjective *the lectures have been interesting as well as illuminating* INFORMATIVE, enlightening, explanatory, instructive, instructional, edifying, helpful, educational, revealing; *informal* tell-all.

**illumination** noun **1** *a floodlight provided illumination* LIGHT, lighting, radiance, gleam, glow, glare; shining, gleaming, glowing; brilliance, luminescence; *literary* illumining, irradiance, lucency, lambency, effulgence, refulgence. ANTONYM darkness.

**2** *the illumination of a manuscript* DECORATION, illustration, embellishment, adornment, ornamentation.

**3** *these books give illumination on the subject* CLARIFICATION, elucidation, explanation, revelation, explication.

**4** *it was an era of great illumination* ENLIGHTENMENT, insight, understanding, awareness; learning, education, edification. ANTONYM ignorance.

**illusion** noun **1** *he had destroyed her illusions* DELUSION, misapprehension, misconception, false impression; fantasy, fancy, dream, chimera; fool's paradise, self-deception.

**2** *the lighting increases the illusion of depth* APPEARANCE, impression, semblance; misperception, false appearance; *rare* simulacrum.

**3** *it's just an illusion* MIRAGE, hallucination, apparition, figment of the imagination, trick of the light, trompe l'oeil; deception, trick, smoke and mirrors.

**4** *Copperfield's amazing illusions* (MAGIC) TRICK, conjuring trick; **(illusions)** magic, conjuring, sleight of hand, legerdemain.

**illustrate** verb **1** *the photographs that illustrate the book* DECORATE, adorn, ornament, accompany, embellish; add pictures/drawings to, provide artwork for.

**2** *this can be illustrated through a brief example* EXPLAIN, explicate, elucidate, clarify, make plain, demonstrate, show, emphasize; *informal* get across.

**3** *his sense of humor was illustrated by his screen saver* EXEMPLIFY, typify, epitomize, show, demonstrate, display, represent, encapsulate.

**illustration** noun **1** *the illustrations in children's books* PICTURE, drawing, sketch, figure, image, plate, print, artwork; visual aid.

**2** *by way of illustration* EXEMPLIFICATION, demonstration, showing; example, typical case, case in point, object lesson, analogy.

**illustrative** adjective *the parables are wonderfully illustrative* EXEMPLIFYING, explanatory, elucidative, explicative, expository, exegetical; demonstrative, descriptive, representative, indicative, emblematic, symbolic, typical; *rare* evincive.

**illustrious** adjective *the book falls short of its illustrious cinematic predecessor* EMINENT, distinguished, acclaimed, notable, noteworthy, prominent, preeminent, foremost, leading, important, influential; renowned, famous, famed, well-known, celebrated, legendary; esteemed, honored, respected, venerable, august, highly regarded, well-thought-of, of distinction; brilliant, glorious, stellar. ANTONYMS lackluster, unknown.

**ill will** noun *the ill will between the two families predates anyone's memory* ANIMOSITY, hostility, enmity, acrimony, animus, hatred, hate, loathing, antipathy; ill feeling, bad feeling, bad blood, antagonism, unfriendliness, dislike; spite, spitefulness, resentment, hard feelings, bitterness, malice, rancor; *informal* grudge, friction. ANTONYM goodwill.

**image** noun **1** *an image of St. Bartholomew* LIKENESS, resemblance; depiction, portrayal, representation; statue, statuette, sculpture, bust, effigy; painting, picture, portrait, drawing, sketch.

**2** *images of the planet Neptune* PICTURE, photograph, snapshot, photo.

**3** *he contemplated his image in the mirror* REFLECTION, mirror image, likeness.

**4** *the image of this country as democratic* CONCEPTION, impression, idea, perception, notion; mental picture, vision; character, reputation; appearance, semblance. See note at EMBLEM.

**5** *biblical images* SIMILE, metaphor, metonymy; figure of speech, trope, turn of phrase; imagery.

**6** *his heartthrob image* PUBLIC PERCEPTION, persona, profile, reputation, stature, standing; face, front, facade, mask, guise.

**7** *I'm the image of my grandfather* DOUBLE, living image, look-alike, clone, copy, twin, duplicate, exact likeness, mirror image, doppelgänger; *informal* spitting image, dead ringer, carbon copy; *archaic* similitude.

**8** *a graven image* IDOL, icon, fetish, totem.

▸ verb *she imaged imposing castles* ENVISAGE, envision, imagine, picture, see in one's mind's eye.

**imaginable** adjective *they did everything imaginable to save the farm* THINKABLE, conceivable, supposable, believable, credible, creditable; possible, plausible, feasible, tenable, within reason, under the sun.

**imaginary** adjective *his imaginary friends* UNREAL, nonexistent, fictional, fictitious, pretend, make-believe, mythical, mythological, fabulous, fanciful, storybook, fantastic; made-up, dreamed-up, invented, concocted, fancied; illusory, illusive, a figment of one's imagination, *archaic* visionary. ANTONYMS real, actual.

**imagination** noun **1** *a vivid imagination* CREATIVE POWER, fancy, vision; *informal* mind's eye.

**2** *you need imagination in dealing with these problems* CREATIVITY, imaginativeness, creativeness; vision, inspiration, inventiveness, invention, resourcefulness, ingenuity; originality, innovation, innovativeness.

**3** *the album captured the public's imagination* INTEREST, fascination, attention, passion, curiosity.

**imaginative** adjective *imaginative writers | an imaginative solution* CREATIVE, visionary, inspired, inventive, resourceful, ingenious; original, innovative, innovatory, unorthodox, unconventional; fanciful, whimsical, fantastic; *informal* offbeat, off the wall, zany. See note at CREATIVE.

**imagine** verb **1** *imagine sitting through five hours of steady air turbulence* VISUALIZE, envisage, envision, picture, see in the mind's eye; dream up, think up/of, conjure up, conceive, conceptualize; *formal* ideate.

**2** *I imagine he was at home* ASSUME, presume, expect, take it, presuppose; suppose, think (it likely), dare say, surmise, believe, be of the view, figure; *informal* guess, reckon; *formal* opine.

**imbecile** noun. See FOOL noun sense 1.

**imbed** verb. See EMBED.

**imbibe** verb *formal* **1** *they'd imbibed too much whiskey* DRINK, consume, quaff, guzzle, gulp (down); *informal* knock back, down, swill, chug.

**2** *he had imbibed liberally* DRINK (ALCOHOL), take strong drink, tipple; *informal* booze, knock a few back, hit the bottle, bend one's elbow.

**3** *imbibing local history* ASSIMILATE, absorb, soak up, take in, drink in, digest, learn, acquire, grasp, pick up, familiarize oneself with.

**imbroglio** noun *the company may not survive another legal imbroglio* COMPLICATED SITUATION, complication, problem, difficulty, predicament, trouble, confusion, quandary, entanglement, muddle, mess, quagmire, morass, sticky situation; *informal* bind, jam, pickle, fix, corner, hole, scrape.

**imbue** verb *the painting has become deeply imbued with the idea of Basque separatism* PERMEATE, saturate, diffuse, suffuse, pervade, bathe, drench, steep; impregnate, inject, inculcate, ingrain, instill, invest, inspire, breathe; fill.

**imitate** verb **1** *other artists have imitated her style* EMULATE, copy, model oneself on, follow, echo, parrot; *informal* rip off, knock off, pirate.

**2** *he imitated Richard Nixon* MIMIC, do an impression of, impersonate, ape; parody, caricature, burlesque, travesty; *informal* take off, send up, make like, mock; *formal* personate.

THE RIGHT WORD **imitate, ape, copy, impersonate, mimic, mock**

A young girl might **imitate** her mother by answering the phone in exactly the same tone of voice, while a teenager who deliberately *imitates* the way her mother talks for the purpose of irritating her would more accurately be said to **mimic** her. *Imitate* implies following something as an example or model (*he imitated the playing style of his music teacher*), while *mimic* suggests imitating someone's mannerisms for fun or ridicule (*they liked to mimic the teacher's southern drawl*). To **copy** is to imitate or reproduce something as closely as possible (*he copied the style of dress and speech used by the other gang members*). When someone assumes another person's appearance or mannerisms, sometimes for the purpose of perpetrating a fraud, he or she is said to **impersonate** (*arrested for impersonating a police officer; a comedian well known for impersonating political figures*). **Ape** and **mock** both imply an unflattering imitation. Someone who mimics in a contemptuous way is said to *ape* (*he entertained everyone in the office by aping the boss's phone conversations with his wife*), while someone who imitates with the intention of belittling or irritating is said to *mock* (*the students openly mocked their teacher's attempt to have a serious discussion about sex*).

**imitation** noun **1** *an imitation of a sailor's hat* COPY, simulation, reproduction, replica; counterfeit, forgery, rip off.

**2** *learning by imitation* EMULATION, copying, echoing, parroting.

**3** *a perfect imitation of Elvis* IMPERSONATION, impression, parody, mockery, caricature, burlesque, travesty, lampoon, pastiche; mimicry, mimicking, imitating, aping; *informal* send-up, takeoff, spoof.

▸ adjective *imitation ivory* ARTIFICIAL, synthetic, simulated, man-made, manufactured, ersatz, substitute; mock, sham, fake, faux, bogus, knockoff, pseudo, phony. ANTONYMS real, genuine.

**imitative** adjective **1** *imitative crime* SIMILAR, like, mimicking; *informal* copycat.

**2** *I found the film empty and imitative* DERIVATIVE, unoriginal, unimaginative, uninspired, uninventive, plagiarized, plagiaristic, slavish; clichéd, hackneyed, stale, trite, banal, rehashed; *informal* cribbed, old hat. ANTONYM original.

**imitator** noun *she has many imitators* COPIER, emulator, follower, mimic, plagiarist, ape, parrot; *informal* copycat.

**immaculate** adjective **1** *an immaculate white shirt* CLEAN, spotless, ultraclean, pristine, unsoiled, unstained, unsullied; shining, shiny, gleaming; neat, tidy, spick-and-span; *informal* squeaky clean, as clean as a whistle. ANTONYM dirty.

**2** *a guitar in immaculate condition* PERFECT, pristine, mint, as good as new; flawless, faultless, unblemished, unspoiled, undamaged; excellent, impeccable; *informal* tip-top, A1. ANTONYMS worn, damaged.

**3** *his immaculate service record* UNBLEMISHED, spotless, impeccable, unsullied, undefiled, untarnished, stainless; pure, virtuous, incorrupt, above reproach; *informal* squeaky clean, as pure as the driven snow. ANTONYMS defiled, reproachable.

**immaterial** adjective **1** *the difference in our ages was immaterial* IRRELEVANT, unimportant, inconsequential, insignificant, of no matter/consequence, of little account, beside the point, neither here nor there. ANTONYMS significant, important.

**2** *the immaterial soul* INTANGIBLE, incorporeal, bodiless, disembodied, impalpable, ethereal, insubstantial, metaphysical; spiritual, unearthly, supernatural. ANTONYMS tangible, physical.

**immature** adjective **1** *an immature Stilton cheese* UNRIPE, not mature, premature, unmellowed; undeveloped, unformed, unfinished, raw, embryonic. ANTONYM ripe.

**2** *an extremely immature girl* CHILDISH, babyish, infantile, juvenile, adolescent, puerile, sophomoric, jejune, callow, green, tender, young, inexperienced, unsophisticated, unworldly, naive; *informal* wet behind the ears. See note at YOUTHFUL. ANTONYMS mature, worldly.

**immeasurable** adjective *the immeasurable riches provided to us by nature* INCALCULABLE, inestimable, innumerable, untold; limitless, boundless, unbounded, unlimited, illimitable, infinite, countless, never-ending, interminable, endless, inexhaustible; vast, immense, extensive, great, abundant; *informal* no end of; *literary* myriad.

**immediate** adjective **1** *the UN called for immediate action* INSTANT, instantaneous, swift, prompt, fast, speedy, rapid, brisk, quick, expeditious; sudden, hurried, hasty, precipitate; *informal* snappy. ANTONYMS delayed, gradual.

**2** *their immediate concerns* CURRENT, present, existing, actual; urgent, pressing, exigent. ANTONYMS past, future.

**3** *the immediate past* RECENT, not long past, just gone, latest. ANTONYM remote.

**4** *our immediate neighbors* NEAREST, near, close, closest, next-door; adjacent, adjoining, contiguous. ANTONYM distant.

**5** *the immediate cause of death* DIRECT, primary. ANTONYM indirect.

**immediately** adverb **1** *it was necessary to make a decision immediately* STRAIGHTAWAY, at once, right away, instantly, now, directly, promptly, forthwith, this/that (very) minute, this/that instant, there and then, then and there, on the spot, here and now, without delay, without further ado, posthaste; quickly, as fast as possible, speedily, as soon as possible; *informal* ASAP, pronto, double-quick, on the double, PDQ, in/like a flash, like a shot, tout de suite; *humorous* toot sweet; *archaic* forthright.

2 *I sat immediately behind him* DIRECTLY, right, exactly, precisely, squarely, just, dead; *informal* smack dab.

**immemorial** adjective *immemorial customs* ANCIENT, (very) old, age-old, antediluvian, timeless, archaic, venerable, long-standing, timeworn, time-honored, tried and true; traditional; *literary* of yore.

**immense** adjective *an immense brick church | immense jars of mayonnaise* HUGE, vast, massive, enormous, gigantic, colossal, great, very large/big, monumental, towering, tremendous; giant, elephantine, monstrous, mammoth, titanic, king-size(d), economy-size(d); *informal* mega, monster, whopping, humongous, jumbo, astronomical, cosmic, ginormous, Brobdingnagian. ANTONYM tiny.

**immerse** verb 1 *litmus paper turns red on being immersed in acid* SUBMERGE, dip, dunk, duck, sink, plunge; soak, drench, saturate, marinate, wet, douse, souse, steep.

2 *Elliot was **immersed in** his work* ABSORB IN, engross in, occupy by/with, engage in, involve in/with, bury in, swamp with, lose (oneself) in; busy with, preoccupy with, fixate on/upon.

**immigrant** noun *they will convene to discuss the civil liberties of immigrants* NEWCOMER, settler, migrant, emigrant; nonnative, foreigner, alien, outsider; expatriate; *informal* expat. ANTONYM native.

**imminent** adjective *a cease-fire was imminent* IMPENDING, close (at hand), near, (fast) approaching, coming, forthcoming, on the way, in the offing, in the pipeline, on the horizon, in the air, just around the corner, coming down the pike, expected, anticipated, brewing, looming, threatening, menacing; *informal* in the cards. See note at EMINENT.

**immobile** adjective 1 *she sat immobile for a long time* MOTIONLESS, without moving, still, stock-still, static, stationary; rooted to the spot, rigid, frozen, transfixed, like a statue, not moving a muscle. ANTONYM moving.

2 *I dreaded being immobile* UNABLE TO MOVE, immobilized; paralyzed, crippled. ANTONYM mobile.

**immobilize** verb *the virus has immobilized the House's internal communication system | it is important to immobilize the injured part of the body* PUT OUT OF ACTION, disable, make inoperative, inactivate, deactivate, paralyze, freeze, cripple; bring to a standstill, halt, stop; restrain, stabilize.

**immoderate** adjective *immoderate spending* EXCESSIVE, heavy, intemperate, unrestrained, unrestricted, uncontrolled, unlimited, unbridled, uncurbed, overindulgent, imprudent, reckless; undue, inordinate, unreasonable, unjustified, unwarranted, uncalled for, outrageous; extravagant, lavish, exorbitant, prodigal, profligate, wanton, dissipated.

**immodest** adjective *the deputy minister complained that the dance was too immodest for the memorial ceremony* INDECOROUS, improper, indecent, indelicate, immoral; forward, bold, brazen, impudent, shameless, loose, wanton; *informal* fresh, cheeky, saucy, brassy.

**immoral** adjective *the legality of the fugitive slave laws does not alter the fact that they were deeply immoral* UNETHICAL, bad, morally wrong, wrongful, wicked, evil, foul, unprincipled, unscrupulous, dishonorable, dishonest, unconscionable, iniquitous, disreputable, corrupt, depraved, vile, villainous, nefarious, base, miscreant; sinful, godless, impure, unchaste, unvirtuous, shameless, degenerate, debased, debauched, dissolute, reprobate, lewd, obscene, perverse, perverted; licentious, wanton, promiscuous, loose; *informal* shady, lowdown, crooked, sleazy. ANTONYMS ethical, chaste.

**immorality** noun *he charged that the overseas press was prone to lies and immorality* WICKEDNESS, immoral behavior, badness, evil, vileness, corruption, dishonesty, dishonorableness; sinfulness, ungodliness, unchastity, sin, depravity, villainy, vice, degeneracy, debauchery, dissolution, perversion, lewdness, obscenity, wantonness, promiscuity; *informal* shadiness, crookedness; *formal* turpitude.

**immortal** adjective 1 *our souls are immortal* UNDYING, deathless, eternal, everlasting, never-ending, endless, lasting, enduring, ceaseless; imperishable, indestructible, inextinguishable, immutable, perpetual, permanent, unfading.

2 *an immortal children's classic* TIMELESS, perennial, classic, time-honored, enduring; famous, famed, renowned, legendary, great, eminent, outstanding, acclaimed, celebrated.

▸ noun 1 *Greek temples of the immortals* GOD, GODDESS, deity, divine being, supreme being, divinity.

2 *one of the immortals of literature* GREAT, hero, legend, god, celebrity, star, Olympian.

**immortality** noun 1 *the immortality of the gods* ETERNAL LIFE, everlasting life, deathlessness; indestructibility, imperishability.

2 *the book has achieved immortality* TIMELESSNESS, legendary status, lasting fame/renown.

**immortalize** verb *the battle was immortalized by Pushkin* COMMEMORATE, memorialize, eternalize; celebrate, deify, exalt, glorify; eulogize, pay tribute to, honor, salute.

**immovable** adjective 1 *lock your bike to something immovable* FIXED, secure, stable, moored, anchored, rooted, braced, set firm, set fast; stuck, jammed, stiff, unbudgeable, foursquare. ANTONYM mobile.

2 *there he was, silent and immovable* MOTIONLESS, unmoving, immobile, stationary, still, stock-still, not moving a muscle, rooted to the spot; transfixed, paralyzed, frozen. ANTONYMS moving, in motion.

3 *she was immovable in her loyalties* STEADFAST, unwavering, unswerving, resolute, determined, firm, unshakable, adamant, unfailing, dogged, tenacious, inflexible, unyielding, unbending, uncompromising, obdurate, obstinate, iron-willed; *informal* rock-steady, diehard. ANTONYMS fickle, unsure.

**immune** adjective *they are **immune to** hepatitis B | this company seems to be **immune to** fluctuations in the economy* RE-

SISTANT TO, not subject to, not liable to, unsusceptible to, not vulnerable to; protected from, safe from, secure against, not in danger of; impervious to, invulnerable to, unaffected by. ANTONYM susceptible.

**immunity** noun **1** *an* ***immunity to*** *malaria* RESISTANCE TO, nonsusceptibility to; ability to fight off, protection against, defenses against; immunization against, inoculation against.

**2** *immunity from prosecution* EXEMPTION, exception, freedom, release, dispensation, amnesty.

**3** *diplomatic immunity* INDEMNITY, privilege, prerogative, right, liberty, license; legal exemption, impunity, protection.

**immunize** verb *have these children been* ***immunized against*** *rubella?* VACCINATE AGAINST, inoculate against; protect from, safeguard against.

**imp** noun **1** *our neighborhood imps are, for the most part, harmless* RASCAL, monkey, devil, troublemaker, urchin; *informal* scamp, brat, monster, horror, terror, tyke, whippersnapper, hellion, varmint, rapscallion; *archaic* scapegrace.

**2** *this trickster of Indian myth is an inscrutable imp possessed of satanic charisma* HOBGOBLIN, goblin, elf, sprite, pixie, brownie, fairy, puck; demon, little devil; *archaic* bugbear.

**impact** noun **1** *the force of the impact* COLLISION, crash, smash, bump, bang, knock.

**2** *the job losses will have a major impact* EFFECT, influence, significance, meaning; consequences, repercussions, ramifications, reverberations.

▸ verb **1** *a comet impacted the earth sixty million years ago* CRASH INTO, smash into, collide with, hit, strike, ram, smack into, bang into, slam into.

**2** *high interest rates have impacted retail spending* AFFECT, influence, have an effect on, make an impression on; hit, touch, change, alter, modify, transform, shape.

**USAGE NOTE impact**

*Impact* has traditionally been only a noun. In recent years, however, it has undergone a semantic shift that has allowed it to act as a verb. Such use has become widespread (and also widely condemned by stylists)—e.g.: "The researchers concluded that this low level of intensity may have impacted [read *affected*] the results." (*Tampa Tribune*; July 17, 1997.) This use of the word would be perfectly acceptable if *impact* were performing any function not as ably performed by *affect* or *influence*. If *affect* as a verb is not sufficiently straightforward in context, then the careful writer might use *have an impact on*, which, though longer, is probably better than the jarring impact of *impacted*. Reserve *impact* for noun uses and *impacted* for wisdom teeth.

Interestingly, *impact* as a verb might have arisen partly in response to widespread diffidence about the spelling of *affect* (often confused with *effect*). —BG

**impair** verb *sagging eyelid skin can impair eyesight* HAVE A NEGATIVE EFFECT ON, damage, harm, diminish, reduce, weaken, lessen, decrease, impede, hinder, hobble; undermine, compromise; *formal* vitiate. ANTONYMS improve, enhance.

**impale** verb *her knife impaled the counter like a javelin* STICK, skewer, spear, spike, transfix, harpoon; pierce, stab, run through; *literary* transpierce.

**impalpable** adjective *his skin was sallow and his pulse impalpable | impalpable clouds* INTANGIBLE, insubstantial, incorporeal, immaterial; indefinable, elusive, imperceptible, indescribable.

**impart** verb **1** *she had news to impart* COMMUNICATE, pass on, convey, transmit, relay, relate, recount, tell, make known, make public, report, announce, proclaim, herald, spread, disseminate, circulate, promulgate, broadcast; disclose, reveal, divulge; *informal* let on about, blab, blurt.

**2** *the picture imparts some color to the drab office* GIVE, bestow, confer, grant, lend, afford, provide, supply.

**impartial** adjective *can the United Nations be trusted as an impartial arbiter of world affairs?* UNBIASED, unprejudiced, neutral, nonpartisan, nondiscriminatory, disinterested, detached, dispassionate, objective, open-minded, equitable, evenhanded, fair, fair-minded, just; without favoritism, without fear or favor. ANTONYMS biased, partisan.

**impassable** adjective *the farm-to-market roads were impassable* UNPASSABLE, unnavigable, untraversable, impenetrable; closed, blocked, barricaded; dense, thick, blind.

**impasse** noun *an impasse in the peace talks poses new challenges* DEADLOCK, dead end, stalemate, standoff; standstill, halt, stoppage, stop; *informal* Catch-22.

**impassioned** adjective *an impassioned commentary about the state of American politics* EMOTIONAL, heartfelt, wholehearted, earnest, sincere, fervent, ardent, passionate, fervid, intense, burning; vehement, zealous, heated; *literary* perfervid.

**impatience** noun **1** *he was shifting in his seat with impatience* RESTLESSNESS, restiveness, agitation, nervousness, anxiety; eagerness, keenness; *informal* jitteriness.

**2** *a burst of impatience* IRRITABILITY, testiness, tetchiness, irascibility, querulousness, peevishness, petulance, frustration, exasperation, annoyance, pique.

**impatient** adjective **1** *Elaine grew impatient* RESTLESS, restive, agitated, nervous, anxious, tense, ill at ease, edgy, jumpy, keyed up; *informal* twitchy, jittery, uptight, high-strung. ANTONYMS calm, indifferent.

**2** *they are impatient to get back home* ANXIOUS, eager, keen, yearning, longing, aching, agog; *informal* itching, dying, raring, gung-ho, straining at the leash. ANTONYM reluctant.

**3** *why must you be so impatient with the children?* IRRITATED, annoyed, angry, testy, tetchy, snappy, cross, querulous, peevish, piqued, short-tempered; abrupt, curt, brusque, terse, short; *informal* peeved. ANTONYMS even-tempered, pleased.

**impeach** verb **1** *congressional moves to impeach the president* INDICT, charge, accuse, lay charges against, arraign, take to court, put on trial, prosecute.

2 *the headlines impeached their clean image* CHALLENGE, question, disparage, criticize, call into question, raise doubts about, cast aspersions on. ANTONYM confirm.

**impeccable** adjective *the lieutenant's record is impeccable* FLAWLESS, faultless, unblemished, spotless, immaculate, stainless, perfect, exemplary; sinless, irreproachable, blameless, guiltless; *informal* squeaky clean. ANTONYMS imperfect, sinful.

**impecunious** adjective *she left Evansville to escape the solicitations of her impecunious relatives* PENNILESS, poor, impoverished, indigent, insolvent, hard up, poverty-stricken, needy, destitute; in straitened circumstances, unable to make ends meet; *informal* (flat) broke, strapped (for cash); *formal* penurious. ANTONYM wealthy.

**impede** verb *your efforts to impede our progress will be unsuccessful* HINDER, obstruct, hamper, hold back/up, delay, interfere with, disrupt, retard, slow (down), hobble, cripple; block, check, stop, scupper, scuttle, thwart, frustrate, balk, foil, derail; *informal* stymie, throw a (monkey) wrench in the works of; *dated* cumber. See note at HINDER. ANTONYM facilitate.

**impediment** noun 1 *an impediment to economic improvement* HINDRANCE, obstruction, obstacle, barrier, bar, block, handicap, check, curb, restriction, limitation; setback, difficulty, snag, hitch, hurdle, stumbling block; *informal* fly in the ointment, hiccup, (monkey) wrench in the works, glitch; *archaic* cumber.

2 *a speech impediment* DEFECT; stammer, stutter, lisp.

**impel** verb 1 *financial difficulties impelled her to seek work* FORCE, compel, constrain, oblige, require, make, urge, exhort, press, pressurize, drive, push, spur, prod, goad, incite, prompt, persuade.

2 *vital energies impel him in unforeseen directions* PROPEL, drive, move, get going, get moving.

**impending** adjective *a smarter grid could warn of impending blackouts* IMMINENT, close (at hand), near, nearing, approaching, coming, forthcoming, upcoming, to come, on the way, about to happen, in store, in the offing, on the horizon, in the air/wind, brewing, looming, threatening, menacing; *informal* coming down the pike, in the cards.

**impenetrable** adjective 1 *impenetrable armor* IMPERVIOUS, impermeable, indestructible, solid, thick, unyielding; impregnable, inviolable, invulnerable, unassailable, unpierceable; *informal* bulletproof. ANTONYMS permeable, vulnerable.

2 *a dark, impenetrable forest* IMPASSABLE, unpassable, inaccessible, unnavigable, untraversable; dense, thick, overgrown; *archaic* thickset. ANTONYMS sparse, accessible.

3 *an impenetrable clique* EXCLUSIVE, closed, secretive, secret, private; restrictive, restricted, limited. ANTONYM open.

4 *impenetrable statistics* INCOMPREHENSIBLE, unfathomable, inexplicable, unintelligible, inscrutable, unclear, baffling, bewildering, puzzling, perplexing, enigmatic, cryptic, confusing, abstruse, opaque; complex, complicated, difficult. ANTONYM clear.

**impenitent** adjective *the hardness of their impenitent hearts* UNREPENTANT, unrepenting, uncontrite, remorseless, unashamed, unapologetic, unabashed.

**imperative** adjective 1 *it is imperative that you find him* VITALLY IMPORTANT, of vital importance, all-important, vital, crucial, critical, essential, necessary, indispensable, urgent; compulsory, obligatory, mandatory. ANTONYMS unimportant, optional.

2 *the imperative note in her voice* PEREMPTORY, commanding, imperious, authoritative, masterful, dictatorial, magisterial, assertive, firm, insistent. ANTONYM submissive.

**imperceptible** adjective *the imperceptible shift of constellations | an imperceptible rustle of cellophane* UNNOTICEABLE, undetectable, indistinguishable, indiscernible, invisible, inaudible, inappreciable, impalpable, unobtrusive, inconspicuous, unseen; slight, small, tiny, minute, microscopic, infinitesimal, subtle, faint, fine, negligible, inconsequential; indistinct, unclear, obscure, vague, indefinite, hard to make out. ANTONYMS noticeable, obvious.

**imperfect** adjective 1 *the goods were returned as imperfect* FAULTY, flawed, defective, shoddy, unsound, inferior, second-rate, below standard, substandard; damaged, blemished, torn, broken, cracked, scratched; *informal* not up to snuff, not up to scratch, crummy, lousy. ANTONYM flawless.

2 *an imperfect form of the manuscript* INCOMPLETE, unfinished, half-done; unpolished, unrefined, rough. ANTONYM complete.

3 *she spoke imperfect Arabic* BROKEN, faltering, halting, hesitant, rudimentary, limited. ANTONYMS flawless, fluent.

**imperfection** noun 1 *the glass is free from imperfections* DEFECT, fault, flaw, deformity, discoloration, disfigurement; crack, scratch, chip, nick, pit, dent; blemish, stain, spot, mark, streak. ANTONYM strength.

2 *he was aware of his imperfections* FLAW, fault, failing, deficiency, weakness, vice, weak point, fallibility, shortcoming, foible, inadequacy, frailty, limitation, chink in one's armor. ANTONYM perfection.

3 *the imperfection of the fossil record* INCOMPLETENESS, patchiness, deficiency; roughness, crudeness. ANTONYM completeness.

**imperial** adjective 1 *imperial banners* ROYAL, regal, monarchical, sovereign, kingly, queenly, princely.

2 *her imperial bearing* MAJESTIC, grand, august, dignified, proud, stately, noble, aristocratic, regal; magnificent, imposing, impressive.

3 *our customers thought we were imperial.* See IMPERIOUS.

**imperil** verb *allowing access to the detainee would imperil national security* ENDANGER, jeopardize, risk, put in danger, put in jeopardy, expose to danger, hazard; threaten, pose a threat to; *archaic* peril.

**imperious** adjective *Black tells stories of imperious judges and duplicitous witnesses* PEREMPTORY, high-handed, commanding, imperial, overbearing, overweening, domineering, authoritarian, dictatorial, autocratic, authoritative, lordly, assertive, bossy, arrogant, haughty, presumptuous; *informal* pushy, high and mighty.

**impermanent** adjective *the methods they're proposing for reforestation are risky and impermanent* TEMPORARY, transient, transitory, passing, fleeting, momentary, ephemeral, fugitive; short-lived, brief, here today and gone tomorrow; *literary* evanescent.

**impersonal** adjective **1** *an impersonal judgment* NEUTRAL, unbiased, nonpartisan, unprejudiced, objective, detached, disinterested, dispassionate, without favoritism. ANTONYM biased.

**2** *their impersonal relationships extended even to their own wives and children* ALOOF, distant, remote, reserved, withdrawn, unemotional, unsentimental, dispassionate, cold, cool, indifferent, unconcerned; formal, stiff, businesslike; *informal* starchy, standoffish, wooden. ANTONYMS emotional, warm.

**impersonate** verb *impersonating the boss during a meeting was not your smartest move* IMITATE, mimic, do an impression of, ape, copy, parrot; parody, caricature, burlesque, travesty, satirize, lampoon; masquerade as, pose as, pass oneself off as; *informal* take off, send up, make like; *formal* personate. See note at IMITATE.

**impersonation** noun *the president seemed genuinely amused by the impersonations of the first family* IMPRESSION, imitation; parody, caricature, burlesque, travesty, lampoon, pastiche; *informal* takeoff, send-up; *formal* personation.

**impertinence** noun *I'll refrain from answering with the impertinence your question deserves* RUDENESS, insolence, impoliteness, bad manners, discourtesy, disrespect, incivility; impudence, cheek, cheekiness, audacity, presumption, temerity, effrontery, nerve, gall, boldness, cockiness, brazenness; *informal* brass, sauce, sass, sassiness, chutzpah, lip, back-talk, guff; *archaic* assumption.

**impertinent** adjective *impertinent remarks* RUDE, insolent, impolite, ill-mannered, bad-mannered, uncivil, discourteous, disrespectful; impudent, cheeky, audacious, bold, brazen, brash, presumptuous, forward; tactless, undiplomatic; *informal* saucy, pert, sassy, smart-alecky. ANTONYM polite.

THE RIGHT WORD **impertinent, impudent, insolent, intrusive, meddlesome, obtrusive**

All of these adjectives mean exceeding the bounds of propriety; the easiest way to distinguish **impertinent** from the others is to think of its root: *impertinent* behavior is not pertinent—in other words, it is in or out of place. The *impertinent* individual has a tendency to be rude or presumptuous toward those who are entitled to deference or respect (*it was an impertinent question to ask a woman who had just lost her husband*). The **intrusive** person is unduly curious about other people's affairs (*her constant questions about the state of their marriage were intrusive and unwelcome*), while **obtrusive** implies objectionable actions rather than an objectionable disposition. The *obtrusive* person has a tendency to thrust himself or herself into a position where he or she is conspicuous and apt to do more harm than good (*they tried to keep him out of the meeting because his presence would be obtrusive*). To be **meddlesome** is to have a prying or inquisitive nature and a tendency to interfere in an annoying way in other people's affairs (*a meddlesome neighbor*). **Impudent** and **insolent** are much stronger words for in behavior. Young people are often accused of being *impudent*, which means to be *impertinent* in a bold and shameless way (*an impudent young man who had a lot to learn about tact*). Anyone who is guilty of insulting and contemptuously arrogant behavior might be called *insolent* (*he was so insolent to the arresting officer that he was handcuffed*).

---

**imperturbable** adjective *the guide dogs are trained to be imperturbable* SELF-POSSESSED, composed, calm, cool, and collected, coolheaded, self-controlled, serene, relaxed, unexcitable, even-tempered, placid, phlegmatic; unperturbed, unflustered, unruffled; *informal* unflappable, unfazed, nonplussed, laid-back; *rare* equanimous. ANTONYMS excitable, edgy.

**impervious** adjective **1** *he seemed* ***impervious to*** *the chill wind* UNAFFECTED BY, untouched by, immune to, invulnerable to, insusceptible to, resistant to, indifferent to, heedless of, insensible to, unconscious of, oblivious to; proof against.

**2** *an impervious rain jacket* IMPERMEABLE, impenetrable, impregnable, waterproof, watertight, water-resistant, repellent; (hermetically) sealed, zip-locked. ANTONYM permeable.

**impetuous** adjective **1** *an impetuous decision* IMPULSIVE, rash, hasty, overhasty, reckless, heedless, careless, foolhardy, bullheaded, headstrong, incautious, imprudent, injudicious, ill-considered, unthought-out; spontaneous, impromptu, spur-of-the-moment, precipitate, precipitous, hurried, rushed; *informal* devil-may-care, harum-scarum, hotheaded. See note at TEMERITY. ANTONYMS considered, cautious.

**2** *an impetuous flow of water* TORRENTIAL, powerful, forceful, vigorous, violent, raging, relentless, uncontrolled; rapid, fast, fast-flowing, swift. ANTONYM sluggish.

**impetus** noun **1** *the flywheel lost all its impetus* MOMENTUM, propulsion, impulsion, motive force, driving force, drive, thrust; energy, force, power, push, strength.

**2** *the sales force were given fresh impetus* MOTIVATION, stimulus, incitement, incentive, inducement, inspiration, encouragement, boost, fillip, springboard; *informal* a shot in the arm.

**impiety** noun **1** *a world of impiety and immorality* GODLESSNESS, ungodliness, unholiness, irreligion, irreverence, sinfulness, sin, vice, transgression, wrongdoing, immorality, unrighteousness, blasphemy, sacrilege; apostasy, atheism, agnosticism, paganism, heathenism, nonbelief, unbelief. ANTONYM holiness.

**2** *not even motherhood was immune to impiety* IRREVERENCE, disrespect, impertinence, insolence, mockery, derision. ANTONYM reverence.

**impinge** verb **1** *these issues* ***impinge on*** *all of us* AFFECT, have an effect on, touch, have a bearing on, influence, have/make an impact on, leave a mark on.

**2** *the proposed highway would* ***impinge on*** *parkland* ENCROACH ON, intrude on, infringe (on), invade, trespass on, obtrude, cut through, interfere with; violate; *informal* horn in on.

**impious** adjective *the impious magistrate of the Sung dynasty* GODLESS, ungodly, unholy, irreligious, sinful, wicked, immoral, unrighteous, sacrilegious, heretical, profane, blasphemous, irreverent; apostate, atheistic, agnostic, pagan, heathen, faithless, nonbelieving, unbelieving, *rare* nullifidian.

**impish** adjective **1** *he takes an impish delight in shocking the press* MISCHIEVOUS, naughty, wicked, devilish, rascally, roguish, playful, sportive; mischief-making, full of mischief.

**2** *an impish grin* ELFIN, elflike, pixieish, puckish; mischievous, roguish, sly.

**implacable** adjective *the computer hacker has become the new implacable foe* UNAPPEASABLE, unforgiving, unsparing; inexorable, intransigent, inflexible, unyielding, unbending, uncompromising, unrelenting, relentless, ruthless, remorseless, merciless, heartless, pitiless, cruel, hard, harsh, stern, tough, iron-fisted.

**implant** verb **1** *the microchip is implanted under the skin* INSERT, embed, bury, lodge, place; graft.

**2** *he implanted the idea in my mind* INSTILL, inculcate, insinuate, introduce, inject, plant, sow, root, lodge.

▸ noun *a silicone implant* TRANSPLANT, graft, implantation, insert.

**implausible** adjective *a swift conclusion to the negotiations is implausible | another one of his implausible excuses* UNLIKELY, improbable, questionable, doubtful, debatable; unrealistic, unconvincing, far-fetched, incredible, unbelievable, unimaginable, inconceivable, fantastic, fanciful, ridiculous, absurd, preposterous, outrageous; *informal* hard to swallow, cock and bull. ANTONYM convincing.

**implement** noun *garden implements* TOOL, utensil, instrument, device, apparatus, gadget, contraption, appliance, machine, contrivance; *informal* gizmo; **(implements)** equipment, kit, tackle, accoutrements, paraphernalia. See note at TOOL.

▸ verb *the cost of implementing the new law* EXECUTE, apply, put into effect, put into action, put into practice, carry out/through, perform, enact; fulfill, discharge, accomplish, bring about, achieve, realize, actualize, phase in; *formal* effectuate.

**implicate** verb **1** *he had been implicated in a financial scandal* INCRIMINATE, compromise; involve, connect, link, embroil, enmesh, ensnare, entangle; *archaic* inculpate; *informal* finger.

**2** *viruses are* ***implicated in*** *the development of cancer* INVOLVE IN, concern with, associate with, connect to/with.

**implication** noun **1** *he was smarting at their implication* SUGGESTION, insinuation, innuendo, hint, intimation, imputation.

**2** *important political implications* CONSEQUENCE, result, ramification, repercussion, reverberation, effect, significance.

**3** *his implication in the murder case* INCRIMINATION, involvement, connection, entanglement, association; *dated* inculpation.

**implicit** adjective **1** *implicit assumptions* IMPLIED, hinted at, suggested, insinuated; unspoken, unexpressed, undeclared, unstated, tacit, unacknowledged, taken for granted; inherent, latent, underlying, inbuilt, incorporated; understood, inferred, deducible. ANTONYM explicit.

**2** *an implicit trust in human nature* ABSOLUTE, complete, total, wholehearted, perfect, utter; unqualified, unconditional, categorical; unshakable, unquestioning, firm, steadfast. ANTONYM limited.

**implicitly** adverb *a man in whom they implicitly believed* COMPLETELY, absolutely, totally, wholeheartedly, utterly, unconditionally, unreservedly, without reservation.

**implied** adjective. See IMPLICIT.

**implore** verb *his mother implored him to continue studying* PLEAD WITH, beg, entreat, beseech, appeal to, ask, request, call on; exhort, urge, enjoin, press, push, petition, bid, importune; supplicate. See note at BEG.

**imply** verb **1** *are you implying he is mad?* INSINUATE, suggest, hint (at), intimate, say indirectly, indicate, give someone to understand, convey the impression, signal. See note at INFER.

**2** *the forecasted traffic increase implies more roads* INVOLVE, entail; mean, point to, signify, indicate, signal, connote, denote; necessitate, require, presuppose.

**impolite** adjective *Devon was consistently impolite, always interrupting and making the most doltish remarks* RUDE, bad-mannered, ill-mannered, discourteous, uncivil, disrespectful, inconsiderate, boorish, churlish, ill-bred, ungentlemanly, unladylike, ungracious; insolent, impudent, impertinent, cheeky; loutish, rough, crude, vulgar, indelicate, indecorous, tactless, gauche, uncouth; *informal* ignorant, lippy, saucy; *archaic* contumelious. ANTONYMS polite, well-mannered.

**impolitic** adjective *it was impolitic of you to alienate the very people who could finance our program* IMPRUDENT, unwise, injudicious, incautious, irresponsible; ill-judged, ill-advised, misguided, rash, reckless, foolhardy, foolish, shortsighted; undiplomatic, tactless, thoughtless. ANTONYMS prudent, wise.

**import** verb **1** *Greenland imports just about everything that is consumed* BUY FROM ABROAD, bring in, ship in. ANTONYM export.

**2** *practices imported from the business world* DERIVE, obtain, take, extract, glean; *informal* steal, crib, filch.

▸ noun **1** *a tax on* ***imports*** IMPORTED GOODS, foreign goods, imported merchandise, foreign merchandise, imported commodities, foreign commodities.

**2** *the import of foreign books* IMPORTATION, importing, introduction, bringing in, bringing from abroad, shipping in.

**3** *a matter of great import* IMPORTANCE, significance, consequence, momentousness, magnitude, substance, weight, note, gravity, seriousness; *formal* moment. ANTONYM insignificance.

**4** *the full import of her words* MEANING, sense, essence, gist, drift, purport, connotation, message, thrust, point, substance, implication.

**importance** noun **1** *the signing of the treaty was an event of immense importance* SIGNIFICANCE, momentousness, import, consequence, note, noteworthiness, substance; seriousness, gravity, weightiness, urgency.

**2** *she had a fine sense of her own importance* POWER, influence, authority, sway, weight, dominance; prominence, eminence, preeminence, prestige, notability, worth, stature; *informal* clout, pull.

**important** adjective **1** *an important meeting* SIGNIFICANT, consequential, momentous, of great import, major; critical, crucial, vital, pivotal, decisive, urgent, historic; serious, grave, weighty, material; *formal* of great moment. ANTONYM trivial.

**2** *the important thing is that you do well in your exams* MAIN, chief, principal, key, major, salient, prime, foremost, paramount, overriding, crucial, vital, critical, essential, significant; central, fundamental; *informal* number-one. ANTONYM inessential.

**3** *the school was important to the community* OF VALUE, valuable, (highly) prized, beneficial, necessary, essential, indispensable, vital; of concern, of interest, relevant, pertinent. ANTONYMS irrelevant, of no concern.

**4** *he was an important man* POWERFUL, influential, of influence, well-connected, high-ranking, high-powered; prominent, eminent, preeminent, notable, noteworthy, of note; distinguished, esteemed, respected, prestigious, celebrated, famous, great; *informal* affluential, major league. ANTONYM insignificant.

**importune** verb *he importuned her for some spare change* BEG, beseech, entreat, implore, plead with, appeal to, call on, lobby; harass, pester, press, badger, bother, nag, harry; *informal* hassle, bug. See note at BEG.

**impose** verb **1** *he imposed his ideas on the art director* FOIST, force, inflict, press, urge; *informal* saddle someone with, land someone with.

**2** *new taxes will be imposed* LEVY, charge, apply, enforce; set, establish, institute, introduce, bring into effect.

**3** *it was never my intention to* ***impose on*** *you* TAKE ADVANTAGE OF, exploit, take liberties with, treat unfairly; bother, trouble, disturb, inconvenience, put out, put to trouble, be a burden on; *informal* walk all over.

**imposing** adjective *an imposing mansion* IMPRESSIVE, striking, arresting, eye-catching, dramatic, spectacular, stunning, awesome, awe-inspiring, formidable, splendid, grand, grandiose, majestic, stately, august. ANTONYM modest.

**imposition** noun **1** *the imposition of an alien culture* IMPOSING, foisting, forcing, inflicting.

**2** *the imposition of tax on consumables* LEVYING, charging, application, applying, enforcement, enforcing, enjoining; setting, establishment, introduction, institution.

**3** *it would be no imposition* BURDEN, encumbrance, strain, bother, worry; *informal* hassle, drag.

**impossible** adjective **1** *gale-force winds made fishing impossible* NOT POSSIBLE, out of the question, unfeasible, impractical, impracticable, nonviable, unworkable; unthinkable, unimaginable, inconceivable, absurd. ANTONYM easy.

**2** *an impossible dream* UNATTAINABLE, unachievable, unobtainable, unwinnable, hopeless, impractical, implausible, far-fetched, outrageous, preposterous, ridiculous, absurd, impracticable, unworkable, futile. ANTONYM attainable.

**3** *informal* *an impossible customer* UNREASONABLE, objectionable, difficult, awkward; intolerable, unbearable, unendurable; exasperating, maddening, infuriating, irritating; *informal* high maintenance. ANTONYM bearable.

**imposture** noun *Barton's imposture was recognized as such only after he had fled town* MISREPRESENTATION, pretense, deceit, deception, trickery, artifice, subterfuge, feint; hoax, trick, ruse, dodge; *informal* con, scam, flimflam.

**impotent** adjective **1** *the legal sanctions are impotent* POWERLESS, ineffective, ineffectual, inadequate, weak, feeble, useless, worthless, futile; *literary* impuissant. ANTONYMS powerful, effective.

**2** *natural forces that humans are impotent to control* UNABLE, incapable, powerless, helpless. ANTONYM able.

**impound** verb **1** *officials began impounding documents* CONFISCATE,, take possession of, seize, commandeer, expropriate, requisition, sequester, sequestrate; *Law* distrain.

**2** *the cattle were impounded* PEN IN, shut up/in, fence in, enclose, cage, confine, corral.

**3** *criminals impounded in prison* LOCK UP, incarcerate, imprison, confine, intern, immure, hold captive, hold prisoner.

**impoverished** adjective **1** *an impoverished peasant farmer* POOR, poverty-stricken, penniless, destitute, indigent, impecunious, needy, beggared, beggarly, pauperized, down-and-out, bankrupt, ruined, insolvent; *informal* (flat) broke, hard up, dirt poor, on skid row; *formal* penurious. ANTONYMS rich, wealthy.

**2** *the soil is impoverished* WEAKENED, exhausted, drained, sapped, depleted, spent; barren, unproductive, unfertile, unfruitful. ANTONYMS rich, fertile.

**impracticable** adjective *a repeat autopsy would be impracticable* UNWORKABLE, unfeasible, nonviable, unachievable, unattainable, unrealizable; impractical, impossible. ANTONYMS workable, feasible.

**impractical** adjective **1** *an impractical suggestion* UNREAL-

ISTIC, unworkable, unfeasible, nonviable, impracticable; ill-thought-out, impossible, absurd, wild; *informal* cockeyed, crackpot, crazy. ANTONYMS practical, sensible.

**2** *impractical white ankle boots* UNSUITABLE, not sensible, inunserviceable. ANTONYMS practical, sensible.

**3** *an impractical scholar* IDEALISTIC, unrealistic, romantic, dreamy, fanciful, quixotic; *informal* ivory-tower, blue-sky, starry-eyed; *chiefly Brit. informal* airy-fairy. ANTONYMS practical, down-to-earth.

**imprecation** noun. See CURSE noun senses 1, 4.

**imprecise** adjective **1** *a rather imprecise definition* VAGUE, loose, indefinite, inexplicit, indistinct, nonspecific, unspecific, sweeping, broad, general; hazy, fuzzy; *informal* loosey-goosey, woolly, sketchy, nebulous, ambiguous, equivocal, uncertain. ANTONYM narrow.

**2** *an imprecise estimate* INEXACT, approximate, estimated, rough, ballpark. ANTONYM exact.

**impregnable** adjective **1** *the fortress is impregnable* INVULNERABLE, impenetrable, unassailable, inviolable, secure, strong, well fortified, well defended; invincible, unconquerable, unbeatable, indestructible. ANTONYM vulnerable.

**2** *he displayed a calm, impregnable certainty* UNASSAILABLE, unbeatable, undefeatable, unshakable, invincible, unconquerable, invulnerable. ANTONYMS shaky, vulnerable.

**impregnate** verb **1** *a pad impregnated with natural oils* INFUSE, soak, steep, saturate, drench; permeate, pervade, suffuse, imbue.

**2** *the woman he had impregnated* MAKE/GET PREGNANT, inseminate, fertilize; *informal* get/put in the family way; *informal, vulgar* knock up; *informal, dated* get into trouble; *archaic* fecundate, get with child.

**impresario** noun *a theatrical impresario* ORGANIZER, (stage) manager, producer; promoter, publicist, showman; director, conductor, maestro.

**impress** verb **1** *Hazel had impressed him* MAKE AN IMPRESSION ON, have an impact on, influence, affect, move, stir, rouse, excite, inspire; dazzle, awe, overawe, take someone's breath away, amaze, astonish; *informal* grab, blow someone away, stick in someone's mind. ANTONYM disappoint.

**2** *goldsmiths impressed his likeness on medallions* IMPRINT, print, stamp, mark, emboss, punch.

**3** *you must* ***impress upon*** *her the need to save* EMPHASIZE TO, stress to, bring home to, instill in, inculcate into, drum into.

**impression** noun **1** *he got the impression that she was hiding something* FEELING, feeling in one's bones, sense, fancy, (sneaking) suspicion, inkling, premonition, intuition, presentiment, hunch; notion, idea, funny feeling, gut feeling.

**2** *a favorable impression* OPINION, view, image, picture, perception, judgment, verdict, estimation. See note at IDEA.

**3** *school made a profound impression on me* IMPACT, effect, influence.

**4** *the cap had left a circular impression* INDENTATION, dent, mark, outline, imprint.

**5** *he did a good impression of their science teacher* IMPERSONATION, imitation; parody, caricature, burlesque, travesty, lampoon; *informal* takeoff, send-up, spoof; *formal* personation.

**6** *an artist's impression of the gardens* REPRESENTATION, portrayal, depiction, rendition, interpretation, picture, drawing.

**impressionable** adjective *his music has anxious parents concerned about what impressionable children may hear and think* EASILY INFLUENCED, suggestible, susceptible, persuadable, pliable, malleable, pliant, trusting, naive, innocent, wide-eyed, credulous, gullible.

**impressive** adjective **1** *an impressive building* MAGNIFICENT, majestic, imposing, splendid, spectacular, grand, awe-inspiring, striking, stunning, breathtaking; *informal* mind-blowing, jaw-dropping. ANTONYM ordinary.

**2** *it was an impressive performance* ADMIRABLE, masterly, accomplished, expert, skilled, skillful, consummate; excellent, outstanding, first-class, first-rate, fine, superb; *informal* awesome, great, mean, nifty, ace, crackerjack, bang-up. ANTONYM mediocre.

**imprint** verb **1** *patterns can be imprinted in the clay* STAMP, print, impress, mark, emboss, brand, inscribe, etch.

**2** *the image was imprinted into his mind* FIX, establish, stick, lodge, implant, plant, embed, instill, impress, inculcate.

▸ noun **1** *her feet left imprints on the floor* IMPRESSION, print, mark, indentation.

**2** *colonialism has left its imprint* IMPACT, lasting effect, influence, impression, mark, trace.

**imprison** verb *we expect to imprison another two dozen individuals by the end of this month alone* INCARCERATE, send to prison, jail, lock up, put away, intern, detain, hold prisoner, hold captive; confine, shut up, cage; *informal* put behind bars. ANTONYMS free, release.

**improbable** adjective **1** *it seemed improbable that the hot weather would continue* UNLIKELY, doubtful, dubious, debatable, questionable, uncertain; unthinkable, inconceivable, unimaginable, incredible; *informal* iffy. ANTONYM certain.

**2** *an improbable explanation* UNCONVINCING, unbelievable, incredible, ridiculous, absurd, preposterous, outrageous; far-fetched, fantastic, fanciful. ANTONYM believable.

**impromptu** adjective *an impromptu lecture* UNREHEARSED, unprepared, unscripted, extempore, extemporized, extemporaneous, improvised, spontaneous, unplanned; *informal* off-the-cuff, offhand, spur-of-the-moment, ad-lib. See note at SPONTANEOUS. ANTONYMS prepared, rehearsed.

▸ adverb *they played the song impromptu* EXTEMPORE, spontaneously, extemporaneously, without preparation, without rehearsal; *informal* off the cuff, off the top of one's head, on the spur of the moment, ad lib.

**improper** adjective **1** *it is improper for policemen to accept* *gifts* IN, unacceptable, unsuitable, unprofessional, irregular; unethical, corrupt, immoral, dishonest, dishonorable. ANTONYMS appropriate, acceptable.

2 *it was improper for young ladies to drive a young man home* UNSEEMLY, indecorous, unfitting, unbecoming, undignified, unladylike, ungentlemanly; indecent, immodest, immoral; scandalous, shocking, offensive. ANTONYMS proper, fitting.

3 *improper limericks* INDECENT, risqué, off color, indelicate, naughty, suggestive, smutty, vulgar, crude, obscene; *informal* raunchy, steamy, blue, X-rated. ANTONYM decent.

4 *improper installation will affect performance* INCORRECT, wrong, inaccurate, erroneous, mistaken. ANTONYM correct.

**impropriety** noun 1 *a suggestion of impropriety* WRONGDOING, misconduct, dishonesty, corruption, unscrupulousness, unprofessionalism, irregularity; unseemliness, indecorousness, indelicacy, indecency, immorality.

2 *fiscal improprieties* TRANSGRESSION, misdemeanor, offense, misdeed, misconduct, crime; indiscretion, mistake, peccadillo, solecism; *archaic* trespass.

**improve** verb 1 *ways to improve the service* MAKE BETTER, better, ameliorate, upgrade, update, refine, enhance, boost, build on, raise, polish, fix (up), amend; *informal* tweak; *formal* meliorate. ANTONYM worsen.

2 *communications improved during the eighteenth century* GET BETTER, advance, progress, develop; make headway, make progress, pick up, look up. ANTONYM deteriorate.

3 *the dose is not repeated if patient improves* RECOVER, get better, recuperate, gain strength, rally, revive, get back on one's feet, get over something; be on the road to recovery, be on the mend; *informal* turn the corner, take a turn for the better, bounce back. ANTONYM deteriorate.

4 *resources are needed to improve the offer* INCREASE, make larger, raise, augment, enhance, boost, supplement, top up; *informal* up, hike up, bump up, soup up, beef up. ANTONYMS decrease, diminish.

PHRASE: **improve on** *how could anyone improve on his brilliant analysis?* SURPASS, better, do better than, outdo, exceed, beat, top, cap.

**improvement** noun *identifying the areas most in need of improvement | passengers will notice many new improvements* ADVANCE, development, upgrade, refinement, renovation, enhancement, advancement, upgrading, amelioration, betterment; boost, lift, rise, augmentation, raising, step up; rally, recovery, upswing, upturn.

**improvident** adjective *one consequence of a healthy economy may be a generation of improvident youth* SPENDTHRIFT, thriftless, wasteful, prodigal, profligate, extravagant, lavish, free-spending, immoderate, excessive; imprudent, irresponsible, careless, reckless, heedless. ANTONYMS thrifty, conservative.

**improvise** verb 1 *she was improvising in front of the cameras* EXTEMPORIZE, ad lib, speak impromptu; *informal* speak off the cuff, speak off the top of one's head, wing it; jam, scat.

2 *she improvised a playhouse for the kids* CONTRIVE, devise, throw together, cobble together, rig up; *informal* whip up, rustle up.

**improvised** adjective 1 *an improvised speech* IMPROMPTU, unrehearsed, unprepared, unscripted, extempore, extemporized, spontaneous, unplanned; *informal* off-the-cuff, ad-libbed, spur-of-the-moment. See note at SPONTANEOUS. ANTONYMS prepared, rehearsed.

2 *an improvised shelter* MAKESHIFT, thrown together, cobbled together, rough and ready, crude, make-do, temporary, jerry-built, jury-rigged, slapdash.

**imprudent** adjective *a series of imprudent marriages* UNWISE, injudicious, incautious, indiscreet, misguided, ill-advised, ill-judged; thoughtless, unthinking, improvident, irresponsible, shortsighted, foolish; rash, reckless, heedless. ANTONYM sensible.

**impudence** noun *her irrepressible impudence landed her in the principal's office about a million times* IMPERTINENCE, insolence, effrontery, audacity, cheek, cheekiness, cockiness, brazenness, brass, boldness; presumption, presumptuousness, disrespect, flippancy, bumptiousness, brashness; rudeness, impoliteness, ill manners, gall; *informal* chutzpah, nerve, sauce, sass, sassiness.

**impudent** adjective *the oblivious couple and their impudent children were asked to leave* IMPERTINENT, insolent, cheeky, cocky, brazen, bold, audacious; presumptuous, forward, disrespectful, insubordinate, bumptious, brash; rude, impolite, ill-mannered, discourteous, ill-bred; *informal* saucy, lippy, sassy, brassy, smart-alecky; *archaic* contumelious. See note at IMPERTINENT. ANTONYM polite.

**impugn** verb *are you impugning my judgment?* CALL INTO QUESTION, challenge, question, dispute, query, take issue with.

**impulse** noun 1 *she had an impulse to run and hide* URGE, instinct, drive, compulsion, itch; whim, desire, fancy, notion, inclination, temptation.

2 *passions provide the main impulse of poetry* INSPIRATION, stimulation, stimulus, incitement, motivation, encouragement, incentive, spur, catalyst, impetus, thrust.

3 *impulses from the spinal cord to the muscles* PULSE, current, wave, signal. PHRASE: **on (an) impulse** *I agreed to bungee-jump on an impulse | they claimed the robbery was not planned, that they did it on impulse* IMPULSIVELY, spontaneously, on the spur of the moment, without forethought, without premeditation.

**impulsive** adjective 1 *he had an impulsive nature* IMPETUOUS, spontaneous, hasty, passionate, emotional, uninhibited; rash, reckless, careless, imprudent, foolhardy, unwise, madcap, devil-may-care, daredevil. ANTONYM cautious.

2 *an impulsive decision* IMPROMPTU, snap, spontaneous, unpremeditated, spur-of-the-moment, extemporaneous; impetuous, precipitate, hasty, rash; sudden, ill-considered,

ill-thought-out, whimsical. See note at SPONTANEOUS. ANTONYM premeditated.

**impunity** noun *the lawsuit attempts to fight the impunity that these military officials have enjoyed for too long* IMMUNITY, indemnity, exemption (from punishment), freedom from liability, nonliability, license; amnesty, dispensation, reprieve, pardon, exoneration; stay of execution; privilege, favoritism, special treatment, carte blanche. ANTONYM liability.

PHRASE: **with impunity** *they boldly break laws at will, and do so with impunity* WITHOUT PUNISHMENT, with no ill consequences, scot-free, unpunished.

**impure** adjective **1** *impure gold* ADULTERATED, mixed, combined, blended, alloyed; *technical* admixed. ANTONYM pure.

**2** *the water was impure* CONTAMINATED, polluted, tainted, unwholesome, poisoned; dirty, filthy, foul, unclean, defiled; unhygienic, unsanitary; *literary* befouled. ANTONYM clean.

**3** *impure thoughts* IMMORAL, sinful, wrongful, wicked; unchaste, lustful, lecherous, lewd, lascivious, prurient, obscene, indecent, ribald, risqué, improper, crude, coarse, debased, degenerate; *formal* concupiscent. ANTONYM chaste.

**impurity** noun **1** *the impurity of the cast iron* ADULTERATION, debasement, degradation, corruption; contamination, pollution.

**2** *the impurities in beer* CONTAMINANT, pollutant, foreign body, foreign matter; dross, dirt, filth.

**3** *sin and impurity* IMMORALITY, sin, sinfulness, wickedness; unchastity, lustfulness, lechery, lecherousness, lewdness, lasciviousness, prurience, obscenity, dirtiness, crudeness, indecency, ribaldry, impropriety, vulgarity, depravity, coarseness; *formal* concupiscence.

**impute** verb *the worst of these mistakes have been unfairly* ***imputed to*** *Dr. Irvine* ATTRIBUTE TO, ascribe to, assign to, credit to; connect with, associate with.

**in** preposition **1** *she was hiding in the closet* INSIDE, within, in the middle of; surrounded by, enclosed by.

**2** *he was covered in mud* WITH, by.

**3** *he put a candy in his mouth* INTO, inside.

**4** *they met in 1921* DURING, in the course of, over.

**5** *I'll see you in half an hour* AFTER, at the end of, following; within, in less than, in under.

▸ adverb **1** *his mom walked in* INSIDE, indoors, into the room, into the house/building.

**2** *the tide's in* HIGH, at its highest level, rising.

▸ adjective **1** *no one is in* PRESENT, (at) home; inside, indoors, in the house/room.

**2** *informal sculpted beards are in* FASHIONABLE, in fashion, in vogue, popular, stylish, modern, modish, chic, à la mode, de rigueur, trendy, cool, all the rage, du jour, with it, the in thing, hip, hot. ANTONYMS unfashionable, unpopular.

PHRASES: **in for** *we're probably in for some rain* DUE FOR, in line for; expecting, about to undergo/receive.

**in for it** *when Dad gets home, you're gonna be in for it* IN TROUBLE, about to be punished; *informal* in hot/deep water.

**in on** *we were never in on the whole story* PRIVY TO, aware of, acquainted with, informed about/of, apprised of; *informal* wise to, in the know about, hip to.

**ins and outs** *informal no one expects you to learn all the ins and outs on your first day of work* DETAILS, particulars, facts, features, characteristics, nuts and bolts; *informal* nitty gritty.

**in with** *her principal mission was to get in with as many senior executives as possible* IN FAVOR WITH, popular with, friendly with, friends with, on good terms with; liked by, admired by, accepted by.

**inability** noun *the state's inability to build a credible case against him* LACK OF ABILITY, incapability, incapacity, powerlessness, impotence, helplessness; incompetence, ineptitude, unfitness, inefficacy.

**inaccessible** adjective **1** *inaccessible woodlands* UNREACHABLE, out of reach, unapproachable; cutoff, isolated, remote, insular, in the back of beyond, out of the way, lonely, solitary, godforsaken.

**2** *the book was elitist and inaccessible* INCOMPREHENSIBLE, impenetrable, inscrutable, baffling; obscure, esoteric, abstruse, recondite, arcane; elitist, exclusive, pretentious.

**3** *the lecturer was inaccessible to students* UNAPPROACHABLE, aloof, distant, unfriendly, standoffish.

**inaccuracy** noun **1** *the inaccuracy of recent opinion polls* INCORRECTNESS, inexactness, imprecision, erroneousness, mistakenness, fallaciousness, faultiness. ANTONYM correctness.

**2** *the article contained a number of inaccuracies* ERROR, mistake, fallacy, slip, slip-up, oversight, fault, blunder, gaffe; erratum, solecism; *informal* howler, typo, blooper, goof.

**inaccurate** adjective *inaccurate reports* INEXACT, imprecise, incorrect, wrong, erroneous, careless, faulty, imperfect, flawed, defective, unsound, unreliable; fallacious, false, mistaken, untrue; *informal* wide of the mark.

**inactive** adjective **1** *I was terribly inactive over the holidays* IDLE, indolent, lazy, lifeless, slothful, lethargic, inert, sluggish, unenergetic, listless, torpid, sedentary.

**2** *the computer is currently inactive* INOPERATIVE, nonfunctioning, idle; not working, out of service, unused, not in use; dormant.

**inadequacy** noun **1** *the inadequacy of available resources* INSUFFICIENCY, deficiency, deficit, scarcity, sparseness, dearth, paucity, shortage, want, lack, undersupply; paltriness, meagerness. ANTONYMS abundance, surplus.

**2** *her feelings of personal inadequacy* INCOMPETENCE, incapability, unfitness, ineffectiveness, inefficiency, inefficacy, inexpertness, ineptness, uselessness, impotence, powerlessness; inferiority, mediocrity. ANTONYM competence.

**3** *the inadequacies of the present system* SHORTCOMING, defect, fault, failing, weakness, weak point, limitation, flaw, imperfection. ANTONYM strength.

**inadequate** adjective **1** *inadequate water supplies* INSUFFICIENT, deficient, poor, scant, scanty, scarce, sparse, in short supply; paltry, meager, niggardly, beggarly, limited; *informal* measly, pathetic; *formal* exiguous. ANTONYM sufficient.

**2** *an inadequate typist* INCOMPETENT, incapable, unsatisfactory, unfit, unacceptable, ineffective, ineffectual, inefficient, unskillful, inexpert, inept, amateurish, substandard, poor, useless, inferior; *informal* not up to scratch, not up to snuff, no great shakes, lame, shabby. ANTONYM competent.

**inadmissible** adjective *inadmissible evidence* UNALLOWABLE, not allowed, invalid, unacceptable, impermissible, disallowed, forbidden, prohibited, precluded.

**inadvertent** adjective *an inadvertent omission* UNINTENTIONAL, unintended, accidental, unpremeditated, unplanned, innocent, uncalculated, unconscious, unthinking, unwitting, involuntary; careless, negligent. ANTONYM deliberate.

**inadvisable** adjective *traveling to the village is inadvisable for the president at this time* UNWISE, ill-advised, imprudent, ill-judged, ill-considered, injudicious, impolitic, foolish, misguided; *Medicine* contraindicated. ANTONYMS wise, shrewd.

**inalienable** adjective *China of course contends that Taiwan is an inalienable part of China* INVIOLABLE, absolute, sacrosanct; untransferable, nontransferable, nonnegotiable; *Law* indefeasible.

**inane** adjective *another one of Craig's inane schemes* SILLY, foolish, stupid, fatuous, idiotic, ridiculous, ludicrous, absurd, senseless, asinine, frivolous, vapid; childish, puerile; *informal* dumb, moronic, ditzy, daft. ANTONYM sensible.

**inanimate** adjective *in the dream sequence, several of the inanimate objects in his bedroom come to life* LIFELESS, insentient, without life, inorganic; dead, defunct. ANTONYM living.

**inapplicable** adjective *they argued that executive privilege was simply inapplicable in the face of the grand jury subpoena* IRRELEVANT, immaterial, not germane, not pertinent, unrelated, unconnected, extraneous, beside the point; unsuitable, inapposite; *formal* impertinent. ANTONYM relevant.

**inappropriate** adjective *children's access to the Internet may expose them to inappropriate material* UNSUITABLE, unfitting, unseemly, unbecoming, unbefitting, improper, impolite; incongruous, out of place/keeping, inapposite, inapt, infelicitous, ill-suited; ill-judged, ill-advised; *informal* out of order/line; *formal* malapropos. ANTONYM suitable.

**inapt** adjective. See INAPPROPRIATE.

**inarticulate** adjective **1** *an inarticulate young man* TONGUE-TIED, lost for words, unable to express oneself. ANTONYM silver-tongued.

**2** *an inarticulate reply* UNINTELLIGIBLE, incomprehensible, incoherent, unclear, indistinct, mumbled, muffled. ANTONYM fluent.

**3** *inarticulate rage* UNSPOKEN, silent, unexpressed, wordless, speechless, unvoiced. ANTONYM vocal.

**inattentive** adjective **1** *an inattentive student* DISTRACTED, lacking concentration, preoccupied, absentminded, daydreaming, dreamy, abstracted, distrait; *informal* miles away, spaced out. ANTONYM alert.

**2** *inattentive service.* See NEGLIGENT.

**inaudible** adjective *inaudible voices* UNHEARD, out of earshot; indistinct, imperceptible, faint, muted, soft, low, muffled, whispered, muttered, murmured, mumbled; silent, soundless, noiseless, hushed; ultrasonic.

**inaugural** adjective *the inaugural meeting of the Geographic Society* OPENING, FIRST, launching, initial, introductory, initiatory, maiden. ANTONYM final.

**inaugurate** verb **1** *he inaugurated a new trade policy* INITIATE, begin, start, commence, institute, launch, start off, get going, get underway, set in motion, get off the ground, establish, found, lay the foundations of; bring in, usher in, introduce; *informal* kick off.

**2** *the new president will be inaugurated in January* ADMIT TO OFFICE, install, instate, swear in; invest, ordain; crown, enthrone.

**3** *the library was inaugurated on Jefferson's birthday* OPEN, declare open, unveil; dedicate, consecrate.

**inauspicious** adjective *after an inauspicious start, the Giants ended the season in first place* UNPROMISING, unpropitious, unfavorable, unfortunate, infelicitous, unlucky, ill-omened, ominous; discouraging, disheartening, bleak. ANTONYM promising.

**inborn** adjective *inborn allergic reactions* INNATE, congenital, connate, instinctive, inherent, natural, inbred, inherited, hereditary, in one's genes. See note at INHERENT.

**incalculable** adjective *artifacts of incalculable value | incalculable losses* INESTIMABLE, untold, indeterminable, immeasurable, incomputable; infinite, endless, limitless, boundless, measureless; enormous, immense, huge, vast, innumerable, countless.

**incandescent** adjective **1** *incandescent fragments of lava* WHITE-HOT, red-hot, burning, fiery, blazing, ablaze, aflame; glowing, aglow, radiant, bright, brilliant, luminous, sparkling; *literary* fervid, lucent; *rare* igneous.

**2** *an incandescent speech* PASSIONATE, ardent, fervent, fervid, intense, impassioned, spirited, fiery.

**incantation** noun *I was more amused than entranced by the flickering candles and spooky incantations* CHANT, invocation, conjuration, magic spell/formula, charm, hex, enchantment, mojo; intonation, recitation.

**incapable** adjective **1** *the job should never have been assigned to an incapable crew* INCOMPETENT, inept, inadequate, lacking ability, not good enough, leaving much to be desired, inexpert, unskillful, ineffective, ineffectual, inefficacious, feeble, unfit, unqualified, unequal to the task; *informal* not up to it, not up to snuff, useless, hopeless. ANTONYM competent.

**2** *he was judged to be mentally incapable* INCAPACITATED, incompetent, helpless, powerless, impotent. ANTONYM competent.

**3** *they are incapable of supporting themselves* UNABLE TO (BE), not capable of, lacking the ability to (be), not equipped to (be), lacking the experience to (be). ANTONYM able.

**incapacitated** adjective *Ivan did not expect to be incapacitated for more than a few days* DISABLED, debilitated, indisposed, unfit, impaired; immobilized, paralyzed, out of action, out of commission, hors de combat; *informal* laid up. ANTONYM fit.

**incapacity** noun *the doctors were baffled by the severity of her physical incapacity* DISABILITY, incapability, inability, debility, impairment, indisposition; impotence, powerlessness, helplessness; incompetence, inadequacy, ineffectiveness. ANTONYM capability.

**incarcerate** verb *Luckins returned to the site where she had been incarcerated nearly fifty years earlier* IMPRISON, put in prison, send to prison, jail, lock up, put under lock and key, put away, intern, confine, detain, hold, immure, put in chains, hold prisoner, hold captive; *informal* put behind bars. ANTONYMS release, set free.

**incarceration** noun *eight years of incarceration* IMPRISONMENT, internment, confinement, detention, custody, captivity, restraint; *informal* time; *archaic* durance, duress.

**incarnate** adjective *the chairman has been labeled "evil incarnate" by various conservationists* IN HUMAN FORM, in the flesh, in physical form, in bodily form, made flesh; corporeal, physical, fleshly, embodied, personified.

**incarnation** noun **1** *the incarnation of artistic genius* EMBODIMENT, personification, exemplification, type, epitome; manifestation, bodily form, avatar.

**2** *a previous incarnation* LIFETIME, life, existence.

**incautious** adjective *my uncle's history of incautious behavior is hardly a secret* RASH, unwise, careless, heedless, thoughtless, reckless, unthinking, imprudent, misguided, ill-advised, ill-judged, injudicious, impolitic, unguarded, foolhardy, foolish. ANTONYM circumspect.

**incendiary** adjective **1** *an incendiary bomb* COMBUSTIBLE, flammable, inflammable.

**2** *an incendiary speech* INFLAMMATORY, rabble-rousing, provocative, seditious, subversive; contentious, controversial.

▸ noun *a political incendiary* AGITATOR, demagogue, rabble-rouser, firebrand, troublemaker, agent provocateur, revolutionary, insurgent, subversive.

**incense** verb. See ENRAGE.

**incentive** noun *only financial incentives will curb the polluting activities of major industries* INDUCEMENT, motivation, motive, reason, stimulus, stimulant, spur, impetus, encouragement, impulse; incitement, goad, provocation; attraction, lure, bait; *informal* carrot, sweetener, come-on. ANTONYM deterrent.

**inception** noun *the airline plans to file for bankruptcy, seven years after its inception* BEGINNING, commencement, start, birth, dawn, genesis, origin, outset; establishment, institution, foundation, founding, formation, initiation, setting up, origination, constitution, inauguration, opening, debut, day one; *informal* kickoff. See note at ORIGIN. ANTONYM end.

**incessant** adjective *their dog's incessant barking* CEASELESS, unceasing, constant, continual, unabating, interminable, endless, unending, never-ending, everlasting, eternal, perpetual, continuous, nonstop, around/round-the-clock, uninterrupted, unbroken, unremitting, persistent, relentless, unrelenting, unrelieved, sustained. ANTONYMS intermittent, occasional.

**incidence** noun *an increased incidence of heart disease* OCCURRENCE, prevalence; rate, frequency; amount, degree, extent.

**incident** noun **1** *incidents in his youth* EVENT, occurrence, episode, experience, happening, occasion, proceeding, eventuality, affair, business; adventure, exploit, escapade; matter, circumstance, fact, development.

**2** *police were investigating the incident* DISTURBANCE, fracas, melee, commotion, rumpus, scene; fight, skirmish, clash, brawl, free-for-all, encounter, conflict, ruckus, confrontation, altercation, contretemps; *informal* ruction.

**3** *the journey was not without incident* EXCITEMENT, adventure, drama; danger, peril.

**incidental** adjective **1** *incidental details* LESS IMPORTANT, secondary, subsidiary; minor, peripheral, background, nonessential, inessential, unimportant, insignificant, inconsequential, tangential, extrinsic, extraneous, superfluous. ANTONYMS essential, crucial.

**2** *an incidental discovery* CHANCE, accidental, by chance, by accident, random; fortuitous, serendipitous, adventitious, coincidental, unlooked-for, unexpected, fluky. See note at ACCIDENTAL. ANTONYM deliberate.

**3** *the risks* ***incidental to*** *the job* CONNECTED WITH, related to, associated with, accompanying, attending, attendant on, concomitant to/with. ANTONYM unrelated.

**incidentally** adverb **1** *incidentally, I haven't had a reply yet* BY THE WAY, by the by, by the bye, in passing, en passant, speaking of which; parenthetically; *informal* BTW, as it happens.

**2** *the infection was discovered incidentally* BY CHANCE, by accident, accidentally, fortuitously, by a fluke, by happenstance; coincidentally, by coincidence.

**incinerate** verb *we would incinerate our household trash in a barrel in the backyard.* BURN, reduce to ashes, consume by fire, carbonize; cremate.

**incipient** adjective *the system detects incipient problems early* DEVELOPING, growing, emerging, emergent, dawning, just beginning, inceptive, initial, inchoate; nascent, embryonic, fledgling, in its infancy, germinal. ANTONYM full-blown.

**incision** noun **1** *a surgical incision* CUT, opening, slit.

2 *incisions on the marble* NOTCH, carving, etching, engraving, inscription, score; nick, scratch, scarification.

**incisive** adjective *an incisive commentator* PENETRATING, acute, sharp, sharp-witted, razor-sharp, keen, astute, trenchant, shrewd, piercing, cutting, perceptive, insightful, percipient, perspicacious, discerning, analytical, clever, smart, quick; concise, succinct, pithy, to the point, brief, crisp, clear, effective; *informal* punchy, heads-up, on the ball; *rare* sapient. ANTONYMS rambling, vague.

**incite** verb 1 *we're hoping that last night's incident will not incite altercations in the stadium today* STIR UP, whip up, encourage, fan the flames of, stoke up, fuel, kindle, ignite, inflame, stimulate, instigate, provoke, excite, arouse, awaken, inspire, engender, trigger, spark off, ferment, foment; *literary* enkindle. ANTONYM suppress.

2 *she incited him to commit murder* EGG ON, encourage, urge, goad, provoke, spur on, drive, stimulate, push, prod, prompt, induce, impel; arouse, rouse, excite, inflame, sting, prick; *informal* put up to. ANTONYMS discourage, deter.

THE RIGHT WORD **incite, arouse, exhort, foment, instigate, provoke**

The best way to start a riot is to **incite** one, which means to urge or stimulate to action, either in a favorable or an unfavorable sense. If you **instigate** an action, however, it implies that you are responsible for initiating it and that the purpose is probably a negative or evil one (*the man who instigated the assassination plot*). **Foment** suggests agitation or incitement over an extended period of time (*foment a discussion; foment the rebellion that leads to war*). An instigator, in other words, is someone who initiates the idea, while a fomenter is someone who keeps it alive. You can **provoke** a riot in the same way that you instigate one, but the emphasis here is on spontaneity rather than on conscious design (*her statement provoked an outcry from animal rights activists*). To **arouse** is to awaken a feeling or elicit a response (*my presence in the junkyard aroused suspicion*), or to open people's eyes to a situation (*we attempted to arouse public awareness*). But once you've aroused people, you may have to **exhort** them, meaning to urge or persuade them, by appealing to their sympathy or conscience, to take constructive action.

**incivility** noun *Cadet Anderson was reprimanded for incivility* RUDENESS, discourtesy, impoliteness, bad manners, disrespect, boorishness, ungraciousness; insolence, impertinence, impudence. ANTONYM politeness.

**inclement** adjective *inclement weather* COLD, chilly, bleak, wintry, freezing, snowy, icy; wet, rainy, drizzly, damp; stormy, blustery, wild, rough, squally, windy; unpleasant, bad, foul, nasty, brutal, severe, extreme, harsh. ANTONYMS fine, sunny.

**inclination** noun 1 *his political inclination* TENDENCY, propensity, proclivity, leaning, predisposition, disposition, predilection, desire, wish, impulse, bent, bias; liking, affection, penchant, partiality, preference, appetite, fancy, interest, affinity; stomach, taste; *informal* yen. ANTONYM aversion.

2 *an inclination of his head* BOWING, bow, bending, nod, nodding, lowering.

**incline** verb 1 *his prejudice inclines him to overlook obvious facts* PREDISPOSE, lead, make, make of a mind, dispose, prejudice, bias; prompt, induce, influence, sway; persuade, convince.

2 *I **incline to** the opposite view* PREFER, favor, go for; tend to, lean to, swing to, veer to, gravitate to, be drawn to.

3 *he inclined his head* BEND, bow, nod, bob, lower, dip.

▸ noun *a steep incline* SLOPE, gradient, pitch, ramp, bank, ascent, rise, upslope, dip, descent, declivity, downslope; hill, grade, downgrade.

**include** verb 1 *activities include sports and drama* INCORPORATE, comprise, encompass, cover, embrace, involve, take in, number, contain; consist of, be made up of, be composed of; *formal* comprehend. ANTONYM exclude.

2 *don't forget to include the cost of repairs* ALLOW FOR, count, take into account, take into consideration. ANTONYMS omit, leave out.

THE RIGHT WORD **include, comprise**

**Include** has a broader meaning than **comprise**. In the sentence *the accommodations comprise two bedrooms, bathroom, kitchen, and living room*, the word **comprise** implies that there are no accommodations other than those listed. **Include** can be used in this way too, but it is also used in a nonrestrictive way, implying that there may be other things not specifically mentioned that are part of the same category, as in *the price includes a special welcome pack*. Careful writers will avoid superfluous uses of "including . . . and more," commonly found in advertising. The 'and more' is superfluous because **including** or **includes** implies that there is more than what is listed.

**inclusive** adjective *an inclusive travel package* ALL-INCLUSIVE, with everything included, comprehensive, in toto; overall, full, all-around, umbrella, blanket, across-the-board, catch-all, all-encompassing.

**incognito** adverb & adjective *you'll be traveling incognito* UNDER AN ASSUMED NAME, under a false name, in disguise, disguised, under cover, in plain clothes, camouflaged, unidentified; secretly, anonymously.

**incoherent** adjective 1 *a long, incoherent speech* UNCLEAR, confused, unintelligible, incomprehensible, hard to follow, disjointed, disconnected, disordered, mixed up, garbled, jumbled, scrambled, muddled; rambling, wandering, disorganized, illogical; inarticulate, mumbling, slurred. ANTONYM intelligible.

2 *she was incoherent and shivering* DELIRIOUS, raving, babbling, hysterical, irrational. ANTONYM lucid.

**income** noun *annual income* EARNINGS, salary, pay, remuneration, wages, stipend; revenue, receipts, takings, profits, gains, proceeds, turnover, yield, dividend, means, take; *formal* emolument. ANTONYM expenditure.

**incoming** adjective 1 *the incoming train* ARRIVING, entering; approaching, coming (in), inbound. ANTONYM outgoing.

2 *the incoming president* NEWLY ELECTED, newly appointed,

succeeding, new, next, future; elect, to-be, designate. ANTONYM outgoing.

**incomparable** adjective *the incomparable Maggie Smith is once again the deputy headmistress of Hogwarts* WITHOUT EQUAL, beyond compare, unparalleled, matchless, peerless, unmatched, without parallel, beyond comparison, second to none, in a class of its/one's own, unequaled, unrivaled, inimitable, nonpareil, par excellence; transcendent, superlative, surpassing, unsurpassed, unsurpassable, supreme, top, best, outstanding, consummate, singular, unique, rare, perfect; *informal* one-in-a-million; *formal* unexampled. ANTONYMS ordinary, commonplace.

**incompatible** adjective **1** *she and McBride are totally incompatible* UNSUITED, mismatched, ill-matched; worlds apart, poles apart, like night and day. ANTONYMS well-matched, suited.

**2** *incompatible economic objectives* IRRECONCILABLE, conflicting, opposed, opposing, opposite, contradictory, antagonistic, antipathetic; clashing, inharmonious, discordant; mutually exclusive; poles apart, worlds apart, night and day. ANTONYMS compatible, complementary.

**3** *his theory was* ***incompatible with*** *that of his predecessor* INCONSISTENT WITH, at odds with, out of keeping with, at variance with, inconsonant with, different to, divergent from, contrary to, in conflict with, in opposition to, antithetical to, (diametrically) opposed to, counter to, irreconcilable with. ANTONYM consistent.

**incompetent** adjective *not only is the staff overpaid, they're incompetent* INEPT, unskillful, unskilled, inexpert, amateurish, unprofessional, bungling, blundering, clumsy, inadequate, substandard, inferior, ineffective, deficient, inefficient, ineffectual, wanting, lacking, leaving much to be desired; incapable, unfit, unqualified; *informal* useless, pathetic, ham-fisted, not up to it, not up to scratch, bush league.

**incomplete** adjective **1** *the project is still incomplete* UNFINISHED, uncompleted, partial, half-finished, half-done, half-completed.

**2** *inaccurate or incomplete information* DEFICIENT, insufficient, imperfect, defective, partial, patchy, sketchy, fragmentary, fragmented.

**incomprehensible** adjective *the patient's muttering was incomprehensible | the judge ruled that the original contract was too incomprehensible to be binding* UNINTELLIGIBLE, impossible to understand, impenetrable, unclear, indecipherable, inscrutable, beyond one's comprehension, beyond one, beyond one's grasp, complicated, complex, involved, baffling, bewildering, mystifying, unfathomable, puzzling, cryptic, confusing, perplexing; abstruse, esoteric, recondite, arcane, mysterious, Delphic; *informal* over one's head, all Greek. ANTONYMS intelligible, clear.

**inconceivable** adjective *even his oldest rivals thought the charges of treason against him were inconceivable* UNBELIEVABLE, beyond belief, incredible, unthinkable, unimaginable, extremely unlikely; impossible, beyond the bounds of possibility, out of the question, preposterous, ridiculous, ludicrous, absurd, incomprehensible; *informal* hard to swallow. ANTONYM likely.

**inconclusive** adjective *the defendant was confident that the evidence would be inconclusive* INDECISIVE, proving nothing; indefinite, indeterminate, unresolved, unproved, unsettled, still open to question/doubt, debatable, unconfirmed; moot; vague, ambiguous; *informal* up in the air, left hanging.

**incongruous** adjective **1** *the women visiting the mission looked incongruous in their smart hats and fur coats* OUT OF PLACE, out of keeping, inappropriate, unsuitable, unsuited; wrong, strange, odd, curious, queer, absurd, bizarre. ANTONYM appropriate.

**2** *an incongruous collection of objects* ILL-MATCHED, ill-assorted, mismatched, unharmonious, discordant, dissonant, conflicting, clashing, jarring, incompatible, different, dissimilar, contrasting, disparate. ANTONYM harmonious.

**inconsequential** adjective *their efforts to save the Bixner Building were ultimately inconsequential* INSIGNIFICANT, unimportant, of little/no consequence, neither here nor there, incidental, inessential, nonessential, immaterial, irrelevant; negligible, inappreciable, inconsiderable, slight, minor, trivial, trifling, petty, paltry, measly; *informal* piddling, piffling. ANTONYMS significant, important, of great consequence.

**inconsiderate** adjective *she reproached her son for being routinely inconsiderate to his wife* THOUGHTLESS, unthinking, insensitive, selfish, self-centered, unsympathetic, uncaring, heedless, unmindful, unkind, uncharitable, ungracious, impolite, discourteous, rude, disrespectful; tactless, undiplomatic, indiscreet, indelicate. ANTONYM thoughtful.

**inconsistent** adjective **1** *his inconsistent behavior* ERRATIC, changeable, unpredictable, variable, varying, changing, inconstant, unstable, irregular, fluctuating, unsteady, unsettled, uneven; self-contradictory, contradictory, paradoxical; capricious, fickle, flighty, whimsical, unreliable, mercurial, volatile, blowing hot and cold, ever-changing, chameleonlike; *technical* labile.

**2** *he had done nothing* ***inconsistent with*** *his morality* INCOMPATIBLE WITH, conflicting with, in conflict with, at odds with, at variance with, differing from, contrary to, in opposition to, (diametrically) opposed to, irreconcilable with, out of keeping with, out of step with; antithetical to.

**inconsolable** adjective *those left homeless by the fire were inconsolable* HEARTBROKEN, broken-hearted, grief-stricken, beside oneself with grief, devastated, wretched, sick at heart, desolate, despairing, distraught, comfortless; miserable, unhappy, sad; *literary* heartsick.

**inconspicuous** adjective *the flaw in the carpeting is inconspicuous | wearing inconspicuous street clothes, Swann escaped through the crowd* UNOBTRUSIVE, unnoticeable, unremarkable, unspectacular, unostentatious, undistinguished, unexceptional, modest, unassuming, discreet, hidden, concealed; unseen, in the background, low-profile. ANTONYM noticeable.

**inconstant** adjective *an inconstant friend* FICKLE, faithless, unfaithful, false, wayward, unreliable, untrustworthy, capricious, volatile, flighty, unpredictable, erratic, blowing hot and cold; changeable, mutable, mercurial, variable, irregular; *informal* cheating, two-timing. ANTONYM faithful.

**incontestable** adjective. See INCONTROVERTIBLE.

**incontinent** adjective *incontinent hysteria* UNRESTRAINED, lacking self-restraint, uncontrolled, unbridled, unchecked, unfettered; uncontrollable, ungovernable. ANTONYM restrained.

**incontrovertible** adjective *he realizes that his forensic findings are not incontrovertible* INDISPUTABLE, incontestable, undeniable, irrefutable, unassailable, beyond dispute, unquestionable, beyond question, indubitable, beyond doubt, unarguable, undebatable; certain, sure, definite, definitive, proven, decisive, conclusive, demonstrable, emphatic, categorical, airtight, watertight. ANTONYM questionable.

**inconvenience** noun **1** *we apologize for any inconvenience caused by the delay* TROUBLE, bother, problems, disruption, difficulty, disturbance; vexation, irritation, annoyance; *informal* aggravation, hassle.

**2** *his early arrival was clearly an inconvenience* NUISANCE, trouble, bother, problem, vexation, worry, trial, bind, bane, irritant, thorn in someone's side; *informal* headache, pain, pain in the neck, pain in the butt, drag, aggravation, hassle.

▸ verb *I don't want to inconvenience you* TROUBLE, bother, put out, put to any trouble, disturb, impose on, burden, incommode; *informal* hassle, plague; *formal* discommode.

**inconvenient** adjective *symptoms can range from merely inconvenient to downright life-changing* AWKWARD, difficult, inopportune, untimely, ill-timed, unsuitable, inappropriate, unfortunate; tiresome, troublesome, irritating, annoying, vexing, bothersome; *informal* aggravating.

**incorporate** verb **1** *the region was incorporated into Moldavian territory* ABSORB, include, subsume, assimilate, integrate, take in, swallow up.

**2** *the model incorporates some advanced features* INCLUDE, contain, comprise, embody, embrace, build in, encompass.

**3** *literary references were incorporated with photographs* BLEND, mix, mingle, meld; combine, unite, join.

**incorrect** adjective **1** *an incorrect answer* WRONG, erroneous, in error, mistaken, inaccurate, imprecise, wide of the mark, off target; untrue, false, fallacious; *informal* out, way out.

**2** *incorrect behavior* INAPPROPRIATE, wrong, unsuitable, inapt, inapposite; ill-advised, ill-considered, ill-judged, injudicious, unacceptable, unfitting, out of keeping, improper, unseemly, unbecoming, indecorous; *informal* out of line, out of order.

**incorrigible** adjective *an incorrigible flirt* INVETERATE, habitual, confirmed, hardened, dyed-in-the-wool, incurable, chronic, irredeemable, hopeless, beyond hope; impenitent, unrepentant, unapologetic, unashamed; bad, naughty, terrible. ANTONYM repentant.

**incorruptible** adjective **1** *an incorruptible man* HONEST, honorable, trustworthy, principled, high-principled, unbribable, moral, ethical, good, virtuous. ANTONYM venal.

**2** *an incorruptible substance* IMPERISHABLE, indestructible, indissoluble, enduring, everlasting. ANTONYM perishable.

**increase** verb **1** *demand is likely to increase* GROW, get bigger, get larger, enlarge, expand, swell; rise, climb, escalate, soar, surge, rocket, shoot up, spiral; intensify, strengthen, extend, heighten, stretch, spread, widen; multiply, snowball, mushroom, proliferate, balloon, build up, mount up, pile up, accrue, accumulate; *literary* wax. ANTONYM decrease.

**2** *higher expectations will increase user demand* ADD TO, make larger, make bigger, augment, supplement, top up, build up, extend, raise, swell, inflate; magnify, maximize, intensify, strengthen, heighten, amplify; *informal* up, jack up, hike up, bump up, torque up, crank up. ANTONYM reduce.

▸ noun *the increase in size* | *an increase in demand* GROWTH, rise, enlargement, expansion, extension, multiplication, elevation, inflation; increment, addition, augmentation; magnification, intensification, amplification, climb, escalation, surge, upsurge, upswing, spiral, spurt; *informal* hike. ANTONYMS decrease, reduction.

**increasingly** adverb *the regime became increasingly draconian* MORE AND MORE, progressively, to an increasing extent, ever more.

**incredible** adjective **1** *I find his story incredible* UNBELIEVABLE, beyond belief, hard to believe, unconvincing, far-fetched, implausible, improbable, highly unlikely, dubious, doubtful; inconceivable, unthinkable, unimaginable, impossible; *informal* hard to swallow, cock-and-bull.

**2** *an incredible feat of engineering* MAGNIFICENT, wonderful, marvelous, spectacular, remarkable, phenomenal, prodigious, breathtaking, extraordinary, unbelievable, amazing, stunning, astounding, astonishing, awe-inspiring, staggering, formidable, impressive, supreme, great, awesome, superhuman; *informal* fantastic, terrific, tremendous, stupendous, mind-boggling, mind-blowing, jaw-dropping, out of this world, far-out; *literary* wondrous.

**incredulous** adjective *Chung was incredulous when the congressman was not more forthcoming in his first broadcast interview about the case* DISBELIEVING, skeptical, unbelieving, distrustful, mistrustful, suspicious, doubtful, dubious, unconvinced; cynical. See note at INCREDIBLE.

**increment** noun *the three-percent increment is unlikely to make much difference to the price* INCREASE, addition, supplement, gain, augmentation, accretion, addendum; enlargement, enhancement, boost; *informal* hike. ANTONYM reduction.

**incriminate** verb *no witnesses to last night's shooting have incriminated Mr. Jackson* IMPLICATE, involve, enmesh; blame, accuse, denounce, inform against, point the finger at; entrap; *informal* frame, set up, stick/pin the blame on, rat on; *archaic* inculpate.

**inculcate** verb *the beliefs* ***inculcated in*** *him by his father* IN-

STILL IN, implant in, fix in, impress in, imprint in; hammer into, drum into, drive into, drill into.

**incumbent** adjective **1** *it is **incumbent on** you **to** tell them* NECESSARY FOR ONE TO, essential that, required that, imperative that; compulsory for one to, binding on one to, mandatory that.

**2** *the incumbent president* CURRENT, present, in office, in power; reigning.

▸ noun *the first incumbent of the post* HOLDER, bearer, occupant.

**incur** verb *it is astonishing how many expenses they incurred in just one evening | these actions are likely to incur the coach's wrath* BRING UPON ONESELF, expose oneself to, lay oneself open to; run up; attract, invite, earn, arouse, cause, give rise to, be liable/subject to, meet with, sustain, experience, contract.

**incurable** adjective **1** *an incurable illness* UNTREATABLE, inoperable, irremediable; terminal, fatal, mortal; chronic.

**2** *an incurable romantic* INVETERATE, dyed-in-the-wool, confirmed, established, long-established, long-standing, absolute, complete, utter, thorough, out-and-out, through and through; unashamed, unapologetic, unrepentant, incorrigible, hopeless.

**incursion** noun *an Israeli **incursion into** the Palestinian camp left nine dead* ATTACK ON, assault on, raid on, invasion of, storming of, overrunning of, foray into, blitz on, sortie into, sally into/against, advance on/into, push into, thrust into, infiltration of. ANTONYM retreat.

**indebted** adjective *nations we assumed would be indebted to us have turned a blind eye* BEHOLDEN, under an obligation, obliged, obligated, grateful, thankful, in debt, owing a debt of gratitude.

**indecent** adjective **1** *indecent photographs* OBSCENE, dirty, filthy, rude, coarse, naughty, vulgar, gross, crude, lewd, salacious, improper, smutty, off-color; pornographic, offensive, prurient, sordid, scatological; ribald, risqué, racy; *informal* porn, porno, X-rated, XXX, raunchy, blue; *euphemistic* adult.

**2** *they left the dinner table with indecent haste* UNSEEMLY, improper, indecorous, unceremonious, indelicate, unbecoming, ungentlemanly, unladylike, unfitting, unbefitting; untoward, unsuitable, inappropriate; in bad taste, tasteless, unacceptable, offensive, crass.

**indecipherable** adjective *indecipherable handwriting* ILLEGIBLE, unreadable, hard to read, unintelligible, unclear; scribbled, scrawled, hieroglyphic, cramped, crabbed.

**indecision** noun *many an opportunity has been lost to indecision* INDECISIVENESS, irresolution, hesitancy, hesitation, tentativeness; ambivalence, doubt, doubtfulness, uncertainty, incertitude; vacillation, wavering, equivocation, second thoughts; shilly-shallying, dithering, temporizing, hemming and hawing, dilly-dallying, sitting on the fence; *formal* dubiety.

**indecisive** adjective **1** *an indecisive result* INCONCLUSIVE, proving nothing, settling nothing, open, indeterminate, undecided, unsettled, borderline, indefinite, unclear, ambiguous, vague; *informal* up in the air.

**2** *an indecisive leader* IRRESOLUTE, hesitant, tentative, weak; vacillating, equivocating, dithering, wavering, faltering; ambivalent, divided, blowing hot and cold, of two minds, in a dilemma, in a quandary, torn; doubtful, unsure, uncertain; undecided, uncommitted; *informal* iffy, sitting on the fence, wishy-washy, shilly-shallying, waffling, waffly.

**indecorous** adjective *they swaggered in sporting wild hair and the most indecorous attire* IMPROPER, unseemly, unbecoming, undignified, immodest, indelicate, indecent, unladylike, ungentlemanly; inappropriate, incorrect, unsuitable, undesirable, unfitting, in bad taste, ill-bred, vulgar.

**indeed** adverb **1** *there was, indeed, quite a furor* AS EXPECTED, to be sure; in fact, in point of fact, as a matter of fact, in truth, actually, as it happens/happened, if truth be told, admittedly; *archaic* in sooth.

**2** *"May I join you?" "Yes, indeed."* CERTAINLY, assuredly, of course, naturally, without (a) doubt, without question, by all means, yes; *informal* you bet, I'll say; *informal* indeedy.

**3** *you are indeed clever* VERY, extremely, exceedingly, tremendously, immensely, singularly, decidedly, particularly, remarkably, really.

**indefatigable** adjective *the indefatigable Cosby spoke at eight different colleges* TIRELESS, untiring, unflagging, unwearied; determined, tenacious, dogged, single-minded, assiduous, industrious, hard-working, unswerving, unfaltering, unwavering, unshakable, resolute, indomitable; persistent, relentless, unremitting.

**indefensible** adjective *Smith admitted that her remarks about Collins were indefensible* INEXCUSABLE, unjustifiable, unjustified, unpardonable, unforgivable; uncalled for, unprovoked, gratuitous, unreasonable, unnecessary; insupportable, unacceptable, unwarranted, unwarrantable; flawed, wrong, untenable, unsustainable.

**indefinable** adjective *the flavor is indefinable* HARD TO DEFINE, hard to describe, indescribable, inexpressible, nameless; vague, obscure, nebulous, impalpable, intangible, elusive.

**indefinite** adjective **1** *an indefinite period* INDETERMINATE, unspecified, unlimited, unrestricted, undecided, undetermined, undefined, unfixed, unsettled, unknown, uncertain; limitless, infinite, endless, immeasurable. ANTONYMS fixed, limited.

**2** *an indefinite idea* VAGUE, ill-defined, unclear, imprecise, inexact, loose, general, nebulous, fuzzy, hazy, obscure, ambiguous, equivocal. ANTONYM clear.

**indelible** adjective *indelible memories* INERADICABLE, permanent, lasting, ingrained, persisting, enduring, unfading, unforgettable, haunting, never to be forgotten.

**indelicate** adjective **1** *an indelicate question* INSENSITIVE, tactless, inconsiderate, undiplomatic, impolitic. ANTONYM tactful.

**2** *an indelicate sense of humor* VULGAR, rude, crude, tasteless, bawdy, racy, risqué, ribald, earthy, indecent, improper, naughty, indecorous, off-color, dirty, smutty, raunchy. ANTONYMS polite, clean.

**indemnity** noun **1** *indemnity against loss* INSURANCE, assurance, protection, security, indemnification, surety, guarantee, warranty, safeguard.

**2** *the company was paid $100,000 in indemnity* COMPENSATION, reimbursement, recompense, repayment, restitution, payment, redress, reparation(s), damages.

**3** *legislative indemnity* SALARY, wages, pay, remuneration, earnings.

**indent** verb *the shoreline is indented by marshes, harbors, and tidal inlets* NOTCH, make an indentation in, nick; depress, impress, mark, imprint; scallop, groove, furrow.

▸ noun. See INDENTATION.

**indentation** noun *the indentation in the side of the refrigerator is barely visible* HOLLOW, depression, dip, dent, indent, cavity, concavity, pit, trough; dimple, cleft; nick, notch, groove; impression, imprint, mark; recess, bay, inlet, cove.

**indenture** noun *the validity of the indenture was in question* CONTRACT, agreement, compact, deal, covenant, bond.

▸ verb *Taylor was indentured by the age of twelve* BIND, contract, employ, apprentice; *Law* article.

**independence** noun **1** *the struggle for Quebec independence* SELF-GOVERNMENT, self-rule, home rule, separation, self-determination, sovereignty, autonomy, freedom, liberty.

**2** *he valued his independence* SELF-SUFFICIENCY, self-reliance, autonomy, freedom, liberty. See note at LIBERTY.

**3** *financial independence* FREEDOM, comfort, ease.

**independent** adjective **1** *an independent country* SELF-GOVERNING, self-ruling, self-determining, sovereign, autonomous, free, nonaligned. ANTONYMS subservient, dependent.

**2** *two independent groups of biologists verified the results* SEPARATE, different, unconnected, unrelated, dissociated, discrete. ANTONYM connected.

**3** *independent schools* PRIVATE, private-sector, non-state-run, fee-paying; privatized, denationalized. ANTONYMS public, state-run.

**4** *her grown-up, independent children* SELF-SUFFICIENT, self-supporting, self-reliant, standing on one's own two feet. ANTONYM dependent.

**5** *independent advice* IMPARTIAL, unbiased, unprejudiced, neutral, disinterested, uninvolved, uncommitted, detached, dispassionate, objective, nonpartisan, nondiscriminatory. ANTONYM biased.

**6** *an independent spirit* FREETHINKING, free, individualistic; unconventional, maverick, bold, unconstrained, unfettered, untrammeled. ANTONYMS orthodox, constrained.

**indescribable** adjective *indescribable joy* INEXPRESSIBLE, indefinable, beyond words/description, ineffable, incommunicable; unutterable, unspeakable.

**indestructible** adjective *indestructible plastics* UNBREAKABLE, shatterproof, durable; lasting, enduring, everlasting, perennial, deathless, undying, immortal, inextinguishable, imperishable; *informal* heavy-duty, industrial-strength; *literary* adamantine. ANTONYMS fragile, breakable.

**indeterminate** adjective **1** *an indeterminate period of time* UNDETERMINED, uncertain, unknown, unspecified, unstipulated, indefinite, unfixed. ANTONYM known.

**2** *some indeterminate figures* VAGUE, indefinite, unspecific, unclear, nebulous, indistinct; amorphous, shapeless, formless; hazy, faint, fuzzy, shadowy, dim. ANTONYMS definite, clear.

**index** noun **1** *the library's subject index* LIST, listing, inventory, catalog, register, directory.

**2** *literature is an index to its time* GUIDE, sign, indication, indicator, gauge, measure, signal, mark, evidence, symptom, token; clue, hint.

▸ verb *he indexed his sources* LIST, catalog, make an inventory of, itemize, inventory, record.

**indicate** verb **1** *sales indicate a growing market* POINT TO, be a sign of, be evidence of, evidence, demonstrate, show, testify to, bespeak, be a symptom of, be symptomatic of, denote, connote, mark, signal, signify, suggest, imply; manifest, reveal, betray, display, reflect, represent; *formal* evince; *literary* betoken.

**2** *the president indicated his willingness to use force* STATE, declare, make known, communicate, announce, mention, express, reveal, divulge, disclose; put it on record; admit.

**3** *please indicate your preferences on the form* SPECIFY, designate, mark, stipulate; show.

**4** *he indicated the direction we needed to go* POINT TO, point out, gesture toward.

**indication** noun *there was no indication of injury* SIGN, signal, indicator, symptom, mark, manifestation, demonstration, show, evidence, attestation, proof; pointer, guide, hint, clue, intimation, omen, augury, portent, warning, forewarning. See note at SIGN.

**indicative** adjective *the results are indicative of a possible warming trend* SYMPTOMATIC, expressive, suggestive, representative, emblematic, symbolic; typical, characteristic.

**indicator** noun *the test is used as an indicator of performance* MEASURE, gauge, barometer, guide, index, mark, sign, signal, symptom; bellwether, herald, hint; standard, touchstone, yardstick, benchmark, criterion, point of reference, guideline, test, litmus test.

**indict** verb *the teenager was **indicted for** second-degree robbery* CHARGE WITH, accuse of, arraign for, take to court for, put on trial for, bring to trial for, prosecute for; cite for, impeach for. ANTONYM acquit.

**indifference** noun **1** *his apparent indifference infuriated her*

LACK OF CONCERN, unconcern, disinterest, lack of interest, lack of enthusiasm, apathy, nonchalance, insouciance; boredom, unresponsiveness, impassivity, dispassion, detachment, coolness.

**2** *a matter of indifference* UNIMPORTANCE, insignificance, irrelevance, inconsequentiality.

**indifferent** adjective **1** *an indifferent shrug* UNCONCERNED, uninterested, uncaring, casual, nonchalant, offhand, uninvolved, unenthusiastic, apathetic, lukewarm, phlegmatic, blasé, insouciant; unimpressed, bored, unmoved, unresponsive, impassive, dispassionate, detached, cool. ANTONYMS heedful, caring.

**2** *an indifferent performance* MEDIOCRE, ordinary, average, middling, middle-of-the-road, uninspired, undistinguished, unexceptional, unexciting, unremarkable, run-of-the-mill, pedestrian, prosaic, lackluster, forgettable, amateur, amateurish; *informal* OK, so-so, 'comme ci, comme ça,' fair-to-middling, no great shakes, bush-league. ANTONYM brilliant.

**indigenous** adjective *indigenous species* NATIVE, original, aboriginal, autochthonous; local, domestic, homegrown; earliest, first. See note at NATIVE.

**indigent** adjective *indigent families* POOR, impecunious, destitute, penniless, impoverished, insolvent, poverty-stricken; needy, in need, hard up, disadvantaged, badly off; *informal* (flat) broke, strapped (for cash), on skid row, down-and-out; *formal* penurious. ANTONYM rich.

▸ noun *a shelter for the city's indigents* VAGRANT, homeless person, down-and-out, beggar, pauper, derelict, have-not; *informal* bum.

**indigestion** noun *my indigestion was probably caused by the fried shrimp* DYSPEPSIA, heartburn, hyperacidity, stomachache; upset stomach; *informal* bellyache, tummy ache, collywobbles; *technical* pyrosis.

**indignant** adjective *after the shabby way you've treated me, why shouldn't I be indignant?* AGGRIEVED, resentful, affronted, disgruntled, displeased, cross, angry, mad, annoyed, offended, exasperated, irritated, piqued, nettled, in high dudgeon, chagrined; *informal* peeved, vexed, irked, put out, miffed, aggravated, riled, in a huff, huffy, ticked off, sore.

**indignation** noun *she was filled with indignation at having been blamed unjustly* RESENTMENT, umbrage, affront, disgruntlement, displeasure, anger, outrage, annoyance, irritation, exasperation, vexation, offense, pique; *informal* aggravation; *literary* ire.

**indignity** noun *the indignity of being dumped by one's wife* SHAME, humiliation, loss of self-respect, loss of pride, loss of face, embarrassment, mortification, ignominy; disgrace, dishonor, stigma, discredit; affront, insult, abuse, mistreatment, injury, offense, injustice, slight, snub, discourtesy, disrespect; *informal* slap in the face, kick in the teeth.

**indirect** adjective **1** *an indirect effect* INCIDENTAL, accidental, unintended, unintentional, secondary, subordinate, ancillary, concomitant.

**2** *the indirect route* ROUNDABOUT, circuitous, wandering, meandering, serpentine, winding, tortuous, zigzag.

**3** *an indirect answer* OBLIQUE, inexplicit, implicit, implied, allusive, mealy-mouthed; backhanded.

**indirectly** adverb **1** *we're all affected, if only indirectly* INCIDENTALLY, secondarily, concomitantly, consequentially, contingently, accidentally.

**2** *I heard about it indirectly* SECONDHAND, at second hand, from others, in a roundabout way; *informal* through the grapevine.

**3** *he referred to the subject indirectly* OBLIQUELY, by implication, allusively, by hinting.

**indiscernible** adjective. See IMPERCEPTIBLE.

**indiscreet** adjective *indiscreet office romances* IMPRUDENT, unwise, impolitic, injudicious, incautious, irresponsible, ill-judged, ill-advised, misguided, ill-considered, careless, thoughtless, rash, unwary, hasty, reckless, precipitate, impulsive, foolhardy, foolish, shortsighted; undiplomatic, indelicate, tactless, insensitive; untimely, infelicitous; immodest, indecorous, unseemly, improper.

**indiscretion** noun **1** *he was prone to indiscretion* IMPRUDENCE, injudiciousness, incaution, irresponsibility; carelessness, rashness, recklessness, impulsiveness, foolhardiness, foolishness, folly; tactlessness, thoughtlessness, insensitivity; *humorous* foot-in-mouth disease.

**2** *his past indiscretions* BLUNDER, lapse, gaffe, mistake, faux pas, error, slip, impropriety; misdemeanor, transgression, peccadillo, solecism, misdeed; *informal* slip-up. See note at SIN.

**indiscriminate** adjective *their choice of furnishings is appallingly indiscriminate* NONSELECTIVE, unselective, undiscriminating, uncritical, aimless, hit-or-miss, haphazard, random, arbitrary, unsystematic, undirected; wholesale, general, sweeping, blanket; thoughtless, unthinking, inconsiderate, casual, careless. ANTONYM selective.

**indispensable** adjective *the volunteers' help has been indispensable* ESSENTIAL, necessary, all-important, of the utmost importance, of the essence, vital, must-have, crucial, key, needed, required, requisite, imperative; invaluable. See note at NECESSARY. ANTONYM superfluous.

**indisposed** adjective **1** *my wife is indisposed* ILL, unwell, sick, on the sick list, poorly, ailing, not (very) well, out of sorts, out of action, hors de combat; *informal* under the weather, laid up. ANTONYM well.

**2** *she was indisposed to help him* RELUCTANT, unwilling, disinclined, loath, unprepared, not disposed, not keen. ANTONYM willing.

**indisposition** noun. See ILLNESS.

**indisputable** adjective *the photographs are what really made the facts indisputable* INCONTROVERTIBLE, incontestable, undeniable, irrefutable, beyond dispute, unassailable, unquestionable, beyond question, indubitable, not in doubt, beyond doubt, beyond a shadow of a doubt, unarguable, airtight, watertight; unequivocal, unmistakable, certain, sure, definite, definitive, proven, decisive, conclusive, demonstrable, self-evident, clear, clear-cut, plain, obvious, manifest, patent, palpable. ANTONYM questionable.

**indistinct** adjective **1** *the distant shoreline was indistinct* BLURRED, out of focus, fuzzy, hazy, misty, foggy, cloudy, shadowy, dim, nebulous; unclear, obscure, vague, faint, indistinguishable, indiscernible, barely perceptible, hard to see, hard to make out. ANTONYM clear.

**2** *the last two digits are indistinct* INDECIPHERABLE, illegible, unreadable, hard to read. ANTONYM legible.

**3** *indistinct sounds* MUFFLED, muted, low, quiet, soft, faint, inaudible, hard to hear; muttered, mumbled. ANTONYMS audible, clear.

**indistinguishable** adjective **1** *the two girls were indistinguishable* IDENTICAL, difficult to tell apart, like (two) peas in a pod, like Tweedledum and Tweedledee, very similar, two of a kind. ANTONYM dissimilar.

**2** *the image had become indistinguishable | the voices are indistinguishable* UNINTELLIGIBLE, incomprehensible, hard to make out, indistinct, unclear; inaudible. ANTONYM clear.

**individual** adjective **1** *exhibitions devoted to individual artists* SINGLE, separate, discrete, independent, solo; sole, lone, solitary, isolated.

**2** *the fashion world was eager to be rocked by her individual style* CHARACTERISTIC, distinctive, distinct, typical, particular, peculiar, personal, personalized, special; original, unique, exclusive, singular, idiosyncratic, different, unusual, novel, unorthodox, atypical, out of the ordinary, one of a kind.

▸ noun **1** *Ed was never a particularly happy individual* PERSON, human being, mortal, soul, creature; man, boy, woman, girl; character, personage; *informal* type, sort, customer, guy.

**2** *the anthology is dedicated to the math professor who most encouraged her to be an individual* INDIVIDUALIST, free spirit, nonconformist, original, eccentric, character, maverick, rare bird, something else.

**individualistic** adjective *an individualistic approach to symphonic composition* UNCONVENTIONAL, unorthodox, atypical, singular, unique, original, nonconformist, independent, individual, freethinking; eccentric, maverick, strange, odd, peculiar, quirky, queer, idiosyncratic; *informal* off-the-wall.

**individuality** noun *the need to assert our individuality* DISTINCTIVENESS, distinction, uniqueness, originality, singularity, particularity, peculiarity, differentness, separateness; personality, character, identity, self, ego.

**individually** adverb *the applications will be reviewed individually* ONE AT A TIME, one by one, singly, separately, severally, independently, apart. ANTONYM together.

**indoctrinate** verb *armed with an evil political agenda, they set out to indoctrinate the nation's idealistic youth* BRAINWASH, propagandize, proselytize, inculcate, instill, reeducate, persuade, convince, condition, program, mold, discipline; instruct, teach, train, school, drill.

**indolent** adjective *those who choose to remain aimless and indolent will never benefit from our self-help programs* LAZY, idle, slothful, loafing, do-nothing, sluggardly, shiftless, lackadaisical, languid, inactive, inert, sluggish, lethargic, torpid; slack, good-for-nothing, feckless. ANTONYMS industrious, energetic.

**indomitable** adjective *the indomitable spirit of this team* INVINCIBLE, unconquerable, unbeatable, unassailable, invulnerable, unshakable, unsinkable; indefatigable, unyielding, unbending, stalwart, stout-hearted, lionhearted, strong-willed, strong-minded, steadfast, staunch, resolute, firm, determined, intransigent, inflexible, adamant; unflinching, courageous, brave, valiant, heroic, intrepid, fearless, plucky, gritty. ANTONYM submissive.

**indubitable** adjective *indubitable testimony* UNQUESTIONABLE, undoubtable, indisputable, unarguable, undebatable, incontestable, undeniable, irrefutable, incontrovertible, unmistakable, unequivocal, certain, sure, positive, definite, absolute, conclusive, watertight, ironclad; beyond doubt, beyond the shadow of a doubt, beyond dispute, beyond question, not in question, not in doubt; *informal* sure as shootin'. ANTONYM doubtful.

**induce** verb **1** *the pickets induced many workers to stay away* PERSUADE, convince, prevail upon, get, make, prompt, move, inspire, influence, encourage, motivate; coax into, wheedle into, cajole into, talk into, prod into; *informal* twist someone's arm. ANTONYM dissuade.

**2** *how to induce hypnosis* BRING ABOUT, cause, produce, effect, create, give rise to, generate, instigate, engender, occasion, set in motion, lead to, result in, trigger, whip up, stir up, kindle, arouse, rouse, foster, promote, encourage; *literary* beget, enkindle; *rare* effectuate. ANTONYM prevent.

**inducement** noun *customers responded best to such inducements as rebates and low interest rates* INCENTIVE, encouragement, attraction, temptation, stimulus, bait, lure, pull, draw, spur, goad, impetus, motive, motivation, provocation; bribe, reward; *informal* carrot, come-on, sweetener. ANTONYM deterrent.

**indulge** verb **1** *Seth indulged his passion for vintage stemware* SATISFY, gratify, fulfill, feed, accommodate; yield to, give in to, give way to.

**2** *she seldom* **indulged in** *sentimentality* WALLOW IN, give oneself up to, give way to, yield to, abandon oneself to, give free rein to; luxuriate in, revel in, lose oneself in.

**3** *she did not indulge her children* PAMPER, spoil, overindulge, coddle, mollycoddle, cosset, baby, spoon-feed, pander to, wait on hand and foot, cater to someone's every whim, kill with kindness. PHRASE: **indulge oneself** *it's healthy to indulge yourself once in a while* TREAT ONESELF, give oneself a treat; go on a spree; *informal* go to town, splurge.

**indulgence** noun **1** *the indulgence of all his desires* SATISFAC-

TION, gratification, fulfillment, satiation, appeasement; accommodation; slaking, quenching. ANTONYMS denial, withholding.

2 *excessive indulgence contributed to his ill health* SELF-GRATIFICATION, self-indulgence, overindulgence, intemperance, immoderation, excess, excessiveness, lack of restraint, extravagance, decadence; *rare* sybaritism. ANTONYMS moderation, restraint.

3 *they viewed vacations as an indulgence* EXTRAVAGANCE, luxury, treat, nonessential, extra, frill. ANTONYM necessity.

4 *his mother's indulgence made him ungovernable* PAMPERING, coddling, mollycoddling, spoiling, cosseting, babying. ANTONYM strictness.

5 *I ask for your indulgence* TOLERANCE, forbearance, understanding, kindness, compassion, sympathy, forgiveness, leniency, mercy, clemency, liberality. ANTONYMS severity, harshness.

**indulgent** adjective *the children took advantage of their indulgent sitter* PERMISSIVE, easygoing, liberal, tolerant, forgiving, forbearing, lenient, kind, kindly, generous, softhearted, compassionate, understanding, sympathetic; fond, doting, soft; compliant, obliging, accommodating. See note at LENIENT. ANTONYM strict.

**industrial** adjective 1 *industrial areas of the city* MANUFACTURING, factory; commercial, business, trade.

2 *industrial plastic* HEAVY-DUTY, durable, strong, tough, rugged.

**industrialist** noun *nineteenth-century industrialists* MANUFACTURER, factory owner; captain of industry, big businessman, magnate, tycoon, capitalist, financier.

**industrious** adjective *the industrious immigrants who founded our town in 1826* HARD-WORKING, diligent, assiduous, conscientious, steady, painstaking, sedulous, persevering, unflagging, untiring, tireless, indefatigable, studious; busy, as busy as a bee, active, bustling, energetic, on the go, vigorous, determined, dynamic, zealous, productive; with one's shoulder to the wheel, with one's nose to the grindstone. See note at BUSY. ANTONYM indolent.

**industry** noun 1 *Canadian industry* MANUFACTURING, production; construction.

2 *the publishing industry* BUSINESS, trade, field, line (of business); *informal* racket.

3 *the kitchen was a hive of industry* ACTIVITY, busyness, energy, vigor, productiveness; hard work, industriousness, diligence, application, dedication. ANTONYM inactivity.

**inebriated** adjective *an apparently inebriated boater stunned diners at a waterfront restaurant when he docked his craft in the buff* DRUNK, intoxicated, inebriate, impaired, drunken, tipsy, under the influence; *informal* plastered, smashed, bombed, sloshed, sozzled, sauced, lubricated, well-oiled, wrecked, juiced, blasted, stinko, blitzed, half-cut, fried, gassed, polluted, tanked (up), soaked, out of one's head/skull, loaded, trashed, buzzed, befuddled, besotted, pickled, pixilated, canned, cockeyed, blotto, blind drunk, roaring drunk, dead drunk, punch-drunk, ripped, stewed, tight, the worse for wear, far gone, pie-eyed, three sheets to the wind; *vulgar slang* shit-faced; *Brit. informal* bladdered, lashed; *informal, dated* in one's cups, merry; *literary* crapulous. See note at DRUNK. ANTONYM sober.

**inedible** adjective *the stew looked fabulous but it was inedible* UNEATABLE, indigestible, unsavory, unpalatable, unappetizing, unwholesome; stale, rotten, off, bad, unfit to eat.

**ineffable** adjective 1 *the ineffable, surging joy of the Beatles* INDESCRIBABLE, inexpressible, beyond words, beyond description, begging description; indefinable, unutterable, untold, unimaginable; overwhelming, breathtaking, awesome, marvelous, wonderful, staggering, amazing.

2 *the ineffable name of God* UNUTTERABLE, not to be uttered, not to be spoken, unmentionable, forbidden, taboo.

**ineffective** adjective 1 *an ineffective scheme* UNSUCCESSFUL, unproductive, fruitless, unprofitable, abortive, futile, purposeless, useless, worthless, ineffectual, inefficient, inefficacious, inadequate; feeble, inept, lame; *archaic* bootless.

2 *an ineffective president* INEFFECTUAL, inefficient, inefficacious, unsuccessful, powerless, impotent, lame-duck; inadequate, incompetent, incapable, unfit, inept, bungling, weak, poor; *informal* useless, hopeless.

**ineffectual** adjective. See INEFFECTIVE senses 1, 2.

**inefficient** adjective 1 *an inefficient worker* INEFFECTIVE, ineffectual, unproductive, incompetent, inept, incapable, unfit, unskillful, inexpert, amateurish, unprofessional; disorganized, unprepared; negligent, lax, sloppy, slack, careless; *informal* lousy, useless, good-for-nothing.

2 *inefficient processes* UNECONOMICAL, wasteful, unproductive, time-wasting, slow; deficient, disorganized, unsystematic.

**inelegant** adjective 1 *an inelegant laugh* UNREFINED, uncouth, unsophisticated, unpolished, uncultivated; ill-bred, coarse, vulgar, rude, impolite, unmannerly, tasteless. ANTONYM refined.

2 *an inelegant maneuver* GRACELESS, ungraceful, ungainly, uncoordinated, awkward, clumsy, lumbering; inept, unskillful, inexpert; *informal* having two left feet, clunky. ANTONYM graceful.

**ineligible** adjective *the aforementioned agencies will be ineligible to participate in any federally funded assistance program* UNQUALIFIED, unsuitable, unacceptable, undesirable, inappropriate, unworthy; ruled out, disqualified, disentitled; *Law* incompetent. ANTONYM qualified.

**inept** adjective *his mother could pitch a wicked fastball, but she was completely inept in the kitchen* INCOMPETENT, unskillful, unskilled, inexpert, amateurish; clumsy, awkward, maladroit, bungling, blundering; unproductive, unsuccessful, ineffectual, not up to scratch; *informal* ham-handed, ham-fisted, butterfingered, klutzy, all thumbs. ANTONYM competent.

**inequality** noun *Dominicans spoke out against the social inequality in their country* IMBALANCE, inequity, inconsistency, variation, variability; divergence, polarity, disparity, discrepancy, dissimilarity, difference; bias, prejudice, discrimination, unfairness.

**inequitable** adjective *inequitable salaries for similar positions* UNFAIR, unjust, unequal, uneven, unbalanced, one-sided, discriminatory, preferential, biased, partisan, partial, prejudiced. ANTONYM fair.

**inequity** noun *the inequity of the law* UNFAIRNESS, injustice, unjustness, discrimination, partisanship, partiality, favoritism, bias, prejudice.

**inert** adjective *forces that once drove the economy have become inert* UNMOVING, motionless, immobile, inanimate, still, stationary, static; dormant, sleeping; unconscious, comatose, lifeless, insensible, insensate, insentient; idle, inactive, sluggish, lethargic, indolent, stagnant, listless, torpid. ANTONYM active.

**inertia** noun *by the nature of its own inertia, the coal industry has remained an unshakable constant* INACTIVITY, inaction, inertness; unchanged state, stationary condition, stasis.

**inescapable** adjective *meeting the future in-laws is inescapable* UNAVOIDABLE, inevitable, ineluctable, inexorable; assured, sure, certain, guaranteed; necessary, required, compulsory, mandatory; *rare* ineludible. ANTONYM avoidable.

**inestimable** adjective *inestimable damage* IMMEASURABLE, incalculable, innumerable, unfathomable, indeterminable, measureless, countless, untold; limitless, boundless, unlimited, infinite, endless, inexhaustible; *informal* no end of; *literary* myriad. ANTONYM few.

**inevitable** adjective *at this point, war is inevitable* UNAVOIDABLE, inescapable, inexorable, ineluctable; assured, certain, sure, fixed; fated, destined, predestined, predetermined; *rare* ineludible. ANTONYM uncertain.

**inexact** adjective *inexact diagnostic practices* IMPRECISE, inaccurate, approximate, rough, crude, general, vague, fuzzy, ill-defined; *informal* off-base, ballpark.

**inexcusable** adjective *our report found inexcusable national security weaknesses* INDEFENSIBLE, unjustifiable, unwarranted, unpardonable, unforgivable; blameworthy, censurable, reprehensible, deplorable, unconscionable, disgraceful, unacceptable, unreasonable.

**inexhaustible** adjective **1** *her patience is inexhaustible* UNLIMITED, limitless, illimitable, infinite, boundless, endless, never-ending, unfailing, everlasting; immeasurable, incalculable, inestimable, untold; copious, abundant, plentiful, bottomless. ANTONYM limited.

**2** *the dancers were inexhaustible* TIRELESS, indefatigable, untiring, unwearied, unwearying, unfaltering, unflagging, unremitting, persevering, persistent, dogged. ANTONYMS weary, lacking stamina.

**inexorable** adjective **1** *the inexorable advance of science* RELENTLESS, unstoppable, inescapable, inevitable, unavoidable, irrevocable, unalterable; persistent, continuous, nonstop, steady, interminable, incessant, unceasing, unremitting, unrelenting.

**2** *inexorable creditors* INTRANSIGENT, unbending, unyielding, inflexible, adamant, obdurate, immovable, unshakable; implacable, unappeasable, severe, hard, unforgiving, unsparing, uncompromising, ruthless, relentless, pitiless, merciless.

**inexpensive** adjective *inexpensive wine* CHEAP, low-priced, low-cost, modest, economical, competitive, affordable, reasonable, budget, bargain, cut-rate, reduced, discounted, discount, rock-bottom, giveaway, downmarket, low-end; *informal* bargain-basement, dirt cheap.

**inexperienced** adjective *she's inexperienced, but we expect her to become an excellent teacher* UNSEASONED, unpracticed, untrained, unschooled, unqualified, unskilled, amateur; ignorant, unversed, inexpert; ill-equipped, ill-prepared; naive, unsophisticated, callow, immature, green, unworldly; *informal* wet behind the ears.

**inexpert** adjective *inexpert installation spoils the windows irreparably* UNSKILLED, unskillful, amateur, amateurish, unprofessional, inexperienced; inept, incompetent, maladroit, uncoordinated, clumsy, bungling, blundering; *informal* ham-handed, ham-fisted, butterfingered.

**inexplicable** adjective *these inexplicable acts of vandalism have left the community stunned* UNACCOUNTABLE, unexplainable, incomprehensible, unfathomable, impenetrable, insoluble; baffling, puzzling, perplexing, mystifying, bewildering, confusing; mysterious, strange. ANTONYM understandable.

**inexpressible** adjective *my grief is inexpressible* INDESCRIBABLE, indefinable, unutterable, unspeakable, ineffable, beyond words, nameless; unimaginable, inconceivable, unthinkable, untold.

**inexpressive** adjective *a room of inexpressive faces* EXPRESSIONLESS, impassive, emotionless; inscrutable, unreadable, blank, vacant, glazed, glassy, lifeless, deadpan, wooden, stony; poker-faced, straight-faced.

**inextinguishable** adjective *his inextinguishable passion for literature* IRREPRESSIBLE, unquenchable, indestructible, undying, immortal, imperishable, unfailing, unceasing, ceaseless, enduring, everlasting, eternal, persistent.

**inextricable** adjective **1** *our lives are inextricable* INSEPARABLE, indivisible, entangled, tangled, mixed up.

**2** *an inextricable situation* INESCAPABLE, unavoidable, ineluctable.

**infallible** adjective **1** *an infallible sense of timing* UNERRING, unfailing, faultless, flawless, impeccable, perfect, precise, accurate, meticulous, scrupulous.

**2** *an infallible remedy* UNFAILING, unerring, guaranteed, dependable, trustworthy, reliable, sure, certain, safe, foolproof, effective; *informal* sure-fire; *formal* efficacious.

**infamous** adjective **1** *an infamous train robber* NOTORIOUS, disreputable; legendary, fabled, famed. ANTONYM reputable.

**2** *infamous misconduct* ABOMINABLE, outrageous, shocking, shameful, disgraceful, dishonorable, discreditable, contemptible, unworthy; monstrous, atrocious, nefarious, appalling, dreadful, terrible, heinous, egregious, detestable, despicable, loathsome, hateful, vile, unspeakable, unforgivable, iniquitous, scandalous; *informal* dirty, filthy, lowdown. ANTONYM honorable.

**infancy** noun **1** *his twin died in infancy* BABYHOOD, early childhood.

**2** *music video was in its infancy* BEGINNINGS, early days, early stages; seeds, roots; start, commencement, rise, emergence, genesis, dawn, birth, inception. ANTONYM end.

**infant** noun *a fretful infant* BABY, newborn, young child, (tiny) tot, little one, papoose; *Medicine* neonate; *informal* tiny; *literary* babe, babe in arms, suckling.

▸ adjective *an infant stage* DEVELOPING, emergent, emerging, embryonic, nascent, incipient, new, fledgling, budding, up-and-coming.

**infantile** adjective *it's time you outgrew your infantile behavior* CHILDISH, babyish, immature, puerile, juvenile, adolescent, jejune; silly, inane, fatuous.

**infantry** noun *the infantry, as usual, took the worst of the battle* INFANTRYMEN, foot soldiers, foot guards; the ranks; *informal* GIs; cannon fodder; *Military slang* grunts; *historical* footmen.

**infatuated** adjective *Kyle was hopelessly **infatuated with** his cousin's girlfriend* BESOTTED WITH, in love with, head over heels about, obsessed with, taken with, lovesick for, moonstruck over; enamored of, attracted to, devoted to, captivated by, enthralled by, enchanted by, bewitched by, under the spell of; *informal* smitten with, sweet on, keen on, hot for, gone on, hung up on, mad about, crazy about, nuts about, stuck on, carrying a torch for.

**infect** verb **1** *he didn't want to infect others with his chicken pox* PASS INFECTION TO, spread disease to, contaminate.

**2** *nitrates were infecting rivers* CONTAMINATE, pollute, taint, foul, dirty, blight, damage, ruin; poison.

**3** *his high spirits infected everyone* AFFECT, influence, have an impact on, touch; excite, inspire, stimulate, animate.

**infection** noun *a treatable skin infection* DISEASE, virus; disorder, condition, affliction, complaint, illness, ailment, sickness, infirmity; contamination, poison, septicemia, suppuration; *informal* bug; *dated* contagion; *Medicine* sepsis.

**infectious** adjective **1** *infectious disease* CONTAGIOUS, communicable, transmittable, transferable, spreadable; epidemic; *informal* catching; *dated* infective.

**2** *her laughter is infectious* IRRESISTIBLE, compelling, persuasive, contagious, catching.

**infer** verb *is it really possible to infer that a crime was committed, given this flimsy evidence?* DEDUCE, conclude, conjecture, surmise, reason, interpret; gather, understand, presume, assume, take it, extrapolate; read between the lines, figure (out); *informal* reckon.

**USAGE NOTE infer**

Properly used, *infer* means "deduce; reason from premises to a conclusion"—e.g.: "We get no sense of the man himself from this book except what we can infer from the biographical facts that Mr. Magida presents." (*New York Times*; Aug. 18, 1996.)

Writers frequently misuse *infer* when *imply* (= hint at; suggest) would be the correct word—e.g.: "And no team is, of course, inferring [read *implying*] that Dallas isn't talented." (*New York Times*; Jan. 12, 1996.) Remember: a speaker or writer *implies* something without putting it expressly. A listener or reader *infers* beyond what has been literally expressed. Or, as Theodore Bernstein put it, "The *implier* is the pitcher; the *inferrer* is the catcher." (*The Careful Writer*; 1965.) Stylists agree that the important distinction between these words deserves to be maintained. —*BG*

**inference** noun *there should be no inference drawn from the fact that he chooses not to be a witness* DEDUCTION, conclusion, reasoning, conjecture, speculation, guess, presumption, assumption, supposition, reckoning, extrapolation.

**inferior** adjective **1** *poorer people were thought to be innately inferior* SECOND-CLASS, lesser, lower in status, lower-ranking, subordinate, second-fiddle, junior, minor; subservient, lowly, humble, menial, beneath one. ANTONYM superior.

**2** *inferior accommodations* SECOND-RATE, substandard, low-quality, low-grade, downmarket, bush-league, unsatisfactory, shoddy, deficient; poor, bad, awful, dreadful, wretched; *informal* crummy, scuzzy, rotten, lousy, third-rate, tinpot, rinky-dink. ANTONYM luxury.

▸ noun *how dare she treat him as an inferior?* SUBORDINATE, junior, underling, minion, menial, peon. ANTONYM superior.

**infernal** adjective **1** *the infernal regions* HELLISH, nether, subterranean, underworld, chthonic, Tartarean; satanic, devilish, diabolical, fiendish, demonic.

**2** *informal an infernal nuisance* DAMNABLE, wretched, confounded; annoying, irritating, infuriating, irksome, detestable, exasperating; *informal* damned, damn, blasted, blessed, pesky, aggravating; *informal, dated* cursed.

**infertile** adjective **1** *infertile soil* BARREN, unfruitful, unproductive; sterile, impoverished, arid.

**2** *she was infertile* STERILE, barren; childless, unable to procreate/reproduce, impotent; *Medicine* infecund.

**infest** verb *without follow-up treatment, a new horde of ants will infest the building* OVERRUN, spread through, invade, infiltrate, pervade, permeate, inundate, overwhelm; beset, plague, swarm.

**infidel** noun *a holy war against the infidels* UNBELIEVER, disbeliever, nonbeliever, agnostic, atheist; heathen, pagan, idolater, heretic, freethinker, dissenter, nonconformist; *archaic* paynim; *rare* nullifidian.

**infidelity** noun *even after reconciliation, she could not forgive* *his infidelity* UNFAITHFULNESS, adultery, cuckoldry, disloyalty, extramarital sex; deceit, falseness; affair, liaison, fling, amour; *informal* fooling/playing around, cheating, two-timing, hanky-panky; *formal* fornication. ANTONYM faithfulness.

**infiltrate** verb *spies were prepared to infiltrate the enemy camp* INSINUATE ONESELF INTO, worm one's way into, sneak into, slip into, get into, invade, penetrate, enter; permeate, pervade, seep into/through, soak into.

**infinite** adjective **1** *the universe is infinite* BOUNDLESS, unbounded, unlimited, limitless, never-ending, interminable; immeasurable, fathomless, imponderable; extensive, vast; immense, great, huge, enormous. ANTONYMS limited, small.

**2** *infinite resources* COUNTLESS, uncountable, inestimable, innumerable, numberless, immeasurable, incalculable, untold, myriad. ANTONYM limited.

**infinitesimal** adjective *these infinitesimal organisms can cause monstrously huge problems* MINUTE, tiny, minuscule, very small; microscopic, imperceptible, indiscernible; *informal* teeny, wee, teeny-weeny, itsy-bitsy, little-bitty. ANTONYM enormous.

**infinity** noun **1** *the infinity of space* ENDLESSNESS, infinitude, infiniteness, boundlessness, limitlessness; vastness, immensity.

**2** *an infinity of accessories* INFINITE NUMBER, great number; abundance, profusion, host, multitude, mass, wealth; *informal* heap, stack.

**infirm** adjective *how long has he been so infirm?* FRAIL, weak, feeble, debilitated, decrepit, disabled; ill, unwell, sick, sickly, indisposed, ailing. See note at WEAK. ANTONYM healthy.

**infirmity** noun *the family would never openly discuss Aunt Erma's infirmity* ILLNESS, malady, ailment, disease, disorder, sickness, affliction, complaint, indisposition, frailty, weakness; disability, impairment.

**inflame** verb **1** *his opinions inflamed his rival* ENRAGE, incense, anger, madden, infuriate, exasperate, provoke, antagonize, rile; *informal* make someone see red, make someone's blood boil. ANTONYM placate.

**2** *the case inflamed passions against the pit bull* INCITE, arouse, rouse, provoke, stir up, whip up, kindle, ignite, touch off, foment, inspire, stimulate, agitate. ANTONYMS calm, dampen.

**3** *he inflamed an already tense situation* AGGRAVATE, exacerbate, intensify, worsen, compound. ANTONYM soothe.

**inflamed** adjective **1** *the cut became inflamed* SWOLLEN, puffed up; red; raw, sore, painful, tender; infected, septic.

**2** *inflamed feelings* ANGRY, infuriated, furious, enraged; excited, aroused, stimulated, titillated.

**inflammation** noun *apply ice to the inflammation* SWELLING, puffiness; redness; rawness, soreness, tenderness; infection, festering, suppuration, septicity.

**inflammatory** adjective *neither senator condemned the inflammatory language used by Sharpton* PROVOCATIVE, incendiary, inflaming, inciting, agitating, stirring, rousing, provoking, fomenting, rabble-rousing, seditious, subversive, mutinous; fiery, passionate; controversial, contentious.

**inflate** verb **1** *she inflated the mattress* BLOW UP, fill up, fill with air, aerate, pump up; dilate, distend, swell. ANTONYM deflate.

**2** *the demand inflated prices* INCREASE, raise, boost, escalate, put up; *informal* hike up, jack up, bump up, boost (up). ANTONYMS decrease, depress.

**3** *the figures were inflated by the press* EXAGGERATE, magnify, overplay, overstate, enhance, embellish, increase, amplify, augment. ANTONYMS play down, understate, soft-pedal.

**inflated** adjective **1** *an inflated balloon* BLOWN UP, aerated, filled, puffed up/out, pumped up; distended, expanded, engorged, swollen.

**2** *inflated prices* HIGH, sky-high, excessive, unreasonable, prohibitive, outrageous, exorbitant, extortionate; *informal* steep, stiff, pricey.

**3** *an inflated opinion of himself* EXAGGERATED, magnified, aggrandized, immoderate, overblown, overstated.

**4** *inflated language* HIGH-FLOWN, extravagant, exaggerated, elaborate, flowery, ornate, overblown, overwrought, grandiloquent, magniloquent, lofty, grandiose; affected, pretentious, bombastic, tumid; *informal* windy, highfalutin.

**inflection** noun *when I read my lines, he'd gently correct my pronunciation and inflection.* STRESS, cadence, rhythm, accent, intonation, pitch, emphasis, modulation, lilt, tone.

**inflexible** adjective **1** *his inflexible attitude* STUBBORN, obstinate, obdurate, intractable, intransigent, unbending, immovable, unaccommodating; hidebound, single-minded, pigheaded, mulish, uncompromising, adamant, firm, resolute, diehard, dyed-in-the-wool; *formal* refractory. ANTONYMS accommodating, flexible.

**2** *inflexible rules* UNALTERABLE, unchangeable, immutable, unvarying; firm, fixed, set, established, entrenched, hard and fast, carved in stone; stringent, strict, hardline, ironclad. ANTONYM flexible.

**3** *inflexible plastic* RIGID, stiff, unyielding, unbending, unbendable; hard, firm, inelastic. ANTONYMS pliable, flexible.

**inflict** verb **1** *he **inflicted** an injury **on** James* ADMINISTER TO, deliver to, deal out to, dispense to, mete out to; impose on, exact on, wreak on; cause to, give to; *informal* dish out to.

**2** *I won't inflict myself on you any longer* IMPOSE, force, thrust, foist; saddle someone with, burden someone with.

**influence** noun **1** *the influence of parents on their children* EFFECT, impact; control, sway, hold, power, authority, mastery, domination, supremacy; guidance, direction; pressure.

**2** *a bad **influence on** young girls* EXAMPLE TO, (role) model for, guide for, inspiration to.

**3** *political influence* POWER, authority, sway, leverage, weight, pull, standing, prestige, stature, rank; *informal* clout, muscle, teeth.

▸ verb **1** *bosses can influence our careers* AFFECT, have an impact on, impact, determine, guide, control, shape, govern, decide; change, alter, transform.

**2** *an attempt to influence the jury* SWAY, bias, prejudice, suborn; pressure, coerce; dragoon, intimidate, browbeat, brainwash; *informal* twist someone's arm, lean on, put ideas into one's head.

**influential** adjective **1** *an influential leader* POWERFUL, dominant, controlling, strong, authoritative, persuasive; important, affluential, prominent, distinguished, eminent. ANTONYMS unimportant, impotent.

**2** *she was influential in shaping his career* INSTRUMENTAL, significant, important, crucial, pivotal. ANTONYM insignificant.

**influx** noun **1** *an influx of tourists* INUNDATION, rush, stream, flood, incursion; invasion, intrusion.

**2** *influxes of river water* INFLOW, inrush, flood, inundation.

**inform** verb **1** *she informed him that she was ill* TELL, notify, apprise, advise, impart to, communicate to, let someone know; brief, prime, enlighten, send word to, give/supply information to; *informal* fill someone in, clue someone in.

**2** *he* ***informed on*** *two of the suspects* DENOUNCE, give away, betray, incriminate, inculpate, report, finger; sell out, stab in the back; *informal* rat on/out, squeal on, tell on, blab on, tattle on, blow the whistle on, sell down the river, snitch on.

**3** *the articles were informed by feminism* SUFFUSE, pervade, permeate, infuse, imbue, inspire; characterize.

**informal** adjective **1** *an informal chat* UNOFFICIAL, casual, relaxed, easygoing, unceremonious; open, friendly, intimate; simple, unpretentious, easy; *informal* unstuffy, laid-back, chummy. ANTONYMS official, formal.

**2** *informal language* COLLOQUIAL, vernacular, idiomatic, demotic, popular; familiar, everyday, unofficial; simple, natural, unpretentious; *informal* slangy, chatty, folksy. ANTONYMS literary, formal.

**3** *informal clothes* CASUAL, relaxed, comfortable, everyday, sloppy, leisure; *informal* comfy, cazh. ANTONYM formal.

**information** noun *we'll give you the latest information* DETAILS, particulars, facts, figures, statistics, data; knowledge, intelligence; instruction, advice, guidance, direction, counsel, enlightenment; news, word; *informal* info, lowdown, dope, dirt, inside story, scoop, poop. See note at KNOWLEDGE.

**informative** adjective *he hosts TV's most informative game show* INSTRUCTIVE, instructional, illuminating, enlightening, revealing, explanatory; factual, educational, educative, edifying, didactic; *informal* newsy.

**informed** adjective *our informed listeners tell us we've reported the wrong concert dates* KNOWLEDGEABLE, enlightened, literate, educated; sophisticated, cultured; briefed, versed, up to date, up to speed, in the know, au courant, au fait; *informal* hip, in the loop. ANTONYM ignorant.

**informer** noun *a Libyan informer for the CIA* INFORMANT, betrayer, traitor, Judas, double-crosser, collaborator, spy, double agent, fifth columnist, infiltrator, plant, tattletale; *informal* rat, squealer, whistle-blower, snake in the grass, snitch, fink, stool pigeon, stoolie, canary.

**infraction** noun *leaving the grounds before noon is an infraction of the rules | Hurley has been cited for another infraction* VIOLATION, contravention, breach, transgression, infringement, offense; neglect, dereliction, noncompliance; *Law* contumacy.

**infrequent** adjective *her infrequent visits* RARE, uncommon, unusual, exceptional, few (and far between), as rare/scarce as hen's teeth; unaccustomed, unwonted; isolated, scarce, scattered; sporadic, irregular, intermittent, seldom; *informal* once in a blue moon. ANTONYM common.

**infringe** verb **1** *the statute infringed constitutionally guaranteed rights* CONTRAVENE, violate, transgress, break, breach; disobey, defy, flout, fly in the face of; disregard, ignore, neglect; go beyond, overstep, exceed; *Law* infract. ANTONYMS obey, comply with.

**2** *the surveillance* ***infringed on*** *his rights* RESTRICT, limit, curb, check, encroach on; undermine, erode, diminish, weaken, impair, damage, compromise. ANTONYM preserve.

**infuriate** verb *the governor's veto is likely to infuriate child-care providers statewide* ENRAGE, incense, anger, inflame; exasperate, antagonize, provoke, rile, annoy, irritate, aggravate, madden, nettle, gall, irk, vex, get on someone's nerves, try someone's patience, rankle; *informal* make someone see red, get someone's back up, make someone's blood boil, needle, ride, tick off, tee off, piss off, PO, wind up, get to, bug. ANTONYMS please, humor.

**infuriating** adjective *it's infuriating that they leave that dog outside to bark all day* EXASPERATING, maddening, annoying, irritating, irksome, vexatious, trying, tiresome; *informal* aggravating, pesky, infernal.

**ingenious** adjective *an ingenious economist | the kids in her science class have devised an ingenious machine for sorting recyclables* INVENTIVE, creative, imaginative, original, innovative, pioneering, resourceful, enterprising, inspired; clever, intelligent, smart, brilliant, masterly, talented, gifted, skillful; astute, sharp-witted, quick-witted, shrewd; elaborate, sophisticated. See note at CREATIVE.

**ingenuous** adjective *she had never before met a grown man so ingenuous* NAIVE, innocent, simple, childlike, trusting, unwary; unsuspicious, unworldly, wide-eyed, inexperienced, green; open, sincere, honest, frank, candid, forthright, artless, guileless, genuine, upfront. See note at GULLIBLE. ANTONYM artful.

**inglorious** adjective *her association with the blackmailers brought an inglorious end to an otherwise brilliant career* SHAMEFUL, dishonorable, ignominious, discreditable, disgraceful, scandalous; humiliating, mortifying, demeaning, ignoble, undignified, wretched, shabby.

**ingrained**, **engrained** adjective **1** *ingrained attitudes* ENTRENCHED, established, deep-rooted, deep-seated, fixed, firm, unshakable, ineradicable; inveterate, dyed-in-the-wool, abiding, enduring, stubborn. See note at INHERENT. ANTONYM transient.

**2** *ingrained dirt* GROUND-IN, fixed, implanted, embedded; permanent, indelible, ineradicable. ANTONYM superficial.

**ingratiate** PHRASE: **ingratiate oneself** *he has **ingratiated himself with** President Jiang by running ideological education campaigns* CURRY FAVOR WITH, cultivate, win over, get in good with; toady to, grovel to, fawn over, kowtow to, play up to, pander to, flatter, court, wheedle, schmooze; *informal* suck up to, lick someone's boots, butter up, brown-nose.

**ingratiating** adjective *a forced and ingratiating smile* SYCOPHANTIC, toadying, fawning, unctuous, obsequious; flattering, insincere; smooth-tongued, slick; greasy, oily, saccharine; *informal* smarmy, slimy.

**ingratitude** noun *these sanctions have sent a message of ingratitude to the many honest and hard-working officers* UNGRATEFULNESS, thanklessness, lack of appreciation, nonrecognition.

**ingredient** adjective *crystallized iodine is a legal ingredient of an illegal drug* CONSTITUENT, component, element; part, piece, bit, strand, portion, unit, feature, aspect, attribute; (**ingredients**) contents, makings.

**ingress** noun *two doors offer ingress to the station* ENTRY, entrance, entryway, entrée, access, admittance, admission; way in, approach, passage. ANTONYM exit.

**inhabit** verb *outside of the research team, humans do not inhabit this island* LIVE IN/ON, occupy; settle (in/on), people, populate, colonize; dwell in/on, reside in/on, tenant, lodge in/on, have one's home in/on; *formal* be domiciled in/on, abide in/on.

**inhabitant** noun *the inhabitants have organized a protest* RESIDENT, occupant, occupier, dweller, squatter, settler; local, native; *formal* denizen; **(inhabitants)** population, populace, people, public, community, citizenry, townsfolk, townspeople.

**inhale** verb *inhale deeply | we'd rather not inhale your cigar smoke* BREATHE IN, inspire, draw in, suck in, take in, sniff in, drink in.

**inharmonious** adjective **1** *inharmonious sounds* UNMELODIOUS, discordant, unharmonious, unmusical, dissonant, off-key; grating, harsh, cacophonous; *rare* absonant. ANTONYM musical.

**2** *once you've endured a dinner with her family you will never again think that your relatives are inharmonious* ANTAGONISTIC, argumentative, quarrelsome, captious, disputatious, belligerent, confrontational, combative. ANTONYM congenial.

**inherent** adjective *inherent traits* INTRINSIC, innate, immanent, built-in, indwelling, inborn, ingrained, deep-rooted; essential, fundamental, basic, structural, organic; natural, instinctive, instinctual, congenital, native. ANTONYM acquired.

**THE RIGHT WORD inherent, congenital, essential, inborn, ingrained, innate, intrinsic**

A quality that is **inherent** is a permanent part of a person's nature or essence (*an inherent tendency to fight back*). If it is **ingrained**, it is deeply wrought into his or her substance or character (*ingrained prejudice against women*). **Inborn** and **innate** are nearly synonymous, sharing the basic sense of existing at the time of birth, but *innate* is usually preferred in an abstract or philosophical context (*innate defects; innate ideas*), while *inborn* is reserved for human characteristics that are so deep-seated they seem to have been there from birth (*an inborn aptitude for the piano*). **Congenital** also means from the time of one's birth, but it is primarily used in medical contexts and refers to problems or defects (*congenital color-blindness; a congenital tendency toward schizophrenia*). **Intrinsic** and **essential** are broader terms that can apply to things as well as people. Something that is *essential* is part of the essence or constitution of something (*an essential ingredient; essential revisions in the text*), while an *intrinsic* quality is one that belongs naturally to a person or thing (*her intrinsic fairness; an intrinsic weakness in the design*).

**inherit** verb **1** *she inherited his farm* BECOME HEIR TO, come into/by, be bequeathed, be left, be willed, receive; *Law* be devised.

**2** *Richard inherited the title* SUCCEED TO, assume, take over, come into; *formal* accede to.

**inheritance** noun **1** *a comfortable inheritance* LEGACY, bequest, endowment, bestowal, provision; birthright, heritage, patrimony; *Law* devise.

**2** *his **inheritance of** the title* SUCCESSION TO, accession to, assumption of, elevation to.

**inhibit** verb **1** *the obstacles that inhibit change* IMPEDE, hinder, hamper, hold back, discourage, interfere with, obstruct, slow down, retard; curb, check, suppress, restrict, fetter, cramp, frustrate, stifle, prevent, block, thwart, foil, stop, halt. See note at THWART. ANTONYMS encourage, allow.

**2** *she feels inhibited from taking part* PREVENT, disallow, exclude, forbid, prohibit, preclude, ban, bar, interdict. ANTONYM encourage.

**inhibited** adjective *witnesses should not be inhibited to reveal what they know | she was so inhibited that most people thought she was cold and unfeeling* SHY, reticent, reserved, self-conscious, diffident, bashful, coy; wary, reluctant, hesitant, insecure, unconfident, unassertive, timid; withdrawn, repressed, constrained, undemonstrative; *informal* uptight, anal-retentive.

**inhibition** noun **1** *they overcame their inhibitions* SHYNESS, reticence, self-consciousness, reserve, diffidence; wariness, hesitancy, hesitation, insecurity; timidity; repression, reservation; psychological block; *informal* hang-up.

**2** *writing without inhibition* HINDRANCE, hampering, discouragement, obstruction, impediment, suppression, repression, restriction, restraint, constraint, cramping, stifling, prevention; curb, check, bar, barrier.

**inhospitable** adjective **1** *the inhospitable landscape* UNINVITING, unwelcoming; bleak, forbidding, cheerless, hostile, savage, wild, harsh, inimical; uninhabitable, barren, bare, austere, desolate, stark, spartan. ANTONYMS welcoming, cheery.

**2** *forgive me if I seem inhospitable* UNWELCOMING, unfriendly, unsociable, antisocial, unneighborly, uncongenial; aloof, cool, cold, frosty, distant, remote, indifferent, uncivil, discourteous, ungracious; ungenerous, unkind, unsympathetic; *informal* standoffish. ANTONYMS welcomng, warm, friendly.

**inhuman** adjective **1** *inhuman treatment* CRUEL, harsh, inhumane, brutal, callous, sadistic, severe, savage, vicious, barbaric; monstrous, heinous, egregious; merciless, ruthless, pitiless, remorseless, cold-blooded, heartless, hard-hearted, dastardly; unkind, inconsiderate, unfeeling, uncaring; *informal* beastly. ANTONYM humane.

**2** *he ran at an inhuman pace* SUPERHUMAN, unearthly, extraordinary, phenomenal, exceptional, incredible, unbelievable.

**inhumane** adjective. See INHUMAN sense 1.

**inimical** adjective *an inimical gaze | policies inimical to democracy* HARMFUL, injurious, detrimental, deleterious, prejudicial, damaging, hurtful, destructive, ruinous, pernicious; antagonistic, contrary, antipathetic, unfavorable, adverse, opposed; hostile, unkind, unsympathetic, unfriendly, ill-disposed, malevolent; unwelcoming, cold, frosty; *literary* malefic. See note at HOSTILE. ANTONYMS friendly, favorable.

**inimitable** adjective *after years of trying to imitate Hitchcock, I finally accepted the fact that the master is inimitable* INCOMPARABLE, unparalleled, unrivaled, peerless, matchless, unequaled, unsurpassable, superlative, supreme, perfect, beyond compare, second to none, in a class of one's own; unique, distinctive, individual, sui generis; *formal* unexampled.

**iniquity** noun **1** *many runaways become the pawns of these merchants of iniquity* WICKEDNESS, sinfulness, immorality, impropriety; vice, evil, sin; villainy, criminality; odiousness, atrocity, egregiousness; outrage, monstrosity, obscenity, reprehensibility; *formal* turpitude. ANTONYMS morality, virtue.

**2** *I will forgive their iniquity* SIN, crime, transgression, wrongdoing, wrong, violation, offense, vice. ANTONYMS goodness, virtue.

**initial** adjective *the initial stages* BEGINNING, opening, commencing, starting, inceptive, embryonic, fledgling; first, early, primary, preliminary, elementary, foundational, preparatory; introductory, inaugural. ANTONYM final.

▸ verb *he initialed the warrant* PUT ONE'S INITIALS ON, initialize, sign, ink, countersign, autograph, endorse, inscribe, witness, verify.

**initially** adverb *initially, we thought it might be pilot error* AT FIRST, at the start, at the outset, in/at the beginning, to begin with, to start with, originally.

**initiate** verb **1** *the government initiated the scheme* BEGIN, start (off), commence; institute, inaugurate, launch, instigate, establish, set up, start the ball rolling on; originate, pioneer; *informal* kick off, spark. ANTONYM finish.

**2** *he was initiated into a cult* ADMIT, induct, install, incorporate, enlist, enroll, recruit, sign up, swear in; ordain, invest. ANTONYM expel.

**3** *she was* ***initiated into*** *the business of publishing* TEACH ABOUT, instruct in, tutor in, school in, prime in, ground in; familiarize with, acquaint with; indoctrinate; *informal* show someone the ropes in/within.

▸ noun *the initiates were put through the customary opening-day paces* NOVICE, starter, beginner, newcomer; student, pupil, learner, trainee, apprentice; recruit, new recruit, raw recruit, tyro, neophyte; postulant, novitiate; *informal* rookie, newbie, new kid (on the block), greenhorn.

**initiation** noun **1** *the initiation of the program* BEGINNING, starting, commencement; institution, inauguration, launch, opening, instigation, actuation, origination, devising, inception; establishment, setting up; *informal* kickoff. ANTONYM finish.

**2** *a rite of initiation into the tribe* INDUCTION, introduction, admission, admittance, installation, incorporation, ordination, investiture, enlistment, enrollment, recruitment; baptism. ANTONYM expulsion.

**initiative** noun **1** *employers are looking for people with initiative* SELF-MOTIVATION, resourcefulness, inventiveness, imagination, ingenuity, originality, creativity, enterprise; drive, dynamism, ambition, motivation, spirit, energy, vision; *informal* get-up-and-go, pep, moxie, spunk, gumption.

**2** *a recent initiative on recycling* PLAN, scheme, strategy, stratagem, measure, proposal, step, action, approach.

**inject** verb **1** *he injected a painkiller* ADMINISTER, introduce; *informal* shoot (up), mainline.

**2** *a pump injects air into the valve* INSERT, introduce, feed, push, force, shoot. See note at INSERT.

**3** *he injected new life into the team* INTRODUCE, instill, infuse, imbue, breathe.

**4** *she injected a note of realism into the debate* INTERJECT, interpose, throw in, add, contribute.

**injection** noun **1** *every time I go to the doctor's, I seem to be due for another injection* INOCULATION, vaccination, immunization, booster (shot); *informal* jab, shot, needle, hypo, fix.

**2** *her injection of humor into the discussion was a godsend* INTRODUCTION, infusion, instilling, imbuing, inculcation.

**injudicious** adjective *he now regrets his injudicious comments* IMPRUDENT, unwise, inadvisable, ill-advised, misguided; ill-considered, ill-judged, incautious, hasty, rash; inappropriate, impolitic, inexpedient; foolish, foolhardy, hare-brained. ANTONYM prudent.

**injunction** noun *the injunction prevents Sunday trading* ORDER, ruling, directive, command, instruction; decree, edict, dictum, dictate, fiat, mandate, writ; warning, caution, admonition.

**injure** verb **1** *he injured his foot* HURT, wound, damage, harm; cripple, lame, disable; maim, mutilate, deform, mangle, break.

**2** *his comments injured her reputation* DAMAGE, mar, impair, spoil, ruin, blight, blemish, tarnish, blacken.

**3** *dated my actions have injured no one* WRONG, abuse, do an injustice to, offend against, maltreat, mistreat, ill-use.

**injured** adjective **1** *his injured arm* HURT, wounded, damaged, sore, bruised; crippled, lame, disabled; maimed, mutilated, deformed, mangled, broken, fractured. ANTONYM healthy.

**2** *the injured party* WRONGED, offended, maltreated, mistreated, ill-used, harmed; defamed, maligned, insulted, dishonored. ANTONYM offending.

**3** *an injured tone* UPSET, hurt, wounded, offended, reproachful, pained, aggrieved; displeased, unhappy, put out, disgruntled, cut to the quick. ANTONYMS healthy, offending.

**injurious** adjective *the searing summer sun could prove injurious | an injurious story* HARMFUL, damaging, deleterious, detrimental, hurtful, baleful; disadvantageous, unfavorable, undesirable, adverse, inimical, unhealthy, pernicious; insulting, libelous, wrongful; *literary* malefic.

**injury** noun **1** *minor injuries* WOUND, bruise, cut, gash, laceration, scratch, graze, abrasion, contusion, lesion; *Medicine* trauma.

**2** *they escaped without injury* HARM, hurt, damage, pain, suffering, impairment, affliction; disfigurement.

**3** *the injury to her feelings* OFFENSE, abuse; affront, insult, slight, snub, indignity, slap in the face; wrong, wrongdoing, injustice.

**injustice** noun **1** *the injustice of the world* UNFAIRNESS, unjustness, inequity, corruption; cruelty, tyranny, repression, exploitation; bias, prejudice, discrimination, intolerance.

**2** *his sacking was an injustice* WRONG, offense, crime, sin, misdeed, outrage, atrocity, scandal, disgrace, affront; *informal* raw deal.

**inkling** noun *I had no inkling of their intentions* IDEA, notion, sense, impression, conception, suggestion, indication, whisper, glimmer; (sneaking) suspicion, fancy, hunch, feeling; hint, clue, intimation, sign; *informal* the foggiest (idea), the faintest (idea).

**inky** adjective **1** *the inky darkness* BLACK, jet-black, pitch-black; sable, ebony, dark, raven; *literary* Stygian.

**2** *inky fingers* INK-STAINED, stained, blotchy, smudged.

**inlaid** adjective *an inlaid design of glass beads in the tile | an inlaid floor* INSET, set, studded, lined, paneled, laid; ornamented, decorated; mosaic, intarsia, marquetry.

**inland** adjective **1** *inland areas* INTERIOR, inshore, central, internal, upcountry, upriver; landlocked. ANTONYM coastal.

**2** *inland trade* DOMESTIC, internal, home, local; national, provincial. ANTONYM international.

▸ adverb *the goods were carried inland* UPCOUNTRY, upriver, inshore, to the interior.

**inlet** noun **1** *we drifted toward a marshy inlet* COVE, bay, bight, estuary, fjord, sound, armlet, salt chuck.

**2** *a fresh-air inlet* VENT, flue, shaft, duct, channel, passage, pipe, pipeline, opening.

**inmate** noun **1** *at least two dozen inmates were treated for minor injuries following the prison fire* PRISONER, convict, captive, detainee, internee; *informal* jailbird, con, yardbird, lifer.

**2** *from our treehouse we would watch the inmates of Twin Oaks Hospital tending to their pretty little gardens* PATIENT, inpatient; convalescent; resident, inhabitant, occupant.

**inn** noun *the inn where Longfellow stayed* HOTEL, guest house, lodge, bed and breakfast, B&B, hostel; tavern, bar, hostelry, taproom, pub, public house, watering hole; *French* auberge; *dated* alehouse.

**innate** adjective *an innate talent for woodworking* INBORN, inbred, inherent, indwelling, natural, intrinsic, instinctive, intuitive, unlearned; hereditary, inherited, in the blood, in the family; inbuilt, deep-rooted, deep-seated, hard-wired, connate. See note at INHERENT. ANTONYM acquired.

**inner** adjective **1** *the inner gates* INTERNAL, interior, inside, inmost, innermost. ANTONYM external.

**2** *the premier's inner circle* PRIVILEGED, restricted, exclusive, private, confidential, intimate.

**3** *inner feelings* HIDDEN, secret, deep, underlying, unapparent; veiled, unrevealed. ANTONYM apparent.

**4** *one's inner life* MENTAL, intellectual, psychological, spiritual, emotional.

**innkeeper** noun *relatively few innkeepers maintain a constant Internet connection* LANDLORD, landlady, hotelier, hotel owner, proprietor, manager, host, hostess; licensee, barkeeper, barkeep; publican, restaurateur.

**innocence** noun **1** *he protested his innocence* GUILTLESSNESS, blamelessness, irreproachability.

**2** *the innocence of Sleeping Beauty is beyond the comprehension of these young girls* VIRGINITY, chastity, chasteness, purity; integrity, morality, decency; *dated* honor; *archaic* virtue.

**3** *she took advantage of his innocence* NAIVETÉ, ingenuousness, credulity, inexperience, gullibility, simplicity, unworldliness, guilelessness, greenness.

**innocent** adjective **1** *he was entirely innocent* GUILTLESS, blameless, in the clear, unimpeachable, irreproachable, above suspicion, faultless; honorable, honest, upright, law-abiding; *informal* squeaky clean. ANTONYM guilty.

**2** *innocent fun* HARMLESS, benign, innocuous, safe, inoffensive. ANTONYM harmful.

**3** *Alcott's depiction of innocent girls* VIRTUOUS, pure, moral, decent, righteous, upright, wholesome; demure, modest, chaste, virginal; impeccable, spotless, sinless, unsullied, incorrupt, undefiled; *informal* squeaky clean, lily-white, pure as the driven snow. ANTONYM sinful.

**4** *she is* ***innocent of*** *guile* FREE FROM, without, lacking (in), clear of, ignorant of, unaware of, untouched by.

**5** *at the innocent age of twelve* NAIVE, ingenuous, trusting, credulous, unsuspicious, unwary, unguarded; impressionable, gullible, easily led; inexperienced, unworldly, unsophisticated, green; simple, artless, guileless, wide-eyed; *informal* wet behind the ears, born yesterday. ANTONYMS worldly, seasoned.

▸ noun *an innocent in a strange land* INGÉNUE, unworldly person; child, baby, babe; novice; *informal* greenhorn; *literary* babe in arms.

**USAGE NOTE innocent**

**Innocent** properly means 'harmless,' but it has long been extended in general language to mean 'not guilty.' The jury (or judge) in a criminal trial does not, strictly speaking, find a defendant 'innocent.' Rather, a defendant may be *guilty* or *not guilty* of the charges brought. In common use, however, owing perhaps to the concept of the *presumption of innocence*, which instructs a jury to consider a defendant free of wrongdoing until proven guilty on the basis of evidence, *not guilty* and *innocent* have come to be thought of as synonymous.

**innocuous** adjective **1** *an innocuous fungus* HARMLESS, safe, nontoxic, innocent; edible, eatable. ANTONYMS harmful, toxic.

**2** *an innocuous comment* INOFFENSIVE, unobjectionable, unexceptionable, harmless, mild, tame, anodyne, soft-focus. ANTONYM offensive.

**innovation** noun *no appliance manufacturer can survive without an ongoing commitment to innovation* CHANGE, alteration, revolution, upheaval, transformation, metamorphosis, breakthrough; new measures, new methods, modernization, novelty, newness; creativity, originality, ingenuity, inspiration, inventiveness; *informal* a shake up.

**innuendo** noun *his innuendoes were usually just thinly veiled sexual remarks* INSINUATION, suggestion, intimation, implication, hint, overtone, undertone, allusion, reference; aspersion, slur.

**innumerable** adjective *innumerable letters and telegrams flooded the courtroom during the trial* COUNTLESS, untold, legion, without number, numberless, unnumbered, multitudinous, incalculable, limitless; *informal* umpteen, a slew of, no end of, loads of, stacks of, heaps of, masses of, oodles of, zillions of, gazillions of; *literary* myriad. ANTONYM few.

**inoculation** noun *the school nurse has no record of your child's most recent inoculation* IMMUNIZATION, vaccination, vaccine; injection, booster; *informal* jab, shot, hypo, needle.

**inoffensive** adjective *many people are challenging your contention that these were inoffensive remarks* HARMLESS, innocuous, unobjectionable, unexceptionable; nonviolent, nonaggressive, mild, peaceful, peaceable, gentle; tame, innocent.

**inoperative** adjective **1** *the fan is inoperative* DEFECTIVE, out of order, out of service, down, unserviceable, unusable, inoperable, bust/busted, out of action, shot, broken, faulty, on the blink, on the fritz, out of commission, acting up, kaput. ANTONYM working.

**2** *the contract is inoperative* VOID, null and void, invalid, ineffective, nonviable; canceled, revoked, terminated; worthless, valueless, unproductive, abortive. ANTONYM valid.

**inopportune** adjective *the embassy's decision to release that statement was unfortunate and inopportune* INAPPROPRIATE, unsuitable, malapropos, unfavorable, unfortunate, infelicitous, inexpedient; untimely, ill-timed, ill-chosen, unseasonable; awkward, difficult, inconvenient, disruptive. ANTONYM appropriate.

**inordinate** adjective *don't you think this is an inordinate amount of luggage for one weekend?* EXCESSIVE, undue, unreasonable, unjustifiable, unwarrantable, disproportionate, unwarranted, unnecessary, needless, uncalled for, gratuitous, exorbitant, extreme; outrageous, immoderate, extravagant, intemperate; *informal* over the top. ANTONYMS moderate, conservative.

**inquest** noun. See INQUIRY sense 2.

**inquire** verb **1** *I inquired about part-time training courses* ASK, make inquiries, question someone, request/solicit information.

**2** *the commission will* ***inquire into*** *the state of health care* INVESTIGATE, conduct an inquiry into/about/regarding, probe, look into; research, examine, explore, delve into, study; *informal* check out.

**inquiring** See INQUISITIVE.

**inquiry** noun **1** *an inquiry about our location* QUESTION, query.

**2** *an inquiry into alleged security leaks* INVESTIGATION, probe, examination, review, analysis, exploration; inquest, hearing.

**inquisition** noun *what started as a few friendly questions soon turned into a not-so-friendly inquisition* INTERROGATION, questioning, quizzing, cross-examination; investigation, inquiry, inquest, hearing; *informal* grilling; *Law* examination.

**inquisitive** adjective *we laughed when Brian said his sister was studying journalism—she was always such an inquisitive little pest* CURIOUS, interested, intrigued, prying, spying, eavesdropping, intrusive, busybody, meddlesome, snooping; inquiring, questioning, probing, searching; *informal* nosy, Nosy Parker, snoopy. ANTONYM uninterested.

**insane** adjective **1** *she was declared insane* MENTALLY ILL, mentally disordered, of unsound mind, certifiable; psychotic, schizophrenic; mad, deranged, demented, out of one's mind, non compos mentis, unhinged, unbalanced, unstable, disturbed, crazed; *informal* crazy, (stark) raving mad, not all there, bushed, bonkers, cracked, psycho, batty, cuckoo, loony, loopy, loco, nuts, screwy, bananas, crackers, wacko, off one's rocker, out of one's tree, around the bend, mad as a hatter, buggy. ANTONYM sane.

**2** *insane laughter* MANIACAL, psychotic, crazed, hysterical. ANTONYM normal.

**3** *an insane suggestion* FOOLISH, idiotic, stupid, silly, senseless, nonsensical, absurd, ridiculous, ludicrous, lunatic, preposterous, fatuous, inane, asinine, hare-brained, half-baked; impracticable, implausible, irrational, illogical; *informal* crazy, mad, cockeyed, daft. ANTONYM sensible.

**4** *I just looked at next week's schedule, and now I'm completely insane* MAD, crazy; angry, furious, annoyed; *informal* aggravated, foaming at the mouth, hot under the collar. ANTONYMS calm, contented.

**insanity** noun **1** *insanity runs in her family* MENTAL ILLNESS, madness, dementia; lunacy, instability; mania, psychosis; *informal* craziness.

**2** *it would be insanity to take this loan* FOLLY, foolishness, madness, idiocy, stupidity, lunacy, silliness; *informal* craziness.

**insatiable** adjective *an insatiable appetite for expensive jewelry* UNQUENCHABLE, unappeasable, uncontrollable; voracious, gluttonous, greedy, hungry, ravenous, wolfish; avid, eager, keen; *informal* piggy; *literary* insatiate.

**inscribe** verb **1** *his name was inscribed above the door* CARVE, write, engrave, etch, cut, incise; imprint, stamp, impress, mark.

**2** *a book inscribed to him by the author* DEDICATE, address, name, sign.

**inscription** noun **1** *the inscription on the sarcophagus* ENGRAVING, etching; wording, writing, lettering, legend, epitaph, epigraph.

**2** *the book had an inscription* DEDICATION, message; signature, autograph.

**inscrutable** adjective *John Law was a financial genius with inscrutable motives* ENIGMATIC, mysterious, unreadable, inexplicable, unexplainable, incomprehensible, impenetrable, unfathomable, unknowable; opaque, abstruse, arcane, obscure, cryptic. ANTONYM transparent.

**insecure** adjective **1** *an insecure young man* UNCONFIDENT, uncertain, unsure, doubtful, hesitant, self-conscious, unassertive, diffident, unforthcoming, shy, timid, retiring, timorous, inhibited, introverted; anxious, fearful, worried; *informal* mousy. ANTONYM confident.

**2** *an insecure railing* UNSTABLE, rickety, rocky, wobbly, shaky, unsteady, precarious; weak, flimsy, unsound, unsafe; *informal* jerry-built. ANTONYM stable.

**insecurity** noun **1** *he hid his insecurity* LACK OF CONFIDENCE, self-doubt, diffidence, unassertiveness, timidity, uncertainty, nervousness, inhibition; anxiety, worry, unease.

**2** *the insecurity of our situation* VULNERABILITY, defenselessness, peril, danger; instability, fragility, frailty, shakiness, unreliability.

**insensible** adjective **1** *she was insensible on the floor* UNCONSCIOUS, insensate, senseless, insentient, inert, comatose, knocked out, passed out, blacked out; stunned, numb, numbed; *informal* out (cold), down for the count, out of it, zonked out, dead to the world. ANTONYM conscious.

**2** *he was **insensible to** the risks* UNAWARE OF, ignorant of, unconscious of, unmindful of, oblivious to, incognizant of; indifferent to, impervious to, deaf to, blind to, unaffected by; *informal* in the dark about. ANTONYM aware.

**3** *he showed insensible disregard* INSENSITIVE, dispassionate, cool, emotionless, unfeeling, unconcerned, detached, indifferent, hardened, tough, callous; *informal* hard-boiled. ANTONYM sensitive.

**insensitive** adjective **1** *an insensitive bully* HEARTLESS, unfeeling, inconsiderate, thoughtless, thick-skinned; hardhearted, cold-blooded, uncaring, unconcerned, unsympathetic, unkind, callous, cruel, merciless, pitiless. ANTONYM compassionate.

**2** *he was **insensitive to** her feelings* IMPERVIOUS TO, oblivious to, unaware of, unresponsive to, indifferent to, unaffected by, unmoved by, untouched by; *informal* in the dark about.

**inseparable** adjective **1** *inseparable friends* DEVOTED, bosom, close, fast, firm, good, best, intimate, faithful; *informal* as thick as thieves, joined at the hip.

**2** *the laws are inseparable* INDIVISIBLE, indissoluble, inextricable, entangled; (one and) the same.

**insert** verb **1** *he inserted a tape in the machine* PUT, place, push, thrust, slide, slip, load, fit, slot, lodge, install; *informal* pop, stick. ANTONYMS extract, take out.

**2** *she inserted a clause* ENTER, introduce, add, incorporate, interpolate, interpose, interject. ANTONYM remove.

▸ noun *the newspaper carried an insert* ENCLOSURE, insertion, supplement; circular, advertisement, pamphlet, leaflet; *informal* ad.

**THE RIGHT WORD insert, inject, interject, interpolate, introduce, mediate**

If you want to put something in a fixed place between or among other things, you can **insert** it (*insert a new paragraph in an essay; insert photographs in the text of a book*). If it's a liquid, you'll probably want to **inject** it (*inject the flu vaccine*), although to inject can also mean to add something new or different (*inject some humor into an otherwise dreary speech*). If it's a person, you should **introduce** him or her, which suggests placing the individual in the midst of a group so as to become part of it. You can also introduce things (*introduce a new subject into the curriculum*), but if the thing you're introducing is extraneous or lacks authorization, you may have to **interpolate** it (*interpolate editorial comments*). If you have remarks, statements, or questions to introduce in an abrupt or forced manner, you'll have to **interject** them (*in the midst of his speech, she interjected what she felt were important details*). If you interject too often, however, you risk offending the speaker and may have to ask someone to **mediate**, which means to settle a dispute or bring about a compromise by taking a stand midway between extremes.

---

**inside** noun **1** *the inside of a volcano* INTERIOR, inner part; center, core, middle, heart. ANTONYM exterior.

**2** *informal my insides are aching* STOMACH, gut, internal organs, bowels, intestines; *informal* belly, tummy, guts, innards, viscera.

▸ adjective **1** *his inside pocket* INNER, interior, internal, innermost. ANTONYM outer.

**2** *inside information* CONFIDENTIAL, classified, restricted, privileged, private, secret, exclusive; *informal* hush-hush. ANTONYM public.

▸ adverb **1** *she ushered me inside* INDOORS, within, in.

**2** *how do you feel inside?* INWARDLY, within, secretly, privately, deep down, at heart, emotionally, intuitively, instinctively.

**3** *informal if I get caught again I'll be back inside* IN PRISON, in jail, in custody; locked up, imprisoned, incarcerated; *informal* behind bars, doing time.

**insidious** adjective *the insidious bond between big money and political decisions* STEALTHY, subtle, surreptitious, cunning, crafty, treacherous, artful, sly, wily, shifty, underhanded, indirect; *informal* sneaky.

**insight** noun **1** *your insight has been invaluable* INTUITION, discernment, perception, awareness, understanding, comprehension, apprehension, appreciation, penetration, acumen, perspicacity, judgment, acuity; vision, wisdom, prescience; *informal* savvy.

**2** *an* ***insight into*** *the government* UNDERSTANDING OF, appreciation of, revelation about; introduction to; *informal* eye-opener about.

**insignia** noun *I thought from the insignia that he was at least a colonel* BADGE, crest, emblem, symbol, sign, device, mark, seal, logo, colors.

**insignificant** adjective *the raises the kitchen staff received were insignificant* UNIMPORTANT, trivial, trifling, negligible, inconsequential, of no account, inconsiderable; nugatory, paltry, petty, insubstantial, frivolous, pointless, worthless, meaningless, irrelevant, immaterial, peripheral; *informal* piddling.

**insincere** adjective *voters respond favorably to even the most insincere campaign promises, as long as they hear just what they want* FALSE, fake, hollow, artificial, feigned, pretended, put-on, inauthentic; disingenuous, hypocritical, cynical, deceitful, deceptive, duplicitous, double-dealing, two-faced, lying, untruthful, mendacious; *informal* phony, pretend.

**insinuate** verb *he insinuated that she lied* IMPLY, suggest, hint, intimate, indicate, let it be known, give someone to understand; *informal* make out. PHRASE: **insinuate oneself into** *he is trying to insinuate himself into their family* WORM ONE'S WAY INTO, ingratiate oneself with, curry favor with; foist oneself on, introduce oneself into, edge one's way into, insert oneself into; infiltrate, invade, sneak into, maneuver oneself into, intrude on, impinge on; *informal* muscle in on.

**insinuation** noun *she made many unkind insinuations regarding Lewis's parental ability* IMPLICATION, inference, suggestion, hint, intimation, connotation, innuendo, reference, allusion, indication, undertone, overtone; aspersion, slur, allegation.

**insipid** adjective **1** *insipid coffee* TASTELESS, flavorless, bland, weak, wishy-washy; unappetizing, unpalatable. ANTONYM tasty.

**2** *insipid pictures* UNIMAGINATIVE, uninspired, uninspiring, characterless, flat, uninteresting, lackluster, dull, drab, boring, dry, humdrum, ho-hum, monochrome, tedious, run-of-the-mill, commonplace, pedestrian, trite, tired, hackneyed, stale, lame, wishy-washy, colorless, anemic, lifeless. ANTONYMS interesting, imaginative.

**insist** verb **1** *she insisted that they pay up* DEMAND, command, require, dictate; urge, exhort.

**2** *he insisted that he knew nothing* MAINTAIN, assert, hold, contend, argue, protest, claim, vow, swear, declare, stress, repeat, reiterate; *formal* aver. PHRASE: **insist on** *she insisted on her children's going to college* BE SET ON, be intent on, persist in, stand firm about, stand one's ground about, be resolute about, be emphatic about, be adamant about, not take no for an answer about; *informal* stick to one's guns about.

**insistent** adjective **1** *Tony's insistent questioning* PERSISTENT, determined, adamant, importunate, tenacious, unyielding, dogged, unrelenting, tireless, inexorable; demanding, pushy, forceful, urgent; clamorous, vociferous; emphatic, firm, assertive.

**2** *the insistent rattle of the fan* INCESSANT, constant, unremitting, repetitive; obtrusive, intrusive, loud.

**insolent** adjective *Dan is an inveterate wise guy who can't help making insolent cracks as he narrates the tale* IMPERTINENT, impudent, cheeky, ill-mannered, bad mannered, unmannerly, rude, impolite, uncivil, discourteous, disrespectful, insubordinate, contemptuous; audacious, bold, cocky, brazen; insulting, abusive; *informal* fresh, lippy, saucy, pert, sassy, smart-alecky; *archaic* contumelious. See note at IMPERTINENT. ANTONYM polite.

**insoluble** adjective **1** *some problems are insoluble* UNSOLVABLE, unanswerable, unresolvable; unfathomable, impenetrable, unexplainable, inscrutable, inexplicable.

**2** *these minerals are insoluble in water* INDISSOLUBLE, incapable of dissolving.

**insolvency** noun. See BANKRUPTCY.

**insolvent** adjective *even his family never suspected that Chet was insolvent* BANKRUPT, ruined, wiped out, in receivership; penniless, poor, impoverished, impecunious, destitute, without a penny (to one's name), in debt, in arrears; *informal* bust, (flat) broke, belly up, in the red, hard up, strapped (for cash), cleaned out; *formal* penurious.

**insomnia** noun *I've tried every wild remedy for insomnia, including cinnamon baths and standing on my head* SLEEPLESSNESS, wakefulness, restlessness, inability to sleep.

**insouciant** adjective *only outwardly did he possess an insouciant attitude about the disease* NONCHALANT, untroubled, unworried, unruffled, unconcerned, indifferent, blasé, heedless, careless; relaxed, calm, equable, serene, composed, easy, easygoing, carefree, free and easy, happy-go-lucky, lighthearted, airy, blithe, mellow; *informal* cool, laid-back, slaphappy.

**inspect** verb *by all means, inspect any part of the house you wish* EXAMINE, check, scrutinize, investigate, vet, test, monitor, survey, study, look over, peruse, scan, explore, probe; assess, appraise, review, audit; *informal* check out, give something a/the once-over.

**inspection** noun *on further inspection, we detected a slight crack in the pipe* EXAMINATION, checkup, survey, scrutiny, probe, exploration, observation, investigation; assessment, appraisal, review, evaluation; *informal* once-over, going-over, look-see.

**inspector** noun *the inspector's report is due here by noon* EXAMINER, scrutineer, investigator, surveyor, assessor, appraiser, reviewer, analyst; observer, overseer, supervisor, monitor, watchdog, ombudsman; auditor.

**inspiration** noun **1** *her work is a real inspiration to others* GUIDING LIGHT, example, model, muse, motivation, encouragement, influence, spur, stimulus, lift, boost, incentive, impulse, catalyst.

**2** *his work lacks inspiration* CREATIVITY, inventiveness, innovation, ingenuity, genius, imagination, originality; artistry, insight, vision; finesse, flair.

**3** *she had a sudden inspiration* BRIGHT IDEA, revelation, flash; *informal* brainwave, brainstorm, eureka moment.

**inspire** verb **1** *the landscape inspired him to write* STIMULATE, motivate, encourage, influence, rouse, move, stir, energize, galvanize, incite; animate, fire, excite, spark, inspirit, incentivize, affect. See note at ENCOURAGE.

**2** *the film inspired a musical* GIVE RISE TO, lead to, bring about, cause, prompt, spawn, engender; *literary* beget.

**3** *Charles inspired awe in her* AROUSE, awaken, prompt, induce, ignite, trigger, kindle, produce, bring out; *literary* enkindle.

**inspired** adjective *toe-tapping melodies and inspired lyrics* OUTSTANDING, wonderful, marvelous, excellent, magnificent, fine, exceptional, first-class, first-rate, virtuoso, supreme, superlative, brilliant; innovative, ingenious, imaginative, original; *informal* tremendous, superb, super, ace, wicked, awesome, out of this world. ANTONYMS dull, poor.

**instability** noun **1** *the instability of political life* UNRELIABILITY, uncertainty, unpredictability, insecurity, riskiness; impermanence, inconstancy, changeability, variability, fluctuation, mutability, transience. ANTONYMS certainty, steadiness.

**2** *emotional instability* VOLATILITY, unpredictability, variability, capriciousness, flightiness, fickleness, changeability, vacillation. ANTONYM steadiness.

**3** *the instability of the foundations* UNSTEADINESS, unsoundness, shakiness, frailty, fragility, weakness. ANTONYM soundness.

**install** verb **1** *a photocopier was installed in the office* PUT, position, place, locate, situate, station, site, lodge; insert. ANTONYM remove.

**2** *the college installs its new president this afternoon* SWEAR IN, induct, instate, inaugurate, invest; appoint; ordain, consecrate, anoint; enthrone, crown. ANTONYM remove.

**3** *she installed herself behind the table* ENSCONCE, establish, position, settle, seat, lodge, plant; sit (down); *informal* plonk, park.

**4** *you'll need to install new software* LOAD, store.

**installment** noun **1** *I pay monthly installments* PART PAYMENT; deferred payment, premium.

**2** *a story published in installments* PART, portion, section, segment, bit; chapter, episode, volume, issue.

**instance** noun *an instance of racism* EXAMPLE, exemplar, occasion, occurrence, case; illustration.

▸ verb *they instanced the previous case as an example* CITE, quote, refer to, mention, allude to, give; specify, name, identify, draw attention to, put forward, offer, advance.

**instant** adjective **1** *instant access to your money* IMMEDIATE, instantaneous, on-the-spot, prompt, swift, speedy, rapid, quick, express, lightning; sudden, precipitate, abrupt; *informal* snappy, PDQ (pretty damn/darn quick). ANTONYM delayed.

**2** *instant meals* PREPREPARED, precooked, ready-made, ready-mixed, heat-and-serve, fast; microwaveable.

▸ noun **1** *come here this instant!* MOMENT, minute, second; juncture, point.

**2** *it all happened in an instant* MOMENT, minute, trice, (split) second, wink/blink/twinkling of an eye, flash, no time (at all), heartbeat; *informal* sec, jiffy, jiff, snap.

**instantaneous** adjective *it doesn't have the instantaneous delivery aspect of the Internet but you'll get much higher resolution* IMMEDIATE, instant, on-the-spot, prompt, swift, speedy, rapid, quick, express, expedutious, lightning; sudden, hurried, precipitate; *informal* snappy, PDQ (pretty damn/darn quick); *literary* fleet. ANTONYM delayed.

**instead** adverb *instead, let's take the train* AS AN ALTERNATIVE, alternatively, alternately; on second thought, all things being equal. PHRASE: **instead of** *I'll have the blue instead of the yellow, please* AS AN ALTERNATIVE TO, as a substitute for, as a replacement for, in place of, in lieu of, in preference to; rather than, as opposed to, as against, as contrasted with, before.

**instigate** verb **1** *the committee instigated formal proceedings* SET IN MOTION, get underway, get off the ground, start, commence, begin, initiate, launch, institute, set up, inaugurate, establish, organize; actuate, generate, bring about; start the ball rolling on, kick off. See note at ENCOURAGE. ANTONYM halt.

2 *the liberal clergy is instigating a movement of political reform* INCITE, encourage, urge, provoke, goad, spur (on), initiate, stimulate, push (for), prompt, induce; arouse, rouse, inflame, excite, stir up; *informal* root on. See note at INCITE. ANTONYMS dissuade, quell.

**instigation** noun 1 *it was primarily Aaron's instigation that brought the festival into being* PROMPTING, suggestion, recommendation; request, entreaty, demand, insistence; wish, desire, persuasion; *formal* instance.

2 *foreign instigation is suspected to be at the root of this disturbance* INCITEMENT, initiation, provocation, stirring up, fomentation, inducement, encouragement.

**instigator** noun *the instigators behind the crime wave* INITIATOR, prime mover, motivator, architect, designer, planner, inventor, mastermind, originator, author, creator, agent; founder, pioneer, founding father; agitator, fomenter, troublemaker, ringleader, rabble-rouser.

**instill** verb 1 *we instill vigilance in our children* INCULCATE, implant, ingrain, impress, imprint, introduce; engender, produce, generate, induce, inspire, promote, foster; drum (into), drill (into).

2 *he instilled Monet with a love of nature* IMBUE, inspire, infuse, inculcate, inject; indoctrinate; teach.

**instinct** noun 1 *some instinct told me to be careful* NATURAL TENDENCY, inherent tendency, inclination, urge, drive, compulsion, need; intuition, feeling, hunch, sixth sense, insight; nose.

2 *his instinct for music* TALENT, gift, ability, aptitude, faculty, skill, flair, feel, genius, knack, bent.

**instinctive** adjective *an instinctive understanding of machinery* | *an instinctive urge to scream* INTUITIVE, natural, instinctual, innate, inborn, inherent; unconscious, subconscious, intuitional; automatic, reflex, knee-jerk, mechanical, spontaneous, involuntary, impulsive; *informal* gut, second nature. ANTONYMS learned, voluntary.

**institute** noun. See INSTITUTION sense 1.

▸ verb *Ingersoll has asked us to institute the new hiring policies before December 31* INITIATE, set in motion, get underway, get off the ground, get going, start, commence, begin, launch; set up, inaugurate, found, establish, organize, generate, bring about; start the ball rolling on; *informal* kick off. ANTONYM end.

**institution** noun 1 *an academic institution* ESTABLISHMENT, organization, institute, foundation, center; academy, school, college, university; society, association, body, guild, federation, consortium.

2 *how much do we know about the quality of medical care in these institutions?* HOSPITAL, NURSING HOME, retirement home, old-age home, old folks' home, (residential) home; asylum, mental institution; sanatorium.

3 *the institution of marriage* PRACTICE, custom, convention, tradition, habit; phenomenon, fact; system, policy; idea, notion, concept, principle.

4 *the institution of legal proceedings* INITIATION, instigation, launch, start, commencement, beginning, inauguration, generation, origination.

**institutional** adjective 1 *an institutional framework for discussions* ORGANIZED, established, bureaucratic, conventional, procedural, prescribed, set, routine, formal, systematic, systematized, methodical, businesslike, orderly, coherent, structured, regulated.

2 *the rooms are rather institutional* IMPERSONAL, formal, regimented, uniform, unvaried, monotonous; insipid, bland, uninteresting, dull; unappealing, uninviting, unattractive, unwelcoming, dreary, drab, colorless; stark, spartan, bare, clinical, sterile, austere.

**instruct** verb 1 *the union instructed them to strike* ORDER, direct, command, tell, enjoin, require, call on, mandate, charge; *literary* bid.

2 *do not attempt to operate the binder until you've been thoroughly instructed* TEACH, school, coach, train, enlighten, inform, educate, tutor, guide, prepare, prime.

3 *the judge instructed the jury to consider all of the facts* INFORM, tell, notify, apprise, advise, brief, prime; *informal* fill someone in, clue someone in.

**instruction** noun 1 *my instructions are to be obeyed at all times* ORDER, command, directive, direction, decree, edict, injunction, mandate, dictate, commandment, bidding; requirement, stipulation; *informal* marching orders; *literary* behest.

2 **(instructions)** *read the instructions* DIRECTIONS, key, rubric, specification, how-tos; handbook, manual, guide, tutorial.

3 *most of the instruction we received was combat-related* TEACHING, coaching, schooling, education, tutelage, tuition; lessons, classes, lectures; training, preparation, grounding, guidance.

**instructive** adjective *the manual is not sufficiently instructive* INFORMATIVE, instructional, informational, illuminating, enlightening, explanatory; educational, educative, edifying, didactic, pedagogic, heuristic; improving, moralistic, homiletic; useful, helpful.

**instructor** noun *Heilbrun was briefly an instructor at Brooklyn College* TEACHER, schoolteacher, educator, professor; mentor, tutor; coach, trainer; adviser, counselor, guide; *formal* pedagogue.

**instrument** noun 1 *a wound made with a sharp instrument* IMPLEMENT, tool, utensil; device, apparatus, contrivance, gadget. See note at TOOL.

2 *check all the cockpit instruments* MEASURING DEVICE, gauge, meter; indicator, dial, display; avionics.

3 *Tony tuned his instruments* MUSICAL INSTRUMENT.

4 *drama can be an instrument of learning* AGENT, agency, cause, channel, medium, means, mechanism, vehicle, organ.

5 *he is a mere instrument* PAWN, puppet, creature, dupe, cog; tool, cat's paw; *informal* stooge.

**instrumental** adjective *the space program has always been instrumental in our efforts to make medical advances* INVOLVED, active, influential, contributory; helpful, useful, of service; significant, important, crucial, critical, essential, pivotal, key; (**be instrumental in**) play a part in, contribute to, be a factor in, have a hand in; add to, help, promote, advance, further; be conducive to, lead to, cause.

**insubordinate** adjective *she defended her insubordinate behavior by exposing corruption in high places* DISOBEDIENT, unruly, wayward, errant, badly behaved, disorderly, undisciplined, delinquent, troublesome, rebellious, defiant, recalcitrant, uncooperative, willful, intractable, unmanageable, uncontrollable; awkward, difficult, perverse, contrary; disrespectful, cheeky. ANTONYM obedient.

**insubordination** noun *one quickly learns at West Point that insubordination is a serious matter* DISOBEDIENCE, unruliness, indiscipline, bad behavior, misbehavior, misconduct, delinquency, insolence; rebellion, defiance, mutiny, revolt; recalcitrance, willfulness, awkwardness, perversity; *informal* acting-up; *Law* contumacy.

**insubstantial** adjective 1 *an insubstantial structure* FLIMSY, fragile, breakable, weak, frail, slight, unstable, shaky, wobbly, rickety, ramshackle, jerry-built. ANTONYM sturdy.

2 *insubstantial evidence* WEAK, flimsy, feeble, poor, inadequate, insufficient, tenuous, insignificant, unconvincing, implausible, unsatisfactory, paltry. ANTONYM sound.

3 *insubstantial visions* INTANGIBLE, impalpable, untouchable, discarnate, unsubstantial, incorporeal; imaginary, unreal, illusory, spectral, ghostlike, vaporous, immaterial. ANTONYM tangible.

4 *an insubstantial amount* SMALL, negligible, inconsequential, inconsiderable, trifling, measly; *informal* piddling. ANTONYMS ample, generous.

**insufferable** adjective 1 *the heat was insufferable* INTOLERABLE, unbearable, unendurable, insupportable, unacceptable, oppressive, overwhelming, overpowering; *informal* too much. ANTONYM bearable.

2 *his win made him insufferable* CONCEITED, arrogant, boastful, cocky, cocksure, full of oneself, self-important, swaggering; vain, puffed up, self-satisfied, self-congratulatory, smug; *informal* bigheaded, too big for one's britches, too big for one's boots; *literary* vainglorious. ANTONYM modest.

**insufficient** adjective *the emergency lighting is insufficient* | *insufficient funds* INADEQUATE, deficient, poor, scant, scanty; not enough, too little, too few, too small; scarce, sparse, in short supply, lacking, wanting; paltry, meager, niggardly; incomplete, restricted, limited; *informal* measly, pathetic, piddling.

**insular** adjective 1 *insular attitudes* NARROW-MINDED, small-minded, inward-looking, parochial, provincial, small-town, shortsighted, hidebound, blinkered; set in one's ways, inflexible, rigid, entrenched; illiberal, intolerant, prejudiced, bigoted, biased, partisan, xenophobic; *informal* redneck. ANTONYMS broad-minded, tolerant.

2 *an insular existence* ISOLATED, inaccessible, cutoff, segregated, detached, solitary, lonely, hermitic. ANTONYM cosmopolitan.

**insulate** verb 1 *pipes must be insulated* WRAP, sheathe, cover, coat, encase, enclose, envelop; heatproof, soundproof; pad, cushion.

2 *they were insulated from the impact of the war* PROTECT, save, shield, shelter, screen, cushion, buffer, cocoon; isolate, segregate, sequester, detach, cut off.

**insult** verb *he insulted my wife* ABUSE, be rude to, slight, disparage, discredit, libel, slander, malign, defame, denigrate, cast aspersions on, call someone names, put someone down; offend, affront, hurt, humiliate, wound; *informal* badmouth, dis; *formal* derogate, calumniate; *rare* asperse. ANTONYM compliment.

▸ noun *he hurled insults at us* ABUSIVE REMARK, jibe, affront, slight, barb, slur, indignity; injury, libel, slander, defamation; abuse, disparagement, aspersions; *informal* dig, crack, putdown, slap in the face, kick in the teeth, cheap shot, low blow.

**insulting** adjective *once you send that insulting message, there's no taking it back* ABUSIVE, rude, offensive, disparaging, belittling, derogatory, deprecatory, disrespectful, uncomplimentary, pejorative; disdainful, derisive, scornful, contemptuous; defamatory, slanderous, libelous, scurrilous, blasphemous; *informal* bitchy, catty, snide. See note at OFFENSIVE.

**insupportable** adjective 1 *his arrogance was insupportable* INTOLERABLE, insufferable, unbearable, unendurable; oppressive, overwhelming, overpowering; *informal* too much. ANTONYM bearable.

2 *this view is insupportable* UNJUSTIFIABLE, indefensible, inexcusable, unwarrantable, unreasonable, untenable; unjustified, baseless, groundless, unfounded, unsupported, unsubstantiated, unconfirmed, uncorroborated, invalid; implausible, weak, flawed, specious, defective. ANTONYMS defensible, justified.

**insurance** noun 1 *insurance for his new car* INDEMNITY, indemnification, assurance, (financial) protection, security, coverage.

2 *insurance against a third world war* PROTECTION, defense, safeguard, security, hedge, precaution, provision, surety; immunity; guarantee, warranty; *informal* backstop.

**insure** verb *the high cost of insuring a teenage driver* PROVIDE INSURANCE FOR, indemnify, cover, assure, protect, underwrite; guarantee, warrant.

**insurgent** adjective *insurgent forces* REBELLIOUS, rebel, revolutionary, mutinous, insurrectionist; renegade, seditious, subversive. ANTONYM loyal.

▸ noun *the insurgents are gaining popularity* REBEL, revolutionary, revolutionist, mutineer, insurrectionist, agitator, subversive, renegade, incendiary; guerrilla, freedom fighter, anarchist, terrorist. ANTONYM loyalist.

**insurmountable** adjective *I refuse to believe that any of the problems mentioned here today are insurmountable* INSUPERABLE, unconquerable, invincible, unassailable; overwhelming, hopeless, impossible.

**insurrection** noun *Spann later died in a prison insurrection by Taliban and al Qaeda prisoners* REBELLION, revolt, uprising, mutiny, revolution, insurgence, riot, sedition, subversion; civil disorder, unrest, anarchy; coup (d'état).

**intact** adjective *we expect to find the house intact when we get back* WHOLE, entire, complete, unbroken, undamaged, unimpaired, faultless, flawless, unscathed, untouched, unspoiled, unblemished, unmarked, perfect, pristine, inviolate, undefiled, unsullied, virgin, in one piece; sound, solid. ANTONYM damaged.

**intangible** adjective **1** *the shadows were more intangible than usual as they shifted with each quavering bough and passing cloud* IMPALPABLE, untouchable, incorporeal, discarnate, abstract; ethereal, insubstantial, immaterial, airy; ghostly, spectral, unearthly, supernatural.

**2** *team spirit may be intangible, but we wouldn't have gotten to the finals without it* INDEFINABLE, indescribable, inexpressible, nameless; vague, obscure, abstract, unclear, indefinite, undefined, subtle, elusive.

**integral** adjective **1** *an integral part of human behavior* ESSENTIAL, fundamental, basic, intrinsic, inherent, constitutive, innate, structural; vital, necessary, requisite. ANTONYMS peripheral, incidental.

**2** *the dryer has integral cord storage* BUILT-IN, integrated, incorporated, included. ANTONYM peripheral.

**3** *an integral approach to learning* UNIFIED, integrated, comprehensive, composite, combined, aggregate; complete, whole. ANTONYMS partial, fragmented.

**integrate** verb *reserve forces will be more closely integrated with the regular forces* COMBINE, amalgamate, merge, unite, fuse, blend, mingle, coalesce, consolidate, meld, intermingle, mix; incorporate, unify, assimilate, homogenize; desegregate. ANTONYM separate.

**integrated** adjective **1** *an integrated package of services* UNIFIED, united, consolidated, amalgamated, combined, merged, fused, homogeneous, assimilated, cohesive, complete; *Brit.* joined-up.

**2** *an integrated school* DESEGREGATED, nonsegregated, unsegregated, mixed, multicultural.

**integrity** noun **1** *I never doubted his integrity* HONESTY, probity, rectitude, honor, good character, principle(s), ethics, morals, righteousness, morality, virtue, decency, fairness, scrupulousness, sincerity, truthfulness, trustworthiness. ANTONYM dishonesty.

**2** *the integrity of the federation* UNITY, unification, coherence, cohesion, togetherness, solidarity. ANTONYM division.

**3** *the structural integrity of the aircraft* SOUNDNESS, strength, sturdiness, solidity, durability, stability, stoutness, toughness. ANTONYM fragility.

**intellect** noun **1** *a film that appeals to one's intellect* MIND, brain(s), intelligence, reason, understanding, thought, brainpower, sense, judgment, wisdom, wits; *informal* gray matter, IQ, brain cells, smarts.

**2** *one of the finest intellects* THINKER, intellectual, sage; mind, brain.

**intellectual** adjective **1** *her intellectual capacity* MENTAL, cerebral, cognitive, psychological; rational, abstract, conceptual, theoretical, analytical, logical; academic. ANTONYM physical.

**2** *an intellectual man* INTELLIGENT, clever, academic, educated, well-read, lettered, erudite, cerebral, learned, knowledgeable, literary, bookish, highbrow, scholarly, studious, enlightened, sophisticated, cultured, donnish; *informal* brainy. ANTONYM stupid.

▸ noun *"The Simpsons" is among the most revered TV shows among intellectuals* HIGHBROW, learned person, academic, bookworm, man/woman of letters, bluestocking; thinker, brain, scholar, genius, Einstein, polymath, mastermind; *informal* egghead, brains, brainiac, rocket scientist. ANTONYM dunce.

**intelligence** noun **1** *a man of great intelligence* INTELLECTUAL CAPACITY, mental capacity, intellect, mind, brain(s), IQ, brainpower, judgment, reasoning, understanding, comprehension; acumen, wit, sense, insight, perception, penetration, discernment, smartness, canniness, astuteness, intuition, acuity, cleverness, brilliance, ability; *informal* braininess.

**2** *we're awaiting the latest intelligence from our operatives* INFORMATION, facts, details, particulars, data, knowledge, reports, inside story; *informal* info, dope, skinny, lowdown.

**3** *intelligence operation* INFORMATION GATHERING, surveillance, observation, reconnaissance, spying, espionage, infiltration, ELINT, humint; *informal* recon.

**intelligent** adjective **1** *an intelligent writer* CLEVER, bright, brilliant, quick-witted, quick on the uptake, smart, canny, astute, intuitive, insightful, perceptive, perspicacious, discerning; knowledgeable; able, gifted, talented; *informal* brainy.

**2** *an intelligent being* RATIONAL, higher-order, capable of thought.

**intelligentsia** plural noun *this antidemocratic system is supported by the political intelligentsia who call themselves democratic, even progressive* INTELLECTUALS, intelligent people, academics, scholars, literati, cognoscenti, illuminati, highbrows, thinkers, brains; intelligent; *informal* eggheads. ANTONYM masses.

**intelligible** adjective *finally, an owner's manual that's actually intelligible* COMPREHENSIBLE, understandable; accessible, digestible, user-friendly, penetrable, fathomable; lucid, clear, coherent, plain, simple, explicit, precise, unambiguous, self-explanatory; *formal* exoteric.

**intemperate** adjective *a man of intemperate taste may soon find himself with little left to taste* IMMODERATE, excessive, undue, inordinate, extreme, unrestrained, uncontrolled; self-indulgent, overindulgent, extravagant, lavish, prodigal, profligate; imprudent, reckless, wild; dissolute, debauched, wanton, dissipated. ANTONYM moderate.

**intend** verb *I intend to lease a car | what does Mark intend to do about the broken gate?* PLAN, mean, have in mind, have the intention, aim, propose; aspire, hope, expect, be resolved, be determined; want, wish; contemplate, think of, envisage, envision; design, earmark, designate, set aside; *formal* purpose.

THE RIGHT WORD **intend, aim, design, mean, plan, propose, purpose**

If you **intend** to do something, you may or may not be serious about getting it done (*I intend to clean out the garage some day*) but at least you have a goal in mind. Although **mean** can also imply either a firm resolve (*I mean to go, with or without her permission*) or a vague intention (*I've been meaning to write her for weeks*), it is a less formal word that usually connotes a certain lack of determination or a weak resolve. **Plan**, like *mean* and *intend*, may imply a vague goal (*I plan to tour China some day*), but it is often used to suggest that you're taking active steps (*I plan to leave as soon as I finish packing*). **Aim** indicates that you have an actual goal or purpose in mind and that you're putting some effort behind it (*I aim to be the first woman president*), without the hint of failure conveyed by *mean*. If you **propose** to do something, you declare your intention ahead of time (*I propose that we set up a meeting next week*), and if you **purpose** to do it, you are even more determined to achieve your goal (*I purpose to write a three-volume history of baseball in America*). **Design** suggests forethought in devising a plan (*design a strategy that will keep everyone happy*).

**intense** adjective **1** *intense heat* EXTREME, great, acute, fierce, severe, high; exceptional, extraordinary; harsh, strong, powerful, potent, overpowering, vigorous; *informal* serious. ANTONYM mild.

**2** *a very intense young man* PASSIONATE, impassioned, ardent, fervent, zealous, vehement, fiery, emotional; earnest, eager, animated, spirited, vigorous, energetic, fanatical, committed. ANTONYM apathetic.

THE RIGHT WORD **intense, intensive**

**Intense** and **intensive** are similar in meaning, but they differ in emphasis. **Intense** tends to relate to subjective responses—emotions and how we feel—while **intensive** tends to relate to objective descriptions. Thus *an intensive course* simply describes the type of course: one that is designed to cover a lot of ground in a short time. On the other hand, in *the course was intense*, the word **intense** describes how someone felt about the course.

**intensify** verb *leaders here are fearful that yesterday's bombing will intensify the fighting north of the city* ESCALATE, increase, step up, boost, raise, strengthen, augment, reinforce; pick up, build up, heighten, deepen, extend, expand, amplify, magnify; aggravate, exacerbate, worsen, inflame, compound. ANTONYMS abate, lessen.

**intensity** noun **1** *the intensity of the sun* STRENGTH, power, potency, force; severity, ferocity, vehemence, fierceness, harshness; magnitude, greatness, acuteness, extremity.

**2** *many here today remember the intensity in Dr. King's voice* PASSION, ardor, fervor, fervency, zeal, vehemence, fire, heat, emotion; eagerness, animation, spirit, vigor, strength, energy; fanaticism. ANTONYMS apathy, indifference.

**intensive** adjective *an intensive search of the area | an intensive course in Russian* THOROUGH, thoroughgoing, in-depth, rigorous, exhaustive; all-inclusive, comprehensive, all-embracing, all-encompassing, complete, full; vigorous, strenuous; concentrated, condensed, accelerated; detailed, minute, close, meticulous, scrupulous, painstaking, methodical, careful. See note at INTENSE. ANTONYMS cursory, superficial.

**intent** noun *he tried to figure out his father's intent* AIM, intention, purpose, objective, object, goal, target; design, plan, scheme; wish, desire, ambition, idea, aspiration.

▸ adjective **1** *he was* ***intent on*** *proving his point* BENT ON, set on, insistent on, hell-bent on; committed to, obsessive about, obsessed with fanatical about, fixated on; determined to; anxious to, resolved to, impatient to.

**2** *an intent expression* ATTENTIVE, absorbed, engrossed, fascinated, enthralled, rapt, riveted; focused, earnest, concentrating, intense, studious, preoccupied; alert, watchful.

PHRASE: **for/to all intents and purposes** *if you sublet your apartment, realize that you are—for all intents and purposes—a landlord* IN EFFECT, effectively, in essence, essentially, virtually, practically; more or less, just about, all but, as good as, in all but name, almost, nearly; *informal* pretty much, pretty well; *literary* nigh on. ANTONYMS by no means, in no way.

**intention** noun **1** *it is his intention to be leader.* See INTENT noun.

**2** *he managed, without intention, to upset me* INTENT, intentionality, deliberateness, design, calculation, meaning; premeditation, forethought, preplanning; *Law* malice aforethought.

**intentional** adjective *intentional contamination of our food supply is a real threat* DELIBERATE, calculated, conscious, intended, planned, meant, studied, knowing, willful, purposeful, purposive, done on purpose, premeditated, preplanned, preconceived; *rare* witting.

**intentionally** adverb *she would never intentionally hurt anyone* DELIBERATELY, on purpose, purposely, purposefully, by design, knowingly, wittingly, consciously; premeditatedly, calculatedly, in cold blood, willfully, wantonly; *Law* with malice aforethought. ANTONYM accidentally.

**inter** verb. See BURY sense 1.

**intercede** verb *a third party was called in to intercede* MEDIATE, intermediate, arbitrate, conciliate, negotiate, moderate; intervene, interpose, step in, act; plead, petition, advocate.

**intercept** verb *the ball was intercepted | a nearby Coast*

*Guard cutter was able to intercept the gunrunners before they reached the harbor* STOP, head off, cut off; catch, seize, grab, snatch; obstruct, impede, interrupt, block, check, detain; ambush, challenge, waylay.

**intercession** noun *four Serbs were released after intercession by NATO-led peacekeepers in Kosovo* MEDIATION, intermediation, arbitration, conciliation, negotiation; intervention, involvement; pleading, petition, entreaty, agency; diplomacy.

**interchange** verb *the watch comes with five different straps, which can be interchanged to match your outfit* SUBSTITUTE, transpose, switch, alternate; exchange, swap, trade; reverse, invert, replace.

▸ noun **1** *the interchange of ideas* EXCHANGE, trade, swap, barter, give and take, traffic, reciprocation, reciprocity; *archaic* truck.

**2** *a highway interchange* JUNCTION, intersection, crossing; overpass, exit (ramp), cloverleaf.

**interchangeable** adjective *the attachments for these two vacuum cleaners are interchangeable* SIMILAR, identical, indistinguishable, alike, the same, uniform, twin, undifferentiated; corresponding, commensurate, equivalent, synonymous, comparable, equal; transposable.

**intercourse** noun **1** *social intercourse* DEALINGS, relations, relationships, association, connections, contact; interchange, communication, communion, correspondence; negotiations, bargaining, transactions; trade, traffic, commerce; *informal* doings, truck.

**2** *she did not consent to intercourse* SEXUAL INTERCOURSE, sex, lovemaking, sexual relations, intimacy, coupling, mating, copulation, penetration; *informal* nookie, whoopee; *technical* coitus, coition; *formal* fornication; *dated* carnal knowledge.

**interdict** noun *they breached an interdict* PROHIBITION, ban, bar, veto, proscription, interdiction, embargo, moratorium, injunction. ANTONYM permission.

▸ verb **1** *they interdicted foreign commerce* PROHIBIT, forbid, ban, bar, veto, proscribe, embargo, disallow, debar, outlaw; stop, suppress; *Law* enjoin. See note at PROHIBIT. ANTONYM permit.

**2** *efforts to interdict the flow of heroin* INTERCEPT, stop, head off, cut off; obstruct, impede, block; detain. ANTONYM facilitate.

**interest** noun **1** *we listened with interest* ATTENTIVENESS, attention, absorption; heed, regard, notice; curiosity, inquisitiveness; enjoyment, delight, enthusiasm. ANTONYM boredom.

**2** *places of interest* ATTRACTION, appeal, fascination, charm, beauty, allure. ANTONYM repulsion.

**3** *this will be of interest to those involved* CONCERN, consequence, importance, import, significance, note, relevance, value, weight; *formal* moment. ANTONYM irrelevance.

**4** *her interests include reading* HOBBY, pastime, leisure pursuit, recreation, diversion, amusement; passion, enthusiasm; *informal* thing, bag, cup of tea.

**5** *a financial interest in the firm* STAKE, share, claim, investment, stock, equity; involvement, concern.

**6** *what is your interest in the case?* INVOLVEMENT, partiality, partisanship, preference, loyalty; bias, prejudice.

**7** *his attorney guarded his interests* CONCERN, business, affair.

**8** *her savings earned interest* DIVIDENDS, profits, returns; a percentage.

▸ verb **1** *a topic that interests you* APPEAL TO, be of interest to, attract, intrigue, fascinate; absorb, engross, rivet, grip, captivate; amuse, divert, entertain; arouse one's curiosity, whet one's appetite; *informal* float someone's boat, tickle someone's fancy. ANTONYM bore.

**2** *can I* ***interest*** *you* ***in*** *a drink?* persuade to have, tempt to have; sell.

PHRASE: **in someone's best interests** *there was bitter disagreement over which treatment would be in their father's best interest* OF (THE MOST) BENEFIT TO, to the advantage of; for the sake of, for the benefit of.

**interested** adjective **1** *an interested crowd* ATTENTIVE, intent, absorbed, engrossed, fascinated, riveted, gripped, captivated, rapt, agog; intrigued, inquisitive, curious; keen, eager; *informal* all ears, nosy, snoopy. ANTONYMS uninterested, bored.

**2** *the government consulted with interested groups* CONCERNED, involved, affected, connected, related. ANTONYM uninvolved.

**3** *no interested party can judge the contest* PARTISAN, partial, biased, prejudiced, preferential. ANTONYMS disinterested, nonpartisan.

**interesting** adjective *a dramatic look inside the classroom that makes for some interesting television* ABSORBING, engrossing, fascinating, riveting, gripping, compelling, compulsive, captivating, engaging, enthralling; appealing, attractive; amusing, entertaining, stimulating, thought-provoking, diverting, intriguing. ANTONYM boring.

**interfere** verb **1** *we don't let emotion* ***interfere with*** *our duty* IMPEDE, obstruct, stand in the way of, hinder, inhibit, restrict, constrain, hamper, handicap, cramp, check, block; disturb, disrupt, influence, impinge on, affect, confuse.

**2** *she tried not to* ***interfere in*** *his life* BUTT INTO, barge into, pry into, intrude into, intervene in, get involved in, encroach on, impinge on; meddle in, tamper with; *informal* poke one's nose into, horn in on, muscle in on, stick one's oar in.

**interference** noun **1** *they resent state interference* INTRUSION, intervention, intercession, involvement, trespass, meddling, prying; *informal* butting in.

**2** *radio interference* DISRUPTION, disturbance, distortion, static.

**interim** noun *in the interim they did more research* MEANTIME, meanwhile, intervening time; interlude, interval.

▸ adjective *an interim advisory body* PROVISIONAL, temporary, pro tem, stopgap, short-term, fill-in, caretaker, acting, transitional, makeshift, improvised, impromptu. ANTONYM permanent.

**interior** adjective 1 *the house has interior paneling* INSIDE, inner, internal, intramural. ANTONYM exterior.

2 *the interior waterways of British Columbia* INLAND, inshore, noncoastal, inner, innermost, central, upcountry, upland. ANTONYM outer.

3 *an interior monologue* INNER, mental, spiritual, psychological; private, personal, intimate, secret.

▸ noun 1 *the yacht's interior* INSIDE, inner part, inner area, depths, recesses, bowels, belly; center, core, heart, nucleus; *informal* innards. ANTONYMS exterior, outside.

2 *the interior of the province* CENTER, heartland, hinterland, backcountry, bush. ANTONYM borderland.

**interject** verb 1 *may I interject a comment?* INTERPOSE, introduce, throw in, interpolate, add, insert. See note at INSERT.

2 *please refrain from interjecting during each speaker's two-minute introductory remarks* INTERRUPT, intervene, cut in, break in, butt in, chime in; have one's say; *informal* put one's oar in, put one's two cents in.

**interloper** noun *we were made to feel more like interlopers than vacationers* INTRUDER, encroacher, trespasser, invader, infiltrator; uninvited guest; outsider, stranger, alien; *informal* gatecrasher, buttinsky.

**interlude** noun *the scene in the hospital room was a welcome interlude in this relentlessly high-paced adventure* INTERVAL, intermission, break, recess, pause, respite, rest, breathing space, halt, gap, stop, stoppage, hiatus, lull; *informal* breather, time out.

**intermediary** noun *the deal was concluded through an intermediary* MEDIATOR, go-between, negotiator, intervenor, intercessor, arbitrator, arbiter, conciliator, peacemaker; middleman, broker.

**intermediate** adjective *an intermediate stage in the cell's development* IN-BETWEEN, middle, mid, midway, halfway, median, medial, intermediary, intervening, transitional.

**interment** noun. See BURIAL.

**USAGE NOTE interment, internment**

*Interment* = burial (*interment will take place just after the funeral service*). *Internment* = detention, esp. of aliens in wartime (*the internment of Japanese Americans during World War II*). *Interment* is sometimes, especially in obituaries, confounded with *internment*—e.g.: "Graveside ceremony and internment [read *interment*] will be at Hillside Cemetery in Peekskill immediately following." (*Times Union* [Albany]; Aug. 22, 2000.)

**interminable** adjective *the interminable silence was finally broken by the plaints of her crying infant* (SEEMINGLY) ENDLESS, never-ending, unending, nonstop, everlasting, ceaseless, unceasing, incessant, constant, continual, uninterrupted, sustained; monotonous, tedious, long-winded, overlong, rambling. See note at ETERNAL.

**intermingle** verb *marinating overnight allows the flavors to intermingle* MIX, intermix, mingle, blend, fuse, merge, combine, amalgamate, integrate, unite; *rare* commix, admix; *literary* commingle.

**intermission** noun *refreshments are available during the intermission* INTERVAL, interlude, halftime, entr'acte, break, recess, pause, rest, respite, breathing space, lull, gap, stop, stoppage, halt, hiatus; cessation, suspension; *informal* breather, time out.

**intermittent** adjective *intermittent bursts of gunfire* SPORADIC, irregular, fitful, spasmodic, broken, fragmentary, discontinuous, isolated, random, patchy, scattered; occasional, infrequent, periodic, episodic, on and off; *informal* herky-jerky. ANTONYM continuous.

**intern** verb 1 *the refugees were interned in camps* CONFINE, detain, hold (captive), lock up, imprison, incarcerate, impound, jail; *informal* put away.

2 *she's interning with an accounting firm* APPRENTICE, train; *Law* article.

▸ noun *an intern at a local firm* TRAINEE, apprentice, probationer, (summer) student, novice, beginner.

**internal** adjective 1 *the internal structure of the building* INNER, interior, inside, intramural; central. ANTONYM external.

2 *Canada's internal affairs* DOMESTIC, home, interior, civil, local; national, federal, provincial, state. ANTONYM foreign.

3 *an internal battle with herself* MENTAL, psychological, emotional; personal, private, secret, hidden.

**international** adjective *international business concerns* GLOBAL, worldwide, intercontinental, universal; multinational. ANTONYMS national, local.

**interpolate** verb *language models can be interpolated online* INSERT, interpose, interject, enter, add, incorporate, inset, put, introduce. See note at INSERT.

**interpose** verb 1 *he interposed himself between the girls* INSINUATE, insert, place, put.

2 *I must interpose a note of caution* INTRODUCE, insert, interject, add, put in; *informal* slip in.

3 *they interposed to uphold the truce* INTERVENE, intercede, step in, involve oneself; interfere, intrude, butt in, cut in, meddle; *informal* barge in, horn in, muscle in.

**interpret** verb 1 *the rabbis interpret the Jewish laws* EXPLAIN, elucidate, expound, explicate, clarify, illuminate, shed light on. See note at CLARIFY.

2 *the remark was interpreted as an invitation* UNDERSTAND, construe, take (to mean), see, regard.

3 *the symbols are difficult to interpret* DECIPHER, decode, unscramble, make intelligible; understand, comprehend, make sense of, figure out; *informal* crack.

4 *he interpreted the role of Hamlet* PERFORM, act, play, render, depict, portray.

**interpretation** noun 1 *the interpretation of the Bible's teach-*

*ings* EXPLANATION, elucidation, expounding, exposition, explication, exegesis, clarification.

**2** *they argued over interpretation* MEANING, understanding, construal, connotation, explanation, inference.

**3** *the interpretation of experimental findings* ANALYSIS, evaluation, review, study, examination.

**4** *his interpretation of the sonata* RENDITION, rendering, execution, presentation, performance, portrayal.

**interpreter** noun **1** *he spoke through an interpreter | interpreters were brought in to read the German messages* TRANSLATOR, transcriber, transliterator.

**2** *a fine interpreter of this role* PERFORMER, presenter, exponent; singer, player, actor, dancer.

**3** *interpreters of Soviet history* ANALYST, evaluator, reviewer, critic.

**interrogate** verb *the suspects were interrogated in separate rooms* QUESTION, cross-question, cross-examine, quiz, catechize; interview, examine, debrief, give someone the third degree; *informal* pump, grill.

**interrogation** noun *he was taken to the police station for interrogation* QUESTIONING, cross-questioning, cross-examination, quizzing; interview, debriefing, inquiry, the third degree; *informal* grilling; *Law* examination.

**interrupt** verb **1** *she opened her mouth to interrupt* CUT IN (ON), break in (on), barge in (on), intervene (in), put one's oar in, put one's two cents in, interject; *informal* butt in (on), chime in (with).

**2** *the band had to interrupt their tour* SUSPEND, adjourn, discontinue, break off, put on hold; stop, halt, cease, end, bring to an end/close; *informal* put on ice, put on the back burner.

**3** *the coastal plain is* ***interrupted by*** *large lagoons* BREAK (UP) BY, punctuate by/with; pepper with, strew with, dot with, scatter with, sprinkle with.

**4** *their view was interrupted by houses* OBSTRUCT, impede, block, restrict, hamper.

**interruption** noun **1** *he was not pleased at her interruption* CUTTING IN, barging in, intervention, intrusion; *informal* butting in.

**2** *an interruption of the power supply* DISCONTINUATION, breaking off, suspension, disruption, stopping, stoppage, halting, cessation.

**3** *an interruption in her career* INTERVAL, interlude, break, pause, gap, hiatus.

**intersect** verb **1** *the lines intersect at right angles* CROSS, crisscross; *technical* decussate.

**2** *the cornfield is intersected by a track* BISECT, divide, cut in two/half, cut across/through, crosscut; cross, traverse.

**intersection** noun **1** *the intersection of two lines* CROSSING, crisscrossing; meeting.

**2** *the driver stopped at an intersection* JUNCTION, interchange, crossroads, corner, cloverleaf.

**intersperse** verb **1** *giant poppies were interspersed among the rocks* SCATTER, disperse, spread, strew, dot, sprinkle, pepper.

**2** *the beech trees are interspersed with pines* INTERMIX, mix, mingle, diversified, punctuate.

**intertwine** verb *a wreath of laurel, intertwined with daffodils* ENTWINE, interweave, interlace, twist, braid, plait, splice, knit, weave, mesh.

**interval** noun **1** *Baldwin made two speeches in the interval* INTERIM, interlude, intervening time, intervening period, meantime, meanwhile.

**2** *short intervals between contractions* STRETCH, period, time, spell; break, pause, gap.

**3** *intervals of still water* OPENING, distance, span, space, area.

**intervene** verb **1** *had the war not intervened, they might have married* OCCUR, happen, take place, arise, crop up, come about; *literary* come to pass, befall, betide.

**2** *she intervened in the dispute* INTERCEDE, involve oneself, get involved, interpose oneself, step in; mediate, referee; interfere, intrude, meddle, interrupt.

**interview** noun *all applicants will be called for an interview* MEETING, discussion, conference, examination, interrogation; audience, talk, dialogue, exchange, conversation.

▸ verb *we interviewed seventy subjects for the survey* TALK TO, have a discussion with, have a dialogue with; question, interrogate, cross-examine, meet with; poll, canvass, survey, sound out; *informal* grill, pump; *Law* examine.

**interviewer** noun *her first stint as an interviewer was for her fifth-grade newsletter* QUESTIONER, interrogator, examiner, assessor, appraiser; journalist, reporter.

**interweave** verb **1** *the threads are interwoven* INTERTWINE, entwine, interlace, splice, braid, plait; twist together, weave together, wind together; *Nautical* marry.

**2** *their fates were interwoven* INTERLINK, link, connect; intermix, mix, merge, blend, interlock, bind together, knit together, fuse.

**intestinal** adjective *he was treated for an intestinal complaint* ENTERIC, gastro-enteric, duodenal, celiac, gastric, ventral, stomach, abdominal.

**intestines** plural noun *the intestines are used in pet foods* GUT, guts, entrails, viscera; *informal* insides, innards.

**intimacy** noun **1** *the sisters reestablished their old intimacy* CLOSENESS, togetherness, affinity, rapport, attachment, familiarity, friendliness, friendship, amity, affection, warmth, confidence; *informal* chumminess.

**2** *the memory of their intimacy* SEXUAL RELATIONS, (sexual) intercourse, sex, lovemaking; *dated* carnal knowledge; *formal* copulation, (sexual) congress; *technical* coitus.

**intimate**[1] adjective **1** *an intimate friend of Picasso's* CLOSE, bosom, dear, cherished, faithful, devoted, fast, firm, familiar; *informal* chummy. ANTONYM distant.

**2** *an intimate atmosphere* FRIENDLY, warm, welcoming, hospitable, relaxed, informal; cozy, comfortable, snug; *informal* comfy. ANTONYMS formal, cold.

3 *intimate thoughts* PERSONAL, private, confidential, secret; innermost, inner, inward, deep, deepest; unspoken, undisclosed.

4 *an intimate knowledge of the music industry* DETAILED, thorough, exhaustive, deep, in-depth, profound; direct, personal, immediate, firsthand; *informal* up-close-and-personal. ANTONYMS sketchy, superficial.

5 *intimate relations* SEXUAL, carnal, romantic, amorous, amatory. ANTONYMS nonsexual, platonic.

▸ noun *his circle of intimates* CLOSE FRIEND, best friend, bosom friend, confidant, confidante; *informal* chum, pal, crony, buddy, bosom buddy, bud; *chiefly Brit. informal* mate.

**intimate**[2] verb 1 *he intimated to the committee his decision to retire* ANNOUNCE, state, proclaim, declare, make known, make public, publicize, disclose, reveal, divulge, set forth.

2 *her feelings were subtly intimated* IMPLY, suggest, hint at, insinuate, indicate, signal, allude to, refer to, convey; *informal* get at, drive at.

**intimation** noun *the first intimation of trouble came when the police began going door to door* SUGGESTION, hint, indication, sign, signal, inkling, suspicion, impression; clue, undertone, whisper, wind; communication, notification, notice, warning.

**intimidate** verb *Rico sent his goons to intimidate the local merchants* FRIGHTEN, menace, terrify, scare, terrorize, cow, dragoon, subdue; THREATEN, browbeat, bully, pressure, harass, harry, hassle, hound, torment, tyrannize, persecute; *informal* lean on, push around, bulldoze, railroad, twist someone's arm, strong-arm.

**intolerable** adjective *the drilling noise had become intolerable* UNBEARABLE, insufferable, unsupportable, insupportable, unendurable, beyond endurance, too much to bear; unacceptable; *informal* too much. ANTONYM bearable.

**intolerance** 1 *clearly she had not inherited her parents' racial intolerance* BIGOTRY, narrow-mindedness, small-mindedness, illiberality, parochialism, provincialism; prejudice, bias, partisanship, partiality, discrimination; injustice, inequality. See note at BIAS.

2 *lactose intolerance* SENSITIVITY, hypersensitivity; allergy.

**intolerant** adjective 1 *intolerant in religious matters* BIGOTED, narrow-minded, small-minded, parochial, provincial, illiberal; prejudiced, biased, partial, partisan, discriminatory.

2 *foods to which you are intolerant* ALLERGIC, sensitive, hypersensitive.

**intonation** noun 1 *she read with the wrong intonation* INFLECTION, pitch, tone, timbre, cadence, lilt, rise and fall, modulation, speech pattern; accentuation, accent, emphasis, stress.

2 *the intonation of hymns* CHANTING, intoning, incantation, recitation, singing.

**intoxicate** verb 1 *one glass of wine intoxicated him* INEBRIATE, make drunk, make someone's head spin, befuddle, go to someone's head; *informal* make someone woozy.

2 *she became intoxicated by sci-fi literature at age ten* EXHILARATE, thrill, elate, delight, captivate, enthrall, entrance, enrapture, excite, stir, rouse, invigorate, inspire, fire with enthusiasm, electrify, transport; *informal* give someone a buzz, give someone a kick, give someone a thrill, bowl over.

**intoxicated** adjective *several passengers later said they suspected the driver of being intoxicated* DRUNK, inebriated, inebriate, impaired, drunken, tipsy, under the influence; *informal* plastered, smashed, bombed, sloshed, sozzled, hammered, sauced, lubricated, well-oiled, wrecked, juiced, blasted, stinko, blitzed, half-cut, fried, gassed, polluted, pissed, tanked (up), soaked, out of one's head, out of one's skull, loaded, trashed, buzzed, befuddled, hopped up, besotted, pickled, pixilated, canned, cockeyed, wasted, blotto, blind drunk, roaring drunk, dead drunk, punch-drunk, ripped, stewed, tight, high, merry, the worse for wear, far gone, pie-eyed, in one's cups, three sheets to the wind; *Brit. informal* bladdered, lashed; *literary* crapulous. See note at DRUNK. ANTONYM sober.

**intoxicating** adjective 1 *intoxicating drink* ALCOHOLIC, strong, hard, fortified, potent, stiff, intoxicant; *formal* spirituous.

2 *an intoxicating sense of freedom* HEADY, exhilarating, thrilling, exciting, rousing, stirring, stimulating, invigorating, electrifying; strong, powerful, potent; *informal* mind-blowing. ANTONYM nonalcoholic.

**intractable** adjective 1 *intractable problems* UNMANAGEABLE, uncontrollable, difficult, awkward, troublesome, demanding, burdensome. ANTONYM manageable.

2 *an intractable man* STUBBORN, obstinate, obdurate, inflexible, headstrong, willful, unbending, unyielding, uncompromising, unaccommodating, uncooperative, difficult, awkward, perverse, contrary, pigheaded, stiff-necked. See note at STUBBORN. ANTONYM compliant.

**intransigent** adjective *both Palestinian and Israeli leaders have grown increasingly intransigent* UNCOMPROMISING, inflexible, unbending, unyielding, diehard, unshakable, unwavering, resolute, rigid, unaccommodating, uncooperative, stubborn, obstinate, obdurate, pigheaded, single-minded, iron-willed, stiff-necked. ANTONYM compliant.

**intrepid** adjective *our intrepid leader inspired us to forge ahead* FEARLESS, unafraid, undaunted, unflinching, unshrinking, bold, daring, gallant, audacious, adventurous, heroic, dynamic, spirited, indomitable; brave, courageous, valiant, valorous, stouthearted, stalwart, plucky, doughty; *informal* gutsy, spunky, ballsy. See note at BOLD. ANTONYM timid.

**intricate** adjective *intricate designs etched into the glass* | *an intricate plot* COMPLEX, complicated, convoluted, tangled, entangled, twisted; elaborate, ornate, detailed, baroque, delicate; involuted; bewildering, confusing, perplexing, labyrinthine, Byzantine; *informal* fiddly.

**intrigue** verb *her answer intrigued him* INTEREST, be of interest to, fascinate, arouse someone's curiosity, arouse someone's interest, pique someone's curiosity, pique someone's interest, attract.

▸ noun **1** *political intrigue* SECRET PLAN, plotting, plot, conspiracy, collusion, conniving, scheme, scheming, stratagem, machination, trickery, double-dealing, underhandedness, subterfuge; *informal* dirty tricks. See note at PLOT.

**2** *Rick's intrigue with his brother's wife caused the family immeasurable grief* (LOVE) AFFAIR, affair of the heart, liaison, amour, fling, flirtation, dalliance, tryst; adultery, infidelity, unfaithfulness, indiscretion; *informal* fooling around, playing around, hanky-panky.

**intriguing** adjective *intriguing stories* INTERESTING, fascinating, absorbing, compelling, gripping, riveting, captivating, engaging, enthralling, enchanting, attractive, appealing.

**intrinsic** adjective *an intrinsic eye for fashion* INHERENT, innate, inborn, inbred, congenital, connate, natural; deep-rooted, deep-seated, indelible, ineradicable, ingrained; integral, basic, fundamental, essential; built-in. See note at INHERENT.

**introduce** verb **1** *she has introduced a new system* INSTITUTE, initiate, launch, inaugurate, establish, found; bring in, usher in, set in motion, start, begin, commence, get going, get underway, originate, pioneer, kick off.

**2** *she introduced new legislation* PROPOSE, put forward, suggest, bring to the table, submit; set forth, raise, broach, bring up, mention, air, float; *informal* run something up the flagpole.

**3** *she introduced Lindsey to the young man* PRESENT (FORMALLY), make known, acquaint with.

**4** *introducing nitrogen into canned beer* INSERT, inject, put, force, shoot, feed. See note at INSERT.

**5** *she introduced a note of severity into her voice* INSTILL, infuse, inject, add, insert.

**6** *Clayton introduces the program each week* ANNOUNCE, present, give an introduction to; start off, begin, open.

**introduction** noun **1** *the introduction of democratic reforms* INSTITUTION, establishment, initiation, launch, inauguration, foundation; start, commencement, debut, inception, origination. ANTONYM abolition.

**2** *an **introduction to** the king* (FORMAL) PRESENTATION TO; meeting with, audience with.

**3** *the book's introduction* FOREWORD, preface, preamble, prologue, prelude; opening (statement), beginning; *informal* intro, lead-in, prelims; *formal* proem, prolegomenon. ANTONYM afterword.

**4** ***an introduction to*** *hothouse gardening* A PRIMER OF, a basic explanation of, a brief account of; the basics of, the rudiments of, the fundamentals of.

**5** *freshmen would soon experience the traditional **introduction to** school life* INITIATION INTO, induction into, inauguration into, baptism into.

**introductory** adjective **1** *the introductory chapter* OPENING, initial, starting, initiatory, first; prefatory, preliminary, leadoff. ANTONYM final.

**2** *an introductory course* ELEMENTARY, basic, rudimentary, primary; initiatory, preparatory, entry-level, survey; *informal* 101. ANTONYM advanced.

**introspective** adjective *an introspective poet* INWARD-LOOKING, self-analyzing, introverted, introvert, brooding; contemplative, thoughtful, pensive, meditative, reflective; *informal* navel-gazing.

**introverted** adjective *his introverted parents were uncomfortable with the rowdy friends he brought home from college* SHY, reserved, withdrawn, reticent, diffident, retiring, quiet; introspective, introvert, inward-looking, self-absorbed; pensive, contemplative, thoughtful, meditative, reflective. ANTONYM extroverted.

**intrude** verb *there will never be a consensus on just how entitled the press is to **intrude on** the lives of celebs* ENCROACH ON, impinge on, interfere in, trespass on/upon, infringe on, obtrude on/into, invade, violate, disturb, disrupt, interrupt; meddle in, barge in on; *informal* horn in on, muscle in on, poke one's nose into.

**intruder** noun *the intruder turned out to be a raccoon in the garage* TRESPASSER, interloper, invader, infiltrator; burglar, housebreaker, thief, prowler.

**intrusion** noun *victims of illegal computer intrusion* ENCROACHMENT, invasion, incursion, intervention, infringement, impingement; disturbance, disruption, interruption.

**intrusive** adjective *an intrusive journalist* INTRUDING, invasive, obtrusive, unwelcome, pushy; meddlesome, prying, impertinent, interfering; *informal* nosy, snoopy. See note at IMPERTINENT.

**intuition** noun **1** *he works according to intuition* INSTINCT, intuitiveness; sixth sense, clairvoyance, second sight.

**2** *this confirms an intuition I had* HUNCH, feeling (in one's bones), inkling, (sneaking) suspicion, idea, sense, notion; premonition, presentiment; *informal* gut feeling, gut instinct.

**intuitive** adjective *an intuitive grasp of the truth* INSTINCTIVE, instinctual; innate, inborn, inherent, natural, congenital; unconscious, subconscious, right-brained, involuntary, visceral; *informal* gut.

**inundate** verb **1** *a flood inundated the temple* FLOOD, deluge, overrun, swamp, drown, submerge, engulf.

**2** *we have been inundated with complaints* OVERWHELM, overrun, overload, bog down, swamp, besiege, snow under, bombard, glut.

**inure** verb *they had become inured to poverty* HARDEN, toughen, season, temper, condition; accustom, habituate, familiarize, acclimatize, adjust, adapt, desensitize. ANTONYM sensitize.

**invade** verb **1** *the army invaded the town* OCCUPY, conquer, capture, seize, take (over), annex, win, gain, secure; march into, storm. ANTONYM withdraw from.

2 *someone had invaded our privacy* INTRUDE ON, violate, encroach on, infringe on, trespass on, obtrude on, disturb, disrupt; *informal* horn in on, muscle in on, barge in on. ANTONYM respect.

3 *every summer, tourists invaded the beach* OVERRUN, swarm, overwhelm, inundate.

**invader** noun *invaders surprised them at dawn* ATTACKER, aggressor, raider, marauder; occupier, conqueror; intruder, interloper.

**invalid**[1] noun *a home for invalids* ILL PERSON, sick person, valetudinarian; patient, convalescent, shut-in.

▸ adjective *her invalid husband* ILL, sick, sickly, ailing, unwell, infirm, in poor health, indisposed; incapacitated, bedridden, housebound, frail, feeble, weak, debilitated. ANTONYM healthy.

**invalid**[2] adjective 1 *the law was invalid* (LEGALLY) VOID, null and void, unenforceable, not binding, illegitimate, inapplicable. ANTONYM binding.

2 *the theory is invalid* FALSE, untrue, inaccurate, faulty, fallacious, spurious, unconvincing, unsound, weak, wrong, wide of the mark, off target; untenable, baseless, ill-founded, groundless; *informal* full of holes. ANTONYM true.

**invalidate** verb 1 *the court invalidated the statute* RENDER INVALID, void, nullify, annul, negate, cancel, disallow, overturn, overrule; *informal* nix. See note at VOID.

2 *this case invalidates the general argument* DISPROVE, refute, contradict, negate, belie, discredit, debunk; weaken, undermine, explode; *informal* poke holes in; *formal* confute.

**invaluable** adjective *an invaluable member of the organization* INDISPENSABLE, crucial, critical, key, vital, necessary, irreplaceable, all-important; immeasurable, incalculable, inestimable, priceless. ANTONYM dispensable.

**invariably** adverb *we say we'll order light, but we invariably end up with platters of fried food* ALWAYS, on every occasion, at all times, without fail, without exception; everywhere, in all places, in all cases, in all instances; regularly, consistently, repeatedly, habitually, unfailingly, religiously; constantly, steadily. ANTONYMS sometimes, never.

**invasion** noun 1 *the invasion of the island* OCCUPATION, capture, seizure, annexation, annexing, takeover; storming, incursion, attack, assault. ANTONYM withdrawal.

2 *an invasion of tourists* INFLUX, inundation, flood, rush, torrent, deluge, avalanche, juggernaut.

3 *an invasion of my privacy* VIOLATION, infringement, interruption, intrusion, encroachment, disturbance, disruption, breach. ANTONYM respect.

**invective** noun *the invective that spewed from Claude's lips left everyone speechless* ABUSE, insults, expletives, swear words, swearing, curses, foul language, foul language, vituperation; denunciation, censure, vilification, revilement, reproach, castigation, recrimination; *informal* tongue-lashing, trash talk; *formal* obloquy, contumely. ANTONYM praise.

**inveigh** verb *he was one of the few Wall Streeters willing to* ***inveigh against*** *corporate greed* FULMINATE AGAINST, declaim against, protest (against), rail against/at, rage at, remonstrate against; denounce, censure, condemn, decry, criticize; disparage, denigrate, run down, abuse, vituperate, vilify, impugn; *informal* sound off about, blast, dis, slam. ANTONYM support.

**inveigle** verb *planted in colleges throughout the country are brainwashed members whose only mission is to inveigle unsuspecting students into the cult* ENTICE, tempt, lure, seduce, beguile; wheedle, cajole, coax, persuade; *informal* sweet-talk, soft-soap, con, sucker, snow. See note at TEMPT.

**invent** verb 1 *Louis Braille invented an alphabet for the blind* ORIGINATE, create, design, devise, contrive, develop, innovate; conceive, think up, dream up, come up with, pioneer; coin.

2 *they invented the story for a laugh* MAKE UP, fabricate, concoct, hatch, dream up, conjure up; *informal* cook up.

**invention** noun 1 *the invention of the telescope* ORIGINATION, creation, innovation, devising, development, design.

2 *medieval inventions* INNOVATION, creation, design, contraption, contrivance, construction, device, gadget; *informal* brainchild.

3 *she played with taste and invention* INVENTIVENESS, originality, creativity, imagination, inspiration.

4 *the story was a total invention* FABRICATION, concoction, (piece of) fiction, story, tale; lie, untruth, falsehood, fib, myth, fantasy, make-believe; *informal* tall tale, cock-and-bull story.

**inventive** adjective *a well-intentioned and fairly inventive kids' movie* CREATIVE, original, innovative, imaginative, ingenious, resourceful; unusual, fresh, novel, new, newfangled; experimental, avant-garde, groundbreaking, revolutionary, unorthodox, unconventional. See note at CREATIVE. ANTONYMS unimaginative, hackneyed.

**inventor** noun *the inventor of the separating zipper* ORIGINATOR, creator, innovator; designer, deviser, developer, maker, producer; author, architect; pioneer, mastermind, father, progenitor.

**inventory** noun *an inventory of all their belongings | our inventory of leaf rakes is low* LIST, listing, catalog, record, register, checklist, log, archive; stock, supply, store.

▸ verb *I inventoried his collection of music boxes* LIST, catalog, record, register, log, document.

**inverse** adjective *inverse snobbery.* See REVERSE adjective sense 2.

▸ noun *alkalinity is the inverse of acidity.* See OPPOSITE noun.

**invert** verb *the crew inverted the mast* TURN UPSIDE DOWN, upend, upturn, turn around/about, turn inside out, turn back to front, transpose, reverse, flip (over).

**invest** verb 1 *he* ***invested in*** *a soap company* PUT MONEY

INTO, provide capital for, fund, back, finance, subsidize, bankroll, underwrite; buy into, buy shares in; *informal* grubstake.

2 *they invested $18 million* SPEND, expend, put in, venture, speculate, risk; *informal* lay out.

3 *they* ***invested in*** *a new car* PURCHASE, buy, procure.

4 *the scene was invested with magic* IMBUE, infuse, charge, steep, suffuse, permeate, pervade.

5 *the powers* ***invested in*** *the bishop* VEST IN, confer on, bestow on, grant to, entrust to, put in the hands of.

**investigate** verb *police are still investigating this apparent murder* INQUIRE INTO, look into, go into, probe, explore, scrutinize, conduct an investigation into, make inquiries about; inspect, analyze, study, examine, consider, research; *informal* check out, suss out, scope out, dig, get to the bottom of.

**investigation** noun *we cannot determine the cause of the fire without further investigation* EXAMINATION, inquiry, study, inspection, exploration, consideration, analysis, appraisal; research, scrutiny, perusal; probe, review, (background) check, survey.

**investigator** noun *investigators searching the ship on Monday found a cache of weapons* INSPECTOR, examiner, inquirer, inquisitor, explorer, analyzer; researcher, fact-finder, scrutineer, prober, searcher, auditor; detective.

**investiture** noun *the investiture of archbishops* INAUGURATION, appointment, installation, initiation, swearing in; ordination, consecration, crowning, enthronement.

**investment** noun 1 *some tips for responsible investment* INVESTING, speculation; funding, backing, financing, underwriting; buying shares.

2 *it's a good investment* VENTURE, speculation, risk, gamble; asset, acquisition, holding, possession; *informal* grubstake.

3 *an investment of $305,000* STAKE, share, money/capital invested.

4 *a substantial investment of time* CONTRIBUTION, surrender, loss, forfeiture, sacrifice.

**inveterate** adjective 1 *an inveterate gambler* CONFIRMED, hardened, incorrigible, addicted, habitual, compulsive, obsessive; *informal* pathological, chronic.

2 *an inveterate liberal* STAUNCH, steadfast, committed, devoted, dedicated, dyed-in-the-wool, out and out, diehard, hard-core.

3 *inveterate corruption* INGRAINED, deep-seated, deep-rooted, entrenched, congenital, ineradicable, incurable.

**invidious** adjective 1 *that put her in an invidious position* UNPLEASANT, awkward, difficult; undesirable, unenviable; odious, hateful, detestable. ANTONYM pleasant.

2 *an invidious comparison* UNFAIR, unjust, iniquitous, unwarranted; deleterious, detrimental, discriminatory. ANTONYM fair.

**invigorate** verb *invigorated by the chilly autumn air | the need to invigorate the peace process in the Middle East* REVITALIZE, energize, refresh, revive, vivify, brace, rejuvenate, enliven, liven up, perk up, wake up, animate, galvanize, fortify, stimulate, rouse, exhilarate; *informal* buck up, pep up, breathe new life into. See note at QUICKEN. ANTONYM tire.

**invincible** adjective *invincible superheroes* INVULNERABLE, indestructible, unconquerable, unbeatable, indomitable, unassailable; impregnable, inviolable; *informal* bulletproof. ANTONYM vulnerable.

**inviolable** adjective. See INALIENABLE.

**inviolate** adjective *the insignia of the Red Cross was regarded as virtually inviolate* UNTOUCHABLE, inviolable, safe from harm; UNTOUCHED, undamaged, unhurt, unharmed, unscathed; unspoiled, unflawed, unsullied, unstained, undefiled, unprofaned, perfect, pristine, pure; intact, unbroken, whole, entire, complete.

**invisible** adjective *when the glue dries, it is invisible* UNABLE TO BE SEEN, not visible; undetectable, indiscernible, inconspicuous, imperceptible; unseen, unnoticed, unobserved, hidden, veiled, obscured, out of sight.

**invitation** noun 1 *an invitation to dinner* REQUEST TO ATTEND, call, summons; offer; card, note; *informal* invite.

2 *an open door is an invitation to a thief* ENCOURAGEMENT, provocation, temptation, lure, magnet, bait, enticement, attraction, allure; *informal* come-on.

**invite** verb 1 *they invited us to Sunday brunch* ASK, summon, have someone over, request someone's company, request the pleasure of someone's company.

2 *we invite your comments* ASK FOR, request, call for, appeal for, solicit, seek, summon.

3 *airing such views invites trouble* PROVOKE, induce, cause, create, generate, engender, foster, encourage, lead to; incite, elicit, bring on oneself, arouse, call forth.

**inviting** adjective *the inviting aromas wafting from her kitchen* TEMPTING, enticing, alluring, beguiling; attractive, appealing, pleasant, agreeable, delightful; appetizing, mouthwatering; fascinating, enchanting, entrancing, captivating, intriguing, irresistible, seductive. ANTONYM repellent.

**invoice** noun *an invoice for the goods* BILL, account, statement (of charges), check; *informal* tab; *archaic* reckoning.

▸ verb *we'll invoice you for the damage* BILL, charge, send an invoice/bill to.

**invoke** verb 1 *he invoked his statutory rights* CITE, refer to, adduce, instance; resort to, have recourse to, turn to.

2 *I invoked the Madonna* APPEAL TO, pray to, call on, supplicate, entreat, solicit, beg, implore; *literary* beseech.

3 *invoking spirits* SUMMON, call (up), conjure (up).

**involuntary** adjective *an involuntary urge* SPONTANEOUS, instinctive, unconscious, unintentional, uncontrollable; reflex, automatic; *informal* knee-jerk. ANTONYM deliberate.

**involve** verb 1 *the inspection involved a lot of work* REQUIRE, necessitate, demand, call for; entail, mean, imply, presuppose. ANTONYM preclude.

2 *I try to involve everyone in key decisions* INCLUDE, count in, bring in, take into account, take note of; incorporate, encompass, touch on, embrace, comprehend, cover. ANTONYM exclude.

**involved** adjective 1 *social workers* ***involved in*** *the case* ASSOCIATED WITH, connected with, concerned in/with. ANTONYM unconnected.

2 *he had been involved in drug dealing* IMPLICATED, incriminated, inculpated, embroiled, entangled, caught up; *informal* mixed up.

3 *a long and involved story* COMPLICATED, intricate, complex, elaborate; convoluted, impenetrable, unfathomable. ANTONYM straightforward.

4 *very* ***involved with*** *the organization* ENGROSSED IN, absorbed in, immersed in, caught up in, preoccupied by, busy with, engaged in/with, intent on. ANTONYM uninterested.

**invulnerable** adjective *acts of terrorism have reminded us that no nations are invulnerable* IMPERVIOUS, insusceptible, immune; indestructible, impenetrable, impregnable, unassailable, inviolable, invincible, secure; proof (against); *informal* bulletproof.

**inward** adjective 1 *an inward curve* TOWARD THE INSIDE, going in; concave. ANTONYM outward.

2 *an inward smile* INTERNAL, inner, interior, innermost; private, personal, hidden, secret, veiled, masked, concealed, unexpressed. ANTONYM external.

▸ adverb *the door opened inward.* INSIDE, into the interior, inwards, within.

**inwardly** adverb *inwardly, George blamed himself* INSIDE, internally, within, deep down (inside), in one's heart (of hearts); privately, secretly, confidentially; *literary* inly.

**iota** noun *nothing she said made an iota of difference* BIT, speck, mite, scrap, shred, ounce, scintilla, atom, jot, grain, whit, trace; *informal* smidgen, smidge, tad; *archaic* scruple.

**irascible** adjective *this hot weather has put everyone in an irascible mood* IRRITABLE, quick-tempered, short-tempered, hot-tempered, testy, touchy, tetchy, edgy, crabby, petulant, waspish, dyspeptic, snappish; cross, surly, crusty, grouchy, grumpy, cranky, cantankerous, curmudgeonly, ill-natured, peevish, querulous, fractious; *informal* prickly, snippy. ANTONYMS even-tempered, good-natured.

**irate** adjective *several irate customers demanded a full refund* ANGRY, furious, infuriated, incensed, enraged, fuming, seething, cross, mad, livid; raging, ranting, raving, in a frenzy, beside oneself, outraged, up in arms; indignant, exasperated, annoyed, irritated, irked, vexed, piqued, choleric; *informal* foaming at the mouth, hot under the collar, seeing red, cheesed off, hopping mad, PO'd, fit to be tied; *literary* wrathful; *archaic* wroth. ANTONYMS calm, contented.

**ire** noun *literary the plans provoked the ire of conservationists* ANGER, rage, fury, wrath, outrage, temper, crossness, spleen; annoyance, exasperation, irritation, displeasure, indignation, vexation, chagrin, pique; *literary* choler.

**iridescent** adjective *an iridescent film of oil on the puddle* OPALESCENT, nacreous; shimmering, luminous, glittering, sparkling, dazzling, shining, gleaming, glowing, lustrous, scintillating; kaleidoscopic, rainbow-colored, multicolored; *literary* glistering, coruscating, effulgent, scintillant.

**irk** verb *clearly, the prosecutor's opening questions irked him* IRRITATE, annoy, gall, pique, nettle, exasperate, try someone's patience; anger, infuriate, madden, incense, get on someone's nerves; antagonize, provoke; *informal* get someone's dander up, ruffle someone's feathers, make someone's hackles rise; rub the wrong way, get (someone's goat), get/put someone's back up, make someone's blood boil, peeve, miff, frost, rile, aggravate, needle, get to, bug, drive mad/crazy, tee off, tick off, piss off, PO, rankle, ride, drive up the wall, make someone see red. ANTONYM please.

**irksome** adjective *the irksome babbling of the couple upstairs* IRRITATING, annoying, vexing, vexatious, galling, exasperating, disagreeable; tiresome, wearisome, tedious, trying, troublesome, bothersome, nettlesome, obnoxious, awkward, difficult, boring, uninteresting; infuriating, maddening; *informal* infernal.

**iron** noun 1 *a ship built of iron* metal, pig iron, cast iron, wrought iron.

2 **(irons)** *they were clapped in irons* MANACLES, shackles, fetters, chains, handcuffs; *informal* bracelets, cuffs.

▸ adjective 1 *an iron law of politics* INFLEXIBLE, unbreakable, absolute, unconditional, categorical, incontrovertible, infallible. ANTONYM flexible.

2 *an iron will* UNCOMPROMISING, unrelenting, unyielding, unbending, resolute, resolved, determined, firm, rigid, steadfast, unwavering, steely; *literary* adamantine. ANTONYM flexible.

PHRASE: **iron out** *it's time we iron out our differences* RESOLVE, straighten out, sort out, smooth out, clear up, settle, put right, solve, remedy, rectify, fix, mend, eliminate, eradicate, erase, get rid of; harmonize, reconcile.

**ironic** adjective 1 *Edward's tone was ironic* SARCASTIC, sardonic, cynical, mocking, satirical, caustic, wry. ANTONYM sincere.

2 *it's ironic that a former illiterate is now a successful writer* PARADOXICAL, incongruous. ANTONYM logical.

**irony** noun 1 *that note of irony in her voice* SARCASM, causticity, cynicism, mockery, satire, sardonicism. See note at WIT. ANTONYM sincerity.

2 *the irony of the situation* PARADOX, incongruity, incongruousness. ANTONYM logic.

**irradiate** verb 1 *her smile irradiated the room* ILLUMINATE, light (up), cast light upon, brighten, shine on; *literary* illumine, illume.

**2** *irradiated with gamma rays* RADIATE, charge, blast, shoot; infuse, permeate, saturate, flood; *informal* zap, nuke.

**irrational** adjective *an irrational fear of insects* UNREASONABLE, illogical, groundless, baseless, unfounded, unjustifiable; absurd, ridiculous, ludicrous, preposterous, silly, foolish, senseless. ANTONYMS reasonable, logical.

**irreconcilable** adjective **1** *irreconcilable views about religion* INCOMPATIBLE, at odds, at variance, conflicting, clashing, antagonistic, mutually exclusive, diametrically opposed; disparate, poles apart. ANTONYMS compatible, similar.

**2** *irreconcilable enemies* IMPLACABLE, unappeasable, uncompromising, inflexible; mortal, bitter, deadly, sworn, out-and-out.

**irrefutable** adjective *irrefutable evidence* INDISPUTABLE, undeniable, unquestionable, incontrovertible, incontestable, beyond question, beyond doubt, conclusive, definite, definitive, decisive, certain, positive, sure; *informal* sure as shootin'.

**irregular** adjective **1** *irregular features* | *an irregular coastline* ASYMMETRICAL, nonuniform, uneven, crooked, misshapen, lopsided, twisted; unusual, peculiar, strange, bizarre; jagged, ragged, serrated, indented. ANTONYM straight.

**2** *irregular surfaces* ROUGH, bumpy, uneven, pitted, rutted; lumpy, knobbly, gnarled. ANTONYM smooth.

**3** *an irregular heartbeat* INCONSISTENT, unsteady, uneven, fitful, patchy, variable, varying, changeable, changing, inconstant, erratic, unstable, unsettled, spasmodic, intermittent, fluctuating; *informal* herky-jerky. ANTONYM steady.

**4** *irregular financial dealings* AGAINST THE RULES, out of order, improper, illegitimate, unscrupulous, unethical, unprofessional, unacceptable; *informal* shady. ANTONYM aboveboard.

**5** *irregular clothing* FLAWED, damaged, imperfect, discarded, rejected, throwaway.

**irregularity** noun **1** *the irregularity of the coastline* ASYMMETRY, nonuniformity, unevenness, crookedness, lopsidedness; jaggedness, raggedness, indentation.

**2** *the irregularity of the surface* ROUGHNESS, bumpiness, unevenness; lumpiness.

**3** *irregularity in the fabric* FLAW, damage, imperfection; blemish, mark, spot, stain.

**4** *the irregularity of the bus service* INCONSISTENCY, unsteadiness, unevenness, fitfulness, patchiness, instability, variability, changeableness, fluctuation, unpredictability, unreliability.

**5** *financial irregularities* IMPROPRIETY, wrongdoing, misconduct, dishonesty, corruption, immorality; *informal* shadiness, crookedness, dodginess.

**6** *the staff noted any irregularity in operation* ABNORMALITY, unusualness, strangeness, oddness, singularity, anomaly, deviation, aberration, peculiarity, idiosyncrasy.

**irrelevant** adjective *the judge ruled that the victim's use of drugs was irrelevant* BESIDE THE POINT, immaterial, not pertinent, not germane, off the subject, unconnected, unrelated, peripheral, extraneous, inapposite, inapplicable; unimportant, inconsequential, insignificant, trivial; *formal* impertinent.

**irreligious** adjective *it was a great miscalculation to assess America as an irreligious society* ATHEISTIC, unbelieving, nonbelieving, agnostic, heretical, faithless, godless, ungodly, impious, profane, infidel, barbarian, heathen, pagan; secular, humanist. ANTONYMS pious, God-fearing.

**irreparable** adjective *irreparable damage to the landing module* IRREVERSIBLE, irrevocable, irrecoverable, unrepairable, beyond repair, unrectifiable; hopeless. ANTONYM repairable.

**irreplaceable** adjective *an irreplaceable set of engraved wine glasses* UNIQUE, invaluable, priceless, unrepeatable, one-of-a-kind, incomparable, unparalleled; treasured, prized, cherished.

**irrepressible** adjective **1** *the desire for freedom is irrepressible* INEXTINGUISHABLE, unquenchable, uncontainable, uncontrollable, indestructible, undying, everlasting.

**2** *his irrepressible personality* EBULLIENT, exuberant, buoyant, sunny, breezy, jaunty, lighthearted, high-spirited, vivacious, animated, full of life, lively; *informal* bubbly, bouncy, peppy, chipper.

**irreproachable** adjective *her irreproachable character* IMPECCABLE, above/beyond reproach, blameless, faultless, flawless, unblemished, untarnished, spotless, immaculate, exemplary, model, outstanding, exceptional, admirable, perfect; *informal* squeaky clean; *trademark* Teflon. ANTONYM reprehensible.

**irresistible** adjective **1** *irresistible snakeskin stilettos* | *his irresistible smile* ENTICING, tempting, alluring, inviting, seductive; attractive, desirable, fetching, glamorous, appealing, delightful; ravishing, captivating, beguiling, tantalizing, enchanting, charming, fascinating, magnetic. ANTONYMS undesirable, off-putting.

**2** *an irresistible impulse to scream* UNCONTROLLABLE, overwhelming, overpowering, compelling, compulsive, irrepressible, ungovernable, besetting; unavoidable, inexorable, unpreventable, inescapable, driving, potent, forceful, urgent, imperative; obsessive. ANTONYM controllable.

**irresolute** adjective *once again, faced with an important issue, this legislative body sits irresolute and utterly useless* INDECISIVE, hesitant, vacillating, equivocating, dithering, wavering, shilly-shallying; ambivalent, blowing hot and cold, of two minds, hemming and hawing, in a dilemma, in a quandary, torn; doubtful, in doubt, unsure, uncertain, undecided, wishy-washy; *informal* sitting on the fence. ANTONYM decisive.

**irrespective** adjective *each member has one vote, **irrespective of** the number of shares held* REGARDLESS OF, without regard to/for, notwithstanding, whatever, no matter what, without consideration of.

**irresponsible** adjective *such irresponsible behavior is un-*

*thinkable for a man your age* RECKLESS, rash, careless, thoughtless, foolhardy, foolish, impetuous, impulsive, devil-may-care, delinquent, derelict, negligent, hare-brained; unreliable, undependable, untrustworthy, flighty, immature. ANTONYM sensible.

**irreverent** adjective *no one was amused by his irreverent joke-telling* DISRESPECTFUL, disdainful, scornful, contemptuous, derisive, disparaging; impertinent, impudent, cheeky, saucy, flippant, rude, discourteous. ANTONYM respectful.

**irreversible** adjective *irreversible damage* IRREPARABLE, beyond repair, irremediable, irrevocable, permanent; unalterable, unchangeable, immutable, carved in stone; *Law* peremptory. ANTONYM temporary.

**irrevocable** adjective *an irrevocable commitment* IRREVERSIBLE, unalterable, unchangeable, immutable, final, binding, permanent, carved in stone; *Law* peremptory. ANTONYM temporary.

**irritable** adjective *being out of work made him irritable* BAD-TEMPERED, short-tempered, irascible, tetchy, testy, touchy, grumpy, grouchy, moody, crotchety, in a (bad) mood, cantankerous, bilious, curmudgeonly, ill-tempered, annoyed, cross, ill-humored, peevish, fractious, pettish, crabby, bitchy, waspish, prickly, splenetic, dyspeptic, choleric; *informal* cranky, ornery, shirty, on a short fuse, soreheaded. ANTONYM easygoing.

**irritate** verb **1** *they seem to enjoy irritating me* ANNOY, vex, make angry, make cross, anger, exasperate, irk, gall, pique, nettle, put out, antagonize, get on someone's nerves, try someone's patience, ruffle someone's feathers, make someone's hackles rise; infuriate, madden, provoke, pester, rub the wrong way; *informal* aggravate, hassle, miff, rile, needle, get to, bug, get in someone's hair, get under someone's skin, get someone's dander up, rattle someone's cage, get/put someone's back up, drive mad/crazy, drive someone around the bend, drive up the wall, drive bananas, tee off, tick off, burn up, rankle, ride. See note at AGGRAVATE. ANTONYM pacify.

**2** *paint fumes irritate my throat* INFLAME, aggravate; pain, hurt; chafe, abrade, scratch, rasp; *rare* excoriate. ANTONYM soothe.

**irritating** adjective *a slow Web site is irritating to your customers* ANNOYING, infuriating, exasperating, maddening, trying, tiresome, vexing, vexatious, obnoxious, irksome, nagging, niggling, galling, grating, aggravating, pestilential.

**irritation** noun **1** *she tried not to show her irritation* ANNOYANCE, exasperation, vexation, indignation, impatience, crossness, displeasure, chagrin, pique; anger, rage, fury, wrath, aggravation; *literary* ire. ANTONYM delight.

**2** *I realize my presence is an irritation for you* IRRITANT, annoyance, thorn in someone's side/flesh, bother, trial, torment, plague, inconvenience, nuisance, aggravation, pain (in the neck), headache, burr under someone's saddle. ANTONYM pleasure.

**island** noun *she lived on an island* ISLE, islet; atoll; (**islands**) archipelago.

▸ verb *he was islanded from the problems of real life* ISOLATE, cloister, seclude; separate, detach, cut off.

**isolate** verb **1** *the police isolated the area* CORDON OFF, seal off, close off, fence off.

**2** *doctors isolated the patients* separate, set/keep apart, segregate, detach, cut off, shut away, keep in solitude, quarantine, cloister, seclude, sequester. ANTONYM integrate.

**3** *I have isolated the problem* IDENTIFY, single out, pick out, point out, spot, recognize, distinguish, pinpoint, locate.

**isolated** adjective **1** *isolated communities* REMOTE, out of the way, outlying, off the beaten track/path, secluded, lonely, godforsaken, far-flung, inaccessible, cutoff, incommunicado, in the backwoods, in the back of beyond, in the back concessions, in the boonies/boondocks, in the middle of nowhere, in the sticks, in the tall timbers, in the hinterland. ANTONYM accessible.

**2** *he lived an isolated existence* SOLITARY, lonely, companionless, friendless; secluded, cloistered, segregated, unsociable, reclusive, hermitic, lonesome. ANTONYM sociable.

**3** *an isolated incident* UNIQUE, lone, solitary; unusual, uncommon, exceptional, anomalous, abnormal, untypical, atypical, freak. ANTONYMS common, everyday.

**issue** noun **1** *the committee discussed the issue* MATTER, matter in question, question, point, point at issue, affair, case, subject, topic; problem, bone of contention.

**2** *the issue of a special stamp* ISSUING, publication, publishing, printing; circulation, distribution.

**3** *the latest issue of our magazine* EDITION, number, copy, installment, volume, publication.

**4** *Law* *she died without issue* OFFSPRING, descendants, heirs, successors, children, progeny, family; *archaic* seed, fruit (of one's loins).

**5** *an issue of water* DISCHARGE, emission, release, outflow, outflowing, secretion, emanation, exudation, effluence; *technical* efflux.

▸ verb **1** *the mayor issued a statement* SEND OUT, put out, release, deliver, publish, announce, pronounce, broadcast, communicate, circulate, distribute, disseminate, transmit.

**2** *the students were issued with new uniforms* SUPPLY, provide, furnish, arm, equip, fit out, rig out; *Brit.* kit out; *informal* fix up.

**3** *the smell of onion issued from the kitchen* EMANATE, emerge, exude, flow (out/forth), pour (out/forth); be emitted.

**4** *large profits might* ***issue from*** *the deal* RESULT FROM, follow, ensue from, stem from, spring (forth) from, arise from, proceed from, come (forth) from; be the result of, be brought on/about by, be produced by.

PHRASES: **at issue** *at issue here is what constitutes 'art'* IN QUESTION, in dispute, under discussion, under consideration, for debate.

**take issue with** *we'll get nowhere if you have to take issue with everything that anybody says* DISAGREE WITH, be in dispute with, be in contention with, be at variance with, be at odds with, argue with, quarrel with; challenge, dispute, (call into) question. ANTONYM agree with.

**itch** noun **1** *I have an itch on my back* tingling, irritation, prickle, prickling, tickle, tickling, itchiness.

**2** *informal the itch to travel* LONGING, yearning, craving, ache, hunger, thirst, keenness, urge, hankering; wish, fancy, desire; *informal* yen.

▸ verb **1** *my scar really itches* tingle, prickle, tickle, be irritated, be itchy.

**2** *informal he itched to help her* LONG, yearn, ache, burn, crave, hunger, thirst, be eager, be desperate; want, wish, desire, pine, fancy; *informal* have a yen, be dying.

**item** noun **1** *an item of farm equipment | the main item in a moose's diet* THING, article, object, artifact, piece, product; element, constituent, component, ingredient.

**2** *a news item* REPORT, story, account, article, piece, write-up, bulletin, feature.

**3** *I hear they are an item* COUPLE, twosome, partners, lovers; *informal* thing.

**itemize** verb *they itemized thirty-two design flaws in the reactor type* LIST, catalog, inventory, record, document, register, detail, specify, identify; enumerate, number.

**itinerant** adjective *itinerant traders* TRAVELING, peripatetic, wandering, roving, roaming, touring, saddlebag, nomadic, gypsy, migrant, vagrant, vagabond, of no fixed address.

▸ noun *an encampment of itinerants* TRAVELER, wanderer, roamer, rover, nomad, gypsy, migrant, transient, drifter, vagabond, hobo, vagrant, tramp.

**itinerary** noun *the old stone chapel should be on every visitor's itinerary* TRAVEL PLAN, schedule, timetable, agenda, program, tour; (planned) route.

**jab** verb *he jabbed the officer with his finger* POKE, prod, dig, nudge, butt, ram; thrust, stab, push.

▸ noun **1** *a jab in the ribs* POKE, prod, dig, nudge, butt; thrust, stab, push.

**2** *felled by a left jab* PUNCH, blow, hit, whack, smack, cuff.

**3** *exchanging verbal jabs* INSULT, cutting remark, barb; *informal* dig, put-down.

**jabber** verb *they jabbered nonstop* PRATTLE, babble, chatter, twitter, prate, yap, gabble, rattle on, blather; *informal* yak, yammer, yabber, yatter, blab, blabber.

▸ noun *stop your jabber!* PRATTLE, babble, chatter, chattering, twitter, twittering, gabble, blather; *informal* yabbering, yatter, blabber.

**jack** noun *a phone jack* SOCKET, outlet, plug, connection. PHRASE: **jack something up 1** *they jacked up the car* RAISE, hoist, lift (up), winch up, lever up, hitch up, elevate.

**2** *informal they may need to jack up interest rates* INCREASE, raise, up, mark up; *informal* hike (up), bump up, boost.

**jacket** noun.

**jackpot** noun *this week's lottery jackpot* TOP PRIZE, first prize; pool, kitty, pot, gold mine, bonanza. PHRASE: **hit the jackpot** *informal Ingalls may have hit the jackpot with this latest novel* STRIKE IT RICH, strike gold, succeed; *informal* clean up, hit the big time, score.

**jaded** adjective *a taste exotic enough for the most jaded palate | the uninspired writing of a jaded journalist* SURFEITED, sated, satiated, glutted; dulled, blunted, deadened, inured; TIRED, weary, wearied; unmoved, blasé, apathetic. ANTONYM fresh.

**jagged** adjective *don't give your dog a jagged bone* SPIKY, barbed, ragged, rough, uneven, irregular, broken; jaggy, snaggy; serrated, sawtooth, sawtoothed, indented. ANTONYM smooth.

**jail** noun *he was thrown into the local jail* PRISON, penitentiary, penal institution, lockup, detention center, jailhouse, stockade, correctional facility, reformatory, reform school; *informal* clink, slammer, big house, jug, brig, can, pen, hoosegow, cooler, cage, slam, pokey.

▸ verb *she was jailed for killing her husband* IMPRISON, put in prison, send to prison, incarcerate, lock up, put away, intern, detain, hold (prisoner/captive), put into detention, put behind bars, put inside. ANTONYMS acquit, release.

**jailer** noun WARDEN, prison officer, guard; captor; *informal* screw.

**jam**[1] verb **1** *he jammed a finger in each ear* STUFF, shove, force, ram, thrust, press, push, stick, squeeze, cram.

**2** *hundreds of people jammed into the hall* CROWD, pack, pile, press, squeeze, squish, cram, wedge; throng, mob, occupy, fill, overcrowd, obstruct, block, congest.

**3** *the rudder had jammed* STICK, become stuck, catch, seize (up), become trapped.

**4** *dust can jam the mechanism* IMMOBILIZE, paralyze, disable, cripple, put out of action, bring to a standstill; clog.

**5** *we were just jamming and his amp blew* IMPROVISE, play (music), extemporize, ad lib.

▸ noun **1** *a traffic jam* CONGESTION, holdup, bottleneck, gridlock, backup, tie-up, snarl-up.

**2** *informal we are in a real jam* PREDICAMENT, plight, tricky situation, difficulty, problem, quandary, dilemma, muddle, mess, imbroglio, mare's nest, dire straits; *informal* pickle, stew, fix, hole, scrape, bind, tangle, spot, tight spot, corner, tight corner, hot/deep water, can of worms.

**jam**[2] noun *raspberry jam* PRESERVE, conserve, jelly, marmalade, fruit spread, compote, (fruit) butter.

**jamboree** noun *the community's annual jamboree* RALLY, gathering, convention, conference; festival, fête, fiesta, gala, carnival, celebration; *informal* bash, shindig, hoedown.

**jangle** verb *keys jangled at his waist* CLANK, clink, jingle, tinkle.

▸ noun *the jangle of his chains* CLANK, clanking, clink, clinking, jangling, jingle, jingling, tintinnabulation.

**janitor** noun *the janitor's supply closet* CUSTODIAN, caretaker, cleaner, maintenance man/worker, superintendent.

**jar**[1] noun *a jar of honey* (GLASS) CONTAINER, pot, crock, receptacle, cookie jar, mason jar, ginger jar.

**jar**[2] verb **1** *each step jarred my whole body* JOLT, jerk, shake, shock, concuss, rattle, vibrate.

**2** *the play's symbolism jarred with the realism of its setting* CLASH, conflict, contrast, be incompatible, be at variance, be at odds, be inconsistent, be discordant.

**jargon** noun *the brochure is written in legal jargon* SPECIALIZED LANGUAGE, slang, cant, idiom, argot, patter; *informal* -speak, -ese, -babble, newspeak, journalese, bureaucratese, technobabble, psychobabble; double-talk, doublespeak; gibberish, gobbledygook, blather. See note at DIALECT.

**jaundiced** adjective *a jaundiced view of the world* BITTER, resentful, cynical, soured, disenchanted, disillusioned, disappointed, pessimistic, skeptical, distrustful, suspicious, misanthropic; envious, jealous.

**jaunt** noun *a jaunt around Manhattan* TRIP, pleasure trip, outing, excursion, day trip, day out; tour, drive, ride, run; *informal* spin. See note at JOURNEY.

**jaunty** adjective *Kevin looked pretty jaunty for the awards show* | *a jaunty musical score* CHEERFUL, cheery, happy, merry, jolly, joyful; lively, perky, bright, buoyant, bubbly, bouncy, breezy, in good spirits, exuberant, ebullient; carefree, blithe, airy, lighthearted, nonchalant, insouciant, happy-go-lucky; *informal* bright-eyed and bushy-tailed, chirpy. ANTONYMS depressed, serious.

**jaw** noun **1** *a broken jaw* JAWBONE, lower/upper jaw, jowl; *Anatomy* mandible, maxilla.

**2** (**jaws**) *the wolf held the rat in its jaws* MOUTH, maw, muzzle; teeth, fangs; *informal* chops.

**jazz** noun *their band plays mostly jazz* SWING, bebop, big band, boogie woogie.

PHRASE: **jazz up** *informal let's jazz up this boring decor* ENLIVEN, liven up, brighten up, make more interesting/exciting, add (some) color to, ginger up, spice up; *informal* perk up, pep up.

**jazzy** adjective *that's one jazzy bedspread* FUNKY, hip, vibrant, lively, spirited, bold, exciting, flamboyant, showy, gaudy, flashy; bright, colorful, brightly colored, striking, eye-catching, vivid. ANTONYM dull.

**jealous** adjective **1** *he was jealous of his sister's popularity* ENVIOUS, covetous, desirous; resentful, grudging, begrudging, green (with envy). ANTONYMS proud, admiring.

**2** *a jealous lover* SUSPICIOUS, distrustful, mistrustful, doubting, insecure, anxious; possessive, overprotective. ANTONYM trusting.

**3** *they are very jealous of their rights* PROTECTIVE, vigilant, watchful, heedful, mindful, careful, solicitous. ANTONYM careless.

THE RIGHT WORD **jealous, covetous, envious**

**Envious** implies wanting something that belongs to another and to which one has no particular right or claim (*envious of her good fortune*). **Jealous** may refer to a strong feeling of envy (*it is hard not to be jealous of a man with a job like his*), or it may imply an intense effort to hold on to what one possesses (*jealous of what little time she has to herself*); it is often associated with distrust, suspicion, anger, and other negative emotions (*a jealous wife*). Someone who is **covetous** has fallen prey to an inordinate or wrongful desire, usually for a person or thing that rightfully belongs to another. In other words, a young man might be *jealous* of the other men who flirt with his girlfriend, while they might be *envious* of her obvious preference for him. But the young man had better not be *covetous* of his neighbor's wife.

**jealousy** noun **1** *he was consumed with jealousy* ENVY, covetousness; resentment, resentfulness, bitterness, spite; *informal* the green-eyed monster.

**2** *the jealousy of his long-suffering wife* SUSPICION, suspiciousness, distrust, mistrust, insecurity, anxiety; possessiveness, overprotectiveness.

**jeans** plural noun. See note below.

**jeer** verb *the demonstrators* ***jeered at*** *the police* TAUNT, mock, scoff at, ridicule, sneer at, deride, insult, abuse, heckle, catcall at, boo, whistle at, jibe at, hiss at. ANTONYM cheer.

▸ noun *the jeers of the crowd* TAUNT, sneer, insult, shout, jibe, boo, hiss, catcall; derision, teasing, scoffing, abuse, scorn, heckling, catcalling; *informal* raspberry, Bronx cheer. ANTONYM applause.

**jell**, **gel** verb **1** *leave the mixture to jell* SET, stiffen, solidify, thicken, harden; cake, congeal, jellify, coagulate, clot.

**2** *things started to jell very quickly* TAKE SHAPE, fall into place, come together, take form, work out; crystallize.

**jeopardize** verb *accused of jeopardizing the health of their children* THREATEN, endanger, imperil, risk, put at risk, put in danger/jeopardy; hazard, stake; leave vulnerable; compromise, be a danger to, pose a threat to. ANTONYM safeguard.

**jeopardy** noun *the peace talks are* ***in jeopardy*** IN DANGER, in peril; at risk. ANTONYMS safety, security.

**jerk** noun **1** *she gave the reins a jerk* YANK, tug, pull, wrench, tweak, twitch.

**2** *the elevator stopped with a jerk* JOLT, lurch, bump, start, jar, bang, bounce, shake, shock.

**3** *informal I showed up for the party on the wrong night and felt like a complete jerk.* See FOOL noun sense 1.

**4** *informal Tim is such a jerk for screaming at her in public.* See BASTARD noun sense 2.

▸ verb **1** *she jerked her arm free* YANK, tug, pull, wrench, wrest, drag, pluck, snatch, seize, rip, tear.

**2** *the car jerked along* JOLT, lurch, bump, rattle, bounce, shake, jounce.

**jerky** adjective *it was a very jerky ride* CONVULSIVE, spasmodic, fitful, twitchy, shaky; JOLTING, lurching, bumpy, bouncy, jarring. ANTONYM smooth.

**jerry-built** adjective *we entered our jerry-built monstrosity in the raft race and won second prize* SHODDY, makeshift, badly built, gimcrack, flimsy, insubstantial, rickety, ramshackle, crude, chintzy; inferior, poor-quality, second-rate, third-rate, tinpot, low-grade. ANTONYM sturdy.

**jest** verb *I think he's jesting* fool around, play a practical joke, tease, kid, pull someone's leg, pull/jerk/yank someone's chain, have someone on; fun; joke, quip, gag, tell jokes, crack jokes; *informal* wisecrack.

▸ noun *jests were bandied about freely* JOKE, witticism, funny remark, gag, quip, sally, pun; crack, wisecrack, one-liner.

PHRASE: **in jest** *those sarcastic remarks were made in jest* IN FUN, as a joke, tongue in cheek, playfully, jokingly, facetiously, frivolously, for a laugh.

**jester** noun **1** *historical a court jester* FOOL, court fool, court jester, clown, harlequin, pantaloon; *archaic* buffoon, merry-andrew.

**2** *the class jester* JOKER, clown, comedian, comic, humorist, wag, wit, prankster, jokester, trickster, buffoon; *informal* card, hoot, scream, laugh, wisecracker, barrel of laughs, smart-ass, smart aleck.

**jet**[1] noun **1** *a jet of water* STREAM, spurt, squirt, spray, spout; gush, rush, surge, burst.

**2** *an executive jet* JET PLANE, jetliner; aircraft, plane, jumbo jet.

**jet**[2] adjective *her glossy jet hair* BLACK, jet-black, pitch-black, ink-black, ebony, raven, sable, sooty.

**jettison** verb **1** *six aircraft jettisoned their loads* DUMP, drop, ditch, discharge, throw out, unload, throw overboard.

**2** *he jettisoned his unwanted papers | the scheme was jettisoned* DISCARD, dispose of, throw away/out, get rid of; reject, scrap, abandon, drop; *informal* chuck (out), dump, ditch, ax, trash, junk, deep-six. ANTONYMS keep, retain.

**jetty** noun *we'd walk out on the jetty at low tide to look for starfish* PIER, landing stage, landing, quay, wharf, dock; breakwater, mole, groin, dike, dockominium, levee.

**jewel** noun **1** *priceless jewels* GEM, gemstone, (precious) stone, brilliant; baguette; *informal* sparkler, rock; *archaic* bijou.

**2** *the jewel of his collection* FINEST EXAMPLE/SPECIMEN, showpiece, pride (and joy), cream, crème de la crème, jewel in the crown, masterpiece, nonpareil, glory, prize, boast, pick, ne plus ultra.

**jewelry** noun *a locked box for her jewelry* JEWELS, gems, gemstones, precious stones; costume jewelry, trinkets; *informal* bling; *archaic* bijoux.

**jiffy** , **jiff** PHRASE: **in a jiffy/jiff** *informal I'll be there in a jiffy* (VERY) SOON, in a second, in a minute, in a moment, momentarily, in a trice, in a flash, shortly, any second, any minute (now), in no time (at all), directly; *informal* in a sec, in a snap, in two shakes (of a lamb's tail), in a wink, in a twinkle; *archaic* anon.

**jilt** verb *do you think she's jilted him?* LEAVE, walk out on, throw over, finish with, break up with, spurn, chuck, ditch, dump, drop, run out on, give someone the old heave-ho; *literary* forsake.

**jingle** noun **1** *the jingle of money* CLINK, chink, tinkle, jangle, ding-a-ling, ring, ding, ping, chime, tintinnabulation.

**2** *advertising jingles* SLOGAN, catchphrase; ditty, song, rhyme, tune.

▸ verb *the keys jingled* CLINK, chink, tinkle, jangle, ring, ding, ping, chime.

**jingoism** noun *a newspaper known for its jingoism* EXTREME PATRIOTISM, chauvinism, extreme nationalism, xenophobia, flag-waving; hawkishness, militarism, belligerence, bellicosity. See note at CHAUVINISM.

**jinx** noun *after years of bad luck they finally broke the jinx* CURSE, spell, malediction; evil eye, black magic, voodoo, bad luck, hex.

▸ verb *the family is jinxed* CURSE, cast a spell on, put the evil eye on, hex.

**jittery** adjective *informal the company's accounting troubles left stock investors jittery* NERVOUS, on edge, edgy, tense, anxious, agitated, ill at ease, uneasy, keyed up, overwrought, jumpy, on tenterhooks, worried, apprehensive; *informal* with butterflies in one's stomach, twitchy, uptight, het up, in a tizzy, spooky, squirrelly, antsy. ANTONYM calm.

**job** noun **1** *my job involves a lot of traveling* OCCUPATION, profession, trade, position, career, work, line of work, livelihood, post, situation, appointment, métier, craft; vocation, calling; vacancy, opening; *humorous* McJob.

**2** *this job will take three months* TASK, piece of work, assignment, project; chore, errand; undertaking, venture, operation, enterprise, business.

**3** *it's your job to protect her* RESPONSIBILITY, duty, charge, task; role, function, mission; *informal* department.

**4** *informal a bank job* ROBBERY, theft, holdup, burglary, break-in; *informal* stickup, heist.

**jobless** adjective *as of today, Young is among the jobless* UNEMPLOYED, out-of-work, out of a job, between jobs, laid off, unwaged, on the dole; *Brit.* redundant. ANTONYM employed.

**jockey** noun *legendary jockey Willie Shoemaker won his first horse race when he was 17* RIDER, horseman, horsewoman, equestrian.

▸ verb *on the eve of the primary, with McCain running even with Bush in New Hampshire polls, both men jockeyed for position* MANEUVER, ease, edge, work, steer; compete, contend, vie; struggle, fight, scramble, jostle.

**jocular** adjective *my jocular uncle* HUMOROUS, funny, witty, comic, comical, amusing, droll, waggish, jokey, hilarious, facetious, tongue-in-cheek, teasing, playful; lighthearted, jovial, cheerful, cheery, merry; *formal* jocose, ludic. ANTONYM solemn.

**jocund** adjective *formal*. See CHEERFUL sense 1.

**jog** verb **1** *he jogged along the road* RUN SLOWLY, trot, lope, dog-trot; *dated* jog-trot.

**2** *something jogged her memory* STIMULATE, prompt, stir, activate, refresh; prod, jar, nudge.

▸ noun **1** *he set off at a jog* RUN, trot, lope, dog-trot; *dated* jog trot.

**2** *a jog in the road* BEND, turn, curve, corner, zigzag, kink, dog-leg.

**join** verb **1** *we joined a bunch of sticks together* FASTEN, attach, tie, bind, couple, connect, unite, link, yoke, weld, fuse, glue.

**2** *the two clubs have joined together* COMBINE, amalgamate, merge, join forces, unify, unite.

**3** *we joined them in their venture* TEAM UP WITH, band together with, cooperate with, collaborate with.

**4** *she joined the volleyball team* SIGN UP WITH, enlist in, enroll in, enter, become a member of, be part of.

**5** *where the Ottawa River joins the St. Lawrence* MEET, reach, abut, touch, adjoin, border on, connect with.

THE RIGHT WORD **join, combine, conjoin, connect, consolidate, unite**

It is possible for an individual to **join** an investment club, to **consolidate** his or her financial resources, and to **combine** a background in economics with a strong interest in retirement planning. All of these words mean to bring together or to attach two or more things. *Join* is the general term for bringing into contact or conjunction two discrete things (*join two pieces of wood; join one's friends in celebration*), while **conjoin** emphasizes both the separateness of the things that are joined and the unity that results (*her innate brilliance, conjoined with a genuine eagerness to learn, made her the ideal candidate for the job*). In contrast, to *combine* is to mix or mingle things together, often to the point where they merge with one another (*combine the ingredients for a cake*). *Consolidate* also implies a merger of distinct and separate elements, but the emphasis here is on achieving greater compactness, strength, or efficiency (*consolidate their furnishings and buy a new house together*). **Connect** implies a loose or obvious attachment of things to each other, but with each thing's identity or physical separateness preserved (*the two families were connected by blood; she connected the computer to the printer*). In a physical context, it differs from *join* in that it implies an intervening element that permits movement; in other words, the bones are *connected* by ligaments, but bricks are *joined* by mortar. When things are joined or combined so closely that they form a single thing, they are said to **unite** (*the parties were united in their support of the new law*).

**joint** noun **1** *cracks in the joint* JUNCTURE, junction, join, intersection, confluence, nexus, link, linkage, connection; weld, seam; *Anatomy* commissure.

**2** *the hip joint* ball-and-socket joint, hinge joint, articulation.

**3** *informal a classy joint* ESTABLISHMENT, restaurant, bar, club, nightclub, place; hole, dump, dive. See also BAR sense 4.

**4** *informal he rolled a joint* marijuana cigarette, cannabis cigarette; *informal* reefer, doobie, roach, jay, blunt, spliff.

▸ adjective *matters of joint interest | a joint effort* COMMON, shared, communal, collective; mutual, cooperative, collaborative, concerted, combined, united, bilateral, multilateral. ANTONYM separate.

**jointly** adverb *Hitachi and NEC will jointly develop business software* TOGETHER, in partnership, in cooperation, cooperatively, in conjunction, in collaboration, in concert, as one, in combination, mutually; in league, in alliance; in collusion.

**joke** noun **1** *they were telling jokes* FUNNY STORY, jest, witticism, quip; pun, play on words; *informal* gag, wisecrack, crack, one-liner, rib-tickler, knee-slapper, thigh-slapper, punch-line, groaner.

**2** *playing stupid jokes* TRICK, practical joke, prank, lark, stunt, hoax, jape; *informal* spoof.

**3** *informal he soon became a joke to us* LAUGHINGSTOCK, object of ridicule, stooge, butt; *Brit. informal* Aunt Sally.

**4** *informal the present system is a joke* FARCE, travesty, waste of time.

▸ verb **1** *she laughed and joked with the guests* TELL JOKES, crack jokes; jest, banter, quip; *informal* wisecrack, josh.

**2** *they didn't realize you were only joking* FOOL, fool around, play a trick, play a practical joke, tease; *informal* kid, fun, pull (someone's leg), pull/jerk/yank someone's chain, make a monkey out of someone, put someone on.

**joker** noun HUMORIST, comedian, comedienne, comic, wit, clown, card, jokester, jester, wisecracker, wag; prankster, practical joker, hoaxer, trickster.

**jolly** adjective *he returned in a jolly mood* CHEERFUL, happy, cheery, good-humored, jovial, merry, sunny, joyful, joyous, lighthearted, in high spirits, bubbly, exuberant, ebullient, gleeful, mirthful, genial, affable, fun-loving; *informal* chipper, chirpy, perky, bright-eyed and bushy-tailed, hail-fellow-well-met; *formal* jocund, jocose; *dated* gay; *literary* blithe. ANTONYM miserable.

▸ noun **(jollies)** *people who get their jollies reading the tabloids* PLEASURE, thrill, enjoyment, excitement, titillation; *informal* kicks.

**jolt** verb **1** *the train jolted the passengers to one side* PUSH, thrust, jar, bump, knock, bang; shake, joggle, jog.

**2** *the car jolted along* BUMP, bounce, jerk, rattle, lurch, shudder, jounce; *Brit.* judder.

**3** *she was jolted out of her reverie* STARTLE, surprise, shock, stun, shake, take aback; astonish, astound, amaze, stagger, stop someone in their tracks; *informal* rock, floor.

▸ noun **1** *a series of sickening jolts* BUMP, bounce, shake, jerk, lurch.

**2** *he woke up with a jolt* START, jerk, jump.

**3** *the sight of the dagger gave him a jolt* FRIGHT, the fright of one's life, shock, scare, surprise; wake-up call.

**jostle** verb **1** *jostled by the crowd* BUMP INTO/AGAINST, knock into/against, bang into, collide with, plow into, jolt; PUSH, shove, elbow, mob, shoulder; *informal* barrel into, bulldoze.

**2** *media empires jostle to catch the eye of Asian readers and viewers* STRUGGLE, vie, jockey, scramble, crowd one another.

**jot** verb *I've **jotted down** a few details* WRITE DOWN, note down, make a note of, take down, put on paper; scribble, scrawl.

▸ noun *not a jot of evidence* IOTA, scrap, shred, whit, grain, crumb, ounce, (little) bit, jot or tittle, speck, atom, particle, scintilla, trace, hint; *informal* smidgen, tad.

**journal** noun **1** *a medical journal* PERIODICAL, magazine, gazette, digest, review, newsletter, bulletin; newspaper, paper, tabloid, broadsheet; daily, weekly, monthly, quarterly.

**2** *he keeps a journal* DIARY, daily record, daybook, log, logbook, chronicle.

**journalism** noun *a career in journalism* THE PRESS, the fourth estate, REPORTING, news writing, news broadcasting, news coverage, reportage, feature writing, photojournalism, sensationalism, the newspaper business; articles, reports, features, pieces, stories.

**journalist** noun *another journalist has been wounded in Bosnia* REPORTER, correspondent, columnist, writer, commentator, reviewer; investigative journalist, photojournalist, newspaperman, newspaperwoman, newsman, newswoman, newshound, newshawk, hack, stringer.

**journey** noun *their journey around the world* TRIP, expedition, excursion, tour, trek, voyage, junket, cruise, ride, drive, jaunt; crossing, passage, flight; travels, wandering, globe-trotting; odyssey, pilgrimage; peregrination.

▸ verb *they journeyed south* TRAVEL, go, voyage, sail, cruise, fly, hike, trek, ride, drive, make one's way; take/go on a trip, go on an expedition, tour, rove, roam.

THE RIGHT WORD **journey, excursion, expedition, jaunt, pilgrimage, trip, voyage**

While all of these nouns refer to a course of travel to a particular place, usually for a specific purpose, there is a big difference between a **jaunt** to the nearest beach and an **expedition** to the rainforest. While a **trip** may be either long or short, for business or pleasure, and taken at either a rushed or a leisurely pace (*a ski trip; a trip to Europe*), a **journey** suggests that a considerable amount of time and distance will be covered and that the travel will take place over land (*a journey into the Australian outback*). A long trip by water or through air or space is a **voyage** (*a voyage to the Galapagos Islands; a voyage to Mars*), while a short, casual trip for pleasure or recreation is a *jaunt* (*a jaunt to the local shopping mall*). **Excursion** also applies to a brief pleasure trip, usually no more than a day in length, that returns to the place where it began (*an afternoon excursion to the zoo*). Unlike the rest of these nouns, *expedition* and **pilgrimage** apply to *journeys* that are undertaken for a specific purpose. An *expedition* is usually made by an organized group or company (*a scientific expedition; an expedition to locate new sources of oil*), while a *pilgrimage* is a journey to a place that has religious or emotional significance (*the Muslims' annual pilgrimage to Mecca; a pilgrimage to the place where her father died*).

**jovial** adjective *his jovial manner* CHEERFUL, jolly, happy, cheery, good-humored, convivial, genial, good-natured, friendly, amiable, affable, sociable, outgoing; smiling, merry, sunny, joyful, joyous, high-spirited, exuberant; chipper, chirpy, perky, bright-eyed and bushy-tailed, hail-fellow-well-met; *formal* jocund, jocose; *dated* gay; *literary* blithe. ANTONYM miserable.

**joy** noun **1** *whoops of joy* DELIGHT, great pleasure, joyfulness, jubilation, triumph, exultation, rejoicing, happiness, gladness, glee, exhilaration, exuberance, elation, euphoria, bliss, ecstasy, rapture; enjoyment, felicity, joie de vivre, jouissance; *literary* jocundity. ANTONYM misery.

**2** *it was a joy to be with her* PLEASURE, source of pleasure, delight, treat, thrill. ANTONYM trial.

**joyful** adjective **1** *his joyful mood* CHEERFUL, happy, jolly, merry, sunny, joyous, lighthearted, in good spirits, bubbly, exuberant, ebullient, cheery, smiling, mirthful, radiant; jubilant, overjoyed, thrilled, ecstatic, euphoric, blissful, on cloud nine, elated, delighted, gleeful; jovial, genial, good-humored; *informal* chipper, chirpy, peppy, over the moon, on top of the world, upbeat; *dated* gay; *formal* jocund; *literary* blithe. ANTONYMS sad, miserable.

**2** *joyful news* PLEASING, happy, good, cheering, gladdening, welcome, heartwarming. ANTONYM distressing.

**3** *a joyful occasion* HAPPY, cheerful, merry, jolly, festive, joyous. ANTONYMS sad, depressing.

**joyless** adjective **1** *a joyless man* GLOOMY, melancholy, morose, lugubrious, glum, somber, saturnine, sullen, dour, humorless. ANTONYM cheerful.

**2** *a joyless room* DEPRESSING, cheerless, gloomy, dreary, bleak, dispiriting, drab, dismal, desolate, austere, somber; unwelcoming, uninviting, inhospitable; *literary* drear. ANTONYMS cheerful, welcoming.

**joyous** adjective. See JOYFUL senses 1, 3.

**jubilant** adjective *a jubilant crowd* OVERJOYED, exultant, triumphant, joyful, rejoicing, exuberant, elated, thrilled, gleeful, euphoric, ecstatic, enraptured, in raptures, walking on air, in seventh heaven, on cloud nine; *informal* over the moon, on top of the world, tickled pink, on a high. ANTONYM despondent.

**jubilation** noun *we couldn't conceal our jubilation* EXULTATION, joy, joyousness, elation, euphoria, rejoicing, ecstasy, rapture, glee, gleefulness, exuberance.

**jubilee** noun *Queen Elizabeth II's golden jubilee* ANNIVERSARY, commemoration; celebration, festival, jamboree; festivities, revelry.

**judge** noun **1** *the judge sentenced him to five years* JUSTICE, magistrate, sheriff, jurist.

**2** *a panel of judges will select the winner* ADJUDICATOR, arbiter, arbitrator, assessor, evaluator, referee, ombudsman, ombudsperson, appraiser, examiner, moderator, mediator.

▸ verb **1** *we judged that it was too late to proceed* FORM THE OPINION, conclude, decide; consider, believe, think, deem, view; deduce, gather, infer, gauge, estimate, guess, surmise, conjecture; regard as, look on as, take to be, rate as, class as; *informal* reckon, figure.

**2** *the case was judged by a tribunal* TRY, hear; adjudicate, decide, give a ruling on, give a verdict on.

**3** *she was judged innocent of murder* ADJUDGE, pronounce, decree, rule, find.

**4** *the competition will be judged by last year's winner* ADJUDICATE, arbitrate, mediate, moderate.

**5** *entries were judged by a panel of experts* ASSESS, appraise, evaluate; examine, review.

**judgment** noun **1** *his temper could affect his judgment* DISCERNMENT, acumen, shrewdness, astuteness, sense, common sense, perception, perspicacity, percipience, acuity, discrimination, reckoning, wisdom, wit, judiciousness, prudence, canniness, sharpness, sharp-wittedness, powers of reasoning, reason, logic; savvy, horse sense, street smarts, gumption.

**2** *a court judgment* VERDICT, decision, adjudication, ruling, pronouncement, decree, finding; sentence.

**3** *critical judgment* ASSESSMENT, evaluation, appraisal; review, analysis, criticism, critique. PHRASE: **against one's better judgment** *I paid the asking price, against my better judgment* RELUCTANTLY, unwillingly, grudgingly.

**judicial** adjective *a judicial inquiry* LEGAL, juridical, judicatory; official.

**judicious** adjective *following a judicious course of action* WISE, sensible, prudent, politic, shrewd, astute, canny, sagacious, commonsensical, sound, well-advised, discerning, percipient, intelligent, smart; *informal* heads-up. See note at JUDICIAL. ANTONYM ill-advised.

**jug** noun *a jug of cider* PITCHER, carafe, flask, flagon, bottle, decanter, ewer, crock, jar, urn; *historical* amphora.

**juggle** verb **1** *juggling three part-time jobs* HANDLE, manage, deal with, multitask.

**2** *the auditors suspect that the books had been juggled* TAMPER WITH, manipulate, falsify, alter, rig; *informal* fudge, fix, doctor, cook.

**juice** noun **1** *the juice from two lemons* LIQUID, fluid, sap; extract; nectar.

**2** *informal he ran out of juice on the last lap* ENERGY, power, stamina, steam.

**juicy** adjective **1** *a juicy peach* SUCCULENT, tender, moist; ripe; *archaic* mellow. ANTONYM dry.

**2** *informal juicy gossip* SENSATIONAL, very interesting, fascinating, lurid; scandalous, racy, risqué, spicy; *informal* hot. ANTONYM dull.

**3** *informal juicy profits a juicy role* SUBSTANTIAL, large, sizable, generous; profitable, lucrative, remunerative; DESIRABLE, appealing, attractive; *informal* tidy, whopping, to die for. ANTONYMS insignificant, undesirable.

**jumble** noun *a jumble of books and toys* UNTIDY HEAP, clutter, muddle, mess, confusion, disarray, tangle, imbroglio; HODGEPODGE, mishmash, miscellany, motley collection, mixed bag, medley, jambalaya, farrago, gallimaufry.

▸ verb *the photographs are all* ***jumbled up*** MIX UP, muddle up, disarrange, disorganize, disorder, put in disarray.

THE RIGHT WORD **jumble, confusion, conglomeration, disarray, farrago, hodgepodge, mlange, muddle**

**Confusion** is a very broad term, applying to any indiscriminate mixing or mingling that makes it difficult to distinguish individual elements or parts (*a confusion of languages*). The typical teenager's bedroom is usually a **jumble** of books, papers, clothing, CDs, and soda cans—the word suggests physical disorder and a mixture of dissimilar things. If the disorder exists on a figurative level, it is usually called a **hodgepodge** (*a hodgepodge of ideas, opinions, and quotations, with a few facts thrown in for good measure*). **Conglomeration** refers to a collection of dissimilar things, but with a suggestion that the collection is random or inappropriate (*a conglomeration of decorating styles*). A **mélange** can be a mixture of foods (*add peppers or zucchini to the mélange*), but it can also be used in a derogatory way (*an error-filled mélange of pseudoscience, religion, and fanciful ideas*). A **farrago** is an irrational or confused mixture of elements and is usually worse than a *conglomeration* (*a farrago of doubts, fears, hopes, and desires*), while a **muddle** is less serious and suggests confused thinking and lack of organization (*their bank records were in a complete muddle*). **Disarray** implies disarrangement and is most appropriately used when order or discipline has been lost (*his unexpected appearance threw the meeting into disarray*).

**jumbo** adjective *informal*. See HUGE.

**jump** verb **1** *the cat jumped off his lap | Flora began to jump around* LEAP, spring, bound, hop; skip, caper, dance, prance, frolic, cavort.

**2** *he jumped the fence* VAULT (OVER), leap over, clear, sail over, hop over, hurdle.

**3** *pretax profits jumped* RISE, go up, shoot up, soar, surge, climb, increase; *informal* skyrocket.

**4** *the noise made her jump* START, jerk, jolt, flinch, recoil; *informal* jump out of one's skin.

**5** *Polly* ***jumped at*** *the chance* ACCEPT EAGERLY, leap at, welcome with open arms, seize on, snap up, grab, pounce on.

**6** *the place was jumping* ROCK, hop, buzz, be lively, be wild.

**7** *two guys jumped him in the alley* ASSAULT, assail, set upon, mug, attack, pounce on.

▸ noun **1** *a short jump across the ditch* LEAP, spring, vault, bound, hop.

2 *a jump in profits* RISE, leap, increase, upsurge, upswing, upturn; *informal* hike.

3 *I woke up with a jump* START, jerk, involuntary movement, spasm.

PHRASES: **jump the gun** *informal several radio stations have jumped the gun by announcing winners long before the polls have closed in certain districts* ACT PREMATURELY, act too soon, be too/overly hasty, be precipitate, be rash; *informal* be ahead of oneself.

**jump to it** *informal this year, students will really have to jump to it if they hope to get a hot meal before the kitchen closes* HURRY UP, get a move on, be quick; *informal* get cracking, shake a leg, look lively, look sharp, get the lead out; *dated* make haste.

**jumpy** adjective 1 *informal he was tired and jumpy* NERVOUS, on edge, edgy, tense, anxious, ill at ease, uneasy, restless, fidgety, keyed up, overwrought, on tenterhooks; *informal* a bundle of nerves, jittery, uptight, het up, in a tizzy; strung out; squirrelly, antsy. ANTONYMS calm, relaxed.

2 *jumpy black-and-white footage* JERKY, jolting, lurching, bumpy, jarring; fitful, convulsive.

**junction** noun 1 *the junction between the roof and the wall* JOINT, intersection, join, bond, seam, connection, juncture; *Anatomy* commissure.

2 *the junction of the two rivers* CONFLUENCE, convergence, meeting point, juncture.

3 *turn right at the next junction* INTERSECTION, crossroads, crossing, interchange; turn, turnoff, exit; traffic circle, cloverleaf.

**juncture** noun 1 *at this juncture, I am unable to tell you* POINT, point in time, time, moment, moment in time; period, occasion, phase.

2 *the juncture of the pipes.* See JUNCTION sense 1.

3 *the juncture of the rivers.* See JUNCTION sense 2.

**jungle** noun 1 *the Amazon jungle* TROPICAL FOREST, (tropical) rain forest, wilderness.

2 *the jungle of bureaucracy* COMPLEXITY, confusion, complication, chaos, mess; labyrinth, maze, tangle, web.

**junior** adjective 1 *the junior members of the family* YOUNGER, youngest. ANTONYMS senior, older.

2 *a junior position in the firm* LOW-RANKING, lower-ranking, entry-level, subordinate, lesser, lower, minor, secondary. ANTONYMS senior, higher-ranking.

**junk** *informal* noun *an attic full of junk* RUBBISH, clutter, odds and ends, bric-a-brac, bits and pieces; garbage, trash, refuse, litter, scrap, waste, debris, detritus, dross; *informal* crap.

▸ verb *time to junk the old pickup* THROW AWAY/OUT, discard, get rid of, dispose of, scrap, toss out, jettison; *informal* chuck, dump, ditch, deep-six, trash.

**junket** noun *informal the company sponsored a New Year's Eve gambling junket* excursion, outing, spree, trip, jaunt; celebration, party, jamboree, feast, festivity; *informal* bash, shindig.

**jurisdiction** noun 1 *an area under French jurisdiction* AUTHORITY, control, power, dominion, rule, administration, command, sway, leadership, sovereignty, hegemony.

2 *foreign jurisdictions* TERRITORY, region, province, district, area, domain, realm.

THE RIGHT WORD **jurisdiction, authority, command, dominion, power, sovereignty, sway**

The **authority** of our elected officials refers to their *power* (often conferred by rank or office) to give orders, require obedience, or make decisions. Their authority is normally limited by their **jurisdiction**, which is a legally predetermined division of a larger whole, within which someone has a right to rule or decide (*the matter was beyond his jurisdiction*). The president of the United States has more **power** than any other American official, which means that he has the ability to exert force or control over something. He does not, however, have the *authority* to make laws on his own. As commander in chief, he does have **command** over the nation's armed forces, implying that he has the kind of authority that can enforce obedience. Back in the days when Great Britain had **dominion**, or supreme authority, over the American colonies, it was the king of England who held **sway** over this country's economic and political life—an old-fashioned word that stresses the sweeping scope of one's power. But his **sovereignty**, which emphasizes absolute or autonomous rule over something considered as a whole, was eventually challenged. The rest, as they say, is history.

**just** adjective 1 *a just and democratic society* FAIR, fair-minded, equitable, evenhanded, impartial, unbiased, objective, neutral, disinterested, unprejudiced, open-minded, nonpartisan; honorable, upright, decent, honest, righteous, moral, virtuous, principled. ANTONYM unfair.

2 *a just reward* DESERVED, well deserved, well earned, earned, merited; rightful, due, fitting, appropriate, suitable; *formal* condign; *archaic* meet. ANTONYM undeserved.

3 *just criticism* VALID, sound, well-founded, justified, justifiable, warranted, legitimate. ANTONYMS unfair, wrongful.

▸ adverb 1 *I just saw him* A MOMENT AGO, a second ago, a short time ago, very recently, not long ago.

2 *she's just right for him* EXACTLY, precisely, absolutely, completely, totally, entirely, perfectly, utterly, wholly, thoroughly, in all respects; *informal* to a T, dead.

3 *we just made it* NARROWLY, only just, by a hair's breadth; barely, scarcely, hardly; *informal* by the skin of one's teeth, by a whisker.

4 *she's just a child* ONLY, merely, simply, but, nothing but, no more than.

5 *the color's just fantastic* REALLY, absolutely, completely, positively, entirely, totally, quite; indeed, truly.

PHRASE: **just about** *informal that's just about all I can eat at one meal* NEARLY, almost, practically, all but, virtually, as good as, more or less, to all intents and purposes; *informal* pretty much; *literary* well-nigh, nigh on.

**justice** noun **1** *I appealed to his sense of justice* FAIRNESS, justness, fair play, fair-mindedness, equity, evenhandedness, impartiality, objectivity, neutrality, disinterestedness, honesty, righteousness, morals, morality.

**2** *they were determined to exact justice* PUNISHMENT, judgment, retribution, compensation, just deserts.

**3** *an order made by the justices* JUDGE, magistrate, jurist. PHRASE: **do justice to** *the movie didn't do justice to the book* CONSIDER FAIRLY, be worthy of.

**justifiable** adjective *justifiable criticism* VALID, legitimate, warranted, well-founded, justified, just, reasonable; defensible, tenable, supportable, acceptable. ANTONYM indefensible.

**justification** noun *there's no justification for their rudeness* GROUNDS, reason, basis, rationale, premise, rationalization, vindication, explanation; defense, argument, apologia, apology, case.

**justify** verb **1** *directors must justify the expenditure* GIVE GROUNDS FOR, give reasons for, give a justification for, explain, give an explanation for, account for; defend, answer for, vindicate.

**2** *the situation justified further investigation* WARRANT, be good reason for, be a justification for.

**justly** adverb **1** *he is justly proud of his achievement* JUSTIFIABLY, with (good) reason, legitimately, rightly, rightfully, deservedly. ANTONYM unjustifiably.

**2** *they were treated justly* FAIRLY, with fairness, equitably, evenhandedly, impartially, without bias, objectively, without prejudice, fairly and squarely. ANTONYM unfairly.

**jut** verb *the face of the cliff is sheer, except for one shelf of rock that* ***juts out*** STICK OUT, project, protrude, bulge out, overhang.

**juvenile** adjective **1** *juvenile offenders* YOUNG, teenage, adolescent, boyish, girlish, junior, pubescent, prepubescent, youthful. See note at YOUTHFUL. ANTONYM adult.

**2** *juvenile behavior* CHILDISH, immature, puerile, infantile, babyish; jejune, inexperienced, callow, green, unsophisticated, sophomoric, naive, foolish, silly. ANTONYM mature.

▸ noun *two juveniles fled the scene* YOUNG PERSON, youngster, child, teenager, adolescent, youth, boy/girl, minor, junior; *informal* kid, punk. ANTONYM adult.

**juxtapose** verb *the exhibit juxtaposes works by Van Gogh and Gauguin* PLACE SIDE BY SIDE, set side by side, collocate, mix; compare, contrast.

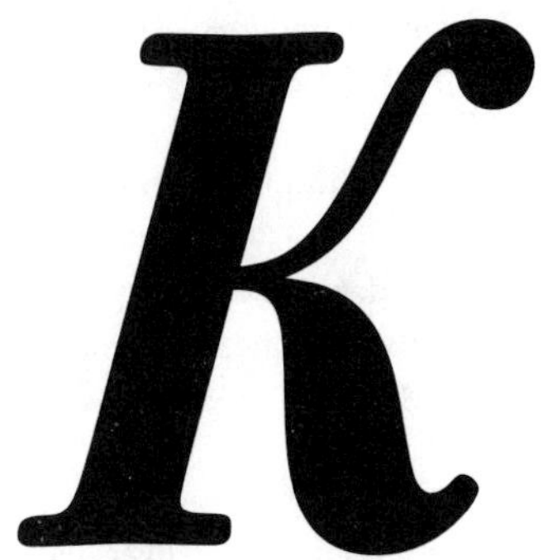

**kaleidoscopic** adjective **1** *kaleidoscopic swirls in the puddles* MULTICOLORED, many-colored, multicolor, many-hued, variegated, parti-colored, varicolored, psychedelic, rainbow, polychromatic. ANTONYM monochrome.

**2** *the kaleidoscopic political landscape* EVER-CHANGING, changeable, shifting, fluid, protean, variable, inconstant, fluctuating, unpredictable, impermanent. ANTONYMS fixed, constant.

**keel** PHRASES: **on an even keel** *finally, the relationship seems to be on an even keel* steady, on track, on course, untroubled. **keel over 1** *the boat keeled over* CAPSIZE, turn turtle, turn upside down, founder; overturn, turn over, flip (over), tip over.

**2** *the slightest activity made him keel over* COLLAPSE, faint, pass out, black out, lose consciousness, swoon.

**keen** adjective **1** *his publishers were keen to capitalize on his success* EAGER, anxious, intent, impatient, determined, ambitious, champing at the bit; *informal* raring, itching, dying. See note at EAGER. ANTONYM reluctant.

**2** *a keen birdwatcher* ENTHUSIASTIC, avid, eager, ardent, passionate, fervent, impassioned; conscientious, committed, dedicated, zealous. ANTONYMS apathetic, halfhearted.

**3** *they are* ***keen on*** *horses* | *a girl he was* ***keen on*** ENTHUSIASTIC ABOUT, interested in, passionate about; attracted to, fond of, taken with, smitten with, enamored of, infatuated with; *informal* struck on, hot on/for, mad about, crazy about, nuts about. ANTONYMS indifferent, unenthusiastic.

**4** *a keen cutting edge* SHARP, sharpened, honed, razor-sharp. ANTONYM blunt.

**5** *keen eyesight* ACUTE, sharp, discerning, sensitive, perceptive, clear. ANTONYM weak.

**6** *a keen mind* ACUTE, penetrating, astute, incisive, sharp, perceptive, piercing, razor-sharp, perspicacious, shrewd, discerning, clever, intelligent, brilliant, bright, smart, wise, canny, percipient, insightful. ANTONYMS dull, stupid.

**7** *a keen wind* COLD, icy, freezing, harsh, raw, bitter; penetrating, piercing, biting. ANTONYM gentle.

**8** *a keen sense of duty* INTENSE, acute, fierce, passionate, burning, fervent, ardent, strong, powerful.

THE RIGHT WORD **keen, acute, astute, penetrating, perspicacious, sharp, shrewd**

A knife can be **sharp**, even **keen**, but it can't be **astute**. While *keen* and *sharp* mean having a fine point or edge, they also pertain to mental agility and perceptiveness. You might describe someone as having a *keen* mind, which suggests the ability to grapple with complex problems, or to observe details and see them as part of a larger pattern (*a keen appreciation of what victory would mean for the Democratic party*) or a *keen* wit, which suggests an incisive or stimulating sense of humor. Someone who is *sharp* has an alert and rational mind, but is not necessarily well grounded in a particular field and may in some cases be cunning or devious (*sharp enough to see how the situation might be turned to her advantage*). An **astute** mind, in contrast, is one that has a thorough and profound understanding of a given subject or field (*an astute understanding of the legal principles involved*). Like *sharp*, **shrewd** implies both practicality and cleverness, but with an undercurrent of self-interest (*a shrewd salesperson*). **Acute** is close in meaning to *keen*, but with more emphasis on sensitivity and the ability to make subtle distinctions (*an acute sense of smell*). While a keen mind might see only superficial details, a **penetrating** mind would focus on underlying causes (*a penetrating analysis of the plan's feasibility*). **Perspicacious** is the most formal of these terms, meaning both perceptive and discerning (*a perspicacious remark; perspicacious judgment*).

**keep** verb **1** *you should keep all the old forms* RETAIN, hold on to, keep hold of, retain possession of, keep possession of, not part with; save, store, conserve, put aside, set aside; *informal* hang on to, stash away. ANTONYMS throw away, lose.

**2** *I tried to keep calm* REMAIN, continue to be, stay, carry on being, persist in being.

**3** *he keeps talking about the Super Bowl* PERSIST IN, keep on, carry on, continue, do something constantly. ANTONYMS stop, give up.

**4** *I won't keep you long* DETAIN, keep waiting, delay, hold up, retard, slow down.

**5** *most people kept the rules* | *he had to keep his promise* COMPLY WITH, obey, observe, conform to, abide by, adhere to, stick to, heed, follow; fulfill, carry out, act on, make good, honor, keep to, stand by. ANTONYMS disobey, break.

**6** *keeping the old traditions* PRESERVE, keep alive/up, keep going, carry on, perpetuate, maintain, uphold, sustain. ANTONYMS discard, abandon.

7 *that's where we keep the linen* STORE, house, stow, put (away), place, deposit.

8 *she keeps rabbits* BREED, rear, raise, farm; own, have as a pet.

9 *God keep you | keep them from harm* LOOK AFTER, care for, take care of, mind, watch over; PRESERVE, protect, keep safe, shield, shelter, safeguard, defend, guard. ANTONYMS neglect, endanger.

10 *she kept their whereabouts from us* KEEP SECRET, keep hidden, hide, conceal, withhold.

11 *worry kept her from sleeping* PREVENT, stop, restrain, hold back. ANTONYMS enable, allow.

▸ noun *money to pay for his keep* MAINTENANCE, upkeep, sustenance, board, room and board, lodging, food, livelihood.

PHRASES: **keep at** *she's determined to keep at her studies until she passes the bar exam* PERSEVERE WITH/IN/AT, persist in/with, keep going with, carry on with, press on with, work away at, continue with; *informal* stick at, plug away at, hammer away at.

**keep something back** 1 *she kept back some of the money* RESERVE, keep in reserve, put aside/by, set aside; retain, hold back, hold on to, not part with; *informal* stash away.

2 *she kept back the details* WITHHOLD, keep secret, keep hidden, conceal, suppress, keep quiet about.

3 *she could hardly keep back her tears* SUPPRESS, stifle, choke back, fight back, hold back/in, repress, keep in check, contain, smother, swallow, bite back.

**keep from** *it's hard to keep from smoking* REFRAIN FROM, stop oneself, restrain oneself from, prevent oneself from, forbear from, avoid.

**keep off** 1 *we ask that you please keep off the playing field* STAY OFF, not enter, keep away from, stay away from, not trespass on.

2 *Maud tried to keep off political subjects* AVOID, steer clear of, stay away from, evade, dodge, sidestep, bypass, skirt around; *informal* duck.

3 *you should keep off alcohol* ABSTAIN FROM, do without, refrain from, give up, forgo, not touch; *informal* swear off; *formal* forswear.

**keep on** *they kept on working | despite our exhaustion, we agreed to keep on* CONTINUE, go on, carry on, persist in, persevere in; soldier on, struggle on, keep going.

**keep something up** *keep up the good work* CONTINUE (WITH), keep on with, keep going with, carry on with, persist with, persevere with.

**keep up with** *she walked fast to keep up with them* KEEP PACE WITH, keep abreast of; match, equal.

**keeper** noun *Gregor is the keeper of the tennis courts and adjacent grounds* GUARDIAN, custodian, curator, administrator, overseer, steward, caretaker.

**keeping** PHRASE: **in keeping with** *in keeping with the patriotic theme, we've asked the band to conclude with a Sousa medley* CONSISTENT WITH, in harmony with, in accord with, in agreement with, in line with, in character with, compatible with; appropriate to, befitting, suitable for.

**keepsake** noun *a box with concert programs, pressed corsages, and other keepsakes* MEMENTO, souvenir, reminder, remembrance, token; party favor, bomboniere.

**keg** noun *the beer is delivered in kegs* BARREL, cask, vat, butt, tun, hogshead; *historical* firkin.

**kernel** noun 1 *the kernel of a nut* seed, grain, core; nut.

2 *the kernel of the argument* ESSENCE, core, heart, essentials, quintessence, fundamentals, basics, nub, gist, substance; *informal* nitty-gritty.

3 *a kernel of truth* NUCLEUS, germ, grain, nugget.

**key** noun 1 *I put my key in the lock* door key, latchkey, pass key, master key.

2 *the key to the mystery | the key to success* ANSWER, clue, solution, explanation; basis, foundation, requisite, precondition, means, way, route, path, passport, secret, formula.

▸ adjective *a key figure* CRUCIAL, central, essential, indispensable, pivotal, critical, dominant, vital, principal, prime, primary, chief, major, leading, main, important, significant. ANTONYM peripheral.

**keynote** noun *the keynote of this year's conference is 'Adequate and Affordable Health Care'* THEME, salient point, gist, substance, burden, tenor, pith, marrow, essence, heart, core, basis, essential feature/element, crux.

**keystone** noun *the keystone of the government's policy* FOUNDATION, basis, linchpin, cornerstone, base, principle, guiding principle, core, heart, center, crux, fundament.

**kibosh** PHRASE: **put the kibosh on** *informal inclement weather can put the kibosh on a promising vintage* PUT A STOP TO, stop, halt, put an end to, quash, block, cancel, scotch, thwart, prevent, suppress; *informal* stymie; scuttle.

**kick** verb 1 *she kicked the ball over the fence* BOOT, punt, drop-kick; *informal* hoof.

2 *informal he was struggling to kick his drug habit* GIVE UP, break, abandon, end, stop, cease, desist from, renounce; *informal* shake, pack in, leave off, quit.

▸ noun 1 *that kick landed the ball across the street* BLOW WITH THE FOOT, punt; *informal* boot.

2 *informal I get a kick out of driving a race car* THRILL, excitement, stimulation, tingle; fun, enjoyment, amusement, pleasure, gratification; *informal* buzz, high, rush, charge.

3 *informal a drink with a powerful kick* POTENCY, stimulant effect, strength, power; tang, zest, bite, piquancy, edge, pungency; *informal* punch.

4 *informal a health kick* CRAZE, enthusiasm, obsession, mania, passion; fashion, vogue, trend; *informal* fad.

PHRASES: **kick someone/something around** *informal* 1 *I'm tired of getting kicked around* ABUSE, mistreat, maltreat, push around, trample on, take for granted; *informal* boss around, walk all over.

2 *they began to kick around some ideas* DISCUSS, talk over, debate, thrash out, consider, toy with, play with.

**kick back** *informal I just wanna kick back and watch some TV*

RELAX, unwind, take it easy, rest, slow down, let up, ease up/off, sit back, chill (out), hang loose.

**kick off** *informal we'll kick off with a brief description of how a timeshare works | they kicked off the ceremony with a parade of cadets* START, commence, begin, get going, get off the ground, get underway; open, start off, set in motion, launch, initiate, introduce, inaugurate, usher in.

**kick someone out** *informal most of us were given one-week suspensions from school, but Andy and Olivia were actually kicked out* EXPEL, eject, banish, exile, throw out, oust, evict, get rid of, ax; dismiss, discharge; *informal* chuck (out), send packing, boot out, give someone their marching orders, give someone their walking papers, give someone the gate, give someone the (old) heave-ho, sack, bounce, fire, give someone the bum's rush.

**kickoff** noun *informal breakfast on the boat was a great kickoff to the weekend* BEGINNING, start, commencement, launch, outset, opening.

**kid**1 noun *informal they have three kids* CHILD, youngster, little one, baby, toddler, tot, infant, boy/girl, young person, minor, juvenile, adolescent, teenager, youth, stripling; offspring, son/daughter; *informal* kiddie, shaver, young 'un, rug rat, ankle-biter, munchkin, whippersnapper; *derogatory* brat; *literary* babe.

**kid**2 verb *informal* **1** *I'm not kidding | stop kidding me* JOKE, tease, jest, chaff, be facetious, fool around, pull (someone's) leg, pull/jerk/yank someone's (chain), have (someone) on, rib.

**2** *don't kid yourself* DELUDE, deceive, fool, trick, hoodwink, hoax, beguile, dupe, gull; *informal* con, pull the wool over (someone's) eyes.

**kidnap** verb *they attempted to kidnap the president's child* ABDUCT, carry off, capture, seize, snatch, take hostage.

**kill** verb **1** *gangs killed twenty-seven people* MURDER, take/end the life of, assassinate, eliminate, terminate, dispatch, finish off, put to death, execute; slaughter, butcher, massacre, wipe out, annihilate, exterminate, mow down, shoot down, cut down, cut to pieces; *informal* bump off, polish off, do away with, do in, knock off, take out, croak, stiff, blow away, liquidate, dispose of, ice, snuff, rub out, waste, whack, smoke; *euphemistic* neutralize; *literary* slay.

**2** *this would kill all hopes of progress* DESTROY, put an end to, end, extinguish, dash, quash, ruin, wreck, shatter, smash, crush, scotch, thwart; *informal* put the kibosh on, stymie, scuttle.

**3** *we had to kill several hours at the airport* WHILE AWAY, fill (up), occupy, pass, spend, waste.

**4** *informal you must rest or you'll kill yourself* EXHAUST, wear out, tire out, overtax, overtire, fatigue, weary, sap, drain, enervate, knock out.

**5** *informal my feet were killing me* HURT, cause pain to, torture, torment, cause discomfort to; be painful, be sore, be uncomfortable.

**6** *a shot to kill the pain* ALLEVIATE, assuage, soothe, allay, dull, blunt, deaden, stifle, suppress, subdue.

**7** *informal an opposition attempt to kill the bill* VETO, defeat, vote down, rule against, reject, throw out, overrule, overturn, put a stop to, quash, squash.

**8** *informal Noel killed the engine* TURN OFF, switch off, stop, shut off/down, cut.

▸ noun **1** *the hunter's kill* PREY, quarry, victim, bag.

**2** *the wolf was moving in for the kill* DEATH BLOW, killing, dispatch, finish, end, coup de grâce.

THE RIGHT WORD **kill, assassinate, dispatch, execute, massacre, murder, slaughter, slay**

When it comes to depriving someone or something of life, the options are seemingly endless. To **kill** is the most general term, meaning to cause the death of a person, animal, or plant, with no reference to the manner of killing, the agent, or the cause (*killed in a car accident*). Even inanimate things may be killed (*Congress killed the project when they vetoed the bill*). To **slay** is to kill deliberately and violently; it is used more often in written than in spoken English (*a novel about a presidential candidate who is slain by his opponent*). **Murder** implies a malicious and premeditated killing of one person by another (*a gruesome murder carried out by the son-in-law*), while **assassinate** implies that a politically important person has been murdered, often by someone hired to do the job (*assassinate the head of the guerilla forces*). Someone who is put to death by a legal or military process is said to be **executed** (*execute by lethal injection*), but if someone is killed primarily to get rid or him or her, the appropriate verb is **dispatch**, which also suggests speed or promptness (*after delivering the secret documents, the informer was dispatched*). While **slaughter** is usually associated with the killing of animals for food, it can also apply to a mass killing of humans (*the slaughter of innocent civilians provoked a worldwide outcry*). **Massacre** also refers to the brutal murder of large numbers of people, but it is used more specifically to indicate the wholesale destruction of a relatively defenseless group of people (*the massacre of Bethlehem's male children by King Herod*).

**killer** noun **1** *police are searching for the killer* MURDERER, assassin, slaughterer, butcher, serial killer, gunman; executioner, hit man, cutthroat; *literary* slayer; *dated* homicide.

**2** *a major killer* CAUSE OF DEATH, fatal illness, deadly illness, threat to life, scourge.

**killing** noun *a brutal killing* MURDER, assassination, homicide, manslaughter, elimination, putting to death, execution; slaughter, massacre, butchery, carnage, bloodshed, extermination, annihilation; *literary* slaying.

▸ adjective **1** *a killing blow* DEADLY, lethal, fatal, mortal, death-dealing; murderous, homicidal; *literary* deathly.

**2** *informal a killing schedule* EXHAUSTING, grueling, punishing, taxing, draining, wearing, prostrating, crushing, tiring, fatiguing, debilitating, enervating, arduous, tough, demanding, onerous, strenuous, rigorous; *informal* murderous.

PHRASE: **make a killing** *informal Tess made a killing in real estate* MAKE A LARGE PROFIT, make a/one's fortune, make money, rake it in, clean up, cash in, make a pretty penny, make big bucks.

**killjoy** noun *uh-oh, here comes that killjoy Walter* SPOILSPORT, wet blanket, damper, party pooper; prophet of doom.

**kilter** PHRASE: **out of kilter** *jet lag has left me completely out of kilter* AWRY, off balance, unbalanced, out of order, disordered, confused, muddled, disoriented, out of tune, out of whack, out of step; *humorous* discombobulated.

**kin** noun *their own kin* RELATIVES, relations, family (members), kindred, kith and kin; flesh and blood, nearest and dearest; kinsfolk, kinsmen, kinswomen, people; *informal* folks.

**kind** adjective *she is such a kind and caring person* KINDLY, good-natured, kindhearted, warmhearted, caring, affectionate, loving, warm; considerate, helpful, thoughtful, obliging, unselfish, selfless, altruistic, good, attentive; compassionate, sympathetic, understanding, big-hearted, benevolent, benign, friendly, neighborly, hospitable, well-meaning, public-spirited. ANTONYMS inconsiderate, mean.

▸ noun **1** *all kinds of gifts | the kinds of bird that could be seen* SORT, type, variety, style, form, class, category, genre; genus, species, race, breed; flavor.

**2** *they were different in kind | the first of its kind* CHARACTER, nature, essence, quality, disposition, makeup; type, style, stamp, manner, description, mold, cast, temperament, ilk, stripe.

PHRASE: **kind of** *informal it was kind of spicy* RATHER, quite, fairly; somewhat, a little, slightly, a shade; *informal* pretty, sort of; a bit, kinda, a touch, a tad.

**kindle** verb **1** *he kindled a fire* LIGHT, ignite, set alight, set light to, set fire to, put a match to. ANTONYMS extinguish, douse.

**2** *the Beatles kindled my interest in music* ROUSE, arouse, wake, awake, awaken; stimulate, inspire, stir (up), excite, evoke, provoke, fire, inflame, trigger, activate, spark off; *literary* waken, enkindle.

**kindly** adjective *a kindly old lady* BENEVOLENT, kind, kindhearted, warm-hearted, generous, gentle, warm, good-natured, compassionate, caring, loving, benign, well meaning; helpful, thoughtful, considerate, good-hearted, nice, friendly, neighborly. ANTONYMS unkind, cruel.

▸ adverb **1** *she spoke kindly* BENEVOLENTLY, good-naturedly, warmly, affectionately, tenderly, lovingly, compassionately; considerately, thoughtfully, helpfully, obligingly, generously, selflessly, unselfishly, sympathetically. ANTONYMS unkindly, harshly.

**2** *kindly explain what you mean* PLEASE, if you please, if you wouldn't mind; *archaic* prithee, pray.

**kindness** noun *he thanked her for her kindness* KINDLINESS, kindheartedness, warmheartedness, affection, warmth, gentleness, concern, care; consideration, helpfulness, thoughtfulness, unselfishness, selflessness, altruism, compassion, sympathy, understanding, big-heartedness, benevolence, benignity, friendliness, hospitality, neighborliness; generosity, magnanimity, charitableness.

**kindred** noun *his mother's kindred* FAMILY, relatives, relations, kin, kith and kin, one's own flesh and blood; kinsfolk, kinsmen/kinswomen, people; *informal* folks.

▸ adjective **1** *industrial relations and kindred subjects* RELATED, allied, connected, comparable, similar, like, parallel, associated, analogous. ANTONYM unrelated.

**2** *a kindred spirit* LIKE-MINDED, in sympathy, in harmony, in tune, of one mind, akin, similar, like, compatible; *informal* on the same wavelength. ANTONYMS unsympathetic, alien.

**king** noun **1** *the king of France* RULER, sovereign, monarch, crowned head, Crown, emperor, prince, potentate, lord. See also the table at RULER.

**2** *informal the king of country music* STAR, leading light, luminary, superstar, giant, master; *informal* supremo, megastar.

**kingdom** noun **1** *his kingdom stretched to the sea* REALM, domain, dominion, country, empire, principality, duchy, land, nation, state, sovereign state, province, territory.

**2** *the third floor was Henderson's little kingdom* DOMAIN, province, realm, sphere, dominion, territory, arena, zone.

**3** *the plant kingdom* DIVISION, category, classification, grouping, group.

**kink** noun **1** *your fishing line should have no kinks in it* CURL, twist, twirl, loop, crinkle; knot, tangle, entanglement.

**2** *there are still some kinks to iron out* FLAW, defect, imperfection, problem, complication, hitch, snag, shortcoming, weakness; *informal* hiccup, glitch.

**3** *a kink in my neck* CRICK, stiffness, pinch, knot.

**kinky** adjective **1** *informal kinky underwear* PROVOCATIVE, sexy, erotic, titillating, naughty, indecent, immodest.

**2** *informal a kinky relationship* PERVERSE, abnormal, deviant, unconventional, unnatural, degenerate, depraved, perverted; *informal* pervy.

**3** *Catriona's long kinky hair* CURLY, crimped, curled, curling, frizzy, frizzed, wavy.

**kinship** noun **1** *the value of kinship in society* family ties, blood ties, common ancestry, consanguinity.

**2** *she felt kinship with the others* AFFINITY, sympathy, rapport, harmony, understanding, empathy, closeness, fellow feeling, bond, compatibility; similarity, likeness, correspondence, concordance.

**kiosk** noun *the kiosks along the boardwalk* BOOTH, stand, stall, concession, counter, newsstand; information booth.

**kiss** verb **1** *he kissed her on the lips | they kissed* give a kiss to, brush one's lips against, blow a kiss to; *informal* peck, smooch, canoodle, neck, buss, make out, lock lips; *formal/humorous* osculate.

**2** *allow your foot just to kiss the floor* BRUSH (AGAINST), caress, touch (gently), stroke, skim over.

▸ noun 1 *a kiss on the cheek | a passionate kiss* peck, smack, smooch, buss, French kiss; X; *formal/humorous* osculation.

2 *the kiss of the flowers against her cheeks* GENTLE TOUCH, caress, brush, stroke.

**kit** noun 1 *the sculptor's kit* EQUIPMENT, tools, implements, instruments, gadgets, utensils, appliances, tools of the trade, gear, tackle, hardware, paraphernalia; *informal* things, stuff, (the) necessaries; *Military* accoutrements.

2 *a model airplane kit* SET (OF PARTS), do-it-yourself kit.

**knack** noun 1 *a knack for making money* GIFT, talent, flair, genius, instinct, faculty, ability, capability, capacity, aptitude, aptness, bent, forte, facility; TECHNIQUE, method, trick, skill, adroitness, art, expertise; (**a knack for**) *informal* the hang of.

2 *his **knack of** getting injured at the wrong time* TENDENCY TO, propensity for, habit of, proneness to, aptness to, bent for, liability to, predisposition to, inclination to.

**knave** noun *archaic*. See JERK noun sense 3.

**knead** verb *kneading the dough* PUMMEL, work, pound, squeeze, shape, mold.

**kneel** verb *they knelt to pray* FALL TO ONE'S KNEES, get down on one's knees, genuflect; *historical* kowtow.

**knell** noun *literary* 1 *the knell of the ship's bell* TOLL, tolling, dong, resounding, reverberation; death knell; *archaic* tocsin.

2 *this sounded the knell for the project* END, beginning of the end, death knell, death warrant.

**knickknack** noun *it's no fun dusting all her knickknacks* TRINKET, novelty, gewgaw, bibelot, ornament, trifle, bauble, gimcrack, curio, tchotchke; memento, souvenir, kickshaw; *archaic* gaud.

**knife** noun *a sharp knife* CUTTING TOOL, blade, cutter.

▸ verb *the victims had been knifed* STAB, hack, gash, run through, slash, lacerate, cut, pierce, jab, stick, spike, impale, transfix, bayonet, spear.

**knight** noun *knights in armor* CAVALIER, cavalryman, horseman; lord, noble, nobleman; *historical* chevalier, paladin, banneret. PHRASE: **knight in shining armor** *she clung to the fantasy of her knight in shining armor* SIR GALAHAD, knight on a white charger/horse/steed, rescuer, savior, champion, hero, liberator, defender, protector, guardian, guardian angel.

**knit** verb 1 *he learned to knit in medical school, to keep his fingers nimble* loop, weave, interweave, crochet.

2 *disparate regions began to knit as one* UNITE, unify, come together, draw together, become closer, bond, fuse, coalesce, merge, meld, blend.

3 *Marcus knitted his brows* FURROW, tighten, contract, gather, wrinkle.

▸ noun *silky knits in pretty shades* KNITTED GARMENT, knitwear, woolen; sweater, pullover, jersey, cardigan.

**knob** noun 1 *the drake has a black bill with a knob at the base* LUMP, bump, protuberance, protrusion, bulge, swelling, knot, node, nodule, ball, boss.

2 *the knobs on the radio* DIAL, button.

3 *she turned the knob on the door* DOORKNOB, handle, door handle.

**knock** verb 1 *he knocked on the door* BANG, tap, rap, thump, pound, hammer; strike, hit, beat.

2 *she knocked her knee on the table* BUMP, bang, hit, strike, crack; injure, hurt, bruise; *informal* bash, thwack.

3 *he **knocked into** an elderly man* COLLIDE WITH, bump into, bang into, be in collision with, run into, crash into, smash into, plow into, bash into.

4 *informal I'm not knocking the company.* See CRITICIZE.

▸ noun 1 *a sharp knock at the door* TAP, rap, rat-tat-tat, knocking, bang, banging, pounding, hammering, drumming, thump, thud.

2 *the casing is tough enough to withstand knocks* BUMP, blow, bang, jolt, jar, shock; collision, crash, smash, impact.

3 *informal this isn't a knock on Dave.* See CRITICISM sense 1.

4 *life's hard knocks* SETBACK, reversal, defeat, failure, difficulty, misfortune, bad luck, mishap, blow, disaster, calamity, disappointment, sorrow, trouble, hardship; *informal* kick in the teeth.

PHRASES: **knock something back** *informal we can watch the game and knock back a few beers* SWALLOW, gulp down, drink (up), quaff, guzzle, slug, down, swig, drain, swill (down), toss off, scarf (down).

**knock someone/something down** *he deliberately knocked down the display of toilet paper in aisle 3* FELL, floor, flatten, bring down, knock to the ground; knock over, run over/down; DEMOLISH, pull down, tear down, destroy; raze (to the ground), level, bulldoze.

**knock it off!** *informal it's not funny anymore, so just knock it off!* STOP IT; *informal* cut it out, give it a rest, pack it in, that's enough, lay off.

**knock someone out** 1 *I hit him and knocked him out* KNOCK UNCONSCIOUS, knock senseless; floor, prostrate, put out cold, KO, kayo.

2 *in the second match, Canada was knocked out* ELIMINATE, beat, defeat, vanquish, overwhelm, trounce.

3 *informal walking that far knocked her out* EXHAUST, wear out, tire (out), overtire, fatigue, weary, drain; *informal* do in, take it out of.

4 *informal the view knocked me out* OVERWHELM, stun, stupefy, amaze, astound, astonish, stagger, take someone's breath away; impress, dazzle, enchant, awe, entrance; *informal* bowl over, flabbergast, blow away.

**knock someone up** *informal, vulgar she's not the first girl he's knocked up* GET/MAKE PREGNANT, impregnate; *informal* put in the family way.

**knockout** noun 1 *the match was won by a knockout* KO, finishing blow, coup de grâce, stunning blow, kayo, TKO (technical knockout).

2 *informal* *she's a knockout!* BEAUTY, babe, bombshell, vision, dream, hottie, dish, looker, eye-catcher, peach, heartthrob, fox, arm candy.

3 *informal* *the performance was a knockout* MASTERPIECE, sensation, marvel, wonder, triumph, success, feat, coup, master stroke, tour de force; *informal* humdinger, doozy, stunner.

**knoll** noun *she walked up the grassy knoll* MOUND, hillock, rise, hummock, hill, drumlin, hump, bank, ridge, elevation.

**knot** noun 1 *make a small knot* TIE, twist, loop, bow, hitch, half hitch, clove hitch, join, fastening; square knot, reef knot, slip knot, overhand knot, granny knot; tangle, entanglement.

2 *a knot in the wood* NODULE, gnarl, node; lump, knob, swelling, gall, protuberance, bump, burl.

▸ verb *a long blue scarf was knotted around her waist* TIE (UP), fasten, secure, bind, do up.

**knotty** adjective 1 *a knotty legal problem* COMPLEX, complicated, involved, intricate, convoluted, involuted; difficult, hard, thorny, taxing, awkward, tricky, problematic, troublesome. ANTONYMS straightforward, simple.

2 *knotty roots* GNARLED, knotted, knurled, nodular, knobbly, lumpy, bumpy.

3 *a knotty piece of thread* KNOTTED, tangled, tangly, twisted, entangled, snarled, matted.

**know** verb 1 *who knows I'm here?* BE AWARE, realize, be conscious, be informed; notice, perceive, see, sense, recognize; *informal* be clued in, savvy.

2 *I think Mary knows his address* HAVE KNOWLEDGE OF, be informed of, be apprised of; *formal* be cognizant of.

3 *you should know the rules beforehand* BE FAMILIAR WITH, be conversant with, be acquainted with, have knowledge of, be versed in, have mastered, have a grasp of, understand, comprehend; have learned, have memorized, be up to speed on.

4 *I know only a few people here* BE ACQUAINTED WITH, have met, be familiar with; be friends with, be friendly with, be on good terms with, be close to, be intimate with.

5 *he had known better times* EXPERIENCE, go through, live through, undergo, taste.

6 *my brothers don't know a saucepan from a frying pan* DISTINGUISH, tell (apart), differentiate, discriminate; recognize, pick out, identify.

**know-how** noun *informal* *good old American know-how* KNOWLEDGE, expertise, skill, skillfulness, expertness, proficiency, understanding, mastery, technique; ability, capability, competence, capacity, adeptness, dexterity, deftness, aptitude, adroitness, ingenuity, faculty; *informal* savvy.

**knowing** adjective 1 *a knowing smile* SIGNIFICANT, meaningful, eloquent, expressive, suggestive; ARCH, sly, mischievous, impish, teasing, playful.

2 *she's a very knowing child* SOPHISTICATED, worldly, worldly-wise, urbane, experienced; knowledgeable, well-informed, enlightened; shrewd, astute, canny, sharp, wily, perceptive.

3 *a knowing infringement of the rules* DELIBERATE, intentional, conscious, calculated, willful, done on purpose, premeditated, planned, preconceived.

**knowingly** adverb *a civil court jury agreed that the auto maker did not knowingly design a faulty vehicle* DELIBERATELY, intentionally, consciously, wittingly, on purpose, by design, premeditatedly, willfully.

**knowledge** noun 1 *his knowledge of history* | *technical knowledge* UNDERSTANDING, comprehension, grasp, command, mastery; expertise, skill, proficiency, expertness, accomplishment, adeptness, capacity, capability; *informal* know-how. ANTONYM ignorance.

2 *people anxious to display their knowledge* LEARNING, erudition, education, scholarship, schooling, wisdom. ANTONYMS ignorance, illiteracy.

3 *he slipped away without my knowledge* AWARENESS, consciousness, realization, cognition, apprehension, perception, appreciation; *formal* cognizance. ANTONYM unawareness.

4 *an intimate* ***knowledge of*** *the countryside* FAMILIARITY WITH, acquaintance with, intimacy with.

5 *inform the police of your knowledge* INFORMATION, facts, intelligence, news, reports; *informal* info, (the) lowdown.

THE RIGHT WORD **knowledge, erudition, information, learning, pedantry, scholarship, wisdom**

How much do you know? **Knowledge** applies to any body of facts gathered by study, observation, or experience, and to the ideas inferred from these facts (*an in-depth knowledge of particle physics; firsthand knowledge about the company*). **Information** may be no more than a collection of data or facts (*information about vacation resorts*) gathered through observation, reading, or hearsay, with no guarantee of their validity (*false information that led to the arrest*). **Scholarship** emphasizes academic knowledge or accomplishment (*a special award for scholarship*), while **learning** is knowledge gained not only by study in schools and universities but by individual research and investigation (*a man of education and learning*), which puts it on a somewhat higher plane. **Erudition** is on a higher plane still, implying bookish knowledge that is beyond the average person's comprehension (*exhibit extraordinary erudition in a doctoral dissertation*). **Pedantry**, on the other hand, is a negative term for a slavish attention to obscure facts or details or an undue display of learning (*the pedantry of modern literary criticism*). You can have extensive *knowledge* of a subject and even exhibit *erudition*, however, without attaining **wisdom**, the superior judgment and understanding that is based on both knowledge and experience.

**knowledgeable** adjective 1 *Beryl was a knowledgeable woman* WELL-INFORMED, learned, well-read, educated, well-educated, erudite, scholarly, cultured, cultivated, enlightened. ANTONYM ignorant.

2 *he is* ***knowledgeable about*** *modern art* ACQUAINTED WITH, familiar with, (well) versed in, conversant with, au courant with, au fait with; having a knowledge of, up on, up to date with, up to speed on, abreast of, plugged in to, (well) grounded in. ANTONYM ill-informed.

**known** adjective **1** *a known criminal* RECOGNIZED, well-known, widely known, noted, celebrated, notable, notorious; acknowledged, self-confessed, declared, overt.

**2** *the known world* FAMILIAR, known about, well-known; studied, investigated.

**kowtow** verb **1** *they **kowtowed to** the emperor* PROSTRATE ONESELF BEFORE, bow (down) to/ before, genuflect to/before, do/make obeisance to/before, fall on one's knees before, kneel before.

**2** *she didn't have to **kowtow to** a boss* GROVEL TO, be obsequious to, be servile to, be sycophantic to, fawn over/on, cringe to, bow and scrape to, toady to, truckle to, abase oneself before, humble oneself to; curry favor with, dance attendance on, ingratiate oneself with, suck up to, kiss up to, brown-nose, lick someone's boots.

**kudos** noun *kudos to you, Mrs. DeHaven, for a lifetime of quiet courage and unwavering generosity | much kudos comes with the job* PRAISE, glory, honor, status, standing, distinction, fame, celebrity; admiration, respect, esteem, acclaim, prestige, cachet, credit, full marks, props.

**label** noun **1** *the price is clearly stated on the label* TAG, ticket, sticker, marker, tab.

**2** *a designer label* BRAND, brand name, trade name, trademark, make, logo.

**3** *the label the media came up with for me* DESIGNATION, description, tag; name, epithet, nickname, title, sobriquet, pet name, cognomen; *formal* denomination, appellation.

▸ verb **1** *label each jar with the date* TAG, put labels on, ticket, mark.

**2** *tests labeled him an underachiever* CATEGORIZE, classify, class, describe, designate, identify; mark, stamp, brand, condemn, pigeonhole, stereotype, typecast; call, name, term, dub, nickname.

**labor** noun **1** *manual labor* WORK, hard work, toil, exertion, industry, drudgery, effort, menial work; *informal* slog, grind, sweat, scut work; *literary* travail, moil. ANTONYMS rest, leisure.

**2** *management and labor need to cooperate* WORKERS, employees, workmen, workforce, staff, working people, blue-collar workers, laborers, labor force, proletariat. ANTONYM management.

**3** *the labors of Hercules* TASK, job, chore, mission, assignment.

**4** *a difficult labor* CHILDBIRTH, birth, delivery, nativity; contractions, labor pains; *formal* parturition; *literary* travail; *dated* confinement; *archaic* lying-in, accouchement, childbed.

▸ verb **1** *a project on which he had labored for many years* WORK, work hard, toil, slave (away), grind away, struggle, strive, exert oneself, work one's fingers to the bone, work like a dog, work like a Trojan; *informal* slog away, plug away; *literary* travail, moil.

**2** *she labored to unite the party* STRIVE, struggle, endeavor, work, try, work hard, try hard, make every effort, do one's best, do one's utmost, do all one can, give one's all, go all out, fight, put oneself out, apply oneself, exert oneself; *informal* bend/lean/fall over backwards, pull out all the stops, bust a gut, bust one's chops.

**3** *there is no need to labor the point* OVEREMPHASIZE, belabor, overstress, overdo, strain, overplay, make too much of, exaggerate, dwell on, harp on.

**4** *Rex was **laboring under** a misapprehension* SUFFER FROM, be a victim of, be deceived by, be misled by.

THE RIGHT WORD **labor, drudgery, grind, toil, travail, work**

Most people have to **work** for a living, meaning that they have to exert themselves mentally or physically in return for a paycheck. But *work* is not always performed by humans (*a machine that works like a charm*). **Labor** is not only human but usually physical work (*the labor required to build a stone wall*), although it can also apply to intellectual work of unusual difficulty (*the labor involved in writing a symphony*). Anyone who has been forced to perform **drudgery** knows that it is the most unpleasant, uninspiring, and monotonous kind of labor (*a forklift that eliminates the drudgery of stacking boxes; the drudgery of compiling a phone book*). A **grind** is even more intense and unrelenting than drudgery, emphasizing work that is performed under pressure in a dehumanizing way (*the daily grind of classroom teaching*). **Toil** suggests labor that is prolonged and very tiring (*farmers who toil endlessly in the fields*), but not necessarily physical (*mothers who toil to teach their children manners*). Those who **travail** endure pain, anguish, or suffering (*his hours of travail ended in heartbreak*).

**labored** adjective **1** *labored breathing* STRAINED, difficult, forced, laborious.

**2** *Wang's labored alibi only hurt his defense* CONTRIVED, strained, stilted, forced, stiff, unnatural, artificial, overdone, ponderous, overelaborate, laborious, unconvincing, overwrought.

**laborer** noun *auto-industry laborers* WORKMAN, worker, working man/woman, manual worker, unskilled worker, day laborer, blue-collar worker, hired hand, hand, peon, roustabout, drudge, menial; *informal* grunt; *archaic* mechanic, cottier.

**laborious** adjective **1** *a laborious job* ARDUOUS, hard, heavy, difficult, strenuous, grueling, punishing, exacting, tough, onerous, burdensome, back-breaking, labor-intensive, trying, challenging; tiring, fatiguing, exhausting, wearying, wearing, taxing, demanding, wearisome, tedious, boring, time-consuming; *archaic* toilsome. See note at HARD. ANTONYM easy.

**2** *Doug's laborious writing style* LABORED, strained, forced, contrived, affected, stiff, stilted, unnatural, artificial, overwrought, heavy, ponderous, convoluted. ANTONYMS natural, effortless.

**labyrinth** noun **1** *a labyrinth of little streets* MAZE, warren, network, complex, web, entanglement.

2 *the labyrinth of conflicting regulations* TANGLE, web, morass, jungle, confusion, entanglement, convolution; jumble, mishmash.

**labyrinthine** adjective 1 *labyrinthine corridors* MAZELIKE, winding, twisting, serpentine, meandering, wandering, rambling.

2 *a labyrinthine system* COMPLICATED, intricate, complex, involved, tortuous, convoluted, involuted, tangled, elaborate; confusing, puzzling, mystifying, bewildering, baffling.

**lace** noun 1 *a dress trimmed with white lace* openwork, lacework, tatting; passementerie, needlepoint (lace), filet, bobbin lace, pillow lace, torchon lace, needle lace, point lace, Battenberg lace, Chantilly lace, Mechlin lace, Valenciennes.

2 *brown shoes with laces* SHOELACE, bootlace, shoestring, lacing, tie.

▸ verb 1 *he* ***laced up*** *his running shoes* FASTEN, do up, tie up, secure, knot. ANTONYM untie.

2 *he laced his fingers into mine* ENTWINE, intertwine, twine, entangle, interweave, link; braid, plait.

3 *tea laced with rum* FLAVOR, mix (in), blend, fortify, strengthen, stiffen, season, spice (up), enrich, liven up; doctor, adulterate; *informal* spike.

4 *her brown hair was laced with gray* STREAK, stripe, striate, line.

PHRASE: **lace into** *informal* 1 *Danny laced into him.* See BEAT SOMEONE UP at BEAT.

2 *the newspaper laced into the prime minister.* See CRITICIZE.

**lacerate** verb *the nail has lacerated his left arm* CUT (OPEN), gash, slash, tear, rip, rend, shred; score, scratch, scrape, graze; wound, injure, hurt.

**laceration** noun *a bleeding laceration* GASH, cut, wound, injury, tear, slash; scratch, scrape, abrasion, graze.

**lachrymose** adjective See TEARFUL sense 1. ANTONYMS cheerful, comic.

**lack** noun *a lack of cash* ABSENCE, want, need, deficiency, dearth, insufficiency, shortage, shortfall, scarcity, paucity, unavailability, deficit. ANTONYM abundance.

▸ verb *they lack sufficient resources* BE WITHOUT, be in need of, need, be lacking, require, want, be short of, be deficient in, be bereft of, be low on, be pressed for, have insufficient; *informal* be strapped for. ANTONYMS have, possess.

THE RIGHT WORD **lack, absence, dearth, privation, shortage, want**

To suffer from a **lack** of food means to be partially or totally without it; to be in **want** of food also implies a lack, but with an emphasis on the essential or desirable nature of what is lacking; for example, you may experience a complete *lack* of pain following surgery, but you would be in *want* of medication if pain were suddenly to occur. **Absence**, on the other hand, refers to the complete nonexistence of something or someone. A *lack* of dairy products in your diet implies that you're not getting enough; an *absence* of dairy products implies that you're not getting any at all. If the scarcity or lack of something makes it costly, or if something is in distressingly low supply, the correct word is **dearth** (*a dearth of water in the desert; a dearth of nylon stockings during World War II*). A **shortage** of something is a partial insufficiency of an established, required, or accustomed amount (*a shortage of fresh oranges after the late-season frost*), while **privation** is the negative state or absence of a corresponding positive (*they suffered from hunger, cold, and other privations*).

**lackadaisical** adjective *I was lackadaisical about my training* LETHARGIC, apathetic, listless, sluggish, spiritless, passionless; careless, lazy, lax, unenthusiastic, halfhearted, lukewarm, indifferent, unconcerned, casual, offhand, blasé, insouciant, relaxed; *informal* laid-back, easygoing, couldn't-care-less. ANTONYM enthusiastic.

**lackey** noun 1 *lackeys helped them from their carriage* SERVANT, flunky, footman, manservant, valet, steward, butler, attendant, houseboy, domestic; *archaic* scullion.

2 *one of the manager's lackeys* TOADY, flunky, sycophant, flatterer, minion, hanger-on, lickspittle, brown-noser, spaniel, pawn, underling, stooge; *informal* yes-man, trained seal, bootlicker, doormat, drudge, peon.

**lackluster** adjective *a lackluster performance* UNINSPIRED, uninspiring, unimaginative, dull, humdrum, colorless, characterless, bland, dead, insipid, vapid, flat, dry, lifeless, tame, prosaic, spiritless, lusterless; boring, monotonous, dreary, tedious; *informal* blah. ANTONYM inspired.

**laconic** adjective 1 *his laconic comment* BRIEF, concise, terse, succinct, short, pithy. See note at TERSE. ANTONYM verbose.

2 *their laconic press agent* TACITURN, uncommunicative, reticent, quiet, reserved, silent, unforthcoming, brief. ANTONYM loquacious.

**lad** noun *informal a lad of eight* BOY, schoolboy, youth, youngster, juvenile, stripling; *informal* kid, whippersnapper; *derogatory* brat. See also CHILD.

**ladder** noun 1 *she climbed down the ladder* steps, set of steps; rope ladder, stepladder, extension ladder.

2 *the academic ladder* HIERARCHY, scale, grading, ranking, pecking order.

**laden** adjective *a tray laden with plates* LOADED, burdened, weighed down, encumbered, overloaded, piled high, fully charged; full, filled, packed, stuffed, crammed; *informal* chock-full, chockablock.

**ladle** verb *he was* ***ladling out*** *the contents of the pot* SPOON OUT, scoop out, dish up/out, serve.

▸ noun *a soup ladle* SPOON, scoop, dipper.

**lady** noun 1 *several ladies were present* WOMAN, female; *informal* dame; *derogatory* broad; *literary* maid, damsel; *archaic* wench.

2 *lords and ladies* NOBLEWOMAN, duchess, countess, peeress, viscountess, baroness; *archaic* gentlewoman.

**ladylike** adjective *as ladylike as Audrey Hepburn* GENTEEL, polite, refined, well-bred, cultivated, polished, decorous, proper, respectable, seemly, well-mannered, cultured, sophisticated, elegant, modest; feminine, womanly. ANTONYM coarse.

**lag** verb *I'm sorry to be **lagging behind*** FALL BEHIND, straggle, fall back, trail (behind), hang back, not keep pace, bring up the rear; dawdle, dilly-dally. See note at LOITER. ANTONYM keep up.

**laggard** noun *there'll be no laggards on my watch, Mr. Tyler* STRAGGLER, loiterer, lingerer, dawdler, sluggard, snail, idler, loafer; *informal* lazybones, slacker, slowpoke, foot-dragger.

**lagoon** noun *swimming in the moonlit lagoon* BAY, inland sea, lake, bight, pool.

**laid-back** adjective *informal you must try to be more laid-back* RELAXED, easygoing, free and easy, casual, nonchalant, unexcitable, imperturbable, unruffled, blasé, cool, equable, even-tempered, low-maintenance, insouciant, calm, unperturbed, unflustered, unflappable, unworried, unconcerned, unbothered; leisurely, unhurried, Type-B; stoical, phlegmatic, tolerant. ANTONYM uptight.

**lair** noun **1** *the lair of a large python* DEN, burrow, hole, tunnel, cave.

**2** *a villain's lair* HIDEOUT, hiding place, hideaway, refuge, sanctuary, haven, shelter, retreat.

**laissez-faire** noun *an agenda that embraces the concept of laissez-faire* FREE ENTERPRISE, free trade, nonintervention, free-market capitalism, market forces.

▸ adjective *he has argued for a laissez-faire policy regarding the Internet | Elliott's laissez-faire approach to parenting* NONINTERVENTIONIST, noninterventional, noninterfering; uninvolved, indifferent; lax, loose, permissive, nonrestrictive, liberal, libertarian; *informal* hands-off.

**lake** noun *the frozen lake* POND, pool, tarn, reservoir, slough, lagoon, water, waterhole, watering hole, inland sea; oxbow (lake), pothole (lake), glacial lake; *Scottish* loch; *literary* mere.

**lambaste** verb *the coach was lambasted in the media* CRITICIZE, chastise, censure, take to task, harangue, rail at, rant at, fulminate against; upbraid, scold, reprimand, rebuke, castigate, chide, reprove, admonish, berate; *informal* lay into, tear into, give someone a dressing-down, dress down, give someone what for, give someone a tongue-lashing, tell off, bawl out, chew out; *formal* excoriate.

**lame** adjective **1** *the mare was lame* LIMPING, hobbling; crippled, disabled, incapacitated; *dated* game. ANTONYM able-bodied.

**2** *a lame excuse* FEEBLE, weak, thin, flimsy, poor, sorry; unconvincing, implausible, unlikely. ANTONYM convincing.

**lament** noun **1** *the widow's laments* WAIL, wailing, lamentation, moan, moaning, weeping, crying, sob, sobbing, keening; jeremiad; complaint.

**2** *a lament for the dead* DIRGE, requiem, elegy, threnody, monody; keen.

▸ verb **1** *the mourners lamented* MOURN, grieve, sorrow, wail, weep, cry, sob, keen, beat one's breast. See note at MOURN. ANTONYMS celebrate, rejoice.

**2** *he lamented the modernization of the buildings* BEMOAN, bewail, complain about, deplore, rue; protest against, object to, oppose, fulminate against, inveigh against, denounce.

**lamentable** adjective *lamentable living conditions* DEPLORABLE, regrettable, sad, terrible, awful, wretched, woeful, dire, disastrous, grave, appalling, dreadful, pitiful, shameful, sorrowful, unfortunate. ANTONYM wonderful.

**lamentation** noun *the survivors' lamentation* WEEPING, wailing, crying, sobbing, moaning, lament, keening, grieving, mourning.

**lamp** noun *we had plenty of illumination from our lamps* LIGHT, lantern; floor lamp, table lamp, bedside lamp, banker's lamp, gooseneck lamp; chandelier; candelabra; *trademark* Tiffany lamp; floodlight, spotlight, strobe light, arc lamp; fluorescent lamp, track lights; lava lamp; sunlamp; flashlight; streetlight, streetlamp; Chinese lantern, Japanese lantern; storm lantern, hurricane lamp, oil lamp, kerosene lamp; *trademark* Coleman lamp.

**lampoon** verb *he was mercilessly lampooned* SATIRIZE, mock, ridicule, make fun of, caricature, burlesque, parody, tease; *informal* roast, send up.

▸ noun *a lampoon of student life* SATIRE, burlesque, parody, skit, caricature, impersonation, travesty, mockery; *informal* send-up, takeoff, spoof. See note at CARICATURE.

**lance** noun *a knight with a lance* SPEAR, pike, javelin; harpoon.

**land** noun **1** *publicly owned land* GROUNDS, fields, terrain, territory, open space; property, landholding, acres, acreage, lands, real estate, realty, estate; *historical* demesne.

**2** *fertile land* SOIL, earth, loam, topsoil, humus; tillage.

**3** *many people are leaving **the land*** THE COUNTRYSIDE, the country, rural areas, farmland, agricultural land.

**4** *Tunisia is a land of variety* COUNTRY, nation, nation state, state, realm, kingdom, province; region, area, domain.

**5** *the lookout sighted land to the east* TERRA FIRMA, dry land; coast, coastline, shore. ANTONYM sea.

▸ verb **1** *Canadian troops landed at Juno Beach* DISEMBARK, go ashore, debark, alight, get off. ANTONYM embark.

**2** *our ship landed at New London* DOCK, moor, berth, put in, anchor, drop anchor. ANTONYM set sail.

**3** *their plane landed in Chicago* TOUCH DOWN, make a landing, come in to land, come down. ANTONYM take off.

**4** *a bird landed on the branch* PERCH, settle, come to rest, alight. ANTONYM fly off.

**5** *informal Nick landed the job of editor* OBTAIN, get, acquire, secure, be appointed to, gain, net, win, achieve, attain, carry off; *informal* bag.

**6** *informal Joanne's drug habit **landed** her **in** big trouble* BRING, lead to, drive to, cause to be in.

7 informal *he landed a left hook that staggered Curry* INFLICT, deal, deliver, administer, dispense, score, mete out.

**landmark** noun 1 *the cliff is a landmark for hikers* MARKER, mark, indicator, beacon, cairn.

2 *one of Arizona's most famous landmarks* MONUMENT, distinctive feature, prominent feature.

3 *the ruling was hailed as a landmark* TURNING POINT, milestone, watershed, critical point, benchmark.

▸ adjective *a landmark decision* PRECEDENT-SETTING, normative, consequential, historic.

**landscape** noun *the landscape of Tahiti* SCENERY, countryside, topography, country, terrain; outlook, view, vista, prospect, aspect, panorama, perspective, sweep.

**landslide** noun 1 *floods and landslides* rockslide, mudslide; avalanche.

2 *the Democrats enjoyed a landslide* DECISIVE VICTORY, overwhelming majority, triumph, sweep.

**lane** noun 1 *country lanes* road, street, byroad, byway, alley, alleyway, back alley, back lane, track.

2 *bicycle lanes* | *a three-lane highway* TRACK, way, course; road division; express lane.

**language** noun 1 *the structure of language* SPEECH, writing, communication, conversation, speaking, talking, talk, discourse; words, vocabulary.

2 *the English language* TONGUE, mother tongue, native tongue; dialect, patois, slang, idiom, jargon, argot, cant; informal lingo.

3 *the booklet is written in simple, everyday language* WORDING, phrasing, phraseology, style, vocabulary, terminology, expressions, turns of phrase, parlance, form/mode of expression, usages, locutions, choice of words, idiolect; informal lingo.

**languid** adjective 1 *a languid wave of the hand* RELAXED, unhurried, languorous, slow; listless, lethargic, sluggish, lazy, idle, indolent, apathetic; informal laid-back. ANTONYM energetic.

2 *languid days in the sun* LEISURELY, languorous, relaxed, restful, lazy. ANTONYM action-packed.

3 *she was pale and languid* SICKLY, weak, faint, feeble, frail, delicate; tired, weary, fatigued. ANTONYM vigorous.

**languish** verb 1 *the plants languished and died* WEAKEN, deteriorate, decline; wither, droop, wilt, fade, waste away; informal go downhill. ANTONYMS thrive, flourish.

2 *the general is now languishing in prison* WASTE AWAY, rot, be abandoned, be neglected, be forgotten, suffer, experience hardship.

**languor** noun 1 *the sultry languor that was stealing over her* LASSITUDE, lethargy, listlessness, torpor, fatigue, weariness, sleepiness, drowsiness; laziness, idleness, indolence, inertia, sluggishness, apathy. ANTONYM vigor.

2 *the languor of a hot day* STILLNESS, tranquility, calm, calmness; oppressiveness, heaviness.

**lap**[1] noun *Liam sat on Santa's lap* KNEE, knees, thighs.

**lap**[2] noun *a race of eight laps* CIRCUIT, leg, circle, revolution, round; length.

▸ verb 1 *she lapped the other runners* OVERTAKE, outstrip, leave behind, pass, go past; catch up with; informal leapfrog.

2 literary *he was lapped in blankets* WRAP, swathe, envelop, enfold, swaddle.

**lap**[3] verb 1 *waves lapped against the sea wall* SPLASH, wash, swish, slosh, break, beat, strike, dash, roll; literary plash.

2 *the dog lapped water out of a puddle* DRINK, lick up, swallow, slurp, gulp. PHRASE: **lap something up** *he was lapping up the accolades* RELISH, revel in, savor, delight in, glory in, enjoy.

**lapse** noun 1 *a lapse of concentration* FAILURE, failing, slip, error, mistake, blunder, fault, omission, hiccup; informal slip-up.

2 *his lapse into petty crime* DECLINE, fall, falling, slipping, drop, deterioration, degeneration, backsliding, regression, retrogression, descent, sinking, slide.

3 *a lapse of time* INTERVAL, gap, pause, interlude, lull, hiatus, break.

▸ verb 1 *our membership has lapsed* EXPIRE, become void, become invalid, run out.

2 *she lapsed into self-pity* REVERT, relapse; drift, slide, slip, sink; deteriorate, decline, fall, degenerate, backslide, regress, retrogress.

**lapsed** adjective 1 *a lapsed Catholic* NONPRACTICING, backsliding, apostate; former. ANTONYM practicing.

2 *a lapsed membership* EXPIRED, void, invalid, out of date. ANTONYM valid.

**larceny** noun *his police record included two counts of larceny* THEFT, stealing, robbery, pilfering, thieving; burglary, housebreaking, breaking and entering; informal filching, swiping, pinching; formal peculation.

**large** adjective 1 *a large house* | *large numbers of people* BIG, great, huge, sizable, substantial, immense, enormous, colossal, massive, mammoth, vast, prodigious, tremendous, gigantic, giant, monumental, stupendous, gargantuan, elephantine, titanic, mountainous, monstrous; towering, tall, high; mighty, voluminous; king-size(d), economy-size(d), family-size(d), man-size(d), giant-size(d); informal jumbo, whopping, mega, humongous, monster, astronomical, ginormous. ANTONYM small.

2 *a large man* BIG, burly, heavy, tall, bulky, thickset, chunky, strapping, hulking, hefty, muscular, brawny, solid, powerful, sturdy, strong, rugged; full-figured, buxom; fat, plump, overweight, chubby, stout, meaty, fleshy, portly, rotund, flabby, paunchy, obese, corpulent; informal hunky, roly-poly, beefy, tubby, well-upholstered, pudgy, well-fed, big-boned, cornfed. ANTONYMS small, thin.

3 *a large supply of wool* ABUNDANT, copious, plentiful, ample,

liberal, generous, lavish, bountiful, bumper, boundless, good, considerable, superabundant; *literary* plenteous. ANTONYM meager.

4 *the measure has large economic implications* WIDE-REACHING, far-reaching, wide, sweeping, large-scale, broad, extensive, comprehensive, exhaustive. ANTONYM trivial.

PHRASES: **at large** 1 *fourteen criminals are still at large* AT LIBERTY, free, loose, on the loose, on the run, fugitive, on the lam.

2 *society at large* AS A WHOLE, generally, in general.

**by and large** *the children, by and large, treated him well* ON THE WHOLE, generally, in general, all things considered, all in all, for the most part, in the main, as a rule, overall, almost always, mainly, mostly; on average, on balance.

**largely** adverb *the population in this district is largely of retirement age* MOSTLY, mainly, to a large/great extent, chiefly, predominantly, primarily, principally, for the most part, in the main; usually, typically, commonly.

**large-scale** adjective *a large-scale program* EXTENSIVE, wide-ranging, far-reaching, exhaustive, comprehensive; mass, nationwide, global.

**largesse** noun 1 *Bob took advantage of his friend's largesse* GENEROSITY, liberality, munificence, bounty, bountifulness, beneficence, altruism, charity, philanthropy, magnanimity, benevolence, charitableness, openhandedness, kindness, bigheartedness; *formal* benefaction. ANTONYM stinginess.

2 *distributing largesse to the locals* GIFTS, presents, handouts, grants, aid; patronage, sponsorship, backing, help; alms. See note at PRESENT[3].

**lark** noun *informal we were just having a bit of* ***a lark*** FUN, good fun, amusement, a laugh, a joke; an escapade, a prank, a trick, a jape, a practical joke.

**lascivious** adjective *his lascivious jokes are not funny* LECHEROUS, lewd, lustful, licentious, libidinous, salacious, lubricious, prurient, dirty, smutty, naughty, indecent, ribald; *informal* blue; *formal* concupiscent.

**lash** verb 1 *he lashed the beast repeatedly* WHIP, flog, flagellate, beat, thrash, horsewhip, scourge, birch, belt, strap, cane, switch; strike, hit; *informal* wallop, whack, tan (someone's hide), larrup, whale.

2 *rain lashed the windowpanes* BEAT AGAINST, dash against, pound, batter, strike, hit, knock.

3 *the tiger began to lash its tail* SWISH, flick, twitch, whip.

4 *two boats were lashed together* FASTEN, bind, tie (up), tether, hitch, knot, rope, make fast.

▸ noun 1 *he brought the lash down upon the prisoner's back* WHIP, horsewhip, scourge, thong, flail, strap, birch, cane, switch; *historical* cat-o'-nine-tails, cat, knout.

2 *twenty lashes* STROKE, blow, hit, strike, welt, thwack; *archaic* stripe.

PHRASE: **lash out at** *the president lashed out at the opposition* CRITICIZE, chastise, censure, attack, condemn, denounce, lambaste, rail at/against, harangue, pillory; berate, upbraid, rebuke, reproach; *informal* lay into, tear into, blast; *formal* castigate.

**last**[1] adjective 1 *the last woman in line* REARMOST, hindmost, endmost, at the end, at the back, furthest (back), final, ultimate. ANTONYMS first, leading.

2 *Rembrandt spent his last years in Amsterdam* CLOSING, concluding, final, ending, end, terminal; later, latter. ANTONYMS initial, early.

3 *I'd be the last person to say anything against him* LEAST LIKELY, most unlikely, most improbable; least suitable, most unsuitable, most inappropriate, least appropriate. ANTONYMS first, most likely.

4 *we met last year* THE PREVIOUS, the preceding; the prior, the former. ANTONYM next.

5 *this was his last chance* FINAL, only remaining.

▸ adverb *the entrant arriving last is eliminated* AT THE END, at/in the rear.

▸ noun *the most important business was left to the last* END, ending, finish, close, conclusion, finale, termination. ANTONYM beginning.

PHRASES: **at last** *at last, the rain stopped* FINALLY, at long last, after a long time, in the end, eventually, ultimately, in (the fullness of) time.

**last word** 1 *that's my last word* FINAL DECISION, definitive statement, conclusive comment.

2 *she was determined to have the last word* CONCLUDING REMARK, final say, closing statement.

3 *the last word in luxury and efficiency* BEST, peak, acme, epitome, latest; pinnacle, apex, apogee, ultimate, height, zenith, nonpareil, crème de la crème; *archaic* nonsuch.

**last hurrah** *Sunday's performance was Shelley's last hurrah* SWAN SONG, grand finale, finale, curtain call.

**last**[2] verb 1 *the hearing lasted for six days* CONTINUE, go on, carry on, keep on, keep going, proceed; stay, remain, persist.

2 *how long will he last as manager?* SURVIVE, endure, hold on, hold out, keep going, persevere; *informal* stick it out, hang on.

3 *the car is built to last* ENDURE, wear well, stand up, bear up; *informal* go the distance.

**last-ditch** adjective *a last-ditch effort to save the old church* LAST-MINUTE, last-chance, eleventh-hour, last-resort, desperate, do-or-die, last-gasp, final.

**lasting** adjective *a lasting friendship* ENDURING, long-lasting, long-lived, abiding, continuing, long-term, surviving, persisting, permanent; durable, constant, stable, established, secure, long-standing; unchanging, irreversible, immutable, eternal, undying, everlasting, unending, never-ending, unfading, changeless, indestructible, unceasing, unwavering, unfaltering. ANTONYM ephemeral.

**lastly** adverb *lastly, I would like to thank my parents* FINALLY, in conclusion, to conclude, to sum up, to end, last, ultimately. ANTONYM firstly.

**latch** noun *he lifted the latch* FASTENING, catch, fastener, clasp, lock.

▸ verb *Jess latched the back door* FASTEN, secure, make fast, lock.

**late** adjective **1** *the train was late* BEHIND SCHEDULE, behind time, behindhand; tardy, running late, overdue, belated, delayed. ANTONYMS punctual, early.

**2** *her late husband* DEAD, departed, lamented, passed on/away, deceased. ANTONYMS alive, existing.

▸ adverb **1** *she had arrived late* BEHIND SCHEDULE, behind time, behindhand, belatedly, tardily, at the last minute, at the buzzer. ANTONYM early.

**2** *I was working late* AFTER HOURS, after office hours, overtime.

**3** *don't stay out late* LATE AT NIGHT; *informal* till all hours. PHRASE: **of late** *he's not felt well of late.* See LATELY.

**lately** adverb *we haven't seen much of you lately* RECENTLY, of late, latterly, in recent times, in the past few days, in the last couple of weeks.

**latent** adjective *his latent skills* DORMANT, untapped, unused, undiscovered, hidden, concealed, underlying, invisible, unseen, undeveloped, unrealized, unfulfilled, potential.

THE RIGHT WORD **latent, abeyant, dormant, quiescent, potential**

All of these words refer to what is not currently observable or showing signs of activity. A **latent** talent is one that has not yet manifested itself, while **potential** suggests a talent that exists in an undeveloped state (*a potential concert violinist*). A child may have certain *latent* qualities of which his or her parents are unaware; but teachers are usually quick to spot a *potential* artist or poet in the classroom. **Dormant** and **quiescent** are less frequently associated with people and more often associated with things. A volcano might be described as *dormant*, which applies to anything that is currently inactive but has been active in the past and is capable of becoming active again in the future. *Dormant* carries the connotation of sleeping (*plants that are dormant in the winter*), while *quiescent* means motionless (*a quiescent sea*), emphasizing inactivity without referring to past or future activity. **Abeyant**, like *dormant*, means suspended or temporarily inactive, but it is most commonly used as a noun (*personal rights and privileges kept in abeyance until the danger had passed*).

**later** adjective *a later chapter* SUBSEQUENT, following, succeeding, future, upcoming, to come, ensuing, next; *formal* posterior; *archaic* after. ANTONYM earlier.

▸ adverb **1** *later, the film rights were sold* SUBSEQUENTLY, eventually, then, next, later on, after this/that, afterward, at a later date, in the future, in due course, by and by, in a while, in time.

**2** *two days later a letter arrived* AFTERWARD, later on, after, after that, subsequently, following; *formal* thereafter.

**lateral** adjective **1** *lateral movements* SIDEWAYS, sidewise, sideward, edgewise, edgeways, oblique, horizontal.

**2** *lateral thinking* UNORTHODOX, inventive, creative, imaginative, original, innovative, nonlinear.

**latest** adjective **1** *the latest reports from Iraq* MOST RECENT, newest, just released, up-to-the-minute.

**2** *the latest Paris designs* NEWEST, just out, fresh, freshest, up-to-date, state-of-the-art, au courant, dernier cri, current, modern, contemporary, fashionable, in fashion, in vogue; newfangled; *informal* in, with it, trendy, hip, hot, big, funky, happening, cool. See note at LAST. ANTONYMS old, unfashionable.

**lather** noun *rich, soapy lather* FOAM, froth, suds, soapsuds; bubbles; *literary* spume. PHRASE: **in a lather** *Hannah is in a lather over the chemistry exam* AGITATED, flustered, distressed, worked up, strung out, keyed up, in a state, in a tizzy, in a dither, in a twitter, upset.

**latitude** noun **1** *Toronto and Nice are on the same latitude* PARALLEL. ANTONYM longitude.

**2** *he gave them a lot of latitude* FREEDOM, scope, leeway, space, breathing space, flexibility, liberty, independence, free rein, license, room to maneuver, elbow room, wiggle room, freedom of action. See note at RANGE. ANTONYM restriction.

**latter** adjective **1** *the latter stages of development* LATER, closing, end, concluding, final; latest, most recent. ANTONYM initial.

**2** *Russia chose the latter option* LAST-MENTIONED, second, last, later. ANTONYM former.

**latter-day** adjective *a latter-day puritan* MODERN, present-day, current, contemporary.

**lattice** noun *the ivy-covered lattice* GRID, latticework, fretwork, open framework, openwork, trellis, trelliswork, espalier, grille, network, mesh.

**laud** verb *a single lauded by the music press* PRAISE, extol, hail, applaud, acclaim, commend, sing the praises of, speak highly of, pay tribute to, lionize, eulogize, rhapsodize over/about; *informal* rave about; *archaic* magnify, panegyrize. See note at PRAISE. ANTONYM criticize.

**laudable** adjective *thanked for their laudable contributions of time and talent* PRAISEWORTHY, commendable, admirable, meritorious, worthy, deserving, creditable, estimable. ANTONYM shameful.

**laudatory** adjective *a laudatory front-page endorsement* COMPLIMENTARY, praising, congratulatory, extolling, adulatory, commendatory, approbatory, flattering, celebratory, eulogizing, panegyrical; *informal* glowing; *formal* encomiastic. ANTONYM disparaging.

**laugh** verb **1** *Norma started to laugh excitedly* CHUCKLE, chortle, guffaw, cackle, giggle, titter, twitter, snigger, snicker, yuk, tee-hee, burst out laughing, roar/hoot/howl with laughter, crack up, dissolve into laughter, split one's sides, be (rolling) on the floor, be doubled up, be killing oneself (laughing); *informal* be in stitches, be rolling in the aisles.

**2** *people **laughed at** his theories* RIDICULE, mock, deride, scoff at, jeer at, sneer at, jibe at, make fun of, poke fun at, scorn; lampoon, satirize, parody; dismiss; *informal* send up, pooh-pooh.

▸ noun **1** *he gave a short laugh* CHUCKLE, chortle, guffaw, giggle, titter, twitter, tee-hee, snigger, snicker, yuk, roar/hoot/howl of laughter, belly laugh, horse laugh.

**2** *informal he was a laugh* JOKER, jokester, wag, wit, clown, jester, prankster, character; *informal* card, hoot, scream, riot, gas, barrel of laughs.

**3** *informal I entered the contest for a laugh* JOKE, prank, jest, escapade, caper, practical joke; *informal* hoot, lark.

PHRASE: **laugh something off** *you have to just laugh off their stupid remarks* DISMISS, make a joke of, make light of, shrug off, brush aside, scoff at; *informal* pooh-pooh.

**laughable** adjective **1** *the government's new education policy is laughable* RIDICULOUS, ludicrous, absurd, risible, preposterous; foolish, silly, idiotic, stupid, asinine, nonsensical, crazy, insane, outrageous, harebrained, cockamamie; *informal* cockeyed, daffy.

**2** *if it weren't so tragic, it'd be laughable* AMUSING, funny, humorous, hilarious, uproarious, comical, comic, farcical.

**laughingstock** noun *their new airport has been called the laughingstock of world air travel* BUTT, dupe, spectacle, figure of fun, stooge, fall guy.

**laughter** noun *the sound of laughter* LAUGHING, chuckling, chortling, guffawing, giggling, tittering, twittering, cackling, sniggering; *informal* hysterics.

**launch** verb **1** *they've launched the shuttle | the rocket has launched* SEND INTO ORBIT, blast off, take off, lift off.

**2** *he launched the boat* SET AFLOAT, put to sea, put into the water.

**3** *a chair was launched at him* THROW, hurl, fling, pitch, lob, let fly; fire, shoot; *informal* chuck, heave, sling.

**4** *the government launched a new campaign* SET IN MOTION, get going, get underway, start, commence, begin, embark on, initiate, inaugurate, set up, organize, introduce, bring into being; *informal* kick off, roll out.

**5** *he* ***launched into*** *a tirade* START, commence, burst into.

**launder** verb *the linens are laundered each Thursday* WASH, wash and iron, clean; dry-clean.

**laundry** noun **1** *a big pile of laundry* WASHING, wash, dirty clothes.

**2** *the facilities include a laundry* LAUNDRY ROOM, launderette; *trademark* Laundromat; cleaners, dry cleaners.

**laurels** plural noun *enjoying all the laurels befitting such an accomplished young woman* HONORS, tributes, praise, plaudits, accolades, kudos, acclaim, acclamation, credit, glory, honor, distinction, fame, renown, prestige, recognition.

**lavatory** noun. See BATHROOM.

**lavish** adjective **1** *lavish parties* SUMPTUOUS, luxurious, costly, expensive, opulent, grand, splendid, rich, fancy, posh; *informal* fancy-schmancy. ANTONYM meager.

**2** *lavish hospitality* GENEROUS, liberal, bountiful, openhanded, unstinting, unsparing, free, munificent, extravagant, prodigal. ANTONYM frugal.

**3** *lavish amounts of champagne* ABUNDANT, copious, plentiful, liberal, prolific, generous; *literary* plenteous. See note at PROFUSE. ANTONYM scant.

▸ verb *she* **lavished** *money* **on** *her children* GIVE FREELY TO, spend generously on, bestow on, heap on, shower with.

**law** noun **1** *a new law was passed* REGULATION, statute, enactment, act, bill, decree, edict, bylaw, rule, ruling, ordinance, dictum, command, order, directive, pronouncement, proclamation, dictate, fiat.

**2** *a career in law* THE LEGAL PROFESSION, the bar.

**3** *informal on the run from the law.* See POLICE noun.

**4** *the laws of the game* RULE, regulation, principle, convention, instruction, guideline.

**5** *a moral law* PRINCIPLE, rule, precept, directive, injunction, commandment, belief, creed, credo, maxim, tenet, doctrine, canon.

**law-abiding** adjective *law-abiding citizens* HONEST, righteous, honorable, upright, upstanding, good, decent, virtuous, moral, dutiful, obedient, compliant. ANTONYM criminal.

**lawbreaker** noun *to her dying day, Bobbie never believed that her son was a lawbreaker* CRIMINAL, offender, wrongdoer, malefactor, evildoer, transgressor, miscreant; villain, rogue, ruffian, felon; *Law* malfeasant; *informal* crook, con, jailbird, hood; *archaic* miscreant.

**lawful** adjective *the lawful seizure of weapons* LEGITIMATE, legal, licit, just, permissible, permitted, allowable, allowed, rightful, sanctioned, authorized, warranted, within the law; *informal* legit. ANTONYMS illegal, criminal.

**lawless** adjective *a lawless country* UNGOVERNABLE, unruly, disruptive, anarchic, disorderly, rebellious, insubordinate, riotous, mutinous; uncivilized, wild. ANTONYM orderly.

**lawsuit** noun *the actor is now involved in a lawsuit against his former business manager* LEGAL ACTION, suit, case, action, legal proceedings, judicial proceedings, proceedings, litigation, trial, legal dispute, legal contest.

**lawyer** noun *O'Donnell's lawyers are confident that the case will be dismissed* ATTORNEY, counsel, counselor, legal practitioner, legal professional, legal adviser, member of the bar, litigator, advocate; *chiefly Brit.* barrister, solicitor; *informal* ambulance chaser, mouthpiece, legal eagle, legal beagle.

**lax** adjective *lax discipline in schools* SLACK, slipshod, negligent, remiss, careless, heedless, unmindful, slapdash, offhand, casual; easygoing, lenient, permissive, liberal, indulgent, overindulgent; *informal* sloppy. See note at LENIENT. ANTONYM strict.

**lay**[1] verb **1** *Curtis laid the newspaper on the table* PUT, place, set, put down, set down, deposit, rest, situate, locate, position; *informal* stick, dump, park, plunk.

**2** *the act laid the foundation for the new system* SET IN PLACE, put in place, set out; set up, establish.

**3** *I'll lay money that Michelle will be there* BET, wager, gamble, stake, risk, hazard, venture; **(lay money)** give odds, speculate.

**4** *they are going to lay charges* BRING, press, bring forward, lodge, register, place, file.

**5** *she* ***laid*** *the blame* ***on*** *Maxwell* ASSIGN TO, attribute to, ascribe to, allot to, attach to; **(lay the blame on)** hold someone accountable, hold someone responsible, find guilty.

**6** *we* ***laid out*** *plans for the next voyage* DEVISE, arrange, make, make ready, prepare, work out, hatch, design, plan, scheme, plot, conceive, put together, draw up, produce, develop, concoct, formulate, cook up.

**7** *this will lay responsibility on the court* IMPOSE, apply, entrust, vest, place, put; inflict, encumber, saddle, charge, burden.

**8** *we laid the trap and waited* SET, prepare, devise, bait. See note at LIE[2]. PHRASES: **lay something aside 1** *farmers laying aside areas for conservation* PUT ASIDE, put to one side, keep, save.

**2** *developers must lay aside their conservatism* ABANDON, cast aside, set aside, reject, renounce, repudiate, disregard, forget, discard; *literary* forsake.

**lay something bare** *his private life has been laid bare* REVEAL, disclose, divulge, show, expose, exhibit, uncover, unveil, unmask, make known, make public.

**lay something down 1** *he laid down his glass* PUT DOWN, set down, place down, deposit, rest; *informal* plunk down.

**2** *they were forced to lay down their weapons* RELINQUISH, surrender, give up, yield, cede.

**3** *the ground rules have been laid down* FORMULATE, stipulate, set down, draw up, frame; prescribe, ordain, dictate, decree; enact, pass, decide, determine, impose, codify.

**lay down the law** *too many parents have relinquished their right to lay down the law* BE DOGMATIC, be in charge (of the rules), set the rules, be domineering, be the boss, call the shots.

**lay eyes on** *informal something clicked the first time they laid eyes on each other* SEE, spot, observe, regard, view, catch sight of, set eyes on; *literary* behold, espy, descry.

**lay hands on** *wait till I lay my hands on you!* CATCH, lay/get hold of, get one's hands on, seize, grab, grasp, capture.

**lay into** *informal* **1** *the general's henchmen were encouraged to publicly lay into dissenters.* See ASSAULT verb sense 1.

**2** *he laid into her with a string of insults.* See CRITICIZE.

**lay it on thick** *informal oh, brother, can he lay it on thick when he wants to impress a girl* EXAGGERATE, overdo it, embellish the truth; flatter, praise, soft-soap, pile it on, sweet-talk.

**lay off** *informal* **1** *I have to lay off beer* GIVE UP, abstain from, desist from, cut out.

**2** *I lay off work at 5* QUIT, pack in, leave off, stop.

**3** *lay off, you big jerk!* BACK OFF, give it a rest, enough already, shut up, stop it.

**4** *three more couriers were laid off today* DISMISS, let go, discharge, give notice to, release; *informal* sack, fire, ax, give someone their marching orders, pink-slip, give someone the boot, give someone the (old) heave-ho.

**lay out 1** *Robyn laid the plans out on the desk* SPREAD OUT, set out, display, exhibit.

**2** *a paper laying out our priorities* OUTLINE, sketch out, rough out, detail, draw up, formulate, work out, frame, draft.

**3** *informal he had to lay out $70.* See PAY verb sense 2.

**lay waste to** *any further testing at this site will lay waste to an irreplaceable ecosystem* DEVASTATE, wipe out, destroy, demolish, annihilate, raze, ruin, wreck, level, flatten, ravage, pillage, sack, despoil.

**USAGE NOTE**

The verb **lay** means, broadly, 'put something down': *they are going to lay the carpet*. The past tense and the past participle of **lay** is **laid**: *they laid the groundwork; she had laid careful plans*.

The verb **lie**, on the other hand, means 'assume a horizontal or resting position': *why don't you lie on the floor?*

In practice, many speakers inadvertently get the **lay** forms and the **lie** forms into a tangle of right and wrong usage. Here are some examples of typical incorrect usage: *have you been laying on the sofa all day?* (should be **lying**); *he lay the books on the table* (should be **laid**); *I had laid in this position so long, my arm was stiff* (should be **lain**).

**lay**[2] adjective **1** *a lay preacher* NONCLERICAL, nonordained, secular, temporal.

**2** *a lay audience* NONPROFESSIONAL, amateur, nonspecialist, nontechnical, untrained, unqualified.

**layabout** noun *I want Carmen and the rest of these layabouts out of here by noon* IDLER, loafer, slacker, lazybones, lounger, flâneur, shirker, sluggard, laggard, slugabed, malingerer, good-for-nothing; *informal* lazybones, couch potato; *literary* wastrel.

**layoff** noun *a companywide layoff* DISMISSAL, discharge; *informal* sacking, firing; downsizing; the sack, the boot, the ax. ANTONYM recruitment.

**layout** noun **1** *the layout of the house* ARRANGEMENT, geography, design, organization; plan, map; blueprint.

**2** *the magazine's layout* DESIGN, arrangement, presentation, style, format; structure, organization, composition, configuration.

**layperson** noun **1** *a prayer book for laypeople* UNORDAINED PERSON, member of the congregation, layman, laywoman, member of the laity.

**2** *engineering sounds highly specialized to the layperson* LAYMAN, nonexpert, nonprofessional, amateur, nonspecialist, dilettante.

**laze** verb *lazing by the river* RELAX, unwind, idle, do nothing, loaf (around/about), lounge (around/about), loll (around/about), lie (around/about), take it easy; *informal* hang around, veg (out), bum (around).

**lazy** adjective *the lazy volunteers were sent home* IDLE, indolent, slothful, work-shy, shiftless, inactive, sluggish, lethargic; remiss, negligent, slack, lax, lackadaisical. ANTONYM industrious.

**lead**[1] verb **1** *Michelle led them into the house* GUIDE, conduct, show, show the way, lead the way, usher, escort, steer, pilot, shepherd; accompany, see, take. ANTONYM follow.

**2** *he led us to believe they were lying* CAUSE, induce, prompt, move, persuade, influence, drive, condition, make; incline, dispose, predispose.

**3** *this might* ***lead to*** *job losses* RESULT IN, cause, bring on/about, give rise to, be the cause of, make happen, create, produce, occasion, effect, generate, contribute to, promote; provoke, stir up, spark off, arouse, foment, instigate; involve, necessitate, entail; *formal* effectuate. ANTONYM prevent.

**4** *he led a march to the city center* BE AT THE HEAD OF, be at the front of, head, spearhead; precede. ANTONYM follow.

**5** *she led a coalition of radicals* BE THE LEADER OF, be the head of, preside over, head, command, govern, rule, be in charge of, be in command of, be in control of, run, control, direct, be at the helm of; administer, organize, manage; reign over, be in power over; *informal* head up. ANTONYM serve in.

**6** *the Bengals were leading at halftime* BE AHEAD, be winning, be (out) in front, be in the lead, be first, be on top. ANTONYM trail.

**7** *the champion was leading the field* BE AT THE FRONT OF, be first in, be ahead of, head; outrun, outstrip, outpace, leave behind, draw away from; outdo, outclass, beat; *informal* leave standing. ANTONYM trail.

**8** *I just want to lead a normal life* EXPERIENCE, have, live, spend.

▸ noun **1** *I was in* ***the lead*** *early on* THE LEADING POSITION, first place, the van, the vanguard; ahead, in front, winning.

**2** *they took the lead in the personal computer market* FIRST POSITION, forefront, primacy, dominance, superiority, ascendancy; preeminence, supremacy, advantage, upper hand, whip hand.

**3** *playing the lead* LEADING ROLE, star/starring role, title role, principal part; principal character, male lead, female lead, leading man, leading lady.

**4** *a Labrador on a lead* LEASH, tether, rope, chain, cord.

**5** *detectives were following up a new lead* CLUE, hint, tip, tip-off, suggestion, indication, sign, pointer.

▸ adjective *the lead position* LEADING, first, top, foremost, front, head; chief, principal, main, premier.

PHRASES: **lead something off** *let's lead off the meeting with a few words from Mr. Diaz* BEGIN, start (off), commence, open; *informal* kick off.

**lead someone on** *were you leading her on with that talk about marriage?* DECEIVE, mislead, delude, hoodwink, dupe, trick, fool, pull the wool over someone's eyes; *informal* string along, lead up the garden path, take for a ride, fleece, inveigle, hornswoggle, scam.

**lead the way 1** *he led the way to the kitchen* GUIDE SOMEONE, conduct someone, show someone the way.

**2** *our corporation is leading the way in new technologies* TAKE THE INITIATIVE, break (new) ground, blaze a trail, prepare the way, be at the forefront.

**lead up to** *perhaps these informal meetings will lead up to a more formal relationship* PREPARE THE WAY FOR, pave the way for, lay the groundwork for, set the scene for, work up/around to.

**lead**[2] noun *informal get that lead down to forensics immediately* BULLET, slug, pellet; shot, buckshot, ammunition PHRASE: **get the lead out** *come on you guys—get the lead out!* HURRY UP, get a move on, be quick; *informal* get cracking, shake a leg, look lively, look sharp; *dated* make haste.

**leaden** adjective **1** *he moved on leaden feet* SLUGGISH, heavy, lumbering, slow, burdensome, cumbersome.

**2** *leaden prose* BORING, dull, unimaginative, uninspired, monotonous, heavy, labored, wooden, lifeless, plodding; depressing.

**3** *a leaden sky* GRAY, grayish, black, dark; cloudy, gloomy, overcast, dull, sunless, oppressive, threatening; *literary* tenebrous.

**leader** noun **1** *the leader of the Democratic Party* | *world leaders have agreed to meet in Geneva* CHIEF, head, principal; commander, captain; superior, headman; chairman, chairwoman, chairperson, chair; (managing) director, CEO, manager, superintendent, supervisor, overseer, administrator, employer, master, mistress; president, premier, governor; ruler, monarch, king, queen, sovereign, emperor; *informal* boss, skipper, number one, numero uno, honcho, sachem, padrone. ANTONYMS follower, supporter.

**2** *the uncontested leader in genetic engineering* PIONEER, front runner, world leader, world-beater, innovator, trailblazer, groundbreaker, trendsetter, torchbearer, pathfinder.

**leadership** noun **1** *firm leadership* GUIDANCE, direction, control, management, superintendence, supervision; organization, government.

**2** *the leadership of the Rainbow Coalition* DIRECTORSHIP, governorship, governance, administration, captaincy, control, ascendancy, supremacy, rule, command, power, dominion, influence.

**leading** adjective **1** *he played the leading role* MAIN, chief, major, prime, most significant, most important, principal, foremost, key, central, focal, preeminent, paramount, dominant, essential. ANTONYMS subordinate, secondary.

**2** *the nation's leading steel companies* MOST IMPORTANT, most powerful, affluential, foremost, chief, preeminent, outstanding, dominant, most influential. ANTONYMS minor, secondary

**3** *last season's leading scorer* TOP, highest, best, first; front, lead; unparalleled, matchless, star. ANTONYMS worst, last.

**leaf** noun **1** *sycamore leaves* LEAFLET, frond, blade, needle; *Botany* cotyledon, blade, bract.

**2** *a leaf in a book* PAGE, sheet, folio.

▸ verb *he* ***leafed through*** *the documents* FLIP THROUGH, thumb through, flick through, skim through/over, browse through, glance through/over, riffle through, rifle through; scan, run one's eye over, peruse.

PHRASE: **turn over a new leaf** *how many released prisoners actually turn over a new leaf?* REFORM, improve, mend one's ways, make a fresh start, change for the better; *informal* go straight.

**leaflet** noun *leaflets about fire prevention* PAMPHLET, booklet, brochure, handbill, circular, flyer, fact sheet, handout, bulletin.

**league** noun **1** *a league of nations* ALLIANCE, confederation, confederacy, federation, union, association, coalition, consortium, affiliation, guild, cooperative, partnership, fellowship, syndicate.

**2** *the best team in the league* big league(s), major league(s), minor league(s), American League, National League, intramural league, Little League, bush league.

**3** *the store is not in the same league* CLASS, group, circle, category, level.

▸ verb *they* ***leagued together*** *with other companies* ALLY, join forces, join together, unite, band together, affiliate, combine, amalgamate, confederate, team up, join up.

PHRASE: **in league with** *in league with the drug cartel* COLLABORATING WITH, cooperating with, in alliance with, allied with, conspiring with, hand in glove with; *informal* in cahoots with, in bed with.

**leak** verb **1** *oil leaking from the tanker* SEEP (OUT), escape, ooze (out), secrete, bleed, emanate, issue, drip, dribble, drain; discharge, exude.

**2** *civil servants leaked information to the press* DISCLOSE, divulge, reveal, make public, tell, impart, pass on, relate, communicate, expose, broadcast, publish, release, let slip, bring into the open; *informal* blab; **(leak news/information)** let the cat out of the bag, spill the beans.

▸ noun **1** *check that there are no leaks in the pipe* HOLE, opening, aperture, puncture, perforation, gash, slit, nick, rent, break, crack, fissure, rupture.

**2** *a gas leak* DISCHARGE, leakage, seepage, drip, escape.

**3** *leaks to the media* DISCLOSURE, revelation, exposé, leakage, tip-off.

**lean**[1] verb **1** *Polly* ***leaned against*** *the door* REST ON/AGAINST, recline on/against, be supported by.

**2** *trees leaning in the wind* SLANT, incline, bend, tilt, be at an angle, slope, tip, list.

**3** *he* ***leans toward*** *existentialist philosophy* TEND TOWARD, incline toward, gravitate toward; have a preference for, have a penchant for, be partial to, have a liking for, have an affinity with.

**4** *a strong shoulder to* ***lean on*** DEPEND ON, be dependent on, rely on, count on, bank on, have faith in, trust (in).

**5** *informal he* ***leaned on*** *me to change my mind* INTIMIDATE, coerce, browbeat, bully, threaten, put pressure on, harass, hassle; *informal* twist someone's arm, put the screws on, hold a gun to someone's head.

**lean**[2] adjective **1** *a tall, lean man* SLIM, thin, slender, spare, wiry, lanky, skinny. See note at THIN. ANTONYM fat.

**2** *a lean harvest* MEAGER, sparse, poor, mean, inadequate, insufficient, paltry, scanty, deficient, insubstantial. ANTONYMS plentiful, abundant.

**3** *lean times* HARD, bad, difficult, tough, impoverished, poverty-stricken. ANTONYM prosperous.

**leaning** noun *my leaning is definitely toward a more liberal agenda* INCLINATION, tendency, bent, proclivity, propensity, penchant, predisposition, predilection, partiality, preference, bias, attraction, liking, fondness, taste; *informal* yen.

**leap** verb **1** *he* ***leaped over*** *the gate* JUMP OVER, jump, vault over, vault, spring over, bound over, hop (over), hurdle, leapfrog, clear.

**2** *Claudia leapt to her feet* SPRING, jump, jump up, hop, bound.

**3** *we leapt into the car* RUSH, hurry, hasten.

**4** *she* ***leaped at*** *the chance* ACCEPT EAGERLY, grasp (with both hands), grab, take advantage of, seize (on), jump at.

**5** *don't* ***leap to*** *conclusions* FORM HASTILY, reach hurriedly; hurry to, hasten to, jump to, rush to.

**6** *profits leapt in January* INCREASE RAPIDLY, soar, rocket, skyrocket, shoot up, escalate.

▸ noun **1** *an easy leap* JUMP, vault, spring, bound, hop, skip.

**2** *a leap of 33%* SUDDEN RISE, surge, upsurge, upswing, upturn.

PHRASE: **by/in leaps and bounds** *his health has improved by leaps and bounds* RAPIDLY, swiftly, quickly, speedily.

**learn** verb **1** *learning a foreign language* ACQUIRE A KNOWLEDGE OF, acquire skill in, become competent in, become proficient in, grasp, master, take in, absorb, assimilate, digest, familiarize oneself with; study, read up on, be taught, have lessons in; *informal* get the hang of, bone up on.

**2** *she learned the poem in just a few minutes* MEMORIZE, learn by heart, commit to memory, get down pat; *archaic* con.

**3** *he learned that the school would shortly be closing* DISCOVER, find out, become aware, be informed, hear, hear tell; gather, understand, ascertain, establish; *informal* get wind of the fact, get wise to the fact; *Brit. informal* suss out.

**learned** adjective *the most learned man in their community* SCHOLARLY, erudite, well-educated, knowledgeable, well-read, well-informed, lettered, cultured, intellectual, academic, literary, bookish, highbrow, studious; *informal* brainy. ANTONYM ignorant.

**learner** noun. See NOVICE sense 1.

**learning** noun **1** *a center of learning* STUDY, studying, education, schooling, tuition, teaching, academic work; research.

**2** *the astonishing range of his learning* SCHOLARSHIP, knowledge, education, erudition, intellect, enlightenment, illumination, edification, book learning, information, understanding, wisdom. See note at KNOWLEDGE. ANTONYM ignorance.

**lease** noun *a 15-year lease* RENTAL AGREEMENT, leasehold, charter; rental, tenancy, tenure, period of occupancy.

▸ verb **1** *the film crew leased a large hangar* RENT, charter.

**2** *they leased the mill to a reputable family* RENT, rent out, let, let out; sublet, sublease.

**leash** noun *keep your dog on a leash* LEAD, tether, rope, chain, restraint.

▸ verb **1** *she leashed the dog* PUT A/THE LEASH ON, put a/the lead on, tether, tie up, secure, restrain.

**2** *the fury in her face was barely leashed* CURB, control, keep under control, check, restrain, hold back, suppress, rein in. PHRASE: **straining at the leash** *thousands of young actors are straining at the leash just for the chance to audition* EAGER, impatient, anxious, enthusiastic; *informal* itching, dying.

**leathery** adjective **1** *leathery skin* ROUGH, rugged, leathered, hard, hardened, wrinkled, furrowed, lined, weather-beaten, callous, gnarled.

**2** *a leathery cut of beef* TOUGH, hard, gristly, chewy, stringy, rubbery.

**leave**[1] verb **1** *I left the hotel* DEPART FROM, go away from, go from, withdraw from, retire from, take oneself off from, exit from, take one's leave of, pull out of, be gone from, decamp from, disappear from, vacate, absent oneself from; say one's farewells/goodbyes to, quit; *informal* push off from, shove off from, clear out/off of, cut and run from, split, vamoose from, scoot from. ANTONYMS arrive, stay.

**2** *the next morning we left for Taipei* SET OFF, head, make; set sail.

**3** *he's left his wife* ABANDON, desert, cast aside, jilt, throw over; *informal* dump, ditch, drop, walk/run out on; *literary* forsake. ANTONYM stay with.

**4** *he left his job in November* QUIT, resign from, retire from, step down from, withdraw from, pull out of, give up; pack it in, call it quits.

**5** *she left her purse on a bus* LEAVE BEHIND, forget, lose, mislay.

**6** *I thought I'd leave it to the experts* ENTRUST, hand over, pass on, refer; delegate.

**7** *he left her $100,000* BEQUEATH, will, endow, hand down to, make over to.

**8** *the speech left some feelings of disappointment* CAUSE, produce, generate, give rise to. PHRASE: **leave someone/something out 1** *Adam left out the address* OMIT, fail to include, overlook, forget; skip, miss.

**2** *when the roster for Game 2 was drawn up, Harvey was left out* EXCLUDE, omit, pass over; eliminate, cut, drop.

**leave**[2] noun **1** *the judge granted leave to appeal* PERMISSION, consent, authorization, sanction, warrant, dispensation, approval, clearance, blessing, assent, license; *informal* the go-ahead, the green light, the OK, the rubber stamp, the nod.

**2** *he was on leave* VACATION, break, time off, holiday, furlough, sabbatical, leave of absence. PHRASE: **take one's leave of** *he took his leave of us* BID FAREWELL TO, say goodbye to.

**leaven** verb **1** *yeast leavens the bread* RAISE, make rise, puff up, expand.

**2** *formal proceedings leavened by humor* PERMEATE, infuse, pervade, imbue, suffuse, transform; enliven, liven up, invigorate, energize, electrify, ginger up, season, spice (up), perk up, brighten up, lighten, lift; *informal* buck up, pep up.

**lecher** noun *her blind date turned out to be a lecher* LECHEROUS MAN, libertine, womanizer, debauchee, rake, roué, profligate, wanton; Don Juan, Casanova, Lothario, Romeo; *informal* lech, dirty old man, (old) goat, wolf, skirt-chaser; *archaic* fornicator.

**lecherous** adjective *the lecherous creep who lives in our building* LUSTFUL, licentious, lascivious, libidinous, prurient, lewd, salacious, lubricious, debauched, dissolute, wanton, dissipated, degenerate, depraved, dirty, filthy; *formal* concupiscent. ANTONYM chaste.

**lecture** noun **1** *a lecture on children's literature* SPEECH, talk, address, discourse, disquisition, presentation, oration, lesson.

**2** *Dave got a lecture about his daydreaming* SCOLDING, chiding, reprimand, rebuke, reproof, reproach, upbraiding, berating, admonishment, sermon; *informal* dressing-down, talking-to, tongue-lashing, roasting; *formal* castigation.

▸ verb **1** *lecturing on the dangers of drugs* GIVE A LECTURE, give a talk, talk, make a speech, speak, give an address, discourse, hold forth, declaim, expatiate; *informal* spout, sound off.

**2** *she lectures at Colgate University* TEACH, give instruction, give lessons.

**3** *she was lectured for her gossiping* SCOLD, chide, reprimand, rebuke, reprove, reproach, upbraid, berate, chastise, admonish, lambaste, rake/haul over the coals, take to task; *informal* give someone a dressing-down, give someone a talking-to, tell off, bawl out; *formal* castigate.

**lecturer** noun *a guest lecturer from Yale* UNIVERSITY TEACHER, college teacher, professor, tutor, educator; academic, academician, preceptor; *formal* pedagogue.

**ledge** noun *a collection of teapots on the ledge | a rock ledge* SHELF, sill, mantel, mantelpiece, shelving; projection, protrusion, overhang, ridge, prominence.

**ledger** noun *a sales ledger* BOOK, account book, record book, register, log, accounts; records, books; balance sheet, financial statement.

**lee** noun *the lee of the wall* SHELTER, protection, cover, refuge, safety, security.

**leech** noun *the welfare system is supposed to help the needy,* *not to feed the leeches* PARASITE, bloodsucker; *informal* scrounger, sponger, bottom feeder, freeloader.

**leer** verb *Henry* **leered at** *her* OGLE, look lasciviously at, look suggestively at, eye, check out; *informal* give someone a/the once-over, lust after/over.

▸ noun *a sly leer* LECHEROUS LOOK, lascivious look, ogle; *informal* the once-over, the eye.

**leery** adjective *be leery of these slick salesmen* WARY, cautious, careful, guarded, chary, suspicious, distrustful; worried, anxious, apprehensive, hesitant, uncertain.

**leeway** noun *enforcement officials now have more leeway in prosecuting offenders* FREEDOM, scope, latitude, space, room, liberty, flexibility, license, free hand, free rein.

**left** adjective *it's in my left pocket | move to the left side* LEFT-HAND, sinistral; *Nautical* port, larboard; *Heraldry* sinister. ANTONYMS right, starboard.

**left-handed** adjective **1** *a left-handed golfer* sinistral; *informal* southpaw. ANTONYM right-handed.

**2** *a left-handed compliment* BACKHANDED, ambiguous, equivocal, double-edged; dubious, ironic, sardonic, insincere, hypocritical. ANTONYM forthright.

**leftover** noun **1** *a leftover from the 60s* RESIDUE, SURVIVOR, vestige, legacy, throwback.

**2** **(leftovers)** *put the leftovers in the fridge* UNEATEN FOOD, leavings, remainder, scraps, remnants, remains; excess, surplus.

▸ adjective *leftover food* REMAINING, left, uneaten, unconsumed; excess, surplus, superfluous, unused, unwanted, spare.

**leg** noun **1** *Lee broke his leg* LOWER LIMB, limb, shank; *informal* pin.

**2** *the first leg of a European tour* PART, stage, portion, segment, section, phase, stretch, lap. PHRASES: **give someone a leg up** *we all want to give our kids a leg up in the world* HELP/ASSIST SOMEONE, give someone assistance, lend someone a helping hand, give someone a boost.
**leg it** *informal* See RUN verb sense 1.
**on its/one's last legs** *the barn is on its last legs* DILAPIDATED, worn out, rickety, about to fall apart, about to become obsolete; failing, dying, terminal, on one's deathbed.
**pull someone's leg** *is Julie really sick or is she just pulling my leg?* TEASE SOMEONE, make fun of someone, tease, joke, make fun, fool, jest, joke with someone, play a (practical) joke on someone, play a trick on someone, make a monkey out of someone; hoax someone, fool someone, deceive someone, lead someone on, hoodwink someone, dupe someone, beguile someone, gull someone; *informal* kid someone, have someone on, rib someone, take someone for a ride, put someone on.
**stretch one's legs** *we always like to stretch our legs after dinner* GO FOR A WALK, take a stroll, walk, stroll, move about, get some exercise.

**legacy** noun **1** *a legacy from a great aunt* BEQUEST, inheritance, heritage, endowment, gift, patrimony, settlement, birthright; *formal* benefaction.

**2** *a legacy of the residential schools* CONSEQUENCE, effect, upshot, spin-off, repercussion, aftermath, by-product, result.

**legal** adjective *the legal sale of alcoholic beverages* LAWFUL, legitimate, licit, within the law, legalized, valid; permissible, permitted, allowable, allowed, aboveboard, admissible, acceptable; authorized, sanctioned, licensed, constitutional; *informal* legit. ANTONYM criminal.

**legalize** verb *where do you stand on legalizing marijuana?* MAKE LEGAL, decriminalize, legitimize, legitimate, permit, allow, authorize, sanction, license, validate; regularize, normalize; *informal* OK. ANTONYM prohibit.

**legatee** noun. See BENEFICIARY.

**legend** noun **1** *Arthurian legends* MYTH, saga, epic, tale, story, folk tale, folk story, fairy tale, fable, mythos, folklore, lore, mythology, fantasy, oral history, folk tradition; urban myth.

**2** *film legends* CELEBRITY, star, superstar, icon, phenomenon, luminary, leading light, giant; *informal* celeb, megastar.

**legendary** adjective **1** *legendary knights* FABLED, heroic, traditional, fairy-tale, storybook, mythical, mythological. ANTONYMS factual, historical.

**2** *a legendary figure in sports* FAMOUS, celebrated, famed, renowned, acclaimed, illustrious, esteemed, honored, exalted, venerable, well-known, popular, prominent, distinguished, great, eminent, preeminent, high-profile; *formal* lauded.

**legerdemain** noun **1** *stage magicians practicing legerdemain* SLEIGHT OF HAND, conjuring, magic, wizardry; *formal* prestidigitation; *rare* thaumaturgy.

**2** *a piece of management legerdemain* TRICKERY, cunning, artfulness, craftiness, chicanery, skulduggery, deceit, deception, artifice.

**legible** adjective *large, legible handwriting* READABLE, easy to read, easily deciphered, clear, plain, neat, decipherable, intelligible.

**legion** noun **1** *a military legion* BRIGADE, regiment, battalion, company, troop, division, squadron, squad, platoon, phalanx, unit, force.

**2** *the legions of TV cameras* HORDE, throng, multitude, host, crowd, mass, mob, gang, swarm, flock, herd, score, army, pack.

▸ adjective *her fans are legion* NUMEROUS, countless, innumerable, incalculable, many, abundant, plentiful; *literary* myriad.

**legislate** verb *we urge Congress to legislate against human cloning* MAKE LAWS, pass laws, enact laws, formulate laws; authorize, decree, order, sanction.

**legislation** noun *pushing for stronger gun legislation* LAW(S), body of laws, rules, rulings, regulations, acts, bills, statutes, enactments, ordinances.

**legislative** adjective *a legislative assembly* LAWMAKING, judicial, juridical, parliamentary, governmental, policy-making.

**legislator** noun *let your legislators know how you feel about the state income tax* LAWMAKER, lawgiver; representative, congressman, congresswoman, senator; parliamentarian.

**legitimate** adjective **1** *the only form of legitimate gambling* LEGAL, lawful, licit, legalized, authorized, permitted, permissible, allowable, allowed, admissible, sanctioned, approved, licensed, statutory, constitutional; *informal* legit, street legal. ANTONYM illegal.

**2** *the legitimate heir* RIGHTFUL, lawful, genuine, authentic, real, true, proper, authorized, sanctioned, acknowledged, recognized. See note at GENUINE. ANTONYMS false, fraudulent.

**3** *legitimate grounds for doubt* VALID, sound, well-founded, justifiable, reasonable, sensible, just, fair, bona fide. ANTONYM illegal.

**legitimize** verb *China's revised constitution will legitimize citizens' rights to hold private property* VALIDATE, legitimate, permit, authorize, sanction, license, condone, justify, endorse, support; legalize. ANTONYM outlaw.

**leisure** noun *the balance between leisure and work* FREE TIME, spare time, time off; recreation, relaxation, inactivity, pleasure; *informal* R and R, downtime. ANTONYM work.

PHRASE: **at your leisure** *Form A may be completed at your leisure* AT YOUR CONVENIENCE, when it suits you, in your own (good/sweet) time, without haste, unhurriedly.

**leisurely** adjective *a leisurely stroll through town* UNHURRIED, relaxed, easy, gentle, sedate, comfortable, restful, undemanding, slow, lazy. ANTONYM hurried.

**lend** verb **1** *I'll lend you my towel* LOAN, let someone use; advance. See note at LOAN. ANTONYM borrow.

**2** *these examples lend weight to his assertions* ADD, impart, give, bestow, confer, provide, supply, furnish, contribute. ANTONYM detract.

PHRASES: **lend an ear** *when Travers gets up to speak, I hope you'll lend an ear* LISTEN, pay attention, take notice, be attentive, concentrate, heed, pay heed; *informal* be all ears; *archaic* hearken.

**lend a hand** *I'm here to lend a hand with the harvest* HELP, help out, give a helping hand, assist, give assistance, make a contribution, do one's bit; *informal* pitch in.

**lend itself to** *the terrain lends itself to downhill skiing* BE SUITABLE FOR, be suited to, be appropriate for, be applicable for.

**length** noun **1** *a length of three or four yards | the whole length of the valley* EXTENT, distance, linear measure, span, reach; area, expanse, stretch, range, scope.

**2** *a considerable length of time* PERIOD, duration, stretch, span.

**3** *a length of blue silk* PIECE, swatch, measure.

**4** *the press criticized the length of her speech* LENGTHINESS, extent, prolixity, wordiness, verbosity, long-windedness.

PHRASE: **at length 1** *the preacher spoke at length* FOR A LONG TIME, for ages, for hours, interminably, endlessly, ceaselessly, unendingly.

**2** *Everett was questioned at length* THOROUGHLY, fully, in detail, in depth, comprehensively, exhaustively, extensively.

**3** *his search led him, at length, to Seattle* AFTER A LONG TIME, eventually, in time, finally, at last, at long last, in the end, ultimately.

**lengthen** verb *he lengthened his stride to keep up | as the spring days lengthen* ELONGATE, make longer, extend, prolong, protract, stretch out, drag out; expand, widen, broaden, enlarge; grow/get longer, draw out. ANTONYM shorten.

**lengthy** adjective **1** *a lengthy civil war* LONG, very long, long-lasting, prolonged, extended; *informal* marathon. ANTONYM short.

**2** *lengthy discussions* PROTRACTED, overlong, long-drawn-out; verbose, wordy, prolix, long-winded; tedious, boring, interminable. ANTONYM brief.

**lenient** adjective *Brother Andrew was a lenient teacher* MERCIFUL, clement, forgiving, forbearing, tolerant, charitable, humane, indulgent, easygoing, magnanimous, sympathetic, compassionate, mild. See note at MERCY. ANTONYM severe.

THE RIGHT WORD **lenient, forbearing, indulgent, lax, merciful, permissive**

Not all parents approach discipline in the same way. Someone who is **lenient** is willing to lower his or her standards of strictness when it comes to imposing discipline (*the principal was lenient with the students who had been caught playing hooky*). A parent who is **forbearing** struggles against giving in to negative feelings and is therefore able to abstain from hasty or ill-tempered actions, no matter what the provocation (*her father's forbearing attitude meant that she escaped with only a lecture*). **Indulgent** goes beyond forbearing and suggests catering to someone's whims (*an indulgent parent who seldom denied her child anything*). **Lax** is a negative kind of leniency involving laziness or indifference (*a lax mother who never imposed a curfew*), while **merciful** suggests a relaxing of standards on the basis of compassion (*a merciful mother who understood her daughter's anger*). To be **permissive** is also to be extremely lenient—an approach that connotes tolerance to the point of passivity (*the children's utter disregard for the rules was the result of their permissive upbringing*).

**lesbian** noun *the title character is a nineteen-year-old lesbian* HOMOSEXUAL WOMAN, gay woman; *informal* butch, femme; *offensive* dyke, bulldyke, queer. ANTONYMS heterosexual, straight woman.

▸ adjective *a long-term lesbian partnership* HOMOSEXUAL, gay, same-sex; Sapphic, homoerotic; *informal* butch; *offensive* dykey, queer. ANTONYM straight.

**lesion** noun *symptoms include clusters of red lesions* WOUND, injury, bruise, abrasion, contusion; ulcer, ulceration, sore, running sore, abscess; *Medicine* trauma.

**less** pronoun *the fare is **less than** $1* A SMALLER AMOUNT THAN, not so/as much as, under, below. ANTONYM more.

▸ adjective *there was less noise now* NOT SO MUCH, smaller, slighter, shorter, reduced; fewer.

▸ adverb *we must use the car less* TO A LESSER DEGREE, to a smaller extent, not so/as much.

▸ preposition *figure the list price less 10 percent* MINUS, subtracting, excepting, without. ANTONYM plus.

USAGE NOTE **less, fewer**

Strictly, *less* applies to singular nouns (*less tonic water, please*) or units of measure (*less than six ounces of epoxy*). *Fewer* applies to plural nouns (*fewer guests arrived than expected*) or numbers of things (*we have three fewer members this year*). The exception in using *fewer* occurs when count nouns essentially function as mass nouns because the units are so very numerous or they aren't considered discrete items (the idea of individual units becomes meaningless). Hence *less* is used correctly with time and money: one isn't, ordinarily, talking about the number of years or the number of dollars but rather the amount of time or the amount of money—e.g.:

• "On that mantra, Larry Clark has built a $45 million-a-year company in less than five years." (*Arizona Business Gazette*; Nov. 30, 1995.)

• "Okay, how about $50 a month for such an apartment—less than two dollars a day?" (*Village Voice*; Apr. 29, 1997.)

*Fewer*, in fact, is incorrect when intended to refer to a period of time—e.g.: "You can run from sea level to the sky and back to earth in as fast as 45 minutes (so far), but even today, going round-trip in fewer [read *less*] than 60 minutes carries a special cachet." (*Anchorage Daily News*; June 29, 1997.) But if the units of time are thought of as wholes, and not by fractions, then *fewer* is called for (*fewer days abroad* ¦ *fewer weeks spent apart*). Hence we say *less documentation* but *fewer documents*; *less whispering* but *fewer remarks*; *less of a burden* but *fewer burdens*; *less fattening* but *fewer calories*.

Fastidious writers and editors preserve the old distinction. But the loose usage crops up often—e.g.: "You will have less [read *fewer*] people to call and haunt about paying for their outfits and buying their accessories." (*Boston Herald* [magazine]; Oct. 19, 1997.) The linguistic hegemony by which *less* has encroached on *fewer*'s territory is probably now irreversible. What has clinched this development is something as mundane as the express checkout lines in supermarkets. They're typically bedecked with signs cautioning, "15 items or less." These signs are all but ubiquitous in the United States. But the occasional more literate supermarket owner uses a different sign: "15 or fewer items."

Finally, even with the strict usage, it's sometimes a close call whether a thing is a mass noun or a count noun, and hence whether *less* or *fewer* is proper. Take, for example, a percentage: should it be "less than 10% of the homeowners were there" or "fewer than 10% of the homeowners were there"? One could argue that a percentage is something counted (i.e., 10 out of 100), and thus requires *fewer*. One could also argue that a percentage is a collective mass noun (akin, e.g., to money), and thus requires *less*. The latter is the better argument because most percentages aren't whole numbers anyway. And even if it were a toss-up between the two theories, it's sound to choose *less*, which is less formal in tone than *fewer*.

If, in strict usage, *less* applies to singular nouns and *fewer* to plural nouns, the choice is clear: "one less golfer on the course," not "one fewer golfer." This is tricky only because *less* is being applied to a singular count noun, whereas it usually applies to a mass noun. Lyricist Hal David got it right in "One Less Bell to Answer" (1970). Nearly a quarter of the time, however, writers use *one fewer*, an awkward and unidiomatic phrase. One can't help thinking that this is a kind of hypercorrection induced by underanalysis of the *less*-vs.-*fewer* question.

*Lesser*, like *less*, refers to quantity, but is confined to use as an adjective before a singular noun and following an article (*the lesser crime*) or alone before a plural noun (*lesser athletes*), thus performing a function no longer idiomatically possible with less. Dating from the thirteenth century, this formal usage allows *lesser* to act as an antonym of *greater*. —*BG*

**lessen** verb **1** *the new law did little to lessen the stigma* REDUCE, make less/smaller, minimize, decrease; allay, assuage, alleviate, attenuate, palliate, ease, dull, deaden, blunt, moderate, mitigate, dampen, soften, tone down, dilute, weaken. ANTONYM increase.

**2** *the pain began to lessen* GROW LESS, grow smaller, decrease, diminish, decline, subside, abate; fade, die down/off, let up, ease off, tail off, drop (off/away), fall, dwindle, ebb, wane, recede. ANTONYM increase.

**3** *his behavior lessened him in their eyes* DIMINISH, degrade, discredit, devalue, belittle. ANTONYM aggrandize.

**lesser** adjective **1** *a lesser offense* LESS IMPORTANT, minor, secondary, subsidiary, marginal, ancillary, auxiliary, supplementary, peripheral; inferior, insignificant, unimportant, petty. ANTONYMS greater, primary.

**2** *you look down at us lesser mortals* SUBORDINATE, minor, inferior, second-class, subservient, lowly, humble. ANTONYM superior.

**lesson** noun **1** *a math lesson* CLASS, session, seminar, tutorial, lecture, period, period of instruction/teaching.

**2** **(lessons)** *they should be industrious at their lessons* EXERCISES, assignments, schoolwork, homework, study.

**3** *reading the lesson in church* BIBLE READING, scripture, text, reading, passage.

**4** *Stuart's accident should be a lesson to all parents* WARNING, deterrent, caution; example, exemplar, message, moral.

**let** verb **1** *let him sleep for now* ALLOW TO, permit to, give permission to, give leave to, authorize to, sanction to, grant the right to, license to, empower to, enable to, entitle to; *archaic* suffer to. ANTONYMS prevent, prohibit.

**2** *Wilcox opened the door to let her through* ALLOW TO GO, permit to pass; make way for. PHRASES: **let someone down** *I'm afraid I've let the team down* FAIL, fail to support, disappoint, disillusion; abandon, desert, leave stranded, leave in the lurch.

**let something down** *Maryann let down the hem on her mother's old prom dress* LENGTHEN, make longer.

**let fly 1** *he* ***let fly with*** *a brick* HURL, fling, throw, propel, pitch, lob, toss, launch; shoot, fire, blast; *informal* chuck, sling, heave.

**2** *she* ***let fly at*** *Geoffrey* LOSE ONE'S TEMPER WITH, lash out at, scold, chastise, chide, rant at, inveigh against, rail against; explode at, burst out at, let someone have it; *formal* excoriate.

**let go** *don't let go of the steering wheel* RELEASE, release one's hold on, loose/loosen one's hold on, relinquish; archaic unhand.

**let someone go** *they let half of the warehouse crew go* DISMISS, discharge, lay off, give notice to; informal sack, fire, ax, give someone their marching orders, send packing, give someone the boot, give someone the (old) heave-ho, can, pink-slip.

**let someone in** *they seemed reluctant to let me in* ALLOW TO ENTER, allow in, admit, open the door to; receive, welcome, greet.

**let someone in on something** *we can't let you in on the details just yet* INCLUDE IN, count in on, admit in on, allow to share in, let participate in, inform about, tell about.

**let someone off** **1** informal *I'll let you off this time* PARDON, forgive, grant an amnesty to; deal leniently with, be merciful to, have mercy on; acquit, absolve, exonerate, clear, vindicate; informal let someone off the hook; formal exculpate.

**2** *he let me off work* EXCUSE FROM, exempt from, spare from.

**let on** informal **1** *I never let on that I felt anxious* REVEAL, make known, tell, disclose, mention, divulge, let slip, give away, make public; blab; informal let the cat out of the bag, give the game away.

**2** *he let on that he'd won* PRETEND, feign, affect, make out, make believe, simulate.

**let something out** **1** *I let out a cry of triumph* UTTER, emit, give, give vent to, produce, issue, express, voice, release.

**2** *she let out that he'd given her a lift home* REVEAL, make known, tell, disclose, mention, divulge, let slip, give away, let it be known, blurt out.

**let someone out** *they let me out of the hospital on Monday* RELEASE, liberate, (set) free, let go, discharge; set/turn loose, allow to leave.

**let up** informal **1** *the rain has let up* ABATE, lessen, decrease, diminish, subside, relent, slacken, die down/off, ease (off), tail off; ebb, wane, dwindle, fade; stop, cease, finish.

**2** *you never let up, do you?* RELAX, ease up/off, slow down; pause, break (off), take a break, rest, stop; informal take a breather.

**3** *I promise I'll let up on him* TREAT LESS SEVERELY, be more lenient with, be kinder to; informal go easy on.

**letdown** noun *the movie was a big letdown after reading the book* DISAPPOINTMENT, anticlimax, comedown, nonevent, fiasco, setback, blow, disadvantage; informal washout.

**lethal** adjective *a lethal dose of arsenic* FATAL, deadly, mortal, death-dealing, life-threatening, murderous, killing; poisonous, toxic, noxious, venomous; dangerous, destructive, harmful, pernicious; literary deathly, nocuous. ANTONYMS harmless, safe.

**lethargic** adjective *feeling depressed and lethargic* SLUGGISH, inert, inactive, slow, torpid, lifeless; languid, listless, lazy, idle, indolent, shiftless, slothful, apathetic, weary, tired, fatigued.

**lethargy** noun *the lethargy may be related to his latest medication* SLUGGISHNESS, inertia, inactivity, inaction, slowness, torpor, torpidity, lifelessness, listlessness, languor, laziness, idleness, indolence, shiftlessness, sloth, apathy, passivity, weariness, tiredness, lassitude, fatigue, inanition; literary hebetude. ANTONYMS vigor, energy.

**letter** noun **1** *capital letters* ALPHABETICAL CHARACTER, character, sign, symbol, mark, figure, rune; Linguistics grapheme.

**2** *he wrote Len a letter* WRITTEN MESSAGE, message, written communication, communication, note, line, missive, dispatch; correspondence, news, information, intelligence, word; post, mail; formal epistle.

**3 (letters)** *a man of letters* LEARNING, scholarship, erudition, education, knowledge; intellect, intelligence, enlightenment, wisdom, sagacity, culture. PHRASE: **to the letter** *he followed her instructions to the letter* STRICTLY, precisely, exactly, accurately, closely, faithfully, religiously, punctiliously, literally, verbatim, in every detail.

**lettered** adjective *in colonial Brattleboro, this household of lettered young women was quite a curiosity* LEARNED, erudite, academic, educated, well-educated, well-read, widely read, knowledgeable, intellectual, well-schooled, enlightened, cultured, cultivated, scholarly, bookish, highbrow, studious, cerebral. ANTONYM ill-educated.

**letup** noun informal *there can be no letup in the war against drugs* ABATEMENT, lessening, decrease, diminishing, diminution, decline, relenting, remission, slackening, weakening, relaxation, dying down, easing off, tailing off, dropping away/off; respite, break, breather, interval, hiatus, suspension, cessation, stop, pause.

**level** adjective **1** *a smooth and level surface* FLAT, smooth, even, uniform, plane, flush, plumb. ANTONYMS uneven, bumpy.

**2** *he kept his voice level* UNCHANGING, steady, unvarying, even, uniform, regular, constant, invariable, unaltering; calm, unemotional, composed, equable, unruffled, serene, tranquil. ANTONYMS shaky, unsteady.

**3** *his eyes were **level with** hers* ALIGNED WITH, on the same level as, on a level with, at the same height as, in line with. ANTONYMS uneven, above, below.

▸ noun **1** *she is at a managerial level* RANK, standing, status, position; echelon, degree, grade, gradation, stage, standard, rung; class, stratum, group, grouping, set, classification.

**2** *a high level of unemployment* QUANTITY, AMOUNT, extent, measure, degree, volume, size, magnitude, intensity, proportion.

**3** *the level of water is rising* HEIGHT, altitude, elevation.

**4** *the sixth level* FLOOR, story, deck.

▸ verb **1** *tilt the pan to level the mixture* MAKE LEVEL, level out/off, make even, even out, make flat, flatten, smooth, smooth out, make uniform.

**2** *bulldozers leveled the building* RAZE, demolish, flatten, topple, destroy; tear down, knock down, pull down, bulldoze.

**3** *he leveled his opponent with a single blow* KNOCK DOWN, lay out, flatten, floor, fell; knock out; informal KO, kayo.

**4** *Carl leveled the playing field* EQUALIZE, make equal, equal, even, even up, make level.

**5** *he leveled his pistol at me* AIM, point, direct, train, focus, turn, sight.

**6** informal *I knew you'd **level with** me* BE FRANK WITH, be open with, be honest with, be aboveboard with, tell the truth to, tell all to, hide nothing from, be straightforward with, be upfront with; informal come clean with, set the record straight with.

PHRASE: **on the level** informal *Urbana is such a smooth talker, we never know for sure if she's on the level* GENUINE, straight, honest, aboveboard, fair, true, sincere, straightforward, trustworthy; informal upfront, on the up and up.

**levelheaded** adjective *how did those nitwits end up with such levelheaded children?* SENSIBLE, practical, realistic, prudent, pragmatic, wise, reasonable, rational, mature, judicious, sound, sober, businesslike, no-nonsense, composed, calm, 'calm, cool, and collected', confident, well-balanced, equable, coolheaded, self-possessed, having one's feet on the ground; informal unflappable, together, grounded. ANTONYMS excitable, foolish.

**lever** noun **1** *you can insert a lever and pry the rail off* CROWBAR, bar, jimmy.

**2** *he pulled the lever* HANDLE, grip, pull, switch.

▸ verb *he levered the door open* PRY, prize, force, wrench, pull, wrest, heave; informal jimmy.

**leverage** noun **1** *the long handles provide increased leverage* GRIP, purchase, hold; support, anchorage, force, strength.

**2** *the union's leverage at the bargaining table* INFLUENCE, power, authority, weight, sway, pull, control, say, dominance, advantage, pressure; informal clout, muscle, teeth, bargaining chip.

**levitate** noun *the spaceship slowly levitated over the cornfield* FLOAT, rise, rise into the air, hover, be suspended, glide, hang, fly, soar up.

**levity** noun *without some occasional levity, the working environment is no better than a sweatshop* LIGHTHEARTEDNESS, high spirits, vivacity, liveliness, cheerfulness, cheeriness, humor, gaiety, fun, jocularity, hilarity, frivolity, amusement, mirth, laughter, merriment, glee, comedy, wit, wittiness, jollity, joviality. ANTONYM seriousness.

**levy** verb *the government's right to levy taxes* IMPOSE, charge, exact, raise, collect; rare mulct.

▸ noun **1** *the levy of taxes* IMPOSITION, raising, collection; formal exaction.

**2** *the levy on alcohol* TAX, tariff, toll, excise, duty, imposition, impost; rare mulct.

**lewd** adjective **1** *a lewd old man* LECHEROUS, lustful, licentious, lascivious, dirty, prurient, salacious, lubricious, libidinous; debauched, depraved, degenerate, decadent, dissipated, dissolute, perverted, wanton; formal concupiscent; archaic lickerish. ANTONYM chaste.

**2** *a lewd song* VULGAR, crude, smutty, dirty, filthy, obscene, pornographic, coarse, off-color, unseemly, indecent, salacious; rude, racy, risqué, naughty, bawdy, ribald; informal blue, raunchy, X-rated, XXX, porno; euphemistic adult. ANTONYM clean.

**liability** noun **1** *journalists' liability for defamation* ACCOUNTABILITY, responsibility, legal responsibility, answerability; blame, culpability, guilt, fault. ANTONYM immunity.

**2** *they have big liabilities* FINANCIAL OBLIGATIONS, debts, arrears, dues. ANTONYM asset.

**3** *she was proving to be a liability* HINDRANCE, encumbrance, burden, handicap, nuisance, inconvenience; obstacle, impediment, disadvantage, weakness, weak link, shortcoming; millstone around one's neck, albatross, Achilles heel. ANTONYMS advantage, asset.

**liable** adjective **1** *they are liable for negligence* RESPONSIBLE, legally responsible, accountable, answerable, chargeable, blameworthy, at fault, culpable, guilty. See note at RESPONSIBLE.

**2** *my income is liable to fluctuate wildly* LIKELY, inclined, tending, disposed, apt, predisposed, prone, given.

**3** *areas **liable to** flooding* EXPOSED TO, prone to, subject to, susceptible to, vulnerable to, in danger of, at risk of.

**liaison** noun **1** *Dave was my liaison with the district manager* INTERMEDIARY, mediator, middleman, contact, link, connection, go-between, representative, agent.

**2** *a secret liaison* LOVE AFFAIR, affair, relationship, romance, attachment, fling, amour, romantic entanglement, entanglement, tryst; informal hanky-panky.

**liar** noun *even in a court of law, Jeff was a shameless liar* DECEIVER, fibber, perjurer, false witness, fabricator, equivocator; fabulist; informal storyteller.

**libation** noun **1** *they pour libations into the holy well* LIQUID OFFERING, offering, tribute, oblation.

**2** humorous *would you like a libation?* (ALCOHOLIC) DRINK, beverage, liquid refreshment; dram, draft, nip, shot; informal tipple, nightcap, pick-me-up; archaic potation.

**libel** noun *she sued two newspapers for libel* DEFAMATION, defamation of character, character assassination, calumny, misrepresentation, scandalmongering; aspersions, denigration, vilification, disparagement, derogation, insult, slander, malicious gossip; lie, slur, smear, untruth, false report; informal mudslinging, bad-mouthing.

▸ verb *she alleged the magazine had libeled her* DEFAME, malign, slander, blacken someone's name, sully someone's reputation, speak ill/evil of, traduce, smear, cast aspersions on, drag someone's name through the mud, besmirch, tarnish, taint, tell lies about, stain, impugn someone's character/integrity, vilify, denigrate, disparage, run down, stigmatize, discredit, slur; informal dis, bad-mouth; formal derogate, calumniate. See note at MALIGN.

**liberal** adjective **1** *the values of a liberal society* TOLERANT, unprejudiced, unbigoted, broad-minded, open-minded, enlightened; permissive, free, free and easy, easygoing, libertarian, indulgent, lenient. ANTONYMS narrow-minded, bigoted.

2 *a liberal social agenda* PROGRESSIVE, advanced, modern, forward-looking, forward-thinking, progressivist, enlightened, reformist, radical. ANTONYMS reactionary, conservative.

3 *a liberal education* WIDE-RANGING, broad-based, general.

4 *a liberal interpretation of divorce laws* FLEXIBLE, broad, loose, rough, free, general, nonliteral, nonspecific, imprecise, vague, indefinite. ANTONYMS strict, to the letter.

5 *a liberal coating of paint* ABUNDANT, copious, ample, plentiful, generous, lavish, luxuriant, profuse, considerable, prolific, rich; *literary* plenteous. ANTONYM scant.

6 *they were liberal with their cash* GENEROUS, openhanded, unsparing, unstinting, ungrudging, lavish, free, munificent, bountiful, beneficent, benevolent, bighearted, philanthropic, charitable, altruistic, unselfish; *literary* bounteous. ANTONYMS careful, miserly.

**liberate** verb 1 *they liberated the prisoners* SET FREE, free, release, let out, let go, set/let loose, save, rescue; emancipate, enfranchise. ANTONYMS imprison, enslave.

2 *he liberated a trinket from her jewelry box* STEAL, take; *informal* swipe, nab, pinch, borrow.

**libertine** noun *an unrepentant libertine* PHILANDERER, playboy, rake, roué, Don Juan, Lothario, Casanova, Romeo; lecher, seducer, womanizer, adulterer, debauchee, profligate, wanton; *informal* skirt-chaser, ladykiller, lech, wolf; *formal* fornicator.

**liberty** noun 1 *personal liberty* FREEDOM, independence, free rein, license, self-determination, free will, latitude. ANTONYMS constraint, slavery.

2 *the fight for liberty* INDEPENDENCE, freedom, autonomy, sovereignty, self-government, self-rule, self-determination; civil liberties, human rights. ANTONYM tyranny.

3 *the liberty to go where you please* RIGHT, birthright, prerogative, entitlement, privilege, permission, sanction, authorization, authority, license, power. ANTONYM constraint.

PHRASES: **at liberty** 1 *he was at liberty for three months* FREE, on the loose, loose, at large, unconfined; escaped, out, on the lam.

2 *you are at liberty to leave* FREE, permitted, allowed, authorized, able, entitled, eligible.

**take liberties with** *I'd appreciate it if you would refrain from taking liberties with me* ACT WITH FAMILIARITY TOWARD, show disrespect to/toward, act with impropriety with/toward, act indecorously with, be impudent with, act with impertinence to/toward; take advantage of, exploit.

PHRASE: **take the liberty** *may I take the liberty to order champagne?* PRESUME, venture, be so bold as.

**THE RIGHT WORD liberty, freedom, independence, license, permission**

The Fourth of July is the day on which Americans commemorate their nation's **independence**, a word that implies the ability to stand alone, without being sustained by anything else. While *independence* is usually associated with countries or nations, **freedom** and **liberty** more often apply to individuals. But unlike *freedom*, which implies an absence of restraint or compulsion (*the freedom to speak openly*), *liberty* implies the power to choose among alternatives rather than merely being unrestrained (*the liberty to select their own form of government*). *Freedom* can also apply to many different types of oppressive influences (*freedom from interruption; freedom to leave the room at any time*), while *liberty* often connotes deliverance or release (*he gave the slaves their liberty*). **License** may imply the *liberty* to disobey rules or regulations imposed on others, especially when there is an advantage to be gained in doing so (*poetic license*). But more often it refers to an abuse of *liberty* or the power to do whatever one pleases (*a license to sell drugs*). **Permission** is an even broader term than *license*, suggesting the capacity to act without interference or censure, usually with some degree of approval or authority (*permission to be absent from his post*).

**libidinous** adjective *libidinous impulses* LUSTFUL, lecherous, lascivious, lewd, carnal, salacious, prurient, licentious, libertine, lubricious, dissolute, debauched, depraved, degenerate, decadent, dissipated, wanton, promiscuous; *informal* wolfish; *formal* concupiscent.

**libido** noun *alcohol may impair your libido* SEX DRIVE, sexual appetite; sexual desire, desire, passion, sensuality, sexuality, lust, lustfulness; *informal* horniness; *formal* concupiscence.

**license** noun 1 *a driver's license* PERMIT, certificate, document, documentation, authorization, warrant; certification, credentials; pass, papers.

2 *you have license to make changes* PERMISSION, authority, right, a free hand, leave, authorization, entitlement, privilege, prerogative; liberty, freedom, power, latitude, scope, free rein, carte blanche, a blank check, the go-ahead. See note at LIBERTY.

3 *poetic license* DISREGARD FOR THE FACTS, inventiveness, invention, creativity, imagination, fancy, freedom, looseness.

▸ verb *we're licensed to sell beer* PERMIT, allow, authorize, grant/give authority, grant/give permission, grant/give a license; certify, empower, entitle, enable, give approval, let, qualify, sanction; *informal* rubber stamp. ANTONYM ban.

**licentious** adjective *a book that exaggerates the licentious behavior of the rich and famous* DISSOLUTE, dissipated, debauched, degenerate, immoral, naughty, wanton, decadent, depraved, sinful, corrupt; lustful, lecherous, lascivious, libidinous, prurient, lubricious, lewd, promiscuous, lickerish; *formal* concupiscent. ANTONYM moral.

**licit** adjective. See LEGITIMATE sense 1.

**lick** verb 1 *the spaniel licked his face* PASS ONE'S TONGUE OVER, touch with one's tongue, tongue; lap.

2 *informal they licked the home team 3–0.* See DEFEAT verb sense 1.

3 *informal we've got that problem licked* OVERCOME, get the better of, find an answer/solution to, conquer, beat, control, master, curb, check.

▸ noun *informal* **1** *a lick of paint* DAB, bit, drop, dash, spot, touch, splash; *informal* smidgen.

**2** *a guitar lick* SHORT SOLO, riff, line, theme.

PHRASE: **lick someone's boots/shoes** *nobody licks the boss's boots with more finesse than Little Miss* SUCK UP TO, toady to, be servile to, be obsequious to, fawn over, flatter, butter up, ingratiate oneself with, brown-nose with/to.

**licking** noun *informal* **1** *the Mariners took a licking* DEFEAT, beating, trouncing, thrashing; *informal* hiding, pasting, hammering, drubbing, shellacking.

**2** *Ray got the worst licking of his life* THRASHING, beating, flogging, whipping; *informal* walloping, hiding, pasting, whaling.

**lid** noun *the lid of a saucepan* COVER, top, cap, covering.
PHRASES: **put a lid on it** *hey, chatterbox, put a lid on it* STOP TALKING, BE QUIET, hold your tongue; *informal* shut up, hush up, shut your mouth, shut your face, shut your trap, button your lip, pipe down, put a sock in it, give it a rest, save it, not another word.
**blow the lid off** *informal intelligence officials have blown the lid off the so-called crusade against corruption* EXPOSE, reveal, make known, make public, bring into the open, disclose, divulge; *informal* spill the beans, blab.

**lie**[1] noun *loyalty had made him tell lies* UNTRUTH, falsehood, fib, fabrication, deception, invention, fiction, piece of fiction, falsification; (little) white lie, half-truth, exaggeration; *informal* tall tale, whopper, taradiddle. ANTONYM truth.

▸ verb *he lied to the police* TELL AN UNTRUTH, TELL A LIE, fib, dissemble, dissimulate, misinform, mislead, tell a white lie, perjure oneself, commit perjury, prevaricate; *informal* lie through one's teeth, stretch the truth; *formal* forswear oneself.

**THE RIGHT WORD lie, equivocate, fabricate, fib, prevaricate, rationalize**

If your spouse asks you whether you remembered to mail the tax forms and you say "Yes," even though you know they're still sitting on the passenger seat of your car, you're telling a **lie**, which is a deliberately false statement. If you launch into a lengthy explanation of the day's frustrations and setbacks, the correct word would be **prevaricate**, which is to quibble, dodge the point, or confuse the issue so as to avoid telling the truth. If you tell your spouse that you would have mailed the taxes, but then you started thinking about an important deduction you might be entitled to take and decided it would be unwise to mail them without looking into it, you're **rationalizing**, which is to come up with reasons that put your own behavior in the most favorable possible light. If you say that there was an accident in front of the post office that prevented you from finding a parking space and there really wasn't, **fabricate** is the correct verb, meaning that you've invented a false story or excuse without the harsh connotations of *lie* (*she fabricated an elaborate story about how they got lost on their way home*). **Equivocate** implies saying one thing and meaning another; it usually suggests the use of words that have more than one meaning, or whose ambiguity may be misleading. For example, if your spouse says, "Did you take care of the taxes today?" you might equivocate by saying "Yes," you took care of them—meaning that you finished completing the forms and sealing them in the envelope, but that you didn't actually get them to the post office. To **fib** is to tell a falsehood about something unimportant; it is often used as a euphemism for *lie* (*a child who fibs about eating his vegetables*).

**lie**[2] verb **1** *he was lying on a bed* RECLINE, lie down, lie back, be recumbent, be prostrate, be supine, be prone, be stretched out, sprawl, rest, repose, lounge, loll. ANTONYM stand.

**2** *her handbag lay on a chair* BE PLACED, be situated, be positioned, rest.

**3** *lying on the border of Switzerland and Austria* BE SITUATED, be located, be placed, be found, be sited.

**4** *the difficulty lies in building real quality into the products* CONSIST, be inherent, be present, be contained, exist, reside.
PHRASES: **lie heavy on** *keeping these secrets from her family lies heavy on her* TROUBLE, worry, bother, torment, oppress, nag, prey on one's mind, plague, niggle at, gnaw at, haunt; *informal* bug.
**lie low** *Nate and Rizzo will have to lie low until the trial is over* HIDE, go into hiding, conceal oneself, keep out of sight, go underground, hide out; *informal* hole up. See note at LAY.

**USAGE NOTE lie**

In the sense of telling an untruth, the verb is inflected *lie, lied, lied*.

The more troublesome inflections belong to the senses of reclining, being placed, and being situated: *lie, lay, lain*. A murderer may *lie in wait*. Yesterday he *lay in wait*. And for several days he *has lain in wait*—e.g.: "The Ramseys say an intruder may have lay [read *lain*] in wait for hours before killing the 6-year-old beauty queen." (*Austin American-Statesman*; Mar. 18, 2000.) —*BG*

**life** noun **1** *the joy of giving life to a child* EXISTENCE, being, living, animation; sentience, creation, viability. ANTONYMS death, nonexistence.

**2** *threats to life on the planet* LIVING THINGS, living beings, living creatures, the living; human/animal/plant life, fauna, flora, ecosystems; human beings, humanity, humankind, mankind, man.

**3** *an easy life* WAY OF LIFE, lifestyle, situation, fate, lot.

**4** *the last nine months of his life* LIFETIME, life span, days, time on earth, existence.

**5** *he is full of life* VIVACITY, animation, liveliness, vitality, verve, high spirits, exuberance, zest, buoyancy, enthusiasm, energy, vigor, dynamism, élan, gusto, brio, bounce, spirit, fire; movement; *informal* oomph, pizzazz, pep, zing, zip, vim.

**6** *the life of the party* MOVING SPIRIT, vital spirit, spirit, life force, lifeblood, heart, soul.

**7** *more than 1,500 lives were lost in the accident* PERSON, human being, individual, soul.

**8** *I really wanted a new car, but that's life* THE WAY OF THE WORLD, the way things go, the human condition; fate, destiny, providence, kismet, karma, fortune, luck, chance; *informal* the way the cookie crumbles, the breaks. PHRASES: **come to**

**life** 1 *the kids are finally coming to life* BECOME ACTIVE, come alive, wake up, awaken, arouse, rouse, stir; *literary* waken.

2 *the carved angel suddenly came to life* BECOME ANIMATE, come alive.

**for dear life** *we held on to the rope for dear life* DESPERATELY, with all one's might, for all one is worth, as fast/hard as possible, like the devil.

**give one's life** 1 *he would **give his life for** her* DIE FOR, lay down one's life for, sacrifice oneself for, offer one's life for, die to save.

2 *he gave his life to the company* DEDICATE ONESELF, devote oneself, give oneself, surrender oneself.

**life-and-death** adjective *a life-and-death decision* VITAL, of vital importance, crucial, critical, urgent, pressing, pivotal, momentous, important, all-important, key, serious, grave, significant; *informal* earth-shattering; *formal* of great moment. ANTONYM trivial.

**lifeblood** noun *the lifeblood of Hong Kong is trade, especially with China* LIFE FORCE, life, essential constituent, driving force, vital spark, inspiration, stimulus, essence, crux, heart, soul, core.

**lifeless** adjective 1 *a lifeless body* DEAD, departed, perished, gone, no more, passed on/away, stiff, cold, (as) dead as a doornail; *formal* deceased; *rare* demised. ANTONYM alive.

2 *a lifeless rag doll* INANIMATE, without life, inert, insentient. ANTONYM animate.

3 *a lifeless landscape* BARREN, sterile, bare, desolate, stark, arid, infertile, uncultivated, uninhabited; bleak, colorless, characterless, soulless.

4 *a lifeless performance* LACKLUSTER, spiritless, apathetic, torpid, lethargic; dull, monotonous, boring, tedious, dreary, unexciting, expressionless, emotionless, colorless, characterless. ANTONYMS vibrant, lively.

**lifelike** adjective *the doll is so lifelike* REALISTIC, true to life, representational, faithful, exact, precise, detailed, vivid, graphic, natural, naturalistic; *Art* kitchen-sink. ANTONYM unrealistic.

**lifelong** adjective *a lifelong commitment* LASTING, long-lasting, long-term, constant, stable, established, steady, enduring, permanent. ANTONYM ephemeral.

**lifestyle** noun *their privileged lifestyle* WAY OF LIFE, way of living, life, situation, fate, lot; conduct, behavior, customs, culture, habits, ways, mores; *Anthropology* lifeway.

**lifetime** noun 1 *he did a lot in his lifetime* LIFE SPAN, life, days, duration of life, one's time (on earth), existence, one's career.

2 *it would take **a lifetime*** ALL ONE'S LIFE, a very long time, an eternity, years (on end), eons; *informal* ages (and ages), an age.

**lift** verb 1 *lift the pack onto your back* RAISE, hoist, heave, haul up, heft, raise up/aloft, elevate, hold high; pick up, grab, take up, scoop up, snatch up; winch up, jack up, lever up; *informal* hump; *literary* upheave. ANTONYMS drop, put down.

2 *the news lifted his spirits* BOOST, raise, buoy up, elevate, cheer up, perk up, uplift, brighten up, gladden, encourage, stimulate, revive; *informal* buck up. ANTONYM subdue.

3 *the fog had lifted* CLEAR, rise, disperse, dissipate, disappear, vanish, dissolve. ANTONYM appear.

4 *the ban has been lifted* CANCEL, remove, withdraw, revoke, rescind, annul, void, discontinue, end, stop, terminate. ANTONYMS establish, impose.

5 *he lifted his voice* AMPLIFY, raise, make louder, increase. ANTONYMS soften, quiet.

6 *informal he lifted sections from a 1986 article* PLAGIARIZE, pirate, copy, reproduce, poach, steal; *informal* crib, rip off, pinch.

7 *informal she lifted a wallet.* See STEAL verb sense 1.

▸ noun 1 *give me a lift up* PUSH, boost, hoist, heave, thrust, shove.

2 *he gave me **a lift** to the airport* A RIDE, a drive, transportation.

3 *that goal will give his confidence a real lift* BOOST, fillip, stimulus, impetus, encouragement, spur, push; improvement, enhancement; *informal* shot in the arm, pick-me-up.

PHRASE: **lift off** *the helicopters lifted off at 1030 hours* TAKE OFF, become airborne, take to the air, take wing; be launched, blast off, rise.

**light**[1] noun 1 *the light of candles* ILLUMINATION, brightness, luminescence, luminosity, shining, gleaming, gleam, brilliance, radiance, luster, glowing, glow, blaze, glare, dazzle; sunlight, moonlight, starlight, lamplight, firelight; ray of light, beam of light; *literary* effulgence, refulgence, lambency. ANTONYM darkness.

2 *there was a light on in the hall* LAMP, wall light; headlight, headlamp, sidelight; streetlight, floodlight; lantern; flashlight.

3 *have you got a light?* MATCH, (cigarette) lighter.

4 *we'll wait for the light* DAYLIGHT, daylight hours, daytime, day; dawn, morning, daybreak, sunrise; natural light, sunlight. ANTONYMS darkness, nighttime.

5 *he saw the problem in a different light* ASPECT, angle, slant, approach, interpretation, viewpoint, standpoint, context, hue, complexion.

6 *light dawned on Loretta* UNDERSTANDING, enlightenment, illumination, comprehension, insight, awareness, knowledge. ANTONYM ignorance.

7 *an eminent legal light* EXPERT, authority, master, leader, guru, leading light, luminary.

▸ verb *Alan lit the kindling* SET ALIGHT, set light to, set burning, set on fire, set fire to, put/set a match to, ignite, kindle, spark (off). ANTONYM extinguish.

▸ adjective 1 *a light, cheerful room* BRIGHT, full of light, well-lit, well-illuminated, sunny. ANTONYMS dark, gloomy.

2 *light shades of blue and rose* LIGHT-COLORED, light-toned, pale, pale-colored, pastel. ANTONYMS dark, deep.

3 *light hair* FAIR, light-colored, blond/blonde, golden, flaxen. ANTONYMS dark, brunette.

PHRASES: **bring something to light** *the surprise inspection brought some incriminating evidence to light* REVEAL, disclose, expose, uncover, unearth, dig up/out, bring to notice, identify.

**come to light** *a fact important to this case has just come to light* BE DISCOVERED, be uncovered, be unearthed, come out, become known, become apparent, appear, materialize, emerge.

**in (the) light of** *in light of this new information, there is no reason to continue our questioning* TAKING INTO CONSIDERATION, taking into account, considering, bearing in mind, taking note of, in view of.

**light into** *informal* 1 *we started lighting into our attackers.* See SET ON/UPON at SET[1].

2 *my father lit into me for being late.* See SCOLD verb.

**light on/upon** *we'd almost given up when we lit upon this article about Mathew's murder trial* COME ACROSS, chance on/upon, hit on/upon, happen on/upon, stumble on/upon/across, find, discover, uncover, come up with.

**light up** 1 *the dashboard lit up* BECOME BRIGHT, brighten, lighten, shine, gleam, flare, blaze, glint, sparkle, shimmer, glisten, scintillate.

2 *he lit up outside the bar* START SMOKING, light a cigarette.

**light something up** 1 *a flare lit up the night sky* MAKE BRIGHT, brighten, illuminate, lighten, throw/cast light on, shine on, irradiate; *literary* illumine, illume.

2 *her enthusiasm lit up her face* ANIMATE, irradiate, brighten, cheer up, enliven.

**throw/cast/shed (some) light on** *perhaps I can shed some light on this problem* EXPLAIN, elucidate, clarify, clear up, interpret.

**out like a light** *after a day at the beach, these kids will be out like a light by eight o'clock* ASLEEP, unconscious, comatose; *informal* out cold, dead to the world.

**light**[2] adjective 1 *it's light enough to carry* EASY TO LIFT, not heavy, lightweight; easy to carry, portable. ANTONYM heavy.

2 *a light cotton robe* FLIMSY, lightweight, insubstantial, thin; delicate, floaty, gauzy, gossamer, diaphanous. ANTONYMS heavy, thick.

3 *she is light on her feet* NIMBLE, agile, lithe, limber, lissome, graceful; light-footed, fleet-footed, quick, quick-moving, spry, sprightly; *informal* twinkle-toed; *literary* fleet, lightsome. ANTONYM clumsy.

4 *a light soil* FRIABLE, sandy, easily dug, workable, crumbly, loose. ANTONYMS dense, heavy.

5 *a light dinner* SMALL, modest, simple, easily digested; *informal* low-cal. ANTONYMS heavy, rich.

6 *light duties* EASY, simple, undemanding, untaxing; *informal* cushy. ANTONYMS hard, burdensome.

7 *his eyes gleamed with light mockery* GENTLE, mild, moderate, slight; playful, lighthearted. ANTONYM serious.

8 *light reading* ENTERTAINING, lightweight, diverting, undemanding, frivolous, superficial, trivial. ANTONYMS serious, deep.

9 *a light heart* CAREFREE, lighthearted, cheerful, cheery, happy, merry, jolly, blithe, bright, sunny; buoyant, bubbly, jaunty, bouncy, breezy, optimistic, positive, upbeat, ebullient; *dated* gay.

10 *this is no light matter* UNIMPORTANT, insignificant, trivial, trifling, petty, inconsequential, superficial. ANTONYMS serious, important.

11 *light footsteps* GENTLE, delicate, soft, dainty; faint, indistinct. ANTONYM heavy.

12 *her head felt light* DIZZY, giddy, lightheaded, faint, vertiginous; *informal* woozy.

**lighten**[1] verb 1 *the first touch of dawn lightened the sky* MAKE LIGHTER, make brighter, brighten, light up, illuminate, throw/cast light on, shine on, irradiate; *literary* illumine, illume. ANTONYM darken.

2 *he used lemon juice to lighten his hair* WHITEN, make whiter, bleach, blanch, make paler. ANTONYM darken.

**lighten**[2] verb 1 *lightening the burden of taxation* MAKE LIGHTER, lessen, reduce, decrease, diminish, ease; alleviate, mitigate, allay, relieve, palliate, assuage. ANTONYMS increase, intensify.

2 *his smile lightened her spirits* CHEER (UP), brighten, gladden, hearten, perk up, lift, enliven, boost, buoy (up), uplift, revive, restore, revitalize. ANTONYM depress.

**light-fingered** adjective *our light-fingered cashier* THIEVING, stealing, pilfering, shoplifting, dishonest; *informal* sticky-fingered, crooked. ANTONYM honest.

**lightheaded** adjective *sit down if you're feeling lightheaded* DIZZY, giddy, faint, light in the head, vertiginous, reeling; *informal* woozy.

**lighthearted** adjective *a lighthearted musical* CAREFREE, cheerful, cheery, happy, merry, glad, playful, jolly, jovial, joyful, gleeful, ebullient, high-spirited, lively, blithe, bright, sunny, buoyant, vivacious, bubbly, jaunty, bouncy, breezy; entertaining, amusing, diverting; *informal* chirpy, upbeat; *dated* gay. ANTONYM miserable.

**lightly** adverb 1 *Hermione kissed him lightly on the cheek* SOFTLY, gently, faintly, delicately. ANTONYMS hard, heavily.

2 *season very lightly with paprika* SPARINGLY, slightly, sparsely, moderately, delicately. ANTONYMS intensely, abundantly.

3 *he has gotten off lightly* WITHOUT SEVERE PUNISHMENT, easily, leniently, mildly. ANTONYM severely.

4 *her views are not to be dismissed lightly* CARELESSLY, airily, heedlessly, without consideration, indifferently, unthinkingly, thoughtlessly, uncaringly, flippantly, breezily, frivolously. ANTONYM seriously.

**lightweight** adjective 1 *a lightweight jacket* THIN, light, flimsy, insubstantial; summery. ANTONYMS heavy, thick.

2 *lightweight entertainment* TRIVIAL, insubstantial, superfi-

cial, shallow, unintellectual, undemanding, frivolous; of little merit/value; *informal* Mickey Mouse. ANTONYM profound.

▸ noun *he's no lightweight* AMATEUR, second-rater, unimportant person, insignificant person, nobody, nonentity, no-name, small fry.

**like**[1] verb **1** *I like Tony* BE FOND OF, be attached to, have a soft spot for, have a liking for, have regard for, think well of, admire, respect, esteem; be attracted to, fancy, find attractive, be keen on, be taken with; be infatuated with, carry a torch for; *informal* be crazy about, have a crush on, have a thing for, have the hots for, dig, take a shine to. ANTONYM hate.

**2** *she likes gardening* ENJOY, have a taste for, have a preference for, have a liking for, be partial to, find/take pleasure in, be keen on, find agreeable, have a penchant for, have a passion for, find enjoyable; appreciate, love, adore, relish; *informal* have a thing about, be into, be mad about, be hooked on, get a kick out of. ANTONYM hate.

**3** *feel free to say what you like* CHOOSE, please, wish, want, see fit, think fit, care to, will.

**4** *how would she like it if someone did that to her?* FEEL ABOUT, regard, think about, consider.

**like**[2] preposition **1** *you're just like a teacher* SIMILAR TO, the same as, identical to.

**2** *the figure landed like a cat* IN THE SAME WAY AS, in the same manner as, in the manner of, in a similar way to.

**3** *cities like Joplin* SUCH AS, for example, for instance; in particular, namely.

**4** *he sounded mean, which isn't like him* CHARACTERISTIC OF, typical of, in character with.

▸ noun *we'll never see his like again* EQUAL, match, equivalent, counterpart, twin, parallel; *rare* compeer.

▸ adjective *a like situation* SIMILAR, much the same, comparable, corresponding, resembling, alike, analogous, parallel, equivalent, cognate, related, kindred; identical, same, matching. ANTONYM dissimilar.

**likelihood** noun *the likelihood of getting a fair trial in this court is slim | smoking greatly increases the likelihood of lung disease* PROBABILITY, chance, prospect, possibility, likeliness, odds, feasibility; risk, threat, danger; hope, promise.

**likely** adjective **1** *it seemed likely that a scandal would break* PROBABLE, distinctly possible, to be expected, odds-on, possible, plausible, imaginable; expected, anticipated, predictable, predicted, foreseeable; *informal* in the cards. ANTONYMS improbable, impossible.

**2** *a likely explanation* PLAUSIBLE, reasonable, feasible, acceptable, believable, credible, tenable, conceivable. ANTONYMS incredible, unbelievable.

**3** *a likely story!* UNLIKELY, implausible, unbelievable, incredible, untenable, unacceptable, inconceivable. ANTONYM believable.

**4** *a likely place for a picnic* SUITABLE, appropriate, apposite, fit, fitting, acceptable, right; promising, hopeful.

▸ adverb *he was likely dead* PROBABLY, in all probability, presumably, no doubt, doubtlessly; *informal* (as) like as not, chances are.

**likeness** noun **1** *her likeness to Anne is quite uncanny* RESEMBLANCE, similarity, similitude, correspondence. ANTONYM dissimilarity.

**2** *she appeared in the likeness of a ghost* SEMBLANCE, guise, appearance, outward form, form, shape, image.

**3** *a likeness of the president* REPRESENTATION, image, depiction, portrayal; picture, drawing, sketch, painting, portrait, photograph, study; statue, sculpture.

THE RIGHT WORD **likeness, affinity, analogy, resemblance, similarity, similitude**

Two sisters who are only a year apart in age and who are very similar to each other in terms of appearance and personality would be said to bear a **likeness** to one another. **Similarity** applies to people or things that are merely somewhat alike (*there was a similarity between the two women, both of whom were raised in the Midwest*), while **resemblance** suggests a similarity only in appearance or in superficial or external ways (*with their short hair and blue eyes, they bore a strong resemblance to each other*). **Affinity** adds to *resemblance* a natural kinship, temperamental sympathy, common experience, or some other relationship (*she has an affinity for young children*). **Similitude** is a more literary word meaning *likeness* or *similarity* in reference to abstract things (*a similitude of the truth*). An **analogy** is a comparison of things that are basically unlike but share certain attributes or circumstances (*he drew an analogy between the human heart and a bicycle pump*).

**likewise** adverb **1** *an ambush was out of the question, likewise poison* ALSO, in addition, too, as well, to boot; besides, moreover, furthermore.

**2** *encourage your family and friends to do likewise* THE SAME, similarly, correspondingly, in the same way, in similar fashion.

**liking** noun *his* ***liking for*** *fine wine* FONDNESS FOR, love of, affection for, penchant for, attachment to; enjoyment of, appreciation of, taste for, passion for; preference for, partiality to, predilection to; desire for, fancy for.

**lilt** noun *the lilt of her Scottish accent* CADENCE, rise and fall, inflection, intonation, rhythm, swing, beat, pulse, tempo.

**limb** noun **1** *his sore limbs* ARM, LEG, appendage; *archaic* member.

**2** *the limbs of the tree* BRANCH, bough, offshoot, shoot. PHRASE: **go out on a limb** *the government would not go out on a limb* BE PUT IN A PRECARIOUS POSITION, become vulnerable, be put in a risky situation; *informal* be sticking one's neck out.

**limber** adjective *I have to practice to keep myself limber* LITHE, supple, nimble, lissome, flexible, fit, agile, acrobatic, loose-jointed, loose-limbed. See note at FLEXIBLE. ANTONYM stiff.

PHRASE: **limber up** *limbering up for the marathon* WARM UP, loosen up, get into condition, get into shape, practice, train, stretch.

**limbo** PHRASE: **in limbo** *our mortgage approval is in limbo* IN ABEYANCE, unattended to, unfinished; suspended, deferred, postponed, put off, pending, on ice, in cold storage; unresolved, undetermined, up in the air, uncertain; *informal* on the back burner, on hold, treading water, in the balance.

**limelight** noun *she was once again enjoying the limelight* FOCUS OF ATTENTION, public attention, public interest, media attention, public eye, glare of publicity, prominence, spotlight; center stage. ANTONYM obscurity.

**limit** noun **1** *the city limits* BOUNDARY, border, bound, frontier, edge, demarcation line; perimeter, outside, confine, periphery, margin, rim.

**2** *a limit of 4,500 people* MAXIMUM, ceiling, limitation, upper limit; restriction, check, control, restraint.

**3** *resources are stretched to the limit* UTMOST, breaking point, greatest extent.

**4** *informal I've reached* ***my limit!*** ONE'S/THE BREAKING POINT, the last straw; *informal* the end, it, one's wits' end, one's/the max.

▸ verb *the pressure to limit costs* RESTRICT, curb, cap, check, hold in check, restrain, put a brake on, freeze, regulate, control, govern, delimit.

PHRASE: **off limits** *access to their mother's workshop was strictly off limits* OUT OF BOUNDS, forbidden, banned, restricted, unacceptable, taboo.

**limitation** noun **1** *a limitation on the number of guests* RESTRICTION, curb, restraint, control, check; bar, barrier, block, deterrent. ANTONYM increase.

**2** *he is aware of his own limitations* IMPERFECTION, flaw, defect, failing, shortcoming, weak point, deficiency, failure, frailty, weakness, foible. ANTONYM strength.

**limited** adjective **1** *limited resources* RESTRICTED, finite, little, tight, slight, in short supply, short; meager, scanty, sparse, few, insubstantial, deficient, inadequate, insufficient, paltry, poor, minimal. ANTONYMS ample, boundless.

**2** *the limited powers of the council* RESTRICTED, curbed, checked, controlled, restrained, delimited, rangebound, qualified. ANTONYM absolute.

**limitless** adjective *a seemingly limitless supply of free software* BOUNDLESS, unbounded, unlimited, illimitable; infinite, endless, never-ending, unending, everlasting, untold, immeasurable, bottomless, fathomless; unceasing, interminable, inexhaustible, constant, perpetual.

**limp**[1] verb *she limped out of the house* HOBBLE, walk with a limp, walk lamely, walk unevenly, walk haltingly, hitch, falter, stumble, lurch.

▸ noun *walking with* ***a limp*** LAMENESS, a hobble, an uneven gait; *Medicine* claudication.

**limp**[2] adjective **1** *a limp handshake* SOFT, flaccid, loose, slack, lax; floppy, drooping, droopy, sagging. ANTONYM firm.

**2** *we were all limp with exhaustion* TIRED, fatigued, weary, exhausted, worn out; lethargic, listless, spiritless, weak. ANTONYM energetic.

**limpid** adjective **1** *a limpid pool* CLEAR, transparent, glassy, crystal clear, crystalline, translucent, pellucid, unclouded. ANTONYM opaque.

**2** *his limpid prose* LUCID, clear, plain, understandable, intelligible, comprehensible, coherent, explicit, unambiguous, simple, vivid, sharp, crystal clear; *formal* perspicuous. ANTONYM unintelligible.

**line**[1] noun **1** *he drew a line through the name* dash, rule, bar, score; underline, underscore, stroke, slash; *technical* stria, striation.

**2** *there were lines around her eyes* WRINKLE, furrow, crease, groove, crinkle, crow's foot, laugh line.

**3** (usu. **lines**) *the classic lines of the exterior* CONTOUR, outline, configuration, shape, figure, delineation, profile.

**4** *the line between Canada and the United States* BOUNDARY, boundary line, limit, border, borderline, demarcation line, dividing line, edge, margin, perimeter, frontier.

**5** (usu. **lines**) *behind enemy lines* POSITION, formation, defense, fieldwork, front (line); trenches.

**6** *he put the wash on the line* CLOTHESLINE; cord rope, string, cable, wire, thread, twine, strand.

**7** *they waited in a line* ROW, file, lineup, queue.

**8** *a line of figures* COLUMN, row.

**9** *a long line of bad decisions* SERIES, sequence, succession, chain, string, set, cycle.

**10** *a line of flight* COURSE, route, track, path, way, run.

**11** *they took a very tough line with the industry | the party line* COURSE OF ACTION, course, procedure, technique, tactic, tack; policy, practice, approach, plan, program, position, stance, philosophy.

**12** *her own line of thought* COURSE, direction, drift, tack, tendency, trend.

**13** *informal he fed me a line* STORY, piece of fiction, fabrication; *informal* spiel.

**14** (**lines**) *he couldn't remember his lines* WORDS, part, script, speech.

**15** *my line is engineering* LINE OF WORK, work, line of business, business, field, trade, occupation, employment, profession, job, career, specialty, forte, province, department, sphere, area, area of expertise.

**16** *a new line of cologne* BRAND, kind, sort, type, variety, make.

**17** *a noble line* ANCESTRY, family, parentage, birth, descent, lineage, extraction, genealogy, roots, origin, background; stock, bloodline, pedigree.

**18** *the opening line of the poem* SENTENCE, phrase, clause, utterance; passage, extract, quotation, quote, citation.

**19** *I should drop Ralph a line* NOTE, letter, card, postcard, e-mail, message, communication, missive, memorandum; correspondence, word; *informal* memo; *formal* epistle.

▸ verb 1 *her face was lined with age* FURROW, wrinkle, crease, pucker, mark with lines.

2 *the driveway was lined by poplars* BORDER, edge, fringe, bound, rim.

PHRASES: **draw the line at** *we draw the line at keg parties* STOP SHORT OF/AT, refuse to accept, balk at; object to, take issue with, take exception to.
**in line** 1 *they stood in line for food* IN A ROW, in a file, in a lineup; *chiefly Brit.* in a queue.

2 *the advertisements are in line with the editorial style* IN AGREEMENT, in accord, in accordance, in harmony, in step, in compliance.

3 *he stood in line with the target* IN ALIGNMENT, aligned, level, at the same height; side by side.

4 *the referee kept him in line* UNDER CONTROL, in order, in check.
**in line for** *Laine is in line for a senior position* A CANDIDATE FOR, in the running for, on the short list for, being considered for.
**get a line on** *were you able to get a line on their upcoming projects?* learn something about, find out about, be informed about, hear about, hear tell about.
**lay it on the line** *go ahead, lay it on the line, I can take it* SPEAK FRANKLY, speak honestly, be direct, pull no punches, be blunt, not mince one's words, call a spade a spade; *informal* give it to someone straight.
**line up** 1 *line up for inspection* FORM A LINE, get into rows/columns, fall in; *chiefly Brit.* queue up; *Military* dress.

2 *they lined them up against the wall* ARRANGE IN LINES, put in rows, arrange in columns, align, range; *Military* dress.

3 *we've lined up an all-star cast* ASSEMBLE, put together, organize, prepare, arrange, prearrange, fix up; book, schedule.
**on the line** *a firefighter's life is on the line every day* AT RISK, in danger, in jeopardy, endangered, imperiled.
**toe the line** *the choice is yours: toe the line or pack your bags* CONFORM, obey the rules, observe the rules, comply with the rules, abide by the rules, follow the rules; *informal* play by the rules.

**line**[2] verb *they lined the handbags with a quilted rayon* PUT A LINING IN, interline, face, back, pad. PHRASE: **line one's pockets** *informal he had lined his pockets with campaign funds* MAKE MONEY, accept bribes, embezzle money; *informal* feather one's nest, graft, grift, be on the make.

**lineage** noun *tracing his paternal lineage* ANCESTRY, family, parentage, birth, descent, line, extraction, derivation, genealogy, roots, origin, background; stock, bloodline, breeding, pedigree.

**lineup** noun 1 *a star-studded lineup* LIST OF PERFORMERS, cast, company, bill, program, schedule.

2 *the Oilers' lineup* LIST OF PLAYERS, roster, team, squad, side.

**linger** verb 1 *the crowd lingered for a long time* WAIT AROUND, stay, remain, wait, stay put; loiter, dawdle, dally, take one's time; *informal* stick around, hang around, hang on; *archaic* tarry. ANTONYM leave.

2 *the infection can linger for many years* PERSIST, continue, remain, stay, endure, carry on, last, keep on/up. ANTONYMS vanish, disappear.

**lingerie** noun *fine silk lingerie* WOMEN'S UNDERWEAR, underclothes, underclothing, undergarments, foundation garments; nightwear, nightclothes; *informal* undies, underthings. See also the table at UNDERWEAR.

**lingering** adjective 1 *lingering doubts* REMAINING, surviving, persisting, abiding, nagging, niggling.

2 *a slow, lingering death* PROTRACTED, prolonged, long-drawn-out, long-lasting.

**lingo** noun *informal he quickly picked up the musicians' lingo* LANGUAGE, tongue, dialect; jargon, terminology, slang, argot, cant, patter; *informal* -ese, -speak, mumbo-jumbo. See note at DIALECT.

**link** noun 1 *a chain of steel links* LOOP, ring, connection, connector, coupling, joint.

2 *the links between transport and the environment* CONNECTION, relationship, association, linkage, tie-up.

3 *their links with the labor movement* BOND, tie, attachment, connection, relationship, association, affiliation.

4 *he was an important link in our operation* COMPONENT, constituent, element, part, piece.

▸ verb 1 *four boxes were linked together* JOIN, connect, fasten, attach, bind, unite, combine, amalgamate; clamp, secure, fix, tie, couple, yoke, hitch.

2 *the evidence linking him with the murder* ASSOCIATE, connect, relate, join, bracket.

**lionhearted** adjective *the lionhearted champion of freedom* BRAVE, courageous, valiant, gallant, intrepid, valorous, fearless, bold, daring; stouthearted, stalwart, heroic, doughty, plucky, manly; *informal* gutsy, spunky, ballsy. ANTONYM cowardly.

**lionize** verb *popular myths have lionized a man who was in fact little more than a petty thief* CELEBRATE, fête, glorify, honor, exalt, acclaim, admire, praise, extol, applaud, hail, venerate, eulogize; *formal* laud. ANTONYM vilify.

**lip** noun 1 *the lip of the crater* EDGE, rim, brim, border, verge, brink.

2 *informal don't give me any lip!* INSOLENCE, impertinence, impudence, cheek, cheekiness, rudeness, audacity, effrontery, disrespect; *informal* mouth, back-talk, guff, sauce. PHRASES: **bite one's lip** *I wanted to say something about that hideous dress, but I bit my lip* KEEP QUIET, keep one's mouth shut, say nothing, bite one's tongue.
**keep a stiff upper lip** *in my neighborhood, you learned early to keep a stiff upper lip when life ain't all sweetness and roses* KEEP CONTROL OF ONESELF, not show emotion, appear unaffected; *informal* keep one's cool.

**liquid** adjective 1 *liquid fuels* FLUID, liquefied; melted, molten, thawed, dissolved; *Chemistry* hydrous. ANTONYMS solid, gaseous.

2 *her liquid eyes* CLEAR, limpid, crystal clear, crystalline, pellucid, unclouded, bright. ANTONYMS cloudy, opaque.

3 *liquid sounds* PURE, clear, mellifluous, dulcet, mellow, sweet, sweet-sounding, soft, melodious, harmonious. ANTONYMS disharmonious, cacophonous.

4 *liquid assets* CONVERTIBLE, disposable, usable, spendable. ANTONYMS tied up, unavailable.

▸ noun *a vat of liquid* FLUID, moisture; liquor, solution, juice.

**liquidate** verb 1 *the company was liquidated* CLOSE DOWN, wind up, put into liquidation, dissolve, disband.

2 *he liquidated his share portfolio* CONVERT TO CASH, convert, cash in, sell off, sell up.

3 *liquidating the public debt* PAY OFF, pay, pay in full, settle, clear, discharge, square, honor.

4 *informal they were liquidated in bloody purges.* See KILL verb sense 1.

**liquor** noun 1 *he liked his liquor* ALCOHOL, spirits, drink, alcoholic drink, intoxicating liquor, intoxicant; *informal* grog, firewater, rotgut, the hard stuff, the bottle, hooch, moonshine; juice, the sauce.

2 *strain the liquor into the sauce* STOCK, broth, bouillon, juice, liquid.

**list**[1] noun *a list of the world's wealthiest people* CATALOG, inventory, record, register, roll, file, index, directory, listing, checklist, enumeration.

▸ verb *the accounts are listed alphabetically* RECORD, register, make a list of, enter; itemize, enumerate, catalog, file, log, categorize, inventory; classify, group, sort, rank, alphabetize, index.

**list**[2] verb *the boat listed to one side* LEAN, lean over, tilt, tip, heel, heel over, keel over, careen, cant, pitch, incline, slant, slope, bank.

**listen** verb 1 *are you listening?* HEAR, pay attention, be attentive, attend, concentrate; keep one's ears open, prick up one's ears; *informal* be all ears, lend an ear; *literary* hark; *archaic* hearken.

2 *policy-makers should* ***listen to*** *popular opinion* PAY ATTENTION TO, take heed of, heed, take notice of, take note of, mind, mark, bear in mind, take into consideration, take into account, tune in to. PHRASE: **listen in** *she handed him a note that said that the police were listening in* EAVESDROP, spy, overhear, tap, wiretap, bug, monitor.

**listless** adjective *this heat makes me listless* | *a listless performance* LETHARGIC, enervated, spiritless, lifeless, languid, languorous, inactive, inert, sluggish, torpid. ANTONYM energetic.

**litany** noun 1 *reciting the litany* PRAYER, invocation, supplication, devotion; *archaic* orison.

2 *a litany of complaints* RECITAL, recitation, enumeration; list, listing, catalog, inventory.

**literacy** noun *testing for literacy* ABILITY TO READ AND WRITE, reading/writing proficiency; learning, book learning, education, scholarship, schooling.

**literal** adjective 1 *the literal sense of the word "dreadful"* STRICT, factual, plain, simple, exact, straightforward; unembellished, undistorted; objective, correct, true, accurate, genuine, authentic. ANTONYM figurative.

2 *a literal translation* WORD-FOR-WORD, verbatim, letter-for-letter; exact, precise, faithful, close, strict, accurate. ANTONYM loose.

**literary** adjective 1 *literary works* WRITTEN, poetic, artistic, dramatic.

2 *her literary friends* SCHOLARLY, learned, intellectual, cultured, erudite, bookish, highbrow, bluestocking, lettered, academic, cultivated; well-read, widely read, educated, well-educated.

3 *literary language* FORMAL, written, poetic, dramatic; elaborate, ornate, flowery; inkhorn.

**literate** adjective 1 *many of the workers were not literate* ABLE TO READ/WRITE, educated, schooled. ANTONYM illiterate.

2 *her literate friends* EDUCATED, well-educated, well-read, widely read, scholarly, learned, knowledgeable, lettered, cultured, cultivated, sophisticated, well-informed. ANTONYM ignorant.

3 *he was computer literate* KNOWLEDGEABLE, well-versed, savvy, smart, conversant, competent; *informal* up on, up to speed on. ANTONYM ignorant.

**literature** noun 1 *English literature* WRITTEN WORKS, writings, writing, creative writing, literary texts, compositions.

2 *the literature on prototype theory* PUBLICATIONS, published writings, texts, reports, studies.

3 *election literature* PRINTED MATTER, brochures, leaflets, pamphlets, circulars, flyers, handouts, handbills, bulletins, fact sheets, publicity, propaganda, notices.

**lithe** adjective *lithe dancers* AGILE, graceful, supple, limber, lithesome, loose-limbed, nimble, deft, flexible, lissome, slender, slim, willowy. ANTONYM clumsy.

**litigation** noun *his attorneys advised him to avoid the litigation that Comstock was suggesting* LEGAL PROCEEDINGS, legal action, lawsuit, legal dispute, legal case, case, suit, prosecution, indictment.

**litter** noun 1 *never drop litter* GARBAGE, refuse, junk, waste, debris, scraps, leavings, fragments, detritus, trash, rubbish.

2 *the litter of papers around her* CLUTTER, jumble, muddle, mess, heap, disorder, untidiness, confusion, disarray; *informal* shambles.

3 *a litter of kittens* BROOD, family.

4 *she was carried on a litter* SEDAN CHAIR, palanquin; stretcher.

▸ verb 1 *clothes littered the floor* MAKE UNTIDY, mess up, make a mess of, clutter up, be strewn about, be scattered about; *informal* make a shambles of.

2 *a paper littered with quotes* FILL, pack, load, clutter.

**little** adjective 1 *a little writing desk* SMALL, small-scale, compact; mini, miniature, tiny, minute, minuscule; toy, baby, pocket, undersized, dwarf, midget, wee; *informal* teeny-weeny, teensy-weensy, itsy-bitsy, itty-bitty, little-bitty, half-pint, vest-pocket, li'l, micro. See note at SMALL. ANTONYMS big, large.

2 *a little man* SHORT, small, slight, petite, diminutive, tiny; elfin, dwarfish, midget, pygmy, Lilliputian; *informal* teeny-weeny, pint-sized, peewee. ANTONYMS big, large.

3 *my little sister* YOUNG, younger, junior, small, baby, infant. ANTONYMS big, elder.

4 *I was a bodyguard for a little while* BRIEF, short, short-lived; fleeting, momentary, transitory, transient; fast, quick, hasty, cursory. ANTONYM long.

5 *a few little problems* MINOR, unimportant, insignificant, trivial, trifling, petty, paltry, inconsequential, nugatory; *informal* dinky, piddling. ANTONYMS important, significant.

6 *they have little political influence* HARDLY ANY, not much, slight, scant, limited, restricted, modest, little or/to no, minimal, negligible. ANTONYM considerable.

7 *you little sneak* CONTEMPTIBLE, mean, spiteful, petty, small-minded.

▸ adverb 1 *he is little known as a singer* | *they little thought* HARDLY, barely, scarcely, not much, not at all, slightly, only slightly. ANTONYM well.

2 *his art has been little seen in Canada* RARELY, seldom, infrequently, hardly, hardly ever, scarcely, scarcely ever, not much. ANTONYM often.

PHRASES: **a little** 1 *add a little vinegar* SOME, a small amount of, a bit of, a touch of, a soupçon of, a dash of, a taste of, a spot of; a shade of, a suggestion of, a trace of, a hint of, a suspicion of; a dribble of, a splash of, a pinch of, a sprinkling of, a speck of; *informal* a smidgen of, a tad of.

2 *after a little, Oliver came in* A SHORT TIME, a little while, a bit, an interval, a short period; a minute, a moment, a second, an instant; *informal* a sec, a mo, a jiffy.

3 *this reminds me a little of the Adriatic* SLIGHTLY, faintly, remotely, vaguely; somewhat, a little bit, to some degree.

**little by little** *little by little, the house fell into disrepair* GRADUALLY, slowly, by degrees, by stages, step by step, bit by bit, progressively; subtly, imperceptibly.

**liturgy** noun *the Anglican liturgy* RITUAL, worship, service, ceremony, rite, observance, celebration, sacrament; tradition, custom, practice, rubric; *formal* ordinance.

**live**[1] verb 1 *the greatest mathematician who ever lived* EXIST, be alive, be, have life; breathe, draw breath, walk the earth. ANTONYMS die, be dead.

2 *I live in Arkansas* RESIDE IN, have one's home in, have one's residence in, be settled in; be housed in, lodge in; inhabit, occupy, populate; *formal* dwell in, be domiciled in.

3 *they lived quietly* PASS/SPEND ONE'S LIFE, have a lifestyle; behave, conduct oneself; *formal* comport oneself.

4 *she had lived a difficult life* EXPERIENCE, spend, pass, lead, have, go through, undergo.

5 *Fred lived by his wits* SURVIVE, make a living, earn one's living, eke out a living; subsist, support oneself, sustain oneself, make ends meet, keep body and soul together.

6 *you should get out there and live* ENJOY ONESELF, enjoy life, have fun, live life to the full/fullest. PHRASES: **live it up** *informal* *they're living it up in Hawaii* LIVE EXTRAVAGANTLY, live in the lap of luxury, live in clover; carouse, revel, enjoy oneself, have a good time, go on a spree; *informal* party, paint the town red, have a ball, live high on/off the hog; *archaic* wassail.

**live off/on** *the gulls live off discarded fish* SUBSIST ON, feed on/off, eat, consume.

**live**[2] adjective 1 *live bait* LIVING, alive, having life, breathing, animate, sentient. ANTONYMS dead, inanimate.

2 *a live performance* IN THE FLESH, personal, in person, not recorded. ANTONYM recorded.

3 *a live wire* ELECTRIFIED, charged, powered, active; *informal* hot. ANTONYM inactive.

4 *live coals* HOT, glowing, red hot, aglow; burning, alight, flaming, aflame, blazing, ignited, on fire; *literary* afire.

5 *a live grenade* UNEXPLODED, explosive, active; unstable, volatile. ANTONYM inactive.

PHRASE: **live wire** *informal* *that Goldie is a real live wire* ENERGETIC PERSON; *informal* fireball, human dynamo, powerhouse, life of the party.

**livelihood** noun *thousands of people relied on that one factory for their livelihood* INCOME, source of income, means of support, living, subsistence, keep, maintenance, sustenance, nourishment, daily bread; job, work, employment, occupation, vocation; *informal* bread and butter.

**lively** adjective 1 *a lively young woman* ENERGETIC, active, animated, dynamic, full of life, outgoing, spirited, high-spirited, vivacious, enthusiastic, vibrant, buoyant, exuberant, effervescent, cheerful; bouncy, bubbly, perky, sparkling, zestful; *informal* full of beans, chirpy, chipper, peppy. ANTONYMS listless, lifeless.

2 *a lively bar* BUSY, crowded, bustling, buzzing; vibrant, boisterous, jolly, festive; *informal* buzzy, hopping. ANTONYMS quiet, dead.

3 *a lively debate* HEATED, vigorous, animated, spirited, enthusiastic, forceful; exciting, interesting, memorable. ANTONYMS lifeless, dull.

4 *a lively portrait of the local community* VIVID, colorful, striking, graphic, bold, strong. ANTONYMS lifeless, dull.

**liven** PHRASES: **liven up** *we livened up when Edie arrived* BRIGHTEN UP, cheer up, perk up, revive, rally, pick up, bounce back; *informal* buck up.

**liven someone/something up** *the new sofa livens up the whole room* BRIGHTEN UP, cheer up, enliven, animate, raise someone's spirits, perk up, spice up, make lively, wake up, invigorate, revive, refresh, vivify, galvanize, stimulate, stir up, get going; *informal* buck up, pep up.

**livid** adjective **1** *informal Mom was absolutely livid.* See FURIOUS sense 1.

**2** *a livid bruise* PURPLISH, bluish, dark, discolored, purple, grayish-blue; bruised; angry, black and blue. See note at PALE[2].

**living** noun **1** *she cleaned floors for a living* LIVELIHOOD, (source of) income, means of support, subsistence, keep, maintenance, sustenance, nourishment, daily bread; job, work, employment, occupation, vocation; *informal* bread and butter.

**2** *healthy living* WAY OF LIFE, lifestyle, way of living, life; conduct, behavior, activities, habits.

▸ adjective **1** *living organisms* ALIVE, live, having life, animate, sentient; breathing, existing, existent; *informal* alive and kicking. See note at ALIVE. ANTONYMS dead, extinct.

**2** *a living language* CURRENT, contemporary, present; in use, active, surviving, extant, persisting, remaining, existing, in existence. ANTONYMS dead, extinct.

**3** *a living hell* COMPLETE, total, utter, absolute, real, veritable, perfect, out-and-out, downright.

**living room** noun *there is no phone in the living room* SITTING ROOM, front room, family room, living area, great room, den, lounge.

**load** noun **1** *he has **a load** to deliver* CARGO, freight, a consignment, a delivery, a shipment, goods, merchandise; a pack, a bundle, a parcel; a truckload, a shipload, a boatload, a vanload.

**2** *informal I bought **a load of** clothes* A LOT OF, a great deal of, a large amount/quantity of, an abundance of, a wealth of, a mountain of; many, plenty of; *informal* a heap of, a mass of, a pile of, a stack of, a ton of, lots of, heaps of, masses of, piles of, stacks of, tons of.

**3** *a heavy teaching load* COMMITMENT, responsibility, duty, obligation, charge, burden; trouble, worry, strain, pressure.

▸ verb **1** *we quickly loaded the van* FILL, fill up, pack, charge, stock, stack, lade.

**2** *Larry loaded boxes into the jeep* PACK, stow, store, stack, bundle; place, deposit, put away.

**3** *loading the committee with responsibilities* BURDEN, weigh down, saddle, charge; overburden, overwhelm, encumber, tax, strain, trouble, worry.

**4** *Richard loaded Marshal with honors* REWARD, ply, regale, shower.

**5** *he loaded a gun* PRIME, charge, prepare to fire/use.

**6** *load the cassette into the camcorder* INSERT, put, place, slot.

**7** *the dice are loaded against him* BIAS, rig, fix; weight.

**loaded** adjective **1** *a loaded freight train* FULL, filled, laden, packed, stuffed, crammed, brimming, stacked; *informal* chock-full, chockablock.

**2** *a loaded gun* PRIMED, charged, armed, ready to fire.

**3** *informal they have no money worries, they're loaded.* See RICH sense 1.

**4** *informal he came home from the party loaded.* See INTOXICATED.

**5** *loaded dice* BIASED, rigged, fixed; juiced; weighted.

**6** *a loaded question* CHARGED, sensitive, delicate.

**loaf** verb *he was just loafing all day at the beach* LAZE, lounge, loll, idle, waste time; *informal* hang around, bum around, futz around.

**loan** noun *a loan of $7,000* CREDIT, advance; mortgage, overdraft; lending, moneylending.

▸ verb **1** *he loaned me his car* LEND, advance, give credit; give on loan, lease, charter.

**2** *the majority of exhibits have been loaned* BORROW, receive/take on loan.

**loath** adjective *they were loath to take risks* RELUCTANT, unwilling, disinclined, ill-disposed; averse, opposed, resistant. ANTONYM willing.

**loathe** verb *I loathe their so-called music* HATE, detest, abhor, execrate, have a strong aversion to, feel repugnance toward, not be able to bear/stand, be repelled by. See note at DESPISE. ANTONYM love.

**loathing** noun *the loathing she feels for Karyn is understandable* HATRED, hate, detestation, abhorrence, abomination, execration, odium; antipathy, dislike, hostility, animosity, ill feeling, bad feeling, malice, animus, enmity, aversion; repugnance.

**loathsome** adjective *his first wife was a loathsome creature* HATEFUL, detestable, abhorrent, repulsive, odious, repugnant, repellent, disgusting, revolting, sickening, abominable, despicable, contemptible, reprehensible, execrable, damnable; vile, horrible, hideous, nasty, obnoxious, gross, foul, horrid; *informal* yucky.

**lob** verb *they lobbed grenades onto the gun platform* THROW, toss, fling, pitch, hurl, pelt, sling, launch, propel; *informal* chuck, heave.

**lobby** noun **1** *the hotel lobby* ENTRANCE HALL, hallway, entrance, hall, vestibule, foyer, reception area.

**2** *the antigun lobby* SPECIAL INTEREST GROUP, interest group, pressure group; movement, campaign, crusade; lobbyists, supporters; faction, camp.

▸ verb **1** *readers are urged to lobby their legislators* SEEK TO INFLUENCE, try to persuade, bring pressure to bear on, importune, sway; petition, solicit, appeal to, pressurize.

**2** *a group **lobbying for** better rail services* CAMPAIGN FOR, crusade for, press for, push for, ask for, call for, demand; promote, advocate, champion.

**local** adjective **1** *local government* COMMUNITY, district, neighborhood, regional, city, town, municipal, county. ANTONYMS national, global.

**2** *a local restaurant* NEIGHBORHOOD, nearby, near, at hand, close by; accessible, handy, convenient.

**3** *a local infection* CONFINED, restricted, contained, localized. ANTONYMS general, widespread.

▸ noun *complaints from the locals* LOCAL PERSON, native, inhabitant, resident. ANTONYM outsider.

**locale** noun *the advantages of living in a rural locale* PLACE, site, spot, area; position, location, setting, scene, venue, background, backdrop, environment; neighborhood, district, region, locality.

**localize** verb *our efforts to localize the conflict* LIMIT, restrict, confine, contain, circumscribe, concentrate, delimit. ANTONYM generalize.

**locate** verb **1** *help me locate this photograph* FIND, discover, pinpoint, detect, track down, unearth, sniff out, smoke out, search out, ferret out, uncover.

**2** *a company located near Pittsburgh* SITUATE, site, position, place, base; put, build, establish, found, station, install, settle.

**location** noun *we've found the perfect location for our family reunion* POSITION, place, situation, site, locality, locale, spot, whereabouts, point; scene, setting, area, environment; bearings, orientation; venue, address; *technical* locus.

**lock** noun *the lock on the door* BOLT, catch, fastener, clasp, bar, hasp, latch.

▸ verb **1** *he locked the door* BOLT, fasten, bar, secure, seal; padlock, latch, chain. ANTONYMS unlock, open.

**2** *they locked arms* JOIN, interlock, intertwine, link, mesh, engage, unite, connect, yoke, mate; couple. ANTONYMS separate, divide.

**3** *the wheels locked* BECOME STUCK, stick, jam, become/make immovable, become/make rigid.

**4** *he locked her in an embrace* CLASP, grasp, embrace, hug, squeeze, clench.

PHRASES: **lock horns** *he's locked horns with every boss he's ever had* ARGUE, quarrel, fight, disagree, squabble, bicker.
**lock lips** *informal I saw you locking lips with Quinn* KISS; *informal* smooch, peck, neck, canoodle, make out.
**lock someone out of** *we were locked out of the conference* KEEP OUT OF, shut out of/from, refuse entrance to, deny admittance to; exclude from, bar from, debar from, ban from.
**lock someone up** *take him away and lock him up* IMPRISON, jail, incarcerate, send to prison, put behind bars, put under lock and key, put in chains, clap in irons, cage, pen, coop up; *informal* put away, put inside.

**lockup** noun *Eileen spent the night in lockup | the lockup in this town is a historical landmark* JAIL, prison, cell, detention center, jailhouse, penitentiary; *informal* slammer, jug, can, brig, clink, big house, cooler, hoosegow, cage, pen, pokey.

**locomotion** noun *the lemur's amusingly agile locomotion* MOVEMENT, motion, moving; travel, traveling; mobility, motility; walking, running; progress, progression, passage; *formal* perambulation.

**lodge** noun **1** *a hunting lodge* HOUSE, cottage, cabin, chalet.

**2** *we'll eat up at the lodge* MAIN HALL, main building, dining hall.

**3** *a beaver's lodge* DEN, lair, hole, set; retreat, haunt, shelter.

**4** *a Masonic lodge* HALL, clubhouse, meeting room.

**5** *the porter's lodge* GATEHOUSE, cottage.

▸ verb **1** *William lodged at our house* RESIDE, board, stay, live, rent rooms, be put up, be quartered, room; *formal* dwell, be domiciled, sojourn; *archaic* abide.

**2** *they were lodged at an inn* ACCOMMODATE, put up, take in, house, board, billet, quarter, shelter.

**3** *we lodged a complaint* SUBMIT, register, enter, put forward, advance, lay, present, tender, proffer, put on record, record, file.

**4** *the bullet lodged in his back* BECOME FIXED, embed itself, become embedded, become implanted, get/become stuck, stick, catch, become caught, wedge.

**lodging** noun *the lodging provided at the farm was charming* ACCOMMODATIONS, rooms, chambers, living quarters, place to stay, a roof over one's head, housing, shelter; *informal* digs, pad, nest; *formal* abode, residence, dwelling, dwelling place, habitation.

**lofty** adjective **1** *a lofty tower* TALL, high, giant, towering, soaring, skyscraping. ANTONYMS low, short.

**2** *lofty ideals* NOBLE, exalted, high, high-minded, worthy, grand, fine, elevated, sublime. ANTONYMS base, lowly.

**3** *lofty disdain* HAUGHTY, arrogant, disdainful, supercilious, condescending, scornful, patronizing, contemptuous, self-important, conceited, snobbish; aloof, standoffish; *informal* stuck-up, snooty, snotty, hoity-toity. ANTONYM modest.

**log** noun **1** *a fallen log* BRANCH, trunk; piece of wood; **(logs)** timber, firewood.

**2** *a log of phone calls* RECORD, register, logbook, journal, diary, minutes, chronicle, daybook, record book, ledger, account, tally.

▸ verb **1** *all complaints are logged* REGISTER, record, make a note of, note down, write down, jot down, put in writing, enter, file.

**2** *the pilot had logged 95 hours* ATTAIN, achieve, chalk up, make, do, go.

**3** *he was injured while logging* CUT DOWN TREES, chop down trees, fell trees, clear cut, harvest trees.

PHRASE: **log in** *just go to our Web site and log in* SIGN IN, register, enter, log on.

**logic** noun **1** *this case appears to defy all logic* REASON, judgment, logical thought, rationality, wisdom, sense, good sense, common sense, sanity; *informal* horse sense.

**2** *the logic of their argument* REASONING, line of reasoning, rationale, argument, argumentation.

**logical** adjective **1** *information displayed in a logical fashion* REASONED, well-reasoned, reasonable, rational, left-brained, sound, cogent, well-thought-out, valid; coherent, clear, well-organized, systematic, orderly, methodical, analytical, consistent, objective. ANTONYMS illogical, irrational.

**2** *the logical outcome* NATURAL, reasonable, sensible, understandable; predictable, unsurprising, only to be expected, most likely, likeliest, obvious. ANTONYMS unlikely, surprising.

**logistics** plural noun *the logistics of deploying forces in Afghanistan* ORGANIZATION, planning, plans, management, arrangement, administration, orchestration, coordination, execution, handling, running.

**logo** noun *a sweatshirt with the company logo* EMBLEM, trademark, brand, device, figure, symbol, design, sign, mark; insignia, crest, seal.

**loiter** verb **1** *he loitered at bus stops* LINGER, wait, skulk; loaf, lounge, idle, laze, waste time, lollygag; *informal* hang around; *archaic* tarry.

**2** *they loitered along the river bank* DAWDLE, dally, stroll, amble, saunter, meander, drift, putter, take one's time; *informal* dilly-dally, mosey.

THE RIGHT WORD **loiter, dally, dawdle, idle, lag**

Someone who hangs around downtown after the stores are closed and appears to be deliberately wasting time is said to **loiter**, a verb that connotes improper or sinister motives (*the police warned the boys not to loiter*). To **dawdle** is to pass time leisurely or to pursue something halfheartedly (*dawdle in a stationery shop; dawdle over a sinkful of dishes*). Someone who **dallies** dawdles in a particularly pleasurable and relaxed way, with connotations of amorous activity (*he dallied with his girlfriend when he should have been delivering papers*). **Idle** suggests that the person makes a habit of avoiding work or activity (*idle away the hours of a hot summer day*), while **lag** suggests falling behind or failing to maintain a desirable rate of progress (*she lagged several yards behind her classmates as they walked to the museum*).

**loll** verb **1** *he lolled in an armchair* LOUNGE, sprawl, drape oneself, stretch oneself; slouch, slump; laze, luxuriate, put one's feet up, lean back, sit back, recline, relax, take it easy, take a load off.

**2** *her head lolled to one side* HANG DOWN, hang loosely, hang, droop, dangle, sag, drop, flop.

**lone** adjective *a lone police officer* SOLITARY, single, solo, unaccompanied, unescorted, alone, by oneself/itself, sole, companionless; detached, isolated.

**lonely** adjective **1** *I felt very lonely* ISOLATED, alone, lonesome, friendless, with no one to turn to, forsaken, abandoned, rejected, unloved, unwanted, outcast; gloomy, sad, depressed, desolate, forlorn, cheerless, down, blue. ANTONYM popular.

**2** *the lonely life of a writer* SOLITARY, unaccompanied, lone, by oneself/itself, companionless. ANTONYM sociable.

**3** *a lonely road* DESERTED, uninhabited, unfrequented, unpopulated, desolate, isolated, remote, out of the way, secluded, off the beaten track/path, in the back of beyond, godforsaken; *informal* in the middle of nowhere. ANTONYMS populous, crowded.

**loner** noun *a loner from parts unknown* RECLUSE, introvert, lone wolf, hermit, solitary, misanthrope, outsider; *historical* anchorite.

**long**[1] adjective *a long silence* LENGTHY, extended, prolonged, extensive, protracted, long-lasting, long-drawn-out, drawn-out, spun out, dragged out, seemingly endless, lingering, interminable. ANTONYMS short, brief.

PHRASE: **before long** *we'll be in Kentucky before long* SOON, shortly, presently, in the near future, in a little while, by and by, in a minute, in a moment, in a second; *informal* anon, in a jiffy; *dated* directly; *literary* ere long.

**long**[2] verb *I* ***longed for*** *a vacation* YEARN FOR, pine for, ache for, hanker for/after, hunger for, thirst for, itch for, be eager for, be desperate for; crave, dream of, set one's heart on; *informal* have a yen for, be dying for.

**longing** noun *a longing for the countryside* YEARNING, pining, craving, ache, burning, hunger, thirst, hankering; *informal* yen, itch.

▸ adjective *a longing look* YEARNING, pining, craving, hungry, thirsty, hankering, wistful, covetous.

**long-lasting** adjective *our long-lasting friendship* ENDURING, lasting, abiding, long-lived, long-running, long-established, long-standing, lifelong, deep-rooted, time-honored, traditional, permanent. ANTONYMS short-lived, ephemeral.

**long-standing** adjective *a long-standing business partnership* WELL-ESTABLISHED, long-established; time-honored, traditional, age-old; abiding, enduring, long-lived, surviving, persistent, prevailing, perennial, deep-rooted, long-term, confirmed. ANTONYMS new, recent.

**long-suffering** adjective *her long-suffering parents* PATIENT, forbearing, tolerant, uncomplaining, stoic, stoical, resigned; easygoing, indulgent, charitable, accommodating, forgiving, understanding. ANTONYMS impatient, complaining.

**long-winded** adjective *long-winded speeches* VERBOSE, wordy, lengthy, long, overlong, prolix, prolonged, protracted, long-drawn-out, interminable; discursive, diffuse, rambling, tortuous, meandering, repetitious, maundering; *informal* windy. ANTONYMS concise, succinct, laconic.

**look** verb **1** *Mrs. Wright* ***looked at*** *him* GLANCE AT, gaze at, stare at, gape at, peer at; peep at, peek, take a look at; watch, observe, view, regard, examine, inspect, eye, scan, scrutinize, survey, study, contemplate, consider, take in, ogle; *informal* take a gander at, rubberneck, goggle, give someone/something a/the once-over, get a load of, eyeball; *literary* behold. ANTONYM ignore.

**2** *her room* ***looked out on*** *Broadway* COMMAND A VIEW OF, face, overlook, front.

**3** *they looked shocked* SEEM, seem to be, appear, appear to be, have the appearance/air of being, give the impression of being, give every appearance/indication of being, strike someone as being.

▸ noun **1** *here's the latest analysis—let's give it a look* GLANCE, view, examination, study, inspection, observation, scan, survey, peep, peek, glimpse, gaze, stare; *informal* eyeful, gander, look-see, once-over, squint.

**2** *the look on her face* EXPRESSION, mien.

**3** *that rustic look* APPEARANCE, air, aspect, bearing, cast, manner, mien, demeanor, facade, impression, effect.

**4** *this year's look* FASHION, style, vogue, mode.

PHRASES: **look after** *Janie looks after our goats and llamas* TAKE CARE OF, care for, attend to, minister to, tend, mind, keep an eye on, keep safe, be responsible for, protect; nurse, babysit, house-sit.

**look back on** *those songs really make me look back on my college days* REFLECT ON, think back to, remember, recall, reminisce about, harken back to.

**look down on** *we never understood why Papa looked down on the Italian families in our building* DISDAIN, scorn, regard with contempt, look down one's nose at, sneer at, despise.

**look for** *he's looking for a book about begonias* SEARCH FOR, hunt for, try to find, seek, try to track down, forage for, scout out, quest for/after.

**look forward to** *I look forward to Rebecca's call* AWAIT WITH PLEASURE, eagerly anticipate, lick one's lips over, be unable to wait for, count the days until.

**look into** *they promised to look into our complaints* INVESTIGATE, inquire into, ask questions about, go into, probe, explore, follow up, research, study, examine; *informal* check out, give something a/the once-over, scope out.

**look like** *in his overcoat he looks like an undertaker* RESEMBLE, bear a resemblance to, look similar to, take after, have the look of, have the appearance of, remind one of, make one think of; *informal* be the spitting image of, be a dead ringer for.

**look on/upon** *people he looked on as friends took advantage of him* REGARD, consider, think of, deem, judge, see, view, count, reckon.

**look out** *you'll get burned if you don't look out* BEWARE, watch out, be on (one's) guard, be alert, be wary, be vigilant, be careful, take care, be cautious, pay attention, take heed, keep one's eyes open/peeled, keep an eye out; watch your step.

**look something over** *he looked over the engineer's reports* INSPECT, examine, scan, cast an eye over, take stock of, vet, view, look through, peruse, read through, check out; *informal* give something a/the once-over, eyeball.

**look to 1** *we must look to the future* CONSIDER, think about, turn one's thoughts to, focus on, take heed of, pay attention to, attend to, address, mind, heed.

**2** *they look to the government for help* TURN TO, resort to, have recourse to, fall back on, rely on.

**look up 1** *things are looking up* IMPROVE, get better, pick up, come along/on, progress, make progress, make headway, perk up, rally, take a turn for the better.

**2** *she looked up his number* SEARCH FOR, look for, try to find.

**look someone up** *informal I'll look you up next time I'm in Tacoma* GO TO VISIT, pay a visit to, call on, go to see, look in on, visit with, go see; *informal* drop in on, drop by, pop by.

**look up to** *some of the more self-centered ballplayers resent the responsibility of having thousands of kids look up to them* ADMIRE, have a high opinion of, think highly of, hold in high regard, regard highly, rate highly, respect, esteem, value, venerate.

**look-alike** noun *a contest to see who is the most convincing Alfred E. Neuman look-alike* DOUBLE, twin, clone, duplicate, exact likeness, replica, copy, facsimile, doppelgänger; *informal* spitting image, dead ringer.

**lookout** noun **1** *he saw the smoke from the lookout* OBSERVATION POST, lookout point, lookout station, lookout tower, watchtower.

**2** *a scenic lookout* VIEW, vista, prospect, panorama, scene, aspect, outlook.

**3** *he agreed to act as lookout* WATCHMAN, watch, guard, sentry, sentinel. PHRASE: **be on the lookout/keep a lookout** *be on the lookout for enemy aircraft* KEEP WATCH, keep an eye out, keep one's eyes peeled, keep a vigil, be alert, be vigilant, be on the qui vive.

**loom** verb **1** *ghostly shapes loomed out of the fog* EMERGE, appear, come into view, take shape, materialize, reveal itself.

**2** *the church loomed above him* SOAR, tower, rise, rear up; overhang, overshadow, dominate.

**3** *without reforms, disaster looms* BE IMMINENT, be on the horizon, impend, threaten, brew, be just around the corner, be in the air/wind. PHRASE: **loom large** *the impending cutbacks loom large* DOMINATE, be important, be significant, be of consequence; count, matter.

**loop** noun *a loop of rope* COIL, hoop, ring, circle, noose, oval, spiral, curl, bend, curve, arc, twirl, whorl, twist, hook, helix, convolution.

▸ verb **1** *Dave looped rope around their hands* COIL, wind, twist, snake, wreathe, spiral, curve, bend, turn.

**2** *he looped the cables together* FASTEN, tie, join, connect, knot, bind.

**loophole** noun *a loophole in the regulations* MEANS OF EVASION, means of avoidance; window, gap, opening.

**loose** adjective **1** *a loose floorboard* NOT FIXED IN PLACE, not secure, unsecured, unattached; detached, unfastened, untied; wobbly, unsteady, movable. ANTONYMS secure, tight.

**2** *she wore her hair loose* UNTIED, unpinned, unbound, hanging free, down, flowing.

**3** *there's a wolf loose* FREE, at large, at liberty, on the loose, escaped; unconfined, untied, unchained, untethered, stray. ANTONYM secure.

**4** *a loose interpretation* VAGUE, indefinite, inexact, imprecise, approximate; broad, general, rough; liberal; *informal* ballpark. ANTONYMS literal, narrow.

**5** *a loose jacket* BAGGY, generously cut, slack, roomy; oversized, shapeless, sagging, saggy, sloppy. ANTONYMS tight, form-fitting.

**6** *dated a loose woman* PROMISCUOUS, of easy virtue, fast, wanton, unchaste, immoral; licentious, dissolute; *dated* fallen. ANTONYM chaste.

7 *loose talk* INDISCREET, unguarded, free, gossipy, gossiping. ANTONYMS discreet, guarded.

▸ verb 1 *loose the dogs* FREE, set free, unloose, turn loose, set loose, let loose, let go, release; untie, unchain, unfasten, unleash. ANTONYM confine.

2 *the fingers loosed their hold* RELAX, slacken, loosen; weaken, lessen, reduce, diminish, moderate. ANTONYM tighten.

PHRASES: **at loose ends** *ever since the factory closed, Don has been at loose ends* WITH NOTHING TO DO, unoccupied, unemployed, at leisure, idle, adrift, with time to kill; bored, twiddling one's thumbs, hanging/kicking around.
**on the loose** *an inmate from Wickham Hall is on the loose* FREE, at liberty, at large, escaped; on the run, fugitive, wanted; *informal* on the lam.

**loose-limbed** adjective *loose-limbed gymnasts* SUPPLE, limber, lithe, lissome, willowy; agile, nimble, flexible.

**loosen** verb 1 *loosen the clothesline | you simply loosen two screws* MAKE SLACK, slacken, unstick; UNFASTEN, detach, release, disconnect, undo, unclasp, unlatch, unbolt. ANTONYM tighten.

2 *her fingers loosened* BECOME SLACK, slacken, become loose, let go, ease; work loose, work free. ANTONYM tighten.

3 *Philip loosened his grip* WEAKEN, relax, slacken, loose, lessen, reduce, moderate, diminish. ANTONYM tighten.

PHRASE: **loosen up** *you need to loosen up* RELAX, unwind, ease up, calm down; *informal* lighten up, go easy, chill out, kick back.

**loot** noun *a bag full of loot* BOOTY, spoils, plunder, stolen goods, contraband, pillage; *informal* swag, hot goods, ill-gotten gains, take.

▸ verb *troops looted the cathedral* PLUNDER, pillage, despoil, ransack, sack, raid, rifle, rob, burgle, burglarize.

**lop** verb *they've* ***lopped off*** *the dead branches* CUT (OFF), chop off, hack off, saw off, hew (off), ax; prune, sever, clip, trim, snip (off), dock, crop.

**lopsided** adjective *my gingerbread house is lopsided* CROOKED, askew, awry, off-center, uneven, out of line, asymmetrical, tilted, at an angle, aslant, slanting; off-balance, off-kilter; *informal* cockeyed. ANTONYMS even, level, balanced.

**loquacious** adjective *a loquacious little boy* TALKATIVE, voluble, communicative, expansive, garrulous, unreserved, chatty, gossipy, gossiping; *informal* having the gift of gab, gabby, gassy, motormouthed, talky, windy. See note at TALKATIVE. ANTONYMS reticent, taciturn.

**lord** noun 1 *the lord of the manor* MASTER, ruler, leader, chief, superior, monarch, sovereign, king, emperor, prince, governor, commander, suzerain, liege, liege lord. ANTONYMS servant, inferior.

2 *let us pray to* ***the Lord*** GOD, the Father, the Almighty, the Creator; Jehovah, Adonai, Yahweh, Elohim, Allah; Jesus Christ, the Messiah, the Savior, the Son of God, the Redeemer, the Lamb of God, the Prince of Peace, the King of Kings; *informal* the Man Upstairs.

3 *a press lord* MAGNATE, tycoon, mogul, captain, baron, king; industrialist, proprietor; *informal* big shot, (head) honcho; *derogatory* fat cat. PHRASE: **lord it over someone** *in our schooldays, you used to lord it over us* ORDER ABOUT/AROUND, dictate to, domineer, ride roughshod over, pull rank on, tyrannize, have under one's thumb; *informal* boss around, walk all over, push around; throw one's weight around.

**lore** noun 1 *Arthurian lore* MYTHOLOGY, myths, legends, stories, traditions, folklore, fables, oral tradition, mythos.

2 *baseball lore* KNOWLEDGE, learning, wisdom; *informal* know-how.

**lose** verb 1 *I've lost my watch* MISLAY, misplace, be unable to find, lose track of, leave (behind), fail to keep/retain, fail to keep sight of. ANTONYM find.

2 *he's lost a lot of blood* BE DEPRIVED OF, suffer the loss of; no longer have. ANTONYMS keep, regain.

3 *he lost his pursuers* ESCAPE FROM, evade, elude, dodge, avoid, give someone the slip, shake off, throw off, throw off the scent; leave behind, outdistance, outstrip, outrun.

4 *they lost their way* STRAY FROM, wander from, depart from, go astray from, fail to keep to.

5 *you've lost your chance* MISS, waste, squander, fail to grasp, fail to take advantage of, let pass, neglect, forfeit; *informal* pass up, lose out on. ANTONYM seize.

6 *they always lose at lacrosse* BE DEFEATED, be beaten, suffer defeat, be the loser, be conquered, be vanquished, be trounced; *informal* go down, take a licking, be bested. ANTONYM win.

7 *you can lose the phony accent* DISCARD, get rid of, dispose of, dump, jettison, throw out, drop. PHRASES: **lose out** *if we don't act soon, we'll lose out* BE DEPRIVED OF AN OPPORTUNITY, fail to benefit, be disadvantaged, be the loser.
**lose out on** *the town has lost out on a tourist opportunity* BE UNABLE TO TAKE ADVANTAGE OF, fail to benefit from; *informal* miss out on.

**loser** noun 1 *the loser still gets the silver medal* DEFEATED PERSON, also-ran, runner-up. ANTONYM winner.

2 *informal he's a complete loser* FAILURE, underachiever, ne'er-do-well, write-off, has-been; MISFIT, freak, unpopular person; *informal* geek, dweeb, nerd, hoser; flop, no-hoper, washout, lemon. ANTONYM success.

**loss** noun 1 *the loss of the documents* MISLAYING, misplacement, forgetting. ANTONYMS recovery, finding.

2 *loss of earnings* DEPRIVATION, disappearance, privation, forfeiture, diminution, erosion, reduction, depletion.

3 *the loss of her husband* DEATH, dying, demise, passing (away/on), end; *formal* decease; *archaic* expiry.

4 **(losses)** *Canadian losses in the war* CASUALTIES, fatalities, victims; dead; missing; death toll, number killed/dead.

5 *a loss of $15,000* DEFICIT, debit, debt, indebtedness, deficiency. ANTONYMS gain, profit.

PHRASE: **at a loss** *I'm at a loss about what just happened* BAFFLED, nonplussed, mystified, puzzled, perplexed, bewildered, bemused, at sixes and sevens, confused, dumbfounded, stumped, stuck, blank; *informal* clueless, flummoxed, bamboozled, fazed, floored, beaten, discombobulated.

**lost** adjective **1** *her lost keys* MISSING, mislaid, misplaced, vanished, disappeared, gone missing, gone astray, forgotten, nowhere to be found; absent, not present, strayed; irretrievable, unrecoverable.

**2** *I think we're lost* OFF COURSE, off track, disorientated, having lost one's bearings, going around in circles, adrift, at sea, astray.

**3** *a lost opportunity* MISSED, forfeited, neglected, wasted, squandered, gone by the boards; *informal* down the drain.

**4** *lost traditions* BYGONE, past, former, one-time, previous, old, olden, departed, vanished, forgotten, consigned to oblivion, extinct, dead, gone.

**5** *lost species and habitats* EXTINCT, died out, defunct, vanished, gone; DESTROYED, wiped out, ruined, wrecked, exterminated, eradicated.

**6** *a lost cause* HOPELESS, beyond hope, futile, forlorn, failed, beyond remedy, beyond recovery.

**7** *lost souls* DAMNED, fallen, irredeemable, irreclaimable, irretrievable, past hope, past praying for, condemned, cursed, doomed; *literary* accursed. ANTONYM saved.

**8** *lost in thought* ENGROSSED, absorbed, rapt, immersed, deep, intent, engaged, wrapped up.

**lot** pronoun ***lots** of friends* | ***a lot** of money* A LARGE AMOUNT, a fair amount, a good/great deal, a great quantity, quantities, an abundance, a wealth, a profusion, plenty, a mass; a large number, a considerable number, scores; *informal* hundreds, thousands, millions, billions, gazillions, loads, masses, heaps, a pile, a stack, piles, oodles, stacks, scads, reams, wads, pots, oceans, a mountain, mountains, miles, tons, zillions, gobs, a bunch; (**lots of/a lot of**) many, a great many, numerous, more —— than one can shake a stick at. ANTONYMS a little, not much, a few, not many.

▸ noun **1** *the books were auctioned in lots* ITEM, article; batch, set, collection, group, bundle, quantity, assortment, parcel.

**2** *his lot in life* FATE, destiny, fortune, doom; situation, circumstances, state, condition, position, plight, predicament.

**3** *playing ball in a vacant lot* PATCH OF GROUND, piece of ground, plot, area, tract, parcel, plat.

▸ adverb *I work in pastels **a lot*** A GREAT DEAL, a good deal, to a great extent, much; often, frequently, regularly. ANTONYM a little.

PHRASES: **draw/cast lots** *we drew lots to see who gets to drive* toss/flip a coin, draw straws, throw/roll (the) dice.

**throw in one's lot with** *he threw in his lot with the conspirators* JOIN FORCES WITH, join up with, form an alliance with, ally with, align oneself with, link up with, make common cause with.

**lotion** noun *scented hand lotion* OINTMENT, cream, salve, balm, rub, emollient, moisturizer, lubricant, gel, unguent, liniment, embrocation.

**lottery** noun **1** *play the lottery* RAFFLE, drawing, prize drawing, sweepstake(s), lotto.

**2** *life is a lottery* GAMBLE, speculation, venture, risk, game of chance, matter of luck; *informal* crapshoot.

**loud** adjective **1** *loud music* NOISY, blaring, booming, deafening, roaring, thunderous, thundering, ear-splitting, ear-piercing, piercing; carrying, clearly audible; lusty, powerful, forceful, stentorian; *Music* forte, fortissimo. ANTONYMS quiet, soft.

**2** *loud complaints* VOCIFEROUS, clamorous, insistent, vehement, emphatic, urgent. ANTONYM gentle.

**3** *a loud T-shirt* GARISH, gaudy, flamboyant, lurid, glaring, showy, ostentatious; vulgar, tasteless; *informal* flash, flashy, kitsch, kitschy, tacky. ANTONYMS sober, tasteful.

**loudmouth** noun *informal coworkers characterize him as an egocentric loudmouth* BRAGGART, boaster, bragger, blusterer, swaggerer; *informal* blabbermouth, big mouth, blowhard, show-off.

**loudspeaker** noun *a message came over the loudspeaker* PUBLIC ADDRESS SYSTEM, PA (system), intercom; SPEAKER, monitor, woofer, tweeter; megaphone; *informal* squawk box.

**lounge** verb *he just lounges in his room* LAZE, lie, loll, lie back, lean back, recline, stretch oneself, drape oneself, relax, rest, repose, take it easy, put one's feet up, unwind, luxuriate; sprawl, slump, slouch, flop; loaf, idle, do nothing; *informal* take a load off, kick back.

▸ noun **1** *a hotel lounge* BAR, pub, club, barroom, taproom.

**2** *an airport lounge* WAITING AREA, reception room.

**3** *she sat in the lounge* LIVING ROOM, sitting room, front room, salon, family room; *dated* parlor, drawing room.

**lousy** *informal* adjective **1** *a lousy film.* See AWFUL sense 2.

**2** *the lousy, double-crossing snake!* See DESPICABLE.

**3** *I felt lousy.* See ILL adjective sense 1. PHRASE: **be lousy with** *the restaurant was lousy with screaming little brats.* See CRAWL sense 3.

**lout** noun *drunken louts* RUFFIAN, hooligan, thug, boor, barbarian, oaf, hoodlum, rowdy, lubber; *informal* tough, roughneck, bruiser, yahoo, lug. ANTONYM gentleman.

**lovable** adjective *lovable baby gorillas* ADORABLE, dear, sweet, cute, charming, darling, lovely, likable, delightful, captivating, enchanting, engaging, bewitching, pleasing, appealing, winsome, winning, fetching, endearing. ANTONYMS hateful, loathsome.

**love** noun **1** *his friendship with Helen grew into love* DEEP AFFECTION, fondness, tenderness, warmth, intimacy, attachment, endearment; devotion, adoration, doting, idolization, worship; passion, ardor, desire, lust, yearning, infatuation, besottedness. ANTONYM hatred.

**2** *her **love for** fashion* | *a **love of** good food* LIKING OF/FOR, enjoyment of, appreciation of/for, taste for, delight for/in, relish of, passion for, zeal for, appetite for, zest for, enthusiasm for, keenness for, fondness for, soft spot for, weakness for, bent for, proclivity for, inclination for, disposition for, partiality for, predilection for, penchant for.

**3** *their love for their fellow human beings* COMPASSION, care, caring, regard, solicitude, concern, friendliness, friendship, kindness, charity, goodwill, sympathy, kindliness, altruism, unselfishness, philanthropy, benevolence, fellow feeling, humanity.

**4** *he was her one true love* BELOVED, loved one, love of one's life, dear, dearest, dear one, darling, sweetheart, sweet, angel, honey; lover, inamorato, inamorata, amour; *archaic* paramour.

**5** *their love will survive* RELATIONSHIP, love affair, romance, liaison, affair of the heart, amour.

**6** *my mother sends her love* BEST WISHES, regards, good wishes, greetings, kind/kindest regards.

▸ verb **1** *she loves him* CARE VERY MUCH FOR, feel deep affection for, hold very dear, adore, think the world of, be devoted to, dote on, idolize, worship; be in love with, be infatuated with, be smitten with, be besotted with; *informal* be mad/crazy/nuts/wild about, have a crush on, carry a torch for. ANTONYM hate.

**2** *Laura loved painting* LIKE VERY MUCH, delight in, enjoy greatly, have a passion for, take great pleasure in, derive great pleasure from, relish, savor; have a weakness for, be partial to, have a soft spot for, have a taste for, be taken with; *informal* get a kick out of, have a thing about, be mad/crazy/nuts/wild about, be hooked on, get off on. ANTONYM hate.

PHRASES: **fall in love with** *she didn't mean to fall in love with him* BECOME INFATUATED WITH, give/lose one's heart to; *informal* fall for, be bowled over by, be swept off one's feet by, develop a crush on.

**in love with** *he's in love with Gillian* INFATUATED WITH, besotted with, enamored of, smitten with, consumed with desire for; captivated by, bewitched by, enthralled by, entranced by, moonstruck by; devoted to, doting on; *informal* mad/crazy/nuts/wild about.

**lovelorn** adjective *my lovelorn son thinks the world has come to an end* LOVESICK; pining, languishing; spurned, jilted, rejected, forsaken.

**lovely** adjective **1** *a lovely young woman* BEAUTIFUL, pretty, attractive, good-looking, appealing, handsome, adorable, exquisite, sweet, personable, charming; enchanting, engaging, winsome, seductive, sexy, gorgeous, alluring, ravishing, glamorous; *informal* tasty, knockout, stunning, drop-dead gorgeous; killer, cute, foxy, hot; *formal* beauteous; *archaic* comely, fair. ANTONYMS ugly, hideous.

**2** *a lovely view* SCENIC, picturesque, pleasing, easy on the eye; magnificent, stunning, splendid.

**3** *informal we had a lovely day* DELIGHTFUL, very pleasant, very nice, very agreeable, marvelous, wonderful, sublime, superb, magical; *informal* terrific, fabulous, heavenly, divine, amazing, glorious. ANTONYM horrible.

**lover** noun **1** *she had a secret lover* BOYFRIEND, GIRLFRIEND, beloved, love, darling, sweetheart, inamorata, inamorato; mistress; partner, significant other, main squeeze; *informal* bit on the side, toy boy, boy toy; *dated* ladylove, beau; *archaic* swain, concubine, paramour.

**2** *a dog lover* DEVOTEE, admirer, fan, enthusiast, aficionado; *informal* buff, freak, nut, junkie.

**loving** adjective *her loving husband* AFFECTIONATE, fond, devoted, adoring, doting, solicitous, demonstrative; caring, tender, warm, warmhearted, close; amorous, ardent, passionate, amatory. ANTONYMS cold, cruel.

**low** adjective **1** *a low fence* SHORT, small, little; squat, stubby, stunted, dwarf; shallow. ANTONYM high.

**2** *low prices* CHEAP, economical, moderate, reasonable, modest, bargain, budget, bargain-basement, rock-bottom, cut-rate. ANTONYMS high, expensive.

**3** *supplies were low* SCARCE, scanty, scant, skimpy, meager, sparse, few, little, paltry; reduced, depleted, diminished. ANTONYMS plentiful, abundant.

**4** *low quality* INFERIOR, substandard, poor, bad, low-grade, low-end, below par, second-rate, unsatisfactory, deficient, defective, shoddy. ANTONYMS high, superior.

**5** *of low birth* HUMBLE, lowly, low-ranking, plebeian, proletarian, peasant, poor; common, ordinary. ANTONYMS superior, noble.

**6** *low expectations* UNAMBITIOUS, unaspiring, modest. ANTONYMS high, ambitious.

**7** *a low opinion* UNFAVORABLE, poor, bad, adverse, negative. ANTONYMS high, favorable, good.

**8** *a low blow.* See LOWDOWN adjective.

**9** *low humor* UNCOUTH, uncultured, unsophisticated, rough, rough-hewn, unrefined, tasteless, crass, common, vulgar, coarse, crude. ANTONYMS high, exalted.

**10** *a low voice* QUIET, soft, faint, gentle, muted, subdued, muffled, hushed, quieted, whispered, stifled. ANTONYM loud.

**11** *a low note* BASS, baritone, low-pitched, deep, rumbling, booming, sonorous.

**12** *she was feeling low* DEPRESSED, dejected, despondent, downhearted, downcast, low-spirited, down, morose, miserable, dismal, heavy-hearted, mournful, forlorn, woebegone, gloomy, glum, crestfallen, dispirited; without energy, enervated, flat, sapped, weary; *informal* down in/at the mouth, down in the dumps, blue. ANTONYM cheerful.

▸ noun *the dollar fell to an all-time low* NADIR, low point, lowest point, lowest level, minimum, depth, rock bottom. ANTONYMS high, zenith.

**lowdown** *informal* adjective *a lowdown trick* UNFAIR, mean, despicable, reprehensible, contemptible, lamentable, disgusting, shameful, low, cheap, underhanded, foul, unworthy, shabby, base, dishonorable, unprincipled, sordid; *informal* rotten, dirty; beastly; *dated* dastardly. ANTONYMS kind, honorable.

▸ noun *he gave us the lowdown* FACTS, information, story, intelligence, news, inside story; *informal* info, rundown, score, scoop, word, dope, dirt, poop, skinny.

**lower** adjective **1** *the lower house of Parliament* SUBORDINATE, inferior, lesser, junior, minor, secondary, lower-level, subsidiary, subservient. ANTONYMS upper, senior.

**2** *her lower lip* BOTTOM, bottommost, nether, under; underneath, further down, beneath. ANTONYMS upper, higher, top.

**3** *a lower price* CHEAPER, reduced, cut, slashed. ANTONYMS higher, increased.

▸ verb **1** *she lowered the mask* MOVE DOWN, let down, take down, haul down, drop, let fall. ANTONYMS raise, lift up.

**2** *lower your voice* SOFTEN, modulate, quiet, hush, tone down, muffle, turn down, mute. ANTONYMS raise, intensify.

**3** *they are lowering their prices* REDUCE, decrease, lessen, bring down, mark down, cut, slash, ax, diminish, curtail, prune, pare (down). ANTONYM increase.

**4** *the water level lowered* SUBSIDE, fall (off), recede, ebb, wane; abate, die down, let up, moderate, diminish, lessen.

**5** *don't lower yourself to their level* DEGRADE, debase, demean, abase, humiliate, downgrade, discredit, shame, dishonor, disgrace; belittle, cheapen, devalue; **(lower oneself)** stoop, sink, descend. ANTONYM boost.

**low-grade** adjective *low-grade building materials* POOR-QUALITY, inferior, substandard, second-rate; shoddy, cheap, reject, trashy, gimcrack, chintzy, rubbishy; *informal* two-bit, schlocky, bum, cheapjack. ANTONYMS top-quality, first-class.

**low-key** adjective *she conducted a low-key campaign* RESTRAINED, modest, understated, muted, subtle, quiet, low-profile, inconspicuous, unostentatious, unobtrusive, discreet, toned-down; casual, informal, mellow, laid-back. ANTONYMS ostentatious, obtrusive.

**lowly** adjective *that's right Mrs. Tynesdale, I used to be your lowly stable boy* HUMBLE, low, low-born, low-ranking, plebeian, proletarian; common, ordinary, plain, average, modest, simple; inferior, ignoble, subordinate, obscure. ANTONYMS aristocratic, exalted.

**loyal** adjective *she was loyal to her country* FAITHFUL, true, devoted; constant, steadfast, staunch, dependable, reliable, trusted, trustworthy, trusty, dutiful, dedicated, unchanging, unwavering, unswerving; patriotic. ANTONYM treacherous.

**loyalty** noun *my grandparents never doubted each other's loyalty* ALLEGIANCE, faithfulness, obedience, adherence, homage, devotion; steadfastness, staunchness, trueheartedness, dependability, reliability, trustworthiness, duty, dedication, commitment; patriotism; *historical* fealty. ANTONYM treachery.

**lubricant** noun *tubes of lubricant* GREASE, oil, lubrication, emollient, lotion, unguent; *informal* lube.

**lubricate** verb *lubricating the hinges* OIL, GREASE; wax, polish; facilitate, smooth, ease; *informal* lube.

**lucid** adjective **1** *a lucid description* INTELLIGIBLE, comprehensible, understandable, cogent, coherent, articulate; clear, transparent; plain, simple, vivid, sharp, straightforward, unambiguous; *formal* perspicuous. ANTONYMS confusing, ambiguous.

**2** *he was not lucid enough to explain* RATIONAL, sane, in one's right mind, in possession of one's faculties, compos mentis, able to think clearly, balanced, clearheaded, sober, sensible; *informal* all there. See note at SENSIBLE. ANTONYMS muddled, confused.

**luck** noun **1** *with luck you'll make it* GOOD FORTUNE, good luck; a fluke, a stroke of luck; *informal* a lucky break. ANTONYMS bad luck, misfortune.

**2** *I wish you luck* SUCCESS, prosperity, good fortune, good luck. ANTONYMS failure, misfortune.

**3** *it is a matter of luck whether it hits or misses* FORTUNE, fate, destiny, Lady Luck, lot, the stars, karma, kismet; fortuity, serendipity; chance, accident, a twist of fate. PHRASES: **in luck** *you're in luck, there's one blue sweater left in your size* FORTUNATE, lucky, blessed with good luck, born under a lucky star; successful, having a charmed life.

**out of luck** *sorry, you're out of luck—the bus left just five minutes ago* UNFORTUNATE, unlucky, luckless, hapless, unsuccessful, cursed, jinxed, ill-fated; *informal* down on one's luck; *literary* star-crossed.

**luckily** adverb *luckily, we took the Great Elms Bridge, which was not flooded over* FORTUNATELY, happily, providentially, opportunely, by good fortune, as luck would have it, propitiously; mercifully, thankfully. ANTONYM unfortunately.

**luckless** adjective *his luckless father died penniless and alone* UNLUCKY, unfortunate, unsuccessful, hapless, out of luck, cursed, jinxed, doomed, ill-fated; *informal* down on one's luck, losingest; *literary* star-crossed. ANTONYM lucky.

**lucky** adjective **1** *the lucky winner* FORTUNATE, in luck, blessed, favored, born under a lucky star, charmed; successful, prosperous. ANTONYM unfortunate.

**2** *a lucky escape* PROVIDENTIAL, fortunate, advantageous, timely, opportune, serendipitous, expedient, heaven-sent, auspicious; chance, fortuitous, fluky, accidental. ANTONYM untimely.

**lucrative** adjective *a lucrative business* PROFITABLE, profit-making, gainful, remunerative, moneymaking, paying, high-income, well-paid, bankable; rewarding, worthwhile; thriving, flourishing, successful, booming. ANTONYM unprofitable.

**ludicrous** adjective *a ludicrous idea* ABSURD, ridiculous, farcical, laughable, risible, preposterous, foolish, mad, insane, idiotic, stupid, inane, silly, asinine, nonsensical; *informal* crazy. See note at ABSURD. ANTONYM sensible.

**lug** verb *she lugged her groceries to the door* CARRY, lift, bear, tote, heave, hoist, shoulder; haul, drag, tug, tow, transport, move, convey, shift; *informal* hump, schlep.

▸ noun *informal you big lug!* See OAF.

**luggage** noun *a rack for the luggage* BAGGAGE; bags, suitcases, cases, trunks. See also BAG noun sense 2.

**lugubrious** adjective *lugubrious hymns | their lugubrious aunt* MOURNFUL, gloomy, sad, unhappy, doleful, glum, melancholy, woeful, miserable, woebegone, forlorn, somber, solemn, serious, sorrowful, morose, dour, cheerless, joyless, dismal; funereal, sepulchral; *informal* down in/at the mouth; *literary* dolorous. See note at GLUM. ANTONYM cheerful.

**lukewarm** adjective **1** *lukewarm coffee* TEPID, slightly warm, warmish, at room temperature, chambré. ANTONYMS hot, cold.

**2** *a lukewarm response* INDIFFERENT, cool, halfhearted, apathetic, unenthusiastic, tepid, perfunctory, noncommittal, lackadaisical; *informal* laid-back, unenthused, couldn't-care-less. ANTONYM enthusiastic.

**lull** verb **1** *the sound of the bells lulled us to sleep* SOOTHE, calm, hush; rock. ANTONYMS waken, agitate.

**2** *his honeyed words lulled their suspicions* ASSUAGE, allay, ease, alleviate, soothe, quiet, quieted; reduce, diminish; quell, banish, dispel. ANTONYM aggravate.

**3** *they lulled us into a false sense of security* DECEIVE, dupe, trick, fool, hoodwink.

▸ noun **1** *a lull in the fighting* PAUSE, respite, interval, break, hiatus, suspension, interlude, intermission, breathing space; *informal* letup, breather.

**2** *the lull before the storm* CALM, stillness, quiet, tranquility, peace, silence, hush. ANTONYM activity.

**lullaby** noun. *Mother's sweet lullabies* CRADLE SONG, berceuse.

**lumber** verb *elephants lumbered past* LURCH, stumble, trundle, shamble, shuffle, waddle; trudge, clump, stump, plod, tramp, tromp; *informal* galumph.

▸ noun *a truckload of quality lumber* TIMBER, wood, boards, planks.

**lumbering** adjective *he was a lumbering bear of a man* CLUMSY, awkward, heavy-footed, slow, blundering, bumbling, inept, maladroit, uncoordinated, ungainly, ungraceful, gauche, lumpish, hulking, ponderous; *informal* clodhopping. ANTONYMS nimble, agile.

**luminary** noun *the luminaries of the art world* LEADING LIGHT, guiding light, inspiration, role model, hero, heroine, leader, expert, master; lion, legend, celebrity, personality, great, giant; *informal* bigwig, rainmaker, VIP. ANTONYM nobody.

**luminous** adjective *the luminous face of the alarm clock* SHINING, bright, brilliant, radiant, dazzling, glowing, gleaming, scintillating, lustrous; luminescent, phosphorescent, fluorescent, incandescent. See note at BRIGHT. ANTONYM dark.

**lump**[1] noun **1** *a lump of coal* CHUNK, hunk, piece, mass, block, wedge, slab, cake, nugget, ball, brick, cube, pat, knob, clod, gobbet, dollop, wad; *informal* glob, gob.

**2** *a lump on his head* SWELLING, bump, bulge, protuberance, protrusion, growth, outgrowth, nodule, hump; goose egg.

**3 (lumps)** *take your lumps* HARD KNOCKS, defeats, losses.

▸ verb *it is out of ignorance that they* ***lump together*** *all modern artists* COMBINE, put together, group, bunch, aggregate, unite, pool, merge, collect, throw together, consider together.

**lump**[2] verb *informal like it or lump it* PUT UP WITH, bear, endure, suffer, take, tolerate, accept.

**lunacy** noun **1** *originality demands a degree of lunacy* INSANITY, madness, mental illness, dementia, mania, psychosis; *informal* craziness. ANTONYM sanity.

**2** *the lunacy of gambling* FOLLY, foolishness, stupidity, silliness, idiocy, madness, recklessness, foolhardiness, imprudence, irresponsibility; *informal* craziness. ANTONYMS sense, prudence.

**lunatic** noun *he drives like a lunatic* MANIAC, madman, madwoman, imbecile, psychopath, psychotic; fool, idiot; eccentric; *informal* loony, nut, nutcase, head case, psycho, moron, screwball, crackpot, fruitcake, loon.

▸ adjective **1** *a lunatic prisoner.* See MAD sense 1.

**2** *a lunatic idea.* See MAD sense 3.

**lunch** noun *my usual lunch includes soup and a sandwich* MIDDAY MEAL, luncheon, brunch, light meal, snack. PHRASE: **out to lunch** *some of these therapists are more out to lunch than their patients* CRAZY, out of one's mind, mad; out of touch, out of it, unaware, absentminded; cuckoo, batty, flaky, spacey, nutty, wingy, off one's rocker.

**lunge** noun *Darren made a lunge at his attacker* THRUST, jab, stab, dive, rush, charge.

▸ verb *he lunged at Finn with a knife* THRUST, dive, spring, launch oneself, rush, make a grab.

**lurch** verb **1** *he lurched into the kitchen* STAGGER, stumble, wobble, sway, reel, roll, weave, pitch, totter, blunder.

**2** *the ship lurched* SWAY, reel, list, heel, rock, roll, pitch, toss, jerk, shake, flounder, swerve, teeter. PHRASE: **leave someone in the lurch** *Wally talked us into taking part in the protest, and then he just left us in the lurch* LEAVE IN TROUBLE, let down, leave stranded, leave high and dry, abandon, desert.

**lure** verb *consumers are frequently lured into debt* TEMPT, entice, attract, induce, coax, persuade, inveigle, allure, seduce, win over, cajole, beguile, bewitch, ensnare. See note at TEMPT. ANTONYMS deter, put off.

▸ noun *the lure of the stage* TEMPTATION, enticement, attraction, pull, draw, appeal; inducement, allurement, fascination, interest, magnet; *informal* come-on.

**lurid** adjective **1** *lurid colors* BRIGHT, brilliant, vivid, glaring, shocking, fluorescent, flaming, dazzling, intense; gaudy, loud, showy, bold, garish, tacky. ANTONYMS muted, subtle.

**2** *the lurid details* SENSATIONAL, sensationalist, exaggerated, overdramatized, colorful; salacious, graphic, explicit, unrestrained, prurient, shocking; gruesome, gory, grisly; *informal* juicy, full-frontal. ANTONYMS discreet, restrained.

**lurk** verb *is someone lurking in the bushes?* SKULK, loiter, lie in wait, lie low, hide, conceal oneself, take cover, keep out of sight.

**luscious** adjective **1** *luscious fruit* DELICIOUS, succulent, lush, juicy, mouthwatering, lip-smacking, sweet, tasty, appetizing; *informal* scrumptious, yummy, nummy; *literary* ambrosial. ANTONYM unappetizing.

**2** *a luscious well-tanned beauty* SEXY, sexually attractive, nubile, ravishing, gorgeous, seductive, alluring, sultry, beautiful, stunning; *informal* drop-dead gorgeous, hot, curvy, foxy, cute. ANTONYMS plain, scrawny.

**lush** adjective **1** *lush vegetation* LUXURIANT, rich, abundant, profuse, exuberant, riotous, prolific, vigorous; dense, thick, rank, rampant; *informal* jungly. See note at PROFUSE. ANTONYMS barren, meager.

**2** *a lush, ripe peach* SUCCULENT, luscious, juicy, soft, tender, ripe. ANTONYM shriveled.

**3** *a lush apartment* LUXURIOUS, deluxe, sumptuous, palatial, opulent, lavish, elaborate, extravagant, fancy; *informal* plush, ritzy, posh, swanky, swank. ANTONYM austere.

**lust** noun **1** *his lust for her* SEXUAL DESIRE, sexual appetite, sexual longing, ardor, desire, passion; libido, sex drive, sexuality, biological urge; lechery, lasciviousness, concupiscence; *informal* horniness, the hots, randiness.

**2** *a lust for power* GREED, desire, craving, covetousness, eagerness, avidity, cupidity, longing, yearning, hunger, thirst, appetite, hankering. ANTONYM aversion.

▸ verb **1** *he **lusted after** his employer's wife* DESIRE, be consumed with desire for, find sexually attractive, crave, covet, ache for, burn for; *informal* have the hots for, fancy, have a thing about/for, drool over.

**2** *she **lusted after** adventure* CRAVE, desire, covet, want, wish for, long for, yearn for, dream of, hanker for, hanker after, hunger for, thirst for, ache for. ANTONYMS dread, avoid.

**luster** noun **1** *her hair lost its luster* SHEEN, gloss, shine, glow, gleam, shimmer, burnish, polish, patina. See note at POLISH. ANTONYM dullness.

**2** *the luster of the Milky Way* BRILLIANCE, brightness, radiance, sparkle, dazzle, flash, glitter, glint, gleam, luminosity, luminescence.

**lustful** adjective *a lustful look* LECHEROUS, lascivious, libidinous, licentious, salacious, goatish; wanton, unchaste, impure, naughty, immodest, indecent, dirty, prurient; passionate, sensual, sexy, erotic; *informal* horny, randy, raunchy, lusty; *formal* concupiscent. ANTONYMS chaste, pure.

**lustrous** adjective *lustrous black hair* SHINY, shining, satiny, glossy, gleaming, shimmering, burnished, polished; radiant, bright, brilliant, luminous; dazzling, sparkling, glistening, twinkling. See note at BRIGHT. ANTONYM dull.

**lusty** adjective **1** *a lusty baby* HEALTHY, strong, fit, vigorous, robust, hale and hearty, energetic; rugged, sturdy, muscular, muscly, strapping, hefty, husky, burly, powerful; *informal* beefy; *dated* stalwart. ANTONYMS feeble, weak.

**2** *lusty singing* LOUD, vigorous, hearty, strong, powerful, forceful. ANTONYMS feeble, weak.

**3** *informal lusty young men.* See LUSTFUL.

**luxuriant** adjective *luxuriant vegetation* LUSH, rich, abundant, profuse, exuberant, riotous, prolific, vigorous; dense, thick, rank, rampant; *informal* jungly. See note at PROFUSE. ANTONYMS barren, sparse.

**luxuriate** verb *luxuriating in a bubble bath* REVEL, bask, delight, take pleasure, wallow; (**luxuriate in**) enjoy, relish, savor, appreciate; *informal* get a kick out of, get a thrill out of. ANTONYM dislike.

**luxurious** adjective **1** *a luxurious hotel* OPULENT, sumptuous, deluxe, rich, grand, palatial, splendid, magnificent, well appointed, extravagant, fancy, upscale, upmarket, five-star; *informal* plush, posh, classy, ritzy, swanky, swank. ANTONYMS poor, austere, spartan.

**2** *a luxurious lifestyle* SELF-INDULGENT, sensual, pleasure-loving, pleasure-seeking, epicurean, hedonistic, sybaritic. See notes at LUXURIANT, SENSUOUS. ANTONYM abstemious.

**luxury** noun **1** *we'll live in luxury* OPULENCE, luxuriousness, sumptuousness, grandeur, magnificence, splendor, lavishness, the lap of luxury, a bed of roses, (the land of) milk and honey; *informal* the life of Riley. ANTONYMS austerity, poverty.

**2** *a TV is his only luxury* INDULGENCE, extravagance, self-indulgence, nonessential, treat, extra, frill. ANTONYM necessity.

**lying** noun *she was no good at lying* UNTRUTHFULNESS, fabrication, fibbing, perjury, white lies; falseness, falsity, dishonesty, mendacity, telling stories, invention, misrepresentation, deceit, duplicity; *literary* perfidy. ANTONYM honesty.

▸ adjective *he was a lying womanizer* UNTRUTHFUL, false, dishonest, mendacious, deceitful, deceiving, duplicitous, double-dealing, two-faced; *literary* perfidious. ANTONYM truthful.

**lynch** verb *DeLuca was lynched by Yardley's mob* EXECUTE ILLEGALLY, hang, kill; *informal* string up.

**lyrical** adjective **1** *lyrical love poetry* EXPRESSIVE, emotional, deeply felt, personal, subjective, passionate, lyric.

**2** *she was lyrical about her success* ENTHUSIASTIC, rhapsodic, effusive, rapturous, ecstatic, euphoric, carried away. ANTONYM unenthusiastic.

**lyrics** plural noun *Cole Porter wrote the music and lyrics* WORDS, libretto, book, text, lines.

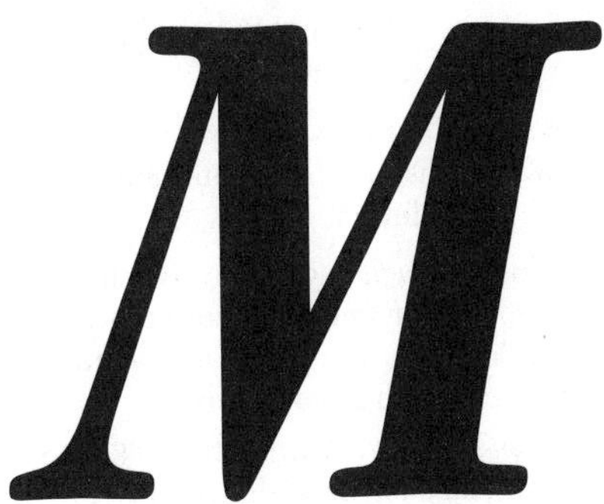

**macabre** adjective **1** *a macabre ritual* GRUESOME, grisly, grim, gory, morbid, ghastly, unearthly, grotesque, hideous, horrific, shocking, dreadful, loathsome, repugnant, repulsive, sickening.

**2** *a macabre joke* BLACK, weird, unhealthy; *informal* sick.

**mace** noun *the thug wielded a mace* CLUB, cudgel, stick, staff, shillelagh, bludgeon, truncheon, nightstick, billy club, blackjack.

**Machiavellian** adjective *their Machiavellian plot to inherit Aunt Lorinda's estate* DEVIOUS, cunning, crafty, artful, wily, sly, scheming, treacherous, two-faced, tricky, double-dealing, unscrupulous, deceitful, dishonest; *literary* perfidious; *informal* foxy. ANTONYMS straightforward, ingenuous.

**machinations** plural noun *they were always wary of the machinations of rival gangs* SCHEMING, schemes, plotting, plots, intrigues, conspiracies, ruses, tricks, wiles, stratagems, tactics, maneuvering. See note at PLOT.

**machine** noun **1** *a threshing machine* APPARATUS, appliance, device, contraption, contrivance, mechanism, engine, gadget, tool.

**2** *an efficient publicity machine* ORGANIZATION, system, structure, arrangement, machinery; *informal* setup.

**3** *he's an eating machine* POWERHOUSE, human dynamo; wonder, phenomenon, sensation; automaton.

**machinery** noun **1** *printing machinery* EQUIPMENT, apparatus, hardware, gear, tackle, plant; mechanism; instruments, tools; gadgetry, technology.

**2** *the machinery of government* WORKINGS, organization, system, structure, administration, institution; *informal* setup.

**machismo** noun *don't be struttin' your machismo around here, buster* (AGGRESSIVE) MASCULINITY, toughness, male chauvinism, sexism, virility, manliness; bravado; *informal* testosterone, macho.

**mad** adjective **1** *he felt he was going mad* INSANE, mentally ill, certifiable, deranged, demented, of unsound mind, out of one's mind, not in one's right mind, sick in the head, crazy, crazed, lunatic, non compos mentis, unhinged, disturbed, raving, psychotic, psychopathic, mad as a hatter, mad as a March hare; *informal* CRAZY, mental, off one's nut, nuts, nutty, nutty as a fruitcake, nutso, off one's rocker, not right in the head, round/around the bend, (stark) raving mad, bats, batty, buggy, bonkers, dotty, cuckoo, cracked, loopy, loony, bananas, loco, screwy, schizoid, psycho, touched, gaga, not all there, not right upstairs, crackers, out of one's tree, meshuga, wacko, gonzo; **(be mad)** have a screw loose, have bats in the/one's belfry; **(go mad)** lose one's reason, lose one's mind, take leave of one's senses, lose one's marbles, crack up. ANTONYM sane.

**2** *I'm still mad at him* | *don't get mad* ANGRY, furious, infuriated, irate, raging, enraged, fuming, incensed, seeing red, beside oneself; *informal* livid, sore; *literary* wrathful; **(get mad)** lose one's temper, get in a rage, rant and rave; *informal* explode, go off the deep end, go ape, flip, flip out, flip one's wig. ANTONYMS unruffled, calm.

**3** *some mad scheme* FOOLISH, insane, stupid, lunatic, foolhardy, idiotic, senseless, absurd, impractical, silly, inane, asinine, wild, unwise, imprudent; *informal* crazy, crackpot, crack-brained, daft. ANTONYM sensible.

**4** *informal he's* ***mad about*** *jazz* ENTHUSIASTIC ABOUT, passionate about; ardent about, fervent about, avid about, fanatical about; devoted to, infatuated with, in love with, hot for; *informal* crazy about, nuts about, wild about, hooked on, gone on, nutso about. ANTONYM indifferent.

**5** *it was a mad dash to get ready* FRENZIED, frantic, frenetic, feverish, wild, hectic, manic. PHRASE: **like mad** *informal* **1** *I ran like mad* FAST, quickly, rapidly, speedily, hastily, hurriedly.

**2** *he had to fight like mad* ENERGETICALLY, enthusiastically, madly, furiously, with a will, for all one is worth, passionately, intensely, ardently, fervently; *informal* like crazy, hammer and tongs.

**madcap** adjective **1** *a madcap scheme* RECKLESS, rash, foolhardy, foolish, harebrained, wild, hasty, imprudent, ill-advised; *informal* crazy, crackpot, crack-brained.

**2** *a madcap comedy* ZANY, eccentric, unconventional.

▸ noun *she was a boisterous madcap* ECCENTRIC, crank, madman/madwoman, maniac, lunatic; oddity, character; *informal* crackpot, oddball, weirdo, loony, nut, screwball, loon.

**madden** verb **1** *what maddens people most is his vagueness* INFURIATE, exasperate, irritate; incense, anger, enrage, provoke, upset, agitate, vex, irk, make someone's hackles rise, make someone see red; *informal* aggravate, make someone's blood boil, make livid, get someone's goat, get someone's back up, tee off, tick off, steam someone up.

**2** *they were maddened with pain* DRIVE MAD, drive insane, derange, unhinge, unbalance; *informal* drive round/around the bend.

**made-up** adjective **1** *a made-up story* INVENTED, fabricated, trumped up, concocted, fictitious, fictional, false, untrue, specious, spurious, bogus, apocryphal, imaginary, mythical.

**2** *she was made up for the evening* WEARING MAKEUP; *informal* dolled up, decked out.

**madhouse** noun *informal* **1** *his father is shut up in a madhouse* MENTAL HOSPITAL, mental institution, psychiatric hospital, asylum; *informal* nuthouse, funny farm, loony bin; *dated* lunatic asylum.

**2** *when we arrived, it was* ***a madhouse*** BEDLAM, mayhem, chaos, pandemonium, an uproar, turmoil, disorder, madness, all hell broken loose, a (three-ring) circus, a zoo.

**madly** adverb **1** *she was smiling madly* INSANELY, deliriously, wildly, like a lunatic; *informal* crazily. ANTONYM sanely.

**2** *madly snapping pictures* FAST, furiously, hurriedly, quickly, speedily, hastily, energetically; *informal* like mad, like crazy. ANTONYM slowly.

**3** *informal she was madly in love with him* INTENSELY, fervently, wildly, unrestrainedly, to distraction. ANTONYM slightly.

**4** *informal a madly eccentric pair* VERY, extremely, really, exceedingly, exceptionally, remarkably, extraordinarily, immensely, tremendously, wildly, hugely; *informal* awfully, terribly, terrifically, fantastically. ANTONYM slightly.

**madman, madwoman** noun *there was a madman on the loose* LUNATIC, maniac, psychotic, psychopath, sociopath; *informal* loony, nut, nutcase, head case, psycho, screwball, loon.

**madness** noun **1** *today madness is called mental illness* INSANITY, mental illness, dementia, derangement; lunacy, instability; mania, psychosis; *informal* craziness. ANTONYM sanity.

**2** *it would be madness to do otherwise* FOLLY, foolishness, idiocy, stupidity, insanity, lunacy, silliness; *informal* craziness. ANTONYMS common sense, good sense.

**3** *it's absolute madness in here* BEDLAM, mayhem, chaos, pandemonium, craziness, uproar, turmoil, disorder, all hell broken loose, (three-ring) circus. ANTONYM calm.

**maelstrom** noun **1** *a maelstrom in the sea* WHIRLPOOL, vortex, eddy, swirl; *literary* Charybdis.

**2** *the maelstrom of war* TURBULENCE, tumult, turmoil, disorder, disarray, chaos, confusion, upheaval, pandemonium, bedlam, whirlwind.

**maestro** noun **1** *blues maestro Eric Clapton* VIRTUOSO, master, expert, genius, wizard, prodigy; *informal* ace, whiz, pro, hotshot. ANTONYMS novice, beginner.

**2** *the maestro took the podium* CONDUCTOR, (music) director.

**magazine** noun *a monthly fashion magazine* JOURNAL, periodical, serial, supplement, quarterly, monthly, weekly, newsmagazine; *informal* glossy, mag, zine, fanzine.

**magenta** adjective *the blouse is white with magenta pinstripes* REDDISH-PURPLE, purplish-red, crimson, plum, carmine red, fuchsia; *literary* incarnadine.

**magic** noun **1** *do you believe in magic?* SORCERY, witchcraft, wizardry, necromancy, enchantment, the supernatural, occultism, the occult, black magic, the black arts, voodoo, hoodoo, mojo, shamanism; charm, hex, spell, jinx.

**2** *he does magic at children's parties* CONJURING TRICKS, sleight of hand, legerdemain, illusion, prestidigitation.

**3** *the magic of the stage* ALLURE, attraction, excitement, fascination, charm, glamour.

**4** *her dancing is pure magic* SKILL, brilliance, ability, accomplishment, adeptness, adroitness, deftness, dexterity, aptitude, expertise, art, finesse, talent.

▸ adjective **1** *a magic spell* SUPERNATURAL, enchanted, occult.

**2** *a magic place* FASCINATING, captivating, charming, glamorous, magical, enchanting, entrancing, spellbinding, magnetic, irresistible, hypnotic.

**3** *informal we were magic together* MARVELOUS, wonderful, excellent, admirable; *informal* terrific, fabulous, brilliant.

**magician** noun **1** *she imagined she was a magician* SORCERER, sorceress, witch, wizard, warlock, enchanter, enchantress, necromancer, shaman.

**2** *Houdini was a great magician* CONJUROR, illusionist, prestidigitator.

**3** *he is a magician on the ice* GENIUS, marvel, wizard.

**magisterial** adjective **1** *a magisterial pronouncement* AUTHORITATIVE, masterful, assured, lordly, commanding, assertive. ANTONYM humble.

**2** *his magisterial style of questioning* DOMINEERING, dictatorial, autocratic, imperious, overbearing, peremptory, high-handed, arrogant, supercilious, patronizing; *informal* bossy. ANTONYMS hesitant, tentative.

**magnanimous** adjective *her magnanimous contributions to the art world* GENEROUS, charitable, benevolent, beneficent, big-hearted, handsome, princely, altruistic, philanthropic, unselfish, chivalrous, noble; forgiving, merciful, lenient, indulgent, clement. ANTONYMS mean-spirited, selfish.

**magnate** noun *the industrial magnates of the nineteenth century* TYCOON, mogul, captain of industry, baron, lord, king, magnifico; industrialist, proprietor; *informal* big shot, big cheese, (head) honcho; *derogatory* fat cat.

**magnet** noun **1** *you can test if it's steel by using a magnet* LODESTONE; electromagnet, solenoid.

**2** *a magnet for tourists* ATTRACTION, focus, draw, lure, mecca.

**magnetic** adjective *a magnetic personality* ALLURING, attractive, fascinating, captivating, enchanting, enthralling, appealing, charming, prepossessing, engaging, entrancing, seductive, inviting, irresistible, charismatic.

**magnetism** noun *the sheer magnetism of his physical presence* ALLURE, attraction, fascination, appeal, draw, drawing power, pull, charm, enchantment, seductiveness, magic, spell, charisma.

**magnification** noun *the fine lines are visible only under magnification* ENLARGEMENT, enhancement, increase, augmentation, extension, expansion, amplification, intensification, inflation. ANTONYM reduction.

**magnificence** noun *the magnificence of Broadway* SPLENDOR, grandeur, impressiveness, glory, majesty, nobility, pomp, stateliness, elegance, sumptuousness, opulence, luxury, lavishness, richness, brilliance, dazzle, skill, virtuosity. ANTONYMS modesty, tawdriness, weakness.

**magnificent** adjective **1** *a magnificent view of the mountains* SPLENDID, spectacular, impressive, striking, glorious, superb, majestic, awesome, awe-inspiring, breathtaking. ANTONYM uninspiring.

**2** *a magnificent apartment overlooking the lake* SUMPTUOUS, resplendent, grand, impressive, imposing, monumental, palatial, stately, opulent, luxurious, lavish, rich, dazzling, beautiful, elegant; *informal* splendiferous, ritzy, posh, swanky. ANTONYMS modest, tawdry, cheap.

**3** *a magnificent performance* MASTERLY, skillful, virtuoso, brilliant. ANTONYMS poor, weak.

**magnify** verb **1** *the lens magnifies the image* ENLARGE, boost, enhance, maximize, increase, augment, extend, expand, amplify, intensify; *informal* blow up. ANTONYM reduce.

**2** *they magnified the problem* EXAGGERATE, overstate, overemphasize, overplay, dramatize, color, embroider, embellish, inflate, make a mountain out of (a molehill); *informal* blow up (out of all proportion), make a big thing out of. ANTONYMS minimize, understate.

**magnitude** noun **1** *the magnitude of the task* IMMENSITY, vastness, hugeness, enormity; size, extent, expanse, greatness, largeness, bigness. ANTONYM smallness.

**2** *events of tragic magnitude* IMPORTANCE, import, significance, weight, consequence, mark, notability, note; *formal* moment. ANTONYM triviality.

PHRASE: **of the first magnitude** *we are witnessing a historic event of the first magnitude* OF THE UTMOST IMPORTANCE, of the greatest significance, very important, of great consequence; *formal* of great moment.

**maid** noun **1** *the maid cleared the table* FEMALE SERVANT, maidservant, housemaid, domestic, housekeeper; help, cleaner, cleaning woman/lady; *dated* parlormaid, lady's maid, chambermaid.

**2** *literary a village maid and her swain* GIRL, young woman, young lady, lass, miss, ingenue; *literary* maiden, damsel, nymph; *archaic* wench.

**maiden** noun *literary a pretty young maiden.* See MAID sense 2.

▸ adjective **1** *a maiden aunt* UNMARRIED, spinster, unwed, unwedded, single, husbandless, celibate.

**2** *a maiden voyage* FIRST, initial, inaugural, introductory, initiatory, virgin.

**mail** noun *the mail arrived* letters, correspondence; postal system, postal service, post office; delivery, collection; e-mail; *chiefly Brit.* post; *informal* snail mail.

▸ verb *we mailed the card* SEND, dispatch, post, direct, forward, redirect, ship, express, courier; e-mail.

**maim** verb *a dog maimed by a coyote* INJURE, wound, cripple, disable, incapacitate, impair, mar, mutilate, lacerate, disfigure, deform, mangle.

**main** adjective *the main item* PRINCIPAL, chief, head, leading, foremost, most important, major, ruling, dominant, central, focal, key, prime, master, premier, primary, first, first-line, fundamental, supreme, predominant, (most) prominent, preeminent, paramount, overriding, cardinal, crucial, critical, pivotal, salient, elemental, essential, staple. ANTONYMS subsidiary, minor.

▸ noun *a burst water main* PIPE, channel, duct, conduit.

PHRASE: **in the main** *in the main, we want the menu to offer a nice selection of kosher alternatives.* See MAINLY.

**mainly** adverb *the people on the island are mainly tourists* MOSTLY, for the most part, in the main, on the whole, largely, by and large, to a large extent, predominantly, chiefly, principally, primarily; generally, usually, typically, commonly, on average, as a rule, almost always.

**mainspring** noun *the mainspring of anticommunism* MOTIVE, motivation, impetus, driving force, incentive, impulse, prime mover, reason, fountain, fount, wellspring, root, generator.

**mainstay** noun *agriculture is the mainstay of their economy* CENTRAL COMPONENT, central figure, centerpiece, prop, linchpin, cornerstone, pillar, bulwark, buttress, chief support, backbone, anchor, foundation, base, staple.

**maintain** verb **1** *they wanted to maintain peace* PRESERVE, conserve, keep, retain, keep going, keep alive, keep up, prolong, perpetuate, sustain, carry on, continue. ANTONYMS break (off), discontinue.

**2** *the association maintains its private roads* KEEP IN GOOD CONDITION, keep in (good) repair, keep up, service, care for, take good care of, look after. ANTONYM neglect.

**3** *the cost of maintaining a dog* SUPPORT, provide for, keep, sustain; nurture, feed, nourish. ANTONYM neglect.

**4** *he always maintained his innocence | he maintains that he is innocent* INSIST (ON), declare, assert, protest, affirm, avow, profess, claim, allege, contend, argue, swear (to), hold to; *formal* aver. ANTONYM deny.

**maintenance** noun **1** *the maintenance of peace* PRESERVATION, conservation, keeping, prolongation, perpetuation, carrying on, continuation, continuance. ANTONYMS breakdown, discontinuation.

**2** *car maintenance* UPKEEP, service, servicing, repair(s), care. ANTONYM neglect.

**3** *the maintenance of his children* SUPPORT, keeping, upkeep, sustenance; nurture, feeding, nourishment. ANTONYM neglect.

**4** *absent fathers are forced to pay maintenance* FINANCIAL SUPPORT, child support, alimony, provision; keep, subsistence, living expenses.

**majestic** adjective *the majestic Rocky Mountains | his father's majestic presence* STATELY, dignified, distinguished, solemn, magnificent, grand, splendid, resplendent, glorious, sumptuous, impressive, august, noble, awe-inspiring, monumental, palatial; statuesque, Olympian, imposing, marvelous, sonorous, resounding, heroic. ANTONYMS modest, wretched.

**major** adjective **1** *the major North American writers* GREATEST, best, finest, most important, chief, main, prime, principal, capital, cardinal, leading, star, foremost, outstanding, first-rate, preeminent, arch-; *informal* major league, big league. ANTONYM minor.

**2** *an issue of major importance* CRUCIAL, vital, great, considerable, paramount, utmost, prime; *informal* serious. ANTONYM little.

**3** *a major factor* IMPORTANT, big, significant, weighty, crucial, key, sweeping, substantial. ANTONYM trivial.

**4** *major surgery* SERIOUS, radical, complicated, difficult. ANTONYM minor.

**majority** noun **1** *the majority of cases* LARGER PART/NUMBER, greater part/number, best/better part, most, more than half; plurality, bulk, mass, weight, (main) body, preponderance, predominance, generality, lion's share. ANTONYM minority.

**2** *a majority in the election* (WINNING) MARGIN, superiority of numbers/votes; landslide.

**3** *my youngest child has reached majority* LEGAL AGE, adulthood, manhood/womanhood, maturity; age of consent, coming of age.

**USAGE NOTE majority**

Strictly speaking, **majority** should be used with countable nouns to mean 'the greater number': *the majority of cases*. The use of **majority** with uncountable nouns to mean 'the greatest part' (*I spent the majority of the day reading*), although common in informal contexts, is not considered good standard English.

**make** verb **1** *he makes models* CONSTRUCT, build, assemble, put together, manufacture, produce, fabricate, create, form, fashion, model. ANTONYM destroy.

**2** *I didn't want to go but she made me* FORCE, compel, coerce, press, drive, pressure, oblige, require; have someone do something, prevail on, dragoon, bludgeon, strong-arm, impel, constrain; *informal* railroad.

**3** *don't make such a noise* CAUSE, create, give rise to, produce, bring about, generate, engender, occasion, effect, set up, establish, institute, found, develop, originate; *literary* beget.

**4** *she made a little bow* PERFORM, execute, give, do, accomplish, achieve, bring off, carry out, effect.

**5** *they made him chairman* APPOINT, designate, name, nominate, select, elect, vote in, install; induct, institute, invest, ordain.

**6** *he had made a will* FORMULATE, frame, draw up, devise, make out, prepare, compile, compose, put together; draft, write, pen.

**7** *I've made a mistake* PERPETRATE, commit, be responsible for, be guilty of, be to blame for.

**8** *he's made a lot of money* ACQUIRE, obtain, gain, get, realize, secure, win, earn; gross, net, clear; bring in, take (in), rake in. ANTONYM lose.

**9** *he made dinner* PREPARE, get ready, put together, concoct, cook, dish up, throw together, whip up, brew; *informal* fix.

**10** *we've got to make a decision* REACH, come to, settle on, determine on, conclude.

**11** *she made a short announcement* UTTER, give, deliver, give voice to, enunciate, recite, pronounce.

**12** *the sofa makes a good bed* BE, act as, serve as, function as, constitute, do duty for.

**13** *he'll make the team* GAIN A PLACE IN, get into, gain access to, enter; achieve, attain.

**14** *he just made his train* CATCH, get, arrive/be in time for, arrive at, reach; get to. ANTONYM miss.

▸ noun **1** *what make is the car?* BRAND, marque, label.

**2** *a man of a different make from his brother* CHARACTER, nature, temperament, temper, disposition, kidney, mold, stamp.

PHRASES: **make as if/though** *he made as if to run away* FEIGN, pretend, make a show/pretense of, affect, feint, make out.

**make believe** *we encourage the children to make believe* PRETEND, fantasize, daydream, build castles in the air, dream, imagine, play-act, play.

**make do** *we have precious little but we make do | we'll have to make do with just one income* SCRAPE BY, get by, manage, cope, survive, muddle through, improvise, make ends meet, keep the wolf from the door, keep one's head above water; *informal* make out; (**make do with**) make the best of, get by on, put up with.

**make for 1** *she made for the door* GO FOR/TOWARD, head for/toward, aim for, make one's way toward, move toward, direct one's steps toward, steer a course toward, be bound for, make a beeline for.

**2** *constant arguing doesn't make for a happy marriage* CONTRIBUTE TO, be conducive to, produce, promote, facilitate, foster.

**make it 1** *he'll never make it as a singer* SUCCEED, be a success, distinguish oneself, get ahead, make good; *informal* make the grade, arrive.

**2** *she's very ill—is she going to make it?* SURVIVE, come through, pull through, get better, recover.

**make love.** See HAVE SEX WITH at SEX.

**make off with** *they made off with all the wedding gifts* TAKE, steal, purloin, pilfer, abscond with, run away/off with, carry off, snatch; kidnap, abduct; *informal* walk away/off with, swipe, filch, nab, lift, "liberate," "borrow," snitch, pinch; heist.

**make out** *informal* **1** *how did you make out?* GET ON/ALONG, fare, do, proceed, go, progress, manage, survive, cope, get by.

**2** *I could just make out a figure in the distance* SEE, discern, distinguish, perceive, pick out, detect, observe, recognize; *literary* descry, espy.

**3** *he couldn't make out what she was saying* UNDERSTAND, comprehend, follow, grasp, fathom, work out, make sense of, interpret, decipher, make head(s) or tail(s) of, get, get the drift of, catch.

**4** *she made out that he was violent* ALLEGE, claim, assert, declare, maintain, affirm, suggest, imply, hint, insinuate, indicate, intimate, impute; *formal* aver.

**5** *he made out a receipt for $20* WRITE OUT, fill out, fill in, complete, draw up.

**6** *they made out in the back seat* KISS, neck, caress, pet; *informal* smooch, canoodle, fool around.

**make over** *Grandpa made over the deed to Uncle Marc* TRANSFER, sign over, turn over, hand over/on/down, give, leave, bequeath, bestow, pass on, assign, consign, entrust; *Law* devolve.

**make up** **1** *let's kiss and make up* BE FRIENDS AGAIN, bury the hatchet, declare a truce, make peace, forgive and forget, shake hands, become reconciled, settle one's differences, mend fences, call it quits.

**2** *exports make up 42% of earnings* CONSTITUTE, form, compose, account for.

**3** *Gina brought a friend to make up a foursome* COMPLETE, round off/out, finish.

**4** *the pharmacist made up the prescription* PREPARE, mix, concoct, put together.

**5** *he made up an excuse* INVENT, fabricate, concoct, dream up, think up, hatch, trump up; devise, manufacture, formulate, coin; *informal* cook up.

**6** *she made up her face* APPLY MAKEUP/COSMETICS TO, powder; **(make oneself up)** *informal* put on one's face, do/paint one's face, apply one's war paint, doll oneself up.

**make up for** **1** *she tried to make up for what she'd said* ATONE FOR, make amends for, compensate for, make recompense for, make reparation for, make redress for, make restitution for, expiate.

**2** *job satisfaction can make up for low pay* OFFSET, counterbalance, counteract, compensate for; balance, neutralize, cancel out, even up, redeem.

**make up one's mind** *you need to make up your mind about the job offer* DECIDE, come to a decision, make/reach a decision; settle on a plan of action, come to a conclusion, reach a conclusion; determine, resolve.

**make way** *make way for the paramedics* MOVE ASIDE, clear the way, make a space, make room, stand back.

**make-believe** noun *that was sheer make-believe* FANTASY, pretense, daydreaming, imagination, invention, fancy, dream, fabrication, play-acting, dreaming in technicolor, charade, masquerade, dress-up. ANTONYM reality.

▸ adjective *make-believe adventures* IMAGINARY, imagined, made-up, fantasy, dreamed-up, fanciful, fictitious, fictive, feigned, fake, mock, sham, simulated; *informal* pretend, phony. ANTONYMS real, actual.

**maker** noun *the makers of fine furniture* CREATOR, manufacturer, constructor, builder, producer, fabricator, inventor, architect, designer.

**makeshift** adjective *we stayed dry under some makeshift shelter* TEMPORARY, provisional, interim, stopgap, make-do, standby, rough and ready, improvised, ad hoc, extempore, jury-rigged, jerry-built, thrown together, cobbled together. ANTONYM permanent.

**makeup** noun **1** *she used excessive makeup* COSMETICS, maquillage; greasepaint, face paint; *informal* war paint.

**2** *the cellular makeup of plants* COMPOSITION, constitution, structure, configuration, arrangement, organization, formation.

**3** *jealousy isn't part of his makeup* CHARACTER, nature, temperament, personality, disposition, mentality, persona, psyche; *informal* what makes someone tick.

**making** noun **1** *the making of cars* MANUFACTURE, mass-production, building, construction, assembly, production, creation, putting together, fabrication, forming, molding, forging. ANTONYM destruction.

**2** **(makings)** *she has the makings of a champion* QUALITIES, characteristics, ingredients; potential, promise, capacity, capability; essentials, essence, beginnings, rudiments, basics, stuff. PHRASE: **in the making** *a hero in the making* BUDDING, up and coming, emergent, developing, nascent, potential, promising, incipient.

**maladjusted** adjective *a home for maladjusted kids* DISTURBED, unstable, neurotic, unbalanced, unhinged, dysfunctional; *informal* mixed up, screwed up, messed up. ANTONYMS normal, stable.

**maladroit** adjective *the judge reprimanded Palermo for his maladroit handling of the case* BUNGLING, awkward, inept, clumsy, bumbling, incompetent, unskillful, heavy-handed, gauche, tactless, inconsiderate, undiplomatic, impolitic; *informal* ham-fisted, all thumbs, klutzy. ANTONYMS adroit, skillful.

**malady** noun *every time we visit Jerry, he has a new malady* ILLNESS, sickness, disease, infection, ailment, disorder, complaint, indisposition, affliction, infirmity, syndrome; *informal* bug, virus.

**malaise** noun *he showed no sign of emerging from his grief and malaise* UNHAPPINESS, uneasiness, unease, discomfort, melancholy, depression, despondency, dejection, angst, ennui; lassitude, listlessness, languor, weariness; indisposition, ailment, infirmity, illness, sickness, disease. ANTONYMS comfort, well-being.

**malapropism** noun *she's famous for her hilarious mala-*

*propisms* WRONG WORD, solecism, misuse, misapplication, infelicity, slip of the tongue, Freudian slip, blunder.

**malcontent** noun *a group of malcontents* TROUBLEMAKER, mischief-maker, agitator, dissident, rebel, rabble-rouser; discontent, complainer, grumbler, moaner, whiner; *informal* grouch, grump, bellyacher, kvetch, squeaky wheel.

▸ adjective *a malcontent employee.* See DISCONTENTED.

**male** adjective *it's his male jealousy, which is nearly always unfounded* MASCULINE, virile, manly, macho; red-blooded. ANTONYM female.

▸ noun *two males walked past.* See MAN noun sense 1.

THE RIGHT WORD **male, manful, manly, mannish, masculine, virile**

We speak of a **male** ancestor, a **masculine** scent, and a **manly** activity, but only of women as **mannish**. While all of these adjectives apply to what is characteristic of the male of the species (particularly the human species), *male* can refer to plants or animals as well as human beings and is used to describe whatever is biologically distinguished from the female sex (*an all-male choir; a male cat; a male holly bush*). *Masculine* refers to the qualities, characteristics, and behaviors associated with or thought to be appropriate to men and boys (*a masculine handshake*). *Manly* emphasizes the desirable qualities that a culture associates with a mature man, such as courage and independence (*the manly virtues; the manly sport of football*). **Manful** differs from *manly* primarily in its emphasis on sturdiness and resoluteness (*a manful effort to hold back tears*). **Virile** is a stronger word than *masculine* or *manly* and is applied only to mature men; it suggests the vigor, muscularity, and forcefulness—and especially the sexual potency—associated with mature manhood (*a virile man who looked like Charlton Heston in his youth*).

**malediction** noun *the maledictions of the evil Dr. Krepling* CURSE, damnation, oath; spell, hex, jinx; *formal* imprecation; *literary* anathema; *archaic* execration. ANTONYM blessing.

**malefactor** noun *she is studying the psychological profiles of three teenage malefactors* WRONGDOER, miscreant, offender, criminal, culprit, villain, lawbreaker, felon, evildoer, delinquent, hooligan, hoodlum; sinner, transgressor; *informal* crook, thug; *archaic* trespasser.

**malevolent** adjective *a malevolent glare* MALICIOUS, hostile, evil-minded, baleful, evil-intentioned, venomous, evil, malign, malignant, rancorous, vicious, vindictive, vengeful; *literary* malefic, maleficent. ANTONYM benevolent.

**malformed** adjective *a mythical island of malformed creatures* DEFORMED, misshapen, misproportioned, ill-proportioned, disfigured, distorted, crooked, contorted, twisted, warped; abnormal, grotesque, dysmorphic, monstrous. ANTONYMS perfect, normal, healthy.

**malfunction** verb *the computer has malfunctioned* CRASH, go wrong, break down, fail, stop working, go down; *informal* conk out, go kaput, blow up, act up.

▸ noun *a computer malfunction* CRASH, breakdown, fault, failure, bug; *informal* glitch.

**malice** noun *she had intended no malice toward him* SPITE, malevolence, ill will, vindictiveness, vengefulness, revenge, malignity, evil intentions, animus, enmity, rancor; *informal* bitchiness, cattiness; *literary* maleficence. ANTONYM benevolence.

**malicious** adjective *their malicious cousin Charles would mysteriously disappear at sea* SPITEFUL, malevolent, evil-intentioned, vindictive, vengeful, malign, mean, nasty, hurtful, mischievous, wounding, cruel, unkind; *informal* bitchy, catty; *literary* malefic, maleficent. ANTONYM benevolent.

**malign** adjective *a malign influence* HARMFUL, evil, bad, baleful, hostile, inimical, destructive, malignant, injurious; *literary* malefic, maleficent. ANTONYM beneficial.

▸ verb *he maligned an innocent man* DEFAME, slander, libel, blacken someone's name/character, smear, vilify, speak ill of, cast aspersions on, run down, traduce, denigrate, disparage, slur, abuse, revile; *informal* badmouth, dis, knock; *formal* derogate, calumniate. ANTONYM praise.

THE RIGHT WORD **malign, calumniate, defame, libel, slander, vilify**

Do you want to ruin someone's life? You can **malign** someone, which is to say or write something evil without necessarily lying (*she was maligned for her past association with radical causes*). To **calumniate** is to make false and malicious statements about someone; the word often implies that you have seriously damaged that person's good name (*after leaving his job, he spent most of his time calumniating and ridiculing his former boss*). To **defame** is to cause actual injury to someone's good name or reputation (*he defamed her by accusing her of being a spy*). If you don't mind risking a lawsuit, you can **libel** the person, which is to write or print something that defames him or her (*the tabloid libeled the celebrity and ended up paying the price*). **Slander**, which is to defame someone orally, is seldom a basis for court action but can nevertheless cause injury to someone's reputation (*after a loud and very public argument, she accused him of slandering her*). If all else fails, you can **vilify** the person, which is to engage in abusive name-calling (*even though he was found innocent by the jury, he was vilified by his neighbors*).

**malignant** noun **1** *a malignant disease* VIRULENT, very infectious, invasive, uncontrollable, dangerous, deadly, fatal, incurable, life-threatening. ANTONYM curable.

**2** *a malignant growth* CANCEROUS; *technical* metastatic. ANTONYM benign.

**3** *a malignant thought* SPITEFUL, malicious, malevolent, evil-intentioned, vindictive, vengeful, malign, mean, nasty, hurtful, mischievous, wounding, cruel, unkind; *informal* bitchy, catty; *literary* malefic, maleficent. ANTONYM benevolent.

**malinger** verb *he was put on report for malingering* PRETEND TO BE ILL, feign (an) illness, fake (an) illness; shirk; *informal* goof off.

**mall** noun *we met at the mall to get our ears pierced* SHOPPING CENTER, (shopping) plaza, shopping complex, strip mall, mini-mall, galleria, megamall, marketplace.

**malleable** adjective **1** *a malleable substance* PLIABLE, ductile, plastic, pliant, soft, workable. ANTONYM hard.

**2** *a malleable young woman* EASILY INFLUENCED, suggestible, susceptible, impressionable, pliable, amenable, compliant, tractable; biddable, complaisant, manipulable, persuadable, like putty in someone's hands. ANTONYM intractable.

**malnutrition** noun *the malnutrition of millions around the world is shameful* UNDERNOURISHMENT, malnourishment, poor diet, inadequate diet, unhealthy diet, lack of food; hunger, starvation.

**malodorous** adjective *several tenants in the building had complained about the malodorous apartment on the second floor* FOUL-SMELLING, evil-smelling, fetid, smelly, stinking (to high heaven), reeking, rank, high, putrid, noxious; *informal* stinky, funky; *literary* noisome, mephitic. ANTONYM fragrant.

**malpractice** noun *her foot surgeon was found guilty of malpractice* WRONGDOING, (professional) misconduct, breach of ethics, unprofessionalism, unethical behavior; negligence, carelessness, incompetence.

**maltreat** verb. See MISTREAT.

**mammoth** adjective *a crisis of mammoth proportions* HUGE, enormous, gigantic, giant, colossal, massive, vast, immense, mighty, stupendous, monumental, Herculean, epic, prodigious, mountainous, monstrous, titanic, towering, elephantine, king-size(d), economy-size(d), gargantuan, Brobdingnagian; *informal* mega, monster, whopping, honking, humongous, bumper, jumbo, astronomical, ginormous. ANTONYM tiny.

**man** noun **1** *a handsome man* MALE, adult male, gentleman; *informal* guy, fellow, fella, joe, geezer, gent, bloke, chap, dude, hombre; **(men)** menfolk.

**2** *all men are mortal* HUMAN BEING, human, person, mortal, individual, personage, soul.

**3** *the evolution of man* THE HUMAN RACE, the human species, *Homo sapiens*, humankind, humanity, human beings, humans, people, mankind.

**4** *the men voted to go on strike* WORKER, workman, laborer, hand, blue-collar worker; staff.

**5** *have you met her new man?* BOYFRIEND, partner, husband, spouse, lover, admirer, fiancé; common-law husband, live-in lover, significant other, main squeeze; *informal* toy boy, sugar daddy, intended; *dated* beau, steady, young man.

▸ verb **1** *the office is manned from 9 to 5* STAFF, crew, occupy, people.

**2** *firefighters manned the pumps* OPERATE, work, use, utilize.

PHRASES: **man to man** *can we speak man to man?* FRANKLY, openly, honestly, directly, candidly, plainly, forthrightly, without beating about the bush; woman to woman.

**to a man** *the squad volunteered, to a man, to work another full shift in the rescue mission* WITHOUT EXCEPTION, with no exceptions, bar none, one and all, everyone, each and every one, unanimously, as one.

**USAGE NOTE man**

Traditionally, the word **man** has been used to refer not only to adult males but also to human beings in general, regardless of sex. There is a historical explanation for this: in Old English, the principal sense of **man** was 'a human being,' and the words *wer* and *wif* were used to refer specifically to 'a male person' and 'a female person,' respectively. Subsequently, **man** replaced *wer* as the normal term for 'a male person,' but the older sense 'a human being' remained in use.

In the second half of the twentieth century, the generic use of **man** to refer to 'human beings in general' (*reptiles were here long before man appeared on the earth*) became problematic; the use is now often regarded as sexist or old-fashioned. In some contexts, terms such as **the human race** or **humankind** may be used instead of **man** or **mankind**.

---

**manacles** plural noun *he claimed there were no manacles that could hold him* HANDCUFFS, shackles, chains, irons, fetters, restraints, bonds; *informal* cuffs, bracelets.

**manage** verb **1** *she manages a staff of 80 people* BE IN CHARGE OF, run, be head of, head, direct, control, preside over, lead, govern, rule, command, superintend, supervise, oversee, administer, organize, conduct, handle, guide, be at the helm of; *informal* head up.

**2** *he managed a smile* ACCOMPLISH, achieve, do, carry out, perform, undertake, bring about/off, effect, finish; succeed in, contrive, engineer.

**3** *will you be able to manage without him?* COPE, get along/on, make do, be/fare/do all right, carry on, survive, get by, muddle through/along, fend for oneself, shift for oneself, make ends meet, weather the storm; *informal* make out, hack it.

**4** *she can't manage that horse* CONTROL, handle, master; cope with, deal with.

**manageable** adjective **1** *a manageable amount of work* ACHIEVABLE, doable, practicable, possible, feasible, reasonable, attainable, viable. ANTONYMS impractical, impossible.

**2** *a manageable child* COMPLIANT, tractable, pliant, pliable, malleable, biddable, docile, amenable, governable, controllable, accommodating, acquiescent, complaisant, yielding. ANTONYM unmanageable.

**3** *a manageable program* USER-FRIENDLY, easy to use, handy. ANTONYM unwieldy.

**management** noun **1** *he's responsible for the management of the firm* ADMINISTRATION, running, managing, organization; charge, care, direction, leadership, control, governing, governance, ruling, command, superintendence, supervision, overseeing, conduct, handling, guidance, operation.

**2** *workers are disputing with management* MANAGERS, employers, directors, board of directors, board, directorate, executives, administrators, administration; owners, proprietors; *informal* bosses, top brass.

**manager** noun **1** *the plant manager* EXECUTIVE, head of department, supervisor, principal, administrator, head, director, managing director, CEO, employer, superintendent, foreman, forewoman, overseer; proprietor; *informal* boss, chief, head honcho.

2 *the band's manager* ORGANIZER, controller, comptroller; impresario.

**mandate** noun 1 *they won a mandate to form the government* AUTHORITY, approval, acceptance, ratification, endorsement, sanction, authorization.

2 *a mandate from the UN* INSTRUCTION, directive, decree, command, order, injunction, edict, charge, commission, bidding, ruling, fiat; *formal* ordinance.

▸ verb 1 *catalytic converters were mandated in 1975* MAKE MANDATORY, legislate, authorize, require by law; designate.

2 *they were mandated to strike* INSTRUCT, order, direct, command, tell, require, charge, call on.

**mandatory** adjective *a high school diploma is mandatory* OBLIGATORY, compulsory, binding, required, requisite, necessary, essential, imperative. ANTONYM optional.

**maneuver** verb 1 *I maneuvered the car into the space* STEER, guide, drive, negotiate, navigate, pilot, direct, manipulate, move, work, jockey.

2 *he maneuvered things to suit himself* MANIPULATE, contrive, manage, engineer, devise, plan, fix, organize, arrange, set up, orchestrate, choreograph, stage-manage; *informal* wangle.

3 *he began maneuvering for the party leadership* INTRIGUE, plot, scheme, plan, lay plans, conspire, pull strings.

▸ noun 1 *a tricky parking maneuver* OPERATION, exercise, activity, move, movement, action.

2 *diplomatic maneuvers* STRATAGEM, tactic, gambit, ploy, trick, dodge, ruse, plan, scheme, operation, device, plot, machination, artifice, subterfuge, intrigue.

3 **(maneuvers)** *military maneuvers* TRAINING EXERCISES, exercises, war games, operations.

**manger** noun *they laid fresh hay in the manger* TROUGH, feeding trough, feeder, crib.

**mangle** verb 1 *the bodies were mangled beyond recognition* MUTILATE, maim, disfigure, damage, injure, crush; hack, cut up, lacerate, tear apart, butcher, maul.

2 *he's mangling the English language* SPOIL, ruin, mar, mutilate, make a mess of, wreck; *informal* murder, make a hash of, butcher.

**mangy** adjective 1 *a mangy cat* SCABBY, scaly, scabrous, diseased.

2 *a mangy old armchair* SCRUFFY, moth-eaten, shabby, worn; dirty, squalid, sleazy, seedy, flea-bitten; *informal* tatty, raggedy-ass, the worse for wear, scuzzy.

**manhandle** verb 1 *tourists were manhandled by the protestors* PUSH, shove, jostle, hustle; maltreat, ill-treat, mistreat, maul, molest; *informal* paw, rough up, roust.

2 *we manhandled the piano down the stairs* HEAVE, haul, push, shove; pull, tug, drag, lug, carry, lift, maneuver; *informal* hump.

**manhood** noun 1 *the transition from boyhood to manhood* MATURITY, sexual maturity, adulthood.

2 *an insult to his manhood* VIRILITY, manliness, machismo, masculinity, maleness; mettle, spirit, strength, fortitude, determination, bravery, courage, intrepidity, valor, heroism, boldness.

**mania** noun 1 *fits of mania* MADNESS, derangement, dementia, insanity, lunacy, psychosis, mental illness; delirium, frenzy, hysteria, raving, wildness.

2 *his mania for gadgets* OBSESSION, compulsion, fixation, fetish, fascination, preoccupation, infatuation, passion, enthusiasm, desire, urge, craving; craze, fad, rage; *informal* thing, yen.

**maniac** noun 1 *a homicidal maniac* LUNATIC, madman, madwoman, psychopath; *informal* loony, fruitcake, nutcase, nut, psycho, mental case, head case, sicko, screwball, crazy, loon.

2 *informal a techno maniac* ENTHUSIAST, fan, devotee, aficionado; *informal* freak, fiend, fanatic, nut, buff, bum, addict.

**manifest** verb 1 *she manifested signs of depression* DISPLAY, show, exhibit, demonstrate, betray, present, reveal; *formal* evince. ANTONYM hide.

2 *his positive potential* ***is manifested by*** *his art* BE EVIDENCE OF, be a sign of, indicate, show, attest to, reflect, bespeak, prove, establish, evidence, substantiate, corroborate, confirm; *literary* betoken. ANTONYM mask.

▸ adjective *his manifest lack of interest* OBVIOUS, clear, plain, apparent, evident, patent, palpable, distinct, definite, blatant, overt, glaring, barefaced, explicit, transparent, conspicuous, undisguised, unmistakable, noticeable, perceptible, visible, recognizable. ANTONYM secret.

**manifestation** noun 1 *the manifestation of anxiety* DISPLAY, demonstration, show, exhibition, presentation.

2 *manifestations of global warming* SIGN, indication, evidence, token, symptom, testimony, proof, substantiation, mark, reflection, example, instance. See note at SIGN.

3 *a supernatural manifestation* APPARITION, appearance, materialization, visitation.

**manifesto** noun *a party manifesto that would change the course of world politics* POLICY STATEMENT, mission statement, platform, (little) red book, program, declaration, proclamation, pronouncement, announcement.

**manifold** adjective *the problems are manifold* MANY, numerous, multiple, multifarious, legion, diverse, various, several, varied, different, miscellaneous, assorted, sundry; *literary* myriad, divers.

**manipulate** verb 1 *he manipulated some knobs and levers* OPERATE, work; turn, pull.

2 *she manipulated the muscles of his back* MASSAGE, rub, knead, feel, palpate.

3 *the government tried to manipulate the situation* CONTROL, influence, use/turn to one's advantage, exploit, maneuver, en-

gineer, steer, direct, gerrymander; twist someone around one's little finger.

4 *they accused him of manipulating the data* FALSIFY, rig, distort, alter, change, doctor, massage, juggle, tamper with, tinker with, interfere with, misrepresent; *informal* cook, fiddle with.

**manipulator** noun *a ruthless political manipulator* EXPLOITER, user, maneuverer, conniver, puppet master, wheeler-dealer; *informal* operator.

**mankind** noun *for the good of all mankind* THE HUMAN RACE, man, humanity, human beings, humans, *Homo sapiens*, humankind, people, men and women.

**manly** adjective 1 *his manly physique* VIRILE, masculine, strong, muscular, muscly, strapping, well-built, sturdy, robust, rugged, tough, powerful, brawny, red-blooded, vigorous; *informal* hunky. See note at MALE. ANTONYM effeminate.

2 *their manly deeds* BRAVE, courageous, bold, valiant, valorous, fearless, plucky, macho, manful, intrepid, daring, heroic, lionhearted, gallant, chivalrous, swashbuckling, adventurous, stouthearted, dauntless, doughty, resolute, determined, stalwart; *informal* gutsy, spunky, ballsy. ANTONYM cowardly.

**man-made** adjective *man-made fabrics* ARTIFICIAL, synthetic, manufactured, fabricated; imitation, ersatz, simulated, mock, fake, phony, counterfeit, plastic. ANTONYMS natural, real.

**manner** noun 1 *it was dealt with in a very efficient manner* WAY, fashion, mode, means, method, system, style, approach, technique, procedure, process, methodology, modus operandi, form.

2 *what manner of creature is it?* KIND, sort, type, variety, nature, breed, brand, stamp, class, category, genre, order.

3 *her rather unfriendly manner* DEMEANOR, air, aspect, attitude, bearing, cast, behavior, conduct; mien; *formal* comportment.

4 **(manners)** *aristocratic manners* CUSTOMS, habits, ways, practices, conventions, usages.

5 **(manners)** *it's bad manners to stare* BEHAVIOR, conduct, way of behaving; form.

6 **(manners)** *you ought to teach him some manners* CORRECT BEHAVIOR, etiquette, social graces, good form, protocol, politeness, decorum, propriety, gentility, civility, Ps and Qs.

**mannered** adjective *his highly mannered style of prose* AFFECTED, pretentious, unnatural, artificial, contrived, stilted, stiff, forced, put-on, theatrical, precious, stagy, camp; *informal* pseudo. ANTONYM natural.

**mannerism** noun *she built an act around the mannerisms she'd picked up from her Jewish mother and Italian aunts* IDIOSYNCRASY, quirk, oddity, foible, trait, peculiarity, habit, characteristic, tic.

**mannish** adjective *she adopted a mannish appearance for the stage* UNFEMININE, unwomanly, masculine, unladylike, Amazonian; *informal* butch. See note at MALE. ANTONYMS feminine, girlish.

**mansion** noun *a tour of Beverly Hills mansions* STATELY HOME, hall, manor, manor house, country house; *informal* palace; *formal* residence. ANTONYM hovel.

**manslaughter** noun *the jury will decide if she is guilty of manslaughter* KILLING, murder, homicide, assassination; *literary* slaying.

**mantle** noun 1 *a dark green velvet mantle* CLOAK, cape, shawl, wrap, stole; *historical* pelisse.

2 *a thick mantle of snow* COVERING, layer, blanket, sheet, veil, curtain, canopy, cover, cloak, pall, shroud.

3 *the mantle of leadership* ROLE, burden, onus, duty, responsibility.

▸ verb *heavy mists mantled the forest* COVER, envelop, veil, cloak, curtain, shroud, swathe, wrap, blanket, conceal, hide, disguise, mask, obscure, surround, clothe; *literary* enshroud.

**manual** adjective 1 *manual work* DONE WITH ONE'S HANDS, by hand, laboring, physical, blue-collar.

2 *a manual drill* HAND-OPERATED, hand, nonelectric, nonautomatic.

▸ noun *a training manual* HANDBOOK, instruction book, instructions, guide, how-to book, companion, ABC, primer, guidebook, A to Z; *informal* bible.

**manufacture** verb 1 *the company manufactures laser printers* MAKE, produce, mass-produce, build, construct, assemble, put together, create, fabricate, turn out, process, engineer.

2 *a story manufactured by the press* MAKE UP, invent, fabricate, concoct, hatch, dream up, think up, trump up, devise, formulate, frame, contrive; *informal* cook up.

▸ noun *the manufacture of aircraft engines* PRODUCTION, making, manufacturing, mass-production, construction, building, assembly, creation, fabrication, prefabrication, processing.

**manufacturer** noun *local manufacturers are important sources of tax revenue* MAKER, producer, builder, constructor, creator; factory owner, industrialist, captain of industry.

**manure** noun *spread composted manure over the strawberry plants* DUNG, muck, excrement, droppings, ordure, guano, cow pats; fertilizer; *informal* cow chips, road apples, horse apples, buffalo chips, cow-pies, cow patties, cow flops; turds, scat.

**many** adjective 1 *many animals were killed* NUMEROUS, a great/good deal of, a lot of, plenty of, countless, innumerable, scores of, crowds of, droves of, an army of, a horde of, a multitude of, a multiplicity of, multitudinous, multiple, untold; several, various, sundry, diverse, assorted, multifarious; copious, abundant, profuse, an abundance of, a profusion of; *informal* lots of, umpteen, loads of, masses of, stacks of, scads of, heaps of, piles of, bags of, tons of, oodles of, dozens of, hundreds of, thousands of, millions of, billions of, zillions of, gazillions of, a slew of, a boatload of, more —— than one can shake a stick at; *literary* myriad, divers. ANTONYM few.

2 *sacrificing the individual for the sake of the many* PEOPLE,

common people, masses, multitude, populace, public, rank and file; *informal* hoi polloi, common herd, mob, proletariat, riffraff, great unwashed, proles. ANTONYM few.

**map** noun *we'll never find their house without a map* PLAN, chart, cartogram, survey, plat, plot; road map, street map, guide; atlas, globe; relief map, contour map; Mercator projection, Peters projection.

▸ verb *the region was mapped from the air* CHART, plot, delineate, draw, depict, portray.

PHRASE: **map out** *he mapped out the plan for our campaign* OUTLINE, set out, lay out, sketch out, trace out, rough out, block out, delineate, detail, draw up, formulate, work out, frame, draft, plan, plot out, arrange, design, program.

**mar** verb **1** *an ugly scar marred his features* SPOIL, impair, disfigure, detract from, blemish, scar; mutilate, deface, deform. ANTONYM enhance.

**2** *the celebrations were marred by violence* SPOIL, ruin, impair, damage, wreck; harm, hurt, blight, taint, tarnish, sully, stain, pollute; *informal* foul up; *formal* vitiate.

**marauder** noun *they placed chains across the river to keep out marauders* RAIDER, plunderer, pillager, looter, robber, pirate, freebooter, bandit, highwayman, rustler; *literary* brigand; *archaic* buccaneer, corsair, reaver.

**march** verb **1** *the men marched past* STRIDE, walk, troop, step, pace, tread; footslog, slog, tramp, tromp, hike, trudge; parade, file, process.

**2** *she marched in without even knocking* STRIDE, strut, stalk, flounce, storm, stomp, sweep.

**3** *time **marches on*** ADVANCE, progress, move on, roll on.

▸ noun **1** *a long march* HIKE, trek, tramp, slog, footslog, walk; route march, forced march.

**2** *police in riot gear charged the march* PARADE, procession, cortège; demonstration, protest.

**3** *the march of technology* PROGRESS, advance, progression, development, evolution; passage.

**margin** noun **1** *the margin of the lake* EDGE, side, verge, border, perimeter, brink, brim, rim, fringe, boundary, limits, periphery, bound, extremity; *literary* bourn, skirt. See note at BORDER.

**2** *there's no margin for error* LEEWAY, latitude, scope, room, room to maneuver, space, allowance, extra, surplus.

**3** *they won by a narrow margin* GAP, majority, amount, difference.

**marginal** adjective **1** *the difference is marginal* SLIGHT, small, tiny, minute, insignificant, minimal, negligible.

**2** *a marginal case* BORDERLINE, disputable, questionable, doubtful.

**marijuana** noun *the illegal cultivation of marijuana* CANNABIS, hashish, hemp, sinsemilla; informal POT, dope, grass, weed, Mary Jane, bud, hash, bhang, kef, ganja, locoweed; reefer, doob, spliff, toke, roach.

**marinate** verb *marinate the ribs in a mixture of beer, honey, and orange rind* STEEP, soak, souse, immerse, marinade, bathe.

**marine** adjective **1** *marine plants* SEAWATER, sea, saltwater, oceanic; aquatic; *technical* pelagic.

**2** *a marine vessel* MARITIME, nautical, naval; seafaring, seagoing, oceangoing.

**mariner** noun *an old mariner from Gloucester* SAILOR, seaman, seafarer; *informal* sea dog, salt, bluejacket; *Brit.* matelot, shellback.

**marital** adjective *Fred was unable to cope with Leah's desire to dissolve their marital bond* MATRIMONIAL, married, wedded, conjugal, nuptial, marriage, wedding; spousal; *literary* connubial.

**maritime** adjective **1** *maritime law* NAVAL, marine, nautical; seafaring, seagoing, sea, oceangoing.

**2** *maritime regions* COASTAL, seaside, littoral.

**mark** noun **1** *a dirty mark* BLEMISH, streak, spot, fleck, dot, blot, stain, smear, speck, speckle, blotch, smudge, smut, fingermark, fingerprint; bruise, discoloration; birthmark; *informal* splotch; *technical* stigma.

**2** *a punctuation mark* SYMBOL, sign, character; diacritic.

**3** *books bearing the mark of a well-known bookseller* LOGO, seal, stamp, imprint, symbol, emblem, device, insignia, badge, brand, trademark, monogram, hallmark, logotype, watermark.

**4** *unemployment passed the three million mark* POINT, level, stage, degree.

**5** *a mark of respect* SIGN, token, symbol, indication, badge, emblem; symptom, evidence, proof.

**6** *the war left its mark on him* IMPRESSION, imprint, traces; effect, impact, influence.

**7** *the mark of a civilized society* CHARACTERISTIC, feature, trait, attribute, quality, hallmark, calling card, badge, stamp, property, indicator.

**8** *he got good marks for math* GRADE, grading, rating, score, percentage.

**9** *the bullet missed its mark* TARGET, goal, aim, bull's-eye; objective, object, end.

▸ verb **1** *be careful not to mark the woodwork* DISCOLOR, stain, smear, smudge, streak, blotch, blemish; dirty, pockmark, bruise; *informal* splotch; *literary* smirch.

**2** *her possessions were clearly marked* PUT ONE'S NAME ON, name, initial, label, identify; hallmark, watermark, brand.

**3** *I've marked the relevant passages* INDICATE, label, flag, tick, check off, highlight; show, identify, designate, delineate, denote, specify.

**4** *a festival to mark the town's 200th anniversary* CELEBRATE, observe, recognize, acknowledge, keep, honor, solemnize, pay tribute to, salute, commemorate, remember, memorialize.

**5** *the incidents marked a new phase in their campaign* REPRESENT, signify, be a sign of, indicate, herald.

6 *his style is marked by simplicity and concision* CHARACTERIZE, distinguish, identify, typify, brand, signalize, stamp.

7 *I have a pile of essays to mark* ASSESS, evaluate, grade, appraise, correct.

8 *it'll cause trouble, you mark my words!* TAKE HEED OF, heed, listen to, take note of, pay attention to, attend to, note, mind, bear in mind, take into consideration.

PHRASES: **make one's mark** *she intends to make her mark in Hollywood* BE SUCCESSFUL, distinguish oneself, succeed, be a success, prosper, get ahead, make good; *informal* make it, make the grade.
**mark down** *the prices will be marked down after Christmas* REDUCE, decrease, lower, cut, put down, discount; *informal* slash.
**mark up** *they were accused of marking up the cost before offering a discount* INCREASE, raise, up, put up, hike (up), escalate; *informal* jack up.
**quick off the mark** *an elite force that was more quick off the mark than any fighting element in the sector* ALERT, quick, quick-witted, bright, clever, perceptive, sharp, sharp-witted, observant, wide awake, on one's toes; *informal* on the ball, quick on the uptake.
**wide of the mark** *his answer was wide of the mark* INACCURATE, incorrect, wrong, erroneous, off target, out, mistaken, misguided, misinformed.

**marked** adjective *we see a marked improvement in Sally's grades* NOTICEABLE, pronounced, decided, distinct, striking, clear, glaring, blatant, unmistakable, obvious, plain, manifest, patent, palpable, prominent, signal, significant, conspicuous, notable, recognizable, identifiable, distinguishable, discernible, apparent, evident; written all over one. ANTONYM imperceptible.

**market** noun 1 *I'll get some sugar when I'm at the market* GROCERY STORE, supermarket, store, convenience store; farmers' market.

2 *browsing through old postcards at the antiques market* MARKETPLACE, mart, flea market, bazaar, fair; *archaic* emporium.

3 *there's no market for such goods* DEMAND, call, want, desire, need, requirement.

4 *the market is sluggish* STOCK MARKET, trading, trade, business, commerce, buying and selling, dealing.

▸ verb *the product was marketed worldwide* SELL, retail, vend, merchandise, trade, peddle, hawk; advertise, promote.

PHRASE: **on the market** *these are the finest pearls on the market today* ON SALE, (up) for sale, available, obtainable, on the block.

**maroon** verb *schoolboys marooned on a desert island* STRAND, cast away, cast ashore, shipwreck; abandon, leave behind, leave, leave in the lurch, desert, forsake; *informal* leave high and dry.

**marriage** noun 1 *a proposal of marriage* (HOLY) MATRIMONY, wedlock.

2 *the marriage took place at St. Margaret's* WEDDING, wedding ceremony, marriage ceremony, nuptials, union. ANTONYMS divorce, separation.

3 *a marriage of jazz, pop, and gospel* UNION, alliance, fusion, mixture, mix, blend, amalgamation, combination, merger. ANTONYM separation.

**married** adjective 1 *a married couple* WEDDED, wed; *informal* spliced, hitched, coupled. ANTONYM single.

2 *married bliss* MARITAL, matrimonial, conjugal, nuptial; *Law* spousal; *literary* connubial.

**marry** verb 1 *the couple married last year* GET/BE MARRIED, wed, be wed, become man and wife; *informal* tie the knot, walk down the aisle, take the plunge, get spliced, get hitched, say "I do"; *dated* plight/pledge one's troth.

2 *John wanted to marry her* WED; *informal* make an honest woman of; *archaic* espouse. ANTONYM divorce.

3 *the show marries poetry with art* JOIN, unite, combine, fuse, mix, blend, merge, amalgamate, link, connect, couple, knit, yoke. ANTONYM separate.

**marsh** noun *a pair of great blue herons made regular visits to the marsh* SWAMP, marshland, bog, peat bog, muskeg, swampland, morass, mire, moor, quagmire, slough, fen, fenland, wetland, bayou.

**marshal** verb 1 *they marshaled an army* ASSEMBLE, gather (together), collect, muster, call together, draw up, line up, align, array, organize, group, arrange, deploy, position, order, dispose; mobilize, rally, round up. See note at GATHER.

2 *guests were marshaled to their seats* USHER, guide, escort, conduct, lead, shepherd, steer, take.

**martial** adjective *their martial exploits* MILITARY, soldierly, soldier-like, army, naval; warlike, fighting, combative, bellicose, hawkish, pugnacious, militaristic.

**martyrdom** noun *the martyrdom of Peter* DEATH, suffering, torture, torment, persecution, agony, ordeal; killing, sacrifice, self-sacrifice, crucifixion, immolation, burning, auto-da-fé; *Christianity* Passion.

**marvel** verb *she marveled at their courage* BE AMAZED, be astonished, be surprised, be awed, stand in awe, wonder; stare, gape, goggle, not believe one's eyes/ears, be dumbfounded; *informal* be flabbergasted.

▸ noun *he's a marvel* WONDER, miracle, sensation, spectacle, phenomenon; *informal* something else, something to shout about.

**marvelous** adjective 1 *his solo climb was marvelous* AMAZING, astounding, astonishing, awesome, breathtaking, sensational, remarkable, spectacular, stupendous, staggering, stunning; phenomenal, prodigious, miraculous, extraordinary, incredible, unbelievable; *literary* wondrous. ANTONYM commonplace.

2 *marvelous weather* EXCELLENT, splendid, wonderful, magnificent, superb, glorious, sublime, lovely, delightful, too good to be true; *informal* super, great, amazing, fantastic, terrific, tremendous, sensational, heavenly, divine, gorgeous, grand, fab-

ulous, fab, marvy, awesome, to die for, magic, ace, killer, wicked, mind-blowing, jaw-dropping, far out, out of this world; smashing, brilliant, boss; *informal, dated* swell, dreamy. ANTONYM awful.

**masculine** adjective **1** *a masculine trait* MALE, man's, men's; male-oriented. See note at MALE. ANTONYM feminine.

**2** *a powerfully masculine man* VIRILE, macho, manly, muscular, muscly, strong, strapping, well built, rugged, robust, brawny, powerful, red-blooded, vigorous; *informal* hunky. ANTONYMS weak, effeminate.

**3** *a rather masculine woman* MANNISH, boyish, unfeminine, unwomanly, Amazonian; *informal* butch.

**masculinity** noun *he's the picture of masculinity* VIRILITY, manliness, maleness, machismo, vigor, strength, muscularity, ruggedness, robustness; *informal* testosterone.

**mash** verb *mash the potatoes* SMASH, crush, purée, cream, pulp, squash, pound, beat, rice.

▸ noun *first pound the garlic to a mash* PULP, purée, mush, paste.

**mask** noun **1** *she wore a mask to conceal her face* DISGUISE, false face; *historical* domino, visor.

**2** *he dropped his mask of good humor* PRETENSE, semblance, veil, screen, front, false front, facade, veneer, blind, disguise, guise, concealment, cover, cover-up, cloak, camouflage.

▸ verb *poplar trees masked the factory* HIDE, conceal, disguise, cover up, obscure, screen, cloak, camouflage, veil.

**Mass** noun *we attended the six o'clock Mass* EUCHARIST, Holy Communion, Communion, service, liturgy.

**mass** noun **1** *a soggy mass of fallen leaves* PILE, heap; accumulation, aggregation, accretion, concretion, buildup; *informal* batch, wad.

**2** *a mass of cyclists* CROWD, horde, large group, throng, host, troop, army, herd, flock, drove, swarm, mob, pack, press, crush, flood, multitude.

**3** *the mass of our students are licensed drivers* MAJORITY, greater part/number, best/better part, major part, bulk, main body, lion's share; **(the mass)** most.

**4** **(masses)** *bringing the news to the masses* COMMON PEOPLE, populace, public, people, rank and file, crowd, third estate; *derogatory* hoi polloi, mob, proletariat, common herd, great unwashed.

**5** *informal a mass of food.* See LOT noun sense 1.

▸ adjective *mass hysteria* WIDESPREAD, general, wholesale, universal, large-scale, extensive, pandemic.

▸ verb *they began massing troops in the region* ASSEMBLE, marshal, gather together, muster, round up, mobilize, rally.

**massacre** noun **1** *a cold-blooded massacre of innocent civilians* SLAUGHTER, wholesale/mass slaughter, indiscriminate killing, mass murder, mass execution, annihilation, liquidation, decimation, extermination; carnage, butchery, bloodbath, bloodletting, pogrom, genocide, ethnic cleansing, holocaust, night of the long knives; *literary* slaying.

**2** *informal the game was an 8–0 massacre.* See ROUT noun sense 2.

▸ verb **1** *thousands were brutally massacred* SLAUGHTER, butcher, murder, kill, annihilate, exterminate, execute, liquidate, eliminate, decimate, wipe out, mow down, cut down, put to the sword, put to death; *literary* slay. See note at KILL.

**2** *informal they were massacred in the final round.* See TROUNCE.

**massage** noun *her physical therapy includes massage* RUB, rubdown, rubbing, kneading, palpation, manipulation, pummeling; body rub, back rub; shiatsu, reflexology, acupressure, hydromassage, Swedish massage, osteopathy; effleurage, tapotement.

▸ verb **1** *he massaged her tired muscles* RUB, knead, palpate, manipulate, pummel, work.

**2** *the statistics have been massaged* ALTER, tamper with, manipulate, doctor, falsify, juggle, fiddle with, tinker with, distort, change, rig, interfere with, misrepresent; *informal* fix, cook, fiddle.

**massive** adjective *a massive iceberg* HUGE, enormous, vast, immense, large, big, mighty, great, colossal, tremendous, prodigious, gigantic, gargantuan, mammoth, monstrous, monumental, giant, towering, elephantine, mountainous, titanic; epic, Herculean, Brobdingnagian; *informal* monster, jumbo, mega, whopping, humongous, hulking, honking, bumper, astronomical, ginormous. See note at HEAVY. ANTONYM tiny.

**mast** noun **1** *a ship's mast* spar, boom, yard, gaff, foremast, mainmast, topmast, mizzen-mast, mizzen, royal mast.

**2** *the mast on top of the building* FLAGPOLE, flagstaff, pole, post, rod, upright; aerial, transmitter, pylon.

**master** noun **1** *historical he acceded to his master's wishes* LORD, overlord, lord and master, ruler, sovereign, monarch, liege (lord), suzerain. ANTONYMS servant, underling.

**2** *the dog's master* OWNER, keeper.

**3** *a chess master* EXPERT, adept, genius, past master, maestro, virtuoso, professional, doyen, authority, champion; *informal* ace, pro, wizard, whiz, hotshot, maven, crackerjack. ANTONYMS novice, amateur.

**4** *the master of the ship* CAPTAIN, commander; *informal* skipper.

**5** *their spiritual master* GURU, teacher, leader, guide, mentor; rabbi, swami, Maharishi. ANTONYMS acolyte, disciple.

▸ verb **1** *I managed to master my fears* OVERCOME, conquer, beat, quell, quash, suppress, control, overpower, triumph over, subdue, vanquish, subjugate, prevail over, govern, curb, check, bridle, tame, defeat, get the better of, get a grip on, get over; *informal* lick.

**2** *it took ages to master the technique* LEARN, become proficient in, know inside out, know (frontward and) backwards; pick up, grasp, understand; *informal* get the hang of.

▸ adjective **1** *a master craftsman* EXPERT, adept, proficient, skilled, skillful, deft, dexterous, adroit, practiced, experienced, masterly, accomplished, complete, demon, brilliant; *informal* crack, ace, mean, crackerjack.

2 *the master bedroom* PRINCIPAL, main, chief; biggest.

**masterful** adjective 1 *a masterful man* COMMANDING, powerful, imposing, magisterial, lordly, authoritative; dominating, domineering, overbearing, overweening, imperious. ANTONYM weak.

2 *their masterful handling of the situation* EXPERT, adept, clever, masterly, skillful, skilled, adroit, proficient, deft, dexterous, accomplished, polished, consummate; *informal* crack, ace. ANTONYM inept.

THE RIGHT WORD **masterful, masterly**

**Masterful** and **masterly** overlap in meaning and are sometimes confused. **Masterful** can mean 'domineering,' but it also means 'very skillful, masterly.' Note, however, that **masterful** used in this 'masterly' sense generally describes a person ( *he has limited talent, but he's masterful at exploiting it*), while **masterly** usually describes an achievement or action ( *that was a masterly response to our opponents' arguments*).

**masterly** adjective. See note at MASTERFUL.

**mastermind** verb *he masterminded the whole campaign* PLAN, control, direct, be in charge of, run, conduct, organize, arrange, preside over, orchestrate, stage-manage, engineer, manage, coordinate; conceive, devise, originate, initiate, think up, frame, hatch, come up with; *informal* be the brains behind.

▸ noun *the mastermind behind the project* GENIUS, mind, intellect, author, architect, organizer, originator, prime mover, initiator, inventor; *informal* brain, brains, idea man.

**masterpiece** noun *Vivaldi's masterpiece* PIÈCE DE RÉSISTANCE, chef-d'œuvre, masterwork, magnum opus, finest/best work, tour de force.

**mastery** noun 1 *her mastery of the language* PROFICIENCY, ability, capability; knowledge, understanding, comprehension, familiarity, command, grasp, grip.

2 *they played with tactical mastery* SKILL, skillfulness, expertise, dexterity, finesse, adroitness, virtuosity, prowess, deftness, proficiency; *informal* know-how.

3 *man's mastery over nature* CONTROL, domination, command, ascendancy, supremacy, preeminence, superiority; triumph, victory, the upper hand, the whip hand, rule, government, power, sway, authority, jurisdiction, dominion, sovereignty.

**masticate** verb *strong jaws enable them to masticate the bones of their prey* CHEW, munch, champ, chomp, crunch, eat; *formal* manducate.

**mat** noun 1 *the fat cat sat on the mat* RUG, runner, carpet, doormat, welcome mat, bath mat, hearth rug, floor cloth; dhurrie, numdah; kilim, flokati, tatami.

2 *he placed his glass on the mat* COASTER, placemat, table mat.

3 *a thick mat of hair* MASS, tangle, knot, mop, thatch, shock, mane.

▸ verb *his hair was matted with blood* TANGLE, entangle, knot, snarl up.

**match** noun 1 *we won the match* CONTEST, competition, game, tournament, event, trial, test, meet, matchup; bout, fight; derby; playoff, replay, rematch, engagement; *Scottish & Canadian* bonspiel.

2 *he was no match for the champion* EQUAL, rival, equivalent, peer, counterpart; *formal* compeer.

3 *the vase was an exact match of the one she already owned* LOOK-ALIKE, double, twin, duplicate, mate, fellow, companion, counterpart; replica, copy; *informal* spitting image, dead ringer.

4 *a love match* MARRIAGE, betrothal, relationship, partnership, union.

▸ verb 1 *the curtains matched the duvet cover* GO WITH, coordinate with, complement, suit; be the same as, be similar to.

2 *did their statements match?* CORRESPOND, be in agreement, tally, agree, match up, coincide, accord, conform, square.

3 *no one can match him at chess* EQUAL, be a match for, measure up to, compare with, parallel, be in the same league as, be on a par with, touch, keep pace with, keep up with, emulate, rival, vie with, compete with, contend with; *informal* hold a candle to.

**matching** adjective *red suede boots with a matching handbag | pick the two matching blocks from the pile* CORRESPONDING, equivalent, parallel, analogous; coordinating, complementary; paired, twin, identical, like, like (two) peas in a pod, alike. ANTONYMS different, clashing.

**matchless** adjective *her sister's matchless beauty* INCOMPARABLE, unrivaled, inimitable, beyond compare/comparison, unparalleled, unequaled, without equal, peerless, second to none, unsurpassed, unsurpassable, nonpareil, unique, consummate, perfect, rare, transcendent, surpassing; *formal* unexampled.

**mate** noun 1 *she's finally found her ideal mate* PARTNER, life partner, husband, wife, spouse, lover, live-in lover, significant other, companion, helpmate, helpmeet, consort; *informal* better half, other half, main squeeze, hubby, missus, missis, old lady, old man.

2 *this sock has lost its mate* MATCH, fellow, twin, companion, other half, equivalent.

3 *informal he's gone out with his mates.* See CHUM.

▸ verb *pandas rarely mate in captivity* BREED, couple, copulate.

**material** noun 1 *the decomposition of organic material* MATTER, substance, stuff, medium.

2 *the materials for a new building* CONSTITUENT, raw material, element, component.

3 **(materials)** *cleaning materials* THINGS, items, articles, stuff, necessaries.

4 *curtain material* FABRIC, cloth, textiles.

5 *material for a magazine article* INFORMATION, data, facts,

facts and figures, statistics, evidence, details, particulars, background, notes; *informal* info, dope, lowdown.

▸ adjective **1** *the material world* PHYSICAL, corporeal, tangible, nonspiritual, mundane, worldly, earthly, secular, temporal, concrete, real, solid, substantial. ANTONYMS spiritual, abstract.

**2** *she was too fond of material comforts* SENSUAL, physical, carnal, corporal, fleshly, bodily, creature. ANTONYMS intellectual, aesthetic.

**3** *information that could be material to the inquiry* RELEVANT, pertinent, important, applicable, germane; apropos, to the point; vital, essential, key. ANTONYMS immaterial, irrelevant.

**4** *the storms caused material damage* SIGNIFICANT, major, important. ANTONYM insignificant.

**materialize** verb **1** *the forecasted rain did not materialize* HAPPEN, occur, come about, take place, come into being, transpire; *informal* come off; *formal* eventuate; *literary* come to pass.

**2** *Harry materialized at the door* APPEAR, turn up, arrive, make/put in an appearance, present oneself/itself, emerge, surface, reveal oneself/itself, show one's face, pop up; *informal* show up.

**maternal** adjective **1** *her maternal instincts* MOTHERLY, protective, caring, nurturing, loving, devoted, affectionate, fond, warm, tender, gentle, kind, kindly, comforting.

**2** *his maternal grandparents* ON ONE'S MOTHER'S SIDE; *dated* on the distaff side.

**mathematical** adjective **1** *mathematical symbols* ARITHMETICAL, numerical; statistical, algebraic, geometric, trigonometric.

**2** *mathematical precision* RIGOROUS, meticulous, scrupulous, punctilious, scientific, strict, precise, exact, accurate, pinpoint, correct, careful, unerring.

**matrimonial** adjective. See MARITAL.

**matrimony** noun *the sacrament of holy matrimony* MARRIAGE, wedlock, union; nuptials. ANTONYM divorce.

**matted** adjective *the cat's matted fur* TANGLED, tangly, knotted, knotty, tousled, disheveled, uncombed, unkempt; *informal* ratty, mussy.

**matter** noun **1** *decaying vegetable matter* MATERIAL, substance, stuff.

**2** *the heart of the matter* AFFAIR, business, proceeding, situation, circumstance, event, happening, occurrence, incident, episode, experience; subject, topic, issue, question, point, point at issue, case, concern.

**3** *it is of little matter now* IMPORTANCE, consequence, significance, note, import, weight; *formal* moment.

**4** *what's the matter?* PROBLEM, trouble, difficulty, complication; upset, worry.

**5** *the matter of the book* CONTENT, subject matter, text, argument, substance.

▸ verb *it doesn't matter what you wear* BE IMPORTANT, make any/a difference, be of importance, be of consequence, be relevant, count; *informal* cut any ice.

PHRASES: **as a matter of fact** *as a matter of fact, I was the one who sent the flowers* ACTUALLY, in (actual) fact, in point of fact, as it happens, really, believe it or not, in reality, in truth, to tell the truth.

**no matter** *I ordered a blue tablecloth, but no matter, the green one looks just fine* IT DOESN'T MATTER, it makes no difference, it's not important, never mind, don't worry about it.

**matter-of-fact** adjective *Desmond is too creative and fanciful to fit in with such matter-of-fact people* UNEMOTIONAL, practical, down-to-earth, sensible, realistic, rational, sober, unsentimental, pragmatic, businesslike, commonsensical, levelheaded, hardheaded, no-nonsense, factual, literal, straightforward, straight-out, plain, unembellished, unvarnished, unadorned; unimaginative, prosaic.

**mature** adjective **1** *a mature woman* ADULT, grown-up, grown, fully grown, full-grown, of age, fully developed, in one's prime, middle-aged. ANTONYM adolescent.

**2** *he's very mature for his age* SENSIBLE, responsible, adult, levelheaded, reliable, dependable; wise, discriminating, shrewd, sophisticated. ANTONYM childish.

**3** *mature cheese* RIPE, ripened, mellow; ready to eat/drink. ANTONYMS fresh, unripe.

**4** *on mature reflection, he decided not to go* CAREFUL, thorough, deep, considered. ANTONYMS impulsive, unthinking.

▸ verb **1** *kittens mature when they are about a year old* BE FULLY GROWN, be full-grown; come of age, reach adulthood, reach maturity.

**2** *he's matured since he left home* GROW UP, become more sensible, become more adult; blossom.

**3** *leave the cheese to mature* RIPEN, mellow; age.

**4** *their friendship didn't have time to mature* DEVELOP, grow, evolve, bloom, blossom, flourish, thrive.

THE RIGHT WORD **mature, age, develop, mellow, ripen**

Most of us would prefer to **mature** rather than simply **age**. *Mature* implies gaining wisdom, experience, or sophistication as well as adulthood; when applied to other living things, it indicates fullness of growth and readiness for normal functioning (*a mature crop of strawberries*). To *age*, on the other hand, is to undergo the changes that result from the passage of time, often with an emphasis on the negative or destructive changes that accompany growing old (*the tragedy aged him five years*). **Develop** is like *mature* in that it means to undergo a series of positive changes to attain perfection or effectiveness, but it can refer to a part as well as a whole organism (*the kitten's eyesight had begun to develop at three weeks*). **Ripen** is a less formal word meaning to *mature*, but it usually applies to fruit (*the apples ripened in the sun*). **Mellow** suggests the tempering or moderation of harshness that comes with time or experience. With its connotations of warmth, mildness, and sweetness, it is a more positive word than *mature* or *age* (*to mellow as one gets older*).

**maturity** noun **1** *her progress from childhood to maturity* ADULTHOOD, majority, coming-of-age, manhood, womanhood.

**2** *he displayed a maturity beyond his years* RESPONSIBILITY, sense, levelheadedness; wisdom, discrimination, shrewdness, sophistication.

**maudlin** adjective **1** *maudlin self-pity* SENTIMENTAL, oversentimental, emotional, overemotional, tearful, lachrymose; *informal* weepy, misty-eyed. See note at SENTIMENTAL.

**2** *a maudlin ballad* MAWKISH, sentimental, oversweet, oversentimental; *informal* tearjerker, tearjerking, mushy, slushy, sloppy, schmaltzy, cheesy, corny, soppy, cornball, three-hankie.

**maul** verb **1** *he had been mauled by a lion* SAVAGE, attack, tear to pieces, lacerate, claw, scratch.

**2** *the customers are not allowed to maul our dancers* MOLEST, feel, fondle, manhandle; *informal* grope, paw.

**3** *informal* *his book was mauled by the critics.* See CRITICIZE.

**mausoleum** noun *the Dirkson family mausoleum dates back to 1878* TOMB, sepulcher, crypt, vault, charnel house, burial chamber, catacomb.

**maverick** noun *Torrey was the maverick in the family, the only one who valued freedom over an inheritance* INDIVIDUALIST, nonconformist, free spirit, unorthodox person, original, eccentric; rebel, dissenter, dissident, enfant terrible; *informal* cowboy, loose cannon. ANTONYM conformist.

**mawkish** adjective *he keeps sending her these mawkish greeting cards* SENTIMENTAL, oversentimental, maudlin, cloying, sickly, saccharine, sugary, oversweet, syrupy, nauseating; *informal* mushy, slushy, sloppy, schmaltzy, weepy, cutesy, lovey-dovey, cheesy, corny, soppy, cornball, hokey, tearjerker, tearjerking, three-hankie. See note at SENTIMENTAL.

**maxim** noun *the maxim "you can't cheat an honest man" is posted on the wall above his desk* SAYING, adage, aphorism, proverb, motto, saw, axiom, dictum, precept, epigram; truism, cliché. See note at SAYING.

**maximum** adjective *the maximum amount* GREATEST, highest, biggest, largest, top, topmost, most, utmost, maximal. ANTONYM minimum.

▸ noun *production levels are near their maximum* UPPER LIMIT, limit, utmost, uttermost, greatest, most, extremity, peak, height, ceiling, top, apex; *informal* max. ANTONYM minimum.

**maybe** adverb *maybe the bus will be on time today* PERHAPS, possibly, conceivably, it could be (that), it is possible (that), for all one knows; *literary* peradventure, perchance.

**mayhem** noun *no one would confess to how the mayhem started* CHAOS, disorder, havoc, bedlam, pandemonium, tumult, uproar, turmoil, commotion, all hell broken loose, maelstrom, trouble, disturbance, confusion, riot, anarchy, violence, insanity, madness; *informal* madhouse.

**maze** noun *the mainland's city streets were a baffling maze to the islanders* LABYRINTH, complex network, warren; web, tangle, jungle, snarl; puzzle.

**meadow** noun *Holsteins and Guernseys grazed lazily in the meadows along Route 24* FIELD, paddock; pasture, pastureland, prairie; *literary* lea, mead.

**meager** adjective **1** *their meager earnings* INADEQUATE, scanty, scant, paltry, limited, restricted, modest, insufficient, sparse, deficient, negligible, skimpy, slender, poor, miserable, pitiful, puny, miserly, niggardly, beggarly; *informal* measly, stingy, pathetic, piddling; *formal* exiguous. ANTONYM abundant.

**2** *a tall, meager man* THIN, lean, skinny, spare, scrawny, gangling, gangly, spindly, stringy, bony, rawboned, gaunt, underweight, underfed, undernourished, emaciated, skeletal. ANTONYM fat.

**meal** noun *each meal on the cruise ship was spectacular* SNACK; *informal* bite (to eat), spread, blowout, feed; *formal* repast, collation; *literary* refection.

**mean**[1] verb **1** *flashing lights mean the road is blocked* SIGNIFY, convey, denote, designate, indicate, connote, show, express, spell out; stand for, represent, symbolize; imply, suggest, intimate, hint at, insinuate, drive at, refer to, allude to, point to; *literary* betoken.

**2** *she didn't mean to break it* INTEND, aim, plan, design, have in mind, contemplate, purpose, propose, set out, aspire, desire, want, wish, expect. See note at INTEND.

**3** *he was hit by a bullet meant for a soldier* INTEND, design; destine, predestine.

**4** *the closures will mean a rise in unemployment* ENTAIL, involve, necessitate, lead to, result in, give rise to, bring about, cause, engender, produce.

**5** *this means a lot to me* MATTER, be important, be significant.

**6** *a red sky in the morning usually means rain* PRESAGE, portend, foretell, augur, promise, foreshadow, herald, signal, bode; *literary* betoken.

**mean**[2] adjective **1** *a mean trick* UNKIND, nasty, unpleasant, spiteful, malicious, unfair, cruel, shabby, foul, despicable, contemptible, obnoxious, vile, odious, loathsome, base, low; *informal* horrible, horrid, hateful, rotten, lowdown; beastly. ANTONYM kind.

**2** *he's too mean to leave a tip* MISERLY, niggardly, close-fisted, parsimonious, penny-pinching, cheeseparing, Scroogelike; *informal* tightfisted, stingy, tight, mingy, money-grubbing, cheap; *formal* penurious. ANTONYMS generous, munificent.

**3** *the truth was obvious to even the meanest intelligence* INFERIOR, poor, limited, restricted.

**4** *their mean origins* LOWLY, humble, ordinary, low, low-born, modest, common, base, proletarian, plebeian, obscure, ignoble, undistinguished; *archaic* baseborn. ANTONYM noble.

**5** *informal* *he's a mean cook.* See EXCELLENT.

**mean**[3] noun *a mean between frugality and miserliness* MID-

DLE COURSE, middle way, midpoint, happy medium, golden mean, compromise, balance; median, norm, average.

▸ adjective *the mean temperature* AVERAGE, median, middle, medial, medium, normal, standard.

**meander** verb **1** *the river meandered gently* ZIGZAG, wind, twist, turn, curve, curl, bend, snake.

**2** *we meandered along the path* STROLL, saunter, amble, wander, ramble, drift, maunder; *informal* mosey, tootle, toodle.

**meandering** adjective **1** *a meandering stream* WINDING, windy, zigzag, zigzagging, twisting, turning, curving, serpentine, sinuous, twisty. ANTONYM straight.

**2** *meandering reminiscences* RAMBLING, maundering, circuitous, roundabout, digressive, discursive, indirect, tortuous, convoluted. ANTONYM succinct.

**meaning** noun **1** *the meaning of his remark* SIGNIFICANCE, sense, signification, import, gist, thrust, drift, implication, tenor, message, essence, substance, purport, intention.

**2** *the word has several different meanings* DEFINITION, sense, explanation, denotation, connotation, interpretation, nuance.

**3** *my life has no meaning* VALUE, validity, worth, consequence, account, use, usefulness, significance, point.

**4** *his smile was full of meaning* EXPRESSIVENESS, significance, eloquence, implications, insinuations.

▸ adjective *a meaning look.* See MEANINGFUL sense 3.

**meaningful** adjective **1** *a meaningful remark* SIGNIFICANT, relevant, important, consequential, telling, material, valid, worthwhile. ANTONYM inconsequential.

**2** *a meaningful relationship* SINCERE, deep, serious, in earnest, significant, important.

**3** *a meaningful glance* EXPRESSIVE, eloquent, pointed, significant, meaning; pregnant, speaking, telltale, revealing, suggestive, charged, loaded.

**meaningless** adjective **1** *a jumble of meaningless words* UNINTELLIGIBLE, incomprehensible, incoherent.

**2** *she felt her life was meaningless* FUTILE, pointless, aimless, empty, hollow, blank, vain, purposeless, valueless, useless, of no use, worthless, senseless, trivial, trifling, unimportant, insignificant, inconsequential. ANTONYM worthwhile.

**means** plural noun **1** *the best means to achieve your goal* METHOD, way, manner, mode, measure, technique, expedient, agency, medium, instrument, channel, vehicle, avenue, course, process, procedure.

**2** *she doesn't have the means to support herself* MONEY, resources, capital, income, finance, funds, cash, wherewithal, assets; *informal* dough, bread, moola.

**3** *a man of means* WEALTH, riches, affluence, substance, fortune, property, money, capital. PHRASES: **by all means** *by all means you must have dinner with us* OF COURSE, certainly, definitely, surely, absolutely, with pleasure; *informal* sure thing.
**by means of** *the load was raised by means of a crane* USING, utilizing, employing, through, with the help of; as a result of, by dint of, by way of, by virtue of.
**by no means** *the result is by no means certain* NOT AT ALL, in no way, not in the least, not in the slightest, not the least bit, not by a long shot, certainly not, absolutely not, definitely not, on no account, under no circumstances; *informal* no way.

**meantime** PHRASE: **in the meantime** See MEANWHILE sense 1.

**meanwhile** adverb **1** *meanwhile, I'll stay here* FOR NOW, for the moment, for the present, for the time being, meantime, in the meantime, in the interim, in the interval.

**2** *cook for a further half hour; meanwhile, make the stuffing* AT THE SAME TIME, simultaneously, concurrently.

**measurable** adjective **1** *a measurable amount* QUANTIFIABLE, computable.

**2** *a measurable improvement* APPRECIABLE, noticeable, significant, visible, perceptible, definite, obvious.

**measure** verb **1** *they measured the length of the room* CALCULATE, compute, count, meter, quantify, weigh, size, evaluate, assess, gauge, plumb, determine.

**2** *she did not need to **measure** herself **against** some ideal* COMPARE WITH, pit against, set against, test against, judge by.

▸ noun **1** *cost-cutting measures* ACTION, act, course (of action), deed, proceeding, procedure, step, means, expedient; maneuver, initiative, program, operation.

**2** *the House passed the measure* STATUTE, act, bill, law, legislation.

**3** *the original dimensions were in metric measure* SYSTEM, standard, units, scale.

**4** *a measure of egg white* QUANTITY, amount, portion.

**5** *the students retain **a measure** of independence* A CERTAIN AMOUNT, an amount, a certain degree, a degree; some.

**6** *sales are the measure of the company's success* YARDSTICK, test, standard, barometer, touchstone, litmus test, criterion, benchmark.

PHRASES: **beyond measure** *it irritates him beyond measure that she is always right* IMMENSELY, extremely, vastly, greatly, excessively, immeasurably, incalculably, infinitely.
**for good measure** *she added a couple of chili peppers for good measure* AS A BONUS, as an extra, into the bargain, to boot, in addition, besides, as well.
**get/have the measure of** *she wants to get the measure of Kate before they meet at the Olympics* EVALUATE, assess, gauge, judge, understand, fathom, read, be wise to, see through; *informal* have someone's number.
**measure up** *he was cut from the Corps because he just couldn't measure up* PASS MUSTER, match up, come up to standard, fit/fill the bill, be acceptable; *informal* come up to scratch, make the grade, cut the mustard, be up to snuff.
**measure up to** *we didn't measure up to their standards* MEET, come up to, equal, match, bear comparison with, be on a level with; achieve, satisfy, fulfill.

**measured** adjective **1** *his measured steps* REGULAR, steady, even, rhythmic, rhythmical, unfaltering; slow, dignified, stately, sedate, leisurely, unhurried.

2 *his measured tones* THOUGHTFUL, careful, carefully chosen, studied, calculated, planned, considered, deliberate, restrained.

**measurement** noun 1 *measurement of the effect is difficult* QUANTIFICATION, computation, calculation, mensuration; evaluation, assessment, gauging.

2 *all measurements are given in metric units* SIZE, dimension, proportions, magnitude, amplitude; mass, bulk, volume, capacity, extent; value, amount, quantity, area, length, height, depth, weight, width, range.

**meat** noun 1 *you need to cut down on your consumption of meat.* FLESH, animal flesh.

2 archaic *meat and drink* FOOD, nourishment, sustenance, provisions, rations, fare, foodstuff(s), provender, daily bread; informal grub, eats, chow, nosh, vittles; formal comestibles; dated victuals; literary viands.

3 *the meat of the matter* SUBSTANCE, pith, marrow, heart, kernel, core, nucleus, nub, essence, essentials, gist, fundamentals, basics; informal nitty-gritty.

**meaty** adjective 1 *a tall, meaty man* BEEFY, brawny, burly, muscular, muscly, powerful, sturdy, strapping, well-built, solidly built, thickset; fleshy, stout.

2 *a good, meaty story* INTERESTING, thought-provoking, three-dimensional, stimulating; substantial, satisfying, meaningful, deep, profound.

**mechanical** adjective 1 *a mechanical device* MECHANIZED, machine-driven, automated, automatic, power-driven, robotic. ANTONYM manual.

2 *a mechanical response* AUTOMATIC, unthinking, unconscious, robotic, involuntary, reflex, knee-jerk, gut, habitual, routine, unemotional, unfeeling, lifeless; perfunctory, cursory, careless, casual. ANTONYM conscious.

**mechanism** noun 1 *an electrical mechanism* MACHINE, piece of machinery, appliance, apparatus, device, instrument, contraption, gadget; informal gizmo.

2 *the train's safety mechanism* MACHINERY, workings, works, movement, action, gears, components.

3 *a formal mechanism for citizens to lodge complaints* PROCEDURE, process, system, operation, method, technique, means, medium, agency, channel.

**meddle** verb 1 *don't* ***meddle in*** *my affairs* INTERFERE IN/WITH, butt in/into, intrude on/into, intervene in, pry into; informal poke one's nose in, horn in on, muscle in on, snoop into, stick one's oar in, kibitz in.

2 *someone had been meddling with her things* FIDDLE, interfere, tamper, tinker, fool around.

**meddlesome** adjective *my meddlesome neighbor is peering out the window at us* INTERFERING, meddling, intrusive, prying, busybody; informal nosy. See note at IMPERTINENT.

**mediate** verb 1 *the UN tried to mediate between the two countries* ARBITRATE, conciliate, moderate, act as peacemaker, make peace; intervene, step in, intercede, act as an intermediary, liaise.

2 *a tribunal was set up to mediate disputes* RESOLVE, settle, arbitrate in, umpire, reconcile, referee; mend, clear up; informal patch up. See note at INSERT.

3 *he attempted to mediate a solution to the conflict* NEGOTIATE, bring about, effect; formal effectuate.

**mediation** noun *mediation between victims and offenders* ARBITRATION, conciliation, reconciliation, intervention, intercession, good offices; negotiation, shuttle diplomacy.

**mediator** noun *the mediator in their salary dispute* ARBITRATOR, arbiter, negotiator, conciliator, peacemaker, go-between, middleman, intermediary, moderator, intervenor, intercessor, broker, honest broker, liaison officer; umpire, referee, adjudicator, judge.

**medicinal** adjective *an infusion of medicinal herbs* CURATIVE, healing, remedial, therapeutic, restorative, corrective, health-giving; medical.

**medicine** noun *take your medicine* MEDICATION, medicament, drug, prescription, pharmaceutical, dose, treatment, remedy, cure; nostrum, panacea, cure-all; informal meds; archaic physic.

**medieval** adjective 1 *medieval times* OF THE MIDDLE AGES, of the Dark Ages, Dark-Age; Gothic. ANTONYM modern.

2 informal *his attitudes are positively medieval* PRIMITIVE, antiquated, archaic, antique, antediluvian, old-fashioned, out of date, outdated, outmoded, anachronistic, passé, obsolete; informal horse-and-buggy. ANTONYM modern.

**mediocre** adjective *a mediocre performance* ORDINARY, average, middling, middle-of-the-road, uninspired, undistinguished, indifferent, unexceptional, unexciting, unremarkable, run-of-the-mill, pedestrian, prosaic, lackluster, forgettable, amateur, amateurish; informal OK, so-so, 'comme ci, comme ça,' plain-vanilla, fair-to-middling, no great shakes, not up to much, bush-league. ANTONYM excellent.

**meditate** verb *please allow me more time to meditate* CONTEMPLATE, think, consider, ponder, muse, reflect, deliberate, ruminate, chew the cud, brood, mull something over; be in a brown study, be deep/lost in thought, debate with oneself; pray; informal put on one's thinking cap; formal cogitate.

**meditation** noun *cultivating the presence of God through meditation* CONTEMPLATION, thought, thinking, musing, pondering, consideration, reflection, deliberation, rumination, brooding, reverie, brown study, concentration; prayer; formal cogitation.

**medium** noun 1 *using technology as a medium for job creation* radio was the first great medium of mass communication MEANS, method, way, form, agency, avenue, channel, vehicle, organ, instrument, mechanism.

2 *organisms growing in their natural medium* HABITAT, element, environment, surroundings, milieu, setting, conditions.

**3** *she consulted a medium* SPIRITUALIST, spiritist, necromancer, channeler; fortune teller, clairvoyant, psychic.

**4** *a happy medium* MIDDLE WAY, middle course, middle ground, middle, mean, median, midpoint; compromise, golden mean.

▸ adjective *medium height* AVERAGE, middling, medium-sized, middle-sized, moderate, normal, standard.

**medley** noun *a medley of Beatles songs | a vegetable medley* ASSORTMENT, miscellany, mixture, mélange, variety, mixed bag, grab bag, mix, collection, selection, potpourri, patchwork, bricolage; motley collection, ragbag, gallimaufry, mishmash, jumble, hodgepodge, salmagundi.

**meek** adjective *they called her Miss Mouse because she was so meek* SUBMISSIVE, yielding, obedient, compliant, tame, biddable, tractable, acquiescent, deferential, timid, unprotesting, unresisting, like a lamb to the slaughter; quiet, mild, gentle, docile, lamblike, shy, diffident, unassuming, self-effacing. ANTONYM assertive.

**meet** verb **1** *I met an old friend on the train* ENCOUNTER, meet up with, come face to face with, run into, run across, come across/upon, chance on, happen on, stumble across/on; *informal* bump into.

**2** *she first met Paul at a party* GET TO KNOW, be introduced to, make the acquaintance of.

**3** *the committee met on Saturday* ASSEMBLE, gather, come together, get together, congregate, convene.

**4** *the place where three roads meet* CONVERGE, connect, touch, link up, intersect, cross, join.

**5** *she met death bravely* FACE, encounter, undergo, experience, go through, suffer, endure, bear; cope with, handle.

**6** *the announcement was met with widespread hostility* GREET, receive, answer, treat.

**7** *he does not meet the job's requirements* FULFILL, satisfy, fill, measure up to, match (up to), conform to, come up to, comply with, answer.

**8** *shipowners would meet the cost of oil spills* PAY, settle, clear, honor, discharge, pay off, square.

▸ noun *a track meet* EVENT, tournament, game, match, contest, competition.

PHRASE: **meet someone halfway** See HALFWAY.

**meeting** noun **1** *he stood up to address the meeting* GATHERING, assembly, conference, congregation, convention, summit, forum, convocation, conclave, council, rally, caucus; *informal* get-together.

**2** *she demanded a meeting with the councilman* CONSULTATION, audience, interview.

**3** *he intrigued her on their first meeting* ENCOUNTER, contact; appointment, assignation, rendezvous; *literary* tryst.

**4** *the meeting of land and sea* CONVERGENCE, coming together, confluence, conjunction, union, junction, abutment; intersection, T-junction, crossing.

**melancholy** adjective *a melancholy expression* SAD, sorrowful, unhappy, desolate, mournful, lugubrious, gloomy, despondent, dejected, depressed, downhearted, downcast, disconsolate, glum, miserable, wretched, dismal, morose, woeful, woebegone, doleful, joyless, heavy-hearted; *informal* down in the dumps, down in/at the mouth, blue; *literary* atrabilious. See note at GLUM. ANTONYM cheerful.

▸ noun *a feeling of melancholy* SADNESS, sorrow, unhappiness, woe, desolation, melancholia, dejection, depression, despondency, cafard, gloom, gloominess, misery; *informal* the dumps, the blues.

**melee** noun *people were trampled in the melee* FRACAS, disturbance, rumpus, tumult, commotion, ruckus, disorder, fray; brawl, fight, scuffle, struggle, skirmish, scrimmage, free-for-all, tussle; *informal* scrap, set-to, ruction, slugfest.

**mellifluous** adjective *mellifluous dinner music* SWEET-SOUNDING, dulcet, honeyed, mellow, soft, liquid, silvery, soothing, rich, smooth, euphonious, harmonious, tuneful, musical. ANTONYM cacophonous.

**mellow** adjective **1** *a mellow mood* GENIAL, affable, amiable, good-humored, good-natured, amicable, pleasant, relaxed, easygoing, low-maintenance, placid; jovial, jolly, cheerful, happy, merry.

**2** *the mellow tone of his voice* DULCET, sweet-sounding, tuneful, melodious, mellifluous; soft, smooth, warm, full, rich.

**3** *a mellow wine* FULL-BODIED, mature, well matured, full-flavored, rich, smooth. See note at MATURE. PHRASE: **mellow out** *you need to mellow out* RELAX, unwind, loosen up, de-stress, slow down, take it easy; *informal* chill (out), take a (chill) pill, decompress.

**melodious** adjective *the pleasure of hearing her melodious singing voice* TUNEFUL, melodic, musical, mellifluous, dulcet, sweet-sounding, silvery, harmonious, euphonious, lyrical; *informal* easy on the ear. ANTONYM discordant.

**melodramatic** adjective *the early soap operas of radio days were exceedingly melodramatic* EXAGGERATED, histrionic, overdramatic, overdone, operatic, sensationalized, overemotional, overwrought, sentimental, extravagant; theatrical, stagy, actressy; *informal* hammy.

**melody** noun *familiar melodies* TUNE, air, strain, theme, song, refrain, piece of music; *informal* ditty.

**melt** verb **1** *the snow was beginning to melt* THAW, liquefy, defrost, soften, dissolve, deliquesce.

**2** *his smile melted her heart* SOFTEN, disarm, touch, affect, move.

**3** *his anger **melted away*** VANISH, disappear, fade away, dissolve, evaporate; *literary* evanesce.

**member** noun **1** *a member of the club* SUBSCRIBER, associate, affiliate, life member, card-carrying member.

**2** *a member of a mathematical set* CONSTITUENT, element, component, part, portion, piece, unit.

**3** archaic *many victims had injured members* LIMB, organ; arm, leg, appendage.

**membrane** noun *the sensitive membranes in the mouth* LAYER, sheet, skin, film, tissue, integument, overlay; *technical* pellicle.

**memento** noun *she kept the painted clamshell as a memento from our trip to Cape Cod* SOUVENIR, keepsake, reminder, remembrance, token, memorial bomboniere; trophy, relic.

**memoir** noun **1** *a touching memoir of her childhood* ACCOUNT, history, record, chronicle, narrative, story, portrayal, depiction, sketch, portrait, profile, biography, monograph.

**2** (**memoirs**) *he published his memoirs in 1955* AUTOBIOGRAPHY, life story, memories, recollections, reminiscences; journal, diary.

**memorable** adjective *thank you for making our visit so memorable* | *a memorable theme song* UNFORGETTABLE, indelible, catchy, haunting; momentous, significant, historic, notable, noteworthy, important, consequential, remarkable, special, signal, outstanding, extraordinary, striking, vivid, arresting, impressive, distinctive, distinguished, famous, celebrated, renowned, illustrious, glorious.

**memorandum** noun *a memorandum from the general* MESSAGE, communication, note, e-mail, letter, missive, directive; reminder, aide-mémoire; *informal* memo.

**memorial** noun **1** *the war memorial* MONUMENT, cenotaph, mausoleum; statue, plaque, cairn; shrine; tombstone, gravestone, headstone.

**2** *the festival is a memorial to his life's work* TRIBUTE, testimonial; remembrance, memento.

▸ adjective *a memorial service* COMMEMORATIVE, remembrance, commemorating.

**memorize** verb *we have to memorize a poem in French* COMMIT TO MEMORY, remember, learn by heart, get off by heart, learn, learn by rote, become word-perfect in, get something down pat; *archaic* con.

**memory** noun **1** *she is losing her memory* ABILITY TO REMEMBER, powers of recall.

**2** *happy memories of her young days* RECOLLECTION, remembrance, reminiscence; impression.

**3** *the town built a statue in memory of him* COMMEMORATION, remembrance; honor, tribute, recognition, respect.

**4** *a computer's memory* MEMORY BANK, store, cache, disk, RAM, ROM, hard drive.

**menace** noun **1** *an atmosphere full of menace* THREAT, ominousness, intimidation, warning, ill omen.

**2** *a menace to urban society* DANGER, peril, risk, hazard, threat; jeopardy.

**3** *that dog is a menace* NUISANCE, pest, annoyance, plague, torment, terror, troublemaker, mischief-maker, thorn in someone's side/flesh.

▸ verb **1** *gorillas are still menaced by poaching* THREATEN, be a danger to, put at risk, jeopardize, imperil.

**2** *a gang of skinheads menaced local residents* INTIMIDATE, threaten, terrorize, frighten, scare, terrify.

**menacing** adjective *a menacing driver forced me to take the nearest exit* THREATENING, ominous, intimidating, frightening, terrifying, alarming, forbidding, black, thunderous, glowering, unfriendly, hostile, sinister, baleful, warning; *formal* minatory. ANTONYM friendly.

**mend** verb **1** *workmen were mending faulty cabling* REPAIR, fix, put back together, piece together, restore; sew (up), stitch, darn, patch, cobble; rehabilitate, renew, renovate; *informal* patch up. ANTONYMS break, worsen.

**2** *they mended their quarrel* PUT/SET RIGHT, set straight, straighten out, sort out, rectify, remedy, cure, right, resolve, square, settle, put to rights, correct, retrieve, improve, make better. ANTONYMS break, worsen.

**mendacious** adjective *politicians and their mendacious spin doctors* LYING, untruthful, dishonest, deceitful, false, dissembling, insincere, disingenuous, hypocritical, fraudulent, double-dealing, two-faced, two-timing, duplicitous, perjured; untrue, fictitious, falsified, fabricated, fallacious, invented, made up; *informal* full of crap; *literary* perfidious. ANTONYM truthful.

**mendicant** noun. See BEGGAR noun sense 1.

**menial** adjective *a menial job* UNSKILLED, lowly, humble, low-status, inferior, degrading; routine, humdrum, boring, dull.

▸ noun *they were treated like menials* SERVANT, drudge, minion, joe-boy, factotum, lackey, hired hand; *informal* wage slave, gofer, peon, grunt; *archaic* scullion.

**menstruation** noun *tribal ceremonies regarding menstruation* PERIOD, menses, menorrhea, menstrual cycle; menarche; *informal* one's/that time of the month; *informal, dated* the curse.

**mental** adjective **1** *mental faculties* INTELLECTUAL, cerebral, brain, rational, cognitive. ANTONYM physical.

**2** *a mental disorder* PSYCHIATRIC, psychological, psychogenic.

**3** *informal he's completely mental.* See MAD sense 1.

**mentality** noun **1** *I can't understand the mentality of these people* WAY OF THINKING, mind set, cast of mind, frame of mind, turn of mind, mind, psychology, mental attitude, outlook, disposition, makeup.

**2** *a person of limited mentality* INTELLECT, intellectual capabilities, intelligence, IQ, (powers of) reasoning, rationality; *informal* brains, smarts.

**mentally** adverb *mentally, I was prepared to deal with the situation* IN ONE'S MIND, in one's head, inwardly, intellectually, cognitively.

**mention** verb **1** *don't mention the war* ALLUDE TO, refer to, touch on/upon; bring up, raise, broach, introduce, moot.

**2** *Jim mentioned that he'd met them before* STATE, say, indicate, let someone know, disclose, divulge, reveal.

**3** *I'll gladly mention your work to my friends* RECOMMEND, commend, put in a good word for, speak well of.

▸ noun **1** *he made no **mention of** your request* REFERENCE TO, allusion to, remark of/about/regarding, statement about/regarding, announcement of, indication of.

**2** *my book got a mention on the show* RECOMMENDATION, commendation, a good word.

PHRASES: **don't mention it** *"Sorry for being late." "Oh, don't mention it."* DON'T APOLOGIZE, it doesn't matter, it makes no difference, it's not important, never mind, don't worry.
**not to mention** *if the party's canceled, we'll have to notify the guests, not to mention the caterers* IN ADDITION TO, as well as; not counting, not including, to say nothing of, aside from, besides.

**mentor** noun **1** *his political mentors* ADVISER, guide, guru, counselor, consultant; confidant(e).

**2** *regular meetings between mentor and trainee* TRAINER, teacher, tutor, instructor.

**mercantile** adjective *her grandfather had invested in several mercantile interests at the turn of the century* COMMERCIAL, trade, trading, business, merchant, sales.

**mercenary** adjective **1** *mercenary self-interest* MONEY-ORIENTED, grasping, greedy, acquisitive, avaricious, covetous, bribable, venal, materialistic; *informal* money-grubbing.

**2** *mercenary soldiers* HIRED, paid, bought, professional.

▸ noun *a group of mercenaries* SOLDIER OF FORTUNE, professional soldier, hired soldier, gunman; *informal* hired gun; *historical* condottiere.

**merchandise** noun *a wide range of merchandise* GOODS, wares, stock, commodities, lines, produce, products.

▸ verb *a new product that can be easily merchandised* PROMOTE, market, sell, retail; advertise, publicize, push; *informal* plug.

**merchant** noun *a tea merchant from Bombay* TRADER, dealer, wholesaler, broker, agent, seller, buyer, buyer and seller, vendor, distributor, peddler, retailer, shopkeeper, storekeeper.

**merciful** adjective **1** *God is merciful* FORGIVING, compassionate, clement, pitying, forbearing, lenient, humane, mild, kind, softhearted, tenderhearted, gracious, sympathetic, humanitarian, liberal, tolerant, indulgent, generous, magnanimous, benign, benevolent. See note at LENIENT. ANTONYM cruel.

**2** *a merciful silence fell* WELCOME, blessed. PHRASE: **be merciful to** *the judge was inclined to be merciful to first offenders* HAVE MERCY ON, have pity on, show mercy to, spare, pardon, forgive, be lenient to; *informal* go/be easy on, let off.

**merciless** adjective *the merciless Cossacks who invaded Siberia* RUTHLESS, remorseless, pitiless, unforgiving, unsparing, implacable, inexorable, relentless, unremitting, inflexible, inhumane, inhuman, unsympathetic, unfeeling, intolerant, rigid, severe, cold-blooded, hard-hearted, stony-hearted, heartless, harsh, callous, cruel, brutal, barbarous, cutthroat. ANTONYM compassionate.

**mercurial** adjective *a mercurial temperament* VOLATILE, capricious, temperamental, excitable, fickle, changeable, unpredictable, variable, protean, mutable, erratic, quicksilver, inconstant, inconsistent, unstable, unsteady, fluctuating, ever-changing, moody, flighty, wayward, whimsical, impulsive; *technical* labile. ANTONYM stable.

**mercy** noun **1** *he showed no mercy to the others* LENIENCY, clemency, compassion, grace, pity, charity, forgiveness, forbearance, quarter, humanity; soft-heartedness, tenderheartedness, kindness, sympathy, liberality, indulgence, tolerance, generosity, magnanimity, beneficence. ANTONYMS ruthlessness, cruelty.

**2** *we must be thankful for small mercies* BLESSING, godsend, boon, favor, piece/stroke of luck, windfall. PHRASE: **at the mercy of 1** *they found themselves at the mercy of the tyrant* IN THE POWER OF, under/in the control of, in the clutches of, subject to.

**2** *he was at the mercy of the elements* DEFENSELESS AGAINST, vulnerable to, exposed to, susceptible to, prey to, (wide) open to.

THE RIGHT WORD **mercy, benevolence, charity, clemency, compassion, leniency**

If you want to win friends and influence people, it's best to start with **benevolence**, a general term for goodwill and kindness (*a grandfather's benevolence*). **Charity** is even better, suggesting generous giving (*the baker gave him bread out of charity*) but also meaning tolerance and understanding of others (*she viewed his selfish behavior with charity*). **Compassion** is a feeling of sympathy or sorrow for someone else's misfortune (*he has shown compassion for the homeless*), and often includes showing **mercy**. Aside from its religious overtones, *mercy* means compassion or kindness in our treatment of others, especially those who have offended us or who deserve punishment (*mercy toward the pickpocket*). **Clemency** is mercy shown by someone whose duty or function it is to administer justice or punish offenses (*the judge granted clemency*), while **leniency** emphasizes gentleness, softness, or lack of severity, even if it isn't quite deserved (*a father's leniency in punishing his young son*).

**mere** adjective *it costs **a mere** $11.00* NO MORE THAN, just, only, merely; no better than; a paltry, a measly, an insignificant, an ordinary, a minor, a little, a piddling, a piffling.

**merge** verb **1** *the company merged with a firm based in Peoria* JOIN (TOGETHER), join forces, amalgamate, unite, affiliate, team up, link (up). ANTONYM separate.

**2** *the two organizations were merged* AMALGAMATE, bring together, join, consolidate, conflate, unite, unify, combine, incorporate, integrate, link (up), knit, yoke. ANTONYM separate.

**3** *the two colors merged* MINGLE, blend, fuse, mix, intermix, intermingle, coalesce; *literary* commingle.

**merger** noun *a pending merger between two Russian oil companies* AMALGAMATION, combination, union, fusion, coalition, affiliation, unification, incorporation, consolidation, link-up, alliance. ANTONYM split.

**merit** noun **1** *composers of outstanding merit* EXCELLENCE, quality, caliber, worth, worthiness, credit, value, distinction, eminence. ANTONYM inferiority.

2 *the merits of the scheme* GOOD POINT, strong point, advantage, benefit, value, asset, plus. ANTONYMS fault, disadvantage.

▸ verb *the accusation did not merit a response* DESERVE, earn, be deserving of, warrant, rate, justify, be worthy of, be worth, be entitled to, have a right to, have a claim to/on.

**meritorious** adjective *an award for meritorious conduct* PRAISEWORTHY, laudable, commendable, admirable, estimable, creditable, worthy, deserving, excellent, exemplary, good. ANTONYM discreditable.

**merriment** noun *we got caught up in the merriment of the occasion* HIGH SPIRITS, high-spiritedness, exuberance, cheerfulness, gaiety, fun, effervescence, verve, buoyancy, levity, zest, liveliness, cheer, joy, joyfulness, joyousness, jolliness, jollity, happiness, gladness, jocularity, conviviality, festivity, merrymaking, revelry, mirth, glee, gleefulness, laughter, hilarity, lightheartedness, amusement, pleasure. ANTONYM misery.

**merry** adjective *merry throngs of students* CHEERFUL, cheery, in high spirits, high-spirited, bright, sunny, smiling, lighthearted, buoyant, lively, carefree, without a care in the world, joyful, joyous, jolly, convivial, festive, mirthful, gleeful, happy, glad, laughing; *informal* chirpy; *formal* jocund; *dated* gay; *literary* blithe. ANTONYM miserable.

PHRASE: **make merry** *I'm afraid we may have made merry a bit too long last night* HAVE FUN, have a good time, enjoy oneself, have a party, celebrate, carouse, feast, 'eat, drink, and be merry,' revel, roister; *informal* party, have a ball.

**mesh** noun *wire mesh* NETTING, net, network; web, webbing, lattice, latticework.

▸ verb 1 *one gear meshes with the other* ENGAGE, connect, lock, interlock.

2 *our ideas just do not mesh* HARMONIZE, fit together, match, dovetail.

**mesmerize** verb *the dancers mesmerized us* ENTHRALL, hold spellbound, entrance, dazzle, bedazzle, bewitch, charm, captivate, enchant, fascinate, transfix, grip, hypnotize.

**mess** noun 1 *please clear up the mess* UNTIDINESS, disorder, disarray, clutter, shambles, jumble, muddle, chaos.

2 *don't step in the dog mess* EXCREMENT, muck, feces, excreta.

3 *I've got to get out of this mess* PLIGHT, predicament, tight spot/corner, difficulty, trouble, quandary, dilemma, problem, muddle, mix-up, imbroglio; *informal* jam, fix, pickle, stew, scrape. PHRASES: **make a mess of** *he made a mess of the project* MISMANAGE, mishandle, bungle, fluff, spoil, ruin, wreck; *informal* mess up, botch, make a hash of, foul up.

**mess around** *don't mess around with any of the equipment* FOOL AROUND, fiddle about/around, play around; fidget, toy, trifle, tamper, tinker, interfere, meddle, monkey (around/about).

**mess up** *he messed up my kitchen* DIRTY; clutter up, disarrange, jumble, dishevel, rumple; *informal* muss up; *literary* befoul.

**message** noun 1 *are there any messages for me?* COMMUNICATION, piece of information, news, note, memorandum, memo, e-mail, letter, missive, report, bulletin, communiqué, dispatch.

2 *the message of his teaching* MEANING, sense, import, idea; point, thrust, gist, essence, content, subject (matter), substance, implication, drift, lesson. PHRASE: **get the message** *informal what do I have to say to make you get the message?* UNDERSTAND, get the point, comprehend; *informal* catch on, get the picture.

**messenger** noun *the messenger arrived by motorcycle* COURIER, runner, envoy, emissary, agent, go-between, messagebearer; postman, letter carrier, mailman; *historical* herald; *archaic* legate.

**messy** adjective 1 *messy oil spills* | *messy hair* DIRTY, filthy, grubby, soiled, grimy; mucky, muddy, slimy, sticky, sullied, spotted, stained, smeared, smudged; disheveled, scruffy, unkempt, rumpled, matted, tousled, bedraggled, tangled; *informal* yucky, grungy. ANTONYM clean.

2 *a messy kitchen* DISORDERLY, disordered, in a muddle, chaotic, confused, disorganized, in disarray, disarranged; untidy, cluttered, in a jumble; *informal* like a bomb's hit it, shambolic. ANTONYMS orderly, tidy.

3 *a messy legal battle* COMPLEX, intricate, tangled, confused, convoluted; unpleasant, nasty, bitter, acrimonious. ANTONYMS straightforward, amicable.

**metallic** adjective 1 *a metallic sound* TINNY, jangling, jingling; grating, harsh, jarring, dissonant.

2 *metallic paint* METALIZED, burnished; shiny, glossy, lustrous.

**metamorphosis** noun *his amazing metamorphosis from gawky hayseed to sexy pop star* TRANSFORMATION, mutation, transmutation, change, alteration, conversion, modification, remodeling, reconstruction; *humorous* transmogrification; *formal* transubstantiation.

**metaphor** noun *the profusion of metaphors in her everyday speech has gotten pretty tiresome* FIGURE OF SPEECH, image, trope, analogy, comparison, symbol, word painting/picture.

**mete** PHRASE: **mete out** *they were instructed to mete out harsh punishment* DISPENSE, hand out, allocate, allot, apportion, issue, deal out, dole out, dish out, assign, administer.

**meteoric** adjective *her meteoric rise to fame* RAPID, lightning, swift, fast, quick, speedy, accelerated, instant, sudden, spectacular, dazzling, brilliant. ANTONYM gradual.

**method** noun 1 *they use very old-fashioned methods* PROCEDURE, technique, system, practice, routine, modus operandi, process; strategy, tactic, plan.

2 *there's a method to his madness* ORDER, orderliness, organization, structure, form, system, logic, planning, design, sense. ANTONYM disorder.

**methodical** adjective *a methodical approach to the evaluation* ORDERLY, well-ordered, well-organized, (well) planned, efficient, businesslike, systematic, structured, logical, analytic, disciplined; meticulous, punctilious.

**meticulous** adjective *the etchers give meticulous attention to each piece* CAREFUL, conscientious, diligent, scrupulous, punctilious, painstaking, accurate; thorough, studious, rigorous, detailed, perfectionist, fastidious, methodical, particular. ANTONYM careless.

**metropolis** noun *their trip to the booming metropolis made them eager to return to their little house in the sticks* CAPITAL (CITY), chief town, county town; big city, conurbation, megalopolis, megacity.

**mettle** noun **1** *a man of mettle* SPIRIT, fortitude, strength of character, moral fiber, steel, determination, resolve, resolution, backbone, grit, true grit, courage, courageousness, bravery, valor, fearlessness, daring; *informal* guts, spunk, balls.

**2** *Frazer was of a very different mettle* CALIBER, character, disposition, nature, temperament, personality, makeup, stamp.

**microscopic** adjective *microscopic fibers found in the suspect's car* TINY, very small, minute, infinitesimal, minuscule; little, micro, diminutive; *informal* teeny, weeny, teeny-weeny, teensy-weensy, itsy-bitsy, little-bitty; *Scottish* wee. ANTONYM huge.

**midday** noun *the bells chime at midday* NOON, twelve noon, high noon, noontide, noonday. ANTONYM midnight.

**middle** noun **1** *a shallow dish with a spike in the middle* CENTER, midpoint, halfway point, dead center, focus, hub; eye, heart, core, kernel. ANTONYM outside.

**2** *he had a towel around his middle* MIDRIFF, waist, belly, stomach, abdomen; *informal* tummy, tum, gut.

▸ adjective **1** *the middle point* CENTRAL, mid, mean, medium, medial, median, midway, halfway.

**2** *the middle level* INTERMEDIATE, intermediary.

**middleman** noun *I'd rather avoid the middleman and buy direct from the manufacturer* INTERMEDIARY, intercessor, go-between, liaison, mediator; dealer, broker, agent, factor, wholesaler, distributor.

**middling** adjective *a town of the middling kind, neither rich nor poor* AVERAGE, standard, normal, middle-of-the-road; moderate, ordinary, commonplace, everyday, workaday, tolerable, passable; run-of-the-mill, fair, mediocre, undistinguished, unexceptional, unremarkable; *informal* OK, so-so, 'comme ci, comme ça,' fair-to-middling, plain-vanilla.

**midget** noun *the inhabitants must have been midgets* SMALL PERSON, dwarf, homunculus, Lilliputian, gnome, pygmy; *informal* shrimp.

▸ adjective **1** *a story about midget matadors* DIMINUTIVE, dwarfish, petite, very small, pygmy; *informal* pint-sized, peewee. ANTONYM giant.

**2** *a midget camera* MINIATURE, pocket, dwarf, baby, mini. ANTONYM giant.

**midnight** noun *we'll meet under the clock tower at midnight* TWELVE MIDNIGHT, the middle of the night, the witching hour. ANTONYM midday.

**midst** noun *literary in the midst of the confusion, one strong and sturdy voice broke through and was heard* MIDDLE, center, heart, core, midpoint, kernel, nub; depth(s), thick; **(in the midst of)** in the course of, halfway through, at the heart/core of. PHRASE: **in our midst** *there is a hero in our midst* AMONG US, in our group, with us.

**midway** adverb *he was explaining what happened and then just stopped midway* HALFWAY, in the middle, at the midpoint, in the center; part-way, at some point.

**mien** noun *a scowling mien that did nothing to boost our confidence* APPEARANCE, look, expression, countenance, aura, demeanor, attitude, air, manner, bearing; *formal* comportment.

**might** noun *she hit him with all her might* STRENGTH, force, power, vigor, energy, brawn, powerfulness, forcefulness.

**mighty** adjective **1** *a mighty blow* POWERFUL, forceful, violent, vigorous, hefty, thunderous. ANTONYM feeble.

**2** *a mighty warrior* FEARSOME, ferocious; big, tough, robust, muscular, strapping. ANTONYMS puny, tiny.

**3** *mighty industrial countries* DOMINANT, influential, strong, powerful, important, predominant. ANTONYM insignificant.

**4** *mighty oak trees* HUGE, enormous, massive, gigantic, big, large, giant, colossal, mammoth, immense; *informal* monster, whopping, humongous, jumbo(-sized), ginormous. ANTONYM tiny.

▸ adverb *informal I'm mighty pleased to see you* EXTREMELY, exceedingly, enormously, immensely, tremendously, hugely, mightily, very (much); *informal* awfully, majorly, mega, plumb, right; *informal, dated* frightfully.

**migrant** noun *they exploited the Puerto Rican migrants who toiled in their orchards for dismal wages* IMMIGRANT, EMIGRANT; nomad, itinerant, traveler, vagrant, transient, rover, wanderer, drifter.

▸ adjective *migrant workers* TRAVELING, wandering, drifting, nomadic, roving, roaming, itinerant, vagrant, transient.

**migrate** verb **1** *cities grew rapidly as rural populations migrated in search of jobs* RELOCATE, resettle, move (house); immigrate; emigrate, go abroad, go overseas, pull up stakes; *dated* remove.

**2** *wildebeest migrate across the Serengeti* ROAM, wander, drift, rove, travel (around).

**migratory** adjective *a winter haven for migratory species* MIGRANT, migrating, moving, traveling.

**mild** adjective **1** *a mild tone of voice* GENTLE, tender, softhearted, tenderhearted, sensitive, sympathetic, warm, placid, calm, tranquil, serene, peaceable, good-natured, mild-mannered, amiable, affable, genial, easygoing. ANTONYM harsh.

**2** *a mild punishment* LENIENT, light; compassionate, merciful, humane. ANTONYMS harsh, cruel.

**3** *he was eyeing her with mild interest* SLIGHT, faint, vague, minimal, nominal, moderate, token, feeble. ANTONYM strong.

**4** *mild weather* WARM, balmy, temperate, clement. ANTONYMS cold, severe.

**5** *a mild curry* BLAND, insipid, tame. ANTONYMS spicy, piquant.

**milieu** noun *the political milieu in New England* ENVIRONMENT, sphere, background, backdrop, setting, context, atmosphere; location, conditions, surroundings, environs; *informal* stomping grounds, stamping grounds, turf.

**militant** adjective *militant supporters* AGGRESSIVE, violent, belligerent, bellicose, vigorous, forceful, active, fierce, combative, pugnacious; radical, extremist, extreme, zealous, fanatical.

▸ noun *the demands of the militants* ACTIVIST, extremist, radical, young turk, zealot.

**military** adjective *military activity* FIGHTING, service, army, armed, defense, martial. ANTONYM civilian.

▸ noun *the military took power* (ARMED) FORCES, services, militia; army, navy, air force, marines.

**militate** verb *his resentment of others in the company* ***militates against*** *his own chances for advancement* TEND TO PREVENT, work against, hinder, discourage, prejudice, be detrimental to.

**milk** verb **1** *Pam was milking the cows* DRAW MILK FROM, express milk from.

**2** *milk a little of the liquid* DRAW OFF, siphon (off), pump off, tap, drain, extract.

**3** *milking rich clients* EXPLOIT, take advantage of, cash in on, suck dry; *informal* bleed, squeeze, fleece.

**milky** adjective *a milky complexion* PALE, white, milk-white, whitish, off-white, cream, creamy, chalky, pearly, nacreous, ivory, alabaster; cloudy, frosted, opaque. ANTONYM swarthy.

**mill** noun **1** *a steel mill* FACTORY, (processing) plant, works, workshop, shop, foundry.

**2** *a pepper mill* GRINDER, crusher, quern.

▸ verb *the wheat is milled into flour* GRIND, pulverize, powder, granulate, pound, crush, press; *technical* comminute, triturate.

PHRASE: **mill around/about** *people were milling about in the streets* THRONG, swarm, crowd.

**millstone** noun *a lifetime of lying and stealing had become the very millstone that would crush him* BURDEN, encumbrance, dead weight, cross to bear, albatross, load; duty, responsibility, obligation, liability, misfortune.

**mime** noun *a mime of someone fencing* PANTOMIME, charade, dumb show.

▸ verb *she mimed picking up a phone* ACT OUT, pantomime, gesture, simulate, represent.

**mimic** verb **1** *she mimicked his accent* IMITATE, copy, impersonate, do an impression of, ape, caricature, parody, lampoon, burlesque, parrot; *informal* send up, take off, spoof. See note at IMITATE.

**2** *most hoverflies mimic wasps* RESEMBLE, look like, have the appearance of, simulate; *informal* make like.

▸ noun *he was a superb mimic* IMPERSONATOR, impressionist, imitator, parodist, caricaturist, lampooner, lampoonist; *informal* copycat; *archaic* ape.

**mince** verb **1** *mince the meat and onions* GRIND, chop up, cut up, dice, hash, chop fine.

**2** *she minced out of the room* WALK AFFECTEDLY; *informal* sashay, flounce, strut. PHRASE: **not mince (one's) words** *I'll not mince words: you need to stick to this exercise program or you're looking at serious health problems* TALK STRAIGHT, not beat around the bush, call a spade a spade, speak straight from the heart, pull no punches, not put too fine a point on it, tell it like it is, talk turkey.

**mincing** adjective *no one dared to laugh at the young master's mincing walk* AFFECTED, dainty, effeminate, pretentious, dandified, foppish; *informal* camp.

**mind** noun **1** *expand your mind* BRAIN, intelligence, intellect, intellectual capabilities, brains, brainpower, wits, understanding, reasoning, judgment, sense, head; *informal* gray matter, brain cells, smarts.

**2** *he kept his mind on the job* ATTENTION, thoughts, concentration, attentiveness.

**3** *the tragedy affected her mind* SANITY, mental faculties, senses, wits, reason, reasoning, judgment; *informal* marbles.

**4** *Justin's words stuck in her mind* MEMORY, recollection.

**5** *the country's great minds* INTELLECT, thinker, brain, scholar, academic.

**6** *I've a mind to complain* INCLINATION, desire, wish, urge, notion, fancy, intention, will.

**7** *we're of the same mind* OPINION, way of thinking, outlook, attitude, view, viewpoint, point of view.

▸ verb **1** *do you mind if I smoke?* CARE, object, be bothered, be annoyed, be upset, take offense, disapprove, dislike it, look askance; *informal* give a damn, give a hoot.

**2** *mind the step!* BE CAREFUL OF, watch out for, look out for, beware of, be on one's guard for, be wary of.

**3** ***mind you*** *wipe your feet* BE/MAKE SURE (THAT) YOU, see (that) you; remember to, don't forget to.

**4** *her husband was minding the baby* LOOK AFTER, take care of, keep an eye on, attend to, care for, tend, babysit.

**5** *mind what your mother says* PAY ATTENTION TO, heed, pay heed to, attend to, take note/notice of, note, mark, listen to, be mindful of; obey, follow, comply with.

PHRASES: **be of two minds** *I am of two minds about going to law school* BE UNDECIDED, be uncertain, be unsure, hesitate, waver, vacillate, hem and haw; *informal* dilly-dally, shilly-shally.

**bear/keep in mind** *just bear in mind that I've never used a Mac* REMEMBER, note, be mindful of, take note of; *formal* take cognizance of.

**cross one's mind** *did it ever cross your mind that he just does-*

*n't want to go?* OCCUR TO ONE, enter one's mind/head, strike one, hit one, dawn on one.

**give someone a piece of one's mind.** *I'd really like to give that lying Patterson a piece of my mind.* See REPRIMAND verb.

**have in mind** *now, for the curtains, do you have a specific pattern in mind?* THINK OF, contemplate; intend, plan, propose, desire, want, wish.

**never mind** 1 *never mind the cost* DON'T BOTHER ABOUT, don't worry about, disregard, forget.

2 *never mind, it's all right now* DON'T APOLOGIZE, forget it, don't worry about it, it doesn't matter.

**out of one's mind** 1 *you must be out of your mind!* See MAD sense 1.

2 *I've been out of my mind with worry* FRANTIC, beside oneself, distraught, in a frenzy.

**put someone in mind of** *the view here puts me in mind of Amsterdam* REMIND OF, recall, conjure up, suggest; RESEMBLE, look like.

**to my mind** *to my mind, this is a clear case of blackmail* IN MY OPINION, in my view, as I see it, in my estimation, in my book, if you ask me.

**mindful** adjective *with mindful steps we slowly made our way down the gorge* AWARE, conscious, sensible, alive, alert, acquainted, heedful, wary, chary; *informal* wise, hip; *formal* cognizant, regardful. ANTONYM heedless.

**mindless** adjective 1 *a mindless idiot* STUPID, idiotic, brainless, imbecilic, imbecile, asinine, witless, foolish, empty-headed, slow-witted, obtuse, featherbrained, doltish; *informal* dumb, pig-ignorant, brain-dead, cretinous, moronic, thick, birdbrained, pea-brained, dopey, dim, halfwitted, dippy, fatheaded, boneheaded, chowderheaded.

2 *mindless acts of vandalism* UNTHINKING, thoughtless, senseless, gratuitous, wanton, indiscriminate, unreasoning.

3 *a mindless task* MECHANICAL, automatic, routine; tedious, boring, monotonous, brainless, mind-numbing. PHRASE: **mindless of** *the birds flock to the feeders, mindless of the humans nearby* INDIFFERENT TO, heedless of, unaware of, unmindful of, careless of, blind to.

**mine** noun 1 *a coal mine* PIT, excavation, quarry, workings, diggings; strip mine, open-pit mine, placer (mine), hardrock mine.

2 *a mine of information* RICH SOURCE, repository, store, storehouse, reservoir, gold mine, treasure house, treasury, reserve, fund, wealth, stock.

3 *he was killed by a mine* EXPLOSIVE, land mine, limpet mine, magnetic mine, depth charge.

▸ verb 1 *the iron ore was mined from shallow pits* QUARRY, excavate, dig (up), extract, remove; strip-mine, pan.

2 *medical data was mined for relevant statistics* SEARCH, delve into, scour, scan, read through, survey.

3 *the entrance to the harbor had been mined* DEFEND WITH MINES, lay with mines.

**miner** noun *the trapped miners were rescued* DIGGER, collier, gold panner; *dated* sourdough.

**mingle** verb 1 *fact and fiction are skillfully mingled in his novels* MIX, blend, intermingle, intermix, interweave, interlace, combine, merge, fuse, unite, join, amalgamate, meld, mesh; *literary* commingle. ANTONYMS separate, be separated.

2 *wedding guests mingled in the lobby* SOCIALIZE, circulate, fraternize, get together, associate with others; *informal* hobnob, rub elbows. ANTONYMS separate, part.

**miniature** adjective *a miniature railroad* SMALL-SCALE, mini; tiny, little, small, minute, baby, toy, pocket, dwarf, pygmy, minuscule, diminutive, vest-pocket; *informal* teeny, teeny-weeny, teensy, teensy-weensy, itsy-bitsy, eensy, eensy-weensy; *Scottish* wee. See note at SMALL. ANTONYM giant.

**minimal** adjective *with minimal care, you can have a beautiful terrarium* VERY LITTLE, minimum, the least (possible); nominal, token, negligible. ANTONYM maximum.

**minimize** verb 1 *the aim is to minimize costs* KEEP DOWN, keep at/to a minimum, reduce, decrease, cut down, lessen, curtail, diminish, prune; *informal* slash. ANTONYMS maximize, increase.

2 *we should not minimize his contribution* BELITTLE, make light of, play down, underestimate, underrate, downplay, undervalue, understate; *informal* pooh-pooh; *archaic* hold cheap. ANTONYM exaggerate.

**minimum** noun *costs will be kept to the minimum* LOWEST LEVEL, lower limit, bottom level, rock bottom, nadir; least, lowest, slightest. ANTONYM maximum.

▸ adjective *the minimum amount of effort* MINIMAL, least, smallest, least possible, slightest, lowest, minutest.

**minion** noun *if working for you means being your minion, I'm not the person you're looking for* UNDERLING, henchman, flunky, lackey, hanger-on, follower, servant, hireling, vassal, stooge, toady, sycophant; *informal* yes-man, trained seal, bootlicker, brown-noser, suck-up.

**minister** noun 1 *our minister visited me in the hospital* CLERGYMAN, clergywoman, cleric, ecclesiastic, pastor, vicar, rector, priest, parson, deacon, father, man/woman of the cloth, man/woman of God, churchman, churchwoman; curate, chaplain; *informal* reverend, padre, Holy Joe, sky pilot.

2 *a government minister* MEMBER OF THE GOVERNMENT, cabinet minister, secretary of state, undersecretary.

3 *the Canadian minister in Egypt* AMBASSADOR, chargé d'affaires, plenipotentiary, envoy, emissary, diplomat, consul, representative; *archaic* legate.

▸ verb *doctors were* ***ministering to*** *the injured* TEND TO, care for, take care of, look after, nurse, treat, attend to, see to, administer to, help, assist.

**ministry** noun 1 *he's training for the ministry* HOLY ORDERS, the priesthood, the cloth, the church.

2 *the ministry of Jesus* TEACHING, preaching, evangelism.

**3** *the ministry for foreign affairs* (GOVERNMENT) DEPARTMENT, bureau, agency, office.

**minor** adjective **1** *a minor problem* SLIGHT, small; unimportant, insignificant, inconsequential, inconsiderable, subsidiary, negligible, trivial, trifling, paltry, petty, nickel-and-dime; *informal* piffling, piddling. ANTONYM major.

**2** *a minor poet* LITTLE KNOWN, unknown, lesser, unimportant, insignificant, obscure, minor-league; *informal* small-time, two-bit. ANTONYM important.

▸ noun *the heir to the throne was a minor* CHILD, infant, youth, adolescent, teenager, boy, girl; *informal* kid, kiddie. ANTONYM adult.

**minstrel** noun *historical a band of gay minstrels* MUSICIAN, singer, balladeer, poet; *historical* troubadour, jongleur; *literary* bard.

**mint** noun *informal the bank made* ***a mint*** *out of the deal* A VAST SUM OF MONEY, a king's ransom, millions, billions; *informal* a (small) fortune, a tidy sum, a bundle, a pile, big money, big bucks, megabucks.

▸ adjective *in mint condition* BRAND NEW, pristine, perfect, immaculate, unblemished, undamaged, unmarked, unused, first-class, excellent.

▸ verb **1** *the shilling was minted in 1742* COIN, stamp, strike, cast, forge, manufacture.

**2** *the slogan had been freshly minted* CREATE, invent, make up, think up, dream up, coin.

**minute**[1] noun **1** *it'll only take a minute* MOMENT, short time, little while, second, instant; *informal* sec, jiff, jiffy, flash.

**2** *at that minute, Tony walked in* POINT, point in time, moment, instant, juncture.

**3** **(minutes)** *their objection was noted in the minutes* RECORD(S), proceedings, log, notes; transcript, summary, résumé. PHRASES: **in a minute** *the biscuits will be done in a minute* VERY SOON, in a moment, in a second, in an instant, in a trice, shortly, any minute (now), in a short time, in (less than) no time, before long, momentarily; *informal* anon, in two shakes, in a snap; *literary* ere long.
**this minute** *you get in here this minute!* AT ONCE, immediately, directly, this second, instantly, straightaway, right now, right away, forthwith; *informal* pronto, straight off, right off, tout de suite.
**up-to-the-minute** *stay tuned for up-to-the-minute fashion tips* LATEST, newest, up-to-date, modern, fashionable, smart, chic, stylish, all the rage, in vogue, hip; *informal* trendy, with it, in, styling, phat.
**wait a minute** *if you'll just wait a minute, I'm sure we can get to the bottom of this* BE PATIENT, wait a moment/second, hold on; *informal* hang on, hold your horses.

**minute**[2] adjective **1** *minute particles* MINUSCULE.

**2** *a minute chance of success* NEGLIGIBLE, slight, infinitesimal, minimal, insignificant, inappreciable. See note at SMALL. ANTONYM significant.

**3** *minute detail* EXHAUSTIVE, painstaking, meticulous, rigorous, scrupulous, punctilious, detailed, precise, accurate. ANTONYM cursory.

**minutiae** plural noun *the captain cannot be concerned with the minutiae of shipboard life* DETAILS, niceties, finer points, particulars, trivia, trivialities.

**miracle** noun *his recovery was a blessed miracle* WONDER, marvel, sensation, phenomenon, supernatural phenomenon, mystery.

**miraculous** adjective **1** *the miraculous help of St. Blaise* SUPERNATURAL, preternatural, inexplicable, unaccountable, magical.

**2** *a miraculous escape* AMAZING, astounding, remarkable, extraordinary, incredible, unbelievable, sensational, marvelous, phenomenal; *informal* mind-boggling, mind-blowing, out of this world.

**mirage** noun *could it be that her face was just a mirage?* OPTICAL ILLUSION, hallucination, phantasmagoria, apparition, fantasy, chimera, vision, figment of the/one's imagination; *literary* phantasm.

**mire** noun **1** *it's a mire out there* SWAMP, bog, morass, quagmire, slough; swampland, wetland, marshland.

**2** *they were stuck in the mire* MUD, slime, dirt, filth, muck.

**3** *struggling to pull Russia out of the mire* MESS, difficulty, plight, predicament, tight spot, trouble, quandary, muddle; *informal* jam, fix, pickle, hot water.

▸ verb **1** *Frank's horse got mired in a bog* BOG DOWN, sink (down).

**2** *he has become mired in lawsuits* ENTANGLE, tangle up, embroil, catch up, mix up, involve.

**mirror** noun **1** *a quick look in the mirror* reflecting surface; full-length mirror, hand mirror, side mirror, rear-view mirror; *chiefly Brit.* looking glass, glass.

**2** *his life was a mirror of her own* REFLECTION, twin, replica, copy, match, parallel.

▸ verb *her music mirrored the mood of desperation* REFLECT, match, reproduce, imitate, simulate, copy, mimic, echo, parallel, correspond to.

**mirth** noun *we could not hold back our mirth* MERRIMENT, high spirits, cheerfulness, cheeriness, hilarity, glee, laughter, gaiety, buoyancy, blitheness, euphoria, exhilaration, lightheartedness, joviality, joy, joyfulness, joyousness. ANTONYM misery.

**misadventure** noun *their journey to the Olympics began as one misadventure after another* ACCIDENT, problem, difficulty, misfortune, mishap; setback, reversal (of fortune), stroke of bad luck, blow, contretemps; failure, disaster, tragedy, calamity, woe, trial, tribulation, catastrophe.

**misapprehend** verb *I fear you have misapprehended my intentions* MISUNDERSTAND, misinterpret, misconstrue, misconceive, mistake, misread, get the wrong idea about, take something the wrong way.

**misappropriate** verb *he confessed to having misappropriated millions from his clients* EMBEZZLE, expropriate, steal, thieve, pilfer, pocket, help oneself to, make off with; *informal* swipe, filch, rip off, snitch, pinch.

**misbegotten** adjective **1** *a misbegotten scheme* ILL-CONCEIVED, ill-advised, badly planned, badly thought-out, harebrained.

**2** *you misbegotten scoundrel!* CONTEMPTIBLE, despicable, wretched, miserable, confounded; *informal* infernal, damned; *dated* cursed, accursed.

**3** *archaic misbegotten children.* See ILLEGITIMATE sense 2.

**misbehave** verb *our parents would never let us misbehave in public* BEHAVE BADLY, be misbehaved, be naughty, be disobedient, disobey, get up to mischief, get up to no good; be bad-mannered, be rude; *informal* carry on, act up.

**miscalculate** verb *please recheck the bill, as I believe you've miscalculated* MISJUDGE, make a mistake (about), calculate wrongly, estimate wrongly, overestimate, underestimate, overvalue, undervalue; misconstrue, misinterpret, misunderstand; go wrong, err, be wide of the mark.

**miscarriage** noun **1** *she's had a miscarriage* STILLBIRTH, spontaneous abortion.

**2** *the miscarriage of the project* FAILURE, foundering, ruin, ruination, collapse, breakdown, thwarting, frustration, undoing, nonfulfillment, mismanagement.

**miscarry** verb **1** *the shock caused her to miscarry* LOSE ONE'S BABY, have a miscarriage, abort, have a spontaneous abortion.

**2** *our plan miscarried* GO WRONG, go awry, go amiss, be unsuccessful, be ruined, fail, misfire, abort, founder, come to nothing, fall through, fall flat; *informal* flop, go up in smoke. ANTONYM succeed.

**miscellaneous** adjective *he does miscellaneous jobs around the studio* VARIOUS, varied, different, assorted, mixed, sundry, diverse, disparate; diversified, motley, multifarious, ragtag, heterogeneous, eclectic, odd; *literary* divers.

**miscellany** noun *amid the miscellany on these shelves are some rare treasures* ASSORTMENT, mixture, mélange, blend, variety, mixed bag, grab bag, mix, medley, diversity, assemblage, potpourri, pastiche, mishmash, ragbag, salmagundi, gallimaufry, hodgepodge, hash; selection, collection, anthology, treasury.

**mischief** noun **1** *the boys are always getting into mischief* NAUGHTINESS, bad behavior, misbehavior, mischievousness, misconduct, disobedience; pranks, tricks, capers, nonsense, devilry, funny business; *informal* monkey business, shenanigans, carryings-on.

**2** *the mischief in her eyes* IMPISHNESS, roguishness, devilment.

**mischievous** adjective **1** *a mischievous child* NAUGHTY, badly behaved, misbehaving, disobedient, troublesome, full of mischief; rascally, roguish. ANTONYM well-behaved.

**2** *a mischievous smile* PLAYFUL, teasing, wicked, impish, roguish, arch.

**misconception** noun *a popular misconception about science* MISAPPREHENSION, misunderstanding, mistake, error, misinterpretation, misconstruction, misreading, misjudgment, misbelief, miscalculation, false impression, illusion, fallacy, delusion.

**misconduct** noun **1** *allegations of misconduct* WRONGDOING, unlawfulness, lawlessness, crime, felony, criminality, sin, sinfulness; unethical behavior, unprofessionalism, malpractice, negligence, impropriety.

**2** *he was reprimanded for his misconduct* MISBEHAVIOR, bad behavior, misdeeds, misdemeanors, disorderly conduct, mischief, naughtiness, rudeness.

**misconstrue** verb *Pete's shyness is misconstrued as unfriendliness* MISUNDERSTAND, misinterpret, misconceive, misapprehend, mistake, misread; be mistaken about, get the wrong idea about, get it/someone wrong.

**miscreant** noun *the South Street playground has been taken over by a pack of drug-dealing miscreants* CRIMINAL, culprit, wrongdoer, malefactor, offender, villain, lawbreaker, evildoer, delinquent, hoodlum, reprobate; *Law* malfeasant.

**misdeed** noun. See MISDEMEANOR.

**misdemeanor** noun *he turned a blind eye to his son's misdemeanors* WRONGDOING, evil deed, crime, felony; misdeed, misconduct, offense, error, peccadillo, transgression, sin; *informal* no-no; *archaic* trespass, misdoing.

**miser** noun *one wonders how happy a miser could ever be* PENNY-PINCHER, Scrooge, pinchpenny; *informal* skinflint, money-grubber, cheapskate, tightwad, piker. ANTONYM spendthrift.

**miserable** adjective **1** *I'm too miserable to eat* UNHAPPY, sad, sorrowful, dejected, depressed, downcast, downhearted, down, despondent, disconsolate, wretched, glum, gloomy, dismal, melancholy, woebegone, doleful, forlorn, heartbroken; *informal* blue, down in/at the mouth, down in the dumps. ANTONYMS happy, contented.

**2** *their miserable surroundings* DREARY, dismal, gloomy, drab, wretched, depressing, grim, cheerless, bleak, desolate; poor, shabby, squalid, seedy, dilapidated; *informal* flea-bitten. ANTONYM luxurious.

**3** *miserable weather* UNPLEASANT, disagreeable, depressing; wet, rainy, stormy; *informal* rotten. ANTONYMS glorious, lovely.

**4** *a miserable old grouch* GRUMPY, sullen, gloomy, bad-tempered, ill-tempered, ill-natured, dour, surly, sour, glum, moody, unsociable, saturnine, lugubrious, irritable, churlish, cantankerous, crotchety, cross, crabby, cranky, grouchy, testy, peevish, crusty, waspish. ANTONYMS cheerful, good-natured.

**5** *miserable wages* INADEQUATE, meager, scanty, paltry, small, poor, pitiful, niggardly; *informal* measly, stingy, pathetic; *formal* exiguous. ANTONYMS generous, adequate.

**6** *all that fuss about a few miserable dollars* WRETCHED, confounded; *informal* blithering, blessed, damned, blasted; *dated* accursed.

**miserly** adjective **1** *his miserly uncle* MEAN, niggardly, closefisted, parsimonious, penny-pinching, cheeseparing, Scroogelike; *informal* tightfisted, stingy, tight, mingy, moneygrubbing, cheap; *formal* penurious. See note at ECONOMICAL. ANTONYM generous.

**2** *the prize is a miserly $300.* See MEAGER sense 1.

**misery** noun **1** *periods of intense misery* UNHAPPINESS, distress, wretchedness, suffering, anguish, anxiety, angst, torment, pain, grief, heartache, heartbreak, despair, despondency, dejection, depression, desolation, gloom, melancholy, melancholia, woe, sadness, sorrow; *informal* the dumps, the blues; *literary* dolor. ANTONYMS contentment, pleasure.

**2** *the miseries of war* AFFLICTION, misfortune, difficulty, problem, ordeal, trouble, hardship, deprivation; pain, sorrow, trial, tribulation, woe.

**misfire** verb *the plan had misfired* GO WRONG, go awry, be unsuccessful, fail, founder, fall through, fall flat; backfire; *informal* flop, go up in smoke.

**misfit** noun they prided themselves on being the class misfits NONCONFORMIST, eccentric, maverick, individualist, square peg in a round hole; *informal* oddball, odd duck, weirdo, freak, screwball.

**misfortune** noun *the loss of their home in the flood was only the first of several misfortunes* PROBLEM, difficulty, setback, trouble, adversity, stroke of bad luck, reversal (of fortune), misadventure, mishap, blow, failure, accident, disaster, catastrophe; sorrow, misery, woe, trial, tribulation, tragedy.

**misgiving** noun *we finally gave our consent to the marriage, but we still had misgivings* QUALM, doubt, reservation; suspicion; (**misgivings**) distrust, mistrust, lack of confidence, second thoughts; trepidation, skepticism, unease, uneasiness, anxiety, apprehension, disquiet. See note at QUALMS.

**misguided** adjective **1** *the policy is misguided* ERRONEOUS, fallacious, unsound, misplaced, misconceived, ill-advised, ill-considered, ill-judged, ill-founded, inappropriate, unwise, injudicious, imprudent.

**2** *you are quite misguided* MISINFORMED, misled, wrong, mistaken, deluded, confused; *informal* off base.

**mishandle** verb **1** *the officer mishandled the situation* BUNGLE, fumble, make a mess of, mismanage, spoil, ruin, wreck; *informal* botch, make a hash of, mess up, screw up, fluff.

**2** *he mishandled his dog* BULLY, persecute, ill-treat, mistreat, maltreat, manhandle, abuse, knock around, hit, beat; *informal* beat up.

**3** *the equipment could be dangerous if mishandled* MISUSE, abuse, handle/treat roughly.

**mishap** noun *even a minor mishap can have serious consequences* ACCIDENT, trouble, problem, difficulty, setback, adversity, misfortune, blow; failure, disaster, tragedy, catastrophe, calamity, mischance, misadventure.

**mishmash** noun *a mishmash of colors and patterns* JUMBLE, confusion, ragbag, patchwork, farrago, assortment, medley, miscellany, mixture, mélange, blend, mix, potpourri, conglomeration, bricolage, gallimaufry, salmagundi, hodgepodge, hash.

**misinform** verb *we're sorry to tell you that you've been deliberately misinformed* MISLEAD, misguide, give wrong information, delude, take in, deceive, lie to, hoodwink; *informal* lead up the garden path, take for a ride, give someone a bum steer.

**misinterpret** verb *his proposal was misinterpreted* MISUNDERSTAND, misconceive, misconstrue, misapprehend, mistake, misread; confuse, be mistaken, get the wrong idea, take amiss.

**misjudge** verb *she misjudged her opponent's stamina* GET THE WRONG IDEA ABOUT, get wrong, judge incorrectly, estimate wrongly, be wrong about, miscalculate, misread; overestimate, underestimate, overvalue, undervalue, underrate.

**mislay** verb *I've mislaid my keys* LOSE, misplace, put in the wrong place, be unable to find, forget the whereabouts of. ANTONYM find.

**mislead** verb *Caroline deliberately misled her* DECEIVE, delude, take in, lie to, fool, hoodwink, throw off the scent, pull the wool over someone's eyes, misguide, misinform, give wrong information to; *informal* lead up the garden path, take for a ride, give someone a bum steer.

**misleading** adjective *a leaflet full of misleading statements* DECEPTIVE, confusing, deceiving, equivocal, ambiguous, fallacious, specious, spurious, false.

**mismanage** verb *the accountant had mismanaged their personal finances* BUNGLE, make a mess of, mishandle, spoil, ruin, wreck; *informal* botch, make a hash of, mess up, screw up, fluff.

**misogynist** noun *he apparently deserved his reputation as a misogynist* WOMAN-HATER; antifeminist, (male) chauvinist, sexist; *informal* male chauvinist pig.

**misplace** verb *he had misplaced the tickets* LOSE, mislay, put in the wrong place, be unable to find, forget the whereabouts of. ANTONYM find.

**misprint** noun *the book is full of misprints* MISTAKE, error, typographical error, erratum; *informal* typo.

**misquote** verb *my original statement has been misquoted* MISREPORT, misrepresent, misstate, take/quote out of context, distort, twist, slant, bias, put a spin on, falsify.

**misrepresent** verb *you are misrepresenting the views of the government* GIVE A FALSE ACCOUNT, misreport, misquote, quote/take out of context, misinterpret, put a spin on, skew, warp, falsify, distort, misstate, exaggerate.

**miss**[1] verb **1** *the shot missed her by inches* FAIL TO HIT, be/go wide of, fall short of. ANTONYM hit.

**2** *Mandy missed the ball* FAIL TO CATCH, drop, fumble, bobble, fluff, flub, mishandle, screw up. ANTONYM catch.

**3** *I've missed my bus* BE TOO LATE FOR, fail to catch/get. ANTONYM catch.

**4** *I missed what you said* FAIL TO HEAR, mishear.

**5** *you can't miss the station* FAIL TO SEE/NOTICE, overlook. ANTONYMS see, notice.

**6** *she never missed a class* FAIL TO ATTEND, be absent from, play truant from, cut, skip. ANTONYM attend.

**7** *don't miss this exciting opportunity!* LET SLIP, fail to take advantage of, let go, let pass, pass up.

**8** *I left early to miss rush hour* AVOID, beat, evade, escape, dodge, sidestep, elude, circumvent, steer clear of, find a way around, bypass.

**9** *she missed him when he was away* PINE FOR, yearn for, ache for, long for, long to see.

▸ noun *one hit and three misses* FAILURE, omission, slip, blunder, error, mistake.

**miss**[2] noun *a lovely miss* YOUNG WOMAN, young lady, girl, schoolgirl, missy; *Scottish* lass, lassie; *French* mademoiselle; *informal* girlie, chick, doll, gal; *literary* maiden, maid, damsel; *archaic* wench.

**misshapen** adjective *his misshapen feet* DEFORMED, malformed, distorted, crooked, twisted, warped, out of shape, bent, asymmetrical, irregular, misproportioned, ill-proportioned, disfigured, dysmorphic, grotesque.

**missing** adjective **1** *his wallet is missing* LOST, mislaid, misplaced, absent, gone (astray), gone AWOL, unaccounted for; disappeared, vanished. ANTONYM at hand.

**2** *passion was missing from her life* ABSENT, not present, lacking, wanting. ANTONYM present.

**mission** noun **1** *a mercy mission to Africa* ASSIGNMENT, commission, expedition, journey, trip, undertaking, operation; task, job, labor, work, duty, charge, trust.

**2** *her mission in life* VOCATION, calling, goal, aim, quest, purpose, function, life's work.

**3** *a trade mission* DELEGATION, deputation, commission, legation.

**4** *a teacher in a mission* missionary post, missionary station, missionary school.

**5** *a bombing mission* SORTIE, operation, raid.

**missionary** noun *Liddell died in occupied China, where he had been a missionary* EVANGELIST, apostle, proselytizer, preacher, minister, priest; *historical* black robe.

**missive** noun *take this missive to Lieutenant Baxter* MESSAGE, communication, letter, word, note, e-mail, memorandum, line, communiqué, dispatch, news; *informal* memo; *formal* epistle; *literary* tidings.

**misspent** adjective *our misspent youth* WASTED, dissipated, squandered, thrown away, frittered away, misused, misapplied.

**mist** noun *the mist was clearing* HAZE, fog, smog, murk, cloud, drizzle.

**mistake** noun *I assumed it had been a mistake* ERROR, fault, inaccuracy, omission, slip, blunder, miscalculation, misunderstanding, oversight, misinterpretation, gaffe, faux pas, solecism; *informal* slip-up, boo-boo, blooper, boner, goof, flub.

▸ verb **1** *did I mistake your meaning?* MISUNDERSTAND, misinterpret, get wrong, misconstrue, misread.

**2** *children often* ***mistake*** *vitamin pills* ***for*** *candies* CONFUSE WITH, mix up with, take for, misinterpret as.

PHRASES: **be mistaken** *I'm afraid you are mistaken—I've never been here before* BE WRONG, be in error, be under a misapprehension, be misinformed, be misguided; *informal* be barking up the wrong tree.

**make a mistake** *he admits he's made a mistake* GO WRONG, err, make an error, blunder, miscalculate; *informal* slip up, make a boo-boo, drop the ball, goof (up).

THE RIGHT WORD **mistake, blooper, blunder, error, faux pas, goof, slip**

It would be a **mistake** to argue with your boss the day before he or she evaluates your performance, but to forget an important step in an assigned task would be an **error**. Although these nouns are used interchangeably in many contexts, a *mistake* is usually caused by poor judgment or a disregard of rules or principles (*it was a mistake not to tell the truth at the outset*), while an *error* implies an unintentional deviation from standards of accuracy or right conduct (*a mathematical error*). A **blunder** is a careless, stupid, or blatant mistake involving behavior or judgment; it suggests awkwardness or ignorance on the part of the person who makes it (*his blunder that ruined the evening*). A **slip** is a minor and usually accidental mistake that is the result of haste or carelessness (*her slip of the tongue spoiled the surprise*), while a **faux pas** (which means "false step" in French) is an embarrassing breach of etiquette (*it was a faux pas to have meat at the table when so many of the guests were vegetarians*). **Goofs** and **bloopers** are humorous mistakes. A *blooper* is usually a mix-up in speech, while to *goof* is to make a careless error that is honestly admitted (*she shrugged her shoulders and said, "I goofed!"*)

**mistaken** adjective *they were acting on mistaken information* WRONG, erroneous, inaccurate, incorrect, false, fallacious, unfounded, misguided, misinformed. ANTONYM correct.

**mistakenly** adverb **1** *she mistakenly assumed that she knew him* WRONGLY, in error, erroneously, incorrectly, falsely, fallaciously, inaccurately. ANTONYM correctly.

**2** *Matt mistakenly opened the letter* BY ACCIDENT, accidentally, inadvertently, unintentionally, unwittingly, unconsciously, by mistake. ANTONYM intentionally.

**mistreat** verb *he's in prison for mistreating his children* ILL-TREAT, maltreat, abuse, knock about/around, hit, beat, strike, molest, injure, harm, hurt; misuse, mishandle; *informal* beat up, rough up, mess up, kick around.

**mistress** noun *her husband's mistress turned out to be one of her friends* LOVER, girlfriend, kept woman; courtesan, concubine, hetaera; *informal* the other woman; *archaic* paramour.

**mistrust** verb **1** *I mistrust his motives* BE SUSPICIOUS OF, be mistrustful of, be distrustful of, be skeptical of, be wary of, be chary of, distrust, have doubts about, have misgivings about, have reservations about, suspect.

**2** *don't mistrust your impulses* QUESTION, challenge, doubt, have no confidence in, have no faith in.

▸ noun **1** *mistrust of Russia was widespread* SUSPICION, distrust, doubt, misgivings, wariness.

**2** *their mistrust of David's competence* QUESTIONING, lack of confidence in, lack of faith in, doubt about.

**mistrustful** adjective *Sheila's unlikely stories made him even more mistrustful* SUSPICIOUS, chary, wary, distrustful, doubtful, dubious, uneasy, skeptical, leery.

**misty** adjective **1** *misty weather* HAZY, foggy, cloudy; smoggy. ANTONYM clear.

**2** *a misty outline* BLURRY, fuzzy, blurred, clouded, dim, indistinct, unclear, vague. ANTONYMS sharp, distinct.

**3** *misty memories* VAGUE, unclear, indefinite, hazy, nebulous. ANTONYM clear.

**misunderstand** verb *she misunderstood his motives* MISAPPREHEND, misinterpret, misconstrue, misconceive, mistake, misread; be mistaken, get the wrong idea, receive a false impression; *informal* be barking up the wrong tree, miss the boat.

**misunderstanding** noun **1** *a fundamental misunderstanding of juvenile crime* MISINTERPRETATION, misconstruction, misreading, misapprehension, misconception, the wrong idea, false impression.

**2** *we have had some misunderstandings* DISAGREEMENT, difference (of opinion), dispute, falling-out, quarrel, argument, altercation, squabble, wrangle, row, clash; *informal* spat, scrap, tiff, rhubarb.

**misuse** verb **1** *misusing public funds* PUT TO WRONG USE, misemploy, embezzle, use fraudulently; abuse, squander, waste.

**2** *she had been misused by her husband.* See MISTREAT.

▸ noun **1** *a misuse of company assets* WRONG USE, embezzlement, fraud; squandering, waste.

**2** *the misuse of drugs* ILLEGAL USE, abuse.

**mitigate** verb *the worst symptoms have been mitigated* ALLEVIATE, reduce, diminish, lessen, weaken, lighten, attenuate, take the edge off, allay, ease, assuage, palliate, relieve, tone down. See note at ALLEVIATE. ANTONYM aggravate.

**mitigating** adjective *if not for mitigating circumstances, he would have been convicted* EXTENUATING, justificatory, justifying, vindicating, qualifying; face-saving; *formal* exculpatory.

**mix** verb **1** *mix all the ingredients together* BLEND, mix up, mingle, combine, put together, jumble; fuse, unite, unify, join, amalgamate, incorporate, meld, marry, coalesce, homogenize, intermingle, intermix; *technical* admix; *literary* commingle. ANTONYM separate.

**2** *she mixes with all sorts* ASSOCIATE, socialize, fraternize, keep company, consort; mingle, circulate, rub elbows; *informal* hang out/around, hobnob, network.

**3** *we just don't mix* BE COMPATIBLE, get along/on, be in harmony, see eye to eye, agree; *informal* hit it off, click, be on the same wavelength.

▸ noun *a mix of ancient and modern* MIXTURE, blend, mingling, combination, compound, fusion, alloy, union, amalgamation; medley, mélange, collection, selection, assortment, variety, mixed bag, grab bag, miscellany, potpourri, jumble, ragbag, patchwork, bricolage, farrago, gallimaufry, salmagundi, hodgepodge.

PHRASES: **mix up 1** *mix up the ingredients.* See MIX verb sense 1.

**2** *I mixed up the dates* CONFUSE, get confused, muddle (up), get muddled up, mistake.

**mixed up in** *how did she get mixed up in a car-theft ring?* INVOLVED IN, embroiled in, caught up in.

**mixed** adjective **1** *a mixed collection* ASSORTED, varied, variegated, miscellaneous, disparate, diverse, diversified, motley, sundry, jumbled, heterogeneous. ANTONYM homogeneous.

**2** *mixed breeds* HYBRID, cross-bred, interbred, mongrel, half-caste. ANTONYM pure.

**3** *mixed reactions* AMBIVALENT, equivocal, contradictory, conflicting, confused, muddled. ANTONYM unequivocal.

**mixed up** adjective *informal sorry, I'm still a little mixed up* CONFUSED, befuddled, bemused, bewildered, muddled; disturbed, neurotic, unbalanced; *informal* hung up, messed up, at sea.

**mixer** noun **1** *a kitchen mixer* BLENDER, food processor, beater; churn.

**2** *he attended a mixer* GATHERING, social, function, get-together, meet-and-greet.

**mixture** noun **1** *the pudding mixture* BLEND, mix, brew, combination, concoction; composition, compound, alloy, amalgam.

**2** *a strange mixture of people* ASSORTMENT, miscellany, medley, mélange, blend, variety, mixed bag, grab bag, mix, diversity, collection, selection, potpourri, mishmash, ragbag, patchwork, bricolage, farrago, gallimaufry, salmagundi, hodgepodge, hash.

**3** *genetically, the animal is a mixture* CROSS, cross-breed, mongrel, hybrid, half-breed, half-caste.

**mix-up** noun *there was some sort of mix-up in the birth records* CONFUSION, muddle, misunderstanding, mistake, error; *informal* screw-up.

**moan** noun **1** *moans of pain* GROAN, wail, whimper, sob, cry.

**2** *the moan of the wind* SIGH, murmur, sough.

**3** *informal there were moans about the delay* COMPLAINT, complaining, grouse, grousing, grumble, grumbling, whine, whining, carping; *informal* gripe, griping, grouching, bellyaching, bitching, beef, beefing.

▸ verb **1** *he moaned in agony* GROAN, wail, whimper, sob, cry.

**2** *the wind moaned in the trees* SIGH, murmur, sough.

**3** *informal* *you're always moaning about the weather* COMPLAIN, grouse, grumble, whine, carp; *informal* gripe, grouch, bellyache, bitch, beef, kvetch.

**mob** noun **1** *troops dispersed the mob* CROWD, horde, multitude, rabble, mass, throng, group, gang, gathering, assemblage.

**2** (**Mob**) *he was hiding from the Mob* MAFIA, Cosa Nostra, Camorra.

**3** *the mob was excluded from political life* COMMON PEOPLE, masses, rank and file, commonality, third estate, plebeians, proletariat; hoi polloi, lower classes, rabble, riffraff, great unwashed; *informal* proles, plebs.

▸ verb **1** *the band's lead singer was mobbed when he visited Vancouver* SURROUND, swarm, besiege, jostle.

**2** *reporters mobbed her hotel* CROWD (INTO), fill, pack, throng, press into, squeeze into.

**mobile** adjective **1** *both patients are mobile* ABLE TO MOVE (AROUND), moving, walking; *Zoology* motile; *Medicine* ambulant. ANTONYM motionless.

**2** *a mobile library* TRAVELING, transportable, portable, movable; itinerant, peripatetic. ANTONYM stationary.

**3** *highly mobile young people* ADAPTABLE, flexible, versatile, adjustable. ANTONYM static.

**mobilize** verb **1** *the government mobilized the troops* MARSHAL, deploy, muster, rally, call up, assemble, mass, organize, prepare.

**2** *mobilizing support for the party* GENERATE, arouse, awaken, excite, incite, provoke, foment, prompt, stimulate, stir up, galvanize, encourage, inspire, whip up; *literary* enkindle.

**mock** verb **1** *they mocked her accent* RIDICULE, jeer at, sneer at, deride, scorn, make fun of, laugh at, scoff at, tease, taunt; *informal* josh, rag on, pull/jerk/yank someone's chain.

**2** *they mocked the way he speaks* PARODY, ape, take off, satirize, lampoon, imitate, impersonate, mimic; *informal* send up. See note at IMITATE.

▸ adjective *mock leather* IMITATION, artificial, man-made, simulated, synthetic, ersatz, fake, reproduction, dummy, sham, false, faux, spurious, bogus, counterfeit, inauthentic, pseudo; *informal* pretend, phony. ANTONYM genuine.

**mockery** noun **1** *the mockery in his voice* RIDICULE, derision, jeering, sneering, contempt, scorn, scoffing, teasing, taunting, sarcasm.

**2** *the trial was a mockery* TRAVESTY, charade, farce, parody.

**model** noun **1** *a working model* REPLICA, copy, representation, mock-up, dummy, imitation, duplicate, reproduction, facsimile.

**2** *the Canadian model of health care* PROTOTYPE, stereotype, archetype, type, version; mold, template, framework, pattern, design, blueprint.

**3** *she was a model of patience* IDEAL, paragon, perfect example/specimen; perfection, acme, epitome, nonpareil, crème de la crème.

**4** *a runway model* FASHION MODEL, supermodel, mannequin.

**5** *an artist's model* SUBJECT, poser, sitter.

**6** *the latest model of car* VERSION, type, design, variety, kind, sort.

▸ adjective **1** *model trains* REPLICA, TOY, miniature, dummy, imitation, duplicate, reproduction, facsimile.

**2** *model farms* PROTOTYPICAL, prototypal, archetypal.

**3** *a model teacher* IDEAL, perfect, exemplary, classic, flawless, faultless.

THE RIGHT WORD **model, archetype, example, ideal, paradigm, pattern, prototype**

Most parents try to set a good **example** for their children, although they may end up setting a bad one. An *example*, in other words, is a precedent for imitation, either good or bad. Most parents would do better to provide a **model** for their children, which refers to a person or thing that is to be followed or imitated because of its excellence in conduct or character. *Model* also connotes a physical shape to be copied closely (*a ship's model, a model airplane*). Not all children regard their parents as an **ideal** to which they aspire, a word that suggests an imagined perfection or a standard based upon a set of desirable qualities (*the ideal gentleman; the ideal of what an artist should be*); but young people's lives often end up following the **pattern** established by their parents, meaning that their lives follow the same basic configuration or design. While **prototype** and **archetype** are often used interchangeably, they really mean quite different things. An *archetype* is a perfect and unchanging form that existing things or people can approach but never duplicate (*the archetype of a mother*), while a *prototype* is an early, usually unrefined version of something that later versions reflect but may depart from (*a prototype for a hydrogen-fueled car*). **Paradigm** can refer to an example that serves as a model, but today its use is primarily confined to a grammatical context, where it means a set giving all the various forms of a word, such as the conjugation of a verb.

**moderate** adjective **1** *moderate success* AVERAGE, modest, medium, middling, ordinary, common, commonplace, everyday, workaday; tolerable, passable, adequate, fair; mediocre, indifferent, unexceptional, unremarkable, run-of-the-mill; *informal* OK, so-so, 'comme ci, comme ça,' fair-to-middling, plain-vanilla, no great shakes, not up to much. ANTONYMS great, massive.

**2** *moderate prices* REASONABLE, acceptable; inexpensive, low, fair, modest. ANTONYMS outrageous, unreasonable.

**3** *moderate views* MIDDLE-OF-THE-ROAD, nonextreme, nonradical, centrist. ANTONYM extreme.

**4** *moderate behavior* RESTRAINED, controlled, sober; tolerant, lenient. ANTONYM unreasonable.

▸ verb **1** *the wind has moderated somewhat* DIE DOWN, abate, let up, calm down, lessen, decrease, diminish; recede, weaken, subside. ANTONYM increase.

**2** *you can help to moderate her anger* CURB, control, check, temper, restrain, subdue; repress, tame, lessen, decrease, lower, reduce, diminish, alleviate, allay, appease, assuage, ease, soothe, calm, tone down. ANTONYMS exacerbate, aggravate.

**3** *the panel was moderated by one of the writers* CHAIR, take the chair of, preside over.

**moderately** adverb *a moderately successful farmer* SOMEWHAT, quite, rather, fairly, reasonably, comparatively, relatively, to some extent; tolerably, passably, adequately; *informal* pretty.

**moderation** noun **1** *he urged them to show moderation* SELF-RESTRAINT, restraint, self-control, self-discipline; temperance, leniency, fairness. See note at ABSTINENCE.

**2** *a moderation of their confrontational style* RELAXATION, easing (off), reduction, abatement, weakening, slackening, tempering, softening, diminution, diminishing, lessening; decline, modulation, modification, mitigation, allaying; *informal* letup. PHRASE: **in moderation** *I quit drinking because I wasn't able to drink in moderation* IN MODERATE QUANTITIES/AMOUNTS, within (sensible) limits; moderately.

**modern** adjective **1** *modern times* PRESENT-DAY, contemporary, present, current, twenty-first-century, latter-day, modern-day, recent. ANTONYM past.

**2** *her clothes are very modern* FASHIONABLE, in fashion, in style, in vogue, up to date, all the rage, trend-setting, stylish, styling/stylin', voguish, modish, chic, à la mode; the latest, new, newest, newfangled, modernistic, advanced; *informal* trendy, cool, in, with it, now, hip, phat, happening, kicky, tony, fly. ANTONYMS out of date, old-fashioned.

**modernize** verb **1** *they are modernizing their manufacturing facilities* UPDATE, bring up to date, streamline, overhaul; renovate, remodel, refashion, revamp.

**2** *we must modernize to survive* GET UP TO DATE, move with the times, innovate; *informal* get in the swim, get with it, go with the flow.

**modest** adjective **1** *she was modest about her poetry* SELF-EFFACING, self-deprecating, humble, unpretentious, unassuming, unostentatious; shy, bashful, self-conscious, diffident, reserved, reticent, coy. ANTONYMS conceited, boastful.

**2** *modest success* MODERATE, fair, limited, tolerable, passable, adequate, satisfactory, acceptable, unexceptional. ANTONYMS great, runaway.

**3** *a modest house* SMALL, ordinary, simple, plain, humble, inexpensive, unostentatious, unpretentious. ANTONYMS grandiose, grand.

**4** *her modest dress* DECOROUS, decent, seemly, demure, proper. ANTONYM flamboyant.

**modesty** noun **1** *Hannah's modesty cloaks many talents* SELF-EFFACEMENT, humility, unpretentiousness; shyness, bashfulness, self-consciousness, reserve, reticence, timidity.

**2** *the modesty of his aspirations* LIMITED SCOPE, moderation.

**3** *the modesty of his home* UNPRETENTIOUSNESS, simplicity, plainness.

**modicum** noun *I'd like to leave while I still have a modicum of my self-respect* SMALL AMOUNT, particle, speck, fragment, scrap, crumb, grain, morsel, shred, dash, drop, pinch, soupçon, jot, iota, whit, atom, smattering, scintilla, hint, suggestion, tinge; *informal* smidgen, tad.

**modification** noun **1** *the design is undergoing modification* ALTERATION, adjustment, change, adaptation, refinement, revision.

**2** *some minor modifications were made* REVISION, refinement, improvement, amendment, adaptation, adjustment, change, alteration.

**3** *the modification of his views* SOFTENING, moderation, tempering, qualification.

**modify** verb **1** *their economic policy has been modified* ALTER, change, adjust, adapt, amend, revise, reshape, refashion, restyle, revamp, rework, remodel, refine; *informal* tweak, doctor.

**2** *he modified his more extreme views* MODERATE, revise, temper, soften, tone down, qualify.

**modulate** verb **1** *the cells modulate the body's response* REGULATE, adjust, set, modify, moderate.

**2** *she modulated her voice* ADJUST, change the tone of, temper, soften.

**mogul** noun *Hollywood movie moguls* MAGNATE, tycoon, VIP, notable, personage, baron, captain, king, lord, grandee, nabob; *informal* bigwig, big shot, big cheese, top dog, top banana, big kahuna, big enchilada.

**moist** adjective **1** *the air was moist* DAMP, dampish, steamy, humid, muggy, clammy, dank, wet, wettish, soggy, sweaty, sticky. ANTONYM dry.

**2** *a moist fruitcake* SUCCULENT, juicy, soft. ANTONYM dry.

**3** *her eyes grew moist* TEARFUL, watery, misty, dewy.

**moisten** verb *they moisten the towels with almond-scented hot water* DAMPEN, wet, damp, water, humidify; *literary* bedew.

**moisture** noun *too much moisture is bad for the tiny seedlings* WETNESS, wet, water, liquid, condensation, dew, steam, vapor, dampness, damp, humidity, clamminess, mugginess, dankness, wateriness.

**mold** noun *walls stained with mold* MILDEW, fungus, dry rot, must, moldiness, mustiness.

**moldy** adjective *everything in the cellar was moldy* MILDEWED, mildewy, musty, moldering, fusty; decaying, decayed, rotting, rotten, bad, spoiled, far gone, decomposing.

**mole** noun **1** *the mole on his left cheek* MARK, birthmark, freckle, blotch, spot, blemish, beauty spot, beauty mark.

**2** *an undercover mole* SPY, agent, secret agent, undercover agent, operative, plant, infiltrator, sleeper, informant, informer; *informal* spook; *archaic* intelligencer.

**molest** verb **1** *the crowd molested the police* HARASS, harry, hassle, pester, bother, annoy, beset, persecute, torment; *informal* roust.

**2** *he molested a ten-year-old boy* (SEXUALLY) ABUSE, (sexually) assault, interfere with, rape, violate; *informal* grope, paw, fondle; *literary* ravish. See note at ATTACK.

**mollify** verb **1** *they tried to mollify the protesters* APPEASE, placate, pacify, conciliate, soothe, calm (down). See note at PACIFY. ANTONYM enrage.

**2** *mollifying the fears of the public* ALLAY, assuage, alleviate, mitigate, ease, reduce, moderate, temper, tone down, soften; *informal* blunt. ANTONYM inflame.

**mollycoddle** verb *his parents mollycoddle him* PAMPER, cosset, coddle, spoil, indulge, overindulge, pet, baby, nanny, wait on hand and foot.

**moment** noun **1** *he thought for a moment* LITTLE WHILE, short time, bit, minute, instant, second, split second; *informal* sec.

**2** *the moment they met* POINT (IN TIME), time, hour.

**3** *formal* *issues of little moment* IMPORTANCE, import, significance, consequence, note, weight, concern, interest. PHRASE: **in a moment** *the show will start in a moment* VERY SOON, in a minute, in a second, in a trice, shortly, any minute (now), in the twinkling of an eye, in (less than) no time, in no time at all, momentarily; *informal* in a jiff, in a jiffy, in two shakes (of a lamb's tail), in the blink of an eye, in a snap, in a heartbeat, in a flash; *literary* ere long.

**momentarily** adverb **1** *he paused momentarily* BRIEFLY, fleetingly, for a moment, for a second, for an instant.

**2** *my husband will be here momentarily.* See IN A MOMENT at MOMENT.

**momentary** adjective *a momentary lapse in power* BRIEF, short, short-lived, fleeting, passing, transient, transitory, ephemeral; *literary* evanescent. ANTONYM lengthy.

**momentous** adjective *a momentous decision* IMPORTANT, significant, historic, portentous, critical, crucial, life-and-death, decisive, pivotal, consequential, of consequence, far-reaching, earth-shattering, earth-shaking; *formal* of moment. ANTONYM insignificant.

**momentum** noun *we gained momentum going down the Killingworth hill* IMPETUS, energy, force, power, strength, thrust, speed, velocity.

**monarch** noun *Elizabeth II has been Britain's reigning monarch since 1953* SOVEREIGN, ruler, the Crown, crowned head, potentate; king, queen, emperor, empress, prince, princess.

**monastery** noun *the monastery was temporarily occupied by Nazis* RELIGIOUS COMMUNITY; friary, abbey, priory, nunnery, cloister, convent.

**monastic** adjective **1** *a monastic community* CLOISTERED, cloistral, claustral.

**2** *a monastic existence* AUSTERE, ascetic, simple, solitary, monkish, celibate, quiet, cloistered, sequestered, secluded, reclusive, hermitlike, hermitic, incommunicado.

**monetary** adjective *her sharp monetary instincts got us through the recession in very good sharp* FINANCIAL, fiscal, pecuniary, money, cash, economic, budgetary. See note at FINANCIAL.

**money** noun **1** *have you got money for train fare?* CASH, hard cash, ready money; the means, the wherewithal, funds, capital, finances, (filthy) lucre; coins, change, specie, silver, currency, bills, (bank) notes; *informal* dough, bread, bucks, loot, greenbacks, moola, dinero, shekels, mazuma; *archaic* pelf.

**2** *she married him for his money* WEALTH, riches, fortune, affluence, assets, liquid assets, resources, means.

**3** *the money here is better* PAY, salary, wages, remuneration; *formal* emolument. PHRASES: **for my money** *for my money, they are the better team* IN MY OPINION, to my mind, in my view, as I see it, personally, in my estimation, in my judgment, if you ask me.
**in the money** *informal* *we're finally in the money.* See MONEYED.

**moneyed** adjective *she's got two brothers—one is broke and the other is moneyed* RICH, wealthy, affluent, well-to-do, well off, prosperous, in clover, opulent, of means, of substance; *informal* in the money, rolling in it, loaded, stinking/filthy rich, well-heeled, made of money. ANTONYM poor.

**money-making** adjective *it wasn't the moneymaking enterprise we had hoped it would be* PROFITABLE, profit-making, remunerative, lucrative, successful, financially rewarding. ANTONYM loss-making.

**mongrel** noun *a curly-tailed mongrel* CROSS-BREED, cross, mixed breed, half-breed; cur, mutt; *informal* Heinz 57.

▸ adjective *a mongrel bitch* CROSS-BRED, of mixed breed, half-breed, interbred, mixed. ANTONYM pedigree.

**monitor** noun **1** *a fetal monitor* DETECTOR, scanner, recorder; listening device; security camera.

**2** *UN monitors* OBSERVER, watchdog, overseer, supervisor.

**3** *a computer monitor* SCREEN, video display terminal, VDT.

▸ verb *his movements were closely monitored* OBSERVE, watch, track, keep an eye on, keep under observation, keep watch on, keep under surveillance, record, note, oversee; *informal* keep tabs on.

**monk** noun *the monks teach a class in organic gardening* brother, religious, cenobite, contemplative, mendicant; friar; abbot, prior; novice, oblate, postulant; lama, marabout.

**monkey** noun **1** SIMIAN, primate, ape.

**2** *you little monkey!* See RASCAL. PHRASES: **make a monkey (out) of** *she made a monkey out of Clark in front of his friends* MAKE SOMEONE LOOK FOOLISH, make a fool of, make a laughingstock of, ridicule, make fun of, poke fun at.
**monkey with** *don't monkey with those switches* TAMPER WITH, fiddle with, interfere with, meddle with, tinker with, play with; *informal* mess with.

**monkey business** noun *informal they better not try any monkey business when Ms. Bergdahl is around* MISCHIEF, misbehavior, mischievousness, devilry, devilment, tomfoolery; dishonesty, trickery, chicanery, skulduggery; *informal* shenanigans, funny business, hanky-panky, monkeyshines.

**monologue** noun *Letterman's nightly monologue* SOLILOQUY, speech, address, lecture, sermon, homily; *formal* oration.

**monopolize** verb **1** *the company has monopolized the market* CORNER, control, take over, gain control/dominance over; *archaic* engross.

**2** *he monopolized the conversation* DOMINATE, take over; *informal* hog.

**3** *she monopolized the guest of honor* TAKE UP ALL THE ATTENTION OF, keep to oneself; *informal* tie up.

**monotonous** adjective **1** *a monotonous job* TEDIOUS, boring, dull, uninteresting, unexciting, wearisome, tiresome, repetitive, repetitious, unvarying, unchanging, unvaried, humdrum, ho-hum, routine, mechanical, mind-numbing, soul-destroying; colorless, featureless, dreary; *informal* deadly, samey, dullsville. ANTONYM interesting.

**2** *a monotonous voice* TONELESS, flat, uninflected, soporific.

**monotony** noun **1** *the monotony of everyday life* TEDIUM, tediousness, lack of variety, dullness, boredom, repetitiveness, uniformity, routineness, wearisomeness, tiresomeness; lack of excitement, uneventfulness, dreariness, colorlessness, featurelessness; *informal* deadliness.

**2** *the monotony of her voice* TONELESSNESS, flatness.

**monster** noun **1** *legendary sea monsters* FABULOUS CREATURE, mythical creature.

**2** *her husband is a monster* BRUTE, fiend, beast, devil, demon, barbarian, savage, animal; *informal* swine, pig.

**3** *the boy's a little monster* RASCAL, imp, monkey, wretch, devil; *informal* horror, scamp, scalawag, tyke, varmint, hellion; *archaic* scapegrace, rapscallion.

**4** *he's a monster of a man* GIANT, mammoth, colossus, leviathan, titan; *informal* jumbo.

▸ adjective *informal a monster truck.* See HUGE.

**monstrosity** noun **1** *a concrete monstrosity* EYESORE, blot on the landscape, excrescence, horror.

**2** *a biological monstrosity* MUTANT, mutation, freak (of nature), monster, abortion.

**monstrous** adjective **1** *a monstrous creature* GROTESQUE, hideous, ugly, ghastly, gruesome, horrible, horrific, horrifying, grisly, disgusting, repulsive, repellent, dreadful, frightening, terrifying, malformed, misshapen. ANTONYM lovely.

**2** *a monstrous tidal wave.* See HUGE.

**3** *monstrous acts of violence* APPALLING, heinous, egregious, evil, wicked, abominable, terrible, horrible, dreadful, vile, outrageous, shocking, disgraceful; unspeakable, despicable, vicious, savage, barbaric, barbarous, inhuman, beastly. ANTONYMS admirable, good.

**monument** noun **1** *a stone monument* MEMORIAL, statue, pillar, column, obelisk, cross; cenotaph, tomb, mausoleum, shrine.

**2** *a monument was placed over the grave* GRAVESTONE, headstone, tombstone, grave marker, plaque.

**3** *a monument to a past era of aviation* TESTAMENT, record, reminder, remembrance, memorial, commemoration.

**monumental** adjective **1** *a monumental task* HUGE, great, enormous, gigantic, massive, colossal, mammoth, immense, tremendous, mighty, stupendous.

**2** *a monumental error in judgment* TERRIBLE, dreadful, awful, colossal, staggering, huge, enormous, unforgivable, egregious.

**3** *her monumental achievement* IMPRESSIVE, striking, outstanding, remarkable, magnificent, majestic, stupendous, ambitious, large-scale, grand, awe-inspiring, important, significant, distinguished, memorable, immortal.

**mood** noun **1** *she's in a good mood* FRAME/STATE OF MIND, humor, temper; disposition, spirit, tenor.

**2** *he's obviously in **a mood*** A BAD MOOD, a (bad) temper, a sulk, a fit of pique; low spirits, the doldrums, the blues, a blue funk; *informal* the dumps.

**3** *the mood of the film* ATMOSPHERE, feeling, spirit, ambience, aura, character, tenor, flavor, feel, tone. PHRASE: **in the mood** *I don't like to go to the casino unless I'm in the mood* IN THE RIGHT FRAME OF MIND, wanting to, inclined to, disposed to, minded to, eager to, willing to.

**moody** adjective *how can she live with that moody man?* TEMPERAMENTAL, emotional, volatile, capricious, changeable, mercurial; sullen, sulky, morose, glum, depressed, dejected, despondent, doleful, dour, sour, saturnine, manic-depressive; *informal* blue, down in the dumps, down in/at the mouth. ANTONYMS even-tempered, cheerful.

**moon** noun *viewing the eclipse of the moon* SATELLITE.

▸ verb **1** *stop **mooning about*** WASTE TIME, loaf, idle, mope; *informal* lollygag.

**2** *he's mooning over her photograph* MOPE, pine, brood, daydream, fantasize, be in a reverie.

PHRASES: **many moons ago** *informal we stayed at that hotel many moons ago* A LONG TIME AGO, ages ago, years ago.
**once in a blue moon** *informal Donnie brings me flowers once in a blue moon* HARDLY EVER, scarcely ever, rarely, very seldom.
**over the moon** *informal I'm over the moon just thinking about our upcoming cruise.* See ECSTATIC.

**moor** verb *a boat was moored to the quay* TIE UP, secure, make fast, fix firmly, anchor, berth, dock.

**moot** adjective *a moot point* DEBATABLE, open to discussion/question, arguable, questionable, at issue, open to doubt, disputable, controversial, contentious, disputed, unresolved, unsettled, up in the air.

▸ verb *the idea was first mooted in the 1930s* RAISE, bring up, broach, mention, put forward, introduce, advance, propose, suggest.

**mop** noun *her tousled mop of hair* SHOCK, mane, tangle, mass.

▸ verb *a man was mopping the floor* WASH, clean, wipe, swab.

PHRASE: **mop up 1** *I mopped up the spilled coffee* WIPE UP, clean up, sponge up.

**2** *troops mopped up the last pockets of resistance* FINISH OFF, deal with, dispose of, take care of, clear up, eliminate.

**mope** verb **1** *it's no use moping* BROOD, sulk, be miserable, be despondent, pine, eat one's heart out, fret, grieve; *informal* be down in the dumps, be down in/at the mouth; *literary* repine.

**2** *she was moping about the house* LANGUISH, moon, idle, loaf; *informal* lollygag.

**moral** adjective **1** *moral issues* ETHICAL, social, having to do with right and wrong.

**2** *a moral man* VIRTUOUS, good, righteous, upright, upstanding, high-minded, principled, honorable, honest, just, noble, incorruptible, scrupulous, respectable, decent, clean-living, law-abiding. ANTONYM dishonorable.

**3** *moral support* PSYCHOLOGICAL, emotional, mental.

▸ noun **1** *the moral of the story* LESSON, message, meaning, significance, signification, import, point, teaching.

**2** *he has no morals* MORAL CODE, code of ethics, (moral) values, principles, standards, (sense of) morality, scruples.

THE RIGHT WORD **moral, ethical, honorable, righteous, sanctimonious, virtuous**

You can be an **ethical** person without necessarily being a **moral** one, since *ethical* implies conformity with a code of fair and honest behavior, particularly in business or in a profession (*an ethical legislator who didn't believe in cutting deals*), while *moral* refers to generally accepted standards of goodness and rightness in character and conduct—especially sexual conduct (*the moral values she'd learned from her mother*). In the same way, you can be **honorable** without necessarily being **virtuous**, since *honorable* suggests dealing with others in a decent and ethical manner, while *virtuous* implies the possession of moral excellence in character (*many honorable businesspeople fail to live a virtuous private life*). **Righteous** is similar in meaning to **virtuous** but also implies freedom from guilt or blame (*righteous anger*); when the righteous person is also somewhat intolerant and narrow-minded, *self-righteous* might be a better adjective. Someone who makes a hypocritical show of being righteous is often described as **sanctimonious**—in other words, acting like a saint without having a saintly character.

**morale** noun *Bob Hope was the champion of troop morale* CONFIDENCE, self-confidence, self-esteem, spirit(s), team spirit, enthusiasm.

**morality** noun **1** *the morality of nuclear weapons* ETHICS, rights and wrongs, ethicality.

**2** *a sharp decline in morality* VIRTUE, goodness, good behavior, righteousness, rectitude, uprightness; morals, principles, honesty, integrity, propriety, honor, justice, decency; ethics, standards/principles of behavior, mores, standards. See note at GOODNESS.

**morass** noun **1** *the muddy morass* QUAGMIRE, swamp, bog, marsh, muskeg, mire, marshland, wetland, slough, moor.

**2** *a morass of paperwork* CONFUSION, chaos, muddle, tangle, entanglement, imbroglio, jumble, clutter; *informal* logjam.

**moratorium** noun *a moratorium on nuclear testing* EMBARGO, ban, prohibition, suspension, postponement, stay, stoppage, halt, freeze, standstill, respite.

**morbid** adjective **1** *a morbid fascination with contemporary warfare* GHOULISH, macabre, unhealthy, gruesome, unwholesome; abnormal, aberrant, disturbing, worrisome; *informal* sick, weird. ANTONYM wholesome.

**2** *I felt decidedly morbid* GLOOMY, glum, melancholy, morose, dismal, somber, doleful, despondent, dejected, sad, depressed, downcast, down, disconsolate, miserable, unhappy, downhearted, dispirited, low; *informal* blue, down in the dumps, down in/at the mouth. ANTONYM cheerful.

**mordant** adjective *a mordant sense of humor* CAUSTIC, trenchant, biting, cutting, acerbic, sardonic, sarcastic, scathing, acid, sharp, keen; critical, bitter, virulent, vitriolic.

**more** adjective *I could do with some more clothes* ADDITIONAL, further, added, extra, increased, new, other, supplementary. ANTONYMS less, fewer.

▸ adverb **1** *he was able to concentrate more on his writing* TO A GREATER EXTENT, further, some more, better.

**2** *he was rich, and more, he was handsome.* See MOREOVER.

▸ pronoun *we're going to need more* EXTRA, an additional amount, an additional amount, an addition, an increase. ANTONYMS less, fewer.

PHRASE: **more or less** *the jar holds more or less 18 pickles* APPROXIMATELY, roughly, nearly, almost, close to, about, of/on the order of, in the region of.

**moreover** adverb *Lindsey is going to the wedding, and moreover, she'll be singing at the reception* BESIDES, furthermore, what's more, in addition, also, as well, too, to boot, additionally, on top of that, into the bargain, more, likewise; *archaic* withal.

**moribund** adjective **1** *the patient was moribund* DYING, expiring, terminal, on one's deathbed, near death, at death's door, not long for this world. ANTONYMS thriving, recovering.

**2** *the moribund shipbuilding industry* DECLINING, in decline, waning, dying, stagnating, stagnant, crumbling, on its last legs. ANTONYM flourishing.

**morning** noun **1** *I've got a meeting* ***this morning*** BEFORE NOON, before lunch/lunchtime, this a.m.; *literary* this morn, this forenoon.

**2** *morning is on its way* DAWN, daybreak, sunrise, first light, sunup; *literary* dayspring, dawning, aurora, cock crow. PHRASE: **morning, noon, and night** *she stayed at his bedside morning, noon, and night* ALL THE TIME, without a break, constantly, continually, incessantly, ceaselessly, perpetually, unceasingly; *informal* 24–7.

**moron** noun *what moron left ice cream on the stove?* FOOL, idiot, ass, blockhead, dunce, dolt, ignoramus, imbecile, cretin, dullard, simpleton, clod; *informal* nitwit, halfwit, dope, ninny, nincompoop, chump, dimwit, dingbat, dipstick, goober, coot, goon, dumbo, dummy, ditz, dumdum, fathead, numbskull, numbnuts, dunderhead, thickhead, airhead, flake, lamebrain, zombie, nerd, peabrain, birdbrain, jughead, jerk, donkey, twit, goat, dork, twerp, schmuck, bozo, boob, turkey, schlep, chowderhead, dumbhead, goofball, goof, goofus, galoot, lummox, klutz, putz, schlemiel, sap, meatball, dumb cluck. ANTONYM genius.

**morose** adjective *Louis sat alone, looking morose* SULLEN, sulky, gloomy, bad-tempered, ill-tempered, dour, surly, sour, glum, moody, ill-humored, melancholy, melancholic, brooding, broody, doleful, miserable, depressed, dejected, despondent, downcast, unhappy, low, down, grumpy, irritable, churlish, cantankerous, crotchety, cross, crabby, cranky, grouchy, testy, snappish, peevish, crusty; *informal* blue, down in the dumps, down in/at the mouth. ANTONYM cheerful.

**morsel** noun *we sampled morsels of their splendid desserts* MOUTHFUL, bite, nibble, bit, soupçon, taste, spoonful, forkful, sliver, drop, dollop, spot, gobbet, tidbit.

**mortal** adjective **1** *mortal remains | all men are mortal* PERISHABLE, physical, bodily, corporeal, fleshly, earthly; human, impermanent, transient, ephemeral.

**2** *a mortal blow* DEADLY, fatal, lethal, death-dealing, murderous, terminal.

**3** *mortal enemies* IRRECONCILABLE, deadly, sworn, bitter, out-and-out, implacable.

**4** *a mortal sin* UNPARDONABLE, unforgivable. ANTONYM venial.

**5** *living in mortal fear* EXTREME, (very) great, terrible, awful, dreadful, intense, severe, grave, dire, unbearable.

▸ noun *we are mere mortals* HUMAN BEING, human, person, man/woman; earthling.

**mortality** noun **1** *a sense of his own mortality* IMPERMANENCE, transience, ephemerality, perishability; humanity; corporeality.

**2** *the causes of mortality* DEATH, loss of life, dying.

**mortify** verb **1** *I'd be mortified if my friends found out* EMBARRASS, humiliate, chagrin, discomfit, shame, abash, horrify, appall.

**2** *he was mortified at being excluded* HURT, wound, affront, offend, put out, pique, irk, annoy, vex; *informal* rile.

**3** *mortifying the flesh* SUBDUE, suppress, subjugate, control; discipline, chasten, punish.

**mortuary** noun *flowers were sent to the mortuary* funeral parlor, funeral home; morgue.

**most** pronoun *most of the guests brought gifts* NEARLY ALL, almost all, the greatest part/number, the majority, the bulk, the preponderance. ANTONYMS little, few.

PHRASE: **for the most part** See MOSTLY senses 1, 2.

**mostly** adverb **1** *the other passengers were mostly businessmen* MAINLY, for the most part, on the whole, in the main, largely, chiefly, predominantly, principally, primarily.

**2** *I mostly wear jeans* USUALLY, generally, in general, for the most part, as a rule, ordinarily, normally, customarily, typically, most of the time, almost always, on average, on balance.

**mother** noun **1** *I will ask my mother* FEMALE PARENT, materfamilias, matriarch; *informal* mom, mommy, ma, mama; old lady, old woman; *chiefly Brit. informal* mum, mummy.

**2** *the foal's mother* DAM.

**3** *necessity is the mother of invention* SOURCE, origin, genesis, fountainhead, inspiration, stimulus; *literary* wellspring.

**4** *informal a mother of a storm* HUMDINGER, dilly, doozy, lulu, whopper.

▸ verb **1** *she mothered her husband* LOOK AFTER, care for, take care of, nurse, protect, tend, raise, rear; pamper, coddle, cosset, fuss over. ANTONYM neglect.

**2** *she mothered two sets of twins* GIVE BIRTH TO, have, bear, produce, birth; *archaic* be brought to bed of.

▸ adjective *my mother tongue* NATIVE, first, original; ancestral.

**motherly** adjective *thanks for your motherly advice* MATERNAL, maternalistic, protective, caring, loving, devoted, affectionate, fond, warm, tender, gentle, kind, kindly, understanding, compassionate.

**motion** noun **1** *the rocking motion of the boat | a planet's motion around the sun* MOVEMENT, moving, locomotion, rise and fall, shifting; progress, passage, passing, transit, course, travel, traveling.

**2** *a motion of the hand* GESTURE, movement, signal, sign, indication; wave, nod, gesticulation.

**3** *the motion failed to obtain a majority* PROPOSAL, proposition, recommendation, suggestion.

▸ verb *he motioned her to sit down* GESTURE, signal, direct, indicate; wave, beckon, nod, gesticulate.

PHRASES: **in motion** *remain seated while the bus is in motion* MOVING, on the move, going, traveling, running, functioning, operational.

**set/put in motion** *they have set in motion a formal review of the law* START, commence, begin, activate, initiate, launch, get underway, get going, get off the ground; trigger off, set off, spark off, generate, cause.

**motionless** adjective *the leaves were motionless in the still night air* UNMOVING, still, stationary, stock-still, immobile, static, not moving a muscle, rooted to the spot, transfixed, paralyzed, frozen. ANTONYM moving.

**motivate** verb **1** *she was primarily motivated by the desire for profit* PROMPT, drive, move, inspire, stimulate, influence, activate, impel, push, propel, spur (on).

**2** *it's the teacher's job to motivate the child* INSPIRE, stimulate, encourage, spur (on), excite, inspirit, incentivize, fire with enthusiasm.

**motivation** noun **1** *his motivation was financial* MOTIVE, motivating force, incentive, stimulus, stimulation, inspiration, inducement, incitement, spur, reason; *informal* carrot.

**2** *keep up the staff's motivation* ENTHUSIASM, drive, ambition, initiative, determination, enterprise; *informal* get-up-and-go.

**motive** noun **1** *the motive for the attack* REASON, motivation, motivating force, rationale, grounds, cause, basis, object, purpose, intention; incentive, inducement, incitement, lure, inspiration, stimulus, stimulation, spur.

**2** *religious motives in art* MOTIF, theme, idea, concept, subject, topic, leitmotif.

▸ adjective *motive power* KINETIC, driving, impelling, propelling, propulsive, motor.

**motley** adjective *a motley collection of vintage fabrics* MISCELLANEOUS, disparate, diverse, assorted, varied, diversified, heterogeneous; *informal* ragtag, raggle-taggle. ANTONYM homogeneous.

**mottled** adjective *mottled horses* BLOTCHY, blotched, spotted, spotty, speckled, streaked, streaky, marbled, flecked, freckled, dappled, stippled; piebald, skewbald, brindled, brindle, pinto, calico; *informal* splotchy.

**motto** noun *the town's motto is "Tolerance and Prosperity"* MAXIM, saying, proverb, aphorism, adage, saw, axiom, apophthegm, formula, expression, phrase, dictum, precept; slogan, catchphrase, mantra; truism, cliché, platitude.

**mound** noun **1** *a mound of leaves* HEAP, pile, stack, mountain; mass, accumulation, assemblage.

**2** *high on the mound* HILLOCK, hill, knoll, rise, hummock, hump, embankment, bank, ridge, elevation; *Geology* drumlin.

▸ verb *mound up the rice on a serving plate* PILE (UP), heap (up).

**mount** verb **1** *he mounted the stairs* GO UP, ascend, climb (up), scale. ANTONYM descend.

**2** *the committee mounted the platform* CLIMB ON TO, jump on to, clamber on to, get on to.

**3** *they mounted their horses* GET ASTRIDE, bestride, get on to, hop on to.

**4** *the museum is mounting an exhibition* (PUT ON) DISPLAY, exhibit, present, install; organize, put on, stage.

**5** *the company mounted a takeover bid* ORGANIZE, stage, prepare, arrange, set up; launch, set in motion, initiate.

**6** *their losses mounted rapidly* INCREASE, grow, rise, escalate, soar, spiral, shoot up, rocket, climb, accumulate, build up, multiply. ANTONYMS decrease, diminish.

**7** *cameras were mounted above the door* INSTALL, place, fix, set, put up, put in position.

**mountain** noun **1** *a range of mountains* PEAK, height, mount, prominence, summit, pinnacle, alp; (**mountains**) range, sierra, cordillera, massif.

**2** *a mountain of work* A GREAT DEAL, a lot; a profusion, an abundance, a quantity, a backlog; *informal* a heap, a pile, a stack, a slew, lots, loads, heaps, piles, tons, masses; gobs.

PHRASE: **move mountains 1** *faith can move mountains* PERFORM MIRACLES, work/do wonders.

**2** *his fans move mountains to attend his performances* MAKE EVERY EFFORT, pull out all the stops, do one's utmost/best; *informal* bend/lean over backwards.

**mountainous** adjective **1** *a mountainous region* HILLY, craggy, rocky, alpine; upland, highland. ANTONYM flat.

**2** *mountainous waves* HUGE, enormous, gigantic, massive, giant, colossal, immense, tremendous, mighty; *informal* whopping, humongous, ginormous. ANTONYM tiny.

**mourn** verb **1** *Isobel mourned her husband* GRIEVE FOR, sorrow over, lament for, weep for.

**2** *he mourned the loss of the beautiful buildings* DEPLORE, bewail, bemoan, rue, regret.

**THE RIGHT WORD mourn, bemoan, grieve, lament, rue, sorrow**

Not everyone exhibits unhappiness in the same way. **Grieve** is the strongest of these verbs, implying deep mental anguish or suffering, often endured alone and in silence (*she grieved for years over the loss of her baby*). **Mourn** is more formal and often more public; although it implies deep emotion felt over a period of time, that emotion may be more ceremonial than sincere (*the people mourned the loss of their leader*). **Lament** comes from a Latin word meaning to wail or weep, and it therefore suggests a vocal or verbal expression of loss (*The shrieking women lamented their husbands' deaths*). **Bemoan** also suggests suppressed or inarticulate sounds of *grief*, often expressing regret or disapproval (*to bemoan one's fate*). **Sorrow** combines deep sadness with regret and often pertains to a less tragic loss than *grieve* or *mourn* (*sorrow over a lost love*), while **rue** has even stronger connotations of regret and repentance (*she rued the day she was born*).

**mournful** adjective *mournful music* SAD, sorrowful, doleful, melancholy, melancholic, woeful, grief-stricken, miserable, unhappy, heartbroken, broken-hearted, gloomy, dismal, desolate, dejected, despondent, depressed, downcast, disconsolate, woebegone, forlorn, rueful, lugubrious, joyless, cheerless; *literary* dolorous. ANTONYM cheerful.

**mourning** noun **1** *a period of mourning* GRIEF, grieving, sorrowing, lamentation, lament, keening, wailing, weeping.

**2** *she was dressed in mourning* BLACK (CLOTHES), (widow's) weeds; *archaic* sables.

**mousy** adjective **1** *mousy hair* LIGHTISH BROWN, brownish, brownish-gray, dun-colored; dull, lackluster.

**2** *a small, mousy woman* TIMID, quiet, fearful, timorous, shy, self-effacing, diffident, unassertive, unforthcoming, withdrawn, introverted, introvert.

**mouth** noun **1** *open your mouth* lips, jaws; maw, muzzle; *informal* trap, chops, kisser, puss.

**2** *the mouth of the cave* ENTRANCE, opening, entry, way in, access, ingress.

**3** *the mouth of the bottle* OPENING, rim, lip.

**4** *the mouth of the river* OUTFALL, outlet, debouchment; estuary.

**5** *informal don't give me any mouth* IMPUDENCE, insolence, impertinence, effrontery, presumption, presumptuousness, rudeness, disrespect, cheek, cheekiness; *informal* lip, sauce, sass, sassiness, back talk.

▸ verb **1** *he mouthed platitudes* UTTER, speak, say; pronounce, enunciate, articulate, voice, express; say insincerely, say for form's sake, pay lip service to.

**2** *he mouthed the words to the song* LIP-SYNCH.

PHRASES: **down in/at the mouth** *informal.* See UNHAPPY sense 1.

**keep one's mouth shut** *informal just keep your mouth shut and no one will get hurt* SAY NOTHING, keep quiet, not breathe a word, not tell a soul; *informal* keep mum, not let the cat out of the bag.

**mouth off** *informal* **1** *he was mouthing off about politics again* RANT, spout, declaim, sound off.

**2** *the students mouthed off to their teacher* TALK INSOLENTLY, be disrespectful.

**mouthful** noun **1** *a mouthful of pizza* BITE, nibble, taste, bit, piece; spoonful, forkful.

**2** *a mouthful of beer* SIP, swallow, drop, gulp, slug; *informal* swig.

**3** *"sesquipedalian" is a bit of a mouthful* TONGUE-TWISTER, long word, difficult word.

**mouthpiece** noun **1** *the flute's mouthpiece* EMBOUCHURE.

**2** *a mouthpiece for the government* SPOKESPERSON, spokesman, spokeswoman, speaker, agent, representative, propagandist, voice; organ, channel, vehicle, instrument.

**movable** adjective **1** *movable objects* PORTABLE, transportable, transferable; mobile.

**2** *movable dates* VARIABLE, changeable, alterable. ANTONYM fixed.

**move** verb **1** *she moved to the door | don't move!* GO, walk, proceed, progress, advance; budge, stir, shift, change position.

**2** *he moved the chair closer to the fire* CARRY, transport, transfer, shift.

**3** *things were moving too fast* (MAKE) PROGRESS, make headway, advance, develop.

**4** *he urged the council to move quickly* TAKE ACTION, act, take steps, do something, take measures; *informal* get moving.

**5** *she's moved to Rotterdam* RELOCATE, move away, change one's address, leave, go away, go down the road, decamp, pull up stakes.

**6** *I was deeply moved by the story* AFFECT, touch, impress, shake, upset, disturb, make an impression on.

**7** *she was moved to act* INSPIRE, prompt, stimulate, motivate, provoke, influence, rouse, induce, incite.

**8** *they are not prepared to move on this issue* CHANGE, budge, shift one's ground, change one's tune, change one's mind, have second thoughts; make a U-turn, do an about-face.

**9** *she moves in the art world* CIRCULATE, mix, socialize, keep company, associate; *informal* hang out/around.

**10** *I move that we adjourn* PROPOSE, submit, suggest, advocate, recommend, urge.

▸ noun **1** *his eyes followed her every move* MOVEMENT, motion, action; gesture, gesticulation.

**2** *his recent move to Sarasota* RELOCATION, change of address, transfer, posting.

**3** *the latest move in the war against drugs* INITIATIVE, step, action, act, measure, maneuver, tactic, stratagem.

**4** *it's your move* TURN, go; opportunity, chance.

PHRASES: **get a move on** *informal c'mon guys, let's get a move on* HURRY UP, speed (it) up, move faster; *informal* get cracking, get moving, step on it, shake a leg, hop to it; *dated* make haste.

**make a move** *waiting for the other side to make a move* DO SOMETHING, take action, act, take the initiative; *informal* get moving.

**on the move 1** *she's always on the move* TRAVELING, in transit, moving, journeying, on the road; *informal* on the go.

**2** *the economy is on the move* PROGRESSING, making progress, advancing, developing.

**movement** noun **1** *Rachel made a sudden movement | there was almost no movement* MOTION, move; gesture, gesticulation, sign, signal; action, activity.

**2** *the movement of supplies* TRANSPORTATION, shift, shifting, conveyance, moving, transfer.

**3** *the labor movement* POLITICAL GROUP, party, faction, wing, lobby, camp.

**4** *a movement to declare war on poverty* CAMPAIGN, crusade, drive, push.

**5** *there have been movements in the financial markets* DEVELOPMENT, change, fluctuation, variation.

**6** *the movement toward equality* TREND, tendency, drift, swing.

**7** *some movement will be made by the end of the month* PROGRESS, progression, advance.

**8** *a symphony in three movements* PART, section, division.

**moving** adjective **1** *moving parts | a moving train* IN MOTION, operating, operational, working, going, on the move, active; movable, mobile. ANTONYMS fixed, stationary.

**2** *a moving book* AFFECTING, touching, poignant, heartwarming, heart-rending, emotional, disturbing; inspiring, inspirational, stimulating, stirring.

THE RIGHT WORD **moving, affecting, pathetic, poignant, touching**

A movie about the Holocaust might be described as **moving**, since it arouses emotions or strong feelings, particularly feelings of pathos. A movie about a young girl's devotion to her dog might more accurately be described as **touching**, which means arousing tenderness or compassion, while a movie dealing with a young girl's first experience with love would be **poignant**, since it pierces one's heart or keenly affects one's sensibilities. While *poignant* implies a bittersweet response that combines pity and longing or other contradictory emotions, **pathetic** means simply moving one to pity (*a pathetic scene in which the dog struggled to save his drowning mistress*). Almost any well-made film can be **affecting**, a more general term that suggests moving one to tears or some other display of feeling (*the affecting story of a daughter's search for her birth mother*).

---

**mow** verb *she had mown the lawn* CUT (DOWN), trim; crop, clip, prune, manicure. PHRASE: **mow down** *they were ordered to mow down the student protestors* KILL, run down, gun down, shoot down, cut down, cut to pieces, butcher, slaughter, massacre, annihilate, wipe out; *informal* blow away.

**much** adjective *did you get much help?* A LOT OF, a great/good deal of, a great/large amount of, plenty of, ample, copious, abundant, plentiful, considerable; *informal* lots of, loads of, heaps of, masses of, tons of, piles of, mucho. ANTONYM little.

▸ adverb **1** *it didn't hurt much* GREATLY, to a great extent/degree, a great deal, a lot, considerably, appreciably.

**2** *does he come here much?* OFTEN, frequently, many times, repeatedly, regularly, habitually, routinely, usually, normally, commonly; *informal* a lot.

▸ pronoun *he did much for our team* A LOT, a great/good deal, plenty; *informal* lots, loads, heaps, masses.

**muck** noun **1** *I'll just clean off the muck* DIRT, grime, filth, mud, slime, mess; *informal* crud, gunk, grunge, gunge, guck, glop.

**2** *spreading muck on the fields* DUNG, manure, ordure, excrement, excreta, droppings, feces, sewage, sludge, biosolids; *informal* cow chips, horse apples.

**mud** noun *we trekked through the mud* MIRE, sludge, ooze, silt, clay, dirt, soil. PHRASE: **as clear as mud** *Dr. Elena's lectures are as clear as mud* UNCLEAR, unintelligible, opaque, unfathomable, incomprehensible, baffling, perplexing, inscrutable.

**muddle** verb **1** *you've **muddled** things **up*** CONFUSE, mix up, jumble (up), disarrange, disorganize, disorder, disturb, mess up.

**2** *she became muddled* BEWILDER, confuse, bemuse, perplex, puzzle, baffle, mystify.

▸ noun **1** *the files are in a muddle* MESS, confusion, jumble, tangle, mishmash, chaos, disorder, disarray, disorganization, imbroglio, hodgepodge. See note at JUMBLE.

**2** *a bureaucratic muddle* BUNGLE, mix-up, misunderstanding; *informal* foul-up, snafu.

PHRASE: **muddle along/through** *don't worry, we'll muddle through* COPE, manage, get by/along, scrape by/along, make do.

**muddy** adjective **1** *muddy ground* WATERLOGGED, boggy, marshy, swampy, squishy, mucky, slimy, spongy, wet, soft, heavy; *archaic* quaggy.

**2** *muddy shoes* MUD-CAKED, muddied, dirty, filthy, mucky, grimy, soiled; *literary* begrimed. ANTONYM clean.

**3** *muddy water* MURKY, cloudy, muddied, turbid, riled. ANTONYM clear.

**4** *a muddy pink* DINGY, dirty, drab, dull, sludgy.

▸ verb **1** *don't muddy your boots* MAKE MUDDY, dirty, soil, spatter, bespatter; *literary* besmirch, begrime.

**2** *these results muddy the situation* MAKE UNCLEAR, obscure, confuse, obfuscate, blur, cloud, befog. ANTONYM clarify.

**muffle** verb **1** *everyone was muffled up in coats* WRAP (UP), swathe, enfold, envelop, cloak.

**2** *the sound of their footsteps was muffled* DEADEN, dull, dampen, mute, soften, quiet, tone down, mask, stifle, smother.

**muffled** adjective *we thought we heard muffled voices* INDISTINCT, faint, muted, dull, soft, stifled, smothered. ANTONYM loud.

**mug** noun **1** *a china mug* CUP, glass; stein, flagon, tankard; *archaic* stoup.

**2** *informal her ugly mug.* See FACE noun sense 1.

▸ verb *informal he was mugged by three youths* ASSAULT, attack, set upon, beat up, rob; *informal* jump, rough up, lay into, do over.

**muggy** adjective *a muggy August afternoon* HUMID, close, sultry, sticky, oppressive, airless, stifling, suffocating, stuffy, clammy, damp, heavy. ANTONYM fresh.

**mull** PHRASE: **mull over** *I'll have to mull it over before making a final decision* PONDER, consider, think over/about, reflect on, contemplate, turn over in one's mind, chew over, cogitate on, give some thought to.

**multifarious** adjective *our multifarious ethnic traditions* DIVERSE, many, numerous, various, varied, diversified, multiple, multitudinous, multiplex, manifold, multifaceted, different, heterogeneous, miscellaneous, assorted; *literary* myriad, divers. ANTONYM homogeneous.

**multiple** adjective *words with multiple meanings* NUMEROUS, many, various, different, diverse, several, manifold, multifarious, multitudinous; *literary* myriad, divers. ANTONYM single.

**multiply** verb **1** *their difficulties seem to be multiplying* INCREASE, grow, become more numerous, accumulate, proliferate, mount up, mushroom, snowball. ANTONYM decrease.

**2** *the rabbits have multiplied* BREED, reproduce, procreate.

**multitude** noun **1** ***a multitude** of birds* A LOT, a great/large number, a great/large quantity, a host, a horde, a mass, a swarm, an abundance, a profusion; scores, quantities, droves; *informal* a slew, lots, loads, masses, stacks, heaps, piles, tons, dozens, hundreds, thousands, millions, gazillions.

**2** *Father Philip addressed the multitude* CROWD, gathering, assembly, congregation, flock, throng, horde, mob; *formal* concourse.

**3** *political power in the hands of the multitude* COMMON PEO-

PLE, people, populace, masses, rank and file, commonality, plebeians; hoi polloi, mob, proletariat, common herd; *informal* great unwashed, rabble, proles, plebs.

**munch** verb *the rustle we heard turned out to be giraffes munching leaves* CHEW, champ, chomp, masticate, crunch, eat, gnaw, nibble, snack, chow down on.

**mundane** adjective **1** *her mundane life* HUMDRUM, dull, boring, tedious, monotonous, tiresome, wearisome, unexciting, uninteresting, uneventful, unvarying, unremarkable, repetitive, repetitious, routine, ordinary, everyday, day-to-day, run-of-the-mill, commonplace, workaday; *informal* plain-vanilla, ho-hum. ANTONYMS extraordinary, imaginative.

**2** *the mundane world* EARTHLY, worldly, terrestrial, material, temporal, secular, areligious; *literary* sublunary. ANTONYM spiritual.

**municipal** adjective *land use is controlled by the municipal authorities* CIVIC, civil, metropolitan, urban, city, town, borough. ANTONYM rural.

**munificent** adjective *a munificent bequest* GENEROUS, bountiful, openhanded, magnanimous, philanthropic, princely, handsome, lavish, liberal, charitable, big-hearted, beneficent; *literary* bounteous. ANTONYM mean.

**murder** noun **1** *a brutal murder* KILLING, homicide, assassination, liquidation, extermination, execution, slaughter, butchery, massacre; manslaughter; *literary* slaying.

**2** *informal driving there was murder* HELL, hell on earth, a nightmare, an ordeal, a trial, misery, torture, agony.

▸ verb **1** *someone tried to murder him* KILL, put to death, assassinate, execute, liquidate, eliminate, dispatch, butcher, slaughter, massacre, wipe out; *informal* bump off, do in, do away with, knock off, blow away, blow someone's brains out, take out, dispose of, ice, rub out, smoke, waste; *literary* slay. See note at KILL.

**2** *informal Anna was murdering a Mozart sonata.* See MANGLE sense 2.

**3** *informal he murdered his opponent.* See TROUNCE.

**murderer, murderess** noun *the murderer was finally brought to justice* KILLER, assassin, serial killer, butcher, slaughterer; *informal* hit man, gunman, hired gun; *literary* slayer.

**murderous** adjective **1** *a murderous attack* HOMICIDAL, brutal, violent, savage, ferocious, fierce, vicious, bloodthirsty, barbarous, barbaric; fatal, lethal, deadly, mortal, death-dealing; *archaic* sanguinary.

**2** *informal a murderous schedule* ARDUOUS, grueling, strenuous, punishing, onerous, exhausting, taxing, difficult, rigorous; *informal* killing, hellish.

**murky** adjective **1** *a murky winter afternoon* DARK, gloomy, gray, leaden, dull, dim, overcast, cloudy, clouded, sunless, dismal, dreary, bleak; *literary* tenebrous. ANTONYMS bright, sunny.

**2** *murky water* DIRTY, muddy, cloudy, turbid, riled, roily. ANTONYM clear.

**3** *her murky past* QUESTIONABLE, suspicious, suspect, dubious, dark, mysterious, secret; *informal* shady, sketchy. ANTONYMS spotless, innocent.

**murmur** noun **1** *his voice was a murmur* WHISPER, undertone, mutter, mumble.

**2** *they left without a murmur* COMPLAINT, grumble, grouse; *informal* gripe, moan.

**3** *the murmur of bees* HUM, humming, buzz, buzzing, thrum, thrumming, drone; sigh, rustle; *literary* susurration, murmuration.

▸ verb **1** *he heard them murmuring in the hall* MUTTER, mumble, whisper, talk under one's breath, speak softly.

**2** *no one murmured at the delay* COMPLAIN, mutter, grumble, grouse; *informal* gripe, moan.

**3** *the wind was murmuring through the trees* RUSTLE, sigh; burble, purl; *literary* whisper.

**muscle** noun **1** *he had muscle but no brains* STRENGTH, power, muscularity, brawn, burliness; *informal* beef, beefiness; *literary* thew.

**2** *financial muscle* INFLUENCE, power, strength, might, force, forcefulness, weight; *informal* clout. PHRASE: **muscle in on** *informal we don't like people muscling in on our private affairs* INTERFERE WITH, force one's way into, impose oneself on, encroach on; *informal* horn in on, barge in on.

**muscular** adjective **1** *muscular tissue* FIBROUS, sinewy.

**2** *he's very muscular* STRONG, brawny, muscly, sinewy, powerfully built, well muscled, hard-bodied, burly, strapping, sturdy, powerful, athletic; *Physiology* mesomorphic; *informal* hunky, beefy, muscle-bound; *literary* thewy.

**3** *a muscular economy* VIGOROUS, robust, strong, powerful, dynamic, potent, active.

**muse** noun *the poet's muse* INSPIRATION, creative influence, stimulus; *formal* afflatus.

**mushroom** noun *the mushrooms thrive in this warm wet weather* FUNGUS, button mushroom, cep, chanterelle, cremini, enoki, field mushroom, honey mushroom, horse mushroom, matsutake, morel, oyster mushroom, pine mushroom, porcini, portobello, shiitake, death cap, bolete.

▸ verb *ecotourism mushroomed in the 1980s* PROLIFERATE, grow/develop rapidly, burgeon, spread, increase, expand, boom, explode, snowball, rocket, skyrocket; thrive, flourish, prosper. ANTONYM contract.

**musical** adjective *musical poetry* TUNEFUL, melodic, melodious, harmonious, sweet-sounding, sweet, mellifluous, euphonious, euphonic. ANTONYM discordant.

**musing** noun *in my musing of late, I have decided that I need more purpose in my life* MEDITATION, thinking, contemplation, deliberation, pondering, reflection, rumination, introspection, daydreaming, reverie, dreaming, preoccupation, brooding; *formal* cogitation.

**muss** verb *informal don't be mussing your hair before the photo shoot* RUFFLE, tousle, dishevel, rumple, mess up, make a mess of, disarrange, make untidy.

**must**[1] verb *I must go* OUGHT TO, should, have (got) to, need to, be obliged to, be required to, be compelled to.

▸ noun *informal this video is **a must*** NOT TO BE MISSED, very good; a necessity, essential, a requirement, a requisite.

**must**[2] noun *a smell of must* MOLD, mustiness, moldiness, mildew, fustiness, decay, rot.

**muster** verb **1** *they mustered 50,000 troops* ASSEMBLE, mobilize, rally, raise, summon, gather (together), mass, collect, convene, call up, call to arms, recruit, conscript, draft; *archaic* levy. See note at GATHER.

**2** *reporters mustered outside her house* CONGREGATE, assemble, gather together, come together, collect together, convene, mass, rally.

**3** *she mustered her courage* SUMMON (UP), screw up, call up, rally.

▸ noun *the colonel called a muster* ROLL CALL, assembly, rally, meeting, gathering, assemblage, congregation, convention; parade, review.

PHRASE: **pass muster** *as far as Dean's parents are concerned, I'll never pass muster* BE GOOD ENOUGH, come up to standard, come up to scratch, measure up, be acceptable/adequate, fill/fit the bill; *informal* make the grade, come/be up to snuff.

**musty** adjective **1** *the room smelled musty* MOLDY, stale, fusty, damp, dank, mildewy, smelly, stuffy, airless, unventilated; *informal* funky. ANTONYMS fresh, fragrant.

**2** *the play seemed musty* UNORIGINAL, uninspired, unimaginative, hackneyed, stale, flat, tired, banal, trite, clichéd, old-fashioned, outdated; *informal* old hat. ANTONYM fresh.

**mutable** adjective *the mutable nature of fashion* CHANGEABLE, variable, varying, fluctuating, shifting, inconsistent, unpredictable, inconstant, fickle, uneven, unstable, protean; *literary* fluctuant. ANTONYM invariable.

**mutation** noun **1** *cells that have undergone mutation* ALTERATION, change, variation, modification, transformation, metamorphosis, transmutation; *humorous* transmogrification.

**2** *a genetic mutation* MUTANT, freak (of nature), deviant, monstrosity, monster, anomaly.

**mute** adjective **1** *she remained mute* SILENT, speechless, dumb, unspeaking, tight-lipped, taciturn; *informal* mum, tongue-tied. ANTONYMS voluble, talkative.

**2** *a mute appeal* WORDLESS, silent, dumb, unspoken, unvoiced, unexpressed. ANTONYM spoken.

**3** *the forest was mute* QUIET, silent, hushed. ANTONYM noisy.

**4** *he was deaf and mute* DUMB, unable to speak; *Medicine* aphasic.

▸ verb **1** *the noise was muted by the heavy curtains* DEADEN, muffle, dampen, soften, quiet, hush; stifle, smother, suppress. ANTONYM amplify.

**2** *Bruce muted his criticisms* RESTRAIN, soften, tone down, moderate, temper. ANTONYM intensify.

**muted** adjective **1** *the muted hum of traffic* MUFFLED, faint, indistinct, quiet, soft, low.

**2** *muted colors* SUBDUED, pastel, delicate, subtle, understated, restrained.

**mutilate** verb **1** *the bodies had been mutilated* MANGLE, maim, disfigure, butcher, dismember; cripple.

**2** *the painting was mutilated* VANDALIZE, damage, deface, ruin, spoil, destroy, wreck, violate, desecrate; *informal* trash.

**mutinous** adjective *your mutinous scheme has failed* REBELLIOUS, insubordinate, subversive, seditious, insurgent, insurrectionary, rebel, riotous.

**mutiny** noun *there was a mutiny over wages* INSURRECTION, rebellion, revolt, riot, uprising, insurgence, insubordination. See note at UPRISING.

▸ verb *thousands of soldiers mutinied* RISE UP, rebel, revolt, riot, disobey/defy authority, be insubordinate.

**mutter** verb **1** *a group of men stood muttering* TALK UNDER ONE'S BREATH, murmur, mumble, whisper, speak in an undertone.

**2** *the players muttered about the salary freezes* GRUMBLE, complain, grouse, carp, whine; *informal* moan, gripe, beef, whinge, kvetch.

**muzzle** noun **1** *the dog's velvety muzzle* SNOUT, nose, mouth, maw.

**2** *the muzzle of a gun* BARREL, end.

▸ verb *attempts to muzzle the media* GAG, silence, censor, stifle, restrain, check, curb, fetter.

**myopic** adjective **1** *a myopic patient* NEARSIGHTED; *chiefly Brit.* shortsighted. ANTONYM farsighted.

**2** *the government's myopic attitude* UNIMAGINATIVE, uncreative, unadventurous, narrow-minded, small-minded, short-term, shortsighted. ANTONYM farsighted.

**myriad** noun *literary **a myriad** of insects* A MULTITUDE, a large/great number, a large/great quantity, scores, quantities, a mass, a host, droves, a horde; *informal* lots, loads, masses, stacks, scads, tons, hundreds, thousands, millions, gazillions.

▸ adjective *the myriad lights of the city* INNUMERABLE, countless, infinite, numberless, untold, unnumbered, immeasurable, multitudinous, numerous; *literary* divers.

**mysterious** adjective **1** *he vanished in mysterious circumstances* PUZZLING, strange, peculiar, curious, funny, queer, odd, weird, bizarre, mystifying, inexplicable, baffling, perplexing, incomprehensible, unexplainable, unfathomable. ANTONYM straightforward.

**2** *he was being very mysterious* ENIGMATIC, inscrutable, secretive, reticent, evasive, furtive, surreptitious. ANTONYMS straightforward, open.

**mystery** noun **1** *his death remains a mystery* PUZZLE, enigma, conundrum, riddle, secret, problem, unsolved problem. See note at RIDDLE.

**2** *her past is shrouded in mystery* SECRECY, obscurity, uncertainty, mystique.

**3** *reading a classic mystery* THRILLER, murder mystery, detective story/novel, murder story, crime novel; *informal* whodunit.

**mystify** verb *Houdini mystified his audiences* BEWILDER, puzzle, perplex, baffle, confuse, confound, bemuse, bedazzle, throw; *informal* flummox, stump, bamboozle, fox.

**myth** noun **1** *ancient Greek myths* FOLK TALE, folk story, legend, tale, story, fable, saga, mythos, lore, folklore, mythology.

**2** *the myths surrounding childbirth* MISCONCEPTION, fallacy, false notion, old wives' tale, fairy tale/story, fiction; *informal* tall tale, cock-and-bull story, urban myth/legend.

**mythical** adjective **1** *mythical beasts* LEGENDARY, mythological, fabled, fabulous, folkloric, fairy-tale, storybook; fantastical, imaginary, imagined, fictitious, storied.

**2** *her mythical child* IMAGINARY, fictitious, make-believe, fantasy, invented, made-up, nonexistent; *informal* pretend.

**mythology** noun *no ancient culture is without its mythology* MYTH(S), legend(s), folklore, folk tales, folk stories, lore, tradition.

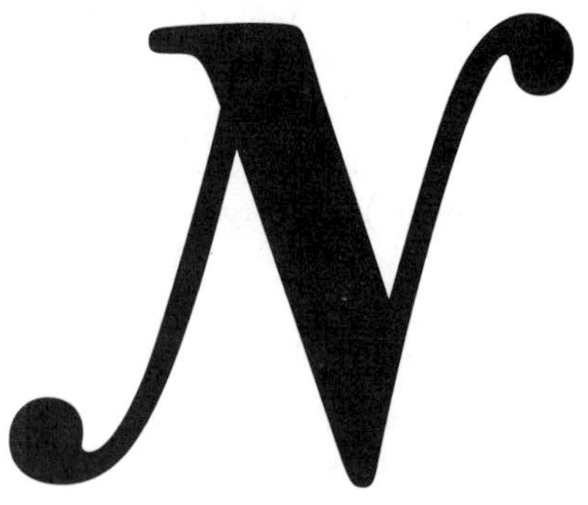

**nadir** noun *the nadir of his career* LOWEST POINT, lowest level, all-time low, bottom, rock-bottom; *informal* pits. ANTONYM zenith.

**nag**[1] verb **1** *she's constantly nagging me* HARASS, badger, give someone a hard time, hound, harry, criticize, carp, find fault with, keep on at, grumble at, go on at; henpeck; *informal* hassle, get on someone's case, ride.

**2** *this has been nagging me for weeks* TROUBLE, worry, bother, plague, torment, niggle, prey on one's mind; annoy, irritate; *informal* bug, aggravate.

▸ noun *don't be such a nag* SHREW, harpy, termagant, harridan; *archaic* scold.

**nag**[2] noun *she rode the nag into town* WORN-OUT HORSE, old horse, hack; *informal* plug; *archaic* jade.

**nagging** adjective **1** *his nagging wife* SHREWISH, complaining, grumbling, fault-finding, scolding, carping, criticizing.

**2** *a nagging pain* PERSISTENT, continuous, niggling, unrelenting, unremitting, unabating.

**nail** noun **1** *fastened with nails* TACK, spike, pin, rivet; finishing nail, roofing nail, hobnail, brad.

**2** *polishing her nails* FINGERNAIL, thumbnail, toenail.

▸ verb **1** *a board was nailed to the wall* FASTEN, attach, fix, affix, secure, tack, hammer, pin.

**2** *informal he nailed the suspect* CATCH, capture, apprehend, arrest, seize; *informal* collar, nab, pull in, pick up.

**3** *she nailed that somersault* PERFORM WELL, succeed in, execute, complete, bring about/off; *informal* land, pull off, score.

PHRASES: **hard as nails** *he regretted having been a father who always acted as if he were hard as nails* CALLOUS, hard-hearted, heartless, unfeeling, unsympathetic, uncaring, insensitive, unsentimental, hard-bitten, tough, lacking compassion.
**hit the nail on the head** *when Arthur said that Donna couldn't be trusted, he really hit the nail on the head* GET IT RIGHT, get it, guess correctly, speak (the) truth.

**naked** adjective **1** *naked sunbathers* NUDE, bare, in the nude, stark naked, having nothing on, stripped, unclothed, undressed; *informal* without a stitch on, in one's birthday suit, in the buff, in the raw, in the altogether, buck-naked, butt-naked, mother-naked. ANTONYMS clothed, dressed.

**2** *a naked flame* UNPROTECTED, uncovered, exposed, unguarded. ANTONYM covered.

**3** *the naked branches of the trees* BARE, barren, denuded, stripped, uncovered.

**4** *I felt naked and exposed* VULNERABLE, helpless, weak, powerless, defenseless, exposed, open to attack.

**5** *the naked truth* | *naked hostility* UNDISGUISED, plain, unadorned, unvarnished, unqualified, stark, bald; overt, obvious, open, patent, evident, apparent, manifest, unmistakable, blatant.

THE RIGHT WORD **naked, bald, bare, barren, nude**

Someone who isn't wearing any clothes is **naked**; this adjective is usually associated with revealing a part or all of the body (*her naked shoulder; a naked man ran from the burning building*). A *naked* person who appears in a painting or photograph is called a **nude**, a euphemistic but more socially acceptable term referring to the unclothed human body. **Bare** can describe the branches of a tree as well as human limbs; it implies the absence of the conventional or appropriate covering (*a bare wooden floor; bare legs; four bare walls*). **Bald** also suggests a lack of covering, but it refers particularly to a lack of natural covering, especially hair (*a bald head*). **Barren** implies a lack of vegetation, and it also connotes destitution and fruitlessness (*a barren wasteland devoid of life*). A *bald* artist might paint a *nude* woman whose *bare* arms are extended against a *barren* winter landscape.

**namby-pamby** adjective *her new boyfriend is the essence of virility—nothing like that namby-pamby guy she used to date* WEAK, feeble, spineless, effeminate, effete; ineffectual; *informal* wimpy, sissy.

**name** noun **1** *her name's Emma* designation, honorific, title, tag, epithet, label; *informal* moniker, handle; *formal* denomination, appellation.

**2** *the top names in the fashion industry* CELEBRITY, star, superstar, VIP, leading light, big name, luminary; expert, authority; *informal* celeb, somebody, megastar, big shot, bigwig, big gun, great, giant.

**3** *the good name of the firm* REPUTATION, character, repute, standing, stature, esteem, prestige, cachet, kudos; renown, popularity, notability, distinction.

▸ verb **1** *they named the baby Phoebe* CALL, give a name to, dub;

label, style, term, title, entitle; baptize, christen; *formal* denominate.

**2** *he named the woman in the photograph* IDENTIFY, specify.

**3** *he has named his successor* CHOOSE, select, pick, decide on, nominate, designate.

**nameless** adjective **1** *a nameless photographer* UNNAMED, unidentified, anonymous, incognito, unspecified, unacknowledged, uncredited; unknown, unsung, uncelebrated.

**2** *nameless fears* UNSPEAKABLE, unutterable, inexpressible, indescribable; indefinable, vague, unspecified.

**namely** adverb *I want to go someplace warm, namely Aruba* THAT IS, that is to say, in other words, to be specific, specifically, viz., to wit.

**nap**[1] verb *they were napping on the sofa* DOZE, sleep, sleep lightly, take a nap, catnap, rest, take a siesta; *informal* snooze, catch forty winks, get some shut-eye, catch some Zs, catch a few Zs.

▸ noun ***a nap*** *will make you feel better* (SOME) SLEEP, a little sleep, a catnap, a siesta, a doze, a lie-down, (a/some) rest, a little rest; *informal* a snooze, forty winks, (some) shut-eye, a little shut-eye, (some) beauty sleep/rest, a little beauty sleep/rest, a power nap.

PHRASE: **catch someone napping** *the teacher had warned us to be ever prepared, but the unannounced test caught most of us napping* CATCH OFF GUARD, catch unawares, surprise, take by surprise, catch out, find unprepared; *informal* catch someone with their pants down.

**nap**[2] noun *the nap of the velvet* PILE, fibers, threads, weave, surface, grain.

**narcissism** noun *his emotional development was hindered by his mother's narcissism* VANITY, self-love, self-admiration, self-absorption, self-obsession, conceit, self-centeredness, self-regard, egotism, egoism. See note at EGOTISM. ANTONYM modesty.

**narcissistic** adjective *she was never happy in the narcissistic life that her press agent and manager had crafted for her* VAIN, self-loving, self-admiring, self-absorbed, self-obsessed, conceited, self-centered, self-regarding, egotistic, egotistical, egoistic; *informal* full of oneself.

**narcotic** noun *addicted to narcotics* SOPORIFIC (DRUG), opiate, sleeping pill; painkiller, pain reliever, analgesic, anodyne, palliative, anesthetic; tranquilizer, sedative; *informal* downer, dope; *Medicine* stupefacient.

▸ adjective *a narcotic sleeping pill* SOPORIFIC, sleep-inducing, opiate; painkilling, pain-relieving, analgesic, anodyne, anesthetic, tranquilizing, sedative; *Medicine* stupefacient.

**narrate** verb *the story is narrated by an English butler* TELL, relate, recount, describe, chronicle, give a report of, report; voice-over.

**narrative** noun *an interesting narrative about her year in Bolivia* ACCOUNT, chronicle, history, description, record, report, story.

**narrator** noun **1** *the narrator of "The Arabian Nights"* STORYTELLER, teller of tales, relater, chronicler, raconteur, anecdotalist. ANTONYMS listener, audience.

**2** *the film's narrator* VOICE-OVER, commentator, speaker.

**narrow** adjective **1** *the path became narrow* SMALL, tapered, tapering, narrowing; *archaic* strait. ANTONYMS wide, broad.

**2** *her narrow waist* SLENDER, slim, slight, spare, attenuated, thin. ANTONYM broad.

**3** *a narrow space* CONFINED, cramped, tight, restricted, limited, constricted. ANTONYM spacious.

**4** *a narrow range of products* LIMITED, restricted, circumscribed, small, inadequate, insufficient, deficient. ANTONYMS wide, broad.

**5** *a narrow view of the world.* See NARROW-MINDED.

**6** *nationalism in the narrowest sense of the word* STRICT, literal, exact, precise. ANTONYM broad.

**7** *a narrow escape* BY A VERY SMALL MARGIN, close, near, by a hair's breadth; *informal* by a whisker.

▸ verb *the path narrowed | narrowing the gap between rich and poor* GET/BECOME/MAKE NARROWER, get/become/make smaller, taper, diminish, decrease, reduce, contract, shrink, constrict; *archaic* straiten.

**narrowly** adverb **1** *one bullet narrowly missed him* ONLY JUST, just, barely, scarcely, hardly, by a hair's breadth; *informal* by a whisker.

**2** *she looked at me narrowly* CLOSELY, carefully, searchingly, attentively.

**narrow-minded** adjective *our school has no place for such narrow-minded teaching* INTOLERANT, illiberal, reactionary, conservative, parochial, provincial, insular, small-minded, petty, blinkered, inward-looking, narrow, hidebound, prejudiced, bigoted; *informal* redneck. See note at BIAS. ANTONYM tolerant.

**narrows** plural noun *these narrows were first navigated in the sixteenth century* STRAIT(S), sound, channel, waterway, passage, sea passage, neck.

**nascent** adjective *the nascent economic recovery* JUST BEGINNING, budding, developing, growing, embryonic, incipient, young, fledgling, evolving, emergent, dawning, burgeoning.

**nastiness** noun **1** *my mother tried to shut herself off from all the nastiness of life* UNPLEASANTNESS, disagreeableness, offensiveness, vileness, foulness.

**2** *her uncharacteristic nastiness* UNKINDNESS, unpleasantness, unfriendliness, disagreeableness, rudeness, churlishness, spitefulness, maliciousness, meanness, ill temper, ill nature, viciousness, malevolence; *informal* bitchiness, cattiness.

**nasty** adjective **1** *a nasty smell* UNPLEASANT, disagreeable, disgusting, distasteful, awful, dreadful, horrible, terrible, vile, foul, abominable, frightful, loathsome, revolting, repulsive, odious, sickening, nauseating, repellent, repugnant, horrendous, appalling, atrocious, offensive, objectionable, obnoxious, unsavory, unappetizing, off-putting; noxious, foul-smelling, smelly, stinking, rank, fetid, malodorous, mephitic; *informal* ghastly, horrid, gruesome, diabolical, yucky, skanky, godawful, gross, beastly, lousy, funky; *literary* miasmal, noisome. ANTONYMS pleasant, delightful.

**2** *the weather turned nasty* UNPLEASANT, disagreeable, foul, filthy, inclement; wet, stormy, cold, blustery, blizzardy. ANTONYMS sunny, pleasant.

**3** *she can be really nasty* UNKIND, unpleasant, unfriendly, disagreeable, rude, churlish, spiteful, malicious, mean, ill-tempered, ill-natured, vicious, malevolent, obnoxious, hateful, hurtful; *informal* bitchy, catty. ANTONYMS nice, charming.

**4** *a nasty accident* | *a nasty cut* SERIOUS, dangerous, bad, awful, dreadful, terrible, severe; painful, ugly. ANTONYMS minor, slight.

**5** *she had the nasty habit of appearing unannounced* ANNOYING, irritating, infuriating, disagreeable, unpleasant, maddening, exasperating.

**6** *they wrote nasty things on the wall* OBSCENE, indecent, offensive, crude, rude, dirty, filthy, vulgar, foul, gross, disgusting, pornographic, smutty, lewd; *informal* sick, X-rated. ANTONYMS polite, decent.

**nation** noun *an independent nation* COUNTRY, sovereign state, state, land, realm, kingdom, republic; fatherland, motherland; people, race.

**national** adjective **1** *national politics* STATE, public, federal, governmental; civic, civil, domestic, internal. ANTONYMS local, international.

**2** *a national strike.* See NATIONWIDE.

▸ noun *a Canadian national* CITIZEN, subject, native; voter.

**nationalism** noun *their extreme nationalism was frightening* PATRIOTISM, patriotic sentiment, flag-waving, xenophobia, chauvinism, jingoism. See notes at CHAUVINISM, JINGOISM.

**nationality** noun **1** *what is your nationality?* CITIZENSHIP.

**2** *all the main nationalities of Ethiopia* ETHNIC GROUP, ethnic minority, tribe, clan, race, nation.

**nationwide** adjective *a nationwide talent search* NATIONAL, countrywide, general, widespread, extensive. ANTONYM local.

**native** noun *a native of Rome, New York* INHABITANT, resident, local; citizen, national; aborigine, autochthon; *formal* dweller. ANTONYM foreigner.

▸ adjective **1** *the native peoples* INDIGENOUS, original, first, earliest, aboriginal, autochthonous. ANTONYM immigrant.

**2** *native produce* | *native plants* DOMESTIC, homegrown, homemade, local; indigenous. ANTONYM imported.

**3** *a native instinct for politics* INNATE, inherent, inborn, instinctive, intuitive, natural; hereditary, inherited, congenital, inbred, connate. ANTONYM acquired.

**4** *her native tongue* MOTHER, vernacular, first.

THE RIGHT WORD **native, aboriginal, endemic, indigenous**

A **native** New Yorker is probably not **indigenous**, although both words apply to persons or things that belong to or are associated with a particular place by birth or origin. *Native* means born or produced in a specific region or country (*native plants; native dances*), but it can also apply to persons or things that were introduced from elsewhere some time ago—which is the case with most New Yorkers who consider themselves natives. *Indigenous*, on the other hand, is more restricted in meaning; it applies only to someone or something that is not only native but was not introduced from elsewhere (*the pumpkin is indigenous to America*). Generally speaking, *native* applies to individual organisms, while *indigenous* applies to races or species. Something that is **endemic** is prevalent in a particular region because of special conditions there that favor its growth or existence (*heather is endemic in the Scottish Highlands; malaria is endemic in Central America*). There are no longer any **aboriginal** New Yorkers, a word that refers to the earliest known inhabitants of a place or to ancient peoples who have no known ancestors and have inhabited a region since its earliest historical time. Australia is known for its *aboriginal* culture, which was preserved for centuries through geographical isolation.

**natty** adjective *informal he's looking pretty darn natty in that new suit* SMART, stylish, fashionable, dapper, debonair, dashing, spruced up, well-dressed, chic, elegant, trim; *informal* snazzy, trendy, snappy, nifty, sassy, spiffy, fly, kicky, styling/stylin', sharp. ANTONYM scruffy.

**natural** adjective **1** *a natural occurrence* NORMAL, ordinary, everyday, usual, regular, common, commonplace, typical, routine, standard, established, customary, accustomed, habitual. See note at NORMAL. ANTONYMS abnormal, exceptional.

**2** *natural produce* UNPROCESSED, organic, pure, wholesome, unrefined, pesticide-free, additive-free. ANTONYMS artificial, refined.

**3** *Alex is a natural leader* BORN, naturally gifted, untaught.

**4** *his natural instincts* INNATE, inborn, inherent, native, instinctive, intuitive; hereditary, inherited, inbred, congenital, connate. ANTONYM acquired.

**5** *she seemed very natural* UNAFFECTED, spontaneous, uninhibited, relaxed, unselfconscious, genuine, open, artless, guileless, ingenuous, unpretentious, without airs. ANTONYMS self-conscious, false, affected.

**6** *it was quite natural to think that* REASONABLE, logical, understandable, (only) to be expected, predictable. ANTONYM unreasonable.

**naturalist** noun *the wildlife preserve employs a team of naturalists from around the world* NATURAL HISTORIAN, life scientist, wildlife expert; biologist, botanist, zoologist, ornithologist, entomologist, ecologist.

**naturalistic** adjective *her sculptures are so naturalistic they seem to breathe* REALISTIC, real-life, true-to-life, lifelike, graphic, representational, faithful, photographic. ANTONYM abstract.

**naturalize** verb **1** *he was naturalized in 1950* GRANT CITIZENSHIP TO, make a citizen, enfranchise, give a passport to.

**2** *they naturalized new species of grass and wildflowers* ESTABLISH, introduce, acclimatize, domesticate; acclimate.

**naturally** adverb **1** *he's naturally shy* BY NATURE, by character, inherently, innately, congenitally.

**2** *try to act naturally* NORMALLY, in a natural manner/way, unaffectedly, spontaneously, genuinely, unpretentiously; *informal* natural. ANTONYM self-consciously.

**3** *naturally, they wanted everything kept quiet* OF COURSE, as might be expected, needless to say; obviously, clearly, it goes without saying. ANTONYM surprisingly.

**nature** noun **1** *the beauty of nature* THE NATURAL WORLD, Mother Nature, Mother Earth, the environment; wildlife, flora and fauna, the countryside; the universe, the cosmos.

**2** *such crimes are, by their very nature, difficult to hide* ESSENCE, inherent/basic/essential qualities, inherent/basic/essential features, character, complexion.

**3** *it was not in her nature to argue* CHARACTER, personality, disposition, temperament, makeup, psyche, constitution.

**4** *experiments of a similar nature* KIND, sort, type, variety, category, ilk, class, species, genre, style, cast, order, kidney, mold, stamp, stripe.

**naughty** adjective **1** *a naughty boy* BADLY BEHAVED, disobedient, bad, misbehaved, misbehaving, wayward, defiant, unruly, insubordinate, willful, delinquent, undisciplined, uncontrollable, ill-mannered, ungovernable, unbiddable, disorderly, disruptive, fractious, recalcitrant, wild, wicked, obstreperous, difficult, troublesome, awkward, contrary, perverse, incorrigible; mischievous, playful, impish, roguish, rascally; *informal* bratty; *formal* refractory. ANTONYM well-behaved.

**2** *naughty jokes* INDECENT, risqué, rude, racy, ribald, bawdy, suggestive, improper, indelicate, indecorous; vulgar, dirty, filthy, smutty, crude, coarse, obscene, lewd, pornographic; *informal* raunchy, saucy; *euphemistic* adult. ANTONYM decent.

**nausea** noun **1** *symptoms include nausea and headaches* SICKNESS, biliousness, queasiness; vomiting, retching, gagging; upset stomach; travel-sickness, seasickness, carsickness, airsickness.

**2** *it induces a feeling of nausea* DISGUST, revulsion, repugnance, repulsion, distaste, aversion, loathing, abhorrence.

**nauseous** adjective *the food made her feel nauseous* SICK, nauseated, queasy, bilious, green around the gills, ill, unwell; seasick, carsick, airsick, travel-sick; *informal* barfy; *rare* qualmish.

**nautical** adjective *a library of nautical history and literature* MARITIME, marine, naval, seafaring; boating, sailing.

**navel** noun **1** *so, does that mean Adam and Eve had no navels? informal* belly button; *Anatomy* umbilicus.

**2** *the navel of Byzantine culture* CENTER, central point, hub, focal point, focus, nucleus, heart, core; *literary* omphalos.

**navigable** adjective *after October, these waters are not navigable by ordinary craft* PASSABLE, negotiable, traversable; clear, open, unobstructed, unblocked.

**navigate** verb **1** *he navigated the yacht across the Atlantic* STEER, pilot, guide, direct, helm, captain; *Nautical* con; *informal* skipper.

**2** *the upper reaches are dangerous to navigate* SAIL ACROSS/OVER, sail, travel/journey/voyage across/over, cross, traverse, negotiate, pass.

**3** *I'll drive—you can navigate* MAP-READ, give directions, plan the route.

**navigator** noun *he had learned to be an able navigator by the time he was twelve* HELMSMAN, steersman, pilot, guide, wheelman.

**navy** noun **1** *a 600-ship navy* FLEET, flotilla, armada, naval force.

**2** *a navy blazer* NAVY BLUE, dark blue, midnight blue, indigo.

**near** adverb **1** *her children live near* NEARBY.

**2** *near perfect conditions* ALMOST, just about, nearly, practically, virtually; *literary* well-nigh.

▸ preposition *a hotel near the seafront* CLOSE TO, close by, a short distance from, in the vicinity of, in the neighborhood of, within reach of, a stone's throw away from; *informal* within spitting distance of.

▸ adjective **1** *the nearest house* CLOSE, nearby, close/near at hand, at hand, a stone's throw away, within reach, accessible, handy, convenient; *informal* within spitting distance. ANTONYM far.

**2** *the final judgment is near* IMMINENT, in the offing, close/near at hand, at hand, (just) around the corner, impending, looming. ANTONYMS remote, distant.

**3** *a near relation* CLOSELY RELATED, close, related. ANTONYM distant.

**4** *a near escape* NARROW, close, by a hair's breadth; *informal* by a whisker.

▸ verb **1** *by dawn we were nearing Moscow* APPROACH, draw near/nearer to, get close/closer to, advance toward, close in on.

**2** *the death toll is nearing 3,000* VERGE ON, border on, approach.

**nearly** adverb *it was nearly midnight* ALMOST, just about, about, more or less, practically, virtually, all but, as good as, not far off, to all intents and purposes; not quite; *informal* pretty much, pretty well; *literary* well-nigh.

**nearsighted** adjective *I'm too nearsighted to go without my glasses* MYOPIC; *informal* as blind as a bat; *archaic* purblind. ANTONYM farsighted.

**neat** adjective **1** *the bedroom was neat and clean* TIDY, orderly, well-ordered, in (good) order, shipshape, in apple-pie order, spick-and-span, uncluttered, straight, trim. ANTONYM untidy.

**2** *he's very neat* SMART, dapper, trim, well-groomed, well-turned-out, spruce; *informal* natty. ANTONYM shabby.

**3** *her neat script* WELL-FORMED, regular, precise, elegant, well-proportioned.

**4** *this neat little gadget* COMPACT, well designed, handy.

**5** *his neat footwork* SKILLFUL, deft, dexterous, adroit, adept, expert; *informal* nifty. ANTONYM clumsy.

**6** *a neat solution* CLEVER, ingenious, inventive.

**7** *neat gin* UNDILUTED, straight, unmixed; *informal* straight up.

**8** *informal we had a really neat time.* See WONDERFUL.

**neatly** adverb **1** *neatly arranged papers* TIDILY, methodically, systematically; smartly, sprucely.

**2** *the point was neatly put* CLEVERLY, aptly, elegantly.

**3** *a neatly executed turn* SKILLFULLY, deftly, adroitly, adeptly, expertly.

**nebulous** adjective **1** *the figure was nebulous* INDISTINCT, indefinite, unclear, vague, hazy, cloudy, fuzzy, misty, blurred, blurry, foggy; faint, shadowy, obscure, formless, amorphous. ANTONYM clear.

**2** *nebulous ideas* VAGUE, ill-defined, unclear, hazy, uncertain, indefinite, indeterminate, imprecise, unformed, muddled, confused, ambiguous. ANTONYM well-defined.

**necessarily** adverb *an increase in fees does not necessarily guarantee a balanced budget* AS A CONSEQUENCE, as a result, automatically, as a matter of course, certainly, surely, definitely, incontrovertibly, undoubtedly, inevitably, unavoidably, inescapably, ineluctably, of necessity; *formal* perforce.

**necessary** adjective **1** *parental permission is necessary* OBLIGATORY, requisite, required, compulsory, mandatory, imperative, needed, de rigueur; essential, indispensable, vital.

**2** *a necessary consequence* INEVITABLE, unavoidable, inescapable, inexorable, ineluctable; predetermined, preordained.

THE RIGHT WORD **necessary, essential, indispensable, requisite**

Food is **essential** to human life, which means that we must have it to survive. *Essential* can also apply to something that makes up the *essence*, or necessary qualities or attributes, of a thing (*a good safecracker is essential to our plan*). Clothing is **indispensable** in Northern climates, which means that it cannot be done without if the specified or implied purpose—in this case, survival—is to be achieved. **Necessary** applies to something without which a condition cannot be fulfilled (*cooperation was necessary to gather the harvest*), although it generally implies a pressing need rather than absolute indispensability. **Requisite** refers to that which is required by the circumstances (*the requisite skills for a botanist*) and generally describes a requirement that is imposed from the outside rather than an inherent need.

**necessitate** verb *the additional enrollment necessitates an additional staff person* MAKE NECESSARY, entail, involve, mean, require, demand, call for, be grounds for, warrant, constrain, force. See note at COMPEL.

**necessitous** adjective *distributing milk to necessitous mothers* NEEDY, poor, short of money, disadvantaged, underprivileged, in straitened circumstances, impoverished, poverty-stricken, penniless, impecunious, destitute, pauperized, indigent, without a cent to one's name; *informal* hard up; *formal* penurious. ANTONYM wealthy.

**necessity** noun **1** *the microwave is now regarded as a necessity* ESSENTIAL, indispensable item, requisite, prerequisite, necessary, basic, sine qua non, desideratum; *informal* must-have.

**2** *political necessity forced him to resign* FORCE OF CIRCUMSTANCE, obligation, need, call, exigency; force majeure.

**3** *the necessity of growing old* INEVITABILITY, certainty, inescapability, inexorability, ineluctability.

**4** *necessity made them steal* POVERTY, need, neediness, want, deprivation, privation, penury, destitution, indigence. PHRASE: **of necessity** *the renovations will, of necessity, require a more aggressive fund-raising campaign* NECESSARILY, inevitably, unavoidably, inescapably, ineluctably; as a matter of course, naturally, automatically, certainly, surely, definitely, incontrovertibly, undoubtedly; *formal* perforce.

**necromancer** noun *a convention of spiritualists and necromancers* SORCERER, sorceress, (black) magician, wizard, warlock, witch, enchantress, occultist, diviner; spiritualist, medium; *rare* thaumaturge, thaumaturgist.

**necromancy** noun *Juma had been a practitioner of necromancy in some small village in Central America* SORCERY, (black) magic, witchcraft, witchery, wizardry, the occult, occultism, voodoo, hoodoo; divination; spiritualism.

**necropolis** noun *overlooking the woeful sea is the home to many a lost soldier, a rolling green necropolis* CEMETERY, graveyard, churchyard, burial ground; *informal* boneyard; *historical* potter's field, God's acre.

**need** verb **1** *do you need money?* REQUIRE, be in need of, have need of, want; be crying out for, be desperate for; demand, call for, necessitate, entail, involve; lack, be without, be short of.

**2** *you needn't come* HAVE TO, be obliged to, be compelled to.

**3** *she needed him so much* YEARN FOR, pine for, long for, desire, miss.

▸ noun **1** *there's no need to apologize* NECESSITY, obligation, requirement, call, demand.

**2** *basic human needs* REQUIREMENT, essential, necessity, want, requisite, prerequisite, demand, desideratum.

**3** *their need was particularly pressing* NEEDINESS, want, poverty, deprivation, privation, hardship, destitution, indigence.

**4** *my hour of need* DIFFICULTY, trouble, distress; crisis, emergency, urgency, extremity.

PHRASE: **in need** *these children are in need* NEEDY, necessitous, deprived, disadvantaged, underprivileged, poor, impoverished, poverty-stricken, destitute, impecunious, indigent; *formal* penurious.

**needful** adjective *formal we'll do whatever is needful* NECESSARY, needed, required, requisite; essential, imperative, vital, indispensable.

**needle** noun **1** *a needle and thread* BODKIN.

**2** *the virus is transmitted via needles* hypodermic needle, syringe; *informal* hypo.

3 *the needle on the meter* INDICATOR, pointer, marker, arrow, hand.

4 *put the needle on the record* STYLUS.

▸ verb *informal he needled her too much* GOAD, provoke, bait, taunt, pester, harass, prick, prod, sting, tease; IRRITATE, annoy, anger, vex, irk, nettle, pique, exasperate, infuriate, get on someone's nerves, rub the wrong way, ruffle someone's feathers, try someone's patience; *informal* aggravate, rile, niggle, get in someone's hair, hassle, get to, bug, miff, peeve, get/put someone's back up, get under someone's skin, get at, ride.

**needless** adjective *needless details* UNNECESSARY, inessential, nonessential, unneeded, undesired, unwanted, uncalled for; gratuitous, pointless; dispensable, expendable, superfluous, redundant, excessive, supererogatory. ANTONYM necessary.

PHRASE: **needless to say** *needless to say, we are grateful for any and all donations* OF COURSE, as one would expect, not unexpectedly, it goes without saying, obviously, naturally; *informal* natch.

**needlework** noun *some of the surgeons keep their fingers nimble with needlework* SEWING, stitching, embroidery, needlepoint, needlecraft, tapestry, crewel (work).

**needy** adjective *collecting food and blankets for needy families* POOR, deprived, disadvantaged, underprivileged, necessitous, in need, needful, hard up, in straitened circumstances, poverty-stricken, indigent, impoverished, pauperized, destitute, impecunious, penniless, moneyless; *informal* broke, strapped (for cash), busted; *formal* penurious. ANTONYM wealthy.

**ne'er-do-well** noun *I don't want to end up a ne'er-do-well like my old man* GOOD-FOR-NOTHING, layabout, loafer, idler, shirker, sluggard, slugabed, drone; *informal* lazybones, bum; *archaic* wastrel.

**nefarious** adjective *the nefarious long-lost brother returns to steal Iris's inheritance* WICKED, evil, sinful, iniquitous, egregious, heinous, atrocious, vile, foul, abominable, odious, depraved, monstrous, fiendish, diabolical, unspeakable, despicable; villainous, criminal, corrupt, illegal, unlawful; *dated* dastardly. ANTONYM good.

**negate** verb 1 *they negated the court's ruling* INVALIDATE, nullify, neutralize, cancel; undo, reverse, annul, void, revoke, rescind, repeal, retract, countermand, overrule, overturn; *informal* nix; *formal* abrogate. See note at VOID. ANTONYMS validate, confirm.

2 *he has never successfully negated Henderson's central theory* DISPROVE, prove wrong, prove false, refute, debunk, discredit, invalidate; *informal* poke holes in; *formal* confute. ANTONYM confirm.

**negation** noun 1 *negation of the findings* DENIAL, contradiction, repudiation, refutation, rebuttal; nullification, cancellation, revocation, repeal, retraction; *formal* abrogation.

2 *evil is not just the negation of goodness* OPPOSITE, reverse, antithesis, contrary, inverse, converse; absence, want.

**negative** adjective 1 *a negative reply* OPPOSING, opposed, contrary, anti-, dissenting, saying "no," in the negative. ANTONYMS positive, affirmative.

2 *stop being so negative* PESSIMISTIC, defeatist, gloomy, cynical, fatalistic, dismissive, antipathetic, critical; unenthusiastic, uninterested, unresponsive. ANTONYMS positive, optimistic.

3 *a negative effect on the economy* HARMFUL, bad, adverse, damaging, detrimental, unfavorable, disadvantageous. ANTONYMS good, favorable.

▸ noun *he murmured a negative* "NO", refusal, rejection, veto; dissension, contradiction; denial; *informal* thumbs-down.

**neglect** verb 1 *she neglected the children* FAIL TO LOOK AFTER, leave alone, abandon, desert; *literary* forsake. ANTONYMS cherish, look after.

2 *he's neglecting his work* PAY NO ATTENTION TO, let slide, not attend to, be remiss about, be lax about, leave undone, shirk. ANTONYM concentrate on.

3 *don't neglect our advice* DISREGARD, ignore, pay no attention to, take no notice of, pay no heed to, overlook; disdain, scorn, spurn. ANTONYM heed.

4 *I neglected to inform her* FAIL, omit, forget. ANTONYM remember.

▸ noun 1 *the place had an air of neglect* DISREPAIR, dilapidation, deterioration, shabbiness, disuse, abandonment; *rare* desuetude.

2 *her doctor was guilty of neglect* NEGLIGENCE, dereliction of duty, carelessness, heedlessness, unconcern, laxity, slackness, irresponsibility; *formal* delinquency. ANTONYM care.

3 *the **neglect of** women's concerns* DISREGARD OF/FOR, ignoring of, overlooking of; inattention to, indifference to, heedlessness to. ANTONYM attention.

THE RIGHT WORD **neglect, disregard, ignore, overlook, slight**

One of the most common reasons why people fail to arrive at work on time is that they **neglect** to set their alarm clocks, a verb that implies a failure to carry out some expected or required action, either intentionally or through carelessness. Some people, of course, choose to **disregard** their employer's rules pertaining to tardiness, which implies a voluntary, and sometimes deliberate, inattention. Others hear the alarm go off and simply **ignore** it, which suggests not only a deliberate decision to **disregard** something but a stubborn refusal to face the facts. No doubt they hope their employers will **overlook** their frequent late arrivals, which implies a failure to see or to take action, which can be either intentional or due to haste or lack of care (*to overlook minor errors*). But they also hope no one will **slight** them for their conduct when it comes to handing out raises and promotions, which means to **disregard** or **neglect** in a disdainful way.

**neglected** adjective 1 *neglected animals* UNCARED FOR, abandoned; mistreated, maltreated; *literary* forsaken.

2 *a neglected cottage* DERELICT, dilapidated, tumbledown, ramshackle, untended.

3 *a neglected masterpiece of prose* DISREGARDED, forgotten,

overlooked, ignored, unrecognized, unnoticed, unsung, underestimated, undervalued, unappreciated.

**neglectful** adjective. See NEGLIGENT.

**negligent** adjective *a negligent safety inspector* NEGLECTFUL, remiss, careless, lax, irresponsible, inattentive, heedless, thoughtless, unmindful, forgetful; slack, sloppy, derelict; *formal* delinquent. ANTONYM dutiful.

**negligible** adjective *the defects are negligible* TRIVIAL, trifling, insignificant, unimportant, minor, inconsequential; minimal, small, slight, inappreciable, infinitesimal, nugatory, petty; paltry, inadequate, insufficient, meager, pitiful; *informal* minuscule, piddling, measly; *formal* exiguous. ANTONYM significant.

**negotiable** adjective **1** *salary is negotiable* OPEN TO DISCUSSION, discussable, flexible, open to modification; unsettled, undecided.

**2** *the pathway was negotiable* PASSABLE, navigable, crossable, traversable; clear, unblocked, unobstructed.

**3** *negotiable checks* transferable; valid.

**negotiate** verb **1** *she refused to negotiate* DISCUSS TERMS, talk, consult, parley, confer, debate; compromise; mediate, intercede, arbitrate, moderate, conciliate; bargain, haggle.

**2** *he negotiated a new contract* ARRANGE, broker, work out, thrash out, agree on; settle, clinch, conclude, pull off, bring off, transact; *informal* sort out, swing.

**3** *I negotiated the obstacles* GET AROUND, get past, get over, clear, cross; surmount, overcome, deal with, cope with.

**negotiation** noun **1** **(negotiations)** *the negotiations resume next week* DISCUSSION(S), talks, deliberations; conference, debate, dialogue, consultation; mediation, arbitration, conciliation.

**2** *the negotiation of the deal* ARRANGEMENT, brokering; settlement, conclusion, completion, transaction.

**negotiator** noun *they brought in an impartial negotiator to help settle the dispute* MEDIATOR, arbitrator, arbiter, moderator, go-between, middleman, intermediary, intercessor, intervener, conciliator; representative, spokesperson, broker, bargainer.

**neighborhood** noun **1** *a quiet neighborhood* DISTRICT, area, locality, locale, quarter, community; part, region, zone; *informal* neck of the woods, hood, nabe, stomping ground, stamping ground.

**2** *in the neighborhood of Greensboro* VICINITY, environs, purlieus, precincts, vicinage. PHRASE: **in the neighborhood of** *a new roof will be in the neighborhood of $4,000* APPROXIMATELY, about, around, roughly, in the region of, of/on the order of, nearly, almost, close to, just about, practically, there or thereabouts, circa.

**neighboring** adjective *the owner of the neighboring property* ADJACENT, adjoining, bordering, connecting, abutting; proximate, near, close, close/near at hand, next-door, nearby, in the vicinity. ANTONYM remote.

**nemesis** noun **1** *they were beaten in the final by their nemesis* ARCHRIVAL, adversary, foe, opponent, arch enemy.

**2** *this could be the bank's nemesis* DOWNFALL, undoing, ruin, ruination, destruction, Waterloo.

**3** *the nemesis that his crime deserved* RETRIBUTION, vengeance, punishment, just deserts; fate, destiny.

**neologism** noun *the delightful neologisms of Lewis Carroll* NEW WORD, new expression, new term, new phrase, coinage; made-up word, nonce word.

**neophyte** noun **1** *a neophyte of the monastery* NOVICE, novitiate; postulant, catechumen.

**2** *cooking classes are offered to neophytes* BEGINNER, learner, novice, newcomer; initiate, tyro, fledgling; trainee, apprentice, probationer, tenderfoot; *informal* rookie, newbie, greenhorn. See note at NOVICE.

**ne plus ultra** noun *the ne plus ultra of jazz pianists* LAST WORD, ultimate, perfect example, height, acme, zenith, epitome, quintessence.

**nepotism** noun *hiring my daughter was not nepotism—it was just good business* FAVORITISM, preferential treatment, the old boy network, looking after one's own, bias, partiality, partisanship. ANTONYM impartiality.

**nerve** noun **1** *the nerves that transmit pain* nerve fiber, neuron, axon, dendrite.

**2** *the match will be a test of nerve* CONFIDENCE, assurance, coolheadedness, self-possession; courage, bravery, pluck, boldness, intrepidity, fearlessness, daring; determination, willpower, spirit, backbone, fortitude, intestinal fortitude, mettle, grit, true grit, stout-heartedness; *informal* guts, spunk, moxie. See note at COURAGE.

**3** *he had the nerve to ask her out again* AUDACITY, cheek, effrontery, gall, temerity, presumption, boldness, brazenness, impudence, impertinence, arrogance, cockiness; *informal* face, front, chutzpah.

**4** *pre-wedding nerves* ANXIETY, tension, nervousness, stress, worry, cold feet, apprehension; *informal* butterflies (in one's stomach), the jitters, the shakes, the heebie-jeebies. PHRASE: **get on someone's nerves** *her squeaky voice gets on my nerves* IRRITATE, annoy, irk, anger, bother, vex, provoke, displease, exasperate, infuriate, gall, pique, needle, ruffle someone's feathers, try someone's patience; jar on, grate on, rankle; rub the wrong way; *informal* aggravate, get to, bug, miff, peeve, rile, nettle, get someone's goat, tick off.

**nerve-racking** adjective *it's the waiting that's the most nerve-racking* STRESSFUL, anxious, worrying, fraught, nail-biting, tense, difficult, trying, worrisome, daunting, frightening; *informal* scary, hairy.

**nervous** adjective **1** *a nervous woman* HIGH-STRUNG, anxious, edgy, tense, excitable, jumpy, skittish, brittle, neurotic; timid, mousy, shy, fearful. ANTONYMS relaxed, calm.

**2** *he was so nervous he couldn't eat* ANXIOUS, worried, apprehensive, on edge, edgy, tense, stressed, agitated, uneasy, restless, worked up, keyed up, overwrought, jumpy; fearful, frightened, scared, shaky, in a cold sweat, gun-shy; *informal* with butterflies in one's stomach, jittery, twitchy, in a state, uptight, wired, in a flap, het up, strung out, having kittens. ANTONYMS relaxed, calm.

**3** *a nervous disorder* NEUROLOGICAL, neural.

**nervous breakdown** noun *the boss's nervous breakdown almost destroyed the company* MENTAL COLLAPSE, breakdown, collapse, crisis, trauma; nervous exhaustion, mental illness; *informal* crack-up.

**nervousness** noun *she began chattering out of nervousness* ANXIETY, edginess, tension, agitation, stress, worry, apprehension, uneasiness, disquiet, fear, trepidation, perturbation, alarm; *informal* butterflies (in one's stomach), the jitters, the willies, the heebie-jeebies, the shakes.

**nervy** adjective *it was a nervy move* AUDACIOUS, impudent, brazen, cheeky, bold, plucky; *informal* gutsy, spunky, ballsy.

**nest** noun **1** *the birds built a nest* ROOST, aerie.

**2** *the animals disperse rapidly from the nest* LAIR, den, burrow.

**3** *a cozy love nest* HIDEAWAY, hideout, retreat, shelter, refuge, den.

**4** *a nest of intrigue* HOTBED, den, breeding ground, cradle.

**nest egg** noun *her nest egg wasn't much, but it was enough to keep the wolves from the door* SAVINGS, life savings, cache, funds, reserve.

**nestle** verb *the little ones nestled under the cozy quilt with their mother* SNUGGLE, cuddle, huddle, nuzzle, settle, burrow.

**Net** noun *their first communication was through* ***the Net*** THE INTERNET, the World Wide Web, the Web; *dated* cyberspace, the information superhighway, the infobahn.

**net**[1] noun **1** *fishermen mending their nets* FISHING NET, dragnet, drift net, trawl (net), landing net, gill net, cast net, seine.

**2** *a dress of green net* NETTING, meshwork, webbing, tulle, fishnet, openwork, lace, latticework.

**3** *he managed to escape the net* TRAP, snare.

▸ verb *they netted big criminals* CATCH, capture, trap, entrap, snare, ensnare, bag, hook, land; *informal* nab, collar.

**net**[2] adjective **1** *net earnings* AFTER TAX, after deductions, take-home, final; *informal* bottom line. ANTONYM gross.

**2** *the net result* FINAL, end, ultimate, closing; overall, actual, effective.

▸ verb *she netted $50,000* EARN, make, get, gain, obtain, acquire, accumulate, clear, take home, bring in, pocket, realize, be paid; *informal* rake in.

**nether** adjective *the nether regions* LOWER, low, bottom, bottommost, under, basal; underground. ANTONYM upper.

**nettle** verb *I try not to be nettled by her, but it isn't easy* IRRITATE, annoy, irk, gall, vex, anger, exasperate, infuriate, provoke; upset, displease, offend, affront, pique, get on someone's nerves, try someone's patience, ruffle someone's feathers; rub the wrong way, rankle; *informal* peeve, aggravate, miff, rile, needle, get to, bug, get someone's goat, tick off.

**network** noun **1** *a network of arteries* WEB, lattice, net, matrix, mesh, crisscross, grid, reticulum, reticulation; *Anatomy* plexus.

**2** *a network of lanes* MAZE, labyrinth, warren, tangle.

**3** *a network of friends* SYSTEM, complex, nexus, web, webwork.

**neurosis** noun *has he been diagnosed with an actual neurosis?* MENTAL ILLNESS, mental disorder, psychological disorder; psychoneurosis, psychopathy; obsession, phobia, fixation; *Medicine* neuroticism.

**neurotic** adjective **1** *Medicine neurotic patients* MENTALLY ILL, mentally disturbed, unstable, unbalanced, maladjusted; psychopathic, phobic, obsessive–compulsive. ANTONYMS stable, well balanced.

**2** *a neurotic, self-obsessed woman* OVERANXIOUS, oversensitive, nervous, tense, high-strung, strung-out, paranoid; obsessive, fixated, hysterical, overwrought, worked-up, irrational, twitchy. ANTONYMS laid-back, calm.

**neuter** adjective *the traumatic abuses of his childhood left him feeling more neuter than masculine* ASEXUAL, sexless, unsexed; androgynous, epicene.

▸ verb *have your pets neutered* STERILIZE, castrate, spay, geld, fix, desex, alter, doctor; *archaic* emasculate.

**neutral** adjective **1** *a neutral judge* IMPARTIAL, unbiased, unprejudiced, objective, open-minded, nonpartisan, disinterested, dispassionate, detached, impersonal, unemotional, indifferent, uncommitted. ANTONYMS biased, partisan.

**2** *Switzerland remained neutral* UNALIGNED, nonaligned, unaffiliated, unallied, uninvolved; noncombatant. ANTONYMS partisan, combatant.

**3** *a neutral topic of conversation* INOFFENSIVE, bland, unobjectionable, unexceptionable, anodyne, unremarkable, ordinary, commonplace; safe, harmless, innocuous. ANTONYMS provocative, offensive.

**4** *a neutral background* PALE, light; beige, cream, taupe, oatmeal, ecru, buff, fawn, gray; colorless, uncolored, achromatic; indeterminate, insipid, nondescript, dull, drab. ANTONYMS bright, colorful.

**neutralize** verb *if the internal dissension is not neutralized, we have no hope of moving forward* COUNTERACT, offset, counterbalance, balance, counterpoise, countervail, compensate for, make up for; cancel out, nullify, negate; equalize.

**never** adverb **1** *his room is never tidy* NOT EVER, at no time, not at any time, not once; *literary* ne'er. ANTONYM always.

**2** *she will never agree to it* NOT AT ALL, certainly not, not for a moment, under no circumstances, on no account, nevermore; *informal* no way, not on your life, not in a million years, when pigs fly, when hell freezes over. ANTONYMS certainly, definitely.

**never-ending** adjective *never-ending noise* INCESSANT, continuous, unceasing, ceaseless, constant, continual, perpetual, uninterrupted, unbroken, steady, unremitting, relentless, persistent, interminable, nonstop, endless, unending, everlasting, eternal. See note at ETERNAL.

**nevertheless** adverb *nevertheless, it makes sense to take a few precautions* NONETHELESS, even so, however, but, still, yet, though; in spite of that, despite that, be that as it may, for all that, that said, just the same, all the same; notwithstanding, regardless, anyway, anyhow, still and all.

**new** adjective **1** *new technology* RECENTLY DEVELOPED, up to date, latest, current, state-of-the-art, contemporary, advanced, recent, modern, cutting-edge, leading-edge. ANTONYMS old, existing.

**2** *new ideas* NOVEL, original, fresh, imaginative, creative, experimental; contemporary, modernist, up to date; newfangled, ultramodern, avant-garde, futuristic; *informal* way out, far out. ANTONYMS old-fashioned, hackneyed.

**3** *is your boat new?* UNUSED, brand new, pristine, fresh, in mint condition. ANTONYMS old, secondhand.

**4** *we have to find a new approach* DIFFERENT, another, alternative; unfamiliar, unknown, strange; unaccustomed, untried. ANTONYM present.

**5** *they had a new classroom built* ADDITIONAL, extra, supplementary, further, another, fresh. ANTONYM existing.

**6** *I came back a new woman* REINVIGORATED, restored, revived, improved, refreshed, regenerated, reborn.

**newborn** adjective *newborn babies* JUST BORN, recently born.

▸ noun *the bacteria are dangerous to newborns* YOUNG BABY, tiny baby, infant; *Medicine* neonate.

**newcomer** noun **1** *a newcomer to the village* (NEW) ARRIVAL, immigrant, settler; stranger, outsider, foreigner, alien; *informal* johnny-come-lately, new kid on the block.

**2** *photography tips for the newcomer* BEGINNER, novice, learner; trainee, apprentice, tyro, initiate, neophyte, tenderfoot; *informal* rookie, newbie, greenhorn.

**newfangled** adjective *newfangled digital technology* NEW, the latest, modern, ultramodern, up-to-the-minute, state-of-the-art, advanced, contemporary, new-generation; *informal* trendy, flash. ANTONYM dated.

**newly** adverb *a newly discovered species of moth* RECENTLY, just, only just, lately, freshly; not long ago, a short time ago, only now, of late; new-.

**news** noun *they were stunned by the news of his death* REPORT, announcement, story, account; article, news flash, newscast, headlines, press release, communication, communiqué, bulletin; message, dispatch, statement, intelligence; disclosure, revelation, word, talk, gossip; *informal* scoop; *literary* tidings.

**newspaper** noun *the front-page story in today's newspaper* PAPER, journal, gazette, tabloid, broadsheet, local (paper), daily (paper), weekly (paper); scandal sheet; *informal* rag, tab.

**next** adjective **1** *the next chapter* FOLLOWING, succeeding, upcoming, to come. ANTONYMS previous, preceding.

**2** *the next house in the street* NEIGHBORING, adjacent, adjoining, next-door, bordering, connected, attached; closest, nearest.

▸ adverb *where shall we go next?* THEN, after, afterward/afterward, after this/that, following that/this, later, subsequently; *formal* thereafter, thereupon. ANTONYM before.

PHRASE: **next to** *she sat down next to a window* BESIDE, by, alongside, by the side of, next door to, adjacent to, side by side with; close to, near, neighboring, adjoining.

**nibble** verb **1** *they **nibbled at** mangoes* TAKE SMALL BITES FROM, pick at, gnaw at, peck at, snack on; toy with; taste, sample; *informal* graze on.

**2** *the mouse nibbled his finger* PECK, nip, bite.

▸ noun **1** *the fish enjoyed a nibble on the lettuce* BITE, gnaw, chew; taste.

**2** *a few nibbles before dinner* MORSEL, mouthful, bite; snack, tidbit, canapé, hors d'oeuvre.

**nice** adjective **1** *have a nice time* ENJOYABLE, pleasant, agreeable, good, satisfying, gratifying, delightful, marvelous; entertaining, amusing, diverting, lovely, great. ANTONYM unpleasant.

**2** *a nice landlord* PLEASANT, likable, agreeable, personable, congenial, amiable, affable, genial, friendly, charming, delightful, engaging; sympathetic, simpatico, compassionate, good. ANTONYM nasty.

**3** *nice manners* POLITE, courteous, civil, refined, polished, genteel, elegant. ANTONYMS unrefined, rough.

**4** *that's a rather nice distinction* SUBTLE, fine, delicate, minute, precise, strict, close; careful, meticulous, scrupulous. ANTONYMS approximate, rough.

**5** *it's a nice day* FINE, pleasant, agreeable; dry, sunny, warm, mild. ANTONYMS stormy, nasty.

**USAGE NOTE nice**

**Nice** originally had a number of meanings, including 'fine, subtle, discriminating' (*they are not very nice in regard to the company they keep*); 'refined in taste, hard to please, fastidious' (*for company so nice, the finest caterers would be engaged*); and 'precise, strict' (*she has a nice sense of decorum*). The popular overuse of **nice** to mean 'pleasant, agreeable, satisfactory' has rendered the word trite: *we had a very nice time*; *this is a nice room*; *he's a nice boy.*

**nicety** noun **1** *legal niceties* SUBTLETY, fine point, nuance, refinement, detail.

**2** *great nicety of control* PRECISION, accuracy, exactness, meticulousness.

**niche** noun **1** *a niche in the wall* RECESS, alcove, nook, cranny, hollow, bay, cavity, cubbyhole, pigeonhole.

**2** *he found his niche in life* IDEAL POSITION, place, function, vocation, calling, métier, job.

**nickname** noun *"Bambi" is the nickname my sister gave me when I was a baby* SOBRIQUET, byname, tag, label, epithet, cognomen; pet name, diminutive, endearment; *informal* moniker; *formal* appellation.

**nifty** adjective *informal* **1** *nifty camerawork* SKILLFUL, deft, agile, capable. ANTONYM clumsy.

**2** *a nifty little gadget* USEFUL, handy, practical.

**3** *a nifty suit* FASHIONABLE, stylish, smart.

**niggardly** adjective **1** *a niggardly person* CHEAP, mean, miserly, parsimonious, close-fisted, penny-pinching, cheeseparing, grasping, ungenerous, illiberal; *informal* stingy, tight, tightfisted. ANTONYM generous.

**2** *niggardly rations* MEAGER, inadequate, scanty, scant, skimpy, paltry, sparse, insufficient, deficient, short, lean, small, slender, poor, miserable, pitiful, puny; *informal* measly, stingy, pathetic, piddling. ANTONYMS lavish, abundant.

**niggle** verb **1** *his behavior does niggle me* IRRITATE, annoy, bother, provoke, exasperate, upset, gall, irk, rankle with; *informal* rile, get to, bug.

**2** *he niggles about the prices* COMPLAIN, quibble, nitpick, fuss, carp, cavil, grumble, gripe, grouse, moan.

▸ noun *niggles about the lack of equipment* QUIBBLE, trivial complaint, criticism, grumble, grouse, cavil; *informal* gripe, moan, beef.

**night** noun *they did all their dirty dealing during the night* nighttime; hours of darkness, darkness, dark; nightfall, sunset. ANTONYM day.

PHRASE: **night and day** *wartime factories ran night and day* ALL THE TIME, around/round the clock, 'morning, noon, and night,' 'day in, day out,' ceaselessly, endlessly, incessantly, unceasingly, interminably, constantly, perpetually, continually, relentlessly; *informal* 24–7.

**nightfall** noun *we lock the doors at nightfall* SUNSET, sundown, dusk, twilight, evening, close of day, dark; *literary* eventide. ANTONYM dawn.

**nightly** adjective **1** *nightly raids* EVERY NIGHT, each night, night after night.

**2** *his nightly wanderings* NOCTURNAL, nighttime.

▸ adverb *a band plays there nightly* EVERY NIGHT, each night, night after night.

**nightmare** noun **1** *she woke from a nightmare* BAD DREAM, night terrors; *archaic* incubus.

**2** *the journey was a nightmare* ORDEAL, trial, torment, horror, hell, misery, agony, torture, murder; curse, bane.

**nihilism** noun *she could not accept Bacon's nihilism, his insistence that man is a futile being* SKEPTICISM, negativity, cynicism, pessimism; disbelief, unbelief, agnosticism, atheism.

**nil** noun *our chances of getting there on time were nil* NOTHING, none; zero, 0, naught/nought; *Tennis* love; *informal* zilch, zip, nada, a goose egg, nix; *dated* cipher.

**nimble** adjective **1** *he was nimble on his feet* AGILE, sprightly, light, spry, lively, quick, graceful, lithe, limber; skillful, deft, dexterous, adroit; *informal* nippy, twinkle-toed; *literary* lightsome. ANTONYM clumsy.

**2** *a nimble mind* QUICK-WITTED, quick, alert, lively, wide awake, observant, astute, adroit, perceptive, penetrating, discerning, shrewd, sharp; intelligent, bright, smart, clever, brilliant; *informal* brainy, quick on the uptake. ANTONYM dull.

**nip** verb *the child nipped her* BITE, nibble, peck; pinch, tweak, squeeze, grip.

▸ noun *a nip in the air* CHILL, biting cold, iciness.

PHRASE: **nip something in the bud** *before your children start spending most of their free time in front of the television or computer, nip it in the bud* CUT SHORT, curtail, check, curb, thwart, frustrate, stop, halt, arrest, stifle, obstruct, block, squash, quash, subdue, crack down on, stamp out; *informal* put the kibosh on.

**nipple** noun *the mother dog's nipples* TEAT; *informal* tit; *Anatomy* mamilla.

**nippy** adjective *it's a bit nippy in here* COLD, chilly, icy, bitter, raw. ANTONYM warm.

**nirvana** noun *there are no shortcuts to nirvana* PARADISE, heaven; bliss, ecstasy, joy, peace, serenity, tranquility; enlightenment. ANTONYM hell.

**nitpicking** adjective *informal*. See PEDANTIC.

**nitty-gritty** noun *informal now let's get to the nitty-gritty of managing your own business* BASICS, essentials, fundamentals, substance, quintessence, heart of the matter; nub, crux, gist, meat, kernel, marrow; *informal* brass tacks, bottom line; nuts and bolts.

**nitwit** noun *informal*. See IDIOT.

**no** exclamation *no, I will not go on a date with your cousin Ralph* absolutely not, most certainly not, of course not, under no circumstances, by no means, not at all, negative, never, not really; *informal* nope, uh-uh, nah, not on your life, no way, no way José, ixnay; *archaic* nay. ANTONYM yes.

**nobility** noun **1** *a member of the nobility* ARISTOCRACY, aristocrats, peerage, peers (of the realm), lords, nobles, noblemen, noblewomen, patricians; *informal* aristos.

**2** *the nobility of his deed* VIRTUE, goodness, honor, decency, integrity; magnanimity, generosity, selflessness.

**noble** adjective **1** *a noble family* ARISTOCRATIC, patrician, blue-blooded, high-born, titled; *archaic* gentle. ANTONYM humble.

**2** *a noble cause* RIGHTEOUS, virtuous, good, honorable, upright, decent, worthy, moral, ethical, reputable; magnanimous, unselfish, generous. ANTONYM dishonorable.

**3** *a noble pine forest* MAGNIFICENT, splendid, grand, stately, imposing, dignified, proud, striking, impressive, majestic, glorious, awesome, monumental, statuesque, regal, imperial. ANTONYM unimpressive.

▸ noun *Scottish nobles* ARISTOCRAT, nobleman, noblewoman, lord, lady, peer, peeress, peer of the realm, patrician; *informal* aristo.

**nod** verb **1** *she nodded her head* INCLINE, bob, bow, dip.

**2** *he nodded to me to start* SIGNAL, gesture, gesticulate, motion, sign, indicate.

▸ noun **1** *she gave a nod to the manager* SIGNAL, indication, sign, cue; gesture.

**2** *a quick nod of his head* INCLINATION, bob, bow, dip.

**3** *Halifax will get the nod as host city* APPROVAL, selection, sanction, endorsement; *informal* OK, A-OK, green light, thumbs up.

PHRASE: **nod off** *give me a pillow and I'll nod off right this second* FALL ASLEEP, go to sleep, doze off, drop off; *informal* drift off, go out like a light, sack out, drift into the arms of Morpheus.

**node** noun *the node of the branches* JUNCTION, intersection, interchange, fork, confluence, convergence, crossing.

**noise** noun *I have a headache from all the noise* SOUND, din, hubbub, clamor, racket, uproar, tumult, commotion, pandemonium, babel; *informal* hullabaloo. ANTONYM silence.

**noisome** adjective. See ODIOUS.

**noisy** adjective **1** *a noisy crowd* ROWDY, clamorous, boisterous, turbulent, uproarious, riotous, rambunctious, rackety; chattering, talkative, vociferous, shouting, screaming. ANTONYM quiet.

**2** *noisy music* LOUD, fortissimo, blaring, booming, overloud, deafening, thunderous, tumultuous, clamorous, ear-splitting, piercing, strident, cacophonous, raucous. ANTONYM soft.

**nomad** noun *a photojournalist who lived with a clan of nomads for six months* ITINERANT, traveler, migrant, wanderer, roamer, rover; gypsy, Bedouin; transient, drifter, vagabond, vagrant, tramp.

**nominal** adjective **1** *the nominal head of the campaign* IN NAME ONLY, titular, formal, official; theoretical, supposed, ostensible, so-called. ANTONYM real.

**2** *a nominal rent* TOKEN, symbolic; tiny, minute, minimal, small, insignificant, trifling; *informal* minuscule, piddling, piffling. ANTONYM considerable.

**nominate** verb **1** *you may nominate a candidate* PROPOSE, recommend, suggest, name, put forward, present, submit.

**2** *he nominated his assistant* APPOINT, select, choose, elect, commission, designate, name, delegate.

**nonbeliever** noun *her family condemned her for marrying a nonbeliever* UNBELIEVER, disbeliever, skeptic, doubter, doubting Thomas, cynic, nihilist; atheist, agnostic, freethinker; infidel, pagan, heathen.

**nonce** PHRASE: **for the nonce** *for the nonce, I'll be the acting chairman* FOR THE TIME BEING, temporarily, pro tem, for now, for the moment, for the interim, for a while, for the present, in the meantime; provisionally.

**nonchalant** adjective *she acts nonchalant, but I think she's quite nervous* CALM, composed, unconcerned, cool, 'calm, cool, and collected,' cool as a cucumber; indifferent, blasé, dispassionate, apathetic, casual, insouciant; *informal* laidback. ANTONYM anxious.

**noncommittal** adjective *please advise your client that this court expects something more substantial than a string of noncommittal responses* EVASIVE, equivocal, guarded, circumspect, reserved; discreet, uncommunicative, tactful, diplomatic, vague; *informal* cagey. PHRASE: **be noncommittal** *he was noncommittal about their chances of success* EQUIVOCATE, give nothing away, dodge the issue, sidestep the issue, hedge, pussyfoot around, beat around the bush, temporize, shilly-shally, vacillate, waver; hem and haw; *informal* duck the question, sit on the fence.

**non compos mentis** adjective. See INSANE sense 1.

**nonconformist** noun *our college has the reputation of being a haven for nonconformists* DISSENTER, dissentient, protester, rebel, renegade, schismatic; freethinker, apostate, heretic; individualist, free spirit, maverick, eccentric, original, deviant, misfit, dropout, outsider, Bohemian.

**nondescript** adjective *he was of average height and build, and even his clothes were nondescript* UNDISTINGUISHED, unremarkable, unexceptional, featureless, characterless, faceless, unmemorable, lackluster; ordinary, commonplace, average, run-of-the-mill, mundane, garden-variety; uninteresting, uninspiring, colorless, bland, dull. ANTONYM distinctive.

**none** pronoun **1** *none of the fish are unusual* NOT ONE, not a (single) one. ANTONYM all.

**2** *none of this concerns me* NO PART, not a bit, not any. ANTONYM all.

**3** *none can know better than you* NOT ONE, no one, nobody, not a soul, not a single person, no man. ANTONYM all.

PHRASE: **none the ——** *we were left none the wiser* NOT AT ALL, not a bit, not the slightest bit, in no way, by no means any.

**nonentity** noun *the tragedy is that, even after all the therapy we can provide, many of these kids will continue to be the nonentities that they've been taught to be* NOBODY, unimportant person, zero, nonperson, no-name, nothing, small fry, mediocrity; *informal* no-hoper, loser. ANTONYM celebrity.

**nonessential** adjective *nonessential items such as colognes and cosmetics are not permitted* UNNECESSARY, inessential, unessential, noncore, needless, unneeded, superfluous, uncalled for, redundant, dispensable, expendable, unimportant, extraneous.

**nonetheless** adverb *I doubt you have much to add—nonetheless, we want to hear your side of the story* NEVERTHELESS, even so, however, but, still, yet, though; in spite of that, despite that, be that as it may, for all that, that said, just the same, all the same; notwithstanding, regardless, anyway, anyhow, still and all.

**nonexistent** adjective *studio honchos would feed the press stories of the nonexistent guy-girl romances of their homosexual stars* IMAGINARY, imagined, unreal, fictional, fictitious, made up, invented, fanciful; fantastic, mythical; illusory, hallucinatory, chimerical, notional, shadowy, insubstantial; missing, absent; *literary* illusive. ANTONYM real.

**nonintervention** noun *a policy of nonintervention is not appropriate when the fundamental freedoms of others are in jeopardy and their very lives at risk* LAISSEZ-FAIRE, nonparticipation, noninterference, inaction, passivity, neutrality; live and let live.

**nonobservance** noun *we take the nonobservance of curfew very seriously* INFRINGEMENT, breach, violation, contravention, transgression, noncompliance, infraction; dereliction, neglect.

**nonpareil** adjective *a nonpareil storyteller* INCOMPARABLE, matchless, unrivaled, unparalleled, unequaled, peerless, beyond compare, second to none, unsurpassed, unbeatable, inimitable; unique, consummate, superlative, supreme; *formal* unexampled. ANTONYM mediocre.

▸ noun *without a doubt, theirs is the nonpareil* BEST, finest, crème de la crème, peak of perfection, elite, jewel in the crown, ne plus ultra, paragon; *archaic* nonesuch.

**nonsense** noun **1** *that's a lot of damn nonsense* RUBBISH, gibberish, claptrap, balderdash, blarney; *informal* hogwash, baloney, rot, moonshine, garbage, jive, tripe, drivel, bilge, bull, guff, bunk, bosh, BS, eyewash, piffle, poppycock, phooey, hooey, malarkey, hokum, twaddle, gobbledygook, codswallop, flapdoodle, hot air; *dated* bunkum, tommyrot; *vulgar slang* bullshit, crap. ANTONYM (good) sense.

**2** *she stands no nonsense* MISCHIEF, naughtiness, bad behavior, misbehavior, misconduct, misdemeanor; pranks, tricks, clowning, buffoonery, funny business; *informal* tomfoolery, monkey business, shenanigans, hanky-panky. ANTONYM good behavior.

**3** *they dismissed the concept as nonsense* ABSURDITY, folly, stupidity, ludicrousness, inanity, foolishness, idiocy, insanity, madness. ANTONYMS (good) sense, wisdom.

▸ exclamation *"Nonsense!" she retorted* RUBBISH, balderdash; *informal* no way, get out of here, get real, phooey, puh-leeze, hooey, poppycock, come off it, like hell; *dated* pshaw.

**THE RIGHT WORD nonsense, bull, bunk, drivel, poppycock, twaddle**

If you write or speak in an obscure, senseless, or unintelligible manner, you'll probably be accused of producing **nonsense**. It is the most general of these nouns and may refer to behavior as well as to what is said (*the demonstrators were told in no uncertain terms to stop this nonsense or leave the room*). **Twaddle** refers to silly, empty utterances from people who know nothing about a subject but who write or talk about it anyway (*I was sick of her twaddle about the dangers of electromagnetic fields*). **Bunk** (short for bunkum) applies to an utterance that strikes the popular fancy even though it is lacking in worth or substance (*the speech, which received enthusiastic applause, was pure bunk*). **Poppycock** applies to nonsense that is full of complex, confused, or clichéd ideas (*the report was a strange combination of logical thinking and outright poppycock*). **Bull** is a slang term for deceitful and often boastful writing or speech (*he gave them a line of bull*). Perhaps the most insulting of these terms is **drivel**, which implies a steady flow of inane, idle, or nonsensical speech or writing similar to what might be expected from a very young child or an idiot (*his first novel was full of romantic drivel*).

**nonsensical** adjective **1** *her nonsensical way of talking* MEANINGLESS, senseless, illogical. ANTONYMS logical, rational.

**2** *a nonsensical generalization* FOOLISH, insane, stupid, idiotic, illogical, irrational, senseless, absurd, silly, inane, harebrained, ridiculous, ludicrous, preposterous; *informal* crazy, crackpot, nutty; daft. ANTONYMS sane, sensible.

**nonstop** adjective *nonstop entertainment* CONTINUOUS, constant, continual, perpetual, incessant, unceasing, ceaseless, endless, uninterrupted, round-the-clock; unremitting, relentless, persistent, never-ending. ANTONYM occasional.

▸ adverb *we worked nonstop* CONTINUOUSLY, continually, incessantly, unceasingly, ceaselessly, all the time, constantly, perpetually, around/round the clock, day and night, steadily, relentlessly, persistently; *informal* 24–7. ANTONYM occasionally.

**nook** noun *the children's library has cozy nooks for quiet reading* RECESS, corner, alcove, niche, cranny, bay, inglenook, cavity, cubbyhole, pigeonhole; opening, gap, aperture; hideaway, hiding place, hideout, shelter.

**noon** noun *the bank closes at noon* MIDDAY, twelve o'clock, twelve hundred hours, twelve noon, high noon, noon hour, noonday; *literary* noontime, noontide.

**no one** pronoun *no one shed a tear when he was fired* NOBODY, not a soul, not anyone, not a single person, never a one, none.

**norm** noun **1** *norms of diplomatic behavior* CONVENTION, standard; criterion, yardstick, benchmark, touchstone, rule, formula, pattern, guide, guideline, model, exemplar.

**2** *such teams are now* ***the norm*** STANDARD, usual, the rule; normal, typical, average, unexceptional, par for the course, expected.

**normal** adjective **1** *they issue books in the normal way* USUAL, standard, ordinary, customary, conventional, habitual, accustomed, expected, wonted; typical, stock, common, everyday, regular, routine, established, set, fixed, traditional, time-honored. ANTONYM unusual.

**2** *a normal couple* ORDINARY, average, typical, run-of-the-mill, middle-of-the-road, common, conventional, mainstream, unremarkable, unexceptional, garden-variety, a dime a dozen.

**THE RIGHT WORD normal, average, natural, ordinary, regular, typical, usual**

Most of us want to be regarded as **normal**, an adjective that implies conformity with established norms or standards and is the opposite of abnormal (*a normal body temperature; normal intelligence*). **Regular**, like *normal*, is usually preferred to its opposite (irregular) and implies conformity to prescribed standards or established patterns (*their regular monthly meeting; a regular guy*), but *normal* carries stronger connotations of conformity within prescribed limits and sometimes allows for a wider range of differences. Few of us think of ourselves as **ordinary**, a term used to describe what is commonplace or unexceptional (*an ordinary person wearing ordinary clothes*), although many people are ordinary in some ways and extraordinary in others. **Average** also implies conformity with what is regarded as normal or ordinary (*a woman of average height*), although it tends to emphasize the middle ground and to exclude both positive and negative extremes. **Typical** applies to persons or things possessing the representative characteristics of a type or class (*a typical teenager*). Someone or something described as **natural** behaves or operates in accordance with an inherent nature or character (*his fears were natural for one so young*), while **usual** applies to that which conforms to common or ordinary use or occurrence (*we paid the usual price*).

---

**normality** noun *after a season of elections, it takes some time to return to normality* NORMALCY, business as usual, the daily round; routine, order, regularity.

**normally** adverb **1** *she wanted to walk normally* NATURALLY, conventionally, ordinarily; as usual, as normal.

**2** *normally we'd keep quiet about this* USUALLY, ordinarily, as a rule, generally, in general, mostly, for the most part, by and large, mainly, most of the time, on the whole; typically, customarily, traditionally.

**north** adjective *the north winds can be brutal* NORTHERN, northerly, polar, Arctic, boreal.

**nose** noun **1** *a punch on the nose* snout, muzzle, proboscis, trunk; *informal* beak, snoot, schnoz, schnozzola, sniffer, honker.

**2** *a nose for scandal* INSTINCT, feeling, sixth sense, intuition, insight, perception.

**3** *wine with a fruity nose* SMELL, bouquet, aroma, fragrance, perfume, scent, odor.

**4** *the plane's nose dipped* nose cone, bow, prow, front end.

▸ verb **1** *the dog nosed the ball* NUZZLE, nudge, push.

**2** *she's **nosing into** my business* PRY INTO, inquire about/into, poke around/about, interfere in/with, meddle in/with; be a busybody about, stick/poke one's nose in/into; *informal* be nosy about, snoop around/into.

**3** *he nosed the car into the traffic* EASE, inch, edge, move, maneuver, steer, guide.

PHRASES: **by a nose** *Harris won the third race by a nose* JUST, only just, barely, narrowly, by a hair's breadth, by the skin of one's teeth, by a whisker.

**nose around/about** *you check the bedrooms and we'll nose around the kitchen* INVESTIGATE, explore, ferret around/through, rummage around/through, search; delve into, peer into; prowl around; *informal* snoop around/about.

**nose out** *a team of trained dogs help us to nose out the armed passengers* DETECT, find, discover, bring to light, track down, dig up, ferret out, root out, uncover, unearth, sniff out.

**on the nose** *informal the plane landed at 7:15 on the nose* EXACTLY, precisely, sharp, on the dot, on the button, promptly, prompt, dead on, bang on.

**nosedive** noun **1** *the plane went into a nosedive* DIVE, descent, drop, plunge, plummet, fall. ANTONYM climb.

**2** *informal the dollar took a nosedive* FALL, drop, plunge, plummet, tumble, decline, slump; *informal* crash.

▸ verb **1** *the device nosedived to earth* DIVE, plunge, pitch, drop, plummet.

**2** *informal costs have nosedived* FALL, take a header, drop, sink, plunge, plummet, tumble, slump, go down, decline; *informal* crash. ANTONYMS soar, rise.

**nosh** *informal* noun *all kinds of nosh.* See FOOD sense 1.

▸ verb *they noshed on smoked salmon.* See EAT sense 1.

**nostalgia** noun *a nostalgia for traditional values* REMINISCENCE, remembrance, recollection; wistfulness, regret, sentimentality; homesickness.

**nostalgic** adjective *music that evokes nostalgic memories of our youth* WISTFUL, evocative, romantic, sentimental; dewy-eyed, misty-eyed, maudlin; homesick.

**nostrum** noun **1** *they have to prove their nostrums work* MEDICINE, patent medicine, potion, elixir, panacea, cure-all, wonder drug, quack remedy; *informal* magic bullet.

**2** *right-wing nostrums* MAGIC FORMULA, recipe for success, remedy, cure, prescription, answer.

**nosy** adjective *informal the nosy guy next door is always peeking out through the curtains* PRYING, inquisitive, curious, spying, eavesdropping, intrusive; *informal* snooping, snoopy.

**notable** adjective **1** *notable examples of workmanship* NOTEWORTHY, remarkable, outstanding, important, significant, momentous, memorable; marked, striking, impressive; uncommon, unusual, special, exceptional, signal. ANTONYMS unremarkable, insignificant.

**2** *a notable author* PROMINENT, important, well-known, famous, affluential, famed, noted, distinguished, great, eminent, illustrious, respected, esteemed, renowned, celebrated, acclaimed, influential, prestigious, of note. ANTONYMS obscure, unknown.

▸ noun *movie stars and other notables* CELEBRITY, public figure, VIP, personage, notability, dignitary, worthy, luminary; star, superstar, icon, name, big name; *informal* celeb, somebody, bigwig, big shot, big cheese, big fish, megastar, big kahuna, high muckamuck. ANTONYMS nonentity, no-name.

**notably** adverb *these are notably short-lived birds* REMARKABLY, especially, specially, very, extremely, exceptionally, singularly, particularly, peculiarly, distinctly, significantly, unusually, extraordinarily, strikingly, uncommonly, incredibly, really, decidedly, surprisingly, conspicuously; in particular, primarily, principally.

**notation** noun **1** *algebraic notation* SYMBOLS, alphabet, syllabary, script; code, cipher, hieroglyphics.

**2** *notations in the margin* ANNOTATION, jotting, comment, footnote, entry, memo, gloss, explanation.

**notch** noun **1** *a notch in the end of the arrow* NICK, cut, incision, score, scratch, slit, slot, groove, cleft, indentation.

**2** *her opinion of Nick dropped a notch* DEGREE, level, rung, point, mark, measure, grade.

▸ verb *notch the plank* NICK, cut, score, incise, carve, scratch, slit, gouge, groove, furrow.

**note** noun **1** *a note in her diary* RECORD, entry, item, notation, jotting, memorandum, reminder, aide-mémoire; *informal* memo.

**2** **(notes)** *his notes were read at the next meeting* MINUTES, records, details; report, account, commentary, transcript, proceedings, transactions; synopsis, summary, outline.

**3** *notes in the margins* ANNOTATION, footnote, commentary, comment; marginalia, exegesis.

**4** *he dropped me a note* MESSAGE, communication, letter, line; *formal* epistle, missive.

**5** *this note is legal tender* BILL; banknote; **(notes)** paper money.

**6** *this is worthy of note* ATTENTION, consideration, notice, heed, observation, regard.

**7** *a composer of note* DISTINCTION, importance, eminence, prestige, fame, celebrity, acclaim, renown, repute, stature, standing, consequence, account.

**8** *a note of hopelessness in her voice* TONE, intonation, inflection, sound; hint, indication, sign, element, suggestion.

▸ verb **1** *we will note your suggestion* BEAR IN MIND, be mindful of, consider, observe, heed, take notice of, pay attention to, take in.

**2** *the letter noted the ministers' concern* MENTION, refer to, touch on, indicate, point out, make known, state.

**3** *note the date in your diary* WRITE DOWN, put down, jot down, take down, inscribe, enter, mark, record, register, pencil (in).

**notebook** noun *a new notebook for French class* NOTEPAD, scratch pad, exercise book, workbook, memo pad, tablet, writing tablet; register, logbook, log, diary, daybook, journal, record.

**noted** adjective *a noted authority on the boll weevil* RENOWNED, well-known, famous, famed, prominent, celebrated; notable, of note, important, eminent, distinguished, illustrious, acclaimed, esteemed; of distinction, of repute. ANTONYM unknown.

**noteworthy** adjective *her work in the field of anthropology is noteworthy* NOTABLE, interesting, significant, important; remarkable, impressive, striking, outstanding, memorable, unique, special; unusual, extraordinary, singular, rare. ANTONYM unexceptional.

**nothing** noun **1** *all my efforts add up to nothing* NOT A THING, not anything, nil, zero, naught/nought; *informal* zilch, zip, nada, diddly-squat, squat. ANTONYM something.

**2** *forget it—it's nothing* A TRIFLING MATTER, a trifle; neither here nor there; *informal* no big deal.

**3** *he treats her as a nothing* NOBODY, unimportant person, nonentity, no-name, nonperson. ANTONYM celebrity.

**4** *the share value fell to nothing* ZERO, naught/nought, 0; *Tennis* love. PHRASES: **be/have nothing to do with** **1** *it has nothing to do with you* BE UNCONNECTED WITH, be unrelated to, not concern; be irrelevant to, be inapplicable to, be inapposite to.

**2** *I'll have nothing to do with him* AVOID, shun, ignore, have no contact with, steer clear of, give a wide berth to.

**for nothing** **1** *she hosted the show for nothing* FREE, free of charge, gratis, without charge, at no cost; *informal* for free, on the house.

**2** *all this trouble for nothing* IN VAIN, to no avail, to no purpose, with no result, needlessly, pointlessly.

**nothing but** *he's nothing but a nuisance* MERELY, only, just, solely, simply, purely, no more than.

**nothingness** noun **1** *the nothingness of death* OBLIVION, nullity, blankness; void, vacuum; *rare* nihility.

**2** *the nothingness of it all overwhelmed him* UNIMPORTANCE, insignificance, triviality, pointlessness, uselessness, worthlessness.

**notice** noun **1** *nothing escaped his notice* ATTENTION, observation, awareness, consciousness, perception; regard, consideration, scrutiny; watchfulness, vigilance, attentiveness.

**2** *a notice on the wall* POSTER, bill, handbill, advertisement, announcement, bulletin; flyer, leaflet, pamphlet; sign, card; *informal* ad.

**3** *show times may change without notice* NOTIFICATION, warning, advance warning, announcement; information, news, communication, word.

**4** *I handed in my notice* RESIGNATION.

**5** *the play got bad notices* REVIEW, write-up, critique, criticism.

▸ verb *I noticed that the door was open* OBSERVE, perceive, note, see, discern, detect, spot, distinguish, mark, remark, descry; *literary* behold. ANTONYM overlook.

PHRASE: **take no notice of** *he took no notice of anything I said* IGNORE, pay no attention to, disregard, pay no heed to, take no account of, brush aside, shrug off, turn a blind eye to, pass over, let go, overlook; look the other way (from).

**noticeable** adjective *a fresh coat of paint will make a noticeable difference* DISTINCT, evident, obvious, apparent, manifest, patent, plain, clear, marked, conspicuous, front-and-center, unmistakable, undeniable, pronounced, prominent, striking, arresting; perceptible, discernible, detectable, observable, visible, appreciable.

THE RIGHT WORD **noticeable, conspicuous, outstanding, prominent, remarkable, striking**

A scratch on someone's face might be **noticeable**, while a scar that runs from cheekbone to chin would be **conspicuous**. When it comes to describing the things that attract our attention, *noticeable* means readily noticed or unlikely to escape observation (*a noticeable facial tic; a noticeable aversion to cock-*

*tail parties*), while *conspicuous* implies that the eye (or mind) cannot miss it (*her absence was conspicuous*). Use **prominent** when you want to describe something that literally or figuratively stands out from its background (*a prominent nose; a prominent position on the committee*). It can also apply to persons or things that stand out so clearly they are generally known or recognized (*a prominent citizen*). Someone or something that is **outstanding** rises above or beyond others and is usually superior to them (*an outstanding student*). **Remarkable** applies to anything that is noticeable because it is extraordinary or exceptional (*remarkable blue eyes*). **Striking** is an even stronger word, used to describe something so out of the ordinary that it makes a deep and powerful impression on the observer's mind or vision (*a striking young woman over six feet tall*).

---

**notification** noun **1** *the notification of the victim's wife* INFORMING, telling, alerting, filling in.

**2** *she received notification that he was on the way* INFORMATION, word, advice, news, intelligence; communication, message; *literary* tidings.

**notify** verb *we will notify you as soon as possible* INFORM, tell, advise, brief, apprise, let someone know, put in the picture, fill in; alert, warn.

**notion** noun **1** *he had a notion that something was wrong* IDEA, belief, conviction, opinion, view, thought, impression, perception; hypothesis, theory; feeling, funny feeling, suspicion, sneaking suspicion, hunch. See note at IDEA.

**2** *Claire had no notion of what he meant* UNDERSTANDING, idea, awareness, knowledge, clue, inkling.

**3** *he got a notion to return* IMPULSE, inclination, whim, desire, wish; *dated* fancy.

**notional** adjective *the notional line between East and West* HYPOTHETICAL, theoretical, speculative, conjectural, suppositional, putative, conceptual; imaginary, fanciful, unreal, illusory. ANTONYM actual.

**notoriety** noun *his undeserved notoriety* INFAMY, disrepute, ill repute, bad name, dishonor, discredit; *dated* ill fame.

**notorious** adjective *a notorious gunman of the Old West* INFAMOUS, scandalous; well known, famous, famed, legendary.

**notwithstanding** preposition *notwithstanding his workload, he is a dedicated father* DESPITE, in spite of, regardless of, for all.

▸ adverb *she is bright and ambitious—notwithstanding, she is now jobless* NEVERTHELESS, nonetheless, even so, all the same, in spite of this, despite this, however, still, yet, that said, just the same, anyway, in any event, at any rate.

▸ conjunction ***notwithstanding that*** *the rain was torrential, they played on* ALTHOUGH, even though, though, in spite of the fact that, despite the fact that.

**nourish** verb **1** *patients must be well nourished* FEED, provide for, sustain, maintain.

**2** *we nourish the talents of children* ENCOURAGE, promote, foster, nurture, cultivate, stimulate, boost, advance, assist, help, aid, strengthen, enrich.

**3** *the hopes Emma nourished* CHERISH, nurture, foster, harbor, nurse, entertain, maintain, hold, have.

**nourishing** adjective *a nourishing snack* NUTRITIOUS, nutritive, wholesome, good for one, healthy, health-giving, healthful, beneficial, sustaining. ANTONYM unhealthy.

**nourishment** noun FOOD, sustenance, nutriment, nutrition, subsistence, provisions, provender, fare; *informal* grub, nosh, chow, eats, vittles, scoff, chuck; *formal* comestibles; *dated* victuals.

**nouveau riche** plural noun *we appeal to the nouveau riche for much of our funding* new rich, parvenus, arrivistes, upstarts, social climbers, vulgarians.

**novel**[1] noun *curl up with a good novel* BOOK, paperback, hardcover; STORY, tale, narrative, romance, roman à clef; piece of fiction; best seller, blockbuster; potboiler, pulp (fiction).

**novel**[2] adjective *a novel way of making money* NEW, original, unusual, unfamiliar, unconventional, unorthodox; different, fresh, imaginative, innovative, innovatory, inventive, modern, neoteric, avant-garde, pioneering, groundbreaking, revolutionary; rare, unique, singular, unprecedented; experimental, untested, untried; strange, exotic, newfangled. ANTONYM traditional.

**novelist** noun *Kafka was a Czech novelist who wrote in German* WRITER, author, fictionist, man/woman of letters, scribe; *informal* penman, scribbler.

**novelty** noun **1** *the novelty of our approach* ORIGINALITY, newness, freshness, unconventionality, unfamiliarity; difference, imaginativeness, creativity, innovation, modernity.

**2** *we sell seasonal novelties* KNICKKNACK, trinket, bauble, toy, trifle, gewgaw, gimcrack, ornament, kickshaw.

**novice** noun **1** *a five-day course for novices* BEGINNER, learner, neophyte, newcomer, initiate, tyro, fledgling; apprentice, trainee, probationer, student, pupil, tenderfoot; *informal* rookie, newbie, greenhorn. ANTONYMS expert, veteran.

**2** *a novice who was never ordained* NEOPHYTE, novitiate; postulant, proselyte, catechumen.

THE RIGHT WORD **novice, apprentice, beginner, neophyte, probationer**

---

All of these nouns are used to describe someone who has not yet acquired the skills and experience needed to qualify for a trade, a career, a profession, or a sphere of life. **Beginner** is the most general and informal term, used to describe someone who has begun to acquire the necessary skills but has not yet mastered them (*violin lessons for beginners*). An **apprentice** is also a beginner, usually a young person, who is serving under a more experienced master or teacher to learn the skills of a trade or profession (*an apprentice to one of the great Renaissance painters*); in a broad sense, *apprentice* refers to any beginner whose efforts are unpolished. **Novice** implies that the person lacks training and experience (*a novice when it came to writing fiction*), while **neophyte** is a less negative term, suggesting that the person is eagerly learning the ways, methods, or principles of something (*he was a neophyte at this type of sailing*). A **pro-**

**bationer** is a beginner who is undergoing a trial period, during which he or she must prove an aptitude for a certain type of work or life (*she was a lowly probationer, with no privileges or status*).

---

**novitiate** noun **1** *his novitiate lasts a year* PROBATIONARY PERIOD, probation, trial period, test period, apprenticeship, training period, traineeship, training, initiation.

**2** *two young novitiates* NOVICE, neophyte; postulant, proselyte, catechumen.

**now** adverb **1** *I'm extremely busy now* AT THE MOMENT, at present, at the present (time/moment), at this moment in time, currently, presently.

**2** *television is now the main source of news* NOWADAYS, today, these days, in this day and age; in the present climate.

**3** *you must leave now* AT ONCE, straightaway, right away, right now, this minute, this instant, immediately, instantly, directly, without further ado, promptly, without delay, as soon as possible; *informal* pronto, straight off, ASAP. PHRASES: **as of now** *as of now, cigarettes are banned in this house* FROM THIS TIME ON, from now on, henceforth, from this day forward, in (the) future; *formal* hereafter.
**for now** *for now, we'll just have salad* FOR THE TIME BEING, for the moment, for the present, for the meantime, for the nonce.
**not now** *I promise I will, but not now* LATER, later on, sometime, one day, some day, one of these days, sooner or later, in due course, by and by, eventually, ultimately.
**(every) now and again** *now and again, we like to visit the gallery* OCCASIONALLY, now and then, from time to time, sometimes, every so often, at times, on occasion(s), (every) once in a while; periodically, once in a blue moon.

**nowadays** adverb *nowadays, it seems as if everyone is obsessed with staying young* THESE DAYS, today, at the present time, in these times, in this day and age, now, currently, at the moment, at present, at this moment in time; in the present climate, presently.

**noxious** adjective *noxious fumes* POISONOUS, toxic, deadly, harmful, dangerous, pernicious, damaging, destructive; unpleasant, nasty, disgusting, awful, dreadful, horrible, terrible; vile, revolting, foul, nauseating, appalling, offensive; malodorous, fetid, putrid; *informal* ghastly, horrid; *literary* noisome. ANTONYM innocuous.

**nuance** noun *the nuances of light are very effective* FINE DISTINCTION, subtle difference; shade, shading, gradation, variation, degree; subtlety, nicety, overtone.

**nucleus** noun *the nucleus of the international banking world* CORE, center, central part, heart, nub, hub, middle, eye, focus, focal point, pivot, crux.

**nude** adjective *nude sunbathers* NAKED, stark naked, bare, unclothed, undressed, disrobed, stripped, unclad, au naturel, without a stitch on, in one's birthday suit, in the raw, in the altogether, in the buff; *informal* buck-naked, butt-naked, mother-naked. See note at NAKED. ANTONYM clothed.

**nudge** verb **1** *he nudged Ben* POKE, elbow, dig, prod, jog, jab.

**2** *the canoe nudged a bank* TOUCH, bump (against), push (against), run into.

**3** *we nudged them into action* PROMPT, encourage, stimulate, prod, galvanize.

**4** *unemployment was nudging 3,000,000* APPROACH, near, come close to, be verging on, border on.

▸ noun **1** *Maggie gave him a nudge* POKE, prod, jog, jab, push, dig (in the ribs).

**2** *after a nudge, she remembered Lillian* REMINDER, prompt, prompting, prod, encouragement.

**nudity** noun *there was one brief moment of nudity* NAKEDNESS, bareness, state of undress, undress; *informal* one's birthday suit.

**nugget** noun *a nugget of gold* | *doughy nuggets in the stew* LUMP, nub, chunk, piece, hunk, wad, gobbet; *informal* gob.

**nuisance** noun *I find these long journeys a nuisance* ANNOYANCE, inconvenience, bore, bother, irritation, problem, trouble, trial, burden; pest, plague, thorn in one's side/flesh; *informal* pain, pain in the neck, hassle, bind, drag, chore, aggravation, headache, nudnik. ANTONYM blessing.

**null** adjective *their marriage was declared null* INVALID, null and void, void; annulled, nullified, canceled, revoked. ANTONYM valid.

**nullify** verb **1** *they nullified the legislation* ANNUL, render null and void, void, invalidate; repeal, reverse, rescind, revoke, disallow, cancel, abolish; countermand, do away with, terminate, quash; *Law* vacate; *formal* abrogate. See note at VOID. ANTONYM ratify.

**2** *the costs would nullify any tax relief* CANCEL OUT, neutralize, negate, negative.

**numb** adjective *his fingers were numb* WITHOUT SENSATION, without feeling, numbed, benumbed, desensitized, insensible, senseless, unfeeling; anesthetized; dazed, stunned, stupefied, paralyzed, immobilized, frozen. ANTONYM sensitive.

▸ verb *the cold numbed her senses* DEADEN, benumb, desensitize, dull; anesthetize; daze, stupefy, paralyze, immobilize, freeze. ANTONYM sensitize.

**number** noun **1** *a whole number* NUMERAL, integer, figure, digit; character, symbol; decimal, unit; cardinal number, ordinal number.

**2** *a large number of complaints* AMOUNT, quantity; total, aggregate, tally; quota.

**3** *the wedding of one of their number* GROUP, company, crowd, circle, party, band, crew, set, gang.

**4** *the band performed another number* SONG, piece (of music), tune, track; routine, sketch, dance, act.

▸ verb **1** *visitors numbered more than two million* ADD UP TO, amount to, total, come to.

**2** *he numbers the fleet at a thousand* CALCULATE, count, total, compute, reckon, tally; assess, tot up; *formal* enumerate.

**3** *each paragraph is numbered* ASSIGN A NUMBER TO, mark with a number; itemize, enumerate.

**4** *he numbers her among his friends* INCLUDE, count, reckon, deem.

**5** *his days are numbered* LIMIT, restrict, fix.

PHRASES: **a number of** *she's collected a number of ashtrays* SEVERAL, various, quite a few, sundry.

**without number** *the nights I've worried about those kids is without number* COUNTLESS, innumerable, unlimited, endless, limitless, untold, numberless, uncountable, uncounted; numerous, many, multiple, manifold, legion.

**numberless** adjective *there are numberless questions to be answered* INNUMERABLE, countless, unlimited, endless, limitless, untold, uncountable, uncounted; numerous, many, multiple, manifold, legion; *informal* more —— than one can shake a stick at; *literary* myriad.

**numbing** adjective **1** *menthol has a numbing effect* DESENSITIZING, deadening, benumbing, anesthetic, anesthetizing; paralyzing.

**2** *numbing cold* FREEZING, raw, bitter, biting, arctic, icy.

**3** *numbing boredom* STUPEFYING, mind-numbing, boring, stultifying, soul-destroying; soporific.

**numeral** noun *your password should have at least one numeral* NUMBER, integer, figure, digit; character, symbol, unit.

**numerous** adjective *numerous studies have been published on the subject* MANY, very many, a lot of, scores of, countless, numberless, innumerable; several, quite a few, various; plenty of, copious, a quantity of, an abundance of, a profusion of, a multitude of; frequent; *informal* umpteen, lots of, loads of, masses of, stacks of, heaps of, bags of, tons of, oodles of, hundreds of, thousands of, millions of, gazillions of, more —— than one can shake a stick at; *literary* myriad. ANTONYM few.

**nuncio** noun *Father Mike was in a dither over the nuncio's visit* (PAPAL) AMBASSADOR, legate, envoy, messenger.

**nuptial** adjective *our nuptial vows* MATRIMONIAL, marital, marriage, wedding, conjugal, bridal; married, wedded; *literary* connubial; *Law* spousal.

**nuptials** plural noun *we attended the young duke's nuptials* WEDDING, wedding ceremony, marriage, union; *archaic* espousal.

**nurse** noun **1** *skilled nurses* CAREGIVER, RN, LPN, nurse practitioner, physician's assistant, health care worker; *informal* Florence Nightingale.

**2** *she had been his nurse in childhood* NANNY, nursemaid, governess, au pair, babysitter; wet nurse.

▸ verb **1** *they nursed smallpox patients* CARE FOR, take care of, look after, tend, minister to.

**2** *I nursed my sore finger* TREAT, medicate, tend; dress, bandage, soothe, doctor.

**3** *Rosa was nursing her baby* BREAST-FEED, suckle, feed; wet-nurse.

**4** *they nursed old grievances* HARBOR, foster, entertain, bear, have, hold (on to), cherish, cling to, retain.

**nurture** verb **1** *she nurtured her children into adulthood* BRING UP, care for, take care of, look after, tend, rear, raise, support, foster; parent, mother. ANTONYM neglect.

**2** *we nurtured these plants* CULTIVATE, grow, keep, tend.

**3** *he nurtured my love of art* ENCOURAGE, promote, stimulate, develop, foster, cultivate, boost, contribute to, assist, help, abet, strengthen, fuel. ANTONYM hinder.

▸ noun **1** *we are what nature and nurture have made us* UPBRINGING, rearing, raising, child care; training, education. ANTONYM nature.

**2** *the nurture of ideas* ENCOURAGEMENT, promotion, fostering, development, cultivation.

**nut** noun **1** *nuts in their shells* kernel, nutmeat.

**2** *informal* *some nut arrived at the office* MANIAC, lunatic, madman, madwoman; eccentric; *informal* loony, nutcase, fruitcake, head case, crank, crackpot, weirdo, screwball, crazy, dingbat, loon.

**3** *informal* *a health nut* ENTHUSIAST, fan, devotee, aficionado; *informal* freak, fiend, fanatic, addict, buff, bum. PHRASE: **off one's nut** *informal.* See MAD sense 1.

**nutrition** noun *the child was not receiving adequate nutrition* NOURISHMENT, nutriment, nutrients, sustenance, food; *informal* grub, chow, nosh, vittles; *literary* viands; *dated* victuals.

**nutritious** adjective *a nutritious fruit drink* NOURISHING, good for one, full of nutrients, nutritive, nutritional, wholesome, healthy, healthful, beneficial, sustaining.

**nuts** adjective *informal* **1** *they thought we were nuts.* See MAD sense 1.

**2** *he's* ***nuts about*** *her* INFATUATED WITH, devoted to, in love with, smitten with, enamored of, hot for, keen on; *informal* mad about, crazy about, nutty about, wild about, hooked on, gone on.

**nuts and bolts** plural noun *the nuts and bolts of running an airline* PRACTICAL DETAILS, fundamentals, basics, practicalities, essentials, mechanics, rudiments, ABCs; *informal* nitty-gritty, ins and outs, brass tacks, meat and potatoes.

**nuzzle** verb **1** *the horse nuzzled at her pocket* NUDGE, nose, prod, push, root.

**2** *she* ***nuzzled up to*** *her boyfriend* SNUGGLE UP TO, cuddle up to, nestle close to, embrace, hug.

**nymph** noun **1** *a nymph with winged sandals* SPRITE, sylph, spirit.

**2** *literary* *a slender nymph with brown eyes* GIRL, belle, nymphet, sylph, ingenue; young woman, young lady; *Scottish* lass; *literary* maid, maiden, damsel.

**oaf** noun *the oaf upstairs with his television on full blast* LOUT, boor, barbarian, Neanderthal, churl, bumpkin, yokel; FOOL, dolt, dullard; *informal* idiot, imbecile, moron, halfwit, cretin, ass, jackass, goon, yahoo, ape, baboon, clod, blockhead, meathead, meatball, bonehead, knucklehead, chucklehead, lamebrain, palooka, lug, bozo, boob, chowderhead, lummox, klutz, goofus, doofus, dork, turkey, dingbat; *Brit. informal* twit, nerk, git, yob; *archaic* lubber.

**oafish** adjective *his oafish brother* STUPID, foolish, idiotic, cretinous; UNGAINLY, loutish, awkward, clumsy, lumbering, apelike, cloddish, Neanderthal, uncouth, uncultured, boorish, rough, coarse, brutish, ill-mannered, unrefined, roughhewn; *informal* blockheaded, moronic, boneheaded, halfwitted, lamebrained, thickheaded; *archaic* lubberly.

**oasis** noun **1** *an oasis near Cairo* WATERING HOLE, watering place, waterhole, spring.

**2** *the park is an oasis filled with half a million flowers and thousands of lights* REFUGE, haven, retreat, sanctuary, sanctum, shelter, harbor, asylum.

**oath** noun **1** *an oath of allegiance* VOW, pledge, sworn statement, promise, avowal, affirmation, word, word of honor, bond, guarantee; *formal* troth.

**2** *he uttered a stream of oaths* SWEAR WORD, profanity, expletive, four-letter word, dirty word, obscenity, vulgarity, curse, malediction, blasphemy; *informal* cuss, cuss word; *formal* imprecation.

**obdurate** adjective *the brass were also obdurate in their opposition to having women in any combat positions* STUBBORN, obstinate, intransigent, inflexible, unyielding, unbending, pigheaded, bullheaded, mulish, stiff-necked; headstrong, unshakable, intractable, unpersuadable, immovable, inexorable, uncompromising, iron-willed, adamant, firm, determined. See note at STUBBORN. ANTONYMS malleable, tractable.

**obedience** noun *the party leadership wants blind obedience to their policies* COMPLIANCE, acquiescence, tractability, amenability; DUTIFULNESS, duty, deference, observance of the law/rules; SUBMISSIVENESS, submission, conformity, docility, tameness, subservience, obsequiousness, servility. ANTONYMS disobedience, rebellion.

**obedient** adjective *obviously, you want an obedient dog for security work* COMPLIANT, acquiescent, tractable, amenable; DUTIFUL, good, law-abiding, deferential, respectful, duteous, well trained, well disciplined, manageable, governable; DOCILE, tame, biddable, meek, passive, submissive, unresisting, yielding; malleable, pliable, pliant, subservient, obsequious, servile. ANTONYMS disobedient, rebellious.

THE RIGHT WORD **obedient; biddable; docile; dutiful; compliant**

Children and animals may be expected to obey, but nowadays **obedient** is seldom used to describe adult human beings without a suggestion that they are allowing someone else to assume too great a degree of authority (*are we to believe that Cinderella became the prince's demure, obedient wife?*). The critical note is stronger in **biddable**. A biddable person is excessively meek and ready to obey any instruction, without questioning either its wisdom or the authority of the person giving it (*he could barely think for herself, having been so biddable to his domineering parents*). **Docile** (from Latin *docilis* 'teachable') has similar implications, but in addition to unquestioning obedience it suggests a general reluctance to complain or rebel, even where such behavior would be justified (*employers depended on the regime for a cheap and docile workforce*). **Dutiful** may evoke a sneer, suggesting the virtuous, yet dull (*his dutiful niece spent most of her life caring for him*) or the perfunctory fulfillment of an obligation (*a dutiful postcard to his mother*). One of the oldest (and still living) meanings of **compliant** is 'reshaping under pressure' (*conversion of the gel to a much less compliant glass*). This helps to explain the principal modern sense of the adjective, '(excessively) disposed to agree with others or obey rules' (*compliant legislators loyally followed party policy*). In the computer age a further sense, 'technically compatible,' has developed (*the system is Windows compliant*).

**obeisance** noun **1** *he made a very formal, elaborate gesture of obeisance* RESPECT, homage, worship, adoration, reverence, veneration, honor, submission, deference. See note at HONOR.

**2** *he made a half-bow, half-curtsy, a sort of unisex obeisance* BOW, curtsy, bob, genuflection, salaam; *historical* kowtow.

**obelisk** noun *an obelisk marks the mass grave where Custer was buried* PILLAR, column, needle, shaft, monolith, monument.

**obese** adjective *a physician would describe her as a young* *obese white female* FAT, overweight, corpulent, gross, stout, fleshy, heavy, portly, plump, paunchy, potbellied, beer-bellied, broad in the beam, bulky, bloated, flabby, Falstaffian; *informal* porky, roly-poly, blubbery, pudgy, well-upholstered. ANTONYMS thin, skinny, emaciated.

**obesity** noun *businesses are developing programs to fight workers' obesity* FATNESS, corpulence, stoutness, portliness, plumpness, chubbiness, rotundity, flabbiness, grossness. ANTONYMS thinness, emaciation.

**obey** verb **1** *I was honor-bound to obey* DO WHAT SOMEONE SAYS, carry out someone's orders; SUBMIT TO, defer to, bow to, yield to, give in to.

**2** *he refused to obey the order* CARRY OUT, perform, act on, execute, discharge, implement, fulfill.

**3** *NRA activists point out that criminals don't obey gun laws* COMPLY WITH, adhere to, observe, abide by, act in accordance with, conform to, respect, follow, keep to, stick to.

**4** *she wants me to just obey and shut up* FOLLOW ORDERS, do as one's told, play it by the book, toe the line. ANTONYMS disobey, defy, ignore.

**obfuscate** verb **1** *mere rationalizations to obfuscate rather than clarify the real issue* OBSCURE, confuse, make unclear, blur, muddle, complicate, muddy, cloud, befog. ANTONYM clarify.

**2** *her work became more and more obfuscated by mathematics and jargon* BEWILDER, mystify, puzzle, perplex, confuse, baffle, confound, bemuse, befuddle, nonplus; *informal* flummox.

**obituary** noun *the local paper ran a full-page obituary* DEATH NOTICE, eulogy; *informal* obit; *rare* necrology.

**object** noun **1** *wooden objects* THING, article, item, device, gadget, entity; *informal* doodad, thingamajig, thingamabob, whatsit, whatchamacallit, thingy, doohickey, dingus.

**2** *he spent five years as the object of a frenzied manhunt* TARGET, butt, focus, recipient, victim.

**3** *the object was to let everyone have a voice in the decision* OBJECTIVE, aim, goal, target, purpose, end, plan; ambition, design, intent, intention, point, idea.

▸ verb *people attending the meeting* ***objected to*** *nearly every element of the new ordinance* PROTEST (AGAINST), lodge a protest against oppose, raise objections to, express disapproval of, take exception to, take issue with, take a stand against, argue against, quarrel with, condemn, draw the line at, demur at, disapprove of, mind, complain about, cavil at, quibble about; beg to differ with; *informal* kick up a fuss/stink about, kvetch about. ANTONYMS approve, accept.

**objection** noun *he lodged an official objection with the town council* PROTEST, protestation, demur, demurral, demurrer, complaint, expostulation, grievance, cavil, quibble; OPPOSITION, argument, counterargument, disagreement, disapproval, dissent; *informal* gripe, beef.

**objectionable** adjective *there is restricted access to objectionable material* UNPLEASANT, offensive, disagreeable, distasteful, displeasing, off-putting, undesirable, obnoxious, unacceptable; NASTY, disgusting, awful, terrible, dreadful, frightful, horrid, appalling, insufferable, intolerable, odious, vile, foul, unsavory, repulsive, repellent, repugnant, revolting, abhorrent, loathsome, hateful, detestable, reprehensible, deplorable; *informal* ghastly, horrible, beastly; *formal* exceptionable, rebarbative. ANTONYMS pleasant, agreeable.

**objective** adjective **1** *I was hoping to get an objective and pragmatic report* IMPARTIAL, unbiased, unprejudiced, nonpartisan, disinterested, neutral, uninvolved, evenhanded, equitable, fair, fair-minded, just, open-minded, dispassionate, detached, neutral. ANTONYMS biased, partial, prejudiced.

**2** *eight objective measurements to track student performance* FACTUAL, actual, real, empirical, evidence-based, verifiable. ANTONYM subjective.

▸ noun *you can't achieve your objectives unless people understand them* AIM, intention, purpose, target, goal, intent, object, end; idea, point, design, plan, ambition, aspiration, desire, hope.

**objectively** adverb *encourage people to look at the information objectively and see how it will affect them* IMPARTIALLY, without bias, without prejudice, evenhandedly, dispassionately, detachedly, equitably, fairly, justly, open-mindedly, with an open mind. ANTONYMS one-sidedly, with prejudice.

**objectivity** noun *the quest for total objectivity is unrealistic* IMPARTIALITY, absence/lack of bias, absence/lack of prejudice, fairness, fair-mindedness, neutrality, evenhandedness, justice, open-mindedness, disinterest, detachment, dispassion, neutrality.

**obligate** verb *signing the agreement does not obligate you to stay through the end of the program* OBLIGE, compel, commit, bind, require, constrain, force, impel.

**obligation** noun **1** *no obligation may be placed upon you without your consent* DUTY, commitment, responsibility moral imperative; FUNCTION, task, job, assignment, commission, burden, charge, onus, liability, accountability, requirement, debt; *literary* trust.

**2** *he felt an obligation to tip well* DUTY, compulsion, indebtedness; duress, necessity, pressure, constraint. PHRASE: **under (an) obligation** *the district attorney is under obligation to investigate | they don't understand that they are under obligation to intervene* BEHOLDEN, obliged, in someone's debt, indebted, obligated, compelled, duty-bound, honor-bound.

**obligatory** adjective *top hat and tails are obligatory for men* COMPULSORY, mandatory, prescribed, required, demanded, statutory, enforced, binding, incumbent; requisite, necessary, imperative, unavoidable, inescapable, essential. ANTONYMS optional, voluntary.

**oblige** verb **1** *it was impractical to oblige taxis to carry infant seats* REQUIRE, compel, bind, constrain, obligate, leave with no option but, force. See note at COMPEL.

**2** *she was kind enough to oblige* DO SOMEONE A FAVOR, accommodate, help, assist, serve; indulge, humor, gratify someone's wishes.

**obliging** adjective *he was obliging enough to carry all the bags* HELPFUL, accommodating, willing, cooperative, considerate, complaisant, agreeable, amenable, generous, kind, neighborly, hospitable, friendly, pleasant, good-natured, amiable, gracious, unselfish, civil, courteous, polite, decent. ANTONYMS inconsiderate, uncooperative.

**oblique** adjective **1** *an oblique line* SLANTING, slanted, sloping, at an angle, angled, diagonal, aslant, slant, slantwise, skew, askew, cater-cornered, kitty-corner. ANTONYM straight.

**2** *an oblique reference to an inside joke* INDIRECT, inexplicit, roundabout, circuitous, circumlocutory, implicit, implied, elliptical, evasive, backhanded. ANTONYMS direct, explicit.

**3** *an oblique glance* SIDELONG, sideways, furtive, covert, sly, surreptitious.

**obliquely** adverb **1** *was the rope, strung across this road obliquely, a real weapon or just a simpleminded booby trap?* DIAGONALLY, at an angle, slantwise, sideways, sidelong, aslant.

**2** *she was an embarrassment, someone who could only be spoken of obliquely* INDIRECTLY, in a roundabout way, not in so many words, circuitously, evasively.

**obliterate** verb **1** *I briefly contemplated trying to obliterate the logo with nail polish remover* ERASE, eradicate, expunge, efface, wipe out, blot out, rub out, block out, remove all traces of.

**2** *I want to see the super-turtle obliterate an entire Japanese district in under a minute* DESTROY, wipe out, annihilate, demolish, eliminate, decimate, liquidate, wipe off the face of the earth, wipe off the map; *informal* zap, nuke. ANTONYM create.

**3** *she slapped her puff over her face, trying to obliterate it with powder* OBSCURE, hide, conceal, blot out, block (out), cover, screen.

**oblivion** noun **1** *they drank themselves into oblivion* UNCONSCIOUSNESS, insensibility, a stupor, stupefaction, senselessness; a coma, a blackout; *literary* the waters of Lethe. ANTONYM consciousness.

**2** *luckily, he was able to rescue that design from oblivion* OBSCURITY, limbo, anonymity, nonexistence, nothingness, neglect, disregard. ANTONYM fame.

**oblivious** adjective ***oblivious to*** *the conversation around the table* | *utterly and happily* ***oblivious of*** *the effect he was having upon his audience* UNAWARE OF, unconscious of, heedless of, unmindful of, insensible of/to, unheeding of, ignorant of, incognizant of, blind to, deaf to, unsuspecting of, unobservant of; INSENSITIVE TO, unconcerned with, impervious to, unaffected by, indifferent to, *informal* clueless. ANTONYMS aware, conscious; sensitive.

**obloquy** noun **1** *he was able to control the press of New York City, so as to hold me up to obloquy* VILIFICATION, opprobrium, vituperation, condemnation, denunciation, abuse, criticism, censure, defamation, denigration, calumny, insults; *informal* flak; *formal* castigation, excoriation; *archaic* contumely. ANTONYM praise.

**2** *there is no moral obloquy connected with getting drunk in Japan* DISGRACE, dishonor, shame, discredit, stigma, humiliation, loss of face, ignominy, odium, opprobrium, disfavor, disrepute, ill repute, infamy, stain, notoriety, scandal. ANTONYM honor.

**obnoxious** adjective **1** *the gasoline-powered pump made an obnoxious racket* UNPLEASANT, disagreeable, nasty, distasteful, offensive, objectionable, unsavory, unpalatable, off-putting, awful, terrible, dreadful, frightful, revolting, repulsive, repellent, repugnant, disgusting, odious, vile, foul, abhorrent, loathsome, nauseating, sickening, hateful, insufferable, intolerable, detestable, abominable, despicable, contemptible; *informal* horrible, horrid, ghastly, gross, putrid, yucky, godawful, beastly, skanky; *literary* noisome. ANTONYMS delightful, fragrant.

**2** *I prayed I could express myself without being obnoxious* ANNOYING, tiresome, irritating; overbearing, bumptious; unpleasant, nasty; *informal* bratty, pesky. ANTONYMS pleasant, charming.

**obscene** adjective **1** *a vengeful lover sent obscene photos of his former girlfriend to her new partner* PORNOGRAPHIC, INDECENT, smutty, salacious, dirty, filthy, X-rated, explicit, lewd, rude, vulgar, coarse, crude, offensive, immoral, improper, impure, off-color, degenerate, depraved, debauched; lubricious, risqué, erotic, carnal, lascivious, licentious, bawdy; scatological, profane; *informal* blue, porn, porno, skin; *euphemistic* adult. ANTONYMS pure, clean, decent.

**2** *I was watching obscene amounts of daytime TV* SHOCKING, scandalous, vile, foul, atrocious, outrageous, heinous, odious, abhorrent, abominable, disgusting, hideous, repugnant, offensive, objectionable, repulsive, revolting, repellent, loathsome, nauseating, sickening, awful, dreadful, terrible, frightful.

**obscenity** noun **1** *the over-the-top obscenity of the musical interludes* INDECENCY, immorality, impropriety, salaciousness, smuttiness, smut, lewdness, impurity, crudeness, vulgarity, dirtiness, dirt, filth, coarseness, crudity; profanity; eroticism, carnality, lasciviousness, licentiousness.

**2** *he attacked, first with obscenities, and then with fists* EXPLETIVE, swear word, oath, profanity, curse, four-letter word, dirty word, blasphemy; *informal* cuss, cuss word; *formal* imprecation.

**3** *they claimed that nearly a third of UN member states practiced human rights obscenities* ATROCITY, (act of) brutality, (act of) cruelty, (act of) savagery, (act of) inhumanity, crime, evil.

**obscure** adjective **1** *the truth is that many aspects of a war's outcome remain obscure for years* UNCLEAR, uncertain, unknown, in doubt, doubtful, dubious, mysterious, hazy, vague, indeterminate, concealed, hidden. ANTONYMS clear, obvious.

**2** *obscure references to Proust* ABSTRUSE, recondite, arcane, esoteric; mystifying, puzzling, perplexing, baffling, ambiguous, cryptic, enigmatic, Delphic, oracular, oblique, opaque, elliptical, unintelligible, incomprehensible, impenetrable, unfathomable; *informal* as clear as mud. ANTONYMS clear, plain.

**3** *rumors from open-mouth radio shows and obscure web sites* LITTLE KNOWN, unknown, unheard of, unnoticed, undistinguished, unimportant, insignificant, inconsequential, minor, lowly; nameless, anonymous; unsung, unrecognized, forgotten. ANTONYMS famous, renowned.

**4** *an obscure shape* INDISTINCT, faint, vague, nebulous, ill-defined, unclear, blurred, blurry, misty, hazy; dark, dim, shadowy; *literary* tenebrous; *archaic* caliginous. ANTONYM distinct.

▸ verb **1** *a shy and abject manner obscured her prettiness* HIDE, conceal, cover, veil, shroud, screen, mask, cloak, cast a shadow over, shadow, block (out), obliterate, eclipse, darken; *literary* bedim, enshroud. ANTONYM reveal.

**2** *human rights are often obscured by the shadow of politics* CONFUSE, complicate, obfuscate, cloud, blur, muddy; muddy the waters of; *literary* befog, becloud. ANTONYMS illuminate, clarify.

THE RIGHT WORD **obscure; abstruse; recondite**

**Obscure** is the general term for something that is unclear or not easy to understand; **abstruse** and **recondite** are more formal terms. **Obscure** often expresses dissatisfaction at one's inability to identify something (*the causation of his mental disorder is obscure*), or, more critically, refers to something that's not sufficiently clearly expressed (*the law is too obscure to interpret correctlywe find it difficult to address your obscure complaints*). A reference to, say, "an obscure congressman" is a dismissive comment, suggesting that this is someone not only little known but perhaps deservedly so. **Abstruse** is more precise in its meaning—'difficult to understand'—and usually implies that the subject would be puzzling to most anyone (*reading her essays, one wonders if even she can understand her abstruse philosophy*). **Recondite** denotes topics that are known and understood by only a few experts: *recondite though their theme may be, they demonstrate that it is not without relevance*. There is often a critical suggestion that difficulty or obscurity has been deliberately sought out or magnified.

**obscurity** noun **1** *the novel plots Carlotta's rise from obscurity to stardom* INSIGNIFICANCE, inconspicuousness, unimportance, anonymity; limbo, twilight, oblivion. ANTONYM fame.

**2** *small-minded intellectuals who had accused him of obscurity* INCOMPREHENSIBILITY, impenetrability, unintelligibility, opacity; abstruseness, arcaneness, esotericism. ANTONYM clarity.

**3** *there may be obscurities but no answerless riddles* ENIGMA, puzzle, mystery, ambiguity.

**obsequies** plural noun *they left the sad obsequies to my men* FUNERAL RITES, funeral service, funeral, burial, interment, entombment, inhumation, last offices; *formal* exequies; *archaic* sepulture.

**obsequious** adjective *an elderly gentlemen surrounded by obsequious heirs* SERVILE, ingratiating, sycophantic, fawning, unctuous, oily, oleaginous, groveling, cringing, subservient, submissive, slavish; *informal* brown-nosing, bootlicking, smarmy; *vulgar slang* ass-kissing. ANTONYM domineering.

THE RIGHT WORD **obsequious, servile, slavish, subservient**

If you want to get ahead with your boss, you might trying being **obsequious**, which suggests an attitude of inferiority that may or may not be genuine, but that is assumed in order to placate a superior in hopes of getting what one wants (*a "goody two shoes" whose obsequious behavior made everyone in the class cringe*). While **subservient** may connote similar behavior, it is more often applied to those who are genuinely subordinate or dependent and act accordingly (*a timid, subservient child who was terrified of making a mistake*). **Servile** is a stronger and more negative term, suggesting a cringing submissiveness (*the dog's servile obedience to her master*). **Slavish**, suggesting the status or attitude of a slave, is often used to describe strict adherence to a set of rules or a code of conduct (*a slavish adherence to the rules of etiquette*).

**observable** adjective *that will certainly cause an observable change in the instrument reading* NOTICEABLE, visible, perceptible, perceivable, detectable, conspicuous, distinguishable, discernible, recognizable, evident, apparent, manifest, obvious, patent, palpable, overt, clear, distinct, plain, unmistakable. ANTONYM hidden.

**observance** noun **1** *elders responsible for the correct observance of sacred rites* COMPLIANCE WITH, adherence to, accordance with, respect for, observation of, obedience to; keeping of, obeying of, fulfillment of, following of, honoring of; *archaic* abidance by. ANTONYM disregard.

**2** *a Catholic calendar of saints' days and religious observances* RITE, ritual, ceremony, ceremonial, celebration, practice, service, office, festival, tradition, custom, convention, formality, form; *formal* praxis.

**observant** adjective **1** *the farmer whose weather eye has been usurped by the radio has become less observant* ALERT, sharp-eyed, sharp, eagle-eyed, hawk-eyed, having eyes like a hawk, watchful, heedful, aware; on the lookout, on the qui vive, on guard, attentive, vigilant, having one's eyes open/peeled; *informal* beady-eyed, not missing a trick, on the ball. ANTONYM inattentive.

**2** *observant Jews* PRACTICING, obedient, conforming, conformist; law-abiding, orthodox, devout.

**observation** noun **1** *the patient has been brought in for observation | whatever the reason, many people are irrationally afraid of snakes, and this makes for poor observation* MONITORING, watching, scrutiny, examination, inspection, survey, surveillance, consideration, study, review.

**2** *who was the recipient of that flattering observation?* REMARK, comment, statement, utterance, pronouncement, declaration; OPINION, impression, thought, reflection; *Law* obiter dictum.

**3** *the **observation of** the law* OBSERVANCE OF, compliance with, adherence to, respect for, obedience to, keeping of, obeying of, heeding of.

**observe** verb **1** *I observed this wheelchair dude in the vestibule waiting for me | other behavioral problems have been observed in our patient population* NOTICE, see, note, perceive, discern, detect, spot; *literary* espy, descry, behold. ANTONYM overlook.

**2** *I may not even observe them unawares* WATCH, look at, eye, contemplate, view, witness, survey, regard, keep an eye on, scrutinize, keep under observation, keep (a) watch on, keep under surveillance, monitor, check out, keep a weather eye on, keep tabs on, spy on; *informal* eyeball.

**3** *She'd observed that the Christmas tree looked underdecorated* REMARK, comment, say, mention, note, declare, announce, state, pronounce; *formal* opine.

**4** *both countries agreed to observe the cease-fire* COMPLY WITH, abide by, keep, obey, adhere to, heed, honor, be heedful of, respect, follow, consent to, acquiesce in, accept, fulfill. ANTONYMS disregard, ignore.

**5** *this year he observed the anniversary at a ceremony on the South Lawn* COMMEMORATE, mark, keep, memorialize, solemnize, remember, recognize, celebrate.

**observer** noun **1** *a casual observer might not have noticed* SPECTATOR, onlooker, watcher, looker-on, fly on the wall, viewer, witness, eyewitness, bystander; *informal* rubberneck; *literary* beholder.

**2** *industry observers expect the deal to be finalized today* COMMENTATOR, reporter; monitor.

**obsess** verb *being thin is obsessing her* PREOCCUPY, be uppermost in someone's mind, prey on someone's mind, prey on, possess, haunt, consume, plague, torment, hound, bedevil, beset, take control of, control, take over, have a hold on, rule, eat up, have a grip on, grip.PHRASE: **be obsessed** ***he was obsessed with*** *his roommate's sister | **I am obsessed by** a desire to win* BE FIXATED ON/UPON, be preoccupied with, be possessed by, be consumed with/by (thoughts of), have an obsession with; be infatuated with, be besotted with, be smitten with; *informal* have a thing about/for, be hung up about/on, have it bad for.

**obsession** noun *that new car has become his obsession* FIXATION, ruling/consuming passion, passion, mania, idée fixe, compulsion, preoccupation, infatuation, addiction, fetish, craze, hobbyhorse; phobia, complex, neurosis; *informal* a bee in one's bonnet, hang-up, thing.

**obsessive** adjective *her obsessive behavior includes relentless tidying* ALL-CONSUMING, consuming, compulsive, controlling, obsessional, fanatic, fanatical, neurotic, excessive, overkeen, besetting, tormenting, inescapable, pathological.

**obsolescent** adjective *much of the business etiquette our parents knew is obsolescent* DYING OUT, on the decline, declining, waning, on the wane, disappearing, past its prime, aging, moribund, on its last legs, old-fashioned, outmoded, downlevel, on the way out; obsolete, outdated, out of date, behind the times.

**obsolete** adjective *most of the machinery in their Somerville plant is obsolete | obsolete hairstyles* OUTDATED, out of date, outmoded, old-fashioned, démodé, passé, out of fashion; no longer in use, disused, fallen into disuse, behind the times, superannuated, outworn, antiquated, antediluvian, anachronistic, discontinued, old, dated, archaic, ancient, fossilized, extinct, defunct, dead, bygone, out; *informal* prehistoric. See note at OLD. ANTONYMS cutting-edge, the latest, modern.

**obstacle** noun *blindness is not the worst obstacle I've had to overcome* BARRIER, hurdle, stumbling block, obstruction, bar, block, impediment, hindrance, snag, catch, drawback, hitch, handicap, deterrent, complication, difficulty, problem, disadvantage, curb, check; *informal* fly in the ointment, monkey wrench (in the works). ANTONYMS advantage, aid.

**obstinacy** noun *Zach's obstinacy contributed to his unfavorable performance evaluation* STUBBORNNESS, inflexibility, intransigence, intractability, obduracy, mulishness, pigheadedness, willfulness, contrariness, perversity, recalcitrance, refractoriness, implacability, rigidity, uncooperativeness; persistence, tenacity, tenaciousness, pertinacity, doggedness, single-mindedness. ANTONYM flexibility.

**obstinate** adjective *it's unusual for two such obstinate people to have a happy marriage* STUBBORN, unyielding, inflexible, unbending, intransigent, intractable, obdurate, mulish, bullheaded, stubborn as a mule, pigheaded, self-willed, strong-willed, headstrong, willful, contrary, perverse, recalcitrant, refractory, uncooperative, unmanageable, stiff-necked, rigid, uncompromising, implacable, unrelenting, immovable, unshakable; persistent, tenacious, pertinacious, dogged, single-minded. See note at STUBBORN. ANTONYM compliant.

**obstreperous** adjective *the hotel manager was accustomed to dealing with obstreperous guests* UNRULY, unmanageable, disorderly, undisciplined, uncontrollable, rowdy, disruptive, truculent, difficult, refractory, rebellious, mutinous, riotous, out of control, wild, turbulent, uproarious, boisterous; noisy, loud, clamorous, raucous, vociferous; *informal* rambunctious. See note at VOCIFEROUS. ANTONYMS quiet, restrained.

**obstruct** verb **1** *ensure that the air vents are not obstructed* BLOCK (UP), clog (up), get in the way of, jam (up), cut off, shut off, bung up, choke, dam up; barricade, bar; *technical* occlude. ANTONYM clear.

**2** *he was charged with obstructing traffic* HOLD UP, bring to a standstill, stop, halt, block.

**3** *fears that the regime would obstruct the distribution of food* IMPEDE, hinder, interfere with, hamper, hobble, block, interrupt, hold up, stand in the way of, frustrate, thwart, balk, inhibit, hamstring, sabotage; slow down, retard, delay, stonewall, stall, stop, halt, stay, restrict, limit, curb, put a brake on, bridle; *informal* stymie. See note at HINDER. ANTONYMS facilitate, further.

**obstruction** noun *wealthy property owners have created one obstruction after another to undermine the low-income housing project* OBSTACLE, barrier, stumbling block, hurdle, bar, block, impediment, hindrance, snag, difficulty, catch, drawback, hitch, handicap, deterrent, curb, check, restriction; blockage, stoppage, congestion, bottleneck, holdup, jam;

*Medicine* occlusion; *informal* fly in the ointment, monkey wrench (in the works).

**obstructive** adjective *he pursued his dreams of being a musician despite the efforts of his obstructive parents* UNHELPFUL, uncooperative, unsupportive, awkward, difficult, unaccommodating, disobliging, perverse, contrary; *archaic* froward, contrarious. ANTONYMS helpful, supportive.

**obtain** verb **1** *the newspaper obtained a copy of the letter* GET, acquire, come by, secure, procure, come into the possession of, pick up, be given; gain, earn, achieve, attain; *informal* get hold of, get/lay one's hands on, get one's mitts on, land, net. See note at GET. ANTONYMS relinquish, lose.

**2** *formal rules obtaining in other jurisdictions* PREVAIL, be in force, apply, exist, be in use, be in effect, stand, hold, be the case.

**obtainable** adjective *use dried herbs only when fresh ones are not obtainable* AVAILABLE, to be had, in circulation, on the market, in season, at one's disposal, at hand, attainable, procurable, accessible, realizable, gettable; *informal* up for grabs, on tap, get-at-able.

**obtrusive** adjective *a car dealership on this stretch of road would be too obtrusive | she wears the most obtrusive outfits* CONSPICUOUS, prominent, noticeable, obvious, unmistakable; intrusive, out of place; bold, loud, showy, gaudy, garish, flashy; *informal* sticking/standing out like a sore thumb. See note at IMPERTINENT. ANTONYMS unobtrusive, inconspicuous.

**obtuse** adjective *he frustrated his teachers by pretending to be obtuse* STUPID, slow-witted, slow, dull-witted, unintelligent, ignorant, simpleminded, witless; insensitive, imperceptive, uncomprehending; *informal* dim, dimwitted, dense, dumb, slow on the uptake, halfwitted, brain-dead, moronic, cretinous, thick, dopey, lamebrained, dumb-ass, dead from the neck up, boneheaded, chowderheaded. See note at STUPID. ANTONYMS clever, astute.

**obvious** adjective *it's obvious that they don't get along | her intentions are obvious* CLEAR, crystal clear, plain, plain to see, evident, apparent, manifest, patent, conspicuous, pronounced, transparent, palpable, prominent, marked, decided, distinct, noticeable, unmissable, perceptible, visible, discernible; unmistakable, indisputable, self-evident, incontrovertible, incontestable, undeniable, beyond doubt, beyond question, as clear as day, staring someone in the face; overt, open, undisguised, unconcealed, frank, glaring, blatant, written all over someone; *informal* as plain as the nose on one's face, sticking/standing out like a sore thumb, right under one's nose. ANTONYMS imperceptible, obscure.

**obviously** adverb *they were obviously thrilled to hear your good news | obviously, I had forgotten her name* CLEARLY, evidently, plainly, patently, visibly, discernibly, manifestly, noticeably; unmistakably, undeniably, incontrovertibly, demonstrably, unquestionably, indubitably, undoubtedly, without doubt, doubtless; of course, naturally, needless to say, it goes without saying. See note at CLEARLY. ANTONYM perhaps.

**occasion** noun **1** *a previous occasion* TIME, instance, moment, juncture, point; event, occurrence, affair, incident, episode, experience; situation, case, circumstance.

**2** *a family occasion* SOCIAL EVENT, event, affair, function, celebration, party, get-together, gathering; *informal* do, bash.

**3** *I doubt if the occasion will arise* OPPORTUNITY, right moment, opportune time, chance, opening, window.

**4** *it's the first time I've had occasion to complain* REASON, cause, call, grounds, justification, need, motive, inducement.

▸ verb *her situation occasioned a good deal of sympathy* CAUSE, give rise to, bring about, result in, lead to, prompt, elicit, call forth, evoke, make for, produce, create, arouse, generate, engender, precipitate, provoke, stir up, inspire, spark (off), trigger; *literary* beget.

PHRASE: **on occasion.** See OCCASIONALLY.

**occasional** adjective *the admiral made occasional appearances on board our ship* INFREQUENT, intermittent, irregular, sporadic, odd, random; periodic; uncommon, rare, isolated, few and far between, sometime. ANTONYMS regular, frequent.

**occasionally** adverb *I occasionally have wine with dinner* SOMETIMES, from time to time, (every) now and then, (every) now and again, at times, every so often, (every) once in a while, on occasion; periodically, at intervals; irregularly, sporadically, infrequently, intermittently, on and off, off and on. ANTONYMS often, frequently.

**occult** noun *his interest in **the occult*** THE SUPERNATURAL, the paranormal, supernaturalism, magic, black magic, witchcraft, sorcery, necromancy, wizardry, the black arts, occultism, diabolism, devil worship, devilry, voodoo, hoodoo, white magic, witchery, mysticism; *rare* theurgy.

▸ adjective **1** *occult powers* SUPERNATURAL, magic, magical, mystical, mystic, psychic, preternatural, paranormal transcendental; Kabbalistic, hermetic.

**2** *the typically occult language of the time* ESOTERIC, arcane, recondite, abstruse, secret; obscure, incomprehensible, impenetrable, puzzling, perplexing, mystifying, mysterious, enigmatic.

**occupancy** noun *our occupancy is temporary* OCCUPATION, tenancy, tenure, residence, residency, inhabitation, habitation, living, lease, holding, possession; *formal* dwelling.

**occupant** noun **1** *the occupants of the houses* RESIDENT, inhabitant, owner, householder, tenant, renter, leaseholder, lessee; addressee, occupier; *formal* dweller.

**2** *the first occupant of the post* INCUMBENT, holder.

**occupation** noun **1** *his father's occupation* JOB, profession, work, line of work, trade, employment, position, post, situation, business, career, field, métier, vocation, calling, craft.

**2** *her leisure occupations* PASTIME, activity, hobby, pursuit, interest, entertainment, recreation, amusement, diversion, divertissement.

**3** *a property suitable for occupation by seniors* RESIDENCE, residency, habitation, inhabitation, occupancy, tenancy, tenure, lease, living in, possession; *formal* dwelling.

**4** *the Roman occupation of Britain* CONQUEST, capture, invasion, seizure, takeover, annexation, overrunning, subjugation, subjection, appropriation; COLONIZATION, rule, control, possession, suzerainty.

**occupational** adjective *occupational hazards | occupational choices* JOB-RELATED, work, professional, vocational, employment, business, career.

**occupied** adjective **1** *tasks that kept her occupied all day* BUSY, engaged, working, at work, active; immersed, preoccupied, absorbed, engrossed; *informal* tied up, wrapped up, hard at it. ANTONYM idle.

**2** *all the tables were occupied* IN USE, full, engaged, taken, unavailable. ANTONYMS available, empty, free.

**3** *only two of the apartments are occupied* INHABITED, lived-in, tenanted, settled. ANTONYMS vacant, empty.

**occupy** verb **1** *Carol occupied the basement apartment* LIVE IN, inhabit, be the tenant of, lodge in; move into, take up residence in, make one's home in; people, populate, settle; *formal* reside in, dwell in.

**2** *two windows occupied almost the whole of the end wall* TAKE UP, fill, fill up, cover, use up.

**3** *he occupies a senior post at the firm* HOLD, fill, be in, have, hold down.

**4** *I need something to occupy my mind* ENGAGE, busy, employ, distract, absorb, engross, preoccupy, hold, interest, involve, entertain, amuse, divert.

**5** *the region was occupied by Soviet troops* CAPTURE, seize, take possession of, conquer; invade, overrun; take over, garrison, hold, annex, subjugate, colonize.

**occur** verb **1** *the accident occurred at about 3:30* HAPPEN, take place, come about, transpire, materialize, arise, crop up; *informal* go down; *literary* come to pass, befall, betide; *formal* eventuate. See note at HAPPEN.

**2** *the disease occurs chiefly in tropical climates* BE FOUND, be present, exist, appear, prevail, present itself, manifest itself, turn up.

**3** *an idea occurred to her* ENTER ONE'S HEAD/MIND, cross one's mind, come to mind, spring to mind, strike one, hit one, dawn on one, suggest itself, present itself.

**occurrence** noun **1** *vandalism used to be a rare occurrence* EVENT, incident, happening, phenomenon, affair, matter, circumstance.

**2** *the occurrence of cancer increases with age* EXISTENCE, instance, appearance, manifestation, materialization, development; frequency, incidence, rate, prevalence; *Statistics* distribution.

**odd** adjective **1** *an odd man* STRANGE, peculiar, weird, queer, funny, bizarre, abnormal, eccentric, unusual, unconventional, outlandish, quirky, zany; *informal* wacky, kooky, screwy, freaky, oddball, offbeat, off the wall, out there. ANTONYMS normal, conventional.

**2** *quite a few odd things had happened* STRANGE, unusual, peculiar, funny, curious, bizarre, weird, uncanny, queer, outré, unexpected, unfamiliar, abnormal, atypical, anomalous, different, out of the ordinary, out of the way, exceptional, rare, extraordinary, remarkable, puzzling, mystifying, mysterious, perplexing, baffling, unaccountable, uncommon, irregular, singular, deviant, aberrant, freak, freakish; *informal* fishy, freaky. ANTONYMS ordinary, usual.

**3** *we have the odd drink together | he does odd jobs for friends* OCCASIONAL, casual, irregular, isolated, random, sporadic, periodic; miscellaneous, various, varied, sundry. ANTONYMS regular, scheduled.

**4** *odd socks* MISMATCHED, unmatched, unpaired; single, lone, solitary, extra, surplus, leftover, remaining.

**5** *when you've got an odd ten minutes, stop by my office* SPARE, free, available, unoccupied; between appointments, between engagements. PHRASE: **odd man out** *no matter what our group planned to do over school vacations, Cassidy was always odd man out* OUTSIDER, exception, oddity, nonconformist, maverick, individualist, misfit, fish out of water, square peg in a round hole.

**oddity** noun **1** *she was regarded as a bit of an oddity* ECCENTRIC, misfit, square peg in a round hole, maverick, nonconformist, odd one, rare bird, crank; *informal* character, oddball, weirdo, crackpot, nut, freak, screwball, kook, queer/odd fish, queer/odd duck. ANTONYMS conformist, average Joe.

**2** *his work remains an oddity in some respects* ANOMALY, aberration, curiosity, rarity.

**3** *there was a real oddity about their artwork* STRANGENESS, peculiarity, oddness, weirdness, bizarreness, eccentricity, queerness, unconventionality, outlandishness, *informal* wackiness, kookiness.

**4** *the oddities of human nature* PECULIARITY, idiosyncrasy, eccentricity, quirk, irregularity, twist.

**odds** plural noun **1** ***odds are*** *that he is no longer alive* THE LIKELIHOOD IS, the probability is, chances are, there's a good chance.

**2** *the odds are in our favor | against all odds* ADVANTAGE, edge; superiority, supremacy, ascendancy. PHRASES: **at odds 1** *Duncan and Eliza have been at odds all week* IN CONFLICT, in disagreement, on bad terms, at cross purposes, at loggerheads, quarreling, arguing, on the outs, at daggers drawn, at each other's throats.

**2** *your behavior is* ***at odds with*** *the interests of the company* AT VARIANCE WITH, not in keeping with, out of keeping with, out of line with, in opposition to, conflicting with, contrary to, incompatible with, inconsistent with, irreconcilable with.

**odds and ends** BITS AND PIECES, bits, pieces, stuff, paraphernalia, things, sundries, miscellanea, bric-a-brac, knickknacks, oddments, junk.

**odious** adjective *the odious procedures of the military government | the dumpsite was especially odious in summer* REVOLT-

ING, repulsive, repellent, repugnant, disgusting, offensive, objectionable, vile, foul, abhorrent, loathsome, nauseating, sickening, hateful, detestable, execrable, abominable, monstrous, appalling, reprehensible, deplorable, insufferable, intolerable, despicable, contemptible, unspeakable, atrocious, awful, terrible, dreadful, frightful, obnoxious, unsavory, unpalatable, unpleasant, disagreeable, nasty, noisome, distasteful; *informal* ghastly, horrible, horrid, gross, godawful; beastly. ANTONYMS delightful, pleasant.

**odium** noun *during the trial, he sensed his family's distrust and odium* DISGUST, abhorrence, repugnance, revulsion, loathing, detestation, hatred, hate, obloquy, dislike, distaste, disfavor, antipathy, animosity, animus, enmity, hostility, contempt; disgrace, shame, opprobrium, discredit, dishonor. ANTONYM approval.

**odor** noun **1** *an odor of sweat* SMELL, stench, stink, reek, whiff, fetor; *informal* funk; *literary* miasma.

**2** *the pleasing odor of fresh-roasted coffee* AROMA, smell, scent, fragrance, bouquet, perfume. See note at SMELL.

**3** *an odor of suspicion* ATMOSPHERE, air, aura, quality, flavor, savor, hint, suggestion, impression, whiff.

**odyssey** noun *Magellan's great odyssey* | *the book details her odyssey from housewife to world leader* JOURNEY, voyage, trek, travels, quest, crusade, pilgrimage, wandering, journeying; *archaic* peregrination.

**off** adverb **1** *Kate's off today* AWAY, absent, out, unavailable, not at work, off duty, on leave, on vacation; free, at leisure; *Brit.* on holiday. ANTONYMS in, at work, working.

**2** *the game's off* CANCELED, postponed, called off, shelved. ANTONYM on.

▸ adjective **1** *the fish was a bit off* ROTTEN, bad, stale, moldy, sour, rancid, turned, spoiled, putrid, putrescent; (of beer) skunky. ANTONYM fresh.

**2** *informal I felt decidedly off* UNWELL, ill, out of sorts, not oneself, sick, indisposed, bad; *informal* under the weather, not up to par, lousy, crummy; *vulgar slang* crappy. ANTONYM well.

PHRASE: **off and on** *I still play tennis, but only off and on* PERIODICALLY, at intervals, on and off, (every) once in a while, every so often, (every) now and then/again, from time to time, occasionally, sometimes, intermittently, irregularly. ANTONYM regularly.

**offbeat** adjective *informal an offbeat suggestion* | *offbeat clothes* UNCONVENTIONAL, unorthodox, unusual, eccentric, idiosyncratic, outré, strange, bizarre, weird, peculiar, odd, freakish, outlandish, out of the ordinary, Bohemian, alternative, zany, quirky; *informal* wacky, freaky, way-out, off the wall, kooky, oddball. ANTONYMS conventional, ordinary.

**off-color** adjective *off-color jokes* SMUTTY, dirty, rude, crude, filthy, suggestive, indecent, indelicate, risqué, racy, bawdy, naughty, blue, vulgar, ribald, broad, salacious, coarse, obscene; *informal* raunchy; *euphemistic* adult.

**offend** verb **1** *I'm sorry if I offended him* HURT SOMEONE'S FEELINGS, give offense to, affront, displease, upset, distress, hurt, wound; annoy, anger, exasperate, irritate, vex, pique, gall, irk, nettle, ruffle someone's feathers, tread on someone's toes; rub the wrong way; *informal* rile, rattle, peeve, needle, miff, put someone's nose out of joint, put someone's back up; *vulgar slang* piss off.

**2** *the smell of cigarette smoke offended him* DISPLEASE, be distasteful to, be disagreeable to, be offensive to, disgust, repel, revolt, sicken, nauseate, be repugnant to; *informal* turn off, gross out. ANTONYMS please, delight.

**3** *criminals who offend again and again* BREAK THE LAW, commit a crime, do wrong, sin, go astray, transgress; *archaic* trespass.

**offended** adjective *he was offended because she had forgotten their anniversary* UPSET, INSULTED, affronted, aggrieved, displeased, hurt, wounded, disgruntled, put out, annoyed, angry, cross, exasperated, indignant, irritated, piqued, vexed, irked, stung, galled, nettled, resentful, in a huff, huffy, in high dudgeon; *informal* riled, miffed, peeved, aggravated, sore, teed off, ticked off; *vulgar slang* pissed off. ANTONYM pleased.

**offender** noun *my client is not the offender in this case* WRONGDOER, CRIMINAL, lawbreaker, miscreant, malefactor, felon, delinquent, culprit, guilty party, outlaw, sinner, transgressor; *Law* malfeasant.

**offense** noun **1** *he denied having committed any offense* CRIME, illegal/unlawful act, misdemeanor, breach of the law, felony, wrongdoing, wrong, misdeed, peccadillo, sin, transgression, infringement; *Law* malfeasance; *informal* no-no; *archaic* trespass; *rare* malefaction. See note at SIN.

**2** *an offense to basic justice* AFFRONT, slap in the face, insult, outrage, violation, slight.

**3** *I do not want to cause offense* ANNOYANCE, anger, resentment, indignation, irritation, exasperation, wrath, displeasure, hard/bad/ill feelings, disgruntlement, pique, vexation, animosity, antipathy.

**4** *planning our next offense* ATTACK, offensive, assault, onslaught, invasion, incursion, foray, sortie. PHRASE: **take offense** *his jokes were very insulting, and many of us took offense* BE/FEEL OFFENDED, take exception, take something personally, feel affronted, be/feel resentful, take something amiss, take umbrage, be/get/feel upset, be/get/feel annoyed, be/get/feel angry, get into a huff.

**offensive** adjective **1** *offensive remarks* INSULTING, insolent, derogatory, disrespectful, hurtful, wounding, abusive; annoying, exasperating, irritating, galling, provocative, outrageous; rude, impertinent, discourteous, uncivil, impolite; crude, vulgar, coarse, improper, indecent; *formal* exceptionable. ANTONYMS complimentary, polite, courteous.

**2** *an offensive smell* UNPLEASANT, disagreeable, nasty, distasteful, displeasing, objectionable, off-putting, awful, terrible, dreadful, frightful, obnoxious, abominable, disgusting, repulsive, repellent, repugnant, revolting, abhorrent, loathsome, detestable, odious, vile, foul, sickening, nauseating; *informal* ghastly, horrible, horrid, gross, putrid, godawful, beastly; *literary* noisome, mephitic. ANTONYMS pleasant, delightful.

**3** *an offensive air strike* HOSTILE, attacking, aggressive, invading, incursive, combative, belligerent, on the attack. ANTONYM defensive.

▸ noun *a military offensive* ATTACK, assault, onslaught, drive, invasion, push, thrust, charge, sortie, sally, foray, raid, incursion, offense, blitz, campaign. PHRASE: **take the offensive** *our fleet will take the offensive within the next 48 hours* LAUNCH AN ATTACK, begin to attack, attack first, strike the first blow.

THE RIGHT WORD **offensive, abhorrent, abominable, detestable, odious, repugnant**

Looking for just the right word to express your dislike, distaste, disgust, or aversion to something? **Offensive** is a relatively mild adjective, used to describe anyone or anything that is unpleasant or disagreeable (*she found his remarks offensive; the offensive sight of garbage piled in the alley*). If you want to express strong dislike for someone or something that deserves to be disliked, use **detestable** (*a detestable man who never had a kind word for anyone*). If something is so offensive that it provokes a physical as well as a moral or intellectual response, use **odious** (*the odious treatment of women during the war in Bosnia*), and if you instinctively draw back from it, use **repugnant** (*the very thought of piercing one's nose was repugnant to her*). If your repugnance is extreme, go one step further and use **abhorrent** (*an abhorrent act that could not go unpunished*). Persons and things that are truly loathsome or terrifying can be called **abominable** (*an abominable act of desecration; the abominable snowman*), although this word is often used as an overstatement to mean "awful" (*abominable taste in clothes*).

**offer** verb **1** *Chris offered another suggestion* PUT FORWARD, proffer, provide, give, present, come up with, suggest, extend, recommend, propose, advance, submit, tender, render. ANTONYMS withdraw, withhold.

**2** *she offered to help | if you're looking for assistance, I'm offering* VOLUNTEER, volunteer one's services, be at someone's disposal, be at someone's service, make oneself available, step/come forward.

**3** *the product is offered at a competitive price* PUT UP FOR SALE, put on the market, sell, market, make available, put under the gavel/hammer; *Law* vend.

**4** *he offered $200* BID, tender, put in a bid of, put in an offer of.

**5** *a job offering good career prospects* PROVIDE, afford, supply, give, furnish, present, purvey, hold out.

**6** *she offered no resistance* ATTEMPT, try, give, show, express; *formal* essay.

**7** *birds were offered to the gods* SACRIFICE, offer up, immolate, give.

▸ noun **1** *a job offer | offers of help* PROPOSAL, proposition, suggestion, submission, approach, overture; *literary* proffer.

**2** *the highest offer* BID, tender, bidding price.

**offering** noun **1** *you may place offerings in the basket* CONTRIBUTION, donation, gift, present, handout, charity; *formal* benefaction; *historical* alms.

**2** *many offerings were made to the goddess* SACRIFICE, oblation, burnt offering, immolation, libation; peace offering, sin offering; *Hinduism* prasad, puja; *Judaism* Omer.

**offhand** adjective *an offhand manner* CASUAL, careless, uninterested, unconcerned, indifferent, cool, nonchalant, blasé, aloof, insouciant, cavalier, glib, perfunctory, cursory, unceremonious, ungracious, dismissive, discourteous, uncivil, impolite, terse, abrupt, curt; *informal* couldn't-care-less, take-it-or-leave-it.

▸ adverb *I can't think of a better answer offhand* ON THE SPUR OF THE MOMENT, without preparation, without consideration, extempore, impromptu, ad lib; extemporaneously, spontaneously; *Latin* ad libitum *informal* off the cuff, off the top of one's head, just like that. See note at SPONTANEOUS.

**office** noun **1** *her office on Union Street* PLACE OF WORK, place of business, workplace; headquarters, base; workroom, studio, workspace, cubicle.

**2** *the newspaper's Paris office* BRANCH, division, section, bureau, department; agency.

**3** *he assumed the office of mayor* POST, position, appointment, job, occupation, role, situation, station, function, capacity.

**4** *he was saved by the good* ***offices*** *of his uncle* ASSISTANCE, help, aid, services, intervention, intercession, mediation, agency, support, backing, patronage, auspices, aegis.

**5** *the offices of a nurse* DUTY, job, task, chore, obligation, assignment, responsibility, charge, commission.

**officer** noun **1** *an officer in the army* MILITARY OFFICER, commissioned officer, noncommissioned officer, NCO, commanding officer, CO.

**2** *all the officers in this precinct carry guns* POLICE OFFICER, policeman, policewoman, officer of the law, law-enforcement officer/agent, peace officer, patrolman, trooper; *informal* cop, copper, flatfoot.

**3** *the officers of the society* OFFICIAL, officeholder, committee member, board member; public servant, administrator, executive, functionary, bureaucrat; *derogatory* apparatchik.

**4** *officers of the court* REPRESENTATIVE, deputy, agent, envoy.

**official** adjective **1** *an official inquiry* AUTHORIZED, approved, validated, authenticated, certified, accredited, endorsed, sanctioned, licensed, recognized, accepted, legitimate, legal, lawful, valid, bona fide, proper, ex cathedra; *informal* kosher. ANTONYMS unofficial, unauthorized.

**2** *an official function* CEREMONIAL, formal, solemn, ceremonious; bureaucratic; *informal* stuffed-shirt. See note at OFFICIOUS. ANTONYM informal.

▸ noun *a union official* OFFICER, officeholder, administrator, executive, appointee, functionary; bureaucrat, mandarin; representative, agent; *derogatory* apparatchik.

**officiate** verb **1** *he officiated the game* PRESIDE OVER, be in charge of, take charge of, direct, head (up); oversee, superintend, supervise, conduct, run; referee, umpire, judge, adjudicate; emcee.

2 *Father Buckley* ***officiated at*** *the wedding service* CONDUCT, perform, celebrate, solemnize.

**officious** adjective *I try to avoid their officious salesclerks* SELF-IMPORTANT, bumptious, self-assertive, overbearing, overzealous, domineering, opinionated, interfering, intrusive, meddlesome, meddling; *informal* pushy, bossy. ANTONYM self-effacing.

**offing** PHRASE: **in the offing** *I knew that a significant change in my life was in the offing* ON THE WAY, coming (soon), (close) at hand, near, imminent, in prospect, on the horizon, in the wings, just around the corner, in the air, in the wind, brewing, upcoming, forthcoming; bound to happen, likely to happen; *informal* in the cards, coming down the pike.

**offload** verb 1 *the cargo was being offloaded* UNLOAD, remove, empty (out), tip (out); *archaic* unlade.

2 *he offloaded 5,000 shares* DISPOSE OF, dump, jettison, get rid of, transfer, shift; palm off, foist; *Brit.* fob off.

**off-putting** adjective 1 *an off-putting aroma* UNPLEASANT, unappealing, uninviting, unattractive, disagreeable, repellent, offensive, distasteful, unsavory, unpalatable, unappetizing, objectionable, nasty, disgusting; *informal* horrid, horrible.

2 *her manner was off-putting* UNINVITING, discouraging, disheartening, demoralizing, dispiriting, daunting, disconcerting, unnerving, unsettling; *formal* rebarbative.

**offset** verb *we were not able to offset our losses over the last quarter* COUNTERBALANCE, balance (out), cancel (out), even out/up, counteract, countervail, neutralize, compensate for, make up for, make good, redeem, indemnify; atone for, make amends for, make restitution for.

**offshoot** noun 1 *the plant's offshoots* SIDE SHOOT, shoot, sucker, tendril, runner, scion, slip, offset, stolon; twig, branch, bough, limb.

2 *an offshoot of Cromwell's line* DESCENDANT, scion, relation.

3 *rap music began as an underground offshoot of disco* OUTCOME, result, (side) effect, corollary, consequence, upshot, product, by-product, spin-off, development, outgrowth, fallout.

4 *the company now controls several offshoots* SUBSIDIARY, branch, adjunct, derivative.

**offspring** noun (usually as plural) *his offspring gathered to mourn his passing* CHILDREN, sons and daughters, progeny, family, youngsters, babies, brood; descendants, heirs, successors, scions; *Law* issue; *informal* kids; *derogatory* spawn; *archaic* fruit of one's loins.

**often** adverb *we go there often* FREQUENTLY, many times, many a time, on many/numerous occasions, a lot, as often as not, repeatedly, again and again, time and (time) again; all the time, regularly, routinely, usually, habitually, commonly, generally, in many cases/instances, ordinarily, oftentimes, recurrently; *informal* lots; *literary* oft, ofttimes. ANTONYMS seldom, never.

**ogle** verb *he never disguised his desire to ogle the young ladies* LEER AT, stare at, eye, make eyes at, check out; *informal* give someone the once-over, lech after, undress with one's eyes.

**oil** noun 1 *make sure the car has enough oil* | *we heat our house with oil* LUBRICANT, lubrication, grease; crude, crude oil, fuel oil, petroleum; *informal* black gold; *humorous* Texas tea.

2 *brown the beef in hot oil* COOKING OIL, vegetable oil; corn oil, olive oil, sunflower oil, safflower oil, canola oil, peanut oil.

3 *add some oil to the bath water* bath oil, essential oil, baby oil, scented oil, suntan oil.

▸ verb *I'll oil that gate for you* LUBRICATE, grease, smear/cover/rub with oil; *informal* lube.

**oily** adjective 1 *oily substances* GREASY, oleaginous, unctuous; *technical* sebaceous; *formal* pinguid.

2 *oily food* GREASY, fatty, buttery, swimming in oil/fat.

3 *he's an oily character* UNCTUOUS, ingratiating, fawning, smooth-talking, fulsome, flattering, obsequious, sycophantic, oleaginous; *informal* smarmy, slimy.

**ointment** noun *apply the ointment twice a day* LOTION, cream, salve, liniment, rub, gel, balm, emollient, unguent; *formal* embrocation; *technical* humectant; *proprietary* Vaseline.

**old** adjective 1 *old ladies* ELDERLY, aged, older, senior, advanced in years, up in years; venerable; in one's dotage, long in the tooth, gray-haired, grizzled, hoary; past one's prime, not as young as one was, ancient, decrepit, doddering, doddery, not long for this world, senescent, senile, superannuated; *informal* getting on, past it, over the hill, no spring chicken. ANTONYM young.

2 *that old barn is an eyesore* DILAPIDATED, broken-down, beat-up, run-down, tumbledown, ramshackle, decaying, crumbling, disintegrating. ANTONYMS new, modern.

3 *old clothes* | *an old sofa* WORN, worn out, shabby, threadbare, holey, torn, frayed, patched, tattered, moth-eaten, ragged; old-fashioned, out of date, outmoded, démodé; castoff, hand-me-down; *informal* tatty. ANTONYMS new, fashionable.

4 *a collector of old cars* | *the city's old architecture* ANTIQUE, historic, vintage, classic; veteran. ANTONYMS new, modern.

5 *she's old for her years* MATURE, wise, sensible, experienced, worldly-wise, knowledgeable. ANTONYMS young, inexperienced.

6 *in the old days* BYGONE, past, former, olden, of old, previous, early, earlier, earliest; medieval, ancient, classical, primeval, primordial, prehistoric, antediluvian. ANTONYMS modern, recent.

7 *the same old phrases* HACKNEYED, hack, banal, trite, overused, overworked, tired, worn out, stale, clichéd, platitudinous, unimaginative, pedestrian, stock, conventional; out of date, outdated, old-fashioned, outmoded, archaic, obsolete, antiquated, hoary; *informal* old hat, corny, played out. ANTONYMS fresh, innovative.

8 *an old girlfriend* FORMER, previous, ex-, one-time, erstwhile, once, then; *formal* quondam. ANTONYM new.

9 *the town has held tight to its old ways* TIME-HONORED, old-time, long-established, age-old; FAMILIAR, established; cus-

tomary, usual, routine, habitual; historic, folk, ancestral, old-world. ANTONYMS modern, progressive.

PHRASES: **old age** *I was not prepared to deal with my father's old age* DECLINING YEARS, advanced years, age, agedness, oldness, winter/autumn of one's life, senescence, senility, dotage. ANTONYMS youth, childhood.

**old person** *the old people in this community deserve our support* SENIOR CITIZEN, senior, elder, retiree, geriatric, dotard, golden ager; crone; Methuselah; septuagenarian, octogenarian, nonagenarian, centenarian; *informal* old-timer, oldie, oldster, codger. ANTONYMS youngster, child.

THE RIGHT WORD **old, aged, ancient, antediluvian, antiquated, archaic, obsolete**

Almost no one likes to be thought of as **old**, which means having been in existence or use for a relatively long time (*an old washing machine*). But those who are **aged**, indicating a longer life span than *old* and usually referring to persons of very advanced years, are often proud of the fact that they have outlived most of their peers. Children may exaggerate and regard their parents as **ancient**, which means dating back to the remote past, often specifically the time before the end of the Roman Empire (*ancient history*), and their attitudes as **antediluvian**, which literally means dating back to the period before the biblical Great Flood and Noah's ark (*an antediluvian transportation system*). Some people seem older than they really are, simply because their ideas are **antiquated**, which means out of vogue or no longer practiced (*antiquated ideas about dating*). Things rather than people are usually described as **archaic**, which means having the characteristics of an earlier, sometimes primitive, period (*archaic words like "thou" and "thine"*). **Obsolete** also refers to things, implying that they have gone out of use or need to be replaced by something newer (*an obsolete textbook; a machine that will be obsolete within the decade*).

---

**old-fashioned** adjective *an old-fashioned hairstyle | old-fashioned thinking* OUT OF DATE, outdated, dated, out of fashion, outmoded, unfashionable, passé, démodé, frumpy; outworn, old, old-time, behind the times, archaic, obsolescent, down-level, obsolete, ancient, antiquated, superannuated, defunct; medieval, prehistoric, antediluvian, old-fogeyish, old-fangled, conservative, backward-looking, quaint, anachronistic, fusty, moth-eaten, old-world, olde-worlde; *informal* old hat, square, not with it; horse-and-buggy, clunky, mossy. ANTONYMS modern, fashionable.

**old-time** adjective *we danced to Grandfather's old-time music | it's an old-time tradition* OLD-STYLE, former, past, bygone, old-fashioned, historic; traditional, folk, ancestral, classical, old-world, quaint. ANTONYM modern.

**omen** noun *the torrential rains on day one of their journey was an omen of things to come* PORTENT, sign, signal, token, forewarning, warning, foreshadowing, prediction, forecast, prophecy, harbinger, augury, auspice, presage; straw in the wind, (hand)writing on the wall, indication, hint; *literary* foretoken. See note at SIGN.

**ominous** adjective *ominous clouds* THREATENING, menacing, baleful, forbidding, sinister, inauspicious, unpropitious, unfavorable, unpromising; portentous, foreboding, fateful, premonitory; black, dark, gloomy; *formal* minatory; *literary* direful; *rare* minacious. ANTONYMS promising, auspicious.

THE RIGHT WORD **ominous, fateful, forbidding, foreboding, portentous, premonitory**

A sky filled with low, dark clouds might look **ominous**, but it probably wouldn't be considered **portentous**, even though the root words *omen* and *portent* are nearly synonymous. What is *ominous* is usually threatening and may imply impending disaster (*an ominous silence*), while *portentous* is more often used to describe something that provokes awe or amazement (*a portentous show of military strength*) or a very important outcome (*a portentous moment for the American people*). Like *ominous*, **foreboding** implies that something evil is coming (*foreboding words that sent shivers through us*), while **forbidding** suggests an unfriendly or threatening appearance (*a dark, forbidding castle*). **Fateful** and **premonitory** are less frightening words. What is *fateful* appears to have been inevitable or decreed by fate, with an emphasis on decisive importance (*a fateful meeting with her ex-boyfriend; a battle that would prove fateful*). Anything that serves to warn beforehand is **premonitory**, whether or not the warning concerns something negative (*a premonitory dream about her father's death; a premonitory feeling about the exam*).

---

**omission** noun **1** *we have read the report, and there seem to be several omissions* EXCLUSION, leaving out, exception; deletion, cut, excision, elimination, erasure; gap, blank, absence; oversight. ANTONYM inclusion.

**2** *the damage was not caused by any omission on behalf of the carrier* NEGLIGENCE, neglect, neglectfulness, dereliction, forgetfulness, oversight, default, lapse, failure. ANTONYM conscientiousness.

**omit** verb **1** *they omitted his name from the list* LEAVE OUT, exclude, leave off, fail to mention, miss, pass over; take out, drop, cut, delete, eliminate, erase, rub out, cross out, expunge, strike out. ANTONYM include.

**2** *I omitted to mention our guest lecturer* FORGET, neglect, fail; leave undone, overlook, ignore, skip. ANTONYM remember.

**omnipotence** noun *the omnipotence of God* ALL-POWERFULNESS, almightiness, supremacy, preeminence, supreme power, absolute power, unlimited power; invincibility. ANTONYM powerlessness.

**omnipotent** adjective *the worship of omnipotent deities* ALL-POWERFUL, almighty, supreme, preeminent, most high; invincible, unconquerable.

**omnipresent** adjective *she was omnipresent in her children's lives long after her death* UBIQUITOUS, all-pervasive, everywhere; boundless, infinite; rife, pervasive, prevalent, far-reaching.

**omniscient** adjective *he thought I was some kind of omniscient guru* ALL-KNOWING, all-wise, all-seeing.

**omnivorous** adjective **1** *most duck species are omnivorous* ABLE TO EAT ANYTHING, having a mixed/varied diet; *rare* omnivorant.

**2** *an omnivorous reader* OF VARIED TASTES, undiscriminating, indiscriminate, unselective.

**on** preposition **1** *your purse is on the hood of my car* RESTING ON, supported by, resting atop, touching the (upper) surface of. ANTONYMS under, underneath.

**2** *put the cushion on the chair* SO AS TO BE RESTING ON, on to, onto, to the (upper) surface.

▸ adjective *the computer's on* FUNCTIONING, in operation, working, in use, operating. ANTONYM off.

▸ adverb *the professor droned on.* See ON AND ON below.

PHRASES: **on and off** *they've been dating, on and off, for years.* See OFF AND ON at OFF.

**on and on** *after a few drinks, he blabbers on and on* FOR A LONG TIME, for ages, for hours, at (great) length, incessantly, ceaselessly, constantly, continuously, continually, endlessly, unendingly, eternally, forever, interminably, unremittingly, relentlessly, indefatigably, without letup, without a pause/break, without cease.

**once** adverb **1** *I spoke to him only once* ON ONE OCCASION, one time, one single time. ANTONYMS twice, many times, often.

**2** *he did not once help* EVER, at any time, on any occasion, at all, under any circumstances, on any account.

**3** *they were friends once* FORMERLY, previously, in the past, at one time, at one point, once upon a time, time was when, in days/times gone by, in times past, in the (good) old days, long ago; *archaic* sometime, erstwhile, whilom; *literary* in days/times of yore, of yore. ANTONYMS now, currently.

▸ conjunction *he'll be all right once she's gone* AS SOON AS, when, after, the instant, the second, the minute, the moment.

PHRASES: **at once 1** *you must leave at once* IMMEDIATELY, right away, right now, this instant, this second, this minute, this moment, now, straightaway, instantly, directly, forthwith, promptly, without delay, without hesitation, without further ado; quickly, as fast as possible, as soon as possible, ASAP, speedily; *informal* like a shot, in a flash, pronto, in two shakes (of a lamb's tail). ANTONYMS later, in due course.

**2** *all the guests arrived at once* AT THE SAME TIME, at one and the same time, (all) together, simultaneously; as a group, in unison, in concert, in chorus. ANTONYMS singly, in dribs and drabs.

**once and for all** *I've made up my mind, once and for all* CONCLUSIVELY, decisively, finally, positively, definitely, definitively, absolutely, irrevocably; for good, for always, forever, permanently; *informal* for keeps.

**once in a while** *we go hiking once in a while* OCCASIONALLY, from time to time, (every) now and then/again, every so often, on occasion, at times, sometimes, off and on, at intervals, periodically, sporadically, intermittently.

**oncoming** adjective *the lights from the oncoming traffic | bracing for the oncoming storm* APPROACHING, advancing, nearing, onrushing; forthcoming, on the way, imminent, impending, looming, gathering, (close) at hand, about to happen, to come.

**one** cardinal number **1** *each one is loosely wrapped* UNIT, item; *technical* monad.

**2** *only one person came* A SINGLE, a solitary, a sole, a lone.

**3** *her one concern was her daughter* ONLY, single, solitary, sole, exclusive.

**4** *they have now become one* UNITED, a unit, unitary, amalgamated, consolidated, integrated, combined, incorporated, allied, affiliated, linked, joined, unified, in league, in partnership; wedded, married.

**5** *I'll get my big break one day* SOME, any.

▸ pronoun *one never knows what tomorrow may bring.* See note below.

**USAGE NOTE one**

**One** is used as a pronoun to mean 'anyone' or 'I (or me) and people in general,' as in *one must try one's best.* In modern English, it is generally used only in formal and written contexts. In informal and spoken contexts, the normal alternative is **you**, as in *you must try your best.*

Until quite recently, sentences in which **one** is followed by **his** or **him** were considered perfectly correct: *one must try his best.* These uses are now held to be less than perfectly grammatical (and possibly sexist as well).

**onerous** adjective *the job had become onerous* BURDENSOME, arduous, strenuous, difficult, hard, severe, heavy, back-breaking, oppressive, weighty, uphill, formidable, laborious, Herculean, exhausting, tiring, taxing, demanding, punishing, grueling, exacting, wearing, wearisome, fatiguing; *archaic* toilsome. ANTONYMS effortless, easy.

**oneself** PHRASE: **by oneself.** See BY.

**one-sided** adjective **1** *a one-sided account* BIASED, prejudiced, partisan, partial, preferential, discriminatory, slanted, colored, inequitable, unfair, unjust. ANTONYMS impartial, fair-minded.

**2** *a one-sided game* UNEQUAL, uneven, unbalanced, lopsided.

**one-time** adjective *a one-time Little League coach* FORMER, ex-, old, previous, sometime, erstwhile; lapsed; *formal* quondam.

**ongoing** adjective **1** *negotiations are ongoing* IN PROGRESS, under way, going on, continuing, taking place, proceeding, progressing, advancing; unfinished. ANTONYMS stalled, finished.

**2** *an ongoing struggle* CONTINUOUS, continuing, uninterrupted, unbroken, nonstop, constant, around/round-the-clock, ceaseless, unceasing, unending, endless, never-ending, unremitting, relentless, unfaltering. ANTONYM intermittent.

**onlooker** noun *onlookers lined the streets* EYEWITNESS, witness, observer, looker-on, fly on the wall, spectator, watcher, viewer, bystander; sightseer; *informal* rubberneck; *literary* beholder.

**only** adverb **1** *there was only enough for two* AT MOST, at best, (only) just, no/not more than; barely, scarcely, hardly, narrowly.

**2** *she works only on one painting at a time* EXCLUSIVELY, solely, to the exclusion of everything else.

**3** *you're only saying that* MERELY, simply, just.

▸ adjective *their only son* SOLE, single, one (and only), solitary, lone, unique; exclusive.

**USAGE NOTE only**

In normal, everyday English, the tendency is to place the word **only** as early as possible in the sentence, generally just before the verb, and the result is rarely ambiguous. Misunderstandings are possible, however, and grammarians have debated the matter for more than two hundred years. Advice varies, but in general, ambiguity is less likely if *only* is placed as close as is naturally possible to the word(s) to be modified or emphasized: The wording *Bill ate* ***only the salad*** explains that the salad was the sole item that Bill ate. There is no doubt what the statement means. The clear implication is that Bill did not eat the ham, the dessert, or anything else that may have been available.
The wording *Bill* ***only ate*** *the salad* almost certainly means the same thing, but in a literal sense, there is indeed some doubt. The linking of *only* with *ate* could imply that what Bill did to the salad was simply eat it; he did not prepare it, or spill it, or throw it across the room, or anything else that one could imagine doing to a salad.

In normal conversation, the second statement would probably not be so misunderstood, but, especially when writing, it's never a mistake to favor the less ambiguous wording.

**onomatopoeic** adjective *several words that describe sounds are onomatopoeic, like 'hiss' and 'buzz'* IMITATIVE, echoic.

**onset** noun *they foolishly ignored the onset of his aggressive behavior* START, beginning, commencement, arrival, (first) appearance, inception, emergence, day one, outbreak, dawn, genesis. ANTONYM end.

**onslaught** noun *the battalion's onslaught was relentless* ASSAULT, attack, offensive, advance, charge, onrush, rush, storming, sortie, sally, raid, descent, incursion, invasion, foray, push, thrust, drive, blitz, bombardment, barrage, salvo; *historical* broadside.

**onus** noun *the onus of single parenting* BURDEN, responsibility, liability, obligation, duty, weight, load, charge, mantle, encumbrance; cross to bear, millstone round one's neck, albatross.

**ooze** verb **1** *blood oozed from the wound* SEEP, discharge, flow, exude, trickle, drip, dribble, issue, filter, percolate, escape, leak, drain, empty, bleed, sweat, well; *Medicine* extravasate.

**2** *she was positively oozing charm* EXUDE, gush, drip, pour forth, emanate, radiate.

▸ noun **1** *the ooze of blood* SEEPAGE, seeping, discharge, flow, exudation, trickle, drip, dribble, percolation, escape, leak, leakage, drainage; secretion, excretion; *Medicine* extravasation.

**2** *the ooze on the ocean floor* MUD, slime, alluvium, silt, mire, sludge, muck, deposit.

**opacity** noun **1** *analyzing the opacity of their drinking water* CLOUDINESS, nontransparency, opaqueness, filminess, blurriness, blurredness, blur, haziness, haze. ANTONYMS transparency, translucence, clarity.

**2** *the opacity of his arguments* OBSCURITY, lack of clarity, abstruseness, unclearness, unintelligibility, density, incomprehensibility. ANTONYM clarity.

**opalescent** adjective *opalescent sequins* IRIDESCENT, prismatic, rainbowlike, kaleidoscopic, multicolored, many-hued, lustrous, shimmering, glittering, sparkling, variegated, scintillating, shot, moiré, opaline, milky, pearly, nacreous.

**opaque** adjective **1** *opaque glass* NONTRANSPARENT, cloudy, filmy, blurred, smeared, smeary, misty, hazy; dirty, muddy, muddied, grimy. ANTONYMS transparent, translucent, clear.

**2** *the technical jargon was opaque to him* OBSCURE, unclear, mysterious, puzzling, perplexing, baffling, mystifying, confusing, unfathomable, incomprehensible, unintelligible, ambiguous, Delphic, impenetrable, oblique, enigmatic, cryptic, hazy, foggy; *informal* as clear as mud. ANTONYM clear.

**open** adjective **1** *the door's open* NOT SHUT, not closed, unlocked, unbolted, unlatched, off the latch, unfastened, unsecured; ajar, gaping, wide open, yawning. ANTONYMS closed, shut.

**2** *a blue silk shirt, open at the neck* UNFASTENED, not done up, undone, loose; unbuttoned, unzipped, unbuckled, untied, unlaced.

**3** *the main roads are open* CLEAR, passable, navigable, unblocked, unobstructed. ANTONYMS blocked, impassable.

**4** *open countryside* | *open spaces* UNENCLOSED, rolling, sweeping, extensive, wide open, unfenced, exposed, unsheltered; spacious, airy, uncrowded, uncluttered; undeveloped, unbuilt-up. ANTONYMS enclosed, developed.

**5** *a map was open beside him* SPREAD OUT, unfolded, unfurled, unrolled; extended, stretched out. ANTONYMS closed (up), folded.

**6** *the bank wasn't open* OPEN FOR BUSINESS, open to the public. ANTONYM closed.

**7** *the position is still open* AVAILABLE, vacant, free, unfilled; *informal* up for grabs. ANTONYMS unavailable, filled.

**8** *the system is* ***open to*** *abuse* VULNERABLE TO, subject to, susceptible to, liable to, exposed to, an easy target for, at risk of, permitting of. ANTONYM immune.

**9** *she was open about her feelings* FRANK, candid, honest, forthcoming, communicative, forthright, direct, unreserved, plain-spoken, outspoken, straightforward, blunt, not afraid to call a spade a spade; *informal* upfront; *archaic* free-spoken. ANTONYMS secretive, withdrawn.

**10** *open hostility* OVERT, obvious, patent, manifest, palpable, conspicuous, plain, undisguised, unconcealed, clear, apparent, evident; blatant, flagrant, barefaced, brazen. ANTONYM concealed.

**11** *the case is still open* UNRESOLVED, undecided, unsettled, yet to be settled, up in the air; open to debate, open for discussion, arguable, debatable, moot. ANTONYMS resolved, concluded.

**12** *an open mind* IMPARTIAL, unbiased, unprejudiced, objective, disinterested, nonpartisan, nondiscriminatory, neutral, dispassionate, detached. ANTONYMS biased, one-sided.

**13** *I'm open to suggestions* RECEPTIVE, amenable, willing to listen, ready to listen, responsive.

**14** *what other options are open to us?* AVAILABLE, accessible, on hand, obtainable.

**15** *an open meeting* PUBLIC, general, unrestricted, nonexclusive, nonrestrictive. ANTONYM private.

▸ verb **1** *she opened the front door* UNFASTEN, unlatch, unlock, unbolt, unbar; throw wide. ANTONYMS close, shut.

**2** *Katherine opened the parcel* UNWRAP, undo, untie, unseal. ANTONYMS wrap, seal.

**3** *shall I open another bottle?* UNCORK, broach, crack (open). ANTONYMS seal, cork.

**4** *Adam opened the map* SPREAD OUT, unfold, unfurl, unroll, straighten out; extend, stretch out. ANTONYMS close, fold up.

**5** *he opened his heart to her* REVEAL, uncover, expose, lay bare, bare, pour out, disclose, divulge.

**6** *we're hoping to open next month* OPEN FOR BUSINESS, start trading, set up shop; *informal* hang out one's shingle.

**7** *Valerie opened the meeting* BEGIN, start, commence, initiate, set in motion, launch, get going, get underway, get the ball rolling, get off the ground; inaugurate; *informal* kick off, get the show on the road. ANTONYMS conclude, end.

**8** *the lounge* ***opens on to*** *a balcony* GIVE ACCESS TO, lead to, be connected to, communicate with; face, overlook, command a view of.

**open-air** adjective *an open-air market* OUTDOOR, out-of-doors, outside, alfresco, al fresco. ANTONYM indoor.

**openhanded** adjective *it was a much-appreciated openhanded contribution* GENEROUS, magnanimous, charitable, benevolent, beneficent, munificent, bountiful, liberal, unstinting; altruistic, philanthropic; *literary* bounteous. ANTONYMS tightfisted, stingy.

**opening** noun **1** *an opening in the center of the roof* HOLE, gap, aperture, orifice, vent; peephole; split, crack, fissure, cleft, crevice, chink, slit; perforation; *Anatomy* foramen.

**2** *the opening in the wall* DOORWAY, gateway, portal, entrance, (means of) entry, entryway, way in, (means of) access; way out, exit, egress.

**3** *their defensive lapse gave Torrez the opening he needed* OPPORTUNITY, chance, window (of opportunity), possibility; *informal* (lucky) break, shot.

**4** *an opening in the sales department* VACANCY, position, job, opportunity.

**5** *the opening of the session* BEGINNING, start, commencement, outset, inception; introduction, prefatory remarks, opening statement; *informal* kickoff; *formal* proem. ANTONYMS close, closure.

**6** *a gallery opening* OPENING CEREMONY, official opening, launch, inauguration; opening night, premiere, first showing, first night; vernissage.

**openly** adverb **1** *drugs were openly on sale* PUBLICLY, for all to see, blatantly, flagrantly, brazenly, boldly, overtly, in full view; shamelessly, immodestly, wantonly. ANTONYMS secretly, covertly.

**2** *the senator spoke openly of his drinking problems* FRANKLY, candidly, explicitly, honestly, sincerely, forthrightly, straightforwardly, bluntly, without constraint, without holding back, straight from the shoulder, straight from the hip. ANTONYMS allusively, indirectly.

**open-minded** adjective **1** *open-minded attitudes* UNBIASED, unprejudiced, nonpartisan, neutral, nonjudgmental, nondiscriminatory; objective, dispassionate, disinterested; tolerant, liberal, permissive, broad-minded. ANTONYMS prejudiced, judgmental.

**2** *it was a progressive school that appealed to parents who were open-minded* RECEPTIVE, open to suggestions, open to new ideas, amenable, flexible, willing to change. ANTONYM narrow-minded.

**operate** verb **1** *he can operate the machine* WORK, run, make go, use, utilize, handle, control, manage; drive, steer, maneuver.

**2** *the machine ceased to operate* FUNCTION, work, go, run, be in working/running order, be operative. ANTONYM break down.

**3** *the way the law operates in practice* TAKE EFFECT, act, apply, be applied, function.

**4** *he operated the mine until 1931* DIRECT, control, manage, run, govern, administer, superintend, head (up), supervise, oversee, preside over, be in control/charge of.

**5** *doctors decided to operate* PERFORM SURGERY, do an operation; *informal* put under the knife.

**operation** noun **1** *the slide bars ensure smooth operation* FUNCTIONING, working, running, performance, action.

**2** *the operation of the factory* MANAGEMENT, running, control, direction, governing, administration, supervision.

**3** *a cardiologist from Atlanta will perform the operation* SURGERY, surgical procedure.

**4** *a military operation* ACTION, activity, exercise, undertaking, enterprise, maneuver, campaign.

**5** *their mining operation in Pennsylvania* BUSINESS, enterprise, company, organization, firm, concern; *informal* outfit, setup. PHRASE: **in operation** *only one of the automatic doors was in operation.* See OPERATIONAL.

**operational** adjective *the new conveyor belts will be operational by tomorrow* UP AND RUNNING, running, working, functioning, operative, in operation, in use, in action; in working order, workable, serviceable, functional, usable, ready for action. ANTONYMS out of order, broken.

**operative** adjective **1** *this piece of legislation is not yet operative* IN FORCE, in operation, in effect, valid. ANTONYM invalid.

**2** *most of our antique machinery is operative.* See OPERATIONAL.

**3** *when I say 'perhaps I'll go,' the operative word is 'perhaps'* KEY, significant, relevant, applicable, pertinent, apposite, germane, crucial, critical, pivotal, central, essential. ANTONYM irrelevant.

▸ noun **1** *the operatives clean the machines* MACHINIST, (machine) operator, mechanic, engineer, worker, workman, blue-collar worker.

**2** *an operative of the CIA* AGENT, secret agent, undercover agent, spy, mole, plant, double agent; *informal* spook; *archaic* intelligencer.

**3** *we hired our own operatives* DETECTIVE, private detective, investigator, private investigator, sleuth; *informal* private eye, bloodhound; *informal, dated* gumshoe, dick, private dick.

**operator** noun **1** *a machine operator* MACHINIST, mechanic, operative, engineer, driver, worker.

**2** *a tour operator* CONTRACTOR, entrepreneur, promoter, arranger, fixer, dealer, outfitter, expediter.

**3** *informal a ruthless operator* MANIPULATOR, maneuverer, mover and shaker, wheeler-dealer, hustler, wirepuller.

**opiate** noun *she refused to take the prescribed opiates* DRUG, narcotic, sedative, tranquilizer, depressant, soporific, anesthetic, painkiller, analgesic, anodyne; morphine, opium, codeine; *informal* dope; *Medicine* stupefacient.

**opinion** noun *she did not share her husband's opinion* BELIEF, judgment, thought(s), (way of) thinking, mind, (point of) view, viewpoint, outlook, attitude, stance, position, perspective, persuasion, standpoint; sentiment, conception, conviction. PHRASES: **a matter of opinion** *whether his art is worthy of an exhibition is a matter of opinion* DEBATABLE, open to question, open to debate, a moot point, up to the individual.
**be of the opinion** *we are of the opinion that his poetry lacks insight* BELIEVE, think, consider, maintain, reckon, estimate, feel, have a/the feeling, contend, be convinced; *informal* allow; *formal* opine.
**in my opinion** *in my opinion, the green tiles clash with the yellow walls* AS I SEE IT, to my mind, (according) to my way of thinking, personally, in my estimation, if you ask me, for my money, in my book.

THE RIGHT WORD **opinion, belief, conviction, persuasion, sentiment, view**

When you give your **opinion** on something, you offer a conclusion or a judgment that, although it may be open to question, seems true or probable to you at the time (*she was known for her strong opinions on women in the workplace*). A **view** is an opinion that is affected by your personal feelings or biases (*his views on life were essentially optimistic*), while a **sentiment** is a more or less settled opinion that may still be colored by emotion (*her sentiments on aging were shared by many other women approaching fifty*). A **belief** differs from an opinion or a view in that it is not necessarily the creation of the person who holds it; the emphasis here is on the mental acceptance of an idea, a proposition, or a doctrine and on the assurance of its truth (*religious beliefs; his belief in the power of the body to heal itself*). A **conviction** is a firmly-held and unshakable belief whose truth is not doubted (*she could not be swayed in her convictions*), while a **persuasion** (in this sense) is a strong belief that is unshakable because you want to believe that it's true rather than because there is evidence proving it so (*she was of the persuasion that he was innocent*).

**opinionated** adjective *she got tired of listening to her opinionated boyfriend* DOGMATIC, of fixed views, dictatorial, pontifical, domineering, pompous, self-important, arrogant; inflexible, uncompromising, prejudiced, bigoted. ANTONYMS open-minded, flexible.

**opponent** noun **1** *his political opponent* RIVAL, adversary, opposer, (the) opposition, fellow contestant, (fellow) competitor, enemy, antagonist, combatant, contender, challenger; *literary* foe. ANTONYMS ally, partner.

**2** *an opponent of the reforms* OPPOSER, objector, dissenter, dissident. ANTONYM supporter.

**opportune** adjective *it seemed like the most opportune occasion to make our announcement* AUSPICIOUS, propitious, favorable, advantageous, golden, felicitous; timely, convenient, suitable, appropriate, apt, fitting. See note at TIMELY. ANTONYMS inopportune, disadvantageous.

**opportunism** noun *she scaled the ladder of success with hard work and opportunism* EXPEDIENCY, pragmatism, exploitation, Machiavellianism, maneuvering; pushing (all) the right buttons striking while the iron is hot, making hay while the sun shines.

**opportunity** noun *this is your opportunity to move on | don't miss another opportunity* CHANCE, lucky chance, favorable time/occasion/moment, time, right set of circumstances, occasion, moment, opening, option, window (of opportunity), turn, go, possibility; *informal* shot, break, new lease on life.

**oppose** verb *most voters opposed the new school budget* BE AGAINST, object to, be hostile to, be in opposition to, disagree with, dislike, disapprove of; resist, take a stand against, put up a fight against, stand up to, fight, challenge; take issue with, dispute, argue with/against, quarrel with; *informal* be anti-; *formal* gainsay; *rare* controvert. ANTONYM support.

**opposing** adjective **1** *two opposing points of view* CONFLICTING, contrasting, opposite, incompatible, irreconcilable, contradictory, antithetical, differing, different, dissimilar clashing, at variance, at odds, divergent, opposed, poles apart, polar. ANTONYMS similar, in agreement, identical.

**2** *opposing sides in the war* RIVAL, opposite, enemy, antagonistic. ANTONYM allied.

**3** *the opposing page* OPPOSITE, facing.

**opposite** adjective **1** *the opposite page* FACING, opposing, reverse.

**2** *opposite views* CONFLICTING, contrasting, incompatible, irreconcilable, antithetical, contradictory, clashing, contrary, at variance, at odds, different, differing, divergent, dissimilar, unalike, disagreeing, opposed, opposing, poles apart, polar. ANTONYMS similar, same, identical.

**3** *opposite sides in a war* RIVAL, opposing, enemy. ANTONYM same.

▸ preposition *they sit opposite one another* FACING, face to face with, across from; *informal* eyeball to eyeball with; *archaic* fronting.

▸ noun *the opposite was also true* REVERSE, converse, antithesis, contrary, inverse, obverse, antipode; the other side of the coin; *informal* flip side.

THE RIGHT WORD **opposite; contradictory; antithetical; contrary; reverse**

All of these adjectives are usually applied to abstractions and are used to describe ideas, statements, qualities, forces, etc., that are so far apart as to seem irreconcilable. **Opposite** refers to ideas or things that are symmetrically opposed in position, direction, or character—in other words, that are set against each other in such a way that the contrast or conflict between them is highlighted (*they sat opposite one another at the table*). **Contradictory** goes a little further, implying that if one of two opposing statements, propositions, or principles is true, the other must be false (*he assured us the fee would be under $500; his partner gave us contradictory information, saying costs could go as high as $800.*). Two contradictory elements are mutually exclusive; for example, *alive* and *dead* are contradictory terms because logically they cannot be applied to the same thing. **Antithetical** implies that the two things being contrasted are diametrically opposed—as far apart or as different from each other as is possible (*they debated the antithetical theories of creationism and evolution*). **Contrary** adds connotations of conflict or antagonism (*the group's discussion was hindered by his contrary remarks*). **Reverse** applies to that which moves or faces in the opposite direction (*he scribbled something on the reverse side of her business card*).

**opposition** noun **1** *the proposal met with opposition* RESISTANCE, hostility, antagonism, enmity, antipathy, objection, dissent, disapproval, criticism, demurral; defiance, noncompliance, obstruction.

**2** *they beat the opposition* OPPONENTS, opposing side, other side, other team, competition, opposers, rivals, adversaries; enemies; *literary* foes.

**3** *the opposition between the public and the private domains* CONFLICT, clash, disparity, antithesis, polarity.

**oppress** verb **1** *the invaders oppressed the people* PERSECUTE, abuse, maltreat, ill-treat, tyrannize, crush, repress, suppress, subjugate, subdue, keep down, grind down, ride roughshod over, rule with an iron fist/hand.

**2** *the darkness of winter oppressed her* DEPRESS, make gloomy, make despondent, weigh down, weigh heavily on, cast down, dampen someone's spirits, dispirit, dishearten, discourage, sadden, get down, bring down; *archaic* deject.

**oppressed** adjective *talk of a revolution spread rapidly among the oppressed masses* PERSECUTED, downtrodden, abused, maltreated, ill-treated, subjugated, tyrannized, repressed, subdued, crushed, browbeaten; disadvantaged, underprivileged.

**oppression** noun *the young people in this country have known nothing but oppression* PERSECUTION, abuse, maltreatment, ill-treatment, tyranny, despotism repression, suppression, subjection, subjugation; cruelty, brutality, injustice, hardship, suffering, misery. ANTONYMS freedom, democracy.

**oppressive** adjective **1** *an oppressive dictatorship* HARSH, cruel, brutal, repressive, tyrannical, tyrannous, iron-fisted, autocratic, dictatorial, despotic, undemocratic; ruthless, merciless, pitiless, draconian. ANTONYMS lenient, humane.

**2** *an oppressive sense of despair* OVERWHELMING, overpowering, unbearable, unendurable, intolerable, burdensome.

**3** *it was gray and oppressive* MUGGY, close, heavy, hot, humid, sticky, steamy, airless, stuffy, stifling, suffocating, sultry. ANTONYMS airy, fresh.

**oppressor** noun *the rebels overthrew their oppressors in a bloody coup* PERSECUTOR, tyrant, despot, autocrat, dictator, subjugator, tormentor, slave driver, taskmaster.

**opprobrium** noun **1** *the government endured months of opprobrium* VILIFICATION, abuse, vituperation, condemnation, criticism, censure, denunciation, defamation, denigration, castigation, disparagement, obloquy, derogation, slander, calumny, execration, lambasting, bad press, invective, libel, character assassination; *informal* flak, mudslinging, bad-mouthing, tongue-lashing; *formal* excoriation; *archaic* contumely; *rare* objurgation. ANTONYM praise.

**2** *the opprobrium of being associated with thugs* DISGRACE, shame, dishonor, stigma, humiliation, discredit, loss of face, ignominy, obloquy, disrepute, infamy, notoriety, scandal; *rare* disesteem. ANTONYM honor.

**opt** verb **1** *I always* ***opt for*** *the better quality* CHOOSE, select, pick (out), decide on, go for, settle on, take.

**2** *she's opted to stay in Richmond* CHOOSE, elect, decide, make/reach the decision, make up one's mind.

**optimistic** adjective **1** *she felt optimistic about the future* HOPEFUL, confident, positive, cheerful, cheery, sanguine, bright, buoyant, full of hope, bullish, Panglossian, Pollyannaish; *informal* upbeat; *dated* of good cheer. ANTONYMS pessimistic, hopeless.

**2** *the forecast is optimistic* ENCOURAGING, promising, hopeful, reassuring, favorable, auspicious, propitious. ANTONYMS ominous, gloomy.

**optimum** adjective *the team is in optimum health | this is the optimum gas-to-oil ratio* (THE) BEST, (the) best of (the) most favorable, (the) most advantageous, ideal, perfect, prime, optimal, model; top, (the) finest, peak, excellent; *informal* tip-top, top-notch, A1.

**option** noun **1** *leave quietly or be forcibly removed—it's your option* CHOICE, alternative, recourse, course of action; power to choose, right to choose.

**2** *there are three options: beef, chicken, fish* CHOICE, selection, alternative, possibility, way to go; *informal* bet.

**optional** adjective *in senior year, phys ed is optional* VOLUN-

TARY, discretionary, not required, elective, noncompulsory, nonmandatory; *Law* permissive; *rare* discretional. ANTONYMS compulsory, mandatory, required.

**opulence** noun 1 *the opulence of the room* LUXURIOUSNESS, sumptuousness, lavishness, richness, luxury, luxuriance, splendor, magnificence, grandeur, splendidness; *informal* plushness, classiness, ritziness, poshness, swankiness. ANTONYMS simplicity, restraint.

2 *a display of opulence* WEALTH, affluence, wealthiness, richness, riches, prosperity, money. ANTONYM poverty.

**opulent** adjective 1 *his opulent home* LUXURIOUS, sumptuous, palatial, lavish, lavishly appointed, rich, splendid, magnificent, grand, grandiose, fancy; *informal* plush, classy, ritzy, posh, swanky, swank. ANTONYMS spartan, stark, ascetic.

2 *an opulent family* WEALTHY, rich, affluent, well off, well-to-do, moneyed, prosperous, of means, of substance; *informal* well-heeled, rolling in money/dough, rolling in it, loaded, stinking/filthy rich, made of money, in clover, (living) on easy street; *dated* in the chips. See note at WEALTHY. ANTONYMS penniless, poor, impoverished.

3 *her opulent red hair* COPIOUS, abundant, profuse, prolific, plentiful, luxuriant; *literary* plenteous. ANTONYMS sparse, thin.

**opus** noun *her latest opus is a critical success* COMPOSITION, work, work of art, oeuvre, piece, creation.

**oracle** noun 1 *the oracle of Apollo* PROPHET, PROPHETESS, sibyl, seer, augur, prognosticator, diviner, soothsayer, fortune teller, sage.

2 *our oracle on Africa* AUTHORITY, expert, specialist, pundit, mentor, adviser, guru.

**oracular** adjective 1 *his every utterance was given oracular significance* PROPHETIC, prophetical, sibylline, predictive, prescient, prognostic, divinatory, augural.

2 *oracular responses* ENIGMATIC, cryptic, abstruse, unclear, obscure, confusing, mystifying, baffling, puzzling, perplexing, mysterious, arcane; ambiguous, equivocal, Delphic. ANTONYMS clear, unambiguous.

**oral** adjective *an oral agreement* SPOKEN, verbal, unwritten, vocal, uttered, said, by mouth, viva voce. ANTONYM written.

▸ noun *studying for French orals* ORAL EXAMINATION; *Brit.* viva, viva voce.

**oration** noun *an oration given in memory of McKinley* SPEECH, address, lecture, talk, homily, sermon, discourse, declamation, valedictory, salutatory; *informal* spiel; *rare* allocution.

**orator** noun *Patrick Henry, the great orator* SPEAKER, public speaker, speech-maker, lecturer, declaimer, rhetorician, rhetor.

**oratorical** adjective *he imitated the oratorical style of Churchill* RHETORICAL, grandiloquent, magniloquent, high-flown, orotund, bombastic, grandiose, pompous, pretentious, overblown, declamatory, turgid, flowery, florid, Ciceronian; *informal*, silver-tongued; *rare* euphuistic, fustian. ANTONYMS plain-spoken, simple.

**orb** noun *the hallway features a display of luminous orbs suspended at various lengths from the ceiling* SPHERE, globe, ball; spheroid, spherule; circle.

**orbit** noun 1 *the monthly orbit of the Moon* COURSE, path, circuit, track, trajectory, rotation, revolution, circle; *rare* circumgyration.

2 *the problem comes outside our orbit* SPHERE, sphere of influence, area of activity, range, scope, ambit, compass, jurisdiction, authority, domain, realm, province, territory, turf; *informal* bailiwick.

▸ verb *Mercury orbits the Sun* REVOLVE AROUND, circle around, go around, travel around.

**orchestrate** verb 1 *the piece was orchestrated by Mozart* ARRANGE, adapt, score.

2 *orchestrating a campaign of civil disobedience* ORGANIZE, arrange, plan, set up, bring about, mobilize, mount, stage, stage-manage, mastermind, coordinate, direct, engineer, choreograph.

**ordain** verb 1 *the Church voted to ordain women* CONFER HOLY ORDERS ON, appoint, anoint, consecrate, install, invest, induct.

2 *the path ordained by fate* PREDETERMINE, predestine, preordain, destine, determine, prescribe, designate, will.

3 *she ordained that anyone found hunting in the forest must pay a fine* DECREE, rule, order, command, enjoin, lay/set down, establish, dictate, legislate, prescribe, pronounce.

**ordeal** noun *the hostages survived the ordeal* UNPLEASANT EXPERIENCE, painful experience, trial, tribulation, nightmare, trauma, hell (on earth), misery, trouble, difficulty, torture, torment, agony.

**order** noun 1 *alphabetical order* SEQUENCE, arrangement, organization, disposition, system, series, succession; grouping, classification, categorization, codification, systematization.

2 *his tidy desk demonstrates his sense of order* TIDINESS, neatness, orderliness, organization, method, system; symmetry, uniformity, regularity; routine. ANTONYMS chaos, disarray.

3 *the police were needed to keep order* PEACE, control, law (and order), lawfulness, discipline, calm, (peace and) quiet, peacefulness, peaceableness.

4 *the equipment was in good order* CONDITION, state, repair, shape.

5 *I had to obey her orders* COMMAND, instruction, directive, direction, decree, edict, injunction, mandate, dictate, commandment, rescript; law, rule, regulation, diktat; demand, bidding, requirement, stipulation; *informal* say-so; *formal* ordinance; *literary* behest. ANTONYM suggestion.

6 *the company has won the order* COMMISSION, contract, purchase order, request, requisition; booking, reservation. ANTONYM chaos.

7 *the lower orders of society* CLASS, level, rank, grade, degree, position, category; *dated* station.

**8** *the established social order* (CLASS) SYSTEM, hierarchy, pecking order, grading, ranking, scale.

**9** *the higher orders of insects* TAXONOMIC GROUP, class, family, species, breed; taxon.

**10** *a religious order* COMMUNITY, brotherhood, sisterhood, organization, association, society, fellowship, fraternity, confraternity, congregation, sodality, lodge, guild, league, union, club; sect.

**11** *skills of a very high order* TYPE, kind, sort, nature, variety; quality, caliber, standard.

▸ verb **1** *he ordered me to return* INSTRUCT, command, direct, enjoin, tell, require, charge; *formal* adjure; *literary* bid.

**2** *the judge ordered that their assets be confiscated* DECREE, ordain, rule, legislate, dictate, prescribe.

**3** *you can order your tickets by phone* REQUEST, apply for, place an order for; book, reserve; *formal* bespeak.

**4** *the messages are ordered chronologically* ORGANIZE, put in order, arrange, sort out, marshal, dispose, lay out; group, classify, categorize, catalog, codify, systematize, systemize.

PHRASES: **in order 1** *list the dates in order* IN SEQUENCE, in series.

**2** *he found everything in order* TIDY, neat, orderly, straight, trim, shipshape, in apple-pie order; in position, in place.

**3** *I think it's in order for me to take the credit* APPROPRIATE, fitting, suitable, acceptable, (all) right, permissible, permitted, allowable; *informal* okay.

**order about/around** *what makes him think he can just waltz in and start ordering us about?* TELL WHAT TO DO, give orders to, dictate to; lay down the law to; *informal* boss around, push around.

**out of order** *the elevator's out of order* NOT WORKING, not in working order, not functioning, broken, broken-down, out of service, out of commission, faulty, defective, inoperative; down; *informal* conked out, bust, busted, (gone) kaput, on the fritz, on the blink, out of whack.

**orderly** adjective **1** *an orderly room* NEAT, tidy, well-ordered, in order, trim, in apple-pie order, spick-and-span, shipshape. ANTONYMS untidy, messy.

**2** *the orderly presentation of information* (WELL) ORGANIZED, efficient, methodical, systematic, meticulous, punctilious; coherent, structured, logical, well-planned, well regulated, systematized. ANTONYM disorganized.

**3** *the crowd was orderly* WELL-BEHAVED, law-abiding, disciplined, peaceful, peaceable, nonviolent. ANTONYM unruly.

**ordinarily** adverb *he ordinarily worked from home* USUALLY, normally, as a (general) rule, generally, in general, for the most part, mainly, mostly, most of the time, typically, habitually, commonly, routinely.

**ordinary** adjective **1** *the ordinary course of events* USUAL, normal, standard, typical, common, customary, habitual, everyday, regular, routine, day-to-day. See note at NORMAL. See also word spectrum at ODD. ANTONYM abnormal.

**2** *my life seemed very ordinary* AVERAGE, normal, run-of-the-mill, standard, typical, middle-of-the-road, conventional, unremarkable, unexceptional, workaday, undistinguished, nondescript, colorless, commonplace, humdrum, mundane, unmemorable, pedestrian, prosaic, quotidian, uninteresting, uneventful, dull, boring, bland, suburban, hackneyed, garden-variety; *informal* plain-vanilla, nothing to write home about, no great shakes. ANTONYMS unusual, exceptional.

PHRASE: **out of the ordinary** *nothing out of the ordinary happened* UNUSUAL, exceptional, remarkable, extraordinary, unexpected, surprising, unaccustomed, unfamiliar, abnormal, atypical, different, special, exciting, memorable, noteworthy, unique, singular, outstanding; unconventional, unorthodox, strange, peculiar, odd, queer, curious, bizarre, outlandish; *informal* offbeat.

**organ** noun **1** *the internal organs* BODY PART, biological structure.

**2** *the official organ of the Communist Party* NEWSPAPER, paper, journal, periodical, magazine, newsletter, gazette, publication, mouthpiece; *informal* rag.

**organic** adjective **1** *organic matter* LIVING, live, animate, biological, biotic.

**2** *organic vegetables* PESTICIDE-FREE, additive-free, natural.

**3** *the love scenes were an organic part of the drama* ESSENTIAL, fundamental, integral, intrinsic, vital, indispensable, inherent.

**4** *a society is an organic whole* STRUCTURED, organized, coherent, integrated, coordinated, ordered, harmonious.

**organism** noun **1** *fish and other organisms* LIVING THING, being, creature, animal, plant, life form.

**2** *a complex political organism* STRUCTURE, system, organization, entity.

**organization** noun **1** *the organization of conferences* PLANNING, arrangement, coordination, administration, organizing, running, management.

**2** *the overall organization of the book* STRUCTURE, arrangement, plan, pattern, order, form, format, framework, composition, constitution.

**3** *his lack of organization* EFFICIENCY, order, orderliness, planning.

**4** *a large international organization* COMPANY, firm, corporation, institution, group, consortium, conglomerate, agency, association, society; *informal* outfit.

**organize** verb **1** *organizing and disseminating information* (PUT IN) ORDER, arrange, sort (out), assemble, marshal, put straight, group, classify, collocate, categorize, catalog, codify, systematize, systemize; *rare* methodize.

**2** *they organized a search party* MAKE ARRANGEMENTS FOR, arrange, coordinate, sort out, put together, fix up, set up, orchestrate, take care of, see to/about, deal with, manage, conduct, administrate, mobilize; schedule, timetable, program; *formal* concert.

**orgy** noun **1** *a drunken orgy* WILD PARTY, debauch,

carousal, carouse, revel, revelry; *informal* binge, jag, bender, love-in, toot; *literary* bacchanal; *archaic* wassail.

**2** *an orgy of violence* BOUT, excess, spree, surfeit; *informal* binge.

**orientation** noun **1** *the orientation of the radar station* POSITIONING, location, position, situation, placement, alignment.

**2** *his orientation to his new way of life* ADAPTATION, adjustment, acclimatization.

**3** *broadly Marxist in orientation* ATTITUDE, inclination.

**4** *freshman orientation begins the week before school starts* INDUCTION, training, initiation, briefing.

**orifice** noun *the orifice must be kept free from debris* OPENING, hole, aperture, slot, slit, cleft.

**origin** noun **1** *the origin of life* BEGINNING, start, commencement, origination, genesis, birth, dawning, dawn, emergence, creation, birthplace, cradle; source, basis, cause, root(s); *formal* radix.

**2** *the Latin origin of the word* SOURCE, derivation, root(s), provenance, etymology.

**3** *her Scottish origin* DESCENT, ancestry, parentage, pedigree, lineage, line (of descent), heritage, birth, extraction, family, stock, blood, bloodline.

THE RIGHT WORD **origin, inception, provenance, root, source**

The **origin** of something is the point from which it starts or sets out, or the person or thing from which it is ultimately derived (*the origin of the custom of carving pumpkins at Halloween; the origin of a word*). It often applies to causes that were in operation before the thing itself was brought into being. **Source**, on the other hand, applies to that which provides a first and continuous supply (*the source of the river; an ongoing source of inspiration and encouragement*). **Root**, more often than *source*, applies to what is regarded as the first or final cause of something; it suggests an origin so fundamental as to be the ultimate cause from which something stems (*money is the root of all evil*). **Inception** refers specifically to the beginning of an undertaking, project, institution, or practice (*she was in charge of the organization from its inception*). **Provenance** is similarly restricted in meaning, referring to the specific place, or sometimes the race or people, from which something is derived or by whom it was invented or constructed (*in digging, they uncovered an artifact of unknown provenance*).

**original** adjective **1** *the original inhabitants* INDIGENOUS, native, aboriginal, autochthonous; first, earliest, early.

**2** *original Rembrandts* AUTHENTIC, genuine, actual, true, bona fide; *informal* kosher.

**3** *the film is highly original* INNOVATIVE, creative, imaginative, inventive; new, novel, fresh, refreshing; unusual, unconventional, unorthodox, groundbreaking, pioneering, avant-garde, cutting-edge, unique, distinctive. See note at CREATIVE.

▸ noun **1** *a copy of the original* ARCHETYPE, prototype, source, master.

**2** *he really is an original* INDIVIDUALIST, individual, eccentric, nonconformist, free spirit, maverick; *informal* character, oddball.

**originality** noun *their animated short won an award for its originality* INVENTIVENESS, ingenuity, creativeness, creativity, innovation, novelty, freshness, imagination, imaginativeness, individuality, unconventionality, uniqueness, distinctiveness.

**originally** adverb *the conference was originally scheduled for November* (AT) FIRST, in/at the beginning, to begin with, initially, in the first place, at the outset.

**originate** verb **1** *the disease originates in Africa* ARISE, have its origin, begin, start, stem, spring, emerge, emanate.

**2** *Tom originated the idea* INVENT, create, initiate, devise, think up, dream up, conceive, formulate, form, develop, generate, engender, produce, mastermind, pioneer; *literary* beget.

**originator** noun *the originator of the Dixie cup* INVENTOR, creator, architect, author, father, mother, initiator, innovator, founder, pioneer, mastermind; *literary* begetter.

**ornament** noun **1** *small tables covered with ornaments* KNICKKNACK, trinket, bauble, bibelot, gewgaw, gimcrack, furbelow; *informal* whatnot, doodad, tchotchke.

**2** *the dress had no ornament at all* DECORATION, adornment, embellishment, ornamentation, trimming, accessories.

▸ verb *the room was highly ornamented* DECORATE, adorn, embellish, trim, bedeck, deck (out), festoon; *literary* bedizen.

**ornamental** adjective *the ornamental trim above the doors gives the room a dramatic lift* DECORATIVE, fancy, ornate, ornamented.

**ornate** adjective **1** *an ornate mirror* ELABORATE, decorated, embellished, adorned, ornamented, fancy, fussy, ostentatious, showy; *informal* flash, flashy. ANTONYM unadorned.

**2** *ornate language* ELABORATE, flowery, florid; grandiose, pompous, pretentious, high-flown, orotund, magniloquent, grandiloquent, rhetorical, oratorical, bombastic, overwrought, overblown; *informal* highfalutin, purple. ANTONYMS plain, simple.

**orotund** adjective **1** *an orotund singing voice* DEEP, sonorous, strong, powerful, full, rich, resonant, loud, booming.

**2** *the orotund rhetoric of his prose* POMPOUS, pretentious, affected, fulsome, grandiose, ornate, overblown, flowery, florid, high-flown, magniloquent, grandiloquent, rhetorical, oratorical; *informal* highfalutin, purple.

**orthodox** adjective **1** *orthodox views* CONVENTIONAL, mainstream, conformist, (well) established, traditional, traditionalist, prevalent, popular, conservative, unoriginal. ANTONYM unconventional.

**2** *an orthodox Hindu* CONSERVATIVE, traditional, observant, devout, strict.

**orthodoxy** noun **1** *a pillar of orthodoxy* CONVENTIONALITY, conventionalism, conformism, conservatism, traditionalism, conformity.

**2** *Christian orthodoxies* DOCTRINE, belief, conviction, creed, dogma, credo, theory, tenet, teaching.

**oscillate** verb **1** *the pendulum started to oscillate* SWING, swing back and forth, swing to and fro, sway; *informal* wigwag.

**2** *oscillating between fear and bravery* WAVER, swing, fluctuate, alternate, seesaw, yo-yo, sway, vacillate, waffle, hover; *informal* wobble.

**oscillation** noun **1** *the oscillation of the pendulum* SWINGING, swinging to and fro, swing, swaying.

**2** *his oscillation between commerce and art* WAVERING, swinging, fluctuation, seesawing, yo-yoing, vacillation.

**ossify** verb **1** *the cartilage may ossify* TURN INTO BONE, become bony, calcify, harden, solidify, rigidify, petrify.

**2** *the old political institutions have ossified* BECOME INFLEXIBLE, become rigid, fossilize, calcify, rigidify, stagnate.

**ostensible** adjective *the ostensible star is Lana Turner, but it's Juanita Moore who makes the movie click* APPARENT, outward, superficial, professed, supposed, alleged, purported. ANTONYM genuine.

THE RIGHT WORD **ostensible, apparent, illusory, seeming**

The **apparent** reason for something is not necessarily the real reason. In this sense the word applies to what appears only on the surface, not to what is borne out by scientific investigation or an examination of the relevant facts and circumstances (*the apparent cause was only an illusion*). The **ostensible** reason for something is the reason that is expressed, declared, or avowed; but it implies that the truth is being concealed (*the ostensible purpose of the meeting was to give the two men a chance to get acquainted*). **Seeming** usually refers to the character of the thing observed rather than to a defect in the observation; it implies even more doubt than either *apparent* or *ostensible* (*her seeming innocence fooled no one*). That which is **illusory** is always deceptive; it has a character or appearance that doesn't really exist (*an illusory beauty that faded quickly in the bright light*).

**ostensibly** adverb *it is ostensibly a book about football* APPARENTLY, seemingly, on the face of it, to all intents and purposes, outwardly, superficially, allegedly, supposedly, purportedly.

**ostentation** noun *most car buyers are looking for a lot more than ostentation* SHOWINESS, show, pretentiousness, vulgarity, conspicuousness, display, flamboyance, gaudiness, brashness, extravagance, ornateness, exhibitionism; *informal* flashiness, glitz, glitziness, ritziness.

**ostentatious** adjective *an ostentatious display of wealth* SHOWY, pretentious, conspicuous, flamboyant, gaudy, brash, vulgar, loud, extravagant, fancy, ornate, overelaborate; *informal* flash, flashy, splashy, over the top, glitzy, ritzy, superfly. ANTONYM restrained.

**ostracize** verb *they were ostracized by their fellow workers* EXCLUDE, shun, spurn, cold-shoulder, reject, shut out, avoid, ignore, snub, cut dead, keep at arm's length, leave out in the cold; blackball, blacklist; *informal* freeze out. ANTONYM welcome.

**other** adjective **1** *these homes use other fuels* ALTERNATIVE, different, dissimilar, disparate, distinct, separate, contrasting.

**2** *are there any other questions?* MORE, further, additional, extra, added, supplementary.

**otherwise** adverb **1** *hurry up, otherwise we'll be late* OR, or else, if not.

**2** *she's exhausted, but otherwise she's fine* IN OTHER RESPECTS, apart from that.

**3** *he could not have acted otherwise* IN ANY OTHER WAY, differently.

**ounce** noun *it took every ounce of courage for her to board the plane* PARTICLE, scrap, bit, speck, iota, whit, jot, trace, atom, shred, crumb, fragment, grain, drop, soupçon, spot; *informal* smidgen.

**oust** verb *armed forces ousted the new coalition government* DRIVE OUT, expel, force out, throw out, remove (from office/power), eject, get rid of, depose, dethrone, topple, unseat, overthrow, bring down, overturn, dismiss, dislodge, displace; *informal* boot out, kick out. See note at EJECT.

**out** adjective & adverb **1** *she's out at the moment* NOT HERE, not at home, not in, (gone) away, elsewhere, absent. ANTONYM in.

**2** *the secret was out* REVEALED, (out) in the open, common knowledge, public knowledge, known, disclosed, divulged. ANTONYM unknown.

**3** *the roses are out* IN FLOWER, flowering, in (full) bloom, blooming, in blossom, blossoming, open.

**4** *the book should be out soon* AVAILABLE, for sale, obtainable, in stores, published, in print.

**5** *the fire was nearly out* EXTINGUISHED, no longer alight.

**6** *informal grunge is out* UNFASHIONABLE, out of fashion, dated, outdated, passé; *informal* old hat, old school, not with it. ANTONYM fashionable.

**7** *smoking and drinking are out* FORBIDDEN, not permitted, not allowed, proscribed, taboo, unacceptable. ANTONYMS permitted, OK.

▸ verb *informal it was not our intention to out him* EXPOSE, unmask.

PHRASE: **out cold** *one swift punch from Max, and Parnell was out cold* UNCONSCIOUS, knocked out, down/out for the count; *informal* KO'd, kayoed.

**out-and-out** adjective *he's an out-and-out chauvinist* UTTER, downright, thoroughgoing, absolute, complete, thorough, total, unmitigated, outright, full-bore, real, perfect, consummate. ANTONYM partial.

**outbreak** noun **1** *the latest outbreak of hostility* ERUPTION, flare-up, upsurge, groundswell, outburst, rash, wave, spate, flood, explosion, burst, flurry.

**2** *on the outbreak of war* START, beginning, commencement, onset, outset.

**outburst** noun *a wild outburst of applause* ERUPTION, explosion, burst, outbreak, flare-up, access, rush, flood, storm, outpouring, surge, upsurge, outflowing.

**outcast** noun *his corrupt practices as an attorney had made him an outcast in the community* PARIAH, persona non grata, reject, black sheep, outsider, leper.

**outclass** verb *even in her freshman year, Taurasi outclassed most everyone on the team* SURPASS, be superior to, be better than, outshine, overshadow, eclipse, outdo, outplay, outmaneuver, outstrip, get the better of, upstage; top, cap, beat, defeat, exceed; *informal* be a cut above, be head and shoulders above, run rings around.

**outcome** noun *the future of the industry could hinge on the outcome of next month's election* RESULT, end result, consequence, net result, upshot, aftereffect, aftermath, conclusion, issue, end, end product.

**outcry** noun **1** *an outcry of passion* SHOUT, exclamation, cry, yell, howl, roar, scream; *informal* holler.

**2** *public outcry* PROTEST(S), protestation(s), complaints, objections, furor, fuss, commotion, uproar, outbursts, opposition, dissent; *informal* hullabaloo, ballyhoo, ructions, stink.

**outdated** adjective *an outdated filing system* OLD-FASHIONED, out of date, outmoded, out of fashion, unfashionable, dated, passé, old, behind the times, behindhand, obsolete, antiquated; *informal* out, old hat, square, not with it, horse-and-buggy, clunky. ANTONYM modern.

**outdistance** verb **1** *the hare outdistanced the fox* OUTRUN, outstrip, outpace, leave behind, get (further) ahead of; overtake, pass.

**2** *the mill outdistanced all its rivals* SURPASS, outshine, outclass, outdo, exceed, transcend, top, cap, beat, better, leave behind; *informal* leave standing.

**outdo** verb *every year, Hank and Oscar try to outdo each other in the triathlon* SURPASS, outshine, overshadow, eclipse, outclass, outmaneuver, get the better of, put in the shade, upstage; exceed, transcend, top, cap, beat, better, leave behind, get ahead of; *informal* be a cut above, be head and shoulders above, run rings around.

**outdoor** adjective *outdoor activities* OPEN-AIR, outdoors, outside, alfresco, field. ANTONYM indoor.

**outer** adjective **1** *the outer layer* OUTSIDE, outermost, outward, exterior, external, surface.

**2** *outer areas of the city* OUTLYING, distant, remote, faraway, furthest, peripheral; suburban. ANTONYM inner.

**outfit** noun **1** *a new outfit* COSTUME, suit, uniform, ensemble, attire, clothes, clothing, dress, garb; *informal* getup, gear, togs, threads; *formal* apparel; *archaic* habit, raiment.

**2** *a studio lighting outfit* KIT, equipment, tools, implements, tackle, apparatus, paraphernalia, things, stuff.

**3** *a local manufacturing outfit* ORGANIZATION, setup, enterprise, company, firm, business; group, band, body, team.

▸ verb *enough swords to outfit an army* EQUIP, kit out, fit out/up, rig out, supply, arm; dress, attire, clothe, deck out; *archaic* apparel, invest, habit.

**outfitter** noun **1** *our outfitters planned the canoe route* supplier, grubstaker; guide.

**2** *the studio has dozens of outfitters at its disposal* CLOTHIER, tailor, couturier, costumer, dressmaker, seamstress; *dated* modiste.

**outflow** noun *the outflow of waste materials is monitored continuously* DISCHARGE, outflowing, outpouring, rush, flood, deluge, issue, spurt, jet, cascade, stream, torrent, gush, outburst; flow, flux; *technical* efflux.

**outgoing** adjective **1** *outgoing children* EXTROVERT, uninhibited, unreserved, demonstrative, affectionate, warm, friendly, genial, cordial, affable, easygoing, sociable, convivial, lively, gregarious; communicative, responsive, open, forthcoming, frank. ANTONYM introverted.

**2** *the outgoing president* DEPARTING, retiring, leaving. ANTONYM incoming.

**outing** noun **1** *family outings* (PLEASURE) TRIP, excursion, jaunt, expedition, day out, (mystery) tour, drive, ride, run; *informal* junket, spin.

**2** *informal the outing of public figures* EXPOSURE, unmasking, revelation.

**outlandish** adjective *he gives the most outlandish excuses* WEIRD, queer, far out, quirky, zany, eccentric, idiosyncratic, unconventional, unorthodox, funny, bizarre, unusual, singular, extraordinary, strange, unfamiliar, peculiar, odd, curious; *informal* offbeat, off the wall, way-out, wacky, freaky, kooky, kinky, oddball, in left field. ANTONYM ordinary.

**outlaw** noun *bands of outlaws* FUGITIVE, (wanted) criminal, public enemy, outcast, exile, pariah; bandit, robber; *dated* desperado.

▸ verb **1** *they voted to outlaw the grizzly hunt* BAN, bar, prohibit, forbid, veto, make illegal, proscribe, interdict. ANTONYM permit.

**2** *she feared she would be outlawed* BANISH, exile, expel.

**outlay** noun *the initial outlay of funds was within their means* EXPENDITURE, expenses, spending, cost, price, payment, investment. ANTONYM profit.

**outlet** noun **1** *a power outlet* SOCKET, receptacle, power bar, power source.

**2** *the outlet of the drain* VENT, way out, egress; outfall, opening, channel, conduit, duct.

**3** *an outlet for farm produce* STORE, market, marketplace, shop, source.

**4** *an outlet for their creative energies* MEANS OF EXPRESSION, (means of) release, vent, avenue, channel.

**outline** noun **1** *the outline of the building* SILHOUETTE, profile, shape, contours, form, line, delineation; diagram, sketch; *literary* lineaments.

**2** *an outline of expenditure for each department* ROUGH IDEA, thumbnail sketch, (quick) rundown, summary, synopsis, résumé, précis; essence, main/key points, gist, (bare) bones, draft, sketch.

▸ verb **1** *the plane was outlined against the sky* SILHOUETTE, define, demarcate; sketch, delineate, trace.

**2** *she outlined the plan briefly* ROUGH OUT, sketch out, draft, give a rough idea of, summarize, précis.

**outlook** noun **1** *the two men were wholly different in outlook* POINT OF VIEW, viewpoint, views, opinion, (way of) thinking, perspective, attitude, standpoint, stance, frame of mind.

**2** *the outlook for the economy* PROSPECTS, expectations, hopes, future, lookout.

**3** *a lovely open outlook* VIEW, vista, prospect, panorama, scene, aspect.

**outlying** adjective *people in the outlying areas had little interest in the politics of the city* DISTANT, remote, outer, out of the way, faraway, extrasolar, far-flung, inaccessible, off the beaten track/path.

**outmoded** adjective *the fax machine we got three years ago is already outmoded* OUT OF DATE, old-fashioned, out of fashion, outdated, dated, behind the times, antiquated, obsolete, passé, unstylish, untrendy, uncool; *informal* old hat, old school.

**out of date** adjective **1** *this design is out of date* OLD-FASHIONED, outmoded, out of fashion, unfashionable, frumpish, frumpy, outdated, dated, old, passé, behind the times, behindhand, obsolete, antiquated; *informal* out, old hat, square, not with it, horse-and-buggy, clunky. ANTONYMS fashionable, modern.

**2** *many of the facts are out of date* SUPERSEDED, obsolete, expired, lapsed, invalid, (null and) void. ANTONYM current.

**out-of-the-way** adjective *an out-of-the-way campsite* OUTLYING, distant, remote, faraway, far-flung, isolated, lonely, godforsaken, inaccessible, off the beaten track/path. ANTONYM accessible.

**out of work** adjective *I'm an actor, currently out of work* UNEMPLOYED, jobless, out of a job; redundant, laid off, on welfare, on the dole; *euphemistic* between jobs.

**outpouring** noun *the defendant received an outpouring of public support* OUTFLOW, outflowing, rush, flood, deluge, discharge, issue, spurt, jet, cascade, stream, torrent, gush, outburst, niagara, flow, flux; *technical* efflux.

**output** noun *our output always increases at the end of summer* PRODUCTION, amount/quantity produced, yield, gross domestic product, works, writings.

**outrage** noun **1** *widespread public outrage* INDIGNATION, fury, anger, rage, disapproval, wrath, resentment.

**2** *it is an outrage* SCANDAL, offense, insult, injustice, disgrace.

**3** *the bomb outrage* ATROCITY, act of violence/wickedness, crime, wrong, barbarism, inhumane act.

▸ verb *his remarks outraged his parishioners* ENRAGE, infuriate, incense, anger, scandalize, offend, give offense to, affront, shock, horrify, disgust, appall.

**outrageous** adjective **1** *outrageous acts of cruelty* SHOCKING, disgraceful, scandalous, atrocious, appalling, monstrous, heinous; evil, wicked, abominable, terrible, horrendous, dreadful, foul, nauseating, sickening, vile, nasty, odious, loathsome, unspeakable; beastly.

**2** *the politician's outrageous promises* FAR-FETCHED, (highly) unlikely, doubtful, dubious, questionable, implausible, unconvincing, unbelievable, incredible, preposterous, extravagant, excessive.

**3** *outrageous clothes* EYE-CATCHING, flamboyant, showy, gaudy, ostentatious; shameless, brazen, shocking; *informal* saucy, flashy.

**outright** adverb **1** *he rejected the proposal outright* COMPLETELY, entirely, wholly, fully, totally, categorically, absolutely, utterly, flatly, unreservedly, in every respect.

**2** *I told her outright* EXPLICITLY, directly, forthrightly, openly, frankly, candidly, honestly, sincerely, bluntly, plainly, in plain language, truthfully, to someone's face, straight from the shoulder, straight up, in no uncertain terms.

**3** *they were killed outright* INSTANTLY, instantaneously, immediately, at once, straightaway, then and there, on the spot.

**4** *paintings have to be bought outright* ALL AT ONCE, in one go.

▸ adjective **1** *an outright lie* OUT-AND-OUT, absolute, complete, downright, utter, sheer, categorical, unqualified, unmitigated, unconditional.

**2** *the outright winner* DEFINITE, unequivocal, clear, unqualified, incontestable, unmistakable.

**outset** noun *at the outset, we had nothing but problems* START, starting point, beginning, commencement, dawn, birth, origin, inception, opening, launch, inauguration; *informal* the word go. ANTONYM end.

**outshine** verb *watching Nadia outshine the other gymnasts was a thrill for viewers around the world* SURPASS, overshadow, eclipse, outclass, put in the shade, upstage, exceed, transcend, top, cap, beat, better; *informal* be a cut above, be head and shoulders above, run rings around.

**outside** noun *the outside of the building* OUTER/EXTERNAL SURFACE, exterior, outer side/layer, case, skin, shell, covering, facade.

▸ adjective **1** *outside lights* EXTERIOR, external, outer, outdoor, out-of-doors.

**2** *outside contractors* INDEPENDENT, hired, temporary, freelance, casual, external, extramural.

**3** *an outside chance* SLIGHT, slender, slim, small, tiny, faint, negligible, remote, vague.

▸ adverb *they went outside* | *shall we eat outside?* OUTDOORS, out of doors, alfresco. ANTONYM inside.

**outsider** noun *after six years, I still feel like an outsider in this town* STRANGER, visitor, nonmember; foreigner, alien, immigrant, emigrant, émigré; newcomer, parvenu.

**outskirts** plural noun *they live in the outskirts of Youngstown* OUTLYING DISTRICTS, edges, fringes, suburbs, suburbia, bedroom community, commutershed; purlieus, borders, environs.

**outsmart** verb *buyers and sellers attempt to outsmart each other* OUTWIT, outmaneuver, outplay, steal a march on, trick, get the better of; *informal* outfox, pull a fast one on, put one over on.

**outspoken** adjective *an outspoken critic of the Reagan administration* FORTHRIGHT, direct, candid, frank, straightforward, honest, open, plain-spoken; blunt, abrupt, bluff, brusque.

**outstanding** adjective **1** *an outstanding painter* EXCELLENT, marvelous, magnificent, superb, fine, wonderful, superlative, exceptional, first-class, first-rate; *informal* great, terrific, tremendous, super, amazing, fantastic, sensational, fabulous, ace, neat, killer, crack, A1, mean, awesome, bang-up, skookum, out of this world; smashing, brilliant. ANTONYM mediocre.

**2** *the outstanding decorative element in this presentation* REMARKABLE, extraordinary, exceptional, striking, eye-catching, arresting, impressive, distinctive, unforgettable, memorable, special, momentous, significant, notable, noteworthy; *informal* out of this world. See note at NOTICEABLE. ANTONYM unexceptional.

**3** *how much work is still outstanding?* TO BE DONE, undone, unattended to, unfinished, incomplete, remaining, pending, ongoing. ANTONYM finished.

**4** *outstanding debts* UNPAID, unsettled, owing, past due, owed, to be paid, payable, due, overdue, undischarged, delinquent. ANTONYM paid.

**outward** adjective *his outward demeanor hides the pain he feels inside* EXTERNAL, outer, outside, exterior; surface, superficial, seeming, apparent, ostensible. ANTONYM inward.

**outwardly** adverb *outwardly, these two products are just about identical* EXTERNALLY, on the surface, superficially, on the face of it, to all intents and purposes, apparently, ostensibly, seemingly.

**outweigh** verb *the costs outweigh the benefits* BE GREATER THAN, exceed, be superior to, prevail over, have the edge on/over, override, supersede, offset, cancel out, (more than) make up for, outbalance, compensate for.

**outwit** verb *the murderers always thought they could outwit Columbo, but of course they couldn't* OUTSMART, outmaneuver, outplay, steal a march on, trick, gull, get the better of, euchre; *informal* outfox, pull a fast one on, put one over on.

**oval** adjective *an oval mirror* EGG-SHAPED, ovoid, ovate, oviform, elliptical.

**ovation** noun *what performer doesn't appreciate an ovation from the crowd?* ROUND OF APPLAUSE, applause, hand-clapping, clapping, cheering, cheers, bravos, acclaim, acclamation, tribute, standing ovation; *informal* (big) hand.

**oven** noun *the roast is in the oven* (kitchen) stove, microwave (oven), (kitchen) range; roaster; kiln.

**over** preposition **1** *there will be clouds over most of the state* ABOVE, on top of, higher (up) than, atop, covering. ANTONYM under.

**2** *he walked over the grass* ACROSS, around, throughout.

**3** *over 200,000 people live in the area* MORE THAN, above, in excess of, upwards of.

**4** *lengthy discussions over what to do next* ON THE SUBJECT OF, about, concerning, apropos of, with reference to, regarding, relating to, in connection with, vis-à-vis.

▸ adverb **1** *a flock of geese flew over* OVERHEAD, on high, above, past, by.

**2** *the relationship is over* AT AN END, finished, concluded, terminated, ended, no more, a thing of the past; *informal* kaput.

**3** *he had some money left over* REMAINING, unused, surplus, in excess, in addition.

PHRASES: **over and above** *we will not pay any costs over and above the original quote* IN ADDITION TO, on top of, plus, as well as, besides, along with.

**over and over** *he tells the same jokes over and over* REPEATEDLY, again and again, over and over again, time and (time) again, many times over, frequently, constantly, continually, persistently, ad nauseam.

**overact** verb *during dramatic scenes, she has a tendency to overact* EXAGGERATE, overdo it, overplay it; *informal* ham it up, camp it up.

**overall** adjective *the overall cost* ALL-INCLUSIVE, general, comprehensive, universal, all-embracing, gross, net, final, inclusive, total; wholesale, complete, across the board, global, worldwide.

▸ adverb *overall, things have improved* GENERALLY (SPEAKING), broadly, in general, altogether, all in all, on balance, on average, for the most part, in the main, on the whole, by and large, to a large extent.

**overawe** verb *Jane was overawed by her landlady* INTIMIDATE, daunt, cow, disconcert, unnerve, subdue, dismay, frighten, alarm, scare, terrify; *informal* psych out.

**overbearing** adjective *his overbearing wife* DOMINEERING, dominating, autocratic, tyrannical, despotic, oppressive, high-handed, bullying; *informal* bossy.

**overblown** adjective *an overblown piece of writing* OVERWRITTEN, florid, grandiose, pompous, overelaborate, flowery, overwrought, pretentious, high-flown, turgid, grandiloquent, magniloquent, orotund; *informal* highfalutin.

**overcast** adjective *she feared it was bad luck to be married on an overcast day* CLOUDY, clouded (over), sunless, darkened, dark, gray, black, leaden, heavy, dull, murky, dismal, dreary. ANTONYM bright.

**overcharge** verb **1** *clients are being overcharged* SWINDLE, charge too much, cheat, defraud, fleece, short-change; *informal* rip off, sting, screw, rob, diddle, have, rook, gouge.

**2** *the decoration is overcharged* OVERSTATE, overdo, exaggerate, overembroider, overembellish; overwrite, overdraw.

**overcome** verb **1** *we overcame the home team* DEFEAT, beat, conquer, trounce, thrash, rout, vanquish, overwhelm, overpower, get the better of, triumph over, prevail over, win over/against, outdo, outclass, worst, crush; *informal* drub, slaughter, clobber, hammer, lick, best, crucify, demolish, wipe the floor with, make mincemeat of, blow out of the water, take to the cleaners, shellac, skunk.

**2** *they overcame their fear of flying* GET THE BETTER OF, prevail over, control, get/bring under control, master, conquer, defeat, beat; get over, get a grip on, curb, subdue; *informal* lick, best.

▸ adjective *I was overcome* OVERWHELMED, emotional, moved, affected, speechless.

**overconfident** adjective *her downfall came through being overconfident* COCKSURE, cocky, smug, conceited, self-assured, brash, blustering, overbearing, presumptuous, heading for a fall, riding for a fall; *informal* too big for one's britches/boots.

**overcritical** adjective *overcritical parents* FAULT-FINDING, hypercritical, captious, carping, caviling, quibbling, hairsplitting, overparticular; fussy, finicky, fastidious, pedantic, overscrupulous, punctilious; *informal* nitpicking, persnickety.

**overcrowded** adjective *an overcrowded bus* OVERFULL, overflowing, full to overflowing/bursting, crammed full, congested, overpopulated, overpeopled, crowded, swarming, teeming; *informal* bursting/bulging at the seams, full to the gunwales, jam-packed. ANTONYM empty.

**overdo** verb **1** *she overdoes the love scenes* EXAGGERATE, overstate, overemphasize, overplay, go overboard with, overdramatize; *informal* ham up, camp up. ANTONYM understate.

**2** *don't overdo the desserts* OVERINDULGE IN, have/use/eat/drink too much of, have/use/eat/drink to excess.

**3** *they overdid the beef* OVERCOOK, burn. PHRASE: **overdo it** *on your first day of an exercise program, you mustn't overdo it* WORK TOO HARD, overwork, do too much, burn the candle at both ends, overtax oneself, drive/push oneself too hard, work/run oneself into the ground, wear oneself out, bite off more than one can chew, strain oneself; *informal* kill oneself, knock oneself out.

**overdone** adjective **1** *the flattery was overdone* EXCESSIVE, too much, undue, immoderate, inordinate, disproportionate, inflated, overstated, overworked, exaggerated, overemphasized, overenthusiastic, overeffusive; *informal* a bit much, over the top. ANTONYM understated.

**2** *overdone food* OVERCOOKED, dried out, burnt. ANTONYM underdone.

**overdue** adjective **1** *the ship is overdue* LATE, behind schedule, behind time, delayed, unpunctual. ANTONYMS early, punctual.

**2** *overdue payments* UNPAID, unsettled, owing, owed, payable, due, outstanding, undischarged, delinquent.

**overeat** verb *it's hard not to overeat at one of their buffets* EAT TOO MUCH, be greedy, gorge (oneself), overindulge (oneself), feast, gourmandize, gluttonize; *informal* binge, make a pig of oneself, pig out, have eyes bigger than one's stomach. ANTONYM starve.

**overemphasize** verb *the importance of regularly testing your smoke alarms cannot be overemphasized* PLACE/LAY TOO MUCH EMPHASIS ON, overstress, place/lay too much stress on, exaggerate, make too much of, overplay, overdo, overdramatize; *informal* make a big thing about/of, blow up out of all proportion. ANTONYMS understate, play down.

**overflow** verb *cream had overflowed the edges of the shallow dish* SPILL OVER, flow over, brim over, well over, pour forth, stream forth, flood.

▸ noun **1** *an overflow from the tank* OVERSPILL, spill, spillage, flood.

**2** *to accommodate the overflow, five more offices were built* SURPLUS, excess, additional people/things, extra people/things, remainder, overspill.

**overhang** verb *above the garage door overhangs a massive cluster of icicles* STICK OUT (OVER), stand out (over), extend (over), project (over), protrude (over), jut out (over), bulge out (over), hang over.

**overhaul** verb *I've been overhauling the engine* SERVICE, maintain, repair, mend, fix up, rebuild, renovate, recondition, refit, refurbish; *informal* do up, patch up.

**overhead** adverb *a burst of thunder erupted overhead* (UP) ABOVE, high up, (up) in the sky, on high, above/over one's head. ANTONYM below.

▸ adjective *overhead lines* AERIAL, elevated, raised, suspended. ANTONYM underground.

▸ noun *subtract your overhead from the gross income* (RUNNING) COSTS, operating costs, fixed costs, expenses.

**overindulge** verb **1** *we overindulged at Christmas* DRINK/EAT TOO MUCH, overeat, overdrink, be greedy, be intemperate, overdo it, drink/eat to excess, gorge (oneself), feast, gourmandize, gluttonize; *informal* binge, stuff oneself, go overboard, make a pig of oneself, pig out. ANTONYM abstain.

**2** *his mother had overindulged him* SPOIL, give in to, indulge, humor, pander to, pamper, mollycoddle, baby.

**overjoyed** adjective *we're just overjoyed to be grandparents* ECSTATIC, euphoric, thrilled, elated, delighted, on cloud nine, in seventh heaven, jubilant, rapturous, jumping for joy, delirious, blissful, in raptures, as pleased as punch; *informal* over the moon, on top of the world, tickled pink, as happy as a clam. ANTONYM unhappy.

**overlay** verb *the area was overlaid with marble* COVER, face, surface, veneer, inlay, laminate, plaster; coat, varnish, glaze.

▸ noun *an overlay of fiberglass* COVERING, cover, layer, face, surface, veneer, lamination; coat, varnish, glaze, wash.

**overload** verb **1** *avoid overloading the ship* OVERBURDEN, put too much in, overcharge, weigh down.

**2** *don't overload the wiring* STRAIN, overtax, overwork, overuse, swamp, oversupply, overwhelm.

▸ noun *there was an overload of demands* EXCESS, overabundance, superabundance, profusion, glut, surfeit, surplus, superfluity; avalanche, deluge, flood.

**overlook** verb **1** *he overlooked the mistake* FAIL TO NOTICE, fail to spot, miss.

**2** *his work has been overlooked* DISREGARD, neglect, ignore, pay no attention/heed to, pass over, forget. See note at NEGLECT.

**3** *she was almost willing to overlook his faults* IGNORE, not take into consideration, disregard, take no notice of, make allowances for, turn a blind eye to, excuse, pardon, forgive.

**4** *the breakfast room overlooks the garden* HAVE A VIEW OF, look over/across, look on to, look out on/over, give on to, command a view of.

**overly** adverb *the guitars here are not overly expensive* UNDULY, excessively, inordinately, too; wildly, absurdly, ridiculously, outrageously, unreasonably, exorbitantly, impossibly.

**overpower** verb **1** *the prisoners might overpower the crew* GAIN CONTROL OVER, overwhelm, prevail over, get the better of, outdo, gain mastery over, overthrow, overturn, subdue, suppress, subjugate, repress, bring someone to their knees, conquer, defeat, triumph over, worst, trounce; *informal* thrash, lick, best, clobber, wipe the floor with.

**2** *he was overpowered by grief* OVERCOME, overwhelm, move, stir, affect, touch, stun, shake, devastate, take aback, leave speechless; *informal* bowl over.

**overpowering** adjective **1** *overpowering disappointment* OVERWHELMING, oppressive, unbearable, unendurable, intolerable, shattering.

**2** *an overpowering smell* STIFLING, suffocating, strong, pungent, powerful; nauseating, offensive, acrid, fetid, mephitic.

**3** *overpowering evidence* IRREFUTABLE, undeniable, indisputable, incontestable, incontrovertible, compelling, conclusive.

**overrate** verb *I think his music is overrated* OVERESTIMATE, overvalue, think too much of, attach too much importance to, praise too highly. ANTONYM underestimate.

**overreach** PHRASE: **overreach oneself** *he waited for his opponents to overreach themselves* TRY TO DO TOO MUCH, overestimate one's ability, overdo it, overstretch oneself, wear/burn oneself out, bite off more than one can chew.

**overreact** verb *before you overreact, let's just calmly discuss this* REACT DISPROPORTIONATELY, act irrationally, lose one's sense of proportion, blow something up out of all proportion, make a mountain out of a molehill.

**override** verb **1** *the court could not override her decision* DISALLOW, overrule, countermand, veto, quash, overturn, overthrow; cancel, reverse, rescind, revoke, repeal, annul, nullify, invalidate, negate, void; *Law* vacate; *formal* abrogate.

**2** *the government can override all opposition* DISREGARD, pay no heed to, take no account of, turn a deaf ear to, ignore, ride roughshod over.

**3** *a positive attitude will override any negative thoughts* OUTWEIGH, supersede, take priority over, take precedence over, offset, cancel out, (more than) make up for, outbalance, compensate for.

**overriding** adjective *safety was the overriding consideration* DECIDING, decisive, most important, of greatest importance, of greatest significance, uppermost, top, first (and foremost), highest, preeminent, predominant, principal, primary, paramount, chief, main, major, foremost, central, key, focal, pivotal; *informal* number-one.

**overrule** verb *this ban was overruled by a federal court* COUNTERMAND, cancel, reverse, rescind, repeal, revoke, retract, disallow, override, veto, quash, overturn, overthrow, annul, nullify, invalidate, negate, void; *Law* vacate; *formal* abrogate; *archaic* recall.

**overrun** verb **1** *guerrillas overran the barracks* INVADE, storm, occupy, swarm into, surge into, inundate, overwhelm.

**2** *the talks overran the deadline* EXCEED, go beyond/over, run over.

**overseer** noun *they finally brought in an overseer that knew how to deal with the workers* SUPERVISOR, foreman, forewoman, team leader, controller, (line) manager, manageress, head (of department), superintendent, captain; *informal* boss, chief, straw boss.

**overshadow** verb **1** *a massive hill overshadows the town* CAST A SHADOW OVER, shade, darken, conceal, obscure, screen; dominate, overlook.

**2** *this feeling of tragedy overshadowed his story* CAST GLOOM OVER, blight, take the edge off, mar, spoil, ruin.

**3** *he was overshadowed by his brilliant elder brother* OUTSHINE, eclipse, surpass, exceed, be superior to, outclass, outstrip, outdo, upstage; *informal* be head and shoulders above.

**oversight** noun **1** *a stupid oversight* MISTAKE, error, omission, lapse, slip, blunder; *informal* slip-up, boo-boo, goof, flub.

**2** *the omission was due to oversight* CARELESSNESS, inattention, negligence, forgetfulness, laxity.

**overt** adjective *an overt attempt to sidestep the truth* UNDISGUISED, unconcealed, plain (to see), clear, apparent, conspicuous, obvious, noticeable, manifest, patent, open, blatant. ANTONYM covert.

**overtake** verb **1** *a green car overtook the taxi* PASS, go past/by, get/pull ahead of, leave behind, outdistance, outstrip.

**2** *tourism overtook lumber as the main revenue source* OUTSTRIP, surpass, overshadow, eclipse, outshine, outclass; dwarf, put in the shade, exceed, top, cap.

**3** *the calamity that overtook us* BEFALL, happen to, come upon, hit, strike, overwhelm, overcome, be visited on; *literary* betide.

**overthrow** verb **1** *the president was overthrown* REMOVE (FROM OFFICE/POWER), bring down, topple, depose, oust, displace, unseat, dethrone.

**2** *an attempt to overthrow military rule* PUT AN END TO, defeat, conquer.

▸ noun **1** *the overthrow of the general* REMOVAL (FROM OFFICE/POWER), downfall, fall, toppling, deposition, ousting, displacement, supplanting, unseating.

**2** *the overthrow of capitalism* ENDING, defeat, displacement, fall, collapse, downfall, demise.

**overtone** noun *there were overtones of flirtatious mischief in her letter* CONNOTATION, hidden meaning, implication, association, undercurrent, undertone, echo, vibrations, hint, suggestion, insinuation, intimation, suspicion, feeling, nuance.

**overture** noun **1** *the overture to "Don Giovanni"* PRELUDE, introduction, opening, introductory movement.

**2** *the overture to a long debate* PRELIMINARY, prelude, introduction, lead-in, precursor, start, beginning.

**3** *peace overtures* (OPENING) MOVE, approach, advances, feeler, signal, proposal, proposition.

**overturn** verb **1** *the boat overturned* CAPSIZE, turn turtle, keel over, tip over, topple over, turn over, flip; *Nautical* pitchpole.

**2** *I overturned the stool* UPSET, tip over, topple over, turn over, knock over, upend.

**3** *the Supreme Court may overturn this ruling* CANCEL, reverse, rescind, repeal, revoke, retract, countermand, disallow, override, overrule, veto, quash, overthrow, annul, nullify, invalidate, negate, void; *Law* vacate; *formal* abrogate; *archaic* recall.

**overweening** adjective *that overweening attitude of his makes my skin crawl* OVERCONFIDENT, conceited, cocksure, cocky, smug, haughty, supercilious, lofty, patronizing, arrogant, proud, vain, self-important, imperious, overbearing; *informal* high and mighty, uppish. ANTONYM unassuming.

**overweight** adjective *the growing number of overweight children is a legitimate health crisis* FAT, obese, stout, full-figured, corpulent, gross, fleshy, plump, portly, chubby, rotund, paunchy, potbellied, flabby, well-upholstered, broad in the beam; *informal* porky, tubby, blubbery, pudgy. ANTONYM skinny.

**overwhelm** verb **1** *advancing sand dunes could overwhelm the village* SWAMP, submerge, engulf, bury, deluge, flood, inundate.

**2** *Canada overwhelmed the U.S. in the hockey final* DEFEAT (UTTERLY/HEAVILY), trounce, rout, beat (hollow), conquer, vanquish, be victorious over, triumph over, worst, overcome, overthrow, crush; *informal* thrash, steamroller, lick, best, massacre, clobber, wipe the floor with.

**3** *she was overwhelmed by a sense of tragedy* OVERCOME, move, stir, affect, touch, strike, dumbfound, shake, devastate, floor, leave speechless; *informal* bowl over, snow under.

**overwhelming** adjective **1** *an overwhelming number of players were unavailable* VERY LARGE, enormous, immense, inordinate, massive, huge.

**2** *the overwhelming desire to laugh* VERY STRONG, forceful, uncontrollable, irrepressible, irresistible, overpowering, compelling.

**overwork** verb **1** *we should not overwork* WORK TOO HARD, work/run oneself into the ground, wear oneself to a shadow, work one's fingers to the bone, burn the candle at both ends, overtax oneself, burn oneself out, do too much, overdo it, strain oneself, overload oneself, drive/push oneself too hard; *informal* kill oneself, knock oneself out.

**2** *my colleagues did not overwork me* DRIVE (TOO HARD), exploit, drive into the ground, tax, overtax, overburden, put upon, impose on.

**overworked** adjective **1** *overworked staff* STRESSED (OUT), stress-ridden, overtaxed, overburdened, overloaded, exhausted, worn out, burned out. ANTONYM relaxed.

**2** *an overworked phrase* HACKNEYED, overused, worn out, tired, played out, clichéd, threadbare, stale, trite, banal, stock, unoriginal. ANTONYM original.

**overwrought** adjective **1** *she was too overwrought to listen* TENSE, agitated, nervous, on edge, edgy, keyed up, worked up, high-strung, neurotic, overexcited, beside oneself, distracted, distraught, frantic, hysterical; *informal* in a state, in a tizzy, uptight, wound up, het up, strung out. ANTONYM calm.

**2** *the painting is overwrought* OVERELABORATE, overornate, overblown, overdone, contrived, overworked, strained. ANTONYM understated.

**owe** verb *I don't want to owe anyone* BE IN DEBT TO, be indebted to, be in arrears to, be under an obligation to.

**owing** adjective *the rent was owing* UNPAID, to be paid, payable, due, past due, overdue, undischarged, owed, outstanding, in arrears, delinquent. ANTONYM paid.

PHRASE: **owing to** *owing to the severity of the weather, tonight's concert will be postponed until next Tuesday* BECAUSE OF, as a result of, on account of, due to, as a consequence of, thanks to, in view of, by dint of; *formal* by reason of.

**own** adjective *he has his own reasons* PERSONAL, individual, particular, private, personalized, unique.

▸ verb **1** *I own this house* BE THE OWNER OF, possess, be the possessor of, have in one's possession, have (to one's name).

**2** *she had to own that she agreed* ADMIT, concede, grant, accept, acknowledge, agree, confess.

PHRASES: **hold one's own** *Britain has begun to hold its own in world markets* STAND FIRM, stand one's ground, keep one's end up, keep one's head above water, compete, survive, cope, get on/along.

**on one's own 1** *I live on my own* (ALL) ALONE, (all) by oneself, solitary, unaccompanied, companionless; *informal* by one's lonesome.

**2** *she works well on her own* UNAIDED, unassisted, without help, without assistance, (all) by oneself, independently.

**own up to** *in the long run, it's always better to own up to your mistakes* CONFESS, admit to, admit the guilt of, accept blame/responsibility for, tell the truth about, make a clean breast of; *informal* come clean about.

**owner** noun *the owner is no longer interested in selling* POSSESSOR, holder, proprietor/proprietress, homeowner, landowner, freeholder, landlord, landlady.

**ownership** noun *there is no question of ownership* POSSESSION, right of possession, freehold, proprietorship, proprietary rights, title.

**ox** noun *a team of oxen* bull, bullock, steer; *Farming* beef.

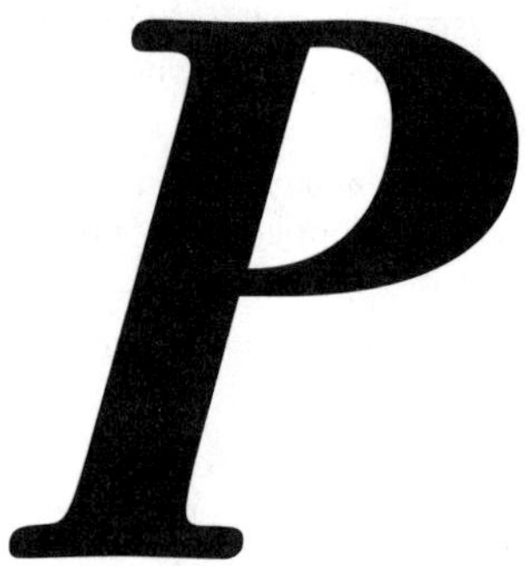

**pace** noun **1** *he stepped back a pace* STEP, stride.

**2** *a slow, steady pace* GAIT, stride, walk, march.

**3** *he drove home at a furious pace* SPEED, rate, velocity; *informal* clip, lick.

▸ verb *she paced up and down* WALK, stride, tread, march, pound, patrol.

**pacific** adjective **1** *a pacific community* PEACE-LOVING, peaceable, pacifist, nonviolent, nonaggressive, nonbelligerent, unwarlike. ANTONYMS aggressive, belligerent.

**2** *their pacific intentions* CONCILIATORY, peacemaking, placatory, propitiatory, appeasing, mollifying, mediatory, dovish; *formal* irenic. ANTONYM warmongering.

**3** *pacific waters* CALM, still, smooth, tranquil, placid, waveless, unruffled, like a millpond. ANTONYM stormy.

**pacifist** noun *you know, even pacifists can support their nation's armed forces* PEACE-LOVER, conscientious objector, passive resister, peacemaker, peace-monger, dove. ANTONYM warmonger.

**pacify** verb *go out there and try to pacify the passengers* PLACATE, appease, calm (down), conciliate, propitiate, assuage, mollify, soothe. ANTONYM enrage.

THE RIGHT WORD **pacify, appease, conciliate, mollify, placate, propitiate**

You might try to **pacify** a crying baby, to **appease** a demanding boss, to **mollify** a friend whose feelings have been hurt, and to **placate** an angry crowd. While all of these verbs have something to do with quieting people who are upset, excited, or disturbed, each involves taking a slightly different approach. *Pacify* suggests soothing or calming (*the mother made soft cooing noises in an attempt to pacify her child*). *Appease* implies that you've given in to someone's demands or made concessions in order to please (*she said she would visit his mother just to appease him*), while *mollify* stresses minimizing anger or hurt feelings by taking positive action (*her flattery failed to mollify him*). *Placate* suggests changing a hostile or angry attitude to a friendly or favorable one, usually with a more complete or long-lasting effect than *appease* (*they were able to placate their enemies by offering to support them*). You can **propitiate** a superior or someone who has the power to injure you by allaying or forestalling their anger (*they were able to propitiate the trustees by holding a dinner party in their honor*). **Conciliate** implies the use of arbitration or compromise to settle a dispute or to win someone over (*the company made every effort to conciliate its angry competitor*).

**pack** noun **1** *a pack of cigarettes* PACKET, container, package, box, carton, parcel.

**2** *with a pack on his back* BACKPACK, knapsack, rucksack, day pack, kit bag, bag.

**3** *a pack of youngsters* CROWD, mob, group, band, troupe, troop, party, set, clique, gang, rabble, horde, herd, throng, huddle, mass, assembly, gathering, host; *informal* crew, bunch.

▸ verb **1** *she helped pack the picnic basket* FILL (UP), put things in, load.

**2** *they packed their belongings* STOW, put away, store, box up.

**3** *the glasses were packed in straw* WRAP (UP), package, parcel, swathe, swaddle, encase, enfold, envelop, bundle.

**4** *Christmas shoppers packed the store* THRONG, crowd (into), fill (to overflowing), cram, jam, squash into, squeeze into.

**5** *pack the cloth against the wall* COMPRESS, press, squash, squeeze, jam, tamp.

PHRASES: **pack off** *informal we packed our youngest son off to college just last week* SEND OFF, dispatch, bundle off.

**pack up 1** *pack up your Legos* PUT AWAY, tidy up/away, clear up/away.

**2** *informal it's time to pack up* STOP, call it a day, finish, cease; *informal* knock off, quit, pack it in.

**package** noun **1** *the delivery of a package* PARCEL, packet, container, box.

**2** *a complete package of services* COLLECTION, bundle, combination.

▸ verb *goods packaged in recyclable materials* WRAP (UP), gift-wrap; pack (up), parcel (up), box, encase.

**packaging** noun *the outer packaging is crucial to consumer appeal* WRAPPING, wrappers, packing, covering.

**packed** adjective *the actors peeked from behind the curtain to see a packed house* CROWDED, full, filled (to capacity), crammed, jammed, solid, overcrowded, overfull, teeming, seething, swarming; *informal* jam-packed, chock-full, standing room only, chockablock, full to the gunwales, bursting/bulging at the seams.

**packet** noun *a small packet of jelly beans* PACK, carton, (cardboard) box, container, case, package.

**pact** noun *the pact was signed at the site of the surrender* AGREEMENT, treaty, entente, protocol, deal, settlement, concordat, accord; armistice, truce; *formal* concord.

**pad**[1] noun **1** *a pad over the eye* piece of cotton, dressing, pack, padding, wadding, wad.

**2** *a seat pad* CUSHION, pillow.

**3** *making notes on a pad* NOTEBOOK, notepad, writing pad, memo pad, sketch pad, steno pad, sketchbook, scratch pad.

▸ verb *a quilted jacket padded with goose down* STUFF, fill, pack, wad.

PHRASE: **pad out** *don't pad out your answer to make it seem impressive* EXPAND UNNECESSARILY, fill out, amplify, increase, flesh out, lengthen, spin out, overdo, elaborate.

**pad**[2] verb *he padded along toward the bedroom* WALK QUIETLY, tread warily, creep, tiptoe, steal, pussyfoot.

**padding** noun **1** *padding around the ankle* WADDING, cushioning, stuffing, packing, filling, lining.

**2** *a concise style with no padding* VERBIAGE, verbosity, wordiness, prolixity, filler.

**paddle**[1] noun *use the paddles to row ashore* OAR, scull, blade.

▸ verb *we paddled around the bay* row gently, pull, scull, canoe, kayak.

**paddle**[2] verb *children were paddling in the water* SPLASH ABOUT, wade; dabble.

**paddock** noun *the horses got out of the paddock* FIELD, meadow, pasture; pen, pound, corral.

**padlock** verb *padlock the shed* LOCK (UP), fasten, secure.

**padre** noun *many of the soldiers requested time with the padre before shipping out* CHAPLAIN, priest, minister, pastor, father, parson, clergyman, cleric, ecclesiastic, man of the cloth, churchman, vicar, rector, curate, preacher; *informal* reverend, Holy Joe, sky pilot.

**paean** noun *a great paean of triumph* SONG OF PRAISE, hymn, alleluia; plaudit, glorification, eulogy, tribute, panegyric, accolade, acclamation; *formal* encomium.

**pagan** noun *pagans worshiped the sun* HEATHEN, infidel, idolater, idolatress; *archaic* paynim.

▸ adjective *the pagan festival* HEATHEN, ungodly, irreligious, infidel, idolatrous.

**page**[1] noun **1** *a book of 672 pages* FOLIO, sheet, side, leaf.

**2** *a glorious page in her life* PERIOD, time, stage, phase, epoch, era, chapter; episode, event.

**page**[2] noun *she worked as a page at the state legislature* MESSENGER, errand boy/girl.

▸ verb *could you please page Mr. Johnson?* CALL (FOR), summon, send for, buzz.

**pageant** noun *people dress up their dogs in wild costumes for the annual pageant* PARADE, procession, cavalcade, tableau (vivant); spectacle, extravaganza, show.

**pageantry** noun *the pageantry of Diana's wedding* SPECTACLE, display, ceremony, magnificence, pomp, splendor, grandeur, show; *informal* razzle-dazzle, razzmatazz.

**pain** noun **1** *she endured great pain* SUFFERING, agony, torture, torment, discomfort.

**2** *a pain in the stomach* ACHE, aching, soreness, throb, throbbing, sting, stinging, twinge, shooting pain, stab, pang, cramps; discomfort, irritation, tenderness.

**3** *the pain of losing a loved one* SORROW, grief, heartache, heartbreak, sadness, unhappiness, distress, desolation, misery, wretchedness, despair; agony, torment, torture, via dolorosa.

**4** *informal that child is a pain.* See NUISANCE.

**5** **(pains)** *he took great pains to hide his feelings* CARE, effort, bother, trouble.

▸ verb **1** *her foot is still* ***paining her*** HURT, cause pain, be painful, be sore, be tender, ache, throb, sting, twinge, cause discomfort; *informal* kill one.

**2** *the memory pains her* SADDEN, grieve, distress, trouble, perturb, oppress, cause anguish to.

**pained** adjective *it troubles us to see you so pained* UPSET, hurt, wounded, injured, insulted, offended, aggrieved, displeased, disgruntled, annoyed, angered, angry, cross, indignant, irritated, resentful; *informal* riled, miffed, aggravated, peeved, teed off, ticked off, sore.

**painful** adjective **1** *a painful arm* SORE, hurting, tender, aching, throbbing, angry.

**2** *a painful experience* DISAGREEABLE, unpleasant, nasty, bitter, distressing, upsetting, traumatic, miserable, sad, heartbreaking, agonizing, harrowing.

**painkiller** noun *these painkillers will make you drowsy* ANALGESIC, pain reliever, anodyne, anesthetic, narcotic; palliative.

**painless** adjective **1** *any killing of animals should be painless* WITHOUT PAIN, pain-free. ANTONYM painful.

**2** *getting rid of him proved to be painless* EASY, trouble-free, effortless, simple, plain sailing; *informal* as easy as pie, a piece of cake, child's play, a cinch. ANTONYM difficult.

**painstaking** adjective *painting these window frames is painstaking work* CAREFUL, meticulous, thorough, assiduous, sedulous, attentive, diligent, industrious, conscientious, punctilious, scrupulous, rigorous, particular; pedantic, fussy. ANTONYM slapdash.

**paint** noun *a gallon of white paint* COLORING, colorant, tint, dye, stain, pigment, color.

▸ verb **1** *paint the ceiling* COLOR, apply paint to, decorate, whitewash, emulsion, gloss, spray-paint, airbrush.

**2** *painting slogans on a wall* DAUB, smear, spray-paint, airbrush.

**3** *Rembrandt painted his mother* PORTRAY, picture, paint a picture of, depict, represent.

**4** *you paint a very stark picture of the suffering* TELL, recount, outline, sketch, describe, depict, evoke, conjure up.

PHRASE: **paint the town red** *informal we're taking the train into Albany, and we're gonna paint the town red* CELEBRATE, carouse, enjoy oneself, have a good/wild time, have a party; *informal* go out on the town, whoop it up, make whoopee, live it up, party, have a ball.

**painting** noun *his paintings are so charming in their simplicity* PICTURE, illustration, portrayal, depiction, representation, image, artwork; oil (painting), watercolor, canvas.

**pair** noun **1** *a pair of gloves* SET (OF TWO), matching set, two of a kind.

**2** *the pair were arrested* TWO, couple, duo, brace, twosome, duplet; twins.

**3** *a pair of lines* COUPLET; *Prosody* distich.

**4** *the happy pair* COUPLE, man/husband and wife.

▸ verb *a cardigan paired with a matching skirt* MATCH, put together, couple, twin.

PHRASE: **pair off/up** *Rachel paired up with Tommy* GET TOGETHER, team up, form a couple, make a twosome, hook up, marry.

**pal** noun *informal my best pal.* See FRIEND sense 1.

**palace** noun *tourists are not allowed in the east wing of the palace* ROYAL/OFFICIAL RESIDENCE, castle, château, mansion, stately home, schloss.

**palatable** adjective **1** *palatable meals* EDIBLE, eatable, digestible, tasty, appetizing, flavorful; *formal* comestible. ANTONYMS tasteless, insipid.

**2** *the truth is not always palatable* PLEASANT, acceptable, pleasing, agreeable, to one's liking. ANTONYMS disagreeable, unpleasant.

**palate** noun **1** *the tea burned her palate* ROOF OF THE MOUTH, hard/soft palate.

**2** *menus to suit the tourist palate* (SENSE OF) TASTE, appetite, stomach.

**3** *wine with a peachy palate* FLAVOR, savor, taste.

**palatial** adjective *a palatial estate on Long Island* LUXURIOUS, deluxe, magnificent, sumptuous, splendid, grand, opulent, lavish, stately, regal; fancy, upscale, upmarket; *informal* plush, swanky, posh, ritzy, swish. ANTONYM modest.

**palaver** noun *informal holy cow, what a palaver we caused in the girls' dormitory!* FUSS, commotion, trouble, rigmarole, folderol; *informal* song and dance, performance, to-do, carrying-on, hoo-ha, hullabaloo, ballyhoo.

**pale**[1] noun **1** *the pales of a fence* STAKE, post, pole, picket, upright.

**2** *outside the pale of decency* BOUNDARY, confines, bounds, limits. PHRASE: **beyond the pale** *his behavior was beyond the pale* UNACCEPTABLE, unseemly, improper, unsuitable, unreasonable, unforgivable, intolerable, disgraceful, deplorable, outrageous, scandalous, shocking; *informal* not on, out of line; *formal* exceptionable.

**pale**[2] adjective **1** *she looked pale and drawn* WHITE, pallid, pasty, wan, colorless, anemic, bloodless, washed out, peaked, ashen, gray, whitish, white-faced, whey-faced, drained, sickly, sallow, as white as a sheet, deathly pale; milky, creamy, cream, ivory, milk-white, alabaster; *informal* like death warmed over. ANTONYMS rosy, flushed.

**2** *pale colors* LIGHT, light-colored, pastel, muted, subtle, soft; faded, bleached, washed out.

**3** *the pale light of morning* DIM, faint, weak, feeble. ANTONYMS dark, bright.

**4** *a pale imitation* FEEBLE, weak, insipid, bland, poor, inadequate; uninspired, unimaginative, lackluster, spiritless, lifeless; *informal* pathetic.

▸ verb **1** *his face paled* GO/TURN WHITE, grow/turn pale, blanch, lose color.

**2** *everything else pales by comparison* DECREASE IN IMPORTANCE, lose significance, pale into insignificance, fade into the background.

**THE RIGHT WORD pale, ashen, livid, pallid, wan**

---

Someone of fair complexion who usually stays indoors and spends little time in the sun is apt to be **pale**, referring to an unusually white or colorless complexion; one can also become *pale* out of fear or illness. Someone who has lost color from being ill or under stress may be described as **pallid**, which suggests a paleness that is the result of some abnormal condition (*she appeared pallid when she left the police station*). **Wan** also connotes an unhealthy condition or sickly paleness (*her wan face smiled at him from the hospital bed*). Someone who is **ashen** has skin the pale grayish color of ashes (*ashen with fear*), while **livid** can mean either bluish to describe loss of normal coloring (*the livid face of a drowned corpse*) or reddish or flushed (*livid with rage*).

---

**pall**[1] noun **1** *a rich velvet pall* FUNERAL CLOTH, coffin covering.

**2** *a pall of black smoke* CLOUD, covering, cloak, veil, shroud, layer, blanket. PHRASE: **cast a pall over** *the bad news from home cast a pall over our honeymoon* SPOIL, cast a shadow over, overshadow, cloud, put a damper on.

**pall**[2] verb *the high life was beginning to pall* BECOME/GROW TEDIOUS, become/grow boring, lose its/their interest, lose attraction, wear off; weary, sicken, nauseate; irritate, irk.

**palliate** verb **1** *the treatment works by palliating symptoms* ALLEVIATE, ease, relieve, soothe, take the edge off, assuage, moderate, temper, diminish, decrease, blunt, deaden.

**2** *there is no way to palliate his dirty deed* DISGUISE, hide, gloss over, conceal, cover (up), camouflage, mask; excuse, justify, extenuate, mitigate.

**pallid** adjective **1** *a pallid child* PALE, white, pasty, wan, colorless, anemic, washed out, peaked, whey-faced, ashen, gray, whitish, drained, sickly, sallow; *informal* like death warmed over. See note at PALE[2].

**2** *pallid watercolors* INSIPID, uninspired, colorless, uninteresting, unexciting, unimaginative, lifeless, spiritless, sterile, bland.

**pallor** noun *her dark hair accentuated her pallor* PALENESS, pallidness, lack of color, wanness, ashen hue, pastiness, grayness, sickliness, sallowness.

**palm** PHRASES: **grease someone's palm** *informal my Uncle Duke would grease the commissioner's palm on Tuesday, and on Wednesday his speakeasy would be serving up booze by the barrel* BRIBE, buy (off), corrupt, suborn, give an inducement to; *informal* give a sweetener to.
**have someone in the palm of one's hand** *can't you see that Dorrey has you in the palm of her hand?* HAVE CONTROL OVER, have influence over, have someone eating out of one's hand, have someone on a string, have someone in one's hip pocket, have someone wrapped around one's finger.
**palm off** *you're not going to palm off that rusty old truck on me* FOIST, fob off, get rid of, dispose of, unload.

**palpable** adjective **1** *a palpable bump* TANGIBLE, touchable, noticeable, detectable. See note at TANGIBLE. ANTONYM imperceptible.

**2** *his reluctance was palpable* PERCEPTIBLE, perceivable, visible, noticeable, discernible, detectable, observable, tangible, unmistakable, transparent, self-evident; obvious, clear, plain (to see), evident, apparent, manifest, staring one in the face, written all over someone. ANTONYM imperceptible.

**USAGE NOTE palpable**

*Palpable* (literally, "touchable") = tangible; apparent. There is nothing wrong with using this word in figurative senses (*palpable weaknesses in the argument*), as it has been used since at least the fifteenth century. What is nonsensical, however, is to say that the *level* of frustration, tension, etc., is *palpable*—e.g.: "When they share a scene, the energy level is palpable [read *the energy is palpable*]." (*Daily News* [New York]; Sept. 24, 2002.) -BG

**palpitate** verb **1** *her heart began to palpitate* BEAT RAPIDLY, pound, throb, pulsate, pulse, thud, thump, hammer, race.

**2** *palpitating with terror* TREMBLE, quiver, quake, shake (like a leaf).

**paltry** adjective **1** *a paltry sum of money* SMALL, meager, trifling, insignificant, negligible, inadequate, insufficient, derisory, pitiful, pathetic, miserable, niggardly, beggarly; *informal* measly, piddling; *formal* exiguous. ANTONYM considerable.

**2** *naval glory struck him as paltry* WORTHLESS, petty, trivial, unimportant, insignificant, inconsequential, of little account. ANTONYM important.

**pamper** verb *Trevor's big sister pampered him* SPOIL, indulge, overindulge, cosset, mollycoddle, coddle, baby, wait on someone hand and foot.

**pamphlet** noun *there's some interesting information in this pamphlet* BROCHURE, leaflet, booklet, circular, flyer, fact sheet, handbill, mailer, folder.

**pan**[1] noun **1** *a heavy pan* SAUCEPAN, skillet, frying pan, pot, wok.

**2** *salt pans* HOLLOW, pit, depression, dip, crater, concavity.

▸ verb **1** *informal the movie was panned by the critics.* See CRITICIZE.

**2** *prospectors panned for gold* SIFT, search, look.

PHRASE: **pan out 1** *Bob's idea hadn't panned out* SUCCEED, be successful, work (out), turn out well, come to fruition.

**2** *the deal panned out badly* TURN OUT, work out, end (up), come out, fall out, evolve; *formal* eventuate.

**pan**[2] verb *the camera panned to the building* SWING (AROUND), sweep, move, turn, circle.

**panacea** noun *a panacea for the country's economic problems* UNIVERSAL CURE, cure-all, cure for all ills, universal remedy, elixir, wonder drug; *informal* magic bullet.

**panache** noun *the chorus line lacks panache* FLAMBOYANCE, confidence, self-assurance, style, flair, élan, dash, verve, zest, spirit, brio, éclat, vivacity, gusto, liveliness, vitality, energy; *informal* pizzazz, oomph, zip, zing.

**pancake** noun *a short stack of pancakes with maple syrup* hotcake, flapjack, griddle cake, crepe, blintz; latke, potato pancake.

**pandemic** adjective *the disease is pandemic in Africa* WIDESPREAD, prevalent, pervasive, rife, rampant. See note at EPIDEMIC.

**pandemonium** noun *we heard a bang and then there was complete pandemonium* BEDLAM, chaos, mayhem, uproar, turmoil, tumult, commotion, confusion, anarchy, furor, hubbub, rumpus; *informal* hullabaloo, hoopla. ANTONYM peace.

**pander** PHRASE: **pander to** *David was always there to pander to her every whim* INDULGE, gratify, satisfy, cater to, give in to, accommodate, comply with.

**panegyric** noun *the panegyric she delivered in Syd's memory brought tears to our eyes* EULOGY, speech of praise, paean, accolade, tribute.

**pang** noun **1** *hunger pangs* PAIN, sharp pain, shooting pain, twinge, stab, spasm.

**2** *a pang of remorse* QUALM, twinge, prick.

**panic** noun *a wave of panic* ALARM, anxiety, nervousness, fear, fright, trepidation, dread, terror, agitation, hysteria, consternation, perturbation, dismay, apprehension; *informal* flap, fluster, cold sweat, funk, tizzy, swivet. ANTONYM calm.

▸ verb **1** *there's no need to panic* BE ALARMED, be scared, be nervous, be afraid, take fright, be agitated, be hysterical, lose one's nerve, get overwrought, get worked up; *informal* flap, get in a flap, lose one's cool, get into a tizzy, freak out, get in a stew, have kittens.

**2** *talk of love panicked her* FRIGHTEN, alarm, scare, unnerve; *informal* throw into a tizzy, freak out.

**panoply** noun **1** *the full panoply of U.S. military might* ARRAY, range, collection.

**2** *all the panoply of religious liturgy* TRAPPINGS, regalia; splendor, spectacle, ceremony, ritual.

**panorama** noun **1** *he surveyed the panorama* VIEW, wide view, scenic view, vista, prospect, scene, scenery, landscape, seascape.

**2** *a panorama of the art scene* OVERVIEW, survey, review, presentation, appraisal.

**panoramic** adjective **1** *a panoramic view* SWEEPING, wide, extensive, scenic, commanding.

**2** *a panoramic look at the twentieth century* WIDE-RANGING, extensive, broad, far-reaching, comprehensive, all-embracing.

**pant** verb **1** *he was panting as they reached the top* BREATHE HEAVILY, breathe hard, puff, huff and puff, gasp, wheeze.

**2** *it makes you* ***pant for*** *more* YEARN FOR, long for, crave, hanker after/for, ache for, hunger for, thirst for, be hungry for, be thirsty for, wish for, desire, want; *informal* itch for, be dying for.

**pants** plural noun *a cashmere sweater with khaki pants* TROUSERS, slacks, britches.

**pap** noun **1** *a plateful of tasteless pap* SOFT FOOD, mush, slop, pulp, purée, mash, *trademark* Pablum; *informal* goo, goop, glop, gook.

**2** *commercial pap* TRIVIA, pulp (fiction), garbage, rubbish, nonsense; *informal* dreck, drivel, trash, twaddle, pablum.

**paper** noun **1** *a sheet of paper* writing paper, notepaper, vellum.

**2** *the local paper* NEWSPAPER, journal, gazette, periodical; tabloid, broadsheet, daily, weekly, evening paper; *informal* rag, tab.

**3** *the paper was peeling off the walls* WALLPAPER, wallcovering.

**4** *a three-hour paper* EXAM, examination, test, quiz.

**5** *she has just published a paper* ESSAY, article, monograph, thesis, work, dissertation, treatise, study, report, analysis, tract, critique, exegesis, review, term paper, theme.

**6 (papers)** *personal papers* DOCUMENTS, certificates, letters, files, deeds, records, archives, paperwork, documentation; *Law* muniments.

**7 (papers)** *they asked us for our papers* IDENTIFICATION PAPERS/DOCUMENTS, identity card, ID, credentials.

▸ verb *we papered the walls* WALLPAPER, hang wallpaper on.

PHRASE: **on paper 1** *he put his thoughts on paper* IN WRITING, in black and white, in print.

**2** *the combatants were evenly matched on paper* IN THEORY, theoretically, supposedly.

**papery** adjective *papery leaves* THIN, paper-thin, flimsy, delicate, insubstantial, light, lightweight.

**par** PHRASES: **below par 1** *their performances have been below par* SUBSTANDARD, inferior, not up to scratch, subpar, under par, below average, second-rate, mediocre, poor, undistinguished; *informal* not up to snuff, bush-league.

**2** *I'm feeling below par* SLIGHTLY UNWELL, not (very) well, not oneself, out of sorts; ill, unwell, poorly, washed out, rundown, peaked, off; *informal* under the weather, not up to snuff, lousy, rough.

**on a par with** *his voice is on a par with Tony Bennett* AS GOOD AS, comparable with, in the same class/league as, equivalent to, equal to, on a level with, of the same standard as.

**par for the course** *long hours are par for the course in catering* NORMAL, typical, standard, usual, what one would expect.

**up to par** *students whose grades are up to par* GOOD ENOUGH, up to the mark, satisfactory, acceptable, adequate, up to scratch; *informal* up to snuff.

**parable** noun *the parable of the prodigal son* ALLEGORY, moral story/tale, fable, exemplum.

**parade** noun **1** *a Memorial Day parade* PROCESSION, march, cavalcade, motorcade, spectacle, display, pageant; review, dress parade, tattoo; march past.

**2** *she made a great parade of doing the housework* EXHIBITION, show, display, performance, spectacle, fuss; *informal* hoo-ha, to-do.

▸ verb **1** *the teams paraded through the city* MARCH, process, file, troop.

**2** *she paraded up and down* STRUT, swagger, stride.

**3** *he was keen to parade his knowledge* DISPLAY, exhibit, make a show of, flaunt, show (off), demonstrate.

**paradigm** noun *why should your sets of values be the paradigm for the rest of us?* MODEL, pattern, example, exemplar, template, standard, prototype, archetype. See note at MODEL.

**paradise** noun **1** *the souls in paradise* HEAVEN, the kingdom of heaven, the heavenly kingdom, Elysium, the Elysian Fields, Valhalla, Avalon. ANTONYM hell.

**2** *Adam and Eve's expulsion from Paradise* THE GARDEN OF EDEN, Eden.

**3** *a tropical paradise* UTOPIA, Shangri-La, heaven, idyll, nirvana.

**4** *this is sheer paradise!* BLISS, heaven, ecstasy, delight, joy, happiness, nirvana, heaven on earth. ANTONYM hell.

**paradox** noun *the paradox of war is that you have to kill people in order to stop people from killing each other* CONTRADICTION, contradiction in terms, self-contradiction, inconsistency, incongruity; oxymoron; conflict, anomaly; enigma, puzzle, mystery, conundrum. See note at RIDDLE.

**paradoxical** adjective *I admit it seems paradoxical for a pacifist such as myself to be in favor of this military action* CONTRADICTORY, self-contradictory, inconsistent, incongruous, anomalous; illogical, puzzling, baffling, incomprehensible, inexplicable.

**paragon** noun *a paragon of cheerfulness* | *your cook is a paragon* PERFECT EXAMPLE, shining example, model, epitome, archetype, ideal, exemplar, nonpareil, embodiment, personification, quintessence, apotheosis, acme; jewel, gem, angel, treasure; *informal* one in a million, the tops; *archaic* a nonesuch.

**paragraph** noun **1** *the concluding paragraph* SECTION, subdivision, part, subsection, division, portion, segment, passage.

**2** *a paragraph in the newspaper* REPORT, article, item, sidebar, piece, write-up, mention.

**parallel** adjective **1** *parallel lines* SIDE BY SIDE, aligned, collateral, equidistant.

**2** *parallel careers* SIMILAR, analogous, comparable, corresponding, like, of a kind, akin, related, equivalent, matching, homologous.

**3** *a parallel universe* COEXISTING, coexistent, concurrent; contemporaneous, simultaneous, synchronous. ANTONYM divergent.

▸ noun **1** *an exact parallel* COUNTERPART, analog, equivalent, likeness, match, twin, duplicate, mirror.

**2** *there is an interesting parallel between these figures* SIMILARITY, likeness, resemblance, analogy, correspondence, equivalence, correlation, relation, symmetry, parity.

▸ verb **1** *his experiences parallel mine* RESEMBLE, be similar to, be like, bear a resemblance to; correspond to, be analogous to, be comparable/equivalent to, equate with/to, correlate with, imitate, echo, remind one of, duplicate, mirror, follow, match.

**2** *her performance has never been paralleled* EQUAL, match, rival, emulate.

**paralysis** noun **1** *the disease can cause paralysis* IMMOBILITY, powerlessness, incapacity, debilitation; *Medicine* paraplegia, quadriplegia, tetraplegia, monoplegia, hemiplegia, diplegia, paresis, paraparesis.

**2** *complete paralysis of the ports* SHUTDOWN, immobilization, stoppage.

**paralytic** adjective *her hands became paralytic* PARALYZED, crippled, disabled, incapacitated, powerless, immobilized, useless.

**paralyze** verb **1** *both of his legs were paralyzed* DISABLE, cripple, immobilize, incapacitate, debilitate; *formal* torpefy.

**2** *Sally was paralyzed by the sight of him* IMMOBILIZE, transfix, become rooted to the spot, freeze, stun, render motionless.

**3** *the capital was paralyzed by a general strike* BRING TO A STANDSTILL, immobilize, bring to a (grinding) halt, freeze, cripple, disable.

**parameter** noun *the parameters of the debate* FRAMEWORK, variable, limit, boundary, limitation, restriction, criterion, guideline.

**paramount** adjective *the safety of the staff is paramount* MOST IMPORTANT, of greatest/prime importance; uppermost, supreme, chief, overriding, predominant, foremost, prime, primary, principal, highest, main, key, central, leading, major, top; *informal* number-one.

**paramour** noun *archaic he was in love with his father's paramour* LOVER, significant other, inamorata; mistress, girlfriend, kept woman, other woman; boyfriend, main squeeze, other man, inamorato; *informal* toy boy, sugar daddy; *archaic* concubine, courtesan.

**paranoid** adjective *all the layoffs in my department have made me paranoid* OVERSUSPICIOUS, paranoiac, suspicious, mistrustful, fearful, insecure.

**parapet** noun **1** *Marian leaned over the parapet* BALUSTRADE, barrier, wall.

**2** *the sandbags making up the parapet* BARRICADE, rampart, bulwark, bank, embankment, fortification, defense, earthwork, breastwork, bastion.

**paraphernalia** plural noun *they have a ton of camping paraphernalia* EQUIPMENT, stuff, things, apparatus, kit, implements, tools, utensils, material(s), appliances, accoutrements, appurtenances, odds and ends, bits and pieces; *informal* gear.

**paraphrase** verb *paraphrasing literary texts* REWORD, rephrase, put/express in other words, rewrite, gloss.

▸ noun *this paraphrase of Frye's words* REWORDING, rephrasing, rewriting, rewrite, rendition, rendering, gloss.

**parasite** noun *she longed to be free of the parasites in her family* HANGER-ON, cadger, leech, passenger; *informal* bloodsucker, sponger, bottom feeder, scrounger, freeloader, mooch.

**parcel** noun **1** *a parcel of clothes* PACKAGE, packet; pack, bundle, box, case, bale.

**2** *a parcel of land* PLOT, piece, patch, tract, allotment, lot, plat.

▸ verb **1** *she* ***parceled up*** *the papers* PACK (UP), package, wrap (up), gift-wrap, tie up, bundle up.

**2** ***parceling out*** *commercial farmland* DIVIDE UP, portion out, distribute, share out, allocate, allot, apportion, hand out, dole out, dish out; *informal* divvy up.

**parched** adjective **1** *the parched earth* (BONE) DRY, dried up/out, arid, desiccated, dehydrated, baked, burned, scorched; withered, shriveled. See note at DRY.

**2** *informal I'm parched.* THIRSTY, longing for a drink, dry, dehydrated.

**pardon** noun **1** *pardon for your sins* FORGIVENESS, absolution, clemency, mercy, leniency, remission.

**2** *he offered them a full pardon* REPRIEVE, free pardon, amnesty, exoneration, release, acquittal, discharge; *formal* exculpation.

▸ verb **1** *I know she will pardon me* FORGIVE, absolve, have mercy on; excuse, condone, overlook. ANTONYM blame.

**2** *they were subsequently pardoned* EXONERATE, acquit, amnesty; reprieve, release, free; *informal* let off; *formal* exculpate. See note at ABSOLVE. ANTONYM punish.

▸ exclamation *Pardon?* WHAT DID YOU SAY, what, what's that, pardon me, I beg your pardon, sorry, excuse me; *informal* come again, say what.

**pardonable** adjective *a pardonable offense* EXCUSABLE, forgivable, condonable, understandable, minor, venial, slight. ANTONYM inexcusable.

**parent** noun *you'll need the signed consent of a parent* MOTHER, FATHER, birth/biological parent, progenitor; adoptive parent, foster-parent, step-parent, guardian; *literary* begetter.

▸ verb *those who parent young children* RAISE, bring up, look after, take care of, rear.

**parentage** noun *Deedham was bound by tradition to marry only a woman of the finest parentage* ORIGINS, extraction, birth, family, ancestry, lineage, heritage, pedigree, descent, blood, stock, roots.

**pariah** noun *they were treated as social pariahs* OUTCAST, persona non grata, black sheep, leper, undesirable, unperson, nonperson.

**parish** noun **1** *the municipal council of the parish of Oka* DISTRICT, community.

**2** *the story scandalized the parish* PARISHIONERS, churchgoers, congregation, fold, flock, community.

**parity** noun *we strive for a parity of wages* EQUALITY, equivalence, uniformity, consistency, correspondence, congruity, levelness, unity, coequality.

**park** noun **1** *we were playing in the park* playground, play area, public garden, garden(s), green.

**2** *a new national park* PARKLAND, wilderness area, protected area, nature reserve, game reserve.

▸ verb **1** *she parked her car* LEAVE, position; stop, pull up, pull over.

**2** *informal* *park your bag by the door* PUT (DOWN), place, deposit, leave, stick, shove, dump; *informal* plonk.

PHRASE: **park oneself** *informal* *park yourself there and we'll be with you in a moment* SIT DOWN, seat oneself, settle (oneself), install oneself; *informal* plunk oneself.

**parlance** noun *for the character of Lyndsay-Ann, she uses her most annoying Valley girl parlance* JARGON, language, phraseology, talk, speech, argot, patois, cant; *informal* lingo, -ese, -speak.

**parliament** noun *the Russian parliament* LEGISLATURE, legislative assembly, congress, senate, (upper/lower) house, (upper/lower) chamber, diet, assembly.

**parliamentary** adjective *parliamentary assemblies* LEGISLATIVE, lawmaking, governmental, congressional, senatorial, democratic, elected, representative.

**parochial** adjective *she was constantly challenging their parochial approach to education* NARROW-MINDED, small-minded, provincial, narrow, small-town, conservative, illiberal, intolerant; *informal* jerkwater. See note at BIAS. ANTONYM broad-minded.

**parody** noun **1** *a parody of the Gothic novel* SATIRE, burlesque, lampoon, pastiche, caricature, imitation, mockery; *informal* spoof, takeoff, send-up. See note at CARICATURE.

**2** *a parody of the truth* DISTORTION, travesty, caricature, misrepresentation, perversion, corruption, debasement.

▸ verb *parodying schoolgirl fiction* SATIRIZE, burlesque, lampoon, caricature, mimic, imitate, ape, copy, make fun of, travesty, take off; *informal* send up.

**paroxysm** noun *paroxysms of coughing* SPASM, attack, fit, burst, bout, convulsion, seizure, outburst, eruption, explosion, access.

**parrot** verb *they parroted slogans without appreciating their significance* REPEAT (MINDLESSLY), repeat mechanically, echo.

**parry** verb **1** *Alfonso parried the blow* WARD OFF, fend off; deflect, hold off, block, counter, repel, repulse.

**2** *I parried her constant questions* EVADE, sidestep, avoid, dodge, answer evasively, field, fend off.

**parsimonious** adjective *Lou's parsimonious mother was horrified by his lavish spending* CHEAP, miserly, mean, niggardly, close-fisted, close, penny-pinching, ungenerous, Scroogelike; *informal* tightfisted, cheeseparing, tight, stingy, mingy; *formal* penurious. See note at ECONOMICAL. ANTONYM generous.

**parsimony** noun *the parsimony of her grandparents had embittered her against the elderly* CHEAPNESS, miserliness, meanness, parsimoniousness, niggardliness, close-fistedness, closeness, penny-pinching; *informal* stinginess, minginess, tightness, tightfistedness, cheeseparing; *formal* penuriousness.

**parson** noun *the new parson brings a youthful joy to the pulpit* VICAR, rector, clergyman, cleric, chaplain, pastor, curate, man of the cloth, ecclesiastic, minister, priest, preacher; *informal* reverend, padre.

**part** noun **1** *the last part of the cake | a large part of their life* BIT, slice, chunk, lump, hunk, wedge, fragment, scrap, piece; portion, proportion, percentage, fraction. See note at FRAGMENT. ANTONYM whole.

**2** *car parts* COMPONENT, bit, constituent, element, module.

**3** *body parts* PART OF THE BODY, organ, limb, member.

**4** *the third part of the book* SECTION, division, volume, chapter, act, scene, installment.

**5** *another part of the country* DISTRICT, neighborhood, quarter, section, area, region.

**6** *the part of Juliet* (THEATRICAL) ROLE, character, persona.

**7** *she's learning her part* LINES, words, script, speech; libretto, lyrics, score.

**8** *he was jailed for his part in the affair* INVOLVEMENT, role, function, hand, work, responsibility, capacity, position, participation, contribution; *informal* bit.

▸ verb **1** *the curtains parted* SEPARATE, divide (in two), split (in two), move apart. ANTONYM join.

**2** *we parted on bad terms* LEAVE, take one's leave, say goodbye/farewell, say one's goodbyes/farewells, go one's (separate) ways, split, go away, depart. ANTONYM meet.

▸ adjective *a part payment* INCOMPLETE, partial, half, semi-, limited, inadequate, insufficient, unfinished. ANTONYM complete.

▸ adverb *it is part finished* TO A CERTAIN EXTENT/DEGREE, to some extent/degree, partly, partially, in part, half, relatively, comparatively, (up) to a point, somewhat; not totally, not entirely, (very) nearly, almost, just about, all but. ANTONYM completely.

PHRASES: **for the most part.** See MOSTLY.
**in part** *the water damage is due in part to the clogged gutters* TO A CERTAIN EXTENT/DEGREE, to some extent/degree, partly, partially, slightly, in some measure, (up) to a point.
**on the part of** *there is increased interest in these coins on the part of collectors* (MADE/DONE) BY, carried out by, caused by, from.
**part with** *Danielle could not part with her stuffed animals* GIVE UP/AWAY, relinquish, forgo, surrender, hand over, deliver up, dispose of.
**take part** *anyone who cares to can take part* PARTICIPATE, join in, get involved, enter, play a part/role, be a participant, contribute, have a hand, help, assist, lend a hand; *informal* get in on the act.
**take part in** *all students must take part in the CPR course before the end of junior year* PARTICIPATE IN, engage in, join in, get involved in, share in, play a part/role in, be a participant in, contribute to, be associated with, have a hand in.

**partake** verb **1** *only senior officers are allowed to* ***partake in*** *the negotiations* PARTICIPATE IN, take part in, engage in, join in, enter into, get involved in, share in, contribute to, play a part in, have a hand in, sit in on. ANTONYMS be excluded from, sit out.

**2** *those averse to sushi can* ***partake of*** *the hot buffet* CONSUME, have, eat, drink, take, ingest, devour; *informal* wolf down, polish off, tuck into. ANTONYMS forgo, abstain from.

**3** *the lyric essay* ***partakes of*** *the poem in its distillation of ideas and musicality of language* HAVE THE QUALITIES/ATTRIBUTES OF, suggest, evoke, be characterized by, hint at, manifest, evince.

**partial** adjective **1** *a partial recovery* INCOMPLETE, limited, qualified, imperfect, fragmentary, unfinished. ANTONYMS complete, total.

**2** *a very partial view of the situation* BIASED, prejudiced, partisan, one-sided, slanted, skewed, colored, unbalanced. ANTONYM unbiased.

PHRASE: **be partial to** *I'm partial to hotdogs and beer* LIKE, love, enjoy, have a liking for, be fond of, be keen on, have a soft spot for, have a taste for, have a penchant for; *informal* adore, be mad about/for, have a thing about, be crazy about, be nutty about, cotton to.

**partiality** noun **1** *his partiality toward their cause* BIAS, prejudice, favoritism, favor, partisanship. See note at BIAS.

**2** *her partiality for brandy* LIKING, love, fondness, taste, soft spot, predilection, penchant, passion.

**partially** adverb *the plan was only partially successful* TO A LIMITED EXTENT/DEGREE, to a certain extent/degree, partly, in part, not totally, not entirely, relatively, moderately, (up) to a point, somewhat, comparatively, slightly.

**participant** noun *the first 100 participants to sign up will get a free T-shirt* PARTICIPATOR, contributor, party, member; entrant, competitor, player, contestant, candidate.

**participate** verb *at least he's willing to* ***participate in*** *town events* TAKE PART IN, engage in, join in, get involved in, share in, play a part/role in, be a participant in, partake in, have a hand in, be associated with; cooperate in, help (out) with, assist in, lend a hand with/to.

**participation** noun *your participation is appreciated* INVOLVEMENT, part, contribution, association.

**particle** noun **1** *minute particles of rock* (TINY) BIT, (tiny) piece, speck, spot, fleck; fragment, sliver, splinter.

**2** *he never showed a particle of sympathy* IOTA, jot, whit, bit, scrap, shred, crumb, drop, hint, touch, trace, suggestion, whisper, suspicion, scintilla; *informal* smidgen.

**particular** adjective **1** *a particular group of companies* SPECIFIC, certain, distinct, separate, discrete, definite, precise; single, individual. ANTONYM general.

**2** *an issue of particular importance* (EXTRA) SPECIAL, especial, exceptional, unusual, singular, uncommon, notable, noteworthy, remarkable, unique; *formal* peculiar. ANTONYM ordinary.

**3** *he was particular about what he ate* FUSSY, fastidious, finicky, meticulous, punctilious, discriminating, selective, painstaking, exacting, demanding; *informal* persnickety, choosy, picky. ANTONYM careless.

▸ noun *the same in every particular* DETAIL, item, point, specific, element, aspect, respect, regard, particularity, fact, feature.

PHRASE: **in particular 1** *nothing in particular* SPECIFIC, special.

**2** *the poor, in particular, were hit by rising prices* PARTICULARLY, specifically, especially, specially.

**particularize** verb *the indictment particularized several incidents* SPECIFY, detail, itemize, list, enumerate, spell out, cite, stipulate, instance.

**particularly** adverb **1** *the acoustics are particularly good* ESPECIALLY, specially, very, extremely, exceptionally, singularly, peculiarly, unusually, extraordinarily, remarkably, outstandingly, amazingly, incredibly, really, seriously.

**2** *he particularly asked that I should help you* SPECIFICALLY, explicitly, expressly, in particular, especially, specially.

**parting** noun **1** *an emotional parting* FAREWELL, leave-taking, goodbye, adieu, departure; valediction.

**2** *they kept their parting quiet* SEPARATION, breakup, split, divorce, rift, estrangement.

**3** *the parting of the Red Sea* DIVISION, dividing, separation, separating, splitting, breaking up/apart, partition, partitioning.

▸ adjective *a parting kiss* FAREWELL, goodbye, last, final, valedictory.

**partisan** noun 1 *conservative partisans* SUPPORTER, follower, adherent, devotee, champion; fanatic, fan, enthusiast, stalwart, zealot, booster.

2 *the partisans opened fire from the woods* GUERRILLA, freedom fighter, resistance fighter, underground fighter, irregular (soldier).

▸ adjective *partisan attitudes* BIASED, prejudiced, one-sided, discriminatory, colored, partial, interested, sectarian, factional. ANTONYM unbiased.

**partition** noun 1 *the partition of Palestine* DIVIDING UP, partitioning, separation, division, dividing, subdivision, splitting (up), breaking up, breakup.

2 *room partitions* SCREEN, (room) divider, (dividing) wall, barrier, panel.

▸ verb 1 *the resolution partitioned Poland* DIVIDE (UP), subdivide, separate, split (up), break up; share (out), parcel out.

2 *the huge hall was partitioned* SUBDIVIDE, divide (up); separate (off), section off, screen off.

**partly** adverb *I admit I am partly responsible* TO A CERTAIN EXTENT/DEGREE, to some extent/degree, in part, partially, a little, somewhat, not totally, not entirely, relatively, moderately, (up) to a point, in some measure, slightly. ANTONYM completely.

**partner** noun 1 *business partners* COLLEAGUE, associate, coworker, fellow worker, collaborator, comrade, teammate; *archaic* compeer.

2 *his partner in crime* ACCOMPLICE, confederate, accessory, collaborator, fellow conspirator, helper; *informal* sidekick.

3 *your relationship with your partner* SPOUSE, husband, wife, consort, life partner; lover, girlfriend, boyfriend, fiancé, fiancée, significant other, live-in lover, common-law husband/wife, man, woman, mate; *informal* hubby, missus, old man, old lady/woman, better half, intended, other half, main squeeze.

**partnership** noun 1 *close partnership* COOPERATION, association, collaboration, coalition, alliance, union, affiliation, relationship, connection.

2 *thriving partnerships* COMPANY, firm, business, corporation, organization, association, consortium, syndicate.

**parturition** noun *formal even today, in many parts of the world, mortality associated with parturition is alarmingly high* CHILDBIRTH, birth, delivery, birthing, labor; *archaic* confinement, travail.

**party** noun 1 *150 people attended the party* (SOCIAL) GATHERING, (social) function, get-together, affair, celebration, festivity, reception, at-home; frolic, soiree, carousal, carouse, fête; *informal* bash, shindig, rave, do, shebang, bop, hop, blast, wingding.

2 *a party of German tourists* GROUP, company, body, gang, band, crowd, pack, contingent; *informal* bunch, crew, load.

3 *the left-wing parties* FACTION, political party, group, grouping, cabal, junta, bloc, camp, caucus.

4 *don't mention a certain party* PERSON, individual, somebody, someone.

▸ verb *informal let's party!* CELEBRATE, have fun, enjoy oneself, have a party, have a good/wild time, go on a spree, rave it up, carouse, make merry; *informal* go out on the town, paint the town red, whoop it up, let one's hair down, make whoopee, live it up, have a ball.

PHRASE: **be a party to** *he refused to be a party to their vandalism* GET INVOLVED IN/WITH, be associated with, be a participant in.

**parvenu** noun make way for our newest little hotshot parvenu UPSTART, social climber, arriviste.

**pass**[1] verb 1 *the traffic passing through the village* GO, proceed, move, progress, make one's way, travel. ANTONYM stop.

2 *a car passed him* OVERTAKE, go past/by, pull ahead of, overhaul, leave behind; *informal* leapfrog.

3 *time passed* ELAPSE, go by/past, advance, wear on, roll by, tick by.

4 *he passed the time writing letters* OCCUPY, spend, fill, use (up), employ, while away.

5 *pass me the salt* HAND (OVER), give, reach.

6 *Max passed the ball back* KICK, hit, throw, lob.

7 *her estate passed to her grandson* BE TRANSFERRED, go, be left, be bequeathed, be handed down/on, be passed on; *Law* devolve.

8 *his death passed almost unnoticed* HAPPEN, occur, take place, come about, transpire, come and go; *literary* befall.

9 *the storm passed* ABATE, fade (away), come to an end, blow over, run its course, die out, finish, end, cease, subside.

10 *nature's complexity passes all human understanding* SURPASS, exceed, transcend.

11 *he passed the exam* BE SUCCESSFUL IN, succeed in, gain a pass in, get through; *informal* sail through, scrape through. ANTONYM fail.

12 *the senate passed the bill* APPROVE, vote for, accept, ratify, adopt, agree to, authorize, endorse, legalize, enact; *informal* OK. ANTONYM reject.

13 *she could not let that comment pass* GO (UNNOTICED), stand, go unremarked, go undisputed.

14 *we should not pass judgment* DECLARE, pronounce, utter, express, deliver, issue.

15 *passing urine* DISCHARGE, excrete, evacuate, expel, emit, release.

▸ noun 1 *you must show your pass* PERMIT, warrant, authorization, license.

2 *a perfectly executed pass* KICK, hit, throw, cross, lateral (pass).

PHRASES: **come to pass** *literary it came to pass that Dorothy left Roberto* HAPPEN, come about, occur, transpire, arise; *literary* befall.

**make a pass at** *are you accusing Mr. Allen of making a pass at you* MAKE (SEXUAL) ADVANCES TO, proposition; *informal* come on to, make a play for, hit on, make time with, put the make on.

**pass away/on.** See DIE sense 1.

**pass as/for** *I really think you could pass for an attorney* BE MISTAKEN FOR, be taken for, be accepted as.

**pass off** *he tried to pass her off as his daughter* MISREPRESENT, falsely represent; disguise.

**pass out** *this heat could make anyone pass out* FAINT, lose consciousness, black out.

**pass over** *many a great movie has been passed over by the Academy* DISREGARD, overlook, ignore, pay no attention to, let pass, gloss over, take no notice of, pay no heed to, turn a blind eye to.

**pass up** *I should never have passed up my chance to go to Rome* TURN DOWN, reject, refuse, decline, give up, forgo, let pass, miss (out on); *informal* give something a miss.

**pass**2 noun *a pass through the mountains* ROUTE, way, road, passage, cut, gap, notch.

**passable** adjective **1** *the beer was passable* ADEQUATE, all right, fairly good, acceptable, satisfactory, moderately good, not (too) bad, average, tolerable, fair; mediocre, middling, ordinary, indifferent, unremarkable, unexceptional; *informal* OK, so-so, 'comme ci, comme ça,' nothing to write home about.

**2** *the road is still passable* NAVIGABLE, traversable, negotiable, unblocked, unobstructed, open, clear.

**passage** noun **1** *their passage through the country* TRANSIT, progress, passing, movement, motion, traveling.

**2** *the passage of time* PASSING, advance, course, march.

**3** *a passage from the embassy* SAFE CONDUCT, warrant, visa; admission, access.

**4** *the overnight passage* VOYAGE, crossing, trip, journey.

**5** *clearing a passage to the front door* WAY (THROUGH), route, path.

**6** *a passage to the kitchen* PASSAGEWAY.

**7** *the nasal passages* DUCT, orifice, opening, channel; inlet, outlet.

**8** *the passage to democracy* TRANSITION, development, progress, move, change, shift.

**9** *the passage of the bill* ENACTMENT, passing, ratification, royal assent, approval, adoption, authorization, legalization.

**10** *a passage from "Macbeth"* EXTRACT, excerpt, quotation, quote, citation, reading, piece, selection.

**passenger** noun *rail passengers* TRAVELER, commuter, fare, rider.

**passerby** noun *several passersby confirmed his description of the collision* BYSTANDER, eyewitness, witness.

**passing** adjective **1** *of passing interest* FLEETING, transient, transitory, ephemeral, brief, short-lived, temporary, momentary; *literary* evanescent.

**2** *a passing glance* HASTY, rapid, hurried, brief, quick; cursory, superficial, casual, perfunctory.

▸ noun **1** *the passing of time* PASSAGE, course, progress, advance.

**2** *Jack's passing* DEATH, demise, passing away/on, end, loss, quietus; *formal* decease.

**3** *the passing of the new bill* ENACTMENT, ratification, approval, adoption, authorization, legalization, endorsement.

PHRASE: **in passing** *in passing, let me add that the new membership directory will be available on Thursday* INCIDENTALLY, by the by/way, en passant.

**passion** noun **1** *the passion of activists* FERVOR, ardor, enthusiasm, eagerness, zeal, zealousness, vigor, fire, fieriness, energy, fervency, animation, spirit, spiritedness, fanaticism. ANTONYM apathy.

**2** *he worked himself up into a passion* (BLIND) RAGE, fit of anger/temper, temper, towering rage, tantrum, fury, frenzy. See note at EMOTION.

**3** *hot with passion* LOVE, (sexual) desire, lust, ardor, infatuation, lasciviousness, lustfulness.

**4** *his passion for football* ENTHUSIASM, love, mania, fascination, obsession, fanaticism, fixation, compulsion, appetite, addiction; *informal* thing.

**5** *French literature is my passion* OBSESSION, preoccupation, craze, mania, hobbyhorse.

**6** *the Passion of Christ* CRUCIFIXION, suffering, agony, martyrdom.

**passionate** adjective **1** *a passionate entreaty* INTENSE, impassioned, ardent, fervent, vehement, heated, emotional, heartfelt, eager, excited, animated, adrenalized, spirited, energetic, fervid, frenzied, fiery, wild, consuming, violent; *literary* perfervid. ANTONYM apathetic.

**2** *Elizabeth is **passionate about** sports* VERY KEEN ON, very enthusiastic about, addicted to; *informal* mad about, crazy about, hooked on, nuts about, nutso for.

**3** *a passionate kiss* AMOROUS, ardent, hot-blooded, aroused, loving, sexy, sensual, erotic, lustful; *informal* steamy, hot, red-hot, turned on. ANTONYM cold.

**4** *a passionate woman* EXCITABLE, emotional, fiery, volatile, mercurial, quick-tempered, high-strung, impulsive, temperamental. ANTONYM phlegmatic.

**passionless** adjective *a room full of passionless faces* UNEMOTIONAL, cold, cold-blooded, emotionless, frigid, cool, unfeeling, unloving, unresponsive, undemonstrative, impassive.

**passive** adjective **1** *a passive role* INACTIVE, nonactive, nonparticipative, uninvolved.

**2** *passive victims* SUBMISSIVE, acquiescent, unresisting, unassertive, compliant, pliant, obedient, docile, tractable, malleable, pliable. ANTONYMS active, assertive.

**3** *the woman's face was passive* EMOTIONLESS, impassive, unemotional, unmoved, dispassionate, passionless, detached, unresponsive, undemonstrative, apathetic, phlegmatic.

**passport** noun *qualifications are the passport to success* KEY, path, way, route, avenue, door, doorway.

**past** adjective **1** *memories of times past* GONE (BY), over (and done with), no more, done, bygone, former, (of) old, olden, long-ago; *literary* of yore.

**2** *the past few months* LAST, recent, preceding.

**3** *a past chairman* PREVIOUS, former, foregoing, erstwhile, one-time, sometime, ex-; *formal* quondam. ANTONYMS present, future.

▸ noun *details about her past* HISTORY, background, life (story).

▸ preposition **1** *she walked past the café* IN FRONT OF, by.

**2** *he's past retirement age* BEYOND, in excess of.

▸ adverb *they hurried past* ALONG, by, on.

PHRASE: **in the past** *in the past, they did not allow women to sit in the bar* FORMERLY, previously, in days/years/times gone by, in former times, in the (good) old days, in days of old, in olden times, once (upon a time); *literary* in days of yore, in yesteryear.

**paste** noun **1** *blend the ingredients to a paste* PURÉE, pulp, mush, mash, blend.

**2** *wallpaper paste* ADHESIVE, glue, gum, fixative, mucilage.

▸ verb *a notice was pasted on the door* GLUE, stick, gum, fix, affix.

**pastel** adjective *we softened the look of the room with pastel paints and fabrics* PALE, soft, light, light-colored, muted, subtle, subdued, soft-hued. ANTONYMS dark, bright.

**pastiche** noun **1** *a pastiche of literary models* MIXTURE, blend, medley, mélange, miscellany, mixed bag, potpourri, mix, compound, composite, collection, assortment, conglomeration, jumble, ragbag, hodgepodge.

**2** *a pastiche of eighteenth-century style* IMITATION, parody; *informal* takeoff.

**pastime** noun *two of my favorite pastimes are softball and street hockey* HOBBY, leisure activity/pursuit, sport, game, recreation, amusement, diversion, avocation, entertainment, interest, sideline.

**past master** noun *when it comes to interior design, Sheri is a past master* EXPERT, master, wizard, genius, old hand, veteran, maestro, connoisseur, authority, grandmaster; *informal* ace, pro, star, hotshot, maven, crackerjack.

**pastor** noun *our pastor is taking a group to Guatemala to help with disaster relief* MINISTER, clergyman, priest, parson, cleric, chaplain, padre, ecclesiastic, man of the cloth, churchman, vicar, rector, curate, preacher, imam; *informal* reverend.

**pastoral** adjective **1** *a pastoral scene* RURAL, country, countryside, rustic, agricultural, bucolic; *literary* sylvan, Arcadian. ANTONYM urban.

**2** *his pastoral duties* PRIESTLY, clerical, ecclesiastical, ministerial.

**pastry** noun **1** *breakfast pastries* cake, doughnut, croissant, cruller, Danish (pastry), eclair, tart, tartlet, pie.

**2** *two layers of pastry* CRUST, piecrust, croute.

**pasture** noun *the cows are in the pasture* GRAZING LAND, grassland, grass, pastureland, pasturage; *Brit.* ley; meadow, field; *literary* lea, mead, greensward.

**pat**[1] verb *Brian patted her on the shoulder* TAP, slap lightly, clap, touch.

▸ noun **1** *a pat on the cheek* TAP, light blow, clap, touch.

**2** *a pat of butter* PIECE, dab, lump, portion, knob, mass, gobbet, ball, curl.

PHRASE: **pat on the back** *Lenny's fellow students were eager to pat him on the back for his amazing test scores* CONGRATULATE, praise, take one's hat off to; commend, compliment, applaud, acclaim.

**pat**[2] adjective *pat answers* GLIB, simplistic, facile, unconvincing.

▸ adverb *his reply came rather pat* OPPORTUNELY, conveniently, at just/exactly the right moment, expediently, favorably, appropriately, fittingly, auspiciously, providentially, felicitously, propitiously.

PHRASES: **down pat** *the understudy knew Lori's lines down pat* WORD-PERFECT, by heart, by rote, by memory.
**get down pat** *I have to get these lyrics down pat within the next two hours* MEMORIZE, commit to memory, remember, learn by heart, learn (by rote).

**patch** noun **1** *a patch over one eye* COVER, eye patch, covering, pad.

**2** *a reddish patch on her wrist* BLOTCH, mark, spot, smudge, speckle, smear, stain, streak, blemish; *informal* splotch.

**3** *a patch of ground* PLOT, area, piece, strip, tract, parcel; bed, allotment, lot, plat.

**4** *informal* *they are going through a difficult patch* PERIOD, time, spell, phase, stretch.

▸ verb *her jeans were neatly patched* MEND, repair, put a patch on, sew (up), stitch (up).

PHRASE: **patch up** *informal* **1** *the houses were being patched up* REPAIR, mend, fix hastily, do a makeshift repair on.

**2** *he's trying to patch things up with his wife* RECONCILE, make up, settle, remedy, put to rights, rectify, clear up, set right, make good, resolve, square.

**patchwork** noun *the exhibit is essentially a patchwork of the students' favorite pieces* ASSORTMENT, miscellany, mixture, mélange, medley, blend, mixed bag, mix, collection, selection, assemblage, combination, potpourri, jumble, mishmash, bricolage, ragbag, hodgepodge.

**patchy** adjective **1** *their education has been patchy* UNEVEN, varying, variable, intermittent, fitful, sporadic, erratic, irregular, haphazard, hit-and-miss. ANTONYM uniform.

**2** *patchy evidence* FRAGMENTARY, inadequate, insufficient, rudimentary, limited, sketchy. ANTONYM comprehensive.

**patent** noun *there is a patent on the drug* COPYRIGHT, license, legal protection, registered trademark.

▸ adjective 1 *patent nonsense* OBVIOUS, clear, plain, evident, manifest, self-evident, transparent, overt, conspicuous, blatant, downright, barefaced, flagrant, undisguised, unconcealed, unmistakable.

2 *patent medicines* PROPRIETARY, patented, licensed, branded.

**paternal** adjective 1 *his face showed paternal concern* FATHERLY, fatherlike, patriarchal; protective, solicitous, compassionate, sympathetic.

2 *his paternal grandfather* ON ONE'S FATHER'S SIDE, patrilineal. ANTONYM maternal.

**paternity** noun *the blood tests are used to determine paternity* FATHERHOOD.

**path** noun 1 *a path down to the beach* TRAIL, pathway, walkway, track, footpath, trackway, bridleway, bridle path, portage trail, lane, alley, alleyway, passage, passageway; sidewalk, bikeway.

2 *journalists blocked his path* ROUTE, way, course; direction, bearing, line; orbit, trajectory.

3 *the best path toward a settlement* COURSE OF ACTION, route, road, avenue, line, approach, tack, strategy, tactic.

**pathetic** adjective 1 *a pathetic groan* PITIFUL, pitiable, piteous, moving, touching, poignant, plaintive, distressing, upsetting, heartbreaking, heart-rending, harrowing, wretched, forlorn. See note at MOVING.

2 *informal a pathetic excuse* FEEBLE, woeful, sorry, poor, pitiful, lamentable, deplorable, contemptible, inadequate, paltry, insufficient, insubstantial, unsatisfactory.

**pathological** adjective 1 *a pathological condition* MORBID, diseased.

2 *informal a pathological liar* COMPULSIVE, obsessive, inveterate, habitual, persistent, chronic, hardened, confirmed.

**pathos** noun *the pathos of Antoine's predicament* POIGNANCY, tragedy, sadness, pitifulness, piteousness, pitiableness.

**patience** noun 1 *she tried everyone's patience* FORBEARANCE, tolerance, restraint, self-restraint, stoicism; calmness, composure, equanimity, serenity, tranquility, imperturbability, phlegm, understanding, indulgence.

2 *a task requiring patience* PERSEVERANCE, persistence, endurance, tenacity, assiduity, application, staying power, doggedness, determination, resolve, resolution, resoluteness.

**patient** adjective 1 *I must ask you to be patient* FORBEARING, uncomplaining, tolerant, resigned, stoical; calm, composed, even-tempered, imperturbable, unexcitable, accommodating, understanding, indulgent; *informal* unflappable, cool.

2 *a good deal of patient work* PERSEVERING, persistent, tenacious, indefatigable, dogged, determined, resolved, resolute, single-minded; *formal* pertinacious.

▸ noun *a doctor's patient* SICK PERSON, case; invalid, convalescent, outpatient, in-patient.

**patio** noun *we had cocktails on the patio* TERRACE, sundeck, deck; courtyard.

**patois** noun *he recognized the patois of New Orleans in her speech* VERNACULAR, (local) dialect, regional language; jargon, argot, cant; *informal* (local) lingo.

**patrician** noun *the great patricians of the British Empire* ARISTOCRAT, grandee, noble, nobleman, noblewoman, lord, lady, peer, peeress; blue blood.

▸ adjective *patrician families* ARISTOCRATIC, noble, titled, blue-blooded, high-born, upper-class, landowning; *informal* upper-crust; *archaic* gentle.

**patriot** noun *would a true patriot abandon a comrade?* NATIONALIST, loyalist; chauvinist, jingoist, flag-waver.

**patriotic** adjective *a patriotic show of support* NATIONALIST, nationalistic, loyalist, loyal; chauvinistic, jingoistic, flag-waving. ANTONYM traitorous.

**patrol** noun 1 *an all-night patrol to protect the witness* VIGIL, guard, watch, monitoring, policing, patroling.

2 *the patrol stopped a suspect* SECURITY GUARD, sentry, sentinel, patrolman; scout, scouting party.

▸ verb *a security guard was patroling the neighborhood* KEEP GUARD (ON), guard, keep watch (on); police, make the rounds (of); stand guard (over), keep a vigil (on), defend, safeguard.

**patron** noun 1 *a patron of the arts* SPONSOR, backer, financier, benefactor, benefactress, contributor, subscriber, donor; philanthropist, promoter, friend, supporter; *informal* angel.

2 *club patrons* CUSTOMER, client, frequenter, consumer, user, visitor, guest; *informal* regular, habitué.

**patronage** noun 1 *art patronage* SPONSORSHIP, backing, funding, financing, promotion, assistance, support.

2 *political patronage* POWER OF APPOINTMENT, favoritism, nepotism, preferential treatment, cronyism, pork-barreling.

3 *thank you for your patronage* CUSTOM, trade, business.

**patronize** verb 1 *don't patronize me!* TREAT CONDESCENDINGLY, condescend to, look down on, talk down to, put down, treat like a child, treat with disdain.

2 *they patronized local merchants* DO BUSINESS WITH, buy from, shop at, be a customer of, be a client of, deal with, trade with, frequent, support.

3 *he patronized a national museum* SPONSOR, back, fund, finance, be a patron of, support, champion.

**patronizing** adjective *your patronizing mother just told me how "adequate" my dress is* CONDESCENDING, disdainful, supercilious, superior, imperious, scornful, contemptuous; *informal* uppity, high and mighty.

**patter**[1] verb 1 *raindrops pattered against the window* GO PITTER-PATTER, tap, drum, beat, pound, rat-a-tat, go pit-a-pat, thrum.

2 *she pattered across the floor* SCURRY, scuttle, skip, trip.

▸ noun *the patter of rain* PITTER-PATTER, tapping, pattering, drumming, beat, beating, pounding, rat-a-tat, pit-a-pat, clack, thrum, thrumming.

**patter**[2] noun **1** *this witty patter* PRATTLE, prating, blather, blither, drivel, chatter, jabber, babble; *informal* yabbering, yatter; *archaic* twaddle.

**2** *the salesman's patter* (SALES) PITCH, sales talk; *informal* line, spiel.

**3** *the local patter* SPEECH, language, parlance, dialect; *informal* lingo.

▸ verb *she pattered on incessantly* PRATTLE, prate, blather, drivel, chatter, jabber, babble; *informal* yabber, yatter.

**pattern** noun **1** *the pattern on the wallpaper* DESIGN, decoration, motif, marking, ornament, ornamentation.

**2** *the patterns of ant behavior* SYSTEM, order, arrangement, form, method, structure, scheme, plan, format, framework.

**3** *this would set the pattern for a generation* MODEL, example, criterion, standard, basis, point of reference, gauge, norm, yardstick, touchstone, benchmark; blueprint, archetype, prototype. See note at MODEL.

**4** *textile patterns* SAMPLE, specimen, swatch.

▸ verb *someone else is patterning my life* SHAPE, influence, model, fashion, mold, style, determine, control.

**patterned** adjective *patterned glassware* DECORATED, ornamented, fancy, adorned, embellished. ANTONYM plain.

**paucity** noun *a paucity of evidence* SCARCITY, sparseness, sparsity, dearth, shortage, poverty, insufficiency, deficiency, lack, want. ANTONYM abundance.

**paunch** noun *I love everything about him, even his cute little paunch* POTBELLY, beer belly, beer gut, spare tire, pot.

**pauper** noun *the story of a lowly pauper who rises to the top of a major crime syndicate* POOR PERSON, indigent, down-and-out; *informal* have-not.

**pause** noun *a pause in the conversation* STOP, cessation, break, halt, interruption, check, lull, respite, breathing space, discontinuation, hiatus, gap, interlude; adjournment, suspension, rest, wait, hesitation; *informal* letup, breather.

▸ verb *Hannah paused for a moment* STOP, cease, halt, discontinue, break off, take a break; adjourn, rest, wait, hesitate, falter, waver; *informal* take a breather, take five.

**pave** PHRASE: **pave the way for** *a document that could pave the way for legislation* PREPARE (THE WAY) FOR, make preparations for, get ready for, lay the foundations for, herald, precede.

**paw** noun *protect their paws from frostbite* FOOT, forepaw, hind paw.

▸ verb **1** *their offspring were pawing each other* HANDLE ROUGHLY, pull, grab, maul, manhandle.

**2** *some Casanova tried to paw her* FONDLE, feel, maul, molest; *informal* grope, feel up, goose.

**pawn** verb *he pawned his watch* PLEDGE, put in pawn, give as security, use as collateral; *informal* hock, put in hock.

▸ noun *a pawn in the battle for the throne* PUPPET, dupe, hostage, tool, cat's paw, instrument.

**pay** verb **1** *I want to pay him for his work* REWARD, reimburse, recompense, give payment to, remunerate.

**2** *Tom must pay a few more dollars* SPEND, expend, pay out, dish out, disburse; *informal* lay out, shell out, fork out, cough up; ante up, pony up.

**3** *he paid his debts* DISCHARGE, settle, pay off, clear, liquidate.

**4** *hard work will pay dividends* YIELD, return, produce.

**5** *he made the buses pay* BE PROFITABLE, make money, make a profit.

**6** *it doesn't pay to get involved* BE ADVANTAGEOUS, be of advantage, be beneficial, benefit.

**7** *paying compliments* BESTOW, grant, give, offer.

**8** *he will pay for his mistakes* SUFFER, suffer the consequences, be punished, atone, pay the penalty/price.

▸ noun *equal pay for women* SALARY, wages, payment; earnings, remuneration, reimbursement, income, revenue; *formal* emolument(s).

PHRASES: **pay back 1** *she has sworn to pay him back for his philandering* GET ONE'S REVENGE ON, be revenged on, avenge oneself on, get back at, get even with, settle accounts with, exact retribution on.

**2** *they eventually paid back the money* REPAY, pay off, give back, return, reimburse, refund.

**pay for** *I'll pay for dinner* FUND, finance, defray the cost of, settle up for, treat someone to; *informal* foot the bill for, shell out for, fork out for, cough up for, ante up for, pony up for.

**pay off 1** *he was busted for trying to pay off a cop* BRIBE, suborn, buy (off); *informal* grease someone's palm.

**2** *she paid off the car loan in less than a year* PAY (IN FULL), settle, discharge, clear, liquidate.

**3** *his hard work paid off* MEET WITH SUCCESS, be successful, be effective, get results.

**pay out** *how much did you have to pay out for that bike?* SPEND, expend, dish out, put up, part with, hand over; *informal* shell out, fork out/up, lay out, cough up.

**pay up** *you have one more week to pay up* MAKE PAYMENT, settle up, pay (in full); *informal* cough up.

**payable** adjective *a notice of payable taxes* DUE, owed, owing, outstanding, unpaid, overdue, in arrears, delinquent.

**payment** noun **1** *discounts for early payment* REMITTANCE, settlement, discharge, clearance, liquidation.

**2** *monthly payments* INSTALLMENT, premium.

**3** *extra payment for good performance* SALARY, wages, pay, earnings, fee(s), remuneration, reimbursement, income; *formal* emolument(s).

**peace** noun **1** *can't a man get any peace around here?* TRANQUILITY, calm, restfulness, peace and quiet, peacefulness, quiet, quietness; privacy, solitude. ANTONYM noise.

2 *peace of mind* SERENITY, peacefulness, tranquility, equanimity, calm, calmness, composure, ease, contentment, contentedness. ANTONYMS agitation, distress.

3 *we pray for peace* LAW AND ORDER, lawfulness, order, peacefulness, peaceableness, harmony, nonviolence; *formal* concord. ANTONYM conflict.

4 *a lasting peace* TREATY, truce, cease-fire, armistice, cessation/suspension of hostilities. ANTONYM war.

**peaceable** adjective 1 *a peaceable man* PEACE-LOVING, nonviolent, nonaggressive, easygoing, placid, gentle, inoffensive, good-natured, even-tempered, amiable, amicable, friendly, affable, genial, pacific, dovelike, dovish, unwarlike, pacifist; *formal* irenic. ANTONYMS aggressive, belligerent.

2 *a peaceable society* PEACEFUL, strife-free, harmonious; law-abiding, disciplined, orderly, civilized. ANTONYMS unruly, warring.

**peaceful** adjective 1 *everything was quiet and peaceful* TRANQUIL, calm, restful, quiet, still, relaxing, soothing, undisturbed, untroubled, private, secluded. See note at CALM. ANTONYMS noisy, bustling.

2 *his peaceful mood* SERENE, calm, tranquil, composed, placid, at ease, untroubled, unworried, content. ANTONYM agitated.

3 *peaceful relations* HARMONIOUS, at peace, peaceable, on good terms, amicable, friendly, cordial, nonviolent. ANTONYM hostile.

**peacemaker** noun *she was regarded as the great peacemaker of her people* ARBITRATOR, arbiter, mediator, negotiator, conciliator, go-between, intermediary, pacifier, appeaser, peacemonger, pacifist, peace-lover, dove; *informal* peacenik.

**peak** noun 1 *the peaks of the mountains* SUMMIT, top, crest, pinnacle, apex, crown, cap.

2 *the highest peak* MOUNTAIN, hill, height, mount, alp.

3 *the peak of a cap* BRIM, visor.

4 *the peak of his career* HEIGHT, high point/spot, pinnacle, summit, top, climax, culmination, apex, zenith, crowning point, acme, capstone, apogee, prime, heyday.

▸ verb *conservative support has peaked* REACH ITS HEIGHT, climax, reach a climax, come to a head.

▸ adjective *peak loads* MAXIMUM, top, greatest, highest; ultimate, best, optimum.

**peaked** adjective *Marjorie, my dear, you look so peaked* PALE, pasty, wan, drained, washed out, drawn, pallid, anemic, ashen, gray, pinched, sickly, sallow, ill, unwell, poorly, indisposed, run down, off; *informal* under the weather, rough, lousy.

**peal** noun 1 *a peal of bells* CHIME, carillon, ring, ringing, tintinnabulation.

2 *peals of laughter* SHRIEK, shout, scream, howl, gale, fit, roar, hoot.

3 *a peal of thunder* RUMBLE, roar, boom, crash, clap, crack.

▸ verb 1 *the bell pealed* RING (OUT), chime (out), clang, sound, ding, jingle.

2 *the thunder pealed* RUMBLE, roar, boom, crash, resound.

**peasant** noun 1 *peasants working the land* AGRICULTURAL WORKER, small farmer, rustic, swain, villein, serf, campesino; *historical* habitant.

2 *informal you peasants!* See BOOR.

**peccadillo** noun *I'm sure we can overlook a few peccadilloes* MISDEMEANOR, petty offense, indiscretion, lapse, misdeed.

**peck** verb 1 *the cockerel pecked my heel* BITE, nip, strike, hit, tap, rap, jab.

2 *he pecked her on the cheek* KISS, give a peck.

3 *informal she* ***pecked at*** *her food* NIBBLE (AT), pick at, take very small bites from, toy with, play with.

**peculiar** adjective 1 *something peculiar began to happen* STRANGE, unusual, odd, funny, curious, bizarre, weird, queer, unexpected, unfamiliar, abnormal, atypical, anomalous, out of the ordinary; exceptional, extraordinary, remarkable; puzzling, mystifying, mysterious, perplexing, baffling; suspicious, eerie, uncanny, unnatural; *informal* freaky, fishy, creepy, spooky. ANTONYM ordinary.

2 *peculiar behavior* BIZARRE, eccentric, strange, odd, weird, queer, funny, unusual, abnormal, idiosyncratic, unconventional, outlandish, quirky; *informal* wacky, freakish, oddball, offbeat, off the wall, wacko.

3 *mannerisms* ***peculiar to*** *the islanders* CHARACTERISTIC OF, typical of, representative of, indicative of, suggestive of, exclusive to, unique to.

4 *their own peculiar contribution* DISTINCTIVE, characteristic, distinct, individual, special, idiosyncratic, unique, personal.

**peculiarity** noun 1 *a legal peculiarity* ODDITY, anomaly, abnormality.

2 *a physical peculiarity* IDIOSYNCRASY, mannerism, quirk, foible.

3 *one of the peculiarities of the city* CHARACTERISTIC, feature, (essential) quality, property, trait, attribute, hallmark, trademark.

4 *the peculiarity of this notion* STRANGENESS, oddness, bizarreness, weirdness, queerness, unexpectedness, unfamiliarity, incongruity.

5 *there is a certain peculiarity about her appearance* OUTLANDISHNESS, bizarreness, unconventionality, idiosyncrasy, weirdness, oddness, eccentricity, unusualness, abnormality, queerness, strangeness, quirkiness; *informal* wackiness, freakiness.

**pecuniary** adjective *free from pecuniary anxieties* FINANCIAL, monetary, money, fiscal, economic. See note at FINANCIAL.

**pedagogic** adjective *Dr. Snow encouraged me in my pedagogic endeavors* EDUCATIONAL, educative, pedagogical, teaching, instructional, instructive, didactic; academic, scholastic.

**pedagogue** *formal* noun *her thirty-two years as a most beloved* *pedagogue* TEACHER, schoolteacher, schoolmaster, schoolmistress, master, mistress, tutor; lecturer, academic, don, professor, instructor, educator, educationist, educationalist.

**pedant** noun *pedants insist that the twenty-first century starts with 2001* DOGMATIST, purist, literalist, formalist, doctrinaire, perfectionist; quibbler, hair-splitter, casuist, sophist; *informal* nitpicker.

**pedantic** adjective *a pedantic interpretation of the rules* OVERSCRUPULOUS, scrupulous, precise, exact, perfectionist, punctilious, meticulous, fussy, fastidious, finicky; dogmatic, purist, literalist, literalistic, formalist; casuistic, casuistical, sophistic, sophistical; captious, hair-splitting, quibbling; *informal* nitpicking, persnickety.

**pedantry** noun *the pedantry in her argument has upset the flow of our discussion* DOGMATISM, purism, literalism, formalism; overscrupulousness, scrupulousness, perfectionism, fastidiousness, punctiliousness, meticulousness; captiousness, quibbling, hair-splitting, casuistry, sophistry; *informal* nitpicking. See note at KNOWLEDGE.

**peddle** verb **1** *they are peddling water filters* SELL, sell from door to door, hawk, tout, vend; trade (in), deal in, traffic in.

**2** *peddling unorthodox views* ADVOCATE, champion, preach, put forward, proclaim, propound, promote, promulgate.

**pedestal** noun *a bust on a pedestal* PLINTH, base, support, mounting, stand, foundation, pillar, column, pier; *Architecture* socle. PHRASE: **put on a pedestal** *if you put me on a pedestal, I'll eventually disappoint you* IDEALIZE, lionize, look up to, respect, hold in high regard, think highly of, admire, esteem, revere, worship.

**pedestrian** noun *accidents involving pedestrians* WALKER, person on foot; **(pedestrians)** foot traffic. ANTONYM driver.

▸ adjective *pedestrian lives* DULL, boring, tedious, monotonous, uneventful, unremarkable, tiresome, wearisome, uninspired, unimaginative, unexciting, uninteresting; unvarying, unvaried, repetitive, routine, commonplace, workaday; ordinary, everyday, run-of-the-mill, mundane, humdrum; *informal* plain-vanilla. ANTONYM exciting.

**pedigree** noun *a long pedigree* ANCESTRY, descent, lineage, line (of descent), genealogy, family tree, extraction, derivation, origin(s), heritage, parentage, bloodline, background, roots.

▸ adjective *a pedigree cat* PURE-BRED, thoroughbred, pure-blooded.

**peek** verb **1** *Hermione peeked from behind the curtains* (HAVE A) PEEP, have a peek, spy, take a sly/stealthy look, sneak a look/peek; *informal* take a gander.

**2** *the deer's antlers* ***peeked out*** *from the trees* APPEAR (SLOWLY/PARTLY), show, come into view/sight, become visible, emerge, peep (out).

▸ noun *a peek at the map* SECRET LOOK, sly look, stealthy look, sneaky look, peep, glance, glimpse, hurried/quick look; *informal* gander, squint.

**peel** verb **1** *peel and core the fruit* PARE, skin, take the skin/rind off; hull, shell, husk, shuck; *technical* decorticate.

**2** *use a long knife to peel the veneer* TRIM (OFF), peel off, pare, strip (off), shave (off), remove.

**3** *the wallpaper was peeling* FLAKE (OFF), peel off, come off in layers/strips.

▸ noun *orange peel* RIND, skin, covering, zest; hull, pod, integument, shuck.

PHRASE: **keep one's eyes peeled** *keep your eyes peeled for a light blue Pontiac* KEEP A (SHARP) LOOKOUT, look out, keep one's eyes open, keep watch, be watchful, be alert, be on the alert, be on the qui vive, be on guard.

**peep**[1] verb **1** *I peeped through the keyhole* LOOK QUICKLY, cast a brief look, take a secret look, sneak a look, (have a) peek, glance; *informal* take a gander.

**2** *the moon peeped through the clouds* APPEAR (SLOWLY/PARTLY), show, come into view/sight, become visible, emerge, peek, peer out.

▸ noun *I'll just take a peep at it* QUICK LOOK, brief look, (sneak) peek, glance; *informal* gander, squint.

**peep**[2] noun **1** *I heard a quiet peep* CHEEP, chirp, chirrup, tweet, twitter, chirr, warble.

**2** *there's been not a peep out of the children* SOUND, noise, cry, word.

**3** *the painting was sold without a peep* COMPLAINT, grumble, mutter, murmur, grouse, objection, protest, protestation; *informal* moan, gripe, grouch.

**peephole** noun *just take a look through this peephole* OPENING, gap, cleft, slit, crack, chink, keyhole, knothole, squint.

**peer**[1] verb *he peered at the manuscript* LOOK CLOSELY, try to see, narrow one's eyes, screw up one's eyes, squint.

**peer**[2] noun **1** *his academic peers* EQUAL, coequal, fellow, confrere; contemporary; *formal* compeer.

**2** *hereditary peers* ARISTOCRAT, lord, lady, peer of the realm, peeress, noble, nobleman, noblewoman, titled man/woman, patrician; duke/duchess, marquess/marchioness, earl/countess, viscount/viscountess, baron/baroness, marquis/marquise, count.

**peerage** noun *she claims to be related to British peerage* ARISTOCRACY, nobility, peers and peeresses, lords and ladies, patriciate; the House of Lords, the Lords.

**peerless** adjective *a peerless performance* INCOMPARABLE, matchless, unrivaled, inimitable, beyond compare/comparison, unparalleled, unequaled, without equal, second to none, unsurpassed, unsurpassable, nonpareil; unique, consummate, perfect, rare, transcendent, surpassing; *formal* unexampled.

**peeve** verb *informal it seems that everything I do peeves her* IRRITATE, annoy, vex, anger, exasperate, irk, gall, pique, nettle, put out, get on someone's nerves, try someone's patience, ruffle someone's feathers; rub the wrong way; *informal* aggravate, rile, needle, get to, bug, get someone's goat, get/put someone's back up, tee off, tick off.

**peevish** adjective *he was embarrassed by his mother's peevish disposition* IRRITABLE, fractious, fretful, cross, petulant, querulous, pettish, crabby, crotchety, cantankerous, curmudgeonly, sullen, grumpy, bad-tempered, short-tempered, touchy, testy, tetchy, snappish, irascible, waspish, prickly, crusty, dyspeptic, splenetic, choleric; *informal* cranky, ornery. ANTONYM good-humored.

**peg** noun *the joints are secured by pegs* PIN, nail, dowel, skewer, spike, rivet, brad, screw, bolt, hook, spigot; *Mountaineering* piton; *Golf* tee.

▸ verb **1** *the tarp is pegged to the ground* FIX, pin, attach, fasten, secure, make fast.

**2** *we decided to peg our prices* HOLD DOWN, keep down, fix, set, hold, freeze.

PHRASE: **take down a peg or two** *wouldn't I just love to take that Mr. Bigshot down a peg or two* HUMBLE, humiliate, mortify, bring down, shame, embarrass, abash, put someone in their place, chasten, subdue, squash, deflate, make someone eat humble pie; *informal* show up, settle someone's hash, cut down to size, make someone eat crow.

**pejorative** adjective *his remarks were considered too pejorative for daytime radio* DISPARAGING, derogatory, denigratory, deprecatory, defamatory, slanderous, libelous, abusive, insulting, slighting; *informal* bitchy. ANTONYM complimentary.

**pellet** noun **1** *a pellet of mud* LITTLE BALL, little piece.

**2** *pellet wounds* BULLET, shot, lead shot, buckshot, slug.

**3** *rabbit pellets* EXCREMENT, excreta, droppings, feces, dung, turd.

**pell-mell** adverb **1** *people streamed pell-mell from the building* HELTER-SKELTER, headlong, (at) full tilt, hotfoot, posthaste, hurriedly, hastily, recklessly, precipitately.

**2** *the sacks' contents were thrown pell-mell to the ground* UNTIDILY, anyhow, in disarray, in a mess, in a muddle; *informal* all over the place, every which way, any old how, all over the map, all over the lot.

**pellucid** adjective **1** *the pellucid waters* TRANSLUCENT, transparent, clear, crystal clear, crystalline, glassy, limpid, unclouded, gin-clear.

**2** *pellucid prose* LUCID, limpid, clear, crystal clear, articulate; coherent, comprehensible, understandable, intelligible, straightforward, simple, clean, well-constructed; *formal* perspicuous.

**pelt**[1] verb **1** *they pelted him with snowballs* BOMBARD, shower, attack, assail, pepper.

**2** *they said we'd get some showers, but it's really* ***pelting down*** POUR (DOWN), come down, teem (down), stream down, rain cats and dogs, rain hard.

**3** *informal* *they pelted into the factory* DASH, run, race, rush, sprint, bolt, dart, career, charge, shoot, hurtle, careen, fly, speed, zoom, streak; hasten, hurry; *informal* tear, belt, hotfoot it, scoot, leg it, go like a bat out of hell, bomb, hightail it.

**pelt**[2] noun *an animal's pelt* SKIN, hide, fleece, coat, fur.

**pen**[1] noun *you'll need a pen and paper* ballpoint (pen), fountain pen, rollerball; felt tip (pen); highlighter, marker (pen).

▸ verb *she penned a number of articles* WRITE, compose, draft, dash off; write down, jot down, set down, take down, scribble.

**pen**[2] noun *a sheep pen* ENCLOSURE, fold, sheepfold, pound, compound, stockade; sty, coop, corral.

▸ verb *the hostages had been penned up in a basement* CONFINE, coop (up), cage, shut in, box up/in, lock up/in, trap, imprison, incarcerate, immure.

**penal** adjective **1** *a penal institution* DISCIPLINARY, punitive, corrective, correctional.

**2** *penal rates of interest* EXORBITANT, extortionate, excessive, outrageous, preposterous, unreasonable, inflated, sky-high.

**penalize** verb **1** *if you break the rules you will be penalized* PUNISH, discipline, inflict a penalty on. ANTONYM reward.

**2** *people with certain medical conditions would be penalized* HANDICAP, disadvantage, put at a disadvantage, cause to suffer. ANTONYM favor.

**penalty** noun **1** *increased penalties for dumping oil at sea* PUNISHMENT, sanction, punitive action, retribution; fine, forfeit, sentence; penance; *formal* mulct. ANTONYM reward.

**2** *a game full of penalties* FOUL, infraction.

**3** *the penalties of old age* DISADVANTAGE, difficulty, drawback, handicap, downside, minus; trial, tribulation, bane, affliction, burden, trouble. ANTONYM advantage.

**penance** noun *true penance requires honest self-examination* ATONEMENT, expiation, self-punishment, self-mortification, self-abasement, amends; punishment, penalty.

**penchant** noun *I have a penchant for small dogs* LIKING, fondness, preference, taste, relish, appetite, partiality, soft spot, love, passion, desire, fancy, whim, weakness, inclination, bent, bias, proclivity, predilection, predisposition.

**pencil** noun **1** *a sharpened pencil* lead pencil, mechanical pencil, colored pencil; grease pencil; eyebrow pencil, lip pencil.

**2** *a pencil of light* BEAM, ray, shaft, finger, gleam.

▸ verb **1** *he penciled his name inside the cover* WRITE, write down, jot down, scribble, note, take down.

**2** *pencil a line along the top of the molding* DRAW, trace, sketch.

**pendant** noun *she wore an antique gold pendant around her neck* NECKLACE, locket, medallion.

**pendent** adjective *the tree's pendent catkins* HANGING, suspended, dangling, pendulous, pensile, pendant, drooping, droopy, trailing.

**pending** adjective **1** *nine cases were still pending* UNRESOLVED, undecided, unsettled, awaiting decision/action, undetermined, open, hanging fire, (up) in the air, on ice, ongoing, outstanding, not done, unfinished, incomplete; *informal* on the back burner.

**2** *with a general election pending* IMMINENT, impending, about to happen, forthcoming, upcoming, on the way, coming, approaching, looming, gathering, near, nearing, close, close at hand, in the offing, to come.

▸ preposition *they were released on bail pending an appeal* AWAITING, until, till, until there is/are.

**penetrate** verb **1** *the knife penetrated his lungs* PIERCE, puncture, make a hole in, perforate, stab, prick, gore, spike.

**2** *they penetrated the enemy territory* INFILTRATE, slip into, sneak into, insinuate oneself into.

**3** *fear penetrated her bones* PERMEATE, pervade, fill, spread throughout, suffuse, seep through.

**4** *he seemed to have penetrated the mysteries of nature* UNDERSTAND, comprehend, apprehend, fathom, grasp, perceive, discern, get to the bottom of, solve, resolve, make sense of, interpret, puzzle out, work out, unravel, decipher, make head(s) or tail(s) of; *informal* crack, get, figure out.

**5** *her words finally penetrated* REGISTER, sink in, be understood, be comprehended, become clear, fall into place; *informal* click.

**penetrating** adjective **1** *a penetrating wind* PIERCING, cutting, biting, stinging, keen, sharp, harsh, raw, freezing, chill, wintry, cold. See note at KEEN. ANTONYMS mild, gentle.

**2** *a penetrating voice* SHRILL, strident, piercing, carrying, loud, high, high-pitched, piping, ear-splitting, screechy, intrusive. ANTONYMS mellow, soft.

**3** *a penetrating smell* PUNGENT, pervasive, strong, powerful, sharp, acrid; heady, aromatic. ANTONYM mild.

**4** *her penetrating gaze* OBSERVANT, searching, intent, alert, shrewd, perceptive, probing, piercing, sharp, keen.

**5** *a penetrating analysis* PERCEPTIVE, insightful, keen, sharp, sharp-witted, intelligent, clever, smart, incisive, piercing, razor-edged, trenchant, astute, shrewd, clear, acute, percipient, perspicacious, discerning, sensitive, thoughtful, deep, profound. ANTONYM dull.

**penetration** noun **1** *skin penetration by infective larvae* PERFORATION, piercing, puncturing, puncture, stabbing, pricking.

**2** *remarks of great penetration* INSIGHT, discernment, perception, perceptiveness, intelligence, sharp-wittedness, cleverness, incisiveness, keenness, sharpness, trenchancy, astuteness, shrewdness, acuteness, clarity, acuity, percipience, perspicacity, discrimination, sensitivity, thoughtfulness, profundity; *formal* perspicuity.

**penitence** noun *the writer prays to God in penitence* REPENTANCE, contrition, regret, remorse, remorsefulness, ruefulness, sorrow, sorrowfulness, pangs of conscience, self-reproach, shame, guilt, compunction; *archaic* rue.

**penitent** adjective *she stood there looking like a penitent child* REPENTANT, contrite, remorseful, sorry, apologetic, regretful, conscience-stricken, rueful, ashamed, shamefaced, abject, in sackcloth and ashes. ANTONYM unrepentant.

**pen name** noun *her pen name was Annabelle Lord* PSEUDONYM, nom de plume, assumed name, alias, professional name.

**pennant** noun *pennants fly from the towers* FLAG, standard, ensign, color(s), banner, banderole, guidon; *Nautical* burgee.

**penniless** adjective *Van Gogh died penniless* DESTITUTE, poverty-stricken, impoverished, poor, indigent, impecunious, in penury, moneyless, necessitous, needy, bankrupt, insolvent, without a cent (to one's name), without a sou; *informal* (flat) broke, cleaned out, strapped for cash, bust; *formal* penurious. ANTONYM wealthy.

**penny** PHRASE: **a pretty penny** *informal I bet that boat cost you a pretty penny* A LOT OF MONEY, millions, billions, a king's ransom; *informal* a (small) fortune, lots/heaps of money, a mint, a killing, a bundle, a tidy sum, big money, big bucks, an arm and a leg.

**penny-pinching** adjective *Zane's penny-pinching aunt gave him five dollars as a wedding gift* MEAN, miserly, niggardly, parsimonious, close-fisted, cheeseparing, grasping, Scroogelike; *informal* stingy, mingy, tight, tightfisted, money-grubbing; *formal* penurious; *archaic* near. ANTONYM generous.

**pension** noun *I doubt I can live on my pension* retirement (benefits), superannuation; Social Security; allowance, benefit, support, welfare.

**pensive** adjective *sorry to interrupt your pensive mood, but we've got to leave* THOUGHTFUL, reflective, contemplative, musing, meditative, introspective, ruminative, absorbed, preoccupied, deep/lost in thought, in a brown study, brooding; *formal* cogitative.

**pent-up** adjective *pent-up anger will eventually explode* REPRESSED, suppressed, stifled, smothered, restrained, confined, bottled up, held in/back, unvented, kept in check, curbed, bridled.

**penurious** adjective *formal* **1** *a penurious student* POOR, poor as a church mouse, poverty-stricken, destitute, necessitous, impecunious, impoverished, indigent, needy, in need/want, badly off, in reduced/straitened circumstances, hard up, unable to make ends meet, penniless, without a cent (to one's name), without a sou; *informal* (flat) broke, strapped for cash. ANTONYM wealthy.

**2** *a penurious old skinflint* MEAN, miserly, niggardly, parsimonious, penny-pinching, close-fisted, Scroogelike; *informal* stingy, mingy, tight, tightfisted, money-grubbing; *archaic* near. ANTONYM generous.

**penury** noun *Dylan was oblivious to his brother's wretched state of penury* EXTREME POVERTY, destitution, pennilessness, impecuniousness, impoverishment, indigence, pauperism, privation, beggary.

**people** noun **1** *crowds of people* HUMAN BEINGS, persons, individuals, humans, mortals, (living) souls, personages, 'men, women, and children'; *informal* folks. See note at PERSON.

**2** *the American people* CITIZENS, subjects, electors, voters, taxpayers, residents, inhabitants, (general) public, citizenry, nation, population, populace.

**3** *a man of the people* COMMON PEOPLE, proletariat, masses, populace, rank and file, commonality, third estate, plebeians; *derogatory* hoi polloi, common herd, great unwashed, proles, plebs.

**4** *her people don't live far away* FAMILY, parents, relatives, relations, folks, kinsmen, kin, kith and kin, kinsfolk, flesh and blood, nearest and dearest.

**5** *the peoples of Africa* RACE, (ethnic) group, tribe, clan. See note at PERSON.

▸ verb *the Beothuk who once peopled Newfoundland* POPULATE, settle (in), colonize, inhabit, live in, occupy; *formal* reside in, be domiciled in, dwell in.

**pep** *informal* noun *a performance full of pep* DYNAMISM, life, energy, spirit, liveliness, animation, bounce, sparkle, effervescence, verve, spiritedness, ebullience, high spirits, enthusiasm, vitality, vivacity, fire, dash, panache, élan, zest, exuberance, vigor, gusto, brio; *informal* feistiness, get-up-and-go, oomph, pizzazz, vim. PHRASE: **pep up** *why don't we pep up this gathering with some tunes?* ENLIVEN, animate, liven up, put some/new life into, invigorate, vitalize, revitalize, vivify, ginger up, energize, galvanize, put some spark into, stimulate, get something going, perk up; brighten up, cheer up; *informal* buck up.

**pepper** verb **1** *salt and pepper the potatoes* ADD PEPPER TO, season, flavor.

**2** *stars peppered the desert skies* SPRINKLE, fleck, dot, spot, stipple; cover, fill.

**3** *a burst of bullets peppered the tank* BOMBARD, pelt, shower, rain down on, attack, assail, batter, strafe, rake, blitz, hit.

**peppery** adjective **1** *a peppery sauce* SPICY, spiced, peppered, hot, highly seasoned, piquant, pungent, sharp. ANTONYMS mild, bland.

**2** *a peppery old man* IRRITABLE, cantankerous, irascible, bad-tempered, ill-tempered, grumpy, grouchy, crotchety, short-tempered, tetchy, testy, crusty, crabby, curmudgeonly, peevish, cross, fractious, pettish, prickly, waspish; *informal* ornery, snappish, cranky. ANTONYM affable.

**perceive** verb **1** *I immediately perceived the flaws in her story* DISCERN, recognize, become aware of, see, distinguish, realize, grasp, understand, take in, make out, find, identify, hit on, comprehend, apprehend, appreciate, sense, divine; *informal* figure out; *Brit. informal* twig; *formal* become cognizant of.

**2** *she perceived a twitch in his nose whenever he lied* SEE, discern, detect, catch sight of, spot, observe, notice.

**3** *she was perceived as too negative* REGARD, look on, view, consider, think of, judge, deem, adjudge.

**perceptible** adjective *I am sure that the flaw in the upholstery is perceptible only to you, my dear* NOTICEABLE, perceivable, detectable, discernible, visible, observable, recognizable, appreciable; obvious, apparent, evident, manifest, patent, clear, distinct, plain, conspicuous. See note at TANGIBLE.

**perception** noun **1** *our perception of our own limitations* RECOGNITION, awareness, consciousness, appreciation, realization, knowledge, grasp, understanding, comprehension, apprehension; *formal* cognizance.

**2** *popular perceptions of old age* IMPRESSION, idea, conception, notion, thought, belief, judgment, estimation.

**3** *he talks with great perception* INSIGHT, perceptiveness, percipience, perspicacity, understanding, sharpness, sharp-wittedness, intelligence, intuition, cleverness, incisiveness, trenchancy, astuteness, shrewdness, acuteness, acuity, discernment, sensitivity, penetration, thoughtfulness, profundity; *formal* perspicuity.

**perceptive** adjective *children are usually more perceptive than their parents think* INSIGHTFUL, discerning, sensitive, intuitive, observant; piercing, penetrating, percipient, perspicacious, penetrative, clear-sighted, farsighted, intelligent, clever, canny, keen, sharp, sharp-witted, astute, shrewd, quick, smart, acute, discriminating; *informal* on the ball, right-brained, heads-up, with it. ANTONYM obtuse.

**perch** noun *the chicken's perch* POLE, rod, branch, roost, rest, resting place.

▸ verb **1** *three swallows perched on the telegraph wire* ROOST, sit, rest; alight, settle, land, come to rest.

**2** *she perched her glasses on her nose* PUT, place, set, rest, balance.

**3** *the church **is perched** on a hill* BE LOCATED, be situated, be positioned, be sited, stand.

**perchance** adverb *literary perchance we shall meet again* MAYBE, perhaps, possibly, for all one knows, it could be, it's possible, conceivably; *literary* peradventure.

**percipient** adjective. See PERCEPTIVE.

**percolate** verb **1** *water percolated through the soil* FILTER, drain, drip, ooze, seep, trickle, dribble, leak, leach.

**2** *these views began to percolate through society as a whole* SPREAD, be disseminated, filter, pass; permeate, pervade.

**3** *he put some coffee on to percolate* BREW; *informal* perk.

**perdition** noun *I hope that lawyer goes to perdition!* DAMNATION, eternal punishment; hell, hellfire, doom.

**peremptory** adjective **1** *a peremptory reply* BRUSQUE, imperious, high-handed, brisk, abrupt, summary, commanding, dictatorial, autocratic, overbearing, dogmatic, arrogant, overweening, lordly, magisterial, authoritarian; emphatic, firm, insistent; *informal* bossy.

**2** *a peremptory order of the court* IRREVERSIBLE, binding, absolute, final, conclusive, decisive, definitive, categorical, irrefutable, incontrovertible; *Law* unappealable.

**perennial** adjective *the perennial fascination with crime* ABIDING, enduring, lasting, everlasting, perpetual, eternal, continuing, unending, unceasing, never-ending, endless, undying, ceaseless, persisting, permanent, constant, continual, unfailing, unchanging, never-changing.

**perfect** adjective **1** *she strove to be the perfect wife* IDEAL, model, without fault, faultless, flawless, consummate, quintessential, exemplary, best, ultimate, copybook; unrivaled, unequaled, matchless, unparalleled, beyond compare, without equal, second to none, too good to be true, Utopian, incomparable, nonpareil, peerless, inimitable, unexcelled, unsurpassed, unsurpassable.

2 *a classic Les Paul guitar in perfect condition* FLAWLESS, mint, as good as new, pristine, impeccable, immaculate, superb, superlative, optimum, prime, optimal, peak, excellent, faultless, as sound as a bell, unspoiled, unblemished, undamaged, spotless, unmarred; *informal* tip-top, A1.

3 *a perfect copy* EXACT, precise, accurate, faithful, correct, unerring, inerrant, right, true, strict; *informal* on the money.

4 *the perfect Christmas present for golfers* IDEAL, just right, right, appropriate, fitting, fit, suitable, apt, made to order, tailor-made; very.

5 *she felt like a perfect idiot* ABSOLUTE, complete, total, real, out-and-out, thorough, thoroughgoing, downright, utter, sheer, arrant, unmitigated, unqualified, veritable, in every respect, unalloyed.

▸ verb *he's busy perfecting his bowling technique* IMPROVE, better, polish (up), hone, refine, put the finishing/final touches to, brush up, fine-tune.

**perfection** noun 1 *the perfection of her technique* IMPROVEMENT, betterment, refinement, refining, honing.

2 *for him, she was still perfection* THE IDEAL, a paragon, the ne plus ultra, a nonpareil, the crème de la crème, the last word, the ultimate, the best; *informal* one in a million, the tops, da bomb; *dated, informal* the bee's knees, the cat's meow/pajamas/whiskers.

**perfectionist** noun *the just-so placement of every little figurine and throw pillow immediately gave him away as a perfectionist* PURIST, stickler for perfection, idealist; pedant.

**perfectly** adverb 1 *a perfectly cooked meal* FAULTLESSLY, superbly, superlatively, excellently, flawlessly, to perfection, without fault, ideally, inimitably, incomparably, impeccably, immaculately, exquisitely, consummately; *informal* like a dream, to a T.

2 *I think we understand each other perfectly* ABSOLUTELY, utterly, completely, altogether, entirely, wholly, totally, thoroughly, fully, in every respect.

3 *you know perfectly well that is not what I meant* VERY, quite, full; *informal* damn, damned, darned, bloody.

**perfidious** adjective *literary a perfidious lover* TREACHEROUS, duplicitous, deceitful, disloyal, faithless, unfaithful, traitorous, treasonous, false, false-hearted, double-dealing, two-faced, untrustworthy. ANTONYM faithful.

**perfidy** noun *literary the perfidy of her husband* TREACHERY, duplicity, deceit, deceitfulness, disloyalty, infidelity, faithlessness, unfaithfulness, betrayal, treason, double-dealing, untrustworthiness, breach of trust; *literary* perfidiousness.

**perforate** verb *a shell fragment perforated his left lung* PIERCE, penetrate, enter, puncture, prick, bore through, riddle.

**perform** verb 1 *I have my duties to perform* CARRY OUT, do, execute, discharge, bring about, bring off, accomplish, achieve, fulfill, complete, conduct, effect, dispatch, work, implement; *informal* pull off; *formal* effectuate; *archaic* acquit oneself of. ANTONYM neglect.

2 *a car that performs well at low speeds* FUNCTION, work, operate, run, go, respond, behave, act, acquit oneself/itself.

3 *the play has been performed in San Francisco* STAGE, put on, present, mount, enact, act, produce.

4 *the band performed live in Central Park* APPEAR, play, be on stage, sing, dance, act.

**performance** noun 1 *the evening performance* SHOW, production, showing, presentation, staging; concert, recital; *informal* gig.

2 *their performance of Mozart's concerto in E flat* RENDITION, rendering, interpretation, reading, playing, acting, representation.

3 *the continual performance of a single task* CARRYING OUT, execution, discharge, accomplishment, completion, fulfillment, dispatch, implementation; *formal* effectuation.

4 *the performance of the processor* FUNCTIONING, working, operation, running, behavior, capabilities, capability, capacity, power, potential.

5 *informal he made a great performance of telling her about it* FUSS, production, palaver, scene, business, pantomime; *informal* song and dance, big deal, to-do, hoo-ha.

**performer** noun *he began his career as a bit performer in B movies* ACTOR, ACTRESS, thespian, artiste, artist, entertainer, trouper, player, musician, singer, dancer, comic, comedian, comedienne.

**perfume** noun 1 *a bottle of perfume* FRAGRANCE, scent, eau de toilette, toilet water, eau de cologne, cologne, aftershave.

2 *the heady perfume of lilacs* SMELL, scent, fragrance, aroma, bouquet, redolence. See note at SMELL.

**perfunctory** adjective *a perfunctory review* CURSORY, desultory, quick, brief, hasty, hurried, rapid, fleeting, token, casual, superficial, careless, halfhearted, sketchy, mechanical, automatic, routine, offhand, inattentive. ANTONYMS careful, thorough.

**perhaps** adverb *perhaps they'll get married* MAYBE, for all one knows, it could be, it may be, it's possible, possibly, conceivably; *literary* peradventure, perchance.

**peril** noun *a situation fraught with peril* DANGER, jeopardy, risk, hazard, insecurity, uncertainty, menace, threat, perilousness; pitfall, problem.

**perilous** adjective *a perilous journey through the mountains* DANGEROUS, fraught with danger, hazardous, risky, unsafe, treacherous; precarious, vulnerable, uncertain, insecure, exposed, at risk, in jeopardy, in danger, touch-and-go; *informal* dicey. ANTONYM safe.

**perimeter** noun **1** *the perimeter of a circle* CIRCUMFERENCE, outside, outer edge.

**2** *the perimeter of the vast estate* BOUNDARY, border, limits, bounds, confines, edge, margin, fringe(s), periphery, borderline, verge; *literary* bourn, marge. See note at PARAMETER.

**period** noun **1** *a six-week period* TIME, spell, interval, stretch, term, span, phase, bout, run, duration, chapter, stage; while, patch.

**2** *the postwar period* ERA, age, epoch, time, days, years; *Geology* eon.

**3** *a double math period* LESSON, class, session.

**4** *women who suffer from painful periods* MENSTRUATION, menstrual flow, menses; *informal* the curse, time of the month, monthlies.

**periodic** adjective *Michael made periodic visits to the hospital* REGULAR, periodical, at fixed intervals, recurrent, recurring, repeated, cyclical, cyclic, seasonal; occasional, infrequent, intermittent, sporadic, spasmodic, odd.

**periodical** noun *he wrote for two periodicals* JOURNAL, publication, magazine, newspaper, paper, review, digest, gazette, newsletter, organ, quarterly, annual, weekly; *informal* mag, glossy.

**peripatetic** adjective *I could never get used to her peripatetic lifestyle* NOMADIC, itinerant, traveling, wandering, roving, roaming, migrant, migratory, unsettled.

**peripheral** adjective **1** *the city's peripheral subdivisions* OUTLYING, outer, on the edge/outskirts, surrounding.

**2** *peripheral issues* SECONDARY, subsidiary, incidental, tangential, marginal, minor, unimportant, lesser, inessential, nonessential, immaterial, ancillary. ANTONYM central.

**periphery** noun *rambling estates on the periphery of the city* EDGE, outer edge, margin, fringe, boundary, border, perimeter, rim, verge, borderline; outskirts, outer limits/reaches, bounds; *literary* bourn, marge. ANTONYM center.

**periphrastic** adjective *the periphrastic nature of legal syntax* CIRCUMLOCUTORY, circuitous, roundabout, indirect, tautological, pleonastic, prolix, verbose, wordy, long-winded, rambling, wandering, tortuous, diffuse.

**perish** verb **1** *millions of soldiers perished* DIE, lose one's life, be killed, fall, expire, meet one's death, be lost, lay down one's life, breathe one's last, pass away, go the way of all flesh, give up the ghost, go to glory, meet one's maker, cross the great divide; *informal* kick the bucket, turn up one's toes, shuffle off this mortal coil, buy it, croak, bite the big one, buy the farm; *archaic* decease, depart this life.

**2** *must these hopes perish so soon?* COME TO AN END, die (away), disappear, vanish, fade, dissolve, evaporate, melt away, wither.

**3** *the wood had perished* GO BAD, go off, spoil, rot, go moldy, molder, putrefy, decay, decompose.

**perjure** PHRASE: **perjure oneself** *he made the regrettable mistake of perjuring himself* LIE UNDER OATH, lie, commit perjury, give false evidence/testimony; *formal* forswear oneself, be forsworn.

**perjury** noun *she was found guilty of perjury* LYING UNDER OATH, giving false evidence/testimony, making false statements, willful falsehood.

**perk**[1] PHRASE: **perk up 1** *you seem to have perked up* CHEER UP, brighten up, liven up, take heart; *informal* buck up.

**2** *the economy has been slow to perk up* RECOVER, rally, improve, revive, take a turn for the better, look up, pick up, bounce back.

**3** *you could do with something to perk you up* CHEER UP, liven up, brighten up, raise someone's spirits, give someone a boost/lift, revitalize, invigorate, energize, enliven, ginger up, put new life/heart into, put some spark into, rejuvenate, refresh, vitalize; *informal* buck up, pep up.

**perk**[2] noun *a job with a lot of perks* FRINGE BENEFIT, additional benefit, benefit, advantage, bonus, extra, plus; *informal* freebie; *formal* perquisite.

**permanence** noun *the permanence of their relationship gives them a mutual sense of security* STABILITY, durability, permanency, fixity, fixedness, changelessness, immutability, endurance, constancy, continuity, immortality, indestructibility, perpetuity, endlessness.

**permanent** adjective **1** *permanent brain damage* LASTING, enduring, indefinite, continuing, perpetual, everlasting, eternal, abiding, constant, irreparable, irreversible, lifelong, indissoluble, indelible, standing, perennial, unending, endless, never-ending, immutable, undying, imperishable, indestructible, ineradicable; *literary* sempiternal, perdurable. ANTONYM temporary.

**2** *a permanent job* LONG-TERM, stable, secure, durable. ANTONYM temporary.

**permanently** adverb **1** *the attack left her permanently disabled* FOR ALL TIME, forever, forevermore, for good, for always, for ever and ever, (for) evermore, until hell freezes over, in perpetuity, indelibly, immutably, until the end of time; *informal* for keeps, until the cows come home, until kingdom come; *archaic* for aye.

**2** *I was permanently hungry* CONTINUALLY, constantly, perpetually, always.

**permeate** verb **1** *the delicious smell permeated the entire apartment* PERVADE, spread through, fill, filter through, diffuse through, imbue, penetrate, pass through, percolate through, perfuse, charge, suffuse, steep, impregnate, inform.

**2** *these resins are able to permeate the timber* SOAK THROUGH, penetrate, seep through, saturate, transfuse, percolate through, leach through.

**permissible** adjective *permissible levels of atmospheric pollution* PERMITTED, allowable, allowed, acceptable, legal, lawful, legitimate, admissible, licit, authorized, sanctioned, tolerated; *informal* legit, OK. ANTONYM forbidden.

**permission** noun *so, do I have permission to use the car?* AU-

THORIZATION, consent, leave, authority, sanction, license, dispensation, assent, acquiescence, agreement, approval, seal/stamp of approval, approbation, endorsement, blessing, imprimatur, clearance, allowance, tolerance, sufferance, empowerment; *informal* the go-ahead, the thumbs up, the OK, the green light, say-so. See note at LIBERTY.

**permissive** adjective *our parents were far less permissive than we are* LIBERAL, broad-minded, open-minded, free, free and easy, easygoing, live-and-let-live, latitudinarian, laissez-faire, libertarian, tolerant, forbearing, indulgent, lenient; overindulgent, lax, soft. See note at LENIENT. ANTONYMS intolerant, strict.

**permit** verb *I cannot permit you to leave | I cannot permit your leaving* ALLOW, authorize, give someone permission, sanction, grant, give someone the right, license, empower, enable, entitle, qualify; give one's blessing to, give the nod to; consent to, assent to, acquiesce in, agree to, tolerate, countenance; legalize, legitimate; *informal* give the go-ahead to, give the thumbs up to, OK, give the OK to, give the green light to; *formal* accede to; *archaic* suffer; (**permit someone to**), let. ANTONYMS ban, forbid.

▸ noun *I need to see your permit* AUTHORIZATION, license, pass, ticket, warrant, document, certification; passport, visa.

**permutation** noun *all the possible permutations were explored* ARRANGEMENT, form, version, configuration, incarnation, order, organization, selection.

**pernicious** adjective *a pernicious influence on society* HARMFUL, damaging, destructive, injurious, hurtful, detrimental, deleterious, dangerous, adverse, inimical, unhealthy, unfavorable, bad, evil, baleful, wicked, malign, malevolent, malignant, noxious, poisonous, corrupting; *literary* maleficent. ANTONYM beneficial.

**perpendicular** adjective **1** *the perpendicular stones* UPRIGHT, vertical, erect, plumb, straight (up and down), on end, standing, upended. ANTONYM horizontal.

**2** *lines perpendicular to each other* AT RIGHT ANGLES, at 90 degrees.

**3** *the perpendicular hillside* STEEP, sheer, precipitous, abrupt, bluff, vertiginous.

**perpetrate** verb *they perpetrated a series of armed robberies* COMMIT, carry out, perform, execute, do, effect, bring about, accomplish; be guilty of, be to blame for, be responsible for, inflict, wreak; *informal* pull off; *formal* effectuate.

**perpetual** adjective **1** *deep caves in perpetual darkness* EVERLASTING, never-ending, eternal, permanent, unending, endless, without end, lasting, long-lasting, constant, abiding, enduring, perennial, timeless, ageless, deathless, undying, immortal; unfailing, unchanging, never-changing, changeless, unfading; *rare* sempiternal, perdurable. ANTONYMS transitory, temporary.

**2** *a perpetual state of fear* CONSTANT, permanent, uninterrupted, continuous, unremitting, unending, unceasing, persistent, unbroken. ANTONYM intermittent.

**3** *her mother's perpetual nagging* INTERMINABLE, incessant, ceaseless, endless, without respite, relentless, unrelenting, persistent, continual, continuous, nonstop, never-ending, recurrent, repeated, unremitting, sustained, around/round-the-clock, chronic, unabating; *informal* eternal.

**perpetuate** verb *must you perpetuate these stupid myths?* KEEP ALIVE, keep going, preserve, conserve, sustain, maintain, continue, extend, carry on, keep up, prolong; immortalize, commemorate, memorialize, eternalize.

**perpetuity** PHRASE: **in perpetuity** *the archive will be preserved in perpetuity as a unified collection* FOREVER, forevermore, permanently, for always, for good, perpetually, for ever and ever, for all time, until the end of time, until hell freezes over, eternally, for eternity, everlastingly; *informal* for keeps; *archaic* for aye.

**perplex** verb *the bizarre notes left at each of these crime scenes perplexed us* PUZZLE, baffle, mystify, bemuse, bewilder, confound, confuse, disconcert, dumbfound, throw, throw/catch off balance, exercise, worry; *informal* flummox, be all Greek to, stump, bamboozle, floor, beat, faze, fox; *informal* discombobulate.

**perplexing** adjective *he was famous for solving the most perplexing cases* PUZZLING, baffling, mystifying, mysterious, bewildering, confusing, disconcerting, worrying, unaccountable, difficult to understand, beyond one, paradoxical, peculiar, funny, strange, weird, odd.

**perplexity** noun **1** *he scratched his head in perplexity* CONFUSION, bewilderment, puzzlement, bafflement, incomprehension, mystification, bemusement; *informal* bamboozlement, discombobulation.

**2** *the perplexities of international relations* COMPLEXITY, complication, intricacy, problem, difficulty, mystery, puzzle, enigma, paradox.

**perquisite** noun *formal*. See PERK[2].

**persecute** verb **1** *they were persecuted for their religious beliefs* OPPRESS, abuse, victimize, ill-treat, mistreat, maltreat, tyrannize, torment, torture; martyr.

**2** *she was persecuted by the press* HARASS, hound, plague, badger, harry, intimidate, pick on, pester, bother, devil, bully, victimize, terrorize; *informal* hassle, give someone a hard time, get on someone's case.

**perseverance** noun *in a competitive environment, perseverance is an invaluable asset* PERSISTENCE, tenacity, determination, staying power, indefatigability, steadfastness, purposefulness; patience, endurance, application, diligence, dedication, commitment, doggedness, assiduity, tirelessness, stamina; intransigence, obstinacy; *informal* stick-to-it-iveness; *formal* pertinacity.

**persevere** verb *she will persevere regardless of the obstacles* PERSIST, continue, carry on, go on, keep on, keep going, struggle on, hammer away, be persistent, be determined, see/follow something through, keep at it, press on/ahead, not take no for an answer, be tenacious, stand one's ground, stand fast/firm, hold on, go the distance, stay the course, plod on, stop at nothing, leave no stone unturned; *informal* soldier on, hang on, plug away, stick to one's guns, stick it out, hang in there. ANTONYM give up.

**persist** verb **1** *Corbett persisted with his questioning.* See PERSEVERE.

**2** *if dry weather persists, water the lawn thoroughly* CONTINUE, hold, carry on, last, keep on, keep up, remain, linger, stay, endure.

**persistence** noun. See PERSEVERANCE.

**persistent** adjective **1** *a very persistent man* TENACIOUS, persevering, determined, resolute, purposeful, dogged, single-minded, tireless, indefatigable, patient, unflagging, untiring, insistent, importunate, relentless, unrelenting; stubborn, intransigent, obstinate, obdurate; *formal* pertinacious. ANTONYM irresolute.

**2** *persistent rain* CONSTANT, continuous, continuing, continual, nonstop, never-ending, steady, uninterrupted, unbroken, interminable, incessant, unceasing, endless, unending, perpetual, unremitting, unrelenting, relentless, unrelieved, sustained. ANTONYMS occasional, intermittent.

**3** *a persistent cough* CHRONIC, permanent, nagging, frequent; repeated, habitual.

**persnickety** adjective *informal my persnickety boss makes us disinfect the drawers in the cash register every night* FUSSY, difficult to please, difficult, finicky, overfastidious, fastidious, overparticular, particular, faddish, punctilious, hair-splitting, critical, overcritical; *informal* nitpicking, choosy, picky. ANTONYM easygoing.

**person** noun *that person over there is the one who called the police* HUMAN BEING, individual, man/woman, child, human, being, (living) soul, mortal, creature; personage, character, customer; *informal* type, sort, cookie; *informal, dated* body, dog; *archaic* wight. PHRASE: **in person** *I hope to talk to you in person before I leave Cleveland* PHYSICALLY, in the flesh, in propria persona, personally; oneself; *informal* as large as life.

**persona** noun *her stage persona is nothing like the real Muriel* IMAGE, face, public face, character, personality, identity, self; front, facade, guise, exterior, role, part.

**personable** adjective *I was blessed with the most personable in-laws* PLEASANT, agreeable, likable, nice, amiable, affable, charming, congenial, genial, simpatico, engaging, pleasing; attractive, presentable, good-looking, nice-looking, pretty, appealing; *Scottish* bonny. ANTONYMS disagreeable, unattractive.

**personage** noun *we always have a table for a personage such as yourself* IMPORTANT PERSON, VIP, luminary, celebrity, personality, name, famous name, household name, public figure, star, leading light, dignitary, notable, notability, worthy, panjandrum; person; *informal* celeb, somebody, big shot, big wheel, big kahuna, big cheese.

**personal** adjective **1** *a highly personal style* DISTINCTIVE, characteristic, unique, individual, one's own, particular, peculiar, idiosyncratic, individualized, personalized. ANTONYMS public, general.

**2** *a personal appearance* IN PERSON, in the flesh, actual, live, physical.

**3** *his personal life* PRIVATE, intimate; confidential, secret.

**4** *a personal friend* INTIMATE, close, dear, great, bosom.

**5** *I have personal knowledge of the family* DIRECT, empirical, firsthand, immediate, experiential.

**6** *personal remarks* DEROGATORY, ad hominem; disparaging, belittling, insulting, critical, rude, slighting, disrespectful, offensive, pejorative.

**personality** noun **1** *her cheerful personality* CHARACTER, nature, disposition, temperament, makeup, persona, psyche.

**2** *she had loads of personality* CHARISMA, magnetism, strength/force of personality, character, charm, presence.

**3** *a famous personality* CELEBRITY, VIP, star, superstar, name, famous name, household name, big name, somebody, leading light, luminary, notable, personage, notability; *informal* celeb.

**personalize** verb **1** *products that can be personalized to your requirements* CUSTOMIZE, individualize.

**2** *attempts to personalize God* PERSONIFY, humanize, anthropomorphize.

**personally** adverb **1** *I'd like to thank you personally* IN PERSON, oneself.

**2** *personally, I think it's a good idea* FOR MY PART, for myself, to my way of thinking, to my mind, in my estimation, as far as I am concerned, in my view/opinion, from my point of view, from where I stand, as I see it, if you ask me, my sense is, for my money, in my book; privately. PHRASE: **take personally** *please don't take this personally, but I think the trim should be a shade darker* TAKE OFFENSE, take something amiss, be offended, be upset, be affronted, take umbrage, take exception, feel insulted, feel hurt.

**personification** noun *Foote is the personification of heroism* EMBODIMENT, incarnation, epitome, quintessence, essence, type, symbol, soul, model, exemplification, exemplar, image, representation.

**personify** verb *the picture on the label should personify good, wholesome American cooking* EPITOMIZE, embody, hypostatize, typify, exemplify, represent, symbolize, stand for, be the incarnation of, body forth, put a face on.

**personnel** noun *sales personnel* STAFF, employees, workforce, workers, labor force, human resources, manpower, wage labor; *informal* liveware.

**perspective** noun **1** *her perspective on things had changed* OUTLOOK, view, viewpoint, point of view, POV, standpoint, position, stand, stance, angle, slant, attitude, frame of mind, frame of reference, approach, way of looking, interpretation.

**2** *a perspective of the whole valley* VIEW, vista, panorama, prospect, bird's-eye view, outlook, aspect.

**perspicacious** adjective *his perspicacious advisers recommended caution* DISCERNING, shrewd, perceptive, astute, penetrating, observant, percipient, sharp-witted, sharp, smart, alert, clear-sighted, farsighted, acute, clever, canny, intelligent, insightful, wise, sage, sensitive, intuitive, understanding, aware, discriminating; *informal* on the ball, heads-up, with it. See note at KEEN. ANTONYM stupid.

**perspiration** noun *you should avoid products that prevent normal perspiration* SWEAT, moisture; *Medicine* diaphoresis.

**perspire** verb *it's natural to perspire under these hot lights* SWEAT, be dripping/pouring with sweat, glow.

**persuade** verb **1** *he tried to persuade her to come with him* PREVAIL ON, coax, convince, get, induce, win over, bring around, coerce, influence, sway, inveigle, entice, tempt, lure, cajole, wheedle; *Law* procure; *informal* sweet-talk, twist someone's arm; (**persuade someone to**) make. See note at CONVINCE. ANTONYMS dissuade, deter.

**2** *a shortage of money persuaded them to abandon the scheme* CAUSE, lead, move, dispose, incline.

**persuasion** noun **1** *Monica needed plenty of persuasion* COAXING, persuading, coercion, inducement, convincing, blandishment, encouragement, urging, inveiglement, cajolery, enticement, wheedling; *informal* sweet-talking, arm-twisting; *formal* suasion.

**2** *various political and religious persuasions* GROUP, grouping, sect, denomination, party, camp, side, faction, affiliation, school of thought, belief, creed, credo, faith, philosophy. See note at OPINION.

**persuasive** adjective *her argument is quite persuasive* CONVINCING, cogent, compelling, potent, forceful, powerful, eloquent, impressive, influential, sound, valid, strong, effective, winning, telling; plausible, credible. ANTONYM unconvincing.

**pert** adjective **1** *a pert little hat* JAUNTY, neat, chic, trim, stylish, smart, perky, rakish; *informal* natty, sassy.

**2** *a young girl with a pert manner* IMPUDENT, impertinent, cheeky, irreverent, forward, insolent, disrespectful, flippant, familiar, presumptuous, bold, as bold as brass, brazen; *informal* fresh, saucy, sassy.

**pertain** verb **1** *developments* ***pertaining to*** *the economy* CONCERN, relate to, be related to, be connected with, be relevant to, regard, apply to, be pertinent to, refer to, have a bearing on, appertain to, bear on, affect, involve, touch on.

**2** *the stock and assets* ***pertaining to*** *the business* BELONG TO, be a part of, be included in.

**3** *the economic situation that pertained at that time* EXIST, be the order of the day, be the case, prevail; *formal* obtain.

**pertinacious** adjective *formal they were quite pertinacious in their demands* DETERMINED, tenacious, persistent, persevering, purposeful, resolute, dogged, indefatigable, insistent, single-minded, unrelenting, relentless, tireless, unshakable; stubborn, obstinate, inflexible, unbending. See note at STUBBORN. ANTONYMS irresolute, tentative.

**pertinent** adjective *he asked a lot of pertinent questions* RELEVANT, to the point, apposite, appropriate, suitable, fitting, fit, apt, applicable, material, germane, to the purpose, apropos; *formal* ad rem. ANTONYM irrelevant.

**perturb** verb *David's appearance perturbs his parents* WORRY, upset, unsettle, disturb, concern, trouble, disquiet; disconcert, discomfit, unnerve, alarm, bother, distress, dismay, gnaw at, agitate, fluster, ruffle, discountenance; *informal* rattle, throw. ANTONYM reassure.

**perturbed** adjective *our pets are perturbed by all the construction going on next door* UPSET, worried, unsettled, disturbed, concerned, troubled, anxious, ill at ease, uneasy, disquieted, fretful; disconcerted, discomposed, distressed, unnerved, alarmed, bothered, dismayed, agitated, flustered, ruffled, shaken, discountenanced; *informal* twitchy, rattled, fazed, unstrung; discombobulated. ANTONYM calm.

**peruse** verb *perusing the racing forms* READ, study, scrutinize, inspect, examine, wade through, look through; browse through, leaf through, scan, run one's eye over, glance through, flick through, skim through, thumb through, dip into.

**pervade** verb *the smell of floor polish pervaded the house* PERMEATE, spread through, fill, suffuse, be diffused through, imbue, penetrate, filter through, percolate through, infuse, perfuse, flow through; charge, steep, saturate, impregnate, inform.

**pervasive** adjective *the low-carb craze is pervasive* PREVALENT, pervading, permeating, extensive, ubiquitous, omnipresent, universal, rife, widespread, general.

**perverse** adjective **1** *he is being deliberately perverse* AWKWARD, contrary, difficult, unreasonable, uncooperative, unhelpful, obstructive, disobliging, recalcitrant, stubborn, obstinate, obdurate, mulish, pigheaded, bullheaded; *formal* refractory. See note at STUBBORN. ANTONYMS accommodating, cooperative.

**2** *a verdict that is manifestly perverse* ILLOGICAL, irrational, unreasonable, wrong, wrong-headed. ANTONYM reasonable.

**3** *an evil life dedicated to perverse pleasure* PERVERTED, depraved, unnatural, abnormal, deviant, degenerate, immoral, warped, twisted, corrupt; wicked, base, evil; *informal* kinky, sick, pervy. See note at DEPRAVED.

**perversion** noun **1** *a twisted perversion of the truth* DISTORTION, misrepresentation, falsification, travesty, misinterpretation, misconstruction, twisting, corruption, subversion, misuse, misapplication, debasement.

**2** *sexual perversion* DEVIANCE, abnormality; depravity, degeneracy, debauchery, corruption, vice, wickedness, immorality.

**perversity** noun **1** *out of sheer perversity, he refused* CONTRARINESS, awkwardness, recalcitrance, stubbornness, obstinacy, obduracy, mulishness, pigheadedness; *formal* refractoriness.

**2** *the perversity of the decision* UNREASONABLENESS, irrationality, illogicality, wrong-headedness.

**pervert** verb **1** *people who attempt to pervert the rules* DIS-

TORT, corrupt, subvert, twist, bend, abuse, misapply, misuse, misrepresent, misinterpret, falsify.

2 *men can be perverted by power* CORRUPT, lead astray, debase, warp, pollute, poison, deprave, debauch.

▸ noun *a sexual pervert* DEVIANT, degenerate; *informal* perv, dirty old man, sicko.

**perverted** adjective *I don't want to hear any more of your perverted stories* UNNATURAL, deviant, warped, corrupt, twisted, abnormal, unhealthy, depraved, perverse, aberrant, immoral, debauched, debased, degenerate, evil, wicked, vile, amoral, wrong, bad; *informal* sick, sicko, kinky, pervy.

**pessimism** noun *Felicia has apparently drawn him out of his pessimism* DEFEATISM, negativity, doom and gloom, gloominess, cynicism, fatalism; hopelessness, depression, despair, despondency, angst.

**pessimist** noun *pessimists have been predicting the doom of the planet for thousands of years* DEFEATIST, fatalist, prophet of doom, cynic, doomsayer, doomster, Cassandra; skeptic, doubter, doubting Thomas; misery, killjoy, Job's comforter; *informal* doom (and gloom) merchant, wet blanket, Chicken Little, gloomy Gus. ANTONYMS optimist, Pollyanna.

**pessimistic** adjective *a pessimistic outlook on life* GLOOMY, negative, defeatist, downbeat, cynical, bleak, fatalistic, dark, black, despairing, despondent, depressed, hopeless; suspicious, distrustful, doubting. See note at OPTIMISTIC. ANTONYM optimistic.

**pest** noun *Dan is dating the girl he used to think was such a pest* NUISANCE, annoyance, irritation, irritant, thorn in one's flesh/side, vexation, trial, the bane of one's life, menace, trouble, problem, worry, bother; *informal* pain (in the neck), aggravation, headache, nudnik.

**pester** verb *is there someplace I can study where no one will pester me?* BADGER, hound, harass, plague, annoy, bother, trouble, keep after, persecute, torment, bedevil, harry, worry, beleaguer, nag, hassle, bug, devil, get on someone's case.

**pestilence** noun *archaic* See PLAGUE noun sense 1.

**pet** noun *the teacher's pet* FAVORITE, darling, the apple of one's eye; *informal* fair-haired boy/girl.

▸ adjective 1 *a pet lamb* TAME, domesticated, domestic, housebroken, house-trained.

2 *his pet theory* FAVORITE, favored, cherished, dear to one's heart; particular, special, personal.

▸ verb 1 *the cats came to be petted* STROKE, caress, fondle, pat.

2 *she had always been petted by her parents* PAMPER, spoil, mollycoddle, coddle, cosset, baby, indulge, overindulge.

3 *couples were petting in their cars* KISS AND CUDDLE, kiss, cuddle, embrace, caress; *informal* make out, canoodle, neck, smooch, get it on.

PHRASE: **pet name** *'Cuddles' is a pet name John gave to me years ago* AFFECTIONATE NAME, term of endearment, endearment, nickname, diminutive; *rare* hypocoristic.

**peter** PHRASE: **peter out** *our enthusiasm eventually petered out* FIZZLE OUT, fade (away), die away/out, dwindle, diminish, taper off, tail off, trail away/off, wane, ebb, melt away, evaporate, disappear, come to an end, subside.

**petition** noun 1 *more than 1,000 people signed the petition* APPEAL, round robin.

2 *petitions to Allah* ENTREATY, supplication, plea, prayer, appeal, request, invocation, suit; *archaic* orison.

▸ verb *they petitioned the governor to revoke the decision* APPEAL TO, request, ask, call on, entreat, beg, implore, plead with, apply to, press, urge; *formal* adjure; *literary* beseech. See note at BEG.

**petrify** verb *the thought of speaking in public petrified her* TERRIFY, horrify, frighten, scare, scare/frighten to death, scare/frighten the living daylights out of, scare/frighten the life out of, strike terror into, put the fear of God into; paralyze, transfix; *informal* scare the pants off, scare the bejesus out of.

**petty** adjective 1 *petty regulations* TRIVIAL, trifling, minor, small, unimportant, insignificant, inconsequential, inconsiderable, negligible, paltry, footling, pettifogging; *informal* piffling, piddling, fiddling. ANTONYMS important, serious.

2 *a petty form of revenge* SMALL-MINDED, mean, ungenerous, shabby, spiteful. ANTONYM magnanimous.

**petulant** adjective *he's as petulant as a spoiled child* PEEVISH, bad-tempered, querulous, pettish, fretful, cross, irritable, sulky, snappish, crotchety, touchy, tetchy, testy, fractious, grumpy, disgruntled, crabby; *informal* grouchy, cranky. ANTONYM good-humored.

**phantom** noun 1 *a phantom who haunts lonely roads* GHOST, apparition, spirit, specter, wraith; *informal* spook; *literary* phantasm, shade.

2 *the phantoms of an overactive imagination* DELUSION, figment of the imagination, hallucination, illusion, chimera, vision, mirage.

**phase** noun 1 *the final phase of the campaign* STAGE, period, chapter, episode, part, step, point, time, juncture.

2 *he's going through a difficult phase* PERIOD, stage, time, spell, patch.

3 *the phases of the moon* ASPECT, shape, form, appearance, state, condition. PHRASES: **phase in** *compliance with the new regulations will be phased in over a six-month period* INTRODUCE GRADUALLY, begin to use, ease in.

**phase out** *we're going to phase out the cash-rebate program* WITHDRAW GRADUALLY, discontinue, stop using, run down, wind down.

**phenomenal** adjective *sales growth has been nothing short of phenomenal* REMARKABLE, exceptional, extraordinary, amazing, astonishing, astounding, sensational, stunning, incredible, unbelievable; marvelous, magnificent, wonderful, outstanding, singular, out of the ordinary, unusual, unprecedented; *informal* fantastic, terrific, tremendous, stupendous, awesome, out of this world; *literary* wondrous. ANTONYM ordinary.

**phenomenon** noun **1** *a rare phenomenon* OCCURRENCE, event, happening, fact, situation, circumstance, experience, case, incident, episode.

**2** *the band was a pop phenomenon* MARVEL, sensation, wonder, prodigy, miracle, rarity, nonpareil; *informal* humdinger, phenom, stunner, doozy, ripsnorter.

**philander** verb *he had no time or inclination to philander* WOMANIZE, have affairs, flirt; *informal* play around, carry on, play the field, sleep around, fool around.

**philanderer** noun *everyone warned me he was a philanderer* WOMANIZER, Casanova, Don Juan, Lothario, flirt, ladies' man, playboy, rake, roué; *informal* stud, skirt-chaser, ladykiller, wolf.

**philanthropic** adjective *a philanthropic millionaire* CHARITABLE, generous, benevolent, humanitarian, public-spirited, altruistic, magnanimous, munificent, openhanded, bountiful, liberal, generous to a fault, beneficent, caring, compassionate, unselfish, kind, kind-hearted, bighearted; *formal* eleemosynary. ANTONYMS selfish, mean.

**philanthropist** noun *the trust was funded by an anonymous philanthropist* BENEFACTOR, benefactress, patron, patroness, donor, contributor, sponsor, backer, helper, good Samaritan; do-gooder, Lady Bountiful; *historical* almsgiver.

**philanthropy** noun *a family noted for its philanthropy* BENEVOLENCE, generosity, humanitarianism, public-spiritedness, altruism, social conscience, charity, charitableness, brotherly love, fellow feeling, magnanimity, munificence, liberality, largesse, openhandedness, bountifulness, beneficence, unselfishness, humanity, kindness, kindheartedness, compassion; *historical* almsgiving.

**philippic** noun *literary no publisher wanted to touch his scathing philippic* TIRADE, diatribe, harangue, lecture, attack, onslaught, denunciation, rant, polemic, broadside, fulmination, condemnation, criticism, censure; *informal* blast.

**philistine** adjective *my only mistake was thinking I could share something culturally uplifting with you philistines* UNCULTURED, lowbrow, anti-intellectual, uncultivated, uncivilized, uneducated, unenlightened, commercial, materialist, bourgeois; ignorant, crass, boorish, barbarian.

**philosopher** noun *when I was young, I failed to appreciate what an insightful philosopher my father was* THINKER, theorist, theorizer, theoretician, metaphysicist, metaphysician; scholar, intellectual, sage, wise man.

**philosophical** adjective **1** *a philosophical question* THEORETICAL, metaphysical.

**2** *a philosophical mood* THOUGHTFUL, reflective, pensive, meditative, contemplative, introspective, ruminative; *formal* cogitative.

**3** *he was philosophical about losing the contract* CALM, composed, cool, collected, 'calm, cool, and collected', self-possessed, serene, tranquil, stoical, impassive, dispassionate, phlegmatic, unperturbed, imperturbable, unruffled, patient, forbearing, long-suffering, resigned, rational, realistic.

**philosophy** noun **1** *the philosophy of Aristotle* THINKING, thought, reasoning.

**2** *her political philosophy* BELIEFS, credo, convictions, ideology, ideas, thinking, notions, theories, doctrine, tenets, principles, views, school of thought; *informal* ism.

**phlegmatic** adjective *I come from a very demonstrative, emotional Italian family—I can't remember one phlegmatic moment from my childhood* CALM, cool, composed, 'calm, cool, and collected', controlled, serene, tranquil, placid, impassive, imperturbable, unruffled, dispassionate, philosophical; stolid, dull, bland, unemotional, lifeless; *informal* unflappable. ANTONYM excitable.

**phobia** noun *fear of spiders is just one of his many phobias* FEAR, irrational fear, obsessive fear, dread, horror, terror, hatred, loathing, detestation, aversion, antipathy, revulsion; complex, neurosis; *informal* thing, hang-up.

**phone** noun *she tried to reach you on your phone* TELEPHONE, cell phone, cell, car phone, cordless phone, speakerphone; extension; *informal* blower, horn.

▸ verb *I'll phone you later* TELEPHONE, call, give someone a call; *informal* call up, give someone a buzz, get someone on the horn/blower.

**phony** *informal* adjective *a phony address* BOGUS, false, fake, fraudulent, spurious; counterfeit, forged, feigned; pseudo, imitation, sham, man-made, mock, ersatz, synthetic, artificial; simulated, pretended, contrived, affected, insincere, inauthentic; *informal* pretend, put-on. ANTONYM authentic.

▸ noun **1** *he's nothing but a phony* IMPOSTOR, sham, fake, fraud, charlatan; *informal* con artist.

**2** *the diamond's a phony* FAKE, imitation, counterfeit, forgery.

**photocopy** noun *we kept a photocopy for our records* COPY, facsimile, duplicate, reproduction; *trademark* Xerox.

**photograph** noun *a photograph of her father* PICTURE, photo, snapshot, shot, image, likeness, print, slide, transparency, still, enlargement, snap; *informal* mug shot, head shot.

▸ verb *she was photographed leaving the castle* TAKE SOMEONE'S PICTURE/PHOTO, snap, shoot, film.

**photographic** adjective **1** *a photographic record* PICTORIAL, in photographs; cinematic, filmic.

**2** *a photographic memory* DETAILED, graphic, exact, precise, accurate, vivid, picture-perfect.

**phrase** noun *familiar words and phrases* EXPRESSION, group of words, construction, locution, term, turn of phrase; idiom, idiomatic expression; saying, tag.

▸ verb *how could I phrase the question?* EXPRESS, put into words, put, word, style, formulate, couch, frame, articulate, verbalize.

**phraseology** noun *no phraseology is more endearing than that of Miss Sallie* WORDING, choice of words, phrasing, way of speaking/writing, usage, idiom, diction, parlance, words, language, vocabulary, terminology; jargon; *informal* lingo, -speak, -ese.

**physical** adjective **1** *physical pleasure* BODILY, corporeal, corporal, somatic; carnal, fleshly, nonspiritual. ANTONYMS mental, spiritual.

**2** *hard physical work* MANUAL, laboring, labor-intensive, blue-collar. ANTONYMS intellectual, clerical.

**3** *the physical universe* MATERIAL, concrete, tangible, palpable, solid, substantial, real, actual, visible. ANTONYMS intangible, abstract.

**physician** noun *consult your physician first* DOCTOR, doctor of medicine, MD, medical practitioner, general practitioner, GP, clinician, family doctor; specialist, consultant; *informal* doc, quack, medic, medico; intern, resident; *informal, dated* sawbones.

**physique** noun *the physique of an athlete* BODY, build, figure, frame, anatomy, shape, form, proportions; muscles, musculature; *informal* vital statistics, bod.

**pick** verb **1** *I got a job picking apples* HARVEST, gather (in), collect, pluck; *literary* cull.

**2** *pick the time that suits you best* CHOOSE, select, pick out, single out, take, opt for, elect, decide on, settle on, fix on, sift out, sort out; name, nominate.

**3** *Beth* ***picked at*** *her food* NIBBLE (AT), toy with, play with, eat like a bird.

**4** *people were picking guitars and singing* STRUM, twang, thrum, pluck.

**5** *he tried to pick a fight* PROVOKE, start, cause, incite, stir up, whip up, instigate, prompt, bring about.

▸ noun **1** *take your pick* CHOICE, selection, option, decision; preference, favorite.

**2** *the pick of the crop* BEST, finest, top, choice, choicest, prime, cream, flower, prize, pearl, gem, jewel, jewel in the crown, crème de la crème, elite.

PHRASES: **pick on** *why don't you pick on somebody your own size?* BULLY, victimize, tyrannize, torment, persecute, criticize, harass, hound, taunt, tease; *informal* get at, have it in for, be down on, needle.

**pick out 1** *one painting was picked out for special mention* CHOOSE, select, single out, opt for, decide on, elect, settle on, fix on, sift out, sort out; name, nominate.

**2** *she picked out Jessica in the crowd* SEE, make out, distinguish, discern, spot, perceive, detect, notice, recognize, identify, catch sight of, glimpse; *literary* espy, behold, descry.

**pick up 1** *business has really picked up* IMPROVE, recover, be on the road to recovery, rally, make a comeback, bounce back, perk up, look up, take a turn for the better, turn the/a corner, be on the mend, make headway, make progress.

**2** *they teach you the proper way to pick up heavy boxes* LIFT, take up, raise, hoist, scoop up, gather up, snatch up.

**3** *I'll pick you up after lunch* FETCH, collect, call for.

**4** *informal she was picked up by the police* ARREST, apprehend, detain, take into custody, seize; *informal* nab, run in, bust.

**5** *we picked it up at a thrift store* FIND, discover, come across, stumble across, happen on, chance on; acquire, obtain, come by, get, procure; purchase, buy; *informal* get hold of, get/lay one's hands on, get one's mitts on, bag, land.

**6** *she picked up a virus* CATCH, contract, get, come down with.

**7** *he told us the bits of gossip he'd picked up* HEAR, hear tell, get wind of, be told, learn; glean, garner.

**8** *we're picking up a distress signal* RECEIVE, detect, get, hear.

**picket** noun **1** *forty pickets were arrested* STRIKER, demonstrator, protester, objector, picketer.

**2** *fences made of cedar pickets* STAKE, post, paling; upright, stanchion, piling.

▸ verb *over 200 people picketed the factory* DEMONSTRATE AT, protest at, strike at, form a picket at, man the picket line at; blockade, shut off.

**pickle** noun *informal they got into a real pickle over this one* PLIGHT, predicament, mess, difficulty, trouble, dire/desperate straits, problem, quandary; *informal* tight corner, tight spot, jam, fix, scrape, bind, hole, hot water, fine kettle of fish.

▸ verb *fish pickled in brine* PRESERVE, souse, marinate, conserve.

**pick-me-up** noun **1** *a drink that's a good pick-me-up* TONIC, restorative, energizer, stimulant, refresher, reviver; *informal* bracer; *Medicine* analeptic.

**2** *his winning goal was a perfect pick-me-up* BOOST, boost to the spirits, fillip, stimulant, stimulus; *informal* shot in the arm.

**pickpocket** noun *a crowded outdoor event is a pickpocket's playground* THIEF, petty thief, purse-snatcher, sneak thief; *archaic* cutpurse.

**picnic** noun **1** *a picnic on the beach* OUTDOOR MEAL, alfresco meal, cookout, barbecue.

**2** *informal working for him was no picnic* EASY TASK/JOB, child's play, five-finger exercise, gift, walkover; *informal* piece of cake, cinch, breeze, kids' stuff, cakewalk, pushover, duck soup.

**pictorial** adjective *a pictorial essay on desegregation* ILLUSTRATED, in pictures, in picture form, in photographs, photographic, graphic. See note at GRAPHIC.

**picture** noun **1** *pictures in an art gallery* PAINTING, DRAWING, sketch, oil painting, watercolor, print, canvas, portrait, portrayal, illustration, artwork, depiction, likeness, representation, image, icon, miniature, landscape; fresco, mural, wall painting; *informal* oil.

**2** *we were told not to take pictures* PHOTOGRAPH, photo, snap, snapshot, shot, print, slide, transparency, exposure, still, enlargement.

**3** *do you have a picture of what your ideal home might look like?* CONCEPT, idea, impression, view, (mental) image, vision, visualization, notion.

**4** *the picture of health* PERSONIFICATION, embodiment, epitome, essence, quintessence, perfect example, soul, model.

**5** *a picture starring Robert de Niro* MOVIE, film, motion picture, feature film; *informal* flick; *dated* moving picture.

▸ verb **1** *he was pictured with his guests* PHOTOGRAPH, take a photograph/photo of, snap, shoot, film.

**2** *in the drawing they were pictured against a snowy background* PAINT, DRAW, sketch, depict, delineate, portray, show, illustrate.

**3** *Anne still pictured Richard as he had been* VISUALIZE, see in one's mind's eye, conjure up a picture/image of, imagine, see, evoke.

PHRASE: **put in the picture** *please come in and sit down, and we'll put you in the picture* INFORM, fill in, explain the situation/circumstances to, bring up to date, update, brief, keep posted, clue in, bring up to speed.

**picturesque** adjective **1** *a picturesque village* ATTRACTIVE, pretty, beautiful, lovely, scenic, charming, quaint, pleasing, delightful, picture-perfect. ANTONYMS ugly, drab.

**2** *a picturesque description* VIVID, graphic, colorful, impressive, striking. See note at GRAPHIC. ANTONYM dull.

**piddling** adjective *informal I'm tired of your piddling complaints* TRIVIAL, trifling, petty, footling, slight, small, insignificant, unimportant, inconsequential, inconsiderable, negligible; meager, inadequate, insufficient, paltry, scant, scanty, derisory, pitiful, miserable, puny, niggardly, beggarly, mere; *informal* measly, pathetic, piffling, mingy, nickel-and-dime.

**pie** noun *the enticing aroma of fresh-baked pies* PASTRY, tart, turnover. PHRASE: **pie in the sky** *informal they thought her dream of fame was just pie in the sky* FALSE HOPE, illusion, delusion, fantasy, pipe dream, daydream, a castle in the air, a castle in Spain.

**piebald** adjective. See PIED.

**piece** noun **1** *a piece of cheese* | *a piece of wood* BIT, slice, chunk, segment, section, lump, hunk, wedge, slab, block, cake, bar, cube, stick, length; offcut, sample, fragment, sliver, splinter, wafer, chip, crumb, scrap, remnant, shred, shard, snippet; mouthful, morsel. See note at FRAGMENT.

**2** *the pieces of a clock* COMPONENT, part, bit, section, segment, constituent, element; unit, module.

**3** *a piece of furniture* ITEM, article, specimen.

**4** *a piece of the profit* SHARE, portion, slice, quota, part, bit, percentage, amount, quantity, ration, fraction, division; *informal* cut.

**5** *pieces from his private collection* WORK (OF ART), creation, production; composition, opus.

**6** *the reporter who wrote the piece* ARTICLE, item, story, report, essay, study, review, composition, column.

**7** *the pieces on a game board* TOKEN, counter, man, disk, chip, marker. PHRASES: **in one piece 1** *the camera was still in one piece* UNBROKEN, entire, whole, intact, undamaged, unharmed.

**2** *I'll bring her back in one piece* UNHURT, uninjured, unscathed, safe, safe and sound.

**in pieces** *the vase was in pieces* BROKEN, in bits, shattered, smashed, in smithereens; *informal* bust, busted.

**go/fall to pieces** *he went to pieces when his wife died* HAVE A BREAKDOWN, break down, go out of one's mind, lose control, lose one's head, fall apart; *informal* crack up, lose it, come/fall apart at the seams, freak, freak out.

**piecemeal** adverb *the reforms were implemented piecemeal* A LITTLE AT A TIME, piece by piece, bit by bit, gradually, slowly, in stages, in steps, step by step, little by little, by degrees, in/by fits and starts.

**pied** adjective *a lovely little pied pony* PARTI-COLORED, multicolored, variegated, black and white, brown and white, piebald, skewbald, dappled, brindle, spotted, mottled, speckled, flecked, pinto, calico, tabby.

**pier** noun **1** *a boat was tied to the pier* JETTY, quay, wharf, dock, levee, landing, landing stage.

**2** *the piers of the bridge* SUPPORT, cutwater, pile, piling, abutment, buttress, stanchion, prop, stay, upright, pillar, post, column.

**pierce** verb **1** *the metal pierced his flesh* PENETRATE, puncture, perforate, prick, lance; stab, spike, stick, impale, transfix, bore through, drill through.

**2** *his anguish pierced her very soul* HURT, wound, pain, sting, sear, grieve, distress, upset, trouble, harrow, afflict; affect, move.

**piercing** adjective **1** *a piercing shriek* SHRILL, ear-splitting, high-pitched, penetrating, strident, loud.

**2** *the piercing wind* BITTER, biting, cutting, penetrating, sharp, keen, stinging, raw; freezing, frigid, glacial, arctic, chill.

**3** *a piercing pain* INTENSE, excruciating, agonizing, sharp, stabbing, shooting, stinging, severe, extreme, fierce, searing, racking.

**4** *his piercing gaze* SEARCHING, probing, penetrating, penetrative, shrewd, sharp, keen.

**5** *his piercing intelligence* PERCEPTIVE, percipient, perspicacious, penetrating, discerning, discriminating, intelligent, quick-witted, sharp, sharp-witted, shrewd, insightful, keen, acute, astute, clever, smart, incisive, razor-edged, trenchant.

**piety** noun *the piety of a saint* DEVOUTNESS, devotion, piousness, religion, holiness, godliness, saintliness; veneration, reverence, faith, religious duty, spirituality, religious zeal, fervor; pietism, religiosity.

**pig** noun **1** *a herd of pigs* HOG, boar, sow, porker, swine, piglet; *children's word* piggy.

**2** *informal he's such a pig, he'll eat us out of house and home* GLUTTON; *informal* hog, greedy guts.

**pigeonhole** verb **1** *they were pigeonholed as an indie guitar band* CATEGORIZE, compartmentalize, classify, characterize, label, brand, tag, typecast, ghettoize, designate.

**2** *the plan was pigeonholed last year* POSTPONE, put off, put back, defer, shelve, hold over, put to one side, put on ice, mothball, put in cold storage; *informal* put on the back burner.

**pigheaded** adjective *you pigheaded old fool* OBSTINATE, stubborn (as a mule), mulish, bullheaded, obdurate, headstrong, self-willed, willful, perverse, contrary, recalcitrant, stiff-necked; uncooperative, inflexible, uncompromising, intractable, intransigent, unyielding, bloody-minded; *formal* refractory.

**pigment** noun *a chestnut brown pigment* COLORING MATTER, coloring, colorant, color, tint, dye, dyestuff.

**pile**[1] noun **1** *a pile of stones* HEAP, stack, mound, pyramid, mass, quantity; collection, accumulation, assemblage, store, stockpile, hoard.

**2** *informal I've got a pile of work to do* GREAT DEAL, lot, large quantity/amount, mountain; abundance, cornucopia; *informal* load, heap, mass, slew, ocean, stack, ton.

**3** *informal he'd made his pile in the fur trade* FORTUNE, millions, billions; *informal* small fortune, bundle, wad.

▸ verb **1** *she **piled up** the plates* HEAP (UP), stack (up).

**2** *he piled his plate with fried eggs* LOAD, heap, fill (up), lade, stack, charge, stock.

**3** *our debts were piling up* INCREASE, grow, mount up, escalate, soar, spiral, leap up, shoot up, rocket, climb, accumulate, accrue, build up, multiply.

**4** *we piled into the car* CROWD, climb, pack, squeeze, push, shove.

PHRASE: **pile it on** *informal if you pile it on like that, no one will believe you* EXAGGERATE, overstate the case, make a mountain out of a molehill, overdo it, overplay it, overdramatize; *informal* lay it on thick.

**pile**[2] noun *a wall supported by timber piles* POST, stake, pillar, column, support, foundation, piling, abutment, pier, cutwater, buttress, stanchion, upright.

**pile**[3] noun *a carpet with a short pile* NAP, fibers, threads.

**pileup** noun *a terrible pileup on I-95* CRASH, multiple crash, collision, multiple collision, smash, accident, road accident, wreck; *informal* smash-up.

**pilfer** verb *the gun was part of a cache pilfered from the air force* STEAL, thieve, take, snatch, purloin, loot; *informal* swipe, rob, nab, rip off, lift, "liberate", "borrow", filch, snaffle; pinch, heist.

**pilgrim** noun *the destination of these weary pilgrims* worshiper, devotee, believer; traveler, crusader; *literary* wayfarer; *historical* palmer.

**pilgrimage** noun *an annual pilgrimage to the Holy City* RELIGIOUS JOURNEY, religious expedition, hajj, crusade, mission. See note at JOURNEY.

**pill** noun *take one pill at bedtime* TABLET, capsule, caplet, cap, gelcap, pellet, lozenge, pastille, horse pill; *Veterinary Medicine* bolus.

**pillage** verb **1** *the abbey was pillaged* RANSACK, rob, plunder, despoil, raid, loot; sack, devastate, lay waste, ravage, rape. See note at RAVAGE.

**2** *columns pillaged from an ancient town* STEAL, pilfer, thieve, take, snatch, purloin, loot; *informal* swipe, rob, nab, rip off, lift, "liberate", "borrow", filch, snaffle, pinch, heist.

▸ noun *the rebels were intent on pillage* ROBBERY, robbing, raiding, plunder, looting, sacking, rape, marauding; *literary* rapine.

**pillar** noun **1** *stone pillars* COLUMN, post, support, upright, baluster, pier, pile, pilaster, stanchion, prop, newel; obelisk, monolith.

**2** *a pillar of the community* STALWART, mainstay, bastion, rock; leading light, worthy, backbone, support, upholder, champion, tower of strength.

**pillory** noun *offenders were put in the pillory* STOCKS.

▸ verb **1** *he was pilloried by the press* ATTACK, criticize, censure, condemn, denigrate, lambaste, savage, stigmatize, denounce; *informal* knock, slam, pan, bash, crucify, hammer, pummel; *formal* excoriate.

**2** *they were pilloried at school* RIDICULE, jeer at, sneer at, deride, mock, scorn, make fun of, poke fun at, laugh at, scoff at, tease, taunt; *informal* rib, josh, razz.

**pillow** noun *his head rested on the pillow* CUSHION, bolster, pad; headrest.

▸ verb *she pillowed her head on folded arms* CUSHION, cradle, rest, lay, support.

**pilot** noun **1** *a fighter pilot* AIRMAN/AIRWOMAN, flyer; captain, commander, co-pilot, wingman, first officer, bush pilot; *informal* skipper; *dated* aviator, aviatrix, aeronaut.

**2** *a harbor pilot* NAVIGATOR, helmsman, steersman, coxswain.

**3** *a pilot for his new TV series* TRIAL EPISODE; sample, experiment, trial run.

▸ adjective *a pilot project* EXPERIMENTAL, exploratory, trial, test, sample, speculative; preliminary.

▸ verb **1** *he piloted the jet to safety* NAVIGATE, guide, maneuver, steer, control, direct, captain, shepherd; fly, drive; sail; *informal* skipper.

**2** *the questionnaire has been piloted* TEST, trial, try out; assess, investigate, examine, appraise, evaluate.

**pimple** noun *the last thing you want on prom night is a pimple* ZIT, pustule, bleb, boil, swelling, eruption, blackhead, whitehead, carbuncle, blister, spot; *technical* comedo, papule; **(pimples)** acne, bad skin.

**pin** noun **1** *fasten the hem with a pin* TACK, safety pin, nail, staple, fastener.

**2** *a broken pin in the machine* BOLT, peg, rivet, dowel, screw.

**3** *souvenir pins* BADGE, brooch.

▸ verb **1** *she pinned the brooch to her dress* ATTACH, fasten, affix, fix, tack, clip; join, secure.

**2** *they pinned him to the ground* HOLD, press, hold fast, hold down; restrain, pinion, immobilize.

**3** *they **pinned** the crime **on** him* BLAME FOR, hold responsible for, attribute to, impute to, ascribe to; lay something at someone's door; *informal* stick on.

PHRASE: **pin down 1** *our troops can pin down the enemy* CON-

FINE, TRAP, hem in, corner, close in, shut in, hedge in, pen in, restrain, entangle, enmesh, immobilize.

**2** *she tried to pin him down to a plan* CONSTRAIN, make someone commit themselves, pressure, tie down, nail down.

**3** *it evoked a memory but he couldn't pin it down* DEFINE, put one's finger on, put into words, express, name, specify, identify, pinpoint, place.

**pinch** verb **1** *he pinched my arm* TWEAK, nip, squeeze, grasp.

**2** *my new shoes pinch my toes* HURT, pain; squeeze, crush, cramp; be uncomfortable.

**3** *I scraped and pinched to afford it* ECONOMIZE, scrimp (and save), be sparing, be frugal, cut back, tighten one's belt, retrench; *informal* be stingy, be tight.

**4** *informal you pinched his baseball cards* STEAL, thieve, take, snatch, pilfer, purloin, loot; *informal* swipe, rob, nab, lift, "liberate," "borrow," filch, heist.

▸ noun **1** *he gave her arm a pinch* TWEAK, nip, squeeze.

**2** *a pinch of salt* BIT, touch, dash, spot, trace, soupçon, speck, taste; *informal* smidgen, tad.

PHRASES: **feel the pinch** *many of our customers are feeling the pinch* SUFFER HARDSHIP, be short of money, be poor, be impoverished.
**in a pinch** *there's room for four adults, five in a pinch* IF NECESSARY, if need be, in an emergency, just possibly, with difficulty.

**pinched** adjective *their pinched faces* STRAINED, stressed, fraught, tense, taut; tired, worn, drained, sapped; wan, peaked, pale, gray, blanched; thin, drawn, haggard, gaunt. ANTONYM healthy.

**pine** verb **1** *I am* ***pining away*** *from love* LANGUISH, decline, weaken, waste away, wilt, wither, fade, sicken, droop; brood, mope, moon.

**2** *he was pining for his son* YEARN, long, ache, sigh, hunger, languish; miss, mourn, lament, grieve over, shed tears for, bemoan, rue, eat one's heart out over; *informal* itch.

**pinion** verb *the hostages were pinioned to each other* HOLD DOWN, pin down, restrain, hold fast, immobilize; tie, bind, truss (up), shackle, fetter, hobble, manacle, handcuff; *informal* cuff.

**pink** adjective *the meat should be slightly pink* ROSE, rosy, rosé, pale red, salmon, coral; flushed, blushing.

▸ noun *informal she's in the pink of condition* PRIME, perfection, best, finest, height; utmost, greatest, apex, zenith, acme, bloom.

PHRASE: **in the pink** *informal I'm finally in the pink again* IN GOOD HEALTH, very healthy, very well, hale and hearty; blooming, flourishing, thriving, vigorous, strong, lusty, robust, in fine fettle, (as) fit as a fiddle, in excellent shape.

**pinnacle** noun **1** *pinnacles of rock* PEAK, needle, crag, tor, aiguille, hoodoo; summit, crest, apex, tip.

**2** *the pinnacles of the clock tower* TURRET, minaret, spire, finial, mirador.

**3** *the pinnacle of the sport* HIGHEST LEVEL, peak, height, high point, top, capstone, apex, zenith, apogee, acme. ANTONYM nadir.

**pinpoint** noun *a pinpoint of light* POINT, spot, speck, dot, speckle.

▸ adjective *pinpoint accuracy* PRECISE, strict, exact, meticulous, scrupulous, punctilious, accurate, careful.

▸ verb *pinpoint the cause of the trouble* IDENTIFY, determine, distinguish, discover, find, locate, detect, track down, spot, diagnose, recognize, pin down, home in on, put one's finger on.

**pioneer** noun **1** *the pioneers of the Wild West* SETTLER, colonist, colonizer, frontiersman, frontierswoman, explorer, trailblazer, bushwhacker.

**2** *an aviation pioneer* DEVELOPER, innovator, trailblazer, groundbreaker, spearhead; founder, founding father, architect, creator.

▸ verb *he pioneered the sale of insurance* INTRODUCE, develop, evolve, launch, instigate, initiate, spearhead, institute, establish, found, be the father/mother of, originate, set in motion, create; lay the groundwork, prepare the way, blaze a trail, break new ground.

**pious** adjective **1** *a pious family* RELIGIOUS, devout, God-fearing, churchgoing, spiritual, prayerful, holy, godly, saintly, dedicated, reverent, dutiful, righteous. ANTONYM irreligious.

**2** *pious platitudes* SANCTIMONIOUS, hypocritical, insincere, self-righteous, holier-than-thou, pietistic, churchy; *informal* goody-goody. ANTONYM sincere.

**3** *a pious hope* FORLORN, vain, doomed, hopeless, desperate; unlikely, unrealistic.

**pipe** noun **1** *a water pipe* TUBE, conduit, hose, main, duct, line, channel, pipeline, drain; tubing, piping, siphon.

**2** *he smokes a pipe* brier (pipe), meerschaum, chibouk; hookah, narghile, bong, churchwarden.

**3** *she was playing a pipe* WHISTLE, pennywhistle, tin whistle, flute, recorder, fife; chanter.

**4** *regimental pipes and drums* BAGPIPES, uillean pipes; pan pipes.

▸ verb **1** *the beer is piped into barrels* SIPHON, feed, channel, run, convey.

**2** *television shows piped in from New York* TRANSMIT, feed, patch.

**3** *he heard a tune being piped* PLAY ON A PIPE, tootle, whistle; *literary* flute.

**4** *a curlew piped* CHIRP, cheep, chirrup, twitter, warble, trill, peep, sing, shrill.

PHRASE: **pipe down** *informal we had to ask that couple in the first row to pipe down* BE QUIET, be silent, hush, stop talking, hold one's tongue, settle down; *informal* shut up, shut one's mouth, zip it, button it, button one's lip, put a sock in it.

**pipe dream** noun *for most aspiring actors, that starring role is just a pipe dream* FANTASY, false hope, illusion, delusion, daydream, chimera; castle in the air, castle in Spain; *informal* pie in the sky.

**pipeline** noun *a gas pipeline* PIPE, conduit, main, line, duct, tube. PHRASE: **in the pipeline** *word of a layoff is in the pipeline* ON THE WAY, coming, forthcoming, upcoming, imminent, about to happen, near, close, brewing, in the offing, in the wind.

**piquant** adjective **1** *a piquant sauce* SPICY, tangy, peppery, hot; tasty, flavorful, appetizing, savory; pungent, sharp, tart, zesty, strong, salty. ANTONYM bland.

**2** *a piquant story* INTRIGUING, stimulating, interesting, fascinating, colorful, exciting, lively; spicy, provocative, racy; *informal* juicy. ANTONYM dull.

**pique** noun *a fit of pique* IRRITATION, annoyance, resentment, anger, displeasure, indignation, petulance, ill humor, vexation, exasperation, disgruntlement, discontent; offense, umbrage.

▸ verb **1** *his curiosity was piqued* STIMULATE, arouse, rouse, provoke, whet, awaken, excite, kindle, stir, galvanize.

**2** *she was piqued by his neglect* IRRITATE, annoy, bother, vex, displease, upset, offend, affront, anger, exasperate, infuriate, gall, irk, nettle; *informal* peeve, aggravate, miff, rile, bug, needle, get someone's back up, get someone's goat, tick off, tee off.

**piracy** noun **1** *piracy on the high seas* FREEBOOTING, robbery at sea; *archaic* buccaneering.

**2** *software piracy* ILLEGAL COPYING, plagiarism, copyright infringement, bootlegging.

**pirate** noun **1** *pirates boarded the ship* FREEBOOTER, marauder, raider; *historical* privateer; *archaic* buccaneer, corsair.

**2** *software pirates* COPYRIGHT INFRINGER, plagiarist, plagiarizer.

▸ verb *designers may pirate good ideas* STEAL, plagiarize, poach, copy illegally, reproduce illegally, appropriate, bootleg; *informal* crib, lift, rip off, pinch.

**pit**[1] noun **1** *a pit in the ground* HOLE, ditch, trench, trough, hollow, excavation, cavity, crater, pothole; shaft, mineshaft, sump.

**2** *pit closures* COAL MINE, colliery, quarry.

**3** *the pits in her skin* POCKMARK, pock, hollow, indentation, depression, dent, dimple.

▸ verb **1** *his skin had been pitted by acne* MARK, pockmark, scar, blemish, disfigure.

**2** *raindrops pitted the bare earth* MAKE HOLES IN, make hollows in, dent, indent.

PHRASES: **pit against** *it's your chance to pit your wits against the world champions* SET AGAINST, match against, put in opposition to, put in competition with; compete with, contend with, vie with, wrestle with.
**the pits** *informal this place is really the pits* HELL, the worst, the lowest of the low, a nightmare; rock-bottom, extremely bad, awful, terrible, dreadful, deplorable; *informal* appalling, lousy, abysmal.

**pit**[2] noun *cherry pits* STONE, pip, seed.

**pitch**[1] noun **1** *her voice rose in pitch* TONE, timbre, key, modulation, frequency.

**2** *the pitch of the roof* GRADIENT, slope, slant, angle, steepness, tilt, incline, inclination.

**3** *her anger reached such a pitch that she screamed* LEVEL, intensity, point, degree, height, extent.

**4** *a pitch of the ball* THROW, fling, hurl, toss, lob; delivery; *informal* heave.

**5** *his sales pitch* PATTER, talk; *informal* spiel, line.

▸ verb **1** *she pitched the crumpled note into the fire* THROW, toss, fling, hurl, cast, lob, flip, propel, bowl; *informal* chuck, sling, heave, peg.

**2** *he pitched overboard* FALL, tumble, topple, plunge, plummet.

**3** *they pitched their tents* PUT UP, set up, erect, raise.

**4** *the boat pitched* LURCH, toss (about), plunge, roll, reel, sway, rock, keel, list, wallow, labor.

PHRASES: **make a pitch for** *we made a pitch for the Loman account, but we lost in the bidding* TRY TO OBTAIN, try to acquire, try to get, bid for, make a bid for.
**pitch in** *if we all pitch in, we can be out of here in thirty minutes* HELP (OUT), assist, lend a hand, join in, participate, contribute, do one's bit, chip in, cooperate, collaborate.

**pitch**[2] noun *cement coated with pitch* bitumen, asphalt, tar.

**pitch-black** adjective *we ventured into the pitch-black tunnel* BLACK, dark, pitch-dark, inky, jet-black, coal-black, jet, ebony; starless, moonless; *literary* Stygian.

**pitcher** noun *a pitcher of beer* JUG, ewer, jar; creamer.

**piteous** adjective *a piteous cry* SAD, pitiful, pitiable, pathetic, heart-rending, heartbreaking, moving, touching; plaintive, poignant, forlorn; poor, wretched, miserable.

**pitfall** noun *home schooling has its pitfalls* HAZARD, danger, risk, peril, difficulty, catch, snag, stumbling block, drawback.

**pith** noun **1** *the pith of the argument* ESSENCE, main point, fundamentals, heart, substance, nub, core, quintessence, crux, gist, meat, kernel, marrow, burden; *informal* nitty-gritty.

**2** *he writes with pith and exactitude* SUCCINCTNESS, conciseness, concision, pithiness, brevity; cogency, weight, depth, force.

**pithy** adjective *pithy comments* SUCCINCT, terse, concise, compact, short (and sweet), brief, condensed, to the point, epigrammatic, crisp, thumbnail; significant, meaningful, expressive, telling; *formal* compendious. See note at TERSE. ANTONYM verbose.

**pitiful** adjective **1** *a child in a pitiful state* DISTRESSING, sad, piteous, pitiable, pathetic, heart-rending, heartbreaking, moving, touching, tearjerking; plaintive, poignant, forlorn; poor, sorry, wretched, abject, miserable.

**2** *a pitiful $500 a month* PALTRY, miserable, meager, insufficient, trifling, negligible, pitiable, derisory; *informal* pathetic, measly, piddling, mingy.

**3** *his performance was pitiful* WOEFUL, deplorable, awful, terrible, lamentable, hopeless, poor, bad, feeble, pitiable, dreadful, inadequate, below par, laughable; *informal* pathetic, useless, appalling, lousy, abysmal, dire.

**pitiless** adjective *a pitiless executioner* MERCILESS, unmerciful, unpitying, ruthless, cruel, heartless, remorseless, hard-hearted, cold-hearted, harsh, callous, severe, unsparing, unforgiving, unfeeling, uncaring, unsympathetic, uncharitable, brutal, inhuman, inhumane, barbaric, sadistic. ANTONYM merciful.

**pittance** noun *the musicians were paid a pittance* A TINY AMOUNT, next to nothing, very little; *informal* peanuts, chicken feed, slave wages, chump change.

**pity** noun **1** *a voice full of pity* COMPASSION, commiseration, condolence, sympathy, fellow feeling, understanding; sorrow, regret, sadness. ANTONYMS indifference, cruelty.

**2** *it's a pity he never had children* SHAME, sad thing, bad luck, misfortune; *informal* crime, bummer, sin.

▸ verb *they pitied me* FEEL SORRY FOR, feel for, sympathize with, empathize with, commiserate with, take pity on, be moved by, grieve for.

PHRASES: **take pity on** *a better person would take pity on them* FEEL SORRY FOR, relent, be compassionate toward, be sympathetic toward, have mercy on, help (out), put someone out of their misery.

**what a pity!** *Cameron lost by less than a tenth of a second? What a pity!* HOW SAD, what a shame, too bad, tant pis, oh dear, bummer.

**pivot** noun **1** *the machine turns on a pivot* FULCRUM, axis, axle, swivel; pin, shaft, hub, spindle, hinge, kingpin, gudgeon.

**2** *the pivot of government policy* CENTER, focus, hub, heart, nucleus, crux, keystone, cornerstone, linchpin, kingpin.

▸ verb **1** *the panel pivots inward* ROTATE, turn, swivel, revolve, spin.

**2** *it all pivoted on his response* DEPEND, hinge, turn, center, hang, rely, rest; revolve around.

**pixie** noun *Loolah was a mischievous little pixie* ELF, fairy, sprite, imp, brownie, puck, leprechaun; *literary* faerie, fay.

**placard** noun *placards with antiwar slogans* NOTICE, poster, sign, bill, advertisement; banner; *informal* ad.

**placate** verb *John did his best to placate her* PACIFY, calm, appease, mollify, soothe, win over, conciliate, propitiate, make peace with, humor. See note at PACIFY. ANTONYM provoke.

**place** noun **1** *an ideal place for dinner* LOCATION, site, spot, setting, position, situation, area, region, locale; venue; *technical* locus.

**2** *foreign places* COUNTRY, state, area, region, town, city; locality, district; *literary* clime.

**3** *a place of her own* HOME, house, flat, apartment; accommodations, property, pied-à-terre; rooms, quarters; *informal* pad, digs; *formal* residence, abode, dwelling (place), domicile, habitation.

**4** *if I were in your place, I'd sell now* SITUATION, position, circumstances; *informal* shoes.

**5** *a place was reserved for her* SEAT, chair, space.

**6** *I offered him a place in the company* JOB, position, post, appointment, situation, office; employment.

**7** *I know my place* STATUS, position, standing, rank, niche; *dated* estate, station.

**8** *it was not her place to sort it out* RESPONSIBILITY, duty, job, task, role, function, concern, affair, charge; right, privilege, prerogative.

▸ verb **1** *books were placed on the table* PUT (DOWN), set (down), lay, deposit, position, plant, rest, stand, station, situate, leave; *informal* stick, dump, park, plonk, pop, plunk.

**2** *the trust you placed in me* PUT, lay, set, invest.

**3** *a survey placed the company sixth* RANK, order, grade, class, classify, categorize; put, set, assign.

**4** *Joe couldn't quite place her* IDENTIFY, recognize, remember, put a name to, pin down; locate, pinpoint.

**5** *we were* ***placed with*** *foster parents* house with, billet to; allocate to, assign to, appoint to.

PHRASES: **in the first place** *in the first place, you're not old enough* INITIALLY, at first, at the start, at the outset, in/at the beginning, in the first instance, to begin with, to start with, originally.

**in place 1** *the veil was held in place by pearls* IN POSITION, in situ.

**2** *the plans are in place* READY, set up, all set, established, arranged, in order.

**in place of** *in place of fresh flowers, use sprays of dried lavender* INSTEAD OF, rather than, as a substitute for, as a replacement for, in exchange for, in lieu of; in someone's stead.

**out of place 1** *she never had a hair out of place* OUT OF POSITION, out of order, in disarray, disarranged, in a mess, messy, topsy-turvy, muddled.

**2** *he said something out of place* INAPPROPRIATE, unsuitable, unseemly, improper, untoward, out of keeping, unbecoming, wrong.

**3** *she seemed out of place at the literary parties* INCONGRUOUS, out of one's element, like a fish out of water; uncomfortable, uneasy.

**put someone in their place** *Marsha's father-in-law finally spoke up and put that hateful woman in her place* HUMILIATE, take down a peg or two, deflate, crush, squash, humble; *informal* cut down to size, settle someone's hash, make someone eat crow.

**take place** *the site where the crash took place* HAPPEN, occur, come about, transpire, crop up, materialize, arise, go down; *literary* come to pass, befall, betide.

**take the place of** *I know I'll never be able to take the place of your father* REPLACE, stand in for, substitute for, act for, fill in for, cover for, relieve.

**placid** adjective 1 *she's normally very placid* EVEN-TEMPERED, calm, tranquil, equable, unexcitable, serene, mild, 'calm, cool, and collected', composed, self-possessed, poised, easygoing, levelheaded, steady, unruffled, unperturbed, phlegmatic; *informal* unflappable. See note at CALM. ANTONYM excitable.

2 *a placid village* QUIET, calm, tranquil, still, peaceful, undisturbed, restful, sleepy. ANTONYM bustling.

**plagiarize** verb *he was fined for plagiarizing a song* COPY, infringe the copyright of, pirate, steal, poach, appropriate; *informal* rip off, crib, "borrow", pinch.

**plague** noun 1 *they died of the plague* BUBONIC PLAGUE, pneumonic plague, Black Death; disease, sickness, epidemic; *dated* contagion; *archaic* pestilence.

2 *a plague of fleas* INFESTATION, epidemic, invasion, swarm, multitude, host.

3 *theft is the plague of restaurants* BANE, curse, scourge, affliction, blight.

▸ verb 1 *he was plagued by poor health* AFFLICT, bedevil, torment, trouble, beset, dog, curse.

2 *he plagued her with questions* PESTER, harass, badger, bother, torment, persecute, bedevil, harry, hound, trouble, irritate, nag, annoy, vex, molest; *informal* hassle, bug, aggravate, devil.

**plain** adjective 1 *it was plain that something was wrong* OBVIOUS, clear, crystal clear, evident, apparent, manifest, patent; discernible, perceptible, noticeable, recognizable, unmistakable, transparent; pronounced, marked, striking, conspicuous, self-evident, indisputable; writ large; *informal* standing/sticking out like a sore thumb.

2 *plain English* INTELLIGIBLE, comprehensible, clear, understandable, coherent, uncomplicated, lucid, unambiguous, simple, straightforward, user-friendly; *formal* perspicuous. ANTONYMS obscure, unclear.

3 *plain speaking* CANDID, frank, outspoken, forthright, direct, honest, truthful, blunt, bald, explicit, unequivocal; *informal* upfront.

4 *a plain dress* SIMPLE, ordinary, unadorned, unembellished, unornamented, unostentatious, unfussy, basic, modest, unsophisticated, without frills, homespun; restrained, muted; everyday, workaday. ANTONYMS elaborate, fancy.

5 *a plain girl* HOMELY, unattractive, unprepossessing, ugly, ill-favored, unlovely, ordinary; *informal* not much to look at. ANTONYM attractive.

6 *it was plain bad luck* SHEER, pure, downright, out-and-out, unmitigated.

▸ adverb *this is just plain stupid* DOWNRIGHT, utterly, absolutely, completely, totally, really, thoroughly, positively, simply, unquestionably, undeniably; *informal* plumb.

▸ noun *the endless grassy plains* GRASSLAND, prairie, flatland, lowland, pasture, meadowland, savanna, steppe; tableland, tundra, pampas, veld.

**plain-spoken** adjective *he's not being rude, he's just plain-spoken* CANDID, frank, outspoken, forthright, direct, honest, truthful, open, blunt, straightforward, explicit, unequivocal, unambiguous, not afraid to call a spade a spade, tell-it-like-it-is; *informal* upfront. ANTONYM evasive.

**plaintive** adjective *a plaintive cry* MOURNFUL, sad, wistful, doleful, pathetic, pitiful, piteous, melancholy, sorrowful, unhappy, wretched, woeful, forlorn, woebegone; *literary* dolorous.

**plan** noun 1 *a plan for raising money* PROCEDURE, scheme, strategy, idea, proposal, proposition, suggestion; project, program, system, method, stratagem, formula, recipe; way, means, measure, tactic.

2 *her plan was to win a medal* INTENTION, aim, idea, intent, objective, object, goal, target, ambition.

3 *plans for the clubhouse* BLUEPRINT, drawing, diagram, sketch, layout; illustration, representation.

▸ verb 1 *plan your route in advance* ORGANIZE, arrange, work out, design, outline, map out, prepare, schedule, formulate, frame, develop, devise, concoct; plot, scheme, hatch, brew, slate.

2 *he plans to buy a house* INTEND, aim, propose, mean, hope, want, wish, desire, envisage; *formal* purpose. See note at INTEND.

3 *I'm planning a new garden* DESIGN, draw up, sketch out, map out.

**plane**[1] noun 1 *a horizontal plane* FLAT SURFACE, level surface; horizontal.

2 *a higher plane of achievement* LEVEL, degree, standard, stratum; position, rung, echelon.

▸ adjective *a plane surface* FLAT, level, horizontal, even; smooth, regular, uniform; *technical* planar.

▸ verb 1 *seagulls planed overhead* SOAR, glide, float, drift, wheel.

2 *boats planed across the water* SKIM, glide.

**plane**[2] noun *the plane took off* AIRCRAFT, airplane, airliner, jet, jumbo jet, jetliner, bush plane, float plane, seaplane, crop duster, water bomber; *dated* flying machine.

**plant** noun 1 *garden plants* flower, vegetable, herb, shrub, weed; **(plants)** vegetation, greenery, flora, herbage, verdure.

2 *the plant commenced production* FACTORY, works, foundry, mill, workshop, shop.

3 *a CIA plant* SPY, informant, informer, agent, secret agent, mole, infiltrator, operative; *informal* spook.

▸ verb 1 *plant the seeds this autumn* SOW, scatter, seed; bed out, transplant.

2 *he planted his feet on the ground* PLACE, put, set, position, situate, settle; *informal* plonk.

3 *she planted the idea in his mind* INSTILL, implant, impress, imprint, put, place, introduce, fix, establish, lodge.

4 *letters were planted to embarrass them* HIDE, conceal, secrete.

**plaque** noun *a plaque in her honor was place on the door to the auditorium* PLATE, tablet, panel, sign, cartouche, brass.

**plaster** noun 1 *the plaster covering the bricks* PLASTERWORK, stucco, pargeting.

2 *a statuette made of plaster* PLASTER OF PARIS, gypsum.

▸ verb 1 *bread plastered with butter* COVER THICKLY, smother, spread, smear, cake, coat, slather.

2 *his hair was* ***plastered down*** *with sweat* FLATTEN (DOWN), smooth down, slick down.

**plastic** adjective 1 *at high temperatures the rocks become plastic* MALLEABLE, moldable, pliable, pliant, ductile, flexible, soft, workable, bendable; *informal* bendy. ANTONYM rigid.

2 *the plastic minds of children* IMPRESSIONABLE, malleable, receptive, pliable, pliant, flexible; compliant, tractable, biddable, persuadable, susceptible, manipulable. ANTONYM intractable.

3 *a plastic smile* ARTIFICIAL, false, fake, superficial, pseudo, bogus, unnatural, insincere; *informal* phony, pretend. ANTONYM genuine.

**plate** noun 1 *a dinner plate* DISH, platter, salver, paten, charger; *historical* trencher.

2 *a plate of spaghetti* PLATEFUL, helping, portion, serving.

3 *steel plates* PANEL, sheet, layer, pane, slab.

4 *a brass plate on the door* PLAQUE, sign, tablet, cartouche.

5 *the book has color plates* PICTURE, print, illustration, photograph, photo.

▸ verb *the roof was plated with steel* COVER, coat, overlay, laminate, veneer; electroplate, galvanize, gild.

**plateau** noun 1 *a windswept plateau* UPLAND, tableland, plain, mesa, highland, coteau.

2 *prices reached a plateau* quiescent period; letup, respite, lull.

**platform** noun 1 *he made a speech from the platform* STAGE, dais, rostrum, podium, soapbox.

2 *the party's platform* POLICY, program, party line, manifesto, plan, principles, objectives, aims.

**platitude** noun *boring us with his platitudes* CLICHÉ, truism, commonplace, banality, old chestnut, bromide, inanity, banal/trite/hackneyed/stock phrase.

**platitudinous** adjective *platitudinous political sound bites* HACKNEYED, overworked, overused, clichéd, banal, trite, commonplace, well-worn, stale, tired, unoriginal; *informal* corny, old hat. ANTONYM original.

**platonic** adjective *the roommates' platonic relationship* NONSEXUAL, nonphysical, chaste; intellectual, friendly. ANTONYM sexual.

**platoon** noun *our platoon lost 200 men on that mission* UNIT, patrol, troop, squad, squadron, team, company, corps, outfit, detachment, contingent.

**platter** noun *a platter of broiled oysters* PLATE, dish, salver, paten, tray; *historical* trencher.

**plaudits** plural noun *the mayor won plaudits for his aggressive campaign against crime* PRAISE, acclaim, commendation, congratulations, accolades, compliments, cheers, applause, tributes, bouquets; a pat on the back; *informal* a (big) hand. ANTONYM criticism.

**plausible** adjective *a plausible explanation* CREDIBLE, reasonable, believable, likely, feasible, tenable, possible, conceivable, imaginable; convincing, persuasive, cogent, sound, rational, logical, thinkable. See note at BELIEVABLE. ANTONYM unlikely.

**play** verb 1 *Aidan and Robert were playing with their toys* AMUSE ONESELF, entertain oneself, enjoy oneself, have fun; relax, occupy oneself, divert oneself; frolic, frisk, romp, caper; *informal* mess around.

2 *I used to play hockey* TAKE PART IN, participate in, be involved in, compete in, do.

3 *St. Joseph's plays Boston on Sunday* COMPETE AGAINST, take on, challenge, vie with, face, go up against.

4 *he was to play Macbeth* ACT (THE PART OF), take the role of, appear as, portray, depict, impersonate, represent, render, perform, enact; *formal* personate.

5 *get your guitar and let's play* PERFORM, make music, jam.

6 *Bryanna played a note on the flute* MAKE, produce, reproduce; blow, toot; plunk, bang out; sound.

7 *the sunlight played on the water* DANCE, flit, ripple, touch; sparkle, glint.

▸ noun 1 *a balance between work and play* AMUSEMENT, entertainment, relaxation, recreation, diversion, distraction, leisure; enjoyment, pleasure, fun, games, fun and games; horseplay, merrymaking, revelry; *informal* living it up.

2 *a Shakespearean play* DRAMA, theatrical work; screenplay, comedy, tragedy; production, performance, show, sketch.

3 *a new tool came into play* ACTION, activity, operation, working, function; interaction, interplay.

4 *there is foul play afoot* BEHAVIOR, goings-on, activity, action, deed.

5 *there was a little play in the rope* MOVEMENT, slack, give; room to maneuver, scope, latitude.

PHRASES: **play around** *informal he's been playing around for years* WOMANIZE, philander, have affairs, flirt; *informal* carry on, mess around, play the field, sleep around, fool around.

**play at being** *she just plays at being the caring one* PRETEND TO BE, pass oneself off as, masquerade as, profess to be, pose as, impersonate; fake, feign, simulate, affect; *informal* make like.

**play ball** *informal if you play ball, I can help you* CO-OPERATE, collaborate, play the game, help, lend a hand, assist, contribute; *informal* pitch in.

**play down** *officials tried to play down the extent of the damage* MAKE LIGHT OF, make little of, gloss over, de-emphasize, downplay, understate; soft-pedal, tone down, diminish, trivialize, underrate, underestimate, undervalue; disparage, belittle, scoff at, sneer at, shrug off; *informal* pooh-pooh.

**play for time** *Nesmith's opponents accused him of playing for* *time in order to pull an election-year coup* STALL, temporize, delay, hold back, hang fire, procrastinate, drag one's feet.

**play it by ear** *when a guest doesn't show up for live radio, you learn quickly how to play it by ear* IMPROVISE, extemporize, ad lib; *informal* wing it.

**play on** *they play on our fears* EXPLOIT, take advantage of, use, turn to (one's) account, profit by, capitalize on, trade on, milk, abuse.

**play the fool** *by the time she was ten, Ronnie knew it was her God-given job to play the fool* CLOWN AROUND, fool around, mess around, monkey around, joke; *informal* horse around.

**play the game** *you find out early on who's willing to play the game, and that's the kind of person this company holds on to* PLAY FAIR, be fair, play by the rules, conform, be a good sport, toe the line.

**play up** *his agents really play up the story of his rise from poverty* EMPHASIZE, accentuate, call attention to, point up, underline, highlight, spotlight, foreground, feature, stress, accent.

**play up to** *wannabes who play up to the boss* INGRATIATE ONESELF WITH, curry favor with, court, fawn over, make up to, toady to, crawl to, pander to, flatter; *informal* soft-soap, suck up to, butter up, lick someone's boots.

**playboy** noun *he claims his days as a playboy are over* SOCIALITE, pleasure-seeker, sybarite; ladies' man, womanizer, philanderer, wolf, rake, roué; *informal* ladykiller.

**player** noun **1** *a tournament for young players* PARTICIPANT, contestant, competitor, contender; sportsman/woman, athlete.

**2** *the players in the orchestra* MUSICIAN, performer, instrumentalist, soloist, virtuoso.

**3** *the players at the Shaw Festival* ACTOR, actress, performer, thespian, entertainer, artist/artiste, trouper.

**playful** adjective **1** *a playful mood* FRISKY, jolly, lively, full of fun, frolicsome, sportive, high-spirited, exuberant, perky; mischievous, impish, clownish, kittenish, rascally, tricksy; *informal* full of beans; *formal* ludic. ANTONYM solemn.

**2** *a playful remark* LIGHTHEARTED, in jest, joking, jokey, teasing, humorous, jocular, good-natured, tongue-in-cheek, facetious, frivolous, flippant, arch; *informal* waggish. ANTONYM serious.

**playground** noun *they need more supervision on the playground* PLAY AREA, park, playing field, recreation ground.

**playwright** noun *we're reading the works of Simon and other modern playwrights* DRAMATIST, dramaturge, scriptwriter, screenwriter, writer, scenarist; tragedian.

**plea** noun **1** *a plea for aid* APPEAL, entreaty, supplication, petition, request, call, suit, solicitation.

**2** *her plea of a headache was unconvincing* CLAIM, explanation, defense, justification; excuse, pretext.

**plead** verb **1** *he* ***pleaded with*** *her to stay* BEG, implore, entreat, appeal to, supplicate, importune, petition, request, ask, call on; *literary* beseech. See note at BEG.

**2** *she pleaded ignorance* CLAIM, use as an excuse, assert, allege, argue, state.

**pleasant** adjective **1** *a pleasant evening* ENJOYABLE, pleasurable, nice, agreeable, pleasing, satisfying, gratifying, good; entertaining, amusing, delightful, charming; fine, balmy; *informal* lovely, great.

**2** *the staff are pleasant* FRIENDLY, agreeable, amiable, nice, genial, cordial, likable, amicable, good-humored, good-natured, personable; hospitable, approachable, gracious, courteous, polite, obliging, helpful, considerate; charming, lovely, delightful, sweet, sympathetic, simpatico. ANTONYM disagreeable.

THE RIGHT WORD **pleasant, agreeable, attractive, congenial, enjoyable, gratifying, pleasing**

One might have a **pleasant** smile and a **pleasing** personality, since the former suggests something that is naturally appealing while the latter suggests a conscious attempt to please. Something that is **enjoyable** is able to give enjoyment or pleasure (*a thoroughly enjoyable evening*), while **agreeable** describes something that is in harmony with one's personal mood or wishes (*an agreeable afternoon spent relaxing in the sun*). **Gratifying** is more intense, suggesting that deeper expectations or needs have been met (*the awards ceremony was particularly gratifying for parents*). Something that is **attractive** gives pleasure because of its appearance or manner (*an attractive house in a wooded setting*), while **congenial** has more to do with compatibility (*a congenial couple*).

**pleasantry** noun **1** *we exchanged pleasantries* BANTER, badinage; polite remark, casual remark.

**2** *he laughed at his own pleasantry* JOKE, witticism, quip, jest, gag, bon mot; *informal* wisecrack, crack.

**please** verb **1** *he'd do anything to please her* MAKE HAPPY, give pleasure to, make someone feel good; delight, charm, amuse, entertain; satisfy, gratify, humor, oblige, content, suit. ANTONYM annoy.

**2** *do as you please* LIKE, want, wish, desire, see fit, think fit, choose, will, prefer.

▸ adverb *please sit down* IF YOU PLEASE, if you wouldn't mind, if you would be so good; kindly, pray; *archaic* prithee.

**pleased** adjective *Edward seemed really pleased to see me* HAPPY, glad, delighted, gratified, grateful, thankful, content, contented, satisfied; thrilled, elated, overjoyed; *informal* over the moon, tickled pink, on cloud nine. ANTONYM unhappy.

**pleasing** adjective **1** *a pleasing day* NICE, agreeable, pleasant, pleasurable, satisfying, gratifying, good, enjoyable, entertaining, amusing, delightful; *informal* lovely, great; *Brit. informal* cushty. See note at PLEASANT.

**2** *her pleasing manner* FRIENDLY, amiable, pleasant, agreeable, affable, nice, genial, likable, good-humored, charming, engaging, delightful; *informal* lovely, simpatico.

**pleasure** noun **1** *she smiled with pleasure* HAPPINESS, delight, joy, gladness, glee, satisfaction, gratification, contentment, enjoyment, amusement.

**2** *his greatest pleasures in life* JOY, amusement, diversion, recreation, pastime; treat, thrill.

**3** *don't mix business and pleasure* ENJOYMENT, fun, entertainment; recreation, leisure, relaxation; *informal* jollies.

**4** *a life of pleasure* HEDONISM, indulgence, self-indulgence, self-gratification, lotus-eating.

**5** *what's your pleasure?* WISH, desire, preference, will, inclination, choice. PHRASES: **take pleasure in** *we're still healthy enough to take pleasure in our retirement years* ENJOY, delight in, love, like, adore, appreciate, relish, savor, revel in, glory in; *informal* get a kick out of, get a thrill out of.

**with pleasure** *certainly I can give you a ride, with pleasure* GLADLY, willingly, happily, readily; by all means, of course; *archaic* fain.

**plebeian** noun *plebeians and gentry lived together* PROLETARIAN, commoner, working-class person, worker; peasant; *informal* pleb, prole. ANTONYM aristocrat.

▸ adjective **1** *people of plebeian descent* LOWER-CLASS, working-class, proletarian, common, peasant; mean, humble, lowly. ANTONYM noble.

**2** *plebeian tastes* UNCULTURED, uncultivated, unrefined, lowbrow, philistine, uneducated; coarse, uncouth, common, vulgar. ANTONYM refined.

**pledge** noun **1** *his election pledge* PROMISE, undertaking, vow, word, word of honor, commitment, assurance, oath, guarantee.

**2** *he gave it as a pledge to a creditor* SURETY, bond, security, collateral, guarantee, deposit.

**3** *a pledge of my sincerity* TOKEN, symbol, sign, earnest, mark, testimony, proof, evidence.

▸ verb **1** *he pledged to root out corruption* PROMISE, vow, swear, undertake, engage, commit oneself, declare, affirm, avow.

**2** *they pledged $10 million* PROMISE (TO GIVE), donate, contribute, give, put up.

**3** *his home is pledged as security against the loan* MORTGAGE, put up as collateral, guarantee, pawn.

**plentiful** adjective *a plentiful supply of food* ABUNDANT, copious, ample, profuse, rich, lavish, generous, bountiful, large, great, bumper, superabundant, inexhaustible, prolific; *informal* galore; *literary* plenteous. See note at PREVALENT. ANTONYM scarce.

**plenty** noun *times of plenty* PROSPERITY, affluence, wealth, opulence, comfort, luxury; plentifulness, abundance; *literary* plenteousness.

▸ pronoun *there are **plenty of** books* A LOT OF, many, a great deal of, enough (and to spare), no lack of, sufficient, a wealth of; *informal* loads of, lots of, heaps of, stacks of, masses of, tons of, oodles of, scads of, a slew of.

**plethora** noun *a plethora of opinion polls* EXCESS, overabundance, superabundance, surplus, glut, superfluity, surfeit, profusion; (**a plethora of**), too many, too much, enough and to spare; *informal* more —— than one can shake a stick at. ANTONYM dearth.

**USAGE NOTE plethora**

According to the *Oxford English Dictionary* (OED) and most other dictionaries, this word refers (and has always referred) to an overabundance, an overfullness, or an excess. The phrase *a plethora of* is essentially a highfalutin equivalent of *too many*—e.g.: "Our electoral politics now is beset with a plethora of [read *too many*] players and a confusing clutter of messages." (*Brookings Review*; Jan. 1, 2002.) But sometimes, when not preceded by the indefinite article, the word is genuinely useful—e.g.: "Critics say the plethora of scrip circulating in Argentina risks running out of control." (*Wall Street Journal*; Dec. 26, 2001.)

Unfortunately, through misunderstanding of the word's true sense, many writers use it as if it were equivalent to *plenty* or *many*. This meaning is unrecorded in the OED and in most other dictionaries. And it represents an unfortunate degeneration of sense—e.g.:

• "Buffalo may seem like a boring city, but we've managed to produce a plethora [read *plenty*] of famous people, the Goo Goo Dolls, Ani Difranco, David Boreanaz and now, Chad Murray." (*Buffalo News*; Jan. 8, 2002.)

• "The old policies did not anticipate a plethora [read *series* or *group* or *lot*] of suicide bombers." (*Orlando Sentinel*; Jan. 10, 2002.) (One suicide bomber is too many—so plethora doesn't work.)

Phrases such as *a whole plethora of* are likewise ill-considered—e.g.: "Then, once you get to the airport ticket counter, there's a whole plethora [read *a whole range* or *a wide variety*] of biometric identifiers you could use to tie the background checks you've done to the individuals who present themselves at the ticket counter." (*Boston Globe*; Jan. 6, 2002.)

The word is pronounced /**pleth**-er-uh/, not /pluh-**thor**-uh/. —*BG*

---

**pliable** adjective **1** *leather is pliable* FLEXIBLE, pliant, bendable, elastic, supple, malleable, workable, plastic, springy, ductile; *informal* bendy. See note at FLEXIBLE. ANTONYM rigid.

**2** *pliable teenage minds* MALLEABLE, impressionable, flexible, adaptable, pliant, compliant, biddable, tractable, yielding, amenable, susceptible, suggestible, persuadable, manipulable, receptive. ANTONYM obdurate.

**plight** noun *the plight of the homeless* PREDICAMENT, quandary, difficult situation, dire straits, trouble, difficulty, extremity, bind; *informal* dilemma, tight corner, tight spot, hole, pickle, jam, fix.

**plod** verb **1** *Mom plodded wearily upstairs* TRUDGE, walk heavily, clump, stomp, tramp, tromp, lumber, slog.

**2** *I have to plod through the whole book* WADE, plow, trawl, toil, labor; *informal* slog.

**plot** noun **1** *a plot to overthrow him* CONSPIRACY, intrigue, secret plan; machinations.

**2** *the plot of her novel* STORY LINE, story, scenario, action, thread; *formal* diegesis.

**3** *a three-acre plot* PIECE OF GROUND, patch, area, tract, acreage, allotment, lot, plat, homesite.

▸ verb **1** *he plotted their downfall* PLAN, scheme, arrange, organize, hatch, concoct, devise, dream up; *informal* cook up.

**2** *his brother was plotting against him* CONSPIRE, scheme, intrigue, collude, connive, machinate.

**3** *the fifty-three sites were plotted* MARK, chart, map, represent, graph.

THE RIGHT WORD **plot, cabal, conspiracy, intrigue, machination**

If you come up with a secret plan to do something, especially with evil or mischievous intent, it's called a **plot** (*a plot to seize control of the company*). If you get other people or groups involved in your plot, it's called a **conspiracy** (*a conspiracy to overthrow the government*). **Cabal** usually applies to a small group of political conspirators (*a cabal of right-wing extremists*), while **machination** (usually plural) suggests deceit and cunning in devising a plot intended to harm someone (*the machinations of the would-be assassins*). An **intrigue** involves more complicated scheming or maneuvering than a plot and often employs underhanded methods in an attempt to gain one's own ends (*she had a passion for intrigue, particularly where romance was involved*).

**plow** verb **1** *the fields were plowed* TILL, furrow, harrow, cultivate, work, break up.

**2** *the streets haven't been plowed yet* CLEAR (OF SNOW), shovel.

**3** *the car plowed into a telephone pole* CRASH, smash, career, plunge, bulldoze, hurtle, careen, cannon, run, drive, barrel.

**4** *they plowed through deep snow* TRUDGE, plod, toil, wade; *informal* slog.

**ploy** noun *perhaps this had been a ploy to revive her husband's fading interest* RUSE, tactic, move, device, stratagem, scheme, trick, gambit, plan, maneuver, dodge, subterfuge, wile.

**pluck** verb **1** *he plucked a thread from his lapel* REMOVE, pick (off), pull (off/out), extract, take (off).

**2** *she **plucked at** his T-shirt* PULL (AT), tug (at), clutch (at), snatch (at), grab, catch (at), tweak, jerk; *informal* yank.

**3** *the turkeys have been plucked* DEPLUME, remove the feathers from.

**4** *Jen plucked the guitar strings* STRUM, pick, plunk, thrum, twang; play pizzicato.

▸ noun *saying those things to her took a lot of pluck* COURAGE, bravery, nerve, backbone, spine, daring, spirit, intrepidity, fearlessness, mettle, grit, true grit, determination, fortitude, resolve, stout-heartedness, dauntlessness, valor, heroism, audacity; *informal* guts, spunk, gumption, moxie. See note at COURAGE.

**plucky** adjective *these plucky young players are still about the game, not about the money* BRAVE, courageous, bold, daring, fearless, intrepid, spirited, game, valiant, valorous, stout-hearted, dauntless, resolute, determined, undaunted, unflinching, audacious, unafraid, doughty, mettlesome; *informal* gutsy, spunky. ANTONYM timid.

**plug** noun **1** *she pulled out the plug* STOPPER, bung, cork, seal, spile.

**2** *a plug of tobacco* WAD, quid, twist, chew, cake, stick.

**3** *informal a plug for her new book* ADVERTISEMENT, promotion, commercial, recommendation, mention, good word; *informal* hype, push, puff piece, ad, boost, ballyhoo.

▸ verb **1** *plug the holes* STOP (UP), seal (up/off), close (up/off), cork, stopper, bung, block (up/off), fill (up).

**2** *informal she plugged her new film* PUBLICIZE, promote, advertise, mention, bang the drum for, draw attention to; *informal* hype (up), push, puff.

**3** *informal don't move or I'll plug you* SHOOT, gun down; *informal* blast, fill/pump full of lead.

PHRASE: **plug away** *informal he plugged away at his novel, unaware of the day or the time* TOIL, labor, slave away, soldier on, persevere, persist, keep on; *informal* slog away, beaver away.

**plum** adjective *informal a plum job* EXCELLENT, very good, wonderful, marvelous, choice, first-class; *informal* great, terrific, cushy.

**plumb** verb *an attempt to plumb her psyche* EXPLORE, probe, delve into, search, examine, investigate, fathom, penetrate, understand.

▸ adverb **1** *informal it went plumb through the screen* RIGHT, exactly, precisely, directly, dead, straight; *informal* bang.

**2** *informal I plumb forgot* COMPLETELY, absolutely, downright, totally, quite, thoroughly.

**3** *the bell hangs plumb* VERTICALLY, perpendicularly, straight down.

▸ adjective *a plumb drop* VERTICAL, perpendicular, straight.

PHRASE: **plumb the depth of** *she had plumbed the depths of depravity* FIND, experience the extremes of, reach the lowest point of; reach rock bottom of.

**plummet** verb **1** *the plane plummeted to the ground* PLUNGE, nosedive, dive, drop, fall, descend, hurtle.

**2** *share prices plummeted* FALL STEEPLY, plunge, tumble, drop rapidly, go down, slump; *informal* crash, nosedive.

**plump** adjective *a plump child* CHUBBY, fat, stout, rotund, well padded, ample, full-figured, pillowy, round, chunky, portly, overweight, fleshy, paunchy, bulky, corpulent; *rare* pulvinate; *informal* tubby, roly-poly, pudgy, beefy, porky, zaftig, corn-fed. ANTONYM thin.

**plunder** verb **1** *they plundered the countryside* PILLAGE, loot, rob, raid, ransack, despoil, strip, ravage, lay waste, devastate, sack, rape. See note at RAVAGE.

**2** *money plundered from pension funds* STEAL, purloin, thieve, seize, pillage; embezzle.

▸ noun **1** *the plunder of the villages* LOOTING, pillaging, plundering, raiding, ransacking, devastation, sacking; *literary* rapine.

**2** *the army took huge quantities of plunder* BOOTY, loot, stolen goods, spoils, ill-gotten gains; *informal* swag.

**plunge** verb **1** *Joy plunged into the sea* DIVE, jump, throw oneself, launch oneself.

**2** *the aircraft plunged to the ground* PLUMMET, nosedive, drop, fall, pitch, tumble, descend, dive-bomb.

**3** *the car plunged down an alley* CHARGE, hurtle, career, plow, cannon, tear; *informal* barrel.

**4** *oil prices plunged* FALL SHARPLY, plummet, drop, go down, tumble, slump; *informal* crash, nosedive.

**5** *he plunged the dagger into her back* THRUST, jab, stab, sink, stick, ram, drive, push, shove, force.

**6** *plunge the pears into boiling water* IMMERSE, submerge, dip, dunk.

**7** *the room was plunged into darkness* THROW, cast, pitch.

▸ noun **1** *a plunge into the deep end* DIVE, jump, nosedive, fall, pitch, drop, plummet, descent.

**2** *a plunge in profits* FALL, drop, slump; *informal* nosedive, crash.

PHRASE: **take the plunge** *she decided to take the plunge and headed for Hollywood* COMMIT ONESELF, go for it, do the deed, throw caution to the wind(s), risk it; *informal* jump in at the deep end, go for broke.

**plus** preposition **1** *three plus three makes six* AND, added to. ANTONYM minus.

**2** *he wrote four novels plus various poems* AS WELL AS, together with, along with, in addition to, and, not to mention, besides.

▸ noun *one of the pluses of the job* ADVANTAGE, good point, asset, pro, (fringe) benefit, bonus, extra, attraction; *informal* perk; *formal* perquisite. ANTONYM disadvantage.

**plush** adjective *informal the car's plush interior* LUXURIOUS, luxury, deluxe, sumptuous, palatial, lavish, opulent, magnificent, lush, rich, expensive, fancy, grand, upscale, upmarket; *informal* posh, ritzy, swanky, classy, swank. ANTONYM austere.

**plutocrat** noun *champagne-swilling plutocrats* RICH PERSON, magnate, millionaire, billionaire, multimillionaire; nouveau riche; *informal* fat cat, moneybags.

**ply** verb **1** *the gondolier plied his oar* USE, wield, work, manipulate, handle, operate, utilize, employ.

**2** *he plied a profitable trade* ENGAGE IN, carry on, pursue, conduct, practice; *archaic* prosecute.

**3** *ferries ply between all lake resorts* GO REGULARLY, travel, shuttle, go back and forth.

**4** *she plied me with chocolate chip cookies* PROVIDE, supply, lavish, shower, regale.

**5** *he plied her with questions* BOMBARD, assail, beset, pester, plague, harass, importune; *informal* hassle, devil.

**poach** verb **1** *he's been poaching salmon* HUNT ILLEGALLY, catch illegally, jacklight, jack; steal.

**2** *workers were poached by other firms* STEAL, appropriate, purloin, take, lure away; *informal* nab, swipe, pinch.

**pocket** noun **1** *a bag with two pockets* POUCH, compartment.

**2** *these donors have deep pockets* MEANS, budget, resources, finances, funds, money, wherewithal, pocketbook.

**3** *pockets of disaffection* AREA, patch, region, isolated area, island, cluster, center.

▸ adjective *a pocket dictionary* SMALL, little, miniature, mini, compact, concise, abridged, portable, vest-pocket.

▸ verb *he pocketed $900,000 of their money* STEAL, take, appropriate, thieve, purloin, misappropriate, embezzle; *informal* filch, swipe, pinch.

**pod** noun *the seeds are formed inside a pod* SHELL, husk, hull, case; shuck; *Botany* pericarp, capsule.

**podium** noun *he was a natural-born speaker, in his glory up at the podium* PLATFORM, stage, dais, rostrum, stand, soapbox.

**poem** noun *Lydia saved every poem that Marshall wrote that year* VERSE, rhyme, piece of poetry, song.

**poet** noun *she has the soul of a poet* WRITER OF POETRY, versifier, rhymester, rhymer, sonneteer, lyricist, lyrist; laureate; *literary* bard; *derogatory* poetaster; *historical* troubadour, balladeer.

**poetic** adjective **1** *poetic compositions* POETICAL, verse, metrical, lyrical, lyric, elegiac.

**2** *poetic language* EXPRESSIVE, figurative, symbolic, flowery, artistic, elegant, fine, beautiful; sensitive, imaginative, creative.

**poetry** noun *a book of Jimmy Carter's poetry* POEMS, verse, versification, metrical composition, rhymes, balladry; *archaic* poesy.

**pogrom** noun *how is that every civilized nation has not formally denounced this pogrom?* MASSACRE, slaughter, mass murder, annihilation, extermination, decimation, carnage, bloodbath, bloodletting, butchery, genocide, holocaust, purge, ethnic cleansing.

**poignancy** noun *his imminent death gave his words a special poignancy* PATHOS, pitifulness, piteousness, sadness, sorrow, mournfulness, wretchedness, misery, tragedy.

**poignant** adjective *they read aloud the poignant letters written by the victims' children* TOUCHING, moving, sad, affecting, pitiful, piteous, pathetic, sorrowful, mournful, wretched, miserable, distressing, heart-rending, tearjerking, plaintive, tragic. See note at MOVING.

**point**[1] noun **1** *the point of a needle* TIP, (sharp) end, extremity; prong, spike, tine, nib, barb.

**2** *points of light* PINPOINT, dot, spot, speck, fleck.

**3** *a meeting point* PLACE, position, location, site, spot, area.

**4** *this point in her life* TIME, stage, juncture, period, phase.

**5** *the tension had reached such a high point* LEVEL, degree, stage, pitch, extent.

**6** *an important point* DETAIL, item, fact, thing, argument, consideration, factor, element; subject, issue, topic, question, matter.

**7** *get to the point* HEART OF THE MATTER, most important part, essence, nub, keynote, core, pith, crux; meaning, significance, gist, substance, thrust, bottom line, burden, relevance; *informal* brass tacks, nitty-gritty.

**8** *what's the point of this?* PURPOSE, aim, object, objective, goal, intention; use, sense, value, advantage.

**9** *he had his good points* ATTRIBUTE, characteristic, feature, trait, quality, property, aspect, side.

▸ verb **1** *she pointed the gun at him* AIM, direct, level, train.

**2** *the evidence* ***pointed to*** *his guilt* INDICATE, suggest, evidence, signal, signify, denote, bespeak, reveal, manifest.

PHRASES: **beside the point** *those accusations are beside the point* IRRELEVANT, immaterial, unimportant, neither here nor there, inconsequential, incidental, out of place, unconnected, peripheral, tangential, extraneous.
**in point of fact** *in point of fact, all three of these gentlemen have immaculate service records* IN FACT, as a matter of fact, actually, in actual fact, really, in reality, as it happens, in truth.
**make a point of** *she made a point of letting us know she was recently divorced* MAKE AN EFFORT TO, go out of one's way to, put emphasis on.
**on the point of** *we were on the point of quitting, but something kept us going* (JUST) ABOUT TO (BE), on the verge of, on the brink of, going to (be), all set to (be).
**point of view** *we have different points of view* OPINION, view, belief, attitude, feeling, sentiment, thoughts; position, perspective, viewpoint, standpoint, outlook.
**point out** *the flaws in the plan have already been pointed out* IDENTIFY, show, designate, draw attention to, indicate, specify, detail, mention.
**point up** *it's as if he deliberately points up every negative aspect of our work* EMPHASIZE, highlight, draw attention to, accentuate, underline, spotlight, foreground, put emphasis on, stress, play up, accent, bring to the fore.
**to the point** *his observations were concise and to the point* RELEVANT, pertinent, apposite, germane, applicable, apropos, appropriate, apt, fitting, suitable, material; *formal* ad rem.
**up to a point** *I agree with you, but only up to a point* PARTLY, to some extent, to a certain degree, in part, somewhat, partially.

**point**[2] noun *the ship rounded the point* PROMONTORY, headland, foreland, cape, spit, peninsula, bluff, ness, horn.

**point-blank** adverb **1** *he fired the pistol point-blank* AT CLOSE RANGE, close up, close to.

**2** *she couldn't say it point-blank* BLUNTLY, directly, straight, frankly, candidly, openly, explicitly, unequivocally, unambiguously, plainly, flatly, categorically, outright.

▸ adjective *a point-blank refusal* BLUNT, direct, straight, straightforward, frank, candid, forthright, explicit, unequivocal, plain, clear, flat, decisive, unqualified, categorical, outright.

**pointed** adjective **1** *a pointed stick* SHARP, tapering, tapered, conical, jagged, spiky, spiked, barbed; *informal* pointy.

**2** *a pointed remark* CUTTING, trenchant, biting, incisive, acerbic, caustic, scathing, venomous, sarcastic; *informal* snarky.

**pointer** noun **1** *the pointer moved to 100 mph* INDICATOR, needle, arrow, hand.

**2** *he used a pointer on the chart* STICK, rod, cane; cursor.

**3** *a pointer to the outcome of the election* INDICATION, indicator, clue, hint, sign, signal, evidence, intimation, inkling, suggestion.

**4** *I can give you a few pointers* TIP, hint, suggestion, guideline, recommendation.

**pointless** adjective *our attempts to help Ryan were pointless* SENSELESS, futile, hopeless, fruitless, useless, needless, in vain, unavailing, aimless, idle, worthless, valueless; absurd, insane, stupid, silly, foolish. ANTONYM valuable.

**poise** noun **1** *poise and good deportment* GRACE, gracefulness, elegance, balance, control.

**2** *in spite of the setback she retained her poise* COMPOSURE, equanimity, self-possession, aplomb, presence of mind, self-assurance, self-control, nerve, calm, sangfroid, dignity; *informal* cool, unflappability.

▸ verb **1** *she was poised on one foot* BALANCE, hold (oneself) steady, be suspended, remain motionless, hang, hover.

**2** *he was poised for action* PREPARE ONESELF, ready oneself, brace oneself, gear oneself up, stand by.

**poison** noun **1** *a deadly poison* TOXIN, toxicant, venom; *archaic* bane.

**2** *Marianne would spread her poison* MALICE, ill will, hate, malevolence, bitterness, spite, spitefulness, venom, acrimony, rancor; bad influence, cancer, corruption, pollution.

▸ verb **1** *her mother poisoned her* GIVE POISON TO; murder.

**2** *a blackmailer poisoning pet food* CONTAMINATE, put poison in, envenom, adulterate, spike, lace, doctor.

**3** *the Amazon is being poisoned* POLLUTE, contaminate, taint, blight, spoil; *literary* befoul.

**4** *they poisoned his mind* PREJUDICE, bias, jaundice, embitter, sour, envenom, warp, corrupt, subvert.

**poisonous** adjective **1** *a poisonous snake* VENOMOUS, deadly. ANTONYM harmless.

**2** *a poisonous chemical* TOXIC, noxious, deadly, fatal, lethal, mortal, death-dealing. ANTONYMS harmless, nontoxic.

**3** *a poisonous glance* MALICIOUS, malevolent, hostile, vicious, spiteful, bitter, venomous, vindictive, vitriolic, rancorous, malign, pernicious, mean, nasty; *informal* bitchy, catty. ANTONYM benevolent.

**poke** verb **1** *she poked him in the ribs* PROD, jab, dig, nudge, butt, shove, jolt, stab, stick.

**2** *leave the cable* ***poking out*** STICK OUT, jut out, protrude, project, extend.

▸ noun *give him a poke* PROD, jab, dig, elbow, nudge, shove, stab.

PHRASES: **poke around/about** *we were just poking around some antique shops* SEARCH, hunt, rummage (around), forage, grub, root about/around, scavenge, nose around, ferret (about/around); sift through, rifle through, scour, comb, probe.

**poke fun at** *I never meant to poke fun at you* MOCK, make fun of, ridicule, laugh at, jeer at, sneer at, deride, scorn, scoff at, pillory, lampoon, tease, taunt, chaff, jibe at; *informal* send up, kid, rib, goof on.

**poke one's nose into** *maybe Barry should stop poking his nose into other people's lives* PRY INTO, interfere in, intrude on, butt into, meddle with; *informal* snoop into.

**poky** adjective *his poky old horse.* See SLOW adjective sense 1.

**polar** adjective **1** *polar regions* ARCTIC, Antarctic, circumpolar, Nearctic.

**2** *polar conditions* COLD, freezing, icy, glacial, chilly, gelid, hypothermic.

**3** *polar opposites* OPPOSITE, opposed, dichotomous, extreme, contrary, contradictory, antithetical.

**polarity** noun *the marked polarity of their political positions* DIFFERENCE, dichotomy, separation, opposition, contradiction, antithesis, antagonism.

**pole**[1] noun *gulls like to perch atop the poles* POST, pillar; telephone pole, utility pole; stanchion, paling, stake, stick, support, prop, batten, bar, rail, rod, beam; staff, stave, cane, baton.

**pole**[2] noun *points of view at opposite poles* EXTREMITY, extreme, limit, antipode. PHRASE: **poles apart** *it would seem that our priorities are poles apart* COMPLETELY DIFFERENT, directly opposed, antithetical, incompatible, irreconcilable, worlds apart, at opposite extremes.

**police** noun *we phoned the police as soon as we heard the collision* POLICE FORCE, police officers, policemen, policewomen, officers of the law, law officers, authorities, constabulary; *informal* COPS, fuzz, law, long arm of the law, boys/men in blue; coppers, force, heat.

▸ verb **1** *we must police the area* GUARD, watch over, protect, defend, patrol; control, regulate.

**2** *the regulations will be policed by the ministry* ENFORCE, regulate, oversee, supervise, monitor, observe, check.

**policy** noun **1** *government policy* PLANS, strategy, stratagem, approach, code, system, guidelines, theory; line, position, stance, attitude.

**2** *it's good policy to listen to your elders* PRACTICE, custom, idea, procedure, conduct, convention.

**polish** verb **1** *I polished his shoes* SHINE, wax, buff, rub up/down; gloss, burnish; varnish, oil, glaze, lacquer, japan, shellac.

**2** ***polish up*** *your essay* PERFECT, refine, improve, hone, enhance; brush up, revise, edit, correct, rewrite, go over, touch up; *informal* clean up.

▸ noun **1** *furniture polish* WAX, glaze, varnish; lacquer, japan, shellac.

**2** *a good surface polish* SHINE, gloss, luster, sheen, sparkle, patina, finish.

**3** *his polish made him stand out* SOPHISTICATION, refinement, urbanity, suaveness, elegance, style, grace, finesse, cultivation, civility, gentility, breeding, courtesy, (good) manners; *informal* class.

PHRASE: **polish off** *informal* **1** *he polished off an apple pie* EAT, finish, consume, devour, guzzle, wolf down, down, bolt; drink up, drain, quaff, gulp (down), binge on, gorge on; *informal* stuff oneself with, put away, scoff, shovel down, pig out on, swill, knock back, scarf (down/up).

**2** *the enemy tried to polish him off* DESTROY, finish off, dispatch, do away with, eliminate, kill, liquidate; *informal* bump off, knock off, do in, take out, dispose of; rub out.

**3** *I'll polish off the last few pages* COMPLETE, finish, deal with, accomplish, discharge, do; end, conclude, close, finalize, round off, wind up; *informal* wrap up, sew up.

THE RIGHT WORD **polish, gloss, luster, sheen**

All of these words refer to a smooth, shining, or bright surface that reflects light. If this surface is produced by rubbing or friction, the correct word is **polish** (*the car's mirrorlike polish was the result of regular waxing and buffing*). **Gloss**, on the other hand, suggests the hard smoothness associated with lacquered, varnished, or enameled surfaces (*a high-gloss paint*). **Luster** is associated with the light reflected from the surfaces of certain materials, such as silk or pearl (*a green stone with a brilliant luster*). **Sheen** describes a glistening or radiant brightness that is also associated with specific materials (*her hair had a rich, velvety sheen*).

**polished** adjective **1** *a polished table* SHINY, glossy, gleaming, lustrous, glassy; waxed, buffed, burnished; varnished, glazed, lacquered, japanned, shellacked. ANTONYMS dull, tarnished.

**2** *a polished performance* EXPERT, accomplished, masterly, masterful, skillful, adept, adroit, dexterous; impeccable, flawless, perfect, consummate, exquisite, outstanding, excellent, superb, superlative, first-rate, fine; *informal* ace. ANTONYM inexpert.

**3** *polished manners* REFINED, cultivated, civilized, well-bred, polite, courteous, genteel, decorous, respectable, urbane, suave, sophisticated. ANTONYM gauche.

**polite** adjective **1** *a very polite girl* WELL-MANNERED, civil, courteous, mannerly, respectful, deferential, well-behaved, well-bred, gentlemanly, ladylike, genteel, gracious, urbane; tactful, diplomatic. ANTONYM rude.

**2** *polite society* CIVILIZED, refined, cultured, sophisticated, genteel, courtly. ANTONYM uncivilized.

**politic** adjective *I do not think it politic to express my reservations* WISE, prudent, sensible, judicious, canny, sagacious, shrewd, astute; recommended, advantageous, beneficial, profitable, desirable, advisable; appropriate, suitable, fitting, apt. ANTONYM unwise.

**political** adjective **1** *the political affairs of the nation* GOVERNMENTAL, government, constitutional, ministerial, parliamentary, diplomatic, legislative, administrative, bureaucratic; public, civic, state.

**2** *he's a political man* POLITICALLY ACTIVE, party; militant, factional, partisan.

**politician** noun *campaigning politicians make more promises than they can keep* LEGISLATOR, elected official, statesman, stateswoman, public servant; senator, congressman, congresswoman; *informal* politico, pol.

**politics** noun **1** *a career in politics* GOVERNMENT, affairs of state, public affairs; diplomacy.

**2** *she studies politics* POLITICAL SCIENCE, civics, statecraft.

**3** *what are his politics?* POLITICAL VIEWS, political leanings, party politics.

**4** *office politics* POWER STRUGGLE, machinations, maneuvering, opportunism, realpolitik.

**poll** noun **1** *a second-round poll* VOTE, ballot, show of hands, referendum, plebiscite; election.

**2** *the poll was unduly low* VOTING FIGURES, vote, returns, count, tally.

**3** *a poll to investigate holiday choices* SURVEY, opinion poll, straw poll, canvass, market research, census.

▸ verb **1** *most of those polled supported the vice president* CANVASS, survey, ask, question, interview, ballot.

**2** *she polled 119 votes* GET, gain, register, record, return.

**pollute** verb **1** *fish farms will pollute the lake* CONTAMINATE, adulterate, taint, poison, foul, dirty, soil, infect; *literary* befoul. ANTONYM purify.

**2** *propaganda polluted this nation* CORRUPT, poison, warp, pervert, deprave, defile, blight, sully; *literary* besmirch.

THE RIGHT WORD **pollute, adulterate, contaminate, defile, taint**

When a factory pours harmful chemicals or wastes into the air or water, it is said to **pollute** the environment. But *pollute* may also refer to impairing the purity, integrity, or effectiveness of something (*a campaign polluted by allegations of sexual impropriety*). To **contaminate** is to spread harmful or undesirable impurities throughout something; unlike *pollute*, which suggests visible or noticeable impurities, **contaminate** is preferred where the change is unsuspected or not immediately noticeable (*milk contaminated by radioactive fallout from a nuclear plant accident*). **Adulterate** often refers to food products to which harmful, low-quality, or low-cost substances have been added in order to defraud the consumer (*cereal adulterated with sawdust*), although this word can apply to any mixture to which the inferior or harmful element is added deliberately and in the hope that no one will notice (*a report adulterated with false statistics*). To **defile** is to pollute something that should be kept pure or sacred (*a church defiled by vandals*), while **taint** implies that a trace of something toxic or corrupt has been introduced (*he contracted the disease from a tainted blood transfusion; the book is tainted by gratuitous violence*).

**pollution** noun **1** *air and water pollution* CONTAMINATION, adulteration, impurity; dirt, filth, toxins, infection; smog.

**2** *the pollution of young minds* CORRUPTION, defilement, poisoning, warping, depravation, sullying, violation.

**pomp** noun *the pomp of a royal wedding* CEREMONY, ceremonial, solemnity, ritual, display, spectacle, pageantry; show, showiness, ostentation, splendor, grandeur, magnificence, majesty, stateliness, glory, opulence, brilliance, drama, resplendence, splendidness; *informal* razzmatazz.

**pompous** adjective *pompous officials* SELF-IMPORTANT, imperious, overbearing, domineering, magisterial, pontifical, sententious, grandiose, affected, pretentious, puffed up, arrogant, vain, haughty, proud, conceited, egotistic, supercilious, condescending, patronizing; *informal* snooty, uppity, uppish. See note at FORMAL. ANTONYM modest.

**pond** noun *snowy egrets visit our pond* POOL, waterhole, lake, tarn, reservoir, slough, beaver pond, lagoon.

**ponder** verb *she had time to* ***ponder over*** *the incident* THINK ABOUT, contemplate, consider, review, reflect on, mull over, meditate on, muse on, deliberate about, cogitate on, dwell on, brood on, ruminate on, chew over, puzzle over, turn over in one's mind.

**ponderous** adjective **1** *a ponderous dance* CLUMSY, heavy, awkward, lumbering, slow, cumbersome, ungainly, graceless, uncoordinated, blundering; *informal* clodhopping, clunky. See note at HEAVY. ANTONYMS light, graceful.

**2** *his ponderous sentences* LABORED, laborious, awkward, clumsy, forced, stilted, unnatural, artificial; stodgy, lifeless, plodding, pedestrian, boring, dull, tedious, monotonous; overelaborate, convoluted, windy. ANTONYM lively.

**pontificate** verb *he pontificated about life and art* HOLD FORTH, expound, declaim, preach, lay down the law, sound off, dogmatize, sermonize, moralize, lecture; *informal* preachify, mouth off.

**pooh-pooh** verb *informal an idea pooh-poohed by the scientific community* DISMISS, reject, spurn, rebuff, wave aside, disregard, discount; play down, make light of, belittle, deride, mock, scorn, scoff at, sneer at.

**pool**[1] noun **1** *pools of water* PUDDLE, pond, slough; *literary* plash.

**2** *the hotel has a pool* SWIMMING POOL, baths, lap pool, natatorium.

**pool**[2] noun **1** *a pool of skilled labor* SUPPLY, reserve(s), reservoir, fund; store, stock, accumulation, cache.

**2** *a pool of money for emergencies* FUND, reserve, kitty, pot, bank, purse.

**3** *the office hockey pool* LOTTERY, bet.

▸ verb *they pooled their skills* COMBINE, amalgamate, group, join, unite, merge; fuse, conglomerate, integrate; share.

**poor** adjective **1** *a poor family* POVERTY-STRICKEN, penniless, moneyless, impoverished, low-income, necessitous, impecunious, indigent, needy, destitute, pauperized, unable to make ends meet, without a sou; insolvent, in debt, without a cent (to one's name); *informal* (flat) broke, hard up, cleaned out, strapped; *formal* penurious. See note at RICH. ANTONYMS rich, wealthy.

**2** *poor workmanship* SUBSTANDARD, below par, bad, deficient, defective, faulty, imperfect, inferior; appalling, abysmal, atrocious, awful, terrible, dreadful, unsatisfactory, second-rate, third-rate, tinpot, shoddy, crude, lamentable, deplorable, inadequate, unacceptable; *informal* crummy, lame, crappy, dismal, bum, rotten. ANTONYM superior.

**3** *a poor crop* MEAGER, scanty, scant, paltry, disappointing, limited, reduced, modest, insufficient, inadequate, sparse, spare, deficient, insubstantial, skimpy, short, small, lean, slender; *informal* measly, stingy, pathetic, piddling; *formal* exiguous. ANTONYMS satisfactory, good.

**4** *poor soil* UNPRODUCTIVE, barren, unyielding, unfruitful; arid, sterile. ANTONYMS fertile, productive.

**5** *the waters are* ***poor in*** *nutrients* DEFICIENT IN, lacking in, wanting in, weak in; short of, low on.

**6** *you poor thing!* UNFORTUNATE, unlucky, luckless, unhappy, hapless, ill-fated, ill-starred, pitiable, pitiful, wretched. ANTONYM lucky.

**poorly** adverb *the text is poorly written* BADLY, deficiently, defectively, imperfectly, incompetently; appallingly, abysmally, atrociously, awfully, dreadfully; crudely, shoddily, inadequately.

▸ adjective *she felt poorly* ILL, unwell, not (very) well, ailing, indisposed, out of sorts, under/below par, peaked; sick, queasy, nauseous; off; *informal* under the weather, funny, peculiar, lousy, rough.

**pop** verb **1** *champagne corks popped* GO BANG, go off; crack, snap, burst, explode.

**2** *I'm just popping home* GO; drop in, stop by, visit.

**3** *pop a lid over the pot* PUT, place, slip, slide, stick, set, lay, install, position, arrange.

▸ noun **1** *the balloons burst with a pop* BANG, crack, snap; explosion, report.

**2** *informal a bottle of pop* SOFT DRINK, soda, carbonated drink.

PHRASE: **pop up** *you never know when a new problem is going to pop up* APPEAR (SUDDENLY), occur (suddenly), arrive, materialize, come along, happen, emerge, arise, crop up, turn up, present itself, come to light; *informal* show up.

**populace** noun *when the populace wants to, it can change the course of history* POPULATION, inhabitants, residents, natives; community, country, (general) public, people, nation; common people, man/woman in the street, masses, multitude, rank and file, commonalty, commonality, third estate, plebeians, proletariat; *informal* proles, plebs; *formal* denizens; *derogatory* hoi polloi, common herd, rabble, riffraff; (**the populace**) Joe Public, John Q. Public.

**popular** adjective **1** *the most popular restaurant in town* WELL-LIKED, favored, sought-after, in demand, desired, wanted; commercial, marketable, fashionable, trendy, in vogue, all the rage, hot; *informal* in, cool, big.

**2** *popular science* NON-SPECIALIST, nontechnical, amateur, lay person's, general, middle-of-the-road; accessible, simplified, plain, simple, easy, straightforward, understandable; mass-market, middlebrow, lowbrow, pop. ANTONYM highbrow.

**3** *popular opinion* WIDESPREAD, general, common, current, prevalent, prevailing, standard, stock; ordinary, usual, accepted, established, acknowledged, conventional, orthodox.

**4** *a popular movement for independence* MASS, general, communal, collective, social, collaborative, group, civil, public.

**popularize** verb **1** *tobacco was popularized by Sir Walter Raleigh* MAKE POPULAR, make fashionable; market, publicize; *informal* hype.

**2** *he popularized the subject* SIMPLIFY, make accessible, give mass-market appeal to, universalize, vulgarize.

**3** *the report popularized the unfounded notion* GIVE CURRENCY TO, spread, propagate, give credence to.

**popularly** adverb **1** *old age is popularly associated with illness* WIDELY, generally, universally, commonly, usually, customarily, habitually, conventionally, traditionally, as a rule.

**2** *the bar was popularly known as "the May"* INFORMALLY, unofficially; by lay people.

**3** *the president is popularly elected* DEMOCRATICALLY, by the people.

**populate** verb **1** *the town is populated by 40,000 people* INHABIT, occupy, people; live in, reside in.

**2** *an attempt to populate the island* SETTLE, colonize, people, occupy, move into, make one's home in.

**population** noun *a new social agenda for the population of these emerging nations* INHABITANTS, residents, people, citizens, citizenry, public, community, populace, society, body politic, natives, occupants; *formal* denizens.

**populous** adjective *a populous island* DENSELY POPULATED, heavily populated, congested, crowded, packed, jammed, crammed, teeming, swarming, seething, crawling; *informal* jam-packed. ANTONYM deserted.

**porch** noun *the chair would be ideal for a porch or patio* VESTIBULE, foyer, entrance (hall), entry, portico, lobby; veranda, terrace; stoop; *Architecture* lanai, tambour, narthex.

**pore**[1] noun *pores in the skin* OPENING, orifice, aperture, hole, outlet, inlet, vent; *Biology* stoma, foramen.

**pore**[2] verb *they* ***pored over*** *the map* STUDY, read intently, peruse, scrutinize, scan, examine, go over.

**pornographic** adjective *pornographic magazines* OBSCENE, indecent, crude, lewd, dirty, vulgar, smutty, filthy; erotic, titillating, arousing, suggestive, sexy, risqué; off-color, adult, X-rated, hard-core, soft-core; *informal* porn, porno, blue, skin. ANTONYM wholesome.

**pornography** noun *selling pornography to minors* erotica, pornographic material, dirty books; smut, filth, vice; *informal* (hard/soft) porn, porno, girlie magazines, skin flicks.

**porous** adjective *porous fibers* PERMEABLE, penetrable, pervious, cellular, holey; absorbent, absorptive, spongy. ANTONYM impermeable.

**port** noun 1 *the German port of Kiel* SEAPORT.

2 *shells exploded down by the port* HARBOR, dock(s), haven, marina; anchorage, moorage, harborage, roads.

**portable** adjective *a portable tape recorder* TRANSPORTABLE, movable, mobile, travel; lightweight, compact, handy, convenient.

**portend** verb *the sight of a dead bird was believed to portend tragedy* PRESAGE, augur, foreshadow, foretell, prophesy; be a sign, warn, be an omen, indicate, herald, signal, bode, promise, threaten, signify, spell, denote; *literary* betoken, foretoken, forebode.

**portent** noun 1 *a portent of things to come* OMEN, sign, signal, token, forewarning, warning, foreshadowing, prediction, forecast, prophecy, harbinger, augury, auspice, presage; writing on the wall, indication, hint; *literary* foretoken.

2 *the word carries terrifying portent* SIGNIFICANCE, importance, import, consequence, meaning, weight; *formal* moment.

**portentous** adjective 1 *portentous signs* OMINOUS, warning, premonitory, threatening, menacing, ill-omened, foreboding, inauspicious, unfavorable. See note at OMINOUS.

2 *portentous dialogue* POMPOUS, bombastic, self-important, pontifical, solemn, sonorous, grandiloquent.

**porter** noun *a porter helped with the bags* carrier, baggage clerk, redcap.

**portion** noun 1 *the upper portion of the chimney* PART, piece, bit, section, segment. See note at FRAGMENT.

2 *her portion of the allowance* SHARE, slice, quota, quantum, part, percentage, amount, quantity, ration, fraction, division, allocation, measure; *informal* cut.

3 *a portion of cake* HELPING, serving, amount, quantity; plateful, bowlful; slice, piece, chunk, wedge, slab, hunk.

4 *archaic* *poverty was certain to be his portion.* See DESTINY sense 1.

▸ verb *she **portioned out** the food* SHARE OUT, allocate, allot, apportion; distribute, hand out, deal out, dole out, give out, dispense, mete out; *informal* divvy up.

**portly** adjective *a portly gentleman showed us the way to the dining room* STOUT, plump, fat, overweight, heavy, corpulent, fleshy, paunchy, potbellied, well padded, rotund, stocky, heavyset, bulky; *informal* tubby, roly-poly, beefy, porky, pudgy; *informal* corn-fed. ANTONYM slim.

**portrait** noun 1 *a portrait of the first lady* PAINTING, picture, drawing, sketch, likeness, image, study, miniature; *informal* oil; *formal* portraiture.

2 *a vivid portrait of Italy* DESCRIPTION, portrayal, representation, depiction, impression, account; sketch, vignette, profile.

**portray** verb 1 *she portrays the older architecture of her province* PAINT, draw, sketch, picture, depict, represent, illustrate, render.

2 *the Newfoundland portrayed by Proulx* DESCRIBE, depict, characterize, represent, present, delineate, evoke, tell of.

3 *the actor portrays a spy* PLAY, act the part of, take the role of, represent, appear as; *formal* personate.

**portrayal** noun 1 *a portrayal of a parrot* PAINTING, picture, portrait, drawing, sketch, representation, depiction, study.

2 *her portrayal of adolescence* DESCRIPTION, representation, characterization, depiction, evocation.

3 *Brando's **portrayal of** Corleone* PERFORMANCE AS, representation of, interpretation of, rendering of, reading of; *formal* personation of.

**pose** verb 1 *pollution poses a threat to health* CONSTITUTE, present, create, cause, produce, be.

2 *the question posed earlier* RAISE, ask, put, set, submit, advance, propose, suggest, moot.

3 *she posed for the artist* MODEL, sit.

4 *he posed her on the sofa* POSITION, place, put, arrange, dispose, locate, situate.

5 *I wonder what poor sucker she's posing for tonight* BEHAVE AFFECTEDLY, strike a pose, posture, attitudinize, put on airs; *informal* show off.

▸ noun 1 *a sexy pose* POSTURE, position, stance, attitude, bearing.

2 *her pose of aggrieved innocence* PRETENSE, act, affectation, facade, show, front, display, masquerade, posture.

PHRASE: **pose as** *they pay us to pose as the celebrities we resemble* PRETEND TO BE, impersonate, pass oneself off as, masquerade as, profess to be, represent oneself as; *formal* personate.

**poser** noun *this situation's a bit of a poser* DIFFICULT QUESTION, vexed question, awkward problem, tough one, puzzle, mystery, conundrum, puzzler, enigma, riddle; *informal* dilemma, toughie, stumper.

**posh** adjective *a posh hotel* SMART, stylish, fancy, high-class, fashionable, chic, luxurious, luxury, deluxe, exclusive, opulent, lavish, grand, showy, upscale, upmarket; *informal* classy, swanky, snazzy, plush, ritzy, flash, la-di-da, fancy-dancy, fancy-schmancy, swank, tony.

**position** noun 1 *the aircraft's position* LOCATION, place, situation, spot, site, locality, setting, area; whereabouts, bearings, orientation; *technical* locus.

2 *a standing position* POSTURE, stance, attitude, pose.

3 *our financial position* SITUATION, state, condition, circumstances; predicament, plight, strait(s).

4 *the two parties jockeyed for position* ADVANTAGE, the upper hand, the edge, the whip hand, primacy; *informal* the catbird seat.

5 *their position in society* STATUS, place, level, rank, standing; stature, prestige, influence, reputation, importance, consequence, class; *dated* station.

6 *a secretarial position* JOB, post, situation, appointment, role,

occupation, employment; office, capacity, duty, function; opening, vacancy, placement.

7 *the government's position on the matter* VIEWPOINT, opinion, outlook, attitude, stand, standpoint, stance, perspective, approach, slant, thinking, policy, feelings.

▸ verb *he positioned a chair between them* PUT, place, locate, situate, set, site, stand, station; plant, stick, install; arrange, dispose; *informal* park.

**positive** adjective 1 *a positive response* AFFIRMATIVE, favorable, good, approving, enthusiastic, supportive, encouraging. ANTONYM negative.

2 *do something positive* CONSTRUCTIVE, practical, useful, productive, helpful, worthwhile, beneficial, effective.

3 *she seems a lot more positive* OPTIMISTIC, hopeful, confident, cheerful, sanguine, buoyant; *informal* upbeat. ANTONYM pessimistic.

4 *positive economic signs* FAVORABLE, good, promising, encouraging, heartening, propitious, auspicious. ANTONYMS negative, unfavorable.

5 *positive proof* DEFINITE, conclusive, certain, categorical, unequivocal, incontrovertible, indisputable, undeniable, unmistakable, irrefutable, reliable, concrete, tangible, clear-cut, explicit, firm, decisive, real, actual. ANTONYM doubtful.

6 *I'm positive he's coming back* CERTAIN, sure, convinced, confident, satisfied, assured. ANTONYMS uncertain, unsure.

**positively** adverb 1 *I could not positively identify the voice* CONFIDENTLY, definitely, emphatically, categorically, with certainty, conclusively, unquestionably, undoubtedly, indisputably, unmistakably, assuredly.

2 *he was positively livid* ABSOLUTELY, really, downright, thoroughly, completely, utterly, totally, extremely, fairly; *informal* plain.

**possess** verb 1 *the only hat she possessed* OWN, have (to one's name), hold.

2 *he does not possess a sense of humor* HAVE, be blessed with, be endowed with; enjoy, boast.

3 *a supernatural force possessed him* TAKE CONTROL OF, take over, control, dominate, influence; bewitch, enchant, enthrall.

4 *she was possessed by a need to talk to him* OBSESS, haunt, preoccupy, consume; eat someone up, prey on one's mind.

**possessed** adjective *he was like a man possessed* MAD, demented, insane, crazed, berserk, out of one's mind; bewitched, enchanted, haunted, under a spell.

**possession** noun 1 *the estate came into their possession* OWNERSHIP, control, hands, keeping, care, custody, charge, hold, title, guardianship.

2 *her possession of the premises* OCCUPANCY, occupation, tenure, holding, tenancy.

3 *she packed her possessions* BELONGINGS, things, property, (worldly) goods, (personal) effects, assets, chattels, movables, valuables; stuff, bits and pieces; luggage, baggage; *informal* gear, junk.

4 *colonial possessions* COLONY, dependency, territory, holding, protectorate. PHRASE: **take possession of** *they were under orders to take possession of the house and all of its contents* SEIZE, appropriate, impound, expropriate, sequestrate, sequester, confiscate; take, get, acquire, obtain, procure, possess oneself of, get hold of, get one's hands on; capture, commandeer, requisition; *Law* distrain; *informal* get one's mitts on.

**possessive** adjective 1 *he was very possessive* PROPRIETORIAL, overprotective, controlling, dominating, jealous, clingy.

2 *kids are possessive of their own property* COVETOUS, selfish, unwilling to share; grasping, greedy, acquisitive, grabby.

**possibility** noun 1 *there is a possibility that he might be alive* CHANCE, likelihood, probability, hope; risk, hazard, danger, fear.

2 *they discussed the possibility of launching a new project* FEASIBILITY, practicability, chances, odds, probability.

3 *buying a smaller house is one possibility* OPTION, alternative, choice, course of action, solution.

4 **(possibilities)** *the idea has distinct possibilities* POTENTIAL, promise, prospects.

**possible** adjective 1 *it's not possible to check the figures* FEASIBLE, practicable, practical, viable, within the bounds/realms of possibility, attainable, achievable, workable; *informal* doable.

2 *a possible reason for his disappearance* CONCEIVABLE, plausible, imaginable, believable, likely, potential, probable, credible. ANTONYM unlikely.

3 *a possible future leader* POTENTIAL, prospective, likely, probable.

**possibly** adverb 1 *possibly he took the boy with him* PERHAPS, maybe, it is possible, for all one knows, very likely; *literary* peradventure, perchance, mayhap.

2 *you can't possibly refuse* CONCEIVABLY, under any circumstances, by any means.

3 *could you possibly help me?* PLEASE, kindly, be so good as to.

**post**[1] noun *wooden posts* POLE, stake, upright, longer, shaft, prop, support, picket, strut, pillar, pale, paling, stanchion; *historical* puncheon.

▸ verb 1 *the notice posted on the wall* AFFIX, attach, fasten, display, pin (up), put up, stick (up), tack (up).

2 *the group posted a net profit* ANNOUNCE, report, make known, publish.

**post**[2] noun *our federally regulated post* MAIL, postal service; airmail, surface mail, registered mail.

▸ verb 1 *post the order form today* MAIL, send (off), put in the mail.

2 *post the transaction in the second column* RECORD, write in, enter, register.

PHRASE: **keep posted** *we have no more news at this moment, but we'll keep you posted* KEEP INFORMED, keep up to date, keep in the picture, keep briefed, update, fill in; *informal* keep up to speed.

**post**[3] noun **1** *there were seventy candidates for the post* JOB, position, appointment, situation, place; vacancy, opening.

**2** *back to your posts!* (ASSIGNED) POSITION, station, observation post.

▸ verb **1** *he'd been **posted to** Berlin* SEND TO, assign to a post in/at, dispatch to.

**2** *armed guards were posted beside the exit* PUT ON DUTY, station, position, situate, locate.

**poster** noun *they put up posters all over town* NOTICE, placard, bill, sign, advertisement, playbill.

**posterity** noun *the names of those who died are recorded for posterity* FUTURE GENERATIONS, the future.

**post-mortem** noun **1** *the hospital carried out a postmortem* AUTOPSY, postmortem examination, necropsy.

**2** *a postmortem of her failed relationship* ANALYSIS, evaluation, assessment, appraisal, examination, review.

**postpone** verb *sorry, we'll have to postpone the relay race* PUT OFF/BACK, delay, defer, reschedule, adjourn, shelve, put over, take a rain check on; *informal* put on ice, put on the back burner; *rare* remit. ANTONYM bring forward.

THE RIGHT WORD **postpone, adjourn, defer, delay, suspend**

All of these verbs have to do with putting things off. **Defer** is the broadest in meaning; it suggests putting something off until a later time (*defer payment; defer a discussion*). If you **postpone** an event or activity, you put it off intentionally, usually until a definite time in the future (*we postponed the party until the next weekend*). If you **adjourn** an activity, you postpone its completion until another day or place; *adjourn* is usually associated with meetings or other formal gatherings that are brought to an end and then resumed (*the judge adjourned the hearing until the following morning*). If you **delay** something, you postpone it because of obstacles (*delayed by severe thunderstorms and highway flooding*) or because you are reluctant to do it (*delay going to the dentist*). **Suspend** suggests stopping an activity for a while, usually for a reason (*forced to suspend work on the bridge until the holiday weekend was over*).

**postponement** noun *a further postponement of the trial* DEFERRAL, deferment, delay, putting off/back, rescheduling, adjournment, shelving.

**postscript** noun **1** *a handwritten postscript* AFTERTHOUGHT, PS, additional remark.

**2** *he added postscripts of his own* ADDENDUM, supplement, appendix, codicil, afterword, addition.

**postulate** verb *a theory postulated by a respected scientist* PUT FORWARD, suggest, advance, posit, hypothesize, propose; assume, presuppose, presume, take for granted.

**posture** noun **1** *a kneeling posture* POSITION, pose, attitude, stance.

**2** *good posture* BEARING, carriage, stance, comportment.

**3** *the unions adopted a militant posture* ATTITUDE, stance, standpoint, point of view, opinion, position, frame of mind.

▸ verb *Keith postured, flexing his biceps* POSE, strike an attitude, strut.

**potency** noun **1** *the potency of his words* FORCEFULNESS, force, effectiveness, persuasiveness, cogency, influence, strength, authoritativeness, authority, power, powerfulness; *literary* puissance.

**2** *the potency of the drugs* STRENGTH, powerfulness, power, effectiveness; *formal* efficacy; efficaciousness.

**potent** adjective **1** *a potent political force* POWERFUL, strong, mighty, formidable, influential, dominant, forceful; *literary* puissant. ANTONYM weak.

**2** *a potent argument* FORCEFUL, convincing, cogent, compelling, persuasive, powerful, strong.

**3** *a potent drug* STRONG, powerful, effective; *formal* efficacious. ANTONYM weak.

**potentate** noun *diplomatic missions to foreign potentates* RULER, monarch, sovereign, king, queen, emperor, empress, sultan, shah, raja, pharaoh.

**potential** adjective *a potential source of conflict* POSSIBLE, likely, prospective, future, probable; latent, inherent, undeveloped. See note at LATENT.

▸ noun *economic potential* POSSIBILITIES, potentiality, prospects; promise, capability, capacity.

**potion** noun *people paid good money to sample her so-called magic potions* CONCOCTION, mixture, brew, elixir, philter, drink, decoction; medicine, tonic; *literary* draft.

**potpourri** noun *the book is a potpourri of curious animal stories* MIXTURE, assortment, collection, selection, assemblage, medley, miscellany, mix, mélange, variety, mixed bag, patchwork, bricolage; ragbag, mishmash, salmagundi, jumble, farrago, hodgepodge, gallimaufry.

**pottery** noun *a collection of antique pottery* CHINA, crockery, ceramics, earthenware, stoneware.

**pouch** noun **1** *a leather pouch* BAG, purse, sack, sac, pocket.

**2** *a kangaroo's pouch* marsupium.

**pounce** verb *two men **pounced on** him* JUMP ON, spring on, leap on, dive on, lunge at, fall on, set on, attack suddenly; *informal* jump, mug.

▸ noun *a sudden pounce* LEAP, spring, jump, dive, lunge, bound.

**pound**[1] verb **1** *the two men pounded him with their fists* BEAT, strike, hit, batter, thump, pummel, punch, rain blows on, belabor, hammer, thrash, set on, tear into; *informal* bash, clobber, wallop, beat the living daylights out of, whack, thwack, lay into, pitch into, light into, whale.

**2** *waves pounded the seafront* BEAT AGAINST, crash against, batter, dash against, lash, buffet.

**3** *gunships pounded the capital* BOMBARD, bomb, shell, fire on; *archaic* cannonade.

**4** *pound the cloves with salt* CRUSH, grind, pulverize, mill, mash, pulp; *technical* triturate.

5 *I heard him pounding along the gangway* WALK/RUN HEAVILY, stomp, lumber, clomp, clump, tramp, tromp, trudge.

6 *her heart was pounding* THROB, thump, thud, hammer, pulse, race, go pit-a-pat; *literary* pant, thrill.

**pound**2 noun *a dog pound* ENCLOSURE, compound, pen, yard, corral.

**pour** verb 1 *blood was pouring from his nose* STREAM, flow, run, gush, course, jet, spurt, surge, spill.

2 *Amy poured wine into his glass* TIP, let flow, splash, spill, decant; *informal* slosh, slop.

3 *it was pouring when we set out* RAIN HEAVILY/HARD, teem down, pelt down, come down in torrents/sheets, rain cats and dogs.

4 *people poured off the train* THRONG, crowd, swarm, stream, flood.

**pout** verb *Crystal pouted sullenly* LOOK PETULANT, pull a face, look sulky.

▸ noun *a childish pout* PETULANT EXPRESSION, sulky expression, moue.

**poverty** noun 1 *abject poverty* PENURY, destitution, pauperism, pauperdom, beggary, indigence, pennilessness, impoverishment, neediness, need, hardship, impecuniousness. ANTONYM wealth.

2 *the poverty of choice* SCARCITY, deficiency, dearth, shortage, paucity, insufficiency, absence, lack. ANTONYM abundance.

3 *the poverty of her imagination* INFERIORITY, mediocrity, poorness, sterility.

**powder** noun *the residue was a pinkish powder* DUST, fine particles; talcum powder, talc.

▸ verb 1 *she powdered her face* DUST, sprinkle/cover with powder.

2 *the grains are powdered* CRUSH, grind, pulverize, pound, mill; *technical* comminute.

3 *powdered milk* dry, freeze-dry; *technical* lyophilize.

**powdery** adjective *a powdery substance floated through the air* FINE, dry, fine-grained, powder-like, dusty, chalky, floury, sandy, crumbly, friable.

**power** noun 1 *the power of speech* ABILITY, capacity, capability, potential, faculty, competence. ANTONYM inability.

2 *the unions wield enormous power* CONTROL, authority, influence, dominance, mastery, domination, dominion, sway, weight, leverage; *informal* clout, teeth, drag; *literary* puissance. See note at JURISDICTION.

3 *police have the power to stop and search* AUTHORITY, right, authorization, warrant, license.

4 *a major international power* STATE, country, nation.

5 *he hit the ball with as much power as he could* STRENGTH, powerfulness, might, force, forcefulness, vigor, energy; brawn, muscle; *informal* punch; *literary* thew.

6 *the power of his arguments* FORCEFULNESS, powerfulness, potency, strength, force, cogency, persuasiveness. ANTONYMS impotence, weakness.

7 *the new engine has more power* DRIVING FORCE, horsepower, h.p., acceleration; *informal* oomph.

8 *generating power from waste* ENERGY, electrical power.

9 *informal the time off did him **a power of** good* A GREAT DEAL OF, a lot of, much; *informal* lots of, loads of. PHRASES: **have someone in/under one's power** *I doubt that Roger will ever have Etta under his power* HAVE CONTROL OVER, have influence over, have under one's thumb, have at one's mercy, have in one's clutches, have in the palm of one's hand, have someone wrapped around one's little finger, have in one's hip pocket; *informal* have over a barrel.

**the powers that be** *the powers that be did nothing to defuse the situation* THE AUTHORITIES, the people in charge, the government.

**powerful** adjective 1 *powerful shoulders* STRONG, muscular, muscly, sturdy, strapping, robust, brawny, burly, athletic, manly, well built, solid; *informal* beefy, hunky; *dated* stalwart; *literary* stark, thewy. ANTONYM weak.

2 *a powerful drink* INTOXICATING, hard, strong, stiff, industrial-strength; *formal* spirituous.

3 *a powerful blow* VIOLENT, forceful, hard, mighty. ANTONYM gentle.

4 *he felt a powerful desire to kiss her* INTENSE, keen, fierce, passionate, ardent, burning, strong, irresistible, overpowering, overwhelming.

5 *a powerful nation* INFLUENTIAL, strong, important, dominant, commanding, potent, forceful, formidable; *literary* puissant. ANTONYMS weak, powerless.

6 *a powerful critique* COGENT, compelling, convincing, persuasive, forceful; dramatic, graphic, vivid, moving. ANTONYM ineffective.

**powerless** adjective *the outgoing administrators are essentially powerless* IMPOTENT, helpless, ineffectual, ineffective, useless, defenseless, vulnerable; lame-duck; *literary* impuissant.

**practicable** adjective *what we need is a practicable solution* REALISTIC, feasible, possible, within the bounds/realms of possibility, viable, reasonable, sensible, workable, achievable; *informal* doable.

**practical** adjective 1 *practical experience* EMPIRICAL, hands-on, actual, active, applied, heuristic, experiential, evidence-based. ANTONYM theoretical.

2 *there are no practical alternatives* FEASIBLE, practicable, realistic, viable, workable, possible, reasonable, sensible; *informal* doable.

3 *practical clothes* FUNCTIONAL, sensible, utilitarian, workaday.

4 *try to be more practical* REALISTIC, sensible, down-to-earth, businesslike, commonsensical, grounded, hardheaded, no-nonsense; *informal* hard-nosed.

5 *a practical certainty* VIRTUAL, effective, near.

**practically** adverb 1 *the theater was practically empty* ALMOST, (very) nearly, virtually, just about, all but, more or less, as good as, to all intents and purposes, verging on, bordering on; *informal* pretty near, pretty well; *literary* well-nigh.

2 *"You can't afford it," he pointed out practically* REALISTICALLY, sensibly, reasonably.

**practice** verb 1 *he practiced the songs every day* REHEARSE, run through, go over/through, work on/at; polish, perfect.

2 *the performers were practicing* TRAIN, rehearse, prepare, go through one's paces.

3 *we still practice these rituals today* CARRY OUT, perform, observe.

4 *she practices medicine* WORK AT, pursue a career in.

▸ noun 1 *the practice of hypnosis* APPLICATION, exercise, use, operation, implementation, execution.

2 *common practice* CUSTOM, procedure, policy, convention, tradition; *formal* praxis.

3 *it takes lots of practice* | *the team's final practice* TRAINING, rehearsal, repetition, preparation; practice session, dummy run, run-through; *informal* dry run.

4 *the practice of medicine* PROFESSION, career, business, work.

5 *a small legal practice* BUSINESS, firm, office, company; *informal* outfit.

PHRASES: **in practice** *it seemed like a good idea, but in practice it just didn't work* IN REALITY, realistically, practically.
**out of practice** *considering how out of practice she was, Elizabeth did very well on the balance beam* RUSTY, unpracticed.
**put into practice** *it's time you put your teaching degree into practice* USE, make use of, put to use, utilize, apply.

**practiced** adjective *a practiced judge of character* EXPERT, experienced, seasoned, skilled, skillful, accomplished, proficient, talented, able, adept, consummate, master, masterly; *informal* crack, ace, mean, crackerjack.

**pragmatic** adjective *she remains pragmatic in the most emotional circumstances* PRACTICAL, matter of fact, sensible, down-to-earth, commonsensical, businesslike, having both/one's feet on the ground, hardheaded, no-nonsense; *informal* hard-nosed. ANTONYM impractical.

**praise** verb 1 *the police praised Pauline for her courage* COMMEND, express admiration for, applaud, pay tribute to, speak highly of, eulogize, compliment, congratulate, sing the praises of, rave about, go into raptures about, heap praise on, wax lyrical about, make much of, pat on the back, take one's hat off to, lionize, admire, hail, ballyhoo; *formal* laud. ANTONYMS criticize, condemn.

2 *we praise God* WORSHIP, glorify, honor, exalt, adore, pay tribute to, give thanks to, venerate, reverence; *formal* laud; *archaic* magnify.

▸ noun 1 *your praise means a great deal to us* APPROVAL, acclaim, admiration, approbation, acclamation, plaudits, congratulations, commendation; tribute, accolade, compliment, a pat on the back, eulogy, panegyric; *formal* encomium.

2 *give praise to God* HONOR, thanks, glory, worship, devotion, adoration, reverence.

THE RIGHT WORD **acclaim, commend, eulogize, extol, laud**

If your dog sits when you tell him to sit, you'll want to **praise** him for his obedience. *Praise* is a general term for expressing approval, esteem, or commendation that usually suggests the judgment of a superior (*the teacher's praise for her students*). If a salesperson goes out of his way to help you, you may want to **commend** him to his superior, which is a more formal, public way of praising someone, either verbally or in writing. If you're watching a performance and want to express your approval verbally or with applause, **acclaim** is the verb you're looking for. **Laud** and **extol** suggest the highest of praise, although *laud* may imply that the praise is excessive (*the accomplishments for which she was lauded were really nothing out of the ordinary*). *Extol*, which comes from the Latin meaning to raise up, suggests that you're trying to magnify whatever or whomever you're praising (*to extol her virtues so that everyone would vote for her*). If you want to praise someone who has died recently, you will **eulogize** him or her, which means to speak or write your praise for a special occasion, such as a funeral.

**praiseworthy** adjective *it was a praiseworthy effort* COMMENDABLE, admirable, laudable, worthy (of admiration), meritorious, estimable, exemplary.

**prance** verb *prancing around in his underpants* CAVORT, dance, jig, trip, caper, jump, leap, spring, bound, skip, hop, frisk, romp, frolic.

**prank** noun *it was just a stupid and childish prank* (PRACTICAL) JOKE, trick, piece of mischief, escapade, stunt, caper, jape, game, hoax, antic; *informal* lark.

**prattle** verb *he **prattled on** for ages.* See CHAT verb.

▸ noun *childish prattle.* See CHATTER noun.

**pray** verb 1 *let us pray* SAY ONE'S PRAYERS, make one's devotions, offer a prayer/prayers.

2 *she prayed God to forgive her* INVOKE, call on, implore, appeal to, entreat, beg, petition, supplicate; *literary* beseech.

**prayer** noun 1 *the priest's murmured prayers* INVOCATION, intercession, devotion; *archaic* orison.

2 *a quick prayer that she wouldn't bump into him* APPEAL, plea, entreaty, petition, supplication, invocation. PHRASE: **not have a prayer** *informal everyone thought this Minnesota team didn't have a prayer against Duke* HAVE NO HOPE, have/stand no chance, not have/stand (the ghost of) a chance; *informal* not have a hope in hell.

**preach** verb 1 *he preached to a large congregation* GIVE/DELIVER A SERMON, sermonize, address, speak.

2 *preaching the gospel* PROCLAIM, teach, spread, propagate, expound.

3 *they preach toleration* ADVOCATE, recommend, advise, urge, teach, counsel.

4 *who are you to preach at me?* MORALIZE, sermonize, pontificate, lecture, harangue; *informal* preachify.

**preacher** noun *the preacher counsels young couples about marital concerns* MINISTER, parson, clergyman, clergywoman, member of the clergy, priest, imam, rabbi, man/woman of the cloth, man/woman of God, cleric, churchman, churchwoman, evangelist; *informal* reverend, padre, Holy Joe, sky pilot.

**preaching** noun *I ain't got no use for your preaching* RELIGIOUS TEACHING, message, sermons; *informal* Bible-thumping.

**preamble** noun *we memorized the preamble to the Constitution* INTRODUCTION, preface, prologue; foreword, prelude, front matter; *informal* intro, lead-in; *formal* exordium, proem, prolegomenon.

**precarious** adjective *those steps look a bit precarious* UNCERTAIN, insecure, unpredictable, risky, parlous, hazardous, dangerous, unsafe; unsettled, unstable, unsteady, shaky; *informal* dicey, chancy, iffy. ANTONYM safe.

**precaution** noun *the guard rails are just a precaution* SAFEGUARD, preventative/preventive measure, safety measure, contingency (plan), insurance.

**precede** verb **1** *commercials preceded the movie* GO/COME BEFORE, lead (up) to, pave/prepare the way for, herald, introduce, usher in. ANTONYM follow.

**2** *Catherine preceded him into the studio* GO AHEAD OF, go in front of, go before, go first, lead the way.

**3** *he preceded the book with a poem* PREFACE, introduce, begin, open.

**precedence** noun *quarrels over precedence* PRIORITY, rank, seniority, superiority, primacy, preeminence, eminence. PHRASE: **take precedence over** *the children's needs take precedence over all the other concerns* TAKE PRIORITY OVER, outweigh, prevail over, come before.

**precedent** noun *there are few precedents for this type of legislation* MODEL, exemplar, example, pattern, previous case, prior instance/example; paradigm, criterion, yardstick, standard.

**preceding** adjective *refer to the preceding chart* FOREGOING, previous, prior, former, precedent, earlier, above, aforementioned, antecedent; *formal* anterior, prevenient.

**precept** noun **1** *the precepts of Orthodox Judaism* PRINCIPLE, rule, tenet, canon, doctrine, command, order, decree, dictate, dictum, injunction, commandment; *Judaism* mitzvah; *formal* prescript.

**2** *precepts that her grandmother used to quote* MAXIM, saying, adage, axiom, aphorism, apophthegm.

**precinct** noun **1** *a pedestrian precinct* AREA, zone, sector.

**2** **(precincts)** *within the precincts of the city* BOUNDS, boundaries, limits, confines.

**3** *the cathedral precinct* ENCLOSURE, close, court.

**4** *the friendliest cop of the 20th precinct* division.

**precious** adjective **1** *precious works of art* VALUABLE, costly, expensive; invaluable, priceless, beyond price.

**2** *her most precious possession* VALUED, cherished, treasured, prized, favorite, dear, dearest, beloved, darling, adored, loved, special.

**3** *his precious manners* AFFECTED, overrefined, pretentious; *informal* la-di-da.

**precipice** noun *it's amazing how these goats can scale such a precipice* CLIFF FACE, cliff, steep cliff, rock face, sheer drop, height, crag, bluff, escarpment, scarp; *literary* steep.

**precipitate** verb **1** *the incident precipitated a crisis* BRING ABOUT/ON, cause, lead to, give rise to, instigate, trigger, spark, touch off, provoke, hasten, accelerate, expedite.

**2** *they were precipitated down the mountain* HURL, catapult, throw, plunge, launch, fling, propel.

▸ adjective **1** *their actions were precipitate* HASTY, overhasty, rash, hurried, rushed; impetuous, impulsive, spur-of-the-moment, precipitous, incautious, imprudent, injudicious, ill-advised, reckless, harum-scarum; *informal* previous; *literary* temerarious.

**2** *a precipitate decline.* See PRECIPITOUS sense 2.

**precipitous** adjective **1** *a precipitous drop* STEEP, sheer, perpendicular, abrupt, sharp, vertical.

**2** *his fall from power was precipitous* SUDDEN, rapid, swift, abrupt, headlong, speedy, quick, fast, precipitate.

**3** *she was too precipitous.* See PRECIPITATE adjective sense 1.

**precise** adjective **1** *precise measurements* EXACT, accurate, correct, specific, detailed, explicit, unambiguous, definite. ANTONYM inaccurate.

**2** *at that precise moment the car stopped* EXACT, particular, very, specific.

**3** *the attention to detail is very precise* METICULOUS, careful, exact, scrupulous, punctilious, conscientious, particular, methodical, strict, rigorous. ANTONYM careless.

**precisely** adverb **1** *at 2 o'clock precisely* EXACTLY, sharp, promptly, prompt, dead on, on the stroke of; *informal* on the button, on the dot, on the nose.

**2** *precisely the kind of man I am looking for* EXACTLY, absolutely, just, in all respects; *informal* to a T.

**3** *fertilization can be timed precisely* ACCURATELY, exactly; clearly, distinctly, strictly.

**4** *"So it's all done?" "Precisely."* YES, exactly, absolutely, (that's) right, quite so, indubitably, definitely; *informal* you bet, I'll say.

**precision** noun *tools crafted with precision* EXACTNESS, exactitude, accuracy, correctness, preciseness; care, carefulness, meticulousness, scrupulousness, punctiliousness, methodicalness, rigor, rigorousness.

**preclude** verb *his difficulties preclude him from leading a normal life* PREVENT, make it impossible for, rule out, stop, prohibit, debar, bar, hinder, impede, inhibit, exclude. See note at PROHIBIT.

**precocious** adjective *some of the boys were extremely preco-*

*cious* ADVANCED FOR ONE'S AGE, forward, mature, gifted, talented, clever, intelligent, quick; *informal* smart. ANTONYM backward.

**preconception** noun *it will be difficult to find jurors who have no preconceptions about this case* PRECONCEIVED IDEA/NOTION, presupposition, assumption, presumption, prejudgment; prejudice.

**precondition** noun *one of the preconditions is a spotless driving record* PREREQUISITE, (necessary/essential) condition, requirement, necessity, essential, imperative, sine qua non; *informal* must.

**precursor** noun **1** *a three-stringed precursor of the guitar* FORERUNNER, predecessor, forefather, father, antecedent, ancestor, forebear.

**2** *a precursor of disasters to come* HARBINGER, herald, sign, indication, portent, omen.

**predatory** adjective **1** *predatory birds* PREDACIOUS, carnivorous, hunting, raptorial; of prey.

**2** *a predatory gleam in his eyes* EXPLOITATIVE, wolfish, rapacious, vulturine, vulturous.

**predecessor** noun **1** *the senator's predecessor* FORERUNNER, precursor, antecedent. ANTONYM successor.

**2** *our Victorian predecessors* ANCESTOR, forefather, forebear, antecedent. ANTONYM descendant.

**predetermined** adjective **1** *a predetermined budget* PREARRANGED, established in advance, preset, set, fixed, agreed.

**2** *our predetermined fate* PREDESTINED, preordained.

**predicament** noun *how did you ever get yourself into such a predicament* DIFFICULT SITUATION, mess, difficulty, plight, quandary, muddle, mare's nest; *informal* hole, fix, jam, pickle, scrape, bind, tight spot/corner, dilemma, can of worms.

**predict** verb *no one can predict the outcome* FORECAST, foretell, foresee, prophesy, anticipate, tell in advance, envision, envisage; *literary* previse; *archaic* augur, presage.

THE RIGHT WORD **predict, augur, divine, forecast, foreshadow, foretell, prognosticate, prophesy**

While all of these words refer to telling something before it happens, **predict** is the most commonly used and applies to the widest variety of situations. It can mean anything from hazarding a guess (*they predicted he'd never survive the year*) to making an astute inference based on facts or statistical evidence (*predict that the Republicans would win the election*). When a meteorologist tells us whether it will rain or snow tomorrow, he or she is said to **forecast** the weather, a word that means *predict* but is used particularly in the context of weather and other phenomena that cannot be predicted easily by the general public (*statistics forecast an influx of women into the labor force*). **Divine** and **foreshadow** mean to suggest the future rather than to predict it, especially by giving or evaluating subtle hints or clues. To *divine* something is to perceive it through intuition or insight (*to divine in the current economic situation the disaster that lay ahead*), while *foreshadow* can apply to anyone or anything that gives an indication of what is to come (*her abrupt departure that night foreshadowed the breakdown in their relationship*). **Foretell**, like *foreshadow*, can refer to the clue rather than the person who gives it and is often used in reference to the past (*evidence that foretold the young girl's violent end*). **Augur** means to foreshadow a favorable or unfavorable outcome for something (*the turnout on opening night augured well for the play's success*). **Prophesy** connotes either inspired or mystical knowledge of the future and suggests more authoritative wisdom than *augur* (*a baseball fan for decades, he prophesied the young batter's rise to stardom*). Although anyone who has inside information or knowledge of signs and symptoms can **prognosticate**, it is usually a doctor who does so by looking at the symptoms of a disease to predict its future outcome.

---

**predictable** adjective *Guido's reaction was predictable* FORESEEABLE, (only) to be expected, anticipated, foreseen, unsurprising; *informal* inevitable.

**prediction** noun *seven months later, his prediction came true* FORECAST, prophecy, prognosis, prognostication, augury; projection, conjecture, guess.

**predilection** noun LIKING, fondness, preference, partiality, taste, penchant, weakness, soft spot, fancy, inclination, leaning, bias, propensity, bent, proclivity, predisposition, appetite. ANTONYM dislike.

**predispose** verb **1** *lack of exercise may predispose an individual to high blood pressure* MAKE SUSCEPTIBLE, make liable, make prone, make vulnerable, put at risk of.

**2** *attitudes which predispose people to behave badly* LEAD, influence, sway, induce, prompt, dispose; bias, prejudice.

**predisposed** adjective INCLINED, prepared, ready, of a mind, disposed, minded, willing.

**predisposition** noun **1** *a predisposition to heart disease* SUSCEPTIBILITY, proneness, tendency, liability, inclination, disposition, vulnerability.

**2** *their political predispositions* PREFERENCE, predilection, inclination, leaning.

**predominance** noun **1** *the predominance of women caregivers* PREVALENCE, dominance, preponderance.

**2** *the superpower's military predominance* SUPREMACY, mastery, control, power, ascendancy, dominance, preeminence, superiority.

**predominant** adjective **1** *our predominant objectives* MAIN, chief, principal, most important, primary, prime, central, leading, foremost, key, paramount; *informal* number-one.

**2** *the predominant political forces* CONTROLLING, dominant, predominating, more/most powerful, preeminent, ascendant, superior, in the ascendancy. ANTONYM subsidiary.

**predominate** verb **1** *small-scale producers predominate* BE IN THE MAJORITY, preponderate, be predominant, prevail, be most prominent.

**2** *private interest predominates over the public good* PREVAIL, dominate, be dominant, carry most weight; override, outweigh.

**preeminence** noun SUPERIORITY, supremacy, greatness,

excellence, distinction, prominence, predominance, eminence, importance, prestige, stature, fame, renown, celebrity.

**preeminent** adjective GREATEST, leading, foremost, best, finest, chief, outstanding, excellent, distinguished, prominent, eminent, important, top, famous, renowned, celebrated, illustrious, supreme, marquee. ANTONYM undistinguished.

**preempt** verb **1** *his action may have preempted war* FORESTALL, prevent.

**2** *many tables were already preempted by family parties* COMMANDEER, occupy, seize, arrogate, appropriate, take over, secure, reserve.

**preen** verb **1** *the robin preened its feathers* CLEAN, tidy, groom, smooth, arrange; *archaic* plume.

**2** *she preened before the mirror* ADMIRE ONESELF, primp oneself, groom oneself, spruce oneself up; *informal* titivate oneself, doll oneself up, gussy oneself up.

**preface** noun *the preface to the novel* INTRODUCTION, foreword, preamble, prologue, prelude; front matter; *informal* prelims, intro, lead-in; *formal* exordium, proem, prolegomenon.

▸ verb *the chapter is prefaced by a poem* PRECEDE, introduce, begin, open, start.

**prefatory** adjective *prefatory text* INTRODUCTORY, preliminary, opening, initial, preparatory, initiatory, precursory. ANTONYM closing.

**prefer** verb **1** *I prefer white wine to red* LIKE BETTER, would rather (have), would sooner (have), favor, be more partial to; choose, select, pick, opt for, go for.

**2** *formal do you want to prefer charges?* BRING, press, file, lodge, lay.

**3** *archaic he was preferred to the post* PROMOTE, upgrade, raise, elevate.

**preferable** adjective *Dom sleeps on a foam pillow, but for me goose down is preferable* BETTER, best, more desirable, more suitable, advantageous, superior, preferred, recommended.

**preferably** adverb *we'd like a table by the window, preferably nonsmoking* IDEALLY, if possible, for preference, from choice.

**preference** noun **1** *her preference for boys' games* LIKING, partiality, predilection, proclivity, fondness, taste, inclination, leaning, bias, bent, penchant, predisposition.

**2** *my preference is rock music* FAVORITE, (first) choice, selection; *informal* cup of tea, thing, druthers.

**3** *preference will be given to applicants speaking Japanese* PRIORITY, favor, precedence, preferential treatment. PHRASE: **in preference to** *the thief chose their home in preference to others* RATHER THAN, instead of, in place of, sooner than.

**preferential** adjective *we were not expecting this preferential treatment* SPECIAL, better, privileged, superior, favorable; partial, discriminatory, partisan, biased.

**pregnancy** noun *how far along is she in the pregnancy?* gestation; *rare* parturiency, gravidity.

**pregnant** adjective **1** *she is pregnant* EXPECTING A BABY, expectant, carrying a child; *informal* expecting, in the family way, with a bun in the oven, knocked up; *chiefly Brit. informal* preggers; *informal, dated* in trouble; *archaic* with child; *technical* parturient, gravid.

**2** *a ceremony pregnant with religious significance* FILLED, charged, heavy; full of.

**3** *a pregnant pause* MEANINGFUL, significant, suggestive, expressive, charged.

**prehistoric** adjective **1** *prehistoric times* PRIMITIVE, primeval, primordial, primal, ancient, early, antediluvian.

**2** *the special effects look prehistoric* OUT OF DATE, outdated, outmoded, old-fashioned, passé, antiquated, archaic, behind the times, primitive, antediluvian; *informal* horse-and-buggy, clunky. ANTONYM modern.

**prejudice** noun **1** *male prejudices about women* PRECONCEIVED IDEA, preconception, prejudgment.

**2** *they are motivated by prejudice* BIGOTRY, bias, partisanship, partiality, intolerance, discrimination, unfairness, inequality. See note at BIAS.

**3** *without prejudice to the interests of others* DETRIMENT, harm, damage, injury, hurt, loss.

▸ verb **1** *the article could prejudice the jury* BIAS, influence, sway, predispose, make biased, make partial, color.

**2** *this could prejudice his chances of victory* DAMAGE, be detrimental to, be prejudicial to, injure, harm, hurt, spoil, impair, undermine, hinder, compromise.

**prejudiced** adjective *his prejudiced views* BIASED, bigoted, discriminatory, partisan, intolerant, narrow-minded, unfair, unjust, inequitable, colored. ANTONYM impartial.

**prejudicial** adjective *disclosure of the information would be prejudicial* DETRIMENTAL, damaging, injurious, harmful, disadvantageous, hurtful, deleterious. ANTONYM beneficial.

**preliminary** adjective *the discussions are still at a preliminary stage* PREPARATORY, introductory, initial, opening, prefatory, precursory; early, exploratory. ANTONYM final.

▸ noun **1** **(preliminaries)** *he began without any preliminaries* INTRODUCTION, preamble, opening/prefatory remarks, formalities.

**2** *a preliminary to the resumption of war* PRELUDE, preparation, preparatory measure, preliminary action.

PHRASE: **preliminary to** *the geese gather in estuaries, preliminary to their flight southward* IN PREPARATION FOR, before, in advance of, prior to, preparatory to.

**prelude** noun **1** *the cease-fire was a prelude to peace negotiations* PRELIMINARY, overture, opening, preparation, introduction, start, commencement, beginning, lead-in, precursor.

**2** *an orchestral prelude* OVERTURE, introductory movement, introduction, opening.

**3** *the passage forms a prelude to Part III* INTRODUCTION, preface, prologue, foreword, preamble; *informal* intro, lead-in; *formal* exordium, proem, prolegomenon.

**premature** adjective **1** *his premature death* UNTIMELY, (too) early, unseasonable, before time. ANTONYM overdue.

**2** *a premature baby* PRETERM. ANTONYM overdue.

**3** *such a step would be premature* RASH, ill-considered, overhasty, hasty, precipitate, precipitous, impulsive, impetuous, inopportune; *informal* previous.

**premeditated** adjective *the premeditated murder of Lady Boswell* PLANNED, intentional, deliberate, preplanned, calculated, cold-blooded, conscious, prearranged. ANTONYM spontaneous.

**premier** adjective *a premier chef* LEADING, foremost, chief, principal, head, top-ranking, top, prime, primary, first, highest, preeminent, nonpareil, senior, outstanding, master, ranking; *informal* top-notch, blue-ribbon, blue-chip.

▸ noun *the Nova Scotian premier* LEADER, head of government, government leader; president, chancellor, prime minister, PM.

**premiere** noun *tickets for a Broadway premiere* FIRST PERFORMANCE, first night, opening night.

**premise** noun *the premise that human life consists of a series of choices* PROPOSITION, assumption, hypothesis, thesis, presupposition, postulation, postulate, supposition, presumption, surmise, conjecture, speculation, assertion, belief.

▸ verb *they premised that the cosmos is indestructible* POSTULATE, hypothesize, conjecture, posit, theorize, suppose, presuppose, surmise, assume.

**premises** plural noun *he was asked to leave the premises* BUILDING(S), property, site, office.

**premium** noun **1** *monthly premiums of $30* (REGULAR) PAYMENT, installment.

**2** *you must pay a premium for organic fruit* SURCHARGE, additional payment, extra amount.

**3** *a foreign service premium* BONUS, extra; incentive, inducement; *informal* perk; *formal* perquisite. PHRASES: **at a premium** *back then, sugar was at a premium* SCARCE, in great demand, hard to come by, in short supply, thin on the ground.

**put/place a premium on 1** *I place a high premium on our relationship* VALUE GREATLY, attach great/special importance to, set great store by, put a high value on.

**2** *the high price of oil put a premium on the coal industry* MAKE VALUABLE, make invaluable, make important.

**premonition** noun *we've learned to take her premonitions seriously* FOREBODING, presentiment, intuition, (funny) feeling, hunch, suspicion, feeling in one's bones; misgiving, apprehension, fear; *archaic* presage. See note at OMINOUS.

**preoccupation** noun **1** *an air of preoccupation* PENSIVENESS, concentration, engrossment, absorption, self-absorption, musing, thinking, deep thought, brown study, brooding; abstraction, absentmindedness, distraction, forgetfulness, inattentiveness, woolgathering, daydreaming.

**2** *their main preoccupation was feeding their family* OBSESSION, concern; passion, enthusiasm, hobbyhorse.

**preoccupied** adjective **1** *officials preoccupied with their careers* OBSESSED, concerned, absorbed, engrossed, intent, involved, wrapped up.

**2** *she looked preoccupied* LOST/DEEP IN THOUGHT, in a brown study, pensive, absentminded, distracted, abstracted.

**preoccupy** verb *the issues that preoccupy environmentalists* ENGROSS, concern, absorb, take up someone's attention, distract, obsess, occupy, prey on someone's mind.

**preparation** noun **1** *the preparation of contingency plans* DEVISING, putting together, drawing up, construction, composition, production, getting ready, development.

**2** **(preparations)** *preparations for the party* ARRANGEMENTS, planning, plans, preparatory measures.

**3** *preparation for exams* INSTRUCTION, teaching, coaching, training, tutoring, drilling, priming.

**4** *a preparation to kill off mites* MIXTURE, compound, concoction, solution, tincture, medicine, potion, cream, ointment, lotion.

**preparatory** adjective *preparatory work* PRELIMINARY, initial, introductory, prefatory, opening, preparative, precursory. PHRASE: **preparatory to** *we locked all the doors and windows preparatory to leaving* IN PREPARATION FOR, before, prior to, preliminary to.

**prepare** verb **1** *I want you to prepare a report* MAKE/GET READY, put together, draw up, produce, arrange, assemble, construct, compose, formulate.

**2** *the meal was easy to prepare* COOK, make, get, put together, concoct; *informal* fix, rustle up.

**3** *preparing for war* GET READY, make preparations, arrange things, make provision, get everything set.

**4** *athletes preparing for the Olympics* TRAIN, get into shape, practice, get ready.

**5** *I must prepare for my exams* STUDY, review.

**6** *this course prepares students for their exams* INSTRUCT, coach, train, tutor, drill, prime.

**7** *prepare yourself for a shock* BRACE, make ready, tense, steel, steady.

**prepared** adjective **1** *he needs to be prepared for the worst* READY, (all) set, equipped, primed; waiting, on hand, poised, in position.

**2** *I'm not prepared to cut the price* WILLING, ready, disposed, predisposed, (favorably) inclined, of a mind, minded.

**preponderance** noun **1** *the preponderance of women among older people* PREVALENCE, predominance, dominance.

**2** *the preponderance of the evidence* BULK, majority, larger part, best/better part.

**3** *the preponderance of the unions* PREDOMINANCE, dominance, ascendancy, supremacy, power.

**prepossessing** adjective *his prepossessing wife turned heads wherever they went* ATTRACTIVE, beautiful, pretty, handsome, good-looking, fetching, charming, delightful, enchanting, captivating; *archaic* fair. ANTONYM ugly.

**preposterous** adjective *at these sessions, no ideas are too preposterous to throw on the table* ABSURD, ridiculous, foolish, stupid, ludicrous, farcical, laughable, comical, risible, nonsensical, senseless, insane; outrageous, monstrous; *informal* crazy. See note at ABSURD. ANTONYM sensible.

**prerequisite** noun *a prerequisite for the course* (NECESSARY) CONDITION, precondition, essential, requirement, requisite, necessity, sine qua non; *informal* must.

▸ adjective *the prerequisite qualifications* NECESSARY, required, called for, essential, requisite, obligatory, compulsory. ANTONYM unnecessary.

**prerogative** noun *it's my prerogative to hold on to the farm* ENTITLEMENT, right, privilege, advantage, due, birthright.

**presage** verb *the owl's hooting presages death* PORTEND, augur, foreshadow, foretell, prophesy, be an omen of, herald, be a sign of, be the harbinger of, warn of, be a presage of, signal, bode, promise, threaten; *literary* betoken, foretoken, forebode.

▸ noun *a somber presage of his final illness* OMEN, sign, indication, portent, warning, forewarning, harbinger, augury, prophecy, foretoken.

**prescribe** verb **1** *the doctor prescribed antibiotics* WRITE A PRESCRIPTION FOR, authorize.

**2** *traditional values prescribe a life of domesticity* ADVISE, recommend, advocate, suggest, endorse, champion, promote.

**3** *rules prescribing your duty* STIPULATE, lay down, dictate, specify, determine, establish, fix.

**prescription** noun **1** *the doctor wrote a prescription* INSTRUCTION, authorization; *informal* scrip; *archaic* recipe.

**2** *he fetched the prescription from the drug store* MEDICINE, drugs, medication.

**3** *a painless prescription for improvement* METHOD, measure; recommendation, suggestion, recipe, formula.

**presence** noun **1** *the presence of a train was indicated electrically* EXISTENCE, being there. ANTONYM absence.

**2** *I requested the presence of a nurse* ATTENDANCE, appearance; company, companionship. ANTONYM absence.

**3** *a woman of great presence* AURA, charisma, (strength/force of) personality; poise, self-assurance, self-confidence.

**4** *she felt a presence in the castle* GHOST, spirit, specter, phantom, apparition, supernatural being; *informal* spook; *literary* shade. PHRASE: **presence of mind** *I didn't have the presence of mind to read his license plate* COMPOSURE, equanimity, self-possession, levelheadedness, self-assurance, calmness, sangfroid, imperturbability; alertness, quick-wittedness; *informal* cool, unflappability.

**present**[1] adjective **1** *a doctor must be present at the ringside* IN ATTENDANCE, here, there, near, nearby, (close/near) at hand, available. ANTONYM absent.

**2** *organic compounds are present in the waste* IN EXISTENCE, existing, existent. See note at ABSENT. ANTONYM absent.

**3** *the present economic climate* CURRENT, present-day, existing. ANTONYMS past, future.

▸ noun *forget the past and think about the present* NOW, today, the present time/moment, the here and now. ANTONYMS past, future.

PHRASES: **at present** *at present, we are offering free installation* AT THE MOMENT, just now, right now, at the present time, currently, at this moment in time.

**for the present** *he can stay in the guest room, but only for the present* FOR THE TIME BEING, for now, for the moment, for a while, temporarily, pro tem.

**present**[2] verb **1** *the president presented a check to the winner* HAND OVER/OUT, give (out), confer, bestow, award, grant, accord.

**2** *the committee presented its report* SUBMIT, set forth, put forward, proffer, offer, tender, table.

**3** *may I present my wife?* INTRODUCE, make known, acquaint someone with.

**4** *I called to present my warmest compliments* OFFER, give, express.

**5** *they presented their new product last month* DEMONSTRATE, show, put on show/display, exhibit, display, launch, unveil.

**6** *presenting good quality opera* STAGE, put on, produce, perform.

**7** *she presents a TV show* HOST, introduce, be the presenter of, emcee.

**8** *the authorities present him as a common criminal* REPRESENT, describe, portray, depict. PHRASE: **present oneself/itself** **1** *he presented himself at ten* BE PRESENT, make an appearance, appear, turn up, arrive.

**2** *an opportunity that presented itself* OCCUR, arise, happen, come about/up, appear, crop up, turn up.

**present**[3] noun *a birthday present* GIFT, donation, offering, contribution; *informal* freebie; *formal* benefaction.

**THE RIGHT WORD present, bonus, donation, gift, gratuity, lagniappe, largesse**

What's the difference between a birthday **present** and a Christmas **gift**? Both words refer to something given as an expression of friendship, affection, esteem, etc. But *gift* is a more formal term, suggesting something of monetary value that is formally bestowed on an individual, group, or institution (*a gift to the university*). *Present*, on the other hand, implies something of less value that is an expression of goodwill (*a housewarming present; a present for the teacher*). **Largesse** is a somewhat pompous term for a very generous gift that is conferred in an ostentatious or condescending way, often on many recipients (*the king's largesse; the largesse of our government*). A **gratuity** is associated with tipping and other forms of voluntary compensation for special attention or service above and beyond what is included in a charge (*known for her generous gratuities, the duchess enjoyed watching the waiters compete with each other to serve her*), while a **lagniappe** is a Southern word, used chiefly in Louisiana and southeast Texas, for either a gratuity or a small gift given to a customer along with a purchase. If you give money or anything else as a gift to a philanthropic, charitable, or religious organization, it is known as a

**donation** (*donations for the poor*). But if your employer gives you money at the end of the year in addition to your regular salary, it isn't a Christmas gift; it's a Christmas **bonus**.

---

**presentable** adjective **1** *I'm making the place look presentable* TIDY, neat, straight, clean, spick-and-span, in good order, shipshape.

**2** *make yourself presentable* NICELY DRESSED, tidily dressed, smartly dressed, tidy, well-groomed, trim, spruce; *informal* natty.

**3** *presentable videos* FAIRLY GOOD, passable, all right, satisfactory, moderately good, not (too) bad, average, fair; *informal* OK.

**presentation** noun **1** *the presentation of his certificate* AWARDING, presenting, giving, handing over/out, bestowal, granting, award.

**2** *the presentation of food* APPEARANCE, arrangement, packaging, disposition, display, layout.

**3** *the presentation of new proposals* SUBMISSION, proffering, offering, tendering, advancing, proposal, suggestion, mooting, tabling.

**4** *a sales presentation* DEMONSTRATION, talk, lecture, address, speech, show, exhibition, display, introduction, launch, launching, unveiling.

**5** *a presentation of his latest play* STAGING, production, performance, mounting, showing.

**presentiment** noun *a presentiment of disaster* PREMONITION, foreboding, intuition, (funny) feeling, hunch, feeling in one's bones, sixth sense; *archaic* presage.

**presently** adverb **1** *I shall see you presently* SOON, shortly, directly, quite soon, in a short time, in a little while, at any moment/minute/second, in next to no time, before long, momentarily; *informal* pretty soon, any moment now, in a jiffy, in two shakes of a lamb's tail; *literary* ere long.

**2** *he is presently abroad* CURRENTLY, at present, at the/this moment, at the present moment/time, now, nowadays, these days.

**preservation** noun **1** *wood preservation* CONSERVATION, protection, care.

**2** *the preservation of the status quo* CONTINUATION, conservation, maintenance, upholding, sustaining, perpetuation.

**3** *the preservation of food* CONSERVING, bottling, canning, freezing, drying; curing, smoking, pickling.

**preserve** verb **1** *oil helps preserve wood* CONSERVE, protect, maintain, care for, look after.

**2** *they wish to preserve the status quo* CONTINUE (WITH), conserve, keep going, maintain, uphold, sustain, perpetuate.

**3** *preserving him from harassment* GUARD, protect, keep, defend, safeguard, shelter, shield.

**4** *spices enable us to preserve food* CONSERVE, bottle, can, freeze, dry, freeze-dry; cure, smoke, pickle.

▸ noun **1** **(preserves)** *strawberry preserves* JAM, jelly, marmalade, conserve, fruit spread.

**2** *the preserve of an educated middle-class* DOMAIN, area, field, sphere, orbit, realm, province, territory; *informal* turf, bailiwick.

**3** *a game preserve* SANCTUARY, (game) reserve, reservation, protected area.

**preside** verb *Dorothy **presides at** the meeting* CHAIR, be chairman/chairwoman/chairperson of/at, officiate (at), conduct, lead. PHRASE: **preside over** *the chief financial officer should preside over these budget talks* BE IN CHARGE OF, be responsible for, be at the head/helm of, head, be head of, manage, administer, be in control of, control, direct, lead, govern, rule, command, supervise, oversee; *informal* head up, be boss of, be in the driver's seat of/at, be in the saddle of/at.

**president** noun **1** *terrorists assassinated the president* HEAD OF STATE, chief executive, premier, prime minister.

**2** *the president of the society* HEAD, chief, director, leader, governor, principal, master; *informal* prez.

**3** *the president of the company* CHAIRMAN, chairwoman, chief executive (officer), CEO; owner, managing director.

**press** verb **1** *press the paper down firmly* PUSH (DOWN), press down, depress, hold down, force, thrust, squeeze, compress.

**2** *his shirt was pressed* SMOOTH (OUT), iron, remove creases from.

**3** *we pressed the grapes* CRUSH, squeeze, squash, mash, pulp, pound, pulverize, macerate.

**4** *she pressed the child to her bosom* CLASP, hold close, hug, cuddle, squeeze, clutch, grasp, embrace.

**5** *Hillary pressed his hand* SQUEEZE, grip, clutch.

**6** *the crowd pressed around* CLUSTER, gather, converge, congregate, flock, swarm, throng, crowd.

**7** *the government pressed its claim* PLEAD, urge, advance insistently, present, submit, put forward.

**8** *they pressed him to agree* URGE, put pressure on, force, push, coerce, dragoon, steamroller, browbeat; *informal* lean on, put the screws on, twist someone's arm, railroad, bulldoze.

**9** *they pressed for a ban on the ivory trade* CALL, ask, advocate, clamor, push, campaign, demand, lobby.

▸ noun **1** *a small literary press* PUBLISHING HOUSE, publisher; printing house/company; printing press.

**2** *the freedom of **the press*** THE MEDIA, the newspapers, the papers, the news media, the fourth estate; journalists, reporters, newspapermen/newspaperwomen, newsmen/newswomen, pressmen; *informal* journos, newshounds, newsies.

**3** *the company had some bad press* (PRESS) REPORTS, press coverage, press articles, (press) reviews, media attention.

PHRASES: **be pressed for** *you shouldn't schedule an interview when you are pressed for time* HAVE TOO LITTLE, be short of, have insufficient, lack, be lacking (in), be deficient in, need, be/stand in need of; *informal* be strapped for.

**press on** *the team regrouped and pressed on* PROCEED, keep going, continue, carry on, make progress, make headway, press ahead, forge on/ahead, soldier on, push on, keep on, struggle on, persevere, keep at it, stay with it, stick with it, plod on, plug away.

**pressing** adjective **1** *a pressing problem* URGENT, critical, crucial, acute, desperate, serious, grave, life-and-death.

**2** *a pressing engagement* IMPORTANT, high-priority, critical, crucial, compelling, inescapable. See note at CRUCIAL.

**pressure** noun **1** *confined gas exerts a constant pressure* PHYSICAL FORCE, load, stress, thrust; compression, weight.

**2** *they put pressure on us to borrow money* COERCION, force, compulsion, constraint, duress; pestering, harassment, nagging, badgering, intimidation, arm-twisting, persuasion.

**3** *she had a lot of pressure from work* STRAIN, stress, tension, trouble, difficulty; *informal* hassle.

▸ verb *they pressured him into resigning* COERCE, pressure, put pressure on, press, push, persuade, force, bulldoze, hound, harass, nag, harry, badger, goad, pester, browbeat, bully, bludgeon, intimidate, dragoon, twist someone's arm, strong-arm; *informal* railroad, lean on, hustle.

**prestige** noun *she missed the prestige of the job, but not the ungodly hours of work* STATUS, standing, stature, reputation, repute, regard, fame, note, renown, honor, esteem, celebrity, importance, prominence, influence, eminence; kudos, cachet; *informal* clout.

**prestigious** adjective **1** *prestigious journals* REPUTABLE, distinguished, respected, esteemed, eminent, august, highly regarded, well-thought-of, acclaimed, authoritative, celebrated, illustrious, leading, renowned. ANTONYM obscure.

**2** *a prestigious job* IMPRESSIVE, important, prominent, high-ranking, influential, affluential, powerful, glamorous; well paid, expensive, upmarket. ANTONYM minor.

**presumably** adverb *presumably, they'll want an ocean view* I PRESUME, I expect, I assume, I take it, I suppose, I imagine, I dare say, I guess, in all probability, probably, in all likelihood, as likely as not, doubtless, undoubtedly, no doubt.

**presume** verb **1** *I presumed that it had once been an attic* ASSUME, suppose, dare say, imagine, take it, expect, believe, think, surmise, guess, judge, conjecture, speculate, postulate, presuppose.

**2** *let me presume to give you some advice* VENTURE, dare, have the audacity/effrontery, be so bold as. PHRASE: **presume on** *he was careful not to presume on their friendship* TAKE (UNFAIR) ADVANTAGE OF, exploit, take liberties with; count on, bank on, place reliance on.

**presumption** noun **1** *this presumption may be easily rebutted* ASSUMPTION, supposition, presupposition, belief, guess, judgment, surmise, conjecture, speculation, hypothesis, postulation, inference, deduction, conclusion.

**2** *he apologized for his presumption* BRAZENNESS, audacity, boldness, audaciousness, temerity, arrogance, presumptuousness, forwardness; cockiness, insolence, impudence, bumptiousness, impertinence, effrontery, cheek, cheekiness; rudeness, impoliteness, disrespect, familiarity; *informal* nerve, chutzpah, sass, sassiness; *archaic* assumption.

**presumptive** adjective **1** *a presumptive diagnosis* CONJECTURAL, speculative, tentative; theoretical, unproven, unconfirmed.

**2** *the heir presumptive* PROBABLE, likely, prospective, assumed, supposed, expected.

**presumptuous** adjective *that was quite a presumptuous remark* BRAZEN, overconfident, arrogant, bold, audacious, forward, familiar, impertinent, insolent, impudent, cocky; cheeky, rude, impolite, uncivil, bumptious; *informal* sassy. See note at BOLD.

**presuppose** verb **1** *this presupposes the existence of a policy-making group* REQUIRE, necessitate, imply, entail, mean, involve, assume.

**2** *I had presupposed that theme parks make people happy* PRESUME, assume, take it for granted, take it as read, suppose, surmise, think, accept, consider.

**presupposition** noun *the presupposition that all enzymes are proteins* PRESUMPTION, assumption, preconception, supposition, hypothesis, surmise, thesis, theory, premise, belief, postulation.

**pretend** verb **1** *they just pretend to listen* MAKE AS IF, profess, affect; dissimulate, dissemble, put it on, put on a false front, go through the motions, sham, fake it.

**2** *I'll* ***pretend to be*** *the dragon* PUT ON AN ACT AS, make believe one is, play at being, act (the part of), play-act (the part of), impersonate.

**3** *it was useless to pretend innocence* FEIGN, sham, fake, simulate, put on, counterfeit, affect.

**4** *he cannot* ***pretend to*** *sophistication* CLAIM, lay claim to, purport to have, profess to have.

▸ adjective *informal a pretend conversation* IMAGINARY, imagined, pretended, make-believe, made-up, fantasy, fantasized, dreamed-up, unreal, invented, fictitious, mythical, feigned, fake, mock, sham, simulated, artificial, ersatz, false, pseudo; *informal* phony.

**pretended** adjective *pretended tears* FAKE, faked, affected, assumed, professed, spurious, mock, imitation, simulated, make-believe, pseudo, sham, false, bogus; *informal* pretend, phony.

**pretender** noun *a pretender to the throne* CLAIMANT, aspirant.

**pretense** noun **1** *cease this pretense* MAKE-BELIEVE, putting on an act, acting, dissembling, shamming, faking, feigning, simulation, dissimulation, play-acting, posturing; deception, deceit, deceitfulness, fraud, fraudulence, duplicity, subterfuge, trickery, dishonesty, hypocrisy, falsity, lying, mendacity. ANTONYM honesty.

**2** *he made a pretense of being unconcerned* (FALSE) SHOW, semblance, affectation, (false) appearance, outward appearance, impression, (false) front, guise, facade, display.

3 *she had dropped any pretense to faith* CLAIM, profession.

4 *he was absolutely without pretense* PRETENTIOUSNESS, display, ostentation, affectation, showiness, posturing, humbug.

**pretension** noun 1 *the author has no pretension to exhaustive coverage* ASPIRATION, claim, assertion, pretense, profession.

2 *she spoke without pretension* PRETENTIOUSNESS, affectation, ostentation, artificiality, airs, posing, posturing, show, flashiness; pomposity, pompousness, grandiosity, grandiloquence, magniloquence.

**pretentious** adjective *Clytemnestra is a pretentious name for a dog* AFFECTED, ostentatious, showy; overambitious, pompous, artificial, inflated, overblown, high-sounding, flowery, grandiose, elaborate, extravagant, flamboyant, ornate, grandiloquent, magniloquent, sophomoric; *informal* flashy, highfalutin, la-di-da, pseudo.

**preternatural** adjective *autumn had arrived with preternatural speed* EXTRAORDINARY, exceptional, unusual, uncommon, singular, unprecedented, remarkable, phenomenal, abnormal, inexplicable, unaccountable; strange, mysterious, fantastic.

**pretext** noun *he used the pretext of looking for his dog to come into our yard* EXCUSE, false excuse, ostensible reason, alleged reason; guise, ploy, pretense, ruse.

**pretty** adjective *a pretty child* ATTRACTIVE, lovely, good-looking, nice-looking, personable, fetching, prepossessing, appealing, charming, delightful, cute, as pretty as a picture; *Scottish* bonny; *informal* easy on the eye; *literary* beauteous; *archaic* fair, comely. ANTONYMS plain, ugly.

▸ adverb *a pretty large sum* QUITE, rather, somewhat, fairly, reasonably, comparatively, relatively.

▸ verb *she's **prettying** herself **up*** BEAUTIFY, make attractive, make pretty, prettify, adorn, ornament, smarten; *informal* do oneself up, titivate.

**prevail** verb 1 *common sense will prevail* WIN, win out/through, triumph, be victorious, carry the day, come out on top, succeed, prove superior, conquer, overcome; rule, reign.

2 *the conditions that prevailed in the 1950s* EXIST, be in existence, be present, be the case, occur, be prevalent, be current, be the order of the day, be customary, be common, be widespread, be in force/effect; *formal* obtain. PHRASE: **prevail on/upon** *they prevailed upon me to emcee their charity affair* PERSUADE, induce, coax, convince, get, urge, pressure, coerce; *informal* sweet-talk, soft-soap.

**prevailing** adjective *prevailing attitudes* CURRENT, existing, prevalent, usual, common, general, widespread. See note at PREVALENT.

**prevalence** noun *the prevalence of smoking among teenagers* COMMONNESS, currency, widespread presence, generality, popularity, pervasiveness, universality, extensiveness; rampancy, rifeness.

**prevalent** adjective *opposition to the war is prevalent* WIDESPREAD, prevailing, frequent, usual, common, current, popular, general, universal; endemic, rampant, rife. ANTONYM rare.

THE RIGHT WORD **prevalent, prevailing, abundant, plentiful, rife, copious, common**

Wildflowers might be **prevalent** in the mountains during the spring months, but a particular type of wildflower might be the **prevailing** one. *Prevalent*, in other words, implies widespread occurrence or acceptance in a particular place or time (*a prevalent belief during the nineteenth century*), while *prevailing* suggests that something exists in such quantity that it surpasses or leads all others in acceptance, usage, or belief (*the prevailing theory about the evolution of man*). Wildflowers might also be **abundant** in the valleys—a word that, unlike *prevalent* and *prevailing*, is largely restricted to observations about a place and may suggest oversupply (*an abundant harvest* ¦ *indications of decay were abundant*). **Plentiful**, on the other hand, refers to a large or full supply without the connotations of oversupply (*a country where jobs were plentiful*). If wildflowers are **rife**, it means that they are not only *prevalent* but spreading rapidly (*speculation was rife among the soldiers*); if they're **copious**, it means they are being produced in such quantity that they constitute a rich or flowing abundance (*weep copious tears*). What often happens, with wildflowers as well as with other beautiful things, is that they become so abundant they are regarded as **common**, a word meaning usual or ordinary (*the common cold*). Like *prevalent*, *common* can apply to a time as well as a place (*an expression common during the Depression*). But neither *abundant* nor *common* connotes dominance as clearly as *prevalent* does.

**prevaricate** verb *you have prevaricated so often through this testimony that the truth has become unrecognizable* BE EVASIVE, beat around the bush, hedge, fence, shilly-shally, dodge (the issue), sidestep (the issue), equivocate, waffle; temporize, stall (for time); hem and haw; *rare* tergiversate. See note at LIE[1].

**prevent** verb *how can any one agency prevent drug trafficking?* STOP, put a stop to, avert, nip in the bud, fend off, stave off, ward off; hinder, impede, hamper, obstruct, balk, foil, thwart, forestall, counteract, inhibit, curb, restrain, preclude, preempt; disallow, prohibit, forbid, proscribe, exclude, debar, bar; *literary* stay. See note at HINDER. ANTONYM allow.

**previous** adjective *the previous commissioner retired after more than 40 years of service* FOREGOING, preceding, antecedent; old, earlier, prior, former, ex-, past, last, sometime, one-time, erstwhile; *formal* quondam, anterior. ANTONYM next.

PHRASE: **previous to** *previous to this, everything was fine* BEFORE, prior to, until, leading up to, up to, earlier than, preceding; *formal* anterior to.

**previously** adverb *previously, only the outermost doors were locked at night* FORMERLY, earlier, earlier on, before, hitherto, once, at one time, in the past, in days gone by, in times gone by, in bygone days, in times past, in former times; in advance, already, beforehand; *formal* heretofore.

**prey** noun **1** *the lions killed their prey* QUARRY, kill. ANTONYMS predator, hunter.

**2** *she was Julia's easy prey* VICTIM, target, dupe, gull; *informal* sucker, soft touch, pushover, patsy, sap, schlemiel. PHRASE: **prey on 1** *certain larvae prey on aphids* HUNT, catch; eat, feed on, live on/off.

**2** *they prey on the elderly* EXPLOIT, victimize, pick on, take advantage of; trick, swindle, cheat, hoodwink, fleece; *informal* con.

**3** *the problem preyed on his mind* OPPRESS, weigh on, weigh heavily on, lie heavy on, gnaw at; trouble, worry, beset, disturb, distress, haunt, nag, torment, plague, obsess.

**price** noun **1** *the purchase price* COST, charge, fee, fare, levy, amount, sum; outlay, expense, expenditure; valuation, quotation, estimate, asking price; *informal, humorous* damage.

**2** *spinsterhood was the price of her career* CONSEQUENCE, result, cost, penalty, sacrifice; downside, snag, drawback, disadvantage, minus.

**3** *he had a price on his head* REWARD, bounty, premium.

▸ verb *we priced each ticket is at $5.00* FIX/SET THE PRICE OF, value, rate cost; estimate.

**priceless** adjective **1** *priceless works of art* INVALUABLE, of incalculable value/worth, of immeasurable value/worth, beyond price; irreplaceable, incomparable, unparalleled. ANTONYMS worthless, cheap.

**2** *informal that's priceless!* See HILARIOUS sense 1.

**prick** verb **1** *prick the potatoes with a fork* PIERCE, puncture, make/put a hole in, stab, perforate, nick, jab.

**2** *her conscience pricked her* TROUBLE, worry, distress, perturb, disturb, cause someone anguish, afflict, torment, plague, prey on, gnaw at.

**3** *ambition pricked him on to greater effort* GOAD, prod, incite, provoke, urge, spur, stimulate, encourage, inspire, motivate, push, propel, impel.

**4** *the horse* ***pricked up*** *its ears* RAISE, erect.

▸ noun **1** *it felt like the prick of a pin* JAB, sting, pinprick, prickle, stab.

**2** *the prick of tears behind her eyelids* STING, stinging, smart, smarting, burning.

**3** *the prick of conscience* PANG, twinge, stab.

PHRASE: **prick up one's ears** *we pricked up our ears when he mentioned the Christmas bonuses* LISTEN CAREFULLY, pay attention, become attentive, begin to take notice, attend; *informal* be all ears.

**prickle** noun **1** *the cactus is covered with prickles* THORN, needle, barb, spike, point, spine.

**2** *Willie felt a cold prickle of fear* TINGLE, tingling, tingling sensation, prickling sensation, chill, thrill; *Medicine* paresthesia.

▸ verb *its tiny spikes prickled his skin* STING, prick.

**prickly** adjective **1** *a prickly hedgehog* SPIKY, spiked, thorny, barbed, spiny; briery, brambly; rough, scratchy; *technical* spiculate, spicular, aculeate, spinose.

**2** *my skin feels prickly* TINGLY, tingling, prickling.

**3** *a prickly character.* See IRRITABLE.

**4** *the prickly question of the refugees* PROBLEMATIC, awkward, ticklish, tricky, delicate, sensitive, difficult, knotty, thorny, irksome, tough, troublesome, bothersome, vexatious.

**pride** noun **1** *their triumphs were a source of pride* SELF-ESTEEM, dignity, honor, self-respect, self-worth, self-regard, pride in oneself. ANTONYM shame.

**2** *take pride in a good job well done* PLEASURE, joy, delight, gratification, fulfillment, satisfaction, a sense of achievement.

**3** *he refused her offer out of pride* ARROGANCE, vanity, self-importance, hubris, conceit, conceitedness, self-love, self-adulation, self-admiration, narcissism, egotism, superciliousness, haughtiness, snobbery, snobbishness; *informal* big-headedness; *literary* vainglory. ANTONYMS modesty, humility.

**4** *the bull is the pride of the herd* BEST, finest, top, cream, pick, choice, prize, glory, jewel in the crown. ANTONYM dregs.

**5** *the rose-covered trellis was the pride of the gardener* SOURCE OF SATISFACTION, pride and joy, treasured possession, joy, delight. PHRASE: **pride oneself on** *Lucas prides himself on his knowledge of wine* BE PROUD OF, be proud of oneself for, take pride in, take satisfaction in, congratulate oneself on, pat oneself on the back for.

THE RIGHT WORD **pride, arrogance, conceit, egotism, self-esteem, vainglory, vanity**

If you take **pride** in yourself or your accomplishments, it means that you believe in your own worth, merit, or superiority—whether or not that belief is justified (*she took pride in her accomplishments*). When your opinion of yourself is exaggerated, you're showing **conceit**, a word that combines *pride* with self-obsession. If you like to be noticed and admired for your appearance or achievements, you're revealing your **vanity**, and if you show off or boast about your accomplishments, you're likely to be accused of **vainglory**, a somewhat literary term for a self-important display of power, skill, or influence. **Arrogance** is an overbearing pride combined with disdain for others (*his arrogance led him to assume that everyone else would obey his orders*), while **egotism** implies self-centeredness or an excessive preoccupation with yourself (*blinded by egotism to the suffering of others*). While no one wants to be accused of *arrogance* or *egotism*, there's a lot to be said for **self-esteem**, which may suggest undue pride but is more often used to describe a healthy belief in oneself and respect for one's worth as a person (*she suffered from low self-esteem*).

**priest** noun *he requested to see a priest.* See CLERGY.

**prig** noun *the notion that librarians are typically prigs is ridiculous* PRUDE, puritan, killjoy; *informal* goody-goody, goody two-shoes.

**priggish** adjective *Miss Sinclair couldn't possibly have been as priggish as she seemed way back then* SELF-RIGHTEOUS, moralistic, holier-than-thou, sanctimonious, prudish, puritanical, prim, straitlaced, stuffy, prissy, governessy, narrow-minded; *informal* goody-goody, starchy. ANTONYM broad-minded.

**prim** adjective *Reverend Cooke had two prim little maids for daughters and one wild little hellion for a son* DEMURE, proper, prim and proper, formal, stuffy, straitlaced, prudish; governessy, prissy, priggish, puritanical; *informal* starchy.

**prima donna** noun **1** LEADING SOPRANO, leading lady, diva, star, opera star, principal singer.

**2** *a city council filled with prima donnas* EGO, self-important person, his nibs, temperamental person, princess, diva, pooh-bah.

**primarily** adverb **1** *the bishop was primarily a leader of the local community* FIRST AND FOREMOST, first, firstly, essentially, in essence, fundamentally, principally, predominantly, basically.

**2** *such work is undertaken primarily for large institutions* MOSTLY, for the most part, chiefly, mainly, in the main, on the whole, largely, to a large extent, especially, generally, usually, typically, commonly, as a rule.

**primary** adjective **1** *our primary role* MAIN, chief, key, prime, central, principal, foremost, first, first-line, most important, predominant, paramount; *informal* number-one. ANTONYMS secondary, subordinate.

**2** *the primary cause* ORIGINAL, earliest, initial, first; essential, fundamental, basic. ANTONYM secondary.

**prime**[1] adjective **1** *his prime reason for leaving* MAIN, chief, key, primary, central, principal, foremost, first, most important, paramount, major; *informal* number-one. ANTONYMS secondary, subordinate.

**2** *the prime cause of flooding* FUNDAMENTAL, basic, essential, primary, central. ANTONYM secondary.

**3** *prime agricultural land* TOP-QUALITY, top, best, first-class, first-rate, grade A, superior, supreme, choice, select, finest; excellent, superb, fine; *informal* tip-top, A1, top-notch, blue-ribbon. ANTONYM inferior.

**4** *a prime example* ARCHETYPAL, prototypical, typical, classic, excellent, characteristic, quintessential.

▸ noun *he is in his prime* HEYDAY, best days, best years, prime of one's life; youth, salad days; peak, pinnacle, zenith.

**prime**[2] verb **1** *he primed the gun* PREPARE, load, get ready.

**2** *Lucy had primed him carefully* BRIEF, fill in, prepare, put in the picture, inform, advise, instruct, coach, drill; *informal* clue in, give someone the lowdown.

**primeval** adjective **1** *primeval forest* ANCIENT, earliest, first, prehistoric, antediluvian, primordial; pristine, original, virgin.

**2** *primeval fears* INSTINCTIVE, primitive, basic, primal, primordial, intuitive, inborn, innate, inherent.

**primitive** adjective **1** *primitive times* ANCIENT, earliest, first, prehistoric, antediluvian, primordial, primeval, primal. ANTONYMS modern, recent.

**2** *primitive peoples* UNCIVILIZED, barbarian, barbaric, barbarous, savage, ignorant, uncultivated. ANTONYM civilized.

**3** *primitive tools* CRUDE, simple, rough, rough and ready, basic, rudimentary, unrefined, unsophisticated, rude, makeshift. ANTONYMS sophisticated, advanced.

**4** *primitive art* SIMPLE, natural, unsophisticated, unaffected, undeveloped, unpretentious. ANTONYMS sophisticated, refined.

**primp** verb *students are encouraged to primp just before the photo session* GROOM, tidy, arrange, brush, comb; smarten (up), spruce up; *informal* titivate, doll up, tart up, gussy up.

**prince** noun *the young prince was the object of much media attention* RULER, sovereign, monarch, king, princeling; crown prince; emir, sheikh, sultan, maharaja, raja.

**princely** adjective **1** *princely buildings.* See SPLENDID sense 1.

**2** *a princely sum.* See HANDSOME sense 3.

**principal** adjective *the principal cause of poor air quality* MAIN, chief, primary, leading, foremost, first, first-line, most important, predominant, dominant, (most) prominent; key, crucial, vital, essential, basic, prime, central, focal; premier, paramount, major, overriding, cardinal, preeminent, uppermost, highest, top, topmost; *informal* number-one. ANTONYM minor.

▸ noun **1** *the principal of the firm* CHIEF, chief executive (officer), CEO, president, chairman, chairwoman, director, managing director, manager, head; *informal* boss.

**2** *the school's principal* headmaster, headmistress; dean, rector, chancellor, president, provost.

**3** *a principal in a soap opera* LEADING ACTOR/ACTRESS, leading player/performer/dancer, leading role, lead, star.

**4** *repayment of the principal* CAPITAL (SUM), debt, loan.

---

USAGE NOTE **principal, principle**

These two words, though often confused and used incorrectly and interchangeably, share no common definitions. Generally, it's enough to remember that *principal* (= chief, primary, most important) is usually an adjective and that *principle* (= a truth, rule, doctrine, or course of action) is virtually always a noun. Although *principle* is not a verb, we have *principled* as an adjective. But *principal* is sometimes a noun—an elliptical form of *principal official* (*Morgan is principal of the elementary school*) or *principal investment* (*principal and interest*).

Substituting *principal* for *principle* is a fairly common blunder—e.g.: "The Ways and Means bill approved today, after more than a month of deliberation and voting, preserves two of the central principals [read *principles*] put forth by the President: universal coverage and the requirement that employers assume 80 percent of its cost for their workers." (*New York Times*; July 1, 1994.)

Substituting *principle* for *principal* is perhaps even more common—e.g.: "Audio CDs are a principle [read *principal*] source of material for making music with samples." (*Electronic Musician*; June 1994.) —*BG*

---

**principally** adverb *the decline is principally due to overfishing* MAINLY, mostly, chiefly, for the most part, in the main, on the whole, largely, to a large extent, predominantly, basically, primarily.

**principle** noun **1** *elementary principles* TRUTH, proposition, concept, idea, theory, assumption, fundamental, essential, ground rule.

**2** *the principle of laissez-faire* DOCTRINE, belief, creed, credo, (golden) rule, criterion, tenet, code, ethic, dictum, canon, law.

**3** *a woman of principle | sticking to one's principles* MORALS, morality, (code of) ethics, beliefs, ideals, standards; integrity, uprightness, righteousness, virtue, probity, (sense of) honor, decency, conscience, scruples. See note at PRINCIPAL.
PHRASE: **in principle 1** *there is no reason, in principle, why we couldn't work together* IN THEORY, theoretically, on paper.

**2** *he has accepted the idea in principle* IN GENERAL, in essence, on the whole, in the main.

**print** verb **1** *the newspaper is printed just after midnight* SEND TO PRESS, set in print, run off, reprint.

**2** *patterns were printed on the cloth* IMPRINT, impress, stamp, mark.

**3** *they printed 30,000 copies* PUBLISH, issue, release, circulate.

**4** *the incident is printed on her memory* REGISTER, record, impress, imprint, engrave, etch, stamp, mark.

▸ noun **1** *small print* TYPE, printing, letters, lettering, characters, type size, typeface, font.

**2** *prints of his left hand* IMPRESSION, fingerprint, footprint.

**3** *Rockwell prints are on sale in the lobby* PICTURE, design, engraving, etching, lithograph, linocut, woodcut.

**4** *prints and negatives* PHOTOGRAPH, photo, snapshot, picture, still.

**5** *soft floral prints* PRINTED CLOTH/FABRIC, patterned cloth/fabric, chintz.

PHRASES: **in print** *I noticed on Amazon.com that the book is still in print* PUBLISHED, printed, available in bookstores.
**out of print** *they will help you track down editions that are out of print* NO LONGER AVAILABLE, unavailable, unobtainable, discontinued.

**prior** adjective *by prior arrangement* EARLIER, previous, preceding, foregoing, antecedent, advance; *formal* anterior. ANTONYM subsequent.

PHRASE: **prior to** *prior to bedtime, set the clocks back an hour* BEFORE, until, till, up to, previous to, earlier than, preceding, leading up to; *formal* anterior to.

**priority** noun **1** *safety is our priority* PRIME CONCERN, most important consideration, primary issue.

**2** *giving priority to elementary schools* PRECEDENCE, greater importance, preference, preeminence, predominance, primacy, first place.

**3** *traffic in the right lane has priority* RIGHT OF WAY.

**priory** noun *the sisters of this priory are famous for their spinning and weaving* RELIGIOUS HOUSE, abbey, cloister; monastery, friary; convent, nunnery.

**prison** noun *the prisons upstate are just as crowded* JAIL, lockup, penal institution, detention center, jailhouse, penitentiary, correctional facility; *informal* clink, slammer, hoosegow, the big house, stir, jug, brig, can, pen, cooler, pokey, slam; **(be in prison)** *informal* be inside, be behind bars, do time.

**prisoner** noun **1** *a prisoner serving a life sentence* CONVICT, detainee, inmate; *informal* jailbird, con, lifer, yardbird.

**2** *the army took many prisoners* CAPTIVE, internee, prisoner of war, POW.

**pristine** adjective *Lurene's clothes are always so pristine* IMMACULATE, perfect, in mint condition, as new, unspoiled, spotless, flawless, clean, fresh, new, virgin, pure, unused. ANTONYMS dirty, spoiled.

**privacy** noun *protecting one's privacy* SECLUSION, solitude, isolation, freedom from disturbance, freedom from interference.

**private** adjective **1** *his private plane* PERSONAL, own, individual, special, exclusive, privately owned. ANTONYM public.

**2** *private talks* CONFIDENTIAL, secret, classified, unofficial, off the record, closet, in camera; backstage, privileged, one-on-one, tête-à-tête, sub rosa. ANTONYMS public, open.

**3** *private thoughts* INTIMATE, personal, secret; innermost, undisclosed, unspoken, unvoiced.

**4** *a very private man* RESERVED, introvert, introverted, self-contained, reticent, discreet, uncommunicative, unforthcoming, retiring, unsociable, withdrawn, solitary, reclusive, hermitic. ANTONYMS extrovert, extroverted.

**5** *they found a private place in which to talk* SECLUDED, solitary, undisturbed, concealed, hidden, remote, isolated, out of the way, sequestered. ANTONYMS busy, crowded.

**6** *we can be private here* UNDISTURBED, uninterrupted; alone, by ourselves.

**7** *the governor attended in a private capacity* UNOFFICIAL, personal. ANTONYM official.

**8** *private industry* INDEPENDENT; privatized, denationalized; commercial, private-enterprise. ANTONYMS public, nationalized.

▸ noun *a private in the army* PRIVATE SOLDIER, common soldier; trooper; sapper, gunner; enlisted personnel; *informal* GI.
PHRASE: **in private** *I'll tell you later, in private* IN SECRET, secretly, privately, behind closed doors, in camera; in confidence, confidentially, between ourselves, entre nous, off the record; *formal* sub rosa.

**privately** adverb **1** *we must talk privately* IN SECRET, secretly, in private, behind closed doors, in camera; in confidence, confidentially, between ourselves, entre nous, off the record; *formal* sub rosa. ANTONYM publicly.

**2** *privately, I am glad* SECRETLY, inwardly, deep down, personally, unofficially.

**3** *he lived very privately* OUT OF THE PUBLIC EYE, out of public view, in seclusion, in solitude, alone.

**privation** noun *years of rationing and privation* DEPRIVA-

TION, hardship, destitution, impoverishment, want, need, neediness, austerity. See note at LACK. ANTONYMS plenty, luxury.

**privilege** noun 1 *senior students have certain privileges* ADVANTAGE, benefit; prerogative, entitlement, right; concession, freedom, liberty.

2 *it was a privilege to meet her* HONOR, pleasure.

3 *congressional privilege* IMMUNITY, exemption, dispensation.

**privileged** adjective 1 *a privileged background* WEALTHY, rich, affluent, prosperous; LUCKY, fortunate, elite, favored; (socially) advantaged. ANTONYMS underprivileged, disadvantaged.

2 *privileged information* CONFIDENTIAL, private, secret, restricted, classified, not for publication, off the record, inside; *informal* hush-hush. ANTONYM public.

3 *these foreign diplomats are privileged* IMMUNE (FROM PROSECUTION), protected, exempt, excepted. ANTONYM liable.

**privy** adjective *he was not* ***privy to*** *the discussions* IN THE KNOW ABOUT, acquainted with, in on, informed of, advised of, apprised of; *informal* wise to; *formal* cognizant of.

▸ noun *dated he went out to the privy.* See BATHROOM.

**prize** noun 1 *an art prize* AWARD, reward, premium, purse; trophy, medal; honor, accolade, crown, laurels, palm.

2 (**prizes**) *the prizes of war* SPOILS, booty, plunder, loot, pickings.

▸ adjective 1 *a prize bull* CHAMPION, award-winning, prize-winning, winning, top, best. ANTONYM second-rate.

2 *a prize example* OUTSTANDING, excellent, superlative, superb, supreme, very good, prime, fine, magnificent, marvelous, wonderful; *informal* great, terrific, tremendous, fantastic.

3 *a prize idiot* COMPLETE, utter, total, absolute, real, perfect, veritable.

▸ verb *many collectors prize his work* VALUE, set great store by, rate highly, attach great importance to, esteem, hold in high regard, think highly of, treasure, cherish. See note at ESTEEM.

**prized** adjective *his prized sheepdog* TREASURED, precious, cherished, much loved, beloved, valued, esteemed, highly regarded.

**probability** noun 1 *the probability of winning* LIKELIHOOD, prospect, expectation, chance, chances, odds.

2 *relegation is a distinct probability* PROBABLE EVENT, prospect, possibility, good/fair/reasonable bet.

**probable** adjective *a recurrence of the symptoms is probable* LIKELY, most likely, odds-on, expected, anticipated, predictable, foreseeable, ten to one; *informal* in the cards, a good/fair/reasonable bet. ANTONYM unlikely.

**probably** adverb *I knew I would probably never see her again* IN ALL LIKELIHOOD, in all probability, as likely as not, (very/most) likely, ten to one, the chances are, doubtless, no doubt; *archaic* like enough.

**probation** noun *during your probation it is imperative that you miss no scheduled meetings* TRIAL PERIOD, test period, experimental period, trial. See note at NOVICE.

**probe** noun *a probe into the air crash* INVESTIGATION, inquiry, examination, inquest, exploration, study, analysis.

▸ verb 1 *alien hands probed his body* EXAMINE, feel, feel around, explore, prod, poke, check.

2 *police probed the tragedy* INVESTIGATE, inquire into, look into, study, examine, scrutinize, go into, carry out an inquest into.

**problem** noun 1 *they ran into a problem* DIFFICULTY, trouble, worry, complication, difficult situation; snag, hitch, drawback, stumbling block, obstacle, hurdle, hiccup, setback, catch; predicament, plight; misfortune, mishap, misadventure; dilemma, quandary; *informal* headache, nightmare.

2 *I don't want to be a problem* NUISANCE, bother, pest, irritant, thorn in one's side/flesh, vexation; *informal* drag, pain, pain in the neck.

3 *mathematical problems* PUZZLE, question, poser, enigma, riddle, conundrum; *informal* teaser, brainteaser.

▸ adjective *a problem child* TROUBLESOME, difficult, unmanageable, unruly, disobedient, uncontrollable, recalcitrant, delinquent. ANTONYMS well-behaved, manageable.

**problematic** adjective *the pest control in this building has gotten very problematic* DIFFICULT, hard, taxing, troublesome, tricky, awkward, controversial, ticklish, complicated, complex, knotty, thorny, prickly, vexed; *informal* sticky. See note at DOUBTFUL. ANTONYMS easy, simple, straightforward.

**procedure** noun *once we establish a procedure, it must be followed* COURSE OF ACTION, plan of action, action plan, policy, series of steps, method, system, strategy, way, approach, formula, mechanism, methodology, MO (modus operandi), technique; routine, drill, practice, operation.

**proceed** verb 1 *she was uncertain how to proceed* BEGIN, make a start, get going, move, set something in motion; TAKE ACTION, act, go on, go ahead, make progress, make headway. ANTONYM stop.

2 *he proceeded down the road* GO, make one's way, advance, move, progress, carry on, press on, push on. ANTONYM stop.

3 *we should proceed with the talks* GO AHEAD, carry on, go on, continue, keep on, get on, get ahead; (**proceed with**) pursue, prosecute.

4 *there is not enough evidence to* ***proceed against*** *him* TAKE SOMEONE TO COURT, start/take proceedings against, start an action against, make a case against, sue.

5 *all power proceeds from God* ORIGINATE, spring, stem, come, derive, arise, issue, flow, emanate.

**proceedings** plural noun 1 *the evening's proceedings are underway* EVENTS, activities, happenings, goings-on, doings.

2 *they published the proceedings of the meeting* REPORT, transactions, minutes, account, record(s); annals, archives.

3 *legal proceedings* LEGAL ACTION, court/judicial proceedings, litigation; lawsuit, case, prosecution.

**proceeds** plural noun *most of the proceeds go to pay salaries* PROFITS, earnings, receipts, returns, takings, take, income, revenue, royalty; *Sports* gate (money/receipts).

**process** noun 1 *investigation is a long process* PROCEDURE, operation, action, activity, exercise, affair, business, job, task, undertaking.

2 *a new canning process* METHOD, system, technique, means, practice, way, approach, methodology.

▸ verb *applications are processed rapidly* DEAL WITH, attend to, see to, sort out, handle, take care of, action.

PHRASE: **in the process of** *we're in the process of updating our files* IN THE MIDDLE OF, in the course of, in the midst of, in the throes of, busy with, occupied in/with, taken up with/by, involved in.

**procession** noun *a procession of marching bands* PARADE, march, march past, cavalcade, motorcade, cortège; column, file, train.

**proclaim** verb 1 *messengers proclaimed the good news* DECLARE, announce, pronounce, state, make known, give out, advertise, publish, broadcast, promulgate, trumpet, blazon. See note at ANNOUNCE.

2 *the men proclaimed their innocence* ASSERT, declare, profess, maintain, protest.

3 *she proclaimed herself president* DECLARE, pronounce, announce.

4 *cheap paint soon proclaims its cheapness* DEMONSTRATE, indicate, show, reveal, manifest, betray, testify to, signify.

**proclamation** noun *the Church issued a proclamation denouncing the movie* DECLARATION, announcement, pronouncement, statement, notification, publication, broadcast, promulgation, blazoning; assertion, profession, protestation; DECREE, order, edict, ruling.

**proclivity** noun *his sexual proclivities are none of your business* INCLINATION, tendency, leaning, disposition, proneness, propensity, bent, bias, penchant, predisposition; predilection, partiality, liking, preference, taste, fondness, weakness.

**procrastinate** verb *fear of failure often causes people to procrastinate* DELAY, put off doing something, postpone action, defer action, be dilatory, use delaying tactics, stall, temporize, drag one's feet/heels, take one's time, play for time, play a waiting game.

**procure** verb 1 *he managed to procure a coat* OBTAIN, acquire, get, find, come by, secure, pick up; buy, purchase, engage; *informal* get hold of, get one's hands on. See note at GET.

2 *the police found that he was procuring* PIMP.

**prod** verb 1 *Cassie prodded him in the chest* POKE, jab, dig, elbow, butt, stab.

2 *they hoped to prod the government into action* SPUR, stimulate, stir, rouse, prompt, drive, galvanize; persuade, urge, chivvy; incite, goad, egg on, provoke.

▸ noun 1 *a prod in the ribs* POKE, jab, dig, elbow, butt, thrust.

2 *they need a prod to get them to act* STIMULUS, push, prompt, reminder, spur; incitement, goad.

**prodigal** adjective 1 *prodigal habits die hard* WASTEFUL, extravagant, spendthrift, profligate, improvident, imprudent. ANTONYM thrifty.

2 *a composer who is prodigal with his talents* GENEROUS, lavish, liberal, unstinting, unsparing; *literary* bounteous. ANTONYM mean.

3 *a dessert prodigal with whipped cream* ABOUNDING IN, abundant in, rich in, covered in, awash with, slathered with. See note at PROFUSE. ANTONYM deficient.

**prodigious** adjective *prodigious quantities of food* ENORMOUS, huge, colossal, immense, vast, great, massive, gigantic, mammoth, tremendous, inordinate, monumental; amazing, astonishing, astounding, staggering, stunning, remarkable, phenomenal, terrific, miraculous, impressive, striking, startling, sensational, spectacular, extraordinary, exceptional, breathtaking, incredible; *informal* humongous, stupendous, fantastic, fabulous, mega, awesome, ginormous; *literary* wondrous. ANTONYMS small, unexceptional.

**prodigy** noun 1 *a seven-year-old prodigy* GENIUS, mastermind, virtuoso, wunderkind, wonder child, boy wonder, girl wonder; *informal* whiz kid, whiz, wizard.

2 *Germany seemed a prodigy of industrial discipline* MODEL, classic example, paragon, paradigm, epitome, exemplar, archetype.

**produce** verb 1 *the company produces furniture* MANUFACTURE, make, construct, build, fabricate, put together, assemble, turn out, create; mass-produce; *informal* churn out.

2 *the vineyards produce excellent wines* YIELD, grow, give, supply, provide, furnish, bear, bring forth.

3 *she produced ten puppies* GIVE BIRTH TO, bear, deliver, bring forth, bring into the world.

4 *he produced five novels* CREATE, originate, fashion, turn out; compose, write, pen; paint.

5 *she produced an ID card* PULL OUT, extract, fish out; present, offer, proffer, show.

6 *no evidence was produced* PRESENT, offer, provide, furnish, advance, put forward, bring forward, come up with.

7 *that will produce a reaction* GIVE RISE TO, bring about, cause, occasion, generate, engender, lead to, result in, effect, induce, set off; provoke, precipitate, breed, spark off, trigger; *literary* beget.

8 *James produced the play* STAGE, put on, mount, present.

▸ noun *fresh produce* FOOD, foodstuff(s), products; harvest, crops, fruit, vegetables, greens.

**producer** noun 1 *a car producer* MANUFACTURER, maker, builder, constructor, fabricator.

2 *coffee producers* GROWER, farmer.

3 *the producer of the show* IMPRESARIO, manager, administrator, promoter, regisseur.

**product** noun 1 *a household product* ARTIFACT, commodity, manufactured article; creation, invention; **(products)** goods, wares, merchandise, produce.

2 *his skill is a product of experience* RESULT, consequence, outcome, effect, upshot, fruit, by-product, spin-off.

**production** noun 1 *the production of washing machines* MANUFACTURE, making, construction, building, fabrication, assembly, creation; mass-production.

2 *the production of literary works* CREATION, origination, fashioning; composition, writing.

3 *literary productions* WORK, opus, creation; publication, composition, piece; work of art, painting, picture; *Law* intellectual property.

4 *agricultural production* OUTPUT, yield; productivity.

5 *admission only on production of a ticket* PRESENTATION, proffering, showing.

6 *a theater production* PERFORMANCE, staging, presentation, show, piece, play.

**productive** adjective 1 *a productive artist* PROLIFIC, inventive, creative; energetic.

2 *productive talks* USEFUL, constructive, profitable, fruitful, gainful, valuable, effective, worthwhile, helpful.

3 *productive land* FERTILE, fruitful, rich, fecund. ANTONYMS sterile, barren.

**productivity** noun 1 *workers have boosted productivity* EFFICIENCY, work rate; output, yield, production.

2 *the productivity of the soil* FRUITFULNESS, fertility, richness, fecundity. ANTONYMS sterility, barrenness.

**profane** adjective 1 *subjects both sacred and profane* SECULAR, lay, nonreligious, temporal; *formal* laic. ANTONYMS religious, sacred.

2 *a profane man* IRREVERENT, irreligious, ungodly, godless, unbelieving, impious, disrespectful, sacrilegious. ANTONYM reverent.

3 *profane language* OBSCENE, blasphemous, indecent, foul, vulgar, crude, filthy, dirty, smutty, coarse, rude, offensive, indecorous. ANTONYM decorous.

▸ verb *invaders profaned our sacred temples* DESECRATE, violate, defile, treat sacrilegiously.

**profanity** noun 1 *he hissed a profanity* | *an outburst of profanity* OATH, swear word, expletive, curse, obscenity, four-letter word, dirty word; blasphemy, swearing, foul language, bad language, cursing; *informal* cuss, cuss word; *formal* imprecation; *archaic* execration.

2 *some traditional festivals were tainted with profanity* SACRILEGE, blasphemy, irreligion, ungodliness, impiety, irreverence, disrespect.

**profess** verb 1 *he professed his love* DECLARE, announce, proclaim, assert, state, affirm, avow, maintain, protest; *formal* aver.

2 *she professed to loathe publicity* CLAIM, pretend, purport, affect; make out; *informal* let on.

3 *the emperor professed Christianity* AFFIRM ONE'S FAITH IN, affirm one's allegiance to, avow, confess.

**professed** adjective 1 *his professed ambition* CLAIMED, supposed, ostensible, self-styled, apparent, pretended, purported.

2 *a professed libertarian* DECLARED, self-acknowledged, self-confessed, confessed, sworn, avowed, confirmed.

**profession** noun 1 *his chosen profession of teaching* CAREER, occupation, calling, vocation, métier, line (of work), walk of life, job, business, trade, craft; *informal* racket.

2 *a profession of allegiance* DECLARATION, affirmation, statement, announcement, proclamation, assertion, avowal, vow, claim, protestation; *formal* averment.

**professional** adjective 1 *people in professional occupations* WHITE-COLLAR, nonmanual. ANTONYM blue-collar.

2 *a professional rugby player* PAID, salaried. ANTONYM amateur.

3 *a thoroughly professional performance* EXPERT, accomplished, skillful, masterly, masterful, fine, polished, skilled, proficient, competent, able, experienced, practiced, trained, seasoned, businesslike, deft; *informal* ace, crack, top-notch. ANTONYM amateurish.

4 *not a professional way to behave* APPROPRIATE, fitting, proper, honorable, ethical, correct, comme il faut. ANTONYMS inappropriate, unethical.

▸ noun 1 *affluent young professionals* WHITE-COLLAR WORKER, office worker. ANTONYM blue-collar worker.

2 *his first season as a professional* PROFESSIONAL PLAYER, paid player, salaried player; *informal* pro. ANTONYM amateur.

3 *she was a real professional on stage* EXPERT, virtuoso, old hand, master, maestro, past master; *informal* pro, ace, wizard, whiz, hotshot, maven, crackerjack. ANTONYM amateur.

**professor** noun *a number of our professors were Rhodes scholars* PROF, tenured faculty member, dean, full/assistant/associate professor, instructor, lecturer, doctor, scholar, academic.

**proffer** verb *Coleman proffered his resignation* OFFER, tender, submit, extend, volunteer, suggest, propose, put forward; hold out. ANTONYMS refuse, withdraw.

**proficiency** noun *her proficiency was obvious to anyone who sailed with her* SKILL, expertise, experience, accomplishment, competence, mastery, prowess, professionalism, deftness, adroitness, dexterity, finesse, ability, facility; *informal* know-how. ANTONYM incompetence.

**proficient** adjective *a proficient equestrian* SKILLED, skillful, expert, experienced, accomplished, competent, masterly, adept, adroit, deft, dexterous, able, professional, consummate, complete, master; *informal* crack, ace, mean. ANTONYM incompetent.

**profile** noun 1 *his handsome profile* SIDE VIEW, outline, silhouette, contour, shape, form, figure, lines.

2 *she wrote a profile of the organization* DESCRIPTION, ac-

count, study, portrait, portrayal, depiction, rundown, sketch, outline.

▸ verb *he was profiled in the local paper* DESCRIBE, write about, give an account of, portray, depict, sketch, outline.

PHRASE: **keep a low profile** *in matters concerning his family, he managed to keep a low profile* LIE LOW, keep quiet, keep out of the public eye, avoid publicity, keep out of sight.

**profit** noun **1** *the firm made a profit* (FINANCIAL) GAIN, return(s), yield, proceeds, earnings, winnings, surplus, excess; *informal* pay dirt, bottom line. ANTONYM loss.

**2** *we could gain no profit by continuing* ADVANTAGE, benefit, value, use, good, avail; *informal* mileage. ANTONYM disadvantage.

▸ verb **1** *this company must not profit from its wrongdoing* MAKE MONEY, make a profit; *informal* rake it in, clean up, make a killing, make a bundle, make big bucks, make a fast/quick buck. ANTONYM lose.

**2** *how will that profit us?* BENEFIT, be beneficial to, be of benefit to, be advantageous to, be of advantage to, be of use to, be of value to, do someone good, help, be of service to, serve, assist, aid. ANTONYM disadvantage.

PHRASE: **profit by/from** *if you're smart, you'll profit from their mistakes* BENEFIT FROM, take advantage of, derive benefit from, capitalize on, make the most of, turn to one's advantage, put to good use, do well out of, exploit, gain from; *informal* cash in on.

**profitable** adjective **1** *a profitable company* MONEYMAKING, profit-making, commercial, successful, solvent, in the black, gainful, remunerative, financially rewarding, paying, lucrative, bankable. ANTONYM loss-making.

**2** *profitable study* BENEFICIAL, useful, advantageous, valuable, productive, worthwhile; rewarding, fruitful, illuminating, informative, well-spent. ANTONYMS fruitless, useless.

**profligate** adjective **1** *profligate local authorities* WASTEFUL, extravagant, spendthrift, improvident, prodigal. ANTONYMS thrifty, frugal.

**2** *a profligate lifestyle* DISSOLUTE, degenerate, dissipated, debauched, corrupt, depraved; PROMISCUOUS, loose, wanton, licentious, libertine, decadent, abandoned, fast; SYBARITIC, voluptuary. ANTONYMS moral, upright.

▸ noun *he was an out-and-out profligate* LIBERTINE, debauchee, degenerate, dissolute, roué, rake, sybarite, voluptuary.

**profound** adjective **1** *profound relief* HEARTFELT, intense, keen, great, extreme, acute, severe, sincere, earnest, deep, deep-seated, overpowering, overwhelming, fervent, ardent. ANTONYMS superficial, mild.

**2** *profound silence* COMPLETE, utter, total, absolute.

**3** *a profound change* FAR-REACHING, radical, extensive, sweeping, exhaustive, thoroughgoing. ANTONYM slight.

**4** *a profound analysis* WISE, learned, clever, intelligent, scholarly, sage, erudite, discerning, penetrating, perceptive, astute, thoughtful, insightful, percipient, perspicacious; *rare* sapient. ANTONYM superficial.

**5** *profound truths* COMPLEX, abstract, deep, weighty, difficult, abstruse, recondite, esoteric. ANTONYM simple.

**profoundly** adverb **1** *she was profoundly grateful that none of her colleagues could see her* EXTREMELY, very, deeply, exceedingly, greatly, immensely, enormously, tremendously, intensely, heartily, keenly, acutely, painfully, from the bottom of one's heart, downright, thoroughly, sincerely, so; *informal* awfully, terribly, seriously, majorly, oh-so, mighty.

**2** *he spoke profoundly on the subject* PENETRATINGLY, discerningly, wisely, sagaciously, thoughtfully, philosophically, weightily, seriously, learnedly, eruditely.

**profuse** adjective **1** *profuse apologies* COPIOUS, prolific, abundant, liberal, unstinting, fulsome, effusive, extravagant, lavish, gushing; *informal* over the top, gushy.

**2** *profuse blooms* LUXURIANT, plentiful, copious, abundant, lush, rich, exuberant, riotous, teeming, rank, rampant; *informal* jungly. ANTONYMS meager, sparse.

THE RIGHT WORD **profuse, extravagant, lavish, lush, luxuriant, prodigal**

Something that is **profuse** is poured out or given freely, often to the point of exaggeration or excess (*profuse apologies*). **Extravagant** also suggests unreasonable excess, but with an emphasis on wasteful spending (*her gift was much too extravagant for the occasion*). Someone who is **prodigal** is so recklessly extravagant that his or her resources will ultimately be exhausted (*the prodigal heir to the family fortune*). Another way to end up impoverished is through **lavish** spending, a word that combines extravagance with generosity or a lack of moderation (*lavish praise; lavish furnishings*). While *lavish*, *extravagant* and *prodigal* are often used to describe human behavior, **lush** and **luxuriant** normally refer to things. What is *luxuriant* is produced in great quantity, suggesting that it is not only profuse but gorgeous (*luxuriant auburn hair*). Something described as *lush* is not only luxuriant but has reached a peak of perfection (*the lush summer grass*).

**profusion** noun *a profusion of crocuses covered the front lawn* ABUNDANCE, mass, host, cornucopia, riot, superabundance; *informal* sea, wealth; *formal* plenitude.

**progeny** noun *genetic traits passed on from parent to progeny* OFFSPRING, young, babies, children, sons and daughters, family, brood; DESCENDANTS, heirs, scions; *Law* issue; *archaic* seed, fruit of one's loins.

**program** noun **1** *our program for the day* SCHEDULE, agenda, calendar, timetable; order of events, lineup.

**2** *the government's reform program* plan of action, series of measures, strategy, scheme.

**3** *a television program* BROADCAST, production, show, presentation, transmission, performance, telecast.

**4** *a program of study* COURSE, syllabus, curriculum.

**5** *a theater program* guide, list of performers, cast list, playbill.

▸ verb *they programmed the day well* ARRANGE, organize, schedule, plan, map out, timetable, line up, slate.

**progress** noun **1** *boulders made progress difficult* FORWARD MOVEMENT, advance, going, progression, headway, passage.

**2** *scientific progress* DEVELOPMENT, advance, advancement, headway, step(s) forward; improvement, betterment, growth.

▸ verb **1** *they progressed slowly down the road* GO, make one's way, move, move forward, go forward, proceed, advance, go on, continue, make headway, work one's way.

**2** *the school has progressed rapidly* DEVELOP, make progress, advance, make headway, take steps forward, move on, get on, gain ground; improve, get better, come on, come along, make strides; thrive, prosper, blossom, flourish; *informal* be getting there. ANTONYM regress.

PHRASE: **in progress** *the game was already in progress* UNDERWAY, going on, ongoing, happening, occurring, taking place, proceeding, continuing; unfinished, in the works.

**progression** noun **1** *progression to the next stage* PROGRESS, advancement, movement, passage, march; development, evolution, growth.

**2** *a progression of peaks on the graph* SUCCESSION, series, sequence, string, stream, chain, concatenation, train, row, cycle.

**progressive** adjective **1** *progressive deterioration* CONTINUING, continuous, increasing, growing, developing, ongoing, accelerating, escalating; gradual, step-by-step, cumulative.

**2** *progressive views* MODERN, liberal, advanced, forward-thinking, enlightened, enterprising, innovative, pioneering, dynamic, bold, avant-garde, reforming, reformist, radical; *informal* go-ahead. ANTONYMS conservative, reactionary.

▸ noun *he is very much a progressive* INNOVATOR, reformer, reformist, liberal, libertarian.

**prohibit** verb **1** *state law prohibits gambling* FORBID, ban, bar, interdict, proscribe, make illegal, embargo, outlaw, disallow, veto; *Law* enjoin. ANTONYMS permit, authorize.

**2** *a cash shortage prohibited the visit* PREVENT, stop, rule out, preclude, make impossible. ANTONYMS facilitate, allow.

THE RIGHT WORD **prohibit, ban, disallow, enjoin, forbid, hinder, interdict, preclude**

There are a number of ways to prevent something from happening. You can **prohibit** it, which assumes that you have legal or other authority and are willing to back up your prohibition with force (*prohibit smoking*); or you can simply **forbid** it and hope that you've got the necessary clout (*forbid teenagers to stay out after midnight*). **Ban** carries a little more weight—both legal and moral—and **interdict** suggests that church or civil authorities are behind the idea. To **enjoin** (in this sense) is to prohibit by legal injunction (*the truckers were enjoined from striking*), which practically guarantees that you'll get what you want. A government or some other authority may **disallow** an act it might otherwise have permitted (*the IRS disallowed the deduction*), but anyone with a little gumption can **hinder** an activity by putting obstacles in its path (*hinder the thief's getaway by tripping him on his way out the door*). Of course, the easiest way to prohibit something is to **preclude** it, which means stopping it before it even gets started.

**prohibition** noun **1** *the prohibition of marijuana* BANNING, forbidding, prohibiting, barring, debarment, vetoing, proscription, interdiction, outlawing.

**2** *a prohibition was imposed* BAN, bar, interdict, veto, embargo, injunction, moratorium.

**prohibitive** adjective **1** *prohibitive costs* EXORBITANT, excessively high, sky-high, overinflated; out of the question, beyond one's means; extortionate, unreasonable; *informal* steep, criminal.

**2** *prohibitive regulations* PROSCRIPTIVE, prohibitory, restrictive, repressive.

**project** noun **1** *an engineering project* PLAN, program, enterprise, undertaking, venture; proposal, idea, concept, scheme.

**2** *a history project* ASSIGNMENT, piece of work, piece of research, task.

▸ verb **1** *profits are projected to rise* FORECAST, predict, expect, estimate, calculate, reckon.

**2** *his projected book* INTEND, plan, propose, devise, design, outline.

**3** *balconies projected over the lake* STICK OUT, jut (out), protrude, extend, stand out, bulge out, poke out, thrust out, cantilever. See note at BULGE.

**4** *seeds are projected from the tree* PROPEL, discharge, launch, throw, cast, fling, hurl, shoot.

**5** *the sun projected his shadow on the wall* CAST, throw, send, shed, shine.

**6** *she tried to project a calm image* CONVEY, put across, put over, communicate, present, promote.

**projectile** noun *the cyclone sent pieces of the house flying like wild projectiles* MISSILE, rocket, bullets.

**projection** noun **1** *a sales projection* FORECAST, prediction, prognosis, outlook, expectation, estimate.

**2** *tiny projections on the cliff face* PROTUBERANCE, protrusion, prominence, eminence, outcrop, outgrowth, jut, jag, snag; overhang, ledge, shelf.

**proletariat** noun *the voice of **the proletariat*** THE WORKERS, working-class people, wage earners, the working classes, the common people, the lower classes, the masses, the rank and file, the third estate, the plebeians; *derogatory* the hoi polloi, the plebs, the proles, the great unwashed, the mob, the rabble. ANTONYM aristocracy.

**proliferate** verb *stories of her trial proliferated* INCREASE RAPIDLY, grow rapidly, multiply, rocket, mushroom, snowball, burgeon, run riot. ANTONYMS decrease, dwindle.

**prolific** adjective **1** *a prolific crop of tomatoes* PLENTIFUL, abundant, bountiful, profuse, copious, luxuriant, rich, lush; fruitful, fecund; *literary* plenteous, bounteous.

**2** *a prolific composer* PRODUCTIVE, creative, inventive, fertile. See note at FERTILE.

**prolix** adjective *his prolix speeches* LONG-WINDED, verbose, wordy, pleonastic, discursive, rambling, long-drawn-out, overlong, lengthy, protracted, interminable; *informal* windy, waffly.

**prologue** noun *Davis wrote the prologue to her brother's autobiography* INTRODUCTION, foreword, preface, preamble, prelude; *informal* intro, lead-in; *formal* exordium, proem, prolegomenon. ANTONYM epilogue.

**prolong** verb *your bickering just prolongs these negotiations* LENGTHEN, extend, draw out, drag out, protract, spin out, stretch out, string out, elongate; carry on, continue, keep up, perpetuate. ANTONYM shorten.

**prominence** noun **1** *his rise to prominence* FAME, celebrity, eminence, preeminence, importance, distinction, greatness, note, notability, prestige, stature, standing, position, rank.

**2** *the press gave prominence to the reports* GOOD COVERAGE, importance, precedence, weight, a high profile, top billing.

**3** *a rocky prominence* HILLOCK, hill, hummock, mound; outcrop, crag, spur, rise; ridge, arête; peak, pinnacle; promontory, cliff, headland.

**prominent** adjective **1** *a prominent surgeon* IMPORTANT, well-known, leading, eminent, distinguished, notable, noteworthy, noted, illustrious, celebrated, famous, renowned, acclaimed, famed, influential, affluential, major-league. ANTONYMS unimportant, unknown.

**2** *prominent cheekbones* PROTUBERANT, protruding, projecting, jutting (out), standing out, sticking out, proud, bulging, bulbous.

**3** *a prominent feature of the landscape* CONSPICUOUS, noticeable, easily seen, obvious, front-and-center, unmistakable, eye-catching, pronounced, salient, striking, dominant; obtrusive. See note at NOTICEABLE. ANTONYM inconspicuous.

**promiscuity** noun *the promiscuity associated with the sixties and seventies* LICENTIOUSNESS, wantonness, immorality; *informal* sleeping around, sluttishness, whorishness; *dated* looseness. ANTONYMS chastity, virtue.

**promiscuous** adjective **1** *a promiscuous teenager* LICENTIOUS, sexually indiscriminate, wanton, immoral, fast; *informal* easy, swinging, sluttish, whorish, bed-hopping; *dated* loose, fallen. ANTONYMS chaste, virtuous.

**2** *promiscuous reading* INDISCRIMINATE, undiscriminating, unselective, random, haphazard, irresponsible, unthinking, unconsidered. ANTONYM selective.

**promise** noun **1** *you broke your promise* WORD (OF HONOR), assurance, pledge, vow, guarantee, oath, bond, undertaking, agreement, commitment, contract, covenant.

**2** *he shows promise* POTENTIAL, ability, aptitude, capability, capacity.

**3** *the promise of fine weather* INDICATION, hint, suggestion, sign.

▸ verb **1** *she promised to go* GIVE ONE'S WORD, swear, pledge, vow, undertake, guarantee, contract, engage, give an assurance, commit oneself, bind oneself, swear/take an oath, covenant; *archaic* plight.

**2** *the skies promised sunshine* INDICATE, lead one to expect, point to, denote, signify, be a sign of, be evidence of, give hope of, bespeak, presage, augur, herald, bode, portend; *literary* betoken, foretoken, forebode.

**promising** adjective **1** *a promising start* GOOD, encouraging, favorable, hopeful, full of promise, auspicious, propitious, bright, rosy, heartening, reassuring. ANTONYM unfavorable.

**2** *a promising actor* WITH POTENTIAL, budding, up-and-coming, rising, coming, in the making.

**promontory** noun *a lone beacon shone from the promontory* HEADLAND, point, cape, head, foreland, horn, bill, peninsula.

**promote** verb **1** *she's been promoted at work* UPGRADE, give promotion to, elevate, advance, move up; *humorous* kick upstairs; *archaic* prefer. ANTONYM demote.

**2** *an organization promoting justice* ENCOURAGE, advocate, further, advance, assist, aid, help, contribute to, foster, nurture, develop, boost, stimulate, forward, work for. ANTONYM obstruct.

**3** *she is promoting her new film* ADVERTISE, publicize, give publicity to, beat/bang the drum for, market, merchandise; *informal* push, plug, hype, boost, ballyhoo. ANTONYM play down.

**promotion** noun **1** *her promotion at work* UPGRADING, preferment, elevation, advancement, step up (the ladder).

**2** *the promotion of justice* ENCOURAGEMENT, advocacy, furtherance, furthering, advancement, assistance, aid, help, contribution to, fostering, boosting, stimulation, boosterism.

**3** *the promotion of her new film* ADVERTISING, publicizing, marketing; publicity, campaign, propaganda; *informal* hard sell, blitz, plug, hype, ballyhoo.

**prompt** verb **1** *curiosity prompted him to look* INDUCE, make, move, motivate, lead, dispose, persuade, incline, encourage, stimulate, prod, impel, spur on, inspire. ANTONYM discourage.

**2** *the statement prompted a hostile reaction* GIVE RISE TO, bring about, cause, occasion, result in, lead to, elicit, produce, bring on, engender, induce, precipitate, trigger, spark off, provoke. ANTONYM restrain.

**3** *the actors needed prompting* REMIND, cue, feed, help out; jog someone's memory.

▸ adjective *a prompt reply* QUICK, swift, rapid, speedy, fast, direct, immediate, instant, expeditious, early, punctual, in good time, on time, timely. ANTONYMS slow, late.

▸ noun *the actor stopped, and Julia supplied a prompt* REMINDER, cue, feed.

**promptly** adverb **1** *William arrived promptly at 7:30* PUNCTUALLY, on time; *informal* bang on, on the button, on the dot, on the nose. ANTONYM late.

**2** *I expect the matter to be dealt with promptly* WITHOUT DELAY, straightaway, right away, at once, immediately, now, as soon as possible; QUICKLY, swiftly, rapidly, speedily, fast, expeditiously, momentarily; *informal* pronto, ASAP, PDQ (pretty damn quick). ANTONYM slowly.

**promulgate** verb **1** *they promulgated their own views* MAKE KNOWN, make public, publicize, spread, communicate, propagate, disseminate, broadcast, promote, preach; *literary* bruit abroad. See note at ANNOUNCE.

**2** *the law was promulgated in 1942* PUT INTO EFFECT, enact, implement, enforce.

**prone** adjective **1** *untreated wood is prone to rotting | prone to disease* SUSCEPTIBLE, vulnerable, subject, open, liable, given, predisposed, likely, disposed, inclined, apt; at risk of. ANTONYMS resistant, immune.

**2** *his prone body* (LYING) FACE DOWN, face downward, on one's stomach/front; LYING FLAT/DOWN, horizontal, prostrate. ANTONYM upright.

**prong** noun *sharpening the prongs of the pitchfork* TINE, spike, point, tip, projection.

**pronounce** verb **1** *his name is difficult to pronounce* SAY, enunciate, articulate, utter, voice, sound, vocalize, get one's tongue around.

**2** *the doctor pronounced that I had a virus* ANNOUNCE, proclaim, declare, affirm, assert; judge, rule, decree.

**pronounced** adjective *a pronounced German accent* NOTICEABLE, marked, strong, conspicuous, striking, distinct, prominent, unmistakable, obvious, recognizable, identifiable. ANTONYM slight.

**pronouncement** noun *we awaited an official pronouncement from Washington* ANNOUNCEMENT, proclamation, declaration, assertion; judgment, ruling, decree; *formal* ordinance.

**pronunciation** noun *the pronunciation of difficult words* ACCENT, manner of speaking, speech, diction, delivery, elocution, intonation; articulation, enunciation, voicing, vocalization, sounding.

**proof** noun **1** *proof of ownership* EVIDENCE, verification, corroboration, authentication, confirmation, certification, documentation, validation, attestation, substantiation.

**2** *the proofs of a book* PAGE PROOF, galley proof, galley.

▸ adjective *no system is proof against theft* RESISTANT, immune, unaffected, invulnerable, impenetrable, impervious, repellent.

**prop** noun **1** *the roof is held up by props* POLE, post, support, upright, brace, buttress, stay, strut, stanchion, shore, pier, pillar, pile, piling, bolster, truss, column.

**2** *a prop for the economy* MAINSTAY, pillar, anchor, backbone, support, foundation, cornerstone.

▸ verb **1** *she propped her bike against the wall* LEAN, rest, stand, balance, steady.

**2** *this post is **propping** the wall **up*** HOLD UP, shore up, bolster up, buttress, support, brace, underpin.

**3** *they **prop up** failing industries* SUBSIDIZE, underwrite, fund, finance.

**propaganda** noun *a so-called documentary that was really socialist propaganda* INFORMATION, promotion, advertising, publicity, spin; disinformation, counter-information; *historical* agitprop; *informal* info, hype, plugging; puff piece; the big lie.

**propagate** verb **1** *an easy plant to propagate* BREED, grow, cultivate.

**2** *these shrubs propagate easily* REPRODUCE, multiply, proliferate, increase, spread, self-seed, self-sow.

**3** *they propagated socialist ideas* SPREAD, disseminate, communicate, make known, promulgate, circulate, broadcast, publicize, proclaim, preach, promote; *literary* bruit abroad.

**propel** verb **1** *a boat propelled by oars* MOVE, power, push, drive.

**2** *he propelled the ball into the air* THROW, thrust, toss, fling, hurl, launch, pitch, project, send, shoot.

**3** *confusion propelled her into action* SPUR, drive, prompt, precipitate, catapult, motivate, force, impel.

**propensity** noun *his propensity for giving long speeches* TENDENCY, inclination, predisposition, proneness, proclivity, readiness, liability, disposition, leaning, weakness.

**proper** adjective **1** *he's not a proper scientist* REAL, genuine, actual, true, bona fide; *informal* kosher. ANTONYM fake.

**2** *the proper channels* RIGHT, correct, accepted, orthodox, conventional, established, official, formal, regular, acceptable, appropriate, de rigueur; *archaic* meet. ANTONYMS inappropriate, wrong.

**3** *they were terribly proper* RESPECTABLE, decorous, seemly, decent, refined, ladylike, gentlemanly, genteel; formal, conventional, correct, comme il faut, orthodox, polite, punctilious. See note at FORMAL. ANTONYM unconventional.

**property** noun **1** *lost property* POSSESSIONS, belongings, things, effects, stuff, gear, chattels, movables; resources, assets, valuables, fortune, capital, riches, wealth; *Law* personalty, goods and chattels.

**2** *private property* BUILDING(S), premises, house(s), land, estates, realty, real estate.

**3** *healing properties* QUALITY, attribute, characteristic, feature, power, trait, mark, hallmark.

**prophecy** noun **1** *her prophecy is coming true* PREDICTION, forecast, prognostication, prognosis, divination, augury.

**2** *the gift of prophecy* DIVINATION, fortune telling, crystal-gazing, prediction, second sight, prognostication, augury, soothsaying.

**prophesy** verb *did those mystical sages ever prophesy anything other than calamity?* PREDICT, foretell, forecast, foresee, forewarn of, prognosticate. See note at PREDICT.

**prophet, prophetess** noun *the queen was disturbed by the prophet's interpretation of her dreams* SEER, soothsayer, fortune teller, clairvoyant, diviner; oracle, augur, sibyl. PHRASE:

**prophet of doom** *if you want to listen to these prophets of doom, you may as well cash it in today* PESSIMIST, doommonger, doomsayer, doomster, Cassandra, Jeremiah; *informal* Chicken Little.

**prophetic** adjective *his words proved prophetic—within a week he was dead* PRESCIENT, predictive, far-seeing, prognostic, divinatory, sibylline, apocalyptic; *rare* vatic.

**prophylactic** adjective *prophylactic measures* PREVENTIVE, preventative, precautionary, protective, inhibitory.

▸ noun **1** *a prophylactic against malaria* PREVENTIVE MEASURE, precaution, safeguard, safety measure; preventive medicine.

**2** *prophylactic dispensers in public washrooms.* See CONDOM.

**prophylaxis** noun *our dental insurance covers twice-yearly prophylaxis* PREVENTIVE TREATMENT, prevention, protection, precaution.

**propitiate** verb *my attempts to propitiate you are useless* APPEASE, placate, mollify, pacify, make peace with, conciliate, make amends to, soothe, calm. See note at PACIFY. ANTONYM provoke.

**propitious** adjective *the timing for such a meeting seemed propitious* FAVORABLE, auspicious, promising, providential, advantageous, optimistic, bright, rosy, heaven-sent, hopeful; opportune, timely. See note at TIMELY. ANTONYMS inauspicious, unfortunate.

**proponent** noun *a proponent of the youth basketball program* ADVOCATE, champion, supporter, backer, promoter, protagonist, campaigner, booster, cheerleader.

**proportion** noun **1** *a small proportion of the land* PART, portion, amount, quantity, bit, piece, percentage, fraction, section, segment, share.

**2** *the proportion of water to alcohol* RATIO, distribution, relative amount/number; relationship.

**3** *the drawing is out of proportion* BALANCE, symmetry, harmony, correspondence, correlation, agreement.

**4** **(proportions)** *men of huge proportions* SIZE, dimensions, magnitude, measurements; mass, volume, bulk; expanse, extent, width, breadth.

**proportional** adjective *a proportional increase in wages* CORRESPONDING, proportionate, comparable, in proportion, pro rata, commensurate, equivalent, consistent, relative, analogous. ANTONYM disproportionate.

**proposal** noun **1** *the proposal was rejected* PLAN, idea, scheme, project, program, manifesto, motion, proposition, suggestion, submission, trial balloon.

**2** *the proposal of a new constitution* PUTTING FORWARD, proposing, suggesting, submitting. ANTONYM withdrawal.

**propose** verb **1** *he proposed a solution* PUT FORWARD, suggest, submit, advance, offer, present, move, come up with, lodge, table, nominate. ANTONYM withdraw.

**2** *do you propose to go?* INTEND, mean, plan, have in mind/view, resolve, aim, purpose, think of, aspire, want. See note at INTEND.

**3** *you've proposed to her!* ASK SOMEONE TO MARRY YOU, make an offer of marriage, offer marriage; *informal* pop the question; *dated* ask for someone's hand in marriage.

**proposition** noun **1** *the analysis derives from one proposition* THEORY, hypothesis, thesis, argument, premise, principle, theorem, concept, idea, statement.

**2** *a business proposition* PROPOSAL, scheme, plan, project, idea, program, bid.

**3** *doing it for real is a very different proposition* TASK, job, undertaking, venture, activity, affair, problem.

▸ verb *he never dared proposition her* PROPOSE SEX WITH, make sexual advances to, make an indecent proposal to, make an improper suggestion to; *informal* hit on.

**propound** verb *exactly what solution are you propounding?* PUT FORWARD, advance, offer, proffer, present, set forth, submit, tender, suggest, introduce, postulate, propose, pose, posit; advocate, promote, peddle, spread.

**proprietor, proprietress** noun *the proprietor is thinking about selling this bar* OWNER, possessor, holder, master/mistress; landowner, landlord/landlady; innkeeper, hotel-keeper, hotelier, storekeeper.

**propriety** noun **1** *she behaves with the utmost propriety* DECORUM, respectability, decency, correctness, protocol, appropriateness, suitability, good manners, courtesy, politeness, rectitude, morality, civility, modesty, demureness; sobriety, refinement, discretion. ANTONYM indecorum.

**2** **(proprieties)** *he was careful to preserve the proprieties in public* ETIQUETTE, convention(s), social grace(s), niceties, one's Ps and Qs, protocol, standards, civilities, formalities, accepted behavior, good form, the done thing, the thing to do, punctilio.

**propulsion** noun *these birds use their wings for propulsion under water* THRUST, motive force, impetus, impulse, drive, driving force, actuation, push, pressure, power.

**prosaic** adjective *a prosaic lecture that had us fighting to stay awake* ORDINARY, everyday, commonplace, conventional, straightforward, routine, run-of-the-mill, by-the-numbers, workaday; UNIMAGINATIVE, uninspired, uninspiring, matter-of-fact, dull, dry, dreary, tedious, boring, humdrum, mundane, pedestrian, tame, plodding; bland, insipid, banal, trite, literal, factual, unpoetic, unemotional, unsentimental. ANTONYMS interesting, imaginative, inspired.

**proscribe** verb **1** *gambling was proscribed* FORBID, prohibit, ban, bar, interdict, make illegal, embargo, outlaw, disallow, veto; *Law* enjoin. ANTONYMS allow, permit.

**2** *the book was proscribed by the Church* CONDEMN, denounce, attack, criticize, censure, damn, reject, taboo. ANTONYMS authorize, accept.

**proscription** noun **1** *the proscription of alcohol* BANNING, forbidding, prohibition, prohibiting, barring, debarment, vetoing, interdiction, outlawing. ANTONYM allowing.

2 *a proscription was imposed* BAN, prohibition, bar, interdict, veto, embargo, moratorium. ANTONYM authorization.

3 *the proscription of his literary works* CONDEMNATION, denunciation, attacking, criticism, censuring, damning, rejection. ANTONYM acceptance.

**prosecute** verb 1 *they prosecute offenders* TAKE TO COURT, bring/institute legal proceedings against, bring an action against, take legal action against, sue, try, impeach, bring to trial, put on trial, put in the dock, bring a suit against, indict, arraign. ANTONYMS defend, let off, pardon.

2 *they helped him prosecute the war* PURSUE, fight, wage, carry on, conduct, direct, engage in, proceed with, continue (with), keep on with. ANTONYM give up.

**proselyte** noun *proselytes are not spiritually mature enough to be counseling others in church matters* CONVERT, new believer, catechumen.

**prospect** noun 1 *there is little prospect of success* LIKELIHOOD, hope, expectation, anticipation, (good/poor) chance, odds, probability, possibility, promise; fear, danger.

2 (**prospects**) *her job prospects* POSSIBILITIES, potential, promise, expectations, outlook.

3 *a daunting prospect* VISION, thought, idea; task, undertaking.

4 *Jack is an exciting prospect* CANDIDATE, possibility; *informal* catch.

5 *there is a pleasant prospect from the lounge* VIEW, vista, outlook, perspective, panorama, aspect, scene; picture, spectacle, sight.

▸ verb *they are prospecting for gold* SEARCH, look, explore, survey, scout, hunt, reconnoiter, examine, inspect.

**prospective** adjective *offering incentives to prospective buyers* POTENTIAL, possible, probable, likely, future, eventual, -to-be, soon-to-be, in the making; intending, aspiring, would-be; forthcoming, approaching, coming, imminent.

**prospectus** noun *nowhere in your prospectus do you list actual costs* BROCHURE, pamphlet, description, particulars, announcement, advertisement; syllabus, curriculum, catalog, program, list, fact sheet, scheme, schedule.

**prosper** verb *the family business continues to prosper* FLOURISH, thrive, do well, bloom, blossom, burgeon, progress, do all right for oneself, get ahead, get on (in the world), be successful; *informal* go places. ANTONYMS fail, flounder.

**prosperity** noun *she deserves all the prosperity she now enjoys* SUCCESS, profitability, affluence, wealth, opulence, luxury, the good life, milk and honey, (good) fortune, ease, plenty, comfort, security, well-being. ANTONYMS hardship, failure.

**prosperous** adjective *a prosperous shipping firm* THRIVING, flourishing, successful, strong, vigorous, profitable, lucrative, expanding, booming, burgeoning; AFFLUENT, wealthy, rich, moneyed, well off, well-to-do, opulent, substantial, in clover; *informal* on a roll, in the money. See note at WEALTHY. ANTONYMS ailing, poor.

**prostitute** noun *undercover cops posing as prostitutes* CALL GIRL, whore; *informal* HOOKER; working girl, lady of the evening, streetwalker, member of the oldest profession, tart, moll, fille de joie, escort, courtesan, hustler; ho; *dated* scarlet woman, camp follower, cocotte, strumpet, harlot, trollop, woman of ill repute, wench.

▸ verb *they prostituted their art* BETRAY, sacrifice, sell, sell out, debase, degrade, demean, devalue, cheapen, lower, shame, misuse, pervert; abandon one's principles (at the expense of).

**prostitution** noun *they claim that the casino industry only encourages prostitution in the area* THE SEX TRADE, the sex industry, whoring, streetwalking, sex tourism; *informal* the oldest profession, hooking, hustling; *dated* whoredom; *archaic* harlotry.

**prostrate** adjective 1 *the prostrate figure on the ground* PRONE, lying flat, lying down, stretched out, spread-eagled, sprawling, horizontal, recumbent; *rare* procumbent. ANTONYM upright.

2 *his wife was prostrate with shock* OVERWHELMED, overcome, overpowered, brought to one's knees, stunned, dazed; speechless, helpless.

3 *the fever left me prostrate* WORN OUT, exhausted, fatigued, tired out, sapped, dog-tired, spent, drained, debilitated, enervated, laid low; *informal* dead, dead beat, dead on one's feet, ready to drop, bushed, frazzled, worn to a frazzle, whacked, pooped. ANTONYM fresh.

▸ verb *she was prostrated by the tragedy* OVERWHELM, overcome, overpower, bring to one's knees, devastate, debilitate, weaken, enfeeble, enervate, lay low, wear out, exhaust, tire out, drain, sap, wash out, take it out of; *informal* frazzle, do in, poop.

PHRASE: **prostrate oneself** *he prostrated himself on the altar mat* THROW ONESELF FLAT/DOWN, lie down, stretch oneself out; throw oneself (at someone's feet).

**protagonist** noun 1 *the protagonist in the plot* CHIEF/CENTRAL/PRINCIPAL/MAIN/LEADING CHARACTER, chief/central/principal/main/leading participant, chief/central/principal/main/leading figure, chief/central/principal/main/leading player, principal, hero/heroine, leading man/lady, title role, lead.

2 *a protagonist of deregulation* CHAMPION, advocate, upholder, supporter, backer, promoter, proponent, exponent, campaigner, fighter, crusader; apostle, apologist, booster. ANTONYM opponent.

**protean** adjective 1 *the protean nature of mental disorders* EVER-CHANGING, variable, changeable, mutable, kaleidoscopic, inconstant, inconsistent, unstable, shifting, unsettled, fluctuating, fluid, wavering, vacillating, mercurial, volatile; *technical* labile. ANTONYMS constant, consistent.

2 *a remarkably protean composer* VERSATILE, adaptable, flex-

ible, all-around, multifaceted, multitalented, many-sided. ANTONYM limited.

**protect** verb *they fought to protect their homes and families* KEEP SAFE, keep from harm, save, safeguard, preserve, defend, shield, cushion, insulate, hedge, shelter, screen, secure, fortify, guard, watch over, look after, take care of, keep; inoculate. ANTONYMS expose, neglect, attack, harm.

**protection** noun **1** *protection against frost* DEFENSE, security, shielding, preservation, conservation, safekeeping, safeguarding, safety, sanctuary, shelter, refuge, lee, immunity, insurance, indemnity.

**2** *under the protection of the Church* SAFEKEEPING, care, charge, keeping, protectorship, guidance, aegis, auspices, umbrella, guardianship, support, patronage, championship, providence.

**3** *good protection against noise* BARRIER, buffer, shield, screen, hedge, cushion, preventative, armor, refuge, bulwark.

**protective** adjective **1** *protective clothing* PRESERVATIVE, protecting, safeguarding, shielding, defensive, safety, precautionary, preventive, preventative.

**2** *he felt protective toward the dog* SOLICITOUS, caring, warm, paternal/maternal, fatherly/motherly, gallant, chivalrous; overprotective, possessive, jealous.

**protector** noun **1** *a protector of the environment* DEFENDER, preserver, guardian, guard, champion, watchdog, ombudsman, knight in shining armor, guardian angel, patron, chaperone, escort, keeper, custodian, bodyguard, minder; *informal* hired gun.

**2** *ear protectors* GUARD, shield, buffer, cushion, pad, screen.

**protest** noun **1** *he resigned as a protest* OBJECTION, complaint, exception, disapproval, challenge, dissent, demurral, remonstration, fuss, outcry. ANTONYMS support, approval.

**2** *women staged a protest* DEMONSTRATION, (protest) march, rally; sit-in, occupation; work-to-rule, industrial action, (work) stoppage, strike, walkout, mutiny, picket, boycott.

▸ verb **1** *residents protested against the plans* EXPRESS OPPOSITION, object, dissent, take issue, make/take a stand, put up a fight, kick, take exception, complain, express disapproval, disagree, demur, remonstrate, make a fuss; cry out, speak out, rail, inveigh, fulminate; *informal* kick up a fuss/stink.

**2** *people protested outside the cathedral* DEMONSTRATE, march, hold a rally, sit in, occupy somewhere; work to rule, take industrial action, stop work, strike, go on strike, walk out, mutiny, picket; boycott something.

**3** *he protested his innocence* INSIST ON, maintain, assert, affirm, announce, proclaim, declare, profess, contend, argue, claim, vow, swear (to), stress; *formal* aver.

**protestation** noun **1** *her protestations of innocence* DECLARATION, announcement, profession, assertion, insistence, claim, affirmation, assurance, oath, vow.

**2** *we helped him despite his protestations* OBJECTION, protest, exception, complaint, disapproval, opposition, challenge, dissent, demurral, remonstration, fuss, outcry; *informal* stink.

**protester** noun *protesters gathers outside of the arena* DEMONSTRATOR, objector, opposer, opponent, complainant, complainer, dissenter, dissident, nonconformist, protest marcher; striker, picket.

**protocol** noun **1** *a stickler for protocol* ETIQUETTE, conventions, formalities, customs, rules of conduct, procedure, ritual, accepted behavior, propriety, proprieties, one's Ps and Qs, decorum, good form, the done thing, the thing to do, punctilio.

**2** *the two countries signed a protocol* AGREEMENT, treaty, entente, concordat, convention, deal, pact, contract, compact; *formal* concord.

**prototype** noun **1** *a prototype of the weapon* ORIGINAL, first example/model, master, mold, template, framework, mock-up, pattern, sample; DESIGN, guide, blueprint. See note at MODEL.

**2** *the prototype of an ideal wife* PARADIGM, typical example, archetype, exemplar, essence.

**protract** verb *the opposition will try to protract the discussion* PROLONG, lengthen, extend, draw out, drag out, spin out, stretch out, string out, elongate; carry on, continue, keep up, perpetuate. ANTONYMS curtail, shorten.

**protracted** adjective *weeks of protracted negotiations* PROLONGED, long-lasting, extended, long-drawn-out, spun out, dragged out, strung out, lengthy, long; *informal* marathon. ANTONYM short.

**protrude** verb *the emergency lever protrudes from the left side* STICK OUT, jut (out), project, extend, stand out, bulge out, poke out, thrust out, cantilever. See note at BULGE.

**protrusion** noun **1** *the neck vertebrae have short vertical protrusions* BUMP, lump, knob; protuberance, projection, prominence, swelling, eminence, outcrop, outgrowth, jut, jag, snag; ledge, shelf, ridge. See note at BUMP.

**2** *protrusion of the lips* STICKING OUT, jutting, projection, obtrusion, prominence; swelling, bulging.

**protuberance** noun **1** *a protuberance can cause drag* BUMP, lump, knob, projection, protrusion, prominence, swelling, eminence, outcrop, outgrowth, jut, jag, snag; ledge, shelf, ridge.

**2** *the protuberance of the incisors* STICKING OUT, jutting, projection, obtrusion, prominence; swelling, bulging.

**protuberant** adjective *his eyes are a little protuberant* STICKING OUT, protruding, projecting, prominent, jutting, overhanging, proud, bulging. ANTONYMS sunken, flush.

**proud** adjective **1** *the proud parents beamed* PLEASED, glad, happy, delighted, joyful, overjoyed, thrilled, satisfied, gratified, content. ANTONYM ashamed.

**2** *a proud day* PLEASING, gratifying, satisfying, cheering, heartwarming; happy, good, glorious, memorable, notable, red-letter. ANTONYM shameful.

**3** *they were poor but proud* SELF-RESPECTING, dignified, noble, worthy; independent. ANTONYM humble.

**4** *I'm not too proud to admit I'm wrong* ARROGANT, conceited, vain, self-important, full of oneself, puffed up, jumped-up, smug, complacent, disdainful, condescending, scornful, supercilious, snobbish, imperious, pompous, overbearing, bumptious, haughty; *informal* big-headed, too big for one's britches/boots, high and mighty, stuck-up, Pooterish, uppity, snooty, highfalutin; *literary* vainglorious; *rare* hubristic. ANTONYMS humble, modest.

**5** *the proud ships* MAGNIFICENT, splendid, resplendent, grand, noble, stately, imposing, dignified, striking, impressive, majestic, glorious, awe-inspiring, awesome, monumental. ANTONYM unimpressive.

**prove** verb **1** *that proves I'm right* SHOW (TO BE TRUE), demonstrate (the truth of), show beyond doubt, manifest, produce proof/evidence; witness to, give substance to, determine, substantiate, corroborate, verify, ratify, validate, authenticate, document, bear out, confirm; *formal* evince. ANTONYM disprove.

**2** *the rumor proved to be correct* TURN OUT, be found, happen. PHRASE: **prove oneself** *I was happy to have the chance to prove myself* DEMONSTRATE ONE'S ABILITIES/QUALITIES, show one's (true) mettle, show what one is made of.

**proverb** noun *Mama didn't just recite proverbs about decency and good sense, she lived by them* SAYING, adage, saw, maxim, axiom, motto, bon mot, aphorism, apophthegm, epigram, gnome, dictum, precept; words of wisdom. See note at SAYING.

**proverbial** adjective *well, the proverbial bad son has returned at last* WELL-KNOWN, famous, famed, renowned, traditional, time-honored, legendary; notorious, infamous.

**provide** verb **1** *the foundation will provide funds* SUPPLY, give, issue, furnish, come up with, dispense, bestow, impart, produce, yield, bring forth, bear, deliver, donate, contribute, pledge, advance, spare, part with, allocate, distribute, allot, put up; *informal* fork out, lay out, ante up, pony up. ANTONYMS refuse, withhold.

**2** *she was provided with enough tools* EQUIP, furnish, issue, supply, outfit; fit out, rig out, arm, provision; *informal* fix up. ANTONYM deprive.

**3** *he had to* ***provide for*** *his family* FEED, nurture, nourish; SUPPORT, maintain, keep, sustain, provide sustenance for, fend for, finance, endow. ANTONYM neglect.

**4** *the test may provide the answer* MAKE AVAILABLE, present, offer, afford, give, add, bring, yield, impart.

**5** *we have provided for further restructuring* PREPARE, allow, make provision, be prepared, arrange, get ready, plan, cater.

**6** *the banks have to provide against bad debts* TAKE PRECAUTIONS, take steps/measures, guard, forearm oneself.

**7** *the legislation provides that factories must be kept clean* STIPULATE, lay down, make it a condition, require, order, ordain, demand, prescribe, state, specify.

**providence** noun **1** *a life mapped out by providence* FATE, destiny, nemesis, kismet, God's will, divine intervention, predestination, predetermination, the stars; one's lot (in life); *archaic* one's portion.

**2** *he had a streak of providence* PRUDENCE, foresight, forethought, farsightedness, judiciousness, shrewdness, circumspection, wisdom, sagacity, common sense; careful budgeting, thrift, economy.

**provident** adjective *Kaye was provident enough to be able to buy her first home at age 24* PRUDENT, farsighted, judicious, shrewd, circumspect, forearmed, wise, sagacious, sensible; thrifty, economical. See note at ECONOMICAL. ANTONYM improvident.

**province** noun **1** *Canada's westernmost province* TERRITORY, region, state, department, canton, area, district, sector, zone, division.

**2** *that's outside my province* RESPONSIBILITY, area of activity, area of interest, knowledge, department, sphere, world, realm, field, domain, territory, orbit, preserve; business, affair, concern; specialty, forte; jurisdiction, authority; *informal* bailiwick, turf.

**provincial** adjective **1** *the provincial government* REGIONAL, state, territorial, district; sectoral, zonal, cantonal. ANTONYM national.

**2** *provincial areas* NONMETROPOLITAN, small-town, nonurban, outlying, rural, country, rustic, backwoods, backwater; *informal* one-horse, hick, jerkwater, freshwater. ANTONYMS national, metropolitan, cosmopolitan.

**3** *provincial attitudes* UNSOPHISTICATED, narrow-minded, parochial, small-town, suburban, insular, bush-league, inward-looking, conservative; small-minded, blinkered, bigoted, prejudiced; *informal* jerkwater, corn-fed. See note at BIAS. ANTONYMS sophisticated, broad-minded.

▸ noun *they were dismissed as provincials* HILLBILLY, (country) bumpkin, country cousin, rustic, yokel, village idiot, peasant, hayseed, hick, rube, redneck. ANTONYM sophisticate.

**provision** noun **1** *the provision of weapons to guerrillas* SUPPLYING, supply, providing, giving, presentation, donation; equipping, furnishing.

**2** *there has been limited provision for gifted children* FACILITIES, services, amenities, resource(s), arrangements; means, funds, benefits, assistance, allowance(s).

**3** **(provisions)** *provisions for the trip* SUPPLIES, food and drink, stores, groceries, foodstuff(s), provender, rations; *informal* grub, vittles, eats, nosh; *formal* comestibles; *literary* viands; *dated* victuals.

**4** *he made no provision for the future* PREPARATIONS, plans, arrangements, prearrangement, precautions, contingency.

**5** *the provisions of the law* TERM, clause; requirement, specification, stipulation; proviso, condition, qualification, restriction, limitation.

**provisional** adjective *a provisional government* INTERIM, temporary, pro tem; transitional, changeover, stopgap, short-term, fill-in, acting, caretaker, subject to confirmation; penciled in, working, tentative, contingent. ANTONYMS permanent, definite.

**proviso** noun *he could use the company car, with the proviso that he would pay for routine maintenance* CONDITION, stipulation, provision, clause, rider, qualification, restriction, caveat.

**provocation** noun **1** *he remained calm despite severe provocation* GOADING, prodding, egging on, incitement, pressure; ANNOYANCE, irritation, nettling; harassment, plaguing, molestation; teasing, taunting, torment; affront, insults; *informal* hassle, aggravation.

**2** *without provocation, Bill punched Mr. Cartwright* JUSTIFICATION, excuse, pretext, occasion, call, motivation, motive, cause, grounds, reason, need; *formal* casus belli.

**provocative** adjective **1** *provocative remarks* ANNOYING, irritating, exasperating, infuriating, maddening, vexing, galling; insulting, offensive, inflammatory, incendiary, controversial; *informal* aggravating, in-your-face. ANTONYMS soothing, calming.

**2** *a provocative pose* SEXY, sexually arousing, sexually exciting, alluring, seductive, suggestive, inviting, tantalizing, titillating; indecent, pornographic, indelicate, immodest, shameless; erotic, sensuous, slinky, coquettish, amorous, flirtatious; *informal* tarty, come-hither. ANTONYMS modest, decorous.

**provoke** verb **1** *the plan has provoked outrage* AROUSE, produce, evoke, cause, give rise to, occasion, call forth, elicit, induce, excite, spark off, touch off, kindle, generate, engender, instigate, result in, lead to, bring on, precipitate, prompt, trigger; *literary* beget. ANTONYM allay.

**2** *she was provoked into replying* GOAD, spur, prick, sting, prod, egg on, incite, rouse, stir, move, stimulate, motivate, excite, inflame, work/fire up, impel. See note at INCITE. ANTONYM deter.

**3** *he wouldn't be provoked* ANNOY, anger, incense, enrage, irritate, infuriate, exasperate, madden, nettle, get/take a rise out of, ruffle, ruffle someone's feathers, make someone's hackles rise; harass, harry, plague, molest; tease, taunt, torment; rub the wrong way; *informal* peeve, aggravate, hassle, miff, needle, rankle, ride, rile, get, bug, make someone's blood boil, get under someone's skin, get in someone's hair, get/put someone's back up, get someone's goat, wind up. ANTONYMS pacify, appease.

**prow** noun *the prow of the skiff* BOW(S), stem, front, nose, head, cutwater.

**prowess** noun **1** *his prowess as a winemaker* SKILL, expertise, mastery, facility, ability, capability, capacity, savoir faire, talent, genius, adeptness, aptitude, dexterity, deftness, competence, accomplishment, proficiency, finesse; *informal* know-how. ANTONYMS inability, ineptitude.

**2** *the knight's prowess in battle* COURAGE, bravery, gallantry, valor, heroism, intrepidity, nerve, pluck, pluckiness, feistiness, boldness, daring, audacity, fearlessness; *informal* guts, spunk, moxie, grit, sand. ANTONYM cowardice.

**prowl** verb *they were seen prowling around the docks late at night* MOVE STEALTHILY, slink, skulk, steal, nose, pussyfoot, sneak, stalk, creep; *informal* snoop.

**proximity** noun *the proximity to her parents' home was a consideration* CLOSENESS, nearness, propinquity; accessibility, handiness; *archaic* vicinity.

**proxy** noun *I am here to vote as Mrs. Carlson's proxy* DEPUTY, representative, substitute, delegate, agent, surrogate, stand-in, attorney, go-between.

**prude** noun *I never knew a boy to be such a prude* PURITAN, prig, killjoy, moralist, pietist; *informal* goody-goody.

**prudence** noun **1** *you have gone beyond the bounds of prudence* WISDOM, judgment, good judgment, common sense, sense, sagacity, shrewdness, advisability. ANTONYMS folly, recklessness.

**2** *financial prudence* CAUTION, care, providence, farsightedness, foresight, forethought, shrewdness, circumspection; thrift, economy. ANTONYM extravagance.

**prudent** adjective **1** *it is prudent to obtain consent* WISE, well judged, sensible, politic, judicious, sagacious, sage, shrewd, advisable, well-advised. ANTONYM unwise.

**2** *a prudent approach to borrowing* CAUTIOUS, careful, provident, farsighted, judicious, shrewd, circumspect; thrifty, economical. See note at ECONOMICAL. ANTONYM reckless.

**prudish** adjective *it's unusual to find someone so young and yet so prudish* PURITANICAL, priggish, prim, prim and proper, moralistic, pietistic, sententious, censorious, strait-laced, Victorian, old-maidish, governessy, fussy, stuffy, strict; *informal* goody-goody, starchy. ANTONYM permissive.

**prune** verb **1** *I pruned the roses* CUT BACK, trim, thin, pinch back, clip, shear, top, dock.

**2** *prune lateral shoots of wisteria* CUT OFF, lop (off), chop off, clip, snip (off), nip off, dock.

**3** *staff numbers have been pruned* REDUCE, cut (back/down), pare (down), slim down, make reductions in, make cutbacks in, trim, decrease, diminish, downsize, ax, shrink; *informal* slash. ANTONYM increase.

**prurient** adjective *she was completely turned off by his prurient remarks* SALACIOUS, licentious, voyeuristic, lascivious, lecherous, lustful, lewd, libidinous, lubricious; *formal* concupiscent.

**pry** verb *I'm not one to pry, but the goings-on at that house are very suspicious* INQUIRE IMPERTINENTLY, be inquisitive, be curious, poke around/about, ferret (about/around), spy, be a busybody; eavesdrop, listen in, tap someone's phone, intrude; *informal* stick/poke one's nose in/into, be nosy, nose, snoop. ANTONYM mind one's own business.

**psalm** noun *one of the psalms attributed to King David* SACRED SONG, religious song, hymn, song of praise; **(psalms)** psalmody, psalter.

**pseudo** adjective *her 'diamonds' are so pseudo* BOGUS, sham, phony, artificial, mock, ersatz, quasi-, fake, false, spurious, deceptive, misleading, assumed, contrived, affected, insincere; *informal* pretend, put-on. ANTONYM genuine.

**pseudonym** noun *Geisel was best known by the pseudonym 'Dr. Seuss'* PEN NAME, nom de plume, assumed name, false name, alias, professional name, sobriquet, stage name, nom de guerre.

**psych** *informal* PHRASES: **psych someone out** *she's trying to psych me out with that demonic stare of hers* INTIMIDATE, daunt, browbeat, bully, cow, tyrannize, scare, terrorize, frighten, dishearten, unnerve, subdue; *informal* bulldoze.
**psych oneself up** *I've really psyched myself up for the marathon* NERVE ONESELF, steel oneself, brace oneself, summon one's courage, prepare oneself, gear oneself up, urge oneself on, gird (up) one's loins.

**psyche** noun *getting in touch with your own psyche* SOUL, spirit, (inner) self, ego, true being, inner man/woman, persona, subconscious, mind, intellect; *technical* anima. ANTONYM body.

**psychiatrist** noun *he's been seeing a psychiatrist for several years* PSYCHOTHERAPIST, psychoanalyst; *informal* shrink, head doctor.

**psychic** adjective **1** *psychic powers* SUPERNATURAL, paranormal, otherworldly, supernormal, preternatural, metaphysical, extrasensory, magic, magical, mystical, mystic, occult.

**2** *I'm not psychic* CLAIRVOYANT, telepathic, having second sight, having a sixth sense.

**3** *psychic development* EMOTIONAL, spiritual, inner; cognitive, psychological, intellectual, mental, psychiatric, psychogenic. ANTONYM physical.

▸ noun *she is a psychic* CLAIRVOYANT, fortune teller, crystal-gazer; medium, channeler, spiritualist; telepath, mind-reader, palmist, palm-reader.

**psychological** adjective **1** *his psychological state* MENTAL, emotional, intellectual, inner, cerebral, brain, rational, cognitive.

**2** *her pain was psychological* (ALL) IN THE MIND, psychosomatic, emotional, irrational, subjective, subconscious, unconscious. ANTONYM physical.

**psychology** noun **1** *a degree in psychology* STUDY OF THE MIND, science of the mind.

**2** *the psychology of the motorist* MINDSET, mind, mental processes, thought processes, way of thinking, cast of mind, mentality, persona, psyche, (mental) attitude(s), makeup, character; *informal* what makes someone tick.

**psychopathic** adjective. See MAD sense 1.

**psychosomatic** adjective *psychosomatic illnesses can produce very real physical symptoms* (ALL) IN THE MIND, psychological, irrational, stress-related, stress-induced, subjective, subconscious, unconscious.

**pub** noun. See BAR sense 4.

**puberty** noun *parents often forget how difficult going through puberty can be* ADOLESCENCE, pubescence, sexual maturity, growing up; youth, young adulthood, the/one's teenage years, the/one's teens, the awkward age; *formal* juvenescence.

**public** adjective **1** *public affairs* state, national, federal, government; constitutional, civic, civil, official, social, municipal, community, communal, local; nationalized. ANTONYM private.

**2** *by public demand* POPULAR, general, common, communal, collective, shared, joint, universal, widespread.

**3** *a public figure* PROMINENT, well-known, important, leading, eminent, distinguished, notable, noteworthy, noted, celebrated, household, famous, famed, influential, major-league. ANTONYMS obscure, unknown.

**4** *public places* OPEN (TO THE PUBLIC), communal, accessible to all, available, free, unrestricted, community. ANTONYM restricted.

**5** *the news became public* KNOWN, published, publicized, in circulation, exposed, overt, plain, obvious. ANTONYMS unknown, secret.

▸ noun **1** *the American public* PEOPLE, citizens, subjects, general public, electors, electorate, voters, taxpayers, residents, inhabitants, citizenry, population, populace, community, society, country, nation, world; everyone.

**2** *his adoring public* AUDIENCE, spectators, followers, following, fans, devotees, aficionados, admirers; patrons, clientele, market, consumers, buyers, customers, readers, viewers, listeners.

PHRASE: **in public** *she didn't like it when he would kiss her in public* PUBLICLY, in full view of people, openly, in the open, for all to see, undisguisedly, blatantly, flagrantly, brazenly, overtly.

**publication** noun **1** *the author of this publication* BOOK, volume, title, work, tome, opus; newspaper, paper, magazine, periodical, newsletter, bulletin, journal, report; organ, booklet, chapbook, brochure, catalog; daily, weekly, monthly, quarterly, annual; *informal* rag, mag, 'zine.

**2** *the publication of her new book* ISSUING, announcement, publishing, printing, notification, reporting, declaration, communication, proclamation, broadcasting, publicizing, advertising, distribution, spreading, dissemination, promulgation, issuance, appearance.

**publicity** noun **1** *the blaze of publicity* PUBLIC ATTENTION, public interest, public notice, media attention/interest, face time, exposure, glare, limelight.

**2** *all this publicity should boost sales* PROMOTION, advertising, propaganda; boost, push; *informal* hype, ballyhoo, puffery, buildup, razzmatazz; plug.

**publicize** verb **1** *I never publicize the fact* MAKE KNOWN, make public, publish, announce, report, post, communicate, broadcast, issue, put out, distribute, spread, promulgate, disseminate, circulate, air; disclose, reveal, divulge, leak. See note at ANNOUNCE. ANTONYM conceal.

**2** *she just wants to publicize her book* ADVERTISE, promote, build up, talk up, push, beat the drum for, boost; *informal* hype, plug, puff (up). ANTONYM suppress.

**publish** verb 1 *we publish novels* ISSUE, bring out, produce, print.

2 *he ought to publish his views* MAKE KNOWN, make public, publicize, announce, report, post, communicate, broadcast, issue, put out, distribute, spread, promulgate, disseminate, circulate, air; disclose, reveal, divulge, leak.

**pucker** verb *she puckered her forehead* WRINKLE, crinkle, crease, furrow, crumple, rumple, ruck up, scrunch up, corrugate, ruffle, screw up, shrivel.

▸ noun *a pucker in the sewing* WRINKLE, crinkle, crumple, corrugation, furrow, line, fold.

**puckish** adjective *he gave her a puckish grin* MISCHIEVOUS, naughty, impish, roguish, playful, arch, prankish; *informal* waggish.

**puddle** noun *puppies and kids are drawn to puddles the way moths are drawn to light* POOL, spill, splash; *literary* plash.

**pudgy** adjective *informal the toddler's pudgy little hands* CHUBBY, plump, fat, stout, rotund, well-padded, ample, round, chunky, portly, overweight, fleshy, paunchy, bulky, corpulent; *informal* tubby, roly-poly, beefy, porky, blubbery, zaftig, corn-fed. ANTONYM thin.

**puerile** adjective *you're too old for these puerile outbursts* CHILDISH, immature, infantile, juvenile, babyish; silly, inane, fatuous, jejune, asinine, foolish, petty. See note at YOUTHFUL. ANTONYMS mature, sensible.

**puff** noun 1 *a puff of wind* GUST, blast, flurry, rush, draft, waft, breeze, breath.

2 *he took a puff at his cigar informal* DRAG, toke.

▸ verb 1 *she walked fast, puffing a little* BREATHE HEAVILY, pant, blow; gasp, fight for breath.

2 *she **puffed on** a cigarette* SMOKE, draw on, suck at/on.

PHRASE: **puff up** *the site of the incision may puff up slightly* BULGE, swell (up), stick out, distend, tumefy, balloon (up/out), expand, inflate, enlarge.

**puffy** adjective *the doctor said his eyes were puffy because of allergies* SWOLLEN, puffed up, distended, enlarged, inflated, dilated, bloated, engorged, bulging, tumid, tumescent.

**pugilist** noun *dated in his neighborhood, guys pretty much had two career choices: drug dealer or pugilist* BOXER, fighter, prizefighter; *informal* bruiser, pug.

**pugnacious** adjective *this looks like the kind of dive that appeals to pugnacious patrons* COMBATIVE, aggressive, antagonistic, belligerent, bellicose, warlike, quarrelsome, argumentative, contentious, disputatious, hostile, threatening, truculent; fiery, hot-tempered. ANTONYM peaceable.

**pull** verb 1 *he pulled the box toward him* TUG, haul, drag, draw, tow, heave, lug, jerk, wrench; *informal* yank. ANTONYM push.

2 *he pulled the bad tooth out* EXTRACT, take out, remove.

3 *she pulled a muscle* STRAIN, sprain, wrench, turn, tear; damage.

4 *race day pulled big crowds* ATTRACT, draw, bring in, pull in, lure, seduce, entice, tempt, beckon, interest, fascinate. ANTONYM repel.

▸ noun 1 *give the chain a pull* TUG, jerk, heave; *informal* yank.

2 *she felt the pull of the sea* ATTRACTION, draw, lure, allurement, enticement, magnetism, temptation, fascination, appeal.

3 *he has a lot of pull in finance* INFLUENCE, sway, power, authority, say, prestige, standing, weight, leverage, muscle, teeth, clout.

PHRASES: **pull apart** *they pulled apart the suitcase looking for hidden drugs* DISMANTLE, disassemble, take/pull to pieces, take/pull to bits, take apart, strip down; demolish, destroy, break up.

**pull back** *the troops were ordered to pull back* WITHDRAW, retreat, fall back, back off; pull out, retire, disengage; flee, turn tail.

**pull in** *pull in here, next to the Camaro* STOP, halt, come to a halt, pull over, pull up, draw up, brake, park.

**pull someone's leg** *are we really getting a snowstorm, or are you pulling my leg?* TEASE, fool, play a trick on, rag, pull the wool over someone's eyes; *informal* kid, rib, take for a ride, have on.

**pull off** *they pulled off a daring crime* ACHIEVE, fulfill, succeed in, accomplish, bring off, carry off, perform, discharge, complete, clinch, fix, effect, engineer.

**pull out** *our forces have begun to pull out* WITHDRAW, resign, leave, retire, step down, bow out, back out, give up; *informal* quit.

**pull through** *we're all praying that Steve will pull through* GET BETTER, get well again, improve, recover, rally, come through, recuperate.

**pull oneself together** *it's just a movie, pull yourself together* REGAIN ONE'S COMPOSURE, recover, get a grip on oneself, get over it; *informal* snap out of it, get one's act together, buck up.

**pulp** noun 1 *he kneaded it into a pulp* MUSH, mash, paste, purée, pomace, pap, slop, slush, mulch; *informal* gloop, goo, glop.

2 *the sweet pulp on cocoa seeds* FLESH, marrow, meat.

▸ verb *pulp the blueberries* MASH, purée, cream, crush, press, liquidize, liquefy, sieve, squash, pound, macerate, grind, mince.

▸ adjective *pulp fiction* TRASHY, cheap, sensational, lurid, tasteless; *informal* tacky, rubbishy.

**pulsate** verb *the alien pods continued to pulsate, as if at any moment writhing creatures would emerge* PALPITATE, pulse, throb, pump, undulate, surge, heave, rise and fall; beat, thump, drum, thrum; flutter, quiver.

**pulse**[1] noun 1 *the pulse in her neck* HEARTBEAT, pulsation, pulsing, throbbing, pounding.

2 *the pulse of the train wheels* RHYTHM, beat, tempo, cadence, pounding, thudding, drumming.

3 *pulses of ultrasound* BURST, blast, spurt, impulse, surge.

▸ verb *music pulsed through the building* THROB, pulsate, vibrate, beat, pound, thud, thump, drum, thrum, reverberate, echo.

**pulse**2 noun *eat plenty of pulses* LEGUME, pea, bean, lentil.

**pulverize** verb 1 *the seeds are pulverized into flour* GRIND, crush, pound, powder, mill, crunch, squash, press, pulp, mash, sieve, mince, macerate; *technical* comminute.

2 *informal he pulverized the opposition.* See TROUNCE.

**pump** verb 1 *I pumped air out of the tube* FORCE, drive, push; suck, draw, tap, siphon, withdraw, expel, extract, bleed, drain.

2 *she* ***pumped up*** *the tire* INFLATE, aerate, blow up, fill up; swell, enlarge, distend, expand, dilate, puff up.

3 *blood was pumping from his leg* SPURT, spout, squirt, jet, surge, spew, gush, stream, flow, pour, spill, well, cascade, run, course.

4 *informal I pumped them for information* INTERROGATE, cross-examine, ask, question, quiz, probe, sound out, catechize, give someone the third degree; *informal* grill.

**pun** noun *"you can make your own antifreeze by stealing her blanket" is a pun guaranteed to get some groans* PLAY ON WORDS, wordplay, double entendre, innuendo, witticism, quip, bon mot.

**punch**1 verb *Diana punched him in the face* HIT, strike, thump, jab, smash, welt, cuff, clip; batter, buffet, pound, pummel; *informal* sock, slug, bop, wallop, clobber, bash, whack, thwack, clout, whomp, cold-cock; *literary* smite.

▸ noun 1 *a punch on the nose* BLOW, hit, knock, thump, box, jab, clip, uppercut, hook; *informal* sock, slug, bop, wallop, bash, whack, clout, belt, knuckle sandwich; *dated* buffet.

2 *the soundtrack is full of punch* VIGOR, liveliness, vitality, drive, strength, zest, verve, enthusiasm; impact, bite, kick; *informal* oomph, zing, pep.

**punch**2 verb *he punched her ticket* MAKE A HOLE IN, perforate, puncture, pierce, prick, hole, spike, skewer; *literary* transpierce.

**punctilio** noun 1 *a stickler for punctilio* CONFORMITY, conscientiousness, punctiliousness; etiquette, protocol, conventions, formalities, propriety, decorum, manners, politesse, good form, the done thing. ANTONYM informality.

2 *the punctilios of court procedure* NICETY, detail, fine point, subtlety, nuance, refinement.

**punctilious** adjective *his punctilious implementation of orders* METICULOUS, conscientious, diligent, scrupulous, careful, painstaking, rigorous, perfectionist, methodical, particular, strict; fussy, fastidious, finicky, pedantic; *informal* nitpicking, persnickety. See note at FORMAL. ANTONYM careless.

**punctual** adjective *she liked her guests to be punctual* ON TIME, prompt, on schedule, in (good) time; *informal* on the dot. ANTONYM late.

**punctuate** verb 1 *how to punctuate direct speech* ADD PUNCTUATION TO, put punctuation marks in.

2 *slides were used to punctuate the talk* BREAK UP, interrupt, intersperse, pepper.

**puncture** noun 1 *the tire developed a puncture* HOLE, perforation, rupture; cut, slit; leak.

2 *my car has a puncture* FLAT TIRE; *informal* flat.

▸ verb 1 *he punctured the child's balloon* MAKE A HOLE IN, pierce, rupture, perforate, stab, cut, slit, prick, spike, stick, lance; deflate.

2 *she knows how to puncture his speeches* PUT AN END TO, cut short, deflate, reduce.

**pundit** noun *an economics pundit* EXPERT, authority, specialist, doyen(ne), master, guru, sage, savant, maven; *informal* buff, whiz.

**pungent** adjective 1 *a pungent marinade* STRONG, powerful, pervasive, penetrating; sharp, acid, sour, biting, bitter, tart, vinegary, tangy; highly flavored, aromatic, spicy, piquant, peppery, hot. ANTONYMS bland, mild.

2 *pungent remarks* CAUSTIC, biting, trenchant, cutting, acerbic, sardonic, sarcastic, scathing, acrimonious, barbed, sharp, tart, incisive, bitter, venomous, waspish. ANTONYMS bland, mild.

**punish** verb 1 *they punished their children* DISCIPLINE, teach someone a lesson; tan someone's hide; *informal* wallop, come down on (like a ton of bricks).

2 *higher charges would punish the poor* PENALIZE, unfairly disadvantage, handicap, hurt, wrong, ill-use, maltreat.

**punishing** adjective *a punishing schedule* ARDUOUS, demanding, taxing, onerous, burdensome, strenuous, rigorous, stressful, trying; hard, difficult, tough, exhausting, tiring, grueling, crippling, relentless; *informal* killing. ANTONYM easy.

**punishment** noun 1 *the punishment of the guilty* PENALIZING, punishing, disciplining; retribution; *dated* chastisement.

2 *the teacher imposed punishments* PENALTY, penance, sanction, sentence, one's just deserts; discipline, correction, vengeance, justice, judgment; *informal* comeuppance.

3 *both boxers took punishment* A BATTERING, a thrashing, a beating, a drubbing.

4 *the ovens take continual punishment* MALTREATMENT, mistreatment, abuse, ill-use, manhandling; damage, harm.

**punitive** adjective 1 *punitive measures* PENAL, disciplinary, corrective, correctional, retributive.

2 *punitive taxes* HARSH, severe, stiff, stringent, burdensome, demanding, crushing, crippling; high, sky-high, inflated, exorbitant, extortionate, excessive, inordinate, unreasonable.

**puny** adjective 1 *he had been a puny kid* UNDERSIZED, undernourished, underfed, stunted, slight, small, little; weak, feeble, sickly, delicate, frail, fragile; informal weedy, pint-sized. ANTONYM sturdy.

2 *puny efforts to save their homes* PITIFUL, pitiable, inadequate, insufficient, derisory, miserable, sorry, meager, paltry, trifling, inconsequential; informal pathetic, measly, piddling; formal exiguous. ANTONYM substantial.

**pupil** noun 1 *former pupils of the school* STUDENT, scholar; schoolchild, schoolboy, schoolgirl.

2 *the guru's pupils* DISCIPLE, follower, student, protégé, apprentice, trainee, novice.

**puppet** noun 1 *a show with puppets* MARIONETTE; hand puppet, finger puppet.

2 *a puppet of the government* PAWN, tool, instrument, cat's paw, creature, dupe; mouthpiece, minion, stooge.

**purchase** verb *we purchased the software* BUY, pay for, acquire, obtain, pick up, snap up, take, procure; invest in; informal get hold of, score. ANTONYM sell.

▸ noun 1 *he's happy with his purchase* ACQUISITION, buy, investment, order, bargain; shopping, goods. ANTONYM sale.

2 *he could get no purchase on the wall* GRIP, grasp, hold, foothold, toehold, anchorage, attachment, support; resistance, friction, leverage.

**pure** adjective 1 *pure gold* UNADULTERATED, uncontaminated, unmixed, undiluted, unalloyed, unblended; sterling, solid, refined, one hundred percent; clarified, clear, filtered; flawless, perfect, genuine, real. ANTONYM adulterated.

2 *the air is so pure* CLEAN, clear, fresh, sparkling, unpolluted, uncontaminated, untainted; wholesome, natural, healthy; sanitary, uninfected, disinfected, germ-free, sterile, sterilized, aseptic. ANTONYMS dirty, polluted.

3 *pure in body and mind* VIRTUOUS, moral, ethical, good, righteous, saintly, honorable, reputable, wholesome, clean, honest, upright, upstanding, exemplary, irreproachable; chaste, virginal, maidenly; decent, worthy, noble, blameless, guiltless, spotless, unsullied, uncorrupted, undefiled; informal squeaky clean. ANTONYM immoral.

4 *pure math* THEORETICAL, abstract, conceptual, academic, hypothetical, speculative, conjectural. ANTONYM practical.

5 *three hours of pure magic* SHEER, utter, absolute, out-and-out, complete, total, perfect, unmitigated.

**purely** adverb *the mission of this weekend is purely recreational* ENTIRELY, completely, absolutely, wholly, exclusively, solely, only, just, merely.

**purge** verb 1 *he purged them of their doubt* CLEANSE, clear, purify, wash, shrive, absolve.

2 *lawbreakers were purged from the army* REMOVE, get rid of, expel, eject, exclude, dismiss, sack, oust, eradicate, clear out, weed out.

▸ noun *the purge of dissidents* REMOVAL, expulsion, ejection, exclusion, eviction, dismissal, sacking, ousting, eradication.

**purify** verb 1 *trees help to purify the air* CLEAN, cleanse, refine, decontaminate; filter, clarify, clear, freshen, deodorize; sanitize, disinfect, sterilize.

2 *they purify themselves before the ceremony* PURGE, cleanse, unburden, deliver; redeem, shrive, exorcise, sanctify.

**purist** noun *the quilting purist doesn't want to hear the words "sewing machine"* PEDANT, perfectionist, formalist, literalist, stickler, traditionalist, doctrinaire, quibbler, dogmatist; informal nitpicker.

**puritanical** adjective *by modern standards, his parents are considered puritanical* MORALISTIC, puritan, pietistic, strait-laced, stuffy, prudish, prim, priggish; narrow-minded, sententious, censorious; austere, severe, ascetic, abstemious; informal goody-goody, starchy. ANTONYM permissive.

**purity** noun 1 *the purity of our tap water* CLEANNESS, clearness, clarity, freshness; sterility, healthiness, safety.

2 *they sought purity in a foul world* VIRTUE, morality, goodness, righteousness, saintliness, piety, honor, honesty, integrity, decency, ethicality, impeccability; innocence, chastity.

**purport** verb *this work* ***purports to be*** *authoritative* CLAIM TO BE, profess to be, pretend to be; appear to be, seem to be; be ostensibly, pose as, impersonate, masquerade as, pass for.

▸ noun 1 *the purport of his remarks* GIST, substance, drift, implication, intention, meaning, significance, sense, essence, thrust, message.

2 *the purport of the attack* INTENTION, purpose, object, objective, aim, goal, target, end, design, idea.

**purpose** noun 1 *the purpose of his visit* MOTIVE, motivation, grounds, cause, occasion, reason, point, basis, justification.

2 *their purpose was to subvert the economy* INTENTION, aim, object, objective, goal, end, plan, scheme, target; ambition, aspiration.

3 *I cannot see any purpose in it* ADVANTAGE, benefit, good, use, value, merit, worth, profit; informal mileage, percentage.

4 *the original purpose of the porch* FUNCTION, role, use.

5 *they started the game with purpose* DETERMINATION, resolution, resolve, steadfastness, backbone, drive, push, enthusiasm, ambition, motivation, commitment, conviction, dedication; informal get-up-and-go.

▸ verb formal *they purposed to reach the summit* INTEND, mean, aim, plan, design, have the intention; decide, resolve, determine, propose, aspire. See note at INTEND.

PHRASE: **on purpose** *we'd like to believe that she didn't start the fire on purpose* DELIBERATELY, intentionally, purposely, by design, willfully, knowingly, consciously, of one's own volition; expressly, specifically, especially, specially.

**purposeful** adjective *she'll need a more purposeful attitude if she wants to succeed in college* DETERMINED, resolute, steadfast, single-minded; enthusiastic, motivated, committed, dedicated, persistent, dogged, tenacious, unfaltering, unshakable. ANTONYM aimless.

**purposely** adverb. See ON PURPOSE at PURPOSE.

**purse** noun 1 *a woman's purse.* See HANDBAG.

fused, bewildered, bemused, baffled, mystified, confounded, nonplussed, at a loss, at sea; *informal* flummoxed, stumped, fazed, clueless, discombobulated.

**puzzling** adjective *his explanation was rather puzzling* BAFFLING, perplexing, bewildering, confusing, complicated, unclear, mysterious, enigmatic, ambiguous, obscure, abstruse, unfathomable, incomprehensible, impenetrable, cryptic. ANTONYM clear.

**pygmy** noun **1** *a Congo pygmy* DWARF, midget, very small person, homunculus, manikin; Lilliputian; *informal* shrimp.

**2** *an intellectual pygmy* LIGHTWEIGHT, mediocrity, nonentity, nobody, no-name, cipher; small fry; *informal* pipsqueak, no-hoper, picayune. ANTONYM giant.

**pyromaniac** noun *the fire marshal has suggested it may be the work of a pyromaniac* ARSONIST, incendiary; *informal* firebug, pyro, torch.

**quack** noun *a quack selling fake medicines* SWINDLER, charlatan, mountebank, trickster, fraud, fraudster, impostor, hoaxer; *informal* con man, snake oil salesman, shark, grifter.

THE RIGHT WORD **quack, charlatan, dissembler, fake, impostor, mountebank**

There are many different ways to describe a **fake**, a colloquial term for anyone who knowingly practices deception or misrepresentation. Someone who sells a special tonic that claims to do everything from curing the common cold to making hair grow on a bald man's head is called a **quack**, a term that refers to any fraudulent practitioner of medicine or law. **Mountebank** sometimes carries implications of quackery, but more often it refers to a self-promoting person who resorts to cheap tricks or undignified efforts to win attention (*political mountebanks*). A **charlatan** is usually a writer, speaker, preacher, professor, or some other "expert" who tries to conceal his or her lack of skill or knowledge by resorting to pretentious displays (*supposedly a leading authority in his field, he turned out to be nothing but a charlatan*). An individual who tries to pass himself or herself off as someone else is an **impostor** (*an impostor who bore a close physical resemblance to the king*), although this term can also refer to anyone who assumes a title or profession that is not his or her own. Although all of these deceivers are out to fool people, it is the **dissembler** who is primarily interested in concealing his or her true motives or evil purpose (*he is a dissembler who weaves a tangled web of lies*).

**quaff** verb *they quaffed a few beers before heading home* DRINK, swallow, gulp (down), guzzle, slurp, down, empty; imbibe, partake of, consume; *informal* kill, swig, swill, slug, knock back, toss off, chug, chugalug, scarf (down).

**quagmire** noun **1** *the field became a quagmire* SWAMP, morass, bog, marsh, muskeg, mire, slough; *archaic* quag.

**2** *a judicial quagmire* MUDDLE, mix-up, mess, predicament, mare's nest, can of worms, quandary, tangle, imbroglio; trouble, confusion, difficulty; *informal* sticky situation, pickle, stew, dilemma, fix, bind.

**quail** verb *the sound of gunfire made us quail* COWER, cringe, flinch, shrink, recoil, shy (away), pull back; shiver, tremble, shake, quake, blench.

**quaint** adjective **1** *a quaint town* PICTURESQUE, charming, sweet, attractive, old-fashioned, old-world, cunning; *pseudoarchaic* olde, olde worlde. ANTONYMS ugly, modern.

**2** *quaint customs* UNUSUAL, different, out of the ordinary, curious, eccentric, quirky, bizarre, whimsical, unconventional; *informal* offbeat. ANTONYMS normal, ordinary.

**quake** verb **1** *the ground quaked* SHAKE, tremble, quiver, shudder, sway, rock, wobble, move, heave, convulse. See note at SHAKE.

**2** *we quaked when we saw the soldiers* TREMBLE, shake, quiver, shiver; blench, flinch, shrink, recoil, cower, cringe.

**qualification** noun **1** *a teaching qualification* CERTIFICATE, diploma, degree, license, document, warrant; eligibility, acceptability, adequacy; proficiency, skill, ability, capability, aptitude.

**2** *I can't accept it without qualification* MODIFICATION, limitation, reservation, stipulation; alteration, amendment, revision, moderation, mitigation; condition, proviso, caveat.

**qualified** adjective *qualified mechanics* CERTIFIED, certificated, chartered, credentialed, licensed, professional; trained, fit, competent, accomplished, proficient, skilled, experienced, expert.

**qualify** verb **1** *I **qualify for** free prescriptions* BE ELIGIBLE FOR, meet the requirements for; be entitled to, be permitted.

**2** *they qualify as refugees* COUNT, be considered, be designated, be eligible.

**3** *she qualified as a doctor* BE CERTIFIED, be licensed; pass, graduate, make the grade, succeed, pass muster.

**4** *the course qualified them to teach* AUTHORIZE, empower, allow, permit, license; equip, prepare, train, educate, teach.

**5** *they qualified their findings* MODIFY, limit, restrict, make conditional; moderate, temper, modulate, mitigate.

**quality** noun **1** *the TV signal is of a poor quality | the quality of life* STANDARD, grade, class, caliber, condition, character, nature, form, rank, value, level; sort, type, kind, variety.

**2** *work of such quality is rare* EXCELLENCE, superiority, merit, worth, value, virtue, caliber, eminence, distinction, incomparability; talent, skill, virtuosity, craftsmanship.

**3** *her good qualities* FEATURE, trait, attribute, characteristic, point, aspect, facet, side, property.

▸ adjective *quality furniture* EXCELLENT, superior, valuable, distinctive, incomparable; well-crafted; *informal* top-notch.

**qualms** plural noun *I have no qualms about overseas travel* MISGIVINGS, doubts, reservations, second thoughts, worries, concerns, anxiety; hesitation, hesitance, hesitancy, demur, reluctance, disinclination, apprehension, trepidation, unease; scruples, remorse, compunction.

THE RIGHT WORD **qualms, compunction, demur, misgiving, scruple**

To have **qualms** is to have an uneasy feeling that you have acted or are about to act against your better judgment (*she had qualms about leaving a nine-year-old in charge of an infant*). **Misgivings** are even stronger, implying a disturbed state of mind because you're no longer confident that what you're doing is right (*his misgivings about letting his 80-year-old mother drive herself home turned out to be justified*). **Compunction** implies a momentary pang of conscience because what you are doing or are about to do is unfair, improper, or wrong (*they showed no compunction in carrying out their devious plans*). **Scruples** suggest a more highly-developed conscience or sense of honor; it implies that you have principles, and that you would be deeply disturbed if you thought you were betraying them (*her scruples would not allow her to participate in what she considered antifeminist activities*). **Demur** connotes hesitation to the point of delay, but the delay is usually caused by objections or indecision rather than a sense of conscience (*they accepted his decision without demur*).

**quandary** noun *conflicting appointments left us in a quandary* PREDICAMENT, plight, difficult situation, awkward situation; trouble, muddle, mess, confusion, difficulty, dilemma, mare's nest; *informal* sticky situation, pickle, hole, stew, fix, bind, jam.

**quantity** noun **1** *the quantity of food collected* AMOUNT, total, aggregate, sum, quota, mass, weight, volume, bulk; quantum, proportion, portion, part.

**2** *a quantity of ammunition* AMOUNT, lot, great deal, good deal, abundance, wealth, profusion; *informal* pile, ton, load, heap, mass, stack.

**quarrel** noun *they had a quarrel about money* ARGUMENT, disagreement, squabble, fight, dispute, wrangle, clash, altercation, feud, contretemps, disputation, falling-out, war of words, shouting match; *informal* tiff, run-in, hassle, blowup, row.

▸ verb *don't quarrel over it* ARGUE, fight, disagree, fall out; differ, be at odds; bicker, squabble, cross swords, lock horns, be at each other's throats; *archaic* altercate.

PHRASE: **quarrel with** *you can't quarrel with the verdict* FIND FAULT WITH, fault, criticize, object to, oppose, take exception to; attack, take issue with, impugn, contradict, dispute, controvert; *informal* knock; *formal* gainsay.

THE RIGHT WORD **quarrel, altercation, dispute, feud, row, spat, squabble, wrangle**

Family feuds come in a variety of shapes and sizes. A husband and his wife may have a **quarrel**, which suggests a heated verbal argument, with hostility that may persist even after it is over (*it took them almost a week to patch up their quarrel*). Siblings tend to have **squabbles**, which are childlike disputes over trivial matters, although they are by no means confined to childhood (*frequent squabbles over who would pick up the check*). A **spat** is also a petty quarrel, but unlike *squabble*, it suggests an angry outburst followed by a quick ending without hard feelings (*another spat in an otherwise loving relationship*). A **row** is more serious, involving noisy quarreling and the potential for physical violence (*a row that woke the neighbors*). Neighbors are more likely to have an **altercation**, which is usually confined to verbal blows but may involve actual or threatened physical ones (*an altercation over the location of the fence*). A **dispute** is also a verbal argument, but one that is carried on over an extended period of time (*an ongoing dispute over who was responsible for taking out the garbage*). Two families who have been enemies for a long time are probably involved in a **feud**, which suggests a bitter quarrel that lasts for years or even generations (*the feud between the Hatfields and the McCoys*). There is no dignity at all in being involved in a **wrangle**, which is an angry, noisy, and often futile dispute in which both parties are unwilling to listen to the other's point of view.

**quarrelsome** adjective *his quarrelsome neighbors* ARGUMENTATIVE, disputatious, confrontational, captious, pugnacious, combative, antagonistic, contentious, bellicose, belligerent, cantankerous, choleric; *informal* scrappy. ANTONYM peaceable.

**quarry** noun *he would not allow his quarry to elude him* PREY, victim; object, goal, target; kill, game.

**quarter** noun **1** *the Italian quarter* DISTRICT, area, region, part, side, neighborhood, precinct, locality, sector, zone; ghetto, community, enclave, Little ——, —— town.

**2** *help from an unexpected quarter* SOURCE, direction, place, location; person.

**3 (quarters)** *the servants' quarters* ACCOMMODATIONS, lodgings, rooms, chambers; home; *informal* pad, digs; *formal* abode, residence, domicile.

**4** *the riot squads gave no quarter* MERCY, leniency, clemency, lenity, compassion, pity, charity, sympathy, tolerance.

▸ verb **1** *they were quartered in a villa* ACCOMMODATE, house, board, lodge, put up, take in, install, shelter; *Military* billet.

**2** *I quartered the streets* PATROL, range over, tour, reconnoiter, traverse, survey, scout.

**quash** verb **1** *the judge may quash the sentence* CANCEL, reverse, rescind, repeal, revoke, retract, countermand, withdraw, overturn, overrule, veto, annul, nullify, invalidate, negate, void; *Law* vacate; *formal* abrogate. ANTONYM validate.

**2** *we want to quash these rumors* PUT AN END TO, put a stop to, stamp out, crush, put down, check, curb, nip in the bud, squash, quell, subdue, suppress, extinguish, stifle; *informal* squelch, put the kibosh on, deep-six. ANTONYM bring about.

**quasi-** combining form **1** *quasi-scientific theories* SUPPOSEDLY, seemingly, apparently, allegedly, ostensibly, on the face of it, on the surface, to all intents and purposes, outwardly, superficially, purportedly, nominally; pseudo-.

**2** *a quasi-autonomous organization* PARTLY, partially, part, to a certain extent, to some extent, half, relatively, comparatively, (up) to a point; almost, nearly, just about, all but.

**quaver** verb *Farnam's voice quavered with emotion* TREMBLE, waver, quiver, shake, vibrate, oscillate, fluctuate, falter, warble.

**queasy** adjective *just the smell of shellfish makes him queasy* NAUSEOUS, nauseated, bilious, sick; ill, unwell, poorly, green around the gills.

**queen** noun **1** *the queen was crowned* MONARCH, sovereign, ruler, head of state; Her Majesty; king's consort, queen consort. See also table at RULER.

**2** *informal the queen of country music* DOYENNE, star, superstar, leading light, big name, queen bee, prima donna, idol, heroine, favorite, darling, goddess.

**queer** adjective **1** *his diction is archaic and queer* ODD, strange, unusual, funny, peculiar, curious, bizarre, weird, uncanny, freakish, eerie, unnatural; unconventional, unorthodox, unexpected, unfamiliar, abnormal, anomalous, atypical, untypical, out of the ordinary, incongruous, irregular; puzzling, perplexing, baffling, unaccountable; *informal* fishy, spooky, bizarro, freaky. ANTONYM normal.

**2** *queer culture.* See GAY adjective sense 1.

USAGE NOTE **queer**

The word **queer** was first used to mean 'homosexual' in the early 20th century: it was originally, and often still is, a deliberately offensive and aggressive term when used by heterosexual people. In recent years, however, many gay people have taken the word **queer** and deliberately used it in place of *gay* or *homosexual*, in an attempt, by using the word positively, to deprive it of its negative power. This use of **queer** is now well established and widely used among gay people (esp. as an adjective or noun modifier, as in *queer rights*; *queer theory*) and at present exists alongside the other, deliberately offensive, use. (This use is similar to the way in which a racial epithet may be used *within* a racial group, but not by outsiders.)

**quell** verb **1** *troops quelled the unrest* PUT AN END TO, put a stop to, end, crush, put down, check, crack down on, curb, nip in the bud, squash, quash, subdue, suppress, overcome; *informal* squelch.

**2** *he quelled his misgivings* CALM, soothe, pacify, settle, quiet, silence, allay, assuage, mitigate, moderate; *literary* stay.

**quench** verb **1** *they quenched their thirst* SATISFY, slake, sate, satiate, gratify, relieve, assuage, take the edge off, indulge; lessen, reduce, diminish, check, suppress, extinguish, overcome.

**2** *the flames were quenched* EXTINGUISH, put out, snuff out, smother, douse.

**query** noun **1** *we are happy to answer any queries* QUESTION, inquiry.

**2** *there was a query as to who owned the hotel* DOUBT, uncertainty, question, reservation; skepticism.

▸ verb **1** *"Why do that?" queried Isobel* ASK, inquire, question.

**2** *some folk may query his credentials* QUESTION, call into question, challenge, dispute, cast aspersions on, doubt, have suspicions about, have reservations about.

**quest** noun **1** *their quest for her killer* SEARCH, hunt.

**2** *Sir Galahad's quest* EXPEDITION, journey, voyage, trek, travels, odyssey, adventure, exploration, search; crusade, mission, pilgrimage; *informal* Holy Grail. PHRASE: **in quest of** *thousands flocked north in quest of gold* IN SEARCH OF, in pursuit of, seeking, looking for, on the lookout for, after.

**question** noun **1** *please answer my question* INQUIRY, query; interrogation. ANTONYMS answer, response.

**2** *there is no question that he is ill* DOUBT, dispute, argument, debate, uncertainty, dubiousness, reservation. ANTONYM certainty.

**3** *the political questions of the day* ISSUE, matter, business, problem, concern, topic, theme, case; debate, argument, dispute, controversy.

▸ verb **1** *the lieutenant questions the suspect* INTERROGATE, cross-examine, cross-question, quiz, catechize; interview, debrief, examine, give the third degree to; *informal* grill, pump.

**2** *she questioned his motives* QUERY, call into question, challenge, dispute, cast aspersions on, doubt, suspect, have suspicions about, have reservations about.

PHRASES: **beyond question 1** *her loyalty is beyond question* UNDOUBTED, beyond doubt, certain, indubitable, indisputable, incontrovertible, unquestionable, undeniable, clear, patent, manifest.

**2** *the results demonstrated this beyond question* INDISPUTABLY, irrefutably, incontestably, incontrovertibly, unquestionably, undeniably, undoubtedly, beyond doubt, without doubt, clearly, patently, obviously.

**in question** *the matter in question* AT ISSUE, under discussion, under consideration, on the agenda, to be decided.

**out of the question** *changing the date of the wedding is out of the question* IMPOSSIBLE, impracticable, unfeasible, unworkable, inconceivable, unimaginable, unrealizable, unsuitable.

**questionable** adjective **1** *the premise to the argument remains questionable* CONTROVERSIAL, contentious, doubtful, dubious, uncertain, debatable, arguable; unverified, unprovable, unresolved, unconvincing, implausible, improbable; borderline, marginal, moot; *informal* iffy. See note at DOUBTFUL. ANTONYMS indisputable, certain.

**2** *questionable financial dealings* SUSPICIOUS, suspect, dubious, irregular, odd, strange, murky, dark, unsavory, disreputable; *informal* funny, fishy, shady, iffy. ANTONYM trustworthy.

**queue** noun *a long queue of people* LINEUP, line, row, column, file, chain, string; procession, train, cavalcade. See note at CUE.

▸ verb *we queued for ice cream* LINE UP, wait in line, form a line, fall in, form a queue, queue up.

**quibble** noun *I have just one quibble* CRITICISM, objection, complaint, protest, argument, exception, grumble, grouse, cavil; *informal* beef, gripe, moan.

▸ verb *no one* ***quibbled with*** *the title* OBJECT TO, find fault with, complain about, cavil at; split hairs about; criticize, query, fault, pick holes in; *informal* nitpick; *archaic* pettifog.

**quick** adjective 1 *a quick pace* FAST, swift, rapid, speedy, high-speed, breakneck, expeditious, brisk, smart; *informal* zippy; *literary* fleet. ANTONYM slow.

2 *she took a quick trip down memory lane* HASTY, hurried, cursory, perfunctory, desultory, superficial, summary; brief, short, fleeting, transient, transitory, short-lived, lightning, momentary, whirlwind, whistle-stop. ANTONYMS careful, long.

3 *a quick end to the recession* SUDDEN, instantaneous, immediate, instant, abrupt, precipitate. ANTONYM gradual.

4 *she isn't quick enough to advance to the next level* INTELLIGENT, bright, clever, gifted, able, astute, quick-witted, sharp-witted, smart; observant, alert, sharp, perceptive; *informal* brainy, on the ball, quick on the uptake. ANTONYM dull-witted.

**quicken** verb 1 *she quickened her pace* SPEED UP, accelerate, step up, hasten, hurry (up).

2 *the film quickened his interest in nature* STIMULATE, excite, arouse, rouse, stir up, activate, galvanize, whet, inspire, kindle; invigorate, revive, revitalize.

THE RIGHT WORD **quicken, animate, enliven, invigorate, stimulate, vitalize**

While all of these verbs mean to make alive or lively, **quicken** suggests the rousing or renewal of life, especially life that has been inert or suspended (*she felt the baby quicken during her second trimester of pregnancy*). **Animate** means to impart life, motion, or activity to something that previously lacked such a quality (*a discussion animated by the presence of so many young people*). **Stimulate** means to goad into activity from a state of inertia, inactivity, or lethargy (*the professor's constant questions stimulated her students to do more research*), while **enliven** refers to a stimulating influence that brightens or makes lively what was previously dull, depressed, or torpid (*a sudden change in the weather enlivened the group's activities*). **Invigorate** and **vitalize** both mean to fill with vigor or energy, but the former refers to physical energy (*invigorated by the climb up the mountain*), while the latter implies that energy has been imparted in a nonphysical sense (*to vitalize an otherwise dull meeting*).

**quickly** adverb 1 *he walked quickly* FAST, swiftly, briskly, rapidly, speedily, at the speed of light, at full tilt, as fast as one's legs can carry one, at a gallop, on the double, posthaste; *informal* PDQ (pretty damn quick), like lightning, like greased lightning, like mad, like blazes, like the wind, lickety-split; *literary* apace.

2 *you'd better leave quickly* IMMEDIATELY, directly, at once, now, straightaway, right away, instantly, forthwith, without delay, without further ado; soon, promptly, early, momentarily; *informal* like a shot, ASAP (as soon as possible), pronto, straight off.

3 *he quickly inspected it* BRIEFLY, fleetingly, briskly; hastily, hurriedly, cursorily, perfunctorily, superficially, desultorily.

**quick-tempered** adjective *they tend to be impulsive and quick-tempered* IRRITABLE, irascible, hot-tempered, short-tempered, snappish, fiery, touchy, volatile; cross, crabby, crotchety, cantankerous, grumpy, ill-tempered, bad-tempered, testy, tetchy, prickly, choleric; *informal* snappy, grouchy, cranky, on a short fuse. ANTONYM placid.

**quick-witted** adjective *Russell was always the quick-witted one in our circle* INTELLIGENT, bright, clever, gifted, able, astute, quick, smart, sharp-witted; observant, alert, sharp, perceptive; *informal* brainy, on the ball, quick on the uptake. ANTONYM slow.

**quid pro quo** noun *the latest agreement between labor and management is a textbook example of quid pro quo* EXCHANGE, trade, trade-off, swap, switch, barter, substitute, reciprocation, return; amends, compensation, recompense, restitution, reparation.

**quiescent** adjective *the volcano is in a quiescent state* INACTIVE, inert, idle, dormant, at rest, inoperative, deactivated, quiet; still, motionless, immobile, passive. See note at LATENT. ANTONYM active.

**quiet** adjective 1 *the whole pub went quiet* SILENT, still, hushed, noiseless, soundless; mute, dumb, speechless. ANTONYM noisy.

2 *a quiet voice* SOFT, low, muted, muffled, faint, indistinct, inaudible, hushed, whispered, suppressed. ANTONYM loud.

3 *a quiet village* PEACEFUL, sleepy, tranquil, calm, still, restful, undisturbed, untroubled; unfrequented. ANTONYMS busy, hectic.

4 *can I have a quiet word?* PRIVATE, confidential, secret, discreet, unofficial, off the record, between ourselves. ANTONYM public.

5 *quiet colors* UNOBTRUSIVE, restrained, muted, understated, subdued, subtle, low-key; soft, pale, pastel. ANTONYM loud.

6 *you can't keep it quiet for long* SECRET, confidential, classified, unrevealed, undisclosed, unknown, under wraps; *informal* hush-hush, mum; *formal* sub rosa. ANTONYM public.

7 *business is quiet* SLOW, stagnant, slack, sluggish, inactive, idle. ANTONYMS busy, active.

▸ noun *the quiet of the countryside* PEACEFULNESS, peace, restfulness, calm, tranquility, serenity; silence, quietness, stillness, still, quietude, hush, soundlessness.

**quietly** adverb 1 *she quietly entered the room* SILENTLY, in silence, noiselessly, soundlessly, inaudibly; mutely.

2 *he spoke quietly* SOFTLY, in a low voice, in a whisper, in a murmur, under one's breath, in an undertone, sotto voce, gently, faintly, weakly, feebly.

3 *some bonds were sold quietly* DISCREETLY, privately, confidentially, secretly, unofficially, off the record.

4 *she is quietly confident* CALMLY, patiently, placidly, serenely.

**quilt** noun DUVET, cover(s), coverlet, comforter; bedspread; *dated* counterpane.

**quintessence** noun 1 *it's the quintessence of the modern home* PERFECT EXAMPLE, exemplar, prototype, stereotype, picture, epitome, embodiment, ideal, apotheosis; best, pick, prime, acme, crème de la crème.

2 *brain scientists are investigating the quintessence of intelli-*

*gence* ESSENCE, soul, spirit, nature, core, heart, crux, kernel, marrow, substance; *informal* nitty-gritty; *Philosophy* quiddity, esse.

**quip** noun *the quip provoked a smile* JOKE, witty remark, witticism, jest, pun, bon mot, sally, pleasantry; *informal* one-liner, gag, crack, wisecrack, funny.

▸ verb *"I think he got the point," quipped Sean* JOKE, jest, pun, sally; *informal* wisecrack.

**quirk** noun **1** *they all know his quirks* IDIOSYNCRASY, peculiarity, oddity, eccentricity, foible, whim, vagary, caprice, fancy, crotchet, habit, characteristic, trait, fad; *informal* hang-up.

**2** *a quirk of fate* CHANCE, fluke, freak, anomaly, twist.

**quit** verb **1** *she quit work at 12:30* LEAVE, vacate, exit, depart from, withdraw from; abandon, desert.

**2** *he's decided to quit his job* RESIGN FROM, leave, give up, hand in one's notice, stand down from, relinquish, vacate, walk out on, retire from; *informal* chuck, pack in; pack it in, call it quits.

**3** *informal quit living in the past* GIVE UP, stop, cease, discontinue, drop, break off, abandon, abstain from, desist from, refrain from, avoid, forgo.

**quite** adverb **1** *two quite different types* COMPLETELY, entirely, totally, wholly, absolutely, utterly, thoroughly, altogether.

**2** *red hair was quite common in Rita's family* FAIRLY, rather, somewhat, slightly, relatively, comparatively, moderately, reasonably, to a certain extent; *informal* pretty, kind of, kinda, sort of.

**quiver** verb **1** *I quivered with terror* TREMBLE, shake, shiver, quaver, quake, shudder. See note at SHIVER.

**2** *the bird quivers its wings* FLUTTER, flap, beat, agitate, vibrate.

▸ noun *a quiver in her voice* TREMOR, tremble, shake, quaver, flutter, fluctuation, waver.

**quiz** noun **1** *there may be a short quiz next class* EXAM, test, pop quiz.

**2** *a music quiz on the radio* COMPETITION, game, game show.

▸ verb *a man was being quizzed by police* QUESTION, interrogate, cross-examine, cross-question, interview, sound out, give someone the third degree; test, examine; *informal* grill, pump.

**quizzical** adjective *a quizzical look on her face* INQUIRING, questioning, curious; puzzled, perplexed, baffled, mystified; amused, mocking, teasing.

**quota** noun *she rarely took her full quota of vacation time* ALLOCATION, share, allowance, limit, ration, portion, dispensation, slice (of the cake); percentage, commission; proportion, fraction, bit, amount, quantity; *informal* cut.

**quotation** noun *a quotation from Jefferson's first inaugural address* CITATION, quote, excerpt, extract, passage, line, paragraph, verse, phrase; reference, allusion.

**quote** verb **1** *he quoted a sentence from the book* RECITE, repeat, reproduce, retell, echo, parrot, iterate; take, extract.

**2** *she quoted one case in which a girl died* CITE, mention, refer to, name, instance, specify, identify; relate, recount; allude to, point out, present, offer, advance.

▸ noun **1** *a Shakespearean quote.* See QUOTATION sense 1.

**2** *a quote from the contractor* ESTIMATE, price, bid, costing, charge, figure, tender.

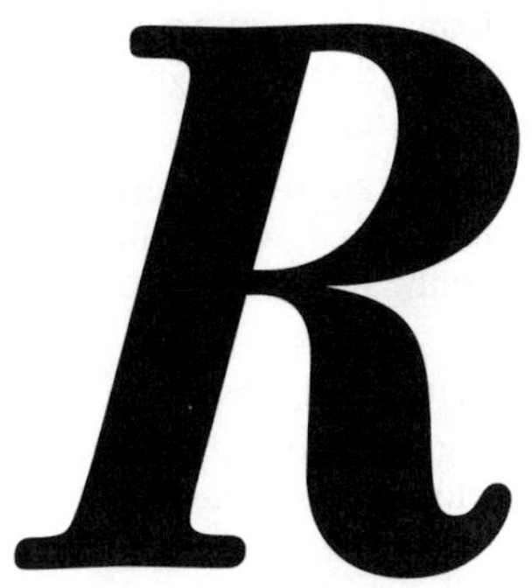

**rabble** noun **1** *a rabble of noisy youths* MOB, crowd, throng, gang, swarm, horde, pack, mass, group.

**2** *rule by the rabble* COMMON PEOPLE, masses, populace, multitude, rank and file, commonality, plebeians, proletariat, peasantry, hoi polloi, lower classes, riffraff; *informal* great unwashed, proles, plebs. ANTONYM nobility.

**rabid** adjective **1** *a rabid dog* rabies-infected, mad, hydrophobic.

**2** *her rabid anti-immigration views | a mecca for rabid shoppers* EXTREME, fanatical, overzealous, extremist, maniacal, passionate, fervent, overkeen, diehard, uncompromising, illiberal; *informal* gung-ho, foaming at the mouth. ANTONYM moderate.

**race**[1] noun **1** *Sasha won the race* CONTEST, competition, event, heat, trial(s).

**2** *the race for naval domination* COMPETITION, rivalry, contention; quest.

**3** *the water in the millrace* CHANNEL, waterway, millrace, raceway, conduit, sluice, chute, spillway.

▸ verb **1** *he will race in the final* COMPETE, contend; run.

**2** *Claire raced after him* HURRY, dash, rush, run, sprint, bolt, dart, gallop, career, charge, shoot, hurtle, careen, hare, fly, speed, scurry; *informal* tear, take off, belt, pelt, scoot, hotfoot it, leg it, hightail it.

**3** *her heart was racing* POUND, beat rapidly, throb, pulsate, thud, thump, hammer, palpitate, flutter, pitter-patter, go pit-a-pat, quiver, pump.

**race**[2] noun **1** *students of many different races* ETHNIC GROUP, racial type, origin, ethnic origin, color.

**2** *a bloodthirsty race* PEOPLE, nation.

**racial** adjective *racial pride* ETHNIC, ethnological, race-related; cultural, national, tribal.

**racism** noun *Aborigines are the main victims of racism is Australia* RACIAL DISCRIMINATION, racialism, racial prejudice, xenophobia, chauvinism, bigotry.

**racist** noun *he was exposed as a racist* RACIAL BIGOT, racialist, xenophobe, chauvinist, supremacist.

▸ adjective *a racist society* (RACIALLY) DISCRIMINATORY, racialist, prejudiced, bigoted.

**rack** noun *put the cake on a wire rack* FRAME, framework, stand, holder, trestle, support, shelf.

▸ verb *she was racked with guilt* TORMENT, afflict, torture, agonize, harrow; plague, bedevil, persecute, wrack, trouble, worry.

PHRASES: **on the rack** *these latest allegations are keeping the Church on the rack* UNDER PRESSURE, under stress, under a strain, in distress; in trouble, in difficulties, having problems.

**rack one's brains** *I've racked my brain, but I still can't think of his name* THINK HARD, concentrate, try to remember; *informal* scratch one's head.

**racket** noun **1** *the engine makes such a racket* NOISE, din, hubbub, clamor, uproar, tumult, commotion, rumpus, pandemonium, babel; *informal* hullabaloo.

**2** *informal a gold-smuggling racket* SCHEME, fraud, swindle; *informal* rip-off, shakedown.

**raconteur** noun *an interviewer with his favorite raconteur, Studs Terkel* STORYTELLER, teller of tales, spinner of yarns, narrator; *rare* anecdotist, anecdotalist.

**racy** adjective *racy lingerie* RISQUÉ, suggestive, naughty, sexy, spicy, ribald; indecorous, indecent, immodest, off-color, dirty, rude, smutty, crude, salacious; *informal* raunchy, blue; *euphemistic* adult. ANTONYM prim.

**radiance** noun **1** *the radiance of the sun* LIGHT, brightness, brilliance, luminosity, beams, rays, illumination, blaze, glow, gleam, luster, glare; luminescence, incandescence.

**2** *her face beamed with radiance* JOY, elation, jubilance, ecstasy, rapture, euphoria, delirium, happiness, delight, pleasure.

**radiant** adjective **1** *the radiant moon* SHINING, bright, illuminated, brilliant, gleaming, glowing, ablaze, luminous, luminescent, lustrous, incandescent, dazzling, shimmering, resplendent; *archaic* splendent. See note at BRIGHT ANTONYMS dark, dull.

**2** *she looked radiant* JOYFUL, elated, thrilled, overjoyed, jubilant, rapturous, ecstatic, euphoric, in seventh heaven, on cloud nine, delighted, very happy; *informal* on top of the world, over the moon. ANTONYM gloomy.

**radiate** verb **1** *the stars radiate energy* EMIT, give off, give out, discharge, diffuse; shed, cast.

**2** *light radiated from the hall* SHINE, beam, emanate.

**3** *their faces radiate hope* DISPLAY, show, exhibit; emanate, breathe, be a picture of.

**4** *four spokes radiate from the hub* FAN OUT, spread out, branch out/off, extend, issue.

**radical** adjective **1** *radical reform* THOROUGHGOING, thorough, complete, total, comprehensive, exhaustive, sweeping, far-reaching, wide-ranging, extensive, across the board, profound, major, stringent, rigorous. ANTONYM superficial.

**2** *radical differences between the two theories* FUNDAMENTAL, basic, essential, quintessential; structural, deep-seated, intrinsic, organic, constitutive. ANTONYM minor.

**3** *a radical political movement* REVOLUTIONARY, progressive, reformist, revisionist, progressivist; extreme, extremist, fanatical, militant, diehard, hard-core. ANTONYMS reactionary, moderate, conservative.

▸ noun *the arrested man was a radical* REVOLUTIONARY, progressive, reformer, revisionist; militant, zealot, extremist, fanatic, diehard; *informal* ultra. ANTONYMS reactionary, moderate, conservative.

**raffish** adjective *donning a raffish cap | her raffish, faithless husband* RAKISH, unconventional, Bohemian; devil-may-care, casual, careless; louche, disreputable, dissolute, decadent.

**raffle** noun *the winner of our raffle was Doris Toomey* LOTTERY, lotto, drawing, prize drawing, sweepstake(s).

**rag** noun **1** *an oily rag* CLOTH, scrap of cloth; *informal* schmatte.

**2** **(rags)** *a man dressed in rags* TATTERS, torn clothing, old clothes; castoffs, hand-me-downs.

**ragamuffin** noun *I always got stuck playing the part of some Dickensian-type ragamuffin* URCHIN, waif, guttersnipe, street kid.

**rage** noun **1** *his rage is due to frustration* FURY, anger, wrath, outrage, indignation, temper, spleen, resentment, pique, annoyance, vexation, displeasure; tantrum, bad mood; *literary* ire, choler.

**2** *the current rage for home improvement* CRAZE, passion, fashion, taste, trend, vogue, fad, enthusiasm, obsession, compulsion, fixation, fetish, mania, preoccupation; *informal* thing.

▸ verb **1** *she raged silently* BE ANGRY, be furious, be enraged, be incensed, seethe, be beside oneself, rave, storm, fume, spit; *informal* be livid, be wild, foam at the mouth, have a fit, be steamed up.

**2** *he* ***raged against*** *the reforms* PROTEST ABOUT, complain about, oppose, denounce; fulminate against, storm about, rail against.

**3** *a storm was raging* THUNDER, rampage, be violent, be turbulent, be tempestuous.

PHRASE: **(all) the rage** *pocket-size digital cameras are all the rage* POPULAR, fashionable, in fashion, in vogue, the (latest) thing, in great demand, sought after, le dernier cri; *informal* in, the in thing, cool, big, trendy, red-hot, hip.

**ragged** adjective **1** *ragged jeans* TATTERED, in tatters, torn, ripped, holey, in holes, moth-eaten, frayed, worn, worn out, falling to pieces, threadbare, scruffy, shabby; *informal* tatty, raggedy-ass.

**2** *a ragged child* SHABBY, scruffy, unkempt, dressed in rags.

**3** *a ragged coastline* JAGGED, craggy, rugged, uneven, rough, irregular; serrated, sawtooth, sawtoothed, indented; *technical* crenulate, crenulated.

**raging** adjective **1** *a raging mob* ANGRY, furious, enraged, incensed, infuriated, irate, fuming, seething, ranting; *informal* livid, wild; *literary* wrathful; *informal* smash-mouth.

**2** *raging seas* STORMY, violent, wild, turbulent, tempestuous.

**3** *a raging headache* EXCRUCIATING, agonizing, painful, throbbing, acute, bad.

**4** *her raging thirst* SEVERE, extreme, great, excessive.

**raid** noun **1** *the raid on Dieppe* ATTACK, assault, descent, blitz, incursion, sortie; onslaught, storming, charge, offensive, invasion, blitzkrieg.

**2** *a police raid* SEARCH; *informal* bust, takedown, shakedown.

▸ verb **1** *they raided shipping in the harbor* ATTACK, assault, set upon, descend on, swoop on, blitz, assail, storm, rush.

**2** *armed men raided the store* ROB, hold up, break into; plunder, steal from, pillage, loot, ransack, sack; *informal* stick up, heist.

**raider** noun *Kelley and his band of raiders* ROBBER, burglar, thief, housebreaker, plunderer, pillager, looter, marauder; attacker, assailant, invader.

**rail** verb *he* ***rails against*** *injustice* PROTEST (AGAINST), fulminate against, inveigh against, rage against, speak out against, make a stand against; expostulate about, criticize, denounce, condemn; object to, oppose, complain about, challenge; *informal* kick up a fuss about.

▸ noun *travel by rail* TRAIN, locomotive; *informal* iron horse.

**railing** noun *hold on to the railing* FENCE, fencing, rail(s), paling, palisade, balustrade, banister.

**raillery** noun *affectionate raillery* TEASING, mockery, chaff, ragging; banter, badinage; *informal* leg-pulling, joshing, ribbing, kidding.

**rain** noun **1** *the rain had stopped* RAINFALL, precipitation, raindrops, wet weather; drizzle, shower, rainstorm, cloudburst, torrent, downpour, deluge, storm.

**2** *a rain of hot ash* SHOWER, deluge, flood, torrent, avalanche, flurry; storm, hail.

▸ verb **1** *it rained heavily* POUR, pour down, come down, pelt down, teem down, beat down, rain cats and dogs; fall, drizzle.

**2** *bombs rained on the city* FALL, hail, drop, shower.

**rainy** adjective *rainy weather* WET, showery, drizzly, damp, inclement.

**raise** verb 1 *he raised a hand in greeting* LIFT, lift up, hold aloft, elevate, uplift, upraise, upthrust; hoist, haul up, hitch up. ANTONYM lower.

2 *he raised himself in the bed* SET UPRIGHT, set vertical; sit up, stand up. ANTONYMS lay down, knock over.

3 *they raised prices* INCREASE, put up, push up, up, mark up, escalate, inflate; *informal* hike (up), jack up, bump up. ANTONYMS lower, reduce.

4 *he raised his voice* AMPLIFY, louden, magnify, intensify, boost, lift, increase, heighten, augment. ANTONYM lower.

5 *the temple was raised in 900 BC* BUILD, construct, erect, assemble, put up. ANTONYMS raze, demolish.

6 *how will you raise the money?* GET, obtain, acquire; accumulate, amass, collect, fetch, net, make. ANTONYMS distribute, spend.

7 *the city raised troops to fight for them* RECRUIT, enlist, sign up, conscript, call up, mobilize, rally, assemble, draft. ANTONYMS demobilize, stand down.

8 *a tax raised on imports* LEVY, impose, exact, demand, charge.

9 *he raised several objections* BRING UP, air, ventilate; present, table, propose, submit, advance, suggest, moot, put forward. ANTONYMS withdraw, keep quiet about.

10 *the disaster raised doubts about safety* GIVE RISE TO, occasion, cause, produce, engender, elicit, create, result in, lead to, prompt, awaken, arouse, induce, kindle, incite, stir up, trigger, spark off, provoke, instigate, foment, whip up; *literary* beget. ANTONYMS allay, end.

11 *most parents try to raise their children well* BRING UP, rear, nurture, look after, care for, provide for, mother, parent, tend, cherish; educate, train.

12 *she raised cattle* BREED, rear, nurture, keep, tend; grow, farm, cultivate, produce.

13 *he was raised to a captaincy* PROMOTE, advance, upgrade, elevate, ennoble; *informal* kick upstairs. ANTONYM demote.

▸ noun *the workers wanted a raise* pay increase, increment.

PHRASE: **raise hell** *informal.* See HELL.

**rake**[1] verb 1 *he raked the leaves into a pile* SCRAPE UP, collect, gather.

2 *she raked the gravel* SMOOTH, smooth out, level, even out, flatten, comb.

3 *the cat raked his arm with its claws* SCRATCH, lacerate, scrape, rasp, graze, grate; *Medicine* excoriate.

4 *she raked a hand through her hair* DRAG, pull, scrape, tug, comb.

5 *I raked through my pockets* RUMMAGE, search, hunt, sift, rifle.

6 *machine-gun fire raked the streets* SWEEP, enfilade, pepper, strafe. PHRASES: **rake something in** *informal his frozen yogurt business is raking in the dough* EARN, make, get, gain, garner, obtain, acquire, accumulate, bring in, pull in, pocket, realize, fetch, return, yield, raise, net, gross.

**rake something up** *I guess I've raked up some bad memories* REMIND PEOPLE OF, recollect, remember, call to mind; drag up, dredge up.

**rake**[2] noun *he was something of a rake* PLAYBOY, libertine, profligate; degenerate, roué, debauchee; lecher, seducer, womanizer, philanderer, adulterer, Don Juan, Lothario, Casanova; *informal* ladykiller, ladies' man, lech.

**rakish** adjective *Felipe's snap-brimmed hat is always cocked at a rakish angle* DASHING, debonair, stylish, jaunty, devil-may-care; raffish, disreputable, louche; *informal* sharp.

**rally** verb 1 *the troops rallied and held their ground* REGROUP, reassemble, re-form, reunite. ANTONYM disperse.

2 *he rallied an army* MUSTER, marshal, mobilize, raise, call up, recruit, enlist, conscript; assemble, gather, round up, draft; *formal* convoke. ANTONYMS demobilize, disband.

3 *team owners rallied to denounce the rumors* GET TOGETHER, band together, assemble, join forces, unite, ally, collaborate, cooperate, pull together. ANTONYMS separate, split up.

4 *share prices rallied* RECOVER, improve, get better, pick up, revive, bounce back, perk up, look up, turn a corner. ANTONYMS deteriorate, slump.

▸ noun 1 *a rally in support of the strike* MEETING, mass meeting, gathering, assembly; demonstration, march, protest march, protest.

2 *a rally in oil prices* RECOVERY, upturn, improvement, comeback, resurgence. ANTONYM slump.

**ram** verb 1 *he rammed his sword into its sheath* FORCE, thrust, plunge, stab, push, sink, dig, stick, cram, jam, stuff, pack.

2 *a van rammed the police car* HIT, strike, crash into, collide with, impact, run into, smash into, smack into, bump (into), butt.

**ramble** verb 1 *we rambled around the village* WALK, hike, tramp, trek, backpack; wander, stroll, saunter, amble, roam, range, rove, traipse; *informal* mosey, tootle; *formal* perambulate.

2 *she does ramble* CHATTER, babble, prattle, prate, blather, jabber, twitter, maunder; *informal* jaw, gas, gab, yak, yabber.

▸ noun *a ramble in the hills* WALK, hike, trek; wander, stroll, saunter, amble, roam, traipse, jaunt, promenade; *informal* mosey, tootle; *formal* perambulation.

**rambler** noun *for two years, he and his dog were a pair of carefree ramblers* WALKER, hiker, backpacker, wanderer, rover; *literary* wayfarer.

**rambling** adjective 1 *a rambling speech* LONG-WINDED, verbose, wordy, prolix; digressive, maundering, roundabout, circuitous, tortuous, circumlocutory; disconnected, disjointed, incoherent. ANTONYM concise.

2 *rambling streets* WINDING, twisting, twisty, tortuous, labyrinthine; sprawling.

3 *a rambling rose* TRAILING, creeping, climbing, vining.

**ramification** noun *the Gulf War of 1991 had ramifications far beyond the Middle East* CONSEQUENCE, result, aftermath, outcome, effect, upshot; development, implication; product, byproduct.

**ramp** noun *they wheeled the appliances down the ramp* SLOPE, bank, incline, gradient, tilt; rise, ascent, drop, descent, declivity.

**rampage** verb *mobs rampaged through the streets* RIOT, run riot, go on the rampage, run amok, go berserk; storm, charge, tear. PHRASE: **go on the rampage** *the prisoners have gone on a rampage* RIOT, go berserk, get out of control, run amok; *informal* go postal.

**rampant** adjective **1** *rampant inflation* UNCONTROLLED, unrestrained, unchecked, unbridled, widespread; out of control, out of hand, rife. ANTONYM controlled.

**2** *rampant dislike* VEHEMENT, strong, violent, forceful, intense, passionate, fanatical. ANTONYM mild.

**3** *rampant vegetation* LUXURIANT, exuberant, lush, rich, riotous, rank, profuse, vigorous; *informal* jungly.

**rampart** noun *the castle's stony ramparts* DEFENSIVE WALL, embankment, earthwork, parapet, breastwork, battlement, bulwark, outwork.

**ramshackle** adjective *their first home was a ramshackle cottage* TUMBLEDOWN, dilapidated, derelict, decrepit, neglected, run-down, gone to rack and ruin, beat-up, crumbling, decaying; rickety, shaky, unsound. ANTONYMS sound, sturdy.

**rancid** adjective *rancid bacon* SOUR, stale, overstored, turned, rank, putrid, foul, rotten, bad, off; gamy, high, fetid, stinking, malodorous, foul-smelling; *literary* noisome. ANTONYM fresh.

**rancor** noun *partisans on both sides have created much rancor* BITTERNESS, spite, hate, hatred, resentment, malice, ill will, malevolence, animosity, antipathy, enmity, hostility, acrimony, venom, vitriol.

**rancorous** adjective *California's rancorous recall campaign* BITTER, spiteful, hateful, resentful, acrimonious, malicious, malevolent, hostile, venomous, vindictive, baleful, vitriolic, vengeful, pernicious, mean, nasty; *informal* bitchy, catty. See note at VINDICTIVE. ANTONYM amicable.

**random** adjective *random spot checks* UNSYSTEMATIC, unmethodical, arbitrary, unplanned, undirected, casual, indiscriminate, nonspecific, haphazard, stray, erratic; chance, accidental. ANTONYM systematic.

PHRASE: **at random** *we chose the names at random* UNSYSTEMATICALLY, arbitrarily, randomly, unmethodically, haphazardly.

**range** noun **1** *his range of vision* SPAN, scope, compass, sweep, extent, area, field, orbit, ambit, horizon, latitude; limits, bounds, confines, parameters.

**2** *a range of mountains* ROW, chain, sierra, ridge, massif; line, string, series.

**3** *a range of quality foods* ASSORTMENT, variety, diversity, mixture, collection, array, selection, choice.

**4** *she put the dish into the range* STOVE, oven.

**5** *cows grazed on the open range* PASTURE, pasturage, pastureland, prairie, grass, grassland, grazing land, veld; *literary* greensward.

▸ verb **1** *interest charges range from 1% to 5%* VARY, fluctuate, differ; extend, stretch, reach, cover, go, run.

**2** *they ranged over the sprawling hills* ROAM, rove, traverse, travel, journey, wander, drift, ramble, meander, stroll, traipse, walk, hike, trek.

**THE RIGHT WORD range, compass, gamut, latitude, reach, scope, sweep**

To say that someone has a wide **range** of interests implies that these interests are not only extensive but varied. Another way of expressing the same idea would be to say that the person's interests run the **gamut** from TV quiz shows to nuclear physics, a word that suggests a graduated scale or series running from one extreme to another. **Compass** implies a range of knowledge or activity that falls within very definite limits reminiscent of a circumference (*within the compass of her abilities*), while **sweep** suggests more of an arc-shaped range of motion or activity (*the sweep of the searchlight*) or a continuous extent or stretch (*a broad sweep of lawn*). **Latitude** and **scope** both emphasize the idea of freedom, although *scope* implies great freedom within prescribed limits (*the scope of the investigation*), while *latitude* means freedom from such limits (*she was granted more latitude than usual in interviewing the disaster victims*). Even someone who has a wide *range* of interests and a broad *scope* of authority, however, will sooner or later come up against something that is beyond his or her **reach**, which suggests the furthest limit of effectiveness or influence.

**rank**[1] noun **1** *she was elevated to an administrative rank* POSITION, level, grade, echelon; class, status, standing; *dated* station.

**2** *a family of rank* HIGH STANDING, blue blood, high birth, nobility, aristocracy; eminence, distinction, prestige; prominence, influence, consequence, power.

**3** *a rank of riflemen* ROW, line, file, column, string, train, procession.

▸ verb **1** *this orchid is ranked as endangered* CLASSIFY, class, categorize, rate, grade, bracket, group, pigeonhole, designate; catalog, file, list.

**2** *he ranked them in order of experience* PRIORITIZE, order, organize, arrange, list; triage.

**3** *she ranked below the others* HAVE A RANK, be graded, have a status, be classed, be classified, be categorized; belong.

PHRASE: **rank and file 1** *the officers and the rank and file* OTHER RANKS, soldiers, NCOs, noncommissioned officers, lower ranks, enlisted personnel; men, troops; *informal* noncoms.

**2** *a speech appealing to the rank and file* PEOPLE, common people, proletariat, masses, populace, commonality, third estate, plebeians; hoi polloi, rabble, riffraff, great unwashed; *informal* proles, plebs.

**rank**[2] adjective **1** *rank vegetation* ABUNDANT, lush, luxuriant, dense, profuse, vigorous, overgrown; *informal* jungly. ANTONYM sparse.

**2** *a rank smell* OFFENSIVE, unpleasant, nasty, revolting, sickening, obnoxious, noxious; foul, fetid, smelly, stinking, reeking, high, off, rancid, putrid, malodorous; *literary* noisome; *Brit. informal* minging, pongy. ANTONYM pleasant.

**3** *rank stupidity* DOWNRIGHT, utter, outright, out-and-out, absolute, complete, sheer, arrant, thoroughgoing, unqualified, unmitigated, positive, perfect, patent, pure, total; *archaic* arrant.

**rankle** verb *Rumsfeld's remarks rankled the Palestinians* CAUSE RESENTMENT TO, annoy, upset, anger, irritate, offend, affront, displease, provoke, irk, vex, pique, nettle, gall; *informal* rile, miff, peeve, aggravate, tick off.

**ransack** verb *Joonie's thugs ransacked Leon's apartment* PLUNDER, pillage, raid, rob, loot, sack, strip, despoil; ravage, devastate, turn upside down; scour, rifle, comb, search.

**ransom** noun *they demanded a huge ransom* PAYOFF, payment, sum, price.

▸ verb *the girl was ransomed for $4 million* RELEASE, free, deliver, liberate, rescue; exchange for a ransom, buy the freedom of.

**rant** verb *she ranted about the unfairness* FULMINATE, go on, hold forth, vociferate, sound off, spout, pontificate, bluster, declaim; shout, yell, bellow; *informal* mouth off.

▸ noun *he went into a rant about them* TIRADE, diatribe, broadside; *literary* philippic.

**rap** verb **1** *she rapped his fingers with a ruler* HIT, strike; *informal* whack, thwack, bash, wallop; *literary* smite.

**2** *I rapped on the door* KNOCK, tap, bang, hammer, pound.

▸ noun **1** *a rap on the knuckles* BLOW, hit, knock, bang, crack; *informal* whack, thwack, bash, wallop.

**2** *a rap at the door* KNOCK, tap, rat-tat, bang, hammering, pounding.

PHRASE: **take the rap** *informal* *why should I take the rap for what Clarence did?* BE PUNISHED, take the blame, suffer, suffer the consequences, pay, pay the price.

**rapacious** adjective *poor Tom has fallen for a rapacious gold digger* GRASPING, greedy, avaricious, acquisitive, covetous; mercenary, materialistic; insatiable, predatory; *informal* money-grubbing, grabby. See note at GREEDY. ANTONYM generous.

**rape** noun **1** *he was charged with rape* SEXUAL ASSAULT, sexual abuse, sexual interference; *archaic* ravishment, defilement.

**2** *the rape of the rain forest* DESTRUCTION, violation, ravaging, pillaging, plundering, desecration, defilement, sacking, sack.

▸ verb **1** *he raped her at knifepoint* SEXUALLY ASSAULT, sexually abuse, violate, force oneself on; *literary* ravish; *archaic* defile.

**2** *they raped our country* RAVAGE, violate, desecrate, defile, plunder, pillage, despoil; lay waste, ransack, sack.

**rapid** adjective *his rapid rise to stardom* QUICK, fast, swift, speedy, expeditious, express, brisk; lightning, meteoric, whirlwind; sudden, instantaneous, instant, immediate; hurried, hasty, precipitate; *informal* PDQ (pretty damn quick); *literary* fleet. ANTONYM slow.

**rapidly** adverb *a new computer worm spread rapidly through the Internet on Tuesday* QUICKLY, fast, swiftly, speedily, at the speed of light, posthaste, at full tilt, briskly; hurriedly, hastily, in haste, in a rush, precipitately; *informal* like a shot, PDQ (pretty damn quick), in a flash, on the double, like a bat out of hell, like lightning, like greased lightning, like mad, like the wind, lickety-split; *literary* apace. ANTONYM slowly.

**rapport** noun *board members fired him for failing to maintain good rapport with the trustees* AFFINITY, close relationship, understanding, mutual understanding, bond, empathy, sympathy, accord.

**rapt** adjective *a rapt teenage audience* FASCINATED, enthralled, spellbound, captivated, riveted, gripped, mesmerized, enchanted, entranced, bewitched, moonstruck; transported, enraptured, thrilled, ecstatic. ANTONYM inattentive.

**rapture** noun *she gazed at him in rapture* ECSTASY, bliss, exaltation, euphoria, elation, joy, enchantment, delight, happiness, pleasure. PHRASE: **go into raptures** *the Cambodian crowd went into raptures over Carreras's rendition of "Some Enchanted Evening"* ENTHUSE, rhapsodize, rave, gush, wax lyrical; *informal* go wild/crazy/mad.

THE RIGHT WORD **rapture, bliss, ecstasy, euphoria, transport**

Happiness is one thing; **bliss** is another, suggesting a state of utter joy and contentment (*marital bliss*). **Ecstasy** is even more extreme, describing a trancelike state in which one loses consciousness of one's surroundings (*the ecstasy of young love*). Although **rapture** originally referred to being raised or lifted out of oneself by divine power, nowadays it is used in much the same sense as *ecstasy* to describe an elevated sensation of bliss (*she listened in speechless rapture to her favorite soprano*). **Transport** applies to any powerful emotion by which one is carried away (*a transport of delight*). When happiness is carried to an extreme or crosses over into mania, it is called **euphoria**. *Euphoria* may outwardly resemble *ecstasy* or *rapture*; but upon closer examination, it is usually found to be exaggerated and out of proportion (*the euphoria that came over him whenever he touched alcohol*).

**rapturous** adjective *Nelson Mandela received a rapturous welcome in London* ECSTATIC, joyful, elated, euphoric, enraptured, on cloud nine, in seventh heaven, transported, enchanted, blissful, happy; enthusiastic, delighted, thrilled, overjoyed, rapt; *informal* over the moon, on top of the world, blissed out.

**rare** adjective **1** *rare moments of privacy* INFREQUENT, scarce, sparse, few and far between, thin on the ground, like gold dust, as scarce as hen's teeth; occasional, limited, odd, isolated, unaccustomed, unwonted. ANTONYMS common, frequent.

**2** *rare stamps* UNUSUAL, recherché, uncommon, unfamiliar, atypical, singular. ANTONYMS ordinary, commonplace.

**3** *a man of rare talent* EXCEPTIONAL, outstanding, unparalleled, peerless, matchless, unique, unrivaled, inimitable, beyond compare, without equal, second to none, unsurpassed; consummate, superior, superlative, first-class; *informal* A1, top-notch. ANTONYMS common, everyday.

**rarely** adverb *we rarely leave the house in the winter* SELDOM, infrequently, hardly ever, hardly, scarcely, not often; once in a while, now and then, occasionally; *informal* once in a blue moon. ANTONYM often.

**rarity** noun **1** *the rarity of earthquakes in Vermont* INFREQUENCY, rareness, scarcity, unusualness, uncommonness.

**2** *this book is a rarity* COLLECTOR'S ITEM, rare thing, rare bird, rara avis; wonder, nonpareil, one of a kind; curiosity, oddity.

**rascal** noun *the title character is a lovable rascal* SCALAWAG, imp, monkey, mischief-maker, wretch; *informal* scamp, tyke, horror, monster, varmint; *archaic* rapscallion.

**rash**[1] noun **1** *he broke out in* ***a rash*** SPOTS, a breakout, an eruption; hives; *Medicine* erythema, exanthema, urticaria.

**2** *a rash of articles in the press* SERIES, succession, spate, wave, flood, deluge, torrent; outbreak, epidemic, flurry.

**rash**[2] adjective *a rash decision* RECKLESS, impulsive, impetuous, hasty, foolhardy, incautious, precipitate; careless, heedless, thoughtless, imprudent, foolish; ill-advised, injudicious, ill-judged, misguided, harebrained, trigger-happy; *literary* temerarious. See note at TEMERITY. ANTONYM prudent.

**rasp** verb **1** *tartar is rasped off the teeth* SCRAPE, rub, abrade, grate, grind, sand, file, scratch, scour; *Medicine* excoriate.

**2** *"Help!" he rasped* CROAK, squawk, caw, say hoarsely.

**rasping** adjective *the rasping voice on the phone sounded familiar* HARSH, grating, jarring; raspy, scratchy, hoarse, rough, gravelly, croaky, gruff, husky, throaty, guttural.

**rate** noun **1** *a fixed rate of interest* PERCENTAGE, ratio, proportion; scale, standard, level.

**2** *an hourly rate of $30* CHARGE, price, cost, tariff, fare, levy, toll; fee, remuneration, payment, wage, allowance.

**3** *the rate of change* SPEED, pace, tempo, velocity, momentum.

▸ verb **1** *they rated his driving ability* ASSESS, evaluate, appraise, judge, estimate, calculate, gauge, measure, adjudge; grade, rank, classify, categorize.

**2** *the scheme was rated effective* CONSIDER, judge, reckon, think, hold, deem, find; regard as, look on as, count as.

**3** *he rated only a brief mention* MERIT, deserve, warrant, be worthy of, be deserving of.

PHRASE: **at any rate** *at any rate, we ask that you remember to vote* IN ANY CASE, anyhow, anyway, in any event, nevertheless; whatever happens, come what may, regardless, notwithstanding.

**rather** adverb **1** *I would rather stay home* SOONER, by preference, preferably, by choice.

**2** *it's rather complicated* QUITE, a bit, a little, fairly, slightly, somewhat, relatively, to some degree, comparatively; *informal* pretty, sort of, kind of, kinda.

**3** *her true feelings—or rather, lack of feelings* MORE PRECISELY, to be precise, to be exact, strictly speaking.

**4** *she seemed sad rather than angry* MORE; as opposed to, instead of.

**5** *it was not impulsive, but rather a considered decision* ON THE CONTRARY, au contraire, instead.

**ratify** verb *they failed to ratify the amendment* CONFIRM, approve, sanction, endorse, agree to, accept, uphold, authorize, formalize, validate, recognize; sign. See note at APPROVE. ANTONYM reject.

**rating** noun *the hotel's four-star rating* GRADE, grading, classification, ranking, rank, category, designation; assessment, evaluation, appraisal; mark, score.

**ratio** noun *the fat ratios in American diets are dangerously askew* PROPORTION, comparative number, correlation, relationship, correspondence; percentage, fraction, quotient.

**ration** noun **1** *a daily ration of chocolate* ALLOWANCE, allocation, quota, quantum, share, portion, helping; amount, quantity, measure, proportion, percentage.

**2 (rations)** *the garrison ran out of rations* SUPPLIES, provisions, food, foodstuffs, eatables, edibles, provender; stores; *informal* grub, eats, vittles; *formal* comestibles; *dated* victuals.

▸ verb *fuel supplies were rationed* CONTROL, limit, restrict; conserve.

**rational** adjective **1** *a rational approach* LOGICAL, reasoned, sensible, reasonable, cogent, intelligent, judicious, shrewd, common-sense, commonsensical, sound, prudent; down-to-earth, practical, pragmatic. See note at SENSIBLE. ANTONYM illogical.

**2** *she was not rational at the time of signing* SANE, compos mentis, in one's right mind, of sound mind; normal, balanced, grounded, lucid, coherent; *informal* all there. ANTONYM insane.

**3** *humans are rational beings* INTELLIGENT, thinking, reasoning; cerebral, logical, analytical; *formal* ratiocinative.

**rationale** noun *Bush outlined his rationale for a national missile defense plan* REASON(S), reasoning, thinking, logic, grounds, sense; principle, theory, argument, case; motive, motivation, explanation, justification, excuse; the whys and wherefores.

**rationalize** verb **1** *he tried to rationalize his behavior* JUSTIFY, explain, explain away, account for, defend, vindicate, excuse. See note at LIE[1].

**2** *an attempt to rationalize the industry* STREAMLINE, reorganize, modernize, update; trim, hone, simplify, downsize, prune.

**rattle** verb **1** *hailstones rattled against the window* CLATTER, patter; clink, clunk.

**2** *he rattled some coins* JINGLE, jangle, clink, tinkle.

**3** *the bus rattled along* JOLT, bump, bounce, jounce, shake.

**4** *the government was rattled by the strike* UNNERVE, disconcert, disturb, fluster, shake, perturb, discompose, discomfit, ruffle, throw; *informal* faze.

▸ noun **1** *the rattle of the bottles* CLATTER, clank, clink, clang; jingle, jangle.

**2** *she gave the baby a rattle* NOISEMAKER, shaker, rain stick, maraca.

PHRASES: **rattle something off** *she can rattle off the complete list of Shakespeare's plays* REEL OFF, recite, list, fire off, run through, enumerate.
**rattle on/away** *rattling on about her grandchildren* PRATTLE, babble, chatter, prate, go on, jabber, gibber, ramble; *informal* gab, yak, yap.

**raucous** adjective **1** *raucous laughter* HARSH, strident, screeching, piercing, shrill, grating, discordant, dissonant; noisy, loud, cacophonous. ANTONYMS soft, dulcet.

**2** *a raucous party* ROWDY, noisy, boisterous, roisterous, wild. ANTONYMS restrained, quiet.

**ravage** verb *they ravaged the countryside* LAY WASTE, devastate, ruin, destroy, wreak havoc on, leave desolate; pillage, plunder, despoil, ransack, sack, loot, rape.

THE RIGHT WORD **ravage, despoil, devastate, pillage, plunder, sack, waste**

**Ravage**, **pillage**, **sack**, and **plunder** are all verbs associated with the actions of a conquering army during wartime. *Ravage* implies violent destruction, usually in a series of raids or invasions over an extended period of time (*the invading forces ravaged the countryside*). *Plunder* refers to the roving of soldiers through recently conquered territory in search of money and goods (*they plundered the city and left its inhabitants destitute*), while *pillage* describes the act of stripping a conquered city or people of valuables (*churches pillaged by ruthless invaders*). *Sack* is even more extreme than *pillage*, implying not only the seizure of all valuables, but total destruction as well (*the army sacked every village along the coast*). **Despoil** also entails the stripping of valuables, but with less violence than *sack*; it is more common in nonmilitary contexts, where it describes a heedless or inadvertent destruction (*forests despoiled by logging companies*). **Devastate** emphasizes ruin and desolation, whether it happens to buildings, forests, or crops (*fields of corn devastated by flooding*). **Waste** comes close in meaning to *devastate*, but it suggests a less violent or more gradual destruction (*a region of the country wasted by years of drought and periodic fires*).

**ravages** plural noun **1** *the ravages of time* DAMAGING EFFECTS, ill effects.

**2** *the ravages carried out by humanity* ACTS OF DESTRUCTION, destruction, damage, devastation, ruin, havoc, depredation(s).

**rave** verb **1** *he was raving about the fires of hell* TALK WILDLY, babble, jabber, talk incoherently.

**2** *I raved and swore at them* RANT, rant and rave, rage, lose one's temper, storm, fulminate, fume; shout, roar, thunder, bellow; *informal* fly off the handle, blow one's top, hit the roof, flip one's wig.

**3** *he **raved about** her singing* PRAISE ENTHUSIASTICALLY, go into raptures about/over, wax lyrical about, sing the praises of, rhapsodize over, enthuse about/over, acclaim, eulogize, extol; *informal* ballyhoo; *formal* laud; *archaic* panegyrize. ANTONYM criticize.

▸ noun *informal* **1** *the food won raves from the critics* ENTHUSIASTIC PRAISE, lavish praise, a rapturous reception, tribute, plaudits, acclaim. ANTONYM criticism.

**2** *an all-night rave.* See PARTY noun sense 1.

▸ adjective *informal rave reviews* VERY ENTHUSIASTIC, rapturous, glowing, ecstatic, excellent, highly favorable.

**ravenous** adjective **1** *I'm absolutely ravenous* VERY HUNGRY, starving, famished; *rare* esurient.

**2** *her ravenous appetite* VORACIOUS, insatiable; greedy, gluttonous; *literary* insatiate.

**ravine** noun *the ravine that runs along Hubble Hollow Road* GORGE, canyon, gully, couloir; chasm, abyss, gulf, gulch, coulee.

**raving** adjective. See MAD sense 1.

**ravings** plural noun *the ravings of a madman* GIBBERISH, rambling, babbling, wild talk, incoherent talk.

**ravish** verb **1** *literary he tried to ravish her* RAPE, sexually assault/abuse, violate, force oneself on, molest; *archaic* dishonor, defile.

**2** *literary you will be ravished by this wine* ENRAPTURE, enchant, delight, charm, entrance, enthrall, captivate.

**3** *archaic her child was ravished from her breast* SEIZE, snatch, carry off/away, steal, abduct.

**ravishing** adjective *you look utterly ravishing* VERY BEAUTIFUL, gorgeous, stunning, wonderful, lovely, striking, magnificent, dazzling, radiant, delightful, charming, enchanting; *informal* amazing, sensational, fantastic, fabulous, terrific, bodacious, hot, red-hot. ANTONYM hideous.

**raw** adjective **1** *raw carrot* UNCOOKED, fresh. ANTONYM cooked.

**2** *raw materials* UNPROCESSED, untreated, unrefined, crude, natural; unedited, undigested, unprepared. ANTONYMS refined, processed.

**3** *raw recruits* INEXPERIENCED, new, untrained, untried, untested, unseasoned; callow, immature, green, naive; *informal* wet behind the ears, raggedy-ass. ANTONYMS experienced, skilled.

**4** *his skin is raw* SORE, red, painful, tender; abraded, chafed; *Medicine* excoriated.

**5** *a raw morning* BLEAK, cold, chilly, bone-chilling, freezing, icy, icy-cold, wintry, bitter, biting; *informal* nippy. ANTONYMS warm, balmy.

**6** *raw emotions* STRONG, intense, passionate, fervent, powerful, violent; undisguised, unconcealed, unrestrained, uninhibited.

**7** *raw images of Latin America* REALISTIC, unembellished, unvarnished, brutal, harsh, gritty, graphic. ANTONYM idealized.

PHRASE: **in the raw** *informal sleeping in the raw.* See NAKED sense 1.

**ray** noun **1** *rays of light* BEAM, shaft, streak, stream.

**2** *a ray of hope* GLIMMER, flicker, spark, hint, suggestion, sign.

**raze** verb *the old library will be razed on Saturday* DESTROY, demolish, raze to the ground, tear down, pull down, knock down, level, flatten, bulldoze, wipe out, lay waste. See note at DESTROY.

**reach** verb **1** *Travis* ***reached out*** *a hand* STRETCH OUT, hold out, extend, outstretch, thrust out, stick out.

**2** *reach me that book* PASS, hand, give, let someone have.

**3** *soon she reached Helen's house* ARRIVE AT, get to, come to; end up at; *informal* make.

**4** *the temperature reached 32 degrees* ATTAIN, get to; rise to, climb to; fall to, sink to, drop to; *informal* hit.

**5** *the leaders reached an agreement* ACHIEVE, attain, work out, draw up, put together, negotiate, thrash out, hammer out.

**6** *I have been trying to reach you all day* GET IN TOUCH WITH, contact, get through to, get, speak to; *informal* get hold of.

**7** *our concern is to reach more people* INFLUENCE, sway, get (through) to, make an impression on, have an impact on.

▸ noun **1** *Bobby moved out of her reach* GRASP, range. See note at RANGE.

**2** *small goals within your reach* CAPABILITIES, capacity.

**3** *beyond the reach of the law* JURISDICTION, authority, influence; scope, range, compass, ambit.

**react** verb **1** *how would he react if she told him the truth?* BEHAVE, act, take it, conduct oneself; respond, reply, answer.

**2** *she* ***reacted against*** *the new regulations* REBEL AGAINST, oppose, rise up against.

**reaction** noun **1** *his reaction had bewildered her* RESPONSE, answer, reply, rejoinder, retort, riposte; *informal* comeback.

**2** *a reaction against modernism* BACKLASH, counteraction.

**reactionary** adjective *a reactionary policy* RIGHT-WING, conservative, rightist, ultraconservative; traditionalist, conventional, old-fashioned, unprogressive; *informal* redneck. ANTONYM progressive.

▸ noun *an extreme reactionary* RIGHT-WINGER, conservative, rightist; traditionalist, conventionalist, dinosaur. ANTONYM radical.

**read** verb **1** *Nadine and Ian were reading the paper by the fireplace* PERUSE, study, scrutinize, look through; pore over, be absorbed in; run one's eye over, cast an eye over, leaf through, scan, flick through, skim through, thumb through.

**2** *he read a passage of the letter* READ OUT/ALOUD, recite, declaim.

**3** *I can't read my own writing* DECIPHER, make out, make sense of, interpret, understand.

**4** *her remark could be read as a criticism* INTERPRET, take, take to mean, construe, see, understand.

**5** *the dial read 70 mph* INDICATE, register, record, display, show.

▸ noun *have a read of this* PERUSAL, study, scan; look (at), browse (through).

PHRASES: **read something into something** *don't read too much into their statistics* INFER FROM, interpolate from, assume from, attribute to; read between the lines.

**read up on** *we'll need to read up on Peruvian culture* STUDY, brush up on; *informal* bone up on.

**readable** adjective **1** *the inscription is perfectly readable* LEGIBLE, easy to read, decipherable, clear, intelligible, comprehensible, reader-friendly. ANTONYM illegible.

**2** *her novels are immensely readable* ENJOYABLE, entertaining, interesting, absorbing, engaging, gripping, enthralling, engrossing, stimulating; *informal* unputdownable. ANTONYM boring.

**readily** adverb **1** *Durkin readily offered to drive him* WILLINGLY, without hesitation, unhesitatingly, ungrudgingly, gladly, happily, eagerly, promptly. ANTONYM reluctantly.

**2** *the island is readily accessible* EASILY, with ease, without difficulty. ANTONYM with difficulty.

**readiness** noun **1** *their readiness to accept change* WILLINGNESS, enthusiasm, eagerness, keenness; promptness, quickness, alacrity.

**2** *a state of readiness* PREPAREDNESS, preparation.

**3** *the readiness of his reply* PROMPTNESS, quickness, rapidity, swiftness, speed, speediness. PHRASE: **in readiness** *there were candles in readiness* READY, at the ready, available, on hand, accessible, handy; prepared, primed, on standby, standing by, on full alert.

**reading** noun **1** *a cursory reading of the financial pages* PERUSAL, study, scan, scanning; browse (through), look (through), glance (through), leaf (through), skim (through).

**2** *a man of wide reading* BOOK LEARNING, book learning, scholarship, education, erudition.

**3** *readings from the Bible* PASSAGE, lesson; section, piece; recital, recitation.

**4** *my reading of the situation* INTERPRETATION, construal, understanding, explanation, analysis.

**5** *a meter reading* RECORD, figure, indication, measurement.

**ready** adjective **1** *are you ready?* PREPARED, set, all set, organized, primed; *informal* fit, psyched up, geared up.

**2** *everything is ready* COMPLETED, finished, prepared, organized, done, arranged, fixed, in readiness.

**3** *he's always ready to help* WILLING, prepared, pleased, inclined, disposed, predisposed; eager, keen, happy, glad; *informal* game.

**4** *she looked* ***ready to*** *collapse* ABOUT TO, on the point of, on the verge of, close to, liable to, likely to.

**5** *a ready supply of food* AVAILABLE, easily available, accessible; handy, close/near at hand, on hand, convenient, within reach, at the ready, near, at one's fingertips.

6 *a ready answer* PROMPT, quick, swift, speedy, fast, immediate, unhesitating; clever, sharp, astute, shrewd, keen, perceptive, discerning.

▸ verb *he needed time to ready himself* PREPARE, get/make ready, organize; gear oneself up; *informal* psych oneself up.

PHRASES: **at the ready** *the fire extinguishers are at the ready* IN POSITION, poised, ready for use/action, waiting, on deck.
**make ready** *making ready for their departure* PREPARE, make preparations, get everything ready, gear up for.

**real** adjective 1 *is she a fictional character or a real person?* ACTUAL, nonfictional, factual, real-life; historical; material, physical, tangible, concrete, palpable. ANTONYM imaginary.

2 *real gold* GENUINE, authentic, bona fide; *informal* kosher, honest-to-goodness, honest-to-God. ANTONYMS imaginary, fake.

3 *my real name* TRUE, actual.

4 *tears of real grief* SINCERE, genuine, true, unfeigned, heartfelt, unaffected. ANTONYMS false, feigned.

5 *a real man* PROPER, true; *informal* regular.

6 *you're a real idiot* COMPLETE, utter, thorough, absolute, total, prize, perfect.

▸ adverb *informal that's real good of you.* See VERY adverb.

**realistic** adjective 1 *you've got to be realistic* PRACTICAL, pragmatic, matter-of-fact, down-to-earth, sensible, commonsensical, grounded; rational, reasonable, levelheaded, clear-sighted, businesslike; *informal* having both/one's feet on the ground, hard-nosed, no-nonsense. ANTONYM idealistic.

2 *a realistic aim* ACHIEVABLE, attainable, feasible, practicable, viable, reasonable, sensible, workable; *informal* doable. ANTONYM impracticable.

3 *a realistic portrayal of war* TRUE TO LIFE, lifelike, truthful, true, faithful, unidealized, real-life, naturalistic, graphic. ANTONYMS fictional, imaginative.

**reality** noun 1 *distinguishing fantasy from reality* THE REAL WORLD, real life, actuality; truth; physical existence. ANTONYM fantasy.

2 *the harsh realities of life* FACT, actuality, truth.

3 *the reality of Steinbeck's detail* VERISIMILITUDE, authenticity, realism, fidelity, faithfulness. ANTONYM idealism.

PHRASE: **in reality** *they got an invitation, but in reality they were not especially welcome* IN FACT, in actual fact, in point of fact, as a matter of fact, actually, really, in truth; in practice; *archaic* in sooth.

**realization** noun 1 *a growing realization of the danger* AWARENESS, understanding, comprehension, consciousness, appreciation, recognition, discernment; *formal* cognizance.

2 *the realization of our dreams* FULFILLMENT, achievement, accomplishment, attainment; *formal* effectuation.

**realize** verb 1 *he suddenly realized what she meant* REGISTER, perceive, discern, be/become aware of (the fact that), be/become conscious of (the fact that), notice; understand, grasp, comprehend, see, recognize, work out, fathom, apprehend; *informal* latch on to, savvy, figure out, get (the message); *Brit.* suss; *formal* be/become cognizant of.

2 *they realized their dream* FULFILL, achieve, accomplish, make a reality, make happen, bring to fruition, bring about/off, carry out/through; *formal* effectuate.

3 *the company realized significant profits* MAKE, clear, gain, earn, return, produce.

4 *the goods realized $3000* BE SOLD FOR, fetch, go for, make, net.

5 *he realized his assets* CASH IN, liquidate, capitalize.

**really** adverb 1 *he is really very wealthy* IN FACT, in actual fact, actually, in reality, in point of fact, as a matter of fact, in truth, to tell the truth; *archaic* in sooth.

2 *he really likes her* GENUINELY, truly, honestly; undoubtedly, without a doubt, indubitably, certainly, assuredly, unquestionably; *archaic* verily.

3 *they were really kind to me* VERY, extremely, thoroughly, decidedly, exceptionally, exceedingly, immensely, monumentally, tremendously, uncommonly, unbelievably, remarkably, eminently, extraordinarily, incredibly, most, downright, terrifically, awfully, so, ever so; *informal* totally, ultra, too —— for words, seriously, real, mighty, awful, plumb, powerful, way.

▸ exclamation *"They've split up." "Really?"* NO KIDDING, for real, is that so, is that a fact, is that right.

**realm** noun 1 *peace in the realm* KINGDOM, country, land, dominion, nation.

2 *the realm of academia* DOMAIN, sphere, area, field, world, province, territory.

**reap** verb 1 *the grain has been reaped* HARVEST, garner, gather in, bring in.

2 *reaping the benefits* RECEIVE, obtain, get, acquire, secure, realize.

**rear**[1] verb 1 *I was reared on a farm* BRING UP, raise, care for, look after, nurture, parent; educate.

2 *he reared cattle* BREED, raise, keep, farm, ranch.

3 *laboratory-reared plants* GROW, cultivate.

4 *the bear reared its head* RAISE, lift (up), hold up, uplift.

5 *Mount Logan reared up before them* RISE, rise up, tower, soar, loom.

**rear**[2] noun 1 *the rear of the building* BACK, back part, hind part, back end; *Nautical* stern. ANTONYM front.

2 *we were standing near the rear of the line* END, tail, rear end, back end, tail, tag end. ANTONYM front.

3 *he slapped the horse on the rear.* See BUTTOCKS.

▸ adjective *the rear bumper* BACK, end, rearmost; hind, hinder, hindmost; *technical* posterior.

**reason** noun 1 *the main reason for his decision* CAUSE, ground(s), basis, rationale; motive, motivation, purpose, point, aim, intention, objective, goal; explanation, justification, argument, defense, vindication, excuse, pretext.

**2** *postmodern voices railing against reason* RATIONALITY, logic, logical thought, reasoning, cognition; *formal* ratiocination.

**3** *he was losing his reason* SANITY, mind, mental faculties; senses, wits; *informal* marbles.

**4** *he continues, against reason, to love her* GOOD SENSE, good judgment, common sense, wisdom, sagacity, reasonableness.

▸ verb **1** *a young child is unable to reason* THINK RATIONALLY, think logically, use one's common sense, use one's head/brain; *formal* cogitate, ratiocinate.

**2** *Scott reasoned that Annabel might be ill* CALCULATE, come to the conclusion, conclude, reckon, think, judge, deduce, infer, surmise; *informal* figure.

**3** *she tried to* ***reason with*** *her husband* BRING AROUND, coax, persuade, prevail on, convince, make someone see the light.

PHRASES: **by reason of** *formal by reason of mental illness, Peterson will not be held in contempt of court* BECAUSE OF, on account of, as a result of, owing to, due to, by virtue of, thanks to.
**reason something out** *we finally reasoned out the cryptic message in chapter twelve* WORK OUT, think through, make sense of, get to the bottom of, puzzle out; *informal* figure out.
**with reason** *he was anxious, with reason, about his own political survival* JUSTIFIABLY, justly, legitimately, rightly, reasonably.

USAGE NOTE **reason is because**

This construction is loose because *reason* implies *because* and vice versa. As Robert W. Burchfield, the distinguished *Oxford English Dictionary* lexicographer, put it: "Though often defended by modern grammarians, the type 'the reason . . . is because' (instead of 'the reason . . . is that') aches with redundancy, and is still as inadmissible in Standard English as it was when H. W. Fowler objected to it in 1926." Points of View 116 (1992). After *reason is*, you'll need a noun phrase, a predicate adjective, or a clause introduced by *that*. The best cure for *reason is because* is to replace *because* with *that*—e.g.: "Marcello (Jean Reno) has one frantic mission in life: to keep anyone from dying in the small Italian village where he lives. The reason is because [read *reason is that*] there are only three plots left in the local cemetery and his terminally ill wife, Roseanna (Mercedes Ruehl), wishes only that she be buried next to their daughter." (*Star-Ledger* [Newark]; June 27, 1997.)

Variations such as *reason is due to* are no better—e.g.: "It's a challenge for any athlete to come back after four years of inactivity. The challenge is even greater when the reason is due to injury [read *the layoff is due to injury* or *injury is the cause*]." (*Tulsa Tribune & Tulsa World*; May 4, 1997.) —*BG*

**reasonable** adjective **1** *a reasonable man* | *a reasonable explanation* SENSIBLE, rational, logical, fair, fair-minded, just, equitable; intelligent, wise, levelheaded, practical, realistic; sound, reasoned, well-reasoned, valid, commonsensical; tenable, plausible, credible, believable.

**2** *you must take all reasonable precautions* WITHIN REASON, practicable, sensible; appropriate, suitable.

**3** *cars in reasonable condition* FAIRLY GOOD, acceptable, satisfactory, average, adequate, fair, all right, tolerable, passable; *informal* OK.

**4** *reasonable prices* INEXPENSIVE, moderate, low, cheap, budget, bargain, downmarket; competitive.

**reasoned** adjective *you have drawn a reasoned conclusion* LOGICAL, rational, well-thought-out, clear, lucid, coherent, cogent, well-expressed, well-presented, considered, sensible.

**reasoning** noun *it is a neurological disorder that results in impaired memory and reasoning* THINKING, reason, thought, train of thought, thought process, logic, analysis, interpretation, explanation, rationalization; reasons, rationale, arguments; *formal* ratiocination.

**reassure** verb *officials hope to reassure tourists in the wake of these latest terrorist attacks* PUT/SET SOMEONE'S MIND AT REST, put someone at ease, encourage, inspirit, hearten, buoy up, cheer up; comfort, soothe. ANTONYM alarm.

**rebate** noun *a 20-percent rebate* REFUND, partial refund, repayment; discount, deduction, reduction, decrease.

**rebel** noun **1** *the rebels took control of the capital* REVOLUTIONARY, insurgent, revolutionist, mutineer, insurrectionist, insurrectionary, guerrilla, terrorist, freedom fighter.

**2** *the concept of the artist as a rebel* NONCONFORMIST, dissenter, dissident, iconoclast, maverick.

▸ verb **1** *the citizens rebelled* REVOLT, mutiny, riot, rise up, take up arms, stage/mount a rebellion, be insubordinate.

**2** *his stomach rebelled at the thought of food* RECOIL, show/feel repugnance.

**3** *teenagers* ***rebelling against*** *their parents* DEFY, disobey, refuse to obey, kick against, challenge, oppose, resist. ANTONYM obey.

▸ adjective **1** *rebel troops* INSURGENT, revolutionary, mutinous, rebellious, insurrectionary, insurrectionist, renegade.

**2** *rebel clergymen* REBELLIOUS, defiant, disobedient, insubordinate, subversive, resistant, recalcitrant; nonconformist, maverick, iconoclastic; *archaic* contumacious. ANTONYMS compliant, conformist.

**rebellion** noun **1** *troops suppressed the rebellion* UPRISING, revolt, insurrection, mutiny, revolution, insurgence, insurgency; rioting, riot, disorder, unrest. See note at UPRISING.

**2** *an act of rebellion* DEFIANCE, disobedience, rebelliousness, insubordination, subversion, subversiveness, resistance.

**rebellious** adjective **1** *rebellious troops* REBEL, insurgent, mutinous, mutinying, rebelling, rioting, riotous, insurrectionary, insurrectionist, revolutionary.

**2** *a rebellious adolescent* DEFIANT, disobedient, insubordinate, unruly, mutinous, wayward, obstreperous, recalcitrant, intractable; *formal* refractory; *archaic* contumacious.

**rebound** verb **1** *the ball rebounded off the wall* BOUNCE, bounce back, spring back, ricochet, boomerang, carom.

**2** *finally the dollar rebounded* RECOVER, rally, pick up, make a recovery.

3 *Thomas's tactics rebounded on him* BACKFIRE, boomerang, have unwelcome repercussions; come back to haunt; *archaic* redound on.

**rebuff** verb *his offer was rebuffed* REJECT, turn down, spurn, refuse, decline, repudiate; snub, slight, repulse, repel, dismiss, brush off, give someone the cold shoulder; *informal* give someone the brush-off, give someone the bum's rush, freeze out. ANTONYM accept.

▸ noun *the rebuff did little to dampen his ardor* REJECTION, snub, slight, repulse; refusal, spurning, cold-shouldering, discouragement; *informal* brush-off, kick in the teeth, slap in the face.

**rebuke** verb *she never rebuked him in front of others* REPRIMAND, reproach, scold, admonish, reprove, chastise, upbraid, berate, take to task, criticize, censure; *informal* tell off, give someone a talking-to, give someone a dressing-down, give someone an earful, chew out, ream out; *formal* castigate. ANTONYM praise.

▸ noun *Damian was silenced by the rebuke* REPRIMAND, reproach, reproof, scolding, admonishment, admonition, upbraiding; *informal* dressing-down; *formal* castigation. ANTONYM compliment.

THE RIGHT WORD **rebuke, admonish, censure, reprimand, reproach, scold**

All of these verbs mean to criticize or express disapproval, but which one you use depends on how upset you are. If you want to go easy on someone, you can **admonish** or **reproach**, both of which indicate mild and sometimes kindly disapproval. To *admonish* is to warn or counsel someone, usually because a duty has been forgotten or might be forgotten in the future (*admonish her about leaving the key in the lock*), while *reproach* also suggests mild criticism aimed at correcting a fault or pattern of misbehavior (*he was reproved for his lack of attention in class*). If you want to express your disapproval formally or in public, use **censure** or **reprimand**. You can *censure* someone either directly or indirectly (*the judge censured the lawyer for violating courtroom procedures; a newspaper article that censured "deadbeat dads"*), while *reprimand* suggests a direct confrontation (*reprimanded by his parole officer for leaving town without reporting his whereabouts*). If you're irritated enough to want to express your disapproval quite harshly and at some length, you can **scold** (*to scold a child for jaywalking*). **Rebuke** is the harshest word of this group, meaning to criticize sharply or sternly, often in the midst of some action (*rebuke a carpenter for walking across an icy roof*).

**rebut** verb *you will have your opportunity to rebut the allegations* DENY, contradict, controvert, repudiate, counter, attempt to refute, attempt to discredit; *informal* poke holes in; *formal* gainsay. ANTONYM confirm.

USAGE NOTE **rebut, refute**

*Rebut* means "attempt to refute." *Refute* means "defeat (countervailing arguments)." Thus one who *rebuts* certainly hopes to *refute*; it is immodest to assume, however, that one has *refuted* another's arguments. See also note at refute.

*Rebut* is sometimes wrongly written *rebutt*. —*BG*

**recalcitrant** adjective *Amy was unprepared to deal with three recalcitrant stepchildren* UNCOOPERATIVE, intractable, obstreperous, truculent, insubordinate, defiant, rebellious, willful, wayward, headstrong, self-willed, contrary, perverse, difficult; *formal* refractory; *archaic* froward, contumacious. ANTONYM amenable.

**recall** verb 1 *he recalled his student days* REMEMBER, recollect, call to mind; think back on/to, look back on, reminisce about. ANTONYM forget.

2 *their exploits recall the days of chivalry* BRING TO MIND, call to mind, put one in mind of, call up, conjure up, evoke.

3 *the ambassador was recalled* SUMMON BACK, order back, call back. ANTONYM prorogue.

▸ noun 1 *the recall of the ambassador* SUMMONING BACK, ordering back, calling back.

2 *their recall of dreams* RECOLLECTION, remembrance, memory.

**recant** verb 1 *he was forced to recant his political beliefs* RENOUNCE, disavow, deny, repudiate, renege on; *formal* forswear, abjure.

2 *he refused to recant* CHANGE ONE'S MIND, be apostate; *rare* tergiversate.

3 *he recanted his testimony* RETRACT, take back, withdraw, unsay.

USAGE NOTE **recant, recount**

*Recant* = publicly repudiate a previous statement, belief, or accusation. *Recount* = narrate a past event, esp. from personal experience. *Recant* sometimes erroneously displaces the similar-sounding *recount*—e.g.: "Dressed in a top hat and tails, Garrett chats with his riders and recants [read *recounts*] tales of Weston's glory days." (*Des Moines Register*; May 19, 2002.) The *Oxford English Dictionary* does give "recount" as one sense of *recant* but labels it obsolete and rare. The most recent example is from 1611.

*Recant* is best reserved for use with personal statements and public positions (think *cant* = sing). Other words are better suited when the thing taken back is something other than words—e.g.:

• "The state's consumer counsel has asked state regulators to recant [read *reverse*] a recent decision under which she said Yankee Gas ratepayers would bear all of the costs of the company's proposed multimillion-dollar system expansion." (*Hartford Courant*; Feb. 14, 2002.)

• "Why do I feel like I'm listening to a deathbed confession by someone who's been a bastard all his life and suddenly, at the 11th hour, is terrified and wants to recant [read *make up for* or *renounce*?] his evil ways?" (*Daily News Leader* [Staunton, VA]; Mar. 5, 2002.)

*Recant* may be transitive (as in the first use in the following example) or intransitive (as in the second): "Police have a follow-up interview scheduled with Olowokandi's former girlfriend, Suzanne Ketcham, who says she plans to recant her original statements to them and a representative of the district attorney's special victims unit. 'It's not unusual for victims of domestic abuse to recant,' Nilsson said." (*Los Angeles Times*; Dec. 7, 2001.) —*BG*

**recapitulate** verb *I will recapitulate the main points* SUMMARIZE, sum up; restate, repeat, reiterate, go over, review; *informal* recap.

**recede** verb **1** *the floodwaters receded* RETREAT, go back, go down, move back, move away, withdraw, ebb, subside, abate. ANTONYMS advance, approach.

**2** *the lights receded into the distance* DISAPPEAR FROM VIEW, fade, be lost to view, pass from sight.

**3** *fears of violence have receded* DIMINISH, lessen, decrease, dwindle, fade, abate, subside, ebb, wane. ANTONYMS intensify, grow.

**receipt** noun **1** *the receipt of a letter* RECEIVING, getting, obtaining, gaining; arrival, delivery.

**2** *make sure you get a receipt* PROOF OF PURCHASE, bill, bill of sale, invoice, sales ticket.

**3** *receipts from house sales* PROCEEDS, takings, money/payment received, income, revenue, earnings; profits, return(s), financial return(s), take.

**receive** verb **1** *Toni received an award | they received $650 in damages* BE GIVEN, be presented with, be awarded, collect, garner; get, obtain, gain, acquire; win, be paid, earn, gross, net. ANTONYMS give, present.

**2** *she received a letter* BE SENT, be in receipt of, accept delivery of, accept. ANTONYM send.

**3** *Alec received the news on Monday* BE TOLD, be informed of, be notified of, hear, discover, find out (about), learn; *informal* get wind of.

**4** *he received her suggestion with a complete lack of interest* HEAR, listen to; respond to, react to.

**5** *she received a serious injury* EXPERIENCE, sustain, undergo, meet with; suffer, bear.

**6** *they received their guests* GREET, welcome, say hello to.

**7** *she's not receiving visitors* ENTERTAIN, see.

**recent** adjective **1** *recent research* NEW, (the) latest, current, fresh, modern, contemporary, up-to-date, up-to-the-minute. ANTONYM old.

**2** *his recent visit* NOT LONG PAST, occurring recently, just gone. ANTONYM former.

**recently** adverb *they recently installed a new flagpole* NOT LONG AGO, a short time ago, in the past few days/weeks/months, a little while back; lately, latterly, just now.

**receptacle** noun *a receptacle for recycling* CONTAINER, holder, repository; box, tin, bin, can, canister, case, bag.

**reception** noun **1** *the reception of the goods* RECEIPT, receiving, getting.

**2** *the reception of foreign diplomats* GREETING, welcoming, entertaining.

**3** *a chilly reception* RESPONSE, reaction, treatment.

**4** *a wedding reception* (FORMAL) PARTY, function, social occasion, soiree, fête, levee; *informal* do, bash.

**receptive** adjective *a receptive audience* OPEN-MINDED, responsive, amenable, well-disposed, flexible, approachable, accessible; *archaic* susceptive. ANTONYM unresponsive.

**recess** noun **1** *two recesses fitted with bookshelves* ALCOVE, bay, niche, nook, corner, hollow, oriel.

**2** **(recesses)** *the deepest recesses of the castle* INNERMOST PARTS/REACHES, remote places, secret places, heart, depths, bowels.

**3** *the Christmas recess* ADJOURNMENT, break, interlude, interval, rest; vacation, holiday; *informal* breather.

▸ verb *let's recess for lunch* ADJOURN, take a recess, stop, pause, break, take a break; *informal* take five, take a time out.

**recession** noun *job losses are symptomatic of the recession* ECONOMIC DECLINE, downturn, depression, slump, slowdown. ANTONYM boom.

**recipe** noun **1** *a tasty recipe* cooking instructions/directions; *archaic* receipt.

**2** *a recipe for success* MEANS/WAY OF ACHIEVING, prescription, formula, blueprint.

**reciprocal** adjective **1** *reciprocal love* GIVEN/FELT IN RETURN, requited, reciprocated.

**2** *reciprocal obligations and duties* MUTUAL, common, shared, joint, corresponding, complementary.

**reciprocate** verb **1** *I was happy to reciprocate* DO THE SAME (IN RETURN), respond in kind, return the favor.

**2** *love that was not reciprocated* REQUITE, return, give back; match, equal.

**recital** noun **1** *a piano recital* CONCERT, performance, musical performance, solo performance, solo; *informal* gig.

**2** *her recital of Bob's failures* ENUMERATION, list, litany, catalog, listing, detailing; account, report, description, recapitulation, recounting.

**3** *a recital of the Lord's Prayer.* See RECITATION sense 1.

**recitation** noun **1** *the recitation of his poem* RECITAL, saying aloud, declamation, rendering, rendition, delivery, performance.

**2** *a recitation of her life story* ACCOUNT, description, narration, narrative, story.

**3** *songs and recitations* READING, passage; poem, verse, monologue.

**recite** verb **1** *he began to recite verses of the Koran* REPEAT FROM MEMORY, say aloud, declaim, quote, deliver, render.

**2** *he stood up and started reciting* GIVE A RECITATION, say a poem.

**3** *Sir John recited the facts they knew* ENUMERATE, list, detail, reel off; recount, relate, describe, narrate, give an account of, recapitulate, repeat.

**reckless** adjective *reckless driving* RASH, careless, thoughtless, heedless, unheeding, hasty, overhasty, precipitate, precipitous, impetuous, impulsive, daredevil, devil-may-care; IRRESPONSIBLE, foolhardy, audacious, overadventurous; ill-advised, injudicious, madcap, imprudent, unwise, ill-considered; *informal* kamikaze; *literary* temerarious. ANTONYM careful.

**reckon** verb 1 *the cost was reckoned at $6,000* CALCULATE, compute, peg, work out, put a figure on, figure; count (up), add up, total; *chiefly Brit.* tot up.

2 *Anselm reckoned Hugh among his friends* INCLUDE, count, consider to be, regard as, look on as.

3 *informal I reckon I can manage that* BELIEVE, think, be of the opinion/view, be convinced, dare say, imagine, guess, suppose, consider, figure.

4 *it was reckoned a failure* REGARD AS, consider, judge, hold to be, think of as; deem, rate, gauge, count.

5 *I* ***reckon to*** *get good value for money* EXPECT TO, anticipate, hope to, be looking to; count on, rely on, depend on, bank on, figure on. PHRASES: **to be reckoned with** *the competition is indeed a force to be reckoned with* IMPORTANT, of considerable importance, significant; influential, estimable, powerful, strong, potent, formidable, redoubtable.
**reckon with** 1 *it's her mother you'll have to reckon with* DEAL WITH, contend with, face, face up to.

2 *they hadn't reckoned with her burning ambition* TAKE INTO ACCOUNT, take into consideration, bargain for/on, anticipate, foresee, be prepared for, consider.

**reckoning** noun 1 *by my reckoning, this comes to $2 million* CALCULATION, estimation, count, computation, working out, summation, addition.

2 *by her reckoning, the train was late* OPINION, view, judgment, evaluation, estimate, estimation.

3 *the terrible reckoning that he deserved* RETRIBUTION, fate, doom, nemesis, punishment. PHRASE: **day of reckoning** *I promise you, the enemy will remember this as their day of reckoning* JUDGMENT DAY, day of retribution, doomsday, D-Day.

**reclaim** verb 1 *traveling expenses can be reclaimed* GET BACK, recoup, claim back, recover, regain, retrieve. See note at RECOVER.

2 *Henrietta had reclaimed him from a life of despair* SAVE, rescue, redeem; reform.

**recline** verb *recline on the sofa* LIE, lie down, lie back, lean back; be recumbent; relax, repose, loll, lounge, sprawl, stretch out; *literary* couch.

**recluse** noun 1 *a religious recluse* HERMIT, ascetic, eremite, marabout; *historical* anchorite, anchoress.

2 *a natural recluse* LONER, solitary, lone wolf, troglodyte; misanthrope; *rare* solitudinarian, solitarian.

**recognition** noun 1 *there was no sign of recognition on his face* IDENTIFICATION, recollection, remembrance.

2 *his recognition of his lack of experience* ACKNOWLEDGMENT, acceptance, admission; realization, awareness, consciousness, knowledge, appreciation; *formal* cognizance.

3 *the sport has finally received the recognition it deserves* OFFICIAL APPROVAL, certification, accreditation, endorsement, validation.

4 *you deserve recognition for the tremendous job you are doing* APPRECIATION, gratitude, thanks, congratulations, credit, commendation, acclaim, acknowledgment; *informal* bouquets.

**recognize** verb 1 *Hannah recognized him at once* IDENTIFY, place, know, put a name to; remember, recall, recollect; know by sight.

2 *they recognized Alan's ability* ACKNOWLEDGE, accept, admit; realize, be aware of, be conscious of, perceive, discern, appreciate; *formal* be cognizant of.

3 *psychotherapists who are recognized* OFFICIALLY APPROVE, certify, accredit, endorse, sanction, validate.

4 *the board recognized their hard work* PAY TRIBUTE TO, show appreciation of/for, appreciate, be grateful for, acclaim, commend.

**recoil** verb 1 *she instinctively recoiled* DRAW BACK, jump back, pull back; flinch, shy away, shrink (back). See note at WINCE.

2 *he recoiled from the thought* FEEL REVULSION AT, feel disgust at, be unable to stomach, shrink from, balk at.

3 *her rifle recoiled* KICK (BACK), jerk back, spring back.

4 *this will eventually* ***recoil on*** *him* HAVE AN ADVERSE EFFECT ON, rebound on, affect badly, backfire on, boomerang on, come back to haunt; *archaic* redound on.

▸ noun *the recoil of the gun* KICKBACK, kick.

**recollect** verb *we recollected many events from our childhood* REMEMBER, recall, call to mind, think of; think back to, look back on, reminisce about. ANTONYM forget.

**recollection** noun *according to my recollection, he was wearing a striped necktie* MEMORY, remembrance, impression, reminiscence.

**recommend** verb 1 *her former employer recommended her for the post* ADVOCATE, endorse, commend, suggest, put forward, propose, nominate, put up; speak favorably of, speak well of, put in a good word for, vouch for; *informal* plug.

2 *the committee recommended a cautious approach* ADVISE, counsel, urge, exhort, enjoin, prescribe, argue for, back, support; suggest, advocate, propose.

3 *there was little to recommend her* HAVE IN ONE'S FAVOR, give an advantage to; *informal* have going for one.

**recommendation** noun 1 *the advisory group's recommendations* ADVICE, counsel, guidance, direction, suggestion, proposal.

2 *a personal recommendation* COMMENDATION, endorsement, good word, favorable mention, testimonial; suggestion, tip; *informal* plug.

3 *a place whose only recommendation is that it has few traffic problems* ADVANTAGE, good point/feature, benefit, asset, boon, attraction, appeal.

**reconcile** verb 1 *the news reconciled us* REUNITE, bring (back) together (again), restore friendly relations between, make peace between; pacify, appease, placate, mollify; *formal* conciliate. ANTONYMS estrange, alienate.

**2** *her divorced parents have reconciled* SETTLE ONE'S DIFFERENCES, make (one's) peace, make up, kiss and make up, bury the hatchet, declare a truce. ANTONYM quarrel.

**3** *trying to reconcile his religious beliefs with his career* MAKE COMPATIBLE, harmonize, square, make congruent, balance; *rare* syncretize.

**4** *the quarrel was reconciled* SETTLE, resolve, sort out, mend, remedy, heal, rectify; *informal* patch up.

**5** *they had to* ***reconcile themselves to*** *drastic losses* ACCEPT, come to accept, resign oneself to, come to terms with, learn to live with, get used to.

**reconciliation** noun **1** *the reconciliation of the disputants* REUNITING, reunion, bringing together (again), conciliation, reconcilement, rapprochement, fence-mending; pacification, appeasement, placating, mollification.

**2** *a reconciliation of their differences* RESOLUTION, settlement, settling, resolving, mending, remedying.

**3** *there was little hope of reconciliation* AGREEMENT, compromise, understanding, peace; *formal* concord.

**4** *the reconciliation of theory with practice* HARMONIZING, harmonization, squaring, balancing.

**recondite** adjective *the recondite realms of Semitic philology* OBSCURE, abstruse, arcane, esoteric, recherché, profound, difficult, complex, complicated, involved; incomprehensible, unfathomable, impenetrable, cryptic, opaque. See note at OBSCURE.

**reconnaissance** noun *unfortunately, our latest reconnaissance has uncovered no new information* PRELIMINARY SURVEY, survey, exploration, observation, investigation, examination, inspection; patrol, search; reconnoitering; *informal* recon.

**reconnoiter** verb *two of our best pilots were sent in to reconnoiter the area* SURVEY, make a reconnaissance of, explore; investigate, examine, scrutinize, inspect, observe, take a look at; patrol; *informal* check out, scope out, recon.

**reconsider** verb *the plaintiff has asked an appeals court to reconsider its decision to order a new trial* RETHINK, review, revise, reexamine, reevaluate, reassess, reappraise; change, alter, modify; have second thoughts, change one's mind.

**reconstruct** verb **1** *the building had to be reconstructed* REBUILD, restore, renovate, recreate, remake, reassemble, remodel, refashion, revamp, recondition, refurbish.

**2** *reconstructing the events of that day* RECREATE, build up a picture/impression of, piece together, reenact.

**record** noun **1** *written records of the past* ACCOUNT(S), document(s), documentation, data, file(s), dossier(s), evidence, report(s); annal(s), archive(s), chronicle(s); minutes, transactions, proceedings, transcript(s); certificate(s), instrument(s), deed(s); register, log, logbook; *Law* muniment(s).

**2** *listening to records* album, vinyl; *dated* phonograph record, LP, single, forty-five, seventy-eight.

**3** *the judge weighed the factor of his good record* PREVIOUS CONDUCT/PERFORMANCE, track record, history, life history, reputation.

**4** *she's got armed robbery on her record* CRIMINAL RECORD, police record; *informal* rap sheet.

**5** *she won the race and set a new record* BEST PERFORMANCE, highest achievement; best time, fastest time; world record.

**6** *a lasting record of what they have achieved* REMINDER, memorial, souvenir, memento, remembrance, testament.

▸ adjective *record profits* RECORD-BREAKING, best ever, unsurpassed, unparalleled, unequaled, second to none.

▸ verb **1** *the doctor recorded her blood pressure* WRITE DOWN, put in writing, take down, note, make a note of, jot down, put down on paper; document, put on record, enter, register, log; list, catalog.

**2** *the thermometer recorded a high temperature* INDICATE, register, show, display.

**3** *the team recorded their fourth win* ACHIEVE, accomplish, chalk up, notch up.

**4** *the recital was recorded live* MAKE A RECORD/RECORDING OF, tape, tape-record; video-record, videotape, video.

PHRASE: **off the record 1** *his comments were off the record* UNOFFICIAL, confidential, in (strict) confidence, not to be made public.

**2** *they admitted, off the record, that they had made a mistake* UNOFFICIALLY, privately, in (strict) confidence, confidentially, between ourselves.

**recorder** noun **1** *he put a cassette in the recorder* tape recorder, cassette recorder; VCR, videocassette recorder, videotape recorder; DVD recorder, digital recorder.

**2** *a recorder of rural life* RECORD KEEPER, archivist, annalist, diarist, chronicler, historian; *rare* chronologer, chronologist.

**recount** verb *Gretchen recounted everything she could remember about what happened that night* TELL, relate, narrate, give an account of, describe, report, outline, delineate, relay, convey, communicate, impart. See note at RECANT.

**recoup** verb *Andalusian health authorities bringing suit against tobacco giants in an attempt to recoup the cost of treating smokers* GET BACK, regain, recover, win back, retrieve, redeem. See note at RECOVER.

**USAGE NOTE recoup, recuperate**

*Recoup*, dating from the fifteenth century as an English word, is a transitive verb with two senses: (1) "get back (lost money, etc.)"; or (2) "pay back (money owed, etc.)." Although sense 2 is older, sense 1 is now predominant. *Recuperate*, dating from the mid-sixteenth century, is almost always an intransitive verb with the sense "get well; regain one's strength after a medical procedure or an illness." The misuse of *recoup* for *recuperate* is not uncommon—e.g.: "Still recouping [read *recuperating*] from foot surgery and planning to strike a long-term performance deal in Las Vegas for early next year, Cassidy kicked back and watched hours of rare footage of the Rats in action." (*Las Vegas Review-Journal*; July 23, 1999.)

A related mistake is the misspelling *recouperate*—e.g.: "Lance Diamond, the godfather of Buffalo soul, is in Mercy Hospital recoupering [read *recuperating*] from a flu-like illness." (*Buffalo News*; Nov. 30, 2000.)

Another error is the misuse of *recuperate* for *recoup*—e.g.:

- "The funeral provider would have to file a civil lawsuit to recuperate [read *recoup*] its money, Yabuno said." (*Press-Enterprise* [Riverside, CA]; July 19, 2000.)
- "They have demanded a jury trial in the hopes of recuperating [read *recouping*] losses they claim are a result of 'incompetence' by the attorneys they are suing." (*South Bend Tribune*; Aug. 4, 2000.) —*BG*

---

**recourse** noun *surgery may be the only recourse* OPTION, possibility, alternative, resort, way out, hope, remedy, choice, expedient. PHRASE: **have recourse to** *we had recourse to the national committee for additional funding* RESORT TO, make use of, avail oneself of, turn to, call on, look to, fall back on.

**recover** verb **1** *he's recovering from a heart attack* RECUPERATE, get better, convalesce, regain one's strength, get stronger, get back on one's feet; be on the mend, be on the road to recovery, pick up, rally, respond to treatment, improve, heal, pull through, bounce back. ANTONYM deteriorate.

**2** *later, shares recovered* RALLY, improve, pick up, make a recovery, rebound, bounce back.

**3** *the stolen material has been recovered* RETRIEVE, regain (possession of), get back, recoup, reclaim, repossess, redeem, recuperate, find (again), track down. ANTONYM lose.

**4** *gold coins recovered from a wreck* SALVAGE, save, rescue, retrieve. PHRASE: **recover oneself** *as nervous as she was, she convincingly recovered herself* PULL ONESELF TOGETHER, regain one's composure, regain one's self-control; *informal* get a grip (on oneself).

THE RIGHT WORD **recover, reclaim, recoup, regain, restore, retrieve**

---

If you lose or let go of something and find it either by chance or with effort, you **recover** it (*recover the stolen artwork*). Although it is often used interchangeably with *recover*, **regain** puts more emphasis on the search or effort involved in getting back something you have been deprived of (*regain one's position as chairperson; regain one's eyesight*). **Recoup** refers to the recovery of something similar or equivalent to what has been lost, usually in the form of compensation (*he tried to recoup his gambling losses*). **Reclaim** and **restore** both involve bringing something back to its original condition or to a better or more useful state. *Reclaim* is usually associated with land (*reclaim neglected farmlands*), while *restore* is linked to buildings or objects of art (*restore an eighteenth-century house*). **Retrieve** implies that something has slipped beyond reach, and that a concerted effort or search is required to recover it (*her desperate efforts to retrieve the family dog from the flooded house*).

---

**recovery** noun **1** *her recovery may be slow* RECUPERATION, convalescence. ANTONYM relapse.

**2** *the economy was showing signs of recovery* IMPROVEMENT, rallying, picking up, upturn, upswing. ANTONYM deterioration.

**3** *the recovery of the stolen goods* RETRIEVAL, regaining, repossession, getting back, reclamation, recouping, redemption, recuperation. ANTONYM loss.

**recreation** noun **1** *she cycles for recreation* PLEASURE, leisure, relaxation, fun, enjoyment, entertainment, amusement; play, sport; *informal* R and R; *archaic* disport. ANTONYM work.

**2** *his favorite recreations* PASTIME, hobby, leisure activity.

**recrimination** noun *this is not a time for recrimination, but a time to come together in solidarity* ACCUSATION(S), counteraccusation(s), countercharge(s), counterattack(s), retaliation(s).

**recruit** verb **1** *more soldiers were recruited* ENLIST, call up, conscript, draft, muster in; *archaic* levy.

**2** *the king recruited an army* MUSTER, form, raise, mobilize. ANTONYM disband.

**3** *the company is recruiting staff* HIRE, employ, take on; enroll, sign up, engage. ANTONYM dismiss.

▸ noun **1** *thousands of recruits were enlisted* CONSCRIPT, new soldier; draftee, yardbird.

**2** *top-quality recruits* NEW MEMBER, new entrant, newcomer, initiate, beginner, novice, tenderfoot, hire; *informal* rookie, newbie, greenhorn.

**rectify** verb *Perry is willing to do anything to rectify the situation with his estranged grandfather* CORRECT, right, put right, put to rights, sort out, deal with, amend, remedy, repair, fix, make good, resolve, settle; *informal* patch up.

**rectitude** noun *not all of his colleagues share his personal frugality and public rectitude* RIGHTEOUSNESS, goodness, virtue, morality, honor, honorableness, integrity, principle, probity, honesty, trustworthiness, uprightness, decency, good character. See note at GOODNESS.

**recuperate** verb **1** *Amanda went to Jackson Hole to recuperate* GET BETTER, recover, convalesce, get well, regain one's strength/health, get over something.

**2** *he recuperated the money*. See note at RECOUP.

**recur** verb *we don't want the termite infestation to recur* HAPPEN AGAIN, reoccur, occur again, repeat (itself); come back (again), return, reappear, appear again.

**recurrent** adjective *a recurrent blood clot in his lung | patriotic feminism is a recurrent theme in her music* REPEATED, recurring, repetitive, periodic, cyclical, seasonal, perennial, regular, frequent; intermittent, sporadic, spasmodic.

**recycle** verb *the UPS Store will recycle those annoying styrofoam peanuts* REUSE, reprocess, reclaim, recover; salvage, save.

**red** adjective **1** *a red dress* scarlet, vermilion, crimson, ruby, cherry, cerise, cardinal, carmine, wine, blood-red; coral, cochineal, rose; brick-red, maroon, rufous; reddish; rusty, cinnamon, fulvous; *literary* damask, vermeil, sanguine.

**2** *he was red in the face* FLUSHED, reddish, crimson, pink, pinkish, florid, rubicund; ruddy, rosy, glowing; burning, feverish; *literary* rubescent; *archaic* sanguine.

3 *his eyes were red* BLOODSHOT, sore.

4 *red hair* reddish, auburn, titian, chestnut, carroty, ginger, sandy. PHRASES: **in the red** *his account is still in the red* OVERDRAWN, in debt, in debit, in deficit, in arrears.

**see red** *informal* *when Kate showed up drunk, Julian saw red* BECOME VERY ANGRY, become enraged, lose one's temper; *informal* go mad, go crazy, go wild, go bananas, hit the roof, fly off the handle, blow one's top, flip out, go ballistic, flip one's wig, blow one's stack.

**redden** verb *the sleet reddened our faces | Sean could feel his cheeks redden* TURN RED, go red, make red, blush, flush, color, burn.

**redeem** verb 1 *the whimsical artwork redeems the book* SAVE, compensate for the defects of, vindicate.

2 *he fully redeemed himself in the next race* VINDICATE, free from blame, absolve.

3 *you cannot redeem their sins* ATONE FOR, make amends for, make restitution for.

4 *who shall redeem these sinners?* SAVE, deliver from sin, convert.

5 *Billy redeemed his drums from the pawnbrokers* RETRIEVE, regain, recover, get back, reclaim, repossess; buy back.

6 *this voucher can be redeemed at any branch* EXCHANGE, give in exchange, cash in, convert, trade in.

7 *they could not redeem their debts* PAY OFF/BACK, clear, discharge, honor.

8 *he made no effort to redeem his promise* FULFILL, carry out, discharge, make good; keep, keep to, stick to, hold to, adhere to, abide by, honor.

**redemption** noun 1 *God's redemption of his people* SAVING, freeing from sin, absolution.

2 *the redemption of their possessions* RETRIEVAL, recovery, reclamation, repossession, return.

3 *the redemption of credit vouchers* EXCHANGE, cashing in, conversion.

4 *the redemption of the mortgage* PAYING OFF, paying back, discharge, clearing, honoring.

5 *the redemption of his obligations* FULFILLMENT, carrying out, discharge, performing, honoring, meeting.

**redolent** adjective *their pubs bear names redolent of the monarchy* EVOCATIVE, suggestive, reminiscent.

**redoubtable** adjective *a redoubtable army commander* FORMIDABLE, awe-inspiring, fearsome, daunting; impressive, commanding, indomitable, invincible, doughty, mighty.

**redound** verb *formal* *such sanctions would not* ***redound to*** *their benefit internationally* CONTRIBUTE TO, be conducive to, result in, lead to, effect; *formal* conduce to.

**redress** verb 1 *we redressed the problem* RECTIFY, correct, right, put to rights, compensate for, amend, remedy, make good, resolve, settle.

2 *we aim to redress the balance* EVEN UP, regulate, equalize.

▸ noun *your best hope of redress* COMPENSATION, reparation, restitution, recompense, repayment, indemnity, indemnification, retribution, satisfaction; justice.

**reduce** verb 1 *the aim to reduce pollution* LESSEN, make smaller, lower, bring down, decrease, diminish, minimize; shrink, narrow, contract, shorten; ax, cut, cut back/down, make cutbacks in, trim, curtail, slim (down), prune; *informal* chop. ANTONYM increase.

2 *she* ***reduced*** *him* ***to*** *tears* BRING TO, bring to the point of, drive to.

3 *he was reduced to the ranks* DEMOTE, downgrade, bring low, lower, lower in rank. ANTONYM promote.

4 *Halloween items have been reduced* DISCOUNT, mark down, lower the price of, cut, cut in price, make cheaper, put on sale; *informal* slash, knock down. ANTONYM mark up.

PHRASE: **in reduced circumstances** *Quinlan was shocked to find his brother in reduced circumstances* IMPOVERISHED, broke, in straitened circumstances, ruined, bankrupted; poor, indigent, impecunious, in penury, poverty-stricken, destitute; needy, badly off, hard up; *informal* without two cents to rub together, strapped for cash; *formal* penurious.

**reduction** noun 1 *a reduction in pollution* LESSENING, lowering, decrease, diminution, fade-out.

2 *a staff reduction* CUTBACK, cut, downsizing, scaling down, trimming, pruning, axing, chopping.

3 *a reduction in inflationary pressure* EASING, lightening, moderation, alleviation.

4 *a reduction in status* DEMOTION, downgrading, lowering.

5 *substantial reductions* DISCOUNT, markdown, deduction, cut, price cut.

**redundant** adjective *many churches are now redundant* UNNECESSARY, not required, inessential, unessential, needless, unneeded, uncalled for; surplus, superfluous. ANTONYMS essential, necessary.

**reel** verb 1 *he reeled as the ship began to roll* STAGGER, lurch, sway, rock, stumble, totter, wobble, falter.

2 *the room reeled* GO ROUND, go round and round, whirl, spin, revolve, swirl, twirl, turn, swim. PHRASES: **reel something off** *she can reel off all the U.S. vice presidents in less than a minute* RECITE, rattle off, list rapidly, run through, enumerate, detail, itemize.

**reeling from** *we were reeling from the crisis* SHAKEN BY, stunned by, in shock from, shocked by, taken aback by, staggered by, aghast at, upset by.

**refer** verb 1 *he* ***referred to*** *errors in the article* MENTION, make reference to, allude to, touch on, speak of/about, talk of/about, write about, comment on, deal with, point out, call attention to.

2 *the matter has been referred to my insurers* PASS, hand over, hand, send on, transfer, remit, entrust, assign.

3 *these figures* ***refer to*** *only the year 2001* APPLY TO, be relevant to, concern, relate to, be connected with, pertain to, appertain to, be pertinent to, have a bearing on, cover.

4 *the name* ***refers to*** *a native village* DENOTE, describe, indicate, mean, signify, designate.

5 *the doctor* ***referred to*** *his notes* CONSULT, turn to, look at, have recourse to.

**referee** noun 1 *the referee blew his whistle* UMPIRE, judge, linesman; *informal* ref, ump.

2 *include the names of two referees* SUPPORTER, character witness, advocate.

▸ verb 1 *he refereed the game* UMPIRE, judge; *informal* ump.

2 *they asked him to referee in the dispute* ARBITRATE, mediate.

**reference** noun 1 *his journal contains many* ***references to*** *railroads* MENTION OF, allusion to, comment on, remark about.

2 *references are given in the bibliography* SOURCE, citation, authority, credit; bibliographical data.

3 *reference to a higher court* REFERRAL, transfer, remission.

4 *a glowing reference* TESTIMONIAL, character reference, recommendation; credentials. PHRASE: **with reference to** *with reference to your latest request for funding, the directors will submit their final decision on Friday* APROPOS TO, with regard to, regarding, with respect to, on the subject of, re; in relation to, relating to, vis-à-vis, in connection with.

**referendum** noun *he called for a referendum on the death penalty* POPULAR VOTE, vote, public vote, plebiscite, ballot, poll.

**refine** verb 1 *refining our cereal foods* PURIFY, process, treat.

2 *helping students to refine their language skills* IMPROVE, perfect, polish (up), hone, fine-tune.

**refined** adjective 1 *refined sugar* PURIFIED, processed, treated. ANTONYM crude.

2 *a refined lady* CULTIVATED, cultured, polished, stylish, elegant, sophisticated, urbane; polite, gracious, well-mannered, well-bred, gentlemanly, ladylike, genteel. ANTONYMS boorish, coarse.

3 *a person of refined taste* DISCRIMINATING, discerning, fastidious, exquisite, impeccable, fine.

**refinement** noun 1 *the refinement of sugar* PURIFICATION, refining, processing, treatment, treating.

2 *all writing needs endless refinement* IMPROVEMENT, polishing, honing, fine-tuning, touching up, finishing off, revision, editing, reworking.

3 *a woman of refinement* STYLE, elegance, finesse, polish, sophistication, urbanity; politeness, grace, graciousness, good manners, good breeding, gentility; cultivation, taste, discrimination.

**reflect** verb 1 *the snow reflects light* SEND BACK, throw back, cast back.

2 *their expressions reflected their feelings* INDICATE, show, display, demonstrate, be evidence of, register, reveal, betray, disclose; express, communicate; *formal* evince.

3 *he* ***reflected on*** *his responsibilities* THINK ABOUT, give thought to, consider, give consideration to, review, mull over, contemplate, cogitate about/on, meditate on, muse on, brood on/over, turn over in one's mind; *archaic* pore on. PHRASE: **reflect badly on** *stunts like these reflect badly on our school* DISCREDIT, disgrace, dishonor, shame, put in a bad light, damage, tarnish the reputation of, give a bad name to, bring into disrepute.

**reflection** noun 1 *the reflection of light* SENDING BACK, throwing back, casting back.

2 *her reflection in the pond* IMAGE, mirror image, likeness.

3 *your hands and nails are a reflection of your well-being* INDICATION, display, demonstration, manifestation; expression, evidence.

4 *a sad reflection on society* SLUR, aspersion, imputation, reproach, shame, criticism.

5 *after some reflection, he turned it down* THOUGHT, thinking, consideration, contemplation, deliberation, pondering, meditation, musing, rumination; *formal* cogitation.

6 *write down your reflections* OPINION, thought, view, belief, feeling, idea, impression, conclusion, assessment; comment, observation, remark.

**reflex** adjective *sneezing is a reflex action* INSTINCTIVE, automatic, involuntary, reflexive, impulsive, intuitive, spontaneous, unconscious, unconditioned, untaught, unlearned. ANTONYM conscious.

**reform** verb 1 *a plan to reform the system* IMPROVE, better, make better, ameliorate, refine; alter, make alterations to, change, adjust, make adjustments to, adapt, amend, revise, reshape, refashion, redesign, restyle, revamp, rebuild, reconstruct, remodel, reorganize.

2 *after his marriage he reformed* MEND ONE'S WAYS, change for the better, turn over a new leaf, improve.

▸ noun *the reform of the prison system* IMPROVEMENT, amelioration, refinement; alteration, change, adaptation, amendment, revision, reshaping, refashioning, redesigning, restyling, revamp, revamping, renovation, rebuilding, reconstruction, remodeling, reorganizing, reorganization.

**refractory** adjective *formal their refractory children* OBSTINATE, stubborn, mulish, pigheaded, obdurate, headstrong, self-willed, wayward, willful, perverse, contrary, recalcitrant, obstreperous, disobedient, difficult; *informal* balky; *archaic* contumacious, froward. ANTONYM obedient.

**refrain** verb *the demonstrators have promised to* ***refrain from*** *violent behavior* ABSTAIN FROM, desist from, hold back from, stop oneself from, forbear (from), avoid, eschew, shun, renounce; *informal* swear off; *formal* forswear, abjure.

**refresh** verb 1 *the cool air will refresh me* REINVIGORATE, revitalize, revive, restore, fortify, enliven, perk up, stimulate, freshen, energize, exhilarate, reanimate, wake up, revivify, inspirit; blow away the cobwebs; *informal* buck up, pep up. ANTONYM weary.

2 *let me refresh your memory* JOG, stimulate, prompt, prod.

3 *I refreshed his glass* REFILL, top up, replenish, recharge.

**refreshing** adjective 1 *a refreshing drink* INVIGORATING, revitalizing, reviving, restoring, bracing, fortifying, enlivening, inspiriting, stimulating, energizing, exhilarating.

2 *a refreshing change of direction* WELCOME, stimulating, fresh, imaginative, innovative, innovatory.

**refrigerate** verb *don't refrigerate the bananas* KEEP COLD, cool, cool down, chill; freeze. ANTONYM heat.

**refuge** noun 1 *homeless people seeking refuge in subway stations* SHELTER, protection, safety, security, asylum, sanctuary.

2 *a refuge for mountain gorillas* SANCTUARY, shelter, place of safety, haven, safe haven, sanctum; retreat, hiding place, hideaway, hideout.

**refugee** noun *collecting blankets for the refugees* ÉMIGRÉ, fugitive, exile, displaced person, asylum seeker; (**refugees**) boat people.

**refund** verb 1 *we will refund your money if you're not satisfied* REPAY, give back, return, pay back.

2 *they refunded the subscribers* REIMBURSE, compensate, recompense, remunerate, indemnify.

▸ noun *a full refund* REPAYMENT, reimbursement, rebate.

**refurbish** verb *the airfield plans to refurbish its museum* RENOVATE, recondition, rehabilitate, revamp, overhaul, restore, renew, redevelop, rebuild, reconstruct; redecorate, spruce up, upgrade, refit, retrofit, bring up to code; *informal* do up, rehab.

**refusal** noun 1 *we had one refusal to our invitation* NONACCEPTANCE, no, dissent, demurral, negation, turndown; regrets.

2 *you can have first refusal* OPTION, choice, opportunity to purchase.

3 *the refusal of a zoning variance* WITHHOLDING, denial, turndown.

**refuse**[1] verb 1 *he refused their invitation* DECLINE, turn down, say no to; reject, spurn, rebuff, dismiss; send one's regrets; *informal* pass up. ANTONYM accept.

2 *the city refused planning permission* WITHHOLD, deny, refuse to grant; *informal* give thumbs down to. ANTONYM grant.

**refuse**[2] noun *piles of refuse* GARBAGE, trash, waste, debris, litter, detritus, dross; dregs, leftovers; *informal* junk.

**regain** verb 1 *government troops regained the capital* RECOVER, get back, win back, recoup, retrieve, reclaim, repossess; take back, retake, recapture, reconquer. See note at RECOVER.

2 *they regained dry land* RETURN TO, get back to, reach again, rejoin.

**regal** adjective 1 *a regal feast.* See SPLENDID sense 1.

2 *his regal forebears* ROYAL, kingly, queenly, princely.

**regale** verb 1 *they were lavishly regaled* ENTERTAIN, wine and dine, fête, feast, serve, feed.

2 *he regaled her with colorful stories* ENTERTAIN, amuse, divert, delight, fascinate, captivate.

**regard** verb 1 *we regard these results as encouraging* CONSIDER, look on, view, see, think of, judge, deem, estimate, assess, reckon, adjudge, rate, gauge.

2 *he regarded her coldly* LOOK AT, contemplate, eye, gaze at, stare at; watch, observe, view, study, scrutinize; *literary* behold.

▸ noun 1 *she has no regard for human life* CONSIDERATION, care, concern, thought, notice, heed, attention.

2 *doctors are held in high regard* ESTEEM, respect, acclaim, admiration, approval, approbation, estimation. See note at ESTEEM.

3 (**regards**) *Jamie sends his regards* BEST WISHES, good wishes, greetings, kind/kindest regards, felicitations, salutations, respects, compliments, best, love.

4 *his steady regard* LOOK, fixed look, gaze, stare; observation, contemplation, study, scrutiny.

5 *in this regard I disagree with you* RESPECT, aspect, point, item, particular, detail, specific; matter, issue, topic, question.

PHRASE: **with/in regard to.** See REGARDING.

**USAGE NOTE regard**

As a noun in *with regard to* and *in regard to*, the singular noun is correct. The plural form (as in with regards to and in regards to) is, to put it charitably, poor usage—e.g.: "Single men and women are overwhelmed and confused by a barrage of information and advice on what to do and what not to do in regards to [read *in regard to*] finding Mr. Right and Ms. Girl-of-My-Dreams." (*Ebony*; Dec. 1997.) The acceptable forms are best used as introductory phrases. But even these may be advantageously replaced by a single word such as *concerning*, *regarding*, or *considering*, or even *in*, *about*, or *for*.

The plural *regards* is acceptable in this sense only in the phrase *as regards*, a traditional literary idiom (though now a little old-fashioned). But some writers mistakenly use with *regards to*—e.g.: "He became furious at the mere mention of . . . the columnist who accused him recently of 'judicial exhibitionism' with regards to [read *with regard to*] his trade-agreement ruling." (*New York Times*; Sept. 17, 1993.)

The verb *regard* commonly appears in two combinations. The one phrase, *highly regarded*, is a vague expression of praise; the other, *widely regarded as*, usually leads to words of praise—though it would certainly be possible to say that someone is "widely regarded as beneath contempt." It's a mistake, however, to truncate the latter phrase—to say *widely regarded* in place of *highly regarded*: "Crotty has published four novels since leaving the newspaper, and he's widely regarded [read *highly regarded*] by both fiction writers and journalists." —*BG*

**regarding** preposition *the condo commission has called a special meeting regarding pet ownership* CONCERNING, as regards, with/in regard to, with respect to, with reference to, relating to, respecting, re, about, apropos, on the subject of, in connection with, vis-à-vis.

**regardless** adverb *he decided to go, regardless* ANYWAY, anyhow, in any case, nevertheless, nonetheless, despite everything, in spite of everything, even so, all the same, in any event, come what may; *informal* still and all, irregardless.

PHRASE: **regardless of** *the race will be held on Saturday, regardless of the weather* IRRESPECTIVE OF, without regard to, without reference to, disregarding, without consideration of, discounting, ignoring, notwithstanding, no matter.

**regenerate** verb *Marion's daily walks really seem to regenerate her* REVIVE, revitalize, renew, restore, breathe new life into, revivify, rejuvenate, reanimate, resuscitate; *informal* give a shot in the arm to.

**regime** noun **1** *the former Communist regime* GOVERNMENT, system of government, authorities, rule, authority, control, command, administration, leadership.

**2** *a health regime* SYSTEM, arrangement, order, pattern, method, procedure, routine, course, plan, program.

**regiment** noun *the regiment was fighting in Europe* UNIT, outfit, force, corps, division, brigade, battalion, squadron, company, platoon.

▸ verb *their life is strictly regimented* ORGANIZE, order, systematize, control, regulate, manage, discipline.

**region** noun *the western region of the country* DISTRICT, province, territory, division, area, section, sector, zone, belt, part, quarter; *informal* parts. PHRASE: **in the region of.** See APPROXIMATELY.

**regional** adjective **1** *regional variations* GEOGRAPHICAL, territorial; by region.

**2** *a regional government* LOCAL, localized, provincial, district, parochial. ANTONYM national.

**register** noun **1** *the register of electors* OFFICIAL LIST, listing, roll, roster, index, directory, catalog, inventory.

**2** *the parish register* RECORD, chronicle, log, logbook, ledger, archive; annals, files.

**3** *the lower register of the piano* RANGE, reaches; notes, octaves.

▸ verb **1** *I wish to register a complaint* RECORD, put on record, enter, file, lodge, write down, put in writing, submit, report, note, log.

**2** *it is not too late to register* ENROLL, put one's name down, enlist, sign on, sign up, apply.

**3** *the dial registered a speed of 100 mph* INDICATE, read, record, show, display.

**4** *her face registered anger* DISPLAY, show, express, exhibit, betray, evidence, reveal, manifest, demonstrate, bespeak; *formal* evince.

**5** *the content of her statement did not register* MAKE AN IMPRESSION, get through, sink in, penetrate, have an effect, strike home.

**regress** verb *he regressed to his former state of madness* REVERT, retrogress, relapse, lapse, backslide, slip back; deteriorate, decline, worsen, degenerate, get worse; *informal* go downhill. ANTONYM progress.

**regret** verb **1** *they came to regret their decision* BE SORRY ABOUT, feel contrite about, feel remorse about/for, be remorseful about, rue, repent (of), feel repentant about, be regretful at/about. ANTONYMS welcome, applaud.

**2** *regretting the passing of youth* MOURN, grieve for/over, feel grief at, weep over, sigh over, feel sad about, lament, sorrow for, deplore.

▸ noun **1** *both players later expressed regret* REMORSE, sorrow, contrition, contriteness, repentance, penitence, guilt, compunction, remorsefulness, ruefulness. ANTONYM satisfaction.

**2** **(regrets)** *please give your grandmother my regrets* APOLOGY, apologies; refusal.

**3** *they left with genuine regret* SADNESS, sorrow, disappointment, unhappiness, grief. ANTONYM happiness.

**regretful** adjective *when your abandoned children grow up, will they care that you claim to be regretful?* SORRY, remorseful, contrite, repentant, rueful, penitent, conscience-stricken, apologetic, guilt-ridden, ashamed, shamefaced. ANTONYM unrepentant.

**regrettable** adjective *a regrettable mistake* UNDESIRABLE, unfortunate, unwelcome, sorry, woeful, disappointing; deplorable, lamentable, shameful, disgraceful.

**regular** adjective **1** *plant them at regular intervals* UNIFORM, even, consistent, constant, unchanging, unvarying, fixed. ANTONYM erratic.

**2** *a regular beat* RHYTHMIC, steady, even, uniform, constant, unchanging, unvarying. ANTONYM unsteady.

**3** *the subject of regular protests* FREQUENT, repeated, continual, recurrent, periodic, constant, perpetual, numerous. ANTONYM occasional.

**4** *regular methods of business* ESTABLISHED, conventional, orthodox, proper, official, approved, bona fide, standard, usual, traditional, tried and tested. ANTONYM experimental.

**5** *a regular procedure* METHODICAL, systematic, structured, well-ordered, well-organized, orderly, efficient. ANTONYM haphazard.

**6** *his regular route to work* USUAL, normal, customary, habitual, routine, typical, accustomed, established. See note at NORMAL. ANTONYM unusual.

**regulate** verb **1** *the flow of the river has been regulated* CONTROL, adjust, manage.

**2** *a new act regulating businesses* SUPERVISE, police, monitor, check, check up on, be responsible for; control, manage, direct, guide, govern.

**regulation** noun **1** *they obey all the regulations* RULE, ruling, order, directive, act, law, bylaw, statute, edict, canon, pronouncement, dictate, dictum, decree, fiat, command, precept.

**2** *the regulation of blood sugar* ADJUSTMENT, control, management, balancing.

**3** *the regulation of financial services* SUPERVISION, policing, superintendence, monitoring, inspection; control, management, ordering.

▸ adjective *regulation dress* OFFICIAL, prescribed, set, fixed, mandatory, compulsory, obligatory, de rigueur. ANTONYM unofficial.

**rehabilitate** verb **1** *efforts to rehabilitate patients* RESTORE TO NORMALITY, reintegrate, readapt; *informal* rehab.

**2** *former dissidents were rehabilitated* REINSTATE, restore, bring back; pardon, absolve, exonerate, forgive; *formal* exculpate.

**3** *rehabilitating vacant housing* RECONDITION, restore, renovate, refurbish, revamp, overhaul, redevelop, rebuild, reconstruct; redecorate, spruce up; upgrade, refit, modernize; *informal* do up, rehab.

**rehearsal** noun *our first concert rehearsal is Monday evening* PRACTICE, practice session, trial performance, read-through, run-through, walk-through; dress rehearsal; *informal* dry run.

**rehearse** verb **1** *I rehearsed the role* PREPARE, practice, read through, run through/over, go over.

**2** *he rehearsed the Vienna Philharmonic* TRAIN, drill, prepare, coach, put someone through their paces.

**3** *the document rehearsed all the arguments* ENUMERATE, list, itemize, detail, spell out, catalog, recite, rattle off; restate, repeat, reiterate, regurgitate, recapitulate, go over, run through; *informal* recap.

**reign** verb **1** *Robert II reigned for nineteen years* BE KING/QUEEN, be monarch, be sovereign, sit on the throne, wear the crown, rule.

**2** *chaos reigned* PREVAIL, exist, be present, be the case, occur, be prevalent, be current, be rife, be rampant, be the order of the day, be in force, be in effect; *formal* obtain.

▸ noun **1** *during Henry's reign* RULE, sovereignty, monarchy. See note at REIN.

**2** *his reign as manager* PERIOD IN OFFICE, incumbency, managership, leadership.

**rein** noun *there is no rein on his behavior* RESTRAINT, check, curb, constraint, restriction, limitation, control, brake. See note at REIGN.

▸ verb *they* ***reined back*** *costs* RESTRAIN, check, curb, constrain, hold back/in, keep under control, regulate, restrict, control, curtail, limit. See note at REIGN.

PHRASES: **free rein** *the sponsors gave the writers free rein* FREEDOM, a free hand, leeway, latitude, flexibility, liberty, independence, free play, license, room to maneuver, carte blanche, a blank check. See note at REIGN.

**keep a tight rein on** *he's a coach who likes to keep a tight rein on his players* EXERCISE STRICT CONTROL OVER, regulate, discipline, regiment, keep in line. See note at REIGN.

**USAGE NOTE rein, reign**

Like many homophones, these words are frequently mistaken for each other in print—but perhaps no other pair is confused in so many different ways. *Rein in*, not *reign in*, is the correct phrase for "check, restrain." The metaphorical image is of the rider pulling on the reins of the horse to slow down (i.e., "hold your horses")—e.g.: "With every disclosure it becomes clearer that Yeltsin is unwilling or unable to reign in [read *rein in*] his protégé." (*Times Magazine* [London]; Mar. 11, 1995.)

The error also occurs with the noun forms: one holds the *reins*, not the *reigns*—e.g.:

• "Ron Low has a hold of the Oilers' reigns [read *reins*] for now, but should he not work out, look for former Canucks and Flyers coach Bob McCammon to take over as coach next season." (*Tampa Tribune*; Apr. 16, 1995.)

• "In other cases, the computer recommended keeping tighter reign [read *rein*] on inventory, pressing the vendor for more discounts, or raising prices." (*New York Times*; May, 20, 2001.)

The opposite error (*rein* for *reign*) occurs as well—e.g.:

• "His rein [read *reign*] as Fort Meade's tobacco-chewing, play-calling leader ended abruptly in September 1993." (*Tampa Tribune*; Sept. 1, 1995.)

• "Confusion reined [read *reigned*] when everyone within a five-mile radius was asked to evacuate." (*Houston Chronicle*; Jan. 4, 2003.) —*BG*

**reinforce** verb **1** *troops reinforced the dam* STRENGTHEN, fortify, bolster up, shore up, buttress, prop up, underpin, brace, support.

**2** *reinforcing links between colleges and companies* STRENGTHEN, fortify, support; cement, boost, promote, encourage, deepen, enrich, enhance, intensify, improve.

**3** *the need to reinforce NATO troops* AUGMENT, increase, add to, supplement, boost, top up.

**reinforcement** noun **1** *the reinforcement of our defenses* STRENGTHENING, fortification, bolstering, shoring up, buttressing, bracing.

**2** *reinforcement of the bomber force* AUGMENTATION, increase, supplementing, boosting, topping up.

**3** *they returned later with reinforcements* ADDITIONAL TROOPS, fresh troops, auxiliaries, reserves; support, backup, help.

**reiterate** verb *he reiterated his concerns* REPEAT, say again, restate, retell, recapitulate, go over (and over), rehearse.

**reject** verb **1** *the loggers rejected the offer* TURN DOWN, refuse, decline, say no to, spurn; *informal* give the thumbs down to. ANTONYM accept.

**2** *Jamie rejected her* REBUFF, spurn, shun, snub, repudiate, cast off/aside, discard, abandon, desert, turn one's back on, have nothing (more) to do with, wash one's hands of; *informal* give someone the brush-off; *literary* forsake. ANTONYM welcome.

▸ noun **1** *a bin of factory rejects* SUBSTANDARD ARTICLE, discard, second.

**2** *what a reject!* FAILURE, loser, incompetent.

**rejection** noun **1** *a rejection of the offer* REFUSAL, declining, turning down, dismissal, spurning.

**2** *Madeleine's rejection of him* REPUDIATION, rebuff, spurning, abandonment, desertion; *informal* brush-off; *literary* forsaking.

**rejoice** verb **1** *they rejoiced when she returned* BE JOYFUL, be happy, be pleased, be glad, be delighted, be elated, be ecstatic, be euphoric, be overjoyed, be as pleased as punch, be jubilant, be in raptures, be beside oneself with joy, be delirious, be thrilled, be on cloud nine, be in seventh heaven; celebrate, make merry; *informal* be over the moon, be on top of the world; *literary* joy; *archaic* jubilate. ANTONYM mourn.

2 *he* ***rejoiced in*** *their success* TAKE DELIGHT IN, find/take pleasure in, feel satisfaction in, find joy in, enjoy, revel in, glory in, delight in, relish, savor.

**rejoicing** noun *news of the war's end unleashed a spectacle of rejoicing in the streets* HAPPINESS, pleasure, joy, gladness, delight, elation, jubilation, exuberance, exultation, celebration, revelry, merrymaking.

**rejoinder** noun *what serious rejoinder could I possibly offer when you make such a ludicrous accusation?* ANSWER, reply, response, retort, riposte, counter; *informal* comeback.

**relapse** verb 1 *a few patients relapse* GET ILL/WORSE AGAIN, have/suffer a relapse, deteriorate, degenerate, take a turn for the worse. ANTONYM improve.

2 *she relapsed into silence* REVERT, lapse; regress, retrogress, slip back, slide back, degenerate.

▸ noun 1 *Dr. Bergdahl's pneumonia patient suffered a relapse* DETERIORATION, turn for the worse, setback.

2 *a relapse into alcoholism* DECLINE, lapse, deterioration, degeneration, reversion, regression, retrogression, fall, descent, slide.

**relate** verb 1 *he related many stories* TELL, recount, narrate, report, chronicle, outline, delineate, retail, recite, repeat, communicate, impart.

2 *suicide rates are* ***related to*** *unemployment levels* CONNECT TO/WITH, associate with, link to/with, correlate to/with, ally with, couple with.

3 *the charges* ***relate to*** *offenses committed in August* APPLY TO, be relevant to, concern, pertain to, be pertinent to, have a bearing on, appertain to, involve.

4 *she cannot* ***relate to*** *her stepfather* HAVE A RAPPORT WITH, get on (well) with, sympathize with, feel for, identify with, empathize with, understand; *informal* hit it off with.

**related** adjective 1 *related ideas* CONNECTED, interconnected, associated, linked, coupled, allied, affiliated, concomitant, corresponding, analogous, kindred, parallel, comparable, homologous, equivalent. ANTONYM unconnected.

2 *are you two related?* OF THE SAME FAMILY, kin, akin, kindred; *formal* cognate, consanguineous. ANTONYM unrelated.

**relation** noun 1 *the relation between church and state* CONNECTION, relationship, association, link, correlation, correspondence, parallel, alliance, bond, interrelation, interconnection.

2 *this had no relation to national security* RELEVANCE, applicability, reference, pertinence, bearing.

3 *are you a relation of his?* | *she has relations in Pennsylvania* RELATIVE, member of the family, kinsman, kinswoman; (**relations**) family, kin, kith and kin, kindred.

4 (**relations**) *improving relations with China* DEALINGS, communication, relationship, connections, contact, interaction.

5 *sexual relations.* See SEX sense 1.

**relationship** noun 1 *the relationship between diet and diabetes* CONNECTION, relation, association, link, correlation, correspondence, parallel, alliance, bond, interrelation, interconnection.

2 *evidence of their relationship to Buffalo Bill Cody* FAMILY TIES, family connections, blood ties, blood relationship, kinship, affinity, consanguinity, common ancestry, common lineage.

3 *the end of their relationship* ROMANCE, (love) affair, love, liaison, amour, partnership.

**relative** adjective 1 *the relative importance of each factor* COMPARATIVE, respective, comparable, correlative, parallel, corresponding.

2 *the food required is relative to body weight* PROPORTIONATE, proportional, in proportion, commensurate, corresponding.

3 *relative ease* MODERATE, reasonable, a fair degree of, considerable, comparative.

▸ noun *he's a relative of mine* RELATION, member of someone's/the family, kinsman, kinswoman; (**relatives**) family, kin, kith and kin, kindred, kinsfolk.

**relatively** adverb *today's puzzle is relatively easy* COMPARATIVELY, by comparison; quite, fairly, reasonably, rather, somewhat, to a (certain) degree, tolerably, passably; *informal* pretty, kind of, kinda, sort of.

**relax** verb 1 *yoga is helpful in learning to relax* UNWIND, loosen up, ease up/off, slow down, de-stress, unbend, rest, put one's feet up, take it easy; *informal* unbutton, hang loose, chill, chill out, take a load off. ANTONYM be tense.

2 *a leisurely walk will relax you* CALM, calm down, unwind, loosen up, make less tense/uptight, soothe, pacify, compose.

3 *he relaxed his grip* LOOSEN, loose, slacken, unclench, weaken, lessen. ANTONYM tighten.

4 *her muscles relaxed* BECOME LESS TENSE, loosen, slacken, unknot. ANTONYMS contract, tighten.

5 *they relaxed the restrictions* MODERATE, modify, temper, ease, ease up on, loosen, lighten, dilute, weaken, reduce, decrease; *informal* let up on. ANTONYM tighten up.

**relaxation** noun 1 *a state of relaxation* MENTAL REPOSE, repose, calm, tranquility, peacefulness, loosening up, unwinding.

2 *I just play for relaxation* RECREATION, enjoyment, amusement, entertainment, fun, pleasure, leisure; *informal* R and R, downtime.

3 *muscle relaxation* LOOSENING, slackening.

4 *relaxation of censorship rules* MODERATION, easing, loosen-

ing, lightening; alleviation, mitigation, dilution, weakening, reduction; *informal* letting up.

**relay** noun *a live relay of the performance* BROADCAST, transmission, showing.

▸ verb *relaying messages through a third party* PASS ON, hand on, transfer, repeat, communicate, send, transmit, disseminate, spread, circulate.

**release** verb **1** *all prisoners were released* FREE, set free, let go/out, allow to leave, liberate, set at liberty; *historical* manumit. ANTONYM imprison.

**2** *Burke released the animal* UNTIE, undo, loose, let go, unleash, unfetter. ANTONYM tie up.

**3** *this released staff for other duties* MAKE AVAILABLE, free, free up, put at someone's disposal, supply, furnish, provide. ANTONYM detain.

**4** *she released Stephen from his promise* EXCUSE, exempt, discharge, deliver, absolve; *informal* let off.

**5** *police released the news yesterday* MAKE PUBLIC, make known, issue, break, announce, declare, report, reveal, divulge, disclose, publish, broadcast, circulate, communicate, disseminate. ANTONYMS suppress, withhold.

**6** *the film has been released on video* LAUNCH, put on the market, put on sale, bring out, make available.

▸ noun **1** *the release of political prisoners* FREEING, liberation, deliverance, bailout; freedom, liberty.

**2** *the release of the news* ISSUING, announcement, declaration, reporting, revealing, divulging, disclosure, publication, communication, dissemination.

**3** *a press release* ANNOUNCEMENT, bulletin, news flash, dispatch, proclamation.

**4** *the hot new band's latest release* CD, album, single, record; video, film; book.

**relent** verb **1** *the government finally relented* CHANGE ONE'S MIND, backpedal, do a U-turn, back down, give way/in, capitulate; become merciful, become lenient, agree to something, allow something, concede something; *formal* accede.

**2** *the rain has relented* EASE OFF/UP, slacken, let up, abate, drop, die down, lessen, decrease, subside, weaken.

**relentless** adjective **1** *their relentless pursuit of quality* PERSISTENT, continuing, constant, continual, continuous, nonstop, never-ending, unabating, interminable, incessant, unceasing, endless, unending, unremitting, unrelenting, unrelieved; unfaltering, unflagging, untiring, unwavering, dogged, tenacious, single-minded, tireless, indefatigable; *formal* pertinacious.

**2** *a relentless taskmaster* HARSH, grim, cruel, severe, strict, remorseless, merciless, pitiless, ruthless, unmerciful, heartless, hard-hearted, unforgiving; inflexible, unbending, uncompromising, obdurate, unyielding.

**relevant** adjective *the relevant page numbers* PERTINENT, applicable, apposite, material, apropos, to the point, germane; connected, related, linked.

**reliable** adjective **1** *reliable evidence* DEPENDABLE, good, well-founded, authentic, valid, genuine, sound, true.

**2** *a reliable friend* TRUSTWORTHY, dependable, good, true, faithful, devoted, steadfast, staunch, constant, loyal, trusty, dedicated, unfailing; truthful, honest. ANTONYM untrustworthy.

**3** *reliable brakes* DEPENDABLE, safe, fail-safe.

**4** *a reliable company* REPUTABLE, dependable, trustworthy, honest, responsible, established, proven. ANTONYM disreputable.

**reliance** noun **1** *reliance on the state* DEPENDENCE, dependency.

**2** *reliance on his own judgment* TRUST, confidence, faith, belief, conviction.

**relic** noun **1** *a Viking relic* ARTIFACT, historical object, ancient object, antiquity, antique.

**2** *a saint's relics* REMAINS, corpse, bones, *Medicine* cadaver.

**relief** noun **1** *it was such a relief to share my worries* REASSURANCE, consolation, comfort, solace.

**2** *the relief of pain* ALLEVIATION, alleviating, relieving, assuagement, assuaging, palliation, allaying, soothing, easing, lessening, reduction. ANTONYM intensification.

**3** *relief from her burden* FREEDOM, release, liberation, deliverance.

**4** *a little light relief* RESPITE, amusement, diversion, entertainment, jollity, jollification, recreation. ANTONYM solemnity.

**5** *bringing relief to the starving* HELP, aid, assistance, succor, sustenance, TLC; charity, gifts, donations.

**6** *his relief arrived to take over* REPLACEMENT, substitute, deputy, reserve, cover, stand-in, supply, locum, locum tenens, understudy. PHRASE: **throw into relief** *we hope these photos will throw into relief the gravity of their plight* HIGHLIGHT, spotlight, give prominence to, point up, show up, emphasize, bring out, stress, accent, underline, underscore, accentuate.

**relieve** verb **1** *this helps relieve pain* ALLEVIATE, mitigate, assuage, ease, dull, reduce, lessen, diminish. See note at ALLEVIATE. ANTONYM aggravate.

**2** *relieving the boredom* COUNTERACT, reduce, alleviate, mitigate; interrupt, vary, stop, dispel, prevent. ANTONYM exacerbate.

**3** *the helpers relieved us* REPLACE, take over from, stand in for, fill in for, substitute for, deputize for, cover for.

**4** *this relieves the teacher of a heavy load* FREE, set free, release, exempt, excuse, absolve, let off, discharge.

**religious** adjective **1** *a religious person* DEVOUT, pious, reverent, godly, God-fearing, churchgoing, faithful, devoted, committed. ANTONYMS atheistic, irreverent.

**2** *religious beliefs* SPIRITUAL, theological, scriptural, doctrinal, ecclesiastical, church, faith-based, churchly, holy, divine, sacred. ANTONYM secular.

**3** *religious attention to detail* SCRUPULOUS, conscientious, meticulous, sedulous, punctilious, strict, rigorous, close. ANTONYM slapdash.

**relinquish** verb 1 *he relinquished control of the company* RENOUNCE, give up/away, hand over, let go of. ANTONYMS retain, keep.

2 *she relinquished her post* LEAVE, resign from, stand down from, bow out of, give up; *informal* quit, chuck.

3 *he relinquished his pipe-smoking* DISCONTINUE, stop, cease, give up, desist from; *informal* quit, kick; *formal* forswear. ANTONYM continue.

4 *she relinquished her grip* LET GO OF, release, loose, loosen, relax.

THE RIGHT WORD **relinquish, abandon, cede, surrender, waive, yield**

Of all these verbs meaning to let go or give up, **relinquish** is the most general. It can imply anything from simply releasing one's grasp (*she relinquished the wheel*) to giving up control or possession reluctantly (*after the defeat, he was forced to relinquish his command*). **Surrender** also implies giving up, but usually after a struggle or show of resistance (*the villagers were forced to surrender to the guerrillas*). **Yield** is a milder synonym for *surrender*, implying some concession, respect, or even affection on the part of the person who is surrendering (*she yielded to her mother's wishes and stayed home*). **Waive** means to give up voluntarily a right or claim to something (*she waived her right to have a lawyer present*), while **cede** is to give up by legal transfer or according to the terms of a treaty (*the French ceded the territory that is now Louisiana*). If one *relinquishes* something finally and completely, often because of weariness or discouragement, the correct word is **abandon** (*they were told to abandon all hope of being rescued*).

**relish** noun 1 *he dug into his food with relish* ENJOYMENT, gusto, delight, pleasure, glee, rapture, satisfaction, contentment, appreciation, enthusiasm, appetite; *humorous* delectation. ANTONYM dislike.

2 *a hot relish* CONDIMENT, sauce, dressing, flavoring, seasoning, dip, chutney, chili sauce.

▸ verb 1 *she was relishing her moment of glory* ENJOY, delight in, love, adore, take pleasure in, rejoice in, appreciate, savor, revel in, luxuriate in, glory in.

2 *I don't relish the drive* LOOK FORWARD TO, fancy, anticipate with pleasure.

**reluctance** noun *he said he was glad to go, but she sensed his reluctance* UNWILLINGNESS, disinclination; hesitation, wavering, vacillation; doubts, second thoughts, misgivings.

**reluctant** adjective 1 *when it came to trying something new, her parents were usually reluctant* UNWILLING, disinclined, unenthusiastic, resistant, resisting, opposed; hesitant. ANTONYMS willing, eager.

2 *a reluctant smile* SHY, bashful, coy, diffident, reserved, timid, timorous. ANTONYM eager.

3 *he was **reluctant to** leave* LOATH TO, unwilling to, disinclined to, indisposed to; not in favor of, against, opposed to. ANTONYMS willing, eager.

**rely** verb 1 *we can **rely on** his discretion* DEPEND ON, count on, bank on, place reliance on, reckon on; be confident of, be sure of, believe in, have faith in, trust in; *informal* swear by, figure on.

2 *we* rely on *government funding* BE DEPENDENT ON, depend on, be unable to manage without.

**remain** verb 1 *the problem will remain* CONTINUE TO EXIST, endure, last, abide, carry on, persist, stay, stay around, prevail, survive, live on.

2 *he remained in the hospital* STAY, stay behind, stay put, wait, wait around, be left, hang on; *informal* hang around.

3 *union leaders remain skeptical* CONTINUE TO BE, stay, keep, persist in being, carry on being.

4 *the few minutes that remain* BE LEFT, be left over, be still available, be unused; have not yet passed.

**remainder** noun *the remainder of the materials should be itemized on a separate list* RESIDUE, balance, remaining part/number, rest, others, those left, remnant(s), surplus, extra, excess, overflow; *technical* residuum.

**remains** plural noun 1 *the remains of her drink* REMAINDER, residue, remaining part/number, rest, remnant(s); *technical* residuum.

2 *Roman remains* ANTIQUITIES, relics.

3 *the saint's remains* CORPSE, body, dead body, carcass; bones, skeleton; *Medicine* cadaver. See note at BODY.

**remark** verb 1 *"You're quiet," he remarked* COMMENT, say, observe, mention, reflect, state, declare, announce, pronounce, assert; *formal* opine.

2 *many critics **remarked on** their rapport* COMMENT ON, mention, refer to, speak of, pass comment on.

3 *she remarked the absence of policemen* NOTE, notice, observe, take note of, perceive, discern.

▸ noun 1 *his remarks have been misinterpreted* COMMENT, statement, utterance, observation, declaration, pronouncement.

2 *worthy of remark* ATTENTION, notice, comment, mention, observation, acknowledgment.

**remarkable** adjective *a remarkable coincidence* EXTRAORDINARY, exceptional, amazing, astonishing, astounding, marvelous, wonderful, sensational, stunning, incredible, unbelievable, phenomenal, outstanding, momentous; out of the ordinary, unusual, uncommon, surprising; *informal* fantastic, terrific, tremendous, stupendous, awesome; *literary* wondrous. See also note at NOTICEABLE. ANTONYM ordinary.

**remedy** noun 1 *herbal remedies* TREATMENT, cure, medicine, medication, medicament, drug; *archaic* physic.

2 *a remedy for all kinds of problems* SOLUTION, answer, cure, antidote, curative, nostrum, panacea, cure-all; *informal* magic bullet.

▸ verb 1 *remedying the situation* PUT/SET RIGHT, put/set to rights, right, rectify, solve, sort out, straighten out, resolve, correct, repair, mend, make good.

**2** *anemia can be remedied by iron pills* CURE, treat, heal, make better; relieve, ease, alleviate, palliate.

**remember** verb **1** *remembering happy times* RECALL, call to mind, recollect, think of; reminisce about, look back on; *archaic* bethink oneself of. ANTONYM forget.

**2** *can you remember all that?* MEMORIZE, commit to memory, retain; learn by heart. ANTONYM forget.

**3** *you must remember that she's only five* BEAR/KEEP IN MIND, be mindful of the fact; take into account, take into consideration. ANTONYM overlook.

**4** *remember to feed the cat* BE SURE, be certain; mind that you, make sure that you. ANTONYM neglect.

**5** ***remember me** to Alice* SEND ONE'S BEST WISHES, send one's regards, give one's love, send one's compliments, say hello.

**6** *the nation remembered those who gave their lives* COMMEMORATE, pay tribute to, honor, salute, pay homage to.

**7** *she remembered them in her will* BEQUEATH SOMETHING TO, leave something to, bestow something on.

**remembrance** noun **1** *an expression of remembrance* RECOLLECTION, reminiscence; remembering, recalling, recollecting, reminiscing.

**2** *she smiled at the remembrance* MEMORY, recollection, reminiscence, thought.

**3** *we sold poppies in remembrance* COMMEMORATION, memory, recognition.

**4** *a remembrance of my father* MEMENTO, reminder, keepsake, souvenir, memorial, token.

**remind** verb **1** *I left a note to remind him* JOG SOMEONE'S MEMORY, help someone remember, prompt.

**2** *the song **reminded me of** my sister* MAKE ONE THINK OF, cause one to remember, put one in mind of, bring/call to mind, evoke.

**reminisce** verb *we reminisced about Freddy's first Christmas with us* REMEMBER, remember with pleasure, cast one's mind back to, look back on, be nostalgic about, recall, recollect, reflect on, call to mind.

**reminiscences** plural noun *her reminiscences of a wartime childhood* MEMORIES, recollections, reflections, remembrances.

**reminiscent** adjective *the smell of fresh apple pies was reminiscent of the aromas from Gramma's kitchen in Middlefield* SIMILAR TO, comparable with, evocative of, suggestive of, redolent of.

**remiss** adjective *I would be remiss if I did not thank my sister* NEGLIGENT, neglectful, irresponsible, careless, thoughtless, heedless, lax, slack, slipshod, lackadaisical, derelict; *informal* sloppy; *formal* delinquent. ANTONYM careful.

**remission** noun **1** *the remission of all fees* CANCELLATION, setting aside, suspension, revocation; *formal* abrogation.

**2** *the cancer is in remission* RESPITE, abeyance.

**3** *the wind howled without remission* RESPITE, lessening, abatement, easing, decrease, reduction, diminution, dying down, slackening, lull; *informal* letup.

**4** *the remission of sins* FORGIVENESS, pardoning, absolution, exoneration; *formal* exculpation.

**remit** verb **1** *the fines were remitted* CANCEL, set aside, suspend, revoke; *formal* abrogate.

**2** *remitting duties to the authorities* SEND, dispatch, forward, hand over; pay.

**3** *the case was remitted to the Supreme Court* PASS (ON), refer, send (on), transfer.

**4** rare *we remitted all further discussion* POSTPONE, defer, put off/back, shelve, delay, suspend, table; *informal* put on the back burner, put on ice.

**5** *remitting their sins* PARDON, forgive; excuse.

**remittance** noun **1** *send the form with your remittance* PAYMENT, money, fee; check; *formal* monies.

**2** *a monthly remittance* ALLOWANCE, sum of money.

**remnant** noun **1** *the remnants of the picnic* REMAINS, remainder, leftovers, residue, rest; *technical* residuum.

**2** *remnants of cloth* SCRAP, piece, bit, fragment, shred, offcut, oddment. See note at TRACE.

**remonstrate** verb **1** *"I'm not a child!" he remonstrated* PROTEST, complain, expostulate; argue with, take issue with.

**2** *we remonstrated against this proposal* OBJECT STRONGLY TO, complain vociferously about, protest against, argue against, oppose strongly, make a fuss about, challenge; deplore, condemn, denounce, criticize; *informal* kick up a fuss/stink about.

**remorse** noun *have you no remorse for what you did to your friends?* CONTRITION, deep regret, repentance, penitence, guilt, compunction, remorsefulness, ruefulness, contriteness; pangs of conscience, self-condemnation, self-reproach.

**remorseful** adjective *remorseful criminals* SORRY, full of regret, regretful, contrite, repentant, penitent, guilt-ridden, conscience-stricken, guilty, chastened. ANTONYM unrepentant.

**remote** adjective **1** *areas remote from hospitals* FARAWAY, distant, far, far off, far removed, extrasolar. ANTONYMS close, near.

**2** *a remote mountain village* ISOLATED, out of the way, off the beaten track/path, secluded, lonely, in the back of beyond, godforsaken, inaccessible, far-flung, in the backwoods, lonesome; *informal* in the sticks, in the middle of nowhere. ANTONYM central.

**3** *events **remote from** modern times* IRRELEVANT TO, unrelated to, unconnected to, unconcerned with, not pertinent to, immaterial to, unassociated with; foreign to, alien to. ANTONYM relevant.

**4** *a remote possibility* UNLIKELY, improbable, implausible, doubtful, dubious; faint, slight, slim, small, slender. ANTONYMS likely, strong.

**5** *she seems very remote* ALOOF, distant, detached, withdrawn, reserved, uncommunicative, unforthcoming, unapproachable, unresponsive, unfriendly, unsociable, introspective, introverted; *informal* standoffish. ANTONYMS friendly, approachable.

**removal** noun **1** *the removal of heavy artillery* TAKING AWAY, moving, carrying away. ANTONYM installation.

**2** *his removal from office* DISMISSAL, ejection, expulsion, ousting, displacement, deposition, ouster; *informal* firing, sacking. ANTONYMS installation, appointment.

**3** *the removal of customs barriers* WITHDRAWAL, elimination, taking away.

**4** *the removal of errors in the copy* DELETION, elimination, erasing, effacing, obliteration.

**5** *the removal of weeds* UPROOTING, eradication.

**6** *the removal of old branches from the tree* CUTTING OFF, chopping off, hacking off.

**7** *her removal to the West Coast* MOVE, transfer, relocation.

**8** *the removal of a rival* DISPOSAL, elimination, killing, murder, dispatch; *informal* liquidation.

**remove** verb **1** *remove the plug* DETACH, unfasten; pull out, take out, disconnect. ANTONYM attach.

**2** *she removed the lid* TAKE OFF, undo, unfasten. ANTONYM put on.

**3** *he removed a twenty from his wallet* TAKE OUT, produce, bring out, get out, pull out, withdraw. ANTONYM insert.

**4** *police removed boxes of documents* TAKE AWAY, carry away, move, transport; confiscate; *informal* cart off. ANTONYMS put back, replace.

**5** *Sheila removed the mud* CLEAN OFF, wash off, wipe off, rinse off, scrub off, sponge out.

**6** *Harry removed his coat* TAKE OFF, pull off, slip out of, peel off; *dated* doff. ANTONYMS put on, don.

**7** *she was removed from her post* DISMISS, discharge, dislodge, displace, expel, oust, depose; *informal* fire, sack, kick out, boot out. ANTONYMS install, appoint.

**8** *tax relief was removed* WITHDRAW, abolish, eliminate, get rid of, do away with, stop, cut; *informal* ax. ANTONYM introduce.

**9** *Gabriel removed two words* DELETE, erase, rub out, cross out, strike out, obliterate; *informal* deep-six. ANTONYM add.

**10** *weeds have to be removed* UPROOT, pull out, eradicate.

**11** *removing branches* CUT OFF, chop off, lop off, hack off.

**remuneration** noun *you will receive adequate remuneration for the work you have done* PAYMENT, pay, salary, wages; earnings, fee(s), reward, compensation, recompense, reimbursement; *formal* emolument(s).

**remunerative** adjective *a remunerative position in his father's firm* LUCRATIVE, well-paid, financially rewarding; profitable.

**renaissance** noun *the renaissance of Byzantine art* REVIVAL, renewal, resurrection, reawakening, reemergence, rebirth, reappearance, resurgence, regeneration; *formal* renascence.

**render** verb **1** *her fury rendered her speechless* MAKE, cause to be/become, leave.

**2** *rendering assistance* GIVE, provide, supply, furnish, contribute; offer, proffer.

**3** *the invoices rendered by the accountants* SEND IN, present, submit.

**4** *the jury rendered its verdict* DELIVER, return, hand down, give, announce.

**5** *paintings rendered in muted colors* PAINT, draw, depict, portray, represent, execute; *literary* limn.

**6** *she rendered all three verses* PERFORM, sing.

**7** *the characters are vividly rendered* ACT, perform, play, depict, interpret.

**8** *the phrase was rendered into English* TRANSLATE, put, express, rephrase, reword.

**9** *the fat can be rendered* MELT DOWN, clarify.

**rendezvous** noun *Eleanor was late for their rendezvous* MEETING, appointment, assignation; *informal* date; *literary* tryst.

▸ verb *the bar where they had agreed to rendezvous* MEET, come together, gather, assemble.

**renegade** noun **1** *he was denounced as a renegade* TRAITOR, defector, deserter, turncoat, rebel, mutineer.

**2** *archaic a religious renegade* APOSTATE, heretic, dissenter.

▸ adjective **1** *renegade troops* TREACHEROUS, traitorous, disloyal, treasonous, rebel, mutinous. ANTONYM loyal.

**2** *a renegade monk* APOSTATE, heretic, heretical, dissident.

**renege** verb *he reneged on his campaign promises* DEFAULT ON, fail to honor, go back on, break, back out of, withdraw from, retreat from, welsh on, backtrack on; break one's word/promise about. ANTONYM honor.

**renounce** verb **1** *Edward renounced his claim to the throne* GIVE UP, relinquish, abandon, abdicate, surrender, waive, forego; *Law* disclaim; *formal* abnegate. ANTONYM assert.

**2** *Hungary renounced the agreement* REJECT, refuse to abide by, repudiate. ANTONYMS abide by, accept.

**3** *she renounced her family* REPUDIATE, deny, reject, abandon, wash one's hands of, turn one's back on, disown, spurn, shun; *literary* forsake. ANTONYM embrace.

**4** *he renounced alcohol* ABSTAIN FROM, give up, desist from, refrain from, keep off, eschew; *informal* quit, pack in, lay off; *formal* forswear. ANTONYM turn to.

PHRASE: **renounce the world** *you can't just renounce the world* BECOME A RECLUSE, turn one's back on society, cloister oneself, hide oneself away.

**renovate** verb *the hotel has been renovated* MODERNIZE, restore, refurbish, revamp, recondition, rehabilitate, overhaul, redevelop; update, upgrade, refit, bring something up to code; *informal* do up, rehab.

**renown** noun *born to a family of political renown* FAME, distinction, eminence, preeminence, prominence, repute, reputation, prestige, acclaim, celebrity, notability.

**renowned** adjective *a renowned Indian filmmaker* FAMOUS, celebrated, famed, eminent, distinguished, acclaimed, illustrious, preeminent, prominent, great, esteemed, of note, of repute, well-known, well-thought-of. ANTONYM unknown.

**rent**[1] noun *I can't afford to pay the rent* RENTAL, fee, lease.

▸ verb **1** *she rented a car* lease, charter.

**2** *why don't you **rent** it **out**?* LET (OUT), lease (out), hire (out); sublet, sublease.

**rent**[2] noun **1** *the rent in his pants* RIP, tear, split, hole, slash, slit.

**2** *a vast rent in the mountains* GORGE, chasm, fault, rift, fissure, crevasse.

**renunciation** noun **1** *the queen's renunciation of her throne* RELINQUISHMENT, giving up, abandonment, abdication, surrender, waiving, foregoing; *Law* disclaimer; *rare* abnegation.

**2** *his **renunciation of** luxury* ABSTENTION FROM, refraining from, going without, giving up, eschewal of; *formal* forswearing of.

**3** *their renunciation of terrorism* REPUDIATION, rejection, abandonment; *rare* abjuration.

**repair**[1] verb **1** *the car was repaired* MEND, fix (up), put/set right, restore, restore to working order, overhaul, service; *informal* patch up.

**2** *they repaired the costumes* MEND, darn; *informal* patch up.

**3** *repairing relations with other countries* PUT/SET RIGHT, mend, fix, straighten out, smooth, improve, warm up; *informal* patch up.

**4** *she sought to repair the wrong she had done* RECTIFY, make good, right, put right, correct, make up for, make amends for, make reparation for.

▸ noun **1** *in need of repair* RESTORATION, fixing (up), mending, renovation; *archaic* reparation.

**2** *an invisible repair* MEND, darn.

**3** *in good repair* CONDITION, working order, state, shape, fettle.

PHRASE: **beyond repair** *the front wheel is beyond repair | their marriage appears to be beyond repair* IRREPARABLE, irreversible, irretrievable, irremediable, irrecoverable, past hope.

**repair**[2] verb *formal we **repaired to** the sitting room* GO TO, head for, adjourn to, wend one's way to; *formal* remove to; *literary* betake oneself to.

**reparation** noun *the victims are seeking reparation* AMENDS, restitution, redress, compensation, recompense, repayment, atonement.

**repartee** noun *an evening of wit and repartee* BANTER, badinage, bantering, raillery, witticism(s), ripostes, sallies, quips, joking, jesting; *formal* persiflage. See note at WIT.

**repast** noun *formal a sumptuous repast* MEAL, feast, banquet; *informal* spread, feed, bite, bite to eat; *formal* collation, refection.

**repay** verb **1** *they promised to repay customers who had been cheated* REIMBURSE, refund, pay back/off, recompense, compensate, indemnify.

**2** *the grants have to be repaid* PAY BACK, return, refund, reimburse.

**3** *I'd like to repay her generosity* RECIPROCATE, return, requite, recompense, reward.

**repeal** verb *the Eighteenth Amendment was repealed in 1933* REVOKE, rescind, cancel, reverse, annul, nullify, declare null and void, quash, abolish; *Law* vacate; *formal* abrogate; *archaic* recall. ANTONYM enact.

▸ noun *the repeal of the law* REVOCATION, rescinding, cancellation, reversal, annulment, nullification, quashing, abolition; *formal* abrogation; *archaic* recall.

**repeat** verb **1** *she repeated her story* SAY AGAIN, restate, reiterate, go/run through again, recapitulate; *informal* recap.

**2** *children can repeat large chunks of text* RECITE, quote, parrot, regurgitate.

**3** *Steele was invited to repeat his work* DO AGAIN, redo, replicate, rehash, duplicate.

**4** *the episodes were repeated* REBROADCAST, rerun.

▸ noun **1** *a repeat of the previous year's final* REPETITION, duplication, replication, duplicate, rehash.

**2** *repeats of the classic sitcom* RERUN, rebroadcast.

PHRASE: **repeat itself** REOCCUR, recur, occur again, happen again.

**repeated** adjective *his repeated complaints about the noise* RECURRENT, frequent, persistent, continual, incessant, constant; regular, periodic, numerous, many, very many. ANTONYM occasional.

**repeatedly** adverb *he tried repeatedly to hit that low note* FREQUENTLY, often, again and again, over and over (again), time and (time) again, time after time, many times, many a time; persistently, recurrently, constantly, continually, regularly, oftentimes; *literary* oft, ofttimes.

**repel** verb **1** *the rebels were repelled* FIGHT OFF, repulse, drive back/away, force back, beat back, push back; hold off, ward off, keep at bay; *archaic* rebut.

**2** *the coating will repel water* BE IMPERVIOUS TO, be impermeable to, keep out, resist, be ——proof.

**3** *the thought of kissing him repelled me* REVOLT, disgust, repulse, sicken, nauseate, turn someone's stomach, be repulsive, be distasteful, be repugnant; *informal* turn off, gross out.

**repellent** adjective **1** *a repellent stench* REVOLTING, repulsive, disgusting, repugnant, sickening, nauseating, stomach-turning, nauseous, vile, nasty, foul, horrible, awful, dreadful, terrible, obnoxious, loathsome, offensive, objectionable; abhorrent, despicable, reprehensible, contemptible, odious, hateful, execrable, vomitous; *informal* ghastly, horrid, gross, yucky, icky, funky; *literary* noisome. See note at REPULSIVE. ANTONYM delightful.

2 *a repellent coating* IMPERMEABLE, impervious, resistant; -proof.

**repent** verb *the senator claims to have repented* FEEL REMORSE, regret, be sorry, rue, reproach oneself, be ashamed, feel contrite; be penitent, be remorseful, be repentant.

**repentance** noun *her lack of repentance angered them* REMORSE, contrition, contriteness, penitence, regret, ruefulness, remorsefulness, shame, guilt.

**repentant** adjective *there are two repentant children in there waiting to talk to you* PENITENT, contrite, regretful, rueful, remorseful, apologetic, chastened, ashamed, shamefaced, guilt-ridden. ANTONYM impenitent.

**repercussion** noun **(repercussions)** *the political repercussions of the scandal* CONSEQUENCE(S), result(s), effect(s), outcome; reverberation(s), backlash, aftermath, fallout, tremors.

**repetition** noun 1 *the facts bear repetition* REITERATION, repeating, restatement, retelling.

2 *endless repetition of passages of poetry* REPEATING, echoing, parroting.

3 *a repetition of the scene in the kitchen* RECURRENCE, reoccurrence, rerun, repeat; *informal* déjà vu, instant replay.

4 *the author is guilty of repetition* REPETITIOUSNESS, repetitiveness, redundancy, tautology.

**repetitive** adjective *repetitive tasks on the assembly line* MONOTONOUS, tedious, boring, humdrum, mundane, dreary, tiresome; unvaried, unchanging, unvarying, recurrent, recurring, repeated, repetitious, routine, mechanical, automatic.

**replace** verb 1 *Eve replaced the receiver* PUT BACK, return, restore. ANTONYM remove.

2 *a new chairman came in to replace him* TAKE THE PLACE OF, succeed, take over from, supersede; stand in for, substitute for, deputize for, cover for, relieve; *informal* step into someone's shoes/boots.

3 *she replaced the spoon with a fork* SUBSTITUTE, exchange, change, swap.

THE RIGHT WORD **replace, displace, supersede, supplant**

When a light bulb burns out, you **replace** it, meaning that you substitute something new or functioning for what is lost, destroyed, or worn out. If something that is obsolete or ineffective is replaced by something that is superior, more up-to-date, or more authoritative, the correct verb is **supersede** (*the computer superseded the electric typewriter*). In contrast, **displace** suggests that someone or something has been ousted or dislodged forcibly, without necessarily implying that it was inferior or ineffective (*a growing number of workers were being displaced by machines*). **Supplant** is more restricted in meaning; it suggests displacement by force, fraud, or innovation (*the democratic government had been supplanted by a power-hungry tyrant*). It can also mean to uproot or wipe out (*the English immigrants gradually supplanted the island's native inhabitants*).

**replacement** noun 1 *we have to find a replacement* SUCCESSOR; SUBSTITUTE, stand-in, locum, relief, cover.

2 *the wiring was in need of replacement* RENEWAL, replacing.

**replenish** verb 1 *she replenished their glasses* REFILL, top up, fill up, recharge, freshen. ANTONYM empty.

2 *their supplies were replenished* RESTOCK, stock up, restore, replace. ANTONYMS use up, exhaust.

**replete** adjective 1 *the guests were replete* WELL-FED, sated, satiated, full, full up; glutted, gorged; *informal* stuffed.

2 *a sumptuous environment replete with antiques* FILLED, full, well-stocked, well-supplied, crammed, packed, jammed, teeming, overflowing, bursting; *informal* jam-packed, chockablock, chock-full.

**replica** noun 1 *is it real or a replica?* COPY, carbon copy, model, duplicate, reproduction, replication; dummy, imitation, facsimile; *informal* knockoff.

2 *a replica of her mother* PERFECT LIKENESS, double, lookalike, mirror image, living image, picture, twin, clone, doppelgänger; *informal* spitting image, dead ringer, ringer.

**reply** verb *Rachel didn't bother to reply* ANSWER, respond, come back, write back, retort, riposte, counter.

▸ noun *"Why would we lie?" she replied* ANSWER, response, rejoinder, retort, riposte; *informal* comeback.

**report** verb 1 *the government reported a fall in inflation* ANNOUNCE, describe, give an account of, detail, outline, communicate, divulge, disclose, reveal, make public, publish, broadcast, proclaim, publicize.

2 *the newspapers* ***reported on*** *the scandal* COVER, write about, describe, give details of, commentate on; investigate, look into, inquire into.

3 *I reported him to the police* INFORM ON, tattle on; *informal* tell on, squeal on, rat on.

4 *Juliet reported for duty* PRESENT ONESELF, arrive, turn up, clock in, sign in, punch in; *informal* show up.

▸ noun 1 *a full report on the meeting* ACCOUNT, review, record, description, statement; transactions, proceedings, transcripts, minutes.

2 *reports of drug dealing* NEWS, information, word, intelligence; *literary* tidings.

3 *newspaper reports* STORY, account, article, piece, item, column, feature, bulletin, dispatch.

4 *a school report* ASSESSMENT, report card, evaluation, appraisal.

5 *reports of his imminent resignation* RUMOR, whisper; *informal* buzz; *archaic* bruit.

6 *the report of a gun* BANG, blast, crack, shot, gunshot, explosion, boom.

**reporter** noun *my client has been instructed not to talk to reporters* JOURNALIST, correspondent, newspaperman, newspaperwoman, newsman, newswoman, columnist, pressman; *informal* newshound, hack, stringer, journo, newsie.

**repose** noun **1** *a face in repose* REST, relaxation, inactivity; sleep, slumber.

**2** *they found true repose* PEACE, peace and quiet, peacefulness, quiet, quietness, calm, tranquility.

**3** *he lost his repose* COMPOSURE, serenity, equanimity, poise, self-possession, aplomb.

▸ verb **1** *the diamond reposed on a bed of velvet* LIE, rest, be placed, be situated.

**2** *the trust he had reposed in her* PUT, place, invest, entrust.

**3** *the beds where we reposed* LIE, lie down, recline, rest, sleep; *literary* slumber.

**repository** noun *a repository for nuclear fuel* | *he's a veritable repository of musical knowledge* STORE, storehouse, depository; reservoir, bank, cache, treasury, fund, mine.

**reprehensible** adjective *his conduct was reprehensible* DEPLORABLE, disgraceful, discreditable, despicable, blameworthy, culpable, wrong, bad, shameful, dishonorable, objectionable, opprobrious, repugnant, inexcusable, unforgivable, indefensible, unjustifiable; criminal, sinful, scandalous, iniquitous; *formal* exceptionable. ANTONYM praiseworthy.

**represent** verb **1** *a character representing a single quality* SYMBOLIZE, stand for, personify, epitomize, typify, embody, illustrate.

**2** *the initials that represent her qualification* STAND FOR, designate, denote; *literary* betoken.

**3** *Hathor is represented as a woman with cow's horns* DEPICT, portray, render, picture, delineate, show, illustrate; *literary* limn.

**4** *he represented himself as the owner of the factory* DESCRIBE AS, present as, profess to be, claim to be, pass oneself off as, pose as, pretend to be.

**5** *aging represents a threat to one's independence* CONSTITUTE, be, amount to, be regarded as.

**6** *a panel representing a cross section of the public* BE A TYPICAL SAMPLE OF, be representative of, typify.

**7** *her lawyer represented her in court* APPEAR FOR, act for, speak on behalf of; *informal* go to bat for.

**8** *the governor general represented the royal family* DEPUTIZE FOR, substitute for, stand in for.

**9** *formal* *I represented the case as I saw it* POINT OUT, state, present, put forward.

**representation** noun **1** *Rossetti's representation of women* PORTRAYAL, depiction, delineation, presentation, rendition.

**2** *representations of the human form* LIKENESS, painting, drawing, picture, illustration, sketch, image, model, figure, figurine, statue, statuette.

**3** *formal* *making representations to the council* STATEMENT, deposition, allegation, declaration, exposition, report, protestation.

**representative** adjective **1** *a representative sample* TYPICAL, prototypical, characteristic, illustrative, archetypal. ANTONYM atypical.

**2** *the red maple leaf is representative of Canada* SYMBOLIC, emblematic, evocative.

**3** *representative government* ELECTED, elective, chosen, democratic, popular. ANTONYM totalitarian.

▸ noun **1** *a representative of Greenpeace* SPOKESPERSON, spokesman, spokeswoman, agent, official, mouthpiece.

**2** *one of our representatives will show you our new line of pop-up books* SALESPERSON, salesman, saleswoman, agent; *informal* rep.

**3** *the Cambodian representative at the UN* DELEGATE, commissioner, ambassador, attaché, envoy, emissary, chargé d'affaires, deputy.

**4** *contact your representatives and urge them to protect our wetlands* LEGISLATOR, lawmaker; senator, congressman, congresswoman, member of Congress, alderman, alderwoman, alderperson, selectman, selectwoman, lawmaker; voice.

**5** *he acted as his father's representative* DEPUTY, substitute, stand-in, proxy.

**6** *fossil representatives of lampreys* EXAMPLE, specimen, exemplar, exemplification.

**repress** verb **1** *the rebellion was repressed* SUPPRESS, quell, quash, subdue, put down, crush, extinguish, stamp out, defeat, conquer, rout, overwhelm, contain.

**2** *the peasants were repressed* OPPRESS, subjugate, keep down, rule with a rod of iron, rule with an iron fist, intimidate, tyrannize, crush.

**3** *these emotions may well be repressed* RESTRAIN, hold back/in, keep back, suppress, keep in check, control, keep under control, curb, stifle, bottle up; *informal* button up, keep the lid on.

**repressed** adjective **1** *a repressed country* OPPRESSED, subjugated, subdued, tyrannized. ANTONYMS democratic, free.

**2** *repressed feelings* RESTRAINED, suppressed, held back/in, kept in check, stifled, pent up, bottled up, unvented. ANTONYMS overt, expressed.

**3** *emotionally repressed* INHIBITED, frustrated, restrained; *informal* uptight, hung up. ANTONYMS relaxed, uninhibited.

**repression** noun **1** *the repression of the protests* SUPPRESSION, quashing, subduing, crushing, stamping out.

**2** *political repression* OPPRESSION, subjugation, suppression, tyranny, despotism, authoritarianism.

**3** *the repression of sexual urges* RESTRAINT, restraining, holding back, keeping back, suppression, keeping in check, control, keeping under control, stifling, bottling up.

**repressive** adjective *a repressive military regime* OPPRESSIVE, authoritarian, despotic, tyrannical, dictatorial, fascist, autocratic, totalitarian, undemocratic.

**reprieve** verb **1** *less than two hours ago the governor reprieved Edgerton* GRANT A STAY OF EXECUTION TO, pardon, spare, grant an amnesty to, amnesty; *informal* let off, let off the hook.

**2** *the project has been reprieved* SAVE, rescue; *informal* take off the hit list.

▸ noun *a last-minute reprieve* STAY OF EXECUTION, remission, pardon, amnesty; *Law* continuance.

**reprimand** verb *was it really necessary to reprimand him in public?* REBUKE, admonish, chastise, chide, upbraid, reprove, reproach, scold, berate, take to task, lambaste, give someone a piece of one's mind, rake/haul over the coals, lecture, criticize, censure; *informal* come down on, give someone a talking-to, tell off, dress down, give someone a dressing-down, give someone an earful, give someone a roasting, rap over the knuckles, rap, slap someone's wrist, bawl out, lay into, lace into, blast, give someone what for, chew out, ream out; *formal* castigate. ANTONYM praise.

▸ noun *they received a severe reprimand* REBUKE, reproof, admonishment, admonition, reproach, scolding, upbraiding, censure; *informal* rap over the knuckles, slap on the wrist, dressing-down, talking-to, earful, roasting, tongue-lashing; *formal* castigation. See note at REBUKE. ANTONYM commendation.

**reprisal** noun *following the ethnic violence in Nigeria, the fear is of reprisal* RETALIATION, counterattack, comeback; revenge, vengeance, retribution, requital; *informal* a taste of one's own medicine.

**reproach** verb *Albert reproached him for being late.* See REPRIMAND verb. See also note at REBUKE.

▸ noun **1** *an expression of reproach.* See REPRIMAND noun.

**2** *this party is a reproach to Canadian politics* DISGRACE, discredit, source of shame, blemish, stain, blot; *literary* smirch.

PHRASE: **beyond/above reproach** *I never claimed to be above reproach* PERFECT, blameless, above suspicion, without fault, faultless, flawless, irreproachable, exemplary, impeccable, immaculate, unblemished, spotless, untarnished, stainless, unsullied, whiter than white; *informal* squeaky clean.

**reproachful** adjective DISAPPROVING, reproving, critical, censorious, disparaging, withering, accusatory, admonitory. ANTONYM approving.

**reproduce** verb **1** *each piece of artwork is reproduced in color* COPY, duplicate, replicate; photocopy, xerox, print.

**2** *this work has not been reproduced in other laboratories* REPEAT, replicate, recreate, redo; simulate, imitate, emulate, mirror, mimic.

**3** *some animals reproduce prolifically* BREED, produce offspring, procreate, propagate, multiply.

**reproduction** noun **1** *color reproduction* COPYING, duplication, duplicating; photocopying, xeroxing, printing.

**2** *a reproduction of the original* PRINT, copy, reprint, duplicate, facsimile, carbon copy, photocopy; *trademark* Xerox.

**3** *the process of reproduction* BREEDING, procreation, multiplying, propagation.

**reproof** noun *he muttered reproof* REBUKE, reprimand, reproach, admonishment, admonition; disapproval, censure, criticism, condemnation; *informal* dressing down.

**reprove** verb *was it necessary to reprove Vicki just for dropping a few crumbs?* REPRIMAND, rebuke, reproach, scold, admonish, chastise, chide, upbraid, berate, take to task, rake/haul over the coals, criticize, censure; *informal* tell off, give someone a talking-to, dress down, give someone a dressing-down, give someone an earful, give someone a roasting, rap over the knuckles, slap someone's wrist; *formal* castigate.

**repudiate** verb **1** *she repudiated communism* REJECT, renounce, abandon, give up, turn one's back on, disown, cast off, lay aside; *formal* forswear, abjure; *literary* forsake. ANTONYM embrace.

**2** *Hansen repudiated the allegations* DENY, contradict, controvert, rebut, dispute, dismiss, brush aside; *formal* gainsay. ANTONYMS acknowledge, confirm.

**3** *Egypt repudiated the treaty* CANCEL, revoke, rescind, reverse, overrule, overturn, invalidate, nullify; disregard, flout, renege on; *Law* disaffirm; *formal* abrogate. ANTONYMS ratify, abide by.

**repugnance** noun *a look of repugnance* REVULSION, disgust, abhorrence, repulsion, loathing, hatred, detestation, aversion, distaste, antipathy, contempt.

**repugnant** adjective **1** *the idea of cannibalism is repugnant* ABHORRENT, revolting, repulsive, repellent, disgusting, offensive, objectionable, cringeworthy, vile, foul, nasty, loathsome, sickening, nauseating, hateful, detestable, execrable, abominable, monstrous, appalling, insufferable, intolerable, unacceptable, contemptible, unsavory, unpalatable; *informal* ghastly, gross, horrible, horrid; *literary* noisome. See note at OFFENSIVE. ANTONYMS attractive, pleasant.

**2** *formal the restriction is* ***repugnant to*** *the tenancy* INCOMPATIBLE WITH, in conflict with, contrary to, at variance with, inconsistent with.

**repulsive** adjective *their bathroom was repulsive* REVOLTING, disgusting, abhorrent, repellent, repugnant, offensive, objectionable, vile, foul, nasty, loathsome, sickening, nauseating, hateful, detestable, execrable, abominable, monstrous, noxious, horrendous, awful, terrible, dreadful, frightful, obnoxious, unsavory, unpleasant, disagreeable, distasteful; ugly, hideous, grotesque; *informal* ghastly, horrible, horrid, gross; *literary* noisome; *archaic* loathly. ANTONYM attractive.

THE RIGHT WORD **repulsive, repellent**

**Repulsive** and **repellent** are very close in meaning, but the former, perhaps because of its sound, is felt to express stronger feeling.

**reputable** adjective *a reputable talent scout* WELL-THOUGHT-OF, highly regarded, respected, well-respected, respectable, of (good) repute, prestigious, established; reliable, dependable, trustworthy. ANTONYM untrustworthy.

**reputation** noun *your careless gossip has ruined my reputation in this town* NAME, GOOD NAME, character, repute, standing, stature, status, position, renown, esteem, prestige; *informal* rep, rap.

**repute** noun **1** *a woman of ill repute* REPUTATION, name, character.

**2** *a firm of international repute* FAME, renown, celebrity, distinction, high standing, stature, prestige.

**reputedly** adverb *this is reputedly the handwriting of Saddam's oldest son* SUPPOSEDLY, by all accounts, so I'm told, so people say, allegedly.

**request** noun **1** *requests for assistance* APPEAL, entreaty, plea, petition, application, demand, call; *formal* adjuration; *literary* behest.

**2** *Charlotte spoke, at Ursula's request* BIDDING, entreaty, demand, insistence.

**3** *indicate your requests on the form* REQUIREMENT, wish, desire; choice.

▸ verb **1** *the government requested military aid* ASK FOR, appeal for, call for, seek, solicit, plead for, apply for, demand; *formal* adjure.

**2** *I requested him to help* CALL ON, beg, entreat, implore; *literary* beseech.

**require** verb **1** *the child required hospital treatment* NEED, be in need of.

**2** *a situation requiring patience* NECESSITATE, demand, call for, involve, entail.

**3** *unquestioning obedience is required* DEMAND, insist on, call for, ask for, expect.

**4** *she was required to pay costs* ORDER, instruct, command, enjoin, oblige, compel, force.

**5** *do you require anything else?* WANT, wish to have, desire; lack, be short of.

**required** adjective **1** *required reading* ESSENTIAL, vital, indispensable, necessary, compulsory, obligatory, mandatory, prescribed; *informal* must-have. ANTONYM optional.

**2** *cut it to the required length* DESIRED, preferred, chosen; correct, proper, right.

**requirement** noun *good spelling is a requirement of the job* NEED, wish, demand, want, necessity, essential, prerequisite, stipulation.

**requisite** adjective *he lacks the requisite skills* NECESSARY, required, prerequisite, essential, indispensable, vital. See note at NECESSARY. ANTONYM optional.

▸ noun *a requisite for a successful career* NECESSITY, essential, essential requirement, prerequisite, precondition, sine qua non; *informal* must.

**requisition** noun **1** *we have submitted our requisition for additional staff* ORDER, request, call, application, claim, demand.

**2** *the requisition of cultural treasures* APPROPRIATION, commandeering, seizure, confiscation, expropriation.

▸ verb **1** *their house was requisitioned by the army* COMMANDEER, appropriate, take over, take possession of, occupy, seize, confiscate, expropriate.

**2** *she requisitioned statements* REQUEST, order, call for, demand.

**rescind** verb *the court can rescind a bankruptcy order* REVOKE, repeal, cancel, reverse, overturn, overrule, annul, nullify, void, invalidate, quash, abolish; *Law* vacate; *formal* abrogate. ANTONYM enforce.

**rescue** verb **1** *an attempt to rescue the hostages* SAVE, save from danger, save the life of, come to the aid of; free, set free, release, liberate.

**2** *Boyd rescued his papers* RETRIEVE, recover, salvage, get back.

▸ noun *the rescue of 10 crewmen* SAVING, rescuing; release, freeing, liberation, bailout, deliverance, redemption.

PHRASE: **come to someone's rescue** *we were stuck in the elevator until Marty came to our rescue* HELP, assist, lend a helping hand to, lend a hand to, bail out; *informal* save someone's bacon, save someone's neck, save someone's skin.

**research** noun **1** *medical research* INVESTIGATION, experimentation, testing, analysis, fact-finding, fieldwork, examination, scrutiny.

**2** *he continued his research* EXPERIMENT(S), experimentation, test(s), testing, inquiry/inquiries, study/studies.

▸ verb **1** *the phenomenon has been widely researched* INVESTIGATE, study, inquire into, look into, probe, explore, analyze, examine, scrutinize, review.

**2** *I researched all the available material* STUDY, read, read up on, sift through, look into; *informal* check out.

**resemblance** noun *Sara says they're twins, but I don't see any resemblance* SIMILARITY, likeness, similitude, correspondence, congruity, congruence, coincidence, conformity, agreement, equivalence, comparability, parallelism, uniformity, sameness. See note at LIKENESS.

**resemble** verb *don't you think he resembles Tom Cruise?* LOOK LIKE, be similar to, be like, bear a resemblance to, remind one of, take after, favor, have the look of; approximate to, smack of, have (all) the hallmarks of, correspond to, echo, mirror, parallel; *archaic* bear semblance to.

**resent** verb *she resented the models who got better assignments* BEGRUDGE, feel aggrieved at/about, feel bitter about, grudge, be annoyed at/about, be resentful of, dislike, take exception to, object to, take amiss, take offense at, take umbrage at, bear/harbor a grudge about. ANTONYM welcome.

**resentful** adjective *constant criticism will make your partner feel resentful* AGGRIEVED, indignant, irritated, piqued, put out, in high dudgeon, dissatisfied, disgruntled, discontented, offended, bitter, jaundiced; envious, jealous; brooding; *informal* miffed, peeved, sore.

**resentment** noun *the lingering Korean resentment of Japanese rule* BITTERNESS, indignation, irritation, pique, dissatisfaction, disgruntlement, discontentment, discontent, resentfulness, bad feelings, hard feelings, ill will, acrimony, rancor, animosity, jaundice; envy, jealousy.

**reservation** noun 1 **(reservations)** *grave reservations about traveling abroad* DOUBTS, qualms, scruples; misgivings, skepticism, unease, hesitation, objection.

2 *the reservation of the room* BOOKING, ordering, securing. PHRASE: **without reservation** *Mr. McNeill apologized without reservation* WHOLEHEARTEDLY, unreservedly, without qualification, fully, completely, totally, entirely, wholly, unconditionally.

**reserve** verb 1 *ask the library to reserve a copy for you* PUT TO ONE SIDE, put aside, set aside, keep, keep back, save, hold, put on hold, keep in reserve, earmark.

2 *he reserved a table* BOOK, make a reservation for, order, arrange for, secure; *formal* bespeak; *dated* engage.

3 *the management reserves the right to alter the program* RETAIN, maintain, keep, hold.

4 *reserve your judgment until you know him better* DEFER, postpone, put off, delay, withhold.

▸ noun 1 *reserves of gasoline* STOCK, store, supply, stockpile, pool, hoard, cache.

2 *the army is calling up reserves* REINFORCEMENTS, the militia, extras, auxiliaries.

3 *a nature reserve* NATIONAL PARK, sanctuary, preserve, conservation area, protected area, wildlife park.

4 *it was difficult to get past his reserve* RETICENCE, detachment, distance, remoteness, coolness, aloofness, constraint, formality; shyness, diffidence, timidity, taciturnity, inhibition; *informal* standoffishness.

5 *she trusted him without reserve* RESERVATION, qualification, condition, limitation, hesitation, doubt.

▸ adjective *a reserve goaltender* BACKUP, substitute, stand-in, relief, replacement, fallback, spare, extra.

PHRASE: **in reserve** *we have four generators in reserve* AVAILABLE, to/on hand, ready, in readiness, set aside, at one's disposal.

**reserved** adjective 1 *Rodney is rather reserved* RETICENT, quiet, private, uncommunicative, unforthcoming, undemonstrative, unsociable, formal, constrained, cool, aloof, detached, distant, remote, unapproachable, unfriendly, withdrawn, secretive, silent, taciturn; shy, retiring, diffident, timid, self-effacing, inhibited, introverted; *informal* buttoned-up, standoffish. ANTONYM outgoing.

2 *that table is reserved* BOOKED, taken, spoken for, prearranged; *dated* engaged; *formal* bespoken. ANTONYM free.

**reservoir** noun 1 *water pumped from the reservoir* pool, pond; water supply, water tower.

2 *an ink reservoir* RECEPTACLE, container, holder, repository, tank.

3 *the reservoir of managerial talent* STOCK, store, stockpile, reserve(s), supply, bank, pool, stable, fund.

**reside** verb 1 *most students* ***reside in*** *apartments* LIVE IN, occupy, inhabit, stay in, lodge in; *formal* dwell in, be domiciled in.

2 *the paintings reside in an air-conditioned vault* BE SITUATED, be found, be located, lie.

3 *executive power* ***resides in*** *the president* BE VESTED IN, be bestowed on, be conferred on, be in the hands of.

4 *the qualities that reside within each individual* BE INHERENT, be present, exist.

**residence** noun 1 *formal her private residence* HOME, house, place of residence, address; quarters, lodgings; *informal* pad, digs; *formal* dwelling, dwelling place, domicile, abode.

2 *the university residence* DORMITORY, dorm.

3 *his place of residence* OCCUPANCY, habitation, residency; *formal* abode.

**resident** noun *the residents of Ivoryton* INHABITANT, local, citizen, native; townsfolk, townspeople; householder, homeowner, occupier, tenant; *formal* denizen.

▸ adjective 1 *is he currently resident in New Brunswick?* LIVING, residing, in residence; *formal* dwelling.

2 *a resident nurse* LIVE-IN, living in.

**residue** noun *the residue of explosives found in the wreckage* REMAINDER, remaining part, rest, remnant(s); surplus, extra, excess; remains, leftovers; *technical* residuum.

**resign** verb 1 *the executive director resigned* LEAVE, hand in one's notice, give notice, stand down, step down; *informal* quit, jump ship.

2 *three state senators resigned their seats* GIVE UP, leave, vacate, stand down from; *informal* quit, pack in.

3 *he resigned his right to the title* RENOUNCE, relinquish, give up, abandon, surrender, forego, cede; *Law* disclaim; *literary* forsake.

4 *we* ***resigned ourselves to*** *a long wait* RECONCILE ONESELF TO, become resigned to, come to terms with, accept.

**resignation** noun 1 *his resignation from his post* DEPARTURE, leaving, standing down, stepping down; *informal* quitting.

2 *she handed in her resignation* NOTICE, notice to quit, letter of resignation.

3 *he accepted his fate with resignation* PATIENCE, forbearance, stoicism, fortitude, fatalism, acceptance, acquiescence, compliance, passivity.

**resigned** adjective *he gave a resigned sigh* PATIENT, long-suffering, uncomplaining, forbearing, stoical, philosophical, fatalistic, acquiescent, compliant, passive, submissive.

**resilient** adjective 1 *resilient materials* FLEXIBLE, pliable, supple; durable, hardwearing, stout, strong, sturdy, tough. See note at FLEXIBLE.

2 *young and resilient* STRONG, tough, hardy; quick to recover, buoyant, irrepressible.

**resist** verb 1 *built to resist cold winters* WITHSTAND, be proof against, combat, weather, endure, be resistant to, keep out. ANTONYMS be harmed by, be susceptible to.

2 *they resisted his attempts to change things* OPPOSE, fight

against, refuse to accept, object to, defy, set one's face against, kick against; obstruct, impede, hinder, block, thwart, frustrate. ANTONYMS welcome, accept.

**3** *I resisted the urge to retort* REFRAIN FROM, abstain from, forbear from, desist from, not give in to, restrain oneself from, stop oneself from. ANTONYMS succumb to, give in to.

**4** *she tried to resist him* STRUGGLE WITH/AGAINST, fight (against), stand up to, withstand, hold off; fend off, ward off. ANTONYMS yield to, submit to.

PHRASE: **cannot resist** *I cannot resist a challenge* LOVE, adore, relish, have a weakness for, be very keen on, like, delight in, enjoy, take great pleasure in; *informal* be mad about, get a kick/thrill out of, cannot help wanting.

**resistance** noun **1** ***resistance to*** *change* OPPOSITION TO, hostility to, refusal to accept.

**2** *a spirited resistance* OPPOSITION, fight, stand, struggle.

**3** *the body's* ***resistance to*** *disease* ABILITY TO FIGHT OFF, immunity from, defenses against.

**4** *the French resistance* RESISTANCE MOVEMENT, freedom fighters, underground, partisans.

**resistant** adjective **1** ***resistant to*** *water* IMPERVIOUS TO, unsusceptible to, immune, invulnerable to, proof against, unaffected by.

**2** ***resistant to*** *change* OPPOSED TO, averse to, hostile to, inimical to, against; *informal* anti.

**resolute** adjective *Israelis and Palestinians held jittery but resolute hopes for peace* DETERMINED, purposeful, resolved, adamant, single-minded, firm, unswerving, unwavering, steadfast, staunch, stalwart, unfaltering, unhesitating, persistent, indefatigable, tenacious, strong-willed, unshakable; stubborn, dogged, obstinate, obdurate, inflexible, intransigent, implacable, unyielding, unrelenting; spirited, brave, bold, courageous, plucky, indomitable; *informal* gutsy, spunky, feisty; *formal* pertinacious. ANTONYM halfhearted.

THE RIGHT WORD **resolute, constant, decisive, determined, faithful, staunch**

Any of the above adjectives might apply to you if you take a stand on something and stick to it, or show your loyalty to a person, country, or cause. If you show unswerving loyalty to someone or something you are tied to (as in marriage, friendship, etc.), you would be described as **faithful** (*a faithful wife; a faithful Republican*). **Constant** also implies a firm or steady attachment to someone or something, but with less emphasis on vows, pledges, and obligations; it is the opposite of fickleness rather than of unfaithfulness (*my grandfather's constant confidant*). To be described as **staunch** carries loyalty one step further, implying an unwillingness to be dissuaded or turned aside (*a staunch friend who refused to believe the rumors that were circulating*). To be called **resolute** means that you are both staunch and steadfast, but the emphasis here is on character and a firm adherence to your own goals and purposes rather than to those of others (*resolute in insisting upon her right to be heard*). **Determined** and **decisive** are less forceful words. You can be *decisive* in almost any situation, as long as you have a choice among alternatives and don't hesitate in taking a stand (*decisive as always, she barely glanced at the menu before ordering*). *Determined*, unlike *resolute*, suggests a stubborn will rather than a conscious adherence to goals or principles (*he was determined to be home before the holidays*).

**resolution** noun **1** *her resolution not to smoke* INTENTION, resolve, decision, intent, aim, plan; commitment, pledge, promise.

**2** *the committee passed the resolution* MOTION, proposal, proposition, resolve.

**3** *she handled the work with resolution* DETERMINATION, purpose, purposefulness, resolve, resoluteness, single-mindedness, firmness, firmness of purpose; steadfastness, staunchness, perseverance, persistence, indefatigability, tenacity, tenaciousness, staying power, dedication, commitment; stubbornness, doggedness, obstinacy, obduracy; boldness, spiritedness, braveness, bravery, courage, pluck, grit, courageousness; *informal* guts, spunk; *formal* pertinacity. See note at COURAGE.

**4** *a satisfactory* ***resolution of*** *the problem* SOLUTION TO, answer to, end to, ending to, settlement of, conclusion to.

**resolve** verb **1** *this matter cannot be resolved overnight* SETTLE, sort out, solve, find a solution to, fix, straighten out, deal with, put right, put to rights, rectify; *informal* hammer out, thrash out, figure out.

**2** *Bob resolved not to wait any longer* DETERMINE, decide, make up one's mind, make a decision.

**3** *the committee resolved that the project should proceed* VOTE, pass a resolution, rule, decide formally, agree.

**4** *the compounds were resolved into their active constituents* BREAK DOWN/UP, separate, reduce, divide.

**5** *the ability to resolve facts into their legal categories* ANALYZE, dissect, break down, categorize.

**6** *the gray smudge resolved into a sandy beach* TURN, change, be transformed, be converted.

▸ noun **1** *their intimidation merely strengthened his resolve.* See RESOLUTION sense 3.

**2** *he made a resolve not to go there again* DECISION, resolution, commitment.

**resort** noun **1** *a seaside resort* VACATION SPOT, tourist center, vacationland; retreat; spa; *informal* tourist trap.

**2** *settle the matter without* ***resort to*** *legal proceedings* RECOURSE TO, turning to, the use of, utilizing.

**3** *strike action is our last resort* EXPEDIENT, measure, step, recourse, alternative, option, choice, possibility, hope. PHRASE: **resort to** *I don't have to resort to such underhanded tricks* HAVE RECOURSE TO, fall back on, turn to, make use of, use, employ, avail oneself of; stoop to, descend to, sink to.

**resound** verb **1** *the explosion resounded around the silent street* ECHO, re-echo, reverberate, ring out, boom, thunder, rumble.

**2** *resounding with the clang of hammers* REVERBERATE, echo, re-echo, resonate, ring.

3 *nothing will resound like their earlier achievements* BE ACCLAIMED, be celebrated, be renowned, be famed, be glorified, be trumpeted.

**resounding** adjective 1 *a resounding voice* REVERBERANT, reverberating, resonant, resonating, echoing, ringing, sonorous, deep, full-throated, rich, clear; loud, booming.

2 *a resounding success* ENORMOUS, huge, very great, tremendous, terrific, colossal; emphatic, decisive, conclusive, outstanding, remarkable, phenomenal.

**resource** noun 1 **(resources)** *use your resources efficiently* ASSETS, funds, wealth, money, capital; staff; supplies, materials, raw materials, store(s), stock(s), reserve(s).

2 *your tutor is there as a resource* FACILITY, amenity, aid, help, support.

3 *tears were her only resource* EXPEDIENT, resort, course, scheme, stratagem; trick, ruse, device.

4 *a person of resource* INITIATIVE, resourcefulness, enterprise, ingenuity, inventiveness; talent, ability, capability; *informal* gumption.

**resourceful** adjective *a group of resourceful fifth graders came up with a workable plan to overhaul the town's inefficient recycling center* INGENIOUS, enterprising, inventive, creative; clever, talented, able, capable; *informal* clueful. See note at CREATIVE.

**respect** noun 1 *the respect due to a great artist* ESTEEM, regard, high opinion, admiration, reverence, deference, honor. ANTONYM contempt.

2 *he spoke to her with respect* DUE REGARD, politeness, courtesy, civility, deference. ANTONYM disrespect.

3 *paying one's respects* REGARDS, kind regards, compliments, greetings, best/good wishes, felicitations, salutations; *archaic* remembrances.

4 *the report was accurate in every respect* ASPECT, regard, facet, feature, way, sense, particular, point, detail.

▸ verb 1 *she is highly respected in the book industry* ESTEEM, admire, think highly of, have a high opinion of, hold in high regard, hold in (high) esteem, look up to, revere, reverence, honor. See note at ESTEEM. ANTONYM despise.

2 *they respected our privacy* SHOW CONSIDERATION FOR, have regard for, observe, be mindful of, be heedful of; *formal* take cognizance of. ANTONYM scorn.

3 *her father respected her wishes* ABIDE BY, comply with, follow, adhere to, conform to, act in accordance with, defer to, obey, observe, keep, keep to. ANTONYMS disregard, disobey.

PHRASE: **with respect to/in respect of** *with respect to the new town garage, the council has decided to accept contractors' bids through the end of the month* CONCERNING, regarding, in/with regard to, with reference to, respecting, re, about, apropos, on the subject of, in connection with, vis-à-vis.

**respectable** adjective 1 *a respectable middle-class background* REPUTABLE, of good repute, upright, honest, honorable, trustworthy, decent, good, well-bred, clean-living. ANTONYM disreputable.

2 *a respectable salary* FAIRLY GOOD, decent, fair, reasonable, moderately good; substantial, considerable, sizable. ANTONYM paltry.

**respective** adjective *please return to your respective classrooms* SEPARATE, personal, own, particular, individual, specific, special, appropriate, different, various.

**respite** noun 1 *a brief respite* REST, break, breathing space, interval, intermission, interlude, recess, lull, pause, time out; relief, relaxation, repose; *informal* breather, letup.

2 *respite from debts* POSTPONEMENT, deferment, delay, reprieve; *Law* continuance.

**respond** verb 1 *they do not **respond to** questions* ANSWER, reply to, make a response to, make a rejoinder to.

2 *"No," she responded* SAY IN RESPONSE, answer, reply, rejoin, retort, riposte, counter.

3 *they were slow to respond* REACT, make a response, reciprocate, retaliate.

**response** noun 1 *his response to the question* ANSWER, reply, rejoinder, retort, riposte; *informal* comeback.

2 *an angry response* REACTION, reply, retaliation, feedback; *informal* comeback.

**responsibility** noun 1 *it was his responsibility to find witnesses* DUTY, task, function, job, role, business.

2 *they denied responsibility for the bomb attack* BLAME, fault, guilt, culpability, liability.

3 *let's show some social responsibility* TRUSTWORTHINESS, common sense, sense, maturity, reliability, dependability.

4 *a job with greater responsibility* AUTHORITY, control, power, leadership.

**responsible** adjective 1 *who is **responsible for** the prisons?* IN CHARGE OF, in control of, at the helm of, accountable for, liable for.

2 *if an error's been made, I'm the one who's responsible* ACCOUNTABLE, answerable, to blame, guilty, culpable, blameworthy, at fault, in the wrong.

3 *a responsible job* IMPORTANT, powerful, executive.

4 *he is responsible to the president* ANSWERABLE, accountable.

5 *a responsible tenant* TRUSTWORTHY, sensible, mature, reliable, dependable.

THE RIGHT WORD **responsible, accountable, answerable, liable**

**Responsible** is an adjective that applies to anyone who is in charge of an endeavor or to whom a duty has been delegated, and who is subject to penalty or blame in case of default (*responsible for getting everyone out of the building in the event of a fire*). **Answerable** implies a legal or moral obligation for which one must answer (*the parents were held to be answerable for their children's behavior*). **Accountable** is more positive than *responsible* or *answerable*, suggesting that something has been entrusted to someone who will be called to account for how that trust has been carried out (*She was directly accountable to the department head for the funds that had been allocated to* *her group*). **Liable** is more restricted in scope than any of the foregoing words; it refers exclusively to the assignment of blame or the payment of monetary damages in the event of a mishap (*because he was responsible for the accident, he was held liable for damages*).

---

**responsive** adjective *several consumers said the company hasn't been* ***responsive to*** *their needs* QUICK TO REACT TO, reactive to, receptive to, open to suggestions about, amenable to, flexible to, sensitive to, sympathetic to; aware of.

**rest**[1] verb **1** *he needed to rest* RELAX, take a rest, ease up/off, let up, slow down, have/take a break, unbend, unwind, recharge one's batteries, be at leisure, take it easy, put one's feet up; lie down, go to bed, have/take a nap, catnap, doze, sleep; *informal* take five, have/take a breather, catch forty winks, get some shut-eye, take a load off, chill, chill out, catch some Zs.

**2** *his hands rested on the rail* LIE, be laid, repose, be placed, be positioned, be supported by.

**3** *she rested her basket on the ground* SUPPORT, prop (up), lean, lay, set, stand, position, place, put.

**4** *the film script* ***rests on*** *an improbable premise* BE BASED ON, depend on, be dependent on, rely on, hinge on, turn on, be contingent on, revolve around, center on.

▸ noun **1** *get some rest* REPOSE, relaxation, leisure, respite, time off, breathing space, downtime; sleep, nap, doze; *informal* shut-eye, snooze, lie-down, forty winks.

**2** *a short rest from work* BREAK, vacation, breathing space, interval, interlude, intermission, time off/out, holiday; *informal* breather.

**3** *she took the poker from its rest* STAND, base, holder, support, rack, frame, shelf.

**4** *passengers queried why the train had come to rest several miles before the next station* A STANDSTILL, a halt, a stop.

**rest**[2] noun *the rest of the board members are appointees* REMAINDER, residue, balance, remaining part/number/quantity, others, those left, remains, remnant(s), surplus, excess; *technical* residuum.

▸ verb *you may rest assured that he is there* REMAIN, continue to be, stay, keep, carry on being.

**restful** adjective *a restful cruise* RELAXED, relaxing, quiet, calm, calming, tranquil, soothing, peaceful, placid, reposeful, leisurely, undisturbed, untroubled. ANTONYM exciting.

**restitution** noun **1** *restitution of the land seized* RETURN, restoration, handing back, surrender.

**2** *restitution for the damage caused* COMPENSATION, recompense, reparation, damages, indemnification, indemnity, reimbursement, repayment, redress, remuneration.

**restive** adjective **1** *Edward is getting restive.* See RESTLESS sense 1.

**2** *the militants are increasingly restive* UNRULY, disorderly, uncontrollable, unmanageable, willful, recalcitrant, insubordinate; *formal* refractory; *archaic* contumacious.

**restless** adjective **1** *Maria was restless throughout the meeting* UNEASY, ill at ease, restive, fidgety, edgy, on edge, tense, worked up, nervous, agitated, anxious, on tenterhooks, keyed up; *informal* jumpy, jittery, twitchy, uptight, antsy.

**2** *a restless night* SLEEPLESS, wakeful; fitful, broken, disturbed, troubled, unsettled.

**restoration** noun **1** *the restoration of democracy* REINSTATEMENT, reinstitution, reestablishment, reimposition, return.

**2** *the restoration of derelict housing* REPAIR, repairing, fixing, mending, whitepainting, refurbishment, reconditioning, rehabilitation, rebuilding, reconstruction, overhaul, redevelopment, renovation; *informal* rehab.

**restore** verb **1** *the aim to restore democracy* REINSTATE, bring back, reinstitute, reimpose, reinstall, reestablish. See note at RECOVER. ANTONYM abolish.

**2** *he restored it to its rightful owner* RETURN, give back, hand back.

**3** *the building has been restored* REPAIR, fix, mend, refurbish, recondition, rehabilitate, rebuild, reconstruct, remodel, overhaul, redevelop, renovate; *informal* do up, rehab. ANTONYM neglect.

**4** *a good sleep can restore you* REINVIGORATE, revitalize, revive, refresh, energize, fortify, revivify, regenerate, stimulate, freshen.

**restrain** verb **1** *Charles restrained his anger* CONTROL, keep under control, check, hold/keep in check, curb, suppress, repress, contain, dampen, subdue, smother, choke back, stifle, bottle up, rein back/in; *informal* keep the lid on.

**2** *she could barely restrain herself from swearing* PREVENT, stop, keep, hold back.

**3** *that beast ought to be restrained* TIE UP, bind, tether, chain (up), fetter, shackle, manacle, put in irons; *informal* hog-tie.

**restrained** adjective **1** *Julie was quite restrained* SELF-CONTROLLED, self-restrained, not given to excesses, sober, steady, unemotional, undemonstrative.

**2** *restrained elegance* MUTED, soft, discreet, subtle, quiet, unobtrusive, unostentatious, understated, tasteful.

**restraint** noun **1** *a restraint on their impulsiveness* CONSTRAINT, check, control, restriction, limitation, curtailment; rein, bridle, brake, damper, impediment, obstacle.

**2** *the protestors showed restraint* SELF-CONTROL, self-restraint, self-discipline, control, moderation, prudence, judiciousness, abstemiousness.

**3** *the room has been decorated with restraint* SUBTLETY, understatedness, taste, tastefulness, discretion, discrimination.

**4** *a child restraint* BELT, harness, strap.

**restrict** verb **1** *a busy working life restricted his leisure activities* LIMIT, keep within bounds, regulate, control, moderate, cut down.

**2** *the cuff supports the ankle without restricting movement* HINDER, interfere with, impede, hamper, obstruct, block, check, curb, shackle.

**3** *he restricted himself to a 15-minute speech* CONFINE, limit.

**restricted** adjective **1** *restricted space* CRAMPED, confined, constricted, small, narrow, tight. ANTONYM roomy.

**2** *a restricted calorie intake* LIMITED, controlled, regulated, reduced, rangebound. ANTONYM unlimited.

**3** *a restricted zone* OUT OF BOUNDS, off limits, private, exclusive. ANTONYM public.

**4** *restricted information* SECRET, top secret, classified; *informal* hush-hush.

**restriction** noun **1** *there is no restriction on the number of places* LIMITATION, limit, constraint, control, check, curb; condition, proviso, qualification.

**2** *the restriction of personal freedom* REDUCTION, limitation, diminution, curtailment.

**3** *restriction of movement* HINDRANCE, impediment, slowing, reduction, limitation.

**result** noun **1** *stress is the result of overwork* CONSEQUENCE, outcome, product, upshot, sequel, effect, reaction, repercussion, ramification, conclusion, culmination. ANTONYM cause.

**2** *having made the calculation, what is your result?* ANSWER, solution; sum, total, product.

**3** *exam results* GRADE, score, mark.

**4** *the result of the trial* VERDICT, decision, outcome, conclusion, judgment, findings, ruling.

▸ verb **1** *differences between species could* ***result from*** *their habitat* FOLLOW FROM, ensue from, develop from, stem from, spring from, arise from, derive from, evolve from, proceed from; occur from, happen from, take place from, come about from; be caused by, be brought about by, be produced by, originate in, be consequent on.

**2** *the shooting* ***resulted in*** *five deaths* END IN, culminate in, finish in, terminate in, lead to, prompt, precipitate, trigger; cause, bring about, occasion, effect, give rise to, produce, engender, generate; *literary* beget.

**resume** verb **1** *the government resumed negotiations* RESTART, recommence, begin again, start again, reopen; renew, return to, continue with, carry on with. ANTONYMS suspend, abandon.

**2** *the priest resumed his kneeling posture* RETURN TO, come back to, take up again, reoccupy. ANTONYM leave.

**resurrect** verb **1** *we believe that Jesus was resurrected* RAISE FROM THE DEAD, restore to life, revive.

**2** *resurrecting his career* REVIVE, restore, regenerate, revitalize, breathe new life into, bring back to life, reinvigorate, resuscitate, rejuvenate, stimulate, reestablish, relaunch.

**resuscitate** verb **1** *medics resuscitated him* BRING AROUND, revive, bring back to consciousness; give CPR (cardiopulmonary resuscitation) to, give the kiss of life to.

**2** *measures to resuscitate the economy* REVIVE, resurrect, restore, regenerate, revitalize, breathe new life into, reinvigorate, rejuvenate, stimulate.

**retain** verb **1** *the government retained a share in the industries* KEEP, keep possession of, keep hold of, hold on to, hang on to. ANTONYM give up.

**2** *existing footpaths are to be retained* MAINTAIN, keep, preserve, conserve. ANTONYM discontinue.

**3** *some students retain facts easily* REMEMBER, memorize, keep in one's mind, keep in one's memory, store. ANTONYM forget.

**4** *we have decided to retain a company lawyer* EMPLOY, contract, secure the services of, sign on, put on the payroll, keep on the payroll. ANTONYM dismiss.

**retainer** noun **1** *they're paid a retainer* RETAINING FEE, fee, periodic payment, advance, standing charge.

**2** *a faithful retainer.* See SERVANT sense 1.

**retaliate** verb *the gang will look for an opportunity to retaliate* FIGHT BACK, hit back, respond, react, reply, reciprocate, counterattack, return like for like, get back at someone, give tit for tat, take reprisals, get even, get one's own back, pay someone back, give someone a taste of their own medicine; have/get/take one's revenge, be revenged, avenge oneself.

**retard** verb *the process is retarded by bureaucratic red tape* DELAY, slow down, slow up, hold back, hold up, set back, postpone, put back, detain, decelerate; hinder, hamper, obstruct, inhibit, impede, check, restrain, restrict, trammel; *literary* stay. ANTONYM accelerate.

**retch** verb **1** *the sour taste made her retch* GAG, heave, almost vomit.

**2** *he went into the bushes to retch.* See VOMIT verb sense 1.

**reticence** noun *security concerns may explain Taylor's reticence* RESERVE, restraint, inhibition, diffidence, shyness; unresponsiveness, quietness, taciturnity, secretiveness.

**reticent** adjective *Smith was reticent about his personal affairs* RESERVED, withdrawn, introverted, inhibited, diffident, shy; uncommunicative, unforthcoming, unresponsive, tight-lipped, buttoned-up, quiet, taciturn, silent, guarded, secretive. ANTONYM expansive.

**retire** verb **1** *he has retired* GIVE UP WORK, stop working, stop work; pack it in, call it quits.

**2** *we've retired him on full pension* force to retire, give someone the golden handshake/parachute.

**3** *Gillian retired to her office* WITHDRAW, go away, take oneself off, decamp, shut oneself away; *formal* repair; *literary* betake oneself.

**4** *their forces retired* RETREAT, withdraw, pull back, fall back, disengage, back off, give ground.

**5** *everyone retired early* GO TO BED, call it a day, go to sleep; *informal* turn in, hit the hay, hit the sack.

**retiring** adjective **1** *the retiring president* DEPARTING, outgoing. ANTONYM incoming.

**2** *a retiring sort of man* SHY, diffident, self-effacing, unassuming, unassertive, reserved, reticent, quiet, timid, modest; private, secret, secretive, withdrawn, reclusive, unsociable. ANTONYM outgoing.

**retract** verb **1** *the sea otter can retract its claws* PULL IN, draw in, pull back.

**2** *she retracted her allegation* TAKE BACK, withdraw, recant, disavow, disclaim, repudiate, renounce, reverse, revoke, rescind, go back on, backtrack on, unsay; *formal* abjure.

**retreat** verb **1** *the army retreated* WITHDRAW, retire, draw back, pull back/out, fall back, give way, give ground, beat a retreat, beat a hasty retreat. ANTONYM advance.

**2** *the tide was retreating* GO OUT, ebb, recede, fall, go down, wane.

**3** *the government had to retreat* CHANGE ONE'S MIND, change one's plans; back down, climb down, do a U-turn, backtrack, backpedal, give in, concede defeat; *informal* pull a U-ey, do a one-eighty.

▸ noun **1** *the retreat of the army* WITHDRAWAL, pulling back.

**2** *the president's retreat* ABOUT-FACE, U-turn; *informal* one-eighty.

**3** *her rural retreat* REFUGE, haven, sanctuary; hideaway, hideout, hiding place, escape.

**4** *a period of retreat from the world* SECLUSION, withdrawal, retirement, solitude, isolation, sanctuary.

**retrench** verb **1** *we have to retrench* ECONOMIZE, cut back, make cutbacks, make savings, make economies, reduce expenditure, be economical, be frugal, tighten one's belt.

**2** *services have to be retrenched* REDUCE, cut, cut back, cut down, pare, pare down, slim down, make reductions in, make cutbacks in, trim, prune; shorten, abridge; *informal* slash.

**retribution** noun *officials condemned the suicide bombing and vowed retribution* PUNISHMENT, penalty, one's just deserts; revenge, reprisal, requital, retaliation, vengeance, an eye for an eye (and a tooth for a tooth), tit for tat, lex talionis; redress, reparation, restitution, recompense, repayment, atonement, indemnification, amends.

**retrieve** verb **1** *I retrieved our balls from their garden* GET BACK, bring back, recover, regain (possession of), recoup, reclaim, repossess, redeem, recuperate. See note at RECOVER.

**2** *they were trying to retrieve the situation* PUT RIGHT, set right, rectify, remedy, restore, sort out, straighten out, resolve, save.

**retrograde** adjective **1** *a retrograde step* FOR THE WORSE, regressive, negative, downhill, unwelcome. ANTONYMS positive, forward-looking.

**2** *retrograde motion* BACKWARD, backwards, reverse, rearward. ANTONYM forward.

**retrospect** PHRASE: **in retrospect** *in retrospect, we can see that more guards should have been installed at the front gate* LOOKING BACK, on reflection, on reexamination, in/with hindsight.

**return** verb **1** *he returned to Halifax* GO BACK, come back, come home. ANTONYM depart.

**2** *the symptoms returned* RECUR, reoccur, occur again, repeat (itself); reappear, appear again. ANTONYM disappear.

**3** *he returned the money* GIVE BACK, hand back; pay back, repay. ANTONYM keep.

**4** *Peter returned the book to the shelf* RESTORE, put back, replace, reinstall.

**5** *he returned the volley* HIT BACK, throw back. ANTONYM miss.

**6** *she returned his kiss* RECIPROCATE, requite, give in return, respond to, repay, give back. ANTONYM ignore.

**7** *"Later," returned Isabel* ANSWER, reply, respond, counter, rejoin, retort, come back.

**8** *the jury returned a unanimous verdict* DELIVER, bring in, hand down.

**9** *the club returned a profit* YIELD, earn, realize, net, gross, clear.

**10** *the Green Party was returned* ELECT, vote in, choose, select.

▸ noun **1** *his return to Oregon* HOMECOMING. ANTONYM departure.

**2** *the return of hard times* RECURRENCE, reoccurrence, repeat, repetition, reappearance, revival, resurrection, reemergence, resurgence, renaissance. ANTONYM disappearance.

**3** *I requested the return of my books* GIVING BACK, handing back, replacement, restoration, reinstatement, restitution.

**4** *a quick return on investments* YIELD, profit, gain, revenue, interest, dividend.

**5** *a census return* STATEMENT, report, submission, record, dossier; document, form.

PHRASE: **in return for** *I'm authorized to show you some leniency in return for information about Sawyer* IN EXCHANGE FOR, as a reward for, as compensation for.

**reveal** verb **1** *the police can't reveal his whereabouts* DIVULGE, disclose, tell, let slip, let drop, give away, give out, blurt (out), release, leak; make known, make public, broadcast, publicize, circulate, disseminate; *informal* let on. ANTONYMS hide, conceal.

**2** *the screen moved back to reveal the new car* SHOW, display, exhibit, disclose, uncover, unveil; *literary* uncloak. ANTONYM hide.

**3** *the data can reveal a good deal of information* BRING TO LIGHT, uncover, lay bare, unearth, expose; *formal* evince; *literary* uncloak.

**revel** verb **1** *they reveled all night* CELEBRATE, make merry, have a party, carouse, roister, go on a spree; *informal* party, live it up, whoop it up, make whoopee, rave, paint the town red.

**2** *she* ***reveled in*** *the applause* ENJOY, delight in, love, like, adore, be pleased by, take pleasure in, appreciate, relish, lap up, savor; *informal* get a kick out of.

▸ noun *late-night revels* CELEBRATION, festivity, jollification, merrymaking, carousing, spree; party, jamboree, hedonism; *informal* rave, shindig, bash, wingding, blast.

**revelation** noun **1** *revelations about his personal life* DISCLOSURE, surprising fact, announcement, report; admission, confession.

2 *the revelation of a secret* DIVULGING, divulgence, disclosure, disclosing, letting slip, letting drop, giving away, giving out, leaking, leak, betrayal, unveiling, making known, making public, broadcasting, publicizing, dissemination, reporting, report, declaring, declaration.

**reveler** noun *the New Year's Eve revelers have poured into Times Square in record numbers* PARTYGOER, merrymaker, carouser, roisterer; *archaic* wassailer.

**revenge** noun 1 *she is seeking revenge* VENGEANCE, retribution, retaliation, reprisal, requital, recrimination, an eye for an eye (and a tooth for a tooth), redress, satisfaction.

2 *they were filled with revenge* VENGEFULNESS, vindictiveness, vitriol, spite, spitefulness, malice, maliciousness, malevolence, ill will, animosity, hate, hatred, rancor, bitterness; *literary* maleficence.

▸ verb *he revenged his brother's murder* AVENGE, take/exact revenge for, exact retribution for, take reprisals for, get redress for, get satisfaction for.

**revenue** noun *this month's revenue is up 5 percent from last month* INCOME, takings, receipts, proceeds, earnings, sales; profit(s). ANTONYM expenditure.

**reverberate** verb *Fred's voice reverberated across the room* RESOUND, echo, re-echo, resonate, ring, boom, rumble, vibrate.

**revere** verb *she is revered as a national hero* RESPECT, admire, honor, think highly of, esteem, hold in high esteem, hold in high regard, look up to, put on a pedestal, lionize, reverence. ANTONYM despise.

THE RIGHT WORD **revere, admire, adore, idolize, venerate, worship**

We might **admire** someone who walks a tightrope between two skyscrapers, **idolize** a rock star, **adore** our mothers, and **revere** a person like Martin Luther King, Jr. Each of these verbs conveys the idea of regarding someone or something with respect and honor, but they differ considerably in terms of the feelings they connote. *Admire* suggests a feeling of delight and enthusiastic appreciation (*admire the courage of the mountain climber*), while *adore* implies the tenderness and warmth of unquestioning love (*he adored babies*). *Idolize* is an extreme form of adoration, suggesting a slavish, helpless love, (*he idolized the older quarterback*). We *revere* individuals and institutions that command our respect for their accomplishments or attributes (*he revered his old English professor*). **Venerate** and **worship** are usually found in religious contexts (*venerate saints and worship God*) but both words may be used in other contexts as well. *Venerate* is usually associated with dignity and advanced age (*venerate the old man who had founded the company more than 50 years ago*), while *worship* connotes an excessive and uncritical respect (*the young girls who waited outside the stage door worshiped the ground he walked on*).

**reverence** noun *reverence for the countryside* HIGH ESTEEM, high regard, great respect, acclaim, admiration, appreciation, estimation, favor. See note at HONOR. ANTONYM scorn.

▸ verb *they reverence modern jazz.* See REVERE.

**reverent** adjective *a reverent silence* RESPECTFUL, reverential, admiring, devoted, devout, dutiful, awed, deferential.

**reversal** noun 1 *there was no reversal on this issue* TURNAROUND, turnabout, about-face, volte-face, change of heart, U-turn, one-eighty, 180, backtracking; *rare* tergiversation.

2 *a reversal of roles* SWAP, exchange, change, swapping, interchange.

3 *the reversal of the decision* ALTERATION, changing; countermanding, undoing, overturning, overthrow, disallowing, overriding, overruling, veto, vetoing, revocation, repeal, rescinding, annulment, nullification, voiding, invalidation, abrogation.

4 *a very slow July was the only reversal we suffered during the entire fiscal year* SETBACK, reverse, upset, failure, misfortune, mishap, disaster, blow, disappointment, adversity, hardship, affliction, vicissitude, defeat; bad luck.

**reverse** verb 1 *the car reversed into a lamppost* BACK, back up, drive back/backward, move back/backward.

2 *reverse the bottle in the ice bucket* TURN UPSIDE DOWN, turn over, upend, upturn, invert.

3 *I reversed my jacket* TURN INSIDE OUT, turn outside in.

4 *reverse your roles* SWAP, change, change around, exchange, interchange, switch, switch around.

5 *the umpire reversed the decision* ALTER, change; overturn, overthrow, disallow, override, overrule, veto, revoke, repeal, rescind, annul, nullify, void, invalidate; *formal* abrogate.

▸ adjective 1 *in reverse order* BACKWARD, reversed, inverted, transposed.

2 *reverse racism* INVERSE, reversed, opposite, converse, contrary, counter, antithetical.

▸ noun 1 *the reverse is the case* OPPOSITE, contrary, converse, inverse, obverse, antithesis. See note at OPPOSITE.

2 *successes and reverses.* See REVERSAL sense 4.

3 *the reverse of the page* OTHER SIDE, reverse side, back, underside, wrong side, verso.

**review** noun 1 *the council undertook a review* ANALYSIS, evaluation, assessment, appraisal, examination, investigation, inquiry, probe, inspection, study.

2 *the rent is due for review* RECONSIDERATION, reassessment, reevaluation, reappraisal; change, alteration, modification, revision.

3 *book reviews* CRITICISM, critique, assessment, evaluation, commentary; *informal* take.

4 *a scientific review* JOURNAL, periodical, magazine, publication.

5 *their review of the economy* SURVEY, report, study, account, description, statement, overview, analysis.

6 *a military review* INSPECTION, parade, tattoo, procession, march past.

▸ verb 1 *I reviewed the evidence* SURVEY, study, research, consider, analyze, examine, scrutinize, explore, look into, probe, investigate, inspect, assess, appraise; *informal* size up.

2 *the referee reviewed his decision* RECONSIDER, reexamine, reassess, reevaluate, reappraise, rethink; change, alter, modify, revise.

3 *he reviewed the day* REMEMBER, recall, reflect on, think through, go over in one's mind, look back on.

4 *reviewing troops* INSPECT, view.

5 *she reviewed the play* COMMENT ON, evaluate, assess, appraise, judge, critique, criticize.

**reviewer** noun *a restaurant reviewer for the local paper* CRITIC, COMMENTATOR, judge, observer, pundit, analyst.

**revile** verb *reviled as a traitor* CRITICIZE, censure, condemn, attack, inveigh against, rail against, castigate, lambaste, denounce; slander, libel, malign, vilify, abuse; *informal* knock, slam, pan, crucify, roast, tear into, badmouth, dis, pummel; *formal* excoriate, calumniate. See note at SCOLD. ANTONYM praise.

**revise** verb 1 *she revised her opinion* RECONSIDER, review, reexamine, reassess, reevaluate, reappraise, rethink; change, alter, modify.

2 *the editor revised the text* AMEND, emend, correct, alter, change, edit, rewrite, redraft, rephrase, rework.

**revision** noun 1 *a revision of the fifth chapter* EMENDATION, correction, alteration, adaptation, editing, rewriting, redrafting.

2 *a new revision* VERSION, edition, rewrite.

3 *a major revision of the system* RECONSIDERATION, review, reexamination, reassessment, reevaluation, reappraisal, rethink; change, alteration, modification.

**revival** noun 1 *a revival in the economy* IMPROVEMENT, recovery, rallying, picking up, amelioration, turn for the better, upturn, upswing, resurgence. ANTONYM downturn.

2 *the revival of traditional crafts* COMEBACK, reestablishment, reintroduction, restoration, reappearance, resurrection, regeneration, renaissance, rejuvenation. ANTONYM disappearance.

**revive** verb 1 *attempts to revive her failed* RESUSCITATE, bring around, bring back to consciousness.

2 *the man soon revived* REGAIN CONSCIOUSNESS, come around, wake up.

3 *a cup of tea revived her* REINVIGORATE, revitalize, refresh, energize, reanimate, resuscitate, revivify, rejuvenate, regenerate, enliven, stimulate.

4 *reviving old traditions* REINTRODUCE, reestablish, restore, resurrect, bring back, regenerate, resuscitate, rekindle.

**revoke** verb *their liquor license was revoked* CANCEL, repeal, rescind, reverse, annul, nullify, void, invalidate, countermand, retract, withdraw, overrule, override; *Law* vacate; *formal* abrogate.

**revolt** verb 1 *the people revolted* REBEL, rise up, rise, take to the streets, riot, mutiny.

2 *the smell revolted him* DISGUST, sicken, nauseate, make nauseous, make someone sick, turn someone's stomach, be repugnant to, be repulsive to, put off, be offensive to, make someone's gorge rise; *informal* turn off, gross out.

▸ noun *an armed revolt* REBELLION, revolution, insurrection, mutiny, uprising, riot, rioting, insurgence, seizure of power, coup, coup d'état.

**revolting** adjective *a number of revolting items in their refrigerator* DISGUSTING, sickening, nauseating, stomach-turning, stomach-churning, repulsive, repellent, repugnant, appalling, abominable, hideous, horrible, awful, dreadful, terrible, obnoxious, vile, nasty, foul, loathsome, offensive, objectionable, off-putting, distasteful, disagreeable, vomitous; *informal* ghastly, putrid, horrid, gross, gut-churning, yucky, icky; *formal* rebarbative; *literary* noisome; *archaic* loathly. ANTONYMS attractive, pleasant, mouthwatering.

**revolution** noun 1 *the French aristocracy was ill-prepared to quell a revolution* REBELLION, revolt, insurrection, mutiny, uprising, riot, rioting, insurgence, seizure of power, coup (d'état). See note at UPRISING.

2 *a revolution in printing techniques* DRAMATIC CHANGE, radical alteration, sea change, metamorphosis, transformation, innovation, reorganization, restructuring; *informal* shake-up, shakedown.

3 *one revolution of a wheel* TURN, single turn, rotation, circle, spin; circuit, lap.

4 *the revolution of the earth* TURNING, rotation, circling; orbit.

**revolutionary** adjective 1 *revolutionary troops* REBELLIOUS, rebel, insurgent, rioting, mutinous, renegade, insurrectionary, insurrectionist, seditious, subversive, extremist.

2 *revolutionary change* THOROUGHGOING, thorough, complete, total, absolute, utter, comprehensive, sweeping, far-reaching, extensive, profound.

3 *a revolutionary kind of wheelchair* NEW, novel, original, unusual, unconventional, unorthodox, newfangled, innovative, modern, state-of-the-art, cutting-edge, futuristic, pioneering.

▸ noun *political revolutionaries* REBEL, insurgent, revolutionist, mutineer, insurrectionist, agitator, subversive.

**revolve** verb 1 *a fan revolved slowly* GO AROUND, turn around, rotate, spin.

2 *the moon revolves around the earth* CIRCLE, travel, orbit.

3 *his life* ***revolves around*** *cars* BE CONCERNED WITH, be preoccupied with, focus on, center on/around.

**revulsion** noun *millions of peaceable Muslims regard the extremists' violence with revulsion* DISGUST, repulsion, abhorrence, repugnance, nausea, horror, aversion, abomination, distaste. ANTONYM delight.

**reward** noun *a reward for its safe return* RECOMPENSE, prize, award, honor, decoration, bonus, premium, bounty, present, gift, payment; *informal* payoff, perk; *formal* perquisite.

▸ verb *they were well rewarded* RECOMPENSE, pay, remunerate, make something worth someone's while; give an award to. ANTONYM punish.

**rewarding** adjective *working in Professor Ott's intern program has been a rewarding experience* SATISFYING, gratifying, pleasing, fulfilling, enriching, edifying, beneficial, illuminating, worthwhile, productive, fruitful.

**rhetoric** noun **1** *a form of rhetoric* ORATORY, eloquence, command of language, way with words.

**2** *empty rhetoric* BOMBAST, turgidity, grandiloquence, magniloquence, pomposity, extravagant language, purple prose; wordiness, verbosity, prolixity; *informal* hot air; *rare* fustian.

**USAGE NOTE rhetoric**

*Rhetoric* = (1) the art of using language persuasively; the rules that help one achieve eloquence; (2) the persuasive use of language; (3) a treatise on persuasive language; (4) prose composition as a school subject. These are the main senses outlined in the *Oxford English Dictionary*. There should probably be added a new sense, related to but distinct from the first sense: (5) the bombastic or disingenuous use of language to manipulate people.

Older books defined *rhetoric* in line with sense 1:

• "Rhetoric is the Art of speaking suitably upon any Subject." (John Kirkby, *A New English Grammar*; 1746.)

• "Rhetoric is the art of adapting discourse, in harmony with its subject and occasion, to the requirements of a reader or hearer." (John F. Genung, *The Working Principles of Rhetoric*; 1902.)

But the slippage toward the pejorative sense 5 began early. In "Some Fruits of Solitude" (1693), William Penn suggested its iniquitous uses: "There is a Truth and Beauty in Rhetorick; but it oftener serves ill Turns than good ones." (Charles W. Eliot, ed., *Harvard Classics*; 1909.) By the twentieth century, some writers with a classical bent were trying hard to reclaim the word—e.g.: "No one who reads [ancient authors] can hold the puerile notions of rhetoric that prevail in our generation. The ancients would have made short work of the cult of the anti-social that lies behind the cult of mystification and the modern hatred of rhetoric. All the great literary ages have exalted the study of rhetoric." (Van Wyck Brooks, *Opinions of Oliver Allston*; 1941.) But T. S. Eliot probably had it right when he acknowledged that the word is essentially ambiguous today—generally pejorative but with flashes of a favorable sense: "The word [*rhetoric*] simply cannot be used as synonymous with bad writing. The meanings which it has been obliged to shoulder have been mostly opprobrious; but if a precise meaning can be found for it this meaning may occasionally represent a virtue." (" 'Rhetoric' and Poetic Drama," in *The Sacred Wood*, 7th ed.; 1950.) —*BG*

**rhetorical** adjective **1** *rhetorical devices* STYLISTIC, oratorical, linguistic, verbal.

**2** *rhetorical hyperbole* EXTRAVAGANT, grandiloquent, magniloquent, high-flown, orotund, bombastic, grandiose, pompous, pretentious, overblown, oratorical, turgid, flowery, florid; *informal* highfalutin; *rare* fustian.

**rhyme** noun an amusing rhyme by Ogden Nash POEM, piece of poetry, verse; **(rhymes)** poetry, doggerel.

**rhythm** noun **1** *the rhythm of the music* BEAT, cadence, tempo, time, pulse, throb, swing.

**2** *poetic features such as rhythm* METER, measure, stress, accent, cadence.

**3** *the rhythm of daily life* PATTERN, flow, tempo.

**ribald** adjective. See CRUDE sense 3.

**rich** adjective **1** *rich people* WEALTHY, affluent, moneyed, well off, well-to-do, prosperous, opulent, silk-stocking; *informal* rolling in money, rolling in it, rolling in (the) dough, in the money, loaded, flush, stinking rich, filthy rich, well-heeled, made of money. See note at WEALTHY. See also word spectrum. ANTONYM poor.

**2** *rich furnishings* SUMPTUOUS, opulent, luxurious, luxury, deluxe, lavish, gorgeous, splendid, magnificent, costly, expensive, fancy; *informal* posh, plush, ritzy, swanky, classy, swank. ANTONYMS plain, austere.

**3** *a garden* ***rich in*** *flowers* ABOUNDING IN, full of, well provided with, well stocked in/with, crammed with, packed with, teeming with, bursting with; *informal* jam-packed with, chockablock with, chock-full of.

**4** *a rich supply of restaurants* PLENTIFUL, abundant, copious, ample, profuse, lavish, liberal, generous, bountiful; *literary* plenteous, bounteous. ANTONYMS poor, meager.

**5** *rich soil* FERTILE, productive, fecund, fruitful. ANTONYM barren.

**6** *a rich sauce* CREAMY, heavy, full-flavored, fatty. ANTONYMS delicate, light.

**7** *a rich wine* FULL-BODIED, heavy, fruity. ANTONYM light.

**8** *rich colors* STRONG, deep, full, intense, vivid, brilliant. ANTONYMS delicate, pastel.

**9** *her rich voice* SONOROUS, full, resonant, deep, clear, mellow, mellifluous, full-throated. ANTONYMS thin, reedy.

**riches** plural noun **1** *his newfound riches* MONEY, wealth, funds, cash, (filthy) lucre, wherewithal, means, assets, liquid assets, capital, resources, reserves; opulence, affluence, prosperity; *informal* dough, bread, loot, shekels, moola, bucks, dinero, jack.

**2** *a cache of underwater riches* RESOURCES, treasure(s), bounty; jewels, gems.

**richly** adverb **1** *the richly furnished chamber* SUMPTUOUSLY, opulently, luxuriously, lavishly, gorgeously, splendidly, magnificently; *informal* plushly, ritzily, swankily, classily. ANTONYMS meanly, shabbily.

**2** *the joy she richly deserves* FULLY, thoroughly, in full measure, well, completely, wholly, totally, entirely, absolutely, amply, utterly.

**rid** verb *ridding the building of asbestos* CLEAR, free, purge, empty, strip. PHRASE: **get rid of 1** *we must get rid of some stuff* DISPOSE OF, throw away, throw out, clear out, discard, scrap, dump, jettison, divest oneself of; *informal* chuck, ditch, junk, trash, deep-six.

**2** *the cats got rid of the rats* DESTROY, eliminate, annihilate, obliterate, wipe out, kill.

**riddle** noun *an answer to the riddle* PUZZLE, conundrum, brainteaser, problem, unsolved problem, question, poser, enigma, mystery, quandary; *informal* stumper.

**THE RIGHT WORD riddle, conundrum, enigma, mystery, paradox, puzzle**

All of these terms imply something baffling or challenging. A **mystery** is anything that is incomprehensible to human reason, particularly if it invites speculation (*the mystery surrounding her sudden disappearance*). An **enigma** is a statement whose meaning is hidden under obscure or ambiguous allusions, so that we can only guess at its significance; it can also refer to a person of puzzling or contradictory character (*he remained an enigma throughout his long career*). A **riddle** is a mystery involving contradictory statements, with a hidden meaning designed to be guessed at (*the old riddle about how many college graduates it takes to change a light bulb*). **Conundrum** applies specifically to a riddle phrased as a question, the answer to which usually involves a pun or a play on words, such as "What is black and white and read all over?"; conundrum can also refer to any puzzling or difficult situation. A **paradox** is a statement that seems self-contradictory or absurd, but in reality expresses a possible truth (*Francis Bacon's well-known paradox, "The most corrected copies are commonly the least correct"*). A **puzzle** is not necessarily a verbal statement, but it presents a problem with a particularly baffling solution or tests one's ingenuity or skill in coming up with a solution (*a crossword puzzle*).

---

**ride** verb **1** *she can ride a horse* SIT ON, mount, bestride; manage, handle, control.

**2** *riding through the town on motorbikes* TRAVEL, move, proceed, make one's way; drive, cycle; trot, canter, gallop.

▸ noun *a ride in the new car* TRIP, journey, drive, run, excursion, outing, jaunt; lift; *informal* spin.

**ridicule** noun *she was subjected to ridicule* MOCKERY, derision, laughter, scorn, scoffing, contempt, jeering, sneering, sneers, jibes, jibing, teasing, taunts, taunting, badinage, chaffing, sarcasm, satire; *informal* kidding, ribbing, joshing, goofing, razzing. ANTONYM respect.

▸ verb *his theory was ridiculed* DERIDE, mock, laugh at, heap scorn on/upon, jeer at, jibe at, sneer at, treat with contempt, scorn, make fun of, poke fun at, scoff at, satirize, lampoon, burlesque, caricature, parody, tease, taunt, chaff; *informal* kid, rib, josh, razz.

**ridiculous** adjective **1** *she looked ridiculous in her dad's oversized shorts and striped socks* LAUGHABLE, absurd, comical, funny, hilarious, risible, droll, amusing, farcical, silly, ludicrous; *rare* derisible. ANTONYM serious.

**2** *a ridiculous suggestion* SENSELESS, silly, foolish, foolhardy, stupid, inane, fatuous, childish, puerile, half-baked, harebrained, cockamamie, ill-thought-out, crackpot, idiotic. ANTONYM sensible.

**3** *a ridiculous exaggeration* ABSURD, preposterous, ludicrous, risible, laughable, nonsensical, senseless, outrageous. See note at ABSURD. ANTONYM reasonable.

**rife** adjective **1** *violence is rife* WIDESPREAD, general, common, universal, extensive, ubiquitous, omnipresent, endemic, inescapable, insidious, prevalent. See note at PREVALENT. ANTONYMS scarce, unknown.

**2** *the village was rife with gossip* OVERFLOWING, bursting, alive, teeming, abounding. ANTONYM devoid.

**riffraff** noun *this government considers its citizens riffraff and is quick to silence the mere whispers of dissent* RABBLE, scum, good-for-nothings, undesirables, lowlifes, hoi polloi, the lowest of the low; *informal* peasants. ANTONYM elite.

**rifle** verb **1** *she rifled through her closet* RUMMAGE, search, hunt, forage.

**2** *a thief rifled her home* BURGLE, burglarize, rob, steal from, loot, raid, plunder, ransack.

▸ noun *he refused to register the rifle* FIREARM, gun, shotgun, 30-30; *trademark* Winchester.

**rift** noun **1** *a deep rift in the ice* CRACK, fault, flaw, split, break, breach, fissure, fracture, cleft, crevice, cavity, opening.

**2** *the rift between them* BREACH, division, split; quarrel, squabble, disagreement, falling-out, row, argument, dispute, conflict, feud; estrangement; *informal* spat, scrap.

**USAGE NOTE riff, rift**

These two are sometimes confused. *Riff* is now largely confined to jazz and pop-music contexts. It refers to a melodic phrase, usually repeated and often played in unison by several instruments; sometimes it's a variation on a tune, and it may be either an accompaniment to a solo or the only melodic element—e.g.: "With guitar riffs so rudimentary they seem to have been made up on the spot, . . . the U.K. sextet played with rude ebullience." (*Chicago Tribune*; Sept. 29, 2000.) The term dates only from the mid-twentieth century—and has little discernible relation to the older, mostly obsolete senses of *riff* (= [1] a string of onions, [2] the diaphragm, or [3] the mange; an itchy rash). That's probably because this particular *riff* seems to have originated as a truncated form of the musical term *refrain*.

*Rift* arose in Middle English in the sense "a fissure or divide; a split or crack"—the meaning it still carries—e.g.: "Word out of Washington is that Bondra wants to change teams because of a rift with coach Ron Wilson." (*Boston Globe*; Oct. 1, 2000.) Occasionally the term also refers to the rapids formed by rocks protruding from the bed of a stream. It formerly also meant "a burp"—a sense long obsolete.

Although the *Oxford English Dictionary* records two early-seventeenth-century uses of *riff* in the obsolete sense "rift, chink," the modern use of the word in that sense appears to be nothing more than rank word-swapping resulting from sound association—e.g.: "The way he sees it, things aren't bad at all. No riffs [read *rifts*] between him and crew chief Todd Parrott." (*USA Today*; May 26, 2000.) —*BG*

---

**rig** verb **1** *the boats were rigged with a single sail* EQUIP, fit out, supply, furnish, provide, arm.

**2** *I **rigged** myself **out** in black* DRESS, clothe, attire, robe, garb, array, deck out, drape, accoutre, outfit, get up, trick out/up; *informal* doll up; *archaic* apparel.

**3** *he will **rig up** a shelter* SET UP, erect, assemble, build; throw together, cobble together, put together, whip up, improvise, contrive.

▸ noun 1 *a CB radio rig* APPARATUS, appliance, machine, device, instrument, contraption, system; tackle, gear, kit, outfit.

2 *the rig of a Civil War cavalry officer* UNIFORM, costume, ensemble, outfit, livery, attire, clothes, clothing, garments, dress, garb, regalia, trappings; *informal* getup, gear, togs, kit; *formal* apparel; *archaic* raiment, vestments.

**right** adjective 1 *it wouldn't be right to do that* JUST, fair, proper, good, upright, righteous, virtuous, moral, ethical, honorable, honest; lawful, legal. ANTONYMS wrong, unjust.

2 *Mr. Hubert had the right answer* CORRECT, accurate, exact, precise; proper, valid, conventional, established, official, formal. ANTONYMS wrong, inaccurate.

3 *the right person for the job* SUITABLE, appropriate, fitting, correct, proper, desirable, preferable, ideal; *archaic* meet. ANTONYMS wrong, unsuitable.

4 *you've come at the right time* OPPORTUNE, advantageous, favorable, propitious, good, lucky, happy, fortunate, providential, felicitous; timely, seasonable, convenient, expedient, suitable, appropriate. ANTONYMS wrong, inopportune.

5 *he's not right in the head* SANE, lucid, rational, balanced, together, compos mentis; healthy, well; *informal* all there. ANTONYMS non compos mentis, insane.

6 *my right hand* DEXTRAL. ANTONYM left.

▸ adverb 1 *she was right at the limit of her patience* COMPLETELY, fully, totally, absolutely, utterly, thoroughly, quite.

2 *right in the middle of the village* EXACTLY, precisely, directly, immediately, just, squarely, dead; *informal* bang, smack, plumb, smack dab.

3 *keep going right ahead* STRAIGHT, directly. ANTONYM indirectly.

4 *informal he'll be right down* STRAIGHT, immediately, instantly, at once, straightaway, now, right now, this minute, directly, forthwith, without further ado, promptly, quickly, as soon as possible, ASAP, in short order; *informal* straight off, PDQ (pretty damn quick), pronto, lickety-split. ANTONYMS sometime, later.

5 *I think I heard right* CORRECTLY, accurately, properly, precisely, aright, rightly, perfectly. ANTONYM wrong.

6 *make sure you're treated right by the authorities* WELL, properly, justly, fairly, nicely, equitably, impartially, honorably, lawfully, legally, ethically. ANTONYM unjustly.

7 *things will turn out right* WELL, for the best, favorably, happily, advantageously, profitably, providentially, luckily, conveniently. ANTONYM badly.

▸ noun 1 *the difference between right and wrong* GOODNESS, righteousness, virtue, integrity, rectitude, propriety, morality, truth, honesty, honor, justice, fairness, equity; lawfulness, legality. ANTONYM wrong.

2 *you have the right to say no* ENTITLEMENT, prerogative, privilege, advantage, due, birthright, liberty, authority, power, license, permission, dispensation, leave, sanction, freedom; *Law, historical* droit.

▸ verb 1 *the way to right a capsized dinghy* SET UPRIGHT, turn back over.

2 *we must right the situation* REMEDY, put right, rectify, retrieve, fix, resolve, sort out, settle, square; straighten out, correct, repair, mend, redress, make good, ameliorate, better.

PHRASES: **by rights** *by rights, these kids should have been offered a decent education* PROPERLY, correctly, technically, in fairness; legally, de jure.

**in the right** *please explain why you think you're in the right* JUSTIFIED, vindicated.

**put right.** See RIGHT verb sense 2.

**right away** *we'll miss the bus if we don't leave right away* AT ONCE, straightaway, now, right now, this minute, this very minute, this instant, immediately, instantly, directly, forthwith, without further ado, promptly, quickly, without delay, as soon as possible, ASAP, in short order; *informal* straight off, PDQ (pretty damn quick), pronto, lickety-split.

**within one's rights** *Mr. Barnes is within his rights to dispute the charges to his account* ENTITLED, permitted, allowed, at liberty, empowered, authorized, qualified, licensed, justified.

**righteous** adjective 1 *righteous living* GOOD, virtuous, upright, upstanding, decent; ethical, principled, moral, high-minded, law-abiding, honest, honorable, blameless, irreproachable, noble; saintly, angelic, pure. See note at MORAL. ANTONYM sinful.

2 *righteous anger* JUSTIFIABLE, justified, legitimate, defensible, supportable, rightful; admissible, allowable, understandable, excusable, acceptable, reasonable. ANTONYM unjustifiable.

**rigid** adjective 1 *a rigid container* STIFF, hard, firm, inflexible, unbending, unyielding, inelastic. ANTONYM flexible.

2 *a rigid routine* FIXED, set, firm, inflexible, unalterable, unchangeable, immutable, unvarying, invariable, hard and fast, cast-iron, ironclad. ANTONYM flexible.

3 *a rigid approach to funding* STRICT, severe, stern, stringent, rigorous, inflexible, uncompromising, intransigent. ANTONYMS flexible, lenient.

**rigor** noun 1 *a mine operated under conditions of rigor* STRICTNESS, severity, stringency, toughness, harshness, rigidity, inflexibility, intransigence.

2 *intellectual rigor* METICULOUSNESS, thoroughness, carefulness, diligence, scrupulousness, exactness, exactitude, precision, accuracy, correctness, strictness.

3 **(rigors)** *the rigors of the journey* HARDSHIP, harshness, severity, adversity; ordeal, misery, trial; discomfort, inconvenience, privation.

**rigorous** adjective 1 *rigorous attention to detail* METICULOUS, conscientious, punctilious, careful, diligent, attentive, scrupulous, painstaking, exact, precise, accurate, thorough, particular, strict, demanding, exacting; *informal* persnickety. ANTONYM slapdash.

2 *the rigorous enforcement of rules* STRICT, severe, stern, stringent, tough, harsh, rigid, relentless, unsparing, inflexible,

draconian, intransigent, uncompromising, exacting. ANTONYM lax.

**3** *rigorous yachting conditions* HARSH, severe, bad, bleak, extreme, inclement; unpleasant, disagreeable, foul, nasty, filthy; stormy, wild, tempestuous. ANTONYMS gentle, mild.

**rim** noun **1** *the rim of her cup* BRIM, edge, lip.

**2** *the rim of the crater* EDGE, border, side, margin, brink, fringe, boundary, perimeter, limits, periphery. See note at BORDER.

**rind** noun *dried lemon rind* SKIN, peel, zest, integument; *Botany* pericarp.

**ring**[1] noun **1** *the rings around Saturn* CIRCLE, band, loop, hoop, halo, disk.

**2** *she wore a ring* WEDDING RING, wedding band, band.

**3** *a circus ring* ARENA, enclosure, field, ground; amphitheater, stadium.

**4** *a ring of onlookers* CIRCLE, group, cluster, bunch, band, throng, crowd, flock, pack.

**5** *a spy ring* GANG, syndicate, cartel, mob, band, circle, organization, association, society, alliance, league, coterie, cabal, cell.

▸ verb *police ringed the building* SURROUND, circle, encircle, encompass, girdle, enclose, hem in, confine, seal off.

**ring**[2] verb **1** *church bells rang all day* TOLL, sound, peal, chime, clang, bong, ding, jingle, tinkle; *literary* knell.

**2** *the room rang with laughter* RESOUND, reverberate, resonate, echo.

▸ noun *the ring of a bell* CHIME, toll, peal, clang, clink, ding, jingle, tinkle, tintinnabulation, sound; *literary* knell.

PHRASE: **ring something in** *our biggest sale of the season will ring in the new year* HERALD, signal, announce, proclaim, usher in, introduce; mark, signify, indicate; *literary* betoken, knell.

**rinse** verb *the campers rinsed their socks and hung them near the fire* WASH, wash out, clean, cleanse, bathe; dip, drench, splash, hose down.

**riot** noun **1** *a riot in the capital* UPROAR, commotion, upheaval, disturbance, furor, tumult, melee, scuffle, fracas, fray, brawl, free-for-all; violence, fighting, vandalism, mayhem, turmoil, lawlessness, anarchy, violent protest.

**2** *the garden was a riot of color* MASS, sea, splash, show, exhibition.

▸ verb *the miners rioted* RAMPAGE, go on the rampage, run riot, fight in the streets, run wild, run amok, go berserk; *informal* raise hell.

PHRASE: **run riot 1** *the children ran riot* GO ON THE RAMPAGE, rampage, riot, run amok, go berserk, go out of control; *informal* raise hell.

**2** *the vegetation has run riot* GROW PROFUSELY, spread uncontrolled, grow rapidly, spread like wildfire; burgeon, multiply, rocket, skyrocket.

**riotous** adjective **1** *the demonstration turned riotous* UNRULY, rowdy, disorderly, uncontrollable, unmanageable, undisciplined, uproarious, tumultuous; violent, wild, ugly, lawless, anarchic. ANTONYM peaceable.

**2** *a riotous party* BOISTEROUS, lively, loud, noisy, unrestrained, uninhibited, uproarious, unruly, rollicking, knockabout; *informal* rambunctious. ANTONYM restrained.

**ripe** adjective **1** *a ripe tomato* MATURE, ripened, full grown, ready to eat; luscious, juicy, tender, sweet. ANTONYM green.

**2** *the dock is ripe for development* READY, fit, suitable, right. ANTONYMS unsuitable, unready.

**3** *the ripe old age of ninety* ADVANCED, hoary, venerable, old.

**4** *the time is ripe for his return* OPPORTUNE, advantageous, favorable, auspicious, propitious, promising, good, right, fortunate, benign, providential, felicitous, seasonable; convenient, suitable, appropriate, apt, fitting. ANTONYM unsuitable.

**ripen** verb *we let the grapes ripen on the vine* BECOME RIPE, mature, mellow. See note at MATURE.

**riposte** noun *an indignant riposte* RETORT, counter, rejoinder, sally, return, answer, reply, response; *informal* comeback.

▸ verb *"Heaven help you," riposted Alicia* RETORT, counter, rejoin, return, retaliate, hurl back, answer, reply, respond, come back.

**rise** verb **1** *the sun rose* MOVE UP/UPWARDS, come up, make one's/its way up, arise, ascend, climb, mount, soar. ANTONYMS fall, descend, set.

**2** *the mountains rising above us* LOOM, tower, soar, rise up, rear (up).

**3** *prices rose* GO UP, increase, soar, shoot up, surge, leap, jump, rocket, escalate, spiral. ANTONYM drop.

**4** *living standards have risen* IMPROVE, get better, advance, go up, soar, shoot up. ANTONYM worsen.

**5** *her voice rose* GET HIGHER, grow, increase, become louder, swell, intensify. ANTONYM drop.

**6** *he rose from his chair* STAND UP, get to one's feet, get up, jump up, leap up; *formal* arise. ANTONYM sit.

**7** *she rises at dawn* GET UP, get out of bed, rouse oneself, stir, bestir oneself, be up and about; *informal* rise and shine, surface; *formal* arise. ANTONYMS retire, go to bed.

**8** *the court rose at midday* ADJOURN, recess, be suspended, pause, take a break; *informal* knock off, take five. ANTONYMS resume, continue.

**9** *he rose through the ranks* MAKE PROGRESS, climb, advance, get on, work one's way, be promoted.

**10** *she wouldn't* ***rise to*** *the bait* REACT TO, respond to; take.

**11** *on the third day, Christ rose* COME BACK TO LIFE, be resurrected, revive. ANTONYM die.

**12** *the dough started to rise* SWELL, expand, enlarge, puff up.

**13** *the nation rose against its oppressors* REBEL, revolt, mutiny, riot, take up arms. ANTONYM kowtow.

**14** *the river* ***rises in*** *the mountains* ORIGINATE IN, begin in, start in, emerge in/from; issue from, spring from, flow from, emanate from.

15 *her spirits rose* BRIGHTEN, lift, cheer up, improve, pick up; *informal* buck up.

16 *the ground rose gently* SLOPE UPWARD, go uphill, incline, climb. ANTONYMS drop away, drop.

▸ noun 1 *a price rise* INCREASE, hike, leap, upsurge, upswing, climb, escalation.

2 *a rise in standards* IMPROVEMENT, amelioration, upturn, leap.

3 *her rise to power* PROGRESS, climb, promotion, elevation, aggrandizement.

4 *we walked up the rise* SLOPE, incline, hillock, hill; *formal* eminence.

**risk** noun 1 *there is a certain amount of risk* CHANCE, uncertainty, unpredictability, precariousness, instability, insecurity, perilousness, riskiness. ANTONYM safety.

2 *the risk of fire* POSSIBILITY, chance, probability, likelihood, danger, peril, threat, menace, fear, prospect. ANTONYM impossibility.

▸ verb 1 *he risked his life to save them* ENDANGER, imperil, jeopardize, hazard, gamble, gamble with, chance; put on the line, put in jeopardy.

2 *you risk getting cold and wet* CHANCE, stand a chance of.

PHRASE: **at risk** *our soldiers are at risk every day* IN DANGER, in peril, in jeopardy, under threat.

**risky** adjective *risky sports* DANGEROUS, hazardous, perilous, high-risk, fraught with danger, unsafe, insecure, precarious, touch-and-go, treacherous, parlous; uncertain, unpredictable; *informal* chancy, dicey, hairy.

**rite** noun *a religious rite practiced for thousands of years* CEREMONY, ritual, ceremonial; service, sacrament, liturgy, worship, office; act, practice, custom, tradition, convention, institution, procedure.

**ritual** noun *an elaborate civic ritual* CEREMONY, rite, ceremonial, observance; service, sacrament, liturgy, worship; act, practice, custom, tradition, convention, formality, procedure, protocol.

▸ adjective *a ritual burial* CEREMONIAL, ritualistic, prescribed, set, formal; sacramental, liturgical; traditional, conventional.

**rival** noun 1 *his rival for the nomination* OPPONENT, challenger, competitor, contender; adversary, antagonist, enemy; *literary* foe. ANTONYM ally.

2 *the tool has no rival* EQUAL, match, peer, equivalent, counterpart, like.

▸ verb *few countries can rival ours for natural resources* MATCH, compare with, compete with, vie with, equal, measure up to, be in the same league as, be on a par with, touch, challenge; *informal* hold a candle to.

▸ adjective *rival candidates* COMPETING, opposing, contending.

**rivalry** noun *a growing rivalry between the two groups* COMPETITIVENESS, competition, contention, vying; opposition, conflict, feuding, antagonism, friction, enmity.

**road** noun 1 *the roads were crowded with traffic* STREET, avenue, boulevard, freeway, highway, parkway, thoroughfare, thruway, turnpike.

2 *a step on the road to recovery* WAY, path, route, course.

PHRASE: **on the road** *the band will be on the road for two months* ON TOUR, touring, traveling.

**roam** verb *he had roamed the countryside for nine years* WANDER, rove, ramble, drift, walk, traipse; range, travel, tramp, traverse, trek; *informal* cruise, mosey around/about; *formal* perambulate; *archaic* peregrinate.

**roar** noun 1 *the roars of the crowd* SHOUT, bellow, yell, cry, howl; clamor; *informal* holler.

2 *the roar of the sea* BOOM, crash, rumble, roll, thundering.

3 *roars of laughter* GUFFAW, howl, hoot, shriek, gale, peal.

▸ verb 1 *"Get out!" roared Angus* BELLOW, yell, shout, bawl, howl; *informal* holler.

2 *thunder roared* BOOM, rumble, crash, roll, thunder.

3 *the movie left them roaring* GUFFAW, laugh, hoot; *informal* split one's sides, be rolling in the aisles, be doubled up, crack up, be in stitches, die laughing.

4 *a motorbike roared past* SPEED, zoom, whiz, flash; belt, tear, zip, bomb.

**rob** verb 1 *the gang robbed the local bank* BURGLE, burglarize, steal from, hold up, break into; raid, loot, plunder, pillage; *informal* knock off, stick up.

2 *he robbed an old woman* STEAL FROM; *informal* mug, jump, roll.

3 *she was robbed of her savings* CHEAT (OUT), swindle (out), defraud (out); *informal* do out, con out, fleece (out); *informal* stiff (out).

4 *informal* *if you paid $300 for that watch, you were robbed* OVERCHARGE; *informal* rip off, sting, have, diddle, gouge.

5 *a dubious call robbed him of his championship title* DEPRIVE, strip, divest; deny.

**robber** noun *the robbers fled the scene in a blue Camaro* BURGLAR, thief, housebreaker, mugger, shoplifter, purse-snatcher; stealer, pilferer, raider, looter, plunderer, pillager; bandit; pirate; *informal* crook, yegg, second-story man; *literary* brigand, highwayman.

**robbery** noun 1 *they were arrested for the robbery* BURGLARY, theft, thievery, stealing, breaking and entering, housebreaking, larceny, shoplifting, purse-snatching; embezzlement, fraud; holdup, break-in, raid; *informal* mugging, stickup, heist.

2 *informal* *Six bucks? That's robbery!* A SWINDLE; *informal* a rip-off, a gyp, a con, a con job.

**robe** noun 1 *they put on their robes after swimming* BATHROBE, dressing gown, kimono, housecoat, kaftan, cover-up, wrapper.

2 *she wore a fur-trimmed red robe* CLOAK, wrap, mantle, cape.

**3 (robes)** *coronation robes* GARB, regalia, costume, finery; garments, clothes; *formal* apparel; *archaic* raiment, habiliments, vestments.

**4 (robes)** *priestly robes* VESTMENT, surplice, cassock, soutane, rochet, alb, dalmatic, chasuble, tunicle, Geneva gown; canonicals.

▸ verb *he robed for Mass* DRESS, vest, clothe oneself; *formal* enrobe.

**robot** noun *robots can perform certain tasks that are considered hazardous for humans* AUTOMATON, android, golem; *informal* bot, droid.

**robust** adjective **1** *a large, robust man* STRONG, vigorous, sturdy, tough, powerful, solid, muscular, sinewy, rugged, hardy, strapping, brawny, burly, husky; healthy, fit, fighting fit, hale and hearty, lusty, in fine fettle; *informal* beefy, hunky. ANTONYMS frail, weak.

**2** *these knives are robust* DURABLE, resilient, tough, hardwearing, long-lasting, sturdy, strong. ANTONYM fragile.

**3** *a robust commodities market* STRONG, healthy, resilient, invulnerable; productive, profitable. ANTONYM vulnerable.

**4** *a robust red wine* STRONG, full-bodied, flavorful, rich. ANTONYMS tasteless, insipid.

**rock**[1] verb **1** *the ship rocked on the water* MOVE TO AND FRO, move back and forth, sway, seesaw; roll, pitch, plunge, toss, lurch, reel, list; wobble, oscillate.

**2** *the building began to rock* SHAKE, vibrate, quake, tremble.

**3** *Wall Street was rocked by the news* STUN, shock, stagger, astonish, startle, surprise, shake, shake up, take aback, throw, unnerve, disconcert.

**4** *informal* *this game totally rocks* BE IMPRESSIVE; *informal* kick butt, blow one away, blow one's mind, rock one's world, be cool, be on fire.

**rock**[2] noun **1** *a gully strewn with rocks* BOULDER, stone, pebble.

**2** *a castle built on a rock* CRAG, cliff, outcrop.

**3** *Toni was the rock on which they relied* FOUNDATION, cornerstone, support, prop, mainstay; tower of strength, bulwark, anchor.

**4** *informal* *she wore a massive rock on her finger* DIAMOND, jewel, precious stone. PHRASE: **on the rocks** *informal* **1** *her marriage is on the rocks* IN DIFFICULTY, in trouble, breaking up, over; in tatters, in ruins, ruined.

**2** *a Scotch on the rocks* WITH ICE, on ice, over ice.

**rocket** noun **1** *guerrillas fired rockets at them* MISSILE, projectile.

**2** *they lit some colorful rockets* FIREWORK, firecracker, Roman candle.

▸ verb **1** *prices have rocketed* SHOOT UP, soar, increase, rise, escalate, spiral; *informal* go through the roof. ANTONYM plummet.

**2** *they rocketed into the alley* SPEED, zoom, shoot, whiz, career; *informal* barrel, tear, bomb, hightail it.

**rocky**[1] adjective *a rocky path* STONY, pebbly, shingly; rough, bumpy; craggy, mountainous.

**rocky**[2] adjective **1** *that table's rocky* UNSTEADY, shaky, unstable, wobbly, tottery, rickety, flimsy. ANTONYMS steady, stable.

**2** *a rocky marriage* DIFFICULT, problematic, precarious, unstable, unreliable, undependable; *informal* iffy, up and down. ANTONYMS solid, stable.

**rod** noun **1** *an iron rod* BAR, stick, pole, baton, staff; shaft, strut, rail, spoke.

**2** *the ceremonial rod* STAFF, mace, scepter.

**3 (the rod)** *instruction was accompanied by the rod* CORPORAL PUNISHMENT, the cane, the lash, the birch; beating, flogging, caning, birching.

**rogue** noun **1** *a rogue without ethics* SCOUNDREL, villain, miscreant, reprobate, rascal, good-for-nothing, ne'er-do-well, wretch; *informal* rat, dog, louse, crook; *dated* cad; *archaic* blackguard, picaroon, knave.

**2** *your boy's a little rogue* RASCAL, imp, devil, monkey; *informal* scamp, scalawag, monster, horror, terror, hellion.

**role** noun **1** *a small role in the film* PART; character, cameo.

**2** *his role as class president* CAPACITY, position, job, post, office, duty, responsibility, mantle, place; function, part.

**roll** verb **1** *the bottle rolled down the table* TURN ROUND AND ROUND, go round and round, turn over and over, spin, rotate.

**2** *waiters rolled in the trolleys* WHEEL, push, trundle.

**3** *we rolled past fields* TRAVEL, go, move, pass, cruise, sweep.

**4** *the months* ***rolled by*** PASS, pass by, go by, slip by, fly by, elapse, wear on, march on.

**5** *tears rolled down her cheeks* FLOW, run, course, stream, pour, spill, trickle.

**6** *the mist rolled in* BILLOW, undulate, tumble.

**7** *he rolled his handkerchief into a ball* WIND, coil, fold, curl; twist.

**8** ***roll out*** *the pastry* FLATTEN (OUT), level (out); even out.

**9** *they rolled about with laughter* STAGGER, lurch, reel, totter, teeter, wobble.

**10** *the ship began to roll* LURCH, toss, rock, pitch, plunge, sway, reel, list, keel.

**11** *thunder rolled* RUMBLE, reverberate, echo, resound, boom, roar, grumble.

▸ noun **1** *a roll of wrapping paper* CYLINDER, tube, scroll; bolt.

**2** *a roll of film* REEL, spool.

**3** *a roll of $20 bills* WAD, bundle.

**4** *a roll of the dice* THROW, toss, turn, spin.

**5** *crusty rolls* BREAD ROLL, bun, bagel, hoagie, kaiser roll.

**6** *the electoral roll* LIST, register, directory, record, file, index, catalog, inventory; census.

**7** *a roll of thunder* RUMBLE, reverberation, echo, boom, clap, crack, roar, grumble.

PHRASES: **roll in** *informal* 1 *money has been rolling in* POUR IN, flood in, flow in.

2 *he rolled in at nine o'clock* ARRIVE, turn up, appear, show one's face; *informal* show up, blow in.

**rolling in it** *informal.* See RICH sense 1.

**roll something out** *she rolled out her towel* UNROLL, spread out, unfurl, unfold, open (out), unwind, uncoil.

**roll something up** *they rolled up the sleeping bags* FOLD (UP), furl, wind up, coil (up), bundle up.

**romance** noun 1 *their romance blossomed* LOVE, passion, ardor, adoration, devotion; affection, fondness, attachment.

2 *he's had many romances* LOVE AFFAIR, relationship, liaison, courtship, attachment; flirtation, dalliance.

3 *an author of historical romances* LOVE STORY, novel; romantic fiction; *informal* tearjerker, bodice-ripper.

4 *the romance of the Far East* MYSTERY, glamour, excitement, exoticism, mystique; appeal, allure, charm. See note at ROMANTIC.

▸ verb 1 *dated he was romancing Carolyn* WOO, chase, pursue; go out with, seduce; *informal* see, go steady with, date; *dated* court, make love to.

2 *I am romancing the past* ROMANTICIZE, idealize, paint a rosy picture of.

**romantic** adjective 1 *he's so romantic* LOVING, amorous, passionate, tender, affectionate; *informal* lovey-dovey.

2 *the book was a bit too romantic for my tastes* SENTIMENTAL, mawkish, saccharine, syrupy; *informal* mushy, schmaltzy, gooey, treacly, cheesy, corny, sappy, soppy, cornball. See note at SENTIMENTAL. ANTONYMS unsentimental, gritty.

3 *a romantic setting* IDYLLIC, picturesque, fairy-tale; beautiful, lovely, charming, pretty.

4 *romantic notions of life in rural communities* IDEALISTIC, idealized, romanticized, unrealistic, fanciful, impractical; head-in-the-clouds, starry-eyed, optimistic, hopeful, visionary, Utopian, fairy-tale. ANTONYMS practical, realistic.

▸ noun *an incurable romantic* IDEALIST, sentimentalist, romanticist; dreamer, visionary, Utopian, Don Quixote, fantasist, fantasizer; *archaic* fantast. ANTONYM realist.

**room** noun 1 *there isn't much room* SPACE; headroom, legroom; area, expanse, extent; *informal* elbow room.

2 *room for improvement* CAPACITY, scope, leeway, latitude, freedom; opportunity, chance.

3 *she wandered around the room* CHAMBER.

4 **(rooms)** *he had rooms at the Plaza* ACCOMMODATIONS, quarters, lodgings; a suite, an apartment, an efficiency unit; *informal* a pad, digs.

▸ verb *she roomed there in September* BOARD, lodge, live, stay; be quartered, be housed, be billeted; *formal* dwell, reside, sojourn.

**roomy** adjective *a roomy apartment* | *roomy pants* SPACIOUS, capacious, sizable, generous, big, large, extensive; voluminous, ample; *formal* commodious. ANTONYMS cramped, tight-fitting.

**root** noun 1 *a plant's roots* rootstock, tuber, rootlet; *Botany* rhizome, radicle.

2 *the root of the problem* SOURCE, origin, germ, beginning(s), genesis; cause, reason, basis, foundation, bottom, seat; core, heart, nub, essence; *informal* ground zero.

3 **(roots)** *he rejected his roots* ORIGINS, beginnings, family, ancestors, predecessors, heritage; birthplace, homeland. See note at ORIGIN.

▸ verb 1 *has the shoot rooted?* TAKE ROOT, grow roots, establish, strike, take.

2 *root the cuttings* PLANT, bed out, sow.

3 *he rooted around in the cupboard* RUMMAGE, hunt, search, rifle, delve, forage, dig, nose, poke.

PHRASES: **put down roots** *they married and put down roots in Yemen* SETTLE, establish oneself, make one's home, set up home.

**root and branch** 1 *the company's accounting department should be eradicated, root and branch* COMPLETELY, entirely, wholly, totally, thoroughly.

2 *a root-and-branch reform* COMPLETE, total, thorough, radical.

**root for** *informal Mollie roots for the Broncos* CHEER, cheer on, applaud, support, encourage.

**root out** 1 *the hedge was rooted out* UPROOT, deracinate, pull up, grub out.

2 *root out corruption* ERADICATE, eliminate, weed out, destroy, wipe out, stamp out, extirpate, abolish, end, put a stop to.

3 *he rooted out a dark secret* UNEARTH, dig up, bring to light, uncover, discover, dredge up, ferret out, expose.

**take root** 1 *leave the plants to take root* GERMINATE, sprout, establish, strike, take.

2 *Christianity took root in Persia* BECOME ESTABLISHED, take hold; develop, thrive, flourish.

**rope** noun *secure the rope to the post* CORD, cable, line, hawser; string; lasso, lariat.

▸ verb *his feet were roped together* TIE, bind, lash, truss; secure, moor, fasten, attach; hitch, tether, lasso.

PHRASES: **know the ropes** *informal you'll spend your first day with someone who knows the ropes* KNOW WHAT TO DO, know the routine, know one's way around, know one's stuff, know what's what; be experienced; *informal* know the drill, know the score, be streetwise.

**rope someone in/into** *why did you let Bruce rope you into this deal?* PERSUADE TO JOIN/PARTICIPATE IN, talk into, trap into, inveigle into; enlist in/into, engage in.

**roster** noun *check to see if your name's on the roster for tomorrow's game* SCHEDULE, list, listing, register, agenda, calendar, table.

**rostrum** noun *the speakers will be seated on either side of the rostrum* DAIS, platform, podium, stage; soapbox.

**rosy** adjective **1** *a rosy complexion* PINK, pinkish, roseate, reddish, peaches-and-cream; glowing, healthy, fresh, radiant, blooming; blushing, flushed; ruddy, high-colored, florid, rubicund; *rare* rubescent, erubescent. ANTONYMS pale, sallow.

**2** *his future looks rosy* PROMISING, optimistic, auspicious, hopeful, encouraging, favorable, bright, golden; *informal* upbeat. ANTONYMS dismal, bleak.

**rot** verb **1** *the floorboards rotted* DECAY, decompose, become rotten; disintegrate, crumble, perish.

**2** *the meat began to rot* GO BAD, spoil, go off; molder, putrefy, fester.

**3** *poor neighborhoods have been left to rot* DETERIORATE, degenerate, decline, decay, go to rack and ruin, go to seed, go downhill; *informal* go to pot, go to the dogs. ANTONYMS improve, recover.

▸ noun **1** *the leaves turned black with rot* DECAY, decomposition, mold, mildew, blight, canker; putrefaction.

**2** *traditionalists said the rot had set in* DETERIORATION, decline; corruption, cancer.

**rotary** adjective *rotary blades* ROTATING, rotational, revolving, turning, spinning, gyrating; *formal* rotatory.

**rotate** verb **1** *the wheels rotate continually* REVOLVE, go around, turn, turn around, spin, gyrate, whirl, twirl, swivel, circle, pivot.

**2** *many nurses rotate jobs* ALTERNATE, take turns, change, switch, interchange, exchange, swap; move around.

**rotation** noun **1** *the rotation of the wheels* REVOLVING, turning, spinning, gyration, circling.

**2** *a rotation of Jupiter* TURN, revolution, orbit, spin.

**3** *each member is chair for six months in rotation* SEQUENCE, succession; alternation, cycle.

**rotten** adjective **1** *rotten meat* DECAYING, rotting, bad, off, far gone, decomposing, putrid, putrescent, perished, moldy, moldering, mildewy, rancid, festering, fetid; maggoty, wormy. ANTONYM fresh.

**2** *rotten teeth* DECAYING, decayed, carious, black; disintegrating, crumbling.

**3** *he's rotten to the core* CORRUPT, unprincipled, dishonest, dishonorable, unscrupulous, untrustworthy, immoral; villainous, bad, wicked, evil, iniquitous, venal; *informal* crooked. ANTONYMS decent, honorable.

**4** *informal a rotten thing to do* NASTY, unkind, unpleasant, obnoxious, vile, contemptible, despicable, shabby, loathsome; spiteful, mean, low, malicious, hateful, hurtful; unfair, uncharitable, uncalled for; *informal* dirty, lowdown. ANTONYMS nice, kind.

**5** *informal he was a rotten singer* BAD, poor, dreadful, awful, terrible, frightful, atrocious, hopeless, inadequate, inferior, substandard; *informal* crummy, pathetic, useless, lousy, appalling, abysmal. ANTONYMS accomplished, good.

**6** *informal she had a rotten time* UNPLEASANT, miserable, awful, dreadful, terrible, frightful, bad, horrible; disappointing, regrettable; *informal* crummy, lousy. ANTONYMS good, delightful.

**7** *informal I feel rotten about it* GUILTY, conscience-stricken, remorseful, ashamed, shamefaced, chastened, contrite, sorry, regretful, repentant, penitent.

**8** *informal I felt rotten with that cold.* See ILL adjective sense 1.

**rotund** adjective **1** *a small, rotund man* PLUMP, chubby, fat, stout, portly, dumpy, round, chunky, overweight, heavy, paunchy, ample; flabby, fleshy, bulky, heavyset, corpulent, obese; *informal* tubby, roly-poly, pudgy, porky, blubbery, zaftig, corn-fed. ANTONYM thin.

**2** *rotund cauldrons* ROUND, bulbous, spherical, spheric.

**3** *the tenor's splendidly rotund tones.* See ROUND adjective sense 3.

**rough** adjective **1** *rough ground* UNEVEN, irregular, bumpy, lumpy, knobbly, stony, rocky, rugged, rutted, pitted, rutty. ANTONYMS smooth, flat.

**2** *the terrier's rough coat* COARSE, bristly, scratchy, prickly; shaggy, hairy, bushy. ANTONYMS smooth, sleek.

**3** *rough skin* DRY, leathery, weather-beaten; chapped, calloused, scaly, scabrous. ANTONYM smooth.

**4** *his voice was rough* GRUFF, hoarse, harsh, rasping, raspy, croaking, croaky, husky, throaty, gravelly, guttural. ANTONYM soft.

**5** *rough red wine* SHARP, sharp-tasting, sour, acidic, acid, vinegary, acidulous. ANTONYMS sweet, mellow.

**6** *he gets rough when he's drunk* VIOLENT, brutal, vicious; AGGRESSIVE, belligerent, pugnacious, thuggish; boisterous, rowdy, disorderly, unruly, riotous. ANTONYMS gentle, passive.

**7** *a machine that can take rough handling* CARELESS, clumsy, inept, unskillful. ANTONYM careful.

**8** *rough manners* BOORISH, loutish, oafish, brutish, coarse, crude, uncouth, vulgar, unrefined, unladylike, ungentlemanly, uncultured; unmannerly, impolite, discourteous, uncivil, ungracious, rude. See note at RUDE. ANTONYMS cultured, refined, civilized.

**9** *rough seas* TURBULENT, stormy, tempestuous, violent, heavy, heaving, choppy. ANTONYM calm.

**10** *informal I've had a rough time* DIFFICULT, hard, tough, bad, unpleasant; demanding, arduous. ANTONYMS easy, pleasant.

**11** *informal you were a bit **rough on** her* HARSH ON/TO, hard on, tough on, stern to, severe to, unfair to, unjust to; insensitive to, nasty to, cruel to, unkind to, unsympathetic to, brutal to, heartless to, merciless to. ANTONYMS gentle, kind.

**12** *a rough draft* PRELIMINARY, hasty, quick, sketchy, cursory, basic, crude, rudimentary, raw, unpolished; incomplete, unfinished. ANTONYMS finished, perfected.

**13** *a rough estimate* APPROXIMATE, inexact, imprecise, vague, estimated, hazy; *informal* ballpark. ANTONYMS exact, precise.

**14** *the accommodations are rather rough* PLAIN, BASIC, simple, rough and ready, rude, crude, primitive, spartan. ANTONYM luxurious.

▸ noun *the artist's initial roughs* SKETCH, draft, outline, mock-up.

▸ verb *rough the surface with sandpaper* ROUGHEN, make rough.

PHRASES: **rough something out** *we roughed out a few drawings of the monument* DRAFT, sketch out, outline, block out, mock up.
**rough someone up** *informal Berman's goons were sent to rough up Donatelli* BEAT UP, attack, assault, knock around/about, batter, manhandle; *informal* do over, beat the living daylights out of.

**rough-and-tumble** adjective *rough-and-tumble play* DISORDERLY, unruly, boisterous, rough, riotous, rowdy, knockabout, noisy, loud.

▸ noun *a political rough-and-tumble* SCUFFLE, fight, brawl, melee, free-for-all, fracas, rumpus; horseplay; *informal* scrap, dust-up, shindy, roughhouse.

**round** adjective **1** *a round window* CIRCULAR, ring-shaped, disk-shaped, hoop-shaped; spherical, spheroidal, globular, globe-shaped, orb-shaped; cylindrical; bulbous, rounded, rotund; *technical* annular, discoid.

**2** *round cheeks* PLUMP, chubby, fat, full. ANTONYM thin.

**3** *his deep, round voice* SONOROUS, full-bodied, full-toned, rich, deep, mellow, resonant, reverberant; grandiloquent, magniloquent, rotund, orotund; pear-shaped; *rare* canorous. ANTONYMS thin, reedy.

**4** *a round dozen* COMPLETE, entire, whole, full.

**5** *dated she berated him in round terms* CANDID, frank, direct, honest, truthful, straightforward, plain, blunt, forthright, bald, explicit, unequivocal, unmistakable, categorical. ANTONYM evasive.

▸ noun **1** *mold the dough into rounds* BALL, sphere, globe, orb, circle, disk, ring, hoop; *technical* annulus.

**2** **(rounds)** *a policeman on his rounds* CIRCUIT, beat, route, tour.

**3** *the first round of the tournament* STAGE, level; heat, game, bout, contest; go-round.

**4** *an endless round of parties* SUCCESSION, sequence, series, cycle.

**5** *the gun fires thirty rounds per second* BULLET, cartridge, shell, shot.

▸ verb *the ship rounded the point* GO AROUND, travel around, skirt, circumnavigate, orbit.

PHRASES: **round about** *the campsite is round about two miles from the main road.* See AROUND preposition sense 3.
**round the bend** *this time, I think Gordon's really gone round the bend.* See MAD sense 1.
**round the clock.** See AROUND THE CLOCK at AROUND.
**round off 1** *the square edges were rounded off* SMOOTH (OFF), plane (off), sand (off), blunt.
**2** *the party rounded off a successful year* COMPLETE, finish off, crown, cap, top; conclude, close, end.
**round up** *go round up your brothers for dinner* GATHER TOGETHER, herd together, muster, marshal, rally, assemble, collect, group, corral.

THE RIGHT WORD **round, annular, circular, globular, spherical**

What do a bicycle wheel, a basketball, and a barrel of oil have in common? All are considered to be **round**, an adjective that may be applied to anything shaped like a circle, a sphere, or a cylinder. But of these three objects, only a basketball is **spherical**, which means having a round body whose surface is equally distant from the center at all points. Something that is **globular** is shaped like a ball or a globe but is not necessarily a perfect sphere (*globular drops of oil leaking from the seam*). A wheel is *circular*, as is a Frisbee; in fact, anything with a round, flat surface in the shape of a ring or a disk may be described as *circular*—whether or not it corresponds to a perfect circle. But only the rings of a tree can be described as **annular**, a word that usually implies having a series of concentric ringlike forms or structures.

**roundabout** adjective **1** *a roundabout route* CIRCUITOUS, indirect, meandering, serpentine, tortuous. ANTONYMS direct, straight.

**2** *I asked in a roundabout sort of way* INDIRECT, oblique, circuitous, circumlocutory, periphrastic, digressive, long-winded; evasive. ANTONYM direct.

**rouse** verb **1** *he roused Ralph at dawn* WAKE, wake up, awaken, arouse; *formal* waken.

**2** *she roused and looked around* WAKE UP, awake, awaken, come to, get up, rise, bestir oneself; *formal* arise. ANTONYM go to sleep.

**3** *he roused the crowd* STIR UP, excite, galvanize, electrify, stimulate, inspire, inspirit, move, inflame, agitate, goad, provoke; incite, spur on, light a fire under. ANTONYM calm.

**4** *he's got a temper when he's roused* PROVOKE, annoy, anger, infuriate, madden, incense, vex, irk; *informal* aggravate. ANTONYMS appease, pacify.

**5** *her disappearance roused my suspicions* AROUSE, awaken, prompt, provoke, stimulate, pique, trigger, spark off, touch off, kindle, elicit. ANTONYM allay.

**rousing** adjective *rousing cheers from the audience* STIRRING, inspiring, exciting, stimulating, moving, electrifying, invigorating, energizing, exhilarating; enthusiastic, vigorous, spirited.

**rout** noun **1** *the army's ignominious rout* RETREAT, flight.

**2** *the game was a rout for the Marlins* CRUSHING DEFEAT, trouncing, annihilation; debacle, fiasco; *informal* licking, hammering, thrashing, drubbing, massacre. ANTONYM victory.

▸ verb **1** *his army was routed* PUT TO FLIGHT, drive off, scatter; defeat, beat, conquer, vanquish, crush, overpower.

**2** *he routed the defending champion.* See DEFEAT verb sense 1.

**route** noun *a different route to school* WAY, course, road, path, direction; passage, journey.

▸ verb *inquiries are routed to the relevant desk* DIRECT, send, convey, dispatch, forward.

**routine** noun **1** *his morning routine* PROCEDURE, practice, pattern, drill, regimen; program, schedule, plan; formula, method, system; customs, habits; wont.

**2** *a stand-up routine* ACT, performance, number, turn, piece; *informal* spiel, patter, shtick.

▸ adjective *a routine safety inspection* STANDARD, regular, customary, normal, usual, ordinary, typical; everyday, common, commonplace, conventional, habitual, wonted. ANTONYM unusual.

**row**[1] noun **1** *rows of children* LINE, column, file, queue; procession, chain, string, succession.

**2** *the middle row of seats* TIER, line, rank, bank. PHRASE: **in a row** *three days in a row* CONSECUTIVELY, in succession; running, straight.

**row**[2] *informal* noun *the siblings were having a row* ARGUMENT, quarrel, squabble, fight, contretemps, falling-out, disagreement, dispute, clash, altercation, shouting match; *informal* tiff, set-to, run-in, blowup, spat. See note at QUARREL.

**rowdy** adjective *rowdy youths* UNRULY, disorderly, obstreperous, riotous, undisciplined, uncontrollable, ungovernable, disruptive, out of control, rough, wild, lawless; boisterous, uproarious, noisy, loud, clamorous; *informal* rambunctious. ANTONYM peaceful.

▸ noun *the bar was full of rowdies* RUFFIAN, troublemaker, lout, hooligan, thug, hoodlum; *informal* tough, yahoo, punk.

**royal** adjective **1** *the royal prerogative* REGAL, kingly, queenly, princely; sovereign, monarchical.

**2** *a royal welcome* EXCELLENT, fine, magnificent, splendid, superb, wonderful, first-rate, first-class; *informal* fantastic, great, tremendous.

**3** *informal she's a royal pain in the neck* COMPLETE, utter, total, absolute, real, thorough.

**rub** verb **1** *Sally rubbed her arm* MASSAGE, knead; stroke, pat.

**2** *he rubbed sunscreen on her back* APPLY, smear, spread, work in.

**3** *my shoes rub badly* CHAFE, pinch; hurt, be painful.

▸ noun **1** *she gave his back a rub* MASSAGE, rubdown.

**2** *I gave the countertop a rub* POLISH, wipe, clean.

**3** *it's too complicated—that's the rub* PROBLEM, difficulty, trouble, drawback, hindrance, impediment; snag, hitch, catch.

PHRASES: **rub something down** *Jake and Pauline are in the stable, rubbing down the horses* CLEAN, sponge, wash; groom.
**rub it in** *informal yes, I screwed up, but you don't have to rub it in* EMPHASIZE IT, stress it, underline it, highlight it; go on (and on) about it, harp on it; *informal* rub someone's nose in it.
**rub off on** *we just don't want his bad habits rubbing off on you* BE TRANSFERRED TO, be passed on to, be transmitted to, be communicated to; affect, influence.
**rub something out** *they promise to rub out your bad credit history* ERASE, delete, remove, efface, obliterate, expunge.
**rub elbows** *it's our chance to rub elbows with the company execs* ASSOCIATE, mingle, fraternize, socialize, mix, keep company, consort; *informal* hang around/out, hobnob.
**rub someone the wrong way** *Regina's roommates rub her boyfriend the wrong way* IRRITATE, annoy, irk, vex, provoke, displease, exasperate, infuriate, get on someone's nerves, put out, pique, upset, nettle, ruffle someone's feathers, make someone's hackles rise, try someone's patience, grate on; *informal* aggravate, get, get to, bug, miff, peeve, rile, needle, tick off, tee off, get under someone's skin, get in someone's hair, get/put someone's back up, get someone's goat, rankle, ride.

**rubbish** noun **1** *throw away that rubbish.* See GARBAGE sense 1.

**2** *she's talking rubbish* NONSENSE, balderdash, gibberish, claptrap, blarney, moonshine, garbage; *informal* hogwash, baloney, jive, guff, tripe, drivel, bilge, bunk, BS, piffle, poppycock, hooey, twaddle, gobbledygook, flapdoodle; *dated* bunkum, tommyrot.

**ruddy** adjective *a ruddy complexion* ROSY, red, pink, roseate, rubicund; healthy, glowing, fresh; flushed, blushing; florid, high-colored; *literary* rubescent. ANTONYM pale.

**rude** adjective **1** *a rude man | rude remarks* ILL-MANNERED, bad-mannered, impolite, discourteous, uncivil, unmannerly, mannerless; impertinent, insolent, impudent, disrespectful, cheeky; churlish, curt, brusque, brash, offhand, short, sharp; offensive, insulting, derogatory, disparaging, abusive; tactless, undiplomatic, uncomplimentary. See note at OFFENSE. ANTONYMS polite, civil.

**2** *rude jokes* VULGAR, coarse, smutty, dirty, filthy, crude, lewd, obscene, off-color, offensive, indelicate, tasteless; risqué, naughty, ribald, bawdy, racy; *informal* blue; *euphemistic* adult. ANTONYM clean.

**3** *a rude awakening* ABRUPT, sudden, sharp, startling; unpleasant, nasty, harsh.

**4** *dated**a rude cabin* PRIMITIVE, crude, rudimentary, rough, simple, basic, makeshift. ANTONYMS classy, luxurious.

**THE RIGHT WORD rude, callow, crude, ill-mannered, rough, uncivil, uncouth**

Someone who lacks consideration for the feelings of others and who is deliberately insolent is **rude** (*It was rude of you not to introduce me to your friends*). **Ill-mannered** suggests that the person is ignorant of the rules of social behavior rather than deliberately rude (*an ill-mannered child*), while **uncivil** implies disregard for even the most basic rules of social behavior among civilized people (*his uncivil response resulted in his being kicked out of the classroom*). **Rough** is used to describe people who lack polish and refinement (*he was a rough but honest man*), while **crude** is a more negative term for individuals and behavior lacking culture, civility, and tact (*he made a crude gesture*). **Uncouth** describes what seems strange, awkward, or unmannerly rather than rude (*his uncouth behavior at the wedding*). Although individuals of any age may be rude, crude, ill-mannered, or uncouth, **callow** almost always applies to those who are young or immature; it suggests naïveté and lack of sophistication (*he was surprisingly callow for a man of almost 40*).

**rudimentary** adjective **1** *rudimentary carpentry skills* BASIC, elementary, primary, fundamental, essential. ANTONYM advanced.

**2** *the equipment was rudimentary* PRIMITIVE, crude, simple, unsophisticated, rough, rough and ready, makeshift. ANTONYM sophisticated.

**3** *a rudimentary thumb* VESTIGIAL, undeveloped, incomplete; *Biology* abortive, primitive. ANTONYM developed.

**rudiments** plural noun *the rudiments of sign language* BASICS, fundamentals, essentials, first principles, foundation; *informal* nuts and bolts, ABCs.

**rue** verb *she may live to rue this impetuous decision* REGRET, be sorry about, feel remorseful about, repent of, reproach oneself for; deplore, lament, bemoan, bewail. See note at MOURN.

**rueful** adjective *his rueful expression said it all* REGRETFUL, apologetic, sorry, remorseful, shamefaced, sheepish, abashed, hangdog, contrite, repentant, penitent, conscience-stricken, sorrowful, sad.

**ruffian** noun *a gang of young ruffians* THUG, lout, hooligan, hoodlum, vandal, delinquent, rowdy, scoundrel, villain, rogue, bully, brute; *informal* tough, roughneck, bruiser, heavy, yahoo, goon.

**ruffle** verb **1** *he ruffled her hair* DISARRANGE, tousle, dishevel, rumple, disorder, mess up, tangle; *informal* muss up. ANTONYM smooth.

**2** *the wind ruffled the water* RIPPLE, riffle. ANTONYM smooth.

**3** *don't let him ruffle you* ANNOY, irritate, vex, nettle, anger, exasperate; disconcert, unnerve, fluster, agitate, harass, upset, disturb, discomfit, put off, perturb, unsettle, bother, worry, trouble; *informal* rattle, faze, throw, get to, rile, needle, aggravate, bug, peeve. ANTONYMS calm, soothe.

▸ noun *a shirt with ruffles* FRILL, flounce, ruff, ruche, jabot, furbelow.

**rugged** adjective **1** *a rugged path* ROUGH, uneven, bumpy, rocky, stony, pitted, jagged, craggy. ANTONYM smooth.

**2** *a rugged vehicle* DURABLE, sturdy, robust, strong, tough, resilient. ANTONYMS fragile, flimsy.

**3** *rugged manly types* WELL-BUILT, burly, strong, muscular, muscly, brawny, strapping, husky, hulking; tough, hardy, robust, sturdy, lusty, solid; *informal* hunky, beefy. ANTONYMS frail, scrawny, weedy.

**4** *his rugged features* STRONG, craggy, rough-hewn; manly, masculine; irregular, weathered. ANTONYM delicate.

**5** *the rugged outdoor life* TOUGH, harsh, rigorous, arduous, onerous, exacting, difficult, hard; austere, spartan. ANTONYM easy.

**6** *the author was captivated by the rugged individualism of these villagers* UNCOMPROMISING, unwavering, unflinching, firm, tenacious, resolute, determined. ANTONYMS feeble, ineffectual.

**ruin** noun **1** *the buildings were saved from ruin* DISINTEGRATION, decay, disrepair, dilapidation, ruination; destruction, demolition, wreckage. ANTONYMS preservation, reconstruction.

**2** (**ruins**) *the ruins of a church* REMAINS, remnants, fragments, relics; rubble, debris, wreckage.

**3** *he was careening toward his ruin* DOWNFALL, collapse, defeat, undoing, failure, breakdown, ruination; Waterloo. ANTONYMS success, triumph.

**4** *local merchants are facing ruin* BANKRUPTCY, insolvency, penury, poverty, destitution, impoverishment, indigence; failure. ANTONYMS success, wealth.

▸ verb **1** *don't ruin my plans* WRECK, destroy, spoil, mar, blight, shatter, dash, torpedo, scotch, mess up; sabotage; *informal* screw up, foul up, put the kibosh on, nix, scupper, scuttle. ANTONYMS save, restore.

**2** *the bank's collapse ruined them all* BANKRUPT, make insolvent, impoverish, pauperize, wipe out, break, cripple, devastate; bring someone to their knees.

**3** *a country ruined by civil war* DESTROY, devastate, lay waste, ravage; raze, demolish, wreck, wipe out, flatten. ANTONYMS repair, rebuild.

PHRASE: **in ruins 1** *the abbey is in ruins* DERELICT, ruined, in disrepair, falling to pieces, dilapidated, tumbledown, ramshackle, decrepit, decaying, ruinous.

**2** *his career is in ruins* DESTROYED, ruined, in pieces, over, finished; *informal* in tatters, on the rocks, done for.

**ruinous** adjective **1** *a ruinous trade war* DISASTROUS, devastating, catastrophic, calamitous, crippling, crushing, damaging, destructive, harmful; costly.

**2** *ruinous interest rates* EXTORTIONATE, exorbitant, excessive, sky-high, outrageous, inflated; *informal* criminal, steep.

**rule** noun **1** *health and safety rules* REGULATION, ruling, directive, order, act, law, statute, edict, canon, mandate, command, dictate, decree, fiat, injunction, commandment, stipulation, requirement, guideline, direction; *formal* ordinance.

**2** *lateness was the general rule* PROCEDURE, practice, protocol, convention, norm, routine, custom, habit, wont; *formal* praxis.

**3** *moderation is the golden rule* PRECEPT, principle, standard, axiom, truth, maxim.

**4** *Punjab came under British rule* CONTROL, jurisdiction, command, power, dominion; government, administration, sovereignty, leadership, supremacy, authority.

▸ verb **1** *El Salvador was ruled by Spain* GOVERN, preside over, control, lead, dominate, run, head, administer, manage.

**2** *Elizabeth has ruled for more than fifty years* BE IN POWER, be in control, be in command, be in charge, govern; reign, be monarch, be sovereign.

**3** *the judge ruled that they be set free* DECREE, order, pronounce, judge, adjudge, ordain; decide, find, determine, resolve, settle.

**4** *chaos ruled* PREVAIL, predominate, be the order of the day, reign supreme; *formal* obtain.

PHRASES: **as a rule** *as a rule, we eat in the kitchen* USUALLY, generally, in general, normally, ordinarily, customarily, for the most part, on the whole, by and large, in the main, mainly, mostly, commonly, typically.
**rule something out** *the gold brocade isn't one of the top choices, but don't yet rule it out* EXCLUDE, eliminate, disregard; preclude, prohibit, prevent, disallow.

**ruler** noun *blessings on our fair ruler* LEADER, sovereign, monarch, potentate, king, queen, emperor, empress, prince, princess; crowned head, head of state, president, premier, governor; overlord, chief, chieftain, lord; dictator, autocrat. ANTONYM subject.

**ruling** noun *the judge's ruling* JUDGMENT, decision, adjudication, finding, verdict; pronouncement, resolution, decree, injunction.

▸ adjective **1** *the ruling class* GOVERNING, controlling, commanding, supreme, leading, dominant, ascendant, reigning.

**2** *hockey was their ruling passion* MAIN, chief, principal, major, prime, dominating, foremost; predominant, central, focal; *informal* number-one.

**ruminate** verb *we* ***ruminated on*** *the nature of existence* THINK ABOUT, contemplate, consider, meditate on, muse on, mull over, ponder on/over, deliberate about/on, chew on, puzzle over; *formal* cogitate about.

**rummage** verb *he* ***rummaged through*** *Stacey's bureau drawers* SEARCH (THROUGH), hunt through, root about/around (in), ferret about/around (in), fish about/around (in), poke around (in), dig through, delve through, go through, explore, sift through, rifle (through).

**rumor** noun *do you think the talk of her resignation is fact or just rumor? | the latest rumors say they're eloping* GOSSIP, hearsay, talk, tittle-tattle, speculation, word; **(rumors)** reports, stories, whispers, canards; *informal* grapevine, word on the street, buzz, dirt, scuttlebutt, loose lips.

**rumple** verb **1** *the sheet was rumpled* CRUMPLE, crease, wrinkle, crinkle, scrunch up. ANTONYM smooth (out).

**2** *Ian rumpled her hair* RUFFLE, disarrange, tousle, dishevel, mess up; *informal* muss up. ANTONYM smooth.

**run** verb **1** *she ran across the road* SPRINT, race, dart, rush, dash, hasten, hurry, scurry, scamper, bolt, fly, gallop, career, charge, shoot, hurtle, speed, zoom, go like lightning, go hell-bent for leather, go like the wind, go like a bat out of hell; jog, trot; *informal* tear, pelt, scoot, hotfoot it, leg it, belt, zip, whip, bomb, hightail it, barrel.

**2** *the robbers turned and ran* FLEE, run away, run off, run for it, take flight, make off, take off, take to one's heels, make a break for it, bolt, make one's getaway, escape; *informal* beat it, clear off, clear out, vamoose, skedaddle, split, leg it, scram, light out, take a powder, make tracks.

**3** *he ran in the marathon* COMPETE, take part, participate.

**4** *a shiver ran down my spine* GO, pass, slide, move, travel.

**5** *he ran his eye down the list* CAST, pass, skim, flick.

**6** *the road runs the length of the valley* EXTEND, stretch, reach, continue.

**7** *water ran from the eaves* FLOW, pour, stream, gush, flood, cascade, roll, course, spill, trickle, drip, dribble, leak.

**8** *a bus runs to Sorrento* TRAVEL, go.

**9** *I'll run you home* DRIVE, take, bring, ferry, chauffeur, give someone a ride/lift.

**10** *he runs a mail-order company* BE IN CHARGE OF, manage, direct, control, head, govern, supervise, superintend, oversee; operate, conduct, own.

**11** *it's expensive to run a car* MAINTAIN, keep, own, possess, have; drive.

**12** *they ran some tests* CARRY OUT, do, perform, execute.

**13** *he left the engine running* OPERATE, function, work, go; idle.

**14** *the lease runs for twenty years* BE VALID, last, be in effect, be operative, continue, be effective.

**15** *the show ran for two years* BE STAGED, be performed, be on, be mounted, be screened.

**16** *he ran for president* BE A CANDIDATE FOR, stand for, be a contender for.

**17** *the paper ran the story* PUBLISH, print, feature, carry, put out, release, issue.

**18** *they run drugs* SMUGGLE, traffic in, deal in.

**19** *they were run out of town* CHASE, drive, hound.

▸ noun **1** *his morning run* SPRINT, jog, dash, gallop, trot.

**2** *she did the school run* ROUTE, journey; circuit, round, beat.

**3** *an unbeaten run of victories* SERIES, succession, sequence, string, chain, streak, spell, stretch, spate.

**4** *a* ***run on*** *umbrellas* DEMAND FOR, rush on.

**5** *they had the* ***run of*** *the house* FREE USE OF, unrestricted access to.

**6** *the usual run of movies* TYPE, kind, sort, variety, class.

**7** *a dog run* ENCLOSURE, pen, coop.

**8** *a toboggan run* SLOPE, track, piste, trail, slide.

**9** *a run in her pantyhose* RIP, tear, snag, hole, pull; *Brit.* ladder.

PHRASES: **in the long run** *in the long run, the move to Spokane may be a really good thing* EVENTUALLY, in the end, ultimately, when all is said and done, in the fullness of time, over the long haul, at the end of the day.
**on the run** *police report that Prentiss has been on the run since early this morning* ON THE LOOSE, at large, loose; running away, fleeing, fugitive; *informal* AWOL, on the lam.
**run across** *we never expected to run across Mrs. Gundlach at the casino* MEET, meet by chance, come across, run into, chance on/upon, stumble on/upon, happen on/upon; *informal* bump into.
**run after** *informal I have no intention of running after him* PURSUE, chase; make advances to, flirt with; *informal* come on to, be all over; *dated* set one's cap for/at.
**run along** *informal it's time for you and your pesky little friends*

*to run along* GO AWAY, be off (with you), shoo; *informal* scram, buzz off, skedaddle, scat, beat it, get lost, shove off, clear off; *literary* begone.
**run around** *informal that creep's been running around since their honeymoon* BE UNFAITHFUL, have affairs, philander; *informal* play the field, sleep around, fool around.
**run away** *her attacker ran away.* See RUN verb sense 2.
**run away with** *she ran away with the championship* WIN EASILY, win hands down; *informal* win by a mile.
**run down** *obviously, this barn didn't start running down yesterday* DECLINE, degenerate, go downhill, go to seed, decay, go to rack and ruin; *informal* go to pot, go to the dogs.
**run someone down 1** *he was run down by a drunk driver* RUN OVER, knock down, knock over; hit, strike.

**2** *she ran him down in front of other people* CRITICIZE, denigrate, belittle, disparage, deprecate, find fault with; *informal* put down, knock, badmouth, dis; *formal* derogate.
**run for it** *they saw the cop car and ran for it.* See RUN verb sense 2.
**run high** *feelings ran high* BE STRONG, be fervent, be passionate, be intense.
**run in 1** *heart disease runs in the family* BE COMMON IN, be inherent in.

**2** *informal you mean they actually ran him in for littering?* See ARREST verb sense 1.
**run into 1** *a car ran into his van* COLLIDE WITH, hit, strike, crash into, smash into, plow into, ram, impact.

**2** *I ran into Hugo the other day.* See RUN ACROSS.

**3** *we ran into a problem* EXPERIENCE, encounter, meet with, be faced with, be confronted with.

**4** *his debts run into six figures* REACH, extend to, be as much as.
**run low** *supplies were running low* DWINDLE, diminish, become depleted, be used up, be in short supply, be tight.
**run off** *the youths ran off.* See RUN verb sense 2.
**run off with** *he ran off with her money.* See STEAL verb sense 1.
**run something off 1** *would you run off that list for me?* COPY, photocopy, xerox, duplicate, print, reproduce.

**2** *run off some of the excess water* DRAIN, bleed, draw off, pump out.
**run on 1** *the call ran on for hours* CONTINUE, go on, carry on, last, keep going, stretch.

**2** *your mother does run on* TALK INCESSANTLY, talk a lot, go on, chatter on, ramble on; *informal* yak, gab, run off at the mouth.
**run out 1** *supplies ran out* BE USED UP, dry up, be exhausted, be finished, peter out.

**2** *her contract ran out* EXPIRE, end, terminate, finish; lapse.
**run out of** *they ran out of their cash* USE UP; be out of, consume, eat up; *informal* be fresh out of.
**run out on** *informal she ran out on her husband.* See ABANDON verb sense 3.
**run over 1** *the bathwater ran over* OVERFLOW, spill over, brim over.

**2** *the project ran over budget* EXCEED, go over, overshoot, overreach.

**3** *he quickly ran over the story* RECAPITULATE, repeat, run through, go over, reiterate, review; look over, read through; *informal* recap.
**run someone over.** See RUN SOMEONE DOWN sense 1.
**run the show** *informal Todd always tries to run the show* BE IN CHARGE, be in control, be at the helm, be in the driver's seat, be at the wheel; *informal* be the boss, call the shots.
**run through 1** *they quickly ran through their money* SQUANDER, spend, fritter away, dissipate, waste, go through, consume, use up; *informal* blow.

**2** *the attitude that runs through his writing* PERVADE, permeate, suffuse, imbue, inform.

**3** *he ran through his notes.* See RUN OVER sense 3.

**4** *let's run through scene three* REHEARSE, practice, go over, repeat; *informal* recap.
**run someone through** *they hung an effigy of Bin Laden and ran it through with sharp sticks* STAB, pierce, transfix, impale.
**run to 1** *the bill ran to $22,000* AMOUNT TO, add up to, total, come to, equal, reach, be as much as.

**2** *he was running to fat* TEND TO, become, get, grow.

**runaway** noun *a teenage runaway* FUGITIVE, escapee; refugee; truant; absconder, deserter.

▸ adjective **1** *a runaway horse* OUT OF CONTROL, escaped, loose, on the loose.

**2** *a runaway victory* EASY, effortless; *informal* as easy as pie.

**3** *runaway inflation* RAMPANT, out of control, unchecked, unbridled.

**rundown** noun *here's the rundown on the latest digital gear* SUMMARY, synopsis, précis, run-through, summarization, summation, review, overview, briefing, sketch, outline; *informal* lowdown, recap.

**run-down** adjective **1** *a run-down area* DILAPIDATED, tumbledown, ramshackle, derelict, ruinous, in ruins, crumbling, beat-up; neglected, uncared-for, depressed, seedy, shabby, slummy, squalid, flea-bitten; *informal* crummy.

**2** *she was feeling rather run-down* UNWELL, ill, poorly, unhealthy, peaked; tired, drained, exhausted, fatigued, worn out, below par, washed out; *informal* under the weather, off; *dated* seedy.

**runner** noun **1** *the runners were limbering up* sprinter, hurdler, racer, jogger; athlete.

**2** *a strawberry runner* SHOOT, offshoot, sprout, tendril; *Botany* stolon.

**3** *he worked as a runner for the mob* MESSENGER, courier, errand boy; *informal* gofer.

**running** noun **1** *his running was particularly fast* SPRINTING, sprint, racing, jogging, jog.

**2** *the running of the school* ADMINISTRATION, management, organization, coordination, orchestration, handling, direction, control, regulation, supervision.

**3** *the smooth running of her department* OPERATION, working, function, performance.

▸ adjective **1** *running water* FLOWING, gushing, rushing, moving.

**2** *a running argument* ONGOING, sustained, continuous, rolling, incessant, ceaseless, constant, perpetual; recurrent, recurring.

**3** *she was late two days running* IN SUCCESSION, in a row, in sequence, consecutively; straight, together.

PHRASE: **in the running for** *he's in the running for a prize* LIKELY TO GET, a candidate for, in line for, on the short list for, up for.

**run-of-the-mill** adjective *even the car he drives is run-of-the-mill* ORDINARY, average, middle-of-the-road, commonplace, humdrum, mundane, standard, nondescript, characterless, conventional; unremarkable, unexceptional, uninteresting, dull, boring, routine, bland, lackluster, garden-variety; *informal* nothing to write home about, nothing special, a dime a dozen. ANTONYM exceptional.

**rupture** noun **1** *pipeline ruptures* BREAK, fracture, crack, breach, burst, split, fissure.

**2** *a rupture due to personal differences* RIFT, estrangement, falling-out, breakup, breach, split, separation, parting, division, schism; *informal* bust-up.

**3** *an abdominal rupture* HERNIA.

▸ verb **1** *the reactor core might rupture* BREAK, fracture, crack, breach, burst, split; *informal* bust.

**2** *the problem ruptured their relationships* SEVER, break off, breach, disrupt; *literary* sunder.

**rural** adjective *the rural backdrop was filmed in Georgia* COUNTRY, countryside, bucolic, rustic, pastoral; agricultural, agrarian; *literary* sylvan, georgic. ANTONYM urban.

**ruse** noun *his offer to help with my presentation was just a clever ruse* PLOY, stratagem, tactic, scheme, trick, gambit, cunning plan, dodge, subterfuge, machination, wile.

**rush** verb **1** *she rushed home* HURRY, dash, run, race, sprint, bolt, dart, gallop, career, charge, shoot, hurtle, careen, hare, fly, speed, zoom, scurry, scuttle, scamper, hasten; *informal* tear, belt, pelt, scoot, zip, whip, hotfoot it, leg it, bomb, hightail it.

**2** *water rushed along gutters* FLOW, pour, gush, surge, stream, cascade, run, course.

**3** *the legislation was rushed through both houses* PUSH, hurry, hasten, speed, hustle, press, force.

**4** *the mob rushed the police* ATTACK, charge, run at, assail, storm.

▸ noun **1** *Tim made a rush for the exit* DASH, run, sprint, dart, bolt, charge, scramble, break.

**2** *the lunch rush* HUSTLE AND BUSTLE, commotion, hubbub, stir; busy time.

**3** *a last-minute rush for flights* DEMAND, clamor, call, request; run on.

**4** *he was in no rush to leave* HURRY, haste, urgency.

**5** *a rush of adrenaline* SURGE, flow, flood, spurt, stream; thrill, flash; *informal* charge, jolt, kick.

**6** *a rush of cold air* GUST, blast, draft.

**7** *I made a sudden rush at him* CHARGE, onslaught, attack, assault, onrush.

▸ adjective *a rush job* URGENT, high-priority, emergency; hurried, hasty, fast, quick, swift; *informal* hurry-up.

**rushed** adjective **1** *a rushed divorce* HASTY, fast, speedy, quick, swift, rapid, hurried.

**2** *he was too rushed to enjoy his stay* PRESSED FOR TIME, busy, in a hurry, run off one's feet.

**rustic** adjective **1** *a rustic setting* RURAL, country, countryside, countrified, pastoral, bucolic; agricultural, agrarian; *literary* sylvan, georgic. ANTONYM urban.

**2** *rustic wooden tables* PLAIN, simple, homely, unsophisticated; rough, rude, crude. ANTONYMS fancy, ornate.

**3** *rustic peasants* UNSOPHISTICATED, uncultured, unrefined, simple; artless, unassuming, guileless, naive, ingenuous; coarse, rough, uncouth, boorish; *informal* hillbilly, hick. ANTONYMS urbane, cultured, sophisticated.

▸ noun *the rustics were carousing* PEASANT, countryman, countrywoman, bumpkin, yokel, country cousin; *informal* hillbilly, hayseed, hick; *archaic* swain, cottier.

**rustle** verb **1** *her dress rustled as she moved* SWISH, whoosh, swoosh, whisper, sigh.

**2** *he was rustling cattle* STEAL, thieve, take; abduct, kidnap; *informal* swipe.

▸ noun *the rustle of the leaves* SWISH, whisper, rustling; *literary* susurration, susurrus.

PHRASE: **rustle something up** *informal* *I'll rustle up some breakfast for us* PREPARE HASTILY, throw together, make; *informal* fix.

**rusty** adjective **1** *rusty wire* RUSTED, rust-covered, corroded, oxidized; tarnished, discolored.

**2** *rusty hair* REDDISH-BROWN, rust-colored, chestnut, auburn, tawny, russet, coppery, copper, Titian, red, ginger, gingery.

**3** *my French is a little rusty* OUT OF PRACTICE, below par; unpracticed, deficient, impaired, weak.

**rut** noun **1** *the car bumped across the ruts* FURROW, groove, trough, ditch, hollow, pothole, crater.

**2** *he was stuck in a rut* BORING ROUTINE, humdrum existence, habit, dead end.

**ruthless** adjective *ruthless killers* MERCILESS, pitiless, cruel, heartless, hard-hearted, cold-hearted, cold-blooded, harsh, callous, unmerciful, unforgiving, uncaring, unsympathetic, uncharitable; remorseless, unbending, inflexible, implacable; brutal, inhuman, inhumane, barbarous, barbaric, savage, sadistic, vicious. ANTONYM merciful.

**sable** adjective *her long sable hair* BLACK, jet-black, pitch-black, ebony, raven, sooty, dusky, inky, coal-black.

**sabotage** noun *the fire may have been an act of sabotage* VANDALISM, wrecking, destruction, impairment, incapacitation, damage; subversion, obstruction, disruption, spoiling, undermining; *informal* a (monkey) wrench in the works.

▸ verb *they were hired to sabotage the competition* VANDALIZE, wreck, damage, destroy, cripple, impair, incapacitate; obstruct, disrupt, spoil, ruin, undermine, threaten, subvert.

**saccharine** adjective *saccharine love songs* SENTIMENTAL, sickly, mawkish, cloying, sugary, sickening, nauseating; *informal* mushy, sappy, schmaltzy, weepy, gooey, drippy, cheesy, corny, soppy, cornball.

**sack**[1] noun **1** *she carried her supplies in a sack* BAG, pouch, pack, satchel; knapsack, backpack, rucksack, packsack, day pack, bookbag, tote bag.

**2** *informal work hard or you'll get* ***the sack*** A DISMISSAL, a discharge; *informal* the boot, the ax, the heave-ho, one's marching orders, a pink slip.

**3** *informal she stayed in* ***the sack*** BED.

▸ verb *informal she was sacked for stealing* DISMISS, discharge, lay off, let go, terminate, get rid of; *Military* cashier; *Brit.* make redundant; *informal* fire, give the sack, give someone their marching orders, give someone the boot, show someone the door, send packing, pink-slip.

PHRASE: **hit the sack** *informal I'm hitting the sack early tonight* GO TO BED, retire, go to sleep; *informal* turn in, hit the hay.

**sack**[2] verb *raiders sacked the town* RAVAGE, lay waste, devastate, raid, ransack, strip, plunder, despoil, pillage, loot, rob. See note at RAVAGE.

**sackcloth** noun *artsy lamps made of castoff materials such as old chicken wire and sackcloth* HESSIAN, sacking, hopsack, burlap; gunny. PHRASE: **in/wearing sackcloth and ashes** *I never thought I'd live to see the day that Josie was wearing sackcloth and ashes* PENITENT, contrite, regretful, sorrowful, rueful, remorseful, apologetic, ashamed, guilt-ridden, chastened, shamefaced, guilty.

**sacred** adjective **1** *the priest entered the sacred place* HOLY, hallowed, blessed, consecrated, sanctified, venerated, revered; *archaic* blest.

**2** *sacred music* RELIGIOUS, spiritual, devotional, church, ecclesiastical. ANTONYMS secular, profane.

**3** *the hill is sacred to the tribe* SACROSANCT, inviolable, inviolate, invulnerable, untouchable, protected, defended, secure.

**sacrifice** noun **1** *the sacrifice of animals* RITUAL SLAUGHTER, offering, oblation, immolation.

**2** *the calf was a sacrifice* (VOTIVE) OFFERING, burnt offering, gift, oblation.

**3** *the sacrifice of sovereignty* SURRENDER, giving up, abandonment, renunciation, forfeiture, relinquishment, resignation, abdication.

▸ verb **1** *two goats were sacrificed* OFFER UP, immolate, slaughter.

**2** *he sacrificed his principles* GIVE UP, abandon, surrender, forgo, renounce, forfeit, relinquish, resign, abdicate; betray.

**sacrilege** noun *any form of gambling on the church grounds, including bingo and raffles, would be sacrilege* DESECRATION, profanity, blasphemy, impiety, irreligion, unholiness, irreverence, disrespect, profanation. ANTONYM piety.

**sacrilegious** adjective *your vile language is sacrilegious* PROFANE, blasphemous, impious, sinful, irreverent, irreligious, unholy, disrespectful.

**sad** adjective **1** *we felt sad when we left* UNHAPPY, sorrowful, dejected, depressed, downcast, miserable, down, despondent, despairing, disconsolate, desolate, wretched, glum, gloomy, doleful, dismal, melancholy, mournful, woebegone, forlorn, crestfallen, heartbroken, inconsolable; *informal* blue, down in/at the mouth, down in the dumps, blah. ANTONYMS happy, cheerful.

**2** *they knew her sad story* TRAGIC, unhappy, unfortunate, awful, miserable, wretched, sorry, pitiful, pathetic, traumatic, heartbreaking, heart-rending, harrowing. ANTONYM cheerful.

**3** *a sad state of affairs* UNFORTUNATE, regrettable, sorry, deplorable, lamentable, pitiful, shameful, disgraceful. ANTONYM fortunate.

**sadden** verb *of course we all saddened by this tragic news* DEPRESS, dispirit, deject, dishearten, grieve, desolate, discourage, upset, get down, bring down, break someone's heart.

**sadness** noun *our sadness cannot be measured* UNHAPPI-

NESS, sorrow, dejection, depression, misery, despondency, despair, desolation, wretchedness, gloom, gloominess, dolefulness, melancholy, mournfulness, woe, heartache, grief; *informal* the blues.

**safe** adjective **1** *the jewels are safe in the bank* SECURE, protected, shielded, sheltered, guarded, out of harm's way. ANTONYMS insecure, at risk.

**2** *the lost children are all safe* UNHARMED, unhurt, uninjured, unscathed, all right, well, in one piece, out of danger, home free; *informal* OK. ANTONYM in danger.

**3** *a safe place to hide* SECURE, sound, impregnable, unassailable, invulnerable. ANTONYM dangerous.

**4** *a safe driver* CAUTIOUS, circumspect, prudent, attentive; unadventurous, conservative, unenterprising. ANTONYM reckless.

**5** *the drug is safe* HARMLESS, innocuous, benign, nontoxic, nonpoisonous. ANTONYM harmful.

▸ noun *I keep the ring in a safe* STRONGBOX, safety-deposit box, safe-deposit box, coffer, strongroom, vault.

**safeguard** noun *a safeguard against terrorism* PROTECTION, defense, guard, screen, buffer, preventive, precaution, provision, security; surety, cover, insurance, indemnity.

▸ verb *the contract will safeguard 1,000 jobs* PROTECT, preserve, conserve, save, secure, shield, guard, keep safe. ANTONYM jeopardize.

**safety** noun **1** *the safety of the residents* WELFARE, well-being, protection, security.

**2** *she worried about the safety of planes* SECURITY, soundness, dependability, reliability.

**3** *we reached the safety of the shore* SHELTER, sanctuary, refuge.

**sag** verb **1** *she sagged in his arms* SINK, slump, loll, flop, crumple.

**2** *the floors all sag* DIP, droop; bulge, bag.

**3** *the markets sagged as the day wore on* DECLINE, fall, drop, slump, plummet; *informal* nosedive.

**saga** noun **1** *Celtic tribal sagas* EPIC, chronicle, legend, folk tale, romance, history, narrative, adventure, myth, fairy story.

**2** *the saga of how they met* LONG STORY, rigmarole; chain of events; *informal* spiel.

**sage** noun *the Chinese sage Confucius* WISE MAN/WOMAN, learned person, philosopher, thinker, scholar, savant; authority, expert, guru.

▸ adjective *some very sage comments* WISE, learned, clever, intelligent, having/showing great knowledge, knowledgeable, sensible, intellectual, scholarly, sagacious, erudite; discerning, judicious, canny, penetrating, perceptive, acute, astute, shrewd, prudent, politic, thoughtful, insightful, percipient, perspicacious, philosophical, profound, deep.

**sail** noun *the ship's sails* canvas, sailcloth.

▸ verb **1** *we sailed across the Atlantic* VOYAGE, travel by water, steam, navigate, cruise.

**2** *you can learn to sail here* YACHT, boat, go sailing; crew, helm.

**3** *we sail tonight* SET SAIL, put to sea, leave port, weigh anchor, shove off.

**4** *he is sailing the ship* STEER, pilot, navigate, con, helm, captain; *informal* skipper.

**5** *clouds were sailing past* GLIDE, drift, float, flow, sweep, skim, coast, flit.

**6** *a pencil sailed past his ear* WHIZ, speed, streak, shoot, whip, buzz, zoom, flash; fly, wing, soar, zip.

PHRASE: **sail through** *she sailed through the exam* SUCCEED EASILY AT, pass easily, romp through, walk through.

**sailor** noun *his mentor at sea was a well-seasoned sailor named Coates* SEAMAN, seafarer, mariner; boatman, yachtsman, hand; *informal* (old) salt, sea dog, rating, bluejacket; *Brit.* matelot, shellback.

**USAGE NOTE sailor, sailer**

A *sailor* is one who sails—always in reference to a person. A *sailer* is a vessel or vehicle that sails, or that moves by the use of a sail—e.g.: "The second part of the project is to launch an operational solar sailer with eight sails to be tested in an 850-km. (528-mi.) circular orbit, also using a Volna rocket." (*Aviation Week & Space Technology*; July 16, 2001.) It isn't unusual to see *sailer* misused for *sailor*—e.g.: "The current exercises involve about 15,000 sailers [read *sailors*] and Marines, and include cruisers and destroyers, with nonexplosive bombs dropped from the air, according to the Associated Press." (*Chicago Sun-Times*; Apr. 30, 2001.) *—BG*

**saintly** adjective *he was a saintly but somewhat ineffective archbishop* HOLY, godly, pious, religious, devout, spiritual, prayerful; virtuous, righteous, good, moral, innocent, sinless, guiltless, irreproachable, spotless, uncorrupted, pure, angelic. ANTONYM ungodly.

**sake** noun **1** *this is simplified for the sake of clarity* PURPOSE, reason, aim, end, objective, object, goal, motive.

**2** *she had to be brave for her daughter's sake* BENEFIT, advantage, good, well-being, welfare, interest, profit.

**salacious** adjective **1** *salacious writing* PORNOGRAPHIC, obscene, indecent, crude, lewd, vulgar, dirty, filthy; erotic, titillating, arousing, suggestive, sexy, risqué, ribald, smutty, bawdy; X-rated; *informal* porn, porno, blue, XXX; *euphemistic* adult.

**2** *salacious women* LUSTFUL, lecherous, licentious, lascivious, libidinous, prurient, lewd; debauched, wanton, loose, fast, impure, unchaste, degenerate, sinful, depraved, promiscuous; *informal* randy, horny, hot to trot.

**salary** noun *a annual raise in his salary* PAY, wages, earnings, payment, remuneration, fee(s), stipend, income; *informal* take-home; *formal* emolument.

**sale** noun **1** *the sale of firearms* SELLING, vending; dealing, trading. ANTONYM purchase.

2 *they make a sale every minute* DEAL, transaction. ANTONYM purchase.

3 *there's a sale on* MARKDOWN, discount, blowout, clearance (sale), fire sale, liquidation (sale). PHRASE: **for sale** *is that picture for sale?* ON THE MARKET, on sale, available, purchasable, obtainable.

**salient** adjective *the most salient point is that the suggested cost is beyond our budget* IMPORTANT, main, principal, major, chief, primary; notable, noteworthy, outstanding, conspicuous, striking, noticeable, obvious, remarkable, prominent, predominant, dominant; key, crucial, vital, essential, pivotal, prime, central, paramount. ANTONYM minor.

**sallow** adjective *a disturbingly sallow complexion* YELLOWISH, jaundiced, pallid, wan, pale, anemic, bloodless, pasty; unhealthy, sickly, washed out; *informal* like death warmed over; *Medicine* icteric.

**sally** noun 1 *the garrison made a sally against us* SORTIE, charge, foray, thrust, drive, offensive, attack, assault, raid, incursion, invasion, onset, onslaught.

2 *a fruitless sally into the city* EXPEDITION, excursion, trip, outing, jaunt, visit.

3 *they exchanged amusing sallies* WITTICISM, smart remark, quip, barb, pleasantry; joke, pun, jest, bon mot; retort, riposte, counter, rejoinder; *informal* gag, wisecrack, comeback.

**salon** noun 1 *he works in an uptown salon* establishment, premises; boutique, store, shop; beauty parlor, beauty shop, hair salon; nail salon; tanning salon.

2 *the chateau's mirrored salon* DRAWING ROOM, sitting room, living room, lounge; *dated* parlor.

3 *he showed his artwork in a salon* EXHIBITION, (public) display, show, showing, showcase, exhibit.

**salt** noun 1 *the potatoes need salt* SODIUM CHLORIDE, table salt, NaCl.

2 *literary he added salt to the conversation* ZEST, spice, piquancy, bite, edge; vitality, liveliness, spirit, sparkle; *informal* zing, punch.

▸ adjective *salt water* SALTY, salted, saline, briny, brackish.

PHRASES: **salt away** *informal Esther salted away most of her allowance* SAVE, put aside, put by, set aside, reserve, keep, store, stockpile, hoard, stow away; *informal* squirrel away, stash away. **with a grain of salt** *he's a spinner of tales, so take what he says with a grain of salt* WITH RESERVATIONS, with misgivings, skeptically, cynically, doubtfully, doubtingly, suspiciously, quizzically, incredulously.

**salty** adjective 1 *salty water* SALT, salted, saline, briny, brackish.

2 *a salty sense of humor* EARTHY, colorful, spicy, racy, risqué, naughty, vulgar, rude; piquant, biting.

**salubrious** adjective 1 *I found the climate salubrious* HEALTHY, health-giving, healthful, beneficial, wholesome; *archaic* salutary. See note at SANITARY. ANTONYM unhealthy.

2 *a salubrious Sunday afternoon* PLEASANT, agreeable, pleasing, enjoyable, pleasurable, nice, delightful; select, high-class, upscale, upmarket; *informal* posh, swanky, classy, swank; *Brit. informal* cushty. ANTONYM unpleasant.

**salutary** adjective 1 *a salutary lesson on the fragility of nature* BENEFICIAL, advantageous, good, profitable, productive, helpful, useful, valuable, worthwhile; timely.

2 *archaic the salutary Atlantic air.* See SALUBRIOUS sense 1.

**salutation** noun *his cheery salutations are a bit too much for a Monday morning* GREETING, salute, address, welcome.

**salute** noun 1 *he gave the captain a salute* GREETING, salutation, gesture of respect, obeisance, acknowledgment, welcome, address.

2 *she raised her hands in salutation* TRIBUTE, testimonial, homage, toast, honor, eulogy; celebration, acknowledgment.

▸ verb 1 *he saluted the ambassadors* GREET, address, hail, welcome, acknowledge, toast; make obeisance to.

2 *we salute a great photographer* PAY TRIBUTE TO, pay homage to, honor, celebrate, acknowledge, take one's hat off to.

**salvage** verb 1 *an attempt to salvage the vessel* RESCUE, save, recover, retrieve, raise, reclaim.

2 *he tried to salvage his reputation* RETAIN, preserve, conserve; regain, recoup, redeem, snatch.

▸ noun 1 *the salvage is taking place off the coast* RESCUE, recovery, reclamation.

2 *she sifted through the salvage* REMAINS, debris, wreckage, rubble, remnants, flotsam and jetsam, scrap.

**salvation** noun 1 *salvation by way of repentance* REDEMPTION, deliverance, reclamation. ANTONYM damnation.

2 *that conviction was her salvation* LIFELINE, preservation; means of escape, help, saving, savior.

**same** adjective 1 *we stayed at **the same** hotel* IDENTICAL, selfsame, very same, one and the same. ANTONYMS another, different.

2 *they had **the same** symptoms* MATCHING, identical, alike, duplicate, carbon copy, twin; indistinguishable, interchangeable, corresponding, equivalent, parallel, like, comparable, similar, congruent, concordant, consonant. ANTONYMS different, dissimilar.

3 *it happened that same month* SELFSAME; aforesaid, aforementioned.

4 *they provide **the same** menu worldwide* UNCHANGING, unvarying, unvaried, invariable, consistent, uniform, regular. ANTONYMS varying, different.

▸ noun *Louise said the same* SAME THING, aforementioned, aforesaid, above-mentioned.

PHRASE: **all the same** 1 *I was frightened all the same* IN SPITE OF EVERYTHING, despite that, nevertheless, nonetheless, even so, however, but, still, yet, though, be that as it may, just the same, at the same time, in any event, notwithstanding, regardless, anyway, anyhow; *informal* still and all.

2 *it's all the same to me* IMMATERIAL, of no importance, of no

consequence, inconsequential, unimportant, of little account, irrelevant, insignificant, trivial, petty.

THE RIGHT WORD **same, equal, equivalent, identical, selfsame, tantamount**

All of these adjectives describe something that is not significantly different from something else. **Same** may imply, and **selfsame** always implies, that what is referred to is one thing and not two or more distinct things (*they go to the same restaurant every Friday night; this is the selfsame house in which the family once lived*). In one sense, **identical** is synonymous with *selfsame* (*the identical place where we first met*); but it can also imply exact correspondence in quality, shape, and appearance (*wearing identical raincoats*). **Equivalent** describes things that are interchangeable or that amount to the same thing in value, force, or significance (*the equivalent of a free hotel room at a luxury resort*), while **equal** implies exact correspondence in quantity, value, or size (*equal portions of food*). **Tantamount** is used to describe one of a pair of things, usually intangible, that are in effect equivalent to each other (*her tears were tantamount to a confession of guilt*).

**sample** noun **1** *a sample of the fabric* SPECIMEN, example, bit, snippet, swatch, representative piece, exemplification; prototype, test piece, dummy, pilot, trial, taste, taster, tester.

**2** *a sample of 10,000 people nationwide* CROSS SECTION, variety, sampling, test.

▸ verb *we sampled the culinary offerings* TRY (OUT), taste, test, put to the test, experiment with; appraise, evaluate, test drive; *informal* check out.

▸ adjective **1** *the sample group is small* REPRESENTATIVE, illustrative, selected, specimen, test, trial, typical.

**2** *a sample copy can be obtained* SPECIMEN, test, trial, pilot, dummy.

**sanctify** verb **1** *he came to sanctify the site* CONSECRATE, bless, make holy, hallow, make sacred, dedicate to God.

**2** *they sanctified themselves* PURIFY, cleanse, free from sin, absolve, unburden, redeem.

**3** *we must not sanctify this outrage* APPROVE, sanction, condone, vindicate, endorse, support, back, permit, allow, authorize, legitimize.

**sanctimonious** adjective *no one wants to hear your sanctimonious hot air* SELF-RIGHTEOUS, holier-than-thou, pious, pietistic, churchy, moralizing, preachy, smug, superior, priggish, hypocritical, insincere; *informal* goody-goody. See note at MORAL.

**sanction** noun **1** *trade sanctions* PENALTY, punishment, deterrent; punitive action, discipline, restriction; embargo, ban, prohibition, boycott. ANTONYM reward.

**2** *the scheme has the sanction of the court* AUTHORIZATION, consent, leave, permission, authority, warrant, license, dispensation, assent, acquiescence, agreement, approval, approbation, endorsement, accreditation, ratification, validation, blessing, imprimatur; *informal* go-ahead, OK, green light. ANTONYM prohibition.

▸ verb **1** *the rally was sanctioned by the government* AUTHORIZE, permit, allow, warrant, accredit, license, endorse, approve, accept, back, support; *informal* OK. See note at APPROVE. ANTONYM prohibit.

**2** *the penalties available to sanction crime* PUNISH, discipline someone for.

**sanctity** noun **1** *the sanctity of St. Francis* HOLINESS, godliness, blessedness, saintliness, spirituality, piety, piousness, devoutness, righteousness, goodness, virtue, purity; *formal* sanctitude.

**2** *the sanctity of the family meal* INVIOLABILITY; importance, paramountcy.

**sanctuary** noun **1** *the sanctuary at Delphi* SANCTUM.

**2** *the island is our sanctuary* REFUGE, haven, harbor, port in a storm, oasis, shelter, retreat, hideaway, hideout.

**3** *he was given sanctuary in the embassy* SAFETY, protection, shelter, immunity, asylum.

**4** *a bird sanctuary* RESERVE, park, reservation, preserve.

**sane** adjective **1** *the accused is presumed to be sane* OF SOUND MIND, in one's right mind, compos mentis, lucid, rational, balanced, stable, normal; *informal* all there, together. ANTONYM mad.

**2** *it isn't sane to use nuclear weapons* SENSIBLE, practical, advisable, responsible, realistic, prudent, wise, reasonable, rational, levelheaded, commonsensical, judicious, politic. See note at SENSIBLE. ANTONYM foolish.

**sang-froid** noun *he recovered his usual sangfroid* COMPOSURE, equanimity, self-possession, equilibrium, aplomb, poise, self-assurance, self-control, nerve, calm, presence of mind; *informal* cool, unflappability.

**sanguine** adjective **1** *he is sanguine about the advance of technology* OPTIMISTIC, bullish, hopeful, buoyant, positive, confident, cheerful, cheery; *informal* upbeat. ANTONYM gloomy.

**2** *archaic a sanguine complexion.* See FLORID sense 1.

**sanitary** adjective *improvements in health are also the result of more sanitary conditions* HYGIENIC, clean, antiseptic, aseptic, sterile, uninfected, disinfected, unpolluted, uncontaminated; salubrious, healthy, wholesome.

THE RIGHT WORD **sanitary, antiseptic, healthful, hygienic, salubrious, sterile**

Americans thrive on cleanliness and the eradication of germs. They try to keep their homes **sanitary**, a term that goes beyond cleanliness to imply that measures have been taken to guard against infections or disease. They demand that their communities provide schools and workplaces that are **hygienic**—in other words, that adhere to the rules or standards promoting public health. But it would be almost impossible to duplicate the conditions found in a hospital, where everything that comes in contact with patients must be **sterile** or free of germs entirely. Most Americans want to make their environment **healthful**, which means conducive to the health or soundness of the body, but they are not interested in making it **antiseptic**, a word that is similar in meaning to *sterile* but implies preventing infections by destroying germs that are already present (*an antiseptic solution*). Many Americans, as they grow older, choose to move to a more **salubrious** climate, a word that means health-giving and applies primarily to an air quality that is invigorating and that avoids harsh extremes.

---

**sanity** noun **1** *she was losing her sanity* MENTAL HEALTH, faculties, reason, rationality, saneness, stability, lucidity; sense, wits, mind.

**2** *sanity has prevailed* (COMMON) SENSE, wisdom, prudence, judiciousness, rationality, soundness, sensibleness.

**sap** noun **1** *sap from the roots of trees* JUICE, secretion, fluid, liquid.

**2** *they're full of youthful sap* VIGOR, energy, drive, dynamism, life, spirit, liveliness, sparkle, verve, ebullience, enthusiasm, gusto, vitality, vivacity, fire, zest, zeal, exuberance; *informal* get-up-and-go, oomph, vim.

▸ verb *they sapped the will of the troops* ERODE, wear away/down, deplete, reduce, lessen, attenuate, undermine, exhaust, drain, bleed.

**sarcasm** noun *well, it's easy to see that she got her biting sarcasm from her mother* DERISION, mockery, ridicule, scorn, sneering, scoffing; irony; cynicism. See note at WIT.

**sarcastic** adjective *I've had enough of your sarcastic comments* SARDONIC, ironic, ironical; derisive, snide, scornful, contemptuous, mocking, sneering, jeering; caustic, scathing, trenchant, cutting, biting, sharp, acerbic; *informal* smart-alecky.

**sardonic** adjective *his sardonic wit* MOCKING, satirical, sarcastic, ironical, ironic; cynical, scornful, contemptuous, derisive, derisory, sneering, jeering; scathing, caustic, trenchant, cutting, sharp, acerbic.

**Satan** noun. See DEVIL sense 1.

**satanic** adjective *a series of satanic messages were written on the wall* DIABOLICAL, fiendish, devilish, demonic, demoniacal, ungodly, hellish, infernal, wicked, evil, sinful, iniquitous, nefarious, vile, foul, abominable, unspeakable, loathsome, monstrous, heinous, hideous, horrible, horrifying, shocking, appalling, dreadful, awful, terrible, ghastly, abhorrent, despicable, damnable.

**satellite** noun **1** *the satellite orbited the earth* SPACE STATION, space capsule, spacecraft; communications satellite, weather satellite.

**2** *the two small satellites of Mars* MOON, secondary planet.

**3** *Bulgaria was then a Russian satellite* BRANCH, colony, protectorate, puppet state, possession, holding; *historical* fief, vassal; *informal* offshoot.

▸ adjective *a satellite state* DEPENDENT, subordinate, subsidiary.

**satiate** verb *here, this stew should satiate you* FILL, satisfy, sate; slake, quench; gorge, stuff, surfeit, glut, cloy, sicken, nauseate.

**satire** noun **1** *a satire on Canadian politics* PARODY, burlesque, caricature, lampoon, skit; *informal* spoof, takeoff, sendup. See note at WIT.

**2** *he has become the subject of satire* MOCKERY, ridicule, derision, scorn, caricature; irony, sarcasm.

**satirical** adjective *satirical essays about American politics* MOCKING, ironic, ironical, satiric, sarcastic, sardonic; caustic, trenchant, mordant, biting, cutting, stinging, acerbic; critical, irreverent, disparaging, disrespectful.

**satirize** verb *a comedy troupe that satirized the conservative establishment of the sixties* MOCK, ridicule, deride, make fun of, poke fun at, parody, lampoon, burlesque, caricature, take off; criticize; *informal* send up.

**satisfaction** noun **1** *he derived great satisfaction from his work* CONTENTMENT, pleasure, gratification, fulfillment, enjoyment, happiness, pride; self-satisfaction, smugness, complacency.

**2** *the satisfaction of consumer needs* FULFILLMENT, gratification; appeasement, assuaging.

**3** *investors turned to the courts for satisfaction* COMPENSATION, recompense, redress, reparation, restitution, repayment, payment, settlement, reimbursement, indemnification, indemnity.

**satisfactory** adjective *the work isn't extraordinary, but it is satisfactory* ADEQUATE, all right, acceptable, good enough, sufficient, reasonable, quite good, competent, fair, decent, average, passable; fine, in order, up to scratch, up to the mark, up to standard, up to par; *informal* OK, jake, hunky-dory, so-so, 'comme ci, comme ça'. ANTONYMS inadequate, poor.

**satisfied** adjective **1** *a satisfied smile* PLEASED, well pleased, content, contented, happy, proud, triumphant; smug, self-satisfied, pleased with oneself, complacent. ANTONYM unhappy.

**2** *the pleasure of satisfied desire* FULFILLED, gratified. ANTONYM unfulfilled.

**3** *I am satisfied that she understands* CONVINCED, certain, sure, positive, persuaded, easy in one's mind. ANTONYM unconvinced.

**satisfy** verb **1** *a last chance to satisfy his hunger for romance* FULFILL, gratify, meet, fill; indulge, cater to, pander to; appease, assuage; quench, slake, satiate, sate, take the edge off. ANTONYM frustrate.

**2** *she satisfied herself that it had been an accident* CONVINCE, persuade, assure; reassure, put someone's mind at rest.

**3** *products that satisfy the criteria* COMPLY WITH, meet, fulfill, answer, conform to; measure up to, come up to; suffice, be good enough, fit/fill the bill.

**4** *there was insufficient collateral to satisfy the loan* REPAY, pay (off), settle, make good, discharge, square, liquidate, clear.

**saturate** verb **1** *heavy rain saturated the ground* SOAK, drench, waterlog, wet through; souse, steep, douse.

**2** *the air was saturated with the stench of incense* PERMEATE, suffuse, imbue, pervade, charge, infuse, fill.

3 *the company has saturated the market* FLOOD, glut, oversupply, overload.

**sauce** noun 1 *a piquant sauce* gravy; relish, condiment, salsa, ketchup; dip, dressing.

2 *informal "I'll have less of your sauce," said Aunt Edie* IMPUDENCE, impertinence, cheek, cheekiness, sauciness, effrontery, forwardness, brazenness; insolence, rudeness, disrespect; *informal* mouth, lip, sass, sassiness.

3 *Uncle Reg was into the sauce again* ALCOHOL, drink, spirits, liquor; *informal* booze, hooch, hard stuff, firewater, rotgut, moonshine, grog, demon rum, bottle, juice.

**saucy** adjective *informal* 1 *you saucy girl!* CHEEKY, impudent, impertinent, irreverent, forward, disrespectful, bold, as bold as brass, brazen, pert; *informal* fresh, lippy, mouthy, sassy. ANTONYMS demure, polite.

2 *the cap sat at a saucy angle* JAUNTY, rakish, sporty, raffish.

**saunter** verb *they sauntered back to the car* STROLL, amble, wander, meander, drift, walk; stretch one's legs, take the air; *informal* mosey, tootle; *formal* promenade.

**savage** adjective 1 *savage dogs* FEROCIOUS, fierce; wild, untamed, untamable, undomesticated, feral. ANTONYM tame.

2 *a savage assault* VICIOUS, brutal, cruel, sadistic, ferocious, fierce, violent, bloody, murderous, homicidal, bloodthirsty; *literary* fell; *archaic* sanguinary; *informal* smash-mouth.

3 *a savage attack on free-trade policy* FIERCE, blistering, scathing, searing, stinging, devastating, mordant, trenchant, caustic, cutting, biting, withering, virulent, vitriolic. ANTONYM mild.

4 *a savage race* PRIMITIVE, uncivilized, unenlightened, nonliterate. ANTONYM civilized.

5 *a savage landscape* RUGGED, rough, wild, inhospitable, uninhabitable.

6 *a savage blow for the town* SEVERE, crushing, devastating, crippling, terrible, awful, dreadful, dire, catastrophic, calamitous, ruinous.

▸ noun 1 *she'd expected mud huts and savages* BARBARIAN, wild man, wild woman, primitive.

2 *she described her son's assailants as savages* BRUTE, beast, monster, barbarian, sadist, animal.

▸ verb 1 *he was savaged by a dog* MAUL, attack, tear to pieces, lacerate, claw, bite.

2 *critics savaged the film* CRITICIZE SEVERELY, attack, lambaste, condemn, denounce, pillory, revile; *informal* pan, tear to pieces, hammer, slam, do a hatchet job on, crucify, trash; *formal* excoriate.

**save** verb 1 *the captain was saved by his crew* RESCUE, come to someone's rescue, save someone's life; set free, free, liberate, deliver, extricate; bail out; *informal* save someone's bacon/neck/skin.

2 *the farmhouse has been saved from demolition* PRESERVE, keep safe, keep, protect, safeguard; salvage, retrieve, reclaim, rescue.

3 *start saving money* PUT ASIDE, set aside, put by, put to one side, save up, keep, retain, reserve, conserve, stockpile, store, hoard, save for a rainy day; *informal* salt away, squirrel away, stash away, hang on to.

4 *asking me first would have saved a lot of trouble* PREVENT, obviate, forestall, spare; stop; avoid, avert.

▸ preposition & conjunction *formal no one needed to know save herself* EXCEPT, apart from, but, other than, besides, aside from, bar, barring, excluding, leaving out, saving; *informal* outside of.

**savior** noun *he was hailed as the country's savior* RESCUER, liberator, deliverer, emancipator; champion, knight in shining armor, friend in need, good Samaritan.

**savoir faire** noun *the French admired Franklin's wit and Jefferson's savoir faire* SOCIAL SKILL, social grace(s), urbanity, suavity, finesse, sophistication, poise, aplomb, adroitness, polish, style, smoothness, tact, tactfulness, diplomacy, discretion, delicacy, sensitivity; *informal* savvy. ANTONYM gaucheness.

**savor** verb 1 *she wanted to savor every moment* RELISH, enjoy (to the full), appreciate, delight in, revel in, luxuriate in, bask in.

2 *such a declaration* ***savored of*** *immodesty* SUGGEST, smack of, have the hallmarks of, seem like, have the air of, show signs of.

▸ noun 1 *the subtle savor of wood smoke* SMELL, aroma, fragrance, scent, perfume, bouquet; TASTE, flavor, tang, smack.

2 *a savor of bitterness seasoned my feelings for him* TRACE, hint, suggestion, touch, smack.

3 *her usual diversions had lost their savor* PIQUANCY, interest, attraction, flavor, spice, zest, excitement, enjoyment, shine; *informal* zing, pizzazz, sparkle.

**savory** adjective 1 *sweet or savory dishes* salty, spicy, piquant, tangy. ANTONYM sweet.

2 *a rich, savory aroma* APPETIZING, mouthwatering, delicious, delectable, luscious; tasty, flavorful, full of flavor, palatable, toothsome; *informal* scrumptious, finger-licking, lip-smacking, melt-in-your/the-mouth, yummy. ANTONYM unappetizing.

3 *one of the less savory aspects of the affair* ACCEPTABLE, pleasant, respectable, wholesome, honorable, proper, seemly. ANTONYMS unpleasant, unacceptable.

**saw** noun *the old saw about when the going gets tough* SAYING, maxim, proverb, aphorism, axiom, adage, epigram.

**say** verb 1 *she felt her stomach flutter as he said her name* SPEAK, utter, voice, pronounce, give voice to, vocalize.

2 *"I must go," she said* DECLARE, state, announce, remark, observe, mention, comment, note, add; reply, respond, answer, rejoin; *informal* come out with.

3 *Newall says he's innocent* CLAIM, maintain, assert, hold, insist, contend; allege, profess; *formal* opine, aver.

4 *I can't conjure up the words to say how I feel* EXPRESS, put into words, phrase, articulate, communicate, make known,

put/get across, convey, verbalize; reveal, divulge, impart, disclose; imply, suggest.

5 *they sang hymns and said a prayer* RECITE, repeat, utter, deliver, perform, declaim, orate.

6 *the clock said one twenty* INDICATE, show, read.

7 *I'd say it's about five miles* ESTIMATE, judge, guess, hazard a guess, predict, speculate, surmise, conjecture, venture; *informal* reckon.

8 *let's say you'd just won a million dollars* SUPPOSE, assume, imagine, presume, hypothesize, postulate, posit.

▸ noun 1 *everyone is entitled to their say* CHANCE TO SPEAK, turn to speak, opinion, view, voice; *informal* two cents, two cents' worth.

2 *don't I have any say in the matter?* INFLUENCE, sway, weight, voice, input, share, part.

PHRASES: **that is to say** *they're inquiring about Miss Leslie—that is to say, they want to know if she's safe and well.* IN OTHER WORDS, to put it another way; i.e., that is, to wit, viz., namely.

**to say the least** *his performance was disappointing to say the least* TO PUT IT MILDLY, putting it mildly, without any exaggeration, at the very least.

**saying** noun *you know the old saying about all work and no play?* PROVERB, maxim, aphorism, axiom, adage, saw, tag, motto, epigram, dictum, expression, phrase, formula; slogan, catchphrase, mantra; platitude, cliché, commonplace, truism, chestnut. PHRASE: **it goes without saying** *it goes without saying we'll need to rent a car when we get there* OF COURSE, naturally, needless to say, it's taken for granted, it's understood/assumed, it's taken as read, it's an accepted fact; obviously, self-evidently, manifestly; *informal* natch.

THE RIGHT WORD **saying, adage, aphorism, apothegm, epigram, epigraph, maxim, proverb**

"Once burned, twice shy" is an old **saying** about learning from your mistakes. In fact, *sayings*—a term used to describe any current or habitual expression of wisdom or truth—are a dime a dozen. **Proverbs**—sayings that are well known and often repeated, usually expressing metaphorically a truth based on common sense or practical experience—are just as plentiful (*her favorite proverb was "A stitch in time saves nine"*). An **adage** is a time-honored and widely known proverb, such as "Where's there's smoke, there's fire." A **maxim** offers a rule of conduct or action in the form of a proverb, such as "Neither a borrower nor a lender be." **Epigram** and **epigraph** are often confused, but their meanings are quite separate. An *epigram* is a terse, witty, or satirical statement that often relies on a paradox for its effect (*Oscar Wilde's well-known epigram that "The only way to get rid of temptation is to yield to it"*). An *epigraph*, on the other hand, is a brief quotation used to introduce a piece of writing (*he used a quote from T. S. Eliot as the epigraph to his new novel*). An **aphorism** requires a little more thought than an *epigram*, since it aims to be profound rather than witty (*she'd just finished reading a book of Mark Twain's aphorisms*). An **apothegm** is a pointed and often startling aphorism, such as Samuel Johnson's remark that "Patriotism is the last refuge of a scoundrel."

**scale**[1] noun 1 *reptiles have scales covering the skin* plate; *technical* lamella, lamina, squama, scute, scutum.

2 *the disease causes scales on the skin* FLAKE; (**scales**) scurf, dandruff; *technical* furfur.

3 *how can I remove the scale from my tea kettle?* BUILDUP, deposit, incrustation.

**scale**[2] noun 1 *the Richter scale* CALIBRATED SYSTEM, calibration, graduated system, system of measurement, measuring system.

2 *we are at opposite ends of the social scale* HIERARCHY, ladder, ranking, pecking order, order, spectrum, progression, succession, sequence, series.

3 *the scale of the map is too small to show details* RATIO, proportion, relative size.

4 *no one foresaw the scale of the disaster* EXTENT, size, scope, magnitude, dimensions, range, breadth, compass, degree, reach, spread, sweep.

▸ verb *thieves scaled the fence* CLIMB, ascend, go up, clamber up, scramble up, mount, shinny (up); *historical* escalade.

PHRASES: **scale down** *manufacturing capacity has been scaled down* REDUCE, cut down, cut back, cut, make cutbacks in, decrease, lessen, lower, trim, slim down, prune, curtail.

**scale up** *the departments intend to scale up their activities* INCREASE, expand, augment, build up, add to; step up, boost, escalate.

**scaly** adjective 1 *the dragon's scaly hide technical* squamous, squamate, squamose, lamellate, lamellar, lamelliform, lamellose.

2 *scaly patches of dead skin* FLAKY, DRY, flaking, scurfy, peeling, rough, scabrous, mangy, scabious; *technical* furfuraceous.

**scamp** noun *informal he was a scamp in his younger days* RASCAL, monkey, devil, imp, wretch, mischief-maker, troublemaker, prankster, rogue; *informal* scalawag, horror, monster, terror, holy terror, hellion, varmint, rapscallion; *archaic* scapegrace.

**scamper** verb *the boy scampered off | his dogs scampered around the yard* SCURRY, scuttle, dart, run, rush, race, dash, sprint, hurry, hasten, make haste, scoot; romp, skip, frolic, gambol; *Brit.* scutter.

**scan** verb 1 *Adam scanned the horizon* SCRUTINIZE, EXAMINE, study, inspect, survey, search, scour, sweep, look at, stare at, look someone/something up and down, gaze at, eye, watch; contemplate, regard, take stock of; *informal* check out, scope (out).

2 *I scanned the pages of his diary* GLANCE THROUGH/OVER, look through/over, have a look at, run/cast/pass one's eye over, skim (through), flick through, flip through, leaf through, thumb through, rifle through, read quickly, browse (through). ANTONYM pore over.

▸ noun 1 *a careful scan of the terrain* INSPECTION, scrutiny, examination, survey.

**2** *a quick scan through the report* GLANCE, look, flick, browse, skim.

**3** *a brain scan* EXAMINATION, screening, MRI, ultrasound.

**scandal** noun **1** *the sex scandal forced him to resign* (OUTRAGEOUS) WRONGDOING, impropriety, misconduct, immoral behavior, unethical behavior, discreditable behavior, outrageous behavior; shocking incident, shocking series of events; offense, transgression, crime, sin; skeleton in the closet; *informal* business, affair, -gate.

**2** *unmarried motherhood at that time was fraught with scandal* SHAME, dishonor, disgrace, disrepute, discredit, infamy, ignominy, embarrassment; odium, opprobrium, censure, obloquy; stigma.

**3** *it's a scandal that the disease is not adequately treated* DISGRACE, outrage, injustice; (crying) shame, pity; affront, insult, reproach.

**4** *no scandal is attached to her name* MALICIOUS GOSSIP, malicious rumor(s), slander, libel, calumny, defamation, aspersions, muckraking, scandalmongering, smear campaign; *informal* dirt.

**scandalize** verb *the audience was scandalized by the speaker's racist remarks* SHOCK, appall, outrage, horrify, disgust, revolt, repel, sicken; offend, give offense to, affront, insult; cause raised eyebrows. ANTONYM impress.

**scandalous** adjective **1** *a scandalous waste of taxpayers' money* DISGRACEFUL, shocking, outrageous, monstrous, criminal, wicked, sinful, shameful, atrocious, appalling, dreadful, deplorable, reprehensible, inexcusable, intolerable, insupportable, unforgivable, unconscionable, unpardonable; *rare* egregious. ANTONYMS acceptable, praiseworthy.

**2** *a series of scandalous liaisons* DISCREDITABLE, disreputable, dishonorable, improper, unseemly, sordid. ANTONYMS proper, seemly.

**3** *scandalous rumors* SCURRILOUS, malicious, slanderous, libelous, defamatory; *rare* calumnious, calumniatory, aspersive.

**scant** adjective *there is only scant evidence to support this hypothesis* LITTLE, little or no, minimal, hardly (any), limited, negligible, barely sufficient, meager; insufficient, too little, inadequate, deficient; *formal* exiguous. ANTONYMS abundant, ample, sufficient.

**scanty** adjective **1** *their scanty wages* | *details of his life are scanty* MEAGER, scant, minimal, limited, modest, restricted, sparse; tiny, small, paltry, negligible, insufficient, inadequate, deficient, too small/little/few, poor, sketchy, thin; scarce, in short supply, few and far between; *informal* measly, piddling, mingy, pathetic; *formal* exiguous. ANTONYMS ample, abundant, plentiful.

**2** *scanty clothing* SKIMPY, revealing, short, brief; low, low-cut; indecent. ANTONYM modest.

**scapegoat** noun *find yourself another scapegoat* WHIPPING BOY; *informal* fall guy, patsy.

**scar** noun **1** *the scar on his left cheek* CICATRIX, mark, blemish, disfigurement, discoloration, defacement; pockmark, pock, pit; lesion, stigma; birthmark, nevus; (**scars**) stigmata.

**2** *deep psychological scars* TRAUMA, damage, injury.

▸ verb **1** *the leg will heal, but he's likely to be scarred for life* DISFIGURE, mark, blemish, discolor; pockmark, pit; stigmatize.

**2** *the landscape has been scarred by strip mining* DAMAGE, spoil, mar, deface, injure; *rare* disfeature.

**3** *she was profoundly scarred by the incident* TRAUMATIZE, damage, injure, wound; distress, disturb, upset.

**USAGE NOTE scarify, scorify**

*Scarify* (from *scar*, but pronounced as if from *scare*) means (1) "make superficial marks or incisions in; cut off skin from"; (2) "break up the surface of (the ground) with a spiked machine [a scarifier] for loosening soil or building roads"; or (3) "pain by severe criticism."

Sense 1 is most common—e.g.: "Rub the seed across some sandpaper to weaken the hard seed coat or scarify it with a knife for better germination." (*Virginian-Pilot* [Norfolk]; Apr. 20, 1997.) This sense applies also to body adornment by cutting and scraping—e.g.: "Worse, once piercing becomes commonplace among people like, well, Leslie, the trendsetters up the ante with other forms of body alteration: cutting (scarification as adornment), branding (searing flesh with high heat in artistic patterns) and—please don't eat during this next sentence—tongue splitting, in which the tongue is cleaved nearly in half so as to cause it to fork like a lizard's." (*Washington Post*; Feb. 11, 2003.)

Sense 3 is also fairly common—e.g.: "With a combination of dazzling philosophical acumen and scarifying wit, Stove does for irrationalism in Karl Popper's philosophy . . . what the Romans did for Carthage in the Third Punic War." (*New Criterion*; Mar. 1997.)

An identically pronounced, but separate, *scarify*, based on the root word *scare*, dates from the late 18th century but remains mostly dialectal. It often carries a lighthearted connotation—e.g.: "The cost-of-living index had taken a scarifying new jump of 1.2 percent in February, to an annual rate of 15 percent." (*Newsweek*; Apr. 2, 1979.)

*Scorify* = reduce to dross or slag. The term surfaces most commonly in cognate forms, such as *scorifier*—e.g.: "Hanging adjacent to the furnace are the specialized tongs for handling crucibles, cupels and the dishlike ceramic containers called scorifiers." (*Bulletin* [Bend, OR]; Apr. 2, 1997.) —*BG*

**scarce** adjective **1** *food was scarce* | *scarce financial resources* IN SHORT SUPPLY, scant, scanty, meager, sparse, short, hard to find, hard to come by, too little, insufficient, deficient, inadequate, lacking, wanting; at a premium, paltry, negligible; *informal* rare/scarce as hen's teeth, rarer/scarcer than hen's teeth, not to be had for love or money; *formal* exiguous. ANTONYMS plentiful, abundant.

**2** *birds that prefer dense forest are becoming scarce* RARE, few and far between; uncommon, unusual. ANTONYM common.

**scarcely** adverb **1** *she could scarcely hear what he was saying* HARDLY, barely, only just; almost not.

**2** *I **scarcely ever** see him* RARELY, seldom, infrequently, not often, hardly ever, almost never, on rare occasions, every once in a while; *informal* once in a blue moon. ANTONYM often.

**3** *this could scarcely be accidental* SURELY NOT, not, hardly, certainly not, definitely not, not at all, on no account, under no circumstances, by no means, in no way, noway, noways.

**scarcity** noun *the scarcity of affordable housing* SHORTAGE, dearth, lack, want, undersupply, insufficiency, paucity, scarceness, scantness, scantiness, meagerness, sparseness, poverty; deficiency, inadequacy; unavailability, absence; *rare* exiguity, exiguousness. ANTONYMS abundance, excess, surplus.

**scare** verb *stop it, you're scaring me* FRIGHTEN, startle, alarm, terrify, petrify, intimidate, terrorize, make afraid, make fearful, fill with fear, give someone a fright, panic, throw into a panic, shock, unnerve, cow; strike terror into, put the fear of God into, chill to the bone/marrow, make someone's blood run cold, scare/frighten to death, scare/frighten someone out of their wits, send into a cold sweat, scare/frighten the living daylights out of, scare/frighten the life out of, scare the hell out of, scare stiff, scare witless, make someone shake in their boots/shoes; *informal* scare the pants off, make someone's hair stand on end, make someone jump out of their skin, make someone's hair curl, spook, scarify, scare the bejesus out of, scare the bejabbers out of, give someone the heebie-jeebies; *vulgar slang* scare shitless, scare the shit out of. ANTONYM reassure.

▸ noun *you gave me a scare—how did you get here?* FRIGHT, shock, start, turn, jump; *informal* heart attack.

**scared** adjective *I've never been so scared in all my life* FRIGHTENED, afraid, fearful, startled, nervous, panicky, alarmed, intimidated; terrified, petrified, terrorized, horrified, unnerved, panic-stricken/-struck, terror-stricken/-struck, horror-stricken/-struck, with one's heart in one's mouth, scared stiff, scared/frightened out of one's wits, scared witless, scared/frightened to death, chilled to the bone/marrow, in a cold sweat; *informal* spooked, scarified; *vulgar slang* scared shitless.

**scarf** noun *she wore a scarf* MUFFLER, headscarf, mantilla, stole, tippet; kerchief, neckerchief, bandanna, babushka.

▸ verb *informal* *stop scarfing your food! we **scarfed down** the entire batch of cookies I can't believe how fast he **scarfed up** his dinner* GOBBLE UP/DOWN, eat greedily, eat hungrily, guzzle, bolt, gulp (down), devour, wolf (down), gorge (oneself) on; *informal* tuck into, put away, pack away, demolish, polish off, shovel in/down, stuff one's face (with), pig out (on); *informal* scoff (down/up), inhale; *rare* gluttonize, gourmandize, ingurgitate. ANTONYM nibble.

**scary** adjective *informal* *that movie is too scary for me* FRIGHTENING, alarming, terrifying, petrifying, hair-raising, spine-chilling, blood-curdling, bone-chilling, chilling, horrifying, nerve-racking, fearsome, unnerving; eerie, sinister; *informal* creepy, spine-tingling, spooky, hairy.

**scathing** adjective *another restaurant has fallen victim to one of her scathing reviews* DEVASTATING, extremely critical, blistering, searing, withering, scorching, fierce, ferocious, savage, severe, stinging, biting, cutting, mordant, trenchant, virulent, caustic, vitriolic, scornful, sharp, bitter, harsh, unsparing; *rare* mordacious. ANTONYMS mild, gentle; complimentary.

**scatter** verb **1** *the papers were scattered by the sudden breeze | scatter the seeds as evenly as possible* THROW, strew, toss, fling; SPRINKLE, spread, distribute, sow, broadcast, disseminate; *literary* bestrew. ANTONYM gather.

**2** *the crowd scattered | onlookers were scattered in all directions* DISPERSE, break up, disband, separate, move/go in different directions, go separate ways; dissipate, dissolve; drive, send, put to flight, chase. ANTONYM assemble.

THE RIGHT WORD **scatter, broadcast, diffuse, dispel, disperse, disseminate, dissipate**

If you **scatter** something, you throw it about in different directions, often using force (*the wind scattered leaves around the yard*). **Disperse** implies a scattering that completely breaks up a mass or assemblage and spreads the units far and wide (*the crowd dispersed as soon as the storm arrived; the ships were so widely dispersed that they couldn't see each other*). To **dispel** is to scatter or to drive away something that obscures, confuses, or bothers (*to dispel her fears*), while to **diffuse** is to lessen the intensity of something by spreading it out over a broader area (*the curtains diffused the bright sunlight pouring in the window*). **Dissipate** suggests that something has completely dissolved, disintegrated, or vanished (*early-morning mist dissipated by the sun*). **Broadcast** originally meant to scatter seed, but it is also used figuratively to mean make public (*The news of the president's defeat was broadcast the next morning*). **Disseminate** also means to publish or make public, but it implies a wider audience and usually a longer duration. You can spend a lifetime *disseminating* knowledge, in other words, but you would *broadcast* the news of the birth of your first grandchild.

**scatterbrained** adjective *my scatterbrained kids left their jackets on the bus* ABSENTMINDED, forgetful, disorganized; dreamy, with one's head in the clouds, with a mind/memory like a sieve, featherbrained, birdbrained, giddy; *informal* dizzy, dippy, ditzy, flaky, scatty, not with it, out to lunch.

**scavenge** verb *they scavenge for food in the restaurant's trash cans* FORAGE, rummage, search, hunt, look, root around/about, grub around/about.

**scavenger** *yesterday he ran the company, today he's a homeless scavenger* FORAGER, rummager, grubber; *historical* ragpicker; *rare* mudlark.

**scenario** noun **1** *Walt wrote scenarios for a major Hollywood studio* PLOT, outline, synopsis, story line, framework; screenplay, script, libretto; *formal* diegesis.

**2** *every possible scenario must be explored* SEQUENCE OF EVENTS, course of events, chain of events, series of developments, situation.

**3** *this film has a more contemporary scenario* SETTING, background, context, scene, milieu.

**scene** noun **1** *the scene of the accident* LOCATION, site, place, position, point, spot; locale, setting, whereabouts; *technical* locus.

2 *the scene is Montreal, in the late 1890s* BACKGROUND, setting, context, milieu, backdrop, mise en scène.

3 *terrible scenes of violence* INCIDENT, event, episode, happening, moment.

4 *an impressive mountain scene* VIEW, vista, outlook, panorama, sight; landscape, scenery; picture, tableau, spectacle.

5 *she created a scene outside the bank* FUSS, exhibition of oneself, performance, tantrum, outburst, commotion, disturbance, upset, furor, brouhaha, row, contretemps; *informal* song and dance, to-do.

6 *the political scene | sorry, fishing just isn't my scene* ARENA, stage, sphere, world, milieu, realm, domain; area of interest, field, field of interest, specialty, province, preserve; *informal* thing.

7 *the last scene of the play* SUBDIVISION, division, section, segment.

8 *a scene from a Laurel and Hardy movie* CLIP, section, segment, part, sequence. PHRASES: **behind the scenes** adverb *informal discussions continued behind the scenes* SECRETLY, in secret, privately, in private, behind closed doors, surreptitiously, off the record; *informal* on the quiet, on the QT; *formal* sub rosa.

**behind-the-scenes** adjective *a behind-the-scenes romance* SECRET, private, clandestine, surreptitious; confidential.

**scenery** noun 1 *the beautiful scenery of the Rockies* LANDSCAPE, countryside, country, terrain, topography, setting, surroundings, environment; view, vista, panorama; cityscape, townscape, roofscape; riverscape, seascape, waterscape, snowscape.

2 *we all helped with the scenery and costumes* STAGE SET, set, mise en scène, backdrop, drop curtain; setting, background, decor.

**scenic** adjective *countless miles of Route 1 are still quite scenic* PICTURESQUE, pretty, pleasing, attractive, lovely, beautiful, charming, pretty as a picture, easy on the eye; impressive, striking, spectacular, breathtaking; panoramic. ANTONYMS dreary, unattractive.

**scent** noun 1 *the scent of freshly cut hay* SMELL, fragrance, aroma, perfume, redolence, savor, odor, whiff; bouquet, nose. See note at SMELL.

2 *that's a lovely scent you're wearing* PERFUME, fragrance, cologne, toilet water.

3 *the hounds picked up the scent of a rabbit* SPOOR, trail, track; *Hunting* foil, wind.

4 *there was a scent of rain in the air* HINT, suggestion, trace, whiff.

▸ verb 1 *a shark can scent blood from over half a mile away* SMELL, detect the smell of, get a whiff of.

2 *Rose looked at him, scenting a threat* SENSE, become aware of, detect, discern, perceive, recognize, get wind of.

**scented** adjective *a hotel with private saunas and scented sheets* PERFUMED, fragranced, perfumy; sweet-smelling, fragrant, aromatic; *rare* aromatized.

**schedule** noun 1 *we need to draw up a production schedule* PLAN, program, timetable, scheme.

2 *I have a very busy schedule* TIMETABLE, agenda, diary, calendar, timeline; itinerary.

▸ verb *another meeting was scheduled for April 20* ARRANGE, organize, plan, program, timetable, set up, line up, slate.

PHRASE: **behind schedule** *the museum renovations are behind schedule* LATE, running late, overdue, behind time, behind, behindhand.

**scheme** noun 1 *crazy fundraising schemes* PLAN, project, plan of action, program, strategy, stratagem, tactic, game plan, course/line of action; system, procedure, design, formula, recipe.

2 *police uncovered a scheme to steal the paintings* PLOT, intrigue, conspiracy; ruse, ploy, stratagem, maneuver, subterfuge; machinations; *informal* game, racket, con, scam.

3 *the sonnet's rhyme scheme* ARRANGEMENT, system, organization, configuration, pattern, format; *technical* schema.

▸ verb *he schemed to bring about the collapse of the government* PLOT, hatch a plot, conspire, intrigue, connive, maneuver, plan.

**scheming** adjective *he finally saw his scheming wife for what she really was* CUNNING, crafty, calculating, devious, designing, conniving, wily, sly, tricky, artful, guileful, slippery, slick, manipulative, Machiavellian, unscrupulous, disingenuous; duplicitous, deceitful, underhanded, treacherous. ANTONYMS ingenuous, honest.

**schism** noun *the schism between her father and his brother* DIVISION, split, rift, breach, rupture, break, separation, severance; chasm, gulf; discord, disagreement, dissension.

**scholar** noun 1 *a leading biblical scholar* ACADEMIC, intellectual, learned person, man/woman of letters, mind, intellect, savant, polymath, highbrow, bluestocking; authority, expert; *informal* egghead.

2 *archaic the school had 28 scholars* STUDENT, pupil, schoolchild, schoolboy, schoolgirl.

**scholarly** adjective 1 *an earnest, scholarly man* LEARNED, erudite, academic, well-read, widely read, intellectual, literary, lettered, educated, knowledgeable, highbrow; studious, bookish, donnish, bluestocking, cerebral; *informal* pointy-headed. ANTONYMS uneducated, illiterate.

2 *a scholarly career* ACADEMIC, scholastic, pedagogic.

**scholarship** noun 1 *a center of medieval scholarship* LEARNING, book learning, knowledge, erudition, education, letters, culture, academic study, academic achievement. See note at KNOWLEDGE.

2 *a scholarship of $200 per semester* GRANT, award, endowment, payment, bursary.

**scholastic** adjective *their scholastic achievements* ACADEMIC, educational, school, scholarly.

**school** noun 1 *their children went to the local school* EDUCA-

TIONAL INSTITUTION; academy, college, university; seminary; alma mater.

**2** *the university's School of Law* DEPARTMENT, faculty, division.

**3** *the Barbizon school* GROUP, set, circle; followers, following, disciples, apostles, admirers, devotees, votaries; proponents, adherents.

**4** *the school of linguistics associated with his ideas* WAY OF THINKING, persuasion, creed, credo, doctrine, belief, faith, opinion, point of view; approach, method, style.

**5** *a school of fish* shoal; pod, gam.

▸ verb **1** *he was born in Paris and schooled in Lyon* EDUCATE, teach, instruct.

**2** *he schooled her in horsemanship* TRAIN, teach, tutor, coach, instruct, drill, discipline, direct, guide, prepare, groom; prime, verse.

**schooling** noun **1** *his parents paid for his schooling* EDUCATION, teaching, tuition, instruction, tutoring, tutelage; lessons; (book) learning.

**2** *the schooling of horses* TRAINING, coaching, instruction, drill, drilling, discipline, disciplining.

**schoolteacher** noun *until 1912, the town had in its employ just one schoolteacher* TEACHER, schoolmaster, schoolmistress, tutor, educationist; *informal* schoolmarm; *formal* pedagogue.

**science** noun **1** *he teaches science at the high school* physics, chemistry, biology; physical sciences, life sciences.

**2** *the science of criminology* BRANCH OF KNOWLEDGE, body of knowledge/information, area of study, discipline, field.

**scientific** adjective **1** *scientific research* technological, technical; research-based, knowledge-based, empirical.

**2** *you need to approach it in a more scientific way* SYSTEMATIC, methodical, organized, well-organized, ordered, orderly, meticulous, rigorous; exact, precise, accurate, mathematical; analytical, rational.

**scintillating** adjective **1** *a scintillating diamond necklace* SPARKLING, shining, bright, brilliant, gleaming, glittering, twinkling, shimmering, glistening; *literary* glistering. ANTONYM dull.

**2** *a scintillating performance* BRILLIANT, dazzling, exciting, exhilarating, stimulating; sparkling, lively, buzzy, vivacious, vibrant, animated, ebullient, effervescent; witty, clever; *literary* coruscating. ANTONYMS dull, boring.

**scion** noun **1** *a scion of the tree* CUTTING, graft, slip; shoot, offshoot, twig.

**2** *the scion of an aristocratic family* DESCENDANT; heir, successor; child, offspring; *Law* issue.

**scoff** verb *they **scoffed at** her article* MOCK, deride, ridicule, sneer at, jeer at, jibe at, taunt, make fun of, poke fun at, laugh at, scorn, laugh to scorn, dismiss, make light of, belittle; *informal* pooh-pooh.

**scold** verb *Mom took Anna away, scolding her for her bad behavior* REBUKE, reprimand, reproach, reprove, admonish, remonstrate with, chastise, chide, upbraid, berate, take to task, read someone the riot act, give someone a piece of one's mind, rake/haul someone over the coals; *informal* tell off, dress down, give someone an earful, rap over the knuckles, let someone have it, bawl out, give someone hell, give someone what for, chew out, ream (out), light into; *formal* castigate. See note at REBUKE. ANTONYM praise.

▸ noun *archaic she is turning into a scold* NAG, shrew, fishwife, harpy, termagant, harridan; complainer, moaner, grumbler; *informal* kvetch.

THE RIGHT WORD **scold, berate, chide, revile, upbraid, vituperate**

A mother might **scold** a child who misbehaves, which means to rebuke in an angry, irritated, and often nagging way, whether or not such treatment is justified. **Chide** is a more formal term than *scold*, and it usually implies disapproval for specific failings (*she was chided by her teacher for using "less" instead of "fewer"*), while **berate** suggests a prolonged scolding, usually aimed at a pattern of behavior or way of life rather than a single misdeed and often combined with scorn or contempt for the person being criticized (*he berated his parents for being too protective and ruining his social life*). **Upbraid** also implies a lengthy expression of displeasure or criticism, but usually with more justification than scold and with an eye toward encouraging better behavior in the future (*the tennis coach upbraided her players for missing so many serves*). **Revile** and **vituperate** are reserved for very strong or even violent displays of anger. To *revile* is to use highly abusive and contemptuous language (*revile one's opponent in the press*), while *vituperate* connotes even more violence in the attack (*the angry hockey players were held apart by their teammates, but they continued to vituperate each other with the foulest possible language*).

**scolding** noun *I'll be in Mr. Kling's office getting my weekly scolding* REBUKE, reprimand, reproach, reproof, admonishment, remonstration, lecture, upbraiding; *informal* talking-to, rap over the knuckles, dressing-down, earful, roasting; *formal* castigation.

**scoop** noun **1** *a measuring scoop* SPOON, ladle, dipper; bailer.

**2** *a scoop of vanilla ice cream* SPOONFUL, ladleful, portion, lump, ball; *informal* dollop.

**3** *informal he got the scoop on the new CEO* EXCLUSIVE (STORY), inside story, exposé, revelation, information.

▸ verb **1** *a hole was **scooped out** in the floor* HOLLOW OUT, gouge out, dig, excavate, cut out.

**2** *cut the tomatoes in half and **scoop out** the flesh* REMOVE, take out, spoon out, scrape out.

**3** *she **scooped up** armfuls of clothes* PICK UP, gather up, lift, take up; snatch up, grab.

**scope** noun **1** *the scope of the investigation* EXTENT, range, breadth, width, reach, sweep, purview, span, horizon; area, sphere, field, realm, compass, orbit, ambit, terms/field of reference, jurisdiction; confine, limit; gamut. See note at RANGE.

2 *the scope for change is limited by political realities* OPPORTUNITY, freedom, latitude, leeway, capacity, liberty, room (to maneuver), elbow room; possibility, chance.

**scorch** verb 1 *the buildings were scorched by the fire* BURN, sear, singe, char, blacken, discolor. See note at BURN.

2 *grass scorched by the sun* DRY UP, desiccate, parch, wither, shrivel; burn, bake.

**scorching** adjective 1 *the scorching July sun* EXTREMELY HOT, red-hot, blazing, flaming, fiery, burning, blistering, searing, sweltering, torrid, broiling; *informal* boiling (hot), baking (hot), sizzling. ANTONYM freezing.

2 *scorching criticism* FIERCE, savage, scathing, withering, blistering, searing, devastating, stringent, severe, harsh, stinging, biting, mordant, trenchant, caustic, virulent, vitriolic. ANTONYM mild.

**score** noun 1 *the final score was 4–3* RESULT, outcome; total, sum total, tally, count.

2 *an IQ score of 161* RATING, grade, mark, percentage.

3 *I've got a score to settle with you* GRIEVANCE, grudge, complaint; dispute, bone of contention; (**score to settle**) bone to pick, ax to grind.

4 *informal he knew* ***the score*** *before he got here* THE SITUATION, the position, the facts, the truth of the matter, the (true) state of affairs, the picture, how things stand, the lay of the land; *informal* what's what, what the deal is/was.

5 (**scores**) *scores of complaints* A GREAT MANY, a lot, a great/good deal, large quantities, plenty; *informal* lots, umpteen, a slew, loads, masses, stacks, scads, heaps, piles, bags, tons, oodles, dozens, hundreds, thousands, millions, billions, gazillions, a bunch.

▸ verb 1 *Lou's already scored 13 goals this season* NET, bag, rack up, chalk up, tally, notch, record; get, gain, achieve, make.

2 *informal his new movie really scored* BE SUCCESSFUL, be a success, triumph, make an impression, go down well; *informal* be a hit, be a winner, be a sellout.

3 *the piece was scored for flute and violin* ORCHESTRATE, arrange, set, adapt; write, compose.

4 *score the wood in crisscross patterns* SCRATCH, cut, notch, incise, scrape, nick, chip, gouge; mark.

5 *informal he was hoping to score on his date tonight* GET LUCKY, have sex, go all the way, do it.

PHRASE: **score points off** *he's obsessed with scoring points off everyone, even his best friends* GET THE BETTER OF, gain the advantage over, outdo, best, have the edge over; have the last laugh on, make a fool of, humiliate; *informal* get/be one up on, get one over on.

**scorn** noun *he was unable to hide the scorn in his voice* CONTEMPT, derision, contemptuousness, disdain, derisiveness, mockery, sneering. ANTONYMS admiration, respect.

▸ verb 1 *critics scorned the painting* DERIDE, hold in contempt, treat with contempt, pour/heap scorn on, look down on, look down one's nose at, disdain, curl one's lip at, mock, scoff at, sneer at, jeer at, laugh at, laugh out of court; disparage, slight; dismiss, thumb one's nose at; *informal* turn one's nose up at. See note at DESPISE. ANTONYMS admire, respect.

2 *"I am a woman scorned," she thought* SPURN, rebuff, reject, ignore, shun, snub.

**scornful** adjective *his scornful remarks* CONTEMPTUOUS, derisive, withering, mocking, scoffing, sneering, jeering, scathing, snide, disparaging, supercilious, disdainful, superior; *archaic* contumelious. ANTONYMS admiring, respectful.

**scoundrel** noun *the lying scoundrel* ROGUE, rascal, miscreant, good-for-nothing, reprobate; cheat, swindler, scam artist, fraudster, trickster, charlatan; *informal* villain, bastard, beast, son of a bitch, SOB, rat, louse, swine, dog, skunk, heel, snake (in the grass), wretch, scumbag, scumbucket, scuzzball, sleazeball, sleazebag, ratfink; *informal, dated* hound; *dated* cad; *archaic* blackguard, knave, varlet, whoreson, picaroon.

**scour** verb *she scoured the oven and cleaned out the cupboards* SCRUB, rub, clean, wash, cleanse, wipe; polish, buff (up), shine, burnish; abrade.

**scourge** noun 1 *historical he was beaten with a scourge* WHIP, horsewhip, lash, strap, birch, switch, bullwhip, rawhide; *historical* cat-o'-nine-tails.

2 *inflation was the scourge of the mid-1970s* AFFLICTION, bane, curse, plague, menace, evil, misfortune, burden, cross to bear; blight, cancer, canker. ANTONYMS blessing, godsend.

▸ verb 1 *historical he was publicly scourged* FLOG, whip, beat, horsewhip, lash, flagellate, strap, birch, cane, thrash, belt, leather; *informal* tan someone's hide, take a strap to.

2 *a disease that scourged North America* AFFLICT, plague, torment, torture, curse, oppress, burden, bedevil, beset.

**scout** noun 1 *scouts reported the enemy's position* LOOKOUT, outrider, advance guard, vanguard; spy.

2 *a lengthy scout around the area* RECONNAISSANCE, reconnoiter; exploration, search, expedition; *informal* recon.

3 *a scout for a major-league team* TALENT SPOTTER, talent scout; *informal* bird dog.

▸ verb 1 *I* ***scouted around*** *for some logs* SEARCH, look, hunt, ferret about/around, root around/about.

2 *a night patrol was sent to* ***scout out*** *the area* RECONNOITER, explore, make a reconnaissance of, inspect, investigate, spy out, survey; examine, scan, study, observe; *informal* check out, case.

**scowl** noun *the scowl on his face* FROWN, glower, glare, grimace, black look; *informal* dirty look.

▸ verb *she* ***scowled at*** *him* GLOWER AT, frown at, glare at, grimace at, lower at, look daggers at, give someone a black look; make a face at, pull a face, turn the corner's of one's mouth down at, pout at; *informal* give someone a dirty look. ANTONYMS smile, grin.

**scraggy** adjective *this scraggy mutt just wandered into our yard* SCRAWNY, thin, as thin as a rake, skinny, skin-and-bones, gaunt, bony, angular, gawky, rawboned. ANTONYM fat.

**scramble** verb 1 *we scrambled over the boulders* CLAMBER, climb, crawl, claw one's way, scrabble, grope one's way, struggle, shinny.

2 *children scrambled for the scattered coins* JOSTLE, scuffle, tussle, struggle, strive, compete, contend, vie, jockey.

3 *the alcohol has scrambled his brains* MUDDLE, confuse, mix up, jumble (up), disarrange, disorganize, disorder, disturb, mess up.

▸ noun 1 *a short scramble over the rocks* CLAMBER, climb, trek.

2 *I lost Tommy in the scramble for a seat* TUSSLE, jostle, scrimmage, scuffle, struggle, free-for-all, competition, contention, vying, jockeying; muddle, confusion, melee.

**scrap**[1] noun 1 *a scrap of paper* FRAGMENT, piece, bit, snippet, shred; offcut, oddment, remnant.

2 *there wasn't a scrap of evidence* BIT, speck, iota, particle, ounce, whit, jot, atom, shred, scintilla, tittle, jot or tittle; *informal* smidgen, tad.

3 *he slept in the streets and lived on scraps* LEFTOVERS, leavings, crumbs, scrapings, remains, remnants, residue, odds and ends, bits and pieces.

4 *the whole thing was made from scrap* WASTE, rubbish, refuse, litter, debris, detritus; flotsam and jetsam, garbage, trash; *informal* junk.

▸ verb 1 *old cars due to be scrapped* THROW AWAY, throw out, dispose of, get rid of, toss out, throw on the scrap heap, discard, remove, dispense with, lose, decommission, recycle, break up, demolish; *informal* chuck, ditch, dump, junk, trash, deep-six. ANTONYMS keep, preserve.

2 *campaigners called for the plans to be scrapped* ABANDON, drop, abolish, withdraw, throw out, do away with, put an end to, cancel, ax, jettison; *informal* ditch, dump, junk, can, scrub. ANTONYMS keep, restore.

**scrap**[2] noun *informal he and Joe had several scraps* QUARREL, argument, row, fight, disagreement, difference of opinion, falling-out, blowup, dispute, squabble, contretemps, clash, altercation, brawl, tussle, conflict, shouting match; *informal* tiff, set-to, run-in, spat, ruction.

▸ verb *the older boys started scrapping with me* QUARREL, argue, row, fight, squabble, brawl, bicker, spar, wrangle, lock horns.

**scrape** verb 1 *we scraped all the paint off the windows* ABRADE, grate, sand, sandpaper, scour, scratch, rub, file, rasp.

2 *their boots scraped along the floor* GRATE, creak, rasp, grind, scratch.

3 *she scraped her hair back behind her ears* RAKE, drag, pull, tug, draw.

4 *he scraped a hole in the ground* SCOOP OUT, hollow out, dig (out), excavate, gouge out.

5 *Ellen had scraped her shins on the wall* GRAZE, scratch, abrade, scuff, rasp, skin, rub raw, cut, lacerate, bark, chafe; *Medicine* excoriate.

▸ noun 1 *the scrape of her key in the lock* GRATING, creaking, grinding, rasp, rasping, scratch, scratching.

2 *there was a long scrape on his leg* GRAZE, scratch, abrasion, cut, laceration, wound.

3 *informal he's always getting into scrapes* PREDICAMENT, plight, tight corner/spot, ticklish/tricky situation, problem, crisis, mess, muddle; *informal* jam, fix, stew, bind, hole, hot water, a pretty/fine kettle of fish.

PHRASE: **scrape by** *when the money's not there, you learn how to scrape by* MANAGE, cope, survive, muddle through/along, make ends meet, get by/along, make do, keep the wolf from the door, keep one's head above water, eke out a living; *informal* make out.

**scratch** verb 1 *the paint was scratched* SCRAPE, abrade, score, scuff.

2 *thorns scratched her skin* GRAZE, scrape, abrade, skin, rub raw, cut, lacerate, bark, chafe; wound; *Medicine* excoriate.

3 *many names had been* ***scratched out*** CROSS OUT, strike out, score out, delete, erase, remove, eliminate, expunge, obliterate.

4 *she was forced to* ***scratch from*** *the race* WITHDRAW FROM, pull out of, back out of, bow out of, stand down from.

▸ noun 1 *he had two scratches on his cheek* GRAZE, scrape, abrasion, cut, laceration, wound.

2 *a scratch on the car door* SCRAPE, mark, line, score.

PHRASE: **up to scratch** *my housekeeper's work is nearly always up to scratch* GOOD ENOUGH, up to the mark, up to standard, up to par, satisfactory, acceptable, adequate, passable, sufficient, all right; *informal* OK, jake, up to snuff.

**scrawl** verb *he scrawled his name at the bottom of the page* SCRIBBLE, write hurriedly, write untidily, dash off.

▸ noun *his writing was a scrawl* SCRIBBLE, chicken scratch, squiggle(s), hieroglyphics.

**scrawny** adjective *scrawny teenage girls addicted to dieting* SKINNY, thin, lean, as thin as a rake, skin-and-bones, gaunt, bony, angular, gawky, scraggy, rawboned, anorexic. ANTONYM fat.

**scream** verb *he screamed in pain* SHRIEK, screech, yell, howl, shout, bellow, bawl, cry out, call out, yelp, squeal, wail, squawk; *informal* holler.

▸ noun 1 *a scream of pain* SHRIEK, screech, yell, howl, shout, bellow, bawl, cry, yelp, squeal, wail, squawk; *informal* holler.

2 *informal the whole thing's a scream* LAUGH, hoot; *informal* gas, giggle, riot, laff riot, bundle of fun/laughs, blast.

3 *informal he's an absolute scream* WIT, hoot, comedian, comic, entertainer, joker, clown, character; *informal* gas, riot; *informal, dated* caution, card.

**screech** verb. See SCREAM verb.

**screen** noun 1 *he dressed hurriedly behind the screen* PARTITION, (room) divider.

2 *a computer with a 15-inch screen* DISPLAY, monitor, video display terminal, VDT, cathode-ray tube, CRT.

3 *the screen keeps out mosquitoes* MESH, net, netting.

**4** *the hedge acts as a screen against the wind* BUFFER, protection, shield, shelter, guard, windbreak.

**5** *sift the dirt through a screen* SIEVE, riddle, strainer, colander, filter.

▸ verb **1** *the end of the hall had been screened off* PARTITION, divide, separate, curtain.

**2** *the cottage was screened by the trees* CONCEAL, hide, veil; shield, shelter, shade, protect, guard, safeguard.

**3** *the prospective candidates will have to be screened* VET, check, check up on, investigate; *informal* check out.

**4** *all donated blood is screened for the virus* CHECK, test, examine, investigate.

**5** *coal used to be screened by hand* SIEVE, riddle, sift, strain, filter, winnow.

**6** *the program is screened on Thursday evenings* SHOW, broadcast, transmit, air, televise, telecast, put on the air.

**screw** noun **1** *stainless steel screws* bolt, fastener; nail, pin, tack, spike, rivet, brad.

**2** *the handle needs a couple of screws to tighten it* TURN, twist, wrench.

**3** *the ship's twin screws* PROPELLER, rotor.

▸ verb **1** *he screwed the lid back on the jar* TIGHTEN, turn, twist, wind.

**2** *the bracket was screwed in place* FASTEN, secure, fix, attach.

**3** *informal she intended to screw money out of them* EXTORT, force, extract, wrest, wring, squeeze; *informal* bleed.

**4** *informal he realized he had been screwed* CHEAT, trick, deceive, swindle, con, scam, dupe, fool; *informal* rip off, hose, gyp, bamboozle, stiff.

PHRASES: **put the screws on** *informal you don't pay up and my pal Bruno here will put the screws on you, see?* PRESSURE, put pressure on, coerce, browbeat, use strong-arm tactics on, strong-arm; hold a gun to someone's head; *informal* turn the heat on, lean on, bulldoze.

**screw up 1** *Tina screwed up her face in disgust* WRINKLE (UP), pucker, crumple, crease, furrow, contort, distort, twist, purse.

**2** *informal they'll screw up the whole economy* WRECK, ruin, destroy, wreak havoc on, damage, spoil, mar; dash, shatter, scotch, make a mess of, mess up; *informal* louse up, foul up, put the kibosh on, scupper, scuttle, do for, nix.

**scribble** verb *he scribbled a few lines on a piece of paper* SCRAWL, write hurriedly, write untidily, scratch, dash off, jot (down); doodle.

▸ noun *a page of scribble* SCRAWL, squiggle(s), jottings; doodle, doodlings.

**scribe** noun **1** *historical a medieval scribe* CLERK, secretary, copyist, transcriber, amanuensis; *historical* penman, scrivener.

**2** *informal a local scribe* WRITER, author, penman; journalist, reporter; *informal* hack, pencil pusher.

**scrimp** verb *I used to criticize my mother for the way she would scrimp* ECONOMIZE, skimp, scrimp and save, save; be thrifty, be frugal, tighten one's belt, cut back, husband one's resources, watch one's pennies, pinch (the) pennies.

**script** noun **1** *her neat, tidy script* HANDWRITING, writing, hand, penmanship, calligraphy.

**2** *the script of the play* TEXT, screenplay; libretto, score; lines, dialogue, words.

**scrounge** verb *they were always scrounging food from the tourists* BEG, borrow, cadge; *informal* sponge, bum, touch someone for, mooch.

**scrounger** noun *don't give your money to that scrounger* BEGGAR, borrower, parasite, cadger; *informal* sponger, freeloader, mooch, moocher, bum, bottom feeder, schnorrer.

**scrub**[1] verb **1** *he scrubbed the kitchen floor* SCOUR, rub; clean, cleanse, wash, wipe.

**2** *informal the plans were scrubbed.* See SCRAP[1] verb sense 2.

**scrub**[2] noun *there the buildings ended and the scrub began* BRUSH, brushwood, scrubland, underbrush, undergrowth, krummholz.

**scruffy** adjective *dressed in scruffy clothes* SHABBY, worn, down-at-heel, down-at-the-heel(s), ragged, tattered, mangy, dirty; untidy, unkempt, bedraggled, messy, disheveled, ill-groomed; *informal* tatty, raggedy-ass, the worse for wear, ratty, raggedy, scuzzy. ANTONYMS smart, tidy.

**scrumptious** adjective *informal scrumptious desserts* DELICIOUS, delectable, mouthwatering, tasty, appetizing, rich, savory, flavorful, toothsome; succulent, luscious; *informal* yummy, lip-smacking, finger-licking, melt-in-your/the-mouth, nummy. ANTONYM unpalatable.

**scruples** plural noun *he had no scruples about eavesdropping* QUALMS, compunction, pangs/twinges of conscience, hesitation, reservations, second thoughts, doubt(s), misgivings, uneasiness, reluctance. See note at QUALMS.

**scrupulous** adjective **1** *scrupulous attention to detail* CAREFUL, meticulous, painstaking, thorough, assiduous, sedulous, attentive, conscientious, punctilious, searching, close, minute, rigorous, particular, strict. ANTONYM careless.

**2** *a scrupulous man* HONEST, honorable, upright, upstanding, high-minded, right-minded, moral, ethical, good, virtuous, principled, incorruptible. ANTONYM dishonest.

**scrutinize** verb *it has become necessary for us to scrutinize the behavior of our staff toward the customers* EXAMINE, inspect, survey, study, look at, peruse; investigate, explore, probe, inquire into, go into, check; *informal* eyeball.

**scrutiny** noun *passengers can expect much more scrutiny at our terminals* EXAMINATION, inspection, survey, study, perusal; investigation, exploration, probe, inquiry; *informal* going-over.

**scuffle** noun *there was a scuffle outside the pub* FIGHT, struggle, tussle, brawl, fracas, free-for-all, scrimmage; *informal* scrap, set-to, roughhouse.

▸ verb *demonstrators scuffled with police* FIGHT, struggle, tussle, exchange blows, come to blows, brawl, clash; *informal* scrap.

**sculpture** noun *a bronze sculpture* MODEL, carving, statue, statuette, figure, figurine, effigy, bust, head, likeness.

**scum** noun **1** *the water was covered with a thick green scum* FILM, layer, covering, froth; filth, dross, dirt.

**2** *informal drug dealers are scum* DESPICABLE PEOPLE, the lowest of the low, the dregs of society, vermin, riffraff, lowlifes; *informal* the scum of the earth, dirt.

**scurrilous** adjective *such scurrilous language!* DEFAMATORY, slanderous, libelous, scandalous, insulting, offensive, gross; abusive, vituperative, malicious; *informal* bitchy.

**scurry** verb *pedestrians scurried for cover* HURRY, hasten, run, rush, dash; scamper, scuttle, scramble; *Brit.*, scutter; *informal* scoot, beetle; *dated* make haste. ANTONYM amble.

▸ noun *there was a scurry to get out* RUSH, race, dash, run, hurry; scramble, bustle.

**sea** noun **1** *the sea sparkled in the sun* OCEAN; *informal* drink, briny, salt chuck; *literary* deep, main, foam.

**2** **(seas)** *the boat overturned in the heavy seas* WAVES, swell, breakers, rollers, combers.

**3** *a sea of roofs and turrets* EXPANSE, stretch, area, tract, sweep, blanket, sheet, carpet, mass; multitude, host, profusion, abundance.

▸ adjective *sea creatures* MARINE, ocean, oceanic; saltwater, seawater; oceangoing, seagoing, seafaring; maritime, naval, nautical; *technical* pelagic.

PHRASE: **at sea** *most of her calculus lectures left me completely at sea* CONFUSED, perplexed, puzzled, baffled, mystified, bemused, bewildered, nonplussed, disconcerted, disoriented, dumbfounded, at a loss, at sixes and sevens; *informal* flummoxed, bamboozled, fazed, discombobulated; *archaic* mazed.

**seal**[1] noun **1** *the seal around the bathtub* SEALANT, sealer, adhesive, caulk, caulking.

**2** *the king put his seal on the letter* EMBLEM, symbol, insignia, device, badge, crest, coat of arms, mark, monogram, stamp.

**3** *the project cannot begin without the committee's seal* RATIFICATION, approval, seal of approval, blessing, consent, agreement, permission, sanction, endorsement, clearance.

▸ verb **1** *she quietly sealed the door behind her* FASTEN, secure, shut, close, lock, bolt.

**2** *seal each bottle while it is hot* STOP UP, seal up, make airtight/watertight, cork, stopper, plug.

**3** **(seal off)** *police sealed off the block* CLOSE OFF, shut off, cordon off, fence off, isolate.

**4** *that seals it* CLINCH, secure, settle, conclude, determine, complete, establish, set the seal on, confirm, guarantee; *informal* sew up.

**seal**[2] noun *seals were basking in the water male* BULL; *female* COW; *young* CALF, pup, whelp.

**seam** noun **1** *the seam was coming undone* JOIN, stitching; *Surgery* suture.

**2** *a seam of coal* LAYER, stratum, vein, lode.

**3** *the seams of his face* WRINKLE, line, crow's foot, furrow, crease, corrugation, crinkle, pucker, groove, ridge.

**sear** verb **1** *the heat of the blast seared his face* SCORCH, burn, singe, char. See note at BURN.

**2** *sear the meat before adding the other ingredients* FLASH-FRY, seal, brown.

**3** *his betrayal had seared her terribly* HURT, wound, pain, cut to the quick, sting; distress, grieve, upset, trouble, harrow, torment, torture.

**search** verb **1** **(search for)** *I searched for the key in my handbag* HUNT (FOR), look for, seek, forage for, fish around/about for, look high and low for, ferret around/about for, root around/about for, rummage around/about for, cast around/about for.

**2** *he searched every room in the house* LOOK THROUGH, hunt through, explore, scour, rifle through, go through, sift through, comb, go through with a fine-tooth comb; turn upside down, turn inside out, leave no stone unturned in.

**3** *the guards searched him for weapons* EXAMINE, inspect, check, frisk.

▸ noun *the police continued their search* HUNT, look, quest; pursuit, manhunt.

PHRASES: **in search of** *they say they are in search of a silver flask with the monogram "DLR"* SEARCHING FOR, hunting for, seeking, looking for, on the lookout for, in pursuit of.

**search me** *informal "Where's my toolbox?" "Search me."* I DON'T KNOW, how should I know?, it's a mystery, I haven't a clue, I haven't the least/slightest idea, I've no idea, who knows; *informal* (I) dunno, don't ask me, I haven't the faintest/foggiest (idea/notion), (it) beats me, you got me.

**searching** adjective *they asked some very searching questions* PENETRATING, piercing, probing, penetrative, keen, shrewd, sharp, intent.

**season** noun *the rainy season* PERIOD, time, time of year, spell, term.

▸ verb **1** *season the casserole to taste* FLAVOR, add flavoring to, add salt (and pepper) to, spice.

**2** *his answers were seasoned with wit* ENLIVEN, leaven, spice (up), liven up; *informal* pep up.

PHRASE: **in season** *we make gallons of sauce when the local tomatoes are in season* AVAILABLE, obtainable, to be had, on the market; plentiful, abundant.

**seasonable** adjective *the Northeast is enjoying seasonable temperatures* USUAL, expected, predictable, normal for the time of year. See note at TIMELY.

**seasoned** adjective *seasoned sportscasters* EXPERIENCED, practiced, well versed, knowledgeable, established, habituated, veteran, hardened, battle-scarred, battle-weary. ANTONYM inexperienced.

**seasoning** noun *we use a secret seasoning made from 12 herbs and spices* FLAVORING, salt (and pepper), herbs, spices, condiments.

**seat** noun **1** *a wooden seat* CHAIR, bench, stool, settle, stall; pew; (**seats**) seating.

**2** *the seat of government* HEADQUARTERS, base, center, nerve center, hub, heart; location, site, whereabouts, place.

▸ verb **1** *they seated themselves around the table* POSITION, put, place; ensconce, install, settle; *informal* plonk, park.

**2** *the hall seats 500* HAVE ROOM FOR, contain, take, sit, hold, accommodate.

**seating** noun *we have seating for 200* SEATS, room, places, chairs, accommodations.

**secede** verb *the southern states seceded from the Union, precipitating the Civil War* WITHDRAW FROM, break away from, break with, separate (oneself) from, leave, split with, split off from, disaffiliate from, resign from, pull out of; *informal* quit. ANTONYM join.

**secluded** adjective *a secluded little park* SHELTERED, private, concealed, hidden, unfrequented, sequestered, tucked away. ANTONYM busy.

**seclusion** noun *she enjoys the seclusion of her cabin* ISOLATION, solitude, retreat, privacy, retirement, withdrawal, concealment, hiding, secrecy.

**second**[1] adjective **1** *the second day of the trial* NEXT, following, subsequent, succeeding. ANTONYMS first, preceding.

**2** *he keeps a second pair of glasses in his office* ADDITIONAL, extra, alternative, another, spare, backup, fallback, alternate. ANTONYM primary.

**3** *he was demoted to the second level* SECONDARY, lower, subordinate, subsidiary, lesser, inferior. ANTONYMS first, top.

**4** *the conflict could turn into a second Vietnam* ANOTHER, new; repeat of, copy of, carbon copy of. ANTONYM original.

▸ noun **1** *Eva had been working as his second.* See SECOND-IN-COMMAND.

**2** *informal* (**seconds**) *he enjoyed the pie and asked for seconds* A SECOND HELPING, a further helping, more.

▸ verb *Hooper seconded the motion* FORMALLY SUPPORT, give one's support to, vote for, back, approve, endorse.

PHRASE: **second to none** *Lori's cheesecake is second to none* INCOMPARABLE, matchless, unrivaled, inimitable, beyond compare/comparison, unparalleled, without parallel, unequaled, without equal, in a class of its own, peerless, unsurpassed, unsurpassable, nonpareil, unique; perfect, consummate, transcendent, surpassing, superlative, supreme; *formal* unexampled.

**second**[2] noun *I'll only be gone for a second* MOMENT, bit, little while, short time, instant, split second, eyeblink, heartbeat; *informal* sec, jiffy, the blink of an eye. PHRASE: **in a second** *I can fix that lamp in a second* VERY SOON, in a minute, in a moment, in a trice, shortly, any minute (now), in the twinkling of an eye, in (less than) no time, in no time at all, momentarily; *informal* in a jiffy, in two shakes (of a lamb's tail), in the blink of an eye, in a snap; *literary* ere long.

**second**[3] verb *he was seconded to my department* ASSIGN TEMPORARILY, lend; transfer, move, shift, relocate, assign, reassign, send.

**secondary** adjective **1** *a secondary issue* LESS IMPORTANT, subordinate, lesser, minor, peripheral, incidental, ancillary, subsidiary, nonessential, inessential, of little account, unimportant. ANTONYM primary.

**2** *secondary infections* ACCOMPANYING, attendant, concomitant, consequential, resulting, resultant. ANTONYM primary.

**second-class** adjective *we were treated like second-class citizens* SECOND-RATE, second-best, inferior, lesser, unimportant.

**secondhand** adjective **1** *secondhand clothes* USED, old, worn, preowned, handed-down, hand-me-down, castoff; *informal* preloved. ANTONYM new.

**2** *secondhand information* INDIRECT, derivative; vicarious. ANTONYM direct.

▸ adverb *I ignore anything I hear secondhand* INDIRECTLY, at secondhand; *informal* on the grapevine. ANTONYM directly.

**second-in-command** noun *while Reade is recuperating, Dunlop will be my second-in-command* DEPUTY, number two, subordinate, right-hand man/woman, second; understudy; *informal* sidekick, second banana.

**secondly** adverb *in the first place you're too young, and secondly it's too dangerous* FURTHERMORE, also, moreover, likewise; second, in the second place, next; secondarily.

**second-rate** adjective *I would never buy second-rate shoes* INFERIOR, substandard, low-quality, below par, bad, poor, deficient, defective, faulty, imperfect, shoddy, chintzy, inadequate, insufficient, unacceptable; *informal* crummy, not up to scratch/snuff, rinky-dink. ANTONYMS first-rate, excellent.

**secrecy** noun **1** *the secrecy of the material* CONFIDENTIALITY, classified nature.

**2** *a government that thrives on secrecy* SECRETIVENESS, covertness, furtiveness, surreptitiousness, stealth, stealthiness.

**secret** adjective **1** *a secret plan* CONFIDENTIAL, top secret, classified, undisclosed, unknown, private, under wraps; *informal* hush-hush; *formal* sub rosa. ANTONYMS public, known.

**2** *a secret drawer in the table* HIDDEN, concealed, disguised; invisible. ANTONYM visible.

**3** *a secret operation to infiltrate terrorist groups* CLANDESTINE, covert, undercover, underground, surreptitious, stealthy, furtive, cloak-and-dagger, hole-and-corner, closet; *informal* hush-hush. ANTONYM overt.

**4** *a secret message* | *a secret code* CRYPTIC, encoded, coded; mysterious, abstruse, recondite, arcane, esoteric, Kabbalistic. ANTONYM open.

**5** *a secret place* SECLUDED, private, concealed, hidden, unfrequented, out of the way, tucked away. ANTONYMS public, known about.

**6** *a very secret person.* See SECRETIVE.

▸ noun **1** *he just can't keep a secret* CONFIDENTIAL MATTER, confidence, private affair; skeleton in the closet.

**2** *the secrets of the universe* MYSTERY, enigma, paradox, puzzle, conundrum, poser, riddle.

**3** *the secret of their success* RECIPE, (magic) formula, blueprint, key, answer, solution.

PHRASE: **in secret** *they met in secret throughout the month of July.* See SECRETLY sense 1.

THE RIGHT WORD **secret, clandestine, covert, furtive, stealthy, surreptitious, underhanded**

While all of these adjectives describe an attempt to do something without attracting attention or observation, **secret** is the most general term, implying that something is being concealed or kept from the knowledge of others (*a secret pact; a secret passageway*). **Covert** suggests that something is being done under cover, or concealed as if with a veil or disguise (*a covert attack; a covert threat*), while **clandestine** suggests that something illicit or immoral is being concealed (*a clandestine meeting between the two lovers*). Someone who is deliberately sneaking around and trying to do something without attracting notice is best described as **stealthy** (*the cat moved toward the bird with a slow, stealthy pace*), and **furtive** connotes even more slyness and watchfulness, as revealed not only by movements but by facial expressions (*a furtive glance; a furtive movement toward the door*). **Surreptitious** connotes guilt on the part of the individual who is acting in a stealthy or furtive manner (*a surreptitious attempt to hide the book before it was noticed*). **Underhanded** is the strongest of these words, implying fraud, deceit, or unfairness (*underhanded business dealings*).

**secrete** verb *a substance secreted by the prostate gland* PRODUCE, discharge, emit, excrete, release, send out. ANTONYM absorb.

**secretive** adjective *I trusted you with this because you're the most secretive person I know* UNCOMMUNICATIVE, secret, unforthcoming, playing one's cards close to one's chest, reticent, reserved, silent, noncommunicative, quiet, tight-lipped, buttoned-up, close-mouthed, taciturn. ANTONYMS open, communicative.

**secretly** adverb **1** *they met secretly for a year* IN SECRET, in private, privately, behind closed doors, in camera, behind the scenes, under cover, under the counter, behind someone's back, furtively, stealthily, on the sly, on the quiet, conspiratorially, covertly, clandestinely, on the side; *informal* on the QT, off the record, hush-hush; *formal* sub rosa.

**2** *he was secretly jealous of Bartholomew* PRIVATELY, in one's heart (of hearts), deep down.

**sect** noun *she had been duped into joining a sect of supposed do-gooders* (RELIGIOUS) CULT, religious group, denomination, persuasion, religious order; splinter group, faction.

**sectarian** adjective *a sectarian society of white supremacists* FACTIONAL, separatist, partisan, parti pris; doctrinaire, dogmatic, extreme, fanatical, rigid, inflexible, bigoted, hidebound, narrow-minded. ANTONYMS tolerant, liberal.

**section** noun **1** *the separate sections of a train* PART, piece, bit, segment, component, division, portion, element, unit, constituent. See note at FRAGMENT.

**2** *the last section of the questionnaire* SUBDIVISION, part, subsection, division, portion, bit, chapter, passage, clause.

**3** *the reference section of the library* DEPARTMENT, area, part, division.

**4** *a residential section of the city.* See SECTOR sense 2.

**sector** adjective **1** *every sector of the industry is affected* PART, branch, arm, division, area, department, field, sphere.

**2** *the northeastern sector of the town* DISTRICT, quarter, part, section, zone, region, area, belt.

**secular** adjective *secular music* NONRELIGIOUS, areligious, lay, temporal, worldly, earthly, profane; *formal* laic. ANTONYMS holy, religious.

**secure** adjective **1** *check to ensure that all bolts are secure* FASTENED, fixed, secured, done up; closed, shut, locked. ANTONYM loose.

**2** *an environment in which children can feel secure* SAFE, protected from harm/danger, out of danger, sheltered, safe and sound, out of harm's way, in a safe place, in safe hands, invulnerable; at ease, unworried, relaxed, happy, confident. ANTONYM vulnerable.

**3** *a secure investment* CERTAIN, assured, reliable, dependable, settled, fixed. ANTONYM uncertain.

▸ verb **1** *pins secure the handle to the main body* FIX, attach, fasten, affix, connect, couple.

**2** *the doors had not been properly secured* FASTEN, close, shut, lock, bolt, chain, seal.

**3** *he leapt out to secure the boat* TIE UP, moor, make fast; anchor.

**4** *they sought to secure the country against attack* PROTECT, make safe, fortify, strengthen; undergird.

**5** *a written constitution would secure the rights of the individual* ASSURE, ensure, guarantee, protect, confirm, establish.

**6** *the division secured a major contract* OBTAIN, acquire, gain, get, get possession of; *informal* get hold of, land. See note at GET.

**security** noun **1** *the security of the nation's citizens* SAFETY, freedom from danger, protection, invulnerability. ANTONYMS vulnerability, danger.

**2** *he could give her the security she needed* PEACE OF MIND, feeling of safety, stability, certainty, happiness, confidence. ANTONYM disquiet.

**3** *security at the court was tight* SAFETY MEASURES, safeguards, surveillance, defense, protection.

**4** *additional security for your loan may be required* GUARANTEE, collateral, surety, pledge, bond.

**sedate**[1] verb *the patient had to be sedated* TRANQUILIZE, put under sedation, drug.

**sedate**[2] adjective **1** *a sedate pace* SLOW, steady, dignified, unhurried, relaxed, measured, leisurely, slow-moving, easy, easygoing, gentle. ANTONYM fast.

**2** *he had lived a sedate life* CALM, placid, tranquil, quiet, uneventful; boring, dull. ANTONYM exciting.

**sedative** adjective *sedative drugs* TRANQUILIZING, calming, calmative, relaxing, soporific, narcotic; depressant; *Medicine* neuroleptic.

▸ noun *the doctor gave him a sedative* TRANQUILIZER, calmative, sleeping pill, narcotic, opiate; depressant; *informal* trank, downer.

**sedentary** adjective *a sedentary job* SITTING, seated, deskbound, stationary; inactive, lethargic, lazy, idle. ANTONYM active.

**sediment** noun *the sediment in the coffee pot* DREGS, lees, precipitate, deposit, grounds; residue, remains; silt, alluvium; *technical* residuum.

**sedition** noun *the on-campus protestors were charged with sedition* RABBLE-ROUSING, incitement to rebel, subversion, troublemaking, provocation; rebellion, insurrection, mutiny, insurgence, civil disorder.

**seditious** adjective *a seditious speech* RABBLE-ROUSING, provocative, inflammatory, subversive, troublemaking; rebellious, insurrectionist, mutinous, insurgent.

**seduce** verb **1** *he took her to his hotel room and tried to seduce her* PERSUADE TO HAVE SEX; *euphemistic* have one's way with, take advantage of; *dated* debauch.

**2** *she was seduced by the smell of coffee* ATTRACT, allure, lure, tempt, entice, beguile, inveigle, maneuver. See note at TEMPT.

**seductive** adjective *a seductive red dress* SEXY, alluring, tempting, irresistible, exciting, provocative, sultry, slinky; coquettish, flirtatious; *informal* vampish, come-hither.

**see** verb **1** *he saw her running across the road* DISCERN, spot, notice, catch sight of, glimpse, catch/get a glimpse of, make out, pick out, spy, distinguish, detect, perceive, note; *informal* lay/set eyes on; *literary* behold, descry, espy.

**2** *I saw a documentary about it last week* WATCH, look at, view; catch.

**3** *would you like to see the house?* INSPECT, view, look round, tour, survey, examine, scrutinize; *informal* give something a/the once-over.

**4** *I finally saw what she meant* UNDERSTAND, grasp, comprehend, follow, take in, realize, appreciate, recognize, work out, get the drift of, perceive, fathom; *informal* get, latch on to, cotton on to, catch on to, savvy, figure out, get a fix on.

**5** *I must go and see what Victor is up to* FIND OUT, discover, learn, ascertain, determine, establish.

**6** *see that no harm comes to him* ENSURE, make sure/certain, see to it, take care, mind.

**7** *I see trouble ahead* FORESEE, predict, forecast, prophesy, anticipate, envisage, picture, visualize.

**8** *about a year later, I saw him in town* ENCOUNTER, meet, run into/across, come across, stumble on/across, happen on, chance on; *informal* bump into.

**9** *they see each other from time to time* MEET, meet up with, get together with, socialize with.

**10** *you'd better see a doctor* CONSULT, confer with, talk to, speak to, have recourse to, call on, call in, turn to, ask.

**11** *he's seeing someone else now* GO OUT WITH, date, take out, be involved with; *informal* go steady with; *dated* court.

**12** *he saw her to her car* ESCORT, accompany, show, walk, conduct, lead, take, usher, attend. PHRASES: **see through 1** *they can see through your dirty little plan* UNDERSTAND, get/have the measure of, read like a book; *informal* be wise to; have someone's number (about).

**2** *Marlon saw us through these long, hard months* SUSTAIN, encourage, buoy up, keep going, support, be a tower of strength to, comfort, help (out), stand by, stick by.

**3** *I'm tired of this campaign, but I promised I would see it through* PERSEVERE WITH, persist with, continue (with), carry on with, keep at, follow through, stay with; *informal* stick to, stick it out, hang in there (with/for).

**see to** *I'll see to the dogs as soon as we finish lunch* ATTEND TO, deal with, see about, take care of, look after, sort out, fix, organize, arrange.

**seed** noun **1** *apple seeds* pip, stone, kernel; ovule.

**2** *each war contains within it the seeds of a fresh war* GENESIS, source, origin, root, starting point, germ, beginnings, potential (for); cause, reason, motivation, motive, grounds.

**3** *Abraham and his seed* DESCENDANTS, heirs, successors, scions; offspring, children, sons and daughters, progeny, family; *Law* issue; *derogatory* spawn; *archaic* fruit of someone's loins. PHRASE: **go/run to seed** *in just two years, this hotel has really gone to seed* DETERIORATE, degenerate, decline, decay, fall into decay, go to rack and ruin, go downhill, molder, rot; *informal* go to pot, go to the dogs, go down the toilet.

**seedy** adjective **1** *the seedy world of prostitution* SORDID, disreputable, seamy, sleazy, squalid, unwholesome, unsavory. ANTONYM high-class.

**2** *a seedy roadside diner* DILAPIDATED, tumbledown, ramshackle, falling to pieces, decrepit, gone to rack and ruin, rundown, down-at-heel, down-at-the-heel(s), shabby, dingy, slummy, insalubrious, squalid; *informal* crummy; scuzzy. ANTONYM classy.

**seek** verb **1** *they sought shelter from the winter snows* SEARCH FOR, try to find, look for, be on the lookout for, be after, hunt for, be in quest of.

**2** *the company is seeking a judicial review of the decision* TRY TO OBTAIN, work toward, be intent on, aim at/for.

**3** *he sought help from the police* ASK FOR, request, solicit, call for, entreat, beg for, petition for, appeal for, apply for, put in for.

**4** *we constantly seek to improve the service* TRY, attempt, endeavor, strive, work, do one's best; *formal* essay.

**seem** verb *they seem friendly* APPEAR (TO BE), have the appearance/air of being, give the impression of being, look, look as though one is, show signs of being, look to be; come across as, strike someone as, sound.

**seeming** adjective *his seeming gentility* APPARENT, ostensible, supposed, outward, surface, superficial; pretended, feigned. See note at OSTENSIBLE. ANTONYMS actual, genuine.

**seemly** adjective *we expect more seemly behavior at our dinner table* DECOROUS, proper, decent, becoming, fitting, suitable, appropriate, apt, apposite, in good taste, genteel, polite, the done thing, right, correct, acceptable, comme il faut. ANTONYMS unseemly, unbecoming.

**seep** verb *a brown substance is seeping into the basement* OOZE, trickle, exude, drip, dribble, flow, issue, escape, leak, drain, bleed, filter, percolate, soak.

**seer** noun *the woeful predictions of an ancient seer* SOOTHSAYER, oracle, prophet(ess), augur, prognosticator, diviner, visionary, fortune teller, crystal-gazer, clairvoyant, psychic, medium; *literary* sibyl.

**seesaw** verb *interest rates continue to seesaw* FLUCTUATE, swing, go up and down, rise and fall, oscillate, alternate, yo-yo, vary.

▸ noun *the seesaws on the playground* TEETER-TOTTER.

**seethe** verb **1** *the brew seethed* BOIL, bubble, simmer, foam, froth, fizz, effervesce.

**2** *the water was seething with fish* TEEM, swarm, boil, swirl, churn, surge.

**3** *I seethed at the injustice of it all* BE ANGRY, be furious, be enraged, be incensed, be beside oneself, boil, simmer, rage, rant, rave, storm, fume, smolder; *informal* be livid, be wild, foam at the mouth, be steamed up, be hot under the collar.

**segment** noun **1** *orange segments* PIECE, bit, section, part, chunk, portion, division, slice; fragment, wedge, lump. See note at FRAGMENT.

**2** *all segments of society* PART, section, sector, division, portion, constituent, element, unit, compartment; branch, wing.

▸ verb *they plan to segment their market share* DIVIDE (UP), subdivide, separate, split, cut up, carve up, slice up, break up; segregate, divorce, partition, section. ANTONYM amalgamate.

**segregate** verb *routes that will segregate passenger cars from tractor trailers* SEPARATE, set apart, keep apart, isolate, quarantine, closet; partition, divide, detach, disconnect, sever, dissociate; marginalize, ghettoize. ANTONYM amalgamate.

**seize** verb **1** *she seized the microphone* GRAB, grasp, snatch, take hold of, get one's hands on; grip, clutch; nab. ANTONYM let go of.

**2** *rebels seized the air base* CAPTURE, take, overrun, occupy, conquer, take over. ANTONYMS relinquish, liberate.

**3** *the drugs were seized by customs* CONFISCATE, impound, commandeer, requisition, appropriate, expropriate, take away; *Law* distrain. ANTONYM release.

**4** *terrorists seized his wife* KIDNAP, abduct, take captive, take prisoner, take hostage, hold for ransom; *informal* snatch. ANTONYMS ransom, release.

PHRASE: **seize on** *they seized on the opportunity* TAKE ADVANTAGE OF, exploit, grasp with both hands, leap at, jump at, pounce on.

**seizure** noun **1** *Napoleon's seizure of Spain* CAPTURE, takeover, annexation, invasion, occupation, colonization.

**2** *the seizure of property* CONFISCATION, appropriation, expropriation, sequestration; *Law* distraint.

**3** *the seizure of UN staff by rebels* KIDNAPPING, kidnap, abduction.

**4** *the baby suffered a seizure* CONVULSION, fit, spasm, paroxysm; *Medicine* ictus; *dated* apoplexy.

**seldom** adverb *we seldom use the dining room* RARELY, infrequently, hardly (ever), scarcely (ever), almost never; now and then, occasionally, sporadically; *informal* once in a blue moon. ANTONYM often.

**select** verb *select the correct tool for the job* CHOOSE, pick (out), single out, sort out, take; opt for, decide on, settle on, determine, nominate, appoint, elect.

▸ adjective **1** *a select group of players* CHOICE, hand-picked, prime, first-rate, first-class, superior, finest, best, top-class, blue-ribbon, supreme, superb, excellent; *informal* A1, top-notch. ANTONYM inferior.

**2** *a select clientele* EXCLUSIVE, elite, favored, privileged; wealthy; *informal* posh. ANTONYM common.

**selection** noun **1** *Jim made his selection of toys* CHOICE, pick; option, preference.

**2** *a wide selection of dishes* RANGE, array, diversity, variety, assortment, mixture.

**3** *a selection of his poems* ANTHOLOGY, assortment, collection, assemblage, compilation; miscellany, medley, potpourri.

**selective** adjective *he's very selective about his coffee* DISCERNING, discriminating, discriminatory, critical, exacting, demanding, particular; fussy, fastidious; *informal* choosy, persnickety, picky, finicky.

**self-assurance** noun *you need to build up your self-assurance* SELF-CONFIDENCE, confidence, assertiveness, self-reliance, composure, self-possession, presence of mind, aplomb. ANTONYM diffidence.

**self-centered** adjective *he's too self-centered to care what his children do* EGOCENTRIC, egotistic, egotistical, egomaniacal, self-absorbed, self-obsessed, self-seeking, self-interested, self-serving; narcissistic, vain; inconsiderate, thoughtless; *informal* looking after number one.

**self-confidence** noun *they told Tom he lacked the self-confidence to make it as a singer* MORALE, confidence, self-assurance, assurance, assertiveness, self-reliance, self-possession, composure.

**self-conscious** adjective *he gave me a self-conscious grin* EMBARRASSED, uncomfortable, uneasy, nervous; unnatural, inhibited, gauche, awkward; modest, shy, diffident, bashful, retiring, shrinking. ANTONYM confident.

**self-control** noun *I had more self-control when I was younger* SELF-DISCIPLINE, restraint, self-possession, willpower, composure, coolness; moderation, temperance, abstemiousness; *informal* cool.

**self-denial** noun *it took years of hard work and self-denial* SELF-SACRIFICE, selflessness, unselfishness; self-discipline, asceticism, self-deprivation, abstemiousness, abstinence, abstention; moderation, temperance. ANTONYM self-indulgence.

**self-esteem** noun *the best thing I ever did for my self-esteem was to divorce Roger* SELF-RESPECT, pride, dignity, self-regard, faith in oneself; morale, self-confidence, confidence, self-assurance. See note at PRIDE.

**self-important** adjective *why, you self-important little toad!* CONCEITED, arrogant, bumptious, full of oneself, puffed up, pompous, overbearing, opinionated, cocky, presumptuous, sententious, vain, overweening, proud, egotistical; *informal* snooty, uppity, uppish; *literary* Pooterish. ANTONYM humble.

**selfish** adjective *he is just selfish by nature* EGOCENTRIC, egotistic, egotistical, egomaniacal, self-centered, self-absorbed, self-obsessed, self-seeking, self-serving, wrapped up in oneself; inconsiderate, thoughtless, unthinking, uncaring, uncharitable; mean, miserly, grasping, greedy, mercenary, acquisitive, opportunistic; *informal* looking after number one. ANTONYM altruistic.

**selfless** adjective *it was very selfless of you to help out your ex-husband like that* UNSELFISH, altruistic, self-sacrificing, self-denying; considerate, compassionate, kind, noble, generous, magnanimous, ungrudging, charitable, benevolent, open-handed. ANTONYM inconsiderate.

**self-possessed** adjective *I'm usually pretty self-possessed during an interview* ASSURED, self-assured, calm, cool, composed, at ease, unperturbed, unruffled, confident, self-confident, poised, imperturbable; *informal* together, unfazed, nonplussed, unflappable. ANTONYM unsure.

**self-respect** noun *if you had any self-respect, you wouldn't be wasting your life in front of the television* SELF-ESTEEM, self-regard, amour propre, faith in oneself, pride, dignity, morale, self-confidence.

**self-righteous** adjective *we listened to Mom because she wasn't as self-righteous as you* SANCTIMONIOUS, holier-than-thou, self-satisfied, smug, priggish, complacent, pious, moralizing, preachy, superior, hypocritical; *informal* goody-goody. ANTONYM humble.

**self-sacrifice** noun *the self-sacrifice of these young men and women is indeed admirable* SELF-DENIAL, selflessness, unselfishness; self-discipline, abstinence, asceticism, abnegation, self-deprivation, moderation, austerity, temperance, abstention.

**self-satisfied** adjective *she's such a self-satisfied Miss Perfect* COMPLACENT, self-congratulatory, smug, superior, puffed up, pleased with oneself; *informal* goody-goody.

**self-seeking** adjective *the self-seeking players would get humbled fast by Coach Higgins* SELF-INTERESTED, self-serving, selfish; egocentric, egotistic, egotistical, self-obsessed, self-absorbed; inconsiderate, thoughtless, unthinking; *informal* looking after number one. ANTONYM altruistic.

**self-styled** adjective *a self-styled poet* WOULD-BE, so-called, self-appointed, self-titled, professed, self-confessed, soi-disant.

**self-willed** adjective *how can you reason with a self-willed teenager?* WILLFUL, contrary, perverse, uncooperative, wayward, headstrong, stubborn, obstinate, obdurate, pigheaded, mulish, intransigent, recalcitrant, intractable; *formal* refractory. ANTONYM biddable.

**sell** verb **1** *they are selling their house* PUT UP FOR SALE, offer for sale, put on sale, dispose of, vend, auction (off); trade, barter. See note at BUY. ANTONYM buy.

**2** *he sells cakes* TRADE IN, deal in, traffic in, stock, carry, offer for sale, peddle, hawk, retail, market.

**3** *the book should sell well* GO, be bought, be purchased; move, be in demand.

**4** *it **sells for** $79.95* COST, be priced at, retail at, go for, be.

**5** *he still has to sell his plan to management* PROMOTE; persuade someone to accept, talk someone into, bring someone around to, win someone over to, win approval for. PHRASES:
**sell down the river** *informal* *my own friends sold me down the river* BETRAY, inform on; be disloyal to, be unfaithful to, double-cross, break faith with, stab in the back, sell out; *informal* tell on, blow the whistle on, squeal on, finger.
**sell out 1** *we **have sold out** of chocolate* HAVE NONE LEFT, be out of stock, have run out; *informal* be fresh out, be cleaned out.

**2** *the edition sold out quickly* BE BOUGHT UP, be depleted, be exhausted.

**3** *they say he has sold out as an artist* ABANDON ONE'S PRINCIPLES, prostitute oneself, sell one's soul, betray one's ideals, be untrue to oneself; debase oneself, degrade oneself, demean oneself.

**4** *he never thought his own brother would sell him out.* See SELL DOWN THE RIVER.
**sell short** *she is always selling herself short* UNDERVALUE, underrate, underestimate, disparage, deprecate, belittle; *formal* derogate.

**seller** noun *the seller does not seem to know the real values of his antiques* VENDOR, retailer, purveyor, supplier, trader, merchant, dealer; shopkeeper, salesperson, salesman, saleswoman, sales assistant, sales associate, clerk, shop assistant, traveling salesperson, peddler, hawker; auctioneer.

**semblance** noun *there remained at least a semblance of discipline* (OUTWARD) APPEARANCE, air, show, facade, front, veneer, guise, pretense.

**send** verb **1** *they sent a message to HQ* DISPATCH, post, mail, address, consign, direct, forward; transmit, convey, communicate; telephone, phone, broadcast, radio, fax, e-mail; *dated* telegraph, wire, cable. ANTONYM receive.

**2** *we* ***sent for*** *a doctor* CALL FOR, summon, contact; ask for, request, order.

**3** *the pump* ***sent out*** *a jet of steam* PROPEL, project, eject, deliver, discharge, spout, fire, shoot, release; throw, let fly; *informal* chuck.

**senile** adjective *she's in her nineties, but she's not a bit senile* DODDERING, doddery, decrepit, senescent, declining, infirm, feeble; aged, long in the tooth, in one's dotage; mentally confused, having Alzheimer's (disease), having senile dementia; *informal* past it, gaga.

**senior** adjective **1** *the senior students can get parking permits* OLDER, elder. ANTONYM junior.

**2** *a senior officer* SUPERIOR, higher-ranking, high-ranking, more important; top, chief, ranking. ANTONYMS junior, subordinate.

**3** *Albert Stone, Senior* SR., the Elder, I. ANTONYMS Junior, Jr.

▸ noun **1** *Angela is a senior at Cal Tech | the seniors are sponsoring a concert* senior student, fourth-year student; **(seniors)** graduating class.

**2** *the quilts are made by a group of seniors at our church.* SENIOR CITIZEN.

**sensation** noun **1** *a sensation of light* FEELING, sense, awareness, consciousness, perception, impression.

**2** *he caused a sensation by donating a million dollars* COMMOTION, stir, uproar, furor, scandal, impact; interest, excitement; *informal* splash, to-do, hullabaloo, hoopla.

**3** *the movie became an instant sensation* TRIUMPH, success, sellout; talking point; *informal* smash (hit), hit, winner, crowd-pleaser, knockout, blockbuster.

**sensational** adjective **1** *a sensational murder trial* SHOCKING, scandalous, appalling; amazing, startling, astonishing, staggering; stirring, exciting, thrilling, electrifying, red-hot; fascinating, interesting, noteworthy, significant, remarkable, momentous, historic, newsworthy. ANTONYM run-of-the-mill.

**2** *sensational stories* OVERDRAMATIZED, dramatic, melodramatic, exaggerated, sensationalist, sensationalistic; graphic, explicit, lurid; *informal* juicy. ANTONYMS dull, understated.

**3** *informal she looked sensational* GORGEOUS, stunning, wonderful, exquisite, lovely, radiant, delightful, charming, enchanting, captivating; striking, spectacular, remarkable, outstanding, arresting, eye-catching; marvelous, superb, excellent, fine, first-class; *informal* great, terrific, tremendous, super, fantastic, fabulous, fab, heavenly, divine, knockout, hot, red-hot, delectable, scrumptious, awesome, magic, wicked, killer, out of this world, smashing, brilliant. ANTONYM unremarkable.

**sense** noun **1** *the sense of touch* SENSORY FACULTY, feeling, sensation, perception; sight, hearing, touch, taste, smell.

**2** *a sense of guilt* FEELING, awareness, sensation, consciousness, recognition.

**3** *a sense of humor* APPRECIATION, awareness, understanding, comprehension, discernment; *informal* nose.

**4** *she had the sense to press the panic button* WISDOM, common sense, sagacity, discernment, perception; wit, intelligence, cleverness, shrewdness, judgment, reason, logic, brain(s); *informal* gumption, horse sense, savvy, (street) smarts. ANTONYM stupidity.

**5** *I can't see the sense in this* PURPOSE, point, reason, object, motive; use, value, advantage, benefit.

**6** *the different senses of "well"* MEANING, definition, import, signification, significance, purport, implication, nuance; drift, gist, thrust, tenor, message.

▸ verb *she sensed their hostility* DISCERN, feel, observe, notice, recognize, pick up (on), be aware of, distinguish, make out, identify; comprehend, apprehend, see, appreciate, realize; suspect, have a funny feeling about, have a hunch about, divine, intuit; *informal* catch on to.

**senseless** adjective **1** *they found him senseless on the floor* UNCONSCIOUS, stunned, insensible, insensate, comatose, knocked out, out cold, out for the count; numb; *informal* KO'd, dead to the world, passed out. ANTONYM conscious.

**2** *a senseless waste* POINTLESS, futile, useless, needless, unavailing, in vain, purposeless, meaningless, unprofitable; absurd, foolish, insane, stupid, idiotic, ridiculous, ludicrous, mindless, illogical. ANTONYM wise.

**sensibility** noun **1** *develop your sensibility* SENSITIVITY, finer feelings, delicacy, taste, discrimination, discernment; understanding, insight, empathy, appreciation; feeling, intuition, responsiveness, receptiveness, perceptiveness, awareness.

**2** **(sensibilities)** *the wording might offend their sensibilities* (FINER) FEELINGS, emotions, sensitivities, moral sense.

**sensible** adjective *isn't this the sensible thing to do? | a sensible young man* PRACTICAL, realistic, responsible, reasonable, commonsensical, rational, logical, sound, balanced, grounded, sober, no-nonsense, pragmatic, levelheaded, thoughtful, down-to-earth, wise, prudent, judicious, sagacious, shrewd. See note at TANGIBLE. ANTONYM foolish.

**THE RIGHT WORD sensible, lucid, rational, sagacious, sane**

A **sensible** person brings an umbrella when rain is forecast. A **rational** one studies the weather map, observes the movement of the clouds across the sky, listens to the forecast on the radio, and then decides whether or not an umbrella is necessary. *Sensible* implies the use of common sense and an appreciation of the value of experience (*a sensible decision not to travel until his injuries had healed*), while *rational* suggests the ability to reason logically and to draw conclusions from inferences (*a rational explanation for why she failed the exam*). **Lucid** and **sane**, like *rational*, are associated with coherent thinking. *Lucid* suggests a mind free of internal pressures or distortions (*lucid intervals during which he was able to recognize his wife and children*), while *sane* indicates freedom from psychosis or mental derangement (*judged to have been sane when she committed the crime*). *Sane* also has a meaning very close to that of *sensible* (*a sane approach to disciplining problem teenagers*). A **sagacious** person is an extremely shrewd one who is both discerning and practical. He or she can look out the window and tell whether it's going to rain by studying the facial expressions of passersby as they glance nervously at the sky.

---

**sensitive** adjective **1** *she's **sensitive to** changes in temperature* RESPONSIVE TO, reactive to, sentient of, sensitized to; aware of, conscious of, alive to; susceptible to, affected by, vulnerable to; attuned to. ANTONYMS impervious, unresponsive.

**2** *sensitive skin* DELICATE, fragile; tender, sore, raw. ANTONYMS resilient, tough.

**3** *the matter needs sensitive handling* TACTFUL, careful, thoughtful, diplomatic, delicate, subtle, kid-glove; sympathetic, compassionate, understanding, intuitive, responsive, insightful. ANTONYM clumsy.

**4** *he's sensitive about his bald patch* TOUCHY, oversensitive, hypersensitive, easily offended, easily upset, easily hurt, thin-skinned, defensive; paranoid, neurotic; *informal* uptight. ANTONYM thick-skinned.

**5** *a sensitive issue* DIFFICULT, delicate, tricky, awkward, problematic, ticklish, precarious; controversial, emotive; *informal* sticky. ANTONYM uncontroversial.

**sensitivity** noun **1** *the sensitivity of the skin* RESPONSIVENESS, sensitiveness, reactivity; susceptibility, vulnerability.

**2** *the job calls for sensitivity* CONSIDERATION, care, thoughtfulness, tact, diplomacy, delicacy, subtlety, finer feelings; understanding, empathy, sensibility, feeling, intuition, responsiveness, receptiveness; perception, discernment, insight; savoir faire.

**3** *her sensitivity on the subject of marriage* TOUCHINESS, oversensitivity, hypersensitivity, defensiveness.

**4** *the sensitivity of the issue* DELICACY, trickiness, awkwardness, ticklishness.

**sensual** adjective **1** *sensual pleasure* PHYSICAL, carnal, bodily, fleshly, animal; hedonistic, epicurean, sybaritic, voluptuary. See note at SENSUOUS. ANTONYM spiritual.

**2** *a beautiful, sensual woman* SEXUALLY ATTRACTIVE, sexy, voluptuous, sultry, seductive, passionate; sexually arousing, erotic, sexual. ANTONYM passionless.

**sensuous** adjective **1** *they lived amid sensuous surroundings* AESTHETICALLY PLEASING, gratifying, rich, sumptuous, luxurious; sensory, sensorial.

**2** *sensuous lips* SEXUALLY ATTRACTIVE, sexy, seductive, voluptuous, luscious, lush.

THE RIGHT WORD **sensuous, epicurean, luxurious, sensual, sybaritic, voluptuous**

---

**Sensuous** and **sensual** are often confused. *Sensuous* implies gratification of the senses for the sake of aesthetic pleasure, or delight in the color, sound, or form of something (*a dress made from a soft, sensuous fabric*), while *sensual* implies indulgence of the appetites or gratification of the senses as an end in itself (*he leads a life of sensual excess*). **Luxurious** implies indulgence in sensuous or sensual pleasures, especially those that induce a feeling of physical comfort or satisfaction (*a luxurious satin coverlet*), while **epicurean** refers to taking delight in the pleasures of eating and drinking (*the epicurean life of a king and his courtiers*). To be **voluptuous** is to give oneself up to the pleasures of the senses (*the symphony is voluptuous in its scoring*), but it carries a suggestion of sensual rather than sensuous enjoyment and can refer to a curvaceous and sexually attractive woman (*he was seen with a voluptuous blonde*). **Sybaritic** implies an overrefined luxuriousness, also suggesting indulgence in good food and drink and the presence of things designed to soothe and charm the senses (*he lived alone, in sybaritic splendor*).

---

**sentence** noun *the judge shortened his sentence to nine months* PRISON TERM, prison sentence; punishment; *informal* time, stretch, stint.

▸ verb *they were sentenced to death* PASS JUDGMENT ON, punish, convict; condemn, doom.

**sententious** adjective *your new churchy friends have certainly made you sententious* MORALISTIC, moralizing, sanctimonious, self-righteous, pietistic, pious, priggish, judgmental; pompous, pontifical, self-important; *informal* preachy.

**sentiment** noun **1** *the comments echo my own sentiments* VIEW, feeling, attitude, thought, opinion, belief. See note at OPINION.

**2** *there's no room for sentiment in this sport* SENTIMENTALITY, sentimentalism, mawkishness, emotionalism; emotion, sensibility, soft-heartedness, tenderheartedness; *informal* schmaltz, mush, slushiness, corniness, soppiness, sappiness. See note at EMOTION.

**sentimental** adjective **1** *she kept the vase for sentimental reasons* NOSTALGIC, tender, emotional, affectionate. ANTONYMS practical, dispassionate.

**2** *the film is too sentimental* MAWKISH, overemotional, cloying, sickly, saccharine, sugary, oversweet; romantic, touching; *informal* slushy, mushy, weepy, tear-jerking, schmaltzy, lovey-dovey, gooey, drippy, cheesy, corny, cornball, sappy, hokey. ANTONYMS realistic, gritty.

**3** *she is sentimental about animals* SOFTHEARTED, tenderhearted, soft.

THE RIGHT WORD **sentimental, effusive, maudlin, mawkish, mushy, romantic**

---

If you are moved to tears by a situation that does not really warrant such a response, you're likely to be called **sentimental**, an adjective used to describe a willingness to get emotional at the slightest prompting (*a sentimental man who kept his dog's ashes in an urn on the mantel*). **Effusive** applies to excessive or insincere displays of emotion, although it may be used in an approving sense (*effusive in her gratitude for the help she had received*). **Maudlin** derives from the name Mary Magdalene, who was often shown with her eyes swollen from weeping. It implies a lack of self-restraint, particularly in the form of excessive tearfulness. **Mawkish** carries sentimentality a step further, implying emotion so excessive that it provokes loathing or disgust (*mawkish attempts to win the audience over*). Although **ro-**

**mantic** at one time referred to an expression of deep feeling, nowadays it is often used disapprovingly to describe emotion that has little to do with the way things actually are and that is linked to an idealized vision of the way they should be (*she had a romantic notion of what it meant to be a "starving artist"*). **Mushy** suggests both excessive emotion or sentimentality and a contempt for romantic love (*a mushy love story*).

---

**sentry** noun *the sentry on the tower signaled to the gatekeeper* GUARD, sentinel, lookout, watch, watchman, patrol.

**separate** adjective **1** *his personal life was separate from his job* UNCONNECTED, unrelated, different, distinct, discrete; detached, divorced, disconnected, independent, autonomous. ANTONYMS linked, interdependent.

**2** *the infirmary was separate from the school* SET APART, detached, fenced off, cut off, segregated, isolated; free-standing, self-contained. ANTONYM attached.

▸ verb **1** *they separated two rioting mobs* SPLIT (UP), break up, part, pull apart, divide; *literary* sunder. ANTONYMS unite, bring together.

**2** *the connectors can be separated* DISCONNECT, detach, disengage, uncouple, unyoke, disunite, disjoin; split, divide, sever; disentangle. ANTONYMS join, connect, combine.

**3** *the wall that separates the two properties* PARTITION, divide, come between, keep apart; bisect, intersect. ANTONYMS link, bridge.

**4** *the south aisle was* ***separated off*** ISOLATE, partition off, section off; close off, shut off, cordon off, fence off, screen off.

**5** *they separated at the airport* PART (COMPANY), go their separate ways, split up; say goodbye; disperse, disband, scatter. ANTONYM meet.

**6** *the road separated* FORK, divide, branch, bifurcate, diverge. ANTONYMS merge, converge.

**7** *her parents separated* SPLIT UP, break up, part, be estranged, divorce. ANTONYMS get together, marry.

**8** *separate fact from fiction* ISOLATE, set apart, segregate; distinguish, differentiate, dissociate; sort out, sift out, filter out, remove, weed out.

**9** *those who* ***separate themselves from*** *society* BREAK AWAY FROM, break with, secede from, withdraw from, leave, quit, dissociate oneself from, resign from, drop out of, repudiate, reject. ANTONYM join.

**separately** adverb *I'll have to interview you all separately* INDIVIDUALLY, one by one, one at a time, singly, severally; apart, independently, alone, by oneself, on one's own.

**separation** noun **1** *the separation of the two companies* DISCONNECTION, detachment, severance, dissociation, disunion, disaffiliation, segregation, partition.

**2** *her parents' separation* BREAKUP, split, parting (of the ways), estrangement, rift, rupture, breach; divorce.

**3** *the separation between art and life* DISTINCTION, difference, differentiation, division, dividing line; gulf, gap, chasm.

**septic** adjective *a septic finger* INFECTED, festering, suppurating, pus-filled, putrid, putrefying, poisoned, diseased; *Medicine* purulent.

**sequel** noun **1** *the film inspired a sequel* FOLLOW-UP, continuation.

**2** *the immediate sequel to the coup was an armed uprising* CONSEQUENCE, result, upshot, outcome, development, issue, postscript; effect, aftereffect, aftermath, by-product; *informal* payoff.

**sequence** noun **1** *the sequence of events* SUCCESSION, order, course, series, chain, train, string, progression, chronology, timeline; pattern, flow; *formal* concatenation.

**2** *a sequence from his film* EXCERPT, clip, extract, episode, section.

**sequester** verb **1** *he sequestered himself from the world* ISOLATE ONESELF, hide away, shut oneself away, seclude oneself, cut oneself off, segregate oneself; closet oneself, cloister oneself, withdraw, retire.

**2** *the government sequestered his property* CONFISCATE, seize, sequestrate, take, appropriate, expropriate, impound, commandeer.

**seraphic** adjective *a look of seraphic contentment on his face* BLISSFUL, beatific, sublime, rapturous, ecstatic, joyful, rapt; serene, ethereal; cherubic, saintly, angelic.

**serendipity** noun *the consequence of serendipity is sometimes a brilliant discovery* (HAPPY) CHANCE, (happy) accident, fluke; luck, good luck, good fortune, fortuity, providence; happy coincidence.

**serene** adjective **1** *on the surface she seemed serene* CALM, composed, tranquil, peaceful, untroubled, relaxed, at ease, unperturbed, unruffled, unworried; placid, equable, centered; *informal* together, unflappable. See note at CALM. ANTONYM agitated.

**2** *serene valleys* PEACEFUL, tranquil, quiet, still, restful, relaxing, undisturbed. ANTONYM turbulent.

**series** noun **1** *a series of lectures* SUCCESSION, sequence, string, chain, run, round; spate, wave, rash; set, course, cycle; row, line; *formal* concatenation.

**2** *a new TV series* SERIAL, program, show, drama; soap opera; *informal* soap, sitcom, miniseries.

**serious** adjective **1** *a serious expression* SOLEMN, earnest, grave, somber, sober, unsmiling, poker-faced, stern, grim, dour, humorless, stony-faced; thoughtful, preoccupied, pensive. ANTONYMS lighthearted, cheerful.

**2** *serious decisions* IMPORTANT, significant, consequential, momentous, weighty, far-reaching, major, grave; urgent, pressing, crucial, critical, vital, life-and-death, high-priority. ANTONYMS unimportant, trivial.

**3** *give serious consideration to this* CAREFUL, detailed, in-depth, deep, profound, meaningful. ANTONYM superficial.

**4** *a serious play* INTELLECTUAL, highbrow, heavyweight, deep, profound, literary, learned, scholarly; *informal* heavy. ANTONYMS lowbrow, light.

**5** *serious injuries* SEVERE, grave, bad, critical, acute, terrible, dire, dangerous, perilous, parlous; *formal* grievous. ANTONYMS minor, negligible.

**6** *we're serious about equality* IN EARNEST, earnest, sincere, wholehearted, genuine; committed, resolute, determined. ANTONYM halfhearted.

**seriously** adverb **1** *Faye nodded seriously* SOLEMNLY, earnestly, gravely, soberly, somberly, sternly, grimly, dourly, humorlessly; pensively, thoughtfully.

**2** *she was seriously injured* SEVERELY, gravely, badly, critically, acutely, dangerously; *formal* grievously.

**3** *do you seriously expect me to come?* REALLY, actually, honestly.

**4** *seriously, I'm very pleased* JOKING ASIDE, to be serious, honestly, truthfully, truly, I mean it; *informal* scout's honor.

**5** *informal "I've resigned." "Seriously?"* REALLY?, is that so?, is that a fact?, you're joking, well I never, go on, you don't say; *informal* you're kidding.

**6** *informal he was seriously rich.* See EXTREMELY.

**sermon** noun **1** *he preached a sermon* HOMILY, address, speech, talk, discourse, oration; lesson.

**2** *her mother gave her a sermon on personal hygiene* LECTURE, tirade, harangue, diatribe; speech, disquisition, monologue; reprimand, reproach, reproof, admonishment, admonition, remonstration, criticism; *informal* talking-to, dressing-down, earful; *formal* castigation.

**serrated** adjective *the serrated edge of the knife* JAGGED, sawtoothed, sawtooth, zigzag, notched, indented, toothed; *Botany* serrate; *technical* crenulated. ANTONYM smooth.

**servant** noun **1** *servants were cleaning the hall* ATTENDANT, retainer; domestic (worker), (hired) help, cleaner; lackey, flunky, minion; maid, housemaid, footman, page (boy), valet, butler, manservant; housekeeper, steward; drudge, menial, slave, water boy; *archaic* scullion.

**2** *a servant of the people* HELPER, supporter, follower.

**serve** verb **1** *they served their masters faithfully* WORK FOR, be in the service of, be employed by; obey.

**2** *this job serves the community* BE OF SERVICE TO, be of use to, help, assist, aid, make a contribution to, do one's bit for, do something for, benefit.

**3** *she **served on** the committee for years* BE A MEMBER OF, work on, be on, sit on, have a place on.

**4** *he served his apprenticeship in Washington* CARRY OUT, perform, do, fulfill, complete, discharge; spend.

**5** *serve the soup hot* DISH UP/OUT, give out, distribute; present, provide, supply.

**6** *she served another customer* ATTEND TO, deal with, see to; ASSIST, help, look after.

**7** *they **served** him **with** a writ* PRESENT WITH, deliver to, give (to), hand over to.

**8** *a plate **serving as** an ashtray* ACT AS, function as, do the work of, be a substitute for.

**9** *these three sizes of brush will serve for most paint jobs* SUFFICE, be adequate, be good enough, fit/fill the bill, do, answer, be useful, meet requirements, suit.

**service** noun **1** *your conditions of service* WORK, employment, employ, labor.

**2** *he has done us a service* FAVOR, kindness, good turn, helping hand; **(services)** ASSISTANCE, help, aid, offices, ministrations.

**3** *the food and service were excellent* WAITING, waitressing, serving, attendance.

**4** *products that give reliable service* USE, usage; functioning.

**5** *the service on the Chevy cost $80* tune-up, maintenance check, servicing, overhaul.

**6** *a marriage service* CEREMONY, ritual, rite, observance; liturgy, sacrament; *formal* ordinance.

**7** *a range of local services* AMENITY, facility, resource, utility.

**8** *soldiers leaving the service* ARMED FORCES, armed services, military; army, navy, air force, marines, coast guard.

▸ verb *the appliances are serviced regularly* check, go over, maintain, overhaul; repair, mend, recondition.

PHRASES: **be of service** *can I be of service to you?* HELP, assist, benefit, be of assistance, be beneficial, serve, be useful, be of use, be valuable; do someone a good turn.

**out of service** *the candy machine is out of service* OUT OF ORDER, broken, broken-down, out of commission, unserviceable, faulty, defective, inoperative, in disrepair; down; *informal* conked out, bust, kaput, on the blink, on the fritz, acting up, shot.

**serviceable** adjective **1** *a serviceable heating system* IN WORKING ORDER, working, functioning, functional, operational, operative; usable, workable, viable. ANTONYM unusable.

**2** *serviceable lace-up shoes* FUNCTIONAL, utilitarian, sensible, practical; HARDWEARING, durable, tough, robust. ANTONYM impractical.

**servile** adjective *here comes Mr. Archer and his servile assistant, Bradley* OBSEQUIOUS, sycophantic, deferential, subservient, fawning, ingratiating, unctuous, groveling, toadyish, slavish, humble, self-abasing; *informal* slimy, bootlicking, smarmy, sucky. See note at OBSEQUIOUS. ANTONYM assertive.

**serving** noun *you should have at least four servings of vegetables* PORTION, helping, plateful, plate, bowlful; amount, quantity, ration.

**servitude** noun *born into a life of servitude* SLAVERY, enslavement, bondage, subjugation, subjection, domination; *historical* serfdom. ANTONYM liberty.

**session** noun **1** *a special session of the committee* MEETING, sitting, *Law* assize, assembly, conclave, plenary; hearing; conference, discussion, forum, symposium, caucus.

**2** *training sessions* PERIOD, time, spell, stretch, bout.

**3** *the next session on campus begins in August* ACADEMIC YEAR, school year; term, semester.

**set**[1] verb **1** *Beth set the bag on the table* PUT (DOWN), place, lay, deposit, position, settle, leave, stand, plant, posit; *informal* stick, dump, park, plunk.

**2** *the cottage is set on a hill* BE SITUATED, be located, lie, stand, be sited, be perched.

**3** *the fence is set in concrete* FIX, embed, insert; mount.

**4** *a ring set with precious stones* ADORN, ornament, decorate, embellish; *literary* bejewel.

**5** *I'll go and set the table* LAY, prepare, arrange.

**6** *we set them some easy tasks* ASSIGN, allocate, give, allot, prescribe.

**7** *just set your mind to it* APPLY, address, direct, aim, turn, focus, concentrate.

**8** *they set a date for the election* DECIDE ON, select, choose, arrange, schedule; fix (on), settle on, determine, designate, name, appoint, specify, stipulate.

**9** *he set his horse toward her* DIRECT, steer, orient, orientate, point, aim, train.

**10** *his jump set a national record* ESTABLISH, create, institute.

**11** *he set his watch* ADJUST, regulate, synchronize; calibrate; put right, correct; program, activate, turn on.

**12** *the adhesive will set in an hour* SOLIDIFY, harden, stiffen, thicken, jell, cake, congeal, coagulate, clot; freeze, crystallize. ANTONYM melt.

**13** *the sun was setting* GO DOWN, sink, dip; vanish, disappear. ANTONYM rise.

PHRASES: **set about** *Mike set about raising $5,000* BEGIN, start, commence, go about, get to work on, get down to, embark on, tackle, address oneself to, undertake.

**set against** *you deliberately set me against my family* ALIENATE FROM, estrange from, set at odds; drive a wedge between (one and another), sow dissension between (one and another).

**set apart 1** *the orchestral background sets this song apart from the rest* DISTINGUISH, differentiate, mark out, single out, separate, demarcate.

**2** *one pew was set apart from the rest* ISOLATE, separate, segregate, put to one side.

**set aside 1** *set aside some money each month* SAVE, put by, put aside, put away, lay by, keep, reserve; store, stockpile, hoard, stow away, cache, withhold; *informal* salt away, squirrel away, stash away.

**2** *he set aside his cup* PUT DOWN, cast aside, discard, abandon, dispense with.

**3** *set aside your differences* DISREGARD, put aside, ignore, forget, discount, shrug off, bury.

**4** *the Supreme Court set aside the decision* OVERRULE, overturn, reverse, revoke, countermand, nullify, annul, cancel, quash, dismiss, reject, repudiate; *Law* disaffirm; *formal* abrogate.

**set back** *the rains have set back the work on the bridge* DELAY, hold up, hold back, slow down/up, retard, check, decelerate; hinder, impede, hobble, obstruct, hamper, inhibit, frustrate, thwart.

**set down 1** *he set down his thoughts* WRITE DOWN, put in writing, jot down, note down, make a note of; record, register, log.

**2** *we set down some rules* FORMULATE, draw up, establish, frame; lay down, determine, fix, stipulate, specify, prescribe, impose, ordain.

**3** *I set it down to the fact that he was drunk* ATTRIBUTE, put down, ascribe, assign, chalk up; blame on, impute.

**set forth** *you have set forth a very credible argument* PRESENT, describe, set out, detail, delineate, explain, expound; state, declare, announce; submit, offer, put forward, advance, propose, propound.

**set free** *the hostages were released just minutes ago* RELEASE, free, let go, turn loose, let out, liberate, deliver, emancipate.

**set in** *bad weather set in* BEGIN, start, arrive, come, develop.

**set off 1** *they set off for America with nothing but the clothes on their backs* SET OUT, start out, sally forth, leave, depart, embark, set sail; *informal* hit the road.

**2** *the bomb was set off* DETONATE, explode, blow up, touch off, trigger; ignite.

**3** *it set off a wave of protest* GIVE RISE TO, cause, lead to, set in motion, occasion, bring about, initiate, precipitate, prompt, trigger (off), spark (off), touch off, provoke, incite.

**4** *the blue dress set off her auburn hair* ENHANCE, bring out, emphasize, show off, throw into relief; complement.

**set on/upon** *the relentless Cossacks set upon village after village* ATTACK, assail, assault, hit, strike, beat, thrash, pummel, wallop, set about, fall on; *informal* lay into, lace into, let someone have it, work over, rough up, knock about/around, have a go at, beat up on, light into.

**set one's heart on** *I think she's set her heart on the orange kitten* WANT DESPERATELY, wish for, desire, long for, yearn for, hanker after, ache for, hunger for, thirst for, burn for; *informal* be itching for, be dying for.

**set out 1** *he set out early.* See SET OFF sense 1.

**2** *the gifts were set out on tables* ARRANGE, lay out, put out, array, dispose, display, exhibit.

**3** *they set out some guidelines* PRESENT, set forth, detail; state, declare, announce; submit, put forward, advance, propose, propound.

**4** *you've done what you set out to do* AIM, intend, mean, seek; hope, aspire, want.

**set up 1** *his father set him up in business* ESTABLISH, finance, fund, back, subsidize.

**2** *informal she set him up for Newley's murder* FALSELY INCRIMINATE, frame, entrap.

**3** *a monument to her memory was set up* ERECT, put up, construct, build, raise, elevate.

**4** *she set up her own business* ESTABLISH, start, begin, initiate, institute, found, create.

**5** *set up a meeting* ARRANGE, organize, fix (up), schedule, timetable, line up.

**6** *set up a committee* ESTABLISH, form.

**set**[2] noun **1** *a set of color postcards* GROUP, collection, series;

assortment, selection, compendium, batch, number; arrangement, array.

2 *the literary set* CLIQUE, coterie, circle, crowd, group, crew, band, company, ring, camp, fraternity, school, faction, league; *informal* gang, bunch.

3 *a chemistry set* KIT, apparatus, equipment, outfit.

4 *a set of china* SERVICE.

5 *the set of his shoulders* POSTURE, position, cast, attitude; bearing, carriage.

6 *a set for the play* SCENERY, setting, backdrop, flats; mise en scène.

7 *the band played two sets* SESSION, time; stretch, bout, round.

**set**[3] adjective 1 *a set routine* FIXED, established, predetermined, hard and fast, prearranged, prescribed, specified, defined; unvarying, unchanging, invariable, unvaried, rigid, inflexible, cast-iron, strict, ironclad, settled, predictable; routine, standard, customary, regular, usual, habitual, accustomed, wonted. ANTONYMS variable, changing.

2 *she had set ideas* INFLEXIBLE, rigid, fixed, firm, deep-rooted, deep-seated, ingrained, entrenched. ANTONYM flexible.

3 *he had a set speech for such occasions* STOCK, standard, routine, rehearsed, well-worn, formulaic, conventional. ANTONYMS original, fresh.

4 *I was all set for the evening* READY, prepared, organized, equipped, primed; *informal* geared up, psyched up. ANTONYM unprepared.

5 *he's **set on** marrying her* DETERMINED TO, intent on, bent on, hell-bent on, resolute about, insistent about. ANTONYM uncertain.

6 *you were dead **set against** the idea* OPPOSED TO, averse to, hostile to, resistant to, antipathetic to, unsympathetic to; *informal* anti.

**setback** noun *this is a team famous for surmounting every setback that fate sends their way* PROBLEM, difficulty, hitch, complication, upset, disappointment, misfortune, mishap, reversal; blow, stumbling block, hurdle, hindrance, impediment, obstruction; delay, holdup; *informal* glitch, hiccup. ANTONYM breakthrough.

**setting** noun 1 *a rural setting* SURROUNDINGS, position, situation, environment, background, backdrop, milieu, environs, habitat; spot, place, location, locale, site, scene; area, region, district.

2 *a garnet in a gold setting* MOUNT, fixture, surround.

**settle** verb 1 *they settled the dispute* RESOLVE, sort out, solve, clear up, end, fix, work out, iron out, straighten out, set right, rectify, remedy, reconcile; *informal* patch up. ANTONYM prolong.

2 *she settled their affairs* PUT IN ORDER, sort out, tidy up, arrange, organize, order, clear up.

3 *they **settled on** a date for the wedding* DECIDE ON, set, fix, agree on, name, establish, arrange, appoint, designate, assign; choose, select, pick.

4 *she went down to the lobby to settle her bill* PAY, settle up, square, clear, defray.

5 *they **settled for** a 4.2% raise* ACCEPT, agree to, assent to; *formal* accede to.

6 *he **settled in** Otsego County* MAKE ONE'S HOME IN, set up home in, take up residence in, put down roots in, establish oneself in; live in, move to, emigrate to.

7 *immigrants settled much of Australia* COLONIZE, occupy, inhabit, people, populate.

8 *Catherine **settled down to** her work* APPLY ONESELF TO, get down to, set about, attack; concentrate on, focus on, devote oneself to.

9 *the class wouldn't **settle down*** CALM DOWN, quiet down, be quiet, be still; *informal* shut up.

10 *a brandy will settle your nerves* CALM, quiet; *Brit.* quieten, soothe, pacify, quell; sedate, tranquilize. ANTONYMS agitate, disturb.

11 *he settled into an armchair* SIT DOWN, seat oneself, install oneself, ensconce oneself, plant oneself; *informal* park oneself, plunk oneself.

12 *a butterfly settled on the flower* LAND, come to rest, alight, descend, perch; *archaic* light.

13 *when the stirring stops, the sediment settles* SINK, subside, fall, gravitate. ANTONYM rise.

**settlement** noun 1 *a pay settlement* AGREEMENT, deal, arrangement, resolution, bargain, understanding, pact.

2 *the settlement of the dispute* RESOLUTION, settling, solution, reconciliation.

3 *a frontier settlement* COMMUNITY, colony, outpost, encampment, post; village, commune; *historical* plantation, clearing.

4 *the settlement of the area* COLONIZATION, settling, populating; *historical* plantation.

5 *the settlement of their debts* PAYMENT, discharge, liquidation, clearance.

**settler** noun *the settlers were ill-prepared for the severe winter ahead* COLONIST, colonizer, frontiersman, frontierswoman, pioneer, bushwhacker; immigrant, newcomer; *historical* homesteader. ANTONYM native.

**set-up** noun 1 *a complicated setup* SYSTEM, structure, organization, arrangement, framework, layout, configuration.

2 *a setup called Film International* ORGANIZATION, group, body, agency, association, operation; company, firm; *informal* outfit.

3 *informal the whole thing was a setup* TRICK, trap; conspiracy; *informal* put-up job, frame-up.

**sever** verb 1 *the head was severed from the body* CUT OFF, chop off, detach, disconnect, dissever, separate, part; amputate; *literary* sunder. ANTONYMS join, attach.

2 *a knife had severed the artery* CUT (THROUGH), rupture, split, pierce.

3 *they severed diplomatic relations* BREAK OFF, discontinue,

suspend, end, terminate, cease, dissolve. ANTONYMS establish, maintain.

**several** adjective **1** *several people* SOME, a number of, a few; various, assorted, sundry, diverse; *literary* divers.

**2** *they sorted out their several responsibilities* RESPECTIVE, individual, own, particular, specific; separate, different, disparate, distinct; various.

**severe** adjective **1** *severe injuries* ACUTE, very bad, serious, grave, critical, dreadful, terrible, awful; dangerous, parlous, life-threatening; *formal* grievous. ANTONYMS minor, negligible.

**2** *severe storms* FIERCE, violent, strong, powerful, intense; tempestuous, turbulent. ANTONYM gentle.

**3** *a severe winter* HARSH, bitter, cold, bleak, freezing, icy, arctic, extreme; *informal* brutal. ANTONYM mild.

**4** *a severe headache* EXCRUCIATING, agonizing, intense, dreadful, awful, terrible, unbearable, intolerable; *informal* splitting, pounding, screaming. ANTONYM slight.

**5** *a severe test of their stamina* DIFFICULT, demanding, tough, arduous, formidable, exacting, rigorous, punishing, onerous, grueling. ANTONYMS easy, simple.

**6** *severe criticism* HARSH, scathing, sharp, strong, fierce, savage, scorching, devastating, trenchant, caustic, biting, withering. ANTONYM mild.

**7** *severe tax penalties* EXTORTIONATE, excessive, unreasonable, inordinate, outrageous, sky-high, harsh, stiff; punitive.

**8** *they received severe treatment* HARSH, stern, hard, inflexible, uncompromising, unrelenting, merciless, pitiless, ruthless, draconian, oppressive, repressive, punitive; brutal, cruel, savage. ANTONYMS lenient, lax.

**9** *his severe expression* STERN, dour, grim, forbidding, disapproving, unsmiling, unfriendly, somber, grave, serious, stony, steely; cold, frosty. ANTONYMS friendly, genial.

**10** *a severe style of architecture* PLAIN, simple, austere, unadorned, unembellished, unornamented, stark, spartan, ascetic; clinical, uncluttered. ANTONYMS fancy, ornate.

THE RIGHT WORD **severe, ascetic, austere, stern, strict, unmitigated**

A storm, a hairdo, and a punishment may all be described as **severe**, which means harsh or uncompromising, without a hint of softness, mildness, levity, or indulgence. **Austere**, on the other hand, primarily applies to people, their habits, their way of life, and the environments they create; it implies coldness, stark simplicity, and restraint (*an austere room with only a table and chair*). **Ascetic** implies extreme self-denial and self-discipline, in some cases to the point of choosing what is painful or disagreeable (*he had an ascetic approach to life and rejected all creature comforts*). **Strict** literally means bound or stretched tight; in extended use, it means strenuously exact (*a strict curfew; strict obedience*). **Stern** combines harshness and authority with strictness or severity (*a stern judge*). **Unmitigated** means unmodified and unsoftened in any way (*a streak of unmitigated bad luck*).

**severely** adjective **1** *he was severely injured* BADLY, seriously, critically; fatally; *formal* grievously.

**2** *she was severely criticized* SHARPLY, roundly, soundly, fiercely, savagely.

**3** *murderers should be treated more severely* HARSHLY, strictly, sternly, rigorously, mercilessly, pitilessly, roughly, sharply; with a rod of iron; brutally, cruelly, savagely.

**4** *she looked severely at Harriet* STERNLY, grimly, dourly, disapprovingly; coldly, frostily.

**5** *she dressed severely in black* PLAINLY, simply, austerely, starkly.

**sew** verb *she sewed the seams of the tunic* STITCH, tack, baste, seam, hem; embroider. PHRASE: **sew up 1** *the tear was sewn up* DARN, mend, repair, patch.

**2** *informal the company sewed up a deal with IBM* SECURE, clinch, pull off, bring off, settle, conclude, complete, finalize, tie up; *informal* swing.

**sex** noun **1** *they talked about sex* SEXUAL INTERCOURSE, intercourse, lovemaking, making love, sex act, (sexual) relations; mating, copulation; *informal* nooky, whoopee, bonking, boinking, boffing, a roll in the hay, quickie; *formal* fornication; *technical* coitus, coition; *dated* carnal knowledge.

**2** *teach your children about sex* THE FACTS OF LIFE, reproduction; *informal* the birds and the bees.

**3** *adults of both sexes* GENDER.

PHRASE: **have sex with** *she had no interest in having sex with Richie* HAVE SEXUAL INTERCOURSE WITH, make love to/with, sleep with, go to bed with; mate with, copulate with; seduce; rape; *informal* do it with, go all the way with, know in the biblical sense; bonk, boink, boff, get it on with; *euphemistic* be intimate with; *literary* ravish; *formal* fornicate with.

**sexuality** noun **1** *she had a powerful sexuality* SENSUALITY, sexiness, seductiveness, desirability, eroticism, physicality; sexual appetite, passion, desire, lust.

**2** *I'm open about my sexuality* SEXUAL ORIENTATION, sexual preference, leaning, persuasion; heterosexuality, homosexuality, lesbianism, bisexuality.

**sexy** adjective **1** *he's so sexy* SEXUALLY ATTRACTIVE, seductive, desirable, alluring, toothsome, sensual, sultry, slinky, provocative, tempting, tantalizing; nubile, voluptuous, luscious, lush, hot, beddable, foxy, cute; *informal* bootylicious.

**2** *sexy videos* EROTIC, sexually explicit, arousing, exciting, stimulating, hot, titillating, racy, naughty, risqué, adult, X-rated; rude, pornographic, crude, lewd; *informal* raunchy, steamy, porno, blue, skin, XXX.

**3** *they weren't feeling sexy* (SEXUALLY) AROUSED, sexually excited, amorous, lustful, passionate; *informal* horny, hot, turned on, sexed up.

**4** *informal a sexy sales promotion* EXCITING, stimulating, interesting, appealing, intriguing, slick, red-hot.

**shabby** adjective **1** *a shabby little bar* RUN-DOWN, down-at-heel, down-at-the-heel(s), scruffy, dilapidated, ramshackle, tumbledown; seedy, slummy, insalubrious, squalid, sordid, flea-bitten; *informal* crummy, scuzzy, raggedy-ass. ANTONYMS smart, upmarket.

**2** *a shabby gray coat* SCRUFFY, old, worn out, threadbare, ragged, frayed, tattered, battered, faded, moth-eaten, mangy; *informal* tatty, ratty, the worse for wear, raggedy. ANTONYM new.

**3** *her shabby treatment of Bill* CONTEMPTIBLE, despicable, dishonorable, discreditable, mean, low, dirty, hateful, shameful, sorry, ignoble, unfair, unworthy, unkind, shoddy, nasty; *informal* rotten, lowdown; beastly. ANTONYMS decent, honorable.

**shackle** verb **1** *he was shackled to the wall* CHAIN, fetter, manacle; secure, tie (up), bind, tether, hobble; put in chains, clap in irons, handcuff.

**2** *journalists were shackled by a new law* RESTRAIN, restrict, limit, constrain, handicap, hamstring, hamper, hinder, impede, obstruct, inhibit, check, curb.

**shackles** plural noun **1** *shackles of iron* CHAINS, fetters, irons, leg irons, manacles, handcuffs; bonds; *informal* cuffs, bracelets.

**2** *the shackles of bureaucracy* RESTRICTIONS, restraints, constraints, impediments, hindrances, obstacles, barriers, obstructions, checks, curbs; *literary* trammels.

**shade** noun **1** *they sat in the shade* SHADOW(S), shadiness, shelter, cover; cool. ANTONYMS light, glare.

**2** *shades of blue* COLOR, hue, tone, tint, tinge.

**3** *shades of meaning* NUANCE, gradation, degree, difference, variation, variety; nicety, subtlety; undertone, overtone.

**4** *her skirt was* ***a shade*** *too short* A LITTLE, a bit, a trace, a touch, a modicum, a tinge; slightly, rather, somewhat; *informal* a tad, a smidgen, a titch, a tinch, a hair.

**5** *the window shade* BLIND, curtain, screen, cover, covering; awning, canopy.

**6** *informal* **(shades)** *he was wearing shades* SUNGLASSES, dark glasses; *proprietary* Polaroids, Raybans.

▸ verb **1** *vines shaded the garden* CAST A SHADOW OVER, shadow, shelter, cover, screen; darken.

**2** *she* ***shaded in*** *the picture* DARKEN, color in, pencil in, block in, fill in; cross-hatch.

**3** *the sky shaded from turquoise to blue* CHANGE, transmute, turn, go; merge, blend, graduate.

PHRASES: **put in the shade** *Candi's clarinet solo puts mine in the shade* SURPASS, outshine, outclass, overshadow, eclipse, transcend, cap, top, outstrip, outdo, put to shame, beat, outperform, upstage; *informal* run rings around, be a cut above. **shades of** *this weekend has been perfectly romantic—you know, shades of our honeymoon* ECHOES OF, a reminder of, memories of, suggestions of, hints of.

**shadow** noun **1** *he saw her shadow in the doorway* SILHOUETTE, outline, shape, contour, profile.

**2** **(shadows)** *he emerged from the shadows* SHADE, darkness, twilight; gloom, murkiness.

**3** *the shadow of war* BLACK CLOUD, cloud, pall; gloom, blight; threat.

**4** *she knew without any shadow of doubt* TRACE, scrap, shred, crumb, iota, scintilla, jot, whit, grain; *informal* smidgen, smidge, tad.

**5** *a shadow of a smile* TRACE, hint, suggestion, suspicion, ghost, glimmer.

**6** *he's a shadow of his former self* INFERIOR VERSION, poor imitation, apology, travesty; remnant.

**7** *the dog became her shadow* CONSTANT COMPANION, alter ego, second self; close friend, bosom friend; *informal* Siamese twin, bosom buddy.

▸ verb **1** *the market is shadowed by the church* OVERSHADOW, shade; darken, dim.

**2** *he is shadowing a poacher* FOLLOW, trail, track, stalk, pursue, hunt; *informal* tail, keep tabs on.

**shadowy** adjective **1** *a shadowy corridor* DARK, dim, gloomy, murky, crepuscular, shady, shaded; *literary* tenebrous. ANTONYM bright.

**2** *a shadowy figure* INDISTINCT, hazy, indefinite, vague, nebulous, ill-defined, faint, blurred, blurry, unclear, indistinguishable, unrecognizable; ghostly, spectral, wraithlike. ANTONYM clear.

**shady** adjective **1** *a shady garden* SHADED, shadowy, dim, dark; sheltered, screened, shrouded; leafy; *literary* bosky, tenebrous. ANTONYMS bright, sunlit.

**2** *informal shady deals* SUSPICIOUS, suspect, questionable, dubious, doubtful, disreputable, untrustworthy, dishonest, devious, dishonorable, underhanded, unscrupulous, irregular, unethical; *informal* fishy, murky. ANTONYMS reputable, honest.

**shaft** noun **1** *the shaft of a golf club* POLE, shank, stick, rod, staff; handle, hilt, stem.

**2** *the shaft of a feather* QUILL; *Ornithology* rachis.

**3** *shafts of sunlight* RAY, beam, gleam, streak, finger.

**4** *a ventilation shaft* mineshaft, tunnel, passage, pit, adit, downcast, upcast; borehole, bore; duct, well, flue, vent.

▸ verb *I think we've just been shafted* DECEIVE, delude, trick, hoodwink, mislead, take in, dupe, fool, double-cross, cheat, defraud, swindle, fleece, catch out, gull, hoax, bamboozle, con, diddle, rook, put one over on, pull a fast one on, pull the wool over someone's eyes, take for a ride, shanghai, flimflam, sucker, snooker.

**shaggy** adjective *his shaggy beard* HAIRY, bushy, thick, woolly; tangled, tousled, unkempt, disheveled, untidy, matted; *formal* hirsute. ANTONYM sleek.

**shake** verb **1** *the whole building shook* VIBRATE, tremble, quiver, quake, shiver, shudder, jiggle, wobble, rock, sway; convulse.

**2** *she shook the bottle* JIGGLE, joggle, agitate.

**3** *he shook his stick at them* BRANDISH, wave, flourish, swing, wield.

**4** *the look in his eyes really shook her* UPSET, distress, disturb, unsettle, disconcert, discompose, disquiet, unnerve, trouble, throw off balance, agitate, fluster; shock, alarm, frighten, scare, worry; *informal* rattle. ANTONYM soothe.

**5** *this will shake their confidence* WEAKEN, undermine, damage, impair, harm; reduce, diminish, decrease. ANTONYM strengthen.

▸ noun **1** *he gave his coat a shake* JIGGLE, joggle.

**2** *a shake of his fist* FLOURISH, brandish, wave.

**3 (shakes)** *it gives me the shakes* TREMORS, delirium tremens; *informal* DTs, jitters, the creeps, the shivers, willies, heebie-jeebies, the jim-jams.

PHRASES: **in two shakes (of a lamb's tail)** *informal I'll be there in two shakes.* See IN A MOMENT at MOMENT.

**no great shakes** *informal that movie was no great shakes* NOT VERY GOOD, unexceptional, unmemorable, forgettable, uninspired, uninteresting, indifferent, unimpressive, lackluster; *informal* nothing to write home about, nothing special.

**shake a leg** *informal c'mon, Ruthie, shake a leg.* See HURRY verb sense 1.

**shake off 1** *I think we shook off that cop* GET AWAY FROM, escape, elude, dodge, lose, leave behind, get rid of, give someone the slip, throw off the scent.

**2** *she can't seem to shake off this virus* RECOVER FROM, get over; get rid of, free oneself from.

**shake up 1** *the accident shook him up.* See SHAKE verb sense 4.

**2** *plans to shake up the legal profession* REORGANIZE, restructure, revolutionize, alter, change, transform, reform, overhaul.

THE RIGHT WORD **shake, quake, quiver, shiver, shudder, tremble**

Does a cool breeze make you **shiver**, **quiver**, **shudder**, or **tremble**? All of these verbs describe vibrating, wavering, or oscillating movements that, in living creatures, are often involuntary expressions of strain or discomfort. **Shake**, which refers to abrupt forward-and-backward, side-to-side, or up-and-down movements, is different from the others in that it can be done to a person or object as well as by one (*shake a can of paint; shake visibly while lifting a heavy load*). *Tremble* applies specifically to the slight and rapid shaking motion the human body makes when it is nervous, frightened, or uneasy (*his hands trembled when he picked up the phone*). To *shiver* is to make a similar movement with the entire body, but the cause is usually cold or fear (*shiver in the draft from an open door*). *Quiver* suggests a rapid and almost imperceptible vibration resulting from disturbed or irregular surface tension; it refers more often to things (*the leaves quivered in the breeze*), although people may quiver when they're under emotional tension (*her lower lip quivered and her eyes were downcast*). *Shudder* suggests a more intense shaking, usually in response to something horrible or revolting (*shudder at the thought of eating uncooked meat*). **Quake** implies a violent upheaval or shaking, similar to what occurs during an earthquake (*the boy's heart quaked at his father's approach*).

**shaky** adjective **1** *shaky legs* TREMBLING, shaking, tremulous, quivering, quivery, unsteady, wobbly, weak; tottering, tottery, teetering, doddery; *informal* trembly. ANTONYM steady.

**2** *I feel a bit shaky* FAINT, dizzy, lightheaded, giddy; weak, wobbly, quivery, groggy, muzzy; *informal* trembly, woozy.

**3** *a shaky table* UNSTEADY, unstable, wobbly, precarious, rocky, rickety, ramshackle. ANTONYM stable.

**4** *the evidence is shaky* UNRELIABLE, untrustworthy, questionable, dubious, doubtful, tenuous, suspect, flimsy, weak, unsound, unsupported, unsubstantiated, unfounded; *informal* iffy. ANTONYM sound.

**shallow** adjective *a shallow analysis of contemporary society* SUPERFICIAL, facile, simplistic, oversimplified; flimsy, insubstantial, lightweight, empty, trivial, trifling; surface, skin-deep, two-dimensional; frivolous, foolish, silly, Mickey Mouse. See note at SUPERFICIAL. ANTONYM profound.

**sham** noun **1** *his tenderness had been a sham* PRETENSE, fake, act, fiction, simulation, fraud, feint, lie, counterfeit; humbug.

**2** *the doctor was a sham* CHARLATAN, fake, fraud, impostor, pretender; quack, mountebank; *informal* phony.

▸ adjective *sham togetherness* FAKE, pretended, feigned, simulated, false, artificial, bogus, insincere, contrived, affected, make-believe, fictitious; imitation, mock, counterfeit, fraudulent; *informal* pretend, put-on, phony, pseudo. ANTONYM genuine.

**shamble** verb *I hear Mr. Billings shambling down the hall* SHUFFLE, drag one's feet, lumber, totter, dodder; hobble, limp.

**shambles** plural noun **1** *we have to sort out this shambles* CHAOS, mess, muddle, confusion, disorder, havoc, mare's nest, dog's breakfast.

**2** *the room was a shambles* MESS, pigsty; *informal* disaster area.

**shame** noun **1** *her face was scarlet with shame* HUMILIATION, mortification, chagrin, ignominy, embarrassment, indignity, discomfort. ANTONYM pride.

**2** *I felt shame at telling a lie* GUILT, remorse, contrition, compunction. ANTONYM indifference.

**3** *he brought shame on the family* DISGRACE, dishonor, discredit, degradation, ignominy, disrepute, infamy, scandal, opprobrium, contempt; *dated* disesteem. ANTONYMS glory, honor.

**4** *it's a shame she never married* PITY, misfortune, sad thing; bad luck; *informal* bummer, crime, sin, crying shame.

▸ verb **1** *you shamed your family's name* DISGRACE, dishonor, discredit, degrade, debase; stigmatize, taint, sully, tarnish, besmirch, blacken, drag through the mud. ANTONYM honor.

**2** *he was shamed in public* HUMILIATE, mortify, chagrin, embarrass, abash, chasten, humble, take down a peg or two, cut down to size; *informal* show up, make someone eat crow.

PHRASE: **put to shame** *these new materials put our old plastics to shame* OUTSHINE, outclass, eclipse, surpass, excel, outstrip, outdo, put in the shade, upstage; *informal* run rings around.

**shamefaced** adjective *Giles looked shamefaced* ASHAMED, abashed, sheepish, guilty, conscience-stricken, guilt-ridden, contrite, sorry, remorseful, repentant, penitent, regretful, rueful, apologetic; embarrassed, mortified, red-faced, chagrined, humiliated; *informal* with one's tail between one's legs. ANTONYM unrepentant.

**shameful** adjective **1** *shameful behavior* DISGRACEFUL, deplorable, despicable, contemptible, dishonorable, discreditable, reprehensible, low, unworthy, ignoble, shabby; shocking, scandalous, outrageous, abominable, atrocious, appalling, vile, odious, heinous, egregious, loathsome, bad; inexcusable, unforgivable; *informal* lowdown, hateful. ANTONYM admirable.

**2** *a shameful secret* EMBARRASSING, mortifying, humiliating, degrading, ignominious.

**shameless** adjective *a shameless display of flirtation* FLAGRANT, blatant, barefaced, overt, brazen, brash, audacious, outrageous, undisguised, unconcealed, transparent; immodest, indecorous; unabashed, unashamed, unblushing, unrepentant. ANTONYM modest.

**shape** noun **1** *the shape of the dining table* FORM, appearance, configuration, formation, structure; figure, build, physique, body; contours, lines, outline, silhouette, profile.

**2** *a spirit in the shape of a fox* GUISE, likeness, semblance, form, appearance, image.

**3** *you're in pretty good shape* CONDITION, health, fettle, order.

▸ verb **1** *the metal is shaped into tools* FORM, fashion, make, mold, model, cast; sculpt, sculpture, carve, cut, whittle.

**2** *attitudes were shaped by his report* DETERMINE, form, fashion, mold, define, develop; influence, affect.

PHRASES: **shape up** *her work is shaping up nicely* IMPROVE, get better, progress, show promise; develop, take shape, come on, come along.
**take shape** *our remodeling plans were really starting to take shape* BECOME CLEAR, become definite, become tangible, crystallize, come together, fall into place.

**shapeless** adjective **1** *shapeless lumps* FORMLESS, amorphous, unformed, indefinite.

**2** *a shapeless dress* BAGGY, saggy, ill-fitting, sacklike, oversized, unshapely, formless.

**shapely** adjective *the shapely models of the forties* WELL-PROPORTIONED, clean-limbed; curvaceous, voluptuous, Junoesque; attractive, sexy; *informal* curvy, bootylicious; *archaic* comely.

**shard** noun *a shard of glass in her heel* FRAGMENT, sliver, splinter, shiver, chip, piece, bit, particle.

**share** noun *her share of the profits* PORTION, part, division, quota, quantum, allowance, ration, allocation, measure, due; percentage, commission, dividend; helping, serving; *informal* cut, slice.

▸ verb **1** *we share the bills* SPLIT, divide, go halves on; *informal* go fifty-fifty on, go Dutch on.

**2** *they **shared out** the bottles of water* APPORTION, divide up, allocate, portion out, ration out, parcel out, measure out; carve up, divvy up.

**3** *we all **share in** the learning process* PARTICIPATE IN, take part in, play a part in, be involved in, contribute to, have a hand in, partake in.

**sharp** adjective **1** *a sharp knife* KEEN, razor-edged; sharpened, honed. See note at KEEN. ANTONYM blunt.

**2** *a sharp pain* EXCRUCIATING, agonizing, intense, stabbing, shooting, severe, acute, keen, fierce, searing; exquisite.

**3** *a sharp taste* TANGY, piquant, strong; ACIDIC, acid, sour, tart, pungent, acrid, bitter, acidulous. ANTONYMS mild, mellow, bland.

**4** *a sharp cry of pain* LOUD, piercing, shrill, high-pitched, penetrating, harsh, strident, ear-splitting, deafening. ANTONYMS soft, quiet.

**5** *a sharp wind* COLD, chilly, chill, brisk, keen, penetrating, biting, icy, bitter, freezing, raw; *informal* nippy, wicked. ANTONYMS warm, balmy.

**6** *sharp words* HARSH, bitter, cutting, scathing, caustic, barbed, trenchant, acrimonious, acerbic, sarcastic, sardonic, spiteful, venomous, malicious, vitriolic, vicious, hurtful, nasty, cruel, abrasive; *informal* bitchy, catty. ANTONYMS amicable, kind.

**7** *a sharp sense of loss* INTENSE, acute, keen, strong, bitter, fierce, heartfelt, overwhelming.

**8** *the lens brings it into sharp focus* DISTINCT, clear, crisp; stark, obvious, marked, definite, pronounced. ANTONYMS blurred, indistinct.

**9** *a sharp increase* SUDDEN, abrupt, rapid; steep, precipitous. ANTONYM gradual.

**10** *a sharp corner* HAIRPIN, tight.

**11** *a sharp drop* STEEP, sheer, abrupt, precipitous, vertical. ANTONYMS gentle, gradual.

**12** *sharp eyes* KEEN, perceptive, observant, acute, beady, hawklike. ANTONYM weak.

**13** *she was sharp and witty* PERCEPTIVE, percipient, perspicacious, incisive, sensitive, keen, acute, quick-witted, clever, shrewd, canny, astute, intelligent, intuitive, bright, alert, smart, quick off the mark, insightful, knowing; *informal* on the ball, quick on the uptake, savvy, heads-up. ANTONYMS slow, dull, stupid.

**14** *informal a sharp suit* SMART, stylish, fashionable, chic, modish, elegant; *informal* trendy, cool, hip, snazzy, classy, snappy, styling/stylin', natty, nifty, fly, spiffy. ANTONYM shabby.

▸ adverb **1** *nine o'clock sharp* PRECISELY, exactly, on the dot; promptly, prompt, punctually, dead on; *informal* on the nose, on the button. ANTONYM roughly.

**2** *the recession pulled people up sharp* ABRUPTLY, suddenly, sharply, unexpectedly.

**sharpen** verb **1** *sharpen the carving knife* HONE, whet, strop, grind, file.

**2** *the players are sharpening their skills* IMPROVE, brush up, polish up, better, enhance; hone, fine-tune, perfect.

**shatter** verb **1** *the glasses shattered* SMASH, break, splinter, crack, fracture, fragment, disintegrate, shiver; *informal* bust.

**2** *the announcement shattered their hopes* DESTROY, wreck, ruin, dash, crush, devastate, demolish, torpedo, scotch; *informal* put the kibosh on, scuttle.

**3** *we were shattered by the news* DEVASTATE, shock, stun, daze, traumatize, crush, distress.

**shave** verb **1** *he shaved his beard* CUT OFF, snip off; crop, trim, barber.

**2** *shave off excess wood* PLANE, pare, whittle, scrape.

**3** *they shaved the deficit by 4 percent* REDUCE, cut, lessen, decrease, pare down, shrink.

**4** *the shot just shaved my arm* GRAZE, brush, touch, glance off, kiss.

**sheath** noun **1** *put the sword in its sheath* SCABBARD, case.

**2** *the wire has a plastic sheath* COVERING, cover, case, casing, envelope, sleeve, wrapper, capsule.

**3** *a contraceptive sheath.* See CONDOM.

**shed**[1] noun *the rabbit lives in the shed* HUT, lean-to, outhouse, outbuilding; shack; potting shed, woodshed, tool shed, garden shed.

**shed**[2] verb **1** *the trees shed their leaves* DROP, scatter, spill.

**2** *the caterpillar shed its skin* SLOUGH OFF, cast off, molt.

**3** *we shed our jackets* TAKE OFF, remove, shrug off, discard, doff, climb out of, slip out of, divest oneself of, peel off. ANTONYM don.

**4** *much blood has been shed* SPILL, discharge.

**5** *she shed 20 pounds* LOSE, get rid of, discard. ANTONYM put on.

**6** *they must shed their illusions* DISCARD, get rid of, dispose of, do away with, drop, abandon, jettison, scrap, cast aside, dump, reject, repudiate; *informal* ditch, junk. ANTONYMS adopt, keep.

**7** *the moon shed a watery light* CAST, radiate, diffuse, disperse, give out. PHRASE: **shed tears** *now, now, there's no need to shed tears* WEEP, cry, sob; lament, grieve, mourn; *informal* blubber, boo-hoo.

**sheen** noun *we were admiring the sheen of your dog's coat* SHINE, luster, gloss, patina, shininess, burnish, polish, shimmer, brilliance, radiance. See note at POLISH.

**sheepish** adjective *stop looking so sheepish and come on in* EMBARRASSED, uncomfortable, hangdog, self-conscious; shamefaced, ashamed, abashed, mortified, chastened, remorseful, contrite, apologetic, rueful, regretful, penitent, repentant.

**sheer**[1] adjective **1** *the sheer audacity of the plan* UTTER, complete, absolute, total, pure, downright, out-and-out, arrant, thorough, thoroughgoing, patent, veritable, unmitigated, plain.

**2** *a sheer drop* PRECIPITOUS, steep, vertical, perpendicular, abrupt, bluff, sharp. ANTONYM gradual.

**3** *a sheer dress* DIAPHANOUS, gauzy, filmy, floaty, gossamer, thin, translucent, transparent, see-through, insubstantial. ANTONYM thick.

**sheer**[2] verb **1** *the boat* ***sheered off*** *from the landing* SWERVE, veer, slew, skew, swing, change course.

**2** *her mind* ***sheered away from*** *his image* TURN AWAY FROM, flinch from, recoil from, shy away from; avoid.

**sheet** noun **1** (often **sheets**) *she changed the sheets* BED LINEN, linen, bedclothes.

**2** *a sheet of ice* LAYER, stratum, covering, blanket, coating, coat, film, skin.

**3** *a sheet of glass* PANE, panel, piece, plate; slab.

**4** *she put a fresh sheet in the typewriter* PIECE OF PAPER, leaf, page, folio.

**5** *a sheet of water* EXPANSE, area, stretch, sweep.

**shelf** noun **1** *the plant on the shelf* LEDGE, sill, bracket, rack; mantelpiece; shelving.

**2** *an ocean shelf* SANDBANK, sandbar, bank, bar, reef, shoal.

**shell** noun **1** *a crab shell* CARAPACE, exterior; armor; *Zoology* exoskeleton.

**2** *peanut shells* POD, husk, hull, casing, case, covering, integument, shuck.

**3** *shells passing overhead* PROJECTILE, bomb, explosive; grenade; bullet, cartridge.

**4** *the metal shell of the car* FRAMEWORK, frame, chassis, skeleton; hull, exterior.

▸ verb **1** *they were shelling peas* HULL, pod, husk, shuck.

**2** *rebel artillery shelled the city* BOMBARD, fire on, shoot at, attack, bomb, blitz, strafe.

PHRASE: **shell out** *informal how much did you shell out for those shoes?* See PAY verb sense 2.

**shelter** noun **1** *the trees provide shelter for animals* PROTECTION, cover, screening, shade; safety, security, refuge, sanctuary, asylum. ANTONYM exposure.

**2** *a shelter for abused women* SANCTUARY, refuge, home, haven, safe house; harbor, port in a storm.

▸ verb **1** *the hut sheltered him from the wind* PROTECT, shield, screen, cover, shade, save, safeguard, preserve, defend, cushion, guard, insulate. ANTONYM expose.

**2** *the anchorage where the convoy sheltered* TAKE SHELTER, take refuge, seek sanctuary, take cover; *informal* hole up.

**sheltered** adjective **1** *a sheltered stretch of water* PROTECTED, screened, shielded, covered; shady; cozy.

**2** *she led a sheltered life* SECLUDED, cloistered, isolated, protected, withdrawn, sequestered, reclusive; privileged, secure, safe, quiet.

**shelve** verb *plans to reopen the school have been shelved* POSTPONE, put off, delay, defer, put back, reschedule, hold over/off, put to one side, suspend, stay, keep in abeyance, mothball; abandon, drop, give up, stop, cancel, jettison, ax, put over, table, take a rain check on; *informal* put on ice, put on the back burner, put in cold storage, ditch, dump, junk. ANTONYM execute.

**shepherd** noun *he worked as a shepherd* herdsman, herder, shepherdess, sheepman.

▸ verb *we shepherded them away* USHER, steer, herd, lead, take, escort, guide, conduct, marshal, walk; show, see, chaperone.

**shield** noun **1** *he used his shield to fend off blows* *Heraldry* escutcheon; *historical* buckler, target.

**2** *a shield against dirt* PROTECTION, guard, defense, cover, screen, security, shelter, safeguard, protector.

▸ verb *he shielded his eyes* PROTECT, cover, screen, shade; save, safeguard, preserve, defend, secure, guard; cushion, insulate. ANTONYM expose.

**shift** verb **1** *she shifted her position* CHANGE, alter, adjust, vary; modify, revise, reverse, retract; do a U-turn. ANTONYM keep.

**2** *the cargo has shifted* MOVE, slide, slip, be displaced.

**3** *the wind shifted* VEER, alter, change, turn, swing round.

▸ noun **1** *the southward shift of people* MOVEMENT, move, transference, transport, transposition, relocation.

**2** *a shift in public opinion* CHANGE, alteration, adjustment, amendment, variation, modification, revision, reversal, retraction, U-turn.

**3** *they worked three shifts* STINT, stretch, spell of work.

**4** *the night shift went home* WORKERS, crew, gang, team, squad, patrol.

**shiftless** adjective *he thought the whole family shiftless and dishonest* LAZY, idle, indolent, slothful, lethargic, lackadaisical; spiritless, apathetic, feckless, good-for-nothing, worthless; unambitious, unenterprising.

**shifty** adjective *informal he had a shifty look about him* DEVIOUS, evasive, slippery, duplicitous, false, deceitful, underhanded, untrustworthy, dishonest, shady, wily, crafty, tricky, sneaky, treacherous, artful, sly, scheming, snide; *informal* hinky. ANTONYM honest.

**shilly-shally** verb *we must not tolerate leaders who shilly-shally over matters of national security* DITHER, be indecisive, be irresolute, vacillate, waver, hesitate, blow hot and cold, falter, drag one's feet, hem and haw; *informal* dilly-dally.

**shimmer** verb *the lake shimmered* GLINT, glisten, twinkle, sparkle, flash, scintillate, gleam, glow, glimmer, glitter, wink; *literary* coruscate.

▸ noun *the shimmer of lights from the traffic* GLINT, twinkle, sparkle, flash, gleam, glow, glimmer, luster, glitter; *literary* coruscation.

**shine** verb **1** *the sun shone* EMIT LIGHT, beam, radiate, gleam, glow, glint, glimmer, sparkle, twinkle, glitter, glisten, shimmer, flash, flare, glare, fluoresce; *literary* glister, coruscate.

**2** *she shone his shoes* POLISH, burnish, buff, wax, gloss.

**3** *they shone at gymnastics* EXCEL, be outstanding, be brilliant, be successful, stand out.

▸ noun **1** *the shine of the moon on her face* LIGHT, brightness, gleam, glow, glint, glimmer, sparkle, twinkle, glitter, glisten, shimmer, beam, glare, radiance, illumination, luminescence, luminosity, incandescence.

**2** *linseed oil restores the shine* POLISH, burnish, gleam, gloss, luster, sheen, patina.

**shining** adjective **1** *a shining expanse of water* GLEAMING, bright, brilliant, illuminated, lustrous, glowing, glinting, sparkling, twinkling, glittering, glistening, shimmering, dazzling, luminous, luminescent, incandescent; *literary* glistering, coruscating. See note at BRIGHT.

**2** *a shining face* GLOWING, beaming, radiant, happy.

**3** *shining chromium tubes* SHINY, bright, polished, gleaming, glossy, sheeny, lustrous. PHRASE: **a shining example** *a shining example of Yankee ingenuity* PARAGON, model, epitome, archetype, ideal, exemplar, nonpareil, paradigm, quintessence, beau ideal, acme, jewel, flower, treasure.

**shiny** adjective *a shiny red apple* GLOSSY, glassy, bright, polished, gleaming, satiny, sheeny, lustrous. ANTONYM matte.

**shirk** verb **1** *she didn't shirk any task* EVADE, dodge, avoid, get out of, sidestep, shrink from, shun, skip, miss; neglect; *informal* duck (out of), cop out of, cut.

**2** *no one shirked* AVOID ONE'S DUTY, be remiss, be negligent, play truant, swing the lead, slack off; *informal* goof off, play hooky.

**shirker** noun *you'll find no shirkers in my crew* DODGER, truant, absentee, layabout, good-for-nothing, loafer, idler; *informal* slacker, bum, lazybones.

**shiver**[1] verb *he was shivering with fear* TREMBLE, quiver, shake, shudder, quaver, quake. See note at SHAKE.

▸ noun *she gave a shiver as the door opened* TREMBLE, quiver, shake, shudder, quaver, quake, tremor, twitch.

**shiver**[2] noun *shivers of glass* SPLINTER, sliver, shard, fragment, chip, shaving, smithereen, particle, bit, piece.

▸ verb *the window shivered into thousands of pieces* SHATTER, splinter, smash, fragment, crack, break.

**shivery** adjective *she felt sick and shivery* TREMBLING, trembly, quivery, shaky, shuddering, shuddery, quavery, quaking; cold, chilly.

**shock**[1] noun **1** *the news came as a shock* BLOW, upset, disturbance; surprise, revelation, a bolt from the blue, thunderbolt, bombshell, rude awakening, eye-opener; *informal* whammy, wake-up call.

**2** *you gave me a shock* FRIGHT, scare, jolt, start; *informal* turn.

**3** *she was suffering from shock* TRAUMA, prostration; collapse, breakdown.

**4** *the first shock of the earthquake* VIBRATION, reverberation, shake, jolt, jar, jerk; impact, blow.

▸ verb *the murder shocked the nation* APPALL, horrify, outrage, revolt, disgust, nauseate, sicken; traumatize, distress, upset, disturb, disquiet, unsettle; stun, rock, stagger, astound, astonish, amaze, startle, surprise, dumbfound, shake, take aback, throw, unnerve.

**shock**[2] noun *a shock of red hair* MASS, mane, mop, thatch, head, crop, bush, frizz, tangle, cascade, halo.

**shocking** adjective *the news from Cambodia was shocking* APPALLING, horrifying, horrific, dreadful, awful, frightful, terrible; scandalous, outrageous, disgraceful, vile, abominable, abhorrent, atrocious; odious, repugnant, disgusting, nauseating, sickening, loathsome; distressing, upsetting, disturbing, disquieting, unsettling; staggering, amazing, astonishing, startling, surprising; *informal* gut-wrenching.

**shoddy** adjective **1** *shoddy goods* POOR-QUALITY, inferior, second-rate, third-rate, tinpot, cheap, cheapjack, trashy, jerry-built; *informal* tacky, chintzy, rubbishy, junky, cheapo, cheesy, schlocky. ANTONYM quality.

**2** *shoddy workmanship* CARELESS, slapdash, sloppy, slipshod, crude; negligent, cursory. ANTONYM careful.

**shoot** verb **1** *they shot him in the street* GUN DOWN, mow down, hit, wound, injure; put a bullet in, pick off, bag, fell, kill; *informal* pot, blast, pump full of lead, plug.

**2** *they shot at the enemy* FIRE, open fire, aim, snipe, let fly; bombard, shell.

**3** *faster than a gun can shoot bullets* DISCHARGE, fire, launch, loose off, let fly, emit.

**4** *a car shot past* RACE, speed, flash, dash, dart, rush, hurtle, careen, streak, whiz, go like lightning, go hell-bent for leather, zoom, charge; career, sweep, fly, wing; *informal* belt, scoot, scorch, tear, zip, whip, step on it, burn rubber, bomb, hightail it, barrel.

**5** *the plant failed to shoot* SPROUT, bud, burgeon, germinate.

**6** *the film was shot in Toronto* FILM, photograph, take, snap, capture, record, tape; videotape, video.

▸ noun *nip off the new shoots* SPROUT, bud, offshoot, scion, sucker, spear, runner, tendril, sprig.

**shop** noun **1** *a shop selling clothes* STORE, (retail) outlet, boutique, emporium, department store, big box store, supermarket, superstore, chain store, market, mart, minimart, convenience store, trading post.

**2** *he works in the machine shop* WORKSHOP, workroom, plant, factory, works, mill, yard.

▸ verb *he was **shopping for** spices* BUY, purchase, get, acquire, obtain, pick up, snap up, procure, stock up on.

**shore**[1] noun *he swam out from the shore* SEASHORE, lakeshore, lakefront, bayfront, beach, foreshore, sand(s), shoreline, waterside, front, coast, seaboard; *literary* strand.

**shore**[2] verb *we had to **shore up** the building* PROP UP, hold up, bolster, support, brace, buttress, strengthen, fortify, reinforce, underpin.

**short** adjective **1** *a short piece of string* SMALL, little, tiny; *informal* teeny. ANTONYM long.

**2** *short people* SMALL, little, petite, tiny, diminutive, stubby, elfin, dwarfish, midget, pygmy, Lilliputian, minuscule, miniature; *informal* pint-sized, vertically challenged, teeny, knee-high to a grasshopper; *Scottish* wee. ANTONYM tall.

**3** *a short report* CONCISE, brief, succinct, compact, summary, economical, crisp, pithy, epigrammatic, laconic, thumbnail, capsule, abridged, abbreviated, condensed, synoptic, summarized, contracted, truncated; *formal* compendious. ANTONYMS long, verbose.

**4** *a short time* BRIEF, momentary, temporary, short-lived, impermanent, cursory, fleeting, passing, fugitive, lightning, transitory, transient, ephemeral, quick. ANTONYM long.

**5** *money is a bit short* SCARCE, in short supply, scant, meager, sparse, insufficient, deficient, inadequate, lacking, wanting, tight; *rare* exiguous. ANTONYM plentiful.

**6** *he was rather short with her* CURT, sharp, abrupt, blunt, brusque, terse, offhand, gruff, surly, testy, rude, uncivil; *informal* snappy, snappish. ANTONYMS patient, courteous.

▸ adverb *she stopped short* ABRUPTLY, suddenly, sharply, all of a sudden, all at once, unexpectedly, without warning, out of the blue.

PHRASES: **in short** *in short, we want you to leave* BRIEFLY, in a word, in a nutshell, in précis, in essence, to come to the point; in conclusion, in summary, to sum up.

**short of 1** *we are short of nurses* DEFICIENT IN, lacking, wanting, in need of, low on, short on, missing; *informal* strapped for, pushed for, minus.

**2** *short of searching everyone, there is nothing we can do* APART FROM, other than, aside from, besides, except (for), excepting, without, excluding, not counting, save (for).

**shortage** noun *the islanders are accustomed to a shortage of fresh water* SCARCITY, sparseness, sparsity, dearth, paucity, poverty, insufficiency, deficiency, inadequacy, famine, lack, want, deficit, shortfall, rarity. See note at LACK. ANTONYM abundance.

**shortcoming** noun *after forty years of marriage, he still claimed she had nary a shortcoming* DEFECT, fault, flaw, imperfection, deficiency, limitation, failing, drawback, weakness, weak point, foible, frailty, vice. See note at FAULT. ANTONYM strength.

**shorten** verb *shorten your essay to a three-paragraph summary | the drapes will have to be shortened* MAKE SHORTER, abbreviate, abridge, condense, précis, synopsize, contract, compress, reduce, shrink, diminish, cut (down); dock, trim, crop, pare down, prune; curtail, truncate. ANTONYM extend.

**short-lived** adjective *it was a short-lived romance* BRIEF, short, momentary, temporary, impermanent, cursory, fleeting, passing, fugitive, lightning, transitory, transient, ephemeral, quick.

**shortly** adverb **1** *she will be with you shortly* SOON, presently, momentarily, in a little while, at any moment, in a minute, in next to no time, before long, by and by; *informal* anon, any time now, pretty soon, in a jiffy; *dated* directly.

**2** *"I know," he replied shortly* CURTLY, sharply, abruptly, bluntly, brusquely, tersely, gruffly, snappily, testily, rudely.

**shortsighted** adjective *shortsighted critics* NARROW-

MINDED, unimaginative, small-minded, insular, parochial, provincial, improvident. ANTONYMS farsighted, imaginative.

**short-staffed** adjective *we're always short-staffed around the holidays* UNDERSTAFFED, short-handed, undermanned, below strength.

**short-tempered** adjective *don't get short-tempered with me, pal!* IRRITABLE, irascible, hot-tempered, quick-tempered, snappish, fiery, touchy, volatile; cross, crabby, crotchety, cantankerous, grumpy, ill-tempered, bad-tempered, testy, tetchy, prickly, choleric; *informal* snappy, grouchy, cranky, on a short fuse, bitchy. ANTONYM placid.

**shot** noun **1** *a shot rang out* report of a gun, crack, bang, blast; (**shots**) gunfire.

**2** *the cannons have run out of shot* BULLETS, cannonballs, pellets, ammunition.

**3** *the winning shot* STROKE, hit, strike; kick, throw, pitch, lob.

**4** *Mike was an excellent shot* MARKSMAN, markswoman, shooter.

**5** *a shot of us on holiday* PHOTOGRAPH, photo, snap, snapshot, picture, print, slide, still.

**6** *informal it's nice to get a shot at driving* ATTEMPT, try; turn, chance, opportunity; *informal* go, stab, crack; *formal* essay.

**7** *tetanus shots* INJECTION, inoculation, immunization, vaccination, booster; *informal* jab, needle. PHRASES: **a shot in the arm** *informal the new sidewalks and landscaping have been a shot in the arm to downtown commerce* BOOST, tonic, stimulus, spur, impetus, encouragement.

**a shot in the dark** *my answer was just a shot in the dark* (WILD) GUESS, surmise, supposition, conjecture, speculation.

**like a shot** *informal when they called his name he ran on to the stage like a shot* WITHOUT HESITATION, unhesitatingly, eagerly, enthusiastically; immediately, at once, right away/now, straightaway, instantly, instantaneously, without delay; *informal* in/like a flash.

**not by a long shot** *he is not yet out of the woods, not by a long shot* BY NO (MANNER OF) MEANS, not at all, in no way, certainly not, absolutely not, definitely not.

**shoulder** verb **1** *he shouldered the burden* TAKE ON (ONESELF), undertake, accept, assume; bear, carry.

**2** *another kid shouldered him aside* PUSH, shove, thrust, jostle, force, bulldoze, elbow. PHRASES: **give the cold shoulder** *ever since Deke's party, Linnie has been giving me the cold shoulder* SNUB, shun, ignore, rebuff, spurn, ostracize, cut out; *informal* freeze out.

**put one's shoulder to the wheel** *it's time to stop talking and start putting your shoulder to the wheel* GET (DOWN) TO WORK, apply oneself, set to work, buckle down, roll up one's sleeves; work hard, be diligent, be industrious, exert oneself.

**shoulder to shoulder** **1** *the regiment lined up shoulder to shoulder* SIDE BY SIDE, abreast, alongside (each other).

**2** *he fought shoulder to shoulder with the others* UNITED, (working) together, jointly, in partnership, in collaboration, in cooperation, side by side, in alliance.

**shout** verb *"Help," he shouted* YELL, cry (out), call (out), roar, howl, bellow, bawl, call at the top of one's voice, clamor, shriek, scream; raise one's voice, vociferate; *informal* holler. ANTONYM whisper.

▸ noun *a shout of pain* YELL, cry, call, roar, howl, bellow, bawl, clamor, vociferation, shriek, scream; *informal* holler.

**shove** verb **1** *she shoved him back into the chair* PUSH, thrust, propel, drive, force, ram, knock, elbow, shoulder; jostle, hustle, manhandle.

**2** *she shoved past him* PUSH (ONE'S WAY), force one's way, barge (one's way), elbow (one's way), shoulder one's way.

▸ noun *a hefty shove* PUSH, thrust, bump, jolt.

PHRASE: **shove off** *informal shove off, you little creep!* GO AWAY, get out (of my sight); get going, take oneself off, be off (with you), shoo; *informal* scram, make yourself scarce, be on your way, beat it, get lost, push off, buzz off, clear off, go (and) jump in the lake, bug off, take a hike; *literary* begone.

**shovel** noun *a pick and shovel* SPADE.

▸ verb *shoveling snow* SCOOP (UP), dig, excavate.

**show** verb **1** *the stitches do not show* BE VISIBLE, be seen, be in view, be obvious. ANTONYM be invisible.

**2** *he wouldn't show the picture* DISPLAY, exhibit, put on show/display, put on view, parade, uncover, reveal. ANTONYM conceal.

**3** *Frank showed his frustration* MANIFEST, exhibit, reveal, convey, communicate, make known; express, proclaim, make plain, make obvious, disclose, betray; *formal* evince. ANTONYM suppress.

**4** *I'll show you how to make a daisy chain* DEMONSTRATE TO, explain to, describe to, illustrate to; teach, instruct, give instructions to.

**5** *recent events show this to be true* PROVE, demonstrate, confirm, show beyond doubt; substantiate, corroborate, verify, establish, attest, certify, testify, bear out; *formal* evince.

**6** *a young woman showed them to their seats* ESCORT, accompany, take, conduct, lead, usher, guide, direct, steer, shepherd.

**7** *informal they never showed* APPEAR, arrive, come, get here/there, put in an appearance, materialize, turn up; *informal* show up.

▸ noun **1** *a spectacular show of fireworks* DISPLAY, array, exhibition, presentation, exposition, spectacle.

**2** *the boat show* EXHIBITION, exposition, fair, extravaganza, spectacle, exhibit.

**3** *they took in a show* (THEATRICAL) PERFORMANCE, musical, play, opera, ballet.

**4** *she's only doing it for show* APPEARANCE, display, impression, ostentation, image.

**5** *Drew made a show of looking busy* PRETENSE, outward appearance, (false) front, guise, semblance, pose, parade.

**6** *informal I don't run the show* UNDERTAKING, affair, operation, proceedings, enterprise, business, venture.

PHRASES: **show off** *informal* **1** *he likes to show off when we have* *company* BEHAVE AFFECTEDLY, put on airs, put on an act, swagger around, swank, strut, strike an attitude, posture; draw attention to oneself; *informal* cop an attitude.

**2** *that dress really shows off your green eyes* DISPLAY, show to advantage, exhibit, demonstrate, parade, draw attention to, flaunt.

**show up 1** *cancers show up on X-rays* BE VISIBLE, be obvious, be seen, be revealed.

**2** *informal only two waitresses showed up.* See SHOW verb sense 7.

**3** *the sun showed up the shabbiness of the room* EXPOSE, reveal, make visible, make obvious, highlight.

**4** *informal they showed him up in front of his friends.* See HUMILIATE.

**showdown** noun *his girlfriend got into a showdown with his ex-wife* CONFRONTATION, clash, face-off.

**shower** noun **1** *a shower of rain* (LIGHT) FALL, drizzle, sprinkling, misting.

**2** *a shower of arrows* VOLLEY, hail, salvo, bombardment, barrage, fusillade, cannonade.

**3** *a shower of awards* AVALANCHE, deluge, flood, spate, flurry; profusion, abundance.

▸ verb **1** *confetti showered down on us* RAIN, fall, hail.

**2** *she showered them with gifts* DELUGE, flood, inundate, swamp, engulf; overwhelm, overload, snow under.

**3** *showering praise on his cronies* LAVISH, heap, bestow freely.

**showing** noun **1** *another showing of the series* PRESENTATION, broadcast, airing, televising, screening.

**2** *the party's present showing* PERFORMANCE, (track) record, results, success, achievement.

**show-off** noun *informal no one minds that Amy's a show-off because she's just so funny* EXHIBITIONIST, extrovert, poser, poseur, peacock, swaggerer, self-publicist, braggart; *informal* showboat, blowhard, grandstander.

**showy** adjective *they spared no sequins or feathers in what may be the most showy finale ever seen on this stage* OSTENTATIOUS, conspicuous, pretentious, flamboyant, gaudy, garish, brash, vulgar, loud, extravagant, fancy, ornate, overelaborate, kitsch, kitschy; pyrotechnical; *informal* flash, flashy, glitzy, ritzy, swanky, fancy-dancy, fancy-schmancy. ANTONYM restrained.

**shred** noun **1** *her dress was torn to shreds* TATTER, scrap, strip, ribbon, rag, fragment, sliver, (tiny) bit/piece.

**2** *not a shred of evidence* SCRAP, bit, speck, iota, particle, ounce, whit, jot, crumb, morsel, fragment, grain, drop, trace, scintilla, spot; *informal* smidgen.

▸ verb *shredding vegetables* CHOP FINELY, cut up, tear up, grate, mince, macerate, grind.

**shrew** noun *my brother has just married a despicable shrew* VIRAGO, dragon, termagant, fishwife, witch, tartar, hag; *informal* battle-ax, old bag, old bat; *archaic* scold.

**shrewd** adjective *a shrewd businessman would never have been so careless about keeping appointments* ASTUTE, sharp-witted, sharp, smart, acute, intelligent, clever, canny, perceptive, perspicacious, sagacious, wise; *informal* on the ball, savvy, heads-up; *formal* sapient. See note at KEEN. ANTONYM stupid.

**shrewdness** noun *he was never known for his shrewdness, but we never thought he could be that stupid* ASTUTENESS, sharp-wittedness, acuteness, acumen, acuity, intelligence, cleverness, smartness, wit, canniness, common sense, discernment, insight, understanding, perception, perceptiveness, perspicacity, discrimination, sagacity, sageness; *informal* horse sense, savvy, (street) smarts; *formal* sapience.

**shriek** verb *she shrieked with fear* SCREAM, screech, squeal, squawk, roar, howl, shout, yelp; *informal* holler.

▸ noun *a shriek of laughter* SCREAM, screech, squeal, squawk, roar, howl, shout, yelp; *informal* holler.

**shrill** adjective *that shrill voice gives me a headache* HIGH-PITCHED, piercing, high, sharp, ear-piercing, ear-splitting, penetrating, screeching, shrieking, screechy.

**shrine** noun **1** *the shrine of St. James* HOLY PLACE, temple, church, chapel, tabernacle, sanctuary, sanctum.

**2** *a shrine to the Beatles* MEMORIAL, monument.

**shrink** verb **1** *the number of competitors shrank* GET SMALLER, become/grow smaller, contract, diminish, lessen, reduce, decrease, dwindle, decline, fall off, drop off. ANTONYMS expand, increase.

**2** *he* ***shrank back*** *against the wall* DRAW BACK, recoil, back away, retreat, withdraw, cringe, cower, quail.

**3** *he doesn't* ***shrink from*** *naming names* RECOIL FROM, shy away from, demur from, flinch from, have scruples about, have misgivings about, have qualms about, be loath to, be reluctant to, be unwilling to, be averse to, fight shy of, be hesitant to, be afraid to, hesitate to, balk at.

**shrivel** verb *the neglected plants shriveled in their pots* WITHER, shrink; wilt; dry up, desiccate, dehydrate, parch, frazzle.

**shroud** noun **1** *the shroud of Turin* WINDING SHEET; *historical* cerements.

**2** *a shroud of mist | a shroud of secrecy* COVERING, cover, cloak, mantle, blanket, layer, cloud, veil.

▸ verb *a mist shrouded the shore* COVER, envelop, veil, cloak, blanket, screen, conceal, hide, mask, obscure; *literary* enshroud.

**shrug** PHRASE: **shrug off** *he just shrugged off all of my advice* DISREGARD, dismiss, take no notice of, ignore, pay no heed to, play down, make light of.

**shudder** verb *she shuddered at the thought* SHAKE, shiver, tremble, quiver, vibrate, palpitate. See note at SHAKE.

▸ noun *a shudder racked his body* SHAKE, shiver, tremor, tremble, trembling, quiver, quivering, vibration, palpitation, spasm.

**shuffle** verb **1** *they shuffled along the passage* SHAMBLE, drag one's feet, totter, dodder.

**2** *she shuffled her feet* SCRAPE, drag, scuffle, scuff.

**3** *he shuffled the cards* MIX (UP), mingle, rearrange, jumble.

**shun** verb *he shunned publicity* AVOID, evade, eschew, steer clear of, shy away from, fight shy of, keep one's distance from, give a wide berth to, have nothing to do with; snub, give someone the cold shoulder, cold-shoulder, ignore, look right through; reject, rebuff, spurn, ostracize; *informal* give someone the brush-off, freeze out, give someone the bum's rush, give someone the brush off. ANTONYM welcome.

**shut** verb *please shut the door* CLOSE, pull/push to, slam, fasten; put the lid on, bar, lock, secure. ANTONYMS open, unlock.

PHRASES: **shut down** *the plant is shutting down in August* CEASE ACTIVITY, close (down), cease operating, cease trading, be shut (down); turn off, switch off; *informal* fold; power down.

**shut in** *shut the goats in for the night* CONFINE, enclose, impound, shut up, pen (in/up), fence in, immure, lock up/in, cage, imprison, intern, incarcerate, corral.

**shut out 1** *he shut me out of the house* LOCK OUT, keep out, refuse entrance to.

**2** *she shut out the memories* BLOCK, suppress.

**3** *the bamboo shut out the light* KEEP OUT, block out, screen, veil.

**4** *they shut out the Blue Jays in three straight games* PREVENT FROM SCORING, blank.

**shut up 1** *informal will you please shut up so we can hear the movie?* BE QUIET, keep quiet, hold one's tongue, keep one's lips sealed; stop talking, quiet (down); *informal* keep mum, button it, hush up, shut it, shut your face/mouth/trap, put a sock in it, give it a rest, save it.

**2** *informal that should shut them up* QUIET (DOWN), silence, hush, shush, gag, muzzle.

**3** *I haven't shut the hens up yet.* See SHUT IN.

**shuttle** verb *they provided a bus to shuttle us to the mall* PLY, run, commute, go/travel back and forth, go/travel to and fro; ferry.

**shy** adjective *I was painfully shy* BASHFUL, diffident, farouche, timid, sheepish, reserved, reticent, introverted, retiring, self-effacing, withdrawn, timorous, mousy, nervous, insecure, unconfident, inhibited, repressed, self-conscious, embarrassed. ANTONYM confident.

PHRASE: **shy away from** *she shied away from success* FLINCH AT, demur at, recoil at, hang back from, have scruples about, have misgivings about, have qualms about, be chary of, be diffident toward, be bashful about, fight shy of, balk at.

**shyness** noun *Gerald's shyness was often mistaken for disinterest* BASHFULNESS, diffidence, sheepishness, reserve, reservedness, introversion, reticence, timidity, timidness, timorousness, mousiness, lack of confidence, self-consciousness, embarrassment, coyness, demureness.

**sick** adjective **1** *the children are sick* ILL, unwell, poorly, ailing, indisposed, not oneself; off; *informal* laid up, under the weather. ANTONYMS well, healthy.

**2** *he was feeling sick* NAUSEOUS, nauseated, queasy, bilious, green around/at the gills; seasick, carsick, airsick, travel-sick; *informal* about to throw up.

**3** *informal we're just sick about it* DISAPPOINTED, depressed, dejected, despondent, downcast, unhappy; angry, cross, annoyed, displeased, disgruntled, fed up. ANTONYM glad.

**4** *I'm* ***sick of*** *this music* FED UP WITH, bored with, tired of, weary of. ANTONYM fond.

**5** *informal a sick joke* MACABRE, black, ghoulish, morbid, perverted, gruesome, sadistic, cruel. PHRASE: **be sick** *I'm going to be sick* VOMIT, throw up, retch, heave, gag; *informal* hurl, puke, spew, spit up, barf, upchuck, toss one's cookies.

**sicken** verb **1** *the stench sickened him* CAUSE TO FEEL SICK/NAUSEOUS, make sick, turn someone's stomach, revolt, disgust; *informal* make someone want to throw up, gross out.

**2** *she sickened and died* BECOME ILL, fall ill, be taken ill/sick, catch something. ANTONYM recover.

**sickening** adjective *ooh, that smell is sickening* NAUSEATING, stomach-turning, stomach-churning, repulsive, revolting, disgusting, repellent, repugnant, appalling, obnoxious, nauseous, vile, nasty, foul, loathsome, offensive, objectionable, off-putting, distasteful, obscene, gruesome, grisly, vomitous; *informal* gross; *formal* rebarbative.

**sickly** adjective **1** *a sickly child* UNHEALTHY, in poor health, delicate, frail, weak. ANTONYM healthy.

**2** *sickly faces* PALE, wan, pasty, sallow, pallid, ashen, anemic. ANTONYM rosy.

**3** *a sickly green* INSIPID, pale, light, light-colored, washed out, faded. ANTONYM deep.

**4** *sickly love songs* SENTIMENTAL, mawkish, cloying, sugary, syrupy, saccharine; *informal* mushy, slushy, schmaltzy, weepy, lovey-dovey, corny, cornball, sappy, hokey, three-hankie.

**sickness** noun **1** *she was absent because of sickness* ILLNESS, disease, ailment, complaint, infection, malady, infirmity, indisposition; *informal* bug, virus.

**2** *a wave of sickness* NAUSEA, biliousness, queasiness.

**3** *he suffers this kind of sickness whenever we travel* VOMITING, retching, gagging; travel-sickness, seasickness, carsickness, airsickness, motion sickness; *informal* throwing up, puking, barfing.

**side** noun **1** *they were standing on the side of the road* EDGE, border, verge, boundary, margin, fringe(s), flank, bank, perimeter, extremity, periphery, (outer) limit, limits, bounds; *literary* marge, bourn. ANTONYM center.

**2** *you're driving on the wrong side of the road* HALF, part; lane.

**3** *the east side of the city* DISTRICT, quarter, area, region, part, neighborhood, sector, section, zone, ward.

**4** *one side of the paper* SURFACE, face, plane.

**5** *his side of the argument* POINT OF VIEW, viewpoint, perspective, opinion, way of thinking, standpoint, position, outlook, slant, angle.

6 *the losing side in the war* FACTION, camp, bloc, party, wing.

7 *the players on their side* TEAM, squad, lineup.

▸ adjective 1 *elaborate side pieces* LATERAL, wing, flanking. ANTONYM front.

2 *a side issue* SUBORDINATE, lesser, lower-level, secondary, minor, peripheral, incidental, ancillary, subsidiary, of little account, extraneous. ANTONYM central.

▸ verb ***siding with*** *the underdog.* See TAKE SOMEONE'S SIDE below.

PHRASES: **side by side** *they worked side by side* ALONGSIDE (EACH OTHER), beside each other, abreast, shoulder to shoulder, close together; in collaboration, in solidarity.
**take someone's side** *I was surprised to see you taking Jack's side* SUPPORT, take someone's part, side with, be on someone's side, stand by, back, give someone one's backing, be loyal to, defend, champion, ally (oneself) with, sympathize with, favor.

**sidelong** adjective *a sidelong glance* INDIRECT, oblique, sideways, sideward; surreptitious, furtive, covert, sly. ANTONYM overt.

▸ adverb *he looked sidelong at her* INDIRECTLY, obliquely, sideways, out of the corner of one's eye; surreptitiously, furtively, covertly, slyly.

**sidestep** verb *he neatly sidestepped the questions about crime* AVOID, evade, dodge, circumvent, skirt around, bypass; *informal* duck, pussyfoot around.

**sidetrack** verb *I'm easily sidetracked by things going on outside my office window* DISTRACT, divert, deflect, draw away.

**sideways** adverb 1 *I slid off sideways* TO THE SIDE, laterally.

2 *the expansion slots are mounted sideways* EDGEWISE, sideward/sidewards, side first, edgeways, end on, broadside.

3 *he looked sideways at her* OBLIQUELY, indirectly, sidelong; covertly, furtively, surreptitiously, slyly.

▸ adjective 1 *sideways force* LATERAL, sideward, on the side, side to side.

2 *a sideways look* OBLIQUE, indirect, sidelong; covert, furtive, sly, surreptitious.

**siege** noun *the siege of the fort lasted into the morning* BLOCKADE, encirclement. ANTONYM relief.

**siesta** noun *he's enjoying a siesta on the terrace* AFTERNOON SLEEP, nap, catnap, doze, rest; *informal* snooze, lie-down, forty winks, bit of shut-eye.

**sieve** noun *use a sieve to strain the mixture* STRAINER, sifter, filter, riddle, screen.

▸ verb 1 *sieve the mixture into a bowl.* See SIFT sense 1.

2 *the coins were sieved from the ash* SEPARATE OUT, filter out, sift, sort out, isolate, part, extract, remove.

**sift** verb 1 *sift the flour into a large bowl* SIEVE, strain, screen, filter, riddle; *archaic* bolt.

2 *we* ***sift out*** *unsuitable applications* SEPARATE OUT, filter out, sort out, put to one side, weed out, get rid of, remove.

3 *investigators are* ***sifting through*** *the wreckage* SEARCH THROUGH, look through, examine, inspect, scrutinize, pore over, investigate, analyze, dissect, review.

**sigh** verb 1 *she sighed with relief* BREATHE OUT, exhale; groan, moan.

2 *the wind sighed in the trees* RUSTLE, whisper, murmur, sough.

3 *he* ***sighed for*** *younger days gone by* YEARN FOR, long for, pine for, ache for, grieve for, cry for/over, weep for/over, rue, miss, mourn, lament, hanker for/after.

**sight** noun 1 *she has excellent sight* EYESIGHT, vision, eyes, faculty of sight, visual perception.

2 *her first sight of it* VIEW, glimpse, glance, look.

3 *within sight of the enemy* RANGE OF VISION, field of vision, view.

4 *dated we are all equal in the sight of God* PERCEPTION, judgment, belief, opinion, point of view, view, viewpoint, mind, perspective, standpoint.

5 *historic sights* LANDMARK, place of interest, monument, spectacle, view, marvel, wonder.

6 *informal I must look a sight* EYESORE, spectacle, mess; *informal* fright.

▸ verb *one of the helicopters sighted wreckage* GLIMPSE, catch/get a glimpse of, catch sight of, see, spot, spy, notice, observe; *literary* espy, descry.

PHRASES: **catch sight of** *we caught sight of a dim flicker of light in the distance* GLIMPSE, catch/get a glimpse of, see, spot, spy, make out, pick out, have sight of; *literary* espy, descry.
**set one's sights on** *she set her sights on a teaching career* ASPIRE TO, aim at/for, try for, strive for/toward, work toward.

**sign** noun 1 *a sign of affection* INDICATION, signal, symptom, pointer, suggestion, intimation, mark, manifestation, demonstration, token, evidence; *literary* sigil.

2 *a sign of things to come* PORTENT, omen, warning, forewarning, augury, presage; promise, threat.

3 *at his sign the soldiers followed* GESTURE, signal, wave, gesticulation, cue, nod.

4 *he read the sign on the wall* NOTICE, signpost, signboard, warning sign, road sign, traffic sign, guidepost, marquee.

5 *the dancers were daubed with signs* SYMBOL, mark, cipher, letter, character, figure, hieroglyph, ideogram, rune, emblem, device, logo. See note at EMBLEM.

▸ verb 1 *he signed the letter* WRITE ONE'S NAME ON, autograph, endorse, initial, countersign, ink; *formal* subscribe.

2 *the government signed the agreement* ENDORSE, validate, certify, authenticate, sanction, authorize; agree to, approve, ratify, adopt, give one's approval to; *informal* give something the go-ahead, give something the green light, give something the thumbs up.

3 *he signed his name* WRITE, inscribe, pen.

**4** *we have signed a new player* RECRUIT, hire, engage, employ, take on, appoint, sign on/up, enlist.

**5** *she signed to Susan to leave.* See SIGNAL[1] verb sense 1.

PHRASES: **sign on/up** **1** *I signed up with Will's committee to raise money for the school library* ENLIST, take a job, join (up), enroll, register, volunteer.

**2** *the Yankees have signed on Rodriguez.* See SIGN verb sense 4.

**sign over** *he signed over the business to his children* TRANSFER, make over, hand over, bequeath, pass on, transmit, cede; *Law* devolve, convey.

THE RIGHT WORD **sign, augury, indication, manifestation, omen, signal, symptom, token**

What's the difference between a **sign** and a **signal**? The former (in this sense) is a general term for anything that gives evidence of an event, a mood, a quality of character, a mental or physical state, or a trace of something (*a sign of approaching rain; a sign of good breeding; a sign that someone has entered the house*). While a sign may be involuntary or even unconscious, a *signal* is always voluntary and is usually deliberate. A ship that shows signs of distress may or may not be in trouble; but one that sends a distress *signal* is definitely in need of help. **Indication**, like *sign*, is a comprehensive term for anything that serves to indicate or point out (*he gave no indication that he was lying*). A **manifestation** is an outward or perceptible indication of something (*the letter was a manifestation of his guilt*), and a **symptom** is an indication of a diseased condition (*a symptom of pneumonia*). An object that proves the existence of something abstract is called a **token** (*she gave him a locket as a token of her love*). **Omen** and **augury** both pertain to foretelling future events, with *augury* being the general term for a prediction of the future and *omen* being a definite sign foretelling good or evil (*they regarded the stormy weather as a bad omen*).

**signal**[1] noun **1** *a signal to stop* GESTURE, sign, wave, gesticulation, cue, indication, warning, motion.

**2** *a clear signal that the company is in trouble* INDICATION, sign, symptom, hint, pointer, intimation, clue, demonstration, evidence, proof. See note at SIGN.

**3** *the encroaching dark is a signal for people to emerge* CUE, prompt, impetus, stimulus; *informal* go-ahead.

▸ verb **1** *the driver signaled to her to cross* GESTURE, sign, give a sign to, direct, motion; wave, beckon, nod.

**2** *they signaled displeasure by refusing to cooperate* INDICATE, show, express, communicate, proclaim, declare.

**3** *his death signals the end of an era* MARK, signify, mean, be a sign of, be evidence of, herald; *literary* betoken, foretoken.

**signal**[2] adjective *a signal victory.* See SIGNIFICANT sense 1.

**significance** noun **1** *a matter of considerable significance* IMPORTANCE, import, consequence, seriousness, gravity, weight, magnitude, momentousness; *formal* moment.

**2** *the significance of his remarks* MEANING, sense, signification, import, thrust, drift, gist, implication, message, essence, substance, point.

**significant** adjective **1** *a significant increase* NOTABLE, noteworthy, worthy of attention, remarkable, important, of importance, of consequence, signal; serious, crucial, weighty, momentous, epoch-making, uncommon, unusual, rare, extraordinary, exceptional, special; *formal* of moment.

**2** *a significant look* MEANINGFUL, expressive, eloquent, suggestive, knowing, telling.

**signify** verb **1** *this signified a fundamental change* BE EVIDENCE OF, be a sign of, mark, signal, mean, spell, be symptomatic of, herald, indicate; *literary* betoken.

**2** *the egg signifies life* MEAN, denote, designate, represent, symbolize, stand for; *literary* betoken.

**3** *signify your agreement by signing below* EXPRESS, indicate, show, proclaim, declare.

**4** *the locked door doesn't signify* MEAN ANYTHING, be of importance, be important, be significant, be of significance, be of account, count, matter, be relevant.

**silence** noun **1** *the silence of the night* QUIETNESS, quiet, quietude, still, stillness, hush, tranquility, noiselessness, soundlessness, peacefulness, peace (and quiet). ANTONYM sound.

**2** *she was reduced to silence* SPEECHLESSNESS, wordlessness, dumbness, muteness, taciturnity. ANTONYMS speech, loquacity.

**3** *the politicians kept their silence* SECRETIVENESS, secrecy, reticence, taciturnity, uncommunicativeness. ANTONYM communicativeness.

▸ verb **1** *he silenced her with a kiss* QUIET, hush, shush; gag, muzzle, censor.

**2** *silencing outside noises* MUFFLE, deaden, soften, mute, smother, dampen, damp down, mask, suppress, reduce.

**3** *this would silence their complaints* STOP, put an end to, put a stop to.

**silent** adjective **1** *the night was silent* COMPLETELY QUIET, still, hushed, inaudible, noiseless, soundless. ANTONYMS audible, noisy.

**2** *the right to remain silent* SPEECHLESS, quiet, unspeaking, dumb, mute, taciturn, uncommunicative, tight-lipped; *informal* mum. ANTONYM loquacious.

**3** *silent thanks* UNSPOKEN, wordless, unsaid, unexpressed, unvoiced, tacit, implicit, understood. ANTONYM spoken.

**silhouette** noun *the silhouette of the dome* OUTLINE, contour(s), profile, form, shape, figure, shadow.

▸ verb *the castle was silhouetted against the sky* OUTLINE, delineate, define; stand out.

**silky** adjective *her long, silky hair* SMOOTH, soft, sleek, fine, glossy, satiny, silken.

**silly** adjective **1** *don't be so silly* FOOLISH, stupid, unintelligent, idiotic, brainless, mindless, witless, imbecilic, doltish; imprudent, thoughtless, rash, reckless, foolhardy, irresponsible; mad, scatterbrained, featherbrained; frivolous, giddy, inane, immature, childish, puerile, empty-headed; *informal* crazy, dotty, scatty, loopy, wingy, ditzy, screwy, thick, thickheaded, birdbrained, pea-brained, dopey, dim, dimwitted, halfwitted, dippy, blockheaded, boneheaded, lamebrained; daft, chowderheaded; *dated* tomfool. ANTONYM sensible.

**2** *that was a silly thing to do* UNWISE, imprudent, thoughtless, foolish, stupid, idiotic, senseless, mindless; rash, reckless, foolhardy, irresponsible, injudicious, misguided, irrational; *informal* crazy; daft. ANTONYM sensible.

**3** *he would brood about silly things* TRIVIAL, trifling, frivolous, footling, petty, small, insignificant, unimportant; *informal* piffling, piddling, small-bore. ANTONYM important.

**4** *he drank himself silly* SENSELESS, insensible, unconscious, stupid, into a stupor, into senselessness, stupefied.

▸ noun *informal you're such a silly!* See FOOL noun sense 1.

**similar** adjective **1** *you two are very similar* ALIKE, (much) the same, indistinguishable, almost identical, homogeneous, homologous; *informal* much of a muchness. ANTONYM different.

**2** *northern India and similar areas* COMPARABLE, like, corresponding, homogeneous, equivalent, analogous. PHRASE: **be similar to** *other towns were similar to this one* BE LIKE, RESEMBLE, look like, have the appearance of, be much the same as, be comparable to.

**similarity** noun *the similarity between John and his daughter* RESEMBLANCE, likeness, sameness, similitude, comparability, correspondence, parallel, equivalence, homogeneity, indistinguishability, uniformity; *archaic* semblance. See note at LIKENESS.

**similarly** adverb *the two vases are similarly flawed at the base* LIKEWISE, in similar fashion, in like manner, comparably, correspondingly, uniformly, indistinguishably, analogously, homogeneously, equivalently, in the same way, the same, identically.

**similitude** noun *Conrad uses a range of constructions that imply similitude* RESEMBLANCE, similarity, likeness, sameness, similar nature, comparability, correspondence, comparison, analogy, parallel, parallelism, equivalence; interchangeability, closeness, nearness, affinity, homogeneity, agreement, indistinguishability, uniformity; community, kinship, relatedness; *archaic* semblance. See note at LIKENESS.

**simmer** verb **1** *the soup was simmering on the stove* BOIL GENTLY, cook gently, bubble, stew.

**2** *she was simmering with resentment* BE FURIOUS, be enraged, be angry, be incensed, be infuriated, seethe, fume, brim, smolder; *informal* be steamed up, be hot under the collar, stew. PHRASE: **simmer down** *we're not going to discuss this until you simmer down* BECOME LESS ANGRY, cool off/down, be placated, control oneself, become calmer, calm down, become quieter, quiet down; *informal* chill out.

**simple** adjective **1** *it's really simple* STRAIGHTFORWARD, easy, uncomplicated, uninvolved, effortless, painless, undemanding, elementary, child's play; *informal* as easy as pie, as easy as ABC, a piece of cake, a cinch, no sweat, a pushover, kids' stuff, a breeze, duck soup, a snap. ANTONYMS difficult, hard, complicated.

**2** *simple language* CLEAR, plain, straightforward, intelligible, comprehensible, uncomplicated, accessible; *informal* user-friendly. ANTONYM complex.

**3** *a simple white blouse* PLAIN, unadorned, undecorated, unembellished, unornamented, unelaborate, basic, unsophisticated, no-frills; classic, understated, uncluttered, restrained. ANTONYMS fancy, elaborate.

**4** *the simple truth* CANDID, frank, honest, sincere, plain, absolute, unqualified, bald, stark, unadorned, unvarnished, unembellished.

**5** *simple country people* UNPRETENTIOUS, unsophisticated, ordinary, unaffected, unassuming, natural, honest-to-goodness, cracker-barrel. ANTONYMS pretentious, affected.

**6** *he's a bit simple* HAVING LEARNING DIFFICULTIES, having special (educational) needs; of low intelligence, simple-minded, unintelligent, backward, (mentally) retarded. ANTONYM gifted.

**7** *simple chemical substances* NONCOMPOUND, noncomplex, uncombined, unblended, unalloyed, pure, single. ANTONYM compound.

**simpleton** noun. See FOOL noun sense 1.

**simplicity** noun **1** *the simplicity of the recipes* STRAIGHTFORWARDNESS, ease, easiness, simpleness, effortlessness.

**2** *the simplicity of the language* CLARITY, clearness, plainness, simpleness, intelligibility, comprehensibility, understandability, accessibility, straightforwardness.

**3** *the building's simplicity* PLAINNESS, lack/absence of adornment, lack/absence of decoration, austerity, spareness, clean lines.

**4** *the simplicity of their lifestyle* UNPRETENTIOUSNESS, ordinariness, lack of sophistication, lack of affectation, naturalness.

**simplify** verb *please simplify your answer* MAKE SIMPLE/SIMPLER, make easy/easier to understand, make plainer, clarify, make more comprehensible/intelligible; paraphrase. ANTONYM complicate.

**simplistic** adjective *the proposed solutions are too simplistic* FACILE, superficial, oversimple, oversimplified; shallow, jejune, naive.

**simply** adverb **1** *he spoke simply and forcefully* STRAIGHTFORWARDLY, directly, clearly, plainly, intelligibly, lucidly, unambiguously.

**2** *she was dressed simply* PLAINLY, without adornment, without decoration, without ornament/ornamentation, soberly, unfussily, unelaborately, classically.

**3** *they lived simply* UNPRETENTIOUSLY, modestly, quietly.

**4** *they are welcomed simply because they have plenty of money* MERELY, just, purely, solely, only.

**5** *Mrs. Marks was simply livid* UTTERLY, absolutely, completely, positively, really; *informal* plain.

**6** *it's simply the best thing ever written* WITHOUT DOUBT, unquestionably, undeniably, incontrovertibly, certainly, categorically.

**simulate** verb **1** *they simulated pleasure* FEIGN, pretend, fake, sham, affect, put on, give the appearance of.

**2** *simulating conditions in space* IMITATE, reproduce, replicate, duplicate, mimic.

**simultaneous** adjective *they carried out simultaneous raids at two houses* CONCURRENT, happening at the same time, contemporaneous, concomitant, coinciding, coincident, synchronous, synchronized.

**simultaneously** adverb *Alison and Frank spoke simultaneously* AT (ONE AND) THE SAME TIME, at the same instant/moment, at once, concurrently, concomitantly; (all) together, in unison, in concert, in chorus.

**sin** noun **1** *a sin in the eyes of God* IMMORAL ACT, wrong, wrongdoing, act of evil/wickedness, transgression, crime, offense, misdeed, misdemeanor; *archaic* trespass.

**2** *the human capacity for sin* WICKEDNESS, wrongdoing, wrong, evil, evildoing, sinfulness, immorality, iniquity, vice, crime. ANTONYM virtue.

**3** *informal they've cut the school music program—it's a sin* SCANDAL, crime, disgrace, outrage.

▸ verb *I have sinned* COMMIT A SIN, commit an offense, transgress, do wrong, commit a crime, break the law, misbehave, go astray; *archaic* trespass.

THE RIGHT WORD **sin, crime, fault, indiscretion, offense, transgression, vice**

If you've ever driven through a red light or chewed with your mouth open, you've committed an **offense**, which is a broad term covering any violation of the law or of standards of propriety and taste. A **sin**, on the other hand, is an act that specifically violates a religious, ethical, or moral standard (*to marry someone of another faith was considered a sin*). **Transgression** is a weightier and more serious word for *sin*, suggesting any violation of an agreed-upon set of rules (*their behavior was clearly a transgression of the terms set forth in the treaty*). A **crime** is any act forbidden by law and punishable upon conviction (*a crime for which he was sentenced to death*). A **vice** has less to do with violating the law and more to do with habits and practices that debase a person's character (*alcohol was her only vice*). **Fault** and **indiscretion** are gentler words, although they may be used as euphemisms for *sin* or *crime*. A *fault* is an unsatisfactory feature in someone's character (*she is exuberant to a fault*), while *indiscretion* refers to an unwise or improper action (*speaking to the media was an indiscretion for which she was chastised*). In recent years, however, *indiscretion* has become a euphemism for such sins as adultery, as if to excuse such behavior by attributing it to a momentary lapse of judgment (*his indiscretions were no secret*).

**sincere** adjective **1** *our sincere gratitude* HEARTFELT, wholehearted, profound, deep; genuine, real, unfeigned, unaffected, true, honest, bona fide.

**2** *a sincere person* HONEST, genuine, truthful, unhypocritical, straightforward, direct, frank, candid; *informal* straight, upfront, on the level, on the up and up.

**sincerely** adverb *we sincerely hope you'll be better soon* GENUINELY, honestly, really, truly, truthfully, wholeheartedly, earnestly, fervently.

**sincerity** noun *there's no reason to doubt her sincerity* HONESTY, genuineness, truthfulness, integrity, probity, trustworthiness; straightforwardness, openness, candor, candidness.

**sinewy** adjective *he was tall, blond, and sinewy* MUSCULAR, muscly, brawny, powerfully built, burly, strapping, sturdy, rugged, strong, powerful, athletic, muscle-bound, hard-bodied; *informal* hunky, beefy; *dated* stalwart; *literary* thewy. ANTONYM puny.

**sinful** adjective **1** *sinful conduct* IMMORAL, wicked, (morally) wrong, wrongful, evil, bad, iniquitous, corrupt, criminal, nefarious, depraved, degenerate. ANTONYM virtuous.

**2** *a sinful waste of money* REPREHENSIBLE, scandalous, disgraceful, deplorable, shameful, criminal. ANTONYM admirable.

**sing** verb **1** *the choir began to sing* croon, carol, trill, chant, intone, chorus; *informal* belt out.

**2** *the birds were singing* WARBLE, trill, chirp, chirrup, cheep, peep.

**3** *Rudy* ***sang out*** *a greeting* CALL (OUT), cry (out), shout, yell; *informal* holler.

**4** *informal he's going to sing to the police* INFORM (ON SOMEONE), confess; *informal* squeal, rat on someone, blow the whistle on someone, snitch (on someone), narc (on someone), finger someone, fink on someone.

**singe** verb *the ends of my hair were singed when I leaned over the candle* SCORCH, burn, sear, char. See note at BURN.

**singer** noun *she's the lead singer* VOCALIST, soloist, songster, songstress, cantor, chorister, cantor; *informal* songbird, siren, diva, chanteuse, chansonnier; *literary* troubadour, minstrel.

**single** adjective **1** *a single red rose* ONE (ONLY), sole, lone, solitary, by itself/oneself, unaccompanied, alone. ANTONYM double.

**2** *she wrote down every single word* INDIVIDUAL, separate, distinct, particular, last.

**3** *is she single?* UNMARRIED, unwed, unwedded, unattached, free, a bachelor, a spinster; partnerless, husbandless, wifeless; separated, divorced, widowed; *informal* solo. ANTONYM married.

PHRASE: **single out** *her watercolors were singled out by the judges* SELECT, pick out, choose, decide on; target, earmark, mark out, separate out, set apart/aside.

**single-handed** adverb *I installed the alarm single-handed* BY ONESELF, alone, on one's own, solo, unaided, unassisted, without help.

**single-minded** adjective *I got where I am with hard work and single-minded determination* DETERMINED, committed, unswerving, unwavering, resolute, purposeful, devoted, dedicated, uncompromising, tireless, tenacious, persistent, indefatigable, dogged; *formal* pertinacious. ANTONYM halfhearted.

**singly** adverb *people, please enter singly into the hallway* ONE BY ONE, one at a time, one after the other, individually, separately, by oneself, on one's own. ANTONYM together.

**singular** adjective **1** *the gallery's singular capacity to attract sponsors* REMARKABLE, extraordinary, exceptional, outstanding, signal, notable, noteworthy; rare, unique, unparalleled, unprecedented, amazing, astonishing, phenomenal, astounding; *informal* fantastic, terrific.

**2** *why was Betty behaving in so singular a fashion?* STRANGE, unusual, odd, peculiar, funny, curious, extraordinary, bizarre, eccentric, weird, queer, unexpected, unfamiliar, abnormal, atypical, unconventional, out of the ordinary, untypical, puzzling, mysterious, perplexing, baffling, unaccountable.

**sinister** adjective **1** *there was a sinister undertone in his words* MENACING, threatening, ominous, forbidding, baleful, frightening, alarming, disturbing, disquieting, dark, black; *formal* minatory; *literary* direful.

**2** *a sinister motive* EVIL, wicked, criminal, corrupt, nefarious, villainous, base, vile, malevolent, malicious; *informal* shady. ANTONYM innocent.

**sink** verb **1** *the coffin sank below the waves* BECOME SUBMERGED, be engulfed, go down, drop, fall, descend. ANTONYMS float, rise.

**2** *the cruise liner sank yesterday* FOUNDER, go under, submerge.

**3** *they sank their ships* SCUTTLE, send to the bottom; scupper.

**4** *the announcement sank hopes of a recovery* DESTROY, ruin, wreck, put an end to, demolish, smash, shatter, dash; *informal* put the kibosh on, put paid to; *informal* scupper; *archaic* bring to naught.

**5** *I sank myself in student life* IMMERSE, submerge, plunge, lose, bury.

**6** *the plane sank toward the airstrip* DESCEND, drop, go down/downward. ANTONYM ascend.

**7** *the sun was sinking* SET, go down/downward. ANTONYM rise.

**8** *Loretta sank into an armchair* LOWER ONESELF, flop, collapse, fall, drop down, slump; *informal* plunk oneself.

**9** *her voice sank to a whisper* FALL, drop, become/get quieter, become/get softer. ANTONYM rise.

**10** *she would never sink to your level* STOOP, lower oneself, descend.

**11** *he was sinking fast* DETERIORATE, decline, fade, grow weak, flag, waste away; be at death's door, be on one's deathbed, be slipping away; *informal* go downhill, be on one's last legs, be giving up the ghost. ANTONYMS recover, improve.

**12** *sink the pots into the ground* EMBED, insert, drive, plant.

**13** *sinking a gold mine* DIG, excavate, bore, drill.

**14** *they sank their life savings into the company* INVEST, venture, risk.

▸ noun *he washed himself at the sink* BASIN, wash basin; *dated* lavabo.

PHRASE: **sink in** *bad news like this often takes time to sink in* REGISTER, be understood, be comprehended, be grasped, get through.

**sinner** noun *on a mission to rescue these sinners from the darkness* WRONGDOER, evildoer, transgressor, miscreant, offender, criminal; *archaic* trespasser.

**sinuous** adjective **1** *a sinuous river* WINDING, windy, serpentine, curving, twisting, meandering, snaking, zigzag, curling, coiling.

**2** *she moved with sinuous grace* LITHE, supple, agile, graceful, loose-limbed, limber, lissome.

**sip** verb *Amanda sipped her coffee* DRINK (SLOWLY).

▸ noun *a sip of whiskey* MOUTHFUL, swallow, drink, drop, dram, nip, taste; *informal* swig.

**siren** noun **1** *a fire engine's siren* ALARM (BELL), warning bell, danger signal; *archaic* tocsin.

**2** *the siren's allure* SEDUCTRESS, temptress, tease, femme fatale; flirt, coquette; *informal* man-eater, home wrecker, vamp.

**sit** verb **1** *here, sit on the comfy chair* TAKE A SEAT, seat oneself, be seated, perch, ensconce oneself, plump oneself, flop; *informal* take the load/weight off one's feet, plunk oneself, take a load off. ANTONYM stand.

**2** *she sat the package on the table* PUT (DOWN), place, set (down), lay, deposit, rest, stand; *informal* stick, dump, park, plunk. ANTONYM lift.

**3** *the church sat about 3,000 people* HOLD, seat, have seats for, have space/room for, accommodate.

**4** *she sat for Picasso* POSE, model.

**5** *a hotel sitting on the mountain* BE SITUATED, be located, be sited, stand.

**6** *the committee sits on Saturday* BE IN SESSION, meet, be convened.

**7** *women jurists* ***sit on*** *the tribunal* SERVE ON, have a seat on, be a member of.

**8** *his shyness doesn't sit easily with Hollywood tradition* BE HARMONIOUS, go, fit in, harmonize.

**9** *Mrs. Hillman will sit for us* BABYSIT. PHRASES: **sit back** *sit back and listen to the music* RELAX, unwind, lie back; *informal* let it all hang out, veg out, hang loose, chill (out), take a load off.

**sit in for** *I'll be sitting in for Tim while he's away* STAND IN FOR, fill in for, cover for, substitute for; *informal* sub for.

**sit in on** *you're welcome to sit in on any of your son's classes* ATTEND, be present at, be an observer at, observe, audit.

**sit tight** *informal* **1** *just sit tight while I call your parents* STAY PUT, wait there, remain in one's place.

**2** *we're advising our clients to sit tight* TAKE NO ACTION, wait, hold back, bide one's time; *informal* hold one's horses.

**site** noun *the site of the battle* LOCATION, place, position, situation, locality, whereabouts; *technical* locus.

▸ verb *garbage cans sited along the street* PLACE, put, position, situate, locate.

**situate** verb *the library is situated just west of the town hall* LOCATE, site, position, place, station, build.

**situation** noun **1** *their financial situation* CIRCUMSTANCES, (state of) affairs, state, condition.

**2** *I'll fill you in on* ***the situation*** THE FACTS, how things stand, the lay of the land, what's going on; *informal* the score, the scoop.

**3** *the hotel's pleasant situation* LOCATION, position, spot, site, setting, environment; *technical* locus.

**4** *he was offered a situation in Canada* JOB, post, position, appointment; employment.

**size** noun *the room was of medium size* DIMENSIONS, measurements, proportions, magnitude, largeness, bigness, area, expanse; breadth, width, length, height, depth; immensity, hugeness, vastness.

▸ verb *the drills are sized in millimeters* SORT, categorize, classify.

PHRASE: **size up** *informal having sized up the competition, I knew I would win* ASSESS, appraise, form an estimate of, take the measure of, judge, take stock of, evaluate.

**skeleton** noun **1** *the human skeleton* BONES.

**2** *she was no more than a skeleton* SKIN AND BONE; *informal* bag of bones.

**3** *a concrete skeleton* FRAMEWORK, frame, shell.

**4** *the skeleton of a report* OUTLINE, (rough) draft, abstract, (bare) bones.

▸ adjective *a skeleton staff* MINIMUM, minimal, basic; essential.

**skeptic** noun **1** *skeptics said the marriage wouldn't last* CYNIC, doubter; pessimist, prophet of doom.

**2** *skeptics who have found faith* AGNOSTIC, atheist, unbeliever, nonbeliever, disbeliever, doubting Thomas.

**skeptical** adjective *she was wisely skeptical about his get-rich-quick scheme* DUBIOUS, doubtful, taking something with a pinch of salt, doubting; cynical, distrustful, mistrustful, suspicious, disbelieving, unconvinced, incredulous, scoffing; pessimistic, defeatist. ANTONYMS certain, convinced.

**skepticism** noun **1** *his ideas were met with skepticism* DOUBT, doubtfulness, a pinch of salt; disbelief, cynicism, distrust, mistrust, suspicion, incredulity; pessimism, defeatism; *formal* dubiety. See note at UNCERTAINTY.

**2** *he passed from skepticism to religious belief* AGNOSTICISM, doubt; atheism, unbelief, nonbelief.

**sketch** noun **1** *a sketch of the proposed design* (PRELIMINARY) DRAWING, outline; diagram, design, plan; *informal* rough.

**2** *she gave a rough sketch of what had happened* OUTLINE, brief description, rundown, main points, thumbnail sketch, (bare) bones; summary, synopsis, summarization, précis, résumé, wrap-up.

**3** *a biographical sketch* DESCRIPTION, portrait, profile, portrayal, depiction.

**4** *a hilarious sketch* SKIT, scene, piece, act, item, routine.

▸ verb **1** *he sketched the garden* DRAW, make a drawing of, draw a picture of, pencil, rough out, outline.

**2** *the company* ***sketched out*** *its plans* DESCRIBE, outline, give a brief idea of, rough out; summarize, précis.

**sketchy** adjective *we have only a sketchy description of the assailant* INCOMPLETE, patchy, fragmentary, cursory, perfunctory, scanty, vague, imprecise, imperfect; hurried, hasty. ANTONYM detailed.

**skill** noun **1** *his skill as a politician* EXPERTISE, skillfulness, expertness, adeptness, adroitness, deftness, dexterity, ability, prowess, mastery, competence, capability, aptitude, artistry, virtuosity, talent. ANTONYM incompetence.

**2** *bringing up a family gives you many skills* ACCOMPLISHMENT, strength, gift.

**skilled** adjective *a skilled architect* EXPERIENCED, trained, qualified, credentialed, proficient, practiced, accomplished, expert, skillful, talented, gifted, adept, adroit, deft, dexterous, able, good, competent; *informal* crack, crackerjack. ANTONYM inexperienced.

**skillful** adjective *the work of a skillful shoemaker* EXPERT, accomplished, skilled, masterly, master, virtuoso, consummate, proficient, talented, gifted, adept, adroit, deft, dexterous, able, good, competent, capable, brilliant, handy; *informal* mean, wicked, crack, ace, wizard, crackerjack, pro.

**skim** verb **1** ***skim off*** *the scum* REMOVE, cream off, scoop off.

**2** *the boat skimmed over the water* GLIDE, move lightly, slide, sail, skate, float.

**3** *he skimmed the pebble across the water* THROW, toss, cast, pitch; bounce.

**4** *she* ***skimmed through*** *the newspaper* GLANCE THROUGH, flick through, flip through, leaf through, riffle through, thumb through, read quickly, scan, run one's eye over.

**5** *Hannah* ***skimmed over*** *this part of the story* MENTION BRIEFLY, pass over quickly, skate over, gloss over. ANTONYM elaborate on.

**skimp** verb **1** *don't* ***skimp on*** *the quantity* STINT ON, scrimp on, economize on, cut back on, be sparing with, be frugal with, be mean with, be parsimonious with, cut corners with; *informal* be stingy with, be mingy with, be tight with.

**2** *the process cannot be skimped* DO HASTILY, do carelessly.

**skimpy** adjective **1** *a skimpy black dress* REVEALING, short, low, low-cut; flimsy, thin, see-through, indecent.

**2** *my information is rather skimpy* MEAGER, scanty, sketchy, limited, paltry, deficient, sparse.

**skin** noun **1** *these chemicals could damage the skin* EPIDERMIS, dermis, derma.

**2** *Mary's fair skin* COMPLEXION, coloring, skin color/tone, pigmentation.

**3** *leopard skins* HIDE, pelt, fleece, *historical* plew; *archaic* fell.

**4** *a banana skin* PEEL, rind, integument.

**5** *milk with a skin on it* FILM, layer, membrane.

**6** *the plane's skin was damaged* CASING, exterior.

▸ verb **1** *skin the tomatoes* PEEL, pare, hull; *technical* decorticate.

**2** *he skinned his knee* GRAZE, scrape, abrade, bark, rub raw, chafe; *Medicine* excoriate.

PHRASES: **by the skin of one's teeth** *he won, but only by the skin of his teeth* (ONLY) JUST, narrowly, barely, by a hair's breadth, by a very small margin; *informal* by a whisker.
**get under someone's skin** *informal* **1** *the children really got under my skin.* See IRRITATE sense 1.

**2** *she got under my skin* OBSESS, intrigue, captivate, charm; enthrall, enchant, entrance.
**it's no skin off my nose** *informal if you want to go swimming in that icy water, it's no skin off my nose* I DON'T CARE, I don't mind, I'm not bothered, it doesn't bother me, it doesn't matter to me; *informal* I don't give a damn, I couldn't/could care less.
**skin alive** *informal Dad would skin me alive if I forgot it* PUNISH SEVERELY; *informal* murder, come down on (like a ton of bricks), give what for.

**skinflint** noun *informal Jodie has the charisma needed to pry those dollar bills from these skinflints' fists* MISER, penny-pincher, Scrooge, pinchpenny; *informal* money-grubber, cheapskate, tightwad, piker.

**skinny** adjective *his extreme height made him look especially skinny* THIN, scrawny, scraggy, bony, angular, rawboned, hollow-cheeked, gaunt, as thin as a rake, skin-and-bones, sticklike, emaciated, waiflike, skeletal, pinched, undernourished, underfed; SLIM, lean, slender, rangy; lanky, spindly, gangly, gangling, gawky; *informal* looking like a bag of bones, anorexic; *dated* spindle-shanked. See note at THIN.

▸ noun *informal everybody wants to know the skinny on Karen's divorce* GOSSIP, (inside) information, intelligence, news, inside story; *informal* lowdown, info, dope, dirt, scoop, poop.

**skip** verb **1** *skipping down the path* CAPER, prance, trip, dance, bound, bounce, gambol, frisk, romp, cavort.

**2** *we skipped the boring stuff* OMIT, leave out, miss out, dispense with, pass over, skim over, disregard; *informal* give something a miss.

**3** *I skipped school* PLAY TRUANT FROM, miss, cut; *informal* play hooky from, ditch.

**4** *informal they* ***skipped off*** *again first chance I get, I'm* ***skipping out*** RUN OFF/AWAY, take off; *informal* beat it, clear off, cut and run, light out, cut out.

**skirmish** noun **1** *the unit was caught up in a skirmish* FIGHT, battle, clash, conflict, encounter, engagement, fray, combat.

**2** *there was a skirmish over the budget* ARGUMENT, quarrel, squabble, contretemps, disagreement, difference of opinion, falling-out, dispute, blowup, clash, altercation; *informal* tiff, spat; row.

▸ verb *they skirmished with enemy soldiers* FIGHT, (do) battle with, engage with, close with, combat, clash with.

**skirt** verb **1** *he skirted the city* GO AROUND, walk around, circle.

**2** *the fields that skirt the highway* BORDER, edge, flank, line, lie alongside.

**3** *he carefully skirted the subject* AVOID, evade, sidestep, dodge, pass over, gloss over; *informal* duck.

**skit** noun *we auditioned by acting out our own three-minute skits* COMEDY SKETCH, comedy act, parody, pastiche, burlesque, satire; *informal* spoof, takeoff, sendup.

**skittish** adjective *going to the dentist makes me skittish* NERVOUS, anxious, on edge, excitable, restive, skittery, jumpy, jittery, high-strung.

**skulk** verb *you're right, I think someone is skulking around behind those cars* LURK, loiter, hide; creep, sneak, slink, prowl, pussyfoot.

**sky** noun *the sun was shining in the sky* the upper atmosphere; *literary* the heavens, the firmament, the blue, the (wide) blue yonder, the welkin, the azure, the empyrean. PHRASE: **to the skies** *he praised Lizzie to the skies* EFFUSIVELY, profusely, very highly, very enthusiastically, unreservedly, fervently, fulsomely, extravagantly.

**slab** noun *slabs of concrete* PIECE, block, hunk, chunk, lump; cake, tablet, brick.

**slack** adjective **1** *the rope went slack* LOOSE, limp, hanging, flexible. ANTONYMS tight, taut.

**2** *slack skin* FLACCID, flabby, loose, sagging, saggy. ANTONYM taut.

**3** *business is slack* SLUGGISH, slow, quiet, slow-moving, flat, depressed, stagnant. ANTONYMS thriving, busy.

**4** *slack accounting procedures* LAX, negligent, remiss, careless, slapdash, slipshod, lackadaisical, inefficient, casual; *informal* sloppy, slaphappy. ANTONYM diligent.

▸ noun **1** *the rope had some slack in it* LOOSENESS, play, give.

**2** *foreign demand will help pick up the slack* SURPLUS, excess, residue, spare capacity.

**3** *a little slack in the daily routine* LULL, pause, respite, break, hiatus, breathing space; *informal* letup, breather.

▸ verb *informal no slacking!* IDLE, shirk, be lazy, be indolent, waste time, lounge about; *informal* goof off.

PHRASES: **slack off 1** *the rain has slacked off* DECREASE, subside, let up, ease off, abate, diminish, die down, fall off.

**2** *you deserve to slack off a bit* RELAX, take things easy, let up, ease up/off, loosen up, slow down; *informal* hang loose, chill (out).
**slack up** *he doesn't slack up until he gets there* SLOW (DOWN), decelerate, reduce speed.

**slacker** noun *informal all right, you slackers, let's get this cargo across the river before the sun sets* LAYABOUT, idler, shirker, malingerer, sluggard, laggard; *informal* lazybones, bum, goof-off.

**slake** verb *we longed for a mountain spring to slake our thirst* QUENCH, satisfy, sate, satiate, relieve, assuage.

**slam** verb **1** *he slammed the door behind him* BANG, shut/close with a bang, shut/close noisily, shut/close with force.

**2** *the car* ***slammed into*** *a post* CRASH INTO, smash into, collide with, hit, strike, ram, plow into, run into, bump into, impact.

**3** *informal he was slammed by the critics.* See CRITICIZE.

**slander** noun *he could sue us for slander* DEFAMATION (OF CHARACTER), character assassination, calumny, libel; scandalmongering, malicious gossip, disparagement, denigration, aspersions, vilification, traducement, obloquy; lie, slur, smear, false accusation; *informal* mudslinging, bad-mouthing; *archaic* contumely.

▸ verb *they were accused of slandering the minister* DEFAME (SOMEONE'S CHARACTER), blacken someone's name, tell lies about, speak ill/evil of, sully someone's reputation, libel, smear, cast aspersions on, spread scandal about, besmirch, tarnish, taint; malign, traduce, vilify, disparage, denigrate, run down, slur; *informal* badmouth, dis, trash; *formal* derogate. See note at MALIGN.

**slanderous** adjective *slanderous accusations* DEFAMATORY, denigratory, disparaging, libelous, pejorative, false, misrepresentative, scurrilous, scandalous, malicious, abusive, insulting; *informal* mudslinging. ANTONYM complimentary.

**slang** noun *the street slang was a bit rough for his uptown ears* INFORMAL LANGUAGE, colloquialisms, patois, argot, cant, jargon. See note at DIALECT.

**slant** verb **1** *the floor was slanting* SLOPE, tilt, incline, be at an angle, tip, cant, lean, dip, pitch, shelve, list, bank.

**2** *their findings were slanted in our favor* BIAS, distort, twist, skew, weight, give a bias to.

▸ noun **1** *the slant of the roof* SLOPE, incline, tilt, gradient, pitch, angle, cant, camber, inclination.

**2** *a feminist slant* POINT OF VIEW, viewpoint, standpoint, stance, angle, perspective, approach, view, attitude, position; bias, leaning.

**slanting** adjective *the slanting angle of the deck* OBLIQUE, sloping, at an angle, on an incline, inclined, tilting, tilted, slanted, aslant, diagonal, canted, cambered.

**slap** verb **1** *he slapped her hard* HIT, strike, smack, clout, cuff, thump, punch, spank; *informal* whack, thwack, wallop, bash, bop, slug, bust; *archaic* smite.

**2** *he slapped down a $10 bill* FLING, throw, toss, slam, bang; *informal* plunk.

**3** *slap on a coat of paint* DAUB, plaster, spread.

**4** *informal they slapped a huge tax on imports* IMPOSE, levy, put.

▸ noun *a slap across the cheek* SMACK, blow, thump, cuff, clout, punch, spank; *informal* whack, thwack, wallop, clip, bash.

PHRASES: **a slap in the face** *your disloyalty was a brutal slap in the face* REBUFF, rejection, snub, insult, put-down, humiliation.

**a slap on the back** *he was always trying to earn a slap on the back from his stepfather* CONGRATULATIONS, commendation, approbation, approval, accolades, compliments, tributes, a pat on the back, praise, acclaim, acclamation.

**a slap on the wrist** *the judge let that bastard go free, with nothing more than a slap on the wrist* REPRIMAND, rebuke, reproof, scolding, admonishment; *informal* rap on/over the knuckles, dressing-down.

**slapdash** adjective *they did a slapdash job on the driveway* CARELESS, slipshod, hurried, haphazard, unsystematic, untidy, messy, hit-or-miss, negligent, neglectful, lax; *informal* sloppy, slaphappy, shambolic. See note at SUPERFICIAL. ANTONYM meticulous.

**slash** verb **1** *her tires had been slashed* CUT (OPEN), gash, slit, split open, lacerate, knife, make an incision in.

**2** *informal the company slashed prices* REDUCE, cut, lower, bring down, mark down.

**3** *informal they have slashed 10,000 jobs* GET RID OF, ax, cut, shed, make redundant.

▸ noun **1** *a slash across his arm* CUT, gash, laceration, slit, incision; wound.

**2** *sentence breaks are indicated by slashes* SOLIDUS, oblique, backslash.

**slaughter** verb **1** *the animals were slaughtered* KILL, butcher.

**2** *innocent civilians are being slaughtered* MASSACRE, murder, butcher, kill (off), annihilate, exterminate, liquidate, eliminate, destroy, decimate, wipe out, put to death; *literary* slay. See note at KILL.

**3** *informal their team was slaughtered.* See DEFEAT verb sense 1.

▸ noun **1** *the slaughter of 20 demonstrators* MASSACRE, murdering, (mass) murder, mass killing, mass execution, annihilation, extermination, liquidation, decimation, carnage, butchery, genocide; *literary* slaying.

**2** *a scene of slaughter* CARNAGE, bloodshed, bloodletting, bloodbath.

**3** *informal their electoral slaughter.* See DEFEAT noun sense 1.

**slave** noun **1** *the work was done by slaves historical* serf, vassal, thrall; *archaic* bondsman, bondswoman. ANTONYMS freeman, master.

**2** *Anna was his willing slave* DRUDGE, servant, lackey, minion; *informal* gofer.

**3** *a fashion slave* DEVOTEE, worshiper, adherent; fan, lover, aficionado; *informal* fanatic, freak, nut, addict.

▸ verb ***slaving away*** *for a pittance* TOIL, labor, grind away, sweat, work one's fingers to the bone, work like a Trojan/dog; *informal* kill oneself, sweat blood, slog away; *literary* travail; *archaic* drudge, moil.

**slaver** verb *her bloodhound loves to slaver on me* DROOL, slobber, dribble, salivate.

**slavery** noun **1** *thousands were sold into slavery* BONDAGE, enslavement, servitude, thralldom, thrall, serfdom, vassalage. ANTONYM freedom.

2 *this work is sheer slavery* DRUDGERY, toil, hard labor, grind; *literary* travail; *archaic* moil.

**slavish** adjective 1 *slavish lackeys of the government* SERVILE, subservient, fawning, obsequious, sycophantic, toadying, unctuous; *informal* bootlicking, forelock-tugging. See note at OBSEQUIOUS.

2 *slavish copying* UNORIGINAL, uninspired, unimaginative, uninventive, imitative.

**slay** verb 1 *literary 8,000 men were slain* KILL, murder, put to death, butcher, cut down, cut to pieces, slaughter, massacre, shoot down, gun down, mow down, eliminate, annihilate, exterminate, liquidate; *informal* wipe out, bump off, do in. See note at KILL.

2 *informal you slay me, you really do* AMUSE GREATLY, entertain greatly, make someone laugh; *informal* have people rolling in the aisles, kill, knock dead, be a hit with.

**sleek** adjective 1 *his sleek dark hair* SMOOTH, glossy, shiny, shining, lustrous, silken, silky.

2 *the car's sleek lines* STREAMLINED, trim, elegant, graceful.

3 *sleek young men in city suits* WELL-GROOMED, stylish, wealthy-looking, suave, sophisticated, debonair.

**sleep** noun *go and have a sleep* NAP, doze, siesta, catnap, beauty sleep; *informal* snooze, forty winks, bit of shut-eye, power nap; *literary* slumber.

▸ verb *she slept for about an hour* BE ASLEEP, doze, take a siesta, take a nap, catnap, sleep like a log; *informal* snooze, catch/snatch forty winks, get some shut-eye, put one's head down, catch some Zs; *humorous* be in the land of Nod, be in the arms of Morpheus; *literary* slumber. ANTONYM wake up.

PHRASES: **go to sleep** *I'm trying to go to sleep* FALL ASLEEP, get to sleep; *informal* drop off, nod off, drift off, crash out, sack out. **put an animal to sleep** *our beloved poodle Maxie had to be put to sleep* PUT DOWN, destroy, euthanize.

**sleepiness** noun *did you tell the doctor about your chronic sleepiness?* DROWSINESS, tiredness, somnolence, languor, languidness, doziness; lethargy, sluggishness, lassitude, enervation.

**sleepless** adjective *he lay sleepless until dawn* WAKEFUL, restless, without sleep, insomniac; (wide) awake, unsleeping, tossing and turning.

**sleepy** adjective 1 *she felt very sleepy* DROWSY, tired, somnolent, languid, languorous, heavy-eyed, asleep on one's feet; lethargic, sluggish, enervated, torpid; *informal* dopey; *literary* slumberous. ANTONYMS awake, alert.

2 *the sleepy heat of the afternoon* SOPORIFIC, sleep-inducing, somnolent. ANTONYM invigorating.

3 *a sleepy little village* QUIET, peaceful, tranquil, placid, slow-moving; dull, boring. ANTONYMS busy, bustling.

**slender** adjective 1 *her tall slender figure* SLIM, lean, willowy, sylphlike, svelte, lissome, graceful; slight, slightly built, thin, skinny. See note at THIN. ANTONYM plump.

2 *slender evidence* MEAGER, limited, slight, scanty, scant, sparse, paltry, insubstantial, insufficient, deficient, negligible; *formal* exiguous. ANTONYM considerable.

3 *we had a slender chance of making it* FAINT, remote, flimsy, tenuous, fragile, slim; unlikely, improbable. ANTONYM strong.

**sleuth** noun *informal I didn't have to be much of a sleuth to catch Irene stealing company funds* (PRIVATE) DETECTIVE, (private) investigator; *informal* private eye, snoop, shamus, gumshoe, (private) dick, PI.

**slice** noun 1 *a slice of fruitcake* PIECE, portion, slab, sliver, wafer, shaving.

2 *a huge slice of public spending* SHARE, part, portion, tranche, piece, proportion, allocation, percentage.

▸ verb 1 *slice the cheese thinly* CUT (UP), shave, carve, julienne, section.

2 *one man had his ear sliced off* CUT OFF, sever, chop off, shear off.

**slick** adjective 1 *a slick advertising campaign* EFFICIENT, smooth, smooth-running, polished, well-organized, well run, streamlined.

2 *his slick use of words* GLIB, smooth, fluent, plausible.

3 *a slick salesman* SUAVE, urbane, polished, assured, self-assured, smooth-talking, glib; *informal* smarmy.

4 *her slick brown hair* SHINY, glossy, shining, sleek, smooth, oiled.

5 *the sidewalks were slick with rain* SLIPPERY, wet, greasy; *informal* slippy.

▸ verb *his hair was slicked down* SMOOTH, sleek, grease, oil, gel.

**slide** verb 1 *the glass slid across the table* GLIDE, move smoothly, slip, slither, skim, skate; skid, slew.

2 *tears slid down her cheeks* TRICKLE, run, flow, pour, stream.

3 *four men slid out of the shadows* CREEP, steal, slink, slip, tiptoe, sidle.

4 *the country is sliding into recession* SINK, fall, drop, descend; decline, degenerate.

▸ noun 1 *the current slide in house prices* FALL, decline, drop, slump, downturn, downswing. ANTONYM rise.

2 *a slide show* TRANSPARENCY.

PHRASE: **let slide** *I guess I let things slide at the office during my wife's illness* NEGLECT, pay little/no attention to, not attend to, be remiss about, let something go downhill.

**slight** adjective 1 *the chance of success is slight* SMALL, modest, tiny, minute, inappreciable, negligible, insignificant, minimal, remote, slim, faint; *informal* minuscule; *formal* exiguous. ANTONYM considerable.

2 *the book is of slight consequence* MINOR, inconsequential, trivial, unimportant, lightweight, superficial, shallow. ANTONYM substantial.

**3** *Elizabeth's slight figure* SLIM, slender, petite, diminutive, small, delicate, dainty. ANTONYM burly.

▸ verb *he had been slighted* INSULT, snub, rebuff, repulse, spurn, treat disrespectfully, give someone the cold shoulder, scorn; *informal* give someone the brush-off, freeze out. See note at NEGLECT. ANTONYM respect.

▸ noun *an unintended slight* INSULT, affront, snub, rebuff; *informal* put-down, dig. ANTONYM compliment.

**slighting** adjective *one more slighting remark from you and I'm walking out that door* INSULTING, disparaging, derogatory, disrespectful, denigratory, pejorative, abusive, offensive, defamatory, slanderous, scurrilous; disdainful, scornful, contemptuous; *archaic* contumelious.

**slightly** adverb *beat the egg whites until they're slightly stiff* A LITTLE, a bit, somewhat, rather, moderately, to a certain extent, faintly, vaguely, a shade, a touch. ANTONYM very.

**slim** adjective **1** *she was tall and slim* SLENDER, lean, thin, willowy, sylphlike, svelte, lissome, trim, slight, slightly built. ANTONYM plump.

**2** *a slim silver bracelet* NARROW, slender, slimline. ANTONYM broad.

**3** *a slim chance of escape* SLIGHT, small, slender, faint, poor, remote, unlikely, improbable. ANTONYM strong.

▸ verb **1** *I'm trying to **slim down*** LOSE WEIGHT, get thinner, lose some pounds/inches, diet, get into shape, slenderize.

**2** *the number of staff had been **slimmed down*** REDUCE, cut (down/back), scale down, decrease, diminish, pare down.

**slime** noun *a greenish slime slowly dripped from the pipe* OOZE, sludge, muck, mud, mire; *informal* goo, gunk, gook, gloop, gunge, guck, glop; *humorous* ectoplasm.

**slimy** adjective **1** *the floor was slimy* SLIPPERY, greasy, muddy, mucky, sludgy, wet, sticky; *informal* slippy, gunky, gooey.

**2** *informal her slimy press agent* OBSEQUIOUS, sycophantic, excessively deferential, subservient, fawning, toadying, ingratiating, unctuous, oily, oleaginous, greasy, toadyish, slavish; *informal* bootlicking, smarmy, forelock-tugging.

**sling** noun **1** *she had her arm in a sling* (SUPPORT) BANDAGE, support, strap.

**2** *armed only with a sling* CATAPULT, slingshot.

▸ verb **1** *a hammock was slung between two trees* HANG, suspend, string, swing.

**2** *informal she slung her jacket on the sofa.* See THROW verb sense 1.

**slink** verb *it's impossible to slink quietly across these squeaky floors* CREEP, sneak, steal, slip, slide, sidle, tiptoe, pussyfoot.

**slip**[1] verb **1** *she slipped on the ice* SLIDE, skid, glide; fall (over), lose one's balance, tumble.

**2** *the envelope slipped through Luke's fingers* FALL, drop, slide.

**3** *we slipped out by a back door* CREEP, steal, sneak, slide, sidle, slope, slink, tiptoe.

**4** *standards have slipped* DECLINE, deteriorate, degenerate, worsen, get worse, fall (off), drop; *informal* go downhill, go to the dogs, go to pot.

**5** *the stock index slipped 30 points* DROP, go down, sink, slump, decrease, depreciate.

**6** *the hours **slipped by*** PASS, elapse, go by/past, roll by/past, fly by/past, tick by/past.

**7** *she slipped the map into her pocket* PUT, tuck, shove; *informal* pop, stick, stuff.

**8** *Sarah **slipped into** a black skirt* PUT ON, pull on, don, dress/clothe oneself in; change into.

**9** *she **slipped out of** her clothes* TAKE OFF, remove, pull off, doff, peel off.

**10** *he slipped the knot of his tie* UNTIE, unfasten, undo.

▸ noun **1** *a single slip could send them plummeting downward* FALSE STEP, misstep, slide, skid, fall, tumble.

**2** *a careless slip* MISTAKE, error, blunder, gaffe, slip of the tongue/pen; oversight, omission, lapse, inaccuracy; *informal* slip-up, boo-boo, howler, goof, blooper. See note at MISTAKE.

**3** *a silk slip* UNDERSKIRT, petticoat.

PHRASES: **give someone the slip** *informal we gave Murphy the slip and headed for the docks* ESCAPE FROM, get away from, evade, dodge, elude, lose, shake off, throw off (the scent), get clear of.

**let something slip** *who let it slip that we were hiding here?* REVEAL, disclose, divulge, let out, give away, blurt out; give the game away; *informal* let on, blab, let the cat out of the bag, spill the beans.

**slip away** **1** *they managed to slip away* ESCAPE, get away, break free; *informal* fly the coop, take a powder.

**2** *she slipped away in her sleep.* See DIE sense 1.

**slip up** *informal Hennie slipped up and left the corral open* MAKE A MISTAKE, (make a) blunder, get something wrong, make an error, err; *informal* make a boo-boo, goof up.

**slip**[2] noun *they took slips from rare plants* CUTTING, graft; scion, shoot, offshoot. PHRASES: **a slip of a ——** *she's just a slip of a girl* SMALL, slender, slim, slight, slightly built, petite, little, tiny, diminutive; *informal* pint-sized.

**slip of paper** *each person takes one slip of paper from the hat* PIECE OF PAPER, scrap of paper, sheet, note; *trademark* Post-it.

**slipper** noun *he pulled on his slippers* bedroom slipper, house shoe, slipper sock, moccasin; mule.

**slippery** adjective **1** *the roads are slippery* ICY, greasy, oily, glassy, smooth, slimy, wet; *informal* slippy.

**2** *a slippery customer* EVASIVE, unreliable, unpredictable; devious, crafty, cunning, unscrupulous, wily, tricky, artful, slick, sly, sneaky, scheming, untrustworthy, deceitful, duplicitous, dishonest, treacherous, two-faced, snide; *informal* shady, shifty, hinky.

**slipshod** adjective *a slipshod sales presentation* CARELESS, lackadaisical, slapdash, disorganized, haphazard, hit-or-miss, untidy, messy, unsystematic, unmethodical, casual, negligent, neglectful, remiss, lax, slack; *informal* sloppy, slaphappy. ANTONYM meticulous.

**slip-up** noun *informal don't worry, everyone makes a slip-up or two* MISTAKE, slip, error, blunder, oversight, omission, gaffe, slip of the tongue/pen, inaccuracy; *informal* boo-boo, howler, goof, blooper, boner.

**slit** noun **1** *three diagonal slits* CUT, incision, split, slash, gash, laceration.

**2** *a slit in the curtains* OPENING, gap, chink, crack, aperture, slot.

▸ verb *he threatened to slit her throat* CUT, slash, split open, slice open, gash, lacerate, make an incision in.

**slither** verb *the garter snake slithered under the shed* SLIDE, slip, glide, wriggle, crawl; skid.

**sliver** noun *slivers of glass | who wants this last sliver of cheesecake?* SPLINTER, shard, shiver, chip, flake, shred, scrap, shaving, paring, piece, fragment.

**slobber** verb *ooh, this mutt keeps slobbering on me* DROOL, slaver, dribble, salivate.

**slogan** noun *familiar advertising slogans* CATCHPHRASE, jingle, byword, motto; *informal* tag line, buzzword, mantra.

**slop** verb *water slopped over the edge* SPILL, flow, overflow, run, slosh, splash.

**slope** noun **1** *the slope of the roof* GRADIENT, incline, angle, slant, inclination, pitch, decline, ascent, declivity, rise, fall, tilt, tip, downslope, upslope, grade, downgrade, upgrade.

**2** *a grassy slope* HILL, hillside, hillock, bank, sidehill, escarpment, scarp; *literary* steep.

**3** *the ski slopes* PISTE, run, trail.

▸ verb *the garden sloped down to a stream* SLANT, incline, tilt; drop away, fall away, decline, descend, shelve, lean; rise, ascend, climb.

**sloping** adjective *a sloping floor* AT A SLANT, on a slant, at an angle, slanting, slanted, leaning, inclining, inclined, angled, cambered, canted, tilting, tilted, dipping. ANTONYM level.

**sloppy** adjective **1** *their defense was sloppy* CARELESS, slapdash, slipshod, lackadaisical, haphazard, lax, slack, slovenly; *informal* slaphappy, shambolic.

**2** *sloppy T-shirts* BAGGY, loose-fitting, loose, generously cut; shapeless, sacklike, oversized.

**3** *a sloppy serving of cereal* RUNNY, watery, thin, liquid, semiliquid, mushy, gloppy.

**4** *sloppy letters* SENTIMENTAL, mawkish, cloying, saccharine, sugary, syrupy; romantic; *informal* slushy, schmaltzy, lovey-dovey, soppy, cornball, corny, sappy, hokey, three-hankie.

**slot** noun **1** *he slid a coin into the slot* APERTURE, slit, crack, hole, opening.

**2** *I have an early time slot* SPOT, time, period, niche, space; *informal* window.

▸ verb *he slotted a cassette into the machine* INSERT, put, place, slide, slip.

**sloth** noun *who is responsible for the sloth of this department?* LAZINESS, idleness, indolence, slothfulness, inactivity, inertia, sluggishness, shiftlessness, apathy, acedia, listlessness, lassitude, lethargy, languor, torpidity; *literary* hebetude. ANTONYM industriousness.

**slothful** adjective *fatigue made him slothful* LAZY, idle, indolent, inactive, sluggish, apathetic, lethargic, listless, languid, torpid; *archaic* otiose.

**slouch** verb **1** *sit up straight—don't slouch!* SLUMP, hunch; loll, droop.

**2** *he just slouched, pretending to work* LOUNGE, loaf, laze, loll, idle, do nothing.

▸ noun *she's no slouch* INCOMPETENT, amateur, bumbler, bungler.

**slovenly** adjective **1** *his slovenly appearance* SCRUFFY, untidy, messy, unkempt, ill-groomed, slatternly, disheveled, bedraggled, tousled, rumpled, frowzy; *informal* slobbish, slobby, raggedy, scuzzy. ANTONYM tidy.

**2** *his work is slovenly* CARELESS, slapdash, slipshod, haphazard, hit-or-miss, untidy, messy, negligent, lax, lackadaisical, slack; *informal* sloppy, slaphappy. ANTONYM careful.

**slow** adjective **1** *their slow walk home | the donkey was annoyingly slow* UNHURRIED, leisurely, steady, sedate, slow-moving, downtempo, plodding, dawdling, sluggish, sluggardly, lead-footed, poky. ANTONYM fast.

**2** *a slow process* LONG-DRAWN-OUT, time-consuming, lengthy, protracted, prolonged, gradual. ANTONYMS brief, short.

**3** *he can be so slow* OBTUSE, stupid, unperceptive, insensitive, bovine, stolid, slow-witted, dull-witted, unintelligent, doltish, witless; *informal* dense, dim, dimwitted, thick, slow on the uptake, dumb, dopey, boneheaded, chowderheaded. See note at STUPID. ANTONYMS astute, bright.

**4** *they were slow to voice their opinions* RELUCTANT, unwilling, disinclined, loath, hesitant, afraid, chary, shy.

**5** *the slow season* SLUGGISH, slack, quiet, inactive, flat, depressed, stagnant, dead. ANTONYMS busy, hectic.

**6** *a slow movie* DULL, boring, uninteresting, unexciting, uneventful, tedious, tiresome, wearisome, monotonous, dreary, lackluster. ANTONYM exciting.

▸ verb **1** *the traffic forced him to* ***slow down*** REDUCE SPEED, go slower, decelerate, brake. ANTONYM accelerate.

**2** *you need to* ***slow down*** TAKE IT EASY, relax, ease up/off, take a break, slack off, let up; *informal* chill (out), hang loose.

**3** *this would* ***slow up*** *our progress* HOLD BACK/UP, delay, retard, set back; restrict, check, curb, inhibit, impede, obstruct, hinder, hamper; *archaic* stay.

**slowly** adverb **1** *Tom walked off slowly* AT A SLOW PACE, without hurrying, unhurriedly, steadily, at a leisurely pace, at a snail's pace; *Music* adagio, lento, largo. ANTONYM quickly.

**2** *her health is improving slowly* GRADUALLY, bit by bit, little by little, slowly but surely, step by step. ANTONYM by leaps and bounds.

**sluggish** adjective **1** *Alex felt tired and sluggish* LETHARGIC, listless, lacking in energy, lifeless, inert, inactive, slow, torpid, languid, apathetic, weary, tired, fatigued, sleepy, drowsy, enervated; lazy, idle, indolent, slothful, sluggardly, logy; *Medicine* asthenic; *informal* dozy, dopey. ANTONYM vigorous.

**2** *the economy is sluggish* INACTIVE, quiet, slow, slack, flat, depressed, stagnant. ANTONYM brisk.

**slumber** verb *literary the child slumbered fitfully.* See SLEEP verb.

▸ noun *literary an uneasy slumber.* See SLEEP noun.

**slump** verb **1** *he slumped into a chair* SIT HEAVILY, flop, flump, collapse, sink, fall; *informal* plunk oneself.

**2** *housing prices slumped* FALL STEEPLY, plummet, tumble, drop, go down; *informal* crash, nosedive.

**3** *reading standards have slumped* DECLINE, deteriorate, degenerate, worsen, slip; *informal* go downhill.

▸ noun **1** *a slump in profits* STEEP FALL, drop, tumble, downturn, downswing, slide, *informal* decline, decrease, nosedive. ANTONYM rise.

**2** *an economic slump* RECESSION, economic decline, depression, slowdown, stagnation. ANTONYM boom.

**slur** verb *she was slurring her words* MUMBLE, speak unclearly, garble.

▸ noun *a gross slur* INSULT, slight, slander, slanderous statement, aspersion, smear, allegation.

**slut** noun *she dressed like a slut and didn't act much better* PROMISCUOUS WOMAN, prostitute, whore; *informal* tart, floozy, tramp, hooker, hustler; *dated* scarlet woman, loose woman, hussy, trollop; *archaic* harlot, strumpet, wanton.

**sly** adjective **1** *she's rather sly* CUNNING, crafty, clever, wily, artful, guileful, tricky, scheming, devious, deceitful, duplicitous, dishonest, underhanded, sneaky; *archaic* subtle.

**2** *a sly grin* ROGUISH, mischievous, impish, playful, wicked, arch, knowing.

**3** *she took a sly sip of water* SURREPTITIOUS, furtive, stealthy, covert. PHRASE: **on the sly** *he's dating Peggy on the sly* IN SECRET, secretly, furtively, surreptitiously, covertly, clandestinely, on the quiet, behind someone's back; *informal* on the QT.

**smack**[1] noun **1** *she gave him a smack* SLAP, clout, cuff, blow, spank, rap, swat, crack, thump, punch, karate chop; *informal* whack, thwack, clip, wallop, swipe, bop, belt, bash, sock.

**2** *the package landed with a smack* BANG, crash, crack, thud, thump.

**3** *informal a smack on the lips* KISS, peck, smooch; *informal* smacker.

▸ verb **1** *he tried to smack her* SLAP, hit, strike, spank, cuff, clout, thump, punch, swat; box someone's ears; *informal* whack, clip, wallop, swipe, bop, belt, bash, sock, slug.

**2** *the waiter smacked a plate down* BANG, slam, crash, thump; sling, fling; *informal* plunk.

▸ adverb *informal smack in the middle* EXACTLY, precisely, straight, right, directly, squarely, dead, plumb, point-blank; *informal* slap, bang, smack dab.

**smack**[2] noun **1** *the beer has a smack of hops* TASTE, flavor, savor.

**2** *a smack of bitterness in his words* TRACE, tinge, touch, suggestion, hint, overtone, suspicion, whisper. PHRASE: **smack of 1** *the tea smacked of tannin* TASTE OF, have the flavor of.

**2** *the plan smacked of self-promotion* SUGGEST, hint at, have overtones of, give the impression of, have the stamp of, seem like; smell of, reek of.

**smack**[3] noun *informal they were shooting smack in the alley* HEROIN.

**small** adjective **1** *a small apartment* LITTLE, compact, bijou, tiny, miniature, mini; minute, microscopic, minuscule; toy, baby; poky, cramped, boxy; *informal* teeny, teensy, itsy-bitsy, itty-bitty, pocket-sized, half-pint, little-bitty; *Scottish* wee. ANTONYMS big, large.

**2** *a very small man* SHORT, little, petite, diminutive, elfin, tiny; puny, undersized, stunted, dwarfish, midget, pygmy, Lilliputian; *Scottish* wee; *informal* teeny, pint-sized. ANTONYMS large, tall, heavily built.

**3** *a few small changes* SLIGHT, minor, unimportant, trifling, trivial, insignificant, inconsequential, negligible, nugatory, infinitesimal; *informal* minuscule, piffling, piddling. ANTONYMS major, substantial.

**4** *small helpings* INADEQUATE, meager, insufficient, ungenerous; *informal* measly, stingy, mingy, pathetic. ANTONYMS ample, generous.

**5** *they made him feel small* FOOLISH, stupid, insignificant, unimportant; embarrassed, humiliated, uncomfortable, mortified, ashamed; crushed. ANTONYM proud.

**6** *a small business* SMALL-SCALE, modest, unpretentious, humble. ANTONYMS big, large-scale, substantial.

**THE RIGHT WORD small, diminutive, little, miniature, minute, petite, tiny**

Why do we call a house **small** and a woman **petite**? *Small* and **little** are used interchangeably to describe people or things of reduced dimensions, but *small* is preferred when describing something concrete that is of less than the usual size, quantity, value, or importance (*a small matter to discuss; a small room; a small price to pay*). *Little* more often refers to concepts (*through little fault of his own; an issue of little importance*) or to a more drastic reduction in scale (*a little shopping cart just like the one her mother used*). **Diminutive** and *petite* intensify the meaning of *small*, particularly with reference to women's figures that are very trim and compact (*with her diminutive figure, she had to shop in stores that specialized in petite sizes*). **Tiny** is used to describe what is extremely small, often to the point where it can be seen only by looking closely (*a tiny flaw in the material; a tiny insect*), while **minute** not only describes what is seen with difficulty but may also refer to a very small amount of something (*minute traces of gunpowder on his glove*). **Miniature** applies specifically to a copy, a model, or a representation of something on a very small scale (*a child's mobile consisting of miniature farm animals*).

**small-minded** adjective *they were too small-minded to listen to our views on interracial marriage* NARROW-MINDED, petty, mean-spirited, uncharitable; close-minded, shortsighted, myopic, blinkered, inward-looking, unimaginative, parochial, provincial, insular, small-town; intolerant, illiberal, conservative, hidebound, dyed-in-the-wool, set in one's ways, inflexible; prejudiced, bigoted. ANTONYM tolerant.

**small-time** adjective *a small-time thief from New Haven* MINOR, small-scale; petty, unimportant, insignificant, inconsequential, minor-league; *informal* penny-ante, piddling, two-bit, bush-league, picayune. ANTONYM major.

**smart** adjective **1** *informal he's the smart one* CLEVER, bright, intelligent, sharp-witted, quick-witted, shrewd, astute, able; perceptive, percipient; *informal* brainy, savvy, quick on the uptake. ANTONYM stupid.

**2** *you look very smart* WELL-DRESSED, stylish, chic, fashionable, modish, elegant, neat, spruce, trim, dapper; *informal* snazzy, natty, snappy, sharp, cool, spiffy, fly, kicky. ANTONYM scruffy.

**3** *a smart restaurant* FASHIONABLE, stylish, high-class, exclusive, chic, fancy, upscale, upmarket, high-toned; *informal* trendy, posh, ritzy, plush, classy, swanky, glitzy, swank. ANTONYM downmarket.

**4** *a smart pace* BRISK, quick, fast, rapid, swift, lively, spanking, energetic, vigorous; *informal* snappy, cracking. ANTONYM slow.

**5** *a smart blow on the snout* SHARP, severe, forceful, violent. ANTONYM gentle.

▸ verb **1** *her eyes were smarting* STING, burn, tingle, prickle; hurt, ache.

**2** *she smarted at the accusations* FEEL ANNOYED, feel upset, take offense, feel aggrieved, feel indignant, be put out, feel hurt.

**smash** verb **1** *he smashed a window* BREAK, shatter, splinter, crack, shiver; *informal* bust.

**2** *she's smashed the car* CRASH, wreck, write off; *informal* total.

**3** *they* ***smashed into*** *a wall* CRASH INTO, collide with, hit, strike, ram, smack into, slam into, plow into, run into, bump into, impact.

**4** *Don smashed him over the head* HIT, strike, thump, punch, smack; *informal* whack, bash, bop, clout, wallop, crown, slug.

**5** *he smashed their hopes of glory* DESTROY, wreck, ruin, shatter, dash, crush, devastate, demolish, overturn, scotch; *informal* put the kibosh on, scuttle.

▸ noun **1** *the smash of glass* BREAKING, shattering, crash.

**2** *it was a terrible smash* CRASH, collision, accident, wreck; *informal* pileup, smash-up.

**3** *informal a box-office smash* SUCCESS, sensation, sellout, triumph; *informal* (smash) hit, blockbuster, winner, knockout, wow, barn burner, biggie.

**smattering** noun *it's mostly modern, with a smattering of art deco* BIT, modicum, touch, soupçon; nodding acquaintance; *informal* smidgen, smidge, tad.

**smear** verb **1** *the table was smeared with grease* STREAK, smudge, mark, soil, dirty; *informal* splotch; *literary* besmear.

**2** *smear the meat with olive oil* COVER, coat, grease; *literary* bedaub.

**3** *she smeared sunblock on her skin* SPREAD, rub, daub, slap, slather, smother, plaster, slick; apply; *literary* besmear.

**4** *they are trying to smear our reputation* SULLY, tarnish, blacken, drag through the mud, taint, damage, defame, discredit, malign, slander, libel, slur; *informal* do a hatchet job on; *formal* calumniate, impugn; *literary* besmirch.

▸ noun **1** *smears of blood* STREAK, smudge, daub, dab, spot, patch, blotch, mark; *informal* splotch.

**2** *they printed smears about his closest aides* FALSE ACCUSATION, lie, untruth, slur, slander, libel, defamation, calumny.

**smell** noun *the smell of the kitchen* ODOR, aroma, fragrance, scent, perfume, redolence; bouquet, nose; stench, fetor, stink, reek, whiff; *informal* funk; *literary* miasma.

▸ verb **1** *he smelled her perfume* get a sniff of, scent, detect.

**2** *the dogs smelled each other* SNIFF, nose.

**3** *the cellar smells* STINK, reek, have a bad smell, whiff.

**4** *it* ***smells like*** *a hoax to me* SMACK OF, have the hallmark(s) of, seem like, have the air of, suggest.

**THE RIGHT WORD smell, aroma, bouquet, fragrance, odor, perfume, scent, stench, stink**

Everyone appreciates the **fragrance** of fresh-cut flowers, but the **stench** from the paper mill across town is usually unwelcome. Both have a distinctive **smell**, which is the most general of these words for what is perceived through the nose, but there is a big difference between a pleasant smell and a foul one. An **odor** may be either pleasant or unpleasant, but it suggests a smell that is clearly recognizable and can usually be traced to a single source (*the pungent odor of onions*). An **aroma** is a pleasing and distinctive odor that is usually penetrating or pervasive (*the aroma of fresh-ground coffee*), while **bouquet** refers to a delicate aroma, such as that of a fine wine (*after swirling the wine around in her glass, she sniffed the bouquet*). A **scent** is usually delicate and pleasing, with an emphasis on the source rather than on an olfactory impression (*the scent of balsam associated with Christmas*). *Fragrance* and **perfume** are both associated with flowers, but *fragrance* is more delicate; a *perfume* may be so rich and strong that it is repulsive or overpowering (*the air was so dense with the perfume of lilacs that I had to go indoors*). *Stench* and **stink** are reserved for smells that are foul, strong, and pervasive, although *stink* implies a sharper sensation, while *stench* refers to a more sickening one (*the stink of sweaty gym clothes; the stench of a rotting animal*).

**smelly** adjective *get that smelly wet dog off the sofa* FOUL-SMELLING, stinking, reeking, fetid, malodorous, pungent, rank, noxious, mephitic; off, gamy, high; musty, fusty; *informal* stinky, humming, funky; *Brit. informal* minging, pongy; *literary* miasmic, noisome.

**smile** verb *he smiled at her* BEAM, grin (from ear to ear), dimple, twinkle; smirk, simper; leer. ANTONYM frown.

▸ noun *the smile on Sara's face* BEAM, grin, twinkle; smirk, simper; leer.

THE RIGHT WORD **smile, grin, smirk, simper**

The facial expression created by turning the corners of the mouth upward is commonly known as a **smile**. It can convey a wide range of emotion, from pleasure, approval, or amusement to insincerity and disinterest (*his complaint was met with a blank smile*). A **grin** is a wide smile that suggests spontaneous cheerfulness, warmth, pleasure, or amusement (*her teasing provoked an affectionate grin*). But *grin* may also describe a ferocious baring of the teeth or an angry grimace (*the grin of a skeleton*). A **simper**, on the other hand, is an expression of smugness and self-righteousness (*her simper of superiority*) as well as a silly or affected smile (*she curtsied with a girlish simper*). **Smirk** also implies an affected or self-conscious smile, but one that expresses derision or hostility (*to trick someone and then smirk as he makes a fool of himself*).

**smirk** verb *I hate the way they just sit there smirking* SMILE SMUGLY, simper, snicker, snigger; leer.

**smitten** adjective **1** *he was smitten with cholera* STRUCK DOWN, laid low, suffering, affected, afflicted, plagued, stricken.

**2** *Jane's* ***smitten with*** *you* INFATUATED WITH, besotted with, in love with, obsessed with, head over heels; enamored of, attracted to, taken with; captivated by, enchanted by, under someone's spell, moonstruck by; *informal* bowled over by, swept off one's feet by, crazy about, mad about, keen on, hot on/for, gone on, sweet on, gaga for.

**smog** noun *the smog in LA is intolerable* FOG, haze; fumes, smoke, pollution.

**smoke** verb **1** *the fire was smoking* SMOLDER, emit smoke; *archaic* reek.

**2** *he smoked his cigarette* PUFF ON, draw on, pull on; inhale; light; *informal* drag on, toke.

**3** *they smoke their salmon* CURE, preserve, dry.

▸ noun *the smoke from the bonfire* FUMES, exhaust, gas, vapor; smog.

**smoky** adjective **1** *the smoky atmosphere* SMOKE-FILLED, sooty, smoggy, hazy, foggy, murky, thick.

**2** *her smoky eyes* GRAY, sooty, dark, black.

**smolder** verb **1** *the bonfire still smoldered* SMOKE, glow, burn.

**2** *she was smoldering with resentment* SEETHE, boil, fume, burn, simmer, be boiling over, be beside oneself; *informal* be livid.

**smooth** adjective **1** *the smooth flat rocks* EVEN, level, flat, plane; unwrinkled, featureless; glassy, glossy, silky, polished. ANTONYMS uneven, rough.

**2** *his face was smooth* CLEAN-SHAVEN, hairless. ANTONYMS rough, hairy.

**3** *a smooth sauce* CREAMY, velvety, blended. ANTONYM lumpy.

**4** *a smooth sea* CALM, still, tranquil, undisturbed, unruffled, even, flat, waveless, like a millpond. ANTONYMS rough, choppy.

**5** *the smooth running of the equipment* STEADY, regular, uninterrupted, unbroken, fluid, fluent; straightforward, easy, effortless, trouble-free, seamless. ANTONYMS irregular, jerky.

**6** *a smooth wine* MELLOW, mild, agreeable, pleasant. ANTONYMS harsh, bitter.

**7** *the smooth tone of the clarinet* DULCET, soft, soothing, mellow, sweet, silvery, honeyed, mellifluous, melodious, lilting, lyrical, harmonious. ANTONYM raucous.

**8** *a smooth, confident man* SUAVE, urbane, sophisticated, polished, debonair; courteous, gracious, glib, slick, ingratiating, unctuous; *informal* smarmy. ANTONYM gauche.

▸ verb **1** *she smoothed the soil* FLATTEN, level (out/off), even out/off; press, roll, steamroll, iron, plane.

**2** *a plan to smooth the way for the agreement* EASE, facilitate, clear the way for, pave the way for, expedite, assist, aid, help, oil the wheels of, lubricate.

**smother** verb **1** *she tried to smother her baby* SUFFOCATE, asphyxiate, stifle, choke.

**2** *we smothered the flames* EXTINGUISH, put out, snuff out, dampen, douse, stamp out, choke.

**3** *we smothered ourselves with sunscreen* SMEAR, daub, spread, cover; *literary* besmear, bedaub.

**4** *their granny always smothers them with affection* OVERWHELM, inundate, envelop, cocoon.

**5** *she smothered a sigh* STIFLE, muffle, strangle, repress, suppress, hold back, fight back, bite back, swallow, contain, bottle up, conceal, hide; bite one's lip; *informal* keep a/the lid on.

**smudge** noun *a smudge of ink* STREAK, smear, mark, stain, blotch, stripe, blob, dab; *informal* splotch.

▸ verb **1** *her face was smudged with dust* STREAK, mark, dirty, soil, blotch, blacken, smear, blot, daub, stain; *informal* splotch; *literary* bedaub, besmirch.

**2** *she smudged her makeup* SMEAR, streak, mess up.

**smug** adjective *he was feeling smug after his win* SELF-SATISFIED, self-congratulatory, complacent, superior, pleased with oneself, self-approving.

**smuggler** noun *it was a small uncharted island frequented by smugglers* TRAFFICKER, runner, courier; *informal* mule, moonshiner, rum-runner.

**snack** noun *she made herself a snack* LIGHT MEAL, collation, treat, refreshments, lunch, nibbles, tidbit(s); *informal* bite (to eat).

▸ verb *don't snack on sugary foods* EAT BETWEEN MEALS, nibble, munch; *informal* graze, nosh.

**snag** noun **1** *the snag is that this might affect inflation* COMPLICATION, difficulty, catch, hitch, hiccup, obstacle, stumbling block, pitfall, problem, impediment, hindrance, inconvenience, setback, hurdle, disadvantage, downside, drawback.

2 *smooth rails with no snags* SHARP PROJECTION, jag; thorn, spur.

3 *a snag in her stocking* TEAR, rip, hole, gash, slash; run.

▸ verb 1 *she snagged her stockings* TEAR, rip.

2 *the zipper snagged on the fabric* CATCH, get caught, hook.

**snap** verb 1 *the ruler snapped* BREAK, fracture, splinter, come apart, split, crack; *informal* bust.

2 *she snapped after years of violence* FLARE UP, lose one's self-control, freak out, go to pieces, get worked up; *informal* crack up, lose one's cool, blow one's top, fly off the handle.

3 *a dog was snapping at his heels* BITE; gnash its teeth.

4 *"Be quiet!" Anna snapped* SAY ROUGHLY, say brusquely, say abruptly, say angrily, bark, snarl, growl; retort, rejoin, retaliate; *informal* jump down someone's throat.

▸ noun 1 *she closed her purse with a snap* CLICK, crack, pop.

2 *a cold snap* PERIOD, spell, time, interval, stretch, patch.

3 *informal vacation snaps* PHOTOGRAPH, picture, photo, shot, snapshot, print, slide, frame, still; *informal* mug shot.

4 *it's **a snap** to put together* AN EASY TASK; *informal* a piece of cake, a cinch, a breeze, child's play, kid's stuff, duck soup.

PHRASES: **snap out of it** *informal you can't tell a clinically depressed person to just snap out of it* RECOVER, get a grip, pull oneself together, get over it, get better, cheer up, perk up; *informal* buck up.

**snap up** *customers are snapping up these DVDs as fast as we can put them out* BUY EAGERLY, accept eagerly, jump at, take advantage of, grab, seize (on), grasp with both hands, pounce on.

**snappy** adjective *informal* 1 *a snappy catchphrase* CONCISE, succinct, memorable, catchy, neat, clever, crisp, pithy, witty, incisive, brief, short. ANTONYM long-winded.

2 *a snappy dresser* SMART, fashionable, stylish, chic, modish, elegant, neat, spruce, trim, dapper; *informal* snazzy, natty, sharp, nifty, cool, hip, styling, spiffy, fly. ANTONYM slovenly.

PHRASE: **make it snappy** *make it snappy, Trina, the Watsons will be here in five minutes* HURRY (UP), be quick (about it), get a move on, look lively, speed up; *informal* get cracking, step on it, move it, buck up, shake a leg; *dated* make haste.

**snare** noun 1 *the hare was caught in a snare* TRAP, gin, net, noose.

2 *avoid the snares of the new law* PITFALL, trap, catch, danger, hazard, peril; web, mesh.

▸ verb 1 *game birds were snared* TRAP, catch, net, bag, ensnare, entrap.

2 *he managed to snare an heiress* ENSNARE, catch, get hold of, bag, hook, land.

**snarl**[1] verb 1 *the wolves are snarling* GROWL, gnash one's teeth.

2 *"Shut up!" he snarled* SAY ROUGHLY, say brusquely, say nastily, bark, snap, growl; *informal* jump down someone's throat.

**snarl**[2] verb 1 *the rope got snarled up in a bush* TANGLE, entangle, entwine, enmesh, ravel, knot, foul.

2 *this case has snarled up the court process* COMPLICATE, confuse, muddle, jumble; *informal* mess up.

**snatch** verb 1 *she snatched the sandwich* GRAB, seize, take hold of, get one's hands on, take, pluck; grasp at, clutch at.

2 *informal someone snatched my bag.* See STEAL verb sense 1.

3 *informal she snatched the newborn from the hospital.* See ABDUCT.

4 *he snatched victory* SEIZE, pluck, wrest, achieve, secure, obtain; scrape.

▸ noun 1 *brief snatches of sleep* PERIOD, spell, time, fit, bout, interval, stretch.

2 *a snatch of conversation* FRAGMENT, snippet, bit, scrap, part, extract, excerpt, portion.

**sneak** verb 1 *I sneaked out* CREEP, slink, steal, slip, slide, sidle, edge, move furtively, tiptoe, pussyfoot, pad, prowl.

2 *she sneaked a camera in* SMUGGLE, bring/take surreptitiously, bring/take secretly, bring/take illicitly, spirit, slip.

3 *he sneaked a doughnut* STEAL, take furtively, take surreptitiously; *informal* snatch.

▸ adjective 1 *a sneak attack* FURTIVE, secret, stealthy, sly, surreptitious, clandestine, covert.

2 *a sneak preview* EXCLUSIVE, private, quick.

**sneaking** adjective 1 *she had a sneaking admiration for him* SECRET, private, hidden, concealed, unvoiced, undisclosed, undeclared, unavowed.

2 *a sneaking feeling* NIGGLING, nagging, lurking, insidious, lingering, gnawing, persistent.

**sneer** noun 1 *she had a sneer on her face* SMIRK, curl of the lip, disparaging smile, contemptuous smile, cruel smile.

2 *the sneers of others* JIBE, barb, jeer, taunt, insult, slight, affront, slur; *informal* dig.

▸ verb 1 *he looked at me and sneered* SMIRK, curl one's lip, smile disparagingly, smile contemptuously, smile cruelly.

2 *it is easy to **sneer at** them* SCOFF AT, scorn, disdain, mock, jeer at, hold in contempt, ridicule, deride, insult, slight, slur.

**snicker** verb *they all snickered at her* GIGGLE, titter, snigger, chortle, simper, laugh.

▸ noun *he could not suppress a snicker* GIGGLE, titter, snigger, chortle, simper.

**sniff** verb 1 *she sniffed and blew her nose* INHALE, breathe in; snuffle.

2 *Sandra sniffed the socks and grimaced* SMELL, scent, get a whiff of.

▸ noun 1 *she gave a loud sniff* SNUFFLE, inhalation.

2 *a sniff of fresh air* SMELL, scent, whiff; lungful.

3 *informal the first sniff of trouble* INDICATION, hint, whiff, inkling, suggestion, whisper, trace, sign, suspicion.

PHRASES: **sniff at** *how dare you sniff at me just because I'm* *poor?* SCORN, disdain, hold in contempt, look down one's nose at, treat as inferior, look down on, sneer at, scoff at; *informal* turn one's nose up at.

**sniff out** *informal McMahon and Romero were sent uptown to sniff out the source of these letters* DETECT, find, discover, bring to light, track down, dig up, hunt out, ferret out, root out, uncover, unearth.

**snip** verb **1** *an usher snipped our tickets* CUT, clip, slit, nick, notch.

**2** ***snip off*** *the faded flowers* CUT OFF, trim (off), clip, prune, chop off, lop (off), dock, crop, sever, detach, remove, take off.

▸ noun **1** *make snips along the edge* CUT, slit, nick, notch, incision.

**2** *snips of wallpaper* SCRAP, snippet, cutting, shred, remnant, fragment, sliver, bit, piece.

**snippet** noun *any snippet of information you can share would be appreciated* PIECE, bit, scrap, fragment, particle, shred; excerpt, extract.

**snivel** verb **1** *he slumped in a chair, sniveling* SNIFFLE, snuffle, whimper, whine, weep, cry; *informal* blubber, boo-hoo.

**2** *don't snivel about what you get* COMPLAIN, mutter, grumble, grouse, groan, carp, bleat, whine; *informal* gripe, moan, grouch, beef, bellyache, whinge, sound off, kvetch.

**snobbery** noun *they were raised in an environment of complacent snobbery* AFFECTATION, pretension, pretentiousness, arrogance, haughtiness, airs and graces, elitism; disdain, condescension, superciliousness; *informal* snootiness, uppitiness.

**snobbish** adjective *the snobbish distinction between art and craft* ELITIST, snobby, superior, supercilious; arrogant, haughty, disdainful, condescending; pretentious, affected; *informal* snooty, uppity, high and mighty, la-di-da, stuck-up, hoity-toity, snotty.

**snoop** *informal* verb **1** *don't* ***snoop into*** *our affairs* PRY INTO, inquire into/about, be inquisitive about/of, be curious about, poke about/around, be a busybody about, poke one's nose into; interfere in/with, meddle in/with, intrude on; *informal* be nosy about.

**2** *they snooped around the building* INVESTIGATE, explore, search, nose, have a good look; prowl around.

▸ noun *he went for a snoop around* SEARCH, nose, look, prowl, ferret, poke, investigation.

**snooze** *informal* noun *a good place for a snooze* NAP, doze, sleep, rest, siesta, catnap; *informal* forty winks; *literary* slumber.

▸ verb *she gently snoozed* NAP, doze, sleep, rest, take a siesta, catnap, drop off; *informal* snatch forty winks, get some shuteye, put one's head down, catch some Zs; *literary* slumber.

**snub** verb *they snubbed their hosts* REBUFF, spurn, repulse, cold-shoulder, brush off, give the cold shoulder to, keep at arm's length; ignore; insult, slight, affront, humiliate; *informal* freeze out, stiff.

▸ noun *a very public snub* REBUFF, repulse, slap in the face; humiliation, insult, slight, affront; *informal* brush-off, kiss-off, put-down.

**snug** adjective **1** *our tents were snug* COZY, comfortable, warm, welcoming, restful, reassuring, intimate, sheltered, secure; *informal* comfy. ANTONYMS bleak, unwelcoming.

**2** *a snug dress* TIGHT, skintight, close-fitting, form-fitting, figure-hugging, slinky. ANTONYM loose.

**snuggle** verb *Kent and Maris snuggled by the fire* NESTLE, curl up, huddle (up), cuddle up, nuzzle, settle.

**soak** verb **1** *soak the beans in water* IMMERSE, steep, submerge, submerse, dip, dunk, bathe, douse, marinate, souse.

**2** *we got soaked outside* DRENCH, wet through, saturate, waterlog, deluge, inundate, submerge, drown, swamp.

**3** *the sweat* ***soaked through*** *his clothes* PERMEATE, penetrate, percolate, seep into, spread through, infuse, impregnate.

**4** *use towels to* ***soak up*** *the water* ABSORB, suck up, blot (up), mop (up), sponge up, sop up.

**soaking** adjective *good Lord, look at these soaking children* DRENCHED, wet (through), soaked (through), sodden, soggy, waterlogged, saturated, sopping wet, dripping wet, wringing wet. ANTONYM parched.

**soar** verb **1** *the bird soared into the air* FLY, wing, ascend, climb, rise; take off, take flight. ANTONYM plummet.

**2** *the gulls soared on the winds* GLIDE, plane, float, drift, wheel, hover.

**3** *the cost of living soared* INCREASE, escalate, shoot up, rise, spiral; *informal* go through the roof, skyrocket.

**sob** verb *must she sob during every romantic scene?* WEEP, cry, shed tears, snivel, whimper; howl, bawl; *informal* blubber, boo-hoo.

**sober** adjective **1** *the driver was clearly sober* NOT DRUNK, clearheaded; teetotal, abstinent, abstemious, dry; *informal* on the wagon. ANTONYM drunk.

**2** *a sober view of life* SERIOUS, solemn, sensible, thoughtful, grave, somber, staid, levelheaded, businesslike, down-to-earth, commonsensical, pragmatic, conservative; unemotional, dispassionate, objective, matter-of-fact, no-nonsense, rational, logical, straightforward. ANTONYM frivolous.

**3** *a sober suit* SOMBER, subdued, severe; conventional, traditional, quiet, drab, plain. ANTONYM flamboyant.

▸ verb **1** *I ought to* ***sober up*** QUIT DRINKING, dry out, become sober.

**2** *his expression sobered her* MAKE SERIOUS, subdue, calm down, quiet, steady; bring down to earth, make someone stop and think, give someone pause for thought.

**sobriety** noun **1** *she noted his sobriety* SOBERNESS, clearheadedness; abstinence, teetotalism, nonindulgence, abstemiousness, temperance.

**2** *the mayor is a model of sobriety* SERIOUSNESS, solemnity, gravity, gravitas, dignity, levelheadedness, common sense, pragmatism, practicality, self-control, self-restraint, conservatism.

**so-called** adjective *your so-called dream date is hitting on our waitress* INAPPROPRIATELY NAMED, supposed, alleged, presumed, ostensible, reputed; nominal, titular, self-styled, professed, would-be, self-appointed, soi-disant.

**sociable** adjective *it was a sociable group, but he would rather have been with his own friends* FRIENDLY, affable, companionable, gregarious, convivial, amicable, cordial, warm, genial; communicative, responsive, forthcoming, open, outgoing, extrovert, hail-fellow-well-met, approachable; *informal* chummy, clubby. ANTONYM unfriendly.

**social** adjective **1** *a major social problem* COMMUNAL, community, collective, group, general, popular, civil, public, societal. ANTONYM individual.

**2** *a social club* RECREATIONAL, leisure, entertainment, amusement.

**3** *a uniquely social animal* GREGARIOUS, interactional; organized.

▸ noun *the club has a social once a month* PARTY, gathering, function, get-together, soiree; celebration, reunion, jamboree; *informal* bash, shindig, do.

**socialize** verb *these are not the type of people we want you socializing with* INTERACT, converse, be sociable, mix, mingle, get together, meet, fraternize, consort; entertain, go out; *informal* hobnob.

**society** noun **1** *a danger to society* THE COMMUNITY, the (general) public, the people, the population; civilization, humankind, mankind, humanity.

**2** *an industrial society* CULTURE, community, civilization, nation, population.

**3** *Sir Paul will help you enter society* HIGH SOCIETY, polite society, the upper classes, the elite, the smart set, the beautiful people, the beau monde, the haut monde; *informal* the upper crust, the top drawer.

**4** *a local history society* ASSOCIATION, club, group, circle, fellowship, guild, lodge, fraternity, brotherhood, sisterhood, sorority, league, union, alliance.

**5** *the society of others* COMPANY, companionship, fellowship, friendship, comradeship, camaraderie.

**sodden** adjective **1** *his clothes were sodden* SOAKING, soaked (through), wet (through), saturated, drenched, sopping wet, wringing wet. ANTONYM dry.

**2** *sodden fields* WATERLOGGED, soggy, saturated, boggy, swampy, miry, marshy; heavy, soft. ANTONYM arid.

**soft** adjective **1** *soft fruit* MUSHY, squashy, pulpy, pappy, slushy, squishy, doughy; *informal* gooey. ANTONYM hard.

**2** *soft ground* SWAMPY, marshy, boggy, miry, oozy; heavy, squelchy. ANTONYM firm.

**3** *a soft cushion* SQUASHY, spongy, compressible, supple, springy, pliable, pliant, resilient, malleable. ANTONYM hard.

**4** *soft fabric* VELVETY, smooth, fleecy, downy, furry, silky, silken, satiny. ANTONYMS rough, harsh.

**5** *a soft wind* GENTLE, light, mild, moderate. ANTONYM strong.

**6** *soft light* DIM, low, faint, subdued, muted, mellow. ANTONYM harsh.

**7** *soft colors* PALE, pastel, muted, understated, restrained, subdued, subtle. ANTONYM lurid.

**8** *soft voices* QUIET, low, faint, muted, subdued, muffled, hushed, whispered, stifled, murmured, gentle, dulcet; indistinct, inaudible. ANTONYMS strident, clear.

**9** *soft outlines* BLURRED, vague, hazy, misty, foggy, nebulous, fuzzy, blurry, indistinct, unclear. ANTONYM sharp.

**10** *he seduced her with soft words* KIND, gentle, sympathetic, soothing, tender, sensitive, affectionate, loving, amorous, warm, sweet, sentimental, pretty; *informal* mushy, slushy, schmaltzy, sappy. ANTONYM harsh.

**11** *she's too soft with her students* LENIENT, easygoing, tolerant, forgiving, forbearing, indulgent, clement, permissive, liberal, lax. ANTONYM strict.

**12** *informal he's soft in the head* FOOLISH, stupid, simple, brainless, mindless; mad, scatterbrained, featherbrained; slow, weak, feeble; *informal* dopey, dippy, scatty, loopy, flaky. ANTONYM sensible.

**soften** verb **1** *she tried to soften the blow of new service cuts* ALLEVIATE, ease, relieve, soothe, take the edge off, assuage, cushion, moderate, mitigate, palliate, diminish, blunt, deaden.

**2** *the winds softened* DIE DOWN, abate, subside, moderate, let up, calm, diminish, slacken, weaken. PHRASE: **soften up** *she knows how to soften up Dad just before reaching into his wallet* CHARM, win over, persuade, influence, weaken, disarm, sweeten, butter up, soft-soap.

**soggy** adjective *the cushions are completely soggy from last night's rain* MUSHY, squashy, pulpy, slushy, squishy; swampy, marshy, boggy, miry; soaking, soaked through, wet, saturated, drenched.

**soil**[1] noun **1** *acid soil* EARTH, loam, dirt, clay, gumbo; ground.

**2** *Canadian soil* TERRITORY, land, domain, dominion, region, country.

**soil**[2] verb **1** *he soiled his tie* DIRTY, stain, splash, spot, spatter, splatter, smear, smudge, sully, spoil, foul; *literary* begrime.

**2** *our reputation is being soiled* DISHONOR, damage, sully, stain, blacken, tarnish, taint, blemish, defile, blot, smear, drag through the mud; *literary* besmirch.

**sojourn** *formal* noun *a sojourn in France* STAY, visit, stop, stopover; vacation.

▸ verb *they sojourned in the monastery* STAY, live, put up, stop (over), lodge, room, board; vacation.

**solace** noun *they found solace in each other* COMFORT, consolation, cheer, support, relief.

▸ verb *she was solaced with tea and sympathy* COMFORT, console, cheer, support, soothe, calm.

**soldier** noun *her daddy was a soldier in the Continental Army* FIGHTER, trooper, serviceman, servicewoman; warrior; GI; peacekeeper; *archaic* man-at-arms. PHRASE: **soldier on** *informal.* See PERSEVERE.

**solecism** noun **1** *a poem marred by solecisms* (GRAMMATICAL) MISTAKE, error, blunder; *informal* howler, blooper.

**2** *it would have been a solecism to answer* FAUX PAS, gaffe, impropriety, social indiscretion, infelicity, slip, error, blunder, lapse; *informal* slip-up, boo-boo, goof, blooper, flub.

**solemn** adjective **1** *a solemn occasion* DIGNIFIED, ceremonious, ceremonial, stately, formal, courtly, majestic; imposing, awe-inspiring, splendid, magnificent, grand. ANTONYM frivolous.

**2** *he looked very solemn* SERIOUS, grave, sober, somber, unsmiling, stern, grim, dour, humorless; pensive, meditative, thoughtful. ANTONYM lighthearted.

**3** *a solemn promise* SINCERE, earnest, honest, genuine, firm, heartfelt, wholehearted, sworn. ANTONYM insincere.

**solicit** verb **1** *Phil tried to solicit his help* ASK FOR, request, seek, apply for, put in for, call for, press for, beg, plead for. See note at BEG.

**2** *they are solicited for their opinions* ASK, petition, importune, implore, plead with, entreat, appeal to, lobby, beg, supplicate, call on, press; *literary* beseech.

**solicitous** adjective *she was always solicitous about the welfare of her students* CONCERNED, caring, considerate, attentive, mindful, thoughtful, interested; anxious, worried.

**solid** adjective **1** *the ice cream was solid* HARD, rock-hard, rigid, firm, solidified, set, frozen, concrete. ANTONYMS liquid, gaseous.

**2** *solid gold* PURE, 24-carat, unalloyed, unadulterated, genuine. ANTONYMS alloyed, plated, hollow.

**3** *a solid line* CONTINUOUS, uninterrupted, unbroken, nonstop, undivided. ANTONYM broken.

**4** *solid houses* WELL-BUILT, sound, substantial, strong, sturdy, durable. ANTONYM flimsy.

**5** *a solid argument* WELL-FOUNDED, valid, sound, reasonable, logical, authoritative, convincing, cogent, plausible, credible, reliable. ANTONYMS untenable, incoherent.

**6** *a solid friendship* DEPENDABLE, reliable, firm, unshakable, trustworthy, stable, steadfast, staunch, constant, rock-steady. ANTONYM unreliable.

**7** *solid citizens* SENSIBLE, dependable, trustworthy, decent, law-abiding, upright, upstanding, worthy.

**8** *the company is very solid* FINANCIALLY SOUND, secure, creditworthy, profit-making, solvent, in credit, in the black.

**9** *solid support from their colleagues* UNANIMOUS, united, consistent, undivided, wholehearted. ANTONYM divided.

**solidarity** noun *our solidarity is what gives us the credibility and power to make changes* UNANIMITY, unity, like-mindedness, agreement, accord, harmony, consensus, concurrence, cooperation, cohesion, fraternity, mutual support; *formal* concord.

**solidify** verb *the mixture will solidify in about nine hours at room temperature* HARDEN, set, freeze, thicken, stiffen, congeal, cake, dry, bake; ossify, calcify, fossilize, petrify. ANTONYM liquefy.

**solitary** adjective **1** *a solitary life* LONELY, companionless, unaccompanied, by oneself, on one's own, alone, friendless; antisocial, unsociable, withdrawn, reclusive, cloistered, hermitic, incommunicado, lonesome. ANTONYM sociable.

**2** *solitary farmsteads* ISOLATED, remote, lonely, out of the way, in the back of beyond, outlying, off the beaten track/path, godforsaken, obscure, inaccessible, cutoff; secluded, private, sequestered, desolate, in the backwoods; *informal* in the sticks, in the middle of nowhere, in the boondocks, in the back woods; *literary* lone. ANTONYM accessible.

**3** *a solitary piece of evidence* SINGLE, lone, sole, unique; only, one, individual; odd.

**solitude** noun **1** *she savored her solitude* LONELINESS, solitariness, isolation, seclusion, sequestration, withdrawal, privacy, peace.

**2** (**solitudes**) *solitudes in the north of the state* WILDERNESS, rural area, wilds, backwoods; desert, emptiness, wasteland; the bush, backcountry; *informal* the sticks, the boondocks.

THE RIGHT WORD **solitude, alienation, desolation, disaffection, estrangement, lonesomeness, solitude**

**Loneliness**, which refers to a lack of companionship and is often associated with unhappiness, should not be confused with **solitude**, which is the state of being alone or cut off from all human contact (*the solitude of the lighthouse keeper*). You can be in the midst of a crowd of people and still experience *loneliness*, but not *solitude*, since you are not physically alone. Similarly, if you enjoy being alone, you can have solitude without loneliness. **Lonesomeness** is more intense than *loneliness*, suggesting the downheartedness you may experience when a loved one is absent (*she experienced lonesomeness following the death of her dog*). **Desolation** is more intense still, referring to a state of being utterly alone or forsaken (*the widow's desolation*). *Desolation* can also indicate a state of ruin or barrenness (*the desolation of the volcanic islands*). **Alienation**, **disaffection**, and **estrangement** have less to do with being or feeling alone and more to do with emotions that change over time. *Alienation* is a word that suggests a feeling of unrelatedness, especially a feeling of distance from your social or intellectual environment (*alienation from society*). *Disaffection* suggests that you now feel indifference or even distaste toward someone of you were once fond of (*a wife's growing disaffection for her husband*), while *estrangement* is a voluntary disaffection that can result in complete separation and strong feelings of dislike or hatred (*a daughter's estrangement from her parents*).

**solution** noun **1** *an easy solution to the problem* ANSWER, result, resolution, way out, fix, panacea; key, formula, explanation, interpretation.

2 *a solution of ammonia in water* MIXTURE, mix, blend, compound, suspension, tincture, infusion, emulsion.

**solve** verb *has anyone ever solved this riddle?* RESOLVE, answer, work out, find a solution to, find the key to, puzzle out, fathom, decipher, decode, clear up, straighten out, get to the bottom of, unravel, piece together, explain; *informal* figure out, crack.

**solvent** adjective *after years in debt, he finally knew what it meant to be solvent* FINANCIALLY SOUND, debt-free, in the black, in credit, creditworthy, solid, secure, profit-making; *Finance* unleveraged.

**somber** adjective 1 *somber clothes* DARK, drab, dull, dingy; restrained, subdued, sober, funereal. ANTONYM bright.

2 *a somber expression* SOLEMN, earnest, serious, grave, sober, unsmiling, stern, grim, dour, humorless; gloomy, depressed, sad, melancholy, dismal, doleful, mournful, lugubrious. ANTONYM cheerful.

**somebody** noun *she wanted to be a somebody* IMPORTANT PERSON, VIP, public figure, notable, dignitary, worthy; someone, (big/household) name, celebrity, star, superstar; grandee, luminary, leading light; *informal* celeb, bigwig, big shot, big cheese, hotshot, megastar. ANTONYMS nonentity, no-name.

**someday** adverb *someday I'll live in the countryside* SOMETIME, one (fine) day, one of these days, at a future date, sooner or later, by and by, in due course, in the fullness of time, in the long run. ANTONYM never.

**somehow** adverb *I knew that somehow I would find a way to buy that car* BY SOME MEANS, by any means, in some way, one way or another, no matter how, by fair means or foul, by hook or by crook, come what may.

**sometime** adverb 1 *I'll visit sometime* SOMEDAY, one day, one of these (fine) days, at a future date, sooner or later, by and by, in due course, in the fullness of time, in the long run. ANTONYM never.

2 *it happened sometime on Sunday* AT SOME TIME, at some point; during, in the course of.

▸ adjective *the sometime editor of the paper* FORMER, past, previous, prior, foregoing, late, erstwhile, one-time, ex-; *formal* quondam.

**sometimes** adverb *sometimes we have supper down on the beach* OCCASIONALLY, from time to time, now and then, every so often, once in a while, on occasion, at times, off and on, at intervals, periodically, sporadically, spasmodically, intermittently.

**somnolent** adjective 1 *he felt somnolent after lunch* SLEEPY, drowsy, tired, languid, dozy, groggy, lethargic, sluggish, enervated, torpid; *informal* snoozy, dopey, yawny; *literary* slumberous.

2 *a somnolent village* QUIET, restful, tranquil, calm, peaceful, relaxing, soothing, undisturbed, untroubled.

**song** noun 1 *a beautiful song* AIR, strain, ditty, melody, tune, number, track, anthem, hymn, chanty, chantey, ballad, aria.

2 *the song of the birds* CALL(S), chirping, cheeping, peeping, chirruping, warble(s), warbling, trilling, twitter; birdsong. PHRASE: **song and dance** *informal why does he have to make such a song and dance out of everything?* See FUSS noun sense 1.

**sonorous** adjective 1 *a sonorous voice* RESONANT, rich, full, round, booming, deep, clear, mellow, orotund, fruity, strong, resounding, reverberant.

2 *sonorous words of condemnation* IMPRESSIVE, imposing, grandiloquent, magniloquent, high-flown, lofty, orotund, bombastic, grandiose, pompous, pretentious, overblown, turgid; oratorical, rhetorical; *informal* highfalutin.

**soon** adverb 1 *we'll be there soon* SHORTLY, presently, in the near future, before long, in a little while, in a minute, in a moment, in an instant, in a bit, in the twinkling of an eye, in no time, before you know it, any minute (now), any day (now), by and by; *informal* pronto, in a jiffy; *dated* directly, anon.

2 *how soon can you get here?* EARLY, quickly, promptly, speedily, punctually.

**soothe** verb 1 *Rachel tried to soothe him* CALM (DOWN), pacify, comfort, hush, quiet, subdue, settle (down), lull, tranquilize; appease, conciliate, mollify. ANTONYM agitate.

2 *an anesthetic to soothe the pain* ALLEVIATE, ease, relieve, take the edge off, assuage, allay, lessen, palliate, diminish, decrease, dull, blunt, deaden. ANTONYM aggravate.

**soothsayer** noun *the most respected of the king's soothsayers* SEER, oracle, augur, prophet/prophetess, sage, prognosticator, diviner, fortune teller, crystal-gazer, clairvoyant, psychic; *literary* sibyl; *rare* haruspex.

**sophisticated** adjective 1 *sophisticated techniques* ADVANCED, modern, state of the art, the latest, new, up-to-the-minute; innovative, trailblazing, revolutionary, futuristic, avant-garde; complex, complicated, intricate, highly evolved. ANTONYM crude.

2 *a sophisticated woman* WORLDLY, worldly-wise, experienced, enlightened, cosmopolitan, knowledgeable; urbane, cultured, cultivated, civilized, polished, refined; elegant, stylish; *informal* cool. See note at URBANE. ANTONYM naive.

**sophistication** noun *the shabbiest of work clothes could not disguise his sophistication* WORLDLINESS, experience; urbanity, culture, civilization, polish, refinement; elegance, style, poise, finesse, savoir faire; *informal* cool.

**sophistry** noun 1 *to claim this is pure sophistry* SPECIOUS REASONING, fallacy, sophism, casuistry.

2 *a speech full of sophistries* FALLACIOUS ARGUMENT, sophism, fallacy; *Logic* paralogism.

**soporific** adjective 1 *soporific drugs* SLEEP-INDUCING, sedative, somnolent, calmative, tranquilizing, narcotic, opiate; drowsy, sleepy, somniferous; *Medicine* hypnotic. ANTONYM invigorating.

2 *a soporific TV drama* BORING, tedious, tired, dreary, turgid, dry, mind-numbing.

▸ noun *she was given a soporific* SLEEPING PILL, sedative, calmative, tranquilizer, narcotic, opiate; *Medicine* hypnotic. ANTONYM stimulant.

**sorcerer, sorceress** noun *he was convinced that a sorceress had cast an evil spell upon his household* WIZARD, witch, magician, warlock, enchanter, enchantress, magus; witch doctor; *archaic* mage.

**sorcery** noun *the practice of sorcery was strictly forbidden* (BLACK) MAGIC, the black arts, witchcraft, wizardry, enchantment, spells, incantation, witching, witchery, thaumaturgy.

**sordid** adjective **1** *a sordid love affair* SLEAZY, dirty, seedy, seamy, unsavory, tawdry, cheap, debased, degenerate, dishonorable, disreputable, discreditable, contemptible, ignominious, shameful, abhorrent. ANTONYM respectable.

**2** *a sordid little street* SQUALID, slummy, insalubrious, dirty, filthy, mucky, grimy, shabby, messy, soiled, scummy, unclean; *informal* cruddy, grungy, crummy, scuzzy. ANTONYM immaculate.

**sore** adjective **1** *a sore leg* PAINFUL, hurting, hurt, aching, throbbing, smarting, stinging, agonizing, excruciating; inflamed, sensitive, tender, raw, bruised, wounded, injured.

**2** *we are in sore need of you* DIRE, urgent, pressing, desperate, parlous, critical, crucial, acute, grave, serious, drastic, extreme, life-and-death, great, terrible; *formal* exigent.

**3** *informal they were sore at us* UPSET, angry, annoyed, cross, furious, vexed, displeased, disgruntled, dissatisfied, exasperated, irritated, galled, irked, put out, aggrieved, offended, affronted, piqued, nettled; *informal* aggravated, miffed, peeved, riled, teed off, ticked off.

▸ noun *a sore on his leg* INFLAMMATION, swelling, lesion; wound, scrape, abrasion, cut, laceration, graze, contusion, bruise; ulcer, boil, abscess, carbuncle.

**sorrow** noun **1** *he felt sorrow at her death* SADNESS, unhappiness, misery, despondency, regret, depression, despair, desolation, dejection, wretchedness, gloom, dolefulness, melancholy, woe, heartache, grief; *literary* dolor. ANTONYM joy.

**2** *the sorrows of life* TROUBLE, difficulty, problem, adversity, misery, woe, affliction, trial, tribulation, misfortune, pain, setback, reverse, blow, failure, tragedy. ANTONYM joy.

▸ verb *they sorrowed over her grave* MOURN, lament, grieve, be sad, be miserable, be despondent, despair, suffer, ache, agonize, anguish, pine, weep, wail. See note at MOURN. ANTONYM rejoice.

**sorrowful** adjective **1** *sorrowful eyes* SAD, unhappy, dejected, regretful, downcast, miserable, downhearted, despondent, despairing, disconsolate, desolate, glum, gloomy, doleful, dismal, melancholy, mournful, woeful, woebegone, forlorn, crestfallen, heartbroken; *informal* blue, down in/at the mouth, down in the dumps.

**2** *sorrowful news* TRAGIC, sad, unhappy, awful, miserable, sorry, pitiful; traumatic, upsetting, depressing, distressing, dispiriting, heartbreaking, harrowing; *formal* grievous.

**sorry** adjective **1** *I was sorry to hear about his accident* SAD, unhappy, sorrowful, distressed, upset, downcast, downhearted, disheartened, despondent; heartbroken, inconsolable, grief-stricken. ANTONYM glad.

**2** *he felt sorry for her* FULL OF PITY, sympathetic, compassionate, moved, consoling, empathetic, concerned. ANTONYM unsympathetic.

**3** *I'm sorry if I was brusque* REGRETFUL, remorseful, contrite, repentant, rueful, penitent, apologetic, abject, guilty, ashamed, sheepish, shamefaced. ANTONYM unrepentant.

**4** *he looks a sorry sight* PITIFUL, pitiable, heart-rending, distressing; unfortunate, unhappy, wretched, unlucky, shameful, regrettable, awful.

▸ exclamation *"Hey, that's my foot!" "Sorry!"* APOLOGIES, excuse me, pardon me, forgive me, my mistake; *informal* my bad.

**sort** noun **1** *what sort of book is it?* TYPE, kind, nature, manner, variety, class, category, style; caliber, quality, form, group, set, bracket, genre, species, family, order, generation, vintage, make, model, brand, stamp, stripe, ilk, cast, grain, mold.

**2** *informal he's a good sort* PERSON, individual, soul, creature, human being; character, customer; *informal* fellow, type.

▸ verb *they sorted things of similar size* CLASSIFY, class, categorize, catalog, grade, group; organize, arrange, order, marshal, assemble, systematize, systemize, pigeonhole, sort out.

PHRASES: **out of sorts 1** *I'm feeling out of sorts* UNWELL, ill, poorly, sick, queasy, nauseous, peaked, run-down, below par; *informal* under the weather, funny, lousy, rotten, awful, crappy, off.

**2** *he's out of sorts because she turned him down* GRUMPY, irritable, crabby; unhappy, sad, miserable, down, depressed, gloomy, glum, forlorn, low, in a blue funk; *informal* blue, down in the dumps.

**sort of** *informal* **1** *you look sort of familiar* SLIGHTLY, faintly, remotely, vaguely; somewhat, moderately, quite, rather, fairly, reasonably, relatively; *informal* pretty, kind of, kinda.

**2** *he sort of pirouetted* AS IT WERE, kind of, somehow.

**sort out** *they must sort out their problems* RESOLVE, settle, solve, fix, work out, straighten out, deal with, put right, set right, rectify, iron out; answer, explain, fathom, unravel, clear up; *informal* sew up, hammer out, thrash out, patch up, figure out.

**sortie** noun **1** *a sortie against their besiegers* FORAY, sally, charge, offensive, attack, assault, onset, onslaught, thrust, drive.

**2** *a bomber sortie* RAID, flight, mission, operation, op.

**so-so** adjective *informal the appetizers were exceptional, but the chowder was so-so* MEDIOCRE, indifferent, average, middle-of-the-road, middling, moderate, ordinary, adequate, fair; uninspired, undistinguished, unexceptional, unremarkable, run-of-the-mill, lackluster, 'comme ci, comme ça'; *informal* no great shakes, not up to much, okay.

**soul** noun **1** *seeing the soul through the eyes* SPIRIT, psyche, (inner) self, inner being, life force, vital force; individuality, makeup, subconscious, anima; *Philosophy* pneuma; *Hinduism* atman.

2 *he is the soul of discretion* EMBODIMENT, personification, incarnation, epitome, quintessence, essence; model, exemplification, exemplar, image, manifestation.

3 *not a soul in sight* PERSON, human being, individual, man, woman, mortal, creature.

4 *their music lacked soul* INSPIRATION, feeling, emotion, passion, animation, intensity, fervor, ardor, enthusiasm, warmth, energy, vitality, spirit.

**sound**[1] noun 1 *the sound of the car* NOISE, note; din, racket, row, hubbub; resonance, reverberation. ANTONYM silence.

2 *she did not make a sound* UTTERANCE, cry, word, noise, peep.

3 *the sound of the flute* MUSIC, tone, notes.

4 *I don't like the sound of that* IDEA, thought, concept, prospect, description.

▸ verb 1 *the buzzer sounded* MAKE A NOISE, resonate, resound, reverberate, go off, blare; ring, chime, peal.

2 *drivers must sound their horns* BLOW, blast, toot, blare; operate, set off; ring.

3 *do you sound the "h"?* PRONOUNCE, verbalize, voice, enunciate, articulate, vocalize, say.

4 *she sounded a warning* UTTER, voice, deliver, express, speak, announce, pronounce.

5 *it* ***sounds like*** *a crazy idea* APPEAR, look (like), seem, strike someone as being, give every indication of being, come across as.

**sound**[2] adjective 1 *your heart is sound* HEALTHY, in good condition, in good shape, fit, hale and hearty, in fine fettle; undamaged, unimpaired. ANTONYM unhealthy.

2 *a sound building* WELL-BUILT, solid, substantial, strong, sturdy, durable, stable, intact, unimpaired. ANTONYMS unsafe, flimsy.

3 *sound advice* WELL-FOUNDED, valid, reasonable, logical, weighty, authoritative, reliable, well-grounded.

4 *a sound judge of character* RELIABLE, dependable, trustworthy, fair; good, sensible, wise, judicious, sagacious, shrewd, perceptive. ANTONYM unreliable.

5 *financially sound* SOLVENT, debt-free, in the black, in credit, creditworthy, secure, solid. ANTONYMS insolvent, light.

6 *a sound sleep* DEEP, undisturbed, uninterrupted, untroubled, peaceful. ANTONYM light.

**sound**[3] verb *sound the depth of the river* MEASURE, gauge, determine, test, investigate, survey, plumb, fathom, probe. PHRASE: **sound out** *if you'll just sound them out, you might learn something useful* INVESTIGATE, test, check, examine, probe, research, look into; canvass, survey, poll, question, interview, sample; *informal* pump.

**sound**[4] noun *an oil spill in the sound* CHANNEL, (sea) passage, strait(s), narrows, waterway; inlet, arm (of the sea), fjord, creek, bay; estuary.

**sour** adjective 1 *sour wine* ACID, acidic, acidy, acidulated, tart, bitter, sharp, vinegary, pungent; *technical* acerbic. ANTONYM sweet.

2 *sour milk* BAD, off, turned, curdled, rancid, rank, foul, fetid; (of beer) skunky. ANTONYM fresh.

3 *a sour old man* EMBITTERED, resentful, rancorous, jaundiced, bitter; nasty, spiteful, irritable, peevish, fractious, cross, crabby, crotchety, cantankerous, disagreeable, petulant, querulous, grumpy, bad-tempered, ill-humored, sullen, surly, sulky, churlish; *informal* grouchy, cranky. ANTONYM amiable.

▸ verb 1 *the war had soured him* EMBITTER, disillusion, disenchant, poison, alienate; dissatisfy, frustrate.

2 *the dispute soured relations* SPOIL, mar, damage, harm, impair, wreck, upset, poison, blight, tarnish. ANTONYM improve.

**source** noun 1 *the source of the river* SPRING, origin, headspring, headwater(s); *literary* wellspring.

2 *the source of the rumor* ORIGIN, birthplace, spring, fountainhead, fount, starting point, ground zero; history, provenance, derivation, root, beginning, genesis, start, rise; author, originator, initiator, inventor. See note at ORIGIN.

3 *a historian uses primary and secondary sources* REFERENCE, authority, material, document, informant.

**souvenir** noun *keep the key ring as a souvenir* MEMENTO, keepsake, reminder, remembrance, token, memorial; bomboniere; trophy, relic.

**sovereign** noun *the daughter of their beloved sovereign* RULER, monarch, crowned head, head of state, potentate, suzerain, overlord, dynast, leader; king, queen, emperor, empress, prince, princess, czar, royal duke, regent, mogul, emir, sheikh, sultan, maharaja, raja.

▸ adjective 1 *sovereign control* SUPREME, absolute, unlimited, unrestricted, boundless, ultimate, total, unconditional, full; principal, chief, dominant, predominant, ruling; royal, regal, monarchical.

2 *a sovereign state* INDEPENDENT, autonomous, self-governing, self-determining; nonaligned, free.

**sovereignty** noun 1 *their sovereignty over the islands* JURISDICTION, rule, supremacy, dominion, power, ascendancy, suzerainty, hegemony, domination, authority, control, influence. See note at JURISDICTION.

2 *the colony demanded full sovereignty* AUTONOMY, independence, self-government, self-rule, home rule, self-determination, freedom.

**sow** verb 1 *sow the seeds in rows* PLANT, scatter, spread, disperse, strew, disseminate, distribute, broadcast; drill, seed.

2 *the new policy has sown confusion* CAUSE, bring about, occasion, create, lead to, produce, spread, engender, generate, prompt, initiate, precipitate, trigger, provoke; culminate in, entail, necessitate; foster, foment; *literary* beget.

**space** noun 1 *there was not enough space* ROOM, capacity, area, volume, expanse, extent, scope, latitude, margin, leeway, play, clearance.

**2** *green spaces in the city* AREA, expanse, stretch, sweep, tract.

**3** *the space between the timbers* GAP, interval, opening, aperture, cavity, cranny, fissure, crack, interstice, lacuna.

**4** *write your name in the appropriate space* BLANK, gap, box; place.

**5** *a space of seven years* PERIOD, span, time, duration, stretch, course, interval.

**6** *the first woman in space* OUTER SPACE, deep space; the universe, the galaxy, the solar system; infinity.

▸ verb *the chairs were spaced widely* POSITION, arrange, range, array, dispose, lay out, locate, situate, set, stand.

**spacious** adjective *spacious accommodations* ROOMY, capacious, palatial, airy, sizable, generous, large, big, vast, immense; extensive, expansive, sweeping, rolling, rambling, open; *formal* commodious. ANTONYM cramped.

**span** noun **1** *a six-foot wing span* EXTENT, length, width, reach, stretch, spread, distance, range.

**2** *the span of one working day* PERIOD, space, time, duration, course, interval.

▸ verb **1** *an arch spanned the stream* BRIDGE, cross, traverse, pass over.

**2** *his career spanned twenty years* LAST, cover, extend, spread over, comprise.

**spank** verb *he would never dream of spanking his children* SMACK, slap, hit, cuff; *informal* wallop, belt, whack, tan someone's hide.

**spar** verb *they sparred over every little thing* QUARREL, argue, fight, disagree, differ, be at odds, be at variance, fall out, dispute, squabble, wrangle, bandy words, cross swords, lock horns, be at loggerheads; *informal* scrap, spat.

**spare** adjective **1** *a spare set of keys* EXTRA, supplementary, additional, second, other, alternative, alternate; emergency, reserve, backup, relief, fallback, substitute; fresh.

**2** *they sold off the spare land* SURPLUS, superfluous, excessive, extra; redundant, unnecessary, inessential, unessential, unneeded, uncalled for, dispensable, disposable, expendable, unwanted; *informal* going begging.

**3** *your spare time* FREE, leisure, own.

**4** *a man of spare build.* See THIN adjective sense 3. See also note at THIN.

▸ verb **1** *sorry, I can't spare a quarter* AFFORD, do without, manage without, dispense with, part with, give, provide.

**2** *their captors eventually spared them* PARDON, let off, forgive, reprieve, release, free; leave uninjured, leave unhurt; be merciful to, show mercy to, have mercy on, be lenient to, have pity on.

**sparing** adjective *a fiercely sparing man, he died rich and friendless* THRIFTY, economical, frugal, canny, careful, prudent, cautious; mean, miserly, niggardly, parsimonious, close-fisted, penny-pinching, ungenerous, close, grasping; *informal* stingy, cheap, tightfisted, tight, mingy, money-grubbing. See note at ECONOMICAL. ANTONYM lavish.

**spark** noun **1** *a spark of light* FLASH, glint, twinkle, flicker, flare, pinprick.

**2** *not a spark of truth in the story* PARTICLE, iota, jot, whit, glimmer, atom, bit, trace, vestige, ounce, shred, crumb, grain, mite, hint, touch, suggestion, whisper, scintilla; *informal* smidgen, tad.

▸ verb *the trial sparked a furious debate* CAUSE, give rise to, lead to, occasion, bring about, start, initiate, precipitate, prompt, trigger (off), provoke, stimulate, stir up.

**sparkle** verb **1** *her earrings sparkled* GLITTER, glint, glisten, twinkle, flash, blink, wink, shimmer, shine, gleam; *literary* coruscate, glister.

**2** *she sparkled as the hostess* BE LIVELY, be vivacious, be animated, be ebullient, be exuberant, be bubbly, be effervescent, be witty, be full of life.

▸ noun *the sparkle of the pool* GLITTER, glint, twinkle, flicker, shimmer, flash, shine, gleam; *literary* coruscation.

**sparse** adjective *areas of sparse population* SCANT, scanty, scattered, scarce, infrequent, few and far between; meager, paltry, skimpy, limited, in short supply. ANTONYM abundant.

**spartan** adjective *the monk's spartan cell* AUSTERE, harsh, hard, frugal, stringent, rigorous, strict, stern, severe; ascetic, abstemious; bleak, joyless, grim, bare, stark, plain. ANTONYM luxurious.

**spasm** noun **1** *a muscle spasm* CONTRACTION, convulsion, cramp; twitch, jerk, tic, shudder, shiver, tremor.

**2** *a spasm of coughing* FIT, paroxysm, attack, burst, bout, seizure, outburst, outbreak, access.

**spasmodic** adjective *the car chugged up the road with spasmodic lurches* INTERMITTENT, fitful, irregular, sporadic, erratic, occasional, infrequent, scattered, patchy, isolated, periodic, periodical, on and off; *informal* herky-jerky.

**spate** noun *a spate of interest in military memorabilia* SERIES, succession, run, cluster, string, rash, epidemic, outbreak, wave, flurry, rush, flood, deluge, torrent.

**spatter** verb *the curtains were spattered with champagne* SPLASH, bespatter, splatter, spray, sprinkle, shower, speck, speckle, fleck, mottle, blotch, mark, cover; *informal* splotch.

**spawn** verb *that one brief statement has spawned a blitz of criticism* GIVE RISE TO, bring about, occasion, generate, engender, originate; lead to, result in, effect, induce, initiate, start, set off, precipitate, trigger; breed, bear; *literary* beget.

**speak** verb **1** *she refused to speak about it* TALK, say anything/something; utter, state, declare, tell, voice, express, pronounce, articulate, enunciate, vocalize, verbalize.

**2** *we spoke the other day* CONVERSE, have a conversation, talk, communicate, chat, pass the time of day, have a word, gossip; *informal* have a confab, chew the fat; natter, shoot the breeze; *formal* confabulate.

**3** *the minister spoke for two hours* GIVE A SPEECH, talk, lecture, hold forth, discourse, expound, expatiate, orate, sermonize, pontificate, declaim; *informal* spout, spiel, speechify, jaw, sound off.

4 *he was **spoken of** as a promising student* MENTION, talk about, discuss, refer to, remark on, allude to, describe.

5 *her expression spoke disbelief* INDICATE, show, display, register, reveal, betray, exhibit, manifest, express, convey, impart, bespeak, communicate, evidence; suggest, denote, reflect; *formal* evince.

6 *you must **speak to** him about his rudeness* REPRIMAND, rebuke, admonish, chastise, chide, upbraid, reprove, reproach, scold, remonstrate with, take to task; *informal* tell off, dress down, rap over the knuckles, come down on, give someone what for; *formal* castigate. PHRASES: **speak for** 1 *she speaks for the Arts Council* REPRESENT, act for, appear for, express the views of, be spokesperson for.

2 *I spoke for the motion* ADVOCATE, champion, uphold, defend, support, promote, recommend, back, endorse, sponsor, espouse.

**speak out** *if you've got a grievance, then speak out* SPEAK PUBLICLY, speak openly, speak frankly, speak one's mind, sound off, stand up and be counted.

**speak up** *speak up so we can hear you* SPEAK LOUDLY, speak clearly, raise one's voice; shout, yell, bellow; *informal* holler.

**speaker** noun *Reverend Graham is one of the guest speakers* SPEECHMAKER, lecturer, talker, speechifier, orator, declaimer, rhetorician; spokesperson, spokesman/woman, mouthpiece; reader, lector, commentator, broadcaster, narrator; *informal* spieler; *historical* demagogue, rhetor.

**spearhead** noun 1 *a Bronze Age spearhead* SPEAR TIP, spear point.

2 *the spearhead of the struggle against fascism* LEADER(S), driving force; forefront, front runner(s), front line, vanguard, van, cutting edge.

▸ verb *she spearheaded the campaign* LEAD, head, front; lead the way, be in the van, be in the vanguard.

**special** adjective 1 *a very special person* EXCEPTIONAL, unusual, singular, uncommon, notable, noteworthy, remarkable, outstanding, unique. ANTONYM ordinary.

2 *our town's special character* DISTINCTIVE, distinct, individual, particular, characteristic, specific, peculiar, idiosyncratic. ANTONYM general.

3 *a special occasion* MOMENTOUS, significant, memorable, signal, important, historic, festive, gala, red-letter.

4 *a special tool for cutting tiles* SPECIFIC, particular, purpose-built, tailor-made, custom-built/made.

**specialist** noun *he's an electronics specialist* EXPERT, authority, pundit, professional; connoisseur; master, maestro, adept, virtuoso; *informal* pro, buff, ace, whiz, hotshot, maven. ANTONYM amateur.

**specialty** noun 1 *his specialty was watercolors* FORTE, strong point, strength, métier, strong suit, talent, skill, bent, gift; *Brit.* speciality; *informal* bag, thing, cup of tea.

2 *a specialty of the region* DELICACY; *Brit.* speciality, fine food/product, traditional food/product.

**species** noun *there are several species of spadefoot toad* TYPE, kind, sort; genus, family, order, breed, strain, variety, class, classification, category, set, bracket; style, manner, form, genre; generation, vintage.

**specific** adjective 1 *a specific purpose* PARTICULAR, specified, fixed, set, determined, distinct, definite; single, individual, peculiar, discrete, express, precise. ANTONYM general.

2 *I gave specific instructions* DETAILED, explicit, express, clear-cut, unequivocal, precise, exact, meticulous, strict, definite. ANTONYM vague.

**specification** noun 1 *the clear specification of objectives* STATEMENT, identification, definition, description, setting out, framing, designation, detailing, enumeration; stipulation, prescription.

2 **(specifications)** *a shelter built to their specifications* INSTRUCTIONS, guidelines, parameters, stipulations, requirements, conditions, provisions, restrictions, order; description, details; *informal* specs.

**specify** verb *specify your color preferences* STATE, name, identify, define, describe, set out, frame, itemize, detail, list, spell out, enumerate, particularize, cite, instance; stipulate, prescribe.

**specimen** noun *a specimen of his handwriting* SAMPLE, example, instance, illustration, demonstration, exemplification; bit, snippet; model, prototype, pattern, dummy, pilot, trial, taster, tester.

**specious** adjective *specious reasoning* MISLEADING, deceptive, false, fallacious, unsound, spurious, casuistic, sophistic.

**speck** noun 1 *a mere speck in the distance* DOT, pinprick, spot, fleck, speckle.

2 *a speck of dust* PARTICLE, grain, atom, molecule; bit, trace.

**speckled** adjective *speckled eggs* FLECKED, speckly, specked, freckled, freckly, spotted, spotty, dotted, mottled, dappled.

**spectacle** noun 1 *a spectacle fit for a monarch* DISPLAY, show, pageant, parade, performance, exhibition, extravaganza, spectacular.

2 *they were rather an odd spectacle* SIGHT, vision, scene, prospect, vista, picture.

3 *don't make a spectacle of yourself* EXHIBITION, laughingstock, fool, curiosity.

**spectacular** adjective 1 *a spectacular victory* IMPRESSIVE, magnificent, splendid, dazzling, sensational, dramatic, remarkable, outstanding, memorable, unforgettable. ANTONYM unimpressive.

2 *a spectacular view* STRIKING, picturesque, eye-catching, breathtaking, arresting, glorious; *informal* out of this world. ANTONYMS unimpressive, dull.

**spectator** noun *the stands are brimming with eager spectators* WATCHER, viewer, observer, onlooker, looker-on, bystander, witness; commentator, reporter, monitor; *literary* beholder. ANTONYM participant.

**specter** noun **1** *the specters in the crypt* GHOST, phantom, apparition, spirit, wraith, shadow, presence; *informal* spook; *literary* phantasm, shade.

**2** *the looming specter of war* THREAT, menace, shadow, cloud; prospect; danger, peril, fear, dread.

**speculate** verb **1** *they speculated about my private life* CONJECTURE, theorize, hypothesize, guess, surmise; think, wonder, muse.

**2** *investors* ***speculate on*** *the stock market* GAMBLE ON, take a risk on, venture in, wager on; invest in, play.

**speculative** adjective **1** *any discussion is largely speculative* CONJECTURAL, suppositional, theoretical, hypothetical, putative, academic, notional, abstract; tentative, unproven, unfounded, groundless, unsubstantiated.

**2** *a speculative investment* RISKY, hazardous, unsafe, uncertain, unpredictable; *informal* chancy, dicey, iffy.

**speech** noun **1** *he doesn't have the power of speech* SPEAKING, talking, verbal expression, verbal communication.

**2** *her speech was slurred* DICTION, elocution, articulation, enunciation, pronunciation; utterance, words.

**3** *an after-dinner speech* TALK, address, lecture, discourse, oration, disquisition, peroration, deliverance, presentation; sermon, homily; monologue, soliloquy; *informal* spiel.

**4** *Spanish popular speech* LANGUAGE, tongue, parlance, idiom, dialect, vernacular, patois; *informal* lingo, patter, -speak, -ese.

**speechless** adjective *her talk of divorce left him speechless* LOST FOR WORDS, at a loss (for words), dumbstruck, dumbfounded, bereft of speech, tongue-tied, inarticulate, mute, dumb, voiceless, silent; *informal* mum. ANTONYM verbose.

**speed** noun **1** *the speed of their progress* RATE, pace, tempo, momentum.

**2** *the speed with which they responded* RAPIDITY, swiftness, speediness, quickness, dispatch, promptness, immediacy, briskness, sharpness; haste, hurry, precipitateness; acceleration, velocity; *informal* lick, clip; *literary* celerity.

▸ verb **1** *I sped home* HURRY, rush, dash, run, race, sprint, bolt, dart, gallop, career, charge, shoot, hurtle, careen, hare, fly, zoom, scurry, scuttle, scamper, hasten; *informal* tear, belt, pelt, scoot, zip, zap, whip, hotfoot it, bomb, hightail it.

**2** *he was caught speeding* DRIVE TOO FAST, exceed the speed limit.

**3** *a holiday will speed his recovery* HASTEN, expedite, speed up, accelerate, advance, further, promote, boost, stimulate, aid, assist, facilitate. ANTONYMS slow, hinder.

**speedy** adjective **1** *a speedy reply* RAPID, swift, quick, fast; prompt, immediate, expeditious, express, brisk, sharp; whirlwind, lightning, meteoric; hasty, hurried, precipitate, breakneck, rushed; *informal* PDQ (pretty damn quick), snappy, quickie. ANTONYM slow.

**2** *a speedy little car* FAST, high-speed; *informal* nippy, zippy, peppy; *literary* fleet. ANTONYM slow.

**spell**[1] verb *the drought spelled disaster for them* SIGNAL, signify, mean, amount to, add up to, constitute; portend, augur, herald, bode, promise; involve; *literary* betoken, foretoken, forebode. PHRASE: **spell out** *allow us to spell out the plan in detail* EXPLAIN, make clear, make plain, elucidate, clarify; specify, itemize, detail, enumerate, list, expound, particularize, catalog.

**spell**[2] noun **1** *the witch recited a spell* INCANTATION, charm, conjuration, formula; (**spells**) magic, sorcery, witchcraft, hex, curse.

**2** *she surrendered to his spell* INFLUENCE, (animal) magnetism, charisma, allure, lure, charm, attraction, enticement; magic, romance, mystique. PHRASE: **cast a spell on** *it's as if this town cast a spell on me* BEWITCH, enchant, entrance; curse, jinx, witch, hex.

**spell**[3] noun **1** *a spell of dry weather* PERIOD, time, interval, season, stretch, run, course, streak, patch.

**2** *a spell of dizziness* BOUT, fit, attack.

**spellbinding** adjective *a spellbinding tale set in the Far East* FASCINATING, enthralling, entrancing, bewitching, captivating, riveting, engrossing, gripping, absorbing, compelling, compulsive, mesmerizing, hypnotic; *informal* unputdownable. ANTONYM boring.

**spellbound** adjective *the audience was spellbound* ENTHRALLED, fascinated, rapt, riveted, transfixed, gripped, captivated, bewitched, enchanted, mesmerized, hypnotized; *informal* hooked.

**spend** verb **1** *she spent $185 on shoes* PAY OUT, dish out, expend, disburse; squander, waste, fritter away; lavish; *informal* fork out, lay out, shell out, cough up, drop, blow, splurge, pony up.

**2** *the morning was spent gardening* PASS, occupy, fill, take up, while away.

**3** *I've spent hours on this essay* PUT IN, devote; waste.

**4** *the storm had spent its force* USE UP, consume, exhaust, deplete, drain.

**spendthrift** noun *he is such a spendthrift* PROFLIGATE, prodigal, squanderer, waster; *informal* big spender. ANTONYM miser.

▸ adjective *his spendthrift father* PROFLIGATE, improvident, thriftless, wasteful, extravagant, prodigal. ANTONYM frugal.

**spent** adjective **1** *a spent force* USED UP, consumed, exhausted, finished, depleted, drained; *informal* burnt out.

**2** *that's enough—I'm spent* EXHAUSTED, tired (out), weary, worn out, dog-tired, on one's last legs, drained, fatigued, ready to drop; *informal* done in, all in, dead on one's feet, dead beat, bushed, wiped out, frazzled, whacked, pooped, tuckered out.

**spew** verb *factories* ***spewed out*** *yellow smoke* EMIT, discharge, eject, expel, belch out, pour out, spout, gush, spurt, disgorge.

**sphere** noun **1** *a glass sphere* GLOBE, ball, orb, spheroid, globule, round; bubble.

**2** *our sphere of influence* AREA, field, compass, orbit; range, scope, extent.

**3** *the sphere of foreign affairs* DOMAIN, realm, province, field, area, territory, arena, department.

**spherical** adjective *a spherical Japanese lantern* ROUND, globular, globose, globoid, globe-shaped, spheroidal, spheric. See note at ROUND.

**spice** noun **1** *the spices in curry powder* SEASONING, flavoring, condiment.

**2** *the risk added spice to their affair* EXCITEMENT, interest, color, piquancy, zest; an edge; *informal* a kick; *literary* salt. PHRASE: **spice up** *they spiced up the party with some wild dancing* ENLIVEN, make more exciting, vitalize, perk up, put some life into, ginger up, galvanize, electrify, boost; *informal* pep up, jazz up, buck up.

**spicy** adjective **1** *a spicy casserole* HOT, peppery, piquant, picante; spiced, seasoned; tasty, zesty, strong, pungent. ANTONYM bland.

**2** *spicy stories* ENTERTAINING, colorful, lively, spirited, exciting, piquant, zesty; risqué, racy, scandalous, ribald, titillating, bawdy, naughty, salacious, dirty, smutty; *informal* raunchy, juicy, saucy. ANTONYM boring.

**spike** noun **1** *a metal spike* PRONG, barb, point; skewer, stake, spit; tine, pin; spur; *Mountaineering* piton.

**2** *the spikes of a cactus* THORN, spine, prickle, bristle; *Zoology* spicule.

▸ verb **1** *she spiked an oyster* IMPALE, spear, skewer; pierce, penetrate, perforate, stab, stick, transfix; *literary* transpierce.

**2** *informal his drink was spiked with drugs* ADULTERATE, contaminate, drug, lace; *informal* dope, doctor, cut.

**spill** verb **1** *Kevin spilled his drink* KNOCK OVER, tip over, upset, overturn.

**2** *the bath water spilled onto the floor* OVERFLOW, flow, pour, run, slop, slosh, splash; leak, escape; *archaic* overbrim.

**3** *students spilled out of the building* STREAM, pour, surge, swarm, flood, throng, crowd.

**4** *the horse spilled its rider* UNSEAT, throw, dislodge, unhorse.

**5** *informal he's spilling out his troubles to her* REVEAL, disclose, divulge, blurt out, babble, betray, tell; *informal* blab.

▸ noun **1** *an oil spill* SPILLAGE, leak, leakage, overflow, flood.

**2** *she took a spill in the opening race* FALL, tumble; *informal* header, cropper, nosedive.

PHRASE: **spill the beans** *informal somebody spilled the beans about the surprise party* REVEAL ALL, tell all, give the game away, talk; *informal* let the cat out of the bag, blab, come clean.

**spin** verb **1** *the bike wheels are spinning* REVOLVE, rotate, turn, go round, whirl, gyrate, circle.

**2** *she spun around to face him* WHIRL, wheel, twirl, turn, swing, twist, swivel, pirouette, pivot.

**3** *her head was spinning* REEL, whirl, go around, swim.

**4** *she spun an amusing yarn* TELL, recount, relate, narrate; weave, concoct, invent, fabricate, make up.

▸ noun **1** *a spin of the wheel* ROTATION, revolution, turn, whirl, twirl, gyration.

**2** *a positive spin on the campaign* SLANT, angle, twist, bias.

**3** *a quick spin to the grocery store* TRIP, jaunt, outing, excursion, journey; drive, ride, run, turn, airing, joyride.

PHRASE: **spin out** *the longer you can spin out the negotiations the better* PROLONG, protract, draw out, drag out, string out, extend, carry on, continue; fill out, pad out.

**spine** noun **1** *he injured his spine* BACKBONE, spinal column, vertebral column; back; *technical* rachis.

**2** *the spine of his philosophy* CORE, center, cornerstone, foundation, basis.

**3** *the spines of a porcupine* NEEDLE, quill, bristle, barb, spike, prickle; thorn; *technical* spicule.

**spine-chilling** adjective *a spine-chilling ghost story* TERRIFYING, blood-curdling, petrifying, hair-raising, frightening, scaring, chilling, horrifying, fearsome; eerie, sinister, bone-chilling, ghostly; eldritch; *informal* scary, creepy, spooky. ANTONYMS comforting, reassuring.

**spineless** adjective *Flora could have smacked him for being so spineless* WEAK, weak-willed, weak-kneed, feeble, soft, ineffectual, irresolute, indecisive; COWARDLY, timid, timorous, fearful, faint-hearted, pusillanimous, craven, unmanly, namby-pamby, lily-livered, chicken-hearted; *informal* wimpish, wimpy, sissy, wussy, chicken, yellow, yellow-bellied, gutless. ANTONYMS bold, brave, strong-willed.

**spiral** adjective *a spiral column of smoke* COILED, helical, corkscrew, curling, winding, twisting, whorled; *technical* voluted, helicoid, helicoidal.

▸ noun *a spiral of smoke* COIL, helix, corkscrew, curl, twist, gyre, whorl, scroll; *technical* volute, volution.

▸ verb **1** *smoke spiraled up* COIL, wind, swirl, twist, wreathe, snake, gyrate; *literary* gyre.

**2** *prices spiraled* SOAR, shoot up, rocket, increase rapidly, rise rapidly, escalate, climb; *informal* skyrocket, go through the roof. ANTONYM fall.

**3** *the economy is **spiraling downward*** DETERIORATE, decline, degenerate, worsen, get worse; *informal* go downhill, take a nosedive, go to pot, go to the dogs, hit the skids, go down the tubes. ANTONYM improve.

**spire** noun *the spire of a nearby church* STEEPLE, flèche.

**spirit** noun **1** *harmony between body and spirit* SOUL, psyche, (inner) self, inner being, inner man/woman, mind, ego, id; *Philosophy* pneuma. ANTONYMS body, flesh.

**2** *a spirit haunts the island* GHOST, presence; *informal* spook.

**3** *that's the spirit* ATTITUDE, frame of mind, way of thinking, point of view, outlook, thoughts, ideas.

**4** *she was in good spirits when I left* MOOD, frame of mind, state of mind, emotional state, humor, temper.

**5** *team spirit* MORALE, esprit de corps.

**6** *the spirit of the age* ETHOS, prevailing tendency, motivating force, essence, quintessence; atmosphere, mood, feeling, climate; attitudes, beliefs, principles, standards, ethics.

**7** *his spirit never failed him* COURAGE, bravery, pluck, valor, strength of character, fortitude, backbone, mettle, stoutheartedness, determination, resolution, resolve, fight, grit; *informal* guts, spunk, sand, moxie.

**8** *they played with great spirit* ENTHUSIASM, eagerness, keenness, liveliness, vivacity, vivaciousness, animation, energy, verve, vigor, dynamism, zest, dash, élan, panache, sparkle, exuberance, gusto, brio, pep, fervor, zeal, fire, passion; *informal* get-up-and-go.

**9** *the spirit of the law* REAL/TRUE MEANING, true intention, essence, substance.

**10** *he drinks spirits* STRONG LIQUOR/DRINK; *informal* hard stuff, firewater, hooch. PHRASE: **spirit away** *they made up a story about having been spirited away by gypsies* WHISK AWAY/OFF, make off with, make disappear, run away with, abscond with, carry off, steal away, abduct, kidnap, snatch, seize.

**spirited** adjective *spirited young dancers* LIVELY, vivacious, vibrant, full of life, vital, animated, high-spirited, sparkling, sprightly, energetic, active, vigorous, dynamic, dashing, enthusiastic, passionate; determined, resolute, purposeful; *informal* feisty, spunky, take-charge, gutsy, peppy. ANTONYMS timid, apathetic, lifeless.

**spiritless** adjective *a spiritless performance* APATHETIC, passive, unenthusiastic, lifeless, listless, weak, feeble, spineless, languid, bloodless, insipid, characterless, submissive, meek, irresolute, indecisive; lackluster, flat, colorless, passionless, uninspired, wooden, dry, anemic, vapid, dull, boring, wishy-washy. ANTONYMS spirited, lively.

**spiritual** adjective **1** *your spiritual self* NONMATERIAL, incorporeal, intangible; inner, mental, psychological; transcendent, ethereal, otherworldly, mystic, mystical, metaphysical; *rare* extramundane. ANTONYM physical.

**2** *spiritual writings* RELIGIOUS, sacred, divine, holy, nonsecular, church, ecclesiastical, faith-based, devotional. ANTONYM secular.

**spit**[1] verb **1** *Cranston coughed and spat* EXPECTORATE; *informal* hawk, gob.

**2** *"Go to hell," she spat* SNAP, say angrily, hiss.

**3** *the fat began to spit* SIZZLE, hiss; crackle, sputter.

▸ noun *I could just retch watching that tobaccoey spit run down his chin* SPITTLE, saliva, sputum, slobber, dribble, drool.

**spit**[2] noun *chicken cooked on a spit* SKEWER, brochette, rotisserie.

**spite** noun *he said it out of spite* MALICE, malevolence, ill will, vindictiveness, vengefulness, revenge, malignity, evil intentions, animus, enmity; *informal* bitchiness, cattiness; *literary* maleficence. ANTONYM benevolence.

▸ verb *he did it to spite me* UPSET, hurt, make miserable, grieve, distress, wound, pain, torment, injure. ANTONYM please.

PHRASE: **in spite of** *in spite of their mutual dislike, he had helped her* DESPITE, notwithstanding, regardless of, for all; undeterred by, in defiance of, in the face of; even though, although.

**spiteful** adjective *they made spiteful remarks about Paula* MALICIOUS, malevolent, evil-intentioned, vindictive, vengeful, malign, mean, nasty, hurtful, mischievous, wounding, cruel, unkind; *informal* bitchy, catty; *literary* malefic, maleficent. See note at VINDICTIVE. ANTONYM benevolent.

**splash** verb **1** *splash your face with cool water* SPRINKLE, spray, shower, splatter, slosh, slop, squirt; daub; wet.

**2** *his boots were splashed with mud* SPATTER, bespatter, splatter, speck, speckle, blotch, smear, stain, mark; *informal* splotch.

**3** *waves splashed against the pier* SWASH, wash, break, lap; dash, beat, lash, batter, crash, buffet; *literary* plash.

**4** *children splashed in the water* PADDLE, wade, slosh; wallow; *informal* splosh; *rare* plash.

**5** *the story was splashed across the front pages* BLAZON, display, spread, plaster, trumpet, publicize; *informal* splatter.

▸ noun **1** *a splash of grease on his shirt* SPOT, blob, dab, daub, smudge, smear, speck, fleck; mark, stain; *informal* splotch.

**2** *a splash of soda water* DROP, dash, bit, spot, soupçon, dribble, driblet.

**3** *a splash of color* PATCH, burst, streak.

PHRASE: **make a splash** *informal he always believed he would make a splash in Washington* CAUSE A SENSATION, cause a stir, attract attention, draw attention to oneself/itself, get noticed, make an impression, make an impact.

**spleen** noun *that doesn't give you the right to vent your spleen on me* BAD TEMPER, bad mood, ill temper, ill humor, anger, wrath, vexation, annoyance, irritation, displeasure, dissatisfaction, resentment, rancor; spite, ill feeling, malice, maliciousness, bitterness, animosity, antipathy, hostility, malevolence, venom, gall, malignance, malignity, acrimony, bile, hatred, hate; *literary* ire, choler. ANTONYM good humor.

**splendid** adjective **1** *splendid costumes* MAGNIFICENT, sumptuous, grand, impressive, imposing, superb, spectacular, resplendent, opulent, luxurious, deluxe, rich, fine, costly, expensive, lavish, ornate, gorgeous, glorious, dazzling, elegant, regal, handsome, beautiful; stately, majestic, princely, noble, proud, palatial; *informal* plush, posh, swanky, spiffy, ritzy, splendiferous, swank; *literary* brave. ANTONYM modest.

**2** *informal we had a splendid holiday* EXCELLENT, wonderful, marvelous, superb, glorious, sublime, lovely, delightful, first-class, first-rate, blue-chip; *informal* super, great, amazing, fantastic, terrific, tremendous, phenomenal, sensational, heavenly, gorgeous, dreamy, grand, fabulous, fab, awesome, magic, ace, cool, mean, wicked, far out, A1, out of this world, killer; smashing, dandy, neat, divine, swell; *archaic* goodly. ANTONYM awful.

**splendor** noun *a wedding long remembered for its splendor* MAGNIFICENCE, sumptuousness, grandeur, impressiveness, resplendence, opulence, luxury, richness, fineness, lavishness, ornateness, glory, beauty, elegance; majesty, stateliness; *informal* ritziness, splendiferousness. ANTONYMS ordinariness, simplicity, modesty.

**splice** verb **1** *the ropes are spliced together* INTERWEAVE, braid, plait, entwine, intertwine, interlace, knit, mesh; *Nautical* marry.

**2** *we had to splice the two sections* JOIN, attach, stick together, unite; blend, mix together.

**splinter** noun *a splinter of wood* SLIVER, shiver, chip, shard; fragment, piece, bit, shred; (**splinters**) matchwood, flinders.

▸ verb *the windshield splintered* SHATTER, break into tiny pieces, smash, smash into smithereens, fracture, split, crack, disintegrate, crumble.

**split** verb **1** *the ax split the wood* BREAK, chop, cut, hew, lop, cleave; snap, crack.

**2** *the ice cracked and split* BREAK APART, fracture, rupture, fissure, snap, come apart, splinter.

**3** *her dress was split* TEAR, rip, slash, slit; *literary* rend.

**4** *the issue could split the party* DIVIDE, disunite, separate, sever; bisect, partition; *literary* tear asunder. ANTONYMS unite, unify.

**5** *they split the money between them* SHARE (OUT), divide (up), apportion, allocate, allot, distribute, dole out, parcel out, measure out; carve up, slice up; *informal* divvy up.

**6** *the path split* FORK, divide, bifurcate, diverge, branch. ANTONYMS converge, merge.

**7** *they **split up** last year* BREAK UP, separate, part, part company, become estranged; divorce, get divorced. ANTONYMS get together, marry.

**8** *informal let's split.* See LEAVE[1] sense 1.

▸ noun **1** *a split in the rock face* CRACK, fissure, cleft, crevice, break, fracture, breach.

**2** *a split in the curtain* RIP, tear, cut, rent, slash, slit.

**3** *a split in the governing party* DIVISION, rift, breach, schism, rupture, partition, separation, severance, scission, breakup.

**4** *the acrimonious split with his wife* BREAKUP, split-up, separation, parting, estrangement, rift; divorce.

PHRASE: **split hairs** *while you're splitting hairs over who's the better parent, no one is watching the kids* QUIBBLE, cavil, carp, niggle, chop logic; *informal* nitpick; *archaic* pettifog.

**spoil** verb **1** *too much sun spoils the complexion* MAR, damage, impair, blemish, disfigure, blight, flaw, deface, scar, injure, harm; ruin, destroy, wreck; be a blot on the landscape. ANTONYMS improve, enhance.

**2** *rain spoiled my plans* RUIN, wreck, destroy, upset, undo, mess up, make a mess of, dash, sabotage, scotch, torpedo; *informal* foul up, louse up, muck up, screw up, put the kibosh on, scuttle, do for, throw a (monkey) wrench in the works of, deep-six; *archaic* bring to naught. ANTONYMS further, help.

**3** *his sisters spoil him* OVERINDULGE, pamper, indulge, mollycoddle, cosset, coddle, baby, wait on hand and foot, kill with kindness; nanny. ANTONYMS neglect, be strict with.

**4** *stockpiled food may spoil* GO BAD, go off, go rancid, turn, go sour, go moldy, go rotten, rot, perish. ANTONYM keep.

PHRASE: **spoiling for** *it's obvious he's spoiling for a fight* EAGER FOR, itching for, looking for, keen to have, after, bent on, longing for.

**spoils** plural noun **1** *the spoils of war* BOOTY, loot, stolen goods, plunder, ill-gotten gains, haul, pickings; *informal* swag, boodle.

**2** *the spoils of office* BENEFITS, advantages, perks, prize; *formal* perquisites.

**spoilsport** noun *what spoilsport turned down the music?* KILLJOY, misery, damper; *informal* wet blanket, party pooper.

**spoken** adjective *spoken communication* VERBAL, oral, vocal, viva voce, uttered, said, stated; unwritten; by word of mouth. ANTONYMS nonverbal, written.

PHRASE: **spoken for 1** *the money is spoken for* RESERVED, set aside, claimed, owned, booked.

**2** *Claudine is spoken for* ATTACHED, going out with someone, in a relationship; *informal* going steady, taken.

**spokesman, spokeswoman** noun *he's the spokesman for our athletics program* SPOKESPERSON, representative, agent, mouthpiece, voice, official; *informal* spin doctor, PR person.

**sponge** verb **1** *I'll sponge your face* WASH, clean, wipe, swab; mop, rinse, sluice, swill.

**2** *informal he lived by **sponging off** others* SCROUNGE OFF/FROM, be a parasite on, beg from; live off; *informal* freeload on, cadge from, bum off, mooch off.

**sponger** noun *informal Ida's good fortune brought out all the spongers in the family* PARASITE, hanger-on, leech, scrounger, beggar; *informal* freeloader, cadger, bum, bloodsucker, mooch, moocher, bottom feeder, schnorrer.

**spongy** adjective *a spongy layer of foam* SOFT, squashy, cushioned, cushiony, compressible, yielding; springy, resilient, elastic; porous, absorbent, permeable; *technical* spongiform. ANTONYMS hard, solid.

**sponsor** noun *the money came from sponsors* BACKER, patron, promoter, benefactor, benefactress, supporter, partner, contributor, subscriber, friend, guarantor, underwriter; *informal* angel.

▸ verb *a bank sponsored the event* FINANCE, put up the money for, fund, subsidize, back, promote, support, contribute to, be a patron of, guarantee, underwrite; *informal* foot the bill for, pick up the tab for, bankroll.

**spontaneous** adjective **1** *a spontaneous display of affection* UNPLANNED, unpremeditated, unrehearsed, impulsive, impetuous, unstudied, impromptu, spur-of-the-moment, extempore, extemporaneous; unforced, voluntary, unconstrained, unprompted, unbidden, unsolicited; *informal* off-the-cuff. ANTONYMS planned, calculated.

**2** *a spontaneous reaction to danger* REFLEX, automatic, mechanical, natural, knee-jerk, involuntary, unthinking, unconscious, instinctive, instinctual, visceral; *informal* gut. ANTONYMS conscious, voluntary.

**3** *a spontaneous kind of person* NATURAL, uninhibited, relaxed, unselfconscious, unaffected, open, genuine, easy, free and easy; impulsive, impetuous. ANTONYM inhibited.

THE RIGHT WORD **spontaneous, impromptu, improvised, impulsive, offhand, spontaneous, unpremeditated**

If you're the kind of person who acts first and thinks about it later, your friends are likely to describe you as **spontaneous**, which means that you behave in a very natural way, without prompting or premeditation (*a spontaneous embrace*; *a spontaneous burst of applause*). Or they may call you **impulsive**, which has somewhat less positive connotations, suggesting someone who is governed by his or her own moods and whims without regard for others. Although *impulsive* behavior may be admirable (*his impulsive generosity prompted him to empty his pockets*), it is just as likely to be ugly or disruptive (*impulsive buying*; *an impulsive temper*). **Offhand** also has negative overtones, implying behavior that is spontaneous to the point of being cavalier or brusque (*her offhand remarks offended them*). **Unpremeditated** is a more formal term, often used in a legal context to describe an impulsive crime committed without forethought (*unpremeditated murder*). In the world of public speaking, an **extemporaneous** speech is one that is delivered without referring to a written text, although the speaker may have been aware that he or she would be called upon to speak, while an **impromptu** speech is one that the speaker was not expecting to give. **Improvised** is often used in the context of a musical or theatrical performance, suggesting a basic structure within which the performers are free to play in a spontaneous manner (*by its very nature, jazz is improvised*). But it has broader applications as well; in fact, anything that is devised on the spur of the moment may be described as *improvised*.

**sporadic** adjective *partly cloudy with sporadic showers* OCCASIONAL, infrequent, irregular, periodic, scattered, patchy, isolated, odd; intermittent, spasmodic, fitful, desultory, erratic, unpredictable. ANTONYMS frequent, steady, continuous.

**sport** noun **1** *we did a lot of sports* (COMPETITIVE) GAME(S), physical recreation, physical activity, physical exercise, athletics; pastime.

**2** *dated**they were rogues out for a bit of sport* FUN, pleasure, enjoyment, entertainment, amusement, diversion.

▸ verb *he sported a beard* WEAR, have on, dress in; DISPLAY, exhibit, show off, flourish, parade, flaunt.

**sporting** adjective *they encourage sporting behavior among the boys* SPORTSMANLIKE, generous, gentlemanly, considerate; fair, just, honorable, decent. ANTONYMS dirty, unfair.

**spot** noun **1** *a grease spot on the wall* MARK, patch, dot, fleck, smudge, smear, stain, blotch, blot, splash; *informal* splotch.

**2** *a secluded spot* PLACE, location, site, position, point, situation, scene, setting, locale, locality, area, neighborhood, region; venue; *technical* locus.

**3** *social policy has a regular spot on the agenda* POSITION, place, slot, space.

**4** *informal in a tight spot* PREDICAMENT, mess, difficulty, trouble, plight, corner, quandary, dilemma; *informal* fix, jam, hole, sticky situation, can of worms, pickle, scrape, hot water, Catch-22.

▸ verb **1** *she spotted him in his car* NOTICE, see, observe, note, discern, detect, perceive, make out, recognize, identify, locate; catch sight of, glimpse; *literary* behold, espy.

**2** *her clothes were spotted with grease* STAIN, mark, fleck, speckle, smudge, streak, splash, spatter; *informal* splotch.

PHRASE: **on the spot** *violators will be arrested on the spot* IMMEDIATELY, at once, right away, without delay, without hesitation, that instant, directly, there and then, then and there, forthwith, instantly, summarily, straightaway, in short order; *archaic* straightway.

**spotless** adjective **1** *the kitchen was spotless* PERFECTLY CLEAN, ultra-clean, pristine, immaculate, shining, shiny, gleaming, spick-and-span. ANTONYM dirty.

**2** *a spotless reputation* UNBLEMISHED, unsullied, untarnished, untainted, unstained, pure, whiter than white, innocent, impeccable, blameless, irreproachable, above reproach; *informal* squeaky clean, Teflon. ANTONYMS tarnished, impure.

**spotlight** noun *she was constantly in the spotlight* PUBLIC EYE, glare of publicity, limelight, center stage; focus of public/media attention.

▸ verb *this article spotlights the problem* FOCUS ATTENTION ON, highlight, point up, draw/call attention to, give prominence to, throw into relief, turn the spotlight on, bring to the fore.

**spotted** adjective **1** *spotted leaves* MOTTLED, dappled, speckled, flecked, freckled, freckly, dotted, stippled, brindle(d); *informal* splotchy. ANTONYM plain.

**2** *a black-and-white spotted dress* POLKA-DOT, dotted. ANTONYM plain.

**spouse** noun *are spouses invited to the office party?* (LIFE) PARTNER, mate, consort; *informal* better half, other half. See also HUSBAND, WIFE.

**spout** verb **1** *lava was spouting from the crater* SPURT, gush, spew, erupt, shoot, squirt, spray; disgorge, discharge, emit, belch forth.

**2** *there he is, **spouting off** about religion, as usual* HOLD FORTH, sound off, go on, talk at length, expatiate; *informal* mouth off, speechify, spiel.

▸ noun *a can with a spout* NOZZLE, lip.

**sprawl** verb **1** *he sprawled on a sofa* STRETCH OUT, lounge, loll, lie, recline, drape oneself, slump, flop, slouch.

**2** *the town sprawled ahead of them* SPREAD, stretch, extend, be strung out, be scattered, straggle, spill.

**spray**[1] noun **1** *a spray of water* SHOWER, sprinkling, sprinkle, jet, mist, drizzle; spume, spindrift; foam, froth.

**2** *a perfume spray* ATOMIZER, vaporizer, aerosol, sprinkler; nebulizer.

▸ verb **1** *water was sprayed around* SPRINKLE, shower, spatter; scatter, disperse, diffuse; mist; douche; *literary* besprinkle.

**2** *water sprayed into the air* SPOUT, jet, gush, spurt, shoot, squirt.

**spray**[2] noun **1** *a spray of holly* SPRIG, twig.

**2** *a spray of flowers* BOUQUET, bunch, posy, nosegay; corsage.

**spread** verb **1** *he spread the map out* LAY OUT, open out, unfurl, unroll, roll out; straighten out, fan out; stretch out, extend; *literary* outspread. ANTONYM fold up.

**2** *the landscape* ***spread out*** *below* EXTEND, stretch (out), open out, be displayed, be exhibited, be on show; sprawl (out).

**3** *papers were spread all over his desk* SCATTER, strew, disperse, distribute.

**4** *he's been spreading rumors* DISSEMINATE, circulate, pass on, put about, communicate, diffuse, make public, make known, purvey, broadcast, publicize, propagate, promulgate; repeat; *literary* bruit about/abroad. ANTONYM suppress.

**5** *she spread cold cream on her face* SMEAR, daub, plaster, slather, lather, apply, put; smooth, rub.

**6** *he spread the toast with butter* COVER, coat, layer, daub; smother.

▸ noun **1** *the spread of learning* EXPANSION, proliferation, extension, growth; dissemination, diffusion, transmission, propagation.

**2** *a spread of six feet* SPAN, width, extent, stretch, reach.

**3** *the immense spread of the heavens* EXPANSE, area, sweep, stretch.

**4** *a wide spread of subjects* RANGE, span, spectrum, sweep; variety.

**5** *informal* *the caterers laid on a huge spread* LARGE/ELABORATE MEAL, feast, banquet; *informal* blowout, nosh.

**spree** noun *a spending spree* BINGE, bout, orgy, splurge, session.

**sprig** noun *a sprig of mistletoe* SMALL STEM, spray, twig.

**sprightly** adjective *sprightly Irish folk dancers* SPRY, lively, agile, nimble, energetic, active, full of energy, vigorous, spirited, animated, vivacious, frisky; *informal* full of vim and vigor. ANTONYMS doddery, lethargic.

**spring** verb **1** *the cat sprang off her lap* LEAP, jump, bound, vault, hop.

**2** *the branch sprang back* FLY, whip, flick, whisk, kick, bounce.

**3** *all art springs from feelings* ORIGINATE, derive, arise, stem, emanate, proceed, issue, evolve, come.

**4** *fifty men sprang from nowhere* APPEAR SUDDENLY, appear unexpectedly, materialize, pop up, shoot up, sprout, develop quickly; proliferate, mushroom.

**5** *he sprang the truth on me* ANNOUNCE SUDDENLY/UNEXPECTEDLY, reveal suddenly/unexpectedly, surprise someone with.

▸ noun **1** *with a sudden spring he leapt on to the table* LEAP, jump, bound, vault, hop; pounce.

**2** *the mattress has lost its spring* SPRINGINESS, bounciness, bounce, resilience, elasticity, flexibility, stretch, stretchiness, give.

**3** *there was a spring in his step* BUOYANCY, bounce, energy, liveliness, jauntiness, sprightliness, confidence.

**4** *a mineral spring* SOURCE, geyser; *literary* wellspring, fount.

**5** *the spring from which all her emotions poured* ORIGIN, source, fountainhead, root, roots, basis; *informal* ground zero.

**springy** adjective *the earth was springy beneath her feet* ELASTIC, stretchy, stretchable, tensile; flexible, pliant, pliable, whippy; bouncy, resilient, spongy. ANTONYMS rigid, squashy.

**sprinkle** verb **1** *he sprinkled water over the towel* SPLASH, trickle, spray, shower; spatter.

**2** *sprinkle sesame seeds over the top* SCATTER, strew; drizzle, pepper.

**3** *sprinkle the cake with powdered sugar* DREDGE, dust.

**4** *the sky was sprinkled with stars* DOT, stipple, stud, fleck, speckle, spot, pepper; scatter, cover.

**sprinkling** noun **1** *a sprinkling of nutmeg* SCATTERING, sprinkle, scatter, dusting; pinch, dash.

**2** *mainly women, but a sprinkling of men* FEW, one or two, couple, handful, small number, trickle, scattering.

**sprint** verb *the lead racers sprinted past our corner at about two o'clock* RUN, race, dart, rush, dash, hasten, hurry, scurry, scamper, hare, bolt, fly, gallop, career, charge, shoot, hurtle, speed, zoom, go like lightning, go hell-bent for leather, go like the wind; jog, trot; *informal* tear, pelt, scoot, hotfoot it, belt, zip, whip, bomb, hightail it, barrel. ANTONYM walk.

**sprite** noun *by light of moon the woodland sprites do dance and play* FAIRY, elf, pixie, imp, brownie, puck, peri, leprechaun; nymph, sylph, naiad.

**sprout** verb **1** *the weeds begin to sprout* GERMINATE, put/send out shoots, bud, burgeon.

**2** *he had sprouted a beard* GROW, develop, put/send out.

**3** *parsley sprouted from the pot* SPRING UP, shoot up, come up, grow, burgeon, develop, appear.

**spruce** adjective *the captain looked very spruce* NEAT, well-groomed, well-turned-out, well-dressed, smart, trim, dapper, elegant, chic; *informal* natty, snazzy, spiffy. ANTONYM untidy.

▸ verb **1** *the cottage had been* ***spruced up*** SMARTEN (UP), tidy, neaten, put in order, clean, upgrade, renovate; *informal* do up, gussy up.

**2** *Sarah wanted to* ***spruce*** *herself* ***up*** GROOM, tidy, smarten (up), preen, primp; *informal* titivate, doll up.

**spry** adjective *isn't Aunt Helen spry for her age?* SPRIGHTLY, lively, agile, nimble, energetic, active, full of energy, full of vim and vigor, vigorous, spirited, animated, vivacious, frisky, peppy. ANTONYMS doddery, lethargic.

**spume** noun *the boat left a wake of white spume* FOAM, froth, surf, spindrift, bubbles.

**spunk** noun *informal it took a lot of spunk to blow the whistle on your own boss* COURAGE, bravery, valor, nerve, confidence, daring, audacity, pluck, spirit, grit, mettle, spine, backbone; *informal* guts, gumption, moxie; *dated, or humorous* derring-do.

**spur** noun **1** *competition can be a spur* STIMULUS, incentive, encouragement, inducement, impetus, prod, motivation, inspiration, catalyst, springboard; *informal* kick up the backside, shot in the arm. ANTONYMS disincentive, discouragement.

**2** *a spur of bone* PROJECTION, spike, point; *technical* process.

▸ verb *the thought spurred him into action* STIMULATE, encourage, prompt, propel, prod, induce, impel, motivate, move, galvanize, inspire, incentivize, urge, drive, egg on, stir; incite, goad, provoke, prick, sting, light a fire under. ANTONYM discourage.

PHRASE: **on the spur of the moment** *the decision had been made on the spur of the moment* IMPULSIVELY, on impulse, impetuously, without thinking, without premeditation, unpremeditatedly, impromptu, extempore, spontaneously; *informal* off the cuff.

**spurious** adjective *an attempt to be excused due to some spurious medical condition* BOGUS, fake, false, counterfeit, forged, fraudulent, sham, artificial, imitation, simulated, feigned, deceptive, misleading, specious; *informal* phony, pretend. ANTONYM genuine.

THE RIGHT WORD **spurious, apocryphal, artificial, counterfeit, ersatz, synthetic**

These adjectives pertain to what is false or not what it appears to be, although not all have negative connotations. **Artificial** implies manmade, especially in imitation of something natural (*artificial flowers; artificial turf*). A **synthetic** substance or material is one produced by a chemical process and used as a substitute for the natural substance it resembles (*boots made from synthetic rubber*). Something that is **counterfeit** is an imitation of something else—usually something rarer, finer, or more valuable—and is intended to deceive or defraud (*counterfeit bills*). **Spurious** also means false rather than true or genuine, but it carries no strong implication of being an imitation (*spurious letters falsely attributed to Winston Churchill*). **Ersatz** refers to an artificial substitute that is usually inferior (*ersatz tea made from tree bark and herbs*). The meaning of **apocryphal**, however, is much more restricted. It applies to accounts of the past that are widely circulated but whose truth or accuracy are doubtful (*an apocryphal story about George Washington as a boy*).

**spurn** verb *he's been spurned by every woman he ever loved* REJECT, rebuff, scorn, turn down, treat with contempt, disdain, look down one's nose at, despise; snub, slight, jilt, dismiss, brush off, turn one's back on; give someone the cold shoulder, cold-shoulder; *informal* turn one's nose up at, give someone the brush-off, kick in the teeth, give someone the bum's rush. ANTONYMS welcome, accept.

**spurt** verb *water spurted from the tap* SQUIRT, shoot, jet, erupt, gush, pour, stream, pump, surge, spew, course, well, spring, burst; disgorge, discharge, emit, belch forth, expel, eject.

▸ noun **1** *a spurt of water* SQUIRT, jet, spout, gush, stream, rush, surge, flood, cascade, torrent.

**2** *a spurt of courage* BURST, fit, bout, rush, spate, surge, attack, outburst, blaze.

**3** *the sprinter put on a spurt* BURST OF SPEED, turn of speed, sprint, rush, burst of energy.

**spy** noun *a foreign spy* SECRET AGENT, intelligence agent, double agent, undercover agent, counterspy, mole, sleeper, plant, scout; *informal* snooper; *archaic* intelligencer.

▸ verb **1** *she spied for the West* BE A SPY, gather intelligence, work for the secret service; *informal* snoop.

**2** *investigators **spied on** them* OBSERVE FURTIVELY, keep under surveillance/observation, watch, keep a watch on, keep an eye on.

**3** *she spied a coffee shop* NOTICE, observe, see, spot, sight, catch sight of, glimpse, make out, discern, detect; *informal* clap/lay/set eyes on; *literary* espy, behold, descry.

**squabble** noun *there was a squabble over which way they should go* QUARREL, disagreement, argument, contretemps, falling-out, dispute, clash, blowup, altercation, shouting match, row, exchange, war of words; *informal* tiff, set-to, run-in, spat, scrap, rhubarb. See note at QUARREL.

▸ verb *the boys were squabbling over a ball* QUARREL, argue, bicker, fall out, disagree, have words, dispute, spar, cross swords, lock horns, be at loggerheads; *informal* scrap.

**squad** noun **1** *an assassination squad* TEAM, crew, gang, band, cell, body, mob, outfit, force.

**2** *a firing squad* DETACHMENT, detail, unit, platoon, battery, troop, patrol, squadron, cadre, commando.

**squalid** adjective **1** *a squalid prison* DIRTY, filthy, grubby, grimy, mucky, slummy, foul, vile, poor, sorry, wretched, miserable, mean, seedy, shabby, sordid, insalubrious; NEGLECTED, uncared-for, broken-down, run-down, down-at-heel, down-at-the-heel(s), depressed, dilapidated, ramshackle, tumbledown, gone to rack and ruin, crumbling, decaying; *informal* scruffy, crummy, ratty, flea-bitten. ANTONYMS clean, pleasant.

**2** *a squalid deal with the opposition* IMPROPER, sordid, unseemly, unsavory, sleazy, seedy, seamy, shoddy, cheap, base, low, corrupt, dishonest, dishonorable, disreputable, despicable, discreditable, disgraceful, contemptible, shameful, underhanded. ANTONYMS proper, decent.

**squalor** noun *they lived in squalor* DIRT, filth, grubbiness, grime, muck, foulness, vileness, poverty, wretchedness, meanness, seediness, shabbiness, sordidness, sleaziness, NEGLECT, decay, dilapidation; *informal* scruffiness, crumminess, grunge, rattiness. ANTONYMS cleanliness, pleasantness, smartness.

**squander** verb *they squander their profits on expensive cars* WASTE, misspend, misuse, throw away, fritter away, spend recklessly, spend unwisely, spend like water; *informal* blow, go through, splurge, drop, pour down the drain. ANTONYMS manage, make good use of, save.

**square** noun 1 *a shop in the square* market square, marketplace, plaza, piazza.

2 *informal you're such a square!* (OLD) FOGEY, conservative, traditionalist, conformist, bourgeois, fossil; *informal* stick-in-the-mud, fuddy-duddy, prig, stuffed shirt. ANTONYM trendy.

▸ adjective 1 *a square table* QUADRILATERAL, rectangular, oblong, right-angled, at right angles, perpendicular; straight, level, parallel, horizontal, upright, vertical, true, plane. ANTONYMS crooked, uneven.

2 *the sides were square at halftime* LEVEL, even, drawn, equal, tied; neck and neck, nip and tuck, side by side, evenly matched; *informal* even-steven(s). ANTONYM uneven.

3 *I'm going to be square with you* FAIR, honest, just, equitable, straight, true, upright, aboveboard, ethical, decent, proper; *informal* on the level. ANTONYM underhanded.

4 *informal don't be square!* OLD-FASHIONED, behind the times, out of date, conservative, traditionalist, conventional, conformist, bourgeois, straitlaced, fogeyish, stuffy; *informal* stick-in-the-mud, fuddy-duddy. ANTONYM trendy.

▸ verb 1 *the theory does not square with the data* AGREE, tally, be in agreement, be consistent, match up, correspond, fit, coincide, accord, conform, be compatible.

2 *his goal squared the match 1–1* LEVEL, even, make equal.

3 *would you **square up** the bill?* PAY, settle, discharge, clear, meet.

4 *Bob squared things with his boss* RESOLVE, sort out, settle, clear up, work out, iron out, smooth over, straighten out, deal with, put right, set right, put to rights, rectify, remedy; *informal* patch up.

**squash** verb 1 *the fruit got squashed* CRUSH, squeeze, flatten, compress, press, smash, distort, pound, trample, stamp on; pulp, mash, cream, liquidize, beat, pulverize; *informal* squish, squoosh.

2 *she squashed her clothes inside the bag* FORCE, ram, thrust, push, cram, jam, stuff, pack, compress, squeeze, wedge, press.

3 *the proposal was immediately squashed* REJECT, block, cancel, scotch, frustrate, thwart, suppress, put a stop to, nip in the bud, put the lid on; *informal* put the kibosh on, stymie, scuttle, deep-six.

▸ noun *a side order of steamed squash* acorn squash, butternut squash, crookneck squash, Hubbard squash, scallop squash, spaghetti squash, summer squash, winter squash, zucchini, pumpkin, (vegetable) marrow.

**squat** verb 1 *I was squatting on the floor* CROUCH (DOWN), hunker (down), sit on one's haunches, sit on one's heels.

2 *they are squatting on private land* OCCUPY ILLEGALLY, set up residence, dwell, settle, live.

▸ adjective *he was muscular and squat* STOCKY, thickset, dumpy, stubby, stumpy, short, small; *informal, humorous* vertically challenged.

▸ noun *informal they gave me squat.* DIDDLY-SQUAT.

**squawk** verb & noun *a pheasant squawked* | *the gull gave a squawk* SCREECH, squeal, shriek, scream, croak, crow, caw, cluck, cackle, hoot, cry, call.

**squeak** noun & verb 1 *the vole's squeak* | *the rat squeaked* PEEP, cheep, pipe, piping, squeal, tweet, yelp, whimper.

2 *the squeak of the hinge* | *the hinges of the gate squeaked* SCREECH, creak, scrape, grate, rasp, jar, groan.

**squeal** noun *the harsh squeal of a fox* SCREECH, scream, shriek, squawk.

▸ verb 1 *a dog squealed* SCREECH, scream, shriek, squawk.

2 *the bookies only squealed because we beat them* COMPLAIN, protest, object, grouse, grumble, whine, wail, carp, squawk; *informal* kick up a fuss, gripe, grouch, bellyache, moan, bitch, beef, whinge.

3 *informal he **squealed on** the rest of the gang to the police* INFORM ON, tell tales on; report, give away, be disloyal to, sell out, stab in the back; *informal* rat on, rat out, snitch on, put the finger on, finger, sell down the river.

**squeamish** adjective 1 *I'm too squeamish to gut fish* | *are you squeamish about a little blood?* EASILY NAUSEATED, nervous; (**squeamish about**) PUT OFF BY, not able to stand the sight of.

2 *less squeamish nations will sell them arms* SCRUPULOUS, principled, fastidious, particular, punctilious, honorable, upright, upstanding, high-minded, righteous, right-minded, moral, ethical.

**squeeze** verb 1 *I squeezed the bottle* COMPRESS, press, crush, squash, pinch, nip, grasp, grip, clutch, flatten.

2 *squeeze the juice from both oranges* EXTRACT, press, force, express.

3 *Sally squeezed her feet into the sandals* FORCE, thrust, cram, ram, jam, stuff, pack, wedge, press, squash.

4 *we all squeezed into Steve's van* CROWD, crush, cram, pack, jam, squash, wedge oneself, shove, push, force one's way.

5 *he would squeeze more money out of Bill* EXTORT, force, extract, wrest, wring, milk; *informal* bleed.

▸ noun 1 *he gave her hand a squeeze* PRESS, pinch, nip; grasp, grip, clutch, hug, clasp; compression.

2 *it was a tight squeeze in the tiny hall* CRUSH, jam, squash, press, huddle; congestion.

3 *a squeeze of lemon juice* FEW DROPS, dash, splash, dribble, trickle, spot, hint, touch.

**squire** noun 1 *the squire of the village* LANDOWNER, landholder, landlord, lord of the manor, country gentleman.

2 *historical his squire carried a banner* ATTENDANT, courtier, equerry, aide, steward, page boy.

**squirm** verb 1 *I tried to squirm away* WRIGGLE, wiggle, writhe, twist, slide, slither, turn, shift, fidget, jiggle, twitch, thresh, flounder, flail, toss and turn.

2 *he squirmed as everyone laughed* WINCE, shudder, feel embarrassed, feel ashamed.

**squirt** verb **1** *a jet of ink squirted out of the tube* SPURT, shoot, spray, fountain, jet, erupt; gush, rush, pump, surge, stream, spew, well, spring, burst, issue, emanate; emit, belch forth, expel, eject.

**2** *she squirted me with cologne* SPLASH, wet, spray, shower, spatter, splatter, sprinkle; *literary* besprinkle.

▸ noun **1** *a squirt of water* SPURT, jet, spray, fountain, gush, stream, surge.

**2** *informal he was just a little squirt* IMPUDENT PERSON, insignificant person, gnat, insect; *informal* pipsqueak, whippersnapper, picayune.

**stab** verb **1** *a soldier stabbed the civilian* KNIFE, run through, skewer, spear, bayonet, gore, spike, stick, impale, transfix, pierce, prick, puncture; *literary* transpierce.

**2** *she stabbed at the earth with a fork* LUNGE, thrust, jab, poke, prod, dig.

▸ noun **1** *a stab in the leg* KNIFE WOUND, puncture, incision, prick, cut, perforation.

**2** *they made stabs into the air* LUNGE, thrust, jab, poke, prod, dig, punch.

**3** *a stab of pain* TWINGE, pang, throb, spasm, cramp, dart, prick, flash, thrill.

**4** *informal he took a stab at writing* ATTEMPT, try, effort, endeavor; guess; *informal* go, shot, crack, bash, whack; *formal* essay.

PHRASE: **stab in the back** *just two months after I got her hired, she stabbed me in the back* BETRAY, be disloyal to, be unfaithful to, desert, break one's promise to, double-cross, break faith with, sell out, play false, inform on/against; *informal* tell on, sell down the river, squeal on, rat out, finger.

**stability** noun **1** *the stability of playground equipment* FIRMNESS, solidity, steadiness, strength, security, safety.

**2** *his mental stability* BALANCE OF MIND, mental health, sanity, normality, soundness, rationality, reason, sense.

**3** *the stability of their relationship* STEADINESS, firmness, solidity, strength, durability, lasting nature, enduring nature, permanence, changelessness, invariability, immutability, indestructibility, reliability, dependability.

**stable** adjective **1** *a stable tent* FIRM, solid, steady, secure, fixed, fast, safe, moored, anchored, stuck down, immovable. ANTONYMS rickety, wobbly.

**2** *a stable person* WELL-BALANCED, of sound mind, compos mentis, sane, normal, right in the head, rational, steady, reasonable, sensible, sober, down-to-earth, matter-of-fact, having both one's feet on the ground; *informal* all there. ANTONYM unbalanced.

**3** *a stable relationship* SECURE, solid, strong, steady, firm, sure, steadfast, unwavering, unvarying, unfaltering, unfluctuating; established, abiding, durable, enduring, lasting, permanent, reliable, dependable. ANTONYMS rocky, changeable.

**stack** noun **1** *a stack of boxes* HEAP, pile, mound, mountain, pyramid, tower.

**2** *a stack of hay* HAYSTACK, rick, hayrick, mow, shock, haycock; *dated* cock.

**3** *informal a stack of money.* See LOT pronoun.

**4** CHIMNEY, smokestack, funnel, exhaust pipe.

▸ verb **1** *Leo was stacking plates* HEAP (UP), pile (up), make a heap/pile/stack of; assemble, put together, collect, hoard, store, stockpile.

**2** *they stacked the shelves* LOAD, fill (up), lade, pack, charge, stuff, cram; stock. ANTONYM empty.

**stadium** noun *many think the Orioles play in the best stadium in the majors* ARENA, field, ground; bowl, amphitheater, coliseum, ring, dome, manège; track, course, racetrack, racecourse, raceway, speedway, velodrome, sportsplex; *Brit.* pitch.

**staff** noun **1** *there is a reluctance to take on new staff* EMPLOYEES, workers, workforce, personnel, human resources, manpower, labor.

**2** *he carried a wooden staff* STICK, stave, pole, crook.

**3** *a staff of office* ROD, tipstaff, cane, mace, wand, scepter, crozier, verge; *Greek Mythology* caduceus.

▸ verb *the center is staffed by teachers* MAN, people, crew, work, operate, occupy.

**stage** noun **1** *this stage of the development* PHASE, period, juncture, step, point, time, moment, instant, level.

**2** *the last stage of the race* PART, section, portion, stretch, leg, lap, circuit.

**3** *a theater stage* PLATFORM, dais, stand, grandstand, staging, apron, rostrum, podium; bandstand, bandshell; catwalk.

**4** *she has written for the stage* THEATER, drama, dramatics, dramatic arts, thespianism; *informal* boards.

**5** *the political stage* SCENE, setting; context, frame, sphere, field, realm, arena, backdrop; affairs.

▸ verb **1** *they staged two plays* PUT ON, put before the public, present, produce, mount, direct; perform, act, give.

**2** *workers staged a protest* ORGANIZE, arrange, coordinate, lay on, put together, get together, set up; orchestrate, choreograph, mastermind, engineer; take part in, participate in, join in.

**stagger** verb **1** *he staggered to the door* LURCH, walk unsteadily, reel, sway, teeter, totter, stumble, wobble.

**2** *I was absolutely staggered* AMAZE, astound, astonish, surprise, startle, stun, confound, dumbfound, stupefy, daze, take aback, leave open-mouthed, leave aghast; *informal* flabbergast, bowl over.

**3** *meetings are staggered throughout the day* SPREAD (OUT), space (out), time at intervals.

**stagnant** adjective **1** *stagnant water* STILL, motionless, static, stationary, standing, dead, slack; FOUL, stale, putrid, smelly. ANTONYMS flowing, fresh.

**2** *a stagnant economy* INACTIVE, sluggish, slow-moving, lethargic, static, flat, depressed, declining, moribund, dying, dead, dormant. ANTONYMS active, vibrant.

**stagnate** verb **1** *obstructions allow water to stagnate* STOP FLOWING, become stagnant, become trapped; stand; become foul, become stale; fester, putrefy. ANTONYM flow.

**2** *exports stagnated* LANGUISH, decline, deteriorate, fall, become stagnant, do nothing, stand still, tread water, be sluggish. ANTONYM boom.

**staid** adjective *I'm not some staid librarian, you know* SEDATE, respectable, quiet, serious, serious-minded, steady, conventional, traditional, unadventurous, unenterprising, set in one's ways, sober, proper, decorous, formal, stuffy, stiff, priggish; *informal* starchy, buttoned-down, stick-in-the-mud. ANTONYMS frivolous, daring, informal.

**stain** verb **1** *her clothing was stained with blood* DISCOLOR, blemish, soil, mark, muddy, spot, spatter, splatter, smear, splash, smudge, blotch, blacken; *literary* imbrue.

**2** *the report stained his reputation* DAMAGE, injure, harm, sully, blacken, tarnish, taint, smear, bring discredit to, dishonor, drag through the mud; *literary* besmirch.

**3** *the wood was stained* COLOR, tint, dye, tinge, pigment.

▸ noun **1** *a mud stain* MARK, spot, spatter, splatter, blotch, smudge, smear.

**2** *a stain on his character* BLEMISH, injury, taint, blot, smear, discredit, dishonor; damage.

**3** *dark wood stain* TINT, color, dye, tinge, pigment, colorant.

**stake**[1] noun *a stake in the ground* POST, pole, stick, spike, upright, support, prop, strut, pale, paling, picket, pile, piling, cane.

▸ verb **1** *the plants have to be staked* PROP UP, tie up, tether, support, hold up, brace, truss.

**2** *he staked his claim* ASSERT, declare, proclaim, state, make, lay, put in.

PHRASE: **stake out 1** *builders staked out the plot* MARK OFF/OUT, demarcate, measure out, delimit, fence off, section off, close off, shut off, cordon off.

**2** *informal the police staked out his apartment* OBSERVE, watch, keep an eye on, keep under observation, keep watch on, monitor, keep under surveillance, surveil; *informal* keep tabs on, keep a tab on, case.

**stake**[2] noun **1** *playing dice for high stakes* BET, wager, ante.

**2** *they are racing for record stakes* PRIZE MONEY, purse, pot, winnings.

**3** *low down in the popularity stakes* COMPETITION, contest, battle, challenge, rivalry, race, running, struggle, scramble.

**4** *a 40 percent stake in the business* SHARE, interest, ownership, involvement.

▸ verb *he staked all his week's pay* BET, wager, lay, put on, gamble, chance, venture, risk, hazard.

**stale** adjective **1** *stale food* OLD, past its best, off, dry, hard, musty, rancid, overstored. ANTONYM fresh.

**2** *stale air* STUFFY, close, musty, fusty, stagnant. ANTONYM fresh.

**3** *stale beer* FLAT, turned, spoiled, off, insipid, tasteless.

**4** *stale jokes* HACKNEYED, tired, worn out, overworked, threadbare, warmed-up, banal, trite, clichéd, platitudinous, unoriginal, unimaginative, uninspired, flat; out of date, outdated, outmoded, passé, archaic, obsolete; warmed-over; *informal* old hat, corny, unfunny, played out. ANTONYM original.

**stalemate** noun *the talks had reached a stalemate* DEADLOCK, impasse, standoff; draw, tie, dead heat.

**stalk**[1] noun *the stalk of a plant* STEM, shoot, trunk, stock, cane, bine, bent; *Brit.* haulm, straw, reed.

**stalk**[2] verb **1** *a cat was stalking a rabbit* CREEP UP ON, trail, follow, shadow, track down, go after, be after, course, hunt; *informal* tail, still-hunt.

**2** *she stalked out* STRUT, stride, march, flounce, storm, stomp, sweep.

**stall** noun **1** *a market stall* STAND, table, counter, booth, kiosk.

**2** *stalls for larger animals* PEN, coop, sty, corral, enclosure, compartment.

▸ verb **1** *the government has stalled the project* OBSTRUCT, impede, interfere with, hinder, hamper, block, interrupt, hold up, hold back, thwart, balk, sabotage, delay, stonewall, check, stop, halt, derail, put a brake on; *informal* stymie.

**2** *the project has stalled* STOP, fizzle, flatline, die, reach an impasse, hit a roadblock.

**3** *quit stalling* USE DELAYING TACTICS, play for time, temporize, gain time, procrastinate, hedge, beat around the bush, drag one's feet, delay, filibuster, stonewall, give someone the runaround.

**4** *stall him for a bit* DELAY, divert, distract; HOLD OFF, stave off, fend off, keep off, ward off, keep at bay.

**stalwart** adjective *a stalwart supporter of the cause* STAUNCH, loyal, faithful, committed, devoted, dedicated, dependable, reliable, steady, constant, trusty, solid, hard-working, steadfast, redoubtable, unwavering. ANTONYMS disloyal, unfaithful, unreliable.

**stamina** noun *I felt my stamina weakening* ENDURANCE, staying power, tirelessness, fortitude, strength, energy, toughness, determination, tenacity, perseverance, grit.

**stammer** verb *he began to stammer* STUTTER, stumble over one's words, hesitate, falter, pause, halt, splutter.

▸ noun *he had a stammer* STUTTER, speech impediment, speech defect.

**stamp** verb **1** *he **stamped on** my toe* TRAMPLE (ON), step on, tread on, tramp on, stomp on; CRUSH, squash, flatten.

**2** *John stamped off, muttering* STOMP, stump, clomp, clump.

**3** *the name is stamped on the cover* IMPRINT, print, impress, punch, inscribe, emboss, brand, frank.

**4** *his face was stamped on Martha's memory* FIX, inscribe, etch, carve, imprint, impress.

**5** *his style stamps him as a player to watch* IDENTIFY, characterize, brand, distinguish, classify, mark out, set apart, single out.

▸ noun **1** *the stamp of authority* MARK, hallmark, indication, sign, seal, sure sign, telltale sign, quality, smack, smell, savor, air.

**2** *he was of a very different stamp* TYPE, kind, sort, variety, class, category, classification, style, description, condition, caliber, status, quality, nature, ilk, kidney, cast, grain, mold, stripe.

PHRASE: **stamp out** *Miller's promise to stamp out crime on these streets is, at best, a naive fantasy* PUT AN END/STOP TO, end, stop, crush, put down, crack down on, curb, nip in the bud, scotch, squash, quash, quell, subdue, suppress, extinguish, stifle, abolish, get rid of, eliminate, eradicate, beat, overcome, defeat, destroy, wipe out; *informal* put the kibosh on, clean house.

**stampede** noun *the noise caused a stampede* CHARGE, panic, rush, flight, rout.

▸ verb *the sheep stampeded* BOLT, charge, flee, take flight; race, rush, career, sweep, run.

**stance** noun **1** *a natural golfer's stance* POSTURE, body position, pose, attitude.

**2** *a liberal stance* ATTITUDE, stand, point of view, viewpoint, opinion, way of thinking, outlook, standpoint, position, angle, perspective, approach, line, policy.

**stand** verb **1** *Lionel stood in the doorway* BE ON ONE'S FEET, be upright, be erect, be vertical. ANTONYMS sit, lie.

**2** *the men* ***stood up*** RISE, get/rise to one's feet, get up, straighten up, pick oneself up, find one's feet, be upstanding; *formal* arise. ANTONYMS sit down, lie down.

**3** *today a house stands on the site* BE, exist, be situated, be located, be positioned, be sited, have been built.

**4** *he stood the book on the shelf* PUT, set, set up, erect, up-end, place, position, locate, prop, lean, stick, install, arrange; *informal* park.

**5** *my decision stands* REMAIN IN FORCE, remain valid/effective/operative, remain in operation, hold, hold good, apply, be the case, exist.

**6** *her heart could not stand the strain* WITHSTAND, endure, bear, put up with, take, cope with, handle, sustain, resist, stand up to.

**7** *informal I can't stand arrogance* ENDURE, tolerate, bear, put up with, take, abide, support, countenance; *informal* swallow, stomach; *formal* brook.

▸ noun **1** *the party's stand on immigration* ATTITUDE, stance, point of view, viewpoint, opinion, way of thinking, outlook, standpoint, position, approach, thinking, policy, line.

**2** *a stand against tyranny* OPPOSITION, resistance, objection, hostility, animosity.

**3** *a large mirror on a stand* BASE, support, mounting, platform, rest, plinth, bottom; tripod, rack, trivet.

**4** *a beer stand* STALL, counter, booth, kiosk, tent.

**5** *a taxi stand* stop, station, park, bay.

**6** *the train drew to a stand* STOP, halt, standstill, dead stop.

**7** *a stand of trees* COPSE, thicket, grove, bush, woodlot.

PHRASES: **stand by 1** *stand by for further instructions* WAIT, be prepared, be in (a state of) readiness, be ready for action, be on full alert, wait in the wings.

**2** *she stood by her husband* REMAIN/BE LOYAL TO, stick with/by, remain/be true to, stand up for, support, back up, defend, stick up for.

**3** *the government must stand by its pledges* ABIDE BY, keep (to), adhere to, hold to, stick to, observe, comply with.

**stand down** *tell the troops to stand down* RELAX, stand easy, come off full alert.

**stand for 1** *BC stands for British Columbia* MEAN, be an abbreviation of, represent, signify, denote, indicate, symbolize.

**2** *informal I won't stand for any nonsense* PUT UP WITH, endure, tolerate, accept, take, abide, support, countenance; *informal* swallow, stomach; *formal* brook.

**3** *we stand for animal welfare* ADVOCATE, champion, uphold, defend, stand up for, support, back, endorse, be in favor of, promote, recommend, urge.

**stand in** *during Coach Clement's absence, Mr. Maynard will stand in* DEPUTIZE, act, act as deputy, substitute, fill in, sit in, do duty, take over, act as locum, be a proxy, cover, hold the fort, step into the breach; replace, relieve, take over from; *informal* sub, fill someone's shoes, step into someone's shoes, pinch-hit.

**stand out 1** *his veins stood out* PROJECT, stick out, bulge (out), be proud, jut (out).

**2** *she stood out in the crowd* BE NOTICEABLE, be visible, be obvious, be conspicuous, stick out, be striking, be distinctive, be prominent, attract attention, catch the eye, leap out, show up; *informal* stick/stand out like a sore thumb.

**stand up 1** *after 200 years, his theory still stands up* REMAIN/BE VALID, be sound, be plausible, hold water, hold up, stand questioning, survive investigation, bear examination, be verifiable.

**2** *that creep Roger stood up his blind date* FAIL TO KEEP A DATE WITH, fail to meet, fail to keep an appointment with, jilt.

**stand up for** *dozens of Mr. Merlin's students stood up for him at the hearing* SUPPORT, defend, back, back up, stick up for, champion, promote, uphold, take someone's part, take the side of, side with.

**stand up to 1** *she stood up to her parents* DEFY, confront, challenge, resist, take on, put up a fight against, argue with, take a stand against.

**2** *the old house has stood up to the war* WITHSTAND, survive, come through (unscathed), outlast, outlive, weather, ride out, ward off.

**standard** noun **1** *the standard of her work* QUALITY, level, grade, caliber, merit, excellence.

**2** *a safety standard* GUIDELINE, norm, yardstick, benchmark, measure, criterion, guide, touchstone, model, pattern, example, exemplar.

**3** *a standard to live by* PRINCIPLE, ideal; (**standards**) code of behavior, code of honor, morals, scruples, ethics.

**4** *the regiment's standard* FLAG, banner, pennant, ensign, color(s), banderole, guidon; *Nautical* burgee.

▸ adjective **1** *the standard way of doing it* NORMAL, usual, typical, stock, common, ordinary, customary, conventional, wonted, established, settled, set, fixed, traditional, prevailing. ANTONYMS unusual, special.

**2** *the standard work on the subject* DEFINITIVE, established, classic, recognized, accepted, authoritative, most reliable, exhaustive.

**standardize** verb *teachers have been asked to standardize their final exams* SYSTEMATIZE, make consistent, make uniform, make comparable, regulate, normalize, bring into line, equalize, homogenize, regiment.

**stand-in** noun *a stand-in for the minister* SUBSTITUTE, replacement, deputy, surrogate, proxy, understudy, locum, supply, fill-in, cover, relief, stopgap; *informal* temp, pinch-hitter; (body) double, stuntman.

▸ adjective *a stand-in goaltender* SUBSTITUTE, replacement, deputy, fill-in, stopgap, supply, surrogate, relief, acting, temporary, provisional, caretaker; *informal* pinch-hitting.

**standing** noun **1** *his standing in the community* STATUS, rank, ranking, position; reputation, estimation, stature; *dated* station.

**2** *a person of some standing* SENIORITY, rank, eminence, prominence, prestige, repute, stature, esteem, importance, account, consequence, influence, distinction; *informal* clout.

**3** *a squabble of long standing* DURATION, existence, continuance, endurance, life, history.

▸ adjective **1** *standing stones* UPRIGHT, erect, vertical, plumb, upended, on end, perpendicular; on one's feet. ANTONYMS flat, lying down, seated.

**2** *standing water* STAGNANT, still, motionless, static, stationary, dead, slack. ANTONYM flowing.

**3** *a standing invitation* PERMANENT, perpetual, everlasting, continuing, abiding, indefinite, open-ended; regular, repeated. ANTONYMS temporary, occasional.

**standoff** noun *a nuclear standoff* DEADLOCK, stalemate, impasse; draw, tie, dead heat; suspension of hostilities, lull.

**standoffish** adjective *informal a standoffish prig* ALOOF, distant, remote, detached, withdrawn, reserved, uncommunicative, unforthcoming, unapproachable, unresponsive, unfriendly, unsociable, introspective, introverted. ANTONYMS friendly, approachable, sociable.

**standpoint** noun *she writes on religion from the standpoint of a believer* POINT OF VIEW, viewpoint, vantage point, attitude, stance, view, opinion, position, way of thinking, outlook, perspective.

**standstill** noun *negotiations have come to a standstill* HALT, stop, dead stop, stand, gridlock.

**staple** adjective *rice is their staple crop* MAIN, principal, chief, major, primary, leading, foremost, first, most important, predominant, dominant, (most) prominent, basic, standard, prime, premier; *informal* number-one.

**star** noun **1** *the sky was full of stars* CELESTIAL BODY, heavenly body, sun; asteroid, planet.

**2** *the stars of the film* PRINCIPAL, leading lady/man, lead, female/male lead, hero, heroine. ANTONYMS extra, bit player.

**3** *a star of the world of chess* CELEBRITY, superstar, big name, famous name, household name, someone, somebody, lion, leading light, VIP, personality, personage, luminary; *informal* celeb, big shot, megastar. ANTONYM nobody.

▸ adjective **1** *a star pupil* BRILLIANT, talented, gifted, able, exceptional, outstanding, bright, clever, masterly, consummate, precocious, prodigious.

**2** *the star attraction* TOP, leading, best, greatest, foremost, major, preeminent, champion. ANTONYMS poor, minor.

**stare** verb *staring out the window* GAZE, gape, goggle, glare, ogle, peer; *informal* gawk, rubberneck.

**stark** adjective **1** *a stark silhouette* SHARP, sharply defined, well-focused, crisp, distinct, obvious, evident, clear, clear-cut, graphic, striking. ANTONYMS fuzzy, indistinct.

**2** *a stark landscape* DESOLATE, bare, barren, arid, vacant, empty, forsaken, godforsaken, bleak, somber, depressing, cheerless, joyless; *literary* drear. ANTONYM pleasant.

**3** *a stark room* AUSTERE, severe, bleak, plain, simple, bare, unadorned, unembellished, undecorated. ANTONYM ornate.

**4** *stark terror* SHEER, utter, complete, absolute, total, pure, downright, out-and-out, outright; rank, thorough, consummate, unqualified, unmitigated, unalloyed.

**5** *the stark facts* BLUNT, bald, bare, simple, basic, plain, unvarnished, harsh, grim. ANTONYM disguised.

▸ adverb *stark naked* COMPLETELY, totally, utterly, absolutely, downright, dead, entirely, wholly, fully, quite, altogether, thoroughly, truly, one hundred percent.

**start** verb **1** *the meeting starts at 7:45* BEGIN, commence, get underway, go ahead, get going; *informal* kick off. ANTONYM finish.

**2** *this was how her illness had started* ARISE, come into being, begin, commence, be born, come into existence, appear, arrive, come forth, establish oneself, emerge, erupt, burst out, originate, develop. ANTONYMS clear up, end.

**3** *she started her own charity* ESTABLISH, set up, found, create, bring into being, institute, initiate, inaugurate, introduce, open, launch, float, kick-start, jump-start, get something off the ground, pioneer, organize, mastermind; *informal* kick something off. ANTONYM end.

**4** *we had better start now if we want to finish the job* COMMENCE, make a start, begin, take the first step, make the first move, get going, go ahead, set things moving, start/get/set the ball rolling, buckle to/down, turn to; *informal* get moving, get cracking, get down to, get to it, get down to business, get the show on the road, take the plunge, kick off, get off one's backside, fire away. ANTONYMS stop, give up, procrastinate.

**5** *he started across the field* SET OFF, set out, start out, set forth, begin one's journey, get on the road, depart, leave, get underway, make a start, sally forth, embark, sail; *informal* hit the road. ANTONYMS arrive, stay.

**6** *you can start the machine* ACTIVATE, set in motion, switch on, start up, turn on, fire up; energize, actuate, set off, start off, set something going/moving. ANTONYMS stop, shut down, close down.

**7** *the machine started* BEGIN WORKING, start up, get going, spring into life. ANTONYM stop.

**8** *"Oh my!" she said, starting* FLINCH, jerk, jump, twitch, recoil, shy, shrink, blench, wince.

▸ noun **1** *the start of the event* BEGINNING, commencement, inception. ANTONYM end.

**2** *the start of her illness* ONSET, commencement, emergence, (first) appearance, arrival, eruption, dawn, birth; *informal* square one.

**3** *a quarter of an hour's start* LEAD, head start, advantage. ANTONYM handicap.

**4** *a start in life* ADVANTAGEOUS BEGINNING, flying start, helping hand, lift, assistance, support, encouragement, boost, kick-start; *informal* break, leg up. ANTONYM handicap.

**5** *she awoke with a start* JERK, twitch, flinch, wince, spasm, convulsion, jump.

**startle** verb *naturally their screaming startled me* SURPRISE, frighten, scare, alarm, give someone a shock/fright/jolt, make someone jump; PERTURB, unsettle, agitate, disturb, disconcert, disquiet; *informal* give someone a turn, make someone jump out of their skin, freak someone out. ANTONYM put at ease.

**startling** adjective *startling news awaited him at Naples* SURPRISING, astonishing, amazing, unexpected, unforeseen, staggering, shocking, stunning; extraordinary, remarkable, dramatic; disturbing, unsettling, perturbing, disconcerting, disquieting; frightening, alarming, scary. ANTONYMS predictable, ordinary.

**starvation** noun *half of the people here face starvation* EXTREME HUNGER, lack of food, famine, undernourishment, malnourishment, fasting; deprivation of food; death from lack of food.

**starving** adjective *the world's starving children* DYING OF HUNGER, deprived of food, undernourished, malnourished, starved, half-starved; very hungry, ravenous, famished, empty, hollow; fasting. ANTONYM full.

**state**[1] noun **1** *the state of the economy* CONDITION, shape, situation, circumstances, position; predicament, plight.

**2** *informal* *don't get into a state* FLUSTER, frenzy, fever, fret, panic, state of agitation/anxiety; *informal* flap, tizzy, dither, stew, sweat.

**3** *informal* *your room is in a state* MESS, chaos, disorder, disarray, confusion, muddle, heap, shambles; clutter, untidiness, disorganization, imbroglio.

**4** *an autonomous state* COUNTRY, nation, land, sovereign state, nation state, kingdom, realm, power, republic, confederation, federation.

**5** *the country is divided into thirty-two states* PROVINCE, federal state, region, territory, canton, department, county, district, shire.

**6** *the power of the state* GOVERNMENT, parliament, administration, regime, authorities.

▸ adjective *a state visit to China* CEREMONIAL, official, formal, governmental, national, public. ANTONYMS unofficial, private, informal.

**state**[2] verb *I stated my views* EXPRESS, voice, utter, put into words, declare, affirm, assert, announce, make known, put across/over, communicate, air, reveal, disclose, divulge, proclaim, present, expound; set out, set down; *informal* come out with.

**stated** adjective *the stated aim of the program* SPECIFIED, fixed, settled, set, agreed, declared, designated, laid down. ANTONYMS undefined, irregular, tacit.

**stately** adjective *a stately mansion on the hill* DIGNIFIED, majestic, ceremonious, courtly, imposing, impressive, solemn, awe-inspiring, regal, elegant, grand, glorious, splendid, magnificent, resplendent; slow-moving, measured, deliberate.

**statement** noun *how do you respond to the president's statement about homeland security?* DECLARATION, expression of views/facts, affirmation, assertion, announcement, utterance, communication, proclamation, presentation, expounding; account, testimony, evidence, report, bulletin, communiqué.

**static** adjective **1** *static prices* UNCHANGED, fixed, stable, steady, unchanging, changeless, unvarying, invariable, constant, consistent. ANTONYM variable.

**2** *a static display* STATIONARY, motionless, immobile, unmoving, still, stock-still, at a standstill, at rest, not moving a muscle, like a statue, rooted to the spot, frozen, inactive, inert, lifeless, inanimate. ANTONYMS mobile, active, dynamic.

**station** noun **1** *a train station* STOPPING PLACE, stop, halt, stage; terminus, terminal, depot.

**2** *a research station* ESTABLISHMENT, base, camp; post, depot; mission; site, facility, installation, yard.

**3** *a police station* OFFICE, depot, base, headquarters, precinct, station house, detachment; *informal* cop shop.

**4** *a radio station* CHANNEL, broadcasting organization; wavelength.

**5** *the watchman resumed his station* POST, position, place.

**6** *dated* *Karen was getting ideas above her station* RANK, place, status, position in society, social class, stratum, level, grade; caste; *archaic* condition, degree.

▸ verb *the regiment was stationed at Camp Pendleton* PUT ON

DUTY, post, position, place; establish, install; deploy, base, garrison.

**stationary** adjective **1** *a stationary car* STATIC, parked, stopped, motionless, immobile, unmoving, still, stock-still, at a standstill, at rest; not moving a muscle, like a statue, rooted to the spot, frozen, inactive, inert, lifeless, inanimate. ANTONYM moving.

**2** *a stationary population* UNCHANGING, unvarying, invariable, constant, consistent, unchanged, changeless, fixed, stable, steady. ANTONYM shifting.

**statue** noun *a statue of Alexander Hamilton* SCULPTURE, figure, effigy, statuette, figurine, idol; carving, bronze, graven image, model; bust, head.

**statuesque** adjective *statuesque beauty queens* TALL AND DIGNIFIED, imposing, striking, stately, majestic, noble, magnificent, splendid, impressive, regal.

**stature** noun **1** *she was small in stature* HEIGHT, tallness; size, build.

**2** *an architect of international stature* REPUTATION, repute, standing, status, position, prestige, distinction, eminence, preeminence, prominence, importance, influence, note, fame, celebrity, renown, acclaim.

**status** noun **1** *the status of women* STANDING, rank, ranking, position, social position, level, place, estimation; *dated* station.

**2** *wealth and status* PRESTIGE, kudos, cachet, standing, stature, regard, fame, note, renown, honor, esteem, image, importance, prominence, consequence, distinction, influence, authority, eminence.

**3** *the current status of the project* STATE, position, condition, shape, stage.

**staunch** adjective *a staunch supporter* STALWART, loyal, faithful, committed, devoted, dedicated, dependable, reliable, steady, constant, trusty, hard-working, steadfast, redoubtable, unwavering, tireless. See note at RESOLUTE. ANTONYMS disloyal, unfaithful, unreliable.

**stave** PHRASE: **stave off** *here, eat some crackers to stave off your hunger* AVERT, prevent, avoid, counter, preclude, forestall, nip in the bud; ward off, fend off, head off, keep off, keep at bay.

**stay**[1] verb **1** *he stayed where he was* REMAIN (BEHIND), stay behind, stay put; wait, linger, stick, be left, hold on, hang on, lodge; *informal* hang around; *archaic* bide, tarry. ANTONYM leave.

**2** *they won't stay hidden* CONTINUE (TO BE), remain, keep, persist in being, carry on being, go on being.

**3** *our aunt is staying with us* VISIT, spend time, put up, stop (off/over); lodge, room, board, have rooms, be housed, be accommodated, be quartered, be billeted, vacation; *formal* sojourn; *archaic* bide.

**4** *legal proceedings were stayed* POSTPONE, put off, delay, defer, put back, hold over/off; adjourn, suspend, prorogue, put over, table, lay on the table, take a rain check on; *Law* continue; *informal* put on ice, put on the back burner. ANTONYM advance.

**5** *literary we must stay the enemy's advance* DELAY, slow down/up, hold back/up, set back, keep back, put back, put a brake on, retard; hinder, hamper, obstruct, inhibit, impede, curb, check, restrain, restrict, arrest; *informal* throw a (monkey) wrench in the works of. ANTONYM promote.

▸ noun **1** *a stay at a hotel* VISIT, stop, stop-off, stopover, overnight, break, vacation; *formal* sojourn.

**2** *a stay of judgment* POSTPONEMENT, putting off, delay, deferment, deferral, putting back; adjournment, suspension, prorogation, tabling.

**stay**[2] noun *the stays holding up the mast* STRUT, WIRE, brace, tether, guy, prop, rod, support, truss; *Nautical* shroud.

▸ verb *her masts were well stayed* BRACE, tether, strut, wire, guy, prop, support, truss.

**steadfast** adjective **1** *a steadfast friend* LOYAL, faithful, committed, devoted, dedicated, dependable, reliable, steady, true, constant, staunch, solid, trusty. ANTONYM disloyal.

**2** *a steadfast policy* FIRM, determined, resolute, relentless, implacable, single-minded; unchanging, unwavering, unhesitating, unfaltering, unswerving, unyielding, unflinching, uncompromising. ANTONYM irresolute.

**steady** adjective **1** *the ladder must be steady* STABLE, firm, fixed, secure, fast, safe, immovable, unshakable, dependable; anchored, moored, jammed, rooted, braced. ANTONYMS unstable, loose.

**2** *keep the camera steady* MOTIONLESS, still, unshaking, static, stationary, unmoving. ANTONYM shaky.

**3** *a steady gaze* FIXED, intent, unwavering, unfaltering. ANTONYM darting.

**4** *a steady young student* SENSIBLE, levelheaded, rational, settled, mature, down-to-earth, full of common sense, reliable, dependable, sound, sober, serious-minded, responsible, serious. ANTONYMS flighty, immature, impulsive.

**5** *a steady income* CONSTANT, unchanging, regular, consistent, invariable; continuous, continual, unceasing, ceaseless, perpetual, unremitting, unwavering, unfaltering, unending, endless, around/round-the-clock, all-year-round. ANTONYMS fluctuating, sporadic.

**6** *a steady boyfriend* REGULAR, usual, established, settled, firm, devoted, faithful. ANTONYM occasional.

▸ verb **1** *he steadied the rifle* STABILIZE, hold steady; brace, support; balance, poise; secure, fix, make fast.

**2** *she needed to steady her nerves* CALM, soothe, quiet, compose, settle; subdue, quell, control, get a grip on.

**steal** verb **1** *the burglars stole a fax machine* PURLOIN, thieve, take, take for oneself, help oneself to, loot, pilfer, run off with, abscond with, carry off, shoplift; embezzle, misappropriate; *informal* walk off with, rob, swipe, snatch, nab, rip off, lift, filch, pinch, heist; *Brit. informal* nick; *formal* peculate.

**2** *his work was stolen by his tutor* PLAGIARIZE, copy, pass off as one's own, pirate, poach, borrow; *informal* rip off, lift, pinch, crib; *Brit. informal* nick.

**3** *he stole a kiss* SNATCH, sneak, get stealthily/surreptitiously.

**4** *he stole out of the room* CREEP, sneak, slink, slip, slide, glide, tiptoe, sidle, edge.

▸ noun *informal at $30 it's a steal.* See BARGAIN noun sense 1.

**stealing** noun *he was convicted of stealing* THEFT, thieving, thievery, robbery, larceny, burglary, shoplifting, pilfering, pilferage, looting, misappropriation; embezzlement; *formal* peculation.

**stealth** noun *the stealth of a cat burglar* FURTIVENESS, secretiveness, secrecy, surreptitiousness, sneakiness, slyness. ANTONYM openness.

**stealthy** adjective she was a natural for such stealthy activities FURTIVE, secretive, secret, surreptitious, sneaking, sly, clandestine, covert, conspiratorial. See note at SECRET. ANTONYM open.

**steam** noun **1** *steam from the kettle* WATER VAPOR, condensation, mist, haze, fog, moisture.

**2** *he ran out of steam* ENERGY, vigor, vitality, stamina, enthusiasm; MOMENTUM, impetus, force, strength, thrust, impulse, push, drive; speed, pace. PHRASES: **steamed up** *informal* **1** *he got steamed up about forgetting his papers* AGITATED.

**2** *they get steamed up about the media.* See ANGRY sense 1.

**let/blow off steam** *informal you'll go nuts if you don't let off steam once in a while* GIVE VENT TO ONE'S FEELINGS, speak one's mind, speak out, sound off, lose one's inhibitions, let oneself go; use up surplus energy.

**steamy** adjective **1** *the steamy jungle* HUMID, muggy, sticky, dripping, moist, damp, clammy, sultry, sweaty, steaming.

**2** *informal a steamy love scene.* See EROTIC.

**3** *informal they had a steamy affair* PASSIONATE, torrid, amorous, ardent, lustful; *informal* sizzling, hot, red-hot.

**steel** PHRASE: **steel oneself** *the coach gives us tips on how to steel ourselves before a game* BRACE ONESELF, nerve oneself, summon (up) one's courage, screw up one's courage, gear oneself up, prepare oneself, get in the right frame of mind; fortify oneself, harden oneself; *informal* psych oneself up; *literary* gird (up) one's loins.

**steely** adjective **1** *steely light* BLUE-GRAY, gray, steel-colored, steel-gray, iron-gray.

**2** *steely muscles* HARD, firm, toned, rigid, stiff, tense, tensed, taut. ANTONYM flabby.

**3** *steely eyes* CRUEL, unfeeling, merciless, ruthless, pitiless, heartless, hard-hearted, hard, stony, cold-blooded, cold-hearted, harsh, callous, severe, unrelenting, unpitying, unforgiving, uncaring, unsympathetic; *literary* adamantine. ANTONYM kind.

**4** *steely determination* RESOLUTE, firm, steadfast, dogged, single-minded; bitter, burning, ferocious, fanatical; ruthless, iron, grim, gritty; unquenchable, unflinching, unswerving, unfaltering, untiring, unwavering. ANTONYM halfhearted.

**steep**[1] adjective **1** *steep cliffs* PRECIPITOUS, sheer, abrupt, sharp, perpendicular, vertical, bluff, vertiginous. ANTONYM gentle.

**2** *a steep increase* SHARP, sudden, precipitate, precipitous, rapid. ANTONYM gradual.

**3** *informal steep prices* EXPENSIVE, costly, high, stiff; unreasonable, excessive, exorbitant, extortionate, outrageous, prohibitive, dear. ANTONYM reasonable.

**steep**[2] verb **1** *the ham is then steeped in brine* MARINADE, marinate, soak, souse, macerate; pickle.

**2** *winding sheets were steeped in mercury sulfate* SOAK, saturate, immerse, wet through, drench; *technical* ret.

**3** *a city steeped in history* IMBUE WITH, fill with, permeate with, pervade with, suffuse with, infuse with, soak in.

**steeple** noun *a solitary gull perched atop the church steeple* SPIRE, tower; bell tower, belfry, campanile; minaret.

**steer** verb **1** *he steered the boat* GUIDE, direct, maneuver, drive, pilot, navigate; *Nautical* con, helm.

**2** *Luke steered her down the path* GUIDE, conduct, direct, lead, take, usher, shepherd, marshal, herd. PHRASE: **steer clear of** *mind my words and steer clear of that man* KEEP AWAY FROM, keep one's distance from, keep at arm's length, give a wide berth to, avoid, avoid dealing with, have nothing to do with, shun, eschew.

**stem**[1] noun *a plant stem* STALK, shoot, trunk, stock, cane, bine. PHRASE: **stem from** *this type of behavior often stems from a childhood of abuse and neglect* HAVE ITS ORIGINS IN, arise from, originate from, spring from, derive from, come from, emanate from, flow from, proceed from; BE CAUSED BY, be brought on/about by, be produced by.

**stem**[2] verb *he stemmed the flow of blood* STAUNCH, stop, halt, check, hold back, restrict, control, contain, curb; block, dam; slow, lessen, reduce, diminish, stanch; *archaic* stay.

**stench** noun the stench from the basement was vile STINK, reek, whiff, fetor, funk; *literary* miasma. See note at SMELL.

**stentorian** adjective *his stentorian voice resonated throughout the theater* LOUD, thundering, thunderous, ear-splitting, deafening; powerful, strong, carrying; booming, resonant; strident. ANTONYMS quiet, soft.

**step** noun **1** *Frank took a step forward* PACE, stride.

**2** *she heard a step on the stairs* FOOTSTEP, footfall, tread.

**3** *she left the room with a springy step* GAIT, walk, tread.

**4** *it is only a step to the river* SHORT DISTANCE, stone's throw, spitting distance; *informal* 'a hop, skip, and jump.'

**5** *the top step* STAIR, tread; **(steps)** STAIRS, staircase, stairway.

**6** *each step of the ladder* RUNG, tread.

**7** *resigning is a very serious step* COURSE OF ACTION, measure, move, act, action, initiative, maneuver, operation, tactic.

**8** *a significant step toward a cease-fire* ADVANCE, development, move, movement; breakthrough.

**9** *the first step on the managerial ladder* STAGE, level, grade, rank, degree; notch, rung.

▸ verb **1** *she stepped gingerly through the snow* WALK, move, tread, pace, stride.

**2** *the bull* ***stepped on*** *the farmer's foot* TREAD ON, stamp on, trample (on); squash, crush, flatten.

PHRASES: **in step** *he is in step with mainstream thinking* IN ACCORD, in accordance, in harmony, in agreement, in tune, in line, in keeping, in conformity, compatible.
**mind/watch one's step** *just watch your step when Mrs. Kline gets here* BE CAREFUL, take care, step/tread carefully, exercise care/caution, mind how one goes, look out, watch out, be wary, be on one's guard, be on the qui vive.
**out of step** *the paper was often out of step with public opinion* AT ODDS, at variance, in disagreement, out of tune, out of line, not in keeping, out of harmony.
**step by step** *I followed the directions step by step* ONE STEP AT A TIME, bit by bit, gradually, in stages, by degrees, slowly, steadily.
**step down** *it's time for Rowland to step down* RESIGN, quit, stand down, give up one's post/job, bow out, abdicate; pack it in, call it quits.
**step in 1** *nobody stepped in to save the bank* INTERVENE, intercede, involve oneself, become/get involved, take a hand.

**2** *I stepped in for a sick colleague* STAND IN, sit in, fill in, cover, substitute, take over; replace, take someone's place; *informal* sub.
**step on it** *informal* *if we don't step on it we'll miss the boat* HURRY UP, get a move on, speed up, go faster, be quick; *informal* get cracking, get moving, step on the gas; *dated* make haste.
**step up 1** *the army stepped up its offensive* INCREASE, intensify, strengthen, augment, escalate; *informal* up, crank up.

**2** *I stepped up my pace* SPEED UP, increase, accelerate, quicken, hasten.

**stereotype** noun *the stereotype of the rancher* STANDARD/CONVENTIONAL IMAGE, received idea, cliché, hackneyed idea, formula.

▸ verb *women in detective novels are often stereotyped as femmes fatales* TYPECAST, pigeonhole, conventionalize, categorize, label, tag.

**stereotyped** adjective *the stereotyped image of a stewardess* STOCK, conventional, stereotypical, standard, formulaic, predictable; hackneyed, clichéd, cliché-ridden, banal, trite, unoriginal; typecast; *informal* corny, old hat. ANTONYMS unconventional, original.

**sterile** adjective **1** *mules are sterile* INFERTILE, unable to reproduce/conceive, unable to have children/young; *archaic* barren. ANTONYMS fertile, fecund.

**2** *sterile desert* UNPRODUCTIVE, infertile, unfruitful, uncultivatable, barren. ANTONYMS fertile, productive, rich.

**3** *a sterile debate* POINTLESS, unproductive, unfruitful, unrewarding, useless, unprofitable, profitless, futile, vain, idle; *archaic* bootless. ANTONYM fruitful.

**4** *sterile academicism* UNIMAGINATIVE, uninspired, uninspiring, unoriginal, stale, lifeless, musty, phlegmatic. ANTONYMS creative, original.

**5** *sterile conditions* ASEPTIC, sterilized, germ-free, antiseptic, disinfected; uncontaminated, unpolluted, pure, clean; sanitary, hygienic. See note at SANITARY. ANTONYM septic.

**sterilize** verb **1** *the scalpel was first sterilized* DISINFECT, fumigate, decontaminate, sanitize; pasteurize; clean, cleanse, purify; *technical* autoclave. ANTONYM contaminate.

**2** *over 6.5 million people were sterilized* MAKE UNABLE TO HAVE CHILDREN, make infertile, hysterectomize, vasectomize, have one's tubes tied, have a tubal ligation, have a salpingectomy.

**3** *sterilizing domestic animals* NEUTER, castrate, spay, geld, cut, fix, desex, alter, doctor.

**sterling** adjective *this is a sterling example of the power of a positive attitude* EXCELLENT, first-rate, first-class, exceptional, outstanding, splendid, superlative, praiseworthy, laudable, commendable, admirable, valuable, worthy, deserving. ANTONYMS poor, unexceptional.

**stern**[1] adjective **1** *a stern expression* SERIOUS, unsmiling, frowning, severe, forbidding, grim, unfriendly, austere, dour, stony, flinty, steely, unrelenting, unforgiving, unbending, unsympathetic, disapproving. ANTONYMS genial, friendly.

**2** *stern measures* STRICT, severe, stringent, harsh, drastic, hard, tough, extreme, rigid, ruthless, rigorous, exacting, demanding, uncompromising, unsparing, inflexible, authoritarian, draconian. See note at SEVERE. ANTONYMS lenient, lax.

**stern**[2] noun *the stern of the ship* REAR (END), back, after end, poop, transom, tail. ANTONYM bow.

**stew** noun **1** *we ate a hearty stew* ragout, casserole, fricassee.

**2** *informal* *she's in a stew about that parking ticket* MOOD, flap, panic, fluster, fret, fuss, sweat, lather, tizzy, dither, twitter, state; *literary* pother.

▸ verb **1** *stew the meat for an hour* BRAISE, simmer, boil.

**2** *informal* *there's no point stewing about it.* See WORRY verb sense 1.

**3** *informal* *the girls sat stewing in the heat* SWELTER, be very hot, perspire, sweat; *informal* roast, bake, cook, be boiling.

**stick**[1] noun **1** *a fire made of sticks* PIECE OF WOOD, twig, small branch.

**2** *he walks with a stick* WALKING STICK, cane, staff, alpenstock, crook, crutch.

**3** *the plants need supporting on sticks* CANE, pole, post, stake, upright.

**4** *he beat me with a stick* CLUB, cudgel, bludgeon, shillelagh; truncheon, baton; cane, birch, switch, rod. PHRASE: **the sticks** *informal* *she didn't want him to know that she'd grown up in the sticks* THE COUNTRY, the countryside, rural areas; the backwoods, the back of beyond, the wilds, the hinterland, a backwater, the backcountry, the backland, the middle of nowhere, the boondocks, the boonies, hicksville.

**stick**[2] verb **1** *he stuck his fork into the sausage* THRUST, push, insert, jab, poke, dig, plunge.

**2** *the bristles* ***stuck into*** *her skin* PIERCE, penetrate, puncture, prick, stab.

**3** *the cup stuck to its saucer* ADHERE, cling, be fixed, be glued.

**4** *stick the stamp there* AFFIX, attach, fasten, fix; paste, glue, gum, tape, Scotch-tape, pin, tack.

**5** *the wheels stuck in the mud* BECOME TRAPPED, become jammed, jam, catch, become wedged, become lodged, become fixed, become embedded.

**6** *that sticks in his mind* REMAIN, stay, linger, dwell, persist, continue, last, endure, burn.

**7** *the charges won't stick* BE UPHELD, hold, be believed; *informal* hold water.

**8** *informal just stick that sandwich on my desk* PUT (DOWN), place, set (down), lay (down), deposit, position; leave, stow; *informal* dump, park, pop, plunk. PHRASES: **stick at** *anything you stick at will eventually get done* PERSEVERE WITH, persist with, keep at, work at, continue with, carry on with, not give up with, hammer away at, stay with; go the distance, stay the course; *informal* soldier on with, hang in there.

**stick by** *Rodney stuck by me when everyone else bailed out* BE LOYAL TO, be faithful to, be true to, stand by, keep faith with, keep one's promise to.

**stick it out** *I think I can stick it out for another two weeks* PUT UP WITH IT, grin and bear it, keep at it, keep going, stay with it, see it through; persevere, persist, carry on, struggle on; *informal* hang in there, soldier on, tough it out, nail one's colors to the mast.

**stick out 1** *his front teeth stuck out* PROTRUDE, jut (out), project, stand out, extend, poke out; bulge, overhang.

**2** *they stuck out in their strange clothes* BE NOTICEABLE, be visible, be obvious, be conspicuous, stand out, be obtrusive, be prominent, attract attention, catch the eye, leap out, show up; *informal* stick/stand out like a sore thumb.

**stick to** *he stuck to his promise* ABIDE BY, keep, adhere to, hold to, comply with, fulfill, make good, stand by.

**stick up for** *after what she did, not even her family would stick up for her* SUPPORT, take someone's side, side with, be on the side of, stand by, stand up for, take someone's part, defend, come to the defense of, champion, speak up for, fight for.

**sticky** adjective **1** *sticky tape* (SELF-)ADHESIVE, gummed, self-stick; *technical* adherent.

**2** *sticky clay* GLUTINOUS, viscous, viscid, gluey, tacky, gummy, treacly, syrupy; mucilaginous; *informal* gooey, icky, gloppy. ANTONYM dry.

**3** *sticky weather* HUMID, muggy, close, sultry, steamy, sweaty, oppressive, heavy. ANTONYMS fresh, cool.

**4** *a sticky situation* AWKWARD, difficult, tricky, ticklish, problematic, delicate, touch-and-go, touchy, embarrassing, sensitive, uncomfortable; *informal* hairy. ANTONYM easy.

**stiff** adjective **1** *stiff cardboard* RIGID, hard, firm, inelastic, inflexible. ANTONYMS flexible, plastic, limp.

**2** *a stiff paste* SEMISOLID, viscous, viscid, thick, stiffened, firm. ANTONYM runny.

**3** *I'm stiff all over* ACHING, achy, painful; arthritic, rheumatic; *informal* creaky, rusty. ANTONYMS supple, limber.

**4** *a rather stiff manner* FORMAL, reserved, unfriendly, chilly, cold, frigid, icy, austere, wooden, forced, strained, stilted; *informal* starchy, uptight, standoffish. ANTONYMS relaxed, informal.

**5** *a stiff fine* HARSH, severe, heavy, crippling, punishing, stringent, drastic, draconian. ANTONYMS lenient, mild.

**6** *stiff resistance* VIGOROUS, determined, full of determination, strong, spirited, resolute, tenacious, steely, four-square, unflagging, unyielding, dogged, stubborn, obdurate, rock-ribbed. ANTONYM halfhearted.

**7** *a stiff climb* DIFFICULT, hard, arduous, tough, strenuous, laborious, uphill, exacting, tiring, demanding, formidable, challenging, punishing, grueling; *informal* killing, hellish. ANTONYM easy.

**8** *a stiff breeze* STRONG, fresh, brisk. ANTONYM gentle.

**9** *a stiff drink* STRONG, potent, alcoholic. ANTONYM weak.

**stiffen** verb **1** *stir until the mixture stiffens* BECOME STIFF, thicken; set, become solid, solidify, harden, jell, congeal, coagulate, clot. ANTONYMS soften, liquefy.

**2** *she stiffened her muscles | without exercise, joints will stiffen* MAKE/BECOME STIFF, tense (up), tighten, tauten. ANTONYM relax.

**3** *intimidation stiffened their resolve* STRENGTHEN, harden, toughen, fortify, reinforce, give a boost to. ANTONYM weaken.

**stifle** verb **1** *she stifled him with a pillow* SUFFOCATE, choke, asphyxiate, smother, gag.

**2** *Eleanor stifled a giggle* SUPPRESS, smother, restrain, fight back, choke back, gulp back, check, swallow, curb, silence. ANTONYM let out.

**3** *cartels stifle competition* CONSTRAIN, hinder, hamper, impede, hold back, curb, check, restrain, prevent, inhibit, suppress. ANTONYM encourage.

**stigma** noun the stigma of bankruptcy SHAME, disgrace, dishonor, ignominy, opprobrium, humiliation, (bad) reputation. ANTONYMS honor, credit.

**still** adjective **1** *the parrot lay still* MOTIONLESS, unmoving, not moving a muscle, stock-still, immobile, inanimate, like a statue, as if turned to stone, rooted to the spot, transfixed, static, stationary. ANTONYMS moving, active.

**2** *a still night* QUIET, silent, hushed, soundless, noiseless, undisturbed; CALM, peaceful, serene, windless; *literary* stilly. ANTONYM noisy.

**3** *the lake was still* CALM, flat, even, smooth, placid, tranquil, pacific, waveless, glassy, like a millpond, unruffled, stagnant. ANTONYMS rough, turbulent.

▸ noun *the still of the night* QUIETNESS, quiet, quietude, silence, stillness, hush, soundlessness; calm, tranquility, peace, serenity. ANTONYMS noise, disturbance, hubbub.

▸ adverb 1 *she's still running in circles* UP TO THIS TIME, up to the present time, until now, even now, yet.

2 *He's crazy. Still, he's good for dinner conversation* NEVERTHELESS, nonetheless, regardless, all the same, just the same, anyway, anyhow, even so, yet, but, however, notwithstanding, despite that, in spite of that, for all that, be that as it may, in any event, at any rate; *informal* still and all, anyhoo.

▸ verb 1 *she stilled the crowd* QUIET, silence, hush; calm, settle, pacify, soothe, lull, allay, subdue. ANTONYM stir up.

2 *the wind stilled* ABATE, die down, lessen, subside, ease up/off, let up, moderate, slacken, weaken. ANTONYM get stronger.

**stilted** adjective *a few minutes of stilted conversation* STRAINED, forced, contrived, constrained, labored, stiff, self-conscious, awkward, unnatural, wooden. ANTONYMS natural, effortless, spontaneous.

**stimulant** noun 1 *caffeine is a stimulant* TONIC, restorative; antidepressant; *informal* pep pill, upper, pick-me-up, bracer, happy pill; *Medicine* analeptic. ANTONYMS sedative, downer.

2 *a stimulant to discussion* STIMULUS, incentive, encouragement, impetus, inducement, boost, spur, prompt; *informal* shot in the arm. ANTONYM deterrent.

**stimulate** verb *we're looking for ways to stimulate tourism* ENCOURAGE, act as a stimulus/incentive/impetus/spur to, prompt, prod, move, motivate, trigger, spark, spur on, galvanize, activate, kindle, fire, fire with enthusiasm, fuel, whet, nourish; inspire, incentivize, inspirit, rouse, excite, animate, electrify, jump-start, light a fire under. See notes at ENCOURAGE, QUICKEN. ANTONYM discourage.

**stimulating** adjective 1 *a stimulating effect on the circulation* RESTORATIVE, tonic, invigorating, bracing, energizing, reviving, refreshing, revitalizing, revivifying; *Medicine* analeptic. ANTONYM sedative.

2 *a stimulating lecture* THOUGHT-PROVOKING, interesting, fascinating, inspiring, inspirational, lively, sparkling, exciting, stirring, rousing, intriguing, giving one food for thought, refreshing; provocative, challenging; *informal* buzzy. ANTONYMS uninspiring, uninteresting, boring.

**stimulus** noun *this sports facility has been a stimulus to the economic restoration of our city* SPUR, stimulant, encouragement, impetus, boost, prompt, prod, incentive, inducement, inspiration; motivation, impulse; *informal* shot in the arm. ANTONYMS deterrent, discouragement.

**sting** noun 1 *a bee sting* PRICK, wound, injury, puncture.

2 *this cream will take the sting away* SMART, pricking; pain, soreness, hurt, irritation.

3 *the sting of his betrayal* HEARTACHE, heartbreak, agony, torture, torment, hurt, pain, anguish.

4 *there was a sting in her words* SHARPNESS, severity, bite, edge, pointedness, asperity; sarcasm, acrimony, malice, spite, venom.

5 *informal* *the victim of a sting* SWINDLE, fraud, deception; trickery, sharp practice; *informal* rip-off, con, fiddle, bunco.

▸ verb 1 *she was stung by a scorpion* PRICK, wound, bite; poison.

2 *the smoke made her eyes sting* SMART, burn, hurt, be irritated, be sore.

3 *the criticism stung her* UPSET, wound, cut to the quick, sear, grieve, hurt, pain, torment, mortify.

4 *he was stung into action* PROVOKE, goad, incite, spur, prick, prod, rouse, drive, galvanize. ANTONYM deter.

5 *informal* *they stung a bank for thousands* SWINDLE, defraud, cheat, fleece, gull; *informal* rip off, screw, shaft, bilk, do, rook, diddle, take for a ride, chisel, gouge.

**stingy** adjective *informal* *you can think I'm stingy all you want, I'm not giving you a penny* MEAN, miserly, niggardly, close-fisted, parsimonious, penny-pinching, cheeseparing, Scroogelike; *informal* tightfisted, cheap, tight, mingy, money-grubbing. ANTONYMS generous, liberal.

**stink** verb 1 *his clothes stank of sweat* REEK, smell (foul/bad/disgusting), stink/smell to high heaven.

2 *informal* *the idea stinks* BE VERY UNPLEASANT, be abhorrent, be despicable, be contemptible, be disgusting, be vile, be foul; *informal* suck.

3 *informal* *the whole affair stinks of a setup* SMACK, reek, give the impression, have all the hallmarks; strongly suggest.

▸ noun 1 *the stink of a dirty diaper* STENCH, reek, fetor, foul/bad smell; *informal* funk; *literary* miasma. See note at SMELL.

2 *informal* *a big stink about the new proposals* FUSS, commotion, rumpus, ruckus, trouble, outcry, uproar, brouhaha, furor; *informal* song and dance, to-do, hoo-ha.

**stint** verb *we saved by* ***stinting on*** *food* SKIMP ON, scrimp on, be economical with, economize on, be sparing with, hold back on, be frugal with; be mean with, be parsimonious with; limit, restrict; *informal* be stingy with, be mingy with, be tight with.

▸ noun *a two-week stint in the office* SPELL, stretch, turn, session, term, shift, tour of duty.

**stipulate** verb *the document stipulates certain conditions* SPECIFY, set down, set out, lay down; demand, require, insist on, make a condition of, prescribe, impose; *Law* provide.

**stipulation** noun *the foundation could use the Lynde name, with the stipulation that a Lynde would always sit on the board of directors* CONDITION, precondition, proviso, provision, prerequisite, specification; demand, requirement; rider, caveat, qualification.

**stir** verb 1 *stir the mixture well* MIX, blend, agitate; beat, whip, whisk, fold in.

2 *Travis stirred in his sleep* MOVE SLIGHTLY, change one's position, shift.

3 *a breeze stirred the leaves* DISTURB, rustle, shake, move, flutter, agitate.

**4** *she finally stirred at ten o'clock* GET UP, get out of bed, rouse oneself, rise; WAKE (UP), awaken; *informal* rise and shine, surface, show signs of life; *formal* arise; *literary* waken. ANTONYMS go to bed, retire.

**5** *I never stirred from here* MOVE, budge, make a move, shift, go away; leave. ANTONYMS stay, stay put.

**6** *symbolism can stir the imagination* AROUSE, rouse, fire, kindle, inspire, stimulate, excite, awaken, quicken; *literary* waken. ANTONYM stultify.

**7** *the war stirred him to action* SPUR, drive, rouse, prompt, propel, prod, motivate, encourage; urge, impel; provoke, goad, prick, sting, incite, light a fire under.

▸ noun *the news caused a stir* COMMOTION, disturbance, fuss, excitement, turmoil, sensation; *informal* to-do, hoo-ha, hullabaloo, flap, splash.

PHRASE: **stir up** *his remarks stirred up a furor* WHIP UP, work up, foment, fan the flames of, trigger, spark off, precipitate, excite, provoke, incite, ignite.

**stirring** adjective *a stirring portrait of his life as a missionary* EXCITING, thrilling, rousing, stimulating, moving, inspiring, inspirational, passionate, impassioned, emotional, heady. ANTONYMS boring, pedestrian.

**stitch** noun *he was panting and had a stitch* SHARP PAIN, stabbing pain, shooting pain, stab of pain, pang, twinge, spasm.

▸ verb *the seams are stitched by hand* SEW, baste, tack; seam, hem; darn.

**stock** noun **1** *the store carries little stock* MERCHANDISE, goods, wares, items/articles for sale, inventory.

**2** *a stock of fuel* STORE, supply, stockpile, reserve, hoard, cache, bank, accumulation, quantity, collection.

**3** *farm stock* ANIMALS, livestock, beasts; flocks, herds.

**4** (**stocks**) *blue-chip stocks* SHARES, securities, equities, bonds.

**5** *her stock is low with most voters* POPULARITY, favor, regard, estimation, standing, status, reputation, name, prestige.

**6** *his mother was of French stock* DESCENT, ancestry, origin(s), parentage, pedigree, lineage, line (of descent), heritage, birth, extraction, family, blood, bloodline.

**7** *chicken stock* BOUILLON, broth, consommé.

**8** *the stock of a weapon* HANDLE, butt, haft, grip, shaft, shank.

▸ adjective **1** *a stock size* STANDARD, regular, normal, established, set; common, readily/widely available; staple. ANTONYM nonstandard.

**2** *the stock response* USUAL, routine, predictable, set, standard, staple, customary, familiar, conventional, traditional, stereotyped, clichéd, hackneyed, unoriginal, formulaic. ANTONYMS original, unusual.

▸ verb **1** *we stock organic food* SELL, carry, keep (in stock), offer, have (for sale), retail, supply.

**2** *the fridge was well stocked with milk* SUPPLY, provide, furnish, provision, equip, fill, load.

PHRASES: **in stock** *what brands of dog food do you have in stock?* FOR/ON SALE, (immediately) available, on the shelf.

**stock up on/with** *people are stocking up on batteries and water* AMASS SUPPLIES OF, stockpile, hoard, cache, lay in, buy up/in, put away/by, put/set aside, collect, accumulate, save; *informal* squirrel away, salt away, stash away.

**take stock of** *let's take stock of our current situation* REVIEW, assess, appraise, evaluate; *informal* size up.

**stockings** plural noun *you'll need a pair of black stockings* NYLONS, pantyhose, tights; hosiery, hose, leotards; knee-highs.

**stockpile** noun *a stockpile of weapons* STOCK, store, supply, accumulation, collection, reserve, hoard, cache; *informal* stash.

▸ verb *food had been stockpiled* STORE UP, amass, accumulate, store (up), stock up on, hoard, cache, collect, lay in, put away, put/set aside, put by, put away for a rainy day, stow away, save; *informal* salt away, stash away.

**stock-still** adjective *two stock-still deer were not more than twenty feet away from us* MOTIONLESS, completely still, unmoving, not moving a muscle, immobile, like a statue/stone, rooted to the spot, transfixed, paralyzed, petrified, static, stationary. ANTONYMS moving, active.

**stocky** adjective *he was short but stocky, and his physical strength was amazing* THICKSET, sturdy, heavily built, chunky, burly, strapping, brawny, solid, heavy, heavyset, hefty, beefy, blocky. ANTONYMS slender, skinny.

**stodgy** adjective **1** *stodgy writing* BORING, dull, uninteresting, dreary, turgid, tedious, dry, unimaginative, uninspired, unexciting, unoriginal, monotonous, humdrum, prosaic, staid, heavy going; *informal* deadly, square. ANTONYMS interesting, lively.

**2** *a stodgy pudding* SOLID, substantial, filling, hearty, heavy, starchy, indigestible. ANTONYM light.

**stoicism** noun *she accepted her sufferings with remarkable stoicism* PATIENCE, forbearance, resignation, fortitude, endurance, acceptance, tolerance, phlegm. ANTONYM intolerance.

**stolid** adjective *her stolid facade is somewhat unnerving* IMPASSIVE, phlegmatic, unemotional, cool, calm, placid, unexcitable; dependable; unimaginative, dull. ANTONYMS emotional, lively, imaginative.

**stomach** noun **1** *a stomach pain* ABDOMEN, belly, gut, middle; *informal* tummy, insides.

**2** *his fat stomach* PAUNCH, potbelly, beer belly, girth; *informal* beer gut, pot, tummy, spare tire, breadbasket, middle-aged spread.

**3** *he had no stomach for it* APPETITE, taste, hunger, thirst; inclination, desire, relish, fancy.

▸ verb **1** *I can't stomach butter* DIGEST, keep down, manage to eat/consume, tolerate, take.

**2** *they couldn't stomach the sight* TOLERATE, put up with, take, stand, endure, bear; *informal* hack, abide.

**stone** noun **1** *someone threw a stone at me* ROCK, pebble, boulder.

**2** *a commemorative stone* TABLET, monument, monolith, obelisk; gravestone, headstone, tombstone.

**3** *paving stones* SLAB, flagstone, flag, cobble.

**4** *what beautiful stones in her tiara* GEM, gemstone, jewel, semiprecious stone, brilliant; *informal* rock, sparkler.

**5** *a peach stone* KERNEL, seed, pip, pit.

**stony** adjective **1** *a stony path* ROCKY, pebbly, gravelly, shingly; rough, hard. ANTONYM smooth.

**2** *a stony stare* UNFRIENDLY, hostile, cold, chilly, frosty, icy; hard, flinty, steely, stern, severe; fixed, expressionless, blank, poker-faced, deadpan; unfeeling, uncaring, unsympathetic, indifferent, cold-hearted, callous, heartless, hard-hearted, stony-hearted, merciless, pitiless. ANTONYMS friendly, sympathetic.

**stooge** noun **1** *a government stooge* UNDERLING, minion, lackey, subordinate; henchman; PUPPET, pawn, cat's paw; *informal* sidekick.

**2** *a comedian's stooge* BUTT, foil, straight man.

**stoop** verb **1** *she stooped to pick up the pen* BEND (OVER/DOWN), lean over/down, crouch (down).

**2** *he stooped his head* LOWER, bend, incline, bow, duck.

**3** *he stoops when he walks* HUNCH ONE'S SHOULDERS, walk with a stoop, be round-shouldered.

**4** *Davis would stoop to committing a crime* LOWER ONESELF, sink, descend, resort; go as far as, sink as low as.

▸ noun **1** *a man with a stoop* HUNCH, round shoulders; curvature of the spine; *Medicine* kyphosis.

**2** *we sat on the front stoop and watched the passers-by* PORCH, steps, platform, veranda, terrace.

**stop** verb **1** *we can't stop the decline* PUT AN END/STOP/HALT TO, bring to an end/stop/halt/close/standstill, end, halt; finish, terminate, discontinue, cut short, interrupt, nip in the bud; deactivate, shut down. ANTONYMS start, begin, continue.

**2** *he stopped smoking* CEASE, discontinue, desist from, break off; give up, abandon, abstain from, cut out; *informal* quit, leave off, knock off, pack in, lay off, give over.

**3** *the car stopped* PULL UP, draw up, come to a stop/halt, come to rest, pull in, pull over; park.

**4** *the music stopped* CONCLUDE, come to an end/stop/standstill, cease, end, finish, draw to a close, be over, terminate; pause, break off; peter out, fade away.

**5** *divers stopped the flow of oil* STEM, staunch, hold back, check, curb, block, dam; *archaic* stay.

**6** *the police stopped her leaving* PREVENT, hinder, obstruct, impede, block, bar, preclude; dissuade from. ANTONYM encourage.

**7** *the council stopped the housing project* THWART, balk, foil, frustrate, stand in the way of; scotch, derail; *informal* put paid to, put the kibosh on, put a stop to, do for, stymie, scuttle, deep-six. ANTONYM expedite.

**8** *just stop the bottle with your thumb* BLOCK (UP), plug, close (up), fill (up); seal, caulk, bung up; *technical* occlude.

▸ noun **1** *all business came to a stop* HALT, end, finish, close, standstill; cessation, conclusion, stoppage, discontinuation. ANTONYMS start, beginning, continuation.

**2** *a brief stop in the town* BREAK, stopover, stop-off, stay, visit; *formal* sojourn.

**3** *the next stop is Central Park* STOPPING PLACE, halt, station.

PHRASES: **put a stop to.** *how can we put a stop to this senseless violence?* See STOP verb senses 1, 7.

**stop off/over** *we decided to stop over in Denver* BREAK ONE'S JOURNEY, take a break, pause, linger; stay, remain, put up, lodge, rest; *formal* sojourn.

**stopgap** noun *that old plane was merely a stopgap* TEMPORARY SOLUTION/FIX, expedient, makeshift; substitute, stand-in, pinch-hitter.

▸ adjective *a stopgap measure* TEMPORARY, provisional, interim, pro tem, short-term, working, makeshift, emergency; caretaker, acting, stand-in, fill-in. ANTONYM permanent.

**stopover** noun *our stopover in Dallas lasted two weeks* BREAK, stop, stop-off, layover, overnight, visit, stay; *formal* sojourn.

**stoppage** noun **1** *the stoppage of production* DISCONTINUATION, stopping, halting, cessation, termination, end, finish; interruption, suspension, breaking off. ANTONYMS start, continuation.

**2** *a stoppage of the blood supply* OBSTRUCTION, blocking, blockage, block; *Medicine* occlusion, stasis.

**3** *a stoppage over pay* STRIKE, walkout; industrial action.

**stopper** noun *the stopper is not keeping the water from running out* PLUG, cork, bung, spigot, spile, seal.

**store** noun **1** *a store of money* STOCK, supply, stockpile, hoard, cache, reserve, bank, pool; *informal* war chest, pork barrel.

**2** *a grain store* STOREROOM, storehouse, repository, depository, stockroom, depot, warehouse, magazine; *informal* lockup.

**3** *ship's stores* SUPPLIES, provisions, stocks, necessities; food, rations, provender; materials, equipment, hardware; *Military* matériel, accoutrements; *Nautical* chandlery.

**4** *a hardware store* SHOP, (retail) outlet, boutique, department store, chain store, emporium; supermarket, superstore, megastore.

▸ verb *rabbits don't store food* KEEP, keep in reserve, stockpile, lay in, put/set aside, put away/by, put away for a rainy day, save, collect, accumulate, hoard, cache; *informal* squirrel away, salt away, stash away. ANTONYMS use, discard.

PHRASE: **set (great) store by** *Gwen set great store by good manners* VALUE, attach great importance to, put a high value on, put a premium on; THINK HIGHLY OF, hold in (high) regard, have a high opinion of; *informal* rate.

**storm** noun **1** *battered by a storm* WINDSTORM, tempest, whirlwind, gale, strong wind, high wind, squall; cyclone, tornado, twister, dust devil, dust storm; rainstorm, thunderstorm, thundershower; monsoon, typhoon, hurricane, tropical storm; hailstorm, snowstorm, blizzard.

**2** *a storm of bullets* VOLLEY, salvo, fusillade, barrage, cannonade; shower, spray, hail, rain.

**3** *there was a storm over his remarks* UPROAR, outcry, fuss, furor, brouhaha, rumpus, trouble, hue and cry, controversy; *informal* to-do, hoo-ha, hullabaloo, ballyhoo, stink, row.

**4** *a storm of protest* OUTBURST, outbreak, explosion, eruption, outpouring, surge, blaze, flare-up, wave.

▸ verb **1** *she stormed out* STRIDE ANGRILY, stomp, march, stalk, flounce, stamp.

**2** *his mother stormed at him* RANT, rave, shout, bellow, roar, thunder, rage.

**3** *police stormed the building* ATTACK, charge, rush, assail, descend on, swoop on. See note at ATTACK.

**stormy** adjective **1** *stormy weather* BLUSTERY, squally, windy, gusty, blowy; rainy, thundery, snowy; wild, tempestuous, turbulent, violent, rough, foul. ANTONYMS calm, fine.

**2** *a stormy debate* ANGRY, heated, fiery, fierce, furious, passionate, lively. ANTONYM peaceful.

**story** noun **1** *a story about his summer in Hawaii* TALE, narrative, account, anecdote; *informal* yarn, spiel.

**2** *the novel has a good story* PLOT, story line, scenario, libretto.

**3** *the story appeared in the papers* NEWS ITEM, news report, article, feature, piece.

**4** *there have been a lot of stories going around* RUMOR, piece of gossip, whisper; speculation.

**5** *Harper changed his story* TESTIMONY, statement, report, account, version.

**6** *Ellie never told stories.* See FALSEHOOD sense 1.

**stout** adjective **1** *a short stout man* FAT, plump, portly, rotund, dumpy, chunky, corpulent; stocky, burly, bulky, hefty, heavyset, solidly built, thickset; *informal* tubby, pudgy, zaftig, corn-fed. ANTONYMS thin, slender.

**2** *stout leather shoes* STRONG, sturdy, solid, substantial, robust, tough, durable, hardwearing. ANTONYMS fragile, flimsy.

**3** *stout resistance* DETERMINED, vigorous, forceful, spirited; staunch, steadfast, stalwart, firm, resolute, unyielding, dogged; brave, bold, courageous, valiant, valorous, gallant, fearless, doughty, intrepid; *informal* gutsy, spunky. ANTONYMS halfhearted, feeble.

**stouthearted** adjective *we stand in awe of these stouthearted heroes* BRAVE, determined, courageous, bold, plucky, spirited, valiant, valorous, gallant, fearless, doughty, intrepid, stalwart; *informal* gutsy, spunky.

**stove** noun *there's a pot of coffee on the stove* OVEN, range, wood stove, wood-burning stove, potbellied stove, Franklin stove; *trademark* Coleman stove.

**stow** verb *Barney stowed her bags in the trunk* PACK, load, store, place, put (away), deposit, stash. ANTONYM unload.

PHRASE: **stow away** *you'd better stow away until the air clears* HIDE, conceal oneself, travel secretly.

**straddle** verb **1** *she straddled the motorbike* SIT/STAND ASTRIDE, bestride, mount, get on.

**2** *a mountain range straddling the border* LIE ON BOTH SIDES OF, extend across, span.

**3** *he straddled the issue of taxes* BE EQUIVOCAL ABOUT, be undecided about, equivocate about, vacillate about, waver about, waffle on; *informal* sit on the fence regarding.

**strafe** verb *enemy aircraft strafed our carriers* BOMB, shell, bombard, fire on, machine-gun, rake with gunfire, enfilade; *archaic* fusillade.

**straggle** verb *we were straggling toward the end, but we weren't the last ones to cross the finish line* TRAIL, lag, dawdle, walk slowly, dally, lollygag; fall behind, bring up the rear.

**straight** adjective **1** *a long, straight road* UNSWERVING, undeviating, linear, as straight as an arrow, uncurving, unbending. ANTONYMS winding, zigzag.

**2** *that picture isn't straight* LEVEL, even, in line, aligned, square; vertical, upright, perpendicular; horizontal. ANTONYMS askew, crooked.

**3** *we must get the place straight* IN ORDER, (neat and) tidy, neat, shipshape, orderly, spick-and-span, organized, arranged, sorted out, straightened out. ANTONYMS untidy, messy.

**4** *a straight answer* HONEST, direct, frank, candid, truthful, sincere, forthright, straightforward, plain-spoken, blunt, straight from the shoulder, unequivocal, unambiguous; *informal* upfront. ANTONYMS indirect, evasive.

**5** *straight thinking* LOGICAL, rational, clear, lucid, sound, coherent. ANTONYMS irrational, illogical.

**6** *three straight wins* SUCCESSIVE, in succession, consecutive, in a row, running.

**7** *straight brandy* UNDILUTED, neat, pure, straight up. ANTONYM diluted.

**8** *informal she's very straight* RESPECTABLE, conventional, conservative, traditional, old-fashioned, straitlaced; *informal* stuffy, square, fuddy-duddy.

▸ adverb **1** *he looked me straight in the eyes* RIGHT, directly, squarely, full; *informal* smack, bang, spang, smack dab.

**2** *she drove straight home* DIRECTLY, right, by a direct route.

**3** *I'll call you straight back* RIGHT AWAY, straightaway, immediately, directly, at once; *archaic* straightway.

**4** *I told her straight* FRANKLY, directly, candidly, honestly, forthrightly, plainly, point-blank, bluntly, flatly, straight from the shoulder, without beating about the bush, without mincing words, unequivocally, unambiguously, in plain English, to someone's face, straight up.

**5** *he can't think straight* LOGICALLY, rationally, clearly, lucidly, coherently, cogently.

PHRASES: **go straight** *maybe a few nights in jail will inspire him to go straight* REFORM, mend one's ways, turn over a new leaf, get back on the straight and narrow.

**straight away** *I'll be there straightaway* AT ONCE, right away, (right) now, this/that (very) minute, this/that instant, immediately, instantly, directly, forthwith, without further/more ado, promptly, quickly, without delay, then and there, here and now, as soon as possible, ASAP, as quickly as possible, in short order; *informal* straight off, PDQ, pretty damn quick, pronto, lickety-split; *archaic* straightway.

**straight from the shoulder** *I have to tell you the truth straight from the shoulder.* See STRAIGHT adverb sense 4.

**straighten** verb **1** *Rory straightened his tie* MAKE STRAIGHT, adjust, arrange, rearrange, (make) tidy, spruce up.

**2** *we must straighten things out with Violet* PUT/SET RIGHT, sort out, clear up, settle, resolve, put in order, regularize, rectify, remedy; *informal* patch up.

**3** *he straightened up* STAND UP (STRAIGHT), stand upright.

**straightforward** adjective **1** *the process was remarkably straightforward* UNCOMPLICATED, simple, easy, effortless, painless, undemanding, plain sailing, child's play; *informal* as easy as pie, a piece of cake, a cinch, a snip, a breeze, a cakewalk, duck soup, a snap. ANTONYM complicated.

**2** *a straightforward man* HONEST, frank, candid, open, truthful, sincere, on the level; forthright, plain-speaking, direct, unambiguous; *informal* upfront, on the up and up. ANTONYM evasive.

**strain**[1] verb **1** *take care that you don't strain yourself* OVERTAX, overwork, overextend, overreach, drive too far; exhaust, wear out; overdo it; *informal* knock oneself out.

**2** *you have strained a muscle* INJURE, damage, pull, wrench, twist, sprain.

**3** *we strained to haul the guns up the slope* STRUGGLE, labor, toil, make every effort, try very hard, break one's back, push/drive oneself to the limit; *informal* pull out all the stops, go all out, bust a gut.

**4** *the flood of refugees is straining the relief services* MAKE EXCESSIVE DEMANDS ON, overtax, be too much for, test, tax, put a strain on.

**5** *the bear strained at the chain* PULL, tug, heave, haul, jerk; *informal* yank.

**6** *archaic she strained the infant to her bosom* CLASP, press, clutch, hold tight; embrace, hug, enfold, envelop.

**7** *strain the mixture* SIEVE, sift, filter, screen, riddle; *rare* filtrate.

▸ noun **1** *the rope snapped under the strain* TENSION, tightness, tautness.

**2** *muscle strain* INJURY, sprain, wrench, twist.

**3** *the strain of her job* PRESSURE, demands, burdens; stress; *informal* hassle.

**4** *Nancy was showing signs of strain* STRESS, (nervous) tension; exhaustion, fatigue, pressure of work, overwork.

**5** *the strains of Brahms's lullaby* SOUND, music; melody, tune.

**strain**[2] noun **1** *a different strain of flu* VARIETY, kind, type, sort; breed, genus.

**2** *McCallum was of Puritan strain* DESCENT, ancestry, origin(s), parentage, lineage, extraction, family, roots.

**3** *there was a strain of insanity in the family* TENDENCY, susceptibility, propensity, proneness; trait, disposition.

**4** *a strain of solemnity* ELEMENT, strand, vein, note, trace, touch, suggestion, hint.

**strained** adjective **1** *relations between them were strained* AWKWARD, tense, uneasy, uncomfortable, edgy, difficult, troubled. ANTONYM friendly.

**2** *Jean's strained face* DRAWN, careworn, worn, pinched, tired, exhausted, drained, haggard.

**3** *a strained smile* FORCED, constrained, unnatural; artificial, insincere, false, affected, put-on. ANTONYM natural.

**strainer** noun *pour the noodles into a strainer* SIEVE, colander, filter, sifter, riddle, screen; *archaic* griddle.

**strait** noun **1** *a strait about six miles wide* CHANNEL, sound, inlet, stretch of water.

**2** *the company is in desperate straits* A BAD/DIFFICULT SITUATION, difficulty, trouble, crisis, a mess, a predicament, a plight; *informal* hot/deep water, a jam, a hole, a bind, a fix, a scrape.

**straitened** adjective *our straitened circumstances improved once Desmond got his first teaching job* IMPOVERISHED, poverty-stricken, poor, destitute, penniless, as poor as a church mouse, in penury, impecunious, unable to make ends meet, in reduced circumstances; *informal* (flat) broke, strapped (for cash); *formal* penurious.

**straitlaced** adjective *our straitlaced relatives were horrified by Stacey's punk hairdo* PRIM (AND PROPER), prudish, puritanical, prissy, conservative, old-fashioned, stuffy, staid, narrow-minded; *informal* starchy, square, fuddy-duddy. ANTONYM broad-minded.

**strand**[1] noun **1** *strands of wool* THREAD, filament, fiber; length, ply.

**2** *the various strands of the ecological movement* ELEMENT, component, factor, ingredient, aspect, feature, strain.

**strand**[2] noun *literary a walk along the strand* SEASHORE, shore, beach, sands, foreshore, shoreline, seaside, waterfront, front, waterside.

**stranded** adjective **1** *a stranded ship* BEACHED, grounded, run aground, high and dry; shipwrecked, wrecked, marooned.

**2** *she was stranded in a strange city* HELPLESS, without resources, in difficulties; in the lurch, abandoned, deserted.

**strange** adjective **1** *strange things have been happening* UNUSUAL, odd, curious, peculiar, funny, bizarre, weird, uncanny, queer, unexpected, unfamiliar, atypical, anomalous, out of the ordinary, extraordinary, puzzling, mystifying, mysterious, perplexing, baffling, unaccountable, inexplicable, singular, freakish; suspicious, questionable; eerie, unnatural; *informal* fishy, bizarro, creepy, spooky. ANTONYMS ordinary, usual.

**2** *strange clothes* WEIRD, eccentric, odd, peculiar, funny, bizarre, unusual; unconventional, outlandish, freakish, quirky, zany; *informal* wacky, way out, freaky, kooky, offbeat, off the wall, screwy, wacko. ANTONYMS normal, conventional.

**3** *visiting a strange house* UNFAMILIAR, unknown, new. ANTONYM familiar.

**4** *Jean was feeling strange* ILL, unwell, poorly, peaked; *informal* under the weather, funny, peculiar, lousy, off; *dated* queer. ANTONYM well.

**5** *she felt strange with him* ILL AT EASE, uneasy, uncomfortable, awkward, self-conscious. ANTONYM relaxed.

**stranger** noun *they were taught to fear strangers* NEWCOMER, new arrival, visitor, outsider, newbie. PHRASE: **a stranger to** *I'm afraid I'm a stranger to these automated methods* UNACCUSTOMED TO, unfamiliar with, unused to, new to, fresh to, inexperienced in; *archaic* strange to.

**strangle** verb **1** *the victim was strangled with a scarf* THROTTLE, choke, garrote; *informal* strangulate.

**2** *she strangled a sob* SUPPRESS, smother, stifle, repress, restrain, fight back, choke back.

**3** *bureaucracy is strangling commercial activity* HAMPER, hinder, impede, restrict, inhibit, curb, check, constrain, squash, crush, suppress, repress.

**strap** noun *thick leather straps* THONG, tie, band, belt.

▸ verb **1** *a bag was strapped to the bicycle* FASTEN, secure, tie, bind, make fast, lash, truss.

**2** *his knee was strapped up* BANDAGE, bind.

**3** *his father strapped him.* See LASH verb sense 1.

**stratagem** noun *Warren devised a series of stratagems to win their confidence* PLAN, scheme, tactic, maneuver, ploy, device, trick, ruse, plot, machination, dodge; subterfuge, artifice, wile; *archaic* shift.

#### USAGE NOTE **stratagem**

The mistaken spelling *strategem* (on the analogy of *strategy*) appears about 20% as often as the correct spelling *stratagem*. Though the words *stratagem* and *strategy* are etymologically related, they came into English by different routes, and their spellings diverged merely as a matter of long-standing convention. What happened is that the Latin *strategema* became *stratagema* in Romance languages such as French. (The *Century Dictionary* calls the Romance spelling "erroneous.") *Stratagem* came into English in the fifteenth century, through French. But it wasn't until the early nineteenth century that English and American writers borrowed *strategy* (originally a Greek term) from Latin. Hence our incongruous spellings today. —*BG*

**strategic** adjective *his lawyers were known for their strategic defense methods* PLANNED, calculated, tactical, politic, judicious, prudent, shrewd.

**strategy** noun **1** *the government's economic strategy* MASTER PLAN, grand design, game plan, plan (of action), action plan, policy, program; tactics.

**2** *military strategy* THE ART OF WAR, (military) tactics.

**stratum** noun **1** *a stratum of flint* LAYER, vein, seam, lode, bed.

**2** *this stratum of society* LEVEL, class, echelon, rank, grade, group, set; caste; *dated* station, estate.

**stray** verb **1** *the gazelle had strayed from the herd* WANDER OFF, go astray, get separated, get lost.

**2** *we strayed from our original topic* DIGRESS, deviate, wander, get sidetracked, go off at a tangent, veer off; get off the subject.

**3** *the young men were likely to stray* BE UNFAITHFUL, have affairs, cheat, philander; *informal* play around, play the field.

**4** *forgive me, Father, for I have strayed* SIN, transgress, err, go astray; *archaic* trespass.

▸ adjective **1** *a stray dog* HOMELESS, lost, strayed, gone astray, abandoned.

**2** *a stray bullet* RANDOM, chance, freak, unexpected, isolated, lone, single.

▸ noun *she adopted three strays* HOMELESS ANIMAL, stray dog/cat, waif.

**streak** noun **1** *a streak of orange light* BAND, line, strip, stripe, vein, slash, ray.

**2** *green streaks on her legs* MARK, smear, smudge, stain, blotch; *informal* splotch.

**3** *a streak of self-destructiveness* ELEMENT, vein, touch, strain; trait, characteristic.

**4** *a winning streak* PERIOD, spell, stretch, run, patch.

▸ verb **1** *the sky was streaked with red* STRIPE, band, fleck.

**2** *overalls streaked with paint* MARK, daub, smear; *informal* splotch.

**stream** noun **1** *a mountain stream* CREEK, river, rivulet, rill, runnel, streamlet, freshet; tributary; bourn; brook.

**2** *a stream of boiling water* JET, flow, rush, gush, surge, torrent, flood, cascade, outpouring, outflow; *technical* efflux.

**3** *a steady stream of visitors* SUCCESSION, flow, series, string.

▸ verb **1** *tears were streaming down her face* FLOW, pour, course, run, gush, surge, flood, cascade, spill.

**2** *children streamed out of the classrooms* POUR, surge, charge, flood, swarm, pile, crowd.

**3** *a flag streamed from the mast* FLUTTER, float, flap, fly, blow, waft, wave.

**streamer** noun *streamers fluttered from every post and pole along the parade route* PENNANT, pennon, flag, banderole, banner.

**streamlined** adjective **1** *streamlined cars* AERODYNAMIC, smooth, sleek.

**2** *a streamlined organization* EFFICIENT, smooth-running, well run, slick; time-saving, labor-saving.

**street** noun *Amsterdam's narrow cobbled streets* ROAD, thoroughfare, avenue, drive, crescent, boulevard; side street/road, lane, highway. PHRASES: **the man/woman in the street** *they* *claim to be interested in what the man in the street has to say, but that hardly seems the case* AN ORDINARY PERSON, Mr./Ms. Average; *informal* Joe Public, John Q. Public, Joe Blow, Joe Schmo, schmo, John Doe, Joe Sixpack.

**on the streets** *many of these teens have parents who don't care that their kids are on the streets* HOMELESS, down and out, of no fixed abode.

**strength** noun **1** *enormous physical strength* POWER, brawn, muscle, muscularity, burliness, sturdiness, robustness, toughness, hardiness; vigor, force, might; *informal* beef; *literary* thew. ANTONYMS weakness, frailty.

**2** *Oliver began to regain his strength* HEALTH, fitness, vigor, stamina. ANTONYM infirmity.

**3** *her great inner strength* FORTITUDE, resilience, spirit, backbone, strength of character; courage, bravery, pluck, pluckiness, courageousness, grit, mettle; *informal* guts, spunk. ANTONYM vulnerability.

**4** *the strength of the retaining wall* ROBUSTNESS, sturdiness, firmness, toughness, soundness, solidity, durability. ANTONYM weakness.

**5** *China's military strength* POWER, influence, dominance, ascendancy, supremacy; *informal* clout; *literary* puissance. ANTONYMS weakness, impotence.

**6** *the strength of feeling against the president* INTENSITY, vehemence, force, forcefulness, depth, ardor, fervor. ANTONYM half-heartedness.

**7** *the strength of their argument* COGENCY, forcefulness, force, weight, power, potency, persuasiveness, soundness, validity. ANTONYMS weakness, ineffectiveness.

**8** *what are your strengths?* STRONG POINT, advantage, asset, forte, aptitude, talent, skill; specialty. ANTONYMS failing, flaw, limitation.

**9** *the strength of the army* SIZE, extent, magnitude. ANTONYM weakness.

PHRASE: **on the strength of** *she got into Princeton on the strength of her essays* BECAUSE OF, by virtue of, on the basis of.

**strengthen** verb **1** *calcium strengthens growing bones* FORTIFY, make strong/stronger, build up, give strength to. ANTONYM weaken.

**2** *engineers strengthened the walls* REINFORCE, make stronger, buttress, shore up, underpin.

**3** *how does this process strengthen the glass?* TOUGHEN, temper, anneal.

**4** *the wind had strengthened* BECOME STRONG/STRONGER, gain strength, intensify, pick up. ANTONYM die down.

**5** *his insistence strengthened her determination* FORTIFY, bolster, make stronger, boost, reinforce, harden, stiffen, toughen, fuel. ANTONYM weaken.

**6** *they strengthened their efforts* REDOUBLE, step up, increase, escalate; *informal* up, crank up, beef up. ANTONYMS relax, decrease.

**7** *the argument is strengthened by this evidence* REINFORCE, lend more weight to; support, substantiate, back up, confirm, bear out, corroborate. ANTONYM undermine.

**strenuous** adjective **1** *a strenuous climb* ARDUOUS, difficult, hard, tough, taxing, demanding, exacting, exhausting, tiring, grueling, back-breaking; *informal* killing; *archaic* toilsome. ANTONYM easy.

**2** *strenuous efforts* VIGOROUS, energetic, zealous, forceful, strong, spirited, intense, determined, resolute, tenacious, tireless, indefatigable, dogged; *formal* pertinacious. ANTONYM halfhearted.

**stress** noun **1** *he's under a lot of stress* STRAIN, pressure, (nervous) tension, worry, anxiety, trouble, difficulty; *informal* hassle.

**2** *laying greater stress on education* EMPHASIS, importance, weight.

**3** *the stress falls on the first syllable* EMPHASIS, accent, accentuation; beat; *Prosody* ictus.

**4** *the stress is uniform across the bar* PRESSURE, tension, strain.

▸ verb **1** *they stressed the need for reform* EMPHASIZE, draw attention to, underline, underscore, point up, place emphasis on, lay stress on, highlight, accentuate, press home. ANTONYM play down.

**2** *the last syllable is stressed* PLACE THE EMPHASIS ON, emphasize, place the accent on.

**3** *all the staff were stressed* OVERSTRETCH, overtax, push to the limit, pressure, make tense, worry, harass; *informal* hassle.

**stretch** verb **1** *this material stretches* BE ELASTIC, be stretchy, be tensile.

**2** *he stretched the elastic* PULL (OUT), draw out, extend, lengthen, elongate, expand.

**3** *stretch your weekend into a vacation* PROLONG, lengthen, make longer, extend, spin out. ANTONYM shorten.

**4** *my budget won't* ***stretch to*** *a new car* BE SUFFICIENT FOR, be enough for, cover; afford, have the money for.

**5** *the court case stretched their finances* PUT A STRAIN ON, overtax, overextend, drain, sap.

**6** *stretching the truth* BEND, strain, distort, exaggerate, embellish.

**7** *she* ***stretched out*** *her hand to him* REACH OUT, hold out, extend, outstretch, proffer; *literary* outreach. ANTONYM withdraw.

**8** *he stretched his arms* EXTEND, straighten (out).

**9** *she* ***stretched out*** *on the sofa* LIE DOWN, recline, lean back, be recumbent, sprawl, lounge, loll.

**10** *the desert stretches for miles* EXTEND, spread, continue.

▸ noun **1** *magnificent stretches of forest* EXPANSE, area, tract, belt, sweep, extent.

**2** *a four-hour stretch* PERIOD, time, spell, run, stint, session, shift.

**3** *informal* *a ten-year stretch* (PRISON) SENTENCE, (prison) term, stint, rap.

▸ adjective *stretch fabrics* STRETCHY, stretchable, elastic.

**strict** adjective **1** *a strict interpretation of the law* PRECISE, exact, literal, faithful, accurate, rigorous, careful, meticulous, pedantic. ANTONYMS loose, imprecise.

**2** *strict controls on spending* STRINGENT, rigorous, severe, harsh, hard, rigid, tough, ironclad. See note at SEVERE. ANTONYM liberal.

**3** *strict parents* STERN, severe, harsh, uncompromising, authoritarian, governessy, firm, austere. ANTONYM lenient.

**4** *this will be treated in strict confidence* ABSOLUTE, utter, complete, total.

**5** *a strict Roman Catholic* ORTHODOX, devout, conscientious. ANTONYMS moderate, liberal.

**stricture** noun **1** *the constant strictures of the nuns* CRITICISM, censure, condemnation, reproof, reproach, admonishment, animadversion. ANTONYM praise.

**2** *the strictures on Victorian women* CONSTRAINT, restriction, limitation, restraint, curb, impediment, barrier, obstacle. ANTONYM freedom.

**3** *an intestinal stricture* NARROWING, constriction.

**stride** verb *she came striding down the path* MARCH, pace, step.

▸ noun *long swinging strides* (LONG/LARGE) STEP, pace.

PHRASE: **take something in one's stride** *he seem to be taking the news in his stride* DEAL WITH EASILY, cope with easily, not bat an eyelid.

**strident** adjective *a strident voice interrupted the consultation* HARSH, raucous, rough, grating, rasping, jarring, loud, shrill, screeching, piercing, ear-piercing. See note at VOCIFEROUS. ANTONYM soft.

**strife** noun *these countries have been immersed in political strife for more than a hundred years* CONFLICT, friction, discord, disagreement, dissension, dispute, argument, quarreling, wrangling, bickering, controversy; ill/bad feeling, falling-out, bad blood, hostility, animosity. ANTONYM peace.

**strike** verb **1** *the teacher struck Mary* HIT, slap, smack, beat, thrash, spank, thump, punch, cuff; cane, lash, whip, club; *informal* clout, schmuck, wallop, belt, whack, thwack, bash, clobber, bop, cold-cock; *literary* smite.

**2** *he struck the gong* BANG, beat, hit; *informal* bash, wallop.

**3** *the car struck a tree* CRASH INTO, collide with, hit, run into, bump into, smash into, impact.

**4** *Jennifer struck the ball* HIT, drive, propel; *informal* clout, wallop, swipe.

**5** *he struck a match* IGNITE, light.

**6** *she was asleep when the killer struck* ATTACK, set upon someone, fall on someone, assault someone.

**7** *the disease is striking 3,000 people a year* AFFECT, afflict, attack, hit.

**8** *striking a balance* ACHIEVE, reach, arrive at, find, attain, establish.

**9** *we have struck a bargain* AGREE (ON), come to an agreement on, settle on; *informal* clinch.

**10** *he struck a heroic pose* ASSUME, adopt, take on/up, affect, cop.

**11** *they have struck oil* DISCOVER, find, come upon, hit.

**12** *a thought struck her* OCCUR TO, come to (mind), dawn on one, hit, spring to mind, enter one's head.

**13** *you strike me as intelligent* SEEM TO, appear to, come across to, give the impression to.

**14** *drivers are striking* TAKE INDUSTRIAL ACTION, go on strike, down tools, walk out, hit the bricks.

**15** *the commodore struck his flag* LOWER, take down, bring down.

**16** *we should strike south* GO, make one's way, head, forge.

▸ noun **1** *a 48-hour strike* INDUSTRIAL ACTION, walkout, job action, stoppage.

**2** *a military strike* (AIR) ATTACK, assault, bombing, raid.

**3** *a gold strike* FIND, discovery.

PHRASES: **strike out** *strike out the old phone number* DELETE, cross out, erase, rub out.

**strike up 1** *the band struck up another tune* BEGIN TO PLAY, start playing.

**2** *we struck up a friendship* BEGIN, start, commence, embark on, establish.

**striking** adjective **1** *Lizzie bears a striking resemblance to her sister* NOTICEABLE, obvious, conspicuous, evident, marked, notable, unmistakable, strong; remarkable, extraordinary, incredible, amazing, astounding, astonishing, staggering. See note at NOTICEABLE. ANTONYM unremarkable.

**2** *Kenya's striking landscape* IMPRESSIVE, imposing, grand, splendid, magnificent, spectacular, breathtaking, superb, marvelous, wonderful, stunning, staggering, sensational, dramatic. ANTONYM unimpressive.

**3** *what a striking young couple* STUNNING, attractive, good-looking, beautiful, glamorous, gorgeous, prepossessing, ravishing, handsome, pretty; *informal* knockout, drop-dead gorgeous; *archaic* fair, comely. ANTONYMS unremarkable, unattractive.

**string** noun **1** *a knotted piece of string* TWINE, cord, yarn, thread, strand.

**2** *a string of convenience stores* CHAIN, group, firm, company.

**3** *a string of convictions* SERIES, succession, chain, sequence, run, streak.

**4** *a string of wagons* LINE, train, procession, queue, file, column, convoy, cavalcade.

**5** *a string of pearls* STRAND, rope, necklace.

**6** *a guaranteed loan with no strings* CONDITION, qualification, provision, proviso, caveat, stipulation, rider, prerequisite, limitation, limit, constraint, restriction; *informal* catch.

▸ verb **1** *lights were strung across the promenade* HANG, suspend, sling, stretch, run; thread, loop, festoon.

**2** *beads strung on a silver chain* THREAD, loop, link.

PHRASES: **string along 1** *must your sister always string along?* GO ALONG, come too, accompany someone, join someone.

**2** *I think Daisy is just stringing poor Dave along* MISLEAD, deceive, take advantage of, dupe, hoax, fool, make a fool of, play with, toy with, dally with, trifle with; *informal* lead up the garden path, take for a ride.

**string out 1** *stringing out a story* SPIN OUT, drag out, lengthen.

**2** *airfields strung out along the Gulf* SPREAD OUT, space out, distribute, scatter.

**string up** *informal Dawes and his boys went after Lucius, threatening to string him up* HANG, lynch, gibbet.

**stringent** adjective *stringent regulations* STRICT, firm, rigid, rigorous, severe, harsh, tough, tight, exacting, demanding, inflexible, hard and fast.

**stringy** adjective **1** *stringy hair* STRAGGLY, lank, thin.

**2** *a stringy brunette* LANKY, gangling, gangly, rangy, wiry, bony, skinny, scrawny, thin, spare, gaunt.

**3** *stringy meat* FIBROUS, gristly, sinewy, chewy, tough, leathery.

**strip**[1] verb **1** *he stripped and got into bed* UNDRESS, strip off, take one's clothes off, unclothe, disrobe, strip naked. ANTONYM dress.

**2** ***stripping off** paint* PEEL (OFF), remove, take off, scrape (off), rub off, clean off.

**3** *they **stripped her of** her doctorate* TAKE AWAY FROM SOMEONE, dispossess someone of, deprive someone of, confiscate, divest someone of, relieve someone of.

**4** *they **stripped down** my engine* DISMANTLE, disassemble, take to bits/pieces, take apart. ANTONYM assemble.

**5** *the house had been stripped* EMPTY, clear, clean out, plunder, rob, burgle, burglarize, loot, pillage, ransack, despoil, sack.

**strip**[2] noun *a strip of paper* (NARROW) PIECE, bit, band, belt, ribbon, slip, shred.

**stripe** noun *it's a red jacket with a white stripe down each sleeve* LINE, band, strip, belt, bar, streak, vein, flash, blaze; *technical* stria, striation.

**striped** adjective *a tropical plant with large striped leaves* barred, lined, banded, stripy; streaky, variegated; *technical* striated.

**stripling** noun *it's natural for these striplings to get into a bit of trouble now and then* YOUTH, adolescent, youngster, boy, schoolboy, lad, teenager, juvenile, minor, young man; *informal* kid, young 'un, whippersnapper, shaver.

**strive** verb **1** *I shall strive to be virtuous* TRY (HARD), attempt, endeavor, aim, venture, make an effort, exert oneself, do one's best, do all one can, do one's utmost, labor, work; *informal* go all out, give it one's best shot, pull out all the stops; *formal* essay.

**2** *scholars must strive against bias* STRUGGLE, fight, battle, combat; campaign, crusade.

**stroke** noun **1** *five strokes of the ax* BLOW, hit, thump, punch, slap, smack, cuff, knock; *informal* wallop, clout, whack, thwack, bash, swipe; *archaic* smite.

**2** *she hit the green in three strokes* SHOT, hit, strike.

**3** *light upward strokes* MOVEMENT, action, motion.

**4** *a stroke of genius* FEAT, accomplishment, achievement, master stroke.

**5** *broad brush strokes* MARK, line.

**6** *the budget was full of bold strokes* DETAIL, touch, point.

**7** *he suffered a stroke* THROMBOSIS, seizure; *Medicine* ictus.

▸ verb *she stroked the cat* CARESS, fondle, pat, pet, touch, rub, massage, soothe.

**stroll** verb *they strolled along the river* SAUNTER, amble, wander, meander, ramble, promenade, walk, go for a walk, stretch one's legs, get some air; *informal* mosey; *formal* perambulate.

▸ noun *a stroll in the park* SAUNTER, amble, wander, walk, turn, promenade; *informal* mosey; *dated* constitutional; *formal* perambulation.

**strong** adjective **1** *Ben is a strong lad* POWERFUL, muscular, brawny, powerfully built, strapping, sturdy, burly, meaty, robust, athletic, tough, rugged, lusty, strong as an ox/horse; *informal* beefy, hunky, husky; *dated* stalwart. ANTONYMS weak, puny.

**2** *a strong character* FORCEFUL, determined, spirited, self-assertive, tough, tenacious, indomitable, formidable, redoubtable, strong-minded; *informal* gutsy, feisty. ANTONYM weak.

**3** *a strong fortress* SECURE, well-built, indestructible, well fortified, well protected, impregnable, solid.

**4** *strong cotton bags* DURABLE, hardwearing, heavy-duty, industrial-strength, tough, sturdy, well-made, long-lasting. ANTONYMS weak, flimsy.

**5** *the current is very strong* FORCEFUL, powerful, vigorous, fierce, intense. ANTONYM gentle.

**6** *a strong interest in literature* KEEN, eager, passionate, fervent.

**7** *strong feelings* INTENSE, forceful, passionate, ardent, fervent, fervid, deep-seated; *literary* perfervid.

**8** *a strong supporter* KEEN, eager, enthusiastic, dedicated, staunch, loyal, steadfast.

**9** *strong arguments* COMPELLING, cogent, forceful, powerful, potent, weighty, convincing, sound, valid, well-founded, persuasive, influential. ANTONYMS weak, unconvincing.

**10** *a need for strong action* FIRM, forceful, drastic, extreme.

**11** *she bore a very strong resemblance to Vera* MARKED, striking, noticeable, pronounced, distinct, definite, unmistakable, notable. ANTONYM slight.

**12** *a strong voice* LOUD, powerful, forceful, resonant, sonorous, rich, deep, booming. ANTONYMS weak, quiet.

**13** *strong language* BAD, foul, obscene, profane.

**14** *a strong blue color* INTENSE, deep, rich, bright, brilliant, vivid. ANTONYM pale.

**15** *strong lights* BRIGHT, brilliant, dazzling, glaring.

**16** *strong black coffee* CONCENTRATED, undiluted, potent. ANTONYMS weak, mild.

**17** *strong cheese* HIGHLY FLAVORED, flavorful, piquant, tangy, spicy. ANTONYM mild.

**18** *strong drink* ALCOHOLIC, intoxicating, hard, stiff; *formal* spirituous. ANTONYMS soft, nonalcoholic.

**strongbox** noun *there was nothing in the strongbox but some worthless old stocks* SAFE, safety deposit box, cash/money box.

**stronghold** noun **1** *the enemy stronghold* FORTRESS, fort, castle, citadel, garrison.

**2** *a liberal stronghold* BASTION, center, hotbed, safe seat.

**strong-minded** adjective *a strong-minded social reformer* DETERMINED, firm, resolute, purposeful, strong-willed, uncompromising, unbending, forceful, persistent, tenacious, dogged; *informal* gutsy, spunky.

**strong-willed** adjective *you strong-willed recruits had better prepare yourselves to get broken* DETERMINED, resolute, stubborn, obstinate, willful, headstrong, strong-minded, self-willed, unbending, unyielding, intransigent, intractable, obdurate, recalcitrant; *formal* refractory.

**structure** noun **1** *a vast Gothic structure* BUILDING, edifice, construction, erection, pile.

**2** *the structure of local government* CONSTRUCTION, form, formation, shape, composition, anatomy, makeup, constitution; organization, system, arrangement, design, framework, configuration, pattern.

▸ verb *the program is structured around periods of home study* ARRANGE, organize, design, shape, construct, build, put together.

**struggle** verb **1** *they struggled to do better* STRIVE, try hard, endeavor, make every effort, do one's best/utmost, bend over backwards, put oneself out; *informal* go all out, give it one's best shot; *formal* essay.

**2** *James struggled with the intruders* FIGHT, grapple, wrestle, scuffle, brawl, spar; *informal* scrap.

**3** *the teams struggled to be first* COMPETE, contend, vie, fight, battle, jockey.

**4** *she struggled over the dunes* SCRAMBLE, flounder, stumble, fight/battle one's way, labor.

▸ noun **1** *the struggle for justice* ENDEAVOR, striving, effort, exertion, labor; campaign, battle, crusade, drive, push.

**2** *they were arrested without a struggle* FIGHT, scuffle, brawl, tussle, wrestling bout, skirmish, fracas, melee; breach of the peace; *informal* scrap.

**3** *many perished in the struggle* CONFLICT, fight, battle, confrontation, clash, skirmish; hostilities, fighting, war, warfare, campaign.

**4** *a struggle within the leadership* CONTEST, competition, fight, clash; rivalry, friction, feuding, conflict, tug-of-war, turf war.

**5** *life has been a struggle for me* EFFORT, trial, trouble, stress, strain, battle; *informal* grind, hassle.

**strut** verb *he strutted around his vast office* SWAGGER, swank, parade, stride, sweep, sashay.

**stub** noun **1** *a cigarette stub* BUTT, (tail) end.

**2** *a ticket stub* COUNTERFOIL, ticket slip, tab.

**3** *a stub of pencil* STUMP, remnant, (tail) end.

**stubborn** adjective **1** *you're too stubborn to admit it* OBSTINATE, headstrong, willful, strong-willed, pigheaded, obdurate, difficult, contrary, perverse, recalcitrant, inflexible, iron-willed, uncompromising, unbending; *informal* stiff-necked, bloody-minded, balky; *formal* pertinacious, refractory, contumacious. ANTONYM compliant.

**2** *stubborn stains* INDELIBLE, permanent, persistent, tenacious, resistant.

THE RIGHT WORD **stubborn, dogged, intractable, obdurate, obstinate, pertinacious**

If you're the kind of person who takes a stand and then refuses to back down, your friends might say you have a **stubborn** disposition, a word that implies an innate resistance to any attempt to change one's purpose, course, or opinion. People who are *stubborn* by nature exhibit this kind of behavior in most situations, but they might be **obstinate** in a particular instance (*a stubborn child, he was obstinate in his refusal to eat vegetables*). *Obstinate* implies sticking persistently to an opinion, purpose, or course of action, especially in the face of persuasion or attack. While *obstinate* is usually a negative term, **dogged** can be either positive or negative, implying both tenacious, often sullen, persistence (*dogged pursuit of a college degree, even though he knew he would end up in the family business*) and great determination (*dogged loyalty to a cause*). **Obdurate** usually connotes a stubborn resistance marked by harshness and lack of feeling (*obdurate in ignoring their pleas*), while **intractable** means stubborn in a headstrong sense and difficult for others to control or manage (*intractable pain*). No matter how stubborn you are, you probably don't want to be called **pertinacious**, which implies persistence to the point of being annoying or unreasonable (*a pertinacious panhandler*).

**stubby** adjective *a small stubby man with glasses* DUMPY, stocky, chunky, chubby, squat; short, stumpy, dwarfish; *informal* vertically challenged. ANTONYMS slender, tall.

**stuck** adjective **1** *a message was stuck to his screen* FIXED, fastened, attached, glued, pinned.

**2** *the gate was stuck* IMMOVABLE, stuck fast, jammed.

**3** *if you get stuck, leave a blank* BAFFLED, beaten, at a loss, at one's wits' end; *informal* stumped, bogged down, flummoxed, fazed, bamboozled. PHRASES: **stuck on** *informal no one knew that Kit was stuck on his brother's wife* INFATUATED WITH, besotted with, smitten with, (head over heels) in love with, obsessed with; *informal* crazy about, mad about, wild about, carrying a torch for.
**stuck with** *she's always getting stuck with the neighbors' kids* LUMBERED WITH, left with, made responsible for.

**stuck-up** adjective *informal*. See CONCEITED.

**student** noun **1** *a college student* SCHOLAR, undergraduate, graduate, grad student, postdoctoral fellow; freshman, sophomore, junior, senior.

**2** *high school student* PUPIL, schoolchild, schoolboy, schoolgirl, scholar.

**3** *a nursing student* TRAINEE, apprentice, probationer, recruit, intern, novice; *informal* rookie.

**studied** adjective *the words were said with studied politeness* DELIBERATE, careful, considered, conscious, calculated, intentional; affected, forced, strained, artificial.

**studio** noun *the artist's studio* WORKSHOP, workroom, atelier, workspace.

**studious** adjective **1** *a studious nature* SCHOLARLY, academic, bookish, intellectual, erudite, learned, donnish.

**2** *studious attention* DILIGENT, careful, attentive, assiduous, painstaking, thorough, meticulous.

**3** *his studious absence from public view* DELIBERATE, willful, conscious, intentional.

**study** noun **1** *two years of study* LEARNING, education, schooling, academic work, scholarship, tuition, research; *informal* cramming.

**2** *a study of global warming* INVESTIGATION, inquiry, research, examination, analysis, review, survey.

**3** *Father was in his study* OFFICE, workroom, studio.

**4** *a critical study* ESSAY, article, work, review, paper, dissertation, disquisition.

▸ verb **1** *Anne studied hard* WORK, review; *informal* cram, hit the books.

**2** *he studied electronics* LEARN, read, be taught.

**3** *Thomas was studying child development* INVESTIGATE, inquire into, research, look into, examine, analyze, explore, review, appraise, conduct a survey of.

**4** *she studied her friend thoughtfully* SCRUTINIZE, examine, inspect, consider, regard, look at, eye, observe, watch, survey; *informal* check out, eyeball.

PHRASE: **in a brown study** *you'll often catch a student in a brown study on a warm spring day like today* LOST IN THOUGHT, in a reverie, musing, ruminating, cogitating, dreaming, daydreaming; *informal* miles away.

**stuff** noun **1** *suede is tough stuff* MATERIAL, fabric, cloth, textile; matter, substance.

**2** *first-aid stuff* ITEMS, articles, objects, goods, equipment; *informal* things, bits and pieces, odds and ends.

**3** *all my stuff is in the suitcase* BELONGINGS, (personal) possessions, effects, goods (and chattels), paraphernalia; *informal* gear, things.

**4** *he knows his stuff* FACTS, information, data, subject.

▸ verb **1** *stuffing pillows* FILL, pack, pad, upholster.

**2** *Robyn stuffed her clothes into a bag* SHOVE, thrust, push, ram, cram, squeeze, force, jam, pack, pile, stick.

**3** *informal they* ***stuffed themselves with*** *chocolate* FILL ONESELF WITH, gorge oneself with/on, overindulge oneself with; gobble, devour, wolf; *informal* pig out on, make a pig of oneself with/on.

**4** *my nose was* ***stuffed up*** BLOCK (UP), congest, obstruct.

**stuffing** noun **1** *the stuffing is coming out of the armchair* PADDING, wadding, filling, upholstery, packing, filler.

**2** *sage and onion stuffing* dressing, filling, forcemeat, salpicon.

PHRASE: **knock the stuffing out of** *informal news of Pam's engagement knocked the stuffing out of Bob* DEVASTATE, shatter, crush, shock.

**stuffy** adjective **1** *a stuffy atmosphere* AIRLESS, close, musty, stale. ANTONYM airy.

**2** *a stuffy young man* STAID, sedate, sober, prim, priggish, straitlaced, conformist, conservative, old-fashioned, governessy; *informal* square, straight, starchy, fuddy-duddy. ANTONYMS laid-back, modern.

**3** *a stuffy nose* BLOCKED, stuffed up, congested. ANTONYM clear.

**stultify** verb **1** *social welfare was stultified by international trade regulations* HAMPER, impede, thwart, frustrate, foil, suppress, smother.

**2** *he stultifies her with too much gentleness* BORE, make bored, dull, numb, benumb, stupefy.

**stumble** verb **1** *she stumbled and fell heavily* TRIP (OVER/UP), lose one's balance, lose/miss one's footing, slip.

**2** *he stumbled back home* STAGGER, totter, teeter, dodder, blunder, hobble, move clumsily.

**3** *she stumbled through her speech* STAMMER, stutter, hesitate, falter, speak haltingly; *informal* fluff/flub one's lines.

PHRASE: **stumble across/on** *I stumbled across these old photographs in the attic* COME ACROSS/UPON, chance on, happen on, bump into, light on; discover, find, unearth, uncover; *informal* dig up.

**stump** verb *we could never stump Mr. Marlowe with our riddles* BAFFLE, perplex, puzzle, confuse, confound, defeat, put at a loss; *informal* flummox, throw, floor, discombobulate.

**stun** verb **1** *a glancing blow stunned Gary* DAZE, stupefy, knock unconscious, knock out, lay out.

**2** *she was stunned by the news* ASTOUND, amaze, astonish, dumbfound, stupefy, stagger, shock, take aback; *informal* flabbergast, bowl over.

**stunning** adjective **1** *a stunning win* REMARKABLE, extraordinary, staggering, incredible, outstanding, amazing, astonishing, marvelous, phenomenal, splendid; *informal* fabulous, fantastic, tremendous, jaw-dropping. ANTONYM ordinary.

**2** *she was looking stunning.* See BEAUTIFUL.

**stunt**[1] verb *a disease that stunts growth* INHIBIT, impede, hamper, hinder, restrict, retard, slow, curb, check. ANTONYM encourage.

**stunt**[2] noun *acrobatic stunts* FEAT, exploit, trick.

**stunted** adjective *a stunted geranium* SMALL, undersize(d), diminutive.

**stupefaction** noun **1** *alcoholic stupefaction* OBLIVION, obliviousness, unconsciousness, insensibility, stupor, daze.

**2** *Don shook his head in stupefaction* BEWILDERMENT, confusion, perplexity, wonder, amazement, astonishment.

**stupefy** verb **1** *the blow had stupefied her* STUN, daze, knock unconscious, knock out, lay out.

**2** *they were stupefied from the wine* DRUG, sedate, tranquilize, intoxicate, inebriate; *informal* dope.

**3** *the cost stupefied us* SHOCK, stun, astound, dumbfound, overwhelm, stagger, amaze, astonish, take aback, take someone's breath away; *informal* flabbergast, bowl over, floor.

**stupendous** adjective **1** *stupendous achievements* AMAZING, astounding, astonishing, extraordinary, remarkable, phenomenal, staggering, breathtaking; *informal* fantastic, mind-boggling, awesome; *literary* wondrous. ANTONYM ordinary.

**2** *a building of stupendous size* COLOSSAL, immense, vast, gigantic, massive, mammoth, huge, enormous. ANTONYM minute.

**stupid** adjective **1** *they're rather stupid* UNINTELLIGENT, ignorant, dense, foolish, dull-witted, slow, simpleminded, vacuous, vapid, idiotic, imbecilic, imbecile, obtuse, doltish; *informal* thick, dim, dimwitted, dumb, dopey, dozy, moronic, cretinous, pea-brained, halfwitted, soft in the head, brain-dead, boneheaded, thickheaded, wooden-headed, mutton-headed, daft. ANTONYM intelligent.

**2** *that was a really stupid thing to do* FOOLISH, silly, unintelligent, idiotic, scatterbrained, nonsensical, senseless, unthinking, ill-advised, ill-considered, unwise, injudicious; inane, absurd, ludicrous, ridiculous, laughable, risible, fatuous, asinine, mad, insane, lunatic; *informal* crazy, dopey, cracked, half-baked, dimwitted, cockeyed, harebrained, lamebrained, nutty, batty, cuckoo, loony, loopy. ANTONYM sensible.

**3** *he drank himself stupid* INTO A STUPOR, into a daze, into oblivion; stupefied, dazed, unconscious. ANTONYM alert.

THE RIGHT WORD **stupid, asinine, dense, dull, dumb, obtuse, slow, unintelligent**

If you want to impugn someone's intelligence, the options are almost limitless. You can call the person **stupid**, a term that implies a sluggish, slow-witted lack of intelligence. **Asinine** is a harsher word, implying asslike or foolish behavior rather than slow-wittedness (*a woman her age looked asinine in a miniskirt*). Calling someone **dumb** is risky, because it is not only an informal word (*you dumb bunny!*), but because it also means mute and is associated with the offensive expression "deaf and dumb," used to describe people who cannot hear or speak. **Dense** implies an inability to understand even simple facts or instructions (*too dense to get the joke*), while **dull** suggests a sluggishness of mind unrelieved by any hint of quickness, brightness, or liveliness (*a dull stare*). **Slow** also implies a lack of quickness in comprehension or reaction and is often used as a euphemistic substitute for *stupid* (*he was a little slow intellectually*). **Obtuse** is a more formal word for slow-wittedness, but with a strong undercurrent of scorn (*it almost seemed as though he were being deliberately obtuse*). You can't go wrong with a word like **unintelligent**, which is probably the most objective term for low mental ability and the least likely to provoke an angry response (*unintelligent answers to the teacher's questions*).

**stupidity** noun **1** *he cursed their stupidity* LACK OF INTELLIGENCE, foolishness, denseness, brainlessness, ignorance, dull-wittedness, slow-wittedness, doltishness, slowness; *informal* thickness, dimness, dopiness.

**2** *the stupidity of the question* FOOLISHNESS, folly, silliness, idiocy, brainlessness, senselessness, injudiciousness, ineptitude, inaneness, inanity, absurdity, ludicrousness, ridiculousness, fatuousness, madness, insanity, lunacy; *informal* craziness.

**stupor** noun *they left him slumped in a drunken stupor* DAZE, state of unconsciousness, torpor, insensibility, oblivion.

**sturdy** adjective **1** *a sturdy lad* STRAPPING, well-built, muscular, athletic, strong, hefty, brawny, powerful, solid, burly, rugged, robust, tough, hardy, lusty; *informal* husky, beefy, meaty; *dated* stalwart; *literary* thewy. ANTONYMS puny, frail.

**2** *sturdy boots* ROBUST, strong, strongly made, well built, solid, stout, tough, resilient, durable, long-lasting, hardwearing. ANTONYMS weak, flimsy.

**3** *sturdy resistance* VIGOROUS, strong, stalwart, firm, determined, resolute, staunch, steadfast. ANTONYM weak.

**stutter** verb *he stuttered over a word* STAMMER, stumble, falter.

▸ noun *a bad stutter* STAMMER, speech impediment, speech defect.

**style** noun **1** *differing styles of management* MANNER, way, technique, method, methodology, approach, system, mode, form, modus operandi; *informal* MO.

**2** *a nondirective style of counseling* TYPE, kind, variety, sort, genre, school, brand, pattern, model.

**3** *wearing clothes with style* FLAIR, stylishness, elegance, grace, gracefulness, poise, polish, suaveness, sophistication, urbanity, chic, dash, panache, élan; *informal* class, pizzazz.

**4** *Laura traveled in style* COMFORT, luxury, elegance, opulence, lavishness.

**5** *modern styles* FASHION, trend, vogue, mode.

▸ verb **1** *sportswear styled by Karl* DESIGN, fashion, tailor.

**2** *men who were styled "knight"* CALL, name, title, entitle, dub, designate, term, label, tag, nickname; *formal* denominate.

**stylish** adjective *a stylish raincoat* FASHIONABLE, modish, voguish, modern, up to date; smart, sophisticated, elegant, chic, dapper, dashing; *informal* trendy, natty, classy, nifty, ritzy, snazzy, fly, kicky, tony, spiffy. ANTONYM unfashionable.

**suave** adjective *your clothes should show what a suave man you are* CHARMING, sophisticated, debonair, urbane, polished, refined, poised, self-possessed, dignified, civilized, gentlemanly, gallant; smooth, polite, well-mannered, civil, courteous, affable, tactful, diplomatic. See note at URBANE. ANTONYM unsophisticated.

**subconscious** adjective *subconscious desires* UNCONSCIOUS, latent, suppressed, repressed, subliminal, dormant, underlying, innermost; *informal* bottled up.

▸ noun *the creative powers of the subconscious* (UNCONSCIOUS) MIND, imagination, inner(most) self, psyche.

**subdue** verb **1** *he subdued all his enemies* CONQUER, defeat, vanquish, overcome, overwhelm, crush, quash, beat, trounce, subjugate, suppress, bring someone to their knees; *informal* lick, thrash, hammer.

**2** *she could not subdue her longing* CURB, restrain, hold back, constrain, contain, repress, suppress, stifle, smother, keep in check, rein in, control, master, quell; *informal* keep a/the lid on.

**subdued** adjective **1** *Lewis's subdued air* SOMBER, low-spirited, downcast, sad, dejected, depressed, gloomy, despondent, dispirited, disheartened, forlorn, woebegone; withdrawn, preoccupied; *informal* down in/at the mouth, down in the dumps, in the doldrums, in a blue funk. ANTONYMS cheerful, lively.

**2** *subdued voices* HUSHED, muted, quiet, low, soft, faint, muffled, indistinct. ANTONYM loud.

**3** *subdued light* DIM, muted, softened, soft, lowered, subtle. ANTONYM bright.

**subject** noun **1** *the subject of this chapter* THEME, subject matter, topic, issue, question, concern, point; substance, essence, gist.

**2** *popular university subjects* BRANCH OF STUDY, discipline, field.

**3** *six subjects did the trials* PARTICIPANT, volunteer; *informal* guinea pig.

**4** *Her Majesty's subjects* CITIZEN, national; taxpayer, voter.

**5** *a loyal subject* LIEGE, liegeman, vassal, henchman, follower.

▸ verb *they were* ***subjected to*** *violence* PUT THROUGH, treat with, expose to.

PHRASE: **subject to** **1** *it is subject to budgetary approval* CONDITIONAL ON, contingent on, dependent on.

**2** *horses are subject to coughs* SUSCEPTIBLE TO, liable to, prone to, vulnerable to, predisposed to, at risk of.

**3** *we are all subject to the law* BOUND BY, constrained by, accountable to.

**subjective** adjective *a subjective analysis* PERSONAL, individual, emotional, instinctive, intuitive. ANTONYM objective.

**subjugate** verb *the Normans had subjugated most of Ireland's Gaelic population* CONQUER, vanquish, defeat, crush, quash, bring someone to their knees, enslave, subdue, suppress. ANTONYM liberate.

**sublime** adjective **1** *sublime music* EXALTED, elevated, noble, lofty, awe-inspiring, majestic, magnificent, glorious, superb, wonderful, marvelous, splendid; *informal* fantastic, fabulous, terrific, heavenly, divine, out of this world.

**2** *the sublime confidence of youth* SUPREME, total, complete, utter, consummate.

**submerge** verb **1** *the U-boat submerged* GO UNDER WATER, dive, sink. ANTONYM surface.

**2** *submerge the bowl in water* IMMERSE, plunge, sink.

**3** *the farmland was submerged* FLOOD, inundate, deluge, swamp.

**4** *she was submerged in work* OVERWHELM, inundate, deluge, swamp, bury, engulf, snow under.

**submission** noun **1** *submission to authority* YIELDING, capitulation, acceptance, consent, compliance. ANTONYM defiance.

**2** *Tim raised his hands in submission* SURRENDER, capitulation, resignation, defeat.

**3** *he wanted her total submission* COMPLIANCE, submissiveness, acquiescence, passivity, obedience, docility, deference, subservience, servility, subjection. ANTONYMS defiance, resistance.

**4** *a report for submission to the Board* PRESENTATION, presenting, proffering, tendering, proposal, proposing.

**5** *his original submission* PROPOSAL, suggestion, proposition, recommendation.

**6** *the judge rejected her submission* ARGUMENT, assertion, contention, statement, claim, allegation.

**submissive** adjective *she's far from being a submissive woman* COMPLIANT, yielding, acquiescent, unassertive, passive, obedient, biddable, dutiful, docile, pliant; *informal* under someone's thumb.

**submit** verb **1** *she submitted under duress* GIVE IN/WAY, yield, back down, cave in, capitulate; surrender, knuckle under. ANTONYMS resist, defy.

**2** *he refused to* ***submit to*** *their authority* BE GOVERNED BY, abide by, be regulated by, comply with, accept, adhere to, be subject to, agree to, consent to, conform to. ANTONYMS resist, defy.

**3** *we submitted an unopposed bid* PUT FORWARD, present, offer, proffer, tender, propose, suggest, float; put in, send in, register. ANTONYM withdraw.

**4** *they submitted that the judgment was inappropriate* CONTEND, assert, argue, state, claim, posit, postulate.

**subnormal** adjective *subnormal trade activity* BELOW AVERAGE, below normal, low, poor, subpar.

**subordinate** adjective **1** *subordinate staff* LOWER-RANKING, junior, lower, supporting. ANTONYM senior.

**2** *a subordinate rule* SECONDARY, lesser, minor, subsidiary, subservient, ancillary, auxiliary, peripheral, marginal; supplementary, accessory. ANTONYM central.

▸ noun *the manager and his subordinates* JUNIOR, assistant, second (in command), number two, right-hand man/woman, deputy, aide, underling, minion; *informal* sidekick, second banana. ANTONYM superior.

**sub rosa** adverb *formal the committee operates sub rosa* IN SECRET, secretly, in private, privately, behind closed doors, in camera. ANTONYM openly.

**subscribe** verb **1** *we* ***subscribe to*** *several news magazines* PAY A SUBSCRIPTION FOR, have a subscription to, take, buy regularly.

**2** *I subscribe to the ballet* HAVE SEASON TICKETS, have a subscription.

**3** *I can't **subscribe to** that theory* AGREE WITH, accept, believe in, endorse, back, support, champion, buy into; *formal* accede to.

**4** *formal he subscribed the document* SIGN, countersign, initial, autograph, witness.

**subsequent** adjective *the subsequent months* FOLLOWING, ensuing, succeeding, later, future, coming, to come, next. ANTONYM previous.

PHRASE: **subsequent to** *tell us what happened in the hours subsequent to the shooting* FOLLOWING, after, at the close/end of.

**subservient** adjective **1** *subservient women* SUBMISSIVE, deferential, compliant, obedient, dutiful, biddable, docile, passive, unassertive, subdued, downtrodden; *informal* under someone's thumb. See note at OBSEQUIOUS. ANTONYM independent.

**2** *individual rights are subservient to the interests of the state* SUBORDINATE, secondary, subsidiary, peripheral, ancillary, auxiliary, less important. ANTONYM superior.

**subside** verb **1** *wait until the storm subsides* ABATE, let up, quiet down, calm, slacken (off), ease (up), relent, die down, recede, lessen, soften, diminish, decline, dwindle, weaken, fade, wane, ebb. ANTONYM intensify.

**2** *the floodwaters have subsided* RECEDE, ebb, fall, go down, get lower, abate. ANTONYM rise.

**3** *the volcano is gradually subsiding* SINK, settle, cave in, collapse, crumple, give way.

**subsidiary** adjective *a subsidiary company* SUBORDINATE, secondary, ancillary, auxiliary, subservient, supplementary, peripheral. ANTONYM principal.

▸ noun *two major subsidiaries* SUBORDINATE COMPANY, branch, branch plant, division, subdivision, derivative, subset, offshoot.

**subsidize** verb *they have agreed to subsidize the after-school program* GIVE MONEY TO, pay a subsidy to, contribute to, invest in, sponsor, support, fund, finance, underwrite; *informal* shell out for, fork out for, cough up for; bankroll.

**subsidy** noun *the theater receives a subsidy of 1.7 million dollars a year* GRANT, allowance, endowment, contribution, donation, bursary, handout; backing, support, sponsorship, finance, funding; *formal* benefaction.

**subsist** verb **1** *he subsists on his pension* SURVIVE, live, stay alive, exist, eke out an existence; support oneself, manage, get along/by, make (both) ends meet.

**2** *the tenant's rights of occupation subsist* CONTINUE, last, persist, endure, prevail, carry on, remain.

**subsistence** noun **1** *they depend on fish for subsistence* SURVIVAL, existence, living, life, sustenance, nourishment.

**2** *the money needed for his subsistence* MAINTENANCE, keep, upkeep, livelihood, room and board, board, nourishment, food.

**substance** noun **1** *an organic substance* MATERIAL, matter, stuff.

**2** *ghostly figures with no substance* SOLIDITY, body, corporeality; density, mass, weight, shape, structure.

**3** *none of the objections has any substance* MEANINGFULNESS, significance, importance, import, validity, foundation; *formal* moment.

**4** *the substance of the tale is very thin* CONTENT, subject matter, theme, message, essence.

**5** *the Huskies are a team of substance* CHARACTER, backbone, mettle.

**6** *independent men of substance* WEALTH, fortune, riches, affluence, prosperity, money, means.

**substantial** adjective **1** *substantial beings* REAL, true, actual; physical, solid, material, concrete, corporeal.

**2** *substantial progress had been made* CONSIDERABLE, real, significant, important, notable, major, valuable, useful.

**3** *substantial damages* SIZABLE, considerable, significant, large, ample, appreciable, goodly.

**4** *substantial oak beams* STURDY, solid, stout, thick, strong, well built, durable, long-lasting, hardwearing.

**5** *rugby players with substantial builds* HEFTY, stout, sturdy, large, solid, bulky, burly, well built, portly.

**6** *substantial landowners* SUCCESSFUL, profitable, prosperous, wealthy, affluent, moneyed, well-to-do, rich; *informal* loaded, stinking rich.

**7** *substantial agreement* FUNDAMENTAL, essential, basic.

**substantially** adverb **1** *the cost has fallen substantially* CONSIDERABLY, significantly, to a great/large extent, greatly, markedly, appreciably. ANTONYM slightly.

**2** *the draft was substantially accepted* LARGELY, for the most part, by and large, on the whole, in the main, mainly, in essence, basically, fundamentally, to all intents and purposes.

**substantiate** verb *can you substantiate your allegations?* PROVE, show to be true, give substance to, support, uphold, bear out, justify, vindicate, validate, corroborate, verify, authenticate, confirm, endorse, give credence to. ANTONYM disprove.

**substitute** noun *substitutes for permanent employees* REPLACEMENT, deputy, relief, proxy, reserve, surrogate, cover, stand-in, locum (tenens), understudy; *informal* sub, pinch-hitter.

▸ adjective *a substitute teacher* ACTING, supply, replacement, deputy, relief, reserve, surrogate, stand-in, temporary, caretaker, interim, provisional. ANTONYM permanent.

▸ verb **1** *cottage cheese can be substituted for yogurt* EXCHANGE, replace, use instead of, use as an alternative to, use in place of, swap.

**2** *the senate was empowered to substitute for the president* DEPUTIZE, act as deputy, act as a substitute, stand in, cover; replace, relieve, take over from; *informal* sub, fill someone's boots/shoes.

**subterfuge** noun **1** *the use of subterfuge by journalists* TRICKERY, intrigue, deviousness, deceit, deception, dishonesty, cheating, duplicity, guile, cunning, craftiness, chicanery, pretense, fraud, fraudulence.

**2** *a disreputable subterfuge* TRICK, hoax, ruse, wile, ploy, stratagem, artifice, dodge, bluff, pretense, deception, fraud, blind, smokescreen; *informal* con, scam.

**subtle** adjective **1** *subtle colors* UNDERSTATED, muted, subdued; delicate, faint, pale, soft, indistinct.

**2** *subtle distinctions* FINE, fine-drawn, nice, hair-splitting.

**3** *a subtle mind* ASTUTE, keen, quick, fine, acute, sharp, shrewd, perceptive, discerning, discriminating, penetrating, sagacious, wise, clever, intelligent.

**4** *a subtle plan* INGENIOUS, clever, cunning, crafty, wily, artful, devious.

**subtlety** noun **1** *the subtlety of the flavor* DELICACY, delicateness, subtleness; understatedness, mutedness, softness.

**2** *classification is fraught with subtlety* FINENESS, subtleness, niceness, nicety, nuance.

**3** *the subtlety of the human mind* ASTUTENESS, keenness, acuteness, sharpness, canniness, shrewdness, perceptiveness, discernment, discrimination, percipience, perspicacity, wisdom, cleverness, intelligence.

**4** *the subtlety of their tactics* INGENUITY, cleverness, skillfulness, adroitness, cunning, guile, craftiness, wiliness, artfulness, deviousness.

**subtract** verb *we'll subtract the cost of shipping* TAKE AWAY/OFF, deduct, debit, dock; *informal* knock off, minus. ANTONYM add.

**suburb** noun *a fast-growing suburb just west of Albany | you'll need a car if you move to the suburbs* RESIDENTIAL AREA, dormitory area, bedroom community, commutershed, commuter belt, exurb; **(suburbs)** suburbia, the burbs.

**suburban** adjective **1** *a suburban area* RESIDENTIAL, commuter, dormitory.

**2** *her drab suburban existence* DULL, boring, uninteresting, conventional, ordinary, commonplace, unremarkable, unexceptional; provincial, unsophisticated, parochial, bourgeois, middle-class, white-picket-fence.

**subversive** adjective *subversive activities* DISRUPTIVE, troublemaking, inflammatory, insurrectionary; seditious, revolutionary, rebellious, rebel, renegade, dissident.

▸ noun *a dangerous subversive* TROUBLEMAKER, dissident, agitator, revolutionary, renegade, rebel.

**subvert** verb **1** *a plot to subvert the state* DESTABILIZE, unsettle, overthrow, overturn; bring down, topple, depose, oust; disrupt, wreak havoc on, sabotage, ruin, undermine, weaken, damage.

**2** *attempts to subvert Soviet youth* CORRUPT, pervert, deprave, contaminate, poison, embitter.

**subway** noun *taking the subway to Yankee Stadium* underground (rail system), metro, train; *Brit. informal* tube.

**succeed** verb **1** *Darwin succeeded where others had failed* TRIUMPH, achieve success, be successful, do well, flourish, thrive; *informal* make it, make the grade, make a name for oneself. ANTONYM fail.

**2** *the plan succeeded* BE SUCCESSFUL, turn out well, work (out), be effective; *informal* come off, pay off. ANTONYMS fail, flop.

**3** *upon Taylor's death, his vice president, Millard Fillmore, succeeded him* REPLACE, take the place of, take over from, follow, supersede; *informal* step into someone's shoes. ANTONYM precede.

**4** *he* ***succeeded to*** *the throne* INHERIT, assume, acquire, attain; *formal* accede to. ANTONYMS renounce, abdicate.

**5** *embarrassment was succeeded by fear* FOLLOW, come after, follow after. ANTONYM precede.

**succeeding** adjective *strands of DNA are reproduced through succeeding generations* SUBSEQUENT, successive, following, ensuing, later, future, coming.

**success** noun **1** *the success of the scheme* FAVORABLE OUTCOME, successfulness, successful result, triumph. ANTONYM failure.

**2** *the trappings of success* PROSPERITY, affluence, wealth, riches, opulence. ANTONYM poverty.

**3** *a box-office success* TRIUMPH, best seller, blockbuster, sellout; *informal* (smash) hit, megahit, winner. ANTONYMS failure, flop.

**4** *an overnight success* STAR, superstar, celebrity, big name, household name; *informal* celeb, megastar. ANTONYM nobody.

**successful** adjective **1** *what can we do to make this campaign successful?* VICTORIOUS, triumphant; fortunate, lucky; effective; *informal* socko, in like Flynn.

**2** *a successful designer* PROSPEROUS, affluent, wealthy, rich; doing well, famous, eminent, top.

**3** *successful companies* FLOURISHING, thriving, booming, buoyant, doing well, profitable, moneymaking, lucrative.

**USAGE NOTE in like Flynn**

This phrase, meaning "assured of success," first became widespread during World War II as an allusion to the actor Errol Flynn's legendary prowess in seducing women. (In 1942, Flynn was prosecuted for the statutory rape of two teenage girls—and was acquitted.) Today the phrase has generally lost any sexual connotation—e.g.: • "By these standards, Gore should be in like Flynn." (*Commercial Appeal* [Memphis]; Feb. 13, 2000.) • "Based on the results of our Triangle Census, you'll be in like Flynn." (*News & Observer* [Raleigh]; Mar. 27, 2000.) • "Follow the formula, and you're in like Flynn." (*BusinessWeek,* Aug. 7, 2000.) The phrase has been the subject of wordplay and consequent confusion. In 1966 appeared *Our Man Flint,* a film starring James Coburn and spoofing the James Bond series; the following year, its sequel, *In Like Flint,* was released. The popularity of these films—especially the latter with its pun on *in like Flynn*—sparked lingering confusion about what the proper phrase should be. Thus, during coverage of the 2000 Republican Convention, Mark Shields, a PBS commentator, said that George W. Bush might be "in like Flynn, or in like

Flint—whatever we say" (PBS Convention Coverage, Aug. 3, 2000). This confusion had already surfaced in print—e.g.: "Yep, with my peacoat, I was in like Flint [read *Flynn*], I thought, able to hubbub with the highbrows or hang with the homeboys." (*News & Observer* [Raleigh]; Jan. 11, 1998) (in this example, *hubbub* should probably be *hobnob*). "If you want to be 'in like Flint [read *Flynn*],' there has to be a measure of exclusivity." Larry Lipson, (*Daily News* [L.A.]; Aug. 27, 1999.) "Finder praises Gawande as a quick learner. If he failed to incorporate advice initially, says Finder, 'the second time he was in like Flint [read *Flynn*].' (*Boston Globe,* Nov. 10, 1999.) Although this usage occasionally appears in tongue-in-cheek references to Flint, Michigan, and to flint as stone, it shouldn't appear in sentences such as those just quoted. Errol Flynn is reported to have resented the phrase, but it will always be linked etymologically to him. —*BG*

---

**succession** noun **1** *a succession of exciting events* SEQUENCE, series, progression, chain, cycle, round, string, train, line, run, flow, stream.

**2** *his succession to the throne* ACCESSION, elevation, assumption. PHRASE: **in succession** *the next four houses went up in succession, in a matter of just a few months* ONE AFTER THE OTHER, in a row, consecutively, successively, in sequence.

**successor** noun *Mary was the rightful successor to the English throne* HEIR (APPARENT), inheritor, next-in-line. ANTONYM predecessor.

**succinct** adjective *what is your succinct appraisal of our situation?* CONCISE, short (and sweet), brief, compact, condensed, crisp, laconic, terse, to the point, pithy, epigrammatic, synoptic, gnomic; *formal* compendious. See note at TERSE. ANTONYM verbose.

**succor** noun *providing succor in times of need* AID, help, a helping hand, assistance; comfort, ease, relief, support, TLC.

▸ verb *the prisoners were succored* HELP, aid, bring aid to, give/render assistance to, assist, lend a (helping) hand to; minister to, care for, comfort, bring relief to, support, take care of, look after, attend to.

**succulent** adjective *succulent black grapes* JUICY, moist, luscious, soft, tender; choice, mouthwatering, appetizing, tasty, delicious; *informal* scrumptious. ANTONYM dry.

**succumb** verb **1** *she succumbed to temptation* YIELD, give in/way, submit, surrender, capitulate, cave in. ANTONYM resist.

**2** *he* ***succumbed to*** *the disease* DIE FROM/OF; catch, develop, contract, fall ill with; *informal* come down with. ANTONYM withstand.

**suck** verb **1** *they sucked orange juice through straws* SIP, sup, siphon, slurp, draw, drink.

**2** *Fran* ***sucked in*** *a deep breath* DRAW, breathe, gasp; inhale, inspire.

**3** *they got* ***sucked into*** *petty crime* IMPLICATE IN, involve in, draw into; *informal* mix up in.

**4** *informal the weather sucks* BE VERY BAD, be awful, be terrible, be dreadful, be horrible; *informal* stink. PHRASE: **suck up to** *informal they suck up to him, hanging on to his every word* GROVEL TO, creep to, toady to, be obsequious to, be sycophantic to, kowtow to, bow and scrape to, truckle to; fawn on; *informal* lick someone's boots, be all over, brown-nose.

**suckle** verb *the lioness sucked her cubs* BREAST-FEED, feed, nurse.

**sudden** adjective *a sudden change in plans* UNEXPECTED, unforeseen, unanticipated, unlooked-for; immediate, instantaneous, instant, precipitous, precipitate, abrupt, rapid, swift, quick.

**suddenly** adverb *suddenly the scene shifts to the year 1954* IMMEDIATELY, instantaneously, instantly, straightaway, all of a sudden, all at once, promptly, abruptly, swiftly; unexpectedly, without warning, without notice, out of the blue; *informal* straight off, in a flash, like a shot. ANTONYM gradually.

**suds** plural noun *a detergent low in suds* LATHER, foam, froth, bubbles, soap.

**sue** verb **1** *he sued the contractor for negligence* TAKE LEGAL ACTION AGAINST, take to court, bring an action/suit against, proceed against, prefer/bring charges against.

**2** ***suing for*** *peace* APPEAL FOR, petition for, ask for, solicit (for), request, seek.

**suffer** verb **1** *I hate to see him suffer* HURT, ache, be in pain, feel pain; be in distress, be upset, be miserable.

**2** *she* ***suffers from*** *asthma* BE AFFLICTED BY/WITH, be affected by, be troubled with, have.

**3** *Brazil suffered a humiliating defeat* UNDERGO, experience, be subjected to, receive, endure, face.

**4** *the school's reputation has suffered* BE IMPAIRED, be damaged, deteriorate, decline.

**5** *archaic he was obliged to suffer her intimate proximity* TOLERATE, put up with, bear, stand, abide, endure; *formal* brook.

**6** *archaic my conscience would not suffer me to accept* ALLOW, permit, let, give leave to, sanction.

**suffering** noun *the suffering of these refugees defied description* HARDSHIP, distress, misery, wretchedness, adversity, tribulation; pain, agony, anguish, trauma, torment, torture, hurt, affliction, sadness, unhappiness, sorrow, grief, woe, angst, heartache, heartbreak, stress; *literary* dolor.

**suffice** verb *a simple yes or no will suffice* BE ENOUGH, be sufficient, be adequate, do, serve, meet requirements, satisfy demands, answer/meet one's needs, answer/serve the purpose; *informal* fit/fill the bill.

**sufficient** adjective *there was sufficient evidence to justify a charge* ENOUGH, plenty of, ample; adequate, satisfactory. ANTONYM inadequate.

**suffocate** verb *it appears that the victim has been suffocated with a bed pillow* SMOTHER, asphyxiate, stifle; choke, strangle.

**suffrage** noun *suffrage for women is not yet a universal condition* FRANCHISE, right to vote, the vote, enfranchisement, ballot.

**suffuse** verb *the room was suffused with soft, pink light* PERMEATE, spread over, spread throughout, cover, bathe, pervade, wash, saturate, imbue.

**sugary** adjective **1** *sugary snacks* SWEET, sugared, sugar-coated, candied. ANTONYM sour.

**2** *sugary romance* SENTIMENTAL, mawkish, cloying, sickly (sweet), saccharine, syrupy; *informal* sappy, schmaltzy, slushy, mushy, sloppy, cutesy, corny.

**suggest** verb **1** *Ruth suggested a vacation* PROPOSE, put forward, recommend, advocate; advise, urge, encourage, counsel.

**2** *evidence suggests that teenagers are responsive to price increases* INDICATE, lead to the belief, argue, demonstrate, show; *formal* evince.

**3** *sources suggest that the prime minister will change his cabinet* HINT, insinuate, imply, intimate, indicate; *informal* put ideas into one's head.

**4** *the seduction scenes suggest his guilt and her loneliness* CONVEY, express, communicate, impart, imply, intimate, smack of, evoke, conjure up; *formal* evince.

**suggestion** noun **1** *some suggestions for tackling this problem* PROPOSAL, proposition, motion, submission, recommendation; advice, counsel, hint, tip, clue, idea, trial balloon.

**2** *the suggestion of a smirk* HINT, trace, touch, suspicion, dash, soupçon, tinge; ghost, semblance, shadow, glimmer, impression, whisper.

**3** *there is no suggestion that he was party to a conspiracy* INSINUATION, hint, implication, intimation, innuendo, imputation.

**suggestive** adjective **1** *suggestive remarks* INDECENT, indelicate, improper, unseemly, sexual, sexy, smutty, dirty, ribald, bawdy, racy, risqué, lewd, vulgar, coarse, salacious.

**2** *an odor suggestive of a brewery* REDOLENT, evocative, reminiscent; characteristic, indicative, typical.

**suit** noun **1** *a pinstriped suit* OUTFIT, set of clothes, ensemble.

**2** *informal suits in faraway boardrooms* BUSINESSMAN, BUSINESSWOMAN, executive, bureaucrat, administrator, manager.

**3** *a medical malpractice suit* LEGAL ACTION, lawsuit, (court) case, action, (legal/judicial) proceedings, litigation.

**4** *they spurned his suit* ENTREATY, request, plea, appeal, petition, supplication, application.

**5** *dated his suit came to nothing* COURTSHIP, wooing, attentions.

▸ verb **1** *blue really suits you* BECOME, work for, look good on, look attractive on, flatter.

**2** *savings plans to suit all customers* BE CONVENIENT FOR, be acceptable to, be suitable for, meet the requirements of; *informal* fit the bill for.

**3** *recipes ideally suited to students* MAKE APPROPRIATE TO/FOR, tailor, fashion, adjust, adapt, modify, fit, gear, design.

**suitable** adjective **1** *suitable employment opportunities* ACCEPTABLE, satisfactory, fitting; *informal* right up someone's alley. ANTONYM inappropriate.

**2** *a drama suitable for all ages* APPROPRIATE, fitting, fit, acceptable, right. ANTONYM inappropriate.

**3** *music **suitable for** a lively dinner party* APPROPRIATE TO/FOR, suited to, befitting, in keeping with; *informal* cut out for. ANTONYM unfit.

**4** *they treated him with suitable respect* PROPER, seemly, decent, appropriate, fitting, befitting, correct, due.

**5** *suitable candidates* WELL QUALIFIED, well-suited, appropriate, fitting. ANTONYM unfit.

**suitcase** noun *the old brown suitcase had survived two ocean voyages and more train and bus trips than she could ever calculate* TRAVEL BAG, traveling bag, case, valise, overnight case, portmanteau, vanity case, garment bag, backpack, duffel bag; **(suitcases)** luggage, baggage.

**suite** noun *we were quite comfortable in our suite at the Biltmore* APARTMENT, rooms, set of rooms; *Brit.* flat.

**suitor** noun *Rosie routinely rejected the suitors who sought her affections, until Laurence came along* ADMIRER, wooer, boyfriend, sweetheart, lover, beau; *literary* swain.

**sulk** verb *Dad was sulking* MOPE, brood, be sullen, have a long face, be in a bad mood, be in a huff, be grumpy, be moody; *informal* be down in the dumps.

▸ noun *she sank into a deep sulk* (BAD) MOOD, fit of ill humor, fit of pique, pet, huff, (bad) temper; the sulks, the blues.

**sulky** adjective *sulky faces* SULLEN, surly, moping, pouting, moody, sour, piqued, petulant, brooding, broody, disgruntled, ill-humored, in a bad mood, out of humor, fed up, put out; bad-tempered, grumpy, huffy, glum, gloomy, morose; *informal* grouchy, crabby, cranky. ANTONYM cheerful.

**sullen** adjective *a bunch of sullen, spoiled brats* SURLY, sulky, pouting, sour, morose, resentful, glum, moody, gloomy, grumpy, bad-tempered, ill-tempered; unresponsive, uncommunicative, farouche, uncivil, unfriendly. See note at GLUM. ANTONYM cheerful.

**sultry** adjective **1** *a sultry day* HUMID, close, airless, stifling, oppressive, muggy, sticky, sweltering, tropical, heavy; hot; *informal* boiling, roasting. ANTONYM refreshing.

**2** *a sultry film star* PASSIONATE, attractive, sensual, sexy, voluptuous, erotic, seductive.

**sum** noun **1** *a large sum of money* AMOUNT, quantity, volume.

**2** *just a small sum* AMOUNT OF MONEY, price, charge, fee, cost.

**3** *the sum of two numbers* (SUM) TOTAL, grand total, tally, aggregate, summation. ANTONYM difference.

**4** *the sum of his wisdom* ENTIRETY, totality, total, whole, aggregate, summation, beginning and end.

**5** *we did sums at school* (ARITHMETICAL) PROBLEM, calculation; **(sums)** arithmetic, mathematics, math, computation. PHRASE: **sum up 1** *one reviewer summed it up as "compelling"*

EVALUATE, assess, appraise, rate, gauge, judge, deem, adjudge, estimate, form an opinion of.

**2** *he summed up his reasons* SUMMARIZE, make/give a summary of, précis, outline, give an outline of, recapitulate, review; *informal* recap.

**summarily** adverb *accused of treason, he was summarily executed* IMMEDIATELY, instantly, right away, straightaway, at once, on the spot, promptly; speedily, swiftly, rapidly, without delay; arbitrarily, without formality, peremptorily, without due process.

**summarize** verb *he summarized these ideas in a single phrase* SUM UP, abridge, condense, encapsulate, outline, give an outline of, put in a nutshell, recapitulate, give/make a summary of, give a synopsis of, précis, synopsize, give the gist of; *informal* recap.

**summary** noun *a summary of the findings* SYNOPSIS, précis, résumé, abstract, digest, encapsulation, abbreviated version; outline, sketch, rundown, review, summing-up, overview, recapitulation, epitome; *informal* recap.

▸ adjective **1** *a summary financial statement* ABRIDGED, abbreviated, shortened, condensed, concise, capsule, succinct, short, brief, pithy; *formal* compendious.

**2** *summary execution* IMMEDIATE, instant, instantaneous, on-the-spot; speedy, swift, rapid, without delay, sudden; arbitrary, without formality, peremptory.

**summit** noun **1** *the summit of Mount Washington* (MOUNTAIN) TOP, peak, crest, crown, apex, tip, cap, hilltop. ANTONYMS base, bottom.

**2** *the summits of world literature* ACME, peak, height, pinnacle, zenith, climax, high point/spot, highlight, crowning glory, capstone, best, finest, nonpareil. ANTONYM nadir.

**3** *the next superpower summit* MEETING, negotiation, conference, talk(s), discussion.

**summon** verb **1** *the embassy summoned her* SEND FOR, call for, request the presence of; ask, invite.

**2** *they were summoned as witnesses* SERVE WITH A SUMMONS, summons, subpoena, cite, serve with a citation.

**3** *the chair summoned a meeting* CONVENE, assemble, order, call, announce; *formal* convoke.

**4** *he summoned the courage to move closer* MUSTER, gather, collect, rally, screw up.

**5** ***summoning up*** *their memories of home* CALL TO MIND, call up/forth, conjure up, evoke, recall, revive, arouse, kindle, awaken, spark (off).

**6** *they summoned spirits of the dead* CONJURE UP, call up, invoke.

**summons** noun **1** *the court issued a summons* WRIT, subpoena, warrant, court order; *Law* citation.

**2** *a summons to go to the boss's office* ORDER, directive, command, instruction, demand, decree, injunction, edict, call, request.

▸ verb *he was summonsed to appear in court* SERVE WITH A SUMMONS, summon, subpoena, cite, serve with a citation.

**sumptuous** adjective *sumptuous brocade drapes* LAVISH, luxurious, opulent, magnificent, resplendent, gorgeous, splendid, grand, lavishly appointed, palatial, rich; *informal* plush, ritzy. ANTONYM plain.

**sunder** verb *literary his father and he were sundered by religious differences* DIVIDE, split, cleave, separate, rend, sever, rive.

**sundry** adjective *wings, radiators, and sundry other items were sent out to various workshops* VARIOUS, varied, miscellaneous, assorted, mixed, diverse, diversified; several, numerous, many, manifold, multifarious, multitudinous; *literary* divers.

**sunken** adjective **1** *sunken eyes* HOLLOWED, hollow, depressed, deep-set, concave, indented.

**2** *a sunken garden* BELOW GROUND LEVEL, at a lower level, lowered.

**sunless** adjective **1** *a cold sunless day* DARK, overcast, cloudy, gray, gloomy, dismal, murky, dull.

**2** *the sunless side of the house* SHADY, shadowy, dark, gloomy.

**sunlight** noun *avoid sunlight when taking this medication* DAYLIGHT, (the) sun, sunshine, the sun's rays, (natural) light.

**sunny** adjective **1** *a sunny day* BRIGHT, sunshiny, sunlit, clear, fine, cloudless, without a cloud in the sky, sun-drenched. ANTONYM cloudy.

**2** *a sunny disposition* CHEERFUL, cheery, happy, lighthearted, bright, merry, joyful, bubbly, blithe, jolly, jovial, animated, buoyant, ebullient, upbeat, vivacious. ANTONYM miserable.

**3** *look on the sunny side* OPTIMISTIC, rosy, bright, hopeful, auspicious, favorable. ANTONYMS sad, pessimistic.

**sunrise** noun *the infantry advanced at sunrise* DAWN, crack of dawn, daybreak, break of day, sun-up, first light, (early) morning, cock crow; *literary* aurora.

**sunset** noun *the blossoms close at sunset* SUNDOWN, nightfall, close of day, twilight, dusk, evening; *literary* eventide, gloaming.

**sunshine** noun **1** *relaxing in the sunshine* SUNLIGHT, sun, sun's rays, daylight, (natural) light.

**2** *his smile was all sunshine* HAPPINESS, cheerfulness, cheer, gladness, laughter, gaiety, merriment, joy, joyfulness, blitheness, joviality, jollity.

**superb** adjective **1** *he scored a superb goal* EXCELLENT, superlative, first-rate, first-class, outstanding, remarkable, marvelous, magnificent, wonderful, splendid, admirable, noteworthy, impressive, fine, exquisite, exceptional, glorious; *informal* great, fantastic, fabulous, terrific, super, awesome, ace, cool, A1, brilliant, killer. ANTONYMS poor, inferior.

**2** *a superb diamond necklace* MAGNIFICENT, majestic, splendid, grand, impressive, imposing, awe-inspiring, breathtaking; gorgeous. ANTONYMS poor, inferior.

**supercilious** adjective *a supercilious young clerk* ARROGANT, haughty, conceited, disdainful, overbearing, pompous, condescending, superior, patronizing, imperious, proud, snobbish, snobby, smug, scornful, sneering; *informal* hoity-toity, high and mighty, uppity, snooty, stuck-up, snotty, snot-nosed, jumped up, too big for one's britches.

**superficial** adjective **1** *superficial burns* SURFACE, exterior, external, outer, outside, slight. ANTONYMS deep, thorough.

**2** *a superficial friendship* SHALLOW, surface, skin-deep, artificial; empty, hollow, meaningless. ANTONYMS deep, significant.

**3** *a superficial investigation* CURSORY, perfunctory, casual, sketchy, desultory, token, slapdash, offhand, rushed, hasty, hurried. ANTONYMS comprehensive, thorough.

**4** *a superficial resemblance* APPARENT, seeming, outward, ostensible, cosmetic, slight. ANTONYMS genuine, authentic.

**5** *a superficial analysis* TRIVIAL, lightweight, two-dimensional. ANTONYM profound.

**6** *a superficial person* FACILE, shallow, flippant, empty-headed, trivial, frivolous, silly, inane. ANTONYMS deep, thoughtful.

THE RIGHT WORD **superficial, cursory, hasty, slapdash, shallow**

No one wants to be accused of being **superficial** or **shallow**, two adjectives that literally indicate a lack of depth (*a superficial wound; a shallow grave*). *Superficial* suggests too much concern with the surface or obvious aspects of something, and it is considered a derogatory term because it connotes a personality that is not genuine or sincere. *Shallow* is even more derogatory because it implies not only a refusal to explore something deeply but an inability to feel, sympathize, or understand. It is unlikely that a *shallow* person, in other words, will ever have more than superficial relationships with his or her peers. **Cursory**, which may or may not be a derogatory term, suggests a lack of thoroughness or attention to detail (*a cursory glance at the newspaper*), while **hasty** emphasizes a refusal or inability to spend the necessary time on something (*a hasty review of the facts*). If you are **slapdash** in your approach, it means that you are both careless and hasty (*a slapdash job of cleaning up*).

**superfluous** adjective **1** *superfluous material* SURPLUS (TO REQUIREMENTS), nonessential, redundant, unneeded, excess, extra, (to) spare, remaining, unused, left over, in excess, waste. ANTONYMS necessary, essential.

**2** *words seemed superfluous* UNNECESSARY, unneeded, redundant, uncalled for, unwarranted. ANTONYM necessary.

**superhuman** adjective **1** *a superhuman effort* EXTRAORDINARY, phenomenal, prodigious, stupendous, exceptional, remarkable, immense, heroic. ANTONYMS average, unremarkable.

**2** *superhuman power* DIVINE, holy, heavenly.

**3** *superhuman beings* SUPERNATURAL, preternatural, paranormal, otherworldly, unearthly; *rare* extramundane. ANTONYM mundane.

**superintend** verb *he was expected to superintend a grand banquet* SUPERVISE, oversee, be in charge of, be in control of, preside over, direct, administer, manage, run, be responsible for.

**superintendent** noun **1** *the superintendent of the museum* MANAGER, director, administrator, supervisor, overseer, controller, chief, head, governor; *informal* boss.

**2** *the building's superintendent* CARETAKER, janitor, warden, porter.

**superior** adjective **1** *a superior officer* HIGHER-RANKING, higher-level, senior, higher, higher-up. ANTONYMS junior, inferior.

**2** *the superior candidate* BETTER, more expert, more skillful; worthier, fitter, preferred. ANTONYMS worse, inferior.

**3** *superior workmanship* HIGH-QUALITY; finer better, higher-grade, of higher quality, greater; accomplished, expert. ANTONYMS low-quality, inferior.

**4** *superior chocolate* GOOD-QUALITY, high-quality, first-class, first-rate, top-quality; choice, select, exclusive, prime, prize, fine, excellent, best, choicest, finest. ANTONYMS low-quality, inferior.

**5** *a superior hotel* HIGH-CLASS, upper-class, select, exclusive, upscale, upmarket, five-star; *informal* classy, posh. ANTONYMS downmarket, inferior.

**6** *Hamish regarded her with superior amusement* CONDESCENDING, supercilious, patronizing, haughty, disdainful, pompous, snobbish; *informal* high and mighty, hoity-toity, snooty, stuck-up. ANTONYMS humble, modest.

▸ noun *my immediate superior* MANAGER, chief, supervisor, senior, controller, foreman; *informal* boss. ANTONYM subordinate.

**superiority** noun *the military superiority of the North* SUPREMACY, advantage, lead, dominance, primacy, ascendancy, eminence.

**superlative** adjective *a superlative photographer* EXCELLENT, magnificent, wonderful, marvelous, supreme, consummate, outstanding, remarkable, fine, choice, first-rate, first-class, premier, prime, unsurpassed, unequaled, unparalleled, unrivaled, preeminent; *informal* crack, ace, wicked, brilliant. ANTONYM mediocre.

**supernatural** adjective **1** *supernatural powers* PARANORMAL, psychic, magic, magical, occult, mystic, mystical, superhuman, supernormal; *rare* extramundane.

**2** *a supernatural being* GHOSTLY, phantom, spectral, otherworldly, unearthly, unnatural.

**supersede** verb *I was superseded by much younger men* REPLACE, take the place of, take over from, succeed; supplant, displace, oust, overthrow, remove, unseat; *informal* fill someone's shoes/boots. See note at REPLACE.

**supervise** verb **1** *he had to supervise the loading* OVERSEE, superintend, be in charge of, preside over, direct, manage, run, look after, be responsible for, govern, organize, handle, micromanage.

**2** *you may need to supervise the patient* WATCH, oversee, keep an eye on, observe, monitor, mind; invigilate.

**supervision** noun **1** *the supervision of the banking system* ADMINISTRATION, management, control, charge; superintendence, regulation, government, governance.

**2** *keep your children under supervision* OBSERVATION, guidance, custody, charge, safekeeping, care, guardianship; control.

**supervisor** noun *the supervisor of sector B* MANAGER, director, overseer, controller, superintendent, governor, chief, head; steward, foreman; *informal* boss.

**supine** adjective **1** *she lay supine on the sand* FLAT ON ONE'S BACK, face upward, facing upward, flat, horizontal, recumbent, stretched out. ANTONYM prostrate.

**2** *the supine media* WEAK, spineless, yielding, effete; docile, acquiescent, pliant, submissive, passive, inert, spiritless. ANTONYM strong.

**supper** noun *I had a bowl of chili for my supper* DINNER, evening meal, main meal; snack, mealtime; *formal* repast; *literary* refection.

**supplant** verb **1** *paved highways supplanted the network of dirt roads* REPLACE, supersede, displace, take over from, substitute for, override.

**2** *the man he supplanted as prime minister* OUST, usurp, overthrow, remove, topple, unseat, depose, dethrone; succeed, come after; *informal* fill someone's shoes/boots.

**supple** adjective **1** *her supple body* LITHE, limber, lissome, willowy, flexible, loose-limbed, agile, acrobatic, nimble, double-jointed. See note at FLEXIBLE. ANTONYM stiff.

**2** *supple leather* PLIANT, pliable, flexible, soft, bendable, workable, malleable, stretchy, elastic, springy, yielding, rubbery. ANTONYMS inflexible, rigid.

**supplement** noun **1** *a mouse is a keyboard supplement* ADDITION, accessory, supplementation, supplementary, extra, add-on, adjunct, appendage; *Computing* peripheral.

**2** *a single room supplement* SURCHARGE, addition, increase.

**3** *a supplement to the essay* APPENDIX, addendum, adhesion, end matter, tailpiece, codicil, postscript, addition, coda.

**4** *a special supplement with today's paper* PULLOUT, insert, extra section.

▸ verb *they supplemented their incomes by waiting tables on weekends* AUGMENT, increase, add to, boost, swell, amplify, enlarge, top up.

**supplementary** adjective **1** *supplementary income* ADDITIONAL, supplemental, extra, more, further; add-on, subsidiary, auxiliary, ancillary.

**2** *a supplementary index* APPENDED, attached, added, extra, accompanying.

**suppliant** noun *they were not mere suppliants* PETITIONER, supplicant, pleader, beggar, applicant.

▸ adjective *those around her were suppliant* PLEADING, begging, imploring, entreating, supplicating; on bended knee.

**supplicate** verb *he supplicated the governor for leniency* ENTREAT, beg, plead with, implore, petition, appeal to, call on, urge, enjoin, importune, sue, ask, request; *literary* beseech.

**supply** verb **1** *they supplied money to rebels* GIVE, contribute, provide, furnish, donate, bestow, grant, endow, impart; dispense, disburse, allocate, assign; *informal* fork out, shell out.

**2** *the lake supplies the city with water* PROVIDE, furnish, endow, serve, confer; equip, arm.

**3** *windmills supply their power needs* SATISFY, meet, fulfill, cater for.

▸ noun **1** *a limited supply of food* STOCK, store, reserve, reservoir, stockpile, hoard, cache; storehouse, repository; fund, mine, bank.

**2** *the supply of liquor* PROVISION, dissemination, distribution, serving.

**3** **(supplies)** *go to the grocery store for supplies* PROVISIONS, stores, stocks, rations, food, foodstuffs, eatables, produce, necessities; *informal* eats; *formal* comestibles.

**support** verb **1** *a roof supported by pillars* HOLD UP, bear, carry, prop up, keep up, brace, shore up, underpin, buttress, reinforce, undergird.

**2** *he struggled to support his family* PROVIDE FOR, maintain, sustain, keep, take care of, look after.

**3** *she supported him to the end* COMFORT, encourage, sustain, buoy up, hearten, fortify, console, solace, reassure; *informal* buck up. ANTONYMS neglect, abandon.

**4** *evidence to support the argument* SUBSTANTIATE, back up, bear out, corroborate, confirm, attest to, verify, prove, validate, authenticate, endorse, ratify, undergird. ANTONYMS contradict, undermine.

**5** *the money supports charitable projects* HELP, aid, assist; contribute to, back, subsidize, fund, finance; *informal* bankroll.

**6** *an independent candidate supported by locals* BACK, champion, help, assist, aid, abet, favor, encourage; vote for, stand behind, defend; sponsor, second, promote, endorse, sanction; *informal* throw one's weight behind. ANTONYM oppose.

**7** *they support human rights* ADVOCATE, promote, champion, back, espouse, be in favor of, recommend, defend, subscribe to.

▸ noun **1** *bridge supports* PILLAR, post, prop, upright, crutch, plinth, brace, buttress; base, substructure, foundation, underpinning.

**2** *she pays support for her ex-husband* MAINTENANCE, keep, sustenance, subsistence; alimony.

**3** *I was lucky to have their support* ENCOURAGEMENT, friendship, strength, consolation, solace, succor, relief.

**4** *he was a great support* COMFORT, help, assistance, tower of strength, prop, mainstay.

**5** *support for community services* CONTRIBUTIONS, backing, donations, money, subsidy, funding, funds, finance, capital.

**6** *they voiced their support for him* BACKING, help, assistance, aid, endorsement, approval; votes, patronage.

**7** *a surge in support for decentralization* ADVOCACY, backing, promotion, championship, espousal, defense, recommendation.

**supporter** noun **1** *supporters of gun control* ADVOCATE, backer, adherent, promoter, champion, defender, upholder, crusader, proponent, campaigner, apologist; *informal* cheerleader.

**2** *Republican supporters* BACKER, helper, adherent, follower, ally, voter, disciple; member.

**3** *the charity relies on its supporters* CONTRIBUTOR, donor, benefactor, sponsor, backer, patron, well-wisher.

**4** *the team's supporters* FAN, follower, enthusiast, devotee, admirer; *informal* buff, addict, groupie.

**supportive** adjective **1** *a supportive teacher* ENCOURAGING, caring, sympathetic, reassuring, understanding, concerned, helpful, kind, kindly; *informal* boosterish

**2** *we are supportive of the proposal* IN FAVOR OF, favorable to, pro, on the side of, sympathetic to, well-disposed to, receptive to.

**suppose** verb **1** *I suppose he's used to this* ASSUME, presume, expect, dare say, take it (as read); believe, think, fancy, suspect, sense, trust; guess, surmise, reckon, conjecture, deduce, infer, gather; *formal* opine.

**2** *suppose you had a spacecraft* ASSUME, imagine, (let's) say; hypothesize, theorize, speculate.

**3** *the theory supposes rational players* REQUIRE, presuppose, imply, assume; call for, need.

**supposed** adjective **1** *the supposed phenomena* APPARENT, ostensible, seeming, alleged, putative, reputed, rumored, claimed, purported; professed, declared, assumed, presumed.

**2** *I'm supposed to meet him at 8:30* MEANT, intended, expected; required, obliged.

**supposition** noun *her supposition is based on previous results* BELIEF, surmise, idea, notion, suspicion, conjecture, speculation, inference, theory, hypothesis, postulation, guess, feeling, hunch, assumption, presumption.

**suppress** verb **1** *they could suppress the rebellion* SUBDUE, repress, crush, quell, quash, squash, stamp out; defeat, conquer, overpower, put down, crack down on; end, stop, terminate, halt. ANTONYMS incite, encourage.

**2** *she suppressed her irritation* CONCEAL, restrain, stifle, smother, bottle up, hold back, control, check, curb, contain, bridle, inhibit, keep a rein on, put a lid on. ANTONYM express.

**3** *the report was suppressed* CENSOR, keep secret, conceal, hide, hush up, gag, withhold, cover up, stifle; ban, proscribe, outlaw; sweep under the carpet. ANTONYMS disclose, publicize.

**suppurate** verb *the lesions are suppurating* FESTER, form pus, discharge, run, weep, become septic.

**supremacy** noun *the supremacy of oppressive leadership anywhere in the world is bad for everyone in the world* ASCENDANCY, predominance, primacy, dominion, hegemony, authority, mastery, control, power, rule, sovereignty, influence; dominance, superiority, advantage, the upper hand, the whip hand, the edge; distinction, greatness.

**supreme** adjective **1** *the supreme commander* HIGHEST RANKING, chief, head, top, foremost, principal, superior, premier, first, prime; greatest, dominant, predominant, preeminent. ANTONYMS subordinate, inferior.

**2** *a supreme achievement* EXTRAORDINARY, remarkable, incredible, phenomenal, rare, exceptional, outstanding, great, incomparable, unparalleled, peerless. ANTONYM minimum.

**3** *the supreme sacrifice* ULTIMATE, final, last; utmost, extreme, greatest, highest. ANTONYM insignificant.

**sure** adjective **1** *I am sure that they didn't know* CERTAIN, positive, convinced, confident, definite, assured, satisfied, persuaded; unhesitating, unwavering, unshakable. ANTONYMS uncertain, doubtful.

**2** *someone was sure to be blamed* BOUND, likely, destined, fated. ANTONYM unlikely.

**3** *a sure winner with the children* GUARANTEED, unfailing, infallible, unerring, assured, certain, inevitable; *informal* surefire. ANTONYMS uncertain, unlikely.

**4** *he entered in the sure knowledge that he would win* UNQUESTIONABLE, indisputable, irrefutable, incontrovertible, undeniable, indubitable, undoubted, absolute, categorical, true, certain; obvious, evident, plain, clear, conclusive, definite.

**5** *a sure sign that he's worried* RELIABLE, dependable, trustworthy, unfailing, infallible, certain, unambiguous, true, foolproof, established, effective; *informal* sure-fire; *formal* efficacious.

**6** *the sure hand of the soloist* FIRM, steady, stable, secure, confident, steadfast, unfaltering, unwavering.

▸ exclamation *"Can I come too?" "Sure."* YES, all right, of course, indeed, certainly, absolutely, agreed; *informal* OK, yeah, yep, uh-huh, you bet, I'll say, sure thing.

PHRASES: **be sure to** *be sure to feed the cat* REMEMBER TO, don't forget to, see that you, mind that you, take care to, be certain to.

**for sure** *informal I'll be there for sure* DEFINITELY, surely, certainly, without doubt, without question, undoubtedly, indubitably, absolutely, undeniably, unmistakably.

**make sure** *make sure that all the doors are locked* CHECK, confirm, make certain, ensure, assure; verify, corroborate, substantiate.

**surely** adverb **1** *surely you remembered?* IT MUST BE THE CASE THAT, assuredly, without question.

**2** *I will surely die* CERTAINLY, for sure, definitely, undoubtedly, without doubt, doubtless, indubitably, unquestionably, without fail, inevitably.

**3** *slowly but surely manipulating the public* FIRMLY, steadily, confidently, assuredly, unhesitatingly, unfalteringly, unswervingly, determinedly, doggedly, tenaciously.

**surety** noun **1** *she's a surety for his obligations* GUARANTOR, sponsor.

**2** *a $10,000 surety* PLEDGE, collateral, guaranty, guarantee, bond, assurance, insurance, deposit; security, indemnity, indemnification; earnest.

**surface** noun **1** *the surface of the door* OUTSIDE, exterior; top, side; finish, veneer. ANTONYMS inside, interior.

**2** *the surface of police culture* OUTWARD APPEARANCE, facade.

**3** *a floured surface* counter, table.

▸ adjective *surface appearances* SUPERFICIAL, external, exterior, outward, ostensible, apparent, cosmetic, skin deep. ANTONYM underlying.

▸ verb **1** *a submarine surfaced* COME TO THE SURFACE, come up, rise. ANTONYM dive.

**2** *the idea first surfaced in the sixties* EMERGE, arise, appear, come to light, crop up, materialize, spring up.

**3** *informal she eventually surfaces for breakfast* GET UP, get out of bed, rise, wake, awaken, appear.

PHRASE: **on the surface** *it sounded plausible enough on the surface* AT FIRST GLANCE, to the casual eye, outwardly, to all appearances, apparently, ostensibly, superficially, externally.

**surfeit** noun *a surfeit of apples* EXCESS, surplus, abundance, oversupply, superabundance, superfluity, glut, avalanche, deluge; overdose; *informal* bellyful. ANTONYM lack.

▸ verb *we'll all be surfeited with food* SATIATE, sate, gorge, overfeed, overfill, glut, cram, stuff, overindulge, fill; saturate.

**surge** noun **1** *a surge of water* GUSH, rush, outpouring, stream, flow.

**2** *a surge in public support* INCREASE, rise, growth, upswing, upsurge, groundswell, escalation, leap.

**3** *a sudden surge of anger* RUSH, uprush, storm, torrent, blaze, outburst, eruption.

**4** *the surge of sea* SWELL, heaving, rolling, roll, swirling; tide.

▸ verb **1** *the water surged into people's homes* GUSH, rush, stream, flow, burst, pour, cascade, spill, overflow, sweep, roll.

**2** *the stock surged 47.63 points* INCREASE, rise, grow, escalate, leap.

**3** *the sea surged* SWELL, heave, rise, roll.

**surly** adjective *we've had complaints from customers about your surly disposition* SULLEN, sulky, moody, sour, unfriendly, unpleasant, scowling, unsmiling; bad-tempered, grumpy, crotchety, prickly, cantankerous, irascible, testy, short-tempered; abrupt, brusque, curt, gruff, churlish, ill-humored, crabby, cranky, uncivil; *informal* grouchy. See note at BRUSQUE. ANTONYM pleasant.

**surmise** verb *I can only surmise that they're plotting against me* GUESS, conjecture, suspect, deduce, infer, conclude, theorize, speculate, divine; assume, presume, suppose, understand, gather, feel, sense, think, believe, imagine, fancy, reckon; *formal* opine.

**surmount** verb **1** *his reputation surmounts language barriers* OVERCOME, conquer, prevail over, triumph over, beat, vanquish; clear, cross, pass over; resist, endure.

**2** *they surmounted the ridge* CLIMB OVER, top, ascend, scale, mount. ANTONYM descend.

**3** *the dome is surmounted by a statue* CAP, top, crown, finish.

**surname** noun *his real surname is MacNeil* FAMILY NAME, last name; patronymic.

**surpass** verb *Hanley has surpassed Rich in the polls* EXCEL, exceed, transcend; outdo, outshine, outstrip, outclass, overshadow, eclipse; improve on, top, trump, cap, beat, better, outperform; *informal* leapfrog.

**surplus** noun *a surplus of grain* EXCESS, surfeit, superabundance, superfluity, oversupply, glut, profusion, plethora; remainder, residue, remains, leftovers. ANTONYM dearth.

▸ adjective *surplus adhesive* EXCESS, leftover, unused, remaining, extra, additional, spare; superfluous, redundant, unwanted, unneeded, dispensable, expendable. ANTONYM insufficient.

**surprise** noun **1** *Kate looked at me in surprise* ASTONISHMENT, amazement, wonder, incredulity, bewilderment, stupefaction, disbelief.

**2** *the test came as a big surprise* SHOCK, bolt from the blue, bombshell, revelation, rude awakening, eye-opener, wake-up call; *informal* shocker.

▸ verb **1** *I was so surprised that I dropped it* ASTONISH, amaze, startle, astound, stun, stagger, shock; leave open-mouthed, take someone's breath away, dumbfound, stupefy, daze, take aback, shake up; *informal* bowl over, floor, flabbergast.

**2** *she surprised a burglar* TAKE BY SURPRISE, catch unawares, catch off guard, catch red-handed, catch in the act.

**surprised** adjective *Lenore's unexpected return surprised everyone* ASTONISHED, amazed, astounded, startled, stunned, staggered, nonplussed, shocked, taken aback, stupefied, dumbfounded, dumbstruck, speechless, thunderstruck, confounded, shaken up; *informal* bowled over, flabbergasted, floored, flummoxed.

**surprising** adjective *the results of the study were surprising* UNEXPECTED, unforeseen, unpredictable; astonishing, amazing, startling, astounding, staggering, incredible, extraordinary, breathtaking, remarkable; *informal* mind-blowing.

**surrender** verb **1** *the army surrendered* CAPITULATE, give in, give (oneself) up, give way, yield, concede (defeat), submit, climb down, back down, cave in, relent, crumble; lay down one's arms, raise the white flag, throw in the towel. ANTONYM resist.

**2** *they surrendered power to the workers* GIVE UP, relinquish, renounce, forgo, forswear; cede, abdicate, waive, forfeit, sacrifice; hand over, turn over, yield, resign, transfer, grant. See note at RELINQUISH. ANTONYM seize.

**3** *don't surrender all hope of changing things* ABANDON, give up, cast aside.

▸ noun *the ordeal ended with their peaceful surrender* CAPITULATION, submission, yielding, succumbing, acquiescence; fall, defeat, resignation.

**surreptitious** adjective *a surreptitious glance* SECRET, secretive, stealthy, clandestine, sneaky, sly, furtive; concealed, hidden, undercover, covert, veiled, cloak-and-dagger. See note at SECRET. ANTONYM blatant.

**surround** verb *we were surrounded by cops* ENCIRCLE, enclose, encompass, ring; fence in, hem in, confine, bound, circumscribe, cut off; besiege, trap. See note at CIRCUMSCRIBE.

**surrounding** adjective *tenants in the surrounding buildings were evacuated as a precaution* NEIGHBORING, nearby, near, neighborhood, local; adjoining, adjacent, bordering, abutting; encircling, encompassing.

**surroundings** plural noun *the surroundings were unfamiliar* ENVIRONMENT, setting, milieu, background, backdrop; conditions, circumstances, situation, context; vicinity, locality, habitat.

**surveillance** noun *we learned later that we had been under surveillance* OBSERVATION, scrutiny, watch, view, inspection, supervision; spying, espionage, infiltration, reconnaissance; *informal* bugging, wiretapping, recon.

**survey** verb **1** *he surveyed his work* LOOK AT, look over, observe, view, contemplate, regard, gaze at, stare at, eye; scrutinize, examine, inspect, scan, study, consider, review, take stock of; *informal* size up; *literary* behold.

**2** *they surveyed 4,000 drug users* INTERVIEW, question, canvass, poll, cross-examine, investigate, research, study, probe, sample.

▸ noun **1** *a survey of the current literature* STUDY, review, consideration, overview; scrutiny, examination, inspection, appraisal.

**2** *a survey of sexual behavior* POLL, review, investigation, inquiry, study, probe, questionnaire, census, research.

**survive** verb **1** *he survived by escaping through a hole* REMAIN ALIVE, live, sustain oneself, pull through, get through, hold on/out, make it, keep body and soul together.

**2** *the theater must survive* CONTINUE, remain, persist, endure, live on, persevere, abide, go on, carry on, be extant, exist.

**3** *he* ***was survived by*** *his sons* OUTLIVE, outlast; live longer than.

**susceptible** adjective **1** *susceptible children* IMPRESSIONABLE, credulous, gullible, innocent, ingenuous, naive, easily led; defenseless, vulnerable; persuadable, tractable; sensitive, responsive, thin-skinned. ANTONYMS skeptical, streetwise.

**2** *people* ***susceptible to*** *blackmail* OPEN TO, receptive to, vulnerable to; an easy target for.

**3** *he is* ***susceptible to*** *ulcers* LIABLE TO, prone to, subject to, inclined to, predisposed to, disposed to, given to, at risk of. ANTONYMS immune, resistant.

**suspect** verb **1** *I suspected she'd made a mistake* HAVE A SUSPICION, have a feeling, feel, (be inclined to) think, fancy, reckon, guess, surmise, conjecture, conclude, have a hunch; suppose, presume, deduce, infer, sense, imagine; fear.

**2** *he had no reason to suspect my honesty* DOUBT, distrust, mistrust, have misgivings about, be skeptical about, have qualms about, be suspicious of, be wary of, harbor reservations about.

▸ noun *a murder suspect* SUSPECTED PERSON, accused, defendant.

▸ adjective *a suspect package* SUSPICIOUS, dubious, doubtful, untrustworthy; odd, queer; *informal* fishy, funny, shady.

**suspend** verb **1** *the court case was suspended* ADJOURN, interrupt, break off, postpone, delay, defer, shelve, put off, put on hold, intermit, prorogue, hold over, hold in abeyance; cut short, discontinue, dissolve, disband, terminate, table; *informal* put on ice, put on the back burner, mothball, take a rain check on. See note at POSTPONE.

**2** *he was suspended from his duties* EXCLUDE, debar, remove, eliminate, expel, eject.

**3** *lights were suspended from the ceiling* HANG, sling, string; swing, dangle.

**suspense** noun *I can't bear the suspense* TENSION, uncertainty, doubt, anticipation, expectation, expectancy, excitement, anxiety, apprehension, strain. PHRASE: **in suspense** *he left us waiting in suspense for hours* EAGERLY, agog, with bated breath, on tenterhooks; on edge, anxious, edgy, jumpy, keyed up, uneasy, antsy, uptight, jittery.

**suspension** noun **1** *the suspension of army operations* ADJOURNMENT, interruption, postponement, delay, deferral, deferment, stay, prorogation; armistice; cessation, end, halt, stoppage, dissolution, disbandment, termination.

**2** *his suspension from school* EXCLUSION, debarment, removal, elimination, expulsion, ejection.

**suspicion** noun **1** *she had a suspicion that he didn't like her* INTUITION, feeling, impression, inkling, hunch, fancy, notion, supposition, belief, idea, theory; presentiment, premonition; *informal* gut feeling, sixth sense.

**2** *I confronted him with my suspicions* MISGIVING, doubt, qualm, reservation, hesitation, question; skepticism, uncertainty, distrust, mistrust.

**3** *wine with a suspicion of soda* TRACE, touch, suggestion, hint, soupçon, tinge, shade, whiff, bit, drop, dash, taste, jot, mite.

**suspicious** adjective **1** *she gave him a suspicious look* DOUBTFUL, unsure, dubious, wary, chary, skeptical, distrustful, mistrustful, disbelieving, cynical. ANTONYM trusting.

**2** *a highly suspicious character* DISREPUTABLE, unsavory, dubious, suspect, dishonest-looking, funny-looking, slippery; *informal* shifty, shady. ANTONYMS upright, reputable.

**3** *she disappeared in suspicious circumstances* QUESTIONA-

BLE, odd, strange, dubious, irregular, queer, funny, doubtful, mysterious, murky; *informal* fishy. ANTONYM innocent.

**sustain** verb **1** *the balcony might not sustain the weight* BEAR, support, carry, stand, keep up, prop up, shore up, underpin.

**2** *her memories sustained her* COMFORT, help, assist, encourage, succor, support, give strength to, buoy up, carry, cheer up, hearten; *informal* buck up.

**3** *they were unable to sustain a coalition* CONTINUE, carry on, keep up, keep alive, maintain, preserve, conserve, perpetuate, retain.

**4** *she had bread and cheese to sustain her* NOURISH, feed, nurture; maintain, preserve, keep alive, keep going, provide for.

**5** *she sustained slight injuries* UNDERGO, experience, suffer, endure.

**6** *the allegation was not sustained* UPHOLD, validate, ratify, vindicate, confirm, endorse; verify, corroborate, substantiate, bear out, prove, authenticate, back up, evidence, justify.

**sustained** adjective *her sustained battle against alcoholism* CONTINUOUS, ongoing, steady, continual, constant, prolonged, persistent, nonstop, perpetual, unabating, relentless, rolling, unrelieved, unbroken, never-ending, incessant, unceasing, ceaseless, around/round-the-clock. ANTONYM sporadic.

**sustenance** noun **1** *the creature needs sustenance* NOURISHMENT, food, nutriment, nutrition, provisions, provender, rations; *informal* grub, chow, vittles; *formal* comestibles; *literary* viands; *dated* victuals.

**2** *the sustenance of his family* SUPPORT, maintenance, keep, living, livelihood, subsistence, income.

**swagger** verb **1** *we swaggered into the arena* STRUT, parade, stride; walk confidently; *informal* sashay.

**2** *try to swagger less and instead show some humility* BOAST, brag, bluster, crow, gloat; strut, posture, blow one's own horn, lord it; *informal* show off, swank.

▸ noun **1** *a slight swagger in his stride* STRUT; confidence, arrogance, ostentation.

**2** *he was full of swagger* BLUSTER, braggadocio, bumptiousness, vainglory; *informal* swank.

**swallow** verb **1** *she couldn't swallow anything* EAT, gulp down, consume, devour, put away; ingest, assimilate; drink, guzzle, quaff, imbibe, sup, slug; *informal* polish off, swig, chug, swill, down, scoff.

**2** *I can't swallow any more of your insults* TOLERATE, endure, stand, put up with, bear, abide, countenance, stomach, take, accept; *informal* hack; *formal* brook.

**3** *he swallowed my story* BELIEVE, credit, accept, trust; *informal* fall for, buy, go for, 'swallow hook, line, and sinker.'

**4** *she swallowed her pride* RESTRAIN, repress, suppress, hold back, fight back; overcome, check, control, curb, rein in; silence, muffle, stifle, smother, hide, bottle up; *informal* keep a/the lid on. PHRASE: **swallow up 1** *the darkness swallowed them up* ENGULF, swamp, devour, overwhelm, overcome.

**2** *the colleges were swallowed up by universities* TAKE OVER, engulf, absorb, assimilate, incorporate.

**swamp** noun *her horse got stuck in a swamp* MARSH, bog, muskeg, quagmire, mire, morass, fen; quicksand, bayou; *archaic* quag.

▸ verb **1** *the rain was swamping the dry roads* FLOOD, inundate, deluge, immerse; soak, drench, saturate.

**2** *he was swamped by media attention* OVERWHELM, inundate, flood, deluge, engulf, snow under, overload, overpower, weigh down, besiege, beset.

**swampy** adjective *the swampy acreage behind the orchard* MARSHY, boggy, fenny, miry; soft, soggy, muddy, spongy, heavy, squelchy, waterlogged, sodden, wet; *archaic* quaggy.

**swap** verb **1** *I swapped my stereo for some hockey equipment* EXCHANGE, trade, barter, interchange, bargain; switch, change, replace.

**2** *we swapped jokes* BANDY, exchange, trade, reciprocate.

▸ noun *a job swap* EXCHANGE, interchange, trade, switch, trade-off, substitution; *informal* switcheroo.

**swarm** noun **1** *a swarm of bees* HIVE, flock, collection.

**2** *a swarm of gendarmes* CROWD, multitude, horde, host, mob, gang, throng, mass, army, troop, herd, pack; *literary* myriad.

▸ verb *reporters were swarming all over the place* FLOCK, crowd, throng, surge, stream.

PHRASE: **be swarming with** *the woods were swarming with biting flies* BE CROWDED WITH, be thronged with, be overrun with, be full of, abound in, be teeming with, be aswarm with, bristle with, be alive with, be crawling with, be infested with, overflow with, be prolific in, be abundant in; *informal* be thick with.

**swarthy** adjective *his swarthy complexion* DARK-SKINNED, olive-skinned, dusky, tanned, saturnine, black; *archaic* swart. ANTONYM pale.

**swashbuckling** adjective *a swashbuckling hero of silent films* DARING, heroic, daredevil, dashing, adventurous, bold, valiant, valorous, fearless, lionhearted, dauntless, devil-may-care; gallant, chivalrous, romantic. ANTONYM timid.

**swathe** verb *his hands were swathed in bandages* WRAP, envelop, bind, swaddle, bandage, cover, shroud, drape, wind, enfold, sheathe.

**sway** verb **1** *the curtains swayed in the breeze* SWING, shake, oscillate, undulate, move to and fro, move back and forth.

**2** *she swayed on her feet* STAGGER, wobble, rock, lurch, reel, roll, list, stumble, pitch.

**3** *we are swayed by the media* INFLUENCE, affect, bias, persuade, win over; manipulate, bend, mold.

**4** *you must not be swayed by emotion* RULE, govern, dominate, control, guide.

▸ noun **1** *the sway of her hips* SWING, roll, shake, oscillation, undulation.

2 *his opinions have a lot of sway* CLOUT, influence, power, weight, authority, control. See note at JURISDICTION.

PHRASE: **hold sway** *they had held sway in France for a quarter of a century* HOLD POWER, wield power, exercise power, have jurisdiction, have authority, have dominion, rule, be in control, predominate; have the upper hand, have the edge, have the whip hand, have mastery; *informal* run the show, be in the driver's seat, be in the saddle.

**swear** verb 1 *they swore to marry each other* PROMISE, vow, pledge, give one's word, take an oath, undertake, guarantee; *Law* depose; *formal* aver.

2 *she swore she would never go back* INSIST, avow, pronounce, declare, proclaim, assert, profess, maintain, contend, emphasize, stress; *formal* aver.

3 *Kate spilled wine and swore* CURSE, blaspheme, utter profanities, utter oaths, use bad language, take the Lord's name in vain; *informal* cuss; *archaic* execrate. PHRASES: **swear by** *informal we swear by these all-weather tires* EXPRESS CONFIDENCE IN, have faith in, trust, believe in; set store by, value; *informal* rate.

**swear off** *informal I swore off hard liquor years ago* RENOUNCE, forswear, forgo, abstain from, go without, shun, avoid, eschew, steer clear of; give up, dispense with, stop, discontinue, drop; *informal* kick, quit.

**swearing** noun *they had to bleep out all the swearing* BAD LANGUAGE, strong language, cursing, blaspheming, blasphemy; profanities, obscenities, curses, oaths, expletives, swear words; *informal* cussing, four-letter words; *formal* imprecation.

**sweat** noun 1 *he was drenched with sweat* PERSPIRATION, moisture, dampness, wetness; *Medicine* diaphoresis.

2 *informal he got into such a sweat about that girl* FLUSTER, panic, frenzy, fever, pother; *informal* state, flap, tizzy, dither, stew, lather.

3 *informal the sweat of the working classes* LABOR, hard work, toil(s), effort(s), exertion(s), industry, drudgery, slog; *informal* grind, elbow grease.

▸ verb 1 *she was sweating heavily* PERSPIRE, swelter, glow; be damp, be wet; secrete.

2 *I've sweated over this for six months* WORK (HARD), work like a Trojan, labor, toil, slog, slave, work one's fingers to the bone; *informal* plug away; *archaic* drudge.

3 *he sweated over his mistakes* WORRY, agonize, fuss, panic, fret, lose sleep; *informal* be on pins and needles, be in a state, be in a flap, be in a stew, torture oneself, torment oneself.

**sweaty** adjective *his sweaty palms* PERSPIRING, sweating, clammy, sticky, glowing; moist, damp.

**sweep** verb 1 *she swept the floor* BRUSH, clean, scrub, wipe, mop, dust, scour; *informal* do.

2 *I swept the crumbs off* REMOVE, brush, clean, clear, whisk.

3 *he was swept out to sea* CARRY, pull, drag, tow.

4 *riots swept the country* ENGULF, overwhelm, flood.

5 *he swept down the stairs* GLIDE, sail, breeze, drift, flit, flounce; stride, stroll, swagger.

6 *a limousine swept past* GLIDE, sail, rush, race, streak, speed, fly, zoom, whiz, hurtle; *informal* tear, whip.

7 *police swept the conference room* SEARCH, probe, check, explore, go through, scour, comb.

▸ noun 1 *a great sweep of his hand* GESTURE, stroke, wave, movement.

2 *a security sweep* SEARCH, hunt, exploration, probe.

3 *a long sweep of golden sand* EXPANSE, tract, stretch, extent, plain.

4 *the broad sweep of our interests* RANGE, span, scope, compass, reach, spread, ambit, gamut, spectrum, extent. See note at RANGE.

PHRASES: **sweep aside** *you can't sweep aside these allegations forever* DISREGARD, ignore, take no notice of, dismiss, shrug off, forget about, brush aside.

**sweep under the carpet** *their grievances could no longer be swept under the carpet* HIDE, conceal, suppress, hush up, keep quiet about, censor, gag, withhold, cover up, stifle.

**sweeping** adjective 1 *sweeping changes* EXTENSIVE, wide-ranging, global, broad, comprehensive, all-inclusive, all-embracing, far-reaching, across the board; thorough, radical; *informal* wall-to-wall. ANTONYMS limited, narrow.

2 *a sweeping victory* OVERWHELMING, decisive, thorough, complete, total, absolute, out-and-out, unqualified, landslide. ANTONYM narrow.

3 *sweeping statements* WHOLESALE, blanket, generalized, all-inclusive, unqualified, indiscriminate, universal, oversimplified, imprecise. ANTONYMS narrow, focused.

4 *sweeping banks of flowers* BROAD, extensive, expansive, vast, spacious, boundless, panoramic. ANTONYM small.

**sweet** adjective 1 *sweet cinnamon buns* SUGARY, sweetened, saccharine; sugared, honeyed, candied, glacé; sickly, cloying. ANTONYMS sour, savory.

2 *the sweet scent of roses* FRAGRANT, aromatic, perfumed; *literary* ambrosial.

3 *her sweet voice* DULCET, melodious, lyrical, mellifluous, musical, tuneful, soft, harmonious, silvery, honeyed, mellow, rich, golden. ANTONYMS harsh, discordant.

4 *life was still sweet* PLEASANT, pleasing, pleasurable, agreeable, delightful, nice, satisfying, gratifying, good, acceptable, fine; *informal* lovely, great. ANTONYMS harsh, disagreeable.

5 *the sweet April air* PURE, wholesome, fresh, clean, clear. ANTONYMS harsh, rotten.

6 *she has a sweet nature* LIKABLE, appealing, engaging, amiable, pleasant, agreeable, genial, friendly, nice, kind, thoughtful, considerate; charming, enchanting, captivating, delightful, lovely. ANTONYM nasty.

7 *she looks quite sweet* CUTE, lovable, adorable, endearing, charming, attractive, dear.

8 *my sweet Lydia* DEAR, dearest, darling, beloved, loved, cherished, precious, treasured.

▸ noun **1** (**sweets**) *trying to cut back on sweets* DESSERTS, treats, cakes, cookies, pastries.

**2** *happy birthday, my sweet!* DEAR, darling, dearest, love, sweetheart, beloved, honey, hon, pet, treasure, angel.

PHRASE: **sweet on** *informal it's obvious that Sam is sweet on Joanie* FOND OF, taken with, attracted to, in love with, enamored of, captivated by, infatuated with, keen on, devoted to, smitten with, moonstruck by; *informal* mad about, bowled over by.

**sweeten** verb **1** *sweeten the milk with honey* MAKE SWEET, add sugar to, sugar, sugar-coat.

**2** *he chewed gum to sweeten his breath* FRESHEN, refresh, purify, deodorize, perfume.

**3** *try to sweeten the bad news* SOFTEN, ease, alleviate, mitigate, temper, cushion; embellish, embroider.

**4** *informal a bigger dividend to sweeten shareholders* MOLLIFY, placate, soothe, soften up, pacify, appease, win over.

**sweetheart** noun **1** *you look lovely, sweetheart* DARLING, dear, dearest, love, beloved, sweet; *informal* honey, hon, sweetie, sugar, baby, babe.

**2** *my high-school sweetheart* LOVER, love, girlfriend, boyfriend, beloved, significant other, lady love, loved one, suitor, admirer; *informal* steady, flame, main squeeze; valentine; *literary* swain; *dated* beau; *archaic* paramour.

**swell** verb **1** *her lip **swelled up*** EXPAND, bulge, distend, inflate, dilate, bloat, puff up, balloon, fatten, fill out, tumefy. ANTONYMS shrink, contract.

**2** *the population swelled* GROW, enlarge, increase, expand, rise, escalate, multiply, proliferate, snowball, mushroom. ANTONYMS wane, decrease.

**3** *she swelled with pride* BE FILLED, be bursting, brim, overflow.

**4** *the program swelled enrollments* INCREASE, enlarge, augment, boost, top up, step up, multiply. ANTONYM decrease.

**5** *the music swelled to fill the house* GROW LOUD, grow louder, amplify, crescendo, intensify, heighten. ANTONYM quiet.

▸ noun **1** *a brief swell in the volume* INCREASE, rise, escalation, surge, boost. ANTONYMS decrease, dip.

**2** *a heavy swell on the sea* SURGE, wave, undulation, roll.

▸ adjective *informal, dated a swell idea* EXCELLENT, marvelous, wonderful, splendid, magnificent, superb; *informal* super, great, fantastic. ANTONYM bad.

**swelling** noun *use ice to reduce the swelling* BUMP, lump, bulge, protuberance, enlargement, distension, prominence, protrusion, node, nodule, tumescence; boil, blister, bunion, carbuncle.

**sweltering** adjective *a sweltering afternoon* HOT, stifling, humid, sultry, sticky, muggy, close, stuffy; tropical, torrid, searing, blistering; *informal* boiling (hot), baking, roasting, sizzling. ANTONYM freezing.

**swerve** verb *a car swerved into her path* VEER, deviate, skew, diverge, sheer, weave, zigzag, change direction; *Sailing* tack.

▸ noun *the bowler regulated his swerve* CURVE, curl, deviation, twist.

**swift** adjective **1** *a swift decision* PROMPT, rapid, sudden, immediate, instant, instantaneous; abrupt, hasty, hurried, precipitate, headlong. ANTONYM unhurried.

**2** *swift runners* FAST, rapid, quick, speedy, high-speed, fast-paced, brisk, lively; express, breakneck; fleet-footed; *informal* nippy, supersonic. ANTONYMS slow, sluggish.

**swill** verb *informal she was swilling beers* DRINK, quaff, swallow, down, gulp, drain, imbibe, sup, slurp, consume, slug; *informal* swig, knock back, toss off, put away, chug, chugalug.

▸ noun **1** *informal she took a swill of coffee* GULP, swallow, drink, draft, mouthful, slug; *informal* swig.

**2** *swill for the pigs* PIGSWILL, mash, slops, scraps, refuse, scourings, leftovers; *archaic* hogwash.

**swim** verb **1** *they swam in the pool* BATHE, take a dip, splash around; float, tread water, paddle.

**2** *his food was **swimming in** gravy* BE SATURATED IN, be drenched in, be soaked in, be steeped in, be immersed in, be covered in, be drowning in, be full of.

**swimmingly** adverb *everything was going swimmingly* WELL, smoothly, easily, effortlessly, like clockwork, without a hitch, as planned, to plan; *informal* like a dream, like magic.

**swindle** verb *I was swindled out of money | he's been swindling clients for years* DEFRAUD, cheat, trick, dupe, deceive, fool, hoax, hoodwink, bamboozle; *informal* fleece, con, bilk, sting, hose, diddle, rip off, take for a ride, pull a fast one on, put one over on, take to the cleaners, gull, stiff, euchre, hornswoggle; *literary* cozen.

▸ noun *an insurance swindle* FRAUD, trick, deception, deceit, cheat, sham, artifice, ruse, dodge, racket, wile; sharp practice; *informal* con, fiddle, diddle, rip-off, flimflam, bunco.

**swindler** noun *the guy collecting for the hospital fund was a swindler* FRAUDSTER, fraud, confidence man, confidence trickster, trickster, cheat, rogue, mountebank, charlatan, impostor, hoaxer; *informal* con man, con artist, scam artist, shyster, gonif, shark, sharp, hustler, phony, crook, snake oil salesman.

**swing** verb **1** *the sign swung in the wind* SWAY, oscillate, move back and forth, move to and fro, wave, wag, rock, flutter, flap.

**2** *Helen swung the bottle* BRANDISH, wave, flourish, wield, shake, wag, twirl.

**3** *this road swings off to the north* CURVE, bend, veer, turn, bear, wind, twist, deviate, slew, skew, drift, head.

**4** *the balance swung from one party to the other* CHANGE, fluctuate, shift, alter, oscillate, waver, alternate, seesaw, yo-yo, vary.

**5** *informal if we keep trying, we can swing this deal* ACCOMPLISH, achieve, obtain, acquire, get, secure, net, win, attain, bag, hook; *informal* wangle, land.

▸ noun **1** *a swing of the pendulum* OSCILLATION, sway, wave.

**2** *a swing to the New Democrats in this constituency* CHANGE, move; turnaround, turnabout, reversal, about face, volte face, change of heart, U-turn, sea change.

**3** *a swing toward plain food* TREND, tendency, drift, movement.

**4** *a mood swing* FLUCTUATION, change, shift, variation, oscillation.

**swirl** verb *the snow swirled around them* WHIRL, eddy, billow, spiral, circulate, revolve, spin, twist; flow, stream, surge, seethe.

**switch** noun **1** *the switch on top of the telephone* BUTTON, lever, control, dial, rocker.

**2** *a switch from direct to indirect taxation* CHANGE, move, shift, transition, transformation; reversal, turnaround, U-turn, changeover, transfer, conversion; substitution, exchange.

**3** *a switch of willow* BRANCH, twig, stick, rod.

▸ verb **1** *he switched sides* CHANGE, shift; reverse; *informal* chop and change.

**2** *he managed to switch envelopes* EXCHANGE, swap, interchange, trade, substitute, replace, rotate.

PHRASES: **switch on** *switch on the air conditioning* TURN ON, put on, flick on, activate, start, power up, set going, set in motion, operate, initiate, actuate, initialize, energize; toggle, flip, throw.
**switch off** *who switched off the fan?* TURN OFF, shut off, flick off, power down, stop, cut, halt, deactivate; toggle, flip.

**swollen** adjective *the rivers are swollen | swollen glands* DISTENDED, expanded, enlarged, bulging, inflated, dilated, bloated, puffed up, puffy, tumescent, tumid; inflamed, varicose.

**swoop** verb **1** *pigeons swooped down after the grain* DIVE, descend, sweep, pounce, plunge, pitch, nosedive; rush, dart, speed, zoom.

**2** *police **swooped on** the building* RAID, pounce on, attack, assault, assail, charge, bust.

**sword** noun *a ceremonial sword* BLADE, foil, broadsword, épée, cutlass, rapier, saber, scimitar; *literary* brand. PHRASE: **cross swords** *Larry is crossing swords with his brother-in-law again* QUARREL, disagree, dispute, wrangle, bicker, be at odds, be at loggerheads, lock horns; fight, contend; *informal* scrap.

**sybaritic** adjective *she regretted having left her homespun past for this sybaritic life with Lanzo* LUXURIOUS, extravagant, lavish, self-indulgent, pleasure-seeking, sensual, voluptuous, hedonistic, epicurean, lotus-eating, libertine, debauched, decadent. See note at SENSUOUS. ANTONYM ascetic.

**sycophant** noun *I thought you wanted a competent assistant, not a nodding sycophant* yes-man, bootlicker, brown-noser, toady, lickspittle, flatterer, flunky, lackey, spaniel, doormat, stooge, cringer, suck, suck-up.

**sycophantic** adjective *his clique of sycophantic friends* OBSEQUIOUS, servile, subservient, deferential, groveling, toadying, fawning, flattering, ingratiating, cringing, unctuous, slavish; *informal* smarmy, bootlicking, brown-nosing.

**symbol** noun **1** *the lotus is the symbol of purity* EMBLEM, token, sign, representation, figure, image; metaphor, allegory; icon.

**2** *the chemical symbol for helium* SIGN, character, mark, letter, ideogram.

**3** *the Red Cross symbol* LOGO, emblem, badge, stamp, trademark, crest, insignia, coat of arms, seal, device, monogram, hallmark, flag, motif, icon. See note at EMBLEM.

**symbolic** adjective **1** *the Colosseum is symbolic of the Roman Empire* EMBLEMATIC, representative, typical, characteristic, symptomatic.

**2** *symbolic language* FIGURATIVE, representative, illustrative, emblematic, metaphorical, allegorical, parabolic, allusive, suggestive; meaningful, significant. ANTONYM literal.

**symbolize** verb *the wheel symbolizes the power of peaceful change* REPRESENT, stand for, be a sign of, exemplify; denote, signify, mean, indicate, convey, express, imply, suggest, allude to; embody, epitomize, encapsulate, personify, typify; *literary* betoken.

**symmetrical** adjective *the two doves on the flag are symmetrical* evenly shaped, aligned, equal; mirror image; regular, uniform, consistent; balanced, proportional, even.

**symmetry** noun *the garden is laid out with perfect symmetry* REGULARITY, evenness, uniformity, consistency, conformity, correspondence, equality; balance, proportions; *formal* concord.

**sympathetic** adjective **1** *a sympathetic listener* COMPASSIONATE, caring, concerned, solicitous, empathetic, understanding, sensitive; commiserative, pitying, consoling, comforting, supportive, encouraging; considerate, kind, tenderhearted; *informal* boosterish. ANTONYM unfeeling.

**2** *the most sympathetic character in the book* LIKABLE, pleasant, agreeable, congenial, friendly, genial, simpatico. ANTONYM unfriendly.

**3** *I was **sympathetic to** his cause* IN FAVOR OF, in sympathy with, pro, on the side of, supportive of, encouraging of; well-disposed to, favorably disposed to, receptive to. ANTONYMS indifferent, opposed.

**sympathize** verb **1** *I do **sympathize with** the poor creature* PITY, feel sorry for, show compassion for, commiserate with, offer condolences to, feel for, show concern for, show interest for; console, comfort, solace, soothe, support, encourage; empathize with, identify with, understand, relate to.

**2** *they **sympathize with** the critique* AGREE WITH, support, be in favor of, go along with, favor, approve of, back, side with.

**sympathizer** noun *his Confederate brothers accused him of being a Yankee sympathizer* SUPPORTER, backer, well-wisher, advocate, ally, partisan; collaborator, fraternizer, conspirator, quisling.

**sympathy** noun **1** *he shows sympathy for the poor* COMPAS-

SION, caring, concern, solicitude, empathy; commiseration, pity, condolence, comfort, solace, support, encouragement; consideration, kindness. ANTONYM indifference.

**2** *sympathy with a fellow journalist* RAPPORT, fellow feeling, affinity, empathy, harmony, accord, compatibility; fellowship, camaraderie. ANTONYM hostility.

**3** *their sympathy with the Communists* AGREEMENT, favor, approval, approbation, support, encouragement, partiality; association, alignment, affiliation. ANTONYM disapproval.

**symptom** noun **1** *the symptoms of the disease* MANIFESTATION, indication, indicator, sign, mark, feature, trait; *Medicine* prodrome.

**2** *a symptom of the country's present turmoil* EXPRESSION, sign, indication, mark, token, manifestation; portent, warning, clue, hint; testimony, evidence, proof; result, consequence, product. See note at SIGN.

**symptomatic** adjective *they worried that her lethargy was symptomatic of depression* INDICATIVE, characteristic, suggestive, typical, representative, symbolic.

**synthesis** noun *the synthesis of their diverse styles makes for a wonderful new sound in country music* COMBINATION, union, amalgam, blend, mixture, compound, fusion, composite, alloy; unification, amalgamation, marrying.

**synthetic** adjective *synthetic leather* ARTIFICIAL, fake, imitation, faux, mock, simulated, ersatz, substitute; pseudo, so-called; man-made, manufactured, fabricated; *informal* phony, pretend. See note at SPURIOUS. ANTONYM natural.

**syrupy** adjective **1** *syrupy medicine* OVERSWEET, sweet, sugary, treacly, honeyed, saccharine; thick, sticky, gluey, viscid, glutinous; *informal* gooey.

**2** *syrupy romantic drivel* SENTIMENTAL, mawkish, cloying, sickly, saccharine, trite; *informal* soppy, schmaltzy, mushy, slushy, sloppy, lovey-dovey, cheesy, corny.

**system** noun **1** *a system of canals* STRUCTURE, organization, arrangement, complex, network; *informal* setup.

**2** *a system for regulating sales* METHOD, methodology, technique, process, procedure, approach, practice; means, way, mode, framework, modus operandi; scheme, plan, policy, program, regimen, formula, routine.

**3** *there was no system in his work* ORDER, method, orderliness, systematization, planning, logic, routine.

**4** *youngsters have no faith in **the system*** THE ESTABLISHMENT, the administration, the authorities, the powers that be; bureaucracy, officialdom; the status quo.

**systematic** adjective *the systematic firing of one department head after another* STRUCTURED, methodical, organized, orderly, planned, systematized, regular, routine, standardized, standard; logical, coherent, consistent; efficient, businesslike, practical; *informal* left-brained. ANTONYM disorganized.

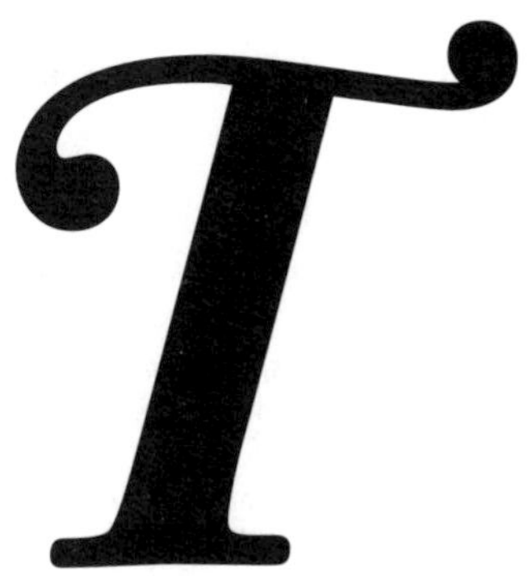

**tab** noun 1 *his name is on the tab of his jacket* TAG, label, flap.

2 *informal the company will pick up the tab* BILL, invoice, account, charge, check, expense, cost.

**table** noun 1 *put the plates on the table* bench, buffet, stand, counter, work surface; desk; bar.

2 *he provides an excellent table* MEAL, food, fare, menu, nourishment; eatables, provisions; *informal* spread, grub, chow, eats, nosh; *literary* viands; *dated* victuals.

3 *the report has numerous tables* CHART, diagram, figure, graph, plan; list, tabulation, index.

▸ verb *the council tabled the rezoning issue until April* POSTPONE, delay, defer, sideline, put on the back burner.

**tableau** noun 1 *mythic tableaux* PICTURE, painting, representation, illustration, image.

2 *the first act consists of a series of tableaux* PAGEANT, tableau vivant, parade, diorama, scene.

3 *a domestic tableau around the fireplace* SCENE, arrangement, grouping, group; picture, spectacle, image, vignette.

**tablet** noun 1 *a carved tablet* SLAB, stone, panel, plaque, plate, sign.

2 *a headache tablet* PILL, capsule, lozenge, caplet, pastille, drop, pilule; *informal* tab.

3 *a writing tablet* PAD, notepad, memo pad, notebook, scratchpad.

**taboo** noun *the taboo against healing on the Sabbath* PROHIBITION, proscription, veto, interdiction, interdict, ban, restriction.

▸ adjective *taboo subjects* FORBIDDEN, prohibited, banned, proscribed, interdicted, outlawed, illegal, illicit, unlawful, restricted, off limits; unmentionable, unspeakable, unutterable, unsayable, ineffable; rude, impolite. ANTONYM acceptable.

**tabulate** verb *we tabulate the phone-in pledges every twenty minutes* CHART, arrange, order, organize, systematize, systemize, catalog, list, index, classify, class, codify; compile, group, log, grade, rate.

**tacit** adjective *tacit promises* IMPLICIT, understood, implied, hinted, suggested; unspoken, unstated, unsaid, unexpressed, unvoiced; taken for granted, taken as read, inferred. ANTONYM explicit.

**taciturn** adjective *our taciturn daughter has suddenly become a little chatty* UNTALKATIVE, uncommunicative, reticent, unforthcoming, quiet, secretive, tight-lipped, buttoned-up, close-mouthed; silent, mute, dumb, inarticulate; reserved, withdrawn. ANTONYM talkative.

**tack** noun 1 *tacks held the carpet down* PIN, thumbtack, pushpin, nail, staple, rivet, stud.

2 *the boat bowled past on the opposite tack* HEADING, bearing, course, track, path, line.

3 *Mitchell wisely changed his tack* APPROACH, way, method; policy, procedure, technique, tactic, plan, strategy, stratagem; path, line, angle, direction, course.

▸ verb 1 *a photo tacked to the wall* PIN, nail, staple, fix, fasten, attach, secure, affix.

2 *the dress was roughly tacked together* STITCH, baste, sew, bind.

3 *the yachts tacked back and forth* ZIGZAG, change direction, change course, swerve, veer; *Nautical* go about, come about, beat.

4 *poems* ***tacked on*** *at the end of the book* ADD (ON), append, join, stick (on).

**tackle** noun 1 *fishing tackle* GEAR, equipment, apparatus, kit, hardware; implements, instruments, accoutrements, paraphernalia, trappings, appurtenances; *informal* things, stuff, bits and pieces; *archaic* equipage.

2 *lifting tackle* PULLEYS, gear, hoist, crane, winch, davit, windlass, sheave.

3 *a tackle by the linebacker* BLOCK, interception, challenge, attack.

▸ verb 1 *we must tackle environmental problems* COME TO GRIPS WITH, address, get to work on, set one's hand to, approach, take on, attend to, see to, try to sort out; deal with, take care of, handle, manage; *informal* have a crack at, have a go at.

2 *he tackled a masked intruder* CONFRONT, face up to, take on, contend with, challenge, attack; seize, grab, grapple with, intercept, block, stop; bring down, floor, fell; *informal* have a go at.

**tacky**[1] adjective *the paint was still tacky* STICKY, wet, gluey, gummy, adhesive, viscous, viscid, treacly; *informal* gooey.

**tacky**[2] adjective *a tacky game show* TAWDRY, TASTELESS, kitsch, kitschy, vulgar, crude, garish, gaudy, showy, trashy, cheesy, cheap, common, second-rate. ANTONYM tasteful.

**tact** noun *Dr. Porter has a lot to learn about timing and tact* DIPLOMACY, tactfulness, sensitivity, understanding, thoughtfulness, consideration, delicacy, discretion, prudence, judiciousness, subtlety, savoir faire; *informal* savvy.

**tactful** adjective *tactful criticism* DIPLOMATIC, discreet, considerate, sensitive, understanding, thoughtful, delicate, judicious, politic, perceptive, subtle; courteous, polite, decorous, respectful; *informal* savvy.

**tactic** noun **1** *a tax-saving tactic* STRATEGY, scheme, stratagem, plan, maneuver; method, expedient, gambit, move, approach, tack; device, trick, ploy, dodge, ruse, machination, contrivance; *informal* wangle; *archaic* shift.

**2** *our fleet's superior tactics* STRATEGY, policy, campaign, battle plans, game plans, maneuvers, logistics; generalship, organization, planning, direction, orchestration.

**tactical** adjective *they met secretly to discuss their next tactical move* CALCULATED, planned, strategic; prudent, politic, diplomatic, judicious, shrewd, cunning, artful.

**tactless** adjective *it was a cruel, tactless thing to say* INSENSITIVE, inconsiderate, thoughtless, indelicate, undiplomatic, impolitic, indiscreet, unsubtle, clumsy, heavy-handed, graceless, awkward, inept, gauche; blunt, frank, outspoken, abrupt, gruff, rough, crude, coarse; imprudent, injudicious, unwise; rude, impolite, uncouth, discourteous, crass, tasteless, disrespectful, boorish.

**tag** noun **1** *a price tag* LABEL, ticket, badge, mark, marker, tab, sticker, stub, counterfoil, flag.

**2** *he gained a "bad boy" tag* DESIGNATION, label, description, characterization, identity; nickname, name, epithet, title, sobriquet; *informal* handle, moniker; *formal* denomination, appellation.

**3** *tags from Shakespeare* QUOTATION, quote, tag line, phrase, platitude, cliché, excerpt; saying, proverb, maxim, adage, aphorism, motto, epigram; slogan, catchphrase.

▸ verb **1** *bottles tagged with colored stickers* LABEL, mark, ticket, identify, flag, indicate.

**2** *she is tagged as a "thinking" actor* LABEL, class, categorize, characterize, designate, describe, identify, classify; mark, stamp, brand, pigeonhole, stereotype, typecast, compartmentalize, typify; name, call, title, entitle, dub, term, style.

**3** *a poem* ***tagged on*** *as an afterthought* ADD, tack on, join; attach, append, stick on.

**4** *he was* ***tagging along*** *behind her* FOLLOW, trail; come after, go after, shadow, dog; accompany, attend, escort; *informal* tail.

**tail** noun **1** *the dog's tail* brush, scut, dock; tail feathers; hindquarters. ANTONYMS head, front.

**2** *the tail of the plane* REAR, end, back, extremity; bottom. ANTONYMS head, front.

**3** *the tail of the hunting season* CLOSE, end, conclusion, tail end. ANTONYMS beginning, start.

**4** *informal put a tail on that suspect* DETECTIVE, investigator, shadow; *informal* sleuth, private eye, gumshoe.

▸ verb *informal the paparazzi tailed them* FOLLOW, shadow, stalk, trail, track, hunt, hound, dog, pursue, chase.

PHRASES: **on someone's tail** *a police car stayed on his tail* CLOSE BEHIND, following closely, (hard) on someone's heels.
**tail off/away** *her voice tailed off* FADE, wane, ebb, dwindle, decrease, lessen, diminish, decline, subside, abate, drop off, peter out, taper off; let up, ease off, die away, die down, come to an end.
**turn tail** *I was so shocked, I just turned tail* RUN AWAY, flee, bolt, make off, take to one's heels, cut and run, beat a (hasty) retreat; *informal* scram, skedaddle, vamoose.

**tailor** noun *the finest tailor in Memphis* OUTFITTER, dressmaker, couturier, fashion designer, designer; clothier, costumer, seamstress.

▸ verb *services can be tailored to customer requirements* CUSTOMIZE, adapt, adjust, modify, change, convert, alter, attune, mold, gear, fit, cut, shape, tune.

**taint** noun *the taint of corruption* TRACE, touch, suggestion, hint, tinge; stain, blot, blemish, stigma, black mark, discredit, dishonor, disgrace, shame.

▸ verb **1** *the wilderness is tainted by pollution* CONTAMINATE, pollute, adulterate, infect, blight, spoil, soil, ruin, destroy; *literary* befoul. See note at POLLUTE. ANTONYM clean.

**2** *those fraudsters taint the reputation of legitimate claimants* TARNISH, sully, blacken, stain, blot, blemish, stigmatize, mar, corrupt, defile, soil, muddy, damage, harm, hurt; drag through the mud; *literary* besmirch. ANTONYM improve.

**take** verb **1** *she took his hand* LAY HOLD OF, get hold of; grasp, grip, clasp, clutch, grab. ANTONYM give.

**2** *he took an envelope from his pocket* REMOVE, pull, draw, withdraw, extract, fish. ANTONYM give.

**3** *a passage taken from my book* EXTRACT, quote, cite, excerpt, derive, abstract, copy, cull.

**4** *she took a little wine* DRINK, imbibe; consume, swallow, eat, ingest.

**5** *many prisoners were taken* CAPTURE, seize, catch, arrest, apprehend, take into custody; carry off, abduct. ANTONYMS liberate, free.

**6** *someone's taken my car* STEAL, remove, appropriate, make off with, pilfer, purloin; *informal* filch, swipe, snaffle, pinch. ANTONYMS give back, restore.

**7** *take four from the total* SUBTRACT, deduct, remove; discount; *informal* knock off, minus. ANTONYM add.

**8** *all the seats had been taken* OCCUPY, use, utilize, fill, hold; reserve, engage; *informal* bag.

**9** *I have taken a room nearby* RENT, lease, hire, charter; reserve, book, engage.

**10** *I took the job* ACCEPT, undertake, take on. ANTONYMS refuse, turn down.

**11** *I'd take this over the other option* PICK, choose, select; prefer, favor, opt for, vote for. ANTONYMS refuse, turn down.

**12** *take, for instance, Altoona* CONSIDER, contemplate, ponder, think about, mull over, examine, study, meditate over, ruminate about.

**13** *she took his temperature* ASCERTAIN, determine, establish, measure, find out, discover; calculate, compute, evaluate, rate, assess, appraise, gauge.

**14** *he took notes* WRITE, note (down), jot (down), scribble, scrawl, record, register, document, minute.

**15** *I took the package to Wilmington* BRING, carry, bear, transport, convey, move, transfer, ferry; *informal* cart, tote.

**16** *the police took her home* ESCORT, accompany, help, assist, show, lead, guide, see, usher, shepherd, convey.

**17** *he took the train* TRAVEL ON/BY, journey on, go via; use.

**18** *the town takes its name from the lake* DERIVE, get, obtain, come by, acquire, pick up.

**19** *she took the prize for best speaker* RECEIVE, obtain, gain, get, acquire, collect, accept, be awarded; secure, come by, win, earn, pick up, carry off; *informal* land, bag, net, scoop.

**20** *I took the chance to postpone it* ACT ON, take advantage of, capitalize on, use, exploit, make the most of, leap at, jump at, pounce on, seize, grasp, grab, accept. ANTONYMS ignore, miss.

**21** *he took great pleasure in painting* DERIVE, draw, acquire, obtain, get, gain, extract, procure; experience, undergo, feel.

**22** *Liz took the news badly* RECEIVE, respond to, react to, meet, greet; deal with, cope with.

**23** *do you* **take** *me* **for** *a fool?* REGARD AS, consider to be, view as, see as, believe to be, reckon to be, imagine to be, deem to be.

**24** *I **take it** that you are hungry* ASSUME, presume, suppose, imagine, expect, reckon, gather, dare say, trust, surmise, deduce, guess, conjecture, fancy, suspect.

**25** *I take your point* UNDERSTAND, grasp, get, comprehend, apprehend, see, follow; accept, appreciate, acknowledge, sympathize with, agree with.

**26** *Shirley was very taken with him* CAPTIVATE, enchant, charm, delight, attract, beguile, enthrall, entrance, infatuate, dazzle; amuse, divert, entertain; *informal* tickle someone's fancy.

**27** *I can't take much more* ENDURE, bear, tolerate, stand, put up with, abide, stomach, accept, allow, countenance, support, shoulder; *formal* brook; *archaic* suffer.

**28** *applicants must take a test* CARRY OUT, do, complete, write, conduct, perform, execute, discharge, accomplish, fulfill.

**29** *I took drama, French, and art history* STUDY, learn, have lessons in; take up, pursue; *informal* do.

**30** *the journey took six hours* LAST, continue for, go on for, carry on for; require, call for, need, necessitate, entail, involve.

**31** *it would take an expert to know that* REQUIRE, need, necessitate, demand, call for, entail, involve.

**32** *I take size six shoes* WEAR, use; require, need.

**33** *the dye did not take* BE EFFECTIVE, take effect, hold, root, be productive, be effectual, be useful; work, operate, succeed, function; *formal* be efficacious.

▸ noun **1** *the whalers' commercial take* CATCH, haul, bag, yield, net.

**2** *the state's tax take* REVENUE, income, gain, profit; takings, proceeds, returns, receipts, winnings, pickings, earnings, spoils; purse.

**3** *a clapperboard for the start of each take* SCENE, sequence, film clip, clip.

**4** *a fresh **take on** gender issues* VIEW OF, reading of, version of, interpretation of, understanding of, account of, analysis of, approach to.

PHRASES: **take after** *Sandy takes after his adventurous Uncle Lenny* RESEMBLE, look like; remind one of, make one think of, recall, conjure up, suggest, evoke; *informal* favor, be a chip off the old block.

**take apart 1** *we took the machine apart* DISMANTLE, pull to pieces, pull apart, disassemble, break up; tear down, demolish, destroy, wreck.

**2** *informal the scene was taken apart by the director.* See CRITICIZE.

**take someone back 1** *the dream **took me back to** Vienna* EVOKE, remind one of, conjure up, summon up; echo, suggest.

**2** *I will never take her back* BE RECONCILED (TO), forgive, pardon, excuse, exonerate, absolve; let bygones be bygones, bury the hatchet.

**take something back 1** *I take back every word* RETRACT, withdraw, renounce, disclaim, unsay, disavow, recant, repudiate; *formal* abjure.

**2** *I must take the keys back* RETURN, bring back, give back, restore.

**take something down** *I took down everything she said* WRITE DOWN, note down, jot down, set down, record, commit to paper, register, draft, document, minute, pen.

**take someone in 1** *she took in paying guests* ACCOMMODATE, board, house, feed, put up, admit, receive; harbor.

**2** *you were taken in by a hoax* DECEIVE, delude, hoodwink, mislead, trick, dupe, fool, cheat, defraud, swindle, outwit, gull, hoax, bamboozle; *informal* con, put one over on.

**take something in 1** *she could hardly take in the news* COMPREHEND, understand, grasp, follow, absorb; *informal* get.

**2** *this route takes in some great scenery* INCLUDE, encompass, embrace, contain, comprise, cover, incorporate, comprehend, hold.

**take someone in hand** *part of your job is to take young Master Jonathon in hand* CONTROL, be in charge of, dominate, master; reform, improve, correct, change, rehabilitate.

**take something in hand** *are you willing to take this project in hand?* DEAL WITH, apply oneself to, come to grips with, set one's hand to, grapple with, take on, attend to, see to, sort out, take care of, handle, manage.

**take it out of someone** *the final lap has taken it out of Johnson* EXHAUST, drain, enervate, tire, fatigue, wear out, weary, debilitate; *informal* poop.

**take off 1** *the horse took off at great speed* RUN AWAY/OFF, flee, abscond, take flight, decamp, leave, go, depart, make off, bolt, take to one's heels, escape; *informal* split, clear off, skedaddle, vamoose.

2 *the plane took off* BECOME AIRBORNE, take to the air, take wing; lift off, blast off.

3 *the idea really took off* SUCCEED, do well, become popular, catch on, prosper, flourish, thrive, boom.

**take someone on 1** *there was no challenger to take him on* COMPETE AGAINST, oppose, challenge, confront, face, fight, vie with, contend with, stand up to.

2 *we took on extra staff* ENGAGE, hire, employ, enroll, enlist, sign up; *informal* take on board.

**take something on 1** *he took on more responsibility* UNDERTAKE, accept, assume, shoulder, acquire, carry, bear.

2 *the study took on political meaning* ACQUIRE, assume, come to have.

**take one's time** *if the place were on fire, Mark would still take his time* GO SLOWLY, dally, dawdle, delay, linger, drag one's feet, waste time, kill time; *informal* dilly-dally, lollygag; *archaic* tarry.

**take someone out 1** *he asked if he could take her out* GO OUT WITH, escort, partner, accompany, go with; romance; *informal* date, see, go steady with; *dated* court, woo.

2 *informal the sniper took them all out* KILL, murder, assassinate, dispatch, execute, finish off, eliminate, exterminate, terminate; *informal* do in, do away with, bump off, rub out, mow down. *literary* slay.

**take something over** *the workers were stunned to learn that a rival corporation had taken over their company* ASSUME CONTROL OF, take charge of, take command of.

**take to 1** *he took to carrying his money in his sock* MAKE A HABIT OF, resort to, turn to, have recourse to (start/begin); start, begin, commence.

2 *Ruth took to the cat instantly* LIKE, get on with, be friendly toward; *informal* take a shine to.

3 *the dog has really taken to racing* BECOME GOOD AT, develop an ability for; like, enjoy.

**take something up 1** *she took up abstract painting* ENGAGE IN, practice; begin, start, commence.

2 *the meetings took up all her time* CONSUME, fill, absorb, use, occupy; waste, squander.

3 *her cousin took up the story* RESUME, recommence, restart, carry on, continue, pick up, return to.

4 *he took up their offer of a job* ACCEPT, say yes to, agree to, adopt; *formal* accede to.

5 *take the skirt up an inch* SHORTEN, turn up; raise, lift.

**take up with** *Burt has taken up with the kids in the ski club* BECOME FRIENDS WITH, (begin to) go around with, fall in with, string along with, get involved with, start seeing; *informal* (begin to) hang out with.

**takeoff** noun **1** *the plane performed a safe takeoff* DEPARTURE, liftoff, launch, blastoff; ascent, flight. ANTONYM touchdown.

2 *informal a takeoff of a talent show* PARODY, pastiche, mockery, caricature, travesty, satire, lampoon, mimicry, imitation, impersonation, impression; *informal* sendup, spoof.

**takings** plural noun *his takings from the race were substantial* PROCEEDS, returns, receipts, earnings, winnings, pickings, spoils; profit, gain, income, revenue; gate, purse.

**tale** noun **1** *a tale of witches* STORY, narrative, anecdote, report, account, history; legend, fable, myth, parable, allegory, saga; *informal* yarn.

2 *she told tales to her mother* LIE, fib, falsehood, story, untruth, fabrication, fiction; *informal* tall story, fairy tale, fairy story, cock-and-bull story.

**talent** noun *a natural talent for dancing* FLAIR, aptitude, facility, gift, knack, technique, touch, bent, ability, expertise, capacity, faculty; strength, forte, genius, brilliance; dexterity, skill, artistry.

**talented** adjective *a talented sculptor* GIFTED, skillful, skilled, accomplished, brilliant, expert, consummate, masterly, adroit, dexterous, able, competent, apt, capable, deft, adept, proficient; *informal* crack, ace. ANTONYM inept.

**talk** verb **1** *I was talking to a friend* SPEAK, chat, chatter, gossip, prattle, babble, rattle on, blather; *informal* yak, gab, jaw, chew the fat, natter, rap.

2 *you're talking garbage* UTTER, speak, say, voice, express, articulate, pronounce, verbalize, vocalize.

3 *they were able to talk in peace* CONVERSE, communicate, speak, confer, consult; negotiate, parley; *informal* have a confab, chew the fat, rap; *formal* confabulate.

4 *he **talked of** suicide* MENTION, refer to, speak about, discuss.

5 *he learned to talk Cree* SPEAK (IN), talk in, communicate in, converse in, express oneself in; use.

6 *nothing would make her talk* CONFESS, speak out, speak up, reveal all, tell tales, give the game away, open one's mouth; *informal* come clean, blab, squeal, let the cat out of the bag, spill the beans, sing, rat.

7 *the others will talk* GOSSIP, pass comment, make remarks; criticize.

▸ noun **1** *he was bored with all this talk* CHATTER, gossip, prattle, jabbering, babbling, gabbling; *informal* yakking, gabbing, nattering.

2 *she needed a talk with Jim* CONVERSATION, chat, discussion, tête-à-tête, heart-to-heart, dialogue, parley, powwow, consultation, conference, meeting; *informal* confab, jaw, chitchat, gossip; *formal* colloquy, confabulation.

3 **(talks)** *peace talks* NEGOTIATIONS, discussions; conference, summit, meeting, consultation, dialogue, symposium, seminar, conclave, parley; mediation, arbitration; *informal* powwow.

**4** *she gave a talk on her travels* LECTURE, speech, address, discourse, oration, presentation, report, sermon; *informal* spiel.

**5** *there was talk of a takeover* GOSSIP, rumor, hearsay, tittle-tattle; news, report.

**6** *informal he's all talk* BOASTING, bragging, idle talk, bombast, braggadocio; *informal* hot air, mouth.

**7** *baby talk* SPEECH, language, slang, idiom, idiolect; words; *informal* lingo, -ese.

PHRASES: **talk back to** *nobody talks back to Mr. Lynde* ANSWER BACK (TO), be impertinent to, be cheeky to, be rude to; contradict, argue with, disagree with.

**talk big** *informal* See BOAST verb sense 1.

**talk down to** *he routinely talks down to women* CONDESCEND TO, patronize, look down one's nose at, put down.

**talk someone into something** *don't even try to talk me into giving you another loan* PERSUADE INTO, argue into, cajole into, coax into, bring around to, inveigle into, wheedle into, sweet-talk into, prevail on someone to; *informal* hustle into, fast-talk into.

**talkative** adjective *the talkative person in the seat next to mine* CHATTY, loquacious, garrulous, voluble, conversational, communicative; gossipy, babbling, blathering; long-winded, wordy, verbose, prolix; *informal* gabby, mouthy, motormouthed, talky. ANTONYM taciturn.

THE RIGHT WORD **talkative, garrulous, glib, loquacious, voluble**

Someone who likes to talk frequently or at length might be described as **talkative** (*He was the most talkative person I'd ever met*). This word implies a readiness to engage in talk, while **loquacious** implies an inclination to talk incessantly or to keep up a constant flow of chatter (*a loquacious woman who never seemed to tire of hearing her own voice*). **Glib** and **voluble** pertain to the ease with which someone is able to converse or speak, although *voluble* may be used in either an approving or a critical sense (*a voluble speaker who was in great demand; a voluble neighbor who could not keep a secret*). *Glib* is almost always negative, referring to a superficial or slick way of speaking (*the glib manner of a used-car salesperson*). **Garrulous** also has negative overtones, implying a tedious or rambling talkativeness, usually about trivial things (*a garrulous old man who bored everyone with his stories about "the old days"*).

**talker** noun *Sue's husband is a real talker* CONVERSATIONALIST, speaker, communicator; chatterbox, motormouth, gossip, flibbertigibbet.

**talking-to** noun *informal if you ask me, that kid needs a good talking-to.* See REPRIMAND noun.

**tall** adjective **1** *a tall man* BIG, large, huge, towering, colossal, gigantic, giant, monstrous; leggy; *informal* long. ANTONYMS short, small.

**2** *tall buildings* HIGH, big, lofty, towering, elevated, sky-high; multistory. ANTONYM low.

**3** *she's five feet tall* IN HEIGHT, high, from head to toe; from top to bottom. ANTONYM wide.

**4** *a tall tale* UNLIKELY, improbable, exaggerated, far-fetched, implausible, dubious, unbelievable, incredible, absurd, untrue; *informal* cock-and-bull. ANTONYMS credible, believable.

**5** *a tall order* DEMANDING, exacting, difficult; unreasonable, impossible. ANTONYM easy.

**tally** noun **1** *he keeps a tally of the score* RUNNING TOTAL, count, record, reckoning, register, account, roll; census, poll.

**2** *her tally of 22 victories* TOTAL, score, count, sum.

▸ verb **1** *these statistics* ***tally with*** *government figures* CORRESPOND WITH, agree with, accord with, concur with, coincide with, match, fit, be consistent with, conform to, equate with, harmonize with, be in tune with, dovetail, correlate with/to, parallel; *informal* square with, jibe with. ANTONYMS disagree, differ.

**2** *votes were tallied with abacuses* COUNT, calculate, add up, total, compute; figure out, work out, reckon, measure, quantify, tot up; *formal* enumerate.

**tame** adjective **1** *a tame elephant* DOMESTICATED, domestic, docile, tamed, broken, trained; gentle, mild; pet, housebroken; *chiefly Brit.* house-trained. ANTONYMS wild, fierce.

**2** *informal he has a tame lawyer* AMENABLE, biddable, cooperative, willing, obedient, tractable, acquiescent, docile, submissive, compliant, meek. ANTONYM uncooperative.

**3** *it was a pretty tame affair* UNEXCITING, uninteresting, uninspiring, dull, bland, flat, insipid, spiritless, pedestrian, colorless, run-of-the-mill, mediocre, ordinary, humdrum, boring; harmless, safe, inoffensive. ANTONYM exciting.

▸ verb **1** *wild rabbits can be tamed* DOMESTICATE, break, train, master, subdue.

**2** *she learned to tame her emotions* SUBDUE, curb, control, calm, master, moderate, overcome, discipline, suppress, repress, mellow, temper, soften, bridle, get a grip on; *informal* lick.

**tamper** verb **1** *she saw them* ***tampering with*** *her car* INTERFERE WITH, monkey around with, meddle with, tinker with, fiddle with, fool around with, play around with; doctor, alter, change, adjust, damage, deface, vandalize; *informal* mess around with.

**2** *the defendant* ***tampered with*** *the jury* INFLUENCE, get at, rig, manipulate, bribe, corrupt, bias; *informal* fix.

**tan** adjective *a tan waistcoat* YELLOWISH-BROWN, light brown, pale brown, beige, tawny.

▸ verb **1** *use a sunscreen to help you tan* BECOME SUNTANNED, get a suntan, brown, go/get/become brown, bronze.

**2** *informal I'll tan his hide.* See THRASH sense 1.

**tang** noun *there's a lovely tang to the glaze* FLAVOR, taste, savor; sharpness, zest, bite, edge, smack, piquancy, spice; smell, odor, aroma, fragrance, perfume, redolence; *informal* kick, pep.

**tangible** adjective *I'd prefer a reward more tangible than praise—say, cash* TOUCHABLE, palpable, material, physical, real, substantial, corporeal, solid, concrete; visible, noticeable; actual, definite, clear, clear-cut, distinct, manifest, evident, unmistakable, perceptible, discernible. ANTONYM abstract.

THE RIGHT WORD **tangible, appreciable, corporeal, palpable, perceptible, sensible**

Anything that can be grasped, either with the hand or with the mind, is **tangible** (*tangible assets; tangible objects*). **Palpable**, like *tangible*, means capable of being touched or felt (*a palpable mist*), but it is often applied to whatever evokes a tactile response from the body (*a palpable chill in the room*). **Perceptible** is used to describe something that just crosses the border between invisibility and visibility or some other sense barrier (*a perceptible change in her tone of voice; a perceptible odor of garlic*). **Sensible** (in this sense) means that which can clearly be perceived through the senses or which makes a strong impression on the mind through the medium of sensations. In contrast to *perceptible*, something that is *sensible* is more obvious or immediately recognized (*a sensible shift in the tenor of the conversation*). **Corporeal** means bodily or material, in contrast to things that are immaterial or spiritual (*corporeal goods*). Something that is **appreciable** is large enough to be measured, valued, estimated, or considered significant. An *appreciable* change in temperature, for example, can be determined by looking at a thermometer; a *palpable* change in temperature may be slight, but still great enough to be felt; and a *perceptible* change in temperature might be so slight that it almost—but not quite—escapes notice.

**tangle** verb **1** *the wool got tangled* ENTANGLE, snarl, catch, entwine, twist, ravel, knot, enmesh, coil, mat, jumble, muddle.

**2** *he tangled with his old rival* COME INTO CONFLICT, dispute, argue, quarrel, fight, wrangle, squabble, contend, cross swords, lock horns.

▸ noun **1** *a tangle of branches* SNARL, mass, knot, mesh, mishmash.

**2** *the defense got into an awful tangle* MUDDLE, jumble, mix-up, confusion, shambles.

**tangled** adjective **1** *tangled hair* KNOTTED, knotty, raveled, entangled, snarled (up), twisted, matted, tangly, messy; tousled, unkempt; *informal* mussed up.

**2** *a tangled bureaucratic mess* CONFUSED, jumbled, mixed up, messy, chaotic, complicated, involved, complex, intricate, knotty, tortuous. ANTONYMS simple, straightforward.

**tank** noun **1** *a hot water tank* CONTAINER, receptacle, vat, cistern, repository, reservoir, basin.

**2** *a tank full of fish* AQUARIUM, bowl.

**3** *the army's use of tanks* ARMORED VEHICLE, armored car, combat vehicle; panzer.

**tantalize** verb *Steve was tantalized by Liliana's exotic eyes* TEASE, torment, torture, bait; tempt, entice, lure, allure, beguile; excite, fascinate, titillate, intrigue.

**tantamount** adjective *this is* ***tantamount to*** *mutiny* EQUIVALENT TO, equal to, as good as, more or less, much the same as, comparable to, on a par with, commensurate with. See note at SAME.

**tantrum** noun *how can you tolerate his tantrums?* FIT OF TEMPER, fit of rage, fit, outburst, pet, paroxysm, frenzy, bad mood, mood, huff, scene; *informal* hissy fit.

**tap**[1] noun **1** *she turned the tap on* FAUCET, valve, stopcock, cock, spout, spigot, spile.

**2** *a phone tap in the embassy* LISTENING DEVICE, wiretap, wire, bug, bugging device, (hidden) microphone, (hidden) mic, receiver.

▸ verb **1** *several barrels were tapped* DRAIN, bleed, milk; broach, open.

**2** *butlers were tapping ale* POUR (OUT), draw off, siphon off, pump out, decant.

**3** *their telephones are tapped* BUG, wiretap, monitor, overhear, eavesdrop on, spy on.

**4** *the resources were to be tapped for our benefit* DRAW ON, exploit, milk, mine, use, utilize, turn to account.

PHRASE: **on tap 1** *beers on tap* ON DRAFT, from barrels, cask-conditioned.

**2** *informal trained staff are on tap* ON HAND, at hand, available, ready, handy, accessible, standing by.

**tap**[2] verb **1** *she tapped on the door* KNOCK, rap, strike, beat, drum.

**2** *Dad tapped me on the knee* PAT, hit, strike, slap, jab, poke, dig.

▸ noun **1** *a sharp tap at the door* KNOCK, rap, drumming.

**2** *a tap on the shoulder* PAT, blow, slap, jab, poke, dig.

**tape** noun **1** *a package tied with tape* BINDING, ribbon, string, braid.

**2** *secure the bandage with tape* ADHESIVE TAPE, sticky tape, masking tape, duct tape; *trademark* Scotch Tape.

**3** *they recorded the interview on tape* AUDIOCASSETTE/VIDEOCASSETTE, (a) reel, (a) spool; video, VHS.

▸ verb **1** *a card was taped to the box* BIND, stick, fix, fasten, secure, attach; tie, strap.

**2** *they* ***taped off*** *the area* CORDON (OFF), seal (off), close (off), shut (off), mark (off), fence (off); isolate, segregate.

**3** *police taped his confession* RECORD, tape-record, capture on tape; video.

**4** *tape your ankle* BIND, wrap, bandage.

**taper** verb **1** *the leaves taper at the tip* NARROW, thin (out), come to a point, attenuate. ANTONYMS thicken, swell.

**2** *the meetings soon* ***tapered off*** DECREASE, lessen, dwindle, diminish, reduce, decline, die down, peter out, wane, ebb, slacken (off), fall off, let up, thin out. ANTONYM increase.

**target** noun **1** *targets at a range of 200 meters* MARK, bull's-eye, goal.

**2** *eagles can spot their target from half a mile* PREY, quarry, game, kill.

**3** *their profit target* OBJECTIVE, goal, aim, end; plan, intention, intent, design, aspiration, ambition, ideal, desire, wish.

**4** *she was the target for a wave of abuse* VICTIM, butt, recipient, focus, object, subject.

▸ verb 1 *he was targeted by a gunman* PICK OUT, single out, earmark, fix on; attack, aim at, fire at.

2 *the product is **targeted at** a specific market* AIM AT, direct at, level at, intend for, focus on.

PHRASE: **on target** 1 *the shot was on target* ACCURATE, precise, unerring, sure, on the mark.

2 *the project was on target* ON SCHEDULE, on track, on course, on time.

**tariff** noun *the lower tariffs across the border* TAX, duty, toll, excise, levy, charge, rate, fee, countervail; price list.

**tarnish** verb 1 *gold does not tarnish easily* DISCOLOR, rust, oxidize, corrode, stain, dull, blacken. ANTONYMS polish, brighten.

2 *it tarnished his reputation* SULLY, blacken, stain, blemish, blot, taint, soil, ruin, disgrace, mar, damage, harm, hurt, undermine, dishonor, stigmatize; *literary* besmirch. ANTONYM enhance.

▸ noun 1 *the tarnish on the candlesticks* DISCOLORATION, oxidation, rust; film.

2 *the tarnish on his reputation* SMEAR, stain, blemish, blot, taint, stigma.

**tart** noun *a lemon tart* PASTRY, flan, tartlet, quiche, pie. See note at PIE.

**task** noun *a daunting task* JOB, duty, chore, charge, assignment, detail, mission, engagement, occupation, undertaking, exercise, business, responsibility, burden, endeavor, enterprise, venture. PHRASE: **take someone to task** *Bryce took me to task for having "borrowed" his car* REBUKE, reprimand, reprove, reproach, remonstrate with, upbraid, scold, berate, castigate, lecture, censure, criticize, admonish, chide, chasten, arraign; *informal* tell off, bawl out, give someone a dressing-down.

**taste** noun 1 *a distinctive sharp taste* FLAVOR, savor, relish, tang, smack.

2 *he was dying for a taste of brandy* MOUTHFUL, drop, bit, sip, nip, swallow, touch, soupçon, dash, modicum.

3 *it's too sweet for my taste* PALATE, taste buds, appetite, stomach.

4 *a taste for adventure* LIKING, love, fondness, fancy, desire, preference, penchant, predilection, inclination, partiality; hankering, appetite, hunger, thirst, relish. ANTONYM dislike.

5 *my first **taste of** prison* EXPERIENCE OF/WITH, impression of; exposure to, contact with, involvement with.

6 *the house was furnished with taste* JUDGMENT, discrimination, discernment, tastefulness, refinement, finesse, elegance, grace, style. ANTONYMS tastelessness, tackiness.

7 *the photo was rejected on grounds of taste* DECORUM, propriety, etiquette, politeness, delicacy, nicety, sensitivity, discretion, tastefulness. ANTONYM dislike.

▸ verb 1 *Adam tasted the wine* SAMPLE, test, try, savor; sip, sup.

2 *he could taste blood on his lip* PERCEIVE, discern, make out, distinguish.

3 *a beer that **tasted of** pumpkin* HAVE A/THE FLAVOR OF, savor of, smack of, be reminiscent of; suggest.

4 *it'll be good to taste real coffee again* CONSUME, drink, partake of; eat, devour.

5 *he tasted defeat* EXPERIENCE, encounter, come face to face with, come up against, undergo; know.

**tasteful** adjective *the decor is simple and tasteful* AESTHETICALLY PLEASING, in good taste, refined, cultured, elegant, stylish, smart, chic, attractive, exquisite. ANTONYMS tasteless, tacky.

**tasteless** adjective 1 *the vegetables are tasteless* FLAVORLESS, bland, insipid, unappetizing, savorless, watery, weak. ANTONYMS tasty, appetizing.

2 *tasteless leather paneling* VULGAR, crude, tawdry, garish, gaudy, loud, trashy, showy, ostentatious, cheap, chintzy, kitschy, kitsch, inelegant; *informal* tacky. ANTONYMS refined, tasteful.

3 *a tasteless remark* CRUDE, vulgar, indelicate, uncouth, unseemly, crass, tactless, gauche, undiplomatic, indiscreet, inappropriate, offensive. ANTONYMS tasteful, seemly.

**tasty** adjective *a tasty meal* DELICIOUS, palatable, luscious, mouthwatering, delectable, ambrosial, toothsome, dainty, flavorful; appetizing, tempting; *informal* yummy, scrumptious, finger-licking, lip-smacking, melt-in-your/the-mouth. ANTONYMS bland, insipid.

**tattle** verb 1 *we were tattling about him* GOSSIP, chatter, chat, prattle, babble, jabber, gabble, rattle on; *informal* chinwag, jaw, yak, gab, natter, tittle-tattle, chitchat.

2 *I would tattle on her if I had evidence* INFORM; report, talk, tell all, spill the beans; *informal* squeal, sing, let the cat out of the bag.

▸ noun *tabloid tattle* GOSSIP, rumor, tittle-tattle, hearsay, scandal.

**taunt** noun *the taunts of his classmates* JEER, jibe, sneer, insult, barb, catcall; *informal* dig, put-down; (**taunts**) teasing, provocation, goading, derision, mockery.

▸ verb *she taunted him about his job* JEER AT, sneer at, scoff at, poke fun at, make fun of, get at, insult, tease, chaff, torment, goad, ridicule, deride, mock, heckle, ride; *informal* rib, needle.

**taut** adjective 1 *the rope was taut* TIGHT, stretched, rigid. ANTONYMS slack, loose.

2 *her muscles remained taut* FLEXED, tense, hard, solid, firm, rigid, stiff. ANTONYM relaxed.

3 *a taut expression* FRAUGHT, strained, stressed, tense; *informal* uptight.

**tautology** noun *avoid such tautology as "let's all work together, everyone, as a team" by saying simply "let's work together"* PLEONASM, repetition, reiteration, redundancy, superfluity, duplication.

**tawdry** adjective *the tawdry rings she wore on her fingers* GAUDY, flashy, showy, garish, loud; tasteless, vulgar, trashy, junky, shoddy, shabby, gimcrack, chintzy, kitsch, kitsch; *informal* tacky, cheesy, schlocky. ANTONYM tasteful.

**tax** noun **1** *they have to pay tax on the interest* DUTY, tariff, excise, customs, dues; levy, toll, impost, tithe, charge, fee. ANTONYM rebate.

**2** *a heavy tax on one's attention* BURDEN, load, weight, demand, strain, pressure, stress, drain, imposition.

▸ verb **1** *they tax foreign companies more harshly* CHARGE (DUTY ON), tithe; *formal* mulct.

**2** *his whining taxed her patience* STRAIN, stretch, overburden, overload, encumber, push too far; overwhelm, try, wear out, exhaust, sap, drain, weary, weaken.

**taxing** adjective *restaurant work can be taxing* DEMANDING, exacting, challenging, burdensome, arduous, onerous, difficult, hard, tough, laborious, back-breaking, strenuous, rigorous, punishing; tiring, exhausting, enervating, wearing, stressful; *informal* murderous. ANTONYM easy.

**teach** verb **1** *Alison teaches small children* EDUCATE, instruct, school, tutor, coach, train; enlighten, illuminate, verse, edify, indoctrinate; drill, discipline.

**2** *I taught yoga* GIVE LESSONS IN, lecture in, be a teacher of; demonstrate, instill, inculcate.

**3** *she taught me how to love* TRAIN, show, guide, instruct, explain to, demonstrate to.

**teacher** noun *the new physics teacher used to be a nun* EDUCATOR, tutor, instructor, master, mistress, governess, educationist, preceptor; coach, trainer; lecturer, professor, don; guide, mentor, guru, counselor; substitute teacher, sub; *informal* teach; *formal* pedagogue; *historical* schoolman, schoolmarm.

**team** noun **1** *the sales team* GROUP, squad, company, party, crew, troupe, band, side, lineup, phalanx; *informal* bunch, gang, posse.

**2** *a team of horses* PAIR, span, yoke, duo, set, tandem.

▸ verb **1** *the horses are teamed in pairs* HARNESS, yoke, hitch, couple.

**2** *you could **team up** with another artist for an exhibition* JOIN (FORCES), collaborate, get together, work together; unite, combine, cooperate, link, ally, associate.

**tear**[1] verb **1** *I **tore up** the letter* RIP UP, rip in two, pull to pieces, shred.

**2** *his flesh was torn* LACERATE, cut (open), gash, slash, scratch, hack, pierce, stab; injure, wound.

**3** *the traumas **tore** her family **apart*** DIVIDE, split, sever, break up, disunite, rupture; *literary* rend, sunder, cleave. ANTONYM unite.

**4** *Gina tore the book from his hands* SNATCH, grab, seize, rip, wrench, wrest, pull, pluck; *informal* yank.

**5** *informal Jack tore down the street* SPRINT, race, run, dart, rush, dash, hasten, hurry, bolt, fly, career, charge, shoot, hurtle, careen, speed, whiz, zoom, go like lightning, go like the wind; *informal* pelt, scoot, hotfoot it, belt, zip, whip, bomb, hightail it. ANTONYMS stroll, amble.

▸ noun *a tear in her dress* RIP, hole, split, slash, slit; snag.

PHRASE: **tear down** *they tore down the old barn* DEMOLISH, knock down, raze, raze to the ground, flatten, level, bulldoze; dismantle, disassemble.

**tear**[2] noun *tears in her eyes* TEARDROP; drop, droplet. PHRASE: **in tears** *he was nearly in tears* CRYING, weeping, sobbing, wailing, howling, bawling, whimpering; tearful, upset; *informal* weepy, teary, blubbering.

**tearful** adjective **1** *Bess was tearful* IN TEARS, with tears in one's eyes, choked up, crying, weeping, sobbing, sniveling; close to tears, emotional, upset, distressed, sad, unhappy; *informal* weepy, teary, misty-eyed; *formal* lachrymose. ANTONYMS laughing, smiling.

**2** *a tearful farewell* EMOTIONAL, upsetting, distressing, sad, heartbreaking, sorrowful; poignant, moving, touching, tear-jerking; *literary* dolorous. ANTONYM cheerful.

**tease** verb *Larry's dentist is the dork he used to tease in sixth grade* MAKE FUN OF, poke fun at, laugh at, guy, make a monkey (out) of; taunt, bait, goad, pick on; deride, mock, ridicule; *informal* rib, josh, pull/yank someone's chain, razz.

**technical** adjective **1** *an important technical achievement* practical, scientific, technological, high-tech.

**2** *this might seem very technical* SPECIALIST, specialized, scientific; complex, complicated, esoteric.

**3** *a technical fault* MECHANICAL.

**technique** noun **1** *different techniques for solving the problem* METHOD, approach, procedure, system, modus operandi, MO, way; means, strategy, tack, tactic, line; routine, practice.

**2** *I was impressed with his technique* SKILL, ability, proficiency, expertise, mastery, talent, genius, artistry, craftsmanship; aptitude, adroitness, deftness, dexterity, facility, competence; performance, delivery; *informal* know-how.

**tedious** adjective *work on the assembly line was tedious* BORING, dull, monotonous, repetitive, unrelieved, unvaried, uneventful; characterless, colorless, lifeless, insipid, uninteresting, unexciting, uninspiring, flat, bland, dry, stale, tired, lackluster, stodgy, dreary, mundane, monochrome; mind-numbing, soul-destroying, wearisome, tiring, tiresome, irksome, trying, frustrating; *informal* deadly, not up to much, humdrum, ho-hum, blah, dullsville, [same old, same old]. ANTONYM exciting.

**tedium** noun **1** *she loathed the tedium of housework* MONOTONY, boredom, ennui, uniformity, routine, dreariness, dryness, banality, vapidity, insipidity. ANTONYM variety.

**2** *I dozed off during the tedium of the third act* TEDIOUS PASSAGE, tedious moments, tedious period of time, flatness, longueur.

**teem** verb *the pond once **teemed with** fish* BE FULL OF, be filled with, be alive with, be brimming with, abound in, be swarming with, be aswarm with; be packed with, be crawling with, be overrun by, bristle with, seethe with, be thick with; be jam-packed with, be chock-full of.

**teenage** adjective *a teenage hairstyle* ADOLESCENT, teenaged, youthful, young, juvenile; *informal* teen.

**teenager** noun *he's been counseling teenagers for twenty years* ADOLESCENT, youth, young person, minor, juvenile; *informal* teen, teenybopper.

**teeter** verb **1** *Daisy teetered toward them* TOTTER, wobble, toddle, sway, stagger, stumble, reel, lurch, pitch.

**2** *the situation teetered between tragedy and farce* SEESAW, veer, fluctuate, oscillate, swing, alternate, waver.

**telegram** noun *the message arrived by telegram* telex; *informal* wire; *dated* radiogram; *historical* cable, cablegram.

**telepathy** noun *he claims he knew about Dylan's past through telepathy* MIND-READING, thought transference; extrasensory perception, ESP; clairvoyance, sixth sense; psychometry.

**telephone** noun *she picked up the telephone* PHONE, cell phone, cellular phone, cell; handset, receiver; *informal* blower, horn.

▸ verb *he telephoned me last night* PHONE, call, ring; get, reach; *dated* dial; *informal* call up, give someone a buzz, get on the blower to, get someone on the horn.

**telescope** noun *a pocket telescope* SPYGLASS, glass; *informal* scope.

▸ verb **1** *the front of the car was telescoped* CONCERTINA, compact, compress, crush, squash.

**2** *his recent employment experience can be telescoped into a short paragraph* CONDENSE, shorten, reduce, abbreviate, abridge, summarize, précis, abstract, shrink, consolidate; truncate, curtail.

**television** noun *what's on television this evening?* TV; *informal* the small screen, the idiot box, the tube, the boob tube, the box.

**tell** verb **1** *why didn't you tell me before?* INFORM, notify, apprise, let know, make aware, acquaint with, advise, put in the picture, brief, fill in; alert, warn; *informal* clue in/up.

**2** *she told the story slowly* RELATE, recount, narrate, unfold, report, recite, describe, sketch, weave, spin; utter, voice, state, declare, communicate, impart, divulge.

**3** *she told him to leave* INSTRUCT, order, command, direct, charge, enjoin, call on, require; *literary* bid.

**4** *I tell you, I did nothing wrong* ASSURE, promise, give one's word, swear, guarantee.

**5** *the figures tell a different story* REVEAL, show, indicate, be evidence of, disclose, convey, signify.

**6** *promise you won't tell?* GIVE THE GAME AWAY, talk, tell tales, tattle; *informal* spill the beans, let the cat out of the bag, blab.

**7** *she was bound to* ***tell on*** *him* INFORM ON, tell tales on, give away, denounce, sell out; *informal* blow the whistle on, rat on, squeal on, finger.

**8** *it was hard to tell what he said* ASCERTAIN, determine, work out, make out, deduce, discern, perceive, see, identify, recognize, understand, comprehend; *informal* figure out; *Brit. informal* suss out.

**9** *he couldn't tell one from the other* DISTINGUISH, differentiate, discriminate.

**10** *the strain began to* ***tell on*** *him* TAKE ITS TOLL, leave its mark; affect. PHRASE: **tell off** *informal oh, brother, did he ever tell you off.* See REPRIMAND verb.

**telling** adjective *a telling critique of the military mind* REVEALING, significant, weighty, important, meaningful, influential, striking, potent, powerful, compelling. ANTONYM insignificant.

**telltale** adjective *the telltale blush on her face* REVEALING, revelatory, suggestive, meaningful, significant, meaning; *informal* giveaway.

**temerity** noun *I doubt they'll have the temerity to print these accusations* AUDACITY, nerve, effrontery, impudence, impertinence, cheek, gall, presumption; daring; *informal* face, front, neck, chutzpah.

THE RIGHT WORD **temerity, audacity, effrontery, foolhardiness, gall, impetuosity, rashness**

The line that divides boldness from foolishness or stupidity is often a fine one. Someone who rushes hastily into a situation without thinking about the consequences might be accused of **rashness**, while **temerity** implies exposing oneself needlessly to danger while failing to estimate one's chances of success (*she had the temerity to criticize her teacher in front of the class*). **Audacity** describes a different kind of boldness, one that disregards moral standards or social conventions (*he had the audacity to ask her if she would mind paying for the trip*). Someone who behaves with **foolhardiness** is reckless or downright foolish (*climbing the mountain after dark was foolhardiness and everyone knew it*), while **impetuosity** describes an eager impulsiveness or behavior that is sudden, rash, and sometimes violent (*his impetuosity had landed him in trouble before*). **Gall** and **effrontery** are always derogatory terms. *Effrontery* is a more formal word for the flagrant disregard of the rules of propriety and courtesy (*she had the effrontery to call the president by his first name*), while *gall* is more colloquial and suggests outright insolence (*he was the only one who had the gall to tell the boss off*).

**temper** noun **1** *he walked out in a temper* FIT OF RAGE, rage, fury, fit of pique, tantrum, bad mood, mood, sulk, huff; *informal* grump, snit, hissy fit.

**2** *a display of temper* ANGER, fury, rage, annoyance, vexation, irritation, irritability, ill humor, spleen, pique, petulance, testiness, tetchiness, touchiness, crabbiness; *literary* ire, choler.

**3** *she struggled to keep her temper* COMPOSURE, equanimity, self-control, self-possession, sangfroid, calm, good humor; *informal* cool.

▸ verb **1** *the steel is tempered by heat* HARDEN, strengthen, toughen, fortify, anneal.

**2** *their idealism is tempered with realism* MODERATE, modify, modulate, mitigate, alleviate, reduce, weaken, lighten, soften. See note at ALLEVIATE.

PHRASE: **lose one's temper** *calm down, there's no need to lose your temper* GET ANGRY, fly into a rage, erupt, lose control, go berserk, breathe fire, flare up, boil over; *informal* go mad, go crazy, go bananas, have a fit, see red, fly off the handle, blow one's top, hit the roof, go off the deep end, go ape, flip, freak out.

**temperament** noun *Haley's dog has the nicest temperament* DISPOSITION, nature, character, personality, makeup, constitution, mind, spirit; stamp, mettle, mold; mood, frame of mind, attitude, outlook, humor.

**temperamental** adjective **1** *a temperamental chef* VOLATILE, excitable, emotional, mercurial, capricious, erratic, unpredictable, changeable, inconsistent; hotheaded, fiery, quick-tempered, irritable, irascible, impatient; touchy, moody, sensitive, oversensitive, high-strung, neurotic, melodramatic. ANTONYM placid.

**2** *a temperamental dislike of conflict* INHERENT, innate, natural, inborn, constitutional, deep-rooted, ingrained, congenital.

**temperance** noun *a strict advocate of temperance* TEETOTALISM, abstinence, abstention, sobriety, self-restraint; prohibition. See note at ABSTINENCE. ANTONYM alcoholism.

**temperate** adjective **1** *temperate climates* MILD, clement, benign, gentle, balmy. ANTONYM extreme.

**2** *he was temperate in his consumption of food* SELF-RESTRAINED, restrained, moderate, self-controlled, disciplined; abstemious, self-denying, austere, ascetic; teetotal, abstinent. ANTONYM immoderate.

**tempest** noun *the skies opened and a tempest erupted* STORM, gale, hurricane; tornado, whirlwind, cyclone, typhoon.

**tempestuous** adjective **1** *the fair weather passed and the day became tempestuous* STORMY, blustery, squally, wild, turbulent, windy, gusty, blowy, rainy; foul, nasty, inclement. ANTONYMS calm, fine.

**2** *the tempestuous political environment* TURBULENT, stormy, tumultuous, wild, lively, heated, explosive, feverish, frenetic, frenzied. ANTONYM peaceful.

**3** *a tempestuous woman* EMOTIONAL, passionate, impassioned, fiery, intense; temperamental, volatile, excitable, mercurial, capricious, unpredictable, quick-tempered. ANTONYMS calm, placid.

**temple** noun *at the altar of the temple* HOUSE OF GOD, house of worship, shrine, sanctuary; church, cathedral, mosque, synagogue, shul; *archaic* fane.

**tempo** noun **1** *the tempo of the music* SPEED, cadence, rhythm, beat, time, pulse; measure, meter.

**2** *the tempo of life in Western society* PACE, rate, speed, velocity.

**temporal** adjective *the temporal aspects of church government* SECULAR, nonspiritual, worldly, profane, material, mundane, earthly, terrestrial; nonreligious, areligious, lay. ANTONYM spiritual.

**temporarily** adverb **1** *the girl was temporarily placed with a foster family* FOR THE TIME BEING, for the moment, for now, for the present, in the interim, for the nonce, in/for the meantime, in the meanwhile; provisionally, pro tem; *informal* for the minute. ANTONYM permanently.

**2** *he was temporarily blinded by the light* BRIEFLY, for a short time, momentarily, fleetingly. ANTONYM permanently.

**temporary** adjective **1** *temporary accommodationss | the temporary captain* NONPERMANENT, short-term, interim; provisional, pro tem, makeshift, stopgap; acting, fill-in, stand-in, caretaker. ANTONYM permanent.

**2** *a temporary loss of self-control* BRIEF, short-lived, momentary, fleeting, passing. ANTONYM lasting.

THE RIGHT WORD **temporary, ephemeral, evanescent, fleeting, transient, transitory**

Things that don't last long are called **temporary**, which emphasizes a measurable but limited duration (*a temporary appointment as chief of staff*). Something that is **fleeting** passes almost instantaneously and cannot be caught or held (*a fleeting thought; a fleeting glimpse*). **Transient** also applies to something that lasts or stays only a short time (*transient house guests*), while **transitory** refers to something that is destined to pass away or come to an end (*the transitory pleasure of eating*). **Evanescent** and **ephemeral** describe what is even more short-lived. *Ephemeral* literally means lasting for only a single day, but is often used to describe anything that is slight and perishable (*his fame was ephemeral*). *Evanescent* is a more lyrical word for whatever vanishes almost as soon as it appears. In other words, a job might be *temporary*, an emotion *fleeting*, a visitor *transient*, a woman's beauty *transitory*, and glory *ephemeral*, but the flash of a bird's wing across the sky would have to be called *evanescent*.

**tempt** verb **1** *the manager tried to tempt him to stay* ENTICE, persuade, convince, inveigle, induce, cajole, coax, woo; *informal* sweet-talk. ANTONYMS discourage, deter.

**2** *more customers are being tempted by credit* ALLURE, attract, appeal to, whet the appetite of; lure, seduce, beguile, tantalize, draw. ANTONYMS repel, put off.

THE RIGHT WORD **tempt, allure, beguile, entice, inveigle, lure, seduce**

When we are under the influence of a powerful attraction, particularly to something that is wrong or unwise, we are **tempted**. **Entice** implies that a crafty or skillful person has attracted us by offering a reward or pleasure (*she was enticed into joining the group by a personal plea from its handsome leader*), while **inveigle** suggests that we are enticed through the use of deception or cajolery (*inveigled into supporting the plan*). If someone **lures** us, it suggests that we have been tempted or influenced for fraudulent or destructive purposes or attracted to something harmful or evil (*lured by gang members*). **Allure** may also suggest that we have been deliberately tempted against our will, but the connotations here are often sexual (*allured by her dark green eyes*). **Seduce** carries heavy sexual connotations (*seduced by an older woman*), although it can simply mean prompted to action against our will (*seduced by a clever sales pitch*). While **beguile** at one time referred exclusively to the use of deception to lead someone astray, nowadays it can also refer to the use of subtle devices to lead someone on (*a local festival designed to beguile the tourists*).

---

**temptation** noun **1** *Mary resisted the temptation to answer back* DESIRE, urge, itch, impulse, inclination.

**2** *the temptations of Las Vegas* LURE, allurement, enticement, seduction, attraction, draw, pull; siren song.

**3** *the temptation of travel to exotic locations* ALLURE, appeal, attraction, fascination.

**tempting** adjective **1** *a tempting opportunity* ENTICING, alluring, attractive, appealing, inviting, captivating, seductive, beguiling, fascinating, tantalizing; irresistible. ANTONYMS off-putting, uninviting.

**2** *a plate of tempting cakes* APPETIZING, mouthwatering, delicious, toothsome; *informal* scrumptious, yummy, lip-smacking. ANTONYM unappetizing.

**tenable** adjective *O'Leary's confession has certainly made Cohn's alibi more tenable* DEFENSIBLE, justifiable, supportable, sustainable, arguable, able to hold water, reasonable, sensible, rational, sound, viable, plausible, credible, believable, conceivable. ANTONYM indefensible.

**tenacious** adjective **1** *his tenacious grip* FIRM, tight, fast, clinging; strong, forceful, powerful, unshakable, immovable, iron. ANTONYMS weak, loose.

**2** *a tenacious opponent* PERSEVERING, persistent, determined, dogged, strong-willed, tireless, indefatigable, resolute, patient, unflagging, staunch, steadfast, untiring, unwavering, unswerving, unshakable, unyielding, insistent; stubborn, intransigent, obstinate, obdurate, stiff-necked; rock-ribbed; pertinacious. ANTONYM irresolute.

**tenacity** noun *she practices her gymnastics routine with the tenacity of a bulldog* PERSISTENCE, determination, perseverance, doggedness, strength of purpose, tirelessness, indefatigability, resolution, resoluteness, resolve, firmness, patience, purposefulness, staunchness, steadfastness, staying power, endurance, stamina, stubbornness, intransigence, obstinacy, obduracy, pertinacity. See note at COURAGE.

**tenant** noun *the tenants' rent is due on the first of each month* OCCUPANT, resident, inhabitant; renter, leaseholder, lessee, lodger, roomer; squatter. ANTONYMS owner, freeholder.

**tend**[1] verb **1** *I tend to get very involved in my work* BE INCLINED, be apt, be disposed, be prone, be liable, have a tendency, have a propensity.

**2** *some of the younger voters tended toward the tabloid press* INCLINE, lean, gravitate, move; prefer, favor, trend.

**tend**[2] verb *she tended her garden* LOOK AFTER, take care of, care for, minister to, attend to, see to, wait on; watch over, keep an eye on, mind, protect, watch, guard, supervise; nurse, nurture, cherish. ANTONYM neglect.

**tendency** noun **1** *his tendency to take the law into his own hands* PROPENSITY, proclivity, proneness, aptness, likelihood, inclination, disposition, predisposition, bent, leaning, penchant, predilection, susceptibility, liability; readiness; habit.

**2** *this tendency toward cohabitation* TREND, movement, drift, swing, gravitation, direction, course; orientation, bias.

**tender**[1] adjective **1** *a gentle, tender man* CARING, kind, kindly, kindhearted, softhearted, tenderhearted, compassionate, sympathetic, warm, warmhearted, solicitous, fatherly, motherly, maternal, gentle, mild, benevolent, generous, giving, humane. ANTONYMS hard-hearted, callous.

**2** *a tender kiss* AFFECTIONATE, fond, loving, emotional, warm, gentle, soft; amorous, adoring; *informal* lovey-dovey.

**3** *simmer until the meat is tender* EASILY CHEWED, chewable, soft; succulent, juicy; tenderized, fork-tender. ANTONYM tough.

**4** *tender plants* DELICATE, easily damaged, fragile, vulnerable. ANTONYM hardy.

**5** *her ankle was swollen and tender* SORE, painful, sensitive, inflamed, raw, red, chafed, bruised, irritated; hurting, aching, throbbing, smarting.

**6** *the tender age of fifteen* YOUNG, youthful, early; impressionable, inexperienced, immature, unseasoned, juvenile, callow, green, raw, unripe, wet behind the ears. ANTONYM advanced.

**7** *the issue of conscription was a particularly tender one* DIFFICULT, delicate, touchy, tricky, awkward, problematic, troublesome, thorny, ticklish; controversial, emotive; *informal* sticky. ANTONYM straightforward.

**tender**[2] verb **1** *she tendered her resignation* OFFER, proffer, present, put forward, propose, suggest, advance, submit, extend, give, render; hand in.

**2** *firms of interior decorators tendered for the work* PUT IN A BID, bid, quote, give an estimate.

▸ noun *six contractors were invited to submit tenders* BID, offer, quotation, quote, estimate, price; proposal, submission, pitch.

**tenderness** noun **1** *I felt an enormous tenderness for her* AFFECTION, fondness, love, devotion, loving kindness, emotion, sentiment.

**2** *with unexpected tenderness, he told her what had happened* KINDNESS, kindliness, kindheartedness, tenderheartedness, compassion, care, concern, sympathy, humanity, warmth, fatherliness, motherliness, gentleness, benevolence, generosity.

**3** *abdominal tenderness* SORENESS, pain, inflammation, irritation, bruising; ache, aching, smarting, throbbing.

**tenet** noun *the fundamental tenet of Marxism* PRINCIPLE, belief, doctrine, precept, creed, credo, article of faith, axiom, dogma, canon; theory, thesis, premise, conviction, idea, view, opinion, position; (**tenets**) ideology, code of belief, teaching(s).

**tenor** noun **1** *the general tenor of his speech* SENSE, meaning, theme, drift, thread, import, purport, intent, intention, burden, thrust, significance, message; gist, tone, essence, substance, spirit, feel.

**2** *the even tenor of life in the village* COURSE, direction, movement, drift, current, trend.

**tense** adjective **1** *the tense muscles of his neck* TAUT, tight, rigid, stretched, strained, stiff. ANTONYMS slack, loose.

**2** *Loretta was feeling tense and irritable* ANXIOUS, nervous, on edge, edgy, antsy, strained, stressed, under pressure, agitated, ill at ease, fretful, uneasy, restless, strung out, worked up, wound up, keyed up, overwrought, jumpy, on tenterhooks, with one's stomach in knots, worried, apprehensive, panicky; *informal* uptight, het up, stressed out, jittery, twitchy, squirrelly, in a state, a bundle of nerves. ANTONYMS relaxed, calm.

**3** *a tense moment* NERVE-RACKING, stressful, anxious, worrying, fraught, charged, strained, nail-biting, suspenseful, uneasy, difficult, uncomfortable; exciting, cliffhanging, knife-edge; *informal* hairy, white-knuckle. ANTONYM relaxing.

▸ verb *Hebden tensed his muscles* TIGHTEN, tauten, tense up, flex, contract, brace, stiffen; screw up, knot, strain, stretch, squinch up. ANTONYM relax.

**tension** noun **1** *the tension of the rope* TIGHTNESS, tautness, rigidity; pull, traction.

**2** *the tension was unbearable* STRAIN, stress, anxiety, pressure; worry, apprehensiveness, apprehension, agitation, nerves, nervousness, jumpiness, edginess, restlessness; suspense, uncertainty, anticipation, excitement; *informal* heebie-jeebies, butterflies (in one's stomach), collywobbles.

**3** *months of tension between the military and the government* STRAINED RELATIONS, strain; ill feeling, friction, antagonism, antipathy, hostility, enmity.

**tentative** adjective **1** *tentative arrangements* | *a tentative conclusion* PROVISIONAL, unconfirmed, penciled in, iffy, preliminary, to be confirmed, subject to confirmation; speculative, conjectural, sketchy, untried, unproven, exploratory, experimental, trial, test, pilot. ANTONYM definite.

**2** *he took a few tentative steps* HESITANT, uncertain, cautious, timid, hesitating, faltering, shaky, unsteady, halting; wavering, unsure. ANTONYM confident.

**tenterhooks** PHRASE: **on tenterhooks** *she's been on tenterhooks ever since the job interview* IN SUSPENSE, waiting with bated breath; anxious, nervous, apprehensive, worried, worried sick, on edge, edgy, antsy, tense, strained, stressed, agitated, restless, worked up, keyed up, jumpy, with one's stomach in knots, with one's heart in one's mouth; *informal* with butterflies in one's stomach, jittery, twitchy, in a state, uptight, het up; squirrelly.

**tenuous** adjective **1** *a tenuous connection* SLIGHT, insubstantial, meager, flimsy, weak, doubtful, dubious, questionable, suspect; vague, nebulous, hazy. ANTONYMS convincing, strong.

**2** *a tenuous thread* FINE, thin, slender, delicate, wispy, gossamer, fragile. ANTONYMS thick, strong.

**tepid** adjective **1** *tepid water* LUKEWARM, warmish, slightly warm; at room temperature. ANTONYMS hot, cold.

**2** *a tepid response* UNENTHUSIASTIC, apathetic, muted, half-hearted, so-so, 'comme ci, comme ça,' indifferent, subdued, cool, lukewarm, uninterested, unenthused. ANTONYMS passionate, enthusiastic.

**term** noun **1** *scientific and technical terms* WORD, expression, phrase, turn of phrase, idiom, locution; name, title, designation, label, moniker; *formal* appellation, denomination, descriptor.

**2 (terms)** *a protest in the strongest terms* LANGUAGE, mode of expression, manner of speaking, phraseology, terminology; words, expressions.

**3 (terms)** *the terms of the contract* CONDITIONS, stipulations, specifications, provisions, provisos, qualifications, particulars, small print, details, points.

**4 (terms)** *a policy offering more favorable terms* RATES, prices, charges, costs, fees; tariff.

**5** *the director is elected for a two-year term* PERIOD, period of time, time, length of time, spell, stint, duration; stretch, run; period of office, incumbency.

**6** *archaic* *the whole term of your natural life* DURATION, length, span.

**7** *the summer term* SESSION, semester, trimester, quarter; intersession.

▸ verb *he has been termed the father of modern theology* CALL, name, entitle, title, style, designate, describe as, dub, label, brand, tag, bill, nickname; *formal* denominate.

PHRASE: **come to terms 1** *the two sides came to terms* REACH AN AGREEMENT/UNDERSTANDING, make a deal, reach a compromise, meet each other halfway.

**2** *she eventually **came to terms with** her situation* ACCEPT, come to accept, reconcile oneself to, learn to live with, become resigned to, make the best of; face up to.

**terminal** adjective **1** *a terminal illness* INCURABLE, untreatable, inoperable; fatal, mortal, deadly; *Medicine* immedicable.

**2** *terminal patients* INCURABLE, dying; near death, on one's deathbed, on one's last legs, with one foot in the grave.

**3** *a terminal bonus may be payable when a policy matures* FINAL, last, concluding, closing, end.

▸ noun **1** *a railroad terminal* STATION, last stop, end of the line; depot; *chiefly Brit.* terminus.

**2** *a computer terminal* WORKSTATION, VDT, visual display terminal.

**terminate** verb **1** *the project was terminated* BRING TO AN END, end, abort, curtail, bring to a close/conclusion, close, conclude, finish, stop, put an end to, wind up, wrap up, discontinue, cease, kill, cut short, ax; *informal* pull the plug on, can. ANTONYMS begin, start, continue.

**2** *ten employees were terminated* FIRE, ax; downsize; *informal* can, cut. ANTONYM hire.

**3** *this bus terminates at Granville Street* END ITS JOURNEY, finish up, stop.

**termination** noun *the termination of the after-school music program* ENDING, end, closing, close, conclusion, finish, stopping, winding up, discontinuance, discontinuation; cancellation, dissolution; *informal* windup. ANTONYMS start, beginning.

**terminology** noun *medical terminology* PHRASEOLOGY, terms, expressions, words, language, lexicon, parlance, vocabulary, wording, nomenclature; usage, idiom; jargon, cant, argot; *informal* lingo, -speak, -ese.

**terrible** adjective **1** *a terrible crime* | *terrible injuries* DREADFUL, awful, appalling, horrific, horrifying, horrible, horrendous, atrocious, abominable, deplorable, egregious, abhorrent, frightful, shocking, hideous, ghastly, grim, dire, unspeakable, gruesome, monstrous, sickening, heinous, vile; serious, grave, acute; *formal* grievous. ANTONYMS minor, negligible.

**2** *a terrible smell* REPULSIVE, disgusting, awful, dreadful, ghastly, horrid, horrible, vile, foul, abominable, frightful, loathsome, revolting, nasty, odious, nauseating, repellent, horrendous, hideous, appalling, offensive, objectionable, obnoxious, gruesome, putrid, noisome, yucky, godawful, gross. ANTONYMS nice, delightful, pleasant.

**3** *he was in terrible pain* SEVERE, extreme, intense, acute, excruciating, agonizing, unbearable, intolerable, unendurable. ANTONYM slight.

**4** *that's a terrible thing to say* UNKIND, nasty, unpleasant, foul, obnoxious, vile, contemptible, despicable, wretched, shabby; spiteful, mean, malicious, poisonous, mean-spirited, cruel, hateful, hurtful; unfair, uncharitable, uncalled for, below the belt, unwarranted. ANTONYMS kind, nice.

**5** *the movie was terrible* VERY BAD, dreadful, awful, deplorable, atrocious, hopeless, worthless, useless, poor, pathetic, pitiful, lamentable, appalling, abysmal; *informal* lame, lousy, brutal, painful, crappy. ANTONYMS brilliant, excellent.

**6** *I feel terrible. I've been in bed all day* ILL, sick, queasy, poorly, unwell, nauseous, nauseated, peaked, green around the gills; dizzy, groggy; *informal* under the weather, lousy, crummy, awful, dreadful, crappy; *rare* peakish. ANTONYM well.

**7** *she still feels terrible about what she did to John* GUILTY, conscience-stricken, remorseful, guilt-ridden, ashamed, chastened, contrite, sorry, sick, bad, awful. ANTONYMS untroubled, unashamed.

**terribly** adverb **1** *she's not terribly upset* VERY, extremely, particularly, hugely, intensely, really, terrifically, tremendously, immensely, dreadfully, incredibly, remarkably, extraordinarily, seriously; *informal* real, mighty, awful, majorly.

**2** *he played terribly* VERY BADLY, atrociously, deplorably, awfully, dreadfully, appallingly, execrably, abysmally, pitifully.

**3** *I shall miss you terribly* VERY MUCH, greatly, a great deal, a lot; *informal* tons, loads, big time.

**terrific** adjective **1** *a terrific all-star cast* MARVELOUS, wonderful, sensational, outstanding, great, superb, excellent, first-rate, first-class, dazzling, out of this world, breathtaking; fantastic, fabulous, super, blue-ribbon, magic; *informal* cool, wicked, awesome, bang-up, dandy, mean.

**2** *a terrific bang* TREMENDOUS, huge, massive, enormous, gigantic, colossal, mighty, great, prodigious, formidable, monstrous, sizable, considerable; intense, extreme, extraordinary; *informal* whopping, humongous; deafening.

**terrify** verb *that crazy driver terrified us* PETRIFY, horrify, frighten, scare, scare stiff, scare/frighten to death, scare/frighten the living daylights out of, scare/frighten the life out of, scare/frighten someone out of their wits, scare witless, strike terror into, put the fear of God into; terrorize, paralyze, transfix; *informal* scare the pants off, scare the bejesus out of.

**territory** noun **1** *the island is a U.S. territory* AREA, area of land, region, enclave; country, state, land, colony, dominion, protectorate, fief, dependency, possession, jurisdiction, holding; section, turf.

**2** *mountainous territory* TERRAIN, land, ground, countryside.

**3** *linguistic puzzles are Stina's territory* DOMAIN, area of concern/interest/knowledge, province, department, field, preserve, bailiwick, sphere, arena, realm, world.

**terror** noun **1** *she screamed in terror* EXTREME FEAR, dread, horror, fear and trembling, fright, alarm, panic.

**2** *informal* *that child is a little terror* RASCAL, rogue, rapscallion, devil, imp, monkey, mischief-maker, troublemaker, scalawag, scamp; *informal* holy terror, horror, hellion, varmint; *archaic* scapegrace.

**terrorize** verb *terrorized by racist thugs* PERSECUTE, victimize, torment, harass, tyrannize, intimidate, menace, threaten, bully, browbeat; scare, frighten, terrify, petrify.

**terse** adjective *we were offended by her terse answers* BRIEF, short, to the point, concise, succinct, crisp, pithy, incisive, trenchant, short and sweet, laconic, elliptical; BRUSQUE, abrupt, curt, clipped, blunt, pointed, ungracious, gruff. ANTONYMS long-winded, polite.

**THE RIGHT WORD terse, concise, laconic, pithy, succinct**

If you don't like to mince words, you'll make every effort to be **concise** in both your writing and speaking, which means to remove all superfluous details (*a concise summary of everything that happened*). **Succinct** is very close in meaning to *concise*, although it emphasizes compression and compactness in addition to brevity (*succinct instructions for what to do in an emergency*). If you're **laconic**, you are brief to the point of being curt, brusque, or even uncommunicative (*his laconic reply left many questions unanswered*). **Terse** can also mean clipped or abrupt (*a terse command*), but it usually connotes something that is both concise and polished (*a terse style of writing that was much admired*). A **pithy** statement is not only succinct but full of substance and meaning (*a pithy argument that no one could counter*).

**test** noun **1** *a series of scientific tests* TRIAL, experiment, test case, case study, pilot study, trial run, tryout, dry run; check, examination, assessment, evaluation, appraisal, investigation, inspection, analysis, scrutiny, study, probe, exploration; screening; *technical* assay.

**2** *candidates may be required to take a test* EXAM, examination, quiz.

▸ verb **1** *a small-scale prototype was tested* TRY OUT, put to the test, put through its paces, experiment with, pilot; check, examine, assess, evaluate, appraise, investigate, analyze, scrutinize, study, probe, explore, trial; sample; screen; *technical* assay.

**2** *such behavior would test any marriage* PUT A STRAIN ON, strain, tax, try; make demands on, stretch, challenge.

**testament** noun *an achievement that is a testament to his professionalism and dedication* TESTIMONY, witness, evidence, proof, attestation; demonstration, indication, symbol, exemplification; monument, tribute.

**testify** verb **1** *you may be required to testify in court* GIVE EVIDENCE, bear witness, be a witness, give one's testimony, attest; *Law* make a deposition.

**2** *he testified that he had been threatened by a fellow officer* ATTEST, swear, state on oath, state, declare, assert, affirm; allege, submit, claim; *Law* depose.

**3** *the exhibits* ***testify to*** *the talents of the local sculptors* BE EVIDENCE/PROOF OF, attest to, confirm, prove, corroborate, substantiate, bear out; show, demonstrate, bear witness to, speak to, indicate, reveal, bespeak.

**testimonial** noun *a glowing testimonial* RECOMMENDATION, reference, character reference, letter of recommendation, commendation, endorsement, blurb.

**testimony** noun **1** *Smith was in court to hear her testimony* EVIDENCE, sworn statement, attestation, affidavit; statement, declaration, assertion, affirmation; allegation, submission, claim; *Law* deposition.

**2** *the work is a* ***testimony to*** *his professional commitment* TESTAMENT TO, proof of, evidence of, attestation to, witness to; confirmation of, verification of, corroboration of; demonstration of, illustration of, indication of.

**testy** adjective *what's made you so testy today?* IRRITABLE, tetchy, cranky, ornery, cantankerous, irascible, bad-tempered, grumpy, grouchy, crotchety, petulant, crabby, crusty, curmudgeonly, ill-tempered, ill-humored, peevish, cross, fractious, pettish, prickly, short-fused, waspish, snappish, snippy. ANTONYM good-humored.

**tether** verb *the horse had been tethered to a post* TIE, tie up, hitch, rope, chain; fasten, bind, fetter, secure. ANTONYM unleash.

▸ noun *a dog on a tether* ROPE, chain, cord, leash, lead; restraint, fetter; halter.

**text** noun **1** *a text that explores pain and grief* BOOK, work, written work, printed work, document.

**2** *the pictures are clear and relate well to the text* WORDS, wording, writing; content, body, main body; narrative, story.

**3** *academic texts* TEXTBOOK, book, material.

**4** *a text from the First Book of Samuel* PASSAGE, extract, excerpt, quotation, verse, line; reading.

**texture** noun *the texture of the burlap is coarse and nubby* FEEL, touch; appearance, finish, surface, grain; quality, consistency; weave, nap.

**thank** verb *the boss thanked us for our special effort* EXPRESS (ONE'S) GRATITUDE TO, express one's thanks to, offer/extend thanks to, say thank you to, show one's appreciation to, credit, recognize, bless.

**thankful** adjective *she was thankful that the evening was over* GRATEFUL, appreciative, filled with gratitude, relieved.

**thankless** adjective **1** *a thankless task* UNENVIABLE, difficult, unpleasant, unrewarding; unappreciated, unrecognized, unacknowledged. ANTONYM rewarding.

**2** *her thankless children* UNGRATEFUL, unappreciative, unthankful, ingrate. ANTONYM grateful.

**thanks** plural noun *they expressed their thanks and wished her well* GRATITUDE, appreciation; acknowledgment, recognition, credit.

▸ exclamation *thanks for being so helpful* THANK YOU, many thanks, thanks very much, thanks a lot, thank you kindly, much obliged, much appreciated, bless you; *informal* thanks a million.

PHRASE: **thanks to** *thanks to the untiring support of my wife, I've gotten back on my feet* AS A RESULT OF, owing to, due to, because of, through, as a consequence of, on account of, by virtue of, by dint of, by reason of.

**thaw** verb *allow the ice cream to thaw for about ten minutes before folding in the other ingredients* MELT, unfreeze, soften, liquefy, dissolve; defrost, warm. ANTONYM freeze.

▸ noun **1** *spring thaw* RUNOFF, debacle, ice-out.

**2** *a thaw in relations* IMPROVEMENT, relaxation, coming-to-terms, rapprochement.

**theater** noun **1** *the local theater* PLAYHOUSE, auditorium, amphitheater; cinema, movie theater, movie house; *dated* nickelodeon.

**2** *what made you want to go into* ***the theater****?* ACTING, performing, the stage; drama, the dramatic arts, dramaturgy, the thespian art; show business, Broadway; *informal* the boards, show biz.

**3** *the lecture theater* HALL, room, auditorium.

**4** *the Pacific theater of the war* SCENE, arena, field/sphere/place of action, setting, site.

**theatrical** adjective **1** *a theatrical career* STAGE, dramatic, thespian, dramaturgical; show-business; *informal* show-biz; *formal* histrionic.

**2** *Henry looked over his shoulder with theatrical caution* EXAGGERATED, ostentatious, stagy, showy, melodramatic, overacted, overdone, histrionic, over-the-top, artificial, affected, mannered; *informal* hammy, ham, camp.

**theft** noun *the theft was reported on Thursday morning* ROB-

BERY, stealing, thieving, larceny, thievery, shoplifting, burglary, misappropriation, appropriation, embezzlement; raid, holdup; *informal* heist, stickup; five-finger discount, rip-off; *formal* peculation.

**theme** noun **1** *the theme of her speech* SUBJECT, topic, subject matter, matter, thesis, argument, text, burden, concern, thrust, message; thread, motif, keynote.

**2** *the first violin takes up the theme* MELODY, tune, air; motif, leitmotif.

**3** *the band played a medley of popular TV show themes* SONG, theme song, jingle.

**then** adverb **1** *I was living in Cairo then* AT THAT TIME, in those days; at that point (in time), at that moment, on that occasion.

**2** *she won the first and then the second game* NEXT, after that, afterward/afterward, subsequently, later.

**3** *and then there's another problem* IN ADDITION, also, besides, as well, additionally, on top of that, over and above that, moreover, furthermore, what's more, to boot; too.

**4** *well, if that's what he wants, then he should leave* IN THAT CASE, that being so, it follows that.

**theological** adjective *theological writings* RELIGIOUS, scriptural, ecclesiastical, doctrinal; divine, holy.

**theoretical** adjective *it's just a theoretical situation* HYPOTHETICAL, abstract, conjectural, academic, suppositional, speculative, notional, postulatory, what-if, assumed, presumed, untested, unproven, unsubstantiated. ANTONYMS actual, real.

**theorize** verb *Darwin theorized that the atolls marked the sites of vanished volcanoes* SPECULATE, conjecture, hypothesize, philosophize, postulate, propose, posit, suppose.

**theory** noun **1** *I reckon that confirms my theory* HYPOTHESIS, thesis, conjecture, supposition, speculation, postulation, postulate, proposition, premise, surmise, assumption, presupposition; opinion, view, belief, contention.

**2** *modern economic theory* PRINCIPLES, ideas, concepts; philosophy, ideology, system of ideas, science. PHRASE: **in theory** *in theory, your idea sounds great, but can it be practically applied?* IN PRINCIPLE, on paper, in the abstract, all things being equal, in an ideal world; hypothetically, theoretically, supposedly.

**therapeutic** adjective *the therapeutic effects of acupuncture* HEALING, curative, remedial, medicinal, restorative, salubrious, health-giving, tonic, reparative, corrective, beneficial, good, salutary. ANTONYM harmful.

**therapy** noun **1** *a wide range of complementary therapies* TREATMENT, remedy, cure.

**2** *he's currently in therapy* PSYCHOTHERAPY, psychoanalysis, analysis, counseling.

**thereabouts** adverb **1** *the land thereabouts* NEAR THERE, around there, in that area.

**2** *they sold it for five million **or thereabouts*** APPROXIMATELY, roughly, or so, give or take, plus or minus, in round numbers, in the ballpark of.

**thereafter** adverb *thereafter their fortunes suffered a deep decline* AFTER THAT, following that, afterward/afterward, subsequently, then, next.

**therefore** adverb *Rodriguez was injured and therefore unable to play* CONSEQUENTLY, so, as a result, hence, thus, accordingly, for that reason, ergo, that being the case, on that account; *formal* whence; *archaic* wherefore.

**thesis** noun **1** *the central thesis of his lecture* THEORY, contention, argument, line of argument, proposal, proposition, idea, claim, premise, assumption, hypothesis, postulation, supposition.

**2** *a doctoral thesis* DISSERTATION, essay, paper, treatise, disquisition, composition, monograph, study.

**thick** adjective **1** *the walls are five feet thick* IN EXTENT/DIAMETER, across, wide, broad, deep.

**2** *his short, thick legs* STOCKY, sturdy, stubby, chunky, blocky, hefty, thickset, burly, beefy, meaty, big, solid; fat, stout, plump. ANTONYMS thin, slender.

**3** *a thick winter sweater* CHUNKY, bulky, heavy; cable-knit, woolly. ANTONYMS thin, lightweight.

**4** *the arena was thick with skaters* CROWDED, swarming, filled, packed, teeming, seething, buzzing, crawling, crammed, solid, overflowing, choked, jammed, congested; *informal* jam-packed, chockablock, stuffed.

**5** *the thick summer vegetation* PLENTIFUL, abundant, profuse, luxuriant, bushy, rich, riotous, exuberant; rank, rampant; dense, impenetrable, impassable; *informal* jungly. ANTONYMS meager, sparse.

**6** *a thick paste* VISCOUS, gooey, syrupy, firm, stiff, heavy; clotted, coagulated, viscid, semisolid, gelatinous; concentrated. ANTONYMS runny, thin.

**7** *thick fog* DENSE, heavy, opaque, impenetrable, soupy, murky. ANTONYM light.

**8** *informal he's a bit thick.* See STUPID sense 1.

**9** *Guy's voice was thick with desire* HUSKY, hoarse, throaty, guttural, gravelly, rough. ANTONYMS clear, shrill.

**10** *a thick Scottish accent* OBVIOUS, pronounced, marked, broad, strong, rich, decided, distinct. ANTONYMS faint, vague.

▸ noun *in the thick of the crisis* MIDST, center, hub, middle, core, heart.

**thicken** verb *stir the sauce as it thickens* BECOME THICK/THICKER, stiffen, condense; solidify, firm up, set, jell, congeal, clot, coagulate, cake, inspissate.

**thicket** noun *rabbits taking refuge in the thicket* COPSE, coppice, grove, brake, covert, clump; wood, woodlot, bush.

**thickness** noun **1** *the wall is several feet in thickness* WIDTH, breadth, depth, diameter.

**2** *several thicknesses of limestone* LAYER, stratum, stratification, seam, vein; sheet, lamina.

**thickset** adjective *a thickset Caucasian male in his thirties* STOCKY, sturdy, big-boned, heavily built, well-built, chunky, burly, strapping, brawny, solid, blocky, heavy, hefty, beefy, meaty. ANTONYM slight.

**thick-skinned** adjective *these guards have gotten pretty thick-skinned over the years* INSENSITIVE, unfeeling, tough, hardened, callous, case-hardened; *informal* hard-boiled. ANTONYM sensitive.

**thief** noun *the thief is at large* ROBBER, burglar, housebreaker, cat burglar, rustler, shoplifter, pickpocket, purse snatcher, sneak thief, mugger; embezzler, swindler, plunderer; criminal, villain; kleptomaniac; bandit, pirate, highwayman; *informal* crook; *literary* brigand.

**thieve** verb *before we were out of diapers, we were learning how to thieve anything that wasn't nailed down* STEAL, take, purloin, help oneself to, snatch, pilfer; embezzle, misappropriate; have one's fingers/hand in the till, rob; swipe, make off with, finagle, lift, "liberate", "borrow", filch, snaffle, pinch, heist; *formal* peculate.

**thin** adjective **1** *a thin white line* NARROW, fine, attenuated. ANTONYMS thick, broad.

**2** *a thin cotton nightdress* LIGHTWEIGHT, light, fine, delicate, floaty, flimsy, diaphanous, gossamer, insubstantial; sheer, gauzy, filmy, transparent, see-through; paper-thin. ANTONYMS thick, heavy.

**3** *a tall, thin woman* SLIM, lean, slender, rangy, willowy, svelte, sylphlike, spare, slight; SKINNY, underweight, scrawny, waiflike, scraggy, bony, angular, rawboned, hollow-cheeked, gaunt, skin-and-bones, emaciated, skeletal, wasted, pinched, undernourished, underfed; lanky, spindly, gangly, gangling, weedy; *informal* anorexic, like a bag of bones. ANTONYMS plump, overweight, fat.

**4** *his thin gray hair* SPARSE, scanty, wispy, thinning. ANTONYMS thick, abundant.

**5** *a bowl of thin soup* WATERY, weak, dilute, diluted; runny. ANTONYMS thick, hearty.

**6** *her thin voice* WEAK, faint, feeble, small, soft; reedy. ANTONYMS strong, loud.

**7** *the plot is very thin* INSUBSTANTIAL, flimsy, slight, feeble, lame, poor, weak, tenuous, inadequate, insufficient, unconvincing, unbelievable, implausible. ANTONYMS meaty, convincing.

▸ verb **1** *some paint must be* ***thinned down*** *before use* DILUTE, water down, weaken.

**2** *the crowds were beginning to* ***thin out*** DISPERSE, dissipate, scatter; become less dense, become less in number, decrease, diminish, dwindle.

THE RIGHT WORD **thin, gaunt, lean, skinny, slender, spare, svelte**

You can't be too rich or too **thin**, but you can be too **skinny**. *Thin* describes someone whose weight is naturally low in proportion to his or her height, although it may also imply that the person is underweight (*she looked pale and thin after her operation*). *Skinny* is a more blunt and derogatory term for someone who is too thin, and it often implies underdevelopment (*a skinny little boy; a tall, skinny fashion model*). Most people would rather be called **slender**, which combines thinness with gracefulness and good proportions (*the slender legs of a Queen Anne table*), or better yet, **svelte**, a complimentary term that implies a slim, elegant figure (*after six months of dieting, she looked so svelte I hardly recognized her*). **Lean** and **spare** are used to describe people who are naturally thin, although *spare* suggests a more muscular leanness (*a tall, spare man who looked like Abraham Lincoln*). **Gaunt**, on the other hand, means so thin that the angularity of the bones can be seen beneath the skin (*looking gaunt after her latest bout with cancer*).

**thing** noun **1** *the room was full of strange things* OBJECT, article, item, artifact, commodity; device, gadget, instrument, utensil, tool, implement; entity, body; *informal* whatsit, whatchamacallit; *Brit.* thingummy, thingy, thingamabob, thingamajig, doohickey, doodad, dingus.

**2** (**things**) *I'll come back tomorrow to collect my things* BELONGINGS, possessions, stuff, property, worldly goods, effects, personal effects, trappings, paraphernalia, bits and pieces, luggage, baggage, bags; *informal* gear, junk; *Law* goods and chattels.

**3** (**things**) *his gardening things* EQUIPMENT, apparatus, gear, kit, tackle, stuff; implements, tools, utensils; accoutrements.

**4** *I've got several things to do today* ACTIVITY, act, action, deed, undertaking, exploit, feat; task, job, chore.

**5** *I've got other things on my mind just now* THOUGHT, notion, idea; concern, matter, worry, preoccupation.

**6** *I keep remembering things he said* REMARK, statement, comment, utterance, observation, declaration, pronouncement.

**7** *quite a few odd things happened* INCIDENT, episode, event, happening, occurrence, phenomenon.

**8** (**things**) *how are things with you?* MATTERS, affairs, circumstances, conditions, relations; state of affairs, situation, life.

**9** *one of the things I like about you is your optimism* CHARACTERISTIC, quality, attribute, property, trait, feature, point, aspect, facet, quirk.

**10** *there's another thing you should know* FACT, piece of information, point, detail, particular, factor.

**11** *the thing is, I'm not sure if it's what I want* FACT OF THE MATTER, fact, point, issue, problem.

**12** *you lucky thing!* PERSON, soul, creature, wretch; *informal* devil, bastard.

**13** *Twylla developed a* ***thing about*** *noise* PHOBIA OF/ABOUT, fear of, dislike of, aversion to, problem with; obsession with, fixation about; *informal* hang-up.

**14** *she had a* ***thing about*** *men who wore glasses* PENCHANT FOR, preference for, taste for, inclination for, partiality for, predilection for, soft spot for, weakness for, fondness for, fancy for, liking for, love for; fetish for, obsession with, fixation on/with.

**15** *books aren't really my thing* WHAT ONE LIKES, what interests one; *informal* one's cup of tea, one's bag, what turns one on.

**16** *it's the latest thing* FASHION, trend, style, rage, fad.

**think** verb **1** *I think he's gone home* BELIEVE, be of the opinion, be of the view, be under the impression; expect, imagine, anticipate; surmise, suppose, conjecture, guess, fancy; conclude, determine, reason; *informal* reckon, figure; *formal* opine.

**2** *his family was thought to be enormously rich* DEEM, judge, hold, reckon, consider, presume, estimate; regard (as), view (as).

**3** *Jack thought for a moment* PONDER, reflect, deliberate, consider, meditate, contemplate, muse, ruminate, be lost in thought, be in a brown study, brood; concentrate, brainstorm, rack one's brains; put on one's thinking cap, sleep on it; *formal* cogitate.

**4** *she* ***thought of*** *all the visits she had made to her father* RECALL, remember, recollect, call to mind, think back to.

**5** *she forced herself to* ***think of*** *how he must be feeling* IMAGINE, picture, visualize, envisage, consider; dream about, fantasize about.

PHRASES: **think better of** *Donnie was going to crash his ex-girlfriend's wedding, but he thought better of it* HAVE SECOND THOUGHTS ABOUT, think twice about, think again about, change one's mind about; reconsider, decide against; *informal* get cold feet about.

**think over** *take a few days to think over the proposal* CONSIDER, contemplate, deliberate about, mull over, ponder, chew over, chew on, reflect on, muse on, ruminate on.

**think up** *I'm sure by Friday we'll have thought up a great idea for the presentation* DEVISE, dream up, conjure up, come up with, invent, create, concoct, make up; hit on.

**thinker** noun *one of the most influential economic thinkers of the century* THEORIST, philosopher, scholar, savant, sage, intellectual, intellect, ideologist, ideologue; mind, brain, brainiac, genius.

**thinking** adjective *he seemed a thinking man* INTELLIGENT, sensible, reasonable, rational; logical, analytical; thoughtful, reflective, meditative, contemplative, pensive, shrewd, philosophical, sagacious. ANTONYMS stupid, irrational.

▸ noun *the thinking behind the campaign* REASONING, logic, idea(s), theory, line of thought, philosophy, beliefs; opinion(s), view(s), thoughts, position, judgment, assessment, evaluation.

**thin-skinned** adjective *you can't benefit from constructive criticism if you're going to be so thin-skinned* SENSITIVE, oversensitive, hypersensitive, easily offended, easily hurt, touchy, defensive. ANTONYMS insensitive, unfeeling.

**third-rate** adjective *a third-rate hotel* SUBSTANDARD, bad, inferior, poor, poor-quality, low-grade, inadequate, unsatisfactory, unacceptable, not up to snuff, not up to scratch; appalling, abysmal, atrocious, awful, terrible, dreadful, execrable, godawful, miserable, pitiful; jerry-built, shoddy, chintzy, tinpot, trashy; cheapjack; *informal* lousy, rotten, bum, crummy, crappy. ANTONYM excellent.

**thirst** noun **1** *I need a drink—I'm dying of thirst* THIRSTINESS, dryness; dehydration.

**2** *his thirst for knowledge* CRAVING, desire, longing, yearning, hunger, hankering, keenness, eagerness, lust, appetite; *informal* yen, itch.

▸ verb *she* ***thirsted for*** *power* CRAVE, want, covet, desire, hunger for, burn for, lust after, hanker after, have one's heart set on; wish, long.

**thirsty** adjective **1** *the boys were hot and thirsty* LONGING FOR A DRINK, dry, dehydrated; *informal* parched, gasping.

**2** *the thirsty soil* DRY, arid, dried up/out, bone-dry, parched, baked, desiccated.

**3** *she was thirsty for power* EAGER, hungry, greedy, thirsting, craving, longing, yearning, lusting, burning, desirous, hankering; *informal* itching, dying.

**thong** noun *leather thongs fastened to the quiver* STRIP, band, cord, string, lash, tie, belt, strap, tape, rope, tether.

**thorn** noun *a thorn in her finger* PRICKLE, spike, barb, spine.

**thorny** adjective **1** *dense thorny undergrowth* PRICKLY, spiky, barbed, spiny, sharp; *technical* spinose, spinous.

**2** *the thorny subject of confidentiality* PROBLEMATIC, tricky, ticklish, touchy, delicate, controversial, awkward, difficult, knotty, tough, taxing, trying, troublesome; complicated, complex, involved, intricate; vexed, sticky.

**thorough** adjective **1** *a thorough investigation* RIGOROUS, in-depth, exhaustive, thoroughgoing, minute, detailed, close, meticulous, methodical, careful, complete, comprehensive, full, extensive, widespread, sweeping, all-embracing, all-inclusive. ANTONYMS superficial, cursory, partial.

**2** *he is slow but thorough* METICULOUS, scrupulous, assiduous, conscientious, painstaking, methodical, careful, diligent, industrious, hard-working. ANTONYM careless.

**3** *the child is being a thorough nuisance* UTTER, downright, thoroughgoing, absolute, complete, total, out-and-out, arrant, real, perfect, sheer, unqualified, unmitigated.

**thoroughbred** adjective *thoroughbred horses* PUREBRED, pedigree, pure, pure-blooded, blooded.

**thoroughfare** noun *avoiding the busy thoroughfares* ROUTE, passageway, waterway, throughway; main road, highway, freeway, street, road, roadway, avenue, boulevard.

**thoroughly** adverb **1** *we will investigate all complaints thoroughly* RIGOROUSLY, in depth, exhaustively, minutely, closely, in detail, meticulously, scrupulously, assiduously, conscientiously, painstakingly, methodically, carefully, comprehensively, fully, from A to Z, from soup to nuts.

**2** *she is thoroughly spoiled* UTTERLY, downright, absolutely, completely, totally, entirely, one-hundred-percent, really, perfectly, positively, in every respect, through and through; *informal* plain, to the hilt.

**though** conjunction *though she smiled bravely, she looked pale and tired* ALTHOUGH, even though/if, in spite of the fact that, despite the fact that, notwithstanding (the fact) that, for all that.

▸ adverb *it seems impossible, but you can try, though* NEVERTHELESS, nonetheless, even so, however, be that as it may, for all that, despite that, having said that; *informal* still and all.

**thought** noun **1** *what are your thoughts on the matter?* IDEA, notion, opinion, view, impression, feeling, theory; judgment, assessment, conclusion. See note at IDEA.

**2** *he gave up any thought of getting a degree* HOPE, aspiration, ambition, dream; intention, idea, plan, design, aim.

**3** *it only took a moment's thought* THINKING, contemplation, musing, pondering, consideration, reflection, introspection, deliberation, rumination, meditation, brooding, reverie, concentration; *formal* cogitation.

**thoughtful** adjective **1** *a thoughtful expression* PENSIVE, reflective, contemplative, musing, meditative, introspective, philosophical, ruminative, absorbed, engrossed, rapt, preoccupied, lost in thought, deep in thought, in a brown study, brooding; *formal* cogitative. ANTONYM vacant.

**2** *how very thoughtful of you!* CONSIDERATE, caring, attentive, understanding, sympathetic, solicitous, concerned, helpful, obliging, neighborly, unselfish, kind, compassionate, charitable. ANTONYM inconsiderate.

**thoughtless** adjective **1** *I'm so sorry—how thoughtless of me* INCONSIDERATE, uncaring, insensitive, uncharitable, unkind, flippant, tactless, undiplomatic, indiscreet, remiss. ANTONYM considerate.

**2** *a few minutes of thoughtless pleasure* UNTHINKING, heedless, careless, unmindful, unguarded, absentminded; injudicious, ill-advised, ill-considered, imprudent, unwise, foolish, frivolous, silly, stupid, reckless, rash, precipitate, negligent, neglectful. ANTONYM careful.

**thrash** verb **1** *she thrashed him across the head and shoulders* HIT, beat, strike, batter, thump, hammer, pound, rain blows on; assault, attack; cudgel, club; *informal* wallop, belt, bash, whup, whack, thwack, clout, clobber, pummel, slug, tan, sock, beat the (living) daylights out of.

**2** *he was thrashing around in pain* FLAIL, writhe, thresh, jerk, toss, twist, twitch. PHRASE: **thrash out 1** *thrash out a problem* RESOLVE, settle, sort out, work out, straighten out, iron out, clear up; talk through, discuss, debate.

**2** *thrash out an agreement* WORK OUT, negotiate, agree on, bring about, hammer out, hammer together, hash out, produce, effect.

**thread** noun **1** *a needle and thread* cotton, filament, fiber; yarn, string, twine.

**2** *literary the Fraser was a thread of silver below them* STREAK, strand, stripe, line, strip, seam, vein.

**3** *she lost the thread of the conversation* GIST, train of thought, drift, direction; theme, motif, tenor; story line, plot.

▸ verb **1** *he threaded the rope through a pulley* PASS, string, work, ease, push, poke.

**2** *she threaded her way through the tables* WEAVE, inch, wind, squeeze, make.

**threadbare** adjective *a threadbare carpet* WORN, well-worn, old, thin, worn out, holey, moth-eaten, mangy, ragged, frayed, tattered, battered; decrepit, shabby, scruffy, unkempt; having seen better days, falling apart at the seams, falling to pieces, tatty, ratty, the worse for wear, raggedy, dog-eared; *informal* raggedy-ass.

**threat** noun **1** *Maggie ignored his threats* THREATENING REMARK, warning, ultimatum.

**2** *a possible threat to aircraft* DANGER, peril, hazard, menace, risk.

**3** *the company faces the threat of liquidation proceedings* POSSIBILITY, prospect, chance, probability, likelihood, risk.

**threaten** verb **1** *how dare you threaten me?* MENACE, intimidate, browbeat, bully, blackmail, terrorize; make/issue threats to.

**2** *these events could threaten the stability of Europe* ENDANGER, be a danger to, be a threat to, jeopardize, imperil, put at risk, put in jeopardy.

**3** *the gray skies threatened snow* FORESHADOW, bode, warn of, presage, augur, portend, herald, be a harbinger of, indicate, point to, be a sign of, signal, spell; *literary* foretoken.

**4** *as rain threatened, the party moved indoors* SEEM LIKELY, seem imminent, be on the horizon, be brewing, be gathering, be looming, be on the way, be impending; hang over someone.

**threatening** adjective **1** *a threatening letter* MENACING, intimidating, bullying, frightening, hostile; *formal* minatory.

**2** *banks of threatening clouds* OMINOUS, sinister, menacing, alarming, portentous, dark, black, thunderous.

**threesome** noun *a talented threesome* TRIO, triumvirate, triad, trinity, troika; triplets.

**threshold** noun **1** *the threshold of the church* DOORSTEP, doorway, entrance, entry, door, gate, gateway, portal, doorsill.

**2** *the threshold of a new era* START, beginning, commencement, brink, verge, cusp, dawn, inception, day one, opening, debut; *informal* kickoff.

**3** *the human threshold of pain* LOWER LIMIT, minimum.

**thrift** noun *she learned her sense of thrift from her mother* FRUGALITY, economy, economizing, thriftiness, providence, prudence, good management, good husbandry, saving, scrimping and saving, abstemiousness; parsimony, penny-pinching, austerity. ANTONYM extravagance.

**thrifty** adjective *these kids have no idea what it means to be thrifty* FRUGAL, economical, sparing, careful with money, penny-wise, provident, prudent, abstemious; parsimonious, penny-pinching, cheap. See note at ECONOMICAL. ANTONYM extravagant.

**thrill** noun **1** *the thrill of jumping out of an airplane* EXCITEMENT, feeling of excitement, stimulation, adrenaline rush, pleasure, tingle; fun, enjoyment, amusement, delight, joy; *informal* buzz, high, rush, kick, charge.

**2** *a thrill of excitement ran through her* WAVE, shiver, rush, surge, flash, blaze, tremor, quiver, flutter, shudder, frisson.

▸ verb **1** *his words thrilled her* EXCITE, stimulate, arouse, rouse, inspire, delight, exhilarate, intoxicate, stir, charge up, electrify, galvanize, move, fire (with enthusiasm), fire someone's imagination; *informal* give someone a buzz, give someone a kick, give someone a charge. ANTONYM bore.

**2** *he thrilled at the sound of her voice* BE/FEEL EXCITED, tingle, quiver; *informal* get a buzz out of, get a kick out of, get a charge out of.

**thrilling** adjective *a thrilling race* EXCITING, stirring, action-packed, breathtaking, rip-roaring, spine-tingling, gripping, riveting, fascinating, dramatic, hair-raising, mind-blowing; rousing, stimulating, moving, inspiring, inspirational, electrifying, heady. ANTONYM boring.

**thrive** verb *the roses in the west garden are thriving | business generally thrives this time of year* FLOURISH, prosper, burgeon, bloom, blossom, mushroom, do well, advance, succeed, boom. ANTONYMS decline, wither.

**thriving** adjective *real estate continues to be a thriving industry* FLOURISHING, prosperous, prospering, growing, developing, burgeoning, blooming, healthy, successful, booming, mushrooming, profitable, expanding; *informal* going strong, going from strength to strength. ANTONYM moribund.

**throat** noun *an inflamed throat* GULLET, esophagus; windpipe, trachea, gorge; maw, neck, jowl.

**throb** verb *her arms and legs throbbed with tiredness* PULSATE, beat, pulse, palpitate, pound, thud, thump, drum, thrum, pitter-patter, go pit-a-pat, quiver; *rare* quop.

▸ noun *the throb of the ship's engines* PULSATION, beat, beating, pulse, palpitation, pounding, thudding, thumping, drumming, thrumming.

**throes** plural noun *the throes of childbirth* AGONY, pain, pangs, spasms, torment, suffering, torture; *literary* travail.
PHRASE: **in the throes of** *we're in the throes of hurricane preparations* IN THE MIDDLE OF, in the process of, in the midst of, busy with, occupied with, taken up with/by, involved in, dealing with; struggling with, wrestling with, grappling with.

**throne** noun *the czar risked losing his throne* SOVEREIGN POWER, sovereignty, rule, dominion.

**throng** noun *a throng of people blocked her way* CROWD, horde, mass, multitude, host, army, herd, flock, drove, swarm, mob, sea, troop, pack, crush; collection, company, gathering, assembly, congregation; *informal* gaggle, bunch, gang.

▸ verb **1** *people thronged to see the play* FLOCK, stream, swarm, troop, pour in.

**2** *visitors thronged around him* CROWD, cluster, mill, swarm, surge, congregate, gather.

**throttle** verb **1** *he tried to throttle her* CHOKE, strangle, strangulate, garrote, gag.

**2** *attempts to throttle the criminal supply of drugs* SUPPRESS, inhibit, stifle, control, restrain, check, contain, choke off, put a/the lid on; stop, put an end to, end, stamp out.

**through** preposition **1** *we drove through the tunnel* INTO AND OUT OF, to the other side of, to the far side of, from one side to the other of.

**2** *he got the job through an advertisement* BY MEANS OF, by way of, by dint of, via, using, thanks to, by virtue of, as a result of, as a consequence of, on account of, owing to, because of.

**3** *he worked through the night* THROUGHOUT, all through, for the whole of, for the duration of, until/to the end of.

▸ adverb *as soon as we opened the gate they came streaming through* FROM ONE SIDE TO THE OTHER, from one end to another, in and out the other side.

▸ adjective *a through train* DIRECT, nonstop.

PHRASE: **through and through** *he was a city kid through and through* IN EVERY RESPECT, to the core; thoroughly, utterly, absolutely, completely, totally, wholly, fully, entirely, unconditionally, unreservedly, altogether, out-and-out.

**throughout** preposition **1** *it had repercussions throughout the Middle East* ALL OVER, across, in every part of, everywhere in, all through, right through, all around.

**2** *she remained fit throughout her life* ALL THROUGH, all, for the duration of, for the whole of, until the end of.

**throw** verb **1** *she threw the ball back* HURL, toss, fling, pitch, cast, lob, launch, catapult, project, propel; bowl; *informal* chuck, heave, sling, peg, let fly with.

**2** *he threw another punch* DELIVER, give, land.

**3** *she threw a withering glance at him* DIRECT, cast, send, dart, shoot.

**4** *the horse threw its rider* UNSEAT, dislodge.

**5** *her question threw me* DISCONCERT, unnerve, fluster, ruffle, agitate, discomfit, put off, throw off balance, discountenance, unsettle, confuse; *informal* rattle, faze, flummox, baffle, befuddle, discombobulate.

**6** *he threw a farewell party for them* GIVE, host, hold, have, provide, put on, lay out, arrange, organize.

**7** *books were thrown all over her desk* STREW, cast, scatter, disperse.

**8** *he threw his keys on the table* TOSS, deposit, throw down, put down, dump, drop, plunk, plonk, plump.

▸ noun **1** *we were allowed two throws each* LOB, pitch; go, turn; bowl, ball.

**2** *the loveseat was decorated with a red throw* BLANKET, afghan, covering, fabric; shawl.

PHRASES: **throw something away 1** *she hated throwing old clothes away* DISCARD, throw out, dispose of, get rid of, do away with, toss out, scrap, clear out, dump, jettison; *informal* chuck (away/out), deep-six, ditch.

**2** *the Tigers threw away a 3–0 lead* SQUANDER, waste, fritter away, fail to exploit, lose, let slip; *informal* blow.
**throw someone out** *the duke and his family were thrown out*

EXPEL, eject, evict, drive out, force out, oust, remove; get rid of, depose, topple, unseat, overthrow, bring down, overturn, dislodge, displace, supplant, show someone the door; banish, deport, exile; *informal* boot out, kick out, give someone the boot.

**throw something out** 1 *throw out this moldy food.* See THROW SOMETHING AWAY sense 1 (above).

2 *his case was thrown out* REJECT, dismiss, turn down, refuse, disallow, veto; *informal* give the thumbs down to.

**throw up** *informal* See VOMIT verb sense 1.

**thrust** verb 1 *she thrust her hands into her pockets* SHOVE, push, force, plunge, stick, drive, propel, ram, poke, jam.

2 *fame had been thrust on him* FORCE, foist, impose, inflict.

3 *he thrust his way past her* PUSH, shove, force, elbow, shoulder, barge, bulldoze.

▸ noun 1 *a hard thrust* SHOVE, push, lunge, poke.

2 *a thrust led by Canadian forces* ADVANCE, push, drive, attack, assault, onslaught, offensive, charge, sortie, foray, raid, sally, invasion, incursion.

3 *only one engine is producing thrust* FORCE, propulsive force, propulsion, power, impetus, momentum.

4 *the thrust of the speech* GIST, substance, drift, burden, meaning, sense, theme, message, import, tenor.

**thud** noun & verb *it landed with a thud | bullets thudded into the ground* THUMP, thunk, clunk, clonk, crash, smack, bang; stomp, stamp, clump, clomp; *informal* wham, whump.

**thug** noun *one of Capone's thugs* RUFFIAN, hooligan, vandal, hoodlum, gangster, villain, criminal; *informal* tough, bruiser, goon, heavy, enforcer, hired gun, hood.

**thumb** noun *the thumb on his left hand* *technical* POLLEX, opposable digit.

▸ verb 1 *he thumbed through his notebook* LEAF, flick, flip, riffle, skim, browse, look.

2 *his dictionaries were thumbed and ink-stained* SOIL, mark, make dog-eared.

3 *he was thumbing his way across Mexico* HITCHHIKE; *informal* hitch, hitch/thumb a lift.

PHRASES: **all thumbs** *don't let Anthony carry the punch bowl—he's all thumbs* CLUMSY, klutzy, awkward, maladroit, inept, unskillful, heavy-handed, inexpert, butterfingered, ham-fisted.

**thumbs down** *informal* *the budget increase has been given a thumbs down* REJECTION, refusal, veto, no, negation, rebuff; *informal* red light.

**thumbs up** *informal* *we got the board's thumbs up for the land grant* APPROVAL, seal of approval, endorsement; permission, authorization, consent, yes, leave, authority, sanction, ratification, license, dispensation, nod, assent, blessing, rubber stamp, clearance; *informal* go-ahead, OK, A-OK, green light, say-so.

**thumbnail** adjective *a thumbnail sketch of the political climate* CONCISE, short, brief, succinct, to the point, compact, crisp, short and sweet, quick, rapid; miniature, mini, small.

**thump** verb 1 *the two men kicked and thumped him* HIT, strike, beat, batter, pound, knock, rap, smack, thwack, pummel, punch, thrash, cuff, box someone's ears; *informal* bash, bop, clout, clobber, sock, swipe, slug, lash, whack, wallop, beat the (living) daylights out of, belt, tan, lay into, let someone have it, whup; *literary* smite.

2 *her heart thumped with fright* THROB, pound, thud, hammer, pulsate, pulse, pump, palpitate, race, beat heavily.

▸ noun *she put the box down with a thump* THUD, thunk, clunk, clonk, crash, smack, bang.

**thunder** noun 1 *thunder and lightning* THUNDERCLAP, peal of thunder, roll of thunder, rumble of thunder, crack of thunder, crash of thunder; *literary* thunderbolt.

2 *the ceaseless thunder of the traffic* RUMBLE, rumbling, boom, booming, roar, roaring, pounding, thud, thudding, crash, crashing, reverberation.

▸ verb 1 *below me the surf thrashed and thundered* RUMBLE, boom, roar, pound, thud, thump, bang; resound, reverberate, beat.

2 *she* ***thundered against*** *the evils of the age* RAIL AGAINST, fulminate against, inveigh against, rage against/about, rant about; condemn, denounce.

3 *"Answer me!" he thundered* ROAR, bellow, bark, yell, shout, bawl; *informal* holler.

**thundering** adjective. See THUNDEROUS.

**thunderous** adjective *a thunderous noise* VERY LOUD, tumultuous, booming, roaring, resounding, reverberating, reverberant, ringing, deafening, ear-splitting, noisy, overloud, stentorian, thundering.

**thunderstruck** adjective *Charles was so thunderstruck that his voice was barely audible* ASTONISHED, amazed, astounded, staggered, surprised, startled, stunned, shocked, aghast, taken aback, dumbfounded, floored, blown away, dumbstruck, stupefied, dazed, speechless; *informal* flabbergasted.

**thus** adverb 1 *the studio handled production, thus cutting its costs* CONSEQUENTLY, as a consequence, in consequence, thereby, so, that being so, therefore, ergo, accordingly, hence, as a result, for that reason, ipso facto, because of that, on that account.

2 *all decent aristocrats act thus* LIKE THAT, in that way, so, like so. PHRASE: **thus far** *thus far, we've avoided any unanticipated expenditures* SO FAR, until now, up until now, up to now, up to this point, hitherto.

**USAGE NOTE thus**

There is never a need to expand the adverb **thus** to "thusly."

**thwack** noun *the plastic ruler made a loud thwack on the desk* SLAP, whack, smack, wallop.

▸ verb. See THUMP verb sense 1.

**thwart** verb *their plans to attack the embassy were thwarted*

FOIL, frustrate, stand in the way of, forestall, derail, dash; stop, check, block, stonewall, prevent, defeat, impede, hinder, obstruct; *informal* put a crimp in, put the kibosh on, scotch, scuttle, do for, stymie. ANTONYM facilitate.

THE RIGHT WORD **thwart, baffle, balk, foil, frustrate, inhibit**

These verbs refer to the various ways in which we can outwit or overcome opposing forces. **Thwart** suggests using cleverness rather than force to bring about the defeat of an enemy or to block progress toward an objective (*thwart a rebellion; have one's goals thwarted by lack of education*). **Balk** also emphasizes setting up barriers (*a sudden reversal that balked their hopes for a speedy resolution*), but it is used more often as an intransitive verb meaning to stop at an obstacle and refuse to proceed (*he balked at appearing in front of the angry crowd*). To **baffle** is to cause defeat by bewildering or confusing (*the police were baffled by the lack of evidence*), while **foil** means to throw off course so as to discourage further effort (*her plan to arrive early was foiled by heavy traffic*). **Frustrate** implies rendering all attempts or efforts useless (*frustrated by the increasingly bad weather, they decided to work indoors*), while **inhibit** suggests forcing something into inaction (*to inhibit wage increases by raising corporate taxes*). Both *frustrate* and *inhibit* are used in a psychological context to suggest barriers that impede normal development or prevent the realization of natural desires (*he was both frustrated by her refusal to acknowledge his presence and inhibited by his own shyness*).

**tic** noun *a tic under his left eye* TWITCH, spasm, jerk, tremor; quirk.

**tick** noun **1** *the tick of his watch* TICKING, tick-tock, click, clicking, tap, tapping.

**2** *put a tick against the item of your choice* CHECK MARK, check, stroke, mark.

▸ verb **1** *the clock ticks* CLICK, tock, tick-tock, tap.

**2** *time is **ticking away*** PASS, elapse, go, continue, advance, wear on, roll on, fly, run out, vanish.

PHRASE: **tick off 1** *that really ticked me off* ANNOY, irritate, rile, rattle, anger, antagonize, make someone mad, get on someone's nerves, get to, get someone's back up.

**2** *tick off a list* CHECK OFF; count off, cross off.

**ticket** noun *present your ticket at the gate* PASS, authorization, permit, token, coupon, voucher; transfer.

**tickle** noun *a tickle in her throat* TINGLE, itch, irritation.

▸ verb **1** *he tried to tickle her under the chin* STROKE, pet, tease, chuck.

**2** *she found something that tickled her imagination* STIMULATE, interest, appeal to, arouse, titillate, excite.

PHRASE: **tickled pink** *the kids were tickled pink when we mentioned Disney World* DELIGHTED, thrilled, tickled to death, jumping for joy, high as a kite, pleased as punch, over the moon.

**ticklish** adjective *the issue has been made more ticklish since the factors of race and gender have entered the picture* DIFFICULT, problematic, tricky, touchy, delicate, sensitive, tender, awkward, prickly, thorny, tough; vexed, sticky.

**tidbit** noun **1** *a tidbit of information* MORSEL, piece, scrap, item, bit, nugget.

**2** *tasty tidbits* DELICACY, dainty, snack, nibble, appetizer, hors d'oeuvre, goody, dipper, finger food, nibbly.

**tide** noun **1** *ships come up the river with the tide* TIDEWATER, ebb and flow, tidal flow.

**2** *the tide of history* COURSE, movement, direction, trend, current, drift, run, turn, tendency, tenor. PHRASE: **tide someone over** *these canned goods should tide us over until the storm is over and the power is restored* SUSTAIN, keep someone going, keep someone afloat, keep someone's head above water, see someone through; keep the wolf from the door; help out, assist, aid.

**tidings** plural noun *literary what tidings do you bring us from across the wide ocean?* NEWS, information, intelligence, word, reports, dispatches, notification, communication, latest; *informal* info, scuttlebutt, lowdown, scoop.

**tidy** adjective **1** *a tidy room* NEAT, neat and tidy, orderly, well-ordered, in (good) order, well-kept, shipshape, in apple-pie order, immaculate, spick-and-span, uncluttered, straight, trim, spruce. ANTONYM messy.

**2** *he's a very tidy person* NEAT, trim, spruce, dapper, well-groomed, organized, well-organized, methodical, meticulous; fastidious; *informal* natty. ANTONYMS scruffy, messy.

**3** *informal a tidy sum* LARGE, sizable, considerable, substantial, generous, significant, appreciable, handsome, respectable, ample, decent, goodly. ANTONYMS small, paltry.

▸ verb **1** *I'd better **tidy up** the living room* PUT IN ORDER, clear up, sort out, straighten (up), clean up, spruce up.

**2** *she **tidied herself up** in the bathroom* GROOM ONESELF, spruce oneself up, freshen oneself up, smarten oneself up; *informal* titivate oneself.

**tie** verb **1** *they tied Max to a chair* BIND, tie up, tether, hitch, strap, truss, fetter, rope, chain, make fast, moor, lash, attach, fasten, fix, secure, join, connect, link, couple.

**2** *he bent to tie his shoelaces* DO UP, lace, knot.

**3** *a bonus deal **tied to** a productivity agreement* LINK TO, connect to, couple to/with, relate to, join to, marry to; make conditional on, bind up with.

**4** *they tied for second place* DRAW, be equal, be even, be neck and neck.

▸ noun **1** *he tightened the ties of his robe* LACE, string, cord, fastening, fastener.

**2** *a collar and tie* NECKTIE, bow tie, string tie, bolo tie.

**3** *family ties* BOND, connection, link, relationship, attachment, affiliation, allegiance, friendship; kinship, interdependence.

**4** *there was a tie for first place* DRAW, dead heat, deadlock.

PHRASES: **tie someone down** *she was afraid of getting tied down* RESTRICT, restrain, limit, constrain, trammel, confine, cramp, hamper, handicap, hamstring, encumber, shackle, inhibit.

**tie in** *how do these revisions tie in with the ultimate plan?* BE CONSISTENT, tally, agree, be in agreement, accord, concur, fit in, harmonize, be in tune, dovetail, correspond, match; square, jibe.

**tie someone/something up** 1 *robbers tied her up and ransacked her home* BIND, bind hand and foot, truss (up), fetter, chain up.

2 *he is tied up in meetings all morning* OCCUPY, engage, keep busy.

3 *her capital is tied up in real estate* LOCK, bind up, trap; entangle.

**tier** noun 1 *tiers of empty seats* ROW, line; layer, level; balcony.

2 *the most senior tier of management* GRADE, gradation, echelon, rank, stratum, level, rung on the ladder.

**tight** adjective 1 *a tight grip* FIRM, fast, secure, fixed, clenched. ANTONYM relaxed.

2 *the rope was tight* TAUT, rigid, stiff, tense, stretched, strained. ANTONYM slack.

3 *tight jeans* TIGHT-FITTING, close-fitting, form-fitting, narrow, figure-hugging, skintight; *informal* sprayed-on. ANTONYMS loose, baggy.

4 *a tight mass of fibers* COMPACT, compacted, compressed, dense, solid. ANTONYM loose.

5 *a tight space* SMALL, tiny, narrow, limited, restricted, confined, cramped, constricted, uncomfortable; *rare* incommodious. ANTONYMS roomy, generous.

6 *tight control over the family's finances* STRICT, rigorous, stringent, tough, rigid, firm, uncompromising. ANTONYM lax.

7 *a tight schedule* BUSY, rigorous, packed, nonstop. ANTONYM open.

8 *he's in a tight spot* DIFFICULT, tricky, delicate, awkward, problematic, worrying, precarious; *informal* sticky. ANTONYM problem-free.

9 *a tight piece of writing* SUCCINCT, concise, pithy, incisive, crisp, condensed, well structured, clean, to the point. ANTONYMS wordy, flowery.

10 *a tight race* CLOSE, even, evenly matched, well-matched; hard-fought, neck and neck. ANTONYM open.

11 *money is tight these days* LIMITED, restricted, in short supply, scarce, depleted, diminished, low, inadequate, insufficient. ANTONYMS plentiful, abundant.

12 *she is tight with the big movie stars* CLOSE, friendly, intimate, connected, close-knit, tight-knit, on good terms, buddy-buddy.

**tighten** verb 1 *she tightened the rope* PULL TAUT, tauten, pull tight, stretch, tense. ANTONYMS loosen, slacken.

2 *he tightened his lips* NARROW, constrict, contract, compress, screw up, pucker, purse, squinch up. ANTONYM relax.

3 *security in the area has been tightened* INCREASE, make stricter, toughen up, heighten, scale up. ANTONYM relax.

**till**[1] noun *she counted the money in the till* CASH REGISTER, cash drawer(s), cashbox, strongbox; checkout.

**till**[2] verb *he went back to tilling the land* CULTIVATE, work, farm, plow, dig, hoe, turn over, prepare.

**till**[3] preposition & conjunction 1 *he'll be in London till July* UNTIL, to, up to, through (to), up until, as late as.

2 *we didn't know about this till yesterday* BEFORE, prior to, previous to, up to, up until, earlier than.

**USAGE NOTE till, until**

*Till* is, like *until,* a bona fide preposition and conjunction. Though less formal than *until, till* is neither colloquial nor substandard. As Anthony Burgess put it, "In nonpoetic English we use 'till' and 'until' indifferently." (*A Mouthful of Air*; 1992.) It's especially common in British English—e.g.:

• "After the First World War, Hatay, named by Attaturk after the Hittites, fell into the hands of the French, who did not return it till 1939." (*Independent* [UK]; Apr. 1, 1995.)

• "He works from dawn till dusk, six days a week." (*Daily Telegraph* [UK]; Mar. 31, 1997.)

And it still occurs in American English—e.g.: "In medium skillet, sauté the garlic till golden. Add onion, wait till brown." (*Palm Beach Post*; Mar. 23, 1995.)

But the myth of the word's low standing persists. Some writers and editors mistakenly think that *till* deserves a bracketed *sic*—e.g.: " 'Trading in cotton futures was not practiced till [sic] after the close of the Civil War, spot cotton being quoted like other stocks in cents, halves, quarters, etc.' " (*School Science and Mathematics*; Apr. 1, 1997 [in which the *sic* appeared in the original source being quoted].)

If a form deserves a *sic*, it's the incorrect *'til*. Worse yet is *'till*, which is abominable—e.g.: "A month or two remain 'till [read *till*] you grab your dancing shoes, plus a crew of pals or that special date." (*Denver Post*; Mar. 21, 1997.) —*BG*

**tilt** verb *you'll have to tilt the sofa to fit it through the door* SLOPE, tip, lean, list, bank, slant, incline, pitch, cant, angle. PHRASE: **(at) full tilt** *our toboggans went down the icy slope at full tilt* (AT) FULL SPEED, at top speed, full bore, as fast as one's legs can carry one, at a gallop, helter-skelter, headlong, pell-mell, at breakneck speed, with great force, with full force; *informal* like crazy, like mad, hell-bent for leather, a mile a minute, like the wind, like a bat out of hell, like (greased) lightning, lickety-split, full blast, all out, with a vengeance; *literary* apace.

**timber** noun *some eighty acres of marketable timber | expertly milled timbers* WOOD, lumber, logs; trees, sawlogs; hardwood, softwood; beam, spar, plank, batten, lath, board, joist, rafter.

**time** noun 1 *what time is it?* HOUR; *dated* o'clock.

2 *late at night was the best time to leave* MOMENT, point, point in time, occasion, hour, minute, second, instant, juncture, stage.

3 *he worked there for a time* WHILE, spell, stretch, stint, span, season, interval, period, period of time, length of time, duration, phase, stage, term, patch.

4 *the time of the dinosaurs* ERA, age, epoch, period, years, days; generation, date.

5 *I've known a lot of cats in my time* LIFETIME, life, life span, days, time on earth, existence.

6 *he had been a professional actor in his time* HEYDAY, day, best days, best years, glory days, prime, peak, Golden Age.

7 **(the times)** *the times are a-changing* CONDITIONS, circumstances; life, the state of affairs, the way of the world.

8 *tunes in waltz time* RHYTHM, tempo, beat; meter, measure, pattern.

▸ verb 1 *the events were timed perfectly* SCHEDULE, set, set up, arrange, organize, coordinate, fix, line up, slot in, prearrange, timetable, plan; slate.

2 *we timed ourselves to prepare for the race* MEASURE, clock, record one's time.

PHRASES: **ahead of time** *get to the airport ahead of time* EARLY, in good time, with time to spare, in advance.

**ahead of one's/its time** *Leonardo was ahead of his time in almost all endeavors | a laser procedure that is ahead of its time* REVOLUTIONARY, avant-garde, futuristic, innovatory, innovative, trailblazing, pioneering, groundbreaking, advanced, cutting edge.

**all the time** *their bleeping dog barks all the time* CONSTANTLY, the entire time, around/round the clock, day and night, night and day, 'morning, noon, and night,' 'day in, day out,' at all times, always, nonstop, without a break, ceaselessly, endlessly, unfailingly, incessantly, perpetually, permanently, interminably, continuously, continually, eternally, unremittingly, remorselessly, relentlessly, unrelentingly; *informal* 24-7; *archaic* without surcease.

**at one time** *she was a nurse at one time* FORMERLY, previously, once, in the past, at one point, once upon a time, time was when, one fine day, in days/times gone by, in times past, in the (good) old days, long ago, back in the day; *literary* in days/times of yore; *archaic* erstwhile, whilom.

**at the same time** 1 *they arrived at the same time* SIMULTANEOUSLY, at the same instant, at the same moment, together, all together, as a group, at once, at one and the same time; in unison, in concert, in chorus, in synchrony, as one, in tandem.

2 *Curt seems like a nice guy—at the same time I'm not sure I would trust him* NONETHELESS, even so, however, but, still, yet, though, on the other hand; in spite of that, despite that, be that as it may, for all that, that said; notwithstanding, regardless, anyway, anyhow, still and all.

**at times** *she is at times cruel and ruthless* OCCASIONALLY, sometimes, from time to time, now and then, every so often, once in a while, on occasion, off and on, at intervals, periodically, sporadically.

**behind the times** *the older I get, the less I think my parents are behind the times* OLD-FASHIONED, out of date, outmoded, outdated, dated, old, passé; *informal* square, not with it, old-school, horse-and-buggy, fusty.

**for the time being** *we're living in the cottage for the time being* FOR NOW, for the moment, for the present, in the interim, for the nonce, in/for the meantime, in the meanwhile, for a short time, briefly; temporarily, provisionally, pro tem.

**from time to time** See AT TIMES (above).

**in no time** *I'll be dressed in no time* (VERY) SOON, in a second, in an instant, in a minute, in a moment, in a trice, in a flash, shortly, any second, any minute (now), momentarily; *informal* in a jiffy, in a sec, in two shakes of a lamb's tail, in a snap; *formal* directly.

**in good time** *don't worry, Father will get here in good time* PUNCTUALLY, promptly, on time, early, with time to spare, ahead of time, ahead of schedule.

**in time** 1 *I came back in time for the party* EARLY ENOUGH, in good time, punctually, on time, not too late, with time to spare, on schedule.

2 *in time, she'll forgot about it* EVENTUALLY, in the end, in due course, by and by, finally, after a while; one day, some day, sometime, sooner or later.

**many a time** *many a time they had gone to bed hungry* FREQUENTLY, regularly, often, very often, all the time, habitually, customarily, routinely; again and again, time and again, over and over again, repeatedly, recurrently, continually, oftentimes; *literary* oft, ofttimes.

**on time** *Rupert never gets to work on time* PUNCTUALLY, in good time, to/on schedule, when expected, on the dot.

**time after time** *the camera produces excellent results time after time* REPEATEDLY, frequently, often, again and again, over and over (again), time and (time) again, many times, many a time; persistently, recurrently, constantly, continually, oftentimes; *literary* oft, ofttimes.

**timeless** adjective *the timeless appeal of a well-crafted rocking chair* LASTING, enduring, classic, ageless, permanent, perennial, abiding, unfailing, unchanging, unvarying, never-changing, changeless, unfading, unending, undying, immortal, eternal, everlasting, immutable. ANTONYM ephemeral.

**timely** adjective *his refresher course on giving CPR proved to be very timely* OPPORTUNE, well-timed, at the right time, convenient, appropriate, expedient, seasonable, felicitous. See note at OPPORTUNE.

THE RIGHT WORD **timely, opportune, propitious, seasonable**

Some people seem to have a knack for doing or saying the right thing at the right time. A **timely** act or remark is one that comes at a moment when it is of genuine value or service (*a timely interruption*), while an **opportune** one comes in the nick of time, as if by accident, and exactly meets the needs of the occasion (*a storm came up at an opportune moment, squelching enthusiasm for the fight*). **Seasonable** applies to whatever is suited to the season of the year or fits in with the needs of the moment or the character of the occasion (*seasonable weather; a seasonable menu for a cold winter day*). **Propitious** means presenting favorable conditions. In other words, while a warm day in December might not be *seasonable*, it might very well be *propitious* for the sailor setting off on a round-the-world cruise.

**timetable** noun *a bus timetable | I have a very full timetable* SCHEDULE, program, agenda, calendar; list, itinerary, timeline.

**timid** adjective *I was too timid to ask for what I wanted* APPREHENSIVE, fearful, easily frightened, afraid, faint-hearted, timorous, nervous, scared, frightened, cowardly, pusillanimous, spineless; shy, diffident, self-effacing; *informal* wimpish, wimpy, yellow, chicken, mousy, gutless, sissy, lily-livered, candy-assed, weak-kneed. ANTONYM bold.

**timorous** adjective. See TIMID.

**tincture** noun **1** *tincture of iodine* SOLUTION, suspension, infusion, elixir.

**2** *a tincture of bitterness.* See TINGE noun sense 2.

**tinge** verb **1** *a mass of white blossom tinged with pink* TINT, color, stain, shade, wash.

**2** *his optimism is tinged with realism* INFLUENCE, affect, touch, flavor, color, modify; taint.

▸ noun **1** *the light had a blue tinge to it* TINT, color, shade, tone, hue.

**2** *a tinge of cynicism* TRACE, note, touch, suggestion, hint, bit, scintilla, savor, flavor, element, modicum, streak, vein, suspicion, soupçon, tincture.

**tingle** verb *her flesh still tingled from the shock* PRICKLE, sting; tremble, quiver, shiver.

▸ noun *she felt a tingle of anticipation* THRILL, buzz, quiver, shiver, tingling, sting, stinging; tremor.

**tinker** verb *a mechanic was* ***tinkering with*** *the engine* FIDDLE WITH, adjust, fix, try to mend, play about with, fool with, futz with; tamper with, interfere with, mess about with, meddle with.

**tinkle** verb **1** *the bell tinkled* RING, jingle, jangle, chime, peal, ding, ping.

**2** *cool water tinkled in the stone fountain* SPLASH, purl, babble, burble; *literary* plash.

▸ noun *the tinkle of sleigh bells* RING, chime, ding, ping, jingle, jangle, tintinnabulation.

**tinsel** noun *the tinsel of Hollywood* OSTENTATION, showiness, show, glitter, flamboyance, gaudiness; attractiveness, glamour; *informal* flashiness, ritz, glitz, garishness, razzle-dazzle, razzmatazz, eye candy.

**tint** noun **1** *the sky was taking on an apricot tint* SHADE, color, tone, hue, pigmentation, tinge, cast, tincture, flush, blush, wash.

**2** *a hair tint* DYE, coloring, rinse, highlights, lowlights.

**tiny** adjective *what are these tiny red insects on my houseplants?* MINUTE, minuscule, microscopic, nanoscale, infinitesimal, very small, little, mini, diminutive, miniature, scaled down, baby, toy, dwarf, pygmy, peewee, Lilliputian; *informal* teeny, teeny-weeny, teensy, teensy-weensy, itty-bitty, itsy-bitsy, eensy, eensy-weensy, little-bitty; bite-sized, pint-sized; *chiefly Scottish* wee. See note at SMALL. ANTONYM huge.

**tip**[1] noun *the swords we use in the play have blunt tips* | *the tip of the iceberg* POINT, end, extremity, head, sharp end, spike, prong, tine, nib; top, summit, apex, cusp, crown, crest, pinnacle, vertex.

**tip**[2] verb **1** *the boat tipped over* OVERTURN, turn over, topple (over), fall (over); keel over, capsize, flip, turn turtle; *Nautical* pitchpole.

**2** *a whale could tip over a small boat* UPSET, overturn, topple over, turn over, knock over, push over, upend, capsize, roll, flip.

**3** *the car tipped to one side* LEAN, tilt, list, slope, bank, slant, incline, pitch, cant, heel, careen.

**tip**[3] noun **1** *a generous tip* GRATUITY, baksheesh; present, gift, reward.

**2** *useful tips* PIECE OF ADVICE, suggestion, word of advice, pointer, recommendation; clue, hint, steer, tip-off; word to the wise.

**tip-off** noun *police have received an anonymous tip-off* PIECE OF INFORMATION, warning, lead, forewarning; hint, clue; advice, information, notification.

**tipsy** adjective *you're too tipsy to be driving home* MERRY, half-drunk, lightheaded, woozy, mellow, slightly drunk, lubricated. See note at DRUNK. ANTONYM sober.

**tirade** noun *both attorneys were stunned when the judge launched into a tirade* DIATRIBE, harangue, rant, onslaught, attack, polemic, denunciation, broadside, fulmination, condemnation, censure, invective, criticism, tongue-lashing; blast; lecture; *literary* philippic.

**tire** verb **1** *he began to tire as the ascent grew steeper* WEAKEN, grow weak, flag, wilt, droop; deteriorate.

**2** *the journey had tired her* FATIGUE, tire out, exhaust, wear out, drain, weary, frazzle, overtire, enervate; *informal* knock out, do in, wear to a frazzle.

**3** *we* ***are tired of*** *your difficult behavior* WEARY OF, get fed up with, get sick of, get bored with, get impatient with; *informal* have had it up to here with, have had enough of.

**tired** adjective **1** *you're just tired from traveling* EXHAUSTED, worn out, weary, fatigued, dog-tired, dead beat, bone-tired, ready to drop, drained, zonked, wasted, enervated, jaded; *informal* done in, bushed, whipped, bagged, knocked out, wiped out, pooped, tuckered out. ANTONYMS energetic, wide awake, fresh.

**2** *are you* ***tired of*** *having him here?* FED UP WITH, weary of, bored with/by, sick (to death) of; *informal* up to here with.

**3** *tired jokes* HACKNEYED, overused, overworked, worn out, stale, clichéd, hoary, stock, stereotyped, predictable, unimaginative, unoriginal, uninspired, dull, boring, routine; *informal* old hat, corny. ANTONYMS lively, fresh.

THE RIGHT WORD **tired, exhausted, fatigued, tuckered, weary**

**Tired** is what you are after you've cleaned the house, spent two hours reading a dull report, or trained for a marathon; it means that you are drained of your strength and energy, without giving any indication of degree. **Weary**, on the other hand, is how you feel after you've had to interrupt your dinner five or six times to answer the phone. It implies not only a depletion of energy but also the vexation that accompanies having to put up with something that is, or has become, disagreeable.

**Exhausted** means that you are totally drained of strength and energy, a condition that may even be irreversible (*exhausted by battling a terminal disease*). **Fatigued** is a more precise word than either *tired* or *weary*; it implies a loss of energy through strain, illness, or overwork to the point where rest or sleep is essential (*fatigued after working a 24-hour shift*). **Tuckered** is an informal word that comes close in meaning to *fatigued* or *exhausted*, but often carries the suggestion of loss of breath (*tuckered out after running up six flights of stairs*).

---

**tireless** adjective *their tireless efforts to reclaim the Hudson have given us a remarkably cleaner river* INDEFATIGABLE, energetic, vigorous, industrious, hard-working, determined, enthusiastic, keen, zealous, spirited, dynamic, dogged, tenacious, persevering, untiring, unwearying, unremitting, unflagging, indomitable. ANTONYM lazy.

**tiresome** adjective *the word is that she just couldn't stand one more day of his tiresome obsession with computer games* BORING, dull, tedious, insipid, wearisome, wearing, uninteresting, uneventful, humdrum, monotonous, mind-numbing; annoying, irritating, trying, irksome, vexing, troublesome, bothersome, nettlesome; *informal* aggravating, pesky. ANTONYMS interesting, pleasant.

**tiring** adjective *it was very tiring work* EXHAUSTING, wearying, taxing, fatiguing, wearing, enervating, draining; hard, heavy, arduous, strenuous, onerous, uphill, demanding, grueling; *informal* murderous.

**tissue** noun **1** *living tissue* MATTER, material, substance; flesh.

**2** *a box of tissues* FACIAL TISSUE; *trademark* Kleenex.

**titillate** verb *the dancers titillated the audience* AROUSE, excite, tantalize, stimulate, stir, thrill, interest, attract, fascinate; *informal* turn on. ANTONYM bore.

**titillating** adjective *a titillating rendition of "Baby, It's Cold Outside"* AROUSING, exciting, stimulating, sexy, thrilling, provocative, tantalizing, interesting, fascinating; suggestive, salacious, erotic. ANTONYM boring.

**title** noun **1** *the title of the work* NAME, heading, legend, label, caption, inscription.

**2** *the company publishes 400 titles a year* PUBLICATION, work, book, newspaper, paper, magazine, periodical.

**3** *the title of governor general* DESIGNATION, name, form of address, honorific; epithet, rank, office, position, job title; *informal* moniker, handle, tag; *formal* appellation, denomination; sobriquet.

**4** *an Olympic title* CHAMPIONSHIP, crown, first place; laurels, palm.

**5** *the landlord is obliged to prove his* ***title to*** *the land* OWNERSHIP OF, proprietorship of, possession of, holding of, freehold of, entitlement to, right to, claim to.

▸ verb *a paper titled "Immigration Today"* CALL, entitle, name, dub, designate, style, term; *formal* denominate.

**titter** verb & noun *she caused a few titters* | *the people at out table started to titter* GIGGLE, snicker, twitter, tee-hee, chuckle, laugh, chortle.

**titular** adjective **1** *the titular head of a university* NOMINAL, in title only, in name only, ceremonial, honorary, so-called; token, puppet.

**2** *the book's titular hero* EPONYMOUS, identifying.

**toady** noun *a conniving little toady* SYCOPHANT, brownnoser, lickspittle, flatterer, flunky, lackey, trained seal, doormat, stooge, cringer; *informal* bootlicker, suck-up, yes-man; *vulgar slang* kiss-ass, ass-kisser.

▸ verb *she imagined him* ***toadying to*** *his rich clients* GROVEL TO, ingratiate oneself with, be obsequious to, kowtow to, pander to, crawl to, truckle to, bow and scrape to, curry favor with, make up to, fawn on/over, slaver over, flatter, adulate, suck up to, lick the boots of, butter up.

**toast** noun **1** *he raised his glass in a toast* TRIBUTE, salute, salutation; *archaic* pledge.

**2** *he was the toast of Toledo* DARLING, favorite, pet, heroine, hero; talk; fair-haired boy/girl.

▸ verb **1** *she toasted her hands in front of the fire* WARM, warm up, heat, heat up.

**2** *we toasted the couple with champagne* DRINK (TO) THE HEALTH OF, drink to, salute, honor, pay tribute to.

**today** adverb **1** *the work must be finished today* THIS DAY, this very day, this morning, this afternoon, this evening.

**2** *the complex tasks demanded of computers today* NOWADAYS, these days, at the present time, in these times, in this day and age, now, currently, at the moment, at present, at this moment in time; in the present climate, presently.

**toddle** verb **1** *the child toddled toward him* TOTTER, teeter, wobble, falter, waddle, stumble.

**2** *informal I toddled down to the quay* AMBLE, wander, meander, stroll, saunter; *informal* mosey, toodle, tootle, putter.

**to-do** noun *informal the to-do in the street finally prompted a call to the police* COMMOTION, fuss, ado, excitement, agitation, stir, palaver, confusion, disturbance, brouhaha, fracas, uproar, furor, tempest in a teapot, much ado about nothing; *informal* hoo-ha, ballyhoo, hullabaloo; *Brit. informal* kerfuffle.

**together** adverb **1** *friends who work together* WITH EACH OTHER, in conjunction, jointly, in cooperation, in collaboration, in partnership, in combination, in league, in tandem, side by side, hand in hand, shoulder to shoulder, cheek by jowl; in collusion, hand in glove; *informal* in cahoots. ANTONYM separately.

**2** *they both spoke together* SIMULTANEOUSLY, at the same time, at one and the same time, at once, all together, as a group, in unison, in concert, in chorus, as one, with one accord. ANTONYM separately.

▸ adjective *informal a very together young woman.* See LEVEL-HEADED.

**toil** verb **1** *she toiled all night* WORK HARD, labor, exert oneself, slave (away), grind away, strive, work one's fingers to the bone, put one's nose to the grindstone; *informal* slog away, plug away, beaver away, work one's butt off, sweat blood; *literary* travail; *archaic* drudge, moil. See note at LABOR. ANTONYMS rest, relax.

**2** *she began to toil up the cliff path* STRUGGLE, trudge, tramp, tromp, traipse, slog, plod, trek, drag oneself; *informal* schlep.

▸ noun *a life of toil* HARD WORK, labor, exertion, slaving, drudgery, effort, industry, [blood, sweat, and tears]; slogging, elbow grease; *literary* travail; *archaic* moil.

**toilet** noun *he left to use the toilet.* See BATHROOM.

**token** noun **1** *a token of our appreciation* SYMBOL, sign, emblem, badge, representation, indication, mark, manifestation, expression, pledge, demonstration, recognition; evidence, proof. See note at SIGN.

**2** *he kept the menu as a token of their wedding anniversary* MEMENTO, souvenir, keepsake, reminder, remembrance, memorial. See note at EMBLEM.

▸ adjective *token resistance* SYMBOLIC, emblematic; perfunctory, slight, nominal, minimal, minor, mild, superficial, inconsequential.

**tolerable** adjective **1** *a tolerable noise level* BEARABLE, endurable, supportable, acceptable. ANTONYM intolerable.

**2** *he had a tolerable voice* FAIRLY GOOD, passable, adequate, all right, acceptable, satisfactory, not (too) bad, average, fair; mediocre, middling, ordinary, indifferent, unremarkable, unexceptional; *informal* OK, so-so, 'comme ci, comme ça,' nothing to write home about, no great shakes. ANTONYMS unacceptable, exceptional.

**tolerance** noun **1** *an attitude of tolerance toward other people* ACCEPTANCE, toleration; open-mindedness, broad-mindedness, forbearance, liberality, liberalism; patience, charity, indulgence, understanding.

**2** *she has a low* ***tolerance to*** *alcohol* ENDURANCE OF, RESISTANCE TO, resilience to, resistance to, immunity to.

**tolerant** adjective *a tolerant attitude toward other religions* OPEN-MINDED, forbearing, broad-minded, liberal, unprejudiced, unbiased; patient, long-suffering, understanding, forgiving, charitable, lenient, indulgent, permissive, easygoing, lax; *informal* laid-back. ANTONYM intolerant.

**tolerate** verb **1** *a regime unwilling to tolerate dissent* ALLOW, permit, condone, accept, swallow, countenance; *formal* brook; *archaic* suffer.

**2** *he couldn't tolerate her mood swings any longer* ENDURE, put up with, bear, take, stand, support, stomach, deal with; abide.

**toleration** noun *her father demonstrated little toleration where her boyfriends were concerned* ACCEPTANCE, tolerance, endurance; forbearance, sufferance, liberality, open-mindedness, broad-mindedness, liberalism; patience, charity, indulgence, understanding.

**toll**[1] noun **1** *a highway toll* CHARGE, fee, payment, levy, tariff, tax.

**2** *the toll of dead and injured* NUMBER, count, tally, total, sum total, grand total, sum; record, list.

**3** *the toll on the environment has been high* ADVERSE EFFECT(S), detriment, harm, damage, injury, impact, hurt; cost, price, loss, disadvantage, suffering, penalty.

**toll**[2] verb *I heard the bell toll* RING (OUT), chime, strike, peal; sound, ding, dong, clang, bong, resound, reverberate; *literary* knell.

**tomb** noun *the tomb of old Mr. Momphreys* BURIAL CHAMBER, sepulcher, mausoleum, vault, crypt, catacomb; last/final resting place, grave, barrow, burial mound; *historical* charnel house.

**tombstone** noun *the writing on the tombstone* GRAVESTONE, headstone, stone; memorial, monument.

**tome** noun *he expects us to read this tome by Monday* VOLUME, book, work, opus, publication, title.

**tomfoolery** noun *Mrs. Marks had no patience for tomfoolery* SILLINESS, fooling around, clowning, shenanigans, capers, antics, pranks, tricks, buffoonery, skylarking, nonsense, horseplay, monkey business, mischief, foolishness, foolery, fandango.

**tone** noun **1** *the tone of the tuba* TIMBRE, sound, sound quality, voice, voice quality, color, tonality.

**2** *the somewhat impatient tone of his letter* MOOD, air, spirit, feel, sound, flavor, note, attitude, character, nature, manner, temper; tenor, vein, drift, gist.

**3** *a dial tone* NOTE, signal, beep, bleep.

**4** *tones of burgundy and firebrick red* SHADE, color, hue, tint, tinge. PHRASE: **tone down** *the pastels in the upholstery will help to tone down the color scheme* SOFTEN, lighten, mute, subdue, mellow; MODERATE, modify, modulate, mitigate, temper, dampen.

**tongue** noun **1** *a foreign tongue* LANGUAGE, dialect, patois, vernacular, mother tongue, native tongue, heritage language, lingua franca; *informal* lingo.

**2** *her sharp tongue* WAY/MANNER OF SPEAKING, speech, choice of words, parlance.

**tongue-tied** adjective *he was tongue-tied with strangers* LOST FOR WORDS, speechless, unable to get a word out, struck dumb, dumbstruck; mute, dumb, silent; *informal* mum. ANTONYM loquacious.

**tonic** noun **1** *ginseng can be used as a natural tonic* STIMULANT, restorative, refresher, medicine; *informal* pick-me-up; *Medicine* analeptic.

**2** *we found the change of scene a tonic* STIMULANT, boost, fillip; *informal* shot in the arm, pick-me-up.

**too** adverb **1** *invasion would be too risky* EXCESSIVELY, overly, over, unduly, immoderately, inordinately, unreasonably, extremely, exorbitantly, very; *informal* too-too.

**2** *he was unhappy, too, you know* ALSO, as well, in addition, additionally, into the bargain, besides, furthermore, moreover, on top of that, to boot, likewise.

**tool** noun **1** *garden tools* IMPLEMENT, utensil, instrument, device, apparatus, gadget, appliance, machine, contrivance, contraption; *informal* gizmo.

**2** *the beautiful Estella is Miss Havisham's tool* PUPPET, pawn, creature, cat's paw; minion, lackey, instrument, organ; *informal* stooge.

▸ verb *tool leather into a saddle* WORK, fashion, shape, cut; ornament, embellish, decorate, chase.

THE RIGHT WORD **tool, apparatus, appliance, implement, instrument, utensil**

A wrench is a **tool**, meaning that it is a device held in and manipulated by the hand and used by a mechanic, plumber, carpenter, or other laborer to work, shape, move, or transform material (*he couldn't fix the drawer without the right tools*). An **implement** is a broader term referring to any tool or mechanical device used for a particular purpose (*agricultural implements*). A washing machine is an **appliance**, which refers to a mechanical or power-driven device, especially for household use (*the newly-married couple went shopping for appliances*). A **utensil** is a hand-held implement for domestic use (*eating utensils*), while an **instrument** is used for scientific or artistic purposes (*musical instrument; surgical instrument*). **Apparatus** refers to a collection of distinct instruments, tools, or other devices that are used in connection or combination with one another for a certain purpose (*the gym was open, but the exercise apparatus had not been set up*).

**top** noun **1** *the top of the cliff* SUMMIT, peak, pinnacle, crest, crown, brow, head, tip, apex, vertex. ANTONYMS bottom, base.

**2** *the top of the table* UPPER PART, upper surface, upper layer.

**3** *the carrots' green tops* LEAVES, shoots, stem, stalk. ANTONYMS root, tuber.

**4** *the top of the coffee jar* LID, cap, cover, stopper, cork.

**5** *a short-sleeved top* SHIRT, jersey, sweatshirt, sweater, pullover, vest; T-shirt, tank top; blouse.

**6** *by 1981 he was at the top of his profession* HIGH POINT, height, peak, pinnacle, zenith, acme, culmination, climax, prime. ANTONYM low point.

▸ adjective **1** *the top floor* HIGHEST, topmost, uppermost. ANTONYMS bottom, lowest.

**2** *the world's top scientists* FOREMOST, leading, principal, preeminent, greatest, best, finest, elite; *informal* top-notch, number one, blue-ribbon, blue-chip.

**3** *the organization's top management* UPPER, chief, principal, main, leading, highest, highest-ranking, ruling, commanding, most powerful, most important.

**4** *a top Paris hotel* PRIME, excellent, superb, superior, choice, select, top-quality, top-grade, first-rate, first-class, grade A, best, finest, premier, superlative, second to none, nonpareil; *informal* A1, top-notch, blue-ribbon, blue-chip, number one. ANTONYMS mediocre, inferior.

**5** *they are traveling at top speed* MAXIMUM, maximal, greatest, utmost. ANTONYMS lowest, minimum.

▸ verb **1** *sales are expected to top $1.3 billion* EXCEED, surpass, go beyond, better, best, beat, outstrip, outdo, outshine, eclipse, go one better than, cap.

**2** *their debut CD is currently topping the charts* LEAD, head, be at the top of.

**3** *chocolate mousse topped with whipped cream* COVER, cap, coat, smother; finish, garnish.

PHRASES: **over the top** *the lavish dessert buffet after that meal was simply over the top* EXCESSIVE, immoderate, inordinate, extreme, exaggerated, extravagant, overblown, too much, unreasonable, hyperbolic, disproportionate, undue, unwarranted, uncalled for, unnecessary, going too far.

**top up** *remember to top up your gas tank before heading back to Houston* FILL, refill, refresh, freshen, replenish, recharge, resupply; supplement, add to, augment.

**topic** noun *today's topic is skin care* SUBJECT, subject matter, theme, issue, matter, point, talking point, question, concern, argument, thesis, text, keynote.

**topical** adjective *let's stick to topical issues* CURRENT, up-to-date, up-to-the-minute, contemporary, recent, relevant; newsworthy, in the news. ANTONYM out-of-date.

**topmost** adjective. See UPPERMOST sense 1.

**top-notch** adjective *informal Rebecca is one of our top-notch salespeople* FIRST-CLASS, first-rate, top-quality, five-star; superior, prime, premier, premium, grade A, blue-chip, blue-ribbon, superlative, best, finest, select, exclusive, excellent, superb, outstanding, unbeatable, splendid, of the highest order, top-of-the-line, top-flight, top-grade; *informal* bang-up, A1.

**topple** verb **1** *she* ***toppled over*** FALL, fall over, tumble, overturn, tip over, keel over, collapse; lose one's balance.

**2** *protesters toppled a huge statue* KNOCK OVER, upset, push over, tip over, fell, upend.

**3** *a plot to topple the government* OVERTHROW, oust, unseat, overturn, bring down, defeat, get rid of, dislodge, eject.

**topsy-turvy** adjective **1** *a topsy-turvy flag* UPSIDE DOWN, wrong side up, inverted, reversed, upset; *informal* bass-ackward, ass-backward. ANTONYM right side up.

**2** *everything in the apartment was topsy-turvy* IN DISARRAY, in a mess, in a muddle, in disorder, disordered, jumbled, in chaos, chaotic, disorganized, awry, upside down, at sixes and sevens; *informal* every which way, higgledy-piggledy. ANTONYMS neat, ordered.

**torment** noun **1** *months of mental and emotional torment* AGONY, suffering, torture, pain, anguish, misery, distress, affliction, trauma, wretchedness; hell, purgatory.

**2** *it was a torment to see him like that* ORDEAL, affliction, scourge, curse, plague, bane, thorn in someone's side/flesh, cross to bear; sorrow, tribulation, trouble.

▸ verb **1** *she was tormented by shame* TORTURE, afflict, rack, harrow, plague, haunt, bedevil, distress, agonize.

**2** *she began to torment the two younger boys* TEASE, taunt, bait, harass, provoke, goad, plague, bother, trouble, persecute; *informal* needle.

**torn** adjective **1** *a torn shirt* RIPPED, rent, cut, slit; ragged, tattered, in tatters, in ribbons.

**2** *she was torn between the two options* WAVERING, vacillating, irresolute, dithering, uncertain, unsure, undecided, split, of two minds.

**tornado** noun. See STORM noun sense 1.

**torpid** adjective *torpid tourists traveled tired through the tropics* LETHARGIC, sluggish, inert, inactive, slow, lifeless; languid, listless, lazy, idle, indolent, slothful, supine, passive, apathetic, phlegmatic, somnolent, sleepy, weary, tired. ANTONYM energetic.

**torpor** noun *the feeling of torpor lingered for weeks* LETHARGY, sluggishness, inertia, inactivity, lifelessness, listlessness, languor, lassitude, laziness, idleness, indolence, sloth, acedia, passivity, somnolence, weariness, sleepiness.

**torrent** noun **1** *a torrent of water* FLOOD, deluge, inundation, spate, cascade, cataract, rush, stream, current, flow, overflow, tide.

**2** *a torrent of abuse* OUTBURST, outpouring, stream, flood, volley, barrage, tide, spate. ANTONYM trickle.

**torrid** adjective **1** *a torrid summer* HOT, dry, scorching, searing, blazing, blistering, sweltering, burning, sultry; *informal* boiling (hot), baking (hot), sizzling. ANTONYMS cold, wet.

**2** *a torrid affair* PASSIONATE, ardent, lustful, amorous; *informal* steamy, sultry, sizzling, hot. ANTONYM passionless.

**tortuous** adjective **1** *a tortuous route* TWISTING, twisty, twisting and turning, winding, windy, zigzag, sinuous, snaky, serpentine, meandering, circuitous. ANTONYM straight.

**2** *a tortuous argument* CONVOLUTED, complicated, complex, labyrinthine, tangled, tangly, involved, confusing, difficult to follow, involuted, lengthy, overlong, circuitous. ANTONYM straightforward.

**torture** noun **1** *acts of torture* INFLICTION OF PAIN, abuse, ill-treatment, maltreatment, persecution; sadism.

**2** *the torture of losing a loved one* TORMENT, agony, suffering, pain, anguish, misery, distress, heartbreak, affliction, scourge, trauma, wretchedness; hell, purgatory.

▸ verb **1** *the security forces routinely tortured suspects* INFLICT PAIN ON, ill-treat, abuse, mistreat, maltreat, persecute.

**2** *he was tortured by grief* TORMENT, rack, afflict, harrow, plague, agonize, scourge, crucify.

**toss** verb **1** *he tossed the ball over the fence* THROW, hurl, fling, sling, cast, pitch, lob, project; *informal* heave, chuck.

**2** *he tossed a coin and it landed heads* FLIP, flick.

**3** *the ship tossed about on the waves* PITCH, lurch, rock, roll, plunge, reel, list, keel, sway, wallow, flounder.

**4** *she tossed about in her sleep* THRASH, squirm, wriggle, writhe, fidget, turn.

**5** *toss the salad ingredients together* SHAKE, stir, turn, mix, combine.

**total** adjective **1** *the total cost* ENTIRE, complete, whole, full, comprehensive, combined, aggregate, gross, overall, final. ANTONYM partial.

**2** *a total success* COMPLETE, utter, absolute, thorough, out-and-out, outright, all-out, sheer, perfect, consummate, arrant, positive, rank, unmitigated, unqualified, unreserved, categorical. ANTONYM partial.

▸ noun *a total of $160,000* SUM, sum total, grand total, aggregate, result; whole, entirety, totality.

▸ verb **1** *the prize money totaled $33,050* ADD UP TO, amount to, come to, run to, make, work out to.

**2** *she totaled up her score* ADD (UP), count, reckon, tot up, tally, compute, work out.

**totalitarian** adjective *Saddam's totalitarian regime* AUTOCRATIC, undemocratic, one-party, dictatorial, tyrannical, despotic, fascist, oppressive, repressive, illiberal; authoritarian, autarchic, absolute, absolutist; dystopian. ANTONYM democratic.

**totality** noun *the concept is difficult to grasp in its totality* ENTIRETY, wholeness, fullness, completeness; whole, total, aggregate, sum, sum total; all, everything.

**totally** adverb *the decor is totally pink* COMPLETELY, entirely, wholly, thoroughly, fully, utterly, absolutely, perfectly, unreservedly, unconditionally, quite, altogether, downright; in every way, in every respect, one hundred percent, every inch, to the hilt; *informal* flat out, to the max. ANTONYM partly.

**totter** verb **1** *arm in arm, they tottered across the lawn* TEETER, dodder, walk unsteadily, stagger, wobble, stumble, shuffle, shamble, toddle; reel, sway, roll, lurch.

**2** *the foundations began to heave and totter* SHAKE, sway, tremble, quiver, teeter, shudder, rock, quake; *chiefly Brit.* judder.

**touch** verb **1** *his shoes were touching the end of the bed* BE IN CONTACT WITH, come into contact with, meet, join, connect with, converge with, be contiguous with, be against.

**2** *he touched her cheek* PRESS LIGHTLY, tap, pat; feel, stroke, fondle, caress, pet; brush, graze, put a hand to.

**3** *nobody can touch her when she's on her game* COMPARE WITH, rival, compete with, come/get close to, be on a par with, equal, match, be a match for, be in the same class/league as, measure up to; better, beat; *informal* hold a candle to.

**4** *you're not supposed to touch the computer* HANDLE, hold, pick up, move; meddle with, play about with, fiddle with, interfere with, tamper with, disturb, lay a finger on; use, employ, make use of.

**5** *people whose lives have been touched by the recession* AFFECT, impact, have an effect on, have an impact on, make a difference to, change.

**6** *years later she wrote to tell them how much their kindnesses had touched her* AFFECT, move, tug at someone's heartstrings; leave an impression on, have an effect on.

▸ noun 1 *he felt her touch on his shoulder* TAP, pat; stroke, caress; brush, graze; hand.

2 *his political touch* SKILL, skillfulness, expertise, dexterity, deftness, adroitness, adeptness, ability, talent, flair, facility, proficiency, mastery, knack, technique, approach, style.

3 *a touch of sadness* TRACE, bit, grain, hint, suggestion, suspicion, scintilla, tinge, overtone, undertone, note; dash, taste, drop, dab, dribble, pinch, speck, soupçon.

4 *the oil lamps are a nice touch* DETAIL, feature, point; addition, accessory.

5 *have you been in touch with him?* CONTACT, communication, correspondence; connection, association, interaction.

PHRASES: **touch down** *the plane is expected to touch down in San Juan* LAND, alight, come down, put down, arrive.
**touch off** *the action touched off a string of protests* CAUSE, spark, trigger, start, set in motion, ignite, stir up, provoke, give rise to, lead to, generate, set off.
**touch on/upon** *his speech is sure to touch on the subject of school vouchers* REFER TO, mention, comment on, speak on, remark on, bring up, raise, broach, allude to; cover, deal with.
**touch something up** 1 *these paints are handy for touching up small areas* REPAINT, retouch, patch, fix; renovate, refurbish, revamp.

2 *the editor touched up my prose* IMPROVE, enhance, make better, refine, give the finishing touches to; *informal* tweak.

**touch-and-go** adjective *his recovery is touch-and-go* UNCERTAIN, precarious, risky, chancy, hazardous, dangerous, critical, suspenseful, cliffhanging, hanging by a thread; *informal* dicey. ANTONYM certain.

**touching** adjective *a touching tribute to their mother* MOVING, affecting, heartwarming, emotional, emotive, tender, sentimental; poignant, sad, tearjerker, tearjerking. See note at MOVING.

**touchstone** noun *the declaration was considered a touchstone for Soviet dissidents* CRITERION, standard, yardstick, benchmark, barometer, bellwether, litmus test; measure, point of reference, norm, gauge, test, guide, exemplar, model, pattern.

**touchy** adjective 1 *Arnie can be so touchy* SENSITIVE, oversensitive, hypersensitive, easily offended, thin-skinned, highstrung, tense; irritable, dyspeptic, tetchy, testy, crotchety, peevish, waspish, querulous, bad-tempered, petulant, pettish, cranky, fractious, choleric. ANTONYMS affable, good-humored.

2 *a touchy subject* DELICATE, sensitive, tricky, ticklish, thorny, prickly, embarrassing, awkward, difficult; contentious, controversial.

**tough** adjective 1 *tough leather gloves* DURABLE, strong, resilient, sturdy, rugged, solid, stout, long-lasting, heavy-duty, industrial-strength, well-built, made to last. ANTONYMS soft, flimsy, fragile.

2 *the steak was tough* CHEWY, leathery, gristly, stringy, fibrous. ANTONYM tender.

3 *she'll survive—she's tough* ROBUST, resilient, strong, hardy, rugged, flinty, fit; stalwart, tough as nails. ANTONYM weak.

4 *another tough report from the auditor* STRICT, stern, severe, stringent, rigorous, hard, firm, hard-hitting, uncompromising; unsentimental, unsympathetic. ANTONYMS soft, light, lenient.

5 *that exercise sure was tough* ARDUOUS, onerous, strenuous, grueling, exacting, difficult, demanding, hard, taxing, tiring, exhausting, punishing, laborious, stressful, back-breaking, Herculean; *archaic* toilsome. ANTONYM easy.

6 *these are tough questions* DIFFICULT, hard, baffling, knotty, thorny, tricky. ANTONYM easy.

▸ noun *a gang of toughs* RUFFIAN, thug, goon, hoodlum, hooligan; *informal* roughneck, hood, heavy, bruiser, yahoo.

**toughen** verb 1 *the process toughens the wood fibers* STRENGTHEN, fortify, reinforce, harden, temper, anneal.

2 *measures to* ***toughen up*** *prison discipline* MAKE STRICTER, make more severe, stiffen, tighten up; *informal* beef up.

**tour** noun 1 *we enjoyed a two-week* ***tour of*** *Italy* TRIP TO/THROUGH, excursion to/through, journey to/through, expedition to/through, jaunt to/through, outing to/through; trek to/through, safari to/through; *archaic* peregrination to/through.

2 *a tour of the factory* VISIT, inspection, guided tour.

▸ verb 1 *this hotel is well placed for touring the Cariboo* TRAVEL AROUND, explore, discover, vacation in, visit.

2 *the governor toured the factory* VISIT, go around/through, walk around/through, inspect; *informal* check out.

PHRASE: **tour of duty** *his tour of duty in Afghanistan* STINT, stretch, spell, turn, assignment, period of service.

**tourist** noun *the islands teem with tourists* VACATIONER, traveler, sightseer, visitor, backpacker, globetrotter, day tripper, out-of-towner. ANTONYM local.

**tournament** noun 1 *a golf tournament* COMPETITION, contest, championship, meeting, tourney, meet, event, match, round robin.

2 *historical* *a knight preparing for a tournament* JOUST, tilt; the lists.

**tousled** adjective *tousled hair* UNTIDY, disheveled, windblown, messy, disordered, disarranged, messed up, rumpled, uncombed, ungroomed, tangled, wild, unkempt; *informal* mussed up. ANTONYMS neat, tidy.

**tout** verb 1 *street merchants were touting their wares* PEDDLE, sell, hawk, offer for sale, promote.

2 *cab drivers were* ***touting for*** *business* SOLICIT, seek, drum up; ask for, petition for, appeal for.

3 *she's being touted as the next party leader* RECOMMEND, speak of, extol, advocate, talk of; predict.

**tow** verb *the car was towed back to the garage* PULL, haul, drag, draw, tug, lug. PHRASE: **in tow** *he arrived with his new girlfriend in tow* IN ATTENDANCE, by one's side, alongside, in one's charge; accompanying, following, tagging along.

**toward, towards** preposition 1 *they were driving toward her apartment* IN THE DIRECTION OF, to; on the way to, on the road to, en route to.

2 *toward evening, dark clouds gathered* JUST BEFORE, shortly before, near, around, approaching, close to, coming to, getting on for.

3 *her attitude toward politics* WITH REGARD TO, as regards, regarding, in/with regard to, respecting, in relation to, concerning, about, apropos, vis-à-vis.

4 *some money toward the cost of a new house* AS A CONTRIBUTION TO, for, to help with.

**tower** noun *a church tower* STEEPLE, spire; minaret; turret; bell tower, belfry, campanile; skyscraper, high-rise, edifice; transmission tower.

▸ verb 1 *snow-capped peaks towered over the valley* SOAR, rise, rear, loom; overshadow, overhang, hang over, dominate.

2 *she* ***towered over*** *most other theologians of her generation* ECLIPSE, overshadow, outshine, outclass, surpass, dominate, be head and shoulders above, put someone/something in the shade.

**towering** adjective 1 *a towering skyscraper* HIGH, tall, lofty, soaring, sky-high, multistory; giant, gigantic, enormous, huge, massive; *informal* ginormous.

2 *a towering intellect* OUTSTANDING, preeminent, leading, foremost, finest, top, surpassing, supreme, great, incomparable, unrivaled, unsurpassed, peerless.

**town** noun *they live in a town just outside Milwaukee* MUNICIPALITY, township, conurbation, urban area; city, capital, metropolis, megalopolis, megacity, burg; small town, whistle-stop.

**toxic** adjective *toxic houseplants* POISONOUS, virulent, noxious, deadly, dangerous, harmful, injurious, pernicious. ANTONYM harmless.

**toy** noun *Santa left a bundle of toys* PLAYTHING, game; gadget, device; trinket, knickknack, gizmo.

▸ adjective 1 *a toy gun* MODEL, imitation, replica, fake; miniature.

2 *a toy poodle* MINIATURE, small, tiny, diminutive, dwarf, midget, pygmy.

PHRASE: **toy with** 1 *I was toying with the idea of writing a book* THINK ABOUT, consider, flirt with, entertain the possibility of; kick around.

2 *Adam toyed with his glasses* FIDDLE WITH, play with, fidget with, twiddle; finger.

3 *she toyed with her food* NIBBLE, pick at, peck at, eat listlessly, eat like a bird.

4 *you are toying with my emotions* TRIFLE WITH, play with, play havoc with, amuse oneself with, mess with, be flippant with.

**trace** verb 1 *police hope to trace the owner of the vehicle* TRACK DOWN, find, discover, detect, unearth, turn up, hunt down, ferret out.

2 *she traced a pattern in the sand with her toe* DRAW, outline, mark, sketch.

3 *the analysis traces the origins of cowboy poetry* OUTLINE, map out, follow, sketch out, delineate, depict, show, indicate.

▸ noun 1 *no trace had been found of the runaways* VESTIGE, sign, mark, indication, evidence, clue; trail, tracks, marks, prints, footprints, spoor; remains, remnant, relic.

2 *a trace of bitterness crept into her voice* BIT, touch, hint, suggestion, suspicion, shadow, whiff; drop, dash, tinge, speck, shred, iota; smidgen, tad.

THE RIGHT WORD **trace, remnant, track, trail, vestige**

You can follow the **track** of a deer in the snow, the **trace** of a sleigh, or the **trail** of someone who has just cut down a Christmas tree and is dragging it back to the car. A *track* is a line or a series of marks left by the passage of something or someone; it often refers specifically to a line of footprints or a path worn into the ground by the feet (*to follow the track of a grizzly bear*). *Trace* may refer to a line or a rut made by someone or something that has been present or passed by; it may also refer to a mark serving as evidence that something has happened or been there (*traces of mud throughout the house; the telephoto shots have a trace of a camera shake*). *Trail* may refer to the track created by the passage of animals or people, or to the mark or marks left by something being dragged along a surface (*they followed the trail of the injured dog*). **Vestige** and **remnant** come closer in meaning to *trace*, as they refer to what remains after something has passed away. A *vestige* is always slight when compared to what it recalls (*the last vestiges of a great civilization*), while a *remnant* is a fragment or scrap of something (*all that remained of the historic tapestry after the fire was a few scorched remnants*).

**track** noun 1 *a gravel track* PATH, pathway, footpath, lane, trail, route, way, course.

2 *the final lap of the track* COURSE, racetrack, raceway; velodrome.

3 **(tracks)** *he found the tracks of a wolverine* TRACES, marks, prints, footprints, trail, spoor.

4 *we followed the track of the hurricane* COURSE, path, line, route, way, trajectory, wake.

5 *railroad tracks* RAIL, line.

6 *the album's title track* SONG, recording, number, piece.

▸ verb *he tracked a bear for 40 miles* FOLLOW, trail, trace, pursue, shadow, stalk, keep an eye on, keep in sight; *informal* tail.

PHRASES: **keep track of** *the electronic log keeps track of your blood-glucose readings* MONITOR, follow, keep up with, keep an eye on; keep in touch with, keep up to date with; *informal* keep tabs on.

**track down** *Captain Pearce vowed that they would track down the killer* DISCOVER, find, detect, hunt down/out, unearth, uncover, turn up, dig up, ferret out, bring to light.

**on track** *the fund-raising is on track* ON COURSE, on an even keel, on schedule.

**tract**[1] noun *large tracts of land* AREA, region, expanse, sweep, stretch, extent, belt, swathe, zone.

**tract**[2] noun *a political tract* TREATISE, essay, article, paper, work, monograph, disquisition, dissertation, thesis, homily, tractate; pamphlet, booklet, chapbook, leaflet.

**tractable** adjective *our preschool teachers disagree with the statement that children are becoming less tractable every year* MALLEABLE, manageable, amenable, pliable, governable, yielding, complaisant, compliant, game, persuadable, accommodating, docile, biddable, obliging, obedient, submissive, meek. ANTONYM recalcitrant.

**trade** noun **1** *the illicit trade in stolen cattle* COMMERCE, buying and selling, dealing, traffic, trafficking, business, marketing, merchandising; dealings, transactions, deal-making.

**2** *we shook hands as we made the trade* EXCHANGE, transaction, swap, trade-off; *archaic* truck.

**3** *the glazier's trade* CRAFT, occupation, job, career, profession, business, line of work, line, métier, vocation, calling, walk of life, field; work, employment, livelihood.

▸ verb **1** *he made his fortune* ***trading in*** *beaver pelts* DEAL (IN), buy and sell, traffic (in), market, merchandise, peddle, vend; *informal* hawk, run.

**2** *the business is trading at a loss* OPERATE, run, do business.

**3** *I traded the old machine for a newer model* SWAP, exchange, switch; barter, trade in.

PHRASE: **trade on** *he trades on his friendship with powerful people* EXPLOIT, take advantage of, capitalize on, profit from, use, make use of; milk; *informal* cash in on.

**trademark** noun **1** *the company's trademark* LOGO, brand, emblem, sign, mark, stamp, symbol, badge, crest, monogram, colophon; brand name, trade name, proprietary name.

**2** *it had all the trademarks of a Mafia hit* CHARACTERISTIC, hallmark, calling card, sign, trait, quality, attribute, feature, peculiarity, idiosyncrasy, quirk.

**trader** noun *a commodities trader* DEALER, merchant, buyer, seller, buyer and seller, marketeer, merchandiser, broker, agent; distributor, vendor, purveyor, monger, supplier, trafficker; retailer, wholesaler; storekeeper, shopkeeper; wheeler-dealer.

**tradition** noun **1** *during a maiden speech, by tradition, everyone keeps absolutely silent* HISTORICAL CONVENTION, unwritten law, mores; oral history, lore, folklore.

**2** *an age-old tradition* CUSTOM, practice, convention, ritual, observance, way, usage, habit, institution; *formal* praxis.

**traditional** adjective **1** *traditional Christmas fare* LONG-ESTABLISHED, customary, time-honored, established, classic, accustomed, standard, regular, normal, conventional, usual, orthodox, habitual, set, fixed, routine, ritual; old, age-old, ancestral.

**2** *traditional beliefs* HANDED-DOWN, folk, unwritten, oral.

**traduce** verb *you dare to traduce my family?* DEFAME, slander, speak ill of, misrepresent, malign, vilify, denigrate, disparage, slur, impugn, smear, besmirch, run down, blacken the name of, cast aspersions on; *informal* badmouth, dis.

**traffic** noun **1** *the bridge is not open to traffic* VEHICLES; cars, trucks.

**2** *they might be stuck in traffic* A TRAFFIC JAM, congestion, a gridlock, a holdup, a bottleneck, a tie-up; *informal* a snarl-up, a logjam.

**3** *the illegal traffic in stolen art* TRADE, trading, trafficking, dealing, commerce, business, buying and selling; smuggling, bootlegging, black market; dealings, transactions.

▸ verb *he confessed to* ***trafficking in*** *narcotics* TRADE (IN), deal (in), do business in, buy and sell; smuggle, bootleg; *informal* run, push.

**tragedy** noun *the flood was the worst tragedy in the city's history* DISASTER, calamity, catastrophe, cataclysm, misfortune, mishap, blow, trial, tribulation, affliction, adversity.

**tragic** adjective **1** *a tragic accident* DISASTROUS, calamitous, catastrophic, cataclysmic, devastating, terrible, dreadful, awful, appalling, dismal, horrendous; fatal, deadly, mortal, lethal. ANTONYMS fortunate, lucky.

**2** *a tragic tale* SAD, unhappy, pathetic, moving, distressing, depressing, painful, harrowing, heart-rending, piteous, wretched, sorry; melancholy, doleful, mournful, miserable, gut-wrenching. ANTONYMS joyful, happy.

**3** *a tragic waste of talent* REGRETTABLE, shameful, terrible, horrible, awful, deplorable, lamentable, piteous, dreadful, grievous.

**trail** noun **1** *he left a trail of clues* | *a trail of devastation* SERIES, string, chain, succession, sequence; aftermath, wake. See note at TRACE.

**2** *wolves on the trail of their prey* TRACK, spoor, path, scent; traces, marks, signs, prints, footprints.

**3** *the airplane's vapor trail* WAKE, contrail, tail, stream.

**4** *a trail of ants* LINE, column, train, file, procession, string, chain, convoy; lineup.

**5** *provincial parks with nature trails* PATH, pathway, way, footpath, walk, track, course, route.

▸ verb **1** *her robe trailed along the ground* DRAG, sweep, swish, be drawn; dangle, hang (down), droop.

**2** *the roses grew wild, their stems trailing over the banks* HANG, droop, fall, spill, cascade.

**3** *Filteau suspected that they were trailing him* FOLLOW, pursue, track, shadow, stalk, hunt (down); *informal* tail.

**4** *the defending champions were trailing 3–1 in the second period* LOSE, be down, be behind, lag behind.

**5** *her voice trailed off* FADE, tail off/away, grow faint, die away, dwindle, taper off, subside, peter out, fizzle out.

**train** verb **1** *an engineer trained in remote-sensing techniques* INSTRUCT, teach, coach, tutor, school, educate, prime, drill, ground; inculcate, indoctrinate, initiate, break in.

**2** *she's training to be a hairdresser* STUDY, learn, prepare, take instruction.

**3** *with the Olympics in mind, athletes are training hard* EXERCISE, do exercises, work out, get into shape, practice, prepare.

**4** *she trained the gun on his chest* AIM, point, direct, level, focus; zero in.

▸ noun **1** *the train for Youngstown* locomotive, subway, monorail; *informal* iron horse; *baby talk* choo choo.

**2** *a minister and his train of attendants* RETINUE, entourage, cortège, following, staff, household.

**3** *a train of elephants* PROCESSION, line, file, column, convoy, cavalcade, caravan, string, succession, trail.

**4** *a bizarre train of events* CHAIN, string, series, sequence, succession, set, course, cycle, concatenation.

**trainer** noun *my personal trainer at the gym* COACH, instructor, teacher, tutor; handler.

**training** noun **1** *in-house training for staff* INSTRUCTION, teaching, coaching, tuition, tutoring, guidance, schooling, education, orientation; indoctrination, inculcation, initiation.

**2** *four months' hard training before the tournament* EXERCISE, exercises, working out, conditioning; practice, preparation.

**trait** noun *elaborating on the truth is just one of her personality traits* CHARACTERISTIC, attribute, feature, quality, property; habit, custom, mannerism, idiosyncrasy, peculiarity, quirk, oddity, foible.

**traitor** noun *convicted traitors will be executed* BETRAYER, backstabber, double-crosser, renegade, fifth columnist; turncoat, defector, deserter; collaborator, informer, mole, snitch, double agent; Judas, Benedict Arnold, quisling; *informal* snake in the grass, two-timer, rat, scab, fink.

**traitorous** adjective *his dealings with a traitorous party* TREACHEROUS, disloyal, treasonous, renegade, backstabbing; double-crossing, double-dealing, faithless, unfaithful, two-faced, duplicitous, deceitful, false; *informal* two-timing; *literary* perfidious. ANTONYM loyal.

**trajectory** noun *the missile's trajectory* COURSE, path, route, track, line, orbit.

**trammel** *literary* noun *the trammels of domesticity* RESTRAINT, constraint, curb, check, impediment, obstacle, barrier, handicap, bar, hindrance, encumbrance, disadvantage, drawback, shackles, fetters, bonds.

▸ verb *those less trammeled by convention than himself* RESTRICT, restrain, constrain, hamper, confine, hinder, handicap, obstruct, impede, hold back, tie down, hamstring, shackle, fetter.

**tramp** verb *we tramped across France* TRUDGE, tromp, plod, galumph, stamp, trample, lumber, clump, clomp, stump, stomp; trek, slog, schlep, drag oneself, walk, hike, march, traipse.

▸ noun **1** *a wandering old tramp* VAGRANT, vagabond, street person, hobo, homeless person, down-and-out; traveler, drifter, derelict, beggar, mendicant, bag lady, bum.

**2** *the regular tramp of the sentry's boots* FOOTSTEP, tromp, step, footfall, tread, stamp, stomp.

**trample** verb **1** *someone had trampled on the tulips* TREAD, tramp, stamp, stomp, walk over; squash, crush, flatten.

**2** *we do nothing but* ***trample over*** *their feelings* TREAT WITH CONTEMPT, disregard, show no consideration for, abuse; encroach on, infringe (on).

**trance** noun *he pretended to be in a trance* DAZE, stupor, hypnotic state, half-conscious state, dream, reverie, fugue state.

**tranquil** adjective **1** *the lake's tranquil waters* PEACEFUL, calm, calming, still, serene, placid, restful, quiet, relaxing, undisturbed, limpid, pacific. ANTONYM disturbed.

**2** *Martha smiled, perfectly tranquil* CALM, serene, relaxed, unruffled, unperturbed, unflustered, untroubled, composed, 'calm, cool, and collected'; equable, even-tempered, placid, unflappable. See note at CALM. ANTONYM excitable.

**tranquilize** verb *the horse was tranquilized* SEDATE, put under sedation, narcotize, anesthetize, etherize, drug.

**tranquilizer** noun *don't have any wine if you're taking tranquilizers* SEDATIVE, barbiturate, calmative, sleeping pill, depressant, narcotic, opiate; *informal* downer. ANTONYM stimulant.

**transact** verb *no business will be transacted on the day after Christmas* CONDUCT, carry out, negotiate, do, perform, execute, take care of, discharge; settle, conclude, finish, accomplish.

**transaction** noun **1** *property transactions* DEAL, business deal, undertaking, arrangement, bargain, negotiation, agreement, settlement; proceedings.

**2** *the bank statement records your transactions* DEBIT, credit, deposit, withdrawal.

**3** *the transaction of government business* CONDUCT, carrying out, negotiation, performance, execution.

**transcend** verb **1** *an issue that transcended party politics* GO BEYOND, rise above, cut across.

**2** *his exploits far transcended those of his predecessors* SURPASS, exceed, beat, cap, tower above, outdo, outclass, outstrip, leave behind, outshine, eclipse, overshadow, throw into the shade, upstage, top.

**transcendent** adjective **1** *the search for a transcendent level of knowledge* MYSTICAL, mystic, transcendental, spiritual, divine; metaphysical.

**2** *a transcendent genius* INCOMPARABLE, matchless, peerless, unrivaled, inimitable, beyond compare/comparison, unparalleled, unequaled, without equal, second to none, unsurpassed, unsurpassable, nonpareil; exceptional, consummate, unique, perfect, rare, surpassing, magnificent.

**transcendental** adjective See TRANSCENDENT sense 1.

**transcribe** verb **1** *each interview was taped and transcribed* WRITE OUT, write down, copy down, put in writing, put on paper, render.

**2** *a person who can take and transcribe shorthand* TRANSLITERATE, interpret, translate.

**transcript** noun **1** *a radio transcript* WRITTEN VERSION, printed version, script, text, transliteration, record, reproduction.

**2** *university transcript* STUDENT RECORD, grades, report card.

**transfer** verb **1** *the hostages were transferred to a safe house* MOVE, convey, take, bring, shift, remove, carry, transport; transplant, relocate, resettle.

**2** *the property was transferred to his wife* HAND OVER, pass on, make over, turn over, sign over, consign, devolve, assign, delegate.

▸ noun **1** *he died shortly after his transfer to hospital* MOVE, conveyance, transferral, transference, shift, relocation, removal, switch, transplantation.

**2** *keep your bus transfer in your pocket* TICKET, pass; receipt, proof of purchase.

**transfix** verb **1** *she was transfixed by the images on the screen* MESMERIZE, hypnotize, spellbind, bewitch, captivate, entrance, enthrall, fascinate, absorb, enrapture, grip, hook, rivet, paralyze.

**2** *a field mouse is transfixed by the owl's curved talons* IMPALE, stab, spear, pierce, spike, skewer, gore, stick, run through.

**transform** verb *the old inn has been transformed into an outpatient medical facility* CHANGE, alter, convert, metamorphose, transfigure, transmute, mutate; revolutionize, overhaul; remodel, reshape, redo, reconstruct, rebuild, reorganize, rearrange, rework, renew, revamp, remake, retool; *informal* transmogrify, morph.

**transformation** noun *the transformation of the sales department has been dramatic* CHANGE, alteration, mutation, conversion, metamorphosis, transfiguration, transmutation, sea change; revolution, overhaul; remodeling, reshaping, redoing, reconstruction, rebuilding, reorganization, rearrangement, reworking, renewal, revamp, remaking, remake; *informal* transmogrification, morphing.

**transgress** verb **1** *if they transgress, the punishment is harsh* MISBEHAVE, behave badly, break the law, err, fall from grace, stray from the straight and narrow, sin, do wrong, go astray; *archaic* trespass.

**2** *she had transgressed an unwritten social law* INFRINGE, breach, contravene, disobey, defy, violate, break, flout.

**transgression** noun **1** *a punishment for past transgressions* OFFENSE, crime, sin, wrong, wrongdoing, misdemeanor, impropriety, infraction, misdeed, lawbreaking; error, lapse, peccadillo, fault; *archaic* trespass.

**2** *Adam's transgression of God's law* INFRINGEMENT, breach, contravention, violation, defiance, disobedience, nonobservance. See note at SIN.

**transgressor** noun *grant these transgressors forgiveness* OFFENDER, miscreant, lawbreaker, criminal, villain, felon, malefactor, guilty party, culprit; sinner, evildoer; *archaic* trespasser, miscreant.

**transient** adjective *our interest in the environment must not be transient* TRANSITORY, temporary, short-lived, short-term, ephemeral, impermanent, brief, short, momentary, fleeting, passing, here today and gone tomorrow; *literary* evanescent, fugitive. See note at TEMPORARY. ANTONYM permanent.

▸ noun *the plight of poor transients* HOBO, vagrant, vagabond, street person, homeless person, down-and-out; traveler, drifter, derelict.

**transit** noun **1** *public transit* TRANSPORTATION, transport, mass transit, bus system, subway system.

**2** *the transit of goods between states* TRANSPORTATION, transport, movement, flow, conveyance, shipping, shipment, trucking, carriage, transfer. PHRASE: **in transit** *the building supplies are in transit* EN ROUTE, on the journey, on the way, on the road.

**transition** noun *the transition from school to work* CHANGE, passage, move, transformation, conversion, metamorphosis, alteration, handover, changeover; segue, shift, switch, jump, leap, progression; progress, development, evolution, flux.

**transitional** adjective **1** *a transitional period* CHANGEOVER, interim; changing, fluid, in flux, unsettled, intermediate, liminal.

**2** *the transitional government* INTERIM, temporary, provisional, pro tem, acting, caretaker.

**transitory** adjective *transitory fashions* TRANSIENT, temporary, brief, short, short-lived, short-term, impermanent, ephemeral, momentary, fleeting, passing, here today and gone tomorrow; *literary* evanescent, fugitive. See note at TEMPORARY. ANTONYM permanent.

**translate** verb **1** *the German original had been translated into English* RENDER, put, express, convert, change; transcribe, transliterate.

**2** *be prepared to translate plenty of jargon* RENDER, paraphrase, reword, rephrase, convert, decipher, decode, gloss, explain.

**3** *interesting ideas cannot always be translated into effective movies* ADAPT, change, convert, transform, alter, turn, transmute; *informal* transmogrify, morph.

**translation** noun *the translation of the Bible into English* RENDITION, rendering, conversion; transcription, transliteration.

**transmission** noun **1** *the transmission of ideas* SPREAD, transferral, communication, conveyance; dissemination, circulation, transference.

**2** *a live transmission* BROADCAST, program, show, airing.

**3** *her car had a faulty transmission* POWER TRAIN, drivetrain.

**transmit** verb **1** *the use of computers to transmit information* TRANSFER, pass on, hand on, communicate, convey, impart, channel, carry, relay, forward, dispatch; disseminate, spread, circulate.

**2** *the program will be transmitted on Sunday* BROADCAST, relay, send out, air, televise.

**transparency** noun **1** *the transparency of the glass* TRANSLUCENCY, limpidity, clearness, clarity.

**2** *color transparencies* SLIDE, acetate.

**3** *the new government aims for better transparency* OPENNESS, accountability, straightforwardness, candor.

**transparent** adjective **1** *transparent blue water* CLEAR, crystal clear, see-through, translucent, pellucid, limpid, glassy, vitreous. ANTONYMS opaque, cloudy.

**2** *fine transparent fabrics* SEE-THROUGH, sheer, filmy, gauzy, diaphanous, translucent. ANTONYM thick.

**3** *a transparent attempt to win favor* OBVIOUS, evident, self-evident, undisguised, unconcealed, conspicuous, patent, clear, crystal clear, plain, (as) plain as the nose on your face, apparent, unmistakable, easily discerned, manifest, palpable, indisputable, unambiguous, unequivocal. ANTONYMS ambiguous, obscure.

**transpire** verb **1** *it transpired that her family had moved away* BECOME KNOWN, emerge, come to light, be revealed, turn out, come out, be discovered, prove to be the case, unfold.

**2** *I'm going to find out exactly what transpired* HAPPEN, occur, take place, arise, come about, materialize, turn up, chance, befall, ensue; *literary* come to pass. See note at HAPPEN.

USAGE NOTE **transpire**

The common use of **transpire** to mean 'occur, happen' (*I'm going to find out exactly what transpired*) is a loose extension of an earlier meaning, 'come to be known' (*it transpired that Mark had been baptized a Catholic*). This loose sense of 'happen,' which is now more common in American usage than the sense of 'come to be known,' was first recorded in American English toward the end of the eighteenth century and has been listed in American dictionaries from the nineteenth century. Careful writers should note, however, that in cases where *occur* or *happen* would do just as well, the use of **transpire** may strike readers as an affectation or as jargon.

**transplant** verb **1** *our headquarters will be transplanted to Pennsylvania* TRANSFER, move, remove, shift, relocate, take.

**2** *the seedlings should be transplanted in larger pots* REPLANT, repot, relocate.

**3** *kidneys must be transplanted within 48 hours of removal* TRANSFER, implant.

**transport** verb *barges transport the lumber from the mill* CONVEY, carry, take, transfer, move, shift, send, deliver, bear, ship, ferry, haul; *informal* cart. See note at RAPTURE.

▸ noun *alternative forms of transport.* See TRANSPORTATION sense 1.

**transpose** verb **1** *the blue and black plates were transposed* INTERCHANGE, exchange, switch, swap (around), reverse, invert, flip.

**2** *the themes are transposed from the sphere of love to that of work* TRANSFER, shift, relocate, transplant, move, displace.

**transverse** adjective *a transverse bar* CROSSWISE, crossways, cross, horizontal, diagonal, oblique, slanted.

**trap** noun **1** *an animal caught in a trap* SNARE, net, mesh, deadfall, leghold (trap), pitfall.

**2** *the question was set as a trap* TRICK, ploy, ruse, deception, subterfuge; booby trap, ambush, setup.

**3** *informal shut your trap!* See MOUTH noun sense 1.

▸ verb **1** *police trapped the two men and arrested them* SNARE, entrap, ensnare, lay a trap for; capture, catch, bag, corner, ambush.

**2** *a rat trapped in a barn* CONFINE, cut off, corner, shut in, pen in, hem in; imprison, hold captive.

**3** *I hoped to trap him into an admission* TRICK, dupe, deceive, lure, inveigle, beguile, fool, hoodwink; catch, trip up.

**trappings** plural noun *surrounded by the trappings of royalty* ACCESSORIES, accoutrements, appurtenances, trimmings, frills, accompaniments, extras, ornamentation, adornment, decoration; regalia, panoply, paraphernalia, apparatus, finery, equipment, gear, effects, things, bits and pieces.

**trash** noun **1** *the subway entrance was blocked with trash* GARBAGE, refuse, waste, litter, junk, debris, detritus, rubbish.

**2** *if they read at all, they read trash* JUNK, dross, dreck, drivel, nonsense, trivia, pulp, pulp fiction, pap, garbage, rubbish; *informal* crap, schlock.

**3** *informal that family is trash* SCUM, vermin, the dregs of society, the lowest of the low; *informal* the scum of the earth, dirt, riffraff.

▸ verb **1** *the apartment had been totally trashed* WRECK, ruin, destroy, wreak havoc on, devastate; vandalize, tear up, bust up, smash; *informal* total.

**2** *his play was trashed by the critics* CRITICIZE, LAMBASTE, censure, attack, insult, abuse, malign, give a bad press to, condemn, flay, savage, pan, knock, take to pieces, take/pull apart, crucify, hammer, slam, bash, trash talk, roast, maul, rubbish, pummel; *informal* bad-mouth, bitch about.

**trauma** noun **1** *the trauma of divorce* SHOCK, upheaval, distress, stress, strain, pain, anguish, suffering, upset, agony, misery, sorrow, grief, heartache, heartbreak, torture; ordeal, trial, tribulation, trouble, worry, anxiety; nightmare, hell, hellishness.

**2** *the trauma to the liver* INJURY, damage, wound; cut, laceration, lesion, abrasion, contusion.

**traumatic** adjective *the enduring pain of this traumatic event* DISTURBING, shocking, distressing, upsetting, heartbreaking, painful, scarring, jolting, agonizing, hurtful, stressful, damaging, injurious, harmful, awful, terrible, devastating, harrowing.

**travel** verb **1** *Tim spent much of his time traveling abroad* JOURNEY, tour, take a trip, voyage, explore, go sightseeing, globe-trot, backpack, gallivant; *archaic* peregrinate.

2 *we traveled the length and breadth of the island* JOURNEY THROUGH, cross, traverse, cover; roam, wander, rove, range, trek.

3 *light travels faster than sound* MOVE, be transmitted.

▸ noun (**travels**) *she amassed great wealth during her travels* JOURNEYS, expeditions, trips, tours, excursions, voyages, treks, safaris, explorations, wanderings, odysseys, pilgrimages, jaunts, junkets; traveling, touring, sightseeing, backpacking, globe-trotting, gallivanting; *archaic* peregrinations.

**traveler** noun *thousands of travelers were left stranded* TOURIST, vacationer, sightseer, visitor, globe-trotter, backpacker; pilgrim, wanderer, drifter, nomad, migrant; passenger, commuter, fare.

**traveling** adjective *in those days, many a tired traveling man would stop at Aunt Dilly's for some hot soup and a warm bath* NOMADIC, itinerant, peripatetic, wandering, roaming, roving, wayfaring, migrant, vagrant, of no fixed address.

**traverse** verb 1 *he traversed the deserts of Iran* TRAVEL OVER/ACROSS, cross, journey over/across, pass over; cover; ply; wander, roam, range.

2 *a ditch traversed by a wooden bridge* CROSS, bridge, span; extend across, lie across, stretch across.

**travesty** noun *a* ***travesty of*** *justice* PERVERSION OF, distortion of, corruption of, misrepresentation of, poor imitation of, poor substitute for, mockery of, parody of, caricature of; farce of, charade of, pantomime of, sham of, spoof of; *informal* apology for, (poor) excuse for. See note at CARICATURE.

**treacherous** adjective 1 *her treacherous brother betrayed her* TRAITOROUS, disloyal, faithless, unfaithful, duplicitous, deceitful, deceptive, false, backstabbing, double-crossing, double-dealing, two-faced, weaselly, untrustworthy, unreliable; apostate, renegade, two-timing; *literary* perfidious. ANTONYMS loyal, faithful.

2 *treacherous driving conditions* DANGEROUS, hazardous, perilous, unsafe, precarious, risky, deceptive, unreliable; *informal* dicey, hairy. ANTONYMS safe, reliable.

**treachery** noun *Myrna never forgave Warren his treachery* BETRAYAL, disloyalty, faithlessness, unfaithfulness, infidelity, breach of trust, duplicity, dirty tricks, deceit, deception, chicanery, stab in the back, backstabbing, double-dealing, untrustworthiness; treason, two-timing; *literary* perfidy.

**tread** verb 1 *he trod purposefully down the hall* WALK, step, stride, pace, go; march, tramp, plod, thump, stomp, trudge.

2 *the snow had been* ***trodden down*** *by the horses* CRUSH, flatten, press down, squash; trample on, tramp on, stamp on, stomp on.

▸ noun *we heard her heavy tread on the stairs* STEP, footstep, footfall, tramp, thump; clip-clop.

**treason** noun *the treason of Benedict Arnold will be recounted for centuries* TREACHERY, disloyalty, betrayal, faithlessness; sedition, subversion, mutiny, rebellion; high treason, lèse-majesté; apostasy; *literary* perfidy. ANTONYMS allegiance, loyalty.

**treasonable** adjective *treasonable offenses against the king* TRAITOROUS, treasonous, treacherous, disloyal; seditious, subversive, mutinous, rebellious; *literary* perfidious. ANTONYM loyal.

**treasure** noun 1 *a casket of treasure* RICHES, valuables, jewels, gems, gold, silver, precious metals, money, cash; wealth, fortune; treasure trove.

2 *art treasures* VALUABLE OBJECT, valuable, work of art, masterpiece, precious item.

3 *informal she's a real treasure* PARAGON, gem, angel, find, star, one of a kind, one in a million.

▸ verb *I treasure the photographs I took of Jack* CHERISH, hold dear, prize, value greatly; adore, dote on, love, be devoted to, worship, venerate.

**treat** verb 1 *Charlotte treated him very badly* BEHAVE TOWARD, act toward; deal with, handle; *literary* use.

2 *police are treating the fires as arson* REGARD, consider, view, look upon, think of.

3 *the book treats its subject with insight and responsibility* TACKLE, deal with, handle, discuss, present, explore, investigate, approach; consider, study, analyze.

4 *she was treated at St. Paul's Hospital* GIVE MEDICAL CARE (TO), nurse, care for, tend (to), help, give treatment (to), attend (to), administer (to); medicate.

5 *the plants may prove useful in treating cancer* CURE, heal, remedy; fight, combat.

6 *she* ***treated him to*** *an expensive meal* BUY (FOR) SOMEONE, take someone out for, give (to) someone; pay for (for someone); foot the bill for, pick up the tab for.

7 *delegates were* ***treated to*** *an Indonesian dance show* REGALE WITH, entertain with/by, fête with, amuse with, divert with.

▸ noun 1 *a birthday treat* CELEBRATION, entertainment, amusement; surprise; party, excursion, outing, special event.

2 *I bought you some chocolate as a treat* PRESENT, gift; delicacy, luxury, indulgence, extravagance, guilty pleasure; *informal* goodie.

3 *it was a real treat to see them* PLEASURE, delight, boon, thrill, joy.

**treatise** noun *a treatise on the principles of democracy* DISQUISITION, essay, paper, work, exposition, discourse, dissertation, thesis, monograph, opus, oeuvre, study, critique; tract, pamphlet, account.

**treatment** noun 1 *the company's treatment of its workers* BEHAVIOR TOWARD, conduct toward; handling of, dealings with, management of.

2 *she's responding well to treatment* MEDICAL CARE, therapy, nursing, ministrations; medication, drugs, medicaments; cure, remedy.

3 *her treatment of the topic* DISCUSSION, handling, investiga-

tion, exploration, consideration, study, analysis, critique; approach, methodology.

**treaty** noun *several terms of the treaty were casually violated* AGREEMENT, settlement, pact, deal, entente, concordat, accord, protocol, convention, contract, covenant, bargain, pledge; concord, compact.

**trek** noun *a three-day trek across the desert* JOURNEY, trip, expedition, safari, odyssey, voyage; hike, march, slog, tramp, walk; long haul.

▸ verb *we trekked through the jungle* HIKE, tramp, march, slog, footslog, trudge, traipse, walk; travel, journey; *informal* hoof it.

**trellis** noun *rambling roses scrambled up the trellis* LATTICE, framework, espalier, arbor; network, mesh; grille, grid, grating; latticework; *technical* reticulation.

**tremble** verb **1** *Joe's hands were trembling* SHAKE, shake like a leaf, quiver, twitch, jerk; quaver, waver.

**2** *the entire building trembled* SHAKE, shudder, quake, wobble, rock, vibrate, move, sway, totter, teeter; *chiefly Brit.* judder. See note at SHAKE.

**3** *she trembled at the thought of what he had in store for her* BE AFRAID, be frightened, be apprehensive, worry, shake in one's boots; quail, quake, shrink, blench.

▸ noun *the slight tremble in her hands* TREMOR, shake, shakiness, trembling, quiver, quaking, twitch, vibration, unsteadiness. ANTONYM steadiness.

**tremendous** adjective **1** *tremendous sums of money* HUGE, enormous, immense, colossal, massive, prodigious, stupendous, monumental, mammoth, vast, gigantic, giant, mighty, epic, titanic, towering, king-size(d), jumbo, gargantuan, Herculean; substantial, considerable, Brobdingnagian; *informal* whopping, astronomical, humongous, ginormous. ANTONYMS tiny, small, slight.

**2** *a tremendous explosion* VERY LOUD, deafening, ear-splitting, booming, thundering, thunderous, resounding. ANTONYM soft.

**3** *informal I've seen him play and he's tremendous* EXCELLENT, splendid, wonderful, marvelous, magnificent, superb, sublime, lovely, delightful, too good to be true; *informal* super, great, amazing, fantastic, terrific, sensational, heavenly, divine, fabulous, awesome, to die for, magic, wicked, mind-blowing, splendiferous, far out, out of this world, brilliant, boss, swell. ANTONYMS bad, poor.

**tremor** noun **1** *the sudden tremor of her hands* TREMBLING, shaking, shakiness, tremble, shake, quivering, quiver, twitching, twitch, tic; quavering, quaver, quake, palpitation.

**2** *a tremor of fear ran through her* SHIVER, frisson, spasm, thrill, tingle, stab, dart, wave, surge, rush, ripple.

**3** *the epicenter of the tremor* EARTHQUAKE, earth tremor, shock; *informal* quake.

**tremulous** adjective **1** *a tremulous voice* SHAKY, trembling, shaking, unsteady, quavering, wavering, quivering, quivery, quaking, weak, warbly, trembly. ANTONYM steady.

**2** *a tremulous smile* TIMID, diffident, shy, hesitant, uncertain, nervous, jittery, timorous, frightened, scared, anxious, apprehensive. ANTONYM confident.

**trench** noun *Chechen fighters steel themselves in their trenches around the city* DITCH, channel, trough, excavation, furrow, rut, conduit, cut, drain, duct, waterway, watercourse; entrenchment, moat; *Archaeology* fosse.

**trenchant** adjective *trenchant criticism of her leadership* INCISIVE, penetrating, sharp, keen, insightful, acute, focused, shrewd, razor-sharp, piercing; vigorous, forceful, strong, potent, telling, emphatic, forthright; mordant, cutting, biting, acerbic, pungent. ANTONYM vague.

**trend** noun **1** *an upward trend in unemployment* TENDENCY, movement, drift, swing, shift, course, current, direction, progression, inclination, leaning; bias, bent.

**2** *the latest trend in dance music* FASHION, vogue, style, mode, craze, mania, rage; *informal* fad, thing, flavor of the month.

▸ verb *interest rates are trending up* MOVE, go, head, drift, gravitate, swing, shift, turn, incline, tend, lean, veer.

**trepidation** noun *he sat in the waiting room, full of trepidation* FEAR, apprehension, dread, fearfulness, fright, agitation, anxiety, worry, nervousness, tension, misgivings, unease, uneasiness, foreboding, disquiet, dismay, consternation, alarm, panic; *informal* butterflies (in one's stomach), jitteriness, the jitters, the creeps, the shivers, a cold sweat, the heebie-jeebies, the willies, the shakes, jim-jams, collywobbles, cold feet. ANTONYMS equanimity, composure.

**trespass** verb **1** *there is no excuse for* ***trespassing on*** *railroad property* INTRUDE ON, encroach on, enter without permission, invade.

**2** *I must not* ***trespass on*** *your good nature* TAKE ADVANTAGE OF, impose on, play on, exploit, abuse; encroach on, infringe on.

**3** *archaic he would be the last among us to trespass* SIN, transgress, offend, do wrong, err, go astray, fall from grace, stray from the straight and narrow.

▸ noun **1** *his alleged trespass on private land* UNLAWFUL ENTRY, intrusion, encroachment, invasion.

**2** *archaic he asked forgiveness for his trespasses* SIN, wrong, wrongdoing, transgression, crime, offense, misdeed, misdemeanor, error, lapse, fall from grace.

**trespasser** noun *trespassers will be prosecuted* INTRUDER, interloper, unwelcome visitor, encroacher.

**tresses** plural noun *her strawberry blonde tresses* HAIR, head of hair, mane, mop of hair, shock of hair, shag of hair; locks, curls, ringlets.

**trial** noun **1** *the trial is expected to last several weeks* COURT CASE, case, assize, lawsuit, suit, hearing, inquiry, tribunal, litigation, legal proceedings, judicial proceedings, proceedings, legal action; court-martial; appeal, retrial.

**2** *the product is undergoing clinical trials* TEST, tryout, experiment, pilot study; examination, check, assessment, evaluation, appraisal; trial/test period, trial/test run, beta test, dry run.

**3** *she could be a bit of a trial at times* NUISANCE, pest, irritant, problem, ordeal, inconvenience, plague, thorn in one's side, one's cross to bear; bore; *informal* pain, pain in the neck, pain in the butt, headache, drag, bother, nightmare, albatross; nudnik, burr under someone's saddle.

**4** *a long account of her trials and tribulations* TROUBLE, anxiety, worry, burden, affliction, ordeal, tribulation, adversity, hardship, trying time, tragedy, trauma, setback, difficulty, problem, misfortune, bad luck, mishap, misadventure; *informal* hassle; *literary* travails.

▸ adjective *a three-month trial period* TEST, experimental, pilot, exploratory, probationary, provisional.

**tribe** noun *nomadic tribes of the Sahara* ETHNIC GROUP, people, band, nation; family, dynasty, house, clan, sept.

**tribulation** noun **1** *the tribulations of her personal life* TROUBLE, difficulty, problem, worry, anxiety, burden, cross to bear, ordeal, trial, adversity, hardship, tragedy, sorrow, trauma, affliction; setback, blow; *informal* hassle; *literary* travail.

**2** *his time of tribulation was just beginning* SUFFERING, distress, trouble, misery, wretchedness, unhappiness, sadness, heartache, woe, grief, sorrow, pain, anguish, agony; *literary* travail.

**tributary** noun *the countless tributaries of the mighty Mississippi* HEADWATER, creek, branch, fork, feeder, side stream, side channel, snye.

**tribute** noun **1** *tributes flooded in from friends and colleagues* ACCOLADE, praise, commendation, salute, testimonial, homage, eulogy, paean, panegyric; congratulations, compliments, plaudits, appreciation; gift, present, offering; bouquet; *formal* encomium. ANTONYMS criticism, condemnation.

**2** *it is a tribute to his courage that he ever played again* TESTIMONY, indication, manifestation, testament, evidence, proof, attestation. PHRASE: **pay tribute to** *the players on both teams paid tribute to the retiring Ripken* PRAISE, sing the praises of, speak highly of, commend, acclaim, tip one's hat to, applaud, salute, honor, show appreciation of, recognize, acknowledge, pay homage to, extol; *formal* laud.

**trick** noun **1** *he's capable of any mean trick | their clever little trick cost us $500* STRATAGEM, ploy, ruse, scheme, device, maneuver, contrivance, machination, artifice, wile, dodge; deceit, deception, trickery, subterfuge, chicanery, swindle, hoax, fraud, confidence trick; *informal* con, setup, rip-off, game, scam, sting, flimflam, bunco; *archaic* shift, fetch, rig.

**2** *I think she's playing a trick on us* PRACTICAL JOKE, joke, prank, jape, spoof, gag, put-on.

**3** *conjuring tricks* FEAT, stunt; **(tricks)** SLEIGHT OF HAND, legerdemain, prestidigitation; magic.

**4** **(tricks)** *the tricks of the trade* KNACK, art, skills, techniques; secrets, shortcuts.

▸ verb *many people have been tricked by con artists with fake IDs* DECEIVE, delude, hoodwink, mislead, take in, dupe, fool, double-cross, cheat, defraud, swindle, gull, hoax, bamboozle, entrap; *informal* con, bilk, diddle, rook, put one over on, pull a fast one on, pull the wool over someone's eyes, take for a ride, shaft, flimflam, sucker, snooker; *literary* cozen, illude; *archaic* chicane.

PHRASES: **do the trick** *informal here, these two aspirins should do the trick* BE EFFECTIVE, work, solve the problem, fill/fit the bill.
**trick of the light** *it was probably just a trick of the light* ILLUSION, optical illusion, figment of the imagination; mirage.

**trickery** noun *she suspects me of trickery* DECEPTION, deceit, dishonesty, cheating, duplicity, double-dealing, legerdemain, sleight of hand, guile, craftiness, deviousness, subterfuge, skulduggery, chicanery, fraud, fraudulence, swindling; *formal* pettifoggery; *informal* monkey business, funny business. ANTONYM honesty.

**trickle** verb *blood was trickling from two cuts in his lip* DRIP, dribble, ooze, leak, seep, percolate, spill. ANTONYMS pour, gush.

▸ noun *trickles of water* DRIBBLE, drip, thin stream, rivulet.

**trickster** noun *she spent her whole life loving and protecting a brother who was never better than the lowest of tricksters* SWINDLER, cheat, fraud, fraudster; charlatan, mountebank, quack, impostor, sham, hoaxer; rogue, villain, shyster, scoundrel; *informal* con man, con artist, sharp, shark, flimflammer, grifter, scam artist, bunco artist, chiseler.

**tricky** adjective **1** *a tricky situation* DIFFICULT, awkward, problematic, delicate, ticklish, sensitive, embarrassing, touchy; risky, uncertain, precarious, touch-and-go; thorny, knotty, complex, complicated; *informal* sticky, hairy, dicey. ANTONYMS straightforward, uncomplicated.

**2** *a tricky and unscrupulous politician* CUNNING, crafty, wily, guileful, artful, devious, sly, scheming, slippery, slick, calculating, designing, sharp, shrewd, astute, canny; duplicitous, dishonest, deceitful. ANTONYM honest.

**trifle** noun **1** *we needn't bother the principal over such trifles* UNIMPORTANT THING, trivial thing, triviality, thing of no importance, thing of no consequence, bagatelle, inessential, nothing; technicality, nonissue; **(trifles)** trivia, minutiae, flummery, small potatoes.

**2** *we wrapped up a few trifles as party favors* BAUBLE, trinket, knickknack, gimcrack, gewgaw, toy; *informal* whatnot.

**3** *he bought it for **a trifle*** NEXT TO NOTHING, a very small amount; a pittance; *informal* peanuts, chump change. PHRASES: **a trifle** *Candace is a trifle miffed at Brad* A LITTLE, a bit, somewhat, a touch, a mite, a whit; *informal* a tad.
**trifle with** *you should never have trifled with her emotions* PLAY WITH, amuse oneself with, toy with, dally with, be flippant with, flirt with, play fast and loose with, mess about with; *dated* sport with.

**trifling** adjective *a trifling matter* TRIVIAL, unimportant, insignificant, inconsequential, petty, minor, of little/no account, of little/no consequence, footling, pettifogging, incidental;

silly, idle, insipid, superficial, small, tiny, inconsiderable, nominal, negligible, nugatory; *informal* piddling; *formal* exiguous. ANTONYM important.

**trigger** verb **1** *the incident triggered an acrimonious debate* PRECIPITATE, prompt, elicit, trigger off, set off, spark (off), touch off, provoke, stir up; cause, give rise to, launch, lead to, set in motion, occasion, bring about, generate, engender, begin, start, initiate; *literary* enkindle.

**2** *thieves triggered the alarm* ACTIVATE, set off, set going, trip.

**trim** verb **1** *his hair had been washed and trimmed* CUT, crop, bob, shorten, clip, snip, shear, barber; neaten, shape, tidy up.

**2** ***trim off*** *the lower leaves using a sharp knife* CUT OFF, remove, take off, chop off, lop off; prune.

**3** *production costs need to be trimmed* REDUCE, decrease, cut down, cut back on, scale down, prune, slim down, pare down, dock.

**4** *the story was severely trimmed for the movie version* SHORTEN, abridge, condense, abbreviate, telescope, truncate.

**5** *a pair of black leather gloves trimmed with fake fur* DECORATE, adorn, ornament, embellish; edge, pipe, border, hem, fringe.

▸ noun **1** *white curtains with a tasteful blue trim* DECORATION, trimming, ornamentation, adornment, embellishment; border, edging, piping, rickrack, hem, fringe, frill, frippery.

**2** *an unruly mop in need of a trim* HAIRCUT, cut, barbering, clip, snip; pruning, tidying up.

▸ adjective **1** *a trim little villa* NEAT, tidy, neat and tidy, orderly, in (good) order, uncluttered, well-kept, well-maintained, shipshape, spruce, in apple-pie order, immaculate, spick-and-span. ANTONYMS untidy, messy.

**2** *she does Pilates to stay trim* SLIM, in shape, slender, lean, sleek, willowy, lissome, svelte; streamlined. ANTONYM fat.

**trimming** noun **1** *a black dress with lace trimming.* See TRIM noun sense 1.

**2** (**trimmings**) *roast turkey with all the trimmings* ACCOMPANIMENTS, extras, frills, fixings, accessories, accoutrements, trappings, paraphernalia; garnishing, garnish.

**trinket** noun *he brought back some lovely little trinkets from the South Seas* KNICKKNACK, bauble, ornament, bibelot, curio, trifle, gimcrack, gewgaw, toy, novelty; *informal* whatnot, doohickey, tchotchke; *dated* kickshaw.

**trio** noun *a talented trio from East Orange will sing the closing hymn* THREESOME, triumvirate, triad, trinity, troika; triplets.

**trip** verb **1** *he tripped on the loose stones* STUMBLE, lose one's footing, catch one's foot, slip, lose one's balance, fall, fall down, tumble, topple, take a spill, wipe out.

**2** *students often* ***trip up*** *by forgetting to add a bibliography* MAKE A MISTAKE, miscalculate, make a blunder, blunder, go wrong, make an error, err; *informal* slip up, screw up, make a boo-boo, goof up, mess up, fluff.

**3** *the question was intended to* trip *him* ***up*** CATCH OUT, trick, outwit, outsmart; throw off balance, disconcert, unsettle, discountenance, discomfit, throw, wrong-foot.

**4** *they tripped merrily along the path* SKIP, run, dance, prance, bound, spring, scamper.

**5** *Hoffman tripped the alarm* SET OFF, activate, trigger; turn on.

▸ noun **1** *a trip to Oahu* EXCURSION, outing, jaunt; VACATION, visit, tour, journey, expedition, voyage; drive, run, day out, day trip, road trip, cruise, junket, spin; *rare* peregrination. See note at JOURNEY.

**2** *a trip down icy front steps can be a devastating accident* STUMBLE, slip, misstep, false step; fall, tumble, spill.

**triple** adjective **1** *a triple alliance* THREE-WAY, tripartite; threefold, trifold.

**2** *they paid her triple the standard fee* THREE TIMES, treble.

**trite** adjective *critics were put off by the trite dialogue* BANAL, hackneyed, clichéd, platitudinous, vapid, commonplace, stock, conventional, stereotyped, overused, overdone, overworked, stale, worn out, timeworn, tired, hoary, hack, unimaginative, unoriginal, uninteresting, dull; *informal* old hat, corny, cornball, cheesy, boilerplate. ANTONYMS original, imaginative.

**triumph** noun **1** *Gretzky's many triumphs* VICTORY, win, conquest, success; achievement, feat, accomplishment. ANTONYM defeat.

**2** *his eyes shone with triumph* JUBILATION, exultation, elation, delight, joy, happiness, glee, pride, satisfaction. ANTONYM disappointment.

**3** *a triumph of their ingenuity* TOUR DE FORCE, masterpiece, coup, wonder, sensation, master stroke, feat. ANTONYM failure.

▸ verb **1** *she triumphed in the tournament* WIN, succeed, come first, clinch first place, be victorious, carry the day, prevail, take the honors, come out on top. ANTONYMS lose, fail.

**2** *they had no chance of* ***triumphing over*** *the Democrats in the third district* DEFEAT, beat, conquer, trounce, vanquish, overcome, overpower, overwhelm, get the better of; bring someone to their knees, prevail against, subdue, subjugate; *informal* lick, best.

**triumphant** adjective **1** *the triumphant Swedish team* VICTORIOUS, successful, winning, conquering, all-conquering; undefeated, unbeaten. ANTONYMS unsuccessful, defeated.

**2** *a triumphant expression* JUBILANT, exultant, elated, rejoicing, joyful, joyous, delighted, gleeful, proud, gloating. ANTONYMS disappointed, despondent.

**trivia** plural noun *his head is overflowing with obscure trivia* MINUTIAE, minor details, petty detail, niceties, technicalities, trivialities, trifles, trumpery, nonessentials, ephemera; *informal* small potatoes, peanuts.

**trivial** adjective **1** *trivial problems* UNIMPORTANT, banal, trite, commonplace, insignificant, inconsequential, minor, of no account, of no consequence, of no importance; incidental, inessential, nonessential, petty, trifling, trumpery, pettifogging, footling, small, slight, little, inconsiderable, negligible, paltry, nugatory; *informal* piddling, picayune, nickel-and-dime, penny-ante; *trademark* Mickey Mouse. ANTONYMS important, significant, life-and-death.

**2** *I used to be quite a trivial person* FRIVOLOUS, superficial, shallow, unthinking, airheaded, featherbrained, lightweight, foolish, silly, trite. ANTONYMS profound, serious.

**triviality** noun **1** *the triviality of the subject matter* UNIMPORTANCE, insignificance, inconsequence, inconsequentiality, pettiness, banality.

**2** *he need not concern himself with such trivialities* MINOR DETAIL, thing of no importance/consequence, trifle, nonessential, nothing; technicality; **(trivialities)** trivia, minutiae.

**troop** noun **(troops)** *Ethiopian troops were stationed there* SOLDIERS, armed forces, servicemen, servicewomen, infantry; peacekeepers; guards, escorts; the services, the army, the military.

▸ verb *we trooped out of the hall* WALK, march, file, proceed; flock, crowd, throng, stream, swarm, surge, spill.

**trophy** noun **1** *a swimming trophy* CUP, medal; prize, award.

**2** *a cabinet full of trophies from his travels* SOUVENIR, memento, keepsake; spoils, booty.

**tropical** adjective *tropical weather* VERY HOT, sweltering, boiling, scorching, humid, sultry, steamy, sticky, oppressive, stifling, suffocating, heavy, equatorial. ANTONYMS cold, arctic.

**trouble** noun **1** *you've caused enough trouble already* PROBLEMS, difficulty, bother, inconvenience, worry, concern, anxiety, distress, stress, strife, agitation, harassment, hassle, unpleasantness.

**2** *she poured out all her troubles* PROBLEM, misfortune, difficulty, trial, tribulation, trauma, burden, pain, woe, grief, heartache, misery, affliction, vexation, suffering.

**3** *he's gone to a lot of trouble to help you* EFFORT, inconvenience, fuss, bother, exertion, work, labor; pains, care, attention, thought.

**4** *Rodney has been no trouble at all* NUISANCE, bother, inconvenience, irritation, irritant, problem, trial, pest, thorn in someone's flesh/side, headache, pain, pain in the neck/backside, drag; *informal* pain in the butt, burr under someone's saddle, nudnik.

**5** *you're too gullible, that's your trouble* SHORTCOMING, flaw, weakness, weak point, failing, fault, imperfection, defect, blemish; problem, difficulty.

**6** *he had a history of heart trouble* DISEASE, illness, sickness, ailments, complaints, problems; disorder, disability.

**7** *the crash was due to engine trouble* MALFUNCTION, dysfunction, failure, breakdown.

**8** *a game marred by serious crowd trouble* DISTURBANCE, disorder, unrest, unruliness, fighting, fracas, breach of the peace.

▸ verb **1** *this matter had been troubling her for some time* WORRY, bother, concern, disturb, upset, agitate, distress, perturb, annoy, irritate, vex, irk, nag, niggle, prey on someone's mind, weigh down, burden; *informal* bug.

**2** *he **was troubled by** bouts of ill health* BE AFFLICTED BY, be burdened with; suffer from, be cursed with, be plagued by.

**3** *there is nothing you need trouble about* WORRY, upset oneself, fret, be anxious, be concerned, concern oneself.

**4** *don't trouble to see me out* BOTHER, take the trouble, go to the trouble, exert oneself, go out of one's way.

**5** *I'm sorry to trouble you* INCONVENIENCE, bother, impose on, disturb, put out, pester, hassle; *formal* discommode.

PHRASE: **in trouble** *he comes to visit only when he's in trouble* IN DIFFICULTY, in difficulties, in a mess, in a bad way, in a predicament, in dire straits; *informal* in a fix, in a pickle, in a tight corner/spot, in a hole, in hot water, up a tree, up a/the creek, up against it.

**troublemaker** noun *I have little use for my former friends, who were, for the most part, troublemakers* RABBLE-ROUSER, rogue, scourge, agitator, agent provocateur, ringleader; incendiary, firebrand, demagogue; scandalmonger, gossipmonger, meddler, nuisance, mischief-maker, hell raiser; *informal* badass.

**troublesome** adjective **1** *a troublesome problem* ANNOYING, irritating, exasperating, maddening, infuriating, irksome, pesky, vexatious, vexing, bothersome, nettlesome, tiresome, worrying, worrisome, disturbing, upsetting, niggling, nagging; difficult, awkward, problematic, taxing; *informal* aggravating. ANTONYMS simple, straightforward.

**2** *a troublesome child* DIFFICULT, awkward, trying, demanding, uncooperative, rebellious, unmanageable, unruly, obstreperous, disruptive, badly behaved, disobedient, naughty, recalcitrant, high-maintenance; *formal* refractory. ANTONYMS obedient, cooperative.

**trough** noun **1** *a large feeding trough* MANGER, feeder, bunk, rack, crib, feed box; waterer.

**2** *a thirty-foot trough* CHANNEL, conduit, trench, ditch, gully, drain, culvert, cut, flume, gutter; rain gutter.

**trounce** verb *Turner scored a season-high 19 points when the UConn women trounced St. Joseph's 87–34* DEFEAT CONVINCINGLY, rout, crush, overwhelm; *informal* hammer, clobber, thrash, whip, drub, shellac, cream, skunk, pulverize, massacre, crucify, demolish, destroy, blow away, annihilate, make mincemeat of, wipe the floor with, walk all over, murder.

**troupe** noun *our theater troupe is on tour* GROUP, company, band, ensemble, set; cast.

**truancy** noun *the Board of Ed wants to know why truancy in the high school is at an all-time high* ABSENTEEISM, nonattendance, playing truant, truanting; *informal* playing hooky, skipping; booking out.

**truant** noun *the truants were sent to Mr. Maurer's office* ABSENTEE, runaway. PHRASE: **play truant** *more than half of the freshman class staged a protest by playing truant on Monday* stay away from school; *informal* skip school, skip, play hooky; book out.

**truce** noun *news of the truce spread quickly among the locals* CEASE-FIRE, armistice, suspension of hostilities, peace, entente; respite, lull; *informal* letup.

**truculent** adjective *a number of staffers have complained that Wilson is too truculent to work with* DEFIANT, aggressive, antagonistic, combative, belligerent, pugnacious, confrontational, ready for a fight, obstreperous, argumentative, quarrelsome, uncooperative; bad-tempered, ornery, short-tempered, cross, snappish, cranky; feisty, spoiling for a fight. ANTONYMS cooperative, amiable.

**trudge** verb *they trudged through two miles of wet snow* PLOD, tramp, tromp, drag oneself, walk heavily, walk slowly, plow, slog, toil, trek; *informal* traipse, galumph.

**true** adjective **1** *you'll see that what I say is true* CORRECT, accurate, right, verifiable, in accordance with the facts, what actually/really happened, well-documented, the case, so; literal, factual, unelaborated, unvarnished. ANTONYMS untrue, false, fallacious.

**2** *people are still willing to pay for true craftsmanship* GENUINE, authentic, real, actual, bona fide, proper; honest-to-goodness, kosher, legit, the real McCoy. ANTONYMS bogus, phony.

**3** *the true owner of the goods* RIGHTFUL, legitimate, legal, lawful, authorized, bona fide, de jure. ANTONYM de facto.

**4** *the necessity for true repentance* SINCERE, genuine, real, unfeigned, heartfelt, hearty, from the heart. ANTONYMS insincere, feigned.

**5** *a true friend* LOYAL, faithful, constant, devoted, staunch, steadfast, true-blue, unswerving, unwavering; trustworthy, trusty, reliable, dependable. ANTONYMS disloyal, faithless.

**6** *a true reflection of life in the 50s* ACCURATE, true to life, faithful, telling it like it is, fact-based, realistic, close, lifelike. ANTONYM inaccurate.

**truly** adverb **1** *tell me truly what you want* TRUTHFULLY, honestly, frankly, sincerely, candidly, openly, to someone's face, laying one's cards on the table; *informal* pulling no punches.

**2** *I'm truly grateful to them* SINCERELY, genuinely, really, indeed, from the bottom of one's heart, heartily, profoundly; very, surely, extremely, immensely, thoroughly, positively, completely, tremendously, totally, incredibly, awfully; *formal* most; *informal* sure.

**3** *this is truly a miracle* WITHOUT (A) DOUBT, unquestionably, undoubtedly, certainly, surely, definitely, beyond doubt, beyond question, indubitably, undeniably, beyond the shadow of a doubt; in truth, really, in reality, actually, in fact; *archaic* forsooth, verily.

**4** *exams do not truly reflect children's abilities* ACCURATELY, correctly, exactly, precisely, faithfully; *informal* to a T.

**trump** verb *by wearing the simplest of dresses, she had trumped them all* OUTSHINE, outclass, upstage, put in the shade, eclipse, surpass, outdo, outperform; beat, better, top, cap; *informal* be a cut above, be head and shoulders above, leave standing.

**trumpet** verb **1** *the elephant trumpeted* call out, bellow, roar, yell, cry out, toot, bugle, holler.

**2** *companies trumpeted their success* PROCLAIM, announce, declare, herald, celebrate, shout from the rooftops.

**truncate** verb *the program may need to be truncated* SHORTEN, cut, cut short, curtail, bring to an untimely end; abbreviate, condense, reduce, prune. ANTONYMS lengthen, extend.

**truncheon** noun. See BLUDGEON noun.

**trunk** noun **1** *the trunk of a tree* MAIN STEM, bole.

**2** *the trunk of her car* LUGGAGE COMPARTMENT, back.

**3** *his powerful trunk* TORSO, body, upper body.

**4** *an elephant's trunk* PROBOSCIS, nose, snout.

**5** *a steamer trunk* CHEST, box, crate, coffer; case.

**truss** noun *three steel trusses* SUPPORT, buttress, joist, brace, beam, prop, strut, stay, stanchion, pier.

▸ verb *she taught us how to truss the hens before roasting* TIE UP, bind, chain up; pinion, fetter, tether, secure; swaddle, wrap.

**trust** noun **1** *good relationships are built on trust* CONFIDENCE, belief, faith, certainty, assurance, conviction, credence; reliance. ANTONYMS distrust, mistrust, doubt.

**2** *a position of trust* RESPONSIBILITY, duty, obligation.

**3** *the money is to be held in trust for his son* SAFEKEEPING, protection, charge, care, custody; trusteeship.

▸ verb **1** *I should never have trusted her* PUT ONE'S TRUST IN, have faith in, have (every) confidence in, believe in, pin one's hopes/faith on, confide in. ANTONYMS distrust, mistrust, doubt.

**2** *he can be trusted to carry out an impartial investigation* RELY ON, depend on, bank on, count on, be sure of.

**3** *I trust we shall meet again* HOPE, expect, take it, assume, presume, suppose.

**4** *they don't like to trust their money to anyone outside the family* ENTRUST, consign, commit, give, hand over, turn over, assign.

**trustworthy** adjective *a trustworthy citizen* RELIABLE, dependable, honest, honorable, upright, principled, true, truthful, as good as one's word, ethical, virtuous, incorruptible, unimpeachable, above suspicion; responsible, sensible, levelheaded; loyal, faithful, staunch, steadfast, trusty; safe, sound, reputable, discreet; *informal* on the level, straight-up. ANTONYM unreliable.

**trusty** adjective *a cowboy and his trusty horse* RELIABLE, dependable, trustworthy, unfailing, fail-safe, trusted, tried and true; loyal, faithful, true, staunch, steadfast, constant, unswerving, unwavering. ANTONYM unreliable.

**truth** noun **1** *he doubted the truth of her statement* VERAC-

ITY, truthfulness, verity, sincerity, candor, honesty; accuracy, correctness, validity, factuality, authenticity. ANTONYMS dishonesty, falseness.

2 *it's **the truth**, I swear* WHAT ACTUALLY HAPPENED, the case, so; the gospel (truth), the honest truth. ANTONYM lies.

3 *truth is stranger than fiction* FACT(S), reality, real life, actuality. ANTONYM fiction.

4 *scientific truths* FACT, verity, certainty, certitude; law, principle. ANTONYMS lie, falsehood.

PHRASE: **in truth** *in truth, their marriage was rocky from the start* IN FACT, in actual fact, as it happens, in point of fact, in reality, really, actually, to tell the truth, if truth be told.

**truthful** adjective 1 *truthful behavior* HONEST, sincere, trustworthy, genuine; candid, frank, straight-shooting, open, forthright, straight, upfront, on the level, on the up and up. ANTONYMS deceitful, deceptive.

2 *a truthful account* TRUE, accurate, correct, factual, faithful, reliable; unvarnished, unembellished, unidealized; *formal* veracious, veridical. ANTONYMS inaccurate, untrue.

**try** verb 1 *try to help him* ATTEMPT, endeavor, venture, make an effort, exert oneself, strive, do one's best, do one's utmost, move heaven and earth; undertake, aim, take it upon oneself; *informal* have a go, give it one's best shot, bend over backwards, bust a gut, do one's damnedest, pull out all the stops, go all out, knock oneself out; *formal* essay.

2 *try it and see what you think* TEST, put to the test, sample, taste, inspect, investigate, examine, appraise, evaluate, assess; *informal* check out, give something a whirl, test drive.

3 *Mary tried everyone's patience* TAX, strain, test, stretch, sap, drain, exhaust, wear out.

4 *the case is to be tried by a jury* ADJUDICATE, consider, hear, adjudge, examine.

▸ noun *I'll have one last try* ATTEMPT, effort, endeavor; *informal* go, shot, crack, stab; *formal* essay.

PHRASE: **try something out** *they volunteered to try out the new system* TEST, trial, experiment with, pilot; put through its paces; assess, evaluate.

**trying** adjective 1 *a trying day* STRESSFUL, taxing, demanding, difficult, tough, hard, pressured, frustrating, fraught; arduous, grueling, tiring, exhausting; *informal* hellish. See note at HARD. ANTONYMS easy, painless.

2 *Steve was very trying* ANNOYING, irritating, exasperating, maddening, infuriating; tiresome, irksome, troublesome, bothersome, vexing; *informal* aggravating. ANTONYM accommodating.

**tuck** verb 1 *he tucked his shirt into his pants* PUSH, insert, slip, fold; thrust, stuff, stick, cram.

2 *the dress was tucked all over* PLEAT, gather, fold, ruffle.

3 *he tucked the knife behind his seat* HIDE, conceal, secrete; store, stow, stash.

▸ noun *a dress with tucks* PLEAT, gather, fold, ruffle.

PHRASE: **tuck in** *Toby tucked the children in after reading them a story* PUT TO BED, settle down, cover up; make comfortable.

**tug** verb 1 *Ben **tugged at** her sleeve* PULL (AT), pluck, tweak, twitch, jerk, wrench; catch hold of, yank (at).

2 *she tugged him toward the door* DRAG, pull, lug, draw, haul, heave, tow.

▸ noun *one good tug would loosen it* PULL, jerk, wrench, heave, yank.

**tuition** noun 1 *students go broke paying the increased tuition* FEES, charges, bill.

2 *her skill improved with tuition* INSTRUCTION, teaching, coaching, tutoring, tutelage, lessons, education, schooling; training, drill, preparation, guidance.

**tumble** verb 1 *he **tumbled over*** FALL (OVER), fall down, topple over, lose one's balance, keel over, take a spill, go headlong, go head over heels, trip, stumble; *informal* come a cropper.

2 *they all tumbled from the room* HURRY, rush, scramble, scurry, bound, pile, bundle.

3 *a creek tumbled over the rocks* CASCADE, fall, flow, pour, spill, stream.

4 *oil prices tumbled* PLUMMET, plunge, fall, dive, nosedive, drop, slump, slide, decrease, decline, crash. ANTONYM rise.

▸ noun 1 *I took a tumble in the bushes* FALL, trip, spill; *informal* nosedive.

2 *a tumble in share prices* DROP, fall, plunge, dive, nosedive, slump, decline, collapse; *informal* crash. ANTONYM rise.

**tumbledown** adjective *a tumbledown shack in the woods* DILAPIDATED, ramshackle, decrepit, neglected, beat-up, rundown, falling to pieces, decaying, derelict, crumbling; rickety, shaky.

**tumor** noun *a biopsy of the tumor* CANCEROUS GROWTH, malignant growth, cancer, malignancy; lump, growth, swelling, fibroid; *Medicine* carcinoma, sarcoma.

**tumult** noun 1 *she added her voice to the tumult* CLAMOR, din, noise, racket, uproar, hue and cry, commotion, ruckus, maelstrom, rumpus, hubbub, pandemonium, babel, bedlam, brouhaha, furor, fracas, melee, frenzy; *informal* hullabaloo. ANTONYM silence.

2 *years of political tumult* TURMOIL, confusion, disorder, disarray, unrest, chaos, turbulence, mayhem, maelstrom, havoc, upheaval, ferment, agitation, trouble. ANTONYM tranquility.

**tumultuous** adjective 1 *tumultuous applause* LOUD, deafening, thunderous, uproarious, noisy, clamorous, vociferous, vehement. ANTONYM soft.

2 *their tumultuous relationship* TEMPESTUOUS, stormy, turbulent, passionate, intense, explosive, violent, volatile, full of ups and downs, roller-coaster. ANTONYMS peaceful, uneventful.

3 *a tumultuous crowd* DISORDERLY, unruly, rowdy, turbulent, boisterous, excited, agitated, restless, wild, riotous, frenzied. ANTONYM orderly.

**tune** noun *she hummed a cheerful tune* MELODY, air, strain, theme; song, jingle, ditty.

▸ verb **1** *they tuned their guitars* ADJUST, fine-tune, tune up.

**2** *a body clock tuned to the lunar cycle* ATTUNE, adapt, adjust, fine-tune; regulate, modulate.

PHRASES: **change one's tune** *our "Bachelor Bob" seems to have changed his tune about settling down and raising a family* CHANGE ONE'S MIND, do a U-turn, have a change of heart; do an about-face; *informal* do a one-eighty, pull a U-ey.
**in tune** *are any of the candidates really in tune with the voters?* IN ACCORD, in keeping, in accordance, in agreement, in harmony, in step, in line, in sympathy, compatible.
**tune up** *most of these old cash registers just need to be tuned up a bit* TWEAK, adjust, fine-tune, calibrate, maintain, improve, ameliorate, enhance.

**tuneful** adjective *an evening of tuneful songs* MELODIOUS, melodic, musical, mellifluous, dulcet, euphonious, harmonious, lyrical, lilting, sweet. ANTONYM discordant.

**tunnel** noun *a tunnel under the hills* UNDERGROUND PASSAGE, underpass, subway; shaft; burrow, hole; *historical* mine.

▸ verb *he tunneled under the fence* DIG, burrow, mine, bore, drill.

**turbulent** adjective **1** *the country's turbulent past* TEMPESTUOUS, stormy, unstable, unsettled, tumultuous, chaotic; violent, anarchic, lawless. ANTONYM peaceful.

**2** *turbulent seas* ROUGH, stormy, tempestuous, storm-tossed, heavy, violent, wild, roiling, raging, seething, choppy, agitated, boisterous. ANTONYM calm.

**turf** noun **1** *they walked over a patch of turf* GRASS, lawn, sod.

**2** *she was keen to protect her turf* TERRITORY, domain, province, preserve, sphere of influence; stomping ground, stamping ground; bailiwick.

**turgid** adjective **1** *his turgid prose* BOMBASTIC, pompous, overblown, inflated, tumid, high-flown, puffed up, affected, pretentious, grandiose, florid, ornate, grandiloquent, orotund; *informal* highfalutin, purple. ANTONYM simple.

**2** *the tissues become turgid* SWOLLEN, distended, tumescent, engorged, bloated, tumid.

**turmoil** noun *political turmoil* CONFUSION, upheaval, turbulence, tumult, disorder, disturbance, agitation, ferment, unrest, disquiet, trouble, disruption, chaos, mayhem; uncertainty. ANTONYM peace.

PHRASE: **in turmoil** *Michel's sudden death left the family in turmoil* CONFUSED, chaotic, in chaos, topsy-turvy, at sixes and sevens; reeling, disorientated; *informal* all over the place.

**turn** verb **1** *the wheels were still turning* GO AROUND, revolve, rotate, spin, roll, circle, wheel, whirl, twirl, gyrate, swivel, pivot.

**2** *I turned and headed back* CHANGE DIRECTION, change course, make a U-turn, about-face, turn around/about; *informal* pull a U-ey, do a one-eighty.

**3** *the car turned the corner* GO AROUND, round, negotiate, take.

**4** *the path turned to right and left* BEND, curve, wind, veer, twist, meander, snake, zigzag.

**5** *he **turned** his gun **on** Lenny* AIM AT, point at, level at, direct at, train on.

**6** *he turned his ankle* SPRAIN, twist, wrench; hurt.

**7** *their honeymoon **turned into** a nightmare* BECOME, develop into, turn out to be; be transformed into, metamorphose into, descend into, grow into.

**8** *Emma turned red* BECOME, go, grow, get.

**9** *he turned the house into apartments* CONVERT, change, transform, make; adapt, modify, rebuild, reconstruct.

**10** *I've just turned forty* REACH, get to, become, hit.

**11** *she **turned to** politics* TAKE UP, become involved in, go into, enter, undertake.

**12** *we can now **turn to** another topic* MOVE ON TO, go on to, proceed to, consider, attend to, address; take up, switch to.

▸ noun **1** *a turn of the wheel* ROTATION, revolution, spin, whirl, gyration, swivel.

**2** *a turn to the left* CHANGE OF DIRECTION, veer, divergence.

**3** *we're approaching the turn* BEND, corner, turning, turnoff, junction, crossroads.

**4** *you'll get your turn in a minute* OPPORTUNITY, chance, say; stint, time; try; *informal* go, shot, stab, crack.

**5** *she did me some good turns* SERVICE, deed, act; favor, kindness.

PHRASES: **at every turn** *her name seemed to come up at every turn* REPEATEDLY, recurrently, all the time, always, constantly, again and again.
**in turn** *let's consider these three points in turn* ONE AFTER THE OTHER, one by one, one at a time, in succession, successively, sequentially.
**take a turn for the better** *his luck took a turn for the better* IMPROVE, pick up, look up, perk up, rally, turn the corner; recover, revive.
**take a turn for the worse** *even the doctors were surprised when Richie took a turn for the worse* DETERIORATE, worsen, decline; *informal* go downhill.
**turn against** *after his father died, Bruce turned against his stepmother* BECOME HOSTILE TO, take a dislike to, betray, double-cross.
**turn away** *I know you're hurt, but please don't turn us away* SEND AWAY, reject, rebuff, repel, cold-shoulder; *informal* send packing.
**turn back** *just before boarding the ferry, Clint changed his mind and turned back* RETRACE ONE'S STEPS, go back, return; retreat.
**turn down 1** *his novel was turned down* REJECT, refuse, decline, spurn, rebuff.

**2** *Pete turned the volume down* REDUCE, lower, decrease, lessen; muffle, mute.
**turn in 1** *he turned in his brother to the police* BETRAY, inform

on, denounce, sell out, stab someone in the back; blow the whistle on, rat on, squeal on, finger.

2 *we turned in the entrance forms just in time* HAND IN/OVER/BACK, give in, submit, surrender, give up; deliver, return.

3 *I usually turn in before 10 o'clock* GO TO BED, retire, go to sleep, call it a day; *informal* hit the hay, hit the sack.

**turn of events** *she was unprepared for this turn of events* DEVELOPMENT, incident, occurrence, happening, circumstance, surprise.

**turn of phrase** *a clever turn of phrase* EXPRESSION, idiom, phrase, term, word, aphorism.

**turn off** 1 *his so-called jokes really turn me off* PUT OFF, leave cold, repel, disgust, revolt, offend; disenchant, alienate; bore, gross out.

2 *please turn off the garage lights* SWITCH OFF, shut off, turn out; extinguish; deactivate; *informal* kill, cut, power down.

**turn on** 1 *the decision turned on the law* DEPEND ON, rest on, hinge on, be contingent on, be decided by.

2 *okay, I admit it—his green eyes turn me on.* See AROUSE sense 3.

3 *I'll turn on the generator* SWITCH ON, start up, activate, trip, power up.

4 *it began as a simple disagreement, but then he turned on us like a mad dog* ATTACK, set on, fall on, let fly at, lash out at, hit out at; *informal* lay into, tear into, let someone have it, bite someone's head off, jump down someone's throat; light into.

**turn on to** *Christie has turned me on to the health benefits of yoga* INTRODUCE SOMEONE TO, get someone into, pique someone's interest in.

**turn out** 1 *a huge crowd turned out* COME, be present, attend, appear, turn up, arrive; assemble, gather, show up.

2 *it turned out that she had been abroad* TRANSPIRE, emerge, come to light, become apparent, become clear.

3 *things didn't turn out as I'd intended* HAPPEN, occur, come about; develop, proceed; work out, come out, end up, pan out, result; *formal* eventuate.

4 *it's about time she turned out that bum of a boyfriend* THROW OUT, eject, evict, expel, oust, drum out, banish; *informal* kick out, send packing, boot out, show someone the door.

5 *turn out the light.* See TURN OFF (above) sense 2.

6 *they turn out a million engines a year* PRODUCE, make, manufacture, fabricate, generate, put out, churn out.

**turn over** 1 *the crate fell off the back of the truck and turned over* OVERTURN, upturn, capsize, keel over, flip, turn turtle, be upended, tip.

2 *I turned over a few pages* FLIP OVER, flick through, leaf through.

3 *she turned the proposal over in her mind* THINK ABOUT, think over, consider, ponder, contemplate, reflect on, chew over, mull over, muse on, ruminate on.

4 *he turned over the business to his brother* TRANSFER, hand over, pass on, consign, commit.

**turn someone's stomach** *the sight of blood turns my stomach* NAUSEATE SOMEONE, sicken someone, make someone sick.

**turn to** *I always had my grandparents to turn to* SEEK HELP FROM, have recourse to, approach, apply to, appeal to; take to, resort to.

**turn up** 1 *the missing documents turned up* BE FOUND, be discovered, be located, reappear.

2 *the police turned up* ARRIVE, appear, present oneself, show up, show, show one's face.

3 *something better will turn up* PRESENT ITSELF, offer itself, occur, happen, crop up, appear.

4 *she turned up the treble* INCREASE, raise, amplify, intensify.

5 *they turned up lots of information* DISCOVER, uncover, unearth, find, dig up, ferret out, root out, expose.

**turning point** noun *the turning point in their relationship* CROSSROADS, critical moment, decisive moment, moment of truth, watershed, crisis, landmark.

**turnout** noun *the producers were overjoyed with the turnout* ATTENDANCE, audience, crowd, gathering, showing, throng, assembly, assemblage, congregation, number; participation.

**turnover** noun 1 *an annual turnover of $2.25 million* (GROSS) REVENUE, income, yield; sales, gross.

2 *a high turnover of staff* RATE OF REPLACEMENT, change, movement.

**tussle** noun *his glasses were smashed in the tussle* SCUFFLE, fight, struggle, skirmish, brawl, scrum, rough-and-tumble, free-for-all, fracas, fray, rumpus, melee; *informal* spat, scrap, roughhouse, tug-of-war.

▸ verb *demonstrators tussled with police* SCUFFLE, fight, struggle, brawl, grapple, wrestle, clash; *informal* scrap, roughhouse.

**tutor** noun *a history tutor* TEACHER, instructor, educator, lecturer, trainer, mentor; *formal* pedagogue.

▸ verb *he was tutored at home* TEACH, instruct, educate, school, coach, train, drill.

**TV** noun. See TELEVISION.

**twaddle** noun *informal* See NONSENSE sense 1. See also note at NONSENSE.

**tweak** verb 1 *she tweaked his nose* PULL, jerk, tug, twist, twitch, pinch, squeeze.

2 *the product can be tweaked to suit your needs* ADJUST, modify, alter, change, adapt; refine.

▸ noun 1 *he gave her hair a tweak* PULL, jerk, tug, twist, pinch, twitch, squeeze.

2 *a few minor tweaks were required* ADJUSTMENT, modification, alteration, change; refinement.

**twig** noun *leafy twigs* STICK, sprig, shoot, stem, branchlet.

**twilight** noun 1 *we arrived at twilight* DUSK, sunset, sundown, nightfall, evening, close of day, day's end; *literary* eventide, gloaming. ANTONYMS dawn, daybreak.

2 *it was scarcely visible in the twilight* HALF-LIGHT, semidarkness, gloom.

**3** *the twilight of his career* DECLINE, waning, ebb; autumn, final years, tail end. ANTONYMS dawn, peak, height.

▸ adjective *a twilight world* SHADOWY, dark, shady, dim, gloomy, obscure, crepuscular, twilit.

**twin** noun *a bedroom that was the twin of her own* DUPLICATE, double, carbon copy, exact likeness, mirror image, replica, look-alike, doppelgänger, clone; counterpart, match, pair; *informal* dead ringer, spitting image.

▸ adjective **1** *twin peaks* MATCHING, identical, matched, paired.

**2** *the twin aims of conservation and recreation* TWOFOLD, double, dual; related, linked, connected; corresponding, parallel, complementary, equivalent.

▸ verb *the company twinned its brewing with distilling* COMBINE, join, link, couple, pair.

**twine** noun *a ball of twine* STRING, cord, thread, yarn.

▸ verb **1** *she twined her arms around him* WIND, entwine, wrap, wreathe.

**2** *ivy twined around the tree* ENTWINE (ITSELF), coil, loop, twist, spiral, curl; weave, interlace, intertwine, braid.

**twinge** noun **1** *twinges in her stomach* PAIN, spasm, ache, throb; cramp, stitch.

**2** *a twinge of guilt* PANG, prick, qualm, scruple, misgiving.

**twinkle** noun & verb *a twinkle in her eye | the lights of the city twinkled below me* GLITTER, sparkle, shine, glimmer, shimmer, glint, gleam, flicker, flash, wink; *literary* glister.

**twinkling** adjective *twinkling white lights graced the gazebo* SPARKLING, glistening, glittering, glimmering, glinting, gleaming, flickering, winking, shining, scintillating, lambent; *literary* coruscating.

**twirl** verb **1** *he twirled the gun around* SPIN, whirl, turn, pivot, swivel, twist, revolve, rotate.

**2** *she twirled her hair around her finger* WIND, twist, coil, curl, wrap.

▸ noun *she did a quick twirl* PIROUETTE, spin, whirl, turn, twist, rotation, revolution, gyration, twizzle.

**twist** verb **1** *the impact twisted the chassis* CRUMPLE, crush, buckle, mangle, warp, deform, distort.

**2** *her face twisted with rage* CONTORT, screw up.

**3** *Ma anxiously twisted a handkerchief* WRING, squeeze.

**4** *he twisted around in his seat* TURN (AROUND), swivel (around), spin (around), pivot, rotate, revolve.

**5** *she twisted out of his grasp* WRIGGLE, squirm, worm one's way, wiggle.

**6** *I twisted my ankle* SPRAIN, wrench, turn.

**7** *you are twisting my words* DISTORT, misrepresent, change, alter, pervert, falsify, warp, skew, misinterpret, misconstrue, misstate, misquote; garble.

**8** *he twisted the radio knob* TWIDDLE, adjust, turn, rotate, swivel.

**9** *she twisted her hair around her finger* WIND, twirl, coil, curl, wrap.

**10** *the wires were twisted together* INTERTWINE, twine, interlace, weave, plait, braid, coil, wind.

**11** *the road twisted and turned* WIND, bend, curve, turn, meander, weave, zigzag, swerve, snake.

▸ noun **1** *a twist of the wrist* TURN, twirl, spin, rotation; flick.

**2** *the twists of the road* BEND, curve, turn, zigzag, kink.

**3** *the twists of the plot* CONVOLUTION, complication, complexity, intricacy; surprise, revelation.

**4** *a modern twist on an old theme* INTERPRETATION, slant, outlook, angle, approach, treatment; variation, change, difference.

PHRASE: **twist someone's arm** *I didn't want to go with them, but Hazel twisted my arm* PRESSURIZE SOMEONE, coerce someone, force someone; persuade someone; *informal* lean on someone, browbeat someone, strong-arm someone, bulldoze someone, railroad someone, put the screws to/on someone.

**twit** noun *informal*. See FOOL noun sense 1.

**twitch** verb *he twitched and then lay still* JERK, convulse, have a spasm, quiver, tremble, shiver, shudder.

▸ noun **1** *a twitch of her lips* SPASM, convulsion, quiver, tremor, shiver, shudder, small movement; tic.

**2** *he gave a twitch at his mustache* PULL, tug, tweak, yank, jerk.

**3** *he felt a twitch in his left side* PANG, twinge, dart, stab, prick.

**twitter** verb **1** *sparrows twittered under the eaves* CHIRP, chirrup, cheep, tweet, peep, chatter, trill, warble, sing.

**2** *stop twittering about Francis* BLATHER, jabber, blabber, chatter, chitter, gabble, go on, blab, rattle, yap, prattle, babble, blither, ramble; *informal* yak, quack, yabber, talk someone's ear off.

▸ noun **1** *a bird's twitter* CHIRP, chirrup, cheep, tweet, peep, trill, warble, song.

**2** *her nonstop twitter* PRATTLE, chatter, babble, talk, gabble, blabber; *informal* yakking.

**two-faced** adjective *her two-faced ex* DECEITFUL, insincere, double-dealing, hypocritical, backstabbing, false, fickle, untrustworthy, duplicitous, deceiving, dissembling, dishonest; disloyal, treacherous, faithless, traitorous, cheating, lying, weaselly; *literary* perfidious. ANTONYM sincere.

**tycoon** noun *a newspaper tycoon* MAGNATE, mogul, industrialist, businessman, financier, entrepreneur, captain of industry, millionaire, multimillionaire, merchant prince; *informal* big shot, bigwig, honcho, supremo, big wheel, kahuna; *derogatory* fat cat, robber baron.

**type** noun **1** *a pastor of the old-fashioned type* KIND, sort, variety, class, category, set, genre, species, order, breed, race; style, nature, manner, rank; generation, vintage; stamp, ilk, cast, grain, mold, stripe, brand, flavor. See note at EMBLEM.

**2** *sporty types* PERSON, individual, character, sort.

**3** *italic type* PRINT, font, typeface, face, characters, lettering, letters.

**typhoon** noun. See STORM noun sense 1.

**typical** adjective **1** *a typical example of art deco* REPRESENTATIVE, classic, quintessential, archetypal, model, prototypical, stereotypical, paradigmatic. ANTONYMS atypical, unusual, abnormal.

**2** *a fairly typical day* NORMAL, average, ordinary, standard, regular, routine, run-of-the-mill, conventional, unremarkable, unsurprising, unexceptional; *informal* blah. See note at NORMAL. ANTONYMS atypical, unusual, exceptional.

**3** *it's typical of him to forget* CHARACTERISTIC, in keeping, usual, normal, par for the course, predictable, true to form; customary, habitual. ANTONYM uncharacteristic.

**typify** verb *the girls basketball team typifies the school spirit of our student body* EPITOMIZE, exemplify, characterize, be representative of; personify, embody, be emblematic of.

**tyrannical** adjective *a tyrannical government* DICTATORIAL, despotic, autocratic, oppressive, repressive, totalitarian, undemocratic, illiberal; authoritarian, high-handed, imperious, harsh, strict, iron-handed, iron-fisted, severe, cruel, brutal, ruthless. ANTONYM liberal.

**tyrannize** verb *she tyrannized her daughter-in-law* DOMINATE, dictate to, browbeat, intimidate, bully, lord it over; persecute, victimize, torment, terrorize; oppress, repress, crush, subjugate; *informal* push around.

**tyranny** noun *they will not soon forget the brutal tyranny of Amin* DESPOTISM, absolute power, autocracy, dictatorship, totalitarianism, Fascism; oppression, repression, subjugation, enslavement; authoritarianism, bullying, severity, cruelty, brutality, ruthlessness.

**tyrant** noun *dare we envision a world free from tyrants?* DICTATOR, despot, autocrat, authoritarian, oppressor; slave driver, martinet, bully, megalomaniac.

**ubiquitous** adjective *the ubiquitous golden arches of burgerdom* OMNIPRESENT, ever-present, everywhere, all over the place, pervasive, universal, worldwide, global; rife, prevalent, far-reaching, inescapable. ANTONYM rare.

**ugly** adjective **1** *an ugly face* UNATTRACTIVE, unappealing, unpleasant, hideous, unlovely, unprepossessing, unsightly, horrible, frightful, awful, ghastly, vile, revolting, repellent, repulsive, repugnant; grotesque, disgusting, monstrous, reptilian, misshapen, deformed, disfigured, plug-ugly, butt-ugly; homely, plain, not much to look at. ANTONYM beautiful.

**2** *things got pretty ugly* UNPLEASANT, nasty, disagreeable, alarming, tense, charged, serious, grave; dangerous, perilous, threatening, menacing, hostile, ominous, sinister. ANTONYM pleasant.

**3** *an ugly rumor* HORRIBLE, despicable, reprehensible, nasty, appalling, objectionable, offensive, obnoxious, vile, dishonorable, rotten, vicious, spiteful.

**ulcer** noun *something to soothe the ulcers in his mouth* SORE, ulceration, abscess, boil, carbuncle, blister, gumboil, cyst; *Medicine* aphtha, chancre, furuncle.

**ulterior** adjective *his ulterior objectives were disguised by feigned concern* UNDERLYING, undisclosed, undivulged, concealed, hidden, covert, secret, personal, private, selfish. ANTONYM overt.

**ultimate** adjective **1** *the ultimate collapse of their empire* EVENTUAL, final, concluding, terminal, end; resulting, ensuing, consequent, subsequent.

**2** *ultimate truths about civilization* FUNDAMENTAL, basic, primary, elementary, elemental, absolute, central, key, crucial, essential, pivotal.

**3** *the ultimate gift for cat lovers* BEST, ideal, perfect, greatest, supreme, paramount, superlative, highest, utmost, optimum, quintessential.

▸ noun *the ultimate in Bohemian chic* UTMOST, optimum, last word, height, epitome, peak, pinnacle, acme, zenith, nonpareil, dernier cri, ne plus ultra; **(the ultimate)** *informal* da bomb; *dated, informal* the bee's knees, the cat's pajamas/whiskers/meow.

**ultimately** adverb **1** *the money will ultimately belong to us* EVENTUALLY, in the end, in the long run, at length, finally, sooner or later, in time, in the fullness of time, when all is said and done, one day, some day, sometime, over the long haul; *informal* when push comes to shove.

**2** *two ultimately contradictory reasons* FUNDAMENTALLY, basically, primarily, essentially, at heart, deep down.

**umbrage** PHRASE: **take umbrage** *I would take umbrage at that if I thought you were serious* TAKE OFFENSE, take exception, be aggrieved, be affronted, be annoyed, be angry, be indignant, be put out, be insulted, be hurt, be piqued, be resentful, be disgruntled, go into a huff, be miffed, have one's nose put out of joint, chafe.

**umbrella** noun **1** *they huddled under the umbrella* parasol, sunshade.

**2** *the groups worked under the umbrella of the Communist Party* AEGIS, auspices, patronage, protection, guardianship, support, backing, agency, guidance, care, charge, responsibility, cover.

**umpire** noun *the umpire reversed his decision* REFEREE, linesman, adjudicator, arbitrator, judge, moderator, official; ref, ump.

▸ verb *he umpired a boat race* REFEREE, adjudicate, arbitrate, judge, moderate, oversee, officiate; *informal* ref, ump.

**umpteen** adjective. See COUNTLESS.

**unable** adjective *I'm unable to fix the leak* POWERLESS, impotent, at a loss, inadequate, incompetent, unfit, unqualified, incapable.

**unabridged** adjective *the unabridged version is in two volumes* COMPLETE, entire, whole, full-length, intact, uncut, unshortened, unexpurgated.

**unacceptable** adjective *the repair job on the gutters was unacceptable* INTOLERABLE, insufferable, unsatisfactory, inadmissible, inappropriate, unsuitable, undesirable, unreasonable, insupportable; offensive, obnoxious, disagreeable, disgraceful, deplorable, beyond the pale, bad; a bit much, too much, not on. ANTONYM satisfactory.

**unaccompanied** adjective *when Howard arrived at the dance he was unaccompanied* ALONE, on one's own, by oneself, solo, lone, solitary, single-handed; unescorted, unattended, unchaperoned; *informal* by one's lonesome.

**unaccountable** adjective **1** *for some unaccountable reason, the dogs have been pacing the floor all evening* INEXPLICABLE, insoluble, incomprehensible, unfathomable, impenetrable, puzzling, perplexing, baffling, bewildering, mystifying, mysterious, inscrutable, peculiar, strange, queer, odd, obscure; *informal* weird, freaky.

**2** *a private company unaccountable to voters* NOT ANSWERABLE, not liable, not responsible; free, exempt, immune; unsupervised.

**unaccustomed** adjective **1** *she was* ***unaccustomed to*** *being bossed around* UNUSED TO, new to, fresh to; unfamiliar with, inexperienced in, unconversant with, unacquainted with. ANTONYM habitual.

**2** *he showed unaccustomed emotion* UNUSUAL, unfamiliar, uncommon, unwonted, exceptional, unprecedented, extraordinary, rare, surprising, abnormal, atypical. ANTONYM habitual.

**unaffected** adjective **1** *they are* ***unaffected by*** *the change in command* UNCHANGED BY, unaltered by, uninfluenced by; untouched by, unmoved by, unresponsive to; proof against, impervious to, immune to. ANTONYM influenced.

**2** *his manner was unaffected* UNASSUMING, unpretentious, down-to-earth, natural, easy, uninhibited, open, artless, guileless, ingenuous, unsophisticated, genuine, real, sincere, honest, earnest, wholehearted, heartfelt, true, bona fide, frank; *informal* upfront. ANTONYMS pretentious, false.

**unanimous** adjective **1** *doctors were unanimous about the effects* UNITED, in agreement, in accord, of one mind, of the same mind, in harmony, concordant, undivided, as one. ANTONYM divided.

**2** *a unanimous vote* UNIFORM, consistent, united, concerted, congruent.

**unanswerable** adjective **1** *an unanswerable case* IRREFUTABLE, indisputable, undeniable, incontestable, incontrovertible, irrefragable; conclusive, absolute, positive. ANTONYMS weak, flawed.

**2** *unanswerable questions* INSOLUBLE, unsolvable, inexplicable, unexplainable. ANTONYM obvious.

**unapproachable** adjective **1** *unapproachable islands* INACCESSIBLE, unreachable, remote, out of the way, isolated, farflung, off the beaten track/path; *informal* in the middle of nowhere, in the sticks, in the boondocks. ANTONYM accessible.

**2** *her boss appeared unapproachable* ALOOF, distant, remote, detached, reserved, withdrawn, uncommunicative, guarded, unresponsive, unforthcoming, unfriendly, unsympathetic, unsociable; cool, cold, frosty, stiff, haughty, superior, formal, intimidating; *informal* standoffish, stuck-up. ANTONYM friendly.

**unarmed** adjective *they fired into a crowd of unarmed civilians* DEFENSELESS, weaponless; unprotected, undefended, unguarded, unshielded, vulnerable, exposed, assailable, open to attack.

**unassailable** adjective **1** *an unassailable fortress* IMPREGNABLE, invulnerable, impenetrable, inviolable, invincible, unconquerable; secure, safe, strong, indestructible. ANTONYM defenseless.

**2** *his logic was unassailable* INDISPUTABLE, undeniable, unquestionable, incontestable, incontrovertible, irrefutable, indubitable, watertight, sound, rock-solid, good, sure, manifest, patent, obvious.

**unassuming** adjective *she's not quite the unassuming ingenue she seems to be* MODEST, self-effacing, humble, meek, bashful, reserved, diffident; unobtrusive, unostentatious, low-key, unpretentious, unaffected, natural, artless, ingenuous.

**unattached** adjective **1** *they were both unattached* SINGLE, unmarried, unwed, uncommitted, available, at large, footloose and fancy free, on one's own; unloved. ANTONYM married.

**2** *we are unattached to any organization* UNAFFILIATED, unallied; autonomous, independent, nonaligned, self-governing, neutral, separate, unconnected, detached. ANTONYM affiliated.

**unattended** adjective **1** *his cries went unattended* IGNORED, disregarded, neglected, passed over, unheeded.

**2** *an unattended vehicle* UNGUARDED, unwatched, alone, solitary; abandoned.

**3** *she had to walk there unattended* UNACCOMPANIED, unescorted, partnerless, unchaperoned, alone, on one's own, by oneself, solo; *informal* by one's lonesome.

**unauthorized** adjective *you can't hold an unauthorized meeting in a town building* UNOFFICIAL, unsanctioned, unaccredited, unlicensed, unwarranted, unapproved, bootleg, pirated; wildcat; disallowed, prohibited, out of bounds, banned, barred, forbidden, outlawed, illegal, illegitimate, illicit, proscribed. ANTONYM official.

**unavoidable** adjective *it was an unavoidable mishap* INESCAPABLE, inevitable, inexorable, assured, certain, predestined, predetermined, fated, ineluctable; necessary, compulsory, required, obligatory, mandatory.

**unaware** adjective *the vice president claimed to be unaware of the arms deal* IGNORANT, unknowing, unconscious, heedless, unmindful, oblivious, incognizant, unsuspecting, uninformed, unenlightened, unwitting, innocent; inattentive, unobservant, unperceptive, blind; *informal* in the dark; *literary* nescient. ANTONYM conscious.

**unawares** adverb **1** *brigands caught them unawares* BY SURPRISE, unexpectedly, without warning, suddenly, abruptly, unprepared, off-guard; *informal* with one's pants down, napping. ANTONYM prepared.

**2** *the chipmunk, unawares, approached the waiting cat* UNKNOWINGLY, unwittingly, unconsciously; unintentionally, inadvertently, accidentally, by mistake. ANTONYM knowingly.

**unbalanced** adjective **1** *he is unbalanced and dangerous* UNSTABLE, mentally ill, deranged, demented, disturbed, unhinged, insane, mad, out of one's mind; *informal* crazy, loopy, loony, nuts, nutso, nutty, cracked, bushed, screwy, batty, dotty, cuckoo, bonkers, squirrelly; *dated* touched. ANTONYM sane.

2 *a most unbalanced article* BIASED, prejudiced, one-sided, partisan, inequitable, unjust, unfair, parti pris. ANTONYM unbiased.

**unbearable** adjective *the cold made the waiting even more unbearable* INTOLERABLE, insufferable, insupportable, unendurable, unacceptable, unmanageable, overpowering; *informal* too much. ANTONYM tolerable.

**unbeatable** adjective *the Cubs were unbeatable in April* INVINCIBLE, unstoppable, unassailable, indomitable, unconquerable, unsurpassable, matchless, peerless, nonpareil; supreme.

**unbecoming** adjective 1 *an unbecoming sundress* UNFLATTERING, unattractive, unsightly, plain, ugly, homely, hideous; unsuitable, ill-fitting. ANTONYM flattering.

2 *as a representative of this state, your conduct was unbecoming* INAPPROPRIATE, unfitting, unbefitting, unsuitable, unsuited, inapt, indecorous, out of keeping, untoward, incorrect, unacceptable; unworthy, improper, unseemly, undignified. ANTONYM appropriate.

**unbelievable** adjective *an unbelievable story | the grandeur of this casino is unbelievable* INCREDIBLE, beyond belief, inconceivable, unthinkable, unimaginable; unconvincing, far-fetched, dubious, implausible, improbable, unrealistic; *informal* hard to swallow. ANTONYM credible.

**unbeliever** noun *a Holy War against the unbelievers* INFIDEL, heretic, heathen, nonbeliever, atheist, agnostic, pagan, nihilist, apostate, freethinker, dissenter, nonconformist; disbeliever, skeptic, cynic, doubter, doubting Thomas, questioner, scoffer. ANTONYM believer.

**unbending** adjective *she resented the demands of her unbending father* INFLEXIBLE, rigid, strict, austere, stern, tough, firm, uncompromising, unyielding, hard line, resolute, determined, unrelenting, relentless, inexorable, intransigent, immovable; unfeeling, unemotional, stiff, forbidding, unfriendly.

**unbiased** adjective *we need an unbiased opinion* IMPARTIAL, unprejudiced, neutral, nonpartisan, disinterested, detached, dispassionate, objective, value-free, open-minded, equitable, evenhanded, fair. ANTONYM prejudiced.

**unborn** adjective *smoking can be harmful to your unborn child* EMBRYONIC, fetal, in utero; expected.

**unbounded** adjective *unbounded enthusiasm* UNLIMITED, boundless, limitless, illimitable; unrestrained, unrestricted, unconstrained, uncontrolled, unchecked, unbridled, rampant; untold, immeasurable, endless, unending, interminable, everlasting, infinite, inexhaustible. ANTONYM limited.

**unbreakable** adjective *unbreakable dishes* INDESTRUCTIBLE, shatterproof, durable, long-lasting; reinforced, sturdy, tough, stout, resistant, infrangible, heavy-duty, industrial-strength. ANTONYM fragile.

**unbridled** adjective *the unbridled spirit in these young players is very contagious* UNRESTRAINED, unconstrained, uncontrolled, uninhibited, unrestricted, unchecked, unmuffled, uncurbed, rampant, runaway, irrepressible, unstoppable, intemperate, immoderate. ANTONYM restrained.

**unbroken** adjective 1 *the last unbroken window* UNDAMAGED, unimpaired, unharmed, unscathed, untouched, sound, intact, whole, perfect.

2 *an unbroken horse* UNTAMED, undomesticated, untrained, wild, feral.

3 *an unbroken chain of victories* UNINTERRUPTED, continuous, endless, constant, unremitting, perpetual; unobstructed.

4 *his record is still unbroken* UNBEATEN, undefeated, unsurpassed, unrivaled, unmatched, supreme, intact.

**unburden** verb *she had a sudden wish to* ***unburden herself*** OPEN ONE'S HEART, confess, confide, tell all; *informal* come clean, fess up, spill one's guts, let it all out.

**uncanny** adjective 1 *the silence was uncanny* EERIE, unnatural, unearthly, preternatural, supernatural, otherworldly, ghostly, mysterious, strange, unsettling, abnormal, weird, bizarre, surreal, eldritch; *informal* creepy, spooky, freakish, freaky.

2 *an uncanny resemblance* STRIKING, remarkable, extraordinary, exceptional, incredible, noteworthy, notable, arresting.

**unceremonious** adjective 1 *an unceremonious dismissal* ABRUPT, sudden, hasty, hurried, summary, perfunctory, undignified; rude, impolite, discourteous, offhand.

2 *an unceremonious man* INFORMAL, casual, relaxed, easygoing, familiar, natural, laid-back. ANTONYM formal.

**uncertain** adjective 1 *the outcome is uncertain* UNKNOWN, debatable, open to question, in doubt, undetermined, unsure, in the balance, up in the air; unpredictable, unforeseeable, incalculable; risky, chancy, dicey; *informal* iffy. ANTONYMS predictable, settled.

2 *its origin is uncertain* VAGUE, unclear, fuzzy, ambiguous, unknown, unascertainable, obscure, arcane.

3 *uncertain weather* CHANGEABLE, variable, irregular, unpredictable, unreliable, unsettled, erratic, fluctuating.

4 *Ed was uncertain about what to do* UNSURE, doubtful, dubious, undecided, irresolute, hesitant, blowing hot and cold, vacillating, vague, unclear, ambivalent, of two minds. ANTONYM sure.

5 *an uncertain smile* HESITANT, tentative, faltering, unsure, unconfident. ANTONYM confident.

**uncertainty** noun 1 *the uncertainty of the stock market* UNPREDICTABILITY, unreliability, riskiness, chanciness, precariousness, changeability, variability, inconstancy, fickleness, caprice. ANTONYM predictability.

2 *uncertainty about the future is always bad for morale* DOUBT, lack of certainty, indecision, irresolution, hesitancy, unsureness, doubtfulness, wavering, vacillation, equivocation, vagueness, haziness, ambivalence, lack of conviction,

disquiet, wariness, chariness, leeriness, skepticism; queries, questions; *formal* dubiety.

**3** *she pushed the anxious uncertainties out of her mind* DOUBT, qualm, misgiving, apprehension, quandary, reservation, scruple, second thought, query, question, question mark, suspicion.

**4** *there was uncertainty in his voice* HESITANCY, hesitation, tentativeness, unsureness, lack of confidence, diffidence, doubtfulness, doubt. ANTONYM confidence.

THE RIGHT WORD **uncertainty, doubt, dubiety, skepticism**

If you're not sure about something, you're probably experiencing a degree of **uncertainty**, which is a general term covering everything from a mere lack of absolute certainty (*uncertainty about the time of the dinner party*) to an almost complete lack of knowledge that makes it impossible to do more than guess at the result or outcome (*uncertainty about the country's future*). **Doubt** implies both uncertainty and an inability to make a decision because the evidence is insufficient (*considerable doubt as to her innocence*). **Dubiety** comes closer in meaning to *uncertainty* than to *doubt*, because it stresses a lack of sureness rather than an inability to reach a decision; but unlike *uncertainty*, it connotes wavering or fluctuating between one conclusion and another (*no one could fail to notice the dubiety in his voice*). If you exhibit **skepticism**, you are not so much uncertain as unwilling to believe. It usually refers to an habitual state of mind or to a customary reaction (*she always listened to his excuses with skepticism*).

**unchangeable** adjective *the political climate in this town is unchangeable* UNALTERABLE, immutable, invariable, changeless, fixed, hard and fast, cast-iron, ironclad, set/cast/carved in stone, dyed-in-the-wool, established, permanent, enduring, abiding, lasting, indestructible, ineradicable, irreversible. ANTONYM variable.

**uncharitable** adjective *in the end, the uncharitable old miser has a change of heart and becomes the benevolent hero* MEAN, mean-spirited, unkind, selfish, self-centered, inconsiderate, thoughtless, insensitive, unfriendly, unsympathetic, hardhearted, uncaring, unfeeling, ungenerous, ungracious, unfair.

**uncharted** adjective *they approached the uncharted territory with some trepidation* UNEXPLORED, undiscovered, unmapped, untraveled, unfamiliar, untrodden, unplumbed, unknown.

**uncivil** adjective *she apologized to her family for Rusty's uncivil words* IMPOLITE, rude, discourteous, disrespectful, unmannerly, bad-mannered, impertinent, impudent, ungracious; brusque, sharp, curt, offhand, gruff, churlish, snippy. See note at RUDE. ANTONYM polite.

**uncivilized** adjective *we had been taught that working-class people were inferior and uncivilized* UNCOUTH, coarse, rough, boorish, vulgar, philistine, uneducated, uncultured, uncultivated, benighted, unsophisticated, unpolished; ill-bred, ill-mannered, thuggish, loutish, redneck; barbarian, primitive, savage, brutish; *archaic* rude.

**unclean** adjective **1** *unclean premises* DIRTY, filthy, grubby, grimy, mucky, foul, impure, tainted, grungy, sullied, soiled, unwashed; polluted, contaminated, infected, unsanitary, unhygienic, unhealthy, disease-ridden. ANTONYMS pure, clean.

**2** *an unclean meat* IMPURE; forbidden, taboo. ANTONYM kosher.

**uncomfortable** adjective **1** *an uncomfortable chair* PAINFUL, disagreeable, intolerable, unbearable, confining, cramped.

**2** *I felt uncomfortable in her presence* UNEASY, awkward, nervous, tense, ill-at-ease, strained, edgy, restless, embarrassed, troubled, worried, anxious, fraught, rattled, twitchy, discombobulated, antsy. ANTONYM relaxed.

**uncommitted** adjective **1** *uncommitted voters* FLOATING, undecided, nonpartisan, unaffiliated, neutral, nonaligned, impartial, independent, undeclared, uncertain; *informal* sitting on the fence. ANTONYM aligned.

**2** *the uncommitted male* UNMARRIED, unattached, unwed, partnerless; footloose and fancy free, available, single, lone. ANTONYM attached.

**uncommon** adjective **1** *an uncommon occurrence* UNUSUAL, abnormal, rare, atypical, unconventional, unfamiliar, strange, odd, curious, extraordinary, outlandish, novel, singular, peculiar, bizarre; alien, weird, oddball, offbeat; scarce, few and far between, exceptional, isolated, infrequent, irregular, seldom seen.

**2** *an uncommon capacity for hard work* REMARKABLE, extraordinary, exceptional, singular, particular, marked, outstanding, noteworthy, significant, especial, special, signal, superior, unique, unparalleled, prodigious, unearthly; *informal* mind-boggling.

**uncommonly** adverb *the cherry blossoms are uncommonly magnificent this year* UNUSUALLY, remarkably, extraordinarily, exceptionally, singularly, particularly, especially, decidedly, notably, eminently, extremely, very.

**uncommunicative** adjective *their uncommunicative dinner guests made the evening seem terribly long* TACITURN, quiet, unforthcoming, reserved, reticent, laconic, tongue-tied, mute, silent, tight-lipped, close-mouthed; guarded, secretive, close, private; distant, remote, aloof, curt, withdrawn, unsociable, farouche; *informal* mum, standoffish. ANTONYM talkative.

**uncompromising** adjective *two uncompromising parties will never reach a common ground* INFLEXIBLE, unbending, unyielding, unshakable, resolute, rigid, hard-line, immovable, intractable, inexorable, firm, determined, obstinate, stubborn, adamant, obdurate, intransigent, headstrong, stiff-necked, pigheaded, single-minded, bloody-minded. ANTONYM flexible.

**unconcerned** adjective **1** *she is unconcerned about their responses* INDIFFERENT, unmoved, apathetic, uninterested, incurious, dispassionate, heedless, impassive, unmindful. ANTONYM interested.

**2** *he tried to look unconcerned* UNTROUBLED, unworried, unruffled, insouciant, nonchalant, blasé, carefree, casual, blithe, relaxed, at ease, 'calm, cool, and collected'; *informal* laid-back, poker-faced. ANTONYM anxious.

**unconditional** adjective *they gave their mom's new husband an unconditional welcome* WHOLEHEARTED, unqualified, unreserved, unlimited, unrestricted, unmitigated, unquestioning; complete, total, entire, full, absolute, out-and-out, unequivocal.

**unconnected** adjective 1 *the ground wire was unconnected* DETACHED, disconnected, loose. ANTONYM attached.

2 *unconnected tasks* UNRELATED, dissociated, separate, independent, distinct, different, disparate, discrete. ANTONYM related.

3 *unconnected chains of thought* DISJOINTED, incoherent, disconnected, rambling, wandering, diffuse, disorderly, haphazard, disorganized, garbled, mixed, muddled, aimless. ANTONYM coherent.

**unconscionable** adjective 1 *the unconscionable use of test animals* UNETHICAL, amoral, immoral, unprincipled, indefensible, unforgivable, wrong; unscrupulous, unfair, underhanded, dishonorable. ANTONYM ethical.

2 *we waited an unconscionable length of time* EXCESSIVE, unreasonable, unwarranted, uncalled for, unfair, inordinate, immoderate, undue, inexcusable, unforgivable, unnecessary, needless; *informal* over the top. ANTONYM acceptable.

**unconscious** adjective 1 *she made sure he was unconscious* INSENSIBLE, senseless, insentient, insensate, comatose, inert, knocked out, stunned; motionless, immobile, prostrate; *informal* out cold, out like a light, out of it, down for the count, passed out, dead to the world.

2 *she was* ***unconscious of*** *the pain* HEEDLESS OF, unmindful of, disregarding of, oblivious to, insensible to, impervious to, unaffected by, unconcerned by, indifferent to; unaware of, unknowing of, ignorant of, incognizant of. ANTONYM aware.

3 *an unconscious desire* SUBCONSCIOUS, latent, suppressed, subliminal, sleeping, dormant, inherent, instinctive, involuntary, uncontrolled, spontaneous; unintentional, unthinking, unwitting, inadvertent; *informal* gut. ANTONYM voluntary.

▸ noun *fantasies raging in the unconscious* SUBCONSCIOUS, psyche, ego, id, inner self.

**uncontrollable** adjective 1 *the crowds were uncontrollable* UNMANAGEABLE, out of control, ungovernable, wild, unruly, disorderly, recalcitrant, turbulent, disobedient, delinquent, defiant, undisciplined; *formal* refractory. ANTONYM compliant.

2 *an uncontrollable rage* UNSTOPPABLE, irrepressible, ungovernable, unquenchable; wild, violent, frenzied, furious, mad, hysterical, passionate, out of control.

**unconventional** adjective *her unconventional sense of humor didn't sit well with some of the audience* UNUSUAL, irregular, unorthodox, unfamiliar, uncommon, unwonted, out of the ordinary, atypical, singular, alternative, different; new, novel, innovative, groundbreaking, pioneering, original, unprecedented; eccentric, idiosyncratic, quirky, odd, strange, bizarre, weird, outlandish, curious; abnormal, anomalous, aberrant, extraordinary; nonconformist, Bohemian, avant-garde; *informal* far out, offbeat, off the wall, wacky, madcap, oddball, zany, hippie, kooky, wacko. ANTONYM orthodox.

**uncoordinated** adjective *you'd be surprised how many uncoordinated hopefuls show up for these dance auditions* CLUMSY, awkward, blundering, bumbling, lumbering, flat-footed, heavy-handed, graceless, gawky, ungainly, ungraceful; inept, unhandy, unskillful, inexpert, maladroit, bungling; *informal* klutzy, butterfingered, ham-fisted, ham-handed, all thumbs. ANTONYM dexterous.

**uncouth** adjective *I was hoping you'd be less uncouth in public* UNCIVILIZED, uncultured, uncultivated, unrefined, unpolished, unsophisticated, bush-league, common, plebeian, low, rough, rough-hewn, coarse, loutish, boorish, oafish, troglodyte; churlish, uncivil, rude, impolite, discourteous, disrespectful, unmannerly, bad-mannered, ill-bred, indecorous, crass, indelicate; vulgar, crude, raunchy. See note at RUDE. ANTONYM refined.

**uncover** verb 1 *she uncovered the new artwork* EXPOSE, reveal, lay bare; unwrap, unveil; strip, denude.

2 *they uncovered a money-laundering plot* DETECT, discover, come across, stumble on, chance on, find, turn up, unearth, dig up; expose, unveil, unmask, disclose, reveal, lay bare, make known, make public, bring to light, blow the lid off, blow the whistle on, pull the plug on.

**unctuous** adjective *she sees through his unctuous manners* SYCOPHANTIC, ingratiating, obsequious, fawning, servile, groveling, subservient, cringing, humble, hypocritical, insincere, gushing, effusive; glib, smooth, slick, slippery, oily, greasy; smarmy, slimy.

**undaunted** adjective *through all our crises, Cal has been the undaunted one* UNAFRAID, undismayed, unflinching, unshrinking, unabashed, fearless, dauntless, intrepid, bold, valiant, brave, courageous, plucky, gritty, indomitable, confident, audacious, daring; *informal* gutsy, spunky. ANTONYM fearful.

**undecided** adjective *Gavin is hoping to win over the majority of undecided voters* UNRESOLVED, uncertain, unsure, unclear, unsettled, indefinite, undetermined, unknown, in the balance, up in the air, debatable, arguable, moot, open to question, doubtful, dubious, borderline, ambiguous, vague; indecisive, irresolute, hesitant, tentative, wavering, vacillating, uncommitted, ambivalent, of two minds, torn, fence-sitting, on the fence; *informal* iffy, wishy-washy. ANTONYM certain.

**undefined** adjective 1 *some matters are still undefined* UNSPECIFIED, unexplained, unspecific, indeterminate, unsettled; unclear, woolly, imprecise, inexact, indefinite, vague, fuzzy. ANTONYMS definite, specific.

2 *undefined shapes* INDISTINCT, indefinite, formless, indistinguishable, vague, amorphous, hazy, misty, shadowy, nebulous, blurred, blurry. ANTONYMS clear, distinct.

**undeniable** adjective *her willingness to work is undeniable* INDISPUTABLE, indubitable, unquestionable, beyond doubt, beyond question, undebatable, incontrovertible, incontestable, irrefutable, unassailable; certain, sure, definite, positive, conclusive, plain, obvious, unmistakable, self-evident, patent, emphatic, categorical, unequivocal. ANTONYM questionable.

**under** preposition **1** *they hid under a bush* BENEATH, below, underneath. ANTONYMS above, over.

**2** *the rent is under $450* LESS THAN, lower than, below. ANTONYMS more than, over.

**3** *branch managers are under the retail director* SUBORDINATE TO, junior to, inferior to, subservient to, answerable to, responsible to, subject to, controlled by. ANTONYMS above, over.

**4** *the town was under water* FLOODED BY, immersed in, submerged by, sunk in, engulfed by, inundated by. ANTONYM above.

**5** *forty homes are under construction* UNDERGOING, in the process of.

**6** *our finances are under pressure* SUBJECT TO, liable to, at the mercy of.

▸ adverb *coughing and spluttering she went under* DOWN, lower, below, underneath, beneath; underwater.

**undercover** adjective *she does undercover work for the insurance company* COVERT, secret, clandestine, incognito, underground, surreptitious, furtive, cloak-and-dagger, stealthy, hidden, concealed, backstairs, closet; *informal* hush-hush, sneaky, on the QT. ANTONYM overt.

**undercurrent** noun **1** *dangerous undercurrents in the cove* UNDERTOW, underflow; riptide.

**2** *the undercurrent of despair in his words* UNDERTONE, overtone, suggestion, connotation, intimation, hint, nuance, trace, suspicion, whisper, tinge; feeling, atmosphere, aura, echo; *informal* vibe.

**undercut** verb **1** *the firm undercut their rivals* CHARGE LESS THAN, undersell, underprice, underbid.

**2** *his authority was being undercut* UNDERMINE, weaken, impair, sap, threaten, subvert, sabotage, ruin, destabilize, wreck.

**underdog** noun *yesterday's underdog is today's champion* LONG SHOT, dark horse, weaker one, little guy, David; downtrodden, victim, loser, fall guy.

**underestimate** verb *underestimating the opposition was our biggest mistake* UNDERRATE, undervalue, lowball, do an injustice to, be wrong about, sell short, play down, understate; minimize, de-emphasize, underemphasize, diminish, gloss over, trivialize; miscalculate, misjudge, misconstrue, misread. ANTONYM exaggerate.

**undergo** verb *she underwent a lengthy cross-examination* GO THROUGH, experience, undertake, face, submit to, be subjected to, come in for, receive, sustain, endure, brave, bear, tolerate, stand, withstand, weather.

**underground** adjective **1** *an underground parking garage* SUBTERRANEAN, buried, sunken, subsurface, basement.

**2** *underground trade* CLANDESTINE, secret, surreptitious, covert, undercover, closet, cloak-and-dagger, back-alley, backstairs, black-market, hidden, sneaky, furtive; resistance, subversive; *informal* hush-hush.

**3** *the underground art scene* ALTERNATIVE, radical, revolutionary, unconventional, unorthodox, avant-garde, counterculture, experimental, innovative.

▸ adverb **1** *the insects live underground* BELOW GROUND, in the earth, subterraneously.

**2** *the rebels went underground* INTO HIDING, into seclusion, undercover, to earth, to ground.

**undergrowth** noun *the undergrowth is a habitat for various small mammals and certain birds* SHRUBBERY, vegetation, underbrush, greenery, ground cover, underwood, brushwood, brush, scrub, bush, covert, thicket, copse; bushes, plants, brambles, herbage; *technical* herbaceous layer.

**underline** verb **1** *she underlined a phrase* UNDERSCORE, mark, pick out, emphasize, highlight.

**2** *the program underlines the benefits of exercise* EMPHASIZE, stress, highlight, accentuate, accent, focus on, spotlight, point up, play up.

**underling** noun *he dishes out orders to his underlings* SUBORDINATE, inferior, junior, minion, lackey, subaltern, flunky, menial, vassal, subject, hireling, servant, henchman, factotum; *informal* gofer. ANTONYM boss.

**underlying** adjective **1** *the underlying aims of the research* FUNDAMENTAL, basic, primary, prime, central, principal, root, chief, cardinal, key, elementary, intrinsic, essential.

**2** *an underlying feeling of irritation* LATENT, repressed, suppressed, unrevealed, undisclosed, unexpressed, concealed, hidden, masked.

**undermine** verb **1** *their integrity is being undermined* SUBVERT, undercut, sabotage, threaten, weaken, compromise, diminish, reduce, impair, mar, spoil, ruin, damage, hurt, injure, cripple, sap, shake; *informal* drag through the mud. ANTONYMS strengthen, enhance.

**2** *rivers undermined their banks* ERODE, wear away, eat away at.

**underprivileged** adjective *he spends his summers backpacking with underprivileged children from his hometown* NEEDY, deprived, disadvantaged, poor, destitute, in need, in straitened circumstances, impoverished, poverty-stricken, on the poverty line, indigent, lower-class; *formal* penurious. ANTONYM wealthy.

**underrate** verb *for years the girls' athletic program was underrated* UNDERVALUE, underestimate, do an injustice to, sell short, play down, understate, minimize, diminish, downgrade, trivialize. ANTONYM exaggerate.

**undersized** adjective *the lack of nutrients will result in undersized tomatoes* UNDERDEVELOPED, stunted, small, short, little, tiny, petite, slight, compact, miniature, mini, diminutive, dwarfish, pygmy, pint-sized, pocket-sized, baby, teeny-weeny, itsy-bitsy, itty-bitty, vertically challenged. ANTONYM overgrown.

**understand** verb **1** *he couldn't understand anything we said* COMPREHEND, grasp, take in, see, apprehend, follow, make sense of, fathom; unravel, decipher, interpret; *informal* figure out, work out, make head(s) or tail(s) of, get one's head around, get the drift of, catch on to, get; *Brit. informal* twig.

**2** *she understood how hard he'd worked* APPRECIATE, recognize, realize, acknowledge, know, be aware of, be conscious of; *informal* be wise to; *formal* be cognizant of.

**3** *I understand that you wish to go* BELIEVE, gather, take it, hear (tell), notice, see, learn; conclude, infer, assume, surmise, fancy.

▸ exclamation *I want out, understand?* get it, get the picture, see, right, know what I mean, get my drift, capisce, comprende.

**understanding** noun **1** *test your understanding of the language* COMPREHENSION, apprehension, grasp, mastery, appreciation, assimilation, absorption; knowledge, awareness, insight, skill, expertise, proficiency; *informal* know-how; *formal* cognizance. ANTONYM ignorance.

**2** *it was my understanding that this was free* BELIEF, perception, view, conviction, feeling, opinion, intuition, impression, assumption, supposition, inference, interpretation.

**3** *she treated me with understanding* COMPASSION, sympathy, pity, feeling, concern, consideration, kindness, sensitivity, decency, humanity, charity, goodwill, mercy, tolerance. ANTONYM indifference.

**4** *we had a tacit understanding* AGREEMENT, arrangement, deal, bargain, settlement, pledge, pact, compact, contract, covenant, bond, meeting of minds.

▸ adjective *an understanding friend* COMPASSIONATE, sympathetic, sensitive, considerate, tender, kind, thoughtful, tolerant, patient, forbearing, lenient, merciful, forgiving, humane; approachable, supportive, perceptive.

**understate** verb *let's not understate the importance of the coaching staff* PLAY DOWN, downplay, underrate, underplay, de-emphasize, trivialize, minimize, diminish, downgrade, brush aside, gloss over, put it mildly; *informal* soft-pedal, sell short. ANTONYM exaggerate.

**understudy** noun *Mark's understudy got better reviews than Mark* STAND-IN, substitute, replacement, reserve, fill-in, locum, proxy, backup, relief, standby, stopgap; *informal* sub, pinch-hitter.

**undertake** verb *are you ready to undertake this challenge?* TACKLE, take on, assume, shoulder, handle, manage, deal with, be responsible for; engage in, take part in, go about, set about, get down to, come to grips with, embark on; attempt, try, endeavor; *informal* have a go at; *formal* essay.

**undertaker** noun *in those days, an epidemic of the flu would have the undertaker working around the clock* FUNERAL DIRECTOR, mortician.

**undertone** noun **1** *he said something in an undertone* LOW VOICE, murmur, whisper, mutter.

**2** *the story's dark undertones* UNDERCURRENT, overtone, suggestion, nuance, vein, atmosphere, aura, tenor, flavor, tinge; vibrations.

**undervalue** verb *I didn't mean to undervalue your contributions* UNDERRATE, underestimate, play down, understate, underemphasize, diminish, minimize, downgrade, reduce, brush aside, gloss over, trivialize, underprice; *informal* sell short.

**underwater** adjective *an underwater laboratory* SUBMERGED, immersed, sunken, subaqueous, subsurface; undersea, subsea, submarine.

**underwear** noun *he always managed to leave half of his underwear at camp* undergarment(s), underthings, underclothes, lingerie; foundation garment(s); *informal* undies, drawers, skivvies.

**underworld** noun **1** *Osiris, god of **the underworld*** THE NETHERWORLD, the nether regions, hell, the abyss; eternal damnation; Sheol, Hades, Gehenna, Tophet; *informal* the other place; *literary* the pit. ANTONYM heaven.

**2** *the city's violent underworld* CRIMINAL WORLD, gangland; criminals, gangsters; *informal* mobsters.

**underwrite** verb *a local businesswoman has agreed to underwrite our charter* SPONSOR, support, back, insure, guarantee, indemnify, subsidize, pay for, finance, fund; *informal* foot the bill for, bankroll.

**undesirable** adjective **1** *undesirable side effects* UNPLEASANT, disagreeable, objectionable, nasty, unwelcome, unwanted, unfortunate, inconvenient, infelicitous. ANTONYM pleasant.

**2** *some very undesirable people* UNPLEASANT, disagreeable, obnoxious, nasty, vile, unsavory, awful, repulsive, repellent, objectionable, abhorrent, loathsome, hateful, detestable, deplorable, appalling, insufferable, intolerable, despicable, contemptible, odious, terrible, dreadful, frightful, ghastly, horrible, horrid. ANTONYMS pleasant, agreeable.

▸ noun *the bar was full of undesirables* OUTCAST, lowlife, misfit, deviant, unsavory character, pariah, leper, untouchable, freak.

**undisciplined** adjective *you've never seen such a bunch of undisciplined kids and pets under one roof* UNRULY, disorderly, disobedient, badly behaved, recalcitrant, restive, wayward, delinquent, rebellious, refractory, insubordinate, disruptive, errant, out of control, uncontrollable, wild, naughty; disorganized, unsystematic, unmethodical, lax, slapdash, slipshod, sloppy.

**undisguised** adjective *he regarded her with undisguised affection* OBVIOUS, evident, patent, manifest, transparent, overt, unconcealed, unhidden, unmistakable, undeniable, plain, clear, clear-cut, explicit, naked, visible; blatant, flagrant, glaring, bold.

**undisputed** adjective *his military preeminence was undisputed* UNCONTESTED, indubitable, undoubted, incontestable, unchallenged, incontrovertible, unequivocal, undeniable, irrefutable, unmistakable, sure, certain, definite, accepted, acknowledged, recognized. ANTONYM doubtful.

**undistinguished** adjective *an undistinguished career as a claims adjuster* UNEXCEPTIONAL, indifferent, run-of-the-mill, middle-of-the-road, ordinary, average, commonplace, mediocre, humdrum, lackluster, forgettable, uninspired, uneventful, unremarkable, inconsequential, featureless, nondescript, middling, moderate; *informal* garden-variety, by-the-numbers, nothing special, no great shakes, nothing to write home about, OK, so-so, 'comme ci, comme ça,' bush-league, blah, plain-vanilla. ANTONYM extraordinary.

**undo** verb **1** *he undid another button* UNFASTEN, unbutton, unhook, untie, unlace; unlock, unbolt; loosen, disentangle, extricate, release, detach, free, open; disconnect, disengage, separate. ANTONYM fasten.

**2** *they will undo a decision by the superior court* REVOKE, overrule, overturn, repeal, rescind, reverse, retract, countermand, cancel, annul, nullify, invalidate, void, negate; *Law* vacate; *formal* abrogate. ANTONYM ratify.

**3** *she undid much of the good work done* RUIN, undermine, subvert, overturn, scotch, sabotage, spoil, impair, mar, destroy, wreck, eradicate, obliterate; cancel out, neutralize, thwart, foil, frustrate, hamper, hinder, obstruct; *informal* blow, put the kibosh on, foul up, scuttle. ANTONYM enhance.

**undoing** noun **1** *she plotted the emperor's undoing* DOWNFALL, defeat, conquest, deposition, overthrow, ruin, ruination, elimination, end, collapse, failure, fall, fall from grace, debasement; Waterloo.

**2** *their complacency was their undoing* FATAL FLAW, Achilles heel, weakness, weak point, failing, nemesis, affliction, curse.

**undone** adjective **1** *some work was left undone* UNFINISHED, incomplete, half-done, unaccomplished, unfulfilled, unconcluded; omitted, neglected, disregarded, ignored; remaining, outstanding, deferred, pending, on ice; *informal* on the back burner. ANTONYM finished.

**2** *formal she had lost and was utterly undone* DONE FOR, finished, ruined, destroyed, doomed, lost, defeated, beaten; *informal* washed up, toast. ANTONYM successful.

**undoubted** adjective *their undoubted friendship* UNDISPUTED, unchallenged, unquestioned, indubitable, incontrovertible, irrefutable, incontestable, sure, certain, unmistakable; definite, accepted, acknowledged, recognized.

**undoubtedly** adverb *they are undoubtedly guilty* DOUBTLESS, indubitably, doubtlessly, no doubt, without (a) doubt, unquestionably, without question, indisputably, undeniably, incontrovertibly, clearly, obviously, patently, certainly, definitely, surely, of course, indeed. See note at CLEARLY.

**undress** verb *he undressed and got into bed* STRIP (OFF), disrobe, take off one's clothes, peel down. PHRASE: **in a state of undress** *she waltzed in while I was in a state of undress* NAKED, (in the) nude, bare, stripped, unclothed, undressed, unclad; *informal* in one's birthday suit, in the raw, in the buff, au naturel, buck-naked, butt-naked, mother-naked.

**undue** adjective *we didn't intend to add undue stress to your situation* EXCESSIVE, immoderate, intemperate, inordinate, disproportionate; uncalled for, unneeded, unnecessary, needless, unwarranted, unjustified, unreasonable; inappropriate, unmerited, unsuitable, improper. ANTONYM appropriate.

**unduly** adverb. See EXCESSIVELY.

**undying** adjective *his undying devotion to Aunt Myrna* ABIDING, lasting, enduring, permanent, constant, infinite; unceasing, perpetual, ceaseless, incessant, unending, never-ending, unfading, amaranthine; immortal, eternal, deathless.

**unearth** verb **1** *workers unearthed an artillery shell* DIG UP, excavate, exhume, disinter, root out, unbury.

**2** *I unearthed an interesting fact* DISCOVER, uncover, find, come across, stumble upon, hit on, bring to light, expose, turn up, hunt out.

**unearthly** adjective *an unearthly chill in the air* OTHERWORLDLY, supernatural, preternatural, alien; ghostly, spectral, phantom, mysterious, spine-chilling, hair-raising; uncanny, eerie, strange, weird, unnatural, bizarre, surreal; eldritch; *informal* spooky, creepy, scary. ANTONYM normal.

**uneasy** adjective **1** *the doctor made him feel uneasy* WORRIED, anxious, troubled, disturbed, agitated, rattled, nervous, tense, overwrought, edgy, jumpy, apprehensive, restless, discomfited, perturbed, fearful, uncomfortable, unsettled; *informal* jittery, antsy. ANTONYMS calm, at ease.

**2** *he had an uneasy feeling* WORRYING, disturbing, troubling, alarming, disquieting, unsettling, disconcerting, upsetting, nagging, niggling.

**3** *the victory ensured an uneasy peace* TENSE, awkward, strained, fraught; precarious, unstable, insecure. ANTONYM stable.

**unemotional** adjective *an effective clinician must remain unemotional when the patient is most out of control* RESERVED, undemonstrative, sober, restrained, passionless, perfunctory, emotionless, unsentimental, unexcitable, impassive, apathetic, phlegmatic, stoical, equable; cool, cold, frigid, unfeeling, callous.

**unemployed** adjective *most of my former colleagues are still unemployed* JOBLESS, out-of-work, between jobs, unwaged, unoccupied, laid off, idle; on welfare; *Brit.* redundant.

**unending** adjective *the unending noise from that construction site is making us crazy* ENDLESS, never-ending, interminable, perpetual, eternal, amaranthine, ceaseless, incessant, unceasing, nonstop, uninterrupted, continuous, continual, constant, persistent, recurring, unbroken, unabating, unremitting, relentless. See note at ETERNAL.

**unenviable** adjective DISAGREEABLE, nasty, unpleasant, undesirable, unfortunate, unlucky, horrible, thankless; unwanted.

**unequal** adjective **1** *they are unequal in length* DIFFERENT, dissimilar, unalike, unlike, disparate, unmatched, uneven, irregular, varying, variable, asymmetrical. ANTONYM identical.

2 *the unequal distribution of wealth* UNFAIR, unjust, disproportionate, inequitable, biased, askew. ANTONYM fair.

3 *an unequal contest* ONE-SIDED, uneven, unfair, ill-matched, unbalanced, lopsided, skewed. ANTONYMS evenly balanced, fair.

4 *she felt* ***unequal to*** *the task* INADEQUATE FOR, incapable of, unqualified for, unsuited to, incompetent at, not up to; *informal* not cut out for. ANTONYM competent.

**unequaled** adjective UNBEATEN, matchless, unmatched, unrivaled, unsurpassed, unparalleled, peerless, incomparable, inimitable, unique, second to none, in a class of its/one's own.

**unequivocal** adjective *the report's advice was unequivocal* UNAMBIGUOUS, unmistakable, indisputable, incontrovertible, indubitable, undeniable; clear, clear-cut, plain, plain-spoken, explicit, specific, categorical, straightforward, blunt, candid, emphatic, manifest. ANTONYM ambiguous.

**unethical** adjective IMMORAL, amoral, unprincipled, unscrupulous, dishonorable, dishonest, wrong, deceitful, unconscionable, unfair, fraudulent, underhanded, wicked, evil, sneaky, corrupt; unprofessional, improper.

**uneven** adjective 1 *uneven ground* BUMPY, rough, lumpy, stony, rocky, rugged, potholed, rutted, pitted, jagged. ANTONYMS flat, smooth.

2 *uneven teeth* IRREGULAR, unequal, unbalanced, misaligned, lopsided, askew, crooked, asymmetrical, unsymmetrical. ANTONYM regular.

3 *uneven quality* INCONSISTENT, variable, varying, fluctuating, irregular, erratic, patchy; choppy, unsteady. ANTONYM consistent.

4 *an uneven contest* ONE-SIDED, unequal, unfair, unjust, inequitable, ill-matched, unbalanced, David and Goliath. ANTONYM fair.

**uneventful** adjective *our flight was, thankfully, quite uneventful* UNEXCITING, uninteresting, monotonous, boring, dull, tedious, humdrum, routine, unvaried, ordinary, run-of-the-mill, pedestrian, mundane, predictable; *informal* blah. ANTONYM exciting.

**unexceptional** adjective *an adequate but unexceptional hotel* ORDINARY, average, typical, everyday, mediocre, run-of-the-mill, middle-of-the-road, indifferent; *informal* OK, blah, so-so, 'comme ci, comme ça,' nothing special, no great shakes, fair-to-middling.

**unexpected** adjective *an unexpected change in plans* UNFORESEEN, unanticipated, unpredicted, unlooked-for, sudden, abrupt, surprising, unannounced.

**unfair** adjective 1 *the trial was unfair* UNJUST, inequitable, prejudiced, biased, discriminatory; one-sided, unequal, uneven, unbalanced, partisan, partial, skewed. ANTONYM just.

2 *his comments were unfair* UNDESERVED, unmerited, uncalled for, unreasonable, unjustified. ANTONYM justified.

3 *unfair play* UNSPORTSMANLIKE, unsporting, dirty, below the belt, underhanded, dishonorable. ANTONYM sporting.

4 *you're being very unfair* INCONSIDERATE, thoughtless, insensitive, selfish, spiteful, mean, unkind, unreasonable; hypercritical, overcritical.

**unfaithful** adjective 1 *her husband had been unfaithful* ADULTEROUS, faithless, fickle, untrue, inconstant; unchaste, cheating, philandering, two-timing.

2 *an unfaithful friend* DISLOYAL, treacherous, traitorous, untrustworthy, unreliable, undependable, fair-weather, false, two-faced, double-crossing, deceitful; *literary* perfidious. ANTONYM loyal.

**unfamiliar** adjective 1 *an unfamiliar part of the city* UNKNOWN, new, strange, foreign, alien; unexplored, uncharted.

2 *the unfamiliar sounds* UNUSUAL, uncommon, unconventional, novel, different, exotic, unorthodox, odd, peculiar, curious, uncharacteristic, anomalous, abnormal, out of the ordinary.

3 *investors* ***unfamiliar with*** *the stock market* UNACQUAINTED WITH, unused to, unaccustomed to, unconversant with, unversed in, inexperienced in, uninformed of, unschooled in, unenlightened of, ignorant of, not cognizant of, new to, a stranger to.

**unfashionable** adjective *a pair of unfashionable shoes will ruin the whole look* OUT, out of date, outdated, old-fashioned, outmoded, out of style, dated, unstylish, passé, démodé, unhip, uncool, nerdy, dowdy, frumpy, lame, unsexy, old hat, square.

**unfasten** verb *Ron unfastened his belt* UNDO, open, disconnect, remove, untie, unbutton, unzip, unlash, loose, loosen, free, unlock, unbolt.

**unfavorable** adjective 1 *unfavorable comments* ADVERSE, critical, hostile, inimical, unfriendly, unsympathetic, negative, scathing; discouraging, disapproving, uncomplimentary, unflattering. ANTONYM positive.

2 *the unfavorable economic climate* GLOOMY, adverse, inauspicious, unpropitious, disadvantageous; unsuitable, inappropriate, inopportune. ANTONYM advantageous.

**unfeeling** adjective *humiliating Don in front of his children was an unfeeling thing to do* UNCARING, unsympathetic, unemotional, uncharitable; heartless, hard-hearted, hard, harsh, austere, cold, cold-hearted, cold-blooded, insensitive, callous. ANTONYM compassionate.

**unfit** adjective 1 *that party is* ***unfit to*** *govern* | ***unfit for*** *service* UNQUALIFIED, unsuitable, unsuited, inappropriate, unequipped, inadequate, not designed; incapable of, unable to, not up to, not equal to, unworthy of; *informal* not cut out for, not up to scratch. ANTONYM suitable.

2 *unfit and overweight children* UNHEALTHY, out of shape, in poor condition/shape. ANTONYM (physically) fit.

**unflattering** adjective 1 *an unflattering review* UNFAVORABLE, uncomplimentary, harsh, unsympathetic, critical, negative, hostile, scathing. ANTONYM complimentary.

2 *an unflattering dress* UNATTRACTIVE, unbecoming, unsightly, ugly, homely, plain, ill-fitting. ANTONYM becoming.

**unfold** verb 1 *May unfolded the map* OPEN OUT, spread out, flatten, straighten out, unroll, unfurl.

2 *I watched the events unfold* DEVELOP, evolve, happen, take place, occur, transpire, progress, play out.

**unforeseen** adjective *the problems with the bus were, of course, unforeseen* UNPREDICTED, unexpected, unanticipated, unplanned, not bargained for, surprising. ANTONYM expected.

**unforgettable** adjective *the trip to Indonesia was unforgettable* MEMORABLE, not/never to be forgotten, haunting, catchy; striking, impressive, outstanding, extraordinary, exceptional. ANTONYM unexceptional.

**unforgivable** adjective *he had committed the unforgivable sin—he had informed on his friends* INEXCUSABLE, unpardonable, unjustifiable, indefensible. ANTONYM venial.

**unfortunate** adjective 1 *unfortunate people* UNLUCKY, hapless, jinxed, out of luck, luckless, wretched, miserable, forlorn, poor, pitiful; *informal* down on one's luck. See note at HAPLESS. ANTONYM lucky.

2 *an unfortunate start to our vacation* ADVERSE, disadvantageous, unfavorable, unlucky, unwelcome, unpromising, inauspicious, unpropitious, bad; *formal* grievous. ANTONYM auspicious.

3 *an unfortunate remark* REGRETTABLE, inappropriate, unsuitable, infelicitous, unbecoming, inopportune, tactless, injudicious. ANTONYMS tactful, appropriate.

**unfounded** adjective *unfounded speculation* GROUNDLESS, baseless, unsubstantiated, unproven, unsupported, uncorroborated, unconfirmed, unverified, unattested, unjustified, without basis, without foundation; specious, speculative, conjectural, idle; false, untrue. ANTONYM proven.

**unfriendly** adjective 1 *an unfriendly look* HOSTILE, disagreeable, antagonistic, aggressive; ill-natured, unpleasant, surly, sour, uncongenial; inhospitable, unneighborly, unwelcoming, unkind, unsympathetic; unsociable, antisocial; aloof, stiff, cold, cool, frosty, distant, unapproachable; *informal* standoffish, starchy. ANTONYM amiable.

2 *an unfriendly wind* UNFAVORABLE, unhelpful, disadvantageous, unpropitious, inauspicious, hostile. ANTONYM favorable.

3 *environmentally unfriendly* HARMFUL, damaging, destructive, disrespectful.

**ungainly** adjective *they were as ungainly as fifth-grade boys taking dance lessons in a foot of snow* AWKWARD, clumsy, klutzy, ungraceful, graceless, inelegant, gawky, maladroit, gauche, uncoordinated; *archaic* lubberly. ANTONYM graceful.

**ungodly** adjective 1 *ungodly behavior* UNHOLY, godless, irreligious, impious, blasphemous, sacrilegious, profane; immoral, corrupt, depraved, sinful, wicked, evil, iniquitous.

2 *he called at an ungodly hour* UNREASONABLE, unsocial, antisocial, unearthly, godforsaken.

**ungrateful** adjective *she's been so generous to those ungrateful children* UNAPPRECIATIVE, unthankful, thankless, ungracious, churlish. ANTONYM thankful.

**unguarded** adjective 1 *an unguarded frontier* UNDEFENDED, unprotected, unfortified; vulnerable, insecure, open to attack.

2 *an unguarded remark* CARELESS, indiscreet, incautious, thoughtless, rash, reckless, foolhardy, foolish, imprudent, injudicious, ill-considered, ill-judged, insensitive; unwary, inattentive, off guard, distracted, absentminded; candid, open; *literary* temerarious.

**unhappy** adjective 1 *the unhappy boy cried all night* SAD, miserable, sorrowful, dejected, despondent, disconsolate, morose, broken-hearted, heartbroken, hurting, down, downcast, dispirited, downhearted, depressed, melancholy, mournful, gloomy, glum, lugubrious, despairing, doleful, forlorn, woebegone, woeful, long-faced, joyless, cheerless; *informal* down in the dumps, down in/at the mouth, blue. ANTONYM cheerful.

2 *in the unhappy event of litigation* UNFORTUNATE, unlucky, luckless; ill-starred, ill-fated, doomed; regrettable, lamentable; *informal* jinxed; *literary* star-crossed.

3 *I was unhappy with the service I received* DISSATISFIED, displeased, discontented, disappointed, disgruntled, angry; *informal* PO'd.

**unhealthy** adjective 1 *an unhealthy lifestyle* HARMFUL, detrimental, destructive, injurious, damaging, deleterious; malign, noxious, poisonous, insalubrious, baleful.

2 *an unhealthy pallor* SICKLY, ill, unwell, in poor health, ailing, sick, indisposed, weak, wan, sallow, frail, delicate, infirm, washed out, run-down.

3 *an unhealthy obsession with toenails* UNWHOLESOME, morbid, macabre, twisted, abnormal, warped, depraved, unnatural; *informal* sick, wrong.

**unheard of** adjective *these medical procedures were unheard of just ten years ago* UNPRECEDENTED, exceptional, extraordinary, out of the ordinary, unthought of, undreamed of, unbelievable, inconceivable, unimaginable, unthinkable; UNKNOWN, unfamiliar, new. ANTONYMS common, well-known.

**unheeded** adjective *he was soon reminded of his parents' unheeded warnings* DISREGARDED, ignored, neglected, overlooked, unnoted, unrecognized.

**unhinged** adjective *he was completely unhinged just because we were a few minutes late* DERANGED, demented, unbalanced, unglued, crazed, mad, insane, disturbed, out of one's mind, out of one's tree; *informal* crazy, mental, nutso, bonkers, batty, loopy, loco, postal, bananas, touched. ANTONYM sane.

**unholy** adjective 1 *a grin of unholy amusement* UNGODLY, godless, irreligious, impious, blasphemous, sacrilegious, pro-

fane, irreverent; wicked, evil, immoral, corrupt, depraved, sinful.

**2** *an unholy alliance* UNNATURAL, unusual, improbable, made in Hell.

**unhurried** adjective *we live at an unhurried pace around here* LEISURELY, easy, easygoing, relaxed, slow, deliberate, measured, calm. ANTONYM hasty.

**unidentified** adjective *an unidentified caller said he knew the whereabouts of Lyle* UNKNOWN, unnamed, anonymous, incognito, nameless, unfamiliar, strange, mysterious. ANTONYM known.

**unification** noun *the costs of German unification* UNION, merger, fusion, fusing, amalgamation, coalition, combination, confederation, federation, synthesis, joining.

**uniform** adjective **1** *a uniform temperature* CONSTANT, consistent, steady, invariable, unvarying, unfluctuating, unchanging, stable, static, regular, fixed, even, equal. ANTONYM variable.

**2** *pieces of uniform size* IDENTICAL, matching, similar, equal; same, like, homogeneous, consistent. ANTONYM varied.

▸ noun *a soldier in uniform* COSTUME, livery, regalia, suit, ensemble, outfit; colors; *informal* getup, monkey suit, rig, gear; *archaic* habit.

**uniformity** noun **1** *uniformity in tax law* CONSTANCY, consistency, conformity, invariability, stability, regularity, evenness, homogeneity, equality, harmony. ANTONYM variation.

**2** *a dull uniformity* MONOTONY, tedium, tediousness, dullness, dreariness, flatness, sameness. ANTONYM variety.

**unify** verb *he unified the confederacy into a powerful entity* UNITE, bring together, join (together), marry, merge, fuse, amalgamate, integrate, coalesce, combine, blend, mix, meld, bind, consolidate. ANTONYM separate.

**unimaginable** adjective *the phone bills have been unimaginable* UNTHINKABLE, inconceivable, indescribable, incredible, unbelievable, unheard of, unthought of, untold, mind-boggling, undreamed of, beyond one's wildest dreams.

**unimaginative** adjective *the biggest letdown is the dessert menu, which is quite unimaginative* UNINSPIRED, uninventive, unoriginal, uncreative, commonplace, pedestrian, mundane, institutional, ordinary, routine, matter-of-fact, humdrum, workaday, run-of-the-mill, by-the-numbers, hackneyed, trite, hoary.

**unimportant** adjective *the details are unimportant at this stage* INSIGNIFICANT, inconsequential, insubstantial, immaterial, trivial, minor, venial, trifling, of little/no importance, of little/no consequence, of no account, no-account, irrelevant, peripheral, extraneous, petty, paltry, derisory, weightless, small; *informal* piddling.

**uninhabited** adjective *most of the village has been uninhabited since the epidemic in the seventies* UNPOPULATED, unpeopled, unsettled, vacant, empty, unoccupied; unlived-in, untenanted.

**uninhibited** adjective **1** *uninhibited dancing* UNRESTRAINED, unrepressed, abandoned, wild, reckless; unrestricted, unmufflered, uncontrolled, unchecked, intemperate, wanton, loose; *informal* gung-ho. ANTONYM controlled.

**2** *I'm pretty uninhibited* UNRESERVED, unrepressed, liberated, unselfconscious, free and easy, free-spirited, relaxed, informal, open, outgoing, extrovert, outspoken, candid, frank, forthright; *informal* upfront, jiggy. ANTONYM repressed.

**unintelligible** adjective **1** *unintelligible sounds* INCOMPREHENSIBLE, indiscernible, mumbled, indistinct, unclear, slurred, inarticulate, incoherent, garbled.

**2** *unintelligible logic* IMPENETRABLE, baffling, perplexing, inscrutable, opaque, cryptic, abstruse, unfathomable, incoherent, incomprehensible, as clear as mud, impossible to follow.

**3** *unintelligible graffiti* ILLEGIBLE, indecipherable, unreadable, hieroglyphic.

**unintentional** adjective *I assure you, the insult was unintentional* UNINTENDED, accidental, inadvertent, involuntary, unwitting, unthinking, unpremeditated, unconscious; random, fortuitous, serendipitous, fluky. ANTONYM deliberate.

**uninterested** adjective *I couldn't live with someone **uninterested in** world affairs* INDIFFERENT TO, unconcerned with, incurious about, uninvolved with/in, apathetic to, lukewarm about, unenthusiastic about, bored with. See notes at DISINTERESTED.

**uninteresting** adjective *an uninteresting book about genealogy* UNEXCITING, boring, dull, tiresome, wearisome, soporific, tedious, jejune, lifeless, lackluster, humdrum, colorless, soulless, bland, insipid, banal, dry, dreary, drab, pedestrian, lacking; *informal* blah, samey. ANTONYM exciting.

**uninterrupted** adjective *an uninterrupted 55 minutes of your favorite music* UNBROKEN, continuous, continual, constant, nonstop, ceaseless; undisturbed, untroubled. ANTONYM intermittent.

**uninviting** adjective *the bed looked cold and uninviting* UNAPPEALING, unattractive, unappetizing, off-putting; bleak, cheerless, dreary, dismal, depressing, grim, inhospitable, forbidding. ANTONYM tempting.

**union** noun **1** *the union of art and nature* UNIFICATION, uniting, joining, merging, merger, fusion, fusing, amalgamation, coalition, combination, synthesis, blend, blending, mingling; MARRIAGE, wedding, alliance; coupling. ANTONYMS separation, parting.

**2** *the workers joined a union* ASSOCIATION, labor union, trade union, league, guild, confederation, federation, brotherhood, organization.

**unique** adjective **1** *each site is unique* DISTINCTIVE, distinct, individual, special, idiosyncratic; single, sole, lone, unrepeated, unrepeatable, solitary, exclusive, rare, uncommon, unusual, sui generis; *informal* one-off, one-of-a-kind, once-in-a-lifetime, one-shot.

**2** *a unique insight* REMARKABLE, special, singular, noteworthy, notable, extraordinary; unequaled, unparalleled, un-

matched, unsurpassed, unrivaled, peerless, nonpareil, incomparable; *formal* unexampled.

**3** *species unique to the island* PECULIAR, specific, limited.

**USAGE NOTE unique**

Strictly speaking, *unique* means "being one of a kind," not "unusual." Hence the phrases *very unique*, *quite unique*, *how unique*, and the like are slovenly. *The Oxford English Dictionary* notes that this tendency to hyperbole—to use *unique* when all that is meant is "uncommon, unusual, remarkable"—began in the nineteenth century. However old it is, the tendency is worth resisting.

Unless the thing is the only one of its kind, rarity does not make it unique. For instance, if a thing is one in a million, logically there would be two things in two million. Rare indeed but not unique. Who can demand responsible use of the language from an ad writer who is reckless enough to say, in a national advertisement, that a certain luxury sedan is "so unique, it's capable of thought"? And what are we to make of the following examples?

- "This year the consensus among the development executives seems to be that there are some fantastically funny, very exciting, very, very unique talents here." (*Time*; Aug. 16, 1993.)
- "Residents of college basketball's most unique unincorporated village were in place yesterday afternoon, the day before their Blue Devils will face North Carolina." (*New York Times*; Feb. 2, 1995.)

Arguably, our modern culture lacks and does not want absolutes, in intellectual life or in language. But stick with the uncomparable *unique*, and you may stand out as almost unique. —*BG*

**unison** PHRASE: **in unison** *they lifted their arms in unison* SIMULTANEOUSLY, at (one and) the same time, (all) at once, (all) together.

**unit** noun **1** *the family is the fundamental unit of society* COMPONENT, element, building block, constituent; subdivision.

**2** *a unit of currency* QUANTITY, measure, denomination.

**3** *a guerrilla unit* DETACHMENT, contingent, division, company, squadron, corps, regiment, brigade, platoon, battalion; cell, faction.

**unite** verb **1** *uniting the municipalities* UNIFY, join, link, connect, combine, amalgamate, fuse, weld, bond, wed, marry, bring together, knit together, splice. See note at JOIN. ANTONYM divide.

**2** *environmentalists and union activists united to demand changes* JOIN TOGETHER, join forces, combine, band together, ally, cooperate, collaborate, work together, pull together, team up, hitch up, hook up, twin. ANTONYM split.

**united** adjective **1** *a united Germany* UNIFIED, integrated, amalgamated, joined, merged; federal, confederate.

**2** *a united response* COMMON, shared, joint, combined, communal, cooperative, collective, collaborative, concerted; *Brit. informal* joined-up.

**3** *they were united in their views* UNANIMOUS, in agreement, agreed, in unison, of the same opinion, like-minded, as one, in accord, in harmony, in unity.

**unity** noun **1** *European unity* UNION, unification, integration, amalgamation; coalition, federation, confederation. ANTONYM division.

**2** *unity between alliance members* HARMONY, accord, cooperation, collaboration, agreement, consensus, solidarity; *formal* concord, concordance. ANTONYMS strife, discord.

**3** *the organic unity of the universe* ONENESS, singleness, wholeness, uniformity, homogeneity.

**universal** adjective *the universal features of language* GENERAL, ubiquitous, comprehensive, common, omnipresent, all-inclusive, all-embracing, across-the-board; global, worldwide, international, widespread; *formal* catholic.

**THE RIGHT WORD universal, catholic, common, ecumenical, general, generic**

Something that is **universal** applies to every case or individual in a class or category (*a universal practice among aboriginal tribesmen; a universal truth*). **General**, on the other hand, is less precise; it implies applicability to all or most of a group or class, whether the members of that group are clearly defined or only casually associated (*a drug that has come into general use among women but has not yet won the universal acceptance of doctors*). **Generic** is often used in place of *general* when referring to every member of a genus or clearly-defined scientific category (*a generic characteristic of insects*); with reference to language, it means referring to both men and women (*a generic pronoun*). **Common** implies participation or sharing by all members of a class (*a common interest in French culture*) or frequently occurring (*a common complaint*). **Catholic** implies a wide-ranging or inclusive attitude (*known for his catholic tastes in music*), while **ecumenical** means pertaining to the whole Christian church or promoting unity among religious groups or divisions (*an ecumenical marriage ceremony*).

**universally** adverb *it was universally accepted that no man married merely for love* GENERALLY, widely, commonly, across the board, all over.

**universe** noun **1** *the physical universe* COSMOS, macrocosm, totality; infinity, all existence, Creation; space, outer space, firmament.

**2** *the universe of computer hardware* WORLD, sphere, domain, preserve, milieu, province.

**unjust** adjective **1** *the assessment was unjust* UNFAIR, prejudiced, prejudicial, biased, inequitable, discriminatory, partisan, partial, one-sided, jaundiced. ANTONYM fair.

**2** *an unjust attack* WRONGFUL, unfair, undeserved, unmerited, unwarranted, uncalled for, unreasonable, unjustifiable, undue, gratuitous. ANTONYMS fair, reasonable.

**unjustifiable** adjective **1** *an unjustifiable extravagance* INDEFENSIBLE, inexcusable, unforgivable, unpardonable, uncalled for, gratuitous, without justification, unwarrantable; excessive, immoderate. ANTONYM reasonable.

**2** *an unjustifiable slur on his character* GROUNDLESS, unfounded, baseless, unsubstantiated, unconfirmed, uncorroborated, indefensible, irrational.

**unkempt** adjective *unkempt hair* UNTIDY, messy, scruffy, straggly, disordered, disheveled, disarranged, rumpled, windblown, ungroomed, bedraggled, in a mess, mussed, messed up; tousled, uncombed. ANTONYM tidy.

**unkind** adjective *everyone was being rude and unkind to him* UNCHARITABLE, unpleasant, disagreeable, nasty, mean, mean-spirited, cruel, vindictive, vicious, spiteful, malicious, callous, unsympathetic, unfeeling, uncaring, unsparing, hurtful, ill-natured, hard-hearted, cold-hearted; unfriendly, uncivil, inconsiderate, insensitive, hostile; *informal* bitchy, catty.

**unknown** adjective **1** *the future is unknown* UNCERTAIN, undisclosed, unrevealed, secret; undetermined, undecided, unresolved, unsettled, unsure, unascertained. ANTONYM decided.

**2** *unknown country* UNEXPLORED, uncharted, unmapped, untraveled, undiscovered, unfamiliar, unheard of, new, novel, strange. ANTONYM familiar.

**3** *persons unknown* UNIDENTIFIED, anonymous, unnamed, nameless; faceless, hidden. ANTONYMS identified, named.

**4** *unknown artists* OBSCURE, unrecognized, unheard of, unsung, overlooked, unheralded, minor, insignificant, unimportant. ANTONYM familiar.

▸ noun *the overseas ballots are a big unknown* MYSTERY, unknown quantity, uncertainty, ambiguity, variable, anyone's guess; *informal* crapshoot.

**unlawful** adjective *unlawful imports of drugs* ILLEGAL, illicit, illegitimate, against the law; criminal, felonious; prohibited, banned, outlawed, proscribed, forbidden. ANTONYM legal.

**unlike** preposition **1** *the familiar artichoke is totally unlike a Jerusalem artichoke* DIFFERENT FROM, dissimilar to. ANTONYM similar to.

**2** *unlike Bob, Regis enjoyed swing dancing* IN CONTRAST TO, as opposed to. ANTONYM similarly to.

▸ adjective *a meeting of unlike minds* DISSIMILAR, unalike, disparate, contrasting, antithetical, different, diverse, incongruous, heterogeneous, mismatched, divergent, at variance, varying, at odds; *informal* poles apart, like night and day, like apples and oranges.

**unlikely** adjective **1** *it is unlikely they will ever recover* IMPROBABLE, doubtful, dubious. ANTONYM probable.

**2** *an unlikely story* IMPLAUSIBLE, improbable, questionable, unconvincing, far-fetched, unrealistic, incredible, unbelievable, inconceivable, unimaginable; absurd, preposterous; *informal* tall. ANTONYM believable.

**unlimited** adjective **1** *unlimited supplies of water* INEXHAUSTIBLE, limitless, illimitable, boundless, immeasurable, incalculable, untold, infinite, endless, bottomless, never-ending. ANTONYM finite.

**2** *unlimited travel* UNRESTRICTED, unconstrained, unrestrained, unchecked, unbridled, uncurbed. ANTONYM restricted.

**3** *unlimited power* TOTAL, unqualified, unconditional, unrestricted, absolute, supreme. ANTONYMS conditional, restricted.

**unload** verb **1** *we unloaded the van* UNPACK, empty.

**2** *they unloaded the cases from the truck* REMOVE, offload, discharge.

**3** *the government unloaded its 20 percent stake* SELL, discard, jettison, offload, get rid of, dispose of; palm something off (on someone), foist something (on someone), fob something off (on someone); *informal* dump, ditch, get shut of.

**4** *she unloaded her troubles* DIVULGE, talk about, open up about, pour out, vent, give vent to, get something off one's chest.

**unlock** verb *I unlocked the door and led the way in* UNBOLT, unlatch, unbar, unfasten, open.

**unloved** adjective *Melanie felt lonely and unloved* UNWANTED, uncared-for, friendless, unvalued; rejected, unwelcome, shunned, spurned, neglected, abandoned.

**unlucky** adjective **1** *he was unlucky not to score* UNFORTUNATE, luckless, out of luck, jinxed, hapless, ill-fated, ill-starred, unhappy; *informal* down on one's luck; *literary* star-crossed. ANTONYM fortunate.

**2** *an unlucky number* UNFAVORABLE, inauspicious, unpropitious, ominous, cursed, ill-fated, ill-omened, disadvantageous, unfortunate. ANTONYM favorable.

**unmanageable** adjective **1** *the huge project was unmanageable* TROUBLESOME, awkward, inconvenient; cumbersome, bulky, unwieldy.

**2** *his behavior was becoming unmanageable* UNCONTROLLABLE, ungovernable, unruly, disorderly, out of hand, difficult, disruptive, undisciplined, wayward, refractory, restive; *archaic* contumacious.

**unmanly** adjective *he was on the verge of tears, but did not wish to appear unmanly* EFFEMINATE, effete, unmasculine, womanish, epicene; weak, limp-wristed, soft, timid, timorous; *informal* sissy, swishy, wimpish, wimpy, nancy, pansy, camp. ANTONYM virile.

**unmarried** adjective *all of my siblings are happily unmarried* SINGLE, unwed, unwedded; spinster, bachelor; unattached, available, eligible, free.

**unmistakable** adjective *the taste of ginger is unmistakable* DISTINCTIVE, distinct, telltale, indisputable, indubitable, undoubted, unambiguous, unequivocal; plain, clear, clear-cut, definite, obvious, unmissable, evident, self-evident, manifest, patent, pronounced, as plain as the nose on your face, as clear as day.

**unmitigated** adjective the raid was an unmitigated disaster ABSOLUTE, unqualified, categorical, complete, total, downright, outright, utter, out-and-out, undiluted, unequivocal, untempered, veritable, perfect, consummate, pure, sheer. See note at SEVERE.

**unmoved** adjective **1** *he was totally unmoved by her outburst* UNAFFECTED, untouched, unimpressed, aloof, cool, cold, dry-eyed; unconcerned, uncaring, unsympathetic, unreceptive, indifferent, impassive, unemotional, stoical, phlegmatic, equable, nonchalant; impervious (to), oblivious (to), heedless (of), deaf to.

2 *he remained unmoved on the crucial issues* STEADFAST, firm, unwavering, unswerving, resolved, resolute, decided, unswayed, uninfluenced, inflexible, unbending, intransigent, implacable, adamant.

**unnatural** adjective 1 *the life of a circus bear is completely unnatural* ABNORMAL, unusual, uncommon, extraordinary, strange, odd, peculiar, unorthodox, exceptional, irregular, atypical, untypical; freakish, freaky, uncanny. ANTONYM normal.

2 *a flash of unnatural color* ARTIFICIAL, man-made, synthetic, manufactured, inorganic, genetically engineered. ANTONYM genuine.

3 *unnatural vice* PERVERTED, warped, aberrant, twisted, deviant, depraved, degenerate; *informal* kinky, sick.

4 *her voice sounded unnatural* AFFECTED, artificial, mannered, stilted, forced, labored, strained, false, fake, theatrical, insincere, ersatz; *informal* put on, phony.

**unnecessary** adjective *extra blankets are unnecessary* UNNEEDED, nonessential, inessential, not required, uncalled for, useless, unwarranted, unwanted, undesired, dispensable, unimportant, optional, extraneous, gratuitous, expendable, noncore, disposable, redundant, pointless, purposeless. ANTONYM essential.

**unnerve** verb *the bleakness of his gaze unnerved her* DEMORALIZE, discourage, dishearten, dispirit, daunt, alarm, frighten, dismay, disconcert, discompose, perturb, upset, discomfit, take aback, unsettle, disquiet, fluster, agitate, shake, ruffle, throw off balance; *informal* rattle, faze, shake up, discombobulate. ANTONYM hearten.

**unobtrusive** adjective *she was unobtrusive and shy* INCONSPICUOUS, unnoticeable, low-key, discreet, circumspect, understated, unostentatious. ANTONYMS extrovert, conspicuous.

**unoccupied** adjective 1 *an unoccupied house* VACANT, empty, uninhabited, unlived-in, untenanted, abandoned; free, available. ANTONYM inhabited.

2 *an unoccupied territory* UNINHABITED, unpopulated, unpeopled, unsettled. ANTONYMS inhabited, populated.

3 *many young people were unoccupied* AT LEISURE, idle, free, with time on one's hands, at a loose end; unemployed, without work. ANTONYM busy.

**unofficial** adjective 1 *unofficial figures* UNCONFIRMED, unauthenticated, uncorroborated, unsubstantiated, provisional, off the record. ANTONYM confirmed.

2 *an unofficial committee* INFORMAL, casual; unauthorized, unsanctioned, unaccredited. ANTONYM formal.

**unorthodox** adjective *Hobson's unorthodox views denied him an academic career* UNCONVENTIONAL, unusual, radical, nonconformist, avant-garde, eccentric, maverick, strange, idiosyncratic; heterodox, heretical, dissenting; *informal* off-the-wall, way out, offbeat, kooky. ANTONYM conventional.

**unpalatable** adjective 1 *unpalatable food* UNAPPETIZING, unappealing, unsavory, inedible, uneatable; disgusting, rancid, revolting, nauseating, tasteless, flavorless, gross. ANTONYM tasty.

2 *the unpalatable truth* DISAGREEABLE, unpleasant, regrettable, unwelcome, lamentable, hard to swallow, hard to take.

**unparalleled** adjective *an unparalleled opportunity to change society* EXCEPTIONAL, unique, singular, rare, unequaled, unprecedented, without parallel, without equal, nonpareil, matchless, peerless, unrivaled, unsurpassed, unexcelled, incomparable, second to none; *formal* unexampled.

**unperturbed** adjective *Daniel was unperturbed by the outburst* UNTROUBLED, undisturbed, unworried, unconcerned, unmoved, unflustered, unruffled, undismayed, impassive; calm, composed, cool, collected, unemotional, self-possessed, self-assured, levelheaded, unfazed, nonplussed, laid-back.

**unpleasant** adjective 1 *a very unpleasant situation* DISAGREEABLE, irksome, troublesome, annoying, irritating, vexatious, displeasing, distressing, nasty, horrible, terrible, awful, dreadful, hateful, miserable, invidious, objectionable, offensive, obnoxious, repugnant, repulsive, repellent, revolting, disgusting, distasteful, nauseating, unsavory. ANTONYM agreeable.

2 *an unpleasant man* UNLIKABLE, unlovable, disagreeable; unfriendly, rude, impolite, obnoxious, nasty, spiteful, mean, mean-spirited; insufferable, unbearable, annoying, irritating. ANTONYM likable.

**unpopular** adjective *he was unpopular at school* DISLIKED, friendless, unliked, unloved, loathed, despised; unwelcome, avoided, ignored, rejected, outcast, shunned, spurned, cold-shouldered, ostracized; unfashionable, unhip, out.

**unprecedented** adjective *warfare on an unprecedented scale* UNHEARD OF, unknown, new, novel, groundbreaking, revolutionary, pioneering, epoch-making; unparalleled, unequaled, unmatched, unrivaled, without parallel, without equal, out of the ordinary, unusual, exceptional, singular, unique; *formal* unexampled.

**unpredictable** adjective 1 *unpredictable results* UNFORESEEABLE, uncertain, unsure, doubtful, dubious, iffy, dicey, in the balance, up in the air.

2 *unpredictable behavior* ERRATIC, moody, volatile, unstable, capricious, temperamental, mercurial, changeable, variable; 'on-again, off-again.'

**unpremeditated** adjective *she later regretted her unpremeditated response* UNPLANNED, spontaneous, unprepared, impromptu, spur-of-the-moment, unrehearsed, ad lib, improvised, extemporaneous; *informal* off-the-cuff, off the top of one's head. See note at SPONTANEOUS. ANTONYM planned.

**unpretentious** adjective 1 *he was thoroughly unpretentious* UNAFFECTED, modest, unassuming, without airs, natural, straightforward, open, honest, sincere, frank, ingenuous.

**2** *an unpretentious hotel* SIMPLE, plain, modest, humble, unostentatious, unsophisticated, folksy, no-frills.

**unprincipled** adjective *he is an unprincipled opportunist* IMMORAL, unethical, amoral, unscrupulous, Machiavellian, dishonorable, dishonest, deceitful, devious, corrupt, crooked, wicked, evil, villainous, shameless, base, low; libertine, licentious. ANTONYM ethical.

**unproductive** adjective **1** *unproductive soil* INFERTILE, sterile, barren, arid, unfruitful, poor. ANTONYM fertile.

**2** *unproductive meetings* FRUITLESS, futile, vain, idle, useless, worthless, valueless, pointless, ineffective, ineffectual, unprofitable, unrewarding. ANTONYM fruitful.

**unprofessional** adjective **1** *unprofessional conduct* IMPROPER, unethical, unprincipled, unscrupulous, dishonorable, disreputable, unseemly, unbecoming, indecorous.

**2** *you don't want to hire unprofessional roofers* AMATEURISH, amateur, unskilled, unskillful, inexpert, unqualified, inexperienced, incompetent, second-rate, inefficient.

**unpromising** adjective *they were not deterred by this unpromising start* INAUSPICIOUS, unfavorable, unpropitious, discouraging, disheartening, gloomy, bleak, black, portentous, ominous, ill-omened. ANTONYM auspicious.

**unqualified** adjective **1** *an unqualified accountant* UNTRAINED, inexperienced; unlicensed, quack.

**2** *those unqualified to look after children* UNSUITABLE, unsuited, unfit, ineligible, incompetent, unable, incapable, unprepared, ill-equipped, ill-prepared.

**3** *unqualified support* UNCONDITIONAL, unreserved, unlimited, without reservations, categorical, unequivocal, unambiguous, wholehearted; complete, absolute, downright, undivided, total, utter.

**unquestionable** adjective *the sincerity of his beliefs is unquestionable* INDUBITABLE, undoubted, beyond question, beyond doubt, indisputable, undeniable, irrefutable, incontestable, incontrovertible, unequivocal; certain, sure, definite, self-evident, evident, manifest, obvious, apparent, patent.

**unravel** verb **1** *he unraveled the strands* UNTANGLE, disentangle, separate out, unwind, untwist, unsnarl, unthread. ANTONYM entangle.

**2** *detectives are trying to unravel the mystery* SOLVE, resolve, clear up, puzzle out, unscramble, get to the bottom of, explain, clarify, make head(s) or tail(s) of; figure out, dope out. ANTONYM complicate.

**3** *society is starting to unravel* FALL APART, fail, collapse, go wrong, deteriorate, go downhill, fray. ANTONYM succeed.

**unreal** adjective **1** *an unreal world of monsters and fairies* IMAGINARY, fictitious, pretend, make-believe, made-up, dreamed-up, mock, false, illusory, chimerical, mythical, fanciful; hypothetical, theoretical; *informal* phony.

**2** *informal that roller coaster was totally unreal* INCREDIBLE, fantastic, unbelievable, out of this world.

**unrealistic** adjective **1** *unrealistic expectations* IMPRACTICAL, impracticable, unfeasible, nonviable; unreasonable, irrational, illogical, senseless, silly, foolish, fanciful, idealistic, quixotic, romantic, starry-eyed, blue-sky, pie in the sky; *chiefly Brit. informal* airy-fairy. ANTONYM pragmatic.

**2** *unrealistic images* UNLIFELIKE, nonrealistic, unnatural, nonrepresentational, abstract; unbelievable, implausible. ANTONYM lifelike.

**unreasonable** adjective **1** *an unreasonable officer* UNCOOPERATIVE, unhelpful, disobliging, unaccommodating, awkward, contrary, difficult; obstinate, obdurate, willful, headstrong, pigheaded, cussed, intractable, intransigent, inflexible; irrational, illogical, prejudiced, intolerant.

**2** *unreasonable demands* UNACCEPTABLE, preposterous, outrageous, ridiculous; excessive, impossible, immoderate, disproportionate, undue, inordinate, intolerable, unjustified, unwarranted, uncalled for. See note at ABSURD.

**unrefined** adjective **1** *unrefined clay* UNPROCESSED, untreated, crude, raw, natural, unprepared, unfinished. ANTONYM processed.

**2** *unrefined people* UNCULTURED, uncultivated, uncivilized, uneducated, unsophisticated; boorish, lumpen, oafish, loutish, coarse, vulgar, rude, rough, uncouth. ANTONYM cultured.

**unrelenting** adjective **1** *the unrelenting heat* CONTINUAL, constant, continuous, relentless, unremitting, unabating, unflagging, uninterrupted, unrelieved, incessant, unceasing, ceaseless, endless, unending, persistent, nonstop. ANTONYM intermittent.

**2** *an unrelenting opponent* IMPLACABLE, inflexible, uncompromising, unyielding, unbending, relentless, determined, dogged, tenacious, steadfast, tireless, indefatigable, unflagging, unshakable, unswerving, unwavering.

**unreliable** adjective **1** *unreliable volunteers* UNDEPENDABLE, untrustworthy, irresponsible, fickle, fair-weather, capricious, erratic, unpredictable, inconstant, faithless, temperamental; *informal* hinky. See note at TRUSTWORTHY.

**2** *an unreliable indicator* QUESTIONABLE, open to doubt, doubtful, dubious, suspect, unsound, tenuous, uncertain, fallible; risky, chancy, inaccurate; *informal* iffy, dicey.

**unrepentant** adjective *how can you expect to be forgiven if you're unrepentant?* REMORSELESS, unrepenting, impenitent, unashamed, shameless, unapologetic, unabashed.

**unreserved** adjective **1** *unreserved support* UNCONDITIONAL, unqualified, without reservations, unlimited, categorical, unequivocal, unambiguous; absolute, complete, thorough, wholehearted, full, total, utter, undivided. ANTONYM qualified.

**2** *unreserved seats* NOT BOOKED, unallocated, unoccupied, free, empty, vacant, available. ANTONYM booked.

**unresolved** adjective *as long as this issue is unresolved we cannot move ahead* UNDECIDED, unsettled, undetermined, uncertain, open, pending, open to debate/question, moot, doubtful, on the table, in play, in doubt, up in the air. ANTONYM decided.

**unrest** noun *social unrest* DISRUPTION, disturbance, trouble, turmoil, turbulence, disorder, chaos, anarchy; discord, disquiet, dissension, dissent, strife, protest, rebellion, uprising, rioting. ANTONYM peace.

**unrestricted** adjective *this area is reserved for unrestricted play* UNLIMITED, open, free, freewheeling, clear, unhindered, unimpeded, unhampered, unchecked, unqualified, unrestrained, unconstrained, unblocked, unbounded, unconfined, rampant. ANTONYM limited.

**unrivaled** adjective *an unrivaled collection of rare coins* UNEQUALED, without equal, unparalleled, without parallel, unmatched, unsurpassed, unexcelled, incomparable, beyond compare, inimitable, second to none, nonpareil.

**unruly** adjective *I can't take care of your unruly brats* DISORDERLY, rowdy, wild, unmanageable, uncontrollable, disobedient, disruptive, undisciplined, restive, wayward, willful, headstrong, irrepressible, obstreperous, difficult, intractable, out of hand, recalcitrant; boisterous, lively, rambunctious, refractory; *archaic* contumacious. ANTONYM disciplined.

**unsaid** adjective *our unsaid feelings for one another* UNSPOKEN, unuttered, unstated, unexpressed, unvoiced, suppressed; tacit, implicit, not spelled out, implied; understood, inferred.

**unsavory** adjective **1** *unsavory portions of food* UNPALATABLE, unappetizing, distasteful, disagreeable, unappealing, repugnant, off-putting, unattractive; inedible, uneatable, disgusting, revolting, nauseating, sickening, foul, raunchy, nasty, vile; tasteless, bland, flavorless; *informal* yucky. ANTONYMS tasty, appetizing.

**2** *an unsavory character* DISREPUTABLE, unpleasant, undesirable, disagreeable, nasty, mean, rough; immoral, degenerate, dishonorable, dishonest, unprincipled, unscrupulous, low, villainous; *informal* shady, crooked. ANTONYM reputable.

**unscrupulous** adjective *we didn't want to believe that someone in our group could be that unscrupulous* UNPRINCIPLED, unethical, immoral, conscienceless, shameless, reprobate, exploitative, corrupt, dishonest, dishonorable, deceitful, devious, underhanded, unsavory, disreputable, evil, wicked, villainous, Machiavellian; *informal* crooked, shady, hinky; *dated* dastardly.

**unseat** verb **1** *the horse unseated his rider* DISLODGE, throw, dismount, upset, unhorse.

**2** *an attempt to unseat the party leader* DEPOSE, oust, remove from office, topple, overthrow, bring down, overturn, eject, dislodge, supplant; usurp.

**unseemly** adjective *their unseemly behavior at Donna's baby shower* IMPROPER, unbecoming, unfitting, unbefitting, unworthy, undignified, indiscreet, indelicate, indecorous, ungentlemanly, unladylike. ANTONYM decorous.

**unselfish** adjective *his unselfish motives* ALTRUISTIC, selfless, self-denying, self-sacrificing; generous, giving, magnanimous, philanthropic, public-spirited, charitable, benevolent, caring, kind, considerate, thoughtful, noble.

**unsettle** verb *all this talk of death was unsettling him* UNNERVE, upset, disturb, disquiet, perturb, discomfit, disconcert, alarm, dismay, trouble, bother, agitate, fluster, ruffle, shake (up), throw, unbalance, destabilize; *informal* rattle, faze, pull the rug (out) from under.

**unsettled** adjective **1** *an unsettled life* AIMLESS, directionless, purposeless, without purpose; rootless, nomadic.

**2** *an unsettled child* RESTLESS, restive, fidgety, anxious, worried, troubled, fretful; agitated, ruffled, uneasy, disconcerted, discomposed, unnerved, ill at ease, edgy, on edge, tense, nervous, apprehensive, disturbed, perturbed, unstrung; *informal* rattled, fazed.

**3** *unsettled weather* CHANGEABLE, changing, variable, varying, inconstant, inconsistent, ever-changing, erratic, unstable, undependable, unreliable, uncertain, unpredictable, protean.

**4** *the question is still unsettled* UNDECIDED, to be decided, unresolved, undetermined, moot, uncertain, open to debate, doubtful, in doubt, up in the air, in a state of uncertainty.

**5** *the debt remains unsettled* UNPAID, payable, outstanding, owing, owed, to be paid, due, undischarged, delinquent, past due.

**6** *unsettled areas* UNINHABITED, unpopulated, unpeopled, unoccupied, desolate, lonely.

**unshakable** adjective *she finally came to trust Hal's unshakable love* STEADFAST, resolute, staunch, firm, decided, determined, unswerving, unwavering; unyielding, inflexible, dogged, obstinate, obdurate, tenacious, persistent, indefatigable, tireless, unflagging, unremitting, unrelenting, relentless.

**unsightly** adjective *unsightly stains on the wall* UGLY, unattractive, unprepossessing, unlovely, disagreeable, displeasing, hideous, horrible, repulsive, revolting, offensive, grotesque, monstrous, gross, ghastly. ANTONYM attractive.

**unskilled** adjective *the unskilled workforce* UNTRAINED, unqualified; manual, blue-collar, laboring, menial; inexpert, inexperienced, unpracticed, amateurish, unprofessional.

**unsociable** adjective *we found him to be stiff and unsociable* UNFRIENDLY, uncongenial, unneighborly, unapproachable, introverted, reticent, reserved, withdrawn, aloof, distant, remote, detached, unsocial, antisocial, asocial, taciturn, silent, quiet; *informal* standoffish. ANTONYM friendly.

**unsolicited** adjective *their unsolicited opinions* UNINVITED, unsought, unasked-for, unrequested.

**unsophisticated** adjective **1** *she seemed a bit unsophisticated* UNWORLDLY, naive, unrefined, simple, innocent, ignorant, green, immature, callow, inexperienced, childlike, artless, guileless, ingenuous, natural, unaffected, unassuming, unpretentious; *informal* cheesy. See note at GULLIBLE.

**2** *unsophisticated software* SIMPLE, crude, low-tech, basic, rudimentary, primitive, rough and ready, homespun, bush-league; straightforward, uncomplicated, uninvolved.

**unsound** adjective **1** *structurally unsound* WEAK, rickety, flimsy, wobbly, unstable, crumbling, damaged, rotten, ramshackle, shoddy, insubstantial, unsafe, dangerous. ANTONYM strong.

**2** *this plan appears unsound* UNTENABLE, flawed, defective, faulty, ill-founded, flimsy, unreliable, questionable, dubious, tenuous, suspect, fallacious, fallible; *informal* iffy.

**3** *of unsound mind* DISORDERED, deranged, disturbed, demented, unstable, unbalanced, unhinged, addled, insane. ANTONYM sane.

**unspeakable** adjective **1** *unspeakable delights* INDESCRIBABLE, beyond description, inexpressible, unutterable, indefinable, unimaginable, inconceivable.

**2** *an unspeakable crime* HORRIFIC, awful, appalling, dreadful, horrifying, horrendous, abominable, frightful, fearful, shocking, ghastly, gruesome, monstrous, heinous, egregious, deplorable, despicable, execrable, vile.

**unspoiled** adjective *the unspoiled landscape* IMMACULATE, perfect, pristine, virgin, unimpaired, unblemished, unharmed, unflawed, undamaged, untouched, unmarked, untainted, as good as new/before.

**unspoken** adjective *they had an unspoken understanding* UNSTATED, unexpressed, unuttered, unsaid, unvoiced, unarticulated, undeclared, not spelt out; tacit, implicit, implied, understood, unwritten. ANTONYM explicit.

**unstable** adjective **1** *that old ladder looks unstable* UNSTEADY, rocky, wobbly, tippy; rickety, shaky, unsafe, insecure, precarious. ANTONYM steady.

**2** *unstable coffee prices* CHANGEABLE, volatile, variable, fluctuating, irregular, unpredictable, capricious, erratic, 'on-again, off-again.' ANTONYMS fixed, firm.

**3** *he was mentally unstable* UNBALANCED, of unsound mind, mentally ill, deranged, demented, disturbed, unhinged, volatile; *informal* kooky. ANTONYMS balanced, of sound mind.

**unstudied** adjective *his unstudied grace* NATURAL, easy, spontaneous, unaffected, unforced, uncontrived, unstilted, unpretentious, ingenuous, without airs, artless.

**unsubstantiated** adjective *unsubstantiated rumors* UNCONFIRMED, unsupported, uncorroborated, unverified, unattested, unproven; unfounded, groundless, baseless, without foundation, unjustified.

**unsuccessful** adjective **1** *an unsuccessful attempt* FAILED, ineffective, fruitless, profitless, unproductive, abortive; vain, futile, useless, pointless, worthless, luckless.

**2** *an unsuccessful business* UNPROFITABLE, loss-making.

**3** *an unsuccessful candidate* FAILED, losing, beaten; unlucky, out of luck; *informal* losingest.

**unsuitable** adjective **1** *the product is unsuitable for your needs* INAPPROPRIATE, unsuited, wrong, ill-suited, inapt, inapplicable, unacceptable, unfitting, unbefitting, incompatible, out of place, out of keeping, misplaced; *formal* inapposite. ANTONYM appropriate.

**2** *an unsuitable moment for belching* INOPPORTUNE, infelicitous, inappropriate, wrong, unfortunate; *formal* malapropos. ANTONYM opportune.

**unsung** adjective *no victory is without its unsung heroes* UNACKNOWLEDGED, uncelebrated, unacclaimed, unapplauded, unhailed, unheralded; neglected, unrecognized, overlooked, forgotten. ANTONYM celebrated.

**unsure** adjective **1** *she felt very unsure* UNCONFIDENT, unassertive, insecure, hesitant, diffident, anxious, apprehensive. ANTONYM confident.

**2** *Sally was unsure what to do* UNDECIDED, irresolute, dithering, equivocating, vacillating, of two minds, wishy-washy, in a quandary. ANTONYM decided.

**3** *some teachers are unsure about the proposed strike* DUBIOUS, doubtful, skeptical, uncertain, unconvinced. ANTONYM convinced.

**4** *the date is unsure* NOT FIXED, undecided, uncertain. ANTONYM fixed.

**unsuspecting** adjective *it's a trap deliberately set for unsuspecting first-time buyers* UNSUSPICIOUS, unwary, unaware, unconscious, ignorant, unwitting; trusting, gullible, credulous, ingenuous, naive, wide-eyed. ANTONYM wary.

**unsympathetic** adjective **1** *unsympathetic staff* UNCARING, unconcerned, unfriendly, unfeeling, apathetic, insensitive, indifferent, unkind, pitiless, thoughtless, heartless, hard-hearted, stony, callous. ANTONYM caring.

**2** *the government was* ***unsympathetic to*** *these views* OPPOSED TO, against, (dead) set against, antagonistic to, ill-disposed to; *informal* anti.

**3** *an unsympathetic character* UNLIKABLE, dislikable, disagreeable, unpleasant, unappealing, off-putting, objectionable, unsavory; unfriendly. ANTONYM likable.

**untangle** verb **1** *I untangled the fishing tackle* DISENTANGLE, unravel, unsnarl, straighten out, untwist, untwine, unknot.

**2** *untangling a mystery* SOLVE, find the/an answer to, resolve, puzzle out, work out, fathom, clear up, clarify, get to the bottom of; *informal* figure out.

**untenable** adjective *these untenable explanations are not helping your case* INDEFENSIBLE, insupportable, unsustainable, unjustified, unjustifiable, flimsy, weak, shaky.

**unthinkable** adjective *winning the lottery is just too unthinkable* UNIMAGINABLE, inconceivable, unbelievable, incredible, beyond belief, implausible, preposterous.

**unthinking** adjective **1** *an unthinking lout* THOUGHTLESS, inconsiderate, insensitive; tactless, undiplomatic, indiscreet. ANTONYM thoughtful.

**2** *an unthinking remark* ABSENTMINDED, heedless, thoughtless, careless, injudicious, imprudent, unwise, foolish, reckless, rash, precipitate; involuntary, inadvertent, unintentional, spontaneous, impulsive, unpremeditated. ANTONYM intentional.

**untidy** adjective **1** *untidy hair* SCRUFFY, tousled, disheveled, unkempt, messy, disordered, disarranged, messed up, rumpled, bedraggled, uncombed, ungroomed, straggly, ruffled, tangled, matted, wind-blown, raddled; *informal* mussed up, raggedy. ANTONYM neat.

**2** *the room was untidy* DISORDERED, messy, in a mess, disorderly, disorganized, in disorder, cluttered, in a muddle, muddled, in chaos, chaotic, haywire, topsy-turvy, in disarray, at sixes and sevens; *informal* higgledy-piggledy. ANTONYMS neat, orderly.

**untie** verb *untie the team of horses* UNDO, unknot, unbind, unfasten, unlace, untether, unhitch, unmoor; (turn) loose, (set) free, release, let go, unshackle.

**untimely** adjective **1** *an untimely interruption* ILL-TIMED, badly timed, mistimed; inopportune, inappropriate, unseasonable; inconvenient, unwelcome, infelicitous; *formal* malapropos. ANTONYM opportune.

**2** *his untimely death* PREMATURE, (too) early, too soon, before time, unexpected. ANTONYM expected.

**untiring** adjective *these kids have been untiring in their efforts to get to the championship* VIGOROUS, energetic, determined, resolute, enthusiastic, keen, zealous, spirited, dogged, tenacious, persistent, persevering, staunch; tireless, unflagging, unfailing, unfaltering, unwavering, indefatigable, unrelenting, unswerving; *formal* pertinacious.

**untold** adjective **1** *untold quantities* BOUNDLESS, immeasurable, incalculable, limitless, unlimited, infinite, measureless; countless, innumerable, endless, numberless, uncountable; numerous, many, multiple; *literary* multitudinous, myriad. ANTONYM limited.

**2** *the untold story* UNREPORTED, overlooked, ignored; hidden, secret, unrecounted, unrevealed, undisclosed, undivulged, unpublished.

**untoward** adjective **1** *an untoward occurrence* INCONVENIENT, unlucky, unexpected, unforeseen, surprising, unusual; unwelcome, unfavorable, adverse, unfortunate, infelicitous; *formal* malapropos.

**2** *untoward behavior* IMPROPER, unseemly; perverse.

**untroubled** adjective *they all thought I was untroubled, but I was really falling to pieces* UNWORRIED, unperturbed, unconcerned, unruffled, undismayed, unbothered, unalarmed, unflustered; insouciant, nonchalant, composed, blasé, carefree, calm, serene, tranquil, relaxed, halcyon, comfortable, at ease, happy-go-lucky, blissful, laid-back, mellow; *informal* supercool.

**untrue** adjective **1** *these suggestions are totally untrue* FALSE, untruthful, fabricated, made up, invented, concocted, trumped up; erroneous, wrong, incorrect, inaccurate; fallacious, fictitious, unsound, unfounded, baseless, misguided. ANTONYM correct.

**2** *he was untrue to his friends* UNFAITHFUL, disloyal, faithless, false, treacherous, traitorous, deceitful, deceiving, duplicitous, double-dealing, insincere, unreliable, undependable, inconstant; *informal* two-timing; *literary* perfidious. ANTONYM faithful.

**untrustworthy** adjective *the group's untrustworthy treasurer* DISHONEST, deceitful, double-dealing, treacherous, traitorous, two-faced, duplicitous, mendacious, dishonorable, unprincipled, unscrupulous, corrupt, slippery; unreliable, undependable, fly-by-night, capricious, fickle; *informal* hinky. ANTONYM reliable.

**untruth** noun **1** *a patent untruth* LIE, falsehood, fib, fabrication, invention, falsification, half-truth, exaggeration; story, myth, piece of fiction; *informal* tall story, fairy tale, cock-and-bull story, whopper.

**2** *the total untruth of the story* FALSITY, falsehood, falseness, untruthfulness, fictitiousness; fabrication, dishonesty, deceit, deceitfulness, inaccuracy, unreliability.

**untruthful** adjective **1** *the answers may be untruthful* FALSE, untrue, fabricated, made up, invented, trumped up; erroneous, wrong, incorrect, inaccurate, fallacious, fictitious.

**2** *an untruthful person* LYING, mendacious, dishonest, deceitful, duplicitous, false, double-dealing, two-faced, untrustworthy, dishonorable; *informal* crooked; *literary* perfidious. ANTONYM honest.

**unusual** adjective *an unusual color for a marigold* UNCOMMON, abnormal, atypical, unexpected, surprising, unfamiliar, different; strange, odd, curious, out of the ordinary, extraordinary, unorthodox, unconventional, outlandish, singular, special, unique, peculiar, bizarre; rare, scarce, few and far between, thin on the ground, exceptional, isolated, occasional, infrequent; *informal* weird, offbeat, out there, freaky. ANTONYM common.

**unutterable** adjective. See UNSPEAKABLE.

**unveil** verb *this afternoon they are unveiling the details of yesterday's invasion* REVEAL, present, display, show, exhibit, put on display; release, launch, bring out; disclose, divulge, make known, make public, publish, broadcast, communicate.

**unwarranted** adjective **1** *the criticism is unwarranted* UNJUSTIFIED, uncalled for, unnecessary, unreasonable, unjust, groundless, excessive, gratuitous, immoderate, disproportionate, undue, unconscionable, unjustifiable, indefensible, inexcusable, unforgivable, unpardonable. ANTONYM justified.

**2** *an unwarranted invasion of privacy* UNAUTHORIZED, unsanctioned, unapproved, uncertified, unlicensed; illegal, unlawful, illicit, illegitimate. ANTONYM legal.

**unwelcome** adjective **1** *I was made to feel unwelcome* UNWANTED, uninvited, unaccepted, excluded, rejected.

**2** *even a small increase is unwelcome* UNDESIRABLE, undesired, unpopular, unfortunate, disappointing, upsetting, distressing, disagreeable, displeasing; regrettable, deplorable, objectionable, lamentable.

**unwell** adjective *I felt unwell as soon as we hit the open sea*

ILL, sick, indisposed, ailing, not (very) well, not too good, lousy, bad, rough, not oneself, under/below par, groggy, peaked, queasy, woozy, nauseous, nauseated; off, poorly, wretched, dead; under the weather; funny, weird; *informal* crappy, pukey.

**unwieldy** adjective *an unwieldy trunk full of old clothes* CUMBERSOME, unmanageable, unmaneuverable; awkward, clumsy, massive, heavy, hefty, ponderous, bulky, weighty. ANTONYM manageable.

**unwilling** adjective **1** *unwilling conscripts* RELUCTANT, unenthusiastic, hesitant, resistant, grudging, involuntary, forced. ANTONYM keen.

**2** *he was unwilling to take on that responsibility* DISINCLINED, reluctant, averse, loath; (**be unwilling to do something**) not have the heart to, balk at, refuse to, demur at, shy away from, flinch from, shrink from, have qualms about, have misgivings about, have reservations about. ANTONYM keen.

**unwind** verb **1** *Ella unwound the scarf from her neck* UNROLL, uncoil, unravel, untwine, untwist, disentangle, open (out), straighten (out).

**2** *he liked to unwind after work* RELAX, loosen up, ease up/off, slow down, de-stress, unbend, rest, put one's feet up, sit back, take it easy, take a load off; *informal* wind down, mellow (out), let it all hang out, veg, hang loose, chill (out).

**unwise** adjective *it would have been unwise to argue* INJUDICIOUS, ill-advised, ill-judged, imprudent, inexpedient, foolish, silly, inadvisable, impolitic, misguided, foolhardy, irresponsible, impetuous, rash, hasty, overhasty, reckless. ANTONYM sensible.

**unwitting** adjective **1** *an unwitting accomplice* UNKNOWING, unconscious, unsuspecting, oblivious, unaware, innocent, in the dark. ANTONYM knowing.

**2** *an unwitting mistake* UNINTENTIONAL, unintended, inadvertent, involuntary, unconscious, accidental. ANTONYM conscious.

**unworldly** adjective **1** *a gauche, unworldly girl* NAIVE, simple, inexperienced, innocent, green, raw, callow, immature, ignorant, gullible, ingenuous, artless, guileless, childlike, trusting, credulous; nonmaterialistic.

**2** *unworldly beauty* UNEARTHLY, otherworldly, ethereal, ghostly, preternatural, supernatural, paranormal, mystical.

**unworthy** adjective **1** *he was unworthy of trust* UNDESERVING, ineligible, unqualified, unfit. ANTONYM deserving.

**2** *unworthy behavior* UNBECOMING, unsuitable, inappropriate, unbefitting, unfitting, unseemly, improper; discreditable, shameful, dishonorable, despicable, ignoble, contemptible, reprehensible. ANTONYM becoming.

**upbraid** verb *we were upbraided for leaving the back door unlocked* REPRIMAND, rebuke, admonish, chastise, chide, reprove, reproach, scold, berate, take to task, lambaste, give someone a piece of one's mind, give someone a tongue-lashing, rake/haul over the coals, lecture; *informal* tell off, give someone a talking-to, tear a strip off (of), dress down, give someone an earful, rap over the knuckles, bawl out, lay into, chew out, ream out; *formal* castigate; *rare* reprehend. See note at SCOLD.

**upbringing** noun *tell us a little about your upbringing* CHILDHOOD, early life, formative years, teaching, education, instruction, tutelage, care, rearing, raising, breeding.

**upgrade** verb **1** *there are plans to upgrade the rail system* IMPROVE, modernize, update, bring up to date, make better, ameliorate, reform; rehabilitate, recondition, refurbish, spruce up, renovate, rejuvenate, overhaul; bring up to code. ANTONYM downgrade.

**2** *he was upgraded to a seat in the cabinet* PROMOTE, give promotion to, elevate, move up, raise. ANTONYM demote.

**upheaval** noun *the upheaval caused by wartime evacuation* DISRUPTION, disturbance, trouble, turbulence, disorder, confusion, turmoil, pandemonium, chaos, mayhem, cataclysm, shakeup, debacle; revolution, change, craziness.

**uphill** adjective **1** *an uphill path* UPWARD, rising, ascending, climbing. ANTONYM downhill.

**2** *an uphill struggle* ARDUOUS, difficult, hard, tough, taxing, demanding, exacting, stiff, formidable, exhausting, tiring, wearisome, laborious, grueling, back-breaking, punishing, burdensome, onerous, Herculean; *informal* no picnic, killing; *archaic* toilsome. ANTONYM easy.

**uphold** verb **1** *the court upheld his claim for damages* CONFIRM, endorse, sustain, approve, agree to, support; champion, defend. ANTONYMS overturn, oppose.

**2** *they've a tradition to uphold* MAINTAIN, sustain, continue, preserve, protect, champion, defend, keep, hold to, keep alive, keep going, back (up), stand by. ANTONYM abandon.

**upkeep** noun *the upkeep of the kennel can be quite expensive* MAINTENANCE, repair(s), service, servicing, preservation, conservation; running; care, support, keep, subsistence.

**uplift** verb *she needs something to uplift her spirits* BOOST, raise, buoy up, lift, cheer up, perk up, enliven, brighten up, lighten, stimulate, inspire, revive, restore; *informal* buck up.

**upper** adjective **1** *the upper floor* HIGHER, superior; top; *informal* nosebleed. ANTONYM lower.

**2** *the upper echelons of the party* SENIOR, superior, higher-level, higher-ranking, top, loftier. ANTONYMS junior, inferior.

PHRASE: **the upper hand** *it remains to be seen which party will have the upper hand in this election* AN ADVANTAGE, the edge, the whip hand, a lead, a head start, ascendancy, superiority, supremacy, sway, control, power, mastery, dominance, command, leverage.

**upper-class** adjective *our upper-class relations look down on us* ARISTOCRATIC, noble, of noble birth, patrician, titled, blue-blooded, high-born, well-born, elite, born with a silver spoon in one's mouth; rich, wealthy; upscale, upmarket, upper-crust, high-class, tony, top-drawer, classy, posh, uptown; landowning, landed; *archaic* gentle, of gentle birth.

**uppermost** adjective **1** *the uppermost branches* HIGHEST, top, topmost.

**2** *their own problems remained uppermost in their minds* PREDOMINANT, of greatest importance, to the fore, foremost, first, primary, dominant, principal, chief, main, paramount, supreme, preponderant, major.

**upright** adjective **1** *an upright position* VERTICAL, perpendicular, plumb, straight (up), straight up and down, standing, bolt upright, erect, on end; on one's feet. ANTONYM horizontal.

**2** *an upright member of the community* HONEST, honorable, upstanding, respectable, high-minded, law-abiding, right-minded, worthy, moral, ethical, righteous, decent, scrupulous, conscientious, good, virtuous, principled, of principle, noble, incorruptible. ANTONYM dishonorable.

**uprising** noun *the uprising was put down by government forces* REBELLION, revolt, insurrection, mutiny, revolution, insurgence, intifada, rioting, riot; civil disobedience, unrest, anarchy, coup, coup d'état, putsch.

THE RIGHT WORD **uprising, insurgency, insurrection, mutiny, putsch, rebellion, revolution**

There are a number of ways to defy the established order or overthrow a government. You can stage an **uprising**, which is a broad term referring to a small and usually unsuccessful act of popular resistance (*uprisings among angry workers all over the country*). An uprising is often the first sign of a general or widespread **rebellion**, which is an act of armed resistance against a government or authority; this term is usually applied after the fact to describe an act of resistance that has failed (*a rebellion against the landowners*). If it is successful, however, a rebellion may become a **revolution**, which often implies a war or an outbreak of violence (*the American Revolution*). Although a *revolution* usually involves the overthrow of a government or political system by the people, it can also be used to describe any drastic change in ideas, economic institutions, or moral values (*the sexual revolution*). An **insurrection** is an organized effort to seize power, especially political power, while an **insurgency** is usually aided by foreign powers. If you're on a ship, you can stage a **mutiny**, which is an insurrection against military or naval authority. But if you're relying on speed and surprise to catch the authorities off guard, you'll want to stage a **putsch**, which is a small, popular uprising or planned attempt to seize power.

**uproar** noun **1** *the uproar in the kitchen continued for some time* TURMOIL, disorder, confusion, chaos, commotion, disturbance, rumpus, ruckus, tumult, turbulence, mayhem, pandemonium, bedlam, noise, din, clamor, hubbub, racket; shouting, yelling, babel; *informal* hullabaloo, hoo-ha, brouhaha. ANTONYM calm.

**2** *there was an uproar when she was dismissed* OUTCRY, furor, protest; fuss, reaction, backlash, commotion, hue and cry; *informal* hullabaloo, stink, rhubarb, firestorm. ANTONYM acquiescence.

**uproarious** adjective **1** *an uproarious party* RIOTOUS, rowdy, noisy, loud, wild, unrestrained, unruly, rip-roaring, rollicking, boisterous, rambunctious, knockabout. ANTONYM quiet.

**2** *an uproarious joke* HILARIOUS, hysterical, rib-tickling, gut-busting, priceless, side-splitting, knee-slapping, thigh-slapping. ANTONYM solemn.

**upset** verb **1** *the accusation upset her* DISTRESS, trouble, perturb, dismay, disturb, discompose, unsettle, disconcert, disquiet, worry, bother, agitate, fluster, throw, ruffle, unnerve, shake; hurt, sadden, grieve.

**2** *he upset a tureen of soup* KNOCK OVER, overturn, upend, tip over, flip, topple (over); spill.

**3** *the dam will upset the ecological balance* DISRUPT, interfere with, disturb, throw out, throw into confusion, throw off balance, mess with/up.

**4** *the Indians upset the Angels 9-0* DEFEAT, beat, topple; surprise, embarrass.

▸ noun **1** *a stomach upset* COMPLAINT, disorder, ailment, illness, sickness, malady; *informal* bug.

**2** *the Oilers' victory was a remarkable upset* SURPRISE WIN, shocker.

▸ adjective **1** *the loss made Jane upset* DISTRESSED, troubled, perturbed, dismayed, disturbed, unsettled, disconcerted, worried, bothered, anxious, agitated, flustered, ruffled, unnerved, shaken, unstrung; hurt, saddened, grieved; *informal* cut up, choked. ANTONYMS unperturbed, calm.

**2** *an upset stomach* DISTURBED, unsettled, queasy, bad, hurting, poorly.

**upshot** noun *the upshot of this conflict of interests was a compromise* RESULT, end result, consequence, outcome, conclusion; effect, repercussion, reverberations, ramification, aftereffect, payoff. ANTONYM cause.

**upside down** adjective *an upside-down canoe* UPTURNED, upended, inverted, wrong side up, overturned; capsized, flipped. PHRASE: **turned upside down** *the apartment was turned upside down* IN DISARRAY, in disorder, jumbled up, in a mess, in a muddle, untidy, disorganized, chaotic, all over the place, in chaos, in confusion, topsy-turvy, at sixes and sevens; *informal* higgledy-piggledy.

**upstanding** adjective *an upstanding citizen* HONEST, honorable, upright, respectable, high-minded, law-abiding, right-minded, worthy, trustworthy, moral, ethical, righteous, decent, good, virtuous, principled, of principle, noble, incorruptible, straightforward. ANTONYM dishonorable.

**upstart** noun *these upstarts, they don't know their place* PARVENU, arriviste, nouveau riche, status seeker, social climber, a jumped-up ——, johnny-come-lately.

**up-to-date** adjective **1** *up-to-date equipment* MODERN, contemporary, the latest, state-of-the-art, cutting-edge, leading-edge, new, present-day, up-to-the-minute; advanced; mod. ANTONYMS out of date, old-fashioned.

**2** *the newsletter will keep you up-to-date* INFORMED, up to speed, in the picture, in touch, au fait, au courant, conversant, familiar, knowledgeable, acquainted, aware, clued in.

**upturn** noun *we've enjoyed an upturn in sales this quarter* IMPROVEMENT, upswing, turn for the better; recovery, revival, rally, resurgence, increase, rise, hike, jump, leap, upsurge, boost, escalation. ANTONYMS fall, slump.

**upward** adjective *an upward trend* RISING, on the rise, ascending, climbing, mounting; uphill. ANTONYM downward.

▸ adverb (also **upwards**) *the smoke drifts upward | he inched his way upwards* UP, upward, higher, uphill, upslope; to the top, skyward, heavenward. ANTONYM downward.

PHRASE: **upward(s) of** *he makes upwards of $500 per session* MORE THAN, above, over, in excess of, exceeding, beyond, greater than.

**urban** adjective *crimes rates are significantly higher in urban areas* TOWN, city, municipal, civic, metropolitan, built-up, inner-city, downtown, suburban; urbanized, citified, townie. ANTONYM rural.

**urbane** adjective *the urbane English professor* SUAVE, sophisticated, debonair, worldly, cultivated, cultured, civilized, cosmopolitan; smooth, polished, refined, self-possessed; courteous, polite, well-mannered, mannerly, civil, charming, gentlemanly, gallant. ANTONYMS uncouth, unsophisticated.

THE RIGHT WORD **urbane, cosmopolitan, genteel, sophisticated, suave**

In his long career as a film star, Cary Grant was known for playing **urbane**, **sophisticated** roles. *Urbane* in this context suggests the social poise and polished manner of someone who is well-traveled and well-bred, while *sophisticated* means worldly-wise as opposed to naïve (*a sophisticated young girl who had spent her childhood in Paris and London*). **Cosmopolitan** describes someone who is at home anywhere in the world and is free from provincial attitudes (*a cosmopolitan man who could charm women of all ages and nationalities*), while **suave** suggests the gracious social behavior of *urbane* combined with a certain glibness or superficial politeness (*she was taken in by his expensive clothes and suave manner*). At one time **genteel** meant well-bred or refined, but nowadays it has connotations of self-consciousness or pretentiousness (*too genteel to drink wine from a juice glass*).

**urchin** noun *Mrs. Duffy made frequent complaints about the urchins who played stickball on her street* RAGAMUFFIN, waif, stray; imp, rascal, street urchin; *derogatory* guttersnipe; scapegrace; *dated* gamin.

**urge** verb **1** *she urged him to try again* ENCOURAGE, exhort, enjoin, press, entreat, implore, call on, appeal to, beg, plead with, coax; egg on, prod, prompt, spur, goad, incite, push, pressure, pressurize; *formal* adjure; *literary* beseech.

**2** *she urged her horse down the lane* SPUR (ON), force, drive, impel, propel.

**3** *I urge caution in interpreting these results* ADVISE, counsel, advocate, recommend, suggest, advance.

▸ noun *his urge to travel* DESIRE, wish, need, compulsion, longing, yearning, hankering, craving, appetite, hunger, thirst; fancy, impulse, impetus; *informal* yen, itch.

**urgent** adjective **1** *the urgent need for more funding* ACUTE, pressing, dire, desperate, critical, serious, grave, intense, crying, burning, compelling, extreme, exigent, high-priority, top-priority; life-and-death. See note at CRUCIAL.

**2** *an urgent whisper* INSISTENT, persistent, importunate, earnest, pleading, begging.

**urinate** verb *it was a bit of a culture shock to see men urinating out on the street* relieve oneself, pass water, make water; *informal* pee, take a leak, piddle, tinkle, (take a) whiz, piss; *formal* micturate.

**usable** adjective *the postage meter on the third floor will not be usable until further notice* READY/FIT FOR USE, able to be used, at someone's disposal, disposable; working, in working order, functioning, functional, serviceable, operational, up and running, accessible.

**usage** noun **1** *energy usage* USE, consumption, utilization.

**2** *the usage of equipment* USE, utilization, operation, manipulation, running, handling.

**3** *the intricacies of English usage* PHRASEOLOGY, parlance, idiom, way of speaking/writing, mode of expression, style; idiolect.

**4** *the usages of polite society* CUSTOM, practice, habit, tradition, convention, rule, observance; way, procedure, form, wont; *formal* praxis; (**usages**) mores.

**use** verb **1** *she used her key to open the front door* UTILIZE, make use of, avail oneself of, employ, work, operate, wield, ply, apply, maneuver, manipulate, put to use, put/press into service.

**2** *the court will use its discretion in making an order* EXERCISE, employ, bring into play, practice, apply, exert, bring to bear.

**3** *he just felt used* TAKE ADVANTAGE OF, exploit, manipulate, take liberties with, impose on, abuse; capitalize on, profit from, trade on, milk; *informal* walk all over.

**4** *we have used all the available funds* CONSUME, get/go through, exhaust, deplete, expend, spend; waste, fritter away, squander, dissipate, run out of.

▸ noun **1** *the use of such weapons* UTILIZATION, usage, application, employment, operation, manipulation.

**2** *what is the use of that?* ADVANTAGE, benefit, service, utility, usefulness, help, good, gain, avail, profit, value, worth, point, object, purpose, sense, reason.

**3** *composers have not found much use for the device* NEED, necessity, call, demand, requirement. See note at USE.

**used** adjective *a used car* SECONDHAND, preowned, nearly new, old; worn, hand-me-down, castoff, recycled, warmed-over; *informal* preloved. ANTONYM new.

PHRASE: **used to** *I'm not used to such fine dining* ACCUSTOMED TO, no stranger to, familiar with, at home with, in the habit of, an old hand at, experienced in, versed in, conversant with, acquainted with.

**useful** adjective **1** *a useful multipurpose tool* FUNCTIONAL, practical, handy, convenient, utilitarian, serviceable, of use, of service. ANTONYM useless.

2 *a useful experience* BENEFICIAL, advantageous, helpful, worthwhile, profitable, rewarding, productive, constructive, valuable, fruitful. ANTONYM disadvantageous.

**useless** adjective 1 *useless attempts* FUTILE, to no avail, (in) vain, pointless, to no purpose, unavailing, hopeless, ineffectual, ineffective, to no effect, fruitless, unprofitable, profitless, unproductive; *archaic* bootless. ANTONYMS useful, beneficial.

2 *useless machines* UNUSABLE, broken, kaput, defunct, dud, faulty.

3 *informal he was a useless worker* INCOMPETENT, inept, ineffective, incapable, unemployable, inadequate, hopeless, no-account, bad; *informal* pathetic. ANTONYM competent.

**usher** verb *she ushered him to a window seat* ESCORT, accompany, take, show, see, lead, conduct, guide, steer, shepherd, marshal.

▸ noun *ushers showed them to their seats* GUIDE, attendant, escort, sidesman.

PHRASE: **usher in** *Henry Ford' assembly line ushered in an era of unprecedented productivity* HERALD, mark the start of, signal, ring in, show in, set the scene for, pave the way for; start, begin, introduce, open the door to, get going, set in motion, get underway, kick off, launch.

**usual** adjective *meatloaf is their usual Wednesday special* HABITUAL, customary, accustomed, wonted, normal, routine, regular, standard, typical, established, set, settled, stock, conventional, traditional, expected, predictable, familiar; average, general, ordinary, everyday. See note at NORMAL. ANTONYM exceptional.

**usually** adverb *he usually arrived home about one o'clock* NORMALLY, generally, habitually, customarily, routinely, typically, ordinarily, commonly, conventionally, traditionally; as a rule, in general, more often than not, in the main, mainly, mostly, for the most part, nine times out of ten.

**usurp** verb 1 *Richard usurped the throne* SEIZE, take over, take possession of, take, commandeer, wrest, assume, expropriate.

2 *the Hanoverian dynasty had usurped the Stuarts* OUST, overthrow, remove, topple, unseat, depose, dethrone; supplant, replace.

**utilitarian** adjective *she traded in her sporty little coupe for a utilitarian station wagon* PRACTICAL, functional, pragmatic, serviceable, useful, sensible, efficient, utility, workaday, no-frills; plain, unadorned, undecorative. ANTONYM decorative.

**utility** noun 1 *we have increased the machine's utility* USEFULNESS, use, benefit, value, advantage, advantageousness, help, helpfulness, effectiveness, avail; *formal* efficacy.

2 *an important public utility* SERVICE, service provider, organization, corporation, institution.

**utilize** verb *the foam pellets are utilized to make lightweight insulation* USE, make use of, put to use, employ, avail oneself of, bring/press into service, bring into play, deploy, draw on, exploit, harness.

**utmost** adjective *a matter of the utmost importance* GREATEST, highest, maximum, most, uttermost; extreme, supreme, paramount.

▸ noun *a plot that stretches credulity to the utmost* MAXIMUM, uttermost, limit; *informal* max.

**utter**[1] adjective *that's utter garbage* COMPLETE, total, absolute, thorough, perfect, downright, out-and-out, outright, thoroughgoing, all-out, sheer, arrant, wholesale, rank, pure, real, veritable, consummate, categorical, unmitigated, unqualified, unadulterated, unalloyed.

**utter**[2] verb 1 *he uttered an exasperated snort* EMIT, let out, give, produce.

2 *he hardly uttered a word* SAY, speak, voice, express, articulate, pronounce, enunciate, verbalize, vocalize.

**utterance** noun *your snide utterances are not appreciated* REMARK, comment, word, statement, observation, declaration, pronouncement; exclamation, assertion.

**utterly** adverb *this is utterly ridiculous* COMPLETELY, totally, absolutely, entirely, wholly, fully, thoroughly, quite, altogether, one hundred percent, downright, outright, in all respects, unconditionally, perfectly, really, to the hilt, to the core; dead.

**vacancy** noun **1** *there are vacancies for computer technicians* OPENING, position, post, job, opportunity, place.

**2** *a hotel vacancy* ROOM AVAILABLE, space for rent.

**vacant** adjective **1** *a vacant house* EMPTY, unoccupied, available, not in use, free, unfilled; uninhabited, untenanted. ANTONYMS full, occupied.

**2** *a vacant look* BLANK, expressionless, unresponsive, emotionless, impassive, uninterested, vacuous, empty, absent, glazed, glassy; unintelligent, dull-witted, dense, brainless, empty-headed; *informal* zombified, lobotomized. ANTONYM expressive.

**vacate** verb **1** *he was forced to vacate the premises* LEAVE, move out of, evacuate, quit, depart from; abandon, desert. ANTONYMS occupy, inhabit.

**2** *he will be vacating his post next year* RESIGN FROM, leave, stand down from, give up, bow out of, relinquish, retire from, quit. ANTONYM take up.

**vacation** noun *their summer vacations in Hawaii* BREAK, time off, recess, leave, leave of absence, furlough, sabbatical; TRIP, tour; *chiefly Brit.* holiday; *formal* sojourn.

▸ verb *I was vacationing in Europe with my family* TRAVEL, tour, stay, visit, stop over; *formal* sojourn.

**vacillate** verb *I vacillated between teaching and journalism* DITHER, waver, be indecisive, be undecided, be ambivalent, hesitate, be of two minds, blow hot and cold, keep changing one's mind, be conflicted; fluctuate, oscillate, hem and haw; *informal* dilly-dally, shilly-shally.

**vacuous** adjective *that vacuous laugh of his drives me nuts* SILLY, inane, unintelligent, insipid, foolish, stupid, fatuous, idiotic, brainless, witless, vapid, vacant, empty-headed; *informal* dumb, moronic, brain-dead, fluffy, fluffball. ANTONYM intelligent.

**vacuum** noun **1** *people longing to fill the spiritual vacuum in their lives* EMPTINESS, void, nothingness, vacancy, absence, black hole.

**2** *the political vacuum left by the emperor's death* GAP, space, lacuna, void.

**3** *informal* *I need to replace the bag in the vacuum* VACUUM CLEANER, vac; *trademark* Dustbuster, Hoover.

**vagabond** noun & adjective. See VAGRANT noun.

**vagary** noun *the vagaries of the weather* CHANGE, fluctuation, variation, quirk, peculiarity, oddity, eccentricity, unpredictability, caprice, foible, whim, whimsy, fancy.

**vagrant** noun *a temporary home for vagrants* STREET PERSON, homeless person, tramp, hobo, drifter, down-and-out, derelict, beggar; itinerant, wanderer, nomad, traveler, vagabond, transient; *informal* bag lady, bum; *literary* wayfarer.

▸ adjective *vagrant beggars* HOMELESS, drifting, transient, roving, roaming, itinerant, wandering, nomadic, traveling, vagabond, rootless, of no fixed address/abode *archaic* errant.

**vague** adjective **1** *a vague shape* INDISTINCT, indefinite, indeterminate, unclear, ill-defined; hazy, fuzzy, misty, blurred, blurry, out of focus, faint, shadowy, dim, obscure, nebulous, amorphous, diaphanous. ANTONYMS clear, precise.

**2** *a vague description* IMPRECISE, rough, approximate, inexact, nonspecific, generalized, ambiguous, equivocal, hazy, woolly. ANTONYMS clear, precise.

**3** *they had only vague plans* HAZY, uncertain, undecided, unsure, unclear, unsettled, indefinite, indeterminate, unconfirmed, up in the air, speculative, sketchy. ANTONYM firm.

**4** *she was so vague in everyday life* ABSENTMINDED, forgetful, dreamy, abstracted, with one's head in the clouds, scatty, scattered, not with it. ANTONYMS organized, together.

**vaguely** adverb **1** *she looks vaguely familiar* SLIGHTLY, a little, a bit, somewhat, rather, in a way; faintly, obscurely; *informal* sort of, kind of, kinda. ANTONYM very.

**2** *he fired his rifle vaguely in our direction* ROUGHLY, more or less, approximately. ANTONYM exactly.

**3** *he smiled vaguely* ABSENTMINDEDLY, abstractedly, vacantly.

**vain** adjective **1** *he was vain about his looks* CONCEITED, narcissistic, self-loving, in love with oneself, self-admiring, self-regarding, self-obsessed, egocentric, egotistic, egotistical; proud, arrogant, boastful, cocky, cocksure, immodest, swaggering; *informal* big-headed; *literary* vainglorious. ANTONYM modest.

**2** *a vain attempt* FUTILE, useless, pointless, to no purpose, hopeless, in vain; ineffective, ineffectual, inefficacious, impotent, unavailing, to no avail, fruitless, profitless, unrewarding, unproductive, unsuccessful, failed, abortive, for nothing; thwarted, frustrated, foiled; *archaic* bootless. ANTONYM successful.

PHRASE: **in vain** 1 *they tried in vain to save him* UNSUCCESSFULLY, without success, to no avail, to no purpose, fruitlessly.

2 *his efforts were in vain.* See VAIN sense 2.

3 *she took the Lord's name in vain* IRREVERENTLY, casually, disrespectfully, flippantly.

**valedictory** noun *at their fifty-year reunion, Estelle Carver read the valedictory that she had delivered in 1954* SPEECH, address, lecture, declamation.

▸ adjective *a valedictory message* FAREWELL, goodbye, leaving, parting; last, final.

**valiant** adjective *a valiant warrior* | *her valiant efforts* BRAVE, courageous, valorous, intrepid, heroic, gallant, lionhearted, bold, fearless, daring, audacious; unflinching, unshrinking, unafraid, dauntless, undaunted, doughty, tough, indomitable, mettlesome, stouthearted, spirited, plucky; *informal* game, gutsy, spunky. ANTONYM cowardly.

**valid** adjective 1 *a valid criticism* WELL-FOUNDED, sound, reasonable, rational, logical, justifiable, defensible, viable, bona fide; cogent, effective, powerful, potent, convincing, credible, forceful, strong, solid, weighty. See note at BELIEVABLE.

2 *a valid contract* LEGALLY BINDING, lawful, legal, legitimate, official, signed and sealed, contractual; in force, current, in effect, effective; *informal* legit.

3 *valid information* LEGITIMATE, authentic, authoritative, reliable, bona fide.

**validate** verb 1 *clinical trials now exist to validate this claim* PROVE, substantiate, corroborate, verify, support, back up, bear out, lend force to, confirm, justify, vindicate, authenticate. ANTONYM disprove.

2 *250 certificates need to be validated* RATIFY, endorse, approve, agree to, accept, authorize, legalize, legitimize, warrant, license, certify, recognize. ANTONYMS reject, revoke.

**valley** noun *the homes in the valley are subject to mudslides* DALE, vale; hollow, basin, gully, gorge, ravine, coulee, trough, canyon, rift; glen; *literary* dell.

**valor** noun *medals awarded for acts of valor* BRAVERY, courage, pluck, nerve, daring, fearlessness, audacity, boldness, dauntlessness, stout-heartedness, heroism, backbone, spirit; *informal* guts, true grit, spunk; moxie. ANTONYM cowardice.

**valuable** adjective 1 *a valuable watch* PRECIOUS, costly, pricey, expensive, dear, high-priced, high-cost, high-end, upscale, big-ticket; worth its weight in gold, priceless. ANTONYMS cheap, worthless.

2 *a valuable contribution* USEFUL, helpful, beneficial, invaluable, crucial, productive, constructive, effective, advantageous, worthwhile, worthy, important. ANTONYM useless.

**value** noun 1 *houses exceeding $250,000 in value* PRICE, cost, worth; market price, monetary value, face value.

2 *the value of adequate preparation cannot be understated* WORTH, usefulness, advantage, benefit, gain, profit, good, help, merit, helpfulness, avail; importance, significance.

3 *society's values are passed on to us as children* PRINCIPLES, ethics, moral code, morals, standards, code of behavior.

▸ verb 1 *his estate was valued at $345,000* EVALUATE, assess, estimate, appraise, price, put/set a price on.

2 *she valued his opinion* THINK HIGHLY OF, have a high opinion of, hold in high regard, rate highly, esteem, set (great) store by, put stock in, appreciate, respect; prize, cherish, treasure.

**valued** adjective *this is my most valued piece of crystal* CHERISHED, treasured, dear, prized; esteemed, respected, highly regarded, appreciated, important.

**vamp** noun *informal a tawny-haired vamp* SEDUCTRESS, temptress, siren, femme fatale, sex kitten, trollop, home wrecker, man-eater; flirt, coquette, tease.

**vanguard** noun *she was in the vanguard of the labor movement* | *they were destined to become the vanguard of space exploration* FOREFRONT, advance guard, spearhead, front, front line, fore, van, lead, cutting edge; avant-garde, leaders, founders, founding fathers, pioneers, trailblazers, trendsetters, innovators, groundbreakers. ANTONYMS rear, followers.

**vanish** verb 1 *he vanished without a trace* DISAPPEAR, be lost to sight/view, become invisible, vanish into thin air, recede from view, dematerialize. ANTONYMS appear, materialize.

2 *all hope of freedom vanished* FADE, fade away, evaporate, vaporize, melt away, come to an end, end, cease to exist, pass away, die out, be no more. ANTONYMS endure, materialize.

**vanity** noun 1 *she had none of the vanity often associated with beautiful women* CONCEIT, narcissism, self-love, self-admiration, self-absorption, self-regard, egotism; pride, arrogance, boastfulness, cockiness, swagger, rodomontade; *informal* bigheadedness; *literary* vainglory. See notes at EGOTISM, PRIDE. ANTONYM modesty.

2 *the vanity of all desires of the will* FUTILITY, uselessness, pointlessness, worthlessness, fruitlessness.

**vanquish** verb *I promise you, we shall vanquish our enemy and reclaim what is rightfully ours* CONQUER, defeat, beat, trounce, rout, triumph over, be victorious over, get the better of, worst, upset; overcome, overwhelm, overpower, overthrow, subdue, subjugate, quell, quash, crush, bring someone to their knees, tear someone apart; *informal* lick, hammer, clobber, thrash, smash, demolish, wipe the floor with, make mincemeat of, massacre, slaughter, annihilate, cream, skunk, shellac.

**vapid** adjective *a tuneful but vapid musical comedy* INSIPID, uninspired, colorless, uninteresting, feeble, flat, dull, boring, tedious, tired, unexciting, uninspiring, unimaginative, lifeless, tame, vacuous, bland, trite, jejune. ANTONYMS lively, colorful.

**variable** adjective *the weather on the shoreline is known for* *being variable* CHANGEABLE, changing, varying, shifting, fluctuating, irregular, inconstant, inconsistent, fluid, unsteady, unstable, unsettled, fitful, mutable, protean, wavering, vacillating, capricious, fickle, volatile, unpredictable, mercurial, unreliable; *informal* up and down. ANTONYM constant.

▸ noun *there are other variables to consider* FACTOR, element, ingredient, quantity, unknown quantity, condition.

**variance** noun *the variance between the two groups is slight* DIFFERENCE, variation, discrepancy, dissimilarity, disagreement, conflict, divergence, deviation, contrast, contradiction, imbalance, incongruity. PHRASE: **at variance 1** *his recollections were* ***at variance with*** *documentary evidence* INCONSISTENT, at odds, not in keeping, out of keeping, out of line, out of step, in conflict, in disagreement.

**2** *science and religion need not be at variance* CONFLICTING, in conflict, in disagreement, in opposition; different, differing, divergent, discrepant, dissimilar, contrary, incompatible, contradictory, irreconcilable, incongruous; at cross purposes, at loggerheads, in dispute.

**variant** noun *there are a number of variants of the same idea* VARIATION, form, alternative, adaptation, alteration, modification, permutation, version, analog.

▸ adjective *a variant spelling* ALTERNATIVE, other, different, substitute, divergent, derived, modified.

**variation** noun **1** *regional variations in farming practice* DIFFERENCE, dissimilarity; disparity, contrast, discrepancy, imbalance; *technical* differential.

**2** *opening times are subject to variation* CHANGE, alteration, modification; diversification.

**3** *there was very little variation from an understood pattern* DEVIATION, variance, divergence, departure, fluctuation.

**4** *hurling is an Irish variation of field hockey* VARIANT, form, alternative form; development, adaptation, alteration, mutation, transformation, diversification, modification.

**varied** adjective *her varied interests keep her extremely busy* DIVERSE, assorted, miscellaneous, mixed, sundry, heterogeneous, wide-ranging, manifold, multifarious; disparate, motley.

**variegated** adjective *variegated leaves* MULTICOLORED, multicolor, many-colored, many-hued, polychromatic, varicolored, colorful, prismatic, rainbow, kaleidoscopic; mottled, striated, marbled, streaked, speckled, flecked, dappled; *informal* splotchy. ANTONYMS plain, monochrome.

**variety** noun **1** *the lack of variety in the curriculum* DIVERSITY, variation, diversification, heterogeneity, multifariousness, change, choice, difference. ANTONYM uniformity.

**2** *a wide variety of flowers and shrubs* ASSORTMENT, miscellany, range, array, collection, selection, mixture, medley, multiplicity; mixed bag, motley collection, potpourri, hodgepodge.

**3** *fifty varieties of pasta* SORT, kind, type, class, category, style, form; make, model, brand; strain, breed, genus.

**various** adjective *there are various styles to choose from* DIVERSE, different, differing, varied, varying, a variety of, assorted, mixed, myriad, sundry, miscellaneous, heterogeneous, disparate, motley; several, a number of, an assortment of; *literary* divers.

**varnish** noun & verb *two coats of varnish | she varnished the woodwork* LACQUER, shellac, finish, japan, enamel, glaze; polish, wax.

**vary** verb **1** *estimates of the development cost vary* DIFFER, be different, be dissimilar, conflict.

**2** *rates of interest can vary over time* FLUCTUATE, rise and fall, go up and down, change, alter, shift, swing, deviate, differ.

**3** *the diaphragm is used for varying the aperture of the lens* MODIFY, change, alter, transform, adjust, regulate, control, set; diversify, reshape; *informal* tweak.

**vast** adjective *a vast holding of farmland* HUGE, extensive, expansive, broad, wide, sweeping, boundless, immeasurable, limitless, infinite; enormous, immense, great, massive, colossal, tremendous, mighty, prodigious, gigantic, gargantuan, mammoth, monumental; giant, towering, mountainous, titanic, Brobdingnagian; *informal* jumbo, mega, monster, whopping, humongous, astronomical, ginormous. ANTONYM tiny.

**vault**[1] noun **1** *the highest Gothic vault in Europe* ARCHED ROOF, dome, arch.

**2** *the vault under the church* CELLAR, basement, underground chamber; crypt, catacomb, burial chamber.

**3** *valuables stored in the vault* SAFE, safety deposit box, repository, coffer, strongroom.

**vault**[2] verb *he* ***vaulted over*** *the gate* JUMP OVER, leap over, spring over, bound over; hurdle, clear.

**vaunt** verb *their much vaunted record of accuracy* BOAST ABOUT, brag about, make much of, crow about, parade, flaunt; acclaim, trumpet, praise, extol, celebrate; *informal* show off about, hype; *formal* laud.

**veer** verb *we then saw the car veer suddenly to the right* TURN, swerve, curve, swing, sheer, career, weave, wheel; change direction, change course, go off course, deviate.

**vegetate** verb *ever since school ended, he just vegetates* DO NOTHING, relax, rest, idle, languish, laze, lounge, loll; stagnate; *informal* veg, bum around, hang out, zone out, lollygag.

**vegetation** noun *lush tropical vegetation* PLANTS, flora; greenery, foliage, herbage, verdure.

**vehemence** noun *the recruiters were told to speak with unwavering vehemence* PASSION, force, forcefulness, ardor, fervor, violence, urgency, strength, vigor, intensity, keenness, feeling, enthusiasm, zeal.

**vehement** adjective *her vehement arguments persuaded them to save the housing project* PASSIONATE, forceful, ardent, impassioned, heated, spirited, urgent, fervent, violent, fierce, fiery, strong, forcible, powerful, emphatic, vigorous, intense, earnest, keen, enthusiastic, zealous. ANTONYMS mild, apathetic.

**vehicle** noun **1** *a stolen vehicle* MEANS OF TRANSPORT, conveyance, motor vehicle.

**2** *a vehicle for the communication of original ideas* CHANNEL, medium, conduit, means, means of expression, agency, agent, instrument, mechanism, organ, apparatus.

**veil** noun **1** *a thin veil of high cloud made the sun hazy* COVERING, cover, screen, curtain, mantle, cloak, mask, blanket, shroud, canopy, cloud, pall.

**2** *the women wore black veils* MASK, scarf, kerchief, head covering, headdress; dupatta, purdah, mantilla, chador, hijab, yashmak.

▸ verb *the peak was veiled in mist* ENVELOP, surround, swathe, enfold, cover, conceal, hide, screen, shield, cloak, blanket, shroud; obscure; *literary* enshroud, mantle.

**veiled** adjective *veiled threats* DISGUISED, camouflaged, masked, covert, hidden, concealed, suppressed, underlying, implicit, implied, indirect. ANTONYM overt.

**vein** noun **1** *a vein in his neck pulsed* BLOOD VESSEL.

**2** *the mineral veins in the rock* LAYER, lode, seam, stratum, stratification, deposit, pipe.

**3** *white marble with gray veins* STREAK, marking, mark, line, stripe, strip, band, thread, strand; *technical* stria, striation.

**4** *he closes the article in a humorous vein* MOOD, frame of mind, temper, disposition, attitude, tenor, tone, key, spirit, character, fashion, feel, flavor, quality, atmosphere, humor; manner, mode, way, style.

**velocity** noun *light travels at a constant velocity* SPEED, pace, rate, tempo, momentum, impetus; swiftness, rapidity; *literary* fleetness, celerity.

**venal** adjective *they ran the town according to their own venal system of "law and order"* CORRUPT, corruptible, bribable, open to bribery; dishonest, dishonorable, untrustworthy, unscrupulous, unprincipled; mercenary, greedy; *informal* crooked. ANTONYMS honorable, honest.

**vendetta** noun *the vendetta between our families is older than our grandparents* FEUD, blood feud, quarrel, argument, falling-out, dispute, fight, war; bad blood, enmity, rivalry, conflict, strife.

**vendor** noun *most of the vendors on Main Street are participating in Saturday's sidewalk sales* RETAILER, seller, dealer, trader, purveyor, storekeeper, shopkeeper, merchant; salesperson, supplier, peddler, hawker; scalper, huckster, trafficker.

**veneer** noun **1** *American cherry wood with a maple veneer* SURFACE, lamination, layer, overlay, facing, covering, finish, exterior, cladding, laminate.

**2** *a veneer of sophistication* FACADE, front, false front, show, outward display, appearance, impression, semblance, guise, disguise, mask, masquerade, pretense, camouflage, cover, window dressing.

**venerable** adjective *the venerable Martin Steed joined our faculty in 1962* RESPECTED, venerated, revered, honored, esteemed, hallowed, august, distinguished, eminent, great, grand.

**vengeance** noun *your appetite for vengeance has destroyed your life* REVENGE, retribution, retaliation, payback, requital, reprisal, satisfaction, an eye for an eye (and a tooth for a tooth). PHRASE: **with a vengeance** *she returned to the stage with a vengeance* VIGOROUSLY, strenuously, energetically, with a will, with all the stops out, for all one is worth, all out, flat out, at full tilt; *informal* hammer and tongs, like crazy, like mad, like gangbusters.

**venial** adjective *the venial indiscretions of my youth* FORGIVABLE, pardonable, excusable, allowable, permissible; slight, minor, unimportant, insignificant, trivial, trifling. See note at VENAL. ANTONYMS unforgivable, mortal.

**venom** noun **1** *snake venom* POISON, toxin; *archaic* bane.

**2** *his voice was full of venom* RANCOR, malevolence, vitriol, spite, vindictiveness, malice, maliciousness, ill will, acrimony, animosity, animus, bitterness, antagonism, hostility, bile, hate, hatred; *informal* bitchiness, cattiness.

**venomous** adjective **1** *a venomous snake* | *the spider's venomous bite* POISONOUS, toxic; dangerous, deadly, lethal, fatal, mortal. ANTONYM harmless.

**2** *venomous remarks* VICIOUS, spiteful, rancorous, malevolent, vitriolic, vindictive, malicious, poisonous, virulent, bitter, acidic, acrimonious, caustic, antagonistic, hostile, cruel; *informal* bitchy, catty; *literary* malefic, maleficent. See note at VINDICTIVE. ANTONYMS kind, benevolent.

**vent** noun *an air vent* DUCT, flue, shaft, well, passage, airway; outlet, inlet, opening, aperture, hole, gap, orifice.

▸ verb *the crowd vented their fury on the police* RELEASE, air, give vent to, give free rein to, let out, pour out, express, give expression to, voice, give voice to, verbalize, ventilate, discuss, talk over, communicate.

**ventilate** verb *ventilate all work areas* AIR, aerate, air out, oxygenate, air-condition, fan; freshen, cool.

**venture** noun *a business venture* ENTERPRISE, undertaking, project, initiative, scheme, operation, endeavor, speculation, plunge, gamble, gambit, experiment.

▸ verb **1** *we ventured across the country* SET OUT, go, travel, journey.

**2** *may I venture an opinion?* PUT FORWARD, advance, proffer, offer, volunteer, air, suggest, submit, propose, moot,

**3** *I ventured to ask her to come and dine with me* DARE, be/make so bold as, presume; take the liberty of, stick one's neck out, go out on a limb.

**veracious** adjective *formal*. See TRUTHFUL sense 2.

**verbal** adjective *a verbal agreement* ORAL, spoken, stated, said, verbalized, expressed; unwritten, word-of-mouth.

**verbatim** adverb *I memorized his monologue verbatim* WORD FOR WORD, letter for letter, line for line, to the letter, literally, exactly, precisely, accurately, closely, faithfully.

**verbose** adjective *try not to be so verbose when you're being interviewed* WORDY, loquacious, garrulous, talkative, voluble; long-winded, flatulent, lengthy, prolix, tautological, pleonastic, periphrastic, circumlocutory, circuitous, wandering, discursive, digressive, rambling; *informal* mouthy, gabby, chatty, motormouthed. ANTONYMS succinct, laconic.

**verdict** noun *the judge's verdict is final* JUDGMENT, adjudication, decision, finding, ruling, decree, resolution, pronouncement, conclusion, opinion; *Law* determination.

**verge** noun **1** *the verge of the lake* EDGE, border, margin, side, brink, rim, lip; fringe, boundary, perimeter, outskirts; *literary* skirt. See note at BORDER.

**2** *Spain was on the verge of an economic crisis* BRINK, threshold, edge, point.

▸ verb *a degree of caution that* ***verged on*** *the obsessive* APPROACH, border on, come close/near to, be tantamount to; tend toward, approximate to, resemble.

**verification** noun *they may require further verification* CONFIRMATION, substantiation, proof, corroboration, support, attestation, validation, authentication, endorsement.

**verify** verb **1** *the evidence verifies my claim* SUBSTANTIATE, confirm, prove, corroborate, back up, bear out, justify, support, uphold, attest to, testify to, validate, authenticate, endorse, certify. ANTONYM refute.

**2** *we need to verify those figures* TEST, double-check, check out, establish the truth of.

**vernacular** noun **1** *he wrote in* ***the vernacular*** *to reach a wider audience* EVERYDAY LANGUAGE, colloquial language, conversational language, common parlance, demotic, lay terms.

**2** *informal the preppy vernacular of Orange County* LANGUAGE, dialect, regional language, regionalisms, patois, parlance; idiom, slang, jargon; *informal* lingo, -speak, -ese. See note at DIALECT.

**versatile** adjective *she's our most versatile player* ADAPTABLE, flexible, all-around, multifaceted, multitalented, resourceful; adjustable, multipurpose, all-purpose, handy; *rare* polytropic.

**verse** noun **1** *Elizabethan verse* POETRY, versification, poetic form; poems, balladry, lyrics, lines, doggerel; *literary* poesy. See also the table at POETRY. ANTONYM prose.

**2** *a verse he'd composed for our anniversary* POEM, lyric, ballad, sonnet, ode, limerick, rhyme, ditty, lay.

**3** *a poem with sixty verses* STANZA, canto, couplet; strophe.

**version** noun **1** *his version of events* ACCOUNT, report, statement, description, record, story, rendering, interpretation, explanation, understanding, reading, impression, side, take.

**2** *the Japanese version will be published next year* EDITION, translation, impression.

**3** *they replaced coal-burning furnaces with gas versions* FORM, sort, kind, type, variety, variant, model.

**vertical** adjective *workers enter through a vertical shaft* UPRIGHT, erect, perpendicular, plumb, straight up and down, on end, standing, upstanding, bolt upright. ANTONYM horizontal.

**vertigo** noun *the steep narrow stairs give me vertigo* DIZZINESS, giddiness, lightheadedness, loss of balance.

**verve** noun *the kids performed with joyful verve* ENTHUSIASM, vigor, energy, pep, dynamism, élan, vitality, vivacity, buoyancy, liveliness, animation, zest, sparkle, charisma, spirit, ebullience, exuberance, life, brio, gusto, eagerness, keenness, passion, zeal, relish, feeling, ardor, fire; *informal* zing, zip, vim, pizzazz, oomph, get-up-and-go.

**very** adverb *that's very kind of you* EXTREMELY, exceedingly, exceptionally, extraordinarily, tremendously, immensely, hugely, intensely, acutely, abundantly, singularly, uncommonly, decidedly, particularly, supremely, highly, remarkably, really, truly, mightily, ever so; *informal* terrifically, awfully, fearfully, terribly, devilishly, majorly, seriously, mega, ultra, damn, damned; dead, real, way, mighty, awful, darned; *archaic* exceeding. ANTONYM slightly.

▸ adjective **1** *those were his very words* EXACT, actual, precise.

**2** *the very thought of food made her feel ill* MERE, simple, pure; sheer.

**vessel** noun **1** *a fishing vessel* BOAT, ship, craft, watercraft; *literary* bark/barque.

**2** *pour the mixture into a heatproof vessel* CONTAINER, receptacle; basin, bowl, pan, pot; urn, tank, cask, barrel, drum, vat.

**vest** verb *executive power is* ***vested in*** *the president* CONFER ON, entrust to, invest in, bestow on, grant to, give to, put in the hands of; endow in, lodge in, lay on, place on.

**vestibule** noun *brochures are available in the vestibule* ENTRANCE HALL, hall, hallway, entrance, porch, portico, foyer, lobby, anteroom, narthex, antechamber, waiting room.

**vestige** noun **1** *the last vestiges of colonialism* REMNANT, fragment, relic, echo, indication, sign, trace, residue, mark, legacy, reminder; remains. See note at TRACE.

**2** *she showed no vestige of emotion* BIT, touch, hint, suggestion, suspicion, shadow, scrap, tinge, speck, shred, jot, iota, whit, scintilla, glimmer; *informal* smidgen, tad, titch, tinch.

**vestigial** adjective **1** *vestigial limbs* RUDIMENTARY, undeveloped; nonfunctional; *Biology* primitive.

**2** *he felt a vestigial flicker of anger from last night* REMAINING, surviving, residual, leftover, lingering.

**veteran** noun *a veteran of 16 political campaigns* OLD HAND, past master, doyen, vet; *informal* old-timer, old stager, old warhorse. ANTONYM novice.

▸ adjective *a veteran diplomat* LONG-SERVING, seasoned, old, hardened; adept, expert, well trained, practiced, experienced, senior; *informal* battle-scarred.

**veto** noun *the president's right of veto* REJECTION, dismissal; prohibition, proscription, embargo, ban, interdict, check; *informal* thumbs down, red light. ANTONYM approval.

▸ verb *China vetoed the proposal* REJECT, turn down, throw out, dismiss; prohibit, forbid, interdict, proscribe, disallow, embargo, ban, rule out, say no to; *informal* kill, put the kibosh on, give the thumbs down to, give the red light to. ANTONYM approve.

**vex** verb *Alice was vexed by his remarks* ANNOY, irritate, anger, infuriate, exasperate, irk, gall, pique, put out, antagonize, nettle, get on someone's nerves, ruffle someone's feathers, rattle someone's cage, make someone's hackles rise, rub the wrong way; *informal* aggravate, peeve, miff, rile, needle, get (to), bug, get someone's goat, get someone's back up, get someone's dander up, tee off, tick off, burn up, rankle.

**vexation** noun *she stamped her foot in vexation* ANNOYANCE, irritation, exasperation, indignation, anger, crossness, displeasure, pique, bile, disgruntlement, bad mood; *informal* aggravation.

**vexed** adjective **1** *a vexed expression* ANNOYED, irritated, cross, angry, infuriated, exasperated, irked, piqued, nettled, displeased, put out, disgruntled; *informal* aggravated, peeved, miffed, riled, hacked off, hot under the collar, teed off, ticked off, sore, bent out of shape; PO'd; *archaic* wroth.

**2** *the vexed issue of immigration* DISPUTED, in dispute, contested, in contention, contentious, debated, at issue, controversial, moot; problematic, difficult, knotty, thorny, ticklish, tense.

**viable** adjective *it doesn't sound like a viable solution* FEASIBLE, workable, practicable, practical, usable, possible, realistic, achievable, attainable, realizable; *informal* doable. ANTONYM impracticable.

**vibrant** adjective **1** *a vibrant and passionate woman* SPIRITED, lively, full of life, energetic, vigorous, vital, full of vim and vigor, animated, sparkling, effervescent, vivacious, dynamic, stimulating, exciting, passionate, fiery; *informal* peppy, feisty. ANTONYMS listless, dull.

**2** *vibrant colors* VIVID, bright, striking, brilliant, strong, rich, colorful, bold. ANTONYMS washed out, pale.

**3** *his vibrant voice* RESONANT, sonorous, reverberant, resounding, ringing, echoing; strong, rich, full, round. ANTONYMS soft, feeble.

**vibrate** verb **1** *the floor beneath them vibrated* QUIVER, shake, tremble, shiver, shudder, throb, pulsate, rattle; rock, wobble, oscillate, waver, swing, sway, move to and fro; *chiefly Brit.* judder.

**2** *a low rumbling sound began to vibrate through the car* REVERBERATE, resonate, resound, ring, echo.

**vibration** noun *loose bolts are causing the vibration* TREMOR, shaking, quivering, quaking, shuddering, throb, throbbing, pulsation; *chiefly Brit.* judder, juddering.

**vicarious** adjective *I had the vicarious thrill of knowing my wife was to be named the next university president* INDIRECT, secondhand, secondary, derivative, derived, surrogate, substitute; empathetic, empathic.

**vice** noun **1** *youngsters driven to vice* IMMORALITY, wrongdoing, wickedness, badness, evil, iniquity, villainy, corruption, misconduct, misdeeds; sin, sinfulness, ungodliness; depravity, degeneracy, dissolution, dissipation, debauchery, decadence, lechery, perversion; crime, transgression; *formal* turpitude; *archaic* trespass. See note at SIN. ANTONYM virtue.

**2** *smoking is my only vice* SHORTCOMING, failing, flaw, fault, bad habit, defect, weakness, deficiency, limitation, imperfection, blemish, foible, frailty. ANTONYM virtue.

**vice versa** adverb *dancers can teach actors a lot and vice versa* CONVERSELY, inversely, contrariwise; reciprocally, the other way around/round.

**vicinity** noun *many female artists and writers live in the vicinity* NEIGHBORHOOD, surrounding area, locality, locale, area, local area, district, region, quarter, zone; environs, surroundings, precincts; *informal* neck of the woods. PHRASE: **in the vicinity of** *his fortune is in the vicinity of four billion dollars* AROUND, about, nearly, circa, approaching, roughly, approximating, approximately, something like, more or less; in the region of, in the neighborhood of, near to, close to.

**vicious** adjective **1** *a vicious killer* BRUTAL, ferocious, savage, violent, dangerous, ruthless, remorseless, merciless, heartless, callous, cruel, harsh, cold-blooded, inhuman, fierce, barbarous, barbaric, brutish, bloodthirsty, fiendish, sadistic, monstrous, murderous, homicidal *informal* smashmouth. ANTONYM gentle.

**2** *a vicious hate campaign* MALICIOUS, malevolent, malignant, malign, spiteful, hateful, vindictive, venomous, poisonous, rancorous, mean, cruel, bitter, cutting, acrimonious, hostile, nasty; defamatory, slanderous; *informal* catty. ANTONYMS benevolent, kindly.

**vicissitude** noun *the vicissitude of our love* CHANGE, alteration, shift, reversal, twist, turn, downturn, variation; inconstancy, instability, uncertainty, chanciness, unpredictability, fickleness, variability, changeability, fluctuation, vacillation; ups and downs.

**victim** noun **1** *a victim of crime* SUFFERER, injured party, casualty; fatality, loss; loser.

**2** *the victim of a con game* TARGET, object, subject, focus, recipient, butt.

**3** *a born victim* LOSER, prey, stooge, dupe, sucker, quarry, fool, fall guy, chump; *informal* patsy, sap.

**4** *he offered himself as a victim* SACRIFICE, offering, burnt offering, scapegoat. PHRASE: **fall victim to** *they fell victim to the flu* FALL ILL WITH, be stricken with, catch, develop, contract, pick up; succumb to.

**victimize** verb *a government that victimizes the most needy and defenseless* PERSECUTE, pick on, push around, bully, abuse, discriminate against, ill-treat, mistreat, maltreat, terrorize, hector; exploit, prey on, take advantage of, dupe, cheat, double-cross, get at, have it in for, give someone a hard time, hassle, lean on, gang up on.

**victor** verb *to the victors go all the sponsorship opportunities*

WINNER, champion, conqueror, conquering hero, vanquisher, hero; prize winner, gold medalist; *informal* champ, top dog. ANTONYM loser.

**victorious** adjective *the victorious Romanians brought home the gold* TRIUMPHANT, conquering, vanquishing, winning, champion, successful, top, first.

**victuals** plural noun *dated*. See FOOD sense 1.

**vie** verb *the brothers had always vied for favoritism* COMPETE, contend, contest, struggle, fight, battle, cross swords, lock horns, buck, jockey; war, feud.

**view** noun **1** *the view from her apartment* OUTLOOK, prospect, panorama, vista, scene, aspect, perspective, spectacle, sight; scenery, landscape.

**2** *we agree with this view* OPINION, point of view, viewpoint, belief, judgment, thinking, notion, idea, conviction, persuasion, attitude, feeling, sentiment, concept, hypothesis, theory; stance, standpoint, philosophy, doctrine, dogma, approach, take. See note at OPINION.

**3** *the church came into view* SIGHT, perspective, vision, visibility.

▸ verb **1** *they viewed the landscape* LOOK AT, eye, observe, gaze at, stare at, ogle, contemplate, watch, scan, regard, take in, survey, inspect, scrutinize; *informal* check out, get a load of, eyeball; *literary* espy, behold.

**2** *the law was viewed as a last resort* CONSIDER, regard, look upon, see, perceive, judge, deem, reckon.

PHRASES: **in view of** *in view of this new evidence, we would like to reconsider our decision* CONSIDERING, bearing in mind, taking into account, on account of, in (the) light of, owing to, because of, as a result of, given.
**on view** *the Garbo memorabilia will be on view until Thursday* ON DISPLAY, on exhibition, on show.

**viewer** noun *one of our lucky viewers will win a trip to Mexico* WATCHER, spectator, onlooker, looker-on, observer, member of the audience; (**viewers**) audience, crowd; *literary* beholder.

**viewpoint** noun *I understand your viewpoint.* See VIEW noun sense 2.

**vigilant** adjective *we've become more vigilant since the neighbors were robbed* WATCHFUL, observant, attentive, alert, eagle-eyed, hawk-eyed, on the lookout, on one's toes, on the qui vive; wide awake, wakeful, unwinking, on one's guard, cautious, wary, circumspect, heedful, mindful; *informal* beady-eyed. ANTONYM inattentive.

THE RIGHT WORD **vigilant, careful, cautious, circumspect, wary, watchful, alert**

All of these adjectives connote being on the lookout for danger or opportunity. **Watchful** is the most general term, meaning closely observant (*a watchful young man who noticed everything*). If you're **vigilant**, you are watchful for a purpose (*to be vigilant in the presence of one's enemies*), and **wary** suggests being on the lookout for treachery or trickery (*wary of his neighbor's motives in offering to move the fence*). If you're **alert**, you are quick to apprehend a danger, an opportunity, or an emergency (*she was much more alert after a good night's sleep*), and if you're **careful**, you may be able to avoid danger or error altogether. **Cautious** and **circumspect** also emphasize the avoidance of danger or unpleasant situations. To be *circumspect* is to be watchful in all directions and with regard to all possible consequences (*these journalists have to be circumspect, not criticizing anyone too harshly*); to be *cautious* is to guard against contingencies (*a cautious approach to treating illness*).

**vigor** noun *they ran with great vigor* ROBUSTNESS, health, hardiness, strength, sturdiness, toughness; bloom, radiance, energy, life, vitality, virility, verve, spirit; zeal, passion, determination, dynamism, zest, pep, drive, force; *informal* oomph, get-up-and-go, zing, piss and vinegar. ANTONYM lethargy.

**vigorous** adjective **1** *the child was vigorous* ROBUST, healthy, hale and hearty, strong, sturdy, fit; hardy, tough, athletic; bouncing, thriving, flourishing, blooming; energetic, lively, active, perky, spirited, vibrant, vital, zestful; *informal* peppy, bouncy, in the pink. ANTONYMS weak, frail.

**2** *a vigorous defense of policy* STRENUOUS, powerful, forceful, spirited, mettlesome, determined, aggressive, two-fisted, driving, eager, zealous, ardent, fervent, vehement, passionate; tough, robust, thorough, blunt, hard-hitting; *informal* punchy. ANTONYMS weak, feeble.

**vigorously** adverb *she pedaled vigorously* STRENUOUSLY, strongly, powerfully, forcefully, energetically, heartily, vehemently, for dear life, for all one is worth, all out, fiercely, hard; *informal* like mad, like crazy, like gangbusters.

**vile** adjective *a vile smell* | *his vile crimes* FOUL, nasty, unpleasant, bad, disagreeable, horrid, horrible, dreadful, abominable, atrocious, offensive, obnoxious, odious, unsavory, repulsive, disgusting, distasteful, loathsome, hateful, nauseating, sickening; disgraceful, appalling, shocking, sorry, shabby, shameful, dishonorable, execrable, heinous, abhorrent, deplorable, monstrous, wicked, evil, iniquitous, nefarious, depraved, debased; contemptible, despicable, reprehensible; *informal* gross, godawful, lowdown, lousy; *archaic* scurvy. See note at DEPRAVED. ANTONYM pleasant.

**vilify** verb *the press has eagerly vilified Smith and her attorneys* DISPARAGE, denigrate, defame, run down, revile, abuse, speak ill of, criticize, condemn, denounce; malign, slander, libel, slur; *informal* tear apart/into, lay into, slam, badmouth, dis, crucify; *formal* derogate, calumniate. See note at MALIGN. ANTONYM commend.

**villain** noun *my favorite Disney villain was Cruella* CRIMINAL, lawbreaker, offender, felon, convict, malefactor, wrongdoer; gangster, gunman, thief, robber; rogue, reprobate, ruffian, hoodlum; miscreant, scoundrel; *Law* malfeasant; *informal* crook, con, bad guy, baddy, lowlife; *dated* cad, knave; *archaic* blackguard.

**villainous** adjective *a taut thriller in which the hero makes a subtle shift from virtuous to villainous* WICKED, evil, iniquitous, sinful, nefarious, vile, foul, monstrous, outrageous, atrocious, abominable, reprehensible, hateful, odious, contemptible, horrible, heinous, egregious, diabolical, flagitious, fiendish, vicious, murderous; criminal, illicit, unlawful, illegal, lawless; immoral, corrupt, degenerate, sordid, depraved, dishonest, dishonorable, unscrupulous, unprincipled; *informal* crooked, bent, lowdown, dirty, shady; *dated* dastardly. ANTONYM virtuous.

**vindicate** verb **1** *he was vindicated by the jury* ACQUIT, clear, absolve, exonerate; discharge, liberate, free; *informal* let off, let off the hook; *formal* exculpate. See note at ABSOLVE.

**2** *I had fully vindicated my contention* JUSTIFY, warrant, substantiate, ratify, authenticate, verify, confirm, corroborate, prove, defend, support, back up, bear out, evidence, endorse.

**vindictive** adjective *in her memoirs she revealed that Drake had been a vindictive ex-lover* VENGEFUL, revengeful, unforgiving, resentful, acrimonious, bitter; spiteful, mean, rancorous, venomous, malicious, malevolent, nasty, mean-spirited, cruel, unkind; *informal* catty. ANTONYM forgiving.

THE RIGHT WORD **vindictive, rancorous, spiteful, vengeful, venomous**

Someone who is motivated by a desire to get even might be described as **vindictive**, a word that suggests harboring grudges for imagined wrongs (*a vindictive person who had alienated friends and neighbors alike*). **Spiteful** is a stronger term, implying a bitter or vicious vindictiveness (*a spiteful child who broke the toy she had been forced to share*). **Vengeful** implies a strong urge to actually seek vengeance (*vengeful after losing her husband in hit-and-run accident*). Someone who is **rancorous** suffers from a deep-seated and lasting bitterness, although it does not imply a desire to hurt or to be vindictive (*his rancorous nature made him difficult to befriend*). **Venomous** takes its meaning from "venom" referring to someone or something of a spiteful, malignant nature and suggesting a poisonous sting (*a critic's venomous attack on the author's first novel*).

**vintage** noun **1** *1986 was a classic vintage for the Cabernet Sauvignon* YEAR.

**2** *furniture of Louis XV vintage* PERIOD, era, epoch, time, origin; genre, style, kind, sort, type.

▸ adjective **1** *vintage French wine* HIGH-QUALITY, quality, choice, select, prime, superior, best.

**2** *vintage automobiles* CLASSIC, ageless, timeless; old, antique, heritage, historic.

**3** *his reaction was vintage Bush* CHARACTERISTIC, typical, pure, prime, trademark.

**violate** verb **1** *this violates fundamental human rights* CONTRAVENE, breach, infringe, break, transgress, overstep, disobey, defy, flout; disregard, ignore, trample on. ANTONYM comply with.

**2** *they felt their privacy had been violated* INVADE, trespass upon, encroach upon, intrude upon; disrespect. ANTONYM respect.

**3** *the tomb was violated* DESECRATE, profane, defile, degrade, debase; damage, vandalize, deface, destroy.

**4** *he drugged and then violated her* RAPE, sexually assault, assault, force oneself on, abuse, attack, molest, interfere with; *archaic* defile, deflower, dishonor, ruin; *literary* ravish.

**violence** noun **1** *violence against women* BRUTALITY, brute force, ferocity, savagery, cruelty, sadism, barbarity, brutishness.

**2** *the protest ended in violence* FIGHTING, fights, bloodshed, brawling, disorder, rioting, hostility, turbulence, mayhem.

**3** *the violence of the blow* FORCEFULNESS, force, power, strength, might, savagery, ferocity, brutality.

**4** *the violence of his passion* INTENSITY, severity, strength, force, vehemence, power, potency, fervency, ferocity, fury, fire.

**violent** adjective **1** *he gets violent when drunk* BRUTAL, vicious, savage, rough, aggressive, abusive, physically abusive, threatening, fierce, physical, wild, ferocious; barbarous, barbaric, thuggish, pugnacious, cutthroat, smash-mouth, homicidal, murderous, cruel. ANTONYM gentle.

**2** *a violent blow* POWERFUL, forceful, hard, sharp, smart, strong, vigorous, mighty, hefty; savage, ferocious, brutal, vicious. ANTONYM weak.

**3** *violent jealousy* INTENSE, extreme, strong, powerful, vehement, intemperate, unbridled, uncontrollable, ungovernable, inordinate, consuming, passionate. ANTONYM mild.

**4** *a violent movie* GORY, gruesome, grisly, full of violence.

**virgin** noun *she remained a virgin* chaste woman/man, celibate; *literary* maiden, maid, vestal, ingenue.

▸ adjective **1** *virgin forest* UNTOUCHED, unspoiled, untainted, immaculate, pristine, flawless; spotless, unsullied, unpolluted, undefiled, perfect; unchanged, intact; unexplored, uncharted, unmapped.

**2** *virgin girls* CHASTE, virginal, celibate, abstinent; maiden, maidenly; pure, uncorrupted, undefiled, unsullied, innocent; *literary* vestal.

**virginal** adjective See VIRGIN adjective sense 2.

**virile** adjective *the strong, virile hero* MANLY, masculine, male; strong, tough, vigorous, robust, muscular, muscly, brawny, rugged, sturdy, lusty, husky; red-blooded, fertile; *informal* macho, butch, beefy, hunky. See note at MALE. ANTONYM effeminate.

**virtual** adjective **1** *a virtual guarantee* EFFECTIVE, in effect, near, near enough, essential, practical, to all intents and purposes.

**2** *a virtual shopping environment* SIMULATED, artificial, imitation, make-believe; computer-generated, online, virtual reality.

**virtually** adverb *the building is virtually empty* EFFECTIVELY, in effect, all but, more or less, practically, almost, nearly, close to, verging on, just about, as good as, essentially, to all intents and purposes, roughly, approximately; *informal* pretty much, pretty well; *literary* well-nigh, nigh on.

**virtue** noun **1** *the simple virtue of farm life* GOODNESS, virtuousness, righteousness, morality, integrity, dignity, rectitude, honor, decency, respectability, nobility, worthiness, purity; principles, ethics. See note at GOODNESS. ANTONYMS vice, iniquity.

2 *promptness was not one of his virtues* STRONG POINT, good point, good quality, asset, forte, attribute, strength, talent, feature. ANTONYM failing.

3 *archaic**she lost her virtue in the city.* See VIRGINITY.

4 *I can see no virtue in this* MERIT, advantage, benefit, usefulness, strength, efficacy, plus, point. ANTONYM disadvantage.

PHRASE: **by virtue of** *they hold the posts by virtue of family connections* BECAUSE OF, on account of, by dint of, by means of, by way of, via, through, as a result of, as a consequence of, on the strength of, owing to, thanks to, due to, by reason of.

**virtuosity** noun *the architect's virtuosity* SKILL, skillfulness, mastery, expertise, prowess, proficiency, ability, aptitude; excellence, brilliance, talent, genius, artistry, flair, panache, finesse, wizardry; *informal* know-how, chops.

**virtuoso** noun *the pianist is clearly a virtuoso* GENIUS, expert, master, past master, maestro, artist, prodigy, marvel, adept, professional, doyen, veteran; star, champion; *informal* hotshot, wizard, magician, pro, ace. ANTONYM beginner.

▸ adjective *a virtuoso violinist* SKILLFUL, expert, accomplished, masterly, master, consummate, proficient, talented, gifted, adept, good, capable; impressive, outstanding, exceptional, magnificent, supreme, first-rate, stellar, brilliant, excellent; *informal* superb, mean, ace. ANTONYM incompetent.

**virtuous** adjective *they were entirely virtuous in their endeavors* RIGHTEOUS, good, pure, whiter than white, saintly, angelic, moral, ethical, upright, upstanding, high-minded, principled, exemplary; law-abiding, irreproachable, blameless, guiltless, unimpeachable, immaculate, honest, honorable, reputable, laudable, decent, respectable, noble, worthy, meritorious; *informal* squeaky clean. See note at MORAL.

**virulent** adjective 1 *virulent herbicides* POISONOUS, toxic, venomous, noxious, deadly, lethal, fatal, dangerous, harmful, injurious, pernicious, damaging, destructive; *literary* deathly. ANTONYMS harmless, nontoxic.

2 *a virulent epidemic* INFECTIOUS, infective, contagious, communicable, transmittable, transmissible, spreading, pestilential; *informal* catching. ANTONYM noncontagious.

3 *a virulent attack on morals* VITRIOLIC, malicious, malevolent, hostile, spiteful, venomous, vicious, vindictive, bitter, sharp, rancorous, acrimonious, scathing, caustic, withering, nasty, savage, harsh. ANTONYMS benevolent, amicable.

**visible** adjective *there are no visible scratches* PERCEPTIBLE, perceivable, seeable, observable, noticeable, detectable, discernible; in sight, in/on view, on display; evident, apparent, manifest, transparent, plain, clear, conspicuous, front-and-center, obvious, patent, unmistakable, unconcealed, undisguised, prominent, salient, striking, glaring.

**vision** noun 1 *her vision was blurred by tears* EYESIGHT, sight, observation, (visual) perception; eyes; view, perspective.

2 *the psychic was troubled by visions of the dead* APPARITION, hallucination, illusion, mirage, specter, phantom, ghost, wraith, manifestation; *literary* phantasm, shade.

3 *visions of a better future* DREAM, daydream, reverie; plan, hope; fantasy, pipe dream, delusion.

4 *his speech lacked vision* IMAGINATION, creativity, inventiveness, innovation, inspiration, intuition, perception, insight, foresight, prescience.

5 *Melissa was a vision in lilac* BEAUTIFUL SIGHT, feast for the eyes, pleasure to behold, delight, dream, beauty, picture, joy, marvel; *informal* sight for sore eyes, stunner, knockout, looker, eye-catcher, peach.

**visionary** adjective 1 *a visionary person* INSPIRED, imaginative, creative, inventive, ingenious, enterprising, innovative; insightful, perceptive, intuitive, prescient, discerning, shrewd, wise, clever, resourceful; idealistic, romantic, quixotic, dreamy; *informal* starry-eyed.

2 *archaic a visionary image.* See IMAGINARY.

▸ noun *a visionary pictured him in hell* SEER, mystic, oracle, prophet/prophetess, soothsayer, augur, diviner, clairvoyant, crystal-gazer, medium; *literary* sibyl.

**visit** verb 1 *I visited my dear uncle* CALL ON, pay a visit to, go to see, look in on; stay with; stop by, drop by; *informal* go see; pop in on, drop in on, look up.

2 *she never visits* STOP BY, drop by, pay a visit, call; *informal* pop in, drop in.

3 *Alex was visiting the Yukon* STAY IN, stop over in, spend time in, vacation in; tour, explore, see.

▸ noun 1 *she paid a visit to her mom* CALL, social call, visitation.

2 *a **visit to** the museum* TRIP TO, tour of, look around; stopover at, stay at; vacation at; *formal* sojourn at.

**visitation** noun 1 *the bishop's visitations* VISIT, official, tour of inspection, survey, examination.

2 *a visitation from God* APPARITION, vision, appearance, manifestation, materialization.

3 *Jehovah punished them by visitations* AFFLICTION, scourge, bane, curse, plague, blight, disaster, tragedy, catastrophe; punishment, retribution, vengeance.

**visitor** noun 1 *I am expecting a visitor* GUEST, caller, house guest; company; *archaic* visitant.

2 *the monument attracts thousands of visitors each month* TOURIST, traveler, vacationer, day tripper, sightseer; pilgrim, habitué; foreigner, outsider, stranger, alien.

**visual** adjective 1 *visual defects* OPTICAL, optic, ocular, eye; vision, sight.

2 *a visual indication that the alarm works* VISIBLE, perceptible, perceivable, discernible.

▸ noun *the speaker used excellent visuals* GRAPHIC, visual aid, image, illustration, diagram, display; show and tell.

**visualize** verb *Grampa's colorful tales made it easy to visualize his childhood adventures* ENVISAGE, envision, conjure up, picture, call to mind, see, imagine, evoke, dream up, fantasize about, conceptualize, contemplate, conceive of.

**vital** adjective **1** *it is vital that action be taken soon* ESSENTIAL, of the essence, critical, crucial, key, indispensable, integral, all-important, imperative, mandatory, requisite, urgent, pressing, burning, compelling, high-priority, life-and-death. ANTONYMS unimportant, peripheral.

**2** *the vital organs* MAJOR, main, chief; essential, necessary. ANTONYMS minor, dispensable.

**3** *he is young and vital* LIVELY, energetic, active, sprightly, spry, spirited, vivacious, exuberant, bouncy, enthusiastic, vibrant, zestful, sparkling, dynamic, virile, vigorous, lusty, hale and hearty; *informal* peppy, spunky, full of beans, bright-eyed and bushy-tailed. See note at ALIVE. ANTONYM listless.

**vitality** noun *the bright weather has revived my vitality* LIVELINESS, life, energy, spirit, vivacity, exuberance, buoyancy, bounce, élan, verve, vim, pep, brio, zest, sparkle, dynamism, passion, fire, vigor, drive, punch; get-up-and-go.

**vitriolic** adjective *a vitriolic attack on the government* ACRIMONIOUS, rancorous, bitter, caustic, mordant, acerbic, trenchant, virulent, spiteful, savage, venomous, poisonous, malicious, splenetic; nasty, mean, cruel, unkind, harsh, hostile, vindictive, vicious, scathing, barbed, wounding, sharp, cutting, withering, sarcastic; *informal* bitchy, catty.

**vituperation** noun *in public he hid well the vituperation he dispensed at home* INVECTIVE, condemnation, opprobrium, scolding, criticism, disapprobation, fault-finding; blame, abuse, insults, vilification, denunciation, obloquy, denigration, disparagement, slander, libel, defamation, slurs, aspersions; vitriol, venom; *informal* flak; *formal* castigation. See note at SCOLD. ANTONYM praise.

**vivacious** adjective *their vivacious daughter had become moody and morose* LIVELY, spirited, bubbly, ebullient, buoyant, sparkling, lighthearted, jaunty, merry, happy, jolly, full of fun, cheery, cheerful, perky, sunny, breezy, enthusiastic, irrepressible, vibrant, vital, zestful, energetic, effervescent, dynamic; *informal* peppy, bouncy, upbeat, chirpy. ANTONYM dull.

**vivid** adjective **1** *a vivid blue sea* BRIGHT, colorful, brilliant, radiant, vibrant, glaring, strong, bold, deep, intense, rich, warm. ANTONYM dull.

**2** *a vivid account of urban poverty* GRAPHIC, evocative, realistic, lifelike, faithful, authentic, clear, detailed, lucid, eloquent, striking, arresting, impressive, colorful, rich, dramatic, lively, stimulating, interesting, fascinating, scintillating; memorable, powerful, stirring, moving, telling, haunting. See note at GRAPHIC. ANTONYM vague.

**vocabulary** noun **1** *technical vocabulary* LANGUAGE, lexicon, lexis, words; diction, terminology, phraseology, nomenclature, terms, expressions, parlance, idiom, jargon, vernacular, argot, cant; *informal* vocab, lingo, -speak, -ese.

**2** *she is improving her vocabulary* WORD POWER, lexicon, command of language; *informal* vocab.

**vocal** adjective **1** *vocal sounds* VOCALIZED, voiced, uttered, articulated, oral; spoken, viva voce, said.

**2** *a vocal critic of the government* VOCIFEROUS, outspoken, forthright, plain-spoken, expressive, blunt, frank, candid, open; vehement, strident, vigorous, emphatic, insistent, forceful, zealous, clamorous, loudmouthed.

▸ **(vocals)** plural noun *we'll record the vocals later* VOICES, singing; harmonies.

**vocation** noun *forestry is my vocation* CALLING, life's work, mission, purpose, function; profession, occupation, career, job, employment, trade, craft, business, line, line of work, métier.

**vociferous** adjective See VOCAL sense 2.

THE RIGHT WORD **vociferous, boisterous, clamorous, obstreperous, strident**

An angry crowd might be **vociferous**, which implies loud and unrestrained shouting or crying out (*a vociferous argument*). A happy crowd might be **boisterous**, which implies noisy exuberance or high-spirited rowdiness (*a boisterous celebration of spring*). A crowd that wants something is likely to be **clamorous**, which suggests an urgent or insistent vociferousness in demanding or protesting something. If people's demands are not met, they might become **obstreperous**, which means noisy in an unruly and aggressive way, usually in defiance of authority (*an obstreperous child*). **Strident** suggests a harsh, grating loudness that is particularly distressing to the ear (*her strident voice could be heard throughout the building*).

**vogue** noun *retro accessories are enjoying a new vogue* FASHION, trend, fad, craze, rage, enthusiasm, passion, obsession, mania; fashionableness, popularity, currency, favor; *informal* trendiness. PHRASE: **in vogue** *denim's been in vogue my whole lifetime* FASHIONABLE, voguish, stylish, modish, up-to-date, up-to-the-minute, du jour, modern, current; prevalent, popular, in favor, in demand, sought-after, all the rage; chic, chi-chi, smart, tony, kicky, le dernier cri; trendy, hip, cool, big, happening, now, in, with it.

**voice** noun **1** *she lost her voice* POWER OF SPEECH.

**2** *he gave voice to his anger* EXPRESSION, utterance, verbalization, vocalization.

**3** *we speak with one voice* OPINION, view, feeling, wish, desire, will; **(voice of the people)** vox populi; *informal* vox pop.

**4** *citizens must have a voice in this* SAY, influence, vote, input, role, representation, seat at the table.

**5** *a powerful voice for conservation* SPOKESPERSON, speaker, champion, representative, mouthpiece, intermediary; forum, vehicle, instrument, channel, organ, agent.

▸ verb *they voiced their opposition* EXPRESS, vocalize, communicate, articulate, declare, state, assert, reveal, proclaim, announce, publish, publicize, make public, make known, table, air, vent; utter, say, speak; *informal* come out with.

**void** noun *the void of space* VACUUM, emptiness, nothingness, nullity, blankness, vacuity; empty space, blank space, space, gap, cavity, chasm, abyss, gulf, pit, black hole.

▸ verb *the contract was voided* INVALIDATE, annul, nullify; negate, quash, cancel, countermand, repeal, revoke, rescind, retract, withdraw, reverse, undo, abolish; *Law* vacate; *formal* abrogate. ANTONYM validate.

▸ adjective **1** *vast void spaces* EMPTY, vacant, blank, bare, clear, free, unfilled, unoccupied, uninhabited. ANTONYM full.

**2** *a country* ***void of*** *man or beast* DEVOID OF, empty of, vacant of, bereft of, free from; lacking, wanting, without, with nary a. ANTONYM occupied.

**3** *the election was void* INVALID, null, ineffective, nonviable, useless, worthless, nugatory. ANTONYM valid.

THE RIGHT WORD **void, abrogate, annul, invalidate, negate, nullify**

To **void** a check, to **invalidate** a claim, to **abrogate** a law, and to **annul** a marriage all refer to the same basic activity, which is putting an end to something or depriving it of validity, force, or authority. But these verbs are not always interchangeable. *Annul* is the most general term, meaning to end something that exists or to declare that it never really existed (*the charter was annulled before it could be challenged*). *Abrogate* implies the exercise of legal authority (*Congress abrogated the treaty between the two warring factions*), while **nullify** means to deprive something of its value or effectiveness (*nullify the enemy's attempt to establish communications*). *Void* and *invalidate* are often used interchangeably as they both mean to make null or worthless (*void a legal document by tearing it up; invalidate a check by putting the wrong date on it*). **Negate** means to prove an assertion false (*her version of the story negated everything her brother had said*) or to nullify or make something ineffective (*the study's findings were negated by its author's arrest for fraud*).

**volatile** adjective **1** *a volatile personality* UNPREDICTABLE, changeable, variable, inconstant, inconsistent, erratic, irregular, unstable, turbulent, blowing hot and cold, varying, shifting, fluctuating, fluid, mutable; mercurial, capricious, whimsical, fickle, flighty, impulsive, temperamental, high-strung, excitable, emotional, fiery, moody, tempestuous. ANTONYMS stable, constant.

**2** *the atmosphere is too volatile for an election* TENSE, strained, fraught, uneasy, uncomfortable, charged, explosive, inflammatory, turbulent; *informal* nail-biting, ready to blow. ANTONYMS stable, calm.

**3** *a volatile organic compound* EVAPORATIVE, vaporous; explosive, inflammable; unstable, labile. ANTONYM stable.

**volition** PHRASE: **of one's own volition** *I joined the army of my own volition* OF ONE'S OWN FREE WILL, of one's own accord, by choice, by preference; voluntarily, willingly, readily, freely, intentionally, consciously, deliberately, on purpose, purposely; gladly, with pleasure.

**volley** noun *a volley of rifle shots* BARRAGE, cannonade, battery, bombardment, salvo, discharge, fusillade; storm, hail, shower, deluge, torrent; *historical* broadside.

**voluble** adjective *she was as voluble as her husband was silent* TALKATIVE, loquacious, garrulous, verbose, wordy, chatty, gossipy, effusive, gushing, forthcoming, conversational, communicative, expansive; articulate, fluent; *informal* mouthy, motormouthed, gabby, gassy, windy, talky. See note at TALKATIVE. ANTONYM taciturn.

**volume** noun **1** *a volume from the library* BOOK, publication, tome, hardback, paperback, title; manual, almanac, compendium.

**2** *a glass syringe of known volume* CAPACITY, cubic measure, size, magnitude, mass, bulk, extent; dimensions, proportions, measurements.

**3** *a huge volume of water* QUANTITY, amount, proportion, measure, mass, bulk.

**4** *she turned the volume down* LOUDNESS, sound, amplification; *informal* decibels.

**voluminous** adjective *the clown's voluminous trousers* CAPACIOUS, roomy, spacious, ample, full, big, large, bulky, extensive, sizable, generous; billowing, baggy, loose-fitting; *formal* commodious.

**voluntarily** adverb *they agreed to leave the country voluntarily* FREELY, of one's own free will, of one's own accord, of one's own volition, by choice, by preference; willingly, readily, intentionally, deliberately, on purpose, purposely, spontaneously; gladly, with pleasure.

**voluntary** adjective **1** *attendance is voluntary* OPTIONAL, discretionary, elective, noncompulsory, volitional; *Law* permissive. ANTONYMS compulsory, obligatory.

**2** *voluntary work* UNPAID, unsalaried, unwaged, for free, without charge, for nothing; honorary, volunteer; *Law* pro bono (publico). ANTONYM paid.

**volunteer** verb **1** *I volunteered my services* OFFER, tender, proffer, put forward, put up, venture.

**2** *he volunteered as a driver* OFFER ONE'S SERVICES, present oneself, make oneself available, sign up.

▸ noun *each volunteer was tested three times* SUBJECT, participant, case, patient; *informal* guinea pig.

**voluptuous** adjective **1** *a voluptuous model* CURVACEOUS, shapely, ample, buxom, full-figured; seductive, alluring, comely, sultry, sensuous, sexy, womanly; Junoesque, Rubenesque; *informal* bodacious, curvy, busty, stacked, built, slinky. See note at SENSUOUS. ANTONYM scrawny.

**2** *she was voluptuous by nature* HEDONISTIC, sybaritic, epicurean, pleasure-loving, self-indulgent; decadent, intemperate, immoderate, dissolute, sensual, licentious. ANTONYM ascetic.

**vomit** verb **1** *he needed to vomit* BE SICK, spew, heave, retch, gag, get sick; *informal* throw up, puke, purge, hurl, barf, upchuck, ralph.

**2** *I vomited my breakfast* REGURGITATE, bring up, spew up, cough up, lose; *informal* throw up, puke, spit up.

▸ noun *a coat stained with vomit* VOMITUS; *informal* puke, spew, barf.

**voracious** adjective. *her voracious appetite* INSATIABLE, unquenchable, unappeasable, prodigious, uncontrollable, compulsive, gluttonous, greedy, rapacious; enthusiastic, eager, keen, avid, desirous, hungry, ravenous; *informal* piggish; *rare* esurient.

**vortex** noun *a whirling vortex of smoke* WHIRLWIND, cyclone, whirlpool, gyre, maelstrom, eddy, swirl, spiral; black hole.

**vote** noun **1** *a rigged vote* BALLOT, poll, election, referendum, plebiscite; show of hands.

**2** *women finally got the vote* SUFFRAGE, voting rights, franchise, enfranchisement; voice, say.

▸ verb **1** *only half of them voted* GO TO THE POLLS, cast one's vote, cast one's ballot.

**2** *he was **voted in** as secretary* ELECT, return, select, choose, pick, adopt, appoint, designate, opt for, decide on.

**3** *I vote we have one more game* SUGGEST, propose, recommend, advocate, move, submit.

**vouch** PHRASE: **vouch for** *I can vouch for his honesty* ATTEST TO, confirm, affirm, verify, swear to, testify to, bear out, back up, support, stick up for, go to bat for, corroborate, substantiate, prove, uphold, sponsor, give credence to, endorse, certify, warrant, validate.

**voucher** noun *present your voucher to the attendant at the front door* COUPON, token, ticket, license, permit, pass; chit, slip, stub; *informal* ducat, comp.

**vow** noun *a vow of silence* OATH, pledge, promise, bond, covenant, commitment, avowal, profession, affirmation, attestation, assurance, guarantee; word, word of honor; *formal* troth.

▸ verb *I vowed to do better* SWEAR, pledge, promise, avow, undertake, engage, make a commitment, give one's word, guarantee; *archaic* plight.

**voyage** noun *the voyage lasted 120 days* JOURNEY, trip, expedition, excursion, tour; hike, trek, travels; pilgrimage, quest, crusade, odyssey; cruise, passage, flight, drive, road trip. See note at JOURNEY.

▸ verb *he voyaged through Peru* TRAVEL, journey, tour, globetrot; sail, steam, cruise, fly, drive; *informal* gallivant; *archaic* peregrinate.

**vulgar** adjective **1** *a vulgar joke* RUDE, indecent, indelicate, offensive, distasteful, coarse, crude, ribald, risqué, naughty, suggestive, racy, earthy, off-color, bawdy, obscene, profane, lewd, salacious, smutty, dirty, filthy, pornographic, X-rated; *informal* sleazy, raunchy, blue, locker-room; saucy, salty; *euphemistic* adult. ANTONYMS decent, inoffensive.

**2** *the decor was lavish but vulgar* TASTELESS, crass, tawdry, ostentatious, flamboyant, overdone, showy, gaudy, garish, brassy, kitsch, kitschy, tinselly, loud; *informal* flash, flashy, tacky. ANTONYMS tasteful, restrained.

**3** *it is vulgar to belch in public* IMPOLITE, ill-mannered, unmannerly, rude, indecorous, unseemly, ill-bred, boorish, uncouth, crude, rough; unsophisticated, unrefined, common, low-minded; unladylike, ungentlemanly. ANTONYMS genteel, decorous.

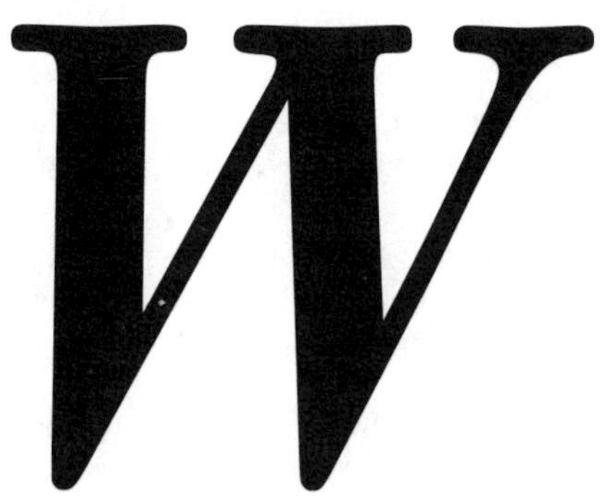

**wad** noun **1** *a wad of cotton* LUMP, clump, mass, pad, swab, hunk, wedge, ball, cake, nugget; bit, piece, plug.

**2** *a wad of $20 bills* BUNDLE, roll, pile, stack, sheaf, bankroll.

**3** *a wad of tobacco* QUID, twist, plug, chew, chaw.

▸ verb *he wadded up his napkin* CRUMPLE, stuff, press, gather, pack, wrap.

**wadding** noun *the wadding in the quilt is all lumpy* STUFFING, filling, filler, packing, padding, cushioning, quilting; (cotton) batting, (cotton) batten.

**waddle** verb *after seven weeks in a hospital bed, it's normal to waddle a bit* TODDLE, dodder, totter, wobble, shuffle; duck-walk.

**wade** verb **1** *they waded in the icy water* PADDLE, wallow, dabble; *informal* splosh.

**2** *I had to wade through some hefty documents* PLOW, plod, trawl, labor, toil; study, browse; *informal* splash, slog.

**waft** verb **1** *smoke wafted through the air* DRIFT, float, glide, whirl, travel.

**2** *a breeze wafted the smell toward us* CONVEY, carry, transport, bear; blow, puff.

**wag**[1] verb **1** *the dog's tail wagged frantically* SWING, swish, switch, sway, shake, quiver, twitch, whip, bob; *informal* waggle.

**2** *he wagged his stick at them* SHAKE, wave, wiggle, waggle, flourish, brandish.

**wag**[2] noun *he's a bit of a wag.* See JOKER.

**wage** noun **1** (usu. **wages**) *the farm workers' wages* | *a fair wage* PAY, payment, remuneration, salary, stipend, fee, honorarium; income, revenue; profit, gain, reward; earnings, paycheck; *Brit.* pay packet; *formal* emolument.

**2** (**wages**) *the wages of sin is death* REWARD, recompense, retribution; returns, deserts.

▸ verb *they waged war on the guerrillas* ENGAGE IN, carry on, conduct, execute, pursue, prosecute, proceed with.

**wager** noun *a wager of $100* BET, gamble, speculation; stake, pledge, ante.

▸ verb *I'll wager ten bucks on the home team* BET, gamble, lay odds, put money on; stake, pledge, risk, venture, hazard, chance.

**waggle** verb *informal*. See WAG[1] .

**waif** noun *a homeless waif* RAGAMUFFIN, urchin; foundling, orphan, stray; *derogatory* guttersnipe; *dated* gamin.

**wail** noun *a wail of anguish* HOWL, bawl, yowl, cry, moan, groan; shriek, scream, holler, yelp.

▸ verb *the children began to wail* HOWL, weep, cry, sob, moan, groan, keen, lament, yowl, snivel, whimper, whine, bawl, shriek, scream, yelp, caterwaul; *informal* blubber.

**wait** verb **1** *Jill waited while Jack fetched the water* STAY (PUT), remain, rest, stop, halt, pause; linger, loiter, dally; *informal* stick around, hang out, hang around, kill time, waste time, kick one's heels, twiddle one's thumbs; *archaic* tarry.

**2** *Joey waited until she nodded* HOLD ON, hold back, bide one's time, hang fire, mark time, stand by, sit tight, hold one's horses.

**3** *they were waiting for the kettle to boil* AWAIT; anticipate, look forward, long, pine, yearn, expect, be ready.

**4** *the movie will have to wait* BE POSTPONED, be delayed, be put off, be deferred; *informal* be put on the back burner, be put on ice.

▸ noun *a long wait* DELAY, holdup, interval, interlude, intermission, pause, break, stay, cessation, suspension, stoppage, halt, interruption, lull, respite, recess, moratorium, hiatus, gap, rest.

PHRASES: **wait on** *he waits on her as if he were a paid servant* SERVE, attend to, tend (to), cater for/to; minister to, take care of, look after, see to.

**wait up 1** *she waited up for him every night* STAY AWAKE, stay up, keep vigil.

**2** *hey, wait up!* STOP, slow down, hold on, wait for me.

**waive** verb **1** *he waived his right to a hearing* RELINQUISH, renounce, give up, abandon, surrender, cede, sign away, yield, reject, dispense with, abdicate, sacrifice, refuse, turn down, spurn. See note at RELINQUISH.

**2** *the manager waived the rules* DISREGARD, ignore, overlook, set aside, forgo, drop.

**wake** verb **1** *at 4:30 am Mark woke up* AWAKE, waken, awaken, rouse oneself, stir, come to, come round, bestir oneself; get up, get out of bed; *formal* arise. ANTONYM sleep.

**2** *she woke her husband* ROUSE, arouse, waken.

**3** *a shock woke him up a bit* ACTIVATE, stimulate, galvanize, enliven, animate, stir up, spur on, buoy, invigorate, revitalize; *informal* perk up, pep up.

**4** *they **woke up to** what we were saying* REALIZE, become aware of, become conscious of, become mindful of, clue in to.

**5** *the name woke an old memory* EVOKE, conjure up, rouse, stir, revive, awaken, rekindle, rejuvenate, stimulate. ANTONYM suppress.

▸ noun *a mourner at a wake* VIGIL, watch; funeral.

**wakeful** adjective **1** *he had been wakeful all night* AWAKE, restless, restive, tossing and turning. ANTONYM asleep.

**2** *I was suddenly wakeful* ALERT, watchful, vigilant, on the lookout, on one's guard, attentive, heedful, wary. ANTONYM inattentive.

**waken** verb. See WAKE verb senses 1, 2.

**walk** verb **1** *they walked along the road* STROLL, saunter, amble, trudge, plod, dawdle, hike, tramp, tromp, slog, stomp, trek, march, stride, sashay, glide, troop, patrol, wander, ramble, tread, prowl, promenade, roam, traipse; stretch one's legs; *informal* mosey, hoof it; *formal* perambulate.

**2** *he walked her home* ACCOMPANY, escort, guide, show, see, usher, take, chaperone, steer, shepherd.

▸ noun **1** *their country walks* STROLL, saunter, amble, promenade; ramble, hike, tramp, march; turn; *dated* constitutional.

**2** *the map shows several nature walks.* See TRAIL noun sense 5.

**3** *he shoveled the front walk* PATH, pathway, walkway, sidewalk.

**4** *her elegant walk* GAIT, step, stride, tread.

PHRASES: **walk all over** *informal* **1** *be firm or he'll walk all over you* TAKE ADVANTAGE OF, impose on, exploit, use, abuse, misuse, manipulate, take liberties with; *informal* take for a ride, run rings around.

**2** *we walked all over the home team.* See TROUNCE.

**walk off/away with** **1** *informal she walked off with my wallet.* See STEAL verb sense 1.

**2** *he walked off with four awards* WIN EASILY, win hands down, attain, earn, gain, garner, receive, acquire, secure, collect, pick up, net; *informal* bag.

**walk of life** *we come from different walks of life* CLASS, status, rank, caste, sphere, arena; profession, career, vocation, job, occupation, employment, business, trade, craft; province, field.

**walk out** **1** *he walked out in a temper* LEAVE, depart, get up and go, storm off/out, flounce out, absent oneself; *informal* take off.

**2** *teachers walked out in protest* (GO ON) STRIKE, stop work; protest, mutiny, revolt.

**walk out on** *did you hear that Sierra walked out on Curt?* DESERT, abandon, leave, betray, throw over, jilt, run out on; *informal* dump, ditch.

**walker** noun *a vigorous walker* HIKER, rambler, traveler, roamer, rover, pedestrian; *literary* wayfarer.

**walkout** noun *workers staged a walkout at 10:45 this morning* STRIKE, stoppage, industrial action, job action, revolt, rebellion.

**walkover** noun *after yesterday's walkover, today's tight game was especially exciting* EASY VICTORY, rout, landslide; *informal* piece of cake, pushover, cinch, breeze, picnic, laugher, whitewash; *informal* duck soup.

**wall** noun **1** *brick walls* BARRIER, partition, enclosure, screen, panel, divider; bulkhead.

**2** *an ancient city wall* FORTIFICATION, rampart, barricade, bulwark, stockade.

**3** *break down the walls that stop world trade* OBSTACLE, barrier, fence; impediment, hindrance, block, roadblock, check.

▸ verb **1** *tenements **walled in** the courtyard* ENCLOSE, bound, encircle, confine, hem, close in, shut in, fence in.

**2** *the doorway had been **walled up*** BLOCK, seal, close, brick up.

PHRASES: **go to the wall for** *informal I never asked you to go the wall for me* RISK EVERYTHING FOR, do anything for, put one's life on the line for.

**off the wall** *informal his outfits are really off the wall.* See UNCONVENTIONAL.

**wallet** noun *I've got maybe two or three dollars in my wallet* PURSE, change purse; billfold, pocketbook, fanny pack.

**wallow** verb **1** *pigs wallow in the mud* LOLL ABOUT/AROUND, roll about/around, lie about/around, splash about/around; slosh, wade, paddle; *informal* splosh.

**2** *a ship wallowing in stormy seas* ROLL, lurch, toss, plunge, pitch, reel, rock, flounder, keel, list; labor.

**3** *she seems to wallow in self-pity* LUXURIATE, bask, take pleasure, take satisfaction, indulge (oneself), delight, revel, glory; enjoy, like, love, relish, savor; *informal* get a kick out of, get off on.

**wan** adjective **1** *she looked so wan and frail* PALE, pallid, ashen, white, gray; anemic, colorless, bloodless, waxen, chalky, pasty, peaked, sickly, washed out, drained, drawn, ghostly. See note at PALE2 . ANTONYM flushed.

**2** *the wan light of the moon* DIM, faint, weak, feeble, pale, watery, washy. ANTONYM bright.

**wand** noun *the magician's wand* BATON, stick, staff, bar, dowel, rod; twig, cane, birch, switch; *historical* caduceus.

**wander** verb **1** *I wandered around the mansion* STROLL, amble, saunter, walk, dawdle, potter, ramble, meander; roam, rove, range, drift, prowl; *informal* traipse, mosey, tootle, mooch.

**2** *we are wandering from the point* STRAY, depart, diverge, veer, swerve, deviate, digress, drift, get sidetracked.

**wanderer** noun *a wanderer in the wilderness* TRAVELER, rambler, hiker, migrant, globetrotter, roamer, rover; itinerant, rolling stone, nomad; tramp, transient, drifter, vagabond, vagrant; *informal* hobo, bum; *literary* wayfarer.

**wane** verb *time-lapse photography shows the moon waning* DECLINE, diminish, decrease, dwindle, shrink, tail off, ebb, fade (away), lessen, peter out, fall off, recede, slump, flag, weaken, give way, wither, crumble, evaporate, disintegrate, die out; *literary* evanesce. ANTONYMS wax, grow.

**want** verb **1** *do you want more coffee?* DESIRE, wish for, hope for, aspire to, fancy, care for, like; long for, yearn for, crave, hanker after, hunger for, thirst for, cry out for, covet; need; *informal* have a yen for, have a jones for, be dying for.

**2** *informal you **want to** be more careful* SHOULD, ought to, need to, must.

**3** *this mollycoddled generation **wants for** nothing* LACK, be without, have need of, be devoid of, be bereft of, be missing. See note at LACK.

▸ noun **1** *his want of vigilance* LACK, absence, nonexistence, unavailability; dearth, deficiency, inadequacy, insufficiency, paucity, shortage, scarcity, deficit.

**2** *a time of want* NEED, neediness, austerity, privation, deprivation, poverty, impoverishment, penury, destitution; famine, drought.

**3** *all her wants would be taken care of* WISH, desire, demand, longing, yearning, fancy, craving, hankering; need, requirement; *informal* yen.

**wanting** adjective **1** *the defenses were found wanting* DEFICIENT, inadequate, lacking, insufficient, imperfect, unacceptable, unsatisfactory, flawed, faulty, defective, unsound, substandard, inferior, second-rate, poor, shoddy. ANTONYM sufficient.

**2** *millions were left* wanting for *food* WITHOUT, lacking, deprived of, devoid of, bereft of, in need of, out of; deficient in, short on; *informal* minus.

**wanton** adjective **1** *wanton destruction* DELIBERATE, willful, malicious, spiteful, wicked, cruel; gratuitous, unprovoked, motiveless, arbitrary, groundless, unjustifiable, needless, unnecessary, uncalled for, senseless, pointless, purposeless, meaningless, empty, random; capricious. ANTONYM justifiable.

**2** *a wanton seductress* PROMISCUOUS, immoral, immodest, indecent, shameless, unchaste, fast, loose, impure, abandoned, lustful, lecherous, lascivious, libidinous, licentious, dissolute, debauched, degenerate, corrupt, whorish, disreputable. ANTONYM chaste.

**war** noun **1** *the Napoleonic wars* CONFLICT, warfare, combat, fighting, (military) action, bloodshed, struggle; battle, skirmish, fight, clash, engagement, encounter; offensive, attack, campaign; hostilities; jihad, crusade. ANTONYM peace.

**2** *the war against drugs* CAMPAIGN, crusade, battle, fight, struggle, movement, drive.

▸ verb *rival empires **warred against** each other* FIGHT (AGAINST), battle (against), combat (against), wage war against, take up arms against; feud with, quarrel with, struggle with/against, contend with, wrangle with, cross swords with; attack, engage (against), take on, skirmish with.

**ward** noun **1** *the surgical ward* ROOM, department, unit, area, wing.

**2** *the majority of voters in our ward are Democrats* DISTRICT, constituency, division, quarter, zone, parish.

**3** *the boy is my ward* DEPENDENT, charge, protégé. PHRASE: **ward off 1** *we use this lotion to ward off gnats* FEND OFF, repel, repulse, beat back, chase away; *informal* send packing.

**2** *she warded off the blow* PARRY, avert, deflect, block; evade, avoid, dodge.

**3** *garlic is worn to ward off evil spirits* REBUFF, avert, keep at bay, fend off, stave off, turn away, repel, resist, prevent, obstruct, foil, frustrate, thwart, check, stop.

**warden** noun **1** *a park warden* RANGER; custodian, keeper, guardian, protector; superintendent, caretaker, supervisor.

**2** *his behavior was reported to the warden* GOVERNOR, executive, president, official; jailer, keeper; *informal* screw.

**wardrobe** noun **1** *she bought new shirts to expand his wardrobe* COLLECTION OF CLOTHES; garments, attire, outfits; trousseau.

**2** *chiefly Brit. she opened the wardrobe* (CLOTHES) CLOSET, armoire, locker, cupboard, cabinet.

**warehouse** noun *twelve DVD players were stolen from the warehouse* DEPOT, distribution center, storehouse, store, storeroom, depository, storage, entrepôt, stockroom; granary; *Military* magazine.

**wares** plural noun *on Saturdays, the weaver would come into town with his wares* MERCHANDISE, goods, products, produce, stock, commodities; lines, range; *informal* stuff.

**warfare** noun *neither side seems ready to end this warfare* FIGHTING, war, combat, conflict, (military) action, hostilities; bloodshed, battles, skirmishes.

**warlike** adjective *warlike leaders* AGGRESSIVE, belligerent, warring, bellicose, pugnacious, combative, bloodthirsty, jingoistic, hostile, threatening, quarrelsome; militaristic, militant, warmongering.

**warlock** noun *Samantha's father, the warlock Maurice* SORCERER, wizard, magus, (black) magician, enchanter; *archaic* mage.

**warm** adjective **1** *a warm kitchen* HOT, cozy, snug; *informal* toasty. ANTONYMS cold, cool.

**2** *a warm day in spring* BALMY, summery, sultry, hot, mild, temperate; sunny, fine. ANTONYMS cold, chilly.

**3** *warm water* HEATED, tepid, lukewarm. ANTONYMS cold, chilled.

**4** *a warm sweater* THICK, thermal, winter, woolly, fleecy, chunky. ANTONYMS light, summery.

**5** *a warm welcome* FRIENDLY, cordial, amiable, genial, kind, pleasant, fond; welcoming, hospitable, benevolent, benign, charitable; sincere, genuine, wholehearted, heartfelt, enthusiastic, eager, hearty. ANTONYMS unfriendly, hostile.

▸ verb *warm the soup in that pan* HEAT (UP), reheat, cook;

thaw (out), melt, warm up, microwave; *informal* zap, nuke. ANTONYM chill.

PHRASES: **warm to 1** *everyone warmed to him* LIKE, take to, get on (well) with, hit it off with, be on good terms with.

**2** *he couldn't warm to the notion* BE ENTHUSIASTIC ABOUT, be supportive of, be excited about, get into.

**warm up 1** *I run in place a bit just to warm up* LIMBER UP, loosen up, stretch, work out, exercise; prepare, rehearse.

**2** *the emcee warmed up the crowd* ENLIVEN, liven, stimulate, animate, rouse, stir, excite; *informal* get going.

**warmth** noun **1** *the warmth of the fire* HEAT, warmness, hotness, fieriness; coziness.

**2** *the warmth of their welcome* FRIENDLINESS, amiability, geniality, cordiality, kindness, tenderness, fondness; benevolence, charity; enthusiasm, eagerness, ardor, fervor, energy, effusiveness.

**warn** verb **1** *David warned her about the cat* NOTIFY, alert, apprise, inform, tell, make someone aware, forewarn, remind, give notice; *informal* tip off.

**2** *police are warning galleries to be alert* ADVISE, exhort, urge, counsel, caution.

**warning** noun **1** *the earthquake came without warning* (ADVANCE) NOTICE, forewarning, alert; hint, signal, sign, alarm bells; *informal* tip-off, heads-up, red flag.

**2** *a health warning* CAUTION, advisory, notification, information; exhortation, injunction; advice.

**3** *a warning of things to come* OMEN, premonition, foreboding, prophecy, prediction, forecast, token, portent, signal, sign; *literary* foretoken.

**4** *his sentence is a warning to other drunk drivers* EXAMPLE, deterrent, lesson, caution, exemplar, message, moral.

**5** *a written warning* ADMONITION, remonstrance, reprimand, censure, caution; *informal* dressing-down, talking-to.

**warrant** noun **1** *a warrant for his arrest* AUTHORIZATION, order, license, permit, document; writ, summons, subpoena; mandate, decree, fiat, edict.

**2** *a travel warrant* VOUCHER, slip, ticket, coupon, pass.

▸ verb **1** *the charges warranted a severe sentence* JUSTIFY, vindicate, call for, sanction, validate; permit, authorize; deserve, excuse, account for, legitimize; support, license, approve of; merit, qualify for, rate, be worthy of, be deserving of.

**2** *we warrant that the texts do not infringe copyright* GUARANTEE, affirm, swear, promise, vow, pledge, undertake, state, assert, declare, profess, attest; vouch, testify, bear witness; *formal* aver.

**warring** adjective *warring tribes* OPPOSING, conflicting, at war, fighting, battling, quarreling; competing, hostile, rival.

**warrior** noun *fearsome warriors* FIGHTER, soldier, serviceman, combatant, mercenary.

**wary** adjective **1** *he was trained to be wary* CAUTIOUS, careful, circumspect, on one's guard, chary, alert, on the lookout, on one's toes, on the qui vive; attentive, heedful, watchful, vigilant, observant; *informal* wide awake. See note at VIGILANT. ANTONYM inattentive.

**2** *we are wary of strangers* SUSPICIOUS, chary, leery, careful, distrustful, mistrustful, skeptical, doubtful, dubious. ANTONYM trustful.

**wash** verb **1** *he is washing in the guest bathroom* CLEAN ONESELF; bathe, take a bath, shower, soak, freshen up; *formal* perform one's ablutions.

**2** *he washed her socks* CLEAN, cleanse, rinse, launder, scour; shampoo, lather, sponge, scrub, wipe; sluice, douse, swab, disinfect; *literary* lave. ANTONYM soil.

**3** *waves washed against the hull* SPLASH, lap, splosh, dash, crash, break, beat, surge, ripple, roll.

**4** *the wreckage was washed downriver* SWEEP, carry, convey, transport.

**5** *it **washed up** on my front lawn* LAND, come to rest, be deposited, be beached.

**6** *guilt **washed over** her* SURGE THROUGH, rush through, course through, flood over, flow over; affect, overcome.

**7** *informal this story just won't wash* BE ACCEPTED, be acceptable, be plausible, be convincing, hold up, hold water, stand up, bear scrutiny; do.

▸ noun **1** *she needs a wash* CLEAN, shower, dip, bath, soak; *formal* ablutions.

**2** *that shirt should go in the wash* LAUNDRY, washing.

**3** *antiseptic skin wash* LOTION, salve, preparation, rinse, liquid; liniment.

**4** *the wash of the boat* BACKWASH, wake, trail, path.

**5** *the wash of the waves on the beach* SURGE, flow, swell, sweep, rise and fall, roll, splash.

**6** *a light watercolor wash* PAINT, stain, film, coat, coating; tint, glaze.

PHRASES: **wash one's hands of** *I'm going to wash my hands of the whole business* DISOWN, renounce, reject, forswear, disavow, give up on, turn one's back on, cast aside, abandon; *formal* abjure.

**wash up** *you kids can wash up after dinner* WASH THE DISHES, do the dishes, clean up.

**washed out** adjective **1** *a washed-out denim jacket* FADED, bleached, decolorized, stonewashed; pale, light, drab, muted. ANTONYM bold.

**2** *he looked washed out after his exams* EXHAUSTED, tired, worn out, weary, fatigued, spent, drained, enervated, rundown; *informal* done in, dog-tired, bushed, beat, zonked, pooped, tuckered out. ANTONYM energetic.

**waspish** adjective *he's a waspish old geezer* IRRITABLE, touchy, testy, cross, snappish, cantankerous, splenetic, short-tempered, bad-tempered, moody, ornery, crotchety, crabby; *informal* grouchy.

**waste** verb **1** *he doesn't like to waste money* SQUANDER, misspend, misuse, fritter away, throw away, lavish, dissipate, throw around; *informal* blow, splurge. ANTONYM conserve.

2 *these children are **wasting away** in the streets* GROW WEAK, grow thin, shrink, decline, wilt, fade, flag, deteriorate, degenerate, languish. ANTONYMS flourish, thrive.

3 *the disease wasted his legs* EMACIATE, atrophy, wither, debilitate, shrivel, shrink, weaken, enfeeble. See note at RAVAGE.

4 *informal I saw them waste the guy.* See MURDER verb sense 1.

▸ adjective 1 *waste material* UNWANTED, excess, superfluous, left over, scrap, useless, worthless; unusable, unprofitable.

2 *waste ground* UNCULTIVATED, barren, desert, arid, bare; desolate, void, uninhabited, unpopulated; wild.

▸ noun 1 *a waste of money* MISUSE, misapplication, misemployment, abuse; extravagance, wastefulness, lavishness.

2 *household waste* GARBAGE, rubbish, trash, refuse, litter, debris, flotsam and jetsam, dross, junk, detritus, scrap; dregs, scraps; sewage, effluent.

3 (usu. **wastes**) *the frozen wastes of the Arctic* DESERT, wasteland, wilderness, wilds, emptiness.

PHRASE: **lay waste** See LAY[1] .

**wasted** adjective 1 *a wasted effort* SQUANDERED, misspent, misdirected, misused, dissipated; pointless, useless, needless, unnecessary; vain, fruitless.

2 *a wasted opportunity* MISSED, lost, forfeited, neglected, squandered, bungled; *informal* down the drain.

3 *I'm **wasted in** this job* UNDEREMPLOYED IN/FOR, underused in, too good for, above.

4 *his wasted legs* EMACIATED, atrophied, withered, shriveled, weak, frail, shrunken, skeletal, rickety, scrawny, wizened.

5 *informal everybody at the party was wasted.* See DRUNK.

**wasteful** adjective *a wasteful use of fuel* PRODIGAL, profligate, uneconomical, inefficient, extravagant, lavish, excessive, imprudent, improvident, intemperate; thriftless, spendthrift; needless, useless. ANTONYM frugal.

**watch** verb 1 *she watched him as he spoke* OBSERVE, view, look at, eye, gaze at, stare at, gape at, peer at; contemplate, survey, keep an eye on; inspect, scrutinize, scan, examine, study, ogle, gawk at, regard, mark; *informal* check out, get a load of, eyeball; *literary* behold. ANTONYM ignore.

2 *he was being watched by the police* SPY ON, keep in sight, track, monitor, survey, follow, keep under surveillance; *informal* keep tabs on, stake out.

3 *will you watch the kids?* LOOK AFTER, mind, keep an eye on, take care of, supervise, tend, attend to; guard, safeguard, protect, babysit. ANTONYM neglect.

4 *we stayed to watch the boat* GUARD, protect, shield, defend, safeguard; cover, patrol, police.

5 *watch what you say* BE CAREFUL, mind, be aware of, pay attention to, consider, pay heed to.

▸ noun 1 *Bill looked at his watch* TIMEPIECE, chronometer; wristwatch, pocket watch, stopwatch.

2 *we kept watch on the yacht* GUARD, vigil, lookout, an eye; observation, surveillance, vigilance.

PHRASE: **watch out/it/yourself** *watch it, Bob, or you'll go over the edge | hey, you kids, watch yourselves!* BE CAREFUL, be watchful, be on your guard, beware, be wary, be cautious, look out, pay attention, take heed, take care, keep an eye open/out, keep one's eyes peeled, be vigilant.

**watchdog** noun 1 *they use watchdogs to ward off trespassers* GUARD DOG.

2 *a consumer watchdog* OMBUDSMAN, monitor, scrutineer, inspector, supervisor; custodian, guardian, protector.

**watcher** noun *the crime scene brought out your typical collection of watchers* ONLOOKER, spectator, observer, viewer, fly on the wall; witness, bystander, looker-on; spy; *informal* rubberneck; *literary* beholder.

**watchful** adjective *the watchful eye of their mother* OBSERVANT, alert, vigilant, attentive, awake, aware, heedful, sharp-eyed, eagle-eyed, hawk-eyed; on the lookout, on the qui vive, wary, cautious, careful, canny, chary. See note at VIGILANT.

**watchman** noun *the morning watchman comes on duty at half past five* SECURITY GUARD, custodian, warden; sentry, guard, patrolman, lookout, sentinel, scout, watch.

**watchword** noun *Quality First is the watchword of our company* GUIDING PRINCIPLE, motto, slogan, maxim, mantra, catchphrase, byword, shibboleth; *informal* buzzword.

**water** noun 1 *a glass of water* $H_2O$; *dated* Adam's ale.

2 *a house down by the water* SEA, ocean; lake, river; drink.

▸ verb 1 *water the plants* SPRINKLE, moisten, dampen, wet, spray, splash; soak, douse, souse, drench, saturate; hose (down).

2 *my mouth watered* MOISTEN, become wet, salivate; *informal* drool.

PHRASES: **hold water** *your story just doesn't hold water* BE TENABLE, ring true, bear scrutiny, make sense, stand up, hold up, be convincing, be plausible, be sound.

**water down** 1 *staff had watered down the drinks* DILUTE, thin (out), weaken; adulterate, doctor, mix; *informal* cut.

2 *the proposals were watered down* MODERATE, temper, mitigate, tone down, soften, tame; understate, play down, soft-pedal.

**waterfall** noun *a family of otters was frolicking in the waterfall* CASCADE, cataract, falls, chute.

**watertight** adjective 1 *a watertight container* IMPERMEABLE, impervious, (hermetically) sealed; waterproof, water-repellent, water-resistant. ANTONYM leaky.

2 *a watertight alibi* INDISPUTABLE, unquestionable, incontrovertible, irrefutable, unassailable, impregnable; foolproof, sound, flawless, airtight, bulletproof, conclusive. ANTONYM flawed.

**watery** adjective 1 *a watery discharge* LIQUID, fluid, aqueous; *technical* hydrous. ANTONYMS solid, thick.

2 *a watery meadow* WET, damp, moist, sodden, soggy, squelchy, slushy, soft; saturated, waterlogged; boggy, marshy, swampy, miry, muddy. ANTONYM dry.

**3** *watery soup* THIN, runny, weak, sloppy, dilute, diluted; tasteless, flavorless, insipid, bland. ANTONYMS thick, hearty.

**4** *the light was watery and gray* PALE, wan, faint, weak, feeble; *informal* wishy-washy, washy. ANTONYM bright.

**5** *watery eyes* TEARFUL, teary, weepy, moist, rheumy; *formal* lachrymose. ANTONYM dry.

**wave** verb **1** *he waved his flag in triumph* BRANDISH, shake, swish, move to and fro, move up and down, wag, sweep, swing, flourish, wield; flick, flutter.

**2** *the grass waved in the breeze* RIPPLE, flutter, undulate, stir, flap, sway, billow, shake, quiver, move.

**3** *the waiter waved them closer* GESTURE, gesticulate, signal, beckon, motion.

▸ noun **1** *she gave him a friendly wave* GESTURE, gesticulation; signal, sign, motion; salute.

**2** *he surfs the Malibu waves* BREAKER, roller, comber, boomer, ripple, white horse, bore, big kahuna; **(waves)** swell, surf, froth; backwash.

**3** *a wave of emigration* FLOW, rush, surge, flood, stream, tide, deluge, spate.

**4** *a wave of self-pity* SURGE, rush, stab, dart, upsurge, groundswell; thrill, frisson; feeling.

**5** *his hair grew in thick waves* CURL, kink, corkscrew, twist, ringlet, coil.

**6** *electromagnetic waves* ripple, vibration, oscillation.

PHRASES: **make waves** *informal just be quiet and don't make waves* CAUSE TROUBLE, be disruptive, be troublesome; make an impression, get noticed.
**wave aside** *he waved aside her protest* DISMISS, reject, brush aside, shrug off, disregard, ignore, discount, play down; *informal* pooh-pooh.
**wave down** *she had no luck waving down a cab* FLAG DOWN, hail, stop, summon, call, accost.

**waver** verb **1** *the candlelight wavered in the draft* FLICKER, quiver, twinkle, glimmer, wink, blink.

**2** *his voice wavered* FALTER, wobble, tremble, quaver, shake.

**3** *he wavered between the choices* BE UNDECIDED, be irresolute, hesitate, dither, equivocate, vacillate, waffle, fluctuate; think twice, change one's mind, blow hot and cold; *informal* shilly-shally, sit on the fence.

**wavy** adjective *wavy hair* | *a screen filled with wavy lines* CURLY, curvy, curved, undulating, squiggly, rippled, crinkly, kinked, zigzag.

**wax** verb *the moon is waxing* GET BIGGER, increase, enlarge. ANTONYM wane.

PHRASE: **wax lyrical** *sorry, I didn't mean to wax lyrical about the good old days* BE ENTHUSIASTIC, enthuse, eulogize, rave, gush, get carried away.

**way** noun **1** *a way of reducing the damage* METHOD, process, procedure, technique, system; plan, strategy, scheme; means, mechanism, approach.

**2** *she kissed him in her brisk way* MANNER, style, fashion, mode; modus operandi, MO.

**3** *I've changed my ways* PRACTICE, wont, habit, custom, policy, procedure, convention, routine, modus vivendi; trait, attribute, peculiarity, idiosyncrasy; conduct, behavior, manner, style, nature, personality, temperament, disposition, character.

**4** *which way leads home?* ROUTE, course, direction; road, street, track, path.

**5** *I'll go out the back way* DOOR, gate, exit, entrance, entry; route.

**6** *a short way downstream* DISTANCE, length, stretch, journey; space, interval, span.

**7** *April is a long way away* TIME, stretch, term, span, duration.

**8** *a car coming the other way* DIRECTION, bearing, course, orientation, line, tack.

**9** *in some ways, he may be better off* RESPECT, regard, aspect, facet, sense, angle; detail, point, particular.

**10** *the country is in a bad way* STATE, condition, situation, circumstances, position; predicament, plight; *informal* shape.
PHRASES: **by the way** *by the way, Roy is back in town* INCIDENTALLY, by the by, in passing, en passant, as an aside.
**give way 1** *the government gave way and passed the bill* YIELD, back down, surrender, capitulate, concede defeat, give in, submit, succumb; acquiesce, agree, assent; *informal* throw in the towel/sponge, cave in.

**2** *the door gave way* COLLAPSE, give, cave in, fall in, come apart, crumple, buckle.

**3** *grief* ***gave way to*** *guilt* BE REPLACED BY, be succeeded by, be followed by, be supplanted by.
**on the way** *help is on the way* COMING, imminent, forthcoming, approaching, impending, close, near, on us; proceeding, en route, in transit.

**wayfarer** noun *literary*. See WANDERER.

**waylay** verb **1** *we were waylaid and robbed* AMBUSH, hold up, attack, assail, rob; *informal* mug, stick up.

**2** *several people waylaid her for an interview* ACCOST, detain, intercept, take aside, pounce on, importune; *informal* buttonhole.

**wayward** adjective *a wayward child* WILLFUL, headstrong, stubborn, obstinate, obdurate, perverse, contrary, disobedient, insubordinate, undisciplined; rebellious, defiant, uncooperative, recalcitrant, unruly, wild, unmanageable, erratic; difficult, impossible; *formal* refractory. ANTONYM docile.

**weak** adjective **1** *they are too weak to move* FRAIL, feeble, delicate, fragile; infirm, sick, sickly, debilitated, incapacitated, ailing, indisposed, decrepit; tired, fatigued, exhausted, anemic; *informal* weedy. ANTONYM strong.

**2** *weak eyesight* INADEQUATE, poor, feeble; defective, faulty, deficient, imperfect, substandard. ANTONYMS strong, powerful, convincing, resolute, bright, loud.

**3** *a weak excuse* UNCONVINCING, untenable, tenuous, implausible, unsatisfactory, poor, inadequate, feeble, flimsy, lame, hollow; *informal* pathetic. ANTONYMS strong, powerful.

**4** *I was too weak to be a rebel* SPINELESS, craven, cowardly, pusillanimous, timid; irresolute, indecisive, ineffectual, inept, effete, meek, tame, ineffective, impotent, soft, faint-hearted; *informal* yellow, weak-kneed, gutless, chicken. ANTONYMS strong, resolute.

**5** *a weak light* DIM, pale, wan, faint, feeble, muted. ANTONYMS strong, bright.

**6** *a weak voice* INDISTINCT, muffled, muted, hushed, low, faint, thready, thin. ANTONYMS strong, loud.

**7** *weak coffee* WATERY, diluted, dilute, watered down, thin, tasteless, flavorless, bland, insipid, wishy-washy. ANTONYMS strong, powerful.

**8** *a weak smile* UNENTHUSIASTIC, feeble, halfhearted, lame.

THE RIGHT WORD **weak, debilitated, decrepit, feeble, frail, infirm**

Someone who is **weak** lacks physical, mental, or moral strength (*a weak heart; a weak excuse; too weak to resist temptation*). But there's nothing to suggest what the cause of this lack of strength might be. Someone who is **frail**, on the other hand, is weak because he or she has a slight build or delicate constitution (*a small, frail man*). Calling someone **feeble** implies that his or her weakness is pitiable (*too feeble to get out of bed*); when applied to things, *feeble* means faint or inadequate (*a feeble light*). **Infirm** suggests a loss of soundness, as from aging or illness (*poverty and illness had made him infirm*). **Debilitated** and **decrepit** also suggest that strength once present has been lost. But while someone who is young may be *debilitated* by disease, *decrepit* specifically refers to a loss of strength due to advanced age or long use (*a decrepit old woman who seldom left her house; a decrepit building that would soon be torn down*).

**weaken** verb **1** *the virus weakened him terribly* ENFEEBLE, debilitate, incapacitate, sap, enervate, tire, exhaust, wear out; wither, cripple, disable, emasculate.

**2** *she tried to weaken the blow for him* REDUCE, decrease, diminish, soften, lessen, moderate, temper, dilute, blunt, mitigate.

**3** *our morale weakened* DECREASE, dwindle, diminish, wane, ebb, subside, peter out, fizzle out, tail off, decline, falter.

**4** *the move weakened her authority* IMPAIR, undermine, erode, eat away at, compromise; invalidate, negate, discredit.

**weakling** noun *a ninety-pound weakling* PUSHOVER, namby-pamby, coward, milksop; *informal* wimp, weed, sissy, twinkie, drip, softie, doormat, chicken, yellow-belly, scaredy-cat, wuss.

**weakness** noun **1** *with old age came weakness* FRAILTY, feebleness, enfeeblement, fragility, delicacy; infirmity, sickness, sickliness, debility, incapacity, impotence, indisposition, decrepitude, vulnerability.

**2** *he has worked on his weaknesses* FAULT, flaw, defect, deficiency, weak point, failing, shortcoming, weak link, imperfection, Achilles heel, foible.

**3** *a weakness for champagne* FONDNESS, liking, partiality, preference, love, penchant, soft spot, predilection, inclination, taste, eye; enthusiasm, appetite; susceptibility.

**4** *the president was accused of weakness* TIMIDITY, cowardliness, pusillanimity; indecision, irresolution, ineffectuality, ineptitude, impotence, meekness, powerlessness, ineffectiveness.

**5** *the weakness of this argument* UNTENABILITY, implausibility, poverty, inadequacy, transparency; flimsiness, hollowness.

**6** *the weakness of the sound* INDISTINCTNESS, mutedness, faintness, feebleness, lowness; dimness, paleness.

**wealth** noun **1** *a gentleman of wealth* AFFLUENCE, prosperity, riches, means, substance, fortune; money, cash, lucre, capital, treasure, finance; assets, possessions, resources, funds; property, stock, reserves, securities, holdings; *informal* wherewithal, dough, moola. ANTONYM poverty.

**2** *a wealth of information* ABUNDANCE, profusion, mine, store, treasury, bounty, bonanza, cornucopia, myriad; *informal* lot, load, heap, mass, mountain, stack, ton; *formal* plenitude. ANTONYM dearth.

**wealthy** adjective *our wealthy neighbors have an indoor swimming pool* RICH, affluent, moneyed, well off, well-to-do, prosperous, comfortable, propertied; of substance; *informal* well-heeled, rolling in it, in the money, made of money, filthy rich, stinking rich, loaded, flush. ANTONYM poor.

THE RIGHT WORD **wealthy, affluent, flush, opulent, prosperous, rich, well-to-do**

If you have an abundance of money, you are **rich**. Another term for *rich* is **wealthy**, which may further imply that you are an established and prominent member of the community whose lifestyle is in keeping with your income (*a wealthy family whose influence on public opinion could not be ignored*). **Affluent** comes from the Latin word meaning to flow, and it connotes a generous income (*an affluent neighborhood*), while **opulent** suggests lavish spending or an ostentatious display of wealth (*an opulent mansion with every imaginable luxury*). One may come from an *affluent* family, in other words, and not have a particularly *opulent* lifestyle. If you're **prosperous**, you are thriving or flourishing (*a prosperous merchant; a prosperous business*). While *prosperous* suggests an economic situation that is on the rise, **flush** means having plenty of money on hand at a particular time (*she was feeling flush after receiving her first paycheck*). **Well-to-do** implies a generous income, enough to support comfortable living but not necessarily enough to be considered rich (*they were known as a well-to-do family with a strong commitment to educating their children*).

**wear** verb **1** *he wore a suit* DRESS IN, be clothed in, have on, sport, model; put on, don.

**2** *Barbara wore a smile* BEAR, have (on one's face), show, display, exhibit; give, put on, assume.

**3** *the bricks have been* ***worn down*** ERODE, abrade, rub away, grind away, wash away, crumble (away), wear down; corrode, eat away (at), dissolve.

**4** *the tires are wearing well* LAST, endure, hold up, bear up, prove durable.

▸ noun **1** *you won't get much wear out of that* USE, wearing, service, utility, value; *informal* mileage.

**2** *evening wear* CLOTHES, clothing, garments, dress, attire, garb, wardrobe; *informal* getup, gear, togs, duds; *formal* apparel; *literary* array.

**3** *the varnish will withstand wear* DAMAGE, friction, erosion, attrition, abrasion; weathering.

PHRASES: **wear down** *he wore down her resistance* GRADUALLY OVERCOME, slowly reduce, erode, wear away, exhaust, undermine.
**wear off** *the novelty soon wore off* FADE, diminish, lessen, dwindle, decrease, wane, ebb, peter out, fizzle out, pall, disappear, run out.
**wear on** *the afternoon wore on* PASS, elapse, proceed, advance, progress, go by, roll by, march on, slip by/away, fly by/past.
**wear out 1** *the fabric will eventually wear out* DETERIORATE, become worn, wear thin, fray, become threadbare, wear through.

**2** *the grandkids wore me out* FATIGUE, tire out, weary, exhaust, drain, sap, overtax, enervate, debilitate, jade, prostrate; *informal* poop, frazzle, do in.

**wearing** adjective. See WEARISOME.

**wearisome** adjective *the wearisome job of shingling the roof* TIRING, exhausting, wearying, fatiguing, enervating, draining, sapping, stressful, wearing, crushing; demanding, exacting, taxing, trying, challenging, burdensome, arduous, grueling, punishing, grinding, onerous, difficult, hard, tough, heavy, laborious, back-breaking, crippling, strenuous, rigorous, uphill; tiresome, irksome, weary, boring, dull, tedious, monotonous, humdrum, prosaic, unexciting, uninteresting.

**weary** adjective **1** *he was weary after cycling* TIRED, worn out, exhausted, fatigued, sapped, burnt-out, dog-tired, spent, drained, prostrate, enervated; *informal* all in, done in, beat, ready to drop, bushed, worn to a frazzle, pooped, tuckered out. See note at TIRED. ANTONYMS fresh, energetic.

**2** *she was* ***weary of*** *the arguments* TIRED OF, fed up with, bored by, sick of, burnt-out on; *informal* have had it up to here with. ANTONYM enthusiastic.

**3** *a weary journey* TIRING, exhausting, wearying, fatiguing, enervating, draining, sapping, wearing, trying, demanding, taxing, arduous, grueling, difficult, hard, tough. ANTONYM refreshing.

**weather** noun *what's the weather like?* FORECAST, outlook; meteorological conditions, climate, atmospheric pressure, temperature; elements.

▸ verb *we weathered the recession* SURVIVE, come through, ride out, pull through; withstand, endure, rise above, surmount, overcome, resist, brave; *informal* stick out.

PHRASE: **under the weather** *informal we were sorry to hear that Dottie's been under the weather.* See ILL adjective sense 1.

**weave** verb **1** *flowers were woven into their hair* ENTWINE, lace, twist, knit, intertwine, braid, plait, loop.

**2** *he weaves colorful plots* INVENT, make up, fabricate, construct, create, contrive, spin; tell, recount, relate.

**3** *he had to weave his way through the crowds* THREAD, wind, wend; dodge, zigzag.

**web** noun **1** *a spider's web* MESH, net, lattice, latticework, lacework, webbing; gauze, gossamer.

**2** *a web of friendships* NETWORK, nexus, complex, set, chain; tissue.

**3** *visit us on the Web* INTERNET, World Wide Web, Net, information superhighway, Infobahn, cyberspace.

▸ adjective *a web environment* ONLINE, Internet, virtual, digital, cyber, web-based, e-.

**wed** verb **1** *they are old enough to wed* MARRY, get married, become husband and wife; *informal* tie the knot, walk down the aisle, get hitched, take the plunge. ANTONYMS divorce, separate.

**2** *he will wed his girlfriend* MARRY, take as one's wife/husband, lead to the altar; *informal* make an honest woman of; *archaic* espouse. ANTONYMS divorce, jilt.

**3** *she wedded the two forms of spirituality* UNITE, unify, join, combine, amalgamate, fuse, integrate, bond, merge, meld, splice.

**wedded** adjective **1** *wedded bliss* MARRIED, matrimonial, marital, conjugal, nuptial; *Law* spousal; *literary* connubial.

**2** *she is* ***wedded to*** *her work* DEDICATED TO, devoted to, attached to, fixated on, single-minded about.

**wedge** noun **1** *the door was secured by a wedge* DOORSTOP, chock, block, stop.

**2** *a wedge of cheese* HUNK, segment, triangle, slice, section; chunk, lump, slab, block, piece.

▸ verb *she wedged her case between two bags* SQUEEZE, cram, jam, ram, force, push, shove; *informal* stuff.

**weed** PHRASE: **weed out** *first we weed out the unqualified candidates* ISOLATE, separate out, sort out, sift out, winnow out, filter out, set apart, segregate; eliminate, get rid of, remove, cut, chop; *informal* lose.

**weekly** adjective *weekly installments* ONCE A WEEK; lasting a week; *formal* hebdomadal.

▸ adverb *the directors meet weekly* ONCE A WEEK, every week, each week, on a weekly basis; by the week, per week, a week.

**weep** verb *even the toughest soldiers wept* CRY, shed tears, sob, snivel, whimper, whine, wail, bawl; *informal* boo-hoo, blubber.

**weepy** adjective *there were a lot a weepy people in the audience* TEARFUL, close to tears, upset, distressed, sad, unhappy; in tears, crying, weeping, sniveling; *informal* teary, misty-eyed, choked-up; *formal* lachrymose.

**weigh** verb **1** *she weighs the fruit* MEASURE THE WEIGHT OF, put on the scales; heft.

**2** *he weighed 170 lbs* HAVE A WEIGHT OF, tip the scales at, weigh in at.

**3** *the situation* ***weighed*** *heavily* ***on*** *him* OPPRESS, lie heavy on, burden, hang over, gnaw at, prey on (one's mind); trouble, worry, bother, disturb, get down, depress, haunt, nag, torment, plague.

**4** *he has to weigh his options* CONSIDER, contemplate, think about, mull over, chew over, reflect on, ruminate about, muse on; assess, appraise, analyze, investigate, inquire into, look into, examine, review, explore, take stock of.

**5** *they need to weigh benefit against risk* BALANCE, evaluate, compare, juxtapose, contrast, measure. PHRASE: **weigh down** *my fishing gear weighed me down* BURDEN, saddle, overload, overburden, encumber, hamper, handicap.

**weight** noun **1** *the weight of the book* HEAVINESS, mass, load, burden, pressure, force; poundage, tonnage.

**2** *his recommendation will carry great weight* INFLUENCE, force, leverage, sway, pull, importance, significance, consequence, value, substance, power, authority; *informal* clout.

**3** *a weight off her mind* BURDEN, load, millstone, albatross, encumbrance; trouble, worry, pressure, strain.

**4** *the weight of the evidence is against him* PREPONDERANCE, majority, bulk, body, lion's share, predominance; most, almost all.

**weighty** adjective **1** *a weighty tome* HEAVY, thick, bulky, hefty, cumbersome, ponderous. See note at HEAVY. ANTONYM light.

**2** *a weighty subject* IMPORTANT, significant, momentous, consequential, far-reaching, key, major, big, vital, critical, crucial; serious, grave, solemn. ANTONYMS unimportant, trivial.

**3** *a weighty responsibility* BURDENSOME, onerous, heavy, oppressive, taxing, troublesome, solemn.

**4** *weighty arguments* COMPELLING, cogent, strong, forceful, powerful, beefy, potent, effective, sound, valid, telling; impressive, persuasive, convincing, influential, authoritative. ANTONYM weak.

**weird** adjective **1** *weird apparitions* UNCANNY, eerie, unnatural, supernatural, unearthly, otherworldly, ghostly, mysterious, strange, abnormal, unusual; eldritch; *informal* creepy, spooky, freaky. ANTONYM normal.

**2** *a weird sense of humor* BIZARRE, quirky, outlandish, eccentric, unconventional, unorthodox, idiosyncratic, surreal, crazy, peculiar, odd, strange, queer, freakish, zany, madcap, outré; *informal* bizarro, wacky, freaky, way-out, offbeat, off the wall, wacko. ANTONYM conventional.

PHRASE: **weird out** *I'm a little weirded out by his spiky blue hair* DISTURB, freak out, unnerve, unsettle, alarm, alienate.

**welcome** noun *I appreciate the welcome I got from your parents* GREETING, salutation; reception, hospitality; red carpet (treatment).

▸ verb **1** *welcome your guests in their own language* GREET, salute, receive, meet, usher in.

**2** *we welcomed their decision* BE PLEASED BY, be glad about, approve of, appreciate, embrace; *informal* give the thumbs up to.

▸ adjective *welcome news* PLEASING, agreeable, encouraging, gratifying, heartening, promising, favorable, pleasant, refreshing; gladly received, wanted, appreciated, popular, desirable.

**welfare** noun **1** *the welfare of children* WELL-BEING, health, comfort, security, safety, protection, prosperity, success, fortune; interest, good.

**2** *we cannot claim welfare* social security, social assistance, benefit, public assistance; pension, credit, support; sick pay, unemployment benefit; *informal* the dole.

**well**[1] adverb **1** *he behaves well* SATISFACTORILY, nicely, correctly, properly, fittingly, suitably, appropriately; decently, fairly, kindly, generously, honestly. ANTONYM badly.

**2** *they get along well* HARMONIOUSLY, agreeably, pleasantly, nicely, happily, amicably, amiably, peaceably; *informal* famously. ANTONYM badly.

**3** *he plays the piano well* SKILLFULLY, ably, competently, proficiently, adeptly, deftly, expertly, admirably, excellently. ANTONYM poorly.

**4** *I know her well* INTIMATELY, thoroughly, deeply, profoundly, personally. ANTONYM barely.

**5** *they studied the recipe well* CAREFULLY, closely, attentively, rigorously, in depth, exhaustively, in detail, meticulously, scrupulously, conscientiously, methodically, completely, comprehensively, fully, extensively, thoroughly, effectively. ANTONYM negligently.

**6** *they speak well of him* ADMIRINGLY, highly, approvingly, favorably, appreciatively, warmly, enthusiastically, positively, glowingly. ANTONYM disparagingly.

**7** *she makes enough money to live well* COMFORTABLY, in (the lap of) luxury, prosperously.

**8** *you may well be right* QUITE POSSIBLY, conceivably, probably; undoubtedly, certainly, unquestionably.

**9** *he is well over forty* CONSIDERABLY, very much, a great deal, substantially, easily, comfortably, significantly. ANTONYM barely.

**10** *she could well afford it* EASILY, comfortably, readily, effortlessly. ANTONYM barely.

▸ adjective **1** *she was completely well again* HEALTHY, fine, fit, robust, strong, vigorous, blooming, thriving, hale and hearty, in good shape, in good condition, in fine fettle; *informal* in the pink. ANTONYM ill.

**2** *all is not well* SATISFACTORY, all right, fine, in order, as it should be, acceptable; *informal* OK, hunky-dory, jake. ANTONYM unsatisfactory.

**3** *it would be well to tell us in advance* ADVISABLE, sensible, prudent, politic, commonsensical, wise, judicious, expedient, recommended, advantageous, beneficial, profitable, desirable; a good idea. ANTONYM inadvisable.

PHRASES: **as well** *I'll have the shrimp cocktail as well* TOO, also, in addition, additionally, into the bargain, besides, furthermore, moreover, likewise, to boot.

**as well as** *we sell books as well as newspapers* TOGETHER

WITH, along with, besides, plus, and, with, on top of, not to mention, to say nothing of, let alone.

**well done** *well done, Robbie, your voice has never been better* CONGRATULATIONS, bravo, right on, congrats, my compliments, good work, three cheers, felicitations.

**well**[2] noun **1** *she drew water from the well* borehole, bore, spring, waterhole.

**2** *he's a bottomless well of forgiveness* SOURCE, supply, fount, reservoir, wellspring, mine, fund, treasury.

▸ verb *tears welled from her eyes* FLOW, spill, stream, run, rush, gush, roll, cascade, flood, spout; seep, trickle; burst, issue, upwell.

**well-advised** adjective *I'm not sure this is a well-advised investment* WISE, prudent, sensible.

**well-being** noun. See WELFARE sense 1.

**well-bred** adjective *a well-bred youngster such as yourself should not be cavorting with people of their station* WELL BROUGHT UP, polite, civil, mannerly, courteous, respectful; ladylike, gentlemanly, genteel, cultivated, urbane, proper, refined, patrician, polished, well-behaved.

**well-built** adjective *we need a couple of well-built guys to move these bookcases* STURDY, strapping, brawny, burly, hefty, muscular, muscly, strong, rugged, lusty, Herculean; *informal* hunky, beefy, husky, hulking. ANTONYM puny.

**well-known** adjective **1** *well-known principles* FAMILIAR, widely known, popular, common, everyday, established. ANTONYM abstruse.

**2** *a well-known family of architects* FAMOUS, famed, prominent, notable, renowned, distinguished, eminent, illustrious, celebrated, acclaimed, recognized, important; notorious. ANTONYM obscure.

**well-nigh** adverb *enforcing the recycling ordinance is well-nigh impossible* ALMOST, nearly, just about, more or less, practically, virtually, all but, as good as, nearing, close to, approaching; roughly, approximately; *informal* pretty much, nigh on.

**well off** adjective **1** *her family's very well off.* See WELL-TO-DO.

**2** *the prisoners were relatively well off* FORTUNATE, lucky, comfortable; *informal* sitting pretty.

**3** *the island is not **well off for** harbors* WELL SUPPLIED WITH, well stocked with, well furnished with, well equipped with; well situated for.

**well-read** adjective *a well-read history professor* KNOWLEDGEABLE, well-informed, well versed, erudite, scholarly, literate, educated, cultured, bookish, studious; *dated* lettered. ANTONYM ignorant.

**well-spoken** adjective *what a bright, well-spoken young man* ARTICULATE, eloquent, coherent, nicely spoken; refined, polite.

**well-to-do** adjective *her well-to-do Uncle Leroy* WEALTHY, rich, affluent, moneyed, well off, prosperous, comfortable, propertied; *informal* rolling in it, in the money, loaded, well-heeled, flush, made of money, on easy street. See note at WEALTHY.

**wet** adjective **1** *wet clothes* DAMP, moist, soaked, drenched, saturated, sopping, dripping, soggy; waterlogged. ANTONYM dry.

**2** *it was cold and wet* RAINY, raining, pouring, teeming, inclement, showery, drizzly, drizzling; damp; humid, muggy. ANTONYM dry.

**3** *the paint is still wet* STICKY, tacky; fresh. ANTONYM dry.

**4** *a wet mortar mix* AQUEOUS, watery, sloppy. ANTONYM dry.

▸ verb *wet the clothes before ironing them* DAMPEN, damp, moisten; sprinkle, spray, splash, spritz; soak, saturate, flood, douse, souse, drench. ANTONYM dry.

▸ noun **1** *the wet of his tears* WETNESS, damp, moisture, moistness, sogginess; wateriness.

**2** *the race was held in the wet* RAIN, drizzle, precipitation; spray, dew, damp.

**wharf** noun *there are no available boat slips at this wharf* QUAY, pier, dock, berth, landing, jetty; harbor, dockyard, marina.

**wheedle** verb *she wheedled us into hiring her brother* COAX, cajole, inveigle, induce, entice, charm, tempt, beguile, blandish, flatter, persuade, influence, win someone over, bring someone around, convince, prevail on, get around; *informal* sweet-talk, soft-soap.

**wheel** noun *a wagon wheel* disk, hoop, ring, circle.

▸ verb **1** *she wheeled the trolley away* PUSH, trundle, roll.

**2** *the flock of doves wheeled around* TURN, go around, circle, orbit.

PHRASE: **at/behind the wheel** *were you at the wheel when the accident occurred?* DRIVING, steering, in the driver's seat.

**wheeze** verb *even with that terrible wheezing, she won't quit smoking* BREATHE NOISILY, gasp, whistle, hiss, rasp, croak, pant, cough.

**whereabouts** plural noun *his whereabouts remain secret* LOCATION, position, site, place, situation, spot, point, vicinity; home, address, locale, neighborhood; bearings, orientation.

**wherewithal** noun *he has the wherewithal to start up his own business* MONEY, cash, capital, finance(s), funds; resources, means, ability, capability; *informal* dough, loot, necessary, boodle, bucks.

**whet** verb **1** *he whetted his knife on a stone* SHARPEN, hone, strop, grind, file. ANTONYM blunt.

**2** *something to whet your appetite* STIMULATE, excite, arouse, rouse, kindle, trigger, spark, quicken, stir, inspire, animate, waken, fuel, fire, activate, tempt, galvanize. ANTONYMS dull, spoil.

**whiff** noun **1** *I caught a whiff of perfume* FAINT SMELL, trace, sniff, scent, odor, aroma.

**2** *the faintest whiff of irony* TRACE, hint, suggestion, impression, suspicion, soupçon, smidgen, nuance, intimation, tinge, vein, shred, whisper, air, element, overtone.

**3** *whiffs of smoke from the boiler* PUFF, gust, flurry, breath, draft, waft.

**while** noun *we chatted for a while* TIME, spell, stretch, stint, span, interval, period; duration, phase, patch.

▸ verb *tennis helped to while away the time* PASS, spend, occupy, use up, fritter, kill.

**whim** noun **1** *she bought it on a whim* IMPULSE, urge, notion, fancy, foible, caprice, conceit, vagary, inclination, megrim.

**2** *human whim* CAPRICIOUSNESS, whimsy, caprice, volatility, fickleness, idiosyncrasy.

**whimper** noun & verb *we heard her whimpers from downstairs* | *why is he whimpering?* WHINE, cry, sob, moan, snivel, wail, groan; mewl, bleat.

**whimsical** adjective **1** *a whimsical sense of humor* FANCIFUL, playful, mischievous, waggish, quaint, quizzical, curious, droll; eccentric, quirky, idiosyncratic, unconventional, outlandish, queer, fey; *informal* offbeat, freaky.

**2** *the whimsical arbitrariness of autocracy* VOLATILE, capricious, fickle, changeable, unpredictable, variable, erratic, mercurial, mutable, inconstant, inconsistent, unstable, protean.

**whine** noun & verb **1** *a whine from the kennel* | *she heard an animal whine* WHIMPER, cry, mewl, howl, yowl.

**2** *the motor's whine* | *the motor whined* HUM, drone.

**3** *his latest whine was about the long hours* | *stop whining!* COMPLAINT [noun], COMPLAIN [verb], grouse, grumble, murmur; *informal* gripe, moan, grouch, whinge, bellyache, beef.

**whip** noun *he would use a whip on his dogs* LASH, scourge, strap, belt, rod, bullwhip; *historical* cat-o'-nine-tails.

▸ verb **1** *he whipped the boy* FLOG, scourge, flagellate, lash, strap, belt, thrash, beat, tan someone's hide.

**2** *whip the cream* WHISK, beat.

**3** *she whipped her listeners into a frenzy* ROUSE, stir up, excite, galvanize, electrify, stimulate, inspire, fire up, get someone going, inflame, agitate, goad, provoke.

**4** *informal* *he whipped around the corner.* See DASH verb sense 1.

**5** *informal* *then she whipped out a revolver* PULL, whisk, pluck, jerk.

**whirl** verb **1** *leaves whirled in eddies* ROTATE, circle, wheel, turn, revolve, orbit, spin, twirl.

**2** *they whirled past* HURRY, race, dash, rush, run, sprint, bolt, dart, gallop, career, charge, shoot, hurtle, fly, speed, scurry; *informal* tear, belt, pelt, scoot, bomb, hightail it.

**3** *his mind was whirling* SPIN, reel, swim.

▸ noun **1** *a whirl of dust* SWIRL, flurry, eddy.

**2** *the mad social whirl* HURLY-BURLY, activity, bustle, rush, flurry, fuss, turmoil, merry-go-round.

**3** *Laura's mind was in a whirl* SPIN, daze, stupor, muddle, jumble; confusion; *informal* dither.

**whirlpool** noun **1** *a river full of whirlpools* EDDY, vortex, maelstrom.

**2** *the health club has a whirlpool* HOT TUB; *trademark* Jacuzzi.

**whirlwind** noun **1** *the building was hit by a whirlwind* TORNADO, hurricane, typhoon, cyclone, vortex, twister, dust devil.

**2** *a whirlwind of activity* MAELSTROM, welter, bedlam, mayhem, babel, swirl, tumult, hurly-burly, commotion, confusion; *informal* madhouse, three-ring circus.

▸ adjective *a whirlwind romance* RAPID, lightning, headlong, impulsive, breakneck, meteoric, sudden, swift, fast, quick, speedy, dizzying; *informal* quickie.

**whisk** verb **1** *the cable car will whisk you to the top* SPEED, hurry, rush, sweep, hurtle, shoot.

**2** *she whisked the cloth away* PULL, snatch, pluck, tug, jerk; *informal* whip, yank.

**3** *he whisked out of sight* DASH, rush, race, bolt, dart, gallop, career, charge, shoot, hurtle, fly, speed, zoom, scurry, scuttle, scamper; *informal* tear, belt, pelt, scoot, zip, whip.

**4** *she whisked the hair from her face* FLICK, brush, sweep, wave.

**5** *whisk the egg yolks* WHIP, beat, mix.

**whisper** verb **1** *Alison whispered in his ear* MURMUR, mutter, mumble, speak softly, breathe; hiss; *formal* susurrate. ANTONYM shout.

**2** *literary* *the wind whispered in the grass* RUSTLE, murmur, sigh, moan, whoosh, whir, swish, blow, breathe. ANTONYM roar.

▸ noun **1** *she spoke in a whisper* MURMUR, mutter, mumble, low voice, undertone; *rare* sibilation, susurration.

**2** *literary* *the wind died to a whisper* RUSTLE, murmur, sigh, whoosh, swish.

**3** *I heard the whisper that he's left town* RUMOR, story, report, speculation, insinuation, suggestion, hint; *informal* buzz.

**4** *not a whisper of interest.* See WHIT.

**whit** noun *they gave him not a whit of consideration* SCRAP, bit, speck, iota, jot, atom, crumb, shred, grain, mite, touch, trace, shadow, suggestion, whisper, suspicion, scintilla, modicum; *informal* smidgen, smidge.

**white** adjective **1** *a clean white bandage* COLORLESS, unpigmented, bleached, natural; snowy, milky, chalky, ivory.

**2** *her face was white with fear* PALE, pallid, wan, ashen, bloodless, waxen, chalky, pasty, washed out, drained, drawn, ghostly, deathly.

**3** *white hair* SNOWY, gray, silver, silvery, hoary, grizzled.

**4** *the early white settlers* CAUCASIAN, European.

**white-collar** adjective *white-collar workers* CLERICAL, administrative, professional, executive, salaried, office.

**whiten** verb *the sun has whitened the pink towels* MAKE WHITE, make pale, bleach, blanch, lighten, fade.

**whitewash** noun **1** *the report was a whitewash* COVER-UP, camouflage, deception, facade, veneer, pretext. ANTONYM exposé.

**2** *informal a four-game whitewash* WALKOVER, rout, landslide; *informal* pushover, cinch, breeze.

▸ verb *don't whitewash what happened* COVER UP, sweep under the carpet, hush up, suppress, draw a veil over, conceal, veil, obscure, keep secret; gloss over, downplay, soft-pedal. ANTONYM expose.

**whittle** verb **1** *he sat whittling a piece of wood* PARE, shave, trim, carve, shape, model.

**2** *his powers were **whittled away*** ERODE, wear away, eat away, reduce, diminish, undermine, weaken, subvert, compromise, impair, impede, hinder, cripple, disable, enfeeble, sap.

**3** *the ten teams have been **whittled down** to six* REDUCE, cut down, cut back, prune, trim, slim down, pare down, shrink, decrease, diminish.

**whole** adjective **1** *the whole report* ENTIRE, complete, full, unabridged, uncut. ANTONYM incomplete.

**2** *they unearthed a whole humanoid skull* INTACT, in one piece, unbroken; undamaged, unmarked, perfect.

▸ noun **1** *a single whole* ENTITY, unit, body, discrete item, ensemble.

**2** ***the whole** of the year* ALL, every part, the lot, the sum, the sum total, the entirety.

PHRASE: **on the whole** *on the whole, they lived peaceably* OVERALL, all in all, all things considered, for the most part, in the main, in general, generally, generally speaking, as a rule, as a general rule, by and large; normally, usually, more often than not, almost always, most of the time, typically, ordinarily.

**wholehearted** adjective *you have my wholehearted support* COMMITTED, positive, emphatic, devoted, dedicated, enthusiastic, unshakable, unswerving; unqualified, unstinting, unreserved, without reservations, unconditional, unequivocal, unmitigated; complete, full, total, absolute. ANTONYM halfhearted.

**wholesale** adverb *the images were removed wholesale* EXTENSIVELY, on a large scale, comprehensively; indiscriminately, without exception, across the board. ANTONYM selectively.

▸ adjective *wholesale destruction* EXTENSIVE, widespread, large-scale, wide-ranging, comprehensive, total, mass; indiscriminate. ANTONYM partial.

**wholesome** adjective **1** *wholesome food* HEALTHY, health-giving, healthful, good (for one), nutritious, nourishing; natural, uncontaminated, organic.

**2** *wholesome fun* GOOD, ethical, moral, clean, virtuous, pure, innocent, chaste; uplifting, edifying, proper, correct, decent, harmless; *informal* squeaky clean.

**wholly** adverb **1** *the measures were wholly inadequate* COMPLETELY, totally, absolutely, entirely, fully, thoroughly, utterly, quite, perfectly, downright, in every respect, in all respects; *informal* one hundred percent, 'lock, stock, and barrel.'

**2** *they rely wholly on you* EXCLUSIVELY, only, solely, purely, alone.

**whoop** noun & verb *whoops of delight | he whooped for joy* SHOUT, cry, call, yell, roar, scream, shriek, screech, cheer, hoot; *informal* holler.

**whore** noun *the whores on the street.* See PROSTITUTE.

▸ verb **1** *she spent her life whoring* WORK AS A PROSTITUTE, sell one's body, sell oneself, be on the streets.

**2** *the men whored and drank* USE PROSTITUTES; *archaic* wench.

**wicked** adjective **1** *wicked deeds* EVIL, sinful, immoral, wrong, morally wrong, wrongful, bad, iniquitous, corrupt, base, mean, vile; villainous, nefarious, erring, foul, monstrous, shocking, outrageous, atrocious, abominable, depraved, reprehensible, hateful, detestable, despicable, odious, contemptible, horrible, heinous, egregious, execrable, fiendish, vicious, murderous, black-hearted, barbarous; criminal, illicit, unlawful, illegal, lawless, felonious, dishonest, unscrupulous; *Law* malfeasant; *informal* crooked; *dated* dastardly. ANTONYM virtuous.

**2** *the wind was wicked* NASTY, harsh, formidable, unpleasant, foul, bad, disagreeable, irksome, troublesome, displeasing, uncomfortable, annoying, irritating, hateful, detestable. ANTONYM agreeable.

**3** *a wicked sense of humor* MISCHIEVOUS, playful, naughty, impish, roguish, arch, puckish, cheeky.

**4** *informal Sophie makes wicked cakes.* See EXCELLENT.

**wide** adjective **1** *a wide river* BROAD, extensive, spacious, vast, spread out. ANTONYM narrow.

**2** *their eyes were wide with shock* FULLY OPEN, dilated, gaping, staring, wide open. ANTONYM closed.

**3** *a wide range of opinion* COMPREHENSIVE, broad, extensive, diverse, full, ample, large, large-scale, wide-ranging, exhaustive, general, all-inclusive. ANTONYMS limited, restricted.

**4** *her shot was wide* OFF TARGET, off the mark, inaccurate. ANTONYM on target.

▸ adverb **1** *he opened his eyes wide* FULLY, to the fullest/furthest extent, as far/much as possible, all the way, completely.

**2** *he shot wide* OFF TARGET, inaccurately.

PHRASE: **wide open 1** *their mouths were wide open* AGAPE, yawning, open wide, fully open.

**2** *the championship is wide open* UNDECIDED, unpredictable, uncertain, unsure, in the balance, up in the air; *informal* anyone's/anybody's guess.

**3** *they were **wide open to** attacks* VULNERABLE TO, exposed to, unprotected from, undefended from, at risk of, in danger of.

**wide-eyed** adjective **1** *the onlookers were wide-eyed as the spaceship descended* SURPRISED, flabbergasted, amazed, astonished, astounded, stunned, staggered, goggle-eyed, pop-eyed, open-mouthed, dumbstruck; enthralled, fascinated, gripped.

2 *a wide-eyed youth in a wicked world* INNOCENT, naive, impressionable, ingenuous, childlike, credulous, trusting, unquestioning, unsophisticated, gullible.

**widen** verb 1 *a proposal to widen the highway* BROADEN, make/become wider, open up/out, expand, extend, enlarge.

2 *the organization must widen its support* INCREASE, augment, boost, swell, enlarge.

**widespread** adjective *widespread starvation* GENERAL, extensive, universal, common, global, worldwide, international, omnipresent, ubiquitous, across the board, blanket, sweeping, wholesale; predominant, prevalent, rife, broad, rampant, pervasive. ANTONYM limited.

**width** noun 1 *the width of the river* BREADTH, broadness, wideness, thickness, span, diameter, girth. ANTONYM length.

2 *the width of experience required* RANGE, breadth, compass, scope, span, spectrum, scale, extent, extensiveness, comprehensiveness. ANTONYM narrowness.

**wield** verb 1 *he was wielding a sword* BRANDISH, flourish, wave, swing; use, employ, handle.

2 *he has wielded power since 1972* EXERCISE, exert, hold, maintain, command, control.

**wife** noun *after seventeen years, he was still madly in love with his wife* SPOUSE, partner, life partner, mate, consort, woman, helpmate, helpmeet, bride; *informal* old lady, wifey, better half, other half, missus, ball and chain, significant other.

**wild** adjective 1 *wild animals* UNTAMED, undomesticated, feral; fierce, ferocious, savage, untamable. ANTONYM tame.

2 *wild flowers* UNCULTIVATED, native, indigenous. ANTONYM cultivated.

3 *wild tribes* PRIMITIVE, uncivilized, uncultured; savage, barbarous, barbaric. ANTONYM civilized.

4 *wild country* UNINHABITED, unpopulated, uncultivated; rugged, rough, inhospitable, desolate, barren.

5 *wild weather* STORMY, squally, tempestuous, turbulent. ANTONYM calm.

6 *her wild black hair* DISHEVELED, tousled, tangled, windswept, untidy, unkempt, mussed up. ANTONYM tidy.

7 *wild behavior* UNCONTROLLED, unrestrained, out of control, undisciplined, unruly, rowdy, disorderly, riotous, corybantic. ANTONYMS self-disciplined, disciplined.

8 *wild with excitement* VERY EXCITED, delirious, in a frenzy; tumultuous, passionate, vehement, unrestrained. ANTONYM calm.

9 *informal* *I was wild with jealousy* DISTRAUGHT, frantic, beside oneself, in a frenzy, hysterical, deranged, berserk; *informal* mad, crazy.

10 *informal* *Hank went wild when he found out.* See FURIOUS sense 1.

11 *informal* *his family wasn't **wild about** me* ENAMORED OF, (very) enthusiastic about, (very) keen on, infatuated with, smitten with; *informal* crazy about, blown away by, mad about, nuts about. ANTONYMS indifferent, unenthusiastic.

12 *Bill's wild schemes* MADCAP, ridiculous, ludicrous, foolish, rash, stupid, foolhardy, idiotic, absurd, silly, ill-considered, senseless, nonsensical; impractical, impracticable, unworkable; *informal* crazy, crackpot, cockeyed, harebrained, cockamamie, loopy. ANTONYMS sensible, practical.

13 *a wild guess* RANDOM, arbitrary, haphazard, hit-or-miss, uninformed. ANTONYM considered.

PHRASE: **run wild** 1 *the children are running wild* RUN AMOK, run riot, get out of control, be undisciplined.

2 *the garden had run wild* GROW UNCHECKED, grow profusely, run riot, ramble.

**wilderness** noun 1 *the Siberian wilderness* WILDS, wastes, bush, bush country, bushland, inhospitable region; desert, backcountry, outback, great outdoors; *informal* boondocks, boonies.

2 *the urban wilderness* WASTELAND, no man's land; *informal* wilds.

▸ adjective *wilderness activities* OUTDOOR RECREATION, ecotourism, adventure, backcountry.

**will**[1] verb *accidents will happen* TEND TO, have a tendency to, are bound to, do, are going to, must.

**will**[2] noun 1 *the will to succeed* DETERMINATION, willpower, strength of character, resolution, resolve, resoluteness, single-mindedness, purposefulness, drive, commitment, dedication, doggedness, tenacity, tenaciousness, staying power.

2 *they stayed against their will* DESIRE, wish, preference, inclination, intention, intent, volition.

3 *God's will* WISH, desire, decision, choice; decree, command.

4 *the dead man's will* TESTAMENT, last will and testament, bequest.

▸ verb 1 *do what you will* WANT, wish, please, see/think fit, think best, like, choose, prefer.

2 *God willed it* DECREE, order, ordain, command.

3 *she willed the money to her husband* BEQUEATH, leave, hand down, pass on, settle on; *Law* devise.

PHRASE: **at will** *he thought he could walk in and out of my life at will* AS ONE PLEASES, as one thinks fit, to suit oneself, at whim.

**willful** adjective 1 *willful destruction* DELIBERATE, intentional, done on purpose, premeditated, planned, conscious. ANTONYMS accidental, unintentional.

2 *a willful child* HEADSTRONG, strong-willed, obstinate, stubborn, pigheaded, recalcitrant, uncooperative, obstreperous, ungovernable, unmanageable; balky; *formal* refractory, contumacious. ANTONYMS biddable, amenable.

**willing** adjective 1 *I'm willing to give it a try* READY, prepared, disposed, inclined, of a mind, minded; happy, glad, pleased, agreeable, amenable; *informal* game. ANTONYMS reluctant, disinclined.

**2** *willing help* READILY GIVEN, willingly given, ungrudging, volunteered. ANTONYM grudging.

**willingly** adverb *I willingly agreed to make a donation* VOLUNTARILY, of one's own free will, of one's own accord; readily, without reluctance, ungrudgingly, cheerfully, happily, gladly, with pleasure.

**willingness** noun *we appreciate your willingness to help* READINESS, inclination, will, wish, desire, alacrity.

**willpower** noun See WILL[2] noun sense 1.

**wilt** verb **1** *the roses had begun to wilt* DROOP, sag, become limp, flop; wither, shrivel (up). ANTONYMS flourish, thrive.

**2** *we wilted in the heat* LANGUISH, flag, droop, become listless, tire, wane. ANTONYM perk up.

**wily** adjective *a wily old rascal* SHREWD, clever, sharp, sharp-witted, astute, canny, smart; crafty, cunning, artful, sly, scheming, calculating, devious; *informal* clueful, tricky, foxy; *archaic* subtle. ANTONYM naive.

**win** verb **1** *he won the race* TAKE, be the victor in, be the winner of, come first in, take first prize in, triumph in, be successful in. ANTONYM lose.

**2** *Claire knew he would win* BE THE WINNER, come in first, be victorious, carry the day, win the day, come out on top, succeed, triumph, prevail. ANTONYM lose.

**3** *he won a cash prize* SECURE, gain, garner, collect, pick up, walk away/off with, carry off; *informal* land, net, bag, scoop.

**4** *she won his heart* CAPTIVATE, steal, snare, capture.

▸ noun *a 1–0 win* VICTORY, triumph, conquest. ANTONYM defeat.

PHRASE: **win over** *do you really believe that flowers and jewelry are enough to win her over?* PERSUADE, convince, sway, prevail on; seduce.

**wince** verb *he winced at the pain* GRIMACE, make a face, flinch, blanch, start.

▸ noun *a wince of pain* GRIMACE, flinch, start.

THE RIGHT WORD **wince, cower, cringe, flinch, recoil**

The same individual might **wince** when receiving a flu shot, **flinch** from a difficult task, and **cower** in fear at the approach of a tornado. All of these verbs mean to draw back in alarm, disgust, faintheartedness, or servility, but there are subtle differences among them. To *wince* is to make a slight recoiling movement, often an involuntary contraction of the facial features, in response to pain or discomfort (*to wince when a singer misses a high note*), while *flinch* may imply a similar drawing-back motion or, more abstractly, a reluctance or avoidance (*to tackle the job without flinching*). *Cower* and **cringe** both refer to stooped postures, although *cower* is usually associated with fearful trembling (*he cowered in the doorway*) while *cringe* is usually linked to servile, cowardly, or fawning behavior (*she cringed before her father's authority*). More than any of the other verbs here, **recoil** suggests a physical movement away from something (*recoil at the sight of a poisonous snake*), although that movement may also be psychological (*recoil at the very thought of a family reunion*).

**wind**[1] noun **1** *the trees were swaying in the wind* BREEZE, current of air; gale, hurricane; *literary* zephyr.

**2** *Jez got his wind back* BREATH.

**3** *the discomfort of holding back one's wind* FLATULENCE, gas; *informal* fart(s), farting; *formal* flatus. PHRASES: **get wind of** *informal White House officials got wind of the plan* HEAR ABOUT/OF, learn about/of, find out about, pick up on, be told about/of, be informed of; *informal* hear (about) through the grapevine.

**in the wind** *we fear that civil war is in the wind* ON THE WAY, coming, about to happen, in the offing, in the air, on the horizon, approaching, looming, brewing, afoot; *informal* in the cards.

**wind**[2] verb **1** *this road winds dangerously* TWIST AND TURN, twist, bend, curve, loop, zigzag, weave, snake.

**2** *she wound a towel around her waist* WRAP, furl, entwine, lace, loop.

**3** *he wound the yarn into a ball* COIL, roll, twist, twine. PHRASES: **wind down 1** *informal* *they needed to wind down* RELAX, unwind, calm down, cool down/off, ease up/off, take it easy, rest, put one's feet up; *informal* take a load off, hang loose, chill, chill out, kick back.

**2** *the summer was winding down* DRAW TO A CLOSE, come to an end, tail off, taper off, slack off, slacken off, slow down, die, die down.

**wind up 1** *let's wind up this meeting and go to lunch* CONCLUDE, bring to an end/close, end, terminate; *informal* wrap up.

**2** *informal I never thought that Jerry would wind up in real estate* END UP, finish up, find oneself.

**winded** adjective *he is winded just from walking up the stairs* OUT OF BREATH, breathless, gasping for breath, panting, hyperventilating; *informal* huffing and puffing.

**windfall** noun *the inheritance from Uncle Larry was an unexpected windfall* BONANZA, jackpot, pennies from heaven, stroke/piece of luck, godsend, manna from heaven.

**winding** noun *the windings of the stream* TWIST, turn, turning, bend, loop, curve, zigzag, meander.

▸ adjective *the winding country roads* TWISTING AND TURNING, meandering, windy, twisty, bending, curving, zigzag, zigzagging, serpentine, sinuous, snaking, tortuous; *rare* flexuous. ANTONYM straight.

**windy** adjective **1** *a windy day* BREEZY, blowy, blustery, gusty; wild, stormy, squally, tempestuous, boisterous. ANTONYM still.

**2** *a windy hillside* WINDSWEPT, exposed, open to the elements, bare, bleak. ANTONYM sheltered.

**wing** noun **1** *a bird's wings literary* pinion.

**2** *the east wing of the house* PART, section, side; annex, extension, ell.

**3** *the radical wing of the party* FACTION, camp, arm, branch, group, section, set, coterie, cabal; side, end.

▸ verb **1** *a seagull winged its way over the sea* FLY, glide, soar.

**2** *the bomb winged past* HURTLE, speed, shoot, whiz, zoom, streak, fly.

**3** *the hunter only winged the hawk* WOUND, graze, hit.

PHRASE: **wing it** *informal if you don't know all the words, just wing it* IMPROVISE, play it by ear, extemporize, ad lib, fly by the seat of one's pants, fake it.

**wink** verb **1** *he winked an eye at her* BLINK, flutter, bat.

**2** *the diamond winked in the moonlight* SPARKLE, twinkle, flash, glitter, gleam, shine, scintillate. PHRASE: **wink at** *too many people on the payroll were willing to wink at the corruption in high places* TURN A BLIND EYE TO, close one's eyes to, ignore, overlook, disregard; connive at, condone, tolerate.

**winner** noun *the winners receive trophies at the closing ceremony* VICTOR, champion, conqueror, vanquisher, hero; medalist; *informal* champ, top dog, world-beater. ANTONYM loser.

**winning** adjective **1** *the winning team* VICTORIOUS, successful, triumphant, vanquishing, conquering; first, first-place, top, leading.

**2** *a winning smile* ENGAGING, charming, appealing, endearing, sweet, cute, winsome, attractive, pretty, prepossessing, fetching, lovely, lovable, adorable, delightful, disarming, captivating, bewitching.

**winnings** plural noun *he put all his winnings into a college fund* PRIZE MONEY, gains, prize, booty, spoils, loot; proceeds, profits, earnings, takings, purse.

**winnow** verb *the chaff is winnowed from the grain* SEPARATE (OUT), divide, segregate, sort out, sift out, filter out; isolate, narrow down; remove, get rid of.

**wintry** adjective **1** *wintry weather* BLEAK, cold, chilly, chill, frosty, freezing, icy, snowy, blizzardy, arctic, glacial, bitter, raw, hypothermic; *informal* nippy. ANTONYMS summery, hot.

**2** *a wintry smile* UNFRIENDLY, unwelcoming, cool, cold, frosty, frigid, dismal, cheerless. ANTONYMS friendly, warm.

**wipe** verb **1** *Beth wiped the table* RUB, mop, sponge, swab; clean, dry, polish, towel.

**2** *he* ***wiped*** *the marks* ***off*** *the window* RUB OFF, clean off, remove from, get rid of from, take off from, erase from, efface from.

**3** *she wiped the memory from her mind* OBLITERATE, expunge, erase, blot out.

▸ noun *he gave the table a wipe* RUB, mop, sponge, swab; clean, polish.

PHRASE: **wipe out 1** *the influenza of 1918 wiped out entire families* DESTROY, annihilate, eradicate, eliminate; slaughter, massacre, kill, exterminate; demolish, raze to the ground; *informal* take out, zap, waste; *literary* slay.

**2** *I wiped out the file accidentally* ERASE, delete, trash, zap, kill, nuke.

**wiry** adjective **1** *a wiry man* SINEWY, athletic, strong; lean, spare, thin, stringy, skinny. ANTONYMS flabby, frail.

**2** *wiry hair* COARSE, rough, stiff; curly, wavy. ANTONYMS straight, smooth.

**wisdom** noun **1** *we questioned the wisdom of the decision* SAGACITY, intelligence, sense, common sense, shrewdness, astuteness, smartness, judiciousness, judgment, prudence, circumspection; logic, rationale, rationality, soundness, advisability. ANTONYMS folly, stupidity.

**2** *the wisdom of the East* KNOWLEDGE, learning, erudition, sophistication, scholarship, philosophy; lore. See note at KNOWLEDGE.

**wise** adjective **1** *a wise old man* SAGE, sagacious, intelligent, clever, learned, knowledgeable, enlightened; astute, smart, shrewd, sharp-witted, canny, knowing; sensible, prudent, discerning, discriminating, sophisticated, judicious, perceptive, insightful, perspicacious; rational, logical, sound, sane; *formal* sapient. ANTONYM foolish.

**2** *wise course of action.* See SENSIBLE. PHRASE: **wise to** *informal countless generations of local fishermen have been wise to these riptides* AWARE OF, familiar with, acquainted with; *formal* cognizant of.

**wisecrack** noun *informal her parents were not amused by Lenny's wisecracks* JOKE, witticism, quip, jest, sally; pun, bon mot; *informal* crack, gag, funny, one-liner, zinger.

**wish** verb **1** *I* ***wished for*** *power* DESIRE, want, hope for, covet, dream of, long for, yearn for, crave, hunger for, lust after; aspire to, be desirous of, set one's heart on, seek, fancy, hanker after; *informal* have a yen for, itch for.

**2** *they can do as they wish* WANT, desire, feel inclined, feel like, care; choose, please, think fit.

**3** *I wish you to send them a message* WANT, desire, require.

**4** *I wished him farewell* BID.

▸ noun **1** *his wish to own a Mercedes* DESIRE, longing, yearning, inclination, urge, whim, craving, hunger; hope, aspiration, aim, ambition, dream; *informal* hankering, yen, itch.

**2** *her parents' wishes* REQUEST, requirement, bidding, instruction, direction, demand, entreaty, order, command; want, desire; will; *literary* behest.

**wishy-washy** adjective **1** *he's so wishy-washy* FEEBLE, ineffectual, weak, vapid, effete, gutless, spineless, limp, namby-pamby, spiritless, indecisive, characterless; pathetic. ANTONYMS strong, decisive.

**2** *wishy-washy soup* WATERY, weak, thin; tasteless, flavorless, insipid. ANTONYM tasty.

**3** *a wishy-washy color* PALE, insipid, pallid, muted, pastel. ANTONYM vibrant.

**wistful** adjective *the old photos gave me a wistful feeling* NOS-

TALGIC, yearning, longing; plaintive, regretful, rueful, melancholy, mournful, elegiac; pensive, reflective, contemplative.

**wit** noun **1** (**wits**) *he needed all his wits to escape* INTELLIGENCE, shrewdness, astuteness, cleverness, canniness, sense, common sense, wisdom, sagacity, judgment, acumen, insight; brains, mind; *informal* gumption, savvy, horse sense, smarts, street smarts.

**2** *my sparkling wit* WITTINESS, humor, funniness, drollery, esprit; repartee, badinage, banter, wordplay; jokes, witticisms, quips, puns.

**3** *she's such a wit* COMEDIAN, humorist, comic, joker, jokester; *informal* wag, card, funnyman.

THE RIGHT WORD **wit, humor, irony, repartee, sarcasm, satire**

If you're good at perceiving analogies between dissimilar things and expressing them in quick, sharp, spontaneous observations or remarks, you have **wit**. **Humor**, on the other hand, is the ability to perceive what is comical, ridiculous, or ludicrous in a situation or character, and to express it in a way that makes others see or feel the same thing. It suggests more sympathy, tolerance, and kindliness than *wit* (*she maintained a sense of humor in the midst of trying circumstances*). **Irony** is the implicit humor in the contradiction between what is meant and what is expressed, or in the discrepancy between appearance and reality. An example would be to shout, in the midst of a hurricane, "What a perfect day for a wedding!" Although **sarcasm** may take the form of irony, it is less subtle and is often used harshly or bitterly to wound or ridicule someone. Unlike irony, however, *sarcasm* depends on tone of voice for its effect (*"a fine friend you turned out to be!" he said, with obvious sarcasm*). **Satire** usually implies the use of sarcasm or irony for the purpose of ridicule or criticism, often directed at institutions or political figures (*she wrote political satire for the comedy team*). If you are good at making quick, witty replies, you will be known for your **repartee**, which is the art of responding pointedly and skillfully with wit or humor in a conversational exchange (*no one could compete with her witty repartee*).

**witch** noun **1** *the witch cast a spell* SORCERESS, enchantress, necromancer; Wiccan; *archaic* pythoness.

**2** *informal she's a nasty old witch* HAG, crone, harpy, harridan, she-devil; *informal* battle-ax.

**witchcraft** noun *they've practiced witchcraft on this island for centuries* SORCERY, black magic, white magic, magic, witching, witchery, wizardry; spells, incantations; Wicca; *rare* thaumaturgy.

**withdraw** verb **1** *she withdrew her hand from his* REMOVE, extract, pull out, take out; take back, take away. ANTONYM insert.

**2** *the ban on advertising was withdrawn* ABOLISH, cancel, lift, set aside, end, stop, remove, reverse, revoke, rescind, repeal, annul, void. ANTONYM introduce.

**3** *she withdrew the allegation* RETRACT, take back, go back on, recant, disavow, disclaim, repudiate, renounce, abjure; back down, climb down, backtrack, backpedal, do a U-turn, eat one's words. ANTONYM put forward.

**4** *the troops* ***withdrew from*** *the city* LEAVE, pull out of, evacuate, quit, (beat a) retreat from. ANTONYM enter.

**5** *his partner* ***withdrew from*** *the project* PULL OUT OF, back out of, bow out of; get cold feet.

**6** *they withdrew to their rooms* RETIRE, retreat, adjourn, decamp; leave, depart, absent oneself; *formal* repair; *dated* remove; *literary* betake oneself.

**withdrawal** noun **1** *the withdrawal of subsidies* REMOVAL, abolition, cancellation, discontinuation, termination, elimination.

**2** *the withdrawal of the troops* DEPARTURE, pullout, exit, exodus, evacuation, retreat.

**3** *she's suffering the effects of withdrawal* DETOXIFICATION; *informal* detox, (going) cold turkey.

**withdrawn** adjective *Kate has become so withdrawn since Lucius left for the Gulf* INTROVERTED, unsociable, inhibited, uncommunicative, unforthcoming, quiet, taciturn, reticent, reserved, retiring, private, reclusive; shy, timid; aloof, indrawn; *informal* standoffish. ANTONYM outgoing.

**wither** verb **1** *the flowers withered in the sun* SHRIVEL (UP), dry up; wilt, droop, go limp, fade, perish; shrink, waste away, atrophy. ANTONYMS thrive, flourish.

**2** *her confidence withered* DIMINISH, dwindle, shrink, lessen, fade, ebb, wane; evaporate, disappear. ANTONYM grow.

**withhold** verb **1** *he withheld the information* HOLD BACK, keep back, refuse to give; retain, hold on to; hide, conceal, keep secret; *informal* sit on.

**2** *she could not withhold her tears* SUPPRESS, repress, hold back, fight back, choke back, control, check, restrain, contain.

**within** preposition **1** *within the prison walls* INSIDE, in, enclosed by, surrounded by; within the bounds of, within the confines of. ANTONYM outside.

**2** *within a few hours* IN LESS THAN, in under, in no more than, after only.

**without** preposition **1** *thousands were without food* LACKING, short of, deprived of, in need of, wanting, needing, requiring.

**2** *I don't want to go without you* UNACCOMPANIED BY, unescorted by; in the absence of; *informal* sans, minus.

**withstand** verb *it was a miracle that they were able to withstand the brutal winter* RESIST, weather, survive, endure, cope with, stand, tolerate, bear, stomach, defy, brave, hold out against, tough out, bear up against; stand up to, face, confront.

**witness** noun **1** *witnesses claimed that he started the fight* OBSERVER, onlooker, eyewitness, spectator, viewer, watcher; bystander, passerby.

**2** *she cross-examined the witness* DEPONENT, testifier.

▸ verb **1** *who witnessed the incident?* SEE, observe, watch, view, notice, spot; be present at, attend; *literary* behold; *informal* get a look at.

**2** *Canada witnessed a cultural explosion* UNDERGO, experience, go through, see; enjoy; suffer.

3 *the will is correctly witnessed* COUNTERSIGN, sign, endorse, validate; notarize. PHRASE: **bear witness to** *his diary bears witness to his lifelong struggle with depression* ATTEST TO, testify to, confirm, evidence, prove, verify, corroborate, substantiate; show, demonstrate, indicate, reveal, bespeak.

**witticism** noun *the publisher asked her to put some of her witticisms in a weekly feature* JOKE, quip, jest, pun, play on words, bon mot; *informal* one-liner, gag, funny, crack, wisecrack, zinger.

**witty** adjective *it was a pleasure to sit and listen to their witty conversations* HUMOROUS, amusing, droll, funny, comic, comical; jocular, facetious, waggish, tongue-in-cheek; sparkling, scintillating, entertaining; clever, quick-witted.

**wizard** noun 1 *the wizard cast a spell over them* SORCERER, warlock, magus, (black) magician, necromancer, enchanter; *archaic* mage.

2 *a financial wizard* GENIUS, expert, master, virtuoso, maestro, marvel, Wunderkind, guru; *informal* hotshot, demon, whiz kid, buff, pro, ace; maven.

**wizened** adjective *their wizened faces said much about the hard lives they had endured* WRINKLED, lined, creased, shriveled (up), withered, weather-beaten, shrunken, gnarled, aged.

**wobble** verb 1 *the table wobbled* ROCK, teeter, jiggle, sway, seesaw, shake.

2 *he wobbled across to the door* TEETER, totter, stagger; lurch.

3 *her voice wobbled* TREMBLE, shake, quiver, quaver, waver.

▸ noun 1 *she stood up with a wobble* TOTTER, teeter, sway.

2 *the operatic wobble in her voice* TREMOR, quiver, quaver, trembling, vibrato.

**woe** noun 1 *a tale of woe* MISERY, sorrow, distress, wretchedness, sadness, unhappiness, heartache, heartbreak, despondency, despair, depression, regret, gloom, melancholy; adversity, misfortune, disaster, suffering, hardship; *literary* dolor. ANTONYMS joy, happiness.

2 *financial woes* TROUBLE, difficulty, problem, trial, tribulation, misfortune, setback, reverse.

**woebegone** adjective *we were not prepared to find Thom in such a woebegone condition* SAD, unhappy, miserable, dejected, disconsolate, forlorn, crestfallen, downcast, glum, gloomy, doleful, downhearted, heavy-hearted, despondent, melancholy, sorrowful, mournful, woeful, plaintive, depressed, wretched, desolate; *informal* down in/at the mouth, down in the dumps, blue. ANTONYM cheerful.

**woeful** adjective 1 *her face was woeful.* See WOEBEGONE.

2 *a woeful ballad* TRAGIC, sad, miserable, cheerless, gloomy, sorry, pitiful, pathetic, traumatic, depressing, heartbreaking, heart-rending, tear-jerking, gut-wrenching. ANTONYMS cheerful, uplifting.

3 *the team's woeful performance* LAMENTABLE, awful, terrible, atrocious, disgraceful, deplorable, shameful, hopeless, dreadful; substandard, poor, inadequate, inferior, unsatisfactory; *informal* rotten, appalling, crummy, pathetic, pitiful, lousy, abysmal, dire, crappy, lame, brutal. ANTONYM excellent.

**wolf** noun *informal he's a bit of a wolf.* See WOMANIZER.

▸ verb *he **wolfed down** his breakfast* DEVOUR, gobble (up), guzzle, gulp down, bolt (down); *informal* put away, demolish, shovel in/down, scoff (down), scarf (up).

**woman** noun 1 *a woman got out of the car* LADY, girl, female; matron; *Scottish* lass, lassie; *informal* chick, girlie, sister, dame, broad, gal; grrrl; *literary* maid, maiden, damsel; *archaic* wench, gentlewoman; (**women**) womenfolk.

2 *he found himself a new woman* GIRLFRIEND, sweetheart, partner, significant other, inamorata, lover, mistress; fiancée; wife, spouse; *informal* missus, better half, main squeeze, squeeze, babe, baby; *dated* lady friend, lady love.

**womanish** adjective *Andrew's first stage role was that of a womanish baker from Brooklyn* EFFEMINATE, girlish, girly, unmanly, unmasculine, epicene. ANTONYM manly.

**womanizer** noun *informal her friends tried to warn her about his reputation as a womanizer* PHILANDERER, Don Juan, Casanova, Romeo, Lothario, playboy, ladies' man, flirt, seducer, rake, roué, lecher, libertine, debauchee; *informal* skirt-chaser, wolf, ladykiller, lech.

**womankind** noun *we are mindful of the plight of womankind throughout the world* WOMEN; woman, the female sex, womenkind, womanhood, womenfolk; *informal* the gentler sex.

**womanly** adjective 1 *womanly virtues* FEMININE, female; *archaic* feminal. ANTONYM masculine.

2 *her womanly figure* VOLUPTUOUS, curvaceous, shapely, ample, buxom, full-figured; Junoesque, Rubenesque; *informal* curvy, busty. ANTONYM boyish.

**wonder** noun 1 *she was speechless with wonder* AWE, admiration, wonderment, fascination; surprise, astonishment, stupefaction, amazement.

2 *the wonders of nature* MARVEL, miracle, phenomenon, sensation, spectacle, beauty; curiosity; *informal* humdinger.

▸ verb 1 *I wondered what was on her mind* PONDER, think about, meditate on, reflect on, muse on, puzzle over, speculate about, conjecture; be curious about.

2 *people wondered at such bravery* MARVEL, be amazed, be astonished, stand in awe, be dumbfounded, gape, goggle; *informal* be flabbergasted.

**wonderful** adjective *a wonderful vacation in Europe* MARVELOUS, magnificent, superb, glorious, sublime, lovely, delightful; *informal* super, great, fantastic, terrific, tremendous, sensational, incredible, fabulous, fab, out of this world, awesome, magic, wicked, far out, killer, brilliant, peachy, dandy, neat, swell. ANTONYM awful.

**wont** adjective *he was wont to arise at 5:30* ACCUSTOMED, used, given, inclined.

▸ noun *Paul drove fast, as was his wont* CUSTOM, habit, way, practice, convention, rule.

**woo** verb *dated* **1** *Richard wooed Joan all through their college years* ROMANTICALLY PURSUE, pursue, chase (after); *dated* court, pay court to, romance, seek the hand of, set one's cap for/at, make love to.

**2** *the party wooed voters with promises* SEEK, pursue, curry favor with, try to win, try to attract, try to cultivate.

**3** *an attempt to woo him out of retirement* ENTICE, tempt, coax, persuade, wheedle; *informal* sweet-talk.

**wood** noun **1** *there should be enough wood left over to make a small shelf* LUMBER, timber, planks, planking; logs, sawlogs.

**2** (usu. **woods**) *a walk through the woods* FOREST, woodland, trees; copse, coppice, grove, bush, woodlot.

**wooded** adjective *the wooded area behind the library* FORESTED, treed, tree-covered, woody; *literary* sylvan.

**wooden** adjective **1** *a wooden door* WOOD, timber, woody; ligneous.

**2** *his wooden posture* STILTED, stiff, unnatural, awkward, leaden; dry, flat, stodgy, lifeless, passionless, spiritless, soulless.

**3** *her face was wooden* EXPRESSIONLESS, impassive, poker-faced, emotionless, blank, vacant, unresponsive.

**woolgathering** noun *lost in her daily woolgathering* DAYDREAMING, reverie, dreaming, musing, abstraction, preoccupation; absentmindedness, forgetfulness.

**woolly** adjective **1** *a woolly hat* WOOLEN, wool, fleecy.

**2** *a sheep's woolly coat* FLEECY, shaggy, hairy, fluffy, flocculent.

**3** *woolly generalizations* VAGUE, ill-defined, hazy, unclear, fuzzy, blurry, foggy, nebulous, imprecise, inexact, indefinite; confused, muddled.

**word** noun **1** *the Italian word for "ham"* TERM, name, expression, designation, locution, vocable; *formal* appellation.

**2** *his words were meant kindly* REMARK, comment, observation, statement, utterance, pronouncement.

**3** (**words**) *I've got three weeks to learn the words* SCRIPT, lyrics, libretto.

**4** *I give you my word* PROMISE, word of honor, assurance, guarantee, undertaking; pledge, vow, oath, bond; *formal* troth.

**5** *I want a word with you* TALK, conversation, chat, tête-à-tête, heart-to-heart, one-to-one, man-to-man; discussion, consultation; *informal* confab, powwow; *formal* confabulation.

**6** *there's no word from the hospital* NEWS, information, communication, intelligence; message, report, communiqué, dispatch, bulletin; *informal* info, dope; *literary* tidings.

**7** *word has it he's turned over a new leaf* RUMOR, hearsay, talk, gossip; *informal* the grapevine, the word on the street.

**8** *I'm waiting for the word from HQ* INSTRUCTION, order, command; signal, prompt, cue, tip-off; *informal* go-ahead, thumbs up, green light.

**9** *Heather's word was law* COMMAND, order, decree, edict; bidding, will.

**10** *our word now must be success* MOTTO, watchword, slogan, catchword, buzzword.

▸ verb *the question was carefully worded* PHRASE, express, put, couch, frame, formulate, style; say, utter.

PHRASES: **have words** *we had words, and Jason walked out* QUARREL, argue, disagree, squabble, bicker, fight, wrangle, dispute, fall out, clash, row.

**in a word** *in a word, it was a miserable day for sailing* BRIEFLY, to be brief, in short, in a nutshell, to come to the point, to cut a long story short, not to put too fine a point on it; to sum up, to summarize, in summary.

**word for word** **1** *they took down the speeches word for word* VERBATIM, letter for letter, to the letter; exactly, faithfully.

**2** *a word-for-word translation* VERBATIM, literal, exact, direct, accurate, faithful; unadulterated, unabridged.

**wordy** adjective *a wordy sermon* LONG-WINDED, verbose, prolix, lengthy, protracted, long-drawn-out, overlong, rambling, circumlocutory, periphrastic, pleonastic; loquacious, garrulous, voluble; *informal* windy. ANTONYM succinct.

**work** noun **1** *a day's work in the fields* LABOR, toil, slog, drudgery, exertion, effort, industry, service; *informal* grind, sweat, elbow grease; *literary* travail. See note at LABOR. ANTONYMS leisure, rest.

**2** *I'm looking for work* EMPLOYMENT, a job, a position, a situation, a post; an occupation, a profession, a career, a vocation, a calling; wage labor; tasks, jobs, duties, assignments, projects; chores. ANTONYMS unemployment, retirement.

**3** *works of literature* COMPOSITION, piece, creation; opus, oeuvre.

**4** (**works**) *the complete works of Shakespeare* WRITINGS, oeuvre, canon, output.

**5** *this is the work of a radical faction* HANDIWORK, doing, act, deed.

**6** (**works**) *a lifetime spent doing good works* DEEDS, acts, actions.

**7** *informal* (**the works**) *for only $60 you can get the works* EVERYTHING, the full treatment; *informal* the lot, the whole shebang, the full nine yards, the whole kit and kaboodle, the whole ball of wax.

▸ verb **1** *staff worked late into the night* TOIL, labor, exert oneself, slave (away); keep at it, put one's nose to the grindstone; *informal* slog (away), plug away, put one's back into it, knock oneself out, sweat blood; *literary* travail. ANTONYMS rest, play.

**2** *he worked in education for years* BE EMPLOYED, have a job, earn one's living, do business.

**3** *farmers worked the land* CULTIVATE, farm, till, plow.

**4** *his car was working perfectly* FUNCTION, go, run, operate; *informal* behave.

**5** *how do I work this machine?* OPERATE, use, handle, control, manipulate, run.

**6** *their ploy worked* SUCCEED, work out, turn out well, go as planned, get results, be effective; *informal* come off, pay off, do/turn the trick. ANTONYM fail.

**7** *makeup can work miracles* BRING ABOUT, accomplish, achieve, produce, perform, create, engender, contrive, effect.

**8** *informal* *can you **work it** so I can get in for free?* ARRANGE IT/THINGS, manipulate it/things, contrive it; pull strings, fix it, swing it, wangle it.

**9** *he worked the crowd into a frenzy* STIR (UP), excite, drive, move, rouse, fire, galvanize; whip up, agitate.

**10** *work the mixture into a paste* KNEAD, squeeze, form; mix, stir, blend. See note at WROUGHT.

**11** *he worked the blade into the padlock* MANEUVER, manipulate, guide, edge.

**12** *her mouth worked furiously* TWITCH, quiver, convulse.

**13** *he worked his way through the crowd* MANEUVER, make, thread, wind, weave, wend.

PHRASES: **work on** *leave Hank to me—I'll work on him* PERSUADE, manipulate, influence; coax, cajole, wheedle, soften up, sweet-talk; *informal* twist someone's arm, lean on.

**work out 1** *the bill works out to $50* AMOUNT TO, add up to, come to, total.

**2** *my idea worked out.* See WORK verb sense 6.

**3** *things didn't work out the way she planned* END UP, turn out, go, come out, develop; happen, occur; *informal* pan out.

**4** *he works out at the local gym* EXERCISE, train.

**5** *work out what you can afford* CALCULATE, compute, determine, reckon (up).

**6** *I'm trying to work out what she meant* UNDERSTAND, comprehend, sort out, make sense of, get to the bottom of, make head(s) or tail(s) of, unravel, decipher, decode, puzzle out; *informal* figure out.

**7** *they worked out a plan* DEVISE, formulate, draw up, put together, develop, construct, arrange, organize, contrive, concoct; hammer out, negotiate.

**work up** *he couldn't work up any enthusiasm* STIMULATE, rouse, raise, arouse, awaken, excite.

**workable** adjective *a workable household budget* PRACTICABLE, feasible, viable, possible, achievable; realistic, reasonable, sensible, practical; *informal* doable. ANTONYM impracticable.

**workaday** adjective *workaday prose | our workaday lives* ORDINARY, average, run-of-the-mill, middle-of-the-road, conventional, unremarkable, unexceptional, humdrum, undistinguished, commonplace, mundane, pedestrian; routine, everyday, day-to-day, garden-variety, standard; *informal* nothing to write home about, dime a dozen. ANTONYM exceptional.

**worker** noun **1** *a strike by 500 workers* EMPLOYEE, member of staff; workman, laborer, hand, operative, operator; proletarian; artisan, craftsman, craftswoman; wage earner, breadwinner.

**2** *informal* *I have a reputation for being a worker* HARD WORKER, toiler, workhorse; *informal* busy bee, eager beaver, workaholic, wheelhorse.

**working** adjective **1** *working mothers* EMPLOYED, in (gainful) employment, in work, waged. ANTONYMS unemployed, out of work.

**2** *a working windmill* FUNCTIONING, operating, running, active, operational, functional, serviceable; *informal* up and running. ANTONYMS broken, faulty.

**3** *a working knowledge of contract law* SUFFICIENT, adequate, viable; useful, effective.

▸ noun **1** *the working of a carburetor* FUNCTIONING, operation, running, action, performance.

**2** (**workings**) *the workings of a watch* MECHANISM, machinery, parts, movement, action, works; *informal* insides.

**workmanship** noun *the workmanship evidenced in these chairs is superb* CRAFTSMANSHIP, artistry, craft, art, artisanship, handiwork; skill, expertise, technique.

**workout** noun *cool down gradually after your workout* EXERCISE SESSION, training session, drill; warm-up; exercises, aerobics, isometrics, callisthenics.

**workshop** noun **1** *the craftsmen had a chilly workshop* WORKROOM, studio, atelier; factory, plant.

**2** *a workshop on combating stress* STUDY GROUP, discussion group, seminar, class; support group.

**world** noun **1** *he traveled the world* EARTH, globe, planet, sphere.

**2** *life on other worlds* PLANET, moon, star, heavenly body, orb.

**3** *the academic world* SPHERE, society, circle, arena, milieu, province, domain, orbit, preserve, realm, field, discipline, area, sector.

**4** *she would show **the world** that she was strong* EVERYONE, everybody, people, mankind, humankind, humanity, the (general) public, the population, the populace, all and sundry, 'every Tom, Dick, and Harry.'

**5** *a world of difference* HUGE AMOUNT, good deal, great deal, abundance, wealth, profusion, mountain; *informal* heap, lot, load, ton.

**6** *she renounced **the world*** SOCIETY, material things, secular interests, temporal concerns, earthly concerns. PHRASES: **on top of the world** *informal* *at age twenty, I was on top of the world.* See OVERJOYED.

**out of this world** *informal* *the scampi at Vinnie's is out of this world.* See WONDERFUL.

**worldly** adjective **1** *his youth was wasted on worldly pursuits* EARTHLY, terrestrial, temporal, mundane; mortal, human, material, materialistic, physical, carnal, fleshly, bodily, corporeal, sensual. ANTONYM spiritual.

**2** *a worldly woman* SOPHISTICATED, experienced, worldly-wise, knowledgeable, knowing, enlightened, shrewd, mature, seasoned, cosmopolitan, streetwise, street-smart, urbane, cultivated, cultured. ANTONYMS unsophisticated, naive.

**worldwide** adjective *a worldwide effort to combat AIDS* GLOBAL, international, intercontinental, universal; ubiquitous, extensive, widespread, far-reaching, wide-ranging, all-embracing. ANTONYM local.

**worn** adjective **1** *his hat was worn* SHABBY, worn out, threadbare, tattered, in tatters, holey, falling to pieces, ragged, frayed, well-used, moth-eaten, scruffy, having seen better days; *informal* tatty, ratty, the worse for wear, raggedy, dog-eared. ANTONYMS smart, new.

2 *her face looked worn* WORN-OUT.

**worried** adjective *Father Douglas came to sit with the worried parents* ANXIOUS, perturbed, troubled, bothered, concerned, upset, distressed, distraught, disquieted, uneasy, fretful, agitated, nervous, edgy, on edge, tense, overwrought, worked up, keyed up, jumpy, stressed, strung out; apprehensive, fearful, afraid, frightened, scared; *informal* uptight, a bundle of nerves, on tenterhooks, jittery, twitchy, in a stew, in a sweat, het up, rattled, antsy, squirrelly. ANTONYMS carefree, unconcerned.

**worry** verb 1 *she worries about his health* FRET, be concerned, be anxious, agonize, brood, panic, lose sleep, get worked up, get stressed, get in a state, stew, torment oneself.

2 *is something worrying you?* TROUBLE, bother, make anxious, disturb, distress, upset, concern, disquiet, fret, agitate, unsettle, perturb, scare, fluster, stress, tax, torment, plague, bedevil; prey on one's mind, weigh down, gnaw at, rattle; *informal* bug, get to, dig at, nag.

▸ noun 1 *I'm beside myself with worry* ANXIETY, perturbation, distress, concern, uneasiness, unease, disquiet, fretfulness, restlessness, nervousness, nerves, agitation, edginess, tension, stress; apprehension, fear, dread, trepidation, misgiving, angst; *informal* butterflies (in the stomach), the willies, the heebie-jeebies.

2 *the rats are a worry* PROBLEM, cause for concern, issue; nuisance, pest, plague, trial, trouble, vexation, bane, bugbear; *informal* pain, pain in the neck, headache, hassle, stress.

**worsen** verb 1 *insomnia can worsen a patient's distress* AGGRAVATE, exacerbate, compound, add to, intensify, increase, magnify, heighten, inflame, augment; *informal* add fuel to the fire of. ANTONYM improve.

2 *the recession worsened* DETERIORATE, degenerate, decline, regress; *informal* go downhill, go to pot, go to the dogs, hit the skids, nosedive. ANTONYMS improve, recover.

**worship** noun 1 *the worship of idols* REVERENCE, veneration, adoration, glorification, glory, exaltation; devotion, praise, thanksgiving, homage, honor; *archaic* magnification.

2 *morning worship* SERVICE, religious rite, prayer, praise, devotion, religious observance.

3 *he contemplated her with worship* ADMIRATION, adulation, idolization, lionization, hero-worship.

▸ verb *they worship pagan gods* REVERE, reverence, venerate, pay homage to, honor, adore, praise, pray to, glorify, exalt, extol; hold dear, cherish, treasure, esteem, adulate, idolize, deify, hero-worship, lionize; follow, look up to; *informal* put on a pedestal; *formal* laud; *archaic* magnify. See note at REVERE.

**worst** verb *they were worsted by the Czechs in the first round* DEFEAT, beat, prevail over, triumph over, trounce, rout, vanquish, conquer, master, overcome, overwhelm, overpower, crush; outdo, outclass, outstrip, surpass; *informal* thrash, smash, lick, best, clobber, drub, slaughter, murder, wipe out, crucify, demolish, wipe the floor with, take to the cleaners, walk all over, make mincemeat of, shellac, cream, whup.

**worth** noun 1 *evidence of the rug's worth* VALUE, price, cost; valuation, quotation, estimate.

2 *the intrinsic worth of education* BENEFIT, advantage, use, value, virtue, utility, service, profit, help, aid; desirability, appeal; significance, sense; *informal* mileage, percentage; *archaic* behoof.

3 *a sense of personal worth* WORTHINESS, merit, value, excellence, caliber, quality, stature, eminence, consequence, importance, significance, distinction.

**worthless** adjective 1 *the item was worthless* VALUELESS; poor quality, inferior, second-rate, third-rate, low-grade, cheap, shoddy, tawdry, cheesy; *informal* crummy, nickel-and-dime. ANTONYMS valuable, precious.

2 *his conclusions are worthless* USELESS, (of) no use, ineffective, ineffectual, fruitless, unproductive, unavailing, pointless, nugatory, valueless, inadequate, deficient, meaningless, senseless, insubstantial, empty, hollow, trifling, petty, inconsequential, lame, paltry, pathetic, no-account. ANTONYM useful.

3 *his worthless son* GOOD-FOR-NOTHING, ne'er-do-well, useless, despicable, contemptible, low, ignominious, corrupt, villainous, degenerate, shiftless, feckless; *informal* no-good, lousy, no-account.

**worthwhile** adjective *a worthwhile expenditure of time* VALUABLE, useful, of use, of service, beneficial, rewarding, advantageous, positive, helpful, profitable, gainful, fruitful, productive, lucrative, constructive, effective, effectual, meaningful, worthy.

**worthy** adjective *a worthy citizen* VIRTUOUS, righteous, good, moral, ethical, upright, upstanding, high-minded, principled, exemplary; law-abiding, irreproachable, blameless, guiltless, unimpeachable, honest, honorable, reputable, decent, respectable, noble, meritorious; pure, saintly, angelic; *informal* squeaky clean. ANTONYM disreputable.

▸ noun *local worthies* DIGNITARY, personage, VIP, notable, notability, pillar of society, luminary, leading light, big name, grandee; *informal* heavyweight, bigwig, top dog, big shot, big cheese, big wheel, big kahuna. ANTONYM nobody.

PHRASE: **be worthy of** *your opinions are worthy of our consideration* DESERVE, merit, warrant, rate, justify, earn, be entitled to, qualify for.

**wound** noun 1 *a chest wound* INJURY, lesion, cut, gash, laceration, tear, slash; graze, scratch, abrasion; bruise, contusion; *Medicine* trauma.

2 *the wounds inflicted by the media* INSULT, blow, slight, offense, affront; hurt, damage, injury, pain, distress, grief, anguish, torment.

▸ verb 1 *he was critically wounded* INJURE, hurt, harm; maim, mutilate, disable, incapacitate, cripple; lacerate, cut, graze, gash, stab, slash.

2 *her words had wounded him* HURT, scar, damage, injure; in-

sult, slight, offend, affront, distress, disturb, upset, trouble; grieve, sadden, pain, cut, sting, shock, traumatize, torment.

**wraith** noun *from a gray and billowy fog the wraith did appear* GHOST, specter, spirit, phantom, apparition, manifestation; *informal* spook; *literary* shade, phantasm.

**wrangle** noun *a wrangle over money* ARGUMENT, dispute, disagreement, quarrel, falling-out, fight, squabble, turf war, altercation, war of words, shouting match, tiff, tug-of-war; *informal* set-to, run-in, row. See note at QUARREL.

▸ verb *we wrangled over the details* ARGUE, quarrel, bicker, squabble, fall out, have words, disagree, be at odds, fight, battle, feud, clash; *informal* scrap.

**wrap** verb **1** *she wrapped herself in a towel* SWATHE, bundle, swaddle, muffle, cloak, enfold, envelop, encase, cover, fold, wind.

**2** *I wrapped the vase carefully* PACKAGE, pack, pack up, bundle, bundle up; gift-wrap.

▸ noun *he put a wrap around her* SHAWL, stole, cloak, cape, mantle, scarf, poncho, serape, pelisse.

PHRASES: **wrap up** *wrap up well—it's cold* DRESS WARMLY, bundle up.

**wrap something up** *informal our objective is to wrap up the Pendleton case by the end of the month* CONCLUDE, finish, end, wind up, terminate, stop, cease, finalize, complete, tie up; *informal* sew up.

**wrapper** noun *a candy wrapper* WRAPPING, wrap, packaging, paper, cover, covering; jacket, sheath.

**wrath** noun *I refuse to subject myself any longer to her wrath* ANGER, rage, fury, outrage, spleen, vexation, (high) dudgeon, crossness, displeasure, annoyance, irritation; *literary* ire, choler. ANTONYM happiness.

**wreath** noun *a wreath of dried flowers* GARLAND, circlet, chaplet, crown, festoon, lei; ring, loop, circle.

**wreathe** verb **1** *a pulpit wreathed in holly* FESTOON, garland, drape, cover, bedeck, deck, decorate, ornament, adorn.

**2** *blue smoke wreathed upward* SPIRAL, coil, loop, wind, curl, twist, snake, curve.

**wreck** noun **1** *salvage teams landed on the wreck* SHIPWRECK, sunken ship, derelict; shell, hull; wreckage.

**2** *the wreck of a stolen car* WRECKAGE, debris, remainder, ruins, remains.

▸ verb **1** *he had wrecked her car* DEMOLISH, crash, smash up, damage, destroy; vandalize, deface, desecrate; *informal* trash, total.

**2** *his ship was wrecked* SHIPWRECK, sink, capsize, run aground.

**3** *the crisis wrecked his plans* RUIN, spoil, disrupt, undo, put a stop to, frustrate, blight, crush, quash, dash, destroy, scotch, shatter, devastate, sabotage; *informal* mess up, screw up, foul up, put paid to, scupper, scuttle, stymie, put the kibosh on, nix.

**wreckage** noun. See WRECK noun senses 1, 2.

**wrench** noun **1** *she felt a wrench on her shoulders* TUG, pull, jerk, jolt, heave; *informal* yank.

**2** *hold the piston with a wrench* monkey wrench.

**3** *leaving was an immense wrench* TRAUMATIC EVENT, painful parting; pang, trauma.

▸ verb **1** *he wrenched the gun from her hand* TUG, pull, jerk, wrest, heave, twist, pluck, grab, seize, snatch, force, pry, jimmy; *informal* yank.

**2** *she wrenched her ankle* SPRAIN, twist, turn, strain, pull; injure, hurt.

**wrest** verb *he wrested the broom from Angela's grasp* WRENCH, snatch, seize, grab, pry, pluck, tug, pull, jerk, dislodge, remove; *informal* yank.

**wrestle** verb *words were exchanged, and then they began wrestling | she wrestled with her conscience* GRAPPLE, fight, struggle, contend, vie, battle, wrangle; scuffle, tussle, brawl; *informal* scrap, wrassle, rassle.

**wretch** noun **1** *the wretches killed themselves* POOR CREATURE, poor soul, poor thing, poor unfortunate; *informal* poor devil.

**2** *I wouldn't trust the old wretch* SCOUNDREL, villain, ruffian, rogue, rascal, reprobate, criminal, miscreant, good-for-nothing; *informal* heel, creep, louse, rat, swine, dog, lowlife, scumbag, scumbucket, scuzzball, sleazeball, sleazebag; *informal, archaic* blackguard, picaroon.

**wretched** adjective **1** *I felt so wretched without you* MISERABLE, unhappy, sad, heartbroken, grief-stricken, sorrowful, sorry for oneself, distressed, desolate, devastated, despairing, disconsolate, downcast, dejected, crestfallen, cheerless, depressed, melancholy, morose, gloomy, mournful, doleful, dismal, forlorn, woebegone; *informal* blue; *literary* dolorous. ANTONYM cheerful.

**2** *I feel wretched* ILL, unwell, poorly, sick, below par; *informal* under the weather, out of sorts. ANTONYM well.

**3** *their living conditions are wretched* HARSH, hard, grim, stark, difficult; poor, impoverished; pitiful, pathetic, miserable, cheerless, sordid, shabby, seedy, unhealthy, insalubrious, dilapidated; *informal* scummy. ANTONYMS comfortable, luxurious.

**4** *the wretched dweller in the chantey town* UNFORTUNATE, unlucky, luckless, ill-starred, blighted, hapless, poor, pitiable, downtrodden, oppressed; *literary* star-crossed. ANTONYMS cheerful, well, comfortable, fortunate, excellent.

**5** *he's a wretched coward* DESPICABLE, contemptible, reprehensible, base, vile, loathsome, hateful, detestable, odious, ignoble, shameful, shabby, worthless; *informal* dirty, rotten, lowdown, lousy. ANTONYM fortunate.

**6** *wretched weather* TERRIBLE, awful, dire, atrocious, dreadful, bad, poor, lamentable, deplorable; *informal* godawful. ANTONYM excellent.

**7** *I don't want the wretched money informal* DAMN, damned, blessed, cursed, flaming, confounded, rotten, blasted, bloody.

**wriggle** verb **1** *she tried to hug him but he wriggled* SQUIRM, writhe, wiggle, jiggle, jerk, thresh, flounder, flail, twitch, twist and turn; snake, worm, slither.

**2** *he* ***wriggled out of*** *his responsibilities* AVOID, shirk, dodge, evade, elude, sidestep; escape from; *informal* duck.

**wring** verb **1** ***wring out*** *the clothes* TWIST, squeeze, screw, scrunch, knead, press, mangle.

**2** *concessions were wrung from the government* EXTRACT, elicit, force, exact, wrest, wrench, squeeze, milk; *informal* bleed.

**3** *his expression wrung her heart* REND, tear at, harrow, pierce, stab, wound, rack; distress, pain, hurt.

**wrinkle** noun **1** *fine wrinkles around her mouth* CREASE, fold, pucker, line, crinkle, furrow, ridge, groove; *informal* crow's feet, laugh line.

**2** *the project has some wrinkles to iron out* DIFFICULTY, snag, hitch, drawback, imperfection, problem.

▸ verb *his coattails* ***wrinkled up*** CREASE, pucker, gather, crinkle, crimp, crumple, rumple, scrunch up.

**writ** noun *they were served with a writ* SUMMONS, subpoena, warrant, arraignment, indictment, citation, court order.

**write** verb **1** *he wrote her name in the book* PUT IN WRITING, write down, jot down, put down, note, take down, record, register, log, list; inscribe, sign, scribble, scrawl, pencil.

**2** *Jacqueline wrote a poem* COMPOSE, draft, think up, formulate, compile, pen, dash off, produce.

**3** *he had her address and promised to write* CORRESPOND, write a letter, communicate, get/stay in touch, keep in contact, e-mail; *informal* drop someone a line. PHRASE: **write off 1** *they have had to write off loans* FORGET ABOUT, disregard, give up on, cancel, annul.

**2** *she wrote off the cost of the computer* DEDUCT, claim.

**3** *who would write off a player of his stature?* DISREGARD, dismiss, ignore.

**writer** noun *my favorite American writer* AUTHOR, wordsmith, man/woman of letters, penman; novelist, essayist, biographer; journalist, columnist, correspondent; scriptwriter, playwright, dramatist, dramaturge, tragedian; poet; *informal* scribbler, scribe, hack.

**writhe** verb *she writhed about in pain* SQUIRM, wriggle, thrash, flail, toss, toss and turn, twist, twist and turn, struggle.

**writing** noun **1** *I can't read his writing* HANDWRITING, script, print, hand; penmanship, calligraphy, chirography; *informal* scribble, scrawl, chicken scratch.

**2** **(writings)** *the writings of Woodrow Wilson* WORKS, compositions, books, publications, oeuvre; papers, articles, essays.

**wrong** adjective **1** *the wrong answer* INCORRECT, mistaken, in error, erroneous, inaccurate, inexact, imprecise, fallacious, wide of the mark, off target, unsound, faulty; *informal* out. See note at RIGHT. ANTONYMS right, correct.

**2** *he knew he had said the wrong thing* INAPPROPRIATE, unsuitable, inapt, inapposite, undesirable; ill-advised, ill-considered, ill-judged, impolitic, injudicious, infelicitous, unfitting, out of keeping, improper; *informal* out of order. ANTONYM appropriate.

**3** *I've done nothing wrong* ILLEGAL, unlawful, illicit, criminal, dishonest, dishonorable, corrupt; unethical, immoral, bad, wicked, sinful, iniquitous, nefarious, blameworthy, reprehensible; *informal* crooked. ANTONYMS ethical, legal.

**4** *there's something wrong with the engine* AMISS, awry, out of order, not right, faulty, flawed, defective.

▸ adverb *she guessed wrong* INCORRECTLY, wrongly, inaccurately, erroneously, mistakenly, in error.

▸ noun **1** *the difference between right and wrong* IMMORALITY, sin, sinfulness, wickedness, evil; unlawfulness, crime, corruption, villainy, dishonesty, injustice, wrongdoing, misconduct, transgression. ANTONYMS right, virtue.

**2** *an attempt to make up for past wrongs* MISDEED, offense, injury, crime, transgression, violation, peccadillo, sin; injustice, outrage, atrocity; *Law* tort; *archaic* trespass.

▸ verb **1** *she was determined to forget the man who had wronged her* ILL-USE, mistreat, do an injustice to, do wrong to, ill-treat, abuse, harm, hurt, injure.

**2** *perhaps I am wronging him* MALIGN, misrepresent, do a disservice to, impugn, defame, slander, libel.

PHRASES: **get wrong** *don't get me wrong, I usually like Italian food* MISUNDERSTAND, misinterpret, misconstrue, mistake, misread, take amiss; get the wrong idea/impression; *informal* be barking up the wrong tree.

**go wrong 1** *I've gone wrong somewhere* MAKE A MISTAKE, make an error, make a blunder, blunder, miscalculate, trip up; *informal* slip up, goof, screw up, make a boo-boo, fluff, flub.

**2** *their plans went wrong* GO AWRY, go amiss, go off course, fail, be unsuccessful, fall through, come to nothing; backfire, misfire, rebound; *informal* come to grief, come a cropper, go up in smoke, go adrift.

**3** *the radio's gone wrong* BREAK DOWN, malfunction, fail, stop working, crash, give out; *informal* be on the blink, conk out, go kaput, go on the fritz.

**in the wrong** *just admit that you're in the wrong* TO BLAME, blameworthy, at fault, reprehensible, responsible, culpable, answerable, guilty; *archaic* peccant.

**wrongdoer** noun *the wrongdoers in our neighborhood were essentially harmless until the Hanovers moved in* OFFENDER, lawbreaker, criminal, felon, delinquent, villain, culprit, evildoer, sinner, transgressor, malefactor, miscreant, rogue, scoundrel; *informal* crook, *Law* malfeasant; *archaic* trespasser.

**wrongful** adjective *a wrongful arrest* UNJUSTIFIED, unwarranted, unjust, unfair, undue, undeserved, unreasonable, groundless, indefensible, inappropriate, improper, unlawful, illegal, illegitimate. ANTONYMS rightful, fair.

**wry** adjective **1** *his wry humor* IRONIC, sardonic, satirical, mocking, sarcastic; dry, droll, witty, humorous.

**2** *a wry expression* UNIMPRESSED, displeased, annoyed, irritated, irked, vexed, piqued, disgruntled, dissatisfied; *informal* peeved.

# XYZ

**X-ray** noun *the X-ray shows a clean break* RADIOGRAPH, radiogram, X-ray image/picture/photograph, roentgenogram.

**yank** verb *informal give the rope a quick yank* JERK, pull, tug, wrench; snatch, seize.

**yap** verb **1** *the dogs yapped at his heels* BARK, woof, yelp, yip.

**2** *informalwhat are they yapping about now?* See BABBLE verb sense 1.

**yardstick** noun *many of the financial yardsticks known to our grandparents are simply not appropriate for today's investors* STANDARD, measure, gauge, scale, guide, guideline, indicator, test, touchstone, barometer, criterion, benchmark, point of reference, model, pattern, template.

**yarn** noun **1** *you need to use a fine yarn* THREAD, cotton, wool, fiber, filament; ply.

**2** *informal a far-fetched yarn* STORY, tale, anecdote, saga, narrative; *informal* tall tale, tall story, fish story, cock-and-bull story, shaggy-dog story, spiel.

**yawning** adjective *a yawning hole where the door once was* GAPING, wide open, wide, cavernous, deep; huge, great, big.

**year** noun *he held the office for one year* TWELVE-MONTH PERIOD, twelve-month session, annum; calendar year, fiscal year, FY; *archaic* twelvemonth. PHRASE: **year in, year out** *we hear the same excuses, year in, year out* REPEATEDLY, again and again, time and (time) again, time after time, over and over (again); 'week in, week out,' 'day in, day out,' inexorably, recurrently; continuously, continually, constantly, nonstop, habitually, regularly, without a break, unfailingly, always.

**yearly** adjective *a yearly payment* ANNUAL, once a year, every year, each year, per annum.

▸ adverb *the guide is published yearly* ANNUALLY, once a year, per annum, by the year, every year, each year.

**yearn** verb *he **yearned for** a second chance* LONG FOR, pine for, crave, desire, want, wish for, hanker for, covet, lust after/for, pant for, hunger for, burn for, thirst for, ache for, eat one's heart out for, have one's heart set on; *informal* have a yen for, itch for.

**yearning** noun *a yearning for the mountains* LONGING, craving, desire, want, wish, hankering, urge, hunger, thirst, appetite, lust, ache; *informal* yen, itch.

**yell** verb *he yelled in agony* CRY OUT, call out, shout, howl, yowl, wail, scream, shriek, screech, yelp, squeal; roar, bawl; *informal* holler.

▸ noun *a yell of rage* CRY, shout, howl, yowl, scream, shriek, screech, yelp, squeal; roar; *informal* holler.

**yen** noun *informal I've got a yen for chocolate cake* HANKERING, yearning, longing, craving, urge, desire, want, wish, hunger, thirst, lust, appetite, ache; fancy, inclination; *informal* itch.

**yes** exclamation *yes, I'll come to your party* ALL RIGHT, very well, of course, by all means, sure, certainly, absolutely, indeed, right, affirmative, in the affirmative, agreed, roger; *Nautical* aye aye; *informal* yeah, yep, yup, ya, uh-huh, okay, OK, okey-dokey, okey-doke; *archaic* yea, aye. ANTONYM no.

**yet** adverb **1** *he hasn't made up his mind yet* SO FAR, thus far, as yet, up till/to now, until now.

**2** *don't celebrate just yet* NOW, right now, at this time; already, so soon.

**3** *he was doing nothing, yet he appeared purposeful* NEVERTHELESS, nonetheless, even so, but, however, still, notwithstanding, despite that, in spite of that, for all that, all the same, just the same, at the same time, be that as it may; *archaic* natheless.

**4** *he supplied yet more unsolicited advice* EVEN, still, further, in addition, additionally, besides, into the bargain, to boot, on top (of that).

**yield** verb **1** *too many projects yield poor returns* PRODUCE, bear, give, supply, provide, afford, return, bring in, earn, realize, generate, deliver, offer, pay out; *informal* rake in.

**2** *the nobility yielded power to the capitalists* RELINQUISH, surrender, cede, remit, part with, hand over; make over, bequeath, leave. See note at RELINQUISH. ANTONYMS withhold, retain.

**3** *the duke was forced to yield* SURRENDER, capitulate, submit, relent, admit defeat, back down, climb down, give in, give up the struggle, lay down one's arms, raise/show the white flag; *informal* throw in the towel, cave in.

**4** *he **yielded to** her demands* GIVE IN TO, give way to, submit to, bow down to, comply with, agree to, consent to, go along with; grant, permit, allow; *informal* cave in to; *formal* accede to. ANTONYMS resist, defy.

**5** *the floorboards yielded underfoot* BEND, give, give way.

▸ noun *risky investments usually have higher yields* PROFIT, gain, return, dividend, earnings.

**yoke** noun **1** *the horses were loosened from the yoke* HARNESS, collar, coupling.

**2** *countries struggling under the yoke of imperialism* TYRANNY, oppression, domination, hegemony, enslavement, servitude, subjugation, subjection, bondage, thrall; bonds, chains, fetters, shackles.

**3** *the yoke of marriage* BOND, tie, connection, link.

▸ verb **1** *a pair of oxen were yoked together* HARNESS, hitch, couple, tether, fasten, attach, join.

**2** *their aim of yoking biology and mechanics* UNITE, join, marry, link, connect; tie, bind, bond.

**yokel** noun *unless you want trouble, don't mess with the local yokels* BUMPKIN, peasant, provincial, rustic, country cousin, countryman, countrywoman; *informal* hayseed, hillbilly, hick, rube, clodhopper, yahoo.

**young** adjective **1** *young people* YOUTHFUL, juvenile; junior, adolescent, teenage; in the springtime of life, in one's salad days. ANTONYMS old, elderly, mature.

**2** *she's very young for her age* IMMATURE, childish, inexperienced, unsophisticated, naive, unworldly; *informal* wet behind the ears. ANTONYMS old, elderly, mature.

**3** *the young microbrewery industry* FLEDGLING, developing, budding, in its infancy, emerging. ANTONYMS old, elderly, mature.

▸ noun **1** *a robin feeding its young* OFFSPRING, progeny, family, babies.

**2 (the young)** *the young don't care nowadays* YOUNG PEOPLE, children, boys and girls, youngsters, youth, the younger generation, juveniles, minors; *informal* young 'uns, kids.

**youngster** noun *a new magazine for youngsters* CHILD, teenager, adolescent, youth, juvenile, minor, junior; boy, girl; lass, lad; whippersnapper, stripling; *informal* kid, young 'un, teen.

**youth** noun **1** *he had been a keen sportsman in his youth* EARLY YEARS, young days, salad days, teens, teenage years, adolescence, boyhood, girlhood, childhood; minority; *formal* juvenescence. ANTONYMS adulthood, old age.

**2** *she had kept her youth and beauty* YOUTHFULNESS, freshness, bloom, vigor, energy. ANTONYM maturity.

**3** *local youths* YOUNG PERSON/MAN/WOMAN, boy, girl, juvenile, teenager, adolescent, junior, minor; *informal* teen, kid.

**4** *the youth of the nation* YOUNG PEOPLE, young, younger generation, next generation. ANTONYM elderly.

**youthful** adjective *a youthful new leader* YOUNG-LOOKING, spry, sprightly, vigorous, active; young, boyish, girlish; fresh-faced, in the springtime of life, in one's salad days. ANTONYMS old, elderly.

THE RIGHT WORD **youthful, adolescent, callow, immature, juvenile, puerile**

Everyone wants to look **youthful**, an adjective that means possessing, or appearing to possess, the qualities associated with youth (*a youthful enthusiasm for the job*). But no one wants to be called **immature**, which means childish or emotionally underdeveloped and usually pertains to behavior and attitudes rather than to physical appearance (*still immature despite the fact that he was almost thirty*). **Juvenile** suggests immaturity of mind or body and is applied especially to things that are designed for boys and girls in their early teens (*juvenile books*), while **adolescent** applies to the period between puberty and maturity and suggests the physical awkwardness and emotional instability associated with the teenage years (*an adolescent response to criticism*). Young men in particular are often described as **callow**, which means immature in terms of experience (*a callow youth who had never lived away from his family*). Of all these words, **puerile** is probably the most insulting, because it is so often used to describe adults who display the immature behavior of a child (*a puerile piece of writing; a puerile revolt against his aging parents*).

**zany** adjective *the zany humor of the Marx Brothers* ECCENTRIC, peculiar, odd, unconventional, strange, bizarre, weird; mad, crazy, comic, madcap, funny, quirky, idiosyncratic; *informal* wacky, screwy, nutty, oddball, off the wall; daft; kooky, wacko, bizarro. ANTONYMS conventional, sensible.

**zap** verb *informal* **1** *they were zapped by antiradar missiles.* See DESTROY sense 5.

**2** *racecars zapped past.* See SPEED verb sense 1.

**3** *she zapped a chicken burger for lunch* NUKE, microwave.

**zeal** noun *Ross's zeal for football* PASSION, ardor, love, fervor, fire, avidity, devotion, enthusiasm, eagerness, keenness, appetite, relish, gusto, vigor, energy, intensity; fanaticism. ANTONYMS apathy, indifference.

**zealot** noun *York was too much of a zealot for the party to endorse seriously* FANATIC, enthusiast, extremist, radical, young Turk, diehard, true believer, activist, militant; bigot, dogmatist, sectarian, partisan; *informal* fiend, maniac, ultra, nut; eager beaver.

THE RIGHT WORD **zealot, bigot, enthusiast, extremist, fanatic**

An **enthusiast** displays an intense and eager interest in something (*a sky-diving enthusiast*). A **fanatic** is not only intense and eager but possibly irrational in his or her enthusiasm; *fanatic* suggests extreme devotion and a willingness to go to any length to maintain or carry out one's beliefs (*a fly-fishing fanatic who hired a helicopter to reach his favorite stream*). A **zealot** exhibits not only extreme devotion but vehement activity in support of a cause or goal (*a feminist zealot who spent most of her time campaigning for women's rights*). An **extremist** is a supporter of extreme doctrines or practices, particularly in a political context (*a paramilitary extremist who anticipated the overthrow of the government*). But it is the **bigot** who causes the most trouble, exhibiting obstinate and often blind devotion to his or her beliefs and opinions. In contrast to *fanatic* and *zealot*, the term *bigot* implies intolerance and contempt for those who do not agree (*a bigot who could not accept his daughter's decision to marry outside her religion*).

---

**zealous** adjective *a zealous worker* FERVENT, ardent, fervid, fanatical, passionate, impassioned, devout, devoted, committed, dedicated, hard-core, enthusiastic, eager, keen, overkeen, avid, card-carrying, vigorous, energetic, intense, fierce; *literary* perfervid. See note at EAGER. ANTONYMS apathetic, indifferent.

**zenith** noun *at the zenith of his power | the view from the mountain's zenith* HIGHEST POINT, high point, crowning point, height, top, acme, peak, pinnacle, apex, apogee, crown, crest, summit, climax, culmination, prime, meridian. ANTONYM nadir.

**zero** noun *I rated my chances at zero* NOTHING, nothing at all, nil, none, naught/nought; *informal* zilch, nix, zip, nada, diddly-squat. PHRASE: **zero in on** *each study group will zero in on a different aspect of the ecosystem* FOCUS ON, focus attention on, center on, concentrate on, home in on, fix on, pinpoint, highlight, spotlight; *informal* zoom in on.

**zero hour** noun *as zero hour approached, thirty ships swung into position* THE APPOINTED TIME, the critical moment, the moment of truth, the point/moment of decision, the Rubicon, the crux; *informal* the crunch.

**zest** noun **1** *she had a great zest for life* ENTHUSIASM, gusto, relish, appetite, eagerness, keenness, avidity, zeal, fervor, ardor, passion; verve, vigor, liveliness, sparkle, fire, animation, vitality, dynamism, energy, brio, pep, spirit, exuberance, high spirits, joie de vivre; *informal* zing, zip, oomph, vim, pizzazz, get-up-and-go. ANTONYMS apathy, indifference.

**2** *the lemon pepper and cilantro will add zest to the sauce | he wanted to put some zest to his life* PIQUANCY, tang, flavor, savor, taste, spice, spiciness, relish, bite; excitement, interest, an edge; *informal* kick, punch, zing, oomph. ANTONYM blandness.

**3** *the grated zest of an orange* RIND, peel, skin.

**zing** noun *informal*. See ZEST sense 1.

**zip** *informal* noun *he's full of zip*. See ENERGY.

▸ verb *I zipped along the highway*. See SPEED verb sense 1.

**zone** noun *the search continued in the zone south of the river* AREA, sector, section, belt, stretch, region, territory, district, quarter, precinct, locality, neighborhood, province.

**zoom** verb *informal a lone car zoomed across the desert road* WHIZ, zip, whip, buzz, hurtle, speed, rush, streak, shoot, race, bolt, dash, run, flash, blast, charge, fly, careen, career, go like the wind; *informal* belt, scoot, tear, go like a bat out of hell, bomb, hightail, clip. PHRASE: **zoom in on** *zoom in on the rabbit in the background* ENLARGE, magnify, close in on, focus in on.

# Language Guide

# Rules of English: Understanding Grammar

Grammar is the system and structure of a language. It embodies all the principles by which the language works. All good writing begins with an understanding of the fundamentals of grammar:

- parts of speech
- parts of sentences
- sentence structures
- sentence functions

## PARTS OF SPEECH

### *Noun*

A **noun** is a word that identifies or names a person, place, thing, action, or quality. There are two types of nouns: proper and common.

#### Proper nouns

A noun that names a particular person, place, or thing is a **proper noun**. It always begins with a capital letter.

Benito Mussolini
Buffy
Mount Everest
Cairo
the Chrysler Building
Jell-O

#### Common nouns

A noun that names a type of person, place, or thing is a **common noun**. There are three kinds of common nouns: concrete, abstract, and collective.

A **concrete noun** names someone or something that you can see or touch.

arm
giraffe
hamburger
lake
photograph
stapler

An **abstract noun** names something intangible (that is, something that cannot be seen nor touched).

awe
assistance
bravery
disappointment
flavor
wit

A **collective noun** names a group of persons or things.

audience
band
colony
herd
platoon
set

SINGULAR AND PLURAL NOUNS

A noun that names one person, place, or thing is **singular**. A noun that names more than one person, place, or thing is **plural**. The spelling of a singular noun almost always changes when it becomes a plural. Most plurals can be formed by adding *-s* or *-es*, but many nouns do not follow this format.

beach/beaches
bean/beans
hairbrush/hairbrushes
leaf/leaves
mouse/mice
party/parties
school/schools
woman/women

If the spelling of a plural noun is in doubt, it is always advisable to consult a dictionary.

APPOSITIVES

An **appositive** is a noun (or a unit of words that acts as a noun) whose meaning is a direct copy or extension of the meaning of the preceding noun in the sentence. In other words, the appositive and the preceding noun refer to the same person, place, or thing. The appositive helps to characterize or elaborate on the preceding noun in a specific way.

The wedding cake, a chocolate masterpiece, was the hit of the reception.
[The noun *cake* and the appositive *masterpiece* are the same thing.]

His primary objective, to write the great American novel, was never realized.
[The noun *objective* and the appositive *to write the great American novel* are the same thing.]

Eleanor's math teacher, Mrs. Kennedy, is retiring next year.
[The noun *teacher* and the appositive *Mrs. Kennedy* are the same person.]

### Possessives

A **possessive** is a noun whose form has changed in order to show possession. Certain rules can be followed to determine how the form should change for any given noun.

In the case of a singular noun, add an apostrophe and an s.

Lincoln's inaugural address
the baby's favorite blanket

*Exception:* Most singular nouns that end in s follow the preceding rule with no difficulty (e.g., Chris's, Dickens's), but some singular nouns that end in *s* may be exempted from the rule because the pronunciation of the plural is less awkward with just an apostrophe and no final *s*.

Ramses' dynasty
Aristophanes' great comedic works

In the case of a plural noun that ends in *s*, add just an apostrophe.

the Lincolns' summer home
our babies' double stroller

In the case of a plural noun that does not end in s, add an apostrophe and an s.

men's footwear
the fungi's rapid reproduction

In the case of a compound noun (a noun made of more than one word), only the last word takes the possessive form.

my sister-in-law's house
the commander in chief's personal staff

In the case of joint possession (that is, two or more nouns possess the same thing together), only the last of the possessing nouns takes the possessive form.

Ryan and Saul's nickel collection
[There is only one nickel collection, and *both* Ryan and Saul own it *together*.]

Gramma and Grampa's photo albums
[However many photo albums there may be, they all belong to *both* Gramma and Grampa *together*.]

In the case of individual possession by two or more nouns (that is, two or more nouns possess the same type of thing, but separately and distinctly), each of the possessing nouns takes the possessive form.

Lenny's and Suzanne's footprints on the beach
[Lenny and Suzanne *each* left *their own distinct* footprints on the beach.]

Strauss's and Khachaturian's waltzes
[Strauss and Khachaturian each composed *their own distinct* waltzes.]

### *Pronoun*

A **pronoun** is a word that represents a person or thing without giving the specific name of the person or thing. There are five classes of pronouns: personal, relative, demonstrative, indefinite, and interrogative.

A **personal pronoun** is used to refer to the person speaking (first person), the person spoken to (second person), or the person or thing spoken about (third person). A pronoun formed from certain personal pronouns by adding the suffix *-self* (singular) or *-selves* (plural) is called "reflexive."

| person | singular | plural | reflexive singular | reflexive plural |
|---|---|---|---|---|
| first person | *I* | *we* | — | — |
| | *my* | *our* | *myself* | *ourselves* |
| | *mine* | *ours* | — | — |
| | *me* | *us* | — | — |
| second person | *you* | *you* | — | — |
| | *your* | *your* | *yourself* | *yourselves* |
| | *yours* | *yours* | — | — |
| | *you* | *you* | — | — |
| third person | masculine: | | | |
| | *he* | *they* | — | — |
| | *his* | *their* | — | — |
| | *his* | *theirs* | — | — |
| | *him* | *them* | *himself* | *themselves* |
| | feminine: | | | |
| | *she* | *they* | — | — |
| | *her* | *their* | — | — |
| | *hers* | *theirs* | — | — |
| | *her* | *them* | *herself* | *themselves* |
| | neuter: | | | |
| | *it* | *they* | — | — |
| | *its* | *their* | — | — |
| | *its* | *theirs* | — | — |
| | *it* | *them* | *itself* | *themselves* |

*Note that the gender designations of masculine, feminine, and neuter apply only to the third person singular.*

**Reflexive personal pronouns** are so-called because they reflect the action of the verb back to the subject. It is incorrect to use a reflexive pronoun by itself; there must be a subject to which it refers.

incorrect: Denise and myself will fix the car.
[The reflexive pronoun *myself* has no subject to refer to; the wording should be "Denise and I."]

correct: I will fix the car myself.
[The reflexive pronoun *myself* refers to the subject I.]

A reflexive pronoun that adds force or emphasis to a noun or another pronoun is called "intensive."

You yourself must return the ladder.
Terri and Phil want to wallpaper the kitchen themselves.

A **relative pronoun** introduces a descriptive clause. The relative pronouns are *which, that, who, whoever, whose, whom,* and *whomever*.

Wendy was the pianist who won the scholarship.
Is Mr. Leonard the teacher whose book was just published?
Whoever wrote the speech is a genius.
I attended the morning meeting, which lasted for three hours.

A **demonstrative pronoun** is specific. It is used to point out particular persons, places, or things. The demonstrative pronouns are *this, that, these,* and *those.*

These are the finest fabrics available.
I'll look at those first.
What is this?

An **indefinite pronoun** is nonspecific. It is used to refer to persons, places, or things without particular identification. There are numerous indefinite pronouns, including the following:

| | | |
|---|---|---|
| all | everybody | none |
| any | everyone | no one |
| anybody | everything | other/others |
| anyone | few | several |
| anything | many | some |
| both | most | somebody |
| each | neither | someone |
| either | nobody | something |

George brought two desserts, but I didn't try either.
Many are called, but few are chosen.
Can somebody please answer the phone?

An **interrogative pronoun** is used to ask a question. The interrogative pronouns are *who, which,* and *what.*

Who wants to buy a raffle ticket?
Which of the two applicants has more practical experience?
What is the purpose of another debate?

PRONOUN CASES

The case of a pronoun is what determines its relation to the other words in the sentence. There are three pronoun cases: nominative, objective, and possessive.

**Nominative case**

The nominative pronouns are *I, we, you, he, she, it, they, who,* and *whoever.*

A pronoun that is the subject (or part of the subject) of a sentence is in the nominative case.

> <u>They</u> loved the movie.
> Mark and <u>I</u> are going to the Bahamas.

A pronoun that is a predicate is in the nominative case.

> It was <u>she</u> who wrote the poem.
> The winner will probably be <u>you</u>.

**Objective case**

The objective pronouns are *me, us, you, him, her, it, them, whom,* and *whomever.*

A pronoun that is the direct object of a verb is in the objective case.

> Stephen already invited <u>them</u>.
> Should we keep <u>it</u>?

A pronoun that is an indirect object of a verb is in the objective case.

> Captain Mackenzie told <u>us</u> many seafaring tales.
> I'll give <u>you</u> the recipe tomorrow.

A pronoun that is the object of a preposition is in the objective case.

> Does she think this job is beneath <u>her</u>?
> To <u>whom</u> was it addressed?

**Possessive case**

A possessive pronoun shows ownership.

The possessive pronouns used as predicate nominatives are *mine, ours, yours, his, hers, its, theirs,* and *whose.*

> The blue station wagon is <u>mine</u>.
> None of the cash was <u>theirs</u>.

The possessive pronouns used as adjectives are *my, our, your, his, her, its, their,* and *whose.*

> <u>Whose</u> test scores were the highest?
> I believe this is <u>your</u> package.

### TIP

A possessive pronoun never has an apostrophe. Remember, the word *it's* is the contraction of *it is* or *it has*—not the possessive form of *it*.

| | |
|---|---|
| possessive: | Life has its ups and downs. |
| contraction: | It's good to see you. |

SINGULAR AND PLURAL AGREEMENT

It is important to identify a pronoun as singular or plural and to make certain that the associated verb form is in agreement. The pronouns that tend to cause the most problems for writers and speakers are the indefinite pronouns.

Some indefinite pronouns are always singular and therefore always require a singular verb. These include *everybody, everyone, somebody, someone, nobody, one, either,* and *neither.*

Nobody wants to leave.
Don't get up unless someone knocks on the door.
Either of these two colors is fine.

Other indefinite pronouns may be singular or plural, depending on the particular reference. These include *any, all, some, most,* and *none.*

If any of these marbles are yours, let me know.
[The noun *marbles* is plural.]

If any of this cake is yours, let me know.
[The noun *cake* is singular.]

Most of the potatoes are already gone.
[The noun *potatoes* is plural.]

Most of the evening is already gone.
[The noun *evening* is singular.]

### *Verb*

A **verb** is a word that expresses an action or a state of being.

An **action verb** expresses a physical or mental action.

break
eat
intercept
operate
unveil
wish

A **state of being verb** expresses a condition or state of being.

be
become
is
lack
seem
smell

TRANSITIVE VERBS

A **transitive verb** expresses an action that is performed on someone or something. The someone or something is the **direct object.** Notice in each of the following examples that the direct object receives the action of the verb.

Ingrid restores antique furniture.
[transitive verb: *restores*; direct object: *furniture*]

Hernandez pitched the ball.
[transitive verb: *pitched*; direct object: *ball*]

Did you feed the animals?
[transitive verb: *feed*; direct object: *animals*]

Sometimes a transitive verb has both a direct object and an indirect object. An **indirect object** is the person or thing to whom or for whom the verb's action is being performed. Notice in each of the following examples that the direct object receives the action of the verb, while the indirect object identifies who or what the action affected.

The captain handed us our orders.
[transitive verb: *handed*; direct object: *orders*; indirect object: *us*]

Did you give the plants some water?
[transitive verb: *give*; direct object: *water*; indirect object: *plants*]

I tossed a pen to Herman.
[transitive verb: *tossed*; direct object: *pen*; indirect object: *Herman*]

INTRANSITIVE VERBS

An **intransitive verb** does not have an object. Notice in each of the following examples that the verb expresses an action that occurs without needing to be received.

We marched in the parade.
The tea kettle whistled.
Heidi and Roy dance in the opening number.

## TIP

Remember: A direct object answers *what?* An indirect object answers *to whom?* (or *to what?*) or *for whom?* (or *for what?*).

| | | |
|---|---|---|
| direct objects: | *What* does Ingrid restore? | furniture |
| | *What* did Hernandez pitch? | ball |
| | Did you feed *what*? | animals |
| | *What* did the captain hand? | orders |
| | Did you give *what*? | water |
| | *What* did I toss? | pen |
| indirect objects: | *To whom* did the captain hand orders? | us |
| | Did you give water *to what*? | plants |
| | *To whom* did I toss a pen? | Herman |

### Linking verbs

A **linking verb** joins a word (or unit of words) that names a person or thing to another word (or unit of words) that renames or describes the person or thing. It is always intransitive and always expresses a state of being. The most common linking verbs are *to be* and all the forms of *to be*, which include *am*, *are*, *is*, *was*, and *were*. Other common linking verbs include the following:

| | | | |
|---|---|---|---|
| act | feel | remain | sound |
| appear | grow | seem | taste |
| become | look | smell | turn |

The air seemed humid yesterday.
What smells so good?
The days grow shorter.
I am a registered voter.
Kim remains a devout Catholic.
Butch and Sundance were the title characters.

## TIP

Remember: Because an intransitive verb does not have an object, the question *what?* will be unanswerable.

*What* did we march?
*What* did the kettle whistle?
*What* do Heidi and Roy dance?

These questions simply cannot be answered; therefore the verbs are intransitive.

### Predicate adjectives and nominatives

The word (or unit of words) that a linking verb joins to the subject can be either an adjective or a noun, but its function is always the same: to tell something about the subject. An adjective that follows a linking verb is a **predicate adjective**. A noun that follows a linking verb is a **predicate nominative**.

predicate adjective: The air seemed humid yesterday.
What smells so good?
The days grow shorter.

predicate nominative: I am a registered voter.
Kim remains a devout Catholic.
Butch and Sundance were the title characters.

### Voice

The subject of a transitive verb either performs or receives the action. A verb whose subject performs is said to be in the **active voice.** A verb whose subject receives is said to be in the **passive voice**.

active voice: Brainerd & Sons built the storage shed.
[The subject *Brainerd & Sons* performed the action of building.]

Lydia will curry the horses.
[The subject *Lydia* will perform the action of currying.]

passive voice: The storage shed was built by Brainerd & Sons.
[The subject *shed* received the action of building.]

The horses will be curried by Lydia.
[The subject *horses* will receive the action of currying.]

### Mood

Verbs have a quality that shows the attitude or purpose of the speaker. This quality is called the **mood**. There are three verb moods: indicative, imperative, and subjunctive.

The **indicative mood** shows a statement or question of fact.

Does Paula know the combination to the safe?
Dr. Sliva is my dentist.

The **imperative mood** shows a command or request.

Make the most of your situation.
Proceed to the third traffic light.

The **subjunctive mood** shows a condition of doubtfulness, possibility, desirability, improbability, or unreality.

Should you decide to return the blouse, you will need the receipt.
If I were rich, I'd quit my job.

PERSON AND NUMBER

The **person** (first, second, or third) of a verb depends on to whom or to what the verb refers: the person speaking (first person), the person spoken to (second person), or the person or thing spoken about (third person).

The **number** (singular or plural) of a verb depends on whether the verb refers to a singular subject or a plural subject.

For nearly all verbs, the form of the verb changes only in the third person singular.

| person | singular | plural |
|---|---|---|
| first person | I *know* | we *know* |
| second person | you *know* | you *know* |
| third person | he *knows*<br>she *knows*<br>it *knows* | they *know*<br>they *know*<br>they *know* |
| | Chris *knows*<br>Mrs. Hansen *knows*<br>God *knows*<br>the teacher *knows*<br>the heart *knows* | Chris and Pat *know*<br>the Hansens *know*<br>the gods *know*<br>the teachers *know*<br>our hearts *know* |

TENSE

The **tense** of a verb shows the time of the verb's action. There are six verb tenses: present, present perfect, past, past perfect, future, and future perfect.

The **present tense** shows action occurring in the present.

I smell fresh coffee.

The present tense can also show the following:

| | |
|---|---|
| action that is typical or habitual: | I design greenhouses.<br>Stuart daydreams during math class. |
| action that will occur: | Lynne retires in six months.<br>Our plane lands at midnight. |
| facts and beliefs: | March follows February.<br>Greed destroys the spirit. |

### TIP

Yet another function of the present tense is what is called the **historical present**. This usage allows the writer or speaker to relate past actions in a present tone, which may enhance the descriptive flow of the text.

> The United States acquires the Oklahoma Territory from France in 1803 as part of the Louisiana Purchase. Following the War of 1812, the U.S. government begins a relocation program, forcing Indian tribes from the eastern United States to move into certain unsettled western areas, including Oklahoma. Because of their opposition to the U.S. government, most of these native people lend their support to the Confederate South during the American Civil War. In 1865, the war ends in utter defeat for the Confederacy, and all of the Oklahoma Territory soon falls under U.S. military rule.

When using the historical present, writers and speakers must be careful not to lapse into the past tense. For example, it would be an incorrect mix of tenses to say, "In 1865, the war ended in utter defeat for the Confederacy, and all of the Oklahoma Territory soon falls under U.S. military rule."

---

The **present perfect tense** is formed with the word *has* or *have*. It shows action begun in the past and completed by the time of the present.

> James has checked the air in the tires at least three times.
> I have read the book you're talking about.

The **past tense** shows action that occurred in the past.

> Greg memorized his speech.
> The mouse scurried across the room.

The **past perfect tense** is formed with the word *had*. It shows action that occurred in the past, prior to another past action.

> Eugene had finished his story by the time we got to the airport.
> The parrot had flown into another room long before we noticed an empty cage.

The **future tense** is formed with the word *will*. It shows action that is expected to occur in the future.

> The president will address the nation this evening.
> Tempers will flare when the truth comes out.

The **future perfect tense** is formed with the words *will have*. It shows action that is expected to occur in the future, prior to another future or expected action.

> Noreen will have finished painting by the time we're ready to lay the carpet.
> The candidates will have traveled thousands of miles before this campaign is over.

VERBALS

A verb form that acts as a part of speech other than a verb is a **verbal**. There are three types of verbals: infinitives, participles, and gerunds.

An **infinitive** is a verb form that can act as a noun, an adjective, or an adverb. It is preceded by the preposition *to*.

noun: To steal is a crime.
[The infinitive *to steal* is the subject.]

Our original plan, to elope, was never discovered.
[The infinitive *to elope* is an appositive.]

adjective: Those are words to remember.
[The infinitive *to remember* modifies the noun *words*.]

adverb: The hill was too icy to climb.
[The infinitive *to climb* modifies the predicate adjective *icy*.]

He lived to golf.
[The infinitive *to golf* modifies the verb *lived*.]

A **participle** is a verb form that has one of two uses: to make a verb phrase ("they were trying"; "the car has died") or to act as an adjective. A participle is a verbal only when it acts as an adjective.

A **present participle** always ends in *-ing*.

catching
laughing
winding

A **past participle** usually ends in *-ed*, *-en*, or *-t*.

given
lost
toasted

In the following examples, each participle acts as an adjective and is therefore a verbal.

Does the zoo have a laughing hyena?
We live on a winding road.
It was a lost opportunity.
Add a cup of toasted coconut.

A **gerund** is a verb form that acts as a noun. It always ends in *-ing*.

Reading is my favorite pastime.
The next step, varnishing, should be done in a well-ventilated area.
The doctor suggested guidelines for sensible dieting.

### TIP

Remember: Both gerunds and present participles always end in –*ing*, but their functions are quite distinct. Also remember that a present participle is only a verbal when it acts as an adjective, *not* when it acts as a verb phrase.

| | |
|---|---|
| verbal: | Her singing has improved this year.<br>[Used as a noun, *singing* is a gerund, which is always a verbal.] |
| | Peterson hired the singing cowboys.<br>[Used as an adjective, *singing* is a present participle that is also a verbal.] |
| not a verbal: | The birds are singing.<br>[Used as a verb phrase, *singing* is a present participle, but not a verbal] |

## *Adjective*

An **adjective** is a word that modifies a noun. There are two basic types of adjectives: descriptive and limiting.

### DESCRIPTIVE ADJECTIVES

A **descriptive adjective** describes a noun. That is, it shows a quality or condition of a noun.

She is an upstanding citizen.
Josh has invited his zany friends.
That was a mighty clap of thunder.
I prefer the white shirt with the long sleeves.

### LIMITING ADJECTIVES

A **limiting adjective** shows the limits of a noun. That is, it indicates the number or quantity of a noun, or it points out a certain specificity of a noun. There are three types of limiting adjectives: numerical adjectives, pronominal adjectives, and articles.

A **numerical adjective** is a number. It may be cardinal ("how many") or ordinal ("in what order").

| | |
|---|---|
| cardinal: | We have served one million customers.<br>There are three prizes.<br>After Arizona was admitted, there were forty-eight states. |
| ordinal: | You are the one millionth customer.<br>We won third prize.<br>Arizona was the forty-eighth state to be admitted. |

A **pronominal adjective** is a pronoun that acts as an adjective. A pronominal adjective may be personal (*my, our, your, his, her, their, its*), demonstrative (*this, that, these, those*), indefinite (*all, any, few, other, several, some*), or interrogative (*which, what*).

personal: We loved her goulash.
The squirrel returned to its nest.

demonstrative: Those directions are too complicated.
This window is broken.

indefinite: Pick any card from the deck.
All luggage will be inspected.

interrogative: Which radios are on sale?
What color is the upholstery?

There are three **articles** in English: *a*, *an*, and *the*. Articles are classified as either indefinite (*a, an*) or definite (*the*).

indefinite: At dawn, a helicopter broke the silence.
An usher seated us.

definite: The paintings lacked imagination.

COMPARISON OF ADJECTIVES

Descriptive adjectives are able to indicate qualities and conditions by three degrees of comparison: positive, comparative, and superlative. Adjectives may be compared in downward or upward order.

For **downward comparisons**, all adjectives use the words *less* (comparative) and *least* (superlative).

***Downward Comparisons***

| **positive** (the quality or condition) | **comparative** (a degree lower than the positive) | **superlative** (the lowest degree of the positive) |
|---|---|---|
| intelligent | less intelligent | least intelligent |
| kind | less kind | least kind |
| salty | less salty | least salty |

For **upward comparisons**, there are three different formats:

***Upward Comparisons***

| **positive** (the quality or condition) | **comparative** (a degree higher than the positive) | **superlative** (the highest degree of the positive) |
|---|---|---|
| 1. Almost all one-syllable adjectives use the endings *-er* (comparative) and *-est* (superlative). Some adjectives with two or more syllables follow this format as well. | | |
| kind | kinder | kindest |
| straight | straighter | straightest |
| salty | saltier | saltiest |
| 2. Most adjectives with two or more syllables use the words *more* (comparative) and *most* (superlative). Most one-syllable adjectives may use this format as an optional alternative to using *-er* and *-est*. | | |
| harmonious | more harmonious | most harmonious |
| impatient | more impatient | most impatient |
| talkative | more talkative | most talkative |
| kind | more kind | most kind |
| 3. Some adjectives have irregular forms. | | |
| bad/ill | worse | worst |
| good/well | better | best |
| far | farther/further | farthest/furthest |
| little | less | least |
| many | more | most |

**TIP**

Never "double compare" an adjective. Remember:

Sometimes a descriptive adjective may use either *-er* or *more*, but it never uses both.

correct: The red grapes are <u>sweeter</u> than the green ones.
The red grapes are <u>more sweet</u> than the green ones.

incorrect: The red grapes are <u>more sweeter</u> than the green ones.

Sometimes a descriptive adjective may use either *-est* or *most*, but it never uses both.

correct: Samson is the <u>friendliest</u> dog in the building.
Samson is the <u>most friendly</u> dog in the building.

incorrect: Samson is the <u>most friendliest</u> dog in the building.

### *Adverb*

An **adverb** is a word that modifies a verb, an adjective, or another adverb.

ADVERB MEANINGS

An adverb usually describes how, where, when, or to what extent something happens.

An **adverb of manner** describes *how.*

They argued loudly.

An **adverb of place** describes *where.*

Please sit near me.

An **adverb of time** describes *when.*

I'll call you later.

An **adverb of degree** describes *to what extent.*

The laundry is somewhat damp.

ADVERB FUNCTIONS

A **relative adverb** introduces a subordinate clause.

I'll be out on the veranda when the clock strikes twelve.

A **conjunctive adverb** (also called a **transitional adverb**) joins two independent clauses.

Dinner is ready; however, you may have to heat it up.

An **interrogative adverb** introduces a question.

Where did Lisa go?

An **independent adverb** functions independently from the rest of the sentence. That is, the meaning and grammatical correctness of the sentence would not change if the independent adverb were removed.

Besides, I never liked living in the city.

COMPARISON OF ADVERBS

Like adjectives, adverbs of manner may be compared in three degrees: positive, comparative, and superlative.

Most adverbs, especially those that end in *–ly*, take on the comparing words "more" and "most."

| **positive** | **comparative** | **superlative** |
|---|---|---|
| nicely | more nicely | most nicely |
| diligently | more diligently | most diligently |

Some adverbs take on the comparing suffixes *–er* and *–est*.

| positive | comparative | superlative |
|---|---|---|
| early | earlier | earliest |
| soon | sooner | soonest |
| close | closer | closest |

Almost all adverbs take on the comparing words "less" and "least."

| positive | comparative | superlative |
|---|---|---|
| nicely | less nicely | least nicely |
| diligently | less diligently | least diligently |
| early | less early | least early |
| soon | less soon | least soon |
| close | less close | least close |

Some adverbs have irregular comparisons.

| positive | comparative | superlative |
|---|---|---|
| much | more | most |
| little | less | least |
| badly | worse | worst |
| well | better | best |
| far | farther | farthest |
| far | further | furthest |

---

## TIP

**Adverbs ending in *–ly***

A great number of adverbs are created by adding the suffix *–ly* to an adjective.

hesitant + *-ly* = hesitantly
strong + *-ly* = strongly

This does not mean, however, that all adverbs end in *–ly*.

adverbs: fast, seldom, now

Nor does it mean that all words ending in *–ly* are adverbs.

adjectives: friendly, homely, dastardly

The way to determine if a word is an adverb or an adjective is to see how it is used in the sentence:

- If it modifies a noun, it is an adjective.
- If it modifies a verb, an adjective, or another adverb, it is an adverb.

---

### *Preposition*

A **preposition** is a word or group of words that governs a noun or pronoun by expressing its relationship to another word in the clause.

> The suspects landed in jail.
> [The relationship between the noun *jail* and the verb *landed* is shown by the preposition *in*.]
>
> Please hide the packages under the bed.
> [The relationship between the noun *bed* and the noun *packages* is shown by the preposition *under*.]
>
> The guitarist playing with our band is Samantha's uncle.
> [The relationship between the noun *band* and the participle *playing* is shown by the preposition *with*.]
>
> I already knew about it.
> [The relationship between the pronoun *it* and the verb *knew* is shown by the preposition *about*.]

---

**TIP**

Many words used as prepositions may be used as other parts of speech as well.

| | |
|---|---|
| The closest village is over that hill. | [preposition] |
| He leaned over and whispered in my ear. | [adverb] |
| I told no one but Corinne. | [preposition] |
| We played our best, but the other team won. | [conjunction] |
| She is but a shadow of her former self. | [adverb] |

---

**Common prepositions**

aboard
about
above
according to
across
after
against
ahead
along
along with
amid
around
as
as far as
as for
as to
aside from
at
because of
before
behind
below
beneath
beside
besides
between
beyond
but
but for
by
by means of
by way of
concerning
contrary to
despite
down
during
except
for
from
in
in accordance with
in addition to
in back of
in case of
in front of
in lieu of
in place of
in regard to
in search of
in spite of
inside

| | | | |
|---|---|---|---|
| instead of | onto | round | unlike |
| into | opposite | since | until |
| like | out | thanks to | up |
| near | out of | through | upon |
| next to | outside | throughout | up to |
| of | over | till | with |
| off | past | to | within |
| on | per | toward | without |
| on account of | prior to | under | |
| on behalf of | regarding | underneath | |

### *Conjunction*

A **conjunction** is a word (or unit of words) that connects words, phrases, clauses, or sentences. There are three kinds of conjunctions: coordinating, subordinating, and correlative.

#### COORDINATING CONJUNCTIONS

A **coordinating conjunction** connects elements that have the same grammatical rank—that is, it connects words to words (nouns to nouns, verbs to verbs, etc.), phrases to phrases, clauses to clauses, sentences to sentences. A coordinating conjunction is almost always one of these seven words: *and, but, for, nor, or, so, yet.*

Would you prefer rice or potatoes?
[The coordinating conjunction *or* connects the two nouns *rice* and *potatoes.*]

I have seen and heard enough.
[The coordinating conjunction *and* connects the two verbs *seen* and *heard.*]

Vinnie's cat lay on the chair purring softly yet twitching its tail.
[The coordinating conjunction *yet* connects the two participial phrases *purring softly* and *twitching its tail.*]

O'Donnell is the reporter whose name is on the story but who denies having written it.
[The coordinating conjunction *but* connects the two subordinate clauses *whose name is on the story* and *who denies having written it.*]

We wanted to see batting practice, so we got to the stadium early.
[The coordinating conjunction *so* connects the two sentences *We wanted to see batting practice* and *We got to the stadium early*, creating one sentence. Notice that a comma precedes the conjunction when two sentences are joined.]

#### SUBORDINATING CONJUNCTIONS

A **subordinating conjunction** belongs to a subordinate clause. It connects the subordinate clause to a main clause.

I could get there on time if only the ferry were still running.
[The subordinating conjunction *if only* connects the subordinate clause *if only the ferry were still running* to the main clause *I could get there on time.*]

**Common subordinating conjunctions**

| | | | |
|---|---|---|---|
| after | but | since | until |
| although | even if | so | when |
| as | even though | so that | whenever |
| as if | how | than | where |
| as long as | if | that | whereas |
| as though | if only | though | wherever |
| because | in order that | till | while |
| before | rather than | unless | why |

### TIP

A noun clause or an adjective clause may or may not be introduced by a subordinating conjunction, but an adverb clause always is introduced by a subordinating conjunction.

- noun clause introduced by subordinating conjunction:
  Jack asked the question even though he knew the answer.
- noun clause with no subordinating conjunction:
  We gave every single detail our fullest attention.
- adjective clause introduced by subordinating conjunction:
  This is the farm where we boarded our horses.
- adjective clause with no subordinating conjunction:
  The people we met last night are Hungarian.
- adverb clause with subordinating conjunction (as always):
  I will speak as soon as the crowd quiets down.

CORRELATIVE CONJUNCTIONS

Two coordinating conjunctions that function together are called a pair of **correlative conjunctions**. These are the most common pairs of correlative conjunctions:

both . . . and
either . . . or
neither . . . nor
not only . . . but
not only . . . but also
whether . . . or

The site in Denver offers the potential for both security and expansion.
[The pair of correlative conjunctions *both . . . and* connects the two nouns *security* and *expansion*.]

I'm running in tomorrow's race whether it is sunny or rainy.
[The pair of correlative conjunctions *whether . . . or* connects the two adjectives *sunny* and *rainy*.]

**TIP**

It would be incorrect to say:

Their dog is neither quiet nor obeys simple commands.

Why? Because the pair of correlative conjunctions *neither . . . nor* is being used to connect the adjective *quiet* to the verb phrase *obeys simple commands*. This is not a grammatically valid connection.

Remember: A pair of correlative conjunctions is comprised of two coordinating conjunctions, and a coordinating conjunction must connect elements that have the same grammatical rank—that is, it must connect words to words (nouns to nouns, verbs to verbs, etc.), phrases to phrases, clauses to clauses, sentences to sentences.

Therefore, the sentence must be reworded to make the grammatical ranks match. Here are two such corrected versions:

Their dog is <u>neither</u> quiet <u>nor</u> obedient.
[The adjective *quiet* is connected to the adjective *obedient*.]

Their dog <u>neither</u> stays quiet <u>nor</u> obeys simple commands.
[The verb phrase *stays quiet* is connected to the verb phrase *obeys simple commands*.]

---

### *Interjection*

An **interjection** is a word or phrase that expresses emotion, typically in an abrupt or emphatic way. It is not connected grammatically to the rest of the sentence. When the emotion expressed is very strong, the interjection is followed by an exclamation point. Otherwise it is followed by a comma.

<u>Stop</u>! I can't let you in here.
<u>Hurray</u>! Dempsey has won another fight.
<u>Ah</u>, that was a wonderful meal.
<u>Oh no</u>, I left my sweater on the train.

---

**TIP**

Interjections occur more often in speech than in writing. It is not wrong to use interjections in writing, but writers should do so sparingly. Remember, an interjection is essentially an interruption, and too many may disrupt the flow of the text.

---

## PHRASES, CLAUSES, SENTENCES, AND PARAGRAPHS

### *Phrases*

A phrase is a unit of words that acts as a single part of speech.

NOUN PHRASES

A phrase made up of a noun and its modifiers is a **noun phrase**.

> The biggest pumpkin won a blue ribbon.
> A magnificent whooping crane flew overhead.

Most noun phrases can be replaced with a pronoun.

> Give the tickets to the tall, dark-haired gentleman.
> Give the tickets to him.

VERB PHRASES

A phrase made up of a main verb and its auxiliaries is a verb phrase (also called a complete verb).

> We have been waiting for three hours.
> What type of music do you prefer?

ADJECTIVE PHRASES

A phrase made up of a participle and its related words is an **adjective phrase** (also called an **adjectival phrase** or a **participial phrase**). Acting as a single adjective, it modifies a noun or pronoun.

> Awakened by the siren, we escaped to safety.
> [The adjective phrase *Awakened by the siren* modifies the pronoun *we*.]
>
> Following his grandmother's directions, Harry baked a beautiful apple pie.
> [The adjective phrase *Following his grandmother's directions* modifies the noun *Harry*.]

PREPOSITIONAL PHRASES

A phrase that begins with a preposition is a **prepositional phrase**. It can act as an adjective or an adverb.

> adjective: The car with the sunroof is mine.
> [The noun *car* is modified by the prepositional phrase *with the sunroof*.]
>
> adverb: After the storm, we gathered the fallen branches.
> [The verb *gathered* is modified by *After the storm*.]

### *Clauses*

A clause is a unit of words that contains a subject and a predicate.

### Independent clauses

A clause that can stand by itself as a complete thought is an **independent clause**. Any independent clause can stand alone as a complete sentence.

The Milwaukee Brewers joined the National League in November 1997.
It is snowing.
Vitus is the patron saint of actors.
Bob called.
The Celts were highly ritualistic.
Read what child development experts have to say.

### Subordinate clauses

A clause that cannot stand by itself as a complete thought is a **subordinate clause** (also called a **dependent clause**). It cannot be a part of a sentence unless it is related by meaning to the independent clause. Essentially, it exists to build upon the information conveyed by the independent clause. A subordinate clause can relate to the independent clause as an adjective, an adverb, or a noun.

adjective: The Milwaukee Brewers, <u>who play at Miller Park</u>, joined the National League in November 1997.

adverb: Bob called <u>when you were at the store</u>.

noun: Read what child development experts have to say <u>about the virtues and drawbacks of homeschooling</u>.

### Elliptical clauses

An **elliptical clause** deviates from the rule that states "a clause contains a subject and a predicate." What an elliptical clause does is *imply* both a subject and a predicate, even though both elements do not in fact appear in the clause.

<u>While vacationing in Spain</u>, Jo received word of her promotion.
[The elliptical clause implies the subject "she" and the predicate "was vacationing"—that is, it implies "While she was vacationing."]

Myers arrived on Saturday the 12th; <u>Anderson, the following Monday</u>.
[The elliptical clause implies the predicate "arrived the following Monday"—that is, it implies "Anderson arrived the following Monday."]

Elliptical clauses are valuable devices, as they allow the writer to avoid excessive wordiness, preserve a sense of variety, and enhance the rhythm of the text.

### Restrictive clauses

A clause that is essential to the meaning of the sentence—that is, it restricts the meaning of the sentence—is a **restrictive clause**. The content of a restrictive clause identifies a particular person, place, or thing. If the restrictive clause were to be removed, the meaning of the sentence would change. A restrictive clause begins with the relative pronoun *that, who,* or *whom*. It should never be set off with commas.

I'm returning the coat that I bought last week.

[The identification of the coat is important. It's not just any coat. It's specifically the one and only coat "that I bought last week." Without the restrictive clause, the identification would be lost.]

The president who authorized the Louisiana Purchase was Thomas Jefferson.

[The point of this sentence is to identify specifically the one and only president responsible for the Louisiana Purchase. Without the restrictive clause, the point of the sentence would be lost.]

NONRESTRICTIVE CLAUSES

A clause that is not essential to the meaning of the sentence—that is, it does not restrict the meaning of the sentence—is a **nonrestrictive clause**. The content of a nonrestrictive clause adds information to what has already been identified. If the nonrestrictive clause were to be removed, the meaning of the sentence would not change. A nonrestrictive clause begins with the relative pronoun *which, who,* or *whom*. It should always be set off with commas.

I'm returning my new coat, which doesn't fit.

President Jefferson, who authorized the Louisiana Purchase, was the third U.S. president.

[The clauses *which doesn't fit* and *who authorized the Louisiana Purchase* are informative but not necessary. Without them, the meaning of each sentence is still clear.]

### *Sentences*

Properly constructed sentences are integral to good communication. By definition, a sentence is "a set of words that is complete in itself, typically containing a subject and predicate, conveying a statement, question, exclamation, or command, and consisting of a main clause and sometimes one or more subordinate clauses." Simply put, a sentence is a group of words that expresses a complete thought.

SUBJECT AND PREDICATE

The primary building blocks of a sentence are the **subject** and the **predicate.**

The **subject** (usually a noun or pronoun) is the part that the sentence is telling about. A **simple subject** is simply the person, place, or thing being discussed. A **complete subject** is the simple subject along with all the words directly associated with it.

The large tropical plant in my office has bloomed every summer.

[Here, the simple subject is *plant*. The complete subject is *The large tropical plant in my office*.]

Two or more subjects that belong to the same verb comprise what is called a **compound subject.**

Stan Garrison and the rest of the department are relocating next week.

[Here, the compound subject consists of *Stan Garrison* and the *rest of the department*.]

The **predicate** (a verb) is the "action" or "being" part—the part that tells something about the subject.]

A **simple predicate** is simply the main verb and its auxiliaries. A **complete predicate** is the simple predicate along with all the words directly associated with it.

The setting sun has cast a scarlet glow across the skyline.
[Here, the simple predicate is *has cast*. The complete predicate is *has cast a scarlet glow across the skyline.* ]

Two or more predicates that have the same subject comprise what is called a **compound predicate**.

I wanted to buy some art but left empty-handed.
[Here, the compound predicate consists of *wanted to buy some art* and *left empty-handed.*]

FOUR SENTENCE STRUCTURES

A **simple sentence** contains one independent clause. Its subject and/or predicate may or may not be compound, but its one and only clause is always independent.

Paula rode her bicycle. [subject + predicate]
Honus Wagner and Nap Lajoie are enshrined in the Baseball Hall of Fame. [compound subject + predicate]
The correspondents traveled across the desert and slept in makeshift shelters. [subject + compound predicate]
Lunch and dinner are discounted on Sunday but are full price on Monday. [compound subject + compound predicate]

A **compound sentence** contains two or more independent clauses. The following examples show the various ways that coordinating conjunctions (e.g., *and, but, yet*), conjunctive adverbs (e.g., *however, therefore*), and punctuation may be used to join the clauses in a compound sentence.

Ken made the phone calls and Maria addressed the envelopes.
The war lasted for two years, but the effects of its devastation will last for decades.
Judges and other officials should sign in by noon; exhibitors will start arriving at 2:00.
I have decided to remain on the East Coast; however, I am willing to attend the monthly meetings in Dallas.
FDR initiated the New Deal, JFK embraced the New Frontier, and LBJ envisioned the Great Society.

A **complex sentence** contains one independent clause and one or more subordinate clauses.

Even though I majored in English, I was hired to teach applied physics.
We can have the party indoors if it gets too windy.
Before I agree, I have to read the final report that you drafted.

The independent clauses are

*I was hired to teach applied physics*
*We can have the party indoors*
*I have to read the final report*

The subordinate clauses are

*Even though I majored in English*
*if it gets too windy*
*Before I agree | that you drafted.*

A **compound-complex sentence** contains two or more independent clauses and one or more subordinate clauses.

Because the candidates have been so argumentative, some voters are confused and many have become disinterested.
We will begin painting tomorrow if the weather's nice; if it rains, we will start on Thursday.

The independent clauses are

*some voters are confused | many have become disinterested*
*We will begin painting tomorrow | we will start on Thursday*

The subordinate clauses are

*Because the candidates have been so argumentative*
*if the weather's nice | if it rains*

FOUR SENTENCE FUNCTIONS

A **declarative sentence** states a fact, an assertion, an impression, or a feeling. It ends with a period.

Florence is a beautiful city.
Lewis Carroll died in 1898.
I'm sorry I missed the end of your speech.

An **interrogative sentence** asks a question. It ends with a question mark.

Did you read the article about migrating geese patterns?
How do spell your last name?
Mr. Young owns a kennel?

An **imperative sentence** makes a request or gives an order. It typically ends with a period but occasionally may end with an exclamation point.

Please lock the doors.
Do not throw trash in the recycling bins.
Think before you speak!

An **exclamatory sentence** expresses surprise, shock, or strong feeling. It ends with an exclamation point.

Look at this mess!
I can't believe how great this is!
I lost my purse!

### *Paragraphs*

A paragraph is a series of sentences that conveys a single theme. Paragraphs help writers organize thoughts, actions, and descriptions into readable units of information. The paragraph, as a unit of text, may have one of several functions. It may be descriptive, giving certain details or impressions about a person, thing, or event. It may be instructive, explaining a method or procedure. It may be conceptual, stating thoughts, feelings, or opinions.

Every paragraph should contain a sentence that states the main idea of a paragraph. This is called the **topic sentence**. The other sentences in the paragraph are the **supporting sentences**, and their function is just that—to support or elaborate on the idea set forth in the topic sentence. Most paragraphs begin with the topic sentence, as in the following example:

> Each Thanksgiving we make place cards decorated with pressed autumn leaves. After gathering the smallest and most colorful leaves from the maples and oaks in our backyard, we place the leaves between sheets of blotter paper, which we then cover with a large, heavy book. In just a day or two, the leaves are ready to be mounted on cards. We use plain index cards, folded in half. Using clear adhesive paper, we put one leaf on each card, leaving room for the guest's name.

Try reading the preceding paragraph without the topic sentence (the first sentence). The supporting information becomes less unified because it has no main idea to support. Now imagine adding to the paragraph the following sentence:

> Last year, three of our guests were snowed in at the airport.

This would be a misplaced addition to the paragraph, as it is unrelated to the topic sentence (that is, it has nothing to do with making Thanksgiving place cards). Because it introduces a new and distinct idea, it should become the topic sentence for a new and distinct paragraph.

## SENTENCE DEVELOPMENT: AVOIDING PROBLEMS

### *Sentence Style*

Getting one's ideas across in words is the core of communication. Sentences provide the means to arrange ideas in a coherent way. Certainly, the rules of grammar should be observed when constructing a sentence, but the general rhythm of the sentence is also important. Sentences may be categorized into three general types: loose, periodic, and balanced. Good writers typically use a combination of these styles in order to create a flow of ideas that will hold the reader's interest.

A **loose sentence** gets to the main point quickly. It begins with a basic and complete statement, which is followed by additional information.

> The power went out, plunging us into darkness, silencing the drone of the television, leaving our dinner half cooked.

[The basic statement is *The power went out*. Everything that follows is additional information. ]

A **periodic sentence** ends with the main point. It begins with additional information, thus imposing a delay before the basic statement is given.

With no warning, like a herd of stampeding bison, a mob of fans crashed through the gate.

[The basic statement is *a mob of fans crashed through the gate*. Everything that precedes is additional information.]

A **balanced sentence** is comprised of grammatically equal or similar structures. The ideas in the sentence are linked by comparison or contrast.

To visit their island villa is to sample nirvana.

As writers become more comfortable with the basic rules of grammar and the general patterns of sentence structure, they are able to remain compliant with the rules while getting more creative with the patterns. Many well-constructed sentences will not agree precisely with any of the three preceding examples, but they should always evoke an answer of "yes" to two fundamental questions:

- Is the sentence grammatically correct?
- Will the meaning of the sentence be clear to the reader?

### *Flawed Sentences*

Three types of "flawed sentences" are sentence fragments, run-on sentences, and sentences with improperly positioned modifiers.

#### SENTENCE FRAGMENTS

A **sentence fragment** is simply an incomplete sentence. Fundamental to every sentence is a complete thought that is able to stand on its own. Because a phrase or subordinate clause is not an independent thought, it cannot stand on its own as a sentence. To be a part of a sentence, it must either be connected to an independent clause or be reworded to become an independent clause. Consider this sentence fragment:

My English guest who stayed on for Christmas.

Here are three possible ways to create a proper sentence from that fragment:

Everyone left on Tuesday except Dan, my English guest who stayed on for Christmas.

[The fragment is added to the independent clause *Everyone left on Tuesday except Dan*.]

My English guest stayed on for Christmas.

[The fragment becomes an independent clause by removing the word *who*.]

Dan was my English guest who stayed on for Christmas.

[The fragment becomes an independent clause by adding the words *Dan was*.]

RUN-ON SENTENCES

A **run-on sentence** results when two or more sentences are improperly united into one sentence. Characteristic of a run-on sentence is the absence of punctuation between the independent clauses or the use of incorrect punctuation (typically a comma) between the independent clauses:

> Our flight was canceled we had to spend the night in Boston.
> Our flight was canceled, we had to spend the night in Boston.

Here are three possible ways to correct the preceding run-on sentences:

> Our flight was canceled; we had to spend the night in Boston.
> [A semicolon provides a properly punctuated separation of the two independent clauses.]

> Our flight was canceled, so we had to spend the night in Boston.
> [A comma followed by a conjunction (*so*) provides a properly worded and punctuated separation of the two independent clauses.]

> Our flight was canceled. We had to spend the night in Boston.
> [The creation of two distinct sentences provides an absolute separation of the two independent clauses.]

MODIFIER PROBLEMS

The improper placement of modifying words, phrases, and clauses is a common mistake. The result is a sentence in which the modifier unintentionally refers to the wrong person or thing. The three principal culprits are dangling modifiers, misplaced modifiers, and squinting modifiers. Writers must be careful to avoid these troublesome errors in sentence construction. Review the following examples to see how an improperly placed modifier can be confusing to the reader. It is important to recognize the subtle differences between the incorrect sentences and their corrected versions.

A **dangling modifier** is an adjectival phrase or clause that lacks a proper connection because the word it is supposed to modify is missing.

| | |
|---|---|
| dangling: | While waiting for my son, a cat jumped onto the hood of my car.<br>[This wrongly implies that "a cat was waiting for my son."] |
| correct: | While I was waiting for my son, a cat jumped onto the hood of my car.<br>While waiting for my son, I saw a cat jump onto the hood of my car.<br>A cat jumped onto the hood of my car while I was waiting for my son.<br>[The word that was missing is "I."] |
| dangling: | At age seven, her grandfather died of diphtheria.<br>[This wrongly implies that "her grandfather died when he was seven."] |
| correct: | When she was seven, her grandfather died of diphtheria.<br>Her grandfather died of diphtheria when she was seven. |

At age seven, she lost her grandfather when he died of diphtheria.
[The word that was missing is "she."]

A **misplaced modifier** is a phrase or clause that is not positioned close enough to the word it is supposed to modify. It will seem to the reader that a different word is being modified.

misplaced: There was an outbreak in our school of chicken pox.
[This wrongly implies that there is "a school of chicken pox."]

correct: There was an outbreak of chicken pox in our school.
In our school there was an outbreak of chicken pox.
Our school experienced an outbreak of chicken pox.

misplaced: I was stopped by a policeman without a driver's license.
[This wrongly implies that there was "a policeman without a driver's license."]

correct: Driving without a license, I was stopped by a policeman.
I was stopped by a policeman, and I did not have a driver's license.

A **squinting modifier** is an adverb placed between two verbs. For the reader, it is often difficult to determine which verb the adverb is supposed to modify.

squinting: The stack of chairs she had arranged carefully collapsed in the wind.
[Was the stack of chairs "arranged carefully" or did it "carefully collapse"?]

correct: The stack of chairs she had carefully arranged collapsed in the wind.
[Of the two possible meanings, this is only one that makes sense.]

squinting: The stack of chairs she had arranged quickly collapsed in the wind.
[Was the stack of chairs "arranged quickly" or did it "quickly collapse"?]

correct: The stack of chairs she had quickly arranged collapsed in the wind.
The stack of chairs she had arranged collapsed quickly in the wind.
[Either meaning could make sense, so only the writer would know which version is correct.]

---

**TIP**

Keep a list of words that you find difficult to spell. Use a dictionary to confirm the correct spellings. Add to your list whenever you encounter a troublesome word. Refer to your list often, and quiz yourself. Make up sentences that include words from the list, writing them without going back and forth to double-check the spelling. Compare the words in your sentences to the words on your list. Make a note of the words that continue to give you trouble, and write these words in sentences every day until you have learned to spell them.

---

# Guide to Spelling

Any reader or writer knows that spelling is an important component of writing. Some individuals seem to have little or no trouble spelling words correctly, while others seem to struggle with spelling, often with the same words over and over.

Those who have experienced the struggle should remember that spelling is a skill that improves with practice. Regular reading and writing, accompanied by a dictionary for consultation, are the best methods for improving one's spelling. Anyone who has encountered trouble with spelling knows that the English language contains numerous irregularities. Even so, there are a number of basic spelling rules that can be followed in most cases.

*For guidelines for plural and possessive nouns, see the "Noun" section under "Parts of Speech."*

## COMPOUND ADJECTIVES AND NOUNS

A compound adjective or noun is a single term formed from two or more distinct words. There are three spelling formats for compounds: open, hyphenated, and closed.

In an **open compound**, the component words are separate, with no hyphen.

well fed
wagon train

In a **hyphenated compound**, the component words are joined by a hyphen.

half-baked
city-state

In a **closed compound**, the component words are joined into a single word.

hardheaded
campfire

### *Compound Adjectives*

For most cases of open compound adjectives, there is a general rule of thumb: the compound is left open when it is not followed by the modified noun; the compound is hyphenated when it is followed by the modified noun.

She was well known in the South for her poetry.
[The compound *well known* is open because it is not followed by the modified noun *She*.]

In the South, she was a well-known poet.
[The compound *well-known* is hyphenated because it is followed by the modified noun *poet*.]

A notable exception occurs when the first part of the compound adjective is an adverb that ends in *-ly*. In this case, the compound remains open, even when it is followed by the noun.

The woman who met us in the lobby was beautifully dressed.
A beautifully dressed woman met us in the lobby.

**TIP**

Different dictionaries often disagree on the preferred spelling formats for a number of compounds, so writers are well advised to consult just one dictionary when establishing a spelling style.

### *Compound Nouns*

For spellers, the least troublesome compound nouns are familiar closed compounds.

| | |
|---|---|
| briefcase | downstairs |
| cupcake | fireplace |

Other compound nouns can be troublesome. Although certain ones, such as *mother-in-law*, are always hyphenated, many compound nouns commonly occur in more than one acceptable format, such as *ice cap* or *icecap* and *vice president* or *vice-president*. For most spelling questions, the best resource is a dictionary; for questions pertaining specifically to compounds, an unabridged edition is recommended.

## PREFIXES

A prefix is a group of letters added to the beginning of a word to adjust its meaning.

In most cases, prefixes are affixed to the root word without hyphenation.

antibacterial
postwar
semicircle

Often, however, a hyphen is customary, necessary, or preferable.

Certain prefixes almost always take a hyphen: *all-*, *ex-*, *full-*, *quasi-*, *self-*.

| | |
|---|---|
| all-encompassing | quasi-liberal |
| ex-partner | self-confidence |
| full-bodied | |

When the root word begins with a capital letter, the prefix takes a hyphen:

anti-American
pre-Conquest

Sometimes, without a hyphen, a word could be easily confused with another.

We recovered our furniture.

Does this mean we *found* our *missing* furniture? Or did we *put new coverings on* our furniture? If the latter is meant, a hyphen would have avoided confusion:

We re-covered our furniture.

### TIP

Regarding the use of optional hyphens, the writer should establish a preferred style. Keeping a running list of hyphenated terms can help writers keep track of which spellings they have already used in their text, thus making the style consistent.

---

Sometimes, a hyphen is not necessary but preferable. Without it, the word may look awkward. One such circumstance is when the last letter of the prefix and the first letter of the root word are both vowels. For each of the following pairs of words, either spelling is acceptable.

antiknock / anti-knock
preadapt / pre-adapt
semiindependent / semi-independent

## SUFFIXES

A suffix is group of letters added to the end of a word to create a derivative of the word.

There are exceptions to the following guidelines on how to spell with suffixes, but in most cases these rules apply:

A root word that ends in *e* drops the *e* when the suffix begins with a vowel.

rehearse / rehearsing

However, most words that end in *ce* or *ge* keep the *e* when the suffix begins with *a* or *o*.

service / serviceable
advantage / advantageous

A root word that ends in *e* keeps the *e* when the suffix begins with a consonant.

wise / wisely

A root word that ends in a *y* preceded by a consonant changes the *y* to *i* when the suffix begins with any letter other than *i*.

satisfy / satisfies / satisfying

A root word that ends in *ie* changes the *ie* to *y* when the suffix is *–ing*.

lie / lying

A root word that ends in *oe* keeps the *e* when the suffix begins with a vowel, unless the vowel is *e*.

toe / toeing / toed

A one-syllable root word that ends in a single consonant preceded by a single vowel doubles the consonant when the suffix is *–ed, -er,* or *–ing*. This rule also applies to root words with two or more syllables if the accent is on the last syllable.

stir / stirred
refer / referring

## WORD DIVISION

Sometimes it is necessary to "break" a word when the line on the page has run out of space. Dividing a word at the end of a line is perfectly acceptable, as long as two conditions are met: the word must be divisible, and the division must be made in the right place.

When a word is properly divided, a hyphen is attached to its first part, so that the hyphen is at the end of the line.

> At the end of the interview, I was given two minutes to summarize my management experiences.

---

**TIP**

When dividing a word at the end of a line, it is always a good idea to use a dictionary to verify the word's proper syllabification.

---

| **What words are never divisible?** | *for example*: |
|---|---|
| • one-syllable words | catch; flutes; strange; through |
| • contractions | didn't; doesn't; wouldn't; you're |
| • abbreviations | Calif.; NASCAR; RSVP; YMCA |
| • numbers written as numerals | 1776; $2,800; 9:45; 0.137 |

| **Where is a correct place to divide a word?** | *good break*: | *bad break*: |
|---|---|---|
| • after a prefix | inter-national | interna-tional |
| • before a suffix that has more than two letters | govern-ment | gov-ernment |
| • between the main parts of a closed compound | nut-cracker | nutcrack-er |
| • at the hyphen of a hyphenated compound | gender-neutral | gen-der-neutral |
| • after double consonants if the root word ends in the double consonants | address-ing | addres-sing |
| • otherwise, between double consonants | rib-bon | ribb-on |
| • in general (for words that don't fall into the previous categories), between syllables | whis-per | whi-sper |

| Where is an incorrect place to divide a word? | *good break*: | *bad break*: |
|---|---|---|
| • before a two-letter suffix | —— | odd-ly |
| • after the first syllable if it has only one letter | Ameri-can | A-merican |
| • before the last syllable if it has only one letter | nu-tria | nutri-a |
| • before the ending *-ed* if the *-ed* is not pronounced | —— | abash-ed |

## NUMBERS

Numbers are an important part of everyday communication, yet they often cause the writer to stumble, particularly over questions of spelling and style. The guidelines on *how* to spell out a number are fairly straightforward. The guidelines on *when* to spell out a number are not so precise.

### *How to Spell Out Numbers*

CARDINAL NUMBERS

The most common problem associated with the spelling of whole cardinal numbers is punctuation. The rules are actually quite simple: Numeric amounts that fall between twenty and one hundred are always hyphenated. No other punctuation should appear in a spelled-out whole number, regardless of its size.

| | |
|---|---|
| 26 | twenty-six |
| 411 | four hundred eleven |
| 758 | seven hundred fifty-eight |
| 6,500 | six thousand five hundred |
| 33,003 | thirty-three thousand three |
| 972,923 | nine hundred seventy-two thousand nine hundred twenty-three |

Note: the word *and* does not belong in the spelling of a number. For example, "758" should not be spelled "seven hundred and fifty-eight."

ORDINAL NUMBERS

The punctuation of spelled-out ordinal numbers typically follows the rules of cardinal numbers.

What should we do for their fifty-fifth anniversary?
He graduated two hundred twenty-ninth out of a class of two hundred thirty.

When ordinal numbers appear as numerals, they are affixed with *-th*, with the exception of those ending with the ordinal *first*, *second*, or *third*.

| | |
|---|---|
| 1st | 581st |
| 2nd | 32nd |
| 3rd | 73rd |
| 4th | 907th |

Note: Sometimes *2nd* is written as *2d*, and *3rd* as *3d*.

FRACTIONS

A fraction can appear in a number of formats, as shown here:

| | |
|---|---|
| $\frac{3}{8}$ | case fraction (*or* split fraction) |
| 3/8 | fraction with solidus |
| 0.375 | decimal fraction |
| three-eighths | spelled-out fraction |

When acting as an adjective, a spelled-out fraction should always be hyphenated.

The Serbian democrats have won a <u>two-thirds</u> majority.

When acting as a noun, a spelled-out fraction may or may not be hyphenated, according to the writer's or publisher's preferred style.

At least <u>four-fifths</u> of the supply has been depleted.
*or*
At least <u>four fifths</u> of the supply has been depleted.

### *When to Spell Out Numbers*

When to spell out a number, whole or fractional, is as much a matter of sense as of style. Text that is heavy with numbers, such as scientific or statistical material, could become virtually unreadable if the numbers were all spelled out. Conversely, conventional prose that occasionally makes mention of a quantity may look unbalanced with an occasional numeral here and there.

Often, the decision to spell or not to spell comes down to simple clarity.

Our standard paper size is 8½ by 11.
Our standard paper size is 8 1/2 by 11.
Our standard paper size is eight and a half by eleven.
Our standard paper size is eight and one-half by eleven.

The preceding four sentences say exactly the same thing, but the best choice for readability is the first.

Even the most comprehensive books of style and usage do not dictate absolute rules regarding the style of numbers in text. When writing, it is most important to be as consistent as possible with a style once one has been established. For example, some writers or publishers may adopt a policy of spelling out the numbers zero through ten. Others may prefer to spell out the numbers zero through ninety-nine. Either style is perfectly acceptable, as long as the style is followed throughout the written work.

Sometimes, even after adopting a basic number style, the writer may wish to incorporate certain style allowances and exceptions. Perhaps the decision has been made to spell out only the numbers zero though ninety-nine. But in one paragraph, a sentence reads, "There must have been more than 1,000,000 people there." In this case, it may be better to write, "There must have been more than a million people there."

## SYMBOLS

In most contexts of formal writing, the use of symbols should be strictly limited, but there are occasions when a symbol may be a better choice than a word. Text that deals largely with commerce, for instance, may rely on the use of various monetary symbols to keep the text organized and readable. In any text, mathematical equations and scientific formulas are much easier to read if written with symbols rather than words. Also, it is usually appropriate to use symbols within tables and charts; as symbols conserve space, they prevent a "cluttered look."

Here are some of the most common symbols found in print:

| Symbol | Meaning |
|---|---|
| @ | at |
| c/o | care of |
| $ | dollar |
| ¢ | cent |
| Can$ | Canadian dollar |
| £ | pound |
| ¥ | yen |
| # | number *or* pound |
| / | per |
| % | percent |
| ° | degree |
| + | plus |
| – | minus |
| ÷ | divided by |
| × | times |
| ± | plus or minus |
| = | equals |
| ≈ | is approximately equal to |
| ≠ | is not equal to |
| < | is less than |
| > | is greater than |
| ⩽ | is less than or equal to |
| ⩾ | is greater than or equal to |
| √ | square root of |
| ∞ | infinity |
| © | copyright |
| ® | registered |
| ™ | trademark |
| ¶ | paragraph |
| § | section |
| * | asterisk |
| † | dagger |
| ‡ | double dagger |
| || | parallels *or* pipes |

Symbols are sometimes used to point out note references to the reader. In a table or chart, for instance, the writer may wish to indicate that an item is further explained or identified elsewhere on the page. A symbol placed with the item signals the reader to look for an identical symbol, which precedes the additional information. Sometimes, numerals are the symbols of choice, but if the material within the table or chart consists of numerals, it is probably better to use non-numeric symbols for the note references. The conventional set of symbols used for this purpose, in the conventional sequence in which to use them, is *, †, ‡, §, ||, #.

### TIP

Numerals and other symbols should never begin a sentence. If the symbol should not or cannot be spelled out, the sentence needs to be reworded.

19 students have become mentors.
*should be:*
Nineteen students have become mentors.

2007 is the year we plan to get married.
*should be:*
We plan to get married in 2007.

$10 was found on the stairs.
*should be:*
Ten dollars was found on the stairs.

6:00 is the earliest I can leave.
*should be:*
Six o'clock is the earliest I can leave.
*or:*
The earliest I can leave is 6:00.

$y = 2x + 1$ is a line with a slope of 2.
*should be:*
The line $y = 2x + 1$ has a slope of 2.

## FOREIGN TERMS

Foreign words and phrases that are likely to be unfamiliar to the reader should be set in italics. When such terms are to be included in writing or speech, a dictionary should be consulted by the writer to insure proper placement of accents and other diacritical marks and by the speaker to insure correct pronunciations. Each of the following sample terms gives the literal translation, the English-usage definition, and an example sentence.

*annus mirabilis:* [Latin, 'wonderful year'] a remarkable or auspicious year.
This has been our team's *annus mirabilis*.

*cause célèbre:* [French, 'famous case'] a controversial issue that attracts a great deal of public attention.
The trial of Lizzie Borden became a *cause célèbre* throughout New England.

*Weltschmerz:* [German, 'world pain'] a feeling of melancholy and world-weariness.
A sense of *Weltschmerz* permeated his later works of art.
[Note that it is correct to capitalize a German noun.]

### FAMILIAR FOREIGN TERMS

Many foreign terms have become so familiar and well-established in standard English usage that it is not necessary to put them in italic type. For most of these words, it is also not necessary to use accents and other diacritical marks, but in certain cases the inclusion of diacritics remains customary. There are, however, no absolute rules regarding when to italicize and when not to italicize, when to use diacritics and when not to use diacritics. Some foreign words may be more familiar to one group of readers than to another; therefore, targeted readership should be considered. Often, the style adopted is a matter of preference. As always, it is important for the writer to be consistent once this preference has been introduced.

Some familiar foreign terms:

ad hoc
ad nauseam
aficionado
à la carte (*or* a la carte)
à la king (*or* a la king)
à la mode (*or* a la mode)
alter ego
apartheid
aperitif
au gratin
au jus
au pair
avant-garde
ballet
basmati
bas-relief
baton
beau
belle
bona fide
bonbon
bouclé
boudoir
bouffant
bouillabaisse
bouillon
bouquet
bouquet garni
bourgeois
bric-a-brac
burka (*or* burkha)
burrito
cabaret
café (*or* cafe)
camisole
canapé
capo
carafe
carte blanche
chaise longue
chalet
chamois
chapeau
chateau (*or* château)
chauffeur
chic
ciao
cognac
coiffeur
connoisseur
consommé
contretemps
corps
crepe (*or* crêpe)
croquette
cul-de-sac
élan
elite
enchilada
en masse
en route
entourage
entrée (*or* entree)
entre nous
eureka
fait accompli
fajita
faux
faux pas
fiancé
fiancée
fiesta
gourmet
hacienda
haute cuisine
hors d'oeuvre
incognito
in vitro
in vivo
jabot
judo
julienne
karma
karate
kasha
kibitz
laissez-faire
lanai
loco
lorgnette
madame
mademoiselle
maître d'
mañana
masseur
masseuse
materiel (*or* matériel)
mea culpa
monsieur
non sequitur
pasha
pâté de foie gras
patio
piccolo
poncho
portière (*or* portiere)
post mortem
pro bono
pronto
protégé (*or* protege)
purée (*or* puree)
rendezvous
repertoire
résumé (*or* resume)
revue
roué
roulette
sachet
salsa
samovar
samurai
seance
serape
siesta
sombrero
soufflé
status quo
suede
tableau
table d'hôte
tabula rasa
taco
tango
tête-à-tête
trousseau
villa
yin/yang
yoga

# COMMONLY MISSPELLED WORDS

absence
absolutely
acceptance
accessible
accidentally
accommodate
accompany
accuracy
ache
achieve
achievement
acquaintance
acquire
acre
across
actually
administration
admittance
adolescent
advantageous
advertisement
advisable
affectionate
affidavit
aficionado
afraid
again aisle
aggravate
aghast
allege
allotment
allotment
ally
amateur
analysis
analyze
anesthetic
angel
angle
annually
answer
anticipate
anxiety
apartheid
aperitif
apology
apparatus
apparent
appearance
appetite
appreciate
approach
appropriate
approximately
argue
argument
arrangement
ascend
ascertain
assistant
athletic
attendance
authority
auxiliary
available
awkward
bachelor
because
beggar
beginning
behavior
believe
benefit
benefited
bicycle
bouillon
boundary
bulletin
bureau
buried
business
cafeteria
calendar
campaign
cancellation
captain
carburetor
career
ceiling
cemetery
census
certificate
chamois
changeable
character
characteristic
chauffeur
chic
chief
chocolate
choice
choose
chose
Christian
clothes
collateral
colonel
color
column
commercial
commission
committee
community
compel
competitor
completely
conceivable
concentrate
condemn
confidence
confidential
confusion
connoisseur
conscience
conscious
continuous
controlled
controversial
convertible
cooperate
copyright
corps
correspondence
counterfeit
courageous
courteous
criticism
criticize
cruelly
curiosity
curious
cylinder
dealt
debtor
deceive
decision
definite
dependent
describe
despair
desperate
despise
develop
difference
dilemma
disappearance
disappoint
disastrous
discipline
discrepancy
disease
doctor
duplicate
easily

## COMMONLY MISSPELLED WORDS *(continued)*

ecclesiastical
ecstasy
effect
efficient
eighth
elementary
eligible
embarrass
eminent
emphasize
encouragement
encumbrances
enforceable
entirely
entourage
envelope
environment
equipped
escape
especially
essential
exaggerate
excellent
exciting
exercise
exhilarating
exhort
existence
expense
experience
experiment
extraordinary
extremely
facsimile
familiar
fantasy
fascinate
fashionable
fasten
fatal
favorite
February
field
fiery
finally
financial
forehead
foreign
forfeit
fortunately
forty
forward
fourth
freight
friend
fulfill
further
gauge
genius
gourmet
government
governor
gracious
grammar
guarantee
guerrilla
guess
guidance
gymnasium
gypsy
handsome
hangar
hanger
happened
happiness
harass
Hawaii
heavily
height
heinous
heroine
hors d'oeuvre
hospital
humor
humorous
hungrily
hygiene
hypocrisy
hypocrite
ignorance
illiterate
imagine
immediately
impossible
incidentally
increase
indefinite
independent
indictment
indispensable
individually
inevitable
influence
ingredient
innocence
inoculate
insurance
intelligence
interference
interrupt
iridescent
irrelevant
itinerary
jealous
knowledge
laboratory
laborer
laid
legitimate
leisure
liaison
library
license
lieutenant
lightning
likely
liquefy
liquidate
listener
literature
livelihood
lively
loneliness
luxury
magazine
magnificent
maintenance
maneuver
manufacturer
marriage
marvelous
mathematics
meant
mechanic
medical
medicine
melancholy
merchandise
millionaire
miniature
minimum
minuscule
minute
miscellaneous
mischief
mischievous
misspell
mortgage
muscle
mysterious

narrative
naturally
necessary
nickel
niece
niece
ninety
noisily
non sequitur
noticeable
obstacle
occasionally
occurrence
offensive
official
often
omission
omit
omitted
once
operate
opponent
opportunity
optimistic
orchestra
ordinarily
organization
originally
outrageous
pageant
paid
parallel
paralleled
paralyze
parliament
particular
pastime
peaceful
peculiar
performance
permanent
perseverance
personality
personnel
perspiration
persuade
pessimistic
phenomenal
Philippines
philosophy
physical
picnicking
pleasant
politician
Portuguese
possession
possibility
practically
practice
prairie
preferred
prejudice
preparation
presence
pressure
pretension
privilege
probably
procedure
proceed
procure
professor
proffered
promissory
pronunciation
propaganda
psychology
pursuit
questionnaire
quiet
quite
realize
really
realtor
realty
receipt
recognize
recommend
referred
reign
relevant
relieve
religious
removal
rendezvous
repertoire
repetition
rescind
reservoir
resistance
resource
responsibility
restaurant
rheumatism
rhythm
ridiculous
roommate
sachet
sacrifice
sacrilegious
safety
satisfied
scarcely
scarcity
scene
schedule
scholar
scissors
scurrilous
seance
secretary
seize
semester
separate
sergeant
shepherd
siege
similar
sincerely
skein
skiing
skillful
sophomore
soufflé
source
souvenir
specifically
specimen
sponsor
statistics
straight
strength
stretch
strictly
stubborn
substitute
subtle
succeed
successful
suede
sufficient
summary
superintendent
supersede
surgeon
surprise
susceptible
suspense
swimming
sympathetic
synonym
temperamental
temperature
tendency
therefore
thorough
though
thoughtful

## COMMONLY MISSPELLED WORDS *(continued)*

tomorrow
tragedy
transferred
tremendous
truly
twelfth
typical
unanimous
unnecessary
useful
useless
usually
vacillate
vacuum
vague
valuable
variety
various
vegetable
vengeance
vilify
villain
warrant
weather
Wednesday
weird
whether
whole
yacht
yield

# Guide to Capitalization and Punctuation

## CAPITALIZATION

### *Beginnings*

The first word in a sentence is capitalized:

> Dozens of spectators lined the street.

The first word in a direct quotation is capitalized:

> Andy stood by the window and remarked, "The view from here is spectacular."

If a colon introduces more than one sentence, the first word after the colon is capitalized:

> We went over our findings, one piece of evidence at a time: The custodian had discovered the body just before midnight. The keys to the victim's office were found in the stairwell. In the adjoining office, three file cabinets had been overturned.

If a colon introduces a formal and distinct statement, the first word after the colon is capitalized:

> All my years on the basketball court have taught me one thing: Winning is more of a process than an outcome.

If a colon introduces a complete statement that is merely an extension of the statement preceding the colon, the first word after the colon is usually lowercased:

> Everything in the house was a shade of pink: the sofa was carnation blush, the tiles were misty mauve, and the carpet was dusty rose.

If a colon introduces an incomplete statement, the first word after the colon is lowercased:

> The caterer provided three choices: chicken, beef, and shrimp.

### *Proper Names*

Proper names are capitalized. This is true of all proper names, including those of persons, places, structures, organizations, vessels, vehicles, brands, etc. Notice from the following examples that when a properly named entity is referred to in a "non-named" general sense, the general sense is almost always lowercased:

Eleanor Roosevelt
J. D. Salinger
Carson City / a city in Nevada
Ural Mountains / a view of the mountain
New York Public Library / borrowing books from the public library
Washington Monument / our photos of the monument
Calvin Leete Elementary School / the rear entrance of the school
Amherst Historical Society / when the society last met
Boeing 747
USS *Missouri* [note that the names of specific ships, aircraft, spacecraft, etc., are italicized]
Chevy Malibu
Slinky

### *Titles*

The titles of works are capitalized. Titled works include:

- written material (books, periodicals, screenplays, etc.)
- components of written material (chapters, sections, etc.)
- filmed and/or broadcast works (movies, television shows, radio programs, etc.)
- works of art (paintings, sculptures, etc.)
- musical compositions (songs, operas, oratorios, etc.)

There are certain rules of convention regarding which words in the titles are capitalized.

Capitalize:

- first word in the title
- last word in the title
- nouns and pronouns
- adjectives
- verbs
- adverbs
- subordinating conjunctions (*although*, *as*, *because*, *if*, *since*, *that*, *whenever*, etc.)

Do not capitalize (unless they are first or last words in the title):

- articles (*a*, *an*, *the*)
- coordinating conjunctions (*and*, *but*, *for*, *nor*, *or*, *so*, *yet*)
- prepositions (although some guides suggest capitalizing prepositions of more than four letters)
- the word *to* in infinitives

The King, the Sword, and the Golden Lantern
A Room within a Room (*or* A Room Within a Room)
Seventy Ways to Make Easy Money from Your Home
The Stars Will Shine Because You Are Mine

If a subtitle is included, it typically follows a colon. It follows the capitalization rules of the main title, thus its first word is always capitalized:

> Aftermath Explored: The Confessions of a Nuclear Physicist

The first element in a hyphenated compound is always capitalized. The subsequent elements are capitalized unless they are articles, prepositions, or coordinating conjunctions. But if the compound is the last word in the title, its final element is always capitalized, regardless of its part of speech:

> Nineteenth-Century Poets
> Over-the-Top Desserts
> The Love-in of a Lifetime
> The Year of the Love-In

An element that follows a hyphenated prefix is capitalized only if it is a proper noun or adjective:

> Pre-Columbian Artifacts
> Memoirs of a Semi-independent Child

### *Education*

An academic title is capitalized (whether it is spelled out or abbreviated) when it directly accompanies a personal name. Otherwise, it is lowercased:

> Professor Sarah McDonald
> Assoc. Prof. Brown
> my chemistry professor

An academic degree or honor is capitalized (whether it is spelled out or abbreviated) when it directly accompanies a personal name. Otherwise, it is lowercased:

> Harold L. Fox, Ph.D.
> Charles Gustafson, Fellow of the Geological Society
> working toward her master's degree

Academic years are lowercased:

> the senior prom
> he's a sophomore
> the fourth grade

The course name of a particular school subject is capitalized. A general field of study is lowercased (unless the word is normally capitalized, such as "English"):

> Astronomy 101
> Algebra II
> taking classes in psychology, French literature, and chemistry

### TIP

Which titles should be set in italics, and which should be set off by quotation marks? In printed material, the distinction can be significant. Here's a handy list of the most common categories of titles and their standard treatments in type:

***italics:***

- books
  *Crossroads of Freedom: Antietam*, by James M. McPherson
- pamphlets
  Thomas Paine's *Common Sense*
- magazines
  *Popular Mechanics*
- newspapers
  *USA Today*
- movies
  *One Flew Over the Cuckoo's Nest*
- television or radio series
  *This Week in Baseball*
- plays
  Neil Simon's *Lost in Yonkers*
- long poems
  *Beowulf*
- collections of poems and other anthologies
  *The Collected Poems of Emily Dickinson*
- operas, oratorios, and other long musical compositions
  *Madame Butterfly*
- paintings, sculptures, and other works of art
  Thomas Cole's *Mount Etna from Taormina*

***quotation marks:***

- articles
  "How to Remove Wallpaper"
- chapters
  "Betsy Saves the Day"
- short stories
  "The Pit and the Pendulum," by Edgar Allan Poe
- short poems
  "Tree at My Window," by Robert Frost
- essays
  Emerson's "Spiritual Laws"
- television or radio episodes
  "Lucy Does a TV Commercial"
- songs and other short musical compositions
  "Are You Lonesome Tonight?"

## *Calendar Terms and Time*

The names of the days of the week and months of the year are capitalized:

| | |
|---|---|
| Sunday | October |
| September | Tuesday |
| Monday | November |

The names of the four seasons are lowercased:

| | |
|---|---|
| winter | spring |
| summer | fall *or* autumn |

The names of holidays (religious and secular) and periods of religious observance are capitalized:

| | |
|---|---|
| Arbor Day | Lent |
| Easter | Memorial Day |
| Halloween | Ramadan |

The names of time zones and the time systems they designate are lowercased (except for any words that are proper names). Their abbreviations are capitalized:

eastern daylight time (EDT)
Greenwich mean time (GMT)
Pacific standard time (PST)

### *Legislation, Treaties, etc.*

The formal name of a policy, treaty, piece of legislation, or similar agreement is capitalized. A general reference to such is lowercased:

Volstead Act
the act sponsored by Congressman Volstead
Treaty of Versailles
the treaty at Versailles
Bottle Bill
Articles of Confederation
Connecticut Constitution
Connecticut's constitution
North American Free Trade Agreement

### *Military Service*

A military title or rank is capitalized (whether it is spelled out or abbreviated) when it directly accompanies a personal name. Otherwise, it is lowercased:

Gen. George Patton
Ensign Irene Mahoney
promoted to admiral
James Kirk, captain of the USS *Enterprise*

There are two significant exceptions to the preceding rule: the U.S. military titles "Fleet Admiral" and "General of the Army" should always be capitalized, even when not directly accompanying a personal name:

became General of the Army in 1950
a visit from the Fleet Admiral

The full official name of a military group or force is capitalized. A general reference to a military group or force is lowercased:

the Royal Air Force
the British air force

the Army Corps of Engineers
the Third Battalion
our battalion
the U.S. Navy
joined the navy

The full name of a battle or war is capitalized. A general reference to a battle or war is lowercased:

the Russian Revolution
fought in the revolution
the Spanish-American War
the war in Vietnam
the Battle of the Bulge
the first battle of the campaign
the Norman Conquest

The official name of a military award or medal is capitalized:

the Purple Heart
the Silver Star
the Victoria Cross
the Congressional Medal of Honor

### *Science*

The capitalization rules governing scientific terminology cover a wide range of categories and applications. Some of the basic rules are discussed here.

Taxonomic nomenclature—that is, the scientific classification of plants and animals—follows specific rules for both capitalization and italics.

The names of the phylum, class, order, and family of a plant or animal are capitalized and set in roman type. This format also applies to the intermediate groupings (suborder, subfamily, etc.) within these divisions:

> The North American river otter belongs to the phylum Chordata, the subphylum Vertebrata, the class Mammalia, the order Carnivora, and the family Mustelidae.

The divisions lower than family—that is, genus, species, and subspecies—are set in italic type. Of these, only the genus is capitalized. When a plant or animal is identified by its "scientific name" or "Latin name," the name given is the genus and species (and, when applicable, the subspecies):

> The scientific name of the river otter is *Lutra canadensis*.
> The Manitoban elk (*Cervus elaphus manitobensis*) is a subspecies of the North American elk.

The common names of plants and animals, as well as their hybrids, varieties, and breeds, are lowercased and set in roman type. A part of the name may be capitalized if that part is a term normally capitalized (that is, a proper name). If there is doubt, a dictionary should be consulted.

Alaskan malamute
Christmas cactus
Johnny-jump-up
maidenhair fern
rainbow trout
rose-breasted grosbeak
Swainson's hawk
Vietnamese potbellied pig

The names of astronomical entities, such as planets, stars, constellations, and galaxies, are capitalized:

Alpha Centauri
Canis Major
Crab Nebula
Ganymede
Mercury
Milky Way
Orion
Sirius

The names of geological eras, periods, epochs, etc., are capitalized. When included with the name, the words *era*, *period*, *epoch*, etc., are lowercased.

Mesozoic era
Quaternary period
Oligocene epoch
Upper Jurassic

### *Abbreviations*

Although the use of abbreviations in formal writing should be limited, abbreviations are legitimate components of the language and deserve the same attention to spelling as do other words. Certain capitalization guidelines for a few types of abbreviations are given below. Because the possible variations are numerous, a standard dictionary should be consulted for more thorough guidance on the spelling, capitalization, and punctuation of a specific abbreviation.

When a capitalized term is abbreviated, the abbreviation is capitalized. If the abbreviation is comprised of initials, all the initials are capitalized:

Professor J. Leggett / Prof. J. Leggett
Sergeant David Potter / Sgt. David Potter
Master of Business Administration / MBA
United States Marine Corps / USMC

### TIP

The names *sun*, *moon*, and *earth* are frequently lowercased. It is customary to capitalize them only when they are being referred to as components of the solar system. Also noteworthy is the fact that, in any context, the words *sun* and *moon* typically are preceded by the definite article, *the*. In non-astronomical contexts, the word *earth* often is preceded by *the*, but it is never preceded by *the* when used specifically as the name of a planet. Hence, *the Earth* would not be an appropriate use of capitalization.

We enjoyed the warmth of the sun.
The glow of the moon has inspired poets for centuries.
Countless species inhabit the earth.
What on earth are you doing?
In size, Venus is comparable to Earth.
The eclipse of the Moon will be visible from the night side of Earth.
They made observations of Neptune's orbit around the Sun.

---

When a lowercased term is abbreviated as a simple shortening, the abbreviation is usually lowercased. But if the abbreviation is comprised of initials, all the initials are usually capitalized. When there is a compound word in the term, the initials may include the first letter of the root word:

especially / esp.
teaspoon / tsp.
deoxyribonucleic acid / DNA
monosodium glutamate / MSG
most favored nation / MFN

Usually, an abbreviation that ends in a capital letter is not followed by a period. An abbreviation that ends in a lowercase letter usually is followed by a period, although the period may be optional, depending on the prevailing style of the particular piece of writing.

One group of abbreviations that never ends with a period is the set of chemical symbols. Also, these abbreviations are always initially capitalized even though the terms they represent are lowercased:

Ar argon
Dy dysprosium
H hydrogen
Kr krypton
Lr lawrencium
Na sodium
Sb antimony
Sn tin
U uranium
Xe xenon

Note that some chemical symbols appear to be straightforward abbreviations (*Ca* for *calcium*) while others seem unrelated to their corresponding terms (*Au* for *gold*). In fact, these symbols are abbreviations of the official scientific, or Latin, names (*Au* for *aurum*, which is Latin for *gold*).

### TIP

If the name of an entity such as an organization, institution, or movement is to be abbreviated, its full name should be identified. Upon first mention, both abbreviation and full name should appear together, with either one being set within parentheses. (Usually the lesser known format goes in the parentheses.) Thereafter in the text, only the abbreviation need appear:

> In February 1909, a group of activists founded what would become the NAACP (National Association for the Advancement of Colored People). For more than ninety years, the NAACP has persevered to honor its founders' vision of racial equality and social justice.
>
> Plans to rebuild at the site of the World Trade Center (WTC) are being discussed today. Various designs for new office space are expected to be considered. Thousands of suggestions for a WTC memorial have already been submitted.

## PUNCTUATION

Punctuation is an essential element of good writing because it makes the author's meaning clear to the reader. Although precise punctuation styles may vary somewhat among published sources, there are a number of fundamental principles worthy of consideration. Discussed below are these punctuation marks used in English:

| | |
|---|---|
| comma | apostrophe |
| semicolon | quotation marks |
| colon | parentheses |
| period | dash |
| question mark | hyphen |
| exclamation point | |

### *Comma*

The **comma** is the most used mark of punctuation in the English language. It signals to the reader a pause, which generally clarifies the author's meaning and establishes a sensible order to the elements of written language. Among the most typical functions of the comma are the following:

1. It can separate the clauses of a compound sentence when there are two independent clauses joined by a conjunction, especially when the clauses are not very short:

   *It never occurred to me to look in the attic, and I'm sure it didn't occur to Rachel either.*

   *The Nelsons wanted to see the canyon at sunrise, but they overslept that morning.*

2. It can separate the clauses of a compound sentence when there is a series of independent clauses, the last two of which are joined by a conjunction:

   *The bus ride to the campsite was very uncomfortable, the cabins were not ready for us when we got there, the cook had forgotten to start dinner, and the rain was torrential.*

3. It is used to precede or set off, and therefore indicate, a nonrestrictive dependent clause (a clause that could be omitted without changing the meaning of the main clause):

   *I read her autobiography, which was published last July.*

   *They showed up at midnight, after most of the guests had gone home.*

   *The coffee, which is freshly brewed, is in the kitchen.*

4. It can follow an introductory phrase:

   *Having enjoyed the movie so much, he agreed to see it again.*

   *Born and raised in Paris, she had never lost her French accent.*

   *In the beginning, they had very little money to invest.*

5. It can set off words used in direct address:

   *Listen, people, you have no choice in the matter.*

   *Yes, Mrs. Greene, I will be happy to feed your cat.*

   *Do you really believe, Eliza, that he will return the fifty dollars?*

6. It can separate two or more coordinate adjectives (adjectives that could otherwise be joined with *and*) that modify one noun:

   *The cruise turned out to be the most entertaining, fun, and relaxing vacation I've ever had.*

   *The horse was tall, lean, and sleek.*

   Note that cumulative adjectives (those not able to be joined with and) are not separated by a comma:

   *She wore bright yellow rubber boots.*

7. It is used to separate three or more items in a series or list:

   *Charlie, Melissa, Stan, and Mark will be this year's soloists in the spring concert.*

   *We need furniture, toys, clothes, books, tools, housewares, and other useful merchandise for the benefit auction.*

   Note that the comma between the last two items in a series is sometimes omitted in less precise style:

   *The most popular foods served in the cafeteria are pizza, hamburgers and nachos.*

8. It is used to separate and set off the elements in an address or other geographical designation:

   *My new house is at 1657 Nighthawk Circle, South Kingsbury, Michigan.*

   *We arrived in Pamplona, Spain, on Thursday.*

9. It is used to set off direct quotations (note the placement or absence of commas with other punctuation):

   *"Kim forgot her gloves," he said, "but we have a pair she can borrow."*

   *There was a long silence before Jack blurted out, "This must be the world's ugliest painting."*

   *"What are you talking about?" she asked in a puzzled manner.*

   *"Happy New Year!" everyone shouted.*

10. It is used to set off titles after a person's name:

    *Katherine Bentley, M.D.*

    *Martin Luther King, Jr., delivered the sermon.*

### *Semicolon*

The **semicolon** has two basic functions:

1. It can separate two main clauses, particularly when these clauses are of equal importance:

   *The crowds gathered outside the museum hours before the doors were opened; this was one exhibit no one wanted to miss.*

   *She always complained when her relatives stayed for the weekend; even so, she usually was a little sad when they left.*

2. It can be used as a comma is used to separate such elements as clauses or items in a series or list, particularly when one or more of the elements already includes a comma:

   *The path took us through the deep, dark woods; across a small meadow into a cold, wet cave; and up a hillside overlooking the lake.*

   *Listed for sale in the ad were two bicycles; a battery-powered, leaf-mulching lawn mower; and a maple bookcase.*

### *Colon*

The **colon** has five basic functions:

1. It can introduce something, especially a list of items:

   *In the basket were three pieces of mail: a postcard, a catalog, and a wedding invitation.*

   *Students should have the following items: backpack, loose-leaf notebook, pens and pencils, pencil sharpener, and ruler.*

2. It can separate two clauses in a sentence when the second clause is being used to explain or illustrate the first clause:

   *We finally understood why she would never go sailing with us: she had a deep fear of the water.*

   *Most of the dogs in our neighborhood are quite large: two of them are St. Bernards.*

3. It can introduce a statement or a quotation:

   *His parents say the most important rule is this: Always tell the truth.*

   *We repeated the final words of his poem: "And such is the plight of fools like me."*

4. It can be used to follow the greeting in a formal or business letter:

   *Dear Ms. Daniels:*

   *Dear Sir or Madam:*

5. It is used in the United States to separate minutes from hours, and seconds from minutes, in showing time of day and measured length of time:

   *Please be at the restaurant before 6:45.*

   *Her best running time so far has been 00:12:35.*

### *Period*

The period has two basic functions:

1. It is used to mark the end of a sentence:

   *It was reported that there is a shortage of nurses at the hospital. Several of the patients have expressed concern about this problem.*

2. It is often used at the end of an abbreviation:

   *On Fri., Sept. 12, Dr. Brophy noted that the patient's weight was 168 lb. and that his height was 6 ft. 2 in.*

   (Note that another period is not added to the end of the sentence when the last word is an abbreviation.)

### *Question Mark and Exclamation Point*

The only sentences that do not end in a period are those that end in either a question mark or an exclamation point.

**Question marks** are used to mark the end of a sentence that asks a direct question (generally, a question that expects an answer):

*Is there any reason for us to bring more than a few dollars?*

*Who is your science teacher?*

**Exclamation points** are used to mark the end of a sentence that expresses a strong feeling, typically surprise, joy, or anger:

*I want you to leave and never come back!*

*What a beautiful view this is!*

### *Apostrophe*

The apostrophe has two basic functions:

1. It is used to show where a letter or letters are missing in a contraction.

   *The directions are cont'd* [continued] *on the next page.*

   *We've* [we have] *decided that if she can't* [cannot] *go, then we aren't* [are not] *going either.*

2. It can be used to show possession:

   The possessive of a singular noun or an irregular plural noun is created by adding an apostrophe and an *s*:

   *the pilot's uniform*
   *Mrs. Mendoza's house*
   *a tomato's bright red color*
   *the oxen's yoke*

   The possessive of a regular plural noun is created by adding just an apostrophe:

   *the pilots' uniforms* [referring to more than one pilot]
   *the Mendozas' house* [referring to the Mendoza family]
   *the tomatoes' bright red color* [referring to more than one tomato]

### *Quotation Marks*

Quotation marks have two basic functions:

1. They are used to set off direct quotations (an exact rendering of someone's spoken or written words):

   *"I think the new library is wonderful," she remarked to David.*

   *We were somewhat lost, so we asked, "Are we anywhere near the gallery?"*

   *"In his letter he had written, "The nights here are quiet and starry. It seems like a hundred years since I've been wakened by the noise of city traffic and squabbling neighbors."*

   Note that indirect quotes (which often are preceded by *that*, *if*, and *whether*) are not set off by quotation marks:

   *He told me that he went to school in Boston.*

   *We asked if we could still get tickets to the game.*

2. They can be used to set off words or phrases that have specific technical usage, or to set off meanings of words, or to indicate words that are being used in a special way in a sentence:

   *The part of the flower that bears the pollen is the "stamen."*

   *When I said "plain," I meant "flat land," not "ordinary."*

*Oddly enough, in the theater, the statement "break a leg" is meant as an expression of good luck.*

*What you call "hoagies," we call "grinders" or "submarine sandwiches."*

*He will never be a responsible adult until he outgrows his "Peter Pan" behavior.*

Note that sometimes single quotation marks, rather than double quotation marks, may be used to set off words or phrases:

*The part of the flower that bears the pollen is the 'stamen.'*

What is most important is to be consistent in such usage. Single quotation marks are also used to set off words or phrases within material already in double quotation marks, as:

*"I want the sign to say 'Ellen's Bed and Breakfast' in large gold letters," she explained.*

### *Parentheses*

**Parentheses** are used, in pairs, to enclose information that gives extra detail or explanation to the regular text. Parentheses are used in two basic ways:

1. They can separate a word or words in a sentence from the rest of the sentence:

   *On our way to school, we walk past the Turner Farm (the oldest dairy farm in town) and watch the cows being fed.*

   *The stores were filled with holiday shoppers (even more so than last year).*

   Note that the period goes outside the parentheses, because the words in the parentheses are only part of the sentence.

2. They can form a separate complete sentence:

   *Please bring a dessert to the dinner party. (It can be something very simple.) I look forward to seeing you there.*

   Note that the period goes inside the parentheses, because the words in the parentheses are a complete and independent sentence.

### *Dash*

A **dash** is used most commonly to replace the usage of parentheses within sentences. If the information being set off is in the middle of the sentence, a pair of long (or "em") dashes is used; if it is at the end of the sentence, just one long dash is used:

*On our way to school, we walk past the Turner Farm—the oldest dairy farm in town—and watch the cows being fed.*

*The stores were filled with holiday shoppers—even more so than last year.*

### *Hyphen*

A **hyphen** has three basic functions:

1. It can join two or more words to make a compound, especially when doing so makes the meaning more clear to the reader:

   *We met to discuss long-range planning.*

   *There were six four-month-old piglets at the fair.*

   *That old stove was quite a coal-burner.*

2. It can replace the word "to" when a span or range of data is given. This kind of hyphen is sometimes keyed as a short (or "en") dash:

   *John Adams was president of the United States 1797–1801.*

   *Today we will look for proper nouns in the L–N section of the dictionary.*

   *The ideal weight for that breed of dog would be 75–85 pounds.*

3. It can indicate a word break at the end of a line. The break must always be between syllables:

   *It is important for any writer to know that there are numerous punctuation prin-
   ciples that are considered standard and proper, but there is also flexibility regard-
   ing acceptable punctuation. Having learned the basic "rules" of good punctuation,
   the writer will be able to adopt a specific and consistent style of punctuation that
   best suits the material he or she is writing.*

## CLICHÉS

A **cliché** is a worn-out expression. It was once fresh and meaningful, but it has lost its original impact through overuse. Numerous clichés have become so familiar that it would be virtually impossible to eradicate them from one's vocabulary. However, writers and speakers should make the effort to avoid using them, especially in formal material.

### *Common clichés to avoid*

above and beyond the call of duty
accident waiting to happen
acid test
add insult to injury
after all is said and done
all hands on deck
all in all
all wet
all's well that ends well
almighty dollar
along the same lines
A-OK
as luck would have it
at a loss for words
at arm's length
avoid like the plague
back in the saddle
back on track

backseat driver
ball is in your court
barking up the wrong tree
be your own worst enemy
beat a dead horse
beat around the bush
been there, done that
beggars can't be choosers
be an open book
believe me
better late than never
between a rock and a hard place
between you, me, and the lamppost
big picture
big spender
bigger fish to fry
bird's-eye view
bitter end
bone of contention
born and bred
both sides of the coin
brain trust
bring home the bacon
broad spectrum
broaden one's horizons
bundle of nerves
bury the hatchet
busy as a bee
buy into
by leaps and bounds
by the skin of one's teeth
call her bluff
can't judge a book by its cover
can't take a joke
cast the net
catbird seat
catch as catch can
center of attention
cheat death
chew the fat
clear as a bell
clear as mud
cloak and dagger
coast is clear
cold as ice
cold shoulder
come full circle
come to no good
come up for air
conspicuous by their absence
cool it
cop out
could eat a horse
counting on you
count your blessings
cover all the bases
crazy like a fox
cream of the crop
creature of habit
crossing the line
cut me some slack
cut to the chase
dead in the water
dead wrong
dog-eat-dog
done deal
done to death
don't know him from Adam
down and dirty
down and out
down in the dumps
down in the mouth
dressed to the nines
due in large measure to
duly noted
dumb luck
easier said than done
easy come, easy go
easy mark
easy target
eat crow
end of discussion
every fiber of my being
face the music

fair and square
fall from grace
fall through the cracks
far and away
feast or famine
few and far between
fighting the tide
fill the bill
find it in your heart
fit as a fiddle
fit to be tied
fits like an old shoe
flat as a pancake
fly in the ointment
fly off the handle
for all intents and purposes
for love or money
for your information
fork it over
free as a bird
from the frying pan into the fire
from time immemorial
game plan
get behind the eight ball
get down to brass tacks
get off scot-free
get our ducks in a row
get the lead out
get the show on the road
get to the bottom of it
give a damn
give rise to
go for the kill
go it alone
go the distance
go the extra mile
go to pieces
go with the flow
goes without saying
good for nothing
goodly number
grass is always greener
green with envy
grist for the mill
hammer out the details
handwriting on the wall
hang in there
has a screw loose
have your heart in your mouth
head over heels
heated argument
his bark is worse than his bite
hit or miss
hit the ceiling
hit the ground running
hit the nail on the head
hold that thought
holding back the tide
hook, line, and sinker
hour of need
I wasn't born yesterday
icing on the cake
if looks could kill
if the price is right
I'm all over it
I'm speechless
in a nutshell
in due course
in hot water
in layman's terms
in one fell swoop
in over their heads
in seventh heaven
in the bag
in the ballpark
in the driver's seat
in the event that
in the final analysis
in the groove
in the near future
in the neighborhood of
in the nick of time
in the same boat
in the zone

in this day and age
irons in the fire
it could be worse
it stands to reason
it takes all kinds
it takes guts
it's your baby
join the club
keep your fingers crossed
keep the home fires burning
keeping score
kill the fatted calf
kiss of death
knock on wood
knock the socks off of
know the ropes
last but not least
last straw
lay an egg
learning curve
leave no stone unturned
left to his own devices
lend me an ear
let the cat out of the bag
let your hair down
letter perfect
lie low
light of day
like a bull in a china shop
like a bump on a log
like greased lightning
like rolling off a log
little does he know
live it up
lock, stock, and barrel
look like a million bucks
low man on the totem pole
make ends meet
make tracks
makes her blood boil
method in (*or* to) my madness
millstone around your neck
mince words
misery loves company
moment of truth
Monday-morning quarterback
monkey on your back
more money than God
more than meets the eye
more than you could shake a stick at
nail to the wall
naked truth
nearing the finish line
needle in a haystack
needs no introduction
never a dull moment
nip and tuck
nip in the bud
no harm, no foul
no skin off my nose
no strings attached
no-brainer
none the worse for wear
nose to the grindstone
not one red cent
nothing new under the sun
off the cuff
old as the hills
old hat
old soldiers never die
older than dirt
on cloud nine
on the one hand/on the other hand
on the road
on the same page
on the same track
on the wagon
on top of the world
out of my league
out of the woods
over a barrel
pan out
par for the course
pass the buck

pay the piper
perish the thought
piece of cake
playing for keeps
powers that be
practice makes perfect
proud as a peacock
pulling my leg
pulling no punches
put faces to names
put on hold
put the bite on
put words in one's mouth
put your money where your mouth is
quick and dirty
rags to riches
rant and rave
reading me like a book
real McCoy
red as a beet
regret to inform you
reign supreme
rings a bell
ripe old age
rise and shine
rolling over in his grave
rub elbows
rule the roost
run circles around
run it up the flagpole
run off at the mouth
sadder but wiser
safe to say
salt of the earth
scarce as hen's teeth
sea of faces
see the forest for the trees
sell like hotcakes
set in stone
shake a leg
sharp as a tack
ships that pass in the night
shoot the breeze
shooting himself in the foot
shot in the arm
shot to hell
sight for sore eyes
sitting duck
skeleton in the closet
skin alive
sleep on it
smells fishy
smooth sailing
snake in the grass
spill the beans
stay in the loop
steal the limelight
stem the tide
stick to your guns
stick your neck out
straight from the horse's mouth
strange bedfellows
strike a balance
strong as an ox
stubborn as a mule
sturdy as an oak
suffice it to say
sweating bullets
take a breather
take into consideration
take on board
take one's word for
take pleasure in
take the bitter with the sweet
take the easy way out
take the liberty of
talk shop
talk the talk
talk through your hat
talk your ear off
that's all she wrote
the die is cast
they'll be sorry
thick as thieves

thin as a rail
think outside the box
think tank
those are the breaks
through thick and thin
throw caution to the wind
thrown to the wolves
tighten our belts
time is money
time marches on
time waits for no man
to each his own
to your heart's content
too funny for words
took the words right out of my mouth
touch base
turn the other cheek
turn up your nose
two peas in a pod
ugly as sin
under the wire
up a creek
upset the applecart
venture a guess
vicious circle
waiting for the other shoe to drop
walk the walk
walking encyclopedia
walking on air
welcome with open arms
when the cows come home
where angels fear to tread
where there's smoke, there's fire
whole nine yards
wild-goose chase
wipe the slate clean
wishful thinking
with bated breath
without further ado
without further delay
wonders never cease
words fail me
wreak havoc
yada, yada, yada
you said a mouthful
you'll never know if you don't try

## REDUNDANT EXPRESSIONS

A **redundant** expression is a group of words (usually a pair) in which at least one word is superfluous—that is, unnecessary. The superfluous element can be removed without affecting the meaning of the expression. In formal speech or writing, redundant expressions should be strictly avoided.

In the following list of common redundant expressions, the superfluous elements have been crossed out.

~~absolute~~ guarantee
~~absolutely~~ certain
~~absolutely~~ essential
~~absolutely~~ necessary
AC ~~current~~
~~actual~~ fact
~~actual~~ truth
add ~~an additional~~
adding ~~together~~
~~advance~~ reservations
~~advance~~ warning
after ~~the end of~~
all meet ~~together~~
alongside ~~of~~
~~already~~ existing
~~and~~ moreover
~~annoying~~ pest
ATM ~~machine~~
~~awkward~~ predicament
bald-~~headed~~

~~basic~~ essentials
~~basic~~ fundamentals
blend ~~together~~
~~brief~~ moment
~~but~~ however
~~but~~ nevertheless
came ~~at a time~~ when
cancel ~~out~~
~~chief~~ protagonist
~~clearly~~ obvious
climb ~~up~~
~~close~~ proximity
~~close~~ scrutiny
collaborate ~~together~~
combine ~~into one~~
commute ~~back and forth~~
~~complete~~ monopoly
~~completely~~ destroyed
~~completely~~ eliminated
~~completely~~ empty
~~completely~~ filled
~~completely~~ random
consensus ~~of opinion~~
continue ~~on~~
~~continue to~~ remain
cooperate ~~together~~
currently ~~today~~
DC ~~current~~
~~decorative~~ garnish
~~deep~~ chasm
~~definitely~~ decided
descend ~~down~~
~~different~~ varieties
~~difficult~~ dilemma
~~direct~~ confrontation
drop ~~down~~
during ~~the course of~~
dwindled ~~down~~
each ~~and every~~
earlier ~~in time~~
~~empty~~ space
~~end~~ result
enter ~~in~~
equal ~~to one another~~
~~established~~ fact
estimated at ~~about~~
estimated ~~roughly~~ at
~~every~~ now and then
~~evil~~ fiend
~~exact~~ duplicate
~~exact~~ opposites
~~fake~~ copy
~~false~~ pretenses
~~fellow~~ classmates
~~fellow~~ teammates
few ~~in number~~
filled ~~to capacity~~
~~final~~ conclusion
~~final~~ outcome
first ~~and foremost~~
~~first~~ began
~~first~~ introduction
first ~~of all~~
~~first~~ started
follow ~~after~~
for ~~a period of~~ six months
for ~~the purpose of~~
~~foreign~~ exports
~~foreign~~ imports
forever ~~and ever~~
foundered ~~and sank~~
~~free~~ gift
~~free~~ pass
~~future~~ prospects
gather ~~together~~
gave birth to a ~~baby~~ girl/boy
~~glowing~~ ember
~~good~~ bargain
~~good~~ benefits
had done ~~previously~~
~~harmful~~ injury
HIV ~~virus~~
~~honest~~ truth
~~hopeful~~ optimism

~~hot~~ water heater
I ~~myself personally~~
if ~~and when~~
~~important~~ breakthrough
in ~~close~~ proximity
~~intense~~ fury
introduced ~~for the first time~~
~~invited~~ guests
ISBN ~~number~~
joined ~~together~~
~~just~~ recently
kneel ~~down~~
last ~~of all~~
lift ~~up~~
look back ~~in retrospect~~
~~major~~ breakthrough
may ~~possibly~~
~~mental~~ telepathy
merged ~~together~~
meshed ~~together~~
~~midway~~ between
might ~~possibly~~
mix ~~together~~
~~mutual~~ cooperation
~~natural~~ instinct
never ~~at any time~~
~~new~~ beginning
~~new~~ bride
~~new~~ innovation
~~new~~ recruit
nine A.M. ~~in the morning~~
no trespassing ~~allowed~~
none ~~at all~~
~~now~~ pending
null ~~and void~~
~~old~~ cliché
~~old~~ proverb
~~opening~~ introduction
~~originally~~ created
over ~~and done with~~
~~over~~exaggerate
~~pair of~~ twins
parched ~~dry~~
~~passing~~ fad
~~past~~ experiences
~~past~~ history
~~past~~ memories
~~past~~ records
penetrate ~~into~~
~~perfect~~ ideal
permeate ~~throughout~~
~~personal~~ friend
~~personal~~ opinion
~~personally~~ believes
PIN ~~number~~
plan ~~in advance~~
~~poisonous~~ venom
~~positively~~ true
~~possibly~~ might
postponed ~~until a later time~~
~~pre~~recorded
~~present~~ incumbent
probed ~~into~~
proceed ~~ahead~~
protest ~~against~~
protrude ~~out~~
~~proven~~ facts
raise ~~up~~
reason ~~why~~
refer ~~back~~
reflect ~~back~~
repeat ~~again~~
reply ~~back~~
revert ~~back~~
Rio Grande ~~River~~
~~sad~~ tragedy
same ~~identical~~
seemed ~~to be~~
share ~~together~~
short ~~in length~~
since ~~the time when~~
~~sincerely~~ mean it
skipped ~~over~~
~~solemn~~ vow

spelled out ~~in detail~~
stacked ~~on top of each other~~
~~still~~ continues
~~still~~ persists
~~still~~ remains
strangled ~~to death~~
~~stupid~~ fool
~~suddenly~~ exploded
sufficient ~~enough~~
~~sum~~ total
summer ~~season~~
~~sworn~~ affidavit
~~temporary~~ recess
~~temporary~~ reprieve
~~terrible~~ tragedy
~~thoughtful~~ contemplation
~~thoughtful~~ deliberation
~~totally~~ eliminated
~~true~~ fact
~~twelve~~ midnight
~~twelve~~ noon
~~two~~ twins
~~ultimate~~ conclusion
~~unexpected~~ surprise
~~unintentional~~ mistake
~~uninvited~~ party crashers
UPC ~~code~~
~~usual~~ custom
~~utter~~ annihilation
~~very~~ unique
ways ~~and means~~
~~well-known old~~ adage
when ~~and if~~
whether ~~or not~~
widow ~~woman~~
written ~~down~~

## Proofreader's Marks

delete

delete and close up

delete and leave space

insert

space

period

comma

semicolon

or colon

apostrophe

quotation marks

parentheses

square brackets

hyphen

em-dash

en-dash

new paragraph

dictionary break line or word

set as superscript

set as subscript

dictionary transpose

transpose (note in margin)

spell out

spell out (note in margin)

dictionary capitalize

set as capitals (note in margin)

Dictionary make lower case

set in lower case (note in margin)

dictionary make boldface

set in boldface (note in margin)

dictionary make italic

set in italic (note in margin)

dictionary small caps

set in small caps (note in margin)

lightface (note in margin)

set in roman (note in margin)